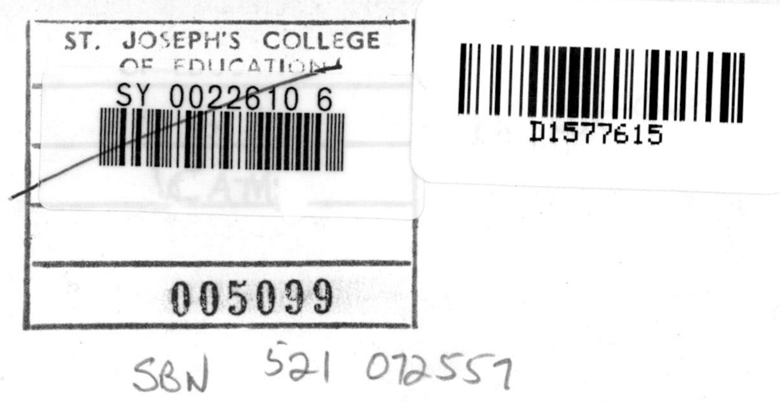

WITHDRAWN FROM STOCK

The New Cambridge Bibliography of English Literature

in five volumes

Volume 3

The New Cambridge Bibliography of English Literature

Edited by
GEORGE WATSON

Volume 3
1800–1900

CAMBRIDGE
AT THE UNIVERSITY PRESS
1969

Published by the Syndics of the Cambridge University Press
Bentley House, 200 Euston Road, London N.W.1
American Branch: 32 East 57th Street, New York, N.Y. 10022

Library of Congress Catalogue Card Number: 69-10199
Standard Book Number: 521 07255 7

Printed in Great Britain
at the University Printing House, Cambridge
(Brooke Crutchley, University Printer)

To F. W. Bateson

CONTENTS

1. INTRODUCTION

I. General works

II. Book production and distribution

III. Literary relations with the Continent

2. POETRY

I. General works

II. Early nineteenth-century poetry

V. Minor fiction 1835–1870

VI. The late nineteenth-century novel

VII. Minor fiction 1870–1900

VIII. Children's books

4. DRAMA

I. General introduction

II. The early nineteenth-century drama

III. The mid-nineteenth-century drama

Other dramatists 1835–1870

IV. The late nineteenth-century drama

Other dramatists 1870–1900

5. PROSE

I. General works

II. Early nineteenth-century prose

III. Minor prose 1800–1835

IV. Mid-nineteenth-century prose

V. Minor prose 1835–1870

VI. Late nineteenth-century prose

VII. Minor prose 1870–1900

VIII. History

IX. Philosophy

X. Religion

A. LIBERAL THEOLOGIANS AND EVANGELICALS

B. THE OXFORD MOVEMENT AND THE HIGH CHURCHMEN

XI. English studies

XII. Travel

XIII. Sport

XIV. Education

XV. Newspapers and magazines

6. ANGLO-IRISH LITERATURE

I. Gaelic sources

II. General works

EDITOR'S PREFACE

This is the first volume of the *New Cambridge Bibliography of English Literature* to appear, and it is massively indebted to volume 3 of *CBEL* (1940), edited by F. W. Bateson, and the Supplement of 1957, of which it represents a total revision. To say this, however, can only confirm a debt that many thousands of scholars and students throughout the world have felt to a book which has proved itself, along with the *Oxford English Dictionary*, as the greatest of all reference-books in English studies. Every contributor to *New CBEL* must have recognized afresh in the course of revision how vast a labour in the less favourable circumstances of the 1930s the achievement of the old Bibliography represented. It is natural to begin *New CBEL* with a tribute to the labours of the editor and contributors of the original work: they have no reason to have been surprised at its success and its influence, and cannot have doubted that the lapse of time would eventually call for a revision.

The largest of all tributes to be paid, perhaps, is to suggest that the design of the work, marshalled according to the literary kinds such as Poetry, Drama and the Novel, has established itself so firmly as a workable solution that it has in all its essentials been retained in this revision. This is the more remarkable when it is remembered how radically nineteenth-century studies have changed in the past thirty years. In the 1930s Victorian literature, and especially the Victorian novel, had with rare exceptions barely entered into the accepted range of scholarly activity. The revision of volume 3, which for this reason among others has been undertaken first, is altogether likely to prove the most radical revision of all. It has raised problems, at times, of an acute kind, and readers who find themselves regretting changes which they observe in a familiar work may console themselves with the reflection that alterations in volume 2 and volume 1 are likely to be both rarer and more conservative. The study of the eighteenth century, and of the Middle Ages and Renaissance, has swollen in extent over the past generation; but it has not transformed the shape of the subject as recent studies of romantic and Victorian literature have done. In spite of this, however, every attempt has been made to proceed cautiously, and it has only been in cases where a decisive advantage was seen to lie in favour of change that a change has been made. In general the task of the fifty contributors and more who have compiled this volume has been to revise and integrate the existing lists of 1940 and 1957, to add materials of the past ten years, to correct and refine the bibliographical details already available, and to reshape the whole according to the new conventions which have been designed to give the Bibliography a clearer and more consistent air.

Inevitably, however, some of the ambitions which seemed realistic in the more limited scholarly world of the 1930s have had to be abandoned. *CBEL* is a bibliography of literature, not of publications in the wider sense; and difficult of definition as this distinction is, it has not been thought practical to preserve such non-literary sections as Political and Social Background. Such sections would have had to be vastly inflated in order to represent modern historical scholarship, and in that event they could only have presumed to rival the bibliographies of historical studies themselves. It is true that the student of literature often finds himself engaged in questions of an extra-literary kind, and in such questions these sections were no doubt designed to assist him; but it no longer seems realistic to suppose that *CBEL* should try to answer questions beyond the range of literary history itself. The student must learn to accept that, when he ranges outside literary history, there are more appropriate works than *CBEL* for him to use. On similar grounds, certain barely literary sections such as Science, Economics, Law, and Classical and Oriental Scholarship have been abandoned, though the new index in the present volume will show which individuals of literary note have been retained from these sections in some other section of the book. On rather different grounds, the final sections on the literatures of certain Commonwealth states have also been dropped—literatures which are, or may soon be, better provided for in their own national bibliographies. *New CBEL* is therefore confined to literary authors native to or mainly resident in the British Isles. But, as in the *Concise CBEL* (1958), no restriction of nationality or language has been imposed on the choice of secondary materials, mainly biography and criticism, concerning the British and Irish authors included here. The effect of this reshaping has been to add Henry James to the Bibliography, on grounds of residence, and to exclude sections on Anglo-Indian, Canadian, South African and Australian and New Zealand literature. The concept of period, however, remains unchanged: a nineteenth-century author, for this purpose, remains an author who was in some sense established after 1800 and before 1900. The remaining four periods of *CBEL* will also be retained: the Old English period (600–1100); the Middle English (1100–1500); the Renaissance to the Restoration (1500–1660); and the Restoration to the Romantic Period (1660–1800). A sixth period, the Earlier Twentieth Century (1900–1950), is now in preparation in a separate volume. It is hoped that the provisional indexes to this and to successive volumes of *New CBEL*, which will include the names of primary authors and certain headings, will answer at a glance any questions concerning which authors the Bibliography does or does not include. A fifth volume will furnish a more detailed index to the whole work.

The scope of the Bibliography in detail remains largely unchanged: it aims to represent the whole of English studies, so far as these concern the literature of the British Isles, both in primary and in secondary materials, 'works by' and 'works about'. The symbols §1 and §2 have been imposed upon author-sections to mark this distinction in an unmistakable way. In addition, the canon of an author's works, or the primary section, has usually been merged into a single chronological list, with the object of demonstrating more clearly the shape of his literary career; though exceptions of convenience have been encouraged, and certain special categories such as letters, diaries and private papers, or contributions to periodicals, have often been allowed sub-sections of their own. Author-sections ordinarily begin with bibliographies, where they exist, and collections, followed by the primary section and its sub-sections, followed in turn by a chronological list of secondary material with works by individual scholars and critics grouped together. In a few instances, for the sake of greater clarity, secondary works have been grouped under the titles of individual primary works.

The Bibliography continues to aim at completeness, but as before this must be understood as completeness in its own terms. Certain categories of material have normally been excluded, notably unpublished dissertations and their published abstracts, ephemeral journalism, encyclopaedia articles, reviews of secondary works, brief notes of less than crucial interest to scholarship, and sections in general works such as literary histories which are listed in their own sections at the head of each major division of the volume. In addition, contributors have been encouraged to drop certain antiquated articles which are now either superseded or absorbed into later studies and editions. But the history of an author's reputation remains an object of study, and articles which represent it memorably have been retained, even where they may have been discredited by later scholarship.

The location of copies and of manuscripts, however, remains essentially outside the scope of the Bibliography, which cannot undertake to rival the *Short-Title Catalogue* in its listing of library holdings. But brief headnotes on manuscripts have sometimes been included; and where a unique copy of a work is known to exist outside the British Museum, such information has at times been admitted into the Bibliography, though in neither case has any attempt at consistency been made.

The page has been newly designed to accommodate about one quarter more than the old *CBEL* page while still presenting a clear and simple aspect to the reader. A radical attempt has been made to simplify and standardize the existing conventions of the Bibliography. Punctuation has been enormously reduced: colons regularly precede subtitles, semi-colons divide titles; and commas rather than semi-colons now ordinarily separate the dates of reprints. Capitalization has been reduced to the level of ordinary prose, which has enabled titles within titles to be distinguished by a capital letter. Roman numerals have been greatly reduced in favour of arabic. Abbreviations, apart from certain indispensable initials to represent major periodicals, have been moderately used, and it is hoped that they are largely self-explanatory. The use of brackets has been much reduced, and headnotes and endnotes which serve as editorial explanations have been allowed to define themselves simply by their position. Titles, as in *CBEL*, are 'short', and omissions are not marked; and, as before, the number of volumes is entered unless it is one, and the place of publication unless it is London; for this purpose books published in England by the Oxford University Press have been entered as 'Oxford'. Such details continue to apply in any given entry until contradicted, and '1 vol' and 'London' may then be used to contradict. In citing periodical articles, monthlies are normally quoted by the month and quarterlies by volume-number. Translations of primary works have been admitted in summary form only, and commonly without details of translator or place of publication, e.g. 'tr French, 1837'. In the case of secondary works, only translations into English have normally been cited.

The provision of bibliographical detail in the primary section, which is perhaps the chief function of the Bibliography, is a matter which eludes definition and which necessarily varies according to the state of knowledge of the subject, and even according to the preoccupations of the contributor. It hardly needs to be emphasized that the Bibliography practices the degressive principle to the full. The detail of an entry tends to be most intense in the early years of the life of a book; late editions are usually cited only when revised or enlarged by the author; and modern reprints may not be included at all unless they justify themselves by reason of an introduction or editorial apparatus. Major authors tend to be more minutely treated than minor, and headnotes to individual sections often define the limits that have been placed. In sum, the proper demands of consistency have not been interpreted as signifying that every author should be treated in the same way. On the contrary, it is recognized that in a bibliography of literature certain authors and subjects are central and others peripheral, and that many intermediate cases exist and demand to be treated as such.

ACKNOWLEDGEMENTS

My deepest acknowledgements are due to the fifty and more contributors in Europe and North America who have sacrificed time and patience to make this volume. Many of them have advised far beyond the scope of their own sections. The Advisory Committee of H. S. Bennett (Chairman), R. W. David, P. G. Burbidge, A. N. L. Munby and Ian Willison initiated the project of a total revision of *CBEL* and have watched benignly over the progress of the volume for three years. Early advice of great benefit to the undertaking was received from members of the staff of the British Museum and of the Bodleian Library; and also from the late Professor John Butt, as well as from Mr John Carter, Professor Philip Harth, Mr J. C. Maxwell, Mr Peter Meade and Mr Arnold Muirhead. Professor Walter E. Houghton gave us a wealth of encouragement based upon his Wellesley index to Victorian periodicals. Many scholars have been generous in their advice relating to sections of the book in which they took a special interest, notably Professor Kathleen Tillotson, Mr Edwin Gilcher, Mr Simon Nowell-Smith, Professor Richard L. Purdy, Professor Donald Smalley and Professor G. W. Stone jr. Others who assisted actively with individual sections include Mr Brian Alderson, Mr R. D. Crinkley, Dr A. G. Cross, Mrs J. I. McDonald, Mr Edward Mendelson, Mr James Ogden and Mr Robert Woodings. Mrs W. J. Harvey generously assisted with her husband's sections after his tragic death in the summer of 1967. The thanks of all who use the section on Book Production and Distribution are due to the Guildhall Library and to the Corporation of the City of London for granting permission to

Mr James Mosley and his staff at the St Bride Printing Library to prepare this section.

The Zeitlin and Ver Brugge Lectureship of 1964 at the University of California, Los Angeles gave me the opportunity to recount the history of the Bibliography and to propose plans for its future in *CBEL: the making of the Cambridge Bibliography* (Los Angeles, 1965). The Cambridge University Library has generously presented us with an office, and in that office Mrs Phyllis Parsons has patiently and heroically undertaken to type the entire volume.

GEORGE WATSON

St John's College, Cambridge
October 1967

LIST OF CONTRIBUTORS TO VOLUME 3

M.A.	Miriam Allott
R.C.A.	R. C. Alston
J.F.A.	J. F. Arnott
G.B.	Gillian Beer
E.B.	Edmund Blunden
B.A.B.	Bradford A. Booth
M.S.B.	Marilyn S. Butler
C.C.	Christophe Campos
G.D.C.	Geoffrey D. Carnall
P.A.W.C.	Philip A. W. Collins
R.L.C.	Rowland L. Collins
C.E.C.	Christina E. Colvin
J.C.C.	J. C. Corson
S.J.C.	S. J. Curtis
H.W.D.	H. W. Donner
G.S.F.	George S. Fayen
W.E.F.	W. E. Fredeman
R.M.G.	Richard M. Gollin
R.L.G.	Roger Lancelyn Green
D.H.G.	David H. Greene
W.J.H.	W. J. Harvey
A.P.H.	A. P. Howse
J.E.J.	John E. Jordan
F.K.	Franz Kuna
C.Y.L.	Cecil Y. Lang
D.H.L.	Dan H. Laurence
D.L.	Donald Low
J.R.M.	J. R. MacGillivray
G.M.M.	G. M. Matthews
O.M.	Oscar Maurer
J.M.	James Mosley
E.L.N.	Eleanor L. Nicholes
W.J.B.O.	W. J. B. Owen
W.D.P.	W. D. Paden
R.P.	Roy Park
M.L.P.	M. L. Pearl
R.B.P.	Robert B. Pearsall
M.P.	Morse Peckham
A.P.	Arthur Pollard
H.G.P.	H. G. Pollard
J.M.R.	John M. Robson
H.M.R.	Henry M. Rosenberg
S.K.R.	Sheila K. Rosenberg
C.R.S.	Charles Richard Sanders
B.C.S.	Brian C. Southam
M.S.	Michael Statham
J.S.	John Sparrow
L.S.	Lionel Stevenson
G.S.	Graham Storey
R.H.S.	R. H. Super
F.G.T.	F. G. Townsend
E. de W.	E. de Waal
G.Wh.	George Whalley
W.W.	William White
C.W.	Cecil Woolf

ABBREVIATIONS

Acad	Academy	HLQ	Huntington Library Quarterly
addn	addition	illustr	illustrated by
Amer	American	Inst	Institute
anon	anonymous	introd	introduction
Archiv	Archiv für das Studium der neueren Sprachen	JEGP	Journal of English and Germanic Philology
AS	Anglo-Saxon	JHI	Journal of the History of Ideas
Assoc	Association	Jnl	Journal
b.	born	Lang	Language
Bibl	Bibliographical	Lib	Library
bk	book	Lit	Literature
BM	British Museum	MAE	Medium Aevum
Br	British	Mag	Magazine
Bull	Bulletin	ME	Middle English
BNYPL	Bulletin of New York Public Library	ML	Muses' Library
		MLN	Modern Language Notes
c.	circa	MLQ	Modern Language Quarterly
ch	chapter	MLR	Modern Language Review
CHEL	Cambridge History of English Literature	MP	Modern Philology
		ms	manuscript
col	column	nd	no date
CQ	Critical Quarterly	no	number
d.	died	N & Q	Notes and Queries
DNB	Dictionary of National Biography	OE	Old English
		OHEL	Oxford History of English Literature
ed	edited by		
edn	edition	OSA	Oxford Standard Authors
E & S	Essays and Studies	p.	page
et al	and others	pbd	published
EC	Essays in Criticism	pbn	publication
EETS	Early English Text Society	PBSA	Publications of the Bibliographical Society of America
EHR	English Historical Review		
EL	Everyman's Library	PMLA	Publications of the Modern Language Association of America
ELH	Journal of English Literary History		
EML	English Men of Letters	PQ	Philological Quarterly
Eng	English	priv	privately
E Studien	Englische Studien	Proc	Proceedings
E Studies	English Studies	prop	proprietor
facs	facsimile	pt	part
fl.	floruit	ptd	printed
GM	Gentleman's Magazine	Quart	Quarterly

REL	Review of English Literature	Soc	Society
rev	revised by	SP	Studies in Philology
Rev	Review	STS	Scottish Text Society
RES	Review of English Studies	suppl	supplement
rptd	reprinted	TLS	Times Literary Supplement
SB	Studies in Bibliography (University of Virginia)	tr	translated by
		trn	translation
SE	Studies in English (University of Texas)	unpbd	unpublished
		UTQ	University of Toronto Quarterly
ser	series	vol	volume
Sh Jb	Shakespeare Jahrbuch	WC	World's Classics

1. INTRODUCTION

I. GENERAL WORKS

(1) BIBLIOGRAPHIES

This section lists bibliographies wholly or largely devoted to the nineteenth century, including general bibliographies of poetry. Non-period lists, including catalogues of books pbd in the provinces, will be found in vol 1, where bibliographies of the principal religious bodies are also listed. Other specialized lists on the nineteenth century will be found in the section on Book Production and Distribution, under Novel, Drama etc, and in sections on individual authors, below.

Hodgkins, L. M. A guide to the study of nineteenth-century authors. Boston 1904.

Amherst (later Cecil), A. M. List of English printed books on gardening to 1837. In her History of gardening, 1910 (rev).

Faxon, F. W. Literary annuals and gift books. Boston 1912.

Woods, G. B. English poetry and prose of the romantic movement. New York 1916 (with bibliography), 1929 (with supplementary bibliography).

[Muddiman, J. G.] The Times tercentenary handlist of English and Welsh newspapers, magazines and reviews. 1920.

Bibliographies of modern authors. London Mercury Nov 1950–Sept 1921. On Birrell, George Moore, Trench, Doughty, Gosse, Hudson, Quiller-Couch.

Danielson, H. Bibliographies of modern authors. 1921. On Crackanthorpe, Gissing, Middleton, Symons.

Summers, M. et al. The nineteenth century and after. Year's Work in Eng Stud 1–1921–. An annual; after 1953 entitled The nineteenth century.

Manly, J. M. and E. Rickert. Contemporary British literature: bibliographies and study outlines. 1922, 1929 (rev), 1935 (rev F. B. Millet).

Morgan, B. Q. A critical bibliography of German literature in English translation. Madison 1922, New York 1965 (rev and enlarged).

Sadleir, M. Excursions in Victorian bibliography. 1922. 1st edns of Trollope, Marryat, Disraeli, Wilkie Collins, Reade, Whyte-Melville, Mrs Gaskell.

Stonehill, C. A. and H. W. Bibliographies of modern authors, ser 2. 1925. On Davidson, Dowson, Alice Meynell, Pater, Francis Thompson.

Williams, J. B. Guide to the printed materials for English social and economic history 1750–1850. 2 vols New York 1926.

Kennedy, A. G. A bibliography of writings on the English language. Cambridge Mass 1927.

Sawyer, C. J. and F. J. H. Darton. English books 1475–1900. 2 vols 1927.

Bernbaum, E. Guide through the romantic movement. New York 1930.

Cutter, B. D. and V. Stiles. Modern British authors: their first editions. New York 1930. On Lewis Carroll, Kipling, Moore, Pater, Stevenson et al.

Muir, P. H., S. Nowell-Smith and A. Mitchell. Bibliographies of modern authors, ser 3. 1931.

Templeman, W. D. et al. Victorian bibliography for 1932. MP 30 1933 (continued annually in MP till 1956); Bibliographies of studies in Victorian literature 1932–44, ed Templeman, Urbana 1945 (collected); Bibliographies of studies in Victorian literature 1945–54, ed. A. Wright, Urbana 1956 (collected).

Jones, H. M. et al. Syllabus and bibliography of Victorian literature. 5 pts Ann Arbor 1934–5.

Brussel, I. R. Anglo-American first editions 1826–1900: describing first editions of English authors whose books were published in America before their publication in England. 1935.

Aubin, R. A. Topographical poetry in eighteenth-century England. New York 1936. Bibliographies (1640–1840), pp. 298–391.

Ehrsam, T. G. and R. H. Deily. Bibliographies of twelve Victorian authors. New York 1936. Supplement by J. G. Fucilla, MP 37 1939. Lists books and articles on E. B. Browning, FitzGerald, D. G. and Christina Rossetti, Clough, Arnold, Tennyson, Morris, Stevenson, Swinburne, Hardy, Kipling.

Kunitz, S. J. and H. Haycraft. British authors of the nineteenth century. New York 1936. An encyclopaedia with brief bibliographies.

Graham, W. et al. The romantic movement: a current selective and critical bibliography for 1936. ELH 4 1937 (continued annually in ELH till 1949, in PQ 1950–64 and in Eng Lang Notes 1965–).

Richards, E. A. Hudibras in the burlesque tradition. New York 1937. Lists Hudibrastic poems 1662–1830.

Batho, E. and B. Dobrée. The Victorians and after 1830–1914. 1938. Introductions to English literature vol 4, with critical bibliography.

Harrold, C. F. Recent trends in Victorian studies 1932–9. SP 37 1940.

Northup, C. S. and J. J. Parry. The Arthurian legends: modern retellings of the old stories—an annotated bibliography [1800–1944]. JEGP 43 1944.

Sadleir, M., J. W. Carter et al. Princeton Univ Lib Chron 8 1946. Essays by various hands on the Morris L. Parrish collections of Victorian literature, notably on Kingsley, Dickens, Hardy, Bulwer-Lytton, Trollope.

Bleiler, E. F. The checklist of fantastic literature: a bibliography of fantasy, weird and science fiction books in English. Chicago 1948.

Green, D. G. and E. G. Wilson. Current bibliography. Keats-Shelley Jnl 1 1950 (continued regularly); Keats, Shelley, Byron, Hunt and their circles: a bibliography July 1 1950–June 30 1962, Lincoln Nebraska 1964 (collected).

Raysor, T. M. et al. The English romantic poets: a review of research. New York 1950, 1956 (rev).

Ray, G. N., C. J. Weber and J. W. Carter. Nineteenth-century books: some problems in bibliography. Urbana 1952.

Townsend, F. G. et al. Recent publications: a selected list. Victorian News Letter no 1 1952 (continued quarterly).

—— et al. Victorian bibliography for 1957. Victorian Stud 1 1958. Continued annually.

Matthews, W. British autobiographies: an annotated bibliography of British autobiographies published or written before 1951. Berkeley 1955.

Faverty, F. E. et al. The Victorian poets: a guide to research. Cambridge Mass 1956, 1968 (rev).

Houtchens, C. W. and L. H. The English romantic poets and essayists: a review of research and criticism. New York 1957, 1966 (rev).

Fogle, R. H. The romantic period. In Contemporary

literary scholarship: a critical review, ed L. Leary, New York 1958.
Stevenson, L. The Victorian period. Ibid.
Houghton, W. E. Victorian periodicals. TLS 6 March 1959.
—— British periodicals of the Victorian age: bibliographies and indexes. Library Trends 7 1959.
—— Reflections on indexing Victorian periodicals. Victorian Stud 7 1963. On plans for the Wellesley index, below.
—— (ed). The Wellesley index to Victorian periodicals 1824–1900. Toronto 1966–.
Altick, R. D. and W. R. Matthews. Guide to dissertations in Victorian literature 1886–1958. Urbana 1960.
Hugh, F. Nineteenth-century pamphlets at Pusey House. 1961.
Strange, G. R. et al. Recent studies in nineteenth-century English literature. Stud in Eng Lit 1500–1900 1– 1961–. Continued annually.
Collins, R. L. The Frederick Tennyson collection. Victorian Stud 1963 (Xmas supplement). On the Tennysons, the Brownings, Mary Brotherton.
Houghton, E. R. The British Critic and the Oxford Movement. SB 16 1963.
Tobias, R. C. The year's work in Victorian poetry 1962. Victorian Poetry 1– 1963–. Continued annually.
Winterich, J. T. The Fales collection: a record of growth. New York 1963.

(2) LITERARY HISTORIES AND SURVEYS

General

Cunningham, A. Biographical and critical history of the British literature of the last fifty years. 1834.
Cleveland, C. D. English literature of the nineteenth century. Philadelphia 1852, 1869 (rev).
Brandes, G. Hovedstrømninger i det 19 aarhundredes litteratur. 6 vols Copenhagen 1872–90, 1901–5; tr as Main currents in nineteenth-century literature: naturalism in England, 1905, New York 1957.
Morley, H. Of English literature in the reign of Victoria. Leipzig 1881.
Oliphant, M. O. The literary history of England in the end of the eighteenth century and beginning of the nineteenth century. 3 vols 1882.
—— The Victorian age of English literature. 2 vols 1892. With F. R. Oliphant.
Garnett, R. Literature 1837–87. In T. H. Ward, The reign of Queen Victoria vol 2, 1887.
Bleibtreu, K. Geschichte der englischen Literatur im 19 Jahrhundert. Leipzig [1888].
Minto, W. The literature of the Georgian era. Ed W. Knight, Edinburgh 1894.
Saintsbury, G. A history of nineteenth-century literature 1780–1895. 1896.
—— The later nineteenth century. Edinburgh 1907.
Graham, R. The masters of Victorian literature 1837–97. 1897.
Herford, C. H. The age of Wordsworth. 1897.
Shorter, C. K. Victorian literature: sixty years of books and bookmen. 1897.
Walker, H. The age of Tennyson. 1897.
—— The literature of the Victorian era. Cambridge 1910, 1913 (abbreviated as Outlines of Victorian literature).
Omond, T. S. The romantic triumph. Edinburgh 1900.
Vaughan, C. E. The romantic revolt. Edinburgh 1907.
Kellner, L. Die englische Literatur im Zeitalter der Königin Viktoria. Leipzig 1909, 1921 (rev as Die englische Literatur der neuesten Zeit).
Magnus, L. English literature in the nineteenth century: an essay in criticism. 1909.
Richter, H. Geschichte der englischen Romantik. 2 vols Halle 1911–16.
Elton, O. A survey of English literature 1780–1830. 2 vols 1912.
—— A survey of English literature 1830–80. 2 vols 1920.
Chesterton, G. K. The Victorian age in literature. 1913.
Hudson, W. H. A short history of English literature in the nineteenth century. 1918.
Williamson, C. C. Writers of three centuries 1789–1914. 1920. On major figures, with Kingsley, Patmore, Mrs H. Ward, Mrs Meynell, R. H. Benson, Lionel Johnson.
Fehr, B. England in Zeitalter des Individualismus 1830–80. St Gall 1921.
—— Die englische Literatur des 19 und 20 Jahrhunderts. 16 pts Berlin 1923–5.
Cazamian, L. Modern times 1660–1914. 1927. Vol 2 of trn of E. Legouis and L. Cazamian, Histoire de la littérature anglaise, Paris 1924, 1954 (rev).
Wyatt, A. J. and H. Clay. Modern English literature 1798–1919. 1927, 1936 (rev).
Miller, G. M. English literature: Victorian period. New York 1933.
Batho, E. C. and B. Dobrée. The Victorians and after 1830–1914. New York 1938, 1951 (rev).
Meissner, P. Englische Literaturgeschichte, vol 3: Romantik und Viktorianismus. Berlin 1938.
Young, G. M. The age of Tennyson. Proc Br Acad 25 1939.
Chew, S. C. The nineteenth century and after. In A literary history of England, ed A. C. Baugh, New York 1948.
van Tieghem, P. Le romantisme dans la littérature européenne. Paris 1948.
Cooke, J. D. and L. Stevenson. English literature of the Victorian period. New York 1949.
Vines, S. A hundred years of English literature [1830–1940]. 1950.
Churchill, R. C. English literature of the nineteenth century. 1951.
Brett-James, A. The triple stream: four centuries of English, French and German literature. 1953.
Ward, A. C. Illustrated history of English literature, vol 3: Blake to Bernard Shaw. 1955.
Ford, B. (ed). The Pelican guide to English literature, vol 5: From Blake to Byron. 1957; vol 6: From Dickens to Hardy, 1958.

Special Periods and Groups

Hamilton, W. The aesthetic movement in England. 1882,
Douglas, G. The Blackwood group. [1897]. On Wilson, Miss Ferrier, Galt, Michael Scott, Moir, Thomas Hamilton.
McCarthy, J. Portraits of the sixties. 1903. On Dickens, Thackeray, Carlyle, Tennyson, the Newmans, Ruskin, Goldwin Smith et al.
Winchester, C. T. A group of English essayists of the early nineteenth century. New York 1910. On Jeffrey, Hazlitt, Lamb, De Quincey, Wilson, Hunt.
Kennedy, J. M. English literature 1880–1905. 1912.
Jackson, H. The eighteen-nineties: a review of art and ideas at the close of the nineteenth century. 1913.
Brailsford, H. N. Shelley, Godwin and their circle. [1913].
Russell, G. W. E. Portraits of the Seventies. 1916. On J. McCarthy, Disraeli, Acton, Labouchere, Liddon, Tennyson, Browning, 'Owen Meredith', Arnold et al.
Pierce, F. E. Currents and eddies in the English romantic generation. New Haven 1918.
Williams, H. Modern English writers 1890–1914. 1918, 1925 (rev).
Hutchinson, H. G. Portraits of the eighties. 1920. On G. W. E. Russell, Huxley, Lubbock, Morris, Swinburne, Meredith, Lang, Gilbert, Wilde et al.

Muddiman, B. The men of the nineties. 1920.
'Raymond, Ernest'. Portraits of the nineties. 1921. On Meredith, Spencer, Wilde, Morley, Stead, Hardy, J. McCarthy et al.
Cunliffe, J. W. English literature during the last half century. New York 1919, 1923 (rev).
Duthuit, G. Le rose et le noir: de Walter Pater à Oscar Wilde. Paris [1923].
Burdett, O. The Beardsley period. [1925].
Le Gallienne, R. The romantic nineties. New York 1925.
Vinciguerra, M. Romantici e decadenti inglesi. Foligno 1926.
Fehr, B. Englische Prosa von 1880 bis zur Gegenwart. Leipzig 1927.
Blunden, E. Leigh Hunt's Examiner examined 1805–25, illustrating the literary history of that period. [1928].
The eighteen-seventies. Ed H. Granville-Barker 1929.
Welby, T. E. The Victorian romantics 1850–70. 1929.
The eighteen-eighties. Ed W. de la Mare 1930.
Farmer, A. J. Le mouvement esthétique et 'décadent' en Angleterre 1873–1900. Paris 1931.
Wilson, E. Axel's castle: a study in the imaginative literature of 1870–1930. New York 1931.
Baring, M. The nineties. In his Lost lectures, 1932.
Bickley, F. The pre-Raphaelite comedy. 1932.
The eighteen-sixties. Ed J. Drinkwater 1932.
Evans, B. I. English poetry in the later nineteenth century. 1933, 1966 (rev).
Nesbitt, G. L. Benthamite reviewing: the first twelve years of the Westminster Review 1824–36. New York 1934.
Elwin, M. Old gods falling. 1939. On popular literature 1887–1914.
Hicks, G. Figures of transition: a study of British literature at the end of the nineteenth century. New York 1939.
Roberts, S. C. At the heart of the nineties. E & S 27 1941.
Taylor, H. W. 'Particular character': an early phase of a literary evolution. PMLA 60 1945.
Hough, G. The last romantics. 1949.
— The romantic poets. 1953.
Bullett, G. The English mystics. 1950.
Warren, A. H. English poetic theory 1825–65. Princeton 1951.
de Sola Pinto, V. Crisis in English poetry 1880–1940. 1951.
Buckley, J. H. The Victorian temper: a study in literary culture. 1952.
Welland, D. S. R. The Pre-Raphaelites in literature and art. 1953.
Altick, R. D. English publishing and the mass audience in 1852. SB 6 1954.
Angeli, H. R. Pre-Raphaelite twilight: the story of Charles Augustus Howell. 1954.
Briggs, A. Victorian people: some reassessments of people, institutions, ideas and events 1851–67. 1954, 1965 (Pelican) (rev).
Crawford, T. The Edinburgh Review and romantic poetry 1802–29. Auckland 1955.
Thomson, P. The Victorian heroine: a changing ideal 1837–73. Oxford 1956.
Clive, J. Scotch reviewers: the Edinburgh Review 1802–15. 1957.
Houghton, W. E. The Victorian frame of mind 1830–70. New Haven 1957.
Brand, C. P. Italy and the English Romantics. 1958.
Perkins, D. The quest for permanence: the symbolism of Wordsworth, Shelley and Keats. Cambridge Mass 1959.
Marshall, W. H. Byron, Shelley, Hunt and the Liberal. Philadelphia 1960.
Fletcher, I. The 1890s: a lost decade. Victorian Stud 4 1961.
Bloom, H. The visionary company: a reading of English romantic poetry. Garden City NY 1961.
Clark, G. K. The making of Victorian England. 1962.

Piper, H. W. The active universe: pantheism and the concept of imagination in the English romantic poets. 1962.
Renwick, W. L. English literature 1789–1815. Oxford 1963 (OHEL vol 9).
Jack, I. English literature 1815–32. Oxford 1963 (OHEL vol 10).
Stanford, D. The poets of the nineties. 1965.

Special Types of Literature

excluding poetry, fiction and drama

Elwood, A. Memoirs of the literary ladies of England from the commencement of the last century. 2 vols 1843.
Kavanagh, J. English women of letters vol 2. Leipzig 1863. On Maria Edgeworth, Jane Austen, Mrs Opie, Lady Morgan.
Queens of literature of the Victorian era. 1886. On Harriet Martineau, Charlotte Brontë, George Eliot et al.
Welsh, C. On some of the books for children of the last century. 1886.
Hamilton, C. J. Women writers: their works and ways. 2 sers 1892–3. Ser 1 on Edgeworth, Opie, Austen, Morgan, Ferrier, Mitford, Blessington; ser 2 on Hemans, Jameson, Martineau, Landon, Norton, Browning, Gaskell, Charlotte Brontë, Eliot, Procter et al.
Mayer, G. T. Women of letters. 2 vols 1894. Vol 2 on Opie, Morgan, Mitford, Shelley, Duff Gordon.
Gausseron, B. H. Les Keepsakes et les annuaires illustrés de l'époque romantique. Paris 1896.
Rickett, A. The vagabond in literature. 1906. On Hazlitt, De Quincey, Borrow, Stevenson, Jefferies.
Fueter, E. Die Geschichte der neueren Historiographie. Berlin 1911, Munich 1936 (rev); tr French, 1914.
Cairns, W. B. British criticisms of American writings 1783–1815 [–1833]. 2 pts Madison 1918–22.
Thayer, W. R. Biography in the nineteenth century. North Amer Rev 211 1920.
Barry, F. V. A century of children's books. [1922].
Bald, M. Women-writers of the nineteenth century. Cambridge 1923. On Jane Austen, the Brontës, Mrs Gaskell, George Eliot, Mrs Browning, Christina Rossetti.
Wilson, Mona. These were Muses. 1924. On Lady Morgan, Jane Porter, Frances Trollope, Sara Coleridge et al.
Casford, E. L. The magazines of the eighteen-nineties. Eugene Oregon 1929.
Hoevel, E. F. Die soziale Herkunft der neuzeitlichen Dialekt-literatur Englands. Leipzig 1929.
Engel, C. E. La littérature alpestre en France et en Angleterre au dix-huitième et au dix-neuvième siècles. Chambéry 1930.
Darton, F. J. H. From Surtees to Sassoon: some English contrasts 1838–1928. 1931. On hunting and war literature.
— Children's books in England. Cambridge 1932, 1958 (rev).
Kitchin, G. A survey of burlesque and parody in English. 1931.
James, P. Children's books of yesterday. 1933.
Law, M. H. The English familiar essay in the early nineteenth century. Philadelphia 1934.
Barnes, H. E. A history of historical writing. Norman Oklahama 1937.
Johnson, E. One mighty torrent: the drama of biography. New York 1937.
Worcester, D. The art of satire. Cambridge Mass 1940.
Thompson, J. W. and B. J. Holm. A history of historical writing. 2 vols New York 1942.
Woodward, E. L. British historians. 1943.
Green, R. L. Tellers of tales. Leicester 1946, 1953 (rev).
Neff, E. E. The poetry of history: the contribution of literature and literary scholarship to the writing of history since Voltaire. New York 1947.

Jefferson, H. A. L. Hymns in Christian worship. 1950.
Borinski, L. Englischer Geist in der Geschichte seiner Prosa. Freiburg 1951.
Egoff, S. A. Children's periodicals of the nineteenth century: a survey and bibliography. 1951 (Lib Assoc).
Keller, E. Kulturbilder aus viktorianischen Autobiographien. Berne 1951.
Gooch, G. P. History and historians in the nineteenth century. 1952 (rev).
Sewell, E. The field of nonsense. 1952.
Wellek, R. A history of modern criticism 1750–1950, vol 2: the romantic age. New Haven 1955.
Wimsatt, W. K. and C. Brooks. Literary criticism: a short history. New York 1957.
Mackerness, E. D. The heeded voice: studies in the literary status of the Anglican sermon 1830–1900. Cambridge 1959.
Walsh, W. Autobiographical literature and educational thought. Leeds 1959.
Kissane, J. Victorian mythology. Victorian Stud 6 1962.
Watson, G. The literary critics: a study of English descriptive criticism. 1962 (Pelican), 1964 (rev).
Preyer, R. Victorian wisdom literature: fragments and maxims. Victorian Stud 6 1963.

(3) SPECIAL STUDIES

Literary Movements and Ideas

Further materials will be found in the sections on Literary relations with the Continent (col 91) and Poetry: general introduction (col 159). See also collections of critical essays listed below, and the corresponding sections in vol 2.

Rushton, W. The classical and romantic school of English literature as represented by Spenser, Dryden, Pope, Scott and Wordsworth. In his Afternoon lectures on English literature, 1863.
Arnold, M. Essays in criticism. 1865. Includes The function of criticism at the present time; The literary influence of academies.
Courthope, W. J. The liberal movement in English literature. 1885.
Pater, W. Appreciations. 1889. Includes Style; Postscript (classicism and romanticism).
Wilson, S. L. The theology of modern literature. Edinburgh 1899.
Beers, H. A. A history of English romanticism in the nineteenth century. New York 1901.
Nordby, C. H. The influence of Old Norse literature upon English literature. New York 1901.
Henley, W. E. Note on romanticism. In his Views and reviews: art, 1902.
Farley, F. E. Scandinavian influences on the English romantic movement. Boston 1903.
Watts-Dunton, T. The renascence of wonder in poetry. Chambers's cyclopaedia of English literature vol 3, 1903.
Babbitt, I. The new Laokoon: an essay on the confusion of the arts. Boston 1910.
— Rousseau and romanticism. Boston 1919. See A. O. Lovejoy, MLN 35 1920.
Chapman, E. M. English literature and religion 1800–1900. Boston 1910.
More, P. E. The drift of romanticism. In his Shelburne essays ser 8, Boston 1913.
Neilson, W. A. The essentials of poetry. New York 1913.
de Meester, M. E. Oriental influences in the English literature of the nineteenth century. Heidelberg 1915.
Richardson, G. F. A neglected aspect of the English romantic revolt. Berkeley 1915.
Raleigh, W. Romance: two lectures. Princeton 1916.
Quiller-Couch, A. T. On the terms 'classic' and 'romantic'. In his Studies in literature ser 1, Cambridge 1918.
Cazamian, L. L'évolution psychologique et la littérature en Angleterre 1660–1914. Paris 1920.
— Le romantisme en France et en Angleterre. Etudes Anglaises 1 1937.
Egan, R. F. The genesis of the theory of 'art for art's sake' in Germany and in England. 2 pts Northampton Mass 1921–4.
Frye, P. H. The terms classic and romantic. In his Romance and tragedy, Boston 1922.
Herford, C. H. Romanticism in the modern world. E & S 8 1922.
Inge, W. R. The Victorian age. Cambridge 1922.
Jones, R. F. Some reflections on the English romantic revival. Washington Univ Stud 9 1922.
Tinker, C. B. Nature's simple plan. Princeton 1922.
Cazamian, M. L. Le roman et les idées en Angleterre [1]: L'influence de la science (1860–90); [2]: L'anti-intellectualisme et l'esthétisme (1880–1900); [3]: Les doctrines d'action et de l'aventure (1880–1914). 3 vols Strasbourg 1923–55.
Grierson, H. J. C. Classical and romantic. Cambridge 1923; rptd in his Background of English literature, 1925.
Murry, J. M. Romanticism. Adelphi 1 1923.
Barker, F. The modern consciousness in English literature. E & S 9 1924.
Lovejoy, A. O. On the discrimination of romanticisms. PMLA 39 1924.
— 'Nature' as aesthetic norm. MLN 42 1927; rptd with above in his Essays, Baltimore 1948.
— Optimism and romanticism. PMLA 42 1927.
— et al. Symposium on romanticism. JHI 2 1941.
Smith, L. P. Four words: romantic, originality, creative, genius. 1924 (Soc for Pure Eng, tract no 17); rptd in his Words and idioms, 1925.
Kaufman, P. Defining romanticism: a survey and a program. MLN 40 1925.
Ker, W. P. Collected essays. Ed C. Whibley 2 vols 1925. Includes Romance; On the value of the terms 'classical' and 'romantic' as applied to literature.
Knickerbocker, W. S. Creative Oxford: its influence in Victorian literature. Syracuse NY 1925.
Robertson, J. G. The reconciliation of classic and romantic. Cambridge 1925.
Abercrombie, L. Romanticism. 1926.
Brinton, C. The political ideas of the English romanticists. Oxford 1926.
Needham, H. A. Le développement de l'esthétique sociologique en France et en Angleterre, au dix-neuvième siècle. Paris 1926.
Powell, A. E. (Dodds). The romantic theory of poetry. 1926.
Shafer, R. Christianity and naturalism. New Haven 1926. On Coleridge, Newman, Huxley, Arnold, Butler, Hardy.
Hussey, C. The picturesque: studies in a point of view. 1927.
Pierce, F. E. Romanticism and other isms. JEGP 26 1927.
Railo, E. The haunted castle: a study of the elements of English romanticism. 1927.
Burgum, E. B. Victorianism. Sewanee Rev 36 1928.
— Romanticism. Kenyon Rev 3 1941.
Clark, K. The Gothic revival. 1928, 1950 (enlarged).
Fairchild, H. N. The noble savage: a study in romantic naturalism. New York 1928.
— The romantic quest. New York 1931.
— The romantic movement in England. PMLA 55 1940.
— Religious trends in English poetry, vol 3: 1780–1830 Romantic faith. New York 1949; vol 4: 1830–80 Christi-

anity and romanticism in the Victorian era, 1957; vol 5: 1880–1920 Gods of a changing poetry, 1962.
Blunden, E. Nature in literature. 1929.
Draper, J. W. The summa of romanticism. Colonnade 14 1929.
Huscher, H. Über Eigenart und Ursprung des englischen Naturgefühls. Leipzig 1929.
Kellett, E. E. The whirligig of taste. 1929.
Priestley, J. B. English humour. 1929.
Rosenblatt, L. L'idée de l'art pour l'art dans la littérature anglaise pendant la période victorienne. Paris 1931.
Yvon, P. Le gothique et la renaissance gothique en Angleterre 1750–1880. Caen 1931.
Sickells, E. M. The gloomy egoist: moods and themes of melancholy from Gray to Keats. New York 1932.
Strehler, E. M. Der Dekadenzgedanke im Yellow Book und Savoy. Turbenthal 1932.
Praz, M. The romantic agony. Tr A. Davidson 1933, 1951, [1954].
Bruce, H. L. Beneath the surface 1800–15. In Essays in criticism ser 2, Berkeley 1934.
Leisering, W. Das Motiv des Einsiedlers in der englischen Literatur des 18 Jahrhunderts und der Hochromantik. Halle 1935.
Routh, H. V. Money, morals and manners as revealed in modern literature. 1935.
—— Towards the twentieth century: essays in the spiritual history of the nineteenth century. 1937.
Beach, J. W. The concept of nature in nineteenth-century English poetry. New York 1936.
Buck, P. M. The world's great age: the story of a century's search for a philosophy of life. New York 1936.
Lucas, F. L. The decline and fall of the romantic ideal. Cambridge 1936.
Mead, G. H. Movements of thought in the nineteenth century. Chicago 1936.
Thurmann, E. Der Niederschlag der evangelischen Bewegung in der englischen Literatur. Münster 1936.
Young, G. M. Victorian England: portrait of an age. Oxford 1936, 1953.
Bush, D. Mythology and the romantic tradition in English poetry. New York 1937, 1963.
Gill, F. C. The romantic movement and Methodism. 1937.
Stevenson, L. Prude's progress. Virginia Quart Rev 13 1937.
Addison, A. Romanticism and the Gothic revival. New York 1938.
Decker, C. R. The aesthetic revolt against naturalism in Victorian criticism. PMLA 53 1938.
Madle, H. Die Maschine und der technische Fortschritt in der englischen Literatur des 19 und 20 Jahrhunderts. Breslau 1938.
Reid, M. J. C. The Arthurian legend: comparison of treatment in modern and medieval literature. Edinburgh [1938].
Schilling, B. Nineteenth-century England and the history of ideas. Eng Jnl 27 1938.
Nitchie, E. Romantic permutations and combinations in England. PMLA 55 1940.
Welker, J. J. The position of the Quarterlies on some classical dogmas. SP 37 1940.
Barzun, J. Darwin, Marx, Wagner: critique of a heritage. Boston 1941.
—— Romanticism and the modern ego. Boston 1943.
Shine, H. Carlyle and the Saint-Simonians: the concept of historical periodicity. Baltimore 1941.
Hook, S. The hero in history. New York 1943.
Baldensperger, F. 1793–94: climacteric times for 'romantic' tendencies in English ideology. JHI 5 1944.
Bentley, E. R. A century of hero-worship: a study of the idea of heroism in Carlyle and Nietzsche. Philadelphia 1944.
Liljegren, S. B. Essence and attitude in English romanticism. Upsala 1945.
Fogle, R. H. A recent attack upon romanticism. College Eng April 1948.
James, D. G. The romantic comedy. Oxford 1948.
Priestley, F. E. L. Newton and the romantic conception of nature. UTQ 17 1948.
Thomson, J. A. K. The classical background of English literature. 1948.
—— Classical influences on English poetry. 1951.
Dingle, H. Science and literary criticism. 1949.
Wellek, R. The concept of 'romanticism' in literary history. Comparative Lit 1 1949.
Willey, B. Nineteenth-century studies: Coleridge to Matthew Arnold. 1949.
—— More nineteenth-century studies: a group of honest doubters. 1956.
Auden, W. H. The enchafèd flood: or the romantic iconography of the sea. New York 1950.
Bowra, C. M. The romantic imagination. Cambridge Mass 1950.
Heath-Stubbs, J. The darkling plain: a study of the later fortunes of romanticism in English poetry from George Darley to W. B. Yeats. 1950.
Steegmann, J. Consort of taste 1830–70. 1950. On Victorian aesthetics.
Culler, A. D. Aspects of Victorian literature. Yale Rev 41 1952.
Houghton, W. E. Victorian anti-intellectualism. JHI 13 1952.
Jump, J. D. Weekly reviewing in the eighteen-sixties. RES new ser 3 1952.
Wallace, M. W. English character and the English literary tradition. 1952.
Abrams, M. H. The mirror and the lamp: romantic theory and the critical tradition. New York 1953.
Holloway, J. The Victorian sage: studies in argument. 1953.
Kirk, R. The conservative mind from Burke to Santayana. Chicago 1953.
Leroy, G. C. Perplexed prophets: six nineteenth-century British authors. Philadelphia 1953. On Carlyle, Arnold, Ruskin, Thomson (BV), Rossetti, Wilde.
Read, H. The true voice of feeling: studies in English romantic poetry. 1953.
Foerster, D. M. The critical attack upon the epic in the English romantic movement. PMLA 69 1954.
—— Critical approval of epic poetry in the age of Wordsworth. PMLA 70 1955.
Gérard, A. L'idée romantique de la poésie de l'Angleterre. Paris 1955.
Roppen, G. Evolution and poetic belief: a study of some Victorian and modern writers. Oslo 1956. On Tennyson, Browning, Swinburne, Meredith, Hardy, Butler, Shaw, Wells.
Williams, R. Culture and society 1780–1950. 1958, 1961 (Pelican), 1963 (with postscript).
Duncan, J. E. The revival of metaphysical poetry: the history of a style, 1800 to the present. Minneapolis 1959.
Eckhoff, L. The aesthetic movement in English literature. Oslo 1959.
Clive, J. The romantic enlightenment. New York 1960.
Pizer, D. Evolutionary ideas in late nineteenth-century English and American literary criticism. Jnl of Aesthetics 19 1961.
Turnell, M. Modern literature and Christian faith. 1961.
Peckham, M. Beyond the tragic vision: the quest for identity in the nineteenth century. New York 1962.
Benziger, J. Images of eternity: studies in the poetry of religious vision from Wordsworth to T. S. Eliot. Carbondale 1963.
Rodway, A. The romantic conflict. 1963.
Miller, J. H. The disappearance of God: five nineteenth-century writers. Cambridge Mass 1964. On De Quincey, Browning, Emily Brontë, Arnold, Hopkins.

Charlesworth, B. Dark passages: the decadent consciousness in Victorian literature. Madison 1965.

Knoepflmacher, U. C. Religious humanism and the Victorian novel: George Eliot, Walter Pater and Samuel Butler. Princeton 1965.

Wilkie, B. Romantic poets and epic tradition. Madison 1965.

Collections of Essays

Miscellaneous unconnected studies, mainly rptd from periodicals. Brief and partial descriptions are given of the contents of some of the earlier collections.

Hazlitt, W. The spirit of the age: or contemporary portraits. 1825. On Bentham, Godwin, Coleridge, Edward Irving, Horne Tooke, Scott, Byron, Southey, Wordsworth, Mackintosh, Malthus, Gifford, Jeffrey, Brougham, Burdett, Eldon, Wilberforce, Canning, Campbell, Crabbe, Moore, Hunt, Lamb, Washington Irving.

Pichot, A. Voyage historique et littéraire en Angleterre et en Ecosse. 3 vols Paris 1825; tr 2 vols 1825. On Joanna Baillie, Wordsworth, Coleridge, Southey, Moore, Byron, Scott et al.

Chorley, H. F. The authors of England: a series of medallion portraits. 1838, 1861. On Mrs. Hemans, Scott, Byron, Southey, Lady Blessington, Coleridge, Lytton, Lady Morgan, Shelley, Moore, Lamb, Miss Mitford, Campbell, Wordsworth.

Macaulay, T. B. Critical and historical essays. 3 vols 1843. On Byron, Southey, Robert Montgomery et al.

Horne, R. H. A new spirit of the age. 2 vols 1844; ed W. Jerrold 1907 (WC). On Dickens, Barham, Landor, the Howitts, Talfourd, Milnes, Hartley Coleridge, Sydney Smith, Jerrold, Wordsworth, Hunt, Tennyson, Macaulay, Hood, Hook, the Brownings, Lytton, Mrs Shelley, Robert Montgomery, Carlyle, Taylor, Ainsworth, Marryat et al.

Jeffrey, F. Contributions to the Edinburgh Review. 4 vols 1844. On Campbell, Hazlitt, Byron, Scott, Keats, Rogers, Moore, Wordsworth, Mrs Hemans, Maria Edgeworth, Galt et al.

Gilfillan, G. A gallery of literary portraits. 3 sers Edinburgh 1845–54; [selection] ed W. R. Nicoll 1909 (EL). On Wilson, Dobell, A. Smith, Massey, Hazlitt, Macaulay, Lytton, Carlyle et al.

Lester, J. W. Criticisms. 1847, 1848, 1853. On Pollok, Alford, Atherstone, Croly, Coleridge, Heber, Carlyle, Irving et al.

Sterling, J. Essays and tales. Ed J. C. Hare 2 vols 1848. Vol 1: Coleridge, Napier, Carlyle, Tennyson et al.

Powell, T. Pictures of the living authors of England. New York 1849. On Macaulay, Henry Taylor, Horne, Mackay, Lytton, Bailey, Mrs Jameson, Jerrold, Forster, Marston.

Chasles, P. Etudes sur la littérature et les moeurs de l'Angleterre au dix-neuvieme siècle. Paris [1850]. On Byron et al.

Richardson, D. L. Literary recreations. 1852. On Lytton, poetry and Utilitarianism, Jeffrey, Dickens and Thackeray, Byron's opinion of Pope, Hartley Coleridge, Carlyle etc.

Hannay, J. Satire and satirists: 6 lectures. 1854. On Byron, Moore et al.

Whipple, E. P. Essays and reviews. 2 vols Boston 1856.

Brimley, G. Essays. Ed W. G. Clark, Cambridge 1858. On Tennyson, Wordsworth, Patmore, Carlyle, Thackeray, Dickens, Kingsley et al.

Hayward, A. Biographical and critical essays. 5 vols 1858–74. On Sydney Smith, Rogers, James Smith, Maria Edgeworth, Canning et al.

—— Sketches of eminent statesmen and writers. 2 vols 1880. On Byron, Tennyson et al.

Bayne, P. Essays, biographical, critical and miscellaneous. Edinburgh 1859. On Tennyson, Mrs Browning, the Brontës, Ruskin et al.

—— Lessons from my masters: Carlyle, Tennyson and Ruskin. New York 1879.

Kingsley, C. Miscellanies. 2 vols 1859. Vol 1: Tennyson, Alexander Smith, Shelley, Byron, Burns et al.

McNicoll, T. Essays on English literature. 1861. On Pollok, Carlyle, Dobell, Alexander Smith, Gilfillan, Tennyson, 'Christopher North', Browning, Landor et al.

Japp, A. H. Three great teachers of our own time: Carlyle, Tennyson and Ruskin. 1865.

Stirling, J. H. Jerrold, Tennyson and Macaulay: critical essays. 1868.

Greg, W. R. Literary and social judgments. 1869 (2nd edn), 1873, 1877 (enlarged). On false morality of lady novelists, Kingsley, Carlyle etc.

Friswell, J. H. Modern men of letters. 1870. On Lemon, Sala, Lever, Ainsworth, Robertson.

Hutton, R. H. Essays, theological and literary. Vol 2, 1871. On Wordsworth, Shelley, Browning, George Eliot, Clough.

—— Essays on some of the modern guides of English thought. 1887. On Carlyle, Newman, Arnold, George Eliot, Maurice.

—— Criticisms on contemporary thought and thinkers. 2 vols 1894. On Carlyle, Dickens, Stephen, Mill, Arnold, Clough, Huxley, Bagehot, Ruskin, Wordsworth, Darwin.

—— Brief literary criticisms. 1906.

Lowell, J. R. My study windows. 1871. On Carlyle, Swinburne et al.

Morley, J. Critical miscellanies. 4 vols 1871–1908. On Byron, Carlyle, Macaulay, Mill, George Eliot, Harriet Martineau, W. R. Greg et al.

—— Studies in literature. 1891. On Wordsworth, Maine, Browning, Macvey Napier.

Minto, W. Manual of English prose literature. Edinburgh 1872.

Buchanan, R. W. Master spirits. 1873. On Dickens, Tennyson, Browning, William Miller et al.

Maginn, W. A gallery of illustrious literary characters (1830–8) drawn by Daniel Maclise and accompanied by notices chiefly by William Maginn. Ed W. Bates [1873], 1883 (as The Maclise portrait-gallery). Rptd from Fraser's Mag 1830–8.

Milnes, R. M. (Baron Houghton). Monographs, personal and social. 1873. On Wiseman, Landor, the Berrys, Sydney Smith, Lady Ashburton et al.

Gosse, Sir E. *See col 1432, below.*

Masson, D. Wordsworth, Shelley, Keats and other essays. 1874.

—— Edinburgh sketches and memories. 1892. On Scott, Carlyle, C. K. Sharpe, J. H. Burton, John Brown.

Stephen, L. Hours in a library. 3 sers 1874–9. On Scott, De Quincey, Hazlitt, Disraeli, the first Edinburgh reviewers, Wordsworth, Landor, Macaulay, Charlotte Brontë, Kingsley et al.

—— Studies of a biographer. 4 vols 1898–1902. On Wordsworth, Scott, Arnold, Jowett, Tennyson, Browning, Ruskin, Bagehot, Huxley, Froude, Southey, Trollope, Stevenson et al.

Smith, G. B. Poets and novelists. 1875. On Thackeray, Peacock, Buchanan, E. B. Browning, the Brontës et al.

Swinburne, A. C. Essays and studies. 1875. On Rossetti, Morris, Arnold, Shelley, Byron, Coleridge et al.

—— Miscellanies. 1886. On Wordsworth and Byron, Landor, Keats, Tennyson, Emily Brontë, Reade et al. Studies in prose and poetry. 1894. On Scott, Jowett, Wilkie Collins, Tennyson, Shelley et al.

Davey, S. Darwin, Carlyle and Dickens, with other essays. 1876.

Lancaster, H. H. Essays and reviews. Edinburgh 1876. On Macaulay, Carlyle, Ruskin, George Eliot, Thackeray et al.

Martineau, H. Biographical sketches. 1869, 1876 (rev). On Mrs Opie, Wilson, Lockhart, Miss Mitford,

Charlotte Brontë, Rogers, Croker, De Quincey, Macaulay, Mrs Jameson, Landor, Procter.

Yates, E. Celebrities at home. 3 sers 1877–9. On Tennyson, Disraeli, Carlyle, 'Ouida', Newman, Miss Braddon, Sala, Milnes, Ruskin, Jowett, Wilkie Collins, Ainsworth et al.

Dowden, E. Studies in literature 1789–1877. 1878.

— Transcripts and studies. 1888.

— New studies in literature. 1895.

Bagehot, W. Literary studies. Ed R. H. Hutton 2 vols 1879; ed G. Sampson 1911 (EL). On the first Edinburgh reviewers, H. Coleridge, Shelley, Thackeray, Scott, Dickens, Macaulay, Clough, Crabb Robinson, Wordsworth, Tennyson, Browning et al.

Spedding, J. Reviews and discussions. 1879. On Peacock, Dickens, Tennyson, H. Coleridge.

Walsh, W. S. Pen pictures of modern authors. New York 1882.

— Pen pictures of earlier Victorian authors. New York 1884.

Skelton, J. Essays in history and biography. Edinburgh 1883. On Macaulay, Thackeray, Charlotte Brontë, Disraeli et al.

Birrell, A. Obiter dicta. 1885.

— Res judicatae. 1892.

— More obiter dicta. 1924.

Montégut, E. Ecrivains modernes de l'Angleterre. 3 sers Paris 1885–92. Ser 1: George Eliot, Charlotte Brontë, 'Guy Livingstone'; ser 2: Mrs Gaskell, Mrs Browning, Borrow, Tennyson.

Smith, J. C. Writings by the way. Edinburgh 1885. On Carlyle, Hamilton, Spalding, Moir et al.

Dawson, G. Biographical lectures. 1886. On Pope and Byron, Lamb, Wordsworth, Coleridge, Carlyle, Thackeray, Hood, Cobbett, Cobden.

Dawson, W. J. Quest and vision. 1886. On Shelley, Wordsworth, Arnold, Browning, Tennyson, George Eliot, J. Thomson et al.

— The makers of modern prose. 1889. On Macaulay, Landor, De Quincey, Lamb, Carlyle, Froude, Ruskin, Newman et al.

Lang, A. Letters to dead authors. 1886.

— Essays in little. 1891.

Buchanan, R. W. A look round literature. 1887. On Peacock, Dobell, George Eliot, Lewes, Rossetti et al.

James, H. Partial portraits. 1888. On Stevenson, George Eliot, Trollope et al.

— Views and reviews. Boston 1908.

— Notes on novelists. 1914.

Salt, H. S. Literary sketches. 1888. On Shelley, Tennyson, J. Thomson, Godwin, De Quincey et al.

Pater, W. Appreciations. 1889. On Wordsworth, Coleridge, Lamb, Rossetti et al.

Robertson, J. M. Essays towards a critical method. 1889.

— Modern humanists: sociological studies of Carlyle, Mill, Emerson, Arnold, Ruskin and Spencer. 1891.

— New essays towards a critical method. 1897. On Shelley, Keats, Clough et al.

— Criticisms. 2 vols 1902–3. On Jane Austen, Lang, Ruskin et al.

Forster, J. Four great teachers: Ruskin, Carlyle, Emerson and Browning. 1890.

Henley, W. E. Views and reviews: literature. 1890.

Saintsbury, G. Essays in English literature 1780–1860. 2 sers 1890–5.

— Corrected impressions. 1895.

Steuart, J. A. Letters to living authors. 1890. On Meredith, Ruskin, Froude, Hardy, Swinburne, Caine, Stevenson, Lang, Black, Buchanan, Blackmore et al.

Jacobs, J. George Eliot, Matthew Arnold, Browning, Newman. 1891.

— Literary studies. 1895.

Scherer, E. Essays on English literature. Tr G. Saintsbury 1891 (with introd). On George Eliot, Mill, Wordsworth, Carlyle, Disraeli et al.

Woodberry, G. E. Studies in letters and life. Boston 1891.

— Makers of literature. New York 1900. On Shelley, Landor, Browning, Byron, Arnold, Coleridge et al.

Watson, W. Excursions in criticism. 1893. On R. H. Hutton, Saintsbury, Dobson et al.

Bridges, R. Overheard in Arcady. 1894. On Meredith, Kipling, Stevenson, Barrie.

Monkhouse, A. Books and plays. 1894. On Meredith, Borrow, Stevenson, Henley.

Harrison, F. Studies in early Victorian literature. 1895. On Thackeray, Disraeli, Dickens, Trollope, the Brontës et al.

— Tennyson, Ruskin, Mill and other literary estimates. 1899.

Le Fère-Deumier, J. Célébrités anglaises. Paris 1895.

Lilly, W. S. Four: English humourists of the nineteenth century. 1895. On Dickens, Thackeray, George Eliot, Carlyle.

Le Gallienne, R. Retrospective reviews: a literary log. 2 vols 1896.

— Attitudes and avowals. 1910. On Grant Allen, Tennyson, Meredith, Stephen Phillips, Symons, Watson.

Quiller-Couch, A. T. Adventures in criticism. 1896. On Reade, H. Kingsley, Kinglake, Calverley, Stevenson.

— Studies in literature. 3 sers Cambridge 1918–30. On Meredith, Hardy, Coleridge, Arnold, Swinburne, Reade et al.

— Charles Dickens and other Victorians. Cambridge 1925. On Thackeray, Disraeli, Mrs Gaskell, Trollope.

Thomson, James. Biographical and critical studies. Ed B. Dobell 1896. On Shelley, Wilson, Hogg, Browning.

Stearns, F. P. Modern English prose writers. 1897. On Macaulay, Carlyle, Froude, Scott, Thackeray, Dickens, George Eliot, Müller, Arnold.

Symons, A. Studies in two literatures. 1897. On Jefferies, J. Thomson, Hake, Symonds.

— Studies in prose and verse. 1904. On De Quincey, Pater, Morris, Buchanan, Yeats, Dobson, Dowson.

— Figures of several centuries. 1916. On Lamb, Beddoes, Hardy, Patmore.

— Dramatis personae. Indianapolis 1923, 1925 (rev). On Emily Brontë, Francis Thompson et al.

Traill, H. D. The new fiction and other essays on literary subjects. 1897.

Clark, J. S. A study of English prose writers. New York 1898.

Dixon, W. M. In the republic of letters. 1898. On Arnold, Meredith, the De Veres, the romantic revival.

Wilson, P. Leaders in literature. Edinburgh 1898. On Carlyle, George Eliot, the Brownings, Arnold, Spencer, Ruskin.

Adams, F. Essays in modernity. 1899. On Tennyson, Kipling, Swinburne, Shelley et al.

Chiarini, G. Studi e ritratti letterari. Leghorn 1900.

Gates, L. E. Studies and appreciations. New York 1900. On Tennyson, Charlotte Brontë et al.

'Rutherford, Mark' (W. H. White). Pages from a journal. 1900. On Carlyle, Scott, Byron, Goethe, Arnold.

— Last pages from a journal. 1915. On George Eliot, William Sewell, Wordsworth, Shelley, Dorothy Wordsworth, Caleb Morris.

Brownell, W. C. Victorian prose masters. New York 1901. On Thackeray, Carlyle, Arnold, Ruskin, Meredith.

Collins, J. C. Ephemera critica: or plain truths about current literature. 1901. On Stevenson, De Quincey, Palgrave, Phillips et al.

— Studies in poetry and criticism. 1905. On Byron, Watson, Massey et al.

— Posthumous essays. Ed L. C. Collins 1912. On Arnold, Browning, Tennyson et al.

Murray, H. Robert Buchanan: a critical appreciation, and other essays. 1901. On Swinburne, Ruskin, Kipling, the Brownings, Marie Corelli et al.
Paul, H. Men and letters. 1901. On Arnold, Macaulay et al.
— Stray leaves. 1906. On George Eliot, Peacock, Lamb, Cory et al.
Burton, R. Forces in fiction and other essays. [1902].
'Paston, George' (E. M. Symonds). Little memoirs of the nineteenth century. 1902. On Haydon, Lady Morgan, Lady Hester Stanhope, the Howitts et al.
Bryce, J. Studies in contemporary biography. 1903. On Disraeli, A. P. Stanley, T. H. Green, Trollope, J. R. Green, Freeman, Sidgwick, Acton, Gladstone et al.
Gould, G. M. Biographic clinics: the origin of the ill-health of De Quincey, Carlyle, Darwin, Huxley and Browning. 2 vols Philadelphia 1903–4. Vol 2: George Eliot, Lewes, Jane Carlyle, Spencer et al.
Lyttleton, A. T. Modern poets of faith, doubt and paganism, and other essays. 1904. On Tennyson, Browning, Arnold, Clough, Carlyle, George Eliot, Swinburne, Thomson.
More, P. E. The Shelburne essays. 8 sers New York 1904, Boston 1913. Ser 2: Hazlitt, Lamb, Kipling, FitzGerald, Crabbe, Meredith; ser 3: Swinburne, Rossetti, Browning, Byron, Shorthouse; ser 4: Keats, Lamb; ser 5: Dickens, Mrs Gaskell, Gissing; ser 7: Shelley, Wordsworth, Hood, Tennyson, Morris; ser 8: Newman, Pater, Huxley.
— New Shelburne essays. Princeton 1928. On Borrow, Trollope.
Ainger, A. Lectures and essays. 2 vols 1905.
Nevinson, H. W. Books and personalities. 1905. On Arnold, Hardy, FitzGerald, Yeats, Lady Gregory, A.E. et al.
Fyvie, J. Some literary eccentrics. 1906. On Landor, Hazlitt, Crabb Robinson, Babbage, Jerrold.
Lord, W. F. The mirror of the century. 1906. On George Eliot, W. E. Norris, Jane Austen, the Brontës, Thackeray, Dickens, Lytton, the Kingsleys, Disraeli, Trollope, Reade.
Rickett, A. Personal forces in modern literature. 1906. On Newman, Martineau, Huxley, Wordsworth, Keats, Rossetti, Dickens, Hazlitt, De Quincey.
Elton, O. Modern studies. 1907. On Tennyson, Swinburne, Meredith et al.
Baker, James. Literary and biographical studies. 1908. On Macaulay, Blackmore, Coleridge, Southey, Tennyson.
Ritchie, A. T. Blackstick papers. 1908. On Mrs Hemans, Mary and Agnes Berry, 'Jacob Omnium' (M. J. Higgins), Mrs Gaskell.
Scott-James, R. A. Modernism and romance. 1908. On Hardy, Stevenson et al.
— The making of literature. 1928. On Arnold, Pater et al.
Laurent, R. Etudes anglaises. Paris 1910. On Pater, Wilde, Pre-Raphaelitism.
Bailey, J. Poets and poetry. Oxford 1911. On Wordsworth, Scott, Keats, Shelley, Swinburne, Pater, FitzGerald, Meredith.
— The continuity of letters. Oxford 1923. On Shelley, Wordsworth, Thackeray et al.
Benson, A. C. The leaves of the tree: studies in biography. 1911. On J. K. Stephen, F. W. H. Myers, C. Kingsley, Arnold.
Jack, A. A. Poetry and prose. 1911. On Wordsworth, Byron, Arnold, Meredith.
Johnson, L. Post liminium: essays and critical papers. Ed. T. Whittemore 1911. On Pater, Borrow, Stevenson et al.
— Reviews and critical papers. Ed R. Shafer 1921. On Stevenson, Davidson, Morris, Mrs H. Ward, Dobson, Kipling et al.
Figgis, D. Studies and appreciations. 1912. On Synge, Yeats, Browning, Watson, Trench, Bridges, Meredith, Dickens, Thackeray, Butler.
Jackson, H. All manner of folk. 1912. On Lear, Synge, Carpenter, Jefferies, Morris, Meredith et al.
Olivero, F. Saggi de letteratura inglese. Bari 1913.
— Studi sul romanticismo inglese. Bari 1914.
Vincent, L. H. Dandies and men of letters. Boston 1913. On Byron, Rogers, Moore, Thomas Hope, Peacock, C. K. Sharpe, Disraeli, Lytton, Crabb Robinson et al.
Freeman, J. The moderns: essays in literary criticism. 1916. On Shaw, Wells, Hardy, Patmore, F. Thompson, Bridges.
— English portraits and essays. 1924. On Stevenson, Cobbett, Hewlett, Gosse, Patmore.
Watts-Dunton, T. Old familiar faces. 1916. On Borrow, Rossetti, Tennyson, Christina Rossetti, Hake, de Tabley, Morris, F. H. Groome.
Meynell, A. Hearts of controversy. 1917. On Dickens, Tennyson, Swinburne.
Sherman, S. P. On contemporary literature. New York 1917. On George Moore, Synge, Austin, Meredith.
Chislett, W. The classical influence in English literature in the nineteenth century, and other essays. Boston 1918.
Waugh, A. Tradition and change: studies in contemporary literature. 1919. On Phillips, Lionel Johnson, Symons, Dickens, Swinburne, Butler, Stevenson.
Clutton-Brock, A. Essays on books. [1920]. On Dickens, Swinburne, Keats et al.
Thorndike, A. H. Literature in a changing age. New York 1920.
Coleridge, S. Letters to my grandson on the glory of English prose. 1922.
Du Bos, C. Approximations. 4 sers Paris 1922–30. On Shelley, Browning, Pater, Hardy et al.
'Lee, Vernon'. The handling of words, and other studies in literary psychology. 1923. On De Quincey, Landor, Carlyle, Meredith, Kipling, Stevenson, Hardy.
Williams, S. T. Studies in Victorian literature. New York [1923].
Ellis, S. M. Mainly Victorian. 1925. On Whyte-Melville, J. Grant, Smedley, Agnes Strickland, Noel, Kenealy, Dobson, Baring-Gould, Lord A. Douglas, Wratislaw, Mrs Antrobus.
Ker, W. P. Collected essays. Ed C. Whibley 2 vols 1925. On Scott, Byron, Keats, Hazlitt, Tennyson, Browning et al.
Larbaud, V. Ce vice impuni, la lecture. Paris 1925. On Henley, Patmore, F. Thompson, Wells, Hardy, Bennett et al.
Marks, J. Genius and disaster. New York 1925. On J. Thomson, Swinburne, F. Thompson.
Vinciguerra, M. Romantici e decadenti inglesi. Foligno 1925. On Carlyle, Wilde, Hardy, Stevenson, Moore, Synge.
Woolf, V. The common reader. 1925. On Jane Austen, George Eliot, Miss Mitford, the Brontës.
— The common reader: second series. 1932. On De Quincey, Hazlitt, Gissing, Hardy et al.
— The death of the moth and other essays. 1942.
— The moment and other essays. 1947.
— The captain's death-bed and other essays. 1950.
Fernandez, R. Messages. Paris 1926. On Newman, Meredith, Pater.
Newbolt, H. Studies green and gray. 1926. On Shorthouse, Peacock, Scott, Alice Meynell, Barham.
Baumann, A. A. The last Victorians. 1927. On Bagehot, Trollope, Jowett, Wyndham, Labouchere.
Bridges, R. Collected essays, papers etc. 9 vols Oxford 1927–35. On Keats, de Tabley, Mary Coleridge, Darley, Kipling.
'Maurois, André'. Etudes anglaises: Dickens, Walpole, Ruskin et Wilde. Paris 1927.
Ralli, A. Critiques. 1927. On the Brontës, Morris, Hardy, Swinburne, Borrow, Pater, FitzGerald et al.
Harper, G. M. Spirit of delight. New York [1928]. On

Coleridge, the Wordsworths, Hardy, Hudson, Housman, Arnold.
— Literary appreciations. Indianapolis 1937.
Weygandt, C. Tuesdays at ten. Philadelphia 1928. On L. Johnson, Doughty, Yeats, F. Thompson, Phillips, Dobson, Hudson et al.
Bradley, A. C. A miscellany. 1929. On Tennyson, Jane Austen, Shelley, Coleridge, Keats et al.
Ince, R. B. Calverley and some Cambridge wits of the nineteenth century. 1929. On Milnes, Sterling, Kinglake.
'Kingsmill, Hugh' (H. K. Lunn). After Puritanism 1850–1900. 1929. From Shakespeare to Dean Farrar, Samuel Butler, Frank Harris, W. T. Stead.
Feiling, K. Sketches in nineteenth-century biography. 1930. On Croker, Southey and Wordsworth, Coleridge, Newman, Lytton, Bagchot.
Blunden, E. Votive tablets. 1931. On Southey, Leigh Hunt, Shelley, Trelawny, Cobbett, Lamb, Hood, Beddoes, H. Coleridge, Darley et al.
Chauvet, P. Sept essais de littérature anglaise. Paris 1931. On Thomson, Wilde, Arnold, Tennyson, E. B. Browning.
Lockhart, J. G. Literary criticism. Ed M. C. Hildyard, Oxford 1931. On Susan Ferrier, Hook, Jeffrey, Tennyson et al.
MacCarthy, D. Portraits. 1931. On Blunt, Burton, Clough, Disraeli, Meredith, George Moore, Raleigh, Ruskin, J. K. Stephen, Stevenson et al.
— Criticism. 1932. On Butler, Browning, Patmore, Yeats.
— Humanities. 1953.
Partridge, E. Literary sessions. 1932. On R. E. Landor, Horne, Mrs Clive et al.
The great Victorians. Ed H. J. and H. Massingham 1932.
Elwin, M. Victorian wallflowers. 1934. On John Wilson, Maginn, Barham, Ainsworth, Forster, Wilkie Collins, Mrs H. Wood, Blackmore, 'Ouida'.
Milner, G. The threshold of the Victorian age. 1934. On Macaulay, Carlyle, Tennyson and Dickens.
Clarke, Isabel C. Six portraits. 1935. On Jane Austen, George Eliot, Mrs Oliphant, John Oliver Hobbes et al.
Forster, E. M. Abinger harvest. 1936. On H. O. Sturgis, Jane Austen, Coleridge, Keats, Wilfrid Blunt.
From Anne to Victoria. Ed B. Dobrée 1937. On Scott, Wordsworth, Coleridge, Keats, Shelley, Byron et al.
Lucas, F. L. Eight Victorian poets. Cambridge 1930, 1940 (as Ten Victorian poets), 1948 (rev).
Abercrombie, L. et al. Revaluations: studies in biography. Oxford 1931.
Abbott, W. C. Adventures in reputation. Cambridge Mass 1935.
Baumann, A. A. Personalities. 1936.
Boas, F. S. From Richardson to Pinero: some innovators and idealists. 1936.
Boyle, E. Biographical essays 1790–1890. Oxford 1936.
Read, H. In defence of Shelley and other essays. 1936.
— Collected essays in literary criticism. 1938, 1951 (rev).
— The tenth Muse: essays in criticism. 1957.
Smith, L. P. Reperusals and re-collections. 1936.
Young, G. M. Daylight and champaign. 1937, 1948 (rev).
— Today and yesterday. 1948.
— Last essays. 1950.
Mackail, J. W. Studies in humanism. 1938.
Murry, J. M. Heaven—and earth. 1938.
— Katherine Mansfield and other literary portraits. 1949.
— John Clare and other studies. 1950.
Lieder, P. R. Eminent British poets of the nineteenth century. 2 vols New York 1938.
Lippincott, B. E. Victorian critics of democracy: Carlyle, Ruskin, Arnold, Stephen, Maine, Lecky. Minneapolis 1938.
Cole, G. D. H. Persons and periods. 1938.
Sitwell, O., E., and S. Trio. 1938.
Bronowski, J. The poet's defence. Cambridge 1939.
Elton, O. Essays and addresses. 1939.
Davis, H. et al. Nineteenth-century studies. Ithaca 1940.
Evans, B. I. Tradition and romanticism. 1940.
Grierson, H. J. C. Essays and addresses. 1940.
Wilson, E. The wound and the bow. Boston 1941.
Pritchett, V. S. In my good books. 1942.
— The living novel. 1946.
— Books in general. 1953.
Tillotson, G. Essays in criticism and research. Cambridge 1942.
— Criticism and the nineteenth century. 1951.
Barfield, O. Romanticism comes of age. 1944.
Gordon, G. S. The discipline of letters. Oxford 1946.
— The lives of authors. 1950.
Laird, J. Philosophical incursions into English literature. Cambridge 1946.
de Selincourt, E. Wordsworthian and other studies. Oxford 1947.
Sampson, G. Seven essays. Cambridge 1947.
Essays mainly on the nineteenth century presented to Humphrey Milford. Oxford 1948.
Grigson, G. The harp of Aeolus. [1948].
— Essays from the air. 1951.
Lovejoy, A. O. Essays in the history of ideas. Baltimore 1948.
Tinker, C. B. Essays in retrospect. New Haven 1948.
Sackville-West, E. Inclinations. 1949.
Cecil, D. Poets and story-tellers. 1949.
Ideas and beliefs of the Victorians. 1949. Broadcast talks by various hands.
Baker, J. E. The reinterpretation of Victorian literature. Princeton 1950.
Denny, M. and W. H. Gilman. The American writer and the European tradition. 1950.
Ellis, H. From Marlowe to Shaw. Ed J. Gawsworth 1950.
Levin, H. Perspectives of criticism. Cambridge Mass 1950.
Shine, H. Booker memorial studies: eight essays on Victorian literature in memory of J. M. Booker. Chapel Hill 1950.
Trilling, L. The liberal imagination. New York 1950.
Quennell, P. C. The singular preference. 1952.
Chesterton, G. K. A handful of authors. Ed D. Collins 1953.
de la Mare, W. Private view. 1953.
Thorpe, C. D., C. Baker and B. Weaver. The major English romantic poets: a symposium in reappraisal. Carbondale 1957.
Shackford, M. H. Talks on ten poets: Wordsworth to Moody. New York 1958. On Wordsworth, Scott, Keats, the Brownings, Emerson, Clough et al.
Appleman, P., W. A. Madden and M. Wolff. 1859: entering an age of crisis. Bloomington 1959.
Glass, B., O. Temkin and W. L. Strauss. Forerunners of Darwin 1745–1859. Baltimore 1960.
Abrams, M. H. English romantic poets: modern essays in criticism. New York 1960.
Ellmann, R. Edwardians and late Victorians. New York 1960. On George Moore and the nineties.
Shapiro, C. Twelve original essays on great English novels. Detroit 1960.
Wright, A. Victorian literature: modern essays in criticism. Oxford 1961.
Clifford, J. L. Biography as an art: selected criticism 1560–1960. Oxford 1962.
Gleckner, R. F. and G. E. Enscol. Romanticism: points of view. New York 1962.
Orel, H. and G. J. Worth. Six studies in nineteenth-century English literature and thought. Lawrence Kansas 1962.
Frye, N. Romanticism reconsidered: selected papers from the English Institute. New York 1963.

Miscellaneous Works

Wotton, M. E. Word portraits of famous writers. 1887. Descriptions of personal appearances of English writers, including 63 nineteenth-century figures.

Rawnsley, H. D. Literary associations of the English lakes. 2 vols 1894.

Nicoll, W. R. and T. J. Wise. Literary anecdotes of the nineteenth century. 2 vols 1895–6.

Spielmann, M. H. The history of Punch. 1895.

Sharp, W. Literary geography. 1907.

Escott, T. H. S. Club makers and club members. New York 1914.

Thomas, E. A literary pilgrim in England. 1917.

Spiller, R. E. The American in England during the first half-century of independence. New York [1926].

Hoevel, E. F. Die soziale Herkunft der neuzeitlichen Dialekt-literatur Englands. Leipzig 1929.

Cruse, A. The Englishman and his books in the early nineteenth century. [1930].

—— The Victorians and their books. 1935.

—— After the Victorians. 1938.

Perugini, M. E. Victorian days and ways. 1932.

Abrams, M. H. The milk of paradise: the effect of opium visions on the works of De Quincey, Crabbe, Francis Thompson and Coleridge. Cambridge Mass 1934.

Thrall, M. Rebellious Fraser's: Nol Yorke's magazine in the days of Maginn, Thackeray and Carlyle. New York 1934.

Early Victorian England 1830–65. Ed G. M. Young 2 vols Oxford 1934.

Smith, B. P. Islam in English literature. Beirut 1939.

Moorman, L. J. Tuberculosis and genius. Chicago 1940.

Lunn, A. Switzerland in English prose and poetry. 1947.

Stuart, D. M. The English abigail. 1947.

Altick, R. D. The scholar adventurers. New York 1950.

—— The sociology of authorship: the social origins, education and occupations of 1,100 British writers 1800–1935. BNYPL June 1962.

Bush, D. Science and English poetry: an historical sketch 1590–1950. New York 1950.

Laski, M. Mrs Ewing, Mrs Molesworth and Mrs Hodgson Burnett. 1950.

Mayhew, H. London's underworld; Mayhew's London; Mayhew's characters. Ed P. C. Quennell 3 vols 1951. Selections from London labour and London poor.

Culler, A. D. Aspects of Victorian literature. Yale Rev 41 1952.

Houghton, W. E. Victorian anti-intellectualism. JHI 13 1952.

Zall, P. M. Lord Eldon's censorship. PMLA 68 1953.

Hartmann, G. The unmeditated vision: an interpretation of Wordsworth, Hopkins, Rilke and Valéry. New Haven 1954.

Laver, J. Victorian vista. 1954.

Ellegard, A. The readership of the periodical press in mid-Victorian Britain. Stockholm 1958.

Foakes, R. A. The romantic assertion: a study of the language of nineteenth-century poets. 1958.

Brightfield, M. F. America and the Americans 1840–60, as depicted in English novels of the period. Amer Lit 31 1959.

Walsh, W. The use of imagination: educational thought and the literary mind. 1959.

Chadwick, O. Victorian minature. 1960.

Amarasinghe, U. Dryden and Pope in the early nineteenth century: a study of changing literary taste 1800–30. Cambridge 1962.

Nelson, J. G. The sublime Puritan: Milton and the Victorians. Madison 1963.

(4) LITERARY MEMOIRS, REMINISCENCES AND LETTERS

Restricted to relatively out-of-the-way material. The standard biographies, collections of letters, etc will be found in the sections devoted to individual writers.

Hunt, L. Lord Byron and some of his contemporaries. 1828.

—— Autobiography. 3 vols 1850; ed R. Ingpen 2 vols 1903; The earliest sketches, ed S. F. Fogle, Gainesville 1959.

—— Table-talk. 1851.

Dibdin, T. F. Reminiscences of a literary life. 2 vols 1836.

Bury, C. Diary illustrative of the times of George IV. 1838.

Hood, T. Literary reminiscences. 1839.

Robberds, J. W. A memoir of the life and writings of William Taylor of Norwich, containing his correspondence with literary men. 2 vols 1843.

Foster, J. Life and correspondence. Ed J. E. Ryland 2 vols 1848.

Jerdan, W. Autobiography. 4 vols 1852–3.

Mitford, M. R. Recollections of a literary life. New York 1852.

Willis, N. P. Pencillings by the way. New York 1836, 1844, 1852 (both enlarged).

—— Famous persons and famous places. New York 1854.

Patmore, P. G. My friends and acquaintances. 3 vols 1854.

Thomson, Mrs A. T. ('Grace Wharton'). Recollections of literary characters. 2 vols 1854.

Madden, R. R. Literary life and correspondence of the Countess of Blessington. 3 vols 1855.

Emerson, R. W. English traits. Boston 1856.

Balmanno, M. Pen and pencil. New York 1858.

Redding, C. Fifty years' recollections, literary and personal. 3 vols [1858].

—— Literary reminiscences and memoirs of Thomas Campbell. 2 vols 1860.

Leslie, C. R. Autobiographical recollections. Ed T. Taylor, Boston 1860. Mainly on painting, Coleridge, Lamb, Irving et al.

Lady Morgan's memoirs: autobiography, diaries and correspondence. Ed W. H. Dixon 2 vols 1862.

Berkeley, G. My life and recollections. 4 vols 1864–6.

Hobhouse, J. C. (Baron Broughton). Recollections of a long life. 5 vols 1865 (priv ptd), 6 vols 1909–11.

Irving, P. M. The life and letters of Washington Irving. 4 vols New York 1865–6.

Duncombe, T. H. Thomas Slingsby Duncombe: life and correspondence. 2 vols 1868.

Godwin, P. Out of the past. New York 1870.

Hall, S. C. A book of memories of great men and women of the age, from personal acquaintance. 1871.

—— Retrospect of a long life. 2 vols 1883.

Meteyard, E. A group of Englishmen 1795–1815: being records of the younger Wedgwoods and their friends. 1871. On Campbell, Coleridge, Godwin et al.

Chambers, W. Memoir of Robert Chambers, with autobiographical reminiscences of William Chambers. 1872.

Fields, J. T. Yesterdays with authors. Boston 1872, 1900 (enlarged).

Hazlitt, W. C. Anecdotes and reminiscences of illustrious men and women of modern times. 1872.

Pebody, C. Our great authors at work. [1872].

Chorley, F. Autobiography, memoir and letters. Ed H. G. Hewlett 2 vols 1873.

Constable, T. Archibald Constable and his literary correspondents. 3 vols Edinburgh 1873.

Hall, S. Biographical sketches of remarkable people, chiefly from personal recollection. 1873.

Paul, C. K. William Godwin, his friends and contemporaries. 2 vols 1876.

— Biographical sketches. 1883.
Ticknor, G. Life, letters and journals. 2 vols Boston Boston 1876.
Bowring, J. Autobiographical recollections. 1877.
Mackay, C. Forty years' recollections of life, literature and public affairs from 1830 to 1870. 2 vols 1877.
— Through the long day: or memorials of a literary life during half a century. 2 vols 1887.
Martineau, H. Autobiography, with memorials by Maria Chapman. 2 vols Boston 1877.
Cowden Clarke, C. and M. Recollections of writers. 1878.
Dobell, S. Life and letters. 2 vols 1878.
Hodgson, J. T. Memoir of the Rev Francis Hodgson, with letters from Byron and others. 2 vols 1878.
Napier, M. Selections from the correspondence. 1879. On Macaulay, Mill, Brougham, Carlyle, Jeffrey et al.
Frost, T. Forty years' recollections, literary and political. 1880.
Fitzgerald, P. Recreations of a literary man. 1882.
Fox, C. Memories of old friends. Ed H. N. Pym 2 vols 1882. Includes letters of J. S. Mill.
Payn, J. Some literary recollections. 1884.
Stuart, J. M. Reminiscences. 1884.
Yates, E. H. Recollections and experiences. 2 vols 1884.
Mason, E. T. Personal traits of British authors. 4 vols New York 1885.
Whipple, E. P. Recollections of eminent men. Boston 1886.
Frith, W. P. My autobiography and reminiscences. 2 vols 1887–8; A Victorian canvas: being the memoirs, ed N. Wallis 1957.
Francis, J. C. John Francis, publisher of the Athenaeum: a literary chronicle of half a century. 2 vols 1888.
Sandford, Mrs H. Thomas Poole and his friends. 2 vols 1888.
Clayden, P. W. Rogers and his contemporaries. 2 vols 1889.
Trollope, T. A. What I remember. 2 vols New York 1888–90.
— Further reminiscences. 1889.
Reid, T. W. The life, letters and friendships of Richard Monckton Milnes, first Lord Houghton. 2 vols 1890.
Smiles, S. A publisher and his friends: memoir and correspondence of John Murray, with an account of the house 1768–1843. 2 vols 1891.
Masson, D. Edinburgh sketches and memories. 1892.
— Memories of London in the 'forties. 1908.
— Memories of two cities, Edinburgh and Aberdeen. 1911. On John Wilson, Hugh Miller, De Quincey et al.
Ritchie, A. T. Records of Tennyson, Ruskin and [Robert and Elizabeth] Browning. 1892.
— Chapters from some unwritten memoirs. New York 1895.
Scott, W. B. Autobiographical notes. 2 vols 1892. On Hunt, Lewes, George Eliot, Ruskin.
Archer-Shee, W. My contemporaries. 1893.
Bertram, J. Some memories of books, authors and events. 1893.
Crosland, Mrs N. Landmarks of a literary life. 1893.
Espinasse, F. Literary recollections and sketches. 1893.
Vizetelly, H. Glances back through seventy years. 2 vols 1893.
Fields, Mrs J. T. A shelf of old books. 1894. Reminiscences of authors.
Correspondence of Joseph Jekyll with Lady Gertrude Sloane Stanley 1818–38. Ed A. Bourke 1894.
Saunders, F. Character studies, with some personal recollections. New York 1894. On Edward Irving, Mrs Jameson.
Hogg, J. De Quincey and his friends: personal recollections. 1895.
Sala, G. A. H. Life and adventures. 2 vols 1895.
Skelton, J. The table-talk of Shirley: reminiscences of, and letters from Froude, Thackeray, Disraeli, Browning, Rossetti, Kingsley, Baynes, Huxley, Tyndall and others. 2 vols Edinburgh 1895.
Black, H. C. Pen, pencil, baton and mask: biographical sketches. 1896.
Hare, A. J. C. Story of my life. 6 vols New York 1896–1901; rptd as The years with mother, In my solitary life, ed M. Barnes 1952–3.
Farrar, F. W. Men I have known. [1897].
Oliphant, M. O. Annals of a publishing house: William Blackwood and his sons, their magazine and friends. 3 vols 1897–8.
— Autobiography and letters. Ed Mrs H. Coghill 1899.
Laughton, J. K. Memoirs of the life and correspondence of Henry Reeve. 2 vols 1898.
[Russell, G. W. E.] Collections and recollections. 1898.
Festing, G. John Hookham Frere and his friends. 1899.
Linton, E. L. My literary life. 1899. On George Eliot et al.
McCarthy, J. Reminiscences. 2 vols 1899.
Palgrave, G. F. Francis Turner Palgrave: his journals and memories of his life. 1899.
Yarnall, E. Wordsworth and the Coleridges, with other memories, literary and political. 1899.
Clark, J. W. Old friends at Cambridge and elsewhere. 1900.
Tinsley, W. Random recollections of an old publisher. 2 vols 1900.
Champneys, B. Memoirs and correspondence of Coventry Patmore. 2 vols 1901.
Kenyon, J. B. Loiterings in old fields: literary sketches. New York [1901]. On Tennyson, Morris, Keats, Rossetti, Stevenson.
'Paston, George' (E. M. Symonds). Side-lights on the Georgian period. 1902.
— At John Murray's: records of a literary circle 1843–92; preface by Lord Ernle. 1932.
Jay, H. Robert Buchanan: some account of his life and literary friendships. 1903.
B[urne]-J[ones], G. Memorials of Sir Edward Burne-Jones. 2 vols 1904.
Fifty years of Fleet Street: being the life and recollections of Sir John R. Robinson. Ed F. M. Thomas 1904.
Betham, E. A house of letters. [1905]. On Coleridge, Lamb, Landor, Southey, Barton et al.
Harrison, F. Memories and thoughts. 1906.
Correspondence of John Whishaw and his friends 1813–40. Ed Lady Seymour 1906.
Brown, J. Letters. Ed J. Brown and D. W. Forrest 1907. Includes letters from Ruskin, Thackeray, Hutton, Brooks et al.
Layard, G. A great Punch editor: being the life, letters and diaries of Shirley Brooks. 1907.
Carr, J. C. Some eminent Victorians: personal recollections. 1908. On Tennyson, Browning, Rossetti et al.
— Coasting Bohemia. 1914. On Rossetti, Meredith, Sullivan, Irving et al.
Sanders, L. The Holland House circle. 1908.
Winter, W. Old friends. New York 1909. On Dickens, Wilkie Collins.
Murdoch, W. G. B. Memories of Swinburne, with other essays. Edinburgh 1910.
Clara Novello's reminiscences, compiled by her daughter, Contessa Valeria Gigliucci, with memoir by A. D. Coleridge. 1910.
Ellis, S. M. William Harrison Ainsworth and his friends. 2 vols 1911.
— George Meredith: his life and friends in relation to his work. 1920.
Hueffer, F. M. Memories and impressions. 1911. Largely on Pre-Raphaelites.
Williams, O. Life and letters of John Rickman. 1911. On Lamb, Coleridge, Hunt, Hazlitt et al.
Collins, L. C. Life and memoirs of John Churton Collins. 1912.
Wedmore, F. Memories. [1912].

Norton, C. E. Letters. 2 vols 1913.
Letters of Edward Dowden and his correspondents. Ed E. D. and H. M. Dowden 1914.
Francillon, R. E. Mid-Victorian memories. 1914. On Lear, Lecky, Stephen et al.
Erskine, Mrs S. Anna Jameson: letters and friendships 1812–60. [1915].
Harris, F. Contemporary portraits. 4 sers New York 1915–23.
— My life and loves. 4 vols 1925–9 (priv ptd), Paris [1946?], New York 1963; His life and adventures, ed G. Richards 1947 (rev and abridged).
— Latest contemporary portraits. New York [1927].
Putnam, G. H. Memories of a publisher 1865–1915. New York 1915.
Whiteing, R. My harvest. New York 1915.
Escott, T. H. S. Great Victorians: memories and personalities. 1916.
Kernahan, C. In good company: some personal recollections of Swinburne, Watts-Dunton, Wilde [et al]. 1917.
Ley, J. W. T. The Dickens circle: a narrative of the novelist's friendships. 1918.
Ward, Mrs. H. A writer's recollections. 2 vols 1918. On Browning, Lewes, John Morley, Goldwin Smith.
Betham-Edwards, M. Mid-Victorian memories. New York 1919. On Patmore, George Eliot et al.
Mallock, W. H. Memoirs of life and literature. 1920.
Aldrich, Mrs T. B. Crowding memories. Boston 1920. On Dickens, Wilde.
Bax, E. B. Reminiscences and reflections of a mid and late Victorian. New York 1920. On Morris, Sharp et al.
Colvin, S. Memories and notes of persons and places 1852–1912. 1921. On Ruskin, Browning, Rossetti, Trelawny, Stevenson et al.
Yeats, W. B. Four years 1887–91. London Mercury June–Aug 1921. On Huxley, Wilde, the Rhymers' Club etc.
Ainslie, D. Adventures social and literary. [1922]. On Swinburne, Wilde, Pater, James et al.
Ticknor, C. Glimpses of authors. Boston 1922. On Anne Thackeray Ritchie, Dickens, Du Maurier et al.
Ridge, W. P. A story teller: forty years in London. [1923].
— I like to remember. [1925].
Sichel, W. The sands of time: recollections and reflections. 1923.
Spencer, W. T. Forty years in my bookshop. Ed T. Moult 1923. On meetings with Pater, Gissing, Jefferies, Tennyson et al.
Benson, A. C. Memories and friends. 1924.
Taylor, U. Guests and memories. 1924. On Henry Taylor, Carlyle, Spedding, Jowett.
Hill, C. Good company in old Westminster and the Temple. [1925]. Founded on the early recollections of Anne (Rickman) Lefroy.
Gray, W. F. An unpublished literary correspondence. Cornhill Mag July 1926. Includes letters of Wordsworth, Southey, Lamb, Landor, Shelley, Keats, Dickens, from the Watson Collection.
Dent, H. R. The memoirs of J. M. Dent 1849–1926. 1928.
Lucas, E. V. The Colvins and their friends. [1928].
Benson, E. F. As we were: a Victorian peep-show. 1930.
A Victorian vintage: being a selection of the best stories from the diaries of the Right Hon Sir Mountstuart E. Grant Duff. Ed A. T. Bassett 1930.
Masson, F. Victorians all. 1931. Reminiscences of Dickens, Carlyle, Browning et al.
Rhys, E. Everyman remembers. 1931.
Rothenstein, W. Men and memories: recollections 1872–1900. 1931; vol 2 (1900–22), 1932.
Whyte, F. A bachelor's London 1889–1914. 1931.
Newbolt, H. My world as in my time: memoirs 1862–1932. 1932. On Ruskin, Burne-Jones, Morris et al.
Roberts, M. Meetings with some men of letters. Queen's Quart 39 1932. On Meredith, Hardy, Doyle.
Tuell, A. K. A Victorian at bay. Boston 1932. On Meredith, Christina Rossetti, Mrs Gaskell.
Pollock, F. Talkers I have known. Quart Rev 261 1933. On Kinglake, Lyall, Maine, Meredith, Huxley, Swinburne, Tennyson.
Jepson, E. Vol 1: Memories of a Victorian. 1933; vol 2: Memories of an Edwardian and neo-Georgian. 1937.
Masson, R. Poets, patriots and lovers: sketches and memories of famous people. 1933.
Compton-Rickett, A. I look back: memories of fifty years. 1933.
— Portraits and personalities. 1937.
Mackenzie, C. Literature in my time. 1933.
Richards, G. Memories of a misspent youth 1872–96. 1933.
— Memories of years spent mainly in publishing 1897–1925. New York 1934.
A great lady's friendships: letters to Mary Marchioness of Salisbury, Countess of Derby 1862–90. Ed Lady Burghclere 1933. Includes letters from Bulwer-Lytton, Lord Cowley et al.
Sharp, E. Unfinished adventure. 1933. Reminiscences of the Yellow Book group et al.
Gougaud, L. La société lettrée de Londres observée par un écrivain français en 1839. Revue d'Histoire Ecclésiastique 30 1934.
Milne, J. The memoirs of a bookman. 1934. On Tennyson, Rossetti, Meredith, Stevenson et al.
Ward, M. The Wilfrid Wards and the transition, vol 1: the nineteenth century, 1934; vol 2: insurrection versus resurrection. 1937. Ward's reminiscences of Gladstone, Jowett, Ruskin, Hutton, Newman et al.
Knox, E. A. Reminiscences of an octogenarian 1847–1934. 1935.
Patmore, D. Portrait of my family. 1935. On Patmore, Carlyle, Hazlitt, Hunt, Browning, Tennyson.
'Anstey, F.' (T. A. Guthrie). A long retrospect. Oxford 1936.
Freeman, J. Letters. Ed G. Freeman and J. C. Squire 1936.
Holmes, C. J. Self and partners: reminiscences. 1936.
May, J. L. John Lane and the nineties. 1936.
Mottram, R. H. Portrait of an unknown Victorian. 1936.
Bell, G. The earlier letters 1876–92. Ed E. Richmond 1937.
Benson, D. M. (Baroness Charnwood). Call back yesterday. 1937.
Birrell, A. Things past redress. 1937.
Blanche, J.-E. Portraits of a lifetime. 1937.
— More portraits of a lifetime. 1939.
Curle, R. Caravansary and conversation. 1937.
Maxwell, W. B. Time gathered. 1937.
Crichton-Browne, J. The doctor remembers. 1938.
Douglas, A. Without apology. 1938.
Sitwell, O. Those were the days. 1938.
— Autobiography. 5 vols 1945–50.
Smith, L. P. Unforgotten years. 1938.
Burke, T. Living in Bloomsbury. 1939.
Ellis, H. My life. Boston 1939.
Lubbock, S. The child in the crystal. 1939.
Marsh, E. A number of people. 1939.
Fisher, H. A. L. An unfinished autobiography. Oxford 1940.
Friends of a lifetime: letters to Sydney Carlyle Cockerell. Ed V. Meynell 1940.
Ingram, A. E. W. Fifty years' work in London 1889–1939. 1940.
Meynell, E. A woman talking. 1940.
Read, H. Annals of innocence and experience. 1940, 1946 (rev and enlarged).
Rhys, E. Wales England wed: an autobiography. 1940.
Two generations. Ed O. Sitwell 1940. Journals of Mrs Campbell Swinton and Florence Sitwell.
Hawthorne, N. English notebooks. Ed R. Stewart, New York 1941.
Lowndes, M. A. I, too, have lived in Arcadia. 1941.

Arnold, J. B. Giants in dressing gowns. Chicago 1942.
Bloom, U. H. Time, tide and I. 1942.
Bowen, E. Bowen's Court. 1942. A family history.
Goldring, D. South lodge: reminiscences of Violet Hunt, Ford Madox Ford and the English Review circle. 1943.
Quiller-Couch, A. T. Memoirs and opinions: an unfinished autobiography. Ed S. C. Roberts, Cambridge 1944.
Colum, M. G. M. Life and the dream. 1947.
The Keats circle: letters and papers 1816–78. Ed H. E. Rollins 2 vols Cambridge Mass 1948.
[Lunn], Hugh Kingsmill. The progress of a biographer. 1949.
Haydon, B. R. Autobiography and journals. Ed M. Elwin 1950.
— The diary. Ed W. B. Pope 2 vols Cambridge Mass 1960.
Barton, B. Letters to Robert Southey. Ed C. R. Woodring, Harvard Lib Bull 4 1950.
Wyndham, H. A. A family history 1688–1837: the Wyndhams of Somerset, Sussex and Wiltshire. 1950.
Noyes, A. Two worlds for memory. 1953.
Adams-Acton, Mrs J. Victorian sidelights. Ed A. M. W. Stirling 1954.
Miss Mitford and Mr Harness: record of a friendship. Ed C. M. Duncan-Jones 1955. On Dickens, Newman, Fanny Kemble et al.
Beaty, F. L. The Lloyd-Manning letters. Bloomington 1957. On Lamb–Wordsworth circle.
Beckford, W. Life at Fonthill 1807–22, with interludes in London and Paris. Ed and tr B. Alexander 1957.
Tennyson, C. Stars and markets. 1957. On Tennyson and Locker.
Stevenson, Mrs. Victoria, Albert and Mrs Stevenson. Ed E. Boykin 1958. Impressions of literati and politicians.
Darwin, C. The autobiography. Ed N. Barlow 1958. On literary quarrels with Samuel Butler.
A Victorian publisher: a study of the Bentley papers. Ed R. A. Gettmann, Cambridge 1960.
Shelley and his circle 1773–1822. Ed K. N. Cameron 2 vols Cambridge Mass 1961.
Lehmann, J. Ancestors and friends. 1962.

R. L. C.

II. BOOK PRODUCTION AND DISTRIBUTION

GENERAL WORKS: *catalogues and surveys.*

BOOK PRODUCTION: *General works; Paper (Bibliographies and dictionaries, History of production, Technique and raw materials, Qualities and trade, Taxation, Directories, Periodicals); Ink; The manufacture of type (Typefounding, Type design, Stereotyping and electrotyping); Printing (General and literary works, Manuals, Business management, Correct composition, Type composing machinery, Presswork, Colour printing); Trade organizations; Graphic processes (General works, Intaglio surfaces, Plane surfaces, Surfaces in relief); Printing Style (Aesthetic considerations, Legibility); Private printing (General works, Particular presses and societies); Printers and printing firms; Printing trade periodicals; Book illustration (General works, Illustrators); Bookbinding.*

BOOK DISTRIBUTION: *General works; Copyright; Authors' guides to publication; The practice of publishing; Individual publishers; General catalogues; Trade periodicals; Circulating libraries; Retail bookselling (General works and the Net Book Agreement, Individual firms); Antiquarian book trade (General works, Periodicals, Book auctions, Individual firms); Private book collecting; Public libraries (The British Museum, Accounts of other libraries, The Free Library movement); Librarianship (Periodicals).*

A. GENERAL WORKS

In addition to the works listed below, much information may be found in the general and special catalogues of the following international exhibitions: London, 1851, 1862, 1872; Paris, 1855, 1867, 1878, 1889, 1900; Vienna, 1873; Philadelphia, 1876; Brussels, 1880, 1888, 1897; Amsterdam, 1883; Antwerp, 1886; Chicago, 1893.

Katalog der Bibliothek des deutschen Börsenvereins. 3 vols Leipzig 1885–1902.
[Peddie, R. A.] Catalogue of the technical reference library of the St Bride Foundation. 1919.
Timperley, C. H. A dictionary of printers and printing. 1839, 1842 (rev as Encyclopaedia of literary and typographical anecdote).
Hodson, W. H. Booksellers, publishers and stationers' directory for London and country. 1855.
Kelly's post office directory of stationers, printers, booksellers, publishers and papermakers of England, Scotland, Wales and Ireland. 1872, 1876, 1880, 1885, 1889, 1893, 1896, 1900.
Catalogue of the Caxton celebration exhibition. Ed G. Bullen 1877.
Hitchcock, F. H. The building of a book. New York 1906, 1927.
Leicester Free Public Libraries. Catalogue of the books on printing, bookbinding and papermaking and related industries. Leicester 1927.
Berry, W. T. The St Bride typographical library. 1932
Hart, H. Bibliotheca typographica: a list of books about books. New York, 1933.
Wellard, J. H. State of reading among the working classes of England during the first half of the nineteenth century. Lib Quart 5 1935.
List of books on printing and the allied trades. Bristol 1936 (Bristol Public Lib).
Jones, G. W. Catalogue of the well-known collection of rare and valuable books illustrating the history of printing, sold by Sotheby & Co 1936.
Winship, G. P. The literature of printing: chapter xv of the history of the printed book. Dolphin 3 1938.
Cleverdon, D. English books 1840–1940: a short catalogue. [1940].
Hogben, L. T. From cave painting to comic strip. 1949.
Lehmann-Haupt, H. (ed). 100 books about bookmaking. New York 1949.
Howe, E. Bibliotheca typographica. Signature new ser 10 1950.
Steinberg, S. H. Five hundred years of printing. 1955 (Pelican), 1961 (rev).
Webb, R. K. The British working class reader 1790–1848. 1955.

B. BOOK PRODUCTION

(1) GENERAL WORKS

The sister arts: or a concise and interesting view of the nature and history of paper-making, printing and bookbinding. Lewes 1809. Attributed to J. Baxter.
British manufacturing industries. Ed G. P. Bevan 1876, 1877, 1892.
Victoria and Albert Museum, South Kensington: catalogue of machinery, models etc. Pt 2 (Paper making and printing machinery), 1897.
Heath, T. C. How books are made. 1900.
Aldis, H. G. The printed book. Cambridge 1916, 1941, 1951 (rev J. Carter and B. Crutchley).
Jackson, H. The printing of books. 1938.
McCoombs, C. F. Printing from the sixteenth to the twentieth century. New York 1940 (New York Public Lib).
Gumuchian, K. Forgotten children's flowers. Print 4 1945.
Book production section. TLS 10 Feb 1950.
Jennett, S. The making of books. 1951.

(2) PAPER

Bibliographies and Dictionaries

Munsell, J. A. A chronology of paper and papermaking. Albany 1857, 1860, 1864, 1870, 1876.
Hopkins, E. A. Taschen-Hilfsbuch unentbehrlicher Wörter des Papierfachs (Deutsch-Englisch). 1903.
Surface, H. E. Bibliography of the pulp and paper industries. Washington 1913 (USA Dept of Agriculture Forest Service Bull no 123).
Paper Makers' Association of Great Britain: Technical Section. Catalogue of the library. 1934.
Labarre, E. J. Dictionary and encyclopaedia of paper and paper-making. Oxford, 1937, 1952 (rev).
The paper industry. 1948 (Assoc of Special Libraries).

History of Production

Koops, M. Historical account of the substances which have been used to describe events and convey ideas from the earliest times. 1800, 1801.
Report from the Select Committee of the House of Commons on M. Koops' petition. 1801. (55). iii. 127.
Minutes of the Proceedings of the Committee of the House of Lords to whom was referred the Bill for prolonging the term of certain Letters Patent assigned to Henry and Sealy Fourdrinier. 10 Aug 1807. xiv. 331.
Fontenelle, J. de and P. Poisson. Der vollkommene Papier- und Schreib-Materialien Händler. Ulm 1831.
Report from the Select Committee of the House of Commons on Fourdrinier's patent. 1837. (331). xx. 35. Report on the recommitted Report. 1837. (405). xx. 91.
Useful arts and manufactures of Great Britain. 1848.
Herring, R. A lecture on the origin, manufacture and importance of paper. 1853.
—— Paper and paper making, ancient and modern. 1855, 1856, 1863.
Planche, G. De l'industrie de la papeterie. Paris 1853.
Tomlinson, C. Cyclopaedia of useful arts etc. [1854].
—— Illustrations of useful arts, manufactures and trades. [1858].
Gamble, J. The origin of the machine for making endless paper, and its introduction into England. Jnl of Soc of Arts 27 Feb 1857.
Patent Office. Abridgements of specifications relating to the manufacture of paper, pasteboard and papier maché. 1858.
—— Abridgements of specifications [illustrated series]: class 96, paper, pasteboard and papier maché. 1858.
Report from the Select Committee of the House of Commons on Paper. Export duty on rags. 1861.
Richardson, W. H. On the manufacture of paper. In W. G. Armstrong, The industrial resources of the Tyne, Wear and Tees, 1864 (2nd edn).
Dropisch, B. Der Papiermaschine: ihre geschichtliche Entwicklung und Construction. Brunswick 1878.
Routledge, T. Minutes of Proc Institution of Civil Engineers 92 1888.
A brilliant page in the history of British papermaking. Mill no 24. St Neot's. British and Colonial Printer 13 Sept 1888.
Vachon, M. Les arts et les industries du papier en France. Paris [1894].
The firm of John Dickinson & Co Ltd. 1896 (priv ptd).
A history of the Fourdrinier machines. World's Paper Trade Rev 1897–8.
Beadle, C. A short account of the history of paper-making. [1897].
—— The development of watermarking in hand made and machine-made papers. Jnl of Soc of Arts 18 May 1906.
[Didot, A. F.] Le centenaire de la machine à papier continu. Paris [1900].
Campredon, E. Le papier. Paris 1901.
Fittica, F. B. Geschichte der Sulfitzellstoff-Fabrikation. Leipzig 1902.
Maddox, H. A. Paper: its history, sources and manufacture. [1916], [1928], [1930], 1933.
Cormack, A. A. Our ancient and honourable craft 1750–1933: being an account of the rise and development of paper-making in Scotland, and at Culter, Aberdeenshire in particular. 1933.
Carter, J. and H. G. Pollard. An enquiry into the nature of certain nineteenth-century pamphlets. 1934. Ch 4.
Clapperton, R. H. Paper: an historical account of its making by hand from the earliest times to the present day. 1934.
—— Paper and its relationship to books. 1935.
—— The paper-making machine: its invention, evolution and development. Oxford 1967.
Esparto papers. Edinburgh 1933 (Assoc of Makers of Esparto).
Albert Spicer 1847–1934: a man of his time, by one of his family. 1938.
The invention of the papermaking machine. Paper & Print 16–18 1943–5.
Bettendorf, J. J. A history of paperboard and paperboard containers. Chicago 1946.
Hunter, D. Papermaking: the history and technique of an ancient craft. 1947 (2nd edn).
Edward Collins & Sons. Over 200 years of papermaking. Paper-Maker 118 1949.
Davies Harvey & Murrell Ltd. The story of D. H. & M. Ltd., incorporating Grimwade & Sons, paper merchants. 1949.
Paper making: a general account of its history, processes and applications. Kenley 1950 (Br Paper & Board Makers Assoc).
Shears, W. S. William Nash of St Pauls Cray: paper-makers. 1950.
A brief history of British paper mills. Paper Making & Paper Selling 70 1951, 72 1953.
Culter Mills Paper Co. History of the Culter Mills: two hundred years of progress. Aberdeen 1951.
Guard Bridge Paper Co. Guard Bridge panorama: the story of a great enterprise founded on the making of paper. Dundee 1951.

Renker, A. Vom Wesen und Werden des Papiers. Wiesbaden 1951.
Shorter, A. H. The distribution of British paper mills in 1851. Paper-Maker 121 1951.
Timaeus, D. E. A century and a half of wire weaving: the story of C. H. Johnson & Sons. 1952.
Balston, T. William Balston: paper maker 1759–1849. 1954.
Chambers, R. S. History of paper making. British Engineer new ser 15 1954.
Evans, J. The endless web: John Dickinson and Co Ltd 1804–1954. 1955.
Carter, H. Wolvercote Mill. Oxford 1957.
Coleman, D. C. The British paper industry 1495–1860: a study in industrial growth. Oxford 1958.
Samuel Jones and Co Ltd: 150 years on paper. [1960]. A pamphlet.

Technique and Raw Materials

Le Normand, L. S. O. Manuel du fabricant de papiers. 3 vols Paris 1833–4.
Rüst, W. A. Papierfabrikation und die technischen Anwendungen des Papiers. Berlin 1838.
Müller, L. Die Fabrikation des Papiers. Berlin 1849, 1855, 1862, 1877.
Saunders, T. H. Illustrations of British paper manufacture. 1855.
Bosworth, T. A few words on paper, flax, hemp and plaintain fibre. 1855.
Royle, J. F. The fibrous plants of India fitted for cordage, clothing and paper, with an account of the cultivation and preparation of flax, hemp and their substitutes. 1855.
Herring, R. A letter on the collection of rags for the manufacture of paper. 1860.
Prouteaux, A. Guide pratique de la fabrication du papier et du carton. Paris 1864, [c. 1885]; tr Philadelphia 1866, 1873.
Hofmann, C. A practical treatise on the manufacture of paper. Philadelphia 1873.
Kerr, H. C. Report on the cultivation of, and trade in, jute in Bengal and on Indian fibres available for the manufacture of paper. Calcutta 1874.
de la Tréhonnais, F. R. Algerian esparto grass for the manufacture of paper. 1874.
Routledge, T. Bamboo considered as a papermaking material. 1875.
— Bamboo and its treatment. Sunderland 1879.
The art of paper making: a guide to the theory and practice of the manufacture of paper by the editor of the Paper mills directory. 1876 (2nd edn).
Archer, T. C. In G. P. Bevan, British manufacturing industries, 1876.
Liotard, L. Memorandum on materials in India suitable for the manufacture of paper. Calcutta 1880.
Maidstone. Industries of Maidstone: being a series of descriptive articles. Maidstone 1881. Describes the Balston paper mills, Hobb's printing office, Amies's paper moulds.
Arnot, W. The technology of the paper trade. 1878; rev J. M. Arnot, British & Colonial Printer 28–30 1891–2.
Dunbar, J. The practical paper-maker. Leith 1881 (2nd edn), 1887.
— Notes on the manufacture of wood pulp and wood pulp papers. Leith 1894.
Hoyer, E. Das Papier: seine Beschaffenheit und deren Prüfung. Munich 1882; tr French, 1884.
Rattray, J. H. et al. Forestry and forest products. Edinburgh 1885.
Stonhill, W. J. Paper pulp from wood, straw and other fibres in the past and present. [c. 1885].
Wyatt, J. W. The art of making paper by the machine. [1885].
Parkinson, R. A treatise on paper. Preston 1886, Clitheroe 1896.
Davis, C. T. The manufacture of paper. Philadelphia 1886.
Mierzinski, S. Handbuch der praktischen Papier-fabrikation. Vienna 1886.
Cross, C. F. and E. J. Bevan. A text-book of papermaking. 1888, 1900, 1907, 1916, 1920.
Herzberg, W. Papier-prüfung. Berlin 1888, 1902; rev R. Korn and B. Schulze, Berlin 1932; tr 1892; French, 1894.
Watt, A. The art of paper-making. 1890, New York 1908.
Bennett, J. B. Paper-making processes and machinery. Edinburgh 1892.
Clapperton, G. Practical paper making. 1894, 1907; rev R. H. Clapperton 1926.
Griffin, R. B. and A. D. Little. The chemistry of paper making. New York 1894.
USA Department of State. Vegetable parchment paper. Consular Reports vol 46 Washington 1894.
Akesson, L., H. Everling and M. Fluckiger. Lexikon der Papier-industrie: Deutsch-Englisch-Französisch. Lucerne 1895, 1905.
Andés, L. E. Papier-Specialitäten. Vienna 1896; tr as The treatment of paper for special purposes, 1907, 1923.
Kirchner, E. Das Papier. 3 vols Biberach 1897–1911.
Robertson, J. Fifty years in paper making. Newcastle 1897.
USA Department of State, Bureau of Foreign Commerce. Paper in foreign countries: uses of wood pulp. Special Consular Reports vol 19, Washington 1900.
Henderson, R. Paper making machinery. 1900.
MacNaughton, J. Factory book-keeping for paper mills. 1900, 1902.
Hubner, J. Cantor lectures on paper manufacture. 1903.
Sindall, R. W. Paper technology. 1906, 1910, 1920 (rev).
— The manufacture of paper. 1908.
Strachan, J. The invention of wood pulp processes in Britain during the nineteenth century. Paper-Maker (annual no) 1949.

Qualities and Trade

Dusautoy, J. A. The paper-maker's ready reckoner. Romsey 1805.
Murray, J. Observations and experiments of the bad composition of modern paper. 1823, 1824.
— Remarks on modern paper. Edinburgh 1829.
The stationer's handbook and guide to the paper trade. 1859, 1859, 1863, 1868, 1869, 1870, 1871, 1872, 1873, 1874, 1875, 1881, 1893 (17th edn).
Herring, R. A practical guide to the varieties and relative values of paper, illustrated with samples. 1860.
Piette, L. Manuel de papeterie. 2 vols Paris 1861.
Haines, E. N. The paper makers' and stationers' calculator. 1862, 1880.
Olmer, G. Du papier mécanique et de ses apprêts dans les diverses impressions. Paris 1882.
Winkler, O. Der Papierkenner: ein Handbuch und Rathgeber für Papier-Käufer und Verkäufer, technische Lehranstalten etc. Leipzig 1887.
Royal Society of Arts. Report of the committee on the deterioration of paper. 1898.
Spicer, A. D. The paper trade. 1907.

Taxation

England—Booksellers' and printers' relief Bill. A Bill for repealing certain duties on paper etc. 1802.
Report from the Committee of the House of Commons on the booksellers' and printers' petition relating to the duty on paper. 1802. ii. 89.
Fourteenth Report of the Commissioners of enquiry into the Excise Establishment. 1835. xxxi. 159.
[McCulloch, J. R.] Observations illustrative of the practical operation and real effect of the duties on paper. 1836.

Edwards, E. The duties on paper, advertisements and newspapers. 1849.
Knight, C. The struggles of a book against excessive taxation. [1850].
— The case of authors as regards the paper duty. 1851.
The paper difficulty. Chambers's Jnl Nov 1854.
England. Report of the Commissioners of Inland Revenue to the Treasury on the repeal of the duty upon paper, dated 1 March 1860. 1860.
England. Report from the Select Committee on paper (export duty on rags). 1861.
Bohn, H. G. The paper duty considered in reference to its action on the literature and trade of Great Britain. 1861 (3 edns).
Petter, G. W. Some objections to the repeal of the paper duty considered in reply to Mr H. G. Bohn's pamphlet. 1860 (for 1861).
Report from the Select Committee of the House of Commons on Paper: export duty on rags. 1861.
Paper. Cornhill Mag Nov 1861.
The rag tax: the paper makers' grievance and how to redress it. 1863 (priv ptd).
Wrigley, T. The case of the paper makers. [1864].
Carey, H. C. The way to outdo England without fighting her: a protective tariff for paper. Philadelphia 1865.
[Bruce, H. and D. Chalmers]. Gladstone and the paper duties by two Midlothian paper makers. 1885.
Collet, C. D. History of the taxes on knowledge. 2 vols 1899, 1 vol 1933 (abridged).

Directories

A new list of paper mills in the United Kingdom. 1859. By G. T. Mickleburgh?
The paper mills directory. 1860. Annually since 1860.
Craig, J. The paper makers' directory and diary. [1876].
Dirctory of paper makers of the United Kingdom. Annually since 1876.
Bryan, C. W. The paper mill directory of the world. Holyoke Mass 1883.
Phillips, S. C. Paper makers' directory of all nations. 1884. Annually since 1884.
The paper trade directory of Great Britain and the colonies. 1886. Annually since 1886.
Alphabetical list of paper and millboard makers in the United Kingdom. Edinburgh 1894.

Periodicals

The paper trade news. No 1, 5 Oct 1860– no 22, 1 July 1861. Continued as The stationers', printers' and bookbinders' monthly journal, no 23, 1 Aug 1861–no 27, 1 Dec 1861. First weekly, then monthly.
The papermakers' circular. No 1, 9 Sept 1861–no 16, 3 Dec 1862. Continued as The papermakers' circular and rag price current, no 17, 3 Feb 1863–no 39, 1 Dec 1864. Monthly.
The paper trade review. No 1, Nov 1862–June 1868. Pbd Edinburgh 1862–5, then London. Monthly.
The papermakers' monthly journal. No 1, Jan 1863–15 March 1932. Monthly.
The paper and printing trades journal. No 1, Dec 1872–no 86, May 1895. Ed A. W. Tuer. Quarterly. Index to nos 1–32 by E. R. Pearce, Taunton 1881.
The paper makers' circular and rag price current. No 1, 19 Jan 1874–no 433, March 1907. Weekly, later monthly.
The paper consumers' circular. No 1, 22 Feb 1879–no 182, 1 Dec 1882. Weekly.
Papermaking. [1881]–1 Nov 1895–. In progress. Monthly.
The paper trade review: new series. No 1, 17 Aug 1883–1 May 1891. Continued as World's paper trade review, 8 May 1891–. In progress; ed W. J. Stonhill. Weekly. Before this new series was started 166 nos had been pbd 1879–83 aa supplements to The British and colonial printer.
The paper record. No 1, 26 Feb 1886–Sept 1895. Some minor changes of title. Fortnightly at first, then weekly.
Stationery world and paper market. No 1, 29 Jan 1892–17 Dec 1927. Continued as Paper market, 17 Jan 1927–. In progress. Monthly.
The paper maker. No 1, 26 Jan 1891–. In progress; ed S. C. Phillips. Monthly.
Amalgamated society of paper makers: first quarterly report. Dartford 1893–. In progress.
The paper exchange news. No 1, April 1895–June 1896.
Wood pulp. No 1, Jan 1896–9 May 1898. Continued as Paper and pulp, 1 June 1898–1 Jan 1906. Incorporated with Paper-making. Fortnightly under first title, then weekly.
Paper box and bag maker. No 1, 7 April 1896–. In progress. Monthly.
World's pulp and paper industry. No 1, 21 Sept 1898–no 80, 2 May 1900. Weekly.
Paper and printing bits. No 1, Oct 1898–no 17, April 1900. Birmingham. Monthly, but irregular.

(3) INK

See W. B. Gamble, Chemistry and manufacture of printing inks: a list of references in the New York Public Library, New York 1926.
Savage, W. On the preparation of printing ink, both black and coloured. 1832.
— Practical hints on decorative printing. 1822.
Haldat, C. N. A. Recherches chimiques sur l'encre. Nancy 1852.
de Champour, — and F. Malepeyre. Nouveau manuel complet de la fabrication des encres. Paris 1856, 1875.
Underwood, J. The history and chemistry of writing, printing and copying inks. [1858].
Davids, Thaddeus & Co. The history of ink. New York [1860].
[Lorilleux, C.] Notice sur la fabrication des encres d'imprimerie noires et de couleur. Paris [1867].
Waldow, A. Kurzer Rathgeber für die Behandlung der Farben. Leipzig 1868, 1884.
Andés, L. E. Oel- und Buchdruckfarben. Vienna 1889; tr as Oil colours and printers' inks, 1903, 1918.
Bannan, J. Modern ink making. Inland Printer (Chicago) 17–18 1896–7.
Goebel, T. Unsere Farbe. St Gallen 1896.
Jennison, F. H. The manufacture of lake pigments from artificial colours. 1900, 1920.
Rubencamp, R. Farbe und Papier im Druckgewerbe. Frankfurt 1900.
Carvalho, D. N. Forty centuries of ink. New York 1904.
Mitchell, C. A. and T. C. Hepworth. Inks: their composition and manufacture. 1904.
Seymour, A. Modern printing inks. 1910.
Underwood, N. and T. V. Sullivan. The chemistry and technology of printing inks. 1915.
Burt, F. L. Printing inks; their history, composition and manufacture. Inland Printer (Chicago) Nov 1919–Feb 1920.
Wiborg, F. B. Printing ink: a history. New York 1926.
Wolf, H. Manufacture of printing and lithographic inks. New York [1931].
Kriegel, H. G. Encyclopaedia of printing, lithographic inks and accessories. New York 1932.
Allen, A. S. Inks for printing. Dolphin 1 1933.
Winstone, B. & Sons. Ink in the making 1849–1948. 1948.
The story of printing inks. Paper & Print 21–2 1948–9.
Hughes, J. H. Printing ink rollers: their history and manufacture. Paper & Print 23 1950.
Coates Bros. Seventy-five years 1877–1952. [1952].
Archambaud, P. L'encre au cours des âges. La France Graphique May 1955.
Bloy, C. H. A history of printing, balls and rollers. 1967.

(4) THE MANUFACTURE OF TYPE

Typefounding

Hansard, T. C. Treatises on printing and typefounding. Edinburgh 1841.
Bower Bros. Proposal for establishing a graduated scale of sizes for the bodies of printing types. Sheffield 1841 (3rd edn).
Henze, A. Handbuch der Schriftgiesserei und der verwandten Nebenzweigen. Weimar 1844.
Mayhew, H. (ed). The type-foundry of Messrs James Marr & Co, Edinburgh and London. Shops & Companies of London 8–9 [1865?].
Bachmann, J. H. Die Schriftgiesserei. Leipzig 1867.
Johnson, J. R. On certain improvements in the manufacture of printing types. Jnl of Soc of Arts 21 March 1873. *See* Printing Times April–May 1873.
Smalian, H. Practisches Handbuch für Buchdrucker im Verkehr mit Schriftgiessereien. Danzig 1874, Leipzig 1877.
Gauthier, V. E. Concordance du point typographique avec la système métrique. Nice 1881 (7th edn).
Boussemaer, A. La fonderie typographique. Lille 1885.
Reed, T. B. A history of the old English letter foundries. 1887, 1952 (rev A. F. Johnson).
Bausa, V. Origines de la fonderie typographique et des machines à fondre. Paris 1893.
Fox, W. W. The printer and the typefounder: a modern view of an ancient grievance. [1897].
de Vinne, T. L. The practice of typography: a treatise on the process of type-making, the point system, the names, sizes and prices of plain printing types. New York 1900.
Figgins, J. Type founding and printing during the nineteenth century. 1901.
Haddon, W. The standardisation and interchangeability of printing types. [1902].
—— Centenary booklet descriptive of the growth of J. Haddon & Co, with personal reminiscences. 1914.
Wightman, J. H. A brief history of typefounding and the point system. 1910.
Legros, L. A. and J. C. Grant. Typographical printing surfaces: the technology and mechanism of their production. 1916.
McRae, J. F. Two centuries of typefounding: annals of the letter foundry established by William Caslon. 1920.
Burdon, C. S. One hundred years: to commemorate the centenary of Pavyer and Bullen's. 1922.
Howe, E. Typefounding and mechanical typesetting in the nineteenth century. Typography 2 1937.
Rollins, C. P. A brief and general discourse on type: part ix of a history of the printed book. Dolphin 3 1938.
Bengtsson, B. Äldre typografisk teknik. Stockholm 1946.
Berry, W. T. and A. F. Johnson. The homes of the London typefounders. Paper & Print 19 1946.
—— British typefounders in 1851. Printing Rev 16 1951.
Bohadti, G. Die Buchdruckletter. Berlin 1954.
Mosley, J. The typefoundry of Vincent Figgins 1792–1836. Motif 1 1958.
Morison, S. Talbot Baines Reed: author, bibliographer, typefounder. Cambridge 1960 (priv ptd).

Type Design

Austin, R. Specimens of printing types cast at Austin's Imperial Foundry. 1819. Preface.
Capelle, P. Manuel de la typographie française. Paris 1826.
de Vinne, T. L. Historic printing types: a lecture. New York 1886 (Grolier Club).
—— The practice of typography: a treatise on the processes of type making, the point system, the names, sizes, styles, and prices of plain printing types. New York 1900, 1925.
Reed, T. B. Old and new fashions in typography. Jnl of Soc of Arts 18 April 1890.
Updike, D. B. Printing types: their history, forms and use. 2 vols Cambridge Mass 1922, 1937 (rev).
Carter, J. and H. G. Pollard. An enquiry into the nature of certain nineteenth century pamphlets. 1934. Ch 5.
Johnson, A. F. Type designs: their history and development. 1934, 1959, 1966.
—— Fat faces: their history, forms and use. Alphabet & Image 5 1947.
—— Some English decorated initials. Alphabet & Image 7 1948.
Berry, W. T. and A. F. Johnson. Catalogue of specimens of printing types by English and Scottish printers and founders 1665–1830. 1935. Suppl in Signature new ser 16 1952.
—— Encyclopaedia of type faces. 1953.
Peddie, R. A. Subject index of books published before 1880: second series. 1935.
Gray, N. Nineteenth-century ornamented types and title-pages. 1938.
Howe, E. and O. Vignettes in typefounders' specimen books 1780–1900. Signature 2 1939.
McLean, R. An examination of Egyptians. Alphabet & Image 1 1946.
Nowell-Smith, S. The phonotypes of Robert Bridges. Alphabet & Image 5 1947.
Thomas, R. A. W. The development of printing types. 1949 (Broadsheet, Baynard Press).
Ornaments. [1951] (Chiswick Press).
Handover, P. M. Letters without serifs. Motif 6 1961.

Stereotyping and Electrotyping

Camus, A. G. Histoire et procédés du polytypage et de la stéréotypie. Paris 1801, 1802.
Wilson, A. Arbitration between the University of Cambridge and A. Wilson. 1806.
—— Stereotype printing. [1811].
Brightly, C. Account of the method of casting stereotype. Bungay 1809.
Hodgson, T. An essay on the origin and progress of stereotype printing; including a description of the various processes. Newcastle 1820.
Le Gentil, J. P. G. (Comte de Paroy). Précis sur la stéréotypie. Paris 1822.
Description des procédés de stéréotypage. Annales de l'Industrie Nationale et Etrangère 12 1823.
Chabert, L. Stéréotypie et polytypie. Paris 1829.
Westreenen van Tiellandt, W. H. Rapport sur les recherches relatives à l'usage le plus ancien de l'imprimerie stéréotype. Hague 1833.
Meyer, H. Handbuch der Stereotypie. Brunswick 1838.
Jordan, C. J. Engraving by Galvanism. Mechanics' Mag 22 May 1839.
Spencer, T. Instructions for the multiplication of works of art in metal by voltaic electricity. Glasgow 1840.
Jacobi, M. H. Die Galvanoplastik. Leningrad 1840.
[Schoenberg, L.] Metallic engravings in relief for letterpress printing: being a greatly improved substitute for wood engravings called acrography by the inventor. 1841.
Smee, A. Elements of electro-metallurgy: or the art of working in metals by the galvanic fluid. 1841, 1843, 1851.
Walker, C. V. Electrotype manipulation. 1841, 1850; tr French, 1843.
Zantedeschi, F. Memorie della elettrotipia. Venice 1841.
Knobloch, M. Der Galvanismus in seiner technischen Anwendung seit dem Jahre 1840: oder Galvanoplastik. Erlangen 1842.
Kobell, F. von. Die Galvanographie. Munich 1842.
Netto, F. A. W. Anweisung zur Galvanoplastik. Quedlinburg 1842.
Sampson, T. Electrotint: or the art of making paintings in such manner that copperplates and blocks can

be taken from them by means of voltaic electricity. 1842.
Palmer, E. Glyphography: or engraved drawing for printing at the type press after the manner of woodcuts. [1843], [c. 1845].
La stéréotypie perfectionnée et de son véritable inventeur [Durouchail]. Paris 1847.
Dircks, H. Jordantype, otherwise called electrotype: being a vindication of the claims of C. J. Jordan as the inventor of electro-metallurgy. 1852.
— Contribution towards a history of electro-metallurgy. 1863.
Martin, A. Repertorium der Galvanoplastik und Galvanostegie. 2 vols Vienna 1856.
Archimowitz, T. Neues französisches Stereotyp-Verfahren. 2 pts Karlsruhe 1856–8.
— Die Papier Stereotypie. Karlsruhe 1862.
Wood, J. and R. M. Papier mâché stereotyping apparatus. 1860.
Collins, H. G. Electro-block printing, especially as applied to enlarging any printing surface. Jnl of Soc of Arts 7 Dec 1860.
Nicholson, T. Instructions for the manipulation of the Nicholson stereotype apparatus. 1874 (2nd edn).
Wilson, F. J. F. Stereotyping and electro-typing. [1880], [1882], [1898].
Urquhart, J. W. Electro-typing. 1881.
Geymet, T. Traité de galvanoplastie et d'électrolyse. Paris 1888.
Bolas, T. Cantor lectures on stereotyping. 1890.
Langbein, G. A complete treatise on the electro-deposition of metals, translated into English by W. T. Braunt. New York 1891, 1920.
Partridge, C. S. Stereotyping. Chicago 1892.
— Electrotyping: a practical treatise. Chicago 1899, 1908, 1909.
Pilworth, E. S. Electrotyping in its relation to the graphic arts. New York 1923.

(5) PRINTING

General and Literary Works

Bigmore, E. C. and C. W. H. Wyman. A bibliography of printing. 3 vols 1880–6.
Bullen, H. L. The literature of typography. Inland Printer (Chicago) 50–5 1913–15.
McCreery, J. The press: a poem. 2 pts Liverpool 1803–27, 1828.
Timperley, C. H. Songs of the press and other poems relative to printing. 1833, 1845.
Brimmer, G. The composing room: a serio-comico-satirico-poetical production. 1835.
Savage, W. A dictionary of the art of printing. 1841.
'Parley, P.' Parley's visit to the printing office. [1843].
Neuburger, H. Encyklopaedie der Buchdruckerkunst. Leipzig 1844.
Knight, C. The old printer and the modern press. 1854.
Patent Office. Abridgements of specifications relating to printing 1617–1857. 1859.
— Abridgements of specifications relating to letterpress and similar printing 1858–66. 1878. (2nd edn).
— Abridgements of specifications relating to letterpress and similar printing 1867–76. 1878.
— Abridgements of specifications [illustrated series], class 100: printing, letterpress and lithographic 1855–66. 1904.
Ringwalt, J. L. American encyclopaedia of printing. Philadelphia 1871.
Southward, J. A dictionary of typography. 1871, 1875.
— Progress in printing and the graphic arts during the Victorian era. 1897.
Waldow, A. Die Buchdruckerkunst in ihren technischen und kaufmannischen Betriebe. 3 vols Leipzig 1874–7.
— Illustrierte Encyklopädie der graphischen Künste. Leipzig 1884.
Wolf, L. Exhibition and market of machinery, implements and material used by printers: official catalogue. 1880.
— 2nd annual exhibition. 1881.
— 3rd printers', stationers' and papermakers' exhibition and market. 1883.
Faulmann, C. Illustrirte Geschichte der Buchdruckerkunst. Vienna 1882.
Lorck, C. B. Handbuch der Geschichte der Buchdruckerkunst. 2 vols Leipzig 1882–3.
Tuer, A. W. Quads for authors, editors and devils. 1884.
Jacobi, C. T. The printer's vocabulary. 1888.
— Gesta typographica: or a medley for printers and others. 1897.
The American dictionary of printing and bookmaking. New York 1894.
[Wilson, J. F.] A few personal recollections by an old printer. 1896.
Thomson, T. Rhymes and songs for printers. Edinburgh 1897.
Plomer, H. R. A short history of English printing. 1900.
Morin, E. Dictionnaire typographique. Lyons 1903.
Maire, A. La technique du livre. Paris 1908.
Times: printing number. 12 Sept 1912.
Peddie, R. A. An outline of the history of printing to which is added the history of printing in colours. 1917.
Arneudo, G. I. Dizionario esegetico, tecnico e storico per le arte grafiche. 3 vols Turin 1917–24.
Thibaudeau, F. La lettre de l'imprimerie. 2 vols Paris 1921.
Jones, I. A history of printing and printers in Wales to 1810, and of successive and related printers to 1923; also a history of printing and printers in Monmouthshire to 1923. 1925.
The catalogue of the collection of broadsides. 1930 (London Univ Lib).
Greenhood, D. and H. Gentry. Chronology of books and printing. New York 1933, 1936 (rev).
Beilenson, P. The nineteenth century: chapter vii of the history of the printed book. Dolphin 3 1938.
London School of printing: a survey of its inception and work, with a few historical notes on its vicinity. 1938.
Fishenden, R. B. Printing and invention. Printing Rev 9 1941.
Corrigan, A. J. A printer and his world. 1944.
— 1851 prototypes of 1951 printing equipment. Paper & Print 24 1951.
Smail, J. C. Printing: Scottish enterprise. Edinburgh [1947].
Simon, O. English typography and the industrial age. Signature new ser 7 1948.
Johnson, A. F. Typographia: or the printer's instructor. Penrose Annual 43 1949.
Sessions, M. The Federation of Master Printers: how it began. 1950.
Berry, W. T. The printed word. In A century of technology 1851–1951, ed P. Dunsheath 1951.
— Printing and related trades. In A history of technology 1850–1900, ed C. Singer et al 1957.
— and H. E. Poole. Annals of printing: a chronological encyclopaedia. 1966.
Hasler, C. The official catalogues of the Great Exhibition of 1851. Penrose Annual 45 1951.
Hazell, R. C. Printing at the turn of the century. Ibid.
Le livre anglais: trésor des collections anglaises. Paris 1951 (Bibliothèque Nationale).
Rosner, C. Printer's progress: a comparative survey of the craft of printing 1851–1951. 1951.
Watson, S. F. Exhibition of early print in East Anglia: sixteenth century to the early years of the nineteenth century. Eastbourne 1951.

Jennett, S. Pioneers in printing. 1958. With brief biographies of Senefelder, Koenig, Mergenthaler, Lanston.
Handover, P. M. Printing in London from 1476 to modern times: competitive practice and technical invention in the trade of book and Bible printing, periodical production, jobbing etc. 1960.
Clair, C. A history of printing in Britain. 1965.
Day, K. (ed). Book typography 1815–1965 in Europe and the United States of America. 1966.

Manuals

See L. C. Wroth, Corpus typographicum: a review of English and American printers' manuals, Dolphin (New York) 2 1935.

Vinçard, B. L'art du typographe. Paris 1806, 1823.
Stower, C. The printer's grammar. 1808.
— The compositor's and pressman's guide to the art of printing. 1808.
Täubel, C. G. Vollständiges theoretisch-praktisches Lehrbuch der Buchdruckerkunst. 2 vols Vienna 1809–10.
Van Winkle, C. S. The printer's guide: or an introduction to the art of printing. New York 1818, 1836.
Flick, J. F. Handbuch der Buchdruckerkunst für angehende und praktische Buchdrucker. Berlin 1820.
Johnson, J. Typographia: or the printer's instructor. 2 vols 1824.
Brun, M. A. Manuel pratique et abrégé de la typographie française. Paris 1825.
Hansard, T. C. Typographia: an historical sketch of the origin and progress of the art of printing; with practical directions for conducting every department in an office. 1825.
Partington, C. F. The printer's complete guide. 1825, [1831].
Fournier, H. Traité de la typographie. Paris 1825, Brussels 1826, Tours 1854 (rev), 1870 (rev). Introd only tr C. E. Keymer, Gloucester 1866.
Krebs, B. Handbuch der Buchdruckerkunst. Frankfurt 1827.
Sherman, A. N. The printer's manual. New York 1834.
Hasper, W. Handbuch der Buchdruckerkunst. Karlsruhe 1835.
Neuburger, H. Praktisches Handbuch der Buchdruckerkunst. Leipzig 1841.
Adams, T. F. Typographia: or the printer's instructor. Philadelphia 1837, 1844 (rev), 1845, 1861.
Timperley, C. H. The printer's manual. 1838.
Hansard, T. C. Treatises on printing and typefounding. Edinburgh 1841.
Holtzapffel & Co. Printing apparatus for the use of amateurs. 1846 (3rd edn).
Pozzoli, G. Manuale di tipografia: ovvero guida practica pei combinatori di caratteri, pei torcolieri e pei legatori di libri. Milan 1861.
The printer. 1865, [c. 1880] (Houlston's Industrial Lib no 31).
MacKellar, T. The American printer: a manual of typography. Philadelphia 1866, 1874, 1879.
Marahrens, A. Vollständiges theoretisch-praktisches Handbuch der Typographie. 2 vols Leipzig 1870.
Morton, C. The cosmopolitan amateur printing office guide. [1873].
Bachmann, J. F. Neues Handbuch der Buchdruckerkunst. Weimar 1876.
Gould, J. The letterpress printer: a complete guide to the art of printing. 1876, [1881], [1888], [1893], [1903], [1927].
Raynor, P. E. Printing for amateurs: a practical guide. [1876].
Fischer, H. Anleitung zum Accidenzsatz. Leipzig 1877.
Trueman, H. P. The eclectic handbook of printing. 1880 (2nd edn).
Southward, J. Practical printing: a handbook of the art of typography. 1882, 1884, 2 vols 1887, 1892, 1900, 1902, 1921.

— Modern printing: a handbook of the principles and practice of typography and the auxiliary arts. 4 vols 1898–1900, 1904–7, 2 vols 1912, 1915.
Jacobi, C. T. The printer's handbook of trade recipes. 1887, 1891, 1905.
— Printing: a practical treatise. 1890, 1893, 1898, 1904, 1908, 1912.
Wilson, F. J. F. and D. Grey. A practical treatise upon modern printing machinery and letterpress printing. 1888.
Oldfield, A. A practical manual of typography. [1890], 1898, [1906].
Dumont, J. Vade-mecum du typographe. Brussels 1891, 1894, 1906.
Sala, C. Manuale pratico di tipografia. 2 vols Milan 1894.
Fisher, T. The elements of letterpress printing, composing and proof reading. Madras 1895, 1906.

Business Management

Rhynd, M. Rhynd's printers' guide: being a new and correct list of master printers in London. 1804 (3rd edn).
Magrath, W. The printer's assistant to which is added a correct list of master printers in London. 1804.
[Mason, W.] The printer's assistant. 1810, 1821 (4th edn).
— The printer's price book for job work in general. 1816, 1820.
Stower, C. The printer's price book. 1814.
Rose, P. and J. Evans. The printer's job price book. Bristol 1814, 1824.
Cowie, G. Cowie's printer's pocket book and manual. [c. 1830], [c. 1835], [c. 1850].
Day, W. J. A series of tables invented and arranged for the use of the practical printer. 1841.
Houghton, T. S. The printer's practical everyday book. 1841, 1843, 1849, Preston [1857] (rev), [1875] (rev G. Marshall).
Feeny, R. Master printer's price manual. 1845.
Howitt, F. E. The country printer's job price book. [1849] (2nd edn).
Fielding, D. The typographical ready reckoner and memorandum book. [1853], [1858].
Cobbett, T. G. The master printer's handbook of prices. Birkenhead 1860.
Ruse, G. and C. Straker. Printing and its accessories: a comprehensive book of charges for the guidance of printers. [c. 1860].
Crisp, W. F. The printer's business guide. 1866, 1867, 1869, [1873], [1874], [1876], [1881].
[Lawton, F. W.] The printer's pocket companion. Rochdale [1870].
Ellis, J. B. and W. Denton. The printer's calculator and practical companion. Leeds 1876.
Manning, J. The printer's vade-mecum and ready reference. Aberdeen 1881.
Ellis, J. B. Hints and tables for the printing office and paper warehouse. Leeds [1887], [c. 1890].
Rowell, G. F. How to start a printing office. 1897.
— Hints on estimating. 1897, 1901.
Gotts, J. B. Estimating, book keeping, system for letterpress and lithographic printers. 1901, 1906 (3rd edn).
Whitehead, T. L. The ideal price list, estimate guide and cost book for commercial letterpress printing. Bury 1901.
Smith, H. L. Printers' accounts. 1903.
Federation of Master Printers. Profit for printers: or what is cost? 1904, 1907, 1909.
Naylor, T. E. How to start in business as a printer. [1905].

Correct Composition

Stower, C. Typographical marks used in correcting proofs. 1805, 1806, 1822.
Graham, J. The compositor's text book: or instructions in the elements of the art of printing. Glasgow 1848.

Wilson, J. A treatise on English punctuation. Boston 1850.
F[ord], T. The compositor's handbook. 1854.
Wilson, W. The compositor's assistant containing all the imposition tables now in use. Exeter 1855.
Beadnell, H. A guide to typography. 2 vols 1859–61.
Ruse, G. Imposition simplified. [1860], 1875.
Goebel, T. Ueber den Satz des Englischen. Leipzig 1865.
Bidwell, G. H. Printer's new handbook: a treatise on the imposition of formes. New York 1866, 1875.
Neill & Co. Guide to authors in correcting the press. Edinburgh [c. 1870], [c. 1880], 1895, 1897.
Newman, E. The author's guide for printing. 1875.
Gould, J. The compositor's guide and pocket book. 1878, 1928.
Jowett, H. Hints to authors: being a handy book of reference in all matters referring to printing. 1889 (3rd edn).
Fletcher, W. C. A simple guide to the art of punctuation for authors and printers. Oxford [c. 1890].
Le Forestier, J. Manuel pratique et bibliographique du correcteur. Paris 1890.
Blades, W. How to correct proofs. 1893.
Hart, H. Rules for compositors and readers at the Clarendon Press. Oxford 1893 (broadside), 1895, 1930 (29th edn).
Mitchell, J. Printers' blunders: their causes, effects and cure. Edinburgh 1894.
Teall, F. H. Punctuation: with chapters on hyphenisation, capitalisation and spelling. New York 1898.
— Proof reading: a series of essays for readers and their employers. Chicago 1899.
De Vinne, T. L. The practice of typography: correct composition. New York 1901.
Collins, F. M. Author and printer: an attempt to codify the best typographical practices of the present day. 1905, 1905, 1909 (rev as Authors' and printers' dictionary), 1912, 1928, 1933.
Brossard, L. E. Le correcteur typographe. Tours 1924.

Type Composing Machinery

Gaubert, E. R. Rénovation de l'imprimerie: notice sur le gérotype, ou machine à distribuer et à composer en typographie. Paris 1843.
Bradbury, H. Hattersley's type composing machine. Jnl of Soc of Arts 7 1859.
Mitchell, W. H. Type-setting by machinery. 1863.
Yeaton, C. C. Manual of the Alden typesetting and distributing machine. New York 1865.
Brown, L. Types: a description of Brown's patent type-setting and distributing machine. Boston 1870.
Mackie, A. Description of patent steam type composing machine. 1871.
Fraser, A. On typesetting machines with a description of Fraser's composing and distributing machines. Edinburgh 1876.
Marchal, J. Rapport sur la machine à composer de M. Kastenbein. [Nancy 1878].
Barnes, W. C., J. W. McCann and A. Duguid. A collation of facts relative to fast typesetting. New York 1887.
Southward, J. The Thorne combined type setting and distributing machine. 1890. Rptd from Printers' Register 6 April 1890.
— Type composing machines of the past, the present and the future. 1890, Leicester 1891.
— The Lanston Monotype machine. [1897].
Linotype Co Ltd. The Linotype composing machine. 1891, 1895, [1897].
— The Linotype: its history, construction and operation. [1893], [1893].
— The solution of a problem of four centuries: the evolution of the Linotype composing machine. [1897].

Report to the American Newspaper Publishers' Association by the committee in charge of the type composition machine tournament held in Chicago 12–17 Oct 1891. New Haven 1892.
Lanston Monotype Machine Co. The Lanston Monotype machine. Washington 1896.
An enquiry into the claims of the Lanston Monotype machine. Manchester 1897.
Steevens, C. W. The Monotype. New Rev Nov 1897.
A revolution in printing: the story of the Linotype. Chambers's Jnl 30 Jan 1897.
Evans, F. The Linotype. Kansas City 1897.
Barclay, E. J. The Linotype operator's companion. Cincinnati 1898.
The Wicks type setter. 1898.
Herrmann, C. Geschichte der Setzmachine und ihre Entwickelung. Vienna [1900].
The Lanston Monotype Corporation Ltd. The Lanston Monotype machine. 1901.
Card, H. C. The Lanston Monotype keyboard. 1902.
Thompson, J. S. The mechanism of the Linotype. Chicago 1902, 1905.
— History of composing machines: a complete record of the art of composing type by machinery. Chicago 1904.
— The origin and development of the Linotype. Inland Printer (Chicago) 35 1905.
de Vinne, T. L. The practice of typography: modern methods of book composition. New York 1904.
Courandy, G. Une étude sur la machine à composer. Brussels 1904.
Legros, L. A. Type casting and composing machines. 1908.
Giraud, H. Nouveau manuel complet de linotypie. Paris 1909.
Blevins, A. E. The evolution of printing and typesetting machines. Jnl of South African Inst of Engineers March–April 1912.
Legros, L. A. and J. C. Grant. Typographical printing surfaces: the technology and mechanism of their production. 1916.
Bullen, H. L. On Lynn Boyd Benton. Inland Printer (Chicago) Oct 1922.
Elliott, R. C. The monotype from infancy to maturity. Monotype Recorder Feb 1932.
Dreier, T. The power of print—and men: commemorating the 50 years of Linotype's contribution to printing and publishing. New York 1936.
Monotype Corporation Ltd: forty years and what they brought about in the composing room. Monotype Recorder 24 1937.
Mossis, C. The Hooker composing machine. Printing Rev 15 1949.
The pioneer days of 'Monotype' composing machines. 1949 (Monotype Corporation Ltd).
Sherman, F. M. The genesis of machine typesetting. Chicago 1950.
Scully, M. Mergenthaler and his Linotype machine: the invention of the first typesetting machine. Amer Printer 134 1953.
Oscar Mergenthaler: the part he played in the development of the Linotype. Linotype & Machinery News 17 1954.
Moran, J. The composition of reading matter. 1965.

Presswork

Giroudot, —. Notice sur les presses mécaniques et celles à la Stanhope. Paris [1835].
Koenig, F. Printing machines 1810: patent specification no 3496. 1856.
Applegath, A. Printing machines 1822: patent specification no 4640. 1857.
— Printing machines 1823: patent specification no 4745. 1857.

— Printing machines 1846: patent specification no 11505. 1857.
Read, J. M. Instructions in the art of making-ready woodcuts. Reading [c. 1860].
Wittig, C. F. and C. F. Fischer. Die Schnellpresse: ihre Mechanik und Vorrichtung zum Druck aller typographischen Arbeiten. Leipzig 1861, 1866, 1878.
Mayhew, H. (ed). Conisbee's printing machine manufactory. Shops & Companies of London 8–9 [1865?].
Eisenmann, A. Die Schnellpresse: ihre Construction, Zusammenstellung und Behandlung. Leipzig 1865, 1872.
Waldow, A. Die Zurichtung und der Druck von Illustrationen. Leipzig 1867, 1879.
— Die Schnellpresse und ihre Behandlung vor und bei dem Drucke. Leipzig 1872.
— Hilfsbuch für Maschinenmeister an Buchdruck-Cylinder-Schnellpressen. 3 vols Leipzig 1887–92.
Myers, J. A few practical hints to printers on the treatment of rollers. 1871.
Monet, A. L. Le conducteur de machines typographiques. Paris 1872.
The Walter Press. 1872, 1876 (enlarged).
Bachmann, J. F. Der Buchdrucker an der Handpresse. Leipzig [1873].
Cummins, R. The pressmen's guide. Brooklyn 1873.
Rigg, A. On type printing machinery and suggestions thereon. Jnl of Soc of Arts 13 Feb 1874.
Goebel, T. Friederich Koenig und die Erfindung der Schnellpresse: ein biographisches Denkmal. Brunswick 1875, Stuttgart 1883, 1906 (rev); tr French, 1885.
Gaskill, J. The printing machine manager's complete practical handbook. 1877, [c. 1880], [1888].
Stevens, C. P. Roller guide: a treatise on rollers and compositions. Boston 1877.
Thompson, J. R. Printers' rollers: how to treat them. Leeds 1880.
Wilson, F. J. F. Typographic printing machines and machine printing. [1880], [c. 1885]; tr French, 1886.
[Wyman, C. W. H.] List of technical terms relating to printing machinery. 1882.
Noble, F. Difficulties in machine printing, and how to overcome them. 1883.
Clowes, E. A. Printing machinery. Minutes of Proc Inst Civil Engineers 89 1887.
Southward, J. The principles and progress of printing machinery. [1888], 1890.
Motteroz, C. Essai sur la mise en train typographique. Paris 1891; tr Inland Printer (Chicago) Dec 1891–Jan 1893.
Patent Office Studies. Br & Colonial Printer 3 Aug 1893–12 April 1894.
Powrie, W. Machinery for book and general printing. 1899.
Hoe, R. A short history of the printing press and of the improvements in printing machinery from the time of Gutenberg. New York 1902.
Thomas, F. W. A concise manual of platen presswork. Chicago 1903.
Beschreibung des Modells der Ersten von Friederich Koenig erfundenen Schnellpresse aus dem Jahre 1811. Würzburg [1908].
Haag, A. Über maschinelle Einrichtungen und Arbeitsmethoden in englischen Buchdruckereien. [Vienna 1910].
Powell, D. T. The inking of the forme. Imprint 17 July 1913.
Isaacs, G. A. The story of the newspaper printing press. 1931.
Dieterichs, K. Die Buchdruckpresse von Johannes Gutenberg bis Friedrich König. Mainz 1930.
Burke, J. Prelum to Albion: a history of the development of the hand press from Gutenberg to Morris. San Francisco 1940.

Dawson, Payne & Elliott Ltd., Otley. Otley's 100 years' service to the printing industry. Paper & Print 22 1949.
Harrild & Sons. The house of Harrild 1801–1948. 1949.
Kainen, J. George Clymer and the Columbian Press. New York 1950.
Berry, W. T. The autobiography of a wooden press. Typographica 8 1953.
Bisset, C. D. A short history of platen presses. Print in Britain 1 1954.

Colour Printing

All methods of colour printing involve separate impressions for each colour used, irrespective of the process by which the printing surface has been made. The only exceptions to this are hand colouring of the plate for each impression, Congreve's patent for interlocking blocks separately inked (c. 1830), and Stenochromy (c. 1875); the last two were never successfully applied to book illustration. This section therefore covers the application of colour to all printing processes including chromolithography. Information on coloured inks is given in some of the books already mentioned cols 31 f., above; historical works not concerned with technique appear in col 53, below; and some further details will be found in the biographies of George Baxter *and* Francis Orpen Morris, *cols 64, 67, below.*

Savage, W. Hints on decorative printing. 1822.
The pictorial album: or cabinet of pictures. 1837. Preface.
Netto, F. A. W. Das Geheimniss des Oelbilder-Drucks erfunden vom Maler Liepmann in Berlin. Quedlinburg 1840.
Rotch, B. Hullmandel's lithotint process. Jnl of Soc of Arts 54 1841.
Liepmann, J. Der Oelgemälde-Druck erfunden und beschrieben. Berlin 1842.
Weishaupt, H. Theoretisch-praktische Anleitung zur Chromolithographie. Quedlinburg 1848.
Digeon, R. H. Cercles chromatiques de M. E. Chevreul reproduits au moyen de la chromo-calcographie, gravure et impression en taille-douce combinées. Paris 1855.
Clerk Maxwell, J. On the theory of compound colours and the relation of the colours of the spectrum. Philosophical Trans of Royal Soc 50 1861.
Chevreul, M. E. Des couleurs et de leurs applications aux arts industriels. Paris 1864.
Ihm, B. A. Die bunten Farben in der Buchdruckerei. Biel 1865, 1874.
The chromolithograph: a journal of art, literature, decoration and the accomplishments. No 1, 23 Nov 1867–27 March 1869. Weekly.
Zenker, W. Lehrbuch der Photochromie. Berlin 1868.
du Hauron, L. D. Les couleurs en photographie. Paris 1869.
— Traité pratique de photographie des couleurs. Paris 1878.
Watt, P. B. A few hints on colour and printing in colours. 1872.
Galton, F. Colour printing and cartography. In Report of the 42nd meeting of the British Association, 1872.
Simpson, W. A glance at the history of chromo-lithography. Lithographer Aug 1873.
Meyerstein, E. Stenochromy: a new process for printing a number of colours at the same time. Jnl of Royal Soc of Arts 15 Dec 1876.
St Victor, P. de. La photochromie. Paris 1876.
Weissenbach, H. von. Der xylographische Farbendruck in den verschiedenen Phasen seiner Herstellung. Nuremberg 1878 (priv ptd).
Noble, F. The principles and practice of colour printing. 1881.
Richmond, W. D. Colour and colour printing as applied to lithography. 1882, [c. 1885], [c. 1890].

Wohlfarth, A. Über Farben. Leipzig 1882 (2nd edn).
Achaintre, A. Etude sur les impressions en couleurs. Paris [1883].
Audsley, G. A. The art of chromolithography. 1883.
Waldow, A. Anleitung zum Farbendruck auf der Buchdruckpresse und Maschine. Leipzig [1883].
Die Heliochromie: das Problem des Photographierens in natürlichen Farben. Düsseldorf 1884.
Meta, O. Der Steindrucker an der Schnellpresse nebst einer Abhandlung über die Farben in der Chromolithographie. Vienna 1884.
Reich, W. Die Farbenmischung für Druckereien: Steindruck, Buchdruck, Lichtdruck. Berlin 1887.
Berget, A. Photographie des couleurs par la méthode intéferentielle de M. Lippmann. Paris 1891.
Earhart, J. F. The color printer: a treatise on the use of colour in typographic printing. Chicago 1892.
Ives, F. E. Handbook to the photochromoscope. 1894.
— The process of three-colour work. Penrose's Pictorial Annual 7 1901.
Morin, E. Essai sur les impressions en couleurs. Paris 1894.
Berthier, A. Manuel de photochromie interférentielle: procédés de reproduction directe des couleurs. Paris 1895.
du Hauron, A. D. La triplice photographique des couleurs et l'imprimerie. Paris 1897.
— La photographie des couleurs et les découvertes de Louis Ducos de Hauron. Paris [1899].
Hesse, F. Die Chromolithographie mit besonderer Berücksichtigung der modernen auf photographischer Grundlage basierten Verfahren. Halle [1896], [1904–6]; tr French, 1897.
Hübl, A. F. von. Die Dreifarbenphotographie mit besonderer Berücksichtigung des Dreifarbendrucks und der photographischen Pigmentbilder in natürlichen Farben. Halle 1897; tr H. O. Klein 1904.
— Die Theorie und Praxis der Farbenphotographie mit Autochromplatten. Halle 1908.
Vidal, L. Photographie des couleurs. Paris 1897.
— Traité pratique de photochromie. Paris 1903.
Mellerio, A. La lithographie en couleurs. Paris 1898.
Clerc, L. P. La photographie des couleurs. Paris [1899].
Zander, C. G. A lecture on the colour principle of trichromatic printing. [1899].
Bolas, T. et al. A handbook of photography in colours. 1900.
Vaughan, W. E. Autobiographica, with a gossip of the art of printing in colours. [Brighton] 1900 (priv ptd).
Horgan, S. H. Three-colour process work. In H. Jenkins, Manual of photo-engraving, 1902.
Shepherd, S. & Co. Photography in natural colours. 1902.
Souillier, E. Nouveau traité sur les impressions modernes en couleurs. Paris 1903.
Dalziel, H. Three-colour printing. Jnl of Royal Soc of Arts 20 Feb 1903.
Klein, H. O. Collodion emulsion and its applications to various photographic and photo-mechanical purposes, with special reference to trichromatic process work. 1905.
Calmels, H. and L. P. Clerc. La reproduction photographique des couleurs. Paris 1907.
Wallon, E. La photographie des couleurs et les plaques autochromes, suivie d'une notice sur le mode d'emploi des plaques autochromes, par MM Lumière. Paris 1907.
Dillaye, F. La photographie des couleurs par les plaques autochromes. Paris 1908.
Goldberg, E. Farbenphotographie und Farbendruck. Leipzig 1908.
Paton, H. Colour etching. 1909.
Preissig, V. Zur Technik der farbigen Radierung und des Farben-Kupferstichs. Leipzig 1909.

Prideaux, S. T. Aquatint engraving: a chapter in the history of book illustration. 1909.
Burch, R. M. Colour printing and colour printers. 1910.
Andrews, E. C. Colour and its application to printing. Chicago 1911.
Martin, L. C. Colour and methods of colour reproduction. 1923.
Wall, E. J. The history of three-color photography. Boston 1925.
Johnson, A. F. Rudolph Ackermann and Thomas Rowlandson. Penrose Annual 1935.
Gray, N. The 19th-century chromo-lithograph. Architectural Rev 84 1938.
Tritton, F. J. A survey of colour photography. 1939.
Heintzelman, A. W. Early English color prints. Bull Boston Public Lib 17 1942.
Friedman, J. F. History of color photography. Boston 1944.
Cordingley, J. Early colour printing and George Baxter 1804–67: a monograph produced in the printing dept of the North-Western Polytechnic. 1949.
Hasler, C. Mid-nineteenth-century colour printing. Penrose Annual 45 1951.
Groschwitz, G. von. The significance of nineteenth-century color lithography. Gazette des Beaux-Arts 44 1954.
Twyman, M. The tinted lithograph. Jnl of Printing Historical Soc 1 1965.

Trade Organizations

Manchester Typographical Society Centenary 1797–1897. 1897.
Head, W. W. The Victoria Press, with an account of the movement for the employment of females in printing. 1869.
Willis, F. The present position and future prospects of the London Society of Compositors. [1881].
Slatter, H. The Typographical Association: a fifty years' record 1849–99. Ed R. Hackett, Manchester [1899].
London Society of Compositors: a brief record of events. 1899.
Scottish Typographical Association: a fifty years' record 1853–1903. 1903.
Cork Typographical Society Centenary 1806–1906. Cork 1906.
Leeds Typographical Society centenary souvenirs 1810–1910. Leeds 1910.
The history and progress of the Amalgamated Society of Lithographic Printers 1880–1930. 1930.
Suthers, R. B. The story of Natsopa. 1930.
Morison, S. Hand list of printing trade documents issued by the London associations of master printers, booksellers, press men and machine men 1795–1919, now preserved at the University Press Cambridge. 1936.
Williamson, H. S. They marched with banners. Signature 6 1937.
Temple, H. S. Printing trade organizations. 1938.
Howe, E. From craft to industry: the London printing trade 1700–1900. Printing Rev 13 1947.
— The London compositor: documents relating to wages, working conditions and customs of the London printing trade 1785–1900. 1947 (Bibl Soc).
— and H. E. Waite. The London Society of Compositors: a centenary history. 1948.
— and J. Child. The London Society of London Bookbinders. 1951.
Rowles, G. E. The line is on: a centenary souvenir of the London Society of Compositors 1848–1948. [1948].
Monotype Casters' and Typefounders' Society diamond jubilee 1889–1949: sixtieth annual report. 1949.
Sessions, M. The Federation of Master Printers: how it began. 1950.

Gillespie, S. C. A hundred years of progress: the records of the Scottish Typographical Association. 1953.
Musson, A. E. The Typographical Association. 1954.
Bundock, C. J. The National Union of Printing, Bookbinding and Paper Workers. 1959.
Moran, J. Seventy-five years of the National Society of Operative Printers and Assistants. 1964.
Child, J. Industrial relations in the British printing industry. 1967.

(6) GRAPHIC PROCESSES

Graphic Processes are here divided into 4 categories according to the nature of the surface from which the impression is taken. Books dealing with impression from relief, plane and intaglio surfaces are separately listed; while those dealing with more than one kind of surface have been grouped under General Works. No attempt has been made to distinguish between books dealing with the autographic and photographic production of the same kinds of surface.

General Works

Clark, L. and W. Brooks. Catalogue of the Camera Club Photographic library. [1894].
Singer, H. W. and S. Strang. Etching, engraving and other methods of printing pictures. 1897.
Levis, H. C. A descriptive bibliography of the most important books in the English language relating to the art and history of engraving. 1912; Supplement and index, 1913.
New York Public Library. List of books on prints. New York 1916.
Columbia University. A catalogue of the Epstean collection on the history and science of photography and its applications to the graphic arts. New York 1937.

Partington, C. F. The engraver's complete guide. 1825.
Pye, J. Evidence relating to the art of engraving taken before the Select Committee on Arts. 1836.
Fielding, T. H. The art of engraving. 1841, 1844.
Donlevy, J. The rise and progress of the graphic arts. New York 1854.
Kessler, G. Photographie auf Stahl, Kupfer und Stein, zur Anfertigung von Druckplatten für den Kupfer-, Stein- und Buchdruck. Berlin 1856.
Fromberg, E. Die graphischen oder zeichnenden Künste der Galvanoplastik. Quedlinburg 1857.
Hammann, J. H. H. Des arts graphiques destinés à multiplier par l'impression considérés sous le double point de vue historique et pratique. Geneva 1857.
Sutton, T. A dictionary of photography. 1858.
James, Sir H. Photo-zincography. Southampton 1860.
Stannard, W. J. The art-exemplar: a guide to distinguish one sort of print from another with pictorial examples. [c. 1860].
Poitevin, A. Traité de l'impression photographique. Paris 1862, 1883.
Scott, A. de C. On photo-zincography and other photographic processes employed at the Ordnance Survey Office. 1862.
Davenport, S. T. On prints and their production. 1869.
Moock, L. Traité pratique complet d'impression photographique aux encres grasses. Paris 1874.
Vogel, H. W. Die chemischen Wirkungen des Lichts und die Photographie in ihrer Anwendung in Kunst, Wissenschaft und Industrie. Leipzig 1874; tr 1875.
—— Handbuch der Photographie. 4 vols Berlin 1890–7.
Tissandier, G. A history and handbook of photography. 1876, 1878.
Wessely, J. E. Anleitung zur Kentniss und zum Sammeln der Werke des Kunstdruckes. Leipzig 1876.
Bolas, T. The application of photography to the production of printing surfaces. 1878.
—— Cantor lectures on the recent improvements in photomechanical printing methods. 1884.
Lostalot, A. de. Les procédés de la gravure. Paris [c. 1880].
Davanne, A. La photographie et les arts graphiques. Paris 1881.
Hamerton, P. G. The graphic arts. 1882.
—— Drawing and engraving. 1892.

Hodson, J. S. An historical and practical guide to art illustration in connection with books, periodicals and general decoration. 1884.
Pettit, J. S. Modern reproductive graphic processes. New York 1884.
Geymet, T. Traité pratique de gravure héliographique et de galvano-plastie. Paris 1885 (3rd edn).
Leslie, A. F. W. Practical instructor of photo-engraving and zinc etching processes. New York 1886, 1888.
Roux, V. Traité de photographie décorative appliquée aux arts industriels. Paris 1887.
Scherer, R. Neueste graphische Verfahren. Vienna 1885.
Les procédés: traité pratique de phototypie etc. Paris 1887
Monet, A. L. Procédés de reproductions graphiques appliquées à l'imprimerie. Paris 1888.
Wilkinson, W. T. Photo-engraving on zinc and copper, in line and half-tone and photolithography. 1886, 1887, New York 1888, London 1890, 1894.
—— Photo-mechanical processes: a practical guide to photozincography, photolithography and collotype. 1892, [1904].
Burbank, W. H. Photographic printing methods. New York 1887.
[Wood, Sir H. T.] Modern methods of illustrating books. 1887, 1898.
Burton, W. K. Practical guide to photographic and photo-mechanical printing. 1887, 1892.
Harrison, W. J. A history of photography. Bradford 1888.
Wall, E. J. The dictionary of photography. 1889; rev F. J. Mortimer [1933].
Waterhouse, J. Practical notes on the preparation of drawings for photographic reproduction, with a sketch of the principal photo-mechanical printing processes. 1890.
Werge, J. The evolution of photography. 1890.
Boston Museum of Fine Arts. Exhibition illustrating the technical methods of the reproductive arts from the xvth century to the present time with special reference to the photo-mechanical processes. Boston 1892. Introd by S. R. Koehler.
Duchochois, P. C. Photographic reproduction processes, edited with additional matter by E. J. Watt. 1892.
Harland, J. W. The printing arts: an epitome of engraving, lithography and printing. 1892.
Eder, J. M. The grammar of photo-engraving; tr New York 1893, 1895.
Process work. Penrose's circular [1893]–Dec 1921. Continued as Process Work and Electrotyping Jan 1922–1929. Ed W. Gamble.
Blackburn, H. The art of illustration. 1894, Edinburgh 1901 (rev).
Hinton, A. H. A handbook of illustration. [1894].
—— Practical pictorial photography. 2 vols 1898.
Adeline, J. Les arts de reproduction vulgarisés. Paris [1894].
Villon, A. M. Nouveau manuel complet du graveur en creux et en relief. 2 vols Paris 1894.
Fraipont, G. Eau-forte, pointe sèche, burin, lithographie. Paris [1895].
Paton, H. Etching, drypoint, mezzotint: the whole art of the painter-etcher. 1895, 1909 (rev).

The photogram. No 1, Jan 1895–Dec 1905. Continued as Process Engraver's Monthly Jan 1906–. Ed H. Snowden Ward, C. W. Ward. Monthly, with varying titles.

The process work year book. Penrose's Pictorial Annual 1 1898–1914. Continued as Penrose's Annual 1915–35. Ed W. Gamble, et al.

Braquemond. Etude sur la gravure sur bois et la lithographie. Paris 1897.

Singer, H. W. and W. Strang. Etching, engraving and other methods of printing pictures. 1897.

Hübl, A. F. von. Die photographischen Reproductionsverfahren. Halle 1898.

Kampmann, C. Die graphischen Künsten. Leipzig 1898.

Albert, A. Verschiedene Reproductions-verfahren. Halle 1900.

Ward, W. H. The printing arts: a description of the methods now in use, more particularly with regard to illustration. 1900.

Fisch, A. Traité pratique des impressions photomécaniques. Paris 1901.

Ribette, A. Traité pratique d'héliogravure en creux sur zinc, au bitume de Judée, accompagné de notions et de quelques procédés lithographiques pour la reproduction. Paris [c. 1902].

Kirkbride, J. Engraving for illustration: historical and practical notes. 1903.

Victoria and Albert Museum, South Kensington. Catalogue of the loan exhibition of process engraving. 1905. Introd by J. Waterhouse.

Amstutz, N. S. Hand-book of photo-engraving. Chicago 1907.

Baker, W. H. A dictionary of engraving. Cleveland 1908.

Hind, A. M. Short history of engraving and etching. 1908, 1910, 1923.

Harrap, C. Textbook of metalography. Leicester 1909, 1912.

Clerc, L. P. Les reproductions photomécaniques monochromes. Paris 1910.

Garrett, A. E. The advance of photography. 1911.

Short, F. Etchings and engravings: what they are, and what they are not. 1911.

Krueger, O. F. W. Die Illustrationsverfahren. Leipzig 1914.

Richter, E. H. Prints: a brief review of their technique and history. 1916.

Gamble, W. Photography and its applications. [1920].

Horgan, S. H. Photo-engraving primer. Boston 1920.

— Souvenirs sur l'histoire des procédés photomécaniques. Bulletin Officiel Union Syndicate (Paris) April, July 1932.

Hackleman, C. W. Commercial engraving and printing. Indianapolis 1924.

Ivins, W. M. Photography and the 'modern' point of view. Metropolitan Museum Stud 1 1928.

Poortenaar, J. Van printen en platten. Amsterdam 1931; tr 1933 (as The technique of prints).

Gamble, C. W. Modern illustration processes. 1933.

Curwen, H. Processes of graphic reproduction. 1934, 1966.

Groesbeck, H. A. Processes for reproduction. Dolphin 1 1933.

Meyer, K. The printing of music 1473–1934. Dolphin 2 1935.

Howe, E. From Bewick to the half-tone: a survey of illustration processes during the nineteenth century. Typography 3 1937.

Eder, J. M. History of photography. Tr E. Epstean, New York 1945.

Figenbaum, M. C. Graphic arts processes. New Books 22 1947.

Newhall, B. History of photography from 1839 to the present day. New York 1950.

Roger-Marx, C. Graphic art of the nineteenth century. 1962.

Cleaver, J. A history of graphic art. 1963.

Intaglio Surfaces

Copperplate engraving, etching, aquatint, photogravure, heliogravure.

[Green, J. H.] The complete aquatinter. Hartfield 1801, 1804, 1810.

Landseer, J. Lectures on the art of engraving. 1807.

Hassell, J. Calcographia: or the art of multiplying with perfection drawings after the manner of chalk, black-lead pencil and pen and ink. 1811.

— Graphic delineation: a practical treatise on the art of etching. 1826, 1827.

Martin, T. The circle of the mechanical arts. 1813.

Eberhard, H. W. Die Anwendung der chemischen Druckart auf Metallplatten. Mainz 1821.

— Die Anwendung des Zinks statt der Stein- und Kupferplatten zu den vertieften Zeichnungsarten. Darmstadt 1822.

Deleschamps, P. Des mordans, des vernis et des planches dans l'art du graveur ou traité complet de la gravure. Paris 1836.

Berthiau and Boitard. Nouveau manuel complet de l'imprimeur en taille-douce. Paris [1837].

Chevreul, M. E. Considérations sur la reproduction par les procédés de M. Niepce de Saint-Victor des images gravées, dessinées ou imprimées. Paris 1847.

Alken, H. The art and practice of etching. 1849.

Ashley, A. The art of etching on copper. [1849], 1851.

Fox Talbot, H. Photographic engraving. Jnl of Photographic Soc 1 1853.

— Description of Mr Fox Talbot's new process of photographic engraving. Photographic News 1 1858.

Salmon and Garnier. The process of photographic engraving. Jnl of Photographic Soc 2 1855.

Niepce de Saint-Victor, C. M. F. Photographic researches. Paris 1855.

— Traité pratique de gravure héliographique sur acier et sur verre. Paris 1856.

Lalanne, M. Traité de la gravure à l'eau-forte. Paris 1866; tr Boston 1880, 1884.

[Sawyer, J. R.] The autotype process. [1867], 1871, 1876, 1878.

Shrubsole, W. G. Etching: its principles and practice. [1870].

Hamerton, P. G. The etcher's handbook. 1871, 1875.

Scamoni, G. Handbuch der Heliogravure nebst praktischen Wegweiser im Gebiete der bezüglichen Gravirkunst. Leningrad 1872.

Hannot, A. Gravure sur cuivre au moyen de la photographie et de galvanoplastik. Brussels 1872.

Martial, A. P. Nouveau traité de la gravure à l'eau-forte pour les peintres et les dessinateurs. Paris 1873.

Tissandier, G. Une conférence sur l'héliogravure et ses applications à la librairie. Paris 1874.

— Histoire de la gravure typographique. Paris 1875.

Edwards, E. The heliotype process. Boston 1876.

Haden, F. S. About etching. 1878.

Husnik, J. Die Heliographie: oder eine Anleitung zur Herstellung druckbarer Metalplatten. Vienna 1878, 1888.

Chattock, R. S. Practical notes on etching. [c. 1880], 1883, 1886.

Vidal, L. Traité pratique de photoglyptie [i.e. Woodburytype]. Paris 1881; tr German, 1897.

— Le progrès de la photogravure. Paris 1900.

— Traité pratique de photogravure. Paris 1900.

Delaborde, H. La gravure. Paris 1882; tr R. A. M. Stevenson 1886.

Davanne, L. A. N. Niepce, inventeur de la photographie. Paris 1885.

Geymet, T. Traité pratique de photogravure sur zinc et sur cuivre. Paris 1886.

— Traité pratique de gravure sur verre par les procédés héliographiques. Paris 1887.

Roux, V. Manuel de l'imprimeur héliographe. Paris 1886.
Fouqué, V. La vérité sur l'invention de la photographie. Paris 1887.
Short, F. On the making of etchings. 1888, 1889, 1893, 1898.
Ferret, J. La photogravure facile et à bon marché. Paris 1889.
Wilkinson, W. T. Photogravure. 1890, 1895.
Dubouchet, H. and G. Précis élémentaire de gravure sur cuivre. Paris 1891.
Robert, K. Traité pratique de la gravure à l'eau-forte. Paris 1891.
Herkomer, H. Etching and mezzotint. 1892.
Kitton, F. G. The art of photo-etching and engraving, describing the works of J. Swain and Son. 1894.
Blaney, H. R. Photogravure. New York 1895.
Wedmore, F. Etching in England. 1895.
—— Cantor lectures: etching. Jnl of Royal Soc of Arts 11 Aug 1911.
Denison, H. A treatise on photogravure by the Talbot-Klic process. 1896.
Huson, T. Photo-aquatint and photogravure. [1897].
Maskell, A. and R. Demachy. Photo-aquatint: or the gum-bichromate process. 1897.
Schiltz, M. Manuel pratique d'héliogravure en taille-douce. Paris 1899.
Ziegler, W. Die Techniken des Tiefdruckes. Halle 1901.
Brown, G. E. Ferric and heliographic processes. 1907.
Hardie, M. Frederick Goulding, master printer of copper plates. Stirling 1910.
Cameron-Swan, D. Pioneers of photogravure. Imprint 17 June 1913.
S[wan], M. E. and K. R. Sir Joseph Wilson Swan. 1929.
Fischer, E. 200 Jahre Naturselbstdruck. Gutenberg-Jahrbuch 1933.
Meier, H. The origin of the printing and roller press. Print Collectors' Quart 28 1941.
Engraving and the graphic arts: bibliography. Paper & Print 20 1947.
Colas, H. Les origines de la photogravure. France Graphique 7 1954.
Lilien, O. M. Die Frühgeschichte des Tiefdruckes bis zur Jahrhundertwende. Frankfurt 1959.
Bain, I. Thomas Ross & Son: copper- and steel-plate printers since 1833. Jnl of Printing Hist Soc 2 1966.
Wakeman, G. Henry Bradbury's nature printed books. Library 5th ser 21 1966.
Cave, R. and G. Wakeman. Typographia naturalis [nature printing]. Wymondham 1967.

Plane Surfaces

Lithography (stone, zinc, aluminium), photolithography, collotype. For chromolithography see col 42, above.

See [F. Weitenkampf], Catalogue of an exhibition illustrative of the centenary of artistic lithography 1796–1896, New York 1896 (Grolier Club); and C. Kampmann, Die Literatur der Lithographie, Vienna 1899.
Senefelder, J. A. A new method and process of performing the various branches of the art of printing. Patent Specification no 2518. 1801, [1856].
—— Vollständiges Lehrbuch der Steindruckerey. 2 pts Munich 1818, 1821, 1827; tr 1819, New York 1911 (as The invention of lithography).
Fisher, T. The process of polyautographic printing. GM March 1808.
—— Curious specimen of polyautography or lithography. GM Oct 1815.
Das Geheimniss der Steindrucks in seinem ganzen Umfange praktisch und nach eigenen Erfahrungen beschrieben von einem Kunstfreunde. Schweinfurt 1810.
Bankes, H. Lithography: or the art of making drawings on stone for the purpose of being multiplied by printing. Bath 1813, London 1816.
Engelmann, G. Rapport sur la lithographie. Paris [1816].
—— Manuel du dessinateur lithographe. Paris 1823, 1824, [1830].
—— Traité théoretique et pratique de lithographie. Mulhouse 1840.
D.— Procédé actuel de la lithographie mise à la portée de l'artiste et l'amateur. Paris 1818.
M[airet], F. Notice sur la lithographie. Dijon 1818, Chatillon-sur-Seine 1824; tr German, 1819.
Peignot, G. Essai historique sur la lithographie. Paris 1819.
Raucourt de Charleville, A. Mémoire sur les expériences lithographiques faites à l'École Royale des Ponts et Chausées de France. Toulon 1819; tr 1820, 1821, 1832.
Ridolfi, C. and F. Tartini. Memoria sulla litografia. Florence 1819.
Ackermann, R. Portable lithographic press. Trans of Soc for Encouragement of Arts, Manufactures & Commerce 37 1820.
Williams, J. F. L. An historical account of inventions and discoveries: lithography. 2 vols 1820.
Eberhard, H. W. Die Anwendung des Zinks statt der Stein- und Kupferplatten zu den vertieften Zeichnungsarten. Darmstadt 1822.
Ruthven, J. A short account of lithography or the art of printing from stone. Edinburgh 1820.
Hullmandel, C. The art of drawing on stone. [1824], 1833, 1835, 1840.
—— On some important improvements in lithographic printing. [c. 1827].
—— On some further improvements in lithographic printing. 1829.
Lithographic pencil drawing: or instructions for imitating aquatinta on stone. 1824.
Houbloup, L. Théorie lithographique: ou manière facile d'apprendre à imprimer soi-même, contenant six planches représentant onze sujets. Paris 1825.
Brégeaut, R. L. Nouveau manuel complet, théorique et pratique du dessinateur et de l'imprimeur lithographe. Paris 1827, 1839.
Phillips, G. F. The art of drawing on stone. 1828.
Croker, T. C. The history of lithography. Foreign Rev July 1829; rev and rptd separately, 1829.
Pescheck, H. E. Das Ganze des Steindrucks, von seiner artischchemisch- und mechanischen Seite betrachtet und dargestellt von H. E. P. Ilmenau 1829.
History and processes of lithography. Library of Fine Arts 1 1831.
View of the present state of lithography in England. Ibid.
Tudot, E. Description de tous les moyens de dessiner sur pierre. Paris 1833, 1834.
—— Traité de lithographie. Paris 1834 (2nd edn).
Senefelder, K. Lehrbuch der Lithographie. Ratisbon 1833, 1834.
Pillou, A. C. Instruction sur l'autographie. Paris 1833.
Desportes, J. Manuel pratique du lithographe. Paris 1834, 1840.
Bautz, J. B. B. Die Lithographie in ihrem ganzen Umfange. Augsburg 1836 (2nd edn).
Chevallier, J. B. A. and Langlume. Traité complet de la lithographie. Paris 1838.
Fielding, T. H. On the theory of painting: also an appendix containing a manual of lithography. 1842.
—— An introduction to painting in watercolours, and a manual of lithography. 1854 (4th edn).
Tissier, L. Historique de la gravure typographique sur pierre et de la Tissiérographie. Paris 1843.
Klinkhardt, F. Die anastatische Druckerei. Quedlinburg 1846.
De la Motte, P. On the various applications of anastatic printing and papyrography. 1849.

Lastegrie, C. de. Lithographie. In Encyclopédie Firmin Didot, Paris 1849.
Cowell, S. H. A brief description of the art of anastatic printing. Ipswich [c. 1851], 1874.
Stanbury, G. Stanbury's practical guide to lithography. 1851, 1854.
Mason, C. Practical lithographer. 1852.
Jordan, C. J. A treatise on anastatic printing. 1853.
Salières, P. N. Gravure diaphane: nouveau procédé à la portée de tous les peintres et de tous les dessinateurs. Montpelier 1853.
[Waterlow, A. C.] Every man his own printer; or lithography made easy. 1854, 1859.
Aresti, J. Lithozôgraphia: or aquatinta stippled gradations produced upon drawings washed or painted on stone. 1856, 1857.
Ferchl, F. M. Übersicht der einzig Incunabeln-Sammlung der Lithographie. Munich 1856.
— Geschichte der Errichtung der ersten lithographischen Kunstanstalt bei der Feierstags-Schule für Künstler und Techniker in München. Munich 1862.
Schenck, F. Short treatise on lithography. Edinburgh 1857.
Scott, A. de C. On photo-zincography and other photographic processes employed at the Ordnance Survey Office. 1862, 1863.
Berri, D. G. The art of lithography. 1864, 1872, 1879.
Straker, C. Instructions in the art of lithography. 1867.
Lemling, J. Die Photoverrotypie. Ludenschied 1870.
Markl, A. Die neuesten Fortschritte der Phototypie. Prague 1870.
Pietsch, L. Alois Senefelder: Erfinder der Lithographie. Berlin 1871.
Sawyer, J. R. Photography in the printing press. Photographic Jnl 15 Jan 1872; rptd in The autotype process, 1876 (5th edn), 1878.
The heliotype process described and illustrated. [1872].
Geymet, T. Photolithographie traits et demi-teintes. Paris 1873.
— Traité pratique de phototypie. Paris 1888 (new edn).
— Traité pratique de photolithographie. Paris 1888 (3rd edn).
Fortier, G. La photolithographie: son origine, ses procédés, ses applications. Paris 1876.
Husnik, J. Das Gesammtgebiet des Lichtdrucks. Vienna 1877, 1880, 1885, 1894.
Doyen, C. Trattato di litografia, storico, teorico, pratico ed economico. Turin 1877.
Richmond, W. D. The grammar of lithography. 1878, 1880, 1886, 1890 (10th edn), 1895, [c. 1901]; tr German, 1880.
Pumphrey, A. Collography for autographic printing. Birmingham 1878.
Vidal, L. Traité pratique de phototypie: ou l'impression à l'encre grasse sur une couche de gelatine. Paris 1879.
Schnauss, J. Der Licht-Druck und die Photolithographie. Düsseldorf [1879], [1880]; tr 1889, [c. 1895].
Mohr, L. Bibliographie der Lithographie, des Steindruckes und der verwandten Zweige. Leipzig 1880.
Allgeyer, J. Handbuch über das Lichtdruck-Verfahren. Leipzig 1881.
Weishaupt, H. Verzeichnis der lithographischen Inkunabeln-Sammlung. Munich 1884.
La gravure sur pierre: traité pratique à l'usage des écrivains et des imprimeurs lithographes. Paris 1887.
Roux, V. Formulaire pratique de phototypie à l'usage de MM les préparateurs et imprimeurs des procédés aux encres grasses. Paris 1887.
Bonnet, G. Manuel de phototypie. Paris 1889.
Lorilleux, C. & Cie. Traité de lithographie: histoire, théorie, pratique. Paris 1889.
Schnauss, J. Collotype and photo-lithography. Tr E. C. Middleton 1889.
Valette, A. A. Manuel pratique du lithographe. Lyons 1891, 1894, Paris 1903.

Villon, A. M. Nouveau manuel complet du dessinateur et de l'imprimerie lithographe. 2 vols Paris 1891.
Trutat, E. Impressions photographiques aux encres grasses: traité pratique de photocollographie à l'usage des amateurs. Paris 1892.
Voirin, J. Manuel pratique de phototypie. Paris 1892, [1910].
Vidal, L. Traité pratique de photolithographie. Paris 1893.
Green, E. The beginnings of lithography. 1894.
— Bath and early lithography. Bath 1894.
Fritz, G. Die Photolithographie. Halle 1894; tr E. J. Wall 1895.
Bouchot, H. La lithographie. Paris [1895].
Wilkinson, W. T. Collotype. 1895.
Spielmann, M. H. The renaissance of lithography. Scribner's Mag Nov 1896.
— The revival of lithography: introduction—its rise and first decline. Mag of Art Dec 1896.
— Original lithography: the present revival in England. Mag of Art April 1897.
Watt, P. B. Early English lithography. Artist May 1896.
Wedmore, F. The revival of lithography. Art Jnl Jan–Feb 1896.
Curtis, A. Some masters of lithography. New York 1897.
Albert, A. Der Lichtdruck an der Hand- und Schnellpresse sammt allen Nebenarbeiten. Halle 1898.
Algraphy Ltd. Instructions to the trade for preparation of aluminium plates for algraphic printing. 1898.
Pennell, J. and E. R. Lithography and lithographers: some chapters in the history of the art. 1898.
Kampmann, C. Die Literatur der Lithographie von 1798–1898. Vienna 1899.
Pennell, J. The truth about lithography. Studio Feb 1899.
Aluminium Plate and Press Co. Aluminography: the aluminium plate versus the lithographic stone. New York 1899.
Haynié, J. Der lithographische Umdruck nach dem heutigen Stande dieser Technik. Frankfurt 1900.
Laynaud, L. La phototypie pour tous. Paris 1900.
Weilandt, C. Algraphy: or the art of printing from aluminium plates, adapted from the German by J. S. Morriss. [1901].
Graul, R. and F. Dornhoffer. Die Lithographie von ihrer Erfindung bis zur Gegenwart. Vienna 1903.
Gerber, C. H. Der praktische Steindrucker an der Hand- und Schnellpresse. Sternberg [1903].
Seymour, A. Practical lithography. 1903.
Cumming, D. Handbook of lithography. 1904.
Jacobi, E. The gelatine process. In F. H. Hitchcock, The building of a book, 1906.
Maurou, P. and A. Broquelet. Traité complet de l'art lithographique au point de vue artistique et pratique. Paris 1907.
Goodman, J. Practical modern metalithography. 1914.
Wagner, C. Alois Senefelder: sein Leben und Wirken. Leipzig 1914.
Halbmeier, C. Senefelder and the history of lithography. New York 1926.
Dussler, L. Die Incunabeln der deutschen Lithographie 1796–1821. 1925, 1955.
Johnson, A. F. Early lithography in England. Penrose Annual 1936.
Gray, N. The nineteenth-century chromolithograph. Architectural Rev 84 1938.
King, A. H. English pictorial music title-pages 1820–85: their style, evolution and importance. Library 5th ser 5 1950.
Man, F. H. 150 years of artists' lithographs 1803–1953. 1953.
— Lithography in England 1801–10. In C. Zigrosser, Prints, New York 1963.
Weber, S. Saxa loquuntur. 1961; tr as History of lithography, 1966.

Surfaces in Relief

Wood engraving, steel engraving, zincography, line blocks, half tone. Some works on electrotyping which deal with the conversion of intaglio into relief surfaces are listed above, under Spencer, Jacobi, Schoenberg, Sampson, Palmer et al.

Stuart, P. A method of engraving and printing [white on black]. Patent Specification no 3,307. 1810, [1856].

Heller, J. Geschichte der Holzschneidekunst. Bamberg 1823.

Dembour, A. Description d'un nouveau procédé de gravure en relief sur cuivre, dite ectypographie métallique. Metz 1835; tr German, 1835.

Modern wood engraving. London & Westminster Rev April–July 1837.

Jackson, J. [and W. A. Chatto]. A treatise on wood engraving, historical and practical. 1839; rev H. G. Bohn 1861.

Palmer, E. Glyphography: or engraved drawing for printing at the type press after the manner of woodcuts. 1843.

Tissier, L. Historique de la gravure typographique sur pierre et de la tissiérographie. Paris 1843.

Chatto, W. A. The history and art of wood engraving. 1848.

—— Gems of wood engraving from the Illustrated London News, with a history of the art, ancient and modern, by W. A. C. 1849.

Michel, V. Specimen des clichés bitumineux inventés par V. Michel. Paris 1851.

Gillot, F. Paniconographie de Gillot. Paris 1852.

Devincenzi, J. Électrographie: ou nouvel art de graver en relief sur métal. Paris 1856.

Wood engraving as an employment for women. Alexandra Mag April 1865.

Fitz-Cook, H. On the Graphotype. Jnl of Soc of Arts 8 Dec 1865.

Gilks, T. The art of wood engraving. 1866, 1867, 1868, [c. 1885].

—— A sketch of the origin and progress of wood-engraving. 1868.

Isermann, A. Anleitung zur Chemitypie. Leipzig 1869.

Fuller, S. E. A manual of instruction in the art of wood engraving. Boston 1867, New York 1879.

The handbook of graphotype. 1868.

Lewis, J. Printing surfaces in relief. Lithographer Feb–June 1871.

Motteroz, C. Essai sur les gravures chimiques en relief. Paris 1871.

Lefman, J. and C. Lourdel. Photo-typographie: gravure en relief. Paris 1872.

Emerson, W. A. Practical instruction in the art of wood engraving. East Douglas 1876, Boston 1881.

Scherer, R. Lehrbuch der Chemigraphie und verwandten Fächer. Vienna 1877.

Linton, W. J. Some practical hints on wood engraving. Boston 1879.

—— Wood engraving: a manual of instruction. 1884.

Marx, G. W. The art of drawing and engraving on wood. 1881 (2nd edn).

Roux, V. Traité pratique de zincographie. Paris 1885, 1891.

Boeck, J. Zincography: guide to the art in connexion with letterpress printing. 1886.

Brown, W. N. A practical manual of wood engraving, with a brief account of the history of the art. 1886.

Delaborde, H. Engraving: its origin, processes and history, translated by R. A. M. Stevenson, with an additional chapter on English engraving by W. Walker. 1886.

Husnik, J. Die Zinkätzung (Chemigraphie, Zinkotypie). Vienna 1886, 1896, 1907.

Geymet, T. Traité de gravure en demi-teinte. Paris 1888.

Schraubstadter, C. Photo-engraving: a practical treatise on the production of printing blocks by modern photographic methods. St Louis 1892.

'Verfasser, Julius' The half-tone process. Bradford 1894, 1895, 1896, London 1904, 1907, [1912]; tr French, 1895; German, 1896.

Volkmer, O. Die Photo-Galvanographie zur Herstellung von Kupferdruck- und Buchdruckplatten nebst den nöthigen Vor- und Nebenarbeiten. Halle 1894.

Meisenbach Co. Ltd. Meisenbach improved process of photo-engraving [half tone]. [1895].

Swan Electric Engraving Co. Specimens of reproductions, press opinions and some criticisms. [1895].

Whittet, R. Photo-engraving by the half-tone enamel process. Ed A. C. Lamoutte, New York 1895.

Jenkins, H. Manual of photo-engraving. Chicago 1896, 1902; rev N. S. Amstutz, Chicago 1907.

Cronenberg, W. Die Praxis der Autotypie auf amerikanischer Basis. Düsseldorf 1895; tr Bradford 1896.

Fraipont, G. Les procédés de reproduction en relief. Paris 1896.

Toifel, W. F. Handbuch der Chemigraphie. Vienna 1896.

Vidal, L. Die Photoglyphie: oder der Woodbury-Druck. Halle 1897.

Ward, W. H. The evolution of half-tone engraving. Artist March 1897.

Austin, A. C. Practical half-tone and tri-colour engraving. Buffalo 1898.

Ives, F. E. Lectures on photo-process work. London Technical Education Gazette Jan 1899.

Cox, A. Half-tone printing. Birmingham [1903].

Gill, E. M. Half-tone, line and colour plates. In F. H. Hitchcock, The building of a book, 1906.

Gamble, W. Line photo-engraving. 1910.

—— The beginning of half-tone. Br & Colonial Printer Dec 1927; rptd New York 1928.

Keppel, F. The golden age of engraving. New York 1910.

D., A. C. A note on the art of mezzotint and mezzotint printing in colours. [1911].

McCabe, L. R. The beginnings of half-tone, from the note books of S. H. Horgan. Chicago [1924].

Horgan, S. H. More about the beginnings of half-tone. Chicago 1925.

Bliss, D. P. A history of wood-engraving. 1928.

(7) PRINTING STYLE

Aesthetic Considerations

Works on individual presses and printers are listed col 55, below.

Hansard, T. C. In his Typographia, 1825 (pp. 609–21).

Jacobi, C. T. On the making and issuing of books. 1891.

Southward, J. Artistic printing. 1892.

Morris, W. The ideal book. Trans Bibl Soc 1 1893; rptd separately 1908.

Arts and Crafts Exhibition Society. Arts and crafts essays. 1893. Printing by William Morris and Emery Walker.

Joyner, G. Fine printing: its inception, development and practice. 1895.

Ricketts, C. and L. Pisarro. De la typographie et de l'harmonie de la page imprimée. 1898.

Ricketts, C. A defence of the revival of printing. 1899.

de Vinne, T. L. The practice of typography: a treatise on title pages. New York 1901 (Grolier Club), 1904.

Cobden Sanderson, T. J. Ecce mundus: industrial ideals and the book beautiful. Hammersmith 1902.

Steele, R. The revival of printing. 1912.

Pevsner, N. Pioneers of modern design. 1936, 1949, 1960 (rev).

Barman, C. Timetable typography. Typography 5 1938.

Beilenson, P. The nineteenth century. In A history of the printed book, Dolphin 3, New York 1938.

Betjeman, J. Ecclesiastical typography. Typography 6 1938.
Ridler, V. Artistic printing: a search for principles. Alphabet & Image 6 1948.
McLean, R. Modern book design. 1951, 1958.
— Victorian book design. 1963.
Ray, P. (ed). Designers in Britain 1851–1951. 1951.
Taylor, J. R. The art nouveau book in Britain. 1966.
Lewis, J. The twentieth-century book. 1967.

Legibility

Babbage, C. Table of logarithms. 1827, 1915. Preface.
Cattell, J. M. Inertia of eye and brain. Brain 8 1885.
Cohn, H. L. Die Hygiene des Auges in den Schulen. Leipzig 1883; tr as Hygiene of the eye in schools, 1886.
Griffing, H. and S. I. Franz. On the conditions of fatigue in reading. Psychological Rev (New York) 3 1896.
Javal, E. Physiologie de la lecture et de l'écriture. Paris 1905.
Huey, E. B. The psychology and pedagogy of reading. New York 1910.
'Typoclastes'. A plea for reform of printing. Imprint 17 June 1913.
Pyke, R. L. The legibility of print. Medical Research Council (Special Report ser) no 110 1926.

(8) PRIVATE PRINTING

General Works

Martin, J. Bibliographical catalogue of privately printed books. 1834, 1854 (rev).
Hume, A. The learned societies and printing clubs of the United Kingdom. 1847, 1853 (rev).
Bohn, H. G. Appendix volume to the Bibliographer's manual by W. T. Lowndes. 1865.
Henning, F. W. J. A few words upon early printing and private presses. [1880].
Quaritch, B. Account of the great learned societies and associations and of the chief printing clubs of Great Britain and Ireland: sette of odde volumes. Miscellany no 14 1886.
Morris, W. A note on his aims in founding the Kelmscott Press. Hammersmith 1898.
Plomer, H. R. Some private presses of the nineteenth century. Library 1 1900.
Dobell, B. Catalogue of books printed for private circulation. 1906.
Terry, C. S. A catalogue of the publications of Scottish historical and kindred clubs and societies 1780–1908. Glasgow 1909.
Ashbee, C. R. The private press: a study in idealism; to which is added a bibliography of the Essex House Press. Broad Campden 1909.
Steele, R. The revival of printing. 1912.
Steeves, H. R. Learned societies and English literary scholarship. New York 1913.
Tomkinson, G. S. A select bibliography of the principal modern presses, public and private in Great Britain and Ireland. 1928.
Williams, H. Book clubs and printing societies of Great Britain and Ireland. 1929.
Ransom, W. Private presses and their books. New York 1929.
— Kelmscott, Doves and Ashendene: the private press credos. Typophile Chapbook (New York) no 27, 1952.
Balston, T. The Cambridge University Press collection of private press types: Kelmscott, Ashendene, Eragny, Cranach. Cambridge 1951 (priv ptd).
Manchester Public Libraries. Reference library subject catalogue, section 094: private press books. Manchester 1959, 1960.

Particular Presses and Societies

Lee Priory Press (Sir Samuel Egerton Brydges, 1812–22)
  Brydges, Sir S. E. The autobiography, times, opinions and contemporaries of Sir Egerton Brydges. 2 vols 1834.
Roxburghe Club (1812 onwards)
  [Scott, Sir W.] Quart Rev 44 1831.
  Haslewood, J. Roxburghe revels and other relative papers. Ed J. Maidment, Edinburgh 1837 (priv ptd).
  Bigham, C. (Baron Mersey). The Roxburghe Club: its history and its members 1812–1927. 1928.
  Barker, N. The publications of the Roxburghe Club 1814–1962. 1964.
Bannatyne Club (1822–67)
  The Bannatyne Club: lists of members, rules and catalogue. Ed D. Laing, Edinburgh 1867.
Abbotsford Club (1833–66)
  The Abbotsford Club: a list of members, the rules and catalogue of books. Ed D. Laing, Edinburgh 1866.
Camden Society (1838–97)
  Nichols, J. G. A descriptive catalogue of the first series of the works of the Camden Society. 1872 (2nd edn).
Daniel Press (C. H. O. Daniel, 1845–1919)
  Madan, F. The Daniel Press: memorials of C. H. O. Daniel with a bibliography of the press. Oxford 1921. Addenda and corrigenda, Oxford 1922.
Kelmscott Press (William Morris, 1891–8)
  Forman, H. B. The books of William Morris described. 1897.
  Morris, W. A note on his aims in founding the Kelmscott Press, together with a short description of the press by S. C. Cockerell and an annotated list of the books printed thereat. Kelmscott 1898.
  Mackail, J. W. The life of William Morris. 2 vols 1899.
  Sparling, H. H. The Kelmscott Press and William Morris. 1924.
  Hewitt, G. et al. Three lectures on Morris. 1934.
  Zapf, H. William Morris: sein Leben und Werk in der Geschichte der Buch- und Schriftkunst. Scharbeutz 1949.
  Gutenberg-Gesellschaft: Ausstellung der Morris-Sammlung. Mainz 1954.
  Schmidt-Kunsemüller, F. A. William Morris und die neuere Buchkunst. Wiesbaden 1955.
  Briggs, R. C. H. William Morris Society: the typographical adventure of William Morris, an exhibition. 1957.
Eragny Press (L. and E. Pissarro, 1894–1914)
  Moore, T. S. A brief account of the origin of the Eragny Press. 1903.
  Pissarro, L. Notes on the Eragny Press and a letter to J. B. Manson. Ed A. Fern, Cambridge 1957 (priv ptd).
Ashendene Press (C. H. St J. Hornby, 1895–1946)
  A handlist of the books printed at the Ashendene Press 1895–1925. 1925.
  A descriptive bibliography of the books printed at the Ashendene Press mdcccxcv–mcmxxxv. 1935.
  Ward, S. The Ashendene Press. Philobiblon 1938.
  C. H. St J. Hornby 1867–1946: an anthology of appreciations. 1946 (priv ptd).
Vale Press (W. L. Hacon and C. Ricketts, 1896–1903)
  Ricketts, C. and L. Pissarro. De la typographie et de l'harmonie de la page imprimée: William Morris et son influence sur les arts et métiers. 1898.
  Ricketts, C. A bibliography of books printed between 1896 and 1903 by Hacon and Ricketts. 1904.
Essex House Press (C. R. Ashbee, 1898–1910)
  Ashbee, C. R. The private press: a study in idealism;

to which is added a bibliography of the Essex House Press. Broad Campden 1909.
Doves Press (T. J. Cobden-Sanderson and Sir Emery Walker, 1899–1916)
Catalogue raisonné of the books printed and published at the Doves Press 1900–16. 1916.
Cobden-Sanderson, T. J. C. Cosmic vision. 1922.
Pollard, A. W. Cobden-Sanderson and the Doves Press: the history of the press and the story of its types. San Francisco 1929.
Schmidt-Kunsemüller, F.-A. Emery Walker. Gutenberg-Jahrbuch (Mainz) 1950.
Rooke, N. Sir Emery Walker 1851–1943. Penrose Annual 1954.
Nordlunde, C. V. Thomas James Cobden-Sanderson. Copenhagen 1957.

(9) PRINTERS AND PRINTING FIRMS

Ballantyne, Hanson & Co, Edinburgh
Lockhart, J. G. The life of Sir Walter Scott. 2 vols Edinburgh 1837–8.
[Lockhart, J. G.] The Ballantyne-humbug handled. Edinburgh 1838.
[Ballantyne, A.] Refutation of the mis-statements and calumnies contained in Mr Lockhart's Life of Sir Walter Scott respecting the Messrs Ballantyne. Edinburgh 1838.
— Reply to Mr Lockhart's pamphlet entitled The Ballantyne-humbug handled. Edinburgh 1839.
The history of the Ballantyne Press and its connexion with Sir Walter Scott. [Edinburgh 1871].
[Dobson, W. T. and W. L. Carrie]. The Ballantyne Press and its founders 1796–1908. Edinburgh 1909.
John Bell, 1754–1831
Morison, S. John Bell: bookseller, printer, typefounder, journalist etc. 1930.
A catalogue of books, newspapers &c, printed by John Bell and John Browne Bell 1779–1855, son of the above, exhibited at the First Editions Club. 1931.
Bemrose & Co, Derby
Bemrose, H. H. The House of Bemrose 1826–1926. Derby 1926.
Thomas Bensley, London. *See* William Bulmer, *below*.
John Brown & Son
The firm of three generations. Glasgow 1908.
George Bradshaw, London
Katin, L. One hundred years of Bradshaw. Printing Rev 8 1939.
William Bulmer, London
Marrot, H. V. William Bulmer–Thomas Bensley: a study in transition. 1930.
Croft, W. The achievement of Bulmer & Bensley, with a handlist of their work. Signature new ser 16–17 1952–3; Supplement 18 1954.
Isaac, P. C. G. William Bulmer: an introductory essay. Library 5th ser 13 1958.
Thomas Bushill & Sons Ltd
Howe, E. Bushills: the story of a Coventry firm of printers and box makers 1856–1956. Coventry 1956.
Butler & Tanner, Frome
Rhode, John. A hundred years of printing 1795–1895. 1927 (priv ptd).
Cambridge University Press, Cambridge
Bowes, R. Biographical notes on the university printers from the commencement of printing in Cambridge to the present time. [Cambridge 1886].
Roberts, S. C. A history of the Cambridge University Press 1521–1921. Cambridge 1921.
Crutchley, E. A. A history and description of the Pitt Press erected to the memory of Mr Pitt for the use of the University Printing Press AD 1833 altered and restored AD 1937. Cambridge 1938.
Rogers, B. Report on the typography of the CUP, prepared in 1917. Cambridge 1950 (priv ptd).
Scurfield, G. A stickful of nonpareil. Cambridge 1956. On the Press in the 1890's under Charles and John Clay.
Cassell & Co, London
McCoy, M. P. A visit to a London printing office. 1881.
Catnach Press, Newcastle; London
Hindley, C. The history of the Catnach Press. 1886.

John Cheney & Sons, Banbury.
Cheney, J. John Cheney and his descendants. Banbury 1936.
William Clowes & Sons, London
Smiles, S. In his Men of invention and industry, 1884.
William Clowes & Sons. Family business. 1953.
Co-operative Printing Society, Manchester
Hall, F. The history of the Co-operative Printing Society, Manchester 1869–1919. Manchester 1920.
S. H. (later W. S.) Cowell Ltd, Ipswich.
Illustrations to the art of printing: being a description of a visit to the steam printing works of S. H. Cowell, Ipswich. Ipswich 1876.
A walk through our works: a short account of a visit to the printing, stationery and bookbinding manufactory of S. H. Cowell, Ipswich. Ipswich 1888.
Ireland, G. The press in the Butter Market. Ipswich 1960.
Thomas de la Rue & Co
Illustrated description of Thos de la Rue and Co's works, with an account of the employees' benefit societies. 1883.
J. M. Dent & Sons Ltd
Thornton, J. A tour of the Temple Press. 1935.
Edinburgh University Press
Fleming, L. An octogenarian printer's recollections. Edinburgh 1893.
W. J. Fowler & Sons, 1898–1948
W. J. Fowler & Sons. 50 years of typographical progress. 1948.
Frank Gaskell, Birmingham
[Gaskell, F.] The experience and maxims of a practical printer. [1890].
Glasgow University Press, Glasgow
Maclehose, J. The Glasgow University Press 1638–1931. Glasgow 1931.
Glasgow University Printing Office
The Glasgow University printing office in 1826. Cambridge 1953 (priv ptd).
Luke Hansard, London
Hansard, J. and L. G. Biographical memoir of Luke Hansard. 1829.
Trewin, J. C. and E. M. King. Printer to the House: the story of Hansard. 1952.
Harrison & Sons, London
The house of Harrisons: being an account of the family and firm of Harrison & Sons, printers to the King. 1914.
Hazell, Watson & Viney Ltd, 1839–1939
Keefe, H. J. A century in print: the story of Hazell's. 1939.
Jarrold & Sons, Norwich
The house of Jarrolds 1823–1923: a brief history of one hundred years. Norwich 1924.
Jarrold & Sons. History of Jarrold & Sons 1823–1948. Norwich 1948.
King's Printing Office, Edinburgh
Kinnear, S. Reminiscences of an aristocratic Edinburgh printing office. Edinburgh 1890.
George W. Jones, 1860–1942
Jay, L. A tribute to the work of George W. Jones. Printing Rev 9 1941.
Rudge, W. E. George W. Jones: superior printer. Print 3 1943.

M. Lownds & Son, London
1855–1905: a record of fifty years' progress. 1905.
Mark & Moody Ltd
Haden, H. J. The story of Mark & Moody Ltd 1840–1957.
William Morris. *See col 56 above, under* Kelmscott Press
Neill & Co, Edinburgh
History of Neill & Co Ltd. Edinburgh 1900.
The house of Neill 1749–1949: bicentenary edition. Edinburgh 1949.
Thomas Nelson & Sons
The story of a famous firm of printer-publishers. Br & Colonial Printer 2nd Suppl 8 June 1951.
Newbery Press
Plough to press 1560–1953.
Bernard Newdigate, 1869–1944
Blackwell, B. Bernard Newdigate, typographer. 1945 (priv ptd).
Thorp, J. Newdigate: scholar-printer 1869–1944. Oxford 1950.
John Nichols, London
Nichols, J. G. Memoirs of John Nichols. In Illustrations of the literary history of the eighteenth century vol 8, 1858.
John Bowyer Nichols, London
Nichols, J. G. Memoir of the late John Bowyer Nichols. 1864.
John Gough Nichols, London
Nichols, R. C. Memoir of the late John Gough Nichols. 1874.
Oxford University Press
Hart, H. Charles Earl Stanhope and the Oxford University Press. Oxford Historical Soc Collectanea 3 1896, 1966.
Batey, C. Horace Hart and the University Press Oxford 1883–1915. Signature new ser no 18 1954.
Pillans & Wilson, Edinburgh
A printing house of old and new Edinburgh 1775–1925. Edinburgh 1925.
Robert Pocock, Gravesend
Arnold, G. M. Robert Pocock: the Gravesend historian, naturalist, antiquarian, botanist and printer. 1883.
William Sessions Ltd, the Ebor Press
The story of a printing house 1865–1965. York 1965.
Robert Skeen
Autobiography of Mr Robert Skeen, printer 1876 (priv ptd).
C. M. Smith
[Smith, C. M.] The working man's way in the world: being the autobiography of a journeyman printer. 1857, 1967.
John Soulby, Ulverston
Twyman, M. John Soulby, printer, Ulverston: a study of the work printed by John Soulby, father and son, between 1796–1827. Reading 1966.
Spottiswoode & Co, London
History of Spottiswoode & Co Ltd 1739–1909. 1909.
Austen-Leigh, R. A. The story of a printing house: being a short account of the Strahans and the Spottiswoodes. [1911], 1912 (rev).
Straker Bros
The house of Straker 1800–1950. 1950.
C. P. Thorn & Sons, Woolwich
Thorns of Woolwich 1881–1953. 1953.
Tillotsons, Bolton
Singleton, F. Tillotsons 1850–1950: centenary of a family business. Bolton 1950.
A. W. Tuer
Johnson, A. F. Old face types in the Victorian age. Monotype Recorder Dec 1931.
Andrew White Tuer. Printing Rev 15 1950.
Unwin Brothers
Unwins. A century of progress: being a record of the rise and present position of the Gresham Press 1826–1926. [1926].
Colebrook, F. The Unwins. Caxton Mag 52 1950.
The Victoria Press (Emily Faithfull), London
Head, W. W. The Victoria Press: its history and vindication with an account of the movement for the employment of females in printing. 1867.
Waterlow Brothers & Layton, London
Smalley, G. The life of Sir Sidney Waterlow. 1909.
The house of Waterlows of Birchin Lane from 1811 to 1911. [1911].
Boon, J. Under six reigns: being some account of 114 years of progress and development of the house of Waterlow. 1925.
Wertheimer, Lea & Co.
A romance of the printing trade. [1914].
C. Whittingham & Co., Chiswick Press, London.
Warren, A. The Charles Whittinghams, printers. New York 1896 (Grolier Club).
Plomer, H. R. A glance at the Whittingham ledgers. Library 2 1901.
Wightman & Co, London
One hundred years. 1936.
C. H. Wyman & Sons, London
Lawrence, A. The story of Wyman & Sons Ltd. [1907].

(10) PRINTING TRADE PERIODICALS

Although this section contains only periodicals issued in Great Britain, two others must be mentioned for their international importance: Journal für Buchdruckerkunst, Brunswick 1834–81; The inland printer, Chicago 1881–.

See F. L. Mohr, Die periodische Fachpresse der Typographie und der verwandten Geschaftszweige, Strasbourg 1879.

The compositors' chronicle. No 1, Sept 1840–no 37, Aug 1843 [–no 39, Oct 1843]. Continued as The Printer no 1, Nov 1843–no 19, June 1845. Monthly.
Printer. No 1, 1843–5.
The typographical gazette. No 1, April, no 2, May 1846–?. Monthly.
The typographical protection circular. No 1, Jan 1849–no 59, Nov 1853 [–no 60, Dec 1853]. Continued as The typographical circular. No 1, Jan 1854–no 54, June 1858. Continued as The London press journal and general trades advocate (late The typographical circular). [1858]–no 4, 21 Jan 1859. Monthly; ed E. S. Mantz.
The provincial typographical circular. No 1, Oct 1852–no 297, June 1877. Continued as The typographical circular, no 298, July 1877–. Manchester. Monthly; ed H. Slatter.
The Scottish typographical circular. No 1, Sept 1857–no 568, Dec 1908. Continued as The Scottish typographical journal, no 569, Jan 1909–. In progress. Edinburgh, later Glasgow, Monthly; ed D. Hunter.
Journal of the typographic arts. No 1, Jan 1860–no 29, May 1862. Monthly.
Typographic advertiser. No 1, June 1862–no 68, Feb 1868. Pbd by J. & R. M. Wood. Monthly.
The printers' register. No 1, July 1863–1952. Monthly; ed W. Dorrington (1863–6), A. J. C. Powell.
The printers' journal and typographical magazine. No 1, 2 Jan 1865–22 March 1869. Fortnightly.
London, provincial and colonial press news. No 1, 15 Jan 1866–no 564, 12 Dec 1912. Monthly; ed W. Dorrington.
The chromolithograph: a journal of art literature, decoration and the accomplishments. No 1, 23 Nov 1867–27 March 1869. Weekly.

The lithographer. No 1, July 1870–no 49, July 1874. Incorporated with The printing times. Monthly; ed P. B. Watt.

The paper and printing trades journal. No 1, Dec 1872–no 86, May 1895. Quarterly; ed A. W. Tuer. Index to nos 1–32 by E. R. Pearce, Taunton 1881.

The printing times. No 1, 1 Jan 1873–no 19, July 1874. Continued as The printing times and lithographer, 1 Aug 1874–Dec 1901. Fortnightly at first, then monthly; ed J. Lovell (1873–4), C. W. H. Wyman (1874–83).

Fleet Street gazette: a journeyman's journal. No 1, 28 Feb–no 7, 23 May 1874. Fortnightly.

Hailing's circular. No 1, Nov 1877–no 24, Autumn 1889. Cheltenham. Quarterly at first, then irregular.

The British and colonial printer and stationer and newspaper press record. No 1, Dec 1878–. The subtitle was altered to 'and paper trades review' in 1879. Fortnightly; ed W. J. Stonhill. In progress as Printing World, 1954.

Paper and print. No 1, 2 Aug 1879–no 87, 26 March 1881–[?] Weekly; ed H. F. Gough.

The printing trades diary and desk-book. 1879–86. Annual; ed C. W. H. Wyman.

The printing review. No 1, Jan 1879–no 11, Nov 1879–[?].

The printers' friend. No 1, 8 Nov 1880–no 8, 30 June 1883.

The printers' international specimen exchange. 16 vols 1880–98. Ed A. W. Tuer.

The printer: a quarterly journal devoted to the interests of printers and printing. No 1, Nov 1883–no 20, Aug 1888.

The British printer. 1888–9. 6 times a year. In progress. Leicester to 1899, Leicester and London 1899–1922, London 1922–.

Salmon's Printing Trades Circular, No 1, 1886–1890. Manchester.

The vigilance gazette: a monthly journal devoted to the interests of the London Society of Compositors. No 1, May 1888–Feb 1889. Continued as The London printers' circular, no 7, May 1889–no 11, May 1890.

The English typographia. 1889–97.

The printing world. No 1, 25 Jan 1891–Sept 1911.

The lithographer. No 1, 15 Sept–no 3, 16 Nov 1891. Incorporated with The printing times.

The British lithographer. 1891–5. Leicester.

Printing news. No 1, Aug 1892–15 June 1894.

The typographic chronicle. No 1, Jan–no 7, Aug 1892–?.

Amalgamated Society of Pressmen: half yearly report. 1892–.

The printer's and kindred traders' weekly advertiser. No 1, 3 June 1893–1 April 1896.

Leeds typographical circular, nos 22–24. 1893–4. Leeds.

Process Work. Penrose's circular no 1, 1893–1929. Ed W. Gamble.

Amalgamated Society of Printers' Warehousemen: report of the committee. 1894–.

The process photogram. No 1, Jan 1895–Dec 1905. Continued as The process engraver's monthly Jan 1906–. Monthly; ed H. Snowden Ward, C. W. Ward. Title varies.

The process work year book. 1895–7. 1900. Continued as Penrose's pictorial annual, 1898–1914.

The British art printer. [1895–6]. Swindon.

Amateur printing. No 1, June 1895–Jan 1909.

The printer's engineer. No 1, Sept 1895–.

Print: a journal for printing-house employés of all grades and departments. No 1, May–no 6, Oct 1896.

The Caxtonian quarterly. No 1, Feb 1898–no 22, May 1904.

Journal of printing and kindred trades of the British Empire. 1 1898–1901.

Paper and printing bits. No 1, Oct 1898–no 10, April 1900. Birmingham. Monthly.

The printers' year book and diary. 1899–?.

The printers' pocket guide, almanack and diary. 1899–[?]. Ed A. C. Couch.

St Bride Foundation Institute: catalogue of the periodicals relating to printing and allied subjects in the technical library. 1951.

Ulrich, C. F. and K. Küp. Books and printing: a selected list of periodicals 1800–1942. Woodstock Vermont 1943.

(11) BOOK ILLUSTRATION

General Works

Orme, E. An essay on transparent prints and on transparencies in general. 1807.

[Plowman, J.] An essay on the illustration of books. 1824.

Jackson, J. and W. A. Chatto. A treatise on wood engraving, historical and practical. 1839, 1861 (rev H. G. Bohn).

Art-circular: a monthly record of illustrated literature and art manufactures. 1850–1.

Hamerton, P. G. Etching and etchers. 1868, 1876, 1880, Boston 1883.

Ruskin, J. Ariadne Florentina. 1872, Orpington 1876, London 1907.

Redgrave, S. A dictionary of artists of the English School. 1874.

Carr, J. C. Cantor lectures on book illustration, old and new. 1882.

Woodberry, G. E. A history of wood engraving. 1883.

Everitt, G. English caricaturists and graphic humourists of the nineteenth century. 1886.

Tuer, A. W. 1,000 quaint cuts from books of other days. [1886].

Linton, W. J. The masters of wood engraving. New Haven 1889.

Crane, W. Cantor lectures on the decoration and illustration of books. 1889.

— Of the decorative illustration of books. 1896, 1901.

Pennell, J. Pen drawing and pen draughtsmen. 1889, 1894, 1897.

— Modern illustration. 1895.

— English book illustration 1860–1870. Jnl of Royal Soc of Arts 3 April 1896.

— The illustration of books. 1896.

Brough, W. S. Book illustration. Leek 1891.

Harper, C. G. English pen artists of to-day: examples of their work, with some criticisms and appreciations. 1892.

— A practical handbook of drawing for modern methods of reproduction. 1894.

Nisbet, H. Illustrative art: past and present. GM March 1892.

Blackburn, H. Cantor lectures on the art of book and newspaper illustration. 1894.

Chapin, W. O. The masters and masterpieces of engraving. New York 1894.

Layard, G. S. Tennyson and his Pre-Raphaelite illustrators. 1894.

Cundall, J. A brief history of wood engraving. 1895.

Meade, E. Pen pictures and how to draw them. 1895.

Vine, C. J. Hints on drawing for process reproduction. 1895.

Wedmore, F. Etching in England. 1895.

White, G. English illustration: the sixties 1855–70, 1897, 1906.

— Children's books and their illustrators. Studio winter 1897.

Slater, J. H. Engravings and their value. 1897 (2nd edn).

— Illustrated sporting books. 1899.

Pennell, J. and E. R. Lithography and lithographers: some chapters in the history of the art. 1898.

Whitman, A. C. The masters of mezzotint, the men and their work. 1898.
Whitman, A. C. Nineteenth-century mezzotinters. 2 vols 1903–4.
Blomfield, R. Of book illustration and book decoration. Arts and Crafts Exhibition Society: arts and crafts essays, 1899.
Kitton, F. G. Dickens and his illustrators. 1899.
Doyen, C. Origini e sviluppo della litografia durante il secolo 19. Milan 1901.
Victoria and Albert Museum. Catalogue of the loan collection of modern illustration. 1901.
Murdoch, T. The early history of lithography in Glasgow. Glasgow 1902.
Bulloch, J. M. The art of extra illustration. 1903.
Pingrenon, R. Les livres ornés et illustrés en couleur depuis le xve siècle en France et en Angleterre. Paris 1903.
Sketchley, R. E. D. English book illustration of to-day: appreciations of living English illustrators with lists of their books. 1903.
'Paston, George' (E. M. Symonds). Old coloured books. 1905.
Hardie, M. English coloured books. 1906.
Prideaux, S. T. Aquatint engraving: a chapter in the history of book illustration. 1909.
Spurrier, S. Black and white: a manual of illustration. 1909.
Salaman, M. C. Old English colour prints. 1909.
—— British book illustration: yesterday and to-day. 1923.
Hammerton, J. A. The Dickens picture book: a record of the Dickens illustrators. 1910.
Blaikie Murdoch, W. G. The renaissance of the nineties. 1911.
Jackson, H. The eighteen-nineties. 1913, 1939.
National Gallery, Millbank. (Tate Gallery). Catalogue: book illustration of the sixties. 1923.
Imeson, W. K. Illustrated music titles and their delineators. 1912.
Nevill, R. H. Old English sporting books. 1924.
Robinson, C. N. Old naval prints. 1924.
Siltzer, F. The story of British sporting prints. 1925, 1929.
Lewis, C. T. C. The story of picture printing in England in the nineteenth century. [1928].
Reid, F. Illustrators of the sixties. [1928].
Newbolt, F. The history of the Royal Society of painter-etchers and engravers 1880–1930. 1930.
Ruemann, A. Das illustrierte Buch des xix Jahrhunderts in England, Frankreich und Deutschland 1790–1860. Leipzig 1930.
Sleigh, B. Wood engraving since 1890. 1932.
Balston, T. English book illustration 1880–1900. In J. Carter, New paths in book collecting, 1934.
Thorpe, J. H. English illustration: the nineties. 1935.
Tooley, R. V. Some English books with coloured plates, their points, collations and values: first half of nineteenth century. 1935.
Burke, W. J. Rudolph Ackermann: promoter of the arts and sciences. BNYPL. 1934.
Gray, B. The English print. 1937.
Pevsner, N. Pioneers of the modern movement, from William Morris to Gropius. 1936, 1960 (rev as Pioneers of modern design).
Reitlinger, H. From Hogarth to Keene. 1938.
Sparrow, W. S. Book illustrators of the sixties. 1939.
Bechtel, E. de T. Illustrated books of the sixties. Print 1 1940.
Council for the encouragement of Music and the Arts. English book illustration since 1800. Ed P. James 1943. An exhibition catalogue.
New York Public Library. Influences and trends in nineteenth-century illustration. New York 1943.
Meynell, F. English printed books. 1946.
Piper, J. British romantic artists. 1946.
—— Picturesque travel illustrated. Signature new ser no 11 1953.
James, P. English book illustration 1800–1900. 1947.
Miller, B. E. Illustrators of children's books 1744–1945. Boston 1947.
Friedman, A. B. English illustrators of the 1860's. Bull Boston Public Lib 23 1948.
Smith, J. A. Children's illustrated books. 1948.
Wallis, N. Fin de siècle. 1948.
Hassall, J. Wood engraving: a reader's guide. 1949.
Abbey, J. R. Scenery of Great Britain and Ireland in aquatint and lithography 1770–1860: a bibliographical catalogue. 1952 (priv ptd).
—— Life in England in aquatint and lithography 1770–1860: a bibliographical catalogue. 1953 (priv ptd).
—— Travel in aquatint and lithography 1770–1860: a bibliographical catalogue. 2 vols 1956–7 (priv ptd).
Ivins, W. M. Prints and visual communication. 1953.
Bland, D. A bibliography of book illustration. 1955.
—— A history of book illustration. 1958.
Barkley, H. 19th-century illustrators—and others. Penrose Annual 1959.
Garvey, E. M. (ed). The artist and the book 1860–1960 in Western Europe and the United States. Boston 1961.
Mahoney, B. E. et al. Illustrators of children's books 1744–1945. 1961.
McLean, R. Victorian book design. 1963.
Pitz, H. Illustrating children's books: history, technique, production. New York 1963.
British Museum. English book illustration 966–1846, I: Illuminated manuscripts; II: Illustrated printed books. 1965.
Sutphen, D. Old engravings and illustrations 1860–1907. Minneapolis 1965.
Taylor, J. R. The art nouveau book in Britain. 1966.

Illustrators

Henry Alken (1787–1851)
Boston Transcript 20 July 1910.
Sparrow, W. S. Henry Alken. 1927.
Francesco Bartolozzi (1727–1815)
Tuer, A. W. Bartolozzi and his works. 2 vols 1881, 1885 (rev).
Brinton, S. Bartolozzi and his pupils in England. 1903, 1906 (2nd edn).
Bailey, J. T. H. Bartolozzi: a biographical study. 1907.
George Baxter (1804–67)
Bullock, C. F. Life of Baxter: engraver, artist and colour printer. Birmingham 1901.
Lewis, C. T. C. Baxter: his life and work. 1908.
—— The picture printer of the nineteenth century: Baxter. 1911.
Colebrook, F. Baxter: his work and method. 1909.
Clarke, H. G. Baxter colour prints: their history and methods of production. 1919.
—— and J. H. Rylatt. The centenary Baxter book with a catalogue résumé of his works. Leamington Spa 1936.
The Baxter times: a journal for xixth-century print collectors (Leamington). Vols 1–3 June 1923–Nov 1925. Continued as The Baxter print collector and Baxter times (Leamington), 10 Dec 1925–.
Aubrey Beardsley (1872–98)
Symons, A. Aubrey Beardsley. 1898, 1905.
The early work of Beardsley. 1899, 1912.
The later work of Beardsley. 1900, 1912.
Ross, R. B. Aubrey Beardsley. 1909.
The uncollected work of Beardsley. 1925.
Walker, R. A. (ed). Letters from Beardsley to Leonard Smithers. 1937.
—— Le morte d'Arthur with Beardsley illustrations: a bibliographical essay. Bedford 1945.
—— The best of Beardsley. 1948.
Gallatin, A. E. Beardsley: a catalogue of drawings and bibliography. New York 1945 (priv ptd).

— and A. D. Wainwright. The Gallatin Beardsley Collection in Princeton University Library: a catalogue. Princeton 1952.
Hoelscher, E. Aubrey Beardsley. Hamburg 1949.
Reade, B. Aubrey Beardsley. 1967.

Thomas Bewick (1753–1828)
Bewick: a memoir written by himself. 1862; ed A. Dobson, Newcastle 1887; ed M. Weekley 1961.
Hugo, T. The Bewick collector: a descriptive catalogue of the works of Thomas and John Bewick. 1866; Supplement, 1868.
Thomson, D. C. The life and works of Bewick. 1882.
Dobson, A. Bewick and his pupils. 1884, 1889 (rev).
Robinson, R. Bewick: his life and times. Newcastle 1887.
Ruemann, A. Thomas Bewick. Philobiblon 10 1938.
Rayner, J. (ed). A selection of engravings on wood by Bewick. 1947.
Bingley, B. Bewickiana. Signature new ser 9 1949.
Reynolds, A. G. Bewick: a résumé of his life and works. 1949.
Roscoe, S. Bewick: a bibliography raisonné of editions of the general history of quadrupeds and the fables of Aesop issued in his lifetime. Oxford 1953.
Stone, R. (ed). Wood engravings of Bewick. 1953.
Weekley, M. Bewick. 1953.

William Blake (1757–1827)
Gilchrist, A. Life of Blake. 2 vols 1868, 1880 (enlarged).
Keynes, G. L. A bibliography of Blake. New York 1921.
— Blake studies. 1949.
— (ed). Blake's engravings. 1950.
— and E. Wolf. Blake's illuminated books: a census. New York 1953 (priv ptd), Paris 1964.
— Blake's illustrations to the Bible. Clairvaux 1957.
Binyon, L. The drawings and engravings of Blake. Ed G. Holme 1922.
Todd, R. Blake's illuminated painting. Print 6 1948.
Butlin, M. Blake: a catalogue of the works of Blake in the Tate Gallery. 1957.

Richard Parkes Bonington (1801–28)
Dubuisson, A. Richard Parkes Bonington. 1924.
Shirley, A. Bonington. 1940.

Thomas Shotter Boys (1803–74)
Stokes, H. Thomas Shotter Boys. 1925.

Ford Madox Brown (1821–93)
Hueffer, F. M. Ford Madox Brown. Life and work. 1896.

Hablot K. Browne (1815–82)
Kitton, F. G. Phiz (Hablot K. Browne): a memoir including a selection from his correspondence. 1882.
Johannsen, A. Phiz: illustrations from the novels of Dickens. 1957.

Sir Edward Burne-Jones (1833–98)
Vallance, A. The decorative art of Burne-Jones. Arts Jnl 1900.

Randolph Caldecott (1846–86)
Blackburn, H. Caldecott: a personal memoir of his early art career. 1886.
Laws, E. Randolph Caldecott. 1947.

Edward Calvert (1799–1883)
Lister, R. Edward Calvert. 1962.

Charles Conder (1868–1909)
Gibson, F. Conder: his life and work. 1904.
Rothenstein, J. The life and death of Conder. 1938.

Samuel Cousins (1801–87)
Pycroft, G. Memoir of Cousins. Exeter 1887 (priv ptd), London 1899.
Whitman, A. C. Samuel Cousins. 1904.

Walter Crane (1845–1915)
Konody, P. G. The art of Crane. 1902.
Crane, W. An artist's reminiscences. 1907.
Massé, G. C. E. Bibliography of the first editions of books illustrated by Crane. 1923.

George Cruikshank (1792–1878)
Jerrold, B. The life of Cruikshank. 1882.
Thackeray, W. M. An essay on the genius of Cruikshank. 1884.
Douglas, R. J. H. The works of Cruikshank. [1903].
Cohn, A. M. Cruikshank: a catalogue raisonné. 1924.
McLean, R. Cruikshank: his life and work as a book illustrator. 1948.

George Dalziel (1815–1902); Edward Dalziel (1817–1905)
Dalziel, G. and E. The brothers Dalziel: a record of 1840–90. 1901.
Colebrook, F. Dalziel and the Dalsprites. 1909.

William Dickes (1815–92)
Docker, A. The colour prints of Dickes. 1924.

Gustave Doré (1833–83)
Roosevelt, B. Life and reminiscences of Doré. 1885.
Valmy-Baysse, J. Gustave Doré. Paris 1930.
Leblanc, H. Catalogue de l'oeuvre complet de Doré. Paris 1931.
Lehmann-Haupt, H. The terrible Doré. New York 1943.
Rose, M. Gustave Doré. 1946.

George du Maurier (1834–96)
Wood, T. M. du Maurier, the satirist of the Victorians. 1913.
Whiteley, D. P. du Maurier's illustrations for Once a week. Alphabet & Image 5 1947.
— du Maurier: his life and work. 1948.
du Maurier, D. (ed). The young du Maurier: a selection of his letters 1860–7, with a biographical appendix by D. P. Whiteley. 1951.

Benjamin Fawcett (1808–93)
Morris, M. C. F. Fawcett: colour printer and engraver. Oxford 1925.

Sir Luke Fildes (1844–1927)
Thomson, D. C. The life and work of Fildes. 1892.

Birket Foster (1823–99)
Huish, M. Birket Foster. 1890.
Cundall, H. M. Birket Foster. 1906.

Alfred Henry Forrester (1804–72)
[Forrester, A. H.] A bundle of crowquills dropped by a crowquill in his eccentric flights over the fields of literature. 1854.

Harry Furniss (1854–1925)
Furniss, H. The confessions of a caricaturist. 2 vols 1901.
— How and why I illustrated Thackeray. 1912.

James Gillray (1757–1815)
[Grego, J.] The works of Gillray with the history of his life and times. Ed T. Wright 1873.
Hill, R. D. Mr Gillray the caricaturist. 1965.

Kate Greenaway (1846–1901)
Spielmann, M. H. and G. S. Layard. Kate Greenaway. 1905.
Muir, P. Notes on the Kate Greenaway centenary. Alphabet & Image 1 1946.

Sir Frank Seymour Haden (1818–1910)
Harrington, H. N. The engraved work of Haden. Liverpool 1910.

Philip Gilbert Hamerton (1834–94)
Hamerton: an autobiography 1834–58, and a memoir by his wife 1858–94. 1897.

Arthur Boyd Houghton (1836–75)
Houghton: a selection from his work in black and white. 1896.
Housman, L. Arthur Boyd Houghton. 1896.

William Holman Hunt (1827–1910)
Schleinitz, O. William Holman Hunt. Leipzig 1907.

Charles Keene (1823–91)
Layard, G. S. The life and letters of Keene. 1892.
Pennell, J. The work of Keene. 1897.
Emmanuel, F. Keene: etcher, draughtsman and illustrator: a lecture to the Print Collectors' Club. 1935.
Hudson, D. Charles Keene. 1947.

Charles Keene (1823–91) *cont.*
Piper, M. Charles Keene. Signature new ser no 16 1952.
Edward Lear (1812–88)
Davidson, A. Lear: landscape painter and nonsense poet. 1930.
Jackson, H. (ed). The complete nonsense of Lear. 1947.
Reade, B. The birds of Lear. Signature new ser no 4 1947.
Murphy, R. (ed). Lear's Indian journal 1873–5. 1953.
Robert Le Blond (1816–63); Abraham Le Blond (1819–94)
Lewis, C. T. C. The Le Blond book: a history of the work of Le Blond & Co. 1920.
John Leech (1817–64)
Kitton, F. G. Leech: artist and humourist. 1883; 1884 (rev).
Frith, W. P. Leech: his life and work. 2 vols 1891.
[Granniss, R. S.] Catalogue of an exhibition of works by Leech. New York 1914.
[Slade, B. C.] Leech on my shelves. Munich 1930 (priv ptd).
Bodkin, T. The noble science: Leech in the hunting field. 1948.
Rose, J. The drawings of Leech. 1950.
Frederic Leighton (1830–96)
Barrington, R. The life, letters and work of Leighton. 2 vols 1906.
William James Linton (1812–98)
Linton, W. J. Threescore and ten years 1820–90. New York 1894, 1895 (as Memoirs).
David Lucas (1802–81)
[Leggatt, E. E. Catalogue of the complete works of Lucas. 1903.
Daniel Maclise (1806–70)
O'Driscoll, W. J. A memoir of Maclise. 1871.
John Martin (1789–1854)
Balston, T. Martin: his life and works. 1947.
Phil May (1864–1903)
Thorpe, J. H. Phil May, master draughtsman and humourist. 1932, 1948 (enlarged).
Sir John Everett Millais (1829–96)
Millais's illustrations: a collection of drawings on wood. 1866.
Spielmann, M. H. Millais and his work. 1898.
Millais, J. G. The life and letters of Millais. 1899, 1905.
Francis Orpen Morris (1810–93)
Morris, M. C. F. Morris: a memoir. 1897.
Samuel Palmer (1805–81)
Palmer, A. H. The life and letters of Palmer. 1892.
Grigson, G. Palmer at Shoreham. Signature no 7 1937.
——Palmer: the visionary years. 1947.
Melville, R. Samuel Palmer. 1956.
Arthur Rackham (1867–1939)
Hudson, D. Rackham: his life and work. 1960.
Abraham Raimbach (1776–1843)
Raimbach, M. T. S. Memoirs and recollections of the late Abraham Raimbach, engraver. 1843.
Samuel William Reynolds (1773–1835)
Whitman, A. C. S. S. W. Reynolds. 1903.

Charles Ricketts
Moore, T. S. Charles Ricketts. 1933.
Robert Traill Rose (1882–1931)
Rose, M. T. S. Alexander Rose and his grandson Robert Traill Rose. Edinburgh 1953.
Dante Gabriel Rossetti (1828–82)
Marillier, H. C. D. G. Rossetti. 1899.
Pissarro, L. Rossetti. 1934.
Thomas Rowlandson (1756–1827)
Grego, J. Rowlandson the caricaturist. 2 vols 1880.
[Granniss, R. S.] A catalogue of books illustrated by Rowlandson. New York 1916.
Roe, E. G. Rowlandson: the life and art of a British genius. Leigh-on-Sea 1947.
Falk, B. Rowlandson, his life and art: a documentary record. 1949.
Frederick Sandys (1829–1904)
Gray, J. M. Sandys and the woodcut designs of thirty years ago. Century Guild Hobby Horse Dec 1888.
Reproductions of woodcuts by Sandys 1860–6. [1919] (priv ptd).
Alois Senefelder (1771–1834)
Nagler, G. K. Senefelder und der geistliche Rath Simon Schmid als Rivalen in der Geschichte der Erfindung des mechanischen Steindruckes. Munich 1862.
Wagner, C. Senefelder, sein Leben und Wirken: ein Beitrag zur Geschichte der Lithographie. Leipzig 1914.
Charles Shannon (1863–1937)
Ricketts, C. A catalogue of Mr Shannon's lithographs. [1909].
Marcus Stone (1840–1921)
Baldry, A. L. The life and work of Stone. 1896.
Thomas Stothard (1755–1834)
Bray, A. E. Life of Stothard. 1851.
Coxhead, A. C. Thomas Stothard. 1906.
William Strang (1859–1921)
[Binyon, L.] Strang: catalogue of his etched work. 1906, 1912.
Dodgson, C. The etchings of Strang and Sir Charles Holroyd. 1933.
Sir John Tenniel (1820–1914)
Monkhouse, W. C. The life and work of Tenniel. 1901.
Sarzano, F. Sir John Tenniel. 1948.
Hugh Thomson (1860–1920)
Spielmann, M. H. and W. Jerrold. Thomson: his art, his letters, his humour and his charm. 1931.
Charles Turner (1774–1857)
Whitman, A. C. Charles Turner. 1907.
J. M. W. Turner (1775–1851)
Mauclair, C. Turner. Paris 1939.
Turner's Liber studiorum reproduced from the original etchings by the Woodbury permanent process. 1875.
Rawlinson, W. G. The engraved work of Turner. 2 vols 1908.
James Abbott McNeill Whistler (1834–1903)
Kennedy, E. G. The etched work of Whistler. New York 1910.

(12) BOOKBINDING

Grolier Club. Commercial bookbinding: an historical sketch. New York 1894.
—— List of books and articles relating to bookbinding to be found in the library. New York 1907.
Mejer, W. Bibliographie der Buchbindereiliteratur. Leipzig 1925; H. Herbst, Supplement 1924–32, Leipzig 1933.
Harthan, J. P. Bookbindings: select bibliography. 1950.

New scale of prices for bookbinding. 1807. A broadside.
Country scale of prices for bookbinding. [1810].
[Minshall, N.] The whole art of bookbinding. Oswestry 1811.
The bookbinder's price-book. 1813.
The art of bookbinding; containing a description of the tools. 1818; tr German, 1819.
[Martin, T.] The bookbinder's complete instructor. Peterhead 1823.
[Cowie, G.] The bookbinder's manual. [1828], 1829, 1832 etc.
The reply of the journeymen bookbinders to remarks on a memorial addressed to their employers on the effects of a machine introduced to supersede manual labour. 1831.
Boteler, W. C. Songs for bookbinders. 1837.
[Hannett, J.] Bibliopegia: or the art of bookbinding in all

its branches by J. A. Arnett. 1835, 1836, 1865 (6th edn).
— The bookbinders' school of design, as applied to the combination of tools in the art of finishing by J. Arnett. 1837.
The handbook of taste in book-binding. [c. 1840].
Foucaud, E. Reliure. In his Les artisans illustres, Paris 1841.
The book-finisher's friendly circular. No 1, Aug 1845–no 19, Sept 1850.
The bookbinders' trade circular, issued by the London Consolidated Society of Journeymen Bookbinders. No 1, Oct 1850–no 154, 20 Nov 1877. Monthly at first, but irregular. Ed T. J. Dunning.
Woolnough, C. W. The art of marbling as applied to book edges and paper. 1853, 1881.
Nicholson, J. B. A manual of the art of bookbinding. Philadelphia 1856, 1882.
Dunning, T. J. Account of the London Consolidated Society of Bookbinders. In National Association for the Promotion of Social Science report, 1860.
Patent Office. Abridgments of specifications relating to books, portfolios, card-cases etc 1768–1866. 1870.
Hatton, J. Printing and bookbinding. In G. P. Bevan, British manufacturing industries, 1876.
Crisp, W. F. Bookbinding made easy: or every man his own binder. Great Yarmouth [1877].
Cox, A. J. & Co. The making of the book: a sketch of the bookbinding art. Chicago 1878.
Lenormand, S. Nouveau manuel complet du relieur en tous genres. Paris 1879.
Zaehnsdorf, J. W. The art of bookbinding. 1880, 1890, 1903 (6th edn).
Wheatley, H. B. Bookbinding considered as a fine art, mechanical art and manufacture. 1882.
— The principles of design as applied to bookbinding. Jnl of Royal Soc of Arts Feb 1888.
Adam, P. Systematisches Lehr- und Handbuch der Buchbinderei. 2 vols Dresden 1883–91.
— Der Bucheinband. Leipzig 1890.
— Practical bookbinding. 1903.
Crane, W. J. E. Bookbinding for amateurs. 1885.
The bookbinder. No 1, Jan 1887–no 36, Dec 1889. Continued as The British bookmaker, no 37, Jan 1890–no 81, March 1894. Monthly.
Michel, M. L'ornamentation des reliures modernes. Paris 1889.
Bosquet, E. Traité de l'art du relieur. Paris 1890.
— La reliure: études d'un practicien. Paris 1894.
Bouchot, H. De la reliure: exemples à imiter ou à rejeter. Paris 1891.
Burlington Fine Arts Club. Exhibition of bookbindings. 1891.
Cobden-Sanderson, T. J. Bookbinding. Eng Illustr Mag Jan 1891.
— Bookbinding: its processes and ideals. Fortnightly Rev Aug 1894.
— Bookbinding. In Arts and Crafts Exhibition Society, Arts and crafts essays, 1899.
Wood, H. F. Bookbinding. In G. P. Bevan, British manufacturing industries, 1892.
Fletcher, W. Y. English bookbindings. In A. H. Church, Some minor arts, 1894.
Matthews, B. Bookbindings of the present. Century Mag June 1894.
— Books in paper covers. Century Mag July 1895.
— Bookbindings, old and new: notes of a book-lover with an account of the Grolier Club, New York. New York 1896.
Gruel, L. Conférence sur la reliure et la dorure des livres. Paris 1896.
Davenport, C. J. Cantor lectures on decorative bookbinding. 1898.
Goupil & Co. Catalogue of exhibition of modern English artistic bookbindings, with historical sketch of bookbinding in England by W. Y. Fletcher. 1898.
Bowdoin, W. G. Decorative achievements of pyrography in bookbindings. Artist June 1899.
Wood, E. et al. Modern bookbindings and their designers. Studio winter no 1899.
Cockerell, D. Bookbinding and the care of books: a textbook for bookbinders and librarians. 1901.
Royal Society of Arts. Report of the committee on leather for bookbinding. 1901.
Stewart, C. J. Bookbinders' arbitration award. 1903.
Loubier, J. Der Bucheinband in alter und neuer Zeit. Berlin [1904].
Prideaux, S. T. Modern bookbindings: their design and decoration. 1906.
Stephen, G. A. Commercial bookbinding. 1910.
Sadleir, M. The evolution of publishers' binding styles 1770–1900. 1930.
— Yellow backs. In New paths in book collecting, ed J. Carter 1934.
Carter, J. Binding variants in English publishing 1820–1900. 1932.
— Publishers' cloth 1820–1900. New York [1935].
Rooke, N. Douglas Cockerell: obituary. Jnl of Royal Soc of Arts 21 Dec 1945.
Diehl, E. Bookbinding: its background and technique. 2 vols New York 1946.
Adams, J. The house of Kitcat: a story of bookbinding 1789–1948. 1948.
Key & Whiting Ltd. The years between 1799–1949. 1949.
Leighton, D. Canvas and bookcloth: an essay on beginnings. Library 5th ser 3 1949.
Rosner, C. The art of the book jacket. 1949.
— The growth of the book jacket. 1954.
Loring, R. B. Decorated book papers: being an account of their design and fashions. 1942, Cambridge Mass 1952 (rev P. Hofer).
Middleton, B. The Zaehnsdorf story. Br & Colonial Printer 25 Dec 1953.
— A history of English craft bookbinding technique. 1963.
Ramsden, C. Bookbinders of the United Kingdom (outside London) 1780–1840. 1954.
Hobson, A. R. A. The literature of bookbinding. 1954.
Hunter and Foulis. A hundred years of publishers' bookbinding 1857–1957. Edinburgh 1958.
Darley, L. S. Bookbinding then and now: a survey of the first hundred and seventy-eight years of James Burn and Co Ltd. 1959.

C. BOOK DISTRIBUTION

(1) GENERAL WORKS

National Book Council. Books about books: a catalogue of the books contained in the National Book Council Library. 1933, 1935, 1955 (as National Book League).
[Phillips, S.] The literature of the rail. 1851.
Britton. J. Autobiography. 2 vols 1850.
Hodson, W. H. Hodson's booksellers', publishers' and stationers' directory for London and country. 1855.
Curwen, H. A history of booksellers, the old and the new. [1873].
'The Bookman' directory of booksellers, publishers and authors. 1893.
Mumby, F. A. The romance of bookselling. 1910, 1930 (rev as Publishing and bookselling), 1940, 1954 (rev).
Shaylor, J. The fascination of books. 1912.
Collins, A. S. The profession of letters 1780–1832. 1928.

Cruse, A. The Englishman and his books in the early 19th century. 1930.
— The Victorians and their books. 1935.
— After the Victorians. 1938.
Darton, F. J. H. Children's books in England. Cambridge 1932.
Flower, D. S. Century of best sellers 1830–1930. 1934.
Craig, A. The banned books of England. 1937.
Turner, E. S. Boys will be boys. 1948. On boys' stories.
Altick, R. D. The English common reader 1800–1900. Chicago 1957.

(2) COPYRIGHT

Solberg, T. Bibliography of literary property. In R. R. Bowker, Copyright: its law and its literature, New York 1886.
List of works on copyright in the Patent Office Library. 1900.
Montefiori, J. The law of copyright. 1802.
Report of the Select Committee [of the House of Commons] on copyright of printed books, and the delivery of them to the public libraries. 1812–13. (292). iv. 999.
— Minutes of evidence on the effect of the law on literary property. 1812–13. (341). iv. 1003; rptd 1818, (177). ix. 389.
[Duppa, R.] An address to the Parliament of Great Britain on the claims of authors to their own copyright. 1813, 1813; rptd in Pamphleteer 2 1813.
[Turner, S.] Reasons for a modification of the Act of Anne respecting the delivery of books and copyright. 1813.
Britton, J. The rights of literature: or an enquiry into the policy and justice of the claims of certain public libraries on all the publishers and authors for eleven copies of every new publication. 1814.
Brydges, E. A summary statement of the great grievance imposed on authors and publishers by the late Copyright Act. 1818.
Report of the Select Committee [of the House of Commons] respecting the amendment of 54 George III. 1818. (402). ix. 249. Minutes of Evidence, 1818, (280). ix. 257.
Godson, R. A practical treatise on the law of patents for inventions and of copyright. 1823, 1840, 1844. Supplements 1832, 1844, 1851.
Maugham, R. A treatise on the laws of literary property. 1828.
Report from the Select Committee [of the House of Commons] appointed to inquire into the laws affecting dramatic literature. 1831–2. (679). vii. 2.
Bossange, H. Opinion nouvelle sur la propriété littéraire. Paris 1836.
Didot, A. F. Note sur la propriété littéraire et sur la répression des contrefaçons faites à l'étranger, particulièrement en Belgique. [Paris c. 1836].
— Observations présentées à la Commission de la propriété littéraire et artistique. Paris 1862.
Hood, T. Copyright and copywrong. Athenaeum 15–29 April 1837, 11–18 June 1842; rptd in Works, vols 4, 6, 1862.
Blanc, E. Traité de contrefaçon et de sa poursuite en justice. Paris 1837, 1838, 1855.
Tegg, T. Remarks on the speech of Sergeant Talfourd. 1837.
Chambers, W. and R. Brief objections to Mr Talfourd's new copyright bill. Edinburgh 1838.
Mudie, R. The copyright question and Mr Sergeant Talfourd's Bill. 1838.
Nicklin, P. H. Remarks on literary property. Philadelphia 1838.
Renouard, A. C. Traité des droits d'auteurs. 2 vols Paris 1838–9.
Webster, G. Observations on the law of copyright in reference to the Bill of Mr Sergeant Talfourd. 1838.
Areopagitica secunda: or speech of the shade of John Milton on Sergeant Talfourd's Copyright Extension Bill. 1838.
A proposed new law of copyright of the highest importance to authors in a letter to T. N. Talfourd. [1838].
A few words on the copyright question shewing it to be one of public interest, with some objections to Sergeant Talfourd's Bill. 1839.
Christie, W. D. A plea for perpetual copyright. 1840.
Lahure, C. Observations sur la demande faite par les libraires, réunies en commission, de reconnaître chez nous, et sans condition, la propriété littéraire des étrangers; et moyen de paralyser les contrefaçons belges sans nuire à aucune des branches de notre industrie. Paris 1840.
Lieber, F. On international copyright. New York 1840.
Lowndes, J. J. An historical sketch of the law of copyright. 1840, 1842.
Talfourd, T. N. Three speeches delivered in the House of Commons in favour of a measure for an extension of copyright, to which are added the petitions in favour of the Bill and remarks on the present state of the copyright question. 1840.
Balzac, H. de. Notes remises à MM. les Députés composant la commission de la loi sur la propriété littéraire [5 March 1841]. In Œuvres complètes vol 22, Paris 1872.
Burke, P. A treatise on the law of copyright in literature. 1842.
— The law of international copyright between England and France. 1852.
— The present state of the law of copyright with a view to its amendment. 1863.
The law of copyright regarding authors, dramatic writers and musical composers as altered by the recent statute. 1842.
Mathews, C. An appeal to American authors and the American press in behalf of an international copyright. New York 1842; rptd in Various writings of C. Mathews, New York 1843.
Campbell, J. Considerations and arguments proving the inexpediency of an international copyright law. New York 1844.
Muquardt, C. De la contrefaçon et de son influence pernicieuse sur la littérature et la librairie. Brussels 1844.
Curtis, G. T. A treatise of the law of copyright in books. Boston 1847.
Boosey versus Purday. Assumed copyright in foreign authors: judgement given in the Court of Exchequer, Westminster Hall 5 June 1849. 1849.
A brief statement on the subject of assumed foreign copyright. 1851.
Bohn, H. G. The question of unreciprocated foreign copyright. 1851.
Villefort, A. De la propriété littéraire et artistique au point de vue internationale. Paris 1851.
Mathews, C. J. Lettre de M. Charles Mathews aux auteurs dramatiques de la France. 1852.
Delalain, A. H. J. Législation de la propriété littéraire. Paris 1852, 1852, 1854, 1855, 1855, 1858 (rev).
— Nouvelle législation de la propriété littéraire. Paris 1868.
Thackeray, W. M. Mr Brown's letters. New York 1853. Author's preface.
Carey, H. C. Letters on international copyright. Philadelphia 1853, New York 1868.
— The international copyright question considered. Philadelphia 1872.
Lacan, A. J. B. and C. P. P. Paulmier. Traité de la législation et de la jurisprudence des théatres. 2 vols Paris 1853.

Leverson, M. R. Copyright and patents: being an investigation of the principles of legal science applicable to property in thought. 1854.
Eisenlohr, C. F. M. Sammlung der Gesetze und internationalen Verträge zum Schutze des literarischen-artischen Eigenthums in Deutschland, Frankreich und England. Heidelberg 1856. 1857.
Laboulaye, E. R. L. Etudes sur la propriété littéraire en France et en Angleterre. Paris 1858.
Compte rendu des travaux du congrès de Bruxelles. Paris 1858.
Reade, C. The eighth commandment. 1860.
— The rights and wrongs of authors. In Readiana, 1863.
Law, S. D. Digest of American cases relating to patents for inventions and copyrights from 1789 to 1862. New York 1862, 1870 (rev), 1877 (rev).
Gastambide, J. A. Histoire et théorie de la propriété des auteurs. Paris 1862.
Phillips, C. P. The law of literature and art. 1863.
Chappell, F. P. and J. Shoard. A handy book of the law of copyright. 1863.
Gambart, E. On piracy of artistic copyright. 1863.
Huard, A. Etude comparative des législations françaises et étrangères en matière de la propriété industriélle, artistique et littéraire. Paris 1863.
Trollope, A. On the best means of extending and securing an international law of copyright. Trans Nat Assoc for Promotion of Social Science 1867.
Le Barrois d'Orgeval, R. La propriété littéraire en France et à l'étranger. Paris 1868.
White, R. G. The American view of the copyright question. Broadway Annual (New York) May 1868; rptd New York 1880.
Howard, A. Copyright: a manual for authors and publishers. 1887.
[Helps, Sir A.] International copyright between England and America. Macmillan's Mag June 1869.
Copinger, W. A. The law of copyright in works of literature and art. 1870, 1881, 1893, 1904 (rev J. M. Easton), 1915, 1927 (rev F. E. Skene Jones).
Booth, W. D. Rights of dramatic authors at Common Law. New York 1871.
Hotten, J. C. Literary copyright: seven letters addressed to Earl Stanhope. 1871.
Klostermann, R. Das Urheberrecht und das Verlagsrecht nach deutschen und ausländischen Gesetzen systematisch und vergleichend dargestellt. Berlin 1871.
Shortt, J. The law relating to literature and art. 1871, 1884.
Memoranda on international and colonial copyright. 1872.
Appleton, W. H. Letters on international copyright. New York 1872.
Coryton, J. Stageright: a compendium of the laws relating to dramatic authors. 1873.
Morgan, J. H. The law of literature. 2 vols New York 1875, 1876.
Dicey, E. The copyright question. Fortnightly Rev 1 Jan 1876.
Purday, C. H. Copyright: a sketch of its rise and progress. 1877.
Copyright Commission. The Royal Commissions and the Report of the Commissioners [evidence and appendix]. 1878.
[Froude, J. A.] The copyright commission. Edinburgh Rev Oct 1878.
Levi, L. International copyright in relation to the USA and other foreign states. 1879.
Macfie, R. A. Copyright and patents for inventions. Vol 1, Edinburgh 1879.
M[arston], E. Copyright national and international from the point of view of a publisher. 1879.
Conant, S. S. and L. H. Courtney. International Copyright. Macmillan's Mag June 1879.
Drone, E. S. A treatise on the law of property in intellectual productions in Great Britain and the USA. Boston 1879.
Putnam, G. H. International copyright considered in some of its relations to ethics and political economy. New York 1879.
— The question of copyright. New York 1891, 1896.
Harper & Bros. Memorandums on international copyright. [New York 1879], [1880] (enlarged).
'Stylus'. American publishers and English authors. Baltimore 1879.
Fliniaux, C. La propriété industrielle et la propriété littéraire et artistique en France et à l'étranger. Tours 1879.
Pouillet, E. Traité théorique et pratique de la propriété littéraire et artistique et du droit de représentation. Paris 1879.
Clunet, E. Concordance des résolutions du Congrès de la Propriété artistique tenu à Paris en 1878. Paris 1879.
Arnold, M. Copyright. Fortnightly Rev 1 March 1880; rptd in his Irish essays, 1882.
Collins, W. W. Considerations on the copyright question addressed to an American friend. International Rev (New York) June 1880; rptd 1880.
Jerrold, S. A handbook of English and foreign copyright in literary and dramatic works. 1881.
Longman, C. J. A publisher's view of international copyright. Fraser's Mag March 1881.
Dawson, S. E. Copyright in books: an insight into its origin and the present state of the law in Canada. Montreal 1882.
Scrutton, T. E. The laws of copyright. 1883, 1890, 1896, 1903.
Thompson, G. C. Remarks on the law of literary property in various countries. 1883.
Lea, H. C. International copyright. [Philadelphia 1884.]
Slater, J. H. The law relating to copyright. 1884.
Bowker, R. R. Copyright: its law and its literature. New York 1886.
— Copyright: its history and its law. 1912.
Matthews, J. B. Cheap books and good books. New York 1888.
— American authors and British pirates. New York 1889.
Association Littéraire Internationale: son histoire 1878–89. Paris 1889.
Lyon-Caen, C. and P. Delalain. Lois françaises et étrangères sur la propriété littéraire. 2 vols Paris 1889.
Cutler, E., T. E. Smith and F. E. Weatherly. The law of musical and dramatic copyright. 1890.
Lely, T. M. Copyright law reform. 1891.
Chamier, D. Law relating to literary copyright. 1895.
Chosson, E. La propriété littéraire. Paris 1895.
Osterreith, A. Die Geschichte des Urheberrechts in England. Leipzig 1895.
Cohen, B. A. The law of copyright. 1896.
Lancefield, R. T. Notes on copyright, domestic and international. Hamilton Ontario 1896.
Rivière, L. Protection internationale des oeuvres littéraires et artistiques. Paris 1897.
Report of the Select Committee of the House of Lords on the Copyright Bills [evidence and appendix]. 1898, 1899, 1900.
Birrell, A. Seven lectures on the law and history of copyright in books. 1899.
Solberg, T. Copyright enactments [in USA] 1783–1900, together with the Presidential proclamations regarding international copyright. Washington 1900.
— Copyright in Congress 1789–1904: a bibliography and chronological record. Washington 1905.
Strong, A. A. The law of copyright for actor and composer. 1901.
Macgillivray, E. J. Treatise upon the law of copyright in the United Kingdom and the Dominions of the Crown and in the USA. 1902, 1906.
Hinkson, H. A. Copyright law. 1903.
Hamlin, A. S. Copyright cases: a summary of leading American decisions. New York 1904.

Recueil des conventions et traités concernant la propriété littéraire. Berne 1904.

Allen, G. Copyright and copywrong: the authentic and the unauthentic Ruskin. 1907.

Report of the Committee on the Law of Copyright. 1909.

Putnam, G. H. George Pamer Putnam. New York 1912.

Potu, E. La convention de Berne. Paris 1914.

Flower, D. Authors and copyright in the xixth century with unpublished letters from Wilkie Collins. Book Collectors' Quart no 7 1932.

Pollard, G. Introduction. In I. R. Brussel, Anglo-American first editions, 1935.

(3) AUTHORS' GUIDES TO PUBLICATION

The following works all profess to instruct an author how to choose and negotiate with a publisher. This function is now fulfilled by the literary agent, who was hardly established as a profession before 1880; and the only work in this list specifically dealing with the literary agent is the collection of testimonials to A. P. Watt, 1893.

[H., T.] The perils of authorship. [c. 1835], [c. 1840] (4th edn).

— The author's advocate and young publishers' friend: a sequel to the perils of authorship. [c. 1840].

The author's printing and publishing assistant. 1839, 1839, New York 1839, 1840, [c. 1848] (7th edn). Attributed to Frederic Saunders; all English edns pbd by Saunders & Otley.

Hints and directions for authors in writing, printing and publishing their works. 1842. Attributed to the publisher Edward Bull.

[Churton, E.] The author's handbook: a complete guide to the art and system of publishing on commission. 1844, 1845 (with addns).

Saunders and Otley. Advice to authors, inexperienced writers and possessors of manuscripts, on the efficient publication of books intended for general circulation or private distribution with select specimens of printing. [1853].

A description of publishing methods and arrangements. New York 1855 (4th edn).

The search for a publisher: or counsels to a young author. 1855, 1859 (4th edn), 1865, 1870, [1873], 1881.

[Judd, J. and A. H. Glass]. Counsels to authors and hints to advertisers. 1856, 1857.

Counsels to authors, plans of publishing, and specimens of types. 1863.

Comprehensive guide to printing and publishing. 1869, 1877 (10th edn), 1897.

Spon, E. How to publish a book. 1872.

[Southward, J.] Authorship and publication: a guide in matters relating to printing and publishing. 1882, 1883, 1884.

[Putnam, G. H. and G. P.] Authors and publishers: a manual of suggestions for beginners in literature. New York 1883, 1897 (7th edn), 1900.

Deacon's composition and style with a complete guide to all matters connected with printing and publishing. Ed R. D. Blackman [1885] (5th edn).

Russell, P. The literary manual: or a complete guide to authorship. 1886.

The author's guide to printing and publishing by a journalist. [1886] (2nd edn).

O'Brien, M. B. A manual for authors, printers and publishers. 1890.

Sprigge, S. S. Methods of publishing. 1890, 1891.

The author. No 1, 15 May 1890–. The monthly organ of the Incorporated Society of Authors; ed Sir Walter Besant.

How to print and publish a book. Winchester 1890.

Jacobi, C. T. On the making and issuing of books. 1891.

— Some notes on books and printing. 1892, 1902.

Besant, W. The Society of Authors: a record of its action from its foundation. 1893.

— The pen and the book. 1899.

Watt, A. P. Letters addressed to A. P. Watt by various writers. 1893, 1894, 1896.

Eisemann, E. Le contrat d'édition et les autres louages d'œuvres intellectuelles. Paris 1894.

Lamb, J. B. Practical hints on writing for the press. 1897.

Wagner, L. How to publish a book or an article. 1898.

Bennett, A. How to become an author. 1903, [1908] 1912.

[Watson, W. L.] The author's progress by Adam Lorimer. Edinburgh 1906.

Booth, W. S. A practical guide to authors in their relations with publishers and printers. Boston 1907.

(4) THE PRACTICE OF PUBLISHING

Memoirs of authors have not been included in this list although they contain much relevant material, particularly the autobiographies of Anthony Trollope, Herbert Spencer, Harriet Martineau, Cyrus Redding and Edmund Yates, and the biographies of Macaulay by Sir G. O. Trevelyan and of Scott by J. G. Lockhart (as well as his Journal and Correspondence). Works relating to publishers' control of the retail price (the Net Book Agreement and its predecessors) have been listed with those on retail bookselling, col 83, below.

Babbage, C. On the economy of machinery and manufactures. 1832.

First Report from the Select Committee on Postage. Minutes of evidence. 1837–8. xx. 278.

Jerdan, W. Illustrations of the plan of a National Association for the encouragement and protection of authors. 1838.

The Aldine magazine of biography, bibliography, criticism and the arts. 1839. Ed William West.

[Grant, J.] Travels in town by the author of Random recollections of the Lords and Commons. 2 vols 1839.

Balzac, H. de. Code littéraire (May 1840). In his Œuvres complètes vol 22, Paris 1872.

James, G. P. R. Some observations on the booktrade as connected with literature in England. Jnl of Statistical Soc of London Feb 1843.

[Petheram, J.] Reasons for establishing an authors publication society. 1843.

The present system of publishing. 1844.

Knight, C. The old printer and the modern press. 1854.

Spedding, J. Publishers and authors. 1867.

Ruskin, J. Fors clavigera. 1871–84. Letters 6, 11, 16, 53, 57, 62, 89; Notes and correspondence, 10, 14–15.

Walker, S. The road: leaves from the sketch book of a commercial traveller. Otley 1872.

Powell, A. The law affecting printers, publishers and newspaper proprietors. 1887, 1889 (rev).

The grievances between authors and publishers: being the report of the conferences of the Incorporated Society of Authors with additional matter and summary. 1887.

Besant, W. Literary conferences. 1888.

— The Society of Authors: a record of its action from its foundation. 1893.

— Literary conferences. Contemporary Rev Jan 1894.

— The pen and the book. 1899.

— Autobiography. 1902.

Jessopp, A. A plea for the publisher. Contemporary Rev March 1890.

Smiles, S. Authors and publishers. Murray's Mag Jan-Feb 1890.

Sprigge, S. S. The methods of publishing. 1890, 1891 (rev).

— The society of French authors. 1890.
The Society of Authors. The cost of production. 1891 (3 edns).
Kegan Paul, C. The life and death of books. In his Faith and unfaith, 1891.
[Heinemann, W.] The hardships of publishing. 1893 (priv ptd).
Jerome, J. K. et al. My first book. 1894.
Buchanan, R. W. Is Barabbas a necessity? a discourse on publishers and publishing. 1896.
Allen, C. E. Publishers' accounts; including a consideration of copyright and the valuation of literary property. 1897.
Spencer, H. Various fragments. 1897, 1900 (rev).
International Publishers' Congress 1899. Report. 1899.
— 1901. Report. Leipzig 1902.
[Bennett, A.] The truth about an author. 1903, 1914.
Publishers and publishing a hundred years ago, from materials collected by Aleck Abrahams, with some notes by E. Marston. Publishers' Circular 6, 13 Jan 1906.
Yard, R. S. The publisher. Boston 1913.
Putnam, G. H. Memories of a publisher 1865–95. 1915.
Unwin, S. The truth about publishing. 1926, 1929 (3rd edn rev), 1946, 1960.
'On the road' one hundred years ago: being an account of a journey made [in 1830] by a traveller of Messrs A. & C. Black's when subscribing the seventh edition of the Encyclopaedia Britannica. Ed J. Cannon, Publishers' Circular 9 Feb–13 April 1935.

(5) INDIVIDUAL PUBLISHERS

Publishers who were also printers may be listed in col 57 above.

Rudolph Ackerman (1764–1834)
P[apworth], W[yatt]. N & Q 7–14 Aug 1869.
Allen & Unwin Ltd
George Allen & Unwin Ltd. 1933.
Samuel Bagster (1772–1851)
The centenary of the Bagster publishing house. 1894.
B. T. Batsford, London
Bolitho, H. A Batsford century: the record of a hundred years of publishing and bookselling 1843–1943. [1943].
George Bell (1814–90)
Bell, E. George Bell, publisher. 1924 (priv ptd).
Richard Bentley (1794–1871)
Richard Bentley & Son: reprinted from Le Livre Oct 1885 with some additional notes. 1886 (priv ptd).
Sadleir, M. Bentley Standard novels. Colophon (New York) April 1932.
Gettman, R. A. A Victorian publisher: a study of the Bentley papers. Cambridge 1960.
Adam Black (1784–1874)
Nicholson, A. Memoirs of A. Black. Edinburgh 1885, 1885.
Adam and Charles Black 1807–1957: some chapters in the history of a publishing house. 1957.
John Blackie (1782–1874)
Blackie, W. G. The origin and progress of the firm of Blackie and Son 1809–74. 1897.
A Scottish student in Leipzig, being the letters of W. G. Blackie, his father and his brothers in the years 1839–40. Ed W. W. Blackie 1932.
Blackie, A. Blackie and Son 1809–1959: a short history of the firm. 1959.
William Blackwood (1776–1834)
Blackwood, J. A selection from the obituary notices. Ed W. Blackwood, Edinburgh 1880 (priv ptd).
Oliphant, M. O. Annals of a publishing house: W. Blackwood and his sons. 2 vols 1897. Vol 3, J. Blackwood by his daughter Mrs G. Porter, 1898.
B., I. C. The early house of Blackwood. Edinburgh 1900 (priv ptd).
Burns & Oates
'Wilberforce, Wilfrid' (Wilfrid Meynell). The house of Burns and Oates. [1908].
Early chapters in the history of Burns & Oates. 1949 (priv ptd).
Cadell and Davies
The publishing firm of Cadell and Davies: select correspondence and accounts 1793–1836. Ed T. Besterman 1938.
Richard Carlile (1790–1843)
Holyoake, G. J. The life and character of Carlile. 1848.
Campbell, T. C. The battle of the press as told in the story of the life of Carlile. 1899.
John Cassell (1817–65)
Kirton, J. W. John Cassell. 1891.
Pike, G. H. John Cassell. 1894.
Flower, N. Just as it happened. 1950.
Nowell-Smith, S. The house of Cassell 1848–1958. 1958.
James Catnach (1792–1841)
Hindley, C. The life and times of Catnach, ballad-monger. 1878.
St Bride Foundation: catalogue of an exhibition of street literature. 1954.
William Chambers (1800–83); Robert Chambers (1802–71)
Chambers, W. Memoir of Robert Chambers with autobiographic reminiscences of William Chambers. Edinburgh 1872, 1884 (12th edn), 1893 (rev).
— The story of a long and busy life. Edinburgh, 1882, 1884 (13th edn).
Payn, J. Some literary recollections. 1886.
Chapman & Hall
Waugh, A. A hundred years of publishing: being the story of Chapman and Hall Ltd. 1930.
— One man's road. 1931.
John W. Chapman
Kegan Paul, C. Biographical sketches. 1883.
Chatto & Windus
A century of writers 1855–1955. 1955. Introd gives a history of the firm.
T. and T. Clark
The publishing house of T. and T. Clark. Edinburgh 1882.
William Cobbett (1763–1833)
See col 1199, below.
William Collins, Sons & Co
William Collins, Sons & Co. The story of a great business 1820–1909. Glasgow 1909.
Keir, D. The house of Collins. 1952.
Archibald Constable (1774–1827)
Constable, T. Constable and his literary correspondents. 3 vols Edinburgh 1873.
J. M. Dent (1849–1926)
Dent, H. R. The memoirs of J. M. Dent, with some additions by H. R. Dent. 1928.
Dent, H. M. and H. R. Dent. The house of Dent 1888–1938. [1938].
G. H. Doran
Chronicles of Barabbas 1884–1934. 1935.
Gerald Duckworth & Co
Fifty years 1898–1948. [1948] (priv ptd).
John Francis (1811–82)
Francis, J. C. Francis: publisher of the Athenaeum. 2 vols 1888.
William Godwin (1756–1836)
Kegan Paul, C. William Godwin: his friends and his contemporaries. 2 vols 1876.
Charles Griffin & Co
The centenary volume of Griffin and Co 1820–1920. 1920.
Harper
Harper, J. H. The house of Harper: a century of publishing in Franklin Square. New York 1912.

C. Harrison
Harrison, C. From office boy to publisher: a record of 43 years of work. [1911].
Hatchard & Co
Humphreys, A. L. Piccadilly bookmen: memorials of the house of Hatchard. 1893.
William Heinemann (1863–1920)
Whyte, F. Heinemann: a memoir. 1928.
Evans, C. S. 1883–1944. Obituary notices. 1945 (priv ptd).
William Hone (1780–1842)
Hackwood, F. W. Hone: his life and times. 1912.
Jarrold & Co
The house of Jarrolds 1823–1923. 1924.
W. & A. K. Johnston
One hundred years of map making: the story of W. and A. K. Johnston. 1925.
Thomas Kelly (1772–1855)
Fell, R. C. Passages from the private and official life of the late Alderman Kelly. 1856.
Charles Knight (1791–1873)
Knight, C. Passages of a working life. 3 vols 1864.
Strahan, A. Knight, publisher. Good Words Sept 1867.
Clowes, A. A. Knight: a sketch. 1892.
Lang, P. H. Charles Knight and The art of printing. Printing Rev 6 1939.
John Lane, The Bodley Head Ltd
May, J. L. John Lane and the nineties. 1936.
H. K. Lewis & Co
Lewis's 1844–1944. 1945.
E. & S. Livingstone Ltd, Edinburgh
Eighty years of publishing 1864–1944. Edinburgh 1944.
Footprints on the sands of time 1863–1963: the story of the House of Livingstone, medical, scientific, nursing and dental publishers. [1963].
Longmans, Green & Co
Rees, T. Reminiscences of literary London from 1779 to 1853, with additions by John Britton. New York 1896.
Cox, H. and J. E. Chandler. The house of Longman 1724–1924. 1925 (priv ptd).
'Indiamen', Three addresses: an essay in publishing ecology 1939–47. 1947.
Blagden, C. Fire more than water: notes for the story of a ship. 1949.
Owen, W. J. B. Letters of Longman & Co to Wordsworth 1814–36. Library 5th ser 9 1954.
Macmillan & Co
Hughes, T. Memoir of Daniel Macmillan. 1882, 1883.
A bibliographical catalogue of Macmillan & Co's publications 1843–89. 1891.
Macmillan, G. A. Letters of Alexander Macmillan. 1908 (priv ptd).
Graves, C. L. Life and letters of Alexander Macmillan. 1910.
Morgan, C. The house of Macmillan 1843–1943. [1943].
Edward Marston (1825–1914)
Marston, E. After work. 1904.
Sir Algernon Methuen (1856–1924)
Methuen: a memoir. 1925.
R. C. Morgan (1827–1908)
Morgan, G. E. A veteran in revival: R. C. Morgan, his life and times. 1909, 1931.
John Murray (I, 1745–1793; II, 1778–1843; III, 1808–92)
Smiles, S. A publisher and his friends [1768–1843]. 2 vols 1891, 1891, 1911 (abridged).
Murray, John (III). The origin and history of Murray's handbooks for travellers. Murray's Mag Nov 1889.
Murray, John [IV]. John Murray III 1808–92. 1919.
'Paston, George' (E. M. Symonds). At John Murray's: records of a literary circle 1843–92. 1932.
William Nelson (1816–87)
Wilson, Sir Daniel. Nelson: a memoir. Edinburgh 1889 (priv ptd).

Sir George Newnes (1851–1910)
Friedrichs, H. The life of Sir George Newnes, Bart. 1911.
James Nisbet (1785–1854)
Wallace, J. A. Lessons from the life of the late James Nisbet. 1867.
Novello, Ewer & Co
A short history of cheap music as exemplified in the records of the house of Novello, Ewer & Co. 1887.
C. Kegan Paul (1828–1902)
Kegan Paul, C. Memories. 1899.
George Philip
Philip, G. The story of the last hundred years: a geographical record. 1934.
Sir Richard Phillips (1767–1840)
Memoirs of the public and private life of Sir Richard Phillips. 1808. Attributed to Phillips himself.
GM Aug 1840. Obituary.
Timbs, J. Recollections of Sir Richard Phillips. In his Walks and talks about London, 1864.
William Pickering (1796–1854)
Keynes, G. L. William Pickering, publisher. 1924.
Sir Isaac Pitman (1813–97)
Reed, T. A. A biography of Isaac Pitman. 1890.
Baker, A. The life of Sir Isaac Pitman. 1908.
The house of Pitman. 1930.
Grant Richards (b. 1872)
Richards, G. Memories of a misspent youth 1872–96. 1932.
—— Author hunting. 1934.
Rivington & Co
Rivington, S. The publishing house of Rivington. 1894.
—— The publishing family of Rivington. 1919.
Holmes, J. C. Self and partners: mostly self. 1936.
Routledge & Co.
Mumby, F. A. The house of Routledge 1834–1934. 1934.
John Sharpe
Bain, I. Sharpe: publisher and bookseller, Piccadilly: a preliminary survey of his activities in the London Book Trade 1800–40. Welwyn 1960.
Joseph Shaylor (1844–1924)
Shaylor, J. Sixty years a bookman. 1923.
Simpkin, Marshall & Co
Simpkins: being some account of the origin and progress of the house of Simpkin, Marshall. 1924.
George Smith (1824–1901)
[Lee, S. and L. Stephen]. Smith: a memoir. 1902 (priv ptd).
[Huxley, L.] The house of Smith, Elder. 1923 (priv ptd).
W. H. Smith (1825–1891)
Maxwell, H. The life and times of the Rt Hon William Henry Smith. 2 vols Edinburgh 1893.
Pocklington, G. R. The story of W. H. Smith & Son. 1921 (priv ptd); rev F. E. K. Foat 1932 (priv ptd).
Society for the Promotion of Christian Knowledge
1698—and after: the story of the SPCK. 1947.
Edward Stanford
Edward Stanford; with a note on the history of the firm 1852–1901. 1902 (priv ptd).
Alexander Strahan
Strahan, A. Twenty years of a publisher's life. Day of Rest Jan–Dec 1881.
Bernard Tauchnitz
Fünfzig Jahre der Verlagshandlung Bernhard Tauchnitz, 1837 bis 1887. Leipzig 1887.
John Taylor (1781–1864)
Taylor, O. M. John Taylor. London Mercury June 1925.
Blunden, E. Keats's publisher: a memoir of John Taylor. 1936.
Thomas Tegg (1776–1845)
[Grant, J.] In his Portraits of public characters vol 2, 1841.

Memoir of the late Thomas Tegg, abridged from his autobiography by permission of his son William Tegg. 1870 (priv ptd). Rptd from City Press 6 Aug 1870.

Temple Press Ltd
Armstrong, A. C. Bouverie Street to Bowling Green Lane: fifty-five years of specialized publishing. 1946.

William Tinsley (1831–1902)
Tinsley, W. Random recollections of an old publisher. 2 vols 1900.
Downey, E. Twenty years ago. 1905.

Nicholas Trubner (1817–84)
Axon, W. E. A. In memoriam Nicholas Trubner. Lib Chron April 1884.

Henry Vizetelly (1820–94)
Vizetelly, H. Glances back through seventy years. 2 vols 1893.

Ward Lock & Co
Liveing, E. Adventure in publishing: the house of Ward, Lock 1854–1954. [1954].

Frederick Warne & Co
King, A. and A. F. Stuart. The house of Warne: one hundred years of publishing. 1965.

Joseph Whitaker (1820–95)
Publishers' circular, 18–25 May 1895.

Effingham Wilson (1783–1868)
[Bagehot, W.] In memoriam Effingham Wilson. 1868 (priv ptd). Rptd from City Press 18 July 1868.

(6) GENERAL CATALOGUES

This section lists general catalogues of books in print over a specified period; it does not include catalogues of individual publishers or any limited to particular subjects. Catalogues issued regularly at intervals of less than a year are listed in cols 81–4 below in the section on Periodicals.

Growoll, A. and W. Eames. Three centuries of English book trade bibliography. New York 1903.

Pollard, G. General lists of books printed in England. Bull Inst of Hist Research Feb 1935.

[Bent, W.] The modern catalogue of books (1792–1803). 1803.
— The new London catalogue (1800–5). 1805.
— The new London catalogue (1800–7). 1807.
— The London catalogue (1700–1811). 1811.
— A modern catalogue of books (1811–12). 1812.
— The London catalogue (1800–14). 1814.
— A catalogue of books (1814–16). 1816.
— The modern London catalogue (1800–18). 1818.
— A catalogue of books (1818–20). 1820.
— The London catalogue (1800–22). 1822.

[Bent, R.] A catalogue of books (1822–4). 1824.
— The London catalogue (1800–27). 1827; Supplement, 1829.
— The London catalogue (1810–31). 1831; Supplement, 1833.
— The London catalogue (1814–34). 1835; Supplement, 1837.
— The London catalogue (1814–39). 1839.

[Low, S.] A catalogue of books. 1838–59. Annually. Incorporated in The English catalogue, below.
— The British catalogue. Vol 1 (1837–52), 1853. Index to the British Catalogue (1837–57), 1858.
— The English catalogue. 1860–. An annual.
— The English catalogue of books (1835–63). 1864. Vol 2 (1863–72), 1873; index to vol 2 (1856–76), 1876; vol 3 (1872–80), 1882; Index to vol 3 (1874–80), 1884; vol 4 (1881–9), 1891; Index to vol 4 (1881–9), 1893; vol 5 (1890–7), 1898; vol 6 (1898–1900), 1901.

[Hodgson, T.] Supplement to the London catalogue (1839–44). 1844.
— The London catalogue (1814–46). 1846; Bibliotheca Londiniensis: a classified index, 1848; Supplement, 1849.
— The London catalogue (1816–51). 1851; Classified index, 1853.
— The London catalogue (1831–55). 1855.

[Whitaker, J.] The reference catalogue of current literature. 1874–. Until 1936 this consisted of publishers' catalogues bound together and indexed. Since 1936 it comprises catalogues of *Authors* and *Titles* compiled from publishers' lists.

Peddie, R. A. and Q. Waddington. The English catalogue of books (1801–36). 1914.

(7) TRADE PERIODICALS

The following periodicals contain either current lists of books pbd or comment and correspondence on trade affairs. Some contain both; but no periodicals of literary criticism intended for general circulation have been included.

The monthly literary advertiser. No 1, 10 May 1805–10 Dec 1828. Continued as Bent's literary advertiser, 10 Jan 1829–16 June 1860. Monthly. Incorporated in Bookseller. Ed William Bent (1805–23), Robert Bent (1823–42), Thomas Hodgson (1842–60).

The retail booksellers' and bookbuyers' advocate. No 1, 1 Dec 1836; no 2, Jan 1837; no 3 [Feb 1837]. Probably ed Edward J. Portwine.

The publishers' circular. No 1, 2 Oct 1837–. Fortnightly at first, then weekly; ed Sampson Low.

The intelligencer for publishers and booksellers. No 1, July 1854–no 7, Jan 1855. Monthly.

The bookseller. Jan 1858–30 March 1928. Continued as Publisher and bookseller 6 April 1928–29 Sept 1933. Continued as Bookseller, 6 Oct 1933–. Weekly. Ed Edward Tucker, Joseph Whitaker.

The stationer. No 1, 1 May 1859–10 Aug 1865. Continued as Stationer, printer, and fancy trades register, 1 Sept 1865–Feb 1912.

Index to current literature. No 1, 30 Sept 1859–no 8, 31 Dec 1860. Quarterly; ed Sampson Low.

The booksellers' record. No 1, 19 Nov–no 7, 31 Dec 1859. Weekly.

The books of the month. No 1, April 1861–no 17, Aug 1862.

The literary gazette: a monthly record of literature. No 1, 14 Jan–no 7, 10 July 1865.

The bookbuyer's guide: being a list of the principal books published in the various departments of literature. No 1, Dec 1869–no 9, March 1872. Quarterly; ed Thomas J. Fenwick from no 4.

The stationer's and bookseller's circular. No 1, 4 March–no 4, 25 March 1871. Weekly.

The booksellers' circular and bookbuyers' guide. No 1, 20 Oct 1874. Monthly; ed W. E. Goulden.

The bookbuyer: a chronicle of, and guide to current literature. New ser no 1, Feb; no 2, March 1875.

The book circular: a monthly record of new books and new editions classified according to subjects. No 1, 1 Jan–no 6, 1 June 1877.

The stationery trades journal. No 1, 18 March 1880–. Monthly; ed J. Whitaker.

The stationery trade review (Edinburgh). No 1, Jan 1881–Dec 1887. Continued at London as Stationery, bookselling and fancy goods, vol 1, no 1, Jan 1888–Sept 1897. Continued as Morriss's Trade journal Oct 1897–April 1903. Continued as British Empire paper, stationery and printing trades journal, vol 23, no 5, May 1903–June 1913. Monthly; ed J. S. Morriss from 1888.

The stationer and bookseller. No 1, 8 May 1883. Continued as Stationers' and booksellers' journal, no 2,

23 June 1883–no 12, 30 April 1884. Monthly; incorporated in Stationery review.

Books. A weekly journal for those who buy them, sell them and read them. No 1, 18 April–no 3, 4 July 1889.

The newsagent and advertisers' record. No 1, July 1889–Dec 1890. Continued as Newsagent and booksellers' review, 31 Jan 1891. Weekly.

The book world: a journal for publishers and booksellers. No 1, Aug 1890–April 1899. Ed 'Boswell'.

The newsman and publication register. No 1, 25 Oct 1890–no 10, 1 Sept 1891. Monthly.

The stationery world and fancy goods review. No 1, 29 Jan 1892–. Monthly; ed S. Phillips.

The book review index. No 1, June 1892. Quarterly.

The book and news trade gazette. [No 1, 1893]–1 Jan 1898–29 Sept 1907.

Bookselling. No 1, Jan 1895–Dec 1896. Continued as Books and bookselling. Jan–Dec 1897. Monthly; ed 'Temple Scott' (J. H. Isaacs).

New book list for bookbuyers, librarians and booksellers. No 1, Sept 1895–Aug 1898. Monthly; ed Cedric Chivers and Armistead Cay.

The stationers' and printers' annual trade book of reference. 1895–1903.

The January monthly part of the English catalogue of books for 1897, Jan 1897–Dec 1900. Monthly.

The booksellers' review. No 1, 11 March 1897–27 Jan 1898.

The Aldine Newsagents' trade journal. Nos 1–92, Dec 1897–Dec 1904. Monthly.

(8) CIRCULATING LIBRARIES

Friswell, J. H. Circulating libraries: their contents and their readers. London Soc Dec 1871.

Moore, G. Literature at nurse: or circulating morals. 1885.

Preston, W. C. Mudie's library. Good Words Oct 1894.

—— W. H. Smith's library. Good Words Nov 1895.

Shaylor, J. Fiction: its issue and classification. Publishers' Circular 14 May 1898; rptd in his Fascination of books, 1912.

Tinsley, W. Random recollections of an old publisher. 2 vols 1900.

John and A. Hallam Murray *v.* Walter and others. 1908 (priv ptd).

Society of Bookmen. Report on the commercial circulating libraries. 1928 (priv ptd).

(9) RETAIL BOOKSELLING

General works and the Net Book Agreement

The stationers' price-book: being a catalogue of every article used or vended in that business. 1800.

Pickering, W. Booksellers' monopoly: address to the trade and to the public. 1832.

Paternoster Row and the bookselling trade. Pinnock's Guide to Knowledge Aug 1834.

The retail booksellers' and bookbuyers' advocate. No 1 L Dec 1836; no 2, Jan 1837; no 3, [Feb 1837]. Ed Edward Portwine?

A manual of book-keeping for booksellers, publishers and stationers, by a bookseller. 1850.

Chapman, J. W. The commerce of literature. Westminster Rev April 1852; rptd as Cheap books and how to get them, 1852, 1852 (rev).

A report of the proceedings at a meeting (consisting chiefly of authors) held 4 May 1852 at the House of Mr John Chapman for the purpose of hastening the removal of the trade restrictions on the commerce of literature. 1852.

The opinions of certain authors on the bookselling question. [Ed John W. Parker] [1852]. Additional letters on the bookselling question, 1852.

[Bigg, J.] The bookselling system: a letter to Lord Campbell respecting the late inquiry into the regulations of the booksellers' Association in reference to the causes which led to its dissolution, by a retired bookseller. 1852.

The intelligencer for publishers and booksellers. No 1, July 1854–no 7, Jan 1855.

Ridge, L. L. Ridge's scheme for promoting the interests of the country booksellers and publishers. Grantham 1868.

[Wyman, C. W. H.] Wyman's dictionary of stationery. [1875], 1876, 1881.

Prouting, F. J. The stationer's guide and practical handbook to the art of window dressing. 1881.

Growoll, A. The profession of bookselling: a handbook of practical hints for the apprentice and bookseller. 2 pts New York 1893–5.

Stott, D. The decay of bookselling. Nineteenth Century Dec 1894.

Heinemann, W. Bookselling: the system adopted in Germany. Taunton 1895.

Bowes, R. The friends of literature. In E. Marston, Sketches of some booksellers of the time of Dr Johnson, 1902.

—— Booksellers' associations, past and present. Taunton 1905.

—— Cambridge bookshops and booksellers 1846–1858. Cambridge 1912.

The successful bookseller: a complete guide to success to all engaged in a retail bookselling, stationery and fancy goods business. 1906.

Net Books Committee. Net books question. 1908.

Macmillan, Sir F. The Net Book Agreement 1899 and the book war 1906–8. 1924.

Gray, G. J. Cambridge bookselling and the older bookshops in the United Kingdom. Cambridge 1925.

Simpson, W. Old Inverness booksellers. Inverness 1931.

Blackwell, B. The nemesis of the Net Book Agreement: an address. 1933.

Corp, W. G. Fifty years: a brief account of the Associated Booksellers of Great Britain and Ireland 1895–1945. Oxford 1945.

Barnes, J. J. Free trade in books. Oxford, 1964.

Individual Firms

Booksellers in alphabetical order

J. Brown & Son. The firm of three generations. Glasgow 1908.

Cowan, S. Humorous episodes in the life of a provincial bookseller. Birmingham 1912.

Fitzgerald, J. The recollections of a book collector (1848–58). Liverpool 1903.

MacAndrew, I. F. Memoir of Isaac Forsyth, bookseller in Elgin 1768–1859. 1889.

Humphreys, C. The life of Charles Humphreys, bookseller, told by himself. [c. 1910].

H. K. Lewis & Co. Ltd. Lewis's 1844–1931: an illustrated account of its foundation and development. 1931.

Miller, G. Later struggles in the journey of life. 1833.

Couper, W. J. The Millers of Haddington, Dunbar and Dunfermline. 1912.

The Parkers of Oxford. Oxford 1914.

Simpson, W. Old Inverness booksellers: men and memories of bygone days. Inverness 1931.

John Smith & Son, Ltd. A short note on a long history 1751–1925. Glasgow 1925.

Burdekin, R. Memoirs of the life and character of Mr R. Spence of York, bookseller. York 1827.

[Thin, J.] Reminiscences of booksellers and bookselling in Edinburgh in the time of William IV. 1905.
Thin, J. A note on the centenary of the firm of J. Thin bookseller 1848–1948. Edinburgh 1948.

[West, W.] Fifty years' recollections of an old bookseller. Cork 1835, 1837.
David Wyllie & Sons. A century of bookselling 1814–1914. Aberdeen 1914.

(10) THE ANTIQUARIAN BOOK TRADE

General Works

[Dibdin, T. F.] Bibliophobia: remarks on the present languid and depressed state of literature and the book trade. 1832.
The directory of second-hand booksellers. Ed A. Gyles, Nottingham 1886; rev J. Clegg, Rochdale 1888, 1891, 1894, 1899, 1903 etc. Later continued by A. J. Philip at Gravesend.
Wheatley, H. B. Prices of books. 1898.
Block, A. A short history of the principal London booksellers and book auctioneers. 1933.

Periodicals

The book exchange: or monthly list of books, odd volumes, mss, wanted to buy, sell or exchange. No 1, Sept 1863–no 11, July 1864.
The literary mart and book exchange. No 1, July 1874–no 22, March 1876. Ed W. E. Goulden.
The clique. Derby. No 1, June 14 1890–. Weekly; ed F. E. Murray. Later at London, and twice a week.

Book Auctions

Sotheby & Co. A list of the original catalogues of the principal libraries which have been sold by auction [1744–1818] by Mr Sotheby. 1818, 1828 (continued to 1828).
Book prices current. 1887. Annually since; ed J. H. Slater. Index, 1887–96, 1901; index 1897–1907, 1909.
Book sales of 1895 [–1897/8]. 4 vols 1896–9. Ed 'Temple Scott' (J. H. Isaacs).
Hodgson & Co. One hundred years of book auctions 1807–1907: being a brief record of the firm of Hodgson's. 1907 (priv ptd).
List of catalogues of English book sales 1676–1900, now in the British Museum. 1915.
Hobson, G. D. Notes on the history of Sotheby's. 1917 (priv ptd).

Individual Firms

Block, A. The book collector's vade mecum. 1932. Appendix B (also rptd separately) contains accounts of many antiquarian booksellers active before 1900.
James Bain Ltd
Booksellers since 1816: retrospectus and prospectus. 1861.
H. G. Bohn
Times 25 Aug 1884.
Book Monthly April 1904.
Gustave David, Cambridge
David of Cambridge: some appreciations. Cambridge 1937.
Bertram Dobell
Bradbury, S. Dobell: bookseller and man of letters. 1909.
Dobell, P. J. In memoriam Bertram Dobell 1842–1914 [1915].
Ellis
Smith, G. and F. Benger. The oldest London bookshop: a history of 200 years. 1928.
Bernard Quaritch
[Wyman, C. W. H.] BQ: a biographical and bibliographical fragment. 1880.
Junk, W. [Memoir in] Internationales Addressbuch der Antiquar-Buchhändler. Berlin 1906.
Thomas Rodd
GM June 1849.
Sotheran & Co
Stonehouse, J. H. In his Piccadilly notes, 1934.
Walter T. Spencer
Spencer, W. T. Forty years in my bookshop. Ed T. Moult 1923.
B. F. Stevens
Manville, Fenn, G. Memoir of Stevens. 1903.
Henry Stevens
Parker, W. W. Stevens of Vermont: American rare book dealer in London 1845–86. Amsterdam 1963.
Waverley Book Store, Edinburgh
Williamson, R. M. Bits from an old book shop. 1904

(11) PRIVATE BOOK COLLECTING

Dibdin, T. F. Bibliomania: or book-madness, containing some account of the history, symptoms and cure of the fatal disease. 1809, 1811 (enlarged), 1842 (rev), 1876 (rev), 4 vols Boston 1903.
— The bibliographical decameron. 3 vols 1817.
— A bibliographical, antiquarian and picturesque tour in France and Germany. 3 vols 1821, 1829; tr French, 1825.
— The library companion: or the young man's guide and the old man's comfort in the choice of a library. 2 vols 1824.
— Reminiscences of a literary life. 2 vols 1836.
— A bibliographical, antiquarian and picturesque tour in the northern counties of England and in Scotland. 3 vols 1838.
[Beresford, J.] Bibliosophia: or Book-wisdom, containing some account of the pride, pleasure and privileges of that glorious vocation, book-collecting. 1810.
[Clarke, W.] Repertorium bibliographicum: or some account of the most celebrated British libraries. 1819.
Goodhugh, W. The English gentleman's library manual. 1827.
Haslewood, J. Roxburghe revels and other relative papers. Ed J. Maidment, Edinburgh 1837 (priv ptd).
The book collector's handbook: a modern library companion. 1845.

Burton, J. H. The book-hunter. Edinburgh 1862, 1863, New York 1863, Edinburgh 1882 (with memoir of the author by K. Burton); ed J. H. Slater [1908].
Power, J. A handy book about books. 1870.
Lang, A. The library. 1881.
— Books and bookmen. 1887, 1892.
Slater, J. H. The library manual: a guide to the formation of a library and the value of rare and standard books. [1883], 1892 (enlarged).
— Round and about the bookstalls. 1891.
— Book collecting: a guide for amateurs. 1892.
— Early editions: a bibliographical survey of some popular modern authors. 1894.
— The romance of book collecting. 1898.
— How to collect books. 1905.
Wheatley, H. B. How to form a library. 1886.
Fitzgerald, P. The book fancier: or the romance of book collecting. 1886, 1887.
Ireland, A. The book-lovers enchiridion. 1890.
Quaritch, B. Contributions towards a dictionary of English book collectors. 13 pts 1892–9.
Roberts, W. The book hunter in London. 1895.
— Rare books and their prices. 1896.
Hazlitt, W. C. The confessions of a collector. 1897.
— Memoirs of book collecting. 1904.

Fletcher, W. Y. English book collectors. 1902.
Jerrold, W. The Autolycus of the bookstalls. 1902.
Bigham, C. The Roxburghe Club: its history and its members 1812–1927. 1928.
de Ricci, S. English collectors of books and mss. Cambridge 1930.
Carter, J. and H. G. Pollard. An enquiry into the nature of certain nineteenth-century pamphlets. 1934.
Partington, W. Thomas J. Wise in the original cloth: the life and records of the forger of nineteenth-century pamphlets, with an appendix by G. B. Shaw. 1946.
Sadleir, M. Book collecting: a reader's guide. 1947.
Winterich, J. T. The Grolier Club 1884–1950: an informal history. New York 1950.
Munby, A. N. L. Phillipps studies. 3 vols Cambridge 1951–60; abridged by N. Barker 1967.
Carter, J. ABC for book-collectors. 1952, 1953, 1961, 1966 (all rev).
— Books and book collectors. 1956.
Barker, N. The publications of the Roxburghe Club 1814–1962. 1964.

(12) PUBLIC LIBRARIES

The British Museum

Acts and votes of Parliament relating to the British Museum with the statutes and rules relating thereto. 1805, 1828.
Report from the Select Committee on the condition, management and affairs of the British Museum [minutes of evidence and appendix] 6 Aug 1835; 14 July 1836.
Edwards, E. A letter to B. Hawes: being strictures on the minutes of evidence taken before the Select Committee on the British Museum. 1836, 1839 (priv ptd as Remarks on the minutes).
— Lives of the founders of the British Museum with notices of its chief augmentors. 1870.
Millard, J. A letter containing a plan for the better management of the British Museum. 1836 (priv ptd).
Panizzi, A. On the collection of printed books at the British Museum: its increase and arrangement. [1845] (priv ptd).
— On the supply of printed books from the Library to the Reading Room of the British Museum. 1846.
Nicolas, N. H. Animadversions on the Library and catalogues of the British Museum. 1846.
Report of the Commissioners appointed to inquire into the constitution and government of the British Museum [minutes of evidence and appendix]. 2 vols 1850.
Cowtan, R. Memoirs of the British Museum. 1872.
— A biographical sketch of Sir Anthony Panizzi. 1873.
Fagan, L. The life of Sir A. Panizzi, late Principal Librarian of the British Museum. 2 vols 1880.
Friggeri, E. La vita, le opere e i tempi di Antonio Panizzi. Belluno 1897.
Rawlings, G. B. The British Museum Library. 1916.
Barwick, G. F. The Reading Room of the British Museum. 1929.
Brooks, C. Antonio Panizzi, scholar and patriot. Manchester 1931.
Esdaile, A. The British Museum Library: a short history and survey. 1946.
Miller, E. Prince of librarians: The life and times of Antonio Parizzi, 1967.

Accounts of Other Libraries

Hartshorne, C. H. The book rarities of the University of Cambridge. 1829.
Edwards, E. Memoirs of libraries: including a handbook of library economy. 2 vols 1859.
— Libraries and founders of libraries. 1864.
Macray, W. D. Annals of the Bodleian Library. 1868, Oxford 1890 (enlarged).
Axon, W. E. A. Handbook of the public libraries of Salford and Manchester. 1877.
Mason, T. The public and private libraries of Glasgow. Glasgow 1885 (priv ptd).
Manchester public libraries. Handbook, historical and descriptive. 1887.
Greenwood, T. Greenwood's library year book. 1897.
— British library year book. 1900.
Credland, W. R. Manchester free libraries. 1899.
Mathews, E. R. N. A survey of the Bristol public libraries. Bristol 1900.
Hunt, F. W. Libraries of Devonport, naval, military and civil. Devonport 1901.
Cowell, P. Liverpool public libraries: a history of fifty years. Liverpool 1903.
Guppy, H. The John Rylands Library, Manchester 1899–1924. Manchester 1924.
Rye, R. A. The libraries of London: a guide for students. 1908, 1927 (enlarged).
Savage, E. A. The story of libraries and book collecting. 1908.
Kenyon, F. G. Libraries and museums. 1930.
Esdaile, A. (ed). The world's great libraries. Vol 1: National libraries, 1934; vol 2: Famous libraries (by M. Burton), 1937.
Davies, W. L. The National Library of Wales: a survey of its history, its contents and its activities. 1937.
Thornton, J. L. The chronology of librarianship. 1941.
Craster, E. History of the Bodleian Library 1845–1945. Oxford 1952.
Birmingham Public Library. Notes on the history of the Birmingham public libraries 1861–1961. Birmingham 1962.

The Free Library Movement

Brougham, H. P. (Baron Brougham). Practical observations on the education of the people. 1825.
Edwards, E. A letter to the Earl of Ellesmere on the desirability of a better provision of public libraries in the British Empire, and particularly in the metropolis. 1848, 1849 (priv ptd as Remarks on the paucity of libraries freely open to the public).
— Free town libraries: their formation, management and history. 1869.
Report of the Select Committee on Public Libraries. 5 pts 1849–52.
Hole, J. An essay on the history and management of literary and scientific and mechanics' institutions. 1853.
Papworth, J. W. and W. Museums, libraries and picture galleries. 1853.
Reed, C. Why not? a plea for a free public library and museum in the City of London. 1855.
Traice, W. H. J. Handbook of Mechanics' Institutions with priced catalogue of books suitable for libraries prepared for the Yorkshire Union of Institutes. 1856.
Feilde, M. H. On the advantage of free public news rooms and lending libraries. 1858.
De Peyster, J. F. The moral and intellectual influence of libraries upon social progress. 1866.
Phillips, J. H. An essay on the advantages of free libraries. 1867.
Mullins, J. D. Free libraries and news rooms. 1869.
Fowler, J. C. On public libraries. 1871.
Chambers, G. F. The law relating to public libraries. 1879.
Hibbert, J. Notes on free public libraries and museums. Preston 1881.
Jevons, W. S. The rationale of free libraries. Contemporary Rev March 1881.
Southward, J. Technical literature in free public libraries. 1883.
Manners, Lady J. Some of the advantages of easily accessible reading and recreation rooms and free libraries with remarks on starting and maintaining them. [1885].

Greenwood, T. Public libraries: a history of the movement and a manual for the organisation and management of rate-supported libraries. [1886], 1894 (rev).
— Sunday schools and village libraries. 1892.
— Edward Edwards: the chief pioneer of municipal public libraries. 1902.
MacAlister, J. Y. W. and T. Mason. Library Association: public library manual, part 1: library legislation 1855–90. 1892.
Fovargue, H. W. Adoption of the Public Library Acts in England and Wales. 1896.
Verney, E. Village libraries. [1897].
Ogle, J. J. The free library: its history and present condition. 1897.
Mullen, B. H. Salford and the inauguration of the public free libraries movement. Salford 1899.
Morel, E. Essai sur le développement des bibliothèques publiques et de la librairie dans les deux mondes. 2 vols Paris 1908.
— La librairie publique. Paris 1910.
Baker, E. A. The public library. 1924.
Greenborough, W. H. The public libraries: a retrospect of 30 years 1882–1912. Reading 1913.
Cruse, A. The Englishman and his books in the nineteenth century. New York 1930.
Shirley, G. W. William Ewart: pioneer of public libraries. Dumfries 1930.
Minto, J. A history of the library movement in Great Britain. 1932.
Hendrick, B. J. The life of Andrew Carnegie. 1933.
Smith, G. A. The British benefactions of Andrew Carnegie. New York 1936.
Leyland, E. The public library: its history, organization and functions. 1937.
Wellard, J. H. The public library comes of age. 1940.
Clough, E. A. On being a hundred years old. 1950.
Munford, W. A. Penny rate: aspects of British public library history 1850–1950. 1951.
— William Ewart 1798–1869: portrait of a radical. 1960.
Bostwick, A. E. (ed). Popular libraries of the world. Chicago 1933.
Thornton, J. L. Selected readings in the history of librarianship. 2 pts 1948–57, 1966 (2nd edn).
Altick, R. D. The English common reader: a social history of the mass reading public 1800–1900. Chicago 1957.
Tylecote, M. The Mechanics' Institutes of Lancashire and Yorkshire before 1851. Manchester 1957.
Irwin, R. The origins of the English library. 1958.
— The heritage of the English library. 1964.
— The English library: sources and history. 1966.
Kelly, T. Early public libraries: a history of public libraries in Great Britain before 1850. 1966.

(13) LIBRARIANSHIP

See M. O. Burton and M. E. Vosburgh. A bibliography of librarianship. 1934.
Namur, P. Manuel du bibliothécaire. Brussels 1834.
Schmidt, J. A. F. Handbuch der Bibliothekwissenschaft, der Litteratur und Bücherkunde. Weimar 1840.
Jewett, C. C. Smithsonian report on the construction of catalogues of libraries and their publication by means of separate stereotyped titles. Washington 1853 (2nd edn).
de Morgan, A. On the difficulty of the correct description of books. Companion to Br Almanack 1853; ed H. Guppy, Library Assoc Record June 1902; rptd Chicago 1902.
Schurtleff, N. B. A decimal system for the arrangement and administration of libraries. 1856.
Petzholdt, J. Katechismus der Bibliothekenlehre. Leipzig 1856, 1871 (enlarged), ed A. Graesel Leipzig 1902 (as Handbuch der Bibliothekslehre).
Guild, R. A. The librarian's manual 1858.
Edwards, E. Memoirs of libraries; together with a handbook of library economy. 2 vols 1859.
Elliot, J. A practical explanation of the method of issuing library books. 1870.
Dewey, M. A classification and subject index for cataloguing and arranging the books and pamphlets of a library. Amherst Mass 1876 (anon), Boston 1885 (as Decimal classification and relative index for arranging, cataloguing and indexing libraries), Boston 1898, New York 1919, 1932 (rev and enlarged).
Transactions and proceedings of the [First International] Conference of librarians held in London 3–5 Oct 1877. 1878.
Hallett, C. H. Parish lending libraries: how to manage and keep them up. 1880.
Wheatley, H. B. How to catalogue a library. 1889.
Rogers, W. T. A manual of bibliography: introduction to the knowledge of books, library management and the art of cataloguing. 1891.
Slater, J. H. The library manual. 1892.
Hoyle, W. E. The Dewey decimal classification and the international catalogue of science. 1896.
Transactions and proceedings of the second International Library Conference held in London 13–16 July 1897. 1898.
Quinn, J. H. Manual of library cataloguing. 1899.
Cotgreave, A. Views and memoranda of public libraries. 1901.
Brown, J. D. Manual of library economy. 1903.
— Manual of practical bibliography. [1906].
Roebuck, G. E. and W. B. Thorne. A primer of library practice for junior assistants. 1904.
Thorne, W. B. The Library Assistants' Association: an outline of its development and work.
Sayers, W. C. B. An introduction to library classification: theoretical, historical and practical. 1918, 1950 (rev).
Dawe, G. Melvil Dewey 1851–1931. New York 1932.
Partridge, R. C. B. The history of the legal deposit of books throughout the British Empire. 1938.
Norris, D. M. A history of cataloguing and cataloguing methods 1100–1850. 1939.
Thornton, J. L. The chronology of librarianship. 1941.
Rider, F. Melvil Dewey. Chicago 1944.

Periodicals

Cannons, H. G. T. Bibliography of library economy: a classified index to the professional periodical literature. 1910, Chicago 1927.
Cole, G. W. Index to bibliographical papers. Chicago [1933].
Transactions and proceedings of the first [-8th] annual meeting of the Library Association of the United Kingdom 1878 [-85]. 7 vols 1879–90.
Monthly notes of the Library Association. 1880–3.
The library chronicle: a journal of librarianship and bibliography. Vols 1–5, 1884–8. Ed E. C. Thomas.
The library. Vol 1, 1889–. Quarterly; ed J. Y. Macalister.
The Library Assistants' Association: first annual report. 1 July 1896–.
The library assistant. No 1, Jan 1898–.
The library world. No 1, July 1898–.
The Library Association record. No 1, Jan 1899–. Monthly; ed H. Guppy, A. Esdaile.
The Library Association year book. 1899–.

J. M.

III. LITERARY RELATIONS WITH THE CONTINENT

This section, which is selective, is divided according to languages or groups of languages: Dutch and Flemish; French; German; Italian; Spanish and Portuguese; Scandinavian; Slavonic; and others. Individual authors, English and foreign, are entered in separate alphabetical lists, linked by cross references, under each language. Trns into English are within the scope of the section; see also under individual authors, below. Secondary works are confined to comparative studies and works essential to the recognition of an author in a foreign country.

Extra-European relations are not considered here. For publishing relations with the United States, see I. R. Brussel, Anglo-American first editions 1826–1900: east to west, 1935; Part 2: west to east 1786–1930, 1936. *Studies of relations with Asian literatures will be found under Edward FitzGerald and W. B. Yeats, cols 483, 1915 below. For general studies see* M. E. de Meester, Oriental influences in the English literature of the nineteenth century, Heidelberg 1915; *and* J. Holloway, Widening horizons in English verse, 1966.

Annual lists may be found in Yearbook of Comparative Lit (Chapel Hill) 1952–.

(1) GENERAL

Anthologies in Translation

Herbert, W. Translations from the Italian, Spanish, Portuguese, German etc. 1806. Poetry.

Laura: or an anthology of sonnets (on the Petrarcan model) and elegiac quatorzains, English, Italian, Spanish, Portuguese, French and German. Ed C. Lofft 5 vols 1813–14.

Thorpe, B. Northern mythology. 3 vols 1851–2.

Half-hours with foreign authors. Tr G. L. 1861. Short stories and extracts from novels.

Waddington, S. The sonnets of Europe. 1886.

Ogden, A. Christmas stories from French and Spanish writers. 1893.

Garnett, R. Dante, Petrarch, Camõens: 124 sonnets translated. 1896.

General Studies

Foreign Quarterly Review. 1827–46.

Foreign Review & Continental Miscellany. 1828–30.

Continental literature. Athenaeum 1869–1904. Yearly surveys; Dec nos until 1884, July nos thereafter.

Cosmopolis. 1896–8.

Ellis, H. The new spirit. 1890.

— Views and reviews. Vol 1, 1932.

Archer, W. The theatrical 'world'. 5 vols 1894–8. An annual collection of review articles.

Merz, J. T. History of European thought in the nineteenth century. 4 vols Edinburgh 1896–1914.

Beers, H. A. A history of English romanticism in the nineteenth century. 1902.

Saintsbury, G. A history of criticism and literary taste in Europe vol 3. Edinburgh 1904.

Omond, T. S. The romantic triumph. 1900; C. E. Vaughan, The romantic revolt, 1907; G. Saintsbury The later nineteenth century, 1907. In Periods of European literature, ed Saintsbury 12 vols Edinburgh 1897–1907.

Brandes, G. Hovedstrømninger i det 19de aarhundredes litteratur. 6 vols Copenhagen 1872–90; tr as Main currents in 19th century literature, 6 vols 1901–5.

Sanders, L. The Holland House circle. 1908.

Richter, H. Geschichte der englischen Romantik. 2 vols Halle 1911–16.

Van Tieghem, P. La littérature comparée. Paris 1931.

— L'ère romantique: le romantisme dans la littérature européene. Paris 1948. With bibliographies.

Block, A. The English novel 1740–1850. 1939. A catalogue, including trns of foreign novels.

Neff, E. E. A revolution in European poetry 1660–1900. New York 1940.

Ullmann, S. Anglicism and anglophobia in continental literature. MP 37 1940.

Lovejoy, A. O. On the discrimination of romanticisms. In his Essays in the history of ideas, Baltimore 1948.

Babits, M. Geschichte der europäischen Literatur. Vienna 1948.

Ernst, F. and K. Wais (ed). Forschungsprobleme der vergleichenden Literaturgeschichte. 2 vols Tübingen 1958.

Wais, K. An den Grenzen der Nationalliteraturen: vergleichende Aufsätze. Berlin 1958.

Lütkens, C. and W. Karbe. Das Bild vom Ausland: fremdsprachliche Lektüre an höheren Schulen in Deutschland, England und Frankreich. Munich 1959.

Zagona, H. G. The legend of Salome and the principle of art for art's sake. Geneva 1960.

Man, P. de Structure intentionnelle de l'image romantique. Revue Internationale de Philosophie 14 1960.

Peckham, M. Toward a theory of romanticism: a reconsideration. Stud in Romanticism 1 1961.

Dietrich, M. Europäische Dramaturgie im 19 Jahrhundert. Graz-Cologne 1961.

Remak, H. H. H. West European romanticism: definition and scope. In Comparative literature: method and perspective, ed N. P. Stallknecht and H. Frenz, Carbondale 1961.

McCutchion, D. Beast or angel? romantic ambiguities in Goethe, Musset, Stendhal and Yeats. Jadavpur Jnl of Comparative Lit 1962.

Wellek, R. Concepts of criticism. New Haven 1963.

Beebe, M. Ivory towers and sacred founts: the artist as hero in fiction from Goethe to Joyce. New York 1964.

Schenk, H. The mind of the European romantics. 1966.

English Authors

Arnold, Matthew

Arnold, M. The popular education of France; with notices of that of Holland and Switzerland. 1861.

— Schools and universities on the Continent. 1868.

Beckford, William

Beckford, W. Italy; with sketches of Spain and Portugal. 2 vols Paris 1834.

Chapman, G. Beckford. 1937.

William Beckford of Fonthill. Ed F. M. Mahmoud, Cairo 1960.

Byron, George Gordon
Axon, W. A. E. Byron's influence on European literature. In his Stray chapters on literature, folklore and archaeology, 1888.
Chiarini, G. Byron nella politica e nella letteratura della prima metà del secolo. Nuova Antologia 1–16 July 1891.
Maychrzak, F. Byron als Übersetzer. E Studien 21–2 1895–6.
Storozhenko, N. J. Byrons Einfluss auf die europäische Literatur. In his Izoblasti Literatury, Moscow 1902.
Farinelli, A. Byron e il Byronismo. Bologna 1924.
Boyd, E. F. Byron's Don Juan: a critical study. New Brunswick 1945.
Borst, W. A. Byron's first pilgrimage. New Haven 1948.

Others
Jacks, W. Burns in other tongues. Glasgow 1896.
Herford, C. H. The age of Wordsworth. 1897.
Baldensperger, F. La grande communion romantique de 1827: sous le signe de Scott. Revue de Littérature Comparée 7 1927.
Jabram-Desrivaux, L. Hardy européen. Point et Virgule July 1928.
Taylor, A. C. Carlyle et la pensée latine. Paris 1938.
Thalmann, L. Dickens in seinen Beziehungen zum Ausland. Zürich 1956.

(2) DUTCH AND FLEMISH

General Studies

Bowring, J. and H. S. Van Dyk. Batavian anthology: or specimens of the Dutch poets etc. 1824.
— Sketch of the language and literature of Holland. 1829.
Invloed der Engelsche taal–en letterkunde op de Nederlandsche. Noord en Zuid (De Bibliotheek) 9 1886.
Worp, J. A. Engelsche letterkunde op ons Tooneel. Tijdspieghel 1887.
Nederlandsche letteren bij Engelsche lezers. Noord en Zuid (De Bibliotheek) 11 1888.
Basse, M. Taal en letteren. Amsterdam 1901. On G. Van de Linde and Ingoldsby's Legends.
De Hoog, W. Studiën over de Nederlandsche en Engelsche taal–en letterkunde en haar wederzijdschen invloed vol 2. Dordrecht 1903.
Dekker, G. Die invloed van Keats en Shelley in Nederland gedurende die negentiende eeu. Groningen 1926.
Russell, J. A. English translations of Dutch novels. Gazette de Hollande 28 Oct 1931.
— Dutch romantic poetry: the English influence. Bradford 1961.
Downs, B. W. Anglo-Dutch literary relations 1867–1900. MLR 31 1936.
Finlay, I. F. Dickens's influence on Dutch literature. Dickensian 53 1957.
Oversteegen, J. J. Nederlandse literatuur in vertaling. Vrij Nederland 1 March 1958.
Weevers, T. Poetry of the Netherlands in its European context 1170–1930. 1960. On Potgieter, Gezelle and English romanticism.
Breugelmans, R. De weerklank van Wilde in Nederland en Vlaanderen 1880–1960. Studia Germanica Gandensia 3 1961.
Baxter, B. M. Verwey's translations from Shelley's poetical works. Leyden 1963.
Colmjon, G. De beweging van tachtig. Utrecht 1963. On the 1880 movement and England.
Gijsen, M. Frank Harris en Maeterlinck. Nieuw Vlaams Tijdschrift April 1964.
Roels, B. Gossaert, Baudelaire, Swinburne. De Nieuwe Taalgids 57 1964.
Willem Kloos: zijn jeugd, zijn leven. Ed H. Michaël, Hague 1965.

Individual Authors

Byron, George Gordon
Popma, T. Byron en het Byronisme in de Nederlandsche letterkunde. Amsterdam 1928.
Schults, U. Het Byronianisme in Nederland. Utrecht 1929.
Conscience, Henrik (1812–83)
Hoe men schilder wordt. Antwerp 1843; Siska van Roosemael, Antwerp 1844; Wat eenne moeder lyden kan, Antwerp 1844; Sketches from Flemish life [tr J. N. Trübner], 1846.
De loteling. Antwerp 1850; Baas Gansendonck, Antwerp 1850; Blinde Rosa, Antwerp 1850; De arme Edelman, Antwerp 1851; Tales of Flemish life, Edinburgh 1854.
Het geluk van ryk te zyn. Antwerp 1855; De gierigaerd, Antwerp 1853; Rikke-tikke-tak, Antwerp 1851; Graef Hugo van Graenhove en zynen vriend Abulfaragus, Antwerp 1845; Houten Clara, Antwerp 1850; Tales, 5 vols 1855.
Het ijzeren graf. Leyden 1879; Levenslust, Antwerp 1868; De jonge doctor, Antwerp 1860; Menschenbloed, Antwerp 1864; in Tales, 10 vols 1888–92.
Simon, I. George Eliot and Conscience. Revue des Langues Vivantes 26 1960.
Couperus, Louis (1863–1923)
Eline Vere. 3 vols Amsterdam 1889; tr J. T. Grein 1892.
Noodlot. Amsterdam 1890; Footsteps of fate, tr C. Bell 1891.
Extaze. Amsterdam 1892; Ecstasy, tr A. Teixeira de Mattos and J. Gray 1892.
Majesteit. Amsterdam 1893; Majesty, tr A. Teixeira de Mattos and E. Dowson 1894.
Psyche. Amsterdam 1898; tr B. S. Berrington 1908.
Russell, J. A. Couperus in English. De Nieuwe Gids May 1927.
Dekker, Eduard Douwes (1820–87)
Max Havelaar. 2 vols Amsterdam 1860; tr Baron A. Nahuijs, Edinburgh 1868; tr W. Siebenhaar with introd by D. H. Lawrence 1927.
Scott, Walter
Prins, J. W. Van Lennep en Scott. Vaderlandsche Letteroefeningen 1874.
Prinsen, J. De oude en de nieuwe historische roman in Nederland. Leyden 1919.
Vissink, H. Scott and his influence on Dutch literature. Zwolle 1922.
Drop, W. Verbeelding en historie: verschijningsvormen van de Nederlandse historische roman in de negentiende eeuw. Assen 1958.
A. S. C. Wallis (A. S. C. Opzoomer) (1857–1925)
In dagen van strijd. 3 vols Amsterdam 1879; In troubled times, tr E. J. Irving 3 vols 1883, 1 vol 1885 (abridged).
Vorstengunst. 3 vols Haarlem 1883; Royal favour, tr E. J. Irving 3 vols 1885, 1902.

(3) FRENCH

General Studies

France
In this section all French titles were pbd in Paris unless otherwise stated.
Croly, G. Paris in 1815. 2 pts 1817–21.
Morgan, Lady. France. 2 vols; La France, 2 vols London and Paris, 1817. Reply by W. Playfair, France as it is, not Lady Morgan's France, 2 vols 1819.
— France in 1829–30. 2 vols 1830.
Trollope, F. Paris and the Parisians in 1835. 2 vols 1836.

Gore, C. G. F. Greville: or a season in Paris 1857.
Pictures of the French. 1850. Trn of a collection of short stories by Balzac, Janin et al.
Senior, N. W. Conversations with Thiers, Guizot and other distinguished persons during the Second Empire. 2 vols 1878.
— Conversations with distinguished persons during the Second Empire. 2 vols 1880.
Hamerton, P. G. French and English. 1889.
Corelli, M. Wormwood: a drama of Paris. 1890.
du Maurier, G. Trilby. 1894.
— The Martian. 1897.
The Yellow Book. 1894–7.
The Savoy. 1896.
The Pageant. 1896–7.
Crackanthorpe, H. Vignettes. 1896.
Conan-Doyle, A. The exploits of Brigadier Gerard. 1896.
Harland, H. Comedies and errors. 1898.
Bodley, J. E. C. France. 1898.
Sherard, R. H. Twenty years in Paris. 1905.
Saroléa, C. Le caractère anglais et le caractère français. Revue de Belgique Aug 1897.

Dowden, E. The French Revolution and English literature. 1897.
Cestre, C. La révolution française et les poètes anglais 1789–1809. Revue Bourguignonne 16 1906.
Moraud, M. La France de la Restauration d'après les visiteurs anglais. 1933.
Mailahn, W. Napoleon in der englischen Geschichtsschreibung von den Zeitgenossen bis zur Gegenwart. Berlin 1937.
Dechamps, J. Napoléon et ses admiratrices britanniques. In Studies in French presented to R. L. Graeme Ritchie, Cambridge 1949.
Ringenson, K. French guests in English literature. Studier i Modern Sprakvetenskap 17 1949.
Campos, C. The view of France from Arnold to Bloomsbury. Oxford 1965. On Thackeray, Arnold, Pater, Swinburne, Meredith, Henry James, G. Moore et al.

Switzerland

Schirmer, G. Die Schweiz im Spiegel englischer und amerikanischer Literatur bis 1848. Zürich 1929.
Löhrer, H. Die Schweiz im Spiegel englischer Literatur 1849–75. Zürich 1952. On Arnold, Ruskin, Stephen et al.
Steffen, W. Die Schweiz im Spiegel englischer Literatur 1875–1900. Zürich 1953.
Lunn, A. Switzerland and the English. 1944. On Wordsworth, Byron and Ruskin.
— Switzerland in English prose and poetry. 1947. An anthology.

French and English Literature

Galignani's Magazine and Paris Monthly Review. Paris 1822–3.
La France et la Grande Bretagne: des rapports littéraires etc. Revue Européenne Aug 1824.
Pichot, A. Voyage historique et littéraire en Angleterre et en Ecosse. 3 vols 1825.
Bissot, L. A. Pichot: a romantic Prometheus. Oxford 1842.
The European library. 20 vols 1846–7. Trns of Thierry, Guizot, Mignet et al.
Chasles, V. E. P. Etudes sur la littérature et les mœurs de l'Angleterre au 19e siècle. 1850. On Scott, Byron, Keats, Shelley et al.
— L'Angleterre littéraire. 1876.
Phillips, E. M. Chasles: critique et historien de la littérature anglaise. 1933.

Ledru-Rollin, (A. A. Ledru) De la décadence de l'Angleterre. 2 vols 1850; tr E. C. as The decline of England, 2 vols 1850.
Forgues, E. D. Originaux et beaux esprits de l'Angleterre contemporaine. 2 vols 1860.
Curwen, H. Echoes from the French poets. 1870. Trns of Lamartine, Musset, Baudelaire, Gautier, Béranger et al.
Lang, A. Ballads and lyrics of old France. 1872.
Mendès, C. Recent French poets. GM Oct–Nov 1879. With trns of Coppée, Verlaine, Sully-Prudhomme, Mendès et al.
D'Heylli, G. La comédie française à Londres journal d'E. Got; journal de F. Sarcey. 1880.
Renard, G. L'influence de l'Angleterre sur la France depuis 1830. Nouvelle Revue 35 1885.
Henley, W. E. Views and reviews. 1890. On Dumas, Hugo, Banville, Balzac, Labiche, Champfleury.
Barlow, G. French plays and English audiences. Contemporary Rev Aug 1893.
Gray, J. Silverpoints. 1893. Trns of Baudelaire, Verlaine, Rimbaud, Mallarmé, Laforgue.
Vizetelly, H. Glances back through seventy years. 2 vols 1893.
Delille, E. Some French writers. 1893. On Bourget, Loti, Baudelaire, Maupassant, Verlaine, Barrès.
Nordau, M. Entartung. 2 vols Berlin 1892; Degeneration, 1895; A. E. Hake, Regeneration: a reply to Nordau, 1895.
Robertson, W. J. A century of French verse. 1895. With trns.
Saroléa, C. Le commerce des idées entre la France et l'Angleterre. Revue de Belgique Oct 1896.
— L'influence de la culture française sur la culture anglaise. Revue Française d'Edimbourg 1 1897.
Potez, H. Le romantisme français et l'influence anglaise. La Quinzaine 1–16 Oct 1899.
Studies in European literature: the Taylorian lectures 1889–99. Oxford 1900. By Mallarmé, Pater, Dowden, W. M. Rossetti, Bourget, Ker et al.

Baldensperger, F. Le moine de Lewis dans la littérature française. Jnl of Comparative Lit 3 1903.
— La mouvement des idées dans l'émigration française 1789–1815. 2 vols 1924.
— English artistic prose and its debt to French writers. Modern Language Forum Dec 1944.
Gosse, E. French profiles. 1905.
— More books on the table. 1923.
Flowers of France: the romantic period etc. Tr J. Payne 2 vols 1906. Trns of Hugo, Musset, Lamartine et al.
Borgerhoff, J.-L. Le théâtre anglais à Paris sous la Restauration. 1913.
Maccunn, F. J. The contemporary English view of Napoleon. 1914.
Ellis, H. Affirmations. 1915.
— From Rousseau to Proust. Boston 1935.
de Nolva, R. Les sources anglaises de Leconte de Lisle. Mercure de France 1 July 1922. On the influence of Shelley and Byron.
Dechamps, J. Il y a cent ans: propos Stendhaliens. Revue des Etudes Napoléoniennes 19 1922.
Draper, F. W. M. The rise and fall of the French romantic drama, with special reference to the influence of Shakespeare, Scott and Byron. 1923.
Cazamian, M. L. Le roman et les idées en Angleterre. Publications de la Faculté des Lettres de Strasbourg 15, 73, 125 1923–54.
Frierson, W. C. L'influence du naturalisme français sur les romanciers anglais de 1885 à 1900. 1925.
— The English controversy over naturalism. In his English novel in transition 1885–1940, Norman Oklahoma 1942.
Reynaud, L. Le romantisme: ses origines anglo-germaniques. 1926. On Scott and Byron.

Needham, H. A. Le développement de l'esthétique sociologique en France et en Angleterre au xix siècle. 1926.

Evans, D. O. French romanticism and British reviewers. French Quart 9 1927.

Lockwood, H. D. Tools and the man: a comparative study of the French working man and English Chartists in the literature of 1830–48. New York 1927.

Devonshire, M. G. The English novel in France 1830–70. 1929. With bibliographies.

Clapton, G. T. Balzac, Baudelaire and Maturin. French Quart 12 1930.

Engel, C. E. Byron et Shelley en Suisse et en Savoie 1816. Chambéry 1930.

Jones, E. Les voyageurs français en Angleterre de 1815 à 1830. 1930.

Liljegren, S. B. Quelques romans anglais comme source partielle d'une religion moderne. In Mélanges Baldensperger vol 2, 1930.

Lehmann, K. Die Auffassung und Gestaltung des Napoleonproblems im englischen Drama. Erlangen 1931.

Moore, M. Shaw et la France. 1933.

Moraud, M. Le romantisme français en Angleterre de 1814 à 1848. 1933.

—— Le théâtre français à Londres sous la Restauration. French Rev 22 1948.

Walton, T. A French disciple of Morris: Jean Lahor. Revue de Littérature Comparée 15 1935.

Delattre, F. S. Butler et le Bergsonisme. Revue Anglo-américaine 13 1936.

van der Vat, D. G. The fabulous opera: a study of continuity in French and English poetry of the nineteenth century. Groningen 1936.

Tronchon, H. Le jeune Quinet. 1937.

Hopkins, A. B. Mrs Gaskell in France 1849–90. PMLA 53 1938. With lists of trns and reviews.

Wais, K. Banville, Chateaubriand, Keats und Mallarmés faun. Zeitschrift für Französische Sprache und Literatur 62 1938.

Jones, K. La Revue Britannique: son histoire et son action littéraire 1825–40. 1939.

McCausland, S. W. Racine vu par les anglais de 1800 à nos jours. Revue de Littérature Comparée 19 1939.

Anderson, G. K. Marie de France and Arthur O'Shaughnessy: a study in Victorian adaptation. SP 36 1939.

Morrissette, B. A. Early English and American critics of French symbolism. In Studies in honor of F. W. Shipley, St Louis 1942.

Bisson, L. A. Proust, Bergson and George Eliot. MLR 40 1945.

Lefèvre, J. L'Angleterre et la Belgique à travers les cinq derniers siècles. 1946.

Voisine, J. Corneille vu par les anglais de 1800 à nos jours. French Stud 3 1949.

Salvan, J.-L. Le romantisme français et l'Angleterre victorienne. 1949.

Goldgar, H. A. de. Axël, de Villiers de l'Isle Adam, et The shadowy waters de Yeats. Revue de Littérature Comparée 24 1950.

Gilman, M. Revival and revolution in English and French romantic poetry. Yale French Stud 6 1950.

McLean, M. D. Poems to the rainbow by Campbell and Hérédia. Hispanic Rev 18 1950.

Häusermann, H. W. The Genevese background. 1952. On Shelley, Maria Edgeworth, Meredith, Conrad et al.

Simon, J. J-E. Blanche et l'Angleterre. Revue de Littérature Comparée 26 1952.

Robinson, J. K. A neglected phase of the aesthetic movement: English Parnassianism. PMLA 68 1953.

Gilsoul, R. Les influences anglo-saxonnes sur les lettres françaises de Belgique de 1850 à 1880. Brussels 1953.

King, N. J. Jane Austen in France. Nineteenth-Century Fiction 8 1954.

Dale, E. H. La poésie française en Angleterre 1850–90, 1954.

Stewart, W. McC. Poésie française, poésie anglaise. Actes de l'Académie Nationale de Bordeaux 4th ser 14 1955.

Jean, R. De Nerval et de quelques humoristes anglais. Revue de Littérature Comparée 29 1955.

Prévost, J. Le dandysme en France 1817–39. Geneva 1957.

Kermode, F. Romantic image. 1957.

Guyard, M.-F. Barrès et les lettres anglaises. In Forschungsprobleme der vergleichenden Literaturgeschichte, 2 vols Tübingen 1958.

Souffrin, E. Gringoire [i.e. Banville] en Angleterre à l'époque victorienne. Revue de Littérature Comparée 33 1959.

Leathers, V. British entertainers in France. Toronto 1959.

Ross Roy, G. A bibliography of French symbolism in English language publications to 1910. Revue de Littérature Comparée 34 1960.

Starkie, E. From Gautier to Eliot. 1960.

Roche, A. Mireille chez les anglo-saxons. In Mirèio. Publications de la Faculté des Lettres de Montpellier 16 1960.

Heppenstall, R. The fourfold tradition. 1961.

Barber, G. Galignani's and the publication of English books in France from 1800 to 1852. Library 5th ser 16 1961.

Underwood, V. P. Rimbaud et les lettres anglo-saxonnes. Revue de Littérature Comparée 35 1961.

Duncan, B. The St James's theatre 1835–1957. 1964.

French Authors

For trns of English plays into French, see M. Horn-Monval, Répertoire bibliographique des traductions et adaptations françaises du théâtre étranger vol 5, 1963. *For selected articles on French authors from A to M in English periodicals, see* H. Talvart and J. Place, Bibliographie des auteurs modernes de langue française 1801–1927, 15 vols 1928–.

Balzac, Honoré de (1799–1850). *See also under De Quincey, James, G. Moore and Scott, cols 112–4 below.*

Les chouans. 1829; The chouans, tr G. Saintsbury 1889.

Les contes drolatiques. 3 vols 1832–7; tr G. Sims 1874; tr R. Whittling 1896.

La recherche de l'absolu. 1834; Balthazar: or science and love, tr W. Robson 1859.

Histoire des treize 2 vols 1834; The mystery of the rue Soly, tr Lady Knutsford 1894. An extract.

Le père Goriot. 1835; Daddy Goriot: or unrequited affection, 1860, 1878.

Histoire de la grandeur et de la décadence de César Birotteau. 2 vols 1838; History of the grandeur and downfall of Cesar Birotteau, tr J. H. Simpson 1860.

Scènes de la vie privée. Vol 1, 1842; The cat and battledore and other tales, tr P. Kent 3 vols 1879.

Le cousin Pons. 1847; Poor relations: cousin Pons, tr P. Kent 1880.

Correspondance 1819–50. 2 vols 1876; Correspondence, with a memoir by his sister, tr C. Lamb Kenney 2 vols 1878.

Public and private life of animals. 1877. Adaptations from Balzac, Janin, Musset, Sand et al by J. Thomson.

Honoré de Balzac. Ed H. van Laun 1869, 1877, 1878, 1880, 1884. A selection, in French.

Shorter stories from Balzac. Tr W. Wilson and Count Stenbock 1890.

Balzac's novels in English. Tr K. P. Wormeley 12 vols 1886–91. A selection.

Comédie humaine. Ed G. Saintsbury 40 vols 1895–8.

The style of Balzac and Thackeray. Dublin Univ Mag Dec 1864.

Walker, H. H. The Comédie humaine and its author. 1879. With trns of La bourse, Gaudissart II and Albert Savarus.

Garnand, H. J. The influence of Scott on the works of Balzac. New York 1926.
Baldensperger, F. Orientations étrangères chez Balzac. Paris 1927.
Decker, C. R. Balzac's literary reputation in Victorian society. PMLA 47 1932.
Astre, G. A. Balzac et l'anglais mangeur d'opium. Revue de Littérature Comparée 15 1935. Balzac and De Quincey.
McNair, L. Balzac and Huxley. French Rev 12 1939.
Pacey, W. C. D. Balzac and Thackeray. MLR 36 1941.
Falconer, J. A. Balzac and Thackeray. E Studies 26 1945.
Maitre, R. Balzac, Thackeray et Charles de Bernard. Revue de Littérature Comparée 24 1950.
Monod, S. La fortune de Balzac en Angleterre. Ibid.
Mallison, V. Balzac and England. Revue des Langues Vivantes 16 1950.
Benson, C. Yeats and Balzac's Louis Lambert. MP 49 1952.
Hunt, H. J. The human comedy: first English reactions. In The French mind: G. Rudler, Oxford 1952.
Carey Taylor, A. and C. Dédéyan. Balzac et l'Angleterre. In Balzac: le livre du centenaire, 1952.
Müller, G. Le père Goriot und Silas Marner. Arhiv 189 1953.
Smith, S. R. B. Balzac et l'Angleterre. 1953.

Baudelaire, Charles (1821–67). *See also under De Quincey and Swinburne, cols 112, 115 below.*
Les fleurs du mal. 1857, 1861 (rev); Some translations from Baudelaire by H.C. [H. Curwen], 1894.
Petits poèmes en prose. 1869; Poems in prose, tr A. Symons 1905.
Les fleurs du mal, Petits poèmes en prose, Les paradis artificiels. Tr A. Symons 1925.
Saintsbury, G. In his Miscellaneous essays, 1892.
Turquet-Milnes, G. The influence of Baudelaire in France and England. 1913. On Swinburne, Wilde, Symons, Moore et al.
Symons, A. Baudelaire. 1920.
Lafourcade, G. Swinburne and Baudelaire. Revue Anglo-américaine 2 1924.
Clapton, G. T. Baudelaire et De Quincey. 1931.
—— Carlyle and some early English critics of Baudelaire. In Miscellany of studies presented to L. E. Kastner, Cambridge 1932.
Ruff, M.-A. L'esprit du mal et l'esthétique Baudelairienne. 1955.
Gargano, J. W. James on Baudelaire. MLN 75 1960.

Chateaubriand, François René de (1768–1848)
Essai historique politique et moral sur les révolutions etc. London 1797; abridged London 1815; Historical, political and moral essay on revolutions, 1815. A trn of the 1815 edn.
Atala. 1801; tr 1802, 1813, 1825, 1844; tr J. S. Harry 1867; tr 'Gerard' 1873 (in verse).
Le génie du christianisme. 5 vols 1802; The beauties of Christianity, tr F. Shoberl 3 vols 1813.
René. 1805; tr 1813.
Les martyrs. 3 vols 1809; The two martyrs, tr W. J. Walter 1819.
Itinéraire de Paris à Jérusalem. 3 vols 1811; Travels in Greece, Palestine, Egypt and Barbary, tr F. Shoberl 2 vols 1811.
De Buonaparte, des Bourbons etc. 1814; On Buonaparte and the Bourbons etc, tr 1814.
De la monarchie selon la Charte. London 1816; The monarchy according to the Charter, 1816.
Recollections of Italy, England and America. 2 vols 1815. A selection from various essays pbd later in Oeuvres, 1826–31.
Les Natchez. 1826; The Natchez, 3 vols 1827.
Les aventures du dernier Abencerage. 1826; Aben-Hamet, tr 1826; The last of the Abencerages, tr I. Hill 1835; The adventures of the last Abencerage, tr H. W. Carter 1870.
Essai sur la littérature anglaise etc. 1836; Sketches of English literature etc, 2 vols 1836.
Mémoires d'outre-tombe. 12 vols 1849–50; Memoirs of Chateaubriand, 1848; An autobiography, 4 vols 1849. Both incomplete.

Prescott, W. H. Chateaubriand's sketches of English literature. North Amer Rev Oct 1839.
Dempsey, M. A contribution to the study of the sources of the Génie du christianisme. 1928.
Roddier, H. Chateaubriand et la Revue d'Edimbourg. Revue de Littérature Comparée 11 1931.
Dechamps, J. Chateaubriand en Angleterre. 1934.
Reboul, P. Chateaubriand et les anglais. Revue de Littérature Comparée 33 1949.
Kahn, E. Chateaubriand in England. Contemporary Rev March 1950.
Weil, A. Chateaubriand à l'étranger: ou le rayonnement du génie français. Information Littéraire 1949–50.
Caddeau, P. Atala et le Voyage aux Amériques ont-ils vu le jour dans les Voyages du capitaine Cook? Revue de la Méditerranée 1961.

Comte, Isidore Auguste (1798–1857). *See also under Mill, col 113 below.*
Système de politique positive. 1824, 4 vols 1851–4; System of positive polity, tr J. H. Bridges, E. S. Beesly, R. Congreve, F. Harrison et al 4 vols 1875–7.
Cours de philosophie positive. 1830–42; The positive philosophy of Comte, tr and abridged by H. Martineau 2 vols 1853, 3 vols 1896.
Discours sur l'esprit positif. 1844; Preliminary discourse on the positive spirit etc, tr W. M. W. Call 1883; tr E. S. Beesly 1903.
Discours sur l'ensemble du positivisme. 1848; A general view of positivism, tr J. H. Bridges 1865.
Calendrier positiviste. 1849; The positivist calendar of 558 worthies of all ages and nations, ed F. Harrison 1894.
Catéchisme positiviste etc. 1852; The catechism of positivist religion, tr R. Congreve 1858.
Bibliothèque du prolétaire au 19e siècle. 1852; The positivist library of Auguste Comte, tr F. Harrison 1886.
Synthèse subjective: ou système universel des conceptions propres à l'état normal de l'humanité. 1856; Religion of humanity etc, tr R. Congreve 1891.

Lewes, G. H. Comte's philosophy of the sciences. 1853.
Mill, J. S. Comte and positivism. 1865. Reply by J. H. Bridges, The unity of Comte's life and doctrine, 1866.
—— Lettres inédites à Auguste Comte avec les réponses de Comte. Ed L. Lévy-Brühl 1899.
Barton, F. B. An outline of the positive religion of humanity etc. 1867.
Bridges, J. H. Five discourses on positive religion. 1882.
—— Comte: the successor of Aristotle and St Paul. 1883.
Spencer, H. Reasons for dissenting from the philosophy of M. Comte. 1864.
Caird, E. The social philosophy and religion of Comte. 1885.
Hutton, H. D. Comte's life and work. 1892.
The positivist review. Ed E. S. Beesly, later S. H. Swinny 1893–1923.
Roberty, E. de. Comte et Spencer. 1894.
Whittaker, T. Comte and Mill. 1908.
Thomas, P. Shelley and Comte. Positivist Rev Jan 1911.

McAleer, E. C. Browning's Cleon and Comte. Comparative Lit 8 1956.

Cousin, Victor (1792–1867)

Rapport sur l'état de l'instruction publique en Prusse. 1833; Report on the state of public instruction in Prussia, tr J. Austin 1834.

De l'instruction publique en Hollande. 1837; On the state of education in Holland etc, tr L. Horner 1838.

Du vrai, du beau et du bien etc. In his Cours de philosophie, 1841; Lectures on the true, the beautiful and the good, tr O. W. Wight 1854; The philosophy of the beautiful, tr J. C. Daniel 1848.

Cours de l'histoire de la philosophie moderne. 3 vols 1847; Course of the history of modern philosophy, tr O. W. Wight 2 vols Edinburgh 1852; Elements of psychology, tr C. S. Henry 1834. The part of the Cours dealing with Locke.

Justice et charité. 1848; Justice and charity, tr W. Hazlitt 1848.

[Hamilton, W.] M. Cousin's Course of philosophy. Edinburgh Rev 50 1829.

Daudet, Alphonse (1840–97)

Le petit chose. 1868; My brother Jack, 1877.

Lettres de mon moulin. 1869; Letters from my mill, tr M. Carey 1880; tr F. H. Potter 1893.

Aventures prodigieuses de Tartarin de Tarascon. 1872; Prodigious adventures of Tartarin of Tarascon, tr 1887, 1887.

Fromont jeune et Risler aîné. 1874; tr E. Vizetelly 1880.

Les femmes d'artistes. 1874; Artists' wives, tr L. Ensor 1890.

Robert Helmont. 1874; tr L. Ensor 1888.

Jack. 1876; tr L. Ensor 1890.

Le nabab. 1877; The nabob, tr E. Clavequin 3 vols 1878.

Les rois en exil. 1879; Kings in exile, tr E. Clavequin 3 vols 1880; tr L. Ensor 1890.

Numa Roumestan. 1881; tr 1884.

L'évangéliste. 1883; Port salvation, tr C. H. Meltzer 2 vols 1883.

Sapho. 1884; tr 1886, 1886.

La Belle Nivernaise. 1886; tr R. Routledge 1887.

Souvenirs d'un homme de lettres. 1888; Recollections of a literary man, tr L. Ensor 1889.

Rose et Ninette. 1892; tr M. J. Serrano 1892.

Sherard, R. H. Daudet. 1894.

Munro, W. A. Dickens et Daudet romanciers de l'enfant et des humbles. Toulouse 1908.

Delattre, F. Daudet et l'Angleterre. In his Dickens et la France, 1927.

Favreau, A. R. British criticism of Daudet 1872–97. PMLA 52 1937.

Dumas, Alexandre (1803–70). *See also under Scott, col 114 below.*

Dumas' historical library. 11 vols 1861. A selection.

The romances of Alexandre Dumas. 60 vols 1893–7. *Before this edn approximately 20 of Dumas' 120 works had been tr and often rptd. For a list, see* R. W. Plummer, Dumas père: a bibliography of English translations, Dumasian 4–6 1957–9.

Parigot, H. Le drame de Dumas. 1899. With ch on Shakespeare, Scott and Byron as sources.

Roberts, W. Dumas and Sue in English. Nineteenth Century Nov 1922.

Schwartz, H. S. The influence of Dumas on Wilde. French Rev 7 1933.

Morley, M. Monte-Christo at Drury Lane: a riot in two parts. Dumasian 4 1957.

—— Dumas plays in London. Dumasian 5 1958.

Dumas, Alexandre, *fils* (1824–95)

La dame aux camélias. 1848; The lady with the camelias, 1856.

La vie à vingt ans. 1850; Paris life at twenty, 1863.

Le régent Mustel. 1851; The resuscitated, tr G. de Croij 1877.

Le fils naturel. 1858; tr 1879.

Affaire Clémenceau: mémoire de l'accusé. 1866; Bella, tr H. L. Williams 1888.

La princesse de Bagdad. 1881; tr 1881.

Denise. 1885; tr 1880.

Francillon. 1887; tr 1887.

Archer, W. Dumas and the English drama. Cosmopolis Feb 1896.

Flaubert, Gustave (1821–80). *See also under De Quincey, col 112 below.*

Madame Bovary. 1857; tr E. Marx-Aveling 1886; with introd by H. James 1902.

Salammbô. 1863; tr M. French Sheldon 1886; tr J. S. Chartres 1886.

L'éducation sentimentale. 1870; Sentimental education, tr D. F. Hannigan 2 vols 1898.

La tentation de Saint Antoine. 1874; The temptation of Saint Antony, tr D. F. Hannigan 1895.

Bouvard et Pécuchet. 1881; tr D. F. Hannigan 1896.

Ferguson, W. D. The influence of Flaubert on George Moore. Philadelphia 1934.

Yvon, P. L'influence de Flaubert en Angleterre. Caen 1939.

Pacey, D. Flaubert and his Victorian critics. UTQ 16 1946.

Heywood, C. Flaubert, Miss Braddon and George Moore. Comparative Lit 12 1960.

Gaboriau, Emile (1835–73)

L'affaire Lerouge. 1866; The widow Lerouge, 1887.

Le dossier 113. 1867; File number 113, tr 1887.

Le crime d'Orcival. 1867; The mystery of Orcival, 1887.

Les esclaves de Paris. 2 vols 1868; The slaves of Paris, 1887, 1889.

Monsieur Lecoq. 1869; tr 1887, 1888.

La corde au cou. 1873; In deadly peril, tr G. Campbell 1888.

L'argent des autres. 1873; Other people's money, 1888.

Les amours d'une empoisonneuse. 1881; Marie de Brinvilliers, 1888.

Gautier, Théophile (1811–72). *See also under De Quincey, col 112 below.*

Mademoiselle de Maupin. 2 vols 1835–6; tr 1887.

Une larme du diable. 1839; The dead Leman and other tales from the French, ed A. Lang and P. Sylvester 1889.

Le roman de la momie. 1858; The romance of a mummy, tr M. Young 1886.

Une nuit de Cléopâtre. 1894; Cleopatra, 1896.

Hugo, Victor-Marie (1802–85). *See also under Arnold, Byron, Hardy and Swinburne, cols 111, 112, 115–6 below.*

Selections, chiefly lyrical etc. Ed H. L. Williams 1895.

Han d'Islande. 1823; Hans of Iceland, 1825, 1845; The demon dwarf, 1847; The outlaw of Iceland, tr G. Campbell 1885 etc.

Bug-Jargal. 1826; The slave king, 1833; The noble rival, 1845.

Cromwell. 1827; *see* A. C. Swinburne, Bothwell, 1874.

Le dernier jour d'un condamné. 1829; The last day of a condemned, tr 1840.

Hernani. 1830; tr 1830, 1832.

Notre-Dame de Paris. 1831; Notre-Dame, tr W. Hazlitt 3 vols 1833; E. Fitzball, Esmeralda: or the hunchback of Notre-Dame, 1844. (A play.)

Marion de Lorme. 1831; The King's edict, adapted by B. Fairclough 1872.

Le roi s'amuse. 1832; tr H. T. Haley 1842; tr F. L. Slous 1843; *see* W. E. Burton, The court fool, 1883; *see* T. Taylor, The fool's revenge, 1869.

Lucrèce Borgia. 1833; tr W. T. Haley 1841; tr W. Young 1847 (in verse).

Claude Gueux. 1834; Capital punishment, tr D. Pyrke 1865.

Angelo, tyran de Padoue. 1835; Angelo, 1851; Angelo and the actress of Padua, adapted by G. H. Davidson 1855; tr E. O. Coe 1880.

Ruy Blas. 1838; adapted by E. O'Rourke 1850; tr W. Alexander 1890; *see* J. Davidson, A queen's romance, 1904.

Les chants du crépuscule. 1841; Songs of twilight, tr G. W. M. Reynolds, Paris 1836.

Châtiments. Brussels 1852; A. C. Swinburne, Dirae, 1873.

Les misérables. 5 vols 1862; tr F. C. L. Wraxall 3 vols 1862; tr C. E. Wilbour 2 vols 1887; tr I. F. Hapgood 5 vols 1897.

Napoléon le petit. Brussels 1852; Napoleon the little, 1852.

William Shakespeare. 1864; tr A. Baillot 1864.

Les travailleurs de la mer. 3 vols 1866; Toilers of the sea, tr W. M. Thomas 3 vols 1866; tr G. Campbell 1887.

L'homme qui rit. 1869; By order of the King, 3 vols 1870, 1 vol 1886; The laughing man, 1887; By the King's command, 1875.

Quatre-vingt treize. 1874; Ninety-three, tr F. L. Benedict 3 vols 1874; tr G. Campbell 1886.

L'art d'être grand-père. 1877; *see* A. C. Swinburne, A dark month, 1882.

Histoire d'un crime. 2 vols 1877–8; The history of a crime 4 vols 1877–78, 1 vol 1886; tr G. Campbell 1888.

Stevenson, R. L. Hugo's romances. In his Familiar studies of men and books, 1882.

Swinburne, A. C. A study of Hugo. 1886.

Bowley, V. E. A. Notre-Dame and Les misérables on the English stage. French Quart 11 1929.

—— English versions of Hugo's plays. Adam International Rev 1952. With appendix listing trns.

Thomas, J. H. L'Angleterre dans l'oeuvre d'Hugo. 1933.

Schinz, A. Hugo, Napoléon III et Elizabeth Browning. Revue de Littérature Comparée 13 1933.

Aubry, G. J. Hugo et Swinburne. Revue Bleue 7 March 1936. On their correspondence.

Hooker, K. W. The fortunes of Hugo in England. New York 1938. With list of articles on Hugo in English periodicals.

Rose, F. Tennyson and Hugo. Poetry Rev 30 1939.

Barrère, J.-B. Hugo et la Grande Bretagne. Revue de Littérature Comparée 28 1954.

Barineau, E. Les feuilles d'automne et les Mémoires de Byron. MP 55 1958.

Huysmans, Joris Karl (1848–1907)

En route. 1895; tr with preface by C. Kegan Paul 1896.

La cathédrale. 1898; The cathedral, tr C. Bell 1898.

Joubert, Joseph (1734–1824)

Pensées, essais et maximes. 2 vols 1842; Pensées of Joubert, tr H. Attwell 1877; tr K. Lyttelton with preface by Mrs H. Ward 1898; tr G. H. Calvert 1903.

Fairclough, G. T. A fugitive and gracious light. Lincoln Nebraska 1961. On Joubert and Arnold.

De Kock, Charles Paul (1793–1871)

Sœur Anne. 4 vols 1825; Sister Anne, tr G. W. M. Reynolds 1840.

André le savoyard. 5 vols 1826; Andrew the savoyard, 1849.

Le barbier de Paris. 4 vols 1826; The barber of Paris, 1839.

Jean. 4 vols 1827; The modern Cymon, 2 vols 1833.

Lamartine, Alphonse de (1790–1869). *See also under Shelley, col 114 below.*

Méditations poétiques. 1820; Solitude and other poems, with translations from the Méditations poétiques by J. Forth, 1830.

Histoire des Girondins. 8 vols 1847; Pictures of the first French Revolution, 1850. A selection.

Les confidences. 2 vols 1849–51; Memoirs of my youth, The wanderer and his home, tr Lady Wilde 1849, 1851.

Christophe Colomb. 1853; The life and times of Columbus, 2 vols 1887.

Lombard, C. M. Portrait of Lamartine in the English periodical 1820–70. MLN 75 1960.

—— Lamartine in America and England 1820–76: a check-list. Bull of Bibliography 23 1961.

Lamennais, Hugues Félicité de (1782–1854)

Paroles d'un croyant. 1833; The words of a believer, 1834, 1845, 1848.

Le livre du peuple. 1838; The book of the people, tr J. H. Lorymer 1838.

De l'esclavage moderne. 1839; Modern slavery, tr W. J. Linton 1840.

Maeterlinck, Maurice (1862–1949)

La Princesse Maleine. Brussels 1889; L'intruse, Brussels 1890; Princess Maleine and the intruder, tr G. Harry and W. Wilson 1892.

Pelléas et Mélisande. Brussels 1892; Les aveugles, Brussels 1890; Pelleas and Melisander, and The sightless, tr L. Alma Tadema 1892.

Alladines et Palomides; Intérieur; La mort de Tintagiles. Brussels 1894; tr A. Sutro and W. Archer 1899.

Aglavaine et Sélysette. 1896; tr A. Sutro 1897.

Le trésor des humbles. 1896; The treasure of the humble, tr A. Sutro 1897.

La sagesse et la destinée. 1898; Wisdom and destiny, tr A. Sutro 1898.

La vie des abeilles. 1901; The life of the bee, tr A. Sutro 1901.

Monna Vanna. 1902; tr A. Sutro 1904.

L'oiseau bleu. 1909; The blue bird, tr A. Teixeira de Mattos 1909.

Rabuse, G. J. M. Synges Verhältnis zur französischen Literatur und besonders zu Maeterlinck. Archiv 184 1938.

Halls, W. D. Some aspects of the relationship between Maeterlinck and Anglo-american literature. Annales de la Fondation Maeterlinck 1955. On Shakespeare, Carlyle and the Pre-Raphaelites.

Pouilliart, R. Maeterlinck et Carlyle. Revue de Littérature Comparée 38 1964.

de Maistre, Joseph Marie (1753–1811)

Holdsworth, F. de Maistre et l'Angleterre. 1935.

Stinglhamber, L. de Maistre, précurseur de Newman. Bulletin de l'Association Guillaume Budé 1944.

Mallarmé, Stéphane (1842–98). *See also under George Moore and Verlaine, cols 109, 113 below.*

The National Observer. 1892–3.

Lhombreaud, R. S. Deuc lettres de Mallarmé à Gosse. Revue de Littérature Comparée 25 1951.

—— Symons' renderings of Mallarmé. Princeton Univ Lib Chron 20 1959.

Souffrin, E. Coup d'oeil sur la bibliothèque anglaise de Mallarmé. Revue de Littérature Comparée 32 1958.

Ryan, M. John Payne et Mallarmé. Ibid.

Maupassant, Guy de (1850–93)

Une vie. 1883; A woman's life 1888; A woman's soul, tr H. Blanchamp 1902.

Yvette. 1885; tr A. G. with a preface by J. Conrad 1904.

Pierre et Jean. 1888; tr C. Bell 1890.

Sur l'eau. 1888; Afloat, tr L. Ensor 1889.

Boule du suif. 1897; tr 1899.

Frierson, W. C. Realism in the 1890's and the Maupassant school in England. French Quart 10 1928; rptd in his English novel in transition, Norman Oklahoma 1942. Reply by G. J. Worth, The English Maupassant school of the 1890's: some reservations, MLN 72 1957.
Worth, G. J. Maupassant in Victorian England. In Literature and society, ed B. Slote, Lincoln Nebraska 1964.

Mérimée, Prosper (1803–70)
Chronique du temps de Charles IX. 1829; A chronicle of the reign of Charles IX, tr A. R. Scoble 1853.
Colomba. 1840; tr A. R. Scoble 1853.
Carmen. 1845; tr 1887; tr E. H. Garrett 1896.
Les faux Démétrius. 1853; Demetrius the imposter, tr A. R. Scoble 1853.
Histoire de don Pèdre I 1848; The history of Peter the Cruel, 2 vols 1849.
Lettres à une inconnue. 2 vols 1874; Letters to an incognita, 1874.

Healy, D. Mérimée et les anglais. 1946.
Decreus, J. Opinions de Mérimée sur la Grande Bretagne et les anglais. Comparative Lit Stud 23–4 1946.

Michelet, Jules (1798–1874)
Histoire romaine: république. 1833; History of the Roman Republic, tr W. Hazlitt 1846.
Histoire de France. 15 vols 1833–65; The history of France [section on Middle Ages], tr W. K. Kelly 2 vols 1844–6; tr G. H. Smith 2 vols 1844–7.
Du prêtre, de la femme et de la famille. 1845; Priests, women and families, tr C. Cocks 1846; 1850.
Le peuple. 1846; The people, tr C. Cocks 1846.
Histoire de la revolution française. 7 vols 1847–53; A history of the French revolution, tr C. Cocks 2 vols 1847–8.
L'oiseau. 1856; The bird, tr A.E. 1868.
L'insecte. 1858; The insect, tr W. H. D. Adams 1875.
La sorcière. 1862; tr L. J. Trotter 1863.
La France devant l'Europe. Florence 1871; France before Europe, 1871.
La montagne. 1868; The mountain, tr W. H. D. Adams 1875.

Musset, Alfred de (1810–57)
Barberine. 1835; Fantasio, 1833; On ne badine pas avec l'amour, 1834; Il faut qu'une porte soit ouverte ou fermée, 1845; Comedies, tr S. L. Gwynn 1890.
Un caprice. 1848: A good little wife, tr 1850.
Jamieson, P. Musset, De Quincey and Piranesi. MLN 71 1956.

Nodier, Jean Emmanuel Charles (1780–1844)
Promenade de Dieppe aux montagnes d'Ecosse. 1821; Promenade from Dieppe to the mountains of Scotland, Edinburgh 1822.

Larat, J. Un voyageur romantique en Angleterre: Nodier. Anglo-French Rev Dec 1920.

Renan, Joseph Ernest (1823–90). *See also under Pater, col 114 below.*
Etudes d'histoire religieuse. 2 sers 1857, 1884; Studies in religious history, tr H. F. Gibbons 1893; tr 1886.
La poésie des races celtiques. In his Essais de morale et de critique, 1859; The poetry of the Celtic races, tr W. G. Hutchison 1892.
Histoire des origines du christianisme. 8 vols 1863–83; The life of Jesus [i.e. vol 1]. 1864; abridged 1887; The apostles [i.e. vol 2], 1869; History of the origins of Christianity, 7 vols 1889–90.
Dialogues et fragments philosophiques. 1876; Philosophical dialogues and fragments, tr R. B. Mukharjî 1883.
Caliban. 1878; tr 1896.
Conférences d'Angleterre. 1880; Lectures on the influence of Rome on Christianity and the development of the Catholic Church, tr C. Beard 1880.
Souvenirs d'enfance et de jeunesse. 1883; Recollections of my youth, tr C. B. Pitman 1883.
Histoire du peuple d'Israël. 5 vols 1887–93; History of the people of Israel, 3 vols 1888–91.
L'avenir de la science. 1890; The future of science, tr A. D. Vandam and C. B. Pitman 1891.
Leaders of Christian and anti-Christian thought. Tr W. M. Thomson 1895. A selection of essays.

Mott, L. F. Renan and Arnold. MLN 33 1918.
Tronchon, H. Renan et l'Angleterre. Revue de Littérature Comparée 7 1927.
Angell, J. W. Arnold's indebtedness to Renan's Essais de morale et de critique. Revue de Littérature Comparée 14 1934.
Smith, H. Renan versus an Anglo-Saxon publisher. Modern Languages Forum 27 1942.
Rivoallan, A. Un admirateur anglais de Renan: Arnold. Nouvelle Revue de Bretagne Sept 1952.
Harding, J. N. Wilde and Renan. Contemporary Rev May 1953.
— Renan and Arnold: two saddened searchers. Hibbert Jnl 57 1959.

Rousseau, Jean-Jacques (1712–78). *See also under Byron, col 112 below.*
Emile. 1762; *see* R. L. Edgeworth, Practical education, 1798; Professional education, 1809; *see* H. Spencer, Education, intellectual moral and physical, 1861.

Schmidt, O. Rousseau und Byron: ein Beitrag zur vergleichenden Literaturgeschichte des Revolutionszeitalters. Oppeln 1890.
Allen, B. S. Godwin as a sentimentalist. PMLA 33 1918. On Godwin, Helvétius and Rousseau.
Gosse, E. Rousseau in England in the nineteenth century. In his Aspects and impressions, 1922.
Barzun, J. Shaw and Rousseau. In Shaw: a critical survey, ed L. Kronenberger 1954.
Voisine, J. Rousseau en Angleterre à l'époque romantique. 1956.

Saint-Simon, Henri de (1760–1825)
Nouveau christianisme. 1825; New Christianity, tr J. E. Smith 1834.

Neff, E. E. Carlyle and Mill. New York 1924.
Murphy, E. M. Carlyle and the Saint-Simonians. SP 33 1936.
Shine, H. Carlyle and the Saint-Simonians: the concept of historical periodicity. Baltimore 1941.

Sainte-Beuve, Charles Augustin de (1804–69). *See also under Arnold, col 465 below.*
Causeries du lundi. 15 vols 1851–62; English portraits, 1875; ed G. Saintebury 1885.
Essays on men and women. Ed W. Sharp 1890. A selection.

Roth, G. Sainte-Beuve, Crabbe et le conte en vers. French Quart 3 1921.
Phillips, E. M. Sainte-Beuve and the Lake poets. French Quart 8 1926.
— Sainte-Beuve's criticism of English prose. French Quart 13 1931.
— Sainte-Beuve et l'Angleterre. In Mélanges offerts à Jean Bonnerot, 1954.
Combe, T. G. S. Sainte-Beuve poète et les poètes anglais. Bordeaux 1937.
Whitridge, A. Arnold and Sainte-Beuve. PMLA 53 1938.
Lehmann, A. G. Sainte-Beuve: critique de la littérature anglaise. Revue de Littérature Comparée 38 1954.

'Sand, George' (Aurore Dupin) (1804–76)
Consuelo. 8 vols 1843; tr 2 vols 1847; 1893.
Le compagnon du tour de France. 2 vols 1841; The journeyman joiner, tr F. G. Shaw, Dublin 1849.
La comtesse de Rudolstadt. 5 vols 1844; The countess of Rudolstadt, 1851; 1862; 1893.

Le meunier d'Angibault. 3 vols 1845; The miller of Angibault, 1853.

La mare au diable. 2 vols 1846; The haunted marsh, 1848; The enchanted lake, tr F. G. Shaw 1850; The devil's pool, 1861.

Francois-le-Champi. Brussels 1848; Francis the waif, tr G. Masson 1888; tr J. M. Sedgwick 1895.

La petite Fadette. 2 vols 1849; Little Fadette, with introd by J. Mazzini 1850.

Correspondance 1812–76. 6 vols 1882–4; Letters, selected and tr R. Ledos de Beaufort 3 vols 1886.

Sardou, Victorien (1831–1908)

Les pattes de mouche. 1860; A scrap of paper, adapted by J. P. Simpson 1861.

Les prés Saint-Gervais. 1862; The meadows of Saint-Gervais, tr J. R. Ware 1871.

Les ganaches. 1863; Progress, adapted by T. W. Robertson 1893.

Nos intimes! 1865; Friends or foes? adapted by H. Wigan nd; Our friends, tr G. March 1879.

Fernande. 1870; tr 1883.

Dora. 1877; tr 1877; *see* B. C. Stephenson and C. Scott, Diplomacy 1878.

Les bourgeois de Pont-Arcy (not pbd in France); The inhabitants of Pontarcy, 1878.

Fédora. 1908 (performed 1882); tr H. Merivale 1883; *see* H. L. Williams, Fedora: a novel, 1883.

Raafat, Z. The literary indebtedness of Wilde's Salome to Sardou's Théodora. Revue de Littérature Comparée 40 1966.

Scribe, Augustin Eugène (Félix Augustin Debersey) (1791–1861)

This list does not include opera libretti and one-act farces based on Scribe.

— and Varner. César: ou le chien du château. 1837; Caesar, the watchdog of the castle, 1886.

La muette de Portici. 1837; Masaniello, adapted by R. B. Brough 1857.

Le verre d'eau. 1840; The glass of water, adapted by W. E. Suter nd.

— and E. Legouvé. Adrienne Lecouvreur. 1849; adapted by H. Herman 1850.

Giralda. 1850. An opera; tr Mrs Davidson 1850; adapted as a play by H. Welstead 1856.

— and E. Legouvé. Bataille de dames. 1851; The ladies' battle, tr T. W. Robertson 1851; tr C. Reade 1851.

— and E. Legouvé. Les doigts de fée. 1858; The world of fashion, tr J. Oxenford 1862.

Stanton, S. S. Shaw's debt to Scribe. PMLA 76 1961.

Sismondi, Jean Charles Léonard Simonde de (1773–1842)

Histoire des républiques italiennes du moyen âge. 8 vols Zürich 1807–9; Italian republics etc, 1832.

De la littérature du midi de l'Europe. 4 vols 1813; Historical view of the literature of the south of Europe, tr T. Roscoe 1823.

Nouveaux principes d'économie politique. 2 vols 1819; Political economy and the philosophy of government, 1847. A selection.

Julia Severa: ou l'an 492. 3 vols 1822; tr 2 vols 1822.

— and A. Renée. Histoire des français. 31 vols 1821–44; History of the crusades against the Albigenses etc, 1826; The battles of Cressy and Poitiers etc, 1831. 2 extracts.

Staël-Holstein, Germaine de (1766–1817)

De l'influence des passions sur le bonheur des individus et des nations. Lausanne 1796; A treatise on the influence of the passions upon the happiness of individuals and nations, 1798.

De la littérature considérée dans ses rapports avec les institutions sociales. 2 vols 1800; A treatise on ancient and modern literature, 2 vols 1803; The influence of literature upon society, 2 vols 1812.

Delphine. 4 vols Geneva 1802; tr 3 vols 1803.

Corinne. 2 vols 1807; Corinna, tr D. Lawler 5 vols 1807; tr I. Hill 1833.

De l'Allemagne. 3 vols 1810, London 1813; Germany, 3 vols 1813.

Réflexions sur le suicide. London and Stockholm 1813; Reflections on suicide, 1813.

An appeal to the nations of Europe against the continental system. 1813.

Considérations sur les principaux évènement de la révolution françoise. London 1818; Considerations on the principal events of the French Revolution, 1818.

Zulma et trois nouvelles: précédé d'un essai sur les fictions. 2 vols London 1813; tr 1813.

Bertaut, J. Madame de Staël et l'Angleterre. Mercure de France 16 July 1917.

Whitford, R. C. Mme de Staël's literary reputation in England. Univ of Illinois Stud 4 1918.

'Stendhal' (Marie-Henri Beyle) (1783–1842). *See also under Browning, Henry James and Thackeray, cols 111, 113, 116 below.*

Rome, Naples et Florence en 1817. 1817; Rome, Naples and Florence in 1817, 1818.

Vie de Rossini. 2 vols 1824; Memoirs of Rossini, 1824.

New Monthly Magazine. 1825–9.

Gunnell, D. Stendhal et l'Angleterre 1909. With list of contributions to English periodicals.

Vigneron, R. Stendhal et Hazlitt. MP 35 1938.

Lafourcade, G. Stendhal et Arnold Bennett. Revue de Littérature Comparée 19 1939.

Imbert, H.-F. Stendhal et Tom Jones. Revue de Littérature Comparée 30 1956.

Del Litto, V. La vie intellectuelle de Stendhal: genèse et évolution de ses idées 1802–21. 1959.

Dechamps, J. A propos d'un centenaire: Leigh Hunt et Stendhal. Stendhal Club 1 1959.

Alciatore, J-C. Quelques remarques sur Stendhal et les héroïnes de Scott. Stendhal Club 8 1966.

Süe, Marie Joseph Eugène (1804–57)

Arthur. 1839; tr 1846.

Jean Cavalier. 2 vols 1840; The Protestant leader, 3 vols 1849.

Le commandeur de Malte. 2 vols 1841; tr A. Doisy 1846.

Mathilde. 3 vols 1841; Matilda, 1846.

Le morne-au-diable (not pbd; performed in 1848); The female Bluebeard, 1845.

Paula Monti. 1842; tr 1845.

Thérèse Dunoyer. 2 vols 1842; tr 1845.

Les mystères de Paris. 5 vols 1842–3; tr J. D. Smith 1844; tr H. D. Williams 1869; etc.

Le juif errant. 10 vols 1844–5; performed as a play in France in 1849; The wandering Jew, 1844; tr D. M. Aird 1845; tr H. D. Mules 1846; tr H. D. Williams 3 vols 1868; *see* G. Landor, The wandering Jew, 1883 (dramatic adaptation).

Martin ou l'enfant trouvé. 1845; Martin the foundling, 1847.

Roberts, W. Dumas and Sue in England. Nineteenth Century Nov 1922.

Taine, Hippolyte (1828–93). *See also under Carlyle, col 112 below.*

Le positivisme anglais: étude sur Stuart Mill. 1864; English positivism: a study on Mill, tr D. Haye 1870.

Histoire de la littérature anglaise. 4 vols 1863–4; History of English literature, tr H. van Laun 2 vols Edinburgh 1871.

Philosophie de l'art. 1865; The philosophy of art, tr J. Durand 1865.

De l'intelligence. 2 vols 1870; On intelligence, tr T. D. Haye 2 vols 1871.

Notes sur l'Angleterre. 1872; Notes on England, tr W. F. Rae 1872.
Carnets de voyage: notes sur la province 1863–5. 1897; Journeys through France, 1897.

Murray, K. Taine und die englische Romantik. Munich 1914.
Roe, F. C. Taine et l'Angleterre. 1923.

Tocqueville, Alexis de (1805–59). *See also under Mill, col 113 below.*
De la démocratie en Amérique. 4 vols 1835–40; Democracy in America, tr H. Reeve 4 vols 1835–40.
L'ancien régime et la Révolution. 1856; On the state of society in France before the Revolution of 1789 etc, tr H. Reeve 1856.
Correspondence and conversations with N. W. Senior. 2 vols 1872.

Verlaine, Paul (1844–96)
The Senate. 1895. Various poems and articles by Verlaine.

Symons, A. Verlaine. Two Worlds March 1926.
Temple, R. Z. Verlaine and his English readers. Comparative Lit Newsletter 3 1945.
Starkie, E. Verlaine and Mallarmé at Oxford. Harlequin 1 1949.
Lhombreaud, R. A. Verlaine et ses amis d'Angleterre. Revue d'Histoire Littéraire de la France 53 1953.
Underwood, V. P. Verlaine et l'Angleterre. 1956.

Verne, Jules Gabriel (1828–1905)
Cinq semaines en ballon. 1863; Five weeks in a balloon, 1870.
Les anglais au pôle nord; Le désert de glace. 2 vols 1866; The English at the North Pole; The field of ice, 2 vols 1875–6.
De la terre à la lune. 1865; Autour de la lune, 1869; From the earth to the moon and a trip around it, tr L. Mercier 2 vols 1876.
Les enfants du capitaine Grant etc. 1868; A voyage around the world etc, 1876.
Vingt mille lieues sous les mers. 1869; Twenty thousand leagues under the seas, 1873, 1874 etc.
Le tour du monde en quatre-vingts jours. 1873; Around the world in eighty days, tr G. M. Towle 1874; tr H. Frith 1879 etc.
L'île mystérieuse. 1874; The mysterious island, tr W. H. G. Kingston 1875.
Le docteur Ox. 1874; Dr Ox's experiment etc, 1874.
Le Chancellor. 1875; The survivors of the Chancellor, tr E. Frewer 1875.
L'île à hélice. 1895; Floating island, tr W. J. Gordon, Edinburgh 1896.
Michel Strogoff. 1875; tr W. H. G. Kingston 1876.
César Cascabel. 2 vols 1890; tr 1891.

Vidocq, François Eugène (1775–1857)
Mémoires. 1828–9; tr H. T. R. 1828–9; *see* Vidocq: a melodrama, 1825.

Vigny, Alfred de (1797–1863). *See also under Byron, Thomas Moore and Scott, cols 111, 113, 114 below.*
Cinq-Mars. 1826; tr W. Hazlitt 1847.
Les consultations du docteur Noir. 1831–2; Servitude et grandeur militaires, 1835; Professional visits of le docteur Noir; Sealed orders. In Tales of the first French Revolution, 1849 (selection).

Poems and romances of Vigny. Westminster Rev 29 1838.
Ascher, J. Vigny and Thomas Campbell. French Quart 4 1922.
Lebbin, E. Vignys Beziehungen zu England und zur englischen Literatur. Halle 1936.
Hope, W. G. The 'suffering humanitarian' theme in Shelley's Prometheus unbound and in certain poems of Vigny. French Rev 12 1939.
Whitridge, A. Vigny and Housman: a study in pessimism. Amer Scholar 10 1941.
Bird, C. W. Vigny's Chatterton: a contribution to the study of its genesis and sources. Los Angeles 1941.
Marshall, J. F. Vigny and W. C. Macready. PMLA 74 1959.

Volney, Comte (Constantin-François de Chasseboeuf) (1757–1820)
Les ruines. 1791; The ruins, 1795.

Kellner, L. Shelley's Queen Mab und Volneys Les ruines. E Studien 22 1896.
Cameron, K. N. A major source of the Revolt of Islam. PMLA 56 1941.

Zola, Emile (1840–1903). *See also under Dickens, Henry James and George Moore, cols 112, 113 below.*
Thérèse Raquin. 1867; tr E. A. Vizetelly 1886.
L'œuvre. 1871; His masterpiece?, 1886.
La fortune des Rougon. 1871; The fortune of the Rougons, 1886.
Nana. 1880; tr 1884.
La curée. 1872; The rush for the spoil, with a preface by George Moore, 1886.
Le ventre de Paris. 1873; Fat and thin, tr E. A. Vizetelly 1888.
La faute de l'abbé Mouret. 1875; Abbé Mouret's transgression, 1886.
Une page d'amour. 1876; A love episode, 1887.
L'assommoir. 1877; The assommoir, 1884; *see* C. Reade, Drink 1879 (play).
Son excellence Eugène Rougon. 1879; His excellency E. Rougon, 1887.
L'attaque du moulin. 1880; The attack on the mill etc, with an essay by E. Gosse, 1892.
Pot-Bouille. 1882; Piping hot! with a preface by George Moore, 1885.
Au bonheur des dames. 1883; The ladies' paradise, tr F. Belmont 3 vols 1883.
La joie de vivre. 1884; How jolly life is!, 1886.
Germinal. 1885; tr 1885.
La terre. 1887; The soil, 1888.
L'argent. 1887; Money, tr E. A. Vizetelly 1894.
Le rêve. 1889; The dream, tr E. E. Chase 1893.
La débâcle 1891; The downfall, tr E. A. Vizetelly 1892.
Le docteur Pascal. 1893; Doctor Pascal: or life and heredity, tr E. A. Vizetelly 1893.

Pernicious literature: debate in the House of Commons, with opinions of the press. 1889 (Nat Vigilance Assoc pamphlet).
Ellis, H. Zola: the man and his work. Savoy 1 1896.
Vizetelly, E. A. With Zola in England. 1899.
—— Zola: novelist and reformer. 1904.
Decker, C. R. Zola's literary reputation in England. PMLA 49 1934. With list of articles in English periodicals.
'Auriant'. Un disciple anglais de Zola: George Moore. Mercure de France 297 1940.
Haines, L. F. Reade, Mill and Zola. SP 40 1943.
Pryme, E. E. Zola's plays in England 1870–1900. French Stud 13 1959.

English Authors

For a selective list of trns of English authors into French, see G. Lanson, Manuel bibliographique de la littérature française moderne 1500–1900, 1931, pt 4, section 2, ch 3. *For a comprehensive list of trns of plays, see* M. Horn-Monval, Répertoire bibliographique des traductions et adaptations françaises du théâtre étranger du XVe siècle à nos jours vol 5, 1962. *For a comprehensive list of trns of novels between 1830 and 1870, see Devonshire, col 97 above.*

Arnold, Matthew. *See also under Joubert, Renan and Sainte-Beuve, cols 103, 106 above.*
A French Eton: or middle-class education and the State. 1864.
Essays in criticism. 2 sers 1865–88.

Mixed essays. 1879.
Irish essays. 1882.

Furrer, P. Der Einfluss Sainte-Beuves auf die Kritik Arnolds. Wetzikon 1920.
Brown, E. K. The French reputation of Arnold. Stud in Eng (Toronto) 1931.
Romer, V. L. Arnold and some French poets. Nineteenth Century June 1926.
Sells, I. E. Arnold and France: the poet. Cambridge 1935.
— Marguerite. MLR 38 1943.
Faverty, F. E. Arnold the ethnologist. Evanston 1951.
Mengers, M. Matters versus man. French Rev 28 1955. On Hugo, Arnold and Régnier.
Allott, K. Arnold's reading-lists in three early diaries. Victorian Stud 2 1959.
Super, R. H. Documents in the Arnold-Sainte-Beuve relationship. MP 60 1963.
Harding, F. S. Arnold the critic and France. Geneva 1964.
Straumann, H. Arnold and the continental idea. In The English mind, ed H. S. Davies and G. Watson, Cambridge 1964.

Bennett, Enoch Arnold. *See also under Stendhal, col 108 above.*
The old wives' tale. 1910.
Paris nights. 1913.
Journals vol 1. 1932.

Evans, R. L. Bennett et la France. Modern Languages 21 1940.
Conacher, W. M. Bennett and the French realists. Queen's Quart 56 1949.

Browning, Robert and Elizabeth Barrett. *See also under Comte and Hugo, cols 101, 102 above.*
Mrs Browning in French. Academy 20 June 1903.
Schmidt, K. Brownings Verhältnis zu Frankreich. Berlin 1909.
Minckwitz, M. J. Einige Beziehungen der englischen Dichterin E. Barrett-Browning zu Frankreich, insbesondere zur französischen Literatur. Zeitschrift für Französische Sprache und Literatur 30 1906.
Hooreman, L. Promenades romaines: la rencontre inopinée de Stendhal et de Browning. Stendhal-Club 6 1964. On Ring and the book.

Burns, Robert
Angellier, A. Burns. Paris 1893.
Power, W. Burns's French interpreter. In Cahier Angellier, Paris 1927. On Angellier and Burns.
Sells, A. L. Leconte de Lisle and Burns. In Studies presented to R. L. Graeme Ritchie, Cambridge 1949.
Ross Roy, G. French translations of Burns. Revue de Littérature Comparée 37 1963.
— French critics of Burns. Revue de Littérature Comparée 38 1964.
Souffrin, E. Burns en France: ou l'image du poète laboureur. In Connaissance de l'étranger: mélanges offerts à la mémoire de J-M Carré, 1964.

Byron, George Gordon. *See also under Dumas père and Rousseau, cols 101, 106 above.*
Vigny, A. de. Œuvres de Byron. Conservateur Littéraire 3 1820.
Hugo, V. Byron et ses rapports avec la littérature actuelle. Annales Romantiques 1827–8.
Pichot, A. Essai sur la vie, le caractère et le génie de Byron. 1830.
Guiccioli, T. Byron jugé par les témoins de sa vie. 1868; My recollections of Lord Byron and those of the eye-witnesses of his life, tr H. Jerningham 2 vols 1869.
[Cléron, L. de]. Les dernières années de Byron, par l'auteur de Robert Emmet. 1874.
Clark, W. J. Byron und die romantische Poesie in Frankreich. Leipzig 1901.
Estève, E. Le Byronisme de Leconte de Lisle. Revue de Littérature Comparée 5 1925.
— Byron et le romantisme français. 1907, 1929.
Dargan, E. P. Byron's fame in France. Virginia Quart 2 1926.
Blanck, A. Floires et Blanceflor et l'épisode de Haïfée dans le Don Juan de Byron. In Mélanges Baldensperger vol 1, 1930.
Baker, A. T. Notes on Byron and Hugo. French Quart 14 1932.
Eggert, G. Byron und Napoleon. Leipzig 1933.
Straumann, H. Byron and Switzerland. Nottingham 1949.
Vandegans, A. Anatole France et Byron avant 1873. Revue de Littérature Comparée 23 1949.
Lowell, E. J. Byron and La nouvelle Héloïse: two parallel paradoxes. MLN 66 1951.
Mortier, R. La réaction d'un critique classique devant Byron. Revue des Langues Vivantes 17 1951.
Escarpit, R. Byron: un tempérament littéraire. 2 vols 1955–7. With comprehensive bibliography.
— La traduction de Byron en français. Cahiers de l'Association Internationale des Etudes Françaises June 1956.
Souffrin, E. Le Byronisme de Banville. Revue de Littérature Comparée 37 1963.

Carlyle, Thomas. *See also under Maeterlinck and Saint-Simon, cols 104, 106 above.*
Voltaire. Foreign Rev 3 1829.
Diderot. Foreign Quart Rev 11 1833.
The French Revolution. 3 vols 1837.

Taine, H. L'idéalisme anglais: étude sur Carlyle. 1864.
Taylor, A. C. Carlyle: sa première fortune littéraire en France 1825–65. 1929.

De Quincey, Thomas. *See also under Balzac, Baudelaire and Musset, cols 99, 99, 105 above.*
Confessions of an English opium eater. 1822; L'anglais mangeur d'opium, tr A. de Musset 1828; Les paradis artificiels, tr C. Baudelaire 1860.

Littlefield, W. Musset and the English opium eater. Bookman (New York) July 1902.
Clapton, G. T. Baudelaire et De Quincey. 1931.
Hughes, R. Vers la contrée de rêve: Balzac, Gautier et Baudelaire disciples de Quincey. Mercure de France 1 Aug 1939.
Dimof, P. Autour d'un projet de roman de Flaubert: La spirale. Revue d'Histoire Littéraire de la France 48 1948.

Dickens, Charles. *See also under Daudet, col 101 above.*
A tale of two cities. 1859.

Delattre, F. Dickens et la France. 1927.
Atkins, S. P. A possible Dickens influence in Zola. MLQ 8 1947.

Hardy, Thomas
The dynasts. 3 pts 1904–8.

Cassidy, J. A. The original source of Hardy's Dynasts. PMLA 69 1954. On Hardy, Buchanan and Hugo.
Starr, W. Romain Rolland and Hardy. MLQ 17 1956.

Hazlitt, William. *See also under Hugo, Michelet, Stendhal and Vigny, cols 102, 105, 108, 109 above.*
Characteristics, in the manner of Rochefoucauld's Maxims. 1823.
Notes of a journey through France and Italy. 1826.
The life of Napoleon Buonaparte. 4 vols 1830.

Dechamps, J. Hazlitt et Napoléon. Revue des Etudes Napoléoniennes 45 1939.
Cohen, B. B. Hazlitt: Bonapartist critic of the Excursion. MLQ 10 1949.

James, Henry. *See also under Baudelaire and Flaubert, cols 99, 102 above.*
The American. Boston 1877.
Madame de Mauves. 1879.

Portraits of places. 1883.
The reverberator. 1888.
The tragic muse. 1890.
Parisian sketches. 1898.
The ambassadors. 1903.

Garnier, M-R. James et la France. 1927.
Cestre, C. La France dans l'œuvre de James. Revue Anglo-américaine 10 1932.
Fay, E. G. James as a critic of French literature. French Amer Rev 2 1949.
— Balzac and James. French Rev Feb 1951.
McFarlane, I. D. A literary friendship: James and Bourget. Cambridge Jnl Oct 1950.
Niess, R. J. James and Zola: a parallel. Revue de Littérature Comparée 30 1956.
Wegelin, C. The image of Europe in James. Dallas 1958.
Cargill, O. The first international novel. PMLA 73 1958. On James and Dumas.
Powers, L. H. James and Zola's Roman expérimental. UTQ 30 1960.
Adams, P. G. James and his master Balzac. Revue de Littérature Comparée 35 1961. With a bibliography.
Dove, J. R. The alienated hero in Le rouge et le noir and the Princess Casamassima. In Studies in comparative literature, ed W. F. McNeir, Baton Rouge 1962.

Bulwer Lytton, Edward
Richelieu. 1839.
The lady of Lyons. 1839.
Zanoni vol 3. 1842.

Qualia, C. B. French dramatic sources of Lytton's Richelieu. PMLA 42 1927.

Meredith, George
Up to midnight. Graphic 1873; Boston 1913.
Beauchamp's career. 1874.
One of our conquerors. 1891.
Odes in contribution to the song of French history. 1898.
Mackay, M. E. Meredith et la France. 1937.

Mill, John Stuart. *See also under Comte, Saint-Simon, Taine and Zola, cols 100, 106, 108, 110, above.*
Letters on the French Revolution of 1830. Ed F. E. Mineka, Victorian Stud 1 1957.
Examiner 1830–4. Various contributions on France by Mill.
Correspondance inédite avec Gustave d'Eichtal [the Saint-Simonian]. Ed E. d'Eichtal 1898.
Letters to Tocqueville. TLS 1–15 Sept 1950.

Littré, E. Comte et Mill. Revue des Deux Mondes 15 Aug 1866.
Whittaker, T. Comte and Mill. 1908.
Mueller, I. Mill and French thought. Urbana 1956.

Moore, Thomas
Baldensperger, F. Moore et Vigny. MLR 1 1906.
Thomas, A. B. Moore en France: la fortune des oeuvres de Moore dans la littérature française 1819–30. 1911.

Moore, George. *See also under Baudelaire, Flaubert and Zola, cols 99, 102, 110 above.*
A modern lover. 1883.
Confessions of a young man. 1888.
Jean-Aubry, G. Zola et George Moore. Nouvelles Littéraires 17 Jan 1925.
Chaikin, M. Balzac, Zola and Moore's A drama in muslin. Revue de Littérature Comparée 29 1955.
— The composition of Moore's A modern lover. Comparative Lit 7 1955.
— Moore's A mummer's wife and Zola. Revue de Littérature Comparée 31 1957.
Collet, G.-P. Moore et la France. Geneva 1957.
Noël, J. Moore et Mallarmé. Revue de Littérature Comparée 32 1958.

Brown, C. S. Balzac as a source of Moore's Sister Teresa. Comparative Lit 11 1959.

Pater, Walter
Renaissance studies. 1873.
Imaginery portraits. 1887.
Gaston de Latour. 1889.

Beyer, A. Paters Beziehungen zur französischen Literatur und Kultur. Halle 1931.
Rosenblatt, L. M. Marius l'épicurien de Pater et ses points de départ français. Revue de Littérature Comparée 15 1935. On Pater, Renan and J. Lemaître's Sérénus.
— The genesis of Pater's Marius the Epicurean. Comparative Lit 14 1962.
Takeda, K. Romanticism by Pater and French literature in the romantic period. Hikaku Bungaku 1962.

Ruskin, John
Milsand, J. L'esthétique anglaise: étude sur Ruskin. 1864.
Audra, E. L'influence de Ruskin en France. Revue des Cours et Conférences Jan 1926.
Souza, S. de. L'influence de Ruskin sur Proust. Montpellier 1932.
Bisson, L. A. Proust and Ruskin reconsidered in the light of the Lettres à une amie. MLR 39 1944.
Delattre, F. Ruskin et Bergson. Oxford 1947.
Autret, J. L'influence de Ruskin sur Proust. Geneva 1955.
— Ruskin and the French before Proust. Geneva 1965.
Carballo, J. R. Proust y la Biblia de Amiens. Insula Oct 1957.
Kolb, P. Proust et Ruskin: nouvelles perspectives. Cahiers de l'Association Internationale des Etudes Françaises 12 1960.

Scott, Walter. *See also under Balzac and Dumas père, cols 99, 101 above.*
Lacroix, P. Soirées de Scott à Paris. 1929.
Maigron, L. Le roman historique à l'époque romantique: essai sur l'influence de Scott. 1898.
François, E. Scott and Vigny. MLN 21 1906. On Quentin Durward and Cinq-Mars.
Devonshire, J. M. The 'decline' of Scott in France. French Quart 1 1919.
Garnand, H. J. The influence of Scott on the works of Balzac. New York 1926.
Smith, M. E. Une anglaise intellectuelle en France sous la Restauration: Mary Clarke. 1927.
Hartland, R. W. Scott et le roman 'frénétique': leur fortune en France. 1928.
Dargan, E. P. Scott and the French romantics. PMLA 49 1934. With list of trns into French.
Genévrier, P. Scott, historien français. Tours 1935. On French material in Quentin Durward.
Cook, D. The Waverleys in French: Scott's authorship revealed in 1822. TLS 17 July 1937.
Latham, E. Dumas and Scott. In Notes et documents littéraires, Mercure de France 1 Jan 1938.
Sells, A. L. Leconte de Lisle and Scott. French Stud 1 1947.
Green, F. C. Scott's French correspondence. MLR 52 1957.
Rinsler, N. Nerval and Scott's Antiquary. Revue de Littérature Comparée 34 1960.

Shelley, Percy Bysshe. *See also under Comte and Volney, cols 100, 110 above.*
de Nolva, R. Shelley et Lamartine. Nouvelle Revue d'Italie 25 Nov 1922.
Meyer, H. Rousseau und Shelley. Würzburg 1934.
Peyre, H. Shelley et la France: lyrisme anglais et lyrisme français au XIXe siècle. Cairo 1935. With full list of Shelley criticism in French.
Amiyakumar Sen. Shelley and the French Revolution. In his Studies in Shelley, Calcutta 1936.
Kapstein, I. J. Shelley and Cabanis. PMLA 52 1937.

Lebois, A. L'influence de Shelley sur Elémir Bourges. Revue de Littérature Comparée 22 1948.

Stevenson, Robert Louis. *See also under Hugo, col 103 above.*
An inland voyage. 1878.
Travels with a donkey in the Cévennes. 1879.
The treasure of a Franchard. In his Merry men and other tales and fables, 1887.
The wrecker. 1892.

Saroléa, C. Stevenson et la France. Edinburgh [1893].
Carré, J-M. Stevenson et la France. In Mélanges Baldensperger vol 1, 1930.
Fabre, F. Stevenson dans le Velay. Revue d'Auvergne 48 1932. With letters.
Maclean, C. La France dans l'œuvre de Stevenson. 1936.

Swinburne, Algernon Charles. *See also under Baudelaire and Hugo, cols 99, 102–3 above.*
Chastelard. 1865.
Ode to France. 1870.
On the proclamation of the French Republic. In his Songs of two nations, 1875.
Poems and ballads: second series. 1878.
Rondeaux parisiens. 1917.

Reul, P. de. Swinburne et la France: essai de littérature comparée. Brussels 1904.
Richter, L. Swinburnes Verhältnis zu Frankreich und Italien. Leipzig 1911.
Delattre, F. Swinburne et la France. Revue des Cours et Conférences 28 Feb 1926.
— Baudelaire et le jeune Swinburne 1861–7. In Mélanges Baldensperger vol 1, 1930.
Nicolson, H. Swinburne and Baudelaire. Oxford 1931.
Fontainas, A. Swinburne et les symbolistes. Yggdrasill 25 April 1937.

Souffrin, E. Swinburne et Les misérables. Revue de Littérature Comparée 34 1960.

Symons, Arthur. *See also under Baudelaire, Mallarmé and Verlaine, cols 99, 104, 109 above.*
Poems. 1898.
The symbolist movement in literature. 1899.
Colour studies in Paris. 1918.

Lhombreaud, R. Symons. 1963.
Leyris, P. Pour Arthur Symons. Mercure de France Jan 1964.

Tennyson, Alfred. *See also under Hugo, col 103 above.*
Dejob, C. Les pauvres gens de Victor Hugo et Enoch Arden de Tennyson. Revue des Cours et Conférences 8 1900.
Bowden, M. Tennyson in France. Manchester 1930.
Pitollet, C. Les fleurs de James et celles de Tennyson. Revue de l'Enseignement des Langues Vivantes 56 1939.

Thackeray, William Makepeace. *See also under Balzac, col 98 above.*
The Paris sketch book. 2 vols 1840.
The history of the next French revolution. Punch March–April 1844.

Walter, E. Entstehungsgeschichte von Thackerays Vanity Fair. Palaestra 79 1908.
Donnelly, J. Stendhal and Thackeray: the source of Henry Esmond. Revue de Littérature Comparée 39 1965.

Wordsworth, William
Texte, J. Wordsworth et la poésie lakiste en France. In his Études de littérature européenne, 1898.
Wright, H. G. The reflection of Wordsworth's personality in his choice of French writers. MLR 42 1947.
Todd, F. M. Wordsworth, Helen Maria Williams et la France. MLR 43 1948.

C. C.

(4) GERMAN

Bibliographies

Morgan, B. Q. A critical bibliography of German literature in English translation 1481–1927. Madison 1922, New York 1965 (rev and enlarged).
— and A. R. Hohlfeld (ed). German literature in British magazines 1750–1860. Madison 1949.
Anglo-German literary bibliography 1933–. Annually in JEGP 1935–.
Schloesser, A. Die englische Literatur in Deutschland von 1895–1934. Jena 1937.
Smith, A. H. and A. T. Hatto. A list of English, Scandinavian and German theses in the University of London. 1939.
Price, L. M. English literature in Germany. Univ of Cal Pbns in Modern Philology 37 1953. On English literature in Germany from 19th century, with bibliography. *See also under Price, col 117 below.*
Mönnig, R. Übersetzungen aus der deutschen Sprache 1948–64: no 1, Deutschland und die Deutschen im englischsprachigen Schrifttum. Göttingen 1957–.
Goedeke, K. *See col 117 below.*

General Studies

The Anti-Jacobin Review and Magazine. [Ed J. Gifford] 1798–1821.
Goede, C. A. G. A foreigner's opinion of England. 1802.
Holcroft, T. Memoirs. 1816.
Carlyle, T. State of German literature. Edinburgh Rev 46 1827.
— German playwrights. Foreign Rev 3 1829.
— Richter's review of Madame de Staël's De l'Allemagne. Fraser's Mag Feb, May 1830.
— The Nibelungenlied. Westminster Rev 15 1831.
— German literature of the fourteenth and fifteenth centuries. Foreign Quart Rev 8 1831.
— Lectures on German literature [May 1837]. Not pbd; *see* Spectator 6 May 1837 for concise report.
— The history of Friedrich II of Prussia, called Frederick the Great. 6 vols 1858–65.
Taylor, W. Historic survey of German poetry. 3 vols 1828–30. *See* also Carlyle's review in Edinburgh Rev 50 1831.
Mann, H. Report of an educational tour in Germany and parts of Great Britain and Ireland. 1846.
Gillies, R. P. Memoirs of a literary veteran. 1851.
'Eliot, George' (M. A. Evans). Three months in Weimar. 1855.
Mackay, R. W. The Tübingen school and its antecedents. 1863.
Deutsche Dichtungen in englischen Übersetzungen. Grenzboten 28 1869.
Henkel. The German influence on the poetry of England and America in the course of the 19th century. Eschwege 1869.
Eitner, K. Ein Engländer über deutsches Geistesleben im ersten Drittel dieses Jahrhunderts. Weimar 1871.
Arnold, M. Higher schools and universities in Germany. 1874.
Payne, J. Pestalozzi: influence of elementary education. 1875.
— Froebel and the Kindergarten. 1876.
— A visit to German schools. 1876.
Weddigen, F. H. O. Vermittler des deutschen Geistes in England und Nordamerika. Archiv 59 1878.
— Geschichte der Einwirkungen der deutschen Literatur auf die Literaturen der übrigen europäischen Kulturvölker der Neuzeit. Leipzig 1882.

Paulsen, F. Die deutschen Universitäten. Berlin 1893; tr E. D. Perry, New York 1895; tr F. Tilly and W. W. Elwang 1906.

Herzfeld, G. William Taylor von Norwich: eine Studie über den Einfluss der neueren deutschen Litteratur in England. Halle 1897.

—— Zur Geschichte der deutschen Literatur in England. Archiv 110 1903.

Stephen, L. The importance of German. In his Studies of a biographer vol 2, 1898.

Bradley, A. C. English poetry and German philosophy in the age of Wordsworth. Manchester 1900; rptd in his A miscellany, 1929.

Zeiger, T. Beiträge zur Geschichte des Einflusses der neueren deutschen Literatur auf die englische. Leipzig 1901.

Batt, M. Contributions to the history of English opinion of German literature, 1: Gillies and the Foreign Quarterly Review; 2: Gillies and Blackwood's Magazine. MLN 17-18 1902-3.

Eichler, A. John Hookham Frere. Vienna 1905.

Jaeck, E. G. Madame de Staël and the spread of German literature. New York 1915.

Goedeke, K. Grundriss zur Geschichte der deutschen Dichtung. Vols 4, Dresden 1916 (rev).

Sigmann, L. Die englische Literatur von 1800-50 im Urteil der zeitgenössischen deutschen Kritik. Heidelberg 1918.

Waddington, M. M. The development of British thought from 1820 to 1890 with special reference to German influences. Toronto 1919.

Block, M. The British and Foreign Review or European Quarterly Journal: ein Beitrag zur Geschichte der Aufnahme deutscher Literatur in England. Zürich 1921.

Egan, R. F. The genesis of the theory of 'art for art's sake' in Germany and in England. 2 vols Northampton Mass 1921-4.

Ziehen, E. Philhelvetism. Die Neueren Sprachen April 1925.

Schwaninger, C. Die Verdienste der Edinburgh Review um die Verbreitung deutscher Literatur in England 1802-29. Zürich 1921.

Ernst, F. La tradition médiatrice de la Suisse aux xviiie et xixe siècles. Revue de Littérature Comparée 6 1926.

Purdie, E. German influence on the literary ballad in England during the Romantic revival. Pbns of Eng Goethe Soc new ser 3 1926.

Stokoe, F. W. German influence in the English Romantic period 1788-1818, with special reference to Scott, Coleridge, Shelley and Byron. Cambridge 1926.

Schirmer, G. Die Schweiz im Spiegel englischer und amerikanischer Literatur bis 1848. Zürich 1929.

—— Der Einfluss der deutschen Literatur auf die englische im 19. Jahrhundert. Halle 1947.

Stockley, V. German literature as known in England 1750-1830. 1929.

Engel, C. E. Byron et Shelley en Suisse et en Savoie (1816). Chambéry 1930.

Wellek, R. Immanuel Kant in England. Princeton 1931.

—— Confrontations: studies in the intellectual and literary relations between Germany, England and the United States during the nineteenth century. Princeton 1965.

Price, L. M. The reception of English literature in Germany. Berkeley 1932.

—— English literature in Germany. Berkeley 1953.

—— Die Aufnahme englischer Literatur in Deutschland 1500-1960. Berne and Munich 1961.

Wenzel, P. Germany and the Germans as seen by English novelists of the 19th and 20th centuries. Bielefeld 1932.

Kornder, T. Der Deutsche im Spiegelbild der englischen Erzählungsliteratur des 19 Jahrhunderts. Erlangen 1934.

Willoughby, L. A. On some German affinities with the Oxford Movement. MLR 29 1934.

Carr, C. T. German grammars in England in the nineteenth century. MLR 30 1935.

Hathaway, L. German literature of the mid-nineteenth century in England and America as reflected in the journals of 1840-1914. Boston 1935.

Weber, C. A. Bristols Bedeutung für die englische Romantik und die deutsch-englischen Beziehungen. Halle 1935.

Stiven, A. B. Englands Einfluss auf den deutschen Wortschatz. Zeulenroda 1936.

Eastlake, A. E. The influence of English literature on the German novel and drama in the period from 1880 to 1900. 1937.

Frehn, P. Der Einfluss der englischen Literatur auf Deutschlands Musiker und Musik im 19 Jahrhundert. Düsseldorf 1937.

Funke, O. Die Schweiz und die englische Literatur. Berne 1937.

Weineck, K. Deutschland und der Deutsche im Spiegel der englischen erzählenden Literatur seit 1830. Halle 1938.

Schultz, F. Der Deutsche in der englischen Literatur vom Beginn der Romantik bis zum Ausbruch des Weltkrieges. Halle 1939.

Wagner, A. Goethe, Carlyle, Nietzsche and the German middle class. Monatshefte für Deutschen Unterricht 31 1939.

Taube, E. German influence on the English vocabulary in the nineteenth century. JEGP 39 1940.

Barzun, J. Darwin, Marx, Wagner: critique of a heritage. Boston 1941, 1958 (rev).

Metz, R. England und die deutsche Philosophie. Stuttgart 1941.

König, E. G. Ruskin und die Schweiz. Berne 1943.

Macphail, J. H. Blake and Switzerland. MLR 38 1943.

Atkins, S. Sir Herbert Croft and German literature. MLQ 5 1944.

Hewett-Thayer, H. W. Ferdinand Lassalle in the novels of Spielhagen and Meredith. Gremanic Rev 19 1944.

Wildi, M. Der angelsächsische Roman und der Schweizer-Leser. Zürich 1944.

Hennig, J. Malvida von Meysenburg and England. Comparative Lit Stud 23-4 1946.

—— Irish-German literary relations: a survey. German Life & Letters 3 1950.

—— Ireland's place in nineteenth-century German poetry. German Life & Letters 8 1955.

Lunn, A. Switzerland in English prose and poetry. 1947.

Schindler, J. Das Bild des Engländers in der Kunst-und Volksliteratur der deutschen Schweiz 1798-1848. Zürich 1950.

Graf, E. Die Aufnahme der englischen und amerikanischen Literatur in der deutschen Schweiz 1800-30. Zürich 1951.

Löhrer, H. Die Schweiz im Spiegel englischer Literatur 1849-75. Zürich 1952.

Steffen, W. Die Schweiz im Spiegel englischer Literatur 1875-1900. Zürich 1953.

Forster, L. England und die deutsche Literatur. Deutsche Akademie für Sprache und Dichtung (Darmstadt) Jahrbuch 1958.

Haas, R. Übersetzungsprobleme im Feld deutsch-englischer Literatur-begegnung. Die Neueren Sprachen Aug 1958.

Mason, E. C. Deutsche und englische Romantik: eine Gegenüberstellung. Göttingen 1959.

Hofmann, C. Die Anglistik-Amerikanistik in der Deutschen Demokratischen Republik. Zeitschrift für Anglistik und Amerikanistik (East Berlin) 8 1960.

Hietsch, O. (ed). Österreich und die angelsächsische Welt. Vienna 1961.

Siegmund-Schultze, D. Zur englandkundigen Literatur in Deutschland. Zeitschrift für Anglistik und Amerikanistik (East Berlin) 9 1961.

Straumann, H. Switzerland and the English-speaking world. In English Studies today, ed G. A. Bonnard, Berne 1961.

— Matthew Arnold and the continental idea. In The English mind, ed H. S. Davies and G. Watson, Cambridge 1964.

Keiser, R. Die Aufnahme englischen Schrifttums in der Schweiz von 1830–60. Zürich 1962.

Oppel, H. Der Einfluss der englischen Literatur auf die deutsche. In Deutsche Philologie im Aufriss vol 3, ed W. Stammler, Berlin 1962.

Shelley, P. A. and A. O. Lewis (ed). Anglo-German and American-German crosscurrents II. Chapel Hill 1962.

Byrne, M. St Clare. Charles Kean and the Meininger myth. Theatre Research 6 1964.

— What we said about the Meiningers in 1881. E & S new ser 18 1965.

Gronbech, V. Religious currents in the nineteenth century. Lawrence Kansas 1964. Mainly on German and English literature.

Enright, D. J. Aimez-vous Goethe?: an enquiry into English attitudes of non-liking towards German literature. Encounter April 1964.

McFarland, G. F. Julius Charles Hare, Coleridge, De Quincey and German Romanticism. Bull John Rylands Lib 47 1964.

Mönke, W. Das literarische Echo in Deutschland auf Friedrich Engels Werk Die Lage der arbeitenden Klasse in England. East Berlin 1965.

Wilkinson, E. M. The inexpressible and the un-speakable: some Romantic attitudes to art and language. German Life & Letters 16 1963.

Anthologies in Translation

Thompson, B. German theatre. 1800–1. Includes trns of Lessing, Goethe, Schiller and Kotzebue.

Taylor, W. Tales of yore. 1810. Includes trns of Wieland's Danischmend and Alxinger's Bliomberis.

Carlyle, T. German romance: specimens of its chief authors [Fouqué, Goethe, Hoffmann, Musäus, Richter]. 1827.

Austin, S. Fragments from German prose writers. New York 1941.

Crossthwaite, G. F. Stories from the German. 1842.

Romantic fiction: Chamisso, Fouqué, Tieck. 1843. Anon.

Oxenford, J. and C. A. Feiling. Tales from the German. 1844.

Mangan, J. C. Anthologica germanica. Dublin 1845.

Baskerville, A. The poetry of Germany. Leipzig and New York 1853.

Winkworth, C. Lyra germanica. 2 vols 1855–8.

Dulcken, H. W. The book of German songs from the 16th to the 19th century. 1856.

Garnett, R. Poems from the german. 1862.

Hedley, F. H. Masterpieces of German poetry, translated in the measure of the original. 1876.

Half hours with foreign novelists. Ed H. and A. Zimmern 1880, 1884 (rev). Includes works by Auerbach, Freytag, Hackländer, Heyse, Keller, Marlitt, Sacher-Masoch, Spielhagen, Stifter.

Müller-Casenov, H. The humour of Germany; with an introduction and biographical index. 1892.

German classics of the nineteenth and twentieth centuries. Ed K. Francke and W. G. Howard, New York 1913–15.

German Authors

For more detailed bibliographies of German writers in their relation to England, see K. Goedeke, col 117, and for trns B. Q. Morgan, col 115 above.

Arnim, Achim von (1781–1831)

Howie, M. D. Arnim and Scotland. MLR 17 1922.

Droste-Hülshoff, Annette Freiin von (1797–1848)

Nettenheim, J. Annette von Droste und die englische Romantik. Jahrbuch der Droste-Gesellschaft 1947.

Eichendorff, Joseph Freiherr von (1788–1857)

Aus dem Leben eines Taugenichts. Berlin 1826; The happy-go-lucky, tr A. L. Wister 1889.

Feuerbach, Ludwig (1804–72)

Das Wesen des Christentums. Leipzig 1841; The essence of Christianity, tr 'George Eliot' 1854.

Fichte, Johann Gottlieb (1762–1814)

Sämmtliche Werke. 8 vols Berlin 1845–6.

Popular writings of Fichte, with a memoir. Tr W. Smith 2 vols 1848–9.

Fontane, Theodor (1819–98)

Rhyn, H. Die Balladendichtung Fontanes. Berne 1914.

Shears, L. A. The influence of Walter Scott on the novels of Fontane. New York 1922.

Paul, A. Der Einfluss Scotts auf die epische Technik Fontanes. Breslau 1934.

Neuendorff, O. Fontanes Gang durch die englische Dichtung. Potsdam 1938.

Barlow, D. Fontane's English journeys. German Life & Letters 6 1953.

Rowley, B. A. Fontane: a German novelist in the European tradition? German Life & Letters 15 1962.

Fouqué, Friedrich Heinrich Karl, Baron de la Motte (1777–1843)

Undine. Berlin 1811; tr G. Soane 1818; tr T. Tracy 1841; tr E. Gosse 1896.

Aslaugas Ritter. Berlin 1813; Aslauga's knight, tr T. Carlyle 1827.

Sintram und seine Gefährten. Berlin 1814; Sintram and his companions, tr J. C. Hare 1820.

Numerous trns of these and other works by Fouqué throughout the century.

Freiligrath, Ferdinand (1810–76)

Weddigen, F. H. O. Freiligrath als Vermittler englischer und französischer Dichtung. Archiv 61 1879.

Liddell, M. F. Freiligrath's debt to English poets. MLR 23 1928.

Spink, G. W. Freiligrath als Verdeutscher der englischen Poesie. Berlin 1925.

— Freiligrath's Verbannungsjahre in London. Berlin 1932.

Freytag, Gustav (1816–95)

Soll und Haben. Leipzig 1854; Debtor and creditor, tr W. J. Stewart 1857; tr Malcolm 1858.

Freymond, R. Der Einfluss von Charles Dickens auf Freytag. Prager Deutsche Studien 19 1912.

Andrews, J. S. The impact on nineteenth-century Britain of Freytag's Soll und Haben. Proc of Leeds Philosophical Soc (Literary and Historical Section) 8 1959.

George, Stefan (1868–1933)

A selection from his works. Tr C. M. Scott 1910.

Breugelmans, R. George und Oscar Wilde: a confrontation. Proc of Pacific Northwest Conference on Foreign Languages 15 1964.

— George and Oscar Wilde: part II of a confrontation—their aesthetic-religious views. Proc of Pacific Northwest Conference on Foreign Languages 17 1966.

Goethe, Johann Wolfgang von (1749–1832)

For his influence in England see J. M. Carré, Bibliographie de Goethe en Angleterre, Lyons 1920, *and* Goethe en Angleterre, Paris 1920; *and review by* A. E. Turner, MLR 16 1921; *also pbns of* Eng Goethe Soc 1886–.

Die Leiden des jungen Werthers. Leipzig 1774.

Long, O. W. English translations of Goethe's Werther. JEGP 14 1915.

Atkins, S. P. The testament of Werther in poetry and drama. Cambridge Mass 1949.

Wilhelm Meisters Lehrjahre. Berlin 1795–6.
Wilhelm Meisters Wanderjahre. Stuttgart 1829; William Meister's apprenticeship, tr T. Carlyle 1824.

Howe, S. Wilhelm Meister and his English kinsmen. New York 1930.
Gottbrath, K. Der Einfluss von Goethes Wilhelm Meister auf die englische Literatur. Munich 1937.
Hennig, J. Englandkunde im Wilhelm Meister. Goethe Jahrbuch, 26 1964.

Faust. 2 pts Tübingen 1808–Stuttgart 1833.
The Urfaust *or original draft (1770–5) of the* First Part *was discovered by Erich Schmidt in 1887 in Dresden and pbd by him in the same year. There are 3 trns of the* Urfaust: (a) by R. McLintock, 1889 (unpbd ms); (b) by W. H. van der Smissen, *below*; (c) by D. M. Scott, *below. The first 35 English trns of* Faust *are discussed by L. Baumann, below. See* B. Q. Morgan, Bibliography of German literature in English translation, *above. The following are the most noteworthy English versions:* Scenes from the Faust of Goethe. Tr P. B. Shelley [1822].
Faust pt 1. Tr A. Hayward 1833. Prose.
Faustus: a dramatic mystery. Tr J. Anster 2 pts 1835–64. A verse imitation.
Faust. Tr Anne Swanwick 2 pts 1849–78. Latest edn, with introd and bibliography by K. Breul, 1928. A popular verse trn.
Faust pt 1. Tr R. McLintock 1897. In original metres.

Carlyle, T. Faustus. New Edinburgh Rev 2 1822.
— Goethe's Helena. Foreign Rev 1 1828.
Courtney, W. L. Faust on the English stage. Fortnightly Rev Jan 1886.
Heinemann, W. Goethes Faust in England und Amerika: bibliographische Zusammenstellung. Berlin 1886.
McLintock, R. The five best English verse translations of Faust. Trans Manchester Goethe Soc 1894.
Tait, J. The literary influence of Goethe's Faust in England 1832–52. Ibid.
Davidson, T. The philosophy of Goethe's Faust. Ed C. M. Bakewell, Boston 1906.
Baumann, L. Die englischen Übersetzungen von Goethes Faust. Halle 1907.
Robertson, J. G. Gillies and Goethe. MLR 4 1908.
Hauhart, W. F. The reception of Goethe's Faust in England in the first half of the nineteenth century. New York 1909.
Montgomery, M. The first English version of Faust part 1 and Dichtung und Wahrheit. Pbns of Eng Goethe Soc new ser 3 1926.
Waterhouse, G. A unique translation of Goethe's Faust [Urfaust]. Discovery Sept 1927.
Nicoll, A. Faust on the English stage. In Das Buch des Goethe-Lessing Jahres, Brunswick 1929.
Bluhm, H. S. The reception of Goethe's Faust in England after the middle of the nineteenth century. JEGP 34 1935.

Simmons, L. van T. Goethe's lyric poems in English translation prior to 1860. Madison 1918.
Fiedler, H. G. Goethe's lyric poems in English translation. MLR 18 1923.
Hinz, S. M. Goethe's lyric poems in English translation after 1860. Madison 1929.
Carlyle, T. Goethe. Foreign Rev 2 1828.
— Goethe's Works. Foreign Quart Rev 10 1832.
— The death of Goethe. New Monthly Mag 34 1832.

Müller, F. M. Goethe and Carlyle. Contemporary Rev June 1886.
Correspondence between Goethe and Carlyle. Ed C. E. Norton 1887.
Flügel, E. Der Briefwechsel zwischen Goethe und Carlyle. Grenzboten 46 1887.
Goethes und Carlyles Briefwechsel. Ed H. Oldenberg, Berlin 1887; ed G. Hecht, Dachau 1914.
Grimm, H. Goethe und Carlyles Briefwechsel. Deutsche Rundschau 4 1887.
Carr, M. Goethe in his connection with English literature. Pbns of English Goethe Soc 4 1890.
Boyesen, H. H. Goethe and Carlyle. In his Essays on German literature, 1892.
Carré, J. M. Goethe en Angleterre. Paris 1920.
Henriot, E. Goethe, Carlyle et Thackeray. L'Europe Nouvelle 15 Oct 1921.

Lewes, G. H. Life of Goethe. 1855.
Brandl, A. Die Aufnahme von Goethes Jugendwerken in England. Goethe-Jahrbuch 3 1882.
— Goethe und Byron. Österreiche Rundschau 1 1883.
— Goethes Verhältnis zu Byron. Goethe-Jahrbuch 20 1899.
— Goethe und England. Fortschritte und Forschungen 31 1932.
Althaus, F. On the personal relations between Goethe and Byron. Pbns of Eng Goethe Soc 2 1888.
Hutton, R. H. Goethe and his influence. In his Literary essays, 1888.
Kaufmann, M. Goethe and modern thought. Scottish Rev no 18 1891.
Alford, R. G. Goethe's earliest critics in England. Pbns of Eng Goethe Soc 7 1893.
Mensch, R. A. J. Goethe and Wordsworth. Ibid.
Seely, J. M. Goethe reviewed after sixty years. 1894.
Sinzheimer, S. Goethe und Lord Byron: eine Darstellung der persönlichen und literarischen Verhältnisse mit Berücksichtigung des Faust und Manfred. Munich 1894.
Bernays, M. Beziehungen Goethes zu Walter Scott. Zur neueren Literaturgeschichte vol 1, Stuttgart 1895.
Heller, O. Goethe and Wordsworth. MLN 14 1899.
Oswald, E. Goethe in England and America: bibliography. Die Neueren Sprachen July 1899–1900; 1909 (separately).
Willoughby, L. A. An early English translation of Goethe's Tasso. MLR 9 1914.
— Goethe and the English language. German Life & Letters 10 1957.
Bode, W. Die Franzosen und Engländer in Goethes Leben und Urteil. Berlin 1915.
Lieder, F. W. C. Goethe in England and America. JEGP 16 1917.
Robertson, J. G. Goethe and Byron. Pbns of Eng Goethe Soc new ser 2 1925.
— Goethe und England. Goethe-Jahrbuch 18 1932.
Strich, F. Goethe und Byron. Die Horen 5 1929.
— Goethe und die Weltliteratur. Berne 1946, 1957 (rev).
Norman, F. Goethe und das heutige England. Goethe-Jahrbuch 17 1931.
Bangs, A. R. Mephistophiles in England. PMLA 47 1932.
Boyd, J. Goethe's knowledge of English literature. Oxford 1932.
Lovett, R. M. Goethe in English literature. Open Court April 1932.
Vollrath, W. Goethe und Grossbritannien. Erlangen 1932.
Koch, J. Goethe und Byron. Archiv 88 1933.
Böschenstein, H. Das literarische Goethebild der Gegenwart in England. Breslau 1932.

Fairley, B. Goethe and Wordsworth. Pbns of Eng Goethe Soc new ser 11 1934.
Henel, H. Ausländische Goethe-Kritik. Deutsche Vierteljahrsschrift für Literaturwissenschaft und Geistesgeschichte 12 1934.
Mennie, D. M. A note on Goethe as a translator of English prose (1830–2). MLR 30 1935.
Poeschel, C. and J. Rosenberg (ed). Goethe über England und die englische Literatur. Leipzig 1936.
Liljegren, S. B. The English source of Goethe's Gretchen tragedy. Lund 1937.
Hayens, K. C. Goethe and English letters. German Life & Letters 3 1939.
Vail, C. C. D. Shelley's translations from Goethe. Germanic Rev 23 1948.
—— Shelley's translations from Goethe's Faust. Symposium 3 1949.
Brie, F. Early English translations of Goethe's essays on Byron. MLR 44 1949.
Bruford, W. H. Goethe and some Victorian humanists. Pbns of Eng Goethe Soc 18 1949.
Carré, J. M. L'Allemagne, la France et l'Angleterre en face de Goethe. Revue de Littérature Comparée 23 1949.
Lemke, V. J. English translations of some major works of Goethe. Virginia Univ Bull 6 1949.
Morgan, B. Q. Goethe in English. In Southwest Goethe Festival, ed J. Dallas 1949.
Scott, D. F. S. Some English correspondents of Goethe. 1949.
Lewisohn, L. Goethe's poetry in the lands of English speech. In Goethe and the modern age, ed A. Bergstraesser, Chicago 1950.
Needler, G. H. Goethe and Scott. Toronto 1950.
Schneider, W. B. Goethe and English literature. In The Southern Illinois Goethe celebration, ed H. A. Hartwig, Carbondale 1950.
Spender, S. Goethe and the English mind. In Goethe and the modern age, ed A. Bergstraesser, Chicago 1950.
Hennig, J. The literary relations between Goethe and Thomas Hood. MLQ 12 1951.
—— Goethes Schottlandkunde. Goethe 25 1963.
Schirmer, W. F. Goethe und Byron: Forschungsprobleme der vergleichenden Literaturgeschichte. Tübingen 1951.
Wolff, E. B. On Goethe's reputation as a scientist in nineteenth-century England. German Life & Letters 6 1953.
Gray, R. D. Turner and Goethe's colour-theory. In German studies presented to Walter H. Bruford, 1962.
Smith, C. J. Goethe's reaction to Byron as a poet and as a personality. Pbns of Eng Goethe Soc 36 1966.

'Gotthelf, Jeremias' (Albert Bitzius) (1797–1854)
Uli der Knecht. Zürich 1841; Ulric the farm hand, tr J. Firth, rev and ed J. Ruskin 1886.
Waidson, H. M. Gotthelf's reception in Britain and America. MLR 43 1948. *See his* Gotthelf: an introduction to the Swiss novelist, Oxford 1953.

Grabbe, Christian Dietrich (1801–36)
Wiehr, J. The relations of Grabbe to Byron. JEGP 7 1908.

Grillparzer, Franz (1791–1872)
Sappho. Vienna 1818; tr J. Bramsen 1820; tr E. Frothingham, Boston 1876.
Medea. Vienna 1822; tr F. W. Thurstan and S. A. Wittmann 1879.
König Ottokars Glück und Ende. Vienna 1825; Ottokar, tr T. Carlyle 1840 (selection).
Trns of Sappho, Der Traum ein Leben, *and* Weh' dem, der lügt, *were made by Archer Thompson Gurney before 1858, but never pbd.*

Wyplel, L. Grillparzer und Byron. Euphorin 9–10 1902–3.
Fiedler, H. G. Notes by Meredith on Grillparzer's Ahnfrau. MLR 26 1931.
Morris, I. V. Grillparzer's impressions of the English. German Life & Letters 14 1960.
Burkhard, A. Grillparzer in England und Amerika. Vienna 1961.

Grimm, Jakob (1778–1863) and Wilhelm (1786–1859)
Kinder- und Hausmärchen. Berlin 1812–22. German popular stories. Tr 1823. Gammer Grethel. Tr E. Taylor 1839. Household stories. Tr 1853. Household tales. Tr M. Hunt 1884. Lang, A. The blue fairy book. 1889.
Briggs, K. M. The influence of the brothers Grimm in England. In Grimm Gedenken, ed. L. Denecke, Marburg 1963.
Brill, E. V. K. The correspondence between Jacob Grimm and Walter Scott. Ibid.

Haeckel, Ernst (1834–1919)
Die Welträtsel. Bonn 1899; The riddle of the universe, tr J. McCabe 1900.

Hauptmann, Gerhart (1862–1946)
Voigt, F. A. Hauptmann und England. Germanisch-romanische Monatsschrift 25 1937.
Hutchins, W. J. and A. C. Weaver. Hauptmann in England: a bibliography. In Hauptmann: centenary lectures, ed K. Knight and F. Norman 1964.

Hebbel, Friedrich (1813–63)
Reichart, W. A. Hebbel in Amerika und England: eine Bibliographie. Hebbel-Jahrbuch 1961.

Hegel, Georg Wilhelm Friedrich (1770–1831)
Phänomenologie des Geistes. Bamberg 1807; The phenomenology of mind, tr J. B. Baillie 1821, New York 1931 (rev).
Wissenschaft der Logik. 2 vols Nuremberg 1812–16; The logic of Hegel, tr W. Wallace 1874; Hegel's doctrine of formal logic, tr H. S. Macran, Oxford 1912.
Enzyklopädie der philosophischen Wissenschaften im Grundriss. Heidelberg 1817; Hegel's philosphy of the mind, tr W. Wallace, Oxford 1894.
Grundlinien der Philosophie des Rechts; Berlin 1821; Hegel's philosophy of right, tr S. W. Dyde 1896.

Ritchie, D. G. Darwin and Hegel, with other philosophical studies. 1894.
Muirhead, J. H. How Hegel came to England. Mind 36 1927.

Heine, Heinrich (1797–1856)
Poems of Heine, complete. Tr E. A. Bowring 1858.
Das Buch der Lieder. Hamburg 1827; Book of songs, tr C. G. Leland 1864; tr T. Brooksbank 1904.
Poems and ballads. Tr T. Martin 1878, 1894 (3rd edn).
Poems. Tr K. Freiligrath-Kroeker 1887.
Prose writings. Ed Havelock Ellis 1887. Includes Reisebilder, The romantic school, Religion and philosophy, Confessions etc.
Reisebilder. Hamburg 1826 etc; Pictures of travel, tr C. G. Leland, Philadelphia 1855; Travel pictures. tr F. Storr 1887; Pictures of travel, tr R. D. Gillman 1907.
Lyrics and ballads. Tr F. Hellman, New York 1892, 1895.
Works. Tr C. G. Leland, T. Brookshank and M. Armour, vols 1892–1905.
Poetical works. Tr J. Payne 1911.

'Eliot, George' (M. A. Evans). German wit: Heine. Westminster Rev new ser 9 1856.
Arnold, M. In his Essays in criticism, 1865.
Katscher, L. Englische Bücher über Heine und Schopenhauer. Magazin 90 1876.
Sharp, W. Life of Heine. 1888. With trns and criticism.
Winternitz, M. Heine in England. Zeit no 178 1900.

Melchior, F. Heines Verhältnis zu Lord Byron. Literarhistorische Forschungen no 27 1903.
Ochsenbein, W. Die Aufnahme Lord Byrons in Deutschland und sein Einfluss auf den jungen Heine. Berne 1905.
Hayens, K. Heine, Hazlitt and Mrs Jameson. MLR 17 1922.
Atkins, H. G. Heine. 1929. With bibliography, especially K. Kirby, Heine in English translation.
Hess, J. A. Heine's appraisal of John Bull. Modern Language Jnl 19 1934.
Black, G. A. James Thomson: his translations of Heine. MLR 31 1936.
Liptzin, S. Heine, Hellenist and cultural pessimist: a late Victorian legend. PQ 22 1943.
—— Heine and the early Victorians. Monatshefte für deutschen Unterricht 25 1943.
—— Heine, blackguard and apostate: a study of the earliest English attitude towards him. PMLA 58 1943.
—— Heine, the continuator of Goethe: a mid-Victorian legend. JEGP 43 1944.
Wormley, S. L. Heine in England. Chapel Hill 1943.
Haber, T. B. Heine and Housman. JEGP 43 1944.
Arnold, A. Heine in England and America: a bibliographical check-list. 1959.

Hoffmann, Ernst Theodor Amadeus (1776–1822)
Der goldene Topf. Bamberg 1814; The golden pot, tr T. Carlyle 1841.
Nachtstücke. Berlin 1817; Hoffmann's strange stories. tr Boston 1855; Weird tales, tr J. T. Bealby, New York 1885.
Die Serapionsbrüder. 4 vols Berlin 1819–21; Serapion brethren, tr A. Ewing 4 vols 1886–92.

Scott, Walter. E. T. A. Hoffmann. 1827.
Gudde, E. Hoffmann's reception in England. PMLA 41 1926.
Koziol, H. Hoffmanns Die Elixiere des Teufels und M. G. Lewis The Monk. Germanisch-romanische Monatsschrift 26 1938.

Hölderlin, Friedrich (1770–1843)
Burwick, F. L. Hölderlin and Arnold: Empedocles on Etna. Comparative Lit 17 1965.

Hofmannsthal, Hugo von (1874–1928)
Gilbert, M. E. Hofmannsthal and England. German Life & Letters 1 1937.
Howarth, H. Eliot and Hofmannsthal. South Atlantic Quart 59 1960. *See his* Notes on some figures behind T. S. Eliot, 1965.
Koziol, H. Zu Thomas Otways Venice preserved und Hofmannsthals Das gerettete Venedig. In Österreich und die angelsächsische Welt, ed H. Hietsch, Vienna and Stuttgart 1961.
Hamburger, M. Hofmannsthals Bibliothek: ein Bericht. Euphorion 55 1961.
—— Hofmannsthal and England. In Hofmannsthal: studies in commemoration, ed F. Norman 1963.
Pick, R. and A. C. Weaver. Hofmannsthal in England and Amerika: a bibliography. Ibid.

Kant, Immanuel (1724–1804)
Kritik der reinen Vernunft. Riga 1781. Critique of pure reason, tr F. Haywood 1838; tr J. M. D. Meiklejohn 1856; tr F. M. Muller 1881; tr N. K. Smith 1929.
Kritik der praktischen Vernunft. Riga 1788; Critique of practical; reason and other works on the theory of ethics, tr T. K. Abbott 1873, 1909 (6th edn).
Kritik der Urteilskraft. Berlin 1790; Critique of judgment, tr J. H. Bernard 1892; Critique of aesthetic judgment, tr J. C. Meredith, Oxford 1911.

Mahaffy, J. P. and J. H. Bernard. Kant's critical philosophy for English readers. 1872.
Duncan, J. M. English translations of Kant's writings. Kantstudien 2 1906.

Schmitt-Wendel, K. Kants Einfluss auf die englische Ethik. Berlin 1912.
Wellek, R. Kant in England 1793–1838. Princeton 1931.

Keller, Gottfried (1819–90)
Romeo und Julia auf dem Dorfe. 1856; A village Romeo and Juliet, tr H. T. and C. Porter 1897.
Kleider machen Leute. 1874; Clothes maketh man, tr K. F. Kroeker 1894. Includes The abused love-letters, Dietegen.

Kleist, Heinrich von (1777–1811)
Michael Kohlhaas. 1810; Michael Kohlhaas, tr J. Oxenford 1844.
Die Heilige Cäcilie oder die Gewalt der Musik. 1810; St Cecilia: or the power of music, tr J. Oxenford 1844.
Prinz Friedrich von Homburg. 1821; Prince Friedrich von Homburg, tr F. Lloyd and W. Newton in Prussia's representative man, 1875.

Peck, L. F. An adaptation of Kleist's Die Familie Schroffenstein. JEGP 44 1945. By M. G. Lewis.

Kotzebue, August (1761–1819)
For the many trns of Kotzebue's works, see B. Q. Morgan, col 115 above.
Koeppel, F. Kotzebue in England. E Studien 13 1891.
Sellier, W. Kotzebue in England. Leipzig 1901.
Süpfle, T. Kotzebue in Frankreich und England. Zeitschrift für Vergleichende Literaturgeschichte 6 1892.
Thompson, L. F. Kotzebue: a survey of his progress in France and England. Paris 1928.
Gosch, M. Translators of Kotzebue in England. Monatshefte für Deutschen Unterricht 31 1939.
Lindsay, D. W. Kotzebue in Scotland 1792–1813. Pbns of Eng Goethe Soc 33 1963.
Jacob, H. Kotzebues Werke in Übersetzungen. In his Studien zur neueren Literatur, Berlin 1964.

Ludwig, Otto (1812–65)
Lohre, H. Ludwig and Charles Dickens. Archiv 124 1910.

Nietzsche, Friedrich (1844–1900)
Complete works. Tr by several hands, ed O. Levy 18 vols 1909–13. This edn based on Works, ed and tr A. Tille, T. Common et al 6 vols New York 1896–9.

Ellis, H. Friedrich Nietzsche. Savoy nos 2–4 1896.
Orage, A. R. Nietzsche: the Dionysian spirit of the age. 1905.
Foerster-Nietzsche, E. Nietzsche in France and England. Open Court 34 1920.
Petzold, G. von. Nietzsche in englisch-amerikanischer Beurteilung bis zum Ausgang des Weltkrieges. Anglia 53 1929.
Hultsch, P. Das Denken Nietzsches in seiner Bedeutung für England. Germanisch-romanische Monatsschrift 26 1938.
Reichert, H. and K. Schlechta. International Nietzsche bibliography. North Carolina Stud in Comparative Lit 29 1960.
KcKenny, J. L. Nietzsche and the Frankenstein creature. Dalhousie Rev 41 1961.
Furness, R. Nietzsche's views on the English and his concept of a European community. German Life & Letters 17 1964.
Sandvoss, E. Nietzsches Kritik an den Angelsachsen. Zeitschrift für Religions- und Geistesgeschichte 17 1965.

'Novalis' (Friedrich Leopold, Freiherr von Hardenberg) (1772–1801)
His life, thoughts and works. Ed and tr M. J. Hope 1891.
Die Lehrlinge zu Sais. 1798; The disciples at Sais and other fragments, tr F.V.M.T. and U.C.B. 1903. Includes Spiritual hymns, Thoughts on philosophy, love and religion, Flower pollen.

Hymnen an die Nacht. Berlin 1800; Hymns and thoughts on religion, tr W. Hastie 1888. Includes Hymns to night, Spiritual songs, Thoughts on religion.
Heinrich von Ofterdingen. Berlin 1802; Henry of Ofterdingen, Cambridge Mass 1842.

Carlyle, T. Novalis. Foreign Rev 4 1829.

Raabe, Wilhelm (1831–1910)
Der Hungerpastor. Berlin 3 vols 1864; The hunger-pastor, tr 'Arnold' 1885.
Abu Telfan oder die Heimkehr vom Mondgebirge. Stuttgart 3 vols 1868; Abu Telfan: or the return from the mountains of the moon, tr S. Delffs 3 vols 1882.

Doernenburg, E. and N. Fehse. Raabe und Dickens. Magdeburg 1921.
Brill, E. V. K. Raabe's reception in England. German Life & Letters 8 1955.

Reuter, Fritz (1810–74)
Ut de Franzosentid. 1859; In the year '13: a tale of Mecklenburg life, tr C. L. Lewes, Leipzig 1867.
Ut mine Strombid, Wismar 1863; An old story of my farming-days, tr M. W. Macdowall, Leipzig 1878.

Geist, H. Reuters literarische Beziehungen zu Charles Dickens. Erfurt 1913.
Andrews, J. S. The reception of Fritz Reuter in Victorian England. MLR 56 1961.

Richter, Johann Paul Friedrich ('Jean Paul') (1763–1825)
Leben des Quintus Fixlein. Bayreuth 1796; Quintus Fixlein, tr T. Carlyle 1864.
Blumen-, Frucht- und Dornenstücke: oder Ehestand, Tod und Hochzeit des Armenadvokaten Fr. St. Siebenkäs. Bayreuth 1796–7; Flower, fruit and thorn pieces: or the married life, death and wedding of Firmian Siebenkäs, tr E. H. Noel 1845.
Levana oder Erziehungslehre. Brunswick 1807; Levana: or the doctrine of education, tr A. H. 1848.

Carlyle, T. Jean Paul Friedrich Richter. Edinburgh Rev 46 1830.
—— Jean Paul Friedrich Richter again. Foreign Rev 5 1830.
Schacht, F. E. Jean Paul im Lichte der englischen und amerikanischen Kritik des 19 Jahrhunderts. In Festgabe für Eduard Berend, ed H. W. Seiffert and B. Zeller, Weimar 1959.

Schiller, Johann Christoph Friedrich von (1759–1805)
Works, historical and dramatic. Tr various hands 1846–9, 1897–1903.
Minor poems. Tr J. H. Merivale 1844.
Poems. Tr E. A. Bowring 1851.
Die Räuber. Stuttgart 1781; The robbers, tr H. G. Bohn in Works, 1846–9.
Don Carlos. Leipzig 1787; tr R. D. Boylan in Works, 1846–9.
Wallenstein. Tübingen 1800; tr S. T. Coleridge 1800 (omits Lager); tr J. A. W. Hunter 1885; tr T. Martin (Lager only), Blackwood's Mag Feb 1892.
Maria Stuart. Tübingen 1801; tr J. C. Mellish 1801.
Wilhelm Tell. Stuttgart 1804; tr S. Robinson 1825; tr T. Martin in Works, 1846–9.
J. S. Knowles. William Tell. 1856. Written 1825.

Carlyle, T. Schiller's life and writings. London Mag 1823–4; 1825 (as The life of Schiller).
—— Schiller. Fraser's Mag March 1831.
—— Schiller, Goethe and Madame de Staël, and Goethe's portrait. Fraser's Mag May 1832.
Machule, P. Coleridges Wallensteinübersetzung. E Studien 31 1902.
Kipka, K. Schillers Maria Stuart im Auslande. Studien zur Vergleichenden Literaturgeschichte 5 1905.
Roscher, H. F. G. Die Wallensteinübersetzung von Samuel T. Coleridge. Leipzig 1905.
Rea, T. Schiller's dramas and poems in England. 1906.
Smith, H. Two English translations of Schiller's Wallenstein. MLR 9 1914.
Cooke, M. W. Schiller's Robbers in England. MLR 11 1915.
Willoughby, L. A. English translation and adaptations of Schiller's Robbers. MLR 16 1921.
—— Schiller's Kabale und Liebe in English translation. Pbns of Eng Goethe Soc new ser 1 1924.
—— Schiller in England and Germany. Pbns of Eng Goethe Soc 12 1935.
Dummer, E. H. Schiller in English. Monatshefte für Deutschen Unterricht 35 1943.
Wilkinson, E. M. Zur Sprache und Struktur der ästhetischen Briefe: Betrachtungen beim Abschluss einer mühevoll verfertigten Übersetzung ins Englische. Akzente 6 1959.
Witte, W. Schiller and Burns and other essays. Oxford 1959.
—— Das neue Schillerbild der britischen Germanistik. Jahrbuch der Schiller-Gesellschaft 5 1961.
Pick, R. (ed). Schiller in England 1787–1960: a bibliography. 1961.
Knepler, H. W. Schiller's Maria Stuart on the stage in England and America. In Anglo-German and American-German crosscurrents vol 2, ed P. A. Shelley and A. O. Lewis jr, Chapel Hill 1962.

Schlegel, August Wilhelm von (1767–1845)
Über dramatische Kunst und Literatur. 3 vols Heidelberg 1809–11; Lectures on dramatic art and literature, tr J. Black 1815; A. W. Schlegel's lectures on German literature from Gottsched to Goethe, taken down by G. Toynbee in 1833, ed H. G. Fiedler, Oxford 1944. Toynbee pbd a trn of his notes in 1838.

Herzfeld, G. August Wilhelm Schlegel in seinen Beziehungen zu englischen Dichtern und Kritikern. Archiv 138 1920.
Schnöckelborg, G. August Wilhelm von Schlegels Einfluss auf William Hazlitt als Shakespeare-Kritiker. Münster 1931.
Schirmer, W. F. A. W. Schlegel und England. Jahrbuch der Shakespeare-Gesellschaft 75 1939.

Schlegel, Friedrich von (1772–1829)
Vorlesungen über die neuere Geschichte. Vienna 1811; A course of lectures on modern history, tr L. Purcell and R. H. Whitelock 1849.
Geschichte der alten und neueren Literatur. Vienna 1815; Lectures on the history of literature ancient and modern, tr J. G. Lockhart, Edinburgh 1818.
Philosophie des Lebens. 1828; The philosophy of life and philosophy of language, tr A. J. W. Morrison 1847.
Philosphie der Geschichte. 1829; The philosophy of history, tr J. B. Robertson 1835.

Schnitzler, Arthur (1862–1931)
Anatol. 1893; Anatol: a sequence of dialogues paraphrased by Granville Barker. 1911.
Most of Schnitzler's works have been tr into English, and have for the greater part appeared in anthologies; see B. Q. Morgan, col 115 above.

Schopenhauer, Arthur (1788–1860)
Die Welt als Wille und Vorstellung. Leipzig 1818; The world as will and idea, tr R. B. Haldane and J. Kemp 4 vols 1883–6.

Goodale, R. H. Schopenhauer and pessimism in nineteenth-century English literature. PMLA 47 1932.

Stifter, Adalbert (1805–68)
Rural life in Austria and Hungary. Tr M. Norman 1850. Includes My great-grandfather's notebook, Abdias

the Jew, The Hochwald, Crazy castle, Maroshely, The village on the heath.
Pictures of life. Tr M. Howitt 1852. Includes Angela, The castle of fools, The village on the heath.

Andrews, J. S. The reception of Stifter in nineteenth-century Britain. MLR 53 1958.
Reichart, W. A. and W. H. Grilk. Stifters Werk in Amerika und England: a bibliography. Adalbert-Stifter-Institut des Landes Österreich 9 1960. Suppl by E. Eisenmeier, ibid.

Storm, Theodor (1817–88)
Immensee. 1849; Immensee; or the old man's reverie, tr H. Clark, Münster 1863; Immen lake, tr M. Briton 1881.

Andrews, J. S. Immensee and Victorian England. MLR 54 1959.

Strauss, David Friedrich (1808–74)
Das Leben Jesu. Tübingen 1835; The life of Jesus, tr 'George Eliot' 1846.

Das Leben Jesu von Strauss in England und Frankreich. Blätter zur Kunde der Litteratur des Auslands 4 1839.

Sudermann, Hermann (1857–1928)
Frau Sorge. Berlin 1886; Dame Care, tr Bertha Overbeck, New York 1891.
Heimat. Stuttgart 1892.
Magda. Tr C. E. A. Winslow, New York 1896.

Suttner, Bertha von (1843–1914)
Die Waffen nieder! Dresden 1889; Lay down your arms, tr T. Holmes 1892, 1906.

Tieck, Ludwig (1773–1853)
Phantasus. 3 vols Berlin 1812–16.
Tales from the Phantasus. Tr J. C. Hare, J. A. Froude et al 1845.

Lüdeke, H. Tieck und das alte englische Theater. Frankfurt 1922.
Zeydel, E. H. Tieck and England. Princeton 1931.
— Tieck as a translator of English. PMLA 51 1936.

Varnhagen von Ense, Karl August (1785–1858)
Carlyle, T. Varnhagen von Ense's Memoirs. Westminster Rev 32 1838.
— Briefwechsel mit Varnhagen von Ense. Ed R. Preuss, Berlin 1892.
Fischer, W. Die Briefe R. Monckton Milnes an Varnhagen von Ense 1844–54. Heidelberg 1922.

Wagner, Wilhelm Richard (1813–83)
Heydet, X. Wagner et Bernard Shaw. Revue de l'Enseignement des Langues Vivantes 1937
Moser, M. Wagner in der englischen Literatur des 19 Jahrhunderts. Berne 1938.

Werner, Zacharias (1768–1823)
Carlyle, T. Life and writings of Werner. Foreign Rev 1 1828.

Wyss, J. D. (1743–1818) and J. R. Wyss (1782–1830)
Der schweizerische Robinson. 2 vols Zürich 1812–13. Many trns in England and America.

Zedlitz, Joseph Christian, Freiherr von (1790–1862)
Totenkränze, Vienna 1828; Poems, tr L. Dick 1843.

Spink, G. W. J. C. von Zedlitz and Byron. MLR 26 1931.

Zschokke, Heinrich (1771–1848)
Abällino der grosse Bandit. Frankfurt 1793 (as a novel), 1795 (as a play); Abaellino the great bandit, tr W. Dunlop, New York 1802; The bravo of Venice, tr M. G. Lewis 1805.

Among the more popular German writers of the century whose works have been widely read in English trn are: Bertha Behrens ('W. Heimburg'), W. Busch (Max und Moritz, 1865) F. W. Carové, Elizabeth, Queen of Roumania ('Carmen Sylva'), G. Ebers, Ernst Eckstein, F. Gerstäcker, Ida Hahn-Hahn, F. Hoffmann, H. Hoffmann (Struwelpeter, 1847), A. H. Lafontaine, G. von Moser, Klara Mundt ('Luise Mühlbach'), G. Nieritz, M. Nordau, Ida Pfeiffer, C. von Schmidt, Lola Kirschner ('Ossip Schubin'), K. A. Postl ('Charles Sealsfield'), F. Spielhagen, Johann Spyri, J. Stinde (Die Familie Buchholz, 1884).

English Authors

Arnold, Matthew
Preisinger, H. Arnold on Goethe. Trans Manchester Goethe Soc 1894.
White, H. C. Arnold and Goethe. PMLA 36 1921.
Orrick, J. B. Arnold and Goethe. Pbns of Eng Goethe Soc new ser 4 1927.
Sells, I. E. Marguerite. MLR 38 1943.

Bailey, Philip James
Black, J. A. Bailey's debt to Goethe's Faust. MLR 28 1933.

Beddoes, Thomas Lovell
Donner, H. W. Echoes of Beddoesian rambles: Edgeworthstown to Zürich. Studia Neophilologica 33 1961.
— Beddoes to Leonhard Tobler: eight German letters. Studia Neophilologica 35 1963.

Browning, Robert
Rhyme, O. P. Browning and Goethe. MLN 44 1929.
Buck, G. Das Nachleben Brownings in Kritik und Forschung. Germanisch-romanische Monatsschrift 21 1933.
Schneider, F. Browning's The ring and the book and Wassermann's Der Fall Maurizius. MLN 48 1933.

Byron, George Gordon, Baron
Flaischlen, C. Lord Byron in Deutschland. Centralblatt für Bibliothekswesen 7–8 1890–1.
Ackermann, R. Sein Leben, seine Werke, sein Einfluss auf die deutsche Litteratur. Heidelberg 1901.
Eimer, M. Byron and Ch.D. Grabbe. Frankfurter Zeitung 15 Jan 1903.
— Byrons Beziehungen zur deutschen Kultur. Anglia 36 1912.
Holzhausen, P. Lord Byron und seine deutschen Biographen. Beilage zur Allgemeinen Zeitung nos 174–5 1903.
Leitzmann, A. Aus der Frühzeit der Byron-Eindeutschung: Knebel als Übersetzer Byrons. Viermonatsschrift der Goethe-Gesellschaft 4 1940.
Straumann, H. Byron and Switzerland. Nottingham 1949.
Korninger, S. Lord Byron und Nikolaus Lenau. Eng Miscellany (Rome) 3 1952.
Dowden, W. S. Byron through Austrian eyes. In Anglo-German and American-German crosscurrents vol 2, ed P. A. Shelley and A. O. Lewis, Chapel Hill 1962.

Carlyle, Thomas. *See under General Studies, cols 115–16, above.*
Streuli, W. Carlyle als Vermittler deutscher Literatur und deutschen Geistes. Zürich 1895.
Kräger, H. Carlyles Stellung zur deutschen Sprache und Literatur. Anglia 22 1899.
Küchler, F. Carlyle und Schiller. Leipzig 1902. *See* Anglia 26 1903.
Pape, H. Jean Paul als Quelle von Carlyles Anschauung und Stil. Rostock 1904.
Blankenagel, J. C. Carlyle as a critic of Grillparzer. PMLA 42 1927.
Harrold, C. F. Carlyle's interpretation of Kant. PQ 27 1928.
— Carlyle and Novalis. SP 27 1930.
— Carlyle and German thought 1819–34. New Haven 1934.
Storrs, M. The relation of Carlyle to Kant and Fichte. Bryn Mawr 1929.

Lotter, K. Carlyle und die deutsche Romantik. Nuremberg 1932.
Shine, H. Carlyle and the German philosophy problem during the year 1826–7. PMLA 50 1935.
— Carlyle's early writings and Herder's Ideen: the concept of history. In Booker Memorial studies, ed H. Shine, Chapel Hill 1950.
Plagens, H. Carlyles Weg zu Goethe. Berlin 1938.
Brooks, R. A. E. (ed). Carlyle: journey to Germany, autumn 1848. New Haven 1940.
Brie, F. Carlyle und Goethes Symbolum. Anglia 66 1942.
Carr, C. T. Carlyle's translations from German. MLR 42 1947.
Fiedler, H. G. The friendship of Carlyle and Varnhagen von Ense. MLR 38 1943.
Cooper, B. A comparison of Quintus Fixlein and Sartor Resartus. Trans of Wisconsin Acad of Sciences, Arts & Letters 48 1959.
Metzger, L. Sartor Resartus: a Victorian Faust. Comparative Lit 13 1961.
Plard, H. Le Sartor Resartus de Carlyle et Jean Paul. Etudes Germaniques 18 1963.
Smeed, J. W. Carlyle and Jean Paul Richter. Comparative Lit 16 1964.
Krohn, M. Carlyle: Friedrich der Grosse-Schlesien. Jahrbuch der Schlesischen Friedrich-Wilhelm-Universität zu Breslau 10 1965.

Coleridge, Samuel Taylor

Ferrier, J. F. The plagiarisms of Coleridge. Blackwood's Mag March 1840.
Haney, J. L. The German influence on Coleridge. Philadelphia 1903.
Helmholtz, A. A. The indebtedness of Coleridge to A. W. Schlegel. Madison 1907.
Pizzo, E. Coleridge als Kritiker. Anglia 28 1916.
Richter, H. Die philosophische Weltanschauung von Coleridge und ihr Verhältnis zur deutschen Philosophie. Anglia 32 1920.
Dunstan, A. C. The German influence on Coleridge. MLR 17–18 1922–3. On Schiller, Goethe, Herder, Schlegel, Schelling.
Winkelmann, E. Coleridge und die Kantische Philosophie. Leipzig 1933.
Wolff, L. Coleridge et l'Allemagne. Revue Anglo-américaine 11 1933.
Willoughby, L. A. Coleridge and his German contemporaries. Pbns of Eng Goethe Soc new ser 12 1935.
Lovejoy, A. O. Coleridge and Kant's two worlds. ELH 7 1940; rptd in his Essays in the history of ideas, Baltimore 1948.
Beach, J. W. Coleridge's borrowings from the German. ELH 9 1942.
Brinkley, R. F. Some unpublished Coleridge marginalia: Richter and Reimarus. JEGP 44 1945.
Benzinger, J. Organic unity: Leibniz to Coleridge. PMLA 66 1951. On Leibniz, Schlegel and Coleridge.
Stahl, E. L. Zur Theorie der Dichtung bei Coleridge im Hinblick auf Goethe. In Festschrift für Fritz Strich, Berne 1952.
Wells, G. A. Man and nature: an elucidation of Coleridge's rejection of Herder's thought. JEGP 51 1952.
Schrickx, W. Coleridge and Friedrich Heinrich Jacobi. Revue Belge de Philologie et d'Histoire 36 1958.
— Coleridge's marginalia in Kant's Metaphysische Anfangsgründe der Naturwissenschaft. Studia Germanica 1 1959.
Wilkinson, E. M. Coleridge und Deutschland 1794–1804; zum ersten Band der Gesamtausgabe seiner Notebooks. In Forschungsprobleme der vergleichenden Literaturgeschichte ser 2, ed F. Ernst and K. Wais, Tübingen 1958.

Greiner, W. Deutsche Einflüsse auf die Dichtungstheorie von Coleridge. Die Neueren Sprachen Aug 1960.
Orsini, G. N. G. Coleridge and Schlegel reconsidered. Comparative Lit 16 1964.

Davidson, John

Petzold, G. von. Davidson und sein geistiges Werden unter dem Einfluss Nietzsches. Leipzig 1928.

Dickens, Charles

Schmidt, J. Bilder aus dem geistigen Leben unserer Zeit. Vols 2, 4, Leipzig 1870–5.
Weizmann, L. Dickens und Daudet in deutscher Übersetzung. Berlin 1880.
Gummer, E. N. Dickens and Germany. MLR 33 1938.
— Dickens's works in Germany 1837–1937. New York 1940.
Hennig, J. Note on Dickens and Goethe. Comparative Lit Stud 23–4 1946.
Thalmann, L. Charles Dickens in seinen Beziehungen zum Ausland. 1956.
Spilka, M. Dickens and Kafka: a mutual interpretation. Bloomington 1963.

'Eliot, George' (Mary Ann Cross, b. Evans)

Conrad, H. George Eliot über die deutsche Literatur. Gegenwart 15 1886.
Pfeiffer, S. George Eliots Beziehungen zu Deutschland. Heidelberg 1925.
Simon-Baumann, L. George Eliot über Heinrich Heine. Anglia 55 1931.

Gissing, George Robert

Francis, C. J. Gissing and Schopenhauer. Nineteenth-Century Fiction 15 1961.
Young, A. C. (ed). The letters of Gissing to Eduard Bertz 1887–1903. London and New Brunswick 1961.

Hardy, Thomas

Steinbach, A. Hardy und Schopenhauer. In Anglica, A. Brandl überreicht vol 2, Leipzig 1925.
Muchnic, H. Hardy and Thomas Mann. Northampton Mass 1939.
Osawa, M. Hardy and the German men of letters. Stud in Eng Lit (Tokyo) 19 1939.

Hopkins, Gerard Manley

Zinnhobler, R. Die Aufnahme des dichterischen Werkes von Hopkins im deutschen Sprachraum. Jahresbuch des Collegium Petrinum 1963–4.

Keats, John

Green, D. B. Keats and Schiller. MLN 66 1951.
de Mann, P. Keats and Hölderlin. Comparative Lit 8 1956.
Bonarius, G. Zum magischen Realismus bei Keats und Novalis. Giessen 1960.

Kingsley, Charles

Jacobsen, A. Kingsleys Beziehungen zu Deutschland. Heidelberg 1917.

Bulwer-Lytton, Edward George Earle Lytton (Baron Lytton)

Schmidt, J. Bilder aus dem geistigen Leben unserer Zeit. Vol 1, Leipzig 1870.
Goldhan, A. H. Über die Einwirkung des Goetheschen Werther und Wilhelm Meister auf die Entwicklung Edward Bulwers. Leipzig 1895.

Meredith, George

Dick, E. Deutschland und die Deutschen bei Meredith. Germanisch-romanische Monatsschrift 6 1914.
Lees, J. Meredith's literary relations with Germany. MLR 12 1917.
Krusemeyer, M. Der Einfluss Goethes auf Meredith. E Studien 59 1925.
Brewer, E. V. The influence of Jean Paul Richter on Meredith's conception of the comic. JEGP 29 1930.
Downs, B. W. Meredith and Fontane. German Life & Letters 2 1938.
Petter, G. B. Meredith and his German critics. 1939.

Stone, J. Meredith and Goethe. UTQ 21 1952.
Green, D. B. Meredith's Austrian poets: a newly identified review essay with translations. MLR 54 1959.

Moore, George
Blisset, W. F. Moore and literary Wagnerism. Comparative Lit 13 1961.

Quincey, Thomas de
Christoph, F. Über den Einfluss Jean Paul Fr. Richters auf De Quincey. Hof 1899.
Dunn, W. A. De Quincey's relation to German literature and philosophy. Strasbourg 1901.
Michelsen, P. De Quincey und die Kantische Philosophie. Revue de Littérature Comparée 33 1959.
—— De Quincey und Jean Paul. JEGP 61 1962.
—— De Quincey und Goethe. Euphorism 50 1956.
—— De Quincey und Schiller. German Life & Letters 9 1956.

Robinson, Henry Crabb
Sadler, T. (ed). Diary, reminiscences and correspondence. 1869.
Morley, E. J. Crabb Robinson in Germany 1800–5. Oxford 1929.
Norman, F. Crabb Robinson and Goethe. Pbns of Eng Goethe Soc new ser 4 1927.
Schulte, E. Crabb Robinson, Goethe e l'Hyperion di Keats. Annali Instituto Universitario Orientale (Naples), Sezione Germanica 6 1963.
Marquardt, H. Crabb Robinson und seine deutschen Freunde. Vol 1, Göttingen 1964.

Rossetti, Dante Gabriel
Willoughby, L. A. Rossetti and German literature. 1912.

Scott, Sir Walter
Gillies, R. P. Recollections of Scott. 1837.
Schmidt, J. Bilder aus dem geistigen Leben unserer Zeit. Vol 1, Leipzig 1870.
Blumenhagen, K. Scott als Übersetzer. Rostock 1900.
Freyl, W. The influence of 'Gothic' literature on Scott. Rostock 1902.
Roesel, L. K. Die literarischen und persönlichen Beziehungen Scotts zu Goethe. Leipzig 1902.
Hohlfeld, A. R. Scott als Übersetzer. Studien zur Vergleichenden Literaturgeschichte 3 1903.
Korff, H. A. Scott und Alexis. Heidelberg 1907.
Kohler, H. F. Walladmor von W. Alexis. Marburg 1915. On the influence of Scott.
MacIntosh, W. Scott and Goethe: German influence on the writings of Scott. Glasgow 1924.
Koch, J. Scotts Beziehungen zu Deutschland. Germanisch-romanische Monatsschrift 15 1927.
Bachmann, F. W. Some German imitators of Scott. Chicago 1933.
Mennie, D. Scott's unpublished translations of German plays. MLR 33 1938.

Ochojski, P. M. Scott's continuous interest in Germany. Stud in Scottish Lit (Texas) 3 1966.

Shelley, Percy Bysshe
Imelmann, R. Shelleys Alastor und Goethe. Zeitschrift für vergleichende Literaturgeschichte 17 1909.
Liptzin, S. Shelley in Germany. New York 1924.
Hess, A. Shelleys Lyrik in deutschen Übertragungen. Zürich 1949.
Steiner, F. Shelley and Goethe's Faust. Rivista di Letterature Moderne 4 1951.

Smith, Adam
Erämetsä, E. Adam Smith als Mittler englisch-deutscher Spracheinflüsse (The Wealth of Nations). Annalis Academiae Scientiarum Fennicae (Helsinki) ser B 1961.

Swinburne, Algernon Charles
Just, K. G. Die Rezeption Swinburnes in der deutschen Literatur der Jahrhundertwende. In Festschrift für Jost Trier, ed W. Foerste and K. H. Borck, Cologne 1964.

Tennyson, Alfred, Baron
Schmitt, K. Tennyson in Deutschland. Deutsches Museum 3 1853.
Asher, D. Lord Tennyson and Goethe. Pbns of Eng Goethe Soc 4 1890.
Meyer, W. Tennysons Jugendgedichte in deutscher Übersetzung. Münster 1914.

Thackeray, William Makepeace
Vulpius, W. Thackeray in Weimar. Century Mag 53 1897.
Kurrelmeyer, W. Thackeray and Friedrich von Heyde. MLN 48 1933.

Wilde, Oscar
Meyerfeld, M. Wilde in Deutschland. Das Literarische Echo 1 Jan 1903.
Sherard, R. H. Life of Wilde. 1911. With bibliography.
Oswald, V. A. Wilde, Stefan George, Heliogabalus. MLQ 10 1940.

Wordsworth, William
Herzberg, M. J. Wordsworth and German literature. PMLA 40 1925.
Stallknecht, N. P. Wordsworth's Ode to duty and the Schöne Seele. PMLA 52 1937.
Hartmann, H. Wordsworth's Lapland night. RES 14 1938.
Willoughby, L. A. Wordsworth and Germany. In German Studies presented to H. G. Fielder, Oxford 1938.
Todd, F. M. Wordsworth in Germany. MLR 47 1952.
Hirsch, E. D. jr. Wordsworth and Schelling: a typological study of Romanticism. New Haven 1960.
de Mann, P. The imagery of heaven and earth in Wordsworth and Hölderlin. MLA Program 1964.

F. K.

(5) ITALIAN

Annual lists are pbd in Italian Studies (Manchester) *and in* Rivista di Letterature Moderne e Comparate (Florence).

General Studies

Italy

For a full list of travel books see C. P. Brand, A bibliography of travel books describing Italy 1800–50, Italian Stud 11 1956. *Others, pbd in the second half of the century, can be found in* S. S. Lodovici, Bibliografia di viaggiatori stranieri in Italia nel secolo XIX, Rome 1938. *On the Risorgimento see Rudman, col 135 below.*

Rogers, S. Italy: a poem. 2 pts 1822–8.
Trollope, F. A visit to Italy. 1842.
Shelley, M. Rambles in Germany and Italy in 1840, 1842 and 1843. 2 vols 1844.
Dickens, C. Pictures from Italy. 1846.
Ruskin, J. Stones of Venice. 3 vols 1851.
Arnold, M. England and the Italian question. 1859.
Corelli, M. Vendetta. 3 vols 1886.
Butler, S. Alps and sanctuaries of Piedmont and the canton Ticino. 1881.
Crawford, F. M. Saracinesca. 3 vols 1887.
—— Sant'Ilario. 1889.
—— Don Orsino. 3 vols 1892. Also many other novels describing Italy, pbd 1883–1900.
Gissing, G. R. By the Ionian sea: notes of a ramble in southern Italy. 1901.

Schuyler, E. Landor and Italy; Dickens in Genoa; Mrs Browning. In his Italian influences, New York 1901.
Wollaston, G. H. The Englishman in Italy. Oxford 1909

Bräm, E. M. Die italienische Renaissance in dem englischen Geistesleben des 19 Jahrhunderts. Zürich 1932. On Ruskin, Symonds and Lee.
Marshall, R. Italy in English literature 1755–1815. New York 1934.
Rudman, H. W. Italian nationalism and English letters. 1940. With full bibliography on the Risorgimento.
Viglione, F. L'Italia nel pensiero degli scrittori inglesi. Milan 1947.
Branchi, E. C. Escursioni letterarie da Londra a Firenze: le fonti italiane della letteratura inglese. Santiago de Chile 1949.
Lloyd, M. Italy and the nostalgia of Gissing. Eng Miscellany (Rome) 2 1951.
Brand, C. P. Italy and the English Romantics. Cambridge 1957.
Hale, J. R. (ed). The Italian journals of Samuel Rogers, with an account of Rogers' life and travel in Italy in 1814–21. 1956.
— Charles Lever and Italy. Eng Miscellany (Rome) 10 1959.
Giddey, E. Samuel Rogers et son poème Italie. Geneva 1959.
Rebora, P. Interpretazioni anglo-italiane. Bari 1961.
Barrows, H. Convention and novelty in the romantic generation's experience of Italy. BNYPL June 1963.
Vita-Finzi, C. Butler and Italy. Italian Stud 18 1963.
Kroeber, K. The artifice of reality. Madison 1964. On Wordsworth, Foscolo, Keats and Leopardi.

English and Italian Literature

For a selected list of works pbd 1800–50 commenting on Italian authors, and a full list of anthologies of Italian literature pbd in 1800–40, see C. P. Brand, above.

Simonde de Sismondi, J. C. L. La littérature du midi de l'Europe. 4 vols Geneva 1818; Historical view of the literature of the south of Europe, tr T. Roscoe 1823.
Roscoe, T. The Italian novelists. Vol 4, 1825.
Lardner, D. Eminent literary and scientific men of Italy, Spain and Portugal. Vol 2, 1837. On Alfieri, Monti, Foscolo.
Merivale, L. A. I poeti italiani moderni. 1865. A selection, with biographical essays, including Alfieri, Monti, Foscolo, Manzoni, Leopardi.
Segrè, C. Lady Holland e i suoi ospiti italiani. In his Relazioni letterarie fra Italia e Inghilterra, Florence 1911.
Gay, H. N. John Keats e gli inglesi a Roma. Nuova Antologia 1 July 1912.
Olivero, F. Saggi di letteratura inglese. Bari 1913. On Wordsworth, Coleridge, Hunt, Shelley, Keats and Italian.
— Studi su poeti e prosatori inglesi. Turin 1925. On Coleridge, Carlyle, Ruskin, Thompson, Morris and Italy.
Benedetti, A. Correnti italiane nella poesia di Keats. Nuova Antologia 16 Feb 1921.
King, R. W. Italian influence on English scholarship and literature during the romantic revival. MLR 20–1 1925–6.
Faggi, A. Swinburne aedo d'Italia. Marzocco May 1926.
Raya, P. N. Italian influences on the poetry of Tennyson. Benares 1936.
Wicks, M. C. W. The Italian exiles in London 1816–48. Manchester 1937.
Rossi, J. I critici inglesi e americani del De Sanctis. Italica 15 1938.
Gabrieli, V. Presentazione italiana di Butler. Civiltà Moderna 12 1940.
Fisch, M. H. The Coleridges, Dr Prati and Vico. MP 41 1943.
Bandy, W. T. Macaulay and his Italian translator. Italica 25 1948.
Sells, A. L. Zanella, Coleridge and Shelley. Comparative Lit 2 1950.
Cline, C. L. Byron, Shelley and their Pisan circle. 1952.
Barksdale, R. K. Arnold and Tennyson on Etna. College Lang Assoc Jnl 2 1958.
Brand, C. P. Italians in England 1800–50: a bibliography of their publications. Italian Stud 15 1960.
Watson, G. The English Petrarchans: a critical bibliography of the Canzoniere. 1967 (Warburg Inst).

Italian Authors

Alfieri, Vittorio (1749–1803)
Tragedie. Paris 1787–9; The tragedies of Alfieri, tr C. Lloyd 3 vols 1815. Contains Philip, Polinices, Antigone, Virginia, Agamemnon, Orestes, Rosamunda, Octavia, Timoleon, Merope, Mary Stuart, The conspiracy of the Pazzi, Don Garcia, Saul, Agis, Sophonisba, The first Brutus, Myrrha, The second Brutus.

Byron, Lord. Marino Faliero. 1821.
— The two Foscari. 1821.
— Sardanapalus. 1821.
Swinburne, A. C. Marino Faliero. 1885.

Krause, F. Byrons Marino Faliero: ein Beitrag zur vergleichenden Literaturgeschichte. Breslau 1897.
Pudbres, A. Lord Byron, admirer and imitator of Alfieri. E Studien 33 1903.
Zanco, A. L'Alfierismo del Byron. Rivista Italiana del Dramma 5 1941.
Vincent, E. R. L'amore londinese di Vittorio Alfieri. Rassegna della Letteratura Italiana 61 1957.

Boccaccio, Giovanni (1313–75). *See under Symonds, col 140 below.*
[Moore, T.] The spirit of Boccaccio's Decameron. 1812. *See* H. G. Wright, Moore as the author of The spirit of Boccaccio's Decameron, RES 23 1947.
Keats, J. Isabella: or the pot of basil. 1818.
'Eliot, George' (M. A. Evans). How Lisa loved the King. Boston 1869.

Wright, H. G. Boccaccio in England from Chaucer to Tennyson. 1957.
Viviani, E. della R. Shelley e Boccaccio. Italica 35 1959.

Carducci, Giosuè (1835–1907). *See under Byron, col 139 below.*
Poems. Tr with introductory essays by F. Sewall. 1893. A selection.

Scalia, S. E. Carducci et la critique anglo-saxonne. Revue de Littérature Comparée 15 1935.
— Carducci: his critics and translators in England and America 1881–1932. New York 1937.
Ferretti, L. Carducci e la letteratura inglese. Milan 1927.

Casti, Giovanni Battista (1721–1803)
Gli animali parlanti. Paris 1802; The court of beasts, [tr W. S. Rose] 1816.
Novelle. Paris 1801; The origin of Rome and of the Papacy, tr D. Whistlecraft 1861.
Li tre Giuli. Naples 1814; The tre Giuli, tr with a memoir of the author 1826.

Fuess, C. M. Lord Byron as a satirist in verse. New York 1912.

Dante Alighieri (1265–1321). *See under Byron, col 138 below.*
Canzionere. Tr C. Lyell 1845.
La divina commedia. Hell, purgatory and paradise, tr H. F. Cary 3 vols 1814, 1819, 1831, 1844, 1850, 1867,

1868, 1869, 1871, 1876, 1883, 1889, 1892, 1894, 1900; tr I. C. Wright 3 vols 1833–40; tr P. Bannerman, Edinburgh 1850; tr E. C. O'Donnell 1845; tr C. B. Cayley 4 vols 1851–55; tr F. Pollock 1854; tr H. W. Longfellow 3 vols 1867, 1886, 1890, 1891; tr D. Johnston 3 vols Bath 1867–8; tr J. I. Minchin 1885; tr F. K. H. Haselfoot 1887; tr C. E. Norton 3 vols 1891–2, 1899; tr A. J. Butler 1880–92. *For a full list see* C. F. Cunningham, The divine comedy in English: a critical bibliography 1782–1900, Edinburgh 1965.

Church, R. W. Dante. Christian Remembrancer 11 1850.
Dobelli, A. Dante e Byron. Giornale Dantesco 6 1898.
Valgimigli, A. Il culto di Dante in Inghilterra. Ibid.
Toynbee, P. Dante in English literature from Chaucer to Cary 1380–1844. Vol 2, 1909. An anthology.
Galimberti, A. Dante nel pensiero inglese. Florence 1921.
Newman, F. M. The Francesca da Rimini episode in English literature. Cambridge Mass 1942.
Friederich, W. P. Dante's fame abroad 1350–1850. Rome 1950. With complete bibliography.
Doughty, O. Dante and the English Romantics. Eng Miscellany (Rome) 2 1951.
Gittings, R. Keat's debt to Dante. In his Mask of Keats, 1956.
Saly, J. Keats's answer to Dante: The fall of Hyperion. Keats-Shelley Jnl 14 1965.

Foscolo, Ugo (1778–1827)
Ultime lettere di Jacopo Ortis. Milan 1802; Letters of Ortis, tr F. B. 1818.
Essays on Petrarch. 1821, 1823.

Viglione, F. Foscolo in Inghilterra, Catania 1910.
Cortese, C. Foscolo e l'Inghilterra. Naples 1935.
Vincent, E. R. Byron, Hobhouse and Foscolo. Cambridge 1949.
— Foscolo and John Allen: unpublished letters. Italian Stud 4 1949.
— Foscolo: an Italian in Regency England. Cambridge 1953. With list of Foscolo's London pbns.
— Overhearing Foscolo. Eng Miscellany (Rome) 7 1956.
Wilkins, E. H. Samuel Carter Hall on Foscolo. Romanic Rev 41 1950.
Limentani, U. Testimonianze inglesi sul Foscolo. Giornale Storico della Letteratura Italiana 3 1956.
Fasano, P. L' 'amicizia' Foscolo—Sterne e la traduzione didimea del Sentimental journey. Eng Miscellany (Rome) 14 1963.

Goldoni, Carlo (1707–93)
La gelosia di Lindoro; Un curioso accidente. In New British theatre vols 1, 3 (as The word of honour; Love, honour and interest).
Un curioso accidente; Il burbero benefico; Il ventaglio; l'avaro fastoso. The comedies of Carlo Goldoni, ed H. Zimmern 1892 (as A curious mishap; The beneficent bear; The fan; The spendthrift miser).

Maddalena, E. Goldoni in Inghilterra e in America. Rivista d'Italia 15 Sept 1923.

Leopardi, Giacomo (1798–1827). *See under Shelley, col 140 below.*
Operette morali. Milan 1826; Pensieri, Milan 1827; Essays and dialogues, tr C. Edwardes 1882; Essays, dialogues and thoughts, tr P. Maxwell 1893; tr J. Thomson ('B.V.') 1905.
Versi. Bologna 1824, Florence 1831; The poems of Leopardi, tr F. H. Cliffe 1893; tr J. M. Morrison 1900; tr T. Martin 1904.

Marchesi, G. Leopardi e la poesia inglese. Iride 3 1899.
Bickersteth, G. L. Leopardi and Wordsworth. 1927.
Olivero, F. La letteratura inglese nei Pensieri di varia filosofia. In his Studi britannici, Turin 1931. Mainly on Byron.
Cotten, L. A. Leopardi and the City of dreadful night. SP 42 1945.
Rhodes, D. E. The composition of Mr Gladstone's essay on Leopardi. Italian Stud 8 1953.
Singh, H. A. E. Housman and Leopardi. Eng Miscellany (Rome) 13 1962.
— Hardy and Leopardi: a study of affinity and contrast. Rivista di Letterature Moderne e Comparate 17 1964.
Corrigan, B. The poetry of Leopardi in Victorian England 1837–78. Eng Miscellany (Rome) 14 1963.

Manzoni, Alessandro (1785–1873). *See under Scott, col 140 below.*
I promessi sposi. 3 vols Milan 1825–6 (for 1827), 1840–2 (rev); The betrothed lovers, tr C. Swan 3 vols Pisa 1828; The betrothed, 1834, 1844, 1845 etc. 1845 alone based on Manzoni's text of 1840–2.

Franzi, T. Promessi sposi giudicati dal primo traduttore inglese. Marzocco 25 Sept 1932.
Neri, N. La fortuna del Manzoni in Inghilterra. Atti della Academia delle Scienze di Torino 74 1939.

Mazzini, Giuseppe (1805?–72)
King, H. E. H. The disciples. 1873.

Galimberti, A. Mazzini nel pensiero inglese. Nuova Antologia 1 July 1919.
Limentani, U. The ideas of Mazzini and Shaw on the function of art. Italian Stud 4 1949.
Daniels, E. A. Collaboration of Mazzini on an article in the Westminster Review. BNYPL Nov 1961.

Pulci, Luigi (1432–84)
Morgante maggiore. Venice 1481; Canto 1, tr G. G. Byron 1822.
Frere, J. H. The monks and the giants. Ed R. D. Waller, Manchester 1926.

English Authors

For a full list of secondary works on Italy and the English Romantics up to 1922, see C. Zacchetti, Shelley e Dante, Milan 1922.

Browning, Robert and Elizabeth Barrett
Browning, R. Sordello. 1840.
— King Victor and King Charles. In his Bells and pomegranates vol 2, 1842.
— Luria. 1846.
— The ring and the book. 4 vols 1868.
— Asolando. 1890.
Browning, E. B. Casa Guidi windows. 1851.

Clarke, H. A. Browning's Italy. New York 1907.
Pratesi, L. L'Italianità nei canti di E. B. Browning. Rocca San Casciano 1928.
Corrigan, B. New documents on Browning's Roman murder case. SP 49 1952.

Byron, George Gordon, Baron. *See under Alfieri, Casti, Dante, Foscolo and Leopardi, above, and under Hunt, col 139 below.*
Childe Harold's pilgrimage. 3 vols 1812–18, 2 vols 1819.
Beppo: a Venetian story. 1818.
Don Juan. 8 vols 1819–24, 2 vols 1826.
The prophecy of Dante. 1821.

Monti, G. G. Leopardi e Byron. In his Studi critici, Florence 1887. On Prisoner of Chillon and Dante's Ugolino.
Muoni, G. La leggenda del Byron in Italia. Milan 1907.

Simhart, M. Byrons Einfluss auf die italienische Literatur. Leipzig 1909.
Zacchetti, C. Byron e l'Italia. Palermo 1920.
'Stendhal' (H. Beyle). In his Mélanges de littérature vol 3, ed H. Martineau 1933.
Messinese, G. Byron and Italy. Tripoli 1937.
Niccolai, B. Bibliografia di atudi inglesi in Italia: Byron. Bollettino di Studi Inglesi in Italia July 1937.
Quennell, P. C. Byron in Italy. 1941.
Borst, W. A. Byron's first pilgrimage 1809–11. New Haven 1948.
Origo, I. The last attachment: the story of Byron and Teresa Guiccioli. 1949.
Wilson Knight, G. Byron: Christian virtues. 1953.
Palacio, J. de. Byron traducteur et les influences italiennes. Rivista di Letterature Moderne e Comparate 1958.
Poli, N. Echi di Byron in Carducci. Ibid.
Melchiori, G. L'Italia di Byron. Lettere Italiane 10 1958.
Lograsso, A. Byron traduttore del Pellico. Lettere Italiane 11 1959.

Hunt, J. H. Leigh
The story of Rimini. 1816. From Dante.
Tasso, T. Gerusalemme liberata. Venice 1580; Jerusalem delivered, tr Hunt 1818.
— Aminta. Venice 1581; Amyntas: a tale of the woods, tr Hunt 1820.
Redi, F. Bacco in Toscana. Florence 1685. Bacchus in Tuscany: a dithyrambic poem, tr Hunt 1825.
Lord Byron and some of his contemporaries, with sketches of Italy etc. 1828.
High and low life in Italy etc by J. J. Pidcock Raikes. Monthly Repository July 1837–April 1838.
A legend of Florence. 1840.
Stories from the Italian poets. 1846. With essays on Dante, Pulci, Boiardo, Ariosto, Tasso.
A jar of honey from Mount Hybla. 1858.

Fischer, E. Hunt und die italienische Literatur. Trute 1936.

James, Henry
Roderick Hudson. Boston 1876.
The portrait of a lady. 3 vols 1881.
The Princess Casamassima. 3 vols 1886.
Italian hours. 1909.

Perry, R. B. James and Italy. Harvard Graduates Mag 41 1933.
Gale, R. L. James and Italy. Studi Americani 3 1957.
Mariani, U. L'esperienza italiana di James. Studi Americani 6 1960; tr Nineteenth-Century Fiction 19 1964.

Landor, Walter Savage
Imaginary conversations. 4 vols 1824–9; ed C. G. Crump 6 vols 1891 (with addns).
The Pentameron, and Pentalogia. 1837.
Andrea of Hungary; Giovanna of Naples; Fra Rupert. 2 vols 1839–40. A trilogy.
The Italics. 1848.

Fornelli, G. Landor e l'Italia. Forlì 1931.
Elkin, F. Landor's studies of Italian life and literature. Philadelphia 1934.

Bulwer-Lytton, E. G. E. L.
The last days of Pompeii. 3 vols 1834.
Rienzi. 3 vols 1835.
Zanoni. 3 vols 1842.

Lloyd, M. Bulwer-Lytton and the idealising principle. Eng Miscellany (Rome) 7 1956.

Meredith, George
Emilia in England. 3 vols 1864.
Vittoria. 3 vols 1867.

Huzzard, J. A. Meredith and the Risorgimento. Italica 35 1959.

Rossetti, Dante Gabriele
The early Italian poets from Ciullo d'Alcamo to Dante Alighieri. 1861, 1874 (rev as Dante and his circle).

Dupré, H. Un italien d'Angleterre: le poète peintre Rossetti. Paris 1922.
Faggi, A. Rossetti. Marzocco 27 May 1928.
Waller, R. D. The Rossetti family. Manchester 1932.
Vincent, E. R. Gabriele Rossetti in England. Oxford 1936. On Rossetti's father.

Scott, Walter
D'Ovidio, F. Appunti per un parallelo tra Manzoni e Scott. In his Discussioni Manzoniane, Lapi 1886.
Dotti, M. Derivazioni nei Promessi sposi di Manzoni dai romanzi di Scott. Pisa 1900.
Agnoli, G. Gli albori del romanzo storico in Italia e i primi imitatori di Scott. Piacenza 1906.
Fassò, L. Saggi e ricerche. Milan 1947.
Gibboni, A. Parallelo tra Manzoni e Scott, ossia The fair maid of Perth e I promessi sposi. Campagna 1950.
Meiklejohn, M. F. M. Scott and Manzoni. Italian Stud 12 1957.

Shelley, Percy Bysshe. *See under Boccaccio, col 136 above.*
Epipsychidion. 1821.
Essays, letters from abroad. Ed M. Shelley 2 vols 1850.
Letters and lyrics on Italy. Ed C. Cucchi, Naples 1934.

Zanella, G. Shelley e Leopardi. Rome 1883; rptd in his Paralleli letterari, Verona 1885.
Olivero, F. Sull'Epipsychidion. In his Nuovi saggi di letteratura inglese, Turin 1919.
Bernheimer, L. Saggio di studi Shelleyani: Shelley in Italia. Piacenza 1920.
Raimondi, R. Shelley in Italia. Padua 1920.
Zacchetti, C. Shelley e Dante. 1922.
Giartosio de Courten, M. L. Shelley e l'Italia. Milan 1923.
Chirpelli, A. Leopardi e Shelley. Marzocco 17 July 1927.
Bini, B. Shelley nel Risorgimento italiano. Fiume 1927.

Swinburne, Algernon Charles
A song of Italy. 1867.
Siena. 1868.
Songs before sunrise. 1871.

Faggi, A. Swinburne aedo d'Italia. Marzocco May 1926.
Brown, C. S. More Swinburne-d'Annunzio parallels. PMLA 55 1940.

Symonds, John Addington
Sketches in Italy and Greece. 1874. With trns of Petrarch and popular songs.
Renaissance in Italy. 7 vols 1875–86.
The sonnets of Michelangelo Buonarroti and Tommaso Campanella. Tr Symonds 1878.
Sketches and studies in Italy. 1879.
Italian byways. 1883.
The life of Benvenuto Cellini, newly translated. 1888.
Giovanni Boccaccio. 1895.
Gozzi, C. Memorie inutili. 3 vols Venice 1797; The memoirs of Count Carlo Gozzi, with essays by the translator, 2 vols 1890.

Wordsworth, William. *See under Leopardi, col 137 above.*
Memorials of a tour on the Continent. 1822.

Shackford, M. H. Wordsworth's Italy. PMLA 38 1923.
Curry, K. Uncollected translations of Michelangelo by Wordsworth and Southey. RES 14 1938.
Vallese, T. Wordsworth in Italy. Symposium 6 1951.
Rossi, S. Wordsworth e l'Italia. Letterature Moderne Sept 1953.
Rossiter Smith, H. Wordsworth and his Italian studies. N & Q June 1953.

(6) SPANISH AND PORTUGUESE

General Studies

For a list of travel books describing the Peninsula, see R. Foulché-Delbosc, Bibliographie des voyages en Espagne et au Portugal, Paris 1896.

Lockhart, J. G. Ancient Spanish ballads, historical and romantic. Edinburgh 1822.

'Leucadio Doblado' (J. Blanco-White). Letters from Spain. 1822.

Méndez Bejarano, M. Vida y obras de don J. M. Blanco y Crespo [J. Blanco-White]. Madrid 1821.

Bowring, J. Ancient poetry and romances of Spain. 1824. Góngora, Camõens et al.

Kennedy, J. Modern poets and poetry of Spain. 1852. With trns of Valdes, Quintana, Martinez de la Rosa, Espronceda, Zorrilla et al.

Gibson, J. Y. The Cid ballads etc. 2 vols 1887.

Ford, J. D. M. English influence on Spanish literature in the early part of the 19th century. PMLA 16 1901.

Mesquita, M. de. Um amigo português de Shelley. Revista de Historia (Coïmbre) 3 1914.

García Morán, C. Influencia de los escritores románticos ingleses en el romantismo español. Madrid 1923.

Peers, E. A. Rivas and romanticism in Spain. Liverpool 1923.

—— Minor English influences on Spanish romanticism. Revue Hispanique 62 1924.

—— The influence of Young and Gray in Spain. MLR 21 1926.

Buceta, E. El entusiasmo por España en algunos románticos ingleses. Revista de Filología Espanola 10 1923. On Southey, Scott, Wordsworth, Shelley, Byron, Landor.

—— Traducciones inglesas de romances en el primer tercio del siglo XIX. Revue Hispanique 62 1924. Continued in Datos suplementarios acerca de las versiones de Lockhart, 68 1926. Continued in Datos suplementarios acerca de J. Bowring, Revista de Filología Española 20 1933.

—— Relaciones anglo-hispanas: apuntes preliminares para un estudio de las traducciones inglesas de romances en el primer tercio del siglo XIX. In Estudios eruditos in memoriam de Adolfo Bonilla y San Martin vol 2, Madrid 1930.

—— El Don Carlos de Lord John Russell. Revista de Filología española 13 1926.

Walter, F. La littérature portugaise en Angleterre à l'époque romantique. Paris 1927. With full bibliography.

Paxeco, F. The intellectual relations between Portugal and Great Britain. Lisbon 1937.

Matthews, E. G. Studies in Spanish-English cultural and literary relations. New York 1938.

Blecua, J. M. Mor de Fuentes y Lord Holland. Boletin del Seminaro de Estudios de Literatura y Filología, Castilla 1940–1.

Umphrey, G. W. Spanish ballads in English. MLQ 6–7 1945–6.

Barker, J. W. Influencia de la literatura espanola en la literatura inglesa. Zaragoza 1946.

Macaulay, R. They went to Portugal. 1946. On Beckford, Southey, Byron, Borrow, Tennyson, Palgrave et al.

Pastor, A. Breve historia del hispanismo inglés. Arbor April 1948.

Weisinger, N. L. José Joaquin de Mora's indebtedness to Blake. Bull of Hispanic Stud 28 1951.

Llorens, V. C. Liberales y románticos: una emigración española en Inglaterra 1823–34. Mexico City 1954.

Parreaux, A. Beckford et le Portugal en 1787. Bulletin des Etudes Portugaises 7 1954.

Spanish and Portuguese Authors

For a full list of trns from the Spanish, see R. U. Pane, English translations from the Spanish 1484–1943, New Brunswick 1944. *In the following list the Spanish originals were all pbd at Madrid unless otherwise stated.*

Calderón de la Barca, Pedro (1600–81)

La dama duende; Nadie fíe su secreto. In Three comedies [tr Lord Holland] 1807, (as The fairy lady; Keep your own secret).

El príncipe constante; El secreto a vozes; El médico de su honra; Amar despues de la muerte; El purgatorio de San Patricio; La vanda y la flor. In Dramas of Calderón, tr D. F. M'Carthy 2 vols 1853 (as The constant prince; The secret in words; The physician of his own honour; Love after death; The purgatory of St Patrick; The scarf and the flower). With a list of previous trns in periodicals.

Justina; La vida es sueño (The wonderful magician). Tr J. H. 1848.

El pinto de su deshonra; Luis Perez el Gallego; Las tres justicias en una; El alcalde de Zalamea; Guardate de la agua mansa. In Six dramas of Calderón, tr E. FitzGerald 1853 (as The painter of his own dishonour; Keep your own secret; Gil perez the Gallician; Three judgments at a blow; The mayor of Zalamea; Beware of smooth water).

Life's a dream, The great theatre of the world etc, tr with an essay on Calderón by R. C. Trench 1856.

Madariaga, S. de. Shelley and Calderón. 1920.

Gates, E. J. Shelley and Calderón. PQ 16 1937.

Camõens, Luis de (c. 1524–1580)

Rhythmas. Lisbon 1595 etc; Poems from the Portuguese of Camoens, tr with remarks on Camoens by Viscount Strangford. 1803.

Os Lusiadas. Lisbon 1572; The Lusiad [bks 1–4] tr E. Quillinan 1853.

Lardner, D. In his Eminent literary and scientific men of Italy, Spain and Portugal vol 3, 1957.

Estorninho, C. O culto de Camoẽs em Inglaterra. Arquivo de Bibliografía Portuguesa 10 1960.

Cervantes, Miguel de (1547–1616). *See also under Wordsworth, col 144 below.*

Peterson, D. E. A note on a probable source of Landor's Metellus and Marius. SP 39 1942.

Cervantes y la literatura inglesa. Realidad 2 1947.

Fernán Caballero (Cecilia Arrom de Ayala) (1796–1877)

Elia. 1850; La familia de Alvareda, 1856; The castle and the cottage in Spain, tr Lady Wallace 1861.

La gaviota. 1849; The seagull, tr A. Bethell 2 vols 1867.

Cuadros de costumbres 1870; National pictures, 1882.

Echegaray y Eizaguirre, José María (1832–1916)

El gran Galeoto. 1881; Ó locura ó santidad; 1877; The great Galeoto; Folly or saintliness, tr with introd by H. Lynch 1895.

El hijo de Don Juan. 1889; The son of Don Juan, tr with introd by J. Graham 1895.

Mariana. 1892; tr J. Graham 1890.

Palacio Valdés, Armando (1853–1916)

El cuarto poder. 1888; The fourth estate, tr R. Challice 1901.

La alegría del capitán Ribot, 1889; The joy of captain Ribot, tr M. C. Smith 1900.

La espuma. Barcelona 1890; Froth, tr C. Bell 1891.

El maestrante. 1893; The grandee, tr with introd by R. Challice 1894.

Pérez Galdós, Benito (1843–1920). *See also under Dickens, col 144 below.*

Episodios nacionales. 1873–1910; Trafalgar, tr C. Bell 1884; Leon Roch, tr C. Bell 2 vols 1886; The Court of Charles IV, tr C. Bell 1888.
Doña Perfecta. 1876; tr D. P. W. 1880; tr M. Wharton 1892; tr M. J. Serrano 1895.
Gloria, 1877; tr N. Wetherhell 2 vols 1879.
Marianela. 1878; tr C. Bell 1883; tr M. Wharton 1893.

Unamuno, Miguel de (1864–1936)
Clavería, C. Temas de Unamuno. Madrid 1953. On Unamuno and Carlyle.
Alberich, J. Temas ingleses en Unamuno y Baroja. Arbor Nov 1956.
Blanco, M. G. Poetas ingleses en la obra de Unamuno. Bull of Hispanic Stud 36 1959.
Earle, P. G. Unamuno and English literature. New York 1960.

English Authors

Borrow, George
The Zincali. 1841.
The Bible in Spain. 1843.

Fréchet, R. Borrow: vagabond, polyglotte, agent biblique—écrivain. Paris 1956.

Byron, George Gordon
Childe Harold's pilgrimage. 1812.

Churchman, P. H. Byron and Espronceda. Revue Hispanique 22 1909.
—— Byron's experience in the Spanish Peninsula in 1809. Bulletin Hispanique 11 1909.
—— The beginnings of Byronism in Spain. Revue Hispanique 23 1910. With critical list of trns.
Rycroft, W. S. Espronceda: la influencia de Byron. Boletín Bibliografico (Lima) 2 1926.
Samuels, D. G. Some Byronic influences in Spanish poetry 1870–80. Hispanic Rev 17 1949.
Pujals, E. Espronceda y Byron. Madrid 1951.
Ribbans, G. W. Bécquer, Byron y Dacarrete. Revista de Literatura 4 1953.
Sarmiento, E. A parallel between Byron and Fray Luis de Leon. RES 29 1953.
Pageard, R. and G. W. Ribbans. Heine and Byron in the Seminario Popular 1862–5. Bull of Hispanic Stud 33 1956.

Dickens, Charles
Burton, J. G. Galdós visto por un inglés y los ingleses vistos por Galdós. Revista de las Indias 17 1943.
Erickson, E. The influence of Dickens on the novels of Pérez Galdós. Hispania 19 1946.

Scott, Walter
The vision of Don Roderick. Edinburgh 1811.

Churchman, P. H. and F. A. Peers. A survey of the influence of Scott in Spain. Revue Hispanique 55 1922. With a list of trns.
Peers, E. A. Studies in the influence of Scott in Spain. Revue Hispanique 58 1926.
Stoudemire, S. A. A note on Scott in Spain. In Romance studies presented to W. M. Day, Chapel Hill 1950.

Southey, Robert
Letters written during a short residence in Spain and Portugal [with poems]. Bristol 1797.
Roderick: the last of the Goths. 1814.
Montalvo, G. O. de. Amadis of Gaul. c. 1500; tr with introd by Southey 1803.
Moraes, F. de. Palmerín de Inglaterra. c. 1550; tr Southey 4 vols 1807. *See* C. I. Patterson, The Keats–Hazlitt–Hunt copy of Palmerin of England in relation to Keats's poetry, JEGP 60 1961.
Poema del Cid. Chronicle of the Cid, tr with introd by Southey 1808.

Pfandl, L. Southey und Spanien. Revue Hispanique 28 1913.
Buceta, E. Opiniones de Southey y de Coleridge acerca del Poema del Cid. Revista de Filología Espanola 9 1922.

Wordsworth, William
The relations of Great Britain, Spain and Portugal to each other and to the common enemy. 1809. *See* Wordsworth's Tract on the Convention of Cintra etc, ed A. V. Dicey 1915.

Sarmiento, E. Wordsworth and Don Quijote. Bull of Hispanic Stud 38 1961.

(7) SCANDINAVIAN

General Studies

Scandinavia

For lists of articles and books in English concerning Denmark and Sweden, see J. C. Bay, Denmark in English and American literature, Chicago 1915, *and* N. Afzelius, Sverige i utländsk och utlandet i svensk litteratur, Biblioteksbladet 1930.

Burchardt, C. B. Norwegian life and literature: English accounts and views. Oxford 1920. With bibliographies.
Thesen, R. Synet på England i norsk litteratur 1830–70. Syn og Segn 7 1935.
Matthews, G. Det viktorianska Englands syn på Finland. Finsk Tidskrift 160 1956.

Scandinavian and English Literature

Wergeland, H. Den engelske lods: et digt. Christiania 1844.
Nicolaysen, S. E. Shelley og Wergeland. Nyt Tidsskrift 1893–4.
Howitt, W. and M. The literature and romance of northern Europe. 2 vols 1852.
Thorpe, B. Yule-tide stories. 1853.
Brandes, G. Benjamin Disraeli. Copenhagen 1878; Lord Beaconsfield, tr G. Sturge 1880.
—— Correspondance vol 2. Copenhagen 1956.
Gosse, E. Studies in the literature of Northern Europe. 1879.
—— Correspondence with Scandinavian writers. Ed E. Bredsdorff, Copenhagen 1960.
Boyesen, H. H. Essays on Scandinavian literature. 1895.
Wright, H. G. Studies in Anglo-Scandinavian literary relations. Bangor 1919. On Borrow, Kingsley, the Howitts, Strindberg et al.
—— Southey's relations with Finland and Scandinavia. MLR 27 1932.
Lindström, E. Scott och den historiska romanen och novelleni Sverige intill 1850. Göteborgs Högskolas Årsskrift 31 1925.
Petersens, H-A. R. P. Gillies, Foreign Quarterly Review och den svenska litteraturen. Samlaren 14 1933.
Barnes, T. Yeats, Synge, Ibsen and Strindberg. Scrutiny 5 1936.
Holst, O. Engelske oversaettelser af Danske folkeviser. Danske Studier 17 1941. On Jamieson, Borrow, Morris.
Downs, B. W. Anglo-Danish literary relations 1867–1900. MLR 39 1944.
—— Anglo-Norwegian literary relations 1867–1900. MLR 47 1952.
Benson, A. B. A list of translations of the Frithiofs saga. In American Scandinavian studies, ed M. W. S. Swan, New York 1952.

Bull, F. The influence of Shakespeare on Wergeland, Ibsen and Bjørnson. Norseman 15 1957.
Eneberg, M. Charles Dickens i sin samtids Finland. Historiska och Litteraturhistoriska Studier (Helsinki) 35 1960.
Rudler, R. De første Shakespeareforestillinger i Norge. Edda 63 1963.
Nelson, W. W. Oscar Wilde och det Svenska nittitalet. Svensk Litteraturtidskrift 33 1964.

Old Norse

General

Nordby, C. H. The influence of Old Norse literature upon English literature. New York 1901.
Leider, P. R. Scott and Scandinavian literature. Smith College Stud in Modern Languages (Northampton Mass) 1920.
Batho, E. C. Sir Walter Scott and the Sagas. MLR 24 1929.
Hoare, D. M. The works of Morris and of Yeats in relation to early saga literature. Cambridge 1937.
Litzenberg, K. The Victorians and the vikings: a bibliographical essay. Ann Arbor 1947.

Translations

For a full list see R. B. Allen, Old Icelandic sources in the English novel, Philadelphia 1933. *For trns of individual poems or parts of the Eddas see* H. Hermannsson, Bibliography of the Eddas, Islandica 13 1923.

Eddas

The prose or younger Edda. Tr G. W. Dasent, Stockholm 1842.
The Edda of Saemund the learned, with a mythological index. [Tr B. Thorpe] 1866.

Sagas

Brennu-Njáls saga. The story of Burnt Njal, tr with introd by G. W. Dasent 2 vols Edinburgh 1861.
Heimskringla. The Heimskringla, tr with introd by S. Laing, 3 vols 1844, 4 vols 1889; T. Carlyle, The early kings of Norway, 1875.
Gísla saga. The story of Gisli the outlaw, tr G. W. Dasent 1866.
Grettis saga. The story of Grettir the strong, tr E. Magnússon and W. Morris 1869.
Völsunga saga. The story of the Volsungs and Niblungs, tr E. Magnússon and W. Morris 1870.
Jómsvíkinga saga. The Vikings of the Baltic, adapted by G. W. Dasent 3 vols 1875.
The saga library. Ed E. Magnússon and W. Morris 6 vols 1891–1905. Hávardar Isfirðings saga; Bandamanna saga; Hœnsa Øóris saga; Eyrbyggja saga; Heiðarvíga saga; Heimskringla.

Others

Select Icelandic poetry. Tr W. Herbert 2 pts 1804–8.
Illustrations of Northern antiquities. Edinburgh 1814. Trns by R. Jamieson, W. Scott, H. Weber.
Icelandic legends selected by J. Arnason. Tr with introd by G. Powell and E. Magnússon 2 sers 1864–6.

William Morris

Morris, W. The lovers of Gudrun. In his Earthly paradise, 1869–70. From Laxdœla saga.
— Poems by the way. 1891.
— The story of Sigurd the Volsung and the fall of the Niblungs. 1876.
— Three northern love stories. 1875.
McDowell, G. T. The treatment of the Volsungasaga by Morris. Scandinavian Stud 7 1923.
Litzenberg, K. The Elder Edda and Haimskringla in Morris's non-Norse poems. Scandinavian Stud 19 1935.
— Morris as a critic of Old Norse literature. Edda 40 1940.
Swannell, J. N. Morris as an interpreter of Old Norse. Saga-book of the Viking Soc 15 1961.
Purkis, J. The Icelandic jaunt. 1962.
Maurer, O. Morris and Laxdœla saga. Texas Stud in Lit & Lang 5 1964.

Scandinavian Authors

For a comprehensive list of trns from the Norwegian, see I. Fæhn and H. Haave, Norwegian literature in English translation since 1742, *in* E. Grönland, Norway in English, Oslo 1961. *For a full list of trns from the Danish, see* E. Bredsdorff, Danish literature in English translation, Copenhagen 1950. *For lists of trns from the Finnish and Swedish, see* S. Haltsonen, Suomalaista kaunokirjallisuutta vierailla kielillä, Helsinki 1961 *and* E. Gustafson, A list of translations of Swedish literature into English, Stockholm 1962. *In the following list the Scandinavian originals were all pbd at Copenhagen unless otherwise stated.*

Andersen, Hans-Christian (1805–1875). Eventyr. 1834–72; A Danish story-book, tr C. Boner 1846; Wonderful stories for children, tr M. Howitt 1846; Stories and tales, tr H. W. Dulcken 1864; The shoes of fortune, tr C. Boner, with biographical sketch by K. R. H. Mackenzie 1883; Fairy tales, tr H. L. Braekstad, introd by E. Gosse 1900. There were over 50 English edns, listed in E. Bredsdorff, above.
Bain, R. B. Hans-Christian Andersen. 1895. With a critical appendix on trns.
Drachmann, A. C. E. B. Browning and Hans Andersen. Edda 33 1933.

Asbjørnsen, Peter Christen (1812–1885) and Jørgen Moe. Norske folkeeventyr. Christiania 1842–4; Norske huldreeventyr og folkesagn, 1845–8; Popular tales from the Norse, with introd by G. W. Dasent, Edinburgh 1859.
Norske folkeeventyr: ny samling. Christiania 1852–71; Tales from the fjeld, tr G. W. Dasent 1874.

Mead, W. R. P. C. Asbjørnsen and his English correspondents. Norseman 10 1952.

Bjørnson, Bjørnstjerne (1832–1910)
The novels of Bjørnson. Ed E. Gosse 13 vols 1895–1909.
Synnøve Solbakken. Christiania 1857; Love and life in Norway, tr A. Bethell 1870.
Arne. Bergen 1858; tr A. Plesner 1866.
En glad gut 1868; Ovind; tr S. and E. Hjerleid 1869.
Smaastykker. Bergen 1860; Brude-slaatten 1873; in Life by the fells and fjords, tr A. Plesner 1879.
De nygifte. 1865; The newly married couple, tr T. Soelfeldt 1868; tr S. and E. Hjerleid 1870.
Fiskerjenten. 1868; The fishing girl, tr A. Plesner 1870.
En hanske. 1883; A gauntlet; tr H. Braekstad 1886; tr O. Edwards 1894.
Brandes, G. Bjørnson och Ibsen. Stockholm 1882.
Ibsen. Bjørnson: a critical study; tr J. Muir 1899.
The later plays of Bjørnson. MacMillan's Mag Dec 1889.

Bremer, Fredrika (1801–65)
Familien H. Stockholm 1830–1; The H... family, 1849.
Presidentens döttrar; Nina. Stockholm 1834, 1835; The president's daughters, and Nina, tr M. Howitt 3 vols 1843.
Grannarne. Stockholm 1837; The neighbours, tr M. Howitt 2 vols 1842.
Hemmet. Stockholm 1839; The home, tr M. Howitt 2 vols 1843.
Trälinnan. Stockholm 1840; The bondmaid, tr M. L. Putnam 1844.
Syskonlif. Stockholm 1848; Brothers and sisters, tr M. Howitt 3 vols 1848.
Hertha. Stockholm 1856; tr M. Howitt 1856.

Fader och dotter. Stockholm 1889; tr M. Howitt 1859.
Skizzer fra England i 1851. 1852; England in 1851, Boulogne 1853.

Gustafson, A. T. English influence in Fredrika Bremer. JEGP 28–30 1931–3.

Goldschmidt, Meïr Aron (1819–87)
En jøde. 1845; The jew of Denmark, tr Mrs Bushby 1852; Jacob Bendixen, tr M. Howitt 3 vols 1852.
Hjemløs. 1857; Homeless: or a poet's inner life, translated by the author, 3 vols 1861.

Ibsen, Henrik (1828–1906). *See also under Byron, col 149 below.*
Kjærlighedens komedie. Christiania 1862; Love's comedy, tr with introd by C. H. Herford 1900.
Brand. 1868; tr W. Wilson 1891.
Peer Gynt. 1867; tr W. and C. Archer 1892.
De unges forbund. 1869; The league of youth, tr W. Archer 1890.
Kejser og Galilaeer. 1873; The emperor and the Galilean, tr C. Ray 1876.
Et dukkehjem. 1880; Nora: or a doll's house, tr with introd by H. F. Lord 1882.
Samfundets støtter. 1877; Gjengangere, 1881; En folkefiende, 1882; The pillars of society and other plays [Ghosts; An enemy of society], tr W. Archer and E. Marx-Aveling, introd by H. Ellis 1888.
Vildanden. 1884; The wild duck, tr F. E. Archer 1890.
Rosmersholm. 1886; tr L. N. Parker 1889.
Fruen fra Havet. 1888; The lady from the sea, tr E. Mark-Aveling, introd by E. Gosse 1890.
Hedda Gabler. 1890; tr E. Gosse 1891.
Bygmester Solness. 1892; The master builder, tr E. Gosse and W. Archer 1893.
Lille Eyolf. 1894; Little Eyolf, tr W. Archer 1894.

Archer, W. Ibsen and English criticism. Fortnightly Rev July 1889.
—— The mausoleum of Ibsen. Fortnightly Rev July 1893.
Archer, C. William Archer. 1931. With bibliography.
Shaw, G. B. The quintessence of Ibsenism. 1892, 1915 (rev). Reply to Shaw's lectures by W. Archer, New Rev 5 1891.
Wicksteed, P. H. Four lectures on Ibsen. 1892.
Courtney, W. L. Ibsen's social dramas. In his Studies at leisure, 1892.
James, H. In his Scenic art, 1949. Two essays of 189 .
Newman, E. The real Ibsen. Free Rev Oct 1893.
Boyesen, H. H. A commentary on the works of Ibsen. 1894.
Filon, A. Ibsen à Londres: le drame de demain. Revue des Deux Mondes Nov 1895.
Russell, E. R. Ibsen on his merits. 1897.
Gosse, E. Ibsen. 1907.
Franc, M. A. Ibsen in England. Boston 1919.
Kröner, J. Die Technik des realistischen Dramas bei Ibsen und Galsworthy. Leipzig 1935.
Qvamme, B. Ibsen og det engelske teater. Edda 42 1942.
Burchardt, C. B. Ibsen and England. Norseman 5 1947.
Irvine, W. Shaw's criticism of Ibsen. South Atlantic Quart 46 1947.
Lamm, M. Ibsen och Shaw. Edda 47 1947.
Setterquist, J. Ibsen and the beginnings of Anglo-Irish drama. Vol 1, J. M. Synge; vol 2, E. Martyn. Upsala 1951–60.
Decker, C. R. Ibsen in England. In his Victorian conscience, New York 1952.
Edwards, H. Henry James and Ibsen. Amer Lit 24 1952.
Wade, A. Ibsen in translation. Drama 39 1955.
Adler, J. H. Ibsen, Shaw and Candida. JEGP 59 1960.
Gerould, D. C. Shaw's criticism of Ibsen. Comparative Lit 15 1963.
Gassner, J. Shaw on Ibsen and the drama of ideas. In his Ideas in the drama, New York 1964.
Stanley, R. Ibsen and his translator Archer. Meanjin 23 1964.

Kielland, Alexander (1849–1907)
Novelletter. 1879–80; Tales of two countries, tr W. Archer 1891; Norse tales and sketches, tr R. L. Cassie 1896.
Garman og Worse. 1880; tr W. Kettlewell 1884.
Skipper Worse. 1882; tr Earl of Ducie 1885.

Lie, Jonas (1833–1907)
Den fremsynte. 1870; The visionary, tr J. Muir 1893.
Kommandørens døttre. 1886; The commodore's daughters, tr H. L. Braekstad 1892.
Trold. 2 vols 1891–2; Weird tales from Northern seas, tr R. N. Bain 1893.

Oehlenschläger, Adam (1779–1850). *See also under Borrow, below.*
Axel og Valborg. 1810; tr R. M. Laing in his Hours in Norway, 1841.
Correggio. 1811; tr T. Martin 1854.
Vaulundurs saga. 1812; tr E. Kinnear in G. B. Depping, Wayland Smith, 1847.
Den lille hyrdedreng. 1818; The little shepherd boy, tr J. Heath 1827.
Nordens guder. 1819; The gods of the North, tr W. E. Frye 1845.
Aladdin. 1820; tr T. Martin 1857.
Haakon Jarl. 1848; tr 1840 (anon).

Rose, E. A northern Hamlet [Oehlenschläger's Amleth]. Fraser's Mag May 1877.

Pontoppidan, Henrik (1857–1943)
Mimoser. 1886; The apothecary's daughters, tr G. Nielsen 1890.
Det forjættede land. 1891–5; Emmanuel: or Children of the soil; and The promised land, tr Mrs E. Lucas 1892, 1896.

Strindberg, August (1849–1912)
Fadren. 1887; The father, tr N. Erichson 1899.

Gustafson, A. Some early English and American Strindberg criticism. In Scandinavian studies presented to George T. Flom, Urbana 1942.
McCarthy, J. H. August Strindberg. Fortnightly Rev Sept 1892.

English Authors

For a comprehensive list of trns into Norwegian, see R. Øksnevad, Det Britiske samvelde og Eire i norsk litteratur, Oslo 1949.

Borrow, George
Romantic ballads translated from the Danish [Kjæmpe viser, Oehlenschläger, Evald etc]. 1826.
The death of Balder [tr from Evald, J. Balders død, 1773]. 1889.
The gold horns [tr from Oehlenschläger, A. Guldhornene, 1802]. 1913.
Hustvedt, S. B. Borrow and his Danish ballads. JEGP 20 1923.
Wright, H. G. Borrow's translations from the Scandinavian languages. Edda 16 1921.
—— Influence of Borrow in Norway and Sweden. MLR 29 1934.

Byron, George Gordon
Beck, R. Grímur Thomsen: a pioneer Byron student. JEGP 25 1928.

— Gisli Brynjúlfsson: an Icelandic imitator of Childe Harold's pilgrimage. JEGP 26 1929.
— Grímur Thomsen og Byron. Reykjavik 1937.
Biller, G. Byron i den svenska litteraturen före Strandberg. Samlaren 33 1912.
Farinelli, A. Byron e Ibsen. Milan 1944.
Holthausen, F. Skandinavische Byron-Übersetzungen. E Studien 25 1898.
Simonsen, P. Om Hedda Gabler, Lille Eyolf og Lord Byron. Edda 62 1962.
Sjöholm, S. Fröding och Byron. Edda 39 1939.
Skard, S. Byron i norsk litteratur. Ibid.

C. C.

(8) SLAVONIC

Bibliographies

Line, M. B. A bibliography of Russian literature in English translation to 1900. 1963.

General Studies

Rossiyskiye Walter Scotty. Delo Nov 1878. Anon.
Veselovsky, A. N. Zapadnoye vliyaniye v novoy russkoy literature. Moscow 1896 (5th edn).
— Etyudy o byronizme. In his Etyudy i kharakteristiki, Moscow 1907.
— Anglo-romansky mir i russkaya literatura: iz istorii mezhdunarodnogo literaturnogo obshcheniya. In Yevropa i voyna vol 2. Moscow 1917.
Spasovich, V. D. Byronizm u Pushkina i Lermontova. Vilna 1911.
Zamotin, I. I. Romantizm dvadtsatykh godov xix stoletiya v russkoy literature, 2 vols St Petersburg 1911–13.
Windakiewicz, S. Walter Scott i Lord Byron w odniesieniu do polskiej poezyi romantycznej. Cracow 1914.
Maslov, V. I. Nachal'nyy period byronizma v Rossii. Kiev 1915.
Kozlowski, W. M. Notes sur les échanges des idées philosophiques entre l'Angleterre et la Pologne. Revue de Littérature Comparée 3 1923.
Grossman, A. P. Russkiye byronisty. In Byron: Sbornik statey, Moscow 1924.
Low, D. H. The first link between English and Serbo-Croat literature. Slavonic Rev 3 1924.
Subotić, D. Serbian popular poetry in English literature. Slavonic Rev 5–6 1927–8.
Vinogradov, V. V. Evolyutsiya russkogo naturalizma: Gogol' i Dostoyevsky. Leningrad 1929.
Simmons, E. J. English literature in Russia. Harvard Stud 13 1931.
— English literature and culture in Russia 1553–1840. Cambridge Mass 1935, New York 1964.
Vočadlo, O. Anglie a Čechy. Lumir 57 1931. With bibliography of Anglo-Bohemian relations.
Osborne, E. A. Early translations from the Russian. Bookman (London) July 1932–June 1933.
Decker, C. Victorian comment on Russian realism. PMLA 52 1937.
— Aesthetic revolt against naturalism in Victorian criticism. PMLA 53 1938.
Dusan, S. The westernization of Russia: the influence of English literature. TLS 13 June 1942.
Kleiner, K. Sedm set lat angloceských vztahu. 1942.
Alekseyev, M. P. Angliyskiy yazyk v Rossii i russkiy yazyk v Anglii. Uchonyye Zapiski Leningradskogo gos Universiteta, 72 (seriya filologicheskikh nauk no 9) 1944.
— Russkiye klassiki v literaturakh anglo-romanskogo mira. Zvezda May–June 1944.
— Angliyskiye memuary o dekabristakh. Issledovaniya po otechestvennomu istochnikovedeniyu: Sbornik statey, posvyashchonnykh 75-letiyu professora S.N. Valka (Akademiya Nauk SSSR, Institut istorii, Trudy no 7), Moscow-Leningrad 1964.
— William Ralston and Russian writers of the later nineteenth century. Oxford Slavonic Papers 11 1964.
Brewster, D. The Russian soul: an English literary pattern. Amer Scholar 17 1948.
— East-west passage: a study in literary relationships. 1954.
Orel, H. The forgotten ambassadors: Russian fiction in Victorian England. Amer Slavic & East European Rev 12 1953.
— English critics and the Russian novel 1850–1917. Slavonic & East European Rev 33 1955.
Phelps, G. The Russian novel in English fiction. 1956. *See* also D. Zhantiyeva, Kniga o russko-angliyskikh literaturnykh svyazyakh, Voprosy Literatury March 1957.
— The early phases of British interest in Russian literature. Slavonic & East European Rev 36 1958, 38 1960.
Gifford, H. Syvazi angliyskoy i russkoy literatur. Kul't ura i zhizn' Feb 1957.
Ordon, E. The reception of the Polish short story in English: reflections on a bibliography. Polish Rev 2 1957.
Desnitsky, V. Zapadnoyevropeyskiye antologii i obozreniya russkoy literatury v pervyye desyatiletiya xix veka. In his Izbrannyye stat'; po russkoy literature xviii–xix vv, Moscow-Leningrad 1958.
Tove, A. Garnett: perevodchik i propagandist russkoy literatury. Russkaya Literatura no 4 1958.
Curran, E. M. The Foreign Quarterly Review on Russian and Polish literature. Slavonic & East European Rev 40 1962.
Wellek, R. Essays on Czech literature. Hague 1963.
Kiparsky, V. English and American characters in Russian fiction. Wiesbaden 1964.
Nazirov, R. G. Dickens, Baudelaire, Dostoyevsky: K istorii odnogo literaturnogo motiva. Uchonyye Zapiski Bashkirskogo Universiteta (seriya filologicheskikh nauk no 7) 1964.
Taborski, B. Polish plays in English translation. Polish Rev 9 1964.
Tregenza, J. M. C. H. Pearson in Russia and his correspondence with Herzen and others. Oxford Slavonic Papers 11 1964.
Davie, D. A. (ed). Russian literature and modern English fiction: a collection of critical essays. Chicago 1965.
Kuleshov, V. I. Literaturnyye svyazi Rossii i zapadnoy Yevropy v xix veke (Pervaya polovina). Moscow 1965.

Anthologies in Translation

Specimens of the Russian poets, with preliminary remarks and biographical notices. Tr J. Bowring 2 vols 1821–3.
The talisman, from the Russian of Alexander Pushkin, with other pieces. Tr G. Borrow, St Petersburg 1835.
Russian lyrics in English verse. Tr C. T. Wilson 1887.
Rhymes from the Russian: being faithful translations of selections from the best Russian poets, Pushkin, Lermontof, Nadson, Nekrasof, Tolstoy, Tyoutchef, Maikof, Lebedef, Fet, K. R. etc. Tr J. Pollen 1891.
The humour of Russia. Tr E. L. Voynich 1895. Contains 5 plays and 14 stories.

Trns from Russian literature, both complete works and extracts, can also be found in the following works:

The universal anthology: a collection of the best literature. Ed R. Garnett 33 vols 1899–1902.
The library of the world's best literature. Ed C. D. Warner 30 vols New York 1896–7.

Single Authors

Russian etc

Aksakov, Sergey Timofeyevich (1791–1858)
Semeynaya khronika. Moscow 1856. Memoirs of the Aksakof family. Tr by a Russian lady, Calcutta 1871; A Russian gentleman, tr J. D. Duff 1917.
Vospominaniya. Moscow 1856.
A Russian schoolboy. Tr J. D. Duff 1917.
Detskiye gody Bagrova-vnuka. Moscow 1858. Years of childhood. Tr J. D. Duff 1917.

Bulgarin, Faddey Venediktovich (1789–1859)
Ivan Vyzhigin. St Petersburg 1829; tr G. Ross 2 vols 1831.

Chekov, Anton Pavlovich (1860–1904)
Tales. Tr C. Garnett 13 vols 1916–23.
Plays. Tr C. Garnett 2 vols 1923; Letters to his family and friends, tr Garnett 1920.

Nabokoff, C. Chekhov on the English stage. Contemporary Rev June 1926.
Heifetz, A. Chekhov in English: a list of works by and about him. New York 1949.
Meister, C. Chekhov's reception in England and America. Amer Slavic & East European Rev 12 1953.
Brewster, D. Chekhov in America and England. Masses & Mainstream 7 1954.
Seresevkaya, M. A. Angliyskiye pisateli i kritiki o Chekhove. In Literaturnoye nasledstvo 68, Moscow and Leningrad 1960.
Yachnin, R. Chekhov in English: a selective list of works by and about him 1949–60. New York 1960.
Erlich, V. (ed). Chekhov and western European drama: a symposium. Yearbook of Comparative Lit 12 1963.
Chukovsky, K. The strongest bridge. TLS 4 June 1964.
Subbotina, K. Tvorchestvo A. P. Chekhova v otsenke angliyskoy kritiki 1910–1920-kh godov. Russkaya Literatura no 2 1964.

Dostoyevsky, Fyodor Mikhaylovich (1821–81)
Novels. Tr C. Garnett 12 vols 1912–20.
Bednyye lyudi. St Petersburg 1846.
Poor folk. Tr L. Milman 1894.
Selo Stepanchikovo. St Petersburg 1859; Igrok, St Petersburg 1866.
The friend of the family and the Gambler. Tr F. Whishaw 1887.
Dyadyushkin son. St Petersburg 1859; Vechnyy muzh, St Petersburg 1870.
Uncle's dream and the Permanent husband. Tr F. Whishaw 1888.
Zapiski iz myortvogo doma. St Petersburg 1860–2.
Buried alive: or ten years of penal servitude in Siberia. Tr M. van Thilo 1881.
Unizhonnyye i oskorblyonnyye. St Petersburg 1861.
Injury and insult. Tr F. Whishaw 1886.
Prestupleniye i nakazaniye. St Petersburg 1866.
Crime and punishment. Tr from the French of V. Derély (1884) 1886.
Idiot. St Petersburg 1868–9; tr F. Whishaw 1887.

Alekseyev, M. P. Dostoyevsky i kniga De Quincey Confessions of an English opium-eater. Uchonyye Zapiski Vysshey Shkoly Odessy 2 1922.
Mirsky, S. Dostojevski in Frankreich und England. Slavische Rundschau 3 1931.
Neuschäffer, W. Dostojewskijs Einfluss auf den englischen Roman. Heidelberg 1935.
Muchnic, H. Dostoevsky's English reputation 1881–1935. Smith College Stud in Modern Languages 20 1939.
Futrell, M. H. Dostoevsky and Dickens. Eng Miscellany (Rome) 7 1956.
Grossman, L. Dostoyevsky i chartistskiy roman. Voprosy Literatury April 1959.
Matlaw, R. E. Dostoevskij and Conrad's political novels. In American contributions to the Fifth International Congress of Slavists, Sofia, Sept 1963, vol 2: Literary contributions, Hague 1963.
Fanger, D. Dostoevsky and romantic realism: a study of Dostoevsky in relation to Balzac, Dickens and Gogol. Cambridge Mass 1965.

Garshin, Vsevolod Mikhaylovich (1855–88)
Stories. Tr E. L. Voynich 1893.

Gogol', Nikolay Vasil'yevich (1809–52)
Works. Tr C. Garnett 6 vols 1922–9.
Revizor. 1836.
The Inspector-General. Tr A. A. Sykes 1892.

Simmons, E. J. Gogol and English literature. MLR 36 1931.
Lefevre, C. Gogol and Anglo-Russian literary relations during the Crimean War. Amer Slavic & East European Rev 34 1956.
Futrell, M. H. Gogol and Dickens. Slavonic & East European Rev 34 1956.
Bryner, C. Gogol, Dickens and the realistic novel. Slavic & East European Stud 8 1963.
Proffer, C. R. Dead souls in translation. Slavonic & East European Jnl 8 1964.

Goncharov, Ivan Aleksandrovich (1812–91)
Obyknovennaya istoriya. Moscow 1847.
A common story. Tr C. Garnett 1894.

Griboyedov, Aleksandr Sergeyevich (1795–1829)
Gore ot uma. 1833; tr N. Benardaky 1857.

Herzen, Aleksandr Ivanovich (1812–70)
Byloye i dumy. 1855.
My past and thoughts. Tr C. Garnett 6 vols 1924–7.

Krasinski, Zygmunt, Count (1812–59)
Lednicki, W. (ed) Zygmunt Krasinski, romantic universalist: an international tribute. New York 1964.

Kozlov, Ivan Ivanovich (1779–1840)
Eyges, I. R. K perevodam Kozlova iz Byrona. In Zven'ya vol 5, Moscow-Leningrad 1935.

Krylov, Ivan Andreyevich (1768–1844)
Krilof and his fables. Tr W. R. S. Ralston 1869. Prose trns of 93 fables. 3rd edn, 1871, contains 148 fables.
Original fables. Tr I. H. Harrison 1883. Verse trns of 149 fables.

Kyukhel'beker, Vil'gel'm Karlovich (1797–1846)
Levin, Y. D. V. K. Kyukhel'beker o poezii Waltera Scotta. Russkaya Literatura no 2 1963.
— Kyukhel'beker and Crabbe. Oxford Slavonic Papers 12 1965.

Lermontov, Mikhail Yur'yevich (1814–41)
Geroy nashego vremeni. 1840.
A hero of our own time. Tr anon 1854.
Demon. 1842; tr F. Storr 1894 (verse).

Bakhtin, N. N. Lermontov i Robert Burns (istoriko-literaturnaya zametka). Minuvshiye Gody Sept 1908.
Dashkevich, N. P. Motivy mirovoy poezil v tvorchestve Lermontova. In his Stat'i po novoy russkoy literature, Petrograd 1914.
Rozanov, M. N. Byronicheskiye motivy v tvorchestve Lermontova. In Venok Lermontovu: sbornik statey, Moscow 1914.
Neyman, B. V. Ispantsy Lermontova i Ivanhoe Walter Scotta. Filologicheskiye Zapiski May–June 1915.
Rozevich, S. I. K voprosu o vliyanii Byrona i A. de Vigny na Lermontova (Yunosheskiye stikhotvoreniya Byrona i Lermontova; Demon i Eloa). Filologicheskiye Zapiski Feb 1915.
Breytman, M. Lermontov, Byron i Chênedollé. Vestnik Literatury Feb–March 1922.
Yakubovich, D. P. Lermontov i Walter Scott. Izvestiya AN SSSR, Otdeleniye Obschchestvennykh Nauk 3 1935.

Chorny, K. Lermontov i Byron. In M. Yu. Lermontov: sbornik statey, Pyatigorsk 1941.
Nol'man, M. Lermontov i Byron. In Zhizn' i tvorchestvo M. Yu. Lermontova, Sbornik 1, Issledovaniya i materialy, Moscow 1941.
Heifetz, A. Lermontov in English: bibliography. BNYPL Sept 1942.
Entwistle, W. J. The Byronism of Lermontov's A hero of our time. Comparative Lit 1 1949.
Grégoire, H. Les sources rythmiques écossaises du Borodino de M. J. Lermontov. Revue des Etudes Slaves 27 1951.
Shaw, J. T. Lermontov's demon and the Byronic oriental verse tale. Indiana Slavic Stud 2 1958.
— Byron, Chênedollé and Lermontov's Dying gladiator. In Studies in honor of John C. Hodges and Alwin Thaler, Knoxville 1962.
Vatsuro, V. Irlandskiye melodii Thomasa Moora v tvorchestve Lermontova. Russkaya Literatura no 3 1965.

Mickiewicz, Adam Bernard (1798–1855)
Windakiewicz, St. The Anglomania of Mickiewicz. Slavonic Rev 8 1929.
Coleman, M. M. Mickiewicz in English 1827–1955. Cambridge 1954.
Bugelski, B. R. (ed). Mickiewicz and the west: a symposium. Buffalo 1956.
Lednicki, W. (ed). Mickiewicz in world literature: a symposium. Berkeley 1956.
Mersereau, J. The influence of James Fenimore Cooper on Adam Mickiewicz. Etudes Slaves et Esteuropéennes 3 1959.

Nekrasov, Nikolay Alekseyevich (1821–77)
Levin, Y. D. Nekrasov v Anglii i Amerike. In N. A. Nekrasov, Stat'i, materialy, referaty i soobshcheniya, Nauchnyy Byulleten' Leningradskogo Universiteta nos 16–17 1947.
— Nekrasov i angliyskiy poet Crabbe. In Nekrasovskiy sbornik vol 2, Moscow-Leningrad 1956.

Ostrovsky, Aleksandr Nikolayevich (1823–86)
Groza. Moscow 1860.
The storm. Tr C. Garnett 1899.

Polezhayev, Aleksandr Ivanovich (1805–38)
Bobrov, Y. Oskar Alvsky Byrona v perevode Polezhayeva. Russkiy Filologicheskiy Vestnik Feb 1905.
— O byronizme Polezhayeva. Warsaw 1906.

Pushkin, Aleksandr Sergeevich (1799–1837)
The queen of spades and other stories, with a biography. Tr S. Edwards 1892.
Prose tales. Tr T. Keane 1894.
Yevgeniy Onegin. Moscow 1825–32; Eugene Onéguine: a romance of Russian life in verse, tr Lt-Col Spalding 1881.

Harnack, O. Pushkin und Byron. Zeitschrift für Vergleichende Literaturgeschichte 1 1888; rptd in his Essays und Studien, Brunswick 1899.
Veselovsky, A. Pushkin i yevropeyskaya poeziya. In his Etyudy i kharakteristiki, Moscow 1907.
Dashkevich, N. P. Otgoloski uvlecheniya Byronom v poezii Pushkina. Sbornik Otdeleniya Russkogo Yazyka i Slovesnosti Imperatorskoy Akademii Nauk (Petrograd) 92 1914.
Sipovsky, V. V. Pushkin i romantizm. In Pushkin i Yego Sovremenniki (Petrograd) 23–4 1916.
Kozmin, N. Pushkin o Byrone. In Pushkin v mirovoy literature: sbornik statey, Leningrad 1926.
Yakovlev, N. Iz razyskaniy o literaturnykh istochnikakh v tvorchestve Pushkina. In Pushkin v mirovoy literature: sbornik statey, Leningrad 1926.
Yakubovich, D. P. Predisloviye k Povestyam Belkina i povestvovatel'nyye priyomy Walter Scotta. In Pushkin v mirovoy literature: sbornik statey Leningrad 1926.
— Reministsentsii iz Walter Scotta v Povestyakh Belkina. In Pushkin i Yego Sovremenniki (Leningrad) 37 1928.
— Iz zametok o Pushkine i Walter Scotte. In Pushkin i Yego Sovremenniki Leningrad 38–9 1930.
— Tragediya W. Scotta Dom aspenov i pushkinskiy romans o rytsare bednom. In Sbornik statey k sorokaletiyu uchonoy deyatel'nosti akad. A. S. Orlova, Leningrad 1934.
— Kapitanskaya dochka i romany Waltera Scotta. Pushkin: Vremennik Pushkinskoy Komissii (Moscow and Leningrad) 4–5 1939.
Svirin, N. K voprosu o byronisme Pushkine. Literaturnyy Sovremennik Feb 1935.
Alekseyev, M. P. Pushkin na zapale. In Pushkin: Vremennik Pushkinskoy Komissii (Moscow and Leningrad) 3 1937.
Cross, S. H. Pouchkine en Angleterre. Revue de Littérature Comparée 17 1937.
Noyes, G. R. Pushkin in world literature. In Centennial essays for Pushkin, ed S. H. Cross and E. J. Simmons, Cambridge Mass.
Simmons, E. J. La littérature anglaise et Pouchkine. Revue de Littérature Comparée 17 1937.
— English translations of Eugene Onegin. Slavonic Rev 17 1938.
Yarmolinsky, A. (ed). Pushkin in English: a list of works by and about Pushkin. New York 1937.
Struve, G. Puškin in early English criticism 1821–38. Amer Slavic & East European Rev 8 1949.
Gifford, H. Pushkin's Feast in time of plague and its original. Ibid.
Greene, M. Pushkin and Sir Walter Scott. Forum for Modern Language Stud 1 1965.

Ryleyev, Kondratiy Fyodorovich (1795–1826)
Voinarofskyi and other poems. Tr into verse by T. Hart-Davies, Calcutta 1879.

Shuvalov, S. V. Ryleyev i Byron. In Svitok 4, Moscow 1926.

Shakhovskoy, Prince Aleksandr Aleksandrovich (1777–1846)
Gozenpud, A. A. Walter Scott i romanticheskiye komedii A. A. Shakovskogo. In Russko-yevropeyskiye literaturnyye svyazi, Moscow-Leningrad 1966.

Shevchenko, Taras Grigor'yevich (1814–61)
Bokjo, J. Shevchenko and western European literature. 1956.
Slavutych, Y. Schevchenko and western European literature. Comparative Lit 10 1958.
Giergielewicz, M. Shevchenko and world literature. In U stolittja, Philadelphia 1962.

Sienkiewicz, Henryk (1846–1916)
Ogniem e mieczem. Warsaw 1884.
With fire and sword. Tr 1890–5.
Quo vadis. 1895; tr 1896.

Segel, H. B. Sienkiewicz's first translator: Jeremiah Curtin. Slavic Rev 24 1965.

Tolstoy, Count Lev Nikolayevich (1828–1910)
Detstvo. Moscow 1852–7.
Childhood, boyhood, youth. Tr I. F. Hapgood, New York 1866, London 1888.
Kazaki. 1852–62.
The Cossacks: a tale of the Caucasus in 1852. Tr E. Schuyler, New York 1878, 2 vols 1878.
Voyna i mir. Moscow 1865–9.
War and peace. Tr N. H. Dole, New York 1889, 4 vols London 1889.
Anna Karenina. Moscow 1873–7.
Anna Karénina. Tr N. H. Dole, New York 1886, London 1886.
Kreitserova sonata. Berlin 1890.
The Kreutzer sonata. Tr H. S. Edwards 1890.
Voskresen'ye. St Petersburg 1899.
Resurrection. Tr L. Maude 1900.

Apostolov, N. N. Tolstoy i Dickens. In Tolstoy i o Tolstom, sbornik i, Moscow 1924.

Yassukovitch, A. Tolstoy in English 1878–1929. BNYPL July 1929.
Zinner, E. P. Tolstoy i angliyskaya realisticheskaya drama kontsa xix i nachala xx stoletiya. Uchonyye Zapiski Irkutskogo Pedagogicheskogo Instituta no 5 1940.
— Tvorchestvo Tolstogo i angliyskaya realisticheskaya literatura kontsa xix i nachala xx stoletiya. Irkutsk 1961.
Clifford, E. War and peace and the Dynasts. MP 54 1956.
Wasiolek, E. Tolstoy's The death of Ivan Ilyich and Jamesian fictional imperatives. Modern Fiction Stud 6 1960.
Buyniak, V. O. Tolstoy and Charles Dickens. Slavic & East European Stud 9 1965.
Zakharov, V. V. Tolstoy i Thomas Hardy: russkiye stseny v Dinastakh. In Russko-yevropeyskiye literaturnyye svyazi, Moscow-Leningrad 1966.

Turgenev, Ivan Sergeyevich (1818–83)
Novels. Tr C. Garnett 15 vols 1894–9.
Nakanune. Moscow 1860.
On the eve. Tr C. E. Turner 1871.
Ottsy i deti. Moscow 1862.
Fathers and sons. Tr E. Schuyler, New York 1867.
Dym. Moscow 1867.
Smoke: or the life at Baden. Tr anon 2 vols 1868.
Nov'. Moscow 1877.
Virgin soil. Tr A. W. Dilke 1878.

Gut'yar, H. Poyezdki I. S. Turgeneva v Angliyu. Izvestiya Kubanskogo Pedagogicheskogo Instituta 2–3 1929.
Gettmann, R. A. Turgenev in England and America. Urbana 1941.
Kain, R. M. The literary reputation of Turgenev in England and America 1867–1906. Madison Quart 2 1942.
Davie, D. Turgenev in England 1850–1950. In Studies in Russian and Polish literature in honour of Waclaw Lednicki, Hague 1962.
Yachnin, R. and D. H. Stam. Turgenev in English: a checklist of works by and about him. New York 1962. *See* G. Watson, Maria Edgeworth and Turgenev, in his edn of Edgeworth, Castle Rackrent, Oxford 1964; Y. Levin, Turgenev na angliyskom yazyke, Russkaya Literatura no 2 1965.

Zogoskin, Mikhail Nikolayevich (1789–1852)
Orlov, A. S. Walter Scott i Zagoskin. In Sergeyu Fyodorovichu Ol'denburgu k 50-letiyu nauchno-obshchestvennoy deyatel'nosti 1882–1932, Moscow and Leningrad 1932.

Zhukovsky, Vasiliy Andreyevich (1783–1852)
Ober, K. H. and W. U. Ober. Žukovskij's early translations of the ballads of Robert Southey. Slavic & East European Jnl 9 1965.
Reizov, B. G. V. A. Zhukovsky, perevodchik Waltera Scotta (Ivanov vecher). In Russko-yevropyeskiye literaturnyye svyazi, Moscow and Leningrad 1966.

English

Burns, Robert
Rudýckyi, J. B. Burns and Shevchenko. Slavistica no 35 1959.
Kepes, G. Burns et Sevcsenko. In La littérature comparée en Europe orientale, ed I. Söter, Budapest 1963.

Byron, George Gordon
Lipnicki, E. Byron im Befreiungskampfe der polnischen Nationalliteratur. Magazin 48 1877.
Byrons Don Juan in polnischer Übersetzung. Magazin 51 1880.
Zdiechowski, M. Karl Hynek Macha und Byrons Einfluss auf die tschechische Dichtkunst. Anzeiger der Akademie der Wissenschaften in Krakau (Cracow) 1893.
— Byron i jego wiek. Studya Porównawczoliterackie (Cracow) 1894–7.
Zhirmunsky, V. M. Byron i Pushkin: Iz istorii romanticheskoy poemy. Leningrad 1924.
Petrovic, I. Byron and the Yugoslavs. Slavonic Rev 8 1929.
Simmons, E. J. Byron and a Greek maid. MLR 27 1932.
Wellek, R. Macha and Byron. Slavonic Rev 16 1937.
Vickery, V. M. Parallelizm v literaturnom razvitii Byrona i Pushkina. In American contributions to the fifth international congress of Slavists, Sofia, Sept 1963 vol 2: literary contributions, Hague 1963.
D'yakonova, N. Ya. Russkiy epizod v poeme Byrona Don Juan. In Russko-yevropeyskiye literaturnyye svyazi, Moscow and Leningrad 1966.

Conrad, Joseph
Maxwell, J. C. Conrad and Turgenev: a minor source for victory. N & Q Oct 1963.

Dickens, Charles
Katkov, G. Steerforth and Stavrogin. Slavonic Rev 27 1949.
Fridlender, Y. V. and I. M. Katarsky (ed). Dickens: bibliografiya russkikh perevodov i kriticheskoy literatury na russkom yazyke (1838–1960). Moscow 1962.
Senelick, L. Dickens and the Russian encyclopaedias. Dickens Stud 1 1965.
Katarsky, I. Dickens v Rossii: seredina xix veka. Moscow 1966.

'Eliot, George' (Mary Ann Cross, b. Evans)
Jones, W. G. George Eliot's Adam Bede and Tolstoy's conception of Anna Karenina. MLR 61 1966.

Gaskell, Elizabeth Cleghorn, Mrs
Johnson, C. A. Russian Gaskelliana. REL 7 1966.

James, Henry
Lerner, D. The influence of Turgenev on James. Slavonic & East European Rev 20 1941.

Moore, Thomas
Alekseyev, M. P. Thomas Moore, yego russkiye sobesedniki i korrespondenty. In Mezhdunarodnyye svyazi russkoy literatury, Moscow and Leningrad 1963.

Ruskin, John
Arthos, J. Ruskin and Tolstoy: The dignity of man. Dalhousie Rev 43 1963.

Scott, Sir Walter
Struve, P. Scott and Russia. Slavonic Rev 11 1933.
Kühne, W. Alexander Branikowski und Scott. Zeitschrift für Slavische Philologie 13 1936.
Razov, Z. Denis Davydov and Scott. Slavonic Yearbook 19 1941.
Klancar, A. J. Josip Jurcie, the Slovene Scott. Amer Slavonic Rev 5 1946.
— Scott in Yugoslavia. Slavonic Rev 27 1949.
Davie, D. The heyday of Sir Walter Scott. 1961. Chs on Scott's influence on Pushkin and Mickiewicz.

Shaw, George Bernard
Breytsburg, S. Shaw v spore c Tolstym o Shakespeare. Literaturnoye Nasledstvo (Moscow and Leningrad) 37–8 1939.
Zinner, E. P. Shaw i russkaya literatura (L. N. Tolstoy, A. P. Chekhov, A. M. Gor'ky). Uchonyye Zapiski Irkutskogo Pedagogicheskogo Instituta no 15 1959.
Mendelsohn, M. J. The heartbreak houses of Shaw and Chekhov. Shaw Rev 6 1963.
Harris, H. J. Shaw, Chekhov and two great ladies of the theatre. Ibid.

Stevenson, Robert Louis
Knowlton, E. C. A Russian influence on Stevenson. MP 11 1916.

Thackeray, William Makepeace
Akmechet, L. Y. Russkaya revolyutsionno-demokraticheskaya kritika o Tekkereye. Uchonyye Zapiski Bashkirskogo Pedagogicheskogo Instituta no 5 1955.

Wilde, Oscar
Abramovich, N. Y. Religiya krasoty i stradaniya: Wilde i Dostoyevsky. St Petersburg 1909.

F. K.

(9) OTHERS

See under Byron and Kinglake, cols 270, 1489 below.

Greek

Gamba, P. A narrative of Byron's last journey to Greece. 1825.

Harrington, L. F. C. S. (Col Leicester Stanhope). Greece in 1823 and 1824. 1825. Letters to Bowring, Byron et al.

Jebb, R. C. Byron in Greece. In his Modern Greece, 1880.

Miller, W. The English in Athens before 1821. 1926.

Spender, H. Byron and Greece. 1924.

Knight, G. W. Byron: Christian virtues. 1953.

Liljegren, S. B. Byron and Greece. In Studies presented to D. M. Robinson vol 2, St Louis 1953.

—— Byron and Greece. Revue de Littérature Comparée 32 1958.

Spencer, T. J. B. Fair Greece, sad relic. 1954.

Rumanian

Doïne: or the national songs and legends of Roumania. 1854. Tr with introd by E. C. Grenville-Murray.

Turdeanu, E. Oscar of Alva de Byron: sources orientales et reflets roumains. Sibiu 1944.

Coleman, M. M. Rumanian materials in English. Bull of Amer Assoc of Teachers of Slavic Languages 5 1947.

Tappe, E. D. The Rumanian anthologies of Grenville-Murray and Stanley. Revue de Littérature Comparée 30 1956.

C. C.

2. POETRY

I. GENERAL WORKS

This section should be used in conjunction with the Introduction, col 1 above

A. HISTORIES AND SURVEYS

(1) GENERAL

Griswold, R. W. The poets and poetry of England in the nineteenth century. Philadelphia 1845 (2nd edn).

Moir, E. M. Sketches of the poetical literature of the past half-century. Edinburgh 1851.

Brandes, G. Hovedstrømninger i det 19de aarhundredes litteratur. 6 vols Copenhagen 1872–90; tr 1901–5.

Sarrazin, G. Poètes modernes de l'Angleterre. Paris 1885.

—— Renaissance de la poésie anglaise 1792–1889. Paris 1889.

Walker, H. The age of Tennyson. 1897.

—— The literature of the Victorian era. Cambridge 1910.

Saintsbury, G. A history of nineteenth-century literature 1780–1900. 1901.

Gosse, E. A history of English literature in the 19th century. 1906.

Payne, W. M. The greater English poets of the nineteenth century. New York 1907.

Schelling, F. E. The English lyric. Boston 1907.

Dixon, W. M. English epic and heroic poetry. 1912.

Rhys, E. Lyric poetry. 1913.

Osmond, P. H. The mystical poets of the English Church. New York 1919.

Cazamian, L. L'évolution psychologique et la littérature en Angleterre 1660–1914. Paris 1920.

Bateson, F. W. English poetry and the English language. Oxford 1934.

—— English poetry: a critical introduction. 1950, 1966 (rev).

Lieder, P. R. Eminent British poets of the nineteenth century. New York 1938.

Read, H. Collected essays in literary criticism. 1938, 1951 (rev).

Bronowski, J. The poet's defence. Cambridge 1939. On Shelley, Wordsworth, Coleridge, Swinburne, Housman, Yeats.

Neff, E. E. A revolution in European poetry 1600–1900. New York 1940.

Chew, S. C. The nineteenth century and after 1789–1939. In A literary history of England, ed A. Baugh, New York 1948.

Grigson, G. The harp of Aeolus and other essays on art, literature and nature. 1948.

Tinker, C. B. Essays in retrospect. New Haven 1948. On the poetry of the Brontës, Morris, the Pre-Raphaelites, Meredith, Housman.

Thompson, F. Minor poets. Ed T. L. Connolly, Los Angeles 1949.

Murry, J. M. John Clare and other studies. 1950.

Tillotson, G. Criticism and the nineteenth century. 1951.

Davie, D. A. Purity of diction in English verse. 1952. Pt 2: Wordsworth, Coleridge, Shelley, Hopkins, Landor.

Hopkins, K. The poets laureate. 1954.

Oliver, J. W. Scottish poetry in the earlier nineteenth century. In Scottish poetry, ed J. Kinsley 1955.

Young, D. Scottish poetry in the later nineteenth century. Ibid.

Ure, P. From Wordsworth to Yeats. Listener 25 July 1957.

Schmerl, R. B. The advance of civilization and the decline of poetry: nineteenth-century statements. Michigan Alumnus Quart Rev 64 1958.

Schackford, M. H. Talks on 10 poets: Wordsworth to Moody. New York 1958.

Schubel, F. Englische Literaturgeschichte III: Romantik und Viktorianismus. Berlin 1960.

Ogawa, J. English poetry. In History of English and American literature VII: the nineteenth century. Tokyo 1961. In Japanese.

Reeves, J. A short history of English poetry. 1961.

Cruttwell, P. Romantics and Victorians. Hudson Rev 14 1962.

Pearsall, R. The archaism that failed. Quart Rev 302 1964.

(2) THE ROMANTIC MOVEMENT

Talfourd, T. N. An attempt to estimate the poetical talent of the present age, including a sketch of the history of poetry and the characters of Southey, Crabbe, Scott, Moore, Lord Byron, Campbell, Lamb, Coleridge and Wordsworth. 1815 (Pamphleteer vol 5).

Hunt, J. H. L. Lord Byron and some of his contemporaries. 1828.

Cunningham, A. Biographical and critical history of the last fifty years. 1833.

Oliphant, M. O. The literary history of England in the end of the eighteenth and the beginning of the nineteenth century. 3 vols 1882.

Courthope, W. J. The liberal movement in English literature. 1885.

—— History of English poetry, vol 6. 1910.

Brandl, A. Samuel Taylor Coleridge und die englische Romantik. Berlin 1886; tr 1887.

Dixon, W. M. English poetry from Blake to Browning. 1894.

Herford, C. H. The age of Wordsworth. 1897.

Omond, T. S. The romantic triumph. Edinburgh 1900.

Vaughan, C. E. The romantic revolt. Edinburgh 1900.

Beers, H. A. A history of English romanticism in the nineteenth century. New York 1901.

Symons, A. The romantic movement in English poetry. 1909.

Richter, H. Geschichte der englischen Romantik. 2 vols Halle 1911–16.

Elton, O. A survey of English literature 1780–1830. 2 vols 1912.

Bernbaum, E. Guide through the romantic movement. New York 1930, 1949, 1954 (both rev and enlarged).

Rogers, W. H. Portraits of romantic poets in contemporary minor fiction. Western Reserve Univ Bull new ser 34 1931.

Cellini, B. Studi sul romanticismo inglese. Leghorn 1932.

Sherwood, M. Undercurrents of influence in English romantic poetry. Cambridge Mass 1934.
'Winwar, Frances' (F. Grebanier). The romantic rebels. Boston 1935.
Leavis, F. R. Revaluation: tradition and development in English poetry. 1936.
Cazamian, L. La poésie romantique anglaise. Paris 1939.
Dyson, H. V. D. and J. Butt. Augustans and romantics 1689–1830. 1940, 1950 (rev). Vol 3 of Introductions to English literature, ed B. Dobrée.
Romanticism: a symposium. PMLA 55 1940.
D'Israeli, I. Unpublished notes on the romantic poets. 1941.
Knight, G. W. The starlit dome. Oxford 1941. On Wordsworth, Coleridge, Shelley, Keats.
van Tieghem, P. La place du romantisme anglais dans le romantisme européen. Lettres 5–6 1946.
de Selincourt, E. Wordsworthian and other studies. Oxford 1947.
Elwin, M. The first romantics. 1947. A collective biography of Wordsworth, Coleridge and Southey.
Fausset, H. I'A. Poets and pundits. 1947.
Klein, F. Anglický romantismus: Wordsowrth, Coleridge, Byron, Shelley, Keats. Prague 1947. In Czech.
James, D. G. The romantic comedy. 1948.
—— Byron and Shelley. Nottingham 1951.
—— Matthew Arnold and the decline of English romanticism. 1961.
Murry, J. M. Katherine Mansfield and other literary portraits. 1949.
White, N. I. Our ancient contemporaries, the romantic poets. Lib Notes July 1950.
Kano, H. English romantic poets. Tokyo 1951.
Armour, R. Survey of the romantic poets. Georgia Rev 6 1952.
Hough, G. The romantic poets. 1953.
Read, H. The true voice of feeling: studies in English romantic poetry. 1953.
—— The romantic revolution. London Mag June 1955.
Murakami, S. The dawn of English romanticism. Tokyo 1956.
Dobrzyckiej, J. (ed). Materialy pomocnicze do historii literatury powszechnej xix wieku: literatura angielska. Warsaw 1957.
Fox, A. English poetry in the reign of George III: continuity and contrast. English 11 1957.
Harding, D. W. The character of literature from Blake to Byron. In Pelican guide to English literature vol 5, ed B. Ford 1957.
Kettle, A. The English romantic movement. Philologica 9 1957.
Battenhouse, H. M. English romantic writers. Great Neck NY 1958.
Brand, C. P. Italy and the English Romantics. Cambridge 1958.
Hirai, M. English romantic poetry. Gakuen [Kōyōkai, Shōwa Woman's College] no 221 1958. In Japanese.
Clark, K. A handlist: the romantic movement. 1959.
James, G. I. The unexplored romanticism. Criticism 1 1959.
Nicolson, H. The romantic revolt. Horizon (New York) 3 1961.
Jack, I. English literature 1815–32. Oxford 1963 (OHEL vol 10).
Dudley, F. A. Dating the term 'Lake School'. Eng Lang Notes 1 1964.
Hewlett, D. On the romantic movement in English poetry. Aryan Path 35 1964.

(3) VICTORIAN POETRY

Stedman, E. C. Victorian poets. 1876, Boston 1903 (rev).
Oliphant, M. O. and F. R. The Victorian age of English literature. 2 vols 1892.
Walker, H. The greater Victorian poets. 1893.
—— The age of Tennyson. 1897.
—— The literature of the Victorian era. Cambridge 1910.
Dixon, W. M. English poetry from Blake to Browning. 1894.
Saintsbury, G. A history of nineteenth-century literature 1780–1900. 1901.
Smith, A. The main tendencies of Victorian poetry. Birmingham 1907.
Chesterton, G. K. The Victorian age in literature. 1913.
Elton, O. A survey of English literature 1830–80. 2 vols 1920.
Weatherhead, L. D. The after-world of the poets: the contribution of Victorian poets to the development of the idea of immortality. 1929.
Lucas, F. L. Eight Victorian poets. Cambridge 1930 (on Tennyson, Browning, Arnold, Clough, Rossetti, Swinburne, Morris, Hardy); rev as Ten Victorian poets, Cambridge 1940 (new chs on Patmore and Christina Rossetti), 1948.
Batho, E. C. The Victorians and after 1830–1914. 1938, 1950 (rev). Vol 4 of Introductions to English literature, ed B. Dobrée.
Merriam, H. G. Edward Moxon, publisher of poets. New York 1938.
Miles, J. Primary language of poetry in the 1740's and 1840's. Berkeley 1950.
Stevenson, L. The pertinacious Victorian poets. UTQ 21 1952.
Yano, H. Victorian poetry. Tokyo 1954.
Parrott, T. M. and R. B. Martin. A companion to Victorian literature. New York 1955.
Jones, H. M. The generation of 1830. Harvard Lib Bull 13 1959.
Müller-Schwefe, G. Fortschrittsglaube und Dichtung im Victorianischen England. Anglia 77 1959.
Rosenbaum, R. A. Earnest Victorians. New York 1961.
Bose, A. Chroniclers of life: studies in early Victorian poetry. 1962.
Davies, H. S. Blake to Browning. 1962. Vol 2 of Poets and their critics. An anthology.
Merivale, P. The 'Death of Pan' in Victorian literature. Victorian Newsletter no 23 1963.
—— The Pan figure in Victorian poetry: Landor to Meredith. PQ 44 1965.
Nelson, J. G. The sublime Puritan: Milton and the Victorians. Madison 1963.
Combecher, H. Drei Victorianische Gedichte. Die Neueren Sprachen 13 1964.
Drew, P. The case for Victorian poetry. Listener 16 July 1964.

(4) LATE VICTORIAN POETRY

Austin, A. The poetry of the period. 1870. On Tennyson, Browning, Swinburne, Arnold, Morris.
Forman, H. B. Our living poets. 1871.
Archer, W. Poets of the younger generation. 1902.
Brooke, S. A. A study of Clough, Arnold, Rossetti and Morris, with an introduction on the course of poetry from 1822 to 1852. 1908.
Kennedy, J. M. English literature 1880–1905. 1912.
Jackson, H. The eighteen-nineties. 1913.
Burdett, O. The Beardsley period. 1925.
Le Gallienne, R. The romantic '90s. 1926.
Granville-Barker, H. et al. The eighteen-seventies. Cambridge 1929.
de la Mare, W. et al. The eighteen-eighties. Cambridge 1930.

Drinkwater, J. et al. The eighteen-sixties. Cambridge 1932.
Wild, F. Die englische Literatur der Gegenwart seit 1870: Versdichtungen. Leipzig 1931.
Braybrooke, P. Some Victorian and Georgian Catholics: their art and outlook. 1932.
Walraf, E. Soziale Lyrik in England 1880–1914. Leipzig 1932.
Evans, B. I. English poetry in the later nineteenth century. 1933, 1966 (rev).
Mégroz, R. L. Modern English poetry 1882–1932. 1933.
Wellek, R. Poesie druhe generace viktorianske. Časopis pro Moderni Filologii 22 1935. The poetical work of the second Victorian generation, with English summary.
Palmer, H. Post-Victorian poetry. 1938.
Hough, G. The last Romantics. 1949.
Salvan, J.-L. Le romantisme français et l'Angleterre victorienne. Paris 1949.
Buckley, J. H. The revolt from 'rationalism' in the seventies and some of its literary consequences. In Booker memorial studies, Chapel Hill 1950.
Heath-Stubbs, J. The darkling plain: a study of the later fortunes of romanticism in English poetry from George Darley to W. B. Yeats. 1950.
Pinto, V. de S. The crisis in English poetry 1880–1940. 1951.
Raymond, W. O. 'The mind's internal heaven' in poetry, UTQ 20 1951. On Hopkins, FitzGerald, Swinburne. Housman, Bridges, Yeats.
Robinson, J. K. A neglected phase of the aesthetic movement: English Parnassianism. PMLA 68 1953.
Temple, R. Z. The critic's alchemy: a study of French symbolism into England. New York 1953.
Thwaite, A. Essays on contemporary English poetry: Hopkins to the present day. Tokyo 1957.
Rodway, A. E. The last phase. In Pelican guide to English literature vol 6, ed B. Ford 1958.
Ryals, C. de L. Toward a definition of *decadent* as supplied to British literature of the nineteenth century. Jnl of Aesthetics 17 1958.
Eckhoff, L. The aesthetic movement in English literature. Oslo 1959.
Peters, R. L. Toward an 'un-definition' of *decadent* as applied to British literature of the nineteenth century. Jnl of Aesthetics 18 1959.
Harris, W. Innocent decadence: the poetry of the Savoy. PMLA 77 1962.
Stanford, D. The poets of the nineties: a note in revision. South Atlantic Quart 64 1965.

B. CRITICAL STUDIES

(1) IDEALS AND POETIC THEORIES OF THE ROMANTIC SCHOOL

Wordsworth, W. Lyrical ballads. 1800, 1815 (with Essay supplementary to the Preface).
Bowles, W. L. Pope's poetical works. 10 vols 1806. Criticism of Pope's standards and methods prefixed.
—— The invariable principles of poetry. 1819.
—— Two letters to Lord Byron. 1821.
Coleridge, S. T. Biographia literaria. 2 vols 1817.
—— Anima poetae: from the unpublished notebooks. Ed E. H. Coleridge 1895.
Hazlitt, W. Lectures on the English poets. 1818.
Campbell, T. An essay on English poetry, prefixed to Specimens of the British poets. 7 vols 1819.
Byron, G. G., Baron. A letter to [John Murray]. 1821.
—— Observations upon Observations. 1821.
de Quincey, T. Letters to a young man whose education has been neglected. London Mag March 1823.
—— The Lake Poets: Wordsworth. Tait's Mag Feb 1839.
—— The Lake Poets: Southey, Wordsworth and Coleridge. Tait's Mag Aug 1839.
—— On Wordsworth's poetry. Tait's Mag Sept 1845.
—— Alexander Pope. North Br Rev 9 1848.
Heine, H. Zur Geschichte der neueren schönen Literatur in Deutschland. In Europe littéraire, Paris 1833; tr German, 1833, 1836 (with addn of bk 3 entitled Die romantische Schule); tr 1883.
Mill, J. S. Thoughts on poetry and its varieties. Monthly Repository new ser Jan, Oct 1833.
—— Autobiography. 1873.
Wilson, J. M. The enthusiast, with a preliminary chapter on poetry. Edinburgh 1834.
Lofft, C. Ernest. 1839, 1868 (with preface on nature of poetry).
Hunt, J. H. L. Imagination and fancy: or selections from the English poets, with an essay in answer to the question What is poetry? 1844; ed A. S. Cook, Boston 1893.
Taylor, H. Philip van Artevelde. 1834, 1846 (3rd edn). Preface.
Mackay, C. Egeria. 1850. Includes essay on poetry.
Lynch, T. T. On poetry. In Essays on some of the forms of literature, 1853.
Shairp, J. Aspects of poetry. Oxford 1881.
Watts-Dunton, T. Essay on poetry. In Encyclopaedia britannica, 1884 (9th edn).
—— The sonnet. In Chambers' Encyclopaedia, 1891.
—— The renascence of wonder in English poetry. Introd to vol 3 of Chambers' cyclopaedia of English literature, ed D. Patrick 1903.
—— Poetry and the renascence of wonder, with a preface by T. Hake. 1916. Based on the foregoing essays, which are rptd, with his contributions to Athenaeum 1876–1902 left unrevised at his death.
Symonds, J. A. The lyricism of the English romantic drama. In his Key of blue, 1893.
Herford, C. H. The age of Wordsworth. 1897.
Texte, J. Keats et le néo-hellénisme dans la poésie anglaise. In Etudes de littérature européenne, Paris 1898.
Campbell, O. W. Shelley and the unromantics. 1923.
Gordon, G. S. Shelley and the oppressors of mankind. Oxford 1923.
Gingerich, S. F. Essays in the romantic poets. New York 1924. Traces growth of their convictions.
—— The conception of beauty in the works of Shelley, Keats and Poe. In Essays and studies in English and comparative literature, Ann Arbor 1932.
Lovejoy, A. O. On the discrimination of romanticisms. PMLA 39 1924; rev and rptd in his Essays in the history of ideas, Baltimore 1948.
—— Romanticism and the principle of plenitude. In his Great chain of being, Cambridge Mass 1936.
—— The meaning of romanticism for the historian of ideas. JHI 2 1941. *See* Wellek *and* Peckham, *below*.
Murry, J. M. Romanticism and the tradition. Criterion 2 1924.
Kauffmann, P. Defining romanticism: a survey and a program. MLN 40 1925.
Powell, A. E. The romantic theory of poetry: an examination in the light of Croce's aesthetic. 1926.
Fairchild, H. N. The noble savage. New York 1928.
—— The romantic quest. New York 1931, 1953.
—— Romanticism: devil's advocate. In the major English romantic poets, ed C. D. Thorpe et al, Carbondale 1957.
Chapman, J. A. Papers on Shelley, Wordsworth and others. Oxford 1929.
Elliott, G. R. The cycle of modern poetry. Princeton 1929.
Praz, M. La carne, la morte e il diavolo nella letteratura romantica. Florence 1930; tr 1933 (as The romantic agony).
Levin, H. The broken column: a study in romantic Hellenism. Cambridge Mass 1931.
Carr, P. Days with the French Romantics in the Paris of 1830. 1932.

Erhardt-Siebold, E. von. Harmony of the senses in English, German and French romanticism. PMLA 47 1932.
Sickells, E. M. The gloomy egoist: moods and themes of melancholy from Gray to Keats. New York 1932.
Jones, R. E. Romanticism reconsidered: humanism and romantic poetry. Sewanee Rev 41 1933.
Sherwood, M. Undercurrents of influence in English romantic poetry. Cambridge Mass 1934.
Morley, E. J. The life and times of Henry Crabb Robinson. Oxford 1935.
Weber, C. A. Bristols Bedeutung für die englische Romantik. Halle 1935.
Batho, E. C. The poet and the past. Proc Br Acad 23 1937.
Bush, D. Mythology and the romantic tradition in English poetry. Cambridge Mass 1937, New York 1963.
Dubois, A. Shelley, Browning and Masters. Personalist 18 1937.
James, D. G. Scepticism and poetry. 1937.
Quennell, P. C. The romantic catastrophe. Horizon 1 1940.
Burgum, E. B. Romanticism. Kenyon Rev 3 1941.
Caldwell, J. R. The solemn romantics. In Studies in the comic, California Univ Pbns in Eng 8 1941.
Earnest, E. Infinity in the palm of your hand. College Eng Jan 1941.
Hungerford, E. B. Shores of darkness. New York 1941.
Blunden, E. Romantic poetry and the fine arts. Proc Br Acad 28 1942.
Barnes, T. Portraits of authors. In Thomas Barnes of the Times, ed D. Hudson, Cambridge 1943. On Moore, Coleridge, Byron, Wordsworth.
Barzun, J. Romanticism and the modern ego. New York 1943, 1961 (rev as Classic, romantic and modern).
Larrabee, S. A. English bards and Grecian marbles. New York 1943.
Bentley, E. A. Romanticism: a revaluation. Antioch Rev 4 1944.
Beach, J. W. A romantic view of poetry. Minneapolis 1944.
Guerard, A. J. Prometheus and the Aeolian lyre. Yale Rev 33 1944.
Bate, W. J. From classic to romantic: premises of taste in eighteenth-century England. Cambridge Mass 1946.
Fogle, R. H. A recent attack on romanticism. College Eng April 1948.
—— A note on romantic oppositions and reconciliations. In The major English romantic poets, ed C. D. Thorpe et al, Carbondale 1957.
Tillotson, G. The manner of proceeding in certain eighteenth and early nineteenth-century poems. Proc Br Acad 34 1948.
—— The methods of description in eighteenth and nineteenth-century poetry. In Restoration and eighteenth-century literature, ed C. Camden, Chicago 1963.
Bowra, C. M. The romantic imagination. Cambridge Mass 1949.
Pottle, F. A. The romantic imagination revisited. Yale Rev 29 1949.
Wellek, R. The concept of romanticism in literary history. Comparative Lit 1 1949.
A source of romanticism. TLS 20 Jan 1950.
Auden, W. H. The enchafèd flood: or the romantic iconography of the sea. New York 1950.
Bullett, G. The English mystics. 1950.
Friederich, W. P. Dante and English romanticism. In his Dante's fame abroad, Chapel Hill 1950.
Grober, L. Shakespeare in der Kritik der englischen Romantik. Neuphilologische Zeitschrift 2 1950.
Havens, R. D. Discontinuity in literary development: the case of English romanticism. SP 47 1950.
—— Simplicity: a changing concept. JHI 14 1953.

Benziger, J. Organic unity: Leibniz to Coleridge. PMLA 66 1951.
Doughty, O. Dante and the English romantic poets. Eng Miscellany (Rome) 2 1951.
Gérard, A. Coleridge, Keats and the modern mind. EC 1 1951.
—— L'idée romantique de la poésie en Angleterre. Paris 1956.
—— On the logic of romanticism. EC 7 1957; tr from L'Athénée 45 1956.
Miles, J. The continuity of poetic language: studies in English poetry from the 1540's to the 1940's. Berkeley 1951.
—— The romantic mode in poetry. ELH 20 1953; rptd in her Eras and modes in English poetry, Berkeley 1957.
Pearce, H. R. The didacticism of the romantics. Dublin Rev 225 1951.
Peckham, M. Toward a theory of romanticism. PMLA 66 1951.
—— The triumph of romanticism. Mag of Art 45 1952.
—— Beyond the tragic vision: the quest for identity in the nineteenth century. New York 1962.
Hardy, B. Keats, Coleridge and negative capability, N & Q 5 July 1952.
Peacock, R. Novalis and Schopenhauer: a critical transition in romanticism, in German studies presented to L. A. Willoughby. Oxford 1952.
Wigod, J. D. Negative capability and wise passiveness. PMLA 67 1952.
Willoughby, L. A. English romantic criticism or fancy and the imagination. In Festgabe für Fritz Strich, ed W. Muschg and E. Staiger, Berne 1952.
Abrams, M. H. The mirror and the lamp: romantic theory and the critical tradition. New York 1953.
—— English romanticism: the spirit of the age. In Romanticism reconsidered, ed N. Frye, New York 1963.
Bronson, B. H. The pre-romantic or post-Augustan mode. ELH 20 1953.
Daniel, R. Odes to dejection. Kenyon Rev 15 1953.
Wain, J. (ed). Contemporary reviews of romantic poetry. 1953.
Watson, G. 'Imagination' and 'fancy'. EC 3 1953.
Poulet, G. Timelessness and romanticism. JHI 15 1954.
Peyre, H. Romantic poetry and rhetoric. Yale French Stud 13 1954.
Crawford, T. The Edinburgh Review and romantic poetry 1802–29. Auckland Univ College Bull 47 (Eng ser 8) 1955.
Dobrée, B. The broken cistern: the Clark lectures 1952–3. 1954.
Cragg, R. C. Romantic revenge. Cambridge Jnl April 1954.
Cohen, R. Association of ideas and poetic unity. PQ 36 1957.
Nitchie, E. Form in romantic poetry. In The major English romantic poets, ed C. D. Thorpe et al, Carbondale 1957.
Adams, R. M. Strains of discord: studies in literary openness. Ithaca 1958.
Foakes, R. A. The romantic assertion: a study of the language of nineteenth-century poets. 1958.
Hennessy, H. The Dial: its poetry and poetic criticism. New England Quart 31 1958.
Hagstrum, J. Romantic skylarks. Newberry Lib Bull 5 1959.
Nicolson, M. H. Mountain gloom and mountain glory: the development of the aesthetics of the infinite. Ithaca 1959.
Oppel, H. The sacred river: Studien und Interpretationen zur Dichtung der englischen Romantik. Die Neueren Sprachen 4 1959.
Perkins, D. The quest for permanence: the symbolism of Wordsworth, Shelley and Keats. Cambridge Mass 1959.
Ryals, C. de L. The nineteenth-century cult of inaction. Tennessee Stud in Lit 4 1959.

Unger, E. J. An aesthetic discussion in the early nineteenth century: the 'ideal'. MLQ 20 1959.

Wasserman, E. R. The subtler language. Baltimore 1959.

—— Romanticism reexamined. In Romanticism reconsidered, ed N. Frye, New York 1963.

—— Shakespeare and the English romantic movement. In The persistence of Shakespeare idolatry, ed H. M. Schueller, Detroit 1964.

—— The English romantics: the grounds of knowledge. Stud in Romanticism 4 1964.

Kroeber, K. Romantic narrative art. Madison 1960.

—— The artifice of reality. Madison 1964.

Bloom, H. The visionary company: a reading of English romantic poetry. Garden City NY 1961.

Pedrini, L. N. and D. T. Serpent imagery and symbolism in the major English romantic poets: Blake, Wordsworth, Coleridge, Byron, Shelley, Keats. Psychiatric Quart suppl 34–5 1960–1.

Viebrock, H. Shakespeare und die englische Romantik. Shakespeare Jahrbuch 97 1961.

Blackstone, B. The lost travellers: a romantic theme with variations. 1962.

Courthion, P. Romanticism. Tr Cleveland 1962.

Frye, N. The drunken boat: the revolutionary element in romanticism. In Romanticism reconsidered, ed Frye, New York 1963.

Hartman, G. H. Romanticism and 'anti-self consciousness'. Centennial Rev of Arts & Science (Michigan State Univ) 6 1962.

Piper, H. W. The active universe: pantheism and the concept of imagination in the English romantic poets. 1962.

Bostetter, E. E. The romantic ventriloquists: Wordsworth, Coleridge, Keats, Shelley, Byron. Seattle 1963.

Empson, W. The active universe. CQ 5 1963.

Godfrey, D. R. Imagination and truth: some romantic contradictions. E Studies 44 1963.

Kreutz, C. Das Prometheus-symbol in der englischen Romantik. Göttingen 1963.

Rodway, A. E. The romantic conflict. 1963.

Runciman, S. Medieval history and the romantic imagination. Essays by Divers Hands 32 1963.

Bentman, R. The romantic poets and critics on Robert Burns. Texas Studies in Lit & Lang 6 1964.

Fischer, H. Die romantische Verserzähling in England. Tübingen 1964.

Hodgart, P., and T. Redpath (ed). Romantic perspectives: the work of Crabbe, Blake, Wordsworth and Coleridge as seen by their contemporaries and by themselves. 1964.

Massey, I. The romantic movement, phrase or fact? Dalhousie Rev 44 1964.

Zwerdling, A. The mythographers and the romantic revival of Greek myth. PMLA 79 1964.

Hertz, R. N. English and American romanticism. Personalist 46 1965.

Kantak, V. Y. Modern appraisal of romantic poetry. Literary Criterion (Univ of Mysore, India) 6 1965.

(2) FRENCH REVOLUTION, BYRONISM AND GOETHE

Goethe, J. W. von. Faust: zweiter Theil. Stuttgart 1833. Especially act 3, pbd separately 1827 as Helena: klassisch-romantische Phantasmagorie. Euphorion, son of Faust and Helen, symbolizes Byron.

Chasles, V. E. P. Vie et influence de Byron sur son époque. In Etudes sur la littérature et les moeurs de l'Angleterre au XIXe siècle, Paris 1850.

Courthope, W. J. The liberal movement in English literature. 1885.

Dowden, E. The French Revolution and English literature. 1897.

Hancock, A. E. The French Revolution and the English poets. 1899.

Cestre, C. La révolution française et les poètes anglais. Dijon 1906.

Graham, W. Politics of the greater romantic poets. PMLA 36 1921.

Chew, S. C. Byron in England: his fame and afterfame. 1924.

Brinton, C. The political ideas of the English romanticists. Oxford 1926.

Estève, E. Byron et le romantisme français. Paris 1929.

Richter, H. Lord Byron: Persönlichkeit und Werk. Halle 1929.

Krug, W. G. Byron als dichterische Gestalt in England, Frankreich, Deutschland und Amerika. Potsdam 1932.

Hentschel, C. The Byronic Teuton: aspects of German pessimism 1800–33. 1939.

Skard, S. Byron i norsk litteratur i det nittande hundrearet. Edda 39 1939.

Hudson, A. P. and V. M. 'The coast of France how near!': French invasion and English literature 1793–1805. South Atlantic Quart 40 1941.

Ward, W. S. Some aspects of the conservative attitude toward poetry in English criticism 1789–1820. PMLA 60 1945.

Frantz, A. I. Half a hundred thralls to Faust: a study based on the British and the American translators of Goethe's Faust 1823–1949. Chapel Hill 1949.

Scott, D. F. S. Some English correspondents of Goethe. 1949.

Link, F. H. Goethe und die Renaissance des neuenglischen Geisteslebens im 19 Jahrhundert. Die Neueren Sprachen 3 1954.

Butler, E. M. Byron and Goethe: analysis of a passion. 1956.

Dédéyan, C. Le thème de Faust II: le préromantisme: le Cain de Byron. Revue des Lettres Modernes 3 1956.

Weinstein, L. The metamorphoses of Don Juan. Stanford 1959.

Bloom, H. Napoleon and Prometheus: the romantic myth of organic energy. Yale French Stud 26 1961.

Thorslev, P. L. The Byronic hero: types and prototypes. Minneapolis 1962.

(3) POETIC FORMS

The Sonnet

Hunt, J. H. L. The book of the sonnet. Ed Leigh Hunt (with an essay on the sonnet) and S. A. Lee (with an essay on American sonnets and sonneteers). 2 vols Boston 1867.

Tomlinson, C. The sonnet: its origin, structure and place in poetry. 1874.

Dennis, J. The English sonnet. In his Studies in English literature, 1876.

Sharp, W. Sonnets of this century. 1886.

Sanderlin, G. The influence of Milton and Wordsworth on the early Victorian sonnet. ELH 5 1938.

—— The repute of Shakespeare's sonnets in the early nineteenth century. MLN 54 1939.

—— A bibliography of English sonnets 1800–50. ELH 8 1941.

Cunningham, J. V. Statius, Keats and Wordsworth. PQ 27 1948.

Steele, M. A. E. The authorship of the Poet and other sonnets: selections from a nineteenth-century ms anthology. Keats-Shelley Jnl 5 1956.

The Spenserian Stanza

Reschke, H. Die Spenserstanze im neunzehnten Jahrhundert. Heidelberg 1918.
Aubin, R. A. Imitations of Childe Harold. E Studien 70 1935.

The Lyric

Dennis, J. English lyrical poetry. In his Studies in English literature, 1876.
du Prell, C. Psychologie der Lyrik. Leipzig 1880.
Sharp, W. (ed). Great odes: English and American. 1890.
Werner, R. M. Lyrik und Lyriker: eine Untersuchung. Hamburg 1890.
Schelling, F. E. The English lyric. Boston 1910.
Hepple, N. Lyrical forms in England. Cambridge 1911.
Reed, E. B. English lyrical poetry. New Haven 1912.
Rhys, E. Lyric poetry. 1913.
Binyon, L. The English ode. Trans Royal Soc of Lit 2 1922.
Grierson, H. J. C. Lyrical poetry from Blake to Hardy. 1928.
Gugler, I. Das Problem der fragmentarischen Dichtung in der englischen Romantik. Berne 1944.
Abrams, M. H. The correspondent breeze: a romantic metaphor. Kenyon Rev 19 1957.
— Structure and style in the greater romantic lyric. In From sensibility to romanticism, ed F. W. Hilles and H. Bloom, New York 1965.
Maddison, C. Apollo and the nine: a history of the ode. Baltimore 1960.
Chayes, I. H. Rhetoric as drama: an approach to the romantic ode. PMLA 79 1964.

Drawing-Room Verse and the Dramatic Monologue

Locker-Lampson, F. Lyra elegantiarum. 1867.
Hewlett, H. G. Poets of society. Contemporary Rev July 1872.
Smith, G. B. English fugitive poets. In his Poets and novelists, 1875.
Gosse, E. A plea for certain exotic forms of verse. Cornhill Mag July 1877.
Dobson, A. Notes on some foreign forms of verse. In W. D. Adams, Latter-day lyrics, 1878.
Lang, A. Letters on literature. 1889. 2 letters on vers de société.
Swinburne, A. C. Social verse. In his Studies in prose and poetry, 1894.
Sessions, I. B. The dramatic monologue. PMLA 62 1947.
Hobman, D. L. Victorian Muses. Hibbert Jnl 48 1950. On L. Aikin, A. and E. Strickland.
Price, J. B. Parody and humour. Contemporary Rev Oct 1951.
Sewell, E. Bats and tea-trays: a note on nonsense. EC 1 1951.
— The field of nonsense. 1952.
Bose, A. The verse of the English Annuals. RES new ser 4 1953.
Disher, M. W. Victorian song: from dive to drawing-room. 1955.
Langbaum, R. The poetry of experience: the dramatic monologue in modern literary tradition. 1958.

Epic, Ballad and Popular Verse

Jordan, W. Epische Briefe no 3. Frankfurt 1876. Is the age of epic composition past?
Beyer, V. Die Begründung der ernsten Ballade durch G. A. Bürger. Quellen und Forschungen 97 1905.
Bradley, C. B. On the distinction between the art-epic and the folk-epic. Univ of California Chron 8 1906.
Hamilton, C. Methods and materials of fiction. New York 1908. The novel compared to poetry.
Dixon, W. M. English epic and heroic poetry. 1912.
Henderson, T. F. The ballad in literature. Cambridge 1912.
Forsythe, R. S. Modern imitations of the popular ballad. JEGP 13 1914.
Elton, O. Poetic romances after 1850. In his A sheaf of papers, 1922.
Bond, W. The art of narrative poetry. Trans Royal Soc of Lit 4 1924.
Van Doorn, W. Of the tribe of Homer: being an enquiry into the theory and practice of English narrative verse since 1833. Amsterdam 1931.
Berlage, H. Über das englische Soldatenlied in der zweiten Hälfte des 19 Jahrhunderts, mit besonderer Berücksichtigung der Soldatenlieder Rudyard Kiplings. Emsdetten 1933.
Bodelsen, C. A. The red, white and blue. E Studies 19 1937. On patriotic ballads of the nineties.
Scott, H. The early doors: origins of the music hall. 1947.
Green, R. L. Tellers of tales. Leicester 1953, London 1965 (rev and enlarged).
Foerster, D. M. The critical attack against the epic in the English romantic movement. PMLA 69 1954.
— Critical approval of epic poetry in the age of Wordsworth. PMLA 70 1955.
— The fortunes of epic poetry. Washington 1962.
Unwin, R. The rural muse: studies in the peasant poetry of England. 1954.
Browne, R. B. Shakespeare in the nineteenth-century songsters. Shakespeare Quart 8 1957.
Montgomerie, W. William Motherwell and Robert A. Smith. RES new ser 9 1958. On Scottish ballads in the 1820's.
Reeves, J. (ed). The idiom of the people: English traditional verse. 1958.
McAleer, J. J. Victorian ballads. South Atlantic Bull 26 1961.
Preyer, R. Sydney Dobell and the Victorian epic. Texas Quart 30 1961.
Friedman, A. B. The ballad revival: studies in the influence of popular on sophisticated poetry. Chicago 1961.
Crawford, T. Scottish popular ballads and lyrics of the eighteenth and early nineteenth centuries: some preliminary conclusions. Stud in Scottish Lit 1 1963.
Wilkie, B. Romantic poets and epic tradition. Madison 1965.

(4) SCOPE AND RANGE OF NINETEENTH-CENTURY POETRY

Philosophy and Religion

Keble, J. Sacred poetry. Quart Rev 32 1825. Review of The star in the east; with other poems by J. Conder 1824.
— De poeticae vi medica. 2 vols Oxford 1844.
Heine, H. Die romantische Schule. Leipzig 1836.
Shairp, J. C. Studies in poetry and philosophy. Edinburgh 1868, 1887.
— Aspects of poetry. Oxford 1881.
Brooke, S. A. Theology in the English poets. 1874.
Courthope, W. J. The liberal movement in English literature. 1885.
Dewey, J. Poetry and philosophy. Andover Rev 16 1891.
Dowden, E. Puritan and Anglican. 1900.
Gingerich, S. F. Wordsworth, Tennyson and Browning: a study in human freedom. Ann Arbor 1911.

Rosteutcher, J. Der Gedanke des kulturellen Fortschritts in der englischen Dichtung. Breslau 1933.
Brockington, A. A. Mysticism and poetry on a basis of experience. 1934. On Browning, Newman, Hopkins et al.
Cerny, V. Essai sur le titanisme dans la poésie romantique occidentale entre 1815 et 1850. Prague 1935.
Vat, D. G. van der. The fabulous opera. Groningen 1936. On the ideas of nineteenth-century poets.
Gill, F. C. The romantic movement and methodism. 1937.
Palmer, H. A brief history of the poetry of despair. English 3 1941.
Woodbridge, B. M. Poets and pessimism: Vigny, Housman et al. Romanic Rev 35 1944.
Grace, W. J. The social idea in the English romantic poets. Thought 22 1947.
Laird, J. Philosophical incursions into English literature. Cambridge 1947.
Hanley, E. A. Stoicism in major English poets of the nineteenth century. New York 1948.
Fairchild, H. N. Religious trends in English poetry, vol 3: 1780–1830, Romantic faith. New York 1949; vol 4: 1830–1880, Christianity and romanticism in the Victorian era, 1957; vol 5: 1880–1920, Gods of a changing poetry, 1962.
— Religious trends in Victorian poetry. Victorian Newsletter no 5 1954.
Dowden, W. S. Metempsychosis and closely related beliefs in English romantic poetry. Univ of North Carolina Record no 478 1950.
MacLean, K. Agrarian age: a background for Wordsworth. New Haven 1950.
Notopoulos, J. A. The Platonism of Shelley: a study of Platonism and the poetic mind. Durham NC 1950.
Hoffman, C. G. Whitehead's philosophy of nature and romantic poetry. Jnl of Aesthetics 10 1952.
Wilder, A. Modern poetry and the Christian tradition: a study in the relation of Christianity to culture. New York 1952.
Daniel, R. Odes to dejection. Kenyon Rev 15 1953. On Coleridge, Keats, Yeats.
Bullough, G. Changing views of the mind in English poetry. Proc Br Acad 41 1955.
— Mirror of minds: changing psychological beliefs in English poetry. 1962.
Kuhn, A. J. English deism and the development of mythological syncretism. PMLA 71 1956.
Abrams, M. H. Belief and disbelief. UTQ 27 1958.
— (ed). Literature and belief. New York 1958.
Kinghorn, A. M. The poet as philosopher. Dalhousie Rev 37 1958.
Buckley, V. Poetry and morality. 1959.
Duncan, J. E. The revival of metaphysical poetry: the history of a style, 1806 to the present. Minneapolis 1959.
Walsh, W. The use of imagination: educational thought and the literary mind. 1959.
Turnell, M. Modern literature and the Christian faith. 1961.
Benziger, J. Images of eternity: studies in the poetry of religious vision from Wordsworth to T. S. Eliot. Carbondale 1962.
Clark, B. B. The spectrum of faith in Victorian literature. Brigham Young Univ Stud 4 1962.
Miller, J. H. The theme of the disappearance of God in Victorian poetry. Victorian Stud 6 1963.
— The disappearance of God. Cambridge Mass 1963.
Randall, J. H., jr. Romantic reinterpretations of religion. Stud in Romanticism 2 1963.
Badger, K. Christianity and Victorian religious confessions. MLQ 25 1964.

Nature and Landscape

Howitt, W. Homes and haunts of the most eminent British poets. 2 vols 1847.
Dowden, E. Poetical feeling for nature. Contemporary Rev Aug 1866.
Brandes, G. Hovedstrømninger i det 19de aarhundredes litteratur. 6 vols Copenhagen 1872–90; tr 1901–5, New York 1957 (vol 4, Naturalism in England).
Shairp, J. C. On the poetic interpretation of nature. 1877.
Laprade, V. de. Histoire du sentiment de la nature. Paris 1883.
Veitch, J. The feeling for nature in Scottish poetry. 2 vols Edinburgh 1887.
Biese, A. Die Entwickelung des Naturgefühls im Mittelalter und in der Neuzeit. Leipzig 1888.
Machie, A. Natural knowledge in modern poetry. 1906.
Brooke, S. A. Naturalism in English poetry. 1920.
Strong, A. T. An essay on nature in Wordsworth and Meredith. Appended to his Three studies in Shelley, 1921.
Foerster, N. Studies in the modern view of nature. New York 1923.
Binyon, L. Landscape in English art and poetry. Tokyo 1927.
Blunden, E. Nature in English literature. 1929.
Huscher, H. Über Eigenart und Ursprung des englischen Naturgefühls. Leipzig 1929.
Beach, J. W. The concept of nature in nineteenth-century English poetry. New York 1936.
Heywood, T. Hopkins and Bridges on trees. Poetry Rev 29 1938.
Johnstone, P. H. Turnips and romanticism. Agricultural History 12 1938.
Miles, J. Pathetic fallacy in the nineteenth century: a study of a changing relation between object and emotion. California Univ Pbns in Eng 12 1942.
Wimsatt, W. K. The structure of romantic nature imagery. In The age of Johnson: essays presented to C. B. Tinker, New Haven 1949.
Badt, K. John Constable's clouds. 1950. Includes a discussion of Wordsworth and Coleridge.
Baker, J. V. The lark in English poetry. Prairie Schooner 24 1950.
Bourke, J. The sea as symbol in British poetry. Eton 1954.
Dahl, C. The Victorian wasteland. College Eng March 1955.
Sells, A. L. Animal poetry in French and English literature and the Greek tradition. Bloomington 1955.
Brumbaugh, T. B. Landscape in nineteenth-century poetry and painting. Mississippi Quart 13 1960.
Immerwahr, R. The first romantic aesthetics. MLQ 21 1960.
Roy, G. R. Le sentiment de la nature dans la poésie canadienne anglaise 1867–1918. Paris 1961.
Street, J. The poets and the English garden. Listener 3 Oct 1963.
Kudo, N. The romantics and nature poetry. Eng Lit (Waseda Univ Engl Lit Soc, Tokyo), no 26 1965.

Science and Poetry

Peacock, T. L. The four ages of poetry. 1820; ed H. F. B. Brett-Smith, Oxford 1921 (with Shelley's Defence of poetry).
Sonnenschein, E. A. Culture and science. Macmillan's Mag Nov 1885.
Scudder, V. D. Effect of the scientific temper in modern poetry. Andover Rev 8 1887.
Bourget, P. Science et poésie. Fortnightly Rev April 1888.
Thomas, C. Poetry and science. Open Court 3 1889.
— Have we still need of poetry? Forum 25 1900.
Watts-Dunton, T. Tennyson as a Nature poet; Tennyson and the scientific movement. Nineteenth Century May, Oct 1893.
Elliott, G. R. The Arnoldian lyric melancholy. PMLA 38 1923.
Stevenson, L. Darwin among the poets. 1932.

Grover, F. Poetry and astronomy. Scientific Monthly (New York) June 1937. On Tennyson et al.
Grabo, C. Science and the romantic movement. Annals of Science 4 1939.
Bush, D. Science and English poetry 1590–1950. New York 1950.
Nelson, N. E. Science and the irresponsible imagination. Yale Rev 43 1953.
Roppen, G. Evolution and poetic belief: a study in some Victorian and modern writers. Oslo 1956.
Gibson, W. Behind the veil: a distinction between poetic and scientific language in Tennyson, Lyell and Darwin. Victorian Stud 2 1958.
Sewell, E. The Orphic voice: poetry and natural history. 1960.
Jones, W. P. John Aikin on the use of natural history in poetry. Jnl of Aesthetics 22 1963.

Exotic Subjects

Brown, W. C. English travel books and minor poetry about the near east 1775–1825. PQ 16 1937.
Garnier, Ch.-M. Les poètes anglais et la Méditerranée. France-Grande-Bretagne Nov 1938.
Gail, M. Persia and the Victorians. 1951.
Kolker, Sr M. D. Spanish legends in English and American literature 1800–1860. Washington 1952.
Yohannan, J. D. The Persian poetry fad in England 1770–1825. Comparative Lit 4 1952.
Hussain, I. Oriental elements in English poetry 1784–1859. Venture 1 1960.
Hulin, J.-P. Exotisme et littérature sociale au début de l'ère victorienne. Etudes Anglaises 16 1963.
Osborn, J. M. Travel literature and the rise of neo-Hellenism in England. BNYPL May 1963.

Partridge, M. Slavonic themes in English poetry of the nineteenth century. Slavonic & East European Rev 41 1963.

Industrialism and Society

Walraf, E. Soziale Lyrik im England 1880–1914. Leipzig 1932.
Bose, A. Early Victorian poetry of social ferment. Raleigh Lit Soc (Aligarh) 1957.
Nikoljukin, A. N. Die Massenpoesie in England am Ende des 18 und zu Beginn des 19 Jahrhunderts. Zeitschrift für Anglistik und Amerikanistik 5 1957; pbd as Massovaia poeziia v Anglii, kontsa 18–nachala 19 vekov (Mass poetry in English at the end of the eighteenth and the beginning of the nineteenth century), Moscow 1961.
—— Byron, Shelley and contemporary English poetry of the masses. Izvestia of Acad of Sciences of USSR, Division of Language and Literature 14 1957. In Russian.
Báti, L. A chartista költéztet szerepe és értékelése. Filológiai Közlöny 4 1958. On Chartist poetry.
Warburg, J. Poetry and industrialism: some refractory material in nineteenth-century and later English verse. MLR 53 1958.
—— (ed). The industrial muse: the industrial revolution in English poetry. 1958.
Arinštejn, L. Progressivnye obščestvenno-političeskie tendencii v Anglijtskojpoezii 50x–70x godov 19 veka (Progressive social-political tendencies in English poetry 1850–70). Moscow 1963.
Mitchell, S. Romanticism and socialism. New Left Rev no 19 1963.

(5) PRE-RAPHAELITISM

Rossetti, W. M. et al. The germ. 1850; ed T. B. Mosher 1898; 1901 (facs).
—— (ed). Ruskin–Rossetti, Pre-Raphaelitism: papers 1854 to 1862. 1899.
—— (ed). The PRB journal. In Pre-Raphaelite diaries and titles, 1900.
Ruskin, J. The Pre-Raphaelites. Times 13, 30 May 1851.
—— Pre-Raphaelitism. 1851.
—— Ruskin as literary critic. Ed A. H. R. Ball, Cambridge 1928.
Buchanan, R. The fleshly school of poetry and other phenomena of the day. Contemporary Rev Oct 1871; 1872.
Forman, H. B. Pre-Raphaelite group. In his Our living poets, 1871.
—— The 'fleshly school' controversy. Tinsley's Mag 10 1872.
Rossetti, D. G. The stealthy school of criticism. Athenaeum 16 Dec 1871.
Hamilton, W. The aesthetic movement in England. 1882.
Myers, F. W. H. Rossetti and the religion of beauty. In his Essays: modern, 1883.
Wilde, O. Intentions. 1891.
Layard, G. S. Tennyson and his Pre-Raphaelite illustrators. 1894.
Bate, P. H. The English Pre-Raphaelite painters: their associates and successors. 1899.
Hunt, W. H. Pre-Raphaelitism and the Pre-Raphaelite brotherhood. 2 vols 1905–6.
Hueffer, F. M. The Pre-Raphaelite brotherhood. 1907.
Brooke, S. A. A study of Clough, Arnold, Rossetti and Morris, with an introduction on the course of poetry from 1822 to 1852. 1908.
Hearn, L. Pre-Raphaelites and other poets: lectures. Ed J. Erskine, New York 1922 (selection).
Mégroz, R. L. Pre-Raphaelite poetry. In his Modern English poetry 1882–1932, 1933.

Burdett, O. The Beardsley period: an essay in perspective. 1925.
Vinciguerra, M. Il preraffaellismo inglese. Bologna 1925.
Reid, F. Illustrators of the sixties. 1928.
Luxardo, L. Preraffaeliti e preraffaellismo in Inghilterra. Bologna 1929.
Welby, T. E. The Victorian romantics 1850–70. 1929.
Axmann, M. Die präraffaelitische Dichtung im Urteile ihrer Zeit. Hildesheim 1930.
Bickley, F. The Pre-Raphaelite comedy. 1932.
Waller, R. D. The Rossetti family 1824–54. Manchester 1932.
Evans, B. I. Minor Pre-Raphaelite poets. In his English poetry in the later nineteenth century. 1933, 1966 (rev).
Housman, L. Pre-Raphaelitism in art and poetry. Essays by Divers Hands new ser 12 1934.
'Winwar, Frances' (F. Grebanier). The Rossettis and their circle. 1934.
Street, A. E. George Price Boyce, with extracts from [his] diaries 1851–75. In The Old Water-Colour Society Club vol 19, 1941
Gaunt, W. The Pre-Raphaelite tragedy. 1942.
Spender, S. The Pre-Raphaelite literary painters. New Writing 6 1945.
De Armond, A. J. What is Pre-Raphaelitism in poetry? Delaware Notes 19th ser 1948.
Ironside, R. (ed). Pre-Raphaelite painters. 1948.
Unwin, R. Keats and Pre-Raphaelitism. English 9 1951.
Cassidy, J. A. Robert Buchanan and the fleshly controversy. PMLA 67 1952.
Dickason, D. H. The daring young men: the story of the American Pre-Raphaelites. Bloomington 1953.
Welland, D. S. R. The Pre-Raphaelites in literature and art. 1953.

Angeli, H. R. Pre-Raphaelite twilight: the story of Charles Augustus Howell. 1954.
House, H. Pre-Raphaelite poetry. In his All in due time, 1955.
Grylls, R. G. The Pre-Raphaelite brotherhood. TLS 12 April 1957.
Robson, W. W. Pre-Raphaelite poetry. In Pelican guide to English literature vol 6, ed. B. Ford 1957.
Greenwood, J. Young and angry, then as now. Listener 3 July 1958.
D'Agostino, N. I preraffaelliti. Belfragor 14 1959.
Gállego, J. P.R.B. Los pre-rafaelistas. Revistas de Ideas Estéticas 17 1959.
Sypher, W. In his Rococo to cubism in art and literature, New York 1960.
Forsyth, R. A. The temper of Pre-Raphaelitism and the concern with natural detail. Eng Stud in Africa 4 1961.
Fredeman, W. E. Pre-Raphaelitism: a bibliocritical study. Cambridge Mass 1965.
Fleming, G. H. Rossetti and the Pre-Raphaelite Brotherhood. 1967.

(6) POST-ROMANTIC IDEALS AND THEORIES OF POETRY

Emerson, R. W. The poet. In his Essays ser 2, Boston 1844.
Poe, E. A. The poet principle. Home Jnl (New York) 31 Aug 1850.
Brimley, G. Poetry and criticism. In Essays, 1858.
Lewes, G. H. The inner life of art. 1865.
Forman, H. B. Our living poets. 1871.
Dobell, S. T. The nature of poetry. In Thoughts on art, philosophy and religion, 1876.
Selkirk, J. B. Ethics and aesthetics of modern poetry. 1878.
Arnold, M. Wordsworth. Macmillan's Mag May, July 1879; rptd in his Essays in criticism ser 2, 1888.
—— The study of poetry. In English poets, ed T. H. Ward vol 4, 1880; rptd in Essays in criticism ser 2, 1888.
—— The study of poetry. In English poets, ed T. H. Ward 1880.
—— Byron. Macmillan's Mag March 1881; rptd in his Essays in criticism ser 2, 1888.
—— Shelley. Nineteenth Century Jan 1888; rptd in his Essays in criticism ser 2, 1888.
Symonds, J. A. Matthew Arnold's selections from Wordsworth. Fortnightly Rev Nov 1879.
Austin, A. Old and new canons of criticism in poetry. Contemporary Rev Dec–Jan 1881–2.
—— The position and prospects of poetry. Preface to 1889 edn of The human tragedy.
Swinburne, A. C. Wordsworth and Byron. Nineteenth Century April–May 1884.
Courthope, W. J. The liberal movement in English literature. 1885.
Bain, A. On teaching English, with an inquiry into the definition of poetry. 1887.
Cook, A. S. (ed). The touchstones of poetry. San Francisco 1887.
Gurney, E. Tertium quid. 2 vols 1887.
Everett, C. C. Poetry, comedy and duty. Boston 1888.
Stedman, E. C. The nature and elements of poetry. Boston 1892.
Dixon, W. M. English poetry from Blake to Browning. 1894.
Woodberry, G. E. The appreciation of literature. New York 1907.
Herford, C. H. A poetical view of the world. 1916.
Grierson, H. J. C. Lord Byron, Arnold and Swinburne. 1920.
Alterton, M. Origin of Poe's critical theory. Iowa Univ Stud 2 1925.
Tucker, T. G. The judgment and appreciation of literature. 1926.
Brémond, H. La poésie pure; avec un débat sur la poésie, par R. de Souza. Paris 1928.
Pelizzi, C. Romanticism and regionalism. Oxford 1929.
Wangelin, A.-M. Die Liebe in der Tristandichtung der viktorianischen Zeit. Bölzle 1937.
Decker, C. R. The aesthetic revolt against naturalism in Victorian criticism. PMLA 53 1938.
Groom, B. On the diction of Tennyson, Browning and Arnold. Soc for Pure Eng Tract no 53 1939.
Fricker, R. Victorian poetry in modern English criticism. E Studies 24 1942.
Ford, G. H. Keats and the Victorians: a study of his influence and rise to fame 1821–95. New Haven 1944.
Stevenson, L. Tennyson, Browning and a romantic fallacy. UTQ 13 1944.
Ong, W. J. J. S. Mill's parish poet. PQ 29 1950.
Maurer, O. Pope and the Victorians. SE 1944.
Warren, A. H. English poetic theory 1825–65. Princeton 1950.
Cox, R. G. Victorian criticism of poetry: the minority tradition. Scrutiny 18 1951.
Perkins, D. Arnold and the function of literature. ELH 18 1951.
Johnson, E. D. H. The alien vision of Victorian poetry: sources of the poetic imagination in Tennyson, Browning and Arnold. Princeton 1952.
Wilcox, J. The beginning of *l'art pour l'art*. Jnl of Aesthetics 11 1953.
Amis, K. Communication and the Victorian poet. EC 4 1954.
Griffith, C. Poe's Ligeia and the English romantics. UTQ 24 1954.
Johnson, R. V. Pater and the Victorian anti-romantics. EC 4 1954.
Super, R. H. Arnold's Oxford lectures on poetry. MLN 70 1955.
Bayley, J. The romantic survival: a study in poetic evolution. 1957.
Kermode, F. Romantic image. 1957.
Peters, R. L. Whistler and the English poets of the 1890's. MLQ 18 1957.
Smidt, K. Point of view in Victorian poetry. E Studies 38 1957.
—— The intellectual quest of the Victorian poets. E Studies 40 1959.
Stevenson, L. The death of love: a touchstone of poetic realism. West Humanities Rev 14 1960.
Gray, D. J. Arthur, Roland, Empedocles, Sigurd and the despair of heroes in Victorian poetry. Boston Univ Stud in English 5 1961.
Hough, G. The muse and her chains. Listener 3–17 May 1962.
Buckler, W. E. A dual quest: the Victorian search for identity and authority. Arts & Sciences 1 1963.
Prynne, J. H. The elegiac world in Victorian poetry. Listener 14 Feb 1963.
Forsyth, R. A. The myth of nature and the Victorian compromise of the imagination. ELH 31 1964.
Johnson, W. S. 'The bride of literature': Ruskin, the Eastlakes and mid-Victorian theories of art. Victorian Newsletter no 26 1964.
Ziff, J. J. M. W. Turner on poetry and painting. Stud in Romanticism 3 1964.
Charlesworth, B. Dark passages: the decadent consciousness in Victorian literature. Madison 1965.
Schneider, E. W. Sprung rhythm: a chapter in the evolution of nineteenth-century verse. PMLA 80 1965.

(7) MODERNISM

This brief list makes no attempt to deal even with major studies of twentieth-century literature. Only representative studies of the transition to modern poetry and of enduring poetic traditions are given.

Whitman, W. The poetry of the future. North Amer Rev 132 1881.
Guyan, M.-J. L'esthétique du vers moderne. Revue Philosophique 17 1884.
Davidson, J. W. The poetry of the future. New York 1888.
Henley, W. E. Views and reviews. 2 vols 1890–1902.
Symons, A. The symbolist movement in literature. 1899.
van Bever, A., and P. Léautaud. Poètes d'aujourd'hui 1880–1900: morceaux choisis, accompagnés de notices biographiques et d'un essai de bibliographie. Paris 1901.
Archer, W. Poets of the younger generation. 1902.
Gosse, E. The future of English poetry. In his Some diversions of a man of letters, 1920.
Olivero, F. Studies in modern poetry. 1921.
Clark, A. M. The realist revolt in modern poetry. Oxford 1922.
Flecker, J. E. Critical studies. In his Collected prose, 1922.
Lowes, J. L. Convention and revolt in poetry. Boston 1922.
Buchan, J. The old and new in literature. Trans Royal Soc of Lit 5 1925.
Burdett, O. Critical essays. 1925.
Williams, H. Modern English writers: being a study of imaginative literature 1890–1914. 1925.
Blodgett, H. Walt Whitman in England. 1934.
Brooks, C. Modern poetry and the tradition. 1939.
Stoll, E. E. Poetry and the passions. PMLA 55 1940. *See* JEGP 40 1941.
Morrissette, B. A. Early English and American critics of French symbolism. In Studies in honor of F. W. Shipley, St Louis 1942. On Moore, Symons, Gosse et al.
Bowra, C. M. The heritage of symbolism. 1943.
Pick, J. Divergent disciples of Walter Pater. Thought 23 1948. On Wilde, Moore, Arthur Symons and Lionel Johnson.
Sergeant, H. Tradition in the making of modern poetry. 1952.
Duncan, J. E. The revival of metaphysical poetry 1872–1912. PMLA 68 1953.
Hartman, G. H. The unmediated vision: an interpretation of Wordsworth, Hopkins, Rilke and Valéry. New Haven 1954.
Chiari, J. Symbolisme from Poe to Mallarmé: the growth of a myth. 1956.
Kato, T. The English romantic school and modern thought. Stud in Eng Lit (Tokyo) 33 1956. In Japanese.
Barzun, J. The energies of art: studies of authors, classic and modern. New York 1957.
Blunden, E. The romantics and ourselves. Stud in Eng Lit (Tokyo) 36 1960.
Gross, H. Sound and form in modern poetry: a study of prosody from Thomas Hardy to Robert Lowell. Ann Arbor 1964.

C. ANTHOLOGIES

(1) ANTHOLOGIES OF ENGLISH POETRY

Aikin, J. The cabinet. Edinburgh 1824, 1825, 1831.
Dyce, A. Specimens of British poetesses. 1825.
The living poets of England, [with an] essay on English poetry. 2 vols Paris 1827.
Hunt, L. Imagination and fancy: or selections from the English poets, illustrative of these first requisites of their art. 1844.
—— and S. A. Lee. The book of the sonnet. 2 vols Boston 1867.
'Giraldus' (W. Allingham). Nightingale Valley: the choicest lyrics and short poems in the English language. 1860.
Palgrave, F. T. The golden treasury of the best songs and lyrical poems in the English language. 1861, 1891 (enlarged).
—— The treasury of sacred song. Oxford 1889.
—— The golden treasury: second series. 1897.
Savile, B. W. Lyra sacra: being a collection of hymns ancient and modern, odes and fragments of sacred poetry. 1861.
Blaikie, J. A. and E. Gosse. Madrigals, songs and sonnets. 1870.
Emerson, R. A. Parnassus. Boston [1874].
Ward, T. H. et al. The English poets. 1880. Vol 4.
Gosse, E. English odes. 1881. Spenser to Swinburne.
Waddington, S. English sonnets by poets of the past and English sonnets by living writers, with a note on the history of the sonnet. 1881.
Caine, T. H. Sonnets of three centuries. 1882.
Linton, W. G. and R. H. Stoddard. Lyrics of the nineteenth century. 1884.
Sharp, W. Sonnets of this century. 1886.
Miles, A. H. et al. The poets and the poetry of the century. 10 vols [1891–7], 1898, 12 vols 1905–7 (rearranged and expanded as The poets and the poetry of the nineteenth century. Selected from some 300 writers; introds by Miles et al.
Henley, W. E. Lyra heroica: a book of verse for boys. 1892.
—— A London garland selected from 5 centuries of English verse. 1897.
—— English lyrics. 1897.
Beeching, H. C. A paradise of English poetry. 2 vols 1893.
—— Lyra sacra. 1895.
—— A book of Christmas verse. 1895.
—— Lyra apostolica. 1901.
Leonard, R. M. The dog in British poetry. 1893.
—— The pageant of English poetry. 1909.
—— A book of light verse, fourteenth to nineteenth century. 1910.
—— The book-lover's anthology. 1911.
—— The poetry of peace. 1918.
Stedman, E. C. A Victorian anthology. Boston 1895.
Lucas, E. V. The open road. 1899.
Quiller-Couch, A. T. The Oxford book of English verse 1250–1900. Oxford 1900.
—— The Oxford book of Victorian verse. Oxford 1912.
Duff, M. E. G. The Victorian anthology. 1902.
Stone, C. Sea songs and ballads 1400–1886. 1906.
Jerrold, W. The book of living poets. 1907.
—— and R. M. Leonard. A century of parody and imitation. 1913.
Knight, W. A Victorian anthology. [1907].
Dixon, W. M. and H. J. C. Grierson. The English Parnassus: an anthology of longer poems (Chaucer to Omar Khayyám). Oxford 1909.
Walker, Mrs H. A book of Victorian prose and poetry. Cambridge 1915.
Nicholson, D. H. S. and A. H. E. Lee. The Oxford book of English mystical verse, thirteenth to twentieth century. Oxford 1916.

Newbolt, H. An English anthology of prose and poetry, showing the main stream of English literature through six centuries. 1921.
Squire, J. C. A book of women's verse. Oxford 1921.
Caldwell, T. The golden book of modern English poetry 1870–1930. 1922.
Brie, F. Englisches Lesebuch: neunzehntes Jahrhundert. Heidelberg 1923.
Crump, G. H. Poets of the romantic revival. 1927.
Lucas, E. V. The joy of life. 1927.
Williams, C. A book of Victorian narrative verse. Oxford 1927.
Wilson, J. D. The poetry of the age of Wordsworth: an anthology of the five major poets. Cambridge 1927.
Milford, H. S. The Oxford book of Regency verse 1798–1837. Oxford 1928, 1935 (rev as The Oxford book of romantic verse).
Bernbaum, E. An anthology of romanticism. 5 vols New York 1929–33, 1948 (rev).
Reed, A. G. The romantic period. New York 1929.
Abdy, G. B. A Victorian potpourri of verses, known, unknown and forgotten. 1930.
Miller, G. M. The Victorian period. New York 1930.
Woods, G. B. Poetry of the Victorian period. Chicago 1930, 1955 (rev with J. H. Buckley).
Jiriczek, O. Victorianische Dichtung. Heidelberg 1931.
Powley, E. B. A hundred years of English poetry. Cambridge 1931.
Sitwell, E. The pleasures of poetry: a critical anthology. Second series: The romantic revival, 1931; Third series: The Victorian age, 1932.
Campbell, O. J., J. F. A. Pyre and B. Weaver. Poetry and criticism of the romantic movement. New York 1932.
Hayward, J. Nineteenth-century poetry: an anthology. 1932.
—— The Oxford book of nineteenth-century verse. Oxford 1964.
Miall, S. Poets at play: anthology of parodies and light verse. 1932.
A little book of Oxford movement poetry. 1932.
Parrott, T. M. and W. Thorp. Poetry of the transition 1850–1914. New York 1932.
Stephens, J., E. L. Beck, and R. H. Snow. English romantic poets. New York 1933.
Davidson, D. British poetry of the eighteen-nineties. New York 1937.
Henderson, W. Victorian street ballads. 1937.
Bowyer, J. W. and J. L. Brooks. The Victorian age. New York 1938, 1954 (rev).
Roberts, D. K. The century's poetry 1837–1937. 2 vols 1938, 1940, 4 vols 1942, 1945, 1950, 1956 (rev).
Bull, C. R. Regency poets. Melbourne 1941, 1957 (rev), 1959.
Brown, E. K. Victorian poetry. New York 1942, 1962 (with J. O. Bailey).
Booth, J. B. Seventy years of song. 1943. Anthology of popular songs.

Spender, S. A choice of English romantic poetry. New York 1947.
Evans, M. R. An anthology of Victorian verse. 1949.
Aldington, R. The religion of beauty: selections from the aesthetes. 1950.
Auden, W. H., and N. H. Pearson. Tennyson to Yeats. New York 1950 (vol 5 of Poets of the English language).
Grigson, G. The Victorians. 1950.
—— The Romantics: an anthology of English prose and poetry. Cleveland 1962.
Heath-Stubbs, J. and D. Wright. The forsaken garden: an anthology of poetry 1824–1909. 1950.
Taylor, G. Irish poets of the nineteenth century. Cambridge Mass 1951.
Blomberg, E. En bukett engelsk lyrik. Stockholm 1952.
Messaien, P. Les romantiques anglais: text anglais et français. Paris 1955.
Noyes, R. English romantic poetry and prose. New York 1956.
Hugo, H. E. The romantic reader. New York 1957.
Pinto, V. de S. and A. E. Rodway. The common muse: an anthology of popular British ballad poetry, fifteenth to twentieth century. 1957.
The preromantic and romantic poets. Paris 1958.
Houghton, W. E. and G. R. Stange. Victorian poetry and poetics. Boston 1959.
Carr, A. J. Victorian poetry: Clough to Kipling. New York 1959.
Bloom, H. English romantic poetry: an anthology. Garden City NY 1961, 2 vols 1963.
Frost, W. Romantic and Victorian poetry. 1961.
Francis Camilla, Sr. The Romantics and Victorians. New York 1961, 1966 (rev.).
Abrams, M. H. The romantic period. In Norton anthology of English literature vol 2, New York 1962.
Ford, G. H. The Victorian age. Ibid.
Hopkins, K. English poetry: a short history. Philadelphia 1963.
Marshall, W. H. The major English romantic poets: an anthology. New York 1963.
—— Victorian poets. 1966.
Creeger, G. R. and J. W. Reed. Selected prose and poetry of the romantic period. New York 1964.
Johnson, E. D. H. The world of the Victorians. New York 1964.
Martin, R. B. Victorian poetry: ten major poets. New York 1964.
Tosswill, T. D. Seven romantic poets. 1964.
Wright, D. Seven Victorian poets. 1964.
Brett, R. L. Poems of faith and doubt: the Victorian age. 1965.
Stanford, D. Poets of the nineties: a biographical anthology. 1965.
Beckson, K. Aesthetes and decadents in the 1890's: an anthology of British poetry and prose. New York 1966.
Merritt, J. D. The pre-Raphaelite poem. New York 1966.
Perkins, D. English romantic writers. New York 1967.

(2) ANTHOLOGIES OF SCOTTISH POETRY

Johnson, J. The Scots musical museum. 5 vols 1787–1803, 6 vols Edinburgh 1833; ed W. Stenhouse, D. Laing and C. K. Sharpe 4 vols Edinburgh 1853.
Thomson, G. Select collection of original Scottish airs, with select and characteristic verses by the most admired Scottish poets. 5 vols Edinburgh 1799–1818.
The Caledonian musical museum. 1801.
The Nithsdale minstrel. Dumfries 1805.
The Caledonian musical repository. 1806, Edinburgh 1809, 1811.
Cromek, R. H. Select Scottish songs ancient and modern. 2 vols 1810.

—— Remains of Nithsdale and Galloway song. 1810, Paisley 1880.
Campbell, A. Albyn's anthology. 2 vols Edinburgh 1816–18.
The harp of Caledonia. 3 vols Glasgow 1819–81.
Motherwell, W. The harp of Renfrewshire. Glasgow 1820, Paisley 1872.
—— Minstrelsy ancient and modern. Glasgow 1827, Paisley 1873.
Smith, R. A. The Scottish minstrel. 6 vols Edinburgh 1821–4.
Cunningham, A. The songs of Scotland, ancient and modern. 4 vols 1825.

Songs of the Edinburgh troop. Edinburgh 1825.
Chambers, R. The Scottish songs. 2 vols 1829–32.
— A miscellany of popular Scottish songs. Edinburgh 1841.
Whistle Binkie. Glasgow 1832–47 etc.
A miscellany of popular Scottish poems. Edinburgh 1841.
Ayrshire ballads and songs. 2 sers Ayr 1846, Edinburgh 1847.
Rogers, C. The modern Scottish minstrel. 6 vols Edinburgh 1856–7.
Wilson, J. G. The poets and poetry of Scotland. 2 vols 1876–7.
Edwards, D. H. Modern Scottish poets. 16 vols Brechin 1880–97.
Douglas, G. Poems of the Scottish minor poets. 1891.
— The book of Scottish poetry. 1910.
Greig, J. Scots minstrelsie: a national monument of Scottish song. 6 vols Edinburgh 1893.
Dixon, W. M. The Edinburgh book of Scottish verse. Edinburgh 1910.
Buchan, J. The northern Muse. 1924.
Young, D. Scottish verse 1851–1951. 1952.

R. L. C.

II. EARLY NINETEENTH-CENTURY POETRY

SAMUEL ROGERS
1763–1855

Collections

The poetical works of Rogers, Campbell [et al]. Paris 1829.
Italy; The pleasures of memory; Human life, and other poems. [1845].
Poetical works. Philadelphia 1852.
Poetical works. 1856; ed E. Bell 1875 (Aldine).

§1

An ode to superstition, with some other poems. 1786. Anon.
The pleasures of memory: a poem in two parts. 1792 (4 edns), 1793, 1794 (illustr T. Stothard), 1806 (15th edn); tr French, 1825; German, 1836.
An epistle to a friend, with other poems. 1798, 1798.
Verses written in Westminster Abbey after the funeral of Charles James Fox. [1806].
The voyage of Columbus: a poem. 1810, [1812].
Miscellaneous poems. 1812. With E. C. Knight et al.
Poems. 1812, 1814, 1816, 1820, 1822, [1833], 1834 (illustr J. M. W. Turner and T. Stothard), 2 vols 1836, 1838 1839, 1840; ed S. Sharpe 1860.
Jacqueline: a poem. 1814, 1814 (both with Byron's Lara).
Human life: a poem. 1819, Cambridge Mass 1820; tr Italian, 1820.
Italy, a poem: part the first. 1822, 1823; part the second, 1828; [both parts] 1830 (illustr J. M. W. Turner and T. Stothard), 1838.
Recollections of the table-talk of Samuel Rogers, with a memoir [by A. Dyce]. 1856 (3 edns), 1887; ed 'Morchard Bishop' (O. Stonor) 1952.
Recollections. [Ed W. Sharpe] 1859, 1859.
Reminiscences and Table-talk, collected by G. H. Powell. 1903.
Italian journal. Ed J. R. Hale 1956.

§2

Jeffrey, F. Edinburgh Rev 31 1819. Review of Human life.
Catalogue of the celebrated collection of works of art, the property of Rogers; also the extensive library. [1856].
The late Samuel Rogers. Illustr London News 22 Dec 1855, 5 Jan 1856; GM Feb 1856. Obituaries.
Hayward, A. In his Biographical and critical essays vol i, 1858.
Leslie, C. R. In his Autobiographical recollections vol 2, 1860.
Roscoe, W. C. Poems and essays. Ed R. H. Hutton, vol 2, 1860.
Martineau, H. In her Biographical sketches, 1877.
Mackay, C. In his Forty years' recollections vol i, 1877.
Hall, S. C. In his Book of memories, 1877.
Bates, W. In his Gallery of illustrious literary characters 1830–8 drawn by the late Daniel Maclise RA, 1873, 1883.
Clayden, P. W. In his Samuel Sharpe, 1883.
— The early life of Rogers. 1887.
— Rogers and his contemporaries. 2 vols 1889.
Eastlake, E. Quart Rev 167 1888. Personal reminiscences.
Schuyler, E. In his Italian influences, 1901.
Lamb, C. Works. Ed E. V. Lucas 7 vols 1903–5.
Roberts, R. E. Rogers and his circle. 1910.
Dobson, A. The books of Rogers. In his De libris, 1911 (2nd edn). On Rogers as a book-collector.
Adorno, C. Italy di Rogers. Florence 1925.
Boyle, E. Rogers the banker poet. Nat Rev Aug 1925; rptd in his Biographical essays 1790–1890, 1936.
Harrold, C. F. Portrait of a saurian: Rogers. Sewanee Rev 37 1929.
Prentiss, M. E. The papers of Rogers. N & Q 22 April 1939.
Firebaugh, J. J. Rogers and American men of letters. Amer Lit 13 1942.
Weeks, D. Rogers, man of taste. PMLA 62 1947.
Werry, R. R. Rogers's approach to the blank-verse dramatic monologue. MLN 62 1947.
Green, D. B. Letters to Rogers from Tom Moore and Sydney Smith. N & Q Dec 1955.
Barbier, C. P. Rogers and William Gilpin: their friendship and correspondence. Oxford 1959.
Hale, J. R. Rogers the perfectionist. HLQ 25 1961.

E. B.

WILLIAM WORDSWORTH
1770–1850

Bibliographies etc

Catalogue of the varied and valuable historical, poetical, theological and miscellaneous library of the late venerated poet-laureate. Preston [1859]; rptd in Trans Wordsworth Soc no 6 [1884?].
Tutin, J. R. The Wordsworth dictionary of persons and places. Hull 1891.
— An index to the animal and vegetable kingdoms of Wordsworth. Hull 1892.
White, W. H. A description of the Wordsworth and Coleridge manuscripts in the possession of Mr T. Norton Longman. 1897.
Cooper, L. A concordance to the poems of Wordsworth. 1911.
Wise, T. J. A bibliography of the writings in prose and verse of Wordsworth. 1916 (priv ptd).
— Two Lake poets: a catalogue of printed books, manuscripts, and autograph letters by Wordsworth and Coleridge. 1927 (priv ptd).
Patton, C. H. The Amherst Wordsworth collection: a descriptive bibliography. Amherst 1936.

Logan, J. V. Wordsworthian criticism: a guide and bibliography. Columbus 1947. *See* Henley and Stam, below.

Bernbaum, E. In Guide through the romantic movement, New York 1949 (2nd edn).

Gordan, J. D. Wordsworth 1770–1850: an exhibition. BNYPL 1950; New York 1950. Catalogue of centennial exhibition in New York Public Lib.

Coe, C. N. Wordsworth and the literature of travel: a bibliography. N & Q 27 Sept, 11 Oct 1952.

Bernbaum, E. and J. V. Logan. In English romantic poets: a review of research, ed T. H. Raysor, New York 1956 (rev).

Healey, G. H. The Cornell Wordsworth collection: a catalogue of books and manuscripts. Ithaca 1957. The most authoritative bibliographical account of works pbd during Wordsworth's lifetime.

Maxwell, J. C. Wordsworth in the Supplement to the Cambridge bibliography of English literature. N & Q Feb 1958.

Barnes, J. C. A bibliography of Wordsworth in American periodicals through 1825. PBSA 52 1958.

Henley, E. F. and D. H. Stam. Wordsworthian criticism 1945–59: an annotated bibliography. New York 1960, 1965 (rev to 1964). Supplements Logan, above.

Swayze, W. E. Early Wordsworthian biography: books and articles containing material on the life and character of Wordsworth that appeared before the publication of the official Memoirs by Christopher Wordsworth in 1851. BNYPL April 1960.

Henley, E. F. A check list of Masters' theses in the United States on Wordsworth. Charlottesville 1962.

Collections

Poems by William Wordsworth: including Lyrical ballads, and the miscellaneous pieces of the author, with additional poems, a new preface and a supplementary essay. 2 vols 1815. In 1820 a leaf was issued in River Duddon for use as the title-page of a third vol, to be made up from River Duddon, Peter Bell, Waggoner, Thanksgiving ode.

The miscellaneous poems of William Wordsworth. 4 vols 1820.

The poetical works of William Wordsworth. 4 vols Boston 1824. First American collected edn, based on 'the latest English edn' (1820), but containing Excursion.

The poetical works of William Wordsworth. 5 vols 1827.

The poetical works of William Wordsworth, complete in one volume. Paris 1828 (pirated).

The poetical works of William Wordsworth: new edition. 4 vols 1832.

The poetical works of William Wordsworth: the first complete American, from the last London edition. New Haven 1836.

The poetical works of William Wordsworth: new edition. 6 vols 1836 [vols 1–2]–1837 [vols 3–6], 1840 (with variations), 1841, 1843. Poems chiefly of early and late years was issued in 1842 with an alternative title-page to form vol 7.

The complete poetical works of William Wordsworth; together with a description of the country of the lakes in the north of England, now published with his works. Ed H. Reed, Philadelphia, Boston, Pittsburgh 1837, 1839.

The sonnets of William Wordsworth, collected in one volume, with a few additional ones, now first published. 1838.

Poems, chiefly of early and late years, including the Borderers: a tragedy, by William Wordsworth. 1842. Contains alternative title-page, presenting the book as vol 7 of the Poetical works 1836–7 and reprints.

The poems of William Wordsworth, DCL, poet laureate: a new edition. 1845, 1847, 1849 etc. Prelude added after 1850.

The poetical works of William Wordsworth, DCL, poet laureate, honorary member of the Royal Society of Edinburgh, and of the Royal Irish Academy. 7 vols 1846, 1849. Similar to the edn of 1836–7 etc, but with the Poems chiefly of early and late years (1842) distributed.

Poems by William Wordsworth; with an introductory essay on his life and writings. New York, Boston 1849 (for 1848).

The poetical works of William Wordsworth, DCL, poet laureate: new edition. 6 vols 1849 [vols 1–2]–1850 [vols 3–6].

The poetical works of William Wordsworth: new edition. Boston 1850.

The poetical works of William Wordsworth. Boston 1854, 1880. With unsigned memoir attributed to James Russell Lowell.

The poetical works of William Wordsworth. 6 vols 1857, 1864, 1865, 1869, 1870 (centenary edn), 1874, 1881, 1882. Includes Fenwick notes.

The poetical works of William Wordsworth. Ed W. M. Rossetti 1870, 1871. Based on one-vol edn of 1845, with Prelude.

The poetical works of William Wordsworth. Ed W. Knight 11 vols Edinburgh 1882–9. Last 3 vols are Knight's Life.

Complete poetical works. Ed J. Morley 1888. Frequently rptd as Globe edn.

The poetical works of William Wordsworth. Ed E. Dowden 7 vols 1892–3 (Aldine).

The poetical works of William Wordsworth. Ed T. Hutchinson, Oxford 1895. Basis of OSA edn, frequently rptd; rev edn, ed E. de Selincourt 1936. Also 5 vols 1895.

The poetical works of William Wordsworth. Ed W. Knight 8 vols 1896.

The poems of William Wordsworth. Ed N. C. Smith 3 vols 1908.

The poetical works of William Wordsworth. Ed E. de Selincourt and H. Darbishire 5 vols Oxford 1940–9; rev edn of vols 1–4, 1952–8. The standard edn.

Wordsworth's poems. Ed P. Wayne 3 vols 1955 (EL). Arranged in order of pbn, but using Wordsworth's final text.

Prose Works

The prose works of William Wordsworth, for the first time collected, with additions from unpublished manuscripts. Ed A. B. Grosart 3 vols 1876.

Prose works. Ed W. Knight 2 vols 1896.

Selections

Selections from the poems of William Wordsworth esq., chiefly for the use of schools and young persons. Ed J. Hine 1831, 1834.

Poems from the poetical works of William Wordsworth. New York 1841, Philadelphia 1842, 1843, 1844, 1846.

Select pieces from the poems of William Wordsworth. 1843. 2 edns from 2 publishers (Moxon and James Burns) and 2 printers, though the contents are the same.

Poems of Wordsworth. Ed M. Arnold 1879. With Arnold's introd; frequently rptd.

Wordsworth's literary criticism. Ed N. C. Smith, Oxford 1905.

Wordsworth: representative poems. Ed A. Beatty, New York 1937.

The critical opinions of Wordsworth. Ed M. L. Peacock jr, Baltimore 1950. Classified extracts, mainly from Wordsworth's prose criticism, letters and reported conversations.

Poetry and prose. Ed W. M. Merchant 1955 (Reynard Lib).

Wordsworth and Coleridge: selected critical essays. Ed T. M. Raysor, New York 1958.

Selected poems. Ed R. Sharrock 1958.

Selected poems. Ed H. M. Margoliouth 1959.

A Wordsworth selection. Ed E. Batho 1962.

Selected poetry and prose. Ed J. Butt, Oxford 1964.

Selected poems and prefaces. Ed J. Stillinger, Boston 1965.

Literary criticism. Ed P. M. Zall, Lincoln Nebraska 1966.

§1

Sonnet, on seeing Miss Helen Maria Williams weep at a tale of distress. European Mag 11 1787. Signed 'Axiologus'; sometimes attributed to Wordsworth.

An evening walk: an epistle in verse, addressed to a young lady from the lakes of the north of England, by W. Wordsworth BA of St John's, Cambridge. 1793.

Descriptive sketches in verse, taken during a pedestrian tour in the Italian, Grison, Swiss and Savoyard Alps, by W. Wordsworth BA of St John's, Cambridge. 1793.

Lyrical ballads, with a few other poems. 1798 (2 issues, the first with imprint 'Bristol: printed by Biggs and Cottle, for T. N. Longman, Paternoster-Row, London.'; the second with imprint 'London: printed for J. & A. Arch, Gracechurch-Street'; *see* R. W. Daniel, The publication of Lyrical ballads, MLR 33 1938. For details of variants in individual copies, see Healey, above, items 3–4); ed E. Dowden 1890, 1891; ed T. Hutchinson 1898, 1920; ed H. Littledale 1911, 1927; Noel Douglas replicas, 1926 (facs); ed F. W. Schulze, Halle 1952; ed W. J. B. Owen, Oxford 1967.

Lyrical ballads, with other poems, in two volumes, by W. Wordsworth. 1800; ed R. L. Brett and A. R. Jones 1963. For the many variants in individual copies, *see* E. L. McAdam, The publication of Lyrical ballads 1800, Yale Univ Lib Gazette 8 1933; J. E. Wells, Lyrical ballads 1800: cancel leaves, PMLA 53 1938; Healey, items 6–11.

Lyrical ballads, with pastoral and other poems, in two volumes, by W. Wordsworth. 1802, 1805 (new edn called the fourth on the title-pages); ed G. Sampson, The lyrical ballads 1798–1805, 1903.

Lyrical ballads, with other poems: in two volumes, by W. Wordsworth. Philadelphia 1802. 2 issues; *see* Healey, items 14–15.

Wordsworth's preface to Lyrical ballads. Ed W. J. B. Owen, Copenhagen 1957.

Poems in two volumes, by William Wordsworth, author of the Lyrical ballads. 1807 (for variants in individual copies, *see* Healey, item 19); ed H. Darbishire 1914, 1952 (rev).

Concerning the relations of Great Britain, Spain and Portugal to each other, and to the common enemy, at this crisis: and specifically as affected by the convention of Cintra: the whole brought to the test of those principles, by which alone the independence and freedom of nations can be preserved or recovered. 1809 (for variants and authentic ms corrections in individual copies, *see* Healey, item 22; early paragraphs appeared in Courier 27 Dec 1808 and 13 Jan 1809, with variant titles over the signature 'G.'); ed A. V. Dicey, Oxford 1915; ed R. J. White, in Political tracts of Wordsworth, Coleridge and Shelley, Cambridge 1953 (with omissions).

[Conversations with Klopstock] [1798]. Ms notes first ptd in part and inaccurately in Coleridge's Friend 18 (21 Dec 1809); rptd in Coleridge, Biographia literaria, 1817.

[Reply to 'Mathetes']. Friend 17, 20 (14 Dec 1809, 4 Jan 1810); rptd 1812, 1818 etc. A reply to an essay attributed to John Wilson and Alexander Blair in Friend 17. Untitled.

Essay upon epitaphs. Friend 25 (22 Feb 1810); rptd as a note to the Excursion bk 5 in 1814 and in subsequent edns. The first essay of 3. The second and third were first pbd in Grosart's edn of the Prose works; Grosart's text unreliable. Extracts in Christopher Wordsworth's Memoirs, 1851.

The excursion, being a portion of the Recluse: a poem, by William Wordsworth. 1814. For variants in individual copies, *see* Healey, item 24. Rptd 1820, and as a vol of Poetical works, 1827, 1832, 1836–7 and reissues, 1849–50 and reissues. Extra copies of the vol concerned were usually ptd and issued separately with appropriate title-pages at each issue of the Poetical works (*see* W. J. B. Owen, Library 5th ser 12 1957) and at other dates, e.g. 1847, Boston 1849.

The white doe of Rylstone: or the fate of the Nortons, a poem by William Wordsworth. 1815 (with The force of prayer: or the founding of Bolton priory); ed A. P. Comparetti, Ithaca 1940.

Original poetry: sonnet addressed in a letter (and published by the poet's permission) to B. R. Haydon, painter, by Wordsworth. A single leaf, reprinting from Champion 31 March 1816) the sonnet High is our calling. Only one copy known (Healey, item 37).

Thanksgiving ode, January 18, 1816, with other short pieces, chiefly referring to recent public events, by William Wordsworth. 1816. Includes various odes and sonnets later collected in the group Poems dedicated to national independence and liberty, and some other poems.

A letter to a friend of Robert Burns, occasioned by an intended republication of the account of the life of Burns, by Dr Currie; and of the selection made by him from his letters, by William Wordsworth. 1816.

Advertisement: to the editor. Kendal Chron 31 Jan 1818. Letter to the editor over the signature 'A friend to consistency'.

To the editor of the Chronicle. Kendal Chron 21 Feb 1818. 2 letters to the editor, over the signature 'A friend to truth', ptd by J. E. Wells, PMLA 55 1940.

To the freeholders of Westmorland. Kendal 1818. Broadsheet dated 28 Feb 1818; part of the text of Two addresses, with variants.

To the editor of the Chronicle. Kendal Chron 14 March 1818. Letter to the editor, over the signature 'A friend to truth'.

Two addresses to the freeholders of Westmorland. Kendal 1818. Previously pbd in part in Kendal Chron 14 Feb 1818, in Carlisle Patriot 7 March 1818, and in the broadsheet above.

Peter Bell: a tale in verse, by William Wordsworth. 1819, 1819. Contains also Sonnets suggested by Mr W. Westall's views of the caves &c in Yorkshire, previously pbd in Blackwood's Mag Jan 1819; later collected in the group Miscellaneous sonnets.

The waggoner: a poem, to which are added sonnets, by William Wordsworth. 1819. Contains 12 sonnets later collected in the group Miscellaneous sonnets.

To the editor of the Westmorland Gazette. Westmorland Gazette 31 Dec 1819. Letter to the editor, over the signature 'An enemy to detraction'.

The river Duddon: a series of sonnets; Vaudracour and Julia; and other poems, to which is annexed A topographical description of the country of the lakes in the north of England, by William Wordsworth. 1820. Also includes Dion, Artegal and Elidure, The prioress's tale, and about 30 shorter poems.

The little maid and the gentleman: or we are seven, embellished with engravings. York [1820?].

Lyrical ballads, with other poems, by W. Wordsworth. 1820. A re-issue of sheets of Lyrical ballads 1800, vol 2 (or, in some copies, of Lyrical ballads 1805, vol 2) with a misleading title-page. *See* J. E. Wells, Wordsworth's Lyrical ballads 1820, PQ 17 1938.

A description of the scenery of the lakes in the north of England: third edition (now first published separately) with additions, and illustrative remarks upon the scenery of the Alps, by William Wordsworth. 1822, 1823 ('fourth'), 1835 ('fifth'); ed E. de Selincourt 1906; ed W. M. Merchant 1951. The 'first' and 'second' edns are Wordsworth's Introduction to Joseph Wilkinson, Select views in Cumberland, Westmoreland and Lancashire, 1810; and The river Duddon, 1820, pp. 213–321. Edns later than 1835 (except that in the American edn of the Poetical works, 1837) contain addns by 'the Rev Professor [Adam] Sedgwick' (1842, 1843, 1846, 1853, 1859).

Ecclesiastical sketches by William Wordsworth. 1822; ed A. F. Potts, New Haven 1922 (as The ecclesiastical sonnets).

Memorials of a tour on the Continent 1820, by William Wordsworth. 1822.

Epitaph. 1835. Priv ptd version of Written after the death of Charles Lamb. Unique copy, BM Ashley 5139. A longer version without title, 1836; *see* Healey, item 95; F. M. Todd, Wordsworth's monody on Lamb: another copy [in Turnbull Library, Wellington, New Zealand], MLR 50 1955.

Yarrow revisited, and other poems, by William Wordsworth. 1835, 1836, 1839, Boston and New York 1835, Boston 1836.

[Speech on laying the foundation stone of the new school in the village of Bowness, Windermere]. Westmorland Gazette & Kendal Advertiser 16 April 1836.

We are seven. [?Alnwick 1840]. A chapbook containing We are seven and another poem, not Wordsworth's; no imprint. *See* H. Hughes, Two Wordsworthian chapbooks, MP 25 1928.

England in 1840! [1840?]. Collection of 8 of Wordsworth's political sonnets, of uncertain occasion. *See* Healey, item 112.

Poems on the loss and re-building of St Mary's church, Cardiff, by William Wordsworth [et al]. Cardiff 1842. Contains sonnet When Severn's sweeping flood.

Grace Darling. Carlisle [1843] (priv ptd), Newcastle [1843].

Verses composed at the request of Jane Wallas Penfold by William Wordsworth esq, poet laureate. [1843]. Unique copy, BM Ashley 5140. Contains Fair lady! can I sing of flowers.

Kendal and Windermere railway: two letters re-printed from the Morning Post, revised with additions. Kendal 1845. Priv ptd, followed by London issue with imprints of Whittaker and Moxon as well as the Kendal imprint, with slight variants; *see* J. E. Wells, Wordsworth and railways in 1844–5, MLQ 6 1945. Earlier, variant versions in Morning Post, 16 Oct, 11, 20 Dec 1844.

To the Queen. Kendal 1846 (priv ptd). Forgery, presumably by T. J. Wise; true date of issue c. 1889. *See* J. Carter and G. Pollard, Enquiry into the nature of certain nineteenth-century pamphlets, 1934, pp. 355–6.

Ode performed in the Senate-House, Cambridge, on the sixth of July MDCCCXLVIII, at the first commencement after the installation of His Royal Highness the Prince Albert, Chancellor of the University. Cambridge 1847. 4 leaves ptd by Univ Press; another issue, 'Metcalfe and Palmer, printers, Cambridge', of 8 leaves, with further information on title-page; another, London, 4 leaves, with frontispiece of Prince Albert, gilt borders etc; another, London 1849, with the music of Thomas Attwood Walmisley, iv+52 pp.

The prelude, or growth of a poet's mind; an autobiographical poem, by William Wordsworth. 1850, New York and Philadelphia 1850; ed E. de Selincourt, Oxford 1926, 1957 (rev H. Darbishire); text of 1805, ed de Selincourt, Oxford 1933, ed E. E. Reynolds 1932.

The recluse. 1888.

A letter to the Bishop of L[l]andaff on the extraordinary avowal of his political principles contained in the appendix to his late sermon: by a republican [1793]. Substantial ms fragment first ptd in Grosart's edn of the Prose works 1876; Grosart's text unreliable.

Preface to the Borderers [1796?]. Ms first ptd by E. de Selincourt, Nineteenth Century Nov 1926; rptd in de Selincourt, Oxford lectures on poetry, Oxford 1934, and in Poetical works, ed de Selincourt, vol 1. None of these ptd versions is wholly accurate.

Essay on morals [1798?]. Ms fragment first ptd in full by G. L. Little, REL 2 1961.

Letters, Diaries etc

Memorials of Coleorton: being letters from Coleridge, Wordsworth and his sister, Southey and Sir Walter Scott to Sir George and Lady Beaumont of Coleorton, Leicestershire, 1803 to 1834. Ed W. Knight 2 vols Edinburgh 1887.

Letters from the Lake poets, Coleridge, Wordsworth, Southey, to Daniel Stuart, editor of the Morning Post and the Courier 1800–38. 1889 (priv ptd).

Unpublished letters of Wordsworth and Coleridge. Athenaeum 8 Dec 1894.

Letters of the Wordsworth family from 1787 to 1855. Ed W. Knight 3 vols 1907.

The law of copyright. 1916 (priv ptd). Originally a letter to Morning Post 23 April 1838.

The correspondence of Henry Crabb Robinson with the Wordsworth circle (1808–66). Ed E. J. Morley 2 vols Oxford 1927.

Wordsworth & Reed: the poet's correspondence with his American editor 1836–50. Ed L. N. Broughton, Ithaca 1933.

The early letters of William and Dorothy Wordsworth. Ed E. de Selincourt, Oxford 1935, 1967 (rev C. L. Shaver).

The letters of William and Dorothy Wordsworth: the middle years. Ed E. de Selincourt 2 vols Oxford 1937.

The letters of William and Dorothy Wordsworth: the later years. Ed E. de Selincourt 3 vols Oxford 1939.

Some letters of the Wordsworth family, now first published, with a few unpublished letters of Coleridge and Southey and others. Ed L. N. Broughton, Ithaca 1941.

The letters of Wordsworth, selected. Ed P. Wayne, Oxford 1954 (WC).

The letters of Sara Hutchinson from 1800 to 1835. Ed K. Coburn 1954.

Letters of Mary Wordsworth 1800–55. Ed M. E. Burton, Oxford 1958.

Journals of Dorothy Wordsworth. Ed W. Knight 2 vols 1897, 1 vol 1930; ed E. de Selincourt 2 vols 1941 (*see* N & Q 16 Jan 1943), 1952; ed H. Darbishire, Oxford 1958 (WC). Selections, with improved text of early journals.

Henry Crabb Robinson on books and their writers. Ed E. J. Morley 3 vols 1938.

Wordsworth's pocket notebook. Ed G. H. Healey, Ithaca 1942.

§2

Jeffrey, F. Southey's Thalaba. Edinburgh Rev 1 1802.

— Wordsworth's Poems in two volumes. Edinburgh Rev 11 1807.

— Crabbe's Poems. Edinburgh Rev 12 1808.

— Cromek's Reliques of Robert Burns. Edinburgh Rev 13 1809.

— Weber's Works of John Ford. Edinburgh Rev 18 1811.

— Wilson's Isle of palms. Edinburgh Rev 19 1812.

— The excursion. Edinburgh Rev 24 1814.

— The white doe of Rylstone. Edinburgh Rev 25 1815.

— Wilson's City of the plague. Edinburgh Rev 26 1816.

Byron, G. G. Poems in two volumes. Monthly Lit Recreations July 1807.

— English bards and Scotch reviewers. 1809.

Hazlitt, W. The excursion. Examiner 21, 28 Aug, 2 Oct 1814.

— In his Lectures on the English poets, 1818.

— My first acquaintance with poets. Liberal 3 1823.

— In his Spirit of the age: or contemporary portraits, 1825.

Lamb, C. The excursion. Quart Rev 12 1814.

Coleridge, S. T. In his Biographia literaria, 1817.

Wilson, J. Observations on Mr Wordsworth's letter relative to a new edition of Burns' works. Blackwood's Mag June 1817.

— Vindication of Mr Wordsworth's letter to Mr Gray, on a new edition of Burns. Blackwood's Mag Oct 1817.

— Letter occasioned by N's vindication of Mr Wordsworth in last number. Blackwood's Mag Nov 1817.
De Quincey, T. Lake reminiscences from 1807 to 1830. Tait's Mag Jan–Feb, April 1839.
— Recollections of Grasmere. Tait's Mag Sept 1839.
— On Wordsworth's poetry. Tait's Mag Sept 1845.
— In his Recollections of the Lakes and the Lake poets, Coleridge, Wordsworth and Southey, Edinburgh 1863.
Wordsworth, C. Memoirs of William Wordsworth. 1851.
Clough, A. H. Lecture on the poetry of Wordsworth. In his Poems and prose remains, 1869.
Graves, R. P. Recollections of Wordsworth and the Lake country. In his Afternoon lectures on literature and art, Dublin 1869.
Pater, W. Wordsworth. Fortnightly Rev April 1874; rptd in his Appreciations, 1889.
Stephen, L. Wordsworth's ethics. Cornhill Mag Aug 1876; rptd in Hours in a library: third series, 1879.
Knight, W. A. (ed). Transactions of the Wordsworth Society. 1882–7. Includes reprint of sale catalogue of Wordsworth's library (1859) and H. D. Rawnsley, Reminiscences of Wordsworth among the peasantry of Westmoreland.
Bussière, G. and E. Legouis. Le général Michel Beaupuy. Paris 1891.
Rawnsley, H. D. Literary associations of the English Lakes. Glasgow 1894.
Legouis, E. La jeunesse de Wordsworth 1770–98. Paris 1896; tr 1897 (as The early life of Wordsworth 1770–98). *See* L. Stephen, Wordsworth's youth, Nat Rev Feb 1897.
— Wordsworth and Annette Vallon. 1922.
— Wordsworth in a new light. Cambridge Mass 1923.
Reynolds, M. The treatment of nature in English poetry between Pope and Wordsworth. Chicago 1896.
White, W. H. An examination of the charge of apostasy against Wordsworth. 1898.
Yarnall, E. Wordsworth and the Coleridges. New York 1899.
Raleigh, W. Wordsworth. 1903.
Cestre, C. In his La révolution française et les poètes anglais, Paris 1906.
Cooper, L. A glance at Wordsworth's reading. MLN 22 1907; rev in his Methods and aims in the study of literature, Boston 1915, in Cornell Stud in Eng 31 1940.
— Some Wordsworthian similes. JEGP 6 1907; rptd in his Aristotelian papers, Ithaca 1939.
— The 'forest hermit' in Coleridge and Wordsworth. MLN 24 1909.
— The making and the use of a verbal concordance. Sewanee Rev 27 1919.
— Matthew Arnold's essay on Wordsworth. Bookman (New York) July 1929.
— Wordsworth on Scott. In his Experiments in education, Ithaca 1943.
Eagleston, A. J. Wordsworth, Coleridge and the spy. Nineteenth Century Aug 1908.
Lienemann, K. Die Belesenheit von Wordsworth. Berlin 1908.
Bradley, A. C. English poetry and German philosophy in the age of Wordsworth. Manchester 1909.
— In his Oxford lectures on poetry, 1909.
More, P. E. In his Shelburne essays: seventh series, Boston 1910.
Robertson, E. S. Wordsworthshire. 1911.
Rice, R. Wordsworth's mind. Bloomington 1913.
Stork, C. W. The influence of the popular ballad on Wordsworth and Coleridge. PMLA 29 1914.
Strunk, W. Some related poems of Wordsworth and Coleridge. MLN 29 1914.
de Selincourt, E. In his English poets and the national ideal, Oxford 1915.
— The hitherto unpublished preface to Wordsworth's Borderers. Nineteenth Century Nov 1926; rptd in his Oxford lectures on poetry, Oxford 1934.
— Dorothy Wordsworth. Oxford 1933.
— Note on the Prelude VI, 160–174 (1805), 142–154 (1850). RES 19 1943.
— The early Wordsworth; Wordsworth and his daughter's marriage; The interplay of literature and science during the last three centuries. In his Wordsworth and other studies, Oxford 1947.
Dicey, A. V. Wordsworth and the war. Nineteenth Century May 1915.
— Wordsworth on the revolution. Nineteenth Century Oct 1915.
— The statesmanship of Wordsworth. Oxford 1917.
Cooke, M. Schiller's Robbers in England. MLR 11 1916. Influence on Borderers.
Harper, G. M. Wordsworth: his life, works and influence. 1916, 1929 (rev).
— Wordsworth at Blois; Wordsworth's love poetry. In his John Morley and other essays, Princeton 1920.
— Wordsworth's French daughter. Princeton 1921.
— The Wordsworth-Coleridge combination. Sewanee Rev 31 1923.
— Did Wordsworth defy the guillotine? Quart Rev 248 1927.
— Wordsworth's 'vast city' [Prelude I.7]. MLN 42 1927.
— Was Wordsworth ever a mystic? Discovery Nov 1928.
— Wordsworth in France [in autumn 1793?]. TLS 1 May 1930. Replies by A. W. Craver, 29 May 1930; J. R. MacGillivray, 12 June 1930.
— The crisis in Wordsworth's life and art. Queen's Quart 40 1933.
— Wordsworth's poetical technique. In his Literary appreciations, Indianapolis 1937.
Simpson, P. Wordsworth's punctuation. TLS 6 Jan 1916. *See* 13–27 Jan, 3–10 Feb 1916.
— An emendation in the text of Wordsworth [Excursion I.43]. RES 18 1942.
Barstow, M. L. Wordsworth's theory of poetic diction. New Haven 1917.
Beatty, A. Joseph Fawcett, The art of war: its relation to the development of Wordsworth. Madison 1918.
— Wordsworth: his doctrine and art in their historical relations. Madison 1922, 1927 (rev).
Baldwin, E. C. Wordsworth and Hermes Trismegistus. PMLA 33 1918.
White, E. A. Wordsworth's knowledge of Plato. MLN 33 1918. Reply by L. Cooper, ibid.
Mead, M. Wordsworth's eye. PMLA 34 1919.
— Four studies in Wordsworth. Menasha 1929.
Whitford, R. C. Another Lucy. JEGP 18 1919.
Broughton, L. N. The Theocritean element in the works of Wordsworth. Halle 1920.
Campbell, O. J. Sentimental morality in Wordsworth's narrative poetry. Univ of Wisconsin Stud in Lang & Lit 11 1920.
— Wordsworth bandies jests with Matthew. MLN 36 1921. Reply by H. S. Pancoast, 37 1922.
Campbell, O. J. and P. Mueschke. Guilt and sorrow: a study in the genesis of Wordsworth's aesthetic. MP 23 1926. Reply by R. D. Havens, RES 3 1927.
— The Borderers as a document in the history of Wordsworth's aesthetic development. MP 23 1926.
— Wordsworth's aesthetic development 1795–1802. Univ of Michigan Pbns in Lang & Lit 10 1933.
Knowlton, E. C. The novelty of Wordsworth's Michael as a pastoral. PMLA 35 1920.
— Wordsworth and Hugh Blair. PQ 6 1927.
Madariaga, S. de. In his Shelley and Calderón, and other essays on English and Spanish poetry, 1920.
Potts, A. F. Wordsworth and the bramble. JEGP 19 1920.
— The date of Wordsworth's first meeting with Hazlitt. MLN 44 1929.
— Wordsworth and William Fleetwood's Sermons. SP 26 1929.

—— The Spenserian and Miltonic influence in Wordsworth's Ode and Rainbow. SP 29 1932.

—— Wordsworth's Prelude: a study of its literary form. Ithaca 1953.

—— The case for internal evidence (7): butterflies and butterfly-hunters. BNYPL March 1959.

Wordsworth, G. G. The boyhood of Wordsworth. Cornhill Mag April 1920.

—— Some notes on the Wordsworths of Peniston. Ambleside 1929 (priv ptd).

Graham, W. The politics of the greater romantic poets. PMLA 36 1921.

Hughes, M. The humanism of Francis Jeffrey. MLR 16 1921.

Lilley, J. P. Wordsworth's interpretation of nature. Hibbert Jnl 19 1921.

Morison, W. Affinities in Wordsworth to Milton. Poetry Rev 12 1921.

Strong, A. T. In his Three studies in Shelley and an essay on nature in Wordsworth and Meredith, Oxford 1921.

Wells, J. E. The story of Wordsworth's Cintra. SP 18 1921.

—— De Quincey's punctuation of Wordsworth's Cintra. TLS 3 Nov 1932.

—— Lyrical Ballads 1800: a paste-in. Library 4th ser 19 1939.

—— Printer's bills for Coleridge's Friend and Wordsworth's Cintra. SP 36 1939.

—— Wordsworth and church building: Airey-force valley. MLR 35 1940.

—— Wordsworth and De Quincey in Westmorland politics. PMLA 55 1940. Addn by L. N. Broughton, 56 1941.

—— De Quincey and the Prelude in 1839. PQ 20 1941.

—— Wordsworth's To the Queen, 1846. PQ 21 1942.

—— Wordsworth and railways in 1844–5. MLQ 6 1945.

Babenroth, A. C. English childhood: Wordsworth's treatment of childhood in the light of English poetry from Prior to Crabbe. New York 1922.

Cerf, B. Wordsworth's gospel of nature. PMLA 37 1922. Reply by J. W. Beach, 40 1925.

Lehman, B. H. The doctrine of leadership in the greater romantic poets. PMLA 37 1922.

Merrill, L. R. Vaughan's influence upon Wordsworth's poetry. MLN 37 1922.

Morley, E. J. Wordsworth's French daughter. TLS 3 Aug 1922, 15 Feb 1923. Replies by E. Legouis, 8 March 1923; A. de Ternant, 15 March 1923.

Adkins, N. F. Wordsworth's Margaret: or the ruined cottage. MLN 38 1923.

Allen, B. S. Analogues of Wordsworth's The Borderers. PMLA 38 1923.

Beatty, J. M. Lord Jeffrey and Wordsworth. PMLA 38 1923.

Garrod, H. W. Wordsworth. Oxford 1923, 1927 (rev).

—— In his Profession of poetry and other lectures, Oxford 1929. On the Lucy poems.

Shackford, M. H. Wordsworth's Italy. PMLA 38 1923.

—— Wordsworth's Michael. Sewanee Rev 31 1923.

—— Wordsworth's interest in painters and pictures. Wellesley 1945.

Snyder, F. B. Wordsworth's favorite words. JEGP 22 1923.

Swaen, A. E. H. Peter Bell. Anglia 47 1923.

Turner, A. M. Wordsworth and Hartley Coleridge. JEGP 22 1923.

—— Wordsworth's influence on Thomas Campbell. PMLA 38 1923.

Elton, O. Wordsworth. 1924.

Gingerich, S. F. In his Essays on the romantic poets, 1924.

Morris, M. A note on Wordsworth and Vaughan. MLN 39 1924.

Weatherhead, L. D. The idea of immortality in Wordsworth. Quart Rev 242 1924.

Wright, H. G. Wordsworth and Wales. Welsh Outlook 11 1924.

—— The reflection of Wordsworth's personality in his choice of French writers. MLR 42 1947.

Bald, R. C. Francis Jeffrey as a literary critic. Nineteenth Century Feb 1925.

Beach, J. W. Expostulation and reply. PMLA 40 1925.

—— In his Concept of nature in nineteenth-century English poetry, New York 1936.

—— Reason and nature in Wordsworth. JHI 1 1940.

Herzberg, M. J. Wordsworth and German literature. PMLA 40 1925.

Moore, J. R. Wordsworth's unacknowledged debt to Macpherson's Ossian. PMLA 40 1925.

Sternberg, T. T. Wordsworth's Happy warrior and Herbert's Constancy. MLN 40 1925.

Whitehead, A. N. Science and the modern world. 1925.

Barber, H. Wordsworth's Ode and personal immortality. Adelphi 3 1926.

Barnard, C. C. Wordsworth and the Ancient mariner. E Studien 60 1926.

Bertram, A. Wordsworth's first love. TLS 15 July 1926. *See* 22 July (G. G. Wordsworth); 11 Nov (Harper); 9 Dec (Legouis); 6 March 1930 (Bertram); MLN 41 1926 (Pennington).

Brinton, C. C. In his Political ideas of the English romanticists, Oxford 1926.

Darbishire, H. Wordsworth's Prelude. Nineteenth Century May 1926.

—— A phrase of Wordsworth's ['along the heart']. RES 21 1945.

—— Milton and Wordsworth. TLS 4 Oct 1947.

—— The ruined cottage and the Excursion. In Essays mainly on the nineteenth century presented to Sir Humphrey Milford, Oxford 1948.

—— Wordsworth's belief in the doctrine of necessity. RES 24 1948.

—— Some variants in Wordsworth's text in the volumes of 1836–7 in the King's Library. Oxford 1949.

—— The poet Wordsworth. Oxford 1950.

—— An approach to Wordsworth's genius. In English studies today, ed C. L. Wrenn and G. Bullough, Oxford 1951. *See* R. S. Woof, TLS 6 July 1962.

—— Wordsworth. 1953 (Br Council pamphlet).

—— Wordsworth's significance for us. In Major English romantic poets: a symposium in reappraisal, ed C. D. Thorpe et al, Carbondale 1957.

—— Wordsworth and the weather. REL 1 1960.

Garstang, W. Wordsworth's interpretation of nature. Nature (supp) 16 Jan 1926.

King, H. Wordsworth's decline. Adelphi Aug 1926.

Meyerstein, E. H. W. Wordsworth and Chatterton. TLS 21 Oct 1926.

—— The mad monk and Wordsworth. TLS 7 Sept 1940.

—— Wordsworth and Coleridge. TLS 29 Nov 1941. *See* 6, 20 Dec 1941.

—— Wordsworth's Ode. TLS 12 Oct 1946.

Powell, A. E. In her Romantic theory of poetry: an examination in the light of Croce's aesthetic, 1926.

Bickersteth, G. L. Leopardi and Wordsworth. Proc Br Acad 13 1927.

Casson, T. E. Wordsworth and the Spectator. RES 3 1927.

Havens, R. D. Wordsworth's Guilt and sorrow. Ibid.

—— A project of Wordsworth's. RES 5 1929. On the Convention of Cintra.

—— Descriptive sketches and the Prelude. ELH 1 1934.

—— Wordsworth's shipwrecked gemometrician. Ibid.

—— The mind of a poet: a study of Wordsworth's thought with particular reference to the Prelude. Baltimore 1941.

—— Discontinuity in literary development: the case of English romanticism. SP 47 1950.

Knaplund, P. Correspondence [between Gladstone and Peele] relating to the grant of a Civil List pension to Wordsworth, 1842. MLN 42 1927.
Maclean, C. M. Dorothy and William Wordsworth. Cambridge 1927.
Muirhead, J. P. A day with Wordsworth. Blackwood's Mag June 1927.
Munk, E. Wordsworth: ein Beitrag zur Erforschung seiner religiösen Entwicklung. Berlin 1927.
Richards, A. E. The day book and ledger of Wordsworth's carpenter. PQ 6 1927.
Thorpe, C. D. Wordsworth and Keats: a study in personal and critical impression. PMLA 42 1927.
—— The imagination: Coleridge versus Wordsworth. PQ 18 1939.
Fairchild, H. N. In his Noble savage: a study in romantic naturalism, New York 1928.
—— In his Romantic quest, New York 1931.
—— Wordsworth's doctrine of creative delusion. South Atlantic Quart 46 1947.
—— In his Religious trends in English poetry, 3: Romantic faith 1780–1830, New York 1948.
Hughes, H. S. Two Wordsworthian chapbooks. MP 25 1928.
Huxley, A. Wordsworth in the tropics. Life & Letters 1 1928: rptd in Yale Rev 18 1929; and in his Do what you will, 1930.
Korteling, J. Mysticism in Blake and Wordsworth. Amsterdam 1928.
Newton, A. Wordsworth in early American criticism. Chicago 1928.
Pierce, F. E. Wordsworth and Thomas Taylor. PQ 7 1928.
Barry, J. A. F. The first review of Wordsworth's poetry. MLN 44 1929. Reply by J. R. MacGillivray, 45 1930.
Chapman, J. A. Papers on Shelley, Wordsworth and others. Oxford 1929.
—— Wordsworth and literary criticism. Oxford 1932.
Cobban, A. In his Edmund Burke and the revolt against the eighteenth century: a study of the political and social thinking of Burke, Wordsworth, Coleridge and Southey, 1929.
Dingle, H. The analytical approach to Wordsworth. Realist 1 1929.
—— Scientific method in criticism: Wordsworth. In his Science and literary criticism, 1949.
Foerster, N. Wordsworth in America. SP 26 1929.
Fraser, W. G. The Prelude, book VI, ll. 592–616. TLS 4 April 1929.
—— The preamble to the Prelude. TLS 6 Oct 1932.
—— A note on Wordsworth's Tintern Abbey, lines 66–83 and the Prelude (1805–6), book XI, lines 171–99. RES 9 1933.
Harrington, J. Wordsworth's Descriptive sketches and the Prelude, book VI. PMLA 44 1929. Reply by E. N. Hooker, 45 1930.
Herford, C. H. Goethe and Wordsworth. Contemporary Rev Oct 1929; rptd in Pbns of Eng Goethe Soc 7 1930.
—— Wordsworth. 1930.
MacGillivray, J. R. Wordsworth and his daughter. TLS 5 Sept 1929. *See* 10 April 1930 (Batho), 17 April 1930 (G. G. Wordsworth), 8 May 1930 (MacGillivray), 7 May 1931 (Weber).
—— Wordsworth's journey from London to Orleans. TLS 24 April 1930.
—— Wordsworth in France. TLS 12 June 1930.
—— The Borderers. TLS 25 Dec 1930.
—— Wordsworth and J. P. Brissot. TLS 29 Jan 1931.
—— The date of the composition of the Borderers. MLN 49 1934.
—— An early poem and letter by Wordsworth. RES new ser 5 1954.
—— The three forms of the Prelude 1798–1805. In Essays in English literature from the Renaissance to the Victorian age, ed M. MacLure and F. W. Watt, Toronto 1964.

Rader, M. M. The transcendentalism of Wordsworth. MP 26 1929.
—— Presiding ideas in Wordsworth's poetry. Univ of Washington Pbns in Lang & Lit 8 1931; Oxford 1967 (rev as Wordsworth: a philosophical approach).
Rea, J. D. Coleridge's intimations of immortality from Proclus. MP 26 1929.
—— Hartley Coleridge and Wordsworth's Lucy. SP 28 1931.
—— Intimations of immortality again. PQ 11 1932.
—— Wordsworth's intimations of palingenesia. RES 8 1932.
Stallknecht, N. P. Wordsworth and philosophy. PMLA 44 1929.
—— The moral of the Ancient mariner. PMLA 47 1932.
—— The doctrine of Coleridge's Dejection and its relation to Wordsworth's philosophy. PMLA 49 1934.
—— Nature and imagination in Wordsworth's meditation upon Mt Snowdon. PMLA 52 1937.
—— Wordsworth's Ode to duty and the Schöne Seele. Ibid.
—— Strange seas of thought: studies in Wordsworth's philosophy of man and nature. Durham NC 1945, Bloomington 1958 (rev).
—— On poetry and geometric truth. Kenyon Rev 18 1956.
—— Wordsworth and the quality of man. In Major English romantic poets: a symposium in reappraisal, ed C. D. Thorpe et al, Carbondale 1957.
Brede, A. Theories of poetic diction in Wordsworth and others and in contemporary poetry. Papers of Michigan Acad of Science, Arts & Letters 14 1930.
Claydon, W. A. The numinous in the poetry of Wordsworth. Hibbert Jnl 28 1930.
Empson, W. [Tintern Abbey]. In his Seven types of ambiguity, 1930.
—— Basic English and Wordsworth. Kenyon Rev 2 1940.
—— Sense in the Prelude. Kenyon Rev 13 1951; rptd in his Structure of complex words, 1952.
Hartman, H. The intimations of Wordsworth's ode. RES 6 1930.
—— Wordsworth's Lucy poems. PMLA 49 1934.
—— Wordsworth's Lapland night. RES 14 1938.
Read, H. Wordsworth. 1930, 1949 (rev).
—— Wordsworth's remorse. In his Coat of many colours, 1945; rptd in Modern literary criticism: an anthology, ed I. Howe, New York 1958.
—— Wordsworth and the Prelude. Listener 4 May 1950.
—— Wordsworth's philosophical faith. Sewanee Rev 58 1950.
—— The true voice of feeling. 1953.
Schumacher, E. Einheit und Totalität bei Wordsworth, unter dem Gesichtpunkt psychologischer Strukturtypologie. Marburg 1930.
Tuckerman, U. V. Wordsworth's plan for his imitation of Juvenal. MLN 45 1930.
Babbitt, I. The primitivism of Wordsworth. Bookman (New York) Sept 1931.
Banerjee, S. Critical theories and poetic practice in the Lyrical ballads. 1931.
Fausset, H. I'A. Wordsworth's Borderers. Adelphi July 1931.
—— The lost leader. 1933.
Hooker, E. N. Wordsworth's letter to the Bishop of Llandaff. SP 28 1931.
Evans, B. and H. Pinney. Racedown and the Wordsworths. RES 8 1932.
Hübner, W. Wordsworths Unsterblichkeitsode. Neuphilologische Monatsschrift 3 1932.
Knight, G. W. Wordsworth's vision of immortality. UTQ 1 1932.
—— The Wordsworthian profundity. In his Starlit dome, Oxford 1941.
Roberts, C. W. The influence of Godwin on Wordsworth's Letter to the Bishop of Llandaff. SP 29 1932.

— Wordsworth, the Philanthropist and Political justice. SP 31 1934.
Smith, E. An estimate of Wordsworth by his contemporaries 1793–1822. Oxford 1932. Excerpts from journals, letters, diaries.
Wellek, R. Wordsworth's and Coleridge's theories of poetic diction. In Charisteria Guilelmo Mathesio quinquagenario a discipulis et circuli linguistici Pragensis sodalibus oblata, Prague 1932.
— In his History of modern criticism 1750–1950 vol 2, 1955.
Williams, C. In his English poetic mind, Oxford 1932.
— Blake and Wordsworth. Dublin Rev April 1941.
Adams, M. R. Joseph Fawcett and Wordsworth's solitary. PMLA 48 1933.
Batho, E. C. The later Wordsworth. Cambridge 1933.
Bush, D. Wordsworth and the Classics. UTQ 2 1933.
— Mythology and the romantic tradition in English poetry. Cambridge Mass 1937.
Dunn, S. G. A note on Wordsworth's metaphysical system. E & S 18 1933.
Eliot, T. S. Wordsworth and Coleridge. In his Use of poetry and use of criticism, 1933.
Griggs, E. L. Hazlitt's estrangement from Coleridge and Wordsworth. MLN 48 1933.
— (ed). Wordsworth and Coleridge: studies in honor of George McLean Harper. Princeton 1939. Includes E. Legouis, Some remarks on the composition of the Lyrical ballads of 1798; R. D. Havens, Solitude, silence and loneliness in the poetry of Wordsworth; O. J. Campbell, Wordsworth's conception of the esthetic experience; N. P. Stallknecht, The tragic flaw in Wordsworth's philosophy; E. de Selincourt, Wordsworth and his daughter's marriage; L. N. Broughton, An imitation of Wordsworth.
— A note on Wordsworth's A character. RES new ser 4 1953.
Hayakawa, S. I. Wordsworth's letter to Mathetes. UTQ 2 1933.
Howard, L. Wordsworth in America. MLN 48 1933. Addns by L. Leary, 58 1943.
Simons, H. The etiology of the Wordsworth case. Symposium 4 1933.
Collis, J. S. Wordsworthian pantheism. Aryan Path 5 1934.
Fairley, B. Goethe and Wordsworth. Pbns of Eng Goethe Soc 10 1934.
Gray, C. H. Wordsworth's first visit to Tintern Abbey. PMLA 49 1934.
Leavis, F. R. Wordsworth. Scrutiny 3 1934; rptd in his Revaluation, 1936.
McCorkell, E. J. The mysticism of Wordsworth. Toronto 1934 (St Michael's College pamphlet).
Mueschke, P. and E. L. Griggs. Wordsworth as the prototype of the poet in Shelley's Alastor. PMLA 49 1934.
Patton, C. H. Important Coleridge and Wordsworth manuscripts acquired by Yale. Yale Univ Lib Gazette 9 1934.
— The rediscovery of Wordsworth. Boston 1935.
Sherwood, M. In her Undercurrents of influence on English romantic poetry, Cambridge Mass 1934.
Smith, J. H. Genesis of the Borderers. PMLA 49 1934. On Gilpin's influence.
Strout, A. L. John Wilson, 'champion' of Wordsworth. MP 31 1934.
— Wordsworth and John Wilson: a review of their relations between 1802 and 1817. PMLA 49 1934.
— Wordsworth versus Brougham. N & Q 28 May 1938.
— Thomas Clarkson as champion of Brougham in 1818. N & Q 4 June 1938.
— De Quincey and Wordsworth. N & Q 11 June 1938.
— Wordsworth's dessication. MLR 35 1940.
Weaver, B. Wordsworth's Prelude: an intimation of certain problems in criticism. SP 31 1934.
— Wordsworth's Prelude: the poetic function of memory. SP 34 1937.
— Wordsworth: forms and images. SP 35 1938.
— Wordsworth: the growth of a poet's mind. Papers of Michigan Acad of Science, Arts & Letters 24 1938.
— Wordsworth: the aesthetic intimation. PQ 19 1940.
— Wordsworth's Prelude: the shaping spirit. SP 37 1940.
— Wordsworth: the property of fortitude. SP 37 1940.
— Wordsworth: poet of the unconquerable mind. PMLA 75 1960.
Willey, B. On Wordsworth and the Locke tradition. In his Seventeenth-century background, 1934.
— Wordsworth's beliefs. Criterion 13 1934.
— 'Nature' in Wordsworth. In his Eighteenth-century background, 1940.
— When men and mountains meet. E Studies 43 1962.
Bishop, D. H. Wordsworth's 'Hermitage': Racedown or Grasmere? SP 32 1935. Reply by R. D. Havens, 33 1936.
— The origin of the Prelude, and the composition of books I and II. SP 38 1941.
Harris, J. R. Wordsworth's Lucy. In his Afterglow essays, 1935.
McMaster, H. N. Vaughan and Wordsworth. RES 11 1935.
Rowland, B. Wordsworth and Mississippi bonds. Jnl of Southern History 1 1935.
— Wordsworth and Pennsylvania state bonds. Pennsylvania Mag of History & Biography 59 1935.
Smith, F. M. The relation of Coleridge's Ode on dejection to Wordsworth's Ode on intimations of immortality. PMLA 50 1935.
Sperry, W. L. Wordsworth's anti-climax. Cambridge Mass 1935.
Watson, H. F. The Borderers and the Ancient mariner. TLS 28 Dec 1935. Reply by A. Beatty, 29 Feb 1936.
— Historic detail in the Borderers. MLN 52 1937.
Wicke, C. Die Tranzendentalpoesie bei Wordsworth. Marburg 1935.
Burra, P. Wordsworth. 1936. Short biography.
Evans, B. I. Variants in Wordsworth's Poems of 1807. TLS 13 June 1936.
— Coleorton manuscripts of Resolution and independence and [Coleridge's] Ode to dejection. MLR 46 1951.
Martin, A. D. The religion of Wordsworth. 1936.
Munby, A. N. L. Wordsworth and Coleridge: early appreciation in the north. TLS 22 Aug 1936. Reply by B. G. Brooks, 29 Aug 1936.
Bartlett, P. Annette and Albertine. Sewanee Rev 45 1937. On Wordsworth and Proust.
Blyton, W. J. Wordsworth's view of Europe in 1837. Nat Rev Nov 1937.
Brooks, B. G. Wordsworth and the Horatian spirit. MLR 32 1937.
Carritt, E. F. Addison, Kant and Wordsworth. E & S 22 1937.
Grierson, H. J. C. Milton and Wordsworth. Cambridge 1937.
Hamilton, M. P. Wordsworth's relation to Coleridge's Osorio. SP 34 1937.
James, D. G. Visionary dreariness. In his Scepticism and poetry, 1937.
— Wordsworth and Tennyson. Proc Br Acad 36 1950.
— Kant's influence on Wordsworth and Coleridge. Listener 31 Aug 1950.
Krüper, A. Wordsworth als politischer Dichter. Die Neueren Sprachen 45 1937.
Monk, S. H. Wordsworth's 'unimaginable touch of time'. MLN 52 1937.
Shearer, E. A. and J. T. Lindsay. Wordsworth and Coleridge marginalia in a copy of Richard Payne Knight's Analytical inquiry into the principles of taste. HLQ 1 1937.

Viebrock, H. Erlebnis und Gestaltung des Schönen in der Dichtung von Wordsworth (1798–1808). Marburg 1937.
— Gott und Natur bei Wordsworth. In Festschrift zum 75 Geburtstag von Theodor Spira, Heidelberg 1961.
Wilcox, S. C. The source of Wordsworth's The force of prayer. MLN 52 1937.
Brewster, P. G. The influence of the popular ballad on Wordsworth's poetry. SP 35 1938.
Burgum, E. B. The myth of impartiality in the teaching of English literature. Eng Jnl 26 1938. On Resolution and independence.
— Wordsworth's reform in poetic diction. College Eng Dec 1940.
Christensen, F. The date of Wordsworth's The birth of love. MLN 53 1938.
— Creative sensibility in Wordsworth. JEGP 45 1946.
— Intellectual love: the second theme of the Prelude. PMLA 80 1965.
Curry, K. Uncollected translations of Michelangelo by Wordsworth and Southey. RES 14 1938.
— Southey's visit to Caroline Wordsworth Baudouin. PMLA 59 1944.
— A note on Wordsworth's Fidelity. PQ 32 1953.
Potter, G. R. Wordsworth and the Traité élémentaire de chimie of Lavoisier. PQ 17 1938. On Excursion IV 941 ff.
Sanderlin, G. The influence of Milton and Wordsworth on the early Victorian sonnet. ELH 5 1938.
Smith, J. Wordsworth: a preliminary survey. Scrutiny 7 1938.
Sutton, D. Unpublished letters from Sir George and Lady Beaumont to the Wordsworths. N & Q 27 Aug 1938.
Willoughby, L. A. Wordsworth and Germany. In German studies presented to Professor H. G. Fiedler, Oxford 1938.
Beatty, F. Wordsworth of Rydal Mount. 1939.
— Wordsworth of Dove Cottage: a study of the poet's most productive decade June 1797–May 1807. New York 1964.
Bradford, C. B. Wordsworth's White doe of Rylstone and related poems. MP 36 1939.
Colledge, E. 'The house of the planets': an obscure passage in the Recluse. MLN 54 1939.
Holmes, E. Some sources of Wordsworth's passages on mythology. MLN 54 1939. On Excursion IV.
Milley, H. J. W. Some notes on Coleridge's Eolian harp. MP 36 1939. Influence on Wordsworth.
Raysor, T. M. Coleridge's criticism of Wordsworth. PMLA 54 1939.
— The themes of immortality and natural piety in Wordsworth's Immortality ode. PMLA 69 1954.
— The establishment of Wordsworth's reputation. JEGP 54 1955.
— Wordsworth's early drafts of the Ruined cottage in 1797–8. JEGP 55 1956.
Wilson, J. D. Leslie Stephen and Matthew Arnold as critics of Wordsworth. Cambridge 1939.
Bernbaum, E. Is Wordsworth's nature-poetry antiquated? ELH 7 1940.
Burton, M. E. Wordsworth's nature philosophy as revealed by his revisions of the Prelude. College Eng Jan 1940.
— How Wordsworth changed the diction of the Prelude. College Eng Oct 1941.
— The one Wordsworth. Chapel Hill 1942.
Crofts, J. Wordsworth and the seventeenth century. Proc Br Acad 26 1940.
Das, P. K. Cowley and Wordsworth's Skylark. MLR 35 1940.
Klimenko, E. I. The language reform in the poetry of the English romanticists Wordsworth and Coleridge. Trans First Leningrad Pedagogical Inst of Foreign Langs 1 1940.

Logan, J. V. Wordsworth and the pathetic fallacy. MLN 55 1940.
— England's peril and Wordsworth. Sewanee Rev 50 1942.
Marjarum, E. W. Wordsworth's view of the state of Ireland. PMLA 55 1940.
Angus, D. R. The relationship of Wordsworth's Ode on the intimations of immortality to Ruskin's theory of the infinite in art. MLR 36 1941.
Lang, V. A lost acquaintance of Wordsworth. ELH 8 1941. On Chauncey Hare Townshend.
Mabbott, T. O. Haydon's letter arranging for Keats to meet Wordsworth. N & Q 10 May 1941.
Noyes, R. Wordsworth and Jeffrey in controversy. Bloomington 1941.
— Wordsworth and Burns. PMLA 59 1944.
— Wordsworth: an unpublished letter to John Kenyon. MLR 53 1958.
— Wordsworth and Pickersgill. N & Q March 1959.
— Wordsworth and the Copyright Act of 1842: addendum. PMLA 76 1961.
— Wordsworth on his brother John: an unpublished letter to Thomas Clarkson, 16 February 1805. N & Q May 1962.
— Wordsworth and Sir George Beaumont's family. TLS 10 Aug 1962.
— Two unpublished Wordsworth letters. N & Q Jan 1964.
Cameron, K. W. Wordsworth, Bishop Doane and the sonnets on the American church. Historical Mag of Protestant Episcopal Church 11 1942.
— Wordsworth and Bishop Doane: new evidence. Emerson Soc Quart nos 23, 29 1961–2.
Daniel, R. Jeffrey and Wordsworth: the shape of persecution. Sewanee Rev 50 1942.
Jordan, J. E. Wordsworth and the Witch of Atlas. ELH 9 1942.
— De Quincey on Wordsworth's theory of diction. PMLA 68 1953.
— Wordsworth's 'minuteness and fidelity'. PMLA 72 1957.
— Wordsworth's humor. PMLA 73 1958.
— De Quincey to Wordsworth: a biography of a relationship, with the letters of Thomas De Quincey to the Wordsworth family. Berkeley and Los Angeles 1962.
Maclean, N. F. An analysis of a lyric poem. Univ Rev 8 1942. On 'It is a beauteous evening'.
Merchant, W. M. Wordsworth's Godwinian period. Comparative Lit Stud 4 1942.
— Wordsworth and the order of nature. Listener 8 June 1950.
— Wordsworth and the doctrine of nature. Die Neueren Sprachen 2 1953.
— Wordsworth and the Gothique taste. Die Neueren Sprachen 3 1954.
Miles, J. Wordsworth and the vocabulary of emotion. Berkeley 1942.
— Wordsworth and 'glitter'. SP 40 1943.
— In her Primary language of poetry in the 1740s and 1840s, Berkeley 1950.
— Wordsworth: the mind's excursive power. In her Eras and modes in English poetry, Berkeley 1957. Shorter version in Major English romantic poets: a symposium in reappraisal, ed C. D. Thorpe et al, Carbondale 1957.
Ralli, A. Wordsworth and his critics. Queen's Quart 49 1942.
Ryan, C. T. The child in Wordsworth's poetry. South Atlantic Quart 41 1942.
Stauffer, D. A. Cooperative criticism. Kenyon Rev 4 1942. On Immortality Ode.
Trilling, L. Wordsworth's Ode: intimations of immortality. Eng Inst Annual 1942; rptd in his Liberal imagination, New York 1950, and in Explication as criticism: selected papers from the English Institute, ed W. K. Wimsatt, New York 1963.

— The fate of pleasure: Wordsworth to Dostoievsky. Partisan Rev 30 1963.
Bagenal, H. On the mysticism of Wordsworth and Blake. Durham Univ Jnl 4 1943.
Geen, E. The concept of grace in Wordsworth's poetry. PMLA 58 1943.
Gordon, R. K. Scott and Wordsworth's Lyrical ballads. Proc & Trans of Royal Soc of Canada 3rd ser 37 1943.
Marsh, G. L. The Peter Bell parodies of 1819. MP 40 1943.
Meyer, G. W. Wordsworth's formative years. Ann Arbor 1943.
— The early history of the Prelude. Tulane Stud in Eng 1 1949.
— Resolution and independence: Wordsworth's answer to Coleridge's Dejection: an ode. Tulane Stud in Eng 2 1950.
— Wordsworth and the spy hunt. Amer Scholar 20 1950.
— A note on the sources and symbolism of the Intimations ode. Tulane Stud in Eng 3 1952.
— Wordsworth: an appreciation. Ibid.
Peek, K. M. Wordsworth in England: studies in the history of his fame. Bryn Mawr 1943.
Pritchard, J. P. Aristotle, Horace and Wordsworth. Amer Philological Assoc Trans & Proc 74 1943.
— On the making of Wordsworth's Dion. SP 49 1952.
Dockhorn, K. Wordsworth und die rhetorische Tradition in England. Göttingen 1944.
— In his Rhetorik als Quelle des vorromantischen Irrationalismus in der Literatur- und Geistesgeschichte, Göttingen 1949.
Housman, L. What happened to Wordsworth? Atlantic Monthly Nov 1944.
McElderry, B. R. jr. Common elements in Wordsworth's Preface and Shelley's Defence of poetry. MLQ 5 1944.
— Southey and Wordsworth's The idiot boy. N & Q Nov 1955.
Metzdorf, R. F. A new Wordsworth letter. MLN 59 1944. To J. W. Croker.
Mounts, C. E. The place of Chaucer and Spenser in the genesis of Peter Bell. PQ 23 1944.
— Wordsworth's transparent sobriquet. HLQ 15 1952. 'Edmund' after Edmund Spenser?
Niblett, W. R. Wordsworth's study of childhood. London Quart 169 1944.
Pfeiffer, K. G. The theme of desertion in Wordsworth. Research Stud of Washington State College 12 1944.
Schubert, L. The realism in romanticism: Hugo and Wordsworth. In Studies in speech and drama in honor of Alexander M. Drummond, Ithaca 1944.
Smith, J. C. A study of Wordsworth. Edinburgh 1944.
Sutherland, J. R. Wordsworth and Pope. Proc Br Acad 30 1944.
Watters, R. E. Wordsworth's 'amaranthine flower of faith'. MLQ 5 1944.
de Selincourt, O. Wordsworth's lodging during his schooldays at Hawkshead. RES 21 1945.
Dyson, H. V. D. The old Cumberland beggar and the Wordsworthian unities. In Essays on the eighteenth century presented to David Nichol Smith, Oxford 1945.
Hartsell, E. H. Wordsworth's 1835 Postscript: an advanced program for labor. SP 42 1945.
McKeehan, I. P. Some observations on the vocabulary of landscape description among the early romanticists. In Elizabethan studies and other essays in honor of George F. Reynolds, Boulder 1945.
McNulty, J. B. Autobiographical vagaries in Tintern Abbey. SP 42 1945.
— Wordsworth's tour of the Wye 1798. MLN 60 1945.
— Milton's influence on Wordsworth's early sonnets. PMLA 62 1947. Reply by R. D. Havens, 63 1948.
Purcell, J. M. A note on the revision of the Prelude. MLQ 6 1945.

Sackville-West, V. M. Wordsworth, especially in relation to modern poetry. Essays by Divers Hands 3rd ser 22 1945.
Ward, W. S. Wordsworth, the Lake poets and their contemporary magazine critics 1798–1820. SP 42 1945.
— An early champion of Wordsworth: Thomas Noon Talfourd. PMLA 68 1953.
Brooks, C. The intimations of the Ode. Kenyon Rev 8 1946; rptd in his Well wrought urn, New York 1947. Replies by W. W. Douglas and Brooks, Western Rev 13 1948.
— Irony and 'ironic' poetry. College Eng Feb 1948.
— Wordsworth and human suffering: notes on two early poems [Old Cumberland beggar, Animal tranquillity and decay, Ruined cottage]. In From sensibility to romanticism: essays presented to Frederick A. Pottle, ed F. W. Hilles and H. Bloom, New York 1965.
Laird, J. Wordsworth's 'natural piety'. In his Philosophical incursions into English literature, Cambridge 1946.
Pittman, C. L. A biographical note on Wordsworth. Bull of Furman Univ 29 1946.
— An introduction to a study of Wordsworth's reading in science. Furman Stud 33 1950.
Rhys, A. Wordsworth as critic: a re-examination. Poetry Rev 37 1946.
Shaver, C. L. A Wordsworth-Pope parallel. MLN 61 1946.
— Wordsworth's adaptation of Pliny in Laodamia. MLN 61 1946.
— Wordsworth's debt to Thomas Newton. MLN 62 1947.
— Wordsworth's Vaudracour. TLS 21 Feb 1958.
— Wordsworth on Byron: an unpublished letter to Southey. MLN 75 1960.
— Wordsworth's Vaudracour and Wilkinson's The wanderer. RES new ser 12 1961.
— The Griffith family: Wordsworth's kinsmen. Trans of Cumberland & Westmorland Antiquarian & Archaeological Soc new ser 63 1963.
Worthington [Smyser], J. Wordsworth's reading of Roman prose. New Haven 1946.
— Coleridge's use of Wordsworth's juvenilia. PMLA 65 1950.
— Wordsworth's dream of poetry and science: the Prelude V. PMLA 71 1956.
Watts, N. Virgil and Wordsworth. Dublin Rev Oct 1946.
Battenhouse, H. M. In his Poets of Christian thought, New York 1947.
Bond, W. H. Wordsworth's Thanksgiving ode: an unpublished postscript. Harvard Lib Bull 1 1947.
Duffin, H. C. The way of happiness: a reading of Wordsworth. 1947.
Elwin, M. In his First romantics, 1947.
Gallie, W. B. Is the Prelude a philosophical poem? Philosophy 22 1947.
Moore, A. K. A folk attitude in Wordsworth's We are seven. RES 23 1947.
Nicolson, H. How Wordsworth passed through France. In his Voyage to Wonderland and other essays, 1947.
Ames, A. C. Contemporary defense of Wordsworth's Pedlar. MLN 63 1948.
Clarke, C. Nature's education of man: some remarks on the philosphy of Wordsworth. Philosophy 23 1948.
— Landscape in the poetry of Wordsworth. Durham Univ Jnl new ser 11 1950.
— Loss and consolation in the poetry of Wordsworth. E Studies 31 1950.
— Romantic paradox: an essay on the poetry of Wordsworth. 1963.
Cunningham, J. V. Statius, Keats and Wordswcrth. PQ 25 1948.
Douglas, W. W. The problem of Wordsworth's conservatism. Science & Soc 12 1948.

— Wordsworth as business man. PMLA 63 1948.
— Wordsworth in politics: the Westmorland election of 1818. MLN 63 1948.
Fink, Z. S. Wordsworth and the English republican tradition. JEGP 47 1948.
— Dion and Wordsworth's political thought. SP 50 1953.
— The early Wordsworthian milieu: a notebook of Christopher Wordsworth with a few entries by William Wordsworth. Oxford 1958.
Lacey, N. Wordsworth's view of nature and its ethical consequences. Cambridge 1948.
Leyburn, E. D. Berkeleian elements in Wordsworth's thought. JEGP 47 1948.
— Recurrent words in the Prelude. ELH 16 1949.
— Radiance in the White doe of Rylstone. SP 47 1950.
Mackerness, E. D. Social interest of Wordsworth's Ecclesiastical sonnets. Theology 51 1948.
— Wordsworth and his American editor. Queen's Quart 67 1960.
MacLean, K. The water symbol in the Prelude (1805–6). UTQ 17 1948.
— Agrarian age: a background for Wordsworth. New Haven 1950.
— Levels of imagination in Wordsworth's Prelude (1805). PQ 38 1959.
Olney, C. Wordsworth and Haydon. N & Q 12 June 1948.
— Lucy revisited. N & Q Dec 1958.
Pottle, F. A. Wordsworth and Freud: or the theology of the unconscious. Bull of General Theological Seminary 34 1948.
— Wordsworth's Lines composed a few miles above Tintern Abbey. Explicator 16 1958. *See* R. S. Swanson and F. M. Combellack, 14 1956.
— An important addition to Yale's Wordsworth-Coleridge collection. Yale Univ Lib Gazette 41 1966. On Lyrical ballads 1800 vol 2 rev for 1802.
Todd, F. M. Wordsworth, Helen Maria Williams and France. MLR 43 1948.
— Wordsworth in Germany. MLR 47 1952.
— Politics and the poet: a study of Wordsworth. 1957.
Bowers, R. H. Wordsworthian solitude. MLQ 10 1949.
Bowra, C. M. In his Romantic imagination, Cambridge Mass 1949.
Cohen, B. B. William Hazlitt: Bonapartist critic of the Excursion. MLQ 10 1949.
— Haydon, Hunt and Scott and six sonnets (1816) by Wordsworth. PQ 29 1950.
— The date of composition of Wordsworth's Thanksgiving ode. N & Q 24 May 1952.
Mathison, J. K. Wordsworth's Ode: intimations of immortality from recollections of early childhood. SP 46 1949.
Maxwell, J. C. Wordsworth and Prospero. N & Q 29 Oct 1949.
Mill, A. J. John Stuart Mill's visit to Wordsworth 1831. MLR 44 1949.
Murry, J. M. Coleridge and Wordsworth. In his Katherine Mansfield and other literary portraits, 1949.
Wormhoudt, A. Demon lover. New York 1949.
Wyman, M. Chinese mysticism and Wordsworth. JHI 10 1949.
— Whitehead's philosophy of science in the light of Wordsworth's poetry. Philosophy of Science 23 1956.
Baker, C. The infinite sea: the development and decline of Wordsworth and Coleridge—an account of Professor [G.M.] Harper's unfinished book. Princeton Univ Lib Chron 11 1950.
Bateson, F. W. The quickest way out of Manchester: four romantic odes. In his English poetry, 1950, 1966 (rev). On Immortality ode.
— Rational irrationality: She dwelt among the untrodden ways. Northern Miscellany 1 1953.
— Wordsworth: a re-interpretation. 1954, 1956 (rev).
— Shelley on Wordsworth: two unpublished stanzas from Peter Bell the third. EC 17 1967.
Benziger, J. Tintern Abbey revisited. PMLA 65 1950.
— The romantic tradition: Wordsworth and T. S. Eliot. Bucknell Rev 8 1959.
— In his Images of eternity, Carbondale 1962.
Bonacina, L. C. W. Wordsworth and the weather of Lakeland. Weather May 1950.
— Wordsworth's responses to natural scenery. Nature 165 1950.
Bonner, F. W. Wordsworth's philosophy of education. Furman Stud 33 1950.
Cecchi, E. Il giovane Wordsworth e la poesia di paesaggio. Eng Miscellany (Rome) 1 1950.
Davies, H. S. Wordsworth and his critics. Listener 15 June 1950.
— Wordsworth and the empirical philosophers. In The English mind, ed Davies and G. Watson, Cambridge 1964.
— A new poem by Wordsworth. EC 15 1965. On A slumber did my spirit seal. Reply by R. F. Storch, ibid; J. Wordsworth and G. W. Ruoff 16 1966.
de Backer, F. Wordsworth en Guido Gezelle. Revue des Langues Vivantes 16 1950.
Denée, M. Survivance de Wordsworth. Ibid.
Dunklin, G. T. Wordsworth's voice of calm. Princeton Univ Lib Chron 11 1950.
— (ed). Wordsworth: centenary studies. Princeton 1951. Contains D. Bush, Wordsworth: a minority report; F. A. Pottle, The eye and the object in the poetry of Wordsworth (also in Yale Rev 39 1950); E. L. Griggs, Wordsworth through Coleridge's eyes; J. C. Ransom, Wordsworth: notes toward an understanding of poetry (also in Kenyon Rev 12 1950); B. I. Evans, Wordsworth and the European problem of the twentieth century; L. Trilling, Wordsworth and the iron time (also in Kenyon Rev 12 1950 and elsewhere); W. L. Sperry, Wordsworth's religion.
Grigson, G. Wordsworth: the man and his character. Listener 18 May 1950.
Huddleston, C. R. Date of a Wordsworth letter. N & Q 1 April 1950.
Lloyd, D. M. Wordsworth and Wales. Nat Lib of Wales Jnl 6 1950.
Lyon, J. S. The Excursion: a study. New Haven 1950.
— Wordsworth and Ticknor. PMLA 66 1951.
Mallaby, G. Wordsworth: a tribute. Oxford 1950.
Margoliouth, H. M. The distributor of stamps. Oxford Mag 26 Oct 1950.
— Wordsworth and Coleridge 1795–1834. Oxford 1953.
— Wordsworth and Coleridge: dates in May and June 1798. N & Q Aug 1953.
Pafford, W. Wordsworth's art of poetry. Emory Univ Quart 6 1950.
Parker, W. M. Wordsworth in Scotland. Scots Mag April 1950.
Sencourt, R. Wordsworth's old age. Contemporary Rev July 1950.
— Wordsworth. TLS 28 April 1950. Marginalia in Barron Field's ms biography.
Sergeant, H. The Cumberland Wordsworth. 1950.
Spark, M. and D. Stanford (ed). Tribute to Wordsworth: a miscellany of opinion for the centenary of the poet's death. 1950. Essays by S. Keyes, M. Spark, J. Heath-Stubbs, G. Woodcock, N. Nicholson, G. S. Fraser, H. Treece, H. Peschmann, W. Gardiner, R. Greacen, P. Hutchins, D. Patmore; foreword by H. Read.
Wordsworth at Cambridge: a record of the commemoration held at St John's College Cambridge in April 1950. Cambridge 1950.
Bland, D. S. Wordsworth and Constable. English 8 1951.
Bullough, G. The Wordsworth-Laing letters. MLR 46 1951.
— In his Mirror of minds, 1962.
Gamble, I. E. Wordsworth and the unit of meaning. Hopkins Rev 4 1951.

Gregory, T. S. Wordsworth unqualified. Month Oct 1951.
Hayden, D. E. After conflict, quiet: a study of Wordsworth's poetry in relation to his life and letters. New York 1951.
— Toward an understanding of Wordsworth's The Borderers. MLN 66 1951.
Hedin, G. Natur och politik i Wordsworths Ungdomsverk. Ed V. Blom, Göteborg 1951.
Muir, K. Centenary eclogue: a conversation about Wordsworth. EC 1 1951.
Owen, W. J. B. Notes on Wordsworth. N & Q 12 May 1951. Reply by H. Darbishire, 26 May 1951. On verse fragments and Essay supplementary to the preface.
— Letters of Longman & Co to Wordsworth 1814–36. Library 5th ser 9 1954.
— The text of Wordsworth's prose. N & Q Jan 1955.
— The major theme of Wordsworth's 1800 Preface. EC 6 1956.
— The text of Wordsworth's Essay upon epitaphs. N & Q May 1956.
— Costs, sales and profits of Longman's editions of Wordsworth. Library 5th ser 12 1957.
— Wordsworth's Essay upon epitaphs. N & Q June 1957.
— Manuscript variants of Wordsworth's poems. N & Q July 1958. In Ode to duty, Epitaphs from Chiabrera.
— Wordsworth and Jeffrey in collaboration. RES new ser 15 1964.
— A Virgilian reminiscence in the Excursion. N & Q May 1964.
— Wordsworth, the problem of communication and John Dennis. In Wordsworth's mind and art, ed A. W. Thomson, Edinburgh 1968.
Raymond, W. O. The mind's 'internal heaven' in poetry. UTQ 20 1951.
Vallese, T. Wordsworth in Italy. Symposium 5 1951.
Woodring, C. L. Peter Bell and 'the pious': a new letter. PQ 30 1951.
— On liberty in the poetry of Wordsworth. PMLA 70 1955.
— Wordsworth. Boston 1965.
Abercrombie, L. The art of Wordsworth. Oxford 1952.
Coombe, D. E. The Wordsworths and botany. N & Q 5 July 1952.
Davie, D. Diction and invention. In his Purity of diction in English verse, 1952.
— Syntax in the blank verse of Wordsworth's Prelude. In his Articulate energy, 1955.
Durrant, G. H. Wordsworth and the sense of fact. Theoria 4 1952.
— Imagination and life: The daffodils. Theoria 19 1962.
— The idiot boy. Theoria 20 1963.
— Wordsworth's metamorphoses. Eng Stud in Africa 7 1964.
— Wordsworth's Peter Bell: a pons asinorum for critics. Wascana Rev 1 1966.
Hartung, C. V. Wordsworth on Westminster bridge: paradox or harmony? College Eng Jan 1952.
Marsh, F. Wordsworth's imagery: a study in poetic vision. New Haven 1952.
— Resolution and independence stanza xviii. MLN 70 1955.
— Wordsworth's Ode: obstinate questionings. Stud in Romanticism 5 1966.
Peckham, M. Constable and Wordsworth. College Art Jnl 12 1952.
— In his Beyond the tragic vision, New York 1962.
Ure, P. Wordsworth's Michael: the picture of a man. Durham Univ Jnl new ser 13 1952.
Wigod, J. D. Negative capability and wise passiveness. PMLA 67 1952.
Abrams, M. H. In his Mirror and the lamp, New York 1953.
— Wordsworth and Coleridge on diction and figures. Eng Inst Essays 1952.
— Belief and disbelief. UTQ 27 1958. On Immortality ode.
Asselineau, R. Wordsworth et les images eidétiques. Revue des Langues Vivantes 19 1953.
Baird, J. R. Wordsworth's 'inscrutable workmanship' and the emblems of reality. PMLA 68 1953.
Bicknell, J. W. A misreading of Wordsworth's Guilt and sorrow. N & Q March 1953.
Carr, B. M. H. On the Prelude, II 399–420. N & Q Feb 1953.
Chorley, K. Wordsworth and Christianity. Month June 1953.
— Wordsworth and nature mysticism. Month April 1953.
— Victorian agnostics and Wordsworth. Month April 1954.
Coe, C. N. Wordsworth and the literature of travel. New York 1953.
Danby, J. F. The simple Wordsworth. Cambridge Jnl Jan 1953.
— The 'nature' of Wordsworth. Cambridge Jnl 7 1954.
— The simple Wordsworth. 1960. Includes articles above.
— Wordsworth: the Prelude and other poems. 1963.
Doherty, K. F. The Vergilian Wordsworth. Classical Jnl 49 1953.
— On Wordsworth's Aeneid. Classical World April 1961.
Hilen, A. The date of Wordsworth's The King of Sweden. E Studies 34 1953.
Rossi, S. Wordsworth e l'Italia. Letterature Moderne 4 1953.
Rudman, H. W. Wordsworth and Admiral Nelson. College Eng Nov 1953. On the Happy warrior.
Seronsy, C. C. Wordsworth's annotations in Daniel's Poetical works. MLN 68 1953.
— Daniel and Wordsworth. SP 56 1959.
Sharrock, R. Wordsworth's revolt against literature. EC 3 1953.
— Wordsworth and John Langhorne's The country justice. N & Q July 1954.
— Speech and prose in Wordsworth's Preface [to Lyrical ballads]. EC 7 1957.
— The chemist and the poet: Sir Humphry Davy and the Preface to Lyrical ballads. Notes & Records of Royal Soc 17 1962; shortened version, Wordsworth on science and poetry, REL 3 1962.
— The Borderers: Wordsworth on the moral frontier. Durham Univ Jnl new ser 25 1964.
Smith, C. J. The effect of Shakespeare's influence on Wordsworth's The Borderers. SP 50 1953.
— The contrarieties: Wordsworth's dualistic imagery. PMLA 69 1954.
— Wordsworth and Coleridge: the growth of a theme. SP 54 1957.
Rossiter-Smith, H. Wordsworth and his Italian studies. N & Q June 1953.
— John Gough 1757–1825: The blind philosopher. N & Q Sept–Oct 1955.
— Wordsworth and pre-existence. Hibbert Jnl 59 1961.
Wilcox, S. C. The sources of Wordsworth's Afterthought sonnet. PQ 32 1953.
— Wordsworth's River Duddon sonnets. PMLA 69 1954.
Zall, P. M. Wordsworth and copyright. TLS 16 Oct 1953.
— Wordsworth and the Copyright Act of 1842. PMLA 70 1955.
— Hazlitt's 'romantic acquaintance': Wordsworth and Charles Lloyd. MLN 71 1956.
— Old Knight revisited. PMLA 71 1956.
— Wordsworth and John Constable. MLN 71 1956.
— Wordsworth edits his editor: by a provincial correspondent. BNYPL Feb 1962. On Hine's Selections, 1831.

— Wordsworth on disinterestedness and on Michelangelo. BNYPL Feb 1965.
Foxon, D. F. The printing of Lyrical ballads 1798. Library 5th ser 9 1954.
Green, D. B. Wordsworth and Edward du Bois. PQ 33 1954.
— Two Wordsworth letters. N & Q Nov 1955.
— An uncollected Wordsworth letter on Shakespeare. RES new ser 15 1964.
— Two Wordsworth letters. N & Q Nov 1965.
— Wordsworth and Lydia Huntley Sigourney. New England Quart 37 1964.
Hartman, G. H. The unmediated vision: an interpretation of Wordsworth, Hopkins, Rilke and Valéry. New Haven 1954.
— Wordsworth's Descriptive sketches and the growth of a poet's mind. PMLA 76 1961.
— A poet's progress: Wordsworth and the via naturaliter negativa. MP 59 1962.
— Wordsworth, the Borderers and 'intellectual murder'. JEGP 62 1963.
— Wordsworth's poetry 1787–1814. New Haven 1964.
— Wordsworth, inscriptions and romantic nature poetry. In From sensibility to romanticism: essays presented to F. A. Pottle, ed F. W. Hilles and H. Bloom, New York 1965.
Jones, J. The egotistical sublime: a history of Wordsworth's imagination. 1954.
Jones, W. P. The captive linnet: a footnote on eighteenth-century sentiment. PQ 33 1954.
Mayo, R. The contemporaneity of the Lyrical ballads. PMLA 69 1954.
Price, M. Imagination in the White doe of Rylstone. PQ 33 1954.
Bates, M. C. A new Wordsworth letter: Lyrical ballads and John Taylor. Harvard Lib Bull 9 1955.
Brown, T. J. Wordsworth and his amanuenses. Book Collector 4 1955. With plates of various hands.
Gérard, A. In his L'idée romantique de la poésie en Angleterre, Paris 1955.
— Wordsworth in our time. Revue des Langues Vivantes 22 1956.
— Resolution and independence: Wordsworth's coming of age. Eng Stud in Africa 3 1960.
— Symbolic landscape in Tintern Abbey. Pbns de l'Université de l'Etat à Elisabethville 4 1962.
— Dark passages: exploring Tintern Abbey. Stud in Romanticism 3 1963.
— Of trees and men: the unity of Wordsworth's The Thorn. EC 14 1964.
Groom, B. In his Diction of poetry from Spenser to Bridges, Toronto 1955.
— The unity of Wordsworth's poetry. 1966.
Hamilton, J. B. Restoration of the Happy warrior. MLQ 16 1955.
Hopkins, K. In his Poets laureate, New York 1955.
Sells, A. L. Wordsworth and the English Romantics. In his Animal poetry in French and English literature, Bloomington 1955.
Morgan, E. A prelude to the Prelude. EC 5 1955. Reply by K. Muir, 6 1956.
Robson, W. W. Resolution and independence. In Interpretations: essays on twelve English poets, ed J. Wain 1955.
Ross, I. Wordsworth and Colthouse near Hawkshead. MLR 50 1955.
Schneider, R. L. The failure of solitude: Wordsworth's Immortality ode. JEGP 54 1955.
Wain, J. The liberation of Wordsworth. Twentieth Century Jan 1955.
Whalley, G. In his Coleridge and Sara Hutchinson and the Asra poems, 1955.
— Preface to Lyrical ballads: a portent. UTQ 25 1956.
— The fields of sleep. RES new ser 9 1958.
Bostetter, E. E. Wordsworth's dim and perilous way. PMLA 71 1956.
— In his Romantic ventriloquists: Wordsworth, Coleridge, Keats, Shelley, Byron, Seattle 1963.
Carnall, G. D. The idiot boy. N & Q Feb 1956.
Coburn, K. Coleridge and Wordsworth on the supernatural. UTQ 25 1956.
Cruttwell, P. Wordsworth, the public and the people. Sewanee Rev 64 1956.
Erdman, D. V. Coleridge, Wordsworth and the Wedgwood fund. BNYPL Sept–Oct 1956.
— A new discovery: the first review of Christabel. SE 37 1958.
— All that mighty heart. BNYPL April 1960.
Kissane, J. A night piece: Wordsworth's emblem of the mind. MLN 71 1956.
Praz, M. Coleridge and Wordsworth. In his Hero in eclipse in Victorian fiction, Oxford 1956.
Schulze, F. W. Wordsworthian and Coleridgian texts (1784–1822) mostly unidentified or displaced. In Strena anglica: [Festschrift für] Otto Ritter, Halle 1956.
Voisine, J. Wordsworth et la révolution poétique. In his J.-J. Rousseau en Angleterre à l'époque romantique: les écrits autobiographiques et la légende, Paris 1956.
Bensimon, P. Wordsworth ou le rêveur en plein midi. Langues Modernes 51 1957.
Coveney, P. Wordsworth's Father of the man. In his Poor monkey: the child in literature, 1957.
Mendilow, A. A. Robert Heron and Wordsworth's critical essays. MLR 52 1957.
— The solitary reaper and the growth of a poet's mind. In Studies in Western literature, ed D. A. Fineman, Jerusalem 1962.
Moorman, C. Wordsworth's Prelude I, l. 269. MLN 72 1957.
Moorman, M. Wordsworth, a biography: the early years 1770–1803. Oxford 1957, 1968 (corrected); The later years 1803–50, Oxford 1965.
— Wordsworth's commonplace book. N & Q Sept 1957.
Parrish, S. M. The Thorn: Wordsworth's dramatic monologue. ELH 24 1957.
— The Wordsworth-Coleridge controversy. PMLA 73 1958.
— Dramatic technique in the Lyrical ballads. PMLA 74 1959.
— Wordsworth and Coleridge on meter. JEGP 59 1960.
— and D. V. Erdman. Who wrote the Mad monk? a debate. BNYPL April 1960.
Patterson, C. I. The meaning and significance of Peele Castle. JEGP 56 1957.
Schneider, B. R., jr. Wordsworth's Cambridge education. Cambridge 1957.
Slote, B. The case of the missing Abbey. Western Humanities Rev 11 1957.
Stout, G. D. Leigh Hunt on Wordsworth and Coleridge. Keats-Shelley Jnl 6 1957.
Towne, F. M. Wordsworth's spiritual autobiography. Research Stud of Washington State College 25 1957.
Warner, A. Wordsworth and the quiet. Theoria 9 1957.
Bonnerot, L. De quelques livres récents sur Wordsworth. Etudes Anglaises 11 1958. Discusses books by M. Moorman, Z. S. Fink, W. J. B. Owen, F. Marsh, F. M. Todd.
Fussell, P., jr. Some observations on Wordsworth's A poet!—he hath put his heart to school. PQ 37 1958.
Greenleaf, R. Emerson and Wordsworth. Science & Soc 22 1958.
Heyworth, N. Purchasing power of the £1 in Wordsworth's early days. N & Q Oct 1958. On Calvert's legacy.
Kroeber, K. The reaper and the sparrow: a study in romantic style. Comparative Lit 10 1958. On Wordsworth and Leopardi.
— A new reading of The world is too much with us. Stud in Romanticism 2 1963.

— Wordsworth: the personal epic. In his Romantic narrative art, Madison 1960.
— In his Artifice of reality, Madison 1964.
Langman, F. H. On the scope of the Prelude. Eng Stud in Africa 1 1958.
— Wordsworth's patriotism. Theoria 18 1962.
— The Thorn: banality or profundity. Theoria 24 1965.
McCanse, R. A. 'The visionary gleam' and 'spots of time'. Trans of Wisconsin Acad 46 1958.
Sastri, P. S. Wordsworth under the influence of Coleridge. Calcutta Rev 149 1958.
Sayers, D. The Beatrician vision in Dante and other poets [Blake, Traherne, Wordsworth]. Nottingham Medieval Stud 2 1958.
Schlüter, K. Wordsworth als Kritiker von Grays poetischer Diktion. Neophilologus 42 1958.
Super, R. H. Landor's letters to Wordsworth and Coleridge. MP 55 1958.
Winkler, R. O. C. Wordsworth's poetry. In From Blake to Byron, ed B. Ford 1958 (Pelican guide to English lit 5).
Worth, G. J. A troublesome Wordsworth sonnet [On a portrait of the Duke of Wellington]. N & Q Nov 1958.
Bishop, J. Wordsworth and the 'spots of time'. ELH 26 1959.
Blanshard, F. Portraits of Wordsworth. 1959.
Brown, J. L. On Wordsworth's Michael. Univ Quart 13 1959.
Everett, B. The Prelude. CQ 1 1959.
Ferry, D. The limits of mortality: an essay on Wordsworth's major poems. Middletown Conn 1959.
Gifford, H. Wordsworth and 'the ballast of familiar life'. Durham Univ Jnl new ser 20 1959.
Hagstrum, J. H. Romantic skylarks. Newberry Lib Bull 5 1959.
Harper, G. Mills. A source of Wordsworth's ages of man. Texas Stud in Lit & Lang 1 1959.
Little, G. L. An important unpublished Wordsworth letter, December 18th 1800. N & Q Sept 1959. To Longman and Rees.
— A note on Wordsworth and Blair. N & Q July 1960.
— An incomplete Wordsworth essay upon moral habits. REL 2 1961.
— James Losh. N & Q Dec 1961.
— Two unpublished Wordsworth letters. N & Q May 1962.
— Wordsworth, Lockhart, Barron Field and the Copyright Act. N & Q Nov 1965.
MacEachen, D. B. Wordsworth's beauteous evening. N & Q Sept 1959.
Maekawa, S. Wordsworth and the philosophy of David Hartley. Stud in Lit (Fukuoka, Japan) 2 1959.
Morton, L. B. Wordsworth's definition of a poet. Southern Univ Bull 46 1959.
Nicolson, M. H. In her Mountain gloom and mountain glory, Ithaca 1959.
Pagnini, M. La poesia di Wordsworth. Milan 1959.
Perkins, D. In his Quest for permanence: the symbolism of Wordsworth, Shelley and Keats, Cambridge Mass 1959.
— Wordsworth and the poetry of sincerity. Cambridge Mass 1964.
Rees, J. Wordsworth and Samuel Daniel. N & Q Jan 1959.
Severs, J. B. Keats's Mansion of many apartments, Sleep and poetry, and Tintern Abbey. MLQ 20 1959.
Walsh, W. The Prelude. In his Autobiographical literature and educational thought, Leeds 1959.
— Wordsworth and the growth of the mind. In his Use of imagination, 1959.
Wildi, M. Wordsworth and the Simplon Pass. E Studies 40 1959, 43 1962.
Wordsworth, J. Wordsworth letters. TLS 8 May 1959.
— Eight early Wordsworthian letters. TLS 5–12 June 1959. Reply by D. B. Green, 17 July 1959.
— Critics who have influenced taste. Times 20 June 1963.
— A ms of Mr Wordsworth. New Statesman 31 July 1964.
— The new Wordsworth poem. College Eng March 1966. On The barberry-tree. Reply by M. L. Reed, Oct 1966.
— A Wordsworth tragedy. TLS 21 July 1966.
Conran, A. E. M. The dialectic of experience: a study of Resolution and independence. PMLA 75 1960.
de Man, P. Structure intentionelle de l'image romantique. Revue Internationale de Philosophie 14 1960.
— Symbolic landscape in Wordsworth and Yeats. In In defense of reading, ed R. A. Brower and R. Poirier, New York 1962.
Garlitz, B. The baby's debut: the contemporary reaction to Wordsworth's poetry of childhood. Boston Univ Stud in Eng 4 1960.
— The Immortality ode: its cultural progeny. Stud in Eng Lit 1500–1900 6 1966.
Harrison, T. P. Bird of paradise: phoenix redivivus. Isis 51 1960.
— Browning's Childe Roland and Wordsworth. Tennessee Stud in Lit 6 1961.
Hirsch, E. D., jr. Wordsworth and Schelling: a typological study of romanticism. New Haven 1960.
Landon, C. Wordsworth, Coleridge and the Morning Post: an early version of the Seven sisters. RES new ser 11 1960.
— Wordsworth's Racedown period: some uncertainties resolved. BNYPL Feb 1964.
Lindenberger, H. The reception of the Prelude. BNYPL April 1960.
— On Wordsworth's Prelude. Princeton 1963.
Misra, T. A note on Wordsworth's sound imagery. Indian Jnl of Eng Stud 1 1960.
Sewell, E. Wordsworth and Rilke: toward a biology of thinking. In her Orphic voice, 1960.
Sonn, C. R. An approach to Wordsworth's earlier imagery. ELH 27 1960.
Turner, P. The parable of the Idiot boy. E Studies 41 1960.
Barnum, P. H. Mythopoesis and the 'poet's mind' in Wordsworth's The prelude. Thoth 2 1961.
Bloom, H. In his Visionary company, Garden City NY 1961.
Brune, R. The origin of Wordsworth's love of man. Thoth 2 1961.
Combecher, H. Zu drei Gedichten von Wordsworth. Die Neueren Sprachen Aug 1961.
— Von der spätklassizistischen zur romantischen Ode: zwei Interpretationen als Beitrag zur Geschichte der englischen Ode. Die Neueren Sprachen Oct 1962. On To the cuckoo.
— The solitary reaper: eine Deutung. Die Neueren Sprachen April 1963.
Copeland, M. W. 'Steady moods of thoughtfulness matured to inspiration': a study of the function of the poetic imagination in the Prelude books iii–vi. Thoth 2 1961.
Grob, A. Process and permanence in Resolution and independence. ELH 28 1961.
— Wordsworth's Nutting. JEGP 61 1962.
— Wordsworth's Immortality ode and the search for identity. ELH 32 1965.
— Wordsworth and Godwin: a reassessment. Stud in Romanticism 6 1967.
Hyman, S. E. A poem of resolution. Centennial Rev of Arts & Science (Michigan State) 5 1961. On Resolution and independence.
Isoda, K. The historical background of the Preface to the Lyrical ballads. Stud in Eng Lit (Tokyo) 38 1961.
Kaul, R. K. Wordsworth's Preface reconsidered. Literary Criterion (Univ of Mysore) 4 1961.
Kregor, K. Meditation, emblem and epiphany in Wordsworth's The prelude (1805). Thoth 2 1961.
Lainoff, S. Wordsworth's final phase: glimpses of eternity. Stud in Eng Lit 1500–1900 1 1961.

— Wordsworth's Answer to Mathetes: a re-appraisal. Eng Lang Notes 3 1966.
Sarmiento, E. Wordsworth and Don Quijote. Bull of Hispanic Stud 33 1961.
Schelp, H. Wordsworth's Daffodils influenced by a Wesleyan hymn? E Studies 42 1961.
Smith, T. V. Wordsworth and the sense of guilt. Ethics 71 1961.
Sternlicht, S. The exile and the quest in the Prelude. Thoth 2 1961.
Stock, A. G. Wordsworth: nature and the revolution. Bull of Dept of English, Univ of Calcutta 2 1961.
Tillotson, G. More about poetic diction. In his Augustan studies, 1961.
— Wordsworth. Sewanee Rev 74 1966.
Aldrich, R. I. The Wordsworths and Coleridge: 'three persons, but not 'one soul'. Stud in Romanticism 2 1962.
Balslev, T. Keats and Wordsworth: a comparative study. Copenhagen 1962.
Blackstone, B. The secondary founts. In his Lost travellers, 1962.
Christensen, N. A Virgilian line in the Prelude. N & Q May 1962.
Doughty, O. The reception of Wordsworth by his contemporaries. Eng Miscellany (Rome) 13 1962.
Hardy, J. E. Wordsworth's The solitary reaper: a music within. In his Curious frame, Notre Dame 1962.
Kaiser, R. Das naturbeschreibende Sonett bei Wordsworth. Die Neueren Sprachen Jan 1962.
— Vier Sonette: eine vergleichende Interpretation. Die Neueren Sprachen June 1963. On Duddon sonnet 21.
Kaufman, P. Wordsworth's 'candid and enlightened friend'. N & Q Nov 1962. Extracts from James Losh's diary.
— To Wordsworth from Archbishop Trench: a volume and a letter. Eng Lang Notes 4 1966.
Knieger, B. Wordsworth and Coleridge as playwrights. College Lang Assoc Jnl 6 1962.
Lal, M. Wordsworth's concept of reason. Indian Jnl of Eng Stud 2 1962.
McAdam, E. L., jr. Wordsworth's shipwreck. PMLA 77 1962.
Partridge, A. C. Biographical evidence and critical understanding. Eng Stud in Africa 5 1962.
— Unpublished Wordsworthiana: the Continental tour of 1820, described in Mary Wordsworth's journal. Eng Stud in Africa 6 1963.
Piper, H. W. In his Active universe, 1962.
Storch, R. F. Wordsworth at Burukuso. Br Jnl of Aesthetics 2 1962. On Resolution and independence.
— Wordsworth and Constable. Stud in Romanticism 5 1966.
Tanner, T. Mountains and depths: an approach to nineteenth-century dualism. REL 3 1962.
Watson, J. R. Wordsworth and Constable. RES new ser 13 1962. *See* 14 1963.
Whittock, T. Wordsworth's poem to Mary Hutchinson. Eng Stud in Africa 5 1962.
Williams, M. G. A new look at Wordsworth's religion. Cithara 2 1962.
Woof, R. S. Wordsworth's poetry and Stuart's newspapers 1797–1803. SB 15 1962.
— Coleridge and Thomasina Dennis. UTQ 32 1963.
Albrecht, W. P. Hazlitt on Wordsworth: the poetry of paradox. In Six studies in nineteenth-century English literature and thought, ed H. Orel and G. J. Worth, Lawrence Kansas 1963.
Beaty, F. L. Mrs Radcliffe's fading gleam. PQ 42 1963. On Immortality ode.
Buchan, A. M. The influence of Wordsworth on Coleridge 1795–1800. UTQ 32 1963.
Godfrey, D. R. Imagination and truth: some romantic contradictions. E Studies 44 1963.
Göller, K. H. Die geistige Entwicklung Wordsworths. Die Neueren Sprachen Aug 1963.
Hamilton, C. C. Wordsworth's decline in poetic power: prophet into high priest. New York 1963.
Jackson, T. H. Wordsworth's 'thought' and his verse. College Eng Jan 1963.
Knoepflmacher, U. C. Dover revisited: the Wordsworthian matrix in the poetry of Matthew Arnold. Victorian Poetry 1 1963.
Reed, M. L. Wordsworth and the Americans: two new letters and visits [1844]. Emerson Soc Quart no 33 1963.
— Two letters of Wordsworth to Richard Monckton Milnes. N & Q Jan 1964.
— Wordsworth's letter to John Gardner, 5 April 1830. N & Q Nov 1965.
— Wordsworth, Coleridge and the 'plan' of the Lyrical ballads. UTQ 34 1965.
— Wordsworth: the chronology of the early years 1770–1799. Cambridge Mass 1967.
Rodway, A. E. Radical romantic poets: Wordsworth. In his Romantic conflict, 1963.
Roger, D. M. Wordsworth's rediscovery of religion 1787–98. Universitas 1 1963.
Smith, G. S. Wordsworth's Socratic irony. Person 44 1963.
Stevenson, L. The unfinished Gothic cathedral: a study of the organic unity of Wordsworth's poetry. UTQ 32 1963.
Stobie, W. G. A reading of the Prelude book v. MLQ 24 1963.
Ball, P. M. Sincerity: the rise and fall of a critical term. MLR 59 1964.
Bentman, R. The romantic poets and critics on Robert Burns. Texas Stud in Lit & Lang 6 1964.
Bernhardt-Kabish, E. Wordsworth's expostulator: Taylor or Hazlitt? Eng Lang Notes 2 1964.
— Wordsworth: the monumental poet. PQ 44 1965.
Black, M. H. On six lines of Wordsworth [Prelude III 58–63]. MLR 59 1964.
Hunting, C. The remarkable suppleness of father William. Discourse 7 1964.
Irwin, M. Wordsworth's 'dependency sublime'. EC 14 1964.
Nabholtz, J. R. Wordsworth and William Mason. RES new ser 15 1964.
— Wordsworth's Guide to the Lakes and the picturesque tradition. MP 61 1964.
— Dorothy Wordsworth and the picturesque. Stud in Romanticism 3 1964.
— Wordsworth's interest in landscape design and an inscription poem of 1800. Papers in Lang & Lit 2 1966.
Watson, M. R. The redemption of Peter Bell. Stud in Eng Lit 1500–1900 4 1964.
Zwerdling, A. Wordsworth and Greek myth. UTQ 33 1964.
Gillis, W. A Scottish source for Wordsworth. Stud in Scottish Lit 3 1965. On To the cuckoo.
Howe, E. M. Lady Beaumont, Wordsworth's friend. Stud in Romanticism 4 1965.
James, G. I. Wordsworth's The solitary reaper. EC 15 1965. Reply by M. Pittock. Ibid.
— and H. Mills. Wordsworth's unknown: two points of view. Anglo Welsh Rev 15 1966. On She dwelt among.
Kliman, B. W. Wordsworth in a small German magazine. N & Q Nov 1965.
Lindsay, J. I. Wordsworth and Haydon. Ibid.
Murray, R. N. Synecdoche in Wordsworth's Michael. ELH 32 1965.
Neft, W. Glory: ein Schlüsselwort in der Dichtung Wordsworths. Die Neueren Sprachen Jan 1965.
Rountree, T. J. This mighty sum of things: Wordsworth's theme of benevolent necessity. Tuscaloosa 1965.

Ruotolo, L. P. Three Prelude events: the growth of a poet's faith. College Eng April 1965.
Ryskamp, C. Wordsworth's Lyrical ballads in their time. In From sensibility to romanticism: essays presented to Frederick A. Pottle, ed F. W. Hilles and H. Bloom, New York 1965.
Salvesen, C. The landscape of memory: a study of Wordsworth's poetry. 1965.
Sellers, W. H. Wordsworth and Spender: some speculations on the use of rhyme. Stud in Eng Lit 1500–1900 5 1965.
Taaffe, J. G. The 'spots of time' passage in the Prelude. Eng Lang Notes 2 1965.
— Poet and lover in Wordsworth's Lucy poems. MLR 61 1966.
Wasserman, E. R. The English romantics: the grounds of knowledge. Stud in Romanticism 4 1965.
Bercovitch, S. Lucy and light: an interpretation of Wordsworth's Lucy poems. English 16 1966.
Buchen, I. H. Wordsworth's exposure and reclamation of the Satanic intellect. Universities Rev 33 1966.
Drabble, M. Wordsworth. 1966.
Echeruo, J. C. Shelley on Wordsworth. Eng Stud in Africa 9 1966.
Garber, F. Wordsworth and the romantic synedoche. Bucknell Rev 14 1966.
Grove, R. Wordsworth. Critical Rev 9 1966.
Hefferman, J. A. W. Wordsworth on imagination: the emblemizing power. PMLA 81 1966.
Hönnighausen, L. Wordsworths 'She was a phantom of delight'. Die Neueren Sprachen April 1966.
King, A. Wordsworth and the artist's vision: an essay in interpretation. 1966.
Kostelanetz, A. Wordsworth's conversations: a reading of The two April mornings and The fountain. ELH 33 1966.
Roy, G. R. Wordsworth on Burns. Stud in Scottish Lit 3 1966.
Ryan, F. L. A Wordsworth sonnet: one phase of a structural linguistic analysis. Stud in Eng Lit (Tokyo) 42 1966.
Stang, R. The false dawn: a study of the opening of Wordsworth's The prelude. ELH 33 1966.
Thorslev, P. L., jr. Wordsworth's Borderers and the romantic villain-hero. Stud in Romanticism 5 1966.
Townsend, R. C. John Wordsworth and his brother's poetic development. PMLA 81 1966.
Welsford, E. Salisbury Plain: a study in the development of Wordsworth's mind and art. Oxford 1966.
Finch, J. A. The ruined cottage restored: three stages of composition 1795–8. JEGP 66 1967.
Scoggins, J. The Preface to Lyrical ballads: a revolution in dispute. In Studies in criticism and aesthetics 1660–1800, ed H. Anderson and J. S. Shea, Minneapolis 1967.
— Imagination and fancy: complementary modes in the poetry of Wordsworth. Lincoln Nebraska 1967.

W. J. B. O.

SAMUEL TAYLOR COLERIDGE

1772–1834

By far the most important collection of mss and of annotated and association books is in the BM; the complementary collection, for many years preserved intact by the Coleridge family, is in the Victoria College Library, Toronto. There are important smaller collections in the Houghton Library Harvard, the Huntington Library, and the Berg Collection of the New York Public Library; and considerable groups of material in several other permanent collections in the United Kingdom and North America. Since the dispersal of Lord Latymer's collection of Coleridge mss there is no private collection of outstanding importance; but there are items in several private collections, and small clusters of Coleridgeana are held in a number of public collections, sometimes embedded in materials primarily devoted to Coleridge's contemporaries—especially Wordsworth, Lamb, Hazlitt, De Quincey, Godwin, Crabb Robinson and the Wedgwoods.

For some account of the dispersal and present location of Coleridge's books, see G. Whalley, Portrait of a bibliophile, Book Collector 10 1961. *There is no corresponding account of the mss of poems, letters and miscellanea.*

Bibliographies etc

Campbell, J. D. Titles, prefaces, contents etc. In Poetical works of Coleridge, 1893. Appendix K.
White, W. H. A description of the Wordsworth and Coleridge mss in the possession of Mr T. Norton Longman. 1897.
Shepherd, R. H. The bibliography of Coleridge, revised, corrected and enlarged by Colonel W. F. Prideaux. 1900. For Prideaux's critical views on Shepherd's work, *see* N & Q 18 Oct 1902; and for the Christabel controversy between Prideaux and T. Hutchinson, N & Q 1902–3.
Coleman, E. H. Coleridge bibliography. N & Q 20 Sept 1902. General review in response to J. L. Haney, referring to earlier bibliographical materials in N & Q.
Haney, J. L. A bibliography of Coleridge. Philadelphia 1903. Includes first comprehensive list of annotated and marked books.
Garnett, R. In his Coleridge, 1904.
Coleridge, E. H. Bibliography of the poetical works. In Complete poetical works, Oxford 1912, appendix 7.
Wise, T. J. A bibliography of the writings in prose and verse of Coleridge. 1913 (priv ptd); Supplement: Coleridgeana, 1919.
— In his Ashley Library: catalogue of printed books, manuscripts and autograph letters collected by Wise, 11 vols 1922–36 (priv ptd). Coleridge items chiefly in vols 1, 8, 10.
— Two Lake poets: a catalogue of printed books, manuscripts and autograph letters by Wordsworth and Coleridge collected by Wise. 1927 (priv ptd).
Catalogue of a unique Coleridge collection. [1913] (with facs). Includes part of the Norton Longman collection.
Dillon, A. E. The Coleridge collection at the Manchester Reference Library. Lib Assoc Record 1 1931.
Coleridge centenary exhibition organized by the University of the South West of England. Exeter [1934].
Kennedy, V. W. and M. N. Barton. Coleridge: a selected bibliography. Baltimore 1935.
Logan, Sr E. A concordance to the poetry of Coleridge. Saint Mary-of-the-Woods Indiana 1940.
Noyes, R. The Oscar L. Watkins Wordsworth-Coleridge collection. Indiana Quart for Bookmen 1 1945.
Coleridge: an excerpt from the general catalogue of printed books in the British Museum. 1947. Prepared before acquisition of the Ottery collection, for which *see* T. C. Skeat, BM Quart 16 1952.
Raysor, T. M. In English romantic poets: a review of research, ed Raysor, New York 1950, 1956 (rev).
Healey, G. H. The Cornell Wordsworth collection: a catalogue of books and manuscripts presented to the University by Mr Victor Emmanuel. Ithaca 1957. Includes Coleridge material.
Metzdorf, R. F. The Tinker library. New Haven 1959. Includes Coleridge material.

Collections

The poetical works of Coleridge, Shelley and Keats. Paris 1829, Philadelphia 1831. The Coleridge sheets also issued separately in 1831 etc.

Poetical works 3 vols 1834. The last issued during Coleridge's lifetime, reissued 1835, 1836, 1837, 1840, 1844. For later authoritative collective edns *see* §1 *below, cols 219–20*.
Poetical and dramatic works, with a life of the author. 1836.
Poetical works, with life of the author. 1837.
Works of Coleridge, prose and verse. Philadelphia 1843.
Poetical works. Ed H. Hooker, Philadelphia 1843, 1844, 1851.
The Ancient mariner and other poems. 1844 (Clarke's Cabinet ser).
Works, prose and verse, complete in one volume. Philadelphia 1846, 1849, 1852 etc.
Poems, with an introductory essay on his life and writings by H. T. Taskerman. New York and Boston 1848.
Poetical works of Coleridge and Keats, with a memoir of each. 2 vols Boston 1852, New York 1878.
Select poetical works. Ed H. G. Bohn 1852.
Complete works, with an introductory essay upon his philosophical and theological opinions. Ed W. G. T. Shedd 7 vols New York 1853, 1871, 1875, 1884. Shedd's introd, Coleridge as a philosopher and theologian, rptd in his Literary essays, New York [1878].
Poetical and dramatic works, with a memoir. 2 vols Boston, New York and Philadelphia 1854.
Poetical and dramatic works. Boston 1857.
The Ancient mariner and other poems. Groombridge 1858.
Poetical works of T. Campbell and Coleridge. Edinburgh [1859].
Poems. 1862 (Bell & Daldy's Pocket Vols), 1864 (Elzevir ser).
Poetical and dramatic works, with a life of the author. Halifax 1864.
Poetical and dramatic works, with a life of the author by C. E. Norton. 3 vols Boston 1864.
Christabel and the lyrical and imaginative poems of Coleridge. Ed A. C. Swinburne 1869.
Coleridge's Ancient mariner and other poems. 1872.
Poetical works. Ed W. M. Rossetti 1872, [1880], 1892, 1912 (with dramatic writings).
Poetical works. Ed W. B. Scott 1874, [1880] (Excelsior ser), [1894].
Favorite poems by Coleridge. Boston 1877. Illustr.
Poetical works, with a life of the author. 1877.
Poetical works. 1878.
Poetical works of Coleridge and Keats, with a memoir of each. New York 1878.
Poetical works, with life. Edinburgh and London [1881] (Landscape ser).
Poems, with a prefatory notice, biographical and critical, by J. Skipsey. 1884 (Canterbury Poets).
Poetical works. Ed T. Ashe 2 vols 1885 (Aldine), 1885 etc (Native edn).
The Ancient mariner, Christabel and miscellaneous poems. London and New York [1886].
Poetical works. Ed W. B. Scott 1889.
Select poems. Ed H. G. Groser. In A. H. M. Miles, Poets and the poetry of the century vol 1, [1891] etc.
Passages from the prose and table talk of Coleridge. Ed W. H. Dircks [1894].
Select poems of Coleridge, Wordsworth etc. Ed F. H. Sykes 1895.
[Select poems]. Ed W. Pakenham and J. Marshall [1895].
The golden book of Coleridge. Ed S. A. Brooke 1895, 1906 (EL).
Poems chosen out of the works of Coleridge. Ed F. S. Ellis, Hammersmith 1896 (Kelmscott Press).
Four poets: poems from Wordsworth, Coleridge, Shelley and Keats. Ed O. J. F. Crawford 1897.
Poetry. Ed R. Garnett 1898 (ML).
Selected poems. Ed A. Lang 1898. Illustr P. Wilson.
Wordsworth, Coleridge and Keats: selections. Ed A. D. Innes 1901.
Select poems. Ed A. J. George 1903. In chronological order.
Christabel, Kubla Khan, Fancy in nubibus and Song from Zapolya. 1904. Designs by L. and E. Pissarro.
Christabel and other poems. Ed H. Bennett 1905.
Poems. Ed A. Symons 1905.
Poems. Ed E. H. Coleridge 1905. Selection.
Poems. Ed A. Meynell [1905].
Poems. Ed E. Dowden, Edinburgh [1906]. Illustr C. Pears.
Poems. Ed A. T. Quiller-Couch 1907 (WC).
Poems. Ed E. H. Coleridge, illustr G. Metcalfe [1907].
Ancient mariner, Kubla Khan and Christabel. Ed T. F. Huntington, New York 1908, 1936 (illustr A. G. Peck).
Coleridge's literary criticism. Ed J. W. Mackail 1908.
Selections from the prose writings. Ed H. A. Beers 1908.
The Ancient mariner and Christabel. Oxford [1909].
Poems of nature and romance 1794–1807. Ed M. A. Keeling, Oxford 1910.
Selected poems. Ed W. Robertson [1915].
Selections from the poems. Ed A. H. Thompson, Cambridge 1916.
Select poems. Ed S. G. Dunn 1916, 1918 (Indian Lib of English Poets).
The table talk and omniana; with a note on Coleridge by Coventry Patmore. 1917. Preface by H. N. Coleridge.
The Ancient mariner and other poems and prose. Ed W. B. Henderson 1920.
The poetry and prose of Coleridge, Lamb and Leigh Hunt. Ed S. E. Winbolt 1920.
The rime of the ancient mariner and other poems. Ed L. Pound, Philadelphia [1920].
[Selected poems]. Ed H. Newbolt [1924].
Poetry and prose, with essays by Hazlitt, Jeffrey, De Quincey, Carlyle and others. Ed H. W. Garrod, Oxford 1925.
Wordsworth and Coleridge. Ed G. Boas 1925. A contrast.
Selected poems and prose. Ed R. B. Hales 1927.
[Select poems]. Ed E. Benn [1928].
[Prose and verse]. Ed B. I. and M. R. Evans 1931.
Selections from the poems. Ed A. H. R. Ball [1931].
The Ancient mariner and other poems. Ed G. E. Hollingworth 1932.
Select poetry and prose. Ed S. Potter 1933, 1950 (with some marginalia added), 1962 (Nonesuch).
The best of Coleridge. Ed E. L. Griggs, New York 1934.
Poems and dramatic works. Ed W. Knight [1934].
Selected poems. 1935 (Nonesuch).
Ancient mariner and Gray's Elegy. 2 pts 1936. Reissues Macmillan edns of 1904 and 1896, with new editorial matter.
The political thought of Coleridge. Ed R. J. White 1938.
Coleridge. Ed D. Wellesley 1942.
Letters of Coleridge, selected. Ed K. Raine 1950 (for 1952).
The portable Coleridge. Ed I. A. Richards, New York 1950, 1961.
Poems. Ed G. Grigson 1951 (ML).
Selected poetry and prose. Ed E. W. Schneider, New York 1951.
Selected poetry and prose. Ed D. A. Stauffer, New York 1951.
Political tracts of Wordsworth, Coleridge and Shelley. Ed R. J. White, Cambridge 1953.
Poems. Ed 'Morchard Bishop' (O. Stonor) 1954.
Selected poems. Ed R. C. Bald, New York 1956.
Selected poems and prose. Ed K. Raine 1957 (Penguin).
William Wordsworth and Coleridge: selected critical essays. Ed T. M. Raysor, New York 1958.

Selected poems. Ed R. Wilbur and G. R. Stange, New York 1959 (Laurel Poetry ser).
Selected poems. Ed J. Reeves 1959 (Poetry Bookshelf).
A Coleridge selection. Ed R. Wilson 1963.
Poems. Ed J. B. Beer 1963 (EL).
Poems, selected. Ed G. Hough 1963.

§ 1

The following list includes successive authoritative edns in which the canon has been amplified or refined, but not edns of material not intended for pbn or separate edns or collections of isolated pieces, for which see Letters, Notebooks etc, below.

The Complete works, ed W. G. T. Shedd 7 vols 1853, *still the only attempt at a collective edn of Coleridge's prose and poetry, is incomplete, devoid of critical commentary, unindexed and silent upon matters of editorial and textual procedure, but still useful, especially for texts not yet available in a modern version. The* Collected works of Coleridge, ed K. Coburn et al, c. 24 vols London and New York 1969–, *will bring together all the writings other than the Letters and Notebooks.*

The fall of Robespierre: an historic drama. Cambridge 1794. Act 1 by Coleridge, acts 2–3 by Southey.

A moral and political lecture delivered at Bristol. Bristol [1795]; expanded in Conciones, below; in Collected works: Lectures 1795.

The plot discovered. Bristol 1795; rptd in Conciones, below; in Collected works: Lectures 1795.

Conciones ad populum: or addresses to the people. [Bristol] 1795. For annotated copy at Harvard *see* C. C. Seronsy, SP 51 1954. In Collected works: Lectures 1795.

The plot discovered: or an address to the people, against ministerial treason. Bristol 1795. In Collected works: Lectures 1795.

An answer to A letter to Edward Long Fox MD. Bristol [1795]; rptd by R. A. Potts, Athenaeum 2 May 1908. Signed C.T.S. (for S.T.C.).

Lectures 1795: on politics and religion. Ed L. Patton and J. P. Mann 1969 (Collected works). Includes Conciones ad populum, The plot discovered, A moral and political lecture etc.

Ode on the departing year. Bristol 1796.

Poems on various subjects. London and Bristol 1796 (ptd in Bristol).

[Sonnets from various authors.] [1796] (priv ptd). 4 sonnets and prefatory essay on the sonnet by Coleridge, 24 sonnets by Bowles, Lamb, Lloyd, Southey et al. Prefatory essay rptd variously in Poems 1797. *For existing marked copies see* G. Whalley, TLS 23 Nov 1956.

The watchman. 10 nos Bristol 1796. Advertised 'to be published every eighth day'; issued 1 March–13 May 1796. Prospectus rptd by J. D. Campbell, Athenaeum 9 Dec 1893. Coleridge's contributions rptd in pt in Essays on his own times, ed S. Coleridge 1853. *See* G. P. Winship, Coleridge bibliography, TLS 19 March 1925.

The watchman. Ed L. Patton, New York 1969 (Collected works).

Poems by S. T. Coleridge, second edition: to which are now added poems by Charles Lamb and Charles Lloyd. Bristol and London 1797 (ptd in Bristol). Includes much of Poems 1796, above, but substantially a new book. For the printer's copy prepared in part from proofs of Poems 1796, *see* J. D. Campbell and W. H. White (ed), Coleridge's poems, 1899; and Collected letters vol 1. For an annotated copy *see* W. E. Gibbs, Unpublished variants in Coleridge's poetry, MLN 46 1931.

Fears in solitude, written in 1798 during the alarm of an invasion; to which are added France: an ode; and Frost at midnight. 1798 (for the ms *see* B. I. Evans, TLS 18 April 1935), [1812] (another edn, perhaps rptd from the Poetical Register 7 1812).

Lyrical ballads, with a few other poems [by W. Wordsworth and S. T. Coleridge]. [Bristol? and] London 1798 (ptd in Bristol). Lewti cancelled in proof and Coleridge's Nightingale substituted. *See* D. F. Foxon, The printing of Lyrical ballads 1798, Library 5th ser 9 1954. *See under Wordsworth, col 185, above. For separate edns of the* Ancient mariner, *see below.*

2 vols 1800 (with Coleridge's poem Love). For ms copy of this edn *see* C. H. Patton, Yale Univ Lib Gazette 9 1934; Collected letters vol 1; G. L. Little, N & Q Sept 1959; M. Peacock, Variants to the preface of Lyrical ballads, MLN 61 1946; F. A. Pottle, An important addition to Yale's Wordsworth–Coleridge collection, Yale Univ Lib Gazette 41 1966.

2 vols 1802 (with omission of Coleridge's Dungeon), 1805.

For separate edns of Lyrical ballads, *see under Wordsworth, col 185, above. The most recent critical edns are* ed R. L. Brett and A. R. Jones 1963 (text of 1798 with the additional 1800 poems and prefaces, with introd, notes and appendixes); ed W. J. B. Owen, Oxford 1967 (text of 1798).

The Ancient Mariner. The rime of the ancyent marinere. In Lyrical ballads, 1798; The rime of the ancient mariner, in Lyrical ballads, 1800 (extensively rev), 1802, 1805; in Sibylline leaves, 1816 (with marginal gloss); in Poetical works, 1828, 1829, 1834 (with minor successive revisions). *See* J. L. Lowes, The road to Xanadu, Boston 1927, 1930 (rev).

Edinburgh and London 1837 (illustr D. Scott); 1857 (illustr); 1863 (illustr J. N. Patton); [1875] (illustr); Boston 1876 (illustr); 1876 (illustr G. Doré); 1878 (Annotated Poems of English Authors); New York 1884 (illustr G. Doré), San Francisco 1952 (ed C. R. Wood, facs edn); ed W. Dent 1895; ed H. Bates 1896; Leeds [1896]; 1899 (decorated by C. Ricketts); 1900 (illustr H. Cole); ed P. Edgar, Toronto 1902; ed C. R. Ashbee 1903; Edinburgh 1903; ed P. T. Creswell 1904, 1936; 1904; ed G. E. Woodberry, New York [1904]; ed N. L. Frazer 1905; [1905]; ed R. M'William [1905]; ed W. J. Alexander, Toronto 1905, 1915; 1906; 1906; ed P. Woodroffe, Edinburgh [1906]; ed A. Guthkelch 1907 (with early English ballads); ed A. Eichler, Wiener Beiträge zur Englischen Philologien 26 1907 (with Christabel); ed W. Pogány 1910; [1910]; ed M. A. Keeling, Oxford 1912; [1912]; ed T. S. Sterling and J. W. Holme 1914; ed E. Smith 1914 (in Milton's sonnets); [1927]; [1928]; Bristol 1929 (illustr D. Jones); Oxford 1930, London 1935; with Gray's poems 1936; 1937 (illustr E. Davies); 1943 (illustr M. Peake); Mt Vernon NY [c. 1950] (illustr H. A. Mueller); Christchurch 1952 (frontispiece by L. Bensemann). Also ptd variously with Kubla Khan, Christabel and other separate poems; *see* Collections, above, 1858, 1872, London and New York [1886], 1908, Oxford [1909], 1920, Philadelphia [1920], 1932, 1936 etc.

Tr French 1858 (Le vieux marin by J. A. X. Michiels, in prose); 1901 (La complainte du vieux marin by V. Larbaud); 1920 (Le dit de l'ancien marinier by O. and G. Lavaud, illustr A. Lhote); 1921 (La ballade du vieux marin by A. Jarry, illustr A. Deslignières); 1926 (La chanson du vieux marin by A. Barbeau).

Tr German, 1877 (Der alte Matrose by F. Freiligrath); Heidelberg 1959 (Der alte Seemann by W. Breitweiser, with Kubla Khan).

Tr Italian 1913 (La ballata del vecchio marinaio by P. Ripari); *see* C. Lutri, Poemetti e liriche, 1953.

Tr Japanese, 1905 (by N. Katagami, Rising Generation 13); 1905 (by N. Kishimoto in One hundred English marine poems); 1934 (by T. Saito).

Tr Latin, 1906 (Carmen Coleridgeianum quod senex nauta by R. Broughton).

Tr Russian, 1930 (Sladkuv preklad stareho namornika by F. Chuduba).

'Morgan O'Doherty' (D. M. Moir), The rime of the auncient waggonere in four parts, Blackwood's Mag Feb 1819 (rptd in W. Maginn's Miscellanies, prose and verse, ed R. W. Montagu 2 vols 1885); The rime of the new-made baccalere: a parody, Oxford 1841, 1867.

Wallenstein: a drama in two parts translated from the German of Frederic Schiller. 1800. The Piccolomini (5 acts) and The death of Wallenstein (5 acts). The one-act prelude, Wallensteins Lager, which made up Schiller's original trilogy, was not tr. For Coleridge's ms *see* F. Freiligrath, Athenaeum 15 June, 31 Aug 1861 (*and* J. Gillman note 18 May 1861); Coleridge's Wallenstein-Uebersetzung, E Studien 31 1902 (collaιion of trn with German original); W. Grossman, The manuscript of Coleridge's Wallenstein, Harvard Lib Bull 9 1957, rptd Euphorion 53 1959.

Rptd in Works of Schiller, historical and dramatic, 1846; Schiller's tragedies, 1853; Complete works of Schiller, ed C. J. Hempel 1870; Dramatic works of Schiller, 1889.

Poems: third edition. 1803. Omits poems by Lamb and Lloyd; a fresh selection and arrangement supervised by Lamb.

The friend: a literary, moral and political weekly paper, excluding personal and party politics and the events of the day. 28 nos Penrith 1809-10. Nos 1-27, with supernumerary no between 20 and 21, issued 1 June 1809-15 March 1810. Includes contributions by Wordsworth et al, but almost entirely Coleridge's composition. Rptd in Collected works.

1812. Re-issue with supplementary matter. For annotated Rose copy *see* J. Wordsworth, TLS 14 June 1957.

3 vols 1818. A new edn, carefully rev and with extensive addns. For annotated Hughes copy *see* H. F. Heineman, N & Q 29 June 1940; for Bristol Library copy, J. Ross, TLS 7 Feb 1948; for Harvard copy, C. C. Seronsy, SP 51 1954.

3 vols 1837, 1844. Ed H. N. Coleridge. With the author's last corrections, an appendix and a synoptical table of the contents of the work by H. N. Coleridge.

1863. Ed D. Coleridge. Rptd 1866 (Bohn's Lib) etc.

The friend. Ed B. E. Rooke 2 vols 1969 (Collected works). Reprints complete texts of 1818 and 1809-10.

Remorse: a tragedy in five acts. 1813 (3 edns), 1884. Prologue by C. Lamb. For first unpbd version *see* Osorio 1873 under Letters etc, below. For Sarah Hutchinson's annotated copy *see* C. S. Bouslog, BNYPL May 1961; and for 2 prompt copies *see* C. Woodring, BNYPL April 1961.

Christabel; Kubla Khan: a vision; The pains of sleep. 1816 (3 edns). *For the annotated Hinves copy see* Christabel, ed E. H. Coleridge 1907, below.

Christabel. 1904 (illustr C. M. Watts), 1920; [1905]; Christabel, illustrated by a facsimile of the ms and by textual and other notes, ed E. H. Coleridge 1907 (Royal Soc of Lit); [1911]; ed T. Saito, Tokyo 1930.

Tr Japanese by Y. Tamato, Muraski 1-2 1934-5.

Christabess, by S. T. Colebritche esq: a right woeful poem, translated from the doggerel by Sir Vinegar Sponge, 1816; 'Morgan O'Doherty' (D. M. Moir), Christabel: the introduction to part the third, Blackwood's Mag June 1819 (rptd in Maginn's Miscellanies, prose and verse, ed R. W. Montagu 2 vols 1885).

M. F. Tupper, Geraldine: a sequel to Coleridge's Christabel, 1838 (rptd in his Ballads for the times [1850], 1851, 1852, 1853), [J. Hogg], Isabelle, The poetic mirror, or The living bards of Britain, 1816; D. B. Lyman, Christobel pts 3-4, suppl to CEA Jnl 15 1953 (Coleridge's pts 1-2, applying the title Christobel to completed poem).

Kubla Khan. For the ms *see* A. D. Snyder, Manuscript of Kubla Khan, TLS 2 Aug 1940; E. H. W. Meyerstein, Kubla Khan, TLS 12 Jan 1951 (the Crewe ms; replies by B. R. Davies 27 Jan 1952 and Meyerstein 9 Feb 1952); The manuscript of Kubla Khan, TLS 16 Feb 1962; T. C. Skeat, BM Quart 26 1963 (on ms now in BM).

1934 (illustr J. Vassos); tr German by H. Hennecke, Neue Rundschau 49 1938 (rhymed metrical trn); by W. Breitweiser, 1959 (with Ancient mariner); completed by H. Sarason 1956.

The statesman's manual, or the Bible the best guide to political skill and foresight: a lay sermon addressed to the higher classes of society, with an appendix containing comments and essays connected with the study of the inspired writings. 1816. Referred to as first Lay sermon. Ed R. J. White in Political tracts of Wordsworth, Coleridge and Shelley, Cambridge 1953.

Biographia literaria: or biographical sketches of my literary life and opinions. 2 vols 1817. For Coleridge's inscription in Derwent's copy, *see* N. F. D. Coleridge, TLS 3 July 1948.

Ed H. N. Coleridge and Sara Coleridge 2 vols 1847 (with long introd and biographical suppl), New York 1848 (from 2nd London edn); ed A. Symons 1898 (Bohn's Lib) (with 2 Lay sermons); ed A. Symons 1906 (EL); ed J. Shawcross 2 vols Oxford 1907 (with the aesthetic essays; text oscillates between 1817 and 1847).

Englischer Besuch in Hamburg im Jahre 1798. Ed D. Loewenfeld, Hamburg 1927. German version of pts of Satyrane's letters, with plates.

Ed G. Watson 1956, 1960, 1965 (with addn) (EL). Excludes Satyrane's letters and the critique of Bertram; text of 1817. *See also his* Text of the Biographia literaria, N & Q June 1954.

Blessed are ye that sow beside all waters: a lay sermon addressed to the higher and middle classes on the existing distresses and discontents. 1817. Second Lay sermon; for marginalia on the Anster copy of Lay sermons *see* M. J. Ryan, Dublin Mag 2 1927; ed D. Coleridge 1852 (with Statesman's manual); 1865 (Bohn's Lib) (with Statesman's manual and Biographia literaria).

A Hebrew dirge, chaunted in the Great Synagogue, St James' Place Aldgate on the day of the funeral of Her Royal Highness Princess Charlotte, by Hyman Hurwitz, with a translation in English verse by S. T. Coleridge esq. 1817.

Sibylline leaves: a collection of poems. 1817. First collective edn, assembled in 1815 omitting contents of the 1816 Christabel vol. For copies with ms addns and corrections *see* J. L. Lowes, The road to Xanadu, Boston 1927, 1930 (rev). For a presentation copy *see* N. van Patten, Library 3rd ser 17 1937. Rptd New York 1962.

Zapolya: a Christmas tale in two parts; the prelude entitled The usurper's fortune and the sequel entitled The usurper's fate. 1817. For a corrected copy, *see* J. Drinkwater, A book for bookmen, 1926 (priv ptd).

[On method.] General introd to Encyclopaedia metropolitana, 1818 (also separate offprint, 1818). Rptd separately [1849], [1850], [1854] (3 edns); as Mental science, 1855, 1873, 1875 (with Whateley's Logic and rhetoric); ed A. D. Snyder 1934 (with ms fragments, detailed introd and notes).

Remarks on the objections which have been urged against the principle of Sir Robert Peel's bill. [1818]. Rptd with the grounds of Sir Robert Peel's bill vindicated, ed E. Gosse as Two addresses on Robert Peel's bill (April 1818), 1913 (priv ptd).

The grounds of Sir Robert Peel's bill vindicated. 1818. Rptd in Two addresses, ed E. Gosse, 1913 (priv ptd).

The tears of a grateful people: a Hebrew dirge and hymn, chaunted in the Great Synagogue, St James' Place Aldgate, on the day of the funeral of his late most gracious Majesty King George III of blessed memory, by Hyman Hurwitz, translated into English verse by a friend [Coleridge]. 1820.

Aids to reflection in the formation of a manly character, on the several grounds of prudence, morality and religion, illustrated by select passages from our elder divines, especially from Archbishop Leighton. 1825, New York 1829, London 1831, 1836. For annotated Harvard copy of 1825, *see* C. C. Seronsy, SP 51 1954. Ed H. N. Coleridge 1839 (4th edn with author's last corrections), H. N. Coleridge 2 vols 1843 (with preliminary essay by J. H. Green and appendixes), 1848; ed D. Coleridge 1854, 1856; ed T. Fenby, Liverpool 1873, 1883, Edinburgh 1896, 1905 (with copious index and trns of Greek and Latin quotations); 1884 etc (Bohn's Lib) (with Confessions of an inquiring spirit etc).

The poetical works, including the dramas of Wallenstein, Remorse and Zapolya. 3 vols 1828. *See* J. D. Campbell, Athenaeum 10, 31 March 1888; replies by T. Ashe 17 March, and T. J. Cobden-Sanderson 7 April 1888.
 3 vols 1829. With a few addns. Guide text for Poetical works, ed J. D. Campbell 1893.

On the constitution of the Church and State according to the idea of each, with aids toward a right judgment on the late Catholic bill. 1830. Ed H. N. Coleridge 1839, 1852; rptd with the 2 Lay sermons in 1839 and after 1852.

The devil's walk: a poem, edited with a biographical memoir and notes by Professor Porson [i.e. Coleridge and Southey]. Ed H. W. Montagu 1830, 1830 (with engravings on wood by Bonner and Slader after R. Cruikshank); 1830, 1830 (with names of Coleridge and Southey in place of Porson's on the titlepage). Rptd in I. Cruikshank, Facetiae, 2 vols 1831. Originally composed by Coleridge and Southey in 1799, ptd anon in Morning Post 6 Sept 1799 as The devil's thoughts; amplified by Southey in 1827 without Coleridge's collaboration.

On the Prometheus of Aeschylus: an essay preparatory to a series of disquisitions respecting the Egyptian in connection with the sacredotal theology, and in contrast to the mysteries of ancient Greece. Read May 18, 1825. Trans Royal Soc of Lit 2 pt 2 1834. Rptd priv in 1834, not in 1825 as stated by T. J. Wise in his Catalogue of the Ashley library and elsewhere. Rptd in Literary remains vol 2, 1836; Notes and lectures upon Shakespeare, 1849; *see* G. Whalley, N & Q Sept 1968.

The poetical works. 3 vols 1834. Probably prepared and arranged by H. N. Coleridge. 66 uncollected pieces added to Poetical works 1829 with some rearrangement. Rptd 1835, 1836, 1840, 1844 (as Poetical and dramatic works). Guide text for Complete poetical works, ed E. H. Coleridge 2 vols 1912. The canon of Coleridge's poetical and dramatic works continued to be clarified and extended in the collective edns of S. Coleridge (1844), D. and S. Coleridge (1852), R. H. Shepherd (1877), J. D. Campbell (1893) and E. H. Coleridge (1912).

Confessions of an inquiring spirit. Ed H. N. Coleridge 1840, 1849, 1853, 1863 (with some miscellaneous pieces and introd by J. H. Green); ed H. N. Coleridge 1884 etc (Bohn's Lib) (with Aids to reflection, above), 1886 (with miscellaneous essays from Friend); ed H. S. Stanford 1957 (with J. H. Green's introd).

The poems. Ed Sara Coleridge 1844, 1848.

Hints toward the formation of a more comprehensive theory of life. Ed S. B. Watson 1848; ed T. Ashe 1885 (in Miscellanies, aesthetic and literary).

Essays on his own times, forming a second series of the Friend. Ed Sara Coleridge 3 vols 1850. Newspaper and periodical articles mostly from Watchman, Morning Post and Courier, and a number of topical and epigrammatic poems.

The poems: a new edition. Ed Derwent and Sara Coleridge. 1852 etc (in later edns associated with Dramatic works 1852, below); Leipzig 1852 (Tauchnitz edn with biographical memoir by F. Freiligrath); in Complete works, ed W. G. T. Shedd, New York 1853 etc; 3 vols Boston 1854, 1863 etc (with addns); 1870 (with introductory essay by Derwent Coleridge, and the 1798 text of the Ancient mariner and a few new poems in an appendix).

The dramatic works. Ed Derwent Coleridge 1852 etc.

The poetical and dramatic works, founded on the author's latest edition of 1834. [Ed R. H. Shepherd] 4 vols London and Boston 1877, 1880 (with addns).

The poetical words. Ed J. D. Campbell 1893 etc. Text based on Poetical works 1829, above. The biographical introd was issued separately 1894 as Coleridge: a narrative of the events of his life.

The complete poetical works, including poems and versions of poems now published for the first time. Ed E. H. Coleridge 2 vols Oxford 1912, 1957, 1962, 1966; I vol Oxford 1912 (OSA) (omitting dramatic writings and bibliographical matter). Text based on Poetical works 1834, above.

The philosophical lectures, hitherto unpublished. Ed K. Coburn 1949. The text, primarily based on a shorthand transcript taken at the lectures, is reconstructed by use of notebooks, marginalia and pbd works; with unpbd marginalia of from Tennemann and Kant. *See her* Coleridge's philosophical lectures, RES 10 1934.

Letters, Notebooks, Marginalia and Fragments

Annual anthology. [Ed. R. Southey] vol 2, Bristol [1800].

Omniana: or horae otiosiores. Ed R. Southey 2 vols 1812 (Coleridge's contributions identified in the contents by asterisks); ed T. Ashe 1884 (Bohn's Lib) (with Table-talk, below). Often rptd with addns from Allsop's Letters etc. Most of the contributions were taken from notebooks.

J., G. [Mr Coleridge's marginalia.] Blackwood's Mag Nov 1819. Transcript, possibly by James Gillman, of Coleridge's letter written in Browne's Pseudodoxia epidemica addressed to Sara Hutchinson, March 1804. Coleridge may have helped prepare letter for pbn.

Specimens of the table-talk of the late Samuel Taylor Coleridge. Ed H. N. Coleridge 2 vols 1835, 1836 (corrected), 1851; ed H. Morley 1874, 1884 (with Ancient mariner, Christabel, Kubla Khan); ed T. Ashe in Table talk and Omniana, 1884 etc (with additional table-talk from Allsop's Recollections and unpbd ms matter); tr Japanese by M. Okamoto, 1943.

The literary remains. Ed H. N. Coleridge 4 vols 1836–9. Vol 1, Uncollected poems, literary lectures, a few marginalia; vol 2, Lectures and notes on Shakespeare and other dramatists; vol 3–4, mostly marginalia, much theological. For H. N. Coleridge's editorial practice, *see* R. F. Brinkley, Coleridge transcribed, RES 24 1938, and P. Elmen, Editorial revisions of Coleridge's marginalia, MLN 67 1952.

Allsop, T. Letters, conversations and recollections of Coleridge. 2 vols 1836, 1858, 1864 (omitting prefaces of 1st and 2nd edns).

Notes and lectures upon Shakespeare and some of the old poets and dramatists, with other literary remains. Ed Mrs H. N. Coleridge 2 vols 1849. Rptd from Literary remains vols 1–2, above, with a few addns. Later edns variously entitled. Ed T. Ashe, Lectures and notes on Shakespeare and other English poets, 1883 etc (Bohn's Lib), Oxford 1931. Text chiefly follows Notes and lectures, 1849, above, but with Collier's Seven lectures and lectures from Bristol newspapers. Rptd 1907 (EL) (as Coleridge's essays and lectures on Shakespeare and some other old poets and dramatists).

'Bonsall'. Coleridge's notes on Pepys's diary. N & Q 4 Sept 1852.

Notes on English divines. Ed Derwent Coleridge 2 vols 1853. Marginalia rptd from Literary remains vols 3–4, above; intended, with the Notes and lectures on Shakespeare, above, and Notes theological, political and miscellaneous, below, to form a fresh and comprehensive arrangement of the marginalia.

Notes theological, political and miscellaneous. Ed Derwent Coleridge 1853. Marginalia, about one-third from Literary remains, the rest unpbd.

G., J. M. [John Matthew Gutch]. Samuel Taylor Coleridge. N & Q 19 March 1853. Marginalia on Parr's Spital sermon.

Ingleby, C. M. On the unpublished manuscripts of Coleridge, N & Q 9 July 1853, 27 May, 24 June 1854. Attacks J. H. Green as literary executor. *See also* Trans Royal Soc of Lit 9 1870.

Collier, J. P. Coleridge's lectures on Shakespeare and Milton; Coleridge and his lectures; Manuscript of Coleridge's lectures in 1812; Coleridge's lectures on Shakespeare. N & Q 1–8, 22 July, 12 Aug 1854. Reply by J. M. G[utch], 5 Aug 1854. *See* W. J. Fitzpatrick, N & Q 4 Aug 1855, with reports of lectures from the Dublin Correspondent.

Seven lectures on Shakespeare and Milton by the late S. T. Coleridge. Ed J. P. Collier 1856. Preface includes a defence against charges that the shorthand notes of Coleridge's lectures were a fabrication. *See* 'Detective' (A. E. Brae), Literary cookery, 1855.

Call, W. M. Unpublished letters written by Coleridge. Westminster Rev 93 1870. Call was Dr Brabant's son-in-law.

Osorio: a tragedy, as originally written in 1797. [Ed R. H. Shepherd] [1873]. Early and unpbd version of Remorse collated with the pbd text.

Garnett, R. Notes on Stillingfleet. Athenaeum 27 March 1875; 1875 (priv ptd). Marginalia on Origines sacrae.

Paul, C. K. In his William Godwin: his friends and contemporaries, 2 vols 1876.

MacCarthy, D. F. Unnoted variations in the text of Coleridge. Athenaeum 28 July 1877. Reply by J. D. Campbell 14 March 1885. 14 poems.

[Zimmern, H.] Coleridge marginalia. Blackwood's Mag Jan 1882. Descriptive account, with quotations from marginalia, of books acquired by Wilson from J. H. Green's library now the foundation for the unparalleled Coleridge collection in BM.

Unpublished letters to the Rev John Prior Estlin. Ed H. A. Bright, Trans Philobiblon Soc 15 1884; 1884 (priv ptd).

Caine, T. H. H. Notes on Coleridge. Athenaeum 11 July 1885. Dating of poems in periodicals.

Miscellanies, aesthetic and literary, to which is added the Theory of life. Ed T. Ashe 1885 (Bohn's Lib).

Anderson, J. R. Books in the library of the British Museum containing ms notes by Coleridge. Bibliography appended to H. Caine, Life of Coleridge, 1887. 66 titles not including works by Coleridge.

Knight, W. G. Memorials of Coleorton: being letters from Coleridge, Wordsworth and his sister, Southey and Sir Walter Scott to Sir George and Lady Beaumont of Coleorton Leicestershire 1803–34. 2 vols Edinburgh 1887.

Campbell, J. D. Coleridge marginalia hitherto unpublished on Grew's Cosmologia sacra. Athenaeum 7 April 1888.

— Coleridge marginalia hitherto unpublished on Jahn's History of the Hebrew commonwealth. Athenaeum 27 June 1888.

— Coleridge's [literary] lectures in 1818. Athenaeum 16 March, 3 May 1889.

— Unpublished verses by Coleridge to Matilda Betham. Athenaeum 15 March 1890. Reply by E. B. de Betham 30 Aug 1890.

— A sonnet by Coleridge, original or translated. Athenaeum 29 Aug 1891.

— Some [philosophical] lectures delivered by Coleridge in the winter of 1818–19. Athenaeum 26 Dec 1891, 2 Jan 1892.

Waugh, F. G. Lines by Coleridge. Athenaeum 28 Jan 1888. Replies by C. A. Ward 4 Feb; W. E. Mozley 11 Feb 1888.

Coleridge, E. H. and M. Stuart. Letters from the Lake Poets to Daniel Stuart. 1889 (priv ptd).

Coleridge, E. H. Notes on Coleridge. Athenaeum 27 Jan 1894. Ms of Wanderings of Cain. *See* W. A. Ward 20 Jan 1895.

Taylor, W. F. Critical annotations: being marginal notes inscribed in volumes formerly in the possession of Coleridge. Harrow 1889. All in BM.

Baker, J. Books read by Coleridge and Southey, from the records of Bristol Library. Chambers's Jnl 1 Feb 1890. *See* also G. Whalley, 1949, below.

Brooke, W. T. Unpublished fragments of Coleridge and Lamb. Newbery House Mag 6 1891.

De Quincey, T. De Quincey memorials, with communications from Coleridge. Ed A. H. Japp 1891.

Smiles, S. A publisher and his friends: memoir and correspondence of the late John Murray. 2 vols 1891.

Young, H. S. Samuel Taylor Coleridge. Athenaeum 2 Sept 1893. Marginalia on Fulke Greville. Reply by J. D. Campbell 9 Sept 1893.

Ward, C. A. Coleridge. Athenaeum 1 July 1893, 26 Oct 1895, 1 Feb 1896. Describes 2 vols of ms Opus maximum. Reply by L. E. Watson 23 Nov 1895.

Anima poetae, from the unpublished notebooks of Coleridge. Ed E. H. Coleridge 1895.

Letters. Ed E. H. Coleridge 2 vols 1895.

Notizbuch aus den Jahren 1795–8. Ed A. L. Brandl, Archiv 97 1896. Edn of Gutch memorandum book.

Aitken, G. A. Coleridge on Gulliver's travels. Athenaeum 15 Aug 1896.

Mathewson, L. Coleridge's notes on comic literature: a find. Athenaeum 16 Jan 1897. Describes his copy of Ralegh's History of the world.

White, W. H. Coleridge on Spinoza. Athenaeum 22 May 1897. Marginalia on Paulus's edn of Spinoza.

Forman, H. B. Coleridge's notes on Flögel. Cosmopolis 9–10 1898. The vols were described anon, Athenaeum 26 Dec 1896.

Higham, C. Coleridge marginalia. N & Q 30 Dec 1899. On Swedenborg vols in the Swedenborg Society, London.

Wheatley, H. B. Marginalia in Defoe's Robinson Crusoe. Hampstead Annual 5 1902. More accurate than Literary remains version. *See* Klingender, 1936, below.

Axon, W. E. A. Coleridge marginalia. N & Q 25 July 1903. Describes 2 edns of Browne's Religio medici and Nodier's Smarra.

Haney, J. L. A bibliography of Coleridge. Philadelphia 1903. Ch 10 lists 341 titles of annotated and marked books, including works by Coleridge.

— The marginalia of Coleridge. In Schelling anniversary papers, ed J. L. Haney, New York 1923.

—— Coleridge the commentator. In Coleridge studies, ed E. Blunden and E. L. Griggs 1934.
Betham, E. A house of letters. [1905]. Includes letters to Matilda Betham.
Biographia epistolaris: being the biographical supplement of Biographia literaria, with additional letters etc. Ed A. Turnbull 2 vols 1911.
Letters hitherto uncollected. Ed W. F. Prideaux 1913 (priv ptd).
Marriage. Ed T. J. Wise 1919 (priv ptd in 30 copies).
Aynard, J. Notes inédites de Coleridge. Revue de Littérature Comparée 2 1922. On Schubert's Allgemeine Naturgeschichte, Richter's Museum and Geist, Schelling's Naturphilosophie, Steffens's Anthropologie.
Latymer, Lord. A Coleridge notebook. TLS 11 Oct 1823. The 'clasped vellum' book. Reply by L. R. M. Strachan 18 Oct 1823.
Lehman, B. H. A paragraph deleted by Coleridge. MLN 39 1924.
Mackall, L. L. Coleridge marginalia on Wieland and Schiller. MLR 19 1924.
Ritter, O. Coleridgiana. E Studien 58 1924. Sources of some Coleridge poems, metrical experiments and epigrams, mostly from German.
Raysor, T. M. Unpublished fragments on aesthetics by Coleridge. SP 22 1925.
—— Some marginalia on Shakespeare by Coleridge. PMLA 42 1927.
—— Coleridge marginalia. MLN 43 1928. On 4 annotated books in Dr Williams's Library: Richter, Schelling, Steffens, with one note from Steffens's Anthropologie.
Drinkwater, J. The notes of Coleridge's in Milton's poems by Thomas Warton. London Mercury Sept 1926; rptd in his A book for bookmen, 1926 (priv ptd), with description of a corrected Zapolya and 2 letters.
Greever, G. A Wiltshire parson and his friends: the correspondence of William Lisle Bowles, together with four hitherto unidentified reviews by Coleridge. Boston 1926. C. I. Patterson questioned the authenticity of all reviews except the Monk, JEGP 50 1951; but D. Roper argues convincingly for their authenticity, MLR 55 1960.
Wright, G. W. A sonnet by Coleridge. N & Q 12 Feb 1927. To poverty, by Joseph Cottle.
Nidecker, H. Notes marginales de Coleridge. Revue de Littérature Comparée 7–8, 10–13 1927–33. Notes on Kant, Schelling, Schubert, Hegel, Steffens, Oersted. All in BM.
Snyder, A. D. Books borrowed by Coleridge from the library of the University of Göttingen 1799. MP 25 1928.
—— Coleridge on logic and learning, with selections from the unpublished manuscripts. New Haven 1929. Includes selections from philosophical notebooks.
—— Coleridge's reading of Mendelssohn's Morgenstunden and Jerusalem. JEGP 28 1929.
—— Coleridge marginalia in the Forster Library. N & Q 24 Nov 1934. On Anderson's British poets.
—— Coleridge's notes. TLS 7 April 1934. *See* 31 May 1934.
Rea, J. D. A letter of Coleridge [1824–5]. MLN 44 1929. On Aids to reflection.
Ashley, A. J. Coleridge on Galt. TLS 25 Sept 1930. Marginalia on Provost.
Coleridge's Shakespearean criticism. Ed T. M. Raysor 2 vols Cambridge Mass 1930, London 1960 (EL) (rev). An extension of the original edns of Notes and lectures on Shakespeare, above, with new material from ms etc.
Koszul, A. Coleridgiana. Revue Anglo-américaine 7 1930. 2 late letters and prospectuses.
Mabbott, T. O. Coleridge mss. N & Q 2 May 1931. Undated letter to Lucius.
Birss, J. H. Coleridge mss. N & Q 2 May 1931. Letter of 3 June 1823.
Dike, E. B. Coleridge marginalia in Henry Brooke's The fool of quality. Huntington Lib Bull 2 1931.
Unpublished letters, including certain letters republished from original sources. Ed E. L. Griggs 2 vols 1932.
Fletcher, E. G. Two Coleridge marginalia. N & Q 30 Sept 1933. Swift's Gulliver, Howie's Biographia Scoticana.
Gibbs, W. E. Two unpublished notes by Coleridge. MLN 48 1933. Marginalia on Cowley and Mandeville's Bees.
Lindsay, J. I. Coleridge marginalia in a volume of Descartes. PMLA 49 1934.
—— Coleridge marginalia in Jacobi's Werke. MLN 50 1935.
Stewart, J. I. M. Some Coleridge letters. RES 10 1934. 6 letters 1818–34 to and from J. G. Lockhart.
Hart, A. A criticism by Coleridge. TLS 19 May 1935. On Parnell's Historical apology.
Coleridge's miscellaneous criticism. Ed T. M. Raysor, Cambridge Mass 1936. Mostly marginalia, some ptd or rev from ms. Correction, TLS 6 Feb 1937.
Klingender, F. G. Coleridge on Robinson Crusoe. TLS 1 Feb 1936.
Potter, G. R. Unpublished marginalia in Coleridge's copy of Malthus's Essay on population. PMLA 51 1936. Reply by K. Curry 54 1939.
de Selincourt, E. Coleridge's Dejection: an ode. E & S 22 1927; rptd in his Wordsworthian and other studies, Oxford 1947. First pbn from the Dove Cottage ms of Letter to Asra; *see* H. House, 1953 and G. Whalley, 1955, under §2, below.
Evans, B. I. Coleridge on slang. TLS 29 May 1937. Marginalia on Marcus Aurelius's Conversations, tr J. Collier.
Griggs, E. L. Diadeste: a fragment of an unpublished play by Coleridge. MP 34 1937.
—— Notes concerning certain poems by Coleridge. MLN 69 1954. Poems of questionable ascription and epigrams.
Patton, L. Coleridge and the soldier. TLS 21 Aug 1937. Marginalia on Stewart's Outlines for the British land forces.
—— The Coleridge canon. TLS 3 Sept 1938. Poems purloined by Coleridge for Watchman. Reply by B. R. Davis, A Southey poem falsely ascribed to Coleridge, 10 Sept 1938.
—— Coleridge marginalia in the Duke University Library: Charles Tennyson Turner's Sonnets. Duke Univ Lib Notes 15 1945. Coleridge's notes not in his hand.
—— Coleridge's marginal comments on Bowles' The spirit of discovery. Duke Univ Lib Notes 19 1948. A ghost?
Shearer, E. A. Wordsworth and Coleridge marginalia in a copy of Richard Payne Knight's Analytical inquiry. HLQ 1 1938. Replies by J. I. Lindsay, and J. H. Wagenblass 13 1950. Includes Wordsworth marginalia.
Coleridge discovers the lake country. Ed G. H. B. Coleridge. In Wordsworth and Coleridge: studies in honor of G. M. Harper, Princeton 1939. Sara Hutchinson's transcript of journal-letters written by Coleridge in 1802. For a more accurate transcript, *see* Inquiring spirit, ed K. Coburn 1951.
Coleridge to a young clergyman. More Books 14 1939. To Rev J. Gillman, 9 Nov 1832.
Davies, D. Coleridge's marginalia in Mather's Magnalia. HLQ 2 1939.
Broughton, L. N. Some early nineteenth-century letters hitherto unpublished. In Nineteenth-century studies, ed H. Davis et al, Ithaca 1940. Letters by Coleridge, Wordsworth, Southey and Allsop.
—— Some letters of the Wordsworth family, now first published, with a few unpublished letters of Coleridge and Southey and others. Ithaca 1942.

Wasserman, E. R. Coleridge's metrical experiments. MLN 55 1940, 63 1948. Coleridge's authorship questioned. *See* O. Ritter, 1924, and W. U. Ober, 1957.
Gordon, I. A. The case-history of Coleridge's Monody on the death of Chatterton, with the text of the unedited second form. RES 18 1942.
Hellman, G. S. Coleridge on trial marriages: text of an unfinished essay. Saturday Rev of Lit 29 Aug 1942.
Kurtz, B. P. Coleridge on Swedenborg, with unpublished marginalia on the Prodromus. California Pbns in Eng 14 1943.
Sparrow, J. Jortin and Coleridge. TLS 3 April 1943. A Coleridge poem tr from Jortin's Votum.
Brinkley, R. F. Coleridge on John Petvin and John Locke. HLQ 8 1945.
— Some notes concerning Coleridge material at the Huntington Library. HLQ 8 1945.
— Some unpublished Coleridge marginalia: Richter and Reimarus. JEGP 44 1945. Vol and marginalia described in Princeton Univ Lib Chron 5 1943.
— Coleridge transcribed. RES 24 1948. On H. N. Coleridge's editorial practice. Includes marginalia.
— Coleridge's criticism of Jeremy Taylor. HLQ 13 1950.
— (ed.) Coleridge on the seventeenth century. Durham NC 1955. Chiefly reprints and fresh transcripts of marginalia in Literary remains; includes notebook material.
Creed, H. H. Coleridge on taste. ELH 13 1946.
Fairchild, H. N. Hartley, Pistorius and Coleridge. PMLA 62 1947.
Finch, J. S. Charles Lamb's copy of the History of Philip de Commines, with autograph notes by Lamb and Coleridge. Princeton Univ Lib Chron 9 1947.
Langford, G. John Barclay's Argenis: a seminal novel. SE 1947.
McElderry, B. R. Coleridge on Blake's Songs. MLQ 9 1948. Quasi-marginalia.
Whalley, G. The Bristol Library borrowings of Southey and Coleridge 1793–8. Library 5th ser 4 1949. Expands P. Kaufman, The reading of Southey and Coleridge: the record of their borrowings from Bristol Library 1793–8, MP 21 1924. *See* J. Baker, 1870, *above*.
[Whalley, G.] The dispersal of Coleridge's books. TLS 28 Oct 1949. Correction 3 Dec 1949.
Whalley, G. Coleridge on classical prosody: an unidentified review of 1797. RES new ser 2 1951.
— A library cormorant. Listener 9 Sept 1954.
Coburn, K. Inquiring spirit: a new presentation of Coleridge from his published and unpublished prose writings. 1951. Includes excerpts from notebooks and marginalia, about one-third unpbd.
Evans, B. I. Coleorton manuscripts of Resolution and independence and Ode to dejection. MLR 46 1951.
Hough, G. Some Coleridge marginalia. MLN 66 1951. Hone's Apocryphal New Testament.
Wells, G. A. Coleridge and Goethe on scientific method in the light of some unpublished Coleridge marginalia in Heinroth's Anthropologie. German Life & Letters 4 1951.
Elmen, P. Editorial revisions of Coleridge's marginalia. MLN 67 1952. H. N. Coleridge's editorial practice.
Hardy, B. Coleridge's marginalia in Fuller's Pisgah-sight of Palestine. MLR 67 1952.
Patterson, C. I. An unidentified criticism by Coleridge related to Christabel. PMLA 67 1952.
Skeat, T. C. Note-books and marginalia of Coleridge. BM Quart 16 1952. Describes the Ottery collection in BM.
— Letters of Charles and Mary Lamb and Coleridge. BM Quart 26 1962.
Renz, M. F. A Coleridge unpublished letter and some remarks concerning the poet's interest in the sound of words. N & Q April 1953. To Mrs Lockhart, 26 July 1833.
Seronsy, C. C. Coleridge marginalia in Lamb's copy of Daniel's poetical works. Harvard Lib Bull 7 1953.
— More Coleridge marginalia. SP 52 1955. On Petrarch, Aristophanes and Walker's rhyming dictionary.

Zall, P. M. A Coleridge inscription. TLS 22 May 1953. In Mary Lamb, Mrs Leicester's school.
Beaty, F. L. Two manuscript poems of Coleridge. RES 7 1956.
Collected letters. Ed E. L. Griggs 6 vols Oxford 1956–68.
Schulze, F. W. Wordsworthian and Coleridgian texts (1784–1822), mostly unidentified or displaced. Festschrift für Otto Ritter, ed G. Dietrich, Halle 1956.
Barnet, S. Coleridge on puns: a note to his Shakespeare criticism. JEGP 56 1957.
— Coleridge's marginalia in Stockdale's Shakespeare of 1784. Harvard Lib Bull 12 1958.
Notebooks. Ed K. Coburn 4 vols New York 1957–61. 11 vols (including index) are projected. *See* her Coleridge's quest for self-knowledge, Listener 8 Sept 1949.
Erdman, D. V. Coleridge on George Washington: newly discovered essays of 1800. BNYPL Feb 1957.
— Reliques of the contemporaries of William Upcott, Emperor of autographs. BNYPL Nov 1960. Includes punning ms by Coleridge.
— Coleridge on Coleridge: the context (and text) of his review of Mr Coleridge's second Lay sermon. Stud in Romanticism 1 1961.
— Lost poem found: the cooperative pursuit and recapture of an escaped Coleridge 'sonnet' of 72 lines. BNYPL April 1961.
Johnson, S. F. An uncollected early poem by Coleridge. BNYPL Oct 1957.
Ober, W. U. Original versions of two Coleridge couplets. N & Q Oct 1957. Epigrams on metres, tr from Schiller. Reply by K. Coburn, May 1959.
— Mohammed: the outline of a proposed poem by Coleridge and Southey. N & Q Oct 1958. Ms in Sydney, Australia.
'Bishop, Morchard' (O. Stonor). Notes of two Coleridges. BNYPL Oct 1959. A Latin tag and an unpbd couplet.
Schrickx, W. Coleridge and F. H. Jacobi 3. Revue Belge de Philologie et d'Historie 36 1958. Marginalia on Jacobi's Ueber die Lehre des Spinoza.
Werkmeister, L., R. Woof and D. V. Erdman. Unrecorded Coleridge variants. SB 11 1958. Addns 14 1961.
Dunlap, R. Verses by Coleridge. PQ 42 1962. 6 unpbd lines.

§2

Hucks, J. A pedestrian tour through North Wales, in a series of letters. 1795. Coleridge accompanied the author.
The observer, part 1st: being a transient glance at about forty youths of Bristol, enumerating what are the prominent traits in their characters, whether they be worthy of imitation or otherwise. Bristol [1795?]. 36 sketches, mostly lampoons, including Southey, Coleridge and Lovell. *See* J. L. Lowes, Coleridge and the forty youths of Bristol, TLS 11 Oct 1928.
Lloyd, C. Edmund Oliver. 1798. Attacks Coleridge, and partly responsible for a serious quarrel with Lamb.
The simpliciad: a satirico-didactic poem, containing hints for the scholars of the new school. 1808. Dedicated to Wordsworth, Southey and Coleridge; parody of their writing, with parallels drawn in footnotes.
Commentary on Coleridge's Three graves. Monthly Mirror July–Sept 1810.
Seward, A. Letters written between the years 1784 and 1807. 6 vols Edinburgh 1811. Vols 4–6 refer to Coleridge.
[Smith, Horace and James.] Rejected addresses: or a new theatrum poetarum. 1812. Play-house musings is a parody of Coleridge.
Lamb, C. Recollections of Christ's Hospital. GM June 1813 (2 pts, signed); rptd in his Works, below.
— Christ's Hospital five and thirty years ago. London Mag Nov 1820; rptd in his Essays of Elia, 1823.
— The two races of men. London Mag Dec 1820; rptd in his Essays of Elia.

—[On the death of Coleridge]. In Charles Lamb: his last words on Coleridge, New Monthly Mag Feb 1835. Lamb's ms note of 21 Nov 1834, perhaps his last composition; rptd in his Works, below.
— In Life and notes of Lamb, ed A. Ainger 12 vols 1899–1900.
— In his Works, ed E. V. Lucas 6 vols 1912.
— In Letters of Charles and Mary Lamb, ed E. V. Lucas 3 vols 1935.
Defence of Coleridge. Literary Gazette 1 1817.
[Hazlitt, W.] Mr Coleridge and Mr Southey. Examiner 6 April 1817.
Hazlitt, W. On the living poets: Coleridge. In his Lectures on the English poets, 1818.
— Coleridge's Lay sermon and Statesman's manual. In his Political essays, with sketches of public characters, 1819.
— My first acquaintance with poets. Liberal April 1823.
— Mr Coleridge. In his Spirit of the age, 1825.
— In his Complete works, ed P. P. Howe 21 vols 1930–4. Reissue, with additional notes and uncollected matter, of Collected works, ed A. R. Waller and A. Glover 13 vols 1902–6, with index by J. Thornton.
Peacock, T. L. Melincourt. 3 vols 1817. Coleridge satirized as Moley Mystic.
— Nightmare Abbey. 1818. Coleridge satirized as Mr Flosky.
— Crotchet Castle. 1831. Coleridge satirized as Mr Skionar.
[Wilson, J.] Some observations on the Biographia literaria. Blackwood's Mag Oct 1817; rptd in A. Mordell, Notorious literary attacks, New York 1926.
— Coleridge's Poetical works. Blackwood's Mag Oct 1834; rptd in his Essays critical and imaginative vol 3, Edinburgh 1857.
Wilson, J. In his Noctes ambrosianae, 4 vols Philadelphia 1843; ed R. S. Mackenzie 5 vols New York 1863.
David Hume charged by Mr Coleridge with plagiarism from St Thomas Aquinas. Blackwood's Mag Sept 1818.
An estimate of the literary character of Mr Coleridge. Monthly Mag Dec 1818.
[Lockhart, J. G.] Essays on the Lake School of poetry no 3: Coleridge. Blackwood's Mag Oct 1819.
— Peter's letters to his kinsfolk. Edinburgh 1819. With postscript, pbd separately New York 1820, addressed to Coleridge.
— Wallenstein, translated by Coleridge. Horae Germanicae no 16, Blackwood's Mag Oct 1823.
— Coleridge's Table talk. Quart Rev 53 1835. Anon review of biographical interest.
W. Memoir of Coleridge. New Monthly Mag April 1819. With portrait by C. R. Leslie.
Hunt, L. Coleridge: sketches of the living poets no 4. Examiner 21 Oct 1821.
— Mr Coleridge, Lord Byron and some of his contemporaries. 1828.
— In his Autobiography, with reminiscences of friends and contemporaries, 3 vols 1850.
— In his Imagination and fancy, 1883.
Irving, E. For missionaries after the apostolical school: a series of orations. 1825. Contains quotations from Coleridge, who annotated a copy.
Kelly, M. In his Reminiscences, 2 vols 1826. Kelly composed the incidental music for Remorse.
Hare, J. C. and A. W. Hare. Guesses at truth by two brothers. 1828.
Hare, J. C. Coleridge and the English opium-eater. Br Mag Jan 1835. Reply to De Quincey's articles in Tait's Mag, below.
— The mission of the comforter. 1846, 1850, 1876, 1877. Contains quotations from Coleridge.
Sterling, J. On Coleridge's Christabel: an appeal apologetic from Philip drunk to Philip sober. Athenaeum 25 June 1828; rptd in his Essays and tales, ed J. C. Hare 2 vols 1848. The earliest understanding criticism of Christabel.
Coleridge and the Germans: a dialogue. Athenaeum 30 Sept 1829. Satiric.
Paris, J. A. In his Life of Sir Humphry Davy, 2 vols 1831, 1 vol 1831 (with variants).
Some account of Coleridge's philosophy. Fraser's Mag June 1832.
'Cergiel' (C. V. Le Grice). College reminiscences of Mr Coleridge. GM Dec 1834; Penzance 1842; rptd in J. Cottle, Reminiscences, 1847.
Coleridge's Unitarianism. Christian Reformer 1 1834.
Coleridge's will. GM Dec 1834.
Heraud, J. A. An oration on the death of Coleridge, delivered at the Russell Institution on Friday August 8 1834. 1834 (3 edns).
[Obituary notices]. Athenaeum, GM, Literary Gazette, New Monthly Mag, Littell's Museum, Annual Register 1834.
Reminiscences of Coleridge, biographical, philosophical, poetical and critical. Fraser's Mag Oct 1834.
Trollope, W. In his History of the royal foundation of Christ's Hospital, 1834.
Withington, L. The present state of metaphysics. Quart Christian Spectator 6 1834. Includes an unfavourable discussion of Coleridge's philosophy.
De Quincey, T. Samuel Taylor Coleridge. Tait's Mag Sept–Nov 1834, Jan 1835. 4 articles, especially on opium, the ser continuing with Sketches of life and manners. Reply by J. C. Hare, above.
— Coleridge and opium eating. Blackwood's Mag Jan 1845. On Gillman's Life.
— In his Collected writings: new and enlarged edition, ed D. Masson 14 vols Edinburgh 1889–90.
— Conversation and Coleridge. Ed A. H. Japp 2 vols 1891.
Coleridgeiana. Fraser's Mag Jan 1835; rptd in Littell's Museum 26 1835.
Jeffrey, J. [Coleridge's thought]. Edinburgh Rev 62 1835. In review of Memoirs of J. Mackintosh.
Carlyon, C. In his Early years and late reflections, 4 vols 1836–58.
Cottle, J. Early recollections, chiefly relating to the late Coleridge during his long residence in Bristol. 2 vols 1837–9, 1847 (rev and enlarged as Reminiscences of Coleridge and R. Southey).
Cooper, J. F. Gleanings in Europe, vol 2: England. New York 1837, 1930. Description of Coleridge in 1828.
Collas, A. In his Authors of England: a series of medallion portraits with illustrative notices, 1838.
Gillman, J. The life of Coleridge. Vol 1, 1838. All pbd.
Remarks on a passage in Coleridge's Aids to reflection. Blackwood's Mag July 1838.
Stuart, D. Anecdotes of the poet Coleridge. In The late Mr Coleridge the poet, GM May–Aug 1838. Reply to H. N. Coleridge.
Ferrier, J. F. The plagiarisms of Coleridge. Blackwood's Mag March 1840.
Mill, J. S. Coleridge. London & Westminster Rev 5 1840; rptd in his Dissertations and discussions vol i, 1859; ed F. R. Leavis 1950 (in Mill on Bentham and Coleridge).
Maurice, F. D. The kingdom of Christ. 1842 (2nd edn). *See also his* Life told in his own letters, 2 vols 1884.
Robberds, J. W. In his A memoir of the life and writings of the late William Taylor of Norwich, 2 vols 1843.
Torrey, J. In his Remains of the Rev James Marsh, Boston 1843. On Marsh's service in introducing Coleridge's philosophy to America.
Gilfillan, G. In his A gallery of literary portraits, Edinburgh 1845.
Hood, T. In his Prose and verse, New York 1845. On his meeting with Coleridge.
Cary, H. In his Memoir of the Rev Henry Francis Cary MA, translator of Dante, 2 vols 1847.

Green, J. H. Mental dynamics, or groundwork of a professional education: the Hunterian Oration, 1847. Regarded by J. D. Campbell as Green's most successful exposition of Coleridge's philosophy.

— Spiritual philosophy founded on the teaching of the late Coleridge. Ed J. Simon 2 vols 1865.

Porter, N. Coleridge and his American disciples. Bibliotheca Sacra 1 1847.

Chasles, V. E. P. Visite à Coleridge. In his Études sur les hommes et les moeurs au 19me siècle, Paris 1849.

Lord, D. N. Coleridge's philosophy of Christianity: an atheistic idealism. Theological & Literary Jnl 1 1849.

Southey, R. In his Life and correspondence, ed C. C. Southey 6 vols 1849–50.

— In Selections from the letters, ed J. W. Warter 4 vols 1856.

Carlyle, T. In his Life of John Sterling, 1851. Pt 1, ch 8.

Coleridge, H. In his Poems, ed D. Coleridge 2 vols 1851.

— In Letters, ed G. E. and E. L. Griggs, Oxford 1937.

Wordsworth, C. In his Memoirs of William Wordsworth, 2 vols 1851.

— Social life at the English universities in the eighteenth century. Cambridge 1874. Includes account of Coleridge as undergraduate.

Coleridge: his philosophy and theology. 1851. Rptd from Eclectic Rev Jan 1851.

Hetherington, W. M. Coleridge and his followers: Exeter Hall lectures, lecture 8. 1853.

Hall, S. C. A book of memories. [1853].

Etienne, L. Poètes contemporains de l'Angleterre: Coleridge, ses amis, ses imitateurs. Revue Contemporaine 2 1854.

Emerson, R. W. A visit to Coleridge. In his English traits, 1856, Boston 1891.

Martineau, J. Personal influences on our present theology: Newman, Coleridge, Carlyle. Nat Rev 3 1856; rptd in his Essays, 1879. On Newman, Hare, Maurice, Davies, Ballantyne.

Rogers, S. In Recollections of the table talk, 1856.

Hort, F. J. A. In Cambridge essays contributed by members of the University [1856].

Rigg, J. H. Modern Anglican theology. 1857, 1859, 1880. Chs on Coleridge, Hare, Maurice, Kingsley, Jowett.

Bayne, P. In his Essays in biography and criticism vol 2, Boston 1858.

Davy, H. In his Fragmentary remains, 1858.

Reed, H. In his Lectures on the British poets vol 2, Philadelphia 1858.

Axon, W. E. A. James Amphlett and Coleridge. Newspaper Press 1860; rptd in Library 3rd ser 2 1911.

— Lancelot Sharpe, Sir R. Philips and Coleridge. N & Q 2 May 1903. Reply by F. H. Reiton 30 May 1903.

Grattan, T. C. A three days' tour with Coleridge and Wordsworth (in Belgium, 1828). In his Beaten paths and those who trod them, 2 vols 1862.

Dallas, E. S. In his Gay science, 2 vols 1866.

Jerdan, W. In his Men I have known, 1866.

Birks, T. R. The victory of divine goodness, including notes on Coleridge's Confessions of an inquiring spirit. 1867.

O'Hagan, T. Coleridge. 1867.

Stirling, J. H. De Quincey and Coleridge upon Kant. Fortnightly Rev Oct 1867.

Shairp, J. C. Coleridge, the man and the poet. In his Studies in poetry and philosophy, Edinburgh 1868.

Robinson, H. C. Diary, reminiscences and correspondence. Ed T. Sadler 3 vols 1869, 2 vols 1872.

— Blake, Coleridge, Wordsworth, Lamb etc: being selections from the remains of Henry Crabb Robinson. Ed E. J. Morley, Manchester 1922.

— Correspondence with the Wordsworth circle. Ed E. J. Morley 2 vols Oxford 1927.

— On books and their writers. Ed E. J. Morley 3 vols 1938.

Meteyard, E. A group of Englishmen (1795–1815): being records of the younger Wedgwoods and their friends. 1871.

Young, J. C. Memoir of Charles Mayne Young, tragedian, with extracts from his son's journal. 1871 (2nd edn). With notes on Coleridge's second visit to Germany (1828).

Brandes, G. M. C. Hovedstromninger i det 19de aarhundredes litteratur. 6 vols Copenhagen 1872–90; tr 1901–5.

Coleridge, E. H. Memoir and letters of Sara Coleridge, by her daughter. 2 vols 1873.

— In Poet's country, ed A. Lang 1907. *See also* his Lake Poets in Somersetshire, Trans Royal Soc of Lit 2nd ser 20 1899, and Coleridge as a Lake Poet, 24 1903.

— The genesis of the Ancient mariner. Poetry Rev 9 1918; rptd in Littell's Living Age 299 1918.

— Biographical notes: being chapters of Ernest Hartley Coleridge's fragmentary and unpublished life of Coleridge. Ed G. H. B. Coleridge in Coleridge studies, ed E. Blunden and E. L. Griggs 1934.

Brooke, S. A. In his Theology in the English poets, 1874.

Swinburne, A. C. In his Essays and studies, 1875. Introd to Christobel etc, 1869.

Paul, C. K. In his William Godwin: his friends and contemporaries, 2 vols 1876.

Vollmer, W. Briefwechsel zwischen Schiller und Cotta. Stuttgart 1876. Contains letters on publisher's arrangements for trn of Wallenstein.

Armstrong, E. J. In his Essays and sketches, 1877.

Procter, B. W. In his An autobiographical fragment and biographical notes, 1877.

Dowden, E. The transcendental movement in literature. In his Studies in literature 1789–1877, 1878.

— Coleridge as a poet. Fortnightly Rev Sept 1889; rptd in Littell's Living Age 183 1889 and in his New studies in literature, 1895.

Rossetti, W. M. In his Lives of famous poets, 1878.

Garrigues, G. Coleridge's Ancient mariner. Jnl of Speculative Philosophy 14 1880.

Calvert, G. H. Coleridge, Shelley, Goethe. In his Biographic aesthetic studies, [1880].

Caine, T. H. H. In his Recollections of Dante Gabriel Rossetti, 1882.

— In his Cobwebs of criticism, 1883.

— Life of Coleridge. 1887.

Cooke, G. W. The influence of Coleridge. Critic 2 1882.

Fox, C. Memories of old friends. Ed H. N. Pym 1882. With references to Coleridge and his children.

Traill, H. D. Coleridge. 1884 (EML).

Browning, R. Sketch of a conversation between Coleridge and Kenyon. Academy 15 Aug 1885.

Tulloch, J. Coleridge and his school: movement of religious thought. New York 1885.

— Coleridge as a spiritual thinker. Fortnightly Rev Jan 1885; rptd in Eclectic Mag new ser 41 1885 and Littell's Living Age 164 1885.

Ainger, A. Coleridge's Ode to Wordsworth. Macmillan's Mag June 1887.

Brandl, A. L. Coleridge and the English romantic school. Ed and tr Lady Eastlake, Berlin 1886, 1887. Unsigned review by J. D. Campbell, Athenaeum 18 June 1887.

— Cowper's Winter evening und Coleridge's Frost at midnight. Archiv 96 1896.

Bourne, H. J. F. Coleridge among the journalists. GM Nov 1887.

Greswell, W. Coleridge and the Quantock Hills. Macmallin's Mag Oct 1887.

Lowell, J. R. Coleridge, democracy and other addresses. Boston 1887. Address on the unveiling of the bust of Coleridge in Westminster Abbey 7 May 1885. *See also* Works of A. G. Mercer [Newport 1889].

Stephen, L. In his Hours in a library ser 3, 1892. Lecture to British Institution 9 March 1888. *See also* his DNB article, 1887.

Campbell, J. D. Coleridge on Cary's Dante. Athenaeum 7 Jan 1888.

— The source of the Ancient mariner. Athenaeum 22 March 1890.

— Coleridge and the Anti-Jacobin. Athenaeum 31 May 1890.

— [An unsigned review of Lyrical ballads, ed F. Dowden]. Athenaeum 10 May 1890.

— Coleridge's Osorio and Remorse. Athenaeum 5 April 1890.

— The Lyrical ballads of 1800. Athenaeum 22 Nov 1890.

— Coleridge's quotations. Athenaeum 20 Aug 1892. Reply by T. Bayne, 3 Sept 1892.

— Scott on Coleridge. Athenaeum 12 Nov, 3 Dec 1892.

— Coleridge on Quaker principles. Athenaeum 16 Sept 1893. Reply to S. C. Thompson, 1893, below.

— Coleridge: a narrative of the events of his life. 1894; ed L. Stephen 1896. A biographical introd to his edn of Poetical works, 1893.

Lloyd, J. H. The history, topography and antiquities of Highgate. Highgate 1888. Sketch and bibliography of Coleridge.

Sandford, Mrs H. Thomas Poole and his friends. 2 vols 1888.

Boyce, A. O. Records of a Quaker family: the Richardsons of Cleveland. 1889.

Sarrazin, G. In his La renaissance de la poésie anglaise 1798–1889, Paris 1889.

Pater, W. H. In his Appreciations, 1890.

— Coleridge's writings. 1910.

— Coleridge as a theologian. In Sketches and reviews, New York 1919.

Taylor, J. The source of the Ancient mariner. Athenaeum 8 March 1890. Against T. James, Strange and dangerous voyage, 1632, as source. Replies by I. James and J. D. Campbell 22 March; S. M. Samuel 29 March 1890. *See* 'Morchard Bishop' (O. Stonor), 1959, below.

Goodwin, A. M. Coleridge as a spiritual philosopher. New Englander 54 1891.

Portraits of English poets from drawings made for Joseph Cottle of Bristol of Charles Lamb, Coleridge etc. 1891.

Birrell, A. In his More obiter dicta, 1891.

Flagg, J. B. The life and letters of Washington Allston. New York 1892. On Coleridge's escape from Rome.

Thompson, S. C. Coleridge on Quaker principles. Friends Quart Bull 27 1893.

Watson, W. Coleridge's supernaturalism. In his Excursions in criticism, 1893.

Bateson, H. D. The rhythm of Coleridge's Christabel. Manchester Quart 13 1894.

— An introduction to the study of English rhythms, with an essay on the metre of Coleridge's Christabel. Ibid; rptd 1896 (priv ptd).

Rawnsley, H. D. In his Literary associations of the English Lakes, 2 vols Glasgow 1894.

Wright, W. A. Coleridge and opium. Academy 24 Feb 1894. *See* T. Hutchinson 3 March 1894.

Hogg, J. In his De Quincey and his friends: personal recollections, 1895.

Saintsbury, G. Coleridge and Southey. In his Essays in English literature ser 2, 1895.

— Wordsworth and Coleridge: their companions and their adversaries. In his History of criticism and literary taste in Europe, Edinburgh 1900–4.

— In his History of English prosody vol 3, 1910.

Smith, N. C. Coleridge and his critics. Fortnightly Rev 1 Sept 1895.

Wedgwood, F. J. Samuel Taylor Coleridge. Contemporary Rev April 1895; rptd in her Nineteenth-century teachers and other essays, 1909.

— The personal life of Josiah Wedgwood the potter, by his great-grand-daughter. Ed C. H. Herford 1915.

Gillman, A. W. The Gillmans of Highgate, with letters from Coleridge etc. [1895].

Dodge, R. E. N. An allusion in Coleridge's First advent of love. Anglia 18 1896.

Forster, M. Wordsworth, Coleridge and Frederike Brun. Academy 27 June 1896.

Johnson, R. B. Christ's Hospital recollections of Lamb, Coleridge and Leigh Hunt. 1896.

De Vere, A. In his Recollections, 1897.

Herzfeld, G. William Taylor von Norwich: eine Studie über den Einfluss der neueren deutschen Literatur in England. Halle 1897.

Higham, C. Coleridge and Swedenborg. New Church Mag 16 1897.

Lang, A. The life and letters of John Gibson. 2 vols 1897.

Robertson, J. M. In his New essays towards a critical method, 1897.

Schnabel, B. Ossian in der schönen Literatur Englands bis 1832. E Studien 23 1897.

Thompson, F. T. S. T. Coleridge. Academy 6 Feb 1897.

Tweedie, W. M. Christabel. MLN 12 1897.

Oliphant, Mrs M. Annals of a publishing house: William Blackwood and his sons, their magazine and friends. 3 vols Edinburgh 1897–8.

Forster, J. Great teachers: Coleridge etc. 1898.

Garnett, R. Introd to Poetry of Coleridge. 1898 (ML); rptd as The poetry of Coleridge in his Essays of an ex-librarian, 1901.

— Coleridge. 1904.

Lucas, E. V. In his Charles Lamb and the Lloyds, 1898.

White, W. H. Coleridge's Mutual passion. Athenaeum 1 Jan 1898.

Festing, G. John Hookham Frere and his friends. 1899.

Hancock, A. E. In his French Revolution and the English poets, New York 1899.

Kuhns, O. Influence of Dante on English poetry in the nineteenth century. MLN 14 1899.

Yarnall, E. Wordsworth and the Coleridges. May Place, Haverford Pa 1899.

Haney, J. L. The color of Coleridge's eyes. Anglia 23 1901.

— The German influence on Coleridge. Philadelphia 1902.

— Early reviews of English poets. Philadelphia 1904.

Pearce, E. H. In his Annals of Christ's Hospital, 1901.

Coleman, E. H. Samuel Taylor Coleridge. N & Q 9 Aug 1902. Ann Coleridge's petition of 1 May 1782 requesting Coleridge's admission to Christ's Hospital.

Gray, A. In his Jesus College, 1902.

Liddell, M. H. An introduction to the scientific study of English poetry. New York 1902. Contains sections on Coleridge's theory of poetry.

Litchfield, R. B. Tom Wedgwood, the first photographer: an account of his life, his discovery, and his friendship with Coleridge, including the letters of Coleridge to the Wedgwoods. 1903.

Cooper, L. Pleonastic compounds in Coleridge. MLN 19 1904; rptd in his Late harvest, 1952, below.

— The forest hermit in Coleridge and Wordsworth. MLN 24 1909; rptd in his Late harvest, 1952, below.

— The power of the eye in Coleridge. In Studies in language and literature in celebration of the seventieth birthday of James Morgan Hart, New York 1910; rptd in his Late harvest, 1952, below.

— Coleridge, Wordsworth and Mr Lowes. MLN 43 1928. Reply by J. L. Lowes in his Road to Xandu, Boston 1930 (rev).

— Late harvest. Ithaca 1952. Includes 6 essays on Coleridge.

Weare, G. E. Coleridge's poetical works: new information etc. 1905.
Cestre, C. In his La Révolution Française et les poètes anglais 1789–1809, Paris 1906.
Ryan, M. J. Coleridge. Catholic Univ Bull 12 1906.
— The philosophy of Coleridge. Catholic Univ Bull 13 1907.
Aynard, H. La vie d'un poète: Coleridge. Paris 1907.
Helmholtz, A. A. The indebtedness of Coleridge to A. W. von Schlegel. Madison 1907.
Eagleston, A. J. Wordsworth, Coleridge and the spy. Nineteenth Century Aug 1908; rptd in Coleridge studies, ed E. Blunden and E. L. Griggs 1934.
Castle, W. R., jr. Newman and Coleridge. Sewanee Rev 17 1909.
Ferrando, G. La critica letteraria di Coleridge. Florence 1909.
— Coleridge: studio critico. Florence [1925].
Rust, J. A. Coleridge: en zijne intuities op het gebied van wijsbegeerte, ethiek en godsdienst. 1909.
Symons, A. In his Romantic movement in English poetry, New York 1909.
Coats, R. H. The mysticism of Coleridge. Quart Rev 116 1911.
Royds (afterwards Innes), K. E. Coleridge and his poetry. 1911.
Douady, J. In his La mer et les poètes anglais, Paris 1912.
Towle, E. A. A poet's children: Hartley and Sara Coleridge. 1912.
Gillington (afterwards Byron), M. C. A day with Coleridge. [1912].
Knight, W. A. Coleridge and Wordsworth in the West Country: their friendship, work and surroundings. 1913.
MacDonagh, M. Coleridge as a parliamentary reporter. In his Reporter's gallery, 1913. Coleridge's report of speech by Pitt favourably compared with other versions.
Wingfield-Stratford, E. C. In his History of English patriotism, 2 vols 1913–28.
Eimer, M. Die Geschichte der Maria Eleonora Schöning und die Characteristik Luthers in Coleridges Friend. E Studien 47 1914.
Escott, T. H. S. Coleridge as a twentieth-century force. Quart Rev 121 1914.
Stork, C. W. The influence of the popular ballad on Wordsworth and Coleridge. PMLA 29 1914.
Strunk, W., jr. Some related poems of Wordsworth and Coleridge. MLN 29 1914.
Vaughan, C. E. In CHEL vol 11, 1914.
Girard, W. De l'influence exercée par Coleridge et Carlyle sur la formation du transcendantalisme: du transcendantalisme considéré essentiellement dans sa définition et ses origines françaises. MP 4 1916.
Pizzo, E. Coleridge als Kritiker. Anglia 40 1916.
Thayer, M. R. In his Influence of Horace on the chief English poets of the nineteenth century, New Haven 1916.
Walters, J. C. Hazlitt's walks with Coleridge. Manchester Quart 35 1916.
Haller, W. The early life of Robert Southey 1774–1803. New York 1917.
Quiller-Couch, A. T. In his Studies in literature, Cambridge 1918.
Snyder, A. D. The critical principle of the reconciliation of opposites as employed by Coleridge. Ann Arbor 1918.
— Coleridge's cosmogony: a note on the poetic 'world-view'. SP 21 1924.
— Coleridge and Mr John Watson. TLS 30 Sept 1926. *See also* J. Drinkwater, Notes of Coleridge, London Mercury Sept 1926; and Snyder, Coleridge and the Watsons, TLS 25 Aug 1927.
— Coleridge and Giordano Bruno. MLN 42 1927.
— Coleridge on Boehme. PMLA 45 1930.
— American comments on Coleridge a century ago (some periodical references to his prose works 1830–40). In Coleridge studies, ed E. Blunden and E. L. Griggs 1934.
— Coleridge and the encyclopedists. MP 38 1941.
Stewart, H. L. The place of Coleridge in English theology. Harvard Theological Rev 11 1918.
Hanford, J. H. Coleridge as a philologian. MP 16 1919.
Wilde, N. The development of Coleridge's thought. Philosophical Rev 28 1919.
Gingerich, S. F. From necessity to transcendentalism in Coleridge. PMLA 35 1920.
— In his Essays in the romantic poets, New York 1924.
Murry, J. M. Coleridge's criticism. In his Aspects of criticism, 1920.
— The metaphysic of poetry. In his Countries of the mind ser 2, 1931.
— Coleridge and Wordsworth. In his Katherine Mansfield and other literary portraits, 1949.
Richter, H. Die philosophische Weltanschauung von Coleridge und ihr Verhältnis zur deutschen Philosophie. Anglia 44 1920.
Graham, W. In his Politics of the greater romantic poets, PMLA 36 1921.
— In his Tory criticism in the Quarterly Review 1809–53, New York 1921.
— Contemporary critics of Coleridge the poet. PMLA 38 1923.
— Henry Nelson Coleridge, expositor of romantic criticism. PQ 4 1925.
Wells, J. E. The story of Wordsworth's Cintra. SP 18 1921.
— Printer's bills for Coleridge's Friend and Wordsworth's Cintra. SP 36 1939.
Blanchard, F. T. Coleridge's estimate of Fielding. In C. M. Gayley anniversary papers, Berkeley 1922.
Lehman, B. H. The doctrine of leadership in the greater romantic poets. PMLA 37 1922.
— Coleridge the statesman: Carlyle's theory of the hero, its sources, development, history and influence on Carlyle's work. Durham NC 1928.
Moore, J. R. The mood of pessimism in nature poetry: Bowles, Coleridge and Arnold. Sewanee Rev 30 1922.
Parsons, H. The source of Coleridge's Kubla Khan. TLS 9 March 1922.
— Coleridge as 'the wedding guest' in the Rime of the ancient mariner. N & Q 10 June 1950.
— The sources of Coleridge's Kubla Khan. N & Q 26 May 1951. In Paradise lost.
— Shakespearian emendations and discoveries. 1953. Includes comments on Ancient mariner, Kubla Khan and Christabel.
White, N. I. English romantic writers as dramatists. Sewanee Rev 30 1922.
Dunstan, A. C. The German influence on Coleridge. MLR 17–18 1922–3.
Harper, G. M. The Wordsworth-Coleridge combination. Sewanee Rev 31 1923.
— Coleridge's conversation poems. Quart Rev 244 1925; rptd in his Spirit of delight, New York 1928 and in English romantic poets: modern essays in criticism, ed M. H. Abrams, New York 1960.
— Gems of purest ray. In Coleridge studies, ed E. Blunden and E. L. Griggs 1934.
— S. T. Coleridge. Quart Rev 263 1934.
— Coleridge's great and dear spirit. In his Literary appreciations, New York 1937.
Nettesheim, J. Das Erlöschen von Coleridges 'dichterischer Produktion' um 1800. Archiv 146 1923.
— Die innere Entwicklung des englischen Romantikers Coleridge. Literaturwissenschaftliches Jahrbuch der Gorresgesellschaft 5 1930.
Draper, J. W. In his William Mason, New York 1924.

Howard, C. Coleridge's idealism: a study of its relationship to Kant and to the Cambridge Platonists. Boston 1924.
Neff, E. E. Carlyle and Mill: mystic and utilitarian. New York 1924.
— Carlyle. New York 1932.
Newdick, R. S. Coleridge on Hazlitt. Texas Rev 9 1924.
Schanck, N. Die sozialpolitischen Anschauungen Coleridges und sein Einfluss auf Carlyle. In Bonner Studien zur englischen Philologie, Bonn 1924.
Ingleby, A. The quarrel between Coleridge and Wordsworth. Adelphi 2 1925.
Potter, G. R. Coleridge and the idea of evolution. PMLA 40 1925.
— Wordsworth and the Traité élémentaire de chimie of Lavoisier. PQ 17 1938. Also on Coleridge's chemical activities.
Ratchford, F. E. Coleridge and the London Philosophical Society. MLR 20 1925.
Watson, L. E. Coleridge at Highgate. 1925.
Barnard, C. C. Wordsworth and the Ancient mariner. E Studien 60 1926.
Brinton, C. C. In his Political ideas of the English romanticists, Oxford 1926, New York 1962.
— In his English political thought in the nineteenth century, 1933.
Brown, F. K. In his Life of William Godwin, New York 1926.
Fausset, H. I'A. Samuel Taylor Coleridge. 1926. A biography.
Howes, R. F. Coleridge and rhetoric. Quart Jnl of Speech 12 1926.
— Importance of Coleridge's talk. Quart Jnl of Speech 14 1928.
Needham, J. Coleridge as a philosophical biologist. Science Progress 20 1926. *See also* A. Arber, The mind and the eye, Cambridge 1954.
Shafer, R. S. In his Christianity and naturalism, New Haven 1926.
Stokoe, F. W. In his German influence in the English romantic period 1788–1818, Cambridge 1926.
Wright, H. G. The tour of Coleridge and his friend Hucks in Wales in 1794. Nineteenth Century May 1926.
— Three aspects of Southey: 1, Reminiscences of Coleridge in Southey's Madoc. RES 9 1933.
— In his Boccaccio in England from Chaucer to Tennyson, Oxford 1957.
Benson, A. C. Coleridge rambles and reflections. [1926].
Charpentier, J. Coleridge, père du romantisme anglais. Mercure de France 15 Sept 1927.
— Coleridge, le somnambule sublime. Paris 1927; tr 1929.
Collins, H. P. The criticism of Coleridge. New Criterion 5 1927.
Morrill, D. I. Coleridge's theory of dramatic illusion. MLN 42 1927.
— An examination of the chronology of Coleridge's lecture notes. PQ 7 1928. Literary remains text made of material from 1802 to 1818–19.
Robinson, F. W. A commentary and questionnaire on the Lyrical ballads. 1927.
Whitting, H. W. The date of Hazlitt's first visit to Coleridge. MLN 42 1927.
Lowes, J. L. The road to Xanadu. Boston 1927, 1930 (rev).
— Coleridge and the Forty youths of Bristol. TLS 11 Oct 1928.
Blunden, E. In his Leigh Hunt's Examiner examined, [1928].
— Coleridge the less. In his Votive tablets, 1931. On the value of annotations and fragments by Coleridge and his son Hartley.
— Coleridge and Christ's Hospital. In Coleridge studies, ed Blunden and E. L. Griggs 1934.
— Lives of the poets: if Dr Johnson had lived rather longer: 1, Wordsworth; 2, Coleridge. TLS 20–7 May 1955. A reply by Johnson submitted by G. W. Dennis, TLS 10 June 1955.
— Coleridge's fellow-Grecian: some account of Charles Valentine Le Grice. Hong Kong [1957].
Scott-James, R. A. The esemplastic imagination: Coleridge and Goethe. In his Making of literature, 1928.
Babbitt, I. Coleridge and imagination. Nineteenth Century Sept 1929.
— Coleridge and the moderns. Bookman (New York) Oct 1929.
Bradley, A. C. Coleridge's use of light and colour. In his A miscellany, 1929.
Carver, P. L. The evolution of the term 'esemplastic'. MLR 24 1929.
— The authorship of a review of Christabel attributed to Hazlitt. JEGP 29 1930. By Brougham.
— 'Inoculation, heavenly maid, descend'. RES 9 1933.
— Coleridge and the theory of imagination. UTQ 9 1940.
Chapman, J. A. In his Papers on Shelley, Wordsworth and others, Oxford 1929.
Garrod, H. W. In his Profession of poetry and other lectures, Oxford 1929.
Griggs, E. L. Hartley Coleridge, his life and work. 1929. *See also* his Coleridge and his son, SP 27 1930; and Hartley Coleridge on his father, PMLA 46 1931.
— Coleridge and Byron. PMLA 45 1930.
— Coleridge and Mrs Mary Robinson. MLN 45 1930.
— Coleridge and the Wedgwood annuity. RES 6 1930.
— Coleridge at Malta. MP 27 1930.
— Notes on a proposed edition of the correspondence of Coleridge. Papers of Michigan Acad 12 1930.
— Coleridge the dragoon. MP 28 1931.
— Hartley Coleridge's unpublished correspondence. London Mercury June 1931.
— Coleridge, De Quincey and nineteenth-century editing. MLN 47 1932. On money obligations to De Quincey.
— Hazlitt's estrangement from Coleridge and Wordsworth. MLN 48 1933.
— James Fenimore Cooper on Coleridge. Amer Lit 4 1933.
— Swinburne on Coleridge. MP 30 1933.
— The death of Coleridge: an unpublished letter from Mrs H. N. Coleridge to her brother. In Coleridge studies, ed E. Blunden and Griggs 1934.
— The Friend: 1809 and 1818 editions. MP 35 1938.
— An early defense of Christabel. In Wordsworth and Coleridge: studies in honor of G. M. Harper, ed Griggs, Princeton 1939.
— Coleridge fille: a biography of Sara Coleridge. Oxford 1940.
— The willing suspension of disbelief. In Elizabethan and other essays in honor of G. F. Reynolds, Boulder 1945.
— Southey's estimate of Coleridge. HLQ 9 1946.
— Date shells and the eye of the critic. Virginia Quart Rev 23 1947. Contains original notes made by H. N. Coleridge on his uncle's conversation.
— Coleridge and Thomas Pringle. Quart Bull of South African Lib 6 1951.
— Wordsworth through Coleridge's eyes. In Wordsworth centenary studies, ed G. T. Dunklin, Princeton 1951, Hamden Conn 1963.
— Coleridge's army experiences. English 9 1953.
— A note on Wordsworth's A character. RES new ser 4 1953.
— Coleridge and opium. HLQ 17 1954.
— Ludwig Tieck and Coleridge. JEGP 54 1955.
Jiriczek, O. L. Zu Coleridges Eolian harp. Anglia Beiblatt 40 1929.

Murray, R. H. Coleridge the philosophic conservative: studies in the English social and political thinkers of the nineteenth century. Cambridge 1929; rptd in Contemporary Rev July 1934.
Raysor, T. M. Coleridge and Asra. SP 26 1929. Includes important notebook entries.
— Coleridge's criticism of Wordsworth. PMLA 54 1939.
— Coleridge's comment on the moral of the Ancient mariner. PQ 31 1952.
— Notes on Coleridge's Lewti. PQ 32 1953. On date of composition.
Rea, J. D. Coleridge's intimations of immortality from Proclus. MP 26 1929.
— Coleridge's health. MLN 45 1930.
Snell, A. L. F. The meter of Christabel. In Fred Newton Scott anniversary papers, ed C. D. Thorpe et al, Chicago 1929.
Cobban, A. The political philosophy of Coleridge. In his Edmund Burke and the revolt against the eighteenth century, 1929, New York 1960.
Babcock, R. W. The direct influence of late eighteenth century Shakespeare criticism on Hazlitt and Coleridge. MLN 45 1930.
Feiling, K. G. In his Sketches in nineteenth-century biography, 1930.
— Coleridge and the English conservatives. In Social and political ideas of some representative thinkers of the age of reaction and reconstruction, ed F. J. C. Hearnshaw 1932.
Gibbs, W. E. An unpublished letter [May 1796] from John Thelwall to Coleridge. MLR 25 1930.
— An autobiographical note of Coleridge's in the Watchman. N & Q 7 Feb 1931.
— Unpublished variants in Coleridge's poetry. MLN 46 1931. On Poems, 1797.
— Coleridge's The Knight's tomb and Youth and age. MLR 28 1933.
— Unpublished letters concerning Cottle's Coleridge. PMLA 49 1934.
Hartman, H. The intimations of Wordsworth's Ode. RES 6 1930. On detailed connexions with Dejection.
— Source of the Lapland night image. RES 14 1938. In Thomson, Maupertuis and Amos Cottle.
Kelley, M. Additional chapters on Thomas Cooper. Orono Maine 1930.
— Thomas Cooper and Pantisocracy. MLN 45 1930.
Logan, Sr E. Coleridge's scheme of Pantisocracy and American travel accounts. PMLA 45 1930.
— An indebtedness of Coleridge to Crashaw. MLN 59 1944. In Coeli enarrant.
Muirhead, J. H. Coleridge as philosopher. 1930.
— Metaphysician or mystic? In Coleridge studies, ed E. Blunden and E. L. Griggs 1934. *See also* his reply to a reviewer, TLS 23 Aug 1934.
Nitchie, E. Coleridge and metre. Saturday Rev of Lit 20 Sept 1930.
— The moral of the Ancient mariner reconsidered. PMLA 48 1933.
Shaaber, M. A. Coleridge as a journalist. Journalism Quart 7 1930.
Fairchild, H. N. Coleridge and transcendentalism; The mediaevalism of Wordsworth and Coleridge; The pantisocratic phase. In his Romantic quest, New York 1931.
— Hartley, Pistorius and Coleridge. PMLA 62 1947.
— In his Religious trends in English poetry vol 3, New York 1949.
— In his Noble savage, New York 1961.
Hawkins, A. Some writers on the Monthly Review. RES 7 1931.
MacGillivray, J. R. The pantisocracy scheme and its immediate background. In Studies in English by members of University College, Toronto 1931.

Morley, E. J. Coleridge in Germany 1799. London Mercury April 1931; addn May 1931; rptd in Wordsworth and Coleridge: studies in honor of G. M. Harper, Princeton 1939.
— Some contemporary allusions to Coleridge's death. In Coleridge studies, ed E. Blunden and E. L. Griggs 1934.
— The rash conjurer. TLS 8 May 1937. Assigns a date before 1813.
Templeman, W. D. A note on the dulcimer. TLS 2 April 1931.
Thorpe, C. D. Some notes on the differentia of prose and poetry, with special reference to the theory of Coleridge. Papers of Michigan Acad 14 1931.
— Some notices of empathy before Lipps. Papers of Michigan Acad 23 1937.
— Coleridge on the sublime. In Wordsworth and Coleridge: studies in honor of G. M. Harper, Princeton 1939.
— The imagination: Coleridge versus Wordsworth. PQ 18 1939.
— Coleridge as aesthetician and critic. JHI 5 1944.
Wellek, R. In his Immanuel Kant in England 1793–1838, Princeton 1931. *See* his reply to B. Muntéano, Revue de Littérature Comparée 14 1934.
— Wordsworth's and Coleridge's theories of poetic diction. In Charisteria Guilelmo Mathesio quinquagenario oblata, Prague 1932.
— Samuel Taylor Coleridge. Listy pro Umeni a Kritiku (Prague) 2 1934.
Zeydel, E. H. In his Ludwig Tieck and England, Princeton 1931.
— In his Ludwig Tieck, the German romanticist, Princeton 1935. Includes account of relations with Coleridge.
Bald, R. C. In his Literary friendships in the age of Wordsworth: an anthology, Cambridge 1932.
— The Ancient mariner. TLS 26 July 1934.
— Coleridge and the Ancient mariner. In Nineteenth-century studies in honor of C. S. Northup, ed H. Davis et al, Ithaca 1940.
Erhardt-Siebold, E. von. Some inventions of the pre-romantic period and their influence upon literature. E Studien 66 1932.
MacElderry, B. R. Coleridge's revision of the Ancient mariner. SP 29 1932.
— Coleridge's plan for completing Christabel. SP 33 1936.
— Walton's lives and Gillman's Life of Coleridge. PMLA 52 1937.
— Coleridge's preface to Christabel. In Wordsworth and Coleridge: studies in honor of G. M. Harper, Princeton 1939.
— Christabel, Coleridge and the commentators. Research Stud (State College of Washington) 9 1941.
Maclean, C. M. In her Dorothy Wordsworth: the early years, 1932.
Patton, L. Coleridge and revolutionary France. South Atlantic Quart 31 1932.
— Coleridge and the Enquirer series. RES 16 1940. *See* D. Coldicutt's query, 15 1939.
Stallknecht, N. P. The moral of the Ancient mariner. PMLA 47 1932.
— The doctrine of Coleridge's Dejection and its relation to Wordsworth's philosophy. PMLA 49 1934.
— Strange seas of thought. Durham NC 1945, Bloomington 1958.
Stewart, J. I. M. Coleridge and Chesterfield. TLS 29 Dec 1932.
Clarke, G. H. Certain symbols in the Ancient mariner. Queen's Quart 40 1933.
de Selincourt, E. In his Dorothy Wordsworth: a biography, 1933.
Eliot, T. S. Wordsworth and Coleridge. In his Use of poetry and use of criticism, 1933. Reply by E. R. Marks, Sewanee Rev 72 1964.

— Shakespearean criticism: 1, From Dryden to Coleridge. In Companion to Shakespeare studies, ed H. Granville-Barker and G. B. Harrison, Cambridge 1934.
Fagin, N. B. In his William Bartram, Baltimore 1933.
Kato, R. Coleridge and his criticism of Milton. Stud in Eng Lit (Tokyo) 13 1933.
— Coleridge as aesthetician. Stud in Eng Lit (Tokyo) 39 1962.
Meyerstein, E. H. W. Coleridge and Sir Eglamour. TLS 6 April 1933.
— Chatterton, Coleridge and Bristol: the sacred river. TLS 21 Aug 1937. Replies by F. W. Sypher and Meyerstein 28 Aug 1937.
— The completeness of Kubla Khan. TLS 30 Oct, 4 Dec 1937.
— Wordsworth and Coleridge. TLS 29 Nov, 6 Dec 1941. On the authorship of Lewti and Beauty and moonlight. Replies by J. R. Sutherland 6 Dec, and E. de Selincourt 20 Dec 1941.
Morse, B. J. Crabb Robinson and Goethe in England. E Studien 67 1933.
Reul, P. de. In his Poésie anglaise de Wordsworth à Keats, Paris 1933.
Schneider, E. W. In her Aesthetics of William Hazlitt, Philadelphia 1933.
— The dream of Kubla Khan. PMLA 60 1945.
— Coleridge, opium and Kubla Khan. Chicago 1953.
— Notes on Christabel. PQ 32 1953.
— The unknown review of Christabel. PMLA 70 1956.
— Tom Moore and the Edinburgh review of Christabel. PMLA 77 1963.
Strout, A. L. Coleridge and John Wilson of Blackwood's Magazine. PMLA 48 1933.
Winkelmann, E. Coleridge und die Kantische Philosophie. Leipzig 1933.
Wolff, L. Coleridge et l'Allemagne. Revue Anglo-américaine 10 1933.
Abrams, M. H. The milk of paradise: the effect of opium visions on the works of De Quincey, Crabbe, Francis Thompson and Coleridge. Cambridge Mass 1934.
— Wordsworth and Coleridge on diction and figures. Eng Inst Stud (New York) 1952.
— In his Mirror and the lamp, New York 1953. Especially chs 5, 7–8.
— The correspondent breeze: a romantic metaphor. Kenyon Rev 19 1957; rev in English romantic poets: modern essays in criticism, ed Abrams, New York 1960.
— Structure and style in the greater romantic lyrics. In From sensibility to romanticism: essays presented to F. A. Pottle, New York 1965.
Ainsworth, E. G., jr. Another source of the 'lonesome road' stanza in the Ancient mariner. MLN 49 1934.
Beeley, H. The political thought of Coleridge. In Coleridge studies, ed E. Blunden and E. L. Griggs 1934.
Bodkin, M. A study of the Ancient mariner and of the rebirth archetype. In her Archetypal patterns in poetry, Oxford 1934.
Bronson, B. H. The willing suspension of disbelief. California Pbns in Eng 4 1934.
Brooks, B. G. Coleridge's poetical technique. Life & Letters Aug 1934.
Chambers, E. K. Some dates in Coleridge's annus mirabilis. E & S 19 1934. Additional comments in his Date of Coleridge's Kubla Khan, RES 11 1935, rptd in his A sheaf of studies, Oxford 1942.
— Samuel Taylor Coleridge. Oxford 1938. A detailed but unsympathetic biography.
Coburn, K. Reports of Coleridge's lectures. TLS 15 Nov 1934.
— Coleridge and Wordsworth on the supernatural. UTQ 25 1956.
— Coleridge redivivus. In Major romantic poets, ed C. D. Thorpe et al, Carbondale 1957.
— Poet into public servant. Trans Royal Soc of Canada 54 1960.
— Critics who have influenced taste: 16, Coleridge. Times 18 July 1963.
— The interpenetration of man and nature. Proc Br Acad 49 1963.
— Reflexions in a Coleridge mirror: some images in his poems. In From sensibility to Romanticism: essays presented to F. A. Pottle, New York 1965.
— Who killed Christabel? TLS 20 May 1965.
— (ed). Coleridge: a collection of critical essays. Englewood Cliffs NJ 1967.
Coleridge is dead. TLS 19 July 1934. A centenary estimate.
Coleridge studies by several hands on the hundredth anniversary of his death. Ed E. Blunden and E. L. Griggs 1934. Essays by H. Beeley, G. H. B. Coleridge, A. J. Eagleston, E. L. Griggs, J. L. Haney, G. M. Harper, J. H. Muirhead, A. D. Snyder, C. H. Wilkinson. For comments on frontispiece portrait *see* W. Pithey, below.
Coleridge, P. M. A short sketch of the life of Coleridge. 1934 (priv ptd).
Coleridge, Sarah (Fricker). Minnow among tritons: Mrs Coleridge's letters to Thomas Poole 1799–1834. Ed S. Potter 1934.
Edwards, O. H. Wordsworth and Coleridge: three odes. [1934].
Cloyn, C. K. Coleridge's theory of the Church in the social order. Church History 3 1934.
Hearnshaw, F. J. C. Coleridge the conservative. Nineteenth Century July 1934.
Hotson, C. P. Coleridge's Hamlet and Emerson's Swedenborg. New Church Mag 53 1934.
'Kingsmill, Hugh' (H. K. Lunn). Samuel Taylor Coleridge. Eng Rev 59 1934.
Moore, J. R. Coleridge's indebtedness to Baltock's Peter Wilkins. MP 31 1934.
Richards, I. A. Coleridge on imagination. 1934, 1950 (rev), Bloomington 1960 (with preface by K. Coburn), London 1962. Reply by F. R. Leavis, Scrutiny 3 1935. *See also* R. Potter, The romanticism of Richards, ELH 26 1959.
— Coleridge the vulnerable poet. Yale Rev 48 1959.
— Coleridge's minor poems: a lecture. Missoula Montana 1960.
Watson, H. F. A note on the Ancient mariner. PQ 13 1934.
Wilkinson, C. H. A note on some early editions of Coleridge. In Coleridge studies, 1934, above.
Willoughby, L. A. Coleridge and his German contemporaries. Pbns of Eng Goethe Soc 10 1934.
— Coleridge as a philologist. MLR 31 1936.
— Coleridge und Deutschland. Germanisch-romanische Monatschrift 24 1936.
— English romantic criticism: or fancy and the imagination. In Weltliteratur: Festgabe für Fritz Strich, Berne 1952.
Wunsche, W. Die Staatsauffassung Coleridges. Leipzig 1934.
Willey, B. In his Eighteenth-century background, 1934.
— Coleridge on imagination and fancy. Proc Br Acad 32 1946.
— In his Nineteenth-century studies: Coleridge to Matthew Arnold, 1949.
Kagey, R. In his Columbia studies in the history of ideas vol 3, 1935.
Pithey, W. A Coleridge portrait. TLS 7 Feb 1935. Replies by W. H. Cam and E. Blunden 14 Feb 1935. Portrait is in Coleridge studies, 1934, above.
Potter, S. Coleridge and STC. 1935.
Rochlin, S. A. Coleridge's A hymn. TLS 17 Jan 1935. On My maker. Quotes ms of 19 June 1814.
Sanders, C. R. Coleridge as a champion of liberty. SP 32 1935.

— Coleridge, F. D. Maurice and the distinction between the reason and the understanding. PMLA 51 1936.
— Maurice as a commentator on Coleridge. PMLA 53 1938.
— Sir Leslie Stephen, Coleridge and two Coleridgeans [F. D. Maurice and J. D. Campbell]. PMLA 55 1940.
— Coleridge, Maurice and the Church universal. Jnl of Religion 21 1941.
— Coleridge and the Broad Church movement. Durham NC 1942.
Smith, F. M. The relation of Coleridge's Ode on dejection to Wordsworth's Ode on intimations of immortality. PMLA 50 1935.
Warne, F. J. Prester John in Coleridge's Kubla Khan. MLR 30 1935.
Weber, C. A. Bristols Bedeutung für die englische Romantik. Halle 1935.
Beach, J. W. Cowper, Blake, Coleridge; Coleridge and Wordsworth; Coleridge, Emerson and naturalism. In his Concept of nature in nineteenth-century English poetry, New York 1936.
— Coleridge's borrowings from the German. ELH 9 1942.
Isaacs, J. Coleridge's critical terminology. E & S 21 1936.
Lindsay, J. I. Coleridge and the University of Vermont. Vermont Alumni Weekly 15 1936.
Mossner, E. C. Coleridge and Bishop Butler. Philosophical Rev 45 1936.
Munby, A. N. L. On the early reputation of Wordsworth and Coleridge. TLS 22 Aug 1936. Reports in Yorkshire periodicals.
Speck, J. Samuel Taylor Coleridge. Archiv 170 1936.
Waples, D. David Hartley in the Ancient mariner. JEGP 35 1936.
Lucas, F. L. A romantic critic. In his Decline and fall of the romantic ideal, Cambridge 1936.
Bateson, F. W. Wordsworth and Coleridge. In From Anne to Victoria, ed B. Dobrée 1937.
Broughton, L. N. Sara Coleridge and Henry Reed's Memoir of Sara Coleridge, her letters to Reed, including her marginalia in Henry Crabb Robinson's copy of Wordsworth's Memoirs. Ithaca 1937.
Bush, D. In his Mythology and the romantic tradition in English poetry, Cambridge Mass 1937.
Hamilton, M. P. Wordsworth's relation to Coleridge's Osorio. SP 34 1937.
James, D. G. In his Scepticism and poetry, 1937.
— In his Romantic comedy, 1948.
— Kant's influence on Wordsworth and Coleridge. Listener 31 Aug 1950.
— The thought of Coleridge. In Major romantic poets, Carbondale 1957.
Johnson, E. C. Lamb and Coleridge. Amer Scholar 6 1937.
Joseph Henry Green, eminent surgeon and literary executor of Coleridge. Annals of Medical History new ser 9 1937.
Pfeiler, W. K. Coleridge and Schelling's Treatise on the Samothracian deities. MLN 52 1937.
Sherwood, M. Coleridge's imaginative conception of the imagination. Wellesley 1937.
Daniel, R. N. The publication of the Lyrical ballads. MLR 33 1938.
— Odes to dejection. Kenyon Rev 15 1953.
Tuttle, D. R. Christabel sources in Percy's Reliques and the Gothic romance. PMLA 53 1938.
Wagner, L. E. Coleridge's use of laudanum and opium as connected with his interest in contemporary investigations concerning stimulation and sensation. Psychoanalytic Rev 25 1938.
'Winwar, F.' Farewell the banner: Coleridge, Wordsworth and Dorothy. 1938.
Hanson, L. The life of Coleridge: the early years. 1938. Vol 1 all pbd.

Beyer, W. W. Coleridge, Wieland's Oberon and the Ancient mariner. RES 15 1939.
— Coleridge, Wieland's Oberon and the Wanderings of Cain. RES 16 1940.
— Coleridge's early knowledge of German. MP 52 1955. *See* Notebooks vol 1, ed K. Coburn, appendix A.
— The background of Coleridge's Cain, precursor of the Ancient mariner. N & Q Jan 1956.
— The enchanted forest. Oxford 1963. Collects articles above.
Bogholm, N. The Ancient mariner. Anglia 63 1939.
— Über die Genesis des Kubla Khan. E Studien 73 1939.
Bronowski, J. Wordsworth and Coleridge. In his Poet's defence, Cambridge 1939.
Coldicutt, D. Was Coleridge the author of the Enquirer series in the Monthly Magazine 1796–9? RES 15 1939. Denied by L. Patton 16 1940.
Mackenzie, G. Organic unity in Coleridge. California Pbns in Eng 7 1939.
Milley, H. J. W. Some notes on Coleridge's Eolian harp. MP 36 1939.
Morgan, R. The philosophic basis of Coleridge's Hamlet criticism. ELH 6 1939.
Scott-Thomas, H. F. The ethics of the Ancient mariner. Dalhousie Rev 18 1939.
Sypher, F. W. Coleridge's Somerset. PQ 18 1939.
Wordsworth and Coleridge: studies in honor of George McLean Harper. Ed E. L. Griggs, Princeton 1939. Coleridge essays by G. H. B. Coleridge, E. L. Griggs, J. R. McElderry, E. J. Morley and C. D. Thorpe.
Nethercot, A. H. The road to Tryermaine: a study of the history, background and purposes of Christabel. Chicago 1939, New York 1963.
— Christabel's wild-flower wine. MLQ 1 1940.
— Coleridge's Ode on the departing year. Explicator 1 1943.
— Coleridge's Christabel and Lefanu's Carmilla. MP 47 1950.
Armour, R. W. and R. F. Howe. Coleridge the talker: a series of contemporary descriptions and comments. Itahca 1940. Addns in Quart Jnl of Speech 32 1946.
Bewley, M. The poetry of Coleridge. Scrutiny 8 1940; rptd in Importance of Scrutiny, ed E. Bentley, New York 1948.
Bonnard, G. The invasion of Switzerland and English public opinion (January to April 1798): the background to Coleridge's France, an ode. E Studies 22 1940.
Howe, H. W. Greta Hall. 1940 (priv ptd).
Klimenko, E. I. The language reform in the poetry of the English romanticists Wordsworth and Coleridge. First Leningrad Pedagogical Inst of Foreign Lang 1 1940. Trn.
Lovejoy, A. O. Coleridge and Kant's two worlds. ELH 7 1940; rptd in his Essays in the history of ideas, Baltimore 1948.
Moore, N. Deism and Coleridge. Personalist 21 1940.
Tauber, E. German influence on the English vocabulary in the nineteenth century. JEGP 39 1940.
Visiak, E. H. Some Coleridge parallels. N & Q 15 June 1940. Chaucer and Milton; correction 29 June 1940.
Woolf, V. The man at the gate; Sara Coleridge. New Statesman 19–26 Oct 1940; rptd in her Death of the moth, 1942.
Burke, K. The Ancient mariner. In his Philosophy of literary form, New York 1941.
Copeland, T. A woman wailing for her demon lover. RES 17 1941.
Dewey, J. James Marsh and American philosophy. JHI 2 1941.
From court to sanctuary: George Herbert's song. TLS 12 July 1941. Echoes of Herbert in Work without hope.
Harding, D. W. The theme of the Ancient mariner. Scrutiny 9 1941; rptd in Importance of Scrutiny, ed E. Bentley, New York 1948 and in his Experience into words, 1963.

Kitzhaber, A. W. David Hartley in Christabel. Research Stud of State College Washington 9 1941.

Knight, G. W. Coleridge's Divine comedy. In his Starlit dome, Oxford 1941; rptd in English romantic poets, ed M. H. Abrams, New York 1960.

Leavis, F. R. Coleridge in criticism. Scrutiny 9 1941; rptd in Importance of Scrutiny, ed E. Bentley, New York 1948.

Mabbott, T. O. Coleridge's Wanderings of Cain and Blake's Death of Abel. N & Q 12 Aug 1941.

Pettit, H. Coleridge's Mount Abora. MLN 56 1941.

Sitwell, O. The sole Arabian tree. TLS 26 April 1941.

Tate, A. Literature and knowledge. In his Reason in madness, New York 1941 and in his On the limits of poetry, New York 1948.

Tuell, A. K. The friendship with Coleridge. In his John Sterling, New York 1941.

Allen, N. B. A note on Coleridge's Kubla Khan. MLN 57 1942.

Bonjour, A. A note on Lewti. E Studies 24 1942.

D., A. E. Zapolya and Merope. N & Q 12 Sept 1942.

Earnest, D. John and William Bartram. Philadelphia 1942. Influence on Coleridge, Wordsworth et al.

Horrell, J. The demonic finale of Christabel. MLR 37 1942.

Basler, R. P. Christabel: a study of its sexual theme. Sewanee Rev 51 1943.

—— Sex, symbolism and psychology in literature. New Brunswick 1948. On Lesbianism in Christabel.

Beck, W. Personne. Virginia Quart Rev 19 1943. On Kubla Khan.

Brogan, H. O. Coleridge's theory and use of the praeter-supernatural. Bull of Citadel 7 1943.

Joughin, G. L. Coleridge's Lewti: the biography of a poem. SE 1943.

Scudder, H. H. Bartram's Travels. N & Q 13 March 1943.

Fisch, M. H. The Coleridges, Dr Prati and Vico. MP 41 1944. Letter of 14 May 1825 with extracts from Prati's Autobiography.

—— and T. G. Bergin. In The autobiography of Giambattista Vico, Ithaca 1944. On Coleridge's part in the dissemination of Vico's philosophy.

Gugler, I. In her Das Problem der fragmentarischen Dichtung in der englischen Romantik, Berne 1944.

Howarth, R. G. Coleridge: a misattribution. N & Q 17 June 1944. On metrical experiment no 12.

Seely, F. F. A footnote to the Road to Xanadu. MLN 59 1944. A Chevy Chase parallel.

Bate, W. J. and J. Bullitt. Distinctions between fancy and imagination in eighteenth-century criticism. MLN 60 1945.

Brinkley, R. F. English book 1808–12: poems by S. T. Coleridge esq. PBSA 39 1945. On so-called Poems of 1812.

—— Coleridge on Locke. SP 46 1949.

Brown, H. The gloss to the Ancient mariner. MLQ 6 1945.

Cameron, K. W. Emerson the essayist. 2 vols Raleigh NC 1945.

—— Emerson's 'capital print' of Coleridge. Emerson Soc Quart 2 1956.

—— Schiller's Die Ideale and the odes of Coleridge and Wordsworth. Emerson Soc Quart 19 1960.

Davis, H. F. Was Newman a disciple of Coleridge? Dublin Rev 217 1945.

Grubb, G. G. Coleridge the metaphysician. Rev & Expositor 42 1945.

McKeehan, I. P. Some observations on the vocabulary of landscape description among the early Romanticists. In Elizabethan studies and other essays in honor of G. F. Reynolds, Boulder 1945.

Bouslog, C. S. The symbol of the sod-seat in Coleridge. PMLA 60 1946.

—— Coleridge and Mithraic symbolism. N & Q Feb 1953.

—— Structure and theme in Coleridge's Dejection: an ode. MLQ 24 1963.

Schilling, B. N. In his Human dignity and the great Victorians, New York 1946.

Tillett, N. S. Is Coleridge indebted to Fielding? SP 43 1946.

Warren, R. P. A poem of pure imagination: the Ancient mariner. Kenyon Rev 8 1946. Adverse replies by E. Olson and E. E. Stoll, 1948, below. Rptd with his edn of Ancient mariner, New York 1946.

Williams, R. M. Coleridge's parody of Dyer's Grongar Hill. MLR 41 1946.

Grigson, G. Kubla Khan in Wales. Cornhill Mag 162 1947. Replies by G. Whalley, TLS 21 June 1947, and K. Rhys 16 Aug 1947.

Kennedy, W. L. The English heritage of Coleridge of Bristol, 1798: the basis in eighteenth-century English thought for his distinction between imagination and fancy. New Haven 1947.

—— Humanist versus economist: the economic thought of Coleridge. Berkeley 1958.

Shapiro, K. English prosody and modern poetry. ELH 14 1947. Christabel and Hopkins.

Starr, N. C. Coleridge's Sir Leoline. PMLA 61 1947.

Whalley, G. The Mariner and the albatross. UTQ 16 1947.

—— Coleridge and Southey in Bristol 1795. RES new ser 1 1950.

—— Coleridge and John Murray. Quart Rev 289 1951.

—— The integrity of Biographia literaria. E & S new ser 6 1953.

—— Two views of imagination [Kant's and Coleridge's]. In his Poetic process, 1953.

—— Coleridge, Southey and Joan of Arc. N & Q Feb 1954.

—— Coleridge and Sara Hutchinson and the Asra poems. 1955. *See* R. S. Woof, A Coleridge-Wordsworth manuscript and Sara Hutchinson's poets, SB 19 1966.

—— Preface to Lyrical ballads: a portent. UTQ 25 1956.

—— Coleridge's debt to Charles Lamb. E & S 11 1958.

—— Coleridge on the Prometheus of Aeschylus. Trans Royal Soc of Canada 54 1960.

—— Portrait of a bibliophile: 7, Coleridge. Book Collector 10 1961.

—— Coleridge unlabyrinthed. UTQ 32 1963.

—— Late autumn's amaranth: Coleridge's late poems. Proc Royal Soc of Canada 4th ser 2 1964.

—— Coleridge's poetical canon: selection and arrangement. REL 7 1966.

Bandy, W. T. Coleridge's friend Joseph Hardman: a bibliographical note. JEGP 47 1948.

Link, A. S. Coleridge and the economic and political crisis in Great Britain 1816–20. JHI 9 1948.

Marcoux, H. The philosophy of Coleridge. Revue de l'Université d'Ottawa 18 1948.

Neumann, J. H. Coleridge on the English language. PMLA 63 1948.

Olsen, E. A symbolic reading of the Ancient mariner. MP 45 1948; rptd in Critics and criticism, ed R. S. Crane, Chicago 1952. Reply to R. P. Warren, above.

Read, H. Coleridge as critic. Sewanee Rev 1948; rptd in his Lectures in criticism, New York 1949 and in his True voice of feeling, 1953.

—— The notion of organic form: Coleridge. In his True voice of feeling, 1953.

Stoll, E. E. Symbolism in Coleridge. PMLA 63 1948. Reply to R. P. Warren, above.

Tillyard, E. M. W. Coleridge: the Ancient mariner 1798. In his Five poems 1470–1870, 1948.

Beatty, F. A by-path along the road to Xanadu. Classical Jnl 44 1949. Echo of Aeneid.

Bowra, C. M. In his Romantic imagination, Cambridge Mass 1949.

Brett, R. L. Coleridge's theory of the imagination. E & S 2 1949.

— In his Third Earl of Shaftesbury, 1951. On Coleridge's concept of imagination.
— In his Reason and imagination, Oxford 1960.
Johnson, S. F. Reflections on the consistency of Coleridge's political views. Harvard Lib Bull 3 1949.
— Coleridge's The watchman: decline and fall. RES new ser 1 1950.
Keynes, G. L. Blake with Lamb and his circle. In his Blake studies, 1949.
Martin, B. The Ancient mariner and the Authentic narrative. 1949.
Stevenson, L. The Ancient mariner as a dramatic monologue. Personalist 30 1949.
Wasserman, E. R. Another eighteenth-century distinction between fancy and imagination. MLN 64 1949.
— The English Romantics: the grounds of knowledge. Stud in Romanticism 3 1964.
— Shakespeare and the English romantic movement. In Persistence of Shakespeare idolatry, ed H. M. Schueller, Detroit 1964.
Willis, R. E. Another source of Christabel. N & Q 19 March 1949. Joseph Warton's Ode to solitude.
Baker, C. The infinite sea: the development and decline of Wordsworth and Coleridge—an account of Professor Harper's unfinished book. Princeton Univ Lib Chron 11 1950.
Bate, W. J. Coleridge on the function of art. In Perspectives of criticism, ed H. Levin, Cambridge Mass 1950.
— In his From classic to romantic, New York 1961.
Ehrenpreis, I. Southey to Coleridge 1799. N & Q 18 March 1950. Letter dated 13 Dec 1799.
Fogle, R. H. The dejection of Coleridge's Ode. ELH 17 1950.
— The romantic unity of Kubla Khan. College Eng Oct 1951.
— Coleridge's conversation poems. Tulane Stud in Eng 5 1955.
— Organic form in American criticism 1840–70. In The development of American literary criticism, ed F. H. Stovall, Chapel Hill 1955.
— Coleridge's critical principles. Tulane Stud in Eng 5 1955.
— The genre of the Ancient mariner. Tulane Stud in Eng 7 1957.
— Coleridge on dramatic illusion. Tulane Drama Rev 4 1960.
— The idea of Coleridge's criticism. Berkeley 1962.
Meyer, G. W. Resolution and independence: Wordsworth's answer to Coleridge's Dejection ode. Tulane Stud in Eng 2 1950.
Mounts, C. E. Coleridge's self-identification with Spenserian characters. SP 47 1950. On Satyrane. *See* Wordsworth's transparent sobriquet, HLQ 15 1952.
Parsons, C. O. The Mariner and the albatross. Virginia Univ Quart 26 1950.
Rulfs, D. J. The romantic writer and Edmund Kean. MLQ 11 1950.
Sells, A. L. Zanella, Coleridge and Shelley. Comparative Lit 2 1950.
Singer, D. W. In his Giordano Bruno, New York 1950. Includes Bruno's influence on Coleridge.
Vivante, L. In his English poetry and its contribution to the knowledge of a creative principle, 1950.
Wagenblass, J. H. Coleridge in dubious battle. HLQ 12 1950.
Warren, A. H. In his English poetic theory 1825–65, Princeton 1950. On Coleridge's influence.
Watson, V. Coleridge's army service. TLS 7 July 1950. With documentary evidence.
Benziger, J. Organic unity: Leibniz to Coleridge. PMLA 66 1951.
Beres, D. A dream, a vision and a poem: a psychoanalytic study of the origins of the Rime of the ancient mariner. International Jnl of Psycho-analysis 32 1951; rptd in Yearbook of Psychoanalysis 8 1952. Reply by D. W. Harding in his Experience into words, 1962.
Breyer, B. R. Towards an interpretation of Kubla Khan. In English studies in honor of J. S. Wilson, ed F. T. Bowers, Charlottesville 1951.
Brooks, E. L. Coleridge's second packet for Blackwood's Magazine. PQ 30 1951. Authorship of articles 1821–2.
Coffin, T. P. Coleridge's use of the ballad stanza in the Ancient mariner. MLQ 12 1951.
Danby, J. F. Coleridge: anima naturaliter christiana. 1951.
Doughty, O. Dante and the English romantic poets. Eng Miscellany (Rome) 2 1951.
— Coleridge and a poets' poet: William Lisle Bowles. Eng Miscellany (Rome) 14 1963.
Fogle, S. F. The design of Coleridge's Dejection. SP 48 1951.
Gérard, A. Coleridge, Keats and the modern mind. EC 1 1951.
— L'idée romantique de la poésie en Angleterre: études sur la théorie de la poésie chez Coleridge, Wordsworth, Keats et Shelley. Belles Lettres (Paris) 1955.
— On the logic of romanticism. EC 7 1957.
— Le romantisme anglais: orientations récentes de l'histoire et de la critique. Revue de Langues Vivantes 25 1959.
— The systolic rhythm: the structure of Coleridge's conversation poems. EC 10 1960.
— Counterfeiting infinity: the Eolian harp and the growth of Coleridge's mind. JEGP 60 1961.
Hardy, B. Distinction without difference: Coleridge's fancy and imagination. EC 1 1951. Replies by L. S. Potts and B. Hardy 2 1952.
— Keats, Coleridge and negative capability. N & Q 5 July 1952.
— 'I have a smack of Hamlet': Coleridge and Shakespeare's characters. EC 8 1958.
Jones, E. A new reading of Christabel. Cambridge Jnl 5 Nov 1951.
Kahn, S. J. Psychology in Coleridge's poetry. Jnl of Aesthetics 9 1951.
Lutz, R. Coleridge: seine Dichtung als Ausdruck ethischen Bewusstseins. Swiss Stud in Lit (Berne) 26 1951.
Milner, R. H. Coleridge's 'sacred river'. TLS 18 May 1951. Hesiod's Styx.
Patterson, C. I. The authenticity of Coleridge's reviews of Gothic romances. JEGP 50 1951. Dismisses all but the Monk. *See* G. Greever, 1926, above, and D. Roper, 1960, below.
— Coleridge's conception of dramatic illusion in the novel. ELH 18 1951.
Rossiter, A. P. Coleridge's Hymn before sunrise. TLS 28 Sept, 26 Oct 1951.
— Coleridge's 'Soother in absence'. TLS 8 May 1953.
Rostvig, M. S. Another source for some stanzas of the Rime of the ancient mariner. MLN 66 1951.
Scherillo, R. Wordsworth and Coleridge's Lyrical ballads. Naples 1951.
Smith, J. P. Criticism of Christabel. UTQ 21 1951.
Smyser, J. W. Coleridge's use of Wordsworth's juvenilia. PMLA 65 1951.
Woodhouse, A. S. P. Romanticism and the history of ideas. In English studies today, ed C. L. Wrenn and G. Bullough 1951.
Benet, L. Coleridge, poet of wild enchantment. New York 1952.
Bramwell, J. Kubla Khan—Coleridge's fall. Neuphilologische Mitteilungen 53 1952.
Davie, D. A. Coleridge and improvised diction. In his Purity of diction in English verse, 1952.
— In his Articulate energy, 1955. On function of syntax in Dejection and Lime tree bower.
Emmet, D. M. Coleridge on the growth of the mind. Bull of John Rylands Lib 34 1952.

Hopwood, V. G. The interpretation of dream and poetry. UTQ 21 1952.
Nethery, W. Coleridge's use of judgment in Shakespearean criticism. Personalist 33 1952.
Oppel, H. Coleridges Kubla Khan—zur Interpretation romantischer Dichtung. Die Neueren Sprachen Sept 1952.
— The sacred river. In his Studien und Interpretationen zur Dichtung der englischen Romantik, Frankfurt 1959.
Stahl, E. L. Coleridges Theorie der Dichtkunst im Hinblick auf Goethe. Berne 1952.
Viebrock, H. 'Einsehen' und 'Einfühlen' in der englischen Romantik. Die Neueren Sprachen Sept 1952.
— Poetic theory of Coleridge and Keats: influence of Shakespeare. Shakespeare Jahrbuch 97 1961.
— A note on Coleridge and memory: Coleridge à la recherche du mot perdu. Archiv 200 1963.
Wells, G. A. Man and nature: an elucidation of Coleridge's rejection of Herder's thought. JEGP 51 1952.
— Herder's and Coleridge's evaluation of the historical approach. MLR 48 1953.
Wiley, M. L. Coleridge and the wheels of intellect. PMLA 67 1952.
Ashe, D. J. Byron's alleged part in the production of Coleridge's Remorse. N & Q Jan 1953.
— Coleridge, Byron and Schiller's Der Geisterseher. N & Q Oct 1956.
Chinol, E. Il pensiero di Coleridge. Collezione di Varia Critica (Venice) 1953.
Contemporary reviews of romantic poetry. Ed J. Wain 1953.
House, H. Coleridge. 1953 (Clark Lectures).
Jordan, J. E. De Quincey on Wordsworth's theory of diction. PMLA 68 1953.
Joseph, M. K. Charles Aders: a biographical note, together with some unpublished letters addressed to him by Coleridge and others, and now in the Grey Collection, Auckland City Library. Auckland Univ College Bull no 43 and Eng Ser no 6 1953.
Kirk, R. Coleridge and conservative ideas. In his Conservative mind, Chicago 1953.
Margoliouth, H. M. Wordsworth and Coleridge: dates in May and June 1798. N & Q Aug 1953.
— Wordsworth and Coleridge 1795–1834. Oxford 1953 (Home Univ Lib).
Raine, K. Coleridge. 1953 (Br Council pamphlet).
— Traditional symbolism in Kubla Khan. Sewanee Rev 72 1964.
Watson, G. 'Imagination' and 'fancy'. EC 3 1953.
— On patronising Coleridge. Listener 24 Oct 1957.
— Coleridge the poet. 1966.
Wilkinson, C. S. The wake of the Bounty. 1953. Possible connection between the mutiny and the Ancient mariner.
Hough, G. In his Romantic poets, 1953.
— Coleridge and the Victorians. In The English mind: studies in the English moralists presented to Basil Willey, ed H. S. Davies and G. Watson, Cambridge 1964.
Arber, A. The mind and the eye: a study of the biologist's standpoint. Cambridge 1954. The standpoint is confessedly Coleridgean.
Creed, H. H. Coleridge's metacriticism. PMLA 69 1954.
— The rime of the ancient mariner: a rereading. Eng Jnl 49 1960.
Foxon, D. F. The printing of Lyrical ballads. Library 5th ser 9 1954.
Fussell, P. Theory of prosody in eighteenth-century England. New London Conn 1954. Frequent comparison of Coleridge with 18th-century theorists.
Glickfield, C. W. Coleridge's prose contributions to the Morning Post. PMLA 69 1954.

Harada, C. An existentialist interpretation of Coleridge's theory of being. Stud in Eng Lit (Tokyo) 29–30 1954.
Hutchinson, S. The letters of Sara Hutchinson 1800–35. Ed K. Coburn, 1954.
Male, R. R., jr. The background of Coleridge's Theory of life. SE 33 1954.
Mary Eleanor, Mother. Strange voyages: Coleridge and Rimbaud. Renascence 8 1954.
Mayo, R. D. The contemporaneity of the Lyrical ballads. PMLA 69 1954. *See* S. M. Parish 74 1959.
Mercer, D. F. The symbolism of Kubla Khan. Jnl of Aesthetics 12 1954.
Peter, J. Symbol and implication: notes apropos of a dictum of Coleridge's. EC 4 1954.
Poulet, G. Timelessness and romanticism. JHI 15 1954.
Rainsberry, F. B. Coleridge and the paradox of the poetic imperative. ELH 21 1954.
Tave, M. The London Magazine 1820–9. MP 52 1954. Includes employment of Coleridge or Lamb.
Werkmeister, L. Coleridge and the work for which poor Palm was murdered. JEGP 53 1954.
— Coleridge on science, philosophy and poetry: their relation to religion. Harvard Theological Rev 52 1959.
— Coleridge's Anthem: another debt to Bowles. JEGP 58 1959.
— Coleridge's Mathematical problem. MLN 74 1959.
— Coleridge's The plot discovered: some facts and a speculation. MP 56 1959.
— Jerdan on Coleridge. N & Q Feb 1959.
— Coleridge and Godwin on the communication of truth. MP 55 1958.
— Coleridge, Bowles and Feelings of the heart. Anglia 78 1960.
— The early Coleridge: his 'rage for metaphysics'. Harvard Theological Rev 54 1961.
— 'High jinks' at Highgate. PQ 40 1961.
— Some whys and wherefores of Coleridge's Lines composed in a concert-room. MP 60 1963.
Wilcox, S. C. The water imagery of the Ancient mariner. Personalist 35 1954.
— The argument and motto of the Ancient mariner. MLQ 22 1961.
Crawford, T. The Edinburgh Review and romantic poetry (1802–29). Auckland Univ College Bull 47 and Eng Ser no 8 1955.
Haven, R. Coleridge and the Greek mysteries. MLN 70 1955.
— Coleridge, Hartley and the mystics. JHI 20 1959.
— Coleridge and Jacob Boehme: a further comment. N & Q May 1966. With marginalia.
[Marsh, F. G.] Christabel and Coleridge's recipe for romance poems. N & Q Nov 1958.
Marsh, F. G. The ocean desert: the Ancient mariner and the Waste land. EC 9 1959.
Mendilow, A. A. Symbolism in Coleridge and the Dantesque element in the Ancient mariner. Scripta Hierosolymitana (Jerusalem) 1955.
Pucelle, J. In his L'Idéalisme en Angleterre de Coleridge à Bradley, Paris 1955.
Schanzer, E. Shakespeare, Lowes and the Ancient mariner. N & Q June 1955.
Walsh, W. Coleridge's 'self-unravelling clue': its meaning for education. Western Humanities Rev (Utah) 9 1955.
— Coleridge's vision of childhood. Listener 24 Feb 1955.
— In his Use of imagination, 1959.
White, A. J. George Dyer 1755–1841: a bicentenary study. Charles Lamb Soc Bull no 124 1955.
Barnet, S. Coleridge on Shakespeare's villains. Shakespeare Quart 7 1956.
Beaty, F. L. Dorothy Wordsworth and the Coleridges: a new letter. MLR 51 1956. D. Wordsworth to Josiah Wade, 27 March 1814.
Beer, J. B. Coleridge's 'great circulating library'. N & Q June 1956.

— Coleridge at school. N & Q March 1958.
— Coleridge the visionary. 1959.
— Coleridge's Watchman. N & Q June 1961.
— Coleridge and Boehme's Aurora. N & Q May 1963.
Bonnerot, L. The two worlds of Coleridge: some aspects of his attitude to nature. Essays by Divers Hands 28 1956.
Erdman, D. V. Coleridge, Wordsworth and the Wedgwood fund. BNYPL Sept–Oct 1956.
— Newspaper sonnets put to the concordance test: can they be attributed to Coleridge? BNYPL Oct, Dec 1957, Jan 1958.
— Coleridge as Nehemiah Higginbottom. MLN 73 1958.
— A new discovery: the first review of Christabel. SE 37 1958.
— The case for internal evidence (6): the signature of style. BNYPL Feb 1959. As evidenced by Coleridge. *See* E. G. Fogel, 1959, below.
— Immoral acts of a library cormorant: the extent of Coleridge's contributions to the Critical Review. BNYPL Sept, Nov 1959.
— Coleridge in Lilliput: the quality of parliamentary reporting in 1800. Speech Monographs 27 1960.
Krieger, M. In his New apologists for poetry, Minneapolis 1956. On Coleridge and the New Critics.
Mann, P. G. Lamb and Coleridge: admission to Christ's Hospital. Charles Lamb Soc Bull 132 1956.
Seronsy, C. C. Dual patterning in the Rime of the ancient mariner. N & Q Nov 1956.
Smith, B. Coleridge's Ancient mariner and Cook's second voyage. Jnl of Warburg & Courtauld Inst 19 1956.
Tomlinson, C. Coleridge: Christabel. In Interpretations, ed J. Wain 1956.
Whitesell, J. E. The rime of the ancient mariner, line 142. N & Q Jan 1956. On the dead albatross.
Will, F. Cousin and Coleridge: the aesthetic ideal. Comparative Lit 8 1956.
Wright, J. K. From Kubla Khan to Florida. Amer Quart 8 1956. Indebtedness to Bartram.
'Bishop, Morchard' (O. Stonor). The farmhouse of Kubla Khan. TLS 10 May 1957.
— Captain James and Ivor James. TLS 16 Jan 1959. *See* J. Taylor, 1890, above.
Bostetter, E. E. Christabel: the vision of fear. PQ 36 1957; rev in his Romantic ventriloquists, 1963, below.
— The man behind the curtain. Western Rev (Iowa) 23 1958.
— The nightmare world of the Ancient mariner. Stud in Romanticism 1 1962.
— In his Romantic ventriloquists, Seattle 1963.
Brand, C. P. In his Italy and the English Romantics, Cambridge 1957.
Cohen, R. Coleridge and William Sotheby's Orestes. MLR 52 1957.
Coveney, P. Coleridge and the 'imaginative child'. In his Poor monkey, 1957.
Dameron, J. L. Emerson and the Edinburgh Review of Coleridge's Statesman's manual. Emerson Soc Quart 8 1957.
Jordan, H. H. Thomas Moore and the review of Christabel. MP 54 1957.
McLuhan, M. Coleridge as artist. In Major romantic poets, Bloomington 1957, below.
The major romantic poets: a symposium in reappraisal. Ed C. D. Thorpe, C. Baker and B. Weaver, Carbondale 1957. Includes essays by K. Coburn, D. G. James, M. McLuhan.
Moorman, M. Wordsworth's commonplace book. N & Q Sept 1957. Includes new information on Ode to the rain.
Nosworthy, J. M. Coleridge on a distant prospect of Faust. E & S 10 1957.
Ober, W. U. The rime of the ancient mariner and Pinckard's Notes on the West Indies. N & Q Sept 1957.

— Southey, Coleridge and Kubla Khan. JEGP 58 1959.
Patrick, J. M. Ammianus and Alpheus: the sacred river. MLN 72 1957.
Preyer, R. O. Julius Hare and Coleridgean criticism. Jnl of Aesthetics 15 1957.
— Bentham, Coleridge and the science of history. Beiträge zur Englischen Philologie 41 1958.
Schrickx, W. Coleridge's vroege contacten met wijsgerige stelsels. Revue des Langues Vivantes 6 1957.
— Coleridge and Friedrich Heinrich Jacobi. Revue Belge de Philologie et d'Histoire 36 1958. On history of the influence; includes marginalia.
— Coleridge, Ernst Platner and the imagination. E Studies 40 1959.
— Coleridge and the Cambridge Platonists. REL 7 1966.
Smith, C. J. Wordsworth and Coleridge: the growth of a theme. SP 54 1957.
Stout, G. D. Leigh Hunt on Wordsworth and Coleridge. Keats–Shelley Jnl 6 1957.
Wilkinson, E. M. Coleridge's knowledge of German as seen in the early notebooks. Notebooks, ed K. Coburn vol 1 (notes) 1957, appendix A.
— The inexpressible and the un-speakable: some romantic attitudes to art and language. German Life & Letters 16 1963.
Woodring, C. R. Coleridge and Mary Hutchinson. N & Q May 1957.
— Coleridge and the Khan. EC 9 1959.
— Politics in the poetry of Coleridge. Madison 1961.
— Christabel of Cumberland. REL 7 1966.
Baker, J. V. The sacred river: Coleridge's theory of the imagination. Baton Rouge 1958.
Barnes, S. G. Was the Theory of life Coleridge's opus maximum? SP 55 1958.
Boulton, J. T. In his edn of Edmund Burke, A philosophical inquiry into the origin of our ideas of the sublime and beautiful, 1958.
Chayes, I. H. Coleridge, metempsychosis and 'almost all the followers of Fénelon'. ELH 25 1958.
— Rhetoric as drama: an approach to the romantic ode. PMLA 79 1964.
— A Coleridgean reading of the Ancient mariner. Stud in Romanticism 4 1965.
— Kubla Khan and the creative process. Stud in Romanticism 6 1967.
Colmer, J. A. An unpublished sermon by Coleridge. N & Q April 1958. College commemoration sermon, summarized with a few extracts.
— Coleridge and the communication of political truth. Eng Stud in Africa 1 1959.
— Coleridge on Addington's administration. MLR 54 1959.
— Coleridge: critic of society. Oxford 1959.
Dilworth, E. N. Fielding and Coleridge: 'poetic faith'. N & Q Jan 1958.
Foakes, R. A. In his Romantic assertion, 1958.
Harper, F. In his edn of Travels of William Bartram, New Haven 1958.
Howes, A. B. In his Yorick and the critics: Sterne's reputation in England 1760–1868, New Haven 1958.
Lang, D. B. Point counterpoint: the emergence of fancy and imagination in Coleridge. Jahrbuch für Amerikastudien 16 1958.
Marks, E. R. The achieve of, the mastery of the thing. Jnl of Aesthetics 16 1958. Aesthetic values in Coleridge, the New Critics et al.
— Means and ends in Coleridge's critical method. ELH 26 1959.
Salingar, L. G. Coleridge: poet and philosopher. In Pelican guide to English literature vol 5: from Blake to Byron, ed B. Ford 1958.
Williams, R. In his Culture and society 1780–1950, 1958, 1961 (rev).
Super, R. H. Landor's letters to Wordsworth and Coleridge. MP 55 1958.

Todd, A. C. Governess to the Wedgwoods. Lettere Italiane 15 May 1958. On unpbd letters of Thomasina Dennis, who discussed poetry with Coleridge. *See* R. S. Woof, 1963, below.

Duncan, J. E. In his Revival of metaphysical poetry, Minneapolis 1959.

Durr, R. A. This lime-tree bower my prison and a recurrent action in Coleridge. ELH 26 1959.

Ewen, F. Coleridge and Wordsworth. Science & Soc 23 1959.

Fogel, E. G. Salmons in both: or some caveats for canonical scholars. BNYPL May–June 1959. Problems of establishing a canon.

Gardner, W. H. The poet and the albatross. Eng Stud in Africa 1 1959.

Parrish, S. M. The Wordsworth-Coleridge controversy. PMLA 74 1959.

— Wordsworth and Coleridge on meter. JEGP 59 1960.

Piper, H. W. The pantheistic sources of Coleridge's early poetry. JHI 20 1959.

— The active universe. 1962.

Ryals, C. de L. The nineteenth-century cult of inaction. Tennessee Stud in Lit 4 1959.

Van Burd, A. Background to Modern painters: the tradition and the Turner controversy. PMLA 74 1959. On Sir G. Beaumont's role in art criticism.

Kaiser, R. Vier Sonnette: eine vergleichende Interpretation. Die Neueren Sprachen 6 1960. Thomas Warton, To the river Lodon; W. L. Bowles, To the river Itchin; Coleridge, To the river Otter; Wordsworth, To the river Duddon 21.

Ahmad, M. Coleridge and the Brahman creed. Indian Jnl of Eng Stud 1 1960.

— A probable Indian source of a Coleridge verse fragment. N & Q June 1961. 'As some vast tropic tree'.

Angus, D. The theme of love and guilt in Coleridge's three major poems. JEGP 59 1960.

Badawi, M. M. Coleridge's formal criticism of Shakespeare's plays. EC 10 1960.

— A note on Coleridge and the acting of Shakespeare's plays. Bull of Faculty of Arts (Alexandria Univ) 14 1960.

Emerson, F. W. Joseph Sterling's Cambuscan in Coleridge's Kubla Khan. N & Q March 1960.

Feeding mind. TLS 1 July 1960.

Fleissner, R. F. Kubla Khan and Tom Jones: an unnoticed parallel. N & Q March 1960.

— The mystical meaning of five: a notelet on Kubla Khan. E Studies 46 1965.

Gose, E. B., jr. Coleridge and the luminous gloom: an analysis of the symbolical language in the Rime of the ancient mariner. PMLA 75 1960.

Greiner, W. Deutsche Einflüsse auf die Dichtungstheorie von Coleridge. Die Neueren Sprachen 2 1960.

Heninger, S. K. A Jungian reading of Kubla Khan. Jahrbuch für Amerikastudien 18 1960.

Kaufman, P. Borrowings from the Bristol Library 1773–84. Charlottesville 1960.

— The Reynolds-Hood commonplace book: a fresh appraisal. Keats-Shelley Jnl 10 1961.

— New light on Coleridge as an undergraduate. REL 7 1966.

Knights, L. C. Idea and symbol. In Metaphor and symbol, ed Knights and B. Cottle 1960; rptd in his Further explorations, 1965.

Kroeber, K. Romantic narrative art. Madison 1960. On Ancient mariner etc.

Marshall, W. H. A Coleridgean borrowing from Plato. Classical Jnl 55 1960.

— Coleridge, the Mariner and dramatic irony. Personalist 12 1961.

— The structure of Coleridge's The eolian harp. MLN 76 1961.

Roper, D. Coleridge and the Critical Review. MLR 55 1960. *See* G. Greever, 1926 and C. I. Patterson, 1951, above.

Suther, M. The dark night of Coleridge. New York 1960.

— Visions of Xanadu. New York 1965.

Ware, M. The rime of the ancient mariner: a discourse on prayer? RES new ser 11 1960.

— Coleridge's spectre-bark: a slave ship? PQ 40 1961.

Pedrini, D. T. and T. V. Serpent imagery and symbolism in the major English romantic poets: Blake, Wordsworth, Coleridge, Byron, Shelley, Keats. Psychiatric Quart Suppl 34–5 1960–1.

Bailey, D. Coleridge's revision of the Friend. MP 59 1961.

Barker, J. R. Some early correspondence of Sarah Stoddart and the Lambs. HLQ 24 1961. On surprise visit to Coleridge at Greta Hall, 10 Aug 1802.

Bloom, H. In his Visionary company: a reading of English romantic poetry, New York 1961.

Boulger, J. D. Coleridge as religious thinker. New Haven 1961.

— Christian skepticism in the Rime of the ancient mariner. In From sensibility to romanticism: essays presented to F. A. Pottle, New York 1965.

— Imagination and speculation in Coleridge's conversation poems. JEGP 64 1965.

Brooke, V. Coleridge's 'true and original realism'. Durham Univ Jnl 22 1961.

Buckley, V. Coleridge: vision and actuality. Melbourne Critical Rev 4 1961.

Calleo, D. P. Coleridge on Napoleon. Yale French Stud 26 1961.

— Coleridge and the idea of the modern state. New Haven 1966.

Deen, L. W. Coleridge and the sources of pantisocracy: Godwin, the Bible and Hartley. Stud in Eng (Boston Univ) 5 1961.

— Coleridge and the radicalism of religious dissent. JEGP 61 1962.

Garvin, K. Snakes in the grass (with particular attention to Satan, Lancia, Christabel). REL 2 1961.

Hussain, I. Orientalism and Coleridge. Venture 1–2 1961.

Little, G. James Losh. N & Q Dec 1961. Reply by R. S. Woof, Feb 1962.

Newell, I. Coleridge and J. G. E. Maas. N & Q June 1961.

Newsome, D. Godliness and good learning: four studies on a Victorian ideal. 1961. With recognition of Coleridge's influence on nineteenth-century educationists.

Schneider, D. B. A note on Coleridge's notebooks. N & Q June 1961. On Boehme's Aurora.

— The structure of Kubla Khan. Amer N & Q 1 1963.

Stuart, J. A. Augustine and the Ancient mariner. MLN 76 1961.

White, R. L. Washington Allston: banditti in Arcadia. Amer Quart 13 1961.

Aldrich, R. I. The Wordsworths and Coleridge: 'three persons' but not 'one soul'. Stud in Romanticism 2 1962.

Amarasinghe, J. In his Dryden and Pope in the early nineteenth century, Cambridge 1962.

Bailey, D. Coleridge's revision of the Friend. MP 59 1962.

Blackstone, B. In his Lost travellers, 1962.

Bullough, G. In his Mirror of minds, 1962.

Dodds, A. E. In his Romantic theory of poetry, New York 1962.

Dowden, W. S. Thomas Moore and the review of Christabel. MP 60 1962.

Elmen, P. The fame of Jeremy Taylor. Anglican Theological Rev 44 1962.

Fox, A. J. Political and biographical backgrounds of Coleridge's Osorio. JEGP 61 1962.

Owen, C. A., jr. Structure in the Ancient mariner. College Eng 23 1962.

Owen, H. P. The theology of Coleridge. CQ 4 1962.

Purves, A. C. Formal structure in Kubla Khan. Stud in Romanticism 1 1962.

Sankey, B. T. Coleridge on Milton's Satan. PQ 41 1962.

— Coleridge and the visible world. Texas Stud in Lit & Lang 6 1964.

Sharrock, R. The chemist and the poet: Sir Humphry Davy and the preface to Lyrical ballads. Notes & Records of Royal Soc 17 1962.
Spacks, P. M. Horror-personification in late eighteenth-century poetry. SP 59 1962.
—— The insistence of horror: aspects of the supernatural in eighteenth-century poetry. Cambridge Mass 1962.
Stevenson, W. Christabel: a reinterpretation. Alphabet 4 1962.
—— The myth and the mind: towards a theory of creativity. Personalist 46 1965.
Ware, J. G. Coleridge's great poems reflecting the mother image. Amer Imago 18 1962.
Woof, R. S. Wordsworth's poetry and Stuart's newspapers 1797–1803. SB 15 1962.
—— Coleridge and Thomasina Dennis. UTQ 32 1963. *See* A. C. Todd, above.
—— A Coleridge-Wordsworth manuscript and Sara Hutchinson's Poets. SB 19 1966.
Braekman, W. Two hitherto unpublished letters of Charles and Mary Lamb to the Morgans. E Studies 44 1963.
—— Letters by Robert Southey to Sir John Taylor Coleridge. Studia Germanica Gandensia 6 1964.
—— A reconsideration of Coleridge's poem On taking leave of... N & Q Jan 1964.
—— The influence of William Collins on Coleridge. Revue des Langues Vivantes 31 1965.
Buchan, A. M. The influence of Wordsworth on Coleridge 1795–1800. UTQ 32 1963.
Delvaille, B. S. T. Coleridge. Paris 1963. Synoptic table of life with extracts etc.
Deutsch, B. Coleridge on himself. Poetry 102 1963.
Gerber, R. Keys to Kubla Khan. E Studies 44 1963.
—— Cybele, Kubla Khan and Keats. E Studies 46 1965.
Godfrey, D. R. Imagination and truth: some romantic contradictions. E Studies 44 1963.
Gottfried, L. In his Matthew Arnold and the Romantics, 1963.
Himmelfarb, G. On Bentham and Coleridge. In her Essays on politics and culture, 1963.
King-Hele, D. Erasmus Darwin. 1963. On Darwin's influence on Coleridge.
McFarland, G. F. The early literary career of Julius Charles Hare. Bull of John Rylands Lib 46 1963.
—— Julius Charles Hare: Coleridge, De Quincey and German literature. Bull of John Rylands Lib 47 1964.
Ridenour, G. M. Source and allusion in some poems of Coleridge. SP 60 1963.
Rodway, A. E. In his Romantic conflict, 1963.
Schulz, M. F. The poetic voices of Coleridge. Detroit 1963.
Sultana, D. Coleridge autographs. TLS 15 Feb 1963. On mss in Malta related to Coleridge and his public service there.
Bagley, C. L. Early American views of Coleridge as poet. Research Stud (Washington State College) 32 1964.
Berkoben, L. D. Christabel: a variety of evil experience. MLQ 25 1964.
—— Coleridge on wit. Humanities Assoc Bull 15 1964.
—— The composition of Coleridge's Hymn before sunrise: some mitigating circumstances. Eng Lang Notes 4 1966.
Déchamps, P. La formation de la pensée de Coleridge 1772–1804. Paris 1964.
Empson, W. The Ancient mariner. CQ 6 1964.
Forstman, H. J. Coleridge's notes toward the understanding of doctrine. Jnl of Religion 44 1964.
Jackson, J. R. de J. Coleridge on dramatic illusion and spectacle in the performance of Shakespeare's plays. MP 62 1964.
—— Coleridge on Shakespeare's preparation. REL 7 1966.
McLaughlin, E. T. Coleridge and Milton. SP 61 1964.
Marcovitz, E. Bemoaning the lost dream: Coleridge's Kubla Khan and addiction. International Jnl of Psychoanalysis 45 1964.
Miller, C. W. Coleridge's concept of nature. JHI 25 1964.
Orsini, G. N. G. Coleridge and Schlegel reconsidered. Comparative Lit 16 1964.
Preston, T. R. Christabel and the mystical tradition. Pittsburgh 1964.
Rapin, R. Coleridge's Dejection: an ode, 76–95. E Studies 45 1964. Reply to H. House, Coleridge, 1953, above.
Rudrum, A. W. Coleridge's This lime tree bower my prison. Southern Rev 1 1964.
Smith, G. S. A reappraisal of the moral stanzas in the Rime of the ancient mariner. Stud in Romanticism 3 1964.
Appleyard, J. A. Coleridge's philosophy of literature: the development of a concept of poetry 1791–1819. Cambridge Mass 1965.
Bryant, E. P. The rime of the ancient mariner: a Coleridgean reading. Standpunte (Cape Town) 18 1965.
Chandler, A. Structure and symbolism in the Rime of the ancient mariner. MLQ 26 1965.
Eiseley, L. Darwin, Coleridge and the theory of unconscious creation. Daedalus 94 1965; Lib Chron 31 1965.
From sensibility to romanticism: essays presented to Frederick A. Pottle. Ed F. W. Hilles and H. Bloom, New York 1965. Essays on Coleridge by J. D. Boulger and K. Coburn above.
Hofstetter, M. La poesia di Coleridge e la letteratura tedesca: una riconsiderazione. Arte e Storia 35 1965.
Meier, H. H. Ancient lights on Kubla's lines. E Studies 46 1965.
Reed, M. L. Wordsworth, Coleridge and the plan of the Lyrical ballads. UTQ 34 1965.
Scarfe, F. Coleridge's nightscapes. Etudes Anglaises 18 1965.
Sen, R. K. Imagination in Coleridge and Abhinavagupta: a critical analysis of Christian and Saiva standpoints. Jnl of Aesthetics 24 1965.
Harrex, S. C. Coleridge's pleasure-dome in Kubla Khan. N & Q May 1966.
Hoyle, J. F. Kubla Khan as an elated experience. Lit & Psychology (Univ of Mass) 16 1966. Comment by M. Worthington, ibid.
Karrfalt, D. H. Another note on Kubla Khan and Coleridge's retirement to Ash Farm. N & Q May 1966.
Lyon, J. S. Romantic psychology and the inner senses: Coleridge. PMLA 81 1966.
Martin, C. G. Coleridge, Edward Rushton and the cancelled note to the Monody on the death of Chatterton. RES new ser 17 1966.
—— Coleridge and Cudworth: a source for the Eolian harp. N & Q May 1966.
—— Coleridge and Crowe's Lewesdon Hill. MLR 62 1967.
Rose, E. S. The anatomy of imagination. College Eng Feb 1966.
Rothman, R. A re-examination of Kubla Khan. Eng Jnl 55 1966.
Shelton, J. The autograph manuscript of Kubla Khan and an interpretation. REL 7 1966.
Ward, P. Coleridge's critical theory of the symbol. Texas Stud in Lit & Lang 8 1966.
Walsh, W. Coleridge: the work and the relevance. 1967.
Yarlott, G. Coleridge and the Abyssinian maid. 1967.

G. Wh.

ROBERT SOUTHEY

1774–1843

Bibliographies

Haller, W. Appendix A, Works of Southey. In his Early life of Southey, New York 1917.
Zeitlin, J. Southey's contributions to the Critical Review. N & Q Feb–May 1918.

Havens, R. D. Southey's contributions to the Foreign Review. RES 8 1932.
Curry, K. Southey's contributions to the Annual Review. Bull of Bibliography 16 1939.
—— The contributors to the Annual Anthology. PBSA 42 1948.
—— Two new works of Southey. SB 5 1953.
—— In The English romantic poets and essayists: a review of research and criticism, ed C. W. and L. H. Houtchens, New York 1957, 1966 (rev).
—— The published letters of Southey: a checklist. BNYPL March 1967.
Shine, H. and H. C. The Quarterly Review under Gifford. Chapel Hill 1949. Identifies Southey's articles 1809–24.
Barber, G. Poems by Robert Southey, 1797. Bodleian Lib Record 6 1960. *See* S. Nowell-Smith, Book Collector 11 1962.

Collections

The minor poems. 3 vols 1815, 1823. A reprint of Poems 1797–9 and Metrical tales 1805, below.
The poetical works, complete in one volume. Paris 1829, [1830?]. Includes some poems not found in other collections.
Selections from the poems. [Ed I. Moxon] 1831, 1833 (as The beauties of the poems).
Selections from the prose works. [Ed I. Moxon] 1832, 1833 (as The beauties of the prose works).
The poetical works of Southey, collected by himself. 10 vols 1837–8, New York 1839. Each vol has a separate preface by Southey. Frequently rptd in whole or in part and dated 1844–59 or nd; 1 vol edns New York 1842, Philadelphia 1846, New York 1848, London 1850, New York 1851, 1853, 1856, London 1863, 1873, 1884.
[Southey's poems] vol 1, Joan of Arc and Madoc: epic poems; vol 2, The curse of Kehama and Ballads and metrical tales; vol 3, Thalaba the destroyer and minor poems. [1854]?.
Joan of Arc, and minor poems. Illustr J. Gilbert 1854. Rptd as Joan of Arc, ballads, lyrics and minor poems, New York 1857, [1870?] London 1881; rptd as Minor poems, ballads and Joan of Arc, 1858.
Poetical works, with a memoir of the author [by H. T. Tuckerman]. 10 vols Boston 1860, 1864, 5 vols [1884].
Selections from the poems. Ed S. R. Thompson 1888.
Poems, chosen and arranged by E. Dowden. 1895.
Poems, containing Thalaba, The curse of Kehama, Roderick, Madoc, A tale of Paraguay and selected minor poems. Ed M. H. Fitzgerald 1909.
Select prose. Ed J. Zeitlin, New York 1916.

§ 1

The fall of Robespierre: an historic drama. Cambridge 1794. Coleridge wrote Act 1, Southey Acts 2 and 3.
Poems: containing The retrospect, odes, elegies, sonnets etc by Robert Lovell and Southey. Bath 1795.
Joan of Arc: an epic poem. Bristol 1796, 2 vols Bristol 1798 (rev), 1 vol Boston 1798, 2 vols 1806 (rev), 1812 (rev), 1817, 1 vol 1853.
Poems. Bristol 1797 (for 1796), 1797 (rev), Boston 1799; vol 2, Bristol 1799; 2 vols 1800, 1801, 1806–8.
Letters written during a short residence in Spain and Portugal, with some account of Spanish and Portugueze poetry. Bristol 1797, 1799, 2 vols 1808 (enlarged as Letters written during a journey in Spain, and a short residence in Portugal).
On the French revolution, by Mr Necker, translated from the French. 2 vols 1797. Vol 2 by Southey.
The annual anthology. 2 vols Bristol 1799–1800. Anon, ed and partly written by Southey.
Thalaba the destroyer. 2 vols 1801, 1809, Boston 1812, London 1814, 1821, 1 vol 1846, 1853, 1856, 1860; tr German, 1837 (in part).

Amadis of Gaul, by Vasco Lobeira. 4 vols 1803, 3 vols 1872. Tr Southey.
The works of Thomas Chatterton. 3 vols 1803. Ed J. Cottle and Southey.
Madoc: a poem, in two parts. 1805, 2 vols Boston 1806, London 1807, 1812, 1815, 1825, 1 vol 1853.
Metrical tales and other poems. 1805, Boston 1811. Poems rptd from Annual Anthology 1799–1800.
Letters from England, by Don Manuel Alvarez Espriella, translated from the Spanish. 3 vols 1807 (anon), 2 vols Boston 1807 (anon), 3 vols 1808 (anon), 2 vols New York 1808 (anon), 3 vols 1814, 2 vols Philadelphia 1818, New York 1836; ed J. Simmons 1951; tr French, 1817; German, 1818.
Palmerin of England, by Francisco de Moraes. 4 vols 1807. Tr A. Munday 1581 from the French version, extensively corrected by Southey from the original.
Specimens of the later English poets, with preliminary notices, by Southey [and G. C. Bedford]. 3 vols 1807.
The remains of Henry Kirke White: with an account of his life. 2 vols 1807, 1811 (5th edn 'corrected'), Philadelphia 1811, London 1813, New York 1815, London 1816, 1819, 1821; vol 3, 1822. The contents of vol 3 were included in the 10th and later edns, 2 vols 1823, 1 vol 1825 etc.
Chronicle of the Cid, from the Spanish. 1808, 1846, Lowell Mass 1846, London 1868, 1883; ed R. Markham, New York 1883; ed V. S. Pritchett, New York 1958.
The geographical, natural and civil history of Chili, translated from the original Italian of the Abbé Don J. Ignatius Molina. Middletown Conn 1808, London 1809. The 2nd edn annotated by Southey.
Memoria sobre a litteratura portugueza, traduzida do inglez. [Hamburg 1809]. Tr from Quart Rev 1 1809.
The curse of Kehama. 1810, 2 vols New York 1811, London 1812, 1818, 1 vol 1853; ed H. Morley 1886.
History of Brazil. Pt 1 1810, 1822; pt 2 1817; pt 3 1819; tr Portuguese, 1862, 1948–54.
The history of Europe [in Edinburgh Annual Register for 1808–11]. Vols 1–4 Edinburgh 1810–13. Anon.
Omniana: or horae otiosores. 2 vols 1812. Anon; 45 contributions by Coleridge, 201 by Southey.
The origin, nature and object of the new system of education. 1812. Anon.
An exposure of the misrepresentations and calumnies in Mr Marsh's review of Sir George Barlow's administration at Madras, by the relations of Sir George Barlow. 1813. Anon.
The life of Nelson. 2 vols 1813, New York 1813, London 1814 (rev), 1825, 1 vol 1830 (rev) etc (at least 30 edns by 1900); ed A. D. Power 1903; ed H. B. Butler, Oxford 1911; ed G. A. R. Callender 1922; ed H. Newbolt 1925; ed E. R. H. Harvey 1953; ed K. Fenwick 1956; ed C. Oman 1962 (EL).
Roderick: the last of the Goths. 1814, 2 vols 1815, 1815, 1 vol Philadelphia 1815, 2 vols 1816, 1818, 1826, 1 vol 1891; tr French, 1820, 1821; Dutch, 1823–4.
Odes to His Royal Highness the Prince Regent, His Imperial Majesty the Emperor of Russia and His Majesty the King of Prussia. 1814.
Carmen triumphale, for the commencement of the year 1814. Rptd with the Odes, above, 1821.
A summary of the life of Arthur Duke of Wellington, from the period of his first achievements in India to his invasion of France and the decisive battle of Waterloo. Dublin 1816. Anon; rptd from Quart Rev 13 1815. Copy in Nat Lib of Ireland.
The poet's pilgrimage to Waterloo. 1816 (12 large paper copies also issued), 1816, New York 1816, Boston 1816.
The lay of the laureate: carmen nuptiale. 1816. On the marriage of the Princess Charlotte.
Wat Tyler: a dramatic poem. 1817 (many pirated edns), Newcastle [1820?], London [1820?], [1825?], Newcastle [1830?], London [1835?], Boston 1850.

A letter to William Smith esq MP. 1817 (4 edns). On the Wat Tyler controversy.

The byrth, lyf and actes of King Arthur, with an introduction and notes. 2 vols 1817.

The life of Wesley, and the rise and progress of Methodism. 2 vols 1820, 1820, New York 1820; ed C. C. Southey 1846 (embodying notes by Coleridge and Remarks on Wesley by A. Knox), New York 1847, London 1858, 1 vol 1864; ed J. A. Atkinson 1889; ed M. H. Fitzgerald 2 vols Oxford 1925; abridged by A. Reynolds 1903; tr German, 1828.

A vision of judgement. 1821, 1822 (as The two visions: or Byron v. Southey: containing The vision of Judgement by Dr Southey LL D; also another Vision of judgement, by Lord Byron), New York 1823 (with Byron's travesty), London 1824 (with Byron). Both poems ed E. M. Earl 1929; ed R. E. Roberts, Harrow Weald 1932.

The expedition of Orsua and the crimes of Aguirre. 1821, Philadelphia 1821. Rptd slightly rev from Edinburgh Annual Register vol 3 pt 2.

Life of John Duke of Marlborough. 1822. Anon; abridged from Quart Rev 23 1820.

History of the Peninsular War. Vol 1 1823, vol 2 1827, vol 3 1832; rptd 6 vols, vols 1–4 1828, vols 5–6 1837.

The book of the church. 2 vols 1824, 1824, 1825, Boston 1825, 1 vol 1837, 1841, 1848, 1859, 1869 (with notes from Vindiciae ecclesiae anglicanae, below), [1885].

A tale of Paraguay. 1825, Boston 1827, London 1828.

Vindiciae ecclesiae anglicanae: letters to Charles Butler esq, comprising Essays on the Romish religion and vindicating the Book of the church. 1826.

All for love; and The pilgrim to Compostella. 1829, Paris 1829.

Sir Thomas More: or colloquies on the progress and prospects of society. 2 vols 1829, 1831, 1 vol 1887.

The pilgrim's progress: with a life of John Bunyan. 1830, Boston 1832, New York 1837, London 1839, 1844, New York 1846, London 1847, 1881.

The devil's walk: a poem by Professor Porson. 1830, 1830, 1830 (as by Coleridge and Southey), 1830. By Coleridge and Southey. Originally ptd as The devil's thoughts, Morning Post 6 Sept 1799, and expanded by Southey alone in 1827.

Select works of the British poets, from Chaucer to Jonson, with biographical sketches. 1831.

Attempts in verse by John Jones, an old servant, with some account of the writer, written by himself, and an introductory essay on the lives and works of our uneducated poets by Robert Southey. 1831, 1836 (as Lives of uneducated poets); [Southey's essay] ed J. S. Childers, Oxford 1925 (as The lives and works of the uneducated poets).

Essays, moral and political, now first collected. 2 vols 1832.

Lives of the British admirals, with an introductory view of the naval history of England. Vol 1 1833, Philadelphia 1835 (as The early naval history of England), London 1839; vol 2 1833; vol 3 1834, 1848; vol 4 1837; vol 5 1840 (continued by R. Bell); ed D. Hannay 1895 (as English seamen), 1904.

Letter to John Murray esq 'touching' Lord Nugent, in reply to a letter from his Lordship, touching an article in the Quarterly Review, by the author of that article. 1833. Anon.

The doctor. Vols 1–2 1834, 1835; vol 3 1834; vol 4 1837; vol 5 1838 (all anon); vols 6–7 ed J. W. Warter 1847. Vols 1–3 rptd in 2 vols New York 1836, 1860; vols 1–7 ed J. W. Warter 1 vol 1848, 1849, 1853, 1856, New York 1856, London 1862, 1864, 1865, New York 1872; abridged by R. B. Johnson [1898]; by M. H. Fitzgerald 1930.

Horae lyricae: poems by Isaac Watts, with a memoir of the author. 1834, 1837, Boston 1854.

The works of William Cowper, with a life of the author. 15 vols 1835–7, 8 vols 1853–5. Life of Cowper rptd Boston 1858.

The life of the Rev Andrew Bell, comprising the history of the rise and progress of the system of mutual tuition. 3 vols 1844. Southey wrote vol 1, C. C. Southey vols 2–3.

Select biographies: Cromwell and Bunyan. 1844. Cromwell rptd from Quart Rev 25 1821, Bunyan from Pilgrim's progress, 1830. Cromwell rptd New York 1854, 1868.

Oliver Newman: a New-England tale (unfinished): with other poetical remains. [Ed H. Hill] 1845.

Robin Hood: a fragment by the late Robert Southey and Caroline Southey, with other fragments and poems. Edinburgh 1847.

Southey's common place book. Ed J. W. Warter 4 sers 1849–50. Ser 1, Choice passages, 1849, 1850; ser 2, Special collections, 1849, 1850; ser 3, Analytical readings, 1850; ser 4, Original memoranda, 1850. Sers 1–2, New York 1849–50, 1860; sers 1–4, 4 vols 1876.

Review of Churchill's poems by the late Mr Southey. [1852] (priv ptd). Rptd from Annual Rev 1804, rptd in Poetical works of Charles Churchill, ed W. Tooke, Boston 1854.

Journal of a tour in the Netherlands in the autumn of 1815. 1902, Boston 1902; ed W. R. Nicoll 1903; tr Dutch, 1946.

Journal of a tour in Scotland in 1819. Ed C. H. Herford 1929.

Journals of a residence in Portugal 1800–1, and a visit to France 1838. Ed A. Cabral, Oxford 1960.

Letters

Robberds, J. W. In his Memoir of the life and writings of the late William Taylor, 2 vols 1843.

Southey, C. C. The life and correspondence of the late Robert Southey. 6 vols 1849–50, 1 vol New York [1850], 1851, 1855.

Selections from the letters of Southey. Ed J. W. Warter 4 vols 1856.

Forster, J. In his Walter Savage Landor: a biography, 2 vols 1869.

The correspondence of Southey with Caroline Bowles: to which are added correspondence with Shelley, and Southey's dreams. Ed E. Dowden, Dublin 1881.

Memorials of Coleorton: being letters from Coleridge, Wordsworth and his sister, Southey and Sir Walter Scott, to Sir George and Lady Beaumont 1803–34. Ed W. Knight 2 vols Edinburgh 1887.

Southey: the story of his life written in his letters. Ed J. Dennis, Boston 1887, London 1894.

Letters from the Lake Poets to Daniel Stuart, editor of the Morning Post and the Courier 1800–38. 1889 (priv ptd). Compiled by M. Stuart, ed E. H. Coleridge. Southey's letters pp. 387–434; poems contributed to Morning Post by Southey pp. 437–48.

Williams, O. Lamb's friend the census-taker: life and letters of John Rickman. 1911.

Letters of Southey: a selection. Ed M. H. Fitzgerald, Oxford 1912 (WC).

New letters of Southey. Ed K. Curry 2 vols New York 1965.

For fuller list see K. Curry, The published letters of Southey: a checklist, BNYPL March 1967; *also*

Conder, E. R. Josiah Conder: a memoir. 1857.

Martin, C. G. Southey: two unpublished letters [to Tom Southey]. N & Q Aug 1967.

Southey contributed to the Flagellent 1795 (*no 5 contains his attack on flogging*), Monthly Mag 1796–1800, Morning Post 1798–9 (poems), Critical Rev 1798–1803, Annual Rev 1802–8, Athenaeum 1807–9, Quart Rev 1809–39, Foreign Rev 1828–30. *For contributions to annuals see* Literary Souvenir 1826–8, Amulet 1829, Anniversary 1829, Keepsake 1829.

§2

[Jeffrey, F.] Southey's Thalaba. Edinburgh Rev 1 1802; rptd (in part) in Famous reviews, ed R. B. Johnson 1914.
Coleridge, S. T. In his Biographia literaria, 2 vols 1817.
The changeling: a poem in two cantos addressed to a Laureat 1817. On pbn of Wat Tyler.
Hazlitt, W. In his Political essays with sketches of public characters, 1819.
— In his Spirit of the age, 1825.
Watson, R. Observations on Southey's Life of Wesley. 1820.
Byron, G. G. The vision of judgment. Liberal 1 1822.
— In his Letters and journals, ed R. E. Prothero 6 vols 1898–1901.
Tilbrook, S. Historical and critical remarks upon the modern hexametrists, and upon Mr Southey's Vision of judgement. 1822.
Landor, W. S. Southey and Porson. In his Imaginary conversations vol 1, 1824; The works of W. S. Landor, 2 vols 1846 (Southey and Porson, Southey and Landor).
— To the Rev C. Cuthbert Southey [on his father's character and public services]. Fraser's Mag Dec 1850; rptd in Works, ed T. E. Welby vol 12, 1931.
Benbow, W. A scourge for the Laureate, in reply to his infamous letter abusive of Lord Byron. [1825?].
Macaulay, T. B. Southey's Colloquies. Edinburgh Rev 50 1830; rptd in Critical and historical essays vol i, 1843.
Cottle, J. In his Early recollections, 2 vols 1837, 1 vol 1847 (rev as Reminiscences of Coleridge and Southey).
Lockhart, J. G. In his Life of Sir Walter Scott, 7 vols Edinburgh 1837–8.
De Quincey, T. In his Lake reminiscences from 1807 to 1830, no 4: Wordsworth and Southey. Tait's Mag 6 1839; rptd in De Quincey's Works, ed D. Masson, vol 2 Edinburgh 1889; and in Reminiscences of the English Lake poets, ed J. E. Jordan 1961 (EL).
Catalogue of the valuable library of the late Robert Southey esq. [1844].
Thackeray, W. M. In his Four Georges, 1861. *See* under George III.
Jerdan, W. In his Men I have known, 1866.
Robinson, H. C. In his Diary, reminiscences and correspondence, ed T. Sadler 3 vols 1869, 2 vols Boston 1869, London 1872.
— In his Correspondence with the Wordsworth circle, ed E. J. Morley 2 vols Oxford 1927.
— In his On books and their writers, ed E. J. Morley 3 vols 1938.
Dowden, E. Southey. 1874 (EML).
— The early revolutionary group. In his French Revolution and English literature, 1895.
Dennis, J. In his Studies in English literature, 1876.
Carlyle, T. In his Reminiscences vol 2, 1881.
Taylor, H. In his Autobiography vol 1, 1885. Ch 17.
Smiles, S. In his A publisher and his friends: memoir of the late John Murray, with an account of the origin and progress of the house 1768–1843, 2 vols 1891.
Scott, W. In his Familiar letters, ed D. Douglas 2 vols Edinburgh 1894.
Saintsbury, G. In his Essays in English literature ser 2, 1895. Essay on Southey rptd in his Collected essays and papers vol 1, 1923.
Stephen, L. Southey's letters. In his Studies of a biographer vol 4, 1902.
Grannis, R. S. An American friend of Southey (Maria Gowen Brooks). 1913.
Pfandl, L. Southey und Spanien. Revue Hispanique 28 1913.
Lounsbury, T. R. Southey as poet and historian. Yale Rev new ser 4 1915.
Haller, W. The early life of Southey 1774–1803. New York 1917.
— Southey's later radicalism. PMLA 37 1922.
Beer, M. In his History of British Socialism vol 1, 1919.
Broadus, E. K. The Laureateship: a study of the office of poet laureate in England. Oxford 1921.
Buceta, E. Una traducción de Lope de Vega hecha por Southey. Romanic Rev 13 1922. On The Madonna's lullaby.
Graham, R. Southey as Tory reviewer. PQ 2 1923.
Kaufman, P. The reading of Southey and Coleridge: the record of their borrowings from the Bristol Library 1793–8. MP 21 1924. *See* G. Whalley, below.
Brinton, C. In his Political ideas of the English romanticists, 1926. Ch 2.
Jakovlev, N. V. In S. Lowré et al, Pushkin v mirowi literature, Leningrad 1926.
Walter, F. In his La littérature portugaise en Angleterre à l'époque romantique, Paris 1927. Ch 3.
Fairchild, H. N. In his Noble savage, New York 1928. Ch 6.
Knowlton, E. C. Southey's eclogues. PQ 7 1928.
— Southey's monodramas. PQ 8 1929.
Cobban, A. In his Edmund Burke and the revolt against the eighteenth century: a study of the political and social thinking of Burke, Wordsworth, Coleridge and Southey, 1929.
Richter, H. Robert Southey. Anglia 53 1929.
Griggs, E. L. Southey and the Edinburgh Review. MP 30 1932.
— Southey's estimate of Coleridge. HLQ 9 1945.
Marcus, H. Unterdrückte Revolutionsverse des jungen Southey. Archiv 161 1932.
Wright, H. G. Southey's relations with Finland and Scandinavia. MLR 27 1932.
— Three aspects of Southey. RES 9 1933.
Peardon, T. P. In his Transition in English historical writing 1760–1830, New York 1933.
Ehrich, E. Southey und Landor. Göttingen 1934.
Weber, C. A. In his Bristols Bedeutung für die englische Romantik, Halle 1935.
Fletcher, I. K. Southey and Miss Seton. TLS 20 Nov, 4 Dec 1937.
Curry, K. Uncollected translations of Michaelangelo by Wordsworth and Southey. RES 14 1938.
— Southey's Madoc: the manuscript of 1794. PQ 22 1943.
— Southey's visit to Caroline Wordsworth Baudouin. PMLA 59 1944.
— The library of Southey. In Studies in honor of J. C. Hodges and A. Thaler, Knoxville 1961.
Feiling, K. Southey and Wordsworth. In his Sketches in nineteenth-century biography, 1930.
Fitzgerald, M. H. Southey's History of Portugal. TLS 30 Oct 1937, 24 April, 8–15 May 1943.
— The dedication of Southey's The doctor. TLS 1 Aug 1952.
Brown, W. C. Southey and the English interest in the Near East. ELH 5 1938.
Hoadley, F. T. The controversy over Southey's Wat Tyler. SP 38 1941.
Cameron, K. N. Shelley vs Southey: new light on an old quarrel. PMLA 57 1942.
Jarrett-Kerr, M. Southey's Colloquies. Nineteenth Century Oct 1942.
Elwin, M. Southey. Quart Rev 281 1943.
— In his First romantics, 1947.
Howe, H. W. Greta Hall. 1943.
Jeffery, S. Southey and Gilbert. TLS 20 March 1943.
Southey: a problem of romanticism—poet who lost his way. TLS 20 March 1943. *See* M. Elwin 27 March, 1943.
Sousa-Leão, J. de. Southey and Brazil. MLR 38 1943.
— Robert Southey. Revista do Instituto Histórico e Geográfico Brasileiro 178 1943.
Shand, J. Robert Southey. Nineteenth Century March 1943.
Davis, S. Centenary appreciation of Southey's Life of Wesley. London Quart 168 1943.

Baughman, R. Southey the schoolboy. HLQ 7 1944.
Havens, R. D. Southey's Specimens of the later English poets. PMLA 60 1945.
— Southey's revision of his Life of Wesley. RES 22 1946.
Simmons, J. Southey. 1945.
The industrious poet: in Southey's workshop. TLS 21 April 1945.
Schilling, B. N. In his Human dignity and the great Victorians, New York 1946.
Macaulay, R. A romantic among the Philistines. In her They went to Portugal, 1946; expanded from Orion: a Miscellany 1 1945.
Shamburger, M. I. and V. R. Lachmann. Southey and The three bears. Jnl Amer Folklore 59 1946.
Wilson, J. L. Washington Irving's 'celebrated English poet'. Amer Lit 18 1946.
Whalley, G. The Bristol Library borrowings of Southey and Coleridge 1793–8. Library 5th ser 4 1949.
— Coleridge and Southey in Bristol 1795. RES new ser 1 1950.
— Coleridge, Southey and Joan of Arc. N & Q Feb 1954.
Dowden, W. S. The source of the metempsychosis motif in Southey's Thalaba. MLN 66 1951.
The three bears. TLS 23 Nov 1951.
Zall, P. M. Lord Eldon's censorship. PMLA 68 1953. On Wat Tyler.
Kaderly, N. L. Southey's borrowings from Celia Fiennes. MLN 69 1954.
— Southey and the Quarterly Review. MLN 70 1955.
Cline, C. L. Byron and Southey: a suppressed rejoinder. Keats-Shelley Jnl 3 1954.
Hopkins, K. In his Poets laureate, 1954.
Carnall, G. D. Southey and Quakerism. Friends Quart 9 1955.
— Southey and his age: the development of a conservative mind. Oxford 1960.
— Robert Southey. 1964 (Br Council pamphlet). With bibliography.
McElderry, B. R. Southey and Wordsworth's The idiot boy. N & Q Nov 1955. *See* G. D. Carnall, Feb 1956.
King, R. W. A note on Shelley, Gibbon, Voltaire and Southey. MLR 51 1956.
Riewald, J. G. Laureates in Elysium: Sir William Davenant and Southey. E Studies 37 1956.
Metzdorf, R. F. Southey manuscripts at Yale. Yale Univ Lib Gazette 30 1956.
Selig, K. L. Sabuco de Nantes, Feijóo and Southey. MLN 71 1956.
Ober, W. U. Southey, Coleridge and Kubla Khan. JEGP 58 1959.
Cabral, A. Southey e Portugal 1774–1801. Lisbon 1959.
Patterson, C. I. The Keats-Hazlitt-Hunt copy of Palmerin of England in relation to Keat's poetry. JEGP 60 1961.
Kryński, S. Angielscy 'poeci jezior'. Wrocław 1963. Polish trn and comment on Wordsworth, Coleridge, Southey.
Beyer, W. W. Southey, orientalism and Thalaba. In his Enchanted forest, Oxford 1963.
Gordan, J. D. New in the Berg Collection 1959–61. BNYPL Dec 1963. Brief account of Southey mss.

G. D. C.

THOMAS CAMPBELL
1777–1844

Bibliographies

Jordan, H. H. In English romantic poets and essayists: a review of research and criticism, ed C. W. and L. H. Houtchens, New York 1957, 1966 (rev).

Collections

Poetical works; biographical sketch by 'a gentleman of New York' (Washington Irving). 2 vols Albany, 1 vol Baltimore 1810, Philadelphia 1815, Paris 1822; 'including Theodric' etc, New York 1825, Philadelphia 1827, 1835, 1847; 2 vols 1828, 1830, 1832, 1833; with Works of Rogers etc, Paris 1829, [1840], Philadelphia 1836, London 1836, 1837, 1839, 1840, 1849, Edinburgh etc 1837; illustr W. Harvey 1840, 1846; illustr J. M. W. Turner 1843; ed W. A. Hill, illustr J. M. W. Turner 1851, 1854; ed W. A. Hill, Boston 1851, 1854, 1856, 1860, 1866, 1874; with Poetical works of Falconer, 1882, nd; illustr W. Harvey, Hartford 1852; with G. Gilfillan's Literary portrait, New York 1852; with Poetical works of Goldsmith and Beattie, 1853, 1858 (with Goldsmith only); Boston 1854, 1858, 1860; with Poetical works of Coleridge, Edinburgh [1859]; illustr J. Gilbert, New York 1862, nd; introd by W. E. Aytoun, Boston 1864; introd by C. Rogers [1870]; introd by W. H. Rossetti, illustr T. Seccombe [1871, 1880], poems only [1878]; Chandos edn [1874] etc; Aldine edn, introd by W. Allingham 1875, 1900; Edinburgh [1880], London 1887; ed J. L. Robertson, Oxford 1907.
The pleasure of hope, Gertrude of Wyoming and other poems. 1852, 1892; Poetical works, ed J. Hogben 1885; Selections, ed W. T. Webb 1902; Poems, ed L. Campbell 1904.

§1

The wounded hussar. Glasgow 1799, Stirling [1800], Newcastle nd, Birmingham nd, London nd. A chapbook.
The pleasures of hope, with other poems. Edinburgh 1799, Glasgow 1800 (4th edn 'corrected and enlarged'), Edinburgh 1801, 1802, 1804 (7th edn), London 1803 (also designated 7th edn 'corrected and enlarged'), Edinburgh 1805 (8th edn), 1806, 1807 (both called 9th edn), New York 1800, 1800, Wilmington 1800 ('third American' edn), New York 1804, Paris 1805 (with Rogers' Pleasures of memory), Cambridge Mass 1807, Edinburgh 1808, 1810, 1811, 1813, Boston 1811, Belfast 1815, London 1815; illustr R. Westall 1820, 1821, 1822, 1825, 1826, Providence 1828, Belfast 1830; Paris 1824, 1825 (with trn by Albert Montémont); illustr B. Foster et al 1855, 1861, [1875]; [1869], 1871, Boston 1877, Dublin 1882, Berlin 1882; tr German, 1838.
Poems. Edinburgh 1803. Contains Lochiel's warning, Hohenlinden.
Gertrude of Wyoming: a Pennsylvanian tale, and other poems. 1809, 1810, 1810, 1812, 1814, 1816, 1819, 1821, 1825, New York 1809; with W. L. Stone's History of Wyoming, New York 1841, 1844, 1864; New York 1856, London 1857; ed H. M. Fitzgibbon, Oxford 1889, 1891; Baden-Baden 1882 (with German trn).
Specimens of the British poets, with biographical and critical notes, and An essay on English poetry. 7 vols 1819; ed P. Cunningham 1841, 1845, 1848 (notices and An essay only); An essay, Boston 1819.
Miscellaneous poems. 1824.
Theodric: a domestic tale, and other poems. 1824, 1824, Philadelphia 1825, Paris 1825.
Inaugural discourse on being installed Lord Rector of the University of Glasgow. Glasgow 1827. Rptd in Inaugural addresses of Lord Rectors of the University of Glasgow, ed J. B. Hay 1839, 1848, which contains also Campbell's Address of 21 May 1827 and his second Inaugural address, 1828.
Poland: a poem; Lines on the view from St Leonard's. 1831, 1831.
Adresse de la société littéraire polonaise de Londres au peuple de la Grande Bretagne. Paris 1832.

The life of Mrs Siddons. 2 vols 1834, 1 vol New York 1834, London 1839.

Letters from the south. 2 vols 1837, 1842 (as The journal of a residence in Algiers).

The dramatic works of William Shakespeare, with remarks on his life and writings by T. Campbell. 1838, 1843, 1848, 1859, 1866; tr French, 1855.

The life of Petrarch. 2 vols London 1841, 1843. Abridged in The sonnets, Triumphs and other poems of Petrarch, 1859, 1875 (Bohn).

The pilgrim of Glencoe, and other poems. 1842.

Periodicals edited by Campbell

The new monthly magazine. 1821–30.

The metropolitan: a monthly journal. 1831–2.

The scenic annual for 1838.

Works of Doubtful Authenticity

Annals of Great Britain from the ascension of George III to the peace of Amiens. 3 vols Edinburgh 1807.

Frederick the Great, his Court and times, edited with an introduction by Thomas Campbell. 4 vols 1842–3, 2 vols 1844.

History of our own times, by the author of the Court and times of Frederick the Great. 2 vols 1843–5.

§2

Jeffrey, F. Edinburgh Rev 14 1809. On Gertrude of Wyoming.

Bowles, W. L. Letters to Mr T. Campbell as far as regards poetical criticism. Pamphleteer 20 1822.

Hazlitt, W. In his Spirit of the age, 1825.

Gilfillan, G. In his First gallery of literary portraits, Edinburgh 1845.

Beattie, W. Life and letters of Campbell. 3 vols 1849, 1850.

Redding, C. Literary reminiscences and memoirs of Campbell. 2 vols 1860.

Madden, R. R. Literary remains of the United Irishmen of 1798, with An essay on the authorship of The exile of Erin. Dublin 1887.

Hadden, J. C. Thomas Campbell. Edinburgh [1899].

Floryan, J. Polish Rev 1 1917. On Campbell and Poland.

Bierstadt, A. M. Gertrude of Wyoming. JEPG 20 1921; Unacknowledged poems by Campbell, MLN 37 1922.

Shumway, D. B. Campbell and Germany. In F. E. Schelling anniversary papers, New York 1923.

Seton, W. Three letters of Campbell. Nineteenth Century Jan 1925.

Dixon, W. M. Campbell: an oration. Glasgow 1928; rptd in his Apology for the arts, 1944.

Duffy, C. 'Hymen's Ball', an unpublished poem by Campbell. N & Q 29 June 1940.

— Campbell's marriage. N & Q 8 Feb 1941. *See* J. Seton-Anderson, 1 March 1941.

— Campbell and America. Amer Lit 13 1942.

— Pelham's widow: a novel by Campbell. N & Q 30 Jan 1943.

— An epigraph by Campbell. N & Q Jan 1959.

Duffy, C. and J. Glennen. Campbell: two letters. N & Q 23 July 1949.

J. R. M

THOMAS MOORE
1779–1852
Bibliographies

Power, J. A catalogue of vocal music by Moore and Sir John Stevenson. 1814, 1815.

Muir, P. H. Moore's Irish melodies 1808–34. Colophon 15 1933.

MacManus, M. J. A bibliographical hand-list of the first editions of Moore. Dublin 1934.

Jordan, H. H. In English romantic poets and essayists: a review of research, ed C. W. and L. H. Houtchens, New York 1957, 1966 (rev).

Collections

Works. 6 vols Paris 1819, 1827, 7 vols 1820, 1823, 1827, 4 vols 1821, 6 vols New York 1825, 1 vol Leipzig 1826, 1833, 1840, Paris 1827, 1829, nd; 2 vols Philadelphia 1829 ('fifth edn'), Paris 1835, 1 vol Philadelphia 1836, 1839, 1845; The poetical works, collected by himself, 10 vols 1840–1, 1853, 1 vol Paris 1841, 1842 ('collected and arranged by himself'), 3 vols 1841 ('collected by the author'), 5 vols Leipzig 1842, 1 vol 1844, 1845, 1850, 1853, 1855, 1860, 1865, New York 1850, 1867, Boston and New York 1854, 1856; ed F. J. Child 6 vols Boston 1856, 1871, [1880]; 1 vol Philadelphia 1856, 1858, London 1859, 1863 [1881], Edinburgh [1859], 1863, [1870], 1874, [1881]; ed W. M. Rossetti, illustr T. Seccombe, [1870], [1872], [1880], [1881]; Glasgow [1870]; memoir by D. Herbert, Edinburgh 1872, 1887, Boston 1872; London 1883 and at least 8 more edns nd before 1900, New York 1884, 1887; memoir by N. A. Dole 2 vols [1895]; ed A. D. Godley, Oxford 1910; ed W. M. Rossetti, 1911; tr German, 1843.

[Extensive selections]. Melodies, songs, sacred songs and national airs. New York 1819, 1821; Selected poetical works, Paris 1847; Songs, ballads and sacred songs, 1849; Melodies, national airs, miscellaneous poems, Boston 1857; 130 of Moore's songs and Irish melodies, [1859]; Irish melodies, Lalla Rookh, National airs etc, [1867]; Prose and verse, humorous, satirical and sentimental, ed R. H. Shepherd 1878; Poetical works, ed J. Dorrian 1888; ed J. R. Tutin [1892]; ed C. L. Falkiner 1903; Lyrics and satires, ed S. O'Faolain, Dublin 1929; tr French, 1820 (with Byron and Scott), 1829, 1841; Italian, 1836 (2nd edn), 1870.

§1

Odes of Anacreon, translated into English verse, with notes. 1800, 2 vols 1802, 1803, 1804, 1805, 1806, 1810, 1815, 1820 (10th edn), 1 vol Dublin 1803, Philadelphia 1804, London 1826, Paris 1835 (with Greek), London [1871].

The poetical works of the late Thomas Little esq. 1801, 1802, 1803, 1804, 1804, 1805, 1806 (8th edn), 1808, 1810, 1812, 1814, 1819 (14th edn), 1822, 1833 (16th edn), Dublin 1804, 1810, 1817, New York 1804, Philadelphia 1804, London 1825, 1828, 1838.

Moore sometimes composed or adapted music for his own lyrical poems. Some early examples are: O lady fair! a ballad for three voices, 1802, 1802, [1804]; When time who steals our years away: a ballad, 1802; Good night, a ballad, 1803; Songs and glees, 1805; A Canadian boat song, arranged for three voices, 1805. *He also collaborated with Michael Kelly to compose* The gypsy prince: a comic opera in thee acts, 1801, *of which little more than the music survives.*

Epistles, odes and other poems. 1806, 2 vols 1807, 1810, 1814, 1817, 1822, 1 vol Philadelphia 1806 (2nd edn).

The works of Sallust, translated into English by the late Arthur Murphy. 1807. With life of Sallust by Moore.

Corruption and Intolerance: two poems with notes, addressed to an Englishman by an Irishman. 1801, 1809.

A selection of Irish melodies, with symphonies and accompaniments by Sir John Stevenson and characteristic words by Moore. 10 pts and suppl 1808 (pts 1–2), 1810, 1811, 1813, 1815, 1818, 1821, 1824, 1834 (pt 10 and suppl). Stevenson was the composer for the first seven parts only, to 1818. For further details *see* P. H.

Muir, Colophon 15 1933. The Irish melodies were not authorized for pbn without musical accompaniment until 1821; *see* below.

The sceptic: a philosophical satire, by the author of Corruption and Intolerance. 1809.

A melologue upon national music. London and Dublin [1810].

A letter to the Roman Catholics of Dublin. 1810, Dublin 1810 (2nd edn).

MP, or the blue-stocking: a comic opera in three acts, by Anacreon Moore. 1811, New York 1812.

Spirit of Boccaccio's Decameron, translated, selected, connected and versified, from the Italian. 1812. Perhaps by Moore.

Intercepted letters: or the two penny post bag, by Thomas Brown the younger. 1813 (at least 11 edns), 1814, 1818 (16th edn), Philadelphia 1813.

Lines on the death of —— [R. B. Sheridan] from the Morning Chronicle of August 5 1816. 1816.

Sacred songs. No 1, 1816; no 2, 1824.

Lalla Rookh: an oriental romance. 1817 (6 edns), 1818 (at least 3 edns), 1826 (13th edn), 1829 (15th edn), 1832, 1838, 1842 (20th edn), Philadelphia 1817, 1826, 1839, 1856, New York 1817, 1818, 1824, 1834, 1844, 1849, 1851, 1860, 1868, [1874], [1884], [1888], 1890, [1891], [1904], Boston 1828, 1885, 1887, [1892], 1899, Paris 1835, London 1823; illustr R. Westall 1840, 1842, 1844; illustr by eminent artists 1846, 1851, 1853, 1856; 1850, 1854, 1859, 1859, 1860, 1884, 1891, 1912, Dublin 1861, nd; illustr J. Tenniel, 1861, New York 1867; Chicago [1900], New York and Toronto 1930; tr (complete, or separate stories) Italian, 1818, 1838, 1872, 1886, 1874; French, 1820 (2 versions), 1887, [1888]; German, 1823, 1825, [1846], 1852 (with music by R. Schumann), 1859, 1878, 1879, [1892, 1901]; [1877] (as an opera by J. Rodenberg), 1881; Polish, 1826 (prose), 1838–43, 1852; Swedish, 1829; Dutch, 1834; Spanish, 1836; Danish, 1878; Telugu, 1920.

The Fudge family in Paris, edited by Thomas Brown the younger. 1818 (at least 9 edns), New York 1818, Philadelphia 1818.

National airs. 6 nos 1818–27.

Tom Crib's memorial to congress, with preface, notes and appendix, by one of the fancy. 1819 (4 edns), New York 1819.

Irish melodies, and A melologue upon national music. Dublin 1820 (unauthorized edn, without music).

Irish melodies, with an appendix containing the original advertisements and the prefatory letter on music. 1821 (first authorized edn of words only), 1822 (at least 3 edns), 1825 (6th edn), 1827 (8th edn), 1832 (10th), 1824 (with National airs), 1846 (with other poems), 1849; illustr D. Maclise 1853, [1858], 1866; 1854, 1856, 1859, [1874], 1887, 1904, 1908, 1912, Dublin 1833 (with other poems), [1846], London 1859, 1862, [1879] (with National airs), Philadelphia 1821, 1850, 1866, 1873, Brussels 1822 (with National airs), Paris 1823, 1843, Pisa [1823] (with National airs), New York [1844], 1874; tr Swedish, 1825, 1858; Latin, 1835, 1856–9; Irish, 1842; French, 1869, 1879 (selection); German, [1874], 1884; Spanish, 1875 (2nd edn); Italian, 1880.

The loves of the angels: a poem. 1823 (4 edns), 1823 (5th edn) (as The loves of the angels: an eastern romance); rev text and notes to make 'machinery and allusions entirely Mahometan', 1824, 1826, Philadelphia 1823, Paris 1823, 1823, 1843, New York [1844]; tr French, 1823 (2 edns, one prose), 1830, 1837; Dutch, 1835; Swedish, 1843, 1864; Italian, 1873, 1882 (prose), 1886, 1898.

Fables for the holy alliance; Rhymes for the road, by Thomas Brown the younger. 1823.

Memoirs of Captain Rock, the celebrated Irish chieftain, with some account of his ancestors, written by himself. 1824 (at least 5 edns), Paris 1824; tr French, 1829.

Memoirs of the life of the Right Honourable Richard Brinsley Sheridan. 1825, 1825, 2 vols 1825, 1826, 1827 (new preface), 1 vol Philadelphia 1825, 2 vols Paris 1825, 1 vol 1835, Leipzig 1833, 2 vols New York 1853, 1858, 1958, Chicago and St Louis 1882; tr French, 1826.

Evenings in Greece: first [second] evening (with music). [1827], [1835], New York 1844; tr German, 1846.

The epicurean: a tale. 1827 (4 edns), 1828, 1864, Philadelphia 1827, Paris 1827, 1828, 1832, 1835, Boston 1831, New York and Boston 1841, New York 1844, 1862; illustr J. M. W. Turner, 1839 (with Alciphron); Chicago 1890, London 1899; tr French, 1827 (2 versions), [1861]; verse by T. Gauthier, illustr G. Doré 1865; German, 1828; Spanish, 1832; Danish, 1844; Italian, 1852 (adaptation by S. Torelli).

Odes upon cash, corn, Catholics and other matters, selected from the columns of the Times journal. 1828, Philadelphia 1828, Paris 1829.

Letters and journals of Lord Byron, with notices of his life. 2 vols 1830, 1831, 1833; tr French, 1830.

The life and death of Lord Edward Fitzgerald. 2 vols 1831, 1 vol Paris 1831, 1835; ed M. MacDermott 1897; abridged as The life and times etc, Dublin 1909 (Irish Lib).

The summer fete: a poem with songs [and music]. 1831, Paris 1832, 1833, Philadelphia 1833.

Travels of an Irish gentleman in search of a religion, with notes and illustrations by the editor of Captain Rock's memoirs. 2 vols 1833, 1 vol Paris 1833, Baltimore and Pittsburgh [186?]; tr French, 1833, 1834, 1835, 1836, 1841; German, 1834; Italian, 1850.

The Fudges in England: being a sequel to the Fudge family in Paris, by Thomas Brown the younger. 1835, 1835, Paris 1835, 1835.

The history of Ireland. 4 vols 1835–46 (in D. Lardner, The cabinet encyclopaedia), Paris 1835–46, 2 vols Philadelphia 1843–6; tr French, 1835 (2 versions), 1836; German, 1846.

Alciphron: a poem. Illustr J. M. W. Turner 1839, Paris 1840.

Letters, Diaries etc

Memoirs, journal and correspondence of Moore. Ed Lord John Russell 8 vols 1853–6; abridged by Russell 1860.

Notes from the letters of Moore to his music publisher, James Power (the publication of which were suppressed in London). Ed T. C. Croker, New York [1854].

'Thomas Moore' anecdotes: being anecdotes, bon-mots and epigrams from the journal. Ed W. Harrison 1899 (2nd edn).

Tom Moore's diary: a selection. Ed J. B. Priestley, Cambridge 1925.

Letters of Moore. Ed W. S. Dowden 2 vols Oxford 1964.

Journal 1818–41. Ed P. C. Quennell, New York 1964. Selection.

§2

Jeffrey, F. Edinburgh Rev 8 1806. Review of Epistles, odes and other poems, and the cause of Moore's duel with Jeffrey.

—— Edinburgh Rev 57 1817. On Lalla Rookh.

—— Edinburgh Rev 89 1826. On Memoirs of Sheridan.

Hazlitt, W. Yellow Dwarf 25 April 1818. On The Fudge family in Paris, rptd in his Complete works, ed P. P. Howe 1930–34, vol 7.

—— In his Spirit of the age, 1825.

—— On the jealousy and the spleen of party. In his Plain speaker, 1826.

Smith, S. Edinburgh Rev 81 1824. On Memoirs of Captain Rock.

Southey, R. Quart Rev 46 1831. On Life of Lord Edward Fitzgerald.

Gilfillan, G. In his A gallery of literary portraits, Edinburgh 1845.
Burke, J. A life of Moore. Dublin 1852.
Montgomery, H. R. Moore: his life, writings and contemporaries. 1860.
Vallat, G. Etude sur la vie et les oeuvres de Moore. Paris 1886.
Gunning, J. P. Moore: poet and patriot. Dublin 1900.
Gwynn, S. Thomas Moore. 1905 (EML).
Clark, J. C. L. Tom Moore in Bermuda: a bit of literary gossip. Lancaster Mass 1897, Boston 1909.
Stockmann, A. Moore: der irische Freiheitssänger. Freiburg 1910.
Thomas, A. B. Moore en France 1819–30. Paris 1911.
Stockley, W. F. P. Essays in Irish biography. Cork 1933. Includes Moore and Ireland, The religion of Thomas Moore.
Trench, W. F. Tom Moore: a lecture. Dublin 1934.
MacCall, S. Thomas Moore. 1935.
Jones, H. M. The harp that once: a chronicle of the life of Moore. New York 1937.
Strong, L. A. G. The minstrel boy: a portrait of Tom Moore. 1937.
Brown, W. C. Moore and English interest in the East. SP 34 1937.
Parker, W. M. Moore in Wiltshire. TLS 16 Oct 1937. *See* E. A. Sadler and W. Roberts 23 Oct 1937.
Brogan, H. O. Moore: Irish satirist and keeper of the English conscience. PQ 24 1945.
Schneider, E. Moore and the Edinburgh Review. MLN 61 1946.
— The unknown reviewer of Christabel: Jeffrey, Hazlitt, Tom Moore. PMLA 70 1955. Attributes review to Moore.
— Tom Moore and the Edinburgh Review of Christabel. PMLA 77 1962. *See* H. H. Jordan, W. S. Dowden and K. Coburn, below.
Wright, H. G. Moore as the author of Spirit of Boccaccio's Decameron. RES 23 1947.
Jordan, H. H. Byron and Moore. MLQ 9 1948.
— Moore and the review of Christabel. MP 54 1956. Against attribution to Moore.
— Moore: artistry in the song lyric. Stud in Eng Lit 1500–1900 2 1962.
Needler, G. H. Moore and his Canadian boat song. Toronto 1950.
Norman, S. Leigh Hunt, Moore and Byron. TLS 2 Jan 1953.
O Hehir, B. P. Moore's The song of Fionnuala. Explicator 15 1957.
Birley, R. R. Lalla Rookh. In his Sunk without trace: some forgotten masterpieces reconsidered, 1962 (Clark Lectures).
Dowden, W. S. Moore and the review of Christabel. MP 60 1962. Against attribution to Moore.
Coburn, K. Who killed Christabel? TLS 20 May 1965. Attributes review to Moore.

J. R. M.

JAMES HOGG
1770–1835

Hogg mss are scattered, but significant collections are available at the Nat Library of Scotland and at Yale Univ Library.

Bibliographies

Hogg, W. D. The first editions of the writings of Hogg. Pbns Edinburgh Bibl Soc 12 1924.
Batho, E. C. In her Ettrick shepherd, Cambridge 1927. Includes Hogg's contributions to periodicals etc, many unrptd.
— Notes on the bibliography of Hogg. Library 4th ser 16 1935.
Pierce, F. E. Hogg: the Ettrick shepherd. Yale Univ Lib Gazette 5 1931.
Simpson, L. In his Hogg: a critical study, 1962.

Collections

Poetical works. 4 vols Edinburgh 1822.
Tales and sketches. 6 vols Glasgow 1837, London 1852.
Poetical works. 5 vols Glasgow 1838–40, 1852.
Works. Ed T. Thomson 2 vols Glasgow 1865–6. Vol 2 contains Autobiography, originally the anon Memoir, in The mountain bard, 1869, 1872.
Tales. 2 vols Glasgow 1880, 1884; ed G. C. Pringle 1909.
Poems, selected by Mrs Garden. Glasgow 1886, 1887.
Selected poems. Ed W. Whyte. In Poets and poetry of the century, ed A. H. Miles 1891.
Selected poems. Ed J. C. Hadden, Glasgow 1893; ed W. Wallace 1903.
Works, letters and manuscripts. Ed R. B. Adam, Buffalo 1930 (priv ptd).
Selected poems. Ed J. W. Oliver, Edinburgh 1940.

§1

For early periodical pbns of collected pieces etc, see Batho, *above.*

Scottish pastorals, poems, songs etc. Edinburgh 1801.
The mountain bard: consisting of ballads and songs, founded on facts and legendary tales. Edinburgh 1807 (with the autobiographical Memoir of the life of James Hogg), 1821 (3rd edn 'greatly enlarged'), 1839 (with The forest minstrel, below), Glasgow 1840.
The shepherd's guide: being a practical treatise on the diseases of sheep. Edinburgh 1807.
The spy. 52 nos Edinburgh 1810–11. Ed and largely written by Hogg.
The forest minstrel: a selection of songs. 1810, Philadelphia 1816.
The Queen's wake: a legendary poem. Edinburgh 1813 (re-issued as 2nd edn), 1814 (re-issued 1815), Boston 1815, Edinburgh 1819, 1819, 1842, [1867]; Selections, 1879.
The hunting of Badlewe: a dramatic tale. Edinburgh 1814.
A selection of German Hebrew melodies. [1815?].
The pilgrims of the sun. Edinburgh 1815, Philadelphia 1816.
The Ettricke garland: being two excellent new songs. Edinburgh 1815. One song by Hogg; the other by Scott.
The poetic mirror: or the living bards of Britain. 1816, 1817; ed T. E. Welby 1929.
Mador of the moor. Edinburgh 1816.
Dramatic tales. 2 vols Edinburgh 1817.
The long pack: a Northumbrian tale. Newcastle 1817, 1818, Glasgow [1840?], [1850?]; ed G. Richardson, Newcastle 1877 etc.
The Brownie of Bodsbeck and other tales. 2 vols Edinburgh 1818; ed G. Lewis, Selkirk 1903.
A border garland. Edinburgh [1819?], nd (as The border garland).
The Jacobite relics of Scotland. 2 sers Edinburgh 1819–21, 1 vol Paisley 1874.
Winter evening tales. 2 vols Edinburgh 1820, 1 vol Glasgow 1821 (selected), 1824.
The three perils of man, or war, women and witchcraft: a border romance. 3 vols 1822, 1837 (as The siege of Roxburgh, in Tales and sketches).
The royal jubilee: a Scottish mask. Edinburgh 1822.
The three perils of woman, or love, leasing and jealousy: a series of domestic Scottish tales. 3 vols Edinburgh 1823; tr French, 1825.
The private memoirs and confessions of a justified sinner, written by himself. 1824 (anon), 1828 (as The suicide's grave), 1837 (rptd with alterations as Confessions of a fanatic, in Tales and sketches), 1895 (as The suicide's grave); ed T. E. Welby 1924; ed A. Gide 1947.

Queen Hynde. 1825.
Select and rare Scottish melodies. [1829].
The shepherd's calendar. 2 vols Edinburgh 1829.
Critical remarks on the psalms of David. Edinburgh 1830. With W. Tennant.
Songs now first collected. Edinburgh 1831, 1855, [1912].
Altrive tales collected among the peasantry of Scotland, and from foreign adventurers. Vol 1 (all pbd), 1832.
A queer book. Edinburgh 1832.
A series of lay sermons on good principles and good breeding. 1834.
The domestic manner and private life of Sir Walter Scott. Glasgow 1834, New York 1834 (as Familiar anecdotes of Sir Walter Scott), Edinburgh 1882; ed J. E. H. Thomson, Stirling 1909.
The works of Robert Burns. 5 vols Glasgow 1834–6 etc (vol 5 contains Hogg's Memoir of Burns), 1847, 1848, 1851, 4 vols 1895. Ed with William Motherwell.
Tales of the wars of Montrose. 3 vols 1835.
A tour in the Highlands in 1803: letters by Hogg to Scott. Paisley 1888.
Kilmeny. 1905, 1911.

§2

[Lockhart, J. G.] In his Peter's letters to his kinsfolk, 1819.
— In his Life of Scott, 1837.
Wilson, J. Some observations illustrated by a comparative view of Burns and the Ettrick shepherd. Blackwood's Mag Feb 1819.
— [?] On Hogg's memoirs. Blackwood's Mag Aug 1821.
— An hour's talk about poetry. In his Works vol 9, 1857.
— et al. In his Noctes ambrosianae, ed R. S. Mackenzie 5 vols New York 1863.
Wordsworth, W. Extempore effusion on the death of the Ettrick shepherd. Athenaeum 30 Nov 1835.
Gillies, R. P. Some recollections of Hogg. Fraser's Mag Oct 1839.
— In his Memoirs of a literary veteran, 1851.
Morrison, J. Random reminiscences of the Ettrick shepherd. Tait's Mag Oct 1843.
Rogers, C. In his Modern Scottish minstrel, 1855.
Mackenzie, R. S. Life of the Ettrick shepherd, in J. Wilson, Noctes ambrosianae vol 4, New York 1863.
Thomson, T. Biographical sketch of the Ettrick shepherd. In his Works vol 2, 1865.
Chambers, W. In his Memoir of R. Chambers, 1872.
Gordon, Mrs. In her Christopher North: a memoir of John Wilson, Edinburgh 1879.
B., J. T. Biographical sketch. In his Tales, 1880.
Bates, W. In his Maclise portrait-gallery of illustrious literary characters, 1883.
Garden, Mrs. Memorials of Hogg. Paisley [1885], 1887, 1893.
Saintsbury, G. In his Essays in English literature 1780–1860, 1890.
Smiles, S. In his A publisher and his friends: memoirs of John Murray, 1891.
— The suicide's grave. Athenaeum 16 Nov 1895. Reply by A. Lang 30 Nov 1895.
Thomson, J. In his Biographical and critical studies, 1896.
Oliphant, Mrs and Mrs Porter. In their Annals of a publishing house: William Blackwood and his sons, 3 vols 1897.
Douglas, G. James Hogg. 1899.
Stephenson, H. T. The Ettrick shepherd: a biography. Bloomington 1922.
Batho, E. C. The Ettrick shepherd. Cambridge 1927.
Carswell, D. Sir Walter. 1930. On Scott, Hogg, Lockhart, Joanna Baillie.
Strout, A. L. Wordsworth and Wilson. PMLA 49 1934.
— Hogg and 'Maga'. TLS 14 Dec 1935.
— Concerning the Noctes ambrosianae. MLN 51 1936.
— Hogg's birthday. TLS 15 Feb 1936.
— Purple patches in the Noctes ambrosianae. ELH 2 1936.
— Hogg's familiar anecdotes of Sir Walter Scott. SP 33 1936.
— Hogg's forgotten satire: John Paterson's mare. PMLA 52 1937.
— The Noctes ambrosianae and Hogg. RES 13 1937.
— Notes on Hogg. N & Q 2 April 1938.
— John Wilson Croker and the Noctes ambrosianae. TLS 9 March 1940.
— Hogg's The spy 1810–11. N & Q 19 April 1941.
— John Aitken, George Goldie and Hogg. N & Q 11 Oct 1941.
— Authorship of On Hogg's memoirs in Blackwood 1821. N & Q 29 Nov 1941.
— Miscellaneous letters to, from and about Hogg. N & Q 13, 27 Dec 1941, 31 Jan, 14 March, 11–18 April, 16 May 1942. Reply by J. C. Corson 16 May 1942.
— Hogg's Domestic manners. N & Q 26 Sept 1942.
— The life and letters of Hogg, vol 1: 1770–1825. Lubbock Texas 1946.
— Hogg's Chaldee manuscript. PMLA 65 1950.
The Ettrick shepherd: a centenary exhibition. TLS 30 Nov 1935.
Cook, D. The Ettrick shepherd. TLS 8 May 1937.
Carr, B. M. H. The Ettrick shepherd: two unnoted articles. N & Q 2 Sept 1950.
Jones, F. L. Hogg's peep at Elizabeth Shelley. PQ 29 1950.
— Shelley's letter of 23 June 1811 to Hogg. Keats-Shelley Memorial Bull 15 1964.
Berry, F. A medieval poem and its secularized derivative. EC 5 1955. On source of Herone.
Kiralis, K. Hogg and William Blake. N & Q Jan 1959.
Riese, T. Hogg und der Roman der englischen Romantik. Archiv 198 1961.
Lehmann, J. In his Ancestors and friends, 1962.
Simpson, L. Hogg: a critical study. 1962.
Parsons, C. O. In his Witchcraft and demonology in Scott's fiction, Edinburgh 1964.
Lee, L. L. The devil's figure: Hogg's Justified sinner. Stud in Scottish Lit 3 1966.

R. L. C.

GEORGE GORDON BYRON, 6th BARON BYRON 1788–1824

Bibliographies

Gerbel, N. V. O russkikh perevodakh iz Byrona. 5 vols Leningrad 1864–7. At end of each vol.
Anderson, J. P. In R. Noel, Life of Lord Byron, 1890. Contains the fullest lists of musical settings and of magazine articles about Byron.
Flaischen, C. Lord Byron in Deutschland. Centralblatt für Bibliothekswesen 7 1890.
Koelbing, E. Bibliographische Notizen. In The prisoner of Chillon and other poems, Weimar 1898. Also contains a list of vols of illustrations of Byron's works.
Lumbroso, A. Saggio di bibliografia Byroniana. In Il Generale Mengaldo, Lord Byron e l'Ode on the Star of the Legion of Honour, Rome 1903; rptd in Pagine Veneziane, Rome 1905.
Coleridge, E. H. A bibliography of the successive editions and translations of Lord Byron's poetical works. In Works of Lord Byron, Poetry vol 7, 1904. The best general bibliography of the poems.
Estève, E. Byron et le romantisme français. Paris 1907.
Churchman, P. H. The beginnings of Byronism in Spain. Revue Hispanique 23 1910. Lists Spanish trns of Byron.

Morvay, G. Byron Magyarországon. In E. Koeppel, Byron fordítótta Esty Jánosné, Budapest 1913.

Intze, O. Byroniana. [Birmingham 1914].

Griffith, R. H. and H. M. Jones. A descriptive catalogue of an exhibition of manuscripts and first editions of Lord Byron. Austin 1924.

Chew, S. C. Byron in England. New York 1924. The fullest list of Byroniana.

— In English romantic poets: a review of research, ed T. M. Raysor, New York 1950, 1956 (rev).

Bibliographical catalogue of first editions, proof copies and manuscripts of books by Lord Byron exhibited at the fourth exhibition of the First Edition Club. 1925.

Wise, T. J. A Byron library. 1928 (priv ptd).

— A bibliography of the writings in verse and prose of Lord Byron. 2 vols 1932–3 (priv ptd). The fullest discussion of the issues of the first edns. *See* J. Carter, TLS 27 April, 4 May 1933.

Elkin Mathews Ltd. Byron and Byroniana: a catalogue of books. 1930.

Nottingham Corporation. The Roe-Byron collection, Newstead Abbey. Nottingham, 1937.

Pollard, H. G. Pirated collections of Byron. TLS 16 Oct 1937.

Niccolai, B. Bibliografia di studi inglesi in Italia: Lord Byron. Bollettino di Studi Inglesi in Italia 6 1937.

Quintana, R. Byron 1788–1938: an exhibition at the Huntington Library. San Marino 1938.

Steffan, T. G. Autograph letters and documents of the Byron circle at the library of the University of Texas. SE 1946. *See* also SP 43 1946 and MLQ 8 1947.

Pratt, W. W. Byron and his circle: a calendar of manuscripts in the University of Texas Library. Austin 1948.

— Lord Byron and his circle: recent acquisitions. Univ of Texas Lib Chron 5 1956.

Hofman, A. Mss de J. J. Rousseau et de Byron à Prague. Philologica 9 1957.

Dwyer, J. T. Check list of primary sources for the Byron-Jeffrey relationship. N & Q July 1960.

Marchand, L. A. Recent Byron scholarship. In Essays in literary history presented to J. Milton French, ed R. Kirk and C. F. Main, New Brunswick 1960.

Brown, T. J. English literary autographs xlii. Book Collector 11 1962.

Collections

Collections in English

The poetical works of Lord Byron. 2 vols Philadelphia 1813, Boston 1814, 3 vols New York 1815, Philadelphia 1815, 2 vols 1815, 4 vols 1815, 1815, 3 vols Philadelphia 1816, 5 vols 1817, New York 1817, Philadelphia 1817, 6 vols 1818; vol 7, 1819, vol 8, 1820; 6 vols Paris 1818, Zwickau 1818–19, 13 vols Leipzig 1818–22, 3 vols 1819, 6 vols Paris 1819, 7 vols Brussels 1819, 4 vols New York 1820, 5 vols 1821, Paris 1821, 16 vols Paris 1822–4 (with life by J. W. Lake), 4 vols 1823, 12 vols Paris 1823, 1823–4 (with life by Sir Cosmo Gordon), 8 vols Philadelphia 1824; vols 5–7, 1824; 30 vols Zwickau 1824–5, 6 vols 1825, 7 vols Paris 1825 (with life by J. W. Lake), 8 vols New York 1825, Philadelphia 1825, 33 vols Zwickau 1825–38, 13 vols Paris 1826, 1826 (with life by Lake), Frankfurt 1826, 6 vols 1827, Paris 1827 (with life by Lake), 4 vols 1828, Paris 1828 (with Life by Lake), Frankfurt 1828, 6 vols 1829, 4 vols 1829, 2 vols Philadelphia 1829, 1829, 1829, Frankfurt 1829, 4 vols 1830, Paris 1830, 6 vols 1831, 1831, Paris 1831 (with abridged life by Lake), Philadelphia 1831 (with life by Lake), 4 vols Paris 1832; The works of Lord Byron, with his letters and journals, and his life by Thomas Moore [ed John Wright] 17 vols 1832–3 (the earlier vols several times rptd); New York, 1833 (with life by FitzGreene Halleck), Paris 1835 (with life by Henry Lytton Bulwer); Paris 1835 (with life by John Galt), 4 vols Paris 1835, 6 vols New York 1836–7 (with life by T. Moore), 1837, 1837, Frankfurt 1837, Paris 1837 (with life by John Galt), 1837, 1837, 7 vols Mannheim 1837, 1 vol 1838, Paris 1839, Philadelphia 1839, 8 vols 1839, 4 vols Paris 1840, 1841, 5 vols Leipzig 1842, 4 vols Philadelphia 1843 (with life by Moore), 1 vol 1845, Frankfurt 1846, Paris 1847, Hartford 1847 (with life by Halleck), London 1848, 2 vols Edinburgh [1850] (with life by William Anderson), 1 vol 1850, Philadelphia 1850, London 1851 (with life by Bulwer), Philadelphia 1851, [1851?] (with life by 'Allan Cunningham') [*see* TLS 14 June 1941], Frankfurt 1852 (with life by Moore), 2 vols Philadelphia, 1853; Philadelphia 1854, Boston 1854; The illustrated Byron [issued in pts 1854–5]; 6 vols 1855–6, Edinburgh [1857] (with 'objectionable pieces' excluded), New York 1857, London 1857, 6 vols 1857, 1 vol 1859, Edinburgh [1859], Philadelphia 1859, Leipzig 1860, 3 vols Leipzig 1860, Edinburgh 1861 (with life by Alexander Leighton), 10 vols Boston 1861 (with life by J. H. Lister), Halifax 1863, 1865, 1865, 1866, 1867, Edinburgh [1868] (with life by Leighton), 1868, 1869, 1869, Philadelphia 1869, New York 1869, 8 vols 1870; [ed W. M. Rossetti] 1870, Philadelphia 1870; [ed Rossetti] [1872], 1873; [ed W. B. Scott] [1874], [1874], Boston 1874, London 1876, [1878], Boston 1878; [ed Rossetti] [1878]; [ed Rossetti and T. Seccombe] [1882]; [ed Scott] 1883, 1883, 3 vols 1883, 12 vols 1885, New York [c. 1886]; [ed Mathilde Blind] 1886, 1886, 1887, 2 vols 1888, 1890, New York [1890], 12 vols 1891–2, 3 vols 1892, 12 vols Philadelphia 1892, 1895, 4 vols 1896, [1897], 1897, 1 vol Edinburgh 1897, 4 vols Philadelphia 1897, 13 vols 1898–1904 (A new revised and enlarged edition: poetry, ed E. H. Coleridge, 7 vols; Letters and journals, ed R. E. Prothero 6 vols), 1904 (Poetical works); [ed E. H. Coleridge] 1905, 1948; [ed P. E. More], New York [1905], 3 vols 1906; [ed W. P. Trent] [1910]; [ed Rossetti and Seccombe] [1911]; [ed N. H. Dole], New York 1927.

Translations of collections

French. By 'A. E. de Chastopalli' (Amédée Pichot and Eusèbe de Salle) 10 vols Paris 1819–21, 5 vols Paris 1820–2, 15 vols Paris 1821–4, 8 vols Paris 1822–5; Œuvres nouvelles 10 vols Paris 1824, 13 vols Paris 1823–4, 20 vols Paris 1827–31 (6th edn), 6 vols Paris 1830, 1830–5, 1836, 1 vol Paris 1837, Paris 1842 (11th edn). By Paulin Paris 3 vols Paris 1827, 13 vols Paris 1830–2, 1835. By Benjamin Laroche 4 vols Paris 1836–7; 1 vol Paris 1837, 1838, 4 vols Paris 1840–1, 1 vol Paris 1842, 4 vols Paris 1847, 1850–1. By Orby Hunter and Pascal Ramé 2 vols Paris 1841–2, 3 vols Paris 1845. By Louis Barré Paris 1856. By 'Daniel le Sueur' (Jeanne Loiseau) 2 vols Paris 1891–2.

German. By Julius Koerner, Wilhelm Reinhold, Heinrich Doering, August Schumann, Christian Karl Meissner 31 vols Zwickau 1821–8. By G. N. Baermann, O. L. B. Wolff, K. L. Kannegiesser, A. Hungari, P. von Haugwitz, P. A. G. von Meyer, J. V. Adrian 12 vols Frankfurt 1830–1, 1837. By Gustav Pfizer, 4 vols Stuttgart 1836–9, 1 vol Stuttgart 1851. By E. Ortlepp, F. Kottenkamp, H. Kurtz,—Duttenhofer,—Bardili, Bernhard von Guseck 10 vols Stuttgart 1839, Pforzheim 1842, Stuttgart 1845, 1846, 12 vols Stuttgart 1856. By Adolf Boettger, Leipzig 1840, 1841, 12 vols 1842, 1844, 1845, 12 vols 1847, 1850, 1852, 8 vols 1854, 12 vols 1856, 1860, 1861, 8 vols 1863, 1864, 1901. Ed O. Gildemeister 6 vols Berlin 1864, 1866, 1877, 1888. By Alexander Neidhart 8 vols Berlin 1865. By Wilhelm Schaeffer, A. H. Janert, W. Gruezmacher, Heinrich Stadelmann, Adolf Strodtmann 7 vols Hildeburghausen 1865–72. By Adolf Seubert 3 vols Leipzig [1874]. By Adalbert Schroeter 6 vols Stuttgart 1885–90. By Henry Tuckermann 8 vols Stuttgart 1886.

Modern Greek. 3 vols Athens 1895 (anon).
Italian. By Carlo Rusconi 2 vols Padua 1842. By Giuseppe Gazzino, Giuseppe Nicolini, Pietro Isola, Pellegrino Rossi, Andrea Maffei, Marcello Mazzoni, P. G. B. Cereseto, Naples 1853. By G. de Stefano, Naples 1857. Naples 1886 (anon), 1891.
Polish. By B. M. Wolff, Leningrad 1857 (vol 1 only, containing Childe Harold). By Piotr Chmielowski, Warsaw 1895.
Russian. By N. V. Gerbel, M. Y. Lermontov, A. Pushkin, V. Jukovsky, K. Batinshkov, D. Minaev, I. Turgenev, L. Meya, P. Kozlov, I. Kozlov, N. Zorin et al 5 vols Leningrad 1864–6, 4 vols Leningrad 1874–7; 3 vols Leningrad 1883–4. By P. I. Veinberg, Leningrad 1876. By S. A. Vengerov (ed), V. Mazurkevitch, P. S. Kogan, S. A. Ilyin, A. M. Federov et al 2 vols Leningrad 1904–5.
Spanish. Madrid, 1880 (anon), 1898. By Francisco Gallach Pales 5 vols Madrid 1930–1.
Swedish. By 'Talis Qualis' (C. W. A. Strandberg) 8 vols Stockholm 1854–6.

Partial Collections in English

Tales. 2 vols 1837, 1 vol Halifax 1845, London 1853, Leipzig 1857, London [1859] (as Eastern tales).
The Corsair, Lara. Paris 1830; ed M. F. Sweetzer, Boston 1893. The Giaour, The bride of Abydos 1844, 1848. Beppo, Don Juan 2 vols 1853. The prisoner of Chillon, The siege of Corinth, ed J. G. C. Schuler, Halle 1886. The prisoner of Chillon, Mazeppa, The lament of Tasso, Oxford [1929].
Dramas. Paris 1832, 2 vols 1837, 1853.
Three poems not included in the works of Lord Byron [Lines to Lady [Jersey], The curse of Minerva, and The enigma (by Catherine Maria Fanshawe)]. 1818; Suppressed poems [English bards, Ode to the land of the Gaul, A sketch, Windsor poetics], Paris 1818 (2nd edn); The works of Lord Byron [English bards, The curse of Minerva, Waltz etc]. 'Philadelphia' 1820; The miscellaneous works [Werner, Heaven and earth, Morgante Maggiore, The age of bronze, The island, The vision of judgement, The deformed transformed], 2 vols 1824, 1830; Poems [Don Juan, Hours of idleness, English bards, Poems on his domestic circumstances], 1825; Don Juan (complete), English bards, Hours of idleness, The waltz, and all the other minor poems, 1826, 1827, 2 vols 1828, 1829; The miscellaneous poems [Hours of idleness, English bards, The curse of Minerva etc], 1829; Miscellanies, 3 vols 1837, 2 vols 1853.

Partial Collections in Translation

Czech. (Corsair, Lara) by Cenek Ibl, Prague 1885.
Danish. (Dramas and tales) by Edvard Lembcke 2 vols Copenhagen 1873; (Manfred, The prisoner of Chillon, Mazeppa) by Alfred Ipsen Copenhagen [1889?]; (Beppo, The vision of judgement) by Alfred Ipsen, Copenhagen 1891.
Dutch. (Mazeppa, Parisina) by Nicholaas Beets (in his Gedichten), Haarlem 1837, 1848; (Poems) by J. J. L. Ten Kate, Leiden [c. 1870].
French. (Childe Harold, cantos iii, iv, Prisoner of Chillon, Corsair, Lara, Giaour, Lament of Tasso, Siege of Corinth), Bibliothèque Universelle (Geneva) 5–9 May 1817–Dec 1818; (Corsair, Mazeppa) by Lucien Méchin, Paris 1848. (Manfred, Lara) by Hya du Pontavice de Henssey, Paris 1856; (Prisoner of Chillon, Lara, Parisina, Poems) by H. Gomont, Nancy 1862; (Corsair, Lara, Siege of Corinth) by Paul Lorencin, Paris 1868; (Two Foscari, Beppo) by Achille Morisseau, Paris 1881; (Corsair, Lara) Paris 1892.
German. (Tales) by J. V. Adrian, Frankfurt 1820; (Prisoner of Chillon, Parisina) by Paul Graf con Haugwitz, Breslau 1821; (Manfred, Dream etc) by E. Koeppe, Berlin 1835; (Bride of Abydos, Mazeppa) by W. Gerhard, Leipzig 1840; (Giaour, Hebrew melodies) by Friederike Friedmann, Leipzig 1854; (Cain, Mazeppa) by Friederike Friedmann, Leipzig 1855; (Manfred, Prisoner of Chillon, Hebrew melodies etc) by A. R. Nielo, Münster 1857; (Giaour, Prisoner of Chillon), Düsseldorf 1859 (anon); (Mazeppa, Corsair, Beppo) by Wilhelm Schaeffer, Leipzig 1864; (Manfred, Cain, Heaven and earth, Sardanapalus) by W. Gruezmacher, Hildburghausen 1870; (Bride of Abydos, Dream) by Otto Riedel, Hamburg 1872; (Prisoner of Chillon, Mazeppa), Leipzig [c. 1875]; (Prisoner of Chillon, Parisina) by Otto Michaeli, Halle 1890; (Tales) by A. Neidhart, Halle [1903].
Hungarian. (Mazeppa, Dream, Poems) by Lázár Horváth, Budapest 1842.
Icelandic. (Prisoner of Chillon etc) by Steingrímur Thorsteinson, Copenhagen 1866.
Italian. (Prisoner of Chillon, Parisina, Siege of Corinth, Lara) by Pietro Isola, Turin 1827; (Corsair, Giaour) by Pietro Isola, Milan 1830; rptd together 2 vols Lugano 1832; (Bride of Abydos, Parisina, Corsair, Lara) by Giuseppe Nicolini, Milan 1834; 2 vols Milan 1837, 1842; (Poems) by Giuseppe Zappala Finocchiaro, Palermo 1837; (Poems) by Marcello Mazzoni, Milan 1838; (Dramas) by P. de Virgilii, Brussels 1841; (Marino Faliero, Two Foscari) by P. G. B. Cereseto, Savona 1845; (Sardanapalus, Marino Faliero, Two Foscari) by Andrea Maffei, Florence 1862; (Cain, Parisina etc) by Andrea Maffei, Milan 1886; (Mysteries, tales, poems) by Andrea Maffei, Florence 1890; (Tales and poems) Milan 1882 (anon); Childe Harold, Parisina, Beppo, Bride of Abydos) by Giacinto Casella (in his Opere edite e postume vol i), Florence 1884; (Parisina, Prisoner of Chillon) by Aldo Ricci, Florence [1924].
Polish. (Siege of Corinth, Corsair) by B[runo hr] K[iciński] in Poemata i powieści vol i, Warsaw 1820; (Mazeppa) by H. Dembiński (Giaour, Parisina etc) by Wandy Maleckićj, Warsaw 1828, 1831; (Parisina, Calmar i Orla) by I. Szydlowski, Vilna 1834; (Giaour) by Adam Mickiewicz, (Corsair) by A. E. Odyniec, Paris 1835, Wroclaw 1839; (Bride of Abydos) by A. E. Odyniec in Tlómaczenia vol 2, Leipzig 1838; (Corsair, Heaven and earth) by A. E. Odyniec in Tlómaczenia vol 3, Leipzig 1841; (Mazeppa) by A. E. Odyniec in Tlómaczenia vol 5, Vilna 1843; (Lament of Tasso, Werner, Bride of Abydos, Island) by A. Zawadzki, Warsaw 1846; (Manfred, Mazeppa, Sieg of Corinth, Parisina, Prisoner of Chillon) by F. D. Morawski, Leszno 1853, (Parisina, Lara, Cain, Poems etc) by Karol Kruzer (in his Przeklady i rymy wlasne vols 3–4), Warsaw 1876.
Portuguese. (Childe Harold, Sardanapalus) by Francisco José Pinheiro Guimarães (in Traduccões Poeticas), Rio de Janeiro 1863.
Roumanian. (Prisoner of Chillon, Beppo, Lament of Tasso) by T. Eliad, Bucharest 1834.
Russian. (Dramas) by I. A. Bunin and N. A. Bruansky, Leningrad 1922.
Spanish. (Ode to Napoleon, Napoleon's Farewell etc) Paris 1830 (anon); (Lara, Siege of Corinth, Parisina, Childe Harold, Mazeppa, Lament of Tasso, Beppo) by Ricardo Canales, Barcelona [c. 1876]; (Parisina, Prisoner of Chillon, Lament of Tasso, Bride of Abydos) by Antonio Sellen, New York 1877; (Don Juan, Lament of Tasso) by J. A. R., Barcelona 1883; (Dramas) by José Alcala Galiano, Madrid 1886.

Selections

Selections in English

The beauties of Byron. Ed T. Parry 1823, 1827.
Life and select poems. Ed C. Hulbert, Shrewsbury [1828].
Beauties of Byron. Ed B. F. French, Philadelphia 1828.
The beauties of Byron. Ed A. Howard [1829].
The beauties of Byron. Ed J. W. Lake, Paris 1829.
Select works of Lord Byron. 6 vols Frankfort 1831–4.
Select works. 1833.
Select poetical works. Paris 1835, 1836.
Lord Byron's select works. Berlin 1837.
Select works. 1837.
The beauties of Byron. Ed A. Howard 1837.
The beauties of Byron and Burns. Hull 1837.
Byron's select works. Paris 1843.
A selection from Byron's poetical works. Ed C. Graeser, Marienwerder 1846.
Select poetical works. 1848.
Lord Byron's select works. Ed F. Breier, Oldenburg 1848.
Selections from the writings of Lord Byron by a clergyman [Whitwell Elwin]. 1854, [1874].
Poems. 1855.
Poems. [1859].
The choice works. Halifax 1864.
A selection from the works of Lord Byron. Ed A. C. Swinburne 1866, [1885].
Songs. 1872.
Beautés de Byron. Ed A. Biard, Paris 1876.
Favourite poems by Lord Byron. Boston 1877.
The Byron birthday book. Ed J. Burrows 1879.
Poems. [1880].
The beauties of Byron. Stuttgart [c. 1880].
The poetry of Byron, chosen and arranged by Matthew Arnold. 1881.
Gems from Byron. Ed H. R. Haweis 1886.
Poems carefully selected. 2 vols [1886].
Shorter poems by Burns, Byron and Campbell. Ed W. Murrison 1893, 1895.
Selections from Wordsworth, Byron, Shelley. Ed A. Ellis 1896.
Selections. Ed F. I. Carpenter, New York 1900, 1908.
Poems selected by C. Linklater Thomson. 1901.
Poems. Ed A. Symons [1904], [1927].
Songs. 1904.
Selected poetry. Ed J. W. Duff 1904.
Love poems of Byron. 1905.
With Byron in Italy: a selection of the poems and letters. Ed A. B. McMahon, Chicago 1906.
Poems selected by Charles Whibley. [1907].
Byron's shorter poems. Ed R. H. Bowles 1907.
Selections from Byron. Ed S. M. Tucker [1907].
Love poems of Byron. 1911.
Selected poems. 1913.
Selections. 1913.
Selected poems. [Ed W. Robertson 1913].
Selections. Ed A. H. Thompson, Cambridge 1920.
Poems. Ed H. J. C. Grierson 1923.
Selections. Ed M. F. Dee [1926].
With Byron in love. Ed W. Littlefield, New York [1926].
An introduction to Byron. Ed G. N. Pocock [1927].
Selections. Ed W. R. Macklin 1927.
Selections. [1927].
The shorter Byron. Ed E. Rhys 1927, [1928].
Selections. Ed H. Miles 1930.
Selections. Ed D. M. Walmsley 1931.
Selections. Ed J. G. Bullocke [1931].
Lyrical poems. Ed E. du Perron, Maastricht 1933.
The best of Byron. Ed R. A. Rice, New York 1933.
Satirical and critical poems. Ed J. Bennet, Cambridge 1937.
Poetry and prose. Ed D. N. Smith, Oxford 1940.
Poems. Ed G. Pocock 3 vols 1848, rev V. de S. Pinto 1963 (EL).
Byron for today. Ed R. Fuller 1948.
Selections from poetry, letters and journals. Ed P. C. Quennell 1950 (Nonesuch Lib).
Poems. Ed P. D. Dickinson 1950.
Poems. Ed A. S. B. Glover 1955 (Penguin).
Selected verse and prose. Ed. P. C. Quennell 1959.
Byronic thoughts. Ed P. C. Quennell 1960.
Selections from poetry and prose. Ed I. Gregor and A. Rutherford 1963.

Selections in translation

Armenian

Beauties of English poets. Venice 1852.
Lord Byron's Armenian exercises and poetry. Venice 1870, 1886.

French

Choix de poésies de Byron, de W. Scott et de Th. Moore. 2 vols Geneva 1820.
Beautés de Lord Byron. Tr Charles Édouard de Léonville, Paris 1825.
Les beautés de Lord Byron. Tr Amédée Pichot, Paris 1838.
Écrin poétique de littérature anglaise. Tr D. Bonnefin, Paris 1841.
Chefs d'oeuvre de Lord Byron. Tr Comte de Hautefeuille, Paris 1847.
Rough hewing of Lord Byron in French by Francis D'Autrey. 1869.
Chefs d'oeuvre de Lord Byron. Tr A. Regnault 2 vols Paris 1874.

German

Byrons Lieder. [Ed A. Friederick], Karlsruhe 1820.
Kleine Gedichte von Byron und Moore. [Ed C. von K.], Berlin 1829.
Lord Byrons Ausgewaehlte Dichtungen. Leipzig 1838.
Dichtungen von Lord Byron. Ed A. Rolein, Crefeld 1841.
Schoenheiten aus Byrons Werken. Ed Adolf Boettger, Leipzig 1841.
Byron-Anthologie. Ed Eduard Hobein, Schwerin 1866.
Lord Byrons Lyrische Gedichte. Ed H. Stadelmann, Hildburghhausen 1872.
Auswahl aus Byron. Ed J. Hengesbach [np] 1892.

Italian

A miei amici [by Pietro Isola]. [Novi c. 1870].

Russian

Vuibor iz sochineny. Ed M. Kachenovsky, Moscow 1821.

Spanish

[Selections by various translators.] Barcelona [1922]; by M. Alfaro, Madrid 1949.

§1

In this section and the following the word 'proof' is used to indicate that the work is known to have been put in type, whether a copy is now extant or not. The word 'counterfeit' is used to indicate edns indistinguishable by normal methods of bibliographical description. Of Byron's earlier works many such were produced for commercial purposes before 1820.

Fugitive pieces. [Newark 1806] (anon); (priv ptd); ed H. Buxton Forman 1886 (facs) ed M. Kessel, New York 1933 (facs).

Roe, H. C. The rare quarto edition of Lord Byron's Fugitive pieces described, with a note on the Pigot family. Nottingham 1919 (priv ptd).

Poems on various occasions. Newark 1807 (priv ptd). Contains 50 pieces of which 12 are new. Anon.

Hours of idleness: a series of poems, original and translated. Newark 1807 (one counterfeit of larger size—*see* Athenaeum 28 May 1898; T. M. B[lagg], Newark as a publishing town, Newark 1898, pp. 20–35; T. J. Wise, Bibliography vol 1 pp. 9–10), 1822, Glasgow 1825. Contains 39 pieces of which 12 are new. Reviewed: Critical Rev Sept 1807 (by Henry Higgs Hunt);

Satirist Oct 1807; Edinburgh Rev 11 1808 (by Henry Brougham; separately rptd 1820, 1820; New Monthly Mag Feb 1819.

Ward, W. S. Byron's Hours of idleness and other than Scottish reviewers. MLN 59 1944.

Poems original and translated: second edition. Newark 1808. Contains 39 pieces of which 5 are new. One counterfeit (*see* Texas exhibition, 1924, pp. 93–7). Rptd as Hours of idleness, Paris 1819, London 1820 (4 edns), Paris 1820, 1822.

The British bards. [Newark 1808] (proof in BM). Largely incorporated in the next entry.

English bards and Scotch reviewers: a satire. [1809] (anon) (2 variants, 3 counterfeits), 1809 ('with considerable additions and alterations'), 1810 (8 counterfeits), Philadelphia 1811, 1810 (4th edn), (one counterfeit), 1811 (4th edn) (6 counterfeits), Boston 1814; ed J. Murray 1936 (Roxburghe Club) (facs of a copy with Byron's ms notes); 1816 ('with additions'), New York 1817, Paris 1818, 1819, Brussels 1819, Geneva 1820, London 1821, Paris 1821, London 1823, 1823, Glasgow 1824, 1825, London 1825, 1826, 1827, 1827, [c. 1830], Halifax 1834; tr French by Raoul (as Les poètes anglais et les auteurs de l'Edinburgh Review), Ghent 1821.

C[ampbell], J. D. et al. Athenaeum 5 May–7 July 1894.

Redgrave, G. R. The first four editions of English bards and Scotch reviewers. Library 2nd ser 1 1899.

Koenig, C. Byrons English bards and Scotch reviewers Entstehung und Beziehungen zur zeitgenoessischen Satire und Kritik. Berlin [1914].

Hints from Horace. 1811 (proof in BM). Extracts were pbd by R. C. Dallas in 1824 and by T. Moore in 1830; the full text was first pbd in the 6-vol edn of Works, 1831, vol 5 pp. 273–327.

Childe Harold's pilgrimage: a romaunt [cantos 1–2]. 1812 (5 edns), Philadelphia 1812, 1813 (6th edn), 1814 (7th–8th edns), 1815 (10th edn), Philadelphia 1816 (3rd Amer edn), 1819 (11th edn).

Childe Harold's pilgrimage, canto the third. 1816 (3 issues), Boston 1817, Philadelphia 1817.

Childe Harold's pilgrimage, canto the fourth. 1818 (7 states. *See* W. H. McCarthy, The printing of canto iv of Childe Harold, Yale Univ Lib Gazette 1 1927); New York 1818, 1818, Philadelphia 1818 (with other poems).

Childe Harold's pilgrimage [cantos 1–4]. 2 vols 1819, Leipzig 1820, 1 vol 1825, 2 vols Paris 1825, 1 vol 1826, 1827, Paris 1827, 2 vols Brussels 1829, [c. 1831], Nuremberg [1831], New York 1836, London 1837, Mannheim 1837, London 1839, 1841, 1842; ed A. Mommsen, Hamburg 1853, Berlin 1885, London 1853; ed F. Brockerhoff, Berlin 1854, London 1859, 1860, 1860, Leipzig 1862; ed W. Spalding [1866]; ed P. Weeg, Münster 1867, London 1869; ed W. Hiley 1877; ed J. Darmesteter, Paris 1882; ed A. Julien, Paris 1883; ed H. F. Tozer, Oxford 1885, 1907; ed W. J. Rolfe, Philadelphia 1886; ed M. Krummacher, Bielefeld 1886, 1891, 1893; ed H. G. Keene 1893; ed E. Chasles, Paris 1893; ed E. C. E. Owen [1897]; ed E. E. Morris 2 vols 1899; ed A. J. George, New York 1900; ed H. Bennett 1905; ed A. H. Thompson, Cambridge 1913; ed D. Frew 1918; [cantos iii–iv] ed B. J. Hayes [1932].

Selections: Glasgow [1882]; ed T. Morrison [1882]; ed T. Morrison [1882]; ed E. D. A. Morshead 1893, 1894, [1900]; ed J. Downie [1901]; ed J. H. Fowler 1906; ed H. F. Tozer, Oxford 1907; ed J. C. Scrimgeour, Calcutta 1914; ed G. A. Sheldon 1933.

Tr Armenian by Gheuond Alíshanian (canto iv only), Venice 1860, 1872; Czech by Eliska Krásnohorská [i.e. Jindřiška Pechová], Prague 1890; Danish by Adolf Hansen, Copenhagen 1880; French [by Pauthier de Censay], Paris 1828; by P. A. Deguer, Paris 1828; by F. Ragon, Paris 1833; by Eugène Quiertant (canto i only), Paris 1852; by Eugène Quiertant (cantos i–iv), Paris 1861; by Lucien Davésiès de Pontès, 2 vols Paris 1862, 1870; by V. R. Jones, St Quentin 1862; by M. Ph. Alard, Dunkirk 1869; by H. Bellet, Paris 1881; by A. Julien, Paris 1883; by M. A. Elwall, Paris 1892; by D. Gibb, Paris 1892; by Roger Martin, Paris 1949; German by K. Baldamus, 3 vols Leipzig 1835; by J. C. von Zedlitz, Stuttgart 1836; By Hermann con Pommer Esche, Stralsund 1839; by C. D. (canto i only), Ansbach 1845; by Adolf Boettger, Leipzig 1846; by Alexander Buechner, Frankfurt 1853, 1855; by Erich von Monbart, Cologne 1865; by A. H. Janert, Hildburghhausen 1868; by F. Schmidt, Berlin 1869; by Adolf Seubert, 2 vols Leipzig 1871–6; by F. Dobbert, [Leipzig?] 1893; Hungarian by Johanna Bickersteth, Geneva 1857; Italian by Michele Leoni (canto iv only), [np] 1819; by Giuseppe Gazzino, Genoa 1836; by Melchior Missirini (canto iv only), Milan 1848; by F. Armenico, Naples 1858; by Giovanni Giovio (cantos i–ii only), Milan 1866; by Pietro Isola (canto iv only), Novi 1870; by Andrea Maffei (canto iv only), Florence 1872, 1874, 1897; by Carlo Faccioli, Florence 1873; by Aldo Ricci, 3 vols Florence [1924–8]; Latin (part only, verse) by N. J. Brennan, Dublin 1894; Polish by M. B. Wolff, Leningrad 1857; by Wiktor z Baworow, Lwow 1857; by Frederyk Krauze, [np] 1865–71; by Jan Kasprowicz, Warsaw 1895; by A. A. K[rajewski], Cracow 1896; Portuguese by F. J. Pinheiro Guimarães, Lisbon 1863; Russian by D. Minaev, Rosskoi Slovo, Leningrad Jan, March, May, Oct 1864; by A. Kozlov, Rosskaya Mysl (Moscow) Jan–Feb, Nov 1890; Spanish, 4 vols Paris 1829 (anon); (canto i only) by Antonio Ledesma, Almeria 1884; Swedish by A. F. Skjoldebrand, Stockholm 1832.

Reviewed: Edinburgh Rev 19 1812 (by Francis Jeffrey); Quart Rev 7 1812 (by George Ellis); O Investigador Portuguez em Ingleterra, 6 April 1812; Quart Rev 16 1816 (by Sir Walter Scott); Edinburgh Rev 27 1816 (by Francis Jeffrey); Quart Rev 19 1818 (by Sir Walter Scott); Yellow Dwarf 2 May 1818 (by William Hazlitt); Edinburgh Rev 30 1818 (by John Wilson).

[Penn, Granville.] Lines to Harold. Stoke Park Bucks [1812] (priv ptd); rptd in Original lines and translations, 1815; rptd as Addresses to Lord Byron on the publication of Childe Harold, Poetical Album ser 2 1829.

Hobhouse, J. C. Historical illustrations of the fourth canto of Childe Harold. 1818, 1818, New York 1818.

[Hodgson, F.] Childe Harold's monitor: or lines occasioned by the last canto of Childe Harold. 1818.

Koelbing, E. Zur Textueberliegerung von Byrons Childe Harold cantos i, ii. Leipzig 1896.

Moll, O. E. E. Der Stil von Byrons Childe Harold's pilgrimage. Berlin 1911.

Maier, H. Enstehungsgeschichte von Byrons Childe Harold's pilgrimage, cantos i, ii. Berlin 1911.

Dalgado, D. G. Childe Harold's pilgrimage to Portugal critically examined. Lisbon 1919.

Murray, J. Two passages in Childe Harold canto iv. TLS 25 Aug 1921.

Lewis, R. T. A commentary and questionnaire on Childe Harold, cantos iii–iv. 1927.

Beck, R. Gisli Brynjúlfson: an Icelandic imitator of Childe Harold's pilgrimage. JEGP 28 1929.

Rutherford, A. The influence of Hobhouse on Childe Harold's pilgrimage canto iv. RES new ser 12 1961.

[Gillies, R. P.] Childe Alarique: a poet's reverie, and other poems. 1813, Edinburgh 1814.

The Baron of Falconberg: or Childe Harold in prose by Mrs Bridget Bluemantle. 3 vols 1815.

The last canto of Childe Harold's pilgrimage, with notes not by Lord Byron. 1818.

The soul's pilgrimage: a poem, written in reference to the sentiments of the noble author of Childe Harold's pilgrimage. Cambridge 1818.

Prodigious!!! or Childe Paddie in London. 3 vols 1818.

Childe Albert: or the misanthrope. Edinburgh 1819.

Harold the exile. 3 vols [1819]. *See* N & Q 13 Oct 1951.

Childe Harold in the shades: an infernal romaunt. 1819.

[Deacon, W. F.] The Childe's pilgrimage by Lord B. In Warreniana, 1824.

Bedford, J. H. Wanderings of Childe Harold. 3 vols 1825.

Lamartine, Alphonse de. Le dernier chant du pèlerinage d'Harold. Paris 1825 (4 edns); tr J. W. Lake, Paris 1826; another trn, 1827; another, Dublin 1848.

Verfèle, D. J. C. Les pèleringes d'un Childe Harold parisien. Paris 1825.

Carry, A. Childe Harold aux ruines de Rome. Paris 1826.

The pilgrimage of Ormonde: or Childe Harold in the New World. Charleston 1831.

Driver, H. A. Harold de Burun. 1835.

B., J. The Childe Harold and the Excursion. [1842].

Brynjúlfson, G. Faraldrð in Nor urfari, Copenhagen 1848; rptd in Lioðmoeli, Copenhagen 1891.

Euthanasia. [1812] (proof). First pbd in the 2nd (first 8vo) edn of Childe Harold (cantos i–ii), 1812; but a proof in 4to exists in the W. A. Clark Library at Pasadena, probably set up in this format for inclusion in the first (4to) edn of Childe Harold. *See* T. J. Wise, Bibliography vol 1, pp. xx–xxii; vol 2 pp. xxx–xxxi.

The curse of Minerva. 1812 (priv ptd) (anon), Philadelphia [=London?] 1815, Paris 1818, 1818, 1820, 1821. A slightly different text was first pbd in New Monthly Mag April 1815, as The malediction of Minerva: or the Athenian marble market and rptd under the original title by William Hone in the 8th edn of Poems on his domestic circumstances, 1816.

Waltz: an apostrophic hymn, by Horace Hornem esq. 1813, 1821, 1821, Paris 1821, London 1826.

The Giaour: a fragment of a Turkish tale. 1813, 1813 ('with some additions'), 1813 ('with considerable additions'), Boston 1813, Philadelphia 1813, 1813 (5th edn) ('with considerable additions'), 1813 (6th edn), 1813 (7th edn) ('with some additions'), 1814 (9th–12th edns), 1815 (13th–14th edns), 1825, 1842, [1844]; tr Dutch by J. J. Ten Kate, Haarlem 1859; French by J. M. H. Bigeon, Paris 1828; by Theodore Carlier (in Voyages poétiques), Paris 1830; by L. Joliet, Paris 1833; by F. Le Bidau and A. Lejourdan, Marseilles 1860; German, Berlin 1819 (anon); by 'A. von Nordstern' [i.e. G. A. E. von Nostiz-Jänkendorf], Leipzig 1820; by Adolf Seubert, Leipzig [1874]; by A. Strodtmann, Leipzig 1887; Modern Greek by A. K. Dosios, Athens 1873, [1898?]; Italian by Pellegrino Rossi, Genoa 1817, Milan 1818; by Andrea Maffei, Milan 1884; Polish by Ladislaus hr Ostrowski, Pulawy 1830; by Adam Mickiewicz, Paris 1835, Wroclaw 1839, Zloczów [1896]; Russian by M. Kachenovsky, Vyestnik Evropui (Moscow), nos 15–17 1821; by N. R., Moscow 1822; by A. Coeikov, Novosti Literatur (Leningrad) Sept–Oct 1826; by E. Mimel, Leningrad 1862; by V. A. Petrov, Leningrad 1873, 1874; Serbian by A. Popovič, Novisad 1860; Spanish, Paris 1828; Swedish by 'Talis Qualis' [i.e. C. W. A. Strandberg], Stockholm 1855. Reviewed: Edinburgh Rev 21 1813 (by Francis Jeffrey); Quart Rev 10 1814 (by George Ellis).

Hoffmann, K. Ueber Lord Byrons The Giaour. Halle 1898.

Fischer, H. Der übertragene Giaur: eine geschmacks-geschichtliche Untersuchung. Die Neueren Sprachen Jan 1961.

The bride of Abydos: a Turkish tale. 1813 (2 issues), 1813 (2nd–5th edns), 1814 (6th–10th edns), Boston 1814, Philadelphia 1814, 1818 (11th edn), [1844]; tr Bulgarian by N. D. Katrapov, Moscow 1850; Czech by Josef V. Frič, Prague 1854; Dutch by J. van Lennep, Amsterdam 1826; French by Léon Thiessé (as Zuleika et Selim), Paris 1816; by August Calvereau, Ghent 1823; German by J. V. Adrian, Frankfurt 1819; by Finck de Bailleul, Landau 1843; by O. Riedel, Hamburg 1872; by F. Kley, Halle 1884; Hungarian by Tercsi, Budapest 1885; Italian, Milan 1828 (anon); by Angelo Fava, Milan 1832; by Giovanni Giovio, Milan 1854; Polish by Ladislaus hr Ostrowski, Warsaw 1828; Russian by M. Kachenovsky, Vyestnik Evropui (Moscow) nos 18–20 1821; by Ivan Kozlov, Leningrad 1826, 1831; by M. Politkovsky, Moscow 1859; Spanish, Paris 1828 (anon), by Joaquin Fiol, Palma de Mallorca 1854; Swedish [by C. W. A. Strandberg], Stockholm [1855].

Reviewed: Edinburgh Rev 23 1814 (by Francis Jeffrey); Quart Rev 10 1814 (by George Ellis).

Dramatized: William Dimond, The bride of Abydos: a tragick play in three acts, 1818, New York 1818, London [1866]; W.O., The bride of Abydos: a tragedy in five acts, 1818. Parodied: The outlaw: a tale, by Erasmus, Edinburgh 1818. Adapted: [J. W. H. Payne], The unfortunate lovers: or the affecting history of Selim and Almena, a Turkish tale from the bride of Abydos, [c. 1821], New York 1822.

The corsair: a tale. 1814 (3 issues), 1814 (2nd–7th edns), New York 1814, Philadelphia 1814, Boston 1814, Baltimore 1814, 1815 (8th–9th edns), 1818 (10th edn), 1825; ed J. W. Lake, Paris 1830, 1835, [1844], 1867; tr Czech by Cenek Ibl, Prague 1885; Danish by H. Schou, Copenhagen 1855; French by Lucile Thomas, Paris 1825; German by F. L. von Tschirsky, Berlin 1816, by Elise von Hohenhausen, Altona 1820, by Caroline Pichler, Vienna 1820, by Friederike Friedmann, Leipzig 1852, by Victor von Arentschild, Mainz 1852, by Adolf Seubert, Leipzig [1874]; Hungarian by Gésa Kacziány, Budapest 1892; Italian by L. C. Turin, 1819, Milan 1820, 1824 (anon), by Giuseppe Nicolini, Milan 1842; by Eritrio Migdonio, Florence 1842, by Luigi Serenelli Honorati, Bologna 1870, by Carlo Rosnati, Pavia 1879; Polish by A. E. Odyniec, Paris 1835; Wroclaw 1839; Russian by A. Boeikov, Novosti Literatur (Leningrad) Oct–Nov 1825, by V. Olin, Leningrad 1827; Spanish, Paris 1827 (anon), Valencia 1832 (anon), by Vicente W. Querol and T. Llorente, Valencia 1863; Swedish by 'Talis Qualis' [i.e. C. W. A. Strandberg], Stockholm 1868.

Reviewed: Edinburgh Rev 23 1814 (by Francis Jeffrey); Quart Rev 11 1814 (by George Ellis).

Adapted or dramatized: [William Hone], Conrad the Corsair: or the pirate's isle, adapted as a romance, 1817; E. F. C. Boulay-Paty and H. J. J. Lucas, Le corsaire, Paris 1830, 1901; G. Galzerani, Il corsaro: azione mimica, Milan 1826; G. Rossetti (senior), Il corsaro: scene melodrammatiche, [c. 1830]; G. Rossetti (senior), Medora e corrado: cantata melodrammatica tratta dal Corsaro di Lord Byron, [c. 1832]; Giacopo Ferretti, Il corsaro: melo-dramma romantico in due atti, Rome [1831].

Uhde, H. Zur Poetik von Byrons Corsair. Leipzig 1907.

Ode to Napoleon Buonaparte. 1814 (anon), 1814 (anon) (2nd–9th edns), Boston 1814, New York 1814, Philadelphia 1814, London 1815 (11th edn), 1816 (12th edn), 1818 (13th edn); tr Spanish, Paris 1830 (anon). Reviewed: Morning Chron 21 April 1814 (by James Perry); Examiner 24 April 1814 (by Leigh Hunt); Anti-Jacobin Rev May 1914.

Lara: a tale; Jacqueline: a tale. 1814 (anon, 2 issues; Jacqueline is by Samuel Rogers), 1814 (anon) (2nd–3rd edns), Boston 1814 (anon), 1814 (4th edn, 1st separate and acknowledged edn), New York 1814, 1817 (5th edn); tr Czech by C. Ibl, Prague 1885; French, Avallon 1840 (anon) (priv ptd); German by J. V. Adrian (in Versmaase des Originals), Frankfurt 1819, by W. Schaeffer and A. Strodtmann, Leipzig 1886; Italian by Girolamo, Count Bazoldo, Paris 1828, by Andrea Maffei, Milan 1882; Polish by J. Korsak, Vilna 1833; Serbian by Atso Popović, Novisad 1860; Spanish, Paris 1828 (anon); Swedish by 'Talis Qualis' [i.e. C. W. A. Strandberg], Stockholm 1869. Reviewed: Quart Rev 11 1814 (by George Ellis); Plagiarisms of Lord Byron, GM Feb 1818 (by A. Dyce).

Hebrew melodies ancient and modern with appropriate symphonies and accompaniments by I. Braham and I. Nathan, the poetry written expressly for the work by Lord Byron. 2 pts [1815], 1 vol 1815 (poetry without the music; 2 issues), Boston 1815, New York 1815, Philadelphia 1815, London 1823, 1825, 1829 (with addns in Fugitive pieces and reminiscences of Lord Byron by I. Nathan); tr Czech by Jaroslen Vrchlický and J. V. Sladek, Prague 1890; Danish by F. Andresen-Halmrast, Oslo 1889; French by J. A. Delérue (in Méandres), Rouen 1845; German by Franz Theremin, Berlin, 1820, by J. E. Hilscher, Laibach 1833, by Eduard Nickles, Karlsruhe 1863, by Heinrich Stadelmann, Memmingen 1866; Hebrew by S. Mandelkern, Leipzig 1890; Italian by P. P. Parzanese, Naples 1837, Ivrea 1855 (anon); Russian by P. Kozlov, Leningrad 1860; Spanish by Tomás Aguiló (in La Fe), Palma de Mallorca 1844, rptd in his Obras en prosa y en versa, Palma de Mallorca 1883; Swedish by Theodor Lind, Helsingfors [1862]; Yiddish by Nathan Horowitz, 1925, 1930. Reviewed: Christian Observer Aug 1815; Analectic Mag (Philadelphia) Dec 1815; Edinburgh Rev 27 1816 (by F. Jeffrey).

Beutler, C. A. Ueber Lord Byrons Hebrew melodies. Leipzig 1912.

Slater, J. Byron's Hebrew melodies. SP 49 1952.

Morel, W. Zu Byrons Hebrew melodies. Anglia 73 1955.

There's not a joy this world can give: a ballad written by Lord Byron, composed by Sir John Stevenson. [1815] (4 leaves with music); rptd in Poems, 1816.

The siege of Corinth: a poem; Parisina: a poem. 1816 (anon), 1816 (2nd–3rd edn) (anon), New York 1816, 1818 (4th edn), 1824, 1826. Reviewed: Monthly Rev Feb 1816; Eclectic Rev March 1816; European Mag May 1816; Literary Panorama June 1816.

The siege of Corinth [alone]. 1824, Paris 1835, Lüneburg 1854, London 1879; ed J. G. C. Schuler, Halle 1886; ed K. Bandow, Bielefeld [c. 1890]; ed K. Koelbing, Berlin 1893; ed P. Hordern 1914; tr Dutch by J. Van Lennep, Amsterdam 1831; French by C. Mancel, Paris 1820; (extracts only) by F. de Reiffenberg in Poésies diverses, Paris 1825; by A. Giron, Brussels 1827; German by A. Wollheim, Hamburg [1817?]; [by F. L. Breuer], Leipzig 1820; by G. E. Schumann, Hamburg 1827; Italian by Vincenzo Padovan, Venice 1838; Spanish, Madrid 1818, Paris 1826, 1828, 1828, Barcelona 1838; Swedish [by C. W. A. Strandberg], Stockholm [1854]. Dramatized by — Soumet and — Balochi, Le siège de Corinth: tragédie lyrique en cinq actes, Paris 1826.

Parisina [alone]. Tr French by Adolphe Krafft, Paris 1900; German by J. V. Cirkel in his Gedichte, Münster 1826; by L. A. Frankel, Vienna 1836; Italian, Milan 1821 (anon), by Andrea Maffei, Milan 1853, by Carlo Dall' Oro, Mantua 1854, by Paolo Pappalardo, Palermo 1855, by A. Canepa, Genoa 1864; Polish by I. Szydlowski, Vilna 1834; Russian by V. Verderevsky, Leningrad 1827; Spanish, Paris 1830 (anon), by H. de V[edia] in El seminario pintoresco (pp. 339, 349), Madrid 1841; Swedish [by C. W. A. Strandberg], Stockholm [1854]. Adapted in Parisina, poème imité de Lord Byron, Montpellier 1829. Dramatized by F. Romani as Parisina: dramma serio, Bologna 1836; as Parisina: melodramma, Venice 1838, Vercelli [c. 1840], Turin 1858; as Parisina: tragedia lirica, Milan 1841.

Wurzbach, W. von. Lord Byrons Parisina und ihre Vorgaengerinnen. E Studien 25 1898.

Stevenson, L. My last Duchess and Parisina. MLN 74 1959.

Fare thee well! 18 March 1816 (52 lines; proof, Murray), [4 April] (60 lines, priv ptd), 7 April 1816 (60 lines, priv ptd). First pbd in Champion 14 April 1816. A list of later appearances in newspapers is given by E. H. Coleridge, Works: poetry, vol 3 pp. 532–5.

A reply to fare thee well: lines addressed to Lord Byron. 1816, 1816.

Lady Byron's responsive fare thee well. 1816 (3 edns), 1825.

Lines addressed to Lady Byron. 1817. Attributed to Mrs Cockle.

Reply to Lord Byron's Fare thee well. 1817. Also attributed to Mrs Cockle.

Reply to fare thee well. Newcastle 1817.

A sketch from private life. 30 March 1816 (proof, Murray), [2 April] (priv ptd). First pbd in Champion 14 April 1816.

A sketch from public life, and A farewell, by Tyro. 1816.

Lines on the departure of a great poet from his country. 1816. Attributed to Charles Thomson.

[Poems on his domestic circumstances.] Fare thee well: a sketch from private life. Bristol (Barry & Son) 1816 (2 poems only), Dublin (W. Espy) 1816 (2 poems); Fare thee well: a sketch etc, Napoleon's farewell, On the star of the Legion of Honour and Ode from the French; (Sherwood Neely & Jones) 1816 (5 poems); An ode: on the star of the Legion of Honour, New York 1816 (the same 5 poems as the previous edn); Fare thee well: a sketch from private life, with other poems, (Rodwell & Martin) 1816 (6 poems); Fare thee well and other poems, Edinburgh (J. Robertson) 1816 (7 poems, 2 of which are not by Byron); Poems on his domestic circumstances (William Hone) 1816 (20 edns, 7 poems, 2 of which are not by Byron; Adieu to Malta was added to the 6th Hone edn, its first appearance in print, and The curse of Minerva to the 8th edn; succeeding edns have the same title as Hone, except where noted); (Richard Edwards) 1816 (10 edns), (Effingham Wilson) 1816 (2nd edn), (Bumpus) 1816 (2 edns, prefatory matter by J. Nightingale); (J. Fairburn) 1816; Boston (J. Eliot) 1816 (from Hone's 6th edn); Bristol (W. Sheppard) 1816 (2nd edn) (20 poems, of which 7 are not by Byron); Miscellaneous poems including those on his domestic circumstances (S. Hodgson) 1823 (25 poems, of which 7 are not by Byron); (J. Bumpus) 1824 (same title as previous edn; 25 poems of which 7 are not by Byron); Miscellaneous poems on his domestic and other circumstances (William Cole) 1825 (29 poems, as in the 1824 edn, with 4 genuine poems added); tr French by Aristide Guilbert, 1826 (Ode from the French only).

Cook, D. Byron's Fare thee well. TLS 18 Sept 1937.

Pollard, H. G. Pirated collections of Byron. TLS 16 Oct 1937.

Poems. (John Murray) 1816 (2 issues), 1816 (2nd edn).

The prisoner of Chillon and other poems. 1816 (2 issues), Lausanne 1818, 1822, London 1824, [1825?], Geneva 1830; ed T. Harvey, Paris 1846, Lausanne 1857, London 1865; ed R. S. Davies [1877]; ed F. Fischer, Berlin 1884; ed T. C. Cann, Florence 1885; ed H.

Evans 1896; ed E. Koelbing, Weimar 1898; ed J. W. Cousins [1910]; ed G. B. Gifford, Lausanne [1939]; tr Czech by Antonin Klásterský, Prague 1895, 1922; Dutch by K. L. Ledeganck in his Gedichten, Ghent 1856; French, Vévey (c. 1870) (anon), Geneva 1892 (anon); German by G. Kreyenberg, Lausanne 1861, by M. von der Marwitz, Vévey [1865], by T. R., Berlin 1886, by J. G. Hagmann, Leipzig 1892; Icelandic by Steingrimur Thorsteinson, Copenhagen 1866, Italian [np] 1830 (anon), by Andrea Maffei, Milan 1853; (Darkness only) by I. Turgenev, Peterburgskii Sbornik 1846, p. 501; Polish by F. D. Morawski (in his Poematów), Leszno 1853, rptd separately Zloczów 1893; Russian by V. Zh[ukovsky], Leningrad 1822; Spanish, Paris 1830 (anon); Swedish [by C. W. A. Strandberg], Stockholm [1854]. Reviewed: Quart Rev 16 1816 (by Sir Walter Scott); Edinburgh Rev 27 1816 (by F. Jeffrey); Critical Rev Dec 1816; Eclectic Rev March 1817. The Dream, originally pbd in this collection, was pbd separately 1849.

Monti, G. In his Studi critici, Florence 1887.

'Amstel, A. van' (J. C. Neuman). The true story of the prisoner of Chillon. Nineteenth Century May 1900.

Monody on the death of the Right Honourable R. B. Sheridan. 1816 (anon) (2 issues), 1817, 1818.

The lament of Tasso. 1817, 1817 (2nd–5th edns), New York 1817, 1818 (6th edn); tr Dutch by J. van Lennep, Amsterdam 1833; French by — Marvaud (in Huit Messéniennes), Paris 1824; Italian by Michele Leoni, Pisa 1818, by P. M. (in Veglie di Torquato Tasso), Venice 1826; by Gaetano Polidori (in La Magion del Terrore), 1843 (priv ptd); by Guglielmo Godio, Turin 1873. Reviewed: GM Aug 1817; Scots Mag Aug 1817; Blackwood's Mag Nov 1817.

Manfred: a dramatic poem. 1817 (3 issues), 1817 (2nd edn), Philadelphia 1817, New York 1817, 1817, London 1824, 1825, Brussels [c. 1830], London 1863 (as Manfred: a choral tragedy in 3 acts); ed G. Ferrando, Florence 1926; ed F. Carter 1929; tr Croatian by Stjepan Mildtić, Zagreb 1894; Czech by Josef V. Frič, Prague 1882; Danish by P. F. Wulff, Copenhagen 1820; by Edvard Lembcke, Copenhagen 1843; Dutch by Johan Rudolph Steinmetz, Amsterdam 1857; by W. Gosler, Heusden 1882; French by the Comtesse de Lalaing, Brussels 1833, 1852; by François Ponsard, Paris 1837; by Emile Moreau, Paris 1887; by C. Trébla, Toulouse 1888; German by Adolf Wagner, Leipzig 1819, by T. Armin, Göttingen 1836, by 'Posgaru' (G. F. W. Suckow), Breslau 1839, by O. S. Seeman, Berlin 1843; Leipzig 1853 (anon), by Hermann von Koesen, Leipzig 1858, by L. Freytag, Berlin 1872, by Adolf Seubert, Leipzig [1874], (with music by Robert Schumann) Leipzig [c. 1880], by Thierry Preyer, Frankfurt 1883; Modern Greek by E. Green, Patras 1864; Hungarian by Lázár Horváth, Budapest 1842, by Imre Kludik, Szolnok 1884, by Emil Abrányi, Budapest 1891, 1897; Icelandic by Matthias Jochumsson, Copenhagen 1875; Italian by Marcello Mazzoni, Milan 1832, by Silvio Pellico, Florence 1859; by Andrea Maffei, Florence 1870; Polish by E. S. Bojanowski, Wroclaw 1835, by F. D. Morawski in Poematów, Leszno 1853, rptd separately Lwow [1885], by Michal Chodźkę, Paris [1859]; Roumanian by T. M. Stoenescu, Bucharest 1896; Russian by O., Moskovski Vyestnik (Moscow) July 1825, by M. Bronchenko, Leningrad 1828, by A. Borodin, Panteon (Leningrad) Feb 1841; by E. Zarin, Biblioteca dlya Chteniya (Leningrad) Aug 1858, by D. Minaev, Russkoi Slovo (Leningrad) April 1853; Spanish, Paris 1830 (anon), by José Alcalá Galiano and Fernandez de las Peñas, Madrid 1861, by Angel R. Chaves, Madrid 1876. Reviewed: Edinburgh Monthly Mag June 1817 (by John Wilson); Critical Rev June 1817; Day & New Times 23 June 1817; Eclectic Rev July 1817; Monthly Rev July 1817; GM July 1817; Edinburgh Rev 28 1817 (by F. Jeffrey); Kunst und Alterthum (Weimar) June 1820 (by Goethe; rptd in Sämtliche Werke vol 37, Stuttgart 1907, pp. 184–7).

B., F. H. Manfred: an address to Lord Byron, with an opinion on some of his writings. 1817.

Duentzer, H. Goethes Faust in seiner Einheit und Ganzheit: ueber Byrons Manfred. Cologne 1836.

Roetscher, H. Manfred in ihren inneren Zusammenhange entwickelt. Berlin 1844, Bamberg 1884.

Lord Byron's Manfred at Drury Lane Theatre, by a dilettante behind the scenes. 1863.

Manfred: peom and drama, by the London hermit. Dublin Univ Mag April 1874.

Anton, H. S. Byrons Manfred. Erfurt 1875.

Koelbing, E. Zu Byrons Manfred. E Studien 22 1898.

Manfred: dramatische Dichtung von Lord Byron von einem Theologen. Oldenburg [1898].

Brandl, A. Goethes Verhaeltniss zur Byron. Goethe-Jahrbuch 20 1899.

Varnhagen, H. De rebus quibusdam compositionem Byronis dramatis quod Manfred inscribitur praecedentibus. Erlangen 1909.

Butterwick, J. C. A note on the first editions of Manfred. Book Collectors' Quart 3 1931.

Evans, B. Manfred's remorse and dramatic tradition. PMLA 62 1947.

Quinland, M. J. Byron's Manfred and Zoroastrianism. JEGP 51 1958.

Allott, K. Arnold's Empedocles on Etna and Byron's Manfred. N & Q Aug 1962.

Butler, M. H. An examination of Byron's revision of Manfred, act III. SP 60 1963.

Beppo: a Venetian story. 1818 (anon), 1818 (2nd–7th edns), Boston 1818, New York 1818, Paris 1821, London 1825.

Additional stanzas to the first, second and third editions of Beppo. [1818] (single sheet). These were first added to the 4th edn; the 5th edn was the first to bear Byron's name. Tr Danish by Alfred Ipsen, Copenhagen 1891; Dutch by J. van Lennep, Amsterdam 1834; French by S. Clogenson, Paris 1865, by A. Morisseau, Paris 1881, Russian by V. Lubich-Romanovich, Sine Otechestva (Leningrad) April 1842; D. Minaev, Sovremennik (Leningrad) Aug 1863; Spanish, Paris 1829 (anon); Swedish by 'Talis Qualis' (C. W. A. Strandberg), Stockholm [1854]. Reviewed: Edinburgh Rev 29 1818 (by F. Jeffrey); Monthly Rev March 1818; Eclectic Rev new ser 9 1818.

A poetical epistle from Alma Mater to Lord Byron occasioned by lines in a tale called Beppo. Cambridge 1819.

Beppo in London: a metropolitan story. 1819.

Steffan, T. G. The Devil a bit of our Beppo. PQ 32 1953.

On John William Rizzo Hoppner born at Venice on 18 January 1818. [Padua 1818].

'My boat is on the shore'. 1818. With music by H. R. Bishop. *See* TLS 16 Oct 1937.

Mazeppa: a poem. 1819 (2 issues), Paris 1819, Boston 1819, Paris 1822, London 1824; ed H. M. Melford, Brunswick 1834; London [1854?]; tr Czech by Antonín Klásterský, Prague [c. 1895], 1922; French by J. Adolphe (in Manuel anglais), Paris 1830; German by T. Hell (Th. Winkler), Leipzig 1820; by Everhard Brauns, Göttingen 1836, by Otto Gildemeister, Bremen 1858, by Ferdinand Freiligath, Stuttgart 1883; Hungarian by Lázár Horváth, Budapest 1842; Italian by Antonio Arioti, Palermo 1847; by T. Virzi, Palermo 1876; by Andrea Maffei, Milan 1886; Polish by Michal Chod kę, Halle 1860; Russian by M. Kachenovsky (in Vuibor iz sochineny Lorda Byrona), Moscow 1821; by A. Voeikov, Novosti Literatur (Leningrad) Nov 1824, by Ya Grot, Sovremennik (Leningrad) 9 1838; by D. Michailovsky, Sovremennik (Leningrad) May 1858, by I. Gogniev, Repertyar i Panteon (Leningrad) Oct 1844, rptd Dramatichesky sbornik (Leningrad) April 1860; Spanish, Paris 1828 (anon), 1830, by J. M. R. Bárcena (in his Ultimas poesías líricas), Mexico City 1888; Swedish [by C. W. A. Strandberg], Stockholm [1853].

Reviewed: Blackwood's Mag July 1819; John Gilpin and Mazeppa [by W. Maginn], ibid; Monthly Rev July 1819; Eclectic Rev Aug 1819.

Adapted: Mazeppa travestied: a poem. 1820; H. M. Milner, Mazeppa: a romantic drama from Lord Byron's poem,[c. 1830], 1874; A. Cortesi, Mazeppa: ballo storico, Milan 1841; C. White, Mazeppa: an equestrian burlesque in two acts, New York [c. 1860].

Englaender, D. Lord Byrons Mazeppa. Berlin 1897.

Holubnychy, L. Mazeppa in Byron's poem and in history. Ukrainian Quart 15 1959.

Don Juan [cantos 1–2]. 1819 (anon), 1819 (2 more edns), Paris 1819, Philadelphia 1819, London 1820 (3 edns), Paris 1821, London 1822, 1823.

Don Juan: cantos 3, 4 and 5. 1821 (anon), 1821 (4 more edns), Paris 1821, New York 1821, 1822 (rev) (5th edn).

Don Juan: cantos 6, 7 and 8. 1823 (anon), 1823 (2 more edns), Paris 1823, Philadelphia 1823, London 1825.

Don Juan: cantos 9, 10 and 11. 1823 (anon), 1823, Paris 1823, Philadelphia 1823.

Don Juan: cantos 12, 13 and 14. 1823 (anon), 1823 (2 more edns), Paris 1824, New York 1824.

Don Juan: cantos 15 and 16. 1824 (anon), 1824 (2 more edns), Paris 1824.

Dedication to Jon Juan. 1833.

Don Juan [cantos 1–5]. 1822 (4 edns), 1823, 1823, 1824, [1826?]; [Cantos 5–11], 1823; [cantos 1–16], 2 vols 1826, 1826 (3 edns), 1827, 1827, 2 vols 1828, 1828, 1828, 1832, Nuremberg [1832], London 1833, 1834, 1835, 1836, 2 vols 1837, Mannheim 1838, London 1845, 1849, [c. 1850], Halifax 1857; ed E. H. Coleridge 1906; ed F. H. Ristine, New York 1927; ed L. I. Bredvold, New York 1935; ed P. C. Quennell 1949; ed T. G. Steffan and W. W. Pratt 4 vols Austin 1957 (variorum).

The beauties of Don Juan. 2 vols 1828.

Tr Danish by H. Schou (canto i only), Fredericia 1854, by Holger Drachmann, 2 vols Copenhagen 1880–1902; French by A[médée] P[ichot] 3 vols Paris 1827, 2 vols Paris 1866, by Paul Lehodey, Paris [1869], by Adolphe Fauvel, Paris 1866, 1868, 1878; (cantos i–v) by A. Digeon, Paris 1854; German (cantos i–iv) by A. von Marées, Essen 1839, by Otto Gildemeister 2 vols Bremen 1845, by Adolf Boettger, Leipzig 1849, 1858, by Wilhelm Schaeffer 2 vols Hildburghausen 1867; Italian by A. Caccia, Turin 1853, by Antonietta Sacchi, Milan 1865 (part as Aidea, Episodio di Don Giovanni) by Vitorio Betteloni, Verona 1875, Milan 1880, by Enrico Casali, Milan 1876; Polish by Wiktor z Baworow (canto i only), Tarnopol 1863, (part of canto ii by same, Cracow 1877, (canto iii by same, Cracow 1877, (cantos ii–iv) by same, Tarnopol 1879, by E. Porebowicz, Warsaw 1885, 2 vols Warsaw 1922; Roumanian by I. Eliade (cantos i–ii), Bucharest 1847; Russian by I. Jand, Leningrad 1846; (cantod i–x) by V. Lubich-Romanovich 2 vols Leningrad [1847], by N. A. Markevitch, Leipzig 1862, (cantos i–x) by D. Minaev, Sovremennik (Leningrad), Jan–Oct 1865, by P. Kozlov, 2nd edn, ed P. Veinberg 2 vols Leningrad 1889, by A. Kozlov 2 vols Leningrad 1892; Serbian by O. Glumchevik 2 vols Belgrade 1888; Spanish 2 vols Paris 1829 (anon), by F. Villalba 2 vols Madrid 1876, [1916], by J. A. R., Barcelona 1883; Swedish (canto i only) Stockholm 1838 (anon), by C. W. A. Strandberg 2 vols Stockholm [1857–62].

Reviewed: Literary Gazette 17–24 July 1819, 11–18 Aug 1821, 19 July 1823, 6 Sept 1823, 6 Dec 1823, 3 April 1824; Monthly Rev July 1819, Aug 1821, July 1823, Oct 1823, April 1824; New Monthly Mag Aug 1819; Br Critic Aug 1819, Sept 1821; Br Rev Aug 1819, Dec 1821; Blackwood's Mag Aug 1819; Don Juan unread [by William Maginn], Blackwood's Mag Nov 1819; Aug 1821, July 1823; Examiner 31 Oct 1819, 26 Aug 1821, 14, 21 March 1824.

[Colton, Charles Caleb]. Remarks, critical and moral, on the talents of Lord Byron and the tendencies of Don Juan. 1819.

[Hone, William?]. Don John: or Don Juan unmasked. 1819 (3 edns).

[Stacy, John?]. A critique on the genius and writings of Lord Byron, with remarks on Don Juan. Norwich 1820.

Cottle, Joseph. An expostulary epistle to Lord Byron. 1820.

Gordon. A tale: a poetical review of Don Juan. 1821.

Goethe, J. W. von. Kunst und Alterthum 3 1821; rptd in Sämtliche Werke vol 37, Stuttgart 1807.

Thomas, J. W. An apology for Don Juan. 1824, 1825, 1850 ('to which is added a third canto'), 1855 (as Byron and the times: or an apology for Don Juan).

[Burgess, G.] Cato to Lord Byron on the immorality of his writings. 1824.

The morality of Don Juan, by the London hermit. Dublin Univ Mag May 1875.

Bévotte, G. G. de. La légende de Don Juan: son évolution dans la littérature des origines au romantisme. Paris 1906.

Pfeiffer, A. Thomas Hopes Anastasius und Byrons Don Juan. Munich 1913.

Alonzo, S. Giorgio Byron: attraverso Don Juan. Acireale 1931.

Austen, J. The story of Don Juan. 1939.

Johnson, E. D. H. Don Juan in England. ELH 11 1944.

Boyd, E. F. Byron's Don Juan. New Brunswick 1945.

Trueblood, P. G. The flowering of Byron's genius. Stanford 1945, New York 1963.

Madariaga, S. de. Don Juan as a European figure. Nottingham 1946.

Ure, P. Beckford's dwarf and Don Juan. N & Q 31 March 1951.

Steffan, T. G. and W. W. Pratt. Don Juan. Austin 1957 (variorum edn, vol i).

Ball, P. M. Byronic re-orientation: Don Juan, the comic vision. Twentieth Century Oct 1960.

Ridenour, G. H. The style of Don Juan. New Haven 1960.

Horn, A. Byron's Don Juan and the eighteenth-century English novel. Berne 1962.

Childers, W. C. A note on the dedication of Don Juan. Keats-Shelley Jnl 12 1963.

Mortenson, R. Another continuation of Don Juan. Stud in Romanticism 2 1963.

Stavrou, C. N. Religion in Byron's Don Juan. Rice Univ Stud in English Lit 3 1963.

Continuations

[Hone, William?]. Don Juan: canto the third. 1819.

Don Juan; with a biographical account of Lord Byron, canto 3. 1819.

A new canto. 1819.

Don Juan, canto 11. 1820.

Don Juan, canto 3. 1821.

[Thompson, W. G.?] A touch at an unpublished canto of Don Juan. Newcastle Mag Jan 1822.

[Clason, Isaac Star?] Don Juan: cantos 9, 10 and 11. Albany 1823.
Continuation of Don Juan: cantos 17 and 18. Oxford 1825, 1825.
Don Juan: cantos 17, 18. 1825.
[Clason, Isaac Star]. Don Juan: cantos 17–18. New York 1825.
Don Juan: canto 17. Rambler July 1825.
Juan secundus: canto the first. 1825.
Don Giovanni: a poem in two cantos. Edinburgh 1825, 1825.
The seventeenth canto of Don Juan. 1829.
Don Juan: canto 17. 1830.
[Clark, Charles?]. Twenty suppressed stanzas of Don Juan in reference to Ireland. In Georgian revel-ations! or the most accomplished gentleman's midnight visit below stairs, Great Totham (Essex) 1838 (priv ptd); priv rptd separately as Some rejected stanzas of Don Juan, Great Totham 1845.
Baxter, G. R. Don Juan junior: a poem by Byron's ghost. 1839.
C[owley], W[illiam]. Don Juan reclaimed: or his peregrination continued from Lord Byron. 1840.
Morford, Henry. The rest of Don Juan. New York 1846.
[Daniel, H. J.?]. Don Juan continued: canto 17. 1849.
Wilberforce, E. and E. F. Blanchard. Don Juan: canto seventeenth. In Poems, 1857.
Wetton, H. W. The termination of the sixteenth canto of Lord Byron's Don Juan. 1864.
The new Don Juan: the introduction by Gerald Noel Byron, the last canto of the original Don Juan from the papers of the Countess Guiccioli, by Lord Byron, never before published. [1880]. The whole book is by G. N. Byron.

Imitations and adaptations

Milner, H. M. The Italian Don Juan: or memoirs of the Devil. 1820.
Thornton, A. Don Juan, volume the first. 1821.
—— Don Juan, volume the second: containing his life in London. 1822.
The Sultana: or a trip to Turkey, a melodrama in three acts, founded on Lord Byron's Don Juan. New York 1822.
Buckstone, J. B. Don Juan: a romantic drama in three acts. [1828], [1887].
—— A new Don Juan. 1828.

Letter to my grandmother's review. 1819 (proof; Murray). First pbd in Liberal no 1 [15 Oct 1822].
Ward, W. S. Lord Byron and my grandmother's review. MLN 64 1949.

Some observations upon an article in Blackwood's Magazine no xxiv, August 1819. [1820] (proof; no copy extant). First pbd in Works of Lord Byron, ed John Wright vol 15, 1833.
Daghlian, P. B. Byron's Observations on an article in Blackwood's Magazine. RES 23 1947.

A letter to [John Murray] on the Rev W. L. Bowles' strictures on the life and writings of Pope. 1821 (2 issues), 1821 (2nd–3rd edns), Paris 1821. Reviewed: Blackwood's Mag May 1821; London Mag June 1821 (by William Hazlitt).
Campbell, T. Essay on English poetry. In Specimens of the British poets vol 1, 1819.
Bowles, W. L. Invariable principles of poetry in a letter addressed to T. Campbell. 1819.
[D'Israeli, I.]. [Review of Spence's Anecdotes]. Quart Rev 1820.
Bowles, W. L. A reply to the charges brought by the reviewer of Spence's Anecdotes. Pamphleteer 17 1820. *See* Bowles, below.
Gilchrist, O. G. Letter to the Rev W. L. Bowles. Stamford 1820.
Bowles, W. L. Observations on the poetical character of Pope. Pamphleteer 17–18 1820.
—— Two letters to Lord Byron in answer to his Lordship's letter. 1821, 1821, 1822 (as Letters to Lord Byron on a question of poetical criticism).
MacDermot, M. A letter to the Rev W. L. Bowles in reply to his letter to T. Campbell, and to his two letters to Lord Byron. 1822.
A letter to Lord Byron protesting against the immolation of Gray, Cowper and Campbell at the shrine of Pope, by Fabius. 1823.
Bowles, W. L. A final appeal to the literary public relative to Pope. 1825.
Rennes, J. J. van. Bowles, Byron and the Pope controversy. Amsterdam 1927.

Observations upon Observations: a second letter to John Murray esq on the Rev W. L. Bowles' strictures on the life and writings of Pope. 1821 (proof; no copy extant). First pbd in Works of Lord Byron, ed John Wright vol 6, 1932.

The Irish avatar. [1821] (priv ptd). The only copy known is in BM (Ashley Library). *See* Athenaeum 26 June 1909. First pbd by Thomas Medwin in his Conversations of Lord Byron, 1824.

Marino Faliero, Doge of Venice: an historical tragedy in five acts, with notes; The prophecy of Dante: a poem. 1821 (2 issues), 1821 (2nd edn), 1823 (3rd edn). Reviewed: Blackwood's Mag April 1821 (by John Wilson); Monthly Rev May 1821; Indicator 2 May 1821 (by Leigh Hunt); Eclectic Rev June 1821; Edinburgh Rev 35 1821 (by F. Jeffrey); Quart Rev 27 1822 (by Reginald Heber).

Marino Faliero [alone]. Paris 1821, Philadelphia 1821, 1821, London 1842; ed F. Brockerhoff, Berlin 1853; tr German by G. von Hardt, Paderborn 1827, by Carl Deahna, Bayreuth 1850, by Thierry Preyer, Frankfurt 1883, by A. Fitger, Oldenburg [1886]; Italian by P. G. B. Cereseto, Savona 1845; Spanish by Marcial Busquetz, Barcelona 1868.
Letter to R. W. Elliston on the injustice and illegality of his conduct in presenting Lord Byron's tragedy Marino Faliero. [1821].
Marino Faliero: or the Doge of Venice: an interesting tale on which is founded the celebrated tragedy of Lord Byron. [c. 1822] (3 edns).
Kaiser, —. Byrons und Delavignes Marino Faliero. Düsseldorf 1870.
Krause, F. Byrons Marino Faliero: ein Beitrag zur vergleichenden Litteratur-geschichte. Breslau 1897.
[Dedication of Marino Faliero to Goethe]. Goethe-Jahrbuch 20 1899.
Schiff, Herman. Ueber Lord Byrons Marino Faliero und seine anderen geschichtlichen Dramen. Marburg 1910.
King, L. The influence of Shakespeare on Byron's Marino Faliero. Texas Univ Stud no 11 1931.
Johnson, E. D. H. A political interpretation of Marino Faliero. MLQ 3 1942.

The prophecy of Dante [alone]. Paris 1821, Philadelphia 1821, London 1825; ed L. W. Potts 1879 (cantos i–ii); tr French by Benjamin Laroche (in Oeuvres de Dante), Paris 1842; Italian by L. da Ponte, New York 1821, by Giovanni Giovio, Milan 1856, by Melchiore Missirini, Milan 1858; Spanish by Antonio Maria Vizcayno, Mexico City 1850.

Sardanapulus: a tragedy; The two Foscari: a tragedy; Cain: a mystery. 1821, Boston 1822. Reviewed: Edinburgh Rev 36 1822 (by F. Jeffrey); Blackwood's Mag Feb 1822; Br Rev March 1822; Eclectic Rev May 1822; Examiner 2 June 1822; Quart Rev 27 1822 (by Reginald Heber); Portfolio (Philadelphia) Dec 1822.

Sardanapalus [alone]. Paris 1822, New York 1822, London 1823, [c. 1825], 1829, Arnsberg 1849, London [1853] (adapted for representation by Charles Kean), Manchester [1875] (adapted by Charles Calvert); tr Czech by Františec Krsek, Prague 1891; Danish by

J. Ruesse, Copenhagen 1827; French by L. Aloin, Brussels 1834, by H. Becque, Paris 1867, by M. P. Berton, Paris 1882; German by Emma Herz, Posen 1854, by C. J. Arnold, Bremen 1854, by Adolf Boettger, Jena 1888, by Josef Kainz, Berlin 1897; Modern Greek by Christos A. Parmenidos, Athens 1865; Italian, Milan 1884 (anon); Polish by Fryderyk Krauze, Warsaw 1872; Russian by E. Zarin, Biblioteka dlya Chteniya (Leningrad) Dec 1860, by O. N. Zhiuminoi, Artist (Moscow) Sept–Oct 1890; Spanish, Madrid 1847 (anon), (part only) by Andres Bello (in his Obras completas vol 3), Santiago de Chile 1883; Swedish by Nils Arfvidsson, Stockholm 1864.

Nieschlag, H. Ueber Lord Byrons Sardanapalus. Halle 1900.

The two Foscari [alone]. Paris 1822, New York 1822; tr French by Escudier frères, 1849, by A. Morisseau, Paris 1881; Italian by P. G. B. Cereseto, Savona 1845; Russian by E. Zarin, Biblioteka dlya Chteniya (Leningrad) Nov 1861; Spanish by Manuel Canete, Madrid 1846, by Manuel Hiraldez de Acosta, Barcelona 1868.

Bebbington, W. G. The two Foscari. English 9 1953.

Cain [alone]. 1822 (6 edns), Paris 1822, New York 1822 London 1824; ed H. Grant 1830; 1832, Breslau 1840, London [1883]; ed B. Uhlmeyer, Nuremberg 1907; tr Czech by Josef Durdík, Prague 1871, Dutch by S. A. Klok, Hague 1906; Esperanto by A. Kofman, Nuremberg 1896; French by Febre D'Olivet, Paris 1823 (D'Olivet's version tr L. Redfield, New York 1923); German by G. Parthey, Berlin 1831, by Frederike Friedmann, Leipzig 1855, by Adolf Seubert, Leipzig [1874]; Greek verse by H. N. de Villiers, Oxford 1925; Hebrew by David Frishmann, Warsaw 1900; Hungarian by Ilona Gyory, [Budapest] 1895, by Lajos Mikes, Budapest 1898; Italian by Andrea Maffei Milan 1852; Polish by Adam Pajgert, Lwow 1868; Russian by E. Baruishev, Leningrad 1881, by P. A. Kalenov, Moscow 1883, Spanish by J. G., Madrid 1873.

[Todd, H. J.] A remonstrance to Mr John Murray respecting a recent publication, by Oxoniensis. 1822.

A letter to Sir Walter Scott in answer to the remonstrance of Oxoniensis on the publication of Cain.

A vindication of the Paradise lost from the charge of exculpating Cain, by Phil-Milton. 1822.

Harness, W. The wrath of Cain. 1822.

Revolutionary causes, with a postscript containing strictures on Cain, by Britannicus. 1822.

A letter of expostulation to Lord Byron. 1822.

Uriel: a poetical address to Lord Byron. 1822, 1825.

Battine, W. Another Cain: a mystery. 1822.

Another Cain: a poem. 1822. Anon.

Adams, T. A scourge for Lord Byron: or Cain, a mystery unmasked. 1823.

Wilkinson, H. Cain: a poem containing an antidote to the impiety and blasphemy of Lord Byron's Cain. 1824.

Goethe, J. W. von. Kunst und Alterthum 5 1824; rptd in his Sämtliche Werke vol 37, Stuttgart 1907, pp. 263–7.

A layman's epistle to a certain nobleman. 1824.

Remarks on Cain. [c. 1825] (priv ptd).

[Reade, J. E.] Cain the wanderer and other poems. 1830.

Monthly Mag May 1830; Fraser's Mag April 1831. Reviews of Harding Grant's edn.

Schaffner, A. Lord Byrons Cain und seine Quellen. Strasbourg 1880.

Blumenthal, F. Lord Byron's mystery Cain and its relation to Milton's Paradise lost and Gessner's Death of Abel. Oldenburg 1891.

Graf, A. La poesia di Caino. Nuova Antologia 16 March, 1 April 1908.

Brooke, S. A. Byron's Cain. Hibbert Jnl 18 1919.

Babcock, R. W. The inception and reception of Byron's Cain. South Atlantic Quart 26 1927.

Heaven and earth. [1821] (proof; no copy extant), Paris 1823 (anon), London 1824 (anon), 1825, [c.1825]. First pbd in Liberal no 2 1823; tr Danish by P. F. Wulff, Copenhagen 1827; French by A[médée P[ichot] in Essai sur le génie et le caractère de Lord Byron, Paris 1824; Italian by Andrea Maffei, Milan 1853. Reviewed: Blackwood's Mag Jan 1823 (by J. Wilson); Edinburgh Rev 38 1823 (by F. Jeffrey).

Mayn, G. Ueber Lord Byrons Heaven and earth. Breslau 1887.

Zuch, J. Thomas Moores The loves of the angels und Lord Byrons Heaven and earth: eine Parallele. Vienna 1905.

The vision of judgement. Paris 1822, London 1822 (with Southey's Vision of judgement, as The two visions), New York 1823, London 1824 (anon), [c. 1830] (anon); ed E. M. Earl 1929; ed F. B. Pinion 1958. First pbd in Liberal no 1 1822. Reviewed: Courier 16 Oct 1822; Literary Gazette 19, 26 Oct, 2 Nov 1822.

The age of bronze: or carmen seculare et annus haud mirabilis. 1823 (anon), 1823 (2nd–3rd edns), Paris 1823, New York 1823, London 1824, 1825. Reviewed: Examiner 30 March 1823; Scots Mag April 1823; Monthly Rev April 1823; Literary Chron 5 April 1823; Literary Gazette 5 April 1823; Monthly Mag May 1823.

The island: or Christian and his comrades. 1823, 1823 (2nd–3rd edns), Paris 1823, New York 1823, London 1826, 1826; tr German [by F. L. Breuer], Leipzig 1827; Italian by — Morrone, Naples 1840; Polish by Adam Pajgert, Cracow 1859; Swedish [by C. W. A. Strandberg], Stockholm [1856]. Reviewed: Literary Chron 21 June 1823; Literary Gazette 21 June 1823; Monthly Rev July 1823; Atlantic Mag (New York) April 1826.

Lotze, C. Quellenstudien ueber Lord Byrons The island. Leipzig 1902.

Werner: a tragedy. 1823 (2 issues), Paris 1823, Philadelphia 1823; ed J. W. S. Howes, New York 1848, London 1865, 1866; tr French, Paris 1844 (anon); German by G. Lotz, Hamburg 1823; Russian by Neizvustn, Leningrad 1829. Reviewed: Blackwood's Mag Dec 1822 (by W. Maginn); Scots Mag Dec 1822; European Mag Jan 1823; Eclectic Rev Feb 1823.

Stoehsel, C. Lord Byrons Trauerspiel Werner und seine Quelle. Erlangen 1891.

Gower, F. L. Did Byron write Werner? Nineteenth Century Aug 1899.

Kluge, W. Lord Byrons Werner: eine dramentechnische Untersuchung mit Quellenstudien. Leipzig 1913.

Motter, T. H. V. Byron's Werner re-estimated. In The Parrott presentation volume by pupils of Prof T. M. Parrott, Princeton 1935.

The deformed transformed: a drama. 1824 (2 variants), 1824 (2nd–3rd edns), Paris 1824, Philadelphia 1824, London [1883]; tr Hungarian by Jośzef Eotvos, Budapest 1840. Reviewed: London Mag March 1824; Scots Mag March 1824; Monthly Mag March 1824; Westminster Rev July 1824.

Varnhagen, H. Ueber Byrons dramatisches Bruchstueck Der umgestaltete Missgestaltete. Erlangen 1905.

The parliamentary speeches of Lord Byron, printed from copies prepared by his Lordship for publication. 1824.

A political ode. 1880. I.e. An ode to the framers of the Frame Bill. First pbd in Morning Chron 2 March 1812.

A version of Ossian's address to the sun. Cambridge Mass [1898] (priv ptd); rptd Atlantic Monthly Dec 1898.

Letters and Journals

[Letter to the editor]. Galignani's Messenger (Paris) May 1819; facs rptd in Works (Galignani), Paris 1826, 1 vol edn.

[Part of journal for Sept 1816]. London Mag March 1820.

[Letter I]. Sir Charles Darell: or the vortex, by R. C. Dallas. 4 vols 1820. Vol 1 pp. 1–6; rptd in Dallas, Recollections, 1824, pp. 259–63.

[Letter on swimming the Hellespont]. Monthly Mag April 1821; rptd in Traveller 3 April 1821.

[Letter to E. D. Clarke]. The life and remains of E. D. Clarke. Ed W. Otter 1824. P. 627.

Correspondence of Lord Byron with a friend, including letters to his mother written from Portugal, Spain, Greece and the shores of the Mediterranean in 1809, 1810 and 1811. Ed R. C. Dallas [1824] (suppressed before pbn), 3 vols Paris 1825, 2 vols Philadelphia 1825; tr French, Paris 1825, 1825.

[Letter to M. H. Beyle et al]. Conversations of Lord Byron at Pisa by Thomas Medwin. 1824.

[Letter to Andreas Londos et al.] A narrative of Lord Byron's last journey to Greece by Count Pietro Gamba. 1825.

[Letter to John Bowring]. Greece in 1823 and 1824 by L. F. C. Stanhope. 1825. P. 550.

[Letters to J. J. Coulmann]. Une visite à Byron à Gênes, suivie d'une lettre du noble Lord sur l'essai sur la vie et ses ouvrages de M. A[médée] P[ichot], par J. J. Coulmann. Paris 1826; tr Paul Pry, 1 April 1826.

[Letter to W. E. West]. The literary souvenir. 1827. Preface p. x.

[Letters to Thomas J. Dibdin]. Reminiscences of Thomas J. Dibdin. 1827. Vol 2 pp. 65, 69–70.

[Letters to Leigh Hunt]. Lord Byron and some of his contemporaries, by Leigh Hunt. 1828.

[Letter to Isaac D'Israeli]. The literary character by Isaac D'Israeli. 1828 (4th edn). Preface.

Letters and journals of Lord Byron, with notices of his life by Thomas Moore. 2 vols 1830, New York [1830], 1 vol Paris 1831, 3 vols 1832, 1833, 1 vol 1837, 1847 (as The life of Lord Byron with his letters and journals), 1850, 1860 (as The life, letters and journals of Lord Byron), 1875; tr French by Louise Swanton Belloc 5 vols Paris 1830. Reviewed: Athenaeum 25 Dec 1830, 1–8 Jan 1831; Blackwood's Mag Feb–March 1831; Quart Rev 44 1831; Fraser's Mag March 1831; Edinburgh Rev 53 1831.

[Letters to Hon Douglas Kinnaird]. Keepsake 1830. Pp. 218–32.

[Letter to Henry Angelo]. Reminiscences of Henry Angelo vol 2, 1830. P. 132.

[Letter to John Galt]. The life of Lord Byron by John Galt. 1830. Pp. 179–80.

[Letters to Col Duffie]. Conversations on religion with Lord Byron by James Kennedy. 1830.

[Letters to Eugenius Roche]. London in a thousand years, with other poems, by Eugenius Roche. 1830. Pp. 5–6.

[Letters to John Hunt]. Literary Guardian 5 Dec 1831–16 June 1832.

[Letters to the Earl of Blessington]. New Monthly Mag July 1832.

[Letter to John Taylor]. Records of my life by John Taylor. 1832. Vol 2 p. 351.

Lord Byron. Discorso di Cesare Cantu; aggiuntevi alcune traduzioni ed un serie di lettere dello stesso Lord Byron ove si narrano i suoi viaggi in Italia e nella Grecia. Milan 1833; tr A. Kinloch as Lord Byron and his works: a biography and essay, 1883.

The works of Lord Byron in verse and prose, including his letters, journals etc. [Ed F. Halleck], New York 1833, Hartford 1847.

[Letter to Sir James Mackintosh]. Life of the Rt Hon Sir James Mackintosh. 1835. Vol 2 p. 268 n.

[Letter to Col Wildman]. The Crayon miscellany no II: Abbotsford and Newstead Abbey, by Washington Irving. Philadelphia 1835, London 1835.

[Letter to Lady Byron]. Memoirs, journal and correspondence of Thomas Moore. Ed Lord John Russell vol 3, 1853. Pp. 114, 115.

[Letters to E. J. Trelawny]. Recollections of the last days of Shelley and Byron, by E. J. Trelawny. 1858; ed J. E. Morpurgo 1952, New York 1961.

[Letters to J. Ridge]. N & Q 10 Nov 1860.

[Letters to Augusta Leigh]. Sharpe's London Mag July–Aug 1869.

[Letter on the separation]. Academy 9 Oct 1869.

[Letters to William Harness]. The literary life of the Rev William Harness by A. G. L'Estrange. 1871.

[Letter to Mrs Parker]. Lord Byron: a biography, by Karl Elze. 1872. Facs p. 1.

[Letter to Andrea Vacci]. Nuova Antologia (Florence) July 1874.

A facsimile of an interesting letter written by Lord Byron 15 Jan 1809. 1876.

Lord Byron: eine autobiographie nach Tagebuechern und Briefen, mit Einleitung und Erlaeuterungen von E. Engel. Berlin 1876, 1876.

[Letter to Francis Hodgson]. Memoirs of the Rev Francis Hodgson, by J. T. Hodgson. 2 vols 1878.

[Letters]. Catalogue of the collection of autograph letters formed by Alfred Morrison [1st ser]. Ed A. W. Thibaudeau vol 1, 1883 (priv ptd). Pp. 142–51.

Letters written by Lord Byron during his residence at Missolonghi Jan–April 1824, to Mr Samuel Barff at Zante. Naples 1884 (priv ptd).

The letters and journals of Lord Byron, selected by Mathilde Blind. 1886.

[Letters to Mary Shelley]. The life and letters of Mary Wollstonecraft Shelley, by Mrs Julian Marshall. 2 vols 1889.

[Letters to Samuel Rogers]. Samuel Rogers and his contemporaries, by P. W. Clayden. 2 vols 1889.

[Letter to R. B. Hoppner]. Archivist April 1889.

[Letter to E. J. Dawkins]. Nineteenth Century Nov 1891.

[Letter to C. J. Barry (28 May 1823)]. E Studien 17 1892.

[Letter to Rev R. Lowe]. Life and letters of Robert Lowe, Viscount Sherbrooke, by A. P. Martin. 1893. Vol 1 p. 46.

[Letters]. The collection of letters formed by Alfred Morrison [2nd ser] vol 1, 1893. Pp. 446–78.

[Letter to Shelley (24 April 1822)]. E Studien 22 1895.

The works of Lord Byron. Vol 1: letters, 1804–13 Ed W. E. Henley 1897. No more pbd.

The works of Lord Byron: letters and journals. Ed R. E. Prothero [Baron Ernle] 6 vols 1898–1904.

Zehn Byroniana. Ed E. Koelbing, E Studien 25 1898.

[Letter to C. Barry]. Anglia Beiblatt April 1898.

[Letter to J. Ridge]. Newark Advertiser 4 May 1898.

[Letters to Elizabeth, Duchess of Devonshire]. The two Duchesses, by Vere Foster. 1898.

[Letters to John Murray]. Reference catalogue of British and foreign autographs and mss. Ed T. J. Wise. Part vii, Byron, by John Murray. 1898. Facs.

[Letter to the Earl of Clare]. Daily Chron 19 April 1900.

[Letters to George Steevens et al, ed C. K. Shorter]. Sphere 17 Sept 1904.

[Letters to Lady Byron]. Astarte, by Ralph Milbanke, Earl of Lovelace. 1905 (priv ptd).

The confessions of Lord Byron: a collection of his private opinions of men and matters. Ed W. A. L. Bettany 1905.

[Letters]. Poems and letters of Lord Byron. Ed from the original mss in the possession of W. K. Bixby by W. N. C. Carlton, Chicago 1912 (Soc of Dofobs) (priv ptd).

[Letters]. Byroniana und anderes aus dem englischen Seminar in Erlangen. Erlangen 1912.

[Letter to C. Barry]. Byroniana, by O. Intze. [Birmingham 1914].

[Letter to W. Baldwin]. Nation (New York) 18 April 1918.

[Letter to Hodgson (20. Jan 1811)]. Annual Report of Br School at Athens (1916–18), 22 1919, pp. 107–9. Facs.
[Letters to Augusta Leigh]. Astarte. 2nd edn with additional letters, ed Mary Countess of Lovelace 1921.
Lord Byron's correspondence, chiefly with Lady Melbourne, Mr Hobhouse, the Hon Douglas Kinnaird and P. B. Shelley. 2 vols 1922.
[Letters to Mrs Stith]. Catherine Potter Stith and her meeting with Byron, by A. B. Benson. South Atlantic Quart 22 1923.
[Letters to Dallas, and to Hodgson]. A descriptive catalogue of an exhibition of mss and first editions of Lord Byron, by R. H. Griffith and H. M. Jones. Austin 1924.
[Letters to Capt Hay and J. Webb. Ed A. Koszul]. Revue Anglo-américaine 2 1925.
[Letters to the Greek Committee]. Nineteenth Century Sept 1926.
Lord Byron in his letters: selections by V. H. Collins. 1927.
The Ravenna journal, mainly compiled at Ravenna in 1821. Ed Lord Ernle [R. E. Prothero] 1928 (First Editions Club) (priv ptd).
[Letters to Lady Byron]. The life and letters of Lady Byron, by E. C. Mayne. 1929.
The letters of George Gordon, Lord Byron, selected by R. G. Howarth. 1933, 1936, 1962 (EL).
[Letter to the Greek Committee]. Ed W. H. McCarthy, Yale Univ Lib Gazette 8 1934.
[Letters to Miss Mercer Elphinstone]. Cornhill Mag April 1934.
Three Byron letters. Ed C. O. Parsons, N & Q 26 May 1934.
[Letters to Lord Holland]. The home of the Hollands, by the Earl of Ilchester. [1937].
[Letters to Leigh Hunt]. L. A. Brewer, My Leigh Hunt library, Iowa City 1938.
Pratt, W. W. Byron at Southwell. Austin 1948. 5 letters.
Origo, I. The last attachment. 1949, 1962. 139 Italian letters.
Borghese, M. L'appassionata di Byron. Milan 1949.
Marchand, L. A. Byron and Count Alborghetti. PMLA 64 1949. 9 letters.
Quennell, P. C. A self portrait: letters and diaries. 2 vols 1950. 56 unpbd letters and 36 first pbd in full.
Jones, F. L. A Byron letter. N & Q 10 June 1960.
Cline, C. L. Byron, Shelley and their Pisan circle. Cambridge Mass 1952. 29 letters.
Forster, H. B. Byron and Nicolas Karvellas. Keats-Shelley Jnl 2 1953.
Selected letters. Ed J. Barzun, New York 1953.
Bates, M. C. Two new letters of Keats and Byron. Keats-Shelley Jnl 3 1954.
Lovell, E. J. His very self and voice: collected conversations of Lord Byron. New York 1954.
Green, D. B. Three new Byron letters. Keats-Shelley Jnl 5 1956.
Marshall, W. H. A news letter from Byron to John Hunt. N & Q March 1957.
de Beer, G. A Byron letter at Leningrad. TLS May 16 1958.
Kendall, L. H. jr. An unpublished letter to Shelley. MLN 76 1961.

Pieces First Published in Periodicals and in Books by Other Writers

Stanzas to Jessy. Monthly Literary Recreations July 1807. With review of Wordsworth's Poems 1807.
Hobhouse, J. C. Imitations and translations from the ancient and modern classics. 1809. Pp. 185–230. 9 poems.
[Review of Gell's Geography of Ithaca]. Monthly Rev Aug 1811.
An ode to the framers of the Frame Bill. Morning Chron 2 March 1812; rptd separately as A political ode, 1880.
Stanzas on a lady weeping. Morning Chron 7 March 1812; rptd in Corsair, 1814 (2nd edn).
Address spoken at the opening of Drury Lane Theatre. Morning Chron 12 Oct 1912; rptd in Genuine rejected addresses, presented to the committee of management for Drury Lane Theatre, preceded by that written by Lord Byron, 1812. Reviewed by Leigh Hunt, Examiner 18 Oct 1812.
[Smith, James and Horace]. Rejected addresses: or the new theatrum poetarum. 1812.
A critique on the address spoken at the opening of the new Theatre Royal, Drury Lane. [1812].
A sequel to the Rejected addresses or the theatrum poetarum minorum, by another author. 1813.
Parenthetical address by Dr Plagiary. Morning Chron 23 Oct 1812; rptd in Works vol 17, 1833 (Murray).
To Sarah, Countess of Jersey. Champion 31 July 1814; rptd in Three poems not included in Byron's works, 1818.
Elegiac stanzas on the death of Sir Peter Parker. Morning Chron 7 Oct 1814; rptd in Hebrew melodies, 1816.
'Bright be the place of thy soul'. Examiner 4 June 1815; rptd with music by I. Nathan, [1815], and in Poems, 1816.
Napoleon's farewell. Examiner 30 July 1815; rptd in Poems, 1816.
'We do not curse thee, Waterloo'. Morning Chron 15 March 1816; rptd in Poems, 1816.
On the star of the Legion of Honour. Examiner 7 April 1816; rptd in Poems, 1816.
[Translations from the Armenian: the epistle of the Corinthians to St Paul etc]. A grammar, Armenian and English, by Yarouthiun Augerean. Venice 1819, 1832, 1873.
'Maid of Athens, ere we part'. In H. W. Williams, Travels in Italy, Greece and the Ionian Isles, Edinburgh 1820. Vol 2, p. 290. *See* TLS 10 Dec 1931.
The vision of judgement; Letter to my grandmother's review; Epigrams on Lord Castlereagh. Liberal no 1, 15 Oct 1822.
Heaven and earth: a mystery; 'Aegle, beauty and poet'; translation from Martial; 'Why how now, Saucy Tom?'. Liberal no 2, 1 Jan 1823.
The blues: a literary eclogue. Liberal no 3, 26 April 1823.
Morgante Maggiore di Messer Luigi Pulci. Liberal no 4, 30 July 1823.
A critique on the Liberal. 1822.
The Illiberal! verse and prose from the North. [1822].
Lord Byron, Leigh Hunt and the Liberal [selections from the Liberal]. Ed L. P. Pickering [1925].
Marshall, W. H. Byron, Shelley, Hunt and the Liberal. Philadelphia 1960.
'And dost thou ask the reason of my sadness?' Nicnac 25 March 1823.
Foscolo, Ugo. In his Essays on Petrarch, 1823. Pp. 215–17.
Notizie estere. El Telegrafo Greco (Missolonghi) no 5, 17 April 1824; rptd Nineteenth Century Sept 1926.
On this day I complete my 36th year. Morning Chron 29 Oct 1824.
Remember thee (1st edn only); Stanzas to the Po; The Irish Avatar. In T. Medwin, Conversations of Lord Byron at Pisa, 1824 (3 edns).
[Stanzas omitted from Childe Harold, canto 2]. In R. C. Dallas, Recollections of the life of Lord Byron, 1824.
Stanzas [on the death of the Duke of Dorset]. Edinburgh Annual Register for 1824, 1825. Pt i p. 265. *See* MLR 44 1949.
[Lines to Lady Blessington]. Annales Romantiques (Paris) 1827–8.
Verses written in compliance with a lady's request to contribute to her album. Casket 1829.
Lines on hearing that Lady Byron was ill. New Monthly Mag Aug 1832; rptd with the next 2 entries in M. Gardiner, Countess of Blessington, Conversations of Lord Byron, 1834.

'Could love for ever'. New Monthly Mag Oct 1832.
'But once I dared to lift my eyes'. New Monthly Mag March 1833.
Question and answer. Fraser's Mag Jan 1833.
Newstead Abbey. In J. T. Hodgson, Memoir of the Rev Francis Hodgson vol 2, 1878. P. 187.
Last words on Greece. Murray's Mag Feb 1887.
'I watched thee when the foe was at our side'. Ibid.
Farewell petition to J. C. H[obhouse]. Murray's Mag March 1887.
My boy Hobbie O! Ibid.
The monk of Athos. In R. Noel, The life of Lord Byron, 1890. Pp. 206–7.
[Epilogue on Wordsworth's Peter Bell]. Philadelphia Record 28 Dec 1891.
To the Hon Mrs George Lamb. In V. Foster, The two Duchesses, 1898, p. 374.
The King of the Humbugs. Good Words Aug–Sept 1904.
Magdalen; Harmodia. In R. Milbanke, Earl of Lovelace, Astarte, 1905 (priv ptd).
[Addn to English bards and Scotch reviewers]. TLS 30 April 1931.
Steffan, T. G. An early Byron ms in the Pierpont Morgan Library. SE 27 1948.
Pratt, W. W. Byron at Southwell. Austin 1948.
—— An Italian notebook of Lord Byron. SE 28 1949.
—— 'To these ladies': an unpublished poem by Byron. Ed W. Pafford, Keats-Shelley Jnl 1 1952.

Works Incorrectly Ascribed to Byron

The spurious continuations of Don Juan *are listed after the edns of that poem, above.*

A farrago libelli: a poem, chiefly imitated from the first satire of Juvenal. 1806. *See* B. Dobell, Eng Rev Aug 1915; S. C. Chew, MLN 31 1916.
Lord Byron's farewell to England, with three other poems. 1816. Included in some later edns of Poems on his domestic circumstances. *See* Prothero, Prose works vol 3, p. 337. Ascribed to John T. Agg. *See* H. M. Jones, The author of two Byron Apocrypha, MLN 41 1926.
Reflections on shipboard by Lord Byron. 1816.
Lord Byron's pilgrimage to the Holy Land. 1816, 1817 (2nd edn, without Byron's name. *See* Prothero vol 4, p. 19. Ascribed to John T. Agg. *See* H. M. Jones, MLN 41 1926.
Clarke, H. Lord Byron, the legal critics refuted: or an essay to prove from the arguments of Lord Byron's Counsel that Childe Harold and the Prisoner of Chillon are mercenary forgeries, and that Pilgrimage to the Holy Land is a genuine production. 1817.
Modern Greece. 1817. By Felicia Hemans.
Poems written by somebody. 1818.
Childe Harold's pilgrimage to the Dead Sea; Death on the pale horse; and other poems. 1818. *See* Prothero vol 4, p. 474.
The vampyre: a tale. 1819 (3 edns; first pbd in New Monthly Mag April 1819); tr French by Amédée Pichot, Paris 1830; dramatized in German by L. Ritter, Brunswick in 1822; tr Spanish, Paris 1829. By J. W. Polidori. *See* Prothero vol 4, p. 286.
Anastasius: or memoirs of a Greek. 1819. By Thomas Hope.
Giuseppino: an Occidental story. 1821, 1821, Philadelphia 1822. Rptd in Arnaldo, Gaddo etc, 1836. By E. N. Shannon.
La mort de Napoléon: dithyrambe traduit de l'anglais de Lord Byron. Paris 1821 (7 edns).
Le cri d'Angeleterre au tombeau de sa Reine: dithyrambe de Lord Byron traduit de l'anglais. Paris 1821.
Irner par Lord Byron. 2 vols Paris 1821.
The Duke of Mantua: a tragedy. 1823, 1833. By John Roby; included in The legendary and poetic remains of John Roby, 1854.

My wedding night: the obnoxious chapter in Lord Byron's memoirs. John Bull Mag July 1824.
The Count Arezzi. 1824. By Robert Eyres Landor.
Lettre de Lord Byron au Grand Turc. Paris 1824.
Arnaldo; Gaddo; and other unacknowledged poems by Lord Byron and some of his contemporaries. Ed 'Odoardo Volpi', Dublin 1836. By E. N. Shannon.
The inedited works of Lord Byron, now first published from his letters, journals and other mss in the possession of his son Major Gordon Byron. 2 pts (all pbd), New York 1849. Some of this is a reprint of genuine originals already pbd.
Don Leon. [Pbd abroad before 1853? *See* N & Q 15 Jan 1853]; 1866, 1866; rptd 1934.
Leon to Annabella: an epistle after the manner of Ovid. Nd, 1865, 1866 (as The great secret revealed), Brussels 1875, Paris [c. 1900], New York 1922 (in Poetica erotica, ed T. R. Smith vol 3).
The unpublished letters of Lord Byron, edited with a critical essay by H. S. Schultess-Young. 1872. Suppressed before pbn. The only letters in this book known to be authentic are those to Byron's mother, and these had been ptd previously.
The bride's confession. Paris 1916 (priv ptd).
Seventeen letters to an unknown lady 1811–17. Ed W. E. Peck, New York 1930. These letters derive from the Schultess-Young edn of 1872. Prothero, vol 6 p. 460, did not accept them as authentic.

Byron in Poetry and Fiction (to 1837)

[Lamb, Lady Caroline]. Glenarvon. 3 vols 1816 (3 edns), 1 vol [1865] (as The fatal passion); tr French, Paris 1819.
Olney, C. Glenarvon revisited. Univ of Kansas City Rev 22 1958.
[Barrett, Eaton Stannard]. Six weeks at Long's, by a late resident. 3 vols 1817.
Three weeks at Fladong's, by a late visitant. 1817.
[Peacock, Thomas Love]. Nightmare Abbey. 1818.
An account of Lord Byron's residence in the Island of Mitylene. 1918. *See* Prothero, vol 4, p. 288; Byron and Col Rooke [by F. W. Hasluck], Saturday Rev 11 June 1921.
Lamartine, Alphonse de. L'homme: à Lord Byron. In his Meditations poétiques, Paris 1820; tr C. Hicks, Whitby 1837. Another English trn, 1843.
Delavigne, Casimir. Messénienne sur Lord Byron. Paris 1824, 1824; rptd in his Nouvelles Messéniennes, Paris 1824; tr Marseilles 1824.
Vigny, Alfred de. Sur la mort de Byron. La Muse Française (Paris) 15 June 1824.
Shelley, P. B. Julian and Maddalo. In his Posthumous poems, 1824.
Narrative of Lord Byron's voyage to Corsica and Sardinia by Capt Benson. 1824, Paris 1825.
Bedford, J. H. Wanderings of Childe Harold. 3 vols 1825.
[Shelley, Mary]. The last man. 3 vols 1826.
—— Lodore. 3 vols 1835.
Taylor, John. Byronna the disappointed. [c. 1830].
[Brydges, Sir S. E.] Modern aristocracy: or the bard's reception. Geneva 1831.
Chamisso, A. von. Lord Byrons letzte Liebe (1827). Chios 1829.
Driver, H. A. Harold de Burun: a semi-dramatic poem. 1835.
Laube, H. Lord Byron: eine Reisenovelle. Mannheim 1835.
Mitford, J. The private life of Lord Byron: comprising his voluptuous amours, secret intrigues and close connection with various ladies of rank. [1836]; tr French, Paris 1837.
Magnien, Édouard. Mortel, ange ou démon. Paris 1836.
[Disraeli, Benjamin]. Venetia: or the poet's daughter. 3 vols 1837.

Hamilton, H. B. Inaugural essay on the portrayal of the life and character of Lord Byron in a novel entitled Venetia. Leipzig 1884.
Cipro, G. B. Lord Byron a Venezia. [Florence?] 1837. A play.

§2

Hobhouse, J. C. (Baron Broughton). A journey through Albania and other provinces of Turkey. 1813, 2 vols 1813, 1855 (as Travels in Albania).
— Lord Byron's residence in Greece. Westminster Rev 2 1824.
— [Review of Dallas's Recollections and Medwin's Conversations]. Westminster Rev 3 1825.
— Italy: remarks made in several visits from 1816 to 1854. 2 vols 1859.
— Recollections of a long life. 5 vols 1865 (priv ptd) (reviewed in Edinburgh Rev 133 1871), 6 vols 1909–11.
— Contemporary account of the separation of Lord and Lady Byron, also of the destruction of Lord Byron's memoirs. 1870 (priv ptd); rptd in Recollections of a long life, 2nd edn vol 2.
[Irving, Washington]. Lord Byron. Analectic Mag (Philadelphia) July 1814; rptd in Poetical works of Lord Byron, Boston 1814.
— An unwritten drama of Lord Byron. Gift for 1836 (New York) [1835]; ed T. O. Mabbott, Metuchen NJ 1925.
A narrative of the circumstances which attended the separation of Lord and Lady Byron. 1816.
A catalogue of books the property of a nobleman [Byron] about to leave England, which will be sold by auction by [Robert H. Evans]. 5 April [1816].
Shelley, P. B. History of a six weeks' tour. 1817.
[Beyle, M. H.] Rome, Naples et Florence en 1817 par M. de Stendhal. Paris 1817; tr 1818.
— Lord Byron en Italie et en France. Revue de Paris March 1830; rptd in his Racine et Shakespeare, Paris 1854; tr as Reminiscences of Lord Byron in Italy, Mirror of Lit 17–24 April 1830.
Hazlitt, W. In his Lectures on the English poets, 1818.
— In his Spirit of the age, 1825.
Wiffen, J. H. The character and poetry of Lord Byron. New Monthly Mag May 1819.
The radical triumvirate: or Infidel Paine, Lord Byron and Surgeon Lawrence colleaguing with the patriotic radicals to emancipate mankind from all laws, human and divine, by an Oxonian. 1820.
Vigny, Alfred de. Littérature anglaise: oeuvres complètes de Lord Byron. Le Conservateur Littéraire (Paris) Dec 1820.
Watts, A. A. Lord Byron's plagiarisms. Literary Gazette 24 Feb–31 March 1821.
[Lockhart, J. G.] A letter to Lord Byron by John Bull. 1821; ed R. L. Strout, Norman Oklahoma 1947. Also ascribed to John Black. *See* Athenaeum 7 March 1905.
[Watkins, John]. Memoirs of the life and writings of Lord Byron. 1822; tr German, Leipzig 1825.
El Telegrafo Greco (Missolonghi) 24 April 1824.
Scott, W. The death of Lord Byron. Edinburgh Weekly Jnl 19 May 1824; rptd in his Miscellaneous prose works vol 1, Edinburgh 1841.
Hugo, V. Sur George Gordon, Lord Byron. La Muse Française 15 June 1824.
— Lord Byron et ses rapports avec la littérature actuelle. Annales Romantiques (Paris) 1827–8.
Full particulars of the much lamented death of Lord Byron with a sketch of his life. 1824.
Gordon, Sir C. The life and genius of Lord Byron. 1824; rptd in Pamphleteer 24 1824.
Medwin, T. Journal of the conversations of Lord Byron at Pisa. 1824 (3 edns). Reviewed in Blackwood's Mag Nov 1824; GM Nov 1824.
Murray, J. Notes on Capt Medwin's Conversations of Lord Byron. 1824 (priv ptd); rptd in Works of Lord Byron (Murray), 1829.
Capt Medwin vindicated from the calumnies of the reviewers by Vindex. 1825.
— The angler in Wales. 2 vols 1834.
Dallas, R. C. Recollections of the life of Lord Byron 1808–14. 1824.
Styles, J. Lord Byron's works viewed in connection with Christianity and the obligations of social life. 1824.
Brydges, S. E. Letters on the character and poetical genius of Lord Byron. 1824.
— An impartial portrait of Lord Byron as a poet and a man. Paris 1825.
Simmons, J. W. An inquiry into the moral character of Lord Byron. New York 1824, London 1826.
[Phillips, W.] A review of the character and writings of Lord Byron. Atlantic Monthly Oct 1825; rptd 1826. Also attributed to Andrews Norton.
Byroniana: Bozzies and Piozzies. 1825.
Pichot, A. Essais sur Lord Byron. Paris 1825. For Byron's comments *see* J. J. Coulmann, Une visite à Byron à Gênes, Paris 1826.
Belloc, L. S. Lord Byron. Paris 1824.
The particulars of the dispute between the late Lord Byron and Mr Southey. Edinburgh 1824.
Tricoupi, S. Funeral oration on Lord Byron, delivered at Missolonghi. 1825, 1836.
Gamba, P. A narrative of Lord Byron's last journey to Greece. 1825.
Parry, W. The last days of Lord Byron. 1825.
Blaquière, E. Narrative of a second visit to Greece, including facts connected with the last days of Lord Byron. 1825.
Stanhope, L. F. C. Greece in 1823 and 1824, to which is added reminiscences of Lord Byron. 1825, Paris 1825.
Clinton, G. Memoirs of the life and writings of Lord Byron. 1825.
Salvo, C. de. Lord Byron en Italie et en Grèce. Paris 1825.
The life, writings, opinions and times of Lord Byron, including copious recollections of the lately destroyed memoirs by an English gentleman in the Greek Military Service. 3 vols 1825. Ascribed to Matthew Iley.
[Kilgour, A.] Anecdotes of Lord Byron from authentic sources. 1825.
Albrizzi, I. T. In her Ritratti scritti, Pisa 1826.
Lake, W. J. The life of Lord Byron. Paris 1826, Frankfurt 1827. First pbd in Galignani's edn of the Works of Lord Byron, Paris 1822.
Catalogue of the library of the late Lord Byron, which will be sold at auction by R. H. Evans, 16 July 1827. Ed G. H. Doane, [Lincoln Nebraska] 1929 (priv ptd).
Hunt, J. H. L. Lord Byron and some of his contemporaries. 1828, 2 vols 1828. Reviewed: Athenaeum 2, 23, 30 Jan 1828; Quart Rev 37 1828.
— Autobiography. 3 vols 1850, 1 vol 1860 (rev); ed R. Ingpen 2 vols 1903.
Moore, T. Letters and journals of Lord Byron, with notices of his life. 2 vols 1830, New York [1830], 1 vol Paris 1831, 3 vols 1832, 1833, 1 vol 1837, 1847, 1850, 6 vols 1851, 1 vol 1860, 1875; tr French, Paris 1830–1. Reviewed: Blackwood's Mag Feb–March 1830; Le National (Paris) 7 March 1830 (by P. Mérimée); Athenaeum 25 Dec 1830, 1–8 Jan 1831; Quart Rev 44 1831 (by J. G. Lockhart); Fraser's Mag March 1831; Br Critic April 1831 (by C. W. Le Bas); Edinburgh Rev 53 1831 (by T. B. Macaulay; rptd in his Critical and miscellaneous works, Philadelphia 1841 vol i).
[Byron, Isabella, Lady]. Remarks occasioned by Mr Moore's notices of Lord Byron's life. [1830] (priv ptd) (3 edns).
Campbell, T. [Lady Byron and Thomas Moore]. New Monthly Mag April 1830.
Lord Byron vindicated and Mr Campbell answered. 1830.
Galt, J. The life of Lord Byron. 1830, [1908]. Reviewed: Athenaeum 4 Sept 1830; GM Sept 1830; Edinburgh Rev 52 1830; Fraser's Mag Oct 1830.

— Pot versus kettle. Fraser's Mag Dec 1830.

— Prose and verse, humorous, satirical and sentimental. Ed R. H. Shepherd 1878. Contains rough notes for the Life.

Kennedy, J. Conversations on religion with Lord Byron and others, held in Cephalonia a short time previous to his Lordship's death. 1830.

Gordon, P. L. In his Personal memoirs or reminiscences, 2 vols 1830.

Milligen, J. Memoirs of the affairs of Greece with various anecdotes of Lord Byron, and an account of his last illness and death. 1831.

Mazure, A. Étude morale sur Lord Byron. Revue Anglo-française (Poitiers) 1 1833.

Gardiner, M. (Countess of Blessington). Conversations of Lord Byron. 1834, 1893 (rev); tr French, Paris 1833. First pbd in New Monthly Mag July 1832–Dec 1833.

Bluemel, M. Die Unterhaltungen Lord Byrons mit der Gräfin Blessington als ein Beitrag zur Byronbiographie kritisch untersucht. Breslau 1900.

— The idler in Italy. 3 vols 1839–40.

Browne, J. H. Voyage from Leghorn to Cephalonia with Lord Byron in 1823. Blackwood's Mag Jan 1834.

— Narrative of a visit to Greece. Fraser's Mag Sept 1834.

Lennep, J. van. Vertalingen en Navolgingen in Poezy. Amsterdam 1834.

Irving, W. The Crayon miscellany, no 2 (Abbotsford and Newstead Abbey). Philadelphia 1835, London 1835.

Niccolini, G. Vita di Giorgio, Lord Byron. Milan 1835.

Conversations of an American with Lord Byron. New Monthly Mag Oct–Nov 1835.

Mordani, F. La vita di Giorgio Lord Byron. Bologna 1839.

'Sand, George' (A. A. L. Dudevant). Essai sur le drame fantastique: Goethe, Byron, Mickiewicz. Revue des Deux Mondes 1 Dec 1839; rptd in Autour de la table, Paris 1862.

Dueringsfeld, I. von. Byrons Frauen. Breslau 1845.

Thomsen, G. On Lord Byron. Copenhagen 1845.

Villemain, A. F. In his Etudes de littératures anciennes et étrangères, Paris 1846.

Mazzini, G. Byron et Goethe. In his Scritti litterari d'un Italiano vivente, Lugano 1847; tr as Life and writings of Mazzini vol 6, 1891.

Hohenhausen, E. von. Rousseau, Goethe, Byron. Cassel 1847.

Nisard, D. Lord Byron et la société anglaise. Revue des Deux Mondes 1 Nov 1850.

Chasles, V. E. P. Vie et influence de Byron sur son époque. In Études sur la littérature et les moeurs de l'Angleterre au 19e siècle, Paris [1850].

Russell, Lord John. Memoirs, journal and correspondence of Thomas Moore. 6 vols 1853–6.

Kingsley, C. Thoughts on Shelley and Byron. Fraser's Mag Nov 1853; rptd in his Miscellanies vol 1, 1859.

Hannay, J. In his Satire and satirists, 1854.

Ferguson, J. C. Lecture on the writings and genius of Byron. Carlisle 1856.

Rogers, S. Recollections of the table talk of Samuel Rogers. 1856.

Trelawny, E. J. Recollections of the last days of Shelley and Byron. 1858; ed E. Dowden 1906; ed J. E. Morpurgo 1952, New York 1961.

— Records of Shelley, Byron and the author. 2 vols 1878, 1 vol 1887, 1905.

— The relations of P. B. Shelley with his two wives and a comment on the character of Lord Byron. 1920 (priv ptd).

— The relations of Lord Byron and Augusta Leigh. 1920 (priv ptd).

Mickiewicz, A. Goethe i Byron. Gazeta Codzienna (Warsaw), 29 April 1860; tr French in Mélanges posthumes vol 1, Paris 1872.

Mondot, A. Hixtoire de la vie et des écrits de Lord Byron. Paris 1860.

Finlay, G. In his History of the Greek revolution, 2 vols 1861.

Gronow, R. H. In his Reminiscences: being anecdotes of the camp, the court and the clubs, 1862.

— Last recollections: being the fourth and final series. 1866.

Coulmann, J. J. In his Réminiscences, 3 vols Strasbourg 1862–9.

Treitschke, H. von. Lord Byron und der Radicalismus. Preussisches Jahrbuch, Berlin 1863; rptd in Historische und politische Aufsaetze, Leipzig 1865.

Guiccioli, Teresa, Countess of (Mme de Boissy). Lord Byron jugé par les témoins de sa vie. Paris 1868; tr 1869, New York 1869.

Martineau, H. In her Biographical sketches, 1869.

Stowe, H. B. The true story of Lady Byron's married life. Macmillan's Mag Sept 1869. Reply by A. Hayward, below.

— Lady Byron vindicated: a history of the Byron controversy. 1870. Reviewed by A. Hayward, below.

Byron painted by his compeers: or all about Lord Byron from his marriage to his death as given in the various newspapers of his day. 1869.

Austin, A. A vindication of Lord Byron. 1869.

Mackay, C. Medora Leigh: a history and an autobiography. 1869.

[Fox, J.] Vindication of Lady Byron. Blackwood's Mag Oct 1869; rptd 1871.

[Hayward, A.] The Byron mystery. Quart Rev 127–8 1869–70. Letters of Lady Byron.

— In his Sketches of eminent statesmen and writers, 2 vols 1880.

[Lucas, S.] The Stowe-Byron controversy: a complete résumé of all that has been written and said on the subject. 1869.

Elze, K. Lord Byron. Berlin 1870, 1881, 1886; tr 1872 (with addns).

Morley, J. Byron and the French Revolution. Fortnightly Rev Dec 1870; rptd in his Miscellanies vol 1, 1886.

L'Estrange, A. G. The literary life of the Rev William Harness. 1871.

Blaze de Bury, H. Lord Byron et le Byronisme. Revue des Deux Mondes 1 Oct 1872.

[Haussonville, Comtesse de]. La jeunesse de Lord Byron. Paris 1872.

— Les dernières années de Lord Byron. Paris 1874.

Tribolati, F. Lord Byron a Pisa. Nuova Antologia July 1874; rptd in his Saggi critici e biografici, Pisa 1891.

Mackay, G. E. Lord Byron at the Armenian Convent. Venice 1876.

Lipnicki, E. Byron in Befreiungskampfe der polnischen National-literatur. Magazin 48 1877.

Torrens, W. M. Memoirs of William, 2nd Viscount Melbourne. 1878.

Hodgson, J. T. Memoirs of the Rev Francis Hodgson. 2 vols 1878.

Telles, A. Lord Byron em Portugal. Lisbon 1879.

Nichol, J. Byron. 1880 (EML).

Ruskin, J. Fiction, fair and foul. Nineteenth Century Sept 1880; rptd in his Works, ed E. T. Cook and A. D. O. Wedderburn vol 34.

Jebb, R. C. In his Modern Greece, 1880.

'Rutherford, Mark' (W. H. White). Byron, Goethe and Mr Matthew Arnold. Contemporary Rev Aug 1881; rptd in Pages from a journal, 1901.

Jeaffreson, J. C. The real Lord Byron. 1883.

Reviewed: Fortnightly Rev April 1883; Quart Rev 156 1883 (by Abraham Hayward); Nineteenth Century Aug 1883 (by J. A. Froude).

Edgecumbe, R. History of the Byron memorial. 1883.

Swinburne, A. C. Wordsworth and Byron. Nineteenth Century April–May 1884; rptd in his Miscellanies, 1886.

Jowett, B. Byron. [Oxford 1884] (priv ptd).

Weddigen, F. H. O. Lord Byrons Einfluss auf die europäische Literatur der Neuzeit. Hanover 1884, Leipzig 1901.
'Gerard, William' (W. G. Smith). Byron re-studied in his dramas. 1886.
Dowden, E. In his Life of P. B. Shelley, 2 vols 1886.
—— The French Revolution and English literature. 1897.
Jerningham, H. E. H. In his Reminiscences of an attaché, 1886.
[Milbanke, Ralph (Viscount Wentworth, later Earl of Lovelace)]. Lady Noel Byron and the Leighs: some authentic records of certain circumstances in the lives of Augusta Leigh and others that concerned Anne Isabella Lady Byron. 1887 (priv ptd).
—— Astarte: a fragment of truth concerning Lord Byron. 1905 (priv ptd); ed Mary, Countess of Lovelace 1921 (with additional letters).
Arnold, M. In his Essays in Criticism ser 2, 1888. Rptd from The poetry of Byron, 1881.
Axon, W. E. A. Byron's influence on European literature. In his Stray chapters on literature, folk-lore and archaeology, 1888.
Lombroso, C. L'uomo di genio. Turin 1888; tr 1891.
Althaus, F. On the personal relations between Goethe and Byron. Pbns of Eng Goethe Soc 2 1888.
Megyery, A. Lord Byron. Budapest 1889.
Noel, R. Life of Lord Byron. 1890.
Westenholtz, F. Ueber Byrons historische Dramen. Stuttgart 1890.
Dallois, J. Etudes morales et littéraires à propos de Lord Byron. Paris 1890.
Rabbé, F. Les maîtresses authentiques de Lord Byron. Paris 1890.
Bancroft, G. History of the battle of Lake Erie and miscellaneous papers. New York 1891.
Ross, J. Byron at Pisa. Nineteenth Century Nov 1891.
Smiles, S. A publisher and his friends: memoir and correspondence of the late John Murray. 2 vols 1891.
Chiarini, G. Lord Byron nella politica e nella letteratura della prima metà del secolo. Nuova Antologia 34 1891.
Lüder, A. Lord Byrons Urtheile über Italien. Dresden 1893.
Roe, J. C. Some obscure and disputed points in Byronic biography. Leipzig 1893.
Hayman, H. Lord Byron and the Greek Patriots. Harper's Mag Feb 1894.
Brandes, G. M. C. Shelley und Lord Byron: zwei literarische Charakterbilder. Leipzig 1894.
Maychrzak, F. Lord Byron als Uebersetzer. Altenburg 1895.
Hamann, A. The life and works of Lord Byron. Berlin 1895, 1910.
Bleibtreu, K. Byron der Uebermensch: sein Leben und sein Dichten. Jena [1896].
Zdiechowski, M. Byron i jego wiek. In his Studya porównawczoliterachie, Cracow 1897.
Donner, J. O. E. Lord Byrons Weltanschauung. Helsingfors 1897.
Holthausen, F. Skandinavische Byron-Übersetzungen. E Studien 25 1898.
—— Tegnér und Byron. Archiv 101 1899.
Graham, W. Last links with Byron, Shelley and Keats. 1898. *See* N & Q 27 Oct 1923.
Foster, V. The two Duchesses. 1898.
Kraeger, H. Der Byronsche Heldentypus. Munich 1898.
Phillips, S. The poetry of Byron. Cornhill Mag Jan 1898.
Harnack, D. In his Essays und Studien, Brunswick 1899.
Biondi, E. La figlia di Lord Byron. Faenza 1899.
Ackermann, R. Lord Byron: sein Leben, seine Werke, sein Einfluss auf die deutsche Literatur. Heidelberg 1901.
Clark, W. J. Byron und die romantische Poesie in Frankreich. Leipzig 1901.
Williams, E. E. The journal of Edward Ellerker Williams, companion of Shelley and Byron in 1821 and 1822. 1902.
Ritter, O. Byron and Chateaubriand. Archiv 109 1902.
Veselovsky, A. N. Byron. Moscow 1902.
Bulloch, J. M. House of Gordon Gight. [1903] (New Spalding Club) (priv ptd).
Lumbroso, A. Il Generale Mengaldo, Lord Byron e l'Ode on the star of the Legion of Honour. Rome 1903; rptd in his Pagine Veneziane, Rome 1905.
Koepel, E. Lord Byron. Berlin 1903; tr Hungarian, Budapest 1913.
Wylpel, L. Grillparzer und Byron. Euphorion 9–10 1902–3.
Pudbres, A. Lord Byron, the admirer and imitator of Alfieri. E Studien 33 1903.
Fuhrmann, L. Die Belesenheit des jungen Byron. Berlin 1903.
Muoni, G. La fama del Byron e il Byronismo in Italia. Milan 1903.
—— La leggenda del Byron in Italia. Milan 1907.
—— Poesia notturna pre-romantica. Florence 1908.
Hoops, J. Lord Byrons Leben und Dichten. Frankfurt 1903.
Melchior, F. Heines Verhältnis zu Lord Byron. Berlin 1903.
Coleridge, E. H. Lord Byron. Trans Royal Soc of Lit 25 1904.
Holzhausen, P. Bonaparte, Byron und die Briten. Frankfurt 1904.
Zabel, E. Byrons Kenntnis von Shakespeare und sein Urteil über ihn. Halle 1904.
Collins, J. C. The works of Lord Byron. In his Studies in poetry and criticism, 1905.
Leonard, W. E. Byron and Byronism in America. Boston 1905.
Ochsenbein, W. Die Aufnahme Lord Byrons in Deutschland und sein Einfluss auf den jungen Heine. Berne 1905.
Wetz, W. Neuere Beiträge zur Byron-Biographie. Cologne 1905.
Prothero, R. E. (Baron Ernle). The Goddess of wisdom and Lady Caroline Lamb. Monthly Rev June 1905.
—— The end of the Byron mystery. Nineteenth Century Aug 1921.
Murray, John [iv], E. H. Pember and R. E. Prothero. Lord Byron and his detractors. 1906 (Roxburghe Club) (priv ptd).
Estève, E. Byron et le romantisme français. Paris 1907, 1929.
—— Le Byronisme de Leconte de Lisle. Revue de Littérature Comparée 5 1925.
Calcano, J. Tres poetas pessimistas del siglo xix. Caracas 1907.
Eimer, M. Lord Byron und die Kunst. Strasbourg 1907.
—— Die persönlichen Beziehungen zwischen Byron und den Shelleys. Heidelberg 1910.
—— Byron und die Kosmos. Heidelberg 1912.
Wiehr, J. The relations of Grabbe to Byron. JEGP 7 1908.
Symons, A. In his Romantic movement in English poetry, 1909.
Edgecumbe, R. Byron: the last phase. 1909.
Churchman, P. H. Lord Byron's experiences in the Spanish Peninsula in 1809. Bulletin Hispanique (Bordeaux) March, June 1909.
—— Byron and Espronceda. Revue Hispanique (Paris) March 1909.
—— The beginnings of Byronism in Spain. Revue Hispanique (Paris) Dec 1910.
Simhart, M. Lord Byrons Einfluss auf die italienische Literatur. Munich 1909.
Austin, A. Byron and Wordsworth. In his Bridling of Pegasus, 1910.
Chesterton, G. K. In his Twelve types, 1910.
Lang, A. Byron and Mary Chaworth. Fortnightly Rev Aug 1910.
Meneghetti, N. Lord Byron a Venezia. Venice [1910].
Miller, B. Leigh Hunt's relations with Byron, Shelley and Keats. New York 1910.

Polidori, J. W. The diary. Ed W. M. Rossetti 1911.
Angeli, H. R. Shelley and his friends in Italy. 1911.
Shaw, W. A. The authentic portraits of Lord Byron. Connoisseur July–Aug 1911.
Brecknock, A. The pilgrim poet: Lord Byron of Newstead. 1911.
— Byron: a study of the poet in the light of new discoveries. [1926].
Dobosal, G. Lord Byron in Deutschland. Zwickau 1911.
Spasowicz, W. Byronism u Pushkina i Lermontova. Vilna 1911.
Fuess, C. M. Lord Byron as a satirist in verse. New York 1912.
Byroniana und anderes aus dem englischen Seminar in Erlangen. Erlangen 1912.
Knott, J. The last illness of Lord Byron. St Paul Minnesota 1912.
Mayne, E. C. Byron. 2 vols 1912, [1924].
— The life and letters of Anne Isabella, Lady Noel Byron. 1929.
Windakiewicz, S. Walter Scott i Lord Byron w odniesieniu do polskiej romantycznij. Cracow 1914.
Chew, S. C. The dramas of Lord Byron. Göttingen 1915.
— Byron in England: his fame and after-fame. 1924.
— Byron in America. Amer Mercury 4 1924.
Ward, J. and G. G. Napier. Lord Byron's lameness. Nottingham 1915 (priv ptd).
Hearn, L. Interpretations of literature. New York 1916.
Northup, C. S. Byron and Gray. MLN 32 1917.
Zacchetti, C. Lord Byron e l'Italia. Palermo 1919.
Fletcher, W. Lord Byron's illness and death as described in a letter to Augusta Leigh. Nottingham 1920 (priv ptd).
Grierson, H. J. C. Lord Byron: Arnold and Swinburne. Proc Br Acad 9 1921.
— In his Essays and addresses, 1940.
Reul, P. de. Byron. Revue de l'Université de Bruxelles May–June 1921.
Goode, C. T. Byron as critic. Weimar 1923.
Draper, F. W. M. The rise and fall of the French romantic drama. 1923.
Porta, A. Byronismo italiano. Milan 1923.
Ker, W. P. Byron: an Oxford lecture. Criterion 2 1923; rptd in his Collected essays vol i, 1925.
Byron the poet: essays by Viscount Haldane, A. T. Quiller-Couch, H. J. C. Grierson, William Archer, Marie Corelli etc. Ed W. A. Briscoe 1924.
Garrod, H. W. Byron. Oxford 1924.
Henson, H. H. Byron. Cambridge 1924.
Prothero, R. E. The poetry of Byron. Quart Rev 241 1924.
Spender, H. Byron and Greece. 1924.
Rice, R. A. Lord Byron's British reputation. Northampton Mass 1924.
Sbornik Byron 1824–1924, by P. S. Kogan, M. N. Pozanov, L. P. Grossman, E. D. Grimm. Moscow 1924.
Zhirmunsky, V. M. Byron i Pushkin. Leningrad 1924.
— Die Gedichte Goethes und Byrons. Weimarer Beiträge 1963.
Berton, R. Une confession de Byron en 1823. La Nouvelle Revue 15 April 1924.
Castelain, M. Byron — en 1924. Revue Anglo-américaine 2 1924.
— Byron. Paris 1931.
Elliott, G. R. Byron and the comic spirit. PMLA 39 1924; rptd in his Cycle of modern poetry, Princeton 1929.
Farinelli, A. Byron e il Byronismo. Bologna 1924.
— Byron e il Byronismo nell'Argentina. Rome 1928.
Teignmouth, Lord. Byron's Suliote bodyguard. Nineteenth Century April 1924.
Cameron, H. C. The mystery of Lord Byron's club foot. N & Q 19 April 1924. *See* Listener 28 April 1949.
Nicolson, H. Byron: the last journey. 1924, 1934, 1940 (rev and enlarged), 1948.
— The poetry of Byron. 1943.
Raymond, D. N. The political career of Lord Byron. [1924].
Bellamy, R. L. Byron the man. 1924.
Fox, J. S. The Byron mystery. 1924.
Symon, J. D. Byron in perspective. 1924.
Boutet de Monvel, R. La vie de Lord Byron. Paris 1924.
Rodocanachi, E. Byron 1788–1824. Paris [1924].
Beck, R. Byron and Byronism in Iceland. Ithaca 1924.
— Grimur Thomsen: a pioneer Byron student. JEGP 27 1928.
— Grimur Thomsen og Byron. Reykjavik 1937.
Elton, O. The present value of Byron. RES 1 1925.
Chambers, R. W. Ruskin (and others) on Byron. 1925.
Drinkwater, J. The pilgrim of eternity: Byron—a conflict. [1925].
Robertson, J. G. Goethe and Byron. Pbns of Eng Goethe Soc 2 1925.
Blacket, J. Joseph Blacket and his links to Byron. London Quart Rev 143 1925.
Lo Gatto, E. Da Lord Byron ai poete slavi. Il Libri del Giorno Sept 1925.
Praz, M. La fortuna di Byron in Inghilterra. Florence 1925.
— Byron e Foscolo. Rivista delle Letterature Moderne e Comparate 11 1961.
de Beer, E. S. and W. W. Seton. Byroniana: the archives of the London Greek Committee. Nineteenth Century Sept 1926.
Cantoni, F. La prima dimora di Lord Byron a Bologna. Il Comune di Bologna March–April 1926.
— Byron e la Guiccioli a Bologna. Ibid April–May 1927.
Gordon, A. G. Allegra: the story of Byron and Miss Clairmont. New York 1926.
Dargan, E. P. Byron's fame in France. Virginia Quart 2 1926.
Stokoe, F. W. In his German influence in the English romantic period, Cambridge 1926.
Rycroft, W. S. Espronceda: la influencia de Byron. Boletín Bibliográfico (Lima) 2 1926.
Treimer, K. Byron und die Albanologie. Séminaire de Philologie Albanoise (Belgrade) 3 1926.
Mayfield, J. S. Notes on Lord Byron's infirmity. [Austin] 1927 (priv ptd).
Popma, T. Byron en het Byronisme in de nederlandsche letterkunde. Amsterdam 1928.
Richter, H. Lord Byron: Persönlichkeit und Werk. Halle 1929.
Rava, L. Byron e Shelley a Ravenna e Teresa Guiccioli Gamba. Rome 1929.
Flower, R. E. W. Byron and Ossian. Nottingham 1929.
Du Bos, C. Byron et le besoin de la fatalité. Paris 1929, 1957 (rev); tr E. C. Mayne [1932].
Doerken, H. Lord Byrons Subjectivismus in seinem Verhalten zur Geschichte. Leipzig 1929.
Schults, U. Het Byronisme in Nederland. Utrecht 1929.
Griggs, E. L. Coleridge and Byron. PMLA 45 1930.
Balslev, C. F. Lord Byron, mennesket og digteren. Copenhagen 1930.
Engel, C. E. Byron et Shelley en Suisse et en Savoie, mai–oct 1816. Chambéry 1930.
'Maurois, André' (E. S. W. Herzog). Byron. Paris 1930; tr [1930], 1963.
— Byron et les femmes. Paris 1934.
Kemble, J. Byron: his lameness and last illness. Quart Rev 257 1931.
Spink, G. W. J. C. von Zedlitz and Byron. MLR 26 1931.
Krug, W. G. Lord Byron als dichterische Gestalt in England, Frankreich, Deutschland und Amerika. Giessen 1931.
Petrović, I. M. Lord Bajron kod Jugoslovena. Pozurevac 1931.
Simmons, E. J. Byron and a Greek maid. MLR 27 1932.
Boyd, J. In his Goethe's knowledge of English literature, Oxford 1932.

Koch, J. Goethe und Byron. Archiv 163 1933.
Eggert, G. Lord Byron und Napoleon. Leipzig 1933, 1939 (rev).
Mifsud Bonnici, C. Lord Byron in Malta, Sept 1809. [Malta 1933].
'Paston, George' (E. M. Symonds). New lights on Byron's lovers. Cornhill Mag April–Sept 1934.
— and P. C. Quennell. 'To Lord Byron': feminine profiles, based upon a collection of unpublished letters 1807–24. 1939.
Clarke, I. C. Shelley and Byron. 1934.
Quennell, P. C. Byron. 1934.
— Byron, the years of fame. 1935, 1950.
— Byron and Harriette Wilson. Cornhill Mag April 1935.
— Byron in Italy. 1941, 1951.
Renzulli, M. Il peccatore: Byron. Naples [1935].
Calvert, W. J. Byron: romantic paradox. Chapel Hill 1935.
Foà, G. Lord Byron: poeta e carbonaro. Florence 1935.
Origo, I. Allegra. 1935.
— The last attachment. 1949, 1962.
— The innocent Miss Francis and the truly noble Lord Byron. Keats-Shelley Jnl 1 1952.
— A measure of love. 1957.
Leavis, F. R. Byron's satire. In his Revaluation, 1936.
Connely, W. Byron as satirist. Nottingham 1936.
Boyle, E. Byron: the last journey of all. In his Biographical essays 1790–1890, Oxford 1956.
Howarth, R. G. Allusions in Byron's letters. N & Q 28 Nov 1936–9 April 1938.
Eliot, T. S. In From Anne to Victoria, ed B. Dobrée 1937.
Kaiser, R. René und Harold. Archiv 170 1937.
Brown, W. C. Byron and English interest in the Near East. SP 34 1937.
Wellek, R. Macha and Byron. Slavonic Rev 16 1937.
McElderry, B. R. Byron's interest in the Americas. Washington State College Research Stud 5 1937.
Harwell, G. Three poems attributed to Byron. MP 35 1937.
Marjarum, E. W. Byron as sceptic and believer. Princeton 1938.
Pope-Hennessy, U. Byron and an American. TLS 23 April 1938.
Caclamanos, D. Some Byron relics. N & Q 11 June 1938.
Barber, T. H. Byron, and where he is buried. Hucknall 1939.
Bottrall, R. Byron and the colloquial tradition in English poetry. Criterion 17 1939.
Brown, H. Influence of Byron on Emily Brontë. MLR 34 1939.
Morphopoulos, P. Byron's translations and use of modern Greek writings. MLN 54 1939.
Messinese, G. Byron and Italy. Tripoli 1939.
Sjoholm, S. Froeding och Byron. Edda 39 1939.
Skard, S. Byron i norsk litteratur. Ibid.
Erdman, D. V. Byron's stage fright: the history of his ambition and fear of writing for the stage. ELH 6 1939.
— Byron and the genteel reformers. PMLA 56 1941.
— Byron as Rinaldo. PMLA 57 1942.
— Byron and revolt in England. Science & Soc 11 1947.
— Byron and 'the new force of the people'. Keats-Shelley Jnl 11 1962.
Wilson Knight, G. The two eternities. In his Burning oracle, 1939.
— Byron: Christian virtues. 1953.
— Byron's dramatic prose. Nottingham 1953.
— Lord Byron's marriage. 1957.
— Shakespeare and Byron's plays. Shakespeare-Jahrbuch 95 1959.
— Byron and Hamlet. Manchester 1963.
— Byron and Shakespeare. 1966.
Russell, B. Byron and the modern world. JHI 1 1940. *See also* his History of Western philosophy, 1946, pp. 774–81.

Wiener, H. S. L. Byron and the East: literary sources of the Turkish tales. In Nineteenth-century studies in honor of C. S. Northup, Ithaca 1940.
Leitzmann, A. Aus der Frühzeit der Byron-eindeutschung: Knebel als Übersetzer Byrons. Viermonatsschrift der Goethe-Gesellschaft 4 1940.
Booth, B. A. Moore to Hobhouse: an unpublished letter. MLN 55 1940.
Jones, J. J. Byron on America. SE 20 1941.
Phillips, W. J. France on Byron. Philadelphia 1941.
Stoll, E. E. Heroes and villains: Shakespeare, Middleton, Byron, Dickens. RES 18 1942.
Pinto, V. de S. Byron and liberty. Nottingham 1944.
Gregory, H. In his Shield of Achilles, New York 1944.
Turdeanu, E. Oscar of Alva de Lord Byron: sources occidentales et reflets roumains. Sibiu 1944.
de Ullmann, S. Romanticism and synaesthesia: a comparative study of sense transfer in Keats and Byron. PMLA 60 1945.
Hudson, A. P. Byron and the ballad. SP 42 1945.
Gray, D. The life and work of Byron. Nottingham 1946.
Cameron, J. Byron's association with Scotland. Dalhousie Rev 26 1946.
de Selincourt, E. In his Wordsworthian and other studies, Oxford 1947.
'Sencourt, Robert' (R. E. G. George). Byron and Shelley in Venice. Quart Rev 285 1947.
Martin, L. C. Byron's lyrics. Nottingham 1948.
Borst, W. A. Byron's first pilgrimage 1809–11. New Haven 1948.
Joyce, M. My friend H. 1948. A biography of Hobhouse.
Jordan, H. H. Byron and Moore. MLQ 9 1948.
Vulliamy, C. E. Byron. 1948.
Pratt, W. W. Byron at Amwell. Austin 1948.
— An Italian notebook of Lord Byron. SE 28 1949.
— Byron's 'fantastic' will of 1811. Texas Univ Lib Chron 4 1951.
Bewley, M. The colloquial mode of Byron. Scrutiny 16 1949.
Straumann, H. Byron and Switzerland. Nottingham 1949.
Vincent, E. R. Byron, Hobhouse and Foscolo. Cambridge 1949.
Lovell, E. J. Byron: the record of a quest. Austin 1949.
— Byron and the Byronic hero in the novels of Mary Shelley. SE 30 1951.
— Byron and Mary Shelley. Keats-Shelley Jnl 2 1953.
— His very self and voice: collected conversations of Lord Byron. New York 1954.
— Captain Medwin, friend of Byron and Shelley. Austin 1962.
Hennig, J. Early English translations of Goethe's essays on Byron. MLR 44 1949.
Borghese, M. L'appassionata di Byron. Milan 1949.
Entwistle, W. J. The Byronism of Lermontov's A hero of our times. Comparative Lit 1 1949.
Vandegans, A. Anatole France et Byron avant 1873. Revue de Littérature Comparée 23 1949.
Samuels, D. G. Some Byronic influences in Spanish poetry. Hispanic Rev 17 1949.
— Critical appreciations of Byron in Spain. Hispanic Rev 18 1950.
Butler, E. M. Goethe and Byron. Nottingham 1950.
Whitton, C. E. Lord Byron on vampires. Queen's Quart 57 1950.
Randi, A. Lord Byron e la Contessa Guiccioli. Ravenna 1950.
Cordié, C. Milano 1816: Byron, Hobhouse e Polidori. Letterature Moderne 1 1950.
Jones, W. P. Sir Egerton Bridges on Lord Byron. HLQ 13 1950.
James, D. G. Byron and Shelley. Nottingham 1951.
Read, H. Byron. 1951.
Schirmer, W. F. Goethe und Byron. Tübingen 1951.

Pujals, E. Espronceda y Lord Byron. Madrid 1951.

Dowden, W. S. A Jacobin journal's view of Lord Byron. SP 48 1951.

— Austrian surveillance of Byron in Greece. Festschrift für Leo von Hibler, ed K. Brunner, Wiener Beiträge zur Englischen Philologie 62 1954.

— Byron through Austrian eyes. Anglo-German & Americo-German Cross Currents (Chapel Hill) 2 1962.

Escarpit, R. Madame de Staël et le ménage Byron. Letterature Moderne 45 1951.

— De quoi vivait Lord Byron? Paris 1952.

— Lord Byron: un tempérament littéraire. Paris 1958.

— Byron et Venise. In Venezia nelle letterature moderne, ed C. Pellegrini, Venice 1961.

Gregor, D. B. Byron's knowledge of Armenian. N & Q 21 July 1951.

Cline, C. L. Byron, Shelley and their Pisan circle. Cambridge Mass 1952.

— Byron and Southey: a suppressed rejoinder. Keats-Shelley Jnl 3 1954.

Lefevre, C. Lord Byron's fiery convert of revenge. SP 49 1952.

Korninger, S. Die geistige Welt Lord Byrons. Rivista di Letterature Moderne 3 1952.

— Lord Byron und Nikolas Lenau. Eng Miscellany (Rome) 3 1952.

Fiess, E. Melville as a reader and student of Byron. Amer Lit 24 1952.

Norman, S. Leigh Hunt, Moore and Byron. TLS 2 Jan 1953.

Ashe, D. J. Byron's alleged part in the production of Coleridge's Remorse. N & Q Jan 1953.

Forster, H. B. Byron and Nicolas Karvellas. Keats-Shelley Jnl 2 1953.

Gates, P. G. A Leigh Hunt-Byron letter. Ibid.

Sarmiento, E. A parallel between Lord Byron and Fray Luis de León. RES new ser 4 1953.

Wain, J. (ed). In Contemporary reviews of romantic poetry, 1963.

— Byron: the search for identity. London Mag July 1958.

Wicker, C. V. Byron as parodist. MLN 69 1954.

Wasserman, E. R. Byron and Sterne. MLN 70 1955.

Manning, C. A. Lesya Ukrainka and Don Juan. MLQ 16 1955.

Greene, M. T. Byron's island refuge. Amer Mercury July 1955.

Blunden, E. A fragment of Byronism. Etudes Anglaises 8 1955.

Elistratova, A. A. Byron. Moscow 1956.

Hough, G. Two exiles: Byron and D. H. Lawrence. Nottingham 1956.

Duncan, R. W. Byron and the London Literary Gazette. Boston Univ Stud in Eng 2 1956.

Brooks, E. A. Byron and the London Magazine. Keats-Shelley Jnl 5 1956.

Bigland, E. Lord Byron. 1956.

Robson, W. W. Byron as poet. Proc Br Acad 43 1957.

Marchand, L. A. Byron: a biography. 3 vols New York 1958.

— Byron's poetry: a critical introduction. Boston 1965.

Barineau, E. Les feuilles d'automne et les Mémoires de Lord Byron. MP 55 1958.

Everett, E. M. Lord Byron's Lakist interlude. SP 55 1958.

Liljegren, J. E. Byron and Greece. In Hommage à L. L. Shücking, Revue de Littérature Comparée 32 1958.

Melchiori, G. Byron and Italy. Nottingham 1958.

de Palacio, J. Byron traducteur et les influences italiennes. Rivista di Letterature Moderne e Comparate 11 1958.

Poli, N. Echi di Byron in Carducci. Ibid.

Carb, N. R. E. Byron as a critic. Philological Papers 11 1958.

Marshall, W. H. Some Byron comments on Pope and Boileau. PQ 38 1959.

— Byron, Shelley, Hunt and the Liberal. Philadelphia 1960.

— The structure of Byron's major poems. Philadelphia 1962.

Langley, D. M. Byron, Leigh Hunt and the Shelleys. Keats-Shelley Memorial Bull 10 1959.

— The burning of Lord Byron's Memoirs. Cornhill Mag 170 1959.

— The late Lord Byron. 1961.

Jannattoni, L. Byron e Dickens agli 'spettacoli' di Mastro Titta. Eng Miscellany (Rome) 10 1959.

Fini, G. Due poeti: Andrea Chénier e Giorgio Byron. Foggia 1959.

Wells, N. K. George Gordon, Lord Byron: a Scottish genius. Abingdon 1960.

Shaver, C. L. Wordsworth on Byron: an unpublished letter to Southey. MLN 75 1960.

Spencer, T. J. B. Byron and the Greek tradition. Nottingham 1960.

Bostetter, E. E. Byron and the politics of paradise. PMLA 75 1960.

Kleinfield, H. L. Infidel on Parnassus: Lord Byron and the North American Review. New England Quart 33 1960.

Coles, W. A. T. N. Talfourd on Byron and the imaginations. Keats-Shelley Jnl 9 1960.

Beaty, F. L. Byron and the story of Francesca da Rimini. PMLA 75 1960.

— Byron's concept of ideal love. Keats-Shelley Jnl 12 1963.

West, P. Byron and the spoiler's art. 1960.

— (ed). Byron: a collection of critical essays. Englewood Cliffs NJ 1963.

Broome, J. H. Autour d'une épigraphe: Byron et Fougeret de Montbrun. Revue de Littérature Comparée 34 1961.

Wayman, D. G. Byron and the Franciscans. Keats-Shelley Memorial Bull 12 1961.

Thompson, K. F. Beckford, Byron and Henley. Etudes Anglaises 14 1961.

Blackstone, B. Guilt and retribution in Byron's sea poems. REL 2 1961.

Woodring, C. R. New light on Byron, Trelawny and Lady Hester Stanhope. Columbia Lib Columns 11 1961.

Shaw, J. J. Byron, Chênedollé and Lermontov's Dying gladiator. In Studies in honor of John C. Hodges and Alwin Thaler, Knoxville 1961.

Pafford, W. Byron and the mind of man. Boston Univ Stud in Romanticism 1 1961.

Hegediis, G. Byron. Budapest 1961.

Mesrep Gianascian, P. Lord Byron à St Lazare. In Venezia nelle letterature moderne, ed C. Pellegrini, Venice 1961.

Thorsley, P. L. The Byronic hero: types and prototypes. Minneapolis 1962.

Rutherford, A. Byron: a critical study. 1962.

Dobrée, B. Byron's dramas. Nottingham 1962.

Elwin, M. Lord Byron's wife. 1962.

Stevenson, R. S. Famous illnesses in history. 1962.

Livermore, A. L. Byron and Emily Brontë. Quart Rev 633 1962.

de Beer, G. Meshes of the Byronic net in Switzerland. E Studies 43 1962.

— Byron on the burning of Shelley. Keats-Shelley Memorial Bull 13 1962.

Simonsen, P. Om Hedda Gabler, Lille Eyolf og Lord Byron. Edda 62 1962.

Comorovski, C. Pe marginea traducerilor romûisti din operele lui Byron si Shelley. Revista de Filologie Romanicà (Bucharest) 6 1962.

de Almeida, P. A escola byroniana no Brasil. Sao Paulo 1962.

Borrow, K. T. and D. Hewlett. Byron: a link with Australia. Keats-Shelley Memorial Bull 14 1963.

Cialfi, M. Byron e il titanismo. Osservatore Politico Letterario 9 1963.
Cogswell, F. Scott-Byron. Stud in Scottish Lit 1 1963.
Green, D. B. Byron's cousin Trevanion. E Studies 44 1963.
Newell, K. B. Paul Elmer More on Byron. Keats-Shelley Jnl 12 1963.
Souffrin, E. Le Byronisme de Théodore de Banville. Revue de Littérature Comparée 37 1963.

H. G. P.

PERCY BYSSHE SHELLEY

1792–1822

Mss of most of Shelley's verse and prose of 1817–22 have survived and are scattered in public and private collections throughout Britain and America. The principal collections are located in: (1) Bodley: 22 notebooks and boxes, including substantial parts in Shelley's or Mary Shelley's hand of Laon and Cythna, Rosalind and Helen, Julian and Maddalo, Prometheus unbound, Peter Bell III, Swellfoot, Sensitive plant, Epipsychidion, Witch of Atlas, Adonais, Hellas, Charles I, Triumph of life, *trns from Euripides, Goethe and Calderón,* Speculations on morals and metaphysics, Coliseum, On manners of the antients, Essay on Christianity, Defence of poetry; *microfilms of this collection are at Duke University. (2) Huntington Library: 3 notebooks (see* Note books of Shelley, ed H. B. Forman, Boston 1911, *below) including drafts of* Mask of anarchy, Vision of the sea, Cyprian, Una favola: *3 poems in Mary Shelley's hand, and* Hellas *in E. Williams's hand. (3) Houghton Library Harvard Univ: a fair-copy notebook, and 7 poems. (4) Pforzheimer Library: the Esdaile notebook of early poems, some 20 other poems and fragments, and* A philosophical view of reform. *(5) BM:* Masque of anarchy *(Wise ms) and 12 minor poems and fragments; transcripts at Duke University. (6) Pierpont Morgan Library:* Julian and Maddalo, *and 4 other poems. (7) Library of Congress:* Mask of anarchy *(Hunt ms) and minor prose. (8) Eton College Library: 6 poems and fragments. The letters are also widely scattered (see F. L. Jones,* Letters, 1964, *below). Collections of more than 20 letters are located in: (1) Bodley (164); (2) Pforzheimer Library (164); (3) BM (59); Huntington Library (28). Microfilms of the 8th Baron Abinger's large collection of material relating to Shelley and his circle are in Bodley and at Duke University; see* Lib Notes no 27 *(Durham NC) April 1953, or* Bodl ms Shelley adds d. 11, *for detailed contents. The R. Ingpen papers, which include transcripts and photostats, are at the University of California Berkeley; the E. Dowden papers, which include transcripts, and the ms of his* Life of Shelley, *are at Trinity College Dublin (no pbd catalogues).*

Bibliographies

Forman, H. B. The Shelley library, i: Shelley's own books, pamphlets and broadsides; posthumous separate issues; and posthumous books wholly or mainly by him. 1886 (Shelley Soc). No pt 2 pbd.
Anderson, J. P. In W. Sharp, Life of Shelley, 1887.
Ellis, F. S. An alphabetical table of contents to Shelley's poetical works. 1888 (Shelley Soc).
—— A lexical concordance to the poetical works of Shelley. 1892 (also in 2 vols), Tokyo 1963 (with appendix by T. Saito).
[Welch, C.] Hand-list of mss, letters, printed books and personal relics of Shelley and his circle, exhibited in the Guildhall Library. 1893.
[Kooistra, J.] Shelley bibliography 1908–22. E Studies 4 1922. Addns by L. Verkoren, 5 1923, 20 1938.
White, W. Fifteen years of Shelley scholarship: a bibliography 1923–38. E Studies 21 1939 (with addns by W. White and L. Verkoren).
—— Shelley scholarship 1939–50. E Studies 32 1951 (with addns by L. Verkoren).
Granniss, R. S. A descriptive catalogue of the first editions in book form of the writings of Shelley. New York 1923 (priv ptd). With 30 plates.
Wise, T. J. A Shelley library. 1924 (priv ptd). Vol 5 of The Ashley library: a catalogue of printed books, mss and autograph letters. *See* also vols 1 (1922) and 11 (1936).
Ricci, S. de. A bibliography of Shelley's letters, published and unpublished. Paris 1927 (priv ptd).
[Griffith, R. H.] An account of an exhibition of books and mss of Shelley, something of their literary history, their present condition and their provenance. [Austin] 1935.
Weaver, B. In English Romantic poets: a review of research, ed T. M. Raysor, New York 1950, 1956 (rev).
The Keats-Shelley journal. New York 1952–. Contains annual bibliography.
Bernbaum, E. Keats, Shelley, Byron, Hunt: a critical sketch of important books and articles 1940–50. Keats-Shelley Jnl 1 1952.
Cameron, K. N. Shelley scholarship 1940–53: a critical survey. Keats-Shelley Jnl 3 1954.
—— (ed). The Carl H. Pforzheimer library: Shelley and his circle 1773–1822. c. 8 vols Cambridge Mass 1961–. Catalogue, full texts and commentary.
Taylor, C. H. The early collected editions of Shelley's poems: a study in the history and transmission of the printed text. New Haven 1958.
Green, D. B., and D. E. G. Wilson. Keats, Shelley, Byron, Hunt and their circles: a bibliography July 1 1950–June 30 1962. Lincoln Nebraska 1964.
Massey, I. The first edition of Shelley's Poetical works 1839: some ms sources. Keats-Shelley Jnl 16 1967.

Collections

Miscellaneous and posthumous poems. Vol 1 (all pbd) 1826. Benbow's unauthorized edn; selections from this were reissued as Miscellaneous poems, 1826.
The poetical works of Coleridge, Shelley and Keats. Paris 1829, Philadelphia 1831 etc. Galignani's edn, with memoir by C. Redding.
The works of Shelley, with his life. 2 vols 1834. Ascham's unauthorized edn; selections from this were reissued as Posthumous poems, 1834.
The poetical works. Ed M. W. Shelley 4 vols 1839 (prints Queen Mab with omissions), 1 vol 1840 (engraved title-page dated 1839; adds Swellfoot, Peter Bell III, and Queen Mab complete), 1841 (omits Queen Mab), 4 vols 1846, 3 vols 1847 (prints cantos 1–2 of Queen Mab), 1 vol 1847, Philadelphia 1847, London 1850, Philadelphia 1851, 3 vols 1853, 1 vol 1853, 1854, 3 vols Boston 1855, 1 vol 1856, 3 vols 1857, 2 vols Boston 1857 (with memoir by J. R. Lowell), 1 vol 1862, 3 vols 1866, 1869, 1 vol 1869, Philadelphia [1884], 3 vols Boston 1889, 1 vol 1889 (including essays and fragments).
The poetical works. Ed G. Cuningham, illustr on steel by G. Standfast 1844.
The poetical works. Ed G. G. Foster, Philadelphia 1845, New York 1850.
The works. Ed M. W. Shelley 1847, 1854. Comprises Poetical works, above, and Essays and letters from abroad, with separate pagination.
The poetical works: including various additional pieces from ms and other sources, the text carefully revised, with notes and a memoir by W. M. Rossetti. 2 vols 1870, 1 vol [1870] (unannotated edn), 3 vols 1878 (rev), 1 vol [1878] (unannotated edn), 3 vols 1881, 1 vol New York [1885], London 1887, 3 vols 1894, 1897, 1 vol 1911, [1951], New York [1953].
The poetical works. Ed W. B. Scott [1874] (with memoir), [1880], 1889, 1895.
The poetical works. [1874].
The poetical works, now first given from the author's original editions with some hitherto inedited pieces,

with memoir by Leigh Hunt. [Ed R. H. Shepherd] 3 vols [1872–]5 (vol 3, and a 4th vol containing the prose, were entitled The works of Shelley), 3 vols 1888, 2 vols 1902, 1912.

The poetical works. Ed H. B. Forman 4 vols 1876–7, 1882 (with notes by M. W. Shelley), 2 vols 1882 (without notes), 1886, 1892, 5 vols 1892 (Aldine).

The prose works. Ed H. B. Forman 4 vols 1880.

The works in verse and prose. Ed H. B. Forman 8 vols 1880. Comprises The poetical works 1876–7 and The prose works, above.

Poetical works. 1888, 1897.

The prose works. Ed R. H. Shepherd 2 vols 1888, 1902, 1912.

Poetical works. Ed E. Dowden 1890, New York 1893 etc.

The complete poetical works. Ed G. E. Woodberry 4 vols Boston 1892, London 1893 (Centenary edn, with memoir, textual notes, and 'contemporary records'), 1 vol Boston 1901 (Cambridge Poets Ser), 1949.

The poetical works, overseen by F. S. Ellis and printed by William Morris at the Kelmscott Press. 3 vols [1894–]5 (priv ptd).

Poems. [Decorated by C. Ricketts] 3 vols 1901–2 (priv ptd).

Poetical works. 1902.

Complete poetical works. Ed T. Hutchinson, Oxford 1904 (OSA), 1905, New York 1933 (introd by B. P. Kurtz), Oxford 1934 (without introd), [1960].

The complete works. Ed N. H. Doyle 8 vols 1904–6.

The poems. Introd by C. D. Locock 4 vols 1906–9.

The poetical works. Ed A. H. Koszul 2 vols [1907], 1 vol 1934, 2 vols (with rev introd) 1953 (EL).

Poetical works. Introd by R. Garnett [1911].

The poems. Ed C. D. Locock with introd by A. Clutton-Brock 2 vols 1911.

The lyrical [dramatic, narrative] poems and translations, arranged in chronological order. Ed C. H. Herford 4 vols 1918–27.

The complete works. Ed R. Ingpen and W. E. Peck 10 vols 1926–30, New York 1965 (Julian edn).

The complete poetical works of Keats and Shelley. New York 1932, London 1935.

Shelley's prose: or the trumpet of a prophecy. Ed D. L. Clark, Albuquerque 1954.

Shelley's poetical works were tr German, 1840–4, 1866; Italian, 1858, 1878, 1902, 1911, 1917, 1925; French, 1885–7; Russian, 1893–5, 1937, 1963; Rumanian, 1957. The prose works were tr Russian, 1895–9; French, 1903; Italian, [1917].

Selections

Miscellaneous poems. 1826. Selected from Miscellaneous and posthumous poems, 1826 (Benbow's edn).

The beauties of Shelley, consisting of miscellaneous selections from his poetical works, the entire poems of Adonais and Alastor and a revised edition of Queen Mab free from all the objectionable passages with a biographical preface. 1830 (S. Hunt's edn), 1832 (Lumley's edn), 1856.

The beauties of Shelley, consisting of Rosalind and Helen, Posthumous and miscellaneous poems, Revolt of Islam, Queen Mab and Prometheus unbound. 1836. Ascham's edn.

The works of Shelley, comprising Queen Mab, The revolt of Islam, The Cenci &c &c &c [with preface]. 1836. Daly's edn, based on Ascham's Works, 1834; reissued as Poetical works of Shelley complete, 1837, 1839.

Einige Dichtungen. Tr F. Prössel, Leipzig 1841.

The minor poems. 1846, 1859.

Queen Mab and other poems. Halifax 1865.

A selection from the poems. Ed M. Blind, Leipzig [1872], 1920 (Tauchnitz).

Poems selected from Shelley. Ed R. Garnett 1880.

Poems. Ed S. A. Brooke 1880.

The lyrics and minor poems, with a prefatory notice by J. Skipsey. 1885, New York 1885.

Essays and letters. Ed E. Rhys 1886, [1905].

Poems and sonnets. Ed 'Charles Alfred Seymour' (T. J. Wise). Philadelphia [i.e. London] 1887 (priv ptd).

The banquet of Plato, and other pieces. Ed H. Morley 1887, 1905.

Prometheus unbound, with Adonais [etc]. Ed H. Morley 1888, 1905, 1906.

The sensitive plant. Ed S. Silvagni, Prato 1888.

The skylark and Adonais, with other poems. Ed J. W. Abernethy, New York [1890].

A defense of poetry. Ed A. S. Cook, Boston 1891.

The lyric poems. Ed E. Rhys [1895].

Select poems. Ed W. J. Alexander, Boston 1898.

Poems: narrative elegiac and visionary. [Ed H. B. Forman] 1899, 1901, 1904 (Temple Classics).

The sensitive plant. [Ed E. Rhys], illustr L. Housman 1899 (priv ptd).

Poems from Shelley and Keats. Ed S. C. Newsom, New York 1900, 1907, 1922.

Poems of Shelley, selected and arranged for use in schools by E. E. Speight. 1901.

Poems. Ed W. Raleigh, illustr R. A. Bell 1902, 1907.

Poems. Ed A. Meynell 1903, 1923.

Thoughts from Shelley. [Selected by V. E. Neale] 1903.

A defence of poetry etc. Ed M. W. Shelley, Indianapolis [1904] (priv ptd). Rptd from Essays, letters from abroad etc, 1845.

With Shelley in Italy: a selection of the poems and letters. Ed. A. B. McMahan, Chicago 1905, London 1907. With 64 photographs.

Poems of Shelley. Ed. H. Bennett 1907, 1924.

Shelley selected. Ed. J. C. Collins [1907], [1915].

Selected poems. Ed G. H. Clarke, New York [1907], London [1910].

Select poems. Ed G. E. Woodberry, Boston 1908.

The banquet of Plato translated by Shelley. Ed B. Rogers 1908 (priv ptd).

Shelley's Defence of poetry; Browning's Essay on Shelley. Ed L. Winstanley, Boston 1911.

Nature poems by Shelley. Illustr W. Hyde 1911.

The sensitive plant. Ed E. Gosse, illustr R. Robinson 1911, Philadelphia [1911].

Selected poems. [1911].

Shelley [prose and verse selections]. Ed R. Ingpen [1912].

Selected poems. Oxford 1913, 1921 (WC).

Selections from the poems. Ed A. H. Thompson, Cambridge 1915, 1919, 1920.

Selected prose works. Ed H. S. Salt 1915, [1922].

Peacock's Four ages of poetry; Shelley's Defence of poetry; Browning's Essay on Shelley. Ed H. F. B. Brett-Smith, Oxford 1921, 1923 (2 issues, one abridged; the abridgment only rptd 1953).

[Poésies choisies]. Tr A. Koszul, Paris 1922, 1927, 1930, 1943.

Odes, poèmes et fragments lyriques choisis. Ed and tr A. Fontaines, Paris 1923.

Poems: an anthology in commemoration of the poet's death. Ed T. J. Cobden-Sanderson 1922.

Selected poems. Ed G. Roth, Paris 1923.

Shelley. Ed H. Newbolt, Edinburgh [1923], 1954.

Select poems and prose. Ed R. Ackermann, Frankfurt 1924 (with glossary).

Shelley and Keats, contrasted by G. Boas. [1925].

Poems. Ed O. W. Campbell 1925.

Poems. Ed N. A. Crawford, Girard Kansas [1925].

Shelley. [Ed E. Thompson 1925] (Augustan Books Ser).

Poems, selected by A. Symons. 1926.

Selections from Shelley. Ed E. H. Blakeney 1926.

Poetry and prose, with essays by Browning, Bagehot, Swinburne, and reminiscences by others. Ed A. M. D. Hughes, Oxford 1931.

The best of Shelley. Ed N. I. White, New York 1932.

Selections from the poems. Ed V. de S. Pinto [1932].

Oeuvres choisies: texte anglais et traduction en vers par M. Castelain 3 vols Paris 1929–35.

Songs: a collection of lyrics and sonnets completed from the minor fragments. Ed C. J. Bostlemann and W. E. Peck, Morristown NJ 1937.
Shelley. Ed D. Wellesley 1941.
The reader's Shelley: selections. Ed. C. H. Grabo and M. J. Freeman, New York [1942].
Selected poems, essays and letters. Ed. E. Barnard, New York 1944.
Selected poems. Ed L. Untermeyer, New York 1944 (priv ptd).
Shelley in Italy: an anthology. Ed J. Lehmann 1947.
A defence of poetry. Ed E. Blunden, Tokyo 1948; ed F. B. Pinion [1955].
The Shelley companion. Ed H. J. Stenning 1948.
Poems. Ed J. Heath-Stubbs 1948.
Poems. Ed R. Church, illustr J. Buckland-Wright 1949 (Folio Soc).
Shelley's poetical works. Ed 'Morchard Bishop' (O. Stonor) 1949.
Selected poetry and prose. Ed C. Baker, New York 1951 (Modern Lib).
Shelley selected poetry, prose and letters. Ed A. S. B. Glover 1951 (Nonesuch Lib).
Selected poems. Ed. E. Blunden 1954.
Selected poetry and prose. Ed K. N. Cameron, New York 1956.
A selection. Ed I. Quigly 1956 (Pelican).
Selected poems. Ed F. L. Jones, New York [1956].
Odes of Keats and Shelley. New York 1957 (priv ptd).
Poems and lyrics. New York 1957 (priv ptd).
Selections from Shelley's poetry. Ed F. B. Pinion 1958.
Poetry and prose. Ed I. G. Neupokoevna, Moscow 1959.
Selected poems. Ed J. Holloway 1960.
Poèmes: traduction, préface et notes par M. L. Cazamian. [Paris 1960].
Selections from Shelley's poetry and prose. Ed D. S. R. Welland 1961.
Selected poems and prose. Ed G. M. Matthews, Oxford 1964.
Choix de textes, suite iconographique et commentaire, étude par Stephen Spender [etc]. Paris 1964.
Selected poetry and prose. Ed H. Bloom, New York 1966.

§1

Zastrozzi: a romance by P.B.S. 1810, 1839; ed P. Hartnoll 1955 (priv ptd); ed E. Chesser 1965.
Original poetry by Victor and Cazire [P.B. and Elizabeth Shelley]. Worthing 1810; ed R. Garnett 1898; ed S. J. Looker in his Shelley, Trelawny and Henley, Worthing 1950 (photofacs).
Posthumous fragments of Margaret Nicholson: being poems found amongst the papers of that noted female who attempted the life of the king in 1786. Ed John Fitzvictor, Oxford 1810; ed H. B. Forman [1877] (priv ptd). Ed Shelley.
St Irvyne or the Rosicrucian: a romance, by a gentleman of the University of Oxford. 1811 (reissue dated 1822), 1840.
The necessity of atheism [anon, by T. J. Hogg and Shelley]. Worthing [1811], London 1906; ed S. J. Looker in his Shelley, Trelawny and Henley, Worthing 1950 (photofacs); ed E. Chesser 1965.
A poetical essay on the existing state of things, by a gentleman of the University of Oxford. [1811]. No known copy.
An address to the Irish people. Dublin 1812; ed T. J. Wise 1886 (Shelley Soc), 1890.
Proposals for an association of those philanthropists, who convinced of the inadequacy of the moral and political state of Ireland to produce benefits which are nevertheless attainable, are willing to unite to accomplish its regeneration. Dublin [1812].
Declaration of rights. [Dublin 1812]. 2 copies of this anon broadside are in the Public Record Office. Rptd in Republican 24 Sept 1819, in Philobiblon Soc Miscellany 12 1868–9, and in Fifty major documents of the nineteenth century, ed L. L. Snyder, Princeton 1955.
The Devil's walk: a ballad. [Barnstaple? 1812]. Pbd as anon broadside; one copy in Public Records Office, one at Univ of Texas. Rptd by W. M. Rossetti, Fortnightly Rev 1 Jan 1871.
A letter to Lord Ellenborough. [1812] (priv ptd), (one copy in Bodley); [ed J. M. Wheeler] 1883; ed T. J. Wise 1887, (Shelley Soc) 1894.
A vindication of natural diet: being one in a series of notes to Queen Mab, a philosophical poem. 1813; [ed H. S. Salt and W. E. A. Axon] 1884; 1884 (Shelley Soc), 1886, 1922.
Queen Mab: a philosophical poem, with notes. 1813 (priv ptd). Numerous unauthorized edns 1821–57, including 1821 (Clark's edn, some copies bowdlerized), 1821 (Benbow's, with false New York imprint), 1822 (Carlile's, some copies without the notes), 1823, 1826, 1829 (Brooks's), 1830 (S. Hunt's bowdlerized edn), New York 1831, London 1847 (Watson's); tr German, [1897].
A refutation of deism, in a dialogue. 1814 (anon); rptd in Theological Inquirer March–April 1815.
[Review of] Hogg's Memoirs of Prince Haimatoff. Critical Rev 6 1814 (anon); ed T. J. Wise 1886, 1886 (rev) (Shelley Soc); rptd in Memoirs of Prince Haimatoff, ed S. Scott 1952 (Folio Soc).
Alastor: or the spirit of solitude, and other poems. 1816; ed H. B. Forman 1876 (priv ptd); ed B. Dobell 1885, 1887 (Shelley Soc); tr French, 1884, 1895; Dutch, [1906], 1909 (Frisian, 1918); Italian, 1923; German, 1909, 1960.
A proposal for putting reform to the vote throughout the kingdom, by the Hermit of Marlow. 1817; ed H. B. Forman 1887 (facs of holograph ms) (Shelley Soc).
An address to the people on the death of Princess Charlotte, by the Hermit of Marlow. [1817], [1843?] ('facsimile reprint', but no copy known of supposed 1817 edn; ptd from a ms?), Edinburgh 1883 (priv ptd).
Remarks on 'Mandeville' and Mr Godwin, by E.K. ['Elfin Knight', i.e. Shelley]. Examiner 28 Dec 1817; rptd by Medwin, Athenaeum 27 Oct 1832.
History of a six weeks' tour through a part of France, Switzerland, Germany and Holland; with letters descriptive of a sail round the Lake of Geneva, and of the glaciers of Chamouni [by Shelley and M. W. Shelley]. 1817 (anon; reissued 1829); ed C. I. Elton 1894 (abridged).
Laon and Cythna, or the revolution of the golden city: a vision of the nineteenth century in the stanza of Spenser. 1818. Suppressed, rev and reissued as The revolt of Islam: a poem in twelve cantos, 1818 (a few copies dated 1817; reissued 1829).
Rosalind and Helen: a modern eclogue; with other poems. 1819; ed H. B. Forman 1876 (priv ptd); ed H. B. Forman 1888 (Shelley Soc).
The Cenci: a tragedy in five acts. 1819 (ptd in Italy), 1821, 1827 (Benbow's unauthorized edn); ed A. and H. B. Forman 1886 (Shelley Soc); New York 1903 (priv ptd); ed G. E. Woodberry, Boston 1909 (with bibliography); Leipzig 1916 (Tauchnitz), 1922, London [1928]; ed A. C. Hicks and R. M. Clark, Caldwell Idaho 1945 (a stage version); tr German, 1837, 1904, 1907, 1924; Italian, 1844, 1892, 1898, 1912, 1916, 1931; Russian, 1864, 1899; French, 1883 (preface by A. C. Swinburne); Polish, 1912; Czech, 1922, 1960; Japanese, 1955.
Prometheus unbound: a lyrical drama in four acts, with other poems. 1820; ed V. Scudder, Boston [1892], London [1892]; ed G. L. Dickinson 1898, 1904 (priv ptd), New York 1904 (priv ptd); ed R. Ackermann, Heidelberg 1908; ed A. M. D. Hughes, Oxford 1910, 1957; ed G. Ferrando, Florence 1922 (notes in Italian); Oxford 1923 (plain text); ed L. J. Zillman, Seattle 1959

(variorum edn, with bibliography); New York [1960]; ed N. K. Basu, Calcutta 1961; tr German, 1876, 1887; French, 1884, 1912, 1942; Italian, 1892, 1892, 1894, 1901, 1904, 1922, 1925, 1946; Danish, 1892; Norwegian, 1892, 1951; Arabic, 1947; Serbo-Croat, 1952; Hebrew, 1953; Japanese, 1957; Hungarian, 1961; Georgian, 1962.

Oedipus tyrannus or Swellfoot the tyrant: a tragedy in two acts, translated from the original Doric. 1820 (anon; edn suppressed); ed H. B. Forman [1876], [1884]; tr Polish, 1912.

Epipsychidion: verses addressed to the noble and unfortunate Lady Emilia V—— now imprisoned in the convent of ——. 1821 (anon, withdrawn); ed H. B. Forman 1876 (priv ptd); ed R. A. Potts 1887 (Shelley Soc) (introd by S. A. Brooke); 1921, Montagnola 1923; tr Italian, 1893, 1928; German, 1900; Japanese, 1923; Polish, [1924].

Adonais: an elegy on the death of John Keats, author of Endymion, Hyperion etc. Pisa 1821, Cambridge 1829; [ed H. B. Forman 1877] (priv ptd); ed T. J. Wise 1886, 1886, 1887 (rev) (Shelley Soc); ed W. M. Rossetti, Oxford 1890; ed W. M. Rossetti, rev A. O. Prickard 1903, 1904 (facs); ed A. R. Weekes [1910]; San Francisco 1922 (facs, priv ptd); ed S. Policardi, Milan 1925 (notes in Italian); ed N. Douglas 1927 (photofacs); ed C. J. Sawyer 1936; ed F. B. Pinion [1955]; tr Italian, 1830, 1899, 1925, 1948, 1956; German, 1900, 1910; Frisian, 1916; Spanish, 1936, 1944, 1947, 1954; Danish, 1950.

Hellas: a lyrical drama. 1822; ed T. J. Wise 1886, 1886, 1887 (Shelley Soc); tr Italian, 1855; French, 1884, 1906.

Poetical pieces by the late Percy Bysshe Shelley: containing Prometheus unmasked, a lyrical drama, with other poems; Hellas: a lyrical drama; The Cenci: a tragedy in five acts; Rosalind and Helen: with other poems. 1823. A reissue of the first edns (second edn of Cenci) with a new title-page; some copies omit Hellas.

Posthumous poems. [Ed M. W. Shelley] 1824. Suppressed.

The masque of anarchy: a poem now first published, with a preface by Leigh Hunt. 1832, 1842; ed H. B. Forman 1887 (Shelley Soc) (photofacs of the holograph ('Wise') ms); ed T. J. Wise 1892 (facs of 1832 edn) (Shelley Soc).

The Shelley papers: memoir by T. Medwin and original poems and papers by Shelley. 1833, 1844. Original material rptd from Athenaeum 28 July, 11, 25 Aug, 1–29 Sept, 20–7 Oct, 10–24 Nov, 8 Dec (by T. F. Kelsall) 1832, 20 April 1833; adds one spurious poem.

Essays, letters from abroad, translations and fragments. Ed M. W. Shelley 2 vols 1840, Philadelphia 1840, London 1841, 1 vol 1845, 2 vols 1852, 1856. First pbn of A defence of poetry; *see* under Selections, above.

Shelley memorials, from authentic sources; to which is added An essay on Christianity. Ed Lady Shelley [and R. Garnett] 1859, 1859, Boston 1859, London 1862 ('2nd edn'), 1875 ('3rd edn').

Relics of Shelley. Ed R. Garnett 1862.

The daemon of the world: the first part as published in 1816 with Alastor; the second part deciphered and now printed from his manuscript revision and interpolations in the newly discovered copy of Queen Mab. Ed H. B. Forman 1876 (priv ptd).

To the Nile; and Shelley fragments. St James Mag March 1876. Pt of Essay on Christianity.

Notes on sculptures in Rome and Florence together with a Lucianic fragment and a criticism on Peacock's poem Rhododaphne. Ed H. B. Forman 1879 (priv ptd) (from ms).

[Fragment of a satire on satire]. Ed E. Dowden in his Correspondence of Robert Southey with Caroline Bowles, 1881.

The wandering Jew [or The victim of the eternal avenger]. Ed B. Dobell 1887 (Shelley Soc). Text conflated from extracts in Edinburgh Literary Jnl 20, 27 June, 4 July, 26 Dec 1829 and from text 'in a complete state' in Fraser's Mag July 1831.

An examination of the Shelley manuscripts in the Bodleian Library, by C. D. Locock. Oxford 1903. New and corrected texts.

Shelley's prose in the Bodleian manuscripts. Ed A. H. Koszul, Oxford 1910.

Note books of Shelley, from the originals in the library of W. K. Bixby [now in Huntington Lib], deciphered, transcribed and edited, with a full commentary, by H. Buxton Forman. 3 vols Boston 1911 (priv ptd).

A philosophical view of reform. Ed T. W. Rolleston, Oxford 1920; ed W. E. Peck 1930 (priv ptd); ed R. J. White in his Political tracts of Wordsworth, Coleridge and Shelley, Cambridge 1953.

New fragments by Shelley. Ed E. Gosse, TLS 24 Feb 1921. Verses from mss now at Eton College.

Inédits italiens de Shelley. [Ed] A. Koszul, Revue de Littérature Comparée 2 1922.

[Prose fragment on the resettlement of the Jews]. Ed T. Saito, in The Shelley memorial volume by members of the English Club, Imperial University of Tokyo, Tokyo 1923. With photofacs of ms, which was probably destroyed in 1945–6.

The celandine. Ed W. E. Peck, Boston Herald 21 Dec 1925; ed E. H. Blakeney, Winchester 1927 (priv ptd).

An unpublished ballad by Shelley ['Young parson Richards']. EdW. E. Peck, PQ 5 1926; ed Peck, Iowa City 1926 (priv ptd).

The Shelley notebook in the Harvard Library. Ed G. E. Woodberry, Cambridge Mass 1929 (photofacs). *See* G. E. Woodberry, Notes on the ms volume of Shelley's poems in the library of Harvard College, Cambridge Mass 1889; autograph ascriptions corrected by M. Kessel, TLS 5 Sept 1936.

On the vegetable system of diet. Ed R. Ingpen 1929 (priv ptd); rptd in his Verse and prose from the mss, 1934, below; 1940, 1947.

Plato's Banquet translated from the Greek: a discourse on the manners of the antient Greeks relative to the subject of love; also A preface to the Banquet. Ed R. Ingpen 1931 (priv ptd) (from ms). *See* Shelley's translations from Plato, below.

Verse and prose from the manuscripts of Shelley. Ed J. C. E. Shelley-Rolls and R. Ingpen 1934 (priv ptd).

Sadak the wanderer: an unknown Shelley poem. Ed D. Cook, TLS 16 May 1936. Rptd from Keepsake 1828.

A Shelley letter. Ed E. H. Blakeney, Winchester 1936 (priv ptd). Verse letter to Feargus Graham.

[Verses from Claire Clairmont's journal]. In N. I. White, Shelley vol 2, New York 1940; ed L. Robertson, MLR 47 1953.

[Translation from Aristotle, Ethics IX viii]. In Shelley at Oxford, ed W. S. Scott 1944 (priv ptd).

Unpublished fragments by Shelley and Mary. Ed F. L. Jones, SP 45 1948. On miracles and the game laws.

Shelley's translations from Plato: a critical edition. Ed J. A. Notopoulos in his Platonism of Shelley: a study of Platonism and the poetic mind, Durham NC 1949. Includes unpbd material.

[A midsummer night's dream poem]. Ed N. Rogers in his Shelley at work, Oxford 1956, 1967 (rev).

[Italian version of Ode to liberty]. Ibid.

Music, when soft voices die. Ed I. Massey, JEGP 59 1960.

A new text of Shelley's scene for Tasso. Ed G. M. Matthews, Keats-Shelley Memorial Bull 11 1960.

The triumph of life: a new text. Ed G. M. Matthews, Studia Neophilologica 32 1960.

The triumph of life apocrypha. Ed G. M. Matthews, TLS 5 Aug 1960.

[An incitement to Satan]. Ed G. M. Matthews, Stand 5 1960. A poem.

[The pursued and the pursuer]. Ed G. M. Matthews, ibid. A poem.

Shelley and Dante: an essay in textual criticism. J. L. de Palacio, Revue de Littérature Comparée 35 1961. New text of Shelley's trn of Dante's Convito.

Shelley traducteur de Dante: le chant xxviii du Purgatoire. Ed J. L. de Palacio, Revue de Littérature Comparée 36 1962. Commentary in French.

Time: an unpublished sequel. Ed I. Massey, Stud in Romanticism 2 1962.

The Esdaile notebook: a volume of early poems. Ed K. N. Cameron, New York 1964, London 1964 (rev); ed N. Rogers as The Esdaile poems, Oxford 1966.

Reiman, D. H. Shelley's The triumph of life: a critical study based on a text newly edited from the Bodleian ms. Urbana 1965.

New texts of Shelley's Plato. Ed J. A. Notopoulos, Keats-Shelley Jnl 15 1966.

Letters

Only the more important collections are listed. For first pbn and present location of individual letters see F. L. Jones, Letters, 1964, vol 2, pp. 452–6, *below*.

Prose works. Ed H. B. Forman 4 vols 1880. The first collected edn of the letters.

The correspondence of Robert Southey with Caroline Bowles; together with his correspondence with Shelley. Ed E. Dowden 1881.

Shelley and Mary. Ed Lady Jane and Sir Percy F. Shelley 3 or 4 vols [1882] (priv ptd).

Select letters. Ed R. Garnett 1882.

Letters to Robert Southey and other correspondents. Ed T. J. Wise 1886 (priv ptd).

Essays and letters. Ed E. Rhys 1886.

Letters from Harriet Shelley to Catherine Nugent. 1889 (priv ptd).

Letters to Jane Clairmont. Ed T. J. Wise 1889 (priv ptd).

Letters to Elizabeth Hitchener. Ed T. J. Wise 2 vols 1890 (priv ptd); ed B. Dobell 1908.

Letters to William Godwin. Ed T. J. Wise 2 vols 1891 (priv ptd).

The best letters. Ed S. C. Hughson, Chicago 1892.

Letters to Leigh Hunt. Ed T. J. Wise 2 vols 1894 (priv ptd).

Letters to T. J. Hogg. Ed T. J. Wise with notes by W. M. Rossetti and H. B. Forman 1897 (priv ptd).

Letters. Ed R. Ingpen 2 vols 1909, 1912 (adds 5 letters), 1914 (rev) (Bohn's Lib).

The Shelley correspondence in the Bodleian Library. Ed R. H. Hill, Oxford 1926. Contains detailed lists of mss, letters and relics.

Complete works: correspondence. Ed R. Ingpen 1926. Vols 8–10 of the Julian edn.

Letters, selected by R. B. Johnson. 1929.

Shelley's lost letters to Harriet. Ed L. Hotson 1930.

Lettere dall'Italia sull'Italia. Ed C. Zacchetti, Naples 1934.

New Shelley letters. Ed W. S. Scott 1948. The letters by Shelley are rptd from Scott's The Athenians, 1943, Harriet and Mary, 1944, Shelley at Oxford, 1944 (all 3 priv ptd).

Letters. Ed F. L. Jones 2 vols Oxford 1964. First complete edn.

Jones, F. L. Shelley's letter of 23 June 1811 to Hogg. Keats-Shelley Memorial Bull 15 1964.

Maxwell, J. C. A Shelley letter: an unrecorded printing. N & Q May 1964. Shelley's letter to Ollier 16 Aug 1818, E Studien 51 1918.

The Collected letters *were tr German, 1840–1.*

§2

All the more important reviews are listed. For a list with summaries and quotations including minor items see G. L. Marsh, The early reviews of Shelley, MP 27 1929. *Nearly all these are rptd in* N. I. White, The unextinguished hearth, Durham NC 1938. *Notices by Hunt are rptd in* E. Blunden, Leigh Hunt's Examiner examined, 1928; *the reviews of* Prometheus unbound *are rptd in* L. J. Zillman, Shelley's Prometheus unbound, Seattle 1959.

Zastrozzi. GM Sept 1810; Critical Rev Nov 1810.

Original poetry. Literary Panorama Oct 1810; Br Critic April 1811; Poetical Register for 1810–11, 1814.

St Irvyne. Br Critic Jan 1811; Literary Panorama Feb 1811; Anti-Jacobin Rev Jan 1812.

Necessity of atheism and A declaration of rights. Brighton Mag May 1822.

Queen Mab. Theological Inquirer or Polemical Mag March, April, May, July 1815 (by R. C. Fair); London Mag & Theatrical Inquisitor March 1821; Literary Gazette 19 May 1821; Windsor, Slough & Eton Express 20–26 May 1821 (by O.N.); Monthly Mag June 1821; Literary Chron 2 June 1821; Beacon 2 June 1821.

Alastor. Monthly Rev April 1816; Br Critic May 1816; Eclectic Rev Oct 1816; Blackwood's Mag Nov 1819 (by J. G. Lockhart).

History of a six weeks' tour. Blackwood's Mag July 1818.

Revolt of Islam. Examiner 1, 22 Feb, 1 March 1818 and 26 Sept, 3, 10 Oct 1819 (by L. Hunt); Man of Kent 21 Nov 1818; Blackwood's Mag Jan 1819 (by J. G. Lockhart); Quart Rev 21 1819 (by J. T. Coleridge).

Rosalind and Helen. Examiner 9 May 1819 (by L. Hunt); London Chron 1 June 1819; Blackwood's Mag June 1819 (by J. G. Lockhart); Monthly Rev Oct 1819.

The Cenci. Literary Gazette 1 April 1820; London Mag & Monthly Critical & Dramatic Rev April 1820; Theatrical Inquisitor April 1820; New Monthly Mag 1 May 1820; London Mag May 1820; Edinburgh Monthly Rev May 1820; Indicator 19, 26 July 1820 (by L. Hunt); Monthly Rev Feb 1821; Independent 17 Feb 1821; Br Rev June 1821.

Prometheus unbound. Blackwood's Mag Sept 1820 (by J. G. Lockhart); Literary Gazette 9 Sept 1820; London Mag & Monthly Critical & Dramatic Rev Sept–Oct 1820; Monthly Rev Feb 1821; Quart Rev 26 1821 (by W. S. Walker); Examiner, 16, 23 June 1822 (by L. Hunt).

Epipsychidion. Gossip 23 June, 14 July 1821; Blackwood's Mag Feb 1822 (by J. G. Lockhart?).

Adonais. Literary Gazette 8 Dec 1821; Blackwood's Mag Dec 1821 (by G. Croly); Examiner 7 July 1822 (by L. Hunt); European Mag April 1825.

Hellas. General Weekly Register of News 30 June 1822; Paris Monthly Rev Aug 1822 (obituary); Rambler's Mag Sept 1822 (obituary).

Posthumous poems. Examiner 13 June 1824; Edinburgh Mag July 1824; Edinburgh Rev 40 1824 (by Hazlitt); Literary Gazette 17 July 1824; Knight's Quart Mag 3 1824; Quart Rev 34 1826 (by J. G. Lockhart).

For modern collections of reviews, see

- Early reviews of English poets. Ed J. L. Haney, Philadelphia 1904. Reviews of Alastor, Cenci, Adonais.
- Famous reviews. Ed R. B. Johnson 1914. On Prometheus unbound.
- Notorious literary attacks. Ed A. Mordell, New York 1926. On Revolt of Islam.
- Contemporary reviews of Romantic poetry. Ed J. Wain 1953. Abridged reviews of Alastor, Revolt of Islam, Prometheus unbound.

Portraits of the metropolitan poets no 3: Mr Shelley. Honeycomb 12 Aug 1820.

Hazlitt, W. On paradox and common-place. In his Table-talk vol 1, 1821.

On the philosophy and poetry of Shelley. London Mag & Theatrical Inquisitor Feb 1821.

Reply to the anti-matrimonial hypothesis and supposed atheism of Shelley as laid down in Queen Mab. 1821. Anon.

Medwin, T. Journal of the conversations of Lord Byron, noted during a residence with his Lordship at Pisa in the years 1821 and 1822. 1824 (3 edns), Paris 1824, 1824, New York 1824, 2 vols 1825, 1 vol Baltimore 1825, London 1832.
—— The Shelley papers: memoir of Shelley. 1833, 1844.
—— Sydney: from the memoranda of a physician. Bentley's Miscellany Feb 1841. Fictionalized biography.
—— Life of Shelley. 2 vols 1847; ed H. B. Forman Oxford 1913 ('from a copy copiously amended and extended by the author').
Stockdale, J. J. In his Budget of 'all that is good, and noble, and amiable, in the country', nos 1–9 1826–7; rptd in Poetical works of Shelley, ed R. H. Shepherd vol 1 [1871], 1888.
Hunt, L. Lord Byron and some of his contemporaries. 1828, 2 vols 1828 (rev), 3 vols Paris 1828.
—— In his Imagination and fancy, 1844.
—— In his Autobiography, 3 vols 1850.
—— In his Correspondence, ed [T. Hunt] 2 vols 1862.
Moore, T. In his Letters and journals of Lord Byron, with notices of his life, 2 vols 1830, 1875 (rev).
Lewes, G. H. Shelley. Westminster Rev 35 1841; partly rptd in his Literary criticism, ed A. R. Kaminsky, Lincoln Nebraska 1964.
[Merle, J. G.] A newspaper editor's reminiscences. Fraser's Mag June 1841.
Gilfillan, G. In his Gallery of literary portraits, Edinburgh 1845, 1851 (3rd edn).
—— Prometheus bound and unbound. In his Third gallery of literary portraits, Edinburgh 1854. Both articles rptd in his Galleries of literary portraits, 2 vols Edinburgh 1856–7.
[Anster, J. H.] Life and writings of Shelley. North Br Rev 8 1847; rptd in Eclectic Mag 13 1848.
A[mos], A. Shelley and his contemporaries at Eton. Athenaeum 15 April 1848.
[Merle, W. H.] Shelley at Eton. Athenaeum 4 March 1848.
Browning, R. In Letters of Shelley, 1852. The letters were forged and the edn suppressed. Browning's introd ed W. T. Harden, 1888 (Shelley Soc); ed R. Garnett 1903, Boston 1911; ed H. F. B. Brett-Smith, Oxford 1921, 1923.
Kingsley, C. Thoughts on Shelley and Byron. Fraser's Mag Nov 1853; rptd in his Literary and general lectures and essays, 1880, 1890.
Bagehot, W. In his Estimates of some Englishmen and Scotchmen, 1858; rptd in his Literary studies vol 1, ed R. H. Hutton, 1879 and in his Collected works vol 1, ed N. St John-Stevas 1965.
Hamm, W. Shelley. Leipzig 1858.
Hogg, T. J. Life of Shelley. 2 vols 1858; ed E. Dowden 1906.
—— Shelley at Oxford. Ed R. A. Streatfeild 1904. Chs 3, 5–8 of his Life, above.
Middleton, C. C. Shelley and his writings. 2 vols 1858.
Peacock, T. L. Memoirs of Shelley. Fraser's Mag June 1858, Jan, March 1860, March 1862; ed H. F. B. Brett-Smith, Oxford 1909; rptd in his Works, ed Brett-Smith and C. E. Jones vol 8, 1934.
—— On the portraits of Shelley. 1911.
Trelawny, E. J. Recollections of the last days of Shelley and Byron. 1858, Boston 1858; ed E. Dowden 1906, Oxford 1923, 1931; ed J. E. Morpurgo, 1952 (Folio Soc) ('with additions from contemporary sources').
—— Records of Shelley, Byron and the author. 2 vols 1878, 1 vol 1887, [1905].
—— Letters. Ed H. B. Forman, Oxford 1910.
Shelley, Lady J. [and R. Garnett]. Shelley memorials: from authentic sources. 1859, 1859, Boston 1859, London 1862, 1875. *See* L. Hunt, Spectator 13 Aug 1859.
Garnett, R. Shelley in Pall Mall. Macmillan's Mag June 1860.
—— Shelley and Lord Beaconsfield; and Shelley's views on art. In his Essays of an ex-librarian, 1901.
—— (ed). Journal of Edward Ellerker Williams. 1902.
[Hunt, T.] Shelley, by one who knew him. Atlantic Monthly Feb 1863; rptd in E. Blunden, Shelley and Keats as they struck their contemporaries, 1925, below.
[Hutton, R. H.] Shelley's poetical mysticism. Nat Rev 16 1863; rptd in his Essays theological and literary vol 2, 1871, 1877 (rev), 1888.
Blind, M. Shelley. Westminster Rev new ser 38 1870.
—— Trelawny on Byron and Shelley. Whitehall Rev Jan 1880.
[Baynes, T. S.] Rossetti's edition of Shelley. Edinburgh Rev 133 1871.
MacCarthy, D. F. Shelley's early life, from original sources. 1872.
Masson, D. In his Wordsworth, Shelley, Keats and other essays, 1874.
Swinburne, A. C. Notes on the text of Shelley. In his Essays and studies, 1875.
—— Les Cenci. In his Studies in prose and poetry, 1894.
—— Percy Bysshe Shelley. Philadelphia 1903.
Paul, C. K. In his William Godwin: his friends and contemporaries, 2 vols 1876.
Sotheran, C. Shelley as a philosopher and reformer. New York 1876.
Smith, G. B. Shelley: a critical biography. Edinburgh 1877.
Scott, R. P. The place of Shelley among the English poets of his time. Cambridge 1878.
Symonds, J. A. Shelley. 1878, 1887 (rev), 1902, 1925 (EML).
'Rutherford, Mark' (W. H. White). Notes on Shelley's birthplace. Macmillan's Mag March 1879; rptd in Bookman (London) June 1912, and in his Last pages from a journal, Oxford 1915.
Stephen, L. Godwin and Shelley. Cornhill Mag March 1879; rptd in his Hours in a library ser 3, 1879.
Calvert, G. H. Coleridge, Shelley, Goethe: biographic aesthetic studies. Boston 1880.
Todhunter, J. A study of Shelley. 1880.
Thomson, J. ('B.V.') Notes on the structure of Prometheus unbound. Athenaeum 17, 24 Sept, 8 Oct, 5, 19 Nov 1881; rptd in his Shelley: a poem, below.
—— Shelley: a poem, with other writings relating to Shelley. 1884 (priv ptd).
—— In his Biographical and critical studies, 1896.
[Reeve, H.] Shelley and Mary. Edinburgh Rev 156 1882.
Rossetti, W. M. Talks with Trelawny. Athenaeum 15, 29 July, 5 Aug 1882.
—— Memoir of Shelley, with new preface. 1886, 1886 (Shelley Soc). Originally prefixed to Poetical works, ed W. M. Rossetti 1870, 1878 (rev).
Salt, H. S. Shelley as a teacher. Temple Bar Nov 1882.
—— A Shelley primer. 1887 (Shelley Soc).
—— Shelley: a monograph. 1888, 1892; rev and rptd as Shelley: poet and pioneer, 1896.
Shelley: his friends and critics. Westminster Rev 119 1883. Letters from Trelawny papers.
Zanella, G. Shelley e G. Leopardi. Nuova Antologia 70 1883; rptd in his Paralleli letterari, Verona 1885.
Birrell, A. Shelley. Athenaeum 3 May 1884. W. C. Gellibrand's recollections.
Druskowitz, H. Percy Bysshe Shelley. Berlin 1884.
Jeaffreson, J. C. The real Shelley. 2 vols 1885.
Sarrazin, G. In his Poètes modernes de l'Angleterre, Paris 1885.
Dowden, E. Life of Shelley. 2 vols 1886, 1 vol 1896 (rev and abridged); ed H. Read 1951.
—— In his Transcripts and studies, 1888.
Preston, S. E. Notes on the first performance of Shelley's Cenci. 1886 (priv ptd).
—— (ed). The Cenci: extracts from reviews of the first performance. 1886 (priv ptd).

Rabbe, F. Shelley: sa vie et ses oeuvres. Paris 1887; tr 2 vols 1888 (as Shelley: the man and the poet).
Sharp, W. Life of Shelley. 1887.
Arnold, M. In his Essays in criticism: second series, 1888.
Hime, H. W. L. The Greek materials of Shelley's Adonais. 1888.
Shelley Society papers, part I. 1888. 9 articles.
Shelley Society note-book, part I. 1888.
S., E. Shelley with Byron. Nation (London) 7 Feb 1889.
Marshall, Mrs J. In her Life and letters of Mary Wollstonecraft Shelley, 2 vols 1889.
Ackermann, R. Quellen, Vorbilder, Stoffe zu Shelleys poetischen Werken. Erlangen 1890.
—— Shelley in Frankreich und Italien. E Studien 17 1892.
—— Lucans Pharsalia in den Dichtungen Shelleys. Zweibrücken 1896.
—— Shelley: der Mann, der Dichter und seine Werke. Dortmund 1906.
Shelley Society papers, part II. 1891. 10 articles.
Biagi, G. Gli ultimi giorni di Shelley. Florence 1892, 1922; tr 1898 (as The last days of Shelley: new details from unpublished documents).
Elton, C. I. An account of Shelley's visits to France, Switzerland and Savoy in the years 1814 and 1816. 1894.
'Twain, Mark' (S. L. Clemens). In defense of Harriet Shelley. North Amer Rev July 1894; rptd in his How to tell a story, New York 1897, and in his Complete essays, ed C. Neider, New York 1963.
Zupitza, J. Zu einigen kleineren Gedichten Shelleys. Archiv 94 1895.
—— and J. Schick. Zu Shelleys Prometheus unbound. Archiv 102 1899.
Kellner, L. Shelley's Queen Mab and Volney's Les ruines. E Studien 22 1896.
Baxter, C. [Reminiscences of Shelley, Mary Shelley and Harriet]. Dundee Advertiser 7 Sept 1897.
Gillardon, H. Shelleys Einwirkung auf Byron. Karlsruhe 1898.
Graham, W. Last links with Byron, Shelley and Keats. 1898.
Kuhns, L. O. Dante's influence on Shelley. MLN 13 1898.
Richter, H. Percy Bysshe Shelley. Weimar 1898.
—— Original poetry by Victor and Cazire. E Studien 26 1899.
—— Zu Shelleys philosophischer Weltanschauung. E Studien 30 1902.
—— Shelley als Dramatiker. Germanisch-romanische Monatschrift Dec 1922.
Edgar, P. A study of Shelley, with special reference to his nature poetry. Toronto 1899.
Bernthsen, S. Der Spinozismus in Shelleys Weltanschauung. Heidelberg 1900.
—— Über den Einfluss des Plinius in Shelleys Jugendwerken. E Studien 30 1902.
Chiarini, G. In his Studi e ritratti letterari, Leghorn 1900.
Cordier, H. Percy Bysshe Shelley. 1900.
Kroder, A. Studien zu Shelleys Epipsychidion. E Studien 28 1900.
—— Shelleys Verskunst. Erlangen 1903.
—— Shelleyana. Erlangen 1906. On Prometheus unbound and Epipsychidion.
Woodberry, G. In his Makers of literature, New York 1900.
—— In his Studies of a littérateur, New York 1908.
Chevrillon, A. La nature dans la poésie de Shelley. In his Études anglaises, Paris 1901.
Zettner, H. Shelleys Mythendichtung. Leipzig [1902].
Slicer, T. R. Shelley: an appreciation with an illustrated bibliography [of early writings only]. New York 1903 (priv ptd).
Yeats, W. B. The philosophy of Shelley's poetry [1900]. In his Ideas of good and evil, 1903; rptd in his Essays and introductions, 1961.
—— Prometheus unbound. Spectator 17 March 1933; rptd in his Essays 1931 to 1936, Dublin 1937, and in his Essays and introductions, 1961.
Jack A. A. Shelley: an essay. 1904.
Winstanley, L. Shelley as nature poet. E Studien 34 1904.
—— Platonism in Shelley. E & S 4 1913.
Forman, H. B. Shelley's stanza-numbering in the Ode to Naples. Athenaeum 22 April 1905. A new ms.
—— Queen Mab and the Daemon of the world. Athenaeum 14 Oct 1905.
—— Shelley's Indian serenade. Athenaeum 31 Aug 1907.
—— Shelley, Metastasio and Mozart: The Indian serenade. Athenaeum 2 Nov 1907.
Koszul, A. The sources of Shelley's romances. Athenaeum 6 May 1905.
—— La jeunesse de Shelley. Paris 1910.
—— Les océanides et le thème de l'amour dans le Prométhée de Shelley. Revue Anglo-américaine June 1925.
Vaughan, P. Early Shelley pamphlets. 1905.
Bradley, A. C. Notes on passages in Shelley. MLR 1 1906.
—— Shelley's view of poetry [1904]. In his Oxford lectures on poetry, 1909.
—— Notes on Shelley's Triumph of life. MLN 9 1914.
—— Shelley and Arnold's critique; Odours and flowers in the poetry of Shelley; Coleridge-echoes in Shelley's poems. In his A miscellany, 1929.
Droop, A. Die Belesenheit Shelleys nach den direkten Zeugnissen und den bisherigen Forschungen. Weimar 1906.
Elsner, P. Shelleys Abhängigkeit von William Godwins Political justice. Berlin 1906.
Maurer, O. Shelley und die Frauen. Berlin 1906.
Young, A. B. Shelley and M. G. Lewis. MLR 1 1906.
—— Shelley and Peacock. MLR 2 1907.
Brooke, S. A. Inaugural address to the Shelley Society; Lyrics of Shelley; Epipsychidion. In his Studies in poetry, 1907.
—— Wordsworth, Shelley, Byron; Poetry of Shelley; Shelley's interpretation of Christianity. In his Naturalism in English poetry, 1920.
Calcaño, J. Tres poetas pessimistas del siglo xix [Byron, Shelley, Leopardi]. Caracas 1907.
Revell, W. F. Shelley's Prometheus unbound: a reading. Westminster Rev 168 1907.
Symons, A. Shelley. Atlantic Monthly Sept 1907.
—— In his Romantic movement in English poetry, 1909.
Yolland, A. B. Shelley's poetry. Budapest 1907.
Bates, E. S. A study of Shelley's drama The Cenci. New York 1908.
—— Mad Shelley: a study in the origins of English romanticism. In The Fred Newton Scott anniversary papers, Chicago 1929.
Catty, C. S. Shelley's I arise from dreams of thee and Miss Sophia Stacey. Athenaeum 18 April 1908.
Böhme, T. Spensers Einfluss auf Shelley. In his Spensers literarisches Nachleben bis zu Shelley, Berlin 1909.
Imelmann, R. Shelleys Alastor und Goethe. Zeitschrift für Vergleichende Literaturgeschichte 17 1909.
Thompson, F. Shelley [1889]. 1909; rptd in his Real Robert Louis Stevenson and other critical essays, ed T. L. Connolly, New York 1959.
Bulletin of the Keats-Shelley memorial, Rome. No 1, ed R. Rodd and H. N. Gay, Rome 1910, London 1961; no 2, Rome 1913, London 1961; no 3, ed D. Hewlett 1950, 1952. Ser in annual progress from no 3.
Clutton-Brock, A. Shelley: the man and the poet. 1910, 1923 (rev).
—— In his Essays on literature and life, New York 1927.
Eimer, M. Die persönliche Beziehungen zwischen Byron und den Shelleys. Heidelberg 1910.
—— Zu Shelleys Dichtung The wandering Jew. Anglia 38 1914.
Miller, B. Leigh Hunt's relations with Byron, Shelley and Keats. New York 1910.

Angeli, H. R. Shelley and his friends in Italy. 1911.
— Two early drawings by Shelley. Keats-Shelley Memorial Bull 13 1962.
Asanger, F. Shelleys Sprachstudien: seine Übersetzungen aus dem Lateinischen und Griechischen. Leipzig 1911.
Godwin, W. The elopement of Shelley and Mary Wollstonecraft Godwin as narrated by William Godwin. Ed H. B. Forman 1911 (priv ptd).
Gribble, F. The romantic life of Shelley and the sequel. 1911.
Polidori, J. W. The diary, 1816. Ed. W. M. Rossetti 1911.
Birkhead, E. Imagery and style in Shelley. In Primitiae: essays in English literature by students of the University of Liverpool, 1912.
Edmunds, E. W. Shelley and his poetry. 1912.
Hughes, A. M. D. Shelley's Zastrozzi and St Irvyne. MLR 7 1912.
— Some recent English Shelley literature. E Studien 45 1912. Contains notes on poems.
— Shelley and nature. North Amer Rev Aug 1918.
— The theology of Shelley. Proc Br Acad 24 1939.
— The nascent mind of Shelley. Oxford 1947.
— Alastor: or the spirit of solitude. MLR 43 1948.
— The triumph of life. Keats-Shelley Memorial Bull 16 1965.
Keats-Shelley memorial souvenir. Bookman (London) June 1912.
MacDonald, D. J. The radicalism of Shelley and its sources. Washington 1912 (priv ptd).
Schmitt, H. Shelley als Romantiker. E Studien 44 1912.
Spurgeon, C. F. E. L'emploi du symbole dans la poésie de Shelley. Revue Germanique July–Aug 1912.
Suddard, M. Keats, Shelley and Shakespeare: studies and essays. Cambridge 1912.
Brailsford, H. N. Shelley, Godwin and their circle. [1913], Oxford 1951 (rev).
Santayana, G. Shelley: or the poetic value of revolutionary principles. In his Winds of doctrine, 1913; rptd in his Essays in literary criticism, ed I. Singer, New York 1956.
Waterlow, S. Shelley. 1913.
Stawell, F. M. Shelley's Triumph of life. E & S 5 1914.
Vaughan, C. E. The influence of English poetry upon the romantic revival on the Continent. Proc Br Acad 6 1914.
Kooistra, J. Shelley's Prometheus unbound. Neophilologus 1 1916.
Garnett, R. S. (ed). Letters about Shelley interchanged by three friends [E. Dowden, R. Garnett, W. M. Rossetti]. 1917.
Ingpen, R. Shelley in England: new facts and letters from the Shelley-Whitton papers. 1917.
— Shelley in London. Bookman (London) July 1922. *See* Sept 1922.
— (ed). The journal of Harriet Grove for 1809–10. 1932 (priv ptd).
Gingerich, S. F. Shelley's doctrine of necessity versus Christianity. PMLA 33 1918.
— In his Essays in the romantic poets, 1924.
Huscher, H. Studien zu Shelleys Lyrik. Leipzig 1919.
— Charles Gaulis Clairmont. Keats-Shelley Memorial Bull 8 1957.
— A new Viviani letter. Keats-Shelley Memorial Bull 14 1963.
Osborn, A. Shelley. 1919.
Madariaga, S. de. In his Shelley and Calderón and other essays, 1920.
Pancoast, H. S. Shelley's Ode to the west wind. MLN 35 1920.
Raymondi, R. Shelley in Italia. Padua 1920.
Hecht, H. Shelley über politische Reformen. Germanisch-romanische Monatsschrift 8 1921.
Peck, W. E. Shelley and the Abbé Barruel. PMLA 36 1921.
— The source-book of Shelley's Adonais? TLS 7 April 1921.
— Shelley's autograph corrections of the Daemon of the world. TLS 23 June 1921.
— Shelley in Edinburgh. Book of Old Edinburgh Club 2 1922.
— (ed). Letters of Elizabeth Hitchener to Shelley. New York 1926 (priv ptd).
— Shelley: his life and work. 2 vols 1927.
Strong, A. T. Three studies in Shelley. Oxford 1921.
Vetter, T. Friedensideale eines Revolutionärs. Zürich 1921.
White, N. I. Shelley's Swellfoot the tyrant in relation to contemporary political satire. PMLA 36 1921.
— The historical and personal background of Shelley's Hellas. South Atlantic Quart 20 1921.
— Shelley's Charles I. JEGP 21 1922.
— Literature and the law of libel: Shelley and the radicals of 1840–2. SP 22 1925.
— The beautiful angel and his biographers. South Atlantic Quart 24 1925; rptd in Fifty years of the South Atlantic Quarterly, ed W. B. Hamilton, Durham NC 1952.
— Shelley's Prometheus unbound: or every man his own allegorist. PMLA 40 1925.
— Shelley and the active radicals of the early nineteenth century. South Atlantic Quart 29 1930.
— Shelley's biography: the primary sources. SP 31 1934.
— The unextinguished hearth: Shelley and his contemporary critics. Durham NC 1938.
— Probable dates of composition of Shelley's Letter to Maria Gisborne and Ode to a skylark. SP 36 1939.
— Shelley. 2 vols New York 1940, London 1947 (rev).
— The development, use and abuse of interpretation in biography. Eng Inst Annual 1942.
— Portrait of Shelley. New York 1945 (abridged from Shelley, 1940, above).
— F. L. Jones and K. N. Cameron. An examination of the Shelley legend. Philadelphia 1951.
Beach, J. W. Latter-day critics of Shelley. Yale Rev 11 1922.
— Shelley's naturalism; and Shelley's 'Platonism'. In his Concept of nature in nineteenth-century English poetry, New York 1936.
— In his Romantic view of poetry, Minneapolis 1944. On Prometheus unbound.
Evans, B. I. The persistent image in Shelley. Nineteenth Century May 1922.
— In his Tradition and romanticism, 1940.
Gordon, G. S. Shelley and the oppressors of mankind. Proc Br Acad 10 1922; rptd in Selected modern English essays 2nd ser, Oxford 1932 (WC), and in his Discipline of letters, Oxford 1946.
Millar, A. H. Mary Godwin in Dundee. Bookman (London) July 1922.
Moore, T. V. Shelley: an introduction to the study of character. Princeton 1922.
Saito, T. (ed). The Shelley memorial volume by members of the English club, Imperial University, Tokyo. Tokyo 1922. In English and Japanese.
Zacchetti, C. Shelley e Dante. Milan 1922.
Allen, A. H. Plagiarism, sources and influences in Shelley's Alastor. MLR 18 1923.
Courten, M. L. G. de. Shelley e l'Italia. Milan 1923.
Kellett, E. E. Suggestions. 1923. Contains essays on Witch of Atlas and Adonais.
Massey, B. W. A. The compound epithets of Shelley and Keats. Poznán 1923.
'Maurois, André'(E. S. W. Herzog). Ariel: ou la vie de Shelley. Paris 1923; tr 1924 (as Ariel: a Shelley romance).
— Ange et démon. Nouvelles Littéraires 6 Aug 1953.
Pottle, F. A. Shelley and Browning: a myth and some facts. Chicago 1923.
— Shelley and Wordsworth. TLS 20 June 1936.

— The case of Shelley. PMLA 67 1952; rev and rptd in English romantic poets: modern essays in criticism, ed M. H. Abrams, New York 1960.
— The role of Asia in the dramatic action of Prometheus unbound. In Shelley: a collection of critical essays, ed G. M. Ridenour, Englewood Cliffs NJ 1965.
Campbell, O. W. Shelley and the unromantics. 1924.
Elton, O. Percy Bysshe Shelley. 1924.
Liptzin, S. Shelley in Germany. New York 1924.
Blunden, E. Shelley and Keats as they struck their contemporaries. 1925.
— G. de Beer and S. Norman. On Shelley. Oxford 1938.
— Harriet Shelley. TLS 13 July 1946.
— Shelley: a life story. 1946.
— The family of Edward Williams. Keats-Shelley Memorial Bull 4 1952.
— Three young poets: critical sketches of Byron, Shelley and Keats. Tokyo 1959.
Carpenter, E., and G. Barnfield. The psychology of the poet Shelley. 1925.
Graham, W. Shelley's debt to Leigh Hunt and the Examiner. PMLA 40 1925.
— Shelley and the Empire of the Nairs. PMLA 40 1925.
Keith, A. L. The imagery of Shelley. South Atlantic Quart 25 1925.
Rolleston, M. Talks with Lady Shelley. 1925.
Walker, S. A. Peterloo, Shelley and reform. PMLA 40 1925.
Brinton, C. In his Political ideas of the English romanticists, 1926.
Burris, E. E. The classical culture of Shelley. Classical Jnl Feb 1926.
Stokoe, F. W. German influence in the English Romantic period 1788–1818, with special reference to Scott, Coleridge, Shelley and Byron. Cambridge 1926.
Bald, M. The psychology of Shelley. Contemporary Rev March 1927.
— Shelley's mental progress. E & S 13 1928.
Solve, M. T. Shelley: his theory of poetry. Chicago 1927.
— Shelley and the novels of Brown. In The Fred Newton Scott anniversary papers, Chicago 1929.
Farrington, B. Shelley's translations from the Greek. Dublin Mag Jan 1928.
Johnson, R. B. (ed). Shelley–Leigh Hunt: how friendship made history—reviews and leaders from the Examiner etc. 1928.
King, R. W. Crabb Robinson's opinion of Shelley. RES 4 1928.
Köhling-O'Sullivan, I. Shelley und die bildende Kunst. Halle-on-Saale 1928.
Banerjee, J. The philosophy of Shelley. Calcutta Rev Feb 1929–May 1930.
Chapman, J. A. In his Papers on Shelley, Wordsworth and others, Oxford 1929.
Elliott, G. R. The solitude of Shelley. In his Cycle of modern poetry, Princeton 1929.
Marsh, G. L. Early reviews of Shelley. MP 27 1929.
Engel, C-E. Byron et Shelley en Suisse et en Savoie (mai–octobre 1916). Chambéry 1930.
Grabo, C. H. A Newton among poets: Shelley's use of science in Prometheus unbound. Chapel Hill 1930.
— Prometheus unbound: an interpretation. Chapel Hill 1935.
— The meaning of the Witch of Atlas. Chapel Hill 1935.
— The magic plant: the growth of Shelley's thought. Chapel Hill 1936.
— Shelley's eccentricities. Albuquerque 1950.
Havens, R. D. Julian and Maddalo. SP 27 1930.
— Shelley's Alastor. PMLA 45 1930. Comments by M. C. Weir and R. D. Havens, 46 1931.
— Rosalind and Helen. JEGP 30 1931.
— Hellas and Charles I. SP 43 1946.
— Structure and prosodic pattern in Shelley's lyrics. PMLA 65 1950.

— Shelley the artist. In Major English romantic poets: a symposium in reappraisal, ed C. D. Thorpe et al, Carbondale 1957.
Massingham, H. J. The friend of Shelley: a memoir of Edward John Trelawny. 1930.
Praz, M. In his La carne, la morte e il diavolo nella letteratura romantica, Milan 1930; tr Oxford 1933 (as The romantic agony).
Rader, M. M. Shelley's theory of evil misunderstood. Western Reserve Univ Bull 33 1930; rev and rptd in Shelley: a collection of critical essays, ed G. M. Ridenour, Englewood Cliffs NJ 1965.
Rechnitz, W. Shelley in Deutschland. Inselschiff (Leipzig) 11 1930.
Sen, A. Godwin and Shelley. Calcutta 1930.
— Studies in Shelley. Calcutta 1933.
Sickels, E. Shelley and Charles Brockden Brown. PMLA 45 1930.
Stovall, F. Shelley's doctrine of love. Ibid.
— Desire and restraint in Shelley. Durham NC 1931.
Ullman, J. R. Mad Shelley. Princeton 1930.
Brett, G. S. Shelley's relation to Berkeley and Drummond. Studies in English by members of University College Toronto, ed M. M. Wallace, Toronto 1931.
Eiloart, A. Shelley's Skylark: the 'silver sphere'. N & Q 4 July 1931.
Fairchild, H. N. In his Romantic quest, New York 1931.
— In his Religious trends in English poetry vol 3, New York 1949.
Shaw, B. Shaming the devil about Shelley [1892]. In his Pen portraits and reviews, 1931.
— Shaw on Shelley. Independent Shavian 1 1962. A review of the Cenci.
Propst, L. An analytical study of Shelley's versification. Iowa City 1932.
Renzulli, M. La poesia di Shelley. Rome 1932.
— To a skylark e il misticismo Shelleyano. Fiera Letteraria 30 June 1957.
Strout, A. L. Maga: champion of Shelley. SP 29 1932.
— Lockhart: champion of Shelley. TLS 12 Aug 1955.
— Blunders about Blackwood. N & Q June 1957.
Weaver, B. Toward the understanding of Shelley. Ann Arbor 1932.
— Shelley's Biblical extracts: a lost book. Papers of Michigan Acad of Science, Arts & Letters 20 1935.
— Pre-Promethean thought in the prose of Shelley. PQ 27 1948.
— Prometheus bound and Prometheus unbound. PMLA 64 1949.
— Shelley: the first beginnings. PQ 32 1953.
— Prometheus unbound. Ann Arbor 1957.
Clark, D. L. Shelley and Bacon. PMLA 48 1933.
— Shelley and Pieces of Irish history. MLN 53 1938.
— The date and source of Shelley's A vindication of natural diet. SP 36 1939.
— Shelley and Shakespeare. PMLA 54 1939. Addns by S. R. Watson, 55 1940.
— Literary sources of Shelley's The witch of Atlas. PMLA 56 1941.
— The dates and sources of Shelley's metaphysical, moral and religious essays. SE 28 1949.
— Shelley's biblical extracts. MLN 66 1951.
Eliot, T. S. Shelley and Keats. In his Use of poetry and use of criticism, 1933.
Harrison, T. P. Spenser and Shelley's Adonais. SE 13 1933.
Hoffman, H. L. An Odyssey of the soul: Shelley's Alastor. New York 1933.
Jones, F. L. The revision of Laon and Cythna. JEGP 33 1933.
— Alastor foreshadowed in St Irvyne. PMLA 49 1934.
— Shelley and Christianity. Crozer Quart 12 1935.
— Shelley's Leonora. MP 32 1935. By Hogg.
— Shelley's boat. TLS 18 Jan 1936.
— Hogg and the Necessity of atheism. PMLA 52 1937.

— Shelley and the Don Juan. TLS 22 April 1939.
— Shelley in Rome. TLS 27 Sept 1941.
— Shelley and Spenser. SP 39 1942.
— Mary Shelley and Claire Clairmont. South Atlantic Quart 42 1943.
— (ed). The letters of Mary Wollstonecraft Shelley. 2 vols Norman Oklahoma 1944.
— Shelley and Shakespeare: a supplement. PMLA 59 1944.
— Shelley's revised will. MLN 59 1944.
— Shelley and Hogg. TLS 23 June 1945.
— The inconsistency of Shelley's Alastor. ELH 13 1946.
— (ed). Mary Shelley's journal. Norman Oklahoma 1947.
— Shelley's On life. PMLA 62 1947.
— The vision theme in Shelley's Alastor and related works. SP 44 1947.
— (ed). Maria Gisborne and Edward E. Williams, Shelley's friends: their journals and letters. Norman Oklahoma 1951.
— Shelley's Essay on war. TLS 4 July 1952.
— Shelley and Milton. SP 49 1952.
— Hogg's peep at Elizabeth Shelley. PQ 29 1950.
— Mary Shelley to Maria Gisborne: new letters 1818–1822. SP 52 1955.
— Canto I of the Revolt of Islam. Keats-Shelley Jnl 9 1960.
— Trelawny and the sinking of Shelley's boat. Keats-Shelley Memorial Bull 16 1965.
Kurtz, B. P. The pursuit of death: a study of Shelley's poetry. New York 1933.
Liedtke, H. A. J. Shelley—durch Berkeley und Drummond beeinflusst? Greifswald 1933.
Wolfe, H. (ed). The life of Shelley, as comprised in the Life of Shelley by T. J. Hogg, the Recollections of Shelley and Byron by E. J. Trelawny, Memoirs of Shelley by T. L. Peacock. 2 vols 1933.
Bailey, R. Shelley. 1934.
Brandt, H. Das protestierende Element in der Dichtung Shelleys. Breslau 1934.
Bush, D. [Textual] Notes on Shelley. PQ 13 1934.
— In his Mythology and the romantic tradition in English poetry, Cambridge Mass 1937.
— In his Science and English poetry, New York 1950.
Clarke, I. C. Shelley and Byron: a tragic friendship. 1934.
Leavis, F. R. Shelley's imagery. Bookman (London) Sept 1934.
— Revaluations viii: Shelley. Scrutiny 4 1935; rptd in his Revaluation, 1936, and in Critiques and essays in criticism 1920–48, ed R. W. Stallman, New York 1949.
Lotspeich, H. G. Shelley's Eternity and Demogorgon. PQ 13 1934.
Meyer, H. Rousseau und Shelley: ein typologischer Vergleich. Würzburg 1934.
Mueschke, P. and E. L. Griggs. Wordsworth as the prototype of the poet in Shelley's Alastor. PMLA 49 1934.
Murry, J. M. In Great democrats, ed A. B. Brown 1934; rev and rptd in his Heaven—and earth, 1938.
— Keats and Shelley. In his Katherine Mansfield and other literary portraits, 1949. On Adonais.
Norman, S. (ed). After Shelley: the letters of T. J. Hogg to Jane Williams. Oxford 1934.
— A forged Shelley letter [16 Dec 1816]. TLS 20 March 1937. Replies by S. de Ricci 27 March, 10, 24 April; by G. Pollard 17 April, 8 May; by T. Besterman 24 April; by M. Kessel 29 May; by S. Norman 3 April, 5 June 1937.
— The bust of Shelley: a lost prospectus. TLS 18 May 1951. Replies by A. Boyle 25 May; by P. G. Gates 29 June 1951.
— Shelley's last residence. Keats-Shelley Jnl 2 1953.
— Flight of the skylark: the development of Shelley's reputation. Norman Oklahoma 1954.
— Critics who have influenced taste: xviii. Times 1 Aug 1963; rptd in Critics who have influenced taste, ed A. P. Ryan 1965.
Ballman, A. B. The dating of Shelley's prose fragments On life, On love, The punishment of death. ELH 2 1935.
Ebeling, E. A probable Paracelsian element in Shelley. SP 32 1935.
Freydorf, R. von. Die bildhafte Sprache in Shelleys Lyrik. Quakenbrück 1935.
Kessel, M. Shelley's To Constantia singing. TLS 17 Jan 1935. Reply by K. Glenn 11 April 1935.
— Shelley–Leigh Hunt. TLS 29 Aug 1936.
— The Harvard Shelley notebook. TLS 5 Sept 1936.
— The poet in Shelley's Alastor: a criticism. PMLA 51 1936. Reply by P. Mueschke and E. L. Griggs, ibid.
— An early review of the Shelleys' Six weeks' tour. MLN 58 1943.
— Lines: When the lamp is shattered. Explicator 3 1944.
— The mark of X in Claire Clairmont's journals. PMLA 66 1951.
Lemmi, C. W. The serpent and the eagle in Spenser and Shelley. MLN 50 1935.
Origo, I. Allegra. 1935.
Peyre, H. Shelley et la France. Paris 1935.
Pratt, W. W. Shelley criticism in England 1810–90. New York 1935.
'Winwar, Frances' (F. Grebanier). The romantic rebels. Boston 1935.
Cowling, G. H. Shelley and other essays. Melbourne 1936.
DuBois, A. E. Alastor: the spirit of solitude. JEGP 35 1936.
Irvine, St J. Shelley as a dramatist. Essays by Divers Hands 15 1936.
Kapstein, I. J. The symbolism of the wind and the leaves in Shelley's Ode to the west wind. PMLA 51 1936.
— Shelley and Cabanis. PMLA 52 1937.
— The meaning of Shelley's Mont Blanc. PMLA 62 1947.
Mousel, M. E. Falsetto in Shelley. SP 33 1936.
Notopoulos, J. A. Shelley and Thomas Taylor. PMLA 51 1936.
— The dating of Shelley's fragment The moral teachings of Jesus Christ. MLR 35 1940.
— The dating of Shelley's prose. PMLA 58 1943.
— A Shelleyan symbol. Classical Jnl Dec 1944. On the serpent.
— The Platonism of Shelley: a study of Platonism and the poetic mind. Durham NC 1949.
— Shelley's 'disinterested love' and Aristotle. PQ 32 1953.
— Two notes on Shelley. MLR 48 1953. On Adonais and Ozymandias.
Read, H. In defence of Shelley and other essays. 1936; rev in The true voice of feeling, 1953.
— Shelley the optimistic philosopher. Listener 21 Sept 1950.
— In his A coat of many colours, 1945.
— The poet and his muse. Br Jnl of Aesthetics 4 1964.
Smith, J. H. Shelley and Milton's 'chariot of paternal deity'. MLN 51 1936.
— Shelley and Claire Clairmont. PMLA 54 1939; Shelley and Claire again, SP 41 1944.
Viviani della Robbia, E. Vita di una donna: l'Emily di Shelley. Florence 1936.
— Shelley e il Boccaccio. Rivista Americana Italica (Evanston) 36 1959.
Barnard, E. Shelley's religion. Minneapolis 1937.
Firkins, O. W. Power and elusiveness in Shelley. Minneapolis 1937.
Freeman, M. J. Introduction to a text [unpbd] of Shelley's Prometheus unbound. Chicago 1937 (priv ptd).
Garnier, C.-M. A metrical study of the lyrical parts in Shelley's Prometheus unbound. Revue de l'Enseignement des Langues Vivantes 54 1937.
Gates, E. J. Shelley and Calderón. PQ 16 1937.
Koller, K. A source for portions of the Witch of Atlas. MLN 52 1937.

Marjarum, E. W. The symbolism of Shelley's To a skylark. PMLA 52 1937.
Mason, F. C. A study in Shelley criticism in England from 1818 to 1860. Mercersburg Pa 1937 (priv ptd).
Spender, S. Keats and Shelley. In From Anne to Victoria, ed B. Dobrée 1937.
— Shelley's Adonais. Listener 22 Jan 1942.
— Shelley. 1952 (Br Council pamphlet).
Thompson, D. W. Ozymandias. PQ 16 1937.
Verkoren, L. A study of Shelley's Defence of poetry: its origin, textual history, sources and significance. Amsterdam 1937.
— Shelley's Prometheus unbound. Levende Talen Oct 1950.
Cappon, A. The scope of Shelley's philosophical thinking. Chicago 1938.
Grylls, R. G. Mary Shelley: a biography. Oxford 1938.
— Claire Clairmont, mother of Byron's Allegra. 1939.
— Trelawny. 1950.
— William Godwin and his world. 1953.
Pettit, H. J. Shelley and Denon's Voyage dans la haute et la basse Egypte. Revue de Littérature Comparée 18 1938.
Roy, P. N. Shelley's Epipsychidion: a study. Calcutta 1938.
— Shelley and Italian literature: a study in poetical derivation. 1943.
Workman, A. M. Percy Bysshe Shelley. Bristol 1938.
Bronowski, J. In his Poet's defence, Cambridge 1939.
Davenport, W. H. Footnote to a political letter of Shelley. N & Q 14 Jan, 8 April 1939. Identifies recipients of A proposal for reform.
— Shelley and Godwin's Essay on sepulchres. N & Q 15 March 1952.
Goodspeed, G. T. The first American Queen Mab. Colophon new ser 1 1939.
Jacobi, W. Bühnen- und Lesedrama: eine Untersuchung an Shelleys Prometheus unbound. Germanisch-romanische Monatsschrift 27 1939.
Lewis, C. S. Shelley, Dryden and Mr Eliot. In his Rehabilitations and other essays, Oxford 1939.
Nitchie, E. Shelley in Fraser's and the annuals. TLS 26 Aug 1939.
— The Reverend Colonel Finch. New York 1940.
— and T. O. Mabbott. Shelley's Adonais. Explicator 1 1943.
— Variant readings in three of Shelley's poems. MLN 59 1944. On To Stella; Methought I was a billow; On Keats.
— Shelley's Hymn to intellectual beauty. PMLA 63 1948.
— Eight letters by Mary Shelley. Keats-Shelley Memorial Bull 3 1950.
— Mary Shelley: author of Frankenstein. New Brunswick 1953.
— Shelley's The sensitive plant, conclusion 23–4. Explicator 15 1956.
— (ed). Mathilda, by Mary Wollstonecraft Shelley. Chapel Hill [1959].
— Shelley at Eton: Mary Shelley vs Jefferson Hogg. Keats-Shelley Memorial Bull 11 1960.
— Mary Shelley, traveler. Keats-Shelley Jnl 10 1961.
— Shelley's Prometheus unbound II v 109–10. Explicator 19 1961.
Oras, A. On some aspects of Shelley's poetic imagery. Acta et Commentationes Universitatis Tartuensis (Estonia) 43 1939.
— The multitudinous orb: some Miltonic elements in Shelley. MLQ 16 1955.
Partington, W. Some marginalia. TLS 28 Jan 1939. Annotations in Shelley memorials.
Alkjaer, N. Studier i Shelleys digtning. Copenhagen 1940.
Armstrong, M. Trelawny: a man's life. New York 1940.
Baker, C. A note on Shelley and Milton. MLN 55 1940.
— The permanent Shelley. Sewanee Rev 48 1940.
— Spenser and Shelley's Witch of Atlas. PMLA 56 1941.
— Spenser, the 18th century and Shelley's Queen Mab. MLQ 2 1941.
— The traditional background of Shelley's ivy-symbol. MLQ 4 1943.
— Shelley's translation from Aristotle. MLN 61 1946.
— Shelley's Ferrarese maniac. Eng Inst Essays 1946. On Julian and Maddalo.
— Shelley's major poetry: the fabric of a vision. Princeton 1948.
— The bottom of the night. In Major English romantic poets, ed C. D. Thorpe et al, Carbondale 1957.
Braunlich, A. F. Parallels to some passages in Prometheus unbound. MLN 55 1940.
Evans, F. B. Shelley, Godwin, Hume and the doctrine of necessity. SP 37 1940.
Knickerbocker, W. S. Arnold, Shelley and Joubert. MLN 55 1940.
Lowes, J. L. The witch of Atlas and Endymion. PMLA 55 1940. Reply by D. L. Clark, 56 1941.
Moorman, L. J. In his Tuberculosis and genius, Chicago 1940.
Noyes, A. In his Pageant of letters, New York 1940.
Power, J. Shelley in America in the 19th century: his relation to American critical thought and his influence. Lincoln Nebraska 1940.
Shuster, G. N. In his English ode from Milton to Keats, New York 1940.
Watson, S. R. A comparison of Othello and the Cenci. PMLA 55 1940.
Beall, C. B. A Tasso quotation in Shelley. MLQ 2 1941.
Cameron, K. N. A major source of the Revolt of Islam. PMLA 56 1941. Volney's Ruins of empire.
— A new source for Shelley's Defence of poetry. SP 38 1941. Rasselas.
— Shelley and Ahrimanes. MLQ 3 1942.
— Shelley and the Conciones ad populum. MLN 57 1942.
— Shelley vs Southey: new light on an old quarrel. PMLA 57 1942.
— The social philosophy of Shelley. Sewanee Rev 50 1942.
— References to Shelley in the Examiner. N & Q 16 Jan 1943.
— The political symbolism of Prometheus unbound. PMLA 58 1943.
— Rasselas and Alastor: a study in transmutation. SP 40 1943.
— Shelley, Cobbett and the national debt. JEGP 42 1943.
— Shelley and the reformers. ELH 13 1945.
— Shelley's use of source-material in Charles I. MLQ 6 1945.
— and H. Frenz. The stage-history of Shelley's The Cenci. PMLA 60 1945.
— The planet-tempest passage in Epipsychidion. PMLA 63 1948.
— The young Shelley: genesis of a radical. New York 1950.
Cluck, J. Elinor Wylie's Shelley obsession. PMLA 56 1941.
Glasheen, F. J. Shelley and Peacock. TLS 18 Oct 1941.
— Shelley's use of Gray's poetry. MLN 56 1941.
— and A. E. The publication of the Wandering Jew. MLR 38 1943.
Hicks, A. C. An American performance of the Cenci. In Stanford studies in language and literature, ed H. Craig, Stanford 1941.
Hungerford, E. B. In his Shores of darkness, New York 1941. On Prometheus unbound and Adonais.
Knight, G. W. The naked seraph. In his Starlit dome, Oxford 1941, London 1959 (rev).
— In his Lord Byron: Christian virtues, 1952; Lord Byron's marriage, 1957. Julian and Maddalo.

Tinker, C. B. Shelley once more. Yale Rev 31 1941; rptd in his Essays in retrospect, New Haven 1948.
— Shelley's Indian serenade. Yale Univ Lib Gazette 25 1950.
Wright, W. F. Shelley's failure in Charles I. ELH 8 1941.
Cherubini, W. Shelley's 'own Symposium': The triumph of life. SP 39 1942.
Jordan, J. E. Wordsworth and the Witch of Atlas. ELH 9 1942.
Larrabee, S. A. In his English bards and Grecian marbles, New York 1942.
Miles, J. Pathetic fallacy in the 19th century. Univ of Cal Pbns in Eng 12 1942.
Pfeiffer, K. G. Landor's critique of the Cenci. SP 39 1942. Addn by R. H. Super, 40 1943.
Woolf, V. 'Not one of us'. In her Death of the moth and other essays, 1942.
Boas, L. S. Lines: when the lamp is shattered. Explicator 1 1943.
— Ode to liberty. Explicator 2 1944.
— Lines written among the Euganean hills. Explicator 3 1944.
— Erasmus Perkins and Shelley. MLN 70 1955.
— Nursemaid to the Shelleys. N & Q May, July 1956.
— Dowden's Life of Shelley. TLS 2 Aug 1957.
— Harriet Shelley: five long years. Oxford 1962. Comments by K. N. Cameron, TLS 23 March; by N. Rogers 27 April; by L. S. Boas 11 May 1962.
— Shelley and Mary. TLS 14 Nov 1963, 20 Feb, 16 July 1964. Addn by A. L. Michell 12 March 1964.
— Shelley: three unpublished lines. N & Q May 1964.
— Edward Dowden, the Esdailes and the Shelleys. N & Q May–June 1965.
Dudley, F. A. Stanzas written in dejection near Naples. Explicator 1 1943.
Mabbott, T. O. Adonais. Ibid.
— and L. S. Friedland. Prometheus unbound III iv. Explicator 2 1943.
Rajan, B. The motivation of Shelley's Prometheus unbound. RES 19 1943.
Roberts, J. H. Epipsychidion. Explicator 1 1943.
Scott, W. S. (ed). The Athenians: being correspondence between T. J. Hogg, T. L. Peacock, Leigh Hunt, Shelley and others. 1943 (priv ptd).
— (ed). Harriet and Mary: being the relations between Shelley, Harriet Shelley, Mary Shelley and T. J. Hogg. 1944 (priv ptd).
— (ed). Shelley at Oxford: the early correspondence of Shelley with T. J. Hogg, together with letters of Mary Shelley and T.L. Peacock and a hitherto unpublished prose fragment by Shelley. 1944 (priv ptd).
Archer, J. W. Kubla Khan, Queen Mab and Alastor. SP 41 1944.
Earp, T. W. Shelley and Stendhal. TLS 22–29 July 1944.
Glasheen, A. E. Shelley's first published review of Mandeville. MLN 59 1954.
Guerard, A. J. Prometheus and the Aeolian lyre. Yale Rev 33 1944.
Kaderly, N. L. The stoppage of Shelley's income in 1821. MLN 59 1944.
McElderry, B. R. Common elements in Wordsworth's Preface and Shelley's Defence of poetry. MLQ 5 1944.
Thomas, G. In his Builders and makers, 1944.
Ward, W. S. Shelley and the reviewers once more. MLN 59 1944.
Fogle, R. H. The abstractness of Shelley. PQ 24 1945.
— Ode to the west wind. Explicator 6 1947.
— The imaginal design of Shelley's Ode to the west wind. ELH 15 1948.
— The imagery of Keats and Shelley. Chapel Hill 1949.
— Image and imageless: a limited reading of Prometheus unbound. Keats-Shelley Jnl 1 1952.
Forman, E. The Cenci. TLS 10 Nov 1945.
— Beatrice Cenci and Alma Murray. Keats-Shelley Memorial Bull 5 1953.
— The Cenci. Times 23 April 1959.
Hamilton, G. R. Shelley's 'own'. English 5 1945; rptd in his Guides and marshals, 1956.
Lea, F. A. Shelley and the romantic revolution. 1945.
Meyerstein, E. H. W. Epipsychidion and the Hound of Heaven. TLS 17 March 1945.
Muir, K. Shelley's heirs. Penguin New Writing 26 1945.
Smith, R. M., M. M. Schlegel, T. G. Ehrsam and L. A. Waters. The Shelley legend. New York 1945. Replies by N. I. White et al in An examination of the Shelley legend, 1951, above.
Thomson, J. S. The unbinding of Prometheus. UTQ 15 1945.
Albrecht, W. P. Queen Mab, Ode to liberty. Explicator 5 1946.
Ehrsam, T. G. Mary Shelley in her letters. MLQ 7 1946.
— Major Byron: the incredible career of a literary forger. 1951.
Hansen, A. Shelley. Copenhagen 1946.
Häusermann, H. W. W. B. Yeats's idea of Shelley. In The mint: a miscellany, ed G. Grigson 1946.
— Shelley's house in Geneva. In his Genevese background, 1952.
Martin-Baynat, R. Shelley: a prelude. Parkstone Dorset 1946.
Barrell, J. Shelley and the thought of his time. New Haven 1947.
Evans, B. Gothic drama from Walpole to Shelley. Berkeley 1947.
Gibson, E. K. Alastor: a reinterpretation. PMLA 62 1947.
Laird, J. Shelley's metaphysics. In his Philosophical incursions into English literature, Cambridge 1947.
Lunn, A. H. M. In his Switzerland in English prose and poetry, 1947.
Mead, D. S. Ode to the west wind. Explicator 5 1947. Comments by R. H. Fogle and A. Wormhoudt, 6 1947.
Prieur, S. Y a-t-il des traces de Platonisme dans Alastor? Langues Modernes 41 1947.
Tyler, H. Hunt and Shelley. TLS 8 Nov 1947.
Aveling, E. B. and E. M. Shelley's socialism: two lectures [1887]. Manchester 1948.
Clemen, W. Shelleys Geisterwelt. Frankfurt 1948.
— Shelleys Ode to the west wind: eine Interpretation. Anglia 69 1950.
Durand, A. Shelley on the nature of poetry. Quebec 1948.
Gates, P. C. Leigh Hunt's review of Shelley's Posthumous poems. PBSA 42 1948.
Griffiths, J. G. Shelley's Ozymandias and Diodorus Siculus. MLR 43 1948.
Himelick, R. Cabell, Shelley and the 'incorrigible flesh'. South Atlantic Quart 47 1948.
James. D. G. Purgatory blind. In his Romantic comedy, Oxford 1948.
— Byron and Shelley. Nottingham 1951.
Kirchner, G. Shelley als revolutionärer Dichter. Iserlohn 1948.
Meldrum, E. The classical background of Shelley. Contemporary Rev March 1948.
Safroni-Middleton, A. Two Shelleys. 1948.
Vail, C. D. Shelley's translations from Goethe. Germanic Rev 23 1948.
Bowra, C. M. Prometheus unbound. In his Romantic imagination, Cambridge Mass 1949.
Hess, A. Shelleys Lyrik in deutschen Uebertragungen. Zürich 1949.
Kairophylas, K. Shelley and Greece. In Hellenike bibliographia, Athens 1949. In Greek.
Langston, B. Shelley's use of Shakespeare. HLQ 12 1949.
Maanen, W. van. A note on Shelley's Ozymandias. Neophilologus 33 1949.
Mayor, A. A suspected Shelley letter [16 Dec 1816]. Library 5th ser 4 1949. Reply by T. G. Ehrsam, 5 1950.

Rogers, N. Keats, Shelley and Rome: an illustrated miscellany. 1949.
—— The Shelley-Rolls gift to the Bodleian. TLS 27 July–10 Aug 1949.
—— Shelley and the skylark. TLS 24 July 1953.
—— Music at Marlow: an unpublished holograph note by Shelley. Keats-Shelley Memorial Bull 5 1953.
—— Shelley's Ginevra. TLS 5 Nov 1954. Reply to letters by B. W. Griffith 15 Jan, N. Rogers 12 Feb 1954.
—— Four missing pages from the Shelley notebook in the Harvard College Library. Keats-Shelley Jnl 3 1954. *See* H. B. Forman, Shelley's Stanzas written in dejection, Athenaeum 10 Aug 1907.
—— Shelley at work: a critical inquiry. Oxford 1956, 1967 (rev).
—— Shelley and the West Wind. London Mag June 1956.
—— A forged Shelley notebook. TLS 15 Nov 1957. Reply by P. G. Muir, 29 Nov 1957.
—— Shelley and the visual arts. Keats-Shelley Memorial Bull 12 1961. On the Medusa.
—— Justice and Harriet Shelley. Keats-Shelley Memorial Bull 15 1964.
—— Shelley's spelling: theory and practice. Keats-Shelley Memorial Bull 16 1965.
—— The punctuation of Shelley's syntax. Keats-Shelley Memorial Bull 17 1966.
Sackville-West, E. The innocent heart. In his Inclinations, 1949.
Scott, N. Shelley: enigma variations. N & Q 5 March, 11 June 1949. Replies by L. M. W. 30 April, M. Philips 25 June 1949.
—— Shelley. N & Q 3 Sept 1949. A Marlow contemporary on Shelley.
—— G. F. Cooke and the Theatre Royal, Windsor. N & Q 29 Oct 1949.
—— Dr Lind. N & Q 12 Nov 1949.
Wilcox, S. C. The sources, symbolism and unity of Shelley's Skylark. SP 46 1949.
—— Adonais xx–xxi. Explicator 8 1949.
—— The prosodic structure of Ode to the west wind. N & Q 18 Feb 1950.
—— Imagery, ideas and design in Shelley's Ode to the west wind. SP 47 1950.
—— Adonais xx 172–7. Explicator 9 1951.
—— and J. M. Raines. Lycidas and Adonais. MLN 67 1952.
—— Present values in Shelley's art. In Major English romantic poets, ed C. D. Thorpe et al, Carbondale. 1957.
Witcutt, W. P. Shelley and introverted intuition. Wind & Rain 5 1949.
Wormhoudt, A. The demon lover. New York 1949.
Bateson, F. W. In his English poetry: a critical introduction, 1950. On Ode to the west wind.
—— Shelley on Wordsworth: two unpublished stanzas from Peter Bell the third. EC 17 1967.
Cronin, J. E. The hag in The cloud. N & Q 5 Aug 1950.
Looker, S. J. Shelley, Trelawny and Henley. Worthing 1950.
Male, R. R. Shelley and the doctrine of sympathy. SE 29 1950.
—— Young Shelley and the ancient moralists. Keats-Shelley Jnl 5 1956. Annotations in Shelley's Diogenes.
—— and J. A. Notopoulos. Shelley's copy of Diogenes Laertius. MLR 54 1959.
McNiece, G. M. Sir Timothy Shelley. TLS 18 Aug 1950.
Nicolini, F. Un' inspiratrice italiana di Shelley: Teresa Viviani Della Robbia. Letterature Moderne 1 1950.
Prins, A. A. Shelley's 'vagueness'. E Studies 31 1950.
—— The religious background of Prometheus unbound. In English studies presented to R. W. Zandvoort: a supplement to English Studies 45 1964. Postscript, 46 1965.
Sells, A. L. Zanella, Coleridge and Shelley. Comparative Lit 2 1950.
Vivante, L. In his English poetry and its contribution to the knowledge of a creative principle, 1950.
Wain, J. Terza rima: a footnote on English prosody. Rivista di Letterature Moderne 2 1950.

Chinol, E. P. B. Shelley. Venice 1951.
Dowden, W. S. Shelley's use of metempsychosis in the Revolt of Islam. Rice Inst Pamphlets 38 1951.
Lohman, C. A. Shelley's Indian serenade. Yale Univ Lib Gazette 25 1951.
Maxwell, J. C. Shelley and Manzoni. MLR 46 1951.
Ogita, S. Shelley in Japan. N & Q 31 March, 28 April, 26 May 1951.
Parr, J. Shelley's Ozymandias again. MLR 46 1951.
Pulos, C. E. Shelley and Malthus. PMLA 67 1952.
—— The deep truth: a study of Shelley's scepticism. Lincoln Nebraska 1954.
Scott, W. Jefferson Hogg. 1951.
Shute, N. Poet pursued. 1951. A biographical novel.
Smith, W. L. An overlooked source [in Ezekiel] for Prometheus unbound. SP 48 1951.
Spark, M. Child of light: a reassessment of Mary Wollstonecraft Shelley. Hadleigh Essex 1951.
—— Mary Shelley: a prophetic novelist. Listener 22 Feb 1952.
—— and D. Stanford (ed). My best Mary: the selected letters of Mary W. Shelley. 1953.
Steiner, F. G. Shelley and Goethe's Faust. Rivista di Letterature Moderne 2 1951.
Bett, W. R. Shelley: neurosis and genius. In his Infirmities of genius, 1952.
Brown, T. J. English literary autographs I. Book Collector 1 1952. Shelley's handwriting.
—— Some Shelley forgeries by 'Major Byron'. Keats-Shelley Memorial Bull 14 1963.
Cline, C. L. Byron, Shelley and their Pisan circle. Cambridge Mass 1952.
Davie, D. A. Shelley's urbanity. In his Purity of diction in English verse, 1952; rptd in English Romantic poets: modern essays in criticism, ed M. H. Abrams, New York 1960. Addn, New Statesman 27 Nov 1964.
Hoffman, C. G. Whitehead's philosophy of nature and Romantic poetry. Jnl of Aesthetics 10 1952.
Kretzel, A. Shelley als Gesellschaftkritiker. Wissenschaftliche Zeitschrift der Universität Leipzig 1 1952.
Mainwaring, M. Arnold on Shelley. MLN 67 1952.
Marchand, L. Trelawny on the death of Shelley. Keats-Shelley Memorial Bull 4 1952.
—— A note on the burning of Shelley's body. Keats-Shelley Memorial Bull 6 1955.
Raymond, E. Two gentlemen of Rome: the story of Keats and Shelley. 1952.
Robertson, L. The journal and notebooks of Claire Clairmont: unpublished passages. Keats-Shelley Memorial Bull 4 1952.
—— Unpublished verses by Shelley. MLR 48 1953. Lines from Claire's journal; for an earlier text *see* N. I. White, Shelley, New York 1940.
Rodway, A. E. In his Godwin and the age of transition, 1952.
—— In his Romantic conflict, 1963.
Rosati, S. Shelley e il romanticismo inglese. Lezioni dell'Anno Accademico 1951–2, Rome 1952.
Ugolini, L. Il naufragio del Don Juan. Nuova Antologia 454 1952.
Watson, M. R. The thematic unity of Adonais. Keats-Shelley Jnl 1 1952.
—— Shelley and tragedy: the case of Beatrice Cenci. Keats-Shelley Jnl 7 1958.
Yohannan, J. D. The Persian poetry fad in England 1770–1825. Comparative Lit 4 1952.
Abrams, M. H. In his Mirror and the lamp: romantic theory and the critical tradition, New York 1953.
Awad, L. In his Essential Prometheus, Cairo 1953.
—— In his Studies in literature, Cairo 1954.
—— Prometheus and Epimetheus. Annual Bull of Eng Stud (Cairo) 1954.
Bebbington, W. G. Shelley's Quaker friend Dr Robert Pope. Keats-Shelley Memorial Bull 5–6 1953–5.
—— G. F. Cooke and Shelley. N & Q April 1955.

— Shelley and the Windsor stage. N & Q May 1956.
— Charles Knight and Shelley. Keats-Shelley Jnl 6 1957.
— A friend of Shelley: Dr James Lind. N & Q March 1960.
Harrison, M. E. The cloud. Explicator 12 1953.
Hough, G. In his Romantic poets, 1953.
Houston, R. Shelley and the principle of association. EC 3 1953. Comments by E. M. M. Taylor, ibid, W. Milgate, D. V. Erdman, V. Pitt, G. M. Matthews 4 1954.
Krabbe, H. Shelleys poesi: sansning—ord og billede, menneske og natur. Copenhagen 1953.
Lovell, E. J. Byron and Mary Shelley. Keats-Shelley Jnl 2 1953.
— Captain Medwin: friend of Byron and Shelley. Austin 1962.
Nabeshima, N. Symbolism in Shelley. Proc of Foreign Langs & Lits (Tokyo) 3 1953. In Japanese.
O'Neill, J. P. and S. C. Wilcox. Adonais. Explicator 12 1953.
Patton, L. The Shelley-Godwin collection of Lord Abinger. Duke Univ Lib Notes 27 1953.
Roe, I. Shelley: the last phase. 1953.
Sato, K. On Shelley's Alastor. Currents of Thought in Eng Lit (Tokyo) 26 1953. In Japanese.
Schrick, W. Shelley's Ode to the west wind: an analysis. Revue des Langues Vivantes 19 1953.
Stephens, P. J. Shelley and Mr Graham. Poetry Book Mag 6 1953.
Wickert, R. A. Adonais. Explicator 12 1953.
Zanco, A. Appunti su Shelley. Rivista di Letterature Moderne 4 1953.
Butter, P. H. Shelley's idols of the cave. Edinburgh 1954.
— Sun and shape in Shelley's The triumph of life. RES new ser 13 1962.
Dobrée, B. In his Broken cistern, 1954.
Dowling, H. M. Shelley's enemy at Tremadoc. N & Q July 1954.
— The alleged attempt to assassinate Shelley. N & Q Sept 1954.
— New letters about Shelley. N & Q Dec 1954.
— Shelley's arrest for debt. N & Q March 1955.
— The attack at Tanyrallt. Keats-Shelley Memorial Bull 12 1961.
Fochi, F. Frammenti postumi di Shelley. Fiera Letteraria 5 1954.
Fuson, B. W. In his Poet and his mask, Parkville Missouri 1954. On the Indian serenade.
Gérard, A. S. Alastor: or the spirit of solipsism. PQ 33 1954.
— In his L'idée romantique de la poésie en Angleterre, Paris 1955.
Griffith, B. W. Another source of the Revolt of Islam. N & Q Jan 1954. D'Ercilla's Araucana?
— Shelley's Ginevra. TLS 15 Jan 1954. Reply by N. Rogers 12 Feb 1954.
— An unpublished Shelley reading list. MLN 69 1954.
— The Keats-Shelley poetry contests. N & Q Aug 1954. Reply by E. Blunden, Dec 1954.
— The removal of incest from Laon and Cythna. MLN 70 1955.
— The revolt of Islam and Byron's The Corsair. N & Q June 1956.
— et al. Music when soft voices die. Explicator 15 1957.
Hildebrand, W. H. A study of Alastor. Kent [Ohio] State Univ Bull 42 1954.
Jarrett-Kerr, M. In his Studies in literature and belief, 1954. On Shelley's trn from Calderón.
McCulloch, W. H. The incident at Tanyrallt on the night of 26 Feb 1813. Explorations (Toronto) 3 1954.
— The last night at Tanyrallt. Keats-Shelley Memorial Bull 8 1957.
Patterson, L. E. Shelley and the way forward. Poetry Book Mag 6 1954.
Scholes, P. A. Shelley and Peterloo. In his God save the Queen!, 1954.
Wasserman, E. R. Adonais: progressive revelation as a poetic mode. ELH 21 1954; rptd in his Subtler language, below.
— Shelley's Adonais 177–9. MLN 69 1954.
— Myth-making in Prometheus unbound. MLN 70 1955.
— In his Subtler language: critical readings of neoclassic and romantic poems, Baltimore 1959. On Mont Blanc, Sensitive plant, Adonais.
— Shelley's last poetics: a reconsideration. In From sensibility to romanticism, ed F. W. Hilles and H. Bloom, New York 1965.
— Shelley's Prometheus unbound: a critical reading. Baltimore 1965.
Bartlett, P. Hardy's Shelley. Keats-Shelley Jnl 4 1955.
— Seraph of heaven: a Shelleyan dream in Hardy's fiction. PMLA 70 1955.
Bhattacherje, M. M. Shelley: the poet of intellectual ideals. Calcutta Rev 135 1955.
Chewning, H. W. M. Rossetti and the Shelley renaissance. Keats-Shelley Jnl 4 1955.
Crawford, T. The Edinburgh Review and romantic poetry 1802–29. Auckland Univ College Bull 47 1955.
Drew, P. Shelley's use of 'recall' [Prometheus unbound I 59]. TLS 16 Dec 1955. Replies by G. Watson, L. S. Boas 6 Jan, G. M. Matthews 20 Jan, F. A. Pottle 15 Feb 1956.
— Browning's Essay on Shelley. Victorian Poetry 1 1963. Addn by T. J. Collins 2 1964.
Furtado, R. de L. Shelley's Platonism. Modern Rev (Calcutta) 90 1955.
— Shelley: concept of nature. Calcutta 1958.
Graves, R. Keats and Shelley. In his Crowning privilege, 1955.
— Poetry's false face. Horizon Nov 1963; rptd as Technique in poetry in his Black goddess, 1965. On To a skylark.
Groom, B. In his Diction of poetry from Spenser to Bridges, 1955.
Hagopian, J. V. A psychological approach to Shelley's poetry. Amer Imago 12 1955.
Harriet Shelley's brother-in-law. TLS 11 Nov 1955. Addn by L. S. Boas 2 Dec 1955.
House, H. In his All in due time, 1955.
Hurukawa, H. A list of the compound epithets in the poetical works of Shelley and Keats. Eng Lit: Essays & Stud (Waseda Univ Tokyo) 10–11 1955. In Japanese.
Kato, T. Notes on the last phase of Shelley's thought. Bull of Kôchi Women's College 3 1955. In Japanese.
— Shelley and didacticism. Shiron Essays [Tohoku Univ, Sendai] 5 1963.
Kline, A. The 'American' stanzas in Shelley's The revolt of Islam: a source. MLN 70 1955.
Kudô, N. A study of Shelley's letters. Waseda Jimbun-Kagaku Kenkyû 16 1955. In Japanese.
Nares, G. Field Place Sussex. Country Life 6–13 Oct 1955.
Neupokoeva, I. G. Shelley in Russian criticism. Vilna Univ Scholarly Notes 2 1955. In Russian.
— Shelley's revolutionary romanticism. Moscow 1959. In Russian.
Norman, A. M. Z. Shelley's heart. Jnl of History of Medicine 10 1955.
Orange, U. Elise, nursemaid to the Shelleys. Keats-Shelley Memorial Bull 6 1955.
— Shuttlecocks of genius: an enquiry into the fate of Shelley's children. Keats-Shelley Memorial Bull 8 1957.
Serdiukov, A. I. The dramaturgy of Shelley. Baku 1955. In Russian.
Suzuki, H. Platonism in Epipsychidion. Eng Lit: Essays & Stud (Waseda Univ Tokyo) 9 1955. In Japanese.
— The veil in Shelley's poetry. Ibid 11 1955. In Japanese.

—— Elysian isles in Shelley's poetry. Ibid 15 1958. In Japanese.
—— An essay on Shelley. Ibid 26 1965. In Japanese.
Vivian, C. H. The one Mont Blanc. Keats-Shelley Jnl 4 1955.
Beck-Friis, J. The Protestant cemetery in Rome. Malmö 1956.
Chiappelli, B. Il pensiero religioso di Shelley: con particolare riferimento alla Necessity of atheism e al Triumph of life. Rome 1956.
Crossett, J. Music when soft voices die. Explicator 14 1956. Replies by B. W. Griffith, W. H. Howard, J. Unterecker 15 1957.
Farago, L. M. Verità e bellezza in Keats e Shelley. Siculorum Gymnasium 9 1956.
Hill, A. Trelawny's strange relations: an account of the domestic life of E. J. Trelawny's mother and sisters in Paris and London 1818–29. Stanford Dingley (Berks) 1956.
—— Trelawny's family background and naval career. Keats-Shelley Jnl 5 1956.
Jeffrey, L. N. Shelley's Triumph of life and the Dhammapada. N & Q March 1956.
—— Shelley's life-images. N & Q Nov 1957.
—— Reptile-lore in Shelley: a study in the poet's use of natural history. Keats-Shelley Jnl 7 1958.
Komiyana, H. Shelley's idealism: with special reference to his view of poetry. Jnl (Shokei Women's Junior College, Sandai) 1 1956. In Japanese.
Ogita, S. A period in Shelley's life: estrangement with Hogg. Ronsô (Kanseigakuin Junior College, Nishinomiya) 5 1956. In Japanese.
Perrine, L. In his Sound and sense: an introduction to poetry, New York 1956. Discusses 4 poems.
Reeves, J. In his Critical sense: practical criticism of prose and poetry, 1956. On Ozymandias.
Rowell, G. In his Victorian theatre: a survey, Oxford 1956. On Shelley's drama.
Steadman, J. M. Errors concerning the publication date [11 Jan 1818] of Ozymandias. N & Q Oct 1956.
Stevens, F. B. Field Place, Warnham. Sussex Notes & Queries 14 1956.
Takeshima, T. Blake's influence on Shelley's Ode to the west wind. Rising Generation 102 1956. In Japanese.
Wallace, I. The fabulous originals: lives of extraordinary people who inspired memorable characters in fiction. 1956. Claire Clairmont and Juliana Bordereau.
Woodhouse, C. M. The unacknowledged legislators (poets and politics). Essays by Divers Hands 28 1956.
Yamaguchi, H. Blake's Europe and Shelley's Ode to the west wind. Rising Generation 102 1956. In Japanese.
Barnett, G. L. Leigh Hunt revises a letter. HLQ 20 1957. To Hazlitt on Shelley.
Brand, C. P. In his Italy and the English Romantics: the Italianate fashion in early 19th-century England, Cambridge 1957.
Harding, D. W. Shelley's poetry. In From Blake to Byron, ed B. Ford 1957 (Pelican).
Jack, I. The poet and his public: Shelley's search for readers. Listener 6 June 1957.
Makirtumova, E. V. Images of the romantic hero-fighters for the liberty of the people in Shelley's Revolt of Islam. Scholarly Notes of Azerbaijan State Univ 9 1957. In Russian.
—— National feeling in the revolutionary-romantic poems of Shelley. Scholarly Notes of Azerbaijan Pedagogical Inst of Foreign Langs 2 1959. In Russian.
Matthews, G. M. A volcano's voice in Shelley. ELH 24 1957.
—— Comments on recent Shelley studies. REL 2 1961.
—— Shelley and Jane Williams. RES new ser 12 1961.
—— On Shelley's The triumph of life. Studia Neophilologica 34 1962.
—— Julian and Maddalo: the draft and the meaning. Studia Neophilologica 35 1963.
Nikoliukin, A. N. Byron, Shelley and contemporary English poetry of the masses. Izvestia of Acad of Sciences of USSR (Division of Lang & Lit) 14 1957. In Russian.
Mori, K. Shelley: The triumph of life. Eibungako Hyôron 4 1957. In Japanese.
Parr, J. Shelley's Ozymandias. Keats-Shelley Jnl 6 1957.
Pruvost, R. André Koszul et la traduction. Bull de la Faculté des Lettres de Strasbourg 36 1957.
Rees, J. The preface to the Cenci. RES new ser 8 1957.
—— Shelley's Orsino: evil in the Cenci. Keats-Shelley Memorial Bull 12 1961.
—— 'But for such faith': a Shelley crux. RES new ser 15 1964. On Mont Blanc.
Sencourt, R. Mary Wollstonecraft Shelley. Contemporary Rev Oct 1957.
Solomon, P. Studiu introductiv la Shelley, opere alese. Bucharest 1957. In Rumanian.
States, B. O. Addendum: the stage history of the Cenci. PMLA 72 1957. Comments by M. Kessel and B. O. States 75 1960.
Tsujumura, K. P. B. Shelley. Gakuin 203 1957. In Japanese.
Wimsatt, W. K. and C. Brooks. Peacock vs Shelley: rhapsodic didacticism. In their Literary criticism: a short history, New York 1957.
Basu, N. K. Aeschylus and Shelley. Calcutta Rev Jan 1958.
—— Shelley's Prometheus and Milton's Satan. Calcutta Rev June 1958.
Battenhouse, H. M. In his English romantic writers, New York 1958.
Bäuerlein, H. Shelley als Publizist. Publizistik 3 1958.
Beer, G. de. An 'atheist' in the Alps. Keats-Shelley Memorial Bull 9 1958.
—— Byron on the burning of Shelley. Keats-Shelley Memorial Bull 13 1962.
Berry, F. Shelley and the future tense. In his Poets' grammar, 1958.
—— The voice of Shelley. In his Poetry and the physical voice, 1962.
Cernuda, L. In his Pensamiento poético en la lírica inglesa (siglo xix), Mexico City 1958.
Foakes, R. A. In his Romantic assertion, 1958. On Adonais.
Good, T. Grandeur et limites de Shelley. Cahiers du Sud 46 1958.
Itō, K. A study of the Revolt of Islam. Jnl, Dept of Lit, Aoyama Gakuen Univ 2–3 1958–9. In Japanese.
Jamison, W. A. Arnold and the Romantics. Anglistica 10 1958.
Kuhn, A. J. Shelley's Demogorgon and eternal necessity. MLN 74 1958.
McAleer, E. C. The sensitive plant: a life of Lady Mount Cashell. Chapel Hill 1958.
Nagai, M. On symbolism and satire in Shelley: the Witch of Atlas. Bull of Aichi Prefecture Women's College 9 1958. In Japanese.
—— Structure and meaning in Lines written among the Euganean hills. Ibid 14 1964.
Saviane, S. I due romanzi di Shelley. Il Mondo 29 1958.
Scott, W. O. Shelley's admiration for Bacon. PMLA 73 1958.
Swaminathan, S. R. Possible Indian influence on Shelley. Keats-Shelley Memorial Bull 9 1958.
—— Some images of process and reality in Shelley. Indian Jnl of Eng Stud 2 1961.
—— The wind and the leaf. In Critical essays on English literature in honour of M. S. Doraiswami, ed S. Ramaswami, Madras 1965.
Varley, D. H. Henry Willey Reveley: first colonial civil engineer at the Cape. Quart Bull of S. Africa Lib 12 1958.
Bigland, E. Mary Shelley. 1959.
Birkinshaw, P. C. Speaking Shelley's Ode to the west wind. Eng Stud in Africa 2 1959.

Bloom, H. Shelley's mythmaking. New Haven 1959. Comment by K. Allott, EC 10 1960.
— In his Visionary company, New York 1961.
Bostetter, E. E. Shelley and the mutinous flesh. Texas Stud in Lit & Lang 1 1959.
— In his Romantic ventriloquists, Seattle 1963.
Daiches, D. Platonism against Plato. In his Critical approaches to literature, 1959.
Emden, C. S. In his Poets in their letters, Oxford 1959.
Gutteling, J. F. C. In her Bezinningen, Hague 1959.
Guzzo, A. In his Scritti critici e studi d'arte religiosa, Turin 1959. On Hellas.
Hagstrum, J. H. Romantic skylarks. Newberry Lib Bull 5 1959.
Kenyon, F. W. The golden years: a novel based on the life and loves of Shelley. New York 1959.
Kojiro, I. The symbolical patterns of necessity in the Ode to the west wind. Thought-currents in Eng Lit (Aoyama Gakuen Univ, Tokyo) 31 1959. In Japanese.
Marshall, W. H. Queen Mab: the inconsistency of Ahasuerus. MLN 74 1959.
— Plato's myth of Aristophanes and Shelley's Panthea. Classical Jnl 55 1959.
— Comments on Shelley in the Beacon and the Kaleidoscope 1821. N & Q June 1959.
— Byron, Shelley, Hunt and the Liberal. Philadelphia 1960.
— Caleb Williams and the Cenci. N & Q July 1960.
— The father-child symbolism in Prometheus unbound. MLQ 22 1961.
Moore, D. L. Byron, Leigh Hunt and the Shelleys: new light on certain old scandals. Keats-Shelley Memorial Bull 10 1959.
Perkins, D. The quest for permanence: the symbolism of Wordsworth, Shelley and Keats. Cambridge Mass 1959.
Richards, I. A. The mystical element in Shelley's poetry. Aryan Path 30 1959.
Schwimmer, E. G. Return to Shelley. Numbers (Wellington) 3 1959.
Sitaramayya, K. B. The fugitives: a lyrical ballad by Shelley. Report of Proc of the All-India Eng Teachers' Conference (Madras) 1959.
Spencer, T. J. Shelley's Alastor and Romantic drama. Trans of Wisconsin Acad of Science, Art & Letters 47 1959.
Stokes, H. S. Shelley's nonsense: an Eton boy in 1810. Street Somerset 1959. On Queen Mab.
Trewin, J. C. Illustr London News 31 Jan, 16 May 1959. On the Old Vic production of the Cenci.
Turner, J. Shelley and Lucretius. RES new ser 10 1959.
Whitman, R. F. Beatrice's 'pernicious mistake' in the Cenci. PMLA 74 1959.
Wilson, M. Shelley's later poetry: a study of his prophetic imagination. New York 1959.
Yoshizumi, K. The sensitive plant: a study. Thought-currents in Eng Lit (Aoyama Gakuen Univ, Tokyo) 32 1959. In Japanese.
Baxter, B. M. Verwey and Shelley: a discussion of Verwey's translations. MLR 55 1960.
— Albert Verwey's translations from Shelley's poetical works. Leyden 1963.
Bhalla, M. M. The myth of the two Shelleys. Indian Jnl of Eng Stud 1 1960.
— Adonais: a note. Eng Miscellany (Delhi) 2 1963.
— Alastor: an interpretation. In Essays presented to Amy G. Stock, ed R. K. Kaul, Jaiphur 1965.
Cartianu, A. Problems of conception and poetic expression in the works of Shelley. Revista de Filologie Romanică şi Germanică 4 1960. In Rumanian, with English abstract.
Draper, J. W. Shelley and the Arabic-Persian lyric style. Rivista di Letterature Moderne e Comparate 13 1960.
Ford, N. F. The symbolism of Shelley's nightingales. MLR 55 1960.

— Shelley's To a skylark. Keats-Shelley Memorial Bull 11 1960.
— Paradox and irony in Shelley's poetry. SP 57 1960.
— The wit in Shelley's poetry. Stud in Eng Lit 1500–1900 1 1961.
Graaf, D. A. de. De dood van Shelley: ongeluk of zelfmoord? Levende Talen April 1960.
Highet, G. In his Powers of poetry, Oxford 1960.
Kegel, C. H. Shelley and Colin Wilson. Keats-Shelley Jnl 9 1960.
King-Hele, D. Shelley: his thought and work. 1960.
— The influence of Erasmus Darwin on Shelley. Keats Shelley Memorial Bull 13 1962.
— In his Erasmus Darwin, 1963.
— Shelley: an address. Charles Lamb Soc Bull 176 1964.
— Erasmus Darwin's influence on Shelley's early poems. Keats-Shelley Memorial Bull 16 1965.
— Shelley and nuclear disarmament demonstrations. Ibid.
Kuić, R. Prijateljstvo izmedju Godvina i Šelija. Zbornik Istorije književnosti (Serbian Acad of Sciences, Belgrade) 1 1960. With English summary.
— Šelijeva poetike. In Veliki pesnici o poeziji, Belgrade 1964.
Massey, I. Shelley's Music, when soft voices die. JEGP 59 1960. Comment by E. D. Hirsch 60 1961.
— Shelley's Time: an unpublished sequel. Stud in Romanticism 2 1962.
— Mary Shelley, Walter Scott and Maga. N & Q Nov 1962.
Newman, C. W. Shelley and Nantgwyllt: three new letters. Radnorshire Soc Trans 30 1960.
Pedrini, L. N. and D. T. Serpent imagery and symbolism in the major English Romantic poets. Psychiatric Quart 34 (suppl, pt 2) 1960, 35 (suppl pt 1) 1961.
Pelletier, R. R. Satan and Prometheus in captivity. N & Q March 1960.
— Shelley's Ahasuerus and Milton's Satan. N & Q 1960.
— Shade and bower images in Milton and Shelley. N & Q Jan 1961.
— Shelley's debt to Milton in the Wandering Jew. N & Q Dec 1961.
— Unnoticed parallels between Ahasuerus and Satan. Keats-Shelley Jnl 11 1962.
— The Revolt of Islam and Paradise lost. Keats-Shelley Jnl 14 1965.
Singh, J. B. The development of Shelley's poetic imagery and a revaluation of his poetry. Uttara Bharahti: Jnl of Research of Univs of Uttar Pradash 7 1960.
Szobotka, T. Shelley. Budapest 1960.
Waters, L. A. Stanzas written in dejection near Naples. Explicator 18 1960.
Woodman, R. G. Shelley's changing attitude to Plato. JHI 21 1960.
— Shelley's Prometheus. Alphabet 3 1961.
— The apocalyptic vision in the poetry of Shelley. Toronto 1964.
Bolton, G. The Olympians. Cleveland 1961. Biography as fiction.
Cacciatore, V. Shelley and Byron in Pisa. Turin [1961].
Chayes, I. H. Plato's statesman myth in Shelley and Blake. Comparative Lit 13 1961. On My soul is an enchanted boat.
Clarke, C. C. Shelley's 'tangled boughs'. Durham Univ Jnl 54 1961.
Henriques, U. In her Religious toleration in England 1787–1833, 1961.
Hughes, D. J. Coherence and collapse in Shelley, with particular reference to Epipsychidion. ELH 28 1961.
— Potentiality in Prometheus unbound. Stud in Romanticism 2 1963.
— Kindling and dwindling: the poetic process in Shelley. Keats-Shelley Jnl 13 1964.
Hutchens, E. N. Cold and heat in Adonais. MLN 76 1961.

Kendall, L. H. Byron: an unpublished letter to Shelley [30 July 1821?]. MLN 76 1961.
Maurice, R. R. In his Au coeur de l'enchantement romantique, Paris 1961.
Palacio, J. L. de. Shelley and Dante: an essay in textual criticism. Revue de Littérature Comparée 35 1961.
— Shelley traducteur de Dante: le chant xxviii du Purgatoire. Revue de Littérature Comparée 36 1962.
— Shelley's library catalogue: an unpublished document. Ibid.
— Music and musical themes in Shelley's poetry. MLR 59 1964.
Park, B. A. The Indian elements of the Indian serenade. Keats-Shelley Jnl 10 1961.
Ranald, M. L. and R. A. Shelley's Magus Zoroaster and the image of the Doppelgänger. MLN 76 1961.
Rivers, C. Three essays on Robert Browning's theory of the poet. Northwest Missouri State College Stud 25 1961.
Russell, B. The importance of Shelley. In his Fact and fiction, 1961.
Saveson, J. E. Shelley's Julian and Maddalo. Keats-Shelley Jnl 10 1961.
Thomas, R. In his How to read a poem, 1961. Ode to the west wind.
Tschumi, R. In his A philosophy of literature, 1961. To a skylark.
Benziger, J. In his Images of eternity, Carbondale 1962.
Blackstone, B. The herd-abandoned deer. In his Lost travellers, 1962.
Cecchi, E. Shelley, analisi e confronti. Osservatore Politico Letterario 8 1962.
Darbishire, H. Didactic poetry. In her Somerville College chapel addresses and other papers, 1962 (priv ptd).
Davies, H. S. (ed). In his Poets and their critics vol 2, 1962.
Hibbard, E. L. Shelley's farewell to the world: a study of the Triumph of life. Bull of Doshisha Women's College 13 1962.
Hirabayashi, K. Shelley's poetical imagination and science. In Science and English literature, ed M. Watanabe, Tokyo 1962. In Japanese.
Kendall, K. E. Some words in the poetry of Shelley and Wordsworth. N & Q Nov 1962. Corrections to OED.
Komatsu, F. Shelley's Epipsychidion. Literary Wagon (Ryukoku Univ Tokyo) 1 1962. In Japanese.
— Shelley's Adonais. Literary Wagon 2 1964. In Japanese.
Lemaitre, H. Shelley, poète des éléments. Paris 1962.
Parsons, C. O. Shelley's prayer to the west wind. Keats-Shelley Jnl 11 1962.
Piper, H. W. In his Active universe, 1962.
Reiman, D. H. Structure, symbol and theme in Lines written among the Euganean hills. PMLA 77 1962.
— Shelley in the encyclopaedias. Keats-Shelley Jnl 12 1963.
— Shelley's The triumph of life: the biographical problem. PMLA 78 1963.
— Shelley's The triumph of life: a critical study based on a text newly edited from the Bodleian ms. Urbana 1965.
— Roman scenes in Prometheus unbound III iv. PQ 46 1967.
Richmond, H. M. Ozymandias and the travelers. Keats-Shelley Jnl 11 1962.
Rovinazzi, R. La poesia drammatica di Shelley. Rimini 1962.
Tillyard, E. M. W. Shelley's Ozymandias. In his Essays literary and educational, 1962.
Barrows, H. Convention and novelty in the Romantic generation's experience of Italy. BNYPL June 1963.
Chatterjee, K. Shelley and modern thought. Calcutta Rev March 1963.
Cialfi, M. Shelley o la sanità del frammento. Osservatore Politico Letterario 9 1963.

Freeman, J. In his Literature and locality: the literary topography of Britain and Ireland, 1963.
Gilenson, B. Shelley in Russian. Soviet Lit 3 1963. Brief survey of Soviet scholarship.
Gilinskii, I. N. A stylistic analysis of Shelley's Song to the men of England. Trudy (Leningrad Gos Bibliotech Inst) 10 1963. In Russian.
Göller, K. H. Shelleys Bilderwelt. Germanisch-romanische Monatsschrift new ser 13 1963.
Gottfried, L. In his Matthew Arnold and the Romantics, 1963.
Green, R. L. In his Authors and places: a literary pilgrimage, 1963.
Kolesnikova, B. Revoliutsionnaia estetika Shelli. Moscow 1963.
Kreutz, C. Das Prometheussymbol in der Dichtung der englischen Romantik. Göttingen 1963.
Levin, R. Shelley's Indian serenade: a re-revaluation. College Eng Jan 1963.
Raben, J. Milton's influence on Shelley's translation of Dante's Matilda gathering flowers. RES new ser 14 1963.
— Shelley's Prometheus unbound: why the Indian Caucasus? Keats-Shelley Jnl 12 1963.
— A computer-aided study of literary influence: Milton to Shelley. Literary Data Processing Conference Proc 11–13 Sept 1964, New York 1964.
— Coleridge as the prototype of the poet in Shelley's Alastor. RES new ser 17 1966.
— Shelley's Invocation to misery: an expanded text. JEGP 65 1966.
— The boat on the Serchio: the evidence of the manuscript. PQ 46 1967.
Raymond, W. O. Browning and the Harriet Westbrook Shelley letters. UTQ 32 1963; rptd in his Infinite moment, Toronto 1965.
Roberts, C. Shelley and Mr Roberts. Keats-Shelley Memorial Bull 14 1963.
Sato, M. Shelley and the Wandering Jew. Eng Lit & Lang 1963 (Sophia Univ, Tokyo) Nov 1963. In Japanese.
Schaar, C. Entangled by locks—entangled by looks [Prometheus unbound II. v. 48–53]. E Studies 44 1963. Addn by M. P. Jackson 45 1964.
Serdiukov, A. I. Esteticheskie vzgliady Shelli. Uchenye Zapiski (Azerbaijan Univ) Istoriia i Filosofia 5 1963.
Smith, L. E. W. In his Twelve poems considered, 1963. Ode to the west wind.
Steensma, R. C. Shelley and the new critics. Proc of Utah Acad of Sciences, Arts & Letters 40 1963.
Tamai, Y. On Shelley's description of nature. Bull of Defence Acad (Yokosuka) 6 1963. In Japanese.
Wojcik, M. In defense of Shelley. Zeitschrift für Anglistik und Amerikanistik 11 1963.
Yamada, C. On Alastor. Stud in Eng Lang & Lit (Kumamoto Univ) 7 1963. In Japanese.
Chayes, I. H. Rhetoric as drama: an approach to the romantic ode. PMLA 79 1964. On Ode to the west wind.
Davies, R. R. Charles Brockden Brown's Ormond: a possible influence upon Shelley's conduct. PQ 43 1964.
Fischer, H. In his Die romantische Verserzählung in England, Tübingen 1964.
Gusmanov, I. G. The problem of the hero in the Cenci. Uchenye Zapiski (Moscow) 218 1964. In Russian.
Hondo, M. Abstract ideas and the inanimate world in Prometheus unbound. In Essays in English literature presented to Professor Kochi Doi, Tokyo 1964. In Japanese.
Mahony, P. J. An analysis of Shelley's craftsmanship in Adonais. Stud in Eng Lit 1500–1900 4 1964.
Mertens, H. Entsprechung von Form und Gehalt in To Jane: The keen stars were twinkling. Die Neueren Sprachen May 1964.

Morita, M. Shelley's idea of love and intellectual beauty in Alastor. Tandai Ronso (Kanto Gakuin Junior College, Yokohama) 24 1964. In Japanese.
— Shelley's idea of necessity and nature's spirit. Tandai Ronso 27 1966.
O'Malley, G. Shelley and synesthesia. [Evanston] 1964.
Pope, W. B. Haydon on Shelley. Keats-Shelley Jnl 13 1964.
Smith, P. Restless casuistry: Shelley's composition of the Cenci. Ibid.
Uesugi, F. Byron and Shelley. Stud in Eng Lang & Lit (Hiroshima Univ) 10 1964. In Japanese.
Whalley, G. Revolution and poetry. Centennial Rev 8 1964.
Whipple, A. B. C. The fatal gift of beauty: the final years of Byron and Shelley. New York 1964.
Adams, C. L. The structure of the Cenci. Drama Survey 4 1965.
Baker, J. E. Shelley's Platonic answer to a Platonic attack on poetry. Iowa City 1965.
Chesser, E. Shelley and Zastrozzi: self-revelation of a neurotic. 1965.
Delasanta, R. Shelley's 'sometimes embarrassing declarations': a defence. Texas Stud in Lit & Lang 7 1965.
Duerksen, R. A. Unidentified Shelley texts [On love] in Medwin's Shelley's papers. PQ 44 1965.
— Shelleyan ideas in Victorian literature. Hague 1966.
Mortenson, P. Image and structure in Shelley's longer lyrics. Stud in Romanticism 4 1965.
Pollin, B. R. Fanny Godwin's suicide re-examined. Etudes Anglaises 18 1965.
Ridenour, G. M. (ed). Shelley: a collection of critical essays. Englewood Cliffs NJ 1965.
Roston, M. Prophet and poet. 1965.
Schaubert, E. von. Shelleys Tragödie The Cenci und Marlowes Doppeldrama Tamburlaine. Paderborn 1965.
St George, P. P. The styles of good and evil in the Sensitive plant. JEGP 64 1965.
Takei, R. An essay on Shelley. Daito Bunka Univ Bull (Tokyo) 3 1965. In Japanese.
Wilkie, B. Shelley: 'holy and heroic verse'. In his Romantic poets and epic tradition, Madison 1965. On Revolt of Islam as an epic.
Woodhouse, A. S. P. In his Poet and his faith, Chicago 1965.
Hunter, P. C. Textual differences in the drafts of Una favola. Stud in Romanticism 6 1966.
Hurt, J. R. Prometheus unbound and Aeschylean dramaturgy. Keats-Shelley Jnl 15 1966.
Klukoff, P. J. Shelley's Hymn of Apollo and Hymn of Pan: the displaced vision. Neuphilologische Mitteilungen 67 1966.
Komatsu, F. Demogorgon in Prometheus unbound. Jnl of Ryukoku Univ (Kyoto) 380 1966. In Japanese.
Leyda, S. Love's rare universe: Eros in Shelley's poetry. In Explorations of literature, ed R. D. Reck, Baton Rouge 1966.
McGann, J. J. The secrets of an elder day: Shelley after Hellas. Keats-Shelley Jnl 15 1966.
Okuda, H. Ode to the west wind: a revaluation of Shelley. Essays (Tokyo) 20 1966. In Japanese.
Rose, E. J. Shelley reconsidered plain. Bucknell Rev 14 1966.
Schulze, E. J. Shelley's theory of poetry: a reappraisal. Hague 1966.
Stempel, D. Shelley and the ladder of love. Keats-Shelley Jnl 15 1966.
Yoshioka, N. Alastor, Epipsychidion and the Triumph of life: on Shelley's idea of love, life and death. Stud in Br & Amer Lit (Univ of Osaka) 13 1966. In Japanese.
Beazley, E. In her Madocks and the wonder of Wales, 1967.
Crompton, M. Shelley's dream women. 1967.
Halliburton, D. G. Shelley's Gothic novels. Keats-Shelley Jnl 16 1967.
Rieger, J. The mutiny within: the heresies of Shelley. New York 1967.

G. M. M.

JOHN KEATS

1795–1821

The largest collection of mss is in the Houghton Library at Harvard, though the BM and the Pierpont Morgan Library New York also have important collections. Mss are described in the introd to Poetical works, ed H. W. Garrod, Oxford 1939, 1958 (rev), *and in the appendix to* C. L. Finney, The evolution of Keats' poetry, Cambridge Mass 1936, New York 1963 (rev).

Bibliographies etc

Baldwin, D. L., L. N. Broughton et al. A concordance of the poems of Keats. Washington 1917, Gloucester Mass 1963.
MacGillivray, J. R. A bibliography and reference guide, with an essay on Keats' reputation. Toronto 1949.
Thorpe, C. D. In English romantic poets: a review of research, ed T. M. Raysor, New York 1950, 1956 (rev).
Keats-Shelley journal. 1952–. Contains annual bibliography. Bibliographies to June 1962 rptd as Keats, Shelley, Byron, Hunt and their circles: a bibliography, Lincoln Nebraska 1964.

Collections

The poetical works of Coleridge, Shelley and Keats. Paris 1829, Philadelphia 1831, 1832, 1835, 1836, 1838, 1839, 1844, 1847, 1853, nd.
The poetical works of Howitt, Milman and Keats. Philadelphia 1840, 1846, 1847, 1849, 1852.
Poetical works. 1840, 1841, 1844, 1846, 1847, 1849, 1850, 1851, 1853.
Poetical works; memoir by R. M. Milnes (Lord Houghton). 1854, 1856, 1858, 1861, 1866, 1868, 1869; illustr G. Scharf 1854, 1862, 1866.
Poetical works. New York 1846, 1848, 1850, 1855, 1857.
Poetical works; memoir by R. M. Milnes, 'elegantly' illustrated. Philadelphia 1855.
Poetical works; life by J. R. Lowell. Boston etc 1854, 1859, 1863, 1863, 1864, 1866, 1871, 1878 (with Coleridge).
Poetical works, reprinted from the early editions. [1868] etc (Chandos Classics), [1874] (as Lansdowne Poets).
Poetical works; memoir by W. M. Rossetti, illustr T. Seccombe. [1872], 1888 (Moxon's Popular Poets), [1878] (not illustr).
Poetical works; memoir and illustrations by W. B. Scott. [1873], 1894, 1880 (not illustr), 1893.
Poetical works; memoir by J. R. Lowell. New York 1873, nd.
Poetical works, chronologically arranged; memoir by Lord Houghton. 1876, 1883, 1886, 1890, 1891, 1892, 1899, 1901, 1906 (Aldine), Boston 1877, 1882, 1887, Toronto 1900, London 1914 (Bohn).
Poetical works. New York 1880, 1881, 1885, 1891, nd.
Poetical works and other writings, now first brought together. Ed H. B. Forman 4 vols 1883, 1889 (rev) (Library edn); Poetry and prose, 1890 (suppl vol).
Letters and poems. Ed J. G. Speed 3 vols New York 1883.
Poetical works. Ed F. T. Palgrave 1884 etc (Golden Treasury).
Poetical works. Ed W. T. Arnold 1884, 1884, 1888, 2 vols New York 1889. Basis of Globe edn 1907 etc.
Poetical works. Ed H. B. Forman 1884, 1885, 1889; illustr W. H. Low 1895, 1896, 1898, 1902, Philadelphia 1895, 3 vols 1891 (not illustr), 2 vols New York 1895, 1 vol 1895.
Poetical works. Ed J. Hogben 1885, 1886, nd (Canterbury Poets).
Poems. Hammersmith 1894 (W. Morris's Kelmscott edn).
Poems. Ed G. T. Drury, introd by R. Bridges 2 vols 1896, London and New York 1896, nd (ML).
Poems. Ed A. Bates, Boston and London 1896.

Poems. Illustr R. A. Bell, introd by W. Raleigh, London and New York 1897, 1898.
Poems. Ed C. J. Holmes 2 vols 1898.
Complete poetical works and letters. Ed H. E. Scudder, Boston and New York 1899, 1925 (without biographical introd).
Complete works. Ed H. B. Forman 5 vols Glasgow 1900–1, 1921–4, New York [1900–1].
Poetical works. 1901 etc, Oxford 1927 (rev) (WC).
Poetical works. Ed W. S. Scott, London and New York 1902, 1903; rev G. Sampson, New York 1903.
Poems. Introd by L. Binyon, notes by J. Masefield 1903.
Poems. Ed G. Sampson 2 vols 1904 (Chiswick Quartos).
Poems. Ed E. de Selincourt 1905, 1906 (rev), 1912, 1920, 1926, 1951, 1954, 1961, New York 1905, 1909, 1921.
Complete works. Ed N. H. Dole 4 vols London and Boston [1905–6] (Laurel edn).
Poetical works. Ed H. B. Forman, Oxford 1906 etc (OSA).
Poetical works. Ed G. Sampson 1906, Edinburgh 1906.
Poems. 1906 (EL), 1944 (rev, with introd by G. Bullett).
Poems. Illustr A. Burleigh [1911].
Poetical works. Introd by A. Lang [1911].
Poems, arranged in chronological order with a preface by S. Colvin. 2 vols 1915, 1924, 1928.
Poetical works. Ed L. Binyon, with essay by R. Bridges, illustr C. A. Shepperson 1916.
Complete poetry. Ed G. R. Elliott, New York 1927.
Poems and verses. Ed J. M. Murry 2 vols 1930, 1 vol New York 1949.
Complete poetical works. Ed H. B. Forman, introd by L. Bacon, New York 1934.
Complete poems and selected letters. Ed C. D. Thorpe 1935.
Poetical works and other writings. Ed H. B. Forman, introd by J. Masefield 8 vols 1938–9 (Hampstead edn).
Poetical works. Ed H. W. Garrod Oxford 1939, 1958 (rev with J. Jones). The definitive edn; full critical apparatus.
Poetical works. Introd by J. Drinkwater [1942].
Complete poetry and selected prose. Ed H. E. Briggs, New York 1951 (Modern Lib).
Poetical works. Ed H. W. Garrod, Oxford 1956 (OSA).
Poems and selected letters. Ed C. Baker, New York 1962 (Bantam).

Selections

Endymion and other poems. 1887, 1892.
Odes and sonnets. Illustr W. H. Low, Philadelphia 1888.
Selections. Ed J. R. Tutin 1889, nd.
Odes, sonnets and lyrics. Oxford 1895.
Odes. Ed A. C. Downer 1897.
Endymion and the longer poems. 1898 (Temple Classics).
Poems. Introd by A. Meynell 1903, New York 1903, 1904.
Endymion and other poems. Introd by H. Morley 1905.
Poems. Ed A. Symons, Edinburgh [1907], Philadelphia 1907.
Odes, sonnets and lyrics. Introd by E. C. Stedman, New York 1908.
Odes, lyrics and sonnets. Ed M. [Robertson] Hills, Oxford 1916.
Poems. Ed W. T. Young, Cambridge 1917.
Poems. 1921 (Commemorative edn).
Poetry and prose, with essays by Charles Lamb, Leigh Hunt, Robert Bridges and others. Ed H. Ellershaw, Oxford 1922.
[Poems]. Ed H. Newbolt, Edinburgh 1923.
Selections. Ed B. Groom 1927.
Poems, with selections from his letters and from criticism. Ed C. W. Thomas, New York 1932.
Poems. Ed J. M. Murry 1948.
[Selections]. Ed R. Church 1948.
Selected poems. Ed G. H. Ford, New York 1950 (Crofts Classics).
Selected poems. Ed L. Whistler 1950.
Poems. Ed R. Vallance, introd by B. I. Evans 1950.
Selected poetry and letters. Ed R. H. Fogle, New York 1951 (Rinehart).
A selection. Ed J. E. Morpurgo 1953 (Penguin).
Selected letters and poems. Ed J. H. Walsh 1954.
Poems and letters. Ed J. R. Caldwell, New York 1954.
Selected poems. Ed E. Blunden 1955.
Poems. Introd by J. Mascarò, Palma de Mallorca 1955.
Selected poems and letters. Ed D. Bush, Boston 1959 (Riverside).
Selected poems and letters. Ed R. Sharrock, Oxford 1964.
Selections of the poems have been tr French, 1907, 1910, 1945, 1950, 1952; and the odes 1933; German, 1897, 1910, 1960; the sonnets and odes 1946; poems and letters 1950; Italian, 1901, 1910, 1911, 1937, 1925 (with Hyperion); *Spanish, 1918, 1946; Norwegian, 1932 (5 poems); Hungarian, 1962; Polish, 1952 (odes), 1962 (selected poems); Czech, 1961.*

§ 1

Poems. 1817, 1927 (photo facs), New York 1934 (photo facs).
Endymion: a poetic romance. 1818; illustr F. Joubert after E. J. Poynter 1873; illustr W. S. Harper 1888, Boston 1888; Rochelle NY 1902 (replica); ed H. C. Notcutt, Oxford 1927 (type facs); illustr J. Buckland-Wright 1947; ed T. Saito, Tokyo 1955.
Lamia, Isabella, the Eve of St. Agnes and other poems. 1820; ed M. Robertson, Oxford 1909 (type facs), 1909, 1920, 1922; 1927 (photo facs), New York 1927, 1928; Famous editions of English poets, ed J. O. Beaty and J. W. Bowyer, New York 1931.
Lamia. Illustr W. H. Low, Philadelphia 1885, 1888, London 1888.
Isabella. Illustr W. B. Macdougall 1898, Philadelphia 1898.
Another version of Keats's Hyperion. [1857]. Rptd by R. M. Milnes from his contribution to Miscellanies of the Philobiblon Society 3 1856–7 (first pbn of The fall of Hyperion: a dream).
Keatsii Hyperionis libri tres. Ed C. Merivale, Cambridge and London 1863 (English with Latin trn; bks 1–2 first pbd 1862); ed J. Hoops, Berlin 1899; Hyperion: a facsimile of Keats's autograph manuscript of The fall of Hyperion, a dream, ed E. de Selincourt, Oxford 1905; tr Dutch, 1888.
Contributions to periodicals. Only first pbns are listed:
Examiner (ed Leigh Hunt). To Solitude, 5 May 1816; On first looking into Chapman's Homer, 1 Dec 1816; To Kosciusko, 16 Feb 1817; After dark vapours, 23 Feb 1817; Haydon: forgive me, On seeing the Elgin marbles, 9 March 1817; On The floure and the lefe, 16 March 1817; [review of J. H. Reynolds, Peter Bell: a lyrical ballad], 25 April 1819; Lines written in the Highlands, 14 July 1822.
Champion. On the sea, 17 Aug 1817; [dramatic reviews], 21, 28 Dec 1817, 4 Jan 1818. Review of 28 Dec perhaps by J. H. Reynolds; *see* L. M. Jones, Keats-Shelley Jnl 3 1954.
The literary pocket-book. Ed Leigh Hunt 1819. The human seasons, To Ailsa rock.
Annals of the fine arts. Ode to a nightingale, July 1819; Ode on a Grecian urn, Dec 1819?
Indicator (ed Leigh Hunt). La belle dame sans merci, 10 May 1820; A dream, after reading Dante's episode of Paolo and Francesca, 28 June 1820; The cap and bells [part only], 23 Aug 1820.
The gem: a literary annual (ed Thomas Hood). On a picture of Leander, 1829.
London literary gazette. In a drear-nighted December, 19 Sept 1829.
The comic annual, by Thomas Hood. To a cat, 1830.
Western messenger. Ode to Apollo ('God of the golden bow'), June 1836.
Ladies' companion. Fame like a wayward girl, 'Hither, hither, love', 'Tis the witching hour of night, Aug 1837.

Portsmouth and Devonport weekly journal. To the Nile, 19 July 1838; Written upon the top of Ben Nevis, 6 Sept; Staffa, 20 Sept; Bright star, 27 Sept; The day is gone, 4 Oct; To sleep, 11 Oct; Shed no tear, 18 Oct; Ah! woe is me, 25 Oct; On sitting down to read King Lear once again, 8 Nov; On seeing a lock of Milton's hair, 15 Nov; Old Meg, 22 Nov.

Hood's magazine and comic miscellany. To a lady seen for a few moments at Vauxhall, vol 2 1844; Hush, hush, tread softly, vol 3 1845.

Milnes, R. M. Life, letters and literary remains. 1848. Many poems and letters first pbd here.

Letters, Diaries etc

Life, letters and literary remains. Ed R. M. Milnes 2 vols 1848. *See* §2, *below*.

Letters to Fanny Brawne. Ed H. B. Forman 1878, 1889 (rev and enlarged), New York 1878. Some copies with the London 1878 title-page have the pagination of 1889, with a note in place of the 1889 preface.

Letters of Keats to his family and friends. Ed S. Colvin 1891, 1891, 1918 (rev), 1921, 1925, 1928. Letters to Fanny Brawne omitted.

Letters: complete revised edition. Ed H. B. Forman 1895.

Letters to Fanny Brawne. New York 1901.

Letters. Ed N. H. Dole 1906.

Letters [selected]. Edinburgh 1908.

The Keats letters, papers and other relics forming the Dilke bequest to the Hampstead Public Library. 1914.

Letters to Fanny Brawne, with three poems and three additional letters. Introd by J. F. Otten, Maastricht 1931.

Keats's anatomical and physiological notebook. Ed M. B. Forman, Oxford 1934.

The letters. Ed M. B. Forman 2 vols Oxford 1931, 1 vol Oxford 1935, 1947, 1952 (rev).

Letters. Introd by H. I'A. Fausset 1938. Selection.

The Keats circle: letters and papers 1816–78. Ed H. E. Rollins 2 vols Cambridge Mass 1948.

The letters: selected passages. Ed H. W. Häusermann, Berne 1949.

Selected letters. Ed L. Trilling, New York 1951.

Letters. Ed F. Page, Oxford 1954 (WC). Selection.

More letters and poems of the Keats circle. Ed H. E. Rollins, Cambridge Mass 1955.

The letters of Keats 1814–21. Ed H. E. Rollins 2 vols Cambridge Mass 1958. The definitive edn.

Letters. Ed S. Gardner 1965. Selection.

There are selections tr French, 1928; Italian, 1945; German, 1949, 1950.

§2

Poems, 1817. Champion 9 March 1817 (J. H. Reynolds); European Mag May 1817 (G. F. Mathew); Examiner 1, 6 June, 13 July 1817 (L. Hunt).

Endymion, 1818. Quart Rev 19 1818 (J. W. Croker); Br Critic June 1818; Blackwood's Mag Aug 1818 (J. G. Lockhart); London Mag April 1820; Edinburgh Rev 34 1820 (F. Jeffrey on the Endymion and Lamia vols); Scots Mag Aug 1820.

Lamia, Isabella, The eve of St Agnes and other poems, 1820. Monthly Rev July 1820; New Times 19 July 1820 (C. Lamb); Indicator 2, 9 Aug 1820 (L. Hunt); London Mag Aug 1820; New Monthly Mag Sept 1820; Br Critic Sept 1820; London Mag Sept 1820; Scots Mag Oct 1820.

Shelley, P. B. Adonais. Pisa 1821, Cambridge 1829.

Dalby, J. W. Remarks on the character and writings of the late John Keats, the poet. Arliss Pocket Mag 1821.

'L'. Death of Mr John Keats. London Mag April 1821.

Hunt, L. Lord Byron and some of his contemporaries. 1828.

—— In his Imagination and fancy: or selections from the English poets, 1844.

—— In his Autobiography, with reminiscences of friends and contemporaries, 3 vols 1853; ed E. Blunden Oxford 1928 (WC); ed J. E. Morpurgo 1948.

Brown, C. A. Walks in the North during the summer of 1818 [with Keats]. Plymouth & Devonport Weekly Jnl 1–22 Oct 1840.

Dendy, W. C. The philosophy of mystery. 1841.

Gilfillan, G. In his Gallery of literary portraits, Edinburgh 1845.

Milnes, R. M. Life, letters and literary remains of Keats. 2 vols 1848, New York 1848, 1 vol 1867; ed R. Lynd 1927 (EL); Oxford 1931 (WC).

Taylor, T. In his Life of Benjamin Robert Haydon, from his autobiography and journals, 3 vols 1853.

De Quincey, T. In his Essays on the poets and other English writers, Boston 1853.

Masson, D. The life and poetry of Keats. Macmillan's Mag Nov 1860; rptd in his Wordsworth, Shelley, Keats and other essays, 1874.

Clarke, C. C. Recollections of Keats. Atlantic Monthly Jan 1861, GM Feb 1874 (rev).

—— and M. Clarke. In their Recollections of writers, 1878.

Haydon, B. R. In his Correspondence and table talk, 2 vols 1876.

Lowell, J. R. In his Among my books: second series, Boston 1876.

Owen, F. M. Keats: a study. 1880.

Arnold, M. Keats. In The English poets, ed T. H. Ward 4 vols 1880; rptd in his Essays in criticism: second series, 1888.

Richardson, B. W. An Esculapian poet: Keats. In his Asclepiad, 1884; rptd in his Disciples of Aesculapius, 1900.

Swinburne, A. C. In his Miscellanies, 1886.

De Vere, A. In his Essays chiefly on poetry, 1887.

Rossetti, W. M. Life of Keats. 1887.

Colvin, S. Keats. 1887 (EML).

—— A morning's walk in a Hampstead garden. Monthly Rev March 1903; rptd in The Keats memorial volume, 1921.

—— Keats and his friends: unpublished poems and letters, TLS 16 April 1914.

—— Keats: his life and poetry, his friends, critics and after-fame. 1917.

Woodberry, G. E. In his Studies in life and letters, Boston 1891.

Sharp, W. In his Life and letters of Joseph Severn, 1892.

Bridges, R. Keats: a critical essay. 1895.

—— A critical introduction to Keats. Oxford 1929.

Hoops, J. Keats Jugend und Jugendgedichte. E Studien 11 1895.

Gothein, M. Keats: Leben und Werke. Halle 1897.

Graham, W. Last links with Byron, Shelley and Keats. 1898.

Symons, A. John Keats. Monthly Rev Oct 1901.

More, P. E. In his Shelburne essays: fourth series. New York 1906.

Brooke, S. A. In his Studies in poetry, 1907.

Hancock, A. E. Keats: a literary biography. 1908.

Wolff, L. An essay on Keats's treatment of the heroic rhythm and blank verse. Paris 1909.

—— Keats: sa vie et son oeuvre. 1910.

—— Keats. 1929.

Bradley, A. C. The letters of Keats. In his Oxford lectures on poetry, 1909.

Miller, B. Leigh Hunt's relations with Byron, Shelley and Keats. New York 1910.

Hudson, W. H. Keats and his poetry. 1911.

The Bookman memorial souvenir. Bookman (London) June 1912.

de Selincourt, E. Keats: recent additions to our knowledge. TLS 21 May 1914. First pbn of two 'laurel crown' sonnets.

— Keats. Proc Br Acad 10 1921; rptd in The Keats memorial volume, 1921, below, and in his Oxford lectures on poetry, 1934.
Thomas, E. Keats. 1916.
Notcutt, H. C. An interpretation of Keats's Endymion. Cape Town 1919; rev as introd to facs of Endymion, 1927.
The Keats memorial volume. 1921. Includes L. Abercrombie, The second version of Hyperion; J. Bailey, The poet of stillness; F. S. Boas, On first looking into Chapman's Homer; A. C. Bradley, Keats and philosophy; B. Harraden, The manuscript of Keats's Hyperion; C. H. Herford, Mountain scenery in Keats; G. B. Shaw, Keats.
Newman, G. Keats: apothecary and poet. Sheffield 1921.
Elliott, G. R. The real tragedy of Keats. PMLA 36 1921; rptd in his Cycle of modern poetry, Princeton 1929.
Fausset, H. I'A. Keats: a study in development. 1922.
Franzinetti-Guastalla, A. John Keats. Rome 1922.
Lowell, A. John Keats. 2 vols Boston 1925, 1 vol Boston 1929 (not illustr), 2 vols 1925.
Murry, J. M. Keats and Shakespeare: a study of Keats's poetic life from 1816 to 1820. 1925.
— Studies in Keats. 1930, 1939 (rev and enlarged as Studies in Keats, new and old), 1949 (rev and 're-arranged' as The mystery of Keats), 1955 ('4th edn rev and enlarged' as Keats).
— Keats's year. TLS 23 April 1954.
Taylor, O. M. John Taylor, author and publisher 1781–1864. London Mercury June–July 1925.
Blunden, E. Shelley and Keats as they struck their contemporaries. 1925.
— Leigh Hunt's Examiner examined. 1928.
— Keats and his predecessors: a note on Ode to a nightingale. London Mercury July 1929.
— Keats and C. A. Brown. TLS 30 Jan 1930.
— Keats's publisher: a memoir of John Taylor. 1936.
— Keats's friend Mathew. English 1 1936.
— John Keats. 1950, 1954 (rev) (Br Council pamphlet).
— Indications of Keats. Keats-Shelley Memorial Bull 11 1960.
— Barry Cornwall and Keats. Keats-Shelley Memorial Bull 14 1963.
Evans, B. I. Keats and the Golden ass. Nineteenth Century Aug 1926.
— Keats. 1934.
— Keats as a medical student. TLS 31 May 1934. *See* R. W. King 21 June 1934.
— Keats and Joseph Severn: a re-estimate with unpublished letters. London Mercury Aug 1934.
Garrod, H. W. Keats. Oxford 1926, 1939 (rev).
— Keats and Miss Mary F—. TLS 5 Sept 1935.
— An unpublished sonnet of Keats. TLS 27 Nov 1937. 'Where didst thou find, young bard, thy sounding lyre' in a Woodhouse scrapbook.
Thorpe, C. D. The mind of Keats. New York 1926.
— Wordsworth and Keats: a study in personal and critical impressions. PMLA 42 1927.
— Keats's interest in politics and world affairs. PMLA 46 1931.
— An early review of Keats [in Time's telescope]. JEGP 43 1944.
— Keats and Hazlitt. PMLA 62 1947.
— and D. Pearce. Recent trends in Keats scholarship and criticism 1941–52. Keats-Shelley Jnl 2 1953.
Dekker, G. Die invloed van Keats en Shelley in Nederland gedurende die negentiende eeu. Groningen 1926.
Lafourcade, G. Swinburne's Hyperion and other poems, with an essay on Swinburne and Keats. 1927.
Weller, E. V. Keats and Mary Tighe: the poems of Mary Tighe with parallel passages from the work of Keats. New York 1928.
Darbishire, H. Keats and Egypt. RES 3 1927.
Erlande, A. (A. J. Brandenburg). La vie de Keats. Paris 1928; tr 1929.

Marsh, G. L. In his John Hamilton Reynolds: poetry and prose, 1928.
— and N. I. White. Keats and the periodicals of his time. MP 31 1934. List of reviews, comments etc.
— Newly identified writings of J. H. Reynolds. Keats-Shelley Jnl 1 1952.
Spurgeon, C. Keats's Shakespeare: a descriptive study based on new material. Oxford 1928, 1929 (rev).
Saito, T. Keats' view of poetry. 1929.
— John Keats. Tokyo 1936. In Japanese.
Turnbull, J. M. Keats, Reynolds and the Champion. London Mercury Feb 1929.
Bush, D. Some notes on Keats. PQ 8 1929.
— The date of Keats's Fall of Hyperion. MLN 49 1934.
— Notes on Keats's reading. PMLA 50 1935.
— In his Mythology and the romantic tradition in English poetry, Cambridge Mass 1937.
— Keats. New York 1966.
Roberts, J. H. Poetry of sensation or of thought? PMLA 45 1930.
— The significance of Lamia. PMLA 50 1935.
Langworthy, C. A. Dryden's influence on the versification of Lamia. Research Stud, State College of Washington Dec 1930.
Crawford, A. W. The genius of Keats: an interpretation. 1932.
Gingerich, S. F. The conception of beauty in the works of Shelley, Keats and Poe. Ann Arbor 1932.
Pope, W. B. A book of Keats. TLS 6 Oct 1932.
— Reynolds or Keats. TLS 26 Oct 1933.
— John Hamilton Reynolds, the friend of Keats. Wessex 11 May 1935.
— (ed). The diary of B. R. Haydon. 5 vols Cambridge Mass 1960–63.
Catel, J. John Keats et les odes (1819). Montpellier 1933.
Ridley, M. R. Keats' craftsmanship: a study in poetic development. Oxford 1933, New York 1962.
Eliot, T. S. In his Use of poetry and use of criticism, 1933.
Williams, C. Reason and beauty in the poetic mind. Oxford 1933.
Lowes, J. L. Keats and the Argonautica. TLS 28 Sept 1933.
— La belle dame sans merci and Dante. TLS 3 May 1934.
— Hyperion and the Purgatorio. TLS 11 Jan 1936.
— Moneta's temple. PMLA 51 1936.
— Keats, Diodorus Siculus and Rabelais. MP 34 1937.
Wright, H. G. Keats and politics. E & S 18 1933.
— Possible indebtedness of Keats' Isabella to the Decameron. RES new ser 2 1951.
Brown, L. The genesis, growth and meaning of Endymion. SP 30 1933.
Forman, M. B. Keats and his family: a series of portraits. Edinburgh 1933.
— Keats and the Richards family. TLS 26 April 1934.
— Some letters and miscellanea of Charles Browne. Oxford 1937.
— Keats's Isabella. TLS 27 June 1942.
— Tributes and allusions to Keats during the years 1816–1920. N & Q 14 June, 16 July, 23 Aug, 4 Oct, 1, 29 Nov 1947, 1 May 1948.
Sherwood, M. In his Undercurrents of influence in English romantic poetry, Cambridge Mass 1934.
O'Loughlin, J. L. N. Coleridge and the Fall of Hyperion. TLS 6 Dec 1934.
Chatterjee, N. A comparative study of Keats and the Pre-Raphaelite poets. Jnl of Dept of Letters, Univ of Calcutta 25 1934.
— Romance and reality in Keats. Ibid 29 1937.
Olney, C. Keats and B. R. Haydon. PMLA 49 1934.
de Geer, V. Keats: en monografi. Stockholm 1935.
'Winwar, F.' (F. V. Grebanier). In her Romantic rebels, Boston 1935.
Havens, R. D. Unreconciled opposites in Keats. PQ 14 1935.

Adami, M. Fanny Keats and her letters. Cornhill Mag Oct 1935, Feb 1936.
— Keats and Elm Cottage. TLS 16 May 1936.
— Fanny Keats. 1937.
Finney, C. L. The evolution of Keats's poetry. 2 vols Cambridge Mass 1936, New York 1963.
Leavis, F. R. In his Revaluation, 1936.
Creek, H. L. Keats and Cortez. TLS 21 March 1936.
Caldwell, J. R. The meaning of Hyperion. PMLA 51 1936.
— Beauty is truth. In Five studies in literature, Berkeley 1940.
— Keats' fancy: the effect on Keats of the psychology of his day. Ithaca 1945.
— Woodhouse's annotations to Keats' first volume of poems. PMLA 63 1948.
Wagenblass, J. H. Keats's Chapman sonnet. TLS 25 Jan 1936.
— Keats and Lucretius. MLR 32 1937.
— Keats's roaming fancy. Harvard Stud & Notes 20 1938.
Letters of Fanny Brawne to Fanny Keats 1820–4. Ed F. Edgecumbe, Oxford 1936.
Bushnell, N. S. A walk after Keats. New York 1936.
Brown, C. A. Life of Keats. Ed D. H. Bodwitha and W. B. Pope 1937.
Hewlett, D. Adonais: a life of Keats. 1937, 1949 (2nd edn rev and enlarged as A life of Keats).
Praz, M. Lettere di Keats. In his Studi e svaghi inglesi, Florence 1937.
Spender, S. Keats and Shelley. In From Anne to Victoria, ed B. Dobrée 1937.
Page, F. Keats and the midnight oil. Dublin Rev July 1937.
Haber, T. B. The unifying influence of love in Keats's poetry. PQ 16 1937.
Diano, F. P. Vita e poesia di Keats. Milan 1938.
Hale-White, W. Keats as doctor and patient. Oxford 1938.
Tillyard, E. M. W. Milton and Keats. In his Miltonic setting past and present, Cambridge 1938.
MacGillivray, J. R. Ode on a Grecian urn. TLS 9 July 1938.
Roberts, W. Ode on a Grecian urn. TLS 20 Aug 1938.
Zillman, L. J. Keats and the sonnet tradition. Los Angeles 1939.
Bate, W. J. Negative capability: the intuitive approach in Keats. Cambridge Mass 1939.
— The stylistic development of Keats. New York 1945.
— John Keats. Cambridge Mass 1963.
Peck, W. E. Love and folly, a poem by Keats and Brown. N & Q 25 Feb 1939.
Moorman, L. J. Tuberculosis and genius. Chicago 1940.
Pershing, J. H. Keats: when was he born and when did he die? PMLA 55 1940. Reply by H. E. Briggs, 56 1941.
Askwith, B. Keats. 1941.
Hungerford, E. B. In his Shores of darkness, New York 1941.
Knight, G. W. In his Starlit dome, 1941.
Stern, M. B. Four letters from George Keats. PMLA 56 1941.
McLuhan, H. M. Aesthetic pattern in Keats's odes. UTQ 12 1943.
Burke, K. Symbolic action in a poem by Keats. Accent 4 1943.
Briggs, H. E. Keats's 'golden-tongued romance'. MLN 58 1943.
— Keats's 'sickly imagination and sick pride'. MLQ 4 1943.
— Keats, Robertson and 'that most hateful land'. PMLA 59 1944.
— Two notes on Hazlitt and Keats. PMLA 59 1944.
— Keats's conscious and unconscious reactions to criticism of Endymion. PMLA 60 1945.
— Swift and Keats. PMLA 61 1946.

Short, C. William Morris and Keats. PMLA 59 1944.
Birkenhead, S. Against oblivion: the life of Joseph Severn. 1943.
Ford, G. H. Keats and the Victorians. New Haven 1944.
LeComte, E. S. Endymion in England: the literary history of a Greek myth. New York 1944.
Webb, S. J. Keats memorial house. TLS 30 Sept 1944.
Thompson, D. W. Keats's To the Nile. MLN 59 1944.
Priestley, F. E. L. Keats and Chaucer. MLQ 5 1944.
Brooks, C. History without footnotes: an account of Keats' urn. Sewanee Rev 52 1944; rptd in his Well wrought urn, New York 1947.
Van Ghent, D. The passion of the groves. Sewanee Rev 52 1944.
Rollins, H. E. Fanny Keats: biographical notes. PMLA 59 1944.
— Keats' reputation in America to 1848. Cambridge Mass 1946.
— Keats's Elgin marbles sonnets. In Studies in honor of A. H. R. Fairchild, Columbia Missouri 1946.
— Keats's letters. JEGP 47 1948.
— The Keats circle: letters and papers 1816–78. 2 vols Cambridge Mass 1948.
— and S. M. Parrish. Keats and the Bostonians: Amy Lowell, Louise I. Guiney, Louis A. Holman and Fred Holland Day. Cambridge Mass 1951.
— Unpublished autograph texts of Keats. Harvard Lib Bull 6 1952.
— Keats's misdated letters. Harvard Lib Bull 7–8 1952–4.
— Keats's letters: observations and notes. Keats-Shelley Jnl 2 1953.
— More letters and poems of the Keats circle. Cambridge Mass 1955.
— Notes on Keats's letters. SB 9 1957.
De Ullmann, S. Romanticism and synaesthesia: a comparative study of sense transfer in Keats and Byron. PMLA 60 1945.
Tate, A. A reading of Keats. Amer Scholar 15 1946.
B., A. G. Keats's Hyperion. N & Q 20 April 1946.
Buys, W. R. V. Keats: een stryd om het dichterschap. Naarden [1946].
Fogle, R. H. Emphatic imagery in Keats and Shelley. PMLA 61 1946.
— Keats's Ode to a nightingale. PMLA 68 1953.
Houghton, W. E. The meaning of Keats's Eve of St Mark. ELH 13 1946.
Beyer, W. W. Keats and the demon king. Oxford 1947.
Clark, E. B. A ms of John Keats at Dumbarton Oaks. Harvard Lib Bull 1 1947. On Spenser a jealous honourer of thine.
Ford, N. F. Endymion—a Neo-Platonic allegory? ELH 14 1947.
— Some Keats echoes and borrowings. MLQ 8 1947.
— The meaning of 'fellowship with essence' in Endymion. PMLA 62 1947.
— Keats, empathy and 'the poetical character'. SP 45 1948.
— Keats's 'O for a life of sensations'. MLN 64 1949.
— The prefigurative imagination of Keats: a study of the beauty-truth identification and its implications. Stanford 1951.
Stubbs, H. H. Keats's 'beauty is truth'. N & Q 31 May 1947. *See* P. Stubbs 20 Sept, R. F. Rashbrook 1 Nov, G. Ryle 15 Nov 1947.
Stallman, R. W. Keats the Apollinian: the time and space logic of his poems as paintings. UTQ 16 1947.
Gorrell, Lord. The principle of beauty. 1948.
Altick, R. D. The Cowden Clarkes. Oxford 1948.
Thorpe, J. A copy of Endymion owned by Haydon. N & Q 27 Nov 1948.
Steele, M. A. E. The Woodhouse transcripts of the poems of Keats. Harvard Lib Bull 3 1949.
— Three early mss of Keats. Keats-Shelley Jnl 1 1952.

— A passport note attributed to Keats: a postscript. Harvard Lib Bull 9 1955.
— The authorship of The poet and other sonnets: selections from a 19th-century ms anthology. Keats-Shelley Jnl 5 1956.
Bebbington, W. G. 'Writ in water'. TLS 26 March 1949. *See* H. A. Hammelmann 2 April, J. C. Maxwell 9 April 1949.
Bellinger, R. R. The first publication of Ode on a Grecian urn. N & Q 29 Oct 1949.
Rogers, N. Keats, Shelley and Rome: an illustrated miscellany. 1949, 1957, New York 1961.
Bowra, C. M. In his Romantic imagination, Cambridge Mass 1949.
Cacciatore, V. The house in war-time. Keats-Shelley Memorial Bull 3 1950.
Strout, A. L. George Croly and Blackwood's Magazine. TLS 6 Oct 1950.
— Knights of the burning epistle: the Blackwood papers in the National Library of Scotland. Neophilologica 26 1954.
Whitely, A. The autograph of Keats's In a drear-nighted December. Harvard Lib Bull 5 1951.
Pratt, W. W. A note on Keats and Camõens. N & Q 9 June 1951.
Atkinson, A. D. Keats and Kamshatka. N & Q 4 Aug 1951.
Richardson, J. Fanny Brawne: a biography. 1952.
— New light on Mr Abbey. Keats-Shelley Memorial Bull 5 1953.
— Richard Woodhouse and his family. Keats-Shelley Memorial Bull 5 1953.
— The everlasting spell: a study of Keats and his friends. 1963.
Holloway, J. The odes of Keats. Cambridge Jnl April 1952; rptd in his Charted mirror, 1960.
Brooks, E. L. 'The poet': an error in the Keats canon? MLN 67 1952.
Wasserman, E. R. Keats' sonnet The poet. MLN 67 1952.
— The finer tone: Keats' major poems. Baltimore 1953.
Wigod, J. D. Negative capability and wise passiveness. PMLA 67 1952.
— The meaning of Endymion. PMLA 68 1953.
— Keats's ideal in the Ode on a Grecian urn. PMLA 72 1957.
Pettet, E. C. Echoes of the Lay of the last minstrel in the Eve of St Agnes. RES new ser 3 1952.
— On the poetry of Keats. Cambridge 1957.
Muir, K. The meaning of Hyperion. EC 2 1952.
— (ed). Keats: a reassessment. Liverpool 1958. Includes J. Grundy, Keats and the Elizabethans; C. Godfrey, Endymion; M. Allott, Isabella, The eve of St Agnes and Lamia; Kenneth Muir, The meaning of the odes, Keats and Hazlitt; K. Allott, The ode to Psyche; A Davenport, A note on To autumn; R. T. Davies, Some ideas and usages; D. I. Masson, The Keatsian incantation.
Green, D. B. More tributes and allusions to Keats 1830–1935. N & Q 15 March, 26 April 1952.
— Further tributes and allusions in verse to Keats 1876–1943. N & Q Jan 1954.
— Keats and La Motte Fouqué's Undine. Delaware Notes 27 1954.
Gittings, R. Keats in Chichester. Keats-Shelley Memorial Bull 5 1953.
— The living year: 21 September 1818 to 21 September 1819. 1954.
— Keats and Chatterton. Keats-Shelley Jnl 4 1955.
— The mask of Keats: a study of problems. 1956.
— Keats at Lulworth Cove. Keats-Shelley Memorial Bull 9 1958.
— Keats's sailor relation. TLS 15 April 1960.
— Mr Keats's origin. TLS 5, 19 March 1964.
— The Keats inheritance. 1964.
Perkins, D. Keats's odes and letters: recurrent diction and imagery. Keats-Shelley Jnl 2 1953.
— The quest of permanence: the symbolism of Wordsworth, Shelley, Keats. Cambridge Mass 1959.
Bates, M. C. Two new letters of Keats and Byron. Keats-Shelley Jnl 3 1954.
Bland, D. S. Logical structure in the Ode to autumn. PQ 33 1954.
Coles, W. A. The proof sheets of Keats's Lamia. Harvard Lib Bull 8 1954.
Hamilton, K. M. Time and the Grecian urn. Dalhousie Rev 34 1954.
Jones, L. M. Keats's theatrical reviews in the Champion. Keats-Shelley Jnl 3 1954.
— New letters, articles and poems by J. H. Reynolds. Keats-Shelley Jnl 6 1957.
— Reynolds and Keats. Keats-Shelley Jnl 7 1958.
— The ode to Psyche. Keats-Shelley Memorial Bull 9 1958.
Patterson, C. I. Passion and permanence in Keats's Ode on a Grecian urn. ELH 21 1954.
— The Keats-Hazlitt-Hunt copy of Palmerin of England in relation to Keats's poetry. JEGP 60 1961.
Parson, D. Portraits of Keats. Cleveland 1954.
Garlitz, B. Egypt and Hyperion. PQ 34 1955.
Grundy, J. Keats and Sandys. N & Q Feb 1955.
— Keats and William Browne. RES new ser 6 1955.
Murchie, G. The spirit of place in Keats: sketches of persons and places known to him, and his reaction to them. 1955.
Spitzer, L. The ode on a Grecian urn: or content vs metagrammar. Comparative Lit 7 1955.
Trilling, L. The poet as hero: Keats in his letters. In his Opposing self, New York 1955.
Ward, A. The date of Keats's Bright star sonnet. SP 52 1955.
— Keats's sonnet Nebuchadnezzar's dream. PQ 34 1955.
— Keats and Burton: a reappraisal. PQ 40 1961.
— Christmas day 1818. Keats-Shelley Jnl 10 1961.
— Keats: the making of a poet. New York 1963.
Shackford, M. H. The Ode on a Grecian urn. Keats-Shelley Jnl 4 1955.
Maxwell, J. C. Keats's sonnet on the tomb of Burns. Ibid.
— A lost Keats letter: genuine or spurious? N & Q Dec 1961.
Allott, K. Keats's Ode to Psyche. EC 6 1956.
Cornelius, R. D. Keats as humanist. Keats-Shelley Jnl 5 1956.
Cooke, A. K. William Maginn on Keats. N & Q March 1956.
Renzulli, M. Keats: l'uomo e il poeta. Rome 1956.
Allen, G. O. The fall of Hyperion: a study in Keats's intellectual growth. Keats-Shelley Jnl 6 1957.
Arnett, C. Thematic structure in Keats's Endymion. SE 36 1957.
Davies, R. T. Keats and Hazlitt. Keats-Shelley Memorial Bull 8 1957.
Goldberg, M. A. The 'fears' of Keats. MLQ 18 1957.
— Keats's Endymion I 1–35. Explicator 15 1957.
Mann, P. G. Keats's Indian allegory. Keats-Shelley Jnl 6 1957.
— Keats's reading. Keats-Shelley Memorial Bull 13 1962.
Muller, R. Some problems concerning Keats and Hazlitt. Keats-Shelley Memorial Bull 8 1957.
Rosenberg, J. D. Keats and Milton: the paradox of rejection. Keats-Shelley Jnl 6 1957.
Severs, J. B. Keats' fairy sonnet. Ibid.
Wicker, B. The 'disputed lines in the Fall of Hyperion'. EC 7 1957.
Adams, R. M. Strains of discord: studies in literary openness. Ithaca 1958.
Bostetter, E. E. The eagle and the truth: Keats and the problem of belief. Jnl of Aesthetics 16 1958.
— In his Romantic ventriloquists, Seattle 1963.
Bradbrook, F. W. Marlowe and Keats. N & Q March 1958.

Davies, R. T. Was 'negative capability' enough for Keats? SP 55 1958.
Lyon, H. T. Keats's well-read urn: an introduction to literary method. New York 1958.
Slote, B. Keats and the dramatic principle. Lincoln Nebraska 1958.
— The climate of Keats's La belle dame sans merci. MLQ 21 1960.
— La belle dame as naiad. JEGP 60 1961.
Stillinger, J. Keats's Grecian urn and the evidence of transcripts. PMLA 73 1958.
— The Brown–Dilke controversy. Keats-Shelley Jnl 11 1962.
— The text of the Eve of St Agnes. SB 16 1963.
Yost, G. A source and interpretation of Keats's Minos. JEGP 57 1958.
— Keats's early religious phraseology. SP 59 1962.
— The poetic drive in the early Keats. Texas Stud in Lit & Lang 5 1964.
Blackstone, B. The consecrated urn: an interpretation of Keats in terms of growth and form. 1959.
Dunbar, G. S. The significance of the humour in Lamia. Keats-Shelley Jnl 8 1959.
Sikes, H. M. The theory and practice of Keats: the record of a debt to Hazlitt. PQ 38 1959.
Wells, W. A. A doctor's life of Keats. New York 1959.
James, D. G. Three odes of Keats. Cardiff 1959.
— Keats and King Lear. Shakespeare Stud 13 1960.
Gérard, A. Keats and the romantic Sehnsucht. UTQ 28 1959.
— Romance and reality: continuity and growth in Keats's view of art. Keats-Shelley Jnl 11 1962.
Stepanik, K. The reflection of social reality in Keats's poems and letters. Brno Stud in Eng 1 1959.
Harrison, R. Symbolism of the cyclical myth in Endymion. Texas Stud in Lit & Lang 1 1960.
Harrison, T. P. Keats and a nightingale. E Studies 41 1960.
Johnson, C. L. 'The realms of gold'. Keats-Shelley Jnl 9 1960.
MacLeish, A. In his Poetry and experience Boston 1960.
Mann, P. G. New light on Keats and his family. Keats-Shelley Memorial Bull 11 1960.
— Keats: further notes. Keats-Shelley Memorial Bull 12 1961.
— Keats's maternal relations. Keats-Shelley Memorial Bull 15 1964.
Schulz, M. F. Keats's timeless order of things. Criticism 2 1960.
Lombardo, A. La poesia di Keats. Milan 1961.
Heinen, H. Interwoven time in Keats's poetry. Texas Stud in Lit & Lang 3 1961.
Manierre, W. R. Versification and imagery in the Fall of Hyperion. Ibid.
Martin, J. S. Keats's new planet. N & Q Jan 1961.
Sharrock, R. Keats and the young lovers. REL 2 1961.
Balslev, T. Keats and Wordsworth: a comparative study. Copenhagen 1962.
Marilla, E. L. Three odes of Keats. Copenhagen 1962.
Bayley, J. Keats and reality. Proc Br Acad 48 1962.
Freeman, A. Keats's Ode on melancholy, 24. N & Q May 1962.
Haeffner, P. Keats and the faery myth of seduction. REL 3 1962.
Haynes, J. John Jennings: Keats's grandfather. Keats-Shelley Memorial Bull 13 1962.
— Keats's paternal relatives. Keats-Shelley Memorial Bull 15 1964.
Kenyon, K. M. R. When did Keats and Fanny Brawne become engaged? Keats-Shelley Memorial Bull 13 1962.
— Keats and the countryside. Keats-Shelley Memorial Bull 14 1963.
Sperry, S. M. Keats, Milton and the Fall of Hyperion. PMLA 77 1962.
— The allegory of Endymion. Stud in Romanticism 2 1962.
— Keats's skepticism and Voltaire. Keats-Shelley Jnl 12 1963.
Kendall, L. H. John Murray to W. J. Croker: an unpublished letter on Keats. Ibid.
Kroeber, K. The commemorative prophecy of Hyperion. Trans of Wisconsin Acad of Sciences, Arts & Letters 52 1963.
— The new humanism of Keats's odes. Proc Amer Philosophical Soc 107 1963.
— The artifice of reality: poetic style in Wordsworth, Foscolo, Keats and Leopardi. Madison 1964.
Robinson, D. E. Ode on a 'new Etrurian' urn: a reflection of Wedgwood ware in the poetic imagery of Keats. Keats-Shelley Jnl 12 1963.
— A question of the imprint of Wedgwood in the longer poems of Keats. Keats-Shelley Jnl 16 1967.
Evert, W. E. Aesthetic and myth in the poetry of Keats. Princeton 1964.
Guy, E. F. Keats's use of 'luxury': a note on meaning. Keats-Shelley Jnl 13 1964.
Hobsbaum, P. The 'philosophy' of the Grecian urn: a consensus of readings. Keats-Shelley Memorial Bull 15 1964.
Miller, B. E. The allusion to Paradise lost in Keats's letter on imagination. N & Q Nov 1964.
— On the meaning of Keats's Endymion. Keats-Shelley Jnl 14 1965.
Wagner, R. D. Ode to Psyche and the second Hyperion. Keats-Shelley Jnl 13 1964.
Wilson, K. M. The nightingale and the hawk: a psychological study of Keats' ode. 1964.
Bloom, H. Keats and the embarrassments of poetic tradition. In From sensibility to romanticism: essays presented to F. A. Pottle, New York 1965.
Saly, J. Keats's answer to Dante: the fall of Hyperion. Keats-Shelley Jnl 14 1965.
Woodring, C. On looking into Keats's voyagers. Ibid.
Inglis, F. Keats. 1966.
Laski, M. The language of the nightingale ode. E & S 29 1966.
Halpern, M. Keats and the 'Spirit that laughest'. Keats-Shelley Jnl 15 1966.
Starr, N. C. Negative capability in Keats's diction. Ibid.
Visick, M. Keats's Epistle to Reynolds and the odes. Ibid.
Notopoulos, J. A. Truth-beauty in the Ode on a Grecian urn and the Elgin marbles. MLR 61 1966.
D'Avanzo, M. L. Keats's metaphors for the poetic imagination. Durham NC 1967.
— Keats's and Vergil's underworlds: source and meaning in Book II of Endymion. Keats-Shelley Jnl 16 1967.

J. R. M.

JOHN CLARE

1793–1864

Mss by or concerning Clare, some unpbd, are in Peterborough Natural Historical Society Museum; Northampton City Library; BM (letters to Clare); and Pierpont Morgan Library, New York. These collections represent his literary life except 1837–41. Poems written at Northampton Asylum, after 1837, are mostly known in transcripts.

Bibliographies

[Dack, C. and J. W. Bodger.] Clare centenary exhibition catalogue. Peterborough 1893.
Smith, C. E. In Poems by Clare, ed N. Gale, Rugby 1901.
[Powell, D.] Catalogue of the Clare Collection in the Northampton Public Library. Northampton 1965.

Collections

Poems. Ed J. W. Tibble 2 vols 1935.
Prose. Ed J. W. and A. Tibble 1951.
Letters. Ed J. W. and A. Tibble 1951.

Selections

Cherry, J. L. Life and remains of Clare. 1873.
Noel, R. In Poets and poetry of the nineteenth century, ed A. H. Miles vol 3 [1892], 1898, 1905.
Poems by Clare. Ed A. Symons, Oxford 1908.
Clare: poems chiefly from manuscript. Ed E. Blunden and A. Porter 1920.
Madrigals and chronicles: newly found poems by Clare. Ed E. Blunden 1924.
Poems of Clare's madness. Ed G. Grigson 1949.
Selected poems. Ed G. Grigson 1950 (ML).
Selected poems. Ed J. Reeves 1954.
Unpublished poems. Ed E. Robinson and G. Summerfield, Listener 20 March 1962.
Later poems. Ed E. Robinson and G. Summerfield, Manchester 1964.
Clare: Northamptonshire poet. Ed J. Carr, Kettering 1964.
Selected poems. Ed L. Clark, Leeds 1964.
Selected poems. Ed J. W. and A. Tibble 1965 (EL).
Spring violets. Northamptonshire Past & Present 3 1965. An unpbd poem.
Poems by Clare. Ed D. Powell 1965.

§1

Proposals for publishing a collection of trifles in verse. Market Deeping 1817.
Poems descriptive of rural life and scenery. 1820 (3 edns), 1821.
The village minstrel. 2 vols 1821, 1823.
The shepherd's calendar. 1827; ed E. Robinson and G. Summerfield, Oxford 1964 (from mss).
Prospectus: The midsummer cushion. Helpston 1832.
The rural muse. 1835.
Sketches in the life of Clare written by himself. Ed E. Blunden 1930.

§2

Gilchrist, O. Clare: an agricultural labourer and poet. London Mag Jan 1820.
[Taylor, J.] A visit to Clare. London Mag Nov 1821.
Allen, W. Four letters to Lord Radstock on the poems of Clare. 1824.
[Galignani, A. and W.] In Living poets of England vol 1, 1827.
Elton, C. A. In his Boyhood with other poems, 1835.
[Wilson, J.] The rural muse. Blackwood's Mag Aug 1835; rptd in his Recreations of Christopher North vol 1, 1842.
Hall, S. C. In his Book of gems vol 3, 1838.
Hood, T. In his Literary reminiscences, Hood's Own May 1839.
De Quincey, T. In his Literary reminiscences, Tait's Mag Dec 1840.
Allen, M. Appeal for Clare. Athenaeum 8 May 1841.
Redding, C. Clare the poet. Eng Jnl May 1841.
Hood, E. P. In his Literature of labour, 1851.
Sternberg, T. In his Northamptonshire glossary, 1851.
Baker, A. E. In his Northamptonshire glossary, 2 vols 1854.
In Men of the time, 1856.
Mitford, M. R. In her Recollections vol 1, 1857.
Chambers, R. Cyclopaedia of English literature vol 2, 1861.
James, T. In his History of Northamptonshire, 1864.
Obituary. GM July 1864.
Martin, F. W. Life of Clare. 1865; ed E. Robinson and G. Summerfield 1964.
Redding, C. In his Past celebrities vol 2, 1866.
Dalby, J. W. In his Tales, songs and sonnets, 1866.
Wilde, G. J. de. In his Rambles round about, 1872.
Hall, S. T. In his Biographical sketches, 1873.
Kingsley, C. Nature in Clare's time and region. 1877. Ed by his wife.
Wainewright, T. G. In his Essays and criticisms, ed W. C. Hazlitt 1 1880.
Strickland, J. M. In her Life of Agnes Strickland, 1887.
Stoddard, R. H. In his Under the evening lamp, 1893.
Heath, R. In his English peasant, 1893.
Symons, A. In his Romantic movement in English poetry, 1908.
Druce, G. C. Northamptonshire botanologia: Clare. Northampton 1912; rptd in his Flora of Northamptonshire, 1930.
Walker, H. In his Literature of the Victorian era, 1913.
Thomas, E. A literary pilgrim in England. 1917.
[Squire, J. C.] Books in general, by Solomon Eagle ser 3, 1920.
Unpublished writings of Clare. Athenaeum 9 April 1920.
Mayer, G. M. T. Clare (includes letter from G. J. de Wilde). TLS 30 June 1921.
Porter, A. John Clare. Spectator 23 Aug 1924.
—— Notes for an autobiography [Clare]. Spectator 19–26 Sept, 3 Oct 1925.
Blunden, E. More footnotes to literary history. Tokyo 1926.
—— In his Nature in English literature, 1929.
Abbott, C. C. In his Life of George Darley, 1928.
Brown, R. W. Clare's library. Northampton 1929.
Kirby, H. T. The Clare country. Saturday Rev 14 March 1931.
—— Notes on Clare. Bookmark spring 1935.
Tibble, J. W. and A. Clare: a life. 1932.
Bell, A. The village minstrel. Spectator 8 March 1935.
[Tomlinson, P.] Clare's dream. TLS 21 Feb 1935.
Lamb, C. and M. In their Letters, ed E. V. Lucas 3 vols 1935.
Park, J. Unpublished poems by Clare. Buffalo 1937.
Channing-Pearce, M. John Clare. Hibbert Jnl 39 1941.
—— Poet in bondage. TLS 27 Dec 1941.
Gregory, H. In his Shield of Achilles, New York 1944.
Heath-Stubbs, J. Clare and the peasant tradition. Penguin New Writing 32 1937; rptd in his Darkling plain, 1950.
Rollins, H. E. A poem by Clare. Harvard Lib Bull 3 1949.
Garfoot Gardner, B. Clare's village. Helpston 1949.
Murry, J. M. In his Clare and other studies, 1950.
Vallette, J. John Clare. Mercure de France Sept 1951.
Wilson, J. Green shadows: the life of Clare. 1951.
Loveman, S. From Clare to Taylor. TLS 13 April 1951.
Wake, J. Early days of the Northamptonshire Natural History Society. Northamptonshire Past & Present 1 1952.
Tennent, D. Reflections on genius. Jnl of Mental Science 99 1953.
Tibble, J. W. and A. Clare: his life and poetry. 1956.
Harrison, T. P. Birds in the poetry of Clare. Peterborough 1957.
Fisher, J. Clare: naturalist and poet. Listener 19 Oct 1961.
Crowson, D. Helpston in the time of Clare. Peterborough 1964.
[Tait, L. (ed)]. Clare: centenary commemoration programme. Peterborough 1964.
Grainger, M. Collector of ballads. 1964.
All Saints' Church, Northampton. Clare: civic memorial service, May 20 1964. 1964.
Tibble, A., J. Fisher, Lord Brain and E. Blunden. Four views of Clare. Chronicle & Echo (Northampton) 20 May 1964.

E. B.

THOMAS HOOD

1799–1845

Bibliographies

The most thorough bibliography is C. Goodrich's unpbd Yale thesis, A bibliography of the works of Hood, 1934, *commented on in the unpbd Harvard dissertation on Hood by A. Whitley, 1950.*

Gilmour, J. Some uncollected authors, VII: Hood. Book Collector 4 1955.

Collections

Poems [serious]. 2 vols 1846, 1846, 1851 (4th edn), 1853 (6th edn), 1857 (9th edn), 1858, 1859 etc.

Poems of wit and humour [excluding those in Hood's Own]. 1847, 1849, 1851, 1856 (7th edn), 1860 (9th edn), 1863 (12th edn), 1866 (16th edn), [1872] (19th edn).

Poetical works, with some account of the author. 4 vols Boston 1856, 1857.

Humorous poems. Ed E. Sargent, Boston 1856.

Passages from the poems. Illustr Jr Etching Club 1858.

[Select poems]. Tr German, 1859; tr Russian, 1864.

Hood's gems. 1861.

Works comic and serious, in prose and verse. Ed with notes by his son [T. Hood jr]. 7 vols 1862–3.

The serious poems. Ed S. Lucas with preface by T. H. the younger [1867], 1870; 2 vols 1876 (with Comic poems, below), 1886; illustr H. G. Fell 1901.

The comic poems. Ed S. Lucas with preface by T. H. the younger [1867], 2 vols 1876 (with Serious poems), 1885.

Works. Ed his son and daughter [F. F. Broderip]. 10 vols 1869–73 (illustr), 11 vols 1882–4.

Early poems and sketches. Ed his daughter 1869.

[Select poems]. Ed J. B. Payne, illustr G. Doré 1870, 1872, 1880.

Songs and etchings. 1871.

Poetical works. Ed W. M. Rossetti, illustr G. Doré 2 sers [1871–5], [1880].

Poems. Glasgow [1889].

The poetical works of Hunt and Hood. 1889.

[Selections]. In Poets and poetry of the century, ed. R. Garnett vol 2, 1891.

Humorous poems. Ed A. Ainger 1893.

Poems. Ed A. Ainger 2 vols 1897.

Poems. Ed W. Jerrold, Oxford 1906 (WC).

Poems, selected by A. Ingram. 1906.

Poems chosen by A. T. Quiller-Couch. [1908].

Selections. 1928.

Poems. Ed C. Dyment 1948.

Other collected edns : Boston [c. 1860]; illustr Foster 1871, 1872; [1874]; [1875]; [1878]; [1880]; 2 vols 1881; 1886; [1886]; 1 vol [1887]; [1890]; ed J. Ashton [1891]; ed F. C. Burnand 1907.

§1

Odes and addresses to great people. 1825 (anon), 1825, 1826. With J. H. Reynolds.

Whims and oddities in prose and verse. 1st ser, 1826, 1829 (4th edn); 2nd ser, 1827, 1829 etc.

National tales. 2 vols 1827.

The plea of the midsummer fairies, Hero and Leander, Lycus the centaur and other poems. 1827.

The Epping hunt. Illustr Cruikshank 1829, 1830, 1889.

The dream of Eugene Aram. Gem 1829; illustr W. Harvey 1831, 1832; tr Welsh, 1853; German, 1861; other edns 1868, 1902.

Tylney hall: a novel. 3 vols 1834, 1840, 1857, [1878].

Hood's own: or laughter from year to year [illustr; contains Literary reminiscences]. 1839, 1855; second ser, with preface by his son 1861; [1882] (both sers).

Up the Rhine. 1840, 1840, Frankrfut 1840, New York 1852.

The loves of Sally Brown and Ben the carpenter. [1840?]. A song, 4to, single sheet.

The song of the shirt. Punch Xmas 1843; tr French, 1895.

Whimsicalities: a periodical gathering, with illustrations by Leech. 2 vols 1844, 1870 (enlarged), [1878].

Lamia: a romance. In W. Jerdan, Autobiography vol 1, 1852. A poem, written c. 1827.

The headlong career and woful ending of precocious piggy. Ed F. F. Broderip, illustr T. H. jr 1859 [1858], [1880].

Fairy land, by the late Thomas and Jane Hood. Ed F. F. Broderip 1861 (for 1860).

Sonnet written in a volume of Shakespeare. Keats-Shelley Jnl 13 1964.

Periodicals edited by Hood

The gem: a literary annual. 1829. Vol 1 only.

The comic annual. 11 vols 1830–42. Literary contributions mainly by Hood. No vol issued 1840–1.

The new monthly magazine. 1841–3.

Hood's magazine. 1–3 1844–5.

The following contain contributions by Hood:

The London magazine. July 1821–July 1823. Ed John Taylor, with Hood as assistant and contributor.

Sporting, with literary contributions by Hood et al. Ed 'Nimrod' (C. J. Apperley) 1838.

The children in the wood. 1865. Preface by Hood.

Letters

Mabbott, T. O. Letters of Leigh Hunt, Hood and Allan Cunningham. N & Q 23 May 1931.

Letters of Hood from the Dilke papers in the British Museum. Ed L. Marchand, New Brunswick 1945.

Whitley A. Hood and Dickens: some new letters. HLQ 14 1951.

Parker, W. M. The stockbroker author. Quart Rev 290 1952. Includes excerpts from unpbd letters.

MS collections in the Columbia University libraries: a descriptive list. New York 1959.

Alexseev, M. P. (ed). In Niezdannye pisma inostrannykh pisateley 18–19 vekov 12 Leningradskikh rukopisnysh sobraniy, Moscow 1960.

Shuman, R. B. A whimsical letter of Hood. N & Q July 1963. Reply by P. F. Morgan, Oct 1963.

Morgan, P. F. Corrections in some letters of Hood. N & Q July 1963.

§2

Horne, R. H. In his A new spirit of the age vol 2, 1844.

Hall, Mrs S. C. A memory of Hood. Littell's Living Age 6 1845.

Gilfillan, G. In his A gallery of literary portraits vol 2, 1852.

Balmanno, Mrs M. Lamb and Hood. In her Pen and pencil, New York 1858.

[Broderip, F. F. and T. Hood jr]. Memorials of Hood collected by his daughter, with a preface and notes by his son. 2 vols 1860.

Masson, D. Hood. Macmillan's Mag Aug 1860.

Thackeray, W. M. On a joke I once heard from the late T. Hood. In his Roundabout papers, 1863.

[Lawrance, H. ?]. Recollections of Hood. Br Quart Rev 46 1867.

Cook, E. Poor Hood. In her Poetical works, 1870.

Lowth, G. T. The Hood controversy on A poem reclaimed. Temple Bar Sept 1872.

Cowden Clarke, C. On the comic writers of England, 15: Hood. GM Jan 1872.

— and M. In their Recollections of writers, 1878.

Lucy, H. W. Hood: a biographical sketch. GM Jan 1875.

Wainewright, T. G. In his Essays and criticisms, ed W. C. Hazlitt 1880.

Mason, E. T. In his Personal traits of British authors vol 4, 1885.
Elliot, A. Hood in Scotland. Dundee 1885.
Fields, J. T. In his Some noted princes, authors and statesmen in our time, ed J. Parton, New York 1885.
Ashton, J. The true story of Eugene Aram. In Eighteenth-century waifs, 1887.
Henley, W. E. In his Views and reviews, 1890.
Dudley, T. U. Hood: punster, poet, preacher. Harper's Mag April 1891.
Saintsbury, G. In his Essays in English literature 1780–1860 ser 2, 1895.
Rolfe, W. J. Hood. Poet-Lore 8 1896.
Spielmann, M. H. Hood and Punch. Bookman (New York) Oct 1899.
Oswald, E. Hood und die soziale Tendenzdichtung seiner Zeit. Wiener Beiträge zur Englischen Philologie 19 1904.
Jerrold, W. Hood: his life and times. 1907.
—— Hood and Charles Lamb: the story of a friendship. 1930. Includes reprint of Literary reminiscences.
Canby, H. S. Hood as a serious poet. Dial 45 1908.
Shelley, H. C. Hood's homes and friends. In his Literary bypaths in old England, Cambridge Mass 1909.
More, P. E. Thomas Hood. Nation (New York) 26 Aug 1909; rptd in his Shelburne essays vol 7, New York 1910.
Olivero, F. Hood and Keats. MLN 28 1913.
Hudson, W. H. Hood: the man, the wit, and the poet. In his A quiet corner in a library, Chicago 1915.
Swann, J. H. The serious poems of Hood. Manchester Quart 51 1925.
Eden, H. Hood. Catholic World Sept 1926.
Shaw, C. B. This fellow of infinite jest. Poet-Lore 40 1929.
Blunden, E. Hood's literary reminiscences. In his Votive tablets, 1931.
—— In his Chaucer to 'B.V.', Tokyo 1950.
—— The poet Hood. REL 1 1960.
Turnbull, J. M. Reynolds, the Hoods and Mary Lamb. TLS 5 Nov 1913.
Gilman, M. Baudelaire and Hood. Romanic Rev 26 1935.
MacIlrath, J. H. Hood. 1935.
Quintus Quiz: Tom Hood. Christian Century 61 1944.
Heath-Stubbs, J. Hood. Time & Tide 28 April 1945.
—— In his Darkling plain, 1950.
Hood: the poet behind the jester's mask. TLS 5 May 1945.
B., L. Hood: a centenary note. N & Q 19 May 1945.
Hudson, D. Hood and Praed. TLS 19 May 1945.
Pritchett, V. S. Our half-Hogarth. In his Living novel, 1946.
Wallis, N. H. Hood. Essays by Divers Hands 23 1947.
Voss, A. Lowell, Hood and the pun. MLN 63 1948.
Cohen, J. M. Thomas Hood. TLS 5 May 1950.
Whitley, A. Hood as a dramatist. SE 30 1951.
—— Keats and Hood. Keats-Shelley Jnl 5 1956.
—— Two hints for Bleak House. Dickensian 52 1956.
—— Hood and the Times. TLS 17 May 1957. Comment by P. F. Morgan 7 June 1957.
Hennig, J. The literary relations between Goethe and Hood. MLQ 12 1951.
Hood: the language of poetry. TLS 19 Sept 1952.
Fielding, K. J. The misfortunes of Hood 1841. N & Q Dec 1953.
Jennings, A. Hood's Autumn. TLS 26 June 1953.
Hobman, D. L. Thomas Hood. Contemporary Rev June 1955.
Morgan, P. F. John Clare again. TLS 7 Feb 1958.
—— Izaak Walton, Lamb and Hood. Charles Lamb Soc Bull May 1961.
—— Author's query. New York Times 3 Sept 1961.
—— John Hamilton Reynolds and Hood. Keats-Shelley Jnl 11 1962.
—— Charles Lamb and Hood: records of a friendship. Tennessee Stud in Lit 9 1964.
Davies, R. E. Hood as playwright and prose writer. Eng Stud in Africa 2 1959.
Kaufman, P. The Reynolds-Hood commonplace book: a fresh appraisal. Keats-Shelley Jnl 10 1961.
Brander, L. Thomas Hood. 1963 (Br Council pamphlet).
Freeman, J. In his Literature and locality, 1963.
Reid, J. C. Thomas Hood. 1963.
Enzensberger, C. Die Fortentwicklung der Romantik am englischen Beispiel: Hood. Deutsche Vierteljahrsschrift für Literaturwissenschaft und Geistesgeschichte 1964.
Lane, W. G. A chord in melancholy: Hood's last years. Keats-Shelley Jnl 13 1964.

R. L. C.

III. MINOR POETRY 1800–1835

References

Rogers The modern Scottish minstrel, ed C. Rogers 6 vols Edinburgh 1855–7.
Miles The poets and poetry of the century, ed A. H. Miles et al 10 vols [1891–7], 12 vols 1905–7 (enlarged).

Numerals refer to vol-nos in these edns; numerals in brackets to the enlarged edn of Miles. Further information about some poets may be found in J. Julian, A dictionary of hymnology, 1892, 1907 (rev).

ROBERT ANDERSON

1770–1833

Collections

The poetical works. 2 vols Carlisle 1820. With autobiography, essay on the peasantry of Cumberland, and Observations on the style and genius of the author by T. Sanderson.
Dialogues, poems, songs and ballads, by various writers, in the Westmoreland and Cumberland dialects. Ed A. Wheeler 1839. Includes 35 poems by Anderson.
The songs and ballads of Cumberland; to which are added dialect and other poems. Ed S. Gilpin 1866, 3 vols 1874 (rev). Includes poems by Anderson.
Cumberland ballads. Ed S. Gilpin 1893.
Anderson's Cumberland ballads and songs. Ed T. Ellwood, Ulverston 1904.
Cumberland dialect: selections from the Cumberland ballads of Anderson. Ed G. Crowther, Ulverston 1907.

§1

Poems on various subjects. Carlisle 1798.
Ballads in the Cumberland dialect. Carlisle 1805, Wigton 1808, 1815 (enlarged), Carlisle 1823, 1828, Wigton 1834, Alnwick [1840], Wigton [1845?] (enlarged), Carlisle [1850?], 1864.

JOHN ANSTER

1793–1868

§1

Ode to fancy, with other poems. Dublin 1815.
Lines on the death of the Princess Charlotte of Wales. Dublin 1818.
Poems with some translations from the German. Edinburgh 1819.
Faustus: a dramatic mystery; The bride of Corinth; The first Walpurgis night, translated from the German of Goethe. 1835. Faustus, i.e. Faust pt 1, has often been rptd, e.g. ed H. Morley 1883; ed A. W. Ward 1907 (WC). Extracts appeared anon in Blackwood's Mag June 1820.
Xeniola: poems, including translations from Schiller and De La Motte Fouqué. Dublin 1837.
Faustus: the second part, from the German of Goethe. 1864; ed H. Morley 1886.
German literature at the close of the last century and the commencement of the present. In Lectures on literature and art delivered in Dublin, ser 2, 1864.
Anster was a contributor, mainly on literary topics, to Blackwood's Mag 1818–24, Dublin Univ Mag 1837–56 and North Br Rev 1847–55.

§2

Baumann, L. In her Die englischen Übersetzungen von Goethes Faust, Halle 1907.

EDWIN ATHERSTONE

1788–1875

Selections

Miles 2.

§1

The last days of Herculaneum; and Abradates and Panthea: poems. 1821.
A midsummer day's dream: a poem. 1824.
The fall of Nineveh: a poem. 2 vols 1828–30, 1847 (enlarged), 1868 (further enlarged).
The sea-kings in England: an historical romance. 3 vols Edinburgh 1830. In prose; anon.
The handwriting on the wall: a story. 3 vols 1858. In prose.
Israel in Egypt: a poem. 1861.
The dramatic works. Ed M. E. Atherstone 1888. Includes Pelopidas; Philip: Love, poetry, philosophy and gout.

§2

[Jeffrey, F.] Atherstone's Fall of Nineveh. Edinburgh Rev 48 1828.
[Wilson, J.] The fall of Nineveh. Blackwood's Mag Feb 1830.

JOANNA BAILLIE

1762–1951

Collections

Complete poetical works. Philadelphia 1832.
Dramatic and poetical works. 1851, 1851 (with memoir), 1853.

§1

Fugitive verses. [1790?], 1840 (enlarged), 1842.
A series of plays in which it is attempted to delineate the stronger passions of the mind. Vol 1 [includes Count Basil; The tryal; De Monfort] 1798 (anon), 1799 (anon), 1800, 1802, 1806; vol 2 [includes The election; Ethwald; The second marriage] 1802, 1802, 1806; vol 3 [includes Orra; The dream; The siege; The beacon] 1812; vols 1–3 1821; vols 1–2 tr German, 1806.
Basil. Philadelphia 1811; tr German, 1807.
De Monfort. 1808 (in British theatre vol 24, with remarks by Mrs Inchbald), New York 1809.
The election. Philadelphia 1811.
Orra. New York 1812.
The siege. New York 1812.
The beacon. New York 1812.
Miscellaneous plays. 1804, 1805. Includes Rayner; The country inn; Constantine Paleologus: or the last of the Caesars.
The family legend: a tragedy. Edinburgh 1810, 1810, New York 1810.
Metrical legends of exalted characters. 1821, 1821.
Poetical miscellanies. 1822. Includes poems by Scott, Mrs Hemans et al.
A collection of poems from living authors, edited by J. Baillie. 1823.
The martyr: a drama. 1826.
The bride: a drama. 1828, 1828.
A view of the general tenour of the New Testament regarding the nature and dignity of Jesus Christ. 1831, 1838.
Dramas. 3 vols 1836. Includes Romiero; The alienated manor; Henriquez; The martyr; The separation; The stripling; The phantom; Enthusiasm; Witchcraft; The homicide; The bride; The match.
Ahalya Baee: a poem. 1849 (priv ptd), Allahabad 1904.

Letters

Plarr, V. G. Sir Walter Scott and Joanna Baillie. Edinburgh Rev 216–17 1912–13.
Unpublished letters of Joanna Baillie to a Dumfriesshire Laird. Ed W. H. O'Reilly, Trans Dumfriesshire & Galloway Natural History & Antiquarian Soc 3rd ser 18 1934.
Sutton, D. Joanna Baillie and Sir George Beaumont. N & Q 26 Feb 1938.
Cunningham, W. R. Mrs Hemans at Mount Rydal. TLS 23 Oct 1943. Letter from Joanna Baillie.

§2

Gilfillan, G. In his Galleries of literary portraits vol 1, 1856.
Pieszczek, R. Joanna Baillie: ihr Leben, ihre dramatischen Theorien und ihre Leidenschaftsspiele. Berlin 1910.
Badstuber, A. Joanna Baillies Plays on the passions. Vienna 1911.
Meynell, A. In her Second person singular and other essays, 1921.
Carhart, M. S. The life and work of Joanna Baillie. New Haven 1923. With bibliography.
Carswell, D. Sir Walter: a four-part study in biography. 1930. On Scott's relations with Hogg, Lockhart, Joanna Baillie.
Evans, B. In his Gothic drama from Walpole to Shelley, Berkeley 1947. Ch 11.
Norton, M. The plays of Joanna Baillie. RES 23 1947.
Insch, A. G. Joanna Baillie's De Monfort in relation to her theory of tragedy. Durham Univ Jnl 54 1962.

JOHN BANIM

1798–1842

See col 707, below.

RICHARD HARRIS BARHAM

1788–1845

§1

Verses spoken at St Paul's School. 1807. Copy in Bodley.

Baldwin, or a miser's heir: a serio-comic tale, by an old bachelor. 2 vols 1820. In prose.

The Ingoldsby legends: or mirth and marvels, by Thomas Ingoldsby esquire. Illustr G. Cruikshank, J. Leech and J. Tenniel 3 sers 1840–7 (many reissues); ser 3, ed R. H. D. Barham 1847 (with memoir); Philadelphia 1860; ed E. A. Bond 3 vols 1894; illustr A. Rackham 1898, 1907 (rev); ed J. B. Atlay 2 vols 1903; selections ed H. Newbolt [1910], ed J. Tanfield and G. Boas 1951. Many other selections and edns of single legends. First ptd in Bentley's Monthly Miscellany and New Monthly Mag from 1837.

Some account of my cousin Nicholas. 3 vols 1841, 1 vol 1846, 1856. A novel rptd from Blackwood's Mag 1834.

Personal reminiscences by Barham, Harness and Hodder. Ed R. H. Stoddard, New York 1875.

The Ingoldsby lyrics, by Thomas Ingoldsby, edited by his son. 1881. Partly from The Ingoldsby legends, partly from other sources.

The Garrick Club: notices of one hundred and thirty-five of its former members. [New York?] 1896 (priv ptd).

Letters

Barham, R. H. D. The life and letters of Barham. 2 vols 1870, 1 vol 1880, 1899.

§2

Horne, R. H. In his A new spirit of the age, 1844.

Saintsbury, G. Three humourists: Hook, Barham, Maginn. In his Essays in English literature 1780–1860 ser 2, 1895.

Elwin, M. In his Victorian wallflowers, 1934.

The Ingoldsby legends. TLS 26 Dec 1936.

Sadleir, M. Ingoldsby legends: first series. TLS 14 April 1945.

Mirth and marvels: Ingoldsby after a hundred years. TLS 16 June 1945.

Gettmann, R. A. Barham and Bentley. JEGP 61 1957.

Lane, W. G. The primitive muse of Thomas Ingoldsby. Harvard Lib Bull 12 1958.

EATON STANNARD BARRETT

1786–1820

See col 709, below.

BERNARD BARTON

1784–1849

Selections

Selections from the poems and letters of Barton. Ed L. Barton 1849 (with memoir by E. FitzGerald), Philadelphia 1850, London 1853.

Miles 10 (11).

§1

Metrical effusions. 1812.

The triumph of the Orwell. Woodbridge [1817].

The convict's appeal. 1818.

Poems by an amateur. 1818.

A day in autumn: a poem. 1820.

Poems. 1820, 1821 (with addns), 1822, 1285, Augusta Maine 1825.

Napoleon, and other poems. 1822.

Verses on the death of P. B. Shelley. 1822.

Minor poems. 1824.

Poetic vigils. 1824.

Devotional verses: founded on, and illustrative of, select texts of Scripture. 1826.

A missionary's memorial: or verses on the death of J. Lawson. 1826.

A widow's tale and other poems. 1827.

A New Year's Eve, and other poems. 1828.

Bible letters for children [by Lucy Barton], with introductory verses by Bernard Barton. 1831, [1857?] (6th edn).

Fisher's juvenile scrap-book. 1836. Ed Barton; the 1837 and 1839 nos ed Barton and Agnes Strickland.

The reliquary, with a prefatory appeal for poetry and poets. 1836. With Lucy Barton.

Household verses. 1845, Philadelphia 1846.

Sea-weeds, gathered at Aldborough. Woodbridge 1846 (priv ptd).

A memorial of J. J. Gurney. 1847.

A brief memorial of Major Edward Moor FRS. Woodbridge 1848.

Birthday verses at sixty-four. Woodbridge 1848.

Ichabod! Woodbridge 1848. Poems.

On the signs of the times. Woodbridge 1848. Poems.

The natural history of the Holy Land [by Lucy Barton], with poetical illustrations by Bernard Barton. [1856].

§2

[Lamb, C.?] London Mag Aug 1820. A review of Poems, 1820.

Lucas, E. V. Barton and his friends. 1893.

Ritchie, J. E. Christopher Crayon's recollections. 1898.

Unpublished letters from Edward FitzGerald to Barton. Scribner's Mag Aug 1922.

Terhune, A. M. The life of Edward FitzGerald. New Haven 1947. Ch 8.

Woodring, C. R. Letters from Barton to Robert Southey. Harvard Lib Bull 4 1950.

NATHANIEL THOMAS HAYNES BAYLY

1797–1839

Collections

Songs, ballads and other poems. Ed H. B. Bayly 2 vols 1844, 1 vol 1857. With memoir.

Miles 9 (10).

Songs of the affections, selected by W. L. Hanchant. 1932.

§1

Rough sketches of Bath, by Q in the corner. Bath 1817, 1817, 1818, London 1819, 1820 (enlarged).

Epistles from Bath: or Q's letters to his Yorkshire relations; and miscellaneous poems by Q in the corner. Bath 1817.

Parliamentary letters, and other poems, by Q in the corner. 1818, 1820.

The dandies of the present, and the macaronies of the past: a rough sketch by Q in the corner. Bath [1818].

The tribute of a friend. Oxford 1819.

Mournful recollections. Oxford 1820.

Outlines of Edinburgh, and other poems. 1822. Anon.

Erin, and other poems. Dublin 1822.

Fifty lyrical ballads. Bath 1829 (priv ptd).

Musings and prosings. Boulogne 1833.

Flowers of loveliness, by various artists, with poetical illustrations by T. H. Bayly. 1837.

Kindness in women: tales. 3 vols 1837, 1 vol 1862. In prose.

Weeds of witchery. 1837. Songs.

Songs and ballads. [1837?].

Bayly also wrote numerous dramatic pieces, including the farce Perfection, *1836; a novel,* The Aylmers *3 vols 1827; collections of songs with music, e.g.* Songs of the days of chivalry, with music by T. H. Severn, *1831; single-sheet quarto issues of popular songs, e.g.* I'd be a butterfly.

§2

Lang, A. In his Essays in little, 1891 (rev).
Sykes, W. The mistletoe bough. N & Q 24 Dec 1948.

ROBERT BLOOMFIELD

1766–1823

Bibliographies

Cranbrook, Earl of, and J. Hadfield. Some uncollected authors, 20: Bloomfield. Book Collector 8 1959.

Collections

The poems of Bloomfield [i.e. The farmer's boy and Rural tales]. Burlington NJ 1803, Wilmington Delaware 1803 (as The farmer's boy; Rural tales etc).
The poems of Bloomfield. 2 vols 1809. With prefaces by Bloomfield.
Collected poems. 2 vols 1817.
The poems of Bloomfield. New York 1821, 3 vols 1827, 1 vol 1831, 1835, Halifax 1847.
Poems by Bloomfield, the farmer's boy (illustrated). 1845.
The farmer's boy, and other poems. Philadelphia 1847.
Poetical works. Ed W. B. Rands [1855].
Poetical works. Illustr Birket Foster 1857, 1864.
The poetical works of Bloomfield and Henry Kirke White. 1871.
Miles 1.
A selection of poems. Ed R. Gant 1947.

§1

The farmer's boy: a rural poem. Ed C. Lofft 1800 (3 edns), 1801, New York 1801, Philadelphia 1801, Leipzig 1801, Baltimore 1803, New York 1803 (5th Amer edn), Paris 1804, London 1827 (15th Br edn), Glasgow 1828, Boston 1877, Darlington 1898, London 1941; tr Latin, 1801 (in part), 1804 (complete); French, 1802.
Rural tales, ballads and songs. 1802, 1802, New York 1802, London 1803, Leipzig 1803, Paris 1804, London 1806, 1826 (10th edn).
Good tidings, or news from the farm: a poem. 1804.
Wild flowers: or pastoral and local poetry. 1806, Philadelphia 1806, London 1809, 1816, 1819, 1826.
Nature's music: consisting of extracts from several authors, in honour of the harp of Aeolus. 1808.
The banks of Wye: a poem. 1811, Philadelphia 1812, London 1813, 1823.
The history of little Davy's new hat. 1815, 1817, Paris 1818, London 1824; ed W. Bloomfield 1878; tr French, 1818.
May day with the muses. 1822, 1822.
Hazelwood-hall: a village drama. 1823. In prose.
The remains of Bloomfield. [Ed J. Weston] 2 vols 1824.

Letters

Selections from the correspondence of Bloomfield. Ed W. H. Hart 1870.

§2

Views in Suffolk, Norfolk and Northamptonshire, illustrative of the works of Robert Bloomfield. 1806, 1818. With memoir by E. W. Brayley.
Hudson, W. H. Afoot in England. 1909. Ch 24.
Fairchild, A. H. R. Robert Bloomfield. SP 16 1919.
Unwin, R. The rural muse. 1954. Ch 5.

SIR ALEXANDER BOSWELL

1775–1822

Collections

The poetical works. Ed R. H. Smith, Glasgow 1871. With memoir.
Rogers 2.

§1

Songs chiefly in the Scottish dialect. Edinburgh 1802, 1803. Anon.
The spirit of Tintoc: a ballad. Edinburgh 1803. Anon.
Epistle to the Edinburgh reviewers. Edinburgh 1803. Anon.
Edinburgh: or the ancient royalty, by Simon Gray. [i.e. Boswell]. Edinburgh 1810. Verse.
Sir Albon: a fragment. [Edinburgh? 1811]. Anon.
Clan-Alpin's vow: a fragment. Edinburgh 1811, 1817 (priv ptd).
The tyrant's fall: a poem on Waterloo. Auchinleck 1815.
Skeldon haughs: or the sow is flitted. Auchinleck 1816.
The woo-creel: or the bill o' Bashan. Auchinleck 1816.
Songs in the justiciary opera, by C- M- and B- I.C.C. Auchinleck 1816. With 'interpolations' by Boswell.
Song for the Harveian anniversary. Edinburgh 1816.
Elegiac ode to the memory of Dr Harvey. In Andrew Duncan, Tribute of regard to the memory of Sir Henry Raeburn, Edinburgh 1824.
Boswell also separately pbd several short poems and satires, and rptd several 16th-century texts, mainly at the Auchinleck Press, under the title Frondes caducae, 1816–18.

CAROLINE ANNE BOWLES later SOUTHEY

1786–1854

Collections

Autumn flowers, and other poems. Boston 1844.
Mrs Southey's (Caroline Bowles) poems. New York [1846?].
The select literary works, prose and verse, of Mrs Caroline Southey. Hartford 1851.
The poetical works of Caroline Bowles Southey. 1867.
Miles 7 (8).

§1

Ellen Fitzarthur: a metrical tale. 1820, 1822. Anon.
The widow's tale and other poems. 1822. Anon; in verse.
Solitary hours. Edinburgh 1826 (anon), 1839. Prose and verse.
Chapters on churchyards. 2 vols Edinburgh 1829 (anon), 1 vol 1841, New York 1842.
The cat's tail, being the history of Childe Merlin: a tale by the Baroness de Katzleben. Edinburgh 1831. Verse.
Tales of the factories. 1833. Anon, in verse.
The birth-day: a poem in three parts, to which are added occasional verses. Edinburgh 1836.
Robin Hood: a fragment, by the late Robert Southey and Caroline Southey, with other fragments and poems by R.S. and C.S. Edinburgh 1847.

Letters

The correspondence of Robert Southey with Caroline Bowles. Ed E. Dowden, Dublin 1881.

§2

Coleridge, H. N. Modern English poetesses. Quart Rev 66 1840.
Courtney, J. In her Adventurous thirties, Oxford 1933. Ch 1.

Warner, O. Miss Bowles visits Southey. Country Life 2 May 1947.
Burnet, J. F. Caroline Bowles. Fortnightly Rev May 1953.

SIR JOHN BOWRING

1792–1872

Selections

Miles 10 (11).

§1

Observations on the state of religion and literature in Spain. 1819.
Specimens of the Russian poets; with preliminary remarks and biographical notices. 1820, Boston 1822, 2 pts 1821–3 (enlarged).
Matins and vespers: with hymns and occasional devotional pieces. 1823, 1824 (enlarged), 1841 ('altered and enlarged'), 1851, Boston 1853, London 1895.
Batavian anthology: or specimens of the Dutch poets; with remarks on the poetical literature and language of the Netherlands, to the end of the seventeenth century. 1824. With H. S. Van Dyk.
Peter Schlemihl: from the German of La Motte Fouqué [i.e. of Chamisso]. Illustr G. Cruikshank 1824, 1861 (3rd edn); illustr G. Browne 1910.
Ancient poetry and romances of Spain: selected and translated. 1824.
Hymns. 1825.
Servian popular poetry translated. 1827.
Specimens of the Polish poets, with notes and observations on the literature of Poland. 1827.
Sketch of the language and literature of Holland: being a sequel to his Batavian anthology. Amsterdam 1829; tr Dutch, 1829. Rptd from Foreign Quart Rev 4 1829.
Brieven van John Bowring, geschreven op eene reize door Holland, Friesland en Groningen. Leeuwarden 1830. Partly tr from letters to the Morning Herald 1828, with sketch of Friesian literature tr from Foreign Quart Rev 3 1829.
Poetry of the Magyars, preceded by a sketch of the language and literature of Hungary and Transylvania. 1830.
Cheskian anthology: being a history of the poetical literature of Bohemia; with translated specimens. 1832.
Minor morals for young people, illustrated in tales and travels, with engravings by G. Cruikshank and W. Heath. 3 pts 1834–9.
Manuscript of the Queen's Court: a collection of old Bohemian lyrics—epic songs, with other ancient Bohemian poems. Prague 1843.
The kingdom and people of Siam: with a narrative of a mission to that country in 1855. 2 vols 1857.
A visit to the Philippine Islands. 1859; tr Dutch, 1861; tr Spanish, 1876.
Ode to the Deity, translated from the Russian of [G.R.] Derzhavin. [Brighton? 1861].
Translations from A. [i.e. S.] Petöfi, the Magyar poet. 1866.
Hwa tsien ki, the flowery scroll: a Chinese novel. 1868.
A memorial volume of sacred poetry: to which is prefixed a memoir of the author, by Lady Bowring. 1873.
Autobiographical recollections; with a brief memoir by L. B. Bowring. 1877.
Bowring edited Westminster Rev *1824–36, and Bentham's* Collected works 1838–43.

Letters

Beer, R. Korrespondence J. Bowringa do Čech. Prague 1904.
Chudoba, F. Listy psané J. Bowringovi ve věcech české a slovanské literatury. Prague 1912.
Filipović, R. Bowring i Kopitar. Slavistična Revija (Ljubljana) 4 1951.

§2

Lulofs, B. H. Eenige toelichtingen en bedenkingen op des geleerden Dr Bowring. Groningen 1829.
Poetry of the Magyars. Fraser's Mag March, May 1830.
Dr Bowring's poetical translations. Edinburgh Rev 52 1831.
Contemporary orators: Dr Bowring. Fraser's Mag Oct 1846.
Jovanović, V. M. Bowring i srpska narodna poezija. Belgrade 1908.
—— La Guzla de Prosper Mérimée' (ch 10). Paris 1911.
Kraushar, A. Bowring, poeta angielski i Kazimierz Brodziński. Cracow 1916.
Subotic, D. P. Serbian popular poetry in English literature. Slavonic Rev 5 1927.
—— In his Yugoslav popular ballads, Cambridge 1932.
Nesbitt, G. L. In his Benthamite reviewing, New York 1934.
Costin, W. C. In his Great Britain and China 1833–60, Oxford 1937.
Wardle, A. C. Benjamin Bowring and his descendants. 1938. Ch 1.
Coleman, A. P. Bowring and the poetry of the Slavs. Proc Amer Philosophical Soc 84 1941. Includes bibliography of articles by Bowring and about him.
Sova, M. Bowring and the Slavs. Slavonic Rev 21 1943.
Scott, D. F. S. In his Some English correspondents of Goethe, 1949. Ch 6.
Bartle, G. F. Bowring and the Arrow War in China. Bull of John Rylands Lib 43 1961.
—— Bowring and the Chinese and Siamese commercial treaties. Bull of John Rylands Lib 44 1962.
—— George Borrow's 'old Radical'. N & Q July 1963. Includes detailed bibliographical notes.
Kowalska, A. Bowring: tłumacz poetów słowiańskich. Slavia Orientalis 12 1963.
—— Bowring. Łodz 1965.
Varannai, A. Bowring and Hungarian literature. Acta Litteraria 6 1963.

HENRY BOYD

1755?–1832

§1

A translation of the Inferno of Dante in English verse; to which is added a specimen of a new translation of the Orlando Furioso of Ariosto. 2 vols 1785.
Poems chiefly dramatic and lyric. Dublin 1793.
The Divina Commedia, translated into English verse. 3 vols 1802.
The penance of Hugo: a vision on the French revolution in the manner of Dante, translated from Vincenzo Monti, with two additional cantos. 1805.
The triumphs of Petrarch. 1807, 1906 (with introd by G. Biagi), San Francisco 1927.
Remarks on the fallen angels of Milton. In Poetical works of Milton, ed H. Todd 1809.

§2

Toynbee, P. In his Dante in English literature, 2 vols 1909.
Cunningham, G. F. In his Divine comedy in English: a critical bibliography, Edinburgh 1965.

BARBARINA BRAND (née WILMOT), Lady DACRE

1768–1854

§1

Ina: a tragedy. 1815 (3 edns). Verse.
Le canzoni di Petrarca. [1815?] (priv ptd). With trns.

Due canzoni del Petrarca. Rome 1818 (priv ptd). With trns.
[Due canzoni del Petrarca.] Naples 1819 (priv ptd). With trns.
Dramas, translations and occasional poems. 2 vols 1821 (priv ptd). Includes Ina and the trns from Petrarch; the latter were rptd in Ugo Foscolo, Essays on Petrarch, 1823.
Translations from the Italian. 1836 (priv ptd).
Frogs and bulls: a Lilliputian piece in three acts. 1838.
Lady Dacre also edited and revised the writings of her daughter Arabella Sullivan.

§2

A family chronicle. Ed G. Lyster 1908.

SIR SAMUEL EGERTON BRYDGES

1762–1837

See col 1269, below.

CHARLES BUCKE

1781–1846

See col 1271, below.

ALFRED BUNN

1796–1860

See col 1128, below.

GEORGE CANNING

1770–1827

See vol 2.

HENRY FRANCIS CARY

1775–1844

§1

An irregular ode to General Elliott. Birmingham [1788].
Sonnets and odes. 1788.
Ode to General Kosciusko. 1797.
The Inferno of Dante: with a translation in blank verse, notes and a life of the author. 2 vols 1805–6.
The vision: or Hell, Purgatory and Paradise of Dante, translated. 3 vols 1814, 1819, 2 vols Philadelphia 1822, 3 vols 1831, 1 vol 1844 etc; illustr G. Doré 2 vols 1866; ed P. Toynbee 1900–2; ed E. Gardner 1908 (EL); illustr J. Flaxman 1910 (with Botticelli drawings and the Italian text), 1928.
The birds of Aristophanes, translated. 1824.
Pindar in English verse. 1833.
Lives of English poets, from Johnson to Kirke White. 1846. Rptd from London Mag Aug 1821–Dec 1824.
The early French poets: notices and translations. 1846; ed T. E. Welby [without French texts] 1923, New York 1925. Rptd from London Mag Nov 1821–April 1824.
Cary edited the poetical works of Pope and Cowper, 1839, and of Milton, Thomson and Young, 1841.

§2

[Foscolo, U.] Dante. Edinburgh Rev 29 1818. Sir J. Mackintosh and Samuel Rogers assisted Foscolo.
[Coleridge, H. N.] Translations of Pindar. Quart Rev 51 1834.
Cary, H. Memoir of the Rev H. F. Cary. 2 vols 1847.
Toynbee, P. In his Dante in English literature from Chaucer to Cary, 2 vols 1909.
—— The centenary of Cary's Dante. MLR 7 1912.
Farinelli, A. Dante in Inghilterra. In his Dante in Spagna, Francia [etc], Turin 1922.
King, R. W. The translator of Dante: the life, work, and friendships of Cary. 1925.
Gosse, E. Cary's Early French poets. In his Silhouettes, 1925.
Cenami, V. La Divina Commedia nelle traduzioni di Longfellow e di Cary. Lucca 1933.
Lowes, J. L. La belle dame sans merci and Dante. TLS 3 May 1934.

JOHN CASTILLO

1792–1845

A specimen of the Bilsdale dialect. Northallerton 1831.
Awd Isaac, The steeple chase and other poems. Whitby 1843.
The bard of the dales, or poems partly in the Yorkshire dialect. 1850, Stokesley 1858 (enlarged, with life).
Jacob's ladder. Filey 1858. A sermon.
Poems in the North Yorkshire dialect. Ed G. M. Tweddell, Stokesley 1878.

RICHARD COBBOLD

1797–1877

See col 717, below.

HARTLEY COLERIDGE

1796–1849

See Samuel Taylor Coleridge, col 211, above.

Collections

Poems, with a memoir by his brother [Derwent Coleridge]. 2 vols 1851, 1851.
The poetical works of Bowles, Lamb and Hartley Coleridge. Ed W. Tirebuck 1887.
Miles 3.
Poems. Ed W. Bailey-Kempling, Ulverston 1903.
Poems. 1907.
Complete poetical works. Ed R. Colles [1908] (ML).

§1

Poems. Vol 1 (all pbd), Leeds 1833, 1833 (as Poems, songs and sonnets).
Biographia borealis: or lives of distinguished northerns. Leeds 1833, London 1836 (as The worthies of Yorkshire and Lancashire); [ed D. Coleridge] 3 vols 1852 (as Lives of northern worthies).
Lives of illustrious worthies of Yorkshire. Hull 1835. Part of the Biographia borealis, above, reissued with new title-page.
The dramatic works of Massinger and Ford, with an introduction by H. Coleridge. 1840, 1848, 1851.
Essays and marginalia. [Ed D. Coleridge] 2 vols 1851.
Ascham, R., The scholemaster, with memoir by H. Coleridge. 1884. Rptd from Biographia, above.

Essays on parties in poetry and on the character of Hamlet. Ed J. Drinkwater, Oxford 1925, New York 1925.
New poems, including a selection from his published poetry. Ed E. L. Griggs 1942.
On the death of Mary Fleming. TLS 15 March 1947. Unpbd poem transcribed by A. S. Whitefield.

Letters

Letters of Hartley Coleridge. Ed G. E. and E. L. Griggs, Oxford 1936.
Hartman, H. A letter of Hartley Coleridge. Colophon new ser 3 1938.
Curry, K. A letter of Hartley Coleridge. RES 20 1944.
Griggs, E. L. Four letters of Hartley Coleridge. HLQ 9 1946.

§2

Horne, R. H. In his A new spirit of the age, 1844.
Bagehot, W. In his Literary studies, 1879.
Turner, A. M. Wordsworth and Hartley Coleridge. JEGP 22 1923.
Williams, S. T. Hartley Coleridge as a critic of literature. Southern Atlantic Quart 23 1924.
Hall, W. C. Hartley Coleridge. Manchester Quart 51 1925.
Pomeroy, M. J. The poetry of Hartley Coleridge. Washington 1927.
Griggs, E. L. Hartley Coleridge: his life and work. 1929. With bibliography.
— Coleridge and his son. SP 27 1930.
— Hartley Coleridge on his father. PMLA 46 1931.
— Hartley Coleridge's unpublished correspondence. London Mercury June 1931.
Blunden, E. Coleridge the less. In his Votive tablets, 1931.
Hartman, H. Hartley Coleridge, poet's son and poet. 1931. With bibliography.
Rea, J. D. Hartley Coleridge and Wordsworth's Lucy. SP 28 1931.
Little, G. L. Hartley Coleridge, Wordsworth and Oxford. N & Q Sept 1959.

GEORGE COLMAN the younger
1762–1836

See vol 2.

JOSIAH CONDER
1789–1855

Selections

Miles 10 (11).

§1

The associate minstrels. 1810 (anon), 1813 (anon). Poems by Conder and others, ed Conder.
Reviewers reviewed: including an enquiry into the moral and intellectual effects of habits of criticism, by J. C. O'Reid [i.e. Conder]. Oxford 1811.
Gloria in excelsis Deo. 1812.
The star in the east, with other poems. 1824.
The law of the sabbath, religious and political. 1830, 1852 (rev), 1853.
The modern traveller. 30 vols 1830.
Italy. 3 vols 1831.
The congregational hymn-book. 1834, 1836.
Illustrations of the Pilgrim's progress; with a sketch of the life and writings of Bunyan. [1836]. Life of Bunyan rptd in Pilgrim's progress, ed W. Mason 1838 etc.
The choir and the oratory: or praise and prayer. 1837. A collection of poems.
The literary history of the New Testament. 1845. Anon.
The poet of the sanctuary: a centenary commemoration of Isaac Watts. 1851.
Hymns of prayer, praise and devout meditation, prepared for publication by the author. Ed E. R. Conder 1856.
Conder wrote a number of other works on religious, political, geographical and literary subjects, and edited Eclectic Rev 1814–36, *and* Patriot 1833–55.

§2

Keble, J. Sacred poetry. Quart Rev 32 1825; rptd in Occasional papers and reviews, ed E. B. Pusey 1877, and in English critical essays: nineteenth century, ed E. D. Jones, Oxford 1916 (WC). A review of The star in the east.
Conder, E. R. Conder: a memoir. 1857.

LOUISA STUART COSTELLO
1799–1870

The maid of the Cyprus isle and other poems. 1815, 1815.
Redwald: a tale of Mona, and other poems. Brentford 1819.
Songs of a stranger. 1825.
Specimens of the early poetry of France, from the time of the troubadours and trouvères to the reign of Henri Quatre. 1835, [1877] (with The book of French songs, tr J. Oxenford).
The rose garden of Persia. 1845, 1899, 1913, 1924. Trns from Persian poetry.
The lay of the stork: a poem. 1856.
Louisa Costello also pbd books of travel and historical memoirs, mainly concerned with France.

JOSEPH COTTLE
1770–1853

§1

Poems, containing John the Baptist; Sir Malcolm and Alla: a tale; War: a fragment; with A monody to John Henderson, and a sketch of his character. Bristol 1795.
Malvern hills: a poem. 1798, 1802 (3rd edn), 2 vols 1829 (with appendix of essays in prose).
Alfred: an epic poem. 1801, 2 vols 1804, Newbury-port 1814, London 1816, 1 vol 1850.
A new version of the Psalms of David. 1801, 1805.
John the Baptist: a poem. 1802. Rptd from Poems, 1795, above.
The fall of Cambria: a poem. 2 vols 1808, 1811.
Messiah: a poem. 1815.
An expostulatory epistle to Lord Byron. 1820.
Dartmoor, and other poems. 1823.
Hymns and sacred lyrics. 1828.
Early recollections, chiefly relating to the late Samuel Taylor Coleridge. 2 vols 1837, 1 vol 1847 (rev as Reminiscences of Coleridge and Southey), New York 1848.
Mr Cottle and the Quarterly Review. [Bristol 1839]. A 'second preface' to Early recollections, 1837, above.
Cottle also edited, with Southey, the works of Thomas Chatterton, 1803, and pbd some theological prose.

§2

Gibbs, W. E. Unpublished letters concerning Cottle's Coleridge. PMLA 49 1934.
Whalley, G. The Bristol Library borrowings of Southey and Coleridge 1793–8. Library 5th ser 4 1949. Appendix B: Borrowings by Joseph Cottle.

JOHN WILSON CROKER

1780–1857

See col 1275, below.

GEORGE CROLY

1780–1860

Collections

The poetical works of the Rev George Croly. 2 vols 1830.

§1

Paris in 1815: a poem. 1817 (anon), 1818 (anon); second part, with other poems, 1821.
Lines on the death of Princess Charlotte. 1818.
The angel of the world: an Arabian tale; Sebastian: a Spanish tale, with other poems. 1820.
Gems principally from the antique, drawn by Richard Dagley, with illustrations in verse by George Croly. 1822.
Catiline: a tragedy, with other poems. 1822.
May Fair, in four cantos. 1827. Verse satire.
The beauties of the British poets, with a few introductory observations. 1828.
Salathiel: a story of the past, the present and the future. 3 vols 1828, 1829, 1842, 1 vol Cincinnati 1847, London 1855 (rev), 1858; ed L. Wallace and I.K.F., New York 1901 (as Tarry thou till I come), 1902; tr French, 1828. Prose.
Tales of the Great St Bernard. 3 vols 1828 (anon), 1829 (anon), 2 vols New York 1829 (anon), 3 vols 1838, 1858 (rev). Prose.
The modern Orlando. Cantos 1–7 (all pbd), 1846, 1848, 1855.
Marston: or the soldier and statesman. 3 vols 1846, 1 vol 1860. A novel.
Scenes from scripture, with other poems. 1851.
Psalms and hymns for public worship. 1854. Partly original, partly compiled.
The Book of Job, with a memoir by F. W. Croly. 1863.
Croly also pbd numerous sermons and other theological works, e.g. The Apocalypse of St John: a new interpretation, 1827; *historical and biographical works, e.g. on George IV, 1830, and Burke, 1840; edns of Jeremy Taylor and Pope's poems; and voluminous contributions to periodicals, including Blackwood's Mag and Literary Gazette. 4 stories were rptd anon in* Tales from Blackwood vols 9–11 [1861].

§2

Gilfillan, G. In his A second gallery of literary portraits, Edinburgh 1850.
Herring, R. A few personal recollections of Croly, with extracts from his speeches and writings. 1861.
Strout, A. L. Croly and Blackwood's Magazine. TLS 6 Oct 1950.
Boyle, A. Portraiture in Lavengro, 4 (2). N & Q 27 Oct 1951.

ALLAN CUNNINGHAM

1784–1842

See col 717, below.

ROBERT CHARLES DALLAS

1754–1824

See col 719, below.

GEORGE DANIEL

1789–1864

See col 1276, below.

GEORGE DARLEY

1795–1846

Bibliographies

Woolf, C. Some uncollected authors, 28: Darley. Book Collector 10 1961.

Collections

Selections from the poems of Darley. Ed R. A. Streatfeild 1904.
Complete poetical works. Ed R. Colles [1908] (ML).

§1

The errors of ecstasie: a dramatic poem, with other pieces. 1822.
The labours of idleness: or seven nights entertainments, by Guy Penseval. 1826, 1829 (as vol 2 of The new sketch book). Prose sketches.
Essays and sketches by the late R. Ayton, with a memoir [by Darley?]. 1825.
A system of popular geometry. 1826, 1844 (5th edn).
A system of popular algebra. 1827, 1836 (3rd edn).
A system of popular trigonometry. 1827, 1835.
Sylvia, or the May queen: a lyrical drama. 1827; ed J. H. Ingram 1892.
The geometrical companion. 1828, 1841.
The sorrows of hope. In The anniversary, ed A. Cunningham 1828.
The new sketch book, by Geoffrey Crayon jun. 2 vols 1829. Vol 2 consists of the unused sheets of Labours of idleness, above.
Familiar astronomy. 1830.
Nepenthe. 1835 (priv ptd); ed R. A. Streatfeild 1897.
Syren songs. In The tribute, ed R. M. Milnes 1837.
Thomas à Becket: a dramatic chronicle. 1840.
The works of Beaumont and Fletcher, with an introduction by G. Darley. 2 vols 1840.
Ethelstan, or the battle of Brunanburh: a dramatic chronicle. 1841.
Poems of the late George Darley, a memorial volume printed for private circulation. Liverpool [1889].

Letters

Abbott, C. C. The life and letters of Darley, poet and critic. Oxford 1928. With bibliography.
— Further letters of Darley. Durham Univ Jnl 33 1940.
Darley contributed to London Mag Dec 1822–March 1825, including 6 letters to the dramatists of the day, signed 'John Lacy'; The characteristic of the present age of poetry, April 1824; *and some lyrics and 'dramaticles'; to Athenaeum 1834–46 (reviews and articles on literature and fine art, and some lyrics); to Bentley's Miscellany 1844 (short stories and poems); and to Illuminated Mag 1844 (short stories and poems).*

§2

Streatfeild, R. A. A forgotten poet: Darley. Quart Rev 196 1902.
Meynell, A. In her Second person singular and other essays, 1921.
Looker, S. J. Cotton and Darley. TLS 29 Jan 1925.
Blunden, E. Darley and his latest biographer [C. C. Abbott]. TLS 14 Feb 1929; rptd in his Votive tablets, 1931.
Greene, G. George Darley: London Mercury March 1929; rptd in his Lost childhood and other essays, 1951.

Bridges, R. In his Collected essays, papers vol 5, Oxford 1931. Written 1906.
Wolff, L. Darley, poète et critique d'art. Revue Anglo-américaine 8 1931.
The poet of solitude. TLS 23 Nov 1946.
Haddow, G. C. George Darley: a centenary sketch. Queen's Quart 53 1946.
Abbott, C. C. The significance of Darley. Durham Univ Jnl 39 1947.
Heath-Stubbs, J. In his Darkling plain: a study of the later fortunes of romanticism in English poetry from Darley to W. B. Yeats, 1950.

THOMAS DERMODY
1775–1803

Collections

The harp of Erin: containing the poetical works of the late Thomas Dermody. [Ed J. G. Raymond] 2 vols 1807.

§1

Poems. Dublin 1789, London 1800 (as Poems moral and descriptive).
Poems: consisting of essays, lyric, elegiac etc. Dublin 1792.
The rights of justice. [Dublin?] 1793. Prose.
Poems on various subjects. 1802.
The histrionade: or theatric tribunal, a poem by Marmaduke Myrtle [i.e. Dermody]. 1802.

Letters

Mabbott, T. O. Dermody: three letters. N & Q 26 May 1934.
— Another letter, N & Q 7 Oct 1939.

§2

Raymond, J. G. The life of Dermody. 2 vols 1806.
[Jeffrey, F.] Raymond's Life of Dermody. Edinburgh Rev 8 1806.
Morgan, S. Memoirs of Lady Morgan. Ed W. H. Dixon and G. E. Jewsbury 2 vols 1862.
Mabbott, T. O. Mrs Browning's possible reminiscence of Dermody. N & Q 21 Oct 1939.

SIR AUBREY DE VERE (originally HUNT)
1788–1846

Selections

Miles 2.

§1

Ode to the Duchess of Angouleme. 1815. Anon.
Julian the apostate: a dramatic poem. 1822, 1823, 1858 (with The Duke of Mercia, below).
The Duke of Mercia: a drama; and other poems. 1823.
A song of faith, devout exercises and sonnets. 1842.
Mary Tudor: an historical drama. 1847, 1884 (with memoir by A. T. De Vere); adapted by A. Mellersh, Torquay [1914].
Sonnets: a new edition. 1875 (with memoir by A. T. De Vere).
For criticism see A. T. De Vere, col 1628, below.

CHARLES DIBDIN the Younger
1768–1833

See col 1129, below.

THOMAS JOHN DIBDIN
1771–1841

See col 1129, below.

ISAAC D'ISRAELI
1766–1848

See col 1277, below.

THOMAS DOUBLEDAY
1790–1870

Sixty-five sonnets, with prefatory remarks on the accordance of the sonnet with the powers of the English language. 1818. Anon.
The fisher's garland for 1821. Newcastle-on-Tyne 1821. With R. Roxby; anon. Doubleday often contributed to this series till 1864. The series was partly collected in the Coquet-dale fishing songs, now first collected by a north country angler [i.e. Doubleday], 1852, and more fully in A collection of right merrie garlands for north country anglers, ed J. Crawhall, Newcastle-on-Tyne 1864.
The Italian wife: a tragedy. 1823. Anon.
Babington: a tragedy. 1825.
Dioclesian: a dramatic poem. 1829.
Caius Marius, the plebeian consul: a historical tragedy. 1836.
On mundane moral government: demonstrating its analogy with the system of material government. 1852.
The political life of Sir Robert Peel. 2 vols 1856.
The eve of St Mark: a romance of Venice. 2 vols 1857, 1 vol 1864. Prose.
A letter to the Duke of Northumberland on the ancient Northumbrian music. 1857.
The touchstone: a series of letters on social, literary and political subjects, originally published in the Newcastle Daily Chronicle under the signature of Britannicus. 1863.
Matter for materialists: a series of letters in vindication and extension of the principles regarding the nature of existence of Dr [George] Berkeley. 1870.
Doubleday also pbd several works on population and other political and social subjects.

GEORGE DYER
1755–1841

§1

An inquiry into the nature of subscription to the 39 Articles. [1789], 1792 (enlarged).
Poems. 1792.
The complaints of the poor people of England. 1793, 1793.
Slavery and famine, punishments for sedition: or an account of the miseries and starvation at Botany Bay. 1794, 1794 (as Slavery etc: an account of New South Wales).
A dissertation on the theory and practice of benevolence. 1795; rptd in Pamphleteer, vols 13–14, 1818–19.
Memoirs of the life and writings of Robert Robinson. 1796.
The poet's fate: a poetical dialogue. 1797, 1797 (rev).
An address to the people of Great Britain on the doctrines of libels. 1799.
Poems. 1801 (BM copy has cancelled title-page and preface, 1800), 2 vols 1802.
Poems and critical essays. 1802.

Poetics: or a series of poems and disquisitions on poetry. 2 vols 1812.
Four letters on the English constitution. 1812, 1817 (3rd edn enlarged); rptd in Pamphleteer, vol 12 1818.
History of the university and colleges of Cambridge. 2 vols 1814.
The privileges of the university and colleges of Cambridge. 2 vols 1824.
Academic unity. 1827.
Dyer contributed to Analytical Rev, Critical Rev, Reflector and Monthly Mag.

§2

Lucas, E. V. The life of Charles Lamb. 2 vols 1905.
Adams, M. R. Dyer and English radicalism. MLR 35 1940; rptd in his Studies in the literary backgrounds of English radicalism, Lancaster Pa 1947.
Payne, E. A. The Baptist connections of Dyer. Baptist Quart new ser 10 1941.
Beales, H. L. Dyer, friend of Charles Lamb. Listener 7 July 1949.
Whalley, G. The date of two letters from Coleridge to Dyer 1795. N & Q 15 Oct 1949.
Shuman, R. B. Southey and Dyer: an unpublished letter. N & Q Jan 1961.

CHARLOTTE ELLIOTT
1789–1871

Selections

Selections from the poems of Charlotte Elliott, with a memoir by E. B[abington]. [1873]. The memoir was reissued [1875].
Miles 10 (11).
Words of hope and grace, with a biographical sketch. [1914].

§1

The invalid's hymn book. 1834, 1841, 1854 (6th edn). Includes Just as I am.
Hours of sorrow. 1836, 1856 (6th edn), 1869 (7th edn).
Morning and evening hymns for a week. Brighton 1836 etc.
Thoughts in verse on sacred subjects. 1869, 1871.
Leaves from the unpublished journals, letters and poems of Charlotte Elliott. [1874], [1878].
Charlotte Elliott also contributed hymns to the Christian Remembrancer pocket book, 1834, *which she edited, and to* Psalms and hymns, ed H. V. Elliott, Brighton 1835.

§2

Winslow, O. The king in his beauty: a tribute to the memory of Miss Charlotte Elliott. [1872].

EBENEZER ELLIOTT
1781–1849

Bibliographies

Eaglestone, A. A., E. R. Seary and G. L. Phillips. Ebenezer Elliott: a commemorative brochure with bibliography. Sheffield 1949. Lists many fugitive pieces.

Collections

[Poetical works] vol 1: The splendid village, Corn Law rhymes and other poems, 1834; vol 2: The village patriarch, Love and other poems, 1834; vol 3: Kerhonah, The vernal walk, Win hill and other poems, 1835. Reissued as The poetical works of Ebenezer Elliott, 3 vols 1844.
The poetical works. Edinburgh 1840.
The poems. Ed R. W. Griswold, Philadelphia 1844, New York 1850. Includes poems not found in other edns.
The poetical works. Ed E. Elliott 2 vols 1876.
Miles 2.
Ward, T. H. In English poets vol 4, 1911. Preface by E. Dowden.

§1

The vernal walk. Cambridge 1801, 1802. Anon.
The soldier and other poems, by Britannicus. Harlow 1810.
Night: a descriptive poem. 1818. Anon.
Peter Faultless to his brother Simon; Tales of night, in rhyme, and other poems, by the author of Night. Edinburgh 1820.
Love: a poem; The giaour: a satirical poem. 1823, 1823, 1831.
Scotch nationality: a vision. 1824, Sheffield 1875 (priv ptd).
The village patriarch: a poem. 1829, 1831.
Corn Law rhymes: the ranter. Sheffield 1830, 1831 (enlarged), 1831, 1904 (selection).
The splendid village: Corn Law rhymes, and other poems. 1833. Reissued 1834 as vol 1 of [Poetical works], above.
More verse and prose by the Cornlaw rhymer. 2 vols 1850. Contains review by Southey.

§2

Carlyle, T. Corn Law rhymes. Edinburgh Rev 55 1832; rptd in his Critical and miscellaneous essays, 1839.
Wilson, J. Poetry of Ebenezer Elliott. Blackwood's Mag May 1834; rptd in vol 6 of Works, Edinburgh 1856. Chiefly on Village patriarch.
Watkins, J. The life, poetry and letters of Ebenezer Elliott. 1850. Includes autobiographical fragment.
'Searle, January' (G. S. Phillips). The life, character and genius of Ebenezer Elliott. 1850, 1852.
Etienne, L. Les poètes des pauvres en Angleterre: 3, Ebenezer Elliott. Revue des Deux Mondes Sept 1856.
Odom, W. Two Sheffield poets: James Montgomery and Ebenezer Elliott. Sheffield 1929.
Phillips, G. L. Elliott's The giaour. RES 15 1939.
Seary, E. R. Robert Southey and Ebenezer Elliott. Ibid.
Hobman, J. B. Ebenezer Elliott: Corn law rhymer. Contemporary Rev Nov 1949.
Corn-Law rhymer. TLS 2 Dec 1949.
Briggs, A. Ebenezer Elliott, the Corn Law rhymer. Cambridge Jnl 3 1950.
James, L. Fiction for the working man. Oxford 1963. Appendix 1: Working-class poets and poetry.

THOMAS ERSKINE, Baron ERSKINE
1750–1823

See col 1280, below.

CATHERINE MARIA FANSHAWE
1765–1834

The aenigma. Ptd as Byron's in Three poems not included in the works of Lord Byron, 1818.
A collection of poems from living authors. Ed J. Baillie 1823. Includes a few poems by Catherine Fanshawe ptd for the first time.
Memorials of Miss C. M. Fanshawe. [Ed W. Harness], Westminster [1865] (priv ptd). Includes most of her poems.
Literary remains, with notes by W. Harness. 1876. Poems.

JOHN HOOKHAM FRERE

1769–1846

See vol 2.

JOHN GALT

1779–1839

See col 721, below.

WILLIAM GILBERT

1760?–1825?

§1

The hurricane: a theosophical and western eclogue; to which is subjoined A solitary effusion in a summer's evening. Bristol 1796.

§2

William Gilbert's Hurricane. Retrospective Rev 10 1824.
Cottle, J. In his Early recollections, 1837. Partly rptd in his Reminiscences of Coleridge and Southey, 1847.
Jeffery, S. Southey and Gilbert. TLS 20 March 1943.

ROBERT GILFILLAN

1798–1850

Original songs. Edinburgh 1831, 1835 (enlarged as Songs), 1839 (as Poems and songs), 1851 (with memoir [by W. Anderson]).
Rogers 3.

WILLIAM GLEN

1787–1826

Collections

Rogers 3.
The poetical remains of William Glen (with memoir by C. Rogers). Edinburgh 1874.

§1

Poems, chiefly lyrical. Glasgow 1815.
Songs on the late battles. Glasgow 1815.
The lonely isle: a south-sea island tale. Glasgow 1816.
Heath flowers: being a collection of poems, chiefly lyrical, written in the Highlands. Glasgow 1817.
The star of Brunswick. Lanark 1818.
The Glasgow Whigs of eighteen hundred and twenty-one. Glasgow 1821.

JAMES GRAHAME

1765–1811

See vol 2.

SIR ROBERT GRANT

1779–1838

Sacred poems. [Ed Charles Lord Glenelg] 1839, 1844, 1868.
Miles 10 (11).
Grant contributed hymns to Christian Observer 1806–15, and to Psalms and hymns, ed H. V. Elliott 1835. *His only separate pbns during his life were a few prose writings on the East India Company, e.g. a sketch of its history, 1813.*

JANET HAMILTON

1795–1873

§1

Poems and essays. Glasgow 1863.
Poems of purpose and sketches in prose of Scottish peasant life and character in auld lang syne. Glasgow 1865.
Poems and ballads. Glasgow 1868, 1873 (with essays by G. Gilfillan and A. Wallace).
Poems, essays and sketches. [Ed J. Hamilton] Glasgow 1870, 1880, 1885.

§2

Young, J. Pictures in prose and verse. Glasgow 1877. Includes Personal recollections of the late Janet Hamilton of Langloan.

REGINALD HEBER

1783–1826

Collections

Poetical works. 1841, Philadelphia 1841, London 1842, 1852 (with poems by F. Hemans and A. Radcliffe), 1854, [1878]. With poetical works of George Herbert [1861], [1881].
Miles 10 (11).

§1

A sense of honour: a prize essay. Oxford 1805, 1836.
Palestine: a prize poem. Oxford 1803 (priv ptd), 1807, London 1809, Oxford 1810, Philadelphia 1828 (with other poems), London 1843 (with other poems); tr Welsh, 1822; Armenian, 1830; Latin, 1844. Set to music by W. Crotch, 1812, Oxford 1827 as Palestine: a sacred oratorio. First pbd in Poetical register for 1802, 1803.
Europe: lines on the present war. 1809, 1809.
Poems and translations. 1812, 1829, Liverpool 1841.
The whole works of Jeremy Taylor. Ed Heber 1822. With life.
Hymns, written and adapted to the weekly church service of the year. [Ed A. Heber] 1827, 1828 (4th edn), 1834 (10th edn), 1849 (12th edn), 1867.
Select portions of psalms and hymns, with some compositions of a late distinguished prelate [i.e. Heber]. Welshpool 1827.
Narrative of a journey through India 1824–5. [Ed A. Heber] 2 vols 1828, 3 vols 1828 (2nd and 3rd edns), 1829 (4th edn), Philadelphia 2 vols 1829, London 2 vols 1844, 1846, 1849, 1873; tr Spanish 1860 (abridged)., Selection ed P. R. Krishnaswami 1923.
Sermons preached in England. [Ed A. Heber] 1829, 1829.
Sermons preached in India. [Ed A. Heber] 1829.
Sermons on the lessons, the Gospel or the Epistle, for every Sunday in the year. 3 vols 1837, 2 vols 1838 (3rd edn).
The lay of the purple falcon: a metrical romance [by R. Heber and R. Curzon, Baron Zouche]. 1847.
Blue-beard: a serio-comic oriental romance in one act. 1868, [1874]. Verse.
A number of sermons and charges were also pbd separately. Some hymns were first pbd in Christian Observer 1811–16.

Letters

The Heber letters 1782–1832. Ed R. H. Cholmondeley 1950. Includes 17 letters from R. Heber.

§2

Kaye, J. A valedictory address to the Bishop of Calcutta, with his Lordship's reply. 1823.

[Blunt, J. J.] The Church in India: Bishop Heber. Quart Rev 35 1827.
[Milman, H. H.] Psalmody. Quart Rev 38 1828.
[Jeffrey, F.] Bishop Heber's journal. Edinburgh Rev 48 1828.
Robinson, T. The last days of Bishop Heber. Madras 1829, 1830.
Some account of the life of Heber. 1829.
Heber, A. The life of Heber, by his widow. 2 vols 1830, 1 vol Boston 1861 (abridged as The life and writings, ed J. W. B.). Includes letters, unpbd poems and prose.
Smyth, T. S. The character and religious doctrines of Bishop Heber. 1831.
Bonner, G. Memoir of the life of Heber. Cheltenham 1833.
Taylor, T. Memoirs of the life and writings of Heber. 1835, 1836 (3rd edn).
Chambers, J. Bishop Heber and Indian missions. 1846.
Smith, G. Bishop Heber: poet and missionary. 1895.
Pittock, M. Cheshire poets: Reginald Heber. Cheshire Round 1 1964.

FELICIA DOROTHEA HEMANS, née BROWNE

1793–1835

Collections

The league of the Alps; The siege of Valencia; The vespers of Palermo; and other poems. Ed A. Norton, Boston 1826.
Poems. Hartford 1827 ('3rd American edn').
Poetical works of Mrs Felicia Hemans. 2 vols New York 1828, Philadelphia 1832, 1 vol Philadelphia 1836, 1836, 1842 (with critical preface and memoir), 1845, 1854.
The works of Mrs Hemans. Ed (with memoir) by her sister [H. Hughes] 7 vols Edinburgh 1839, Philadelphia 1840 (with An essay on her genius by L. H. Sigourney), 8 vols New York 1845, 2 vols New York 1847, 1 vol Edinburgh 1849 etc (chronologically arranged); ed W. M. Rossetti [1873], Oxford 1914.
Poems by Felicia Hemans, with An essay on her genius by H. T. Tuckerman. Ed R. W. Griswold, Philadelphia 1845, 1850.
Poetical works of Felicia Hemans (with memoir by L. H. Sigourney). Boston 1853, Philadelphia [1860?], Boston 1864.
Select poetical works. Leipzig 1865.
Favourite poems. Boston 1877.
Poetical works, reprinted from the early editions. Edinburgh 1886, 1891.
Miles 7 (8).
This list is not complete.

§1

Poems. Liverpool 1808.
England and Spain: or valour and patriotism. 1808. Verse.
The domestic affections, and other poems. 1812, 1843, 1844.
The restoration of the works of art to Italy. Oxford 1816, 1816. Verse.
Modern Greece: a poem. 1817, 1821.
Translations from Camoens and other poets. Oxford 1818.
Tales and historic scenes in verse. 1819, 1824.
Wallace's invocation to Bruce: a poem. Edinburgh 1819.
The sceptic. 1820, 1821 (with the following). Verse.
Stanzas to the memory of the late King. 1820, 1821 (with The sceptic, above).
Dartmoor: a poem. 1821.
Welsh melodies. 1822.
The vespers of Palermo. 1823, [1877?]. Verse tragedy.
The siege of Valencia: a dramatick poem; The last Constantine, with other poems. 1823.
The forest sanctuary, and other poems. 1825, Boston 1827, Edinburgh 1829 (enlarged); tr German, 1871.
Lays of many lands. 1825.
Hymns on the works of nature for the use of children. Boston 1827, 1833.
Records of woman, with other poems. 1828, 1828, Boston 1828, London 1830, 1834, 1837, 1850.
Songs of the affections, with other poems. Edinburgh 1830, Philadelphia 1860, 1873.
Hymns for childhood. Dublin 1834, 1839.
National lyrics and songs for music. Dublin 1834, 1836.
Scenes and hymns of life, with other religious poems. Edinburgh 1834.
Poetical remains. Edinburgh 1836. With memoir by Δ, i.e. D. M. Moir.
Early blossoms of spring, with a life of the authoress. 1840. Juvenile poems.
Mrs Hemans also contributed to numerous periodicals, including Blackwood's Mag, New Monthly Mag and Edinburgh Monthly Mag.

§2

[Jeffrey, F.] Felicia Hemans. Edinburgh Rev 50 1829; rptd in his Contributions to the Edinburgh Review, 1844.
A short sketch of the life of Mrs Hemans. 1835.
Chorley, H. F. Memorials of Mrs Hemans. 2 vols 1836, New York 1836, London 1837.
Gilfillan, G. In his A second gallery of literary portraits, Edinburgh 1850.
Ledderbogen, W. F. D. Hemans Lyrik. Kiel 1913.
Williams, I. A. Wordsworth, Mrs Hemans and R. P. Graves. London Mercury Aug 1922.
Rupprecht, W. K. Felicia Hemans und die englischen Beziehungen zur deutschen Literatur. Anglia 48 1924.
Duméril, E. Une femme poète au déclin du romantisme anglais: Felicia Hemans. Toulouse 1929. With bibliography.
Courtney, J. In her Adventurous thirties, Oxford 1933.
Cunningham, W. R. Mrs Hemans at Mount Rydal. TLS 23 Oct 1943.

JOHN ABRAHAM HERAUD

1799–1887

§1

The legend of St Loy, with other poems. 1820.
Tottenham: a poem. 1820.
The descent into Hell. 1830, 1835 (rev with addns).
An oration on the death of Coleridge. 1834.
The judgement of the flood. 1834, 1857 (rev). A poem.
The substance of a lecture on poetic genius. 1837.
Salvator, the poor man of Naples. 1845 (priv ptd). A dramatic poem.
Videna, or the mother's tragedy: a legend of early Britain. 1854.
Shakspere: his inner life. 1865.
The wreck of the London: a lyrical ballad. 1866.
The in-gathering. 1870. Poems.
The war of ideas: a poem. 1871.
Uxmal; Macé de Léodepart. 1877. Tales in prose and verse.
Only the more important of Heraud's writings in prose are listed here. He edited Sunbeam 1838–9 and Monthly Mag 1839–42, and contributed to Quart Rev, Athenaeum, Fraser's Mag and others.

§2

Heraud, E. Memoirs of Heraud. 1898.

WILLIAM HERBERT

1778–1847

Collections

Works. 3 vols 1842; Supplement, 1846.

§1

Musae etonenses. 3 vols 1795, Eton 1817. Ed Herbert.
Rhenus. [Oxford 1797]; tr in Translations of Oxford Latin prize poems by N. L. Torre, 1831.
Ossiani Darthula Graece reddita. 1801.
Select Icelandic poetry, translated from the originals with notes. 2 pts 1804–6.
Translations from the German, Danish etc; to which is added miscellaneous poetry. 1804.
Translations from the Italian, Spanish, Portuguese, German etc; to which is added miscellaneous poetry: part second. 1806. The above 3 items also pbd as Miscellaneous poetry, 2 vols 1806.
Helga: a poem in seven cantos. 1815, 1820.
Hedin: or the spectre of the tomb, from the Danish history. 1820. Verse.
Pia della Pietra. 1820.
The Guahiba: a tale. 1822. Verse.
The wierd wanderer of Jutland: a tragedy. 1822. Includes Julia Montalban: a tale. Both in verse.
Iris. York 1826. A Latin ode.
Attila: or the triumph of Christianity. 1838, 1841. An epic.
Sylvae recentiores. 1845.
The Christian. 1846. A poem.
Herbert also pbd sermons, and books and articles on botanical subjects, contributing notes to edns of Gilbert White's Selborne.

THEODORE EDWARD HOOK

1788–1841

See col 731, below.

MARY HOWITT

1799–1888

See col 1286, below.

JAMES HENRY LEIGH HUNT

1784–1859

See col 1216, below.

JAMES HYSLOP

1798–1827

Poems; with a sketch of his life, and notes on his poems, by P. Mearns. Glasgow 1887.

SAMUEL WILLIAM HENRY IRELAND

1777–1835

Bibliographies

Lowe, R. W. A bibliographical account of English theatrical literature. 1888. For contemporary pamphlets on Ireland's forgeries.

§1

Miscellaneous papers and legal instruments under the hand and seal of William Shakespeare. Ed S. Ireland 1796.
An authentic account of the Shaksperian manuscripts. 1796.
Vortigern: an historical tragedy; and Henry the Second: an historical drama, supposed to be written by the author of Vortigern. 2 pts 1799. Vortigern was rptd 1832 with facs of portions of the forged ms.
Ballads in imitation of the antient. 1801.
Mutius Scaevola: or the Roman patriot, an historical drama. 1801.
A ballade, written on the feastynge and merrimentes of Easter Maunday, laste paste, by Paul Persius, a learnedd clerke. 1802.
Rhapsodies. 1803.
The angler: a didactic poem. 1804.
The confessions of William Henry Ireland: containing the particulars of his fabrication of the Shakspeare manuscripts; together with anecdotes and opinions of many distinguished persons. 1805; ed R. G. White, New York 1874. An expansion of An authentic account, above.
Effusions of love from Chatelar to Mary, Queen of Scotland: interspersed with songs, sonnets and notes explanatory, by the translator. 1805, 1808.
All the blocks! or an antidote to 'all the talents': a satirical poem. 1807.
Stultifera navis: or the modern ship of fools. 1807.
The fisher boy: a poem. 1808.
The sailor boy: a poem. 1809, 1822.
Neglected genius: a poem, illustrating the untimely and unfortunate fate of many British poets, containing imitations of their different styles. 1812.
Chalcographimania: or the portrait-collector and print-seller's chronicle, a humourous poem. 1814.
Jack Junk: or the sailor's cruise on shore. 1814.
Scribbleomania: or the printer's devil's polichronicon. 1815.
The maid of Orleans. 1822. From Voltaire.
Ireland also pbd several novels and romances and much miscellaneous hackwork. Many of his writings were anon or pseudonymous.

§2

Ingleby, C. M. The Shakspeare fabrications [of J. P. Collier]; with an appendix on the authorship of the Ireland forgeries. 1859.
A., T. J. The Ireland forgeries. Fraser's Mag Aug 1860.
Bodde, D. Shakspere and the Ireland forgeries. Cambridge Mass 1930.
Libbis, G. H. Notes on Samuel and William Henry Ireland and the Shakespeare fabrications. N & Q 21–28 March 1931, 2, 16 April 1932.
Haraszti, Z. The Shakespeare forgeries of Ireland. Boston 1934.
Mair, J. The fourth forger. 1938.
Muir, P. H. The Ireland Shakespeare forgeries. Book Collector 1 1952.
Barnet, S. Charles Lamb and Ireland. N & Q Nov 1953.
Grebanier, B. The great Shakespeare forgery. New York 1965. With bibliography.

JOHN KEBLE

1792–1866

See col 1629, below.

JOHN KENYON
1784–1856

§1

Rhymed plea for tolerance. 1833, 1839 (rev with addns).
Poems, for the most part occasional. 1838.
A day at Tivoli, with other verses. 1849.

§2

Poems by Kenyon. Blackwood's Mag Dec 1838.

JAMES SHERIDAN KNOWLES
1748–1862

See col 1132, below.

LADY CAROLINE LAMB
1785–1828

See col 740, below.

CHARLES LAMB
1775–1834

See col 1223, below.

ROBERT EYRES LANDOR
1781–1869

Collections

Selections from his poetry and prose, with an introduction biographical and critical by E. Partridge. 1927. Also pbd in 2 pts: Selections from Robert Landor; Robert Eyres Landor: a biographical and critical sketch.

§1

An essay on the character and doctrines of Socrates. Oxford 1802. Anon.
Guy's porridge pot. 1808 (anon), 1809 (anon, with The dun cow roasted whole).
The Count Arezzi: a tragedy. 1824. Anon; verse.
The impious feast: a poem in ten books. 1828.
The Earl of Brecon: a tragedy. 1841. Containing also Faith's fraud: a tragedy; and The ferryman: a tragedy.
The fawn of Sertorius. 2 vols 1846. Anon; a novel.
The fountain of Arethusa. 2 vols 1848.

§2

Super, R. H. The authorship of Guy's porridge pot and the Dun cow. Library 5th ser 5 1950.
Czerwinski, R. Robert Landor and Guy's porridge pot. Library 5th ser 16 1961.

WALTER SAVAGE LANDOR
1775–1864

See col 12 10, below.

CHARLES VALENTINE LE GRICE
1773–1858

Bibliographies

Boase, G. C. and W. P. Courtney. Bibliotheca cornubiensis. Vol 1, 1874.

§1

An imitation of Horace's first epistle. Cambridge 1793, Penzance 1824, Truro 1850.
The Tineum. Cambridge 1794. Mock-heroic pieces in prose and verse.
A prize declamation on Richard Cromwell, and a speech to prove that the reign of Anne has been improperly called the Augustan age of English genius. Cambridge 1795.
Analysis of Paley's principles of moral and political philosophy. Cambridge 1795, 1796 (enlarged), London 1822 (8th edn).
A general theorem for a [Trinity] College declamation, with copious notes by Gronovius [i.e. Le Grice]. Cambridge 1796.
Daphnis and Chloe: a pastoral novel, now first selectly translated. Penzance 1803.
Petition of an old uninhabited house in Penzance to its master in town. Penzance [1811], 1823, 1858. A poem.
College reminiscences of Mr Coleridge, reprinted from the Gentleman's Magazine, December 1834, by desire. Penzance [1842]. Also rptd in J. Cottle, Reminiscences of Coleridge and Southey, 1847.

MATTHEW GREGORY LEWIS
1775–1818

See col 742, below.

JOHN LEYDEN
1775–1811

Bibliographies

Sinton, J. Bibliography of the life and writings of Leyden. In Journal of a tour in the Highlands and Western Islands of Scotland in 1800 by John Leyden, Edinburgh 1903.

Collections

Poetical remains. Ed R. Heber 1819. With memoir by J. Morton.
Rogers 2.
Poems and ballads. Kelso 1858, 1875. With memoir by W. Scott and supplement by R. White.
Poetical works. 1875. With memoir by T. Brown.

§1

A historical and philosophical sketch of the discoveries and settlements of the Europeans in northern and western Africa. 1799; tr French, 1804; 2 vols Edinburgh 1817 (enlarged as Historical account of discoveries and travels in Africa), 1818.
The complaynt of Scotland, written in 1548; with a preliminary dissertation and glossary [by J. Leyden]. Edinburgh 1801.
Scotish descriptive poems, with some illustrations of Scotish literary antiquities. Edinburgh 1803. Anthology ed J. Leyden; includes his Biographical sketch of John Wilson, which was rptd 1852, with the text of Wilson's Clyde: a poem.
Scenes of infancy: descriptive of Teviotdale. Edinburgh 1803, 1811, Jedburgh 1844, Kelso 1875 (with memoir by W. M. Tulloch).

Leyden contributed to M. G. Lewis, Tales of wonder, 1801, and assisted Scott with the earlier vols of Minstrelsy of the Scottish border, 1802. He was an authority on several oriental languages, publishing treatises and trns.

§2

[Scott, W.] Biographical memoir of Leyden. Edinburgh Annual Register for 1811, pt 2.
Reith, J. Life of Leyden. Galashiels [1908], [1923].
Aiyangar, S. An Anglo-Indian poet: Leyden. Madras 1912.

CHARLES LLOYD

1775–1839

§1

Poems on various subjects. Carlisle 1795.
Poems on the death of Priscilla Farmer, by her grandson. 1796.
Poems by S. T. Coleridge: second edition; to which are now added poems by Charles Lamb and Charles Lloyd. Bristol 1797. 28 poems by Lloyd.
Blank verse, by Charles Lloyd and Charles Lamb. 1798.
Edmund Oliver. 2 vols Bristol 1798. A novel.
A letter to the Anti-Jacobin reviewers. Birmingham 1799. On Edmund Oliver.
Lines suggested by the fast appointed on Wednesday, February 27, 1799. Birmingham 1799.
The tragedies of Vittorio Alfieri, translated. 3 vols 1815.
Nugae canorae: poems—third edition, with additions. 1819. Mainly new poems.
Isabel: a tale. 2 vols 1820. Prose.
Desultory thoughts in London; Titus and Gisippus, with other poems. 1821.
Memoirs of the life and writings of Vittorio Alfieri. 1821.
Poetical essays on the character of Pope as a poet and moralist, and on the language and objects most fit for poetry. 1821.
The Duke d'Ormond: a tragedy; and Beritola: a tale. 1822. Verse.
Poems. 1823.

Letters

The Lloyd-Manning letters. Ed F. L. Beaty, Bloomington 1957.

§2

[Southey, R.] Alfieri's life and writings. Quart Rev 14 1816.
[Lamb, C.] Nugae canorae: poems by Charles Lloyd. Examiner 24–25 Oct 1819; rptd in his Works, ed T. Hutchinson vol 1, 1908.
De Quincey, T. Reminiscences of Charles Lloyd. Tait's Mag 7 1840; rptd in his Collected writings, ed D. Masson vol 2, Edinburgh 1889.
Lucas, E. V. Charles Lamb and the Lloyds. 1898.
Hunt, H. C. Note on Lloyd. TLS 20 Feb 1937.
Zall, P. M. Hazlitt's 'romantic acquaintance': Wordsworth and Lloyd. MLN 71 1956.
Smith, H. R. Lloyd: the friend of the Lake poets. N & Q Dec 1956, Oct 1957.

SAMUEL LOVER

1797–1868

See col 744, below.

HENRY LUTTRELL

1765?–1851

§1

Lines written at Ampthill Park in the autumn of 1818. 1819, 1822 (with Letters to Julia).
Advice to Julia: a letter in rhyme. 1820, 1820.
Letters to Julia, in rhyme: third edition; to which are added Lines written at Ampthill-Park. 1822. Advice to Julia, above, rehandled and enlarged.
Crockford-House: a rhapsody in two cantos; A rhymer in Rome. 1827. 2 poems.

§2

Dobson, A. A forgotten poet of society. St James's Mag 33 1878; rptd as Luttrell's Letters to Julia in his Paladin of philanthropy, 1899.

HENRY FRANCIS LYTE

1793–1847

Collections

Miles 10 (11).
The poetical works. Ed J. Appleyard 1907.

§1

Tales in verse illustrative of the Lord's prayer. 1826, 1829.
Poems chiefly religious. 1833, 1841, 1845 (enlarged).
The spirit of the Psalms. 1834, 1836 (enlarged), [1864].
Silex scintillans etc, by Henry Vaughan. 1847, Boston 1856, London 1858, 1883. With memoir by Lyte.
Remains, with memoir [by his daughter Mrs Hogg]. 1850.
Miscellaneous poems. 1868, 1875. Reprint of Poems chiefly religious, 1845, above with Abide with me added.

§2

Appleyard, J. Henry Francis Lyte. 1939.
White, F. C. A link with Lyte. N & Q 13 Dec 1941.
Hunt, A. Abide with me. Bradford 1947.
Garland, H. J. Lyte and the story of Abide with me. Manchester 1957.

WILLIAM MAGINN

1793–1842

See col 1293, below.

RICHARD MANT

1776–1848

Selections

Miles 10 (11).

§1

Verses to the memory of Joseph Warton. Oxford 1800.
The poetical works of Thomas Warton, with a memoir by Mant. 2 vols Oxford 1802.
The country curate. Oxford 1804. Poems.
Poems. Oxford 1806.
The slave and other poetical pieces. Oxford 1807. Poems.
The simpliciad: a satirico-didactic poem. 1808. Anon.
The Book of Psalms in an English metrical version. 1824.
The holydays of the Church, with metrical sketches. 2 vols 1828–31.
The Gospel miracles: poetical sketches. 1832.
The happiness of the blessed; Musings on the Church. 1833, 1837 (4th edn), 1870. Prose and verse.
Christmas carols, with an introductory account of the Christmas carol. 1833.
The British months: a poem. 2 vols 1835.
Ancient hymns from the Roman Breviary. 1837, 1871. Includes original hymns by Mant.
The sundial of Armoy: a poem. Dublin 1847.
The matin bell. Oxford 1848. Poem.
The youthful Christian soldier, with spiritual songs and hymns. Dublin 1848. Prose and verse.

Mant also pbd numerous sermons and other prose works, including a History of the Church of Ireland, 2 vols 1840.

§2

Berens, E. Memoir of Bishop Mant. 1849.
Mant, W. R. Memoirs of Mant. Dublin 1857.

JOHN HERMAN MERIVALE

1779–1844

Collections

Poems original and translated, now first collected. 2 vols 1828–38, 3 vols 1844 (corrected).

§1

Translations chiefly from the Greek Anthology; with tales and miscellaneous poems. 1806. With R. Bland.
The minstrel: book the third [continuation of poem by James Beattie]. 1808.
Collections from the Greek Anthology, by R. Bland and others [including Merivale]. 1813, 1833 (3rd edn).
Orlando in Roncevalles: a poem. 1814.
The two first cantos of Richardetto, from the original of N. Fortiguerra. 1820.
The minor poems of Schiller, translated. 1844.
Leaves from the diary of a literary amateur. Ed E. H. A. Koch, Hampstead 1911.
Merivale contributed to Quart Rev, New Monthly Mag and GM. His pbns on legal subjects are not listed here.

RICHARD ALFRED MILLIKEN

1767–1815

See col 1899, below.

HENRY HART MILMAN

1791–1868

See col 1959, below.

JOHN MITFORD

1781–1859

§1

Agnes, the Indian captive; with other poems. 1811.
A letter to R. Heber esq on Mr Weber's edition of Ford. 1812.
Sacred specimens selected from the early English poets, with prefatory verses. 1827.
Lines suggested by a fatal shipwreck. 1855, Woodbridge 1856.
Cursory notes on various passages in the text of Beaumont and Fletcher, as edited by A. Dyce. 1856.
Miscellaneous poems. 1858.
The Rev John Mitford on cricket. Ed F. S. Ashley-Cooper, Nottingham 1921. Writings rptd from GM.
Mitford edited GM 1834–50, contributing frequently to it, and edited numerous edns of the English poets, chiefly in the Aldine ser 1830–9.

§2

Houstoun, M. C. Sylvanus redivivus: the Rev John Mitford. 1889, 1891 (as Letters and reminiscences of John Mitford).

MARY RUSSELL MITFORD

1787–1855

See col 748, below.

DAVID MACBETH MOIR

1798–1851

See col 750, below.

'WILLIAM THOMAS MONCRIEFF'

1794–1857

See col 1134, below.

JAMES MONTGOMERY

1771–1854

Bibliographies

Tallent-Bateman, C. T. James Montgomery: a literary estimate [with bibliography]. Papers of Manchester Lit Club 15 1889. Bibliography ptd in Reports and proceedings.

Collections

The poetical works of Rogers, James Montgomery [and others]. Paris 1829.
The poetical works, collected by himself. 4 vols 1841, 1 vol 1850, Philadelphia 1853, 4 vols 1855, 1858, Edinburgh [1870], London 1873, 1 vol [1879] (Lansdowne poets), [1879] (Chandos poets), [1881] (Landscape edn).
Poetical works. Ed (with memoir) R. W. Griswold 2 vols Philadelphia 1845, Boston 1853.
The poetical works. Ed (with memoir) R. Carruthers 5 vols Boston 1858, London 1860.
Poems, selected by R. A. Willmott, illustr Birket Foster. 1860.
Poems. 1861.

§1

The history of a church and a warming pan. 1793.
Prison amusements, by Paul Positive. 1797.
The whisperer: or tales and speculations by Gabriel Silvertongue. 1798.
The loss of the locks: a Siberian tale. 1800. Poem. No copy extant? Rptd in Memoirs of J. Montgomery by J. Holland and J. Everett vol 1, 1854.
The ocean. 1805. Poem. No copy extant?
The wanderer of Switzerland, and other poems. Sheffield 1806, 1806, London 1806, Boston 1807, Morris-town NJ 1811, Edinburgh 1815 (7th edn), London 1832 (11th edn), 1841 (13th edn).
Poems on the abolition of the slave trade. 1809. With J. Grahame and E. Benger. Illustr R. Smirke. Montgomery's The West Indies: a poem in four parts, was pbd separately in 1809, and also in 1814 as The abolition of the slave trade.
The West Indies and other poems. 1810, New Brunswick NJ 1811, London 1828 (7th edn).
The world before the flood: a poem in ten cantos, with other occasional pieces. 1813, New York 1814, London 1823 (6th edn), 1826 (7th edn).
Verses to the memory of Richard Reynolds. 1816, 1817 (3rd edn).
The state lottery. 1817. By various writers; includes poem Thoughts on wheels.
Greenland, and other poems. 1819, 1819, New York 1819, London 1825.
Abdallah and Labat. 1821. Poem.

Polyhymnia: or select airs of celebrated foreign composers, adapted to English words by James Montgomery. 1822.
Songs of Zion: being imitations of psalms. 1822, Boston 1823, London 1828 (3rd edn).
The chimney-sweeper's friend, and climbing-boy's album. 1824. Ed Montgomery and with poems by him.
Prose, by a poet. 2 vols 1824, Philadelphia 1824. Anon.
The Christian psalmist: or hymns selected and original. Glasgow 1825, 1826 (4th edn), London [1862] (10th edn).
The Christian poet. Glasgow 1827, 1828 (3rd edn).
The pelican island, and other poems. 1827, Philadelphia 1827, London 1828.
Lectures on poetry and general literature. 1833, New York 1838, 1846.
A poet's portfolio: or minor poems. 1835.
Lives of literary and scientific men of Italy, Spain etc. 3 vols 1835–7. Part of D. Lardner, The cabinet cyclopaedia; Ariosto, Dante and Tasso by Montgomery.
Poems on the loss of St Mary's Church Cardiff. 1842. By various writers, including Montgomery.
Liturgy and hymns for the use of the protestant church of the United Brethren: a new and revised edition. 1849. Rev and contributed to by Montgomery.
Original hymns. 1853; ed J. Holland, New York 1854 (as Sacred poems and hymns).
Also minor prose writings, a few poems issued in single-sheet or pamphlet form, and many hymns contributed to collections ed W. B. Collyer 1812, T. Cotterill 1819, and others. Montgomery was editor and proprietor of Sheffield Iris 1794–1825.

§2

The trial of Montgomery for a libel on the war. Sheffield 1795.
[Jeffrey, F.] Montgomery's Poems. Edinburgh Rev 9 1807.
[Southey, R.] Montgomery's Poems. Quart Rev 6 1811.
— Montgomery's World before the flood. Quart Rev 11 1814.
Wilson, J. Sacred poetry. In his Recreations of Christopher North, 1842.
Gilfillan, G. In his A second gallery of literary portraits, Edinburgh 1850.
Holland, J. and J. Everett. Memoirs of Montgomery. 7 vols 1854–6; abridged by H. C. Knight, Boston 1857 (as Life of Montgomery).
King, J. W. Montgomery: a memoir. 1858.
Ellis, S. The life, times and character of Montgomery. 1864.
Wissmann, P. Die grösseren Dichtungen von Montgomery. Königsberg 1914.
Odom, W. Two Sheffield poets: Montgomery and Ebenezer Elliott. Sheffield 1929.
Phillips, G. L. Climbing-girls. N & Q 12 Nov 1949. Illustrates Chimney-sweeper's friend.
Holbrook, A. S. The life and work of Montgomery. London Quart 179 1954.
Kay, J. A. The poetry and hymns of Montgomery. Ibid.

SYDNEY OWENSON, Lady MORGAN
1783?–1859

See col 754, below.

WILLIAM MOTHERWELL
1797–1835

Collections

Poems narrative and lyrical. Glasgow 1832, Boston 1841, 1844, 1846.
Poetical works. Ed J. M'Conechy, Glasgow 1847, Boston 1847, Glasgow 1849 (with 71 addns), Boston 1863, Paisley 1881.
Rogers 3.
Miles 3.

§1

The harp of Renfrewshire: a collection of songs and other poetical pieces (many of which are original), and a short essay on the poets of Renfrewshire. Glasgow 1820, Paisley 1872–3 (with second ser).
Renfrewshire characters and scenery: a poem in three hundred and sixty-five cantos, by Isaac Brown [i.e. Motherwell]. Paisley 1824, 1881. Only one canto pbd.
Minstrelsy ancient and modern. [Ed Motherwell], Glasgow 1827, 2 vols Boston 1846, 1 vol Paisley 1873. Modified by C. Mackay as The legendary and romantic ballads of Scotland, 1861.
Certain curious poems [by] J. M'Alpie. Paisley 1828. Ed Motherwell.
Scottish proverbs, collected and arranged by Andrew Henderson; with an introductory essay by Motherwell. Edinburgh 1832.
The works of Robert Burns, edited by the Ettrick shepherd and Motherwell. 5 vols Glasgow 1834–6 etc.
Posthumous poems. Boston 1851.
Motherwell edited the Paisley Advertiser 1828–30 and Glasgow Courier 1830–5.

§2

Wasserman, E. R. The source of Motherwell's Melancholye. MLN 55 1940.
Montgomerie, W. Motherwell and Robert A. Smith. RES new ser 9 1958.

JOHN MOULTRIE
1799–1874

Collections

Poems; with memoir by Prebendary [Derwent] Coleridge. 2 vols 1876.

§1

Poems. 1837, 1852 (3rd edn).
The dream of life, lays of the English Church and other poems. 1843.
Saint Mary, the virgin and the wife. 1850, 1850, 1856. Poem.
The black fence: a lay of modern Rome. 1850, 1851 (4th edn).
Psalms and hymns. 1851, 1860. Compiled by Moultrie and including about 20 of his hymns.
The song of the Rugby church-builders. [1851].
A pentecostal ode. 1852.
The poetical remains of William Sidney Walker, with a memoir [by Moultrie]. 1852.
Sermons. 1852.
Altars, hearths and graves. 1854. Poems.
Moultrie also contributed poems to Etonian 1820–1, and to Knight's Quart Mag 1823–4.

CAROLINA, Baroness NAIRNE
1766–1845

See vol 2.

JOHN NICHOLSON

1790–1843

Collections

Poems by John Nicholson, the Airedale poet; with a sketch of his life and writings by J. James. 1844; ed W. Dearden 1859 ('4th edn', enlarged); ed A. Holroyd, Bingley 1876; ed W. G. Hird 1876.

§ 1

The siege of Bradford. Bradford 1821, 1831. A verse play.
Airedale in ancient times, and other poems. 1825, 1825.
Lines on the grand musical festival. Bradford 1825.
Lines on the present state of the country. Bradford 1826 (3 edns).
The Airedale poet's walk. Knaresborough 1826. Poem.
The lyre of Ebor, and other poems. 1827.
The vale of Ilkley; and the poet's sick-bed. Bradford 1831.

WILLIAM NICHOLSON

1783–1849

Tales in verse and miscellaneous poems. Edinburgh 1814, 1828 (with memoir by J. Macdiarmid).
Rogers 3.
Poetical works, with a memoir by M. M'L. Harper. Castle-Douglas 1878, Dalbeattie 1897.

AMELIA OPIE

1769–1853

See col 753, below.

HENRY JOHN TEMPLE, Viscount Palmerston

1784–1865

See col 1298, below.

THOMAS PARK

1759–1834

See col 1622, below.

THOMAS LOVE PEACOCK

1785–1866

See col 700, below.

JAMES ROBINSON PLANCHÉ

1796–1880

See cols 1108, 1135, below.

ROBERT POLLOK

1798–1827

Selections

Miles 10 (11).

§ 1

Helen of the glen: a tale for youth. [1825?], Glasgow 1830 (4th edn), 1870, Richmond Va [1900]. Prose.
Ralph Gemmell: a tale. [1825?], Edinburgh 1829 (3rd–4th edns). Prose.
The persecuted family. [1825?], Edinburgh 1828 (with memoir), 1829. Prose.
The course of time: a poem in ten books. 2 vols 1827, Boston 1828, Edinburgh 1829 (9th edn), New York 1831 (12th Amer edn), Portland 1844, New York 1854, London 1867 (25th edn); illustr B. Foster et al 1869, [1898]; tr German, 1830.
Tales of the Covenanters [i.e. Helen of the glen, Ralph Gemmell, The persecuted family]. Edinburgh 1833, 1836; ed A. Thomson, Edinburgh 1895, Kilmarnock [1928].

§ 2

Pollok, D. Life of Pollok. 1843.
Gilfillan, G. In his A gallery of literary portraits, Edinburgh 1845.
Masson, R. O. Pollok and Aytoun. [1898].

THOMAS PRINGLE

1789–1834

Collections

The poetical works of Pringle, with a sketch of his life by L. Ritchie. 1838.
Rogers 3.
Afar in the desert, and other South African poems. Ed J. Noble 1881.
Pringle: his life, times and poems. Ed W. Hay, Cape Town 1912.

§ 1

The institute: a heroic poem. Edinburgh 1811. Anon; with R. Story.
The autumnal excursion: or sketches in Teviotdale, with other poems. Edinburgh 1819.
[African sketches]. In G. Thompson, Travels and adventures in southern Africa, 2 vols 1827. Rptd from South African Jnl.
Ephemerides: or occasional poems, written in Scotland and South Africa. 1828.
The history of Mary Prince, a West Indian slave; with a supplement by the editor [Pringle]. 1831.
African sketches. 1834. Poems, with a prose Narrative of his residence in South Africa; *see* below.
Narrative of a residence in South Africa, with biographical sketch by J. Conder. 1835, 1851; ed W. Hay, Cape Town 1924 (selected, as The Pringle school reader); tr German, 1836.
South African sketches. Edinburgh [1902]. Poems from African sketches.
McLeod, A. L. Two letters of Pringle. N & Q Jan 1961.
Pringle also pbd miscellaneous prose and edited periodicals in Britain and South Africa, including Edinburgh Monthly Mag 1817 and Constable's Edinburgh Mag 1817–18.

§ 2

Pachaly, R. Pringle und Ferdinand Freiligrath. Freiburg 1879.
Hall, A. D. Pringle, Somerset and press freedom. Eng Stud in Africa 3 1960.
Mphahlele, E. In his African image, 1962.

BRYAN WALLER PROCTER ('BARRY CORNWALL')

1787–1874

Collections

Poetical works. 3 vols 1822.
The poetical works of Milman, Barry Cornwall [et al]. Paris 1829.
Miles 2.

§1

Dramatic scenes, and other poems. 1819, 1820, 1857 (enlarged, and illustr Birket Foster, Tenniel et al), Boston 1857.
A Sicilian story, and other poems. 1820, 1820, 1821.
Marcian Colonna: an Italian tale, with three dramatic scenes, and other poems. 1820.
Mirandola: a tragedy. 1821, 1821. Verse.
The flood of Thessaly, The girl of Provence, and other poems. 1823.
Effigies poeticae: or the portraits of the British poets. 1824.
English songs. 1832, 1844 (new edn), Boston 1844, London 1851 (enlarged).
The life of Edmund Kean. 2 vols 1835; tr German, 1836.
The works of Ben Johnson, with a memoir [by Procter]. 1838.
The works of Shakspere, with a memoir and essay on his genius [by Procter]. 3 vols 1843, 2 vols 1853, 1857–9, 3 vols 1875–80.
Essays and tales in prose. 2 vols Boston 1853.
Selections from Robert Browning. 1863. Ed Procter and J. Forster.
Charles Lamb: a memoir. 1866, Boston 1866; rptd in Essays of Elia, with a memoir of Lamb, 1879.
Procter: an autobiographical fragment. Ed C. Patmore 1877; ed R. W. Armour, Boston 1936 (selected as The literary recollections of Barry Cornwall).
Procter made numerous contributions to periodicals, including Literary Gazette, London Mag and Edinburgh Rev.

§2

[Jeffrey, F.] Cornwall's poems. Edinburgh Rev 33 1820.
[Lamb, C.?] New Times 22 July 1820. Review of Marcian Colonna, rptd in Works of Lamb, ed W. Macdonald vol 3, 1903.
[Darley, G.] The characteristic of the present age of poetry. London Mag April 1824.
Armour, R. W. Barry Cornwall: a biography of Bryan Waller Procter, with a selection of hitherto unpublished letters. Boston 1935.
Price, F. Barry Cornwall and Patmore on child-love. N & Q 14 Aug 1943.
Ford, G. H. Keats and Procter: a misdated acquaintance. MLN 66 1951.
Townend, R. G. Barry Cornwall's memoir of Charles Lamb. Charles Lamb Soc Bull March 1953.
Brooks, E. L. B. W. Procter and the genesis of Carlyle's Frederick the Great. Harvard Lib Bull 7 1953.
Blunden, E. Barry Cornwall and Keats. Keats-Shelley Memorial Bull 14 1963.

EDWARD QUILLINAN
1791–1851

Collections

Poems, with a memoir by W. Johnston. 1853, Ambleside 1891.

§1

Ball-room votaries. 1810, 1810. Verse.
Dunluce Castle: a poem. Lee Priory, Kent 1814 (priv ptd).
Stanzas. Lee Priory 1814 (priv ptd).
Consolation: a poem. Lee Priory 1815 (priv ptd).
Monthermer: a poem. 1815.
The sacrifice of Isabel: a poem. 1816, New York 1816.
Elegiac verses, addressed to a lady. Lee Priory 1817 (priv ptd).
Miscellaneous poems. Lee Priory 1820 (priv ptd).
Wood cuts and verses, edited with a preface by E. Quillinan. Lee Priory 1820 (priv ptd).
The retort courteous. 1821. Reply to T. Hamilton's attack on Dunluce Castle in Blackwood's Mag.
Carmina Brugesiana: domestic poems. Geneva 1822 (priv ptd).
The King: the lay of 'a papist'. [1829].
The conspirators. 3 vols 1841. A novel.
The rangers of Connaught. In The Edinburgh tales, ed Mrs C. I. Johnstone vol 1, Edinburgh 1845.
The Lusiad [of Camõens] books 1–5, translated. Ed J. Adamson 1853.

Letters

The correspondence of Henry Crabb Robinson with the Wordsworth circle. Ed E. J. Morley 2 vols Oxford 1927. Includes about 70 letters from Quillinan, and a reprint from Blackwood's Mag April 1843 of his article defending Wordsworth against Landor.

§2

Quillinan, D. Journal of a few months' residence in Portugal. 2 vols 1847.

ANN RADCLIFFE
1764–1823

See col 758, below.

JOHN HAMILTON REYNOLDS
1796–1852

Bibliographies

Marsh, G. L. The writings of Keats's friend Reynolds. SP 25 1928.
—— Newly identified writings by Reynolds. Keats-Shelley Jnl 1 1952. *See* L. M. Jones, below.

Collections

Poetry and prose. Ed G. L. Marsh, Oxford 1928. A selection, with detailed biographical introd.
Selected prose. Ed L. M. Jones, Cambridge Mass 1966. With bibliography.

§1

Safie: an eastern tale. 1814.
The Eden of imagination: a poem. 1814.
An ode. 1815. Anon.
The naiad: a tale, with other poems. 1816. Anon.
Peter Bell: a lyrical ballad. 1819 (3 edns). Signed W.W.; an anticipatory parody of Wordsworth's poem.
Benjamin the waggoner, a ryghte merrie and conceitede tale in verse: a fragment. 1819. Anon; a further burlesque of Wordsworth, possibly by Reynolds.
The fancy: a selection from the poetical remains of the late Peter Corcoran, of Gray's Inn, student-at-law, with a brief memoir of his life. 1820; ed J. Masefield [1905].
The garden of Florence and other poems. 1821.
The press, or literary chit-chat: a satire. 1822.
Odes and addresses to great people. 1825 (anon), 1826 (3rd edn). With Thomas Hood.
One, two, three, four, five, by advertisement: a musical entertainment in one act. In J. Cumberland, British theatre vol 31 1829 (anon). Acted 1819.
Confounded foreigners: a farce in one act. [1838].

Letters

Rollins, H. E. The Keats circle. 2 vols Cambridge Mass 1948. Includes 21 letters by Reynolds.

Reynolds contributed to many periodicals, notably Champion 1815–7 and London Mag 1820–4.

§2

Gosse, E. In his Gossip in a library, 1891. Articles on Peter Bell and Fancy.

Swaen, A. E. H. Peter Bell. Anglia 47 1923. Reprints Reynold's burlesque and considers its relation to Wordsworth.

Gates, W. B. A sporting poet of the regency. Sewanee Rev 35 1927.

Marsh, G. L. New data on Reynolds. MP 25 1928.

— The Peter Bell parodies of 1819. MP 40 1943.

Turnbull, J. M. Keats, Reynolds and the Champion. London Mercury Feb 1929.

Blunden, E. Friends of Keats. In his Votive tablets, 1931. On Reynolds and G. F. Mathew.

Pope, W. B. John Hamilton Reynolds. Wessex 3 1935.

Jones, L. M. New letters, articles and poems by Reynolds. Keats-Shelley Jnl 6 1957.

— Reynolds and Keats. Keats-Shelley Jnl 7 1958.

Kaufman, P. The Reynolds-Hood commonplace book: a fresh appraisal. Keats-Shelley Jnl 10 1961.

Slote, B. La belle dame as naiad. JEGP 60 1961. On Naiad.

Morgan, P. F. Reynolds and Thomas Hood. Keats-Shelley Jnl 11 1962.

Marshall, W. H. Pulpit oratory 1–3: essays by Reynolds in imitation of William Hazlitt. Lib Chron 28 1962.

ALEXANDER RODGER

1784–1846

Selections

Rogers 3.

§1

Scotch poetry: consisting of songs, odes, anthems and epigrams. 1821.

Peter Cornclips: a tale of real life, with other poems. Glasgow 1827.

Poems and songs: humorous and satirical. Glasgow 1838; ed R. Ford 1897, 1901.

Whistle Binkie: or the piper of the party. 2nd ser ed Rodger, Glasgow 1839; 3rd ser Glasgow 1841; 4th ser Glasgow 1842; 5th ser Glasgow 1843; [collected] Glasgow 1846, 1853, 1878, 1890 (enlarged). Songs by various authors.

Stray leaves from the portfolios of Alisander the seer, Andrew Whaup and Humphrey Henkeckle. Glasgow 1842, 1842. Verse and prose.

WILLIAM STANLEY ROSCOE

1782–1843

§1

Poems. 1834.

§2

The poems of Roscoe. Blackwood's Mag June 1835.

Goldman, A. Blake and the Roscoes. N & Q May 1965. Blake's influence on To spring.

See William Roscoe, col 1087, below.

WILLIAM STEWART ROSE

1775–1843

A naval history of the late war. Vol 1 (all pbd), 1802.

Amadis de Gaul, freely translated from the first part of the French version. 1803.

Partenopex de Blois, freely translated from the French. 1807.

The crusade of St Lewis, and King Edward the martyr. 1810. Ballads.

The court and parliament of beasts, freely translated [or rather adapted] from the Animali parlanti of Giambattista Casti: a poem. 1816, 1819.

Letters from the north of Italy, addressed to Henry Hallam esq. 2 vols 1819. Anon.

The Orlando innamorato, translated into prose. Edinburgh 1823. Abridged, and with passages in verse.

Orlando furioso, translated with notes. 8 vols 1823–31, 2 vols 1858 (with brief memoir by C. Townsend), 1864.

Thoughts and recollections. 1825.

Apology addressed to the Travellers' Club: or anecdotes of monkeys. 1825. Anon; authenticity doubtful.

To the Right Honourable J. H. Frere. Brighton [1834]. No title-page; a rhymed epistle.

Rhymes. Brighton 1837 (priv ptd). Includes the preceding poem.

Some verses to Byron (1818) were first ptd in Works of Byron: letters, ed R. E. Prothero vol 4, 1900 pp. 212–4.

HORATIO (HORACE) SMITH

1779–1849

and

JAMES SMITH

1775–1839

§1

Rejected addresses: or the new theatrum poetarum. 1812 (anon), 1812 (rev), 1813 (9th edn), 1813 (15th edn), 1833 (18th edn 'carefully revised'), 1847 (21st edn); ed P. Cunningham 1851; ed E. Sargent, New York 1871 (with memoirs); ed P. Fitzgerald 1890; ed A. D. Godley 1904; ed A. Boyle 1929 (with bibliography).

Horace in London: consisting of imitations of the first two books of the odes of Horace. 1813, 1813, Boston 1813, London 1815 (4th edn). Rptd from Monthly Mirror.

For the poems, novels etc of Horace Smith alone, together with his edn of James Smith's Comic miscellanies in prose and verse, *see col 767, below.*

§2

[Jeffrey, F.] Rejected addresses. Edinburgh Rev 20 1812.

Lowe, R. W. The real rejected addresses. Blackwood's Mag May 1893. On the competition which provided the occasion for the burlesque.

Beavan, A. H. James and Horace Smith. 1899.

Blunden, E. The Rejected addresses. In his Votive tablets, 1931.

Clark, P. O. 'Punch's apotheosis'. PQ 31 1952.

WILLIAM SOTHEBY

1757–1833

§1

Poems: consisting of sonnets, odes etc. Bath 1790, 1794 (as A tour through parts of Wales, sonnets and other poems).

Oberon: a poem, from the German of Wieland. 1798; illustr H. Fuseli 1805.
The battle of the Nile: a poem. 1799.
The Georgics of Virgil, translated. 1800, 1815, 1827, 1830.
The siege of Cuzco: a tragedy. 1800. Verse.
The Cambrian hero. [1800?] A verse tragedy; authenticity doubtful.
A poetical epistle to Sir George Beaumont. 1801.
Julian and Agnes: a tragedy. 1801, 1814 (as The confession), 1816 (as Ellen: or the confession).
Orestes: a tragedy. 1802. Verse.
Oberon: or Huon de Bordeaux, a mask; and Orestes. 1802.
Saul: a poem. 1807, Boston 1808.
Constance de Castile: a poem. 1810, Boston 1812.
A song of triumph. 1814.
Tragedies. 1814. Includes The death of Darnley; Ivan; Zamorin and Zama; The confession; Orestes.
Ivan: a tragedy. 1816. Verse.
Farewell to Italy, and occasional poems. 1818, 1825 (rev and enlarged as Poems), 1828 (as Italy and other poems).
The first book of the Iliad [and 2 other] specimens of a new version of Homer. 1830.
The Iliad of Homer, translated. 1831.
The Odyssey of Homer, translated. 1834.
Lines suggested by the third meeting of the British Association, with a short memoir of his life. 1834.

§2

Wilson, J. Sotheby's Homer. Blackwood's Mag April–May, July, Dec 1831, Feb 1832, Jan–Feb 1834; rptd in his Works vol 8, Edinburgh 1857.
Beyer, W. W. Keats and the daemon king. New York 1947. On Sotheby's trn of Wieland's Oberon.
—— In his Enchanted forest, Oxford 1963.
Cohen, R. S. T. Coleridge and Sotheby's Orestes. MLR 52 1957.

WILLIAM ROBERT SPENCER
1769–1834

Collections

Poems. 1811, 1835 (enlarged, with memoir).
Miles 9 (10).

§1

Leonora, translated from the German of G. A. Bürgher, illustrated. 1796, Dublin 1799, 1809.
Beth-Gêlert: or the grave of the greyhound. Oxford 1800. Anon.
Urania: or the illuminé—a comedy. 1802. Prose.
The year of sorrow. 1804. A poem.
Miscellaneous poems. 1812.

ROBERT STORY
1795–1860

Collections

Poetical works. 1857.
The lyrical and other minor poems of Story, with a sketch of his life and writings by J. James. 1861.

§1

The harvest: a poem. 1816.
Craven blossoms. 1826. Poems.
The magic fountain, with other poems. 1829.
The isles are awake. 1834. Poems.
The outlaw: a drama. 1839. Verse.
Love and literature: being the reminiscences, literary opinions and fugitive pieces of a poet in humble life. 1842.
Songs and lyrical poems. Liverpool [1845?], 1849 (3rd edn, as Songs and poems).
Guthrum the Dane: a tale. 1852, 1853. Verse.
The third Napoleon: an ode. 1854, 1855 (enlarged).
The Alloway [Burns] centenary festival: an ode. 1859.

CHARLES STRONG
1785–1864

§1

Specimens of sonnets from the most celebrated Italian poets; with translations. 1827. Anon.
Sonnets, by the author of Specimens of sonnets from the most celebrated Italian poets, with translations. 1829.
Sonnets. 1835, 1862 (with 15 additional sonnets by 'C.L.').

§2

The sonnets of Strong. Blackwood's Mag Nov 1835.

SIR THOMAS NOON TALFOURD
1795–1854

See col 1140, below.

ROBERT TANNAHILL
1774–1810

§1

The soldier's return: a Scots pastoral, in two acts. Paisley 1807. Rptd in the following.
The soldier's return: a Scottish interlude, in two acts; with other poems and songs, chiefly in the Scottish dialect. Paisley 1807, 1822; ed J. J. Lamb, Paisley 1873.
Poems and songs, chiefly in the Scottish dialect. [Ed J. Muir] 1815, 1815 ('3rd edn' enlarged), 1817 (enlarged), New York 1820.
The poetical works. Glasgow 1825, [1872] (enlarged).
The songs, ballads and fragments of Tannahill; with a sketch of his life. Ed A. Laing, Brechin 1833.
The poems and songs of Tannahill [with memoir of Tannahill and R. A. Smith]. Ed P. A. Ramsey, Glasgow 1838, [1853] (as The works of Tannahill).
The poetical works of Tannahill. Belfast 1844.
Rogers 2.
The songs of Tannahill, complete. Glasgow 1859.
The poems and songs of Tannahill. Ed D. Semple, Paisley 1874. Centenary edn.
The poems and songs and correspondence of Tannahill. Ed D. Semple, Paisley 1875 (with bibliography etc), 1900.
Miles 2.
The songs and poems of Tannahill [with memoir by A. Reekie]. Paisley 1911. Includes some musical settings.

§2

[MacLaren, W.] A life of the Renfrewshire bard Tannahill, by a friend. Paisley 1815.
Douglas, G. B. S. In his James Hogg, Edinburgh [1899].
Crawford, R. L. New light on Tannahill, the weaver-poet of Paisley. N & Q May 1966.

ANN TAYLOR, later GILBERT
1782–1866
and
JANE TAYLOR
1783–1824

See col 1087, below.

WILLIAM TAYLOR
1765–1836

See col 1306, below.

WILLIAM TENNANT
1784–1848

§1

Anster Fair. Edinburgh 1812 (anon), 1814 (other poems added), Baltimore 1815, Boston 1815, Edinburgh 1816, London 1821, 1838 (with memoir), Edinburgh 1871.
Elegy on trottin' Nanny. Edinburgh 1814. Anon.
The dominie's disaster, and other poems. Cupar 1816. Anon.
The thane of Fife: a poem, in six cantos. Edinburgh 1822.
Cardinal Beaton: a drama in five acts. Edinburgh 1823.
John Baliol: a historical drama. Edinburgh 1825.
Papistry storm'd or the dingin' down o' the cathedral: ane poem, in sax sangs. Edinburgh 1827.
Critical remarks on the Psalms of David. Edinburgh 1830. Rptd from Edinburgh Literary Jnl.
Hebrew dramas. Edinburgh 1845.
Miles 2.

§2

Conolly, M. F. Memoirs of the life and writings of Tennant. 1861.

JOHN THELWALL
1764–1834

§1

Poems on various subjects: vol 1 consisting of tales [vol 2 consisting of a dramatic poem, miscellanies etc]. 2 vols 1787.
A speech in rhyme. 1788.
The peripatetic. 1793.
John Gilpin's ghost, or the warning voice of King Chanticleer: an historical ballad dedicated to the treason-hunters of Oakham. 1795.
Poems written in close confinement in the Tower and Newgate upon a charge of treason. 1795.
Poems chiefly written in retirement—The fairy of the lake: a dramatic romance; Effusions of relative and social feeling; and specimens of The hope of Albion, or Edwin of Northumbria: an epic poem; with memoir of the life of the author and notes and illustrations of runic mythology. Hereford 1801, [1805?].
The daughter of adoption: a tale of modern times, by John Beaufort [i.e. Thelwall]. 4 vols 1801.
The black bowl, Feb 3 1208, or tears of Eboracum: an old monkish legend. York 1802.
The trident of Albion: an epic effusion. Liverpool 1805.
Monody on the Right Hon Charles James Fox. 1806, 1806.
The poetical recreations of the Champion, and his literary correspondents; with a selection of essays, literary and critical, which have appeared in the Champion newspaper. 1822. Ed Thelwall; includes 12 poems by Lamb.

Letters

Thelwall to Hardy. TLS 19 June 1953. Extracts from correspondence.
Thelwall also pbd many miscellaneous lectures and tracts, mainly on elocution and political subjects. He was editor of Biographical & Imperial Mag 1789–92, Champion 1818–21 *and* Monthly Mag 1824.

§2

Thelwall, C. B. The life of Thelwall. Vol 1, 1837.
Cestre, C. Thelwall: a pioneer of democracy and social reform in England during the French revolution. 1906.
Haberman, F. W. Thelwall: his life, his school and his theory of elocution. Quart Jnl of Speech 1947; rptd in Historical studies of rhetoric and rhetoricians, ed R. F. Howes, Ithaca 1961.
Boyle, A. Portraiture in Lavengro, 6: the teacher of oratory—Thelwall. N & Q 19 Jan 1952.
Thompson, E. P. In his Making of the English working class, 1963. Ch 5.

WILLIAM THOM
1789–1848

§1

Rhymes and recollections of a hand loom weaver. 1844, 1845 (enlarged); ed W. Skinner, Paisley 1880.
Rogers 3.
Miles 3.

§2

Douglas, G. B. S. In his James Hogg, Edinburgh [1899].

EDWARD THURLOW, afterwards HOVELL-THURLOW, 2nd BARON THURLOW
1781–1829

§1

The defence of poesy, by Sir Philip Sidney. 1810. Ed Thurlow, with 5 original sonnets.
Verses prefixed to the Defence of poesy; the induction to an heroic poem; also verses dedicated to the Prince Regent. 1812. Anon.
Hermilda in Palestine, with other poems. 1812. Anon.
Poems on several occasions. 1813, 1813 (enlarged). An appendix to Poems on several occasions: being a continuation of the Sylva, 1813.
Ariadne: a poem. 1814, 1822.
Carmen britannicum: or the song of Britain, written in honour of his Royal Highness George Augustus Frederick Prince Regent. 1814.
Moonlight; The doge's daughter; Ariadne; Carmen britannicum: or the song of Britain; Angelica: or the rape of Proteus. 1814.
Moonlight: a poem; with several copies of verses. 1814. A different collection.
The sonnets of Edward Lord Thurlow. Brussels 1819 (priv ptd).
Select poems. Chiswick 1821 (priv ptd).
Angelica, or the rape of Proteus: a poem. 1822.
Arcita and Palamon, after Geoffrey Chaucer. 1822.

§2

[Moore, T.] Lord Thurlow's poems. Edinburgh Rev 23 1814; rptd in his Prose and verse, ed R. H. Shepherd 1878.

MARY TIGHE, neé BLACHFORD

1772–1810

Bibliographies

Henchy, P. The works of Mary Tighe: published and unpublished. Bibl Soc of Ireland Pbns 6 no 6 1957.

§1

Psyche: or the legend of love. 1805.
Psyche, with other poems. 1811, 1812 (4th edn), Philadelphia 1812, London 1816, 1843, 1853 (in trn of Apuleius).
Mary: a series of reflections during twenty years. [Ed W. Tighe] 1811 (priv ptd).

§2

Weller, E. V. Keats and Mary Tighe: the poems of Mary Tighe, with parallel passages from the work of John Keats. New York 1928.
Gillam, C. W. Keats, Mary Tighe and others. N & Q Feb 1954.

WILLIAM SIDNEY WALKER

1795–1846

See col 1666, below.

WILLIAM WATT

1793–1859

Comus and Cupid. Glasgow 1835, 1844, 1860 (as Poems and songs).

ALARIC ALEXANDER WATTS

1797–1864

§1

Poetical sketches. 1822 (priv ptd).
Poetical sketches; The profession; The broken heart etc, with stanzas for music and other poems. 1823, 1824, 1828.
Scenes of life and shades of character. 2 vols 1831. Prose.
Lyrics of the heart. 1851, Philadelphia 1853.
Also a few minor prose writings and numerous contributions to periodicals. Watts edited the following periodicals and annuals: Leeds Intelligencer 1822–5; Manchester Courier 1825–6; Literary Souvenir 1825–35; Cabinet of Br Art 1835–8 (continuation of Souvenir, above); Poetical Album 1828–9; United Services Gazette 1833–47; Men of the Time 1856.

§2

Watts, A. A. Watts: a narrative of his life. 2 vols 1884.

CORNELIUS WEBB

1790?–1850?

§1

Sonnets, amatory, incidental and descriptive, with other poems. 1820 (priv ptd).
Summer; An invocation to sleep; Fairy revels; and Songs and sonnets. 1821.
The posthumous papers, facetious and fanciful, of a person lately about town. 1828.
Lyric leaves. 1832.
Glances at life in city and suburb. 1836; ser 2, 1845.
The man about town. 2 vols 1838, Philadelphia 1839, London 1857 (vol 2 as The absent man).

Letters

Green, D. B. Four letters of Webbe. N & Q Jan 1958.

§2

Marsh, G. L. A forgotten cockney poet: Webb. PQ 21 1942.
Blunden, E., J. Richardson, A. Reid, A. Mordell. The obscure Webb(e). TLS 18 Dec 1959, 1, 22 Jan, 19 Feb 1960.

CHARLES JEREMIAH WELLS

1800–79

Selections

Miles 3.

§1

Stories after nature. 1822; ed W. J. Linton 1891. Prose.
Joseph and his brethren: a scriptural drama. 1824; ed A. C. Swinburne 1876, 1908 (WC). Verse, pbd under the pseudonym 'H. L. Howard'. Swinburne's introd is virtually rptd from his article An unknown poet, Fortnightly Rev Feb 1875.
A dramatic scene. Ed H. B. Forman. In Literary anecdotes of the nineteenth century, ed W. R. Nicoll and T. J. Wise vol 1, 1895. Written c. 1876; intended for insertion in Joseph and his brethren, above.

§2

Gosse, E. [Obituary]. Academy 1 March 1879.

HENRY KIRKE WHITE

1785–1806

Bibliographies

Catalogue of portraits, books, mss etc relating to Kirke White [exhibited in Nottingham, Nov 1906]. Ed J. T. Godfrey, Nottingham 1906.

Collections

The remains of Kirke White, with an account of his life by Robert Southey. Vols 1–2, 1807, 1811 (5th edn 'corrected'), Philadelphia 1811, London 1813, New York 1815, London 1816, 1819, 1821; vol 3, 1822. The contents of vol 3 were included in the 10th and later edns, 2 vols 1823, 1 vol 1825 etc; ed R. A. 4 vols 1825; 1 vol 1825 (with a life), 1828; Glasgow 1828 (with a memoir), 1838, 1844.
Poetical remains; the prose remains. 2 vols 1824, 1831.
The poetical works of Rogers, Kirke White [et al]. Paris 1829.
The beauties of White. Ed A. Howard, Philadelphia 1829, Hartford [1830].
The poetical works, with a memoir by Sir H. Nicolas. 1830 (Aldine edn), 1837, 1840, Boston 1854, 1859, 1864, 1871.
Memoir and poetical remains of Kirke White; also Melancholy hours. Ed J. Todd, Philadelphia 1844, Boston 1850.
The poetical works of Kirke White and James Grahame. Ed G. Gilfillan, Edinburgh 1856, 1868, [1878].
The poetical works of Robert Bloomfield and Kirke White. 1871.

Miles 10 (11).
Poems, letters and prose fragments. Ed J. Drinkwater [1907] (ML).
This list is not complete.

§1

Clifton grove: a sketch in verse, with other poems. 1803.
[Uncollected poems and prose, ed T. O. Mabbott]. N & Q 7 Sept 1940, 13 Jan 1945, 15 June, 2 Nov 1946, 4 Sept 1948.

Letters

Mabbott, T. O. Letters of Kirke White. N & Q 16 Nov 1946.

§2

Piggott, S. In his Guide for families, 1818 (2nd edn).
Cary, H. F. Lives of English poets, from Johnson to Kirke White. 1846. Rptd from London Mag Dec 1824.
Godfrey, J. T. and J. Ward. Homes and haunts of Kirke White. 1908.
Ward, W. S. Was Kirke White a victim of the review press? MLN 60 1945.
Blunden, E. A word for Kirke White. N & Q 11–24 Dec 1948.
—— Thoughts on Kirke White. Renaissance & Modern Stud (Nottingham) 6 1962.

JOSEPH BLANCO WHITE
1775–1841

See col 1604, below.

JEREMIAH HOLMES WIFFEN
1792–1836

§1

Poems by three friends. 1813, 1815. With T. Raffles and J. B. Brown.
Elegiac lines. 1818. With B. B. Wiffen.
Aonian hours and other poems. 1819, 1820.
Julia Alpinula, with other poems. 1820, 1820.
Jerusalem delivered: book the fourth. 1821. Specimen of projected verse trn of Tasso, with dissertation on existing ones.
The works of Garcilasso de la Vega, translated [in verse]. 1823. With critical and historical essay on Spanish poetry.
Jeruslem delivered, translated into English Spenserian verse, together with a life of the author. 2 vols 1824–5, 3 vols 1826, 2 vols 1830, 1 vol New York 1846, London 1854, New York 1858, London 1872. Life of Tasso pbd separately, New York 1859.
Verses written on the alameda at Ampthill Park. 1827 (priv ptd).
Historical memoirs of the first race of ancestry whence the house of Russell had its origin. 2 vols 1833.
Appeal for the injured African. Newcastle-on-Tyne 1833. Verse.
Verses written at Woburn Abbey. 1836 (priv ptd).
Also some minor prose writings.

§2

Mr Wiffen's translation of Tasso. Quart Rev 34 1826. A comparison with earlier trns.
The brothers Wiffen [J. H. and B. B. Wiffen]: memoirs. Ed S. R. Pattison 1880. Includes selections from their poems.

ALEXANDER WILSON
1766–1813

See vol 2.

JOHN WILSON
1774–1855

See col 1308, below.

CHARLES WOLFE
1791–1823

Collections

Remains of the late Rev Charles Wolfe. Ed J. A. Russell 2 vols Dublin 1825, 1 vol 1826, Hartford 1828, London 1829 (4th Br edn), 1838 (7th edn), 1846. Poems and sermons, with memoir.
Poems. 1903, 1909. With memoir by C. L. Falkiner and ms facs of Burial of Sir John Moore.

§1

The burial of Sir John Moore. Newry Telegraph 19 April 1817.
The burial of Sir John Moore, with other poems [and a memoir]. 1825.
Sermons of the late Rev Charles Wolfe [with memoir by G. J. Davies]. 1883. Rptd from Remains, above.

§2

[O'Sullivan, S.] College recollections. 1825. Contains personal sketch of Wolfe as 'Waller'.
Small, H. A. The field of his fame: a ramble in the curious history of Wolfe's poem The burial of Sir John Moore. Berkeley 1953.

FRANCIS WRANGHAM
1769–1842

Bibliographies

Sadleir, M. Archdeacon Francis Wrangham. Suppl to Trans of Bibl Soc no 12 1937; *see* Library 4th ser 19 1939.

Collections

Sermons practical and occasional; dissertations, translations, including new versions of Virgil's Bucolica and of Milton's Defensio secunda; Seaton poems etc. 3 vols 1816.

§1

Reform: a farce modernised from Aristophanes by S. Foote jr. 1792.
The restoration of the Jews. Cambridge 1795. Seatonian prize poem, rptd with 1800, below, in Cambridge prize poems.
The destruction of Babylon. 1795. Unsuccessful Seatonian prize poem.
Poems. 1795 (priv ptd) (pbd c. 1802).
The Holy Land. Cambridge 1800. Seatonian prize poem.
Thirteen practical sermons: founded upon Doddridge's Rise and progress of religion in the soul [with 2 more sermons]. 1800, 1802.
The raising of Jaïrus' daughter: a poem; to which is annexed a short memoir interspersed with a few poetical productions of the late Caroline Symmons. 1804.
A poem on the restoration of learning in the east. Cambridge 1805.

A dissertation on the best means of civilizing the subjects of the British Empire in India, and of diffusing the light of the Christian religion throughout the eastern world. 1805.
A volunteer song. York [1805?]. Anon; 11 pieces in verse.
Trafalgar: a song. [1805?] (priv ptd). Rptd from the preceding.
The sufferings of the primitive martyrs. Cambridge 1812. Seatonian prize poem.
Joseph made known to his brethren. Cambridge 1812. Seatonian prize poem.
On the death of Saul and Jonathan: a poem. 1813 (no copy extant?).
Poetical sketches of Scarborough. 1813, 1813. Anon; by Wrangham and others, illustr J. Green, T. Rowlandson.
Poems. [1814?] (priv ptd).
Virgil's Bucolics [translated]. Scarborough 1815, 1830 (rev, in Valpy's classical library vol 8).
Humble contributions to a British Plutarch. 1816.
A few [40] sonnets attempted from Petrarch in early life. Lee Priory, Kent 1817 (priv ptd).
Specimens of a version of Horace's first four books of odes, attempted in octosyllabic verse. 1820. From bk 3 only (priv ptd).
The pleiad: or a series of abridgements of seven distinguished writers, in opposition to the pernicious doctrines of deism. 7 pts 1820, 1 vol Edinburgh 1828.
The lyrics of Horace: being the first four books of his odes. York 1821, Chester [1832?].
Scarborough Castle: a poem. Scarborough 1823.
Sertum Cantabrigiense: on the Cambridge garland. Malton 1824.
Psychae: or songs on butterflies, by T. H. Bayly, attempted in Latin rhyme. Malton 1828 (priv ptd).
The quadrupeds' feast. Chester [1830?] (priv ptd).
Homerics. Chester 1834 (priv ptd). Trns of Odyssey 5 and Iliad 3.
Epithalamia tria Mariana etc. Chester 1837. Trns from George Buchanan *et al.*
A few epigrams attempted in Latin translation by an old pen nearly worn to its stump. [Chester 1842].

G. D. C.

IV. MID-NINETEENTH-CENTURY POETRY

THOMAS LOVELL BEDDOES

1803–49

Collections

Poems posthumous and collected. 2 vols 1851. Vol 1 includes memoir by T. F. Kelsall; vol 2 Death's jest-book, 1850; in 1 vol without Jest-book as Poems by the late Thomas Lovell Beddoes, author of Death's jest-book, with a memoir, 1851.
Poetical works. Ed E. Gosse 2 vols 1890. Memoir rptd in Gosse, Critical kit-kats, 1896.
Poems. Ed R. Colles 1907 (ML).
Complete works. Ed E. Gosse 2 vols 1928, 1 vol 1928 (75 copies).
Works. Ed H. W. Donner, Oxford 1935.
An anthology. Ed F. L. Lucas, Cambridge 1932. Introd rptd in Lucas, Studies French and English, 1934.
Plays and poems. Ed H. W. Donner 1950 (ML).

§1

For single poems etc, see bibliography in Works, 1935, *above.*
The improvisatore, in three fyttes, with other poems. Oxford 1821.
The brides' tragedy. 1822.
Antistraussianischer [Grauss-] Gruss an einen Herrn Antistes von Struthio Camelus. [Zürich 1839, 1839].
Death's jest-book: or the fool's tragedy. 1850. Anon.
Two German poems. Studia Neophilologica 37 1965.

Letters

Letters. Ed E. Gosse 1894.
Todd, A. C. Beddoes and his guardian. TLS 10 Oct 1952. 2 unpbd letters.
Donner, H. W. Echoes of Beddoesian rambles: Edgeworthstown to Zürich. Studia Neophilologica 33 1961. 2 unpbd letters.
Beddoes to Leonhard Tobler: 8 German letters. Studia Neophilologica 35 1963.

§2

Monthly Rev June 1821. Review of Improvisatore.
Procter, B. W. London Mag Feb 1823, March 1924; Edinburgh Rev 38 1823. Reviews of Brides' tragedy.
—— An autobiographical fragment. 1877.
Monthly Rev Jan 1823; Album May 1823; GM Oct 1823; G. Darley, London Mag Dec 1823, May 1824; J. Wilson, Blackwood's Mag Dec 1823. Reviews of Brides' tragedy.
Bayerisches Volksblatt 29 March 1832 (report of speech for Poland); 16 June 1832 (speech for freedom); 24 July, 30 Aug 1832 (deportation).
Der Freisinnige 9 July 1832 (report of speech for freedom).
Nürnberger Correspondent 25, 30 July 1832 (deportation).
Volksbote 23 Jan 1838 (performance of Henry IV): 7 Dec 1838 (Booing Soc); 3 May 1839 (Strauss feud).
Scherr, I. T. Beobachtungen, Bestrebungen und Schicksale. Vols 3, 4. St Gall 1840.
Illuminated Mag May 1844.
Spectator 6 July 1850 (review of Death's jest-book); 13 Sept 1851 (review of Poems posthumous and collected).
Forster, J. Examiner 20 July 1850, 27 Sept 1851, rptd in Littell's Living Age 15 Nov, Eclectic Mag Dec 1851.
Bristol Mirror 23 Dec 1854.
Blackwood's Mag Oct 1856.
Kelsall, T. F. Fortnightly Rev July 1872.
Collins, M. A poet not laureate. Dublin Univ Mag Nov 1879.
Gosse, E. Athenaeum 20 Oct 1883.
—— TLS 11 March 1909.
Symons, A. Academy 15 Aug 1891; rptd in his Figures of several centuries, 1916.
Crosse, A. Temple Bar March 1894.
Hannigan, D. F. Westminster Rev 149 1898.
Miller, B. Sewanee Rev 11 1903.
Strachey, L. The last Elizabethan. New Quart 1 1907; rptd in his Books and characters, 1922.
Wooster, H. D. Bibliophile March 1909.
Feller, A. Thomas Lovell Beddoes. Marburg 1914.
Potter, G. R. Did Beddoes believe in the evolution of the species? MP 21 1923.
Rickword, E. London Mercury 9 1923.
Moldauer, G. Thomas Lovell Beddoes. Vienna 1924.

Snow, R. H. Beddoes: eccentric and poet. New York 1928.
Blunden, E. Beddoes and his contemporaries. TLS 13 Dec 1928; rptd in his Votive tablets, 1931.
Church, R. Beddoes: the last of the alchemists. Spectator 9 Feb 1929.
Bayley, A. R. TLS 16 May 1929. Letter from Bourne to Beddoes.
Lindsay, J. TLS 16 May 1929. Letter from Kelsall to Browning.
Fugô, S. Beddoes rom-kô. Tokyo 1930. Studies on Beddoes.
Sparrow, J. Dr Beddoes. Farrago 3 1930.
Günther, L. Würzburger Chronik 3 1932. On subversive activities in Würzburg.
Weber, C. A. Bristols Bedeutung für die englische Romantik und die deutsch-englischen Beziehungen. Halle 1935.
Donner, H. W. The Browning Box: or the life and works of Beddoes as reflected in letters by his friends and admirers. Oxford 1935.
—— Beddoes: the making of a poet. Oxford 1935.
Burchardt, C. Edda 36 1936.
Meyerstein, E. H. W. English 3 1940.
Abbott, C. C. The parents of Beddoes. Durham Univ Jnl 34 1942.
Johnson, H. K. Psychiatric Quart 17 1943.
Gregory, H. In his Shield of Achilles, New York 1944.
Heath-Stubbs, J. Penguin New Writing 23 1945; rptd in his Darkling plain, 1950.
Sackville-West, E. New Statesman 10 May 1947.
Howarth, R. G. N & Q Sept 1947.
Forster, L. Beddoes's views on German literature. E Studies 30 1949.
Wagner, G. Horizon 19 1949.
Nomachi, S. Stud in Eng Lit (Tokyo) 26 1949.
Coxe, L. O. Beddoes: the mask of parody. Hudson Rev 6 1953.
Todd, A. C. The mother of Beddoes. Studia Neophilologica 29 1957.
Hoyt, C. A. Themes and imagery in the poetry of Beddoes. Studia Neophilologica 35 1963.
Nickerson, C. C. Beddoes' readings in Bodley. Studia Neophilologica 36 1964.
Harrex, A. Death's jest-book and the German contribution. Studia Neophilologica 39 1967.

H. W. D.

WINTHROP MACKWORTH PRAED

1802–39

Collections

The poetical works, now first collected by R. W. Griswold. New York 1844.
Lillian and other poems, now first collected [by R. W. Griswold]. New York 1852, 1853 (as Poetical works), 1854, 1856, 1857.
Poetical works. Ed W. A. Whitmore 2 vols New York [?] 1859–60.
Poems, with a memoir by Derwent Coleridge. 2 vols 1864, 1864, New York 1865, London 1869, 1874, New York 1885. The authorized and standard edn.
Political and occasional poems. Ed G. Young 1888. Supplements Coleridge edn, above.

Selections

Charades. New York 1752 (for 1852).
A selection from the works. Ed G. Young 1866, [1885].
Poems. Ed F. Cooper 1886.
Essays, collected and arranged by G. Young. 1887 (Morley's Univ Lib).
Select poems. Ed A. D. Godley 1909.
Poems. Ed F. Greenslet, Boston 1909.
Selected poems. Ed K. Allott 1953 (ML).

§1

Carmen graecum numismate annuo dignatum 1822 (Pyramides Aegyptiacae). [Cambridge 1822].
Epigrammata numismate annuo dignata 1822 (Nugae seria ducunt in mala). [Cambridge 1822].
Carmen graecum numismate annuo dignatum 1823. In obitum T. F. Middleton, Episcopi Calcuttensis, [Cambridge 1823].
Lillian: a fairy tale. 1823. Verse.
Australasia: a poem which obtained the Chancellor's Medal. Cambridge 1823.
Athens: a poem which obtained the Chancellor's Medal. Cambridge 1824. Rptd with the preceding in Cambridge prize poems, 1828 (4th edn).
Epigrammata numismate annuo dignata 1824 (Scribimus indocti doctique). [Cambridge 1824].
The ascent of Elijah: a poem. Cambridge 1831.
Intercepted letters about the Infirmary Bazaar. Nd. 4 leaflets of 4 pp. each, in verse and ptd on light green paper.
Speech in committee on the Reform Bill, on moving an amendment. 1832.
Trash dedicated without respect to J. Halse esq MP. Penzance 1833.
Political poems. 1835 (priv ptd).
Every-day characters. 1896. First pbd in New Monthly Mag 1828–32 and in Literary Souvenir 1831.
Letters of Praed. Etoniana 1 July 1941–28 Dec 1943. 67 letters dating from Praed's Eton days.

Contributions to Periodicals

The Etonian. 2 vols 1821. Ed and largely written by Praed and W. Blunt, Oct 1820–Aug 1821.
Knight's Quarterly Magazine. 1823–4.
The Brazen Head. 1826. 4 nos only; written and ed by Praed, C. Knight and J. B. B. St Leger.
Praed also contributed to Morning Chron 1823–5, Albion 1830–2, Morning Post 1832–4, Times and other papers, and to Literary Souvenir, ed A. A. Watts 1825 and other poetical annuals.

§2

Saintsbury, G. In his Essays in English literature 1780–1860, 1890.
Kraupa, M. Praed: sein Leben und seine Werke. Vienna 1910.
Previté-Orton, C. W. In his Political satire in English poetry, Cambridge 1910.
Hudson, D. A poet in Parliament. 1939.
—— W. M. Praed. N & Q 3 Jan 1942. Addns to his biography.
Allott, K. The text of Praed's poems. N & Q March 1953.
Paden, W. D. Twenty new poems attributed to Tennyson, Praed and Landor: pt 1. Victorian Stud 4 1961.

G. D. C.

ALFRED, 1st BARON TENNYSON

1809–92

Tennyson's notebooks are in Trinity College Cambridge (those inherited by his son Hallam) and at Harvard (those inherited by the children of his son Lionel). The Tennyson Research Centre at Lincoln holds a ms of In memoriam. *Other mss are widely scattered. In the 1830's his poems circulated in ms among his friends; hence such transcriptions as the Heath ms in the Fitzwilliam Museum Cambridge.*

Bibliographies etc

Brightwell, D. B. A concordance to the entire works of Tennyson. 1869. Pbd by Moxon without Tennyson's sanction or knowledge; *see* Ashley Library vol 7 p. 132.
[Langley, S.] A concordance to the works of Tennyson. Strahan 1870.

[Shepherd, R. H.] A bibliography of the works of Tennyson. 1896.

L[ivingston], L. S. A bibliography of the first editions in book form of Tennyson. New York 1901; Supplement, [1903?].

W[ise], T. J. A bibliography of the writings of Tennyson. 2 vols 1908 (priv ptd). Advance proofs had circulated discreetly since c. 1900 and had been used by both Livingston, above, and Thomson, below. Harvard has a set with the pts in different order; the rev proofs of vol i were ptd in 1907. Wise and the bibliographers who relied upon him are now known to include many forged edns; Shepherd, though incomplete, includes only one forgery (Idylls of the hearth), which may have been inserted by his posthumous editor. Wise may still be trusted on such matters as collected edns and contents of authentic edns.

Thomson, J. C. A bibliography of the writings of Tennyson. Wimbledon 1905.

—— Apocryphal poems of Tennyson. 1905.

Baker, A. E. A concordance to the poetical and dramatic works of Tennyson. 1914, New York 1966; Supplement, 1931 (The devil and the lady).

—— A Tennyson dictionary. [1916].

Wise, T. J. The Ashley Library: a catalogue vol 7. 1925 (priv ptd). A few Tennyson items in vols 8–10.

Ehrsam, T. G. and R. H. Deily. In their Bibliographies of twelve Victorian authors, New York 1936; J. G. Fucilla, Supplement, MP 37 1939.

Baum, P. F. In The Victorian poets: a guide to research, ed F. E. Faverty, Cambridge Mass 1956, 1968 (rev).

The Tennyson collection presented to the University of Virginia. Charlottesville [1961]. *See* W. D. Paden, Library 5th ser 18 1965.

Collections

Collected edns began to appear in 1870; see Wise, Bibliography, *above.*

The canonical text appears in the Eversley edition, ed Hallam Tennyson with annotations by the poet 9 vols 1907–8, 1 vol 1913; American Eversley edition 6 vols New York 1908.

Among the numerous other collected edns pbd since 1902, the best is the Poems, Oxford 1912, 1953 (with the plays) (OSA). *Among the far more numerous edns of selections, none merits particular mention.*

§ 1

Tennyson required 2 successive proofs for Poems chiefly lyrical, 1830, *and later more;* Poems, 1842 *and* The princess, 1847 *were often rev, largely on proofs. He had* In memoriam, 1850 *ptd in a preliminary version and distributed copies to friends, to be recalled or destroyed; incompletely rev, the setting of type was unexpectedly used in several early edns, with successive corrections and revisions by the poet. After 1855 he again commonly used unpbd preliminary versions, each ptd in a few copies and lent to advisers for eventual recall or destruction; single examples survive, used by the poet in revision and later given to trusted friends. The gradual discovery of these practices encouraged forgers to provide numerous 'priv ptd edns' for the rare book market; see* W. B. Todd (ed), T. J. Wise centenary studies, Austin 1959 pp. 111–3.

Decorum led the Laureate to seek approval while in ms of poems proffered to the Court or written at royal request. Tennyson had priv ptd edns made for the Court, e.g. [Stanzas 1858]; A welcome [to Alexandra]; A welcome to Marie Alexandrovna; Carmen saeculare(?); To the Queen [1873]; To HRH Princess Beatrice. *Of the last 2 a few examples in varying format are known, perhaps proofs or impressions retained by a press or publisher as routine required or opportunity offered. Few authentic examples of Court poems survive, and among these so few inscribed, that it is clear Tennyson refrained from distributing them; he is unlikely to have authorized others to do so. Forgers worked here also; for fraudulent and suspicious edns of Court poems see* Todd, *above.*

A first edn here is a vol, offered with the author's consent to the general public, of which a significant portion of the contents had not appeared earlier in the series. This excludes periodical pbns, unpbd preliminary versions, priv ptd edns, copyright edns, and such intermediate pbns as collected edns prior to the final canonical edn. An edn with music or illustrations which was offered to the public preceding pbn of the text in a vol counts as a first edn, as well as (by default) a separate priv ptd pamphlet or leaflet of a poem not rptd in the series of firsts. Edns neither firsts nor in a sequence of revisions are omitted. Known unpbd preliminary versions, authentic priv ptd edns, and copyright edns are noted within the entries; proofs and similar objects, piracies and forgeries are listed where their omission might allow confusion.

Poems by two brothers. Ptd Louth 1827; ed Hallam Tennyson 1893 (adds 4 poems by Alfred from the ms and Timbuctoo). With Charles Tennyson; Frederick contributed 4 poems. *See* C. Ricks for 2 additional poems by Alfred in the ms (from copies of 1893), Victorian Poetry 3 1965.

Prolusiones academicae. Cambridge 1829. Includes Timbuctoo; priv distributed offprint of Timbuctoo, Cambridge 1829.

Poems, chiefly lyrical. 1830, 1842 (partly rptd and rev); *see* below. Reviewed in Westminster Rev 14 1831 (by W. J. Fox); Tatler 24–6 Feb 1831 (by L. Hunt); Englishman's Mag Aug 1831 (by A. H. Hallam); Blackwood's Mag Feb–May 1832 (by 'Christopher North', J. Wilson). On Fox *see* W. D. Paden, Tennyson and the reviewers 1829–35, Stud in Eng (Univ of Kansas Pbns, Humanistic ser 4) 1940; and on North, A. L. Strout, RES 14 1938.

Poems. 1833 (for 1832). Partly rptd and rev in 1842; *see* below. Reviewed in Literary Gazette 8 Dec 1832 (by W. Jordan); Atlas 16 Dec 1832 (by R. Bell?); New Monthly Mag Jan 1833 (by E. Bulwer?); Monthly Repository Jan 1833 (by W. J. Fox); True Sun 19 Jan 1833 (by J. Forster?); Quart Rev 49 1833 (by J. W. Croker); London Rev 1 1835 (by J. S. Mill).

The lover's tale [withdrawn from Poems, 1833]. 1833 (for 1832) (priv circulated edn of c. 12 copies), [1868] (proofs only, rev), 1879 (rev). Piracy by R. H. Shepherd [1870], 1875. Forgery of first piracy '1870' [c. 1890].

[Early poems, suppressed in 1842. Ed J. D. Campbell] 1862; ed J. C. Thomson (with Timbuctoo and The lover's tale of 1833) in The Avon Booklet vol i nos 3–6 1903 and as Suppressed poems 1830–62, Warwick 1904, 1910.

Poems. 2 vols 1842, 1843, 1845, 1846, 1 vol 1848, 1850, 1851, 1853 (some edns rev with addns); partly illustr Millais, Holman Hunt and Rossetti 1857; ed J. C. Collins 1900 (with suppressed poems); ed A. M. D. Hughes, Oxford 1914 (with suppressed poems). Reviewed in Examiner 28 May 1842 (by J. Forster); Christian Remembrancer July 1842 (by F. Gardner?); Tait's Mag Aug 1842; Athenaeum 6 Aug 1842 (by F. H. Chorley); Morning Post 9 Aug 1842; Weekly Dispatch 21 Aug 1842; Quart Rev 70 1842 (by J. Sterling); Cambridge Univ Mag Oct 1842; Westminster Rev 38 1842 (by R. M. Milnes); Church of England Quart Rev 12 1842 (by L. Hunt); Christian Teacher Oct 1842 (by J.J.); Literary Gazette 19 Nov 1842 (by W. Jerdan); London Univ Mag Dec 1842 (by W. A. Case?); Edinburgh Rev 77 1843 (by J. Spedding).

The Princess. 1847, 1850 (rev), 1851 (rev), 1853 (rev); illustr Maclise 1860; ed J. C. Collins 1902 (with In memoriam and Maud).

In memoriam. 1850 (3 edns), 1851, 1851, 1855, 1856 etc. Within the sequence occasional revision (*see* headnote); additional poem in 4th edn, another inserted in 1870.

Preceded by unpbd preliminary version [1850]. Poem ed J. C. Collins, above (with variants).

Ode on the death of the Duke of Wellington. 1852, 1853 (rev).

Maud and other poems. 1855, 1855, 1856 (rev), 1857, 1858, 1859 (rev) etc. Within the sequence occasional revision. No unpbd preliminary version known. Preceded by The charge of the Light Brigade, 1855 (priv ptd) (1,000 copies for soldiers in the Crimea). Maud ed J. C. Collins, above (with variants).

[Stanzas on the marriage of the Princess Royal]. [1858] (priv ptd for Court use). One example known; stanzas pbd in Memoir, 1897.

Idylls of the King. 1859, 1859 etc. Preceded by unpbd preliminary versions called Enid and Nimuë (2 of 1857); The true and the false (1859). Enlarged edns 1862, 1869 (for 1870), 1873, 1889. *See* below, The holy grail; Gareth and Lynette; the last idyll pbd in Tiresias and other poems, 1885. Edn of 1862 preceded by Dedication [1862] (priv ptd) (perhaps a proof of central fold in preliminary gathering of 1862 edn possibly sent to Windsor, in contrast to his later practice of submitting poems in ms); edn of 1873 (in Library edn vols 5 and 6) preceded by To the Queen, for Court use [1873] (priv ptd) single fold, gilt edges (and proofs? with second, outer fold bearing title-page and imprint, smaller pages, no gilt 1873). One version of Enid and Nimuë (1857) pbd without authorization, Guildford 1902.

Ode written expressly for the opening of the International Exhibition, composed by William Sterndale Bennett Op. 40. 1862. Score for soprano, contralto, tenor, bass and piano or organ, here accorded priority to the vocal parts. BM copy bears on last page, which advertises Bennett's compositions, the date 20 Feb 1862; pages of music undated [plate number C. H & Co 3405]; cover dated 1 May 1862, when the Exhibition formally opened.

A welcome to HRH the Princess of Wales from the Poet Laureate. Owen Jones, Illuminator. Day & Son Lithographers to the Queen. 1863. Preceded by priv ptd edn for the Court [1863] (4 states).

Enoch Arden and other poems. 1864 etc; illustr Arthur Hughes 1866.

A selection from the work of Tennyson. 1865 (Moxon's Miniature Poets), 1870. Includes 5 unpbd poems and 2 versions of poems not pbd elsewhere etc; *see* Wise, Bibliography, above, vol 2, pp. 180–1.

The Holy Grail and other poems. 1870 (for 1869). Preceded by unpbd (and undated) preliminary versions of The birth of Arthur; The Holy Grail; Sir Pelleas; The death of Arthur; and Property (i.e. The northern farmer, new style). Also preceded by The victim. Canford Manor, 1867 (priv ptd) (folio; proofs in 8vo).

The window or the songs of the wrens: words written for music by Tennyson, the music by Arthur Sullivan. 1871 (for 1870). Preceded by The window: or the loves of the wrens. Canford Manor 1867 (priv ptd); piracy by R. H. Shepherd '1867' (for 1870).

Gareth and Lynette. 1872. Preceded by unpbd (and undated) preliminary versions of The last tournament; Gareth and Lineth.

A welcome to Marie Alexandrovna. [1874] (priv ptd for Court use) (4to; in some proofs the spelling Alexandro*w*na). Pbd Cabinet edn vol 4 1874. Forgery (8vo) '1874' (for c. 1897).

Queen Mary. 1875, 1875.

Harold. 1877 (for 1876).

Ballads and other poems. 1880.

Hands all round, a national song: the music arranged and edited by C. Villiers Stanford. [1882].

The cup and the falcon. 1884. Preceded by unpbd preliminary version of 1882.

Becket. 1884, 1893 (acting edn).

Tiresias and other poems. 1885. Preceded by Early spring, 1883 (copyright edn); To HRH Princess Beatrice, 1885 (priv ptd for Court use) (4to, gilt edges; proofs? on different paper, larger pages, no gilt).

Gordon boys' morning and evening hymns: the words edited by Lord Tennyson, the music by Lady Tennyson, edited by Dr Bridge. 1885.

An ode written for the opening of the Colonial and Indian Exhibition 1886 by Alfred Lord Tennyson set to music by Arthur Sullivan for solo, chorus and orchestra. Vocal score, the orchestral music reduced to a piano score; nd, BM copy received 2 June 1886.

Locksley Hall sixty years after. 1886. Preceded by unpbd preliminary version of The promise of May of 1883.

Carmen saeculare: an ode for the Jubilee of Her Majesty Queen Victoria written by Alfred Lord Tennyson and set to music by C. Villiers Stanford Op. 26: pianoforte arrangement by the composer. [1887]. On the final page of music dated Feb 1887 [plate number 7432]; title-page and cover undated. Probably followed (in April) by offprint from Macmillan's Mag—perhaps for Court use [1887] (priv ptd).

Demeter and other poems. 1889. Preceded by The throstle, 1889 (copyright edn).

The foresters. 1892, 1892. Preceded by unpbd version, [1881?].

The death of Oenone, Akbar's dream and other poems. 1892. Preceded by The silent voices 1892 (copyright edn). Edn of The silent voices with music by J. F. Bridge 1892. Vol includes Riflemen form!, previously pbd [in earlier version] only in newspapers of 1859; an early version pbd without authorization as Rifle Clubs, New York 1899.

Tennyson's patriotic poems. 1914. Includes A call to arms [also called Arm, arm, arm!—'Oh, where is he, the simple fool'], previously pbd anon in newspapers of 1852; ed C. Ricks MP 62 1964.

The devil and the lady. Ed C. Tennyson 1930, Bloomington 1964 (facs).

Unpublished early poems. Ed C. Tennyson 1931, Bloomington 1964 (facs, with above). Preceded by C. Tennyson, Tennyson's unpublished poems, Nineteenth Century March–June 1931.

Hallam Tennyson, Materials for a life of A.T., 1896 (priv ptd), *his* Memoir, 1897, *the annotations in the* Eversley editions, *and his memoir in the one-vol* Eversley edition, 1913, *all contain poems not pbd elsewhere.* The Christ of Ammergau, *which Tennyson dictated extempore to Knowles in 1870, was pbd from Knowles's papers,* Twentieth Century Jan 1955. *A few early poems remain in ms.*

Letters

Letters of literary men vol 2. Ed F. A. Mumby 1906.

Tennyson and William Kirby: unpublished correspondence. Ed L. Pierce, Toronto 1929.

Ellmann, M. J. Unpublished letters of Tennyson 1833–6. MLN 65 1950.

§2

For further reviews of Tennyson's pbd vols see E. F. Shannon jr, Tennyson and the reviewers 1827–51, Cambridge Mass 1952 *and his* The critical reception of Maud, PMLA 68 1953; *for later reviews see bibliography in* W. M. Dixon, A Tennyson primer, 1901 (rev).

[Fox, W. J.] Westminster Rev 14 1831. On Poems chiefly lyrical.

[Hunt, L.] Tatler 24, 26 Feb 1831. On Poems chiefly lyrical.

[Hallam, A. H.] Englishman's Mag Aug 1831. On Poems chiefly lyrical.

[Wilson, J.] ('Christopher North'). Blackwood's Mag May 1832. On Poems chiefly lyrical. *See* A. L. Strout, 'Christopher North' on Tennyson, RES 14 1938.

[Croker, J. W.] Quart Rev 49 1833. On Poems 1833.
[Mill, J. S.] London Rev I 1835. On Poems 1833.
M[ilnes], R. M. (Baron Houghton). Westminster Rev 38 1842. On Poems 1842.
Horne, R. H. [and E. Barrett]. In Horne, A new spirit of the age, 1844. For E.B.'s contributions *see* E. B. Browning, Tennyson: notes and comments, 1919 (priv ptd).
Gilfillan, G. Alfred Tennyson. Tait's Mag April 1847; rptd in his A second gallery of literary portraits, 1850.
[Kingsley, C.] Tennyson. Fraser's Mag Sept 1850. On In memoriam.
Burke, J. B. Genealogical history of the family of Tennyson D'Eyncourt; and Bayons Manor in the county of Lincoln. In his Visitations of seats and arms, 1852.
Anon. The third Napoleon: an ode to Alfred Tennyson esq. 1854. (Cambridge Univ Lib LO.31.5[14]).
[Bennet, W. C.] Anti-Maud, by a poet of the people. 1855, 1856 (rev).
— Locksley Hall: an appeal. 1887.
Brimley, G. Tennyson's poems. In Cambridge essays for 1855; rptd in his Essays, ed W. G. Clark, Cambridge 1858.
Mann, R. J. Tennyson's Maud vindicated: an explanatory essay. [1855].
[Gladstone, W. E.] Tennyson's poems. Quart Rev 106 1859. On Idylls of the King.
— Locksley Hall and the Jubilee. Nineteenth Century Jan 1887.
Lear, E. Poems and songs by Tennyson, set to music. 1859.
— Poems by Tennyson illustrated. 1889.
Gatty, A. The poetical character illustrated from the works of Tennyson. 1860.
— A key to In memoriam. 1881, 1882 (rev), 1885 (with a few comments by Tennyson).
Arnold, M. In his On translating Homer: last words, 1862. On Tennyson's style.
Robertson, F. W. An analysis of In memoriam. 1862.
Dowden, E. Mr Tennyson and Mr Browning. In his Afternoon lectures on English literature, 1863.
Bagehot, W. Wordsworth, Tennyson and Browning: or pure, ornate and grotesque art in English poetry. Nat Rev Nov 1864; rptd in his Literary studies, ed R. H. Hutton 1879.
Watts, H. E. Tennyson: a lecture. Melbourne 1864.
Japp, A. H. Three great teachers of our time: Carlyle, Tennyson and Ruskin. 1865.
Ludlow, J. M. Mr Tennyson and the Eyre defence fund. Spectator 3 Nov 1866.
[Shepherd, R. H.] Tennysoniana. 1866, 1879 (rev).
— The genesis of Maud. North Amer Rev Oct 1884. Prints passages later cancelled from proofs of second edn of the poem.
Cheetham, S. The Arthurian legends in Tennyson. Contemporary Rev April 1868.
Jebb, R. C. On Mr Tennyson's Lucretius. Macmillan's Mag June 1868.
Smith, G. On three contemporary poets. Bentley's Miscellany 64 1868.
Stirling, J. H. Jerrold, Tennyson and Macaulay. Edinburgh 1868.
[Austin, A.] The poetry of the period: Mr Tennyson. Temple Bar May 1869; rptd in his Poetry of the period, 1870.
— A vindication of Tennyson. In his Bridling of Pegasus, 1910.
— Tennyson's literary sensitiveness [c. 1898]. Nat Rev Jan 1948.
Blair, D. An unacknowledged poem of Tennyson's? (in Good Words Feb 1868, signed T.). N & Q 2 Oct 1869. Reply by G. A. Schrumpf 23 Oct 1869. A trn from the Danish.
Palgrave, F. T. A fortnight in Portugal in 1859. Under the Crown Jan–Feb 1869.
Tainsh, E. C. A study of the works of Tennyson. 1868, 1869 (rev), 1893 (rev).
Alford, H. The Idylls of the King. Contemporary Rev Jan 1870.
[Forman, H. B.] The laureate and his Arthuriad. London Quart Rev 34 1870.
— The building of the Idylls. In Literary anecdotes of the nineteenth century, ed W. R. Nicoll and T. J. Wise vol 2, 1896.
Friswell, J. H. Modern men of letters honestly criticised. 1870.
[Oliphant, M.] The epic of Arthur. Edinburgh Rev 131 1870.
Ranking, B. M. (ed). La mort d'Arthur: the old prose stories whence the Idylls of the King have been taken by Tennyson. [1871].
[Simpson, R.] Mr Tennyson's poetry. North Br Rev 53 1871.
Sir Tray. Blackwood's Mag Jan 1873. An anon parody.
Hutton, R. H. Tennyson. Macmillan's Mag Dec 1872; rptd in his Literary essays, 1888.
— Tennyson's poem on Despair (1881); Locksley Hall in youth and age (1886); rptd in his Criticisms on contemporary thought and thinkers, 1894.
Irving, W. Tennyson. Edinburgh 1873. On the Idylls.
[Rawnsley, H. D.] Lincolnshire scenery and character as illustrated by Mr Tennyson. Macmillan's Mag Dec 1873.
— Memories of the Tennysons. Glasgow 1900.
— In his Homes and haunts of famous authors, 1906.
Brody, G. M. Tennyson's Queen Mary: a criticism. Edinburgh 1875.
McCrie, G. The religion of our literature: essays. 1875.
Stedman, E. C. Tennyson and Theocritus. In his Victorian poets, 1876.
Elsdale, H. Studies in the Idylls. 1878.
Bayne, P. Lessons from my masters: Carlyle, Tennyson and Ruskin. 1879.
Payne, F. T. Essays on Sir Philip Sidney and Tennyson. 1879 (priv ptd).
Tennyson's songs. 1880. 31 settings by composers including Gounod, Liszt, Massenet, Saint-Saens and Sullivan; separately issued.
C[ollins], J. C. A new study of Tennyson. Cornhill Mag Jan, July 1880, July 1881. Incorporated in his Illustrations of Tennyson, 1891.
Conway, M. D. Laureate despair. 1881.
Foote, G. W. Atheism and suicide. [1881].
Genung, J. F. In memoriam: its purpose and structure. 1881.
— The Idylls and the ages. New York 1907.
Stoddard, R. H. A study of Tennyson. North Amer Rev July 1881.
Swinburne, A. C. Tennyson and Musset. Fortnightly Rev 1 Feb 1881; rptd in his Miscellanies, 1886.
— Threnody. Nineteenth Century Jan 1893.
'Wace, W. E.' (W. R. Nicoll). Tennyson: his life and works. Edinburgh 1881.
Dawson, S. E. A study of the Princess. Montreal 1882, 1884 (rev).
Walker, T. Mr Tennyson's despair: its religious significance. 1882.
Wright, A. (ed). Versus Tennysonianos Franklini cenotaphio inscriptos Graece Latine aliter reddendos redditosque. Cambridge 1882.
Wallis, A. A Tennyson forgery. N & Q 23 Feb 1884. On a clumsy forgery of first edn of In memoriam.
G., R. G. A sketch explanatory of the Princess. [1885] (priv ptd).
Hamann, A. An essay on Tennyson's Idylls of the King. Berlin 1887.
MacKay, E. Vox clamantis. [1887]. On supposed plagiarism in Columbus.
Chapman, E. R. A companion to In memoriam. 1888.
— Talks with Tennyson [1889]. Putnam's Mag 7 1910.

Nutt, A. Studies on the legend of the Holy Grail. 1888.
Tennyson's spiritual services to his generation. Andover Rev 12 1889.
Davidson, T. Prolegomena to In memoriam. Boston 1889.
Jennings, H. J. Lord Tennyson: a biographical sketch. 1889, 1892 (rev).
Montégut, É. Essais sur Tennyson. In his Écrivains modernes de l'Angleterre ser 2, Paris 1889.
Myers, F. W. H. Tennyson as a prophet. Nineteenth Century March 1889.
Rodriguez, F. Lord Tennyson. Rome 1889.
Napier, G. G. The homes and haunts of Tennyson. Glasgow 1889 (priv ptd), 1892 (rev).
Robertson, J. M. The art of Tennyson. In his Essays towards a critical method, 1889.
— Browning and Tennyson: two studies. 1903.
Van Dyke, H. The poetry of Tennyson. New York 1889, 1891 (rev), 1898 (rev).
Cooledge, C. E. The sunny side of bereavement as illustrated by In memoriam. Boston [1890].
Henley, W. E. In his Views and reviews, 1890.
Shepherd, H. E. A study of Tennyson's English. MLN 5 1890.
— A commentary upon In memoriam. New York 1908.
Walters, J. C. In Tennyson land. 1890.
— Tennyson: poet, philosopher, idealist. 1893.
— Links with Tennyson's youth. Academy 16 March 1895.
Church, A. J. The Laureate's country. 1891.
Davies, J. J. Tennyson's Lincolnshire farmers. Westminster Rev 136 1891.
Lester, G. Lord Tennyson and the Bible. [1891].
Rhys, J. Studies in the Arthurian legends. Oxford 1891.
Darmesteter, M. Tennyson. Revue Politique 50 1892.
Greswell, W. H. P. Tennyson and our imperial heritage. [1892].
Jacobs, J. Tennyson and In memoriam: an appreciation and a study. 1892.
Jenkinson, A. Alfred Lord Tennyson: Poet Laureate. 1892.
Ritchie, A. T. Records of Tennyson, Ruskin and Browning. 1892.
— Reminiscences. In H. H. H. Cameron, Tennyson and his friends, 1893.
Waugh, A. Alfred Lord Tennyson. 1892, 1893 (rev), 1894 (rev).
Fields, A. Harper's Mag Jan 1893; rptd, with paper on Emily Lady Tennyson, in her Authors and friends, Boston 1896.
— The Tennysons at Farringford. Ed M. A. de W. Howe, Cornhill Mag Oct 1927.
Innes, A. D. Seers and singers: a study of five English poets. 1893.
Luce, M. New studies in Tennyson: including a commentary on Maud. [1893].
— A handbook to the works of Tennyson. 1895.
— Tennyson. 1901.
Salt, H. S. Tennyson as a thinker. 1893. An attack.
Symonds, J. A. Recollections of Tennyson: an evening at Thomas Woolner's. Century Mag 46 1893.
Weld, A. G. Talks with Tennyson. Contemporary Rev March 1893.
— Glimpses of Tennyson, and of some of his relations and friends. 1903.
Littledale, H. Essays on Tennyson's Idylls of the King. 1893, 1907.
Adams, F. New Rev 10 1894; rptd in his Essays in modernity, 1899.
Bellezza, P. La vita e le opere di Tennyson. Florence 1894.
Brooke, S. A. Tennyson: his art and relation to modern life. 1894, 1900.
Brookfield, Mrs W. H. Early recollections of Tennyson. Temple Bar Feb 1894.
Layard, G. S. Tennyson and his Pre-Raphaelite illustrators. 1894.
MacCallum, M. W. Tennyson's Idylls of the King and Arthurian story from the 16th century. 1894.
Teeling, B. A visit to the Tennysons in 1839. Blackwood's Mag May 1894. From the diary of Louisa Lanesborough.
Gurteen, S. H. V. The Arthurian epic: a comparative study of the Cambrian, Breton and Anglo-Norman versions and Tennyson's Idylls of the King. 1895.
Jones, R. The growth of the Idylls of the King. Philadelphia 1895.
Nicoll, W. R. and T. J. Wise (ed). Literary anecdotes of the 19th century. 2 vols 1895–6. A. H. Hallam's letters to Leigh Hunt about Tennyson; H. B. Forman, The building of the Idylls etc.
Oates, J. The teaching of Tennyson. 1895, 1898 (rev).
Saintsbury, G. In his Corrected impressions, 1895.
Walker, H. In his Greater Victorian poets, 1895.
Barera, E. A critical essay on the works of Tennyson. Venice 1896.
Tennyson, H. Materials for a life of A.T., collected for my children. 1896 (priv ptd).
— Alfred Lord Tennyson: a memoir. 1897.
— (ed). Tennyson and his friends. 1911.
Dixon, W. M. A primer of Tennyson, with a critical essay. 1896, 1901 (rev).
Knight, W. A reminiscence of Tennyson. Blackwood's Mag Aug 1897.
Cary, E. L. Tennyson: his homes, his friends and his work. 1898.
Cuthbertson, E. J. Tennyson: the story of his life. 1898.
King, J. M. A critical study of In memoriam. Toronto 1898.
Stephen, L. The life of Tennyson. In his Studies of a biographer, 1898.
Ward, W. G. Tennyson's debt to environment. Boston Lincs 1898.
Beeching, H. C. In memoriam, with an analysis and notes. 1899, 1923.
Fischer, T. A. Leben und Werke Tennysons. Gotha 1899.
— Tennysonstudien. Leipzig 1905.
Gwynn, S. Tennyson: a critical study. 1899.
Koeppel, E. Tennyson. Berlin 1899.
Ragey, R. P. Tennyson. Paris and Lyons 1899.
Harrison, F. In his Tennyson, Ruskin, Mill and other literary estimates, 1899.
— Tennyson: a new estimate (1902). Unpbd ms; *see* Colby Lib Quart 3 1951.
— The centenary of Tennyson. In his Among my books, 1912.
Horton, R. F. Tennyson: a saintly life. 1900.
Looten, C. Une biographie de Tennyson. Arras and Paris [1900].
Masterman, C. F. G. Tennyson as a religious teacher. 1900.
Sneath, E. H. The mind of Tennyson: his thoughts on God, freedom and immortality. New York 1900, 1903.
Bradley, A. C. A commentary on In memoriam. 1901, 1902 (rev), 1930 (rev).
— The reaction against Tennyson (1914). In his A miscellany, 1929.
Carpenter, W. B. In his Religious spirit in the poets, 1901.
Lang, A. Alfred Tennyson. 1901.
Miles, A. H. (ed). The Tennyson reciter. 1901.
Paul, H. The classical poems of Tennyson. In his Men and letters, 1901.
[Warren, T. H.] Virgil and Tennyson: a literary parallel. Quart Rev 193 1901.
— The centenary of Tennyson 1809–1909. Oxford 1909; rptd in his Oxford lectures on literature, 1921.
— Tennyson and Dante. In his Essays of poets and poetry, 1909.

—— The real Tennyson. Nineteenth Century Oct 1923.
Lyall, A. C. Tennyson. 1902 (EML).
McCabe, W. G. Personal recollections of Tennyson. Century Illustr Monthly Mag March 1902.
Potwin, L. S. The source of the Lady of Shalott. MLN 17 1902.
Garnett, R. and G. K. Chesterton. Tennyson. 1903, 1906.
Axon, W. E. A. Tennyson's Lover's tale: original and analogues. Trans Soc of Lit 2nd ser 24 1903.
Blöndal, S. Alfred Tennyson. Reykjavik 1903.
Ward, W. In his Problems and persons, 1903.
—— Tennyson at Freshwater. In his Men and matters, 1914.
Watkins, W. J. G. S. The birds of Tennyson. 1903.
Benson, A. C. Alfred Tennyson. 1904.
Mustard, W. P. Classical echoes in Tennyson. New York 1904.
Pallen, C. B. The meaning of the Idylls of the King. 1904.
Ainger, A. The death of Tennyson. In his Lectures and essays, 1905.
Allingham, H. and A. Paterson. The homes of Tennyson. 1905.
Boegner, A. La pensée religieuse dans In memoriam. Cahors 1905.
Dhaleine, L. A study on Tennyson's Idylls of the King. Bar-le-Duc 1905.
Dyboski, R. Über Wortbildung und Wortgebrauch bei Tennyson. Berlin 1905.
—— Tennysons Sprache und Stil. Vienna and Leipzig 1907.
—— Tennyson: jego życie i dzieta. Cracow 1912.
Jones, H. The immortality of the soul in Tennyson and Browning. 1905.
—— Tennyson. Proc Br Acad 4 1909.
Ellison, E. N. (née Bradley). A child's recollections of Tennyson. New York 1906.
Gordon, W. C. The social ideals of Tennyson as related to his time. Chicago 1906.
Mackie, A. Nature knowledge in modern poetry. 1906.
Whitmell, C. T. Astronomy in Tennyson. Jnl & Trans Leeds Astronomical Soc 14 1906.
Dhruva, A. B. (K. Anandasan). Kant and Tennyson (1907); and Kant and Browning. Bombay 1917.
Elton, O. Tennyson: an inaugural lecture (Liverpool, 1901). In his Modern studies, 1907.
—— Tennyson and Matthew Arnold. 1924.
Giuliano, A. Essai sur Locksley Hall et Locksley Hall sixty years after. In his Commentaires et comparaisons, Turin 1907.
Maynardier, D. In his Arthur of the English poets, 1907.
Hayes, J. W. Tennyson and scientific theology. 1909.
Tennyson centenary exhibition: catalogue. 1909 (Fine Art Soc).
Ker, W. P. Tennyson: Leslie Stephen lecture 1909. 1909; rptd in his Collected essays, ed C. Whibley 1925.
Leveloh, P. Tennyson und Spenser: Spensers Einfluss auf Tennyson mit Berücktsichtigung von Keats. Marburg 1909.
Rawnsley, W. F. Tennyson 1809–1909: a lecture. Ambleside 1909.
—— Personal recollections of Tennyson. Nineteenth Century Jan–Feb 1925.
Sidgwick, A. Tennyson. 1909.
Stork, C. W. Heine and Tennyson. In Haverford essays, Haverford 1909.
Wickham, E. C. The religious value of Tennyson's poetry. 1909.
James, C. C. A Tennyson pilgrimage; Tennyson the imperialist. Toronto 1910.
Jurczyk, O. Tennyson. E Studien 41 1910.
Lauvrière, É. Repetition and parallelism in Tennyson. 1910.
—— La morbidité de Tennyson. Revue Germanique 9 1913.
Lockyer, N. and W. L. Tennyson as a student and poet of nature. 1910.
Mackail, J. W. Theocritus and Tennyson. In his Lectures on Greek poetry, 1910.
—— In his Studies of English poets, 1926.
Gingerich, S. F. Wordsworth, Tennyson and Browning: a study in human freedom. Ann Arbor 1911.
Roz, F. In his Grands écrivains étrangers, Paris 1911.
Silvestri-Falconieri, F. di. Lord Tennyson. Rome 1911.
Choisy, L.-F. Tennyson: son spiritualisme, sa personnalité morale. Geneva and Paris 1912.
Gosse, E. A first sight of Tennyson. In his Portraits and sketches, 1912.
Watson, A. Tennyson. 1912.
Huckel, O. Through England with Tennyson: a pilgrimage to places associated with the great Laureate. New York 1913.
Johnson, R. B. Tennyson and his poetry. 1913.
Way, A. S. Tennyson and Quintus Calaber. E Studies 1 1913. On Death of Oenone.
Description of a collection of holograph mss poems by Tennyson in the possession of B. Quaritch. 1914.
Turnbull, A. The life and writings of Tennyson. 1914.
Jennings, J. G. An essay on metaphor in poetry, with an appendix on In memoriam. 1915.
Lounsbury, T. R. The life and times of Tennyson [to 1850]. 1915, New York 1962.
Olivero, F. Sulla lirica di Tennyson. Bari 1915.
—— La leggenda di Ulisse in Tennyson e in alcuni poeti irlandesi. Giornale Dantesco 25 1922.
Moore, J. K. Sources of In memoriam in Tennyson's early poems. MLN 31 1916.
Alden, R. M. Tennyson: how to know him. Indianapolis 1917.
Bussmann, E. Tennysons Dialektdichtungen, nebst einer Übersicht über den Gebrauch des Dialekts in der englischen Literatur von Tennyson. Weimar 1917.
Robinson, E. M. Tennyson's use of the Bible. Hesperia, Ergänzungsreihe 4 1917.
Osmond, P. H. In his Mystical poets of the English Church, 1919.
Browning, R. An opinion on the writings of Tennyson. 1920 (priv ptd). In a letter of 1870.
Dixon, J. M. The spiritual meaning of In memoriam. New York 1920.
—— The Rubáiyát and In memoriam. Methodist Rev 104 1921.
Sidey, T. K. Some unnoted Latinisms in Tennyson. MLN 35 1920.
Boas, F. S. The Idylls of the King in 1921. Nineteenth Century Nov 1921.
—— Tennyson and the Arthurian legend. In his From Richardson to Pinero, 1937.
Cross, T. P. Tennyson as a Celticist. MP 18 1921.
Engel, H. Taines Urteil über Tennyson. Zeitschrift für Französische und Englische Unterricht 20 1921.
Holmes, M. D. The poet as philosopher: a study of In memoriam. Philadelphia 1921.
Pallis, E. H. Tennysons og Swinburnes Arthurdigte. Edda 15 1921.
Pyre, J. F. A. The formation of Tennyson's style. Wisconsin Univ Stud in Lang & Lit no 12 1921.
Staines, De W. T. The influence of Carlyle upon Tennyson. Texas Rev 6 1921.
Vann, W. H. A prototype of Tennyson's Arthur [Christ]. Sewanee Rev 29 1921.
Arnold, W. H. My Tennysons. Scribner's Mag May 1922; rptd in his Ventures in book collecting, 1923.
Kern, A. A. King Lear and Pelleas and Ettarre. MLN 37 1922.
Ratchford, F. E. The Tennyson collection in the Wren Library. Texas Rev 7 1922.
—— Idylls of the hearth: Wise's forgery of Enoch Arden. Southwest Rev 26 1941.
—— An exhibition of mss and printed books at the University of Texas Library. Austin 1942.
Warre-Cornish, Mrs [née Ritchie]. Memories of Tennyson. London Mercury Dec 1921–Jan 1922.
H., R. W. Bodleian Quart Record 3 1922. On a ms of Gareth and Lynette presented by Hallam Tennyson.

Abbott, C. C. A short view of the case against Tennyson. Humberside 1 1923.
Fausset, H. I'A. Tennyson: a modern portrait. 1923.
—— The young Tennyson. Bookman (London) Jan 1932.
—— The hidden Tennyson. Poetry Rev 33 1942.
Nicolson, H. Tennyson: some aspects of his life, character and poetry. 1923, New York 1962 (with Afterword dated 1960).
—— Tennyson: fifty years after. Poetry Rev 33 1942.
—— Tennyson's two brothers: Leslie Stephen lecture. 1947; rptd in his English sense of humour, 1956.
Shewan, A. Repetition in Homer and Tennyson. Classical Weekly 2–9 April 1923.
Stenberg, T. T. A word on the sources of the Charge of the Light Brigade. MLN 38 1923.
Thomas, G. Tennyson and the Georgians. London Quart Rev 140 1923.
Willcocks, M. P. Tennyson. Eng Rev 36 1923.
Drew, M. Tennyson and Laura Tennant. In her Acton, Gladstone and others, [1924].
Noyes, A. Tennyson and some recent critics. In his Some aspects of modern poetry, 1924.
—— Tennyson. 1932.
—— A tribute. Poetry Rev 30 1939.
—— The real Tennyson. Quart Rev 287 1949.
Boas, G. Tennyson and Browning contrasted. 1925.
Japikse, C. G. H. The dramas of Tennyson. 1926.
Stockley, W. F. P. The faith of In memoriam. Catholic World March 1925.
Eliot, T. S. Whitman and Tennyson. Nation 18 Dec 1926. *See* 4 June 1927.
—— In memoriam. Introd to Poems of Tennyson, Edinburgh 1936; rptd in his Essays ancient and modern, 1936.
—— The voice of his time. Listener 12 Feb 1942. On In memoriam.
Jiriczek, O. L. Die 'neunte Woge'. Anglia Beiblatt 37 1926.
McKeehan, I. P. A neglected example of the In memoriam stanza. MLN 41 1926.
Postma, J. Tennyson as seen by his parodists. Amsterdam 1926.
Fischer, W. Zur neunten Woge. Anglia Beiblatt 38 1927.
Perry, H. ten E. The Tennyson tragedy. Southwest Rev 12 1927.
Giordano-Orsini, G. N. La poesia di Tennyson: saggio critico. Bari 1928.
MacNaughton, G. F. A. Tennyson: an interview [in 1880]. Glasgow [1928].
Cressman, E. D. The classical poems of Tennyson. Classical Jnl Nov 1928.
Daniels, E. The younger generation reads Browning and Tennyson. Eng Jnl 18 1929.
Granville-Barker, H. Some Victorians afield, 2: The poet as dramatist. Theatre Arts Monthly May 1929.
Macy, J. Tennyson: the perfect laureate. Bookman (New York) June 1929.
Magnus, L. Tennyson a hundred years after. Cornhill Mag June 1929.
Wright, H. G. Tennyson and Wales. E & S 14 1929.
Beck, G. Tennysons ethische Anschauungen. Erlangen 1930.
Blos, E. Die politischen Anschauungen Tennysons. Erlangen 1930.
Bowden, M. Tennyson in France. Manchester 1930.
Burton, K. Hallam's review of Tennyson. MLN 45 1930.
Lucas, F. L. In his Eight Victorian poets, Cambridge 1930, 1940 (as Ten Victorian poets), 1948 (rev).
—— (ed). Tennyson: poetry and prose. Oxford 1947. Reprints criticism from Quart Rev, FitzGerald, Arnold, Leslie Stephen, Harold Nicolson.
—— Tennyson. 1957 (Br Council pamphlet).
Möllman, A. Tennysons künstlerische Arbeit an seinen Gedichten. Universitas-Archiv 37 1930.
Scaife, C. H. O. The poetry of Tennyson. 1930.
Schonfield, H. J. (ed). Letters to Frederick Tennyson. 1930. None from the poet.
Sparrow, J. Tennyson and Thomson's shorter poems. London Mercury March 1930.
Wilner, O. L. Tennyson and Lucretius. Classical Jnl Feb 1930.
Wolfe, H. Tennyson. 1930. Mainly on Maud.
Abercrombie, L. In his Revaluations, 1931.
Crum, R. B. In his Scientific thought in poetry, New York 1931.
Brodribb, C. W. and G. Callender. Tennyson and Froude. TLS 15 Oct, 17, 31 Dec 1931, 21 Jan 1932. On the Revenge.
Chauvet, P. In his Sept essais de littérature anglaise, Paris 1931.
Hegner, A. Die Evolutionsidee bei Tennyson und Browning. Freiburg 1931.
Tennyson, C. B. L. Tennyson's unpublished poems. Nineteenth Century March–June 1931.
—— Tennyson papers. Cornhill Mag March–June 1936.
—— Alfred Tennyson. 1949.
—— Six Tennyson essays. 1954.
—— The story of Farringford. 1955.
—— The Idylls of the King. Twentieth Century March 1957.
—— Stars and markets. 1957.
—— Tennyson's conversation. Twentieth Century Jan 1959.
—— Tennyson and his times. Lincolnshire Historian 2 1963.
—— Tennyson collection: Usher Gallery Lincoln. Lincoln 1963.
—— The Somersby Tennysons. Victorian Stud 7 1963; *see* Postscript 9 1966.
—— The dream in Tennyson's poetry. Virginia Quart Rev 40 1964.
—— Bird and beast in Tennyson. Veterinary Record 4 Dec 1965.
—— and F. T. Baker (ed). Some unpublished poems by A. H. Hallam. Victorian Poetry 3 1965.
Auld, W. M. The mount of vision. 1932.
Bradby, G. F. Tennyson's In memoriam. In his Brontës and other essays, 1932.
Evans, B. I. Tennyson and the origins of the Golden treasury. TLS 8 Dec 1932.
Füting, A. Tennyson's Jugenddrama The devil and the lady. Marburg 1932.
Peake, L. S. Tennyson and the search for immortality. Saturday Rev 20 Feb–12 March 1932.
Stevenson, L. In his Darwin among the poets, Chicago 1932.
—— Tennyson, Browning and a romantic fallacy. UTQ 13 1944.
—— The 'highborn maiden' symbol in Tennyson. PMLA 63 1948; rptd in Critical essays, ed J. Killham 1960.
—— The pertinacious Victorian poets. UTQ 21 1952.
—— The Elkins collection in the Philadelphia Library. Victorian Newsletter no 3 1953.
Bird, W. H. B. Tennyson in 1833. TLS 21 Sept 1933. W. H. Thompson on Tennyson's classical attainments.
Gaglio Morana, V. Tennyson: poeta rappresentativo dell' Inghilterra vittoriana. [Rome 1933].
Mabbott, T. O. The correspondence of John Tomlin. N & Q Feb 1933.
—— Tennyson's The poet. Explicator 3 1945.
—— Merlin and the gleam. N & Q 10 Jan 1948.
Madan, G. Tennyson and the letter S. TLS 18 May 1933.
Richardson, R. K. The idea of progress in Locksley Hall. Trans Wisconsin Acad 28 1933.
Tennyson, L. (3rd Baron). From verse to worse. 1933, 1950 (rev as Sticky wickets).
Howe, M. L. D. G. Rossetti's comments on Maud 49 1934.
Motter, T. H. V. Arthur Hallam's centenary: a bibliographical note. Yale Univ Lib Gazette 8 1934.
—— Hallam's Poems of 1830: a census of copies. PBSA 35 1941.

— When did Tennyson meet Hallam? MLN 57 1942.
— Hallam's suppressed allusion to Tennyson. PLMA 57 1942.
Pollard, H. G. and T. J. Wise. Tennyson's A welcome 1863. TLS 15 Feb 1934. Replies, 8–15 March 1934.
Quiller-Couch, A. T. Tennyson in 1833. In his Poet as citizen, Cambridge 1934.
— Tennyson: after fifty years. Poetry Rev 33 1942.
Phelps, W. L. Lancelot and that forward hussy Elaine. Scribner's Mag June 1934. Quotes Godey's Lady's book, 1860.
S. Tennyson: Porcius Licinus. N & Q 17 Feb 1934. On Oenone.
Brie, F. Tennysons Ulysses. Anglia 59 1935.
Bush, D. The personal note in Tennyson's classical poems. UTQ 4 1935.
— In his Mythology and the romantic tradition in English poetry, 1937.
— Tennyson's Ulysses and Hamlet. MLR 38 1943.
— Introduction. In Tennyson: selected poetry, New York 1951.
Thompson, J. W. The true history of Tennyson's Lord Burleigh in Byways in bookland. Berkeley 1935.
Ward, M. Wilfrid Ward and Tennyson. Commonweal 16 Nov 1935.
Carlson, C. L. A French review of Tennyson's 1830 and 1832 volumes. ELH 3 1936. In L'Europe Littéraire 6 March 1833.
Hesse, G. Das politische Element in der Lyrik Swinburnes und Tennysons. Danzig 1936.
Howell, A. C. Tennyson's Palace of art: an interpretation. SP 33 1936.
Jensen, H. Tennysons Ulysses. In Englische Kultur in sprachwissenschaftlicher Deutung: Max Deutschbein Festschrift, ed W. Schmidt, Leipzig 1936.
Raya, P. N. (formerly Roy). Italian influence on the poetry of Tennyson. Benares 1936.
Weygandt, C. The time of Tennyson: English Victorian poetry as it affected America. New York 1936.
Geza, H. Tennyson és a közvélemény. Szeged 1937.
Grierson, H. J. C. Croker and Tennyson. TLS 24 April 1937. *See* M. F. Brightfield, John Wilson Croker, Berkeley 1940; F. L. Lucas, TLS 30 Nov 1946; A. L. Strout, N & Q 26 July, 15 Nov 1947.
Millhauser, M. 'Ringing grooves'. N & Q 16 Jan 1937. On Locksley Hall.
— Tennyson's Princess and Vestiges. PMLA 69 1954.
— Tennyson: artifice and image. Jnl of Aesthetics 14 1956.
— Just before Darwin. Middleton Conn 1959.
— Structure and symbol in Crossing the bar. Victorian Poetry 4 1966.
Pisanti, G. Ulisse nella poesia di Tennyson e in quella di Pascoli. Giuseppe Vesuviano 1937.
Potter, G. H. Tennyson and the biological theory of mutability of species. PQ 16 1937.
Green, J. A sorrow's crown of sorrows. N & Q 18 June 1938.
Hunton, W. A. Tennyson and the Victorian political milieu. New York 1938.
Merriam, H. G. In his Edward Moxon: publisher of poets, New York 1938.
Reid, M. J. C. The Arthurian legend. 1938, 1961.
Starke, F.-J. Tennyson und Vergil. Neuphilologische Monatsschrift 9 1938.
Stewart, S. M. Pope and Tennyson: a possible parallel. N & Q 20 Aug 1938.
Groom, B. On the diction of Tennyson, Browning and Arnold. Soc for Pure Eng tract no 53 1939.
Pike, J. S. Dickens, Carlyle and Tennyson. Ed H. Davis, Atlantic Monthly Dec 1939. Accounts of the 1860's.
Pitollet, C. Les fleurs de Francis Jammes et celles d'Alfred Tennyson. Revue de l'Enseignement des Langues Vivantes 56 1939.
Rose, F. Tennyson and Victor Hugo. Poetry Rev 30 1939.

Young, G. M. The age of Tennyson. Proc Br Acad 25 1939; rptd in Critical essays, ed J. Killham 1960.
Bay, J. C. A Tennyson–Browning association book. In his Fortune of books, 1940 (priv ptd), Chicago 1941. An inscribed copy of Maud.
de la Mare, W. In his Pleasures and speculations, 1940.
DeVane, W. C. and M. P. Introduction. In Selections from Tennyson, New York 1940.
Hull, M. E. The merman lover in ballad and song. Stud in Eng (Univ of Kansas Pbns, Humanistic ser 6) 1940.
Johnson, W. S. 'Musty, fusty Christopher'. Ibid.
Loane, G. G. Echoes in Tennyson and other essays. [1940].
Lumiansky, R. M. Tennyson and Guþrúnarkviþa I. N & Q 13 July 1940.
Mansford, W. Tennyson: the poet-seer. Poetry Rev 31 1940.
McKeon, G. R. Faith in Locksley Hall. Dalhousie Rev 19 1940.
Mooney, E. A., jr. Tennyson's earliest Shakespeare parallels. Shakespeare Assoc Bull 15 1940.
— Tennyson's earliest classical parallels. Classical Jnl Oct 1940.
— A note on astronomy in the Princess. MLN 64 1949.
Paden, W. D. Tennyson and the reviewers 1829–35. Stud in Eng (Univ of Kansas Pbns, Humanistic ser 6) 1940.
— Tennyson in Egypt. Lawrence Kansas 1942.
— Tennyson's The poet. Explicator 2 1944.
— Mt 1, 352: Jacques de Vitry, the Mensa Philosophica, Hödeken and Tennyson. Jnl Amer Folklore 58 1945. On The devil and the lady.
— Photographs of Tennyson. TLS 30 June 1950. Reply by H. Gernsheim 21 July 1950.
— A note on the variants of In memoriam and Lucretius. Library 5th ser 8 1953. Correction by C. Ricks 18 1963.
— Twenty new poems attributed to Tennyson, Praed and Landor. Victorian Stud 4 1961.
— Tennyson's The lover's tale, R. H. Shepherd and T. J. Wise. SB 18 1965.
Rutland, W. R. Tennyson and the theory of evolution. E & S 26 1940.
S., W. W. The miller's daughter. N & Q 3 Feb 1940. Possible source.
Chew, S. C. Introduction. In Tennyson: representative poems, New York 1941.
Kishi, S. (ed). Lafcadio Hearn's lectures on Tennyson. Tokyo 1941.
A great national poet: England at war—Tennyson's mystical imperialism. TLS 10 Oct 1942.
Caclamanos, D. Tennyson's ideal man. TLS 17 Oct 1942.
Harrison, T. P. Tennyson's Maud and Shakespeare. Shakespeare Assoc Bull 17 1942.
Woods, M. L. (née Bradley). My recollections of Tennyson. Poetry Rev 33 1942.
Yohannon, J. D. Tennyson and Persian poetry. MLN 57 1942. Reply by W. D. Paden, 58 1943, 60 1945.
N & Q 11 Sept 1943. On Tennyson and Carlyle in 1881.
Eidson, J. O. Tennyson in America. Athens Georgia 1943.
— Charles Stearns Wheeler: Emerson's 'good Grecian'. New England Quart 27 1954.
— The reception of Tennyson's plays in America. PQ 35 1956.
— The first performance of Tennyson's Harold. New England Quart 37 1964. At Yale.
— Tennyson's first play on the American stage. Amer Lit 35 1964.
— Tennyson's The foresters on the American stage. PQ 43 1964.
— Tennyson's Becket on the American stage. Emerson Soc Quart 39 1965.
— Tennyson's minor plays in America. Amer N & Q 4 1965.

Gettmann, R. A. and J. M. Moore. Tennyson's Ulysses. Explicator 2 1943.
Marie, Sr R. Poetry in the twilight of the classics. College Eng Oct 1943.
Shannon, E. F., jr. Tennyson and the reviewers 1830–42. PMLA 58 1943; included in his Tennyson and the reviewers 1827–51, Cambridge Mass 1952.
— The proofs of Gareth and Lynette in the Widener Collection. PBSA 41 1947.
— The coachman's part in the publication of Poems by two brothers. MLN 64 1949.
— Tennyson's 'balloon stanzas'. PQ 31 1952.
— The critical reception of Maud. PMLA 68 1953.
— (with W. H. Bon). Literary mss of Tennyson in the Harvard College Library. Harvard Lib Bull 10 1956.
— Alfred Tennyson. Victorian Newsletter no 12 1957. On location of mss.
— Locksley Hall and Ivanhoe. N & Q June 1959.
— Tennyson's admission to Cambridge. TLS 6 March 1959. In Nov 1827.
— The history of a poem: Tennyson's Wellington Ode. SB 13 1960.
Auden, W. H. Introduction. In A selection from the poems of Tennyson, New York 1944.
Basler, R. P. Tennyson the psychologist. South Atlantic Quart 43 1944; rptd in Sex, symbolism and psychology in literature, New Brunswick 1948.
Emery, C. The background of Tennyson's 'airy navies'. Isis 35 1944.
Ford, G. H. In his Keats and the Victorians, New Haven 1944.
— The Governor Eyre case in England. UTQ 17 1948.
M[unsterberg], M. From Tennyson's library. More Books 19 1944.
— Letters from Lady Tennyson [to Mrs Gatty]. Boston Public Lib Jnl 7 1955.
Arms, G. Childe Roland and Sir Galahad. College Eng Feb 1945.
Carew, P. One of 'the six hundred'. Blackwood's Mag Jan 1946.
d'Agata, A. Alcuni punti controversi nell' interpretazione dell' In memoriam. Anglica 1 1946.
Fuson, B. W. Tennyson's In memoriam xi. Explicator 4 1946.
Hansen, K. H. (tr). Alfred Lord Tennyson: Oenone. Antike und Abendland 2 1946.
Paraclita, Sr M. Aubrey de Vere, Tennyson and Alice Meynell. Thought 21 1946.
Walcutt, C. C. Tennyson's Ulysses. Explicator 4 1946.
Battenhouse, H. M. In his Poets of Christian thought, New York 1947.
Brooks, C. The motivation of Tennyson's weeper. In his Well-wrought urn, New York 1947; rptd in Critical essays, ed J. Killham 1960.
Terhune, A. M. In his Life of Edward FitzGerald, New Haven 1947.
Fairchild, H. N. Tennyson and Shelley. TLS 11 Jan 1947.
— 'Wild bells' in Bailey's Festus. MLN 64 1949.
— In his Religious trends in English poetry vol 4, New York 1957.
Haight, G. S. Tennyson's Merlin. SP 44 1947.
Hough, G. The natural theology of In memoriam. RES 23 1947.
— Tears, idle tears. Hopkins Rev 4 1951; rptd in Critical essays, ed J. Killham 1960; reply by L. Spitzer, Hopkins Rev 5 1952, also rptd by Killham.
Sessions, I. B. The dramatic monologue. PMLA 62 1947.
Sir Edwin Arnold, Whitman and Tennyson. N & Q 21 Aug 1948.
Baum, P. F. Tennyson sixty years after. 1948.
— Crossing the bar. Eng Lang Notes 1 1964.
Brown, A. W. The Metaphysical Society. New York 1947.
Carter, J. Tennyson's Carmen saeculare. Library 5th ser 2 1947.
Long, M. The Tennysons and the Brownings. College Eng Dec 1947.

Donahue, M. J. Tennyson: two unpublished epigrams. N & Q 27 Nov 1948.
— The revision of Tennyson's Sir Galahad. PQ 28 1949.
— Hail, Briton! and Tithon in the Heath ms. PMLA 64 1949. Correction by C. Ricks, RES 57 1964.
Friedeman, P. B. The Tennyson [Poems] of 1857. More Books 23 1948.
Bowman, M. V. The Hallam–Tennyson Poems (1830). SB 1 1949.
Cohen, J. M. In memoriam a hundred years after. Cornhill Mag 164 1949.
Johnson, E. D. H. The lily and the rose: symbolic meaning in Maud. PMLA 64 1949.
— The alien vision in Victorian poetry. Princeton 1952.
— In memoriam: the way of the poet. Victorian Stud 2 1959.
Meldrum, E. Tennyson and the classical poets. Contemporary Rev May 1949.
Patmore, D. In his Life and times of Coventry Patmore, 1949.
Thaler, A. Tennyson and Whittier. PQ 28 1949.
— Whittier and the English poets. New England Quart 24 1951.
Turner, P. The stupidest English poet. E Studies 29 1949.
— Some ancient light on Tennyson's Oenone. JEGP 61 1962.
Tyler, H. 'I am Mad Tom'. TLS 21 Oct 1949. Verses supposedly written by Dr G. C. Tennyson.
Bergman, H. Whitman on his poetry and some poets. Amer N & Q Feb 1950.
— Whitman and Tennyson. SP 51 1954.
Carr, A. J. Tennyson as a modern poet. UTQ 19 1950; rptd in Critical essays, ed J. Killham 1960.
Ellman, M. J. Revision of In memoriam, section 85. MLN 65 1950.
Fox, A. Tennyson's elegy. Spectator 16 June 1950.
James, D. G. Wordsworth and Tennyson. Proc Br Acad 36 1950.
Knaplund, P. The Poet-Laureateship in 1892: some Acton–Gladstone letters. Quart Rev 288 1950.
Meyerstein, E. H. W. A Drayton echo in Tennyson. TLS 2 June 1950.
Milmed, B. K. In memoriam a century after. Antioch Rev 10 1950.
Priestley, F. E. L. Tennyson's Idylls. UTQ 19 1949; rptd in Critical essays, ed J. Killham 1960.
— Control of tone in the Princess. Langue et Littérature 6 1962.
Robertson, D. A. Tennyson On the Jungfrau, and the mountain-maid. Amer Alpine Jnl 7 1950.
Rudman, H. W. Crossing the bar. Explicator 8 1950.
— Keats and Tennyson on 'Nature red in tooth and claw'. N & Q July 1954.
Rust, J. D. George Eliot's reviews of three Victorian poets. Papers of Michigan Acad 36 1950.
Templeman, W. D. Locksley Hall and Carlyle. In Booker memorial studies, Chapel Hill 1950.
— A consideration of the fame of Locksley Hall [1842–1960]. Victorian Poetry 1 1963.
Buckley, J. H. Tennyson: the two voices. In his Victorian temper, Cambridge Mass 1951.
— Introduction. In Poems of Tennyson, Cambridge Mass 1958.
— Tennyson: the growth of a poet. Cambridge Mass 1960.
Carleton, W. J. Dickens and the two Tennysons. Dickensian 47 1951.
Green, D. B. Keats and Tennyson. N & Q 18 Aug 1951.
— Leigh Hunt's hand in S. C. Hall's Book of gems [vol 3 1838]. Keats-Shelley Jnl 8 1959.
Green, J. Tennyson's development during the 'ten years silence' 1832–42. PMLA 66 1951.
Jump, J. D. Shelley and Tennyson. N & Q 8 Dec 1951.
— Matthew Arnold and Enoch Arden. N & Q Feb 1954.

Kirkwood, K. P. Maud: an essay. Ottawa 1951.
Lloyd, J. E. Victorian writers and the Great Exhibition. N & Q 22 Dec 1951. Addn by C. Evans 2 Feb 1952.
Mattes, E. B. In memoriam: the way of a soul. New York 1951.
McLuhan, H. M. Tennyson and picturesque poetry. EC 1 1951; rptd in Critical essays, ed J. Killham 1960.
— Tennyson and the romantic epic. In Critical essays, ed J. Killham 1960.
Short, C. Edward FitzGerald on some fellow Victorians. Western Humanities Rev 5 1951.
Waterston, E. H. Symbolism in Tennyson's minor poems. UTQ 20 1951; rptd in Critical essays, ed J. Killham 1960.
White, F. E. Unorthodox tendencies in Tennyson. Rev of Religion 15 1951.
Tennyson: or an imitation. N & Q 8 Nov 1952. An exercise in the In memoriam stanza and tone.
Ball, D. The characters in Tennyson. Poetry Rev 43 1952.
Burnam, T. Tennyson's 'ringing grooves' and Captain Ahab's grooved soul. PMLA 67 1952.
Estrich, R. M. and H. Sperber. Personal style and period style: a Victorian poet. In Three keys to language, New York 1952. On the Revenge.
Gwynn, F. L. Tithon, Tears idle tears and Tithonus. PMLA 67 1952.
Jamieson, P. F. Tennyson and his audience in 1832. PQ 31 1952.
Jones, F. L., J. T. Fain and G. G. Langsam. Crossing the bar. Explicator 10 1952.
Stange, G. R. Tennyson's garden of art: a study of the Hesperides. PMLA 67 1952; rptd in Critical essays, ed J. Killham 1960.
— Tennyson's mythology: a study of Demeter and Persephone. ELH 21 1954; rptd in Critical essays, ed J. Killham 1960.
Bose, A. In memoriam: a revaluation. Aligarh 1953.
Burchell, S. C. Tennyson's 'allegory in the distance'. PMLA 68 1953.
Moore, J. R. Conan Doyle, Tennyson and Rasselas. Nineteenth-Century Fiction 7 1953.
Okasawa, T. Tennyson: poetical saint. Tokyo 1953.
Spector, R. D. A Dryden echo in Tennyson. N & Q Nov 1953.
Tillotson, K. and A. L. P. Norrington. Rugby 1850: Arnold, Clough, Walrond and In memoriam. RES new ser 4 1953. Addn by R. H. Super, TLS 28 Oct 1960. Rptd in G. and K. Tillotson, Mid-Victorian studies, 1965, with her article Tennyson's serial poem.
Tryon, W. S. Nationalism and international copyright: Tennyson and Longfellow in America. Amer Lit 24 1953.
Buckler, W. E. Tennyson's Lucretius bowdlerized? RES new ser 5 1954. On the advice of Professor Masson to Macmillan's.
Chiasson, E. J. Tennyson's Ulysses: a re-interpretation. UTQ 23 1954; rptd in Critical essays, ed J. Killham 1960.
Perrine, L. Tennyson's In memoriam. Explicator 12 1954.
Stanford, W. B. In his Ulysses theme, Oxford 1954.
Allott, M. The Lord of Burleigh and Henry James's A landscape painter. N & Q May 1955.
— J. R. Lowell: a link between Tennyson and Henry James. RES new ser 6 1955.
Crossett, J. Tennyson and Catullus. Classical Jnl April 1955.
Engelberg, E. The beast image in Idylls of the King. ELH 22 1955.
Gransden, K. W. Some uncatalogued mss of Tennyson. Book Collector 4 1955. In Palgrave bequest to BM.
— Tennyson: In memoriam. 1964.
Healy, Sr E. T. Virgil and Tennyson. Kentucky Foreign Lang Quart 2 1955.

Lerner, L. D. In memoriam 1955. EC 5 1955.
Miller, B. Somersby and background: a fragment. Cornhill Mag 167 1954.
— Tennyson and the sinful queen. Twentieth Century Oct 1955. Reply by J. Killham, N & Q Dec 1958.
— Camelot at Cambridge. Twentieth Century Feb 1958.
— Tennyson: the early years. Twentieth Century June 1960.
Pierce, A. L. A visit to Farringford [in 1868]. Boston Univ Stud in Eng 1 1955.
Allott, K. An Arnold-Clough letter: references to Carlyle and Tennyson. N & Q June 1956.
Barker, G. The face behind the poem. Encounter May 1956.
Beck, W. Clouds upon Camelot. Eng Jnl 45 1956. On the shorter poems.
de Selincourt, A. In his Six great poets, 1956.
Esher, Viscount. Tennyson's influence on his times. Essays by Divers Hands 28 1956.
Greenberg, R. A. A possible source of Tennyson's 'tooth and claw'. MLN 71 1956. From Carlyle's Past and present.
Hendrick, G. (ed). Enoch Arden in Texas [in 1871]. Texas Univ Lib Chron 5 1956.
Krause, A. Unamuno and Tennyson. Comparative Lit 8 1956.
Roppen, G. Evolution and poetic belief: a study in some Victorian and modern writers. Oslo 1956.
— Tennyson's sea-quest. E Studies 40 1959.
Sharrock, R. A reminiscence of In memoriam in David Copperfield. N & Q Nov 1956.
Willard, C. B. Whitman and Tennyson's Ulysses. Walt Whitman Newsletter no 2 1956.
Willey, B. In his More nineteenth-century studies, 1956.
Fall, C. An index of the letters from papers of Frederick Tennyson. SE 36 1957.
Houghton, W. E. In his Victorian frame of mind, New Haven 1957.
Johnson, W. S. The theme of marriage in Tennyson. Victorian Newsletter no 12 1957.
Langbaum, R. In his Poetry of experience, 1957. On the dramatic monologue.
Marshall, G. O. Textual changes in a presentation copy of Poems 1833. Texas Univ Lib Chron 6 1957.
— Tennyson's The lotus eaters. In his Creativity and the arts, Athens Georgia 1961.
— Tennyson's The poet: mis-seeing Shelley plain. PQ 40 1961.
— Tennyson's Oh! that 'twere possible: a link between In memoriam and Maud. PMLA 77 1962.
— Gift books, Tennyson and The tribute (1837). Georgia Rev 16 1962.
— Tennyson's Ulysses. Explicator 21 1963.
— A Tennyson handbook. New York 1963.
McBurney, W. H. Welty's The burning [and The lady of Shalott]. Explicator 16 1957.
Ostrowski, W. Wczesna poezja Tennysona. Łódź 1957.
Robson, W. W. The dilemma of Tennyson. Listener 13 June 1957; rptd in Critical essays, ed J. Killham 1960.
Sanders, C. R. Tennyson and the human hand. Victorian Newsletter no 11 1957.
— Carlyle and Tennyson. PMLA 76 1961.
Siegenthaler, W. Zum Problem der Anordnung in der Gedichtsammlungen von Wordsworth und Tennyson. Berne 1957.
Wain, J. A stranger and afraid. In his Preliminary essays, 1957.
Woodward, R. H. The journey motif in Whitman and Tennyson. MLN 72 1957.
Assad, T. J. Analogy in Crossing the bar. Tulane Stud in Eng 8 1958.
— Tennyson's Break, break, break. Tulane Stud in Eng 12 1962.
— Tennyson's Tears, idle tears. Tulane Stud in Eng 13 1963.

B., A. C. Extant copies of Timbuctoo (1829). Book Collector 7 1958.
Barksdale, R. K. Arnold and Tennyson on Etna. College Lang Assoc Jnl 2 1958.
Cochrane, R. C. Francis Bacon in early 18th-century literature. PQ 37 1958. On Palace of art.
Dahl, C. A double frame for Tennyson's Demeter? Victorian Stud 1 1958.
Elliott, P. L. Another manuscript version of To the Queen. N & Q Feb 1958.
— Tennyson's To Virgil. N & Q April 1959.
— 'The charge of the Light Brigade'. N & Q July 1963. On the Times.
— In memoriam ii and cxxviii. Eng Lang Notes 2 1965.
— In memoriam xcvi. Victorian Poetry 3 1965.
Gullason, T. P. Tennyson's influence on Stephen Crane. N & Q April 1958.
Jones, H. M. Telemachus and Ulysses. Texas Quart 1 1958.
Killham, J. Tennyson and the Princess: reflections of an age. 1958.
— Maud: the function of the imagery. In Critical essays, below.
— (ed). Critical essays on the poetry of Tennyson. 1960.
Korg, J. The pattern of fatality in Tennyson's poetry. Victorian Newsletter no 14 1958.
MacEachen, D. B. Tennyson and the sonnet. Ibid.
Mayhead, R. The poetry of Tennyson. In Pelican guide to English literature, ed B. Ford vol 6, 1958.
Preyer, R. Tennyson as an oracular poet. MP 55 1958.
— Tennyson: the poetry and politics of conservative vision. Victorian Stud 9 1966.
Warburg, J. Poetry and industrialism: some refractory material in 19th-century and later English verse. MLR 53 1958.
Duncan, E. H. Tennyson: a modern appraisal. Tennessee Stud in Lit 4 1959. Mainly on Ulysses.
Forker, C. R. Tennyson's Tithonus and Marston's Antonio's revenge. N & Q Dec 1959.
Gibson, W. Behind the veil: a distinction between poetic and scientific language in Tennyson, Lyell and Darwin. Victorian Stud 2 1959.
Gossman, A. and G. W. Whiting. King Arthur's farewell to Guinevere. N & Q Dec 1959.
Hartmann, J. E. The mess of Gareth and Lynette. Harvard Lib Bull 13 1959.
Hess, M. W. Tennyson 1809–1959. Contemporary Rev Oct 1959.
Lawry, J. S. Tennyson's The epic: a gesture of recovered faith. MLN 74 1959.
Millgate, M. Tennyson: poet and laureate. Listener 13 Aug 1959.
Rosenberg, J. D. The two kingdoms of In memoriam. JEGP 58 1959.
Ryals, C. de L. The 19th-century cult of inaction. Tennessee Stud in Lit 4 1959.
— The 'fatal woman' symbol in Tennyson. PMLA 74 1959.
— Point of view in Tennyson's Ulysses. Archiv 199 1961.
— The 'heavenly friend': the 'new mythus' of In memoriam. Personalist 43 1962.
— The 'weird seizures' in the Princess. Texas Stud in Lit & Lang 4 1962.
— Tennyson's Maud. Connotation 1 1962.
— The poet as critic: appraisals of Tennyson by his contemporaries. Tennessee Stud in Lit 7 1962.
— The moral paradox of the hero in the Idylls of the King. ELH 30 1963. Reply by S. J. Solomon, Victorian Poetry 1 1963.
— Percivale, Ambrosius and the method of narration in the Holy Grail. Die Neueren Sprachen 12 1963.
— Tennyson's The lotus eaters. Revue des Langues Vivantes 28 1963.
— Theme and symbol in Tennyson's poems to 1850. Philadelphia 1964.
— A non-existent variant in Tennyson's Poems, chiefly lyrical. Book Collector 14 1965.
Smidt, K. The intellectual quest of the Victorian poets. E Studies 40 1959.
Tener, R. H. Bagehot and Tennyson. TLS 21 Aug 1959. Bagehot reviewed Idylls, Nat Rev Oct 1859.
Wilson, C. Mirror of a shire: Tennyson's dialect poems. Durham Univ Jnl 21 1959.
Altick, R. D. Four Victorian poets and an exploding island. Victorian Stud 3 1960.
Brett, R. L. The influence of Darwin upon his contemporaries. South Atlantic Quart 59 1960.
Cameron, K. W. Tennyson to Edward Campbell Tainsh in 1868. Emerson Soc Quart no 19 1960. On Enoch Arden.
Cannon, W. F. The Uniformitarian-catastrophist debate. Isis 51 1960.
Litzinger, B. The genesis of Hopkins' Heaven-haven. Victorian Newsletter no 17 1960. From Mort d'Arthur?
— The structure of the Last tournament. Victorian Poetry 1 1963.
Nowell-Smith, S. In memoriam (1850). Book Collector 9 1960.
— Poems by two brothers (1827). Book Collector 11 1962. Addn 12 1963.
P., L. The palace of art 1–16. Explicator 18 1960. Reply by J. Britton 20 1962.
Rogers, E. G. Birdlore in the poetry of Tennyson. Southern Folklore Quart 24 1960.
Schweik, R. C. The 'peace or war' passages in Maud. N & Q Dec 1960. Addn by C. Ricks, June 1962.
Sewell, E. The orphic voice: poetry and natural history. New Haven 1960.
Sonn, C. R. Poetic vision and religious certainty in Tennyson's earlier poetry. MP 57 1960.
Truss, T. J., jr. Tennysonian aspects of Maud. Univ of Mississippi Stud in Eng 1 1960.
Valette, J. Tennyson et nous. Mercure de France 339 1960.
Ware, M. Hamlet's sullied/solid flesh. Shakespeare Quart 11 1960. On Tennyson's suggestion.
Collins, R. L. Clara Tennyson-D'Eyncourt's copy of Poems, chiefly lyrical: new facts and new queries. N & Q Dec 1961.
— Tennyson's original issues of poems, reviews etc 1842–86: a compilation by Henry Van Dyke. Princeton Univ Lib Chron 24 1963.
— How rare are Montagu Butler's translations of Tennyson? Book Collector 12 1963. Reply by C. S. Bliss, ibid.
— The Frederick Tennyson Collection [at Indiana University]. Victorian Stud 7 1963.
Daiches, D. Imagery and mood in Tennyson and Whitman. Eng Stud Today 2 1961.
Gray, D. J. Arthur, Roland, Empedocles, Sigurd and the despair of heroes in Victorian poetry. Boston Univ Stud in Eng 5 1961.
Kendall, J. L. A neglected theme in In memoriam. MLN 76 1961.
MacLaren, M. Tennyson's epicurean lotos-eaters. Classical Jnl March 1961.
Rand, G. I. Tennyson's gift to Walt Whitman: a new letter. Emerson Soc Quart no 24 1961.
Sanders, C. R. Carlyle and Tennyson. PMLA 76 1961.
Spencer, T. J. B. A new look at In memoriam. Venture 1 1961.
Benziger, J. Images of eternity: studies in the poetry of religious vision from Wordsworth to Eliot. Carbondale 1962.
Bishop, J. The unity of In memoriam. Victorian Newsletter no 21 1962.
Danzig, A. The contraries: a central concept in Tennyson. PM LA77 1962.

— Tennyson's The Princess: a definition of love. Victorian Poetry 4 1966.
Diericks, J. King and Archbishop: Henry II and Becket from Tennyson to Frye. Revue de l'Enseignement des Langues Vivantes 28 1962.
Grant, S. A. The mystical implications of In memoriam. Stud in Eng Lit 1500–1900 2 1962.
Gridley, R. Confusion of the seasons in Tennyson's Last tournament. Victorian Newsletter no 22 1962.
Lewis, N. Palgrave and his Golden treasury. Listener 4 Jan 1962.
Peters, R. L. Swinburne and the use of integral detail. Victorian Stud 5 1962.
Pitt, V. Tennyson Laureate. 1962.
Rader, R. W. Tennyson and Rosa Baring. Victorian Stud 5 1962.
— The composition of Maud. MP 59 1962.
— Tennyson in the year of Hallam's death. PMLA 77 1962.
— Tennyson's Maud: the biographical genesis. Berkeley 1963.
— Tennyson's 'strange' father. N & Q Dec 1963.
Richardson, J. The pre-eminent Victorian: a study of Tennyson. 1962.
Smalley, D. A new look at Tennyson—and especially the Idylls. JEGP 61 1962.
Svaglic, M. J. A framework for In memoriam. Ibid.
Young, A. Tennyson in Lincolnshire. In his Poet and the landscape, 1962.
Ball, P. M. Tennyson and the Romantics. Victorian Poetry 1 1963.
Benton, R. P. Tennyson and Lao Tzu. Philosophy East & West 12 1963.
Burch, F. F. Tennyson and Milton: sources for [L. W.] Reece's Tears. Amer N & Q April 1963.
Cadbury, W. The utility of the poetic mask in Supposed confessions. MLQ 24 1963.
— Tennyson's The palace of art and the rhetoric of structures. Criticism 7 1965.
Fredeman, W. E. Rossetti's impromptu portraits of Tennyson reading Maud. Burlington Mag 105 1963.
Fulweiler, H. W. Mermen and mermaids. Victorian Newsletter no 23 1963.
— Tennyson and the 'summons from the sea'. Victorian Poetry 3 1965.
Goldberg, J. P. Two Tennysonian allusions to a poem of Andrew Marvell. N & Q July 1963.
Brown, T. J. English literary autographs xlv: Tennyson. Book Collector 12 1963.
Hall, P. E. A Latin translation of In memoriam. Ibid. By Oswald Augustus Smith.
Hall, R. Gleanings from Tennyson's Idylls for the OED. N & Q Dec 1963.
Hovey, R. B. Locksley Hall: a reinterpretation. Forum 4 1963.
Huxter, N. E. W. Tennyson and Juvenal. N & Q Dec 1963.
Kissane, J. Victorian mythology. Victorian Stud 6 1963.
— Tennyson: the passion of the past and the curse of time. ELH 32 1965.
Metzger, L. The eternal process: some parallels between Faust and In memoriam. Victorian Poetry 1 1963.
Miller, J. H. The theme of the disappearance of God in Victorian poetry. Victorian Stud 6 1963.
— In his Disappearance of God: five nineteenth-century writers, Cambridge Mass 1963.
Pettigrew, J. Tennyson's Ulysses: a reconciliation of opposites. Victorian Poetry 1 1963.
Pipes, N. A slight meteorological disturbance: the last two stanzas of the Poet. Ibid.
Taafe, J. G. Circle imagery in In memoriam. Ibid.
Taylor, J. R. The Hotten piracy of Poems mdcccxxx–mdcccxxxiii. Book Collector 12 1963.
Brashear, W. R. Tennyson's third voice: a note. Victorian Poetry 2 1964.
Bufkin, E. C. Imagery in Locksley Hall. Ibid.
Combecher, H. Drei victorianische Gedichte. Die Neueren Sprachen [13] 1964. Includes Crossing the bar.
Drew, P. Aylmer's Field: a problem for critics. Listener 2 April 1964.
Engbretsen, N. M. The thematic evolution of the Idylls of the King. Victorian Newsletter no 26 1964.
Grob, A. The lotus eaters: two versions of art. MP 62 1964.
Mitchell, C. The undying will of Tennyson's Ulysses. Victorian Poetry 2 1964.
Moore, C. Faith, doubt and mystical experience in In memoriam. Victorian Stud 7 1964.
Packer, L. M. Sun and shadow: the nature of experience in the Lady of Shalott. Victorian Newsletter no 25 1964.
Poston, L. The argument of the Geraint-Enid books in Idylls of the King. Victorian Poetry 2 1964.
— Pelleas and Ettarre: Tennyson's Troilus. Victorian Poetry 4 1966.
Rehak, L. R. On the use of martyrs: Tennyson and Eliot on Becket. UTQ 33 1964.
Ricks, C. Tennyson: three notes. MP 62 1964. On Come not when I am dead; The vision of sin; O, where is he, the simple fool?
— Incumbency. New Statesman 3 July 1964. On Now lies the earth.
— Tennyson's Rifle Clubs!!! RES new ser 15 1964. From ms of 1852?
— Maud. TLS 31 Dec 1964.
— Hallam's 'youthful letters' and Tennyson. Eng Lang Notes 3 1965.
— Two early poems by Tennyson. Victorian Poetry 3 1965. On The wild bee in the wide parterre; I dare not write an ode (from copies of the mss).
— A note on Tennyson's Ode on the death of the Duke of Wellington. SB 18 1965.
— Tennyson's Lucretius. Library 5th ser 20 1965.
— Tennyson: Armageddon into Timbuctoo. MLR 61 1966.
— Tennyson and Persian. Eng Lang Notes 4 1966.
Smith, E. E. The two voices: a Tennyson study. Lincoln Nebraska 1964.
Stokes, E. The metrics of Maud. Victorian Poetry 2 1964.
Talon, H.-A. Sur un poème de Tennyson. Langues Modernes 58 1964. On In memoriam xiii.
— Tennysoniana. TLS 16 July 1964. On the Tennyson Research Centre in Lincoln City Library.
Todd, W. B. Wise, Wrenn and Enoch Arden. Book Collector 13 1964.
Whiting, G. W. The artist and Tennyson. Rice Univ Stud 50 1964.
Bakaya, K. N. Tennyson's use of the dramatic monologue. In Essays presented to Amy G. Stock, ed R. K. Kaul, Jaipur 1965.
Baldini, G. Tennyson conviviale. Rivista di Cultura Classica e Medievale 8 1965.
Fass, I. L. Green as a motif of Tennyson. Victorian Poetry 3 1965.
Gray, J. M. The lady of Shalott and Tennyson's reading in the supernatural. N & Q Aug 1965.
— Source and symbol in Geraint and Enid: Tennyson's Doorm and Limours. Victorian Poetry 4 1966.
— Tennyson and Nennius. N & Q Sept 1966.
— Tennyson and Geoffrey of Monmouth. N & Q Feb 1967.
Hardie, W. The Light Brigade. TLS 3 June 1965. Reply by C. B. L. Tennyson 15 July 1965.
Hinton, P. F. The 'green Tennysons'. Book Collector 14 1965.
Huebbenthal, J. Growing old; Rabbi ben Ezra; and Tears, idle tears. Victorian Poetry 3 1965.
Kincaid, J. R. Crossing the bar. Ibid.
Legris, M. Structure and allegory in Tennyson's Idylls of the King. Humanities Assoc Bull (Canada) 16 1965.

Mattheisen, P. F. Gosse's candid snapshots. Victorian Stud 8 1965.
Maxwell, J. C. 'Tennysonian'. N & Q Aug 1965.
Mays, J. C. C. In memoriam: an aspect of form. UTQ 35 1965.
Melchiori, G. Locksley Hall revisited: Tennyson and Henry James. REL 6 1965.
Shaw, W. D. and C. W. Gartlein. The aurora: a spiritual metaphor of Tennyson. Victorian Poetry 3 1965.
Battaglia, F. J. The use of contradiction in In memoriam. Eng Lang Notes 4 1966.
Eggers, J. P. Tennyson's Geraint idylls and the Mabinogion. Victorian Poetry 4 1966.
Golffing, F. Tennyson's last phase: the poet as seer. Southern Rev 2 1966.
Kozicki, H. Tennyson's Idylls of the King as tragic drama. Victorian Poetry 4 1966.
Perrine, L. The tone of Crossing the bar. Ibid.
Rackin, P. Recent misreadings of Break, break, break. JEGP 65 1966.
Sendry, J. The Palace of art revisited. Victorian Poetry 4 1966.
Solimine, J. The dialectics of Church and State: Tennyson's historical plays. Personalist 47 1966.
Steane, J. B. Tennyson. 1966.
Wilkenfeld, R. B. The shape of Two voices. Victorian Poetry 4 1966.
Short, C. Tennyson and the Lover's tale. PMLA 82 1967.
Ostriker, A. The three modes in Tennyson's prosody. Ibid.

W. D. P. and D. A. L.

ELIZABETH BARRETT BROWNING
1806–61

Diaries, memo books, ms poems, and nearly a thousand letters (to H. S. Boyd, B. R. Haydon, Anna Jameson, J. Kenyon, Mary Russell Mitford, Robert Browning et al) are in the Wellesley College Library. Most of Mrs Browning's letters to her sisters are in the Berg Collection of the New York Public Library and the collection of A. A. Houghton, New York City. Important ms materials are in the BM, Huntington Library, Folger Library, Pierpont Morgan Library, libraries of Baylor, Harvard and Yale universities and the universities of Illinois and Texas.

Bibliographies

Forman, H. B. Elizabeth Barrett Browning and her scarcer books. 1896; rptd in W. R. Nicoll and T. J. Wise, Literary anecdotes of the nineteenth century, 2 vols 1895–6.
Wise, T. J. Bibliography of the writings of Elizabeth Barrett Browning. 1918.
—— A Browning library. 1929.
Ehrsam, T. G., R. H. Deily and R. M. Smith. In their Bibliographies of twelve Victorian authors, New York 1936. Supplement by J. G. Fucilla, MP 37 1939.
Taplin, G. B. Mrs Browning's contributions to periodicals. PBSA 44 1950; rptd in his Life of Elizabeth Barrett Browning, 1957.
Broughton, L. N., C. S. Northup and R. B. Pearsall. In their Robert Browning: a bibliography, Ithaca 1953.
Jannattoni, L. Elizabeth Barrett Browning, con un saggio di bibliografia italiana. Florence 1953.
Pettit, K. I. By Elizabeth Barrett Browning. Yale Univ Lib Gazette 34 1959. A list of mss and pbns.
Catalogue of the Elizabeth Barrett Browning centenary exhibition. 1961.

Collections

Poems. 2 vols 1844, New York 1844 (as A drama of exile and other poems); ed Robert Browning 1887.
Poems: new edition. 2 vols 1850. Enlarged as Poems, 3 vols 1856, 1862, 4 vols 1864.
Poetical works. 5 vols 1866, 2 vols New York 1871, 1877 ('corrected by the last London edition'), 6 vols 1899 etc.
Poetical works from 1826 to 1844. Ed J. H. Ingram [1887]. With Browning's prefatory note.
Poetical works. Ed F. G. Kenyon 1897.
Poetical works. Ed H. W. Preston, Boston 1900 etc. The Cambridge edn.
Complete poems. 2 vols 1904.
Poetical works. Oxford 1904 (OSA).
Complete poetical works. Ed L. Whiting 2 vols New York York 1919.

Selections

A selection from the poetry of Elizabeth Barrett Browning. 2 sers 1866–80. Ser 1 contains foreword by Robert Browning.
The earlier poems. Ed R. H. Shepherd 1878.
Poems. Ed Mrs D. Ogilvie 1893.
Poems. Ed A. Meynell 1903.
Selected poems. Ed E. Lee, Boston 1904.
Poems by Robert and Elizabeth Browning. Ed C. Charles 1910.
Selections from the Brownings. Ed H. O'B. Boas 1933.
Best known poems of Elizabeth and Robert Browning. Garden City NY 1942.
Love poems of Elizabeth Barrett Browning and Robert Browning. Ed L. Untermeyer, New Brunswick 1946.
The poetry of the Brownings. Ed C. Bax 1947.

§1

For a list of about a hundred periodical contributions, see G. B. Taplin, PBSA 44 1950.
The battle of Marathon: a poem. 1820; ed H. B. Forman 1891 (facs).
Essay on mind, with other poems. 1826.
Prometheus bound, translated from the Greek of Aeschylus; and miscellaneous poems. 1833.
The Seraphim and other poems. 1838.
Queen Annelida and false Arcite. In The poems of Chaucer modernized, 1841.
A new spirit of the age. 2 vols 1844. With R. H. Horne. Articles on Landor and Milnes, and parts of other articles, are by E. B. B. An essay on Carlyle rptd in Nicoll and Wise, Literary anecdotes, 1896.
Sonnets [or] Sonnets from the Portugese. In Poems, 1850 etc; often rptd separately. Earliest independent edn Boston 1886. A famous edn dated Reading, 1847, is a forgery by T. J. Wise. Annotated edn, ed F. E. Ratchford and D. Fulton, New York 1950; tr French, 1905; Spanish, 1954.
Casa Guidi windows: a poem. 1851.
The cry of the children. In Two poems, 1854. The second poem is by Robert Browning.
Aurora Leigh. 1857 (3 edns), 1859, 1860 (rev), 1882 (17th edn), New York 1857 etc; ed A. C. Swinburne 1898; ed H. B. Forman 1899 (Temple Classics).
Poems before congress. 1860, New York 1860 (as Napoleon III in Italy and other poems).
Last poems. 1862.
The Greek Christian poets and the English poets. 1863. First pbd as articles in Athenaeum 1842.
Psyche apocalypte: a lyrical drama. St James Mag Feb 1876; 1876 (separately). A drama 'projected' by E. B. B. and R. H. Horne.
Epistle to a canary. Ed T. J. Wise 1913.
The enchantress, and other poems. Ed T. J. Wise 1913.
Deila: a tale. Ed T. J. Wise 1913.
New poems by Robert and Elizabeth Barrett Browning. Ed F. G. Kenyon 1914.
The poet's enchiridion. Ed H. B. Forman, Boston 1914. Contains 3 items of juvenilia.

Hitherto unpublished poems and stories, with an unedited autobiography. Ed H. B. Forman 2 vols Boston 1914 (pamphlets).
The sorrows of the Muses: an early [unpbd] poem. Ed W. Barnes, Books at Iowa 4 1966.

Letters and Papers

Powell, T. In his Living authors of England, New York 1849. Includes the first pbd correspondence.
Townshend Mayer, S. R. Letters addressed to R. Hengist Horne. 2 vols 1877.
Kind words from a sickroom, to A. P. Paton. Greenock 1891. 4 letters from E. B. B.
Nicholl, W. R. The religious opinions of Elizabeth Barrett Browning. 1896. 4 letters, rptd in Nicoll and T. J. Wise, Literary anecdotes, 1896.
Kenyon, F. G. Letters of Elizabeth Barrett Browning. 2 vols 1897.
Letters of Robert Browning and Elizabeth Barrett Browning 1845–6. 2 vols 1899, New York 1899.
Meynell, A. The art of scansion: letters of E. B. Browning to Uvedale Price. 1916.
Wise, T. J. Letters of Elizabeth Barrett Browning to Robert Browning and other correspondents. 1916.
Huxley, L. Letters to her sister 1846–59. 1929.
Twenty-two unpublished letters of Elizabeth Barrett Browning and Robert Browning (to her sisters). New York, 1935.
Benet, W. R. From Robert and Elizabeth Browning: a further selection. 1936.
Shackford, M. H. Letters to B. R. Haydon. Oxford 1939.
Price, F. Some uncollected letters of Mrs Browning. N & Q 18 Nov 1944. *See* A. Meynell 16 Dec 1944.
Harrod, H. Correspondence of Harriet Beecher Stowe and Elizabeth Barrett Browning. SE 27 1948.
Weaver, B. Twenty unpublished letters of Elizabeth Barrett to H. S. Boyd. PMLA 65 1950.
McAleer, E. C. New letters from Mrs Browning to Isa Blagden. PMLA 66 1951.
Miller, B. Elizabeth Barrett to Miss Mitford: unpublished letters. 1954.
Musgrove, S. Unpublished letters of Thomas de Quincey and E. B. Browning. Auckland Univ College Bull 44 1954.
McCarthy, B. P. Elizabeth Barrett to Mr Boyd: unpublished letters. 1955.
Landis, P. and R. E. Freeman. Letters of the Brownings to George Barrett. Urbana 1958.
Green, D. B. Elizabeth Barrett and R. Shelton Mackenzie. SE 14 1961. 2 unpbd letters; *see* An additional letter, PMLA 76 1961.
Kelley, P. Letters from the Brownings. Listener 17 May 1962. Announces 10,000 new documents.

§2

'North, Christopher' (J. Wilson). The Seraphim and other poems. Blackwood's Mag Aug 1838.
[Coleridge, H. N.] Miss Barrett's poems. Quart Rev 66 1840.
Fuller, Margaret (Ossioli). Poems 1844. New York Tribune 4 Jan 1845; rptd in her Papers on literature and art, New York 1846.
Poe, E. A. Poems, 1844. Broadway Jnl 1845; rptd in his Works, 1895.
Griswold, R. W. In his Poets and poetry of England in the nineteenth century, Philadelphia 1845.
Powell, T. In his Living poets of England, New York 1849.
Poems 1850. Guardian 22 Jan 1851.
Milsand, J. Elizabeth Barrett. Revue des Deux Mondes 15 Jan 1852; rptd in his Littérature anglaise et philosophie, Dijon 1893.
Gilfillan, G. In his Galleries of literary portraits vol i, 1856.
Roscoe, W. C. Aurora Leigh. Nat Rev 4 1857; rptd in his Poems and essays, 1860.

Chorley, H. F. Elizabeth Barrett Browning. Athenaeum 6 July 1861.
Elizabeth Barrett Browning. Saturday Rev 13 July 1861.
Holcombe, S. B. Death of Mrs Browning. Southern Literary Messenger 33 1861.
Conant, C. B. Mrs Browning. North Amer Rev 94 1862.
Taine, H. A. In his Notes sur l'Angleterre, Paris 1872.
Stedman, E. C. Elizabeth Barrett Browning. Boston 1877.
Selden, C. In his Portraits des femmes, Paris 1877.
Bayne, P. Two great Englishwomen: Mrs Browning and Charlotte Bronte. 1881.
Robertson, E. S. In his English poetesses, 1883.
des Guerrois, C. Etude sur Mistress Elizabeth Browning. Paris 1885.
Druskowitz, H. In his Drei englische Dichterinnen, Berlin 1885.
Ingram, J. H. Elizabeth Barrett Browning. 1888.
Ritchie, A. T. In her Records of Tennyson, Ruskin and the Brownings, 1892.
Zampini-Salazar, F. Roberto ed Elizabetta Browning. Naples 1896.
—— La vita e le opere de Roberto e Elizabetta B. Browning. Turin 1907.
Whiting, Lillian. A study of Elizabeth Barrett Browning. 1899.
—— The Brownings: their life and art. 1911.
Stephen, L. The Browning letters. In his Studies of a biographer ser 2, 1902.
Gould, E. P. The Brownings and America. Boston 1904.
Merlette, G. M. La vie et l'oeuvre d'Elizabeth Barrett Browning. Paris 1905.
Lubbock, P. Elizabeth Barrett Browning in her letters. 1906.
Pluviannes, H. et al. Hommage français à Elizabeth Barrett Browning. Vals-les-Bains 1906.
Cunliffe, J. W. Elizabeth Barrett's influence on Browning's poetry. PMLA 23 1908.
Jacobi, B. Elizabeth Barrett Browning als Übersetzerin antiker Dichtungen. Munich 1908.
Nicati, A. B. Femme et poète: Elizabeth Barrett Browning. Paris 1912.
Royds, K. E. Elizabeth Barrett Browning and her poetry. 1912.
Viterbi, B. B. Elizabeth Barrett Browning. Bergamo 1913.
Jameson, A. In her Letters and friendships, 1915.
Symons, A. Some Browning reminiscences. North Amer Rev Oct 1916.
Elton, O. The Brownings. 1924.
Minckwitz, M. J. Zu den Casa Guidi windows. Anglia 38 1926.
Burdett, O. The Brownings. 1928.
Willis, I. C. Elizabeth Barrett Browning. 1928.
Clarke, I. C. Elizabeth Barrett Browning: a portrait. 1929.
Creston, D. Andromeda in Wimpole Street. 1929.
Lenanton, C. Miss Barrett's elopement. 1929.
Loth, D. G. The Brownings: a Victorian idyll. 1929.
Boas, S. Elizabeth Barrett Browning. 1930.
Sim, F. M. Robert Browning and Elizabeth Barrett. 1930.
Gaylord, H. Pompilia and her poet. New York 1931.
Woolf, V. In her Common reader: second series, 1932.
—— Flush: a dog. 1933.
Saludok, E. Stilkritische Untersuchungen der Sonette der E. B. B. im Verhältnis zu Rilkes Übertragung. Marburg 1933.
Shackford, M. H. In her Two studies, Wellesley 1935.
Marks, J. The family of the Barretts: a colonial romance. New York 1938.
McCormick, J. P. As a flame springs: the romance of Robert and Elizabeth Barrett Browning. New York 1940.
Ransom, H. The Brownings in Paris 1858. SE 1941.
Smith, F. M. Mrs Browning's rhymes. PMLA 54 1942.
Smith, G. Petronius Arbiter and Elizabeth Barrett. N & Q 2 Nov 1946.
Turner, P. Aurora versus the angel. RES 24 1948.
Miller, B. The child of Casa Guidi. Cornhill Mag 163 1949.

— Miss Barrett and Mr Hunter. Cornhill Mag 165 1951.
— Elizabeth Barrett and her brother. Cornhill Mag 166 1952.
Boyce, C. K. From Paris to Pisa with the Brownings. New Colophon 1950. On their elopement.
'Winwar, Frances' The immortal lovers. 1950.
Hewlett, D. Elizabeth Barrett Browning. 1953.
Waite, H. E. How do I love thee. 1953.
Burnett, C. B. Silver answer: a romantic biography. 1955.
Sewter, A. C. The Barretts at Hope End: unpublished portraits, sketches and letters. Connoisseur (New York) May 1956.
Treves, G. A. In his Golden ring: the Anglo-Florentines, 1956.
Kenmare, D. The Browning love story. 1957.
Taplin, G. B. Life of Elizabeth Barrett Browning. 1957.
Barbery, Y. La critique moderne face à Elizabeth et Robert Browning. Études Anglaises 13 1960.
Centenary commemorative exhibition. TLS 2 June 1961.
Rosenbaum, R. A. In his Earnest Victorians, New York 1961.
Tompkins, J. M. S. Aurora Leigh. 1961 (Fawcett lecture).
Hayter, A. Mrs Browning: a poet's work and its setting. 1962.
— Elizabeth Barrett Browning. 1965 (Br Council pamphlet).
Phillipson, J. S. How do I love thee: an echo of St Paul. Victorian Newsletter no 22 1962.
Gerard, W. Miss Ba: ou l'immortalité par l'amour. Revue Générale Belge 9 1963.
Davenport, G. In her Great loves in legend and life, New York 1964.
'Bishop, Morchard'. Towards a biography of Flush. TLS 15 Dec 1966.
DeLaura, D. A. Robert Browning letter: the source of Mrs Browning's A curse for a nation. Victorian Poetry 4 1966.
Lohrli, A. Greek slave mystery. N & Q Feb 1966. On pbn of sonnet in Household Words 1850.

R.B.P.

ROBERT BROWNING
1812–89

Some noteworthy collections of ms material relating to Browning are in the Balliol College Library, Bodley, the BM, the Victoria and Albert Museum; in the Keats-Shelley House in Rome and the Biblioteca Nazionale in Florence; in libraries at the universities of Chicago, Illinois and Texas, and at Baylor University, Wellesley College and Yale; and in the Huntington Library, the Pierpont Morgan Library, and the Berg Collection of the New York Public Library.

Bibliographies etc.

Furnivall, F. J. Bibliography of Browning from 1833 to 1881. Browning Soc Papers 1 1881–4. *See* Orr, below.
Orr, A. A handbook to the works of Browning. 1885. Discusses the whole canon in classified groups, as authorized and partly supervised by Browning. A bibliography based on Furnivall's, above, appears in the sixth (1892) and later edns.
Cooke, G. W. A guide book to the poetic and dramatic works of Browning. 1890.
Berdoe, E. The Browning cyclopaedia: a guide to the study of the works of Browning, with copious notes and references on all difficult passages. 1892, 1897 (rev).
Molineux, M. A. Phrase book from the poetic and dramatic works. Boston 1896. Contains also an index of significant words.
Wise, T. J. A complete bibliography of Browning. 1897. First pbd as Materials for a bibliography of Browning in W. R. Nicholl and Wise, Literary anexdotes of the nineteenth century vol i, 1895.
— A Browning library. 1929.
Cook, A. K. A commentary upon Browning's The ring and the book. Oxford 1920, New York 1966.
Broughton, L. N. and B. F. Stelter. A concordance to the poems of Browning. 1924.
Brooks, A. E. Browningiana in Baylor University. Baylor Bull 24 1921. Bibliography of criticism.
Armstrong, A. J. Browning the world over. Waco Texas 1933. Includes extensive bibliography of foreign Browningiana.
Forster, M. and W. Zappe. Browning Bibliographie. Halle 1939.
Raymond, W. O. Browning studies in England and America 1910–49. In his Infinite moment, Toronto 1950.
Broughton, L. N., C. S. Northup and R. B. Pearsall. Browning: a bibliography 1830–1950. Ithaca 1953. The standard bibliography.
Archibald, R. C. Additions to the bibliography. N & Q June 1954. Musical settings.
DeVane, W. C. A Browning handbook. Ithaca 1935, New York 1955 (rev). The standard handbook.
Litzinger, B. and K. L. Knickerbocker. In their Browning critics, Lexington Kentucky 1965. Includes bibliography 1951–65.

Collections

Poems: a new edition. 2 vols 1849. First collected edn containing only Paracelsus, the eight numbers of Bells and Pomegranates, and lines from a version of Home-thoughts.
Poems: a new edition. 2 vols Boston 1850. Most of the subsequent London collected edns were similarly echoed by Boston, and later New York, edns.
Poetical works: third edition. 3 vols 1863.
Poetical works: fourth edition. 3 vols 1865.
Poetical works. 6 vols 1868.
Poetical works. 4 vols Leipzig 1872 (Tauchnitz).
Poetical works. In monthly numbers of American railway guides from 1872. Browning's works were to have been 'continued every month until completed'.
Poetical and dramatic works. Ed G. W. Cooke 6 vols Boston 1887. Became Riverside edn, 1889, 1899 etc.
Poetical works. 17 vols 1888–94. Fourth and complete edition, with closing vols ed by E. Berdoe.
Complete poetic and dramatic works. Boston 1895. Cambridge edn, with apparatus by Cooke and H. E. S[cudder]. Includes some previously uncollected poems.
Poetical works. Ed A. Birrell 2 vols 1896. Often rptd and sometimes rev; issued till 1928 or later in both London and New York.
Complete works. Ed C. Porter and H. A. Clarke, preface by W. L. Phelps, richly illustrated. 14 vols New York 1898. Florentine edn; sold under many bindings and imprints bearing diverse names for 20 years.
Poetical works. 1904 etc. An edn begun by Grant Richards and continued in WC, Oxford edn etc; as Poetical works complete from 1833 to 1868 and shorter poems thereafter, Oxford 1941.
Poems and plays. 2 vols 1906 (EL) (later 4 vols); ed J. Bryson 1954.
Works. Ed F. G. Kenyon 10 vols 1912. Centenary edn.
Complete poetical works, with additional poems first published in 1914. Ed A. Birrell and F. G. Kenyon 1915. Globe edn.
Complete works. Ed J. H. Finley 6 vols 1926.
The poems and plays. Ed S. Commins, New York 1934 (Modern Lib).

Selections

For further selections see L. N. Broughton et al, Bibliography, Ithaca 1953.
Selections. [Ed J. Forster and B. W. Proctor (Barry Cornwall)] 1863; A selection from Browning, 1865 1865 (Moxon's Miniature Poets); Lyrics of life, illustr

S. Eytinge jr, Boston 1865; Selections, [ed Browning] 1872 (dedicated to Tennyson); Favorite poems by Browning, Boston 1877; Selections: second series, [ed Browning] 1880.

A selection for the use of schools. Ed F. Ahn, Berlin 1882; Lyrical and dramatic poems, ed E. T. Mason, New York 1883; Selections, ed R. G. White, New York 1883; A Browning calendar, Chicago 1884 (first of many edns); Bits from Browning, ed Mrs N. V. Walker, Boston 1886; An introduction to the study of Browning, ed H. Corson, Boston 1886.

Christmas-eve and Easter-day, and other poems, with an introductory essay on Browning's theory concerning personal immortality. Ed H. E. Hersey and W. J. Rolfe 1886.

Bits of burnished gold from Browning. Ed R. Porter, New York 1888; Good and true thoughts from Browning, ed A. Cross, New York 1888; The Browning reciter, ed A. H. Miles 1889 ('tenth thousand'); Shorter poems, ed N. Bögholm, New York 1890; Browning year book, ed C. M. Tyths, New York 1892; Fifine at the fair, and other poems, ed J. Morrison, Edinburgh 1892; The Browning primer, ed F. J. Furnivall, New York 1893; A blot, and other dramas, ed F. Rinder 1896; The Brownings for the young, ed F. G. Kenyon 1896; Dramatic romances and other poems, ed E. Dixon 1897; Poems, ed O. Browning 1897; Poems, ed R. Garnett, illustr Byam Shaw 1897.

Saul and other poems. Ed E. H. Turpin, New York 1898; The best of Browning, ed J. Mudge and W. V. Kelley, New York 1898; The lyric poems, ed E. Rhys 1898; Shorter poems, ed F. T. Baker 1899; Earlier monologues, ed H. B. Forman 1900; Select poems, ed E. H. Blakeney 1900; Selections, ed W. Hall Griffin 1902; Browning's poems, ed A. D. Innes 1903; A blot, and other plays, ed A. Bates, Boston 1904; Florence in the poetry of the Brownings, ed A. B. McKahan, Chicago 1904 (lavishly ptd and illustr).

Select poems. Ed A. B. George, Boston 1905; Selections, ed R. M. Lovett, Boston 1906; Selections, ed C. W. French, Chicago 1907; Selections, ed J. C. Saul, Toronto 1907; Lyrical poems, ed A. T. Quiller-Couch, Oxford 1908; Poems, ed A. Birrell, Edinburgh 1908; Selections, ed R. D. Stocker 1908; Selections, ed R. A. S. Rankin, Glasgow 1909; Shorter poems, ed J. W. Cunliffe, New York 1909; A selection, ed W. T. Young, Cambridge 1911; Poems, ed C. W. Hodell 1911; Selections, ed E. F. Hoernle, illustr A. Ross, Edinburgh 1911.

Introduction to Browning. Ed E. B. Halleck, New York 1912; Rabbi Ben Ezra and other poems, illustr B. Partridge 1914; A Browning anthology, ed F. A. Forbes, Oxford 1917; Browning for the trenches, 1918 (Boston Browning Soc) (distributed free to US soldiers; sold as the Victory edn 1919); Poems and plays, ed H. E. Joyce, New York 1922; Browning, humanist, ed E. Compton-Rickett 1924; Select poems, ed R. Ishikawa, Tokyo 1925.

Tennyson and Browning contrasted. Ed G. Boas 1925; Shorter poems, ed F. T. Baker and N. Y. Moffett, New York 1927; Selected poems, ed L. E. Robinson, Philadelphia 1930; The best of Browning, ed C. J. Weber, Fairfield Maine 1930; Poems, ed B. R. Redman, New York 1932; Selections, ed H. Boaz 1933.

Two poets, a dog and a boy. Ed F. T. P. Russell, illustr C. Odell, Philadelphia 1933.

Selected poems. Ed W. T. Hutchins and J. R. Reed 1937.

Poetry and prose, with appreciations by Landor, Bagehot, Swinburne, Henry James, Saintsbury and F. L. Lucas. Ed H. Milford, Oxford 1941.

The best of Browning. Ed W. H. Rogers, New York 1942; Selections, ed W. Fancutt 1944; Selected poems, ed W. C. DeVane, New York 1949; Poetry and prose, ed S. Nowell-Smith 1950; Thirty poems, ed W. S. Mackie 1950; Selected poems, ed K. L. Knickerbocker, New York 1951; Selected poems, ed J. Reeves 1954; Poems, ed D. Smalley, Boston 1956; ed R. Wilbur, New York 1960; ed R. Sprague 1964.

§1

Pauline: a fragment of a confession. 1833; ed T. J. Wise 1886; ed N. H. Wallis 1931 (comparing states of the text).

Sonnet: eyes calm beside thee. Monthly Repository Oct 1834.

Paracelsus. 1835; ed G. Lowes Dickinson 1899 (Temple Classics); ed M. L. Lee and K. B. Locock 1909; ed C. P. Denison, New York 1911.

The King: 'A king lived long ago'. Monthly Repository Nov 1835.

Johannes Agricola. Monthly Repository Jan 1836.

Porphyria. Ibid.

Lines: Still ailing, wind? Monthly Repository May 1836.

Contributions to the Life of Strafford by J. Forster. In Lives of statesmen, 1836; ed C. H. Firth and F. J. Furnivall 1892.

Strafford: an historical tragedy. 1837, 1882 (for North London Collegiate School); ed E. H. Hickey 1884; ed A. Wilson 1901; ed H. B. George, Oxford 1908; 1929 (playbook).

Sordello. 1840; ed H. Buxton Forman 1902; ed A. J. Whyte 1913.

Pippa passes (Bells and pomegranates no I). Often rptd, e.g. illustr L. L. Brooke 1898; illustr M. Armstrong, New York 1903; ed A. Symons 1906; ed A. L. Irvine 1924; ed E. A. Parker 1927.

King Victor and King Charles (Bells and pomegranates no ii). 1842.

Dramatic lyrics (Bells and pomegranates no iii). 1842; ed J. O. Beatty and J. W. Bowyer, New York 1931 (facs). Includes Cavalier tunes (Marching along, Give a rouse, My wife Gertrude); Italy and France (My last Duchess, Count Gismond); Camp and cloister (Incident of the French camp, Soliloquy of the Spanish cloister); In a gondola; Artemis prologizes; Waring; Queen worship (Rudel to the lady of Tripoli, Cristina); Madhouse cells (Johannes Agricola, Porphyria's lover); Through the Metidja to Abd-el-Kadr; The pied piper of Hamelin.

Tasso and Chatteron [essay]. Foreign Quart Rev 29 1842 (anon); ed D. Smalley, Cambridge Mass 1948.

The return of the Druses: a tragedy in five acts (Bells and pomegranates no iv). 1843; ed C. Porter, Boston 1902 (stage version); tr German, 1912.

A blot in the 'scutcheon: a tragedy in five acts (Bells and pomegranates no v). 1843. For so-called second edn [1846] *see* Broughton et al, Bibliography, above. Other edns 1892, 1916, 1923, and in play anthologies; tr French, 1899.

A blot in the 'scutcheon: a tragedy in three acts (Bells and pomegranates no v). 1843, [1846] ('second edition'; *see* Broughton et al, Bibliography). Other edns, 1892, 1916, 1923, and in play anthologies; tr French, 1899.

Colombe's birthday: a play in five acts (Bells and pomegranates no vi). 1844.

Claret and tokay. Hood's Mag June 1844.

The laboratory (Ancien Régime). Ibid.

Garden fancies (The flower's name, and Sibrandus Schafnaburgensis). Hood's Mag July 1844.

Dramatic romances and lyrics (Bells and pomegranates no vii). 1845, 1897; illustr C. Ricketts 1899; illustr E. F. Brickdale, New York 1909. Includes How they brought the good news; Pictor Ignotus; Italy in England; England in Italy; The lost leader; The lost mistress; Home thoughts from abroad; The tomb at St Praxed's; Garden fancies (The flower's name, Sibrandus Schafnaburgensis); France and Spain (The laboratory, The confessional); The flight of the Duchess; Earth's immortalities; Song; The boy and the angel; Night and morning; Claret and tokay; Saul; Time's revenges; The glove.

The tomb at San Praxed's. Hood's Mag March 1845.

The flight of the Duchess: part first. Hood's Mag April 1845.

Luria and A soul's tragedy (Bells and pomegranates no viii). 1846. A soul's tragedy, tr German, 1903; Luria, tr German, 1910; Italian, 1934.

Christmas eve and Easter day. 1850, 1900, 1907; ed O. Smeaton 1918.

Shelley [essay]. In the [spurious] Letters of Percy Bysshe Shelley, 1852; ed F. J. Furnivall 1881 (Browning Soc), 1888 (Shelley Soc), Bibelot 1902; Warwick 1903; ed R. Garnett 1903; ed J. C. Thompson, Hull 1908; ed L. Winstanley, Boston 1911 (with Shelley, Defence of poetry); ed H. F. B. Brett-Smith, Oxford 1921 (with Shelley, Defence; Peacock, Four ages of poetry).

The twins. In Two poems (the other by Elizabeth Barrett Browning), 1854.

Men and women. 2 vols 1855, 1 vol Boston 1856, 1863, 1866, 1869; ed H. B. Forman 1899; 2 vols Westminster 1899; illustr H. Osprovat 1903; ed B. Worsfold 1904; 1908; Oxford 1910; ed G. E. Hadow, Oxford 1911, 1920 (facs); ed F. B. Pinion 1963; tr French (incomplete), 1938. Poems included are (vol i) Love among the ruins; A lovers' quarrel; Evelyn Hope; Up at a villa—down in the city; A woman's last word; Fra Lippo Lippi; A toccata of Galuppi's; By the fireside; Any wife to any husband; An epistle of Karshish the Arab physician; Mesmerism; A serenade at the villa; My star; Instans Tyrannus; A pretty woman; 'Childe Roland to the dark tower came'; Respectability; A light woman; The statue and the bust; Love in a life; Life in a love; How it strikes a contemporary; The last ride together; The patriot; Master Hugues of Saxe-Gotha; Bishop Blougram's apology; Memorabilia; (vol ii) Andrea del Sarto; Before: After; In three days; In a year; Old pictures in Florence; In a balcony; Saul; 'De gustibus'; Women and roses; Protus; Holy-cross day; The guardian angel; Cleon; The twins; Popularity; The heretic's tragedy; Two in the Campagna; A grammarian's funeral; One way of love; Another way of love; 'Transcendentalism'; Misconceptions; One word more.

Ben Karshook's wisdom. Keepsake 1856.

May and death. Ibid

Dramatis personae. 1864, 1864 ('second edn'); ed M. Edwardes 1906 (Temple Classics); 1910; ed J. O. Beatty and J. W. Bowyer, New York 1931 (facs); illustr E. F. Brickdale 1909; tr Italian, 1924. Poems included are James Lee; Gold hair; The worst of it; Dis aliter visum; Too late; Abt Vogler; Rabbi Ben Ezra; A death in the desert; Caliban upon Setebos; Confessions; May and death; Prospice; Youth and art; A face; A likeness; Mr Sludge 'the medium'; Apparent failure; Epilogue.

Euridice to Orpheus: a picture by Leighton. Royal Academy Exhibition Catalogue 1864.

Gold hair: a legend of Pornic. Atlantic Monthly May 1864.

Prospice. Atlantic Monthly June 1864.

Under the cliff (from James Lee). Ibid.

Note on Elizabeth Barrett Browning. In A selection of the poetry of Elizabeth Barrett Browning, 1866. Another note in her Poems, 1887, contradicting her biographer J. H. Ingram. *See* Athenaeum 31 Jan 1891.

The ring and the book: in four volumes. Vols 1–2 1868, vols 3–4 1869; 2 vols Boston 1869, 4 vols 1872 ('second edn'), '2 vols in 1' Boston 1883, 3 vols 1889; ed C. Porter and H. A. Clarke 1897; illustr 1898; ed F. M. Padelford, Boston 1899; ed J. Buchan 1908; ed C. W. Hodell 1911 (EL); ed E. Dowden 1912; New York 1912; London 1919; ed M. J. Moses, New York 1929; ed A. K. Cook, Oxford 1940; ed W. Sypher, New York 1961; tr German, 1927.

Balaustion's adventure, including a transcript from Euripides. 1871, Boston 1871, London 1872 ('second edn'), 1881; ed E. A. Parker 1928.

Prince Hohenstiel-Schwangau, saviour of society. 1871.

Hervé Riel. Cornhill Mag March 1871.

Fifine at the fair. 1872.

Red Cotton night-cap country: or turf and towers. 1873, Boston 1873.

Aristophanes' apology, including a transcript from Euripides: being the last adventures of Balaustion. 1875, Boston 1875.

The inn album. New York Times 14, 21, 28 Nov 1875; London 1875, Boston 1876; tr German, 1877.

Pacchiarotto and how he worked in distemper; with other poems. 1876, Boston 1877. Includes Prologue; Of Pacchiarotto, and how he worked in distemper; At the 'Mermaid'; House; Shop; Pisgah-sights, II; Fears and scruples; Natural magic; Magical nature; Bifurcation; Numpholeptos; Appearances; St Martin's summer; Hervé Riel; A forgiveness; Cenciaja; Filippo Baldinucci on the privilege of burial; Epilogue.

To my critics. Examiner 5 Aug 1876.

The Agamemnon of Aeschylus, transcribed by Browning. 1877.

La Saisiaz, and The two poets of Croisic. 1878.

Dramatic idyls. 1879, 1882 ('second edn'). Includes Martin Relph; Pheidippides; Halbert and Hob; Ivan Ivanovitch; Tray; Ned Bratts.

Dramatic idyls: second series. 1880. Includes Prologue; Echetlos; Clive; Muléykeh; Pietro of Albano; Doctor —; Pan and Luna; Epilogue.

Ten new lines to Touch him ne'er so lightly. Century Mag Nov 1882.

Jocoseria. 1883, Boston 1883, London 1883 ('second edn'), 1884 ('third edn'). Includes Wanting is—what?; Donald; Solomon and Balkis; Cristina and Monaldeschi; Mary Wollstonecraft and Fuseli; Adam, Lilith and Eve; Ixion; Jochanan Hakkadosh; Never the time and the place; Pambo.

Sonnet on Goldoni. Pall Mall Gazette 8 Dec 1883.

Helen's tower. Pall Mall Gazette 28 Dec 1883.

Ferishtah's fancies. 1884, Boston 1885, London 1885 (2nd edn), 1885 (3rd edn). Includes Prologue; The eagle; The melon-seller; Shah Abbas; The family; The sun; Mihrab Shah; A camel-driver; Two camels; Cherries; Plot-culture; A pillar at Sebzevah; A bean-stripe, also apple-eating; Epilogue.

Sonnet on Rawden Brown. Century Mag Feb 1884.

The founder of the feast. World 16 April 1884.

The names ('Shakespeare, to that name's sounding'). In Shakesperian Show book (for an Albert Hall bazaar), 1884; Pall Mall Gazette 29 May 1884.

Introduction to the Divine order and other sermons, by Thomas Jones. 1884.

Sonnet: why I am a Liberal. In Why I am a Liberal, ed A. Reid 1885.

Parleyings with certain people of importance in their day, to wit: Bernard de Mandeville, Daniel Bartoli, Christopher Smart, George Bubb Dodington, Francis Furini, Gerard de Lairesse, and Charles Avison; introduced by a dialogue between Apollo and the Fates; concluded by another between John Fust and his friends. 1887, Boston 1887.

Jubilee memorial lines. Pall Mall Gazette Dec 1887.

The isle's enchantress (on F. Moscheles' painting). Pall Mall Gazette 26 March 1889.

To Edward FitzGerald. Athenaeum 13 July 1889.

Lines for the tomb of L. L. Thaxter. Poet Lore Aug 1889.

Asolando: fancies and facts. 1890, 1890, 1893 (10th edn), Boston 1890. Silently annotated, 1894; tr Italian, 1838. Includes Prologue; Rosny; Dubiety; Now; Humility; Poetics; Summum bonum; A pearl, a girl; Speculative; White witchcraft; Bad dreams I; Bad dreams II; Bad dreams III; Bad dreams IV; Inapprehensiveness; Which?; The Cardinal and the dog; The Pope and the net; The bean-feast; Mucklemouth Meg; Arcades ambo; The lady and the painter; Ponte dell' Angelo, Venice; Beatrice Signorini; Flute-music, with an accompaniment; 'Imperante Augusto natus est—'; Development; Rephan; Reverie; Epilogue.

New poems. Ed F. G. Kenyon 1913. Includes periodical verse previously uncollected, with several short trns, verse squibs and fragmentary poems.
A forest thought. Country Life 10 June 1905.
Epps. Cornhill Mag Oct 1913.
Aeschylus's soliloquy ('I am an old and solitary man'). Cornhill Mag Nov 1913.
The first-born of Egypt. Cornhill Mag Jan 1914.
The dance of death. Ibid.
Lines to the memory of his parents. Cornhill Mag Feb 1914.
Gerousios Oinos. Cornhill Mag April 1914.
The Moses of Michael Angelo. Cornhill Mag Sept 1914.
'A very original poem'. Ed G. Monteiro, N & Q Sept 1966. 5 lines addressed to his son.

Letters and Accounts

Pearsall, R. B. A calendar of letters 1830–89. In L. N. Broughton et al, Bibliography, above. Entries for c. 2,300 letters.
Sanders, B. C. A supplementary calendar of letters. Baylor Browning Interests no 18 1961.
Wise, T. J. Letters from Browning to various correspondents. 2 vols 1895. First of a series of pamphlets ed Wise, each containing a few letters.
Browning, R. B. (ed). Letters of Browning and Elizabeth Barrett Browning. 2 vols 1899.
Rossetti, W. M. Ruskin, Rossetti, Pre-Raphaelite papers. 1899. 7 letters.
Knight, W. A. Retrospects; first series. 1904. 17 letters.
Kenyon, F. G. Browning and Alfred Domett. New York 1906. Chiefly letters.
Benet, W. R. Twenty-two unpublished letters of Robert and Elizabeth Barrett Browning. New York 1935.
Donner, H. W. The Browning box. Oxford 1935. Letters to T. L. Beddoes.
Curle, R. Browning and Julia Wedgwood: a broken friendship as revealed in their letters. New York 1937.
King, R. A. Account book. In Browning's finances from his own account book, Waco Texas 1947.
DeVane, W. C. and K. L. Knickerbocker. New letters of Browning. New Haven 1950.
Armytage, W. H. G. Some new letters of Browning. MLQ 12 1951.
McAleer, E. C. Dearest Isa: Browning's letters to Isa Blagden. Austin 1951.
—— Learned lady: letters from Browning to Mrs Thomas Fitzgerald. New York 1966.
Landis, P. Letters of the Brownings to George Barrett. Urbana 1958.
Bevington, M. M. Three letters of Browning to the editor of the Pall Mall Gazette. MLN 75 1960.
Dougherty, C. T. Browning letters in the Vatican Library. Manuscripta 4 1960.
—— Three Browning letters to his son. Manuscripta 6 1962.
Kelley, L. P. Browning and George Smith. Quart Rev 199 1961. Selections from their correspondence.
Sanders, C. R. Lost and unpublished Carlyle-Browning correspondence. JEGP 62 1963.
Hudson, G. R. Browning to his American friends: letters between the Brownings, the Storys and J. R. Lowell 1841–90. New York 1965.
Ricks, C. Two letters by Browning. TLS 3 June 1965.

§2

[Cunningham, A.] Athenaeum 6 April 1833; Atlas 14 April 1833; [Fox, W. J.], Monthly Repository April 1833. Reviews of Pauline.
[Fox, W. J.] Monthly Repository Nov 1835; Athenaeum 2 Aug 1835; [Forster, J.], Examiner 6 Sept 1835; [Heraud, J.], Fraser's Mag March 1836; [Emerson, R. W.], Dial April 1843. Reviews of Paracelsus.
The poets of the day: batch the third. Fraser's Mag Dec 1833.
[Forster, J.] Evidences of a new genius for dramatic poetry. New Monthly Mag March 1836.
Edinburgh Rev July 1837; Literary Gazette 6 May 1837. Reviews of Strafford, the first by H. Merivale.
Chasles, P. De l'art dramatique et du théâtre actuel en Angleterre. Revue des Deux Mondes 1 April 1840.
Spectator 14 March 1840. Review of Sordello.
Examiner 2 Oct 1841; Spectator 17 April 1841. Reviews of Pippa passes.
Athenaeum 30 April 1842. Review of King Victor and King Charles.
Spectator 5 March 1842. Review of Dramatic lyrics.
Athenaeum 18 Feb 1843; Literary Gazette 18 Feb 1843. Reviews of A blot in the 'scutcheon.
GM Aug 1843. Review of Bells and pomegranates nos 1–4.
Athenaeum 19 Oct 1844. Review of Colombe's birthday.
Horne, R. H. Browning and J. W. Marston. In his A new spirit of the age, 1844.
B[risted], C. A. English poetry and poets of the present day. Knickerbocker Mag June 1845.
English Rev Dec 1845. Review of Paracelsus and other poems 1835–45.
Chorley, H. F. Pippa passes, Colombe's birthday etc. Peoples 18 July, 22 Aug 1846.
Fuller, M. Browning's poems. In her Papers on literature and art, 1846.
Eclectic Rev April 1846. Review of Bells and pomegranates nos 1–7.
Douglas Jerrold's Shilling Mag June 1846. Review of Luria, A soul's tragedy etc.
Forgues, E. D. Poètes et romanciers de la grande Bretagne: Browning. Revue des Deux Mondes 15 Aug 1847.
—— In his Originaux et beaux esprits d'Angleterre contemporaine, Paris 1860.
Browning and the poetry of the age. British Quart Rev 6 1847.
Lowell, J. R. North American Rev April 1848. Review of Paracelsus, Sordello, Bells and pomegranates.
—— Address at the Browning Society meeting 25 April 1884. Browning Soc Papers 1844.
Browning's poems: Paracelsus, Sordello and plays. Church of England Quart Rev 12 1849.
[Edmunds, C.] Eclectic Rev Aug 1849. Review of 1849 Poems and Sordello.
Powell, T. In his Living authors of England, New York 1849.
Rossetti, W. M. Germ May 1850. Review of Christmas-eve and Easter-day.
—— On one word more. Academy 10 Jan 1891.
Mr and Mrs Browning. Fraser's Mag Feb 1851. Review of Sordello, Paracelsus and Poems 1849; and of Poems 1850 by Elizabeth Barrett Browning.
Milsand, J. Revue des Deux Mondes 15 Aug 1851. Review of the 1849 Poems, Christmas-eve and Easter-day.
—— La poésie expressive et dramatique en Angleterre. Revue Contemporaine Sept 1856.
Moir, D. M. Browning: Paracelsus, Sordello, Bells and pomegranates. In his Sketches of the poetical literature of the past half century, 1851.
Athenaeum 21 Feb 1852. Review of Letters of Shelley.
Mitford, M. R. Married poets: Elizabeth Barrett Browning and Robert Browning. In her Recollections of a literary life, 1852.
D., G. M. Monthly Christian Spectator May 1853. Review of Christmas-eve and Easter-day.
Jameson, A. In her Commonplace book of thoughts, memories and fancies, 1854.
Spectator 22 Dec 1855; Saturday Rev 24 Nov 1855; British Quart Rev 23 1856; T. McNicoll, London Quart Rev 6 1856; [W. Morris], Oxford & Cambridge Mag 1 1856; N. P. S. Wiseman, Rambler Jan 1856. Reviews of Men and women.
Taylor, B. The Brownings. In his At home and abroad: a sketchbook, second series, New York 1860.

Evans, F. H. The poems and plays of Browning. North Br Rev 34 1861.

Exon. Historical basis of How they brought the good news. N & Q 1 Feb 1862. Reply by W. M. Rossetti 25 Feb 1862.

Hood, E. P. Eclectic & Congregational Rev May 1863. Review of Selections.

—— Eclectic & Congregational Rev July 1864. Review of Dramatis personae.

—— Eclectic & Congregational Rev Dec 1868. Review of Poetical works.

Hutton, R. H. Nat Rev 47 1863. Review of Works.

Reeve, L. In his Portraits of men of eminence in literature, science and art, with biographical memoirs, 1863.

Skelton, J. ('Shirley'). Robert Browning. Fraser's Mag Feb 1863.

Bagehot, W. Wordsworth, Tennyson and Browning: or pure, ornate and grotesque art in English poetry. Nat Rev 18 1864; rptd in his Literary studies, ed R. H. Hutton 2 vols 1879.

Conway, M. D. Victoria Mag Feb 1864. Review of Works 1863.

—— Atlantic Monthly Feb 1869. Review of Ring and the book.

Edinburgh Rev 120 1864. Review of Works 1863 and Dramatis personae. Rebuttal by G. Massey, Reader 26 Nov 1864.

Wedmore, T. F. New Monthly Mag Feb 1865. Review of Dramatis personae.

Dowden, E. Mr Browning's Sordello: first paper. Fraser's Mag Oct 1867; rptd with the rejected Second paper in his Transcripts and studies, 1888.

Nencioni, E. Robert Browning. Nuova Antologia July 1867. Review of Works 1863 and Dramatis personae.

—— L'anello e il libro: poema di Browning. Nuova Antologia Dec 1885; rptd in his Saggi critici, Florence 1897.

Buchanan, R. W. The ring and the book. Athenaeum 26 Dec 1868; rptd in his Master spirits, 1873.

Nettleship, J. T. Essays on Browning's poetry. 1868, 1890 (enlarged as Essays and thoughts). The first full-scale book on Browning.

Smiles, S. Browning. In his Brief biographies, Boston 1868.

[Stirling, J. H.] The poetical works of Browning. North Br Rev Dec 1868.

Chadwick, J. W. Christian Examiner May 1869. Review of Ring and the book.

Forman, H. B. Browning's poetry. London Quart Rev 32 1869; rptd as Browning and the epic of psychology, 1869; and in his Our living poets, 1871.

—— London Quart Rev 37 1872. Review of Balaustion's adventure.

Morley, J. Fortnightly Rev March 1869. Review of Ring and the book. *See* S. Colvin, G. A. Simcox, *below*.

Symonds, J. A. The ring and the book. Macmillan's Mag Jan 1869.

—— Aristophanes's apology and the Inn album. Academy 17 April, 27 Nov 1875.

Austin, A. Mr Browning. In his Poetry of the period, 1870.

Etienne, L. Une nouvelle forme de poésie dramatique [reviewing Works, 1868 and Ring and the book]. Revue des Deux Mondes Feb 1870.

Trollope, T. A. A very naughty artist. Temple Bar July 1870. On Fra Lippo Lippi.

Colvin, S. Fortnightly Rev Oct 1871. Review of Balaustion's adventure.

—— Fifine at the fair. Fortnightly Rev July 1872.

Simcox, G. A. Academy 1 Sept 1871. Review of Balaustion's adventure.

Everett, C. C. Old & New Nov 1872. Review of Fifine, with other poems.

Home, D. C. In his Incidents in my life: second series, 1872. The medium of Mr Sludge.

Mr Browning's Napoleon III. Literary World 5 Jan 1872. On Prince Hohenstiel-Schwengau.

Mallock, W. H. How to make an imitation of Mr Browning. In his Every man his own poet: or the inspired singer's recipe book, 1872.

Devey, J. Realistic school. In his Comparative estimate of modern English poets, 1873.

Simcox, E. J. Fortnightly Rev July 1873. Review of Red cotton night-cap country.

Balfour-Browne, J. H. Red cotton night-cap country. Jnl of Mental Science July 1874.

Orr, A. Mr Browning's place in literature. Contemporary Rev May 1874.

—— Contemporary Rev May 1879. Review of Dramatic idyls.

—— Life and letters of Browning. 1891, 2 vols Boston 1891 (enlarged).

Gosse, E. W. Examiner 24 April 1875. Review of Aristophanes's apology.

—— The early writings of Browning. Century Mag Dec 1881. Rejoinder by F. J. Furnivall, Academy 10 Dec 1881.

—— Browning: personalia. 1890.

McCrie, G. In his Religion of our literature, 1875.

[Stevenson, R. L.] Mr Browning again. Vanity Fair 11 Dec 1875.

Stedman, E. C. In his Victorian poets, 1875.

Bradley, A. C. Mr Browning's Inn album. Macmillan's Mag Feb 1876.

Howells, W. D. Atlantic Monthly March 1876. Review of the Inn album.

James, H. On a drama of Mr Browning. Nation (New York) 20 Jan 1876. The inn album.

—— The private life. Atlantic Monthly April 1892. Short story modelled on Browning.

—— Browning in Westminster Abbey. In his Essays, New York 1893.

—— In his William Wetmore Story and his friends, 1903.

—— The novel in the Ring and the book. Trans of Royal Soc of Lit 31 1912.

O'Connor, W. A. Mr Browning's Childe Roland. Pbns of Manchester Lit Soc 3 1877.

Lyttelton, A. T. Browning. Church Quart Rev 1878.

[Watts, W. T.] Athenaeum 25 May 1878. Review of La Saisiaz and Two poets.

Allen, G. Fortnightly Rev July 1879. Review of Dramatic idyls.

Bayne, T. Mr Browning's Dramatic idyls. St James' Mag Aug 1880.

Haweis, H. R. Browning: New Year's Eve. In his Poets in the pulpit, 1880.

Furnivall, F. J. (ed). The [London] Browning Society's papers. 13 pts 1881–91. Includes material by Furnivall, W. Sharpe, J. T. Nettleship, A. Orr, H. Corson, W. F. Revell, G. B. Shaw, W. A. Raleigh, J. Morison, E. Marx, L. S. Outram, C. H. Hereford, E. Berdoe, W. M. Rossetti et al. Longer papers are listed in Broughton et al, Bibliography, above, pp. 131–2. Over 200 shorter papers, notes, explications and rptd items are included.

Kirkman, J. The Browning Society: introductory address at the inaugural meeting, 28 October 1881. 1881.

Johnson, E. Conscience and art in Browning. Browning Soc Papers 1882.

Holland, F. M. Stories from Browning, with an introduction by Alexandra Orr. 1882.

Marx, E. An account of Abbé Vogler. Browning Soc Papers 1882.

Sidgwick, A. On the love poems of Browning. Jnl of Education May 1882.

Symons, A. W. Browning as a religious poet. Wesleyan Methodist Mag Dec 1882.

Thaxter, L. L. Browning in the United States. Literary World 11 March 1882.

Thomson, J. Notes on the genius of Browning. Browning Soc Papers 1882.

Cooke, B. An introduction to Browning. 1883. Especially on Browning's earlier works.

Courthope, W. J. Joscoseria and the critics: a plea for the reader. Nat Rev June 1883. Anon reply in Pall Mall Gazette 7 July 1883.
Ker, W. P. Contemporary Rev Sept 1883. Review of Jocoseria.
— Contemporary Rev Jan 1885. Review of Ferishtah's fancies.
— Browning. E & S 1 1910
Noel, R. Robert Browning. Contemporary Rev Nov 1883.
Wescott, B. F. On some points in Browning's view of life. In Browning Soc Papers 1883; Cambridge 1883.
Birrell, A. On the alleged obscurity of Mr Browning's poetry. In his Obiter dicta, 1884.
Le Conte, A. A study of Browning. Overland Monthly June 1884.
[Watts-Dunton, W. T.] Athenaeum 6 Dec 1884. Review of Ferishtah's fancies.
Galton, A. H. In his Urbana scripta: studies of five living poets, 1885.
Cooke, G. W. In his Poets and problems, Boston 1886.
Corson, H. An introduction to the study of Browning's poetry. Boston 1886, 1910 (enlarged).
Symons, A. An introduction to the study of Browning. 1886 (including a Reprint of discarded prefaces to some of Mr Browning's works), 1906 (enlarged). Reviewed by W. Pater, Guardian 9 Nov 1887, rptd in his Essays from the Guardian, 1896.
Burt, M. E. Browning's women. Chicago 1887. Introd by E. E. Hale.
Fotheringham, J. Studies in the poetry of Browning. 1887.
Hale, E. E. In his Lights of two centuries, 1887.
Kingsland, W. G. Browning, chief poet of the age: an essay addressed primarily to beginners in the study of Browning. 1887.
— Some Browning memories. Contemporary Rev Aug 1922.
Thorne, W. H. In his Modern idols: studies in biography and criticism, 1887.
Murray, J. O. The poetry of Browning: its value to clergymen. Homiletic Rev 15 1888.
Simpson, H. B. Wordsworth's successor. In his Cross lights, 1888.
Alexander, W. J. An introduction to the poetry of Browning. Boston 1889.
— Browning once more. Dalhousie Rev 6 1927.
Campbell, J. M. Sordello: an outline analysis of Mr Browning's poem. 1889.
Lang, A. In his Letters on literature, 1889.
— Mr Robert Browning. Contemporary Rev July 1891.
Sarrazin, G. In his La Renaissance de la poésie anglaise 1798–1889, Paris 1889.
Berdoe, E. Browning's message to his time: his religion, philosophy and science. 1890.
— (ed). Browning studies: select papers of the Browning Society. 1895.
— Browning and the Christian faith: the evidences of Christianity from Browning's point of view. 1896.
— A primer of Browning. 1904.
Brooke, S. A. Robert Browning. Contemporary Rev Jan 1890.
— The poetry of Browning. 1902.
Browning's portraits. Critic 4 Jan, 22 Feb, 8–15 March 1890.
[Ernle (Baron), R. E. P.] On Browning. Quart Rev 170 1890.
Forster, J. Four great teachers: Ruskin, Carlyle, Emerson and Browning. 1890, 1898 (enlarged as Great teachers).
Jacobs, J. Browning's theology. Jewish Quart Rev 2 1890.
[Meynell, W.] Robert Browning. Merry England Jan 1890.
Schelling, F. E. Browning and the poetry of the future; Browning and the arabesque in art. In Two essays on Browning, [Philadelphia] 1890.
Sharp, W. Life of Browning. 1890. With bibliography by J. P. Anderson.

Smalley, G. W. In his London letters and some others, 1890.
Wilde, O. The true function and value of criticism. Nineteenth Century July 1890.
Jones, H. Browning as a philosophical and religious teacher. Glasgow 1891.
Stefansson, J. Browning et literaturbillede fra det moderne England. Copenhagen 1891. For Stefansson's pamphlet war with Otto Jesperson, *see* Broughton et al, Bibliography, p. 181.
Wilson, F. M. A primer on Browning 1891. Includes a handbook section, Introduction to the poems.
Brinton, D. G. Browning on unconventional [amatory] relations. Poet Lore May 1892.
Defries, E. P. A Browning primer. 1892. Introd by F. J. Furnivall.
Innes, A. The ring and the book. Monthly packet of Evening Readings for Members of the English Church May 1892.
Revell, W. F. Browning's criticism of life. 1892.
Thackeray, A. T. (Lady Ritchie). In her Records of Tennyson, Ruskin and Browning, 1892.
Sherman, L. A. The art of Browning. In his Analytics of literature, Boston 1893.
Triggs, O. L. Browning and Whitman: a study in democracy. New York 1893.
Walters, F. Studies of some of Browning's poems. 1893.
Saintsbury, G. In his Corrected impressions, 1895.
Hill, A. et al. Notes to the pocket volume of selections from Browning. 1896.
Royce, J. Browning's theism. New World Sept 1896.
Boston Browning Society. Selected papers 1886–97. Boston 1897. Essays by J. Royce, P. S. Grant, J. W. Chadwick, P. Cummings, G. D. Latimer et al.
Hornbrooke, F. B. The Pope of the Ring and the book. Nation (New York) 20 May 1897.
— The ring and the book: an interpretation. Boston 1909.
Quale, W. A. The poet's poet and the Ring and the book. In his Poets and other essays, New York 1897.
Chapman, J. J. In his Emerson and other essays, New York 1898.
Cary, E. L. Browning, poet and man: a survey. New York 1899.
Fisher, C. The idea of evolution in Browning's poetry. Temple Bar Dec 1899.
[Gwynn, S. L.] Discretion and publicity. Edinburgh Rev 189 1899. On the love letters.
Little, M. Essays on Browning. 1899.
Lounsbury, T. R. A Philistine view. Atlantic Monthly Dec 1899. On A blot in the 'scutcheon.
— The early literary career of Browning. New York 1911. 4 lectures.
Stanley, H. M. The love letters and the psychology of love. Open Court Dec 1899.
Stephen, L. The Browning letters. Nat Rev May 1899.
Clark, J. S. In his Study of English and American poets: a laboratory method, New York 1900.
Le Gallienne, R. A propos the Browning love-letters. In his Sleeping beauty and other prose fancies, 1900.
— Old love stories retold. 1924.
Santayana, G. The poetry of barbarism. In his Interpretations of poetry and religion, New York 1900.
Waugh, A. Robert Browning. 1900.
Bushnell, C. C. A study of Browning's Agamemnon. Proc of Amer Philological Assoc 1901.
Goodrich-Freer, A. M. Browning the musician. Nineteenth Century April 1901.
Pigou, A. C. Browning as a religious teacher. Cambridge 1901.
Woodard, H. D. Santayana on Browning: a pessimist criticism. Poet Lore March 1901.
Bronson, K. de K. Browning in Venice. Cornhill Mag Feb 1902.
Corkran, H. In her Celebrities and I, 1902.

MacDonald, C. N. A study of Browning's Saul. 1902.
Benson, E. In his Sordello and Cunizza: fact, legend, poetry concerning Sordello, 1903.
Chesterton, G. K. Robert Browning. 1903 (EML).
Douglas, J. Robert Browning. 1903.
Machen, M. G. The Bible in Browning, with particular reference to the Ring and the book. 1903. Largely a catalogue of Browning's biblical references.
Phelps, W. L. Maeterlinck and Browning. Independent 5 March 1903.
— Browning: how to know him. Indianapolis 1915.
— Browning, Schopenhauer and music. North Amer Rev Oct 1917.
— Browning and Alfred Austin. Yale Rev 8 1918.
— Browning and the two popes. Yale Rev 20 1930.
— Browning on spiritualism. Yale Rev 23 1933.
Robertson, J. M. Browning and Tennyson as teachers. 1903.
Smith, L. W. Browning's place in the evolution of English poetry. Sewanee Rev 11 1903.
Wicksteed, P. H. Robert Browning. Contemporary Rev Jan 1903.
Dowden, E. Robert Browning. 1904.
Flew, J. Studies in Browning. 1904.
Gould, E. P. The Brownings and America. Boston 1904.
Parrott, T. M. The vitality of Browning. In his Studies of a booklover, New York 1904.
Cook, A. S. Abt Vogler. JEGP 5 1905. On ll. 69f.
Gilder, R. W. A romance of the nineteenth century: Robert and Elizabeth Barrett Browning. Century Mag Oct 1905.
Herford, C. H. Robert Browning. 1905. A biography.
Mabie, H. W. In his Essays in literary interpretation, Toronto 1905.
Marzials, F. T. Robert Browning. 1905. A biography.
More, P. E. Why is Browning popular? Evening Post 13 May 1905.
Duff, D. An exposition of Browning's Sordello, with historical and other notes. 1906.
Inge, W. R. The mysticism of Browning. In his Studies of English mystics, 1906.
Padelford, F. M. Browning out west. Cornhill Mag Feb 1907.
Smith, A. W. Poetry or optimism: Browning. In his Main tendencies of Victorian poetry, 1907.
Clarke, H. A. Browning's England: a study of English influences in Browning. New York 1908.
— Browning and his century. New York 1912.
Curry, S. S. Browning and the dramatic monologue. Boston 1908.
Hodell, C. W. The Old Yellow Book: source of Browning's The ring and the book. Washington 1908. Photo-reproduced, with trn and notes.
Lehmann, R. C. In his Memories of half a century, 1908.
Cunliffe, J. W. Browning and the marathon race [in Pheidippides]. PMLA 24 1909.
— Browning's idealism. Trans of Wisconsin Acad 17 1913.
— In his Leaders of the Victorian revolution, New York 1933.
Masson, R. O. Browning in Edinburgh. Cornhill Mag Feb 1909.
Rogers, A. Prophecy and poetry: studies in Isaiah and Browning. 1909 (Bohlen lectures).
Schmidt, K. Brownings Verhältnis zu Frankreich. Berlin 1909.
Bradford, G. jr. Browning and Sainte-Beuve. North Amer Rev April 1910.
Gildersleeve, B. L. On Aristophanes' Apology. Amer Jnl of Philology 31 1910.
— On the Ring and the book. Amer Jnl of Philology 32 1911.
Griffin, W. H. and H. C. Minchin. The life of Browning, with notices of his writings, his family and his friends. 1910. Heavily illustr; the first full biography.

Mill, J. S. In Griffin and Minchin, above, Browning, 1910. An unpbd review of Pauline.
Gingerich, S. F. Wordsworth, Tennyson and Browning: a study in human freedom. Ann Arbor 1911.
Koeppel, E. Robert Browning. Berlin 1911. Chiefly critical.
Lomax, J. A. Karshish and Cleon. Sewanee Rev 19 1911.
Whiting, L. The Brownings: their life and art. Boston 1911.
Berger, P. Robert Browning. Paris 1912.
Hind, W. A. Browning's teaching on faith, life and love. 1912.
Minchin, H. C. Browning and Wordsworth. Fortnightly Rev 1 May 1912.
Pellegrini, L. Studi sulla poesia di Browning: la filosofia, la psicologia, l'arte. Naples 1912.
Pinero, A. W. Browning as a dramatist. Trans of Royal Soc of Lit 31 1912.
Rhys, E. Browning and his poetry. 1912.
Singleton, A. H. Goethe and Browning. Pbns of Eng Goethe Soc 14 1912.
Tupper, T. W. A soul's tragedy: a defence of Chiappino. E Studien 44 1912.
Delattre, F. L'obscurité de Browning. Revue Germanique 9 1913.
— L'anglais de Browning dans Sordello. Revue Anglo-américaine 15 1938.
Mayne, E. C. Browning's heroines. 1913.
Treves, F. The country of the Ring and the book. 1913.
Brockington, A. A. Browning's answers to questions concerning some of his poems. Cornhill Mag March 1914.
— Browning and the twentieth century. New York 1932.
Smith, W. A. Browning and the special interests. Atlantic Monthly Dec 1914.
Craig, H. The mantle of Browning. Mid-West Quart 2 1915. On Romain Rolland.
Harrington, V. C. Browning studies. Toronto 1915. Essays on groups of poems.
Harris, F. In his Contemporary portraits, 1915.
Harris, C. A. Browning as the poet of music. Calcutta Rev new ser 4 1916.
Hearn, L. Studies in Browning. In his Appreciations of poetry, New York 1916.
— In his Complete lectures on poets, Tokyo 1934. 2 lectures on Browning.
Lucy, H. W. Browning and Swinburne. In his Nearing Jordan, 1916.
Symons, A. Some Browning reminiscences. North Amer Rev Oct 1916.
Tisdel, F. M. Balaustion's adventure as an interpretation of the Alcestis of Euripides. PMLA 22 1917.
Sully, J. In his My life and friends: a psychologists' memories, 1918. 3 meetings with Browning.
Wordsworth, E. Andrea del Sarto. In her Essays old and new, Oxford 1919.
Clarke, G. H. Browning's A blot: a defence. Sewanee Rev 28 1920.
Glicksman, H. A legal aspect of the Ring and the book. MLN 28 1920.
Pound, E. In his Instigations, New York 1920. Against Browning's trns from the Greek.
Swisher, W. S. A psychoanalysis of Browning's Pauline. Psychoanalytic Rev 7 1920.
Marshall, A. Balaustion and Mrs Browning. Cornhill Mag Nov 1921.
Nitchie, E. Browning's use of the classics. Classical Weekly 31 Jan 1921.
Beerbohm, M. Browning introduces a great lady. In his Rossetti and his circle, 1922. One of several cartoons on Browning.
Bonnell, J. K. Touch images in the poetry of Browning. PMLA 37 1922.
Grant, P. S. Browning's art in the monologue. In his Essays, New York 1922.

Hood, T. L. Browning's ancient classical sources. Harvard Stud in Classical Philology 33 1922.

Burt, E. J. The seen and unseen in Browning. Oxford 1923.

Drinkwater, J. Some letters from Matthew Arnold to Browning. Cornhill Mag Dec 1923.

Pottle, F. A. Shelley and Browning: a myth and some facts. Chicago 1923, New York 1965. Foreword by W. L. Phelps.

Quiller-Couch, A. T. In The outline of literature, ed J. Drinkwater 1923.

Shaw, C. B. Childe Roland redivivus. South Atlantic Quart 22 1923.

Golder, H. Browning's Childe Roland. PMLA 39 1924.

Göritz, K. Brownings Christmas-eve and Easter-day und das Leben Jesu von Strauss. Archiv 47 1924.

Russell, T. P. The pessimism of Browning. Sewanee Rev 32 1924.

— One word more on Browning. Stanford 1927.

Wallis, N. H. A study of Pauline and Dramatic lyrics. In his Ethics of criticism, 1924.

DeVane, W. C. jr. The landscape of Childe Roland. PMLA 40 1925.

— Browning's Parleyings with certain people: the autobiography of a mind. New Haven 1927.

— Sordello's story retold. SP 27 1930.

— The harlot and the thoughtful young man. SP 29 1932. On Browning's Fifine and Rossetti's Jenny.

— The virgin and the dragon. Yale Rev 37 1947. Browning's preoccupation with the Andromeda situation.

Gest, J. M. The Old Yellow Book: source of Browning's The ring and the book. Boston 1925. New trns, annotated.

MacCallum, M. W. The dramatic monologue in the Victorian period. Proc Br Acad 11 1925.

Massey, B. W. A. Browning's vocabulary. N & Q 8–15 Aug 1925, 12 Sept, 10 Oct 1925, 19–26 Oct 1929; enlarged as Browning's vocabulary: compound epithets, Poznan 1931.

Raymond, W. O. Browning's conception of love as represented in Paracelsus. Papers of Michigan Acad 4 1925.

— Browning's dark mood: a study of Fifine. SP 31 1934.

— Browning's casuists. SP 37 1940.

— The infinite moment and other essays in Browning. Toronto 1950.

— The jewelled bow: a study of Browning's imagery and humanism. PMLA 70 1955.

— The statue and the bust. UTQ 28 1959.

— Browning and the Harriet Westbrook Shelley letters. UTQ 32 1963.

'Torquemada'. A Browning exercise: a cross-word examination on the works of Browning. Poetry Rev 16 1925.

de Reul, P. Fifine à la foire ou le Don Juan de Browning. Revue de l'Université de Bruxelles 32 1926.

— L'art et la pensée de Browning. Brussels 1929.

Dickson, A. Browning's sources for the Pied piper of Hamelin. SP 23 1926.

Havens, R. D. Blake and Browning. MLN 41 1926.

Kirkconnell, W. The epilogue to Dramatis personae. MLN 41 1926.

Roberts, W. W. Music in Browning. Music & Letters 17 1926.

Shaw, J. E. The Donna Angelicata in the Ring and the book. PMLA 41 1926.

Crawford, A. W. Browning's Cleon. JEGP 26 1927.

— Browning's Saul. Queens Quart 34 1927.

Stevenson, L. A French text-book by Browning. MLN 42 1927.

— In his Darwin among the poets, Chicago 1932.

— Tennyson, Browning and a romantic fallacy. UTQ 8 1944.

— The pertinacious Victorian poets. UTQ 21 1952. Source notes on A grammarian's funeral, Childe Roland, My last duchess, The laboratory.

— My last Duchess and Parisina. MLN 74 1959.

Browning, Fannie B. Some memories of Browning by his daughter-in-law. Boston 1928.

Burdett, O. The Brownings. 1928.

Mason, A. E. W. Great rides in literature. Trans of Royal Soc of Lit new ser 8 1928.

Hood, A. Sordello, the poet of a poet. Poetry Rev 20 1929.

Weatherhead, L. D. Browning and man's final destiny. London Quart Rev 151 1929.

Blunden, E. In his Leigh Hunt and his circle, 1930.

Lucas, F. L. In his Eight Victorian poets, Cambridge 1930, 1940 (as Ten Victorian poets), 1948 (rev).

'Kingsmill, Hugh' (H. K. Lunn). Browning and FitzGerald. In his More invective, 1930.

Spindler, R. Browning und die Antike. 2 vols Leipzig 1930.

Alekseev, M. Zur Entstehungsgeschichte der Dramatic Idyls von Browning. E Studien 66 1931.

Duckworth, F. R. G. Browning: background and conflict. 1931. Introd by W. L. Phelps.

Gaylord, H. Pompilia and her poet. New York 1931.

MacDonald, J. F. Inhibitions of Browning's poetry. In Studies in English collected by M. W. Wallace, Toronto 1931. On the monologues.

Abercrombie, L. In The great Victorians, ed H. J. Massingham 1932.

Hovelaque, H. L. La jeunesse de Browning. Paris 1932. On Pauline, Paracelsus, Sordello.

Newbolt, H. J. In his My world as in my time, 1932.

Rea, J. D. My last Duchess. SP 29 1932.

Berlin-Lieberman, J. Browning and Hebraism. Jerusalem 1933. On the poems 'based on sources in Jewish literature'.

Evans, B. I. In his English poetry in the later nineteenth century, 1933, 1966 (rev).

Ley, W. R. The Brownings in Paris. Amer Rev 1 1933. On meetings with George Sand.

Woolf, V. Flush: a biography. 1933.

Knickerbocker, K. L. Browning's Cenciaja. PQ 13 1934.

— An echo from Browning's second courtship. SP 32 1935.

— A tentative apology for Browning. Tennessee Stud in Lit 1 1956.

— Browning: a modern appraisal. Tennessee Stud in Lit 4 1959.

Sherwood, M. The young Browning: Browning and Santayana. In her Undercurrents of influence in English romantic poetry, Cambridge Mass 1934.

Armour, R. W. In his Barry Cornwall: a biography of B. W. Proctor, Boston 1935.

Boas, F. S. Browning's Paracelsus. Quart Rev 1935.

DuBois, A. E. Browning, dramatist. SP 33 1936.

MacCarthy, B. G. The psychology of genius: studies in Browning. 1936.

Friedland, L. S. Ferrara and My last Duchess. SP 33 1936.

Pettigrew, H. P. The early vogue of the Ring and the book. Archiv 169 1936.

Tracy, C. R. Browning's heresies. SP 33 1936.

— Caliban upon Setebos. SP 35 1938.

— Bishop Blougram. MLR 34 1939.

Clemens, C. Father Prout and the Brownings. Dalhousie Rev 17 1937.

Compton-Rickett, A. In his Portraits and personalities, 1937.

Holmes, S. W. The sources of Browning's Sordello. SP 34 1937.

— Sordello in the light of Jung's theory of types. PMLA 56 1941.

— Browning: semantic stutterer. PMLA 60 1945.

Routh, H. V. In his Toward the twentieth century, Cambridge 1937.

'Maurois, André' (E. S. W. Herzog). Browning poète de sa vie: les leçons d'un grand Anglais. Nouvelles Littéraires 2 April 1938.
— Robert et Elizabeth Browning. In his Portraits suivis de quelques autres, Paris 1955.
Faverty, F. E. The absconded abbot in the Ring and the book. SP 36 1939.
— The source of the Jules-Phene episode in Pippa passes. SP 38 1941.
McElderry, B. R. jr. Victorian evaluation of the Ring and the book. Research Stud of State College of Washington 8 1939.
Partington, W. G. Browning: his Pauline and other affairs. In his Forging ahead: the true story of T. J. Wise, New York 1939. On the Browning industry after 1881.
Purcell, J. M. The dramatic failure of Pippa passes. SP 36 1939. Reply by J. M. Ariail 37 1940.
Sone, T. The Brownings. Tokyo 1939.
Senex. Browning queries. N & Q 27 July, 31 Aug 1940. Comments on 23 of Browning's poems dubiously annotated by A. Birrell.
Smalley, D. A parleying with Aristophanes. PMLA 55 1940.
— Browning's view of fact in the Ring and the book. Victorian Newsletter no 16 1960.
— Joseph Arnould and Browning: new letters and a verse epistle (by Arnould). PMLA 80 1965.
Cramer, M. B. What Browning's reputation owed to the Pre-Raphaelites. ELH 8 1941.
Ransom, H. The Brownings in Paris. SE 1941.
Smith, C. M. Proverb-lore in the Ring and the book. PMLA 56 1941.
Smith, C. W. Browning's star-imagery: the study of a detail in poetic design. Princeton 1941.
Wenger, C. N. The masquerade in Browning's dramatic monologues. College Eng Dec 1941.
— Clio's rights in poetry: Browning's Cristina and Monaldeschi. PMLA 60 1945.
Lindsay, J. S. The central episode of By the fireside. SP 39 1942.
Shackford, M. H. The Brownings and Leighton. Wellesley Mass 1942.
— The authorship of Aeschylus's soliloquy. TLS 21 March 1942. Reply by G. D. Hobson 11 April 1942.
Smith, F. M. Elizabeth Barrett and the Flight of the Duchess. SP 39 1942.
Stoll, E. E. Browning's In a balcony. MLQ 3 1942.
D., A. E. Uncollected poems by Browning. N & Q 16, 30 Jan, 13 Feb, 24 April 1943. Reply by S. J. Looker 13 Feb 1943.
E., D. H. Query on A toccata of Galuppi's. Explicator 1 1943. Explications by R. P. Basler, A. Dickson, W. D. Templeman, F. A. Pottle and E. H. Duncan in later issues.
Wilson, G. E. Browning's portraits, photographs and other likenesses, and their makers. Waco Texas 1943.
Charlton, H. B. Poetry and truth: an aspect of the Ring and the book. Bull John Rylands Lib 28 1944.
— The making of the dramatic lyric. Bull John Rylands Lib 35 1953.
Cook, V. Browning and De Lassay. MLN 59 1944. On the Parleying with Daniel Bartoli.
McPeek, J. A. The shaping of Saul. JEGP 44 1945.
Dunsany, Lord. Browning is Blougram. Nineteenth Century April 1946.
Laird, J. Some facets in Browning's poetry. In his Philosophical incursions into English literature, Cambridge 1946.
Greene, H. E. Browning's knowledge of music. PMLA 62 1947.
Hess, M. W. Margaret Fuller and Childe Roland. Personalist Oct 1947.
Bayford, E. G. Poem by Browning. N & Q 12 June 1948. On the posthumous Lines to the memory of his parents.
Cohen, J. M. The young Browning. Cornhill Mag 163 1948.
— Robert Browning. 1952.
Cundiff, P. A. The clarity of Browning's ring metaphor. PMLA 63 1948.
— Browning: 'Our human speech'. Victorian Newsletter no 15 1959.
— Browning: 'Indisputably fact'. Victorian Newsletter no 17 1960.
Dingle, H. In his Science and literary criticism, 1948.
Fuson, B. W. Browning and his predecessors in the dramatic monologue. State Univ of Iowa Humanistic Stud 8 1948.
Page, F. Browning: a conversation. In Essays presented to Humphrey Milford, Oxford 1948. A survey of earlier criticism in dialogue form.
Fairchild, H. N. Browning's heaven. Rev of Religion 14 1949.
— Browning the simple-hearted casuist. UTQ 18 1949.
— La Saisiaz and the Nineteenth Century [Magazine]. MP 48 1950.
— Browning's 'pomegranate heart'. MLN 66 1951.
— Browning's 'Whatever is, is right'. College Eng April 1951.
Hartle, R. W. Gide's interpretation of Browning. SE 28 1949.
Miller, B. The child of Casa Guidi. Cornhill Mag 163 1949.
— Browning: a portrait. 1952.
— The séance at Ealing. Cornhill Mag 169 1957.
Ratcliffe, S. K. Browning's early friends. Cornhill Mag 164 1949.
Altick, B. D. Browning rides the Chicago and Alton. New Colophon 3 1950. The 'railroad edn' of Browning's works.
— The private life of Browning. Yale Rev 41 1951.
— Karshish and St Paul. MLN 72 1957.
— 'Transcendentalism'. JEGP 58 1959.
— Memo to the next annotator of Browning. Victorian Poetry 1 1963.
— The grammarian's funeral: Browning's praise of folly? Stud in Eng Lit 1500–1900 3 1963.
— The symbolism of Master Hugues of Saxe-Gotha. Victorian Poetry 3 1965.
Boyce, G. K. From Paris to Pisa with the Brownings. New Colophon 3 1950. On the elopement.
Thompson, W. L. Greek wisdom and Browning. Classical Jnl Feb 1950. Reply by K. L. Knickerbocker, May.
Willy, M. The indomitable optimist. In her Life was their cry, 1950.
Brown, E. K. The first person in Caliban upon Setebos. MLN 66 1951.
Giersach, W. A serenade at the villa. Explicator 8 1950. Continued by A. Dickson, 9 1951.
Himelick, R. Bayard Taylor and Browning's 'Holy Vitus'. South Atlantic Quart 50 1951.
Rundle, J. U. Burns' Holy Willie's prayer and Browning's Soliloquy of the Spanish cloister. N & Q 9 June 1951.
Wallace, S. A. Browning in London society. MLN 66 1951.
— Curious annals: new documents on Browning's murder case. SP 49 1952.
— New documents relating to Browning's Roman murder story. Toronto 1956.
Coyle, W. Molinos: 'the subject of the day' in the Ring and the book. PMLA 67 1952.
Greer, L. Browning and America. Chapel Hill 1952.
Jamieson, P. F. Pictor ignotus. Explicator 11 1952.
Johnson, E. D. H. In his Alien vision of Victorian poetry, Princeton 1952.
— Browning's pluralistic universe: the Ring and the book. UTQ 31 1961.
Kenmare, D. Ever a fighter. 1952. 6 lectures on Browning.
— An end to darkness: a new approach to Browning. 1962.

Lowe, R. L. Scott, Browning and Kipling. N & Q 1 March 1952.
Pearsall, R. B. Browning's texts in Galatians and Deuteronomy. MLQ 13 1952. Soliloquy of the Spanish cloister.
Super, R. H. A grain of truth about Wordsworth and Browning, Landor and Swinburne. MLN 67 1952.
Bowra, M. C. Dante and Sordello. Comparative Lit 5 1953.
Duncan, J. E. Intellectual kinship of Donne and Browning. SP 50 1953.
Gwynn, F. L. Home-thoughts, from the sea. Explicator 12 1953.
McCormick, J. P. Browning and the experimental drama. PMLA 68 1953.
Parr, J. The date of composition of Love among the ruins. PQ 32 1953.
— Site and ancient city of Love among the ruins. PMLA 68 1953.
— Fra Lippo Lippi, Baldinucci and the Milanese edition of Vasari. Eng Lang Notes 3 1966.
Smith, C. D. How they brought the good news. Explicator 11 1953. Continued by F. V. Lloyd 12 1954.
Stone, W. H. Browning and 'Mark Rutherford'. RES new ser 4 1953. Includes 3 new Browning letters.
Wright, M. Karshish's name. TLS 1 May 1953.
Condee, R. W. Meeting at night, Parting at morning. Explicator 12 1954.
Dahl, C. Ben Karshook's wisdom. MLN 60 1954.
— 'Neblaretai' and 'Rattei' in Aristophanes' apology. MLN 72 1957.
— Who was Browning's Cleon? Cithara 4 1965.
Du Bos, C. Pauline. Études Anglaises 7 1954.
Hilton, E. Sordello as a study of the will. PMLA 69 1954.
Badger, K. See the Christ stand. Boston Univ Stud in Eng 1 1955. On Browning's religion.
Glen, M. E. The meaning and structure of Pippa passes. UTQ 24 1955.
Priestley, F. E. L. A reading of La Saisiaz. UTQ 25 1955.
— The ironic pattern of Paracelsus. UTQ 34 1964.
Ruffin, D. Browning's Childe Roland and Chaucer's House of fame. In Essays in honor of W. C. Curry, Nashville 1955.
Short, C. John Keats and Childe Roland. N & Q May 1955.
Thale, J. Browning's popularity and the Spasmodic poets. JEGP 54 1955.
Beall, C. B. A Dantean simile in Browning. MLN 71 1956.
de Selincourt, A. In his Six great poets, 1956.
Duffin, H. C. Amphibian: a reconsideration of Browning. Cambridge 1956.
Going, W. T. The Ring and the Brownings. MLN 71 1956.
Harrison, T. P. Birds in the poetry of Browning. RES 7 1956.
— Browning's Childe Roland and Wordsworth. Tennessee Stud in Lit 6 1961.
Langbaum, R. The ring and the book: a relativist poem. PMLA 71 1956.
— The importance of fact in the Ring and the book. Victorian Newsletter no 17 1960.
— Browning and the question of myth. PMLA 81 1966.
McAleer, E. C. Browning's Cleon and Auguste Comte. Comparative Lit 8 1956.
— Pasquale Villari and the Brownings. Boston Public Lib Quart 4 1957.
— Nationality in drinks. Explicator 20 1961.
McNeir, W. F. Lucrezia's 'cousin' in Andrea del Sarto. N & Q Nov 1956.
Schneck, J. M. Browning and Mesmerism. Bull of Medical Lib Assoc 44 1956.
Schweik, R. C. Bishop Blougram's miracles. MLN 71 1956.
— The structure of A grammarian's funeral. College Eng 1961.

Baker, J. E. Religious implications in Browning's poetry. PMLA 72 1957.
Dudley, F. A. 'Hy, Zy, Hine'. Research Stud of State College of Washington 25 1957. On the Soliloquy.
Hill, A. A. Pippa's song: two attempts at a structural criticism. SE 35 1957.
Jerman, B. R. Browning's witless duke. PMLA 72 1957. Ferrara in My last Duchess.
King, R. A. The bow and the lyre: the art of Browning. Ann Arbor 1957.
— Browning, mage and maker. Victorian Newsletter no 20 1962.
Litzinger, B. A. Master Hugues of Saxe-Gotha. N & Q June 1957.
— Browning on immortality. N & Q Oct 1958.
— The prior's niece in Fra Lippo Lippi. College Eng 1961.
— The statue and the bust. In Studies in honor of J. C. Hodges and A. Thaler, Knoxville 1962.
— Browning and the Babylonian woman. Baylor Browning Interests no 19 1962.
— Time's revenges: Browning's reputation as a thinker 1889–1962. Knoxville 1964.
Pepperdene, M. W. Fra Lippo Lippi 70–5. Explicator 15 1957. Replies by L. Perrine, E. M. Everett 16 1957.
Praz, M. A grammarian's funeral. TLS 6 Dec 1957. Further comment by H. H. Brown 27 Dec 1957. On a connection with Erasmus.
Szladits, L. L. Browning's French night-cap. BNYPL Sept 1957. Milsand's assistance to Browning.
Adrian, A. A. The Browning–Rossetti friendship: some unpublished letters of Rossetti. PMLA 73 1958.
Cutts, J. P. Soliloquy of the Spanish cloister. N & Q Jan 1958. On the damnations.
de Courten, M. L. G. 'Pen, il figlio dei Browning'. Eng Miscellany (Rome) 8 1958.
Fiorini, N. Robert Browning. Turin 1958.
Marks, E. R. Abt Vogler 43–6. Explicator 16 1958.
Porter, K. H. Through a glass darkly: Spiritualism in the Browning circle. Lawrence Kansas 1958.
Tanzy, C. E. Browning, Emerson and Bishop Blougram's apology. MP 58 1960.
Watkins, C. C. Browning's 'fame within these four years'. MLR 53 1958.
— Browning's Men and women and the Spasmodic School. JEGP 57 1958.
— The 'abstruser themes' of Fifine at the fair. PMLA 74 1959.
— Red cotton nightcap country and Carlyle. Victorian Stud 7 1964.
Zamwalt, E. B. Christian symbolism in My last Duchess. N & Q Oct 1958.
Britton, J. Bishop Blougram's apology. Explicator 17 1959.
Bryson, J. Browning. 1959 (Br Council pamphlet).
Honan, P. Browning's poetic laboratory: the uses of Sordello. MP 56 1959.
— Browning's characters; a study in poetic techniques. New Haven 1961.
— Belial upon Setebos. Tennessee Stud in Lit 9 1964. On his reading of Milton.
— Browning's testimony on his Essay on Shelley. Eng Lang Notes 2 1964.
Hughes, R. E. Childe Roland and the broken taboo. Lit & Psychology 9 1959.
Maxwell, J. C. Browning and Christopher Smart. N & Q Dec 1959.
— Browning's concept of the poet: a revision in Pauline. Victorian Poetry 1 1963.
— A Horatian echo in Saul. Victorian Poetry 3 1965.
Perrine, L. Browning's shrewd duke (Ferrara). PMLA 74 1959.
Preyer, R. Browning: a reading of the early narratives. ELH 26 1959.
— Two styles in the verse of Browning. ELH 32 1965.

Stange, G. R. James Lee's wife. Explicator 17 1959.
Trawick, B. B. The moon metaphor in One word more. N & Q Dec 1959.
Assad, T. J. My last Duchess. Tulane Stud in Eng 10 1960.
Jones, T. H. The disposition of images in the Ring and the book. Australasian Universities Modern Languages Assoc 1960.
Palmer, R. E. jr. The uses of character in Bishop Blougram's apology. MP 58 1960.
Porter, J. L. Physical locale in the Ring and the book. Personalist 41 1960.
Reed, J. W. jr. Browning and Macready: the final quarrel. PMLA 75 1960.
Starkman, M. K. The Manichee in the [Spanish] cloister. MLN 75 1960.
Waters, D. D. Great test in Galatians. MLR 55 1960. The Spanish cloister.
Wilkinson, D. C. The need for disbelief: a comment on Pippa passes. UTQ 29 1960.
Chiarenza, F. J. The Bishop orders his tomb 73–9, 99–100. Explicator 19 1961.
Cox, M. E. The parleying with Bernard de Mandeville. West Virginia Univ Philological Papers 13 1961.
Hagopian, J. V. The mask of Browning's Countess Gismond. PQ 40 1961.
Kilburn, P. E. My last Duchess. Explicator 19 1961. Reply by L. Nathanson, ibid. On 'Fra Pandolf'.
Mendl, R. W. S. Browning, the poet-musician. Music & Letters 42 1961.
Orenstein, I. A fresh interpretation of the Last ride together. Baylor Browning Interests no 18 1961.
Wasserman, G. R. The meaning of Browning's ring-figure. MLN 76 1961.
Clarke, C. C. Humor and wit in Childe Roland. MLQ 23 1962.
Curran, E. M. Browning: tallow and brown sugar? Colby Lib Quart 6 1962. Charles Kingsley's phrase applied to Browning.
Davies, H. S. Browning and the modern novel. Hull 1962 (St John's College lecture).
Kendall, L. H. jr. A new Browning letter. N & Q Aug 1962. To G. B. Smith.
Orel, H. Historical sources in Strafford. In his Six studies, Lawrence Kansas 1962.
Seturman, V. S. By the fireside: 'The path grey heads abhor'. N & Q Aug 1962.
Tilton, J. W. and R. D. Tuttle. A new reading of Count Gismond. SP 59 1962.
Willoughby, J. W. Johannes Agricola in meditation. Explicator 20 1962.
—— Childe Roland to the dark tower came. Victorian Poetry 1 1963.
Woodard, C. R. The road to the dark tower (in Childe Roland). In Studies in honor of J. C. Hodges and A. Thaler, Knoxville 1962.
Balliet, C. A. [Arnold's] Growing old, along with Rabbi Ben Ezra. Victorian Poetry 1 1963.
Bisignano, D. Nencioni and Browning. Eng Miscellany (Rome) 14 1963.
Crowell, N. B. The triple soul: Browning's theory of knowledge. Albuquerque 1963.
Drew, P. Browning's Essay on Shelley. Victorian Poetry 1 1963.
—— Henry Jones on Browning's optimism. Victorian Poetry 2 1964.
Fleisher, D. Rabbi Ben Ezra 49–72: a new key. Victorian Poetry 1 1963.
Fryxell, L. D. The Spanish cloister 65–72. Explicator 21 1963. Reply by V. Adair, ibid.
Gainer, P. W. 'Hy, Zy, Hine' in the Spanish cloister. Victorian Poetry 1 1963.
Guerin, W. L. Irony and tension in the Epistle to Karshish. Ibid.
Holloway, Sr M. M. A further reading of Count Gismond. SP 55 1963.
Howard, J. Caliban's mind. Victorian Poetry 1 1963. Reply by L. Perrine 2 1964.
Kishler, T. C. A note on the Spanish cloister. Victorian Poetry 1 1963.
Leary, L. An American [Elizabeth Dodge] in Florence meets the Brownings. Columbia Lib Columns 7 1963.
Martin, H. The faith of Browning. Richmond Virginia 1963.
Melchiori, B. The tapestry horse: Childe Roland and Metzenerstein. Eng Miscellany (Rome) 14 1963.
—— Where the Bishop ordered his tomb. REL 5 1964.
—— Browning and the Bible: Holy-cross day. REL 7 1966.
—— Andrea del Sarto: a source in de Musset. Victorian Poetry 3 1966.
—— Browning: Don Juan [in Fifine]. EC 16 1966.
Miller, J. H. In his Disappearance of God, Cambridge Mass 1963.
Montiero, G. My last Duchess. Victorian Poetry 1 1963.
—— The grammarian's estate. Victorian Poetry 3 1965.
—— A very original poem by Browning. N & Q Sept 1966.
Paganelli, E. Il teatro di Browning. Convivium 31 1963.
Page, D. And so is Browning. EC 13 1963.
Ridenour, G. M. Browning's music poems: fancy and art. PMLA 78 1963.
Ryan, W. M. Classification of Browning's 'difficult' vocabulary. SP 55 1963.
Whitla, W. The central truth: the incarnation in Browning's poetry. Toronto 1963.
Armstrong, I. Mr Sludge. Victorian Poetry 2 1964.
Bachem, R. M. Musset's and Browning's Andrea del Sarto. Revue de Littérature Comparée 38 1964.
Bonner, F. W. The Bishop orders his tomb. Explicator 22 1964. The Ecclesiastes lines. Reply by L. Perrine 23 1965.
Cadbury, W. Lyric and anti-lyric forms: a method for judging Browning. UTQ 34 1964.
Collins, T. J. Browning's Essay on Shelley in context. Victorian Poetry 2 1964.
—— Shelley and God in Pauline. Victorian Poetry 3 1965.
Columbus, R. R. and C. Kemper. Sordello and the Speaker. Ibid.
Fleming, J. V. Browning's Yankee medium. Amer Stud 39 1964.
Friend, J. H. Euripides Browningized: the meaning of Balaustion's adventure. Victorian Poetry 2 1964.
Irvine, W. Four monologues in Men and women. Ibid.
Jennings, C. W. Diderot: a suggested source of the Jules-Phene episode in Pippa passes. Eng Lang Notes 2 1964.
Kramer, D. Character and theme in Pippa passes. Victorian Poetry 2 1964.
Mendel, S. Andrea del Sarto. Explicator 23 1964.
Poston, L. Ruskin and Browning's artists. Eng Miscellany (Rome) 15 1964.
Shaw, W. D. Character and philosophy in Fra Lippo Lippi. Victorian Poetry 2 1964.
—— The analogical argument of Saul. Ibid.
—— Browning's Duke [of Ferrara] as a theatrical producer. Victorian Newsletter no 29 1966.
Tamagnan, J. Fenêtre ouverte sur Browning. Etudes Anglaises 17 1964.
Tillotson, G. A word for Browning. Sewanee Rev 72 1964; rptd in his Mid-Victorian studies, 1965.
Triesch, G. Der dramatische Monolog in The ring and the book. Die Neueren Sprachen 13 1964.
Truss, T. T., jr. Browning's ambiguities and the Ring and the book. Univ of Mississippi Stud in Eng 5 1964.
Ball, P. M. Browning's Godot. Victorian Poetry 3 1965.
Boo, Sr M. R. The ordeal of Caponsacci. Ibid.
Bennett, J. R. Lazarus in Karshish. Ibid.
Bose, A. The ring and the book. In Essays presented to Amy G. Stock, Jaipur 1965.
Chandler, A. The eve of St Agnes and Porphyria's lover. Victorian Poetry 3 1965.

Day, R. A. Soliloquy of the Spanish Cloister 17–24. Explicator 34 1965.
Goldfarb, R. M. Sexual meaning in the Last ride together. Victorian Poetry 3 1965.
Hoar, V. A note on Childe Roland. Victorian Newsletter no 27 1965.
Jerman, B. R. The death of Browning. UTQ 35 1965.
Kroeber, K. Touchstones for Browning's complexity. Victorian Poetry 3 1965. On Meeting at night and Parting at morning.
Mattheison, P. F. Gosse's candid snapshots. Victorian Stud 8 1965.
Matthews, J. Browning and Neoplatonism. Victorian Newsletter no 28 1965.
Miyoshi, M. J. S. Mill and Browning's Pauline. Victorian Stud 9 1965.
Puhvel, M. Reminiscent bells in the Waste land. Eng Lang Notes 2 1965.
Smith, C. Browning's star imagery. New York 1965.
Sprague, R. Forever in joy: the life of Browning. Philadelphia 1965.
Stemple, D. Sordello: the art of the makers-see. PMLA 80 1965.
Stevens, L. R. Aestheticism in Browning's early Renaissance monologues. Victorian Poetry 4 1966.
—— My last Duchess: a possible source. Victorian Newsletter no 28 1965. Analogue in a book by N. Wanley.
Timko, M. Browning upon Butler: or Natural Theology. Criticism 7 1965.
—— And did you once see Browning plain? Stud in Eng Lit 1500–1900 6 1966.
Camp, D. Pompilia and the truth. Personalist 47 1966.
Friedman, B. R. Imagery of good and evil in the Ring and the book. Stud in Eng Lit 1500–1900 6 1966.
Gabbard, G. N. Browning's metamorphoses. Victorian Poetry 4 1966. On the tapestry in the Ring and the book.
Guskin, P. J. Ambiguities in the structure and meaning of Christmas-eve. Ibid.
Hellstrom, W. Time and type in Saul. ELH 33 1966.
Hitner, J. M. Browning's grotesque period. Victorian Poetry 4 1966.
Huebenthal, J. The dating of Love among the ruins, Women and roses, Childe Roland. Ibid.
Pitts, G. 'Hy Zy Hine'. N & Q Sept 1966. On the expression in the Soliloquy.
Plunkett, P. M. Abt Vogler, stanza 4. Explicator 25 1966.
Malbone, R. G. Fra Lippo Lippi. Ibid. On circumstances of Lippi's near-arrest.
—— That blasted rose-acacia. Victorian Poetry 4 1966. On the expression in the Soliloquy.
Marshall, G. O. Evelyn Hope's lover. Ibid.
Nelson, C. E. Role-playing in the Ring and the book. Ibid.
Penner, A. R. Judgment in the Ring and the book. Xavier Univ Stud 5 1966.
Radner, S. G. Love in Evelyn Hope. Lit & Psychology 16 1966.
Wasserman, G. Johannes Agricola in meditation. Explicator 24 1966. On the satirical point of the poem.

R. B. P.

ARTHUR HUGH CLOUGH
1819–61

The mss of most of Clough's poetry, prose and correspondence are in Bodley; others are in the Houghton Library, Harvard.

Bibliographies

Ehrsam, T. G. and R. H. Deily. In their Bibliographies of twelve Victorian authors, New York 1936; Supplement by Fucilla, MP 37 1939.

Terhune, A. M. In Victorian poets: a guide to research, ed F. E. Faverty, Cambridge Mass 1956, 1967 (rev M. Timko).
Houghton, W. E. The prose works of Clough: a checklist and calendar, with some unpublished passages. BNYPL 1960; rev in Gollin, Houghton and Timko, below.
Gollin, R. M., W. E. Houghton and M. Timko. Clough: a descriptive catalogue. BNYPL Jan–March 1967. Contains unpbd verse and a full list of comment on Clough; rev New York 1967.

Collections

Poems. 1862 (with memoir by F. T. Palgrave), 1863 (slightly rev, with some additional poems), [1906] (ML). *See also* Milford's edn, below.
Poems. Boston 1862 (with memoir by C. E. Norton).
Letters and remains. [Ed Mrs Clough] 1865 (priv ptd). Includes some unpbd poems.
Poems and prose remains. Ed Mrs Clough [and J. A. Symonds]. 2 vols 1869 (with memoir by Mrs Clough), 1 vol 1871 (poems only), 1874, 1877, 1878, 1879, 1880, 1882, 1883, 1885.
The Bothie and other poems. Ed E. Rhys [1884], New York [1884], 1896.
Poems. 1888 (called 'new and revised' from vol 2, 1869, but not significantly so), 1890, 1892, 1895, 1898, 1903, 1909, New York [1911]; ed C. Whibley 1913, 1920.
Prose remains. 1888.
Selections from the poems. Ed Mrs Clough 1894, 1904, 1909.
Poems. Ed H. S. Milford. 1910. A scholarly re-editing of London 1862, above, collated with Ambarvalia.
Poems. Oxford [1912], 1914.
Poems. Ed H. F. Lowry, A. L. P. Norrington and F. L. Mulhauser, Oxford 1951. A definitive edn of the canon with many unpbd poems (but *see* R. M. Gollin, The 1951 edition of Clough's poems, MP 60 1962.)
Selected prose works. Ed B. B. Trawick, Tuscaloosa 1964. Many unpbd essays and lectures.

§ 1

Clough contributed perhaps 24 poems and 13 essays to the Rugby Mag 2 vols 1835–7; see R. M. Gollin et al, Descriptive catalogue, above. *Much of Clough's work was first pbd posthumously; see also the collections listed above.*

The close of the eighteenth century. Rugby 1835; The longest day, Rugby 1836. 2 prize poems, both anon.
A stray valentine. Youth's Literary Messenger 2 1838.
Verses written in a diary. Ibid.
[77 brief biographies]. In Dictionary of Greek and Roman biography and myth, ed W. Smith 3 vols 1844–49.
I give thee joy. Balance 30 Jan 1846.
Differ to agree. Balance 13 Feb 1846.
Illustrations of Latin lyrical metres. Classical Museum 4 1847.
A consideration of objections against the Retrenchment Association. Oxford 1847.
The bothie of Toper-na-fuosich. Oxford 1848, Cambridge Mass 1849.
Ambarvalia. 1849 (with poems by T. Burbidge), 1850 (without Burbidge's poems), 1853.
Last words: Napoleon and Wellington. Fraser's Mag Feb 1853.
Oxford University Commission. North Amer Rev April 1853.
As ships, becalmed. In Thalatta: a book for the sea-side, ed S. Longfellow and T. W. Higginson, Boston 1853.
Recent English poetry. North Amer Rev July 1853.
Recent social theories. Ibid.
Westminster Rev 60 1853. Review of C. E. Norton's recent social theories.
Peschiera. Putnam's Mag 3 1854.

The struggle. Crayon 2 1955.
Amours de voyage. Atlantic Monthly Feb–May 1858.
Poems and ballads of Goethe. Fraser's Mag June 1859.
Plutarch's lives: the translation called Dryden's corrected from the Greek and revised [with a preface] by Clough. 5 vols Boston 1859, 1864, 1874, 1874, 1902; ed E. Rhys 3 vols 1910 (EL).
Greek history from Themistocles to Alexander in a series of lives from Plutarch: revised and arranged [with a preface] by Clough. 1860.

Letters

See also above, Letters and remains, 1865; Poems and prose remains, 1869; Descriptive catalogue, 1967; *and* B. B. Trawick (ed), Selected prose works, *which reprints some of the following.*
[6 letters to the editor]. Balance 23 and 30 Jan, 6 and 13 Feb, 6 and 20 March 1846.
[2 letters]. Spectator 6 and 20 Nov 1847. Signed 'Alpha'.
Letter. In Testimonials in favour of Mr Francis R. Sandford, [Edinburgh 1852].
Letter. In Testimonials in favour of Mr Bonamy Price, [Edinburgh 1852].
Letter in Oxford University Commission: report of her Majesty's Commissioners appointed to inquire into the state, discipline, studies and revenues of the University and colleges of Oxford. 1852.
Two letters of Paripedemus. Putnam's Mag 2 1853.
The letters of Arnold to Clough. Ed H. F. Lowry, Oxford 1932. Contains a letter from Clough. *See* K. Allott, An Arnold-Clough letter: references to Carlyle and Tennyson, N & Q 10 June 1956.
Emerson-Clough letters. Ed H. F. Lowry and R. L. Rusk, Cleveland Ohio 1934; rptd in Correspondence of Emerson and Carlyle, ed J. Slater, New York 1964.
Correspondence. Ed F. L. Mulhauser 2 vols Oxford 1957. Vol 2 contains a 'catalogue of all known letters'.
Peattie, R. W. William Michael Rossetti. TLS 30 July 1964. A letter to Rossetti.
New Zealand letters of Thomas Arnold the younger. Ed J. Bertram, Oxford 1966.

§2

Emerson, R. W. The Bothie. Mass Quart Rev 2 1849; rptd in his Uncollected writings, New York 1912.
[Kingsley, C.] The Bothie. Fraser's Mag Jan 1849.
Powell, T. Burbidge and Clough. In his Living authors of England, New York 1849.
Rossetti, W. M. The Bothie. Germ 1 1850.
[Hutton, R. H., and T. Hughes]. Clough—in memoriam. Spectator 23 Nov 1861.
Bagehot, W. Mr Clough's poems. Nat Rev 13 1862; rptd in his Literary studies vol 2, 1879, and in his Collected works, ed N. St John-Stevas, vol 2 Cambridge Mass 1965.
[Hutton, R. H.] Mr Clough's long-vacation pastoral Spectator 25 Jan 1862.
— Clough. Spectator 11 Sept 1869; rev and rptd in his Essays theological and literary vol 2, 1871, and in his Literary essays, 1888.
— The unpopularity of Clough. Spectator 25 Nov 1882; rptd in his Brief literary criticisms, ed E. M. Roscoe 1906.
[Lewes, G. H.] Clough's poems. Cornhill Mag Sept 1862.
Masson, D. The poems of Clough. Macmillan's Mag Aug 1862.
[Allingham, W.] Clough. Fraser's Mag Oct 1866.
[Lowell, J. R.] Swinburne's tragedies. North Amer Rev April 1866; rptd in his My study windows, 1871.
[Symonds, J. A.] Clough's life and poems. Cornhill Mag Oct 1866.
— Clough. Fortnightly Rev Dec 1868; rptd in his Last and first, ed A. Morell, New York 1919.
[Norton, C. E.] Clough. North Amer Rev Oct 1867.
Sidgwick, H. The poems and prose remains of Clough. Westminster Rev 92 1869; rptd in his Miscellaneous essays and addresses, 1904.
Waddington, S. Clough: a monograph. 1883.
Patmore, C. Clough. St James Gazette 10 Aug 1888; rptd in his Principle in art, 1889.
Swinburne, A. C. Social verse. Forum 12 1891; rptd in his Complete works, ed E. Gosse and T. J. Wise, vol 15, 1926.
Hudson, W. H. In his Studies in interpretation, 1896.
Robertson, J. M. In his New essays toward a critical method, 1897. Reply, Academy 25 Sept 1897.
Arnold, T. Clough: a sketch. Nineteenth Century Jan 1898.
Brooke, S. A. In his Four Victorian poets, New York 1908.
Huth, A. O. Über Clough's the Bothie of Toper-na-fuosich. Leipzig 1911.
Lutonsky, P. Clough. Vienna 1912.
Guyot, E. Essai sur la formation philosophique du poète Clough. Paris 1913.
Osborne, J. I. Clough. 1919.
Shackford, M. H. The Clough centenary: his Dipsychus. Sewanee Rev 27 1919; rev and rptd in her Studies of certain nineteenth-century poets, Natick Mass 1946.
Gosse, E. In his Books on the table, 1921.
Hewlett, M. H. Teufelsdröckh in hexameters. Nineteenth Century Jan 1922; rptd in his Extemporary essays, 1922.
Williams, S. T. Clough's prose. In his Studies in Victorian literature, 1923.
Beatty, J. M., jr. Clough as revealed in his prose. South Atlantic Quart 25 1926.
Lucas, F. L. Thyrsis. Life & Letters 2 1929; rptd as Clough in his Eight Victorian poets, Cambridge 1930, 1940 (as Ten Victorian poets), 1948 (rev).
Turner, A. M. A study of Clough's Mari Magno. PMLA 44 1929.
Garrod, H. W. In his Poetry and the criticism of life, Oxford 1931.
MacCarthy, D. In his Portraits, 1931.
Lowry, H. F. Introductory. In his edn of Letters of Arnold to Clough, Oxford 1932.
Peake, L. S. Clough as religious teacher. Modern Churchman 22 1932.
Wolfe, H. In The eighteen-sixties, ed J. Drinkwater 1932.
Knickerbocker, W. A. Semaphore: Arnold and Clough. Sewanee Rev 41 1933.
Scudder, T. Incredible recoil. Amer Scholar 5 1936; rev and rptd in his Lonely wayfaring man, 1936.
Levy, G. Clough. 1938.
Palmer, F. W. Was Clough a failure? PQ 22 1943.
— The bearing of science on the thought of Clough. PMLA 59 1944.
Mulhauser, F. L. Clough's Love and reason. MP 42 1945.
Turner, P. Dover beach and the Bothie. E Studies 28 1947.
Norrington, A. L. P. 'Say not the struggle nought availeth'. In Essays presented to Sir Humphrey Milford, Oxford 1948.
Trawick, B. B. The sea of faith and the battle by night in Dover beach. PMLA 65 1950. On similarities to the Bothie.
Badger, K. Clough as Dipsychus. MLQ 12 1951.
Johari, G. P. Clough at Oriel and University Hall. PMLA 66 1951.
Robertson, D. A. jr. Clough's 'Say not' in ms. N & Q 10 Nov 1951.
— Dover beach and 'Say not'. PMLA 66 1951.
The poetry of Clough. TLS 23 Nov 1951.
Baum, P. F. Clough and Arnold. MLN 67 1952.
Curvegnen, J. T. Walrond: friend of Arnold and Clough. Durham Univ Jnl 44 1952.
Dalglish, D. N. Clough: the shorter poems. EC 2 1952.

Townsend, F. G. Clough's The struggle: the text, title and date of publication. PMLA 67 1952.
Berlind, B. A curious accomplishment. Poetry 82 1953.
Jump, J. D. Clough's Amours de voyage. English 9 1953.
Pritchett, V. S. The poet of tourism. In his Books in general, 1953.
Tillotson, K. Rugby 1850: Arnold, Clough, Walrond and In memoriam. RES new ser 4 1953; rptd in her Mid-Victorian studies, 1965, with G. Tillotson, Clough's Bothie; Clough: thought and action.
Tompkins, J. M. S. MLR 48 1953. Review of Poems, 1951.
Woodward, F. In her Doctor's disciples, 1954.
Johnson, W. S. Parallel imagery in Arnold and Clough. E Studies 37 1956.
Fairchild, H. N. In his Religious trends in English poetry vol 4, New York 1957.
Allott, K. Clough's letters. EC 8 1958.
Gollin, R. M. Sandford's bid for the Edinburgh professorship and Clough's expectations. N & Q Nov 1958.
Veyriras, P. Un regain d'intérêt pour Clough. Etudes Anglaises 11 1958.
—— Clough 1819–1861. Paris 1964.
Black, I. Was it [Thomas] Arnold's doing? Psychoanalysis & Psychoanalytic Review 48 1961.
Timko, M. Corydon had a rival. Victorian Newsletter no 7 1961.
—— Innocent Victorian: the satiric poetry of Clough. Athens Ohio 1966.
Armstrong, I. Clough. 1962 (Br Council pamphlet).
Burrows, L. R. A mid-Victorian Faust. Westerly 1 1962.
Chorley, K. Clough: the uncommitted mind. Oxford 1962.
Borrie, M. A. F. Three poems of Clough. BM Quart 27 1963.
Brooks, R. L. The genesis of Arnold's Thyrsis. RES new ser 14 1963.
—— Arnold's revision of Tristram and Iseult: Clough's influence. Victorian Poetry 2 1964.
Green, D. B. Clough and the Parkers. N & Q Jan 1963.
Houghton, W. E. The poetry of Clough: an essay in revaluation. New Haven 1963.
Ryals, C. D. L. An interpretation of Clough's Dipsychus. Victorian Poetry 1 1963.
Barish, E. A new Clough ms. RES new ser 15 1964. 4 more stanzas of Solvitur acris hiems.
Cockshut, A. O. J. Clough: the real doubter. In his Unbelievers, 1964.
Bowers, F. Clough: recent revaluations. Humanities Assoc Bull 16 1965.
Miyoshi, M. Clough's poems of self-irony. Stud in Eng Lit 1500–1900 5 1965.
Castan, C. Clough's Epi-Strauss-ium and Carlyle. Victorian Poetry 4 1966.

R. M. G.

MATTHEW ARNOLD

1822–88

Bibliographies etc

Smart, T. B. The bibliography of Arnold. 1892, 1904 (rev and expanded in Works vol 15). Correction by W. F. Prideaux, N & Q 16 April 1892.
Ehrsam, T. G., R. H. Deily and R. M. Smith. In their Bibliographies of twelve Victorian authors, New York 1936. Addn by J. G. Fucilla, MP 37 1940.
Bonnerot, L. Matthew Arnold, poète. Paris 1947. Contains extensive bibliography.
Mainwaring, M. Notes toward a Matthew Arnold bibliography. MP 49 1952.
Townsend, F. G. A neglected edition of Arnold's St Paul and Protestantism. RES new ser 5 1954.
Buckler, W. E. An American edition of Arnold's Poems. PMLA 69 1954. Correction by J. C. Maxwell, ibid. Edn of New York 1878 rev Arnold.
Ullmann, S. O. A. A 'new' version of Arnold's Essay on Wordsworth. N & Q Dec 1955.
Super, R. H. The authenticity of the first edition of Arnold's Alaric at Rome (1840). HLQ 19 1956.
—— Arnold's notebooks and Arnold bibliography. MP 56 1959.
—— The first publication of Thyrsis. N & Q June 1961.
—— American piracies of Arnold. Amer Lit 38 1967.
Neiman, F. Some newly attributed contributions of Arnold to the Pall Mall Gazette. MP 55 1958.
—— Arnold's review of the Lettres et opuscules inédits by Joseph de Maistre. MLN 74 1959.
Metzdorf, R. F. The Tinker library. New Haven 1959.
Parrish, S. M. A concordance to the poems of Arnold. Ithaca 1959.
Wilkins, C. T. The English reputation of Arnold 1840–77. Ann Arbor 1959. With extensive list of reviews.
Brooks, R. L. Arnold's poetry 1849–55; an account of the contemporary criticism and its influence. Ann Arbor 1960.
—— A Septuagenarian poet: an addition to the Arnold bibliography. MP 57 1960.
—— A census of Arnold's Poems (1853). PBSA 54 1960.
—— Arnold and the Pall Mall Gazette. MP 58 1961.
—— A neglected edition [Boston 1856] of Arnold's poetry and a bibliographical correction. PBSA 55 1961.
—— An unrecorded American edition [New York 1878] of the Selected poems of Arnold. Library 5th ser 16 1961.
—— A Deptford poet: an addition and a correction to the Arnold bibliography. PQ 41 1962.
—— The publication of Arnold's early volumes of poetry. Victorian Newsletter no 22 1962.
—— The Strayed reveller myth. Library 5th ser 18 1963.
—— Arnold and Ticknor & Fields. Amer Lit 35 1964.
—— The Story manuscript of Arnold's New Rome. PBSA 58 1964.
—— Arnold's Joseph de Maistre on Russia. HLQ 30 1967.
Lefcowitz, A. B. Arnold's other countrymen: the reputation of Arnold in America from 1853 to 1870. Ann Arbor 1964.
The Poetical works, ed Tinker and Lowry, *and* Complete prose works, ed Super, *below*, *also contain bibliographies.*

Collections

Essays in criticism [first series]. Boston 1865, 1866 etc. Includes On translating Homer, A French Eton.
Poems: a new and complete edition. Boston 1856.
Poems. 2 vols 1869.
Poems: new and complete edition. 2 vols 1877, New York 1878 (rev), London 1881 (new edn), New York 1883.
Selected poems. 1878, 1878, 1880 etc, New York 1878. Chosen by Arnold.
Passages from the prose writings. 1880; ed W. E. Buckler, New York 1963. Chosen by Arnold.
The Arnold birthday book, arranged by his daughter Eleanor Arnold. 1883. From his poems.
Poems. 3 vols. 1885, 1888, 1895 (Library edn).
Poetical works. 1890, 1891 etc.
The strayed reveller, Empedocles on Etna and other poems. Ed W. Sharp [1896].
Poetical works, with introduction by N. H. Dole. New York 1897.
Selections from the prose writings. Ed L. E. Gates, New York 1897.
Works. 15 vols 1903–4 (Deluxe edn). Includes Letters, ed G. W. E. Russell.
Poems 1849–64. Oxford 1906 (WC) (introd by A. T. Quiller-Couch).
Poems 1840–66. Ed R. A. Scott-James 1908 (EL).
Poems 1840–67. Ed H. S. M[ilford], Oxford 1909 (introd by A. T. Quiller-Couch); ed G. St Quintin, Oxford 1926; with addns as Poetical works, Oxford 1942, 1945 (OSA). Complete text in chronological arrangement with variant readings.

Essays, including Essays in criticism 1865, On translating Homer, with F. W. Newman's reply and five other essays now for the first time collected. Oxford 1914 (OSA).

Poetry and prose, with W. Watson's poem and essays by L. Johnson and H. W. Garrod. Ed E. K. Chambers, Oxford 1939.

The portable Arnold. Ed L. Trilling, New York 1949.

Poetical works. Ed C. B. Tinker and H. F. Lowry, Oxford 1950 (OSA). Arnold's arrangement.

Arnold: a selection of his poems. Ed K. Allott 1954.

Poetry and prose. Ed J. Bryson 1954 (Reynard Lib).

Complete prose works. Ed R. H. Super, Ann Arbor 1960–. 11 vols projected; will not include correspondence. I, On the classical tradition, 1960; II, Democratic education, 1962; III, Lectures and essays in criticism, 1962; IV, Schools and universities on the Continent, 1964; V, Culture and anarchy, 1965; VI, Dissent and dogma, 1968. Cited as Super, below.

Selected essays. Ed N. Annan, Oxford 1964 (WC).

An Arnold verse selection. Ed D. Grant 1964.

Selected poems and prose. Ed F. W. Watt, Oxford 1964.

Poems. Ed K. Allott 1965 (EL).

Poems. Ed K. Allott 1965 (Longmans Annotated Eng Poets).

An Arnold prose selection. Ed J. D. Jump 1965.

Essays on English literature. Ed F. W. Bateson 1965.

Culture and the State. Ed P. Nash, New York 1966.

§1

Alaric at Rome: a prize poem. Rugby 1840; ed T. J. Wise 1893 (priv ptd).

Cromwell: a prize poem. Oxford 1843; rptd 1863, 1891 and in Oxford prize poems, Oxford 1846.

The strayed reveller and other poems, by A. 1849.

Empedocles on Etna and other poems, by A. 1852. *See* L. Bonnerot, Empédocle sur l'Etna: étude critique et traduction, Paris 1947.

Poems: a new edition. 1853 (with critical preface), 1854, 1857 (both rev).

Poems: second series. 1855.

Merope: a tragedy. 1858; ed J. C. Collins (with R. Whitelaw's trn of Sophocles's Electra), Oxford 1906, 1917 (rev).

Oratio anniversaria in memoriam publicorum benefactorum academiae Oxoniensis ex instituto N. domini Crewe. 1858.

England and the Italian question. 1859; ed M. M. Bevington, Durham NC 1953 (with F. Stephen's reply). In Super vol I.

The popular education of France, with notices of that of Holland and Switzerland. 1861. In Super vol II. Previously issued in Education Commission report 1860 (confidential), 1861.

On translating Homer: three lectures. 1861; On translating Homer: last words, 1862; New York 1883 (both texts, with On the study of Celtic literature), London 1896 (popular edn); ed W. H. D. Rouse 1905. In Super vol I.

The twice-revised code: reprinted from Fraser's Magazine. 1862. In Super vol II.

Oratio anniversaria in memoriam publicorum benefactorum academiae oxoniensis ex instituto N. domini Crewe. 1862.

Heinrich Heine: reprint from the Cornhill Magazine, August 1863. Philadelphia 1863.

A French Eton: or middle class education and the State. 1864, 1892 (with Schools and universities in France). In Super vol II.

Essays in criticism [ser I]. 1865, 1869, 1875, New York 1883, London 1884, Leipzig 1887; ed G. K. Chesterton 1906 (EL); ed W. Raleigh 1912; ed C. A. Miles and L. Smith, Oxford 1918; ed T. M. Hoctor, Ann Arbor 1958; Super vol III; ed K. Allott 1964 (EL); tr Spanish, 1894.

On the study of Celtic literature. 1867, New York 1883 (with On translating Homer), London 1891 (popular edn); ed E. Rhys 1910 (EL) (with other essays by Arnold and review by Strangford); ed A. Nutt 1910; Super vol III.

New poems. 1867, Boston 1867, London 1868.

Schools and universities on the Continent. 1868. Previously issued in Schools Inquiry Commission report. Partly rptd in his Higher schools and universities in Germany, 1874, 1882, and in A French Eton, to which is added Schools and universities in France, 1892. In Super vol IV.

Culture and anarchy: an essay in political and social criticism. 1869, 1875, 1882, New York 1883 (with Friendship's garland), London 1889 (popular edn); ed J. D. Wilson, Cambridge 1932; Super vol V.

St Paul and Protestantism; with an introduction on Puritanism and the Church of England. 1870, 1870, 1875, New York 1883 (with Last essays on church and religion), London 1887 (popular edn); Super vol VI.

Friendship's garland: being the conversations, letters and opinions of the late Arminius Baron von Thunder-ten-Tronckh collected and edited with a dedicatory letter to Adolescens Leo Esq of the Daily Telegraph. 1871, New York 1883 (with Culture and anarchy), London 1897, 1903 (popular edn); Super vol V.

Literature and dogma: an essay towards a better apprehension of the Bible. 1873 (3 edns), New York 1873, Boston 1873, London 1874 ('fourth edn'), 1876 ('fifth edn'), New York 1876, 1877, 1883, London 1883 (popular edn); Super vol VI; tr French, 1876.

A Bible-reading for schools: the great prophecy of Israel's restoration (Isaiah chs 40–66) arranged and edited for young learners. 1872.

Isaiah 40–66, with the shorter prophecies allied to it, arranged and edited with notes. 1875.

God and the Bible: a review of objections to Literature and dogma. 1875, Boston 1876, New York 1879, 1883, London 1884 (popular edn); Super vol VII.

Last essays on Church and religion. 1877, New York 1883 (with St Paul and Protestantism), London 1903 (popular edn); Super vol VIII.

The six chief lives from Johnson's Lives of the poets, with Macaulay's Life of Johnson edited with a preface. 1878 etc, 1886 (4th edn with notes), 1889.

Mixed essays. 1879, 1880, New York 1880, 1883 (with Irish essays), London 1903 (popular edn); Super vol VIII.

Poems of Wordsworth chosen and edited. 1879, 1879 (with addns), 1880 etc.

On the study of poetry: general introduction; Thomas Gray: critical introduction; John Keats: critical introduction. In English poets, ed T. H. Ward 1880; rptd in Essays in criticism: second series, 1888.

Letters, speeches and tracts on Irish affairs by E. Burke, collected and arranged. 1881.

Poetry of Byron, chosen and arranged. 1881, 1890 etc.

Irish essays and others. 1882, New York 1883 (with Mixed essays), London 1891 (popular edn); Super vol IX.

Isaiah of Jerusalem in the authorised English version, with an introduction, corrections and notes. 1883.

Discourses in America. 1885, New York 1889; ed F. R. Tomlinson, New York 1924; Super vol X.

Education Department: special report on certain points connected with elementary education in Germany, Switzerland and France. 1886, 1888 (with new prefatory note); Super vol XI.

General Grant: an estimate. Boston 1887; ed J. Y. Simon, Carbondale 1966 (with Mark Twain's rejoinder). Rptd from Murray's Mag Jan–Feb 1887.

Schools. In The reign of Queen Victoria, ed T. H. Ward 1887.

Essays in criticism: second series. 1888 (posthumous edn with prefatory note by Lord Coleridge), 1889 etc, Leipzig 1892; ed S. R. Littlewood 1938; ed. K. Allott 1964 (EL); Super vols IX–XI.

Civilization in the United States: first and last impressions of America. Boston 1888; tr French, 1902.
Reports on elementary schools 1852–82. Ed F. Sandford 1889; ed F. S. Marvin 1908.
On Home Rule for Ireland: two letters to the Times. 1891 (priv ptd). With prefatory note by T. B. Smart.
Arnold's notebooks, with a preface by [Eleanor Arnold] Wodehouse. 1902; ed H. F. Lowry, K. Young and W. H. Dunn 1952; Arnold's diaries: the unpublished items transcribed and ed W. B. Guthrie, Ann Arbor 1959.
Arnold as dramatic critic: a reprint of articles signed 'An old playgoer' contributed by him to the Pall Mall Gazette. Ed C. K. Shorter 1903 (priv ptd); Letters of an old playgoer, ed B. Matthews, New York 1919.
Taunt, H. V. The Oxford poems of Arnold illustrated. Oxford [1909?].
Essays in criticism: third series. Ed E. J. O'Brien, Boston 1910.
Thoughts on education chosen from the writings of Arnold. Ed L. Huxley 1912.
Five uncollected essays. Ed K. Allott, Liverpool 1953.
Essays, letters and reviews. Ed F. Neiman, Cambridge Mass 1960.

Letters and Papers

An extensive collection of originals and photographs has been assembled at the Alderman Library, Univ of Virginia.

Galton, A. H. Some letters of Arnold. Century Guild Hobby Horse April 1890; rptd in his Two essays upon Arnold, 1897.
Russell, G. W. E. Letters of Arnold 1848–88. 2 vols 1895, New York 1895, 2 vols in 1 New York 1900, 2 vols 1901 (with new notes); in Works, 1904, vols 13–15.
Letters from Arnold to John Churton Collins. 1910 (priv ptd).
Gosse, E. Arnold and Swinburne. TLS 12 Aug 1920. 6 letters.
Whitridge, A. [J. H.] Newman and Arnold. TLS 10 March 1921; addn, 31 March 1921. Rptd in his Unpublished letters of Arnold, below.
—— Unpublished letters of Arnold. New Haven 1923.
Powell, A. F. Sainte-Beuve and Arnold: an unpublished letter. French Quart 3 1921.
Koszul, A. Une lettre inédite de Matthew Arnold. Revue de Littérature Comparée 3 1923. To Edouard Reuss.
Drinkwater, J. Some letters from Arnold to Robert Browning. Cornhill Mag Dec 1923; rptd in his Book for bookmen, 1926.
Lowry, H. F. The letters of Arnold to Arthur Hugh Clough. Oxford 1932. Correction by J. C. Maxwell, N & Q Oct 1953; addn by K. Allott, N & Q June 1956.
Houghton, R. E. C. Letter of Arnold. TLS 19 May 1932. To Mr Hill, 5 Nov 1852.
Motter, T. H. V. A new Arnold letter and an old Swinburne quarrel. TLS 31 Aug 1933.
—— A check list of Arnold's letters. SP 31 1934.
Gordon, I. A. Three new letters of Arnold. MLN 56 1941. To R. D. Adams of Sydney.
Armytage, W. H. G. Arnold and a liberal minister 1880–5. RES 23 1947. Letters to A. J. Mundella.
—— Arnold and W. E. Gladstone: some new letters. UTQ 18 1949.
—— Arnold and Richard Cobden in 1864: some recently discovered letters. RES 25 1949.
—— Arnold and T. H. Huxley: some new letters 1870–80. RES new ser 4 1953.
—— Arnold and a reviewer. RES new ser 6 1955. Letter to N. MacColl.
Lowe, R. L. Arnold and Percy William Bunting: some new letters 1884–87. SB 7 1955.
—— Two Arnold letters. MP 52 1955. To Thomas Arnold and Sidney Colvin.
Allott, K. Arnold: two unpublished letters. N & Q Aug 1955. To W. H. Lucas.
Buckler, W. E. Arnold's books: toward a publishing diary. Geneva 1958. Letters to publishers.
Brooks, R. L. Arnold and his contemporaries: a check list of unpublished and published letters. SP 56 1959. Addn, 63 1966.
—— Arnold's correspondence. MP 59 1962. Unpbd letters housed in USA.
Neiman, F. 'My dear Sumner': three letters from Arnold. Victorian Newsletter no 17 1960.
DeLaura, D. J. Four Arnold letters. Texas Stud in Lit & Lang 4 1962.
—— Three Arnold letters. Lib Chron 7 1964; Eight more Arnold letters, 8 1965.
—— Arnold and the American 'literary class': unpublished correspondence and some further reasons. BNYPL April 1966.
Mattheisen, P. F. and A. C. Young. Some letters of Arnold. Victorian Newsletter no 24 1963. To E. Gosse.
Monteiro, G. Arnold and John Hay: three unpublished letters. N & Q Dec 1963.
—— An unpublished Arnold letter. Amer N & Q Jan 1964. To G. W. Smalley.
—— Arnold in America 1884. N & Q Feb 1966.
Williamson, E. L. Arnold's letters to G. S. Gibson. Victorian Newsletter no 31 1967.
Davis, A. K. Arnold's letters: a descriptive checklist. Charlottesville 1968.

§2

Rossetti, W. M. The strayed reveller and other poems. Germ Feb 1850; 1901 (facs), New York 1965 (facs).
[Clough, A. H.] Recent English poetry. North Amer Rev 77 1853; rptd in his Poems and prose remains, 1869.
[Lewes, G. H.] Schools of poetry: Arnold's poems. Leader 26 Nov, 3 Dec 1853.
[Froude, J. A.] Arnold's poems. Westminster Rev 61 1854; rptd in his Essays in literature and history, [1906] (EL).
[Coleridge, J. D.] Arnold's poems. Christian Remembrancer new ser 27 1854.
—— Matthew Arnold. New Rev 1 1889.
—— Matthew Arnold. Times 2 Nov 1891.
[Shairp, J. C.] Arnold's Poems. North Br Rev 21 1854.
['Eliot, George']. Arnold's poems. Westminster Rev 64 1855.
[Swinburne, A. C.] Modern Hellenism. Undergraduate Papers (Oxford) 1 Dec 1857. On Arnold's inaugural lecture.
—— Mr Arnold's New poems. Fortnightly Rev Oct 1867; rptd in his Essays and studies, 1875.
—— Wordsworth and Byron. Nineteenth Century April–May 1884; rptd in his Miscellanies, 1886.
Newman, F. W. Homeric translation in theory and practice: a reply to Arnold. 1861.
—— Literature and dogma. Fraser's Mag July 1873.
Spedding, J. Arnold on translating Homer. Fraser's Mag June 1861, June 1862; rptd in his Reviews and discussions, 1879.
Wright, I. C. A letter to the dean of Canterbury on the Homeric lectures of Arnold. 1864.
[James, H.] Arnold's Essays in criticism. North Amer Rev 101 1865; rptd in his Views and reviews, Boston 1908.
—— Matthew Arnold. English Illustr Mag Jan 1884; rptd in his Literary reviews and essays, New York 1957.
Sidgwick, H. The prophet of culture. Macmillan's Mag Aug 1867; rptd in Eclectic Mag Oct 1867 and in his Miscellaneous essays and addresses, 1904.
Harrison, F. Culture: a dialogue. Fortnightly Rev Nov 1867; rptd in his Choice of books, 1886.
—— Matthew Arnold. Nineteenth Century March 1896; rptd in Living Age 9 May 1896 and in his Tennyson, Ruskin, Mill and other literary estimates, 1899.
Dunn, H. Facts, not fairy-tales: brief notes on Mr Arnold's Literature and dogma. 1873.

Mallock, W. H. The new republic: or culture, faith and philosophy in an English country house. Belgravia June–Dec 1876; 1877, 1878; ed J. M. Patrick, Gainesville 1950.

Symonds, J. A. Arnold's selections from Wordsworth. Fortnightly Rev Nov 1879; rptd as Is poetry at bottom a criticism of life? in his Essays speculative and suggestive, 1890.

White, W. H. Byron, Goethe and Mr Arnold. Contemporary Rev Aug 1881; rptd Appleton's Jnl Oct 1881 and in his Pages from a journal with other papers, 1900.

Lang, A. Matthew Arnold. Century Mag April 1882.

Whitman, W. Our eminent visitors. Critic 17 Nov 1883.

Quesnel, L. Un moraliste anglais: Arnold. Bibliothèque Universelle et Revue Suisse Nov 1886.

[Arnold, T.] Matthew Arnold (by one who knew him well). Manchester Guardian 18 May 1888.

Roosevelt, T. Some recent criticism of America. Murray's Mag Sept 1888; rptd in Eclectic Mag Nov 1888.

Robertson, J. M. Science in criticism. In his Essays towards a critical method, 1889.

— In his Modern humanists: sociological studies of Carlyle, Mill, Emerson, Arnold, Ruskin and Spencer, 1891.

— De mortuis: Matthew Arnold [1888]. In his Criticisms: second faggot, 1903.

— In his Modern humanists reconsidered, 1927.

Henley, W. E. In his Views and reviews, 1890. Rptd with addns from Athenaeum 22 Aug 1885.

Duff, M. E. G. The plant allusions in the poems of Arnold. Nature Notes June–July 1890.

— Arnold's writings. Murray's Mag March 1890; Kingston-on-Thames 1890 (priv ptd); rptd in his Out of the past, 1903.

Housman, A. E. Introductory lecture, University College, London. 1892, 1933 (both priv ptd), Cambridge 1937; rptd in Selected prose, below.

— Appendix. In his Selected prose, ed J. Carter, Cambridge 1961. 3 pages from an unpbd paper of c. 1891.

Stephen, L. Matthew Arnold. Nat Rev Dec 1893; rptd in Eclectic Mag March 1894, in Living Age 13 Jan 1894, and in his Studies of a biographer, 1898.

Saintsbury, G. In his Corrected impressions, 1895.

— Matthew Arnold. Edinburgh 1899.

Flexner, A. Arnold's poetry from an ethical standpoint. International Jnl of Ethics 5 1895.

Gladstone, W. E. Bishop Butler and his censors: Mr Arnold. Nineteenth Century Dec 1895.

Morley, J. Matthew Arnold. Ibid.

Hudson, W. H. In his Studies in interpretation: Keats, Clough, Arnold, New York 1896.

Fitch, J. G. Thomas and Matthew Arnold, and their influence on English education. New York 1897.

Palgrave, F. T. The landscape of Browning, Arnold, Barnes and Charles Tennyson. In his Landscape in poetry, 1897.

Gates, L. E. In his Three studies in literature, New York 1899. Rptd from his Selections from Arnold's prose.

— The return to conventional life. Critic March 1900; rptd in his Studies and appreciations, New York 1900.

Brownell, W. C. Matthew Arnold. Scribner's Mag July 1901; rptd with addns in his Victorian prose masters, New York 1901.

Lewisohn, L. A study of Arnold. Sewanee Rev 9–10 1901–2.

Mustard, W. P. Homeric echoes in Balder dead. In Studies in honor of Basil L. Gildersleeve, Baltimore 1902.

Paul, H. W. Matthew Arnold. 1902 (EML).

Chesterton, G. K. Matthew Arnold. Bookman (New York) Oct 1902.

— In his GKC as MC: thirty-seven introductions, ed J. P. de Fonseka 1929. Rptd from Arnold's essays literary and critical (EL).

Clark, C. C. A possible source of Dover beach. MLN 17 1902.

Johnson, W. K. The church of Brou. Athenaeum 18 April 1903.

Dawson, W. H. Arnold and his relation to the thought of our time. New York 1904.

Russell, G. W. E. Matthew Arnold. 1904.

Schrag, A. Arnold, poet and critic. Basle 1904.

Aronstein, P. Matthew Arnold. Zeitschrift für Vergleicende Litteraturgeschichte new ser 15 1904.

Warren, T. H. Matthew Arnold. Quart Rev 202 1905; rptd in his Essays of poets and poetry, 1909.

Rice, R. Arnold and Joubert. Reader Mag (Indianapolis) Nov 1905.

Mackie, A. Arnold as naturalist: Arnold's birds. In his Nature knowledge in modern poets, 1906.

Starbird, R. S. The ethnological in Arnold. Bull Washington Univ Assoc 4 1906.

Pound, L. Arnold's source for Sohrab and Rustum. MLN 21 1906.

Katscher, L. Der Dichter des Empedokles auf dem Aetna. Nord und Süd Sept 1906.

Jouard, F. L. The source of the Sick king in Bokhara. JEGP 6 1906.

Koszul, A. Comment noter les vers anglais à propos d'une édition de la Merope. Revue Germanique 3 1907.

Cestre, C. The church of Brou. Revue Germanique 4 1908.

Boas, F. S. Some poems of Arnold. Trans Royal Soc of Lit new ser 29 1909; rptd in his From Richardson to Pinero, 1936.

Garrod, H. W. The theology of Arnold. Oxford & Cambridge Rev no 6 1909; rptd in Living Age 5 Feb 1910.

— Poetry and the criticism of life. Cambridge Mass 1931.

— Arnold's 1853 preface. RES 17 1941.

Derham, M. G. Borrowings and adaptations from the Iliad and Odyssey in Sohrab and Rustum. Univ of Colorado Stud 7 1909.

More, P. E. Criticism. In his Shelburne essays, 7th ser New York 1910.

Poisblaud, G. La religion fondée sur le vérifiable d'après Arnold. Geneva 1910.

Warshaw, J. Sainte-Beuve's influence on Arnold. MLN 25 1910.

Sharp, W. On Arnold. In his Papers critical and reminiscent, 1912. Rptd from his edn of Arnold's poems.

Omond, T. S. Arnold and Homer. E & S 3 1912.

Hobohm, J. Arnold als Naturschilderer. Halle 1913.

Mobbs, R. Etude comparée des jugements de Mme Humphry Ward, de M. Arnold et W. Pater sur le Journal intime de H.-F. Amiel. Geneva 1913.

Bendz, E. P. The influence of Pater and Arnold in the prose-writings of Oscar Wilde. Gothenburg 1914.

Kelso, A. P. Arnold on continental life and literature. Oxford 1914.

Strachey, G. L. A Victorian critic. New Statesman 1 Aug 1914; rptd in his Characters and commentaries, 1933.

Powys, J. C. In his Visions and revisions, New York 1915.

— In his Enjoyment of literature, New York 1938, London 1938 (as The pleasures of literature).

Raleigh, W. A. An introduction to Arnold's Essays in criticism. 1916; rptd in his Some authors, Oxford 1923.

Sherman, S. P. Arnold: how to know him. Indianapolis 1917.

Goldmark, R. I. The Hellenism of Arnold. In her Studies in the influence of the classics on English literature, New York 1918.

Quiller-Couch, A. T. In his Studies in literature, Cambridge 1918. Rptd from edn of Arnold's poems (WC).

Wright, H. The source of Arnold's Forsaken merman. MLR 13 1918.

— Arnold's East and west. MLR 13 1918.

Mott, L. F. Renan and Arnold. MLN 33 1918.
Courtney, J. E. In her Freethinkers of the nineteenth century, 1920.
Furrer, P. Der Einfluss Sainte-Beuves auf die Kritik Arnolds. Wetzikon 1920.
Grierson, H. J. C. Lord Byron: Arnold and Swinburne. Proc Br Acad 9 1920; rptd in his Background of English literature, 1925.
Scott, J. A. Arnold's interpretation of Odyssey iv 563. Classical Jnl Nov 1920.
Eliot, T. S. The second order mind. Dial Dec 1920.
— The place of Pater. In The eighteen eighties, ed W. de la Mare, Cambridge 1930; rptd as Arnold and Pater, Bookman (New York) Sept 1930; and in his Selected essays, 1932.
— In his Use of poetry and use of criticism, 1933.
Amūlya-Chandra Aikat. On the poetry of Arnold, Robert Browning and Rabindranath Tagore. Calcutta 1921.
Williams, S. T. Some aspects of Arnold's poetry. Sewanee Rev 29 1921; rptd in his Studies in Victorian literature, New York 1923.
— Arnold on men of his day. Literary Rev 20 May 1922; rptd with Theory and practice in the poetry of Arnold in his Studies in Victorian literature, above.
— The founding of Main Street: the letters of Arnold. North Amer Rev Sept 1922.
— A century of Arnold. North Amer Rev Jan 1923; rptd in his Studies in Victorian literature, above.
— Arnold as a critic of literature. Univ of Cal Chron 26 1924.
White, H. C. Arnold and Goethe. PMLA 36 1921.
Maischhofer, A. Arnold als Kritiker der französischen Literatur. Freiburg 1922.
Houghton, R. E. C. The influence of the classics on the poetry of Arnold. Oxford 1923.
Ker, W. P. In his Art of poetry, Oxford 1923.
Lassen, M. Arnolds Verhältnis zu den Deutschen und zur deutschen Literatur. Freiburg 1923.
Sadler, M. E. Matthew Arnold. Nineteenth Century Feb–March 1923.
Boyer, C. V. Self-expression and happiness: a study of Arnold's idea of perfection. International Jnl of Ethics 33 1923.
Clark, F. L. On certain imitations or reminiscences of Homer in Arnold's Sohrab and Rustum. Classical Weekly 1 Oct 1923.
Elliott, G. R. The Arnoldian lyric melancholy. PMLA 38 1923; rptd in his Cycle of modern poetry, Princeton 1929.
Murry, J. M. Arnold the poet. In his Discoveries, 1924.
— The self-silenced poet: Arnold and his ideals. TLS 28 June 1941; rptd with addns in his Looking before and after, 1948.
— Arnold and his ideals. In his Katherine Mansfield and other literary portraits, 1949.
Zorn, P. W. Arnold und seine Beziehungen zu Deutschland. Hamburg 1924.
Gummere, R. M. Matthew Arnold. Quart Rev 241 1924.
Reuschel, K. The forsaken merman und sein deutsches Vorbild. Germanisch-romanische Monatsschrift 12 1924.
Ellis, F. G. Notes on Sohrab and Rustum. [1925].
Knickerbocker, W. S. Creative Oxford. Syracuse NY 1925.
— Arnold's theory of poetry. Sewanee Rev 33 1925.
— Arnold at Oxford: the natural history of a father and son. Sewanee Rev 35 1927.
— Bellwether. Sewanee Rev 41 1933. Compares Arnold's criticism and T. S. Eliot's.
— Semaphore: Arnold and Clough. Ibid.
— Thunder in the index. Sewanee Rev 47 1939.
— Arnold, Shelley and Joubert. MLN 55 1940.
Shafer, R. Matthew Arnold. In his Christianity and naturalism, New Haven 1926.
Tristram, H. [J. H.] Newman and Arnold. Cornhill Mag March 1926.
Romer, V. L. Arnold and some French poets. Nineteenth Century June 1926.
Harper, G. M. Arnold and the Zeitgeist. Virginia Quart Rev 2 1926; rptd in his Spirit of delight, New York 1928.
Renwanz, J. Arnold und Deutschland. Greifswald 1927.
Phillips, E. M. English friendships of Sainte-Beuve. Bull Modern Humanities Research Assoc 1 1927.
Hille, H. Die Kulturgedanken Arnolds und ihre Verwirklichung in der Pädagogik. Halle 1928.
'Kingsmill, Hugh'. Matthew Arnold. 1928.
Orrick, J. B. Arnold and Goethe. Pbns of Eng Goethe Soc new ser 4 1928.
— Hebraism and Hellenism. New Adelphi Sept 1928.
— Arnold and America. London Mercury Aug 1929.
Montague, C. E. Matthew Arnold. Saturday Rev of Lit 12 May 1928; rptd in London Mercury Jan 1929 and in his A writer's notes on his trade, 1930.
Nicolson, M. H. The real scholar gipsy. Yale Rev new ser 18 1929.
Hall, W. P. The three Arnolds and their Bible. In Essays in intellectual history dedicated to James Harvey Robinson, New York 1929.
Woods, M. Matthew Arnold. E & S 15 1929.
Yvon, P. L'inspiration poétique chez Arnold à propos du Scholar gipsy. Revue Anglo-américaine 6 1929.
— Etude sur la pensée intime d'un poète victorien: Arnold et la critique de la vie contemporaine dans sa poésie (1849–72). Caen 1938.
Cooper, L. Arnold's essay on Wordsworth. Bookman (New York) July 1929; rptd in his Evolution and repentance, Ithaca 1935.
McCallum, J. D. The apostle of culture meets America. New England Quart 2 1929.
Levy, H. Arnold und die volkscharakterologische Erkenntnis. Zeitschrift für Völkerpsychologie und Soziologie 5 1929.
Bush, D. The varied hues of pessimism. Dalhousie Rev 9 1929.
Lucas, F. L. In his Eight Victorian poets, Cambridge 1930, 1940 (as Ten Victorian poets).
Sedgewick, G. G. Wordsworth, Arnold and Professor Lane Cooper. Dalhousie Rev 10 1930.
Bonnerot, L. La jeunesse de Matthew Arnold. Revue Anglo-américaine 7 1930.
— Arnold, poète: essai de biographie psychologique. Paris 1947.
Brown, E. K. The critic as xenophobe: Arnold and the international mind. Sewanee Rev 38 1930.
— The French reputation of Arnold. In Studies in English by members of University College Toronto, Toronto 1931.
— Arnold and the Elizabethans. UTQ 1 1932.
— Studies in the text of Arnold's prose works. Paris 1935.
— The scholar gipsy: an interpretation. Revue Anglo-américaine 12 1935.
— Arnold and the eighteenth century. UTQ 9 1940.
— Arnold: a study in conflict. Chicago 1948.
Bradley, A. C. Shelley and Arnold's critique of his poetry. In his A miscellany, 1931.
Chauvet, P. In his Sept essais de littérature anglaise, Paris 1931.
Elias, O. Arnolds politische Grundanschauungen. Leipzig 1931.
Halperin, M. Le roman de Tristan et Iseut dans la littérature anglo-américaine au xixe et au xxe siècles. Paris 1931.
Harvey, C. H. Arnold: a critic of the Victorian period. 1931.
Burgum, E. B. The humanism of Arnold. Symposium 2 1931.
Lawrence, E. P. An apostle's progress: Arnold in America. PQ 10 1931.

Barnard, C. C. Byron: a criticism of Arnold's essay. E Studien 65 1931.
Leonard, C. H. Two notes on Arnold. MLN 46 1931.
— Arnold in America. Ann Arbor 1964.
Blunden, E. In Great Victorians, ed H. J. and H. Massingham 1932.
Chambers, E. K. Matthew Arnold. Proc Br Acad 18 1932; rptd in his Sheaf of studies, Oxford 1942.
— Arnold's Tree. In his A sheaf of studies, Oxford 1942.
— Arnold: a study. Oxford 1947, New York 1964.
Dunn, W. H. Arnold and the conduct of life. In his Lectures on three eminent Victorians, Claremont Cal 1932.
Steinmetz, M. S. Die ideengeschichtliche Bedeutung Arnolds. Schramberg 1932.
Birss, J. H. Whitman on Arnold: an uncollected comment [New York Herald 16 April 1888]. MLN 47 1932.
Wilson, J. D. Arnold and the educationists. In Social and political ideas of some representative thinkers of the Victorian age, ed F. J. C. Hearnshaw 1933.
— Leslie Stephen and Arnold as critics of Wordsworth. Cambridge 1939.
Arakawa, T. T. S. Eliot's interpretation of Arnold and Pater. Stud in Eng Lit (Tokyo) 13 1933. In Japanese.
Harris, A. Arnold: the 'unknown years'. Nineteenth Century April 1933.
Tinker, C. B. Arnold's poetic plans. Yale Rev new ser 22 1933.
— and H. F. Lowry. Arnold's Dover beach. TLS 10 Oct 1935.
— and H. F. Lowry. The poetry of Arnold: a commentary. Oxford 1940.
Ishida, K. Arnold or Carlyle? Stud in Eng Lit (Tokyo) 13 1933.
Wilkins, E. H. The source of Arnold's Jacopone sonnet. MP 31 1933.
Boyd, A. J. Arnold and the grand style. Bombay 1934.
Hock, E. Arnolds Forsaken merman: ein Interpretationsbeispiel. Neuphilologische Monatsschrift April 1934.
Brown, L. Arnold's succession 1850–1914. Sewanee Rev 42 1934.
Connolly, T. L. Matthew Arnold: critic. Thought 9 1934.
Angell, J. W. Arnold's indebtedness to Renan's Essais de morale et de critique. Revue de Littérature Comparée 14 1934.
Hunt, E. L. Arnold: the critic as rhetorician. Quart Jnl of Speech 20 1934.
— Arnold and his critics. Sewanee Rev 44 1936.
Sells, I. E. Arnold and France: the poet. Cambridge 1935. *See* her letter TLS 7 March 1935.
— Marguerite. MLR 38 1943.
Cairncross, A. S. Arnold's Faded leaves and Switzerland. TLS 28 March 1935.
Pettet, E. C. Note on Arnold's poetry. Adelphi Aug 1935.
Loring, M. L. S. T. S. Eliot on Arnold. Sewanee Rev 43 1935.
Leavis, F. R. Arnold, Wordsworth and the Georgians. In his Revaluation, 1936.
— Arnold as critic. Scrutiny 7 1939.
MacNeill, J. E. Arnold and Alexander Burnes. TLS 11 April 1936.
Lippincott, B. E. In his Victorian critics of democracy, Minneapolis 1938.
Stanley, C. W. Matthew Arnold. Toronto 1938.
Whitridge, A. Arnold and Sainte-Beuve. PMLA 53 1938.
— The gaiety of Arnold. [Univ of Penna] Lib Chron 25 1959.
Churchill, R. C. Gray and Arnold. Criterion April 1938.
Wickelgren, F. L. Arnold's literary relations with France. MLR 33 1938.
Corbett, J. A. A Victorian critic in Germany. German Life & Letters 3 1939.
Groom, B. On the diction of Tennyson, Browning and Arnold. Oxford 1939.
Trilling, L. Matthew Arnold. New York 1939, 1949, 1955 (rev).
Moore, T. S. Matthew Arnold. E & S 24 1939.
Montgomery, H. C. Matthew Arnold: classicist. Classical Jnl 34 1939; Supplement by G. L. Hendrickson, 35 1940.
Evans, B. I. Arnold and the later nineteenth century. In his Tradition and romanticism, 1940.
Hull, M. E. The merman lover in ballad and song. In Studies in English in honor of R. D. O'Leary and S. L. Whitcomb, Lawrence Kansas 1940.
Morrison, T. Dover beach revisited: a new fable for critics. Harper's Mag Feb 1940.
Muller, H. J. Arnold: a parable for partisans. Southern Rev 5 1940.
Savage, H. L. The cuckoo's 'parting cry'. MLQ 1 1940.
Lowry, H. F. Arnold and the modern spirit. Princeton 1941.
Russev, R. Poeziyata na Arnold. Godišnik na Sofiiskiya Universitet, Istoriko-filologičeski Fakultet 37 1941.
Beauchamp, W. T. Plato on the prairies: Arnold at Galesburg. Educational Forum March 1941.
Hamilton, H. W. Arnold's Study of poetry sixty years after. College Eng March 1941.
Motter, T. H. V. Culture and the new anarchy. Bull Amer Assoc of Univ Professors June 1941.
Hicks, J. The stoicism of Arnold. Univ of Iowa Stud 6 1942.
Jacobsen, O. Arnold: som aktuel kritiker. Copenhagen 1942.
Lamborn, E. A. G. Sibylla's name. N & Q 24 Jan 1942.
Dudley, F. A. Arnold and science. PMLA 57 1942.
M., A. Arnold and the Cambridge platonists. N & Q 21 Nov 1942.
Page, F. Balder dead (1855). E & S 28 1942.
Tillotson, G. Arnold: the critic and the advocate. Essays by Divers Hands new ser 20 1943.
— Arnold and eighteenth-century poetry. In Essays on the eighteenth century presented to David Nichol Smith, Oxford 1945.
— Arnold and Pater: critics historical, aesthetic and otherwise. E & S new ser 3 1950. All three rptd in his Criticism and the nineteenth century, 1951.
— Arnold in our time; Arnold, the lecturer and journalist. Both in his Mid-Victorian studies, 1965.
Templeman, W. D. A note on Arnold's Civilisation in the United States. MLN 59 1944.
— Arnold's The literary influence of academies, Macaulay and Espinasse. SP 43 1946.
Jones, H. M. Arnold, aristocracy and America. Amer Historical Rev 49 1944; rptd in his History and the contemporary, Madison 1964.
Liptzin, S. Heine, the continuator of Goethe: a mid-Victorian legend. JEGP 43 1944.
— The English legend of Heinrich Heine. New York 1954.
Major, J. C. Arnold and Attic prose style. PMLA 59 1944.
Holman, H. R. Arnold's elocution lessons. New England Quart 18 1945.
Rowse, A. L. Arnold as Cornishman. Welsh Rev 4 1945.
Blackburn, W. The background of Arnold's Literature and dogma. MP 43 1946.
— Arnold and the Oriel noetics. PQ 25 1946.
— Arnold and the Powis Medal at Cambridge. MLN 62 1947.
— Bishop Butler and the design of Arnold's Literature and dogma. MLQ 9 1948.
Schilling, B. N. In his Human dignity and the great Victorians, New York 1946.
Curgenven, J. P. Arnold in two scholarship examinations. RES 22 1946.
— Theodore Walrond: friend of Arnold and Clough. Durham Univ Jnl 44 1952.

— The scholar gipsy: a study of the growth, meaning and integration of a poem. Litera 2–3 1955–6.
— Thyrsis. Litera 4–6 1957–59.
Shelton, H. S. Arnold and the modern church. Hibbert Jnl 44 1946.
Fitzgerald, P. Arnold's summer holiday: notes on the origin of the Forsaken merman. English 6 1946.
Jump, J. D. Arnold and the Saturday Review. RES 22 1946.
— Arnold and the Spectator. RES 25 1949.
— Arnold and Enoch Arden. N & Q Feb 1954.
— Matthew Arnold. 1955.
— In Pelican guide to English literature, ed B. Ford vol 6, 1958.
Bonnerot, C. Matthew Arnold, poète. Paris 1947.
Muir, K. Arnold and the Victorian dilemma. In Penguin new writing, ed J. Lehmann no 31, 1947.
Yano, H. An essay on Arnold. Tokyo 1947.
Robbins, W. Arnold and Ireland. UTQ 17 1947.
— The ethical idealism of Arnold. 1959.
Turner, P. Dover beach and the Bothie of Tober-na-vuolich. E Studies 28 1947.
Nicolson, H. On re-reading Arnold. Essays by Divers Hands new ser 24 1948.
MacDonald, I. The buried self: a background to the poems of Arnold 1848–51. 1949.
Willey, B. In his Nineteenth-century studies, 1949.
Abel, D. Strangers in nature: Arnold and Emerson. Univ of Kansas City Rev 15 1949.
Baum, P. F. Arnold's Marguerite. In Booker memorial studies, ed H. Shine, Chapel Hill 1950; rptd in his Ten studies, below.
— Ten studies in the poetry of Arnold. Durham NC 1958.
Connell, W. F. The educational thought and influence of Arnold. 1950.
Kelleher, J. V. Arnold and the Celtic revival. In Perspectives of criticism, ed H. Levin, Cambridge Mass 1950.
Warren, A. H. In his English poetic theory 1825–65, Princeton 1950.
Rust, J. D. George Eliot's reviews of three Victorian poets. Papers Michigan Acad of Science, Arts & Letters 36 1950.
Tillotson, K. Arnold and Johnson. RES new ser 1 1950.
— Dr Arnold's death and a broken engagement. N & Q 13 Sept 1952. Replies by N. Wymer and K. Tillotson, 8 Nov 1952.
— 'Yes: in the sea of life.' RES new ser 3 1952; rptd in her Mid-Victorian studies, 1965.
— Rugby 1850: Arnold, Clough, Walrond and In memoriam. RES new ser 4 1953; addn by A. L. P. Norrington, ibid; rptd with above.
— Arnold and Carlyle. N & Q March 1955.
— Arnold and Carlyle. Proc Br Acad 42 1956; rptd in her Mid-Victorian Studies, 1965.
Neiman, F. Plotinus and Arnold's Quiet work. MLN 65 1950.
— The Zeitgeist of Arnold. PMLA 72 1957.
Battle, G. A. Heine's Geoffroy Rudèl und Melisande von Tripoli and Arnold's Tristam and Iseult and The church of Brou. MLN 65 1950.
Trawick, B. B. The sea of faith and the battle by night in Dover beach. PMLA 65 1950.
Faverty, F. E. Arnold the ethnologist. Evanston 1951.
Holloway, J. Arnold and the modern dilemma. EC 1 1951; rptd in his Charted mirror, 1960.
— In his Victorian sage, 1953.
Minnick, W. C. Arnold on Emerson. Quart Jnl of Speech 37 1951.
Perkins, D. Arnold and the function of literature. ELH 18 1951.
Robertson, D. A. Dover beach and Say not the struggle nought availeth. PMLA 66 1951. Replies by P. F. Baum, MLN 67 1952; by H. W. Redman, N & Q June 1953; supplemented by F. G. Townsend, Clough's The struggle, PMLA 67 1952.
Johnson, E. D. H. In his Alien vision of Victorian poetry, Princeton 1952.
Lowe, R. L. A note on Arnold in America. Amer Lit 23 1952, 30 1959. Replies by W. E. Buckler 29 1958, R. L. Brooks 31 1960.
— Notes on Arnold. N & Q 25 Oct, 8 Nov 1952.
— Arnold's poetic theory: a history. Ann Arbor 1955.
Pattison, B. In Pioneers of English education, ed A. V. Judges 1952.
Schmezer, G. Das poetische Genus in den Gedichten von Arnold und Clough. Berne 1952. On personifications and the gender ascribed to abstractions.
Cox, R. G. Victorian criticism of poetry: the minority tradition. Scrutiny 18 1952.
Bantock, G. H. Matthew Arnold HMI. Ibid; rptd in his Freedom and authority in education, 1952.
Smallbone, J. A. Arnold's theology. Baptist Quart new ser 14 1952.
— Arnold and the bicentenary of 1862. Ibid.
— Arnold and the nonconformists. Ibid.
Coulling, S. M. B. Renan's influence on Arnold's literary and social criticism. Florida State Univ Stud no 5 1952.
— Arnold and the Daily Telegraph. RES new ser 12 1961.
— The background of the Function of criticism at the present time. PQ 42 1963.
— The evolution of Culture and anarchy. SP 60 1963.
— Arnold's 1853 preface: its origin and aftermath. Victorian Stud 7 1964.
Mainwaring, M. Arnold on Shelley. MLN 67 1952.
— Arnold and Tolstoi. Nineteenth-century Fiction 6 1952.
Allott, K. Pater and Arnold. EC 2 1952.
— Matthew Arnold. 1955.
— Arnold's original version of the River. TLS 28 March 1958. Corrections by K. Allott and A. Harris 11–18 April 1958.
— A birthday exercise by Arnold. N & Q May 1958.
— Arnold's Stagirius and Saint-Marc Girardin. RES new ser 9 1958.
— Arnold's reading-lists in three early diaries. Victorian Stud 2 1959. Comments by E. L. Williamson and K. Allott 3 1960.
— Arnold's Empedocles on Etna and Byron's Manfred. N & Q Aug 1962.
— Arnold's The new sirens and George Sand. Victorian Poetry 1 1963.
— Arnold's Tyrian trader. TLS 18 Oct 1963.
— The motto of Arnold's Thyrsis. N & Q June 1964.
— A new poem by Arnold. TLS 25 Feb 1965.
Hornstein, L. H. Rugby chapel and Exodus. MLR 47 1952.
Johnson, W. S. Arnold's sea of life. PQ 31 1952.
— Arnold's lonely islands. N & Q July 1954.
— Parallel imagery in Arnold and Clough. E Studies 37 1956.
— Arnold's dialogue. Univ of Kansas City Rev 27 1960.
— The voices of Arnold. New Haven 1961.
Smith, C. W. The 'oblique way' in Arnold's The forsaken merman. Bucknell Univ Stud 3 1952.
LeRoy, G. C. Ambivalence in Arnold's prose criticism. College Eng May 1952.
— In his Perplexed prophets, Philadelphia 1953.
— Arnold and aselgeia. BNYPL May 1963.
Cotten, L. A. Arnold's pronunciation of the name Iseult. MLN 67 1952.
Harding, J. N. Poetry of Arnold. Contemporary Rev Aug 1952.
— Renan and Arnold: two saddened searchers. Hibbert Jnl 57 1959.
Temple, R. Z. In her Critic's alchemy: a study of the introduction of French symbolism into England, New York 1953.

Lovelace, R. E. A note on Arnold's Growing old. MLN 68 1953.
Townsend, F. G. The third installment of Arnold's Literature and dogma. MP 50 1953.
— Literature and dogma: Arnold's letters to George Smith. PQ 35 1956.
Roll-Hansen, D. Arnold and the Academy. PMLA 68 1953.
Williams, R. The idea of culture. EC 3 1953; rptd with addns in his Culture and society 1780–1950, 1958.
Gregor, I. The critic and the age: some observations on the social criticism of Arnold and T. S. Eliot. Dublin Rev 227 1953.
Fischer, W. Arnold und Deutschland. Germanisch-romanische Monatsschrift 35 1954.
Walcott, F. G. Arnold, Her Majesty's Inspector of Schools. Michigan Alumnus Quart Rev 60 1954.
Bezanson, W. E. Melville's reading of Arnold's poetry. PMLA 69 1954.
Super, R. H. Emerson and Arnold's poetry. PQ 33 1954.
— Arnold's Rugby prizes. N & Q Aug 1955.
— Arnold's Oxford lectures on poetry. MLN 70 1955.
— Arnold's Tyrian trader in Thucydides. N & Q Sept 1956.
— Arnold and Tennyson. TLS 28 Oct 1960.
— Documents in the Arnold-Sainte-Beuve relationship. MP 60 1963.
— Vivacity and the Philistines. Stud in Eng Lit 1500–1900 6 1966.
— The dating of Dover beach. N & Q Feb 1967. Replies by K. Allott, M. Thorpe and J. C. Maxwell. Oct 1967.
Bevington, M. M. Arnold and John Bright: a typographical error and some ironic consequences. PMLA 70 1955.
Borinski, L. Arnolds Idee einer europäischen Bildung. Die Neueren Sprachen Feb 1955.
Dougherty, C. T. Arnold's 'Barbarians'. N & Q Sept 1955.
Eells, J. S. The touchstones of Arnold. New York 1955.
Knight, G. W. The scholar gipsy: an interpretation. RES new ser 6 1955. Replies by A. E. Dyson 8 1957; V. S. Seturaman 9 1958.
Long, J. P. Arnold visits Chicago. UTQ 24 1955.
Madden, W. A. The religious and aesthetic ideas of Arnold. Ann Arbor 1955.
— The divided tradition of English criticism. PMLA 73 1958.
— Arnold: a study of the aesthetic temperament in Victorian England. Bloomington 1967.
Maxwell, J. C. 'One who most has suffered': Arnold and Leopardi? RES new ser 6 1955.
Müller-Schwefe, G. Das persönliche Menschenbild Arnolds in der dichterischen Gestaltung. Tübingen 1955.
Broadbent, J. B. Milton and Arnold. EC 6 1956. Reply by J. Holloway 7 1957.
Butler, E. M. Heine in England and Arnold. German Life & Letters new ser 9 1956.
Donovan, R. A. The method of Arnold's Essays in criticism. PMLA 71 1956.
— Philomela: a major theme in Arnold's poetry. Victorian Newsletter no 12 1957.
Gérard, A. L'exemple de Matthew Arnold. Revue Nouvelle April 1956.
Gollin, R. M. A testimonial letter from Arnold. N & Q March 1956. Addn by R. L. Brooks, April 1958.
— Gladstone's mistaken praise of Arnold: an old irony and a new letter. Western Humanities Rev 12 1958.
Lloyd-Jones, R. Common speech: a poetic effect for Hopkins, Browning and Arnold. Ann Arbor 1956.
Watson, J. G. Arnold and Oxford. Quart Rev 294 1956.
Greenwood, E. B. Arnold: thoughts on a centenary. Twentieth Century Nov 1957.
Krieger, M. Dover beach and the tragic sense of eternal recurrence. Univ of Kansas City Rev 23 1957.
Raleigh, J. H. Arnold and American culture. Berkeley 1957.
Buckler, W. E. Studies in three Arnold problems. PMLA 73 1958.
Butts, D. Newman's influence on Arnold's theory of poetry. N & Q June 1958.
Carnall, G. D. Arnold's 'great critical effort'. EC 8 1958.
Harding, F. J. W. Botanical interests in the nineteenth century: Arnold. Durham Research Rev 9 1958.
— Arnold and Wales. Trans Honourable Soc of Cymmrodorion 1963.
— Arnold the critic and France. Geneva 1964.
Hoctor, T. M. Arnold and the critical spirit. Greyfriars Lectures (Loudonville NY) 1st ser 1958.
Houghton, W. E. Arnold's Empedocles on Etna. Victorian Stud 1 1958.
Jamison, W. A. Arnold and the Romantics. Copenhagen 1958.
Smith, B. A. Arnold: 'the dandy Isaiah'. Modern Age 1 1958.
Tobias, R. C. Arnold and Edmund Burke. Ann Arbor 1958.
— On dating Arnold's general note-books. PQ 39 1960.
Barksdale, R. K. Arnold and Tennyson on Etna. College Lang Assoc Jnl 2 1959.
Buckley, V. In his Poetry and morality, 1959.
Krook, D. Christian humanism: Arnold's Literature and dogma. In her Three traditions of moral thought, Cambridge 1959.
Stevenson, L. Arnold's poetry: a modern appraisal. Tennessee Stud in Lit 4 1959.
Waller, J. O. The Arnolds and particular truth. N & Q May 1959.
— Matthew and Thomas Arnold: soteriology. Anglican Theological Rev 44 1962.
— Arnold and the American Civil War. Victorian Newsletter no 22 1962.
Westlake, N. Arnold at the University [of Pennsylvania]. Lib Chron 25 1959.
DeLaura, D. J. Arnold's religious and historical vision. Ann Arbor 1960.
— Arnold and Carlyle. PMLA 79 1964.
— Arnold and John Henry Newman: the 'Oxford sentiment' and the religion of the future. Texas Univ Stud in Lit & Lang 6 1965.
— The Wordsworth of Pater and Arnold: the supreme artistic view of life. Stud in Eng Lit 1500–1900 6 1966.
Friedrich, G. A teaching approach to poetry. Eng Jnl Feb 1960. On Dover beach.
Gottfried, L. A. The strayed reveller. RES new ser 11 1960.
— Arnold and the Romantics. 1963.
Hecht, A. The Dover bitch (a criticism of life). Transatlantic Rev no 2 1960.
Kenosian, C. K. The position of Arnold in the religious dilemma of his time. Ann Arbor 1960.
Logu, P. de. Merope: tragedia neo-classica di Arnold. Eng Miscellany (Rome) 11 1960.
— La poetica e la poesia di Arnold. Genoa 1961.
Lucy, S. T. S. Eliot and the idea of tradition. 1960. On Eliot's debt to Arnold.
Nagarajan, S. Arnold and the Bhagavad gita: a reinterpretation of Empedocles on Etna. Comparative Lit 12 1960.
Ryals, C. de L. The two desires: ambivalence towards action in Arnold. Lock Haven Bull 1 1960.
— Arnold's Balder dead. Victorian Poetry 4 1966.
Walde, E. H. S. and T. S. Dorsch. A. E. Housman and Arnold. Boston Univ Stud in Eng 4 1960.
Williamson, E. L. Arnold's 'eternal not ourselves...' MLN 75 1960.
— Significant points of comparison between the biblical criticism of Thomas and Matthew Arnold. PMLA 76 1961.
— Arnold and the archbishops. MLQ 24 1963.

Brick, A. Equilibrium in the poetry of Arnold. UTQ 30 1961.
Brooks, R. L. Arnold and the national Eisteddfod. N & Q Sept 1961.
— A Danish Balder dead. PBSA 56 1962.
— Some unaccomplished projects of Arnold. SB 16 1963.
— A new source for Sohrab and Rustum. PQ 42 1963.
— The genesis of Thyrsis. RES new ser 14 1963. Reply by K. Allott 15 1964.
— Arnold's revision of Tristram and Iseult: some instances of Clough's influence. Victorian Poetry 2 1964.
— Arnold's Stanzas from Carnac and A southern night. Book Collector 14 1965.
— Arnold's Sohrab and Rustum: an oriental detail. Eng Lang Notes 4 1967.
Fairclough, G. T. A fugitive and gracious light: the relation of Joseph Joubert to Arnold's thought. Lincoln Nebraska 1961.
— The sestet of Arnold's Religious isolation. N & Q Aug 1962.
Francis, N. T. The critical reception of Arnold's poetry: the religious issue. Ann Arbor 1961.
Gabrieli, V. Il mirto e l'alloro. Bari 1961.
James, D. G. Arnold and the decline of English romanticism. Oxford 1961.
Kato, T. The quest for the genuine self: Arnold and the modern world. Stud in Eng Lit (Tokyo) 38 1961.
Lubell, A. J. Matthew Arnold: between two worlds. MLQ 22 1961.
Timko, M. Corydon had a rival. Victorian Newsletter no 19 1961.
Wallace, J. M. Landscape and 'the general law'. Boston Univ Stud in Eng 5 1961.
Andrews, P. The Scholar gipsy. Manchester Rev 9 1962.
Angleman, S. W. 'Wandering between the worlds'. Salt Lake City 1962.
Atkin, J. R. An unpublished report on Roman Catholic schools by Arnold. N & Q March 1962.
Benziger, J. In his Images of eternity: studies in the poetry of religious vision from Wordsworth to T. S. Eliot, Carbondale 1962.
Duffin, H. C. Arnold the poet. 1962.
Edwards, P. Hebraism, Hellenism and the Scholar-gipsy. Durham Univ Jnl 54 1962.
Hertz, N. H. Poetry in an age of prose: Arnold and Gray. In In defense of reading, ed R. A. Brower and R. Poirier, New York 1962.
McElderry, B. R. Poetry and religion: a parallel in Whitman and Arnold. Walt Whitman Rev 8 1962.
Polhemus, G. W. An additional variation in Arnold's The terrace at Berne. N & Q Aug 1962.
Robson, J. M. Mill and Arnold: Liberty and culture, friends or enemies? Humanities Assoc Bull 34 1962.
Roper, A. H. The moral landscape of Arnold's poetry. PMLA 77 1962.
Rosenblatt, L. M. The genesis of Pater's Marius the Epicurean. Comparative Lit 14 1962. On Renan and Arnold.
Shumaker, W. Arnold's humanism: literature as a criticism of life. Stud in Eng Lit 1500–1900 2 1962.
Vogeler, M. S. Arnold and Frederic Harrison: the prophet of culture and the prophet of positivism. Ibid.
Truss, T. J. The genre of Dover beach. Univ of Mississippi Stud in Eng 3 1962.
Wilkins, C. T. Arnold's 'ineffectual angel'. N & Q March 1962.
Balliet, C. A. Growing old along with Rabbi ben Ezra. Victorian Poetry 1 1963. Addn by J. Huebenthal 3 1965.
Eaker, J. G. Arnold's biblical criticism. Religion in Life 32 1963.
Feltes, N. N. Arnold and the modern spirit: a reassessment. UTQ 32 1963.
Frierson, J. W. Matthew Arnold, philosophe. Stud on Voltaire 25 1963.

Fulweiler, H. W. Mermen and mermaids: a note on an 'alien vision' in the poetry of Tennyson Arnold and Hopkins. Victorian Newsletter no 23 1963.
— Arnold: the metamorphosis of a merman. Victorian Poetry 1 1963. Reply by K. Allott and Fulweiler 2 1964.
Greenberg, R. A. Arnold's mournful rhymes: a study of the World and the quietist. Victorian Poetry 1 1963.
— Arnold's refuge of art: Tristram and Iseult. Victorian Newsletter no 25 1964.
— Patterns of imagery: Arnold's Shakespeare. Stud in Eng Lit 1500–1900 5 1965.
Hipple, W. J. Matthew Arnold, dialectician. UTQ 32 1963.
Honan, P. Arnold and cacophony. Victorian Poetry 1 1963.
Kendall, J. L. The unity of Arnold's Tristram and Iseult. Ibid.
Kerpneck, H. 'Kings of modern thought'. MLQ 24 1963.
— The road to Rugby Chapel. UTQ 34 1965.
Knoepflmacher, U. C. Dover revisited: the Wordsworthian matrix in the poetry of Arnold. Victorian Poetry 1 1963.
Ludwig, H. W. Die Self-komposita bei Carlyle, Arnold und Hopkins. Tübingen 1963. On words compounded with the determinant 'self'.
Mazzaro, J. L. Corydon in Thyrsis. Victorian Poetry 1 1963.
Osborne, D. G. Arnold 1843–9: a study of the Yale manuscript. Ann Arbor 1963.
Reeves, P. 'Neither saint nor sophist-led': Arnold's Christology. Mississippi Quart 16 1963.
Schrey, H. John Henry Newman, Charles Kingsley, Arnold. Frankfurt 1963.
Stevens, E. E. Arnold's Tyrian trader. Victorian Newsletter no 24 1963.
Stocking, G. W. Arnold, E. B. Tylor and the uses of invention. Amer Anthropologist 65 1963.
Sullivan, J. P. Arnold on classics and classicists. Arion 2 1963.
Sundell, M. G. The intellectual background and structure of Arnold's Tristram and Iseult. Victorian Poetry 1 1963.
— Story and context in the Strayed reveller. Victorian Poetry 3 1965.
Cockshut, A. O. J. In his Unbelievers, 1964.
Coursen, H. R. 'The moon lies fair': the poetry of Arnold. Stud in Eng Lit 1500–1900 4 1964.
Day, P. W. Arnold and the philosophy of Vico. Auckland 1964.
Hanley, E. A. In her Stoicism in major English poets of the nineteenth century, New York 1964.
Lafourcade, F. A propos de Arnold, Un Eton français. Caliban 1 1964.
Leach, M. Arnold and Celtic magic. In The Celtic Cross, ed R. B. Browne, W. J. Roscelli and R. Loftus, Lafayette 1964.
McCarthy, P. J. Arnold and the three classes. New York 1964.
Moews, D. D. Humanism and ideology: a study of Arnold's ideas on man and society. Ann Arbor 1964.
Peterson, W. S. The landscapes of Rugby chapel. Victorian Newsletter no 25 1964.
— Rugby Chapel and Tom Brown's school-days. Eng Lang Notes 3 1966.
Plotinsky, M. L. Help for pain: the narrative verse of Arnold. Victorian Poetry 2 1964.
San Juan, E. Arnold and the poetics of belief: some implications of Literature and dogma. Harvard Theological Rev 57 1964.
Straumann, H. Arnold and the continental idea. In The English mind, ed H. S. Davies and G. Watson, Cambridge 1964.
Wright, C. D. Arnold's response to German culture. Ann Arbor 1964.

— How Arnold altered Goethe on poetry. Victorian Poetry 5 1967.
Alexander, E. Arnold and John Stuart Mill. 1965.
Anderson, W. D. Arnold and the classical tradition. Ann Arbor 1965.
Boo, M. R. Arnold's Stanzas from the Grande Chartreuse. Explicator May 1965.
Bromwich, R. Arnold and Celtic literature: a retrospect 1865–1965. Oxford 1965.
Burwick, F. L. Hölderlin and Arnold: Empedocles on Etna. Comparative Lit 17 1965.
Campos, C. In his View of France from Arnold to Bloomsbury, Oxford 1965.
Carrithers, G. H. Missing persons on Dover beach? MLQ 26 1965.
Giannone, R. The quest motif in Thyrsis. Victorian Poetry 3 1965.
Gordon, J. B. Disenchantment with intimations: a reading of In utrumque paratus. Victorian Poetry 3 1965.
Berryman, C. Arnold's Empedocles on Etna. Victorian Newsletter no 29 1966.
Cadbury, W. Coming to terms with Dover beach. Criticism 8 1966.
Cherry, D. The two cultures of Arnold and T. H. Huxley. Wascana Rev 1 1966.
Culler, A. D. Imaginative reason: the poetry of Arnold. New Haven 1966.
— 'No Arnold could ever write a novel'. Victorian Newsletter no 29 1966.
— Arnold and Etna. In Victorian essays: a symposium, ed W. D. Anderson and T. D. Clareson, Kent Ohio 1967.
Feschbach, S. Empedocles at Dover beach. Victorian Poetry 4 1966.
Frykman, E. 'Bitter knowledge' and 'unconquerable hope': a thematic study of attitudes towards life in Arnold's poetry 1849–53. Gothenburg 1966.
Holland, N. N. Psychological depths and Dover beach. Victorian Stud 9 1966. Replies by W. V. Harris and N. N. Holland 10 1967.
Narita, S. Melville on Arnold. Stud in Eng Lit (Tokyo) 42 1966.
Wolff, M. The uses of context: aspects of the 1860s. Victorian Stud 9 1966. Replies by H. J. Harris and M. Wolff 10 1967.
Eggenschwiler, D. L. Arnold's passive questers. Victorian Poetry 5 1967.
Raymond, M. B. Apollo and Empedocles on Etna. REL 8 1967.
Schneider, M. W. The source of Balder dead. N & Q Feb 1967.
Stange, G. R. Arnold: the poet as humanist. Princeton 1967.
Watson, G. Arnold and the Victorian mind. REL 8 1967.

R. H. S.

EDWARD FitzGERALD
1809–83

Bibliographies

Way, W. I. A chronological list of the more important issues of FitzGerald's version of the Rubáiyát of Omar Khayyám and of other books written, translated, edited or owned by him; with portraits, autograph letters etc; and with ana, other versions of the Rubáiyát [etc]. Chicago 1899.
Prideaux, W. F. Notes for a bibliography of FitzGerald. 1901. List of separate pbns to 1900 and of contributions to books and periodicals, with notes.
Potter, A. G. A bibliography of the Rubáiyát of Omar Khayyám together with kindred matter in prose and verse pertaining thereto. 1929.
Ehrsam, T. G. and R. H. Deily. In their Bibliographies of twelve Victorian authors, New York 1936; supplement by J. G. Fucilla, MP 37 1939.
Rubáiyát of Omar Khayyám: a catalogue of various editions, offered for sale [by] B. Quaritch. 1959.

Collections (including letters)

Works, reprinted from the original impressions, with some corrections derived from his own annotated copies. 2 vols New York 1887.
Letters and literary remains. Ed W. A. Wright 3 vols 1889.
Letters. Ed W. A. Wright 2 vols 1894.
Letters to Fanny Kemble 1871–83. Ed W. A. Wright 1895.
Miscellanies. Ed W. A. Wright 1900.
More letters. Ed W. A. Wright 1901.
The variorum and definitive edition of the poetical and prose writings of FitzGerald, including a complete bibliography and interesting personal and literary notes. Ed G. Bentham 7 vols New York 1902. Preface by E. Gosse.
Letters and literary remains. Ed W. A. Wright 7 vols 1902–3. Absorbs collections of letters made by Wright, above.
Miscellanies. [Ed H. Morley] 1904.
FitzGerald and 'Posh': 'herring merchants', including a number of letters from FitzGerald to Joseph Fletcher or 'Posh' not hitherto published. Ed J. Blyth 1908.
Some new letters of FitzGerald to Bernard Barton, with a foreword by Viscount Grey. Ed F. R. Barton 1923.
Letters to Bernard Quaritch 1853–83. Ed C. Q. Wrentmore 1926.
A FitzGerald friendship: letters from FitzGerald to William Bodham Donne. Ed N. C. Hannay 1932.
Letters of FitzGerald. Ed J. M. Cohen 1960.
Selected works. Ed J. Richardson 1962 (Reynard Lib).

§1

Memoir of Bernard Barton. In Selections from the poems and letters of Barton, ed L. Barton 1849, Philadelphia 1850, London 1853.
Euphranor: a dialogue on youth. 1851, 1855 (rev), [1882] (rev, priv ptd, as Euphranor: a May-Day conversation at Cambridge, 'Tis forty years since'); ed F. Chapman 1906 (from 1851 text).
Polonius: a collection of wise saws and modern instances. 1852, 1854; ed S. S. Allen 1905.
Six dramas of Calderón freely translated. 1853, 1854; ed H. Oelsner 1903, [1928] (EL).
Salámán and Absál: an allegory translated from the Persian of Jámí. 1856 (anon), 1871 (rev, priv ptd), 1879 (rev, with 4th edn of the Rubáiyát, below), Leigh-on-Sea 1946.
Rubáiyát of Omar Khayyám, the astronomer-poet of Persia, translated into English verse. 1859 (anon), 1868 (rev, anon), 1872 (rev, anon), 1879 (rev, anon, with the Salámán and Absál of Jámí, above); ed N. H. Dole 2 vols Boston 1896 (includes French and German versions, with voluminous critical material), 1898 (enlarged), 1 vol Philadelphia 1898 (text of 4th and 1st edns); ed H. M. Batson and E. D. Ross 1900; ed R. A. Nicholson 1900 (text of 1st edn); ed F. Henry, Paris 1903 (text of 4th edn, with French trn); ed E. Heron-Allen 1908 (text of 2nd edn); ed F. H. Evans 1914 (variorum text); rptd photofacs from 1st edn, New York 1934; ed C. Ganz and E. D. Ross 1938 (with unpbd trn into 'monkish Latin' by FitzGerald); ed G. F. Maine 1947 (text of 1st, 2nd and 5th edns with variants); rptd 1953 (with Euphranor, and Salámán and Absál, above); ed A. J. Arberry 1959 (as The romance of the Rubáiyát: text of 1st edn with introduction, notes and bibliography); ed C. J. Weber, Waterville Maine 1959 (critical text with bibliography); for earliest French trn, *see* F. Henry, above, 1903; Italian, [1910]; Latin, 1893; German, 1907; Hebrew,

1907; Irish, 1909; Afrikaans, [1924]; Portuguese, 1935; Sanskrit, 1929; Spanish, 1926; Swahili, 1952; Swedish, 1912; Welsh, 1907; Welsh Romani, 1902; Yiddish, 1911.

Tutin, J. R. A concordance to FitzGerald's translation of the Rubáiyát. 1900.

The mighty magician and Such stuff as dreams are made of: two plays translated from Calderón. 1865 (priv ptd).

Agamemnon: a tragedy taken from Aeschylus. [1869] (priv ptd), London 1876.

Readings in Crabbe's Tales of the Hall. [1879] (priv ptd), 1882, 1883 (with enlarged introd).

The downfall and death of King Oedipus: a drama in two parts, chiefly taken from the Oedipus Tyrannus and Colonaeus of Sophocles. 2 pts 1880–1 (priv ptd).

The two Generals: I, Lucius Aemilius Paullus; II, Sir Charles Napier. nd. 2 poems, priv ptd.

Occasional verses. 1891 (priv ptd).

Eight dramas of Calderón, freely translated. 1906. Consists of Six dramas, 1853, and The mighty magician and Such stuff as dreams, 1865, above.

Dictionary of Madame de Sévigné. Ed M. E. FitzGerald 2 vols 1914.

A FitzGerald medley. Ed C. Ganz 1933.

For contributions to books and periodicals see W. F. Prideaux, Notes for a bibliography of FitzGerald, above, pp. 57–72.

§2

For personal memoirs of FitzGerald, see W. F. Prideaux, above, pp. 72–4.

Groome, F. H. Two Suffolk friends. 1895. FitzGerald and Archdeacon Groome.

Nicoll, W. R. and T. J. Wise. Literary anecdotes of the nineteenth century. 2 vols 1895–6. Vol 2 includes An old commonplace book of FitzGerald's.

Heron-Allen, E. Some sidelights upon FitzGerald's poem The Rubáiyát of Omar Khayyám. 1898.

— FitzGerald's Rubáiyát of Omar Khayyám with their original Persian sources. 1899.

Jackson, H. FitzGerald and Omar Khayyám: an essay and a bibliography. 1899.

More, P. E. In his Shelburne essays ser 2, New York 1899.

Glyde, J. The life of FitzGerald, with an introduction by E. Clodd. 1900.

Campbell, G. Edward and Pamela FitzGerald: being some account of their lives compiled from the letters of those who knew them. 1904.

Wright, T. The life of FitzGerald. 2 vols 1904.

Benson, A. C. Edward FitzGerald. 1905 (EML).

Dutt, W. H. In his Some literary associations of East Anglia, [1907]. The homes and haunts of FitzGerald.

FitzGerald 1809–1909: centenary celebrations souvenir. Ipswich 1909.

The book of the Omar Khayyám Club 1892–1910. 1910 (priv ptd).

Adams, M. Omar's interpreter: a new life of FitzGerald. 1909, 1911 (rev).

— In the footsteps of Borrow and FitzGerald. 1913.

Bailey, J. In his Poets and poetry, Oxford 1911.

Nicholson, R. A. Omar Khayyám: some facts and fallacies. Aberdeen Univ Rev 1 1914.

Browning, R. FitzGerald and Elizabeth Barrett Browning. 1919 (priv ptd). 3 letters from Browning to his son.

Birrell, A. FitzGerald's letters. Empire Rev May 1924.

Thonet, J. M. H. Etude sur FitzGerald et la littérature persane. Liège 1929.

Campbell, A. Y. In Great Victorians, ed H. J. and H. Massingham 1932.

Greeves, F. Omar Khayyám, modern pessimism and Christian thought. London Quart 163 1938.

Lucas, E. V. The delightful fellow: FitzGerald and Frederick Spalding. Cornhill Mag July 1938.

Hendricks, C. H. and L. S. Boas. On a stanza of the Rubáiyát. Explicator 1 1943.

Terhune, A. M. The life of FitzGerald. 1947. With bibliography.

Hekmat, A. A. FitzGerald's translation of Jámí. Asiatic Rev 43 1947.

Coolidge, T. Letters by FitzGerald [to J. R. Lowell and F. Spalding]. More Books 23 1948.

Clark, J. A. On first looking into Benson's FitzGerald. South Atlantic Quart 48 1949; rptd in Fifty years of the South Atlantic Quarterly, ed W. B. Hamilton, Durham NC 1952.

De Polnay, P. Into an old room: a memoir of FitzGerald. New York 1949.

Short, C. FitzGerald on some fellow-Victorians. Western Humanities Rev 5 1951.

Arberry, A. J. The Rubáiyát of Omar Khayyám, with comparative English versions by FitzGerald etc. 1949.

— In his Omar Khayyám, New Haven 1952.

— FitzGerald's Salámán and Absál: a study. Cambridge 1956.

— Omar Khayyám and FitzGerald. 1959.

Piddington, R. A. FitzGerald's Indian colonel. N & Q Dec 1959.

Richardson, J. FitzGerald. 1960 (Br Council pamphlet). With bibliography.

Wolff, M. The Rubáiyát's neglected reviewer: a centennial recovery. Victorian Newsletter no 17 1960.

Parrinder, E. G. Omar Khayyám: cynic or mystic. London Quart 187 1962.

Gittleman, S. FitzGerald's Rubáiyát in Germany. N & Q March 1962.

— An early reference to FitzGerald's Rubáiyát in Germany. N & Q July 1963.

— John Hay as a critic of the Rubáiyát. Victorian Newsletter no 24 1963.

Weber, C. J. The 'discovery' of FitzGerald's Rubáiyát. Lib Chron 7 1963.

Draper, J. W. FitzGerald's Persian local color. West Virginia Univ Philological Papers 14 1964.

Bagley, F. R. C. Omar Khayyám and FitzGerald. Durham Univ Jnl 59 1967.

G. D. C.

COVENTRY KERSEY DIGHTON PATMORE

1823–96

Bibliographies

Courage in politics and other essays 1885–96, now first collected. Ed F. Page 1921. With bibliography of Patmore's prose contributions to periodicals.

Martin, R. B. Patmore. Princeton Univ Lib Chron 14 1952. On Patmore letters etc at Princeton.

Stevenson, L. In Victorian poets: a guide to research, ed F. E. Faverty, Cambridge Mass 1956, 1968 (rev).

Reid, J. C. The mind and art of Patmore. 1957. Bibliography (pp. 330–46) in part based on Page, above.

Collections

Poems. 4 vols [1879]. Vol 1: Amelia, Tamerton Church-tower etc; vol 2: The angel in the house; vol 3: The victories of love; vol 4: The unknown Eros (42 odes).

Florilegium amantis. Ed R. Garnett [1879], 1888. Selected poems.

Poems: collective edition. 2 vols 1886, 1886, 1887 (3rd edn) (with selections from the poems of Henry Patmore), 1890 (4th edn), 1894 (5th edn), 1897 (6th edn) etc.

The poetry of pathos and delight from the works of Patmore. 1896. Passages selected by Alice Meynell.

Works: new uniform edition. 5 vols 1897, 1907.

The angel in the house, together with the Victories of love. Ed A. Meynell [1905].

Poems. Ed B. Champneys 1906, 1909, 1915, 1921, 1928.

Poèmes. Tr P. Claudel, Paris 1912. With an introd by V. Larbaud.
Selected poems. Ed D. Patmore 1931. With introd and bibliography.
Selected verses. 1934.
Mystical poems of nuptial love: The wedding sermon, The unknown Eros and other odes. Ed T. Connolly, Boston 1938.
A selection of poems. Ed D. Patmore 1948.
Poems. Ed F. Page, Oxford 1949 (OSA).

§1

Poems. 1844.
Tamerton church-tower and other poems. 1853 (Pickering), 1854 (Parker) (rev).
The angel in the house: the betrothal. 1854, Boston 1856. Anon.
[The angel in the house]: the espousals. 1856, Boston 1856. Anon.
The angel in the house: bks i–ii The betrothal, The espousals. 2 vols in 1 1854–6 (Parker), 1858 (2nd edn, Parker), 1860 (3rd edn?, Parker), 2 vols 1863 (vol 1 a reissue in a Macmillan case of Parker's sheets and title page, dated 1860 and certified 3rd edn; vol 2 contains The angel in the house pt ii bks i–ii: Faithful for ever and The victories of love, the first combined reprint of the 2 vols below, with title poem and 7 selections from Tamerton church-tower, above), 1863 (Macmillan reprint without certificate of edn), 1866 (4th edn; rev in 1 vol), [1878] (5th edn, Bell, pt 1 only), 1885 (6th edn), 1887 (Cassell's Nat Lib no 70), 1888 (with other poems), 1892, 1896, 1898, 1905, 1920 etc.
Faithful for ever. 1860, Boston 1861, London 1866.
The children's garland from the best poets. 1862 (for 1861) (Golden Treasury); illustr J. Lawson 1873 etc. Anthology selected and arranged by Patmore.
The victories of love. Macmillan's Mag Sept–Nov 1861; Boston 1862, 1863 (Macmillan), 1878 (4th edn) (Bell), 1888 (rev with Faithful for ever) (Cassell's Nat Lib no 122).
Odes: not published. [1868]. Anon; rptd T. Connolly, Boston 1936. Reid, above, identifies another priv ptd edn entitled Nine odes, 1870.
The unknown Eros and other odes. 1877 (odes i–xxxi) (anon), 1878 (odes i–xlvi) (signed), 1890 (3rd edn, rev).
Bryan Waller Procter [Barry Cornwall]: an autobiographical fragment and biographical notes, with personal sketches of contemporaries, unpublished lyrics and letters of literary friends. 1877. Ed Patmore.
Amelia. 1878 (priv ptd black letter edn).
Amelia, Tamerton church-tower etc; with prefatory study on English metrical law. 1878.
Saint Bernard on the love of God. Tr M. C. and C. Patmore 1881, 1884.
How I managed and improved my estate. 1886. Rptd from St James's Gazette.
Hastings, Lewes, Rye and the Sussex marshes. 1887.
Principle in art. 1889, 1890 (2nd edn), 1898 (rev and rearranged). Rptd from St James's Gazette.
Religio poetae. 1893, 1898 (rev and rearranged). Rptd from Fortnightly Rev, Edinburgh Rev etc.
The rod, the root and the flower. 1895, 1907 (2nd edn, rev), 1923; ed D. Patmore 1950.
The wedding sermon. [1911].
Principle in art and other essays. 1912.
Principle in art, Religio poetae and other essays. 1913.
Courage in politics. *See* Bibliographies, above.
Seven unpublished poems to Alice Meynell. 1922 (priv ptd).
Essay on English metrical law: a critical edition with a commentary by M. A. Roth. Washington 1961.

Letters

Further letters of Gerard Manley Hopkins, including his correspondence with Patmore. Ed C. C. Abbott, Oxford 1938, 1956 (rev and enlarged). With nearly 30 letters from Patmore to Hopkins.
Patmore, D. Patmore and Robert Bridges: some letters. Fortnightly Rev March 1948.
— Three poets discuss new verse forms: the correspondence of Hopkins, Bridges and Patmore. Month Aug 1951.
De Vere, A. The angel in the house. Edinburgh Rev 107 1858; rptd in his Essays chiefly literary and ethical, 1889.
Brimley, G. The angel in the house. In his Essays, 1858, 1882 (3rd edn).
Forman, H. B. In his Our living poets, 1871. Patmore is included among the Pre-Raphaelite group.
Garnett, R. In Poets and poetry of the century, ed A. H. Miles 10 vols 1891–7.
Nicoll, W. R. and T. J. Wise. The angel in the house: Emily Augusta Patmore. In their Literary anecdotes of the nineteenth century vol 2, 1896.
Meynell, A. Patmore's odes. In her Rhythm of life and other essays, 1896.
— In her Second person singular and other essays, Oxford 1922.
Garvin, L. Patmore: the praise of the odes. Fortnightly Rev Feb 1897.
Symons, A. In his Studies in two literatures, 1897, 1924 (vol 8 of Collected works).
— In his Figures of several centuries, 1916.
Champneys, B. Memoirs and correspondence of Patmore. 2 vols 1900, 1901.
Gosse, E. Patmore. 1905. Incorporates Gosse's earlier writings on Patmore in Contemporary Rev and North Amer Rev.
— The laureate of wedded love. In his More books on the table, 1923.
Trobridge, G. Patmore and Swedenborg. Westminster Rev 165 1906.
Lubbock, P. Quart Rev 208 1908.
Brégy, K. In his Poet's chantry, 1912. From 2 articles in Catholic World March–April 1910.
Johnson, L. Patmore's genius. In his Post liminium: essays and critical papers, ed T. Whittemore 1912.
Page, F. A neglected great poem: Patmore's Tamerton church-tower. Catholic World July 1912.
— Patmore's Unknown Eros. Catholic World Sept 1917.
— Patmore: points of view. Catholic World June 1921.
— Centenary of Patmore. Dublin Rev 173 1923.
— Patmore: a study in poetry. Oxford 1933.
Freeman, J. Patmore and Francis Thompson. In his Moderns: essays in literary criticism, 1916.
— Quart Rev 240 1923.
— In his English portraits and essays, 1924.
Wheaton, L. Emily Honoria Patmore and Patmore's poetry. Dublin Rev 163 1918.
Burdett, O. The idea of Patmore. Oxford 1921.
— London Mercury July 1923.
— Two footnotes on Patmore. In his Critical essays, New York 1925.
Harris, F. In his Contemporary portraits ser 3, New York 1920.
Shuster, G. N. Poetry and three poets [De Vere, Patmore, Hopkins]. In his Catholic spirit in modern English literature, New York 1922. With separate ch on Patmore.
Baum, P. F. Patmore's literary criticism. Univ of California Chron 25 1923.
Haddow, G. A neglected poet. Queen's Quart 21 1924.
Harper, A. E. Patmore: poet and realist. Holborn Rev 71 1929.
Quiller-Couch, A. T. In his Studies in literature ser 3, Cambridge 1929.
O'Rourke, J. Irish Ecclesiastical Record 37 1931.

Braybrooke, P. Patmore: poet and philosopher. In his Some Victorian and Georgian Catholics, 1932.
Heinrich, G. Patmore: der Dichter der ehelichen Liebe. Hochland 29 1932.
Leslie, S. In his Studies in sublime failure, 1932.
MacCarthy, D. In his Criticism, 1932.
Patmore, F. J. Patmore: a son's recollections. Eng Rev Feb 1932.
Read, H. In Great Victorians, ed H. J. and H. Massingham 1932.
—— In his In defence of Shelley and other essays, 1936.
Evans, B. I. Patmore and allied poets. In his English poetry in the later nineteenth century, 1933, 1966 (rev).
Musser, B. F. The laureate of wedded love. In his Franciscan poets, New York 1933.
Downing, E. A. Patmore's philosophy of love. Thought March, June 1934.
Claudel, P. Lettre sur Patmore. In his Positions et propositions, Paris 1934.
Patmore, D. Portrait of my family. 1935.
—— The life and times of Patmore. 1949.
Bradley, F. H. Revue de l'Université d'Ottawa 6 1936.
Weygandt, C. In his Times of Tennyson, New York 1936.
Du Bos, C. L'amour selon Patmore. In his Approximations 7th ser, Paris 1937.
Alexander, C. In his Catholic literary revival, Milwaukee 1938.
MacColl, D. S. Patmore and Hopkins: sense and nonsense in English prosody. London Mercury July 1938.
Lucas, F. L. In his Ten Victorian poets, Cambridge 1940, 1948 (rev).
Maynard, T. Patmore's doctrine of love. Thought Sept 1945.
—— In his Pillars of the Church, New York 1945.
Guidi, A. Coventry Patmore. Brescia 1946.
Thompson, F. In his Literary criticisms, ed T. L. Connolly, New York 1948. Includes 3 articles on Patmore.
Turner, P. Aurora versus the Angel. RES 24 1948. On Patmore and E. B. Browning.
Stobie, M. R. Patmore's theory and Hopkins's practice. UTQ 19 1949.
Heath-Stubbs, J. Three Roman Catholic poets [Patmore, Thompson and Hopkins]. In his Darkling plain, 1950.
Cohen, J. M. Prophet without responsibility: a study in Patmore's poetry. EC 1 1951.
Larbaud, V. In his Ce vice impuni, la lecture: domaine anglais, Paris 1925; rptd in Oeuvres complètes vol 3, Paris 1951.
Gardner, W. H. The achievement of Patmore. Month Feb, April 1952.
—— The status of Patmore. Month Oct 1958.
Praz, M. L'angelo nella casa di Patmore. Appendix I in his La crisi dell'eroe nel romanzo vittoriano, Florence 1952.
Oliver, E. J. Patmore. New York 1956.
Reid, J. C. The mind and art of Patmore. 1957.
Guyard, M-F. De Patmore à Claudel: histoire et nature d'une influence. Revue de Littérature Comparée 33 1959.
Dunn, J. The insular Catholicism of Patmore. Amer Benedictine Rev 11 1960.
Gilson, E. Patmore et Maine de Brian. Studi Francesi 7 1963.
Maurocordato, A. Anglo-American influence in Paul Claudel, 1: Patmore. Geneva 1964.
Schmiefsky, M. Principle in art as criticism in the mainstream. Victorian Newsletter no 26 1964.
Cadbury, W. The structure of feeling in a poem by Patmore: meter, phonology, form. Victorian Poetry 4 1966.

W. E. F.

DANTE GABRIEL ROSSETTI
1828–82

For mss, see P. F. Baum's edns under § 1, below.

Bibliographies

Anderson, J. P. Appended to J. Knight, Life of Rossetti, 1887.
Rossetti, W. M. Bibliography of the works of Rossetti. 1905. Rptd from Bibliographer 1–2 1902–3. Addns by W. F. Prideaux, Bibliographer 2 1903.
—— Rossetti: classified lists of his writings with the dates. 1906 (priv ptd).
Vaughan, C. E. Bibliographies of Swinburne, Morris, Rossetti. Oxford 1914 (Eng Assoc pamphlet).
Ehrsam, T. G., R. H. Deily and R. M. Smith. In their Bibliographies of twelve Victorian authors, New York 1936. Supplement by J. G. Fucilla, MP 37 1939.
Jones, H. M. The Pre-Raphaelites. In Victorian poets, ed F. E. Faverty, Cambridge Mass 1956, 1968 (rev).
Fredeman, W. E. In his Pre-Raphaelitism: a bibliocritical study, Cambridge Mass 1965 (sections 22–34).

Collections

Collected works. Ed W. M. Rossetti 2 vols 1886, 1887 etc. Vol 1 contains poems (essentially the 1881 text) and literary prose, vol 2 trns and miscellaneous prose, including art notices.
Poetical works. Ed W. M. Rossetti 1891 etc. Same as vol 1 of Collected works, above, without the prose.
Poems of Rossetti, with illustrations from his own pictures and designs. Ed W. M. Rossetti 2 vols 1904. First authorized restoration of Nuptial sleep to House of life; several poems added.
Works. Ed W. M. Rossetti 1911. The standard edn.
Poems and translations 1850–70. Oxford 1913 (OSA).
Rossetti: an anthology. Ed F. L. Lucas, Cambridge 1933.
Poems, ballads and sonnets. Ed P. F. Baum, New York 1937.
Poems. Ed L. I. Howarth 1950.
Poems. Ed O. Doughty 1957.

§ 1

The first pbd poem, the sonnet This is the Blessed Mary, pre-elect, *appeared in the catalogue of the Free Exhibition, 1849.* The blessed damozel, Hand and soul, *and 11 other pieces, mostly sonnets, were pbd in the 4 nos* of Germ, Jan–April 1850. Sister Helen *appeared in the English edn of the* Düsseldorf artists' album, ed M. Howitt, Leipzig 1854; The burden of Nineveh, *the 2nd version of* The blessed damozel, *and* The staff and the scrip *were included in* Oxford and Cambridge Mag nos 8, 11–12 1856, *rptd with many changes in* Crayon 1858 *and* New Path [Blessed damozel *only*] 1863; *3 sonnets on pictures first appeared in* W. M. Rossetti and A. C. Swinburne, Notes on the Royal Academy exhibition, 1868 (pt 2). *Rossetti also contributed substantial portions to* A. Gilchrist, Life of Blake, 1863, *reviews of T. G. Hake to the* Academy 1871, 1873, *and several poems and prose works to* Athenaeum, Century, Critic, Fortnightly Rev, N & Q, Spectator etc. *Poems first appearing in miscellaneous volumes are:* Sudden light, *in* Poems: an offering to Lancashire, ed Isa Craig 1863; Lost days, *in* A welcome: original contributions in verse and prose, 1863; Autumn song (MS), *in* Specimens from a cycle of English songs and lyrics, the music by E. Dannreuther (priv ptd programme of the musicale 18 June 1877); Raleigh's cell in the Tower, *in* Sonnets of three centuries, ed T. Hall Caine 1882; On certain Elizabethan revivals, *in* T. Hall Caine, Recollections of Rossetti, 1882. *Several poems by Rossetti first appeared in vol 2 of* Family letters with a memoir, ed W. M. Rossetti 1895, *below (detailed in* W. M. Rossetti's Bibliography, *above). For*

Sister Helen (1857) *and* Verses (1881), *the first a suspected, the second a confirmed T. J. Wise forgery, see* J. Carter and H. G. Pollard, An enquiry into the nature of certain nineteenth-century pamphlets, 1934.

Sir Hugh the Heron: a legendary tale in four parts, by Gabriel Rossetti Junior. 1843 (priv ptd by G. Polidori).

The early Italian poets from Ciullo d'Alcamo to Dante Alighieri (1100–1200–1300) in the original metres, together with Dante's Vita nuova. 1861, 1874 (rev and re-arranged as Dante and his circle).

Of life, love, and death: sixteen sonnets. Fortnightly Rev March 1869.

Hand and soul. 1869 (priv ptd).

Poems. 1870 (4 edns), 1871, 1872. First appearance of House of life. 2 priv printings (1869, 1870) preceded this vol. For the history of the pbn of Poems 1870 and clarification of the several 'trial books', *see* J. C. Troxell in Colophon, below.

The stealthy school of criticism. Athenaeum 16 Dec 1871. A reply to Buchanan, below.

Poems: a new edition. 1881. A revision of Poems 1870, with 4 new poems and 3 trns, omitting House of life and 3 other sonnets.

Ballads and sonnets. 1881, 1881, 1882, 1882. House of life expanded to 101 sonnets, Nuptial sleep dropped.

Rossetti, W. M. Some scraps of verse and prose by Rossetti. Pall Mall Mag Dec 1898; New York 1898. All but 2 of these scraps appear in Works, 1911, above.

Lenore, by G. Bürger. Ed W. M. Rossetti 1900. Tr Rossetti.

Henry the leper [by Hartmann von Aue], paraphrased by Rossetti. Ed W. P. Trent 2 vols Boston 1905.

The house of life: a sonnet sequence. Ed P. F. Baum, Cambridge Mass 1928.

Rossetti: an analytical list of manuscripts in the Duke University Library, with hitherto unpublished verse and prose. Ed P. F. Baum, Durham NC 1931.

Howe, M. L. Some unpublished stanzas by Rossetti. MLN 48 1933. On Border song.

The blessed damozel: the unpublished manuscript, texts and collation. Ed P. F. Baum, Chapel Hill 1937.

Rossetti's Sister Helen. Ed J. C. Troxell, New Haven 1939.

Jan Van Hunks. Ed J. R. Wahl, New York 1952. 2 earlier edns ed T. Watts-Dunton (1912), and M. Bell (1929).

The Kelmscott love sonnets. Ed J. R. Wahl, Cape Town 1954. From House of life mss in Bodley.

Letters

Letters appearing in memoirs etc are not detailed.

[Horne, H. P.] Rossetti: some extracts from his letters to Frederick Shields. Century Guild Hobby Horse April 1889. Letters rptd in Life and letters of Shields, ed E. Mills 1912.

Prinsep, V. C. A collector's correspondence. Art Jnl Aug 1892. Rossetti's letters to F. Leyland.

Dante Gabriel Rossetti: his family letters, with a memoir. Ed W. M. Rossetti 2 vols 1895. 317 letters in vol 2.

Letters of Rossetti to William Allingham 1854–70. Ed G. B. Hill 1897. Rptd from Atlantic Monthly May–Aug 1896. Expurgated passages restored by M. L. Howe, MLN 39 1934.

Ruskin; Rossetti; Pre-Raphaelitism: papers 1854–62. Ed W. M. Rossetti 1899.

Some early correspondence of Rossetti. In Preraphaelite diaries and letters, ed W. M. Rossetti 1900.

Rossetti papers 1862–70. Ed W. M. Rossetti 1903.

Letters addressed to A. C. Swinburne by Ruskin, Morris, Burne-Jones and Rossetti. 1919 (priv ptd by T. J. Wise).

John Keats: criticism and comment. 1919 (priv ptd by T. J. Wise). 5 letters from Rossetti to H. B. Forman.

A romance of literature. 1919 (priv ptd by T. J. Wise). Reciprocal letters from Swinburne and Rossetti relating to exhumation of Rossetti's poems.

Compton-Rickett, A. Portraits and personalities. 1937. 9 letters rptd from TLS 16 Oct 1919.

Letters from Rossetti to Swinburne regarding the attacks made upon the latter by Mortimer Collins and upon both by Robert Buchanan. 1921 (priv ptd by T. J. Wise).

Letters of Rossetti to his publisher F. S. Ellis. Ed O. Doughty 1928.

Purves, J. Letters of Rossetti to Alice Boyd. Fortnightly Rev May 1928.

Three Rossettis: unpublished letters to and from Dante Gabriel, Christina, William. Ed J. C. Troxell, Cambridge Mass 1937.

Rossetti's letters to Fanny Cornforth. Ed P. F. Baum, Baltimore 1940.

Adrian, A. A. The Browning–Rossetti friendship: some unpublished letters. PMLA 73 1958.

Meyerstein, E. H. W. Rossetti on Patmore's Odes (1868). TLS 28 April 1950. Unpbd letter from Rossetti to Patmore.

[Baum, P. F.] Rossetti to George Eliot. Duke Univ Lib Notes no 34 1959. Unpbd letter from Rossetti.

Sambrook, A. J. Rossetti and R. W. Dixon. Etudes Anglaises 14 1961. Pair of letters exchanged between Rossetti and Dixon, both unpbd.

The Rossetti–Macmillan letters: some 133 unpublished letters written to Alexander Macmillan, F. S. Ellis and others, by Dante Gabriel, Christina and William Michael Rossetti 1861–89. Ed L. M. Packer, Berkeley 1963.

Briggs, R. C. H. Letters to Janey. Jnl of William Morris Soc 1 1964. Excerpts from Rossetti's letters in BM.

Letters of Dante Gabriel Rossetti. Ed O. Doughty and J. R. Wahl 5 vols Oxford 1965–.

§2

Forman, H. B. In his Our living poets, 1871.

Buchanan, R. In his Fleshly school of poetry and other phenomena of the day, 1872. Expanded from article by 'Thomas Maitland' in Contemporary Rev Oct 1871.

Swinburne, A. C. In his Essays and studies, 1875. Rptd from Fortnightly Rev May 1870.

Stedman, E. C. In his Victorian poets, 1876.

Caine, T. H. Recollections of Rossetti. 1882, 1908 (rev in My story), 1928 (rev).

—— In Poets and poetry of the century, ed A. H. Miles 10 vols 1891–7.

Placci, C. Rossetti. Florence 1882.

Sharp, W. Rossetti: a record and a study. 1882.

—— Rossetti and pictorialism in verse. Portfolio 13 1882.

—— Rossetti in prose and verse. In his Papers critical and reminiscent, ed Mrs W. Sharp 1912. Rptd from Nat Rev March 1887.

Tirebuck, W. E. Rossetti: his work and influence. 1882.

Watts-Dunton, T. The truth about Rossetti. Nineteenth Century March 1883.

—— In his Old familiar faces, 1916.

—— Rossetti's unpublished poems. Athenaeum 23 May 1896.

Myers, F. W. H. Rossetti and the religion of beauty. In his Essays: modern, 1883.

Sarrazin, G. In his Poètes modernes de l'Angleterre, Paris 1885.

Swinburne, L. J. Rossetti and the Pre-Raphaelites. New Haven 1885. Rptd from New Englander & Yale Rev new ser 8 1885.

Nicholson, P. W. Rossetti: poet and painter. Edinburgh 1887.

Knight, J. Life of Rossetti. 1887.

Pater, W. In his Appreciations, 1889. Rptd from The English poets vol 4, ed T. H. Ward 1880.

Rossetti, W. M. Rossetti as designer and writer. 1889.

Patmore, C. Rossetti as a poet. In his Principle in art, 1889.

Hardinge, W. A note on the Louvre sonnets of Rossetti. Temple Bar March 1891.

Scott, W. B. Autobiographical notes. Ed W. Minto 2 vols 1892.

Stephens, F. G. Rossetti. 1894.

Wood, E. Rossetti and the Pre-Raphaelite movement. 1894.

[Skelton, J.] Mainly about Rossetti. In his Table talk of Shirley, 1894.

Kingsland, W. Rossetti's Jenny: with extracts from an hitherto unpublished version of the poem. Poet Lore Jan 1895.

Marillier, H. C. Rossetti: an illustrated memorial of his art and life. 1899, 1904 (abridged and rev).

Cary, E. The Rossettis: Dante Gabriel and Christina. New York 1900.

Spens, J. The ethical significance of Rossetti's poetry. International Jnl of Ethics 12 1902.

Hueffer, F. M. [Ford]. Rossetti: a critical essay on his art. 1902.

Dunn, H. T. Recollections of Rossetti and his circle. 1904.

Benson, A. C. Rossetti. 1904 (EML).

Waldschmidt, W. Rossetti der Maler und der Dichter: die Anfänge der Präraphaelitischen Bewegung in England. Jena and Leipzig 1905.

Hunt, W. H. Pre-Raphaelitism and the Pre-Raphaelite Brotherhood. 2 vols 1905, 1913 (2nd edn, rev M. E. Holman Hunt).

Singer, H. Rossetti. 1906.

Brooke, S. A. A study of Clough, Arnold, Rossetti and Morris. 1908.

Rutter, F. Rossetti: painter and man of letters. 1908.

Horn, K. Zur Entstehungsgeschichte von Rossettis Dichtungen. Bernau 1909.

—— The staff and scrip von Rossetti: Uebertragung und Erläuterung. Zeitschrift für Französischen und Englischen Unterricht 26 1927.

Routh, J. Parallels in Coleridge, Keats and Rossetti. MLN 25 1910.

Bassalik-de Vries, J. William Blake in his relation to Rossetti. Basle 1911.

Ulmer, H. Rossettis Verstechnik. Bayreuth 1911.

Suddard, M. The house of life. In her Keats, Shelley and Shakespeare, Cambridge 1912.

Butterworth, W. Rossetti in relation to Dante. 1912.

Willoughby, L. Rossetti and German literature. 1912.

Wagschal, F. E. B. Brownings Sonnets from the Portuguese und Rossettis House of life. Zeitschrift für Französischen und Englischen Unterricht 13 1914.

Villard, L. The influence of Keats on Tennyson and Rossetti. Saint-Etienne 1914.

Taglialatela, E. Rossetti: studio e versione. Rome 1914.

Boas, Mrs F. S. Rossetti and his poetry. 1914.

Symons, A. In his Figures of several centuries, 1916.

—— The Rossettis. In his Dramatis personae, 1923.

—— In his Studies in strange souls, 1929.

Schücking, L. Rossettis Persönlichkeit. E Studien 51 1917.

Tisdel, F. M. Rossetti's House of life. MP 15 1917.

Venkatesan, N. K. Rossetti: the Pre-Raphaelite poet-painter. Madras 1918.

McKillop, A. D. Festus and the Blessed damozel. MLN 34 1919.

Trombly, A. E. Rossetti the poet: an appreciation. Austin 1920.

—— A translation of Rossetti's. MLN 38 1923.

Williams, S. Rossetti's damozels: blessed and otherwise. Texas Rev 6 1921.

—— Two poems by Rossetti. In his Studies in Victorian literature, 1924.

Dupré, H. Un italien d'Angleterre: le poète-peintre Rossetti. Paris 1921.

Hearn, L. In his Pre-Raphaelite and other poets, New York 1922. 2 essays.

Broers, B. C. Dante and Rossetti. In her Mysticism in the neo-romanticists, Amsterdam 1923, New York 1966.

Davies, C. Rossetti. 1925.

Block, L. Rossetti der Malerdichter: eine Untersuchung seines künsterlerischen Schaffens. In Giessner Beiträge zur Erforschung der Sprache und Kultur Englands und Nordamerikas, Giessen 1925.

Holthausen, F. Rossetti und die Bibel. Germanisch-romanische Monatsschrift 13–14 1925–6.

Jones, H. Rossetti: medievalist and poet. Quart Jnl of Univ of North Dakota 16 1926.

Shine, W. H. The influence of Keats upon Rossetti. E Studien 61 1927.

Turner, A. M. Rossetti's reading and his critical opinions. PMLA 42 1927.

Tietz, E. Das Malerische in Rossettis Dichtung. Anglia 51 1927.

Wallerstein, R. Personal experience in Rossetti's House of life. PMLA 42 1927.

—— The Bancroft manuscripts of Rossetti's sonnets, with the text of two hitherto unpublished sonnets. MLN 44 1929.

Mégroz, R. L. Rossetti: painter poet of heaven in earth. 1928.

Waugh, E. Rossetti: his life and works. 1928.

Ghose, S. N. Rossetti and contemporary criticism 1849–82. Dijon 1929.

Hamilton, G. Rossetti: a review of his poetry. Criterion June 1928.

Förster, M. Die älteste Fassung von Rossettis Ballade Sister Helen. In Die Leipziger Neunundneunzig: Festschrift des Leipziger Bibliophilen-Abends, Leipzig 1929.

Bergum, E. B. Rossetti and the ivory tower. Sewanee Rev 37 1929.

Welby, T. E. The Victorian romantics 1850–70: the early work of Rossetti, Morris, Burne-Jones, Swinburne, Simeon Solomon and their associates. 1929, Hamden Conn 1966.

Whiting, M. Dante and Rossetti. Congregational Quart 7 1929.

Lucas, F. L. In his Eight Victorian poets, Cambridge 1930, 1940 (as Ten Victorian poets), 1948 (rev).

Morse, B. J. A note on the autobiographical elements in Rossetti's Hand and soul. Anglia 54 1930.

—— Rossetti and William Blake. E Studien 66 1932.

—— Rossetti and Dante. E Studien 68 1933.

Waller, R. D. The blessed damozel. MLR 26 1931.

—— The Rossetti family 1824–54. Manchester 1932.

Johnson, G. C. The house of life. Poetry Rev 22 1931.

Cecil, D. In The great Victorians, ed H. J. and H. Massingham 1932.

DeVane, W. C. The harlot and the thoughtful young man: a study of the relation between Rossetti's Jenny and Browning's Fifine at the fair. SP 29 1932.

Knickerbocker, K. L. Rossetti's The blessed damozel. SP 29 1932.

Hunt, V. The wife of Rossetti. 1932.

Evans, B. I. In his English poetry in the later nineteenth century, 1933, 1966 (rev).

'Winwar, Frances' Dante Gabriel's or William Michael's? an attempt to establish the authorship of some of Rossetti's sonnets published by the Duke University Press. PMLA 48 1933.

—— The Rossettis and their circle. 1933, New York 1933 (as Poor splendid wings).

Cammell, C. R. Rossetti and the philosophy of love. 1933.

Larg, D. Trial by virgins: fragment of a biography. 1933.

Klinnert, A. Rossetti und Stefan George. Würzburg 1933.

Wolff, L. Rossetti. Paris 1934.
Vincent, E. R. Gabriele Rossetti in England. Oxford 1936.
Sanford, J. A. The Morgan library manuscript of Rossetti's The blessed damozel. SP 35 1938.
Troxell, J. C. The trial books of Rossetti. Colophon 3 1938.
Koziol, H. Rossettis Reime. Archiv new ser 77 1940.
Baum, P. F. The Bancroft manuscript of Rossetti. MP 39 1941.
— Rossetti's The leaf. MLQ 2 1941.
— Rossetti's The white ship. Duke Univ Lib Notes no 20 1948.
Ray, S. N. Rossettiana. Dacca 1941.
Gaunt, W. The Pre-Raphaelite tragedy. 1942, 1943 (as The Pre-Raphaelite dream).
Jackson, E. Notes on the stanza of Rossetti's Blessed damozel. PMLA 58 1943.
Culler, D. and S. Sources of the King's tragedy. SP 41 1944.
Ford, G. H. In his Keats and the Victorians, New Haven 1944, Hamden Conn 1962.
Preston, K. Blake and Rossetti. 1944.
Spender, S. The Pre-Raphaelite literary painters. New Writing & Daylight 6 1945.
Masefield, J. Thanks before going: notes on some of the original poems of Rossetti. 1946.
Gray, N. Rossetti, Dante and ourselves. 1947.
Simonini, R. C., jr. Rossetti's poems in Italian. Italica 25 1948.
Angeli, H. R. Rossetti: his friends and enemies. 1949.
Doughty, O. A Victorian romantic: Rossetti. 1949, 1960.
— Rossetti as translator. Theoria no 5 1953.
— Rossetti's conception of the poetic in poetry and painting. Trans Royal Soc of Lit 26 1953.
— Rossetti. 1957 (Br Council pamphlet).
Bowra, C. M. The house of life. In his Romantic imagination, Cambridge Mass 1949.
Hough, G. Rossetti and the PRB. In his Last Romantics, 1949.
Lang, C. Y. The French originals of Rossetti's John of Tours and My father's close. PMLA 64 1949.
Bellinger, R. Rossetti's two translations from old French. MLN 65 1950.
Cassidy, J. A. Robert Buchanan and the fleshly controversy. PMLA 67 1952.
Metzdorf, R. F. The full text of Rossetti's sonnet on Sordello. Harvard Lib Bull 7 1953.
West, T. Rossetti and Ezra Pound. RES new ser 4 1953.
Le Roy, G. C. In his Perplexed prophets, Philadelphia 1953.
De Pilato, S. Rossetti: poeta e pittore. Rome 1954.
Groom, B. Rossetti, Morris and Swinburne. In his Diction of poetry from Spenser to Bridges, Toronto 1955.
Fairchild, H. N. In his Religious trends in English poetry vol 4: 1830–80, New York 1957.
Lo Schiavo, R. La poesia di Rossetti. Rome 1957.
Lauter, P. The narrator of the Blessed damozel. MLN 73 1958.
Paolucci, A. Ezra Pound and Rossetti as translators of Guido Cavalcanti. Romanic Rev 51 1960.
Ryals, C. The inner experience: the aesthetic of Rossetti and Isak Dinesen. Revue des Langues Vivantes 26 1960.
Savarit, J. Tendances mystiques et ésotériques chez Rossetti. Paris 1961.
Forsyth, R. A. The temper of Pre-Raphaelitism and the concern with natural detail. Eng Stud in Africa 4 1961
Lindberg, J. Rossetti's Cumaean oracle. Victorian Newsletter no 22 1962.
Robillard, D. Rossetti's Willowwood sonnets and the structure of the House of life. Ibid.

Hyder, C. K. Rossetti's Rosemary: a study in the occult. Victorian Poetry 1 1963.
Vogel, J. White rose or white robe in the Blessed damozel. Eng Lang Notes 1 1963.
Bracker, J. Notes on the texts of two poems by Rossetti. Lib Chron of Univ of Texas 7 1963.
Weatherby, H. Problems of form and content in the poetry of Rossetti. Victorian Poetry 2 1964.
Packer, L. M. Maria Francesca to Dante Rossetti: some unpublished letters. PMLA 79 1964.
Franklin, C. The blessed damozel at Penkhill. EC 14 1964.
Grylls, R. G. Portrait of Rossetti. 1964.
Pedrick, G. Life with Rossetti. 1964.
Charlesworth, B. In her Dark passages: the decadent consciousness in Victorian literature, Madison 1965.
Johnson, W. S. Rossetti as painter and poet. Victorian Poetry 3 1965.
Kendall, J. L. The concept of the infinite moment in the House of life. Victorian Newsletter no 28 1965.
Fredeman, W. E. Rossetti's In Memoriam: an elegiac reading of the House of life. Bull John Rylands Lib 47 1965.
Talon, H. Rossett, comme peintre-poète dans La maison de vie. Etudes Anglaises 19 1966.
— Rossetti, The house of life: quelques aspects de l'art, des thèmes et du symbolisme. Paris 1966.
Fleming, G. H. Rossetti and the Pre-Raphaelite Brotherhood. 1967.

W. E. F.

CHRISTINA GEORGINA ROSSETTI 1830–94

Bibliographies

Anderson, J. P. Appended to M. Bell, Christina Rossetti, 1898.
Ehrsam, T. G., R. H. Deily and R. M. Smith. In their Bibliographies of twelve Victorian authors, New York 1936. Supplement by J. G. Fucilla, MP 37 1939.
Jones, H. M. The Pre-Raphaelites. In Victorian poets: a guide to research, ed F. E. Faverty, Cambridge 1956, 1968 (rev).
Packer, L. M. Selective bibliography. In her Christina Rossetti, below.
Fredeman, W. E. In his Pre-Raphaelitism: a bibliocritical study, Cambridge Mass 1965 (section 44).

Collections

Poetical works. Ed W. M. Rossetti 1904 etc (with memoir). Standard edn. Other selected edns by W. M. Rossetti 1904 (Golden Treasury); Alice Meynell 1910; C. B. Burke nd; W. de la Mare 1930; N. Lewis 1959 (Pocket Poets).

§ I

Many of Christina Rossetti's poems and prose works first appeared in periodicals and in anthologies before being incorporated, frequently with significant revisions, into later volumes. A few have never been rptd.

Periodicals: Aiken's Year 1852–4 (one poem rptd); Argosy 1866 (one story, 7 poems, all rptd); Atalanta 1890 (one poem rptd); Athenaeum 1848–90 (8 poems, all rptd); Bouquet Culled from Marylebone Gardens 1851–2 (2 poems and a prose work, Corrispondenza famigliare, signed 'Calta', all rptd); Century Feb 1884 (unrptd article, Dante, the poet illustrated out of the poem); Century Guild Hobby Horse 1887–9 (3 poems, all rptd); Churchman's Shilling Mag 1867 (3 stories all rptd, one unrptd article, Dante, an English classic); Crayon 1856 (one story rptd); Dawn of Day 1882 (2 poems, both rptd); Dublin Univ Mag 1878 (one poem rptd); Germ 1850 (5 poems signed 'Ellen

Alleyn', all rptd); Literary Opinion 1892 (2 poems, both rptd, one unrptd essay The house of DGR); Macmillan's Mag 1861–83 (24 poems, all rptd); Mag of Art 1890–4 (2 poems, both rptd); New and Old 1879 (A harmony on First Corinthians, unrptd); Once a Week 1859 (one poem rptd); Our Paper 1855 (one poem rptd); Scribner's Mag 1872–3 (3 poems, all rptd); Shilling Mag 1865 (one poem rptd).

Anthologies etc: Beautiful poetry 1853 (Death's chill between, rptd from Athenaeum, rptd in Poetical works 1904); Düsseldorf Artists' Album 1854, ed M. Howitt (A summer evening, rptd in Goblin market as Twilight calm); Memoirs of Mallet du Pan, tr W. M. Rossetti and B. H. Paul [1855] (partly her trn); Imperial dictionary of biography, ed J. F. Waller et al 1857–63 (33 unrptd articles, including one of significance on Petrarch); Poems: an offering to Lancashire, ed Isa Craig 1863 (A Royal Princess rptd with major revisions); A welcome: original contributions in poetry and prose 1863 (Dream love, rptd); Lyra eucharistica 1863, 1864 (2nd edn), Lyra messianica 1864, 1865 (2nd edn), Lyra mystica 1865, ed O. Shipley (13 poems, all rptd); Picture poesies: poems chiefly by living authors 1874 (2 poems, both rptd); A masque of poets, Boston 1878 (one poem rptd); The children's hymn book, compiled by Mrs Carey Brock 1881 (one poem rptd); Sonnets of three centuries, ed T. Hall Caine 1882 (one sonnet rptd); DGR: his family letters with a memoir, ed W. M. Rossetti 1895 (3 poems, all rptd).

Verses by Christina G. Rossetti, dedicated to her mother. 1847 (priv ptd by G. Polidori); ed J. D. Symon 1906 (Eragny Press). Contains poem To my mother on the anniversary of her birth, April 27 1842, originally pbd as a single sheet by G. Polidori [1842], her earliest ptd poem.

Goblin market and other poems, with 2 designs by DGR. 1862, 1865; illustr L. Housman 1893; tr Italian by T. P. Rossetti, Florence 1867.

The prince's progress and other poems, with 2 designs by DGR. 1866; rptd with Goblin market as Poems, Boston 1866.

Outlines for illuminating: Consider. New York 1866 (single sheet).

Commonplace and other short stories. 1870.

Sing-song: a nursery rhyme book, with 120 illustrations by A. Hughes. 1872, 1878, 1893 (new and enlarged edn with 5 additional poems).

Annus Domini: a prayer for each day of the year, founded on a text of Holy Scripture. 1874.

Speaking likenesses, with pictures thereof by A. Hughes. 1874.

Goblin market, The prince's progress and other poems: new edition with 4 designs by DGR. 1875, Boston 1876, 1882 (as Poems), London 1879, 1884, 1888. With 37 new poems. *See below* Poems 1890.

Seek and find: a double series of short studies of the Benedicite. 1879.

A pageant and other poems. 1881.

Called to be Saints: the Minor Festivals devotionally studied. 1881. With 13 poems.

Letter and spirit: notes on the Commandments. 1883.

Time flies: a reading diary. 1885. With 130 poems.

Poems: new and enlarged edition, with 4 designs by DGR. 1890, 1890, 1891, 1892, 1894, 1895, 1196. A rpt of Goblin market etc, 1875, together with A pageant 1881, and 13 new poems.

The face of the deep: a devotional commentary on the Apocalypse. 1892. Prose with over 200 poems and verse fragments, many rptd in Reflected lights, ed W. Jay 1900.

Verses reprinted from Called to be saints, Time flies and The face of the deep. 1893. With some alterations and addns.

New poems, hitherto unpublished and uncollected. Ed W. M. Rossetti 1896.

The Rossetti birthday book. Ed Olivia Rossetti [Agresti] 1896.

Maude: a story for girls. Ed W. M. Rossetti 1897. Written in 1850.

Familiar correspondence newly translated from the Italian of Christina G. Rossetti. Stanford Dingley 1962. A trn of her imaginary correspondence pbd in The Bouquet Culled from Marylebone Gardens 1851–2.

Letters

Bell, M. In his Christina Rossetti, 1898, below.

Ruskin: Rossetti: Pre-Raphaelitism. Ed W. M. Rossetti 1899.

Rossetti papers 1862–70. Ed W. M. Rossetti 1903.

Family letters of Christina Rossetti. Ed W. M. Rossetti 1908.

Curti, M. E. A letter of Christina Georgina Rossetti. MLN 51 1936.

Troxell, J. C. Three Rossettis: unpublished letters to and from Dante Gabriel, Christina, William. Cambridge Mass 1937.

Packer, L. M. Christina Rossetti and Alice Boyd of Penkill Castle. TLS 26 June 1959.

— Christina Rossetti's correspondence with her nephew: some unpublished letters. N & Q Dec 1959.

— The Rossetti–Macmillan letters: some 133 unpublished letters written to Alexander Macmillan, F. S. Ellis and others by Dante Gabriel, Christina and William Michael Rossetti 1861–89. Berkeley 1963.

Putt, S. G. Christina Rossetti, almsgiver. English 13 1961.

§2

Forman, H. B. In his Our living poets, 1871.

Symons, A. In Poets and poetry of the century, ed A. H. Miles 10 vols 1891–7.

— In his Studies in two literatures, 1897.

Nash, J. J. G. A memorial sermon for the late Christina Rossetti. 1895.

Noble, J. A. The burden of Christina Rossetti. In his Impressions and memories, 1895.

Procter, E. A. A brief memoir of Christina Rossetti. 1895.

Watts-Dunton, T. Reminiscences of Christina Rossetti. Nineteenth Century Feb 1895.

— In his Old familiar faces, 1916.

Law, A. The poetry of Christina Rossetti. Westminster Rev 143 1895.

Benson, A. C. In his Essays, 1896.

Gosse, E. In his Critical kit-kats, 1896.

Bell, M. Christina Rossetti: a biographical and critical study. 1898.

Westcott, B. F. An appreciation of the late Christina Rossetti. 1899.

Cary, E. L. The Rossettis: Dante Gabriel and Christina. New York 1900.

More, P. E. In his Shelburne essays: third series, New York 1905.

Breme, M. I. Christina Rossetti und der Einfluss der Bibel auf ihre Dichtung. Münster 1907.

Hueffer, F. M. [Ford]. Christina Rossetti and Pre-Raphaelite love. In his Memories and impressions, 1911.

Sharp, W. Some memories of Christina Rossetti. In his Papers critical and reminiscent, ed Mrs W. Sharp 1912. Rptd from Atlantic Monthly June 1895.

Venkatesan, N. K. Christina Rossetti. Madras 1914.

Mason, E. Two Christian poets, Christina Rossetti and Paul Verlaine. In his A book of preferences, 1915.

Wilde, J. F. de. Christina Rossetti: poet and woman. Nijkerk 1923.

de la Mare, W. Christina Rossetti. Trans Royal Soc of Lit 6 1926.

Birkhead, E. Christina Rossetti and her poetry. 1930.

Sanders, M. F. The life of Christina Rossetti. [1930].

Stuart, D. M. Christina Rossetti. 1930 (EML).
— Christina Rossetti. 1931 (Eng Assoc pamphlet no 78).
Rossetti, G. W. Christina Rossetti: a study and some comparisons. Cornhill Mag Dec 1930.
Kent, M. Christina Rossetti: a reconsideration. Contemporary Rev Dec 1930.
Waugh, A. Christina Rossetti. Nineteenth Century Dec 1930.
Shove, F. Christina Rossetti. Cambridge 1931.
Thomas, E. W. Christina Rossetti. New York 1931.
Zabel, M. D. Christina Rossetti and Emily Dickinson. Poetry Jan 1931.
Morse, B. J. Some notes on Christina Rossetti and Italy. Anglia 55 1931.
Woolf, V. 'I am Christina Rossetti'. In her Common reader: second series, 1932.
Teasdale, S. Christina Rossetti. New York 1932.
Waller, R. D. The young Rossettis: Christina. In his Rossetti family 1824–54, Manchester 1932.
Dubslaff, F. Die Sprachform der Lyrik Christina Rossettis. Halle 1933.
Evans, B. I. In his English poetry in the later nineteenth century, 1933, 1966 (rev).
— The sources of Christina Rossetti's Goblin market. MLR 28 1933.
Shipton, I. M. Christina Rossetti: the poetess of the Oxford Movement. Church Quart Rev 116 1933.
Lucas, F. L. In his Ten Victorian poets, Cambridge 1940, 1948 (rev).
Robb, N. A. In her Four in exile, 1948.
Bowra, C. M. In his Romantic imagination, Cambridge Mass 1949.
Zaturenska, M. Christina Rossetti: a portrait with a background. New York 1949.
Sawtell, M. Christina Rossetti: her life and religion. 1955.
Garlitz, B. Christina Rossetti's Sing song and nineteenth-century children's poetry. PMLA 70 1955.
Fairchild, H. N. In his Religious trends in English poetry vol 4, New York 1957.
Packer, L. M. Symbol and reality in Christina Rossetti's Goblin market. PMLA 73 1958.
— The Protestant existentialism of Christina Rossetti. N & Q June 1959.
— F. S. Ellis and the Rossettis: a publishing venture and misadventure, 1870. Western Humanities Rev 16 1962.
— Christina Rossetti. Berkeley 1963.
— Swinburne and Christina Rossetti: atheist and Anglican. UTQ 33 1963.
Swann, T. B. Wonder and whimsey: the fantastic world of Christina Rossetti. Francestown NH 1960.
Bluen, H. The poetry of Christina Rossetti. Aryan Path Feb 1963.
Murciaux, C. Christina Rossetti: la vierge sage des préraphaélites. Revue de Paris Dec 1964.
Battiscombe, G. Christina Rossetti. 1965 (Br Council pamphlet).
Weathers, W. Christina Rossetti: the sisterhood of self. Victorian Poetry 3 1965.

W. E. F.

V. MINOR POETRY 1835–1870

References

Miles — The poets and poetry of the century, ed A. H. Miles et al 10 vols [1891–7], 12 vols 1905–7 (enlarged).
Julian — Julian, J., A dictionary of hymnology, 1892, 1907 (rev).
Wellesley — Wellesley index to Victorian periodicals, ed W. E. Houghton et al, vol 1 Toronto 1966.

SARAH FULLER ADAMS, née FLOWERS
1805–48

Bibliographies

Stephanson, H. W. The author of Nearer, my God, to thee. 1922. Includes lists of Mrs Adams' contributions to periodicals and of references to her.

Selections

Miles 7 (8).

§1

Hymns and anthems. Ed W. J. Fox 1841. Contains 13 pieces by Mrs Adams, including Nearer, my God, to thee (rptd separately Boston 1876, London 1884, New York 1887; ed in facs J. Julian 1911).
Vivia perpetua: a dramatic poem in five acts. 1841, 1893 (priv ptd, with hymns, and memoir by E. F. Briddell-Fox).
The flock at the fountain. 1845. A catechism and hymns for children.
A summer recollection: a poem. In Appendix 2 of The centenary history of the South Place Society by M. D. Conway, 1894.

§2

Fox, W. J. In his Lectures addressed chiefly to the working classes vol 4, 1849.
Taylor, E. In her Memories of some contemporary poets with selections from their writings, 1868.
Garnett, R. In Miles 7 (8).
Julian.
Stephanson, H. W. The author of Nearer, my God, to thee. 1922.
Whitaker, R. Nearer, my God, to thee. Unity 21 Feb 1938.

THOMAS AIRD
1802–76

Collections

Poetical works. 1848, 1856, 1878 (5th edn, with memoir by J. Wallace).
Foster, B. F. Summer scenes: a series of photographs from some of his choicest water-colour drawings, with selections from the poems of Aird etc. 1867.

§1

Murtzoufle: a tragedy in three acts; with other poems. 1826.
Religious characteristics. Edinburgh 1827. Didactic essays.
The captive of Fez: a poem in five cantos. Edinburgh 1830.
Othuriel and other poems. 1839.

The old bachelor in the old Scottish village. Edinburgh 1845, 1857 (rev and enlarged). Essays and sketches.
Poetical works of D. M. Moir. 2 vols 1852. Ed Aird, with memoir.
For 2 articles by Aird, see Wellesley p. 788.

§2

Gilfillan, G. In his Galleries of literary portraits vol 1, Edinburgh 1856.

WILLIAM ALEXANDER
1824–1911

Selections

Selected poems of W. Alexander and C. F. Alexander. Ed A. P. Graves 1930.

§1

Popular lectures and general reading: a lecture. 1862.
Victor Hugo as poet. In The afternoon lectures on English literature ser 2, 1864.
Specimens poetical and critical. 1867 (priv ptd).
Matthew Arnold's poetry. In The afternoon lectures on English literature ser 4, 1867.
Specimen of a translation of Virgil: Aenaeid bk 1, 1–181. 1869.
St Augustine's holiday and other poems. 1886.
Tenebrae. [1896]. Verses.
Poems of C. F. Humphreys. 1896. Ed Alexander, with preface.
The findings of the book and other poems. 1900. Includes St Augustine's holiday, above, etc.
The soldier's prayer (Is war the only thing that has no good in it?). [1900].
Alexander also wrote and edited a number of theological works.

§2

Garrod, H. B. The poems of Alexander. Academy 15 Jan 1887.
Julian.
Primate Alexander, Archbishop of Armagh: a memoir. Ed E. Alexander 1913.

HENRY ALFORD
1810–71

Bibliographies

Life, journals and letters, edited by his widow. 1873, 1874 (3rd edn).

Collections

The school of the heart and other poems. 2 vols Cambridge 1835.
Poetical works. 2 vols 1845, 1851 (as Select poetical works, with several pieces not before published), Boston 1853 (with 12 previously unpbd poems), 1865 (enlarged), 1868 (enlarged).

§1

Poems and poetical fragments. Cambridge 1833. Anon.
Chapters on the poets of ancient Greece. 1841.
The Abbot of Muchelnaye: sonnets. 1841, 1925.
Psalms and hymns adapted to the Sundays and holydays throughout the year; to which are added some occasional hymns. 1844.
Prose hymns, chiefly from Scripture, printed for chanting. 1844.
Memorial of the Rev Henry Alford: consisting of extracts from his correspondence, six selected sermons and a memoir by his eldest son. Ed H. Alford 1854.
English descriptive poetry: a lecture. In Evening recreations, ed J. H. Gurney 1856.
The Odyssey of Homer in hendecasyllabic verse, bks 1–12. 1861.
A plea for the Queen's English: stray notes on speaking and spelling. 1864 (for 1863), New York [1864], 1870 (rev and enlarged), 1888 (7th edn). First pbd as The Queen's English, the first 3 words being omitted by mistake.
The year of praise: being hymns, with tunes, for the Sundays and holydays of the year. Ed H. Alford 1867.
Works of John Donne. 1870. Ed H. Alford, with memoir.
The Riviera: pen and pencil sketches from Cannes to Genoa. 1870.
Alford also pbd numerous sermons and other religious works and edited Contemporary Rev Jan 1866–March 1870. *See* Wellesley p. 789.

Letters and Papers

Letters from abroad. 1865, 1865.
Life, journals and letters. Ed F. Alford 1873, 1874 (3rd edn).

§2

Moon, G. W. A defence of the Queen's English: in reply to A plea for the Queen's English, by the Dean of Canterbury. 1863.
The poems of Alford. Eclectic Rev 123 1866.
Garbett, E. L. God's view of our Babylon shown in slaying Alford. [1885].
Miles, A. H. In Miles 10 (11).
Davidson, J. In Julian.
Hare, A. J. C. In his Biographical sketches, 1895.

WILLIAM ALLINGHAM
1824–89

Bibliographies

Kropf, H. Allingham und seine Dichtung. Biel 1928. Includes a list of articles on, and references to, Allingham.
O'Hegarty, P. S. A bibliography of Allingham. Dublin Mag 22 1945; Dublin 1945 (priv ptd).

Collections

[Works]. 6 vols 1890.
Miles 5.
Sixteen poems, selected by W. B. Yeats. Dundrum 1905.
Poems. Ed H. Allingham 1912.

§1

Poems. 1850, Boston 1861 (enlarged).
Day and night songs. 1854, 1855 (rev and enlarged as The music master, a love story, and two series of day and night songs), 1884 (rearranged and enlarged). Some of the poems were first ptd in Household Words etc.
Peace and war. 1854. An ode rptd from Daily News, and not rptd in later vols.
The poetical works of Edgar Allen Poe. 1858. With introd by Allingham.
Nightingale valley: a collection of the choicest lyrics and short poems, edited by 'Giraldus'. 1860, 1862 (signed).
The ballad book. Ed W. Allingham et al 1864, 1865.
Laurence Bloomfield in Ireland: a modern poem. 1864, 1869 (adds a preface and subtitle: or the new landlord), 1888. An early version appeared in Fraser's Mag.
Fifty modern poems. 1865.
In fairyland. 1870 (for 1869), 1875.
Rambles by 'Patricius Walker'. 1873, 1893 (as vols 1–2 of Varieties in prose). Essays on England and Ireland.
The poetical works of Thomas Campbell; memoir by W. Allingham. 1875, 1890.
Songs, ballads and stories. 1877.

Evil May-day. 1882. An argumentative poem on the relation of religion to dogma and science.
Ashby Manor: a play in two acts. [1883]; rptd in Thought and word, 1890, below.
The fairies: a child's song. 1883, 1912 (as Up the airy mountain). Rptd from Day and night songs, above.
Blackberries picked off many bushes, by 'D. Pollex and others', put in a basket by W. Allingham. 1884, 1890. Poems by Allingham.
Irish songs and poems. 1887, 1890, 1901.
Rhymes for the young folk. [1887], New York [1915], 1930 (as Robin red breast and other verses).
Flower pieces and other poems. 1888. Includes Day and night songs, above. Opening section priv ptd as Flower pieces [1886?].
Life and phantasy. 1889.
Thought and word. 1890. Poems, including Ashby Manor, above.
Varieties in prose. 3 vols 1893. Vols 1–2 contain Rambles, vol 3 contains Irish sketches, Hopgood and Co (a play), and Essays on modern prophets, Painter and Critic, Poetry, Disraeli's monument to Byron, Some curiosities of criticism, and Baudelaire.
By the way: verses, fragments and notes arranged by H. Allingham. 1912, New York 1912.

Letters and Papers

A diary. Ed H. Allingham and D. Radford. 1907.
Letters from William Allingham to Robert and Elizabeth Barrett Browning. [1914].
Cameron, K. W. Allingham and Emerson: some new evidence. Emerson Soc Quart no 6 1957. 5 letters to Emerson.
Allingham also edited Fraser's Mag.

§2

[Rossetti, D. G.] Critic 15 Oct 1850.
Letters of D. G. Rossetti to Allingham 1845–70. Ed G. B. Hill 1897. Many originally appeared in Atlantic Monthly July–Aug 1896.
Yeats, W. B. In Miles 5.
Johnson, L. In A treasury of Irish poetry in the English tongue, ed S. A. Brooke and T. W. Rolleston 1900.
Letters to W. Allingham. Ed H. Allingham and E. B. Williams 1911.
Graves, A. P. William Allingham. Trans Royal Soc of Lit 32 1913.
Kropf, H. Allingham und seine Dichtung. Biel 1928.
Howe, M. L. Notes on the Allingham canon. PQ 12 1933.
Donaghy, J. L. William Allingham. Dublin Mag 22 1945.
Browne, J. N. Poetry in Ulster. In Arts in Ulster, ed S. H. Bell 1951.
White, H. O. An Allingham pamphlet. TLS 17 Aug 1956.

WILLIAM EDMONDSTOUNE AYTOUN

1813–65

Collections

Miles 4, 9 (10).
Poems. Ed F. Page, Oxford 1921.
Stories and verse. Ed W. L. Renwick, Edinburgh 1964 (Scottish Reprints no 2). Contains The Glenmutchkin railway, How I stood for the Dreepdaily burghs, The emerald stud, How we got possession of the Tuilleries, Firmilian, and Bon Gaultier ballads.

§1

Poland, Homer and other poems. 1832. Anon.
The life and times of Richard the first, King of England. 1840.
Our Zion: or Presbyterian popery, by ane of that ilk. Edinburgh 1840. Anon. Tract written in opposition to the veto act.
The book of ballads, edited by 'Bon Gaultier'. 1845, 1849 (enlarged), 1903 (16th edn). With T. Martin.
Lays of the Scottish cavaliers and other poems. 1849, 1849 (adds appendix on Macaulay, also issued separately), 1853 (6th edn); ed H. Morley 1891. Lays often rptd separately, numerous selections also rptd for school use.
Firmilian, or the student of Badajoz: a spasmodic tragedy by 'T. Percy Jones'. Edinburgh 1854, New York 1854.
Bothwell: a poem in six parts. 1856, Boston 1856, Edinburgh 1858 (3rd edn rev).
The Glenmutchkin railway. 1858. A short story rptd from Blackwood's Mag in Tales from Blackwood vol 1 1858, [1868], [1907] (in The Glenmutchkin railway and other humorous Scots stories).
The ballads of Scotland. 2 vols Edinburgh 1858, 1859 (rev and enlarged), 1870 (4th edn rev and enlarged). Ed Aytoun.
Poems and ballads of Goethe. 1859, 1860 (rev and enlarged), 1877. Tr with R. Martin. Many poems first ptd in Blackwood's Mag.
Inaugural address. Edinburgh 1861. On rhetoric and the art of public speaking.
Norman Sinclair: a novel. 3 vols 1861.
Nuptial ode on the marriage of the Prince of Wales. 1863.
The burial march of Dundee and the island of the Scots. Ed W. K. Leask 1897.
Endymion: or a family party of Olympus. In Ixion in heaven and Endymion: Disraeli's skit and Aytoun's burlesque. Ed E. Partridge 1927. Written in 1842.
Aytoun also contributed extensively to Blackwood's Mag; *see* Wellesley pp. 798–800.

§2

Martin, T. Memoir of Aytoun. 1867. The appendix contains several sketches and essays by Aytoun which are inaccessible elsewhere, and reprints The nuptial ode on the marriage of the Prince of Wales.
Bell, M. In Miles 4. *See* 9 (10).
Masson, R. Pollok and Aytoun. Edinburgh 1898.
TLS 25 Aug 1921.
Frykberg, E. Aytoun, pioneer professor of English at Edinburgh. Gothenburg 1963.

PHILIP JAMES BAILEY

1816–1902

Selections

Miles 4.

§1

Festus: a poem. 1839, 1845 (with addns and a selection of press notices), Boston 1845, London 1864 (7th edn, enlarged), 1877 (10th edn), 1889 (with long preface); tr French, [1890] (excerpts). By 1889 the bulk of Angel world, Mystic and Universal hymn, below, had been included in Festus. In 1884 'A student' issued The beauties of Festus, witha descriptive index.
The angel world and other poems. 1850, Boston 1850.
The mystic and other poems. 1855, Boston 1856.
The age: a colloquial satire [and other poems]. 1858. A verse trialogue between author, critic and friend.
The international policy of the great powers. 1861.
Universal hymn. 1867.
Nottingham castle: an ode. 1878.
Causa britannica: a poem in Latin hexameters with English paraphrase. Ilfracombe 1883.

Letters and Papers

Selections from the letters of Philip James Bailey. Ed M. Peckham, Princeton Univ Lib Chron 7 1946.

§2

Gilfillan, G. In his A second gallery of literary portraits, 1850.
Powell, T. In his Living authors of England, New York 1849, London 1851.
Brown, J. H. In Miles 4.
Nicoll, W. R. and T. J. Wise. In Literary anecdotes of the nineteenth century vol 2, 1896.
Obituary. Athenaeum 13 Sept 1902.
Gosse, E. Philip James Bailey. Fortnightly Rev Nov 1902; rptd in his Portraits and sketches, 1912.
Ward, J. Bailey: personal recollections. Nottingham 1905 (priv ptd).
McKillop, A. D. A Victorian Faust. PMLA 40 1925. On Festus.
Goldschmidt, E. Der Gedankegehalt von Baileys Festus. E Studien 117 1932.
Black, G. A. Bailey's debt to Goethe's Faust in his Festus. MLR 28 1933.
Peckham, M. A Bailey collection. Princeton Univ Lib Chron 7 1946.
—— American editions of Festus: a preliminary survey. Princeton Univ Lib Chron 8 1947.
—— English editions of Bailey's Festus. PBSA 44 1950.
Fairchild, H. N. Wild bells in Bailey's Festus? MLN 54 1949.
Birley, R. In his Sunk without trace, 1962.

WILLIAM BARNES
1801–86

Bibliographies

Baxter, L. The life of Barnes by his daughter. 1887. Includes list of pbd and unpbd writings.

Collections

Poems of rural life in the Dorset dialect. 1879, 1883.
Miles 3.
Select poems chosen and edited with a preface and glossarial notes by T. Hardy. 1908.
A selection of poems of rural life in the Dorset dialect. Ed W. M. Barnes 1909.
Twenty poems in common English. Ed J. Drinkwater, Oxford 1925.
Poems grave and gay. Ed G. Dugdale, Dorchester 1949. With bibliographical notes.
Selected poems. Ed G. Grigson 1950 (ML).
Poems. Ed B. Jones 1962. First collected edn.

§1

Poetical pieces. Dorchester 1820.
Orra: a Lapland tale. Dorchester 1822.
An etymological glossary. Shaftesbury 1829.
A catechism of government in general, and of England in particular. Shaftesbury 1833.
The mnemonic manual. 1833.
A few words on the advantages of a more common adoption of the mathematics as a branch of education. 1834.
A mathematical investigation of the principle of hanging doors, gates, swing bridges and other heavy bodies. Dorchester 1835.
An arithmetical and commercial dictionary. 1840.
An investigation of the laws of case in language, exhibited in a system of natural cases. 1840.
A pronouncing dictionary of geographical names. 1841.
The elements of English grammar, with a set of questions and exercises. 1842.
The elements of linear perspective and the projection of shadows. 1842.
Exercises in practical science. Dorchester 1844.
Sabbath lays: six sacred songs. 1844.
Poems of rural life in the Dorset dialect, with a dissertation and glossary. 1844, 1847 (enlarged), 1862, 1866.
Poems, partly of rural life (in national English). 1846.
Outlines of geography and ethnology for youth. Dorchester 1847.
Humilis domis: some thoughts on the abodes, life and social conditions of the poor. [1849?] (priv ptd).
Se gefylsta (the helper): an Anglo-Saxon delectus, serving as a first class-book of the language. 1849, 1866.
A philological grammar, grounded upon English. 1854.
Notes on ancient Britain and the Britons. 1858.
Views of labour and gold. 1859.
Hwomely rhymes: a second collection of poems in the Dorset dialect. 1859, 1863 (as Poems of rural life in the Dorset dialect: second selection).
The song of Solomon in the Dorset dialect. 1859 (priv ptd).
Tiw: or, a view of the roots and stems of the English as a Teutonic tongue. [1861].
Poems of rural life in the Dorset dialect: third collection. 1862, 1869.
A grammar and glossary of the Dorset dialect, with the history, outspreadings and bearings of south-western English. 1864, 1886 (rev).
A guide to Dorchester. Dorchester 1864.
Poole, J. A glossary of the old dialect of the English colony in the baronies of Forth and Bargy. Ed W. Barnes 1867.
Early England and the Saxon English, with some notes on the fatherstock of the Saxon English, the Frisians. 1869.
Poems of rural life in common English. 1868, Boston 1868, 1869.
An outline of English speech-craft. 1878.
An outline of rede-craft (logic), with English wording. 1880.
A glossary of the Dorset dialect, with a grammar of its word shapening and wording. 1886.
Barnes was also a voluminous contributor to GM, Hone's Year Book, Retrospective Rev, Macmillan's Mag, Fraser's Mag etc. See L. Baxter, Life of Barnes, 1887, pp. 350–6; Wellesley p. 804.

§2

Barnes, Dorsetshire poet. Chambers's Jnl 2 May 1863.
A simple singer. Chambers's Jnl 1 Aug 1868.
Doyle, F. H. C. Provincial poetry. In his Lectures, 1868.
Patmore, C. An English classic: Barnes. Fortnightly Rev Nov 1886.
Hardy, T. Obituary. Athenaeum 16 Oct 1886; rptd in L. Johnson, The art of Thomas Hardy, 1894.
Palgrave, F. T. William Barnes. Nat Rev Feb 1887.
Baxter, L. The life of Barnes by his daughter. 1887.
C. Sayle. In Miles 3.
Powys, L. Barnes the Dorset poet. Freeman 12 July 1922.
Grey, P. William Barnes. London Mercury Feb 1923.
Pinto, V. de S. Barnes: an appreciation. Wessex June 1930.
Quiller-Couch, A. T. In his Poet as citizen and other papers, Cambridge 1934.
Forster, E. M. Homage to Barnes. New Statesman 9 Dec 1939; rptd in his Two cheers for democracy, 1951.
Massingham, H. J. William Barnes. Time & Tide 16 May 1942.
A Wessex Virgil: Barnes's Poems of rural life. TLS 1 July 1944.
Grigson, G. In his Harp of Aeolus, 1948.
Heath-Stubbs, J. In his Darkling plain, 1950.

Bayliss, S. A. A propos Barnes. London Quart 175 1950.
Jacobs, W. D. Barnes, linguist. Albuquerque 1952.
Dugdale, G. Barnes of Dorset. 1953.
The story of Mere. Gillingham 1958.
Jacobs, W. D. A word-hoard for folkdom. Arizona Quart 15 1959.
Hynes, S. Hardy and Barnes: notes on literary influence. South Atlantic Quart 108 1959.
Levy, W. T. Barnes: the man and the poems. Dorchester 1960.
Larkin, P. William Barnes. Listener 16 Aug 1962.
Grigson, G. Out of the swim. New Statesman 17 Aug 1962.
Forsyth, R. A. The conserving myth of Barnes. Victorian Stud 7 1963.
Schulze, F. W. William Barnes. Die Neueren Sprachen Dec 1963.

CHARLES DENT BELL

1818–98

§1

Blanche Nevill: a record of married life. 1853. Anon. A novel.
The miners' sons: Martin Luther and Henry Martyn. 1853.
The Bible in English. 1854.
Time redeemed: or the past recalled. [1875].
Voices from the lakes and other poems. 1877 (for 1876).
The four seasons at the lake. 1878. Poems.
Henry Martyn. 1880, New York 1881. A biography.
Songs in the twilight. 1881.
Hymns for the church and the chamber. 1882 (for 1881).
Songs in many keys. 1884.
Verses for Christmas and the New Year. 1885. The title-page has the unexplained words No iv.
Gleanings from a tour of Palestine and the East. 1887.
A winter on the Nile in Egypt and in Nubia. 1888.
Reminiscences of a boyhood in the early part of the century. 1889. Anon.
Poems old and new. 1893. A selection from earlier vols, with new poems.
The Church of England hymnal. Ed C. Bell and H. E. Fox 1894.
Diana's looking-glass and other poems. 1894.
Some of our English poets. 1895. Essays on Gray, Goldsmith, Cowper, Scott, Coleridge and Wordsworth.
Tales told by the fireside. 1896. 7 short stories.
Home sunshine. [1904]. A tale.
Bell also pbd sermons and devotional works.

§2

Julian.

WILLIAM COX BENNETT

1820–95

Selections

Miles 5.

§1

My sonnets. Greenwich 1843 (priv ptd). Anon.
Songs, ballads etc. Greenwich 1845.
[A collection of poems, printed on single sheets]. [1849]? (priv ptd, no title-page).
Poems. 1850.
The triumph for Salamis: a lyrical ballad. Greenwich [1850?] (priv ptd).
Endowed parish schools and high church vicars. Greenwich [1853].
War songs. 1855.
Queen Eleanor's vengeance and other poems. 1857 (for 1856).
Songs by a song-writer: first hundred. 1859 (for 1858). 1876 (adds almost 50 lyrics).
Baby May and other poems on infants. 1859, 1865 (8 poems from Baby May), 1875 (as Baby May, home poems and ballads; includes The worn wedding-ring and other home poems, below, and Narrative poems and ballads).
The worn wedding-ring and other poems. 1861.
Poems. 1862, New York 1862.
Our glory-roll and other national poems. [1867].
Proposals for and contributions to a ballad history of England and the states sprung from her. 1868. Includes several ballads by Bennett. The preface originally pbd 1866 as Shall we have a national history for the English people?
The consecutive narrative series of reading books, by C. Morell, edited by J. R. Morell, to which is also added a selection of the best English poetry edited by W. C. Bennett, nos 1–5. [1870].
Songs for sailors. 1872, 1873.
Prometheus the fire-giver: an attempted restoration of the lost first part of the Promethean trilogy of Aeschylus. 1877.
Sea songs. 1878.
The lark: songs, ballads and recitations for the people. [1885]. Originally pbd in periodical of the same name at Greenwich [1883–4].

§2

Miles, A. H. In Miles 5.

ALEXANDER BETHUNE

1804–43

Collections

Tales of the Scottish peasantry, by A. and J. Bethune, with biography of the authors by J. Ingram. 1884. Includes Tales and sketches and Scottish peasant's fireside, below.

§1

Tales and sketches of the Scottish peasantry. Edinburgh 1838. With J. Bethune.
Lectures on practical economy. 1839. With J. Bethune.
Poems by the late J. Bethune, with a sketch of the author's life by his brother. 1841.
A Scottish peasant's fireside: a series of tales and sketches. Edinburgh 1843.

Letters and Papers

Memoirs of Bethune. Ed W. H. MacCrombie, Aberdeen 1845. Includes selections from his correspondence and literary remains.

§2

Bethune, J. The Bethunes: or the Fifeshire foresters. [1863]. In verse, with notes.

EDWARD HENRY BICKERSTETH

1825–1906

Selections

Miles 10 (12).

§1

The two brothers. 1845 (anon), 1871 (enlarged as The two brothers, and other poems), 1872, New York 1875.
Poems and songs. 1848.

Poems. Cambridge 1849.
Nineveh: a poem. 1851.
Ezekiel: a Seatonian prize poem. 1854.
Psalms and hymns, based on the Christian psalmody of Edward Bickersteth, compiled anew by E. H. Bickersteth. [1858], [1860].
The Tower of London, Caubul, Caesar's invasion of Britain. In A complete collection of the English poems which have obtained the Chancellor's Gold Medal vol 1, Cambridge 1859.
Winged words: a collection of some of his poems made by the author. [1861].
Yesterday, to-day and for ever: a poem in twelve books. 1866, 1867, 1869, New York 1869, London 1885 (17th edn); tr German, 1887.
The annotated hymnal companion to the Book of Common Prayer. 1870, 1871 (4 edns), 1880 (rev and enlarged), 1906.
Ode on the national thanksgiving for the recovery of the Prince of Wales. 1872.
The shadow of the rock and other poems. Ed E. H. Bickersteth 1873. Selected from various authors.
Milton's Paradise lost. In the St James lectures: companions for the devout life, ed J. E. Kempe 1875, 1877.
Songs in the house of pilgrimage. Hampstead [1880?].
From year to year: poems and hymns for all the Sundays and holy days of the Church. 1884 [1883], 1896 (rev and enlarged). Contains Peace, perfect peace.
Bickersteth also pbd many sermons and other religious writings.

§2

Miles, A. H. In Miles 10 (12).
Julian.
Obituary. Times 17 May 1906.
Aglionby, F. K. The life of Bickersteth. 1907.

JOHN STANYAN BIGG
1828–65

§1

The sea-king: a metrical romance in six cantos with notes. 1848.
Night and the soul: a dramatic poem. 1854.
[Burns centenary poem]. In Burns centenary poems, ed G. Anderson and J. Finley, Glasgow 1859.
Alfred Staunton: a novel. 1860 (for 1859).
Shifting scenes and other poems. 1862.

§2

Athenaeum 28 Oct 1854. An unfavourable review of Night and the soul.
Gilfillan, G. In his A third gallery of portraits, Edinburgh 1854.

JOHN STUART BLACKIE
1809–95

Selections

Rogers, C. In his Modern Scottish minstrel vol 4, Edinburgh 1855.
Miles 4.
Selected poems. Ed A. S. Walker 1896.

§1

[Goethe's] Faust [pt 1], translated into English verse, with notes and preliminary remarks. 1834.
The water cure in Scotland. Aberdeen 1849.
The lyrical dramas of Aeschylus translated into English verse. 2 vols 1850, 1 vol 1906, 1911 (EL).
Lays and legends of ancient Greece, with other poems. Edinburgh 1857, 1880.
On beauty: three discourses, with an exposition of the doctrine of the beautiful according to Plato. Edinburgh 1858.
Lyrical poems. Edinburgh 1860.
The Gaelic language: its classical affinities and distinctive character. Edinburgh 1864. A lecture.
Homer and the Iliad. 4 vols Edinburgh 1866. A trn in ballad metre.
On forms of government: a historical review and estimate of the growth of the principal types of political organization in Europe. 1867.
Musa burschicosa: a book of songs for students and university men. Edinburgh 1869.
War songs of the Germans. Edinburgh 1870.
Four phases of morals: Socrates, Aristotle, Christianity, Utilitarianism. Edinburgh 1871.
Lays of the Highlands and islands. 1871.
On self culture, intellectual, physical and moral: a vade mecum for young men and students. Edinburgh 1874.
The language and literature of the Highlands. Edinburgh 1876.
Songs of religion and life. 1876 (for 1875).
The natural history of atheism. 1877.
The wise men of Greece, in a series of dramatic dialogues. 1877.
Altavona: fact and fiction from my life in the Highlands. Edinburgh 1882, 1882.
The wisdom of Goethe. Edinburgh 1883. A critical estimate with Blackie's trns from Goethe's prose and verse.
Essays civil and moral by Francis Bacon; with an introduction by Prof. J. S. Blackie. 1886.
Messis vitae: gleanings of song from a happy life. 1886.
Life of Robert Burns. 1888.
Scottish song: its wealth, wisdom and significance. Edinburgh 1889. Essays.
A song of heroes. 1890.
Christianity and the ideal of humanity in old times and new. Edinburgh 1893.
Blackie also pbd much prose, mainly lectures, on educational, philological, political and religious matters, and also pbd school-books. He contributed to Blackwood's Mag, North Br Rev etc; see Wellesley pp. 812–3.

Letters and Papers

The day-book of Blackie, selected and transcribed from the mss by A. S. Walker. 1901.
Letters to his wife, with a few earlier ones to his parents. Ed A. S. Walker 1909.
Notes of a life. Ed A. S. Walker 1910. Letters and part of an unfinished autobiography.

§2

Whyte, W. In Miles 4.
Stoddart, A. M. Blackie: a biography. 2 vols 1895.
Kennedy, H. A. Professor Blackie, his sayings and doings. 1895.
Carswell, D. In his Brother Scots, 1927.

SAMUEL LAMAN BLANCHARD
1804–45

Collections

Sketches from life: with memoir by E. Bulwer Lytton. 3 vols 1846. Collected essays.
Poetical works. Ed B. Jerrold 1876.
Miles 3.

§1

Lyric offerings. 1828.

Life and literary remains of L. E. Landon. 2 vols 1841.
George Cruikshank's omnibus. Ed L. Blanchard 1842.
The cemetery at Kensal Green: the grounds and monuments with a memoir of the late Duke of Sussex. [1843?].
Literary remains of E. L. Johnson. 1844 (priv ptd).
A memoir of W. H. Ainsworth. In Works of W. H. Ainsworth vol 1, 1850, 1853, 1857, 1884.
Corporation characters. 1855. Prose sketches of civic celebrities.
Finden's gallery of modern art: a series of engravings with original descriptive tales by L. Blanchard et al. 2 vols [1859].
Blanchard also contributed to Monthly Mag, Examiner etc.

§2

Thackeray, W. M. A brother of the press on the history of a literary man, Laman Blanchard, and the chances of the literary profession. Fraser's Mag March 1846; rptd in Works, ed A. T. Ritchie vol 13, 1899.
Japp, A. H. In Miles 3.

HORATIUS BONAR

1808–89

Bibliographies

Horatius Bonar DD: a memorial. 1889.

Collections

Miles 10 (11).
Hymns: selected and arranged by H. N. Bonar, with a brief history of some of the hymns. 1904, 1908.
The land of light and other hymns of faith and hope. [1912].
Fifty-two sermons. Grand Rapids Michigan 1954. Originally pbd as Family sermons.

§1

Songs for the wilderness. 1843–4.
The Bible hymn-book, compiled by H. Bonar. 1845.
Hymns original and selected. 1846.
The morning of joy: being a sequel to the Night of weeping. New York 1854.
Hymns of faith and hope. 3 sers 1857–66, 1867, 1909 (selection).
Words of peace and welcome. 1860.
The nun: or, convent life. [1869].
The song of the new creation and other pieces. 1872.
My old letters. 1877. In verse.
Hymns of the nativity, and other pieces. 1879.
Communion hymns. 1881.
Verses for Christmas and the New Year. With L. A. Bennett, 1885. Bk 2 by Bonar.
Songs of love and joy: poems. [1888].
Garnered grain. 1889. With L. A. Bennett.
Crowned with light: a poem. 1889.
Until the day break and other hymns and poems left behind. Ed H. N. Bonar 1890.
Bonar also pbd sermons, travel books, religious tracts etc, and contributed to North Br Rev; see Wellesley p. 816.

§2

Horatius Bonar DD: a memorial. 1889. Includes autobiographical fragment, first and last sermons, bibliographical data and an unpbd poem.
Bell, M. In Miles 10 (11).
Memories of Dr Horatius Bonar by relatives and public men: addresses delivered at the centenary celebrations. 1909.
Bonar, J. In Julian.

THOMAS EDWARD BROWN

1830–97

Bibliographies

Radcliffe, W. In Brown: a memorial volume, Cambridge 1930. Includes an annotated list of Brown's contributions to periodicals and articles about him.
Cubbon, W. Brown: a bibliography. Douglas 1934; rptd in his A bibliographical account of works relating to the Isle of Man vol 2, Oxford 1939.
Nowell-Smith, S. Some uncollected authors 33: Brown. Book Collector 9 1962.

Collections

Miles 5.
Collected poems. Ed H. F. Brown, H. G. Dakyns and W. E. Henley 1900, 1901 (with introd by W. E. Henley).
Poems: selected and arranged with an introduction and notes by H. F. B[rown] and H. G. D[akyns]. 1908.
Twenty-three poems. 1931.
Poems. Ed A. T. Quiller-Couch 2 vols Liverpool 1952. Reprint of Collected poems 1900, above, with additional poem The Manx Library.

§1

The student's guide to the school of litterae fictitiae, commonly called novel-literature. 1855.
The library: a sermon preached in Clifton College chapel. Clifton 1873.
Betsy Lee: a fo'c'sle yarn. 1873 (anon), 1881 (enlarged as Fo'c'sle yarns, including Betsy Lee and other poems).
The doctor and other poems. 1887. In 1891 unsold sheets were divided into 2 vols as Kitty of the Serragh Vane and The doctor.
The Manx witch and other poems. 1889, New York 1889.
Old John and other poems. 1893, New York 1893.
Rydings, E. Manx tales; introductory preface by Rev T. E. Brown. [1895].
Manx ballads and music, by A. W. Moore, with preface by T. E. Brown. 1896.
Brown also contributed prose to several magazines, including Contemporary Rev, Macmillan's Mag, Nat Rev, New Rev; see Wellesley p. 829. *Some longer poems were priv ptd before pbn.*

Letters

Letters. Ed S. T. Irwin 2 vols 1900, 1900. With memoir.

§2

Whyte, W. In Miles 5.
Storr, W. T. E. Brown. New Rev Dec 1897. Includes a poem, In memoriam, by W. E. Henley.
T. E. Brown. Macmillan's Mag April–Oct 1900, Jan 1901.
Whibley, C. In his Musings without method, 1902.
Strachan, L. R. M. The poet of Manxland. E Studien 34 1904.
Simpson, S. G. Brown the Manx poet: an appreciation. 1906.
—— Brown, le poète de l'Ile de Man. Revue Anglo-américaine 9 1932; tr in Poetry Rev 26 1934.
Morrison, S. and A. M. Williams. Brown calendar. [1913].
Caine, W. R. H. The Rev T. E. Brown. [1915]. Newspaper articles and correspondence.
—— Brown: the last phase. Douglas 1924 (priv ptd).
Cubbon, W. T. E. Brown the patriot. [1917].
Tarvar, J. C. T. E. B.: Manxman, scholar, poet. Nineteenth Century Dec 1920.
Spender, C. The poetry of Brown. Contemporary Rev March 1925.
Abercrombie, L. T. E. Brown. Nineteenth Century May 1930.

Tuell, A. K. T. E. B. Amer Bookman 71 1930.
Boas, F. S. In The eighteen-eighties, 1930 (Royal Soc of Lit).
Brown: a memorial volume 1830–1930. Cambridge 1930. Includes unpbd letters, a bibliography etc.
Norris, S. In his Two men of Manxland, Douglas 1947.

JAMES DRUMMOND BURNS

1823–64

Selections

Miles 10 (12).

§1

The vision of prophecy and other poems. Edinburgh 1854, 1858.
The heavenly Jerusalem: or glimpses within the gates. 1856.
The evening hymn. 1857. A collection of hymns and prayers.

§2

Reminiscences of the late J. D. Burns from the Weekly Review of 17 December 1864. [1864].
Hamilton, J. Memoir and remains of Burns. 1869. Includes hymns and other verse.
Grossart, A. B. In Miles 10 (12).
Mearns, J. In Julian.

WATHEN MARK WILKS CALL

1817–90

Selections

Miles 4.

§1

Lyra hellenica. 1842. Metrical trn of the Prometheus of Aeschylus and some of the Homeric hymns.
Reverberations. 1849, 1875 (rev). Poems.
Golden histories. 1871. Poems.
Final causes: a refutation. [1891].
Call also contributed anon to the Westminster Rev. His criticism includes articles on George Eliot, Carlyle and Kant.

§2

The poems of Call. Westminster Rev 97 1872.
Obituary. Athenaeum 30 Aug 1890.
Japp, A. H. In Miles 4.
Conway, M. D. Religion and progress interpreted by the life and last work of Call. Monist 2 1892. A full-length study.

GEORGE DOUGLAS CAMPBELL, 8th DUKE OF ARGYLL

1823–1900

Address delivered to the members of the Glasgow Athenaeum, on 21 January 1851. In The importance of literature to men of business, 1852.
The reign of law. 1866.
Primeval man. 1869.
The unity of nature. 1884.
Scotland as it was and as it is. 2 vols Edinburgh 1887.
The Highland nurse: a tale. New York [1891], London [1892].
The burdens of belief and other poems. 1894.
Campbell was a prolific writer on economics, theology and popular science; see Wellesley p. 837 *and col 1512, below.*

Letters and Papers

George Douglas, eighth Duke of Argyll: autobiography and memoirs. Ed Dowager Duchess of Argyll 1906.

EDWARD CASWALL

1814–78

§1

Morals from the churchyard, in a series of cheerful fables. 1833.
The art of pluck: being a treatise after the fashion of Aristotle, writ for the use of students in the universities; to which is added fragments from the examination papers, by Scriblerus Redivivus. Oxford 1835, 1874 (12th edn), London 1893.
Pluck examination papers for candidates at Oxford and Cambridge in 1836, by Scriblerus Redivivus. Oxford 1836, 1836.
Sketches of young ladies, in which these interesting members of the animal kingdom are classified according to their several instincts, habits and general characteristics, by Quiz. 1837, 1838 (6th edn), [1869] (with Sketches of young couples, and young gentlemen by Dickens); tr Spanish, 1842.
Lyra catholica: containing all the breviary and missal hymns, with others from various sources. 1849, 1851, 1884, New York 1851, 1884. Tr Caswall.
The masque of Mary and other poems. 1858, [1887].
L'incoronata: a tale of May. Birmingham 1860.
Hymns and poems, original and translated. 1872; ed E. Bellasis 1908.
A May pageant and other poems. 1865, 1873 (with every line reduced by two syllables, as A tale of Tintern), [1907].
Caswall, who became a Roman Catholic in 1847, also wrote and translated devotional works.

§2

Julian.

ELIZABETH CHARLES, née RUNDLE

1828–96

Selections

Selections from the writings of the author of the Schönberg-Cotta family. 1877.
Thoughts and characters: selections from the writings of the author of the Schönberg-Cotta family. 1878.
Comfort and counsel for every day from the writings of E. R. Charles by two of her friends, with a preface by B. Champneys. 1898.

§1

The song without words. 1856.
The cripple of Antioch. 1856.
The voice of Christian life in song: or hymns and hymn-writers in many lands and ages. 1858, 1865, 1872, 1897 (5th edn, rev and enlarged).
The three wakings, with hymns and songs. 1859, 1860, 1868 (enlarged as The woman of the gospels, the three wakings and other verses), 1894 (enlarged as Songs old and new).
The black ship, with other allegories and parables. 1861.
Chronicles of the Schönberg-Cotta family. 1864, 2 vols 1867, [1903], [1910], [1914].
Diary of Mrs Kitty Trevylyan: a story of the times of Whitefield and the Wesleys. 1865.
Winifred Bertram and the world she lived in. 1866, 1886.
The Draytons and the Davenants: a story of the Civil Wars. 1867, 2 vols 1868.
On both sides of the sea: a story of the Commonwealth and the Restoration. 1868 (for 1867), New York [1867].
Watchwords for the warfare of life. 1869.

The victory of the vanquished: a tale of the first century. 1871, New York 1884.
Against the stream: the story of an heroic age in England. 3 vols 1873, 1 vol [1881].
The Bertram family. 1876, 1882.
Conquering and to conquer: a story of Rome in the days of St Jerome. 1876.
Joan the maid. 1879, New York 1879.
Lady Augusta Stanley: reminiscences. 1892.
Attila and his conquerors: a story of the days of St Patrick and St Leo the Great. [1894].
Our seven homes: autobiographical reminiscences. Ed M. Davidson 1896.
Mrs Charles also translated and arranged some selections from Luther and wrote a number of devotional works.

§2

Miller, J. Singers and songs of the church. 1869.
Julian.

SARA COLERIDGE
1802–52

See also S. T. Coleridge, col 211, above.

Selections

Miles 7 (8).

§1

Account of the Abipones, translated from the Latin of M. Dobrizhöffer. 3 vols 1821.
The right joyous and pleasant history of the feats, gests and prowesses of the Chevalier Bayard, translated from the French. 2 vols 1825, 1 vol [1906].
Pretty lessons in verse for good children. 1834, 1845 (4th edn), 1853, 1875, 1927.
Phantasmion. 1837 (anon); ed Lord Coleridge 1874. A fairy tale with lyrics.
For 2 reviews by Sara Coleridge see Wellesley p. 850.

§2

[Coleridge, H. N.] Quart Rev 66 1840. Long review of Sara Coleridge, Caroline Bowles, Elizabeth Barrett et al.
Memoir and letters of Sara Coleridge. Ed E. Coleridge 2 vols 1873, 1 vol New York 1874.
Garnett, R. In Miles 7 (8).
Towle, E. A. A poet's children: Hartley and Sara Coleridge. 1912.
Wilson, M. In his These were Muses, 1924.
Sara Coleridge and Henry Reed. Ed L. N. Broughton, Ithaca 1937. Includes Reed's memoir of Sara Coleridge and her letters to Read.
Griggs, E. L. Coleridge fille: a biography of Sara Coleridge. Oxford 1940.
Woolf, V. In her Death of the moth and other essays, 1942.

JOHN CONINGTON
1825–69

§1

The victory of suffering: a prize poem. 1842.
The Agamemnon, with a translation into English verse and notes. 1848, 1907.
The poetry of Pope. In Oxford essays, 1858.
The works of Virgil, with a commentary. 3 vols 1858. Many selections and abridgements followed.
The Choephoroe translated into English with notes. 1857.
The University of Oxford and the Greek Chair. Oxford 1863.
The odes and Carmen saeculare of Horace, translated. 1863, 1903 (with Latin text).
The Aeneid of Virgil, translated. 1866.
The style of Lucretius and Catullus as compared with that of the Augustan poets: a lecture. 1867.
The satires, epistles and Art of poetry of Horace, translated into English verse. 1870, 1904 (with Latin text).
The satires of A. Persius Flaccus, with a translation and commentary. Oxford 1872.
Miscellaneous writings. Ed J. A. Symonds with a memoir by H. J. S. Smith 2 vols 1872. Includes King Lear, Hamlet, The English translators of Virgil, Six lectures on Latin literature, The poems of Virgil translated into English prose, Fables of Babrius etc.
The poems of Virgil, translated. 1882. Rptd from Miscellaneous writings, above.
See also Wellesley p. 850.

ELIZA COOK
1812–89

Collections

Poems. 4 vols 1846–53.
Poetical works. Philadelphia 1853.
Poems. 3 vols [1858?].
Poems. 1859.
Poems: selected and edited by the author. 1861.
Auswahl englischer Gedichte der Eliza Cook, aus dem Englischen ins Deutsch übertragen von H. Simon. Leipzig 1865.
Poetical works. 1870, New York [1882].
Miles 7 (8).

§1

Lays of a wild harp: a collection of metrical pieces. 1835.
Melaia and other poems. 1838, 1840 (with addns from Lays of a wild harp).
Poems: second series. 1845.
Eliza Cook's journal. 1849–54. A periodical ed and partly written by Eliza Cook.
I'm afloat. [1850?]. Songs.
The Englishman: two songs. [1850?].
Song of the haymakers: Standard bearer and In this old chair my father sat. [1850?].
Mother be proud of your boy in blue. [1860?]. Songs.
Song of the haymakers: gipsy's tent. [1860?].
Jottings from my journal. 1860. Short essays.
New echoes, and other poems. 1864.
Diamond dust. 1865. A collection of aphorisms.
The old armchair. Boston 1886

§2

In Notable women of our own times, [1883?].
Ingram, J. H. In Miles 7 (8).

THOMAS COOPER, 'ADAM HORNBOOK'
1805–92

Collections

Poetical works. 1877, 1886.

§1

Wise Saws and modern instances. 2 vols 1845, 1 vol 1874 (enlarged as Old-fashioned stories). Short stories and sketches.
The purgatory of suicides: a prison-rhyme in ten books. 1845, 1853 (3rd edn).
The Baron's yule feast: a Christmas-rhyme. 1846.

The land for the labourers, and the fraternity of nations: a scheme for a new industrial system, published in Paris, and intended for proposal to the National Assembly. [1848]. Ed Cooper.
The life and character of Henry Hetherington. 1849. Abridged from Cooper's éloge by G. J. Holyoake.
Captain Cobler, or the Lincolnshire rebellion: an historical romance of the reign of Henry VIII. 1850.
Cooper's journal: or unfetterd thinker and plain speaker for truth, freedom and progress. [1850].
Eight letters to the young men of the working-classes. 1851. Rptd from Plain Speaker. Advice on the art of living.
Alderman Ralph: or the history of the borough of Willowacre, by Adam Hornbook. 2 vols 1853.
The family feud: a tale by Adam Hornbook. 1855.
The bridge of history over the gulf of time: a popular view of the historical evidence for the truth of Christianity. 1871.
The life of Thomas Cooper, written by himself. 1872, 1873 (4th edn).
Plain pulpit talk. 1872; The atonement and other discourses: being a second series of Plain pulpit talk, 1880.
The paradise of martyrs: a faith rhyme, part first, in five books. 1873. No further pts pbd.
Evolution, the stone book and the Mosaic record of creation. 1878.
Thoughts at fourscore and earlier: a medley. 1885. Includes the Letters to the young working men.
Cooper also edited Chartist journals and pbd theological works and sermons.

§2

Holyoake, G. J. Cooper delineated as convert and controversialist. [1861].
Cazamian, L. Kingsley et Cooper: étude sur une source d'Alton Locke. Paris 1903.
Conklin, R. J. Cooper the Chartist. 1936.
Hobman, D. L. Cooper, Chartist and poet. Contemporary Rev Oct 1948.

WILLIAM DAVIES
1830–96

§1

Songs of a wayfarer. 1869.
The shepherd's garden. 1873. Poems.
The pilgrimage of the Tiber from its mouth to its source, with some account of its tributaries. 1873.
A fine old English gentleman, exemplified in the life and character of Lord Collingwood: a biographical study. 1875.
Dante Alighieri and his works. 1888.
Letters of James Smetham; memoir by W. Davies. 1891. Ed with S. Smetham et al.
The literary works of James Smetham. 1893. Ed Davies.
See also Wellesley p. 863.

SYDNEY THOMPSON DOBELL
1824–74

Collections

Poems: author's edition. Boston 1860. England in time of war, Sonnets on the war, other poems, Roman, Balder.
Poetical works, with introductory notice and memoir by J. Nichol. 2 vols 1875.
Poems, selected with an introductory memoir by Mrs Dobell. 1887.
Miles 5.
Home in war time: poems selected. Ed W. G. Hutchinson 1900.

§1

The Roman: a dramatic poem by Sydney Yendys. 1850, 1852.
Balder: part the first. 1853, 1854 (adds preface). Pt 2 never completed; fragments are ptd in Thoughts on art, philosophy and religion, below.
Sonnets on the war. 1855. With Alexander Smith.
America. [1869]. 2 sonnets written in 1855.
England in time of war. 1856. Poems.
Love, to a little girl. 1863. In verse.
Of parliamentary reform: a letter to a politician. 1865.
Thoughts on art, philosophy and religion. Ed J. Nichol 1876. Selected from unpbd works of Dobell.

Letters and Papers

Life and letters. Ed E. J[olly] 2 vols 1878.

§2

Balder. Fraser's Mag July 1854.
'Jones, T. P.' (W. E. Aytoun). Firmilian, or the student of Badajoz: a spasmodic tragedy. Edinburgh 1854. Ridicules Dobell and the Spasmodic School of poetry.
Gilfillan, G. In his A third gallery of literary portraits, Edinburgh 1854.
Buchanan, R. W. In his A look around literature, 1887.
Garnett, R. In Miles 5.
Sackville, Lady M. and E. Dobell. Dobell, nature poet. Poetry Rev 35 1944.
Thale, J. Dobell's Roman: the poet's experience and his work. Amer Imago 12 1955.
Preyer, R. Dobell and the Victorian epic. UTQ 30 1961.

ALFRED DOMETT
1811–87

Selections

Miles 4.

§1

Poems. 1833
Venice. 1839. A poem.
Narrative of the Wairoan massacre. 1843.
Petition to the House of Commons for the recall of Governor Fitzroy. 1845.
Ranolf and Amohia: a South-Sea day dream. 1872, 2 vols 1883 (rev). A poem.
Flotsam and jetsam: rhymes old and new. 1877.
It was the calm and silent night: a Christmas hymn. New York 1884.

Letters and Papers

Canadian journal [1833–5]. Ed E. A. Horsman and L. R. Benson, London Ontario 1955.
Diary 1872–85. Ed E. A. Horsman 1953.

§2

Gisbourne, W. In his New Zealand rulers and statesmen 1840–85, 1886.
—— In Miles 4.
Robert Browning and Domett. Ed F. G. Kenyon 1906. Letters from Browning to Domett.

SIR FRANCIS HASTINGS CHARLES DOYLE
1810–88

Selections

Miles 4.

§1

Miscellaneous verses. 1834, 1840.
The two destinies: a poem. 1844.
Oedipus, King of Thebes. 1849. Tr from the Oedipus tyrannus of Sophocles into English verse.
The vision of Er, the Pamphylian. [1850?]. A poem.
The Duke's funeral: a poem. [1852].
The return of the guards and other poems. 1866, 1883.
Lectures delivered before the University of Oxford 1868. 1869. Includes Inaugural lecture, Provincial poetry, and Dr Newman's Dream of Gerontius.
Lectures on poetry delivered at Oxford: second series. 1877. Includes lectures on Wordsworth, Scott and Shakespeare, with 14 original poems.
Robin Hood's bay: an ode. 1878.
To the memory of General Gordon. [1885]. A poem.
Reminiscences and opinions 1813–85. 1886, New York 1887. An autobiography.
Senilia. 1888 (priv ptd). A poem.
Racecourse and hunting field: the Doncaster St Leger by Doyle; and Melton in 1830, probably by B. Osbourne. Ed S. J. Looker 1931.
For 2 brief articles see Wellesley p. 878.

§2

Japp, A. H. In Miles 4.

ROWLAND EYES EGERTON-WARBURTON

1804–91

Poems. Chester 1833.
Hunting songs, ballads etc. 1834, 1846 (enlarged), 1859 (rev and enlarged), 1860, 1873 (enlarged), 1877; ed H. E. Maxwell, Liverpool 1912, London 1925.
The Hawkstone bow-meeting. 1835.
Cheshire chivalry. 1838. Verses describing a hunt.
Rhymes on the rules of the Cheshire bowmen. Northwich [1840?].
Three hunting songs. Chester 1855.
Four new songs. 1859.
Documents and letters relating to the cattle plague in the years 1747–9. Manchester 1866.
Epigrams and humorous verses by Rambling Richard. 1867.
A looking-glass for landlords. 1875. In verse.
Poems, epigrams and sonnets. 1877.
Songs and verses on sporting subjects. 1879.
Twenty-two sonnets, with illustrations. 1883.

JOHN ELLERTON

1826–93

§1

Hymns for schools and Bible classes. Brighton 1859.
Hymns, original and translated. 1888.
Ellerton also pbd sermons and devotional works.

§2

Julian.
Housman, H. Ellerton: being a collection of his writings on hymnology together with a sketch of his life and works. 1896.

HENRY ELLISON

1811–80

Selections

Miles 10 (11).

§1

Madmoments: or first verseattempts by a born natural. Malta 1833, 2 vols 1839.
Touches on the harp of nature. 1839.
The poetry of real life. 1844, 1851.
Stones from the old quarry: or moods of mind, by Henry Browne. 1875. Mainly sonnets.

§2

Brown, J. Henry Vaughan. In Horae subsecivae ser 1, Edinburgh 1882.
Grosart, A. B. In Miles 10 (11).

ANNE EVANS

1820–70

Poems and music, with a memorial preface by A. T. Ritchie. 1880.

SEBASTIAN EVANS

1830–1909

Selections

Miles 5.

§1

Sonnets on the death of the Duke of Wellington. Cambridge 1852.
Rhymes read in the Queen's drawing room at Ashton Hall, in memory of the birth of Robert Burns. [1859].
Brother Fabian's manuscripts and other poems. 1865.
Politics and Protestantism. 1868.
Songs and etchings. 1871.
In the studio: a decade of poems. 1875.
In quest of the Holy Graal: an introduction to the study of the legend. 1898.
The high history of the Holy Graal. 1898, 1903, [1910]. Tr Evans.
To the memory of W. M. Thackeray: a poem. 1899. Appended to Thackeray's writings in Nat Standard and Constitutional.
Lady Chillingham's houseparty: or Margery's romance. 1901. An English version of Le monde oùl'on s'ennuie by E. Pailleion, tr with F. B. Goldney.
Geoffrey of Monmouth. 1904 (Temple Classics). Tr Evans.
Galfridus: histories of the Kings of Britain. 1912. Tr Evans.
Evans pbd other trns and political tracts; see also Wellesley p. 890.

§2

Knight, J. In Miles 5.

FREDERICK WILLIAM FABER

1814–63

Collections

Poems. 1856, 1857 (3rd edn), [1886]; tr German, 1870 (with long biographical and critical introd).

Ausgewählte englische Gedichte von Dr Friedrich Wilhelm Faber. Ed W. Bottmann, Regensburg 1859. Poems in English with notes in German.
Heavenly promises: a selection of devotional poetry from the writings of Faber. 1898.
Characteristics from the writings of Father Faber. Ed J. Fitzpatrick 1903.
Selected poetry of Father Faber. Ed J. Fitzpatrick 1907.
Works, prose and verse. 11 vols 1914.

§1

The knights of St John. 1836. Newdigate prize poem.
The Cherwell water-lily and other poems. 1840.
The Styrian lake and other poems. 1842, [1907].
Sir Lancelot: a poem. 1844, 1857.
The rosary and other poems. 1845.
Hymns. Derby 1848, 1849 (enlarged as Jesus and Mary: or Catholic hymns), 1852 (enlarged), 1854 (enlarged as The oratory hymn book), 1861 (complete edn with 150 hymns).
Ethel's book: or tales of the angels. 1858, 1887, 1901. New York [1907]. Stories for children.
The first Christmas: the infant Jesus. 1889. Verses.
Faber also pbd numerous sermons and religious tracts, as well as contributing 9 lives to The lives of the English saints, 1844–5.

Letters and Papers

Bowden, J. E. The life and letters of Faber. 1869, [1888].

§2

Faber, F. A. A brief sketch of the early life of the late F. W. Faber. 1869, 1901 (rev).
Hall-Patch, W. Father Faber. 1914.
Plus, R. Frédéric William Faber. Études 108 1931.
Faber, G. C. In his Oxford apostles, 1933.
Blunt, H. F. A forgotten masterpiece: Faber's Sir Lancelot. Catholic World 157 1943.
Cassidy, J. F. The life of Father Faber. 1946.

JULIAN HENRY CHARLES FANE
1827–70

§1

Monody on the death of Adelaide the Queen Dowager. [Cambridge 1850]; rptd in A complete collection of the English poems which have obtained the Chancellor's Gold Medal vol 1, 1859.
Poems. 1852, 1852 (enlarged).
Poems by Heinrich Heine, translated. 1854.
Julian Fane, ad matrem 1849–57. [1857] (priv ptd).
Tannhäuser: or the battle of the bards, by Neville Temple [Fane] and Edward Trevor [E. R. B. Lytton]. 1861, Mobile 1863.

§2

Obituary. Times 21 April 1870.
Lytton, E. R. B. Fane: a memoir. 1871.

CHARLES ROBERT FORRESTER
1803–50

Selections

Miles 9 (10).

§1

Castle Baynard: or the days of John, by Hall Willis. 1824.
Absurdities in prose and verse, written and illustrated by Alfred Crowquill. 1827. Illustr A. H. Forrester.
Eccentric tales from the German of W. F. von Kosewitz. 1827. Kosewitz is Forrester.
Sir Roland: a romance of the twelfth century, by Hall Willis. 4 vols 1827.
The battle of the annuals: a fragment. 1835. Anon.
The Lord Mayor's fool. 1840.
Phantasmagoria of fun, edited and illustrated by Alfred Crowquill. 2 vols 1843. Illustr A. H. Forrester.

§2

Obituary. GM May 1850.
Miles, A. H. In Miles 9 (10).

THOMAS HORNBLOWER GILL
b. 1819

Selections

Miles 10 (11).

§1

The fortunes of faith: or Church and State. 1841. Verse.
The anniversaries: poems in commemoration of great men and great events. Cambridge 1858.
The papal drama: a historical essay. 1866.
The golden chain of praise: hymns. [1868], 1894 (greatly enlarged); tr Spanish, [1917].
Luther's birthday: hymns. 1883.
The triumph of Christ: memorials of Franklin Howorth. 1883.
Richard Serjeant: a biographical sketch. 1885.

§2

Julian, J. and W. G. Horder. In Julian.
Horder, W. G. In Miles 9 (10).

DORA GREENWELL
1821–82

Collections

Poems: selected and with biographical introduction by W. Dorling. 1889.
Miles 7 (8).
Poems. 1904.
Selected poems. Ed C. L. Maynard 1906.
Selections from the prose of Dora Greenwell. Ed W. G. Hanson, 1952 (with biographical introd).

§1

Poems. 1848.
Stories that might be true, with other poems. 1850.
A present heaven. 1855, 1867 (as The covenant of life and peace). Letters on the Gospel.
The patience of hope. 1860, 1862 (with preface by J. G. Whittier). A treatise on the spiritual life.
Poems. Edinburgh 1861, 1867 (omits some earlier poems and adds later ones).
Two friends. 1862, 1867; ed C. L. Maynard 1926, 1952. Essays on the spiritual life.
Home thoughts and home scenes, in original poems by J. Ingelow, D. Greenwell et al. 1865.
Essays. 1866. Includes Our single women, Hardened in good, Prayer, Popular religious literature, Christianos ad Leones.
Lacordaire. Edinburgh 1867.
The wow o'Rivven: or the idiot's home, by George MacDonald. 1868. Ed Dora Greenwell.
On the education of the imbecile. 1869. Rptd from North Br Rev and ed for Royal Albert Idiot Asylum, Lancaster.
Harmless Johnny: or the poor outcast of reason, by C. Bowles. 1868. Ed Dora Greenwell.
Carmina Crucis. 1869; ed C. L. Maynard 1906.
Colloquia crucis: a sequel to Two friends. 1871.

John Woolman: a biographical sketch. 1871.
Songs of salvation. 1873.
The soul's legend. 1873. Verse.
Liber humanitatis. 1875. Essays.
Camera obscura. 1876. Verse.
A basket of summer fruit. 1877. Essays.
Miss Greenwell also pbd other religious works. See Wellesley p. 851.

§2

Dorling, W. Memoirs of Dora Greenwell. 1885.
McC., L. S. Dora Greenwell. Aacademy 12 Aug 1905.
Maynard, C. L. The life of Dora Greenwell. 1926.
Bett, H. In his Studies in literature, 1929.
— Dora Greenwell. 1950.

THOMAS GORDON HAKE
1809–95

Selections

Miles 4.
Poems, selected with prefatory note by A. Meynell. 1894.

§1

Poetic lucubrations: containing the Misanthrope and other effusions. 1828.
The piromides: a tragedy. 1839.
A treatise on varicose capillaries. 1839.
Vates: or the philosophy of madness. 4 pts 1840.
The world's epitaph: a poem. 1866 (priv ptd).
On vital force. 1867.
Madeline, with other poems and parables. 1871. Partly rptd from World's epitaph, above.
Parables and tales. 1872; ed T. Hake 1917.
New Symbols. 1876. Poems.
Legends of the morrow. 1879. In verse.
Maiden ecstasy. 1880. Poems.
The serpent play: a divine pastoral, in 5 acts and in verse. 1883.
On the powers of the alphabet, 1. 1883. Only pt 1 pbd.
The new day: sonnets. Ed W. G. Hodgson 1890. With a portrait of Hake by D. G. Rossetti and long critical preface.
Memoirs of eighty years. 1892.

§2

Rossetti, D. G. Dr Hake's poems. Fortnightly Rev April 1873; rptd in Rossetti, Collected works vol 2, 1886 etc.
Bayne, T. In Miles 4.
Rossetti, W. M. In his Memoir of D. G. Rossetti, prefixed to D. G. Rossetti's family letters, 2 vols 1895.
Symons, A. In his Studies in two literatures, 1897.
Watts-Dunton, T. In his Old familiar faces, 1916.

SIR JOHN HANMER, afterwards BARON HANMER
1809–81

§1

Proteus and other poems. 1832 (priv ptd), 1833 (2nd edn).
Poems on various subjects. 1836 (priv ptd).
Era Cipolla and other poems. 1839.
Sonnets. 1840.
A memorial of the parish and family of Hanmer in Flintshire. 1877 (priv ptd). With an appendix of sonnets and epigrams.

§2

Obituary. Times 11, 15 March 1881.

ROBERT STEPHEN HAWKER
1803–75

Bibliographies

Woolf, C. Some uncollected authors 39: Hawker of Morwenstow. Book Collector 14 1965.

Collections

Poetical works. Ed J. G. Godwin 1879.
Poetical works. Ed A. Wallis 1899. Includes full bibliography.
Miles 3.
Twenty poems. Ed J. Drinkwater, Oxford 1925.
A selection of Hawker's Cornish ballads. Ed F. C. Hamlyn, Truro [1928].
Hawker of Morwenstow. [1932].

§1

Tendrils, by Reuben. Cheltenham 1821.
Pompeii: a prize poem. Oxford 1827; rptd in Oxford English prize poems, 1828.
Records of the western shore: first series. Oxford 1832, Camelford Cornwall 1868. Poems.
Poems. Stratton Cornwall 1836. Contains 3rd edn of Pompeii, 2nd edn of Records of the western shore ser 1, and 1st edn of Records of the western shore ser 2.
Minster church. 1836 (priv ptd). Poems.
A welcome to the Prince Albert . Oxford 1840. In verse.
Ecclesia: a volume of poems. Oxford 1840.
The poor man and his parish church. Plymouth 1843 (2nd edn). Poems.
Reeds shaken with the wind. 1843. Poems.
Reeds shaken with the wind: second cluster. Derby 1844.
Echoes from old Cornwall. 1846. Poems.
A voice from the place of S. Morwenna. 1849.
A letter to a friend. 1857. Anon. Poems.
The quest of the sangraal: chant the first. Exeter 1864 (priv ptd).
Cornish ballads and other poems. Oxford 1869 (including 2nd edn of The quest of the sangraal), 1884; ed C. E. Byles 1904.
Footprints of former men in far Cornwall. 1870; ed C. E. Byles [1903], 1948. Prose sketches with some verses.
Prose works. Ed J. G. Godwin 1893. A new edn of Footprints of former men in far Cornwall, with addns.
Hawker also issued a number of sermons and single poems as leaflets.

Letters and Papers

Stones broken from the rocks: extracts from note-books. Ed E. R. Appleton and C. E. Byles, Oxford 1922.

§2

Gould, S. B. The vicar of Morwenstow. 1875, 1876 (rev).
Lee, F. G. Memorials of Hawker. 1876.
Noble, J. A. In Miles 3.
— In his Sonnet in England and other essays, 1893.
Byles, C. E. Life and letters of Hawker. 1905.
Burrows, M. F. Hawker: a study of his thought and poetry. Oxford 1926.
Hawker of Morwenstow. TLS 20 Dec 1934.
Rowse, A. L. Hawker of Morwenstow: a belated medieval. E & S new ser 12 1959.

RICHARD HENRY (or HENGIST) HORNE
1803–84

Bibliographies

Shumaker, E. J. A concise bibliography of the complete works of Horne. Granville Ohio 1943.

Selections

Miles 2.

§1

Exposition of the false medium and barriers excluding men of genius from the public. 1833. Anon.
The spirit of peers and people: a nation tragi-comedy. 1834.
Introduction to characteristics, by W. Hazlitt. 1837. Introd by Horne.
Cosmo de'Medici: an historical tragedy. 1837, 1875 (with added poems). In verse.
The death of Marlowe: a tragedy in one act. 1837, 1870 (5th edn). Chiefly in verse; rptd in Works of Marlow, ed A. H. Bullen vol 3, 1885.
The life of Van Amburgh the brute tamer, with anecdotes of his pupils, by Ephraim Watts. [1838].
Gregory VII: a tragedy in one act. 1840, 1849 (3rd edn). In verse, includes an essay on tragic influence.
The history of Napoleon. 2 vols 1841, 1 vol 1879.
Poems of Chaucer, modernized. 1841. By various writers. Horne contributed the introd and 3 tales.
Orion: an epic poem in three books. 1843 (3 edns), Melbourne 1854 (adds preface), London 1872 (9th and definitive edn); ed E. Partridge 1928 (with introd on Horne's life and work).
A new spirit of the age, edited [and largely written] by Horne. 2 vols 1844, 1 vol 1844; ed W. Jerrold, Oxford 1907 (WC).
Ballad romances. 1846.
The good-natured bear: a story for children of all ages. 1846, 1856, [1878].
Memoirs of a London doll, written by herself. Ed 'Mrs Fairstar' 1846, Boston 1852, London 1855, New York 1922 (introd by C. W. Hart), London 1923.
Judas Iscariot: a miracle play, with other poems. 1848; rptd in Bible tragedies, [1891].
The poor artist: or seven eye-sights and one object. 1850, 1871 (adds preliminary essay on varieties of vision in man).
Memoir of the Emperor Napoleon. [1850?].
The dreamer and the worker: a story of the present time. 2 vols 1851.
The complete works of Shakespeare. [1857]. Ed Horne.
Australian facts and prospects, to which is prefixed the author's Australian autobiography. 1859.
Prometheus the fire bringer: a drama in verse. Edinburgh 1864, Melbourne 1866.
The two Georges: a dialogue of the dead. Melbourne [1865?]. In verse.
The south-sea sisters: a lyric masque. Melbourne [1866]. With trns into French and German verse.
Galatea secunda: an odaic cantata. Melbourne 1867.
Was Hamlet mad? being a series of critiques on the acting of the late W. Montgomery. Ed R.H.H. [1871] Written in Melbourne in 1867.
Parting legacy of R. H. Horne to Australia (John Ferncliff: an Australian narrative poem). Melbourne [1868].
The great peace-maker: a sub-marine dialogue. 1872 (priv ptd), 1872. Poem, rptd from Household Words.
Ode to the Mikado of Japan. 1873.
Psyche apocalypté: a lyric drama. 1876. Drafts and correspondences between Horne and his co-author E. B. Browning, with connecting narrative by Horne, all rptd from St James Mag and United Empire Rev.
Letters of Elizabeth Barrett Browning addressed to Horne. Ed S. R. T. Mayer 2 vols 1877. Connecting narrative by Horne.
The history of duelling in all countries, translated from the French of Coustard de Massi, with introductions and concluding chapter by 'Sir L. O'Trigger'. [1880].
King Nihil's round table: or the regicide's symposium. 1881. A dramatic scene.
Bible tragedies: John the Baptist, or the valour of the soul; Rahman, the apocryphal book of Job's wife; Judas Iscariot, a mystery. [1881]. In prose and verse.
Soliloquium fratris Rogeri Baconis. 1882 (priv ptd). In verse, rptd from Fraser's Mag.
The last words of Cleanthes: a poem. [1883. Rptd from Longman's Mag.
Sithron the star-stricken, translated by Salem ben Uzäir. 1883. Written in English by Horne.
King Penguin: a legend of the south sea isles. Ed F. M. Fox, New York 1925.
Horne edited Monthly Repository of Theology & General Lit 1836–7. *See also* Wellesley pp. 945–6.

§2

Poe, E. A. R. H. Horne. Graham's Mag (Philadelphia) March 1844; rptd in Works, ed C. F. Richardson vol 6, New York 1902.
Powell, T. In his Pictures of the living authors of Britain, 1851. Chiefly on Gregory VII and Orion.
Forman, H. B. In his Our living poets, 1871.
— In Miles 2.
— In Literary anecdotes of the nineteenth century, ed W. R. Nicoll and T. J. Wise vol 1, 1895.
Gosse, E. In his Portraits and sketches, 1912.
Dickens, C. Notes and comments on certain writings by Horne. 1920 (priv ptd). 6 letters from Dickens to Horne.
Letters from A. C. Swinburne to Horne. 1920 (priv ptd).
Mabbott, T. O. Changes in the text of Horne's orion. N & Q 1928.
Partridge, E. In his Literary sessions, 1932.
Shackford, M. E. B. Browning, Horne: two studies. Wellesley Mass 1935.
Mineka, F. E. The dissidence of dissent: the Monthly Repository 1806–38. Chapel Hill 1944.
DeVane, W. C. and K. L. Knickerbocker (ed). New letters of Robert Browning. New Haven 1950. Includes letter to Horne and several references to him.
Fielding, K. J. Dickens and Horne. English 9 1952.
Pearl, C. Always morning: the life of 'Orion' Horne. Melbourne 1960.

WILLIAM WALSHAM HOW
1823–97

Selections

Miles 10 (12).

§1

Psalms and hymns, compiled by T. B. Morrell and How. 1854, 1860, 1872.
Poems: enlarged edition. [1886].
Was lost and is found: a tale of the London mission of 1874. [1886]. In verse.
Public worship. [1894]. In verse.
A sermon in a children's ward in a hospital. 1896. In verse.
A souvenir of the late Bishop Walsham How. [1898]. A poem, To a mother on the death of her boy.
How was one of the compilers of Church hymns, 1871, *and pbd many sermons and tracts; see also* Wellesley p. 947.

§2

Miles, A. H. In Miles 10 (12).
How, F. D. How: a memoir. 1898.
— How: first Bishop of Wakefield. 1909.
Julian.

CECIL FRANCES HUMPHREYS, afterwards ALEXANDER
1818–95

Collections

Poems. Ed W. Alexander 1896.
Selected poems of William Alexander and Cecil Frances Alexander. Ed A. P. Graves 1930.

§1

Nearly all the following works were issued under the initials C.F.H. or (after 1850) C.F.A.

Verses for holy seasons. 1846. Preface by W. F. Hook.
The lord of the forest and his vassals: an allegory. 1848.
Hymns for little children. 1848. Preface by J. Keble.
Moral songs. 1849, [1850?], 1867, 1873, 1880.
Narrative hymns for village schools. 1853.
Poems on subjects in the Old Testament. 1854, 1871.
Hymns descriptive and devotional. 1858, 1880.
The legend of the golden prayers and other poems. 1859.
The Sunday book of poetry, selected by C. F. A. 1864.
Some account of the parish church of St Colmanell, Aloghill by A. T. Lee; with an original poem by C. F. A. [1867].
The Baron's little daughter and other tales. 1875.
Hymns for children. 1894.
Quireach phádruig: or St Patrick's breastplate. 1902. Mrs Alexander's trn and the Irish text.
Mrs Alexander also pbd other religious works.

§2

Dublin Univ Mag Oct 1858, Sept 1859.
Obituary. Times 14, 19 Oct 1893.
Gwynn, S. Sunday Mag Jan 1896.
Davidson, J. In Julian.

JOHN WILLIAM INCHBOLD
1830–88

§1

Annus amoris. 1876.

§2

Obituary. Athenaeum 4 Feb 1888.

JEAN INGELOW
1820–97

Collections

Poetical works. Boston 1880, New York [188?], Troy NY [1887], Boston 1894.
Lyrical and other poems. 1886. Selected poems.
Miles 7 (8).
Poetical works. 1898. Rptd from Poems, 2 vols 1893, and Poems: third series, 1888.
Poems. 1906 (ML).
Poems, selected and arranged by A. Lang. 1908.
Poems 1850–69. Oxford 1913.

§1

A rhyming chronicle of incidents and feelings. Ed E. Harston 1850. Anon.
Allerton and Drieux: or the war of opinion. 2 vols 1857. Anon.
Tales of Orris. Bath 1860, London 1865 (as Stories told to a child; omits one story). Stories, many later rptd separately.
Poems. 1863 (23 edns by 1880).
Studies for stories. 2 vols 1864, 1 vol Boston 1865. Anon.
Home thoughts and home scenes. 1865. Verse.
Songs of seven. Boston 1866, 1881.
The wild duck-shooter, and I have a right. 1867. Stories.
A story of doom and other poems. 1867 (6 edns by 1880).
A sister's bye-hours. 1868. Anon. Stories, many rptd separately.
Mopsa the fairy. 1869. A long fairy story.
The little wonder-horn. 1872. Stories, many rptd separately.
Off the Skelligs. 4 vols 1872, 1879.
Fated to be free. 3 vols 1875. Rptd from Good Words.
One hundred holy songs, carols and sacred ballads. 1878.
Sarah de Berenger: a novel. 1879, 3 vols 1880, 1886.
Poems. 2 vols 1880, New York 1880, London 1893. Vol 1 rptd from 23rd edn of Poems (1863) with addns; vol 2 rptd from 6th edn of A story of doom and other poems.
Don John: a story. 3 vols 1881, 1881.
The high tide on the coast of Lincolnshire 1571. Boston 1883. Verse.
Poem: third series. 1885, 1888.
Poems of the old days and the new. Boston 1885.
John Jerome, his thoughts and ways: a book without beginning. 1886.
Very young and Quite another story. 1890. A story.
A motto changed. New York 1894.
The old man's prayer. [1895]. Drama in verse.

§2

Forman, H. B. In his Our living poets, 1871.
Robertson, E. S. In her English poetesses, 1883.
Bell, M. In Miles 7 (8).
Obituary. Times 21 July 1897; Athenaeum 24 July 1897.
Some recollections of Jean Ingelow. 1901.
Hearn, L. In Appreciations of poetry, ed J. Erskine, New York 1916.
Stedman, E. A. An appreciation. 1935. With extracts from her work.
Singers-Biggers, G. Jean Ingelow. English 3 1940.
King, H. D. Calverley and Jean Ingelow. N & Q 30 Aug 1952.

WILLIAM JOSIAH IRONS
1812–83

§1

Hymn for advent: Dies irae [of Thomas de Celano] translated [as Day of wrath! o day of mourning!]. 1854.
The idea of a national Church. [1862].
Analysis of human responsibility. [1869].
Christianity as taught by S Paul. Oxford 1870.
Psalms and hymns for the church. [1875], 1883.
Irons also pbd many sermons and theological tracts.

§2

Obituary. Times 20 June 1883.
Miles, A. H. In Miles 10 (12).
Julian.

WILLIAM JOHNSON, later CORY
1823–92

Collections

Ionica. 1891. A rptd of Ionica (1858) and Ionica II, with 85 additional poems and biographical introd and notes by A. C. Benson.
Miles 5.

§1

Ionica. 1858 (anon), 1891, 1905.
Plato, written 1843. In A complete collection of the English poems which have obtained the Chancellor's Gold Medal at the University of Cambridge vol 1, Cambridge 1859.
Eton reform. 2 vols 1861.
On the education of the reasoning faculties. In Essays on a liberal education, ed F. W. Farrar 1867.
Nuces: exercises in the syntax of the public school Latin primer. 3 vols 1867–70.
Early modern Europe. Cambridge 1869.
Lucretilis: an introduction to the art of writing Latin lyric verses. 2 vols 1871.
Iophon: an introduction to the art of writing Greek iambic verses. 1873.
Ionica II. 1877 (priv ptd). Anon.
A guide to modern English history [1815–35]. 2 vols 1880–2.
Hints for Eton masters. 1898.

Letters and Papers

Extracts from the letters and journals, selected and arranged by F. W. Cornish. Oxford 1897 (priv ptd).

§2

Nicoll, W. R. and T. J. Wise. In their Literary anecdotes of the nineteenth century vol 2, 1896.
Paul, H. Stray leaves. 1906. With personal reminiscences.
Notes of the table talk of Cory. In Gathered leaves from the prose of Mary E. Coleridge, ed E. Sichel 1910.
Brett, R. B. Ionicus. 1923. A biography and appreciation, including letters and extracts from Ionica and Lucretilis.
Madan, G. William Cory. Cornhill Mag Aug 1928.
Cory, P. In search of a grandfather. Blackwood's Mag Oct 1946.
Mackenzie, F. C. Cory: a biography. 1950. With unpbd poems.

EBENEZER JONES
1820–60

Selections

Miles 5.

§1

Studies of sensation and event: poems. 1843; ed R. H. Shepherd 1879 (with memorial notices by S. Jones and W. J. Linton).
The land monopoly. 1849.

§2

Shepherd, R. H. In his Forgotten books worth remembering, 1878. A series of monographs.
Watts, T. Athenaeum 21–8 Sept, 12 Oct 1878.
Linton, W. J. In Miles 5.
Rees, T. M. Ebenezer Jones, the neglected poet. [1909].

ERNEST CHARLES JONES
1819–68

Selections

Miles 4.
Ernest Jones, Chartist: selections from writings and speeches, with introduction and notes by J. Saville. 1952.

§1

Infantine effusions. Hamburg 1830.
The student of Padua: a domestic tragedy. 1836. A play in verse.
The wood-spirit: a novel. 2 vols 1841, 1855.
My life: a poem. 1846. Introd signed 'Percy-Vere'.
The maid of Warsaw, or the tyrant Czar: a tale of the last Polish revolution. 1854.
The lass and the lady, or love's ladder: a tale of thrilling interest. 1855. Completed by T. Frost. Pbd in parts.
Woman's wrongs: a series of tales. 1855.
The battle-day, and other poems. 1855.
The song of the lower classes: a song of Cromwell's time. 1856.
Songs of democracy. 1856. Song of the day labourers, A song of resurrection, The marriage feast, Song of the factory slave. Pbd separately as flysheets.
The Emperor's vigil, and the waves and the war. 1856.
The revolt of Hindustan, or the new world: a poem. 1857.
Corayda, a tale of faith and chivalry, and other poems. 1860.
Democracy: a debate between Professor Blackie and the late E. Jones. 1885.
Jones also pbd lectures on social and political subjects.

§2

Obituary. Times 27, 29 Jan, 31 March 1868.
Leary, F. The life of Ernest Jones. 1887.
Miles, A. H. In Miles 4.

FRANCES ANNE KEMBLE, afterwards BUTLER
1809–93

Selections

Miles 7 (8).

§1

Francis the first: an historical drama. 1832 (7 edns), New York 1833. In verse.
Journal. 2 vols 1835, 1 vol Brussels 1835 (as Journal of a residence in America).
The star of Seville. 1837, New York 1837. A play.
Poems. Philadelphia 1844, Boston 1859.
Poems. 1844. Contents similar to US edn, above, but arranged differently; later edns follow the US edn.
A year of consolation. 2 vols 1847. Travels in Italy.
Journal of a residence on a Georgian plantation in 1838–9. 1863. Extracts on slavery were rptd by emancipation groups.
Plays: An English tragedy, Mary Stuart (translated from the German of Schiller), Mademoiselle de Belle Isle (translated from the French of Dumas). 1863.
Poems. 1866. Mostly new.
Record of a girlhood: an autobiography. 3 vols 1878, 1879. Rptd in part from Atlantic Monthly.
Notes upon some of Shakespeare's plays. 1882. Includes On the stage, ed G. Arliss, New York 1926.
Records of later life. 3 vols 1882.
Adventures of John Timothy Homespun in Switzerland: a play stolen from the French of Tartarin de Tarascon. 1889.
Far away and long ago. 1889. A novel.
Further records 1848–83. 2 vols 1890. Letters as a sequel to Record of a girlhood and Records of later life.
See also Wellesley p. 965.

§2

Craven, P. M. A.A. La jeunesse de F. Kemble. Paris 1880.
Japp, A. H. In Miles 7 (8).

James, H. In his Essays in London and elsewhere, New York 1893.
Letters of Edward FitzGerald to Fanny Kemble 1871–83. Ed W. A. Wright 1895.
Pope-Hennessy, U. In her Three English women in America, 1929.
Bobbé, D. Fanny Kemble. New York 1931. Includes a full list of books and articles on Fanny Kemble and her period.
Driver, L. S. Fanny Kemble. Chapel Hill 1933.
Armstrong, M. Fanny Kemble: a passionate Victorian. 1936.
Gibbs, H. Affectionately yours, Fanny: Fanny Kemble and the theatre. 1945.
Buckmaster, H. Fire in the heart. New York 1948.
Fanny Kemble in New York. Columbia Lib Columns 11 1961. Excerpt from G. T. Strong's diary.
Myers, A. B. Miss Kemble's keys. Ibid.

CHARLES RANN KENNEDY

1808–67

Classical education reformed. 1837.
Ode on the birth of the Prince. 1842. On Albert Edward, Prince of Wales.
Poems, original and translated. 1843, 1857 (re-arranged and enlarged).
The Olynthiac and other public creations of Demosthenes. 1848. Tr with notes by Kennedy. Frequently rptd.
A letter to the Lord Chancellor on the subject of circuit leagues. 1850.
Specimens of Greek and Latin verse, chiefly translations. 1853. English verse tr into Greek and Latin.
Francis Beaumont: a tragedy. Birmingham [1860?]. In verse.
The works of Virgil. 1861.
Hannibal: a poem. [1866].
Kennedy also wrote on classical and legal subjects.

LAETITIA ELIZABETH LANDON, afterwards MACLEAN

1802–38

Collections

The poetical works of L. E. L. 3 vols 1827.
The poetical works of L. E. L. [1830?] Containing The Venetian bracelet and other poems.
The miscellaneous poetical works of L. E. L. 1835.
Works. 2 vols Philadelphia 1838, 1847.
Poetical works. 4 vols 1839.
Poetical works, with a memoir of the author. 2 vols 1850, 1853, 1855, 1867.
Complete works. 2 vols Boston 1856.
Poetical works. Ed W. B. Scott [1873], [1880].
Miles 7 (8).

§1

The fate of Adelaide: a Swiss romantic tale, and other poems. 1821.
The improvisatrice and other poems. 1824, 1835 (6th edn), 1831.
The troubadour, catalogue of pictures and historical sketches. 1825 (3 ends), 1827.
The golden violet, with its tales of romance and chivalry, and other poems. 1827.
The Venetian bracelet, the lost Pleiad, a history of the lyre and other poems. 1828.
Romance and reality. 3 vols 1831, 1 vol 1856 (with memoir). A novel.
Francesca Carrara. 3 vols 1834. A novel.
The vow of the peacock, and other poems. 1835.
Traits and trials of early life. 1836, 1844. Tales with poems interspersed.
Ethel Churchill: or the two brides. 3 vols 1837, 1847. A novel.
A birthday tribute, addressed to the Princess Alexandrina Victoria. [1837]. In verse.
Duty and inclination: a novel, edited by Miss Landon. 3 vols 1838.
Floers of loveliness. 1838, [1854]. Poems, with Lady Blessington and T. H. Bayly.
The Easter gift: a religious offering. [1838].
The Zenana, and minor poems of L. E. L.; with a memoir by Emma Roberts. 1839.
Lady Anne Granard: or keeping up appearances. 3 vols 1842, 1 vol 1847. A novel.
The gift of friendship, with contributions by L. E. L. [1877].
L.E.L. also edited or contributed to various annuals, scrap-books etc, as well as writing numerous articles and reviews for W. Jerdan's Literary Gazette *from c. 1820.*

Letters and Papers

Blanchard, S. L. Life and literary remains of L.E.L. 2 vols 1841. Vol 2 consists of unpbd works by L.E.L.

§2

S[heppard], S. Characteristics of the genius and writings of L.E.L. 1841.
Elwood, A. K. In his Memoirs of the literary ladies of England vol 2, 1843.
Hall, S. C. and A. M. Memories of authors: Miss Landon. Atlantic Monthly March 1865.
Robertson, E. S. In his English poetesses, 1883.
Bates, W. In his Maclise portrait-gallery of illustrious literary characters, 1883.
Bell, M. In Miles 7 (8).
Lefèvre-Deumier, J. In his Célébrités anglaises: essais et études biographiques et littéraires, Paris 1895.
Enfield, D. E. L.E.L.: a mystery of the thirties. 1928.
Courtney, J. E. Alphabetical graces. London Mercury Aug 1932.
Flower, R. Letitia E. Landon. BM Quart 11 1937.
Stevenson, L. Miss Landon, 'The milk-and-watery moon of our darkness' 1824–30. MLQ 8 1947.
Ashton, H. Letty Landon. 1951.

ROBERT LEIGHTON

1822–69

Selections

Miles 5.

§1

Rimes and poems: by Robin. Glasgow [1850?].
Poems by Robin. 1855.
[Burns centenary poem.] In Burns centenary poems, ed G. Anderson and J. Finlay, Glasgow 1859.
Rhymes and poems. 1861, 1861.
Poems. Liverpool 1866, 1869.
Scotch words, and the bapteesement o' the bairn. 1869 (3 edns), 1870, New York 1873. With biography.
Reuben and other poems. 1875.
Records and other poems. 1880. Reuben and Records together constitute Leighton's collected works.

§2

Miles, A. H. In Miles 5.

WILLIAM JAMES LINTON

1812–98

Collections

Prose and verse: written and published in the course of fifty years 1836–86. 20 vols [1886]. A collection made by Linton and presented to BM.
Poems and translations. 1889.
Miles 4.

§1

Modern slavery by Robert de la Mennais, translated from the French by Linton. 1840.
The life of Thomas Paine. 1840. Anon.
Bob Thin or the poorhouse fugitive. 1845 (priv ptd). A satire.
The lovers' stratagem and other tales. 1849.
The people's land and an easy way to recover it. 1850. Letters on Ireland.
The plaint of freedom. Newcastle-on-Tyne 1852.
Help for Poland. [1854].
The ferns of the English lake country. 1865.
Claribel and other poems. 1865. Claribel is a dramatic poem in 2 acts.
Ireland for the Irish: rhymes and reasons against landlordism. New York 1867.
The flower and the star, and other stories for children. Boston 1868, London [1892].
The religion of organization. Boston 1869. An essay.
The house that Tweed built. 1871. Anon. A political lampoon in verse.
The Paris commune. Boston 1871.
Pot-pouri. New York 1875. Parodies of E. A. Poe.
Famine: a masque. Hamden Conn 1875, [1887].
The American odyssey: adventures of Ulysses: exposed in modest hudibrastic measure by Abel Reid and A. N. Broome. Washington 1876. Reid and Broome are pseudonymous for Linton.
Poetry of America. 1878. Selections from 100 poets, with some Negro melodies.
James Watson: a memoir. Hamden Conn 1879 [priv ptd], Manchester 1880.
Reminiscences of Eben Jones. In Jones' Studies of sensation and event, 1879.
Voices of the dead. [1879?]. A letter to the editor of Nineteenth Century.
Golden apples of Hesperus: poems not in the collections. New Haven 1882. Ed Linton.
Cetewayo and Dean Stanley. [1880].
Wind-falls, two hundred and odd. [1882]. Quotations ed Linton.
Rare poems of the sixteenth and seventeenth centuries. New Haven 1882 (priv ptd), London 1883. Partly a reprint of Golden apples of Hesperus, above.
English verse. 5 vols New York 1883. Ed Linton and R. H. Stoddard.
Love-lore. Hamden Conn 1887 (priv ptd), 1895 (adds other poems).
Catoninetales: a domestic epic by Hattie Brown. Ed [actually written] by W.J.L. 1891. Parodies.
Wells, C. J. Stories after nature, with a preface by W.J.L. 1891.
Heliconundrums. Hamden Conn 1892 (priv ptd).
European republicans: recollections of Mazzini and friends. 1893.
Life of J. G. Whittier. 1893.
A Christmas carol. [Hamden Conn? 1893].
Ultima verba. 1895 (priv ptd).
Memories. 1895.
Darwin's probabilities. Hamden Conn 1896. A review of The descent of man.
Linton also edited English Republic, Illuminated Mag *and* National.

§2

Kitton, F. G. W. J. Linton. Eng Illustr Mag April 1891.
Bullen, A. H. In Miles 4.
Obituary. Times 3 Jan 1898; Athenaeum 8–15 Jan 1898.
Layard, G. S. In his Life of Mrs Lynn Linton, 1901.
Hopson, W. F. Side lights on Linton 1812–97. PBSA 27 1933.

FREDERICK LOCKER-LAMPSON

1821–95

Bibliographies

Livingston, F. V. Bookman's Jnl May, July–Sept 1924. Detailed account of all edns of Locker-Lampson's works.

Selections

A selection from the works of Frederick Locker. 1865. Includes 20 unpbd pieces, the rest rev.
Miles 5.

§1

London lyrics. 1857, 1862 (with alterations and omissions, adds 20 new poems), 1868 (priv ptd as Poems) (adds 6 poems, omits others), 1870 (adds 6 poems), 1872 (adds 10 poems), 1874 (adds 8 poems), 1876 (final revision, adds 6 poems), 1882 (as London rhymes; omits much, but adds 9 poems), New York 1883 (pirated as Poems), 1884 (authorized edn, as Poems, and differing slightly from 1876 edn); ed A. D. Godley 1903 (from 1857 edn); ed A. Dobson 1904 (definitive edn).
Lyra elegantiarum. 1867 (suppressed), 1867 (rev), 1891 (rev and enlarged, with C. Kernahan). A collection of English vers de société and vers d'occasion.
Patchwork. 1879 (priv ptd), 1879. A commonplace book, with 5 poems by Locker-Lampson, 3 of which are new.
The Rowfant library. 1886. A catalogue. An appendix, with preface by A. Birel land memorial verses by A. Dobson, A. Lang, Lord Crewe and W. S. Blunt pbd separately 1900.
My confidences: an autobiographical sketch addressed to my descendents. Ed A. Birell 1896, 1908.

§2

Dobson, A. In Miles 5.
Swinburne, A. C. In his Studies in prose and poetry, 1894.
Birell, A. Locker-Lampson: a character sketch. 1920.
Locker-Lampson, O. Locker-Lampson, with some unpublished sketches and poems. Scribner's Mag April 1921.
—— Recollections of Locker-Lampson. Cornhill Mag Jan–Feb 1921.
Kernahan, C. Austin Dobson and Lyra elegantiarum. London Quart Rev 1922; Living Age 4 March 1922.
Dunbar, J. R. Some letters of Joaquin Miller to Locker. MLQ 11 1950. 10 letters.
Flanagan, J. T. Dr Holmes selects American verse. JEGP 51 1952. Rejected suggestions for Lyra elegantiarum.
Bates, M. C. That delightful man. Harvard Lib Bull 13 1959.
Ketton-Cremer, R. W. Locker-Lampson's Lyra elegantiarum, 1867. Book Collector 8 1959.

CAPEL LOFFT

1806–73

§1

The Whigs: their prospects and policy. 1835.
Self-formation: or the history of an individual mind. 2 vols 1837, 1 vol Boston 1896. Anon. A mental autobiography.

Ernest, or political regeneration: a poem. 1839 (anon), 1868 (as Ernest: the rule of right, adds a long preface on the nature of poetry, and much revision). A long poem on the history of Chartism.
New Testament: suggestions for reformation of Greek text on principles of logical criticism, by 'R. E. Storer'. 1868.

§2

[Millman, H. H.] Quart Rev 65 1840. Review of Ernest.

THOMAS TOKE LYNCH

1818–71

Selections

The rivulet birthday book, compiled by M. Theobald. [1891].
Miles 10 (11).

§1

Thoughts on a day. 1844 (anon), 1856 (adds a morning and an evening hymn).
Memorials of Theophilus, Trinal student. 1850, 1853, 1868 (enlarged), 1882. 54 poems in 1st edn, 81 in 3rd edn.
Essays on some of the forms of literature. 1853.
Lectures in aid of self improvement, addressed to young men and others. 1853.
The rivulet: a contribution to sacred song. 1855, 1856, 1868 (enlarged).
The ethics of quotation, by Silent Long. 1856. With Songs controversial, below, this pamphlet constitutes Lynch's reply to the attack made on Rivulet, above, in Br Banner.
Songs controversial, by Silent Long. 1856.
The Mornington lecture: Thursday evening addresses. 1870.
Lynch also pbd sermons and religious works.

§2

Most of this material, which is selected, concerns the controversy over the supposed pantheism of Rivulet.
Campbell, J. Nonconformist theology. [1856]. 'On the pernicious errors of Mr Lynch's Rivulet'.
Grant, B. What is negative theology? [1856].
—— 'What's it all about?' 1856.
James, J. A. The Rivulet controversy. 1856.
Little, J. The controversy—what results? 1856.
Binney, T. Who is right and who wrong? 1857.
White, W. Memoir of Lynch. 1874. Includes a list of Lynch's writings.
Horder, W. G. In Miles 10 (11).

CHARLES MACKAY

1814–89

Collections

Selected poems. In Modern Scottish minstrel, ed C. Rogers vol 6, 1857. With memoir by F. Bennoch.
Collected songs. 1859 (for 1858). Includes 100 songs pbd for first time.
Poetical works. 1868.
Poetical works. 1876. With introd rptd from Egeria and other poems.
Selected poems and songs. 1888. Introd of short criticisms by D. Jerrold, G. Combe and A. B. Reach, with a long anon review rptd from St James's Mag.
Miles 4.

§1

Songs and poems. 1834.
A history of London. 1838.
The hope of the world and other poems. 1840.
The Thames and its tributaries. 2 vols 1840.
Longbeard, Lord of London: a romance. 3 vols 1841, 1850 (as Longbeard: or the revolt of the Saxons).
Memoirs of extraordinary popular delusions. 3 vols 1841, 2 vols 1852 etc; ed B. M. Baruch, Boston 1932.
The salamandrine: or love and immortality. 1842, 1853, 1856.
Legends of the isles and other poems. Edinburgh 1845, 1857 (as Legends of the isles and Highland gatherings). Some of the poems rptd 1856 as Ballads and lyrical songs.
Voices from the crowd, and other poems. 1846, 1857 (5th edn rev). Rptd from Daily News.
The scenery and poetry of the English lakes. 1846, 1852.
Education of the people, and the necessity for the establishment of a national system. Glasgow 1846, 1852.
Voices from the mountains. 1847, 1857.
[Poem]. In G. Cruickshank, The bottle, [1847].
Town lyrics and other poems. 1848.
[Poem]. In G. Cruickshank, The drunkard's children, 1848.
Egeria: or the spirit of nature; with other poems. 1850. With an introductory essay on poetry.
The life-boat. 1850. A song.
Far, far upon the sea. [1850?], [1860?].
Cheer, boys, cheer. [1850?].
Tubal-Cain. [1850?]; ed L. A. Sloan, Chicago [1916].
The world as it is. 3 vols 1850–4. With W. C. Taylor. A system of modern geography.
Life and times of Sir Robert Peel from the date of his final retirement to his premature death. 1851. Vol 4 of the Life and times of Sir Robert Peel, carried to vol 3 by C. Taylor.
The Mormons: or latter-day saints. 1851, 1852, 1853, 1857.
The reason-why. [1852]. An anti-Corn law ballad.
Songs for music. 1856.
The lump of gold, and other poems. 1856.
Ballads and lyrical poems. 1856, 1859.
The joy-bell and the requiem. In In honorem: songs of the brave, 1856.
Under green leaves. 1857.
Life and liberty in America. 2 vols 1859, New York 1859.
A man's heart: a poem. 1860.
Original songs, by S. Lover, C. Mackay et al. 1861.
The history of the United States of America. 2 vols 1861.
The gouty philosopher. 1862. Essays.
Studies from the antique and sketches from nature. 1864.
The whiskey-demon. 1866.
Street tramways for London. 1868.
The souls of the children. Ramsgate 1869.
Under the blue sky. 1871. Papers rptd from All the Year Round, Robin Goodfellow etc.
Baron Gimbrosh, D Phil and sometime Governor of Barataria. 1872.
Lost beauties of the English language: an appeal to authors. 1874.
Forty years' recollections of life, literature and public affairs. 2 vols 1877.
Gideon Brown: a story of the covenant. 1877. Ed Mackay.
The Gaelic etymology of the languages of western Europe. 1877.
The Liberal Party. 1880.
Luck: and what came of it. 3 vols 1881. A novel.
The poetry and humour of the Scottish language. Paisley 1882. In part rptd from Blackwood's Mag.
Interludes and undertones: or music at twilight. 1884 'for 1883'.
New light on some obscure words and phrases in the works of Shakespeare and his contemporaries. 1884.
The founders of the American republic. Edinburgh 1885.
A glossary of obscure words and phrases in the works of Shakespeare and his contemporaries. 1884.
The founders of the American republic. Edinburgh 1885.

A glossary of obscure words and phrases in the works of Shakespeare and his contemporaries. 1887.
Through the long day. 2 vols 1887.
A dictionary of Lowland Scotch. Edinburgh 1888 (priv ptd), London 1888. With an appendix of Scottish proverbs.
Gossamer and snowdrift: posthumous poems. Ed E. Mackay 1890.
Mackay also edited anthologies and periodicals, was Times correspondent in American Civil War and contributed extensively to Blackwood's Mag; see Wellesley pp. 992–3.

§2

Powell, T. In his Pictures of the living authors of Britain, 1851.
Miles, A. H. In Miles 4.
Wykoff, G. S. England's forgotten Civil War correspondent. South Atlantic Quart 1927.

SIR THEODORE MARTIN
1816–1909

§1

Disputation between the body and soul. 1838. Poem, signed T.M., with other poems by Martin signed E.N., Martinus Scriblerus and I.G.
Dante and Beatrice. [1845?].
The book of ballads, edited by 'Bon Gaultier'. 1845, [1849], (with new ballads), 1857 (5th edn), 1903 (16th edn). By Martin and W. E. Aytoun.
Hertz, King Rene's daughter. 1850. Trn.
Öhlenschläger, Correggio: a tragedy, with notes. 1854. Trn.
Madonna Pia: a tragedy in verse. 1855 (priv ptd), 1860.
Öhlenschläger, Aladdin: or the wonderful lamp. 1857. Trn.
Goethe, Poems and ballads. 1859, 1860 (rev and enlarged), 1877, 1907. Tr with W. E. Aytoun.
The odes of Horace translated into English verse. 1860, 1861.
The poems of Catullus translated into English verse. 1861, 1875.
Dante, The Vita nuova. 1862, 1871. Trn.
Poems, original and translated. 1863 (priv ptd).
Goethe, Faust pt 1. 1865, 1866, 1877. Pts 1–2 1870, 1954. Trn.
Memoir of W. E. Aytoun. 1867.
Horace. 1870.
Schiller, Complete works, ed C. J. Hempel vol 1. William Tell tr Martin. 1870.
The odes, epodes and satires of Horace. 1870, 1881. Trn.
Essays on the drama. 2 vols 1874–89.
The life of his Royal Highness the Prince Consort. 5 vols 1875–80; tr French, 1883.
Heine, Poems and ballads. 1878, 1894, 1907. Trn.
The Crown and the Cabinet. 1878. By 'Verax'.
A life of Lord Lyndhurst. 1883, 1884.
Sketch of the life of Princess Alice. 1885.
'Halm, F.', The gladiator of Ravenna. 1885. Trn.
Shakespeare or Bacon? Edinburgh 1888.
Schiller, The song of the bell and other translations. 1889.
Virgil, The Aeneid books 1–6. 1896. Trn.
Helena Faucit (Lady Martin). Edinburgh 1900, 1900.
Queen Victoria as I knew her. 1902 (priv ptd), 1908.
Leopardi, Poems. 1904. Trn.
Monographs: Garrick, Macready, Rachel and Baron Stockmar. 1906.
Martin pbd several addresses etc. See also Wellesley, p. 1002.

§2

Theodore Martin. Dublin Univ Mag 90 1877.
Whyte, W. In Miles 9 (10). Under Aytoun-Martin, 'Bon Gaultier'.
Obituary. Blackwood's Mag Sept 1909.

Parsons, C. O. The friendship of Martin and William Harrison Ainsworth. N & Q 23 June 1934.

GERALD MASSEY
1828–1907

Collections

Complete poetical works. Boston 1857, 1861. With biographical sketch by S. Smiles.
My lyrical life: poems old and new. 2 vols 1889.
Miles 5.

§1

Poems and chansons. Tring 1848.
Voices of freedom and lyrics of love. 1850.
The ballad of Babe Christabel, with other lyrical poems. 1854, 1854 (4th edn enlarged), 1855.
Craigcrook Castle. 1856, 1856. 7 poems forming one narrative poem.
Robert Burns: a centenary song and other lyrics. 1859, 1859.
Havelock's march and other poems. 1861. Poems on the Indian Mutiny.
Shakespeare's sonnets never before interpreted. 1866, 1872 (priv ptd) (re-written as The secret drama of Shakespeare's sonnets), 1882. Re-written and greatly enlarged from an article in Quart Rev.
In memory of John William Spencer, Earl Brownlow. [1869] (priv ptd).
A tale of eternity and other poems. 1870.
Concerning spiritualism. 1871. Subsequently withdrawn by Massey.
Carmen nuptiale. [1880?] (priv ptd).
A book of the beginnings. 2 vols 1881. Theories of the origins of myths and mysteries. Extracts rptd 1881.
The natural genesis. 2 vols 1883. Pt 2 of A book of the beginnings.
Ancient Egypt the light of the world. 2 vols 1907.
Massey also priv ptd a number of lectures on his theories. See also Wellesley p. 1003.

§2

Dixon, H. Athenaeum 4 Feb 1854. A review of Babe Christabel.
Miles, A. H. In Miles 5.
Collins, J. C. In his Studies in poetry and criticism, 1905.
Milne, J. A silent singer. Book Monthly July 1905.
—— Poet and thinker. Book Monthly Sept 1907.
Wright, D. Gerald Massey. Open Court Aug 1924.
Evans, B. I. In his English poetry in the later nineteenth century, 1933, 1966 (rev).

THOMAS MILLER
1807–74

Songs of the sea nymphs. 1832.
A day in the woods: tales and poems. 1836.
Royston Gower: or the days of King John. 3 vols 1838, [1874]. An historical romance.
Lady Jane Grey: an historical romance. 1840.
Poems. 1841.
Godfrey Malvern. 1843.
The poetical language of flowers: or the pilgrim of love. 1847, 1855.
Original poems for my children. 2 sers 1852.
Birds, bees and blossoms: poems for children. [1858], [1864].
Langley-on-the-lea: or love and duty. 1860.
Original songs for the rifle volunteers. 1861. With S. Lover.
Songs of the seasons for my children. 1865.
Miller also pbd children's books, botanical guides and historical works.

WILLIAM MILLER

1810–72

Scottish nursery songs and other poems. Glasgow 1863.
Willie Winkie and other song and poems. Ed R. Ford 1902.

RICHARD MONCKTON MILNES, 1st BARON HOUGHTON

1809–85

Collections

Memorials of many scenes: poems, legendary and historical. 2 vols 1844. Selected from Memorials of a tour of Greece, Memorials of a residence on the Continent and Poetry of the people, with some new poems.
Selections from the poetical works. 1863.
A selection from the works of Lord Houghton. 1867. Poems.
Poetical works. 2 vols 1876. Includes songs pbd as flysheets and not mentioned separately below.
Miles 4.

§1

The influence of Homer. Cambridge 1829. A prize essay.
Memorials of a tour in some parts of Greece, chiefly poetical. 1834.
Memorials of a residence on the Continent, and historical poems. 1838.
Poems of many years. 1838 (priv ptd), 1840 (for general circulation), 1846.
Poetry for the people, and other poems. 1840.
One tract more, by a layman. 1841. In support of the Anglo-Catholic movement.
Palm leaves. 1844. Poems written during and about a tour in the East.
The life, letters and literary remains of John Keats. 2 vols 1848; ed R. Lynd 1927 (EL), Oxford 1931 (WC). Also pbd, in an abridged form, with Keats's poetical works, 1854 etc.
Miscellanies of the Philobiblon Society. 15 vols 1853–84. Ed Milnes, with numerous contributions by him.
Good night and good morning: a ballad. 1859.
On the present social results of classical education. In Essays on a liberal education, ed F. W. Farrar 1867.
Monographs: personal and social. 1873.
Milnes also wrote on contemporary political and social subjects; see also Wellesley p. 1013.

Letters and Papers

Reid, T. W. The life, letters and friendships of Milnes. 2 vols 1890.
Fischer, W. Die Briefe Milnes. Heidelberg 1922.

§2

Gibbs, H. J. In Miles 4.
Pope-Hennessy, J. Monckton Milnes at Cambridge. Cornhill Mag 163 1947.
—— Monckton Milnes. 2 vols 1950–2.
Wilson, E. G. Edward Moxon and the first two editions of Milne's biography of Keats. Harvard Lib Bull 5 1951.
Clive, J. Some more or less eminent Victorians. Victorian Stud 2 1958.

ROBERT MONTGOMERY

1807–55

Bibliographies

GM March 1856.

Collections

Selections from the poetical works. 1836, 1837.
Poetical works. 3 vols Glasgow 1839.
Poetical works. 6 vols 1839–40, 1841–3; ed J. W. Twycross 1853.
Religion and poetry. Ed S.J.H. 1847.
Lyra Christiana. 1851. Selected by Montgomery.
Christian poetry. Ed E. Farr [1856].

§1

Poetical trifles, by a youth. 1825.
The stage-coach: a poem. 1827.
The age reviewed: a satire in two parts. 1827, 1828 (rev).
The omnipresence of the Deity: a poem. 1828, (28 edns by 1855).
The puffad: a satire. 1828. Anon.
A universal prayer: Death: A vision of Heaven: and A vision of Hell. 1828, 1829 (4th edn), 1846.
Satan: a poem. 1830, 1830, Glasgow 1841 (8th edn), London 1842 (10th edn).
Oxford: a poem. Oxford 1831, 1835 (4th edn, with recollections of Shelley), 1843 (6th edn).
The Messiah: a poem in six books. 1832, 1836 (5th edn), 1842 (8th edn).
Woman, the angel of life: a poem. 1833, 1841 (5th edn).
Ellesmere lake: poems. 1836.
Sacred meditations and moral themes in verse. 1842, [1847] (3rd edn).
Luther: a poem. 1842, 1842, 1845, 1852 (6th and rev edn).
Scarborough: a poetic glance. 1846.
The Christian life: a manual of sacred verse. 1849, [1855] (7th edn).
The hero's funeral: a poem. 1852 (3 edns). On the Duke of Wellington.
The sanctuary: a companion in verse for the prayer book. 1855.
Montgomery also pbd numerous sermons and theological works.

§2

[Macaulay, T. B.] Edinburgh Rev 51 1830. The famous attack on The omnipresence and Satan.
Clarkson, E. Montgomery and his reviewers. 1830, 1830. A defence of Montgomery.
—— The reviewers reviewed. [1830?].
Horne, R. H. In his A new spirit of the age vol 2, 1844. Severe criticism of Satan and Woman.
Obituary. GM March 1856.
Maginn, W. In A gallery of illustrious literary characters, ed W. Bates [1873].
Hopkins, K. Reflections on Satan Montgomery. Texas Stud in Lit & Lang 4 1962.

EDWARD MOXON

1801–58

§1

The prospect and other poems. 1826.
Christmas: a poem. 1829.
Sonnets. 2 pts 1830–5 (priv ptd), 1837 (priv ptd), 1843 (priv ptd), 1871.
Charles Lamb. [1835].
Moxon edited Englishman's Mag Aug–Oct 1831.

§2

Lamb, C. Athenaeum 13 April 1833; rptd in his Works ed E. V. Lucas vol 1, 1903. On the Sonnets.
[Croker, J. W.] Quart Rev 59 1837. A contemptuous review of the Sonnets.

White, N. I. Literature and the law of libel. SP 22 1925. On Moxon's trial for blasphemous libel in 1841.
Merriam, H. G. Moxon: publisher of poets. New York 1939.
Wilson, E. G. Moxon and the first two editions of Milnes's biography of Keats. Harvard Lib Bull 5 1951.

ARTHUR JOSEPH MUNBY
1828–1910

§1

Benoni: poems. 1852.
Elegiacs. In Burns centenary poems, 1859.
Verses new and old. 1865.
A memorial of Joseph Munby of Clifton Holme. [1875].
Dorothy: a country story in elegiac verse. 1880.
Vestigia retrorsum: poems. 1890.
Vulgar verses by 'Jones Brown'. [1890].
Faithful servants: epitaphs and obituaries. 1891. Ed Munby.
Susan: a poem. 1893.
Ann Morgan's love: a pedestrian poem. 1896.
Poems, chiefly lyric and elegiac. 1901.
Relicta: verses. 1909.

§2

Marston, P. B. A realistic poet. Atlantic Monthly April 1882.
Master and servant. GM Jan 1892.
Bayne, T. The poetry of Munby. GM Nov 1904.

JOSEPH JOHN MURPHY
1827–94

§1

Sonnets and other poems, chiefly religious. 1890.
Murphy also wrote several prose works on religious matters.

§2

Grosart, A. B. In Miles 10 (11).

JOHN MASON NEALE
1818–66

Selections

Selections from the writings. 1884, 1887.
Collected hymns, sequences and carols. Ed M. S. Lawson 1914.

§1

The fisherman's song: Speed the plough!; Work over. [1840].
A history of the Jews. 1841; Supplement, 1842.
Hymns for children in accordance with the catechism. 1843, 2 pts 1844–5 (rev), 3 sers 1848 (rev and corrected).
Agnes de Tracy: a tale of the times of S Thomas of Canterbury. 1843, [1906].
Hymns for the sick. 1843, 1849, [1906].
Songs and ballads for the peoples. 1843.
A mirror of faith: lays and legends of the Church in England. 1845.
The triumphs of the cross: tales and sketches of Christian heroism. 1845.
Annals of virgin saints. 1846.
The unseen world. 1847, 1853.
Duchenier: or the revolt of La Vendée. 1848.
Songs and ballads for manufacturers. 1850.
The hymnal noted. 2 pts 1851–4. Mainly tr Neale.
Hymni ecclesiae, a breviariis quibusdam et missalibus Gallicanis, Germanis, Hispanis, Lusitanis desumpti. 1851.
Mediaeval hymns and sequences. 1851, 1863 (with addns and corrections).
Sequentiae ex missalibus Germicis, Anglicis, Gallicis, aliisque medii aevi collectae. 1852.
Carols for Christmas tide. 1853.
Carols for Easter tide. 1854.
The Egyptian wanderers: a story for children. 1854.
Judith: a Seatonian poem. 1856.
Theodora Phranza: or the fall of Constantinople. 1857; ed E. Rhys [1913] (EL).
Egypt: a Seatonian prize poem. 1858.
The disciples at Emmaus: a Seatonian prize poem. 1859.
The rhythm of Bernard de Morlaix on the celestial country. 1859.
Ruth: a Seatonian poem. 1860.
A commentary on the Psalms. 1860. With R. F. Littledale.
The daughters of Pola. [1861].
Hymns of the Eastern Church. 1862, 1882 (4th edn, with addns).
King Josiah: a Seatonian poem. 1862.
Christ was born on Christmas Day: a carol. 1864.
Seatonian poems. 1864.
The celestial country. 1865. Trn of a portion of Bernard de Morlaix, De contemptu mundi; a metrical trn of the Vexilla regis of Fortunatus and of the Cantemus cuncti of Gotteschalcus.
Hymns, chiefly mediaeval, on the joys and glories of paradise. 1865.
Hymn for use during the cattle plague. 1866.
Sequences, hymns and other ecclesiastical verses. [1866].
Hymns suitable for invalids, selected by R. F. Littledale. 1867.
A history of the Holy Eastern Church. 5 vols 1847–73.
A dissolution of the religious houses AD 1536; The curse of the abbeys. [1886]. 2 historical poems.
Good King Wenceslas: a carol. 1895. With introd by W. Morris.
Neale also pbd many sermons, commentaries, historical novels for children, trns etc.

Letters and Papers

Letters. Ed M. S. Lawson 1910.

§2

Moultrie, G. Dr Neale. [1866].
St Margaret's Mag 1–4 1887–95. A memoir in half-yearly pts, with a full account of Neale's life and writings.
Julian.
Towle, E. A. John Mason Neale DD: a memoir. 1906. With a list of his writings.
Lough, A. G. The influence of Neale. 1962.

CHARLES NEAVES, LORD NEAVES
1800–76

Songs and verses, social and scientific. Edinburgh 1868, 1869, 1875.
A glance at some of the principles of comparative philology. Edinburgh 1870.
Some helps to the study of Scoto-Celtic philology. 1872.
The Greek anthology. 1874. An account, with specimens in English.
Neaves also pbd numerous didactic works and contributed to Blackwood's Mag etc; see also Wellesley, p. 1026.

FRANCIS WILLIAM NEWMAN

1805–97

§1

Lectures on logic. 1838.
The difficulties of elementary geometry. 1841.
History of the Hebrew monarchy. 1847.
The soul: her sorrows and her aspirations. 1849. Prose.
Phases of faith. 1850, 1907. Prose.
Regal Rome. 1852. Prose.
The odes of Horace translated. 1853.
The Iliad of Homer translated. 1856.
Theism, doctrinal and practical. 1858.
Homeric translation in theory and practice. 1861. A reply to Arnold; rptd in Essays by Matthew Arnold, Oxford 1914.
Hiawatha rendered into Latin. 1862.
A handbook of modern Arabic. 1866.
Translations of English poetry into Latin verse. 1868.
The cure of the great social evils. 1869.
Miscellanies: chiefly addresses. 3 vols 1869–89.
Anthropomorphism. Ramsgate 1870.
Europe of the near future. 1871.
A dictionary of modern Arabic. 1871.
On the historical depravation of Christianity. 1873.
Hebrew theism: the common basis of Judaism, Christianity and Mohammedism. 1874.
The two theisms. 1874.
Ancient sacrifice. 1874.
Religion not history. 1877.
Libyan vocabulary. 1882.
Comments on the text of Aeschylus. 1884.
Rebilius Cruso. 1884. Robinson Crusoe in Latin.
Life after death? 1886, 1887.
Reminiscences of two exiles. 1888.
Kabai vocabulary. 1887.
Contributions chiefly to the early history of the late Cardinal Newman. 1891.
Hebrew Jesus. Nottingham 1895.
Newman also pbd numerous lectures and educational works. See also Wellesley, p. 1027.

§2

Arnold, M. On translating Homer. 1861.
—— On translating Homer: last words. 1862.
Gribble, F. Francis W. Newman. Fortnightly Rev July 1905.
Harrison, F. In his Collected essays vol 4, 1908.
Sieveking, I. G. Memoir and letters of Francis W. Newman. 1909.
Robbins, W. The Newman brothers. 1966.

ROBERT NICOLL

1814–37

§1

Poems and lyrics. Edinburgh 1835, 1842 (enlarged, with memoir by C. I. Johnstone), Glasgow 1852, Paisley 1877, 1914.
Marion Wilson: a tale of the persecuting tomes. In C. I. Johnstone, The Edinburgh tales vol 2, Edinburgh 1846.

§2

Kingsley, C. Robert Nicoll. North Br Rev Nov 1851.
Smiles, S. The life and work of Nicoll. Good Words 16 1875.
Drummond, P. R. The life of Nicoll, with some hitherto uncollected pieces. 1884.

CAROLINE ELIZABETH SARAH NORTON, née SHERIDAN and afterwards LADY STIRLING-MAXWELL

1808–77

Selections

Miles 7 (8).

§1

The sorrows of Rosalie: a tale with other poems. 1829. Anon.
The undying one and other poems. 1830, 1830, 1853.
Poems. Boston 1833.
The wife and woman's reward. 3 vols 1835. Anon.
A voice from the factories. 1836. Poems.
The dream, and other poems. 1840, 1841.
Lines. [1840]. On Queen Victoria.
The child of the islands: a poem. 1845, 1846.
Aunt Carry's ballads for children: Adventures of a wood sprite; The story of Blanche and Brutikin. 1847.
A residence at Sierra Leone. 1849.
Love not. [1850?]. A song.
Stuart of Dunleath: a story of modern times. 3 vols 1851, 2 vols 1851, 1 vol 1853.
The centenary festival. In G. Anderson and J. Finlay, The Burns centenary poems. 1859.
The lady of La Garaye. Cambridge 1862 [for 1861], 1862, 1862. Poems.
Lost and saved. 3 vols 1863 (4 edns), 1864.
Home thoughts and home themes. 1865. By Mrs Norton et al.
Old Sir Douglas. 3 vols 1868 [for 1867].
The rose of Jericho. 1870.
Bingen on the Rhine. [1888]. Poems.
Mrs Norton also wrote short works on sociological subjects and edited various annuals etc. See also Wellesley, p. 1030.

Letters

Letters etc. [1841?] (priv ptd).
Some unrecorded letters. Ed B. Collidge, Boston 1934 (priv ptd).
Macnaghten, A. I. Some letters of Caroline Norton. N & Q 8, 22 Jan, 5 Feb, 5 March 1949.

§2

The writings of the Hon Mrs Norton. Littell's Museum of Foreign Lit 41 1840.
[Coleridge, H. N.] Quart Rev 66 1845. A long review.
[Lockhart, J. G.] Mrs Norton's Child of the islands. Quart Rev 76 1845.
Mrs Norton's The lady of La Garaye. Edinburgh Rev 115 1861.
Maginn, W. A. In his A gallery of illustrious literary characters, ed W. Bates [1873].
Mrs Norton. Temple Bar Jan 1878.
Robertson, E. S. In his English poetesses, 1883.
Miles, A. H. In Miles 7 (8).
Alexander, A. H. Mrs Norton. In Women novelists of Queen Victoria's reign, 1897.
Hector, A. F. Mrs Norton. 1897.
Perkins, J. G. The life of Mrs Norton. 1909.
Dent, A. The Honourable Mrs Norton. In his Preludes and studies, 1942.
Acland, A. S. Caroline Norton. New York 1948.

JOHN WALKER ORD

1811–53

§1

The wandering bard and other poems. 1833. Anon.

England: a historical poem. 2 vols 1834–5.
Remarks on the sympathetic connection existing between the body and the mind especially during disease. 1836.
The bard and minor poems. 1841.
Rural sketches and poems chiefly relating to Cleveland. 1845.
The history and antiquities of Cleveland. 1846.
Prince Oswy: a legend of Rosebury. 1868. In verse.

§2

Whellan, T. In his York and the North Riding vol 2, 1859.

GEORGE OUTRAM
1805–56

§1

Legal lyrics: or metrical illustrations of the law of Scotland, by Quizdom Rumfunidos, 1871 (priv ptd); ed H. G. Bell, Edinburgh 1874; ed J. H. Stoddard, Edinburgh 1887, 1916 (with addns).

§2

White, W. In Miles 9 (10). With selections.

HENRY NUTCOMBE OXENHAM
1829–83

§1

The sentence of Kaïres and other poems. 1854, 1871 (3rd edn, as Poems).
Recollections of Ober-Ammeragau in 1871. 1871, 1880.
Memoir of Lieutenant R. de Lisle. 1886.
Oxenham pbd or translated a number of controversial and devotional works from the Roman Catholic standpoint. See also Wellesley, p. 1038.

§2

The Rev Henry N. Oxenham. Saturday Rev 31 March 1887.

FRANCIS TURNER PALGRAVE
1824–97

Selections

Miles 5.

§1

Preciosa: a tale. 1852.
Idyls and songs. 1854.
Essay on the first century of Italian engraving. In F. T. Kugler, Handbook of painting, 1855.
The passionate pilgrim: or Eros and Anteros. 1858.
The golden treasury. 1861, 1862, 1878, 1884, 1891 (rev and enlarged), 1896 etc; Second series, 1897. Often rptd.
Handbook to the fine art collection in the International Exhibition of 1862. 1862.
Essays on art. 1866.
Hymns. 1867, 1868 (enlarged).
The five days' entertainments at Wentworth Grange. 1868.
Gems of English art of the century. 1869.
Lyrical poems. 1871.
A Lyme garland. Lyme [1874].
The children's treasury of English song. 2 pts 1875, 1876 (as The children's treasury of lyrical song).
The visions of England, 1880 (priv ptd), 1881 (for general circulation), 1886, 1889, 1891.
The captive child. [1880?]. A poem.
The life of Jesus Christ illustrated from the Italian painters. 1885.
Ode for the twentieth of June 1887. [1887]. Oxford 1887 (as Ode for the twenty-first of June 1887).
The treasury of sacred song. Oxford 1889.
Amenophis and other poems. 1892. Includes all the earlier poems Palgrave wished to preserve, as well as some new poems.
Prothalamion. [1893] (priv ptd).
Landscape in poetry, from Homer to Tennyson. 1897.
[Miscellaneous essays]. 4 vols [1847–97]. Presented to BM.
Palgrave also pbd numerous edns and selections of the poets. See also Wellesley, p. 1038.

§2

Wedmore, T. F. Palgrave as an art critic. Colburn's New Monthly Mag May 1866.
Bayliss, W. The Professor of Poetry at Oxford and the witness of art. 1888.
Gibbs, J. H. In Miles 5.
Horder, W. G. In Julian.
Chamber, E. K. Academy 14 Jan 1893. Review of Amenophis.
Palgrave, G. F. Palgrave: his journals and memories of his life. 1899.
Evans, B. I. Tennyson and the origins of the Golden treasury. TLS 8 Dec 1932.
Horne, C. J. Palgrave's Golden treasury. E Studies 2 1949.
Owens, R. J. Palgrave's marginalia on Landor's works. N & Q June 1961.
Lewis, N. Palgrave and his Golden treasury. Listener 4 Jan 1962.

SIR JOSEPH NOEL PATON
1821–1901

Selections

Miles 5.

§1

Poems by a painter. 1861. Anon.
Spendrift. 1867. Poems.
A Christmas carol. New York [1907].

§2

Miles 5.

EMILY JANE PFEIFFER, née DAVIS
1827–90

Selections

Miles 7 (8).

§1

Valisneria: or a midsummer night's dream. 1857. A tale.
Margaret: or the motherless. 1861.
Gerard's monument and other poems. 1873, 1878 (enlarged).
Poems. 1876.
Glân-Alarch: his silence and song. 1877.
Quarterman's grace and other poems. 1879.
Sonnets and songs. 1880, [1886] (rev and enlarged).
The Wynnes of Wynhavod: a drama of modern life. 1881. In verse.
Under the aspens: lyrical and dramatic. 1882 [for 1881].
The ryme of the lady of the rock, and how it grew. 1884. Prose and verse.

Flying leaves from east and west. 1885. Prose.
Women and work: an essay. [1887].
Flowers of the night. 1889.
For 3 articles, see also Wellesley, p. 1047.

§2

Robertson, E. S. In his English poetesses, 1883.
Obituary. Academy 1 Feb 1890; Athenaeum 1 Feb 1890.
Japp, A. H. In Miles 7 (8).
Emily Pfeiffer. Western Mail 8 Oct 1895.

EDWARD HAYES PLUMPTRE
1821–91

Selection

Miles 10 (12).

§1

Lazarus and other poems. 1864, 1884 (4th edn).
The tragedies of Sophocles. 2 vols 1865, 1 vol 1867 (rev), 1902. Trn with biography.
Master and scholar. 1866, 1884. Poems.
The tragedies of Aeschylos. 2 vols 1868, 1 vol 1901. Trn with biography, and appendix of rhymed choral odes.
Samples of a new translation of the Divina commedia. 1883.
Things new and old. [1884]. Poems.
The Commedia and Canzoniere of Dante: a new translation. 2 vols 1886–7.
The life of Thomas Ken, Bishop of Bath and Wells. 2 vols 1888, 1890.
Life of Dante. Ed A. J. Butler 1900, 1903.
Plumptre also pbd many sermons and other theological works, and contributed a few articles on Dante to Quart Rev and Contemporary Rev; see also Wellesley, p. 1050.

§2

C[otton], J. S. Dean Plumptre. Academy 7 Feb 1891.
Obituary. Times 12 Feb 1891.
Horder, W. G. In Miles 10 (12).
Julian.

JOHN CRITCHLEY PRINCE
1808–66

Collections

Poetical works. Ed R. A. D. Lithgow 2 vols, 1880.

§1

Hours with the Muses. [1841], 1841 (enlarged), 1842 (enlarged), 1847 (enlarged).
Dreams and realities in verse and prose. 1847.
The poetic rosary. 1851.
Autumn leaves: original poems. Hyde 1856, [1865] (with addns).
Miscellaneous poems. Manchester [1861].

§2

Ossoli, M. F. In his Art, literature and the drama, 1874.
Lithgow, R. A. D. The life of Prince. 1880.
Fontane, T. Der Leidensweg eines Dichter. Glocke 10 1924.
Whittaker, G. H. The reed-maker poet. [1936].

ADELAIDE ANNE PROCTER
1825–64

Collections

Ausgewählte Gedichte nach dem Englischen herausgegeben von C. Schlüter und H. Brinckmann. Cologne 1867.
Miles 7 (8).
Complete works, with introduction by C. Dickens. 1905. With unpbd poem.
Legends and lyrics together with A chaplet of verses, with introduction by C. Dickens. [1905]. Oxford 1914 (OSA).
Selected poems. 1911.

§1

Legends and lyrics. 2 vols 1858–61; 1866 (with addns and introd by C. Dickens), 1895 (with addns), 1906 (EL) (omits introd by Dickens). Most of the poems first appeared in Household Words, and many were later rptd separately.
A chaplet of verses. 1862, 1868 (3rd edn).
The Victoria regia. Ed A. A. Procter 1861.

§2

Robertson, E. S. In his English poetesses, 1883.
Gibbs, H. J. In Miles 7 (8).
Julian.
Janku, F. A. A. Procter: ihr Leben und ihre Werke. Vienna 1912.
Duméril, E. Un poète catholique anglais du xixe siècle: A. A. Procter. Nouvelle Revue des Jeunes 25 May 1930.
Maison, M. Queen Victoria's favourite poet. Listener 29 April 1965.

WILLIAM BRIGHTY RANDS
1823–82

Selections

Miles 5.

§1

Robert Bloomfield: a sketch of his life and writings. [1855].
Chain of lilies and other poems. 1857.
Tangled talk: an essayist's holiday, by 'Thomas Talker'. 1864.
Lilliput levee. 1864, 1867, 1868 (enlarged). Poems.
Views and opinions bv 'Matthew Browne'. 1866.
Chaucer's England, by 'Matthew Browne'. 2 vols 1869.
Lilliput lectures. 1871, 1897. Poems.
Lilliput revels. 1871; ed R. B. Johnson 1905. Poems.
Lilliput legends. 1872. Poems.
Rands also pbd fairy tales, essays etc under his own name and under several pseudonyms. For his extensive contributions to Contemporary Rev etc, see Wellesley, pp. 1058–9.

§2

Japp, A. H. In Miles 5.

WILLIAM CALDWELL ROSCOE
1823–59

Collections

Poems and essays. Ed R. H. Hutton 2 vols 1860 (with memoir).
Poems. Ed E. M. Roscoe 1891.
Miles 5.

§1

Eliduc, Counte of Yoeloc. 1846. Drama.
Violenzia: a tragedy. 1851. Anon. Drama.
Roscoe's poems were first pbd in book form in the collections.

§2

The poems of Roscoe. Nat Rev 11 1860.
The writings of Roscoe. Dublin Univ Mag 58 1860.
Le Gallienne, R. In Miles 5.

WILLIAM BELL SCOTT
1811–90

Selections

Miles 4.

§1

Hades: or the transit and The progress of mind. 1838, Edinburgh 1838. 2 poems.
The year of the world: a philosophical poem. 1846, Edinburgh 1846.
Memoir of David Scott. 1850.
Poems. 1854.
Albert Dürer: his life and works. 1869.
Poems: ballads, studies from nature, sonnets etc. 1875.
The little masters: Altdorfer, Beham [etc]. 1879.
A poet's harvest home: being one hundred short poems. 1882, 1893 (with An aftermath of twenty short poems).
Scott also pbd a number of collections of works of art, and edited Byron, Coleridge, Mrs Inchbold, Keats, Miss Landon, Scott, Shakespeare and Shelley. See also Wellesley, p. 1078.

Papers

Autobiographical notes on the life of Scott 1830–82. Ed W. Minto 2 vols 1892.

§2

Forman, H. B. In his Our living poets, 1871.
Rossetti, W. M. Scott and modern British poetry. Macmillan's Mag March 1875.
Obituary. Athenaeum 29 Nov 1890.
Horne, H. P. Scott: poet, painter and critic. 1891.
Knight, J. In Miles 4.
Evans, B. I. In his English poetry in the later nineteenth century, 1933.

LOUISA CATHERINE SHORE
1824–95

Collections

Poems by A[rabella] and L[ouisa Shore]. 1897.
Poems, with a memoir by A. Shore and an appreciation by F. Harrison. 1897.

§1

War lyrics. 1855, 1855 (enlarged). With Arabella Shore.
Gemma of the isles. 1859. With A. Shore.
Hannibal: a drama. 2 pts 1861; ed A. Shore 1898.
Fra Dolcino. 1870. With A. Shore.
Elegies and memorials. 1894. With A. Shore.

MENELLA BUTE SMEDLEY
1820–77

Selections

Miles 7 (8).

§1

The maiden aunt. [1849]. Anon. Prose.
The very woman. In Seven tales by seven authors, 1849.
The use of sunshine: a Christmas narrative. 1852. Prose.
Nina: a tale for the twilight. 1853. Anon. Prose.
Lays and ballads from English history. [1856]. Anon.
The story of Queen Isabel and other verses. 1863.
Twice lost. 1863. Anon. Prose.
A mere story. 1865.
Poems. 1868.
Poems written for a child, by two friends. 1868, [1895]. With Mrs E. A. Hart.
Child-world. 1869. With Mrs E. A. Hart.
Other folks' lives. 1869. Prose.
Linnet's trial. 1871. Prose.
Two dramatic poems. 1874. Blind love and Cyril.
Boarding-out and pauper schools especially for girls. [From] the Blue-book for 1873–4, ed M. B. Smedley 1875.
For 2 articles, see Wellesley, p. 1088.

§2

Forman, H. B. In his Our living poets, 1871.
Robertson, E. S. In his English poetesses, 1883.
Japp, A. H. In Miles 7 (8).

JAMES SMETHAM
1821–89

Collections

Literary works. Ed W. Davies 1893.

§1

Essay on Blake, from the London Quarterly Review. In A. Gilchrist, Life of William Blake vol 2, 1880.
Letters, with an introductory memoir. Ed S. Smetham and W. Davies 1891, 1892.

§2

Beardmore, W. G. Smetham: painter, poet, essayist. [1906].
Robins, A. H. James Smetham. 1936.

ALEXANDER SMITH
1829–67

Collections

Miles 5.
A life drama, City poems etc. Ed R. E. D. Sketchley [1901].
Poetical works. Ed W. Sinclair, Edinburgh 1909.

§1

Poems. 1853, 1853, 1854, 1856.
Sonnets on the war. 1855. With S. Dobell.
City poems. Cambridge 1857.
Edwin of Deira. Cambridge 1861, 1861.
Dreamthorp: a book of essays. 1863, 1881; ed J. Hogben 1906; ed H. Walker and F. A. Cavenagh 1914; ed H. Walker, Oxford 1914 (WC) (with selection from Last leaves).
A summer in Skye. 2 vols 1865, 1 vol 1885; ed L. M. Watt [1907] (with unpbd letter); ed W. F. Gray, Edinburgh 1912.
Alfred Hagart's household. 2 vols 1866.
Miss Oona McQuarrie. [1866].
Last leaves: sketches and criticisms. Ed P. P. Alexander, Edinburgh 1868 (with memoir).
Smith also supervised an edn of Burns's poems and wrote introds for a reprint of John Bunyan, Divine emblems *and for* J. W. S. Howe, Golden leaves from the American poets. *See also* Wellesley, p. 1088.

§2

Kingsley, C. Smith and Alexander Pope. Fraser's Mag Oct 1853.
Aytoun, E. W. Firmilian: or the student of Badajoz. [1854]. Parodies Smith's poems.
Gilfillan, G. In his Galleries of literary portraits vol 1, Edinburgh 1856.

Brisbane, T. The early years of Smith. 1869.
Japp, A. H. In Miles 5.
Looker, S. J. Alexander Smith. Poetry Rev May–June 1921.
Grimsditch, H. B. Smith: poet and essayist. London Mercury July 1925.
Alexander Smith. TLS 25 Dec 1930.
Reilly, J. J. Some Victorian reputations. Catholic World April 1937.
Garrod, H. W. Matthew Arnold's 1853 preface. RES 17 1941.
Murphy, R. Smith on the art of the essay. In If by your art: testament to Percival Hunt, Pittsburgh 1948.

WALTER CHALMERS SMITH
1824–1908

Collections

Miles 10 (12).
Selections from the poems. Glasgow 1893.
Poetical works. 1902.

§1

The Bishop's walk. 1860. Verse.
Hymns of Christ and the Christian life. 1867.
Olrig Grange. Ed 'Hermann Künst' 1872, 1888. Verse.
Borland Hall. 1874. Verse.
Hilda among the broken gods. 1878. Verse.
Raban: or life splinters. Glasgow 1881 [for 1880]. Verse.
North country folk. Glasgow 1883, 1888. Verse.
Kildrostan: a dramatic poem. Glasgow 1884.
Thoughts and fancies for Sunday evenings. Glasgow 1887.
A heretic and other poems. Glasgow 1891 [for 1890].
Smith also pbd a Life of Thomas Chalmers *and lectures and sermons. See also* Wellesley, p. 1092.

§2

Saintsbury, G. Smith's North-Country folk. Academy 23 1882.
The poems of Smith. Scottish Rev 1 1883.
Horder, W. G. In Miles 10 (12).

EDWARD GEORGE GEOFFREY SMITH STANLEY, 14th EARL OF DERBY
1799–1869

§1

Syracuse. In Translations of the Oxford and Cambridge prize poems, 1833. A trn of Stanley's Latin poem.
Translations of poems, ancient and modern. 1862 (priv ptd), 1868. Trns of poems in Greek, Latin, French, Italian and German.
The Iliad of Homer rendered into English blank verse. 2 vols 1864; ed F. M. Stawell [1910] (EL).
Many of Lord Derby's speeches were also pbd.

Papers

Journal of a tour in America 1824–5. 1930 (priv ptd).

§2

Henkel, W. Ilias und Odyssee und ihre Übersetzer in England von Chapman bis auf Lord Derby. Leipzig 1867.
Kebbel, T. E. Life of the Earl of Derby KG. 1890. With ch on Derby as man of letters.
Saintsbury, G. The Earl of Derby. 1892. With ch on his literary work.

THOMAS TOD STODDART
1810–80

§1

The death-wake or lunacy: a necromaunt in three chimeras. Edinburgh 1831; ed A. Lang 1895. In verse.
The art of angling as practised in Scotland. Edinburgh 1835, 1836.
Angling reminiscenses. Edinburgh 1837, London 1887.
Angling songs. 1839, 1889.
Songs and poems in three parts. Edinburgh 1839.
Abel Massinger, or the aëronaut: a romance. Edinburgh 1846.
The angler's companion to the rivers and lochs of Scotland. Edinburgh 1847, 1853, 1892; ed H. Maxwell 1923.
An angler's rambles and angling songs. Edinburgh 1866, 1889 (with memoir by A. M. Stoddart).
Rambles by Tweed. In H. C. Pennell, Fishing gossip, 1866.
Song of the seasons and other poems. Edinburgh 1873, Kelso 1881 (with autobiographical sketch).
The crown jewel. [1898?]. Drama in verse.

§2

Wilson, J. G. In his Poets and poetry of Scotland vol 2, 1876.
Stoddart, Scottish angler. Chambers's Jnl 12 March 1881.
Lang, A. Stoddart: a Scottish romanticist of 1830. In his Adventures among books, 1905.

LADY EMMELINE CHARLOTTE ELIZABETH STUART-WORTLEY
1806–55

§1

Poems. 1833.
London at night and other poems. 1834.
Unloved of earth and other poems. 1834.
The Knight and the enchantress, with other poems. 1835.
Travelling sketches in rhyme. 1835.
The village churchyard and other poems. 1835.
The visionary: a fragment with other poems. 2 pts 1836–9.
Fragments and fancies. 1837.
Hours at Naples and other poems. 1837.
Impressions of Italy and other poems. 1837.
Lays of leisure hours. 2 vols 1838.
Queen Berengaria's courtesy and other poems. 3 vols 1838.
Sonnets, written chiefly during a tour through Holland, Germany, Italy, Turkey and Hungary. 1839.
Eva, or the error: a play in five acts. 1840.
Jairah: a dramatic mystery; and other poems. 1840.
Alphonzo Algarves: a play in five acts. 1841. In verse.
Angiolina del' Albano, or truth and treachery: a play in five acts. 1841. In verse.
Lillia-Bianca: a tale of Italy. 1841. In verse.
The maiden of Moscow: a poem in twenty-one cantos. 1842.
Adelaida: or letters etc of Madame von Regenburg; to which are added poems. 1843.
Moonshine: a comedy in five acts. 1843. In prose.
Ernest Mountjoy: a comedietta. 1844. In prose.
Travels in the United States during 1849 and 1850. 3 vols 1851.
The Great Exhibition: honour to labour—a lay of 1851. [1851].
On the approaching close of the Great Exhibition, and other poems. 1851.
&c [sketches of travel in America]. 1853. In prose.
A visit to Portugal and Madeira. 1854.
Lady Stuart-Wortley edited Keepsake *in 1837 and 1840.*

§2

[Coleridge, H. N.] Quart Rev 66 1840. A long review.
Bethune, G. W. In his British female poets, 1848.
Lady E. Stuart-Wortley's travels in America. Littell's Living Age 29 1851.
Lady Emmeline Stuart-Wortley. Chambers's Jnl 19 Feb 1853.
Obituary. GM Feb 1856.

HENRY SEPTIMUS SUTTON
1825–1901

Selections

Miles 10 (12).
Fragments of verse. [1916].
A Sutton treasury. Manchester 1899, London 1909.

§1

The evangel of love. [1847].
Clifton grove garland. Nottingham 1848.
Quinquenergia: or proposals for a new practical theology. 1854. Contains Rose's diary poems, priv ptd separately, [Glasgow 1889?], Manchester 1899.
Poems. Glasgow 1886.

§2

Horder, W. G. In Miles 10 (12).
Davis, V. D. In Julian.
Obituary. Manchester Guardian 3 May 1901; Times 6 May 1901.

CHARLES SWAIN
1801–74

Collections

Poems. Ed C. C. Smith, Boston 1857 (with a short life).
Selections compiled by his third daughter. 1906.

§1

Metrical essays on subjects of history and imagination. 1827, 1828.
Beauties of the mind: a poetical sketch with lays. 1831. Title poem recast and enlarged in the following.
The mind and other poems. 1832, 1832, 1841, 1870 (5th edn), 1873.
Dryburgh Abbey: a poem on the death of Sir Walter Scott. 1832, 1868 (with other poems).
Memoir of Henry Liverseege. 1835, 1864.
Cabinet of poetry and romance. 1844.
Rhymes for childhood. 1846.
Dramatic chapters, poems and songs. 1847, 1850.
English melodies. 1849.
Letters of Laura d'Auverne. 1853. Poems.
Art and fashion, with other poems. 1863.
Songs and ballads. 1867, 1877 (5th edn).

SIR HENRY TAYLOR
1800–86

Collections

Poetical works. 3 vols 1864. Plays and poems.
Works. 5 vols 1877–8.
Miles 3.

§1

Isaac Comnenus. 1827, 1845 (adds Edwin the fair), 1852, 1875. Verse tragedy.
Philip van Artevelde: a dramatic romance. 2 vols 1834, 1 vol 1844 (3rd edn), 1846, 1852 (6th edn), 1872; tr German, 1852.
The statesman. 1836; ed H. J. Laski, Cambridge 1927; ed L. Silberman 1957.
Edwin the fair: an historical drama. 1842; rptd in Isaac Comnenus, 1845, above. In verse.
The eve of the conquest and other poems. 1847; rptd in A Sicilian summer, 1875, below.
Notes from life in six essays. 1847, 1848, Boston 1853 (7 essays), London 1854. Prose.
Notes from books in four essays. 1849. Chiefly from Quart Rev; 2 essays on Wordsworth.
The virgin widow: a play. 1850, 1875 (as A Sicilian summer). Chiefly in verse.
St Clement's eve: a play. 1862. In verse.
Crime considered. 1869. A letter to Gladstone on the criminal code.
A Sicilian summer: with The eve of the conquest and minor poems. 1875.
Autobiography 1800–75. 1877 (priv ptd), 2 vols 1885.
Taylor also wrote for London Mag c. 1823 and for Quart Rev; see also Wellesley, p. 111.

Letters

Correspondence. Ed E. Dowden 1888.

§2

[Lockhart, J. G.] Quart Rev 51 1834. A favourable notice of Philip van Artevelde.
Some remarks on the preface to Philip van Artevelde. 1835.
Horne, R. H. In his A new spirit of the age vol 2, 1844.
Powell, T. In his Pictures of the living authors of Britain, 1851.
Forman, H. B. In his Our living poets, 1871.
De Vere, A. In his Essays chiefly on poetry vols 1–2, 1887. 5 papers on Taylor.
Bilderbeck, J. B. Taylor and his drama of Philip van Artevelde. 1877.
Japp, A. H. In Miles 3.
Knanth, R. Taylors Leben und Werke. Strasbourg 1913.
Taylur, U. Guests and memories. 1924. Chiefly on Taylor's later life and friendships.
Abercrombie, L. In The eighteen-sixties, ed J. Drinkwater 1932 (Royal Soc of Lit).

CHARLES TENNYSON, afterwards TURNER
1808–79

Selections

Collected sonnets, old and new. 1880, 1898. With preface by Hallam Tennyson, and introd by J. Spedding, rptd from Nineteenth Century.
Miles 4.
Charles Tennyson. [1931].

§1

Poems by two brothers. 1827, 1893 (with addns). With Alfred and Frederick Tennyson. *See also col. 414, above.*
Sonnets and fugitive pieces. Cambridge 1830.
Sonnets 1864.
Small tableaux. 1868.
Sonnets, lyrics and translations. 1873.

§2

S[hepherd], R. H. Tennysoniana: notes bibliographical and critical on early poems of Alfred and Charles Tennyson. 1866–[75].

Japp, A. H. In Miles 4.
Jelinek, K. A. A. Charles Tennyson-Turners Leben und Werke. Leipzig 1909.
Nicolson, H. Tennyson's two brothers. Cambridge 1947.
Tennyson, C. The Vicar of Grasby. English 8 1950.

FREDERICK TENNYSON
1807–98

Selections

Miles 4.
Shorter poems. Ed C. B. L. Tennyson 1913.

§1

Poems by two brothers. 1827, 1893 (with addns). With Alfred and Charles Tennyson. *See col 414, above.*
ΑΙΓΥΠΤΟΣ: carmen Graecum numismate annuo dignatum et in curia Cantabrigiensi recitatum comitiis maximis AD MDCCCXXVIII. In Prolusiones academicae, Cambridge 1828.
Days and hours. 1854.
The isles of Greece; Sappho and Alcaeus. 1890.
Daphne and other poems. 1891.
Poems of the day and year. 1895.

§2

Frederick Tennyson's poems. Fraser's Mag June 1854.
Japp, A. H. In Miles 4.
Rawnsley, H. D. Memories of the Tennysons. Glasgow 1912.
Letters to Frederick Tennyson. Ed H. J. Schonfield 1930.
Nicolson, H. Tennyson's two brothers. Cambridge 1947.
Fall, C. An index of the letters from papers of Frederick Tennyson. SE 36 1957.

GEORGE WALTER THORNBURY
1828–76

Selections

Miles 5.

§1

Lays and legends: or ballads of the new world. 1851.
The monarchs of the main: or adventures of the buccaneers. 3 vols 1855, 1 vol 1858.
Art and nature at home and abroad. 2 vols 1856.
Shakspere's England: or sketches of our social history in the reign of Elizabeth. 2 vols 1856.
Songs of the Cavaliers and Roundheads, Jacobite ballads etc. 1857.
Every man his own trumpeter. 3 vols 1858.
Life in Spain, past and present. 2 vols 1859.
Turkish life and character. 2 vols 1860.
British artists from Hogarth to Turner. 2 vols [1860].
Cross country. 1861.
Ice bound. 1861.
The life of J. M. W. Turner. 2 vols [1861], 1 vol 1877 (rev and mostly re-written).
True as steel. 3 vols 1863.
Wildfire. 3 vols 1864. A novel.
Haunted London. 1865, [1879].
Tales for the marines. [1865].
Great heart. 1866. A novel.
Two centuries of song. 1867. Anthology with notes.
The fables of La Fontaine, translated into English verse. [1867].
The Vicar's courtship. 3 vols 1869. A novel.
A tour round England. 2 vols 1870.
Criss-cross journeys. 2 vols 1873.
Old and new London. 6 vols 1873–8 etc. Vols 1–2 by Thornbury.
Historical and legendary ballads and songs. [1875].
Thornbury also pbd many collections of tales, topographical works, trns etc. He was associated with Dickens in Household Words and All the Year Round.

§2

The writings of Thornbury. Dublin Univ Mag 50 1859.
Kent, C. George Walter Thornbury. Athenaeum 17 June 1876.
Ingram, J. H. In Miles 5.

RICHARD CHENEVIX TRENCH
1807–86

Collections

Poems, collected and arranged anew. Cambridge 1865, London 1885.
Miles 4.
In time of war: poems. 1900. Preface by F. W. H. Myers.
Sonnets. Ed A. J. Romilly, Bristol [1901].
Sonnets and elegiacs. [1909].

§1

The story of Justin Martyr and other poems. 1835.
Sabbation, Honor Neale and other poems. 1838.
Poems. [1841] (priv ptd).
Notes on the parables of our Lord. 1841, 1844, 1845, 1864, 1882, 1886; ed A. S. Palmer 1906.
Genoveva: a poem. 1842.
Poems from eastern sources: the steadfast Prince and other poems. 1842, 1851 (enlarged).
Elegiac poems. 1843. Anon.
The fitness of Holy Scripture for unfolding the spiritual life of men. 1845.
Notes on the miracles of our Lord. 1846, 1847, 1856, 1858, 1872, 1886.
Sacred Latin poetry, chiefly lyrical. 1849–64. An anthology.
On the study of words: five lectures. 1851, 1852, 1856, 1859, 1872, 1886; ed A. S. Palmer 1904, 1927 (EL).
Poems from eastern sources: Genoveva and other poems. 1851.
On the lessons in proverbs: five lectures. 1853; ed A. S. Palmer 1905 (with bibliography of proverbs).
Synonyms of the New Testament. 1854.
English past and present: five lectures. 1855; rev A. L. Mayhew 1889; ed A. S. Palmer 1905.
On teaching by words. 1855.
Alma and other poems. 1855.
On some deficiencies in our English dictionaries. 1857, 1860 (rev and enlarged).
A select glossary of English words, used formerly in senses different from their present. 1859, 1859, 1873; ed A. S. Palmer 1906.
The history of the English sonnet. 1863.
Gustavus Adolphus: social aspects of the Thirty Years' War. 1865, 1887 (3rd edn enlarged).
Studies in the Gospels. 1867.
A household book of English poetry. 1868, 1870. An anthology.
Plutarch: his life, his Lives and his morals. 1873.
Lectures on medieval church history. 1877.
Brief thoughts and meditations on some passages in Holy Scripture. 1884.
Trench also pbd numerous theological tracts and sermons.

Letters

Trench: letters and memorials. Ed M. Trench 2 vols 1888.

§2

Myers, F. W. H. Archbishop Trench's poems. Nineteenth Century Oct 1877.
De Vere, A. Archbishop Trench's poems. Nineteenth Century June 1888.
Silvester, J. Archbishop Trench: a sketch of his life and character. [1891].
Gibbs, H. J. In Miles 4.
Julian.
Pritchett, V. S. Books in general. New Statesman 16 Oct 1943. Discusses On the study of words.

MARTIN FARQUHAR TUPPER

1810–89

Collections

Complete poetical works. Hartford 1850; Complete prose works, Hartford 1850.
Cithara: a selection from the lyrics. 1863.
A selection from the works. 1866.
Select miscellaneous poems. [1874].

§1

Sacra poesis. 1832.
Geraldine: a sequel to Coleridge's Christabel, with other poems. 1838.
Proverbial philosophy: a book of thoughts and arguments, originally treated. 1838; 4 sers [1876?] (complete).
A modern pyramid to commemorate a septuagint of worthies. 1839. A sonnet and an essay on each of 70 famous men.
St Martha's near Guildford, Surrey. [Guildford?] 1841. Not pbd.
A thousand lines now first offered to the world we live in 1845.
Hactenus. 1848.
The loving ballad to Brother Jonathan. [1848].
King Alfred's poems turned into English metres. 1850.
Farley Heath. Guildford 1850.
Ballads for the times. 1850, 1851, 1852 (rev).
Half a dozen no-popery ballads. [1851].
A hymn for all nations. 1851; tr 30 languages, 1851.
A dirge for Wellington. 1852.
Half a dozen ballads for Australian emigrants. 1853.
A batch of war ballads. 1854.
A dozen ballads for the times about Church abuses. 1854.
A dozen ballads for the times about white slavery. 1854.
Lyrics of the heart and mind. 1855, 1855.
A missionary ballad. [1855?].
Alfred: a patriotic play. Westminster 1858 (priv ptd).
Martin Tupper on rifle-clubs. 1859.
Three hundred sonnets. 1860.
Plan of the ritualistic campaign. [1865?] (priv ptd), 1868 (as The anti-ritualistic satire).
Translations of T. Sullivan's La bannière sur le char de la victoire. [1866].
Translations of J. Sullivan's Elégie sur la mort de Lord Palmerston. 1866.
Our Canadian dominion: half a dozen ballads about a King for Canada. 1868.
Twenty-one Protestant ballads published in the Rock. 1868.
A creed etcetera. 1870.
Fifty of the Protestant ballads. 1874.
Washington: a drama in five acts. 1876.
Autobiography. 1886. Prose.
Jubilate! an offering in 1887. [1887]. For Queen Victoria.
Tupper was also a prolific prose writer, but nothing of interest survives except his Autobiography.

§2

[Wilson, J.] Tupper's Geraldine. Blackwood's Mag Dec 1838. A long, unfavourable review.
Drinkwater, J. In The eighteen-eighties, ed W. de la Mare 1930 (Royal Soc of Lit).
Mr Tupper and the poets. TLS 16 Feb 1938.
Salomon, L. B. He gave the Victorians what they wanted. Eng Jnl 27 1938.
Goodchild, R. Martin Tupper. TLS 5 March 1939.
Buchmann, R. Tupper and the Victorian middle-class mind. Berne 1941.
Hudson, D. Tupper: his rise and fall. 1949.
Nicolson, H. Marginal comment. Spectator 18 Feb 1949.

THOMAS WADE

1805–75

Selections

Miles 3.

§1

Tasso and the sisters: poems. 1825.
Woman's love, or the triumph of patience: a drama. 1829. In prose and verse.
The phrenologists: a farce. 1830. In prose.
The Jew of Arragon: a tragedy. 1830. In verse.
Mundi et cordis de rebus sempiternis et temporariis: carmina. 1835. Lyrics and sonnets in English.
The contention of love and death. 1837. A poem rptd in H. B. Forman's second article, below.
Helena: a poem. 1837.
Prothanasia and other poems. 1839.
What does Hamlet mean? a lecture. Jersey [1840?].
Wade edited Bell's Weekly Messenger c. 1838, *and later* The Br Press, Jersey, *and later* Wade's London Rev. *The ms of his unpbd trn of Dante's Inferno (executed 1845–6) is in the Macauley Collection, Univ of Pennsylvania; specimens are given in Forman's second article, below.*

§2

Forman, H. B. In Miles 3.
— Wade: the poet and his surroundings. In Literary anecdotes of the nineteenth century, ed W. R. Nicoll and T. J. Wise vol 1, 1895. Includes unpbd poems.

ANNA LAETITIA WARING

1823–1910

Selections

Miles 10 (11).

§1

Hymns and meditations, by A.L.W. 1850, 1850, 1852, 1854, 1855, 1856, 1858, 1860, 1863, 1863, 1870, 1871, [1883], [1889], 1911. Most of the edns contain some addns.
Additional hymns. 1858.
Miss Waring also pbd a few tracts.

§2

Horder, W. G. In Miles 10 (11).
Crawford, G. A. In Julian.
Talbot, M. S. In remembrance of Anna Laetitia Waring. 1911. Contains additional hymns and other verses.

EDWIN WAUGH

1817–90

Collections

Poesies from a country garden. 2 pts 1866.
Lancashire sketches. 1869, [1871]; ed G. Milner 2 pts [1892].

Samples of Lancashire wares. [1879]. Includes selections from Waugh.
The chimney corner. 1879; ed G. Milner [1892]. Prose sketches, mostly in the Lancashire dialect.
Complete works. 11 vols 1881–9.
Fireside tales. 1885.
Besom Ben stories. Ed G. Milner [1892].
Tufts of heather from the Lancashire moors. Ed G. Milner 2 sers [1892].
Rambles in the Lake Country and other travel sketches. Ed G. Milner 2 sers [1893].

§ 1

Sketches of Lancashire life and localities. 1855.
A ramble from Bury to Rochdale. Manchester 1855.
Come whoam to thy childer an' me. [Manchester? 1856]. Verse.
What ails thee, my son Robin? [1856]. Verse.
Chirrup. 1858. A song.
Poems and Lancashire songs. 1859, 1870 (3rd edn, with addns), 1876 (4th edn, with addns).
Over sands to the lakes. Manchester 1860.
The Birtle carter's tale. Manchester 1861.
Rambles in the Lake Country and its borders. 1861.
Lancashire songs. 1863, [1892], (6th edn).
Fourteen days in Scotland. [1864].
Besom Ben. Manchester 1865, [1892].
Prince's theatre, Manchester: The grand comic Christmas pantomime, for 1866 and 1867, or Robin Hood and ye merrie men of Sherwood. [1866].
Ben an' th' bantam. Manchester 1866.
The birthplace of Tim Bobbin. [1867].
The owd blanket. [1867].
Dules-gate. [1868].
Sneck-bant. Manchester [1868].
Yeth-bobs an' scaplins. Manchester [1868].
Irish sketches. 1869.
Johnny O'Wobbler's an' th' two-wheeled dragon. Manchester [1869].
An old nest. [1869].
Snowed-up. [1869].
Rambles and reveries. 1872. Poems.
Lancashire anecdotes. Manchester [1872].
Jannoch. Manchester 1873.
The old coal man. Manchester [1878].
The hermit-cobbler. Manchester [1878].
Around the Yule-log. [1879]. Prose.
In the Lake Country. Manchester 1880.
Poems and songs (second series). Liverpool 1889; ed G. Milner [1893] (with an introductory essay on the dialect of Lancashire as a vehicle for poetry).

§ 2

Waugh's Besom Ben stories. Saturday Rev 6 May 1882.
Lamb, R. Obituary. Leisure Hour 39 1890.
Obituary. Athenaeum 10 May 1890; Temple Bar Oct 1890.
Watson, W. Lancashire laureate. Nat Rev June 1890.
Espinasse, F. Manchester memories: Waugh. In his Literary recollections and sketches, 1893.

THOMAS WESTWOOD

1814–88

Selections

Miles 4.

§ 1

Poems. 1840.
Beads from a rosary. 1843.
The burden of the bell and other lyrics. 1850.
Berries and blossoms: a verse-book for young people. 1855.
A new bibliotheca piscatoria: or general catalogue of angling and fishing literature. 1861; rev T. Westwood and T. Satchell 1883.
The chronicle of the Compleat angler of Isaac Walton and Charles Cotton: being a bibliographical record. 1864. The essay on Lamb rptd in E. V. Lucas, Life of Charles Lamb vol 2, 1905.
A stream in Arden—Hey for coquet! A lay of the sea. In H. C. Pennell, Fishing gossip, 1866. Poems.
The sword of kingship: a legend of the Mort d'Arthure. 1866 (priv ptd).
The quest of the sancgreall, The sword of kingship and other poems. 1868.
Gathered in the gloaming. 1881 (priv ptd), 1885.
The secrets of angling, by J.D.: a reprint, with introduction by Thomas Westwood. 1883.
In memoriam Isaak Walton, obiit 15th December 1683. [1884]. 12 sonnets and an epilogue.

Letters

A literary friendship: letters to Lady Alwyne Compton. 1914. With preface by Lady Compton and a memoir by Rosa Westwood.

§ 2

Obituary. Athenaeum 24 March 1888.
Watkins, M. G. Obituary. Academy 31 March 1888.
Miles, A. H. In Miles 4.

CHARLES WHITEHEAD

1804–62

Collections

The solitary and other poems. 1849. Includes The cavalier.
Miles 3.

§ 1

The solitary: a poem. 1831.
The autobiography of Jack Ketch. 1834, 1836. Prose burlesque.
The lives and exploits of English highwaymen, pirates and robbers. 2 vols 1834.
The cavalier: a drama. 1836. In verse.
Victoria Victrix. 1838. A poem.
Richard Savage. 3 vols 1842; ed H. Orrinsmith 1896, 1903. Prose romance based partly on Dr Johnson's Life of Savage.
The Earl of Essex. 3 vols 1843.
Smiles and tears. 3 vols 1847.
Whitehead also made numerous contributions to periodicals, particularly Bentley's Miscellany; *and pbd a revision (1846) of Grimaldi's memoirs as originally ed Dickens (1838).*

§ 2

Bell, H. T. M. A forgotten genius: Whitehead. 1884.
—— In Miles 3.
Crump, J. Whitehead: his life and work. Dickensian 48 1952.
Fielding, K. J. Whitehead and Charles Dickens. RES new ser 3 1952.

ISAAC WILLIAMS

1802–65

Selections

Selections from the writings. 1890.

§1

Lyra apostolica. 1836; ed H. S. Holland and H. C. Beeching 1899. Williams contributed 9 poems.
The cathedral: or the Catholic and Apostolic Church of England. 1838, 1839, 1841, 1857, 1859 (8th edn); ed W. Benham 1889. Verse.
Thoughts in past years. 1838, 1848, 1852 (6th edn enlarged). Poems.
Hymns translated from the Parisian breviary. 1839.
Ancient hymns for children. 1842.
The baptistery: or the way of eternal life. 2 vols Oxford 1842–4, 1 vol 1846, 1852, 1858. Verse.
Hymns on the catechism. 1843.
Some meditations and prayers selected from the way of eternal life, in order to illustrate and explain the pictures by Boetius a Bolswert, for the same work. 1845. Trn from Latin of A. Sucquet.
Sacred verses with pictures. 2 pts 1845.
The altar: or meditations in verse on the great Christian sacrifice. 1847 (anon), 1849.
The Christian scholar. 1849. Verse.
The seven days, or the old and new creation. 1850. Verse.
A series of sermons on the Epistle and Gospel. 1853–55.
The Christian seasons. 1854. Verse.
Female characters of Holy Scripture. 1859. Sermons.
Devotional commentary on the Gospel narratives. 8 vols 1869–70.
Williams pbd a number of other sermons, religious tracts and 'harmonies' of the Gospels. He wrote nos 80, 86–7 of Tracts for the times.

Papers

Autobiography. Ed G. Prevost 1892, 1893 (3rd edn).

§2

Griswold, R. W. In his Sacred poets of England and America, 1859.
Miller, J. In his Singers and songs of the Church, 1869 (2nd edn).
Williams and the Oxford Movement. Church Quart Rev 34 1892.
Overton, J. H. In Julian.

ALEXANDER WILSON

d. 1852

The songs of the Wilsons. 1865, 1866, [1873]. Poems by M. T. and A. Wilson.

RICHARD WILTON

1827–1903

Selections

Miles 10 (12).

§1

Wood-notes and church-bells. 1873.
Lyrics: sylvan and sacred. 1878.
Sungleams: rondeaux and sonnets. [1882].
Benedicite and other poems. [1889].
Lyra pastoralis: songs of nature, church and home. 1902.
Wilson also assisted A. B. Grosart in translating into English verse the sacred Latin poems of George Herbert and Richard Crashaw.

§2

Miles, A. H. In Miles 10 (12).

DAVID WINGATE

1828–92

Selections

Select poems and essays. Glasgow 1890.

§1

Poems and songs. 1862, 1863.
Annie Weir and other poems. 1866.
Lily Neil: a poem. 1879.
Poems and songs. 1883. Different from 1862, above.

§2

[Oliphant, M.] David Wingate. Blackwood's Mag July 1862.
Wilson, J. G. In his Poets and poetry of Scotland vol 2, 1877.

CATHERINE WINKWORTH

1827–78

Selections

A selection of hymns from the Lyra germanica. 1859.
Lyra germanica. [1906] (ML). A collected edn.

§1

Lyra germanica: hymns. 1855, New York 1856, London 1862, 1901. Trns from German.
Lyra germanica: second series; The Christian life. 1858, 1865 (6th edn).
The chorale book for England. 1863. Trns of German hymns.
Veni sancti spiritus. 1865. Latin and English.
Christian singers of Germany. 1869. Prose account.
Miss Winkworth also pbd trns of German prose.

§2

Julian.
Shaen, M. J. Memorials of two sisters: Susanna and Catherine Winkworth. 1908.

THOMAS WOOLNER

1825–92

Selections

Miles 5.

§1

My beautiful lady. Ptd in Germ Jan 1850, and separately, in expanded form, 1863, 1864, 1866 (3rd edn illustr). Verse.
Pygmalion. 1881. Verse.
Silenus. 1884. Verse.
Tiresias. 1886. Verse.
Poems; Nelly Dale; Children. 1887.
My beautiful lady; Nelly Dale. 1893. Verse.

§2

Forman, H. B. In his Our living poets, 1871.
Tupper, J. L. Thomas Woolner. Portfolio 2 1871.
Meynell, A. Thomas Woolner's Pygmalion. Art Jnl 34 1882.
Garrod, H. B. Academy 29 May 1886. Review of Tiresias.
Stephens, F. G. Thomas Woolner. Art Jnl 46 1894.
Le Gallienne, R. In Miles 5.

Woolner, A. Woolner: his life in letters. 1917.
Evans, B. I. In his English poetry in the later nineteenth century, 1933.
Woolner: My beautiful lady. Bodleian Lib Record 3 1950.

CHRISTOPHER WORDSWORTH
1807–85

§ 1

The Druids: Chancellor's Medal poem. Cambridge 1827.
The invasion of Russia by Napoleon Buonaparte: a poem which obtained the Chancellor's Medal. Cambridge 1828.
Ode at Cambridge on 7 July 1835 after the installation of the Chancellor of the University. 1835.
Athens and Attica. 1836, 1855 (3rd edn rev). Prose.
Greece: pictorial, descriptive and historical. 1839.
Diary in France. 1845.
Memoirs of William Wordsworth. 2 vols 1851.
The Druids; Invasion of Russia by Napoleon Buonaparte. In Cambridge prize poems, 1859.
The inspiration of the Bible: five lectures. 1861.
The interpretation of the Bible: five lectures. 1861.
The holy year. Ed W. H. Monk 1862. Hymns.
Journal of a tour in Italy. 2 vols 1863.
Additional hymns for the holy year. 1864.
Church history up to AD 451. 4 vols 1881–3.
Wordsworth also pbd a Commentary on the whole Bible, numerous sermons, religious tracts etc.

§ 2

Overton, J. H. and E. Wordsworth. Christopher Wordsworth, Bishop of Lincoln. 1888.
Overton, J. H. In Julian.

R. M. G.

VI. LATE NINETEENTH-CENTURY POETRY

WILLIAM MORRIS
1834–96

Bibliographies

Forman, H. B. The books of Morris described, with some account of his doings in literature and in the allied crafts. 1897.
Scott, T. A bibliography of the works of Morris. 1897. Essentially the same as that appended to A. Vallance, Art of Morris, 1897.
A note by Morris on his aims in founding the Kelmscott Press; together with a short description of the press by S. C. Cockerell and an annotated list of the books printed thereat. Hammersmith 1898 (Kelmscott Press); rptd in H. Sparling, The Kelmscott Press and Morris, master-craftsman, 1924.
Vaughan, C. E. In his Bibliographies of Swinburne, Morris, Rossetti, Oxford 1914 (Eng Assoc).
Ohtsuki, K. List of new contributions, home and foreign, to the W. Morris bibliography in his year. Tokyo 1934.
Litzenberg, K. Morris and Scandinavian literature: bibliographical essay. Scandinavian Stud 13 1935.
Ehrsam, T. G., R. H. Deily and R. M. Smith. In Bibliographies of twelve Victorian authors, New York 1936. Supplement by J. G. Fucilla, MP 37 1939.
Flower, R. The Morris manuscripts. BM Quart 14 1940.
Jones, H. M. The Pre-Raphaelites. In Victorian Poets, ed F. E. Faverty, Cambridge Mass 1956, 1968 (rev).
Briggs, R. C. H. Handlist of the public addresses of Morris to be found in generally accessible publications. 1961.
Fredeman, W. E. Morris and his circle: selective bibliography of publications 1960–2, 1963–5. Jnl of William Morris Soc 1–2 1964–6. A continuing bibliography including the Pre-Raphaelites.
—— In his Pre-Raphaelitism: a bibliocritical study, Cambridge Mass 1965 (section 43).

Collections

A selection from the poems of Morris. Ed F. Hueffer, Leipzig 1886 (Tauchnitz).
The collected works of Morris, with introductions by May Morris. 24 vols 1910–15, New York 1966.
The defence of Guenevere, the Life and death of Jason, and other poems. Oxford 1914 (WC).
Prose and poetry 1856–70. Oxford 1920 (OSA).
William Morris, selected by H. Newbolt. 1923.
Selections from the prose works of Morris. Ed A. H. R. Ball, Cambridge 1931.
Stories in prose, stories in verse, shorter poems, lectures, and essays: centenary edition. Ed G. D. H. Cole 1934.
Morris: artist, writer, Socialist. Ed May Morris 2 vols Oxford 1936, New York 1966. A supplt to the Collected works, above.
On art and Socialism: essays and lectures. Ed H. Jackson 1947.
Selected writings. Ed W. Gaunt 1948.
Selections from Morris. Moscow 1959.
Selected writings and designs. Ed A. Briggs 1962 (Pelican). With a suppl on Morris as designer by G. Shankland.

§ 1

Morris's contributions toperiodicals are detailed in Temple Scott's bibliography, above, including poems, trns and prose. Special subsections are provided, as in H. B. Forman, Books of Morris, *for the four journals with which Morris was most intimately associated:* (1) The Oxford & Cambridge Magazine (Jan–Dec 1856). *This journal was ed W. Fulford, but Morris was its financial mainstay and its principal contributor. With the exception of* Winter weather, *all of Morris's poems were rptd in* The defence of Guinevere, 1858; *his tales in* The hollow land and other contributions to the Oxford and Cambridge Magazine 1903 *and in* Collected works; (2) Justice; (3) The Commonweal; (4) The Architect. *For* Sir Galahad *and* The two sides of the river, *the first a confirmed, the second a suspected T. J. Wise forgery, see* J. Carter and H. G. Pollard, An enquiry into the nature of certain nineteenth-century pamphlets, 1934.
The defence of Guenevere and other poems. 1858, 1875, 1892 (Kelmscott Press).
The life and death of Jason: a poem. 1867, 1868 (for Dec 1867) (2nd edn rev), 1868, 1869, 1872 (5th–7th edn), 1882 (rev), 1895 (Kelmscott Press).
The earthly paradise: a poem. 3 (or 4) vols 1868–70. Vol 1 (pts 1–2), (March–Aug) 1868 (edns 1–4), 2 vols 1870 (for 1869), pt 3 (Sept–Nov) 1870 (for 1869) (3 edns); pt 4 (Dec–Feb) 1870, 1870, 1871 (3rd edn); [completed work], 10 vols 1872 (popular edn), 5 vols 1886 (popular edn), 1890 (rev), 8 vols 1896 (Kelmscott Press).

The lovers of Gudrun. Boston 1870. Excerpt from Earthly paradise.

Love is enough or the freeing of Pharamond: a morality. 1873 (for 1872), 1873, 1889, 1898 (Kelmscott Press).

The two sides of the river, Hapless love, and The first foray of Aristomenes. 1876. Not for sale. A pamphlet suspected by Carter and Pollard. Two sides of the river appeared first in the Fortnightly Rev Oct 1868 and is rptd in Poems by the way, 1891; Hapless love was ptd in Good Words April 1869 and First foray of Aristomenes in Athenaeum 13 May 1876; neither was rptd during Morris's lifetime.

The story of Sigurd the Volsung, and the fall of the Niblungs. 1877 (for 1876) (3 edns), 1887, 1898 (Kelmscott Press).

The decorative arts, their relation to modern life and progress: an address delivered before the Trades' Guild of Learning. [1878]; rptd as The lesser arts in Hopes and fears for art, below.

Wake London lads! 1878. A broadside.

Address delivered in the Town Hall. Birmingham [1879]; rptd as The art of the people in Hopes and fears for art, 1882.

Labour and pleasure versus labour and sorrow: an address. Birmingham [1880]; rptd as The beauty of life in Hopes and fears for art, 1882, below.

The Wedgwood Institute: reports of the Schools of Science & Art for the year 1880–1, with the address delivered by Morris. Burselm 1881; rptd in Lectures, below, as Art and the beauty of the earth.

Hopes and fears for art: five lectures delivered in Birmingham, London and Nottingham 1878–81. 1882, 1883.

Lectures on art delivered in support of the Society for the Protection of Ancient Buildings. 1882. Morris' 2 lectures are The history of pattern design, 1879 and The lesser arts of life, 1882 (as Some of the minor arts of life).

A summary of the principles of Socialism written for the Democratic Federation by H. M. Hyndman and Morris. 1884, 1884, 1896.

Textile fabrics: a lecture. 1884. Delivered at International Health Exhibition.

A review of European society, with an exposition and vindication of the principles of social democracy, by J. Sketchley. 1884. Introd by Morris.

Art and Socialism: a lecture; and Watchman, what of the night? 1884 (Leek Bijou Reprints, no 7). Subtitled The aims and ideals of the English Socialists of to-day.

Chants for Socialists, no 1: The day is coming. [1884].

The voice of toil, All for the cause: two chants for Socialists. [1884]. Rptd from Justice.

The God of the poor. [1884]. Rptd from Fortnightly Rev Aug 1868.

Chants for Socialists. 1885, 1885 (adds Down among the dead men), 1892.

The manifesto of the Socialist League. 1885, 1885 (new edn annotated by Morris and E. B. Bax).

Socialists at play: prologue spoken at the entertainment of the Socialist League. 1885. Rptd from Commonweal.

The Socialist League: constitution and rules adopted at the General Conference. 1885.

Address to Trades' Unions (The Socialist platform—no 1). 1885. Ed with E. B. Bax.

Useful work v. useless toil (The Socialist platform—no 2). 1885, 1893.

For whom shall we vote? addressed to the working-men electors of Great Britain. [1885].

What Socialists want (Socialist League—Hammersmith Branch—no 11). [1885].

The labour question from the Socialist standpoint (Claims of labour lectures—no 5). Edinburgh 1886; rptd in The claims of labour, Edinburgh 1886. Same as True and false society, below.

A short account of the Commune of Paris (The Socialist platform—no 4). 1886. With E. B. Bax and V. Dave.

Socialism. [1886]. Rptd from Daylight.

The pilgrims of hope. 1886. An unauthorized reprint from Commonweal by H. B. Forman.

The aims of art. 1887.

The tables turned, or Nupkins awakened: a Socialist interlude. 1887.

Alfred Linnell, killed in Trafalgar Square, Nov 20 1887: a death song. [1887]. Sold for the benefit of Linnell's orphans, with a memorial design by Walter Crane.

The principles of Socialism made plain; and Objections, methods and quack remedies for poverty considered, by F. Fairman. 1888. With preface by Morris.

True and false society (The Socialist platform—no 6). 1888, 1893. Same as Labour question, above.

The Socialist platform written by several hands for the Socialist League, together with the Manifesto and Chants for Socialists by Morris. 1888, 1890 (enlarged to include Monopoly).

Signs of change: seven lectures delivered on various occasions. 1888, 1902.

A dream of John Ball and A King's lesson. 1888, 1892 (Kelmscott Press). Rptd from Commonweal, illustr E. Burne-Jones. A King's lesson separately rptd Aberdeen 1891.

A tale of the house of the Wolfings and all the kindreds of the Mark, written in prose and verse. 1889.

The roots of the mountains wherein is told somewhat of the lives of the men of Burgdale, their friends, their neighbours, their foemen and their fellows in arms. 1890.

Monopoly: or how labour is robbed (The Socialist platform—no 7). 1890, 1891, 1893, 1898.

News from nowhere, or an epoch of rest: being some chapters from a utopian romance. Boston 1890 (uncorrected and unauthorized 'author's edition' from Commonweal text), London 1891 (in 3 different states), 1892 (Kelmscott Press); tr Italian, 1895.

The legend of the briar rose: a series of pictures painted by E. Burne-Jones. 1890. With 4 quatrains by Morris.

Statement of principles of the Hammersmith Socialist Society. [1890]. Anon.

Poems by the way. 1891 (Kelmscott Press), 1891 (Chiswick Press).

The Socialist ideal of art. 1891. Rptd from New Rev Jan 1891.

The story of the glittering plain which has been also called the land of living men or the acre of the undying. 1891 (Kelmscott Press), 1891 (regular edn, Reeves & Turner), 1894 (Kelmscott Press, rptd with 23 pictures by Walter Crane). Rptd from English Illustr Mag.

Address on the collection of paintings of the English Pre-Raphaelite school. Birmingham 1891.

Under an elm-tree: or thoughts in the country-side. Aberdeen 1891.

The nature of Gothic: a chapter of the Stones of Venice by John Ruskin. 1892 (Kelmscott Press). Preface by Morris.

Manifesto of English Socialists. 1893. Anon, written conjointly with H. M. Hyndman and G. B. Shaw.

The reward of labour: a dialogue. [1893].

Concerning Westminster Abbey. [1893]. Anon.

Utopia by Sir Thomas More. 1893 (Kelmscott Press). Foreword by Morris.

Medieval lore by Robert Steele. 1893. With a preface by Morris.

Socialism: its growth and outcome. 1893. With E. B. Bax; rptd from Commonweal.

Help for the miners: the deeper meaning of the struggle. [1893]. Rptd from Daily Chron.

Gothic architecture: a lecture for the Arts and Crafts Exhibition Society. 1893 (Kelmscott Press).

Arts and crafts essays by members of the Arts and Crafts Exhibition Society. 1893, 1894. With a preface and

three essays by Morris: Textiles, Printing (with Emery Walker), Of dyeing as an art.
The wood beyond the world. 1894 (Kelmscott Press), 1895 (regular edn).
The why I ams: Why I am a Communist [with L. S. Bevington's Why I am an expropriationist]. 1894. Rptd from Liberty Feb 1894.
Good King Wenceslas: a carol, by Dr Neale. 1895. Introd by Morris.
Child Christopher and Goldilind the Fair. 2 vols 1895 (Kelmscott Press).
Gossip about an old house on the upper Thames. Birmingham 1895. Rptd from Quest Nov 1895.
The well at the world's end: a tale. 2 vols 1896 (Kelmscott Press), 1896 (ordinary edn ptd Chiswick Press). H. B. Forman identifies a unique copy with title page dated 1894 (Reeves & Turner).
Of the external coverings of roofs. [1896].
How I became a Socialist; with some account of his [Morris's] connection with the Social-Democratic Federation by H. M. Hyndman. 1896. Rptd from Justice 1894.
Some German woodcuts of the fifteenth century. Ed S. C. Cockerell 1897 (Kelmscott Press). Reprints partial text of Morris' lecture of 1892, The woodcuts of Gothic books.
The water of the wondrous isles. 1897 (Kelmscott Press, pbd posthumously), 1897.
The sundering flood. 1897 (Kelmscott Press, pbd posthumously), 1898.
A note by Morris on his aims in founding the Kelmscott Press, together with a short description of the press by S. C. Cockerell and an annotated list of the books printed thereat. 1898 (Kelmscott Press).
[Lectures printed at Chiswick Press in Golden type of Kelmscott Press, published by Longmans:] Address delivered at the distribution of prizes to students of the Birmingham Mnicipal School of Art on 21 Feb 1894, 1898; Art and the beauty of the earth, 1899; Some hints on pattern-designing, 1899; Architecture and history, and Westminster Abbey, 1900; Art and its producers, and The arts and crafts of today, 1901.
Architecture, industry and wealth: collected papers. 1902. Reprints Morris's lectures.
The ideal book. New York 1902, 1907, London 1957. Lecture delivered in 1893.
Communism (Fabian Tract no 113). 1903.
The revolt of Ghent. [1911]. Lecture delivered in 1888.
Morris and his Praise of wine. Los Angeles 1958 (priv ptd). With transcript of Morris's poem, included in Morris: artist, writer, Socialist, ed May Morris, and of an unpbd sonnet written after 1867.
Mr Morris on art matters. 1961. Lecture delivered in 1882 as The progress of decorative art in England, rptd from Manchester Guardian 1882.
Ellison, R. C. An unpublished poem by Morris. English 15 1964.
DeLaura, D. J. An unpublished poem of Morris. MP 62 1965.

Translations

Grettis Saga: the story of Grettir the strong. 1869. Tr from the Icelandic by Morris and E. Magnússon.
Völsunga Saga: the story of the Volsungs and Niblungs with certain songs from the Elder Edda. 1870; ed H. Sparling 1888, New York 1965. Tr from the Icelandic Morris and Magnússon.
Three northern love stories and other tales. 1875. Tr Morris and Magnússon. Largely rptd from Fortnightly Rev Feb 1871, and Dark Blue March–April 1871.
The Aeneids of Virgil done into English verse. 1876 (for 1875). *See also* A Pre-Raphaelite Aeneid of Virgil in the collection of Mrs E. L. Doheny of Los Angeles: being an essay in honor of the Morris centenary, Los Angeles 1934.
The Odyssey of Homer done into English verse. 2 vols 1887.
The Saga library. 5 vols 1891–5. Tr from the Icelandic by Morris and Magnússon. Vol 1, The story of Howard the Halt, The story of the banded men, The story of Hen Thorir, 1891; vol 2, The story of the Ere-Dwellers (Eyrbyggja Saga) with the story of the Heath-Slayings (Heiðarviga Saga) as appendix, 1892; vols 3–5, The stories of the kings of Norway called the Round World (Heimskringla), by Snorri Sturluson, vol 1–3, 1893–5.
The order of knighthood. In The order of Chivalry, 1893 (Kelmscott Press).
The tale of King Florus and the Fair Jehane. 1893 (Kelmscott Press).
Of the friendship of Amis and Amile. 1894 (Kelmscott Press).
The tale of the Emperor Coustans and of Over Sea. 1894 (Kelmscott Press).
Old French romances. 1896. With introd by J. Jacobs. Rptd from above 3 items.
The tale of Beowulf, sometime King of the folk of the Weder Geats. 1895 (Kelmscott Press). Tr Morris and A. J. Wyatt.

Letters

Letters on Socialism. 1894 (priv ptd by T. J. Wise).
Letters of Morris to his family and friends. Ed P. Henderson 1950.
Unpublished letters of Morris. Ed R. P. Arnot 1951 (Labour pamphlet ser).
Stokes, E. E., jr. Morris letters at Texas. Jnl of William Morris Soc 1 1963.
See also R. P. Arnot *and* E. P. Thompson, *below*.

§2

Austin, A. In his Poetry of the period, 1870.
Forman, H. B. In his Our living poets, 1871.
—— In Poets and poetry of the century, ed A. H. Miles 1891–7.
Swinburne, A. C. In his Essays and studies, 1875.
Hamilton, W. In his Aesthetic movement in England, 1882.
Pater, W. Aesthetic poetry. In his Appreciations, 1889.
Symons, A. Atlantic Monthly Dec 1896.
Vallance, A. The art of Morris. 1897.
—— Morris: his art, his writings and his public life—a record. 1897.
Mackail, J. W. The life of Morris. 2 vols 1899.
Ashbee, C. R. An endeavour towards the teaching of Ruskin and Morris. 1901.
Cary, E. L. Morris: poet, craftsman, Socialist. New York 1902.
Yeats, W. B. The happiest of the poets. In his Ideas of good and evil, 1903. Rptd from Fortnightly Rev March 1903.
[Burne-Jones, G.] Memorials of Burne-Jones. 2 vols 1904.
Brooke, S. A. A study of Clough, Arnold, Rossetti and Morris. 1908.
Jackson, H. Morris: craftsman-Socialist. 1908, 1926 (rev with 4 new chs).
Noyse, A. Morris. 1908 (EML).
Crane, W. Morris to Whistler: papers and addresses on arts and crafts and the commonweal. 1911.
[Marillier, H. C.] Brief sketch of the Morris movement. 1911.
Drinkwater, J. Morris: a critical study. 1912.
Compton-Rickett, A. Morris: a study in personality. 1913.
Clutton-Brock, A. Morris: his work and influence. 1914.
Dyce, A. Sewanee Rev 22 1914.
Watts-Dunton, T. In his Old familiar faces, 1916.
Vidalenc, G. Morris. Paris 1920.
Glasier, J. B. Morris and the early days of the Socialist movement. 1921.

Hearn, L. In his Pre-Raphaelite and other poets, 1922.
Broers, B. C. In her Mysticism and the Neo-Romanticists, Amsterdam 1923, New York 1966.
Sparling, H. H. The Kelmscott Press and Morris, master-craftsman. 1924.
Wilson, S. Morris and France. South Atlantic Quart 23 1924.
Wolff, L. Le sentiment médiéval en Angleterre au XIXe siècle et la première poésie de Morris. Revue Anglo-américaine 1–2 1924.
Evans, B. I. Morris and his poetry. 1925.
— In his English poetry in the later nineteenth century, 1933, 1966 (rev).
— Morris: his influence and reputation. Contemporary Rev March 1934.
Lucas, F. L. In his Eight Victorian poets, Cambridge 1930, 1940 (as Ten Victorian poets, 1948 (rev)).
Litzenberg, K. The social philosophy of Morris and the doom of the gods. In Essays and studies in English of the University of Michigan, Ann Arbor 1933.
— Scandinavian Stud 14 1936.
— Morris and the reviews. RES 12 1936.
— The diction of Morris. Arkiv för Nordisk Filologi 52 1937.
— Tyrfing into Excalibur? a note on Morris' unfinished poem In Arthur's house. Scandinavian Stud 15 1938.
— Morris and the literary tradition. Michigan Alumnus 53 1946.
Addresses commemorating the one-hundredth anniversary of the birth of Morris. New Haven 1934. Includes lectures by C. B. Tinker, Morris as poet, rptd in his Essays in retrospect, New Haven, 1948; C. P. Rollins, The ordeal of Morris.
Bloomfield, P. Life and work of Morris. 1934.
— Life of Morris: two lectures given before the RSA. 1934.
Some appreciations of Morris. Walthamstow 1934. By G. B. Shaw, May Morris, J. W. Mackail, G. K. Chesterton, H. Read, H. C. Marillier, G. D. H. Cole et al.
Speeches in commemoration of Morris. Walthamstow 1934. By H. Jackson, J. Drinkwater and H. J. Laski.
Weekly, M. Morris. 1934.
Walton, T. A French disciple of Morris: Jean Lahor. Revue de Littérature Comparée 15 1935.
Shaw, G. B. Morris as I knew him. New York 1936, London 1966.
Bush, D. In his Mythology and the romantic tradition in English poetry, Cambridge Mass 1937.
Hoare, D. M. The work of Morris and Yeats in relation to early saga literature. Cambridge 1937.
Löhmann, O. Die Rahmenerzählung von Morris Earthly paradise. Archiv 172 1937.
Ullmann, S. Synaesthetic metaphors in Morris: an essay on the decorative art of the Pre-Raphaelites. Stud in Eng Philology (Budapest) 2 1937.
Riddehough, C. B. Morris' translation of the Aeneid. JEGP 37 1937.
— Morris' translation of the Odyssey. JEGP 40 1941.
Ormerod, J. Poetry of Morris. 1938.
Lewis, C. S. In his Rehabilitations and other essays, Oxford 1939.
Eshleman, L. W. A Victorian rebel: the life of Morris. New York 1940, London 1949 (reissued as Morris: prophet of England's new order, by L. E. Grey).
Maurer, O. Morris and the poetry of escape. In Nineteenth century studies, ed H. Davis, W. C. DeVane and R. C. Bald, New York 1940.
— Some sources of Morris' The wanderers. SE 29 1950.
— Morris and Laxdœla Saga. Texas Stud in Lit & Lang 5 1963.
Davis, A. K. Morris and the eastern question, with a fugitive political poem by Morris. In Humanistic studies in honor of J. C. Metcalfe, Charlottesville 1941.
Tillotson, G. Morris and machines; Morris, word spinner. In his Essays in criticism and research, Cambridge 1942.
Ford, G. H. Morris, Swinburne and some others. In his Keats and the Victorians: a study of his influence and rise to fame 1821–95, New Haven 1944, Hamden Conn 1962.
Short, C. Morris and Keats. PMLA 59 1944.
Grennan, M. Morris: medievalist and revolutionary. New York 1945.
Ekstrom, W. E. The social idealism of Morris and W. D. Howells: a study in four utopian novels. Urbana 1947.
Briggs, M. Ruskin and Morris. In his Men of taste, 1947.
de Carlo, G. Morris. Rome 1947.
Godwin, E. and S. Warrior bard: the life of Morris. 1947.
Masefield, J. In his Thanks before going, 1947.
Meynell, E. Portrait of Morris. 1947.
Jackson, H. In his Dreamers of dreams: the rise and fall of 19th-century idealism. 1948.
Thompson, F. Pre-Raphaelite Morris. In his Literary criticisms, ed T. L. Connolly, New York 1948.
Cole, M. The fellowship of Morris. Virginia Quart Rev 24 1948.
Hough, G. In his Last Romantics, 1949.
Henderson, P. William Morris. 1952, 1964 (rev) (Br Council pamphlet).
Dahl, C. Morris' The chapel in Lyoness: an interpretation. SP 51 1954.
Macleod, R. D. Morris without Mackail. 1954, 1956 (as Morris as seen by his contemporaries).
Thompson, E. P. Morris: romantic to revolutionary. 1955, 1961. *See also* J. Kocmanová, *below*.
Transactions and other publications of the William Morris Society: R. P. Arnot, Bernard Shaw and Morris (1957); G. D. H. Cole, Morris as a Socialist (1960); R. F. Jordan, The medieval vision of Morris (1960); J. Lindsay, Morris, writer (1961); J. Purkis, The Icelandic jaunt: a study in the expeditions made by Morris to Iceland in 1871 and 1873 (1962); J. Swannell, Morris and Old Norse literature (1961); J. R. Dunlap, William Caxton and Morris (1964); E. Thompson, The Communism of Morris (1965).
Wahl, J. R. The mood of energy and the mood of idleness: a note on The earthly paradise. Eng Stud in Africa 2 1959.
— No idle singer: The lovers of Gudrun and Sigurd the Volsung. Cape Town 1964.
Perrine, L. Morris's Guenevere: an interpretation. PQ 39 1960.
Faulkner, P. W. B. Yeats and Morris. Threshold 4 1960.
— Morris and Yeats. Dublin 1962.
— Morris and Yeats. Jnl of William Morris Soc 1 1963.
Kocmanová, J. Two uses of the dream form as a means of confronting the present with the national past: Morris and Svatopluk Čeck. Brno Stud in Eng 2 1960.
— Some remarks on E. P. Thompson's opinion of the poetry of Morris. Philologica Pragensia 3 1960.
— The poetic maturing of Morris, from the Earthly paradise to the Pilgrims of hope. Brno Stud in Eng 5 1964.
— The aesthetic purpose of Morris in the context of his late prose romances. Brno Stud in Eng 6 1966.
Stingle, R. In Association of Canadian University Teachers of English Report, 1960.
Stokes, E. E. Morris and Bernard Shaw. Jnl of William Morris Soc 1 1961.
Gray, D. Arthur, Roland, Empedocles, Sigurd and the despair of heroes in Victorian poetry. Boston Univ Stud in Eng 5 1961.
Swannell, J. N. Morris as an interpreter of Old Norse. Saga-Book 15 1961.
Weevers, T. On the origins of an accentual verse form used by Morris and Henriette Roland Holst. Neophilologus 46 1962.
Carson, A. Morris' Guenevere: a further note. PQ 42 1963. *See also* Perrine, *above*.

Arnot, R. P. Morris: the man and the myth. 1964.
Fleissner, R. F. Percute hic: Morris' terrestrial paradise. Victorian Poetry 3 1965.
Raymond, M. B. The Arthurian group in the Defence of Guenevere and other poems. Victorian Poetry 4 1966.
Gordon, W. K. Pre-Raphaelitism and the Oxford and Cambridge Magazine. Jnl Rutgers Univ Lib 29 1966.

W. E. F.

ALGERNON CHARLES SWINBURNE
1837–1909

Bibliographies

Wise, T. J. A bibliography of the writings of Swinburne. 2 vols 1919–20 (priv ptd), 1927 (rev) (vol 20 in Complete works, Bonchurch edn).
— Catalogue of the Ashley library vols 6–10. 1925–30 (priv ptd).
— A Swinburne library. 1925 (priv ptd).
Hyder, C. K. Swinburne's literary career and fame. Durham NC 1933.
— In The Victorian poets: a review of research, ed F. E. Faverty, Cambridge Mass 1956, 1968 (rev).
Carter, J. and H. G. Pollard. An enquiry into the nature of certain nineteenth-century pamphlets. 1934.
— The firm of Charles Ottley, Landon & Co: footnote to an enquiry. 1948.
Ehrsam, T. G., R. H. Deily and R. M. Smith. In their Bibliographies of twelve Victorian authors, New York 1936.
Partington, W. Forging ahead. New York 1939, 1946 (rev as T. J. Wise in the original cloth).
Todd, W. B. Swinburne manuscripts at Texas. Texas Quart 2 1959.
T. J. Wise centenary studies: essays by J. Carter, H. G. Pollard, W. B. Todd. Austin 1959.
Fredeman, W. E. In his Pre-raphaelitism: a bibliographical study, Cambridge Mass 1965.

Collections

Poetical works, including most of the dramas. New York 1884.
Poems. 6 vols 1904 (with Atalanta and Erechtheus).
Tragedies. 5 vols 1905.
Poems and tragedies. 2 vols Philadelphia [1910].
Golden pine edition. 7 vols 1917–25.
Collected poetical works. 2 vols 1924, 1927.
Complete works. 20 vols 1925–7 (Bonchurch edn).
Selections. Ed R. H. Stoddard, New York 1884.
Select poems. 1887.
Lyrical poems. Ed. W. Sharp, Leipzig 1901 (Tauchnitz).
Dead Love and other inedited pieces. Portland Maine 1901.
Selected poems. Ed. W. M. Payne, Boston 1905.
Selected lyrical poems. New York 1906.
Poems. Ed. A. Beatty, New York 1906.
Selected dramas. Ed. A. Beatty, New York 1909.
Springtide of life: poems on childhood. Ed. E. Gosse 1918.
Poems. Ed. E. Rhys, New York 1919 (Modern Lib).
Selections. Ed. E. Gosse and T. J. Wise 1919.
Golden book of Swinburne's lyrics. Ed. E. H. Blakeney 1922.
The triumph of time and other poems. Ed. G. S. Viereck, Girard Kansas 1925.
Selections. Ed. W. O. Raymond, New York 1925.
Selections. Ed. H. M. Burton 1927.
Selections. Ed. H. Wolfe 1928.
The best of Swinburne. Ed. C. K. Hyder and L. Chase, New York 1937.
Selected poems. Ed. L. Binyon, Oxford 1940 (WC).
Poems and prose. Ed. R. Church 1940 (EL).
Selected poems. Ed. H. Treece 1948.
Selected poems. Ed. H. Hare 1950.
Selected poems. Ed. E. Shanks 1950.
A Swinburne anthology: verse, drama, prose, criticism. Ed. K. Foss 1955.
A selection. Ed. E. Sitwell 1960.
Poems. Ed. B. Dobrée 1961.

§1

William Congreve. In The imperial dictionary, ed. J. F. Waller 1857.
Undergraduate papers. Oxford 1858. The early English dramatists and The monomaniac's tragedy rptd in New writings by Swinburne, 1964; Queen Yseult rptd 1918 (priv) and in Bonchurch edn vol 1; Modern Hellenism (ascribed to Swinburne) and Church imperialism rptd in Lafourcade, La jeunesse de Swinburne vol 2.
The Queen-Mother; Rosamond. 1860, 1860 (for 1865, Moxon's reissue), 1866 (Hotten's reissue), 1868 etc.
Pilgrimage of pleasure. In Mary Gordon's Children of the chapel, 1864, 1875, 1910.
Atalanta in Calydon. 1865, 1865, 1866, 1868, 1875, etc, Oxford 1930 (facs).
Chastelard. 1865, 1866 (Hotten's reissue), 1868, 1878, etc.
Poems and ballads. 1866, 1866 (Hotten's reissue), 1866 etc.
Notes on poems and reviews. 1866, 1866.
Byron. 1866.
An appeal to England. 1867.
A song of Italy. 1867, 1868.
Notes on the Royal Academy exhibition. 1868.
William Blake. 1868 (for 1867), 1868, 1906.
Siena. 1868.
Christabel and the poems of Coleridge. 1869.
Ode on the French Republic. 1870.
Songs before sunrise. 1871, 1874 etc.
Bothwell, Act one [an early version]. 1871 (priv ptd).
Under the microscope. 1872.
Le tombeau de Théophile Gautier. 1873.
Bothwell. 1874, 1874, 1882 etc.
George Chapman. 1875.
Songs of two nations. 1875, 1893.
Essays and studies. 1875, 1876, 1888 etc.
Note on the Muscovite crusade. 1876.
Erechtheus. 1876, 1876, 1887, 1896 etc.
Joseph and his brethren. 1876. Introd to C. J. Wells's play.
Lesbia Brandon. 1877 (galleys); ed R. Hughes 1952; ed E. Wilson, New York 1962. *See also* controversy in TLS 10–17, 31 Oct, 7, 28 Nov 1952.
Note on Charlotte Brontë. 1877, 1877, 1894.
William Congreve. In Encyclopaedia britannica, 1877.
Poems and ballads: second series. 1878, 1878, 1880 etc.
Frank Fane: a ballad. Pearl 1 1879. Unsigned; probably by Swinburne.
A study of Shakespeare. 1880, 1880, 1895, 1902, etc.
Songs of the springtides. 1880, 1880, 1891, 1902.
Specimens of modern poets: the heptalogia. 1880.
Studies in song. 1880, 1896, 1907.
Mary Stuart. 1881, 1898, 1909.
Tristram of Lyonesse and other poems. 1882, 1882, 1884, 1892 etc.
A century of roundels. 1883, 1883, 1892 etc.
Les Cenci. Paris 1883. Introd in French to Tola Dorian's trn.
Christopher Marlow. In Encyclopaedia britannica, 1883.
Mary Queen of Scots. In Encyclopaedia britannica, 1883.
A midsummer holiday and other poems. 1884, 1884, 1889.
Marino Faliero. 1885, 1907.
A study of Victor Hugo. 1886, 1909.
Miscellanies. 1886, 1895, 1911.
The commonweal: a song for unionists. 1886 (rptd from Times 1 July 1886), 1889 (pirated). Rptd in Gathered songs (a forgery with a fraudulent imprint and the date July 1887) and in A channel passage and other poems, 1904.

Cleopatra. 1886–7 or –8 (priv ptd). A forgery, fraudulently dated 1866, but nonetheless the first separate printing.
A word for the Navy. 1887 (priv ptd) (Redway edn).
Locrine. 1887, 1896.
Thomas Middleton. 1887. Introd to Mermaid edn.
The jubilee. [1888–90?] (priv ptd). A forgery, with a fraudulent imprint and the date (not proved false) June 1887. The poem was pbd in Nineteenth Century June 1887 and rptd (as The commonweal) in Poems and ballads: third series, pbd 4 April 1889.
The question. [1888–90?] (priv ptd). A forgery, with a fraudulent imprint and the date (not proved false) May 1887. The poem was ptd in Daily Telegraph 29 April 1887 and rptd in A channel passage and other poems, 1904.
Dead love. [1888?] (priv ptd: a forgery, fraulently dated 1864), [1904?] (a counterfeit of the forgery). Rptd in A pilgrimage of pleasure, Boston 1913 and in Bonchurch edn vol 17.
The Whippingham papers. 1888 (priv ptd). About half the vol, including 2 poems, Arthur's flogging and Reginald's flogging, and one piece in prose, A boy's first flogging at Birchminster, is Swinburne's.
Cyril Tourneur. In Encyclopaedia Britannica, 1889.
Poems and ballads: third series. 1889, 1889, 1892, etc.
A study of Ben Jonson. 1889.
Gathered songs. [1888–90?] (priv ptd). A forgery, with a fraudulent imprint and the date (not proved false) July 1887; 3 of the 4 poems pbd in Poems and ballads: third series, 4 April 1889.
A sequence of sonnets on the death of Robert Browning. 1890 (priv ptd; pirated).
Robert Herrick. 1891. Introd to ML edn.
The sisters 1892.
The ballad of Bulgarie. 1893 (priv ptd; pirated).
Grace Darling. 1893 (priv ptd; pirated).
Astrophel and other poems. 1894, 1894.
Studies in prose and poetry. 1894, 1897, 1906, 1915.
The devil's due. [1896?] (priv ptd). A forgery, fraudulently dated 1875.
The tale of Balen. 1896.
Robert Burns. Edinburgh 1896 (priv ptd; pirated).
Aurora Leigh. 1898. Introd to Mrs Browning's poem.
A channel passage. 1899.
Rosamund, Queen of the Lombards. 1899, 1900.
Love's cross-currents: a year's letters. Portland Maine 1901, 1905, 1906; ed E. Wilson, New York 1962; ed M. Zaturenska, New York 1964.
Victor Hugo. In Encyclopaedia Britannica 1902.
Percy Bysshe Shelley. Philadelphia 1903. Also in Chambers's cyclopaedia of English literature, 1903.
A channel passage and other poems. 1904, 1904, 1904.
Pericles. 1907. Introd in vol 13 of Harrap edn of Shakespeare.
The Duke of Gandia. 1908.
The age of Shakespeare. 1909.
Lord Soulis. 1909 (priv ptd).
In the twilight. 1909 (priv ptd).
To W.T.W.D. 1909 (priv ptd).
Lord Scales. 1909 (priv ptd).
M. Prudhomme at the international exhibition. 1909 (priv ptd).
Of liberty and loyalty. 1909 (priv ptd).
The saviour of society. 1909 (priv ptd).
The marriage of Monna Lisa. 1909 (priv ptd).
The portrait. 1909 (priv ptd).
The chronicle of Queen Fredegonde. 1909 (priv ptd).
Burd Margaret. 1909 (priv ptd).
The worm of Spindlestonheugh. 1909 (priv ptd).
Border ballads. 1909 (priv ptd).
Ode to Mazzini. 1909 (priv ptd).
The ballad of truthful Charles and other poems. 1910 (priv ptd).
A criminal case. 1910 (priv ptd).

The ballade of Villon and Fat Madge. 1910 (priv ptd).
A record of friendship. 1910 (priv ptd).
Blest and The centenary of Shelley. 1912 (priv ptd).
Border ballads. Boston 1912 (priv ptd).
Les fleurs du mal and other studies. 1913 (priv ptd).
The cannibal catechism. 1913 (priv ptd).
Charles Dickens. 1913.
A pilgrimage of pleasure, essays and studies. Boston 1913.
A study of Les misérables. 1914 (priv ptd). The first and fifth essays are not by Swinburne.
Pericles and other studies. 1914 (priv ptd).
Thomas Nabbes. 1914 (priv ptd).
Christopher Marlowe in relation to Greene, Peele and Lodge. 1914 (priv ptd).
Théophile. 1915 (priv ptd).
Lady Maisie's bairn and other poems. 1915 (priv ptd).
Félicien Cossu. 1915 (priv ptd).
Ernest Clouët. 1916 (priv ptd).
A vision of bags. 1916 (priv ptd).
Poems from Villon and other fragments. 1916 (priv ptd).
The death of Sir John Franklin. 1916 (priv ptd).
The triumph of Gloriana. 1916 (priv ptd).
Poetical fragments. 1916 (priv ptd).
Wearieswa'. 1917 (priv ptd).
Posthumous poems. Ed. E. Gosse and T. J. Wise 1917.
Rondeaux parisiens. 1917 (priv ptd).
The character and opinions of Dr Johnson. 1918 (priv ptd).
The Italian mother and other poems. 1918 (priv ptd).
The ride from Milan. 1918 (priv ptd).
The two knights and other poems. 1918 (priv ptd).
A lay of lilies and other poems. 1918 (priv ptd).
Queen Yseult. 1918 (priv ptd).
Undergraduate sonnets. 1918 (priv ptd).
Lancelot, the death of Rudel and other poems. 1918 (priv ptd).
Contemporaries of Shakespeare. Ed. E. Gosse and T. J. Wise 1919.
Shakespeare. Oxford 1919.
The queen's tragedy. 1919 (priv ptd).
French lyrics. 1919 (priv ptd).
Ballads of the English border. Ed. W. A. MacInnes 1925.
Swinburne's Hyperion and other poems. Ed. G. Lafourcade 1928.
Lucretia Borgia: the chronicle of Tebaldeo Tebaldei. Ed. R. Hughes 1942.
Changes of aspect and Short notes. Ed. C. K. Hyder, PMLA 58 1943.
Columbus, with a note by J. S. Mayfield. Jacksonville Fla 1944 (priv ptd).
Pasiphaë. Ed. R. Hughes 1950.
A roundel of retreat. [Washington DC 1950] (priv ptd). The imprint, an obvious jest, reads: London, Charles Ottley, Landon & Co, 1950.
Will Drew and Phil Crewe and Frank Fane by a great English literary figure. [1962?] (priv ptd).
Le prince prolétaire. Bethesda Maryland 1963 (priv ptd).
The influence of the Roman censorship on the morals of the people. Brooklyn 1964 (priv ptd).
New writings by Swinburne. Ed. C. Y. Lang, Syracuse NY 1964.

Letters

All the genuine letters listed here were included in The Swinburne letters, ed Lang 1959–62, *below*.

Letters to T. J. Wise, 1909; Letters on Chapman, 1909; Letters to J. C. Collins, 1910; Letters on Morris, Omar Khayyám etc, 1910; Letters to A. H. Bullen, 1910; Letters to Purnell and others, 1910; Letters concerning Poe, 1910; Letters to Gosse, 5 ser 1910–11; Letters to Stedman, 1912; Letters to Burton and others, 1912; Letters to Henry Taylor, 1912; Letters to Locker-Lampson and others, 1912; Letters to the press, 1912; Letters to Lytton, 1913; Letters to Locker, 1913; Letters

to Mallarmé, 1913; Letters to Morley, 1914; Letters to Dowden, 1914; Letters to Milnes and others, 1915; Letters to Lady Trevelyan, 1916; Letters to Nichol, 1917; Letters to Hugo, 1917. All priv ptd.
The boyhood of Swinburne. Ed Mrs D. Leith 1917.
The letters of Swinburne. Ed T. Hake and A. Compton-Rickett 1918.
The letters of Swinburne. Ed E. Gosse and T. J. Wise 2 vols 1918. Rptd, rev and enlarged in vol 18 of Bonchurch edn, above.
A romance of literature. 1919; Letters to Horne, 1920; Autobiographical notes, 1920. All priv ptd.
A letter by Swinburne on Kate Greenaway. Jacksonville Fla 1944 (priv ptd). A forgery.
The Swinburne letters. Ed. C. Y. Lang 6 vols New Haven 1959–62.

§2

[Houghton, Baron (R. M. Milnes)]. Swinburne's Atalanta. Edinburgh Rev 122 1865.
— Swinburne's Chastelard. Fortnightly Rev April 1866.
Buchanan, R. W. Athenaeum 2 1866. Review of Poems and ballads.
— Immorality in authorship. Fortnightly Rev 15 Sept 1866.
— The fleshly school of poetry. 1872.
Lowell, J. R. North Amer Rev 102 1866. Review of Chastelard and Atalanta, rptd in his My study windows, Boston 1871.
[Morley, J.] Mr Swinburne's new poems. Saturday Rev 22 1866.
Rossetti, W. M. Swinburne's Poems and ballads. 1866.
Thomson, J. The Swinburne controversy. National Reformer 23 Dec 1866. Rptd in his Satires and profanities 1884.
Bayne, P. Mr Arnold and Mr Swinburne. Contemporary Rev 6 1867.
Etienne, L. Le paganisme poétique en Angleterre. Revue des Deux Mondes ser 2 69 1867.
Conway, M. D. Fortnightly Rev 3 1868. Review of William Blake.
Austin, A. The poetry of the period: Mr Swinburne. Temple Bar 26 1869. Rptd in his The poetry of the period, 1870.
Friswell, J. H. Modern men of letters honestly criticised. 1870.
Forman, H. B. Our living poets. 1871.
Blémont, E. Swinburne. La Renaissance 1 1872.
Courthope, W. J. The latest development of literary poetry: Swinburne, Rossetti, Morris. Quart Rev 132 1872.
Stedman, E. C. Swinburne. Scribner's Monthly 9 1875.
Clifford, W. K. Cosmic emotion. Nineteenth Century 2 1877. Rptd in his Lectures and essays, 1879.
Harvey, H. Swinburne. Républiques des Lettres 18 Feb 1877.
Sarrazin, G. Poètes modernes de l'Angleterre. Paris 1885.
Villiers de l'Isle Adam, A. Le sadisme anglais. In his Histoires insolites, Paris 1888.
Lang, A. Letters on literature. 1889.
Patmore, C. Principle in art. 1889.
Wilde, O. Pall Mall Gazette 27 June 1889. Review of Poems and ballads: third series; rptd in his Reviews, vol 2 1910.
Maupassant, G. de. Notes sur Swinburne. Preface to Mourey's trn of Poems and ballads, 1891.
Shindler, R. The theology of Swinburne's poems. GM 271 1891.
Waugh, A. Reticence in literature. Yellow Book 1 1894.
Saintsbury, G. In his Corrected impressions, 1895.
Barlow, G. On the spiritual side of Swinburne's genius. Contemporary Rev 88 1905.
Woodberry, G. E. Swinburne. New York 1905.
Elton, O. In his Modern studies, 1907.

Russell, C. E. Swinburne and music. North Amer Rev 186 1907.
Mackail, J. W. Swinburne. Oxford 1909; rptd in his Studies of English poets, 1926.
Meynell, A. Swinburne's lyrical poetry. Dublin Rev 145 1909.
Svanberg, Harald. Swinburne en studie. Goteberg 1909.
Murdoch, W. G. B. Memories of Swinburne. Edinburgh 1910.
Serner, G. The language of Swinburne's lyrics and epics. Lund 1910.
Thomas, E. Swinburne. 1912.
Drinkwater, J. Swinburne. 1913.
Welby, T. E. Swinburne, 1914.
— A study of Swinburne. 1926.
— In his The Victorian romantics, 1929.
Harris, F. In his Contemporary portraits, 1915.
Lyall, A. C. In his Studies in literature and history, 1915.
Lucas, E. V. At the Pines. New Statesman 25 March 1916.
Catalogue of the library of Swinburne. Sotheby, Wilkinson and Hodge, 19–21 June 1916.
Bennett, A. In his Books and persons, 1917.
Gosse, E. Life. 1917; rptd in Bonchurch edn, vol 19 (rev).
— The first draft of Anactoria. MLR 14 1919. Also priv ptd nd, and rptd in his Aspects and impressions, 1922.
— Swinburne. 1925. Pbd in Danish trn in Det Nittende Aarhundrede 1875 and in German, Dutch and Swedish trns 1876.
Jean-Aubry, G. Beaudelaire et Swinburne. Mercure de France 124 1917.
— Hugo et Swinburne. Revue Bleue 74 1936.
Symons, A. Swinburne. Fortnightly Rev May 1917.
— Studies in strange souls. 1929.
— Notes on two manuscripts. Eng Rev 54 1932.
Bailey, J. Swinburne. Quart Rev 228 1917.
Pound, E. Swinburne vs biographers. Poetry 11 1917.
Quiller-Couch, A. T. Swinburne. Edinburgh Rev 225 1917; rptd in his Studies in literature, Cambridge 1918.
Henderson, W. B. D. Swinburne and Landor. 1918.
Kernahan, C. Swinburne as I knew him. 1919.
Eliot, T. S. Swinburne as critic; Swinburne as poet. In his Sacred wood, 1920.
Wier, M. C. The influence of Aeschylus and Euripides on Atalanta and Erechtheus. Ann Arbor 1920.
Grierson, H. J. C. Byron: Arnold and Swinburne. Proc Br Acad 9 1921; rptd in his Background of English literature, 1925.
— Swinburne. 1953.
Praz, M. La trilogia de Maria Stuarda. Rivista di Cultura 15 Feb 1921.
— Le tragedie greche di Swinburne e le fonti dell' Atalanta. Atene e Roma new ser 3 1922.
— Il manoscritto dell' Atalanta. Cultura 8 1929.
— Swinburniana. Cultura 9 1930.
— In his La carne, la morte e il diavolo nella lettura romantica, Florence 1930; tr Oxford 1933 (as The romantic agony).
Watts-Dunton, C. The home life of Swinburne. 1922.
Reul, P. de. L'oeuvre de Swinburne. Brussels 1922.
Broera, B. C. Mysticism in the neo-romanticists. Amsterdam and Paris 1923.
Lafourcade, G. Swinburne et Baudelaire. Revue Anglo-américaine 1 1924.
— Atalanta: le manuscrit, les sources. Revue Anglo-américaine 3 1925.
— Swinburne and Whitman. MLR 22 1927; Revue Anglo-américaine 9 1931 (rev).
— La jeunesse de Swinburne. 2 vols Paris 1928.
— Swinburne: a literary biography. 1932.
— L'algolagnie de Swinburne. Hippocrate March–April 1935.
— Swinburne romancier: la fille du policeman. Minotaure 7 1935.

— Le triomphe du temps: ou la réputation de Swinburne. Etudes Anglaises 1 1937.
— Le centenaire de Swinburne. Etudes Anglaises 2 1938.
— Swinburne vindicated. London Mercury Feb 1938.
Ratchford, F. E. The first draft of Hertha. MLN 39 1924.
— Swinburne's projected triameron. Texas Rev 9 1923.
— Swinburne at work. Sewanee Rev 31 1923.
Dottin, P. La littérature, les légendes et l'histoire anciennes dans la poésie de Swinburne. Revue de l'Enseignement des Langues Vivantes 42 1925.
Galimberti, A. L'aedo d'Italia. Palermo 1925.
Delattre, F. Swinburne et la France. Revue des Cours et des Conférences 27 1926.
— Baudelaire et le jeune Swinburne. Paris 1930.
Nicolson, H. Swinburne and Baudelaire. Trans Royal Soc of Lit 6 1926; Oxford 1930 (rev).
— Swinburne. 1926.
Galland, R. Emerson, Swinburne et Meredith. Revue Anglo-américaine 6 1928.
Chew, S. C. Swinburne. Boston 1929.
Hyder, C. K. Laus veneris and the Tannhäuser legend. PMLA 45 1930.
— The medieval background in the Leper. PMLA 46 1931.
— Swinburne's literary career and fame. Durham NC 1931.
— Emerson on Swinburne: a sensational interview. MLN 48 1933.
— Swinburne and the popular ballad. PMLA 49 1934.
Lucas, F. L. In his Eight Victorian poets, Cambridge 1930, 1940 (as Ten Victorian poets), 1948 (rev).
Rutland, W. R. Swinburne: a nineteenth-century Hellene. Oxford 1931.
Benson, A. C. Swinburne and Watts-Dunton. Living Age 343 1933.
Dingle, H. Swinburne's internal centre. Queen's Quart 40 1933.
— Science and literary criticism. 1949.
Knickerbocker, K. The source of Les noyades. PQ 12 1933.
— Browning and Swinburne: an episode. MLN 62 1947.
Motter, T. H. V. A new Arnold letter and an old Swinburne quarrel. TLS 31 Aug 1933.
Falk, B. The naked lady. 1934.
Wright, H. G. Unpublished letters from Watts-Dunton to Swinburne. RES 10 1934.
Brown, E. K. Swinburne: a centenary estimate. UTQ 6 1937.
Child, R. C. Swinburne's mature standards of criticism. PMLA 52 1937.
Hopkinson, A. The centenary of Swinburne. Contemporary Rev Oct 1937.
Peyre, H. Le centenaire de Swinburne. Revue de Littérature Comparée 17 1937.
Meyerstein, E. W. H. Two scenes from a tragedy. London Mercury Feb 1938.
Larsen, T. Swinburne on Middleton. TLS 17 June 1939. Reply by K. Muir 24 Feb 1945.
Brown, C. S. More Swinburne–D'Annunzio parallels. PMLA 55 1940.
Shahani, R. G. The Asiatic element in Swinburne's poetry. Poetry Rev 33 1942.
Mackay, W. F. Verlaine and Swinburne. Canada Français 30 1943.
Grantham, E. Letters from Symonds to Swinburne. More Books 21 1946.
Mayfield, J. S. These many years, by Swinburne. Washington 1947 (priv ptd) (with facs).
— Swinburne to P. H. Hayne. Autograph Collectors' Jnl 5 1952.
— Swinburne's unpublished erotic verses to a mistress. Amateur Book Collector 2 1952.
— Swinburne's Boo. Bethesda Md 1953 (priv ptd); rptd in Eng Miscellany (Rome) 4 1953 (separately bound priv reissued Washington DC 1954).
— Two presentation copies of Swinburne's Atalanta in Calydon. PBSA 49 1955; rev as A Swinburne puzzle in Book Collector 4 1955.
Lang, C. Y. Swinburne and American literature. Amer Lit 19 1948.
— The first chorus of Atalanta. Yale Univ Lib Gazette 27 1953.
— Some Swinburne manuscripts. Jnl Rutgers Univ Lib 18 1954.
— A manuscript, a mare's-nest and a mystery. Yale Univ Lib Gazette 31 1957.
— Swinburne's lost love. PMLA 74 1959.
— Atalanta in manuscript. Yale Univ Lib Gazette 37 1962.
Hughes, R. Unpublished Swinburne. Life & Letters Jan 1948.
Tillyard, E. M. W. In his Five poems 1470–1870, 1948. On Hertha.
Angeli, H. R. D. G. Rossetti: his friends and enemies. 1949. *See also* letters in TLS 16 Sept 1949, 24 March 1950.
Bowra, C. M. Atalanta in Calydon. In his Romantic imagination, Cambridge Mass 1949; Essays by Divers Hands 25 1950.
Dahl, C. Swinburne's loyalty to the House of Stuart. SP 46 1949.
— Swinburne's Mary Stuart a reading of Ronsard. Papers on Eng Lang & Lit 1 1965.
— Autobiographical elements in Swinburne's trilogy on Mary Stuart. Victorian Poetry 3 1965.
Hare, H. Swinburne: a biographical approach. 1949.
Troxell, J. C. A Rossetti letter. TLS 16 Dec 1949.
Walker, R. Swinburne, Tolstoy and King Lear. English 7 1949.
Knaplund, P. The Poet Laureateship in 1892: some Acton-Gladstone letters. Quart Rev 288 1950.
Souffrin, E. Swinburne et Banville. Revue de Littérature Comparée 24 1950.
— Swinburne et sa légende en France. Revue de Littérature Comparée 25 1951.
— Swinburne et Les misérables. Revue de Littérature Comparée 34 1960.
Pope-Hennessy, J. Monckton Milnes: the flight of youth. 1951.
Cassidy, J. A. Robert Buchanan and the fleshly controversy. PMLA 67 1952.
— A. C. Swinburne. New York 1964.
Connolly, T. E. Swinburne's theory of the end of art. ELH 19 1952.
— Swinburne on the music of poetry. PMLA 72 1957.
— Swinburne's theory of poetry. Albany NY 1964.
Maurer, O. Swinburne vs Furnivall. SE 31 1952.
Super, R. H. A grain of truth about Wordsworth and Browning, Landor and Swinburne. MLN 67 1952.
Marchand, L. The Watts-Dunton letter books. Jnl Rutgers Univ Lib 17 1953.
Robinson, J. K. A neglected phase of the Aesthetic Movement: English Parnassianism. PLMA 68 1953.
Temple, R. T. The critic's alchemy. New York 1953.
Faurot, R. M. Swinburne's poem Love a translation from Hugo. N & Q March 1954.
Marshall, R. T. S. Eliot et le Baudelaire de Swinburne. Bayou no 70 1957.
Noyes, A. Dinner at the Pines: reminiscences of Swinburne. Listener 28 March 1957.
Baum, P. F. Swinburne's A nympholept. South Atlantic Quart 57 1958.
— The Fitzwilliam manuscript of Swinburne's Atalanta, verses 1,038–1,204. MLR 54 1,959.
[Ehrenpreis], A. W. Henry. A reconstructed Swinburne ballad. Harvard Lib Bull 12 1958.

— Swinburne's edition of popular ballads. PMLA 78 1963.
Adams, D. K. Swinburne and Hazlitt. N & Q Dec 1959.
Kerr, L. Swinburne and Correggio. TLS 31 July 1959.
Lockspeiser, E. Debussy and Swinburne. Monthly Musical Record March–April 1959.
Paden, W. D. Footnote to a footnote. TLS 23 Oct 1959. Replies by A. R. Redway 20 Nov, J. C. Troxell 4 Dec 1959.
— A few annotations by Swinburne. N & Q Dec 1961.
Tener, R. H. Swinburne as reviewer. TLS 25 Dec 1959.
Altick, R. D. Four Victorian poets and an exploding island. Victorian Stud 3 1960.
del Re, R. Il classicismo nella poesia di Swinburne. Convivium 28 1960.
Graaf, D. A. de. L'influence de Swinburne sur Verlaine et Rimbaud. Revue des Sciences Humaines no 97 1960.
Maxwell, J. C. The Swinburne letters and OED. N & Q Sept 1960, Sept 1961, Sept 1963.
Hargreaves, H. A. Swinburne's Greek plays and God the supreme evil. MLN 76 1961.
Lucie-Smith, E. The tortured yearned as well: themes of cruelty in current verse. CQ 4 1962.
Peters, R. L. Swinburne and the use of integral detail. Victorian Stud 5 1962.
— Swinburne's idea of form. Criticism 5 1963.
— Swinburne and the moral design of art. Victorian Poetry 2 1964.
— The crowns of Apollo: Swinburne's principles of literature and art. Detroit 1965.
Grosskurth, P. M. Swinburne and Symonds: an uneasy literary relationship. RES new ser 14 1963.
Johnson, W. S. Swinburne and Carlyle. Eng Lang Notes 1 1963.
Packer, L. M. Swinburne and Christina Rossetti: atheist and Anglican. UTQ 33 1963.
Just, K. G. Die Rezeption Swinburnes in der deutschen Literatur der Jahrhundertwende. In Festschrift für Jost Trier zum 70, Cologne 1964.
Nowell-Smith, S. Swinburne's The Queen-Mother and Rosamond, 1860. Book Collector 13 1964.
Seronsy, C. C. An autograph letter by Swinburne on Daniel and Drummond of Hawthornden. N & Q Aug 1965.
Tillotson, G. In his Mid-Victorian studies, 1965.
Bass, E. Swinburne, Greene and the Triumph of time. Victorian Poetry 4 1966.

C. Y. L.

JAMES THOMSON ('B.V.')

1834–82

In 1952 Bodley obtained Bertram Dobell's collection of mss relating to Thomson, containing holograph poems, notebooks, diaries, letters by and to him, other writings and memoranda. The BM contains drafts for two-thirds of the City of dreadful night, 3 other notebooks, and corrected proofs. A ms of this poem is also in the Pierpont Morgan Library, New York.

Bibliographies

Dobell, B. and J. M. Wheeler. In The city of dreadful night, Portland Maine 1892.
Walker, I. B. In his Thomson: a critical study, Ithaca 1950.

Collections

Selections from original contributions of Thomson to Cope's Tobacco plant. Ed W. Lewin, Liverpool 1889.
Poems, essays and fragments. Ed J. M. Robinson 1892.
Poetical works. Ed B. Dobell 2 vols 1895. With memoir by B. Dobell.
The city of dreadful night [and a selection of poems]. Ed B. Dobell 1910.
Poems. Ed G. H. Gerould, New York 1927.
The city of dreadful night and other poems. Ed E. Blunden 1932.
The city of dreadful night and other poems. 1932. Preface by H. S. Salt.

§1

A commission of inquiry on royalty etc. 1876.
The story of a famous old Jewish firm. 1876.
The devil in the Church of England and The one thing. 1876.
The pilgrimage to Saint Nicotine. Liverpool 1878.
The city of dreadful night and other poems. 1880. The City of dreadful night first pbd in Nat Reformer 22 March–17 May 1874.
Vane's story, Weddah and Om-el-Bonain and other poems. 1881 [for 1880].
Address on the opening of the new hall of the Leicester Secular Society, March 6 1881. 1881?.
The story of a famous old Jewish firm etc. In Leek Bijou Freethought Reprints no 6 1881.
Essays and fantasies. 1881.
The story of the famous old Jewish firm and other pieces in prose and rime. 1884 (priv ptd).
Satires and profanities. Ed G. W. Foote 1884.
A voice from the Nile and other poems. 1884. With memoir by B. Dobell.
Shelley: a poem; with other writings relating to Shelley, by the late James Thomson (B.V.); to which is added an essay on the poetry of William Blake by the same author. 1884 (priv ptd). Preface by B. Dobell.
The city of dreadful night. Portland Maine 1892. Introd by E. Cavazza.
Biographical and critical studies. Ed B. Dobell 1896.
Essays, dialogues and thoughts of Giacomo Leopardi. [1905]. Tr, with a memoir of Leopardi, by Thomson; introd by B. Dobell.
Thomson on George Meredith. 1909 (priv ptd).
Walt Whitman: the man and the poet. Ed B. Dobell 1910. Introd by B. Dobell.
Poems and some letters of Thomson. Ed A. Ridler 1963.

§2

Marston, P. B. In English poets, ed T. H. Ward, vol 4. 1880.
Mccall, W. A Nirvana trilogy. 1886.
Noel, R. In Poets and poetry of the century, ed A. H. Miles, vol 5 [1892].
G[rowell], A. Thomson: biographical and bibliographical sketch. New York 1893.
Salt, H. S. The life of Thomson. 1889, 1898, 1914 (rev edn).
— Extracts from Thomson's notebook. Scottish Rev Sept 1889.
Weissel, J. Thomson der jüngere: sein Leben und seine Werke. Vienna 1906.
Dobell, B. The laureate of pessimism. 1910.
Meeker, J. E. The life and poetry of Thomson. New Haven 1917.
Hoffman, H. An angel in the city of dreadful night. Sewanee Rev 32 1924.
Peyre, H. Les sources du pessimisme de Thomson. Revue Anglo-américaine 2 1925.
Hirsch, A. Thomson: ses traducteurs et ses critiques en France. Revue de l'Enseignement des Langues Vivantes Feb–April 1925.
Marks, J. In his Genius and disaster, New York 1926.
Evans, B. I. In his English poetry in the later nineteenth century, 1933, 1966 (rev).
Newberg, V. Thomson. Free Thinker 18 Nov–2 Dec 1934.
Schiller, F. C. S. Thomson: a poet of pessimism. In his Must philosophers disagree? 1934.
Wallis, N. H. Thomson and his City of dreadful night. Essays by Divers Hands 14 1935.

Black, G. A. Thomson: his translations of Heine. MLR 31 1936.
Rebora, P. Thomson e la poesia di Leopardi in Inghilterra. Bolletino degli Studi Inglesi in Italia July 1937.
Wolff, W. Thomson in Central City. Univ of Colorado Stud ser B 1 1940.
Woodbridge, B. M. Poets and pessimism: Vigny, Housman et al. Romanic Rev 35 1944.
Cotten, L. A. Leopardi and the City of dreadful night. SP 42 1945; rptd in Studies in language and literature, ed G. R. Coffman, Chapel Hill 1945.
De Camp, D. Thomson's The city of dreadful night. Explicator 7 1949.
Walker, I. B. Thomson: a critical study. Ithaca 1950.
Harper, G. M. Blake's Nebuchadnezzar in the City of dreadful night. SP 50 1953.
LeRoy, G. C. In his Perplexed prophets, Philadelphia 1953.
Vachot, C. Thomson et l'orient. Revue de Littérature Comparée 27 1953.
— Thomson. Paris 1964.
Birchmeier-Nussbaumer, A. K. Weltbild eines Pessimisten: die Struktur der konkreten Vorstellungswelt von Thomson. Zürich [1957].
Brown, C. S. Thomson and D'Annunzio on Dürer's Melancolia. Jnl of Aesthetics 19 1960.
Forsyth, R. A. Evolutionism and the pessimism of Thomson. EC 12 1962.
— The Victorian self-image and the city sensibility. UTQ 33 1963.
Schaefer, W. D. The two cities of dreadful night. PMLA 77 1962.
— Thomson: beyond 'the City'. 1966.
McGann, J. J. Thomson: the woven hymns of night and day. Stud in Eng Lit 1500–1900 3 1963.
Bysshe Vanolis: Thomson's journey into night. TLS 16 Feb 1967.

W. W.

GERARD MANLEY HOPKINS

1844–89

The mss in Campion Hall Oxford are listed in Journals and papers, ed H. House, *below, appendix 4; others are in the possession of Bodley and of Lord Bridges.*

Bibliographies

Weyand, N. A chronological bibliography. In his Immortal diamond, New York 1949.
Charney, M. A bibliographical study of Hopkins criticism 1918–49. Thought 25 1950.
Patricia, Sr M. Forty years of criticism: a chronological check list of criticism of the works of Hopkins 1909–49. Bull of Bibliography 20 1950.
Bischoff, D. A. The manuscripts of Hopkins. Thought 26 1952.
Pick, J. In The Victorian poets: a guide to research, ed F. E. Faverty, Cambridge Mass 1956, 1968 (rev).

Collections

Poems. Ed R. Bridges, Oxford 1918. Reviews by L. I. Guiney, Month March 1919; H. A. Lappin, Catholic World July 1919; J. M. Murry, Athenaeum 6 June 1919, rptd in his Aspects of literature, 1920; M. Russell, Irish Monthly Aug 1919; F. Page, Dublin Rev 167 1920; E. Sapir, Poetry 18 1921.
Poems: second edition, with additional poems. Ed C. Williams, Oxford 1930; ed W. H. Gardner, Oxford 1948 (3rd edn rev and enlarged); ed Gardner and N. H. Mackenzie, Oxford 1967 (4th edn rev and enlarged).
Letters of Hopkins to Robert Bridges; Correspondence of Hopkins and Richard Watson Dixon. Ed C. C. Abbott 2 vols Oxford 1935.
Further letters of Hopkins. Ed C. C. Abbott, Oxford 1938, 1956 (rev and enlarged). Letters to and from Coventry Patmore et al.
Note-books and papers of Hopkins. Ed H. House, Oxford 1937; 2nd edn rev and enlarged in 2 vols as:
Journals and papers of Hopkins. Ed H. House, completed by G. Storey, Oxford 1959. Includes appendixes on his drawings (J. Piper), music (J. E. Stevens), and philological notes (A. Ward).
Sermons and devotional writings of Hopkins. Ed C. Devlin, Oxford 1959.
Selections from the notebooks. Ed T. Weiss, New York 1945.
Selected poems. Ed J. Reeves 1953.
A Hopkins reader. Ed J. Pick 1953. Prose and verse.
A selection of poems and prose. Ed W. H. Gardner 1953 (Penguin), 1966 (rev and enlarged).
Selected poems and prose. Ed G. Storey, Oxford 1967.
French trns by E. Roditi (4 poems) and G. Landier (selected letters), Mesures (Paris) Jan 1935; *and of poems and prose by P. Leyris, 1957; tr German by M. Brauns,* Der Dichter Hopkins, *1946; I. Behn, 1948; W. and U. Clemen,* Hopkins: Gedichte, Schriften, Briefe, *1954; tr Italian by A. Guidi (The wreck of the Deutschland and The loss of the Eurydice), 1947, 1948, 1952; tr Hungarian,* B. Inecs *(3 poems),* Az angol irodalun Kincseshaza, ed G. Halász [1942]; *4 poems* in Angol Köttak antológiája, ed M. Vajda 1960; *also Spanish, French and Italian trns of some poems in* J. M. G. Mora, Hopkinsiana, Huatabampo Mexico 1954.

§ 1

For single poems, trns and extracts from his journal priv ptd or in miscellanies, see N. Weyand, Chronological bibliography, *above.*

Winter with the gulf stream. Once a Week 14 Feb 1863.
Barnfloor and winepress. Union Rev 3 1865.
Songs from Shakespeare in Latin: 'Full fathom five thy father lies'. Irish Monthly Nov 1886; 'Come unto these yellow sands', Feb 1887.
Poets and poetry of the century. Ed A. H. Miles vol 8 [1893]. Includes texts and extracts of 11 poems, with introd by R. Bridges.
Lyra sacra. Ed H. C. Beeching 1895. Includes 5 poems.
Rosa mystica. Irish Monthly May 1898.
Carmina Mariana. Ed O. Shipley 1902. Includes 2 poems.
The spirit of man. Ed R. Bridges 1916. Includes texts and extracts of 6 poems.
A vision of the mermaids: facsimile edition of full text dated Christmas 1862. Oxford 1929.
Early poems and extracts from the notebooks and papers. [Ed H. House] Criterion 15 1935.
St Thecla (an unpublished poem). Studies 45 1956.
Jesu dulcis memoria. Month Oct 1947. Trn by Hopkins.
Preface to poems. In English literary criticism: romantic and Victorian, ed D. G. Hoffman and S. L. Hynes, New York 1963.

Letters and Papers

A curious halo. Nature 16 Nov 1882; Shadow-beams in the east at sunset, 15 Nov 1883; The remarkable sunsets, 3 Jan 1884. Letters on unusual sunsets, rptd in Correspondence of Hopkins and Dixon, above.
T. Arnold, A manual of English literature, 1885 (5th edn). Includes a notice of R. W. Dixon by Hopkins, rptd in Correspondence of Hopkins and Dixon, above.
Unpublished journal of Hopkins [extracts from 1866–8]. Month Dec 1950.
Storey, G. (ed). Six new letters of Hopkins [to his father and Katharine Tynan]. Month May 1958.
Brégy, K. Hopkins. Catholic World Jan 1909; rptd in her Poet's chantry, 1912.
— Of poets and poetry. Catholic World Feb–April 1939.

Keating, J. Impressions of Fr Hopkins. Month July–Sept 1909.
Kilner, J. The poetry of Hopkins. Poetry Sept 1914; rptd in her Circus and other essays, New York 1921.
Harting, E. M. Hopkins and Digby Dolben. Month April 1919.
'Plures'. Hopkins: his character. Dublin Rev 167 1920.
Porter, A. Difficult beauty. Spectator 13 Jan 1923.
Richards, I. A. Hopkins. Dial 131 1926; rptd in A Dial miscellany, ed W. Wasserstrom, Syracuse 1963.
—— Hopkins. Cambridge Rev 28 Oct 1927.
—— In his Practical criticism, 1929.
Riding, L. and R. Graves. In their A survey of modernist poetry, 1927.
Brown, A. Hopkins and associative form. Dublin Mag 3 1928.
North, J. N. Quality in madness. Poetry Aug 1929.
Empson, W. In his Seven types of ambiguity, 1930, 1947 (rev).
Lahey, G. F. Hopkins. Oxford 1930.
—— Hopkins and Newman. Commonweal 12 1930.
Zabel, M. D. Hopkins: poetry as experiment and unity. Poetry Dec 1930.
Read, H. Hopkins. Criterion April 1931.
—— The poetry of Hopkins. In English critical essays: twentieth century, ed P. M. Jones, Oxford 1933 (WC); rptd in his Defence of Shelley and other essays, 1936 and in his Collected essays in literary criticism, 1938.
—— In his Form in modern poetry, 1932.
—— Poetry and belief in Hopkins. New Verse 1 1933.
—— In his True voice of feeling, 1953.
Grisewood, H. Hopkins. Dublin Rev 189 1931.
Pryce-Jones, A. Hopkins. London Mercury May 1931.
Turner, W. J. Some modern poetry. Nineteenth Century Feb 1931.
Bridges, R. In his Three friends [memoirs of D. M. Dolben, R. W. Dixon and H. Bradley], Oxford 1932.
Leavis, F. R. In his New bearings in English poetry, 1932, 1950 (enlarged).
—— The letters of Hopkins. Scrutiny 4 1935.
—— Hopkins. Scrutiny 12 1944; rptd as Metaphysical isolation in The Kenyon critics, New York 1945. Both articles rptd in his Common pursuit, 1952.
Stonier, G. W. Hopkins. New Statesman 25 June 1932.
—— Hopkins. In his Gog Magog and other critical essays, 1933.
Kelly, B. W. Joy and chastity in the poetry of Hopkins. Blackfriars 14 1933.
—— The mind and poetry of Hopkins. Ditchling Sussex 1935.
—— Gerard Manley Tuncks. Blackfriars 18 1937.
Phare, E. E. (E. E. Duncan-Jones). The poetry of Hopkins. Cambridge 1933.
—— R. W. Dixon's 'terrible crystal'. N & Q June 1956.
Phillipson, W. Hopkins. Downside Rev 51 1933.
Tierney, M., H. Read, R. S. Stanier and H. House. Hopkins's metres. TLS 16–23 Feb, 2–9 March 1933.
Brémond, A. La poésie naïve et savante de Hopkins. Études 221 1934.
—— Art and inspiration in Hopkins. New Verse 14 1935.
—— Quelques réflexions sur la poésie et les styles poétiques. Études 242 1940.
de Sélincourt, E. In his Oxford lectures on poetry, Oxford 1934.
Eliot, T. S. In his After strange gods, 1934.
Lewis, C. D. In his A hope for poetry, Oxford 1934.
—— Hopkins, poet and Jesuit. Left Rev 3 1937.
McGuire, D. P. The poetry of Hopkins. Adelaide 1934 (Eng Assoc pamphlet).
Sitwell, E. In her Aspects of modern poetry, 1934.
Abbott, C. C. Hopkins. TLS 21 March 1935, 13 March 1937.
—— Hopkins: a letter and drafts of early poems. Durham Univ Jnl new ser 1 1940.

Alexander, C. In his Catholic literary revival, Milwaukee 1935.
Behn, I. Hopkins und seine Dichtung. Hochland 32 1935.
Crehan, J. H. Poetry and religious life: the case of Hopkins. Month Dec 1935.
—— More light on Hopkins. Month Oct 1953.
Devlin, C. Hopkins and Duns Scotus. New Verse (Hopkins issue) 14 1935.
—— The Ignatian spirit of Hopkins. Blackfriars 14 1935.
—— An essay on Scotus. Month 182 1946.
—— Time's eunuch. Month May 1949.
—— The image and the word. Month Feb–March 1950.
—— and W. H. Gardner. Hopkins and Scotus. Month Sept 1950.
Downey, H. A poem not understood. Virginia Quart 11 1935. On the Windhover.
—— Hopkins: a study of influences. Southern Rev 1 1936.
Fairley, B. Charles Doughty and modern poetry. London Mercury June 1935. Comparison of Hopkins and Doughty.
Gardner, W. H. The wreck of the Deutschland. E & S 21 1935.
—— A note on Hopkins and Duns Scotus. Scrutiny 5 1936.
—— The religious problem in Hopkins. Scrutiny 6 1937; rptd in Critiques and essays in criticism 1920–48, ed R. W. Stallman, New York 1949.
—— Hopkins as a cywyddwr. Trans Cymmrodorion Soc 1940.
—— Hopkins: a study of poetic idiosyncrasy in relation to poetic tradition. 2 vols 1944–9, 1948 (vol 1 rev).
—— The windhover. TLS 24 June 1955.
—— and D. A. Bischoff. Hopkins's spiritual diaries. TLS 29 March, 7 June 1957.
Griffith, Ll. W. The Welsh influence in Hopkins's poetry. New Verse 14 1935.
Grigson, G. Blood or bran. Ibid.
—— Hopkins and Hopkinese. Ibid.
—— Hopkins. 1955 (Br Council pamphlet).
House, H. A note on Hopkins's religious life. New Verse 14 1935.
—— Hopkins: poet-priest. Listener 22 June 1944; rptd in his All in due time, 1955.
—— The Hopkinses. TLS 4 Nov 1949.
MacNeice, L. A comment [on Hopkins]. New Verse 14 1935.
—— The notebooks and papers of Hopkins. Criterion 16 1937.
—— Rhythm and rhyme. In his Modern poetry, Oxford 1938.
Madge, C. What is all this juice?—Hopkins and Victorian conceptions of nature. New Verse 14 1935.
Plowman, M. Hopkins. TLS 28 Feb 1935.
Roberts, M. Reflections of Hopkins. London Mercury March 1935.
Sargent, D. In his Four independents, 1935.
—— The charm and the strangeness: Hopkins. Atlantic Monthly Aug 1949.
Turnell, G. M. Homage to Hopkins. Colosseum 2 1935.
Vann, G. The mind and poetry of Hopkins. Colosseum 2 1935.
Barrett, A. Critics, Communists and Hopkins. America 56 1936.
Deutsch. B. In her This modern poetry, 1936.
—— The forgèd feature. In her Poetry in our time, New York 1956.
Bliss, G. In a poet's workshop. Month Feb, June 1936. Recensions of On a piece of music, The woodlark.
—— The Hopkins centenary. Month 180 1944.
Clarke, E. Gerard Hopkins, Jesuit. Dublin Rev 198 1936.
Daiches, D. Hopkins and the modern poets. In his New literary values, Edinburgh 1936.
—— In his Poetry and the modern world, Chicago 1940.
Fletcher, J. G. Hopkins—priest or poet? Amer Rev 6 1936.

Ginneken, J. van. Barbarous in beauty. Onze Taaltuing 5 1936.
Leahy, M. A priest-poet: Hopkins. Irish Ecclesiastical Record 47 1936.
Ogden, C. K. Sprung rhythm. Psyche 16 1936.
Young, G. M. Forty years of verse. London Mercury Dec 1936; rptd in his Daylight and champaign, 1937 (in part).
Yeats, W. B. Preface to his Oxford book of modern verse, Oxford 1936.
Blackmur, R. P. Text and texture. Virginia Quart Rev 13 1937.
— Mature intelligence of an artist. Kenyon Rev 1 1939.
Cock, A. A. Bridges and the Testament of beauty, with some references to Hopkins. France-Grande-Bretagne April 1937.
Croce, B. Un gesuita inglese poeta: Hopkins. La Critica (Naples) 35 1937.
Thornton, F. B. Hopkins, major poet or major craftsman? America 56 1937.
Trueblood, C. K. The esthetics of Hopkins. Poetry 50 1937.
Waterhouse, J. F. Hopkins and music. Music & Letters 18 1937.
Weygandt, C. Latest phases of English poetry. In his Time of Yeats, New York 1937.
Daly, J. J. Fr Hopkins and the Society. Thought 13 1938; rptd in his Jesuit in focus, Milwaukee 1940.
D'Arcy, M. C. Hopkins. In Great Catholics, ed C. C. H. Williamson 1938.
— Hopkins. Tablet 24 June 1944.
— In his Mind and heart of love, 1947.
— A note on Hopkins. Month Feb 1954.
Heywood, T. Hopkins and Bridges on trees. Poetry Rev 29 1938.
— On approaching Hopkins. Poetry Rev 30 1939.
— Hopkins's ancestry. Poetry July–Aug 1939; rptd in English 3 1940.
Iyenga, K. R. S. Hopkins. New Rev (Calcutta) 7 1938.
— Hopkins: the man and the poet. Calcutta 1948.
MacColl, D. S. Patmore and Hopkins: sense and nonsense in English prosody. London Mercury July 1938.
Panhuysen, J. De poesie van Hopkins. Boeckenschouw 32 1938.
Binyon, L. Hopkins and his influence. UTQ 7 1939.
Etman, A. Haunting rhythm. Tijdschrift voor Taal en Letteren 27 1939.
Henderson, P. In his Poet and society, 1939.
Jones, G. Hopkins and Welsh prosody. Life & Letters 21 1939.
Kenmare, D. Hopkins. In her Face of truth, Oxford 1939.
Peters, W. A. M. Hopkins: de controverse rond zijn persoon. Studien 132 1939.
— Hopkins: a critical essay towards the understanding of his poetry. Oxford 1948.
Williams, C. and T. Heywood. Hopkins and Milton. Poetry Rev 30 1939.
— Hopkins. Time & Tide 3 Feb 1945.
'Applejoy, Petronius' (D. R. Lock). Hopkins sets a poetic signpost. Catholic World May 1940.
Drew, E. and J. L. Sweeney. In their Directions in modern poetry, New York 1940.
Evans, B. I. Towards the twentieth century: Hopkins and T. S. Eliot. In his Tradition and romanticism, 1940.
Pick, J. The growth of a poet: Hopkins. Month Jan–Feb 1940.
— Hopkins: priest and poet. Oxford 1942, 1966.
— Hopkins: the problem of religious poetry. Stylus (Boston College) 55 1942.
— The inspiration of Hopkins's poetry. America 68 1943.
— Centenary of Hopkins. Thought 19 1944.
— Right directions in criticism. America 74 1946.
— Hopkins's imagery: the relation of his journal to his poetry. Renascence 7 1954.
Southworth, J. G. In his Sowing the spring, Oxford 1940.
Wells, H. W. New poets from old: a study in literary genetics. New York 1940.
Baldi, S. Hopkins. Brescia 1941.
Matthai, A. P. Hopkins the Jesuit. New Rev (Calcutta) 13 1941.
Matthiessen, F. O. In his American renaissance, New York 1941.
Speaight, R. Hopkins: his genius and stature as a major poet. Commonweal 33 1941.
— The price of poetry [Hopkins and Rimbaud]. Dublin Rev 227 1953.
Stanford, W. B. Hopkins and Aeschylus. Studies 30 1941.
Whitridge, A. Hopkins. Univ Rev June 1941.
Bell, D. Introductory essay to Dafydd ap Gwilym. Y Cymmrodor 48 1942. On Hopkins and Welsh poetry.
Taylor, F. The rebellious will of Hopkins. Poetry Feb 1942.
Tillemans, T. Is Hopkins a modern poet? E Studies 24 1942.
Colligan, G. The mysticism of Hopkins. Ave Maria 58 1943.
Darby, H. S. Jesuit poet—Hopkins. Quart Rev 168 1943.
Lienhardt, R. G. Hopkins and Yeats. Scrutiny 11 1943.
Lilly, G. Welsh influence in the poetry of Hopkins. MLR 38 1943.
Little, A. Hopkins and Scotus. Irish Monthly Feb 1943.
— Hopkins: poet and priest. TLS 10 June 1944.
Auden, W. H. A knight of the infinite. New Republic 111 1944; rptd in Literary opinion in America, ed M. D. Zabel, New York 1951 (rev).
Bischoff, D. A. Postscript on Hopkins. America 72 1944.
— Hopkins. Victorian Newsletter no 13 1958.
Boyle, R. R. The teaching of Hopkins. Jesuit Educational Quart 7 1944.
— Hopkins's imagery: the thread for the maze. Thought 35 1960.
— Metaphor in Hopkins. Chapel Hill 1961.
Brooks, C. (ed). Hopkins. Kenyon Rev 6 1944 (2 Hopkins issues); rptd in The Kenyon critics, below.
Lowell, R. A note. Ibid.
McLuhan, H. M. The analogical mirrors. Ibid.
Miles, J. The sweet and lovely language. Ibid.
Mizener, A. Victorian Hopkins. Ibid.
Warren, A. Instress of inscape. Ibid.
Whitehall, H. Sprung rhythm. Ibid.
Churchill, R. C. Hopkins—a Christian Socialist. Tribune 9 June 1944.
Grady, T. J. The windhover's meaning. America 70 1944.
Hanson, W. G. Hopkins and R. W. Dixon. Quart Rev 169 1944.
Hopkins, G. W. S. Correct date of Hopkins's birth. TLS 24 June 1944.
Kliger, S. God's 'plenitude' in the poetry of Hopkins. MLN 59 1944.
Maritain, J. Poetic experience. Rev of Politics 6 1944.
Moore, S. Hopkins and Duns Scotus. Downside Rev 62 1944.
Price, F. Hopkins on Bridges. N & Q 15 Jan 1944.
Reid, J. C. Hopkins, priest and poet. Wellington 1944 (a centenary pamphlet).
Ridler, A. Hopkins. Periodical 26 1944.
Ruggles, E. Hopkins: a life. 1944.
Schoder, R. V. Spelt from Sibyl's leaves. Thought 19 1944; rptd in Immortal diamond, below.
Spencer, T. Poet in search of inscape. Saturday Rev of Lit 2 Sept 1944.
Thornton, F. B. The wreck of the Deutschland. Catholic World Oct 1944.
Turner, V. Hopkins: a centenary article. Dublin Rev 215 1944.
Winstedt, R. and S. J. Davies. Hopkins. Guardian 21 July, 4, 11, 25 Aug 1944.

Brauns, M. Der Dichter Hopkins. Stimmen der Katholischen Welt (Bonn) 1946. With trns of 4 poems into German.

Fausset, H. I'A. In his Poets and pundits, 1945.

Hastings, M. D. More comments on Hopkins. Poetry Rev 36 1945.

Howarth, R. G. Yeats and Hopkins. N & Q 19 May 1945.

— Hopkins's earlier poems: the order of composition. N & Q 14 June 1947.

— Hopkins and Sir Thomas More. N & Q 6 Sept 1947.

— An unconscious prophet of Hopkins [i.e. Edwin Guest, author of A history of English rhythm, 1838]. N & Q Dec 1959.

Kenyon critics. Hopkins. New York 1945. Reprints articles in Kenyon Rev 6 1944, with biographical study by A. Warren and F. R. Leavis, Metaphysical isolation, rptd from Scrutiny 12 1944.

Muñoz Rojas, J. A. En el centenario de Hopkins. Razón y Fe (Madrid) 132 1945.

Noon, W. T. Hopkins, Christian humanist. America 74 1945.

Pepper, S. C. In his Basis of criticism in the arts, Cambridge Mass 1945.

Weiss, T. Hopkins: realist on Parnassus. Accent 16 1945.

Duffy, J. Hopkins. Spirit 13 1946.

Gerard, A. Duns Scotus et Hopkins. Revue des Langues Vivantes 12 1946.

Gordon, G. S. Hopkins and Bridges. In his Discipline of letters, Oxford 1946.

Guidi, A. Introduzione alla poetica di Hopkins. Letteratura 8 1946.

— Persone e cose nella poesia di Hopkins. Humanitas 1 1946.

— Problemi d'interpretazione in Hopkins. Anglica 1 1946.

— Milton e Hopkins. Eng Miscellany (Rome) 6 1955.

Schwartz, D. The poetry of Hopkins. Nation (New York) 1946.

Thomas, M. G. L. Hopkins as critic. E & S 32 1946.

Treece, H. Hopkins and Dylan Thomas. In his How I see apocalypse, 1946; rptd in A casebook on Dylan Thomas, ed J. M. Brinnin, New York 1960.

— Hopkins et 'l'inspect' des choses. Critique 21 1965.

Cattaui, G. Trois poètes: Hopkins, Yeats, Eliot. Paris 1947.

Cohen, S. J. The poetic theory of Hopkins. PQ 26 1947.

— Hopkins's As kingfishers catch fire. MLQ 11 1950.

Collins, J. Philosophical themes in Hopkins. Thought 22 1947.

Elliott, B. Hopkins and Marcus Clarke. Southerly 8 1947.

Mathison, J. K. The poetic theory of Hopkins. PQ 26 1947.

Ghiselin, B. Reading sprung rhythms. Poetry May 1947.

Gibson, W. M. Hopkins's To R.B. Explicator 6 1947.

Holloway, M. M. The prosodic theory of Hopkins. Washington 1947.

— Hopkins's Sonnet 65 (No worst, there is none). Explicator 14 1956.

Purcell, J. M. The poetry of Hopkins. Cronos 1 1947.

Schneider, E. W. Hopkins's My own heart let me more have pity on. Explicator 5 1947.

— Two metaphysical images in the Wreck of the Deutschland. MLN 65 1950.

— Hopkins's The wreck of the Deutschland stanza 33. Explicator 16 1958.

— Hopkins's The windhover. Explicator 18 1960.

— Sprung rhythm. PMLA 80 1965.

— The wreck of the Deutschland: a new reading. PMLA 81 1966.

Shapiro, K. English prosody and modern poetry. ELH 14 1947.

Silverstein, H. On Tom's garland. Accent 7 1947.

Tindall, W. Y. Hunt for a father. In his Forces in modern British literature 1885–1946, New York 1947.

Mims, E. Hopkins: Jesuit scholar. In his Christ of the poets, Nashville 1948.

Pietrkiewicz, J. Introducing Norwid [with comparison between Hopkins and the Polish poet Norwid]. Slavonic & East European Rev 27 1948.

Ryan, F. The wreck of the Deutschland: an introduction and a paraphrase. Dublin Rev 221 1948.

Warren, A. In his Rage for order, Chicago 1948.

Alonso, D. Hopkins. Trivium (Monterey) Jan 1949.

Clemen, W. Die Tagebücher des Hopkins. Merkur 3 1949.

Doyle, L. F. In the valley of the shadow of Hopkins. Catholic World June 1949.

Fussell, P. A note on the Windhover. MLN 64 1949.

Meyerstein, E. H. W. Note on the Loss of the Eurydice. TLS 11 Nov 1949.

Stobie, M. R. Patmore's theory and Hopkins's practice. UTQ 19 1949.

Symes, G. Hopkins, Herbert and contemporary modes. Hibbert Jnl 47 1949.

Vallette, J. Hopkins. Mercure de France 307 1949.

Weyand, N. (ed). Immortal diamond: studies in Hopkins. New York 1949. Includes M. C. Carroll, Hopkins and the Society of Jesus; A. MacGillivray, Hopkins and creative writing; J. L. Bonn, Greco-Roman verse theory and Hopkins; W. J. Ong, Sprung rhythm and the life of English poetry; C. A. Burns, Hopkins, poet of ascetic and aesthetic conflict; R. V. Schoder, An interpretative glossary of difficult words in the poems; What does the Windhover mean?; M. B. McNamee, Hopkins, poet of nature and of the supernatural; W. T. Noon, The three languages of poetry; Y. Watson, The loss of the Eurydice; R. R. Boyle, The thought structure of the Wreck of the Deutschland; N. Weyand, The historical basis of the Wreck of the Deutschland and the Loss of the Eurydice. *See also* Bibliographies, above.

Winters, Y. The poetry of Hopkins. Hudson Rev 1–2 1949; rptd in his Function of criticism, Denver 1957. Reply by J. H. Johnston, Renascence 2 1950. *See also* McDonnell, below.

— In his On modern poets, New York 1959.

Coogan, M. D. Inscape and instress: further analogies with Duns Scotus. PMLA 65 1950.

Corr, G. M. Our Lady's praise in Hopkins. Clergy Rev May 1950.

Heath-Stubbs, J. Three Roman Catholic poets. In his Darkling plain, 1950.

Lees, F. N. The windhover. Scrutiny 17 1950.

— O. Couldrey, W. Empson and W. A. M. Peters. Hopkinsiana. TLS 3, 24 Sept, 1, 22–29 Oct 1954.

— In Pelican guide to English literature, ed B. Ford vol 6, 1958.

— Hopkins. New York 1966.

Owen, B. E. Hopkins. Fortnightly Rev July 1950.

Treneer, A. The criticism of Hopkins. Penguin New Writing 1950.

Woodring, C. R. Once more the Windhover. Western Rev 15 1950.

Davie, D. A. Hopkins, the decadent critic. Cambridge Jnl Sept 1951; rptd in his Purity of diction in English verse, 1952.

Gwynn, F. L. The windhover. MLN 66 1951.

Pearson, W. H. and F. H. A. Micklewright. Hopkins and Provost Fortescue. N & Q 29 Sept 1951, 12 April, 16 Aug 1952.

— Hopkins and 'Gifted Hopkins'. N & Q Dec 1959.

Patmore, D. Three poets discuss new verse forms: the correspondence of Hopkins, Bridges and Patmore. Month Aug 1951.

Pinto, V. de S. Hopkins and Bridges. In his Crisis in English poetry 1880–1940, 1951.

— Hopkins and 'The Trewnesse of the Christian religion'. TLS 10 June 1955.

Raymond, W. O. 'The mind's internal heaven' in poetry. UTQ 20 1951.

Wright, B. Hopkins's God's grandeur. Explicator 10 1951.

Durr, R. A. Hopkins's No worse, there is none. Explicator 11 1952.
Futrell, J. C. Hopkins and God's 'poem of beauty'. Catholic World Feb 1952.
Healy, A. Milton and Hopkins. UTQ 22 1952.
Jeremy, M. Hopkins and St Gertrude. TLS 14 Nov 1952.
Pitchford, L. W. The curtal sonnets of Hopkins. MLN 67 1952.
Ward, D. Hopkins's Spelt from Sibyl's leaves. Month July 1952.
Wilder, A. N. In his Modern poetry and the Christian tradition, New York 1952.
Fraser, G. S. The poetry of Hopkins and Bridges. New Statesman 10 Oct 1953.
Melchiori, G. Due manieristi: Henry James e Hopkins. Spettatore Italiano 6 1953; tr in his Tightrope walkers: studies of mannerism in modern English literature, New York 1956.
Morris, D. The poetry of Hopkins and Eliot in the light of the Donne tradition. Berne 1953.
Amis, K. Communication and the Victorian poet. EC 4 1954.
Goldhurst, R. Translation: sine qua non—Bowra and Hopkins. Classical Jnl Oct 1954.
Hartman, G. H. In his Unmediated vision, New Haven 1954.
— (ed). Hopkins: a collection of critical essays. Englewood Cliffs NJ 1966.
Mora, J. M. G. Hopkinsiana: la vida, la obra y la supervivencia de Hopkins. Huatabampo Mexico 1954.
Templeman, W. D. Hopkins and Whitman. PQ 33 1954.
Wickham, J. F. Mariology in Hopkins. Month Sept 1954.
Adorita, Sr M. Hopkins's 'wings that spell' in the Wreck of the Deutschland. MLN 70 1955.
Bogan, L. In her Selected criticism, New York 1955.
Bowen, R. O. Hopkins and Welsh prosody. Renascence 8 1955.
— Scotism in Hopkins. History of Ideas Newsletter 5 1959.
Donoghue, D. Technique in Hopkins. Studies 44 1955.
— The bird as symbol: Hopkins's Windhover. Ibid.
Hill, A. A. An analysis of the Windhover. PMLA 70 1955. Reply by W. H. Matchett 72 1957.
Humiliata, Sr M. Hopkins and the Prometheus myth. PMLA 70 1955.
Miller, J. H. The creation of the self in Hopkins. ELH 22 1955.
— 'Orion' in the Wreck of the Deutschland. MLN 76 1961.
— The theme of the disappearance of God in Victorian poetry. Victorian Stud 6 1963.
— In his Disappearance of God: five nineteenth-century writers, Cambridge Mass 1963.
Ritz, J.-G., W. Empson, W. H. Gardner and G. L. Nolan. The windhover. TLS 6, 20 May, 24 June, 5 Aug 1955.
— The windhover de Hopkins. Études Anglaises 9 1956.
— The strong fire of love [Bridges and Hopkins]. TLS 6 May 1960.
— Bridges and Hopkins 1863–89: a literary friendship. Oxford 1960.
— Le poète Hopkins. Paris 1963.
Rooney, W. J. Spelt from Sibyl's leaves. Jnl of Aesthetics 13 1955.
Tindall, W. Y. In his Literary symbol, New York 1955.
Ward, D. The windhover. In Interpretations, ed J. Wain 1955.
Wasmuth, E. Hopkins's Asthetik. Neue Rundschau 66 1955.
Ayers, R. W. Hopkins's The windhover. MLN 71 1956.
Baird, M. J. Blake, Hopkins and Thomas Merton. Catholic World April 1956.
Doyle, F. G. A note on Hopkins's Windhover. Studies 45 1956.
Giovannini, M. Hopkins's The caged skylark. Explicator 14 1956.
Kelly, H. The Windhover—and Christ. Studies 45 1956.
King, A. R. Hopkins's Windhover and Blake. E Studies 37 1956.
Schoeck, R. J. Influence and originality in Hopkins. Renascence 9 1956.
— Peine forte et dure and Hopkins's Margaret Clitheroe. MLN 74 1959.
Sherwood, H. C. Hopkins's Spelt from Sibyl's leaves. Explicator 15 1956.
Spira, T. Hopkins: zu einer deutschen Neuerscheinung. Anglia 74 1956.
Tillotson, G. Hopkins and Ruskin. TLS 6 Jan 1956.
Whitlock, B. W. Hopkins's Windhover. N & Q April 1956.
Coanda, R. Hopkins and Donne: 'mystic' and metaphysical. Renascence 9 1957.
Fairchild, H. N. In his Religious trends in English poetry vol 4, 1830–80, New York 1957; vol 5, 1880–1920, New York 1962.
Guzie, T. W. Are modern poets morbid? Catholic World April 1957.
Harrison, T. P. The birds of Hopkins. SP 54 1957.
Lisca, P. The return of the Windhover. College Eng Dec 1957.
Litzinger, B. Hopkins's The habit of perfection. Explicator 16 1957.
— The genesis of Hopkins's Heaven haven. Victorian Newsletter no 17 1960.
— Hopkins's Pied beauty once more. Renascence 13 1961.
— Hopkins's The wreck of the Deutschland stanza 19. Explicator 20 1961.
— The pattern of ascent in Hopkins. Victorian Poetry 2 1964.
Martin, P. M. Mastery and mercy: a study of the Wreck of the Deutschland and Ash-Wednesday. Oxford 1957.
Miles, J. In her Eras and modes in English poetry, Berkeley 1957.
Nowell-Smith, S. Bridges, Hopkins and Dr Daniel. TLS 13 Dec 1957.
— Bridges's debt to Hopkins. TLS 12 May 1961. Replies by J.-G. Ritz and G. Tillotson 30 June; W. H. Gardner 18 Aug; N. H. Mackenzie 1 Sept 1961.
Peel, J. H. B. The echoes in the booming voice [comparison of Hopkins and Dylan Thomas]. New York Times Book Review 20 Oct 1957. Replies by L. Frankenberg et al 10 Nov 1957.
Prasada, S. K. The poetry of Hopkins. Sri Aurobindo Circle 13 1957.
Ratcliff, J. D. Hopkins's The May magnificat. Explicator 16 1957.
Wain, J. 'Stranger and afraid': notes on four Victorian poets. In his Preliminary essays, 1957.
— Hopkins: an idiom of desperation. Proc Br Acad 45 1959; rptd in his Essays on literature and ideas, 1963.
Britton, J. Pied beauty and the glory of God. Renascence 11 1958.
Brooke-Rose, C. In her A grammar of metaphor, 1958.
Gibson, W. Sound and sense in Hopkins. MLN 73 1958.
Green, D. B. A new letter of Bridges to Patmore. MP 55 1958. On Bridges's relations with Patmore and Hopkins.
Heuser, A. E. The shaping vision of Hopkins. Oxford 1958.
Kano, H. In his Crisis and imagination, Tokyo 1958.
Kelly, J. C. Hopkins: piety versus poetry. Studies 47 1958.
Kissane, J. Classical echoes in Hopkins's Heaven-haven. MLN 73 1958.
Magny, O. de. Hopkins et le coeur des choses. Lettres Nouvelles Feb 1958.
Chapman, J. A. In his Critical papers, 1959.
Downes, D. A. Hopkins: a study of his Ignatian spirit. New York 1959.
— The Hopkins enigma. Thought 36 1961.
— Hopkins and Thomism. Victorian Poetry 3 1965.
— In his Victorian portraits, 1966.

Duncan, J. E. In his Revival of metaphysical poetry, Oxford 1959.
Stanzel, F. Hopkins, Yeats, Lawrence und die Spontaneität der Dichtung. In Anglistische Studien, ed K. Brunner et al, Vienna [1958].
Storey, G. The notebooks and papers of Hopkins: a new edition. Month Nov 1958.
Allison, A. W. Hopkins's I wake and feel the fell of dark. Explicator 17 1959.
Assad, T. J. A closer look at Hopkins's Carrion comfort. Tulane Univ Stud in Eng 9 1959.
—— Hopkins's The windhover. Tulane Univ Stud in Eng 11 1961.
Baum, P. F. Sprung rhythm. PMLA 74 1959.
Bolsius, E. Hopkins: de dichter en de religieus. Streven 13 1959.
Goodin, G. Man and nature in Hopkins's Ribblesdale. N & Q Dec 1959.
Johnson, W. S. The imagery of Hopkins: fire, light and the Incarnation. Victorian Newsletter no 16 1959.
Mellown, E. W. Hopkins, Hall Caine and D. G. Rossetti. N & Q March 1959.
—— Hopkins and his public 1889–1918. MP 57 1959.
—— The reception of Hopkins' poems 1918–30. MP 63 1965.
Rathmell, J. C. A. Hopkins, Ruskin and the Sidney Psalter. London Mag Sept 1959.
Stephenson, A. A. Hopkins and John Donne. Downside Rev 77 1959.
Therese, Sr. Hopkins's Spelt from Sibyl's leaves. Explicator 17 1959.
Walsh, W. In his Use of the imagination, 1959.
Altick, R. D. Four Victorian poets and an exploding island. Victorian Stud 3 1960.
Jennings, E. The unity of Incarnation: a study of Hopkins. Dublin Rev 234 1960.
Mooney, S. Hopkins and counterpoint. Victorian Newsletter no 18 1960.
Morati, L. Spiritualità e ispirazione nella poesia di Hopkins. Lettura 15 1960.
Stanford, D. Christian humanist: recent works on Hopkins. Month Sept 1960.
Brophy, J. The noble brute: medieval nuance in the Windhover. MLN 76 1961.
Brown, T. J. English literary autographs: Hopkins. Book Collector 10 1961.
Guardini, R. Ästhetisch-theologische Gedanken zu Hopkins Sonnet Der Turmfalk. In Unterscheidung und Bewahrung: Festschrift für H. Kurisch, Berlin 1961.
Joshi, B. N. Hopkins and T. S. Eliot: a study in linguistic innovation. Osmania Jnl of Eng Stud 1 1961.
McDonnell, T. P. Hopkins as a sacramental poet: a reply to Yvor Winters [in his Function of criticism, 1957, above]. Renascence 14 1961.
Müller-Schwefe, G. Hopkins: der Victorianer. In Festschrift zum 75 Geburtstag von Theodor Spira, ed H. Viebrock et al, Heidelberg 1961.
Nist, J. Hopkins and textural intensity. College Eng April 1961. Reply by W. J. Ong 1962.
O'Brien, A. P. Structure complex of Hopkins's words. Indian Jnl of Eng Stud 1 1960.
Onesta, P. A. The self in Hopkins. English Stud in Africa 4 1961.
Sutherland, D. Hopkins again. Praie Schooner 35 1961.
Thomas, J. D. Hopkins's The windhover. Explicator 20 1961.
Zelocchi, R. La 'barbarica bellezza' di Hopkins. Convivium 29 1961.
Bernad, M. A. Hopkins's Pied beauty: a note on its Ignatian inspiration. EC 12 1962.
Clemen, U. Neue Ausgaben der Werke von Hopkins. Anglia 80 1962.
Eleanor, Mother M. Hopkins's Windhover and Southwell's hawk. Renascence 15 1962.
Gavin, R. J. Hopkins's The candle indoors. Explicator 20 1962.
Greiner, F. J. Hopkins's The habit of perfection. Explicator 21 1962.
—— Hopkins's The windhover viewed as a nature poem. Renascence 15 1962.
McNamee, M. B. Mastery and mercy in the Wreck of the Deutschland. College Eng Jan 1962.
Myers, J. A. Intimations of mortality: an analysis of Hopkins's Spring and fall. Eng Jnl 51 1962.
Norris, C. B. 'Fused images' in the sermons of Hopkins. Tennessee Stud in Lit 7 1962.
—— Hopkins in his sermons and poetry. N & Q Jan 1963.
Sambrook, J. In his A poet hidden: the life of R. W. Dixon, 1962.
Stempel, D. A reading of the Windhover. College Eng 1962.
Templeman, W. D. Ruskin's ploughshare and Hopkins's The windhover. E Studies 43 1962.
Wooton, C. The terrible fire of Hopkins. Texas Stud in Lit & Lang 4 1962.
Astel, A. Ingestalt und Inkraft bei Hopkins. Neue Deutsche Hefte 93 1963.
August, E. R. Hopkins's dangerous fire. Victorian Poetry 1 1963.
Bender, T. K. Hopkins's God's grandeur. Explicator 21 1963.
Campbell, M. M. H. The silent sonnet: Hopkins's Shepherd's brow. Renascence 15 1963.
Chamberlain, R. L. George MacDonald's A Manchester poem and Hopkins's God's grandeur. Personalist 44 1963.
Fulweiler, H. Mermen and mermaids: a note on an 'alien vision' in the poetry of Tennyson, Arnold and Hopkins. Victorian Newsletter no 23 1963.
Graves, W. L. Hopkins as composer: an interpretive postscript. Victorian Poetry 1 1963.
Grennen, J. E. Grammar as thaumaturgy: Hopkins's Heraclitean fire. Renascence 15 1963.
Hines, L. Pindaric imagery in Hopkins. Month May 1963.
Keating, J. E. The wreck of the Deutschland. Kent Ohio 1963.
Louise, Sr R. Hopkins's Spring and fall. Explicator 21 1963.
Ludwig, H.-W. Die Self-Komposita bei Carlyle, M. Arnold und Hopkins. Tübingen 1963.
Masson, D. I. Sound and sense in a line of poetry. Br Jnl of Aesthetics 3 1963.
McQueen, W. A. The windhover and St Alphonsus Rodriguez. Victorian Newsletter no 23 1963.
Milward, P. The underthought of Shakespeare in Hopkins. Stud in Eng Lit (Tokyo) 39 1963.
Montag, G. E. Hopkins's God's grandeur and 'the ooze of oil crushed'. Victorian Poetry 1 1963.
—— The windhover: crucifixion and redemption. Victorian Poetry 3 1965.
Singh, Y. N. Hopkins: a problem of prosody. Eng Miscellany (Delhi) 2 1963.
Spender, S. The modern necessity [Hopkins and D. H. Lawrence]. In his Struggle of the modern, 1963.
Stevens, M. D. Hopkins's That nature is a Heraclitean fire. Explicator 22 1963.
Andreach, R. J. In his Studies in structure, New York 1964.
Bates, R. The windhover. Victorian Poetry 2 1964.
Giovannini, G. A literal gloss of Hopkins' The windhover. In Linguistic and literary studies in honor of H. A. Hatzfeld, Washington 1964.
Gomme, A. A note on two Hopkins sonnets [Spelt from Sibyl's leaves; Thou art indeed just, Lord]. EC 14 1964. Reply on Spelt from Sibyl's leaves by F. Doherty, ibid.
Gross, H. S. In his Sound and form in modern poetry, Ann Arbor 1964.
Huntley, J. F. Hopkins's The windhover as a prayer of request. Renascence 15 1964.
Mackenzie, N. H. Hopkins among the Victorians. In English studies today, ed G. I. Duthie, Edinburgh 1964.

— Hopkins mss: old losses and new finds. TLS 18 March 1965.
— Gerard and Grace Hopkins: some new links. Month June 1965.
McNamara, P. L. Motivation and meaning in the 'terrible sonnets'. Renascence 16 1964.
Miller, B. E. On the Windhover. Victorian Poetry 2 1964.
Shea, F. X. Another look at the Windhover. Ibid.
Watson, T. L. Hopkins's God's grandeur. Explicator 22 1964.
Chard, L. F. Once more into the Windhover. Eng Lang Notes 2 1965.
Chevigny, B. G. Instress and devotion in the poetry of Hopkins. Victorian Stud 9 1965.
Fiore, A. Hopkins' relation to the Deutschland nuns. Renascence 18 1965.
Giovannini, M. Hopkins' God's grandeur. Explicator 24 1965.
Nassar, E. Hopkins, 'figura' and grace: God's better beauty. Renascence 17 1965.
Ochshorn, M. Hopkins the critic. Yale Rev 54 1965.
Thomas, A. Hopkins and the Silver jubilee album. Library 5th ser 20 1965.
— A Hopkins fragment replaced. TLS 20 Jan 1966.
— Hopkins. Dublin Rev 240 1966.
— Hopkins: an unpublished triolet. MLR 61 1966.
Barton, J. M. T. and A. Thomas. Odd priest out. TLS 20–7 Oct 1966.
Bender, T. K. Hopkins: the classical background and critical reception of his work. Baltimore 1966.
Driskell, L. V. The progressive structure of the Windhover. Renascence 19 1966.
Fulweiler, H. W. Hopkins and the 'stanching, quenching ocean of a motionable mind'. Victorian Newsletter 1966.
Hill, A. A. The windhover revisited. Texan Stud 7 1966.
Hufstader, A. The experience of nature in Hopkins' journal and poems. Downside Rev 84 1966.
King, D. R. The vision of 'being' in Hopkins's poetry and Ruskin's Modern painters. Discourse 9 1966.
O'Dea, R. J. The loss of the Eurydice. Victorian Poetry 4 1966.
Reiman, D. H. Hopkins's 'ooze of oil' rises again. Ibid.
Sharples, Sr M. Conjecturing a date for Hopkins' St Thecla. Ibid.
Vickers, B. W. and W. H. Gardner. Hopkins and Newman. TLS 3 March, 15 Sept 1966.
White, G. M. Hopkins' God's grandeur. Victorian Poetry 4 1966.
Winter, J. L. Notes on the Windhover. Ibid.
Doherty, P. C. Hopkins' Spring and fall. Victorian Poetry 5 1967.
Hallgarth, S. A. A study of Hopkins' use of nature. Ibid.
Rader, L. Hopkins' dark sonnets. Victorian Poetry 5 1967.

G. S.

ROBERT SEYMOUR BRIDGES
1844–1930

Bibliographies

[Daniel, C. H. O.] Notes on a bibliography of Bridges. Oxford Mag 19 June 1895.
Chaundy, L. and E. H. M. Cox. Bibliographies of modern authors, no 1: Bridges. 1921.
Madan, F. Bibliography of the Daniel press. In Memorials of C. H. O. Daniel, 1921.
Boutell, H. S. English first editions: Bridges, a bibliographical check-list. Publishers' Weekly 24 May 1930.
McKay, G. L. A bibliography of Bridges. New York 1933.
Nowell-Smith, S. Check-list of the works of Bridges. Book-collector's Quart no 16 1934.
Ritz, J.-G. In Bridges and Gerald Hopkins 1863–89: a literary friendship, Oxford 1960.
Kable, W. S. The Ewelme collection of Bridges: a catalogue. Columbia SC 1967.

Collections

Poetical works. 6 vols 1898–1905. Vol 1, 1898: Prometheus, Eros and Psyche, Growth of love; vol 2, 1899: Shorter poems (bks 1–5), New poems; vol 3, 1901, vols 4–5, 1902, vol 6, 1905: Dramas.
Poetical works excluding the eight dramas, Oxford 1912, 1936 (enlarged) (OSA), 1953 (with Testament of beauty).
Poetry and prose. Ed J. Sparrow, Oxford 1955 (with appreciations by G. M. Hopkins et al).

§1

Poems. 1873; second series 1879 (anon); third series, 1880, Oxford 1884 (H. Daniel) (anon); Shorter poems, 1890 (4 bks in 1 vol), bk 5, Oxford 1893 (H. Daniel), 1894 (rev), 1896 (rev); ed M. M. Bridges, Oxford 1931 (enlarged).
Carmen elegiacum. 1876, 1877 (rev).
The growth of love. 1876, Oxford 1889 (H. Daniel) (rev and enlarged), 1890.
Prometheus the firegiver. Oxford 1883 (H. Daniel), London 1884 (rev).
Nero: an historical tragedy, part 1. 1885; part 2, [1894].
Eros and Psyche. 1885, 1894 (rev).
The feast of Bacchus. Oxford 1889 (H. Daniel), 1894 (rev).
Plays. 1890. No 2, Palicio; no 3, The return of Ulysses; no 4, The Christian captives; no 5, Achilles in Scyros; with Nero, pts 1–2, Humours of the Court, and Feast of Bacchus, as Eight plays, 1894.
Eden: an oratorio. 1891 (with music by C. V. Stanford).
The humours of the Court and other poems. 1893.
Milton's prosody: an examination of the rules of the blank verse in Milton's later poems, with an account of the versification of Samson agonistes. Oxford 1893, 1894, 1901 (enlarged), 1921 (with further addns).
John Keats: a critical essay. 1895 (priv ptd); rptd in Poems of John Keats, ed G. T. Drury 1896; and in Poetical works of John Keats, ed L. Binyon [1916] (rev).
Invocation to music: an ode in honour of Henry Purcell. 1895 (with music by C. H. H. Parry), 1896 (rev as Ode for the bicentenary commemoration of Henry Purcell, with other poems and a preface on the musical setting of poetry). Ode rptd in Later poems, 1912, below; other poems in New poems in Poetical works, above, 1899.
A song of darkness and light. 1898 (with music by C. H. H. Parry); rptd as A hymn of nature in Later poems, 1912, below.
A practical discourse on hymn-singing. Oxford 1901.
Now in wintry delights. Oxford 1903; rptd in Poems in classical prosody, 1912, below.
Peace ode written on the conclusion of the Three years' war. Oxford 1903; rptd in Poems in classical prosody, 1912, below.
Demeter: a masque. Oxford 1905; rptd in Poetical works, 1912, above.
Eton memorial ode. [1908] (with music by C. H. H. Parry); rptd in Later poems, 1912, below.
About hymns. Chilswell 1911.
Sonnet xliv of Michelangelo Buonarroti, translated for Andrew Lang. 1912 (priv ptd).
Later poems and Poems in classical prosody. In Poetical works, Oxford 1912, above.
Poems written in the year mcmxiii. 1914 (priv ptd); rptd in October and other poems, 1920, below.
Ode on the tercentenary of the commemoration of Shakespeare. 1916 (priv ptd); rptd in Shakespeare's England, Oxford 1916 and TLS 6 July 1916.
The chivalry of the sea: naval ode. 1916 (with music by C. H. H. Parry); rptd in October and other poems, 1920, below.
An address to the Swindon branch of the Workers' Educational Association. Oxford 1916.
Ibant obscuri: an experiment in the classical hexameter. Oxford 1916.

The necessity of poetry. Oxford 1918.
Britannia victrix. Oxford 1918; rptd in Times 25 Nov 1918 and New verse, 1925, below.
October and other poems with occasional verses on the war. 1920, Oxford 1929.
Poor Poll. 1923 (priv ptd); rptd in New verse, 1925, below.
The tapestry. 1925 (priv ptd). Rptd in part from October and other poems, 1920, above, and rptd in part in New verse, 1925, below.
New verse written in 1921 with the other poems of that year and a few earlier pieces. Oxford 1925, 1926 (rev).
The influence of the audience. New York 1926 (priv ptd). Rptd from Works of William Shakespeare, Stratford-on-Avon 1907; rptd in Collected essays, papers etc, 1927.
Henry Bradley: a memoir. Oxford 1926; rptd in Collected papers of H. Bradley, Oxford 1928, and in Three friends, 1932.
The testament of beauty: a poem in four books. 5 pts [1927–29] (priv ptd), 1 vol Oxford 1929 (rev), 1930 ('final corrections').
Poetry: the first of the broadcast national lectures. 1929.
On receiving trivia from the author. Stanford Dingley, Berks 1930 (priv ptd).
Verses written for Mrs Daniel. Oxford 1932 (introd by G. S. Gordon).
Three friends: memoirs of Digby Mackworth Dolben, Richard Watson Dixon, Henry Bradley. Oxford 1932.

Letters and Papers

Although Bridges's letters to Gerard Manley Hopkins were destroyed by Bridges, his letters to members of Hopkins's family 1889–1929 are in Bodley, most of them unpbd; there are also other letters.

Collected essays, papers etc. 30 pts Oxford 1927–36. Pt 1, 1927: Influence of audience on Shakespeare's drama; 2–3, 1928: Humdrum and harum-scarum, poetic diction; 4, 1929: Critical introduction to Keats; 5, 1930: George Darley; 6–7, 1931: Poems of Mary Coleridge, Lord de Tabley's poems; 8–10, 1932: Dante in English literature, Poems of Emily Brontë, Dryden on Milton; 11–15, 1933: Studies in poetry, Springs of Helicon, Wordsworth and Kipling, Wordbooks, Letter on English prosody; 16–20, 1934: The Bible, Bunyan's Pilgrim's progress, Sir Thomas Browne, George Santayana, The glamour of grammar; 21–6, 1935: The musical setting of poetry, Some principles of hymn-singing, About hymns, English chanting, Chanting, Psalms noted in speech rhythm; 27–30, 1936: An address to the Swindon WEA, The necessity of poetry, Poetry, An account of the casualty department. Pts 5–30 ed M. M. Bridges.
The letters of G. M. Hopkins to Bridges. Ed C. C. Abbott, Oxford 1935; Further letters of Hopkins, ed C. C. Abbott, Oxford 1956 includes one from Bridges.
Correspondence of Bridges and Henry Bradley 1900–23. Oxford 1940.
Coventry Patmore and Bridges: some letters. Ed D. Patmore, Fortnightly Rev March 1948.
Green, D. B. A new letter of Bridges to Coventry Patmore. MP 55 1958.
Bridges also edited the Yattendon hymnal, Oxford 1895–9, 1920; Yattendon hymns, Oxford 1897 (for 1898); Hymns from the Yattendon hymnal, Oxford 1899; The small hymn book, Oxford 1899, 1914, 1920; Yattendon four-part chants, [1897] (priv ptd); Last poems of R. W. Dixon, Oxford 1905; Poems by R. W. Dixon, with a memoir, 1909; The poems of D. M. Dolben, with memoir, Oxford 1911, 1915 (rev); Society for Pure English [tracts], Oxford 1913–29; The spirit of man, 1916; Poems of G. M. Hopkins, Oxford 1918; The Chilswell book of English poetry, 1924; Selections from the letters of W. Raleigh, 1928 (introd by Bridges); The collected papers of H. Bradley, with a memoir, Oxford 1928.
For a full list of Bridges's contributions to periodicals, SPE tracts etc, see McKay, Bibliography, *above.*

§2

Warren, T. H. In Poets and poetry of the century, ed A. H. Miles vol 8, 1893.
— Bridges, poet laureate: a lecture. Oxford 1913.
Dowden, E. In his New studies in literature, 1895.
Young, F. and E. B. Bridges: a critical study. 1914.
Hearn, L. Appreciations of poetry. Ed J. Erskine, New York 1916.
Squire, J. C. Bridges' lyrical poems. London Mercury April 1920.
Fox, A. W. Bridges: poet laureate. Manchester Quart 167 1923.
Kelshall, T. M. Bridges: poet laureate. 1924.
Davison, E. Bridges: poet laureate of England. Eng Jnl Dec 1925.
— In praise of the poet laureate. Fortnightly Rev July 1928.
Dackweiler, C. Bridges: poète-lauréat. Humanitas 2 1927.
The testament of beauty. TLS 24 Oct 1929.
Twitchett, E. G. The poetry of Bridges. London Mercury Dec 1929.
Abercrombie, L. Technique and the Testament of beauty. Booman (London) Dec 1930.
Boas, C. The metre of the Testament of beauty. London Mercury June 1930.
de Selincourt, E. The testament of beauty. Hibbert Jnl 28 1930.
— In his Oxford lectures of poetry, Oxford 1934.
Grew, E. M. Music in the Testament of beauty. Contemporary Rev Aug 1930.
— The testament of beauty: study of musical passages. Br Musician June–Sept 1936, Jan–Feb 1937.
MacCarthy, D. Notes on the poetry of Bridges. Life & Letters 4 1930.
Magnus, L. The testament of beauty. Cornhill Mag May 1930; rptd in Trans Royal Soc of Lit 10 1931.
Monroe, H. Bridges as a lyrist. Poetry 36 1930.
Sasaki, T. On the language of Bridges' poetry. Tokyo 1930.
Shepard, O. Bridges. Amer Bookman April–May 1930.
Waugh, A. Bridges. Fortnightly Rev June 1930.
Garrod, H. W. In his Poetry and the criticism of life, Oxford 1931.
Pearce, T. M. The legacy of Bridges. New Mexico Quart 1 1931.
Smith, F. Bridges. Holburn Rev April 1931.
Smith, L. P. Bridges. SPE tract no 35 1931. Includes E. Daryush on Bridges's work on the English language.
Smith, N. C. Notes on the Testament of beauty. Oxford 1931, 1932 (rev), 1940 (rev).
Sulkie, T. A. The testament of beauty. Catholic World July 1931.
Elton, O. Bridges and the Testament of beauty. 1932 (English Assoc), rptd in his Essays and addresses, 1939.
Gordon, G. S. Bridges. Cambridge 1932, 1946 (Rede lecture).
— Hopkins and Bridges. In his Discipline of letters, Oxford 1947.
Larrabee, H. A. Bridges and George Santayana. Amer Scholar 1 1932.
Evans, B. I. In his English poetry in the later nineteenth century, 1933, 1966 (rev).
Lipscomb, H. C. Lucretius and the Testament of beauty. Classical Jnl 31 1935.
Guerard, A. Bridges. Virginia Quart Rev 12 1936.
— The dates of some of Bridges' lyrics. MLN 55 1940.
— Bridges: a study of traditionalism in poetry. Cambridge Mass 1942.

Brandl, L. Bridges: das Vermächtnis der Schönheit. Germanische-romanische Monatsschrift 25 1937.
Cock, A. A. Bridges and the Testament of beauty, with some references to Hopkins. France-Grande Bretagne April 1937.
Winters, Y. Bridges and Elizabeth Daryush. Amer Rev 8 1937.
Heywood, T. Hopkins and Bridges on trees. Poetry Rev 29 1938.
Langdon-Brown, W. Bridges: poet of evolution. In his Thus we are men, 1938.
Oberdieck, W. Die Weltanschauung des Testament of beauty. Göttingen 1938.
Eaker, T. G. Bridges' concept of nature. PMLA 54 1939.
Green, A. J. Bridges' odes for music. Sewanee Rev 49 1941.
— Bridges and the spiritual animal. Philosophy Rev 53 1944.
Mackay, J. The religion of Bridges. Expository Times May 1941.
Fox, A. English landscape in Bridges. English 4 1942.
Tindall, W. Y. The Bridges collection. Columbia Univ Quart 33 1942.
Bevan, B. The poetry of Bridges. Poetry Rev 34 1943.
Clough, H. C. The 'unpopularity' of Bridges. Ibid.
Nowell-Smith, S. Bridges' classical prosody: new verses and variants. TLS 28 Aug 1943. *See also* F. Hutchinson, 11 Sept 1943.
— A poet in Walton street. In Essays presented to Humphrey Milford, Oxford 1948.
— Bridges, Hopkins and Dr Daniel. TLS 13 Dec 1957.
— Bridges's debt to Hopkins. TLS 12 May 1961. *See also* 30 June, 18 Aug, 1 Sept 1961.
R., B. Andrew Lang on Bridges. N & Q 18 Dec 1943.
Price, F. Hopkins on Bridges. N & Q 15 Jan 1944.
Thompson, E. Bridges 1844–1930. Oxford 1944.
Church, R. The chemistry of time. Fortnightly Rev March 1945.
Charney, M. A bibliographical study of Hopkins criticism 1918–49. Thought 25 1950.
Baines, A. H. J. Bridges: a source. N & Q 28 Oct 1950.
Cohen, J. M. The road not taken: a study in the poetry of Bridges. Cambridge Jnl 4 1951.
Patmore, D. Three poets discuss new verse forms: the correspondence of Hopkins, Bridges and Patmore. Month Aug 1951.
Wright, E. C. Metaphor sound and meaning in Bridges' The testament of beauty, Philadelphia 1951.
Kellog, G. A. Bridges' Milton's prosody and Renaissance metrical theory. PMLA 68 1953.
Hughes, M. L. V. The philosophy of neighbourliness. London Quart 6th ser 22 1953.
Altick, R. D. Four Victorian poets and an exploding island. Victorian Stud 3 1960.
Ritz, J.-G. Bridges and Gerard Hopkins 1863–89: a literary friendship. Oxford 1960.
Sparrow, J. Robert Bridges. 1962 (Br Council pamphlet).
Berg, M. G. The prosodic structure of Bridges' neo-Miltonic syllabics. Washington 1962.
Beum, R. Profundity revisited: Bridges and his critics. Dalhousie Rev 44 1964.

W. W.

FRANCIS THOMPSON

1859–1907

The largest collection of Thompson mss, notebooks, letters and vols is in the Boston College Library, Mass.

Bibliographies

Stonehill, C. A. and H. W. In their Bibliographies of modern authors ser 2, 1925.
Connolly, T. L. In Poems of Thompson, New York 1941.
— In Literary criticisms of Thompson, ed Connolly, New York 1948.
— In his The real Robert Louis Stevenson, New York 1959.
Reid, J. C. In his Thompson: man and poet, 1959.
Pope, M. P. A critical bibliography of works by and about Thompson. New York 1959. Rptd from BNYPL 1958–9.
Danchin, P. In his Thompson: la vie et l'oeuvre d'un poète, Paris 1959.

Collections

Selected poems. Ed W. Meynell 1908.
A renegade and other essays. Boston 1910. Introd by E. J. O'Brien.
Works. Ed W. Meynell 1913. Vols 1–2 poetry, vol 3 prose; 3 vols in 1 Westminster Maryland 1949.
Collected poetry. 1913.
Essays of today and yesterday: Thompson. 1927. Introd by W. Meynell.
Selected poems and prose. 1929.
Poems. Ed T. L. Connolly, New York 1932, 1941 (rev).
Selected poems. 1934 (rev).
Poems. Ed W. Meynell, Oxford 1937 (OSA), 1955.
Selected poems. Ed P. Beard 1938.
Poems. 1946. Collected edn with a bibliography of 1st printings to 1913.
Literary criticisms newly discovered and collected. Ed T. L. Connolly, New York 1948.
Minor poets newly discovered and collected. Ed T. L. Connolly, Los Angeles 1949.
Poèmes choisis. Ed and tr P. Danchin, Paris 1962.

§ 1

For single essays, poems and trns into French, Norwegian, Irish, Czech and Hebrew, and separate printings of The hound of heaven, *see M. P. Pope,* Bibliography, *above; and for essays, T. L. Connolly,* Bibliography, *above.*

The life and labours of Saint John Baptist de la Salle. 1891, 1911 (preface by W. Meynell).
The child set in the midst. Ed W. Meynell 1892. Contains 4 poems by Thompson.
Poems. 1893.
Sister songs: an offering to two sisters. 1895. Also priv ptd as Songs wing to wing: an offering to two sisters, 1895.
Saint Anthony of Padua, by L. de Chérance. 1895. Contains a poem by Thompson To Saint Anthony of Padua.
New poems. 1897.
Victorian ode for Jubilee Day. 1897 (priv ptd).
Little Jesus [1897] (priv ptd), 1920.
Health and holiness. 1905. Introd by G. Tyrell.
Ode to English martyrs. 1906 (priv ptd).
Eyes of youth [1909]. Foreword by G. K. Chesterton. Contains 4 early poems by Thompson.
Shelley. 1909. Introd by G. Wyndham.
Saint Ignatius Loyola. Ed J. H. Pollen [1909] (preface by W. Meynell), 1951 (introd by H. Kelly).
Poems. Portland Maine 1911. A word on Thompson by A. Symons, foreword by T. B. Mosher.
Sir Leslie Stephen as a biographer. [1915] (priv ptd). Bibliography and chronology by C. Shorter.
Uncollected verses. 1917 (priv ptd).
The mistress of vision. Sussex 1918, London 1966. Commentary by J. O'Connor, preface by V. McNabb.
Le lévrier du ciel etc. Paris 1921. Trn of 5 poems by Thompson, with notes, by A. Morel.
Youthful verses. Preston 1928 (priv ptd).
The man has wings: new poems and plays. Ed T. L. Connolly, New York 1957.
The real Robert Louis Stevenson and other critical essays. Ed T. L. Connolly, New York 1959, New York and London 1961.

§2

Patmore, C. Mr Thompson: a new poet. Fortnightly Rev Jan 1894.
Archer, W. In his Poets of the younger generation, 1902.
White, G. A poetical problem. Sewanee Rev 6 1898.
Lucas, E. V. Thompson's cricket verses. Cornhill Mag July 1908.
Meynell, A. Some memories of Thompson. Dublin Rev 142 1908.
De Lattre, F. Le poète Thompson. Paris 1909. Rptd from Revue Germanique 5 1909; also in his De Byron à Thompson: essais de littérature anglaise, Paris 1913.
Tynan, K. Thompson. Fortnightly Rev Feb 1910.
Cock, A. A. Thompson. Dublin Rev 159 1911.
Beacock, G. A. Thompson. Borna-Leipzig 1912.
O'Conor, J. F. X. A study of Thompson's Hound of heaven. New York 1912.
Thomson, J. Thompson: the Preston-born poet. Preston 1912, 1913 (rev), 1923.
Armstrong, M. D. The poetry of Thompson. Forum 50 1913.
Figgis, D. Thompson. Contemporary Rev Oct 1913; rptd in his Bye-ways of study, Dublin 1918.
Jackson, H. In his The eighteen nineties, 1913.
Harrison, A. The poetry of Thompson. Eng Rev 15 1913.
Meynell, E. The life of Thompson. 1913, 1926 (5th edn rev and condensed).
— The notebooks of Thompson. Dublin Rev Jan 1917; rptd in Living Age 294 1917.
Rooker, J. K. Thompson. 1913. In French.
Jacobson, A. Tuberculosis and genius: a study with special reference to Thompson. Interstate Medical Jnl 21 1914.
Mason, E. A Catholic poet: Thompson and his legend. In A book of preferences in literature, New York 1915.
Allen, H. A. The poet of the return to God. Catholic World June 1918.
Moore, T. V. The hound of heaven. Psychoanalytic Rev 5 1918.
Armstrong, R. The simplicity of Thompson. Poetry Rev 12 1921.
LeBeffe, F. P. The hound of heaven: an interpretation. New York 1921.
Haecker, T. Über Thompson und Sprachkunst. Hochland 22 1924.
Finberg, H. B. R. Thompson. Eng Rev 41 1925.
Madeleva, Sr M. Thompson's prose. In her Chaucer's nuns and other essays, New York 1925.
Symons, A. In his Dramatis personae, 1925.
Hutton, J. A. Guidance from Thompson in matters of faith. 1926.
Shuster, G. N. Notes for a literary study of the Hound of heaven. Catholic Educational Rev 24 1926.
— Thoughts on Thompson. Commonweal 25 1937.
Mégroz, R. L. Thompson: the poet of earth in heaven. 1927.
Wright, T. H. Thompson and his poetry. 1927.
Peterson, E. L. Thompson: a picture biography. Virginia Quart Rev 4 1928.
Pullen, E. Thompson. Catholic World April 1928.
Chapman, J. A. Shelley and Thompson. In his Papers on Shelley, Wordsworth and others, Oxford 1929.
Abercrombie, L. Thompson. Circle 19 1930.
Tardivel, F. L'expérience poétique et l'expérience religieuse de Thompson. Rev Anglo-américaine 8 1930.
Kenealy, A. Thompson: some personal recollections. Carmina May 1931.
— Thompson: the man and his poetry. Capuchin Annual 1933.
de la Gorce, A. Thompson et les poètes catholiques d'Angleterre. Paris 1932; tr 1933.
Gautrey, R. M. This tremendous lover: an exposition of Thompson's Hound of heaven. 1932.
Marz, A. Thompsons dichterische Entwicklung. Münster 1932.
Evans, B. I. In his English poetry in the later nineteenth century, 1933, 1966 (rev).
McNabb, V. In his Thompson and other essays, 1935.
Olivero, F. Thompson. Brescia 1935; tr 1938.
Willson, C. Thompson: poet of childhood. Dalhousie Rev 14 1935.
Williamson, C. Thompson: a new study. Poetry Rev 26–7 1935–6.
Owlett, F. C. Essay on Thompson. 1936.
Bourne, R. Thompson's Shelley: a re-appreciation. Month April 1937.
Connolly, T. L. An account of books and mss of Thompson. Boston 1937.
— Thompson: in his paths—a vist to persons and places associated with the poet. Milwaukee 1944.
— Laudanum or poetry? Renascence 13 1961. *See also* his textual notes to C. Patmore, Mystical poems of nuptial love, Boston 1938.
D'Alessio, E. Thompson. Milan 1937.
Rebora, P. Thompson e la poesie di Leopardi in Inghilterra. Bollettino degli Studi Inglesi in Italia July 1937.
Ketrick, P. J. Thompson: poet of two worlds. Catholic World July 1938.
Caillouette, W. J. Quantitative studies in the poetry of Thompson. Nashville 1940.
John, P. A poet of the church. Catholic World June 1940.
Kehoe, M. Thompson: a poet of religious romanticism. Thought 15 1940.
Moorman, L. J. In Tuberculosis and genius, Chicago 1940.
Tolles, F. B. The praetorian cohorts: a study of the language of Thompson's poetry. E Studies 22 1940.
Wilson, W. G. His fruit not bread. Quart Rev 276 1941.
— Thompson's outlook on science. Contemporary Rev Nov 1957.
Smith, F. Thompson: some sort of derelict! Catholic World Jan 1943.
Barry, J. J. The child who never grew up. Commonweal 43 1945.
Kawa, E. Der Jaghund des Himmels. Berlin 1946.
Dutta, S. K. Thompson: homage from India. English 7 1948.
Pólit, A. E. El lebrel del cielo de Thompson. Quito 1948.
Cohen, J. M. Thompson. Month Dec 1949.
Hennessy, D. Did Thompson attempt suicide? Catholic World Feb 1950.
Williams, G. C. Thompson's Grace of the way 21–28, 53–56. Explicator 9 1951. *See also* T. L. Connolly, ibid.
Catherine Frederick, M. The Franciscan spirit as revealed in the literary contributions of Thompson. Franciscan Stud 9 1951.
Meynell, V. Thompson and Wilfrid Meynell: a memoir. 1952.
Doogan, F. The Catholicity of Thompson. Melbourne [1955?].
Karol, M. Franciscan elements in the life and some essays of Thompson. Franciscan Stud 17 1958.
Alexander, D. Eugene O'Neill, the Hound of heaven and the Hell hole. MLQ 20 1959.
Danchin, P. Thompson: la vie et l'oeuvre d'un poète. Paris 1959.
— Thompson 1859–1907: à propos d'un centenaire. Etudes Anglaises 13 1960.
— Du nouveau sur Thompson, prosateur et critique. Etudes Anglaises 17 1964.
Flanigan, T. M. The Hound and metaphysics. America 101 1959.
Kumar, P. N. Thompson. Aryan Path 30 1959.
Meynell, F. Thompson, my godfather. Poetry Rev 50 1959.
Pope, M. P. Thompson's Sad semele. Explicator 17 1959.

Quinlen, J. The centenary of Thompson. Contemporary Rev Dec 1959.
Reid, J. C. Thompson: man and poet. 1959.
Thompson centenary 1859–1959: catalogue of mss, letters and books in the Harris Public Library. Preston 1959.
Dingle, R. J. Thompson's centenary: the fashionable reaction. Dublin Rev 234 1960.
Lees, F. N. Thompson: 1859–1907. Bull John Rylands Lib 42 1960.
Butter, P. H. Thompson. 1961.
— Thompson. REL 2 1961.
Kraemer, K. W. Thompson: der Dichter der Rückkehr zu Gott. Stimmen der Zeit 167 1961.
Nichols, L. I. Thompson: flight and fall. Thought 36 1961.
Reiman, D. H. Sheeley, De Verre and Thompson's Hound of heaven. Victorian Newsletter no 19 1961.
Thomson, P. van K. Thompson: a critical biography. New York 1961.
Brophy, J. D., jr. Thompson and contemporary readers: a centennial appraisal. Renascence 14 1962.
Buchen, I. H. Source-hunting versus tradition: Thompson's Hound of heaven. Victorian Poetry 2 1964.
Jeune, S. Thompson. Revue de Littérature Comparée 38 1964.

W. W.

ALFRED EDWARD HOUSMAN

1859–1936

The Library of Congress Washington has the substantial remains of the ms notebooks Housman used for composing, correcting and polishing from c. 1890, together with a number of fair copies. The library of Trinity College Cambridge has the ms printer's copy (lacking one poem) of A Shropshire lad, *and the Fitzwilliam Museum the ms copy of* Last poems *from which the printer's copy was typed, lacking 5 poems. Mr John Carter of London and the Lilly Collection of Indiana Univ have mss, letters, juvenilia, light verse, and some fair copies. The BM contains a number of fair copies.*

Bibliographies etc.

Gow, A. S. F. List of writings. In his Housman: a sketch, Cambridge 1936.
Hyder, C. K. A concordance to the poems of Housman. Lawrence Kansas 1940.
Ehrsam, T. G. A bibliography of Housman. Boston 1941.
Stallman, R. W. Annotated bibliography of Housman: a critical study. PMLA 60 1945.
Carter, J. and J. Sparrow. Housman: an annotated hand-list. 1952. Rptd from Library 4th ser 21 1940; for addns *see* W. White, 23 1943, 5th ser 7 1952; G. B. A. Fletcher, 4th ser 23 1943, 5th ser 7 1952, Durham Univ Jnl 37 1946.

Collections

Collected poems. 1939, 1960 (rev, with note on text by J. Carter).
Collected poems. Ed J. Sparrow 1956 (Penguin), 1961.
Complete poems. New York 1959. Centennial edn, introd by B. Davenport, with history of the text by T. B. Haber. Incomplete.
Selected prose. Ed J. Carter, Cambridge 1961, 1962 (corrected).
Collected poems. Ed J. Carter, New York 1965. Authorized and complete. *See* W. White, PBSA 60 1966.

§1

Introductory lecture delivered in University College London. Cambridge 1892 (priv ptd), 1933 (priv ptd), 1937.

A Shropshire lad. 1896; Jubilee edition, ed C. J. Weber, Waterville Maine 1946 (with bibliography).
Last poems. 1922.
Fragment of a Greek tragedy. Amherst 1925 (priv ptd).
Nine essays by Arthur Platt. Cambridge 1927. With preface by Housman.
The name and nature of poetry. Cambridge 1933.
Three poems: the parallelogram, the amphisbaena, the crocodile. 1935 (priv ptd); ed W. White, Los Angeles 1941.
More poems. [Ed L. Housman] 1936.
Additional poems. In L. Housman, A.E.H.: some poems, some letters and a personal memoir, 1937.
A meeting with the Royal Family. Los Angeles 1941.
Selected poems. New York 1942 (Armed services edn).
The manuscript poems. Ed T. B. Haber, Minneapolis 1955.
Housman's Cambridge inaugural [1911]. TLS 9 May 1968.

Letters and Papers

Housman, L. In his A.E.H.: some poems, some letters and a personal memoir, 1937.
Richards, G. In his Housman 1897–1936, Oxford 1941.
Letters from Housman to E. H. Blakeney. Winchester 1941 (priv ptd).
B[lakeney], E. H. A.E.H. W.W. Winchester 1944 (priv ptd). Pamphlet on Sir William Watson, with one letter.
Thirty Housman letters to Witter Bynner. Ed T. B. Haber, New York 1957.
White, W. Housman to Joseph Ishill: five unpublished letters. Berkeley Heights NJ 1959 (priv ptd).
Also critical editions of Manilius (1903–30), Juvenal (1905) and Lucan (1926). For his contributions to classical scholarship etc see Gow, Bibliography, *above. There are unpbd fragments, letters, marginalia and poems in items below: N. Abeel, J. Carter, C. Clemens, T. B. Haber, H. Martin, M. Pollet, K. E. Symons, W. White and P. Withers. For a list of Housman letters see* W. White, Published letters of Housman: a survey, Bull of Bibliography 22 1957.

§2

Gale, N. Some volumes of verse. Academy 11 July 1896.
Archer, W. Housman. Fortnightly Rev 1 Aug 1898; rptd in his Poets of the younger generation, 1902.
The Shropshire lad again. TLS 19 Oct 1922.
Ellis, S. M. Housman. Fortnightly Rev Jan 1923; rptd in his Mainly Victorians, 1925.
Lucas, F. L. Few, but roses. New Statesman 20 Oct 1923.
— 'Fool's errand' to the grave: the personality and poetry of Housman. In his Greatest problem and other essays, 1960.
Macdonald, J. F. The poetry of Housman. Queen's Quart 31 1923.
Priestley, J. B. The poetry of Housman. London Mercury Dec 1922; rptd in his Figures in modern literature, 1924.
Collins, H. P. Housman: a retrospective note. Adelphi 3 1925; rptd in his Modern poetry, 1925.
Evans, B. I. In his English poetry in the later nineteenth century, 1933, 1966 (rev).
Sparrow, J. Echoes in the poetry of Housman. Nineteenth Century Feb 1934. *See* L. R. Lind, Classical Weekly 9 Dec 1935; G. B. A. Fletcher, RES 21 1935; and G. Richards, Housman 1897–1936 Oxford 1941.
— A Housman reminiscence. RES 10 1959, 11 1960.
Mauer, K. W. The poetry of Housman. Neuphilologische Monatsschrift 6 1935.
— Housman. Anglia 63 1939.
Ryan, J. K. Defeatist as poet. Catholic World April 1935.
Tinker, C. B. Housman's poetry. Yale Rev 25 1935; rptd in his Essays in retrospect, New Haven 1948.
Abeel, N. A letter from Housman. Forum 96 1936; rptd in Princeton Lib Chron 13 1951.

Gow, A. S. F. Housman: a sketch together with a list of his writings and indexes to his classical papers. Cambridge 1936.
— A Housman couplet. TLS 24 May 1957. *See* W. White, 12 July 1957.
Martin, H. With letters from Housman. Yale Rev 26 1936.
Pound, E. Mr Housman at little Bethel. Criterion 13 1934; rptd in his Polite essays, 1936.
Richmond, O. L. Housman and Headlam. TLS 31 Oct, 7 Nov 1936.
Symons, K. E. Memories of Housman. Bath 1936.
— More memories. Bath 1936.
— et al. Housman: recollections. Bromsgrove 1936.
Taylor, G. A. Housman. Queen's Quart 43 1936.
Housman number. Mark Twain Quart 1 1936. 42 articles, notes and poems.
Housman: More poems and a memoir. TLS 24 Oct 1936.
Clemens, C. An evening with Housman. Webster Groves Missouri 1937.
— Housman and his publisher: a series of unpublished letters. Mark Twain Quart 4 1941.
— Housman at Cambridge. Dalhousie Rev 22 1942.
— Housman in America. Poet Lore 49 1943.
— Some unpublished Housman letters. Poet Lore 53 1947.
Cooper, M. Sunt lacrimae rerum. London Mercury Jan 1937. On the pessimism of Housman and Leopardi.
Elvin, R. Housman. Mois July 1937.
Flower, R. Three poems by Housman. BM Quart 11 1937.
Gillet, L. Housman. Revue des Deux Mondes 1 May 1937.
Housman, L. A.E.H.: some poems, some letters and a personal memoir. 1937.
— A poet in the making. Atlantic Monthly July 1946.
— Housman's 'De amicitia', annotated by John Carter. Encounter Oct 1967.
Johnson, H. H. Housman: poet and pessimist. Hibbert Jnl 35 1937.
Molson, H. Philosophies of Hardy and Housman. Quart Rev 268 1937.
Pollet, M. Housman. Etudes Anglaises 1 1937.
Tillotson, G. The publication of Housman's comic poems. English 1 1937; rptd in his Essays in criticism and research, Cambridge 1942.
Watts, N. H. Poetry of Housman. Dublin Rev 200 1937.
Wilson, E. The voice sent forth. New Republic 29 Sept 1937; rptd in his Triple Thinkers, New York 1938.
Ashton, T. Housman: a critical study. Poetry Rev 29 1938.
Carter, J. On collecting Housman. Colophon new ser 3 1938; rptd in his Books and book-collectors, 1956.
— A poem of Housman. TLS 5–12 June 1943.
— The Housman mss in the Library of Congress. Book Collector 4 1955.
— The text of Housman's poems. TLS 15 June 1956. *See* 15–22 June, 10–7 July 1956, 29 May, 24 July, 14 Aug 1959, 14 March 1968.
— Housman's contributions to an Oxford magazine. Book Collector 6 1957.
— Housmaniana. Book Collector 11 1962, 14 1965.
— Housman, Shelley and Swinburne. TLS 6 Sept 1963. *See* 13 Sept 1963.
— and J. W. Scott. Housman: catalogue of an exhibition on the centenary of his birth. 1959.
Fletcher, G. B. A. Housman and the NED. N & Q 29 Oct 1938.
Leighton, L. One view of Housman. Poetry 52 1938.
Bronowski, J. In his Poet's defence, Cambridge 1939.
Chambers, R. W. Philologists at University College. In his Man's unconquerable mind, 1939.
Garrod, H. W. Housman 1939. E & S 25 1939.
Jarrell, R. Texts from Housman. Kenyon Rev 1 1939.
Salinger, H. Housman's Last poems and Heine's Lyrische intermezzo 62. MLN 54 1939.
Bishop, J. P. Poetry of Housman. Poetry 56 1940; rptd in his Collected essays, 1948.
Brown, S. G. The poetry of Housman. Sewanee Rev 48 1940.
Caclamanos, D. Source of a poem by Housman. N & Q 24 Feb, 6 April 1940.
Peters, E. C. A cynical classicist. Poetry Rev 31 1940.
Repplier, A. The brothers Housman. Atlantic Monthly Jan 1940.
Spender, S. The essential Housman. Horizon April 1940; rptd in his Making of a poem, 1960.
White, W. Bibliographical notes. PBSA 34–5 1940–41, 37 1943, 45 1951, 48–9 1954–5, 52 1958, 54 1960, 56 1962, 60 1966.
— Housman's riddle: A Shropshire lad lxiii. Mark Twain Quart 4 1941.
— Housman on Blunt and Kipling. N & Q 29 Nov 1941.
— A note on some Housman marginalia. PMLA 58 1943.
— Housman and music. Music & Letters 24 1943. *See* K. E. Symons, 25 1944.
— More Housman letters. Mark Twain Quart 5 1943.
— John Morley and A.E.H. TLS 22 March 1947.
— To Housman: echoes in novels and verses. Bull of Bibliography 19 1947.
— Housman on Galsworthy: more marginalia. RES 24 1948.
— Fifteen unpublished letters of Housman. Dalhousie Rev 29 1950.
— Housman fragments. TLS 4 July 1952. *See* 27 June, 18 July, 1 Aug, 26 Sept, 24 Oct, 7 Nov 1952; 2, 23 Oct 1953; 12 Feb, 5 March, 15 May 1954; 29 April, 1–8 July 1955.
— Variant readings in Housman. Book Collector 2 1953, 6 1957, 12–3 1963–4, 14 1965; AN & Q Oct 1966; Serif Sept 1967.
— Southey borrowings in Housman. N & Q Feb 1953.
— The death of Socrates: Housman's first published poem. PMLA 68 1953.
— Un poëme inédit de Housman: Sir Walter Raleigh. Etudes Anglaises 6 1953.
— A Shropshire lad in process: the textual evolution of some Housman poems. Library 5th ser 9 1955.
— Housman: a father-son collaboration. MLN 70 1955.
— Housman's Latin inscriptions. Classical Jnl 50 1955.
— Colophon notes for Housman collectors. Amer Book Collector Oct 1956, June 1957, March 1961, Sept 1967.
— Housman: a critical and bibliographical review of books about the poet 1936–55. JEGP 56 1957.
— Willa Cather and Housman. N & Q 4 1957. *See* Victorian Newsletter no 13 1958, Prairie Schooner 39 1965.
— Accuracy in Housman biography. TLS 1 Aug 1958.
— Commentary. In A centennial memento with excerpts from A Shropshire lad and Fragments of a Greek tragedy, including five letters to Joseph Ishill, Berkeley Heights NJ 1959 (priv ptd).
— Birth of a poem: A Shropshire lad xliv. Amer Book Collector Oct 1959.
— Housman exhibition. TLS 16 Oct 1959. *See* S. Nowell-Smith, 6 Nov 1959.
— Suicide and the poet: Housman. Today's Japan June 1960.
— Housman's Cambridge inaugural address. Orient West May 1961.
Withers, P. A buried life. 1940.
Gladding, E. B. Housman's More poems vii and Dehmel's Trost. MLN 56 1941. *See* C. B. Beall, Housman, Dehmel and Dante, 57 1942.
Haber, T. B. The spirit of the perverse in A.E.H. South Atlantic Quart 40 1941.
— The influence of the ballads in Housman's poetry. SP 39 1942.
— Heine and Housman. JEGP 43 1944.

— Housman's poetry and the lyrics of Shakespeare. MLQ 6 1945.
— Housman's poetic ear. Poet Lore 54 1948.
— How poetic is Housman's poetry? MLN 67 1952.
— Housman's downward eye. JEGP 53 1954.
— Housman's poetic method. PMLA 69 1954.
— Housman: astronomer-poet. E Studies 35 1954.
— Housman's poetry in book-titles. PBSA 49 1955, 52 1958, 55 1961.
— New Housman Lucretiana. Classical Jnl 51 1956. *See* 58 1963; G. B. A. Fletcher, On Housman Lucretiana, 54 1958.
— Parallels in Juvenal and Housman. Classical Jnl 52 1956.
— Translations and paraphrases in Housman. Zeitschrift für Anglistik und Amerikanstik 5 1957.
— Housman and Ye rounde table. JEGP 61 1962.
— Housman's notebooks and his posthumous poetry. Iowa Eng Yearbook 8 1963.
— Three unreported letters of Housman. PBSA 57 1963.
— The making of A Shropshire lad: a manuscript variorum. Seattle 1960. *See* W. White, ELN 4 1967.
— Housman. New York 1967.
Marcellino, R. E. Vergil and Housman. Classical Jnl 37 1941. *See* P. R. Murphy 37 1941, R. W. Brown, A. P. Dorjahn, E. M. Sanford, H. C. Lipscomb, 37 1942.
— Housman and Propertius. Classical Weekly 23 March 1953.
— Housman's Fragment of a Greek tragedy. Classical Jnl 48 1953.
Richards, G. Housman 1897–1936. Oxford 1941.
Whitridge, A. Vigny and Housman: a study in pessimism. Amer Scholar 10 1941.
Allison, A. F. The poetry of Housman. RES 19 1943.
Fletcher, J. G. The riddle of Housman. Mark Twain Quart 5 1943.
H., R. M. Housman's use of parody. N & Q 11 Sept 1943.
Platnauer, M. Variants in the mss of the poems of Rupert Brooke and Housman. RES 19 1943.
Housman number. Explicator 2 1944. Essays by C. Brooks, L. S. Boas, T. S. K. Scott-Craig, C. C. Walcutt, F. A. Philbrick, R. P. Boas, F. Sullivan, W. L. Werner, R. W. Stallman. For other explications *see* 3–24 1944–66.
Walcutt, C. C. Housman and the Empire: an analysis of 1887. College Eng 5 1944. *See* W. L. Werner 6 1944.
Woodridge, B. M. Poets and pessimism: Vigby, Housman et al. Romanic Rev 35 1944.
Sweeney, F. The ethics of Housman. Thought 20 1945.
Connolly, C. Housman: a controversy. In his Condemned playground, 1946.
Mounts, C. E. Housman's twisting of scripture. MLN 61 1946. *See* D. P. Harding, 65 1950; V. Freimarck, 67 1952.
Wilshire, L. The background of A Shropshire lad. Poetry Rev 38 1947.
Butcher, A. V. Housman and the English composer. Music & Letters 29 1948.
Kane, R. J. Housman and the new prefect of the Ambrosian. MLN 63 1948.
Robb, N. A. Housman. In her Four in exile, 1948.
Robinson, O. Angry dust: the poetry of Housman. Boston 1950.
Macklem, M. The elegiac theme in Housman. Queen's Quart 59 1952.
Hamilton, R. Housman the poet. Exeter 1953. Rev and rptd from London Quart 175 1950.
Edgren, C. H. A Hardy-Housman parallel. N & Q March 1954.
Aldington, R. Housman and Yeats: two lectures. Hurst Berks 1955 (350 copies).
Kaul, J. L. Housman. Jnl of Univ of Jammu & Kashmir 1955.
Marlow, A. N. The earliest influence on A Shropshire lad. RES 6 1955.
— Housman: scholar and poet. 1958.
Scott-Kilvert, L. Housman. 1955, 1965 (rev) (Br Council pamphlet).
Stevenson, J. W. The pastoral setting in the poetry of Housman. South Atlantic Quart 55 1956.
— The martyr as innocent: Housman's lonely lad. South Atlantic Quart 57 1958.
— Housman's lyric tradition. Forum 4 1963.
Drew, F. B. and W. V. Sieller. Housman's comments on Morris Masefield, Wilde, Douglas and Saintsbury. Colby Lib Quart 4 1957.
Gross, S. L. Housman and Pindar. N & Q March 1957.
Rockwell, K. A. Housman, poet-scholar. Classical Jnl 52 1957.
Sinclair, F. O. Housman: an evaluation. Pretoria 1957.
Watson, G. L. Housman: a divided life. 1957.
Anziloti, R. La poesia di Housman. Florence 1958.
Hawkins, M. M. Housman: man behind a mask. Chicago 1958.
Housman's The deserter. N & Q June 1958. *See* J. A. Lavin, March 1952; M. Dean-Smith, July 1962.
Marshall, G. O. Jr. A Miltonic echo in Housman. N & Q June 1958.
Housman Centenary. Publisher's Weekly 9 March 1959.
Bailey, D. R. S. Housman as a classical scholar. Listener 7 May 1959.
Carr, R. Farewell: a study in the domestication of horror. Descant 4 1959.
Kumar, P. N. Housman: an Indian view. Aryan Path 30 1959.
Russell, F. The bard of Bromsgrove. Nat Rev 7 1959.
Scheltma, T. W. L. Housman. Litterair Paspoort Nov 1959.
Campbell, H. Conflicting metaphors: a poem by Housman [The immortal part]. CEA Critic Jan 1960.
Justice, D. A Housman centennial. Poetry 95 1960.
Murray, G. Reminiscences 5: Milking the bull. John O'London's 5 May 1960.
Olivier, F. Housman: in integrum restituere. Etudes de Lettres 3 1960.
Skutch, O. Housman 1859–1936. 1960.
Walde, E. H. S. and T. S. Dorsch. Housman and Matthew Arnold. Boston Univ Stud in Eng 4 1960.
Housman Exhibition April 1–30 1961, Lilly Library. Bloomington 1961. Includes F. B. Drew, The poet as house-guest: some unpublished verse by Housman.
Megata, M. Herodotus and Housman: two versions of Atys. Stud in Eng Lit (Tokyo) 38 1961.
Singh, G. Housman and Leopardi. Eng Miscellany (Rome) 13 1962.
Sullivan, J. P. The leading classicist of his generation. Arion 1 1962. *See* K. A. Rockwell, Sullivan 2 1963.
Wilbur, R. Round about a poem of Housman's. In The moment of poetry, ed D. C. Allen, Baltimore 1962.
Wysong, J. N. Housman's use of astronomy. Anglia 80 1962.
Franklin, R. Housman's Shropshire. MLQ 24 1963.
Lohf, K. A. Housman through the eyes of others. Columbia Lib Columns 13 1963.
Ricks, C. The nature of Housman's poetry. EC 14 1964.
Seigel, J. P. Housman's modification of the flower motif of the pastoral elegy. Victorian Poetry 2 1964.
Le Mire, E. D. The irony and ethics of A Shropshire lad. Univ of Windsor Rev 1 1965.
Sprozier, R. I. Housman: illogic and allusion. Colby Lib Quart 7 1966.
Pearsall, R. B. The vendible values of Housman's soldiery. PMLA 82 1967.

W. W.

VII. MINOR POETRY 1870–1900

References

Miles The poets and poetry of the century, ed A. H. Miles et al 10 vols [1891–7], 12 vols 1905–7 (enlarged).

ALEXANDER ANDERSON
1845–1909

§1

A song of labour and other poems. Dundee 1873.
The two angels. and other poems, with an introductory sketch by G. Gilfillan. 1875.
Songs of the rail. 1878.
Ballads and sonnets. 1879. Partly rptd from A song of labour and Two angels, above, with many new poems.
Later poems of Anderson, Surface man. Ed A. Brown, Glasgow 1912 (with biographical sketch).

§2

Cuthbertson, D. The life-history of Anderson. Inveresk 1929 (priv ptd).
Evans, B. I. In his English poetry in the later nineteenth century, 1933, 1966 (rev).

SIR EDWIN ARNOLD
1832–1904

Collections

Arnold birthday book. Ed K. L. and C. Arnold 1885. From The works of Arnold, with new poems.
Poems, national and non-oriental, with some new pieces, selected from the Works of Arnold. 1888.
Poetical works. 8 vols 1888.
Oriental poems. Ed J. M. Watkins 1904.
Indian poems and Indian idylls. 1915.
The Arnold poetry reader: selections, with memoir and notes by E. L. Arnold. 1920.

§1

The feast of Belshazzar: a prize poem. Oxford 1852.
Poems, narrative and lyrical. Oxford 1853.
Griselda: a tragedy, and other poems. 1856.
The wreck of the northern belle: a poem. Hastings 1857.
Education in India: a letter from the ex-principal of an Indian government college to his appointed successor. 1860.
The Marquis of Dalhousie's administration of British India, 2 vols 1862–5.
The poets of Greece. 1869.
A simple transliteral grammar of the Turkish language with dialogues and vocabulary. 1877.
The light of Asia, or the great renunciation. 1879; ed E. D. Ross 1926.
Poems. Boston 1880.
Indian poetry. 1881.
Pearls of the faith: or Islam's rosary. 1883.
The secret of death, with some collected poems. 1885.
India revisited. 1886. Rptd with addns from Daily Telegraph.
Death—and afterwards. 1887. Rptd with supplement from Fortnightly Rev.
Lotus and jewel. 1887.
With Sa'di in the garden: or the book of love. 1888.
In my lady's praise: being poems, old and new, written in the honour of Fanny, Lady Arnold, and now collected for her memory. 1889.
The light of the world, or the great consummation: a poem. 1891; tr Dutch, 1892.
Seas and lands. 1891. Rptd from Daily Telegraph.
Japonica. 1892. Rptd from Scribner's Mag.
Potiphar's wife and other poems. 1892.
Adzuma, or the Japanese wife: a play in four acts. 1893.
Wandering words. 1894. Rptd from Daily Telegraph etc.
The tenth muse and other poems. 1895.
East and west. 1896. Rptd from Daily Telegraph etc.
Victoria, Queen and Empresss: the sixty years. 1896. Rptd from Daily Telegraph.
The Queen's justice: a true story of Indian village life. 1899.
The voyage of Ithobal: a poem. 1901.
The birth of wine: an unpublished poem. Saturday Rev of Lit 30 Sept 1933.
The two Arnolds. Blackwood's Mag March 1954. Compares Edwin and Matthew Arnold.
Bell, M. Arnold. Miles 5.
Obituary. Times 26 March 1904.
Evans, B. I. In his English poetry in the later nineteenth century, 1933, 1966 (rev).
Arnold and Walt Whitman. N & Q 21 Aug 1948. An 1889 letter from Arnold to Whitman.
Hendrick, G. Whitman and Arnold. Western Humanities Rev 14 1960.

ALFRED AUSTIN
1835–1913

Bibliographies

Crowell, N. B. In his Austin: Victorian, Albuquerque 1953.

Selections

Days of the year: a poetic calendar from the works of Austin. Ed W. Sharp 1886.
English lyrics. Ed W. Watson 1890.
Love poems. 1912.

§1

Randolph: a poem in two cantos. 1854, 1877 (recast as Leszco the bastard: a tale of Polish grief).
Five years of it: a novel. 2 vols 1858.
The season: a satire. 1861, 1861 (rev with preface), 1869 (rev).
The human tragedy: a poem. 1862 (withdrawn), 1876 (rev), 1889 (rev), 1889 (rev with preface On the position and prospects of poetry), 1891 (omits preface).
An artist's proof: a novel. 3 vols 1864.
Won by a head: a novel. 3 vols 1866.
A vindication of Lord Byron. 1869. Reply to Mrs Stowe.
The poetry of the period. 1870. Rptd from Temple Bar.
The golden age: a satire in verse. 1871.
Interludes. 1872.
Madonna's child. 1873. Incorporated as Act 2 in The human tragedy, 1876.
Rome or death! a poem. 1873. Forms Act 3 of The human tragedy. 1876.
The tower of babel: a poetical drama. 1874.
Savonarola: a tragedy. 1881.
Soliloquies in song. 1882.
At the gate of the convent, and other poems. 1885.

Prince Lucifer. 1887, 1887 (adds essay on The end and limits of objective poetry), 1891 (omits essay).
Love's widowhood, and other poems. 1889.
Lyrical poems. 1891.
Narrative poems. 1891. In the heart of the forest, At the gate of the convent, Love's widowhood etc and new poems.
Fortunatus the pessimist: a dramatic poem. 1892.
The garden that I love. 2 ser 1894–1907. In the form of a diary.
In Veronica's garden. 1895. In the form of a diary.
England's darling. 1896, 1901 (as Alfred the Great, England's darling).
The conversion of Winckelmann, and other poems. 1897.
Victoria: June 20 1837, June 20 1897. 1897.
Lamia's winter quarters. 1898. A story.
Songs of England. 1898, 1900, 1900, 1900 (all enlarged).
Spring and autumn in Ireland. 1900. Rptd from Blackwood's Mag.
Polyphemus. 1901.
A tale of true love, and other poems. 1902.
Haunts of ancient peace. 1902. A story.
Flodden field: a tragedy. 1903.
The poet's diary, edited by Lamia. 1904.
The door of humility: a poem. 1906.
Sacred and profane love, and other poems. 1908.
The bridling of Pegasus. 1910. 9 essays on poetry and poets.
Autobiography. 2 vols 1911.
Austin also pbd some political and controversial pamphlets.

§2

Whyte, W. Austin. Miles 6.
O., J. Austin. Athenaeum 7 June 1913.
Sherman, S. P. The complacent Toryism of Austin. In his On contemporary literature, New York 1917.
Welby, T. E. Austin. Bookman (London) Dec 1930.
Evans, B. I. In his English poetry in the later nineteenth century, 1933, 1966 (rev).
May, J. L. A neglected poet. Dublin Rev no 402 1937.
Crowell, N. B. Austin: Victorian. Albuquerque 1953.
The Banjo-Byron. TLS 13 Nov 1953. *See* V. G. Miller, 27 Nov 1953.
Murray, C. C. Austin. TLS 20 Nov 1953.

JOHN EVELYN BARLAS

1860–1914

Several vols were pbd under the pseudonym 'Evelyn Douglas'.

Bibliographies

Lowe, D. In his Barlas: sweet singer and Socialist, Cupar 1915.
Salt, H. S. In his edn, Selections, 1925, below.

Selections

Selections. Ed H. S. Salt 1925.

§1

Poems lyrical and dramatic. 1884.
Queen of the hid isle. 1885.
Punchinello and his wife Judith: a tragedy. Chelmsford 1886.
Phantasmagoria: dream fugues. Chelmsford 1887.
Bird-notes. Chelmsford 1887.
Holy of holies: confession of an archist. Chelmsford 1887.
Love sonnets. Chelmsford 1889.
Songs of a bayadere and songs of a troubadour. Dundee 1893 (priv ptd).

§2

Lowe, D. Barlas: sweet singer and Socialist. Cupar 1915.

GEORGE BARLOW

1847–1913

Collections

Poetical works. 11 vols 1902–14.
Selected poems. 1921. With note by C. W., bibliography and short life.

§1

A life's love. 1873. Sonnets.
An English madonna, by James Hinton. 1874.
Under the dawn. 1875.
The gospel of humanity: or the connection between spiritualism and modern thought. 1876.
The marriage before death, and other poems. 1878.
Through death to life. 1878.
The two marriages: a drama in three acts. 1878.
Love-songs. 1880.
Time's whisperings: sonnets and songs. 1880.
Song-bloom. 1881.
Song-spray. 1882.
An actor's reminiscences, and other poems. 1883.
Love's offering, by James Hinton. 1883.
Poems real and ideal. 1884.
Loved beyond words. 1885.
The pageant of life: an epic poem in five books. 1888.
From dawn to sunset. 1890.
A lost mother. 1892.
The crucifixion of man: a narrative poem. 1893.
Jesus of Nazareth. 1896. Tragedy in prose and verse.
To the women of England, and other poems. 1901.
A coronation poem. 1902.
Vox clamantis: sonnets and poems. 1904.
A man's vengenace, and other poems. 1908.
Songs of England awaking. 1909.
Barlow also pbd a novel and miscellaneous essays.

§2

Miles, A. H. Barlow. Miles 8 (7).
Bennett, E. T. The poetical work of Barlow: a study. 1903

JANE BARLOW

1857–1917

See col 1908, below.

AUBREY VINCENT BEARDSLEY

1872–98

Bibliographies

Gallatin, A. E. Beardsley's drawings. 1903.
— Beardsley: catalogue of drawings and bibliography. New York 1945.
— and A. D. Wainwright. Catalogue of the Beardsley collection in Princeton University Library. Princeton 1952.
Additions to the Beardsley collection. Princeton Univ Lib Chron 19 1958.

Collections

The best of Beardsley. Ed R. A. Walker 1948.
A Beardsley miscellany. Ed R. A. Walker 1949.
For a selection, see Beardsley: his best fifty drawings, ed K. Foss 1955.

§1

Under the hill and other essays in prose and verse. 1904. Rptd from Yellow Book and Savoy.
Last letters, with an introductory note by J. Gray. 1904.
The story of Venus and Tannhäuser: a romantic novel. 1907 (priv ptd; original, unexpurgated version of Under the hill, above), New York 1967 (with introd by P. J. Gillette).
Letters from Beardsley to Leonard Smithers. Ed R. A. Walker 1937.

§2

Symons, A. Beardsley. 1897, 1905 (rev and enlarged).
Gallatin, A. E. In his Whistler's art dicta and other essays, 1904.
— Beardsley. Princeton Univ Lib Chron 10 1949.
Ross, R. Beardsley. 1909, New York 1967.
King, A. W. A Beardsley lecture. 1924. Introd by R. A. Walker. Includes 10 letters.
Myers, J. A. Beardsley. In his Fighters of fate, 1927.
Macfall, H. Beardsley: the man and his work. 1928.
Blunt, H. F. Beardsley: a study in conversion. Catholic World 134 1932.
Evans, B. I. In his English poetry in the later nineteenth century, 1933, 1966 (rev).
Clarke, I. C. In Great Catholics, ed C. C. H. Williamson 1938.
Walker, R. A. Le morte d'Arthur. Bedford 1945.
— How to detect Beardsley forgeries. 1950.
Birnbaum, M. In his Jacovleff and other artists, New York 1946.
Ironside, R. Beardsley. Horizon 14 1946.
Pierrot of the minute. TLS 19 March 1949.
Ross, M. (ed). Robert Ross: friend of friends. 1952. Includes 12 letters from Beardsley.
Weintraub, S. Beardsley. New York 1967.

HENRY CHARLES BEECHING
1859-1919

Bibliographies

Stephen, G. A. Bibliography of Beeching. Norwich Public Lib Readers' Guide 7 1919.

§1

Mensae secundae. Oxford 1879. By Beeching, J. W. Mackail and J. B. B. Nichols.
Love in idleness. 1883 (anon), 1891 (with addns and omissions, as Love's looking glass). By Beeching, J. W. Mackail and J. B. B. Nichols.
In a garden and other poems. 1895.
St Augustine at Ostia: Oxford sacred poem. 1896.
Pages from a private diary. 1898 (anon), 1903 (by Urbanus Sylvan).
Conferences on books and men. 1900. Anon.
Two lectures introductory to the study of poetry. Cambridge 1901.
Religio laici: a series of studies addressed to laymen. 1902.
Provincial letters and other papers. 1906. Anon.
William Shakespeare: player, playmaker and poet. 1908.
Francis Atterbury. 1909.
Beeching also pbd numerous sermons and lectures and edited Milton's poems and several devotional series.

§2

Archer, W. In his Poets of the younger generation, 1902.
Greenwood, G. G. In re Shakespeare: Beeching versus Greenwood—rejoinder on behalf of the defendant. 1909.
Lee, S. Norwich Public Lib Readers' Guide 7 1919.
Huxley, L. Obituary. Cornhill Mag April 1919.

HENRY THOMAS MACKENZIE BELL
1856-1930

Collections

Collected poems. 1901.
Poems. 1909.
Selected poems. 1921.

§1

The keeping of the vow and other verses. 1879.
Verses of varied life. 1882.
Old year leaves: being old verses revived. 1883, 1886.
A forgotten genius, Charles Whitehead: a critical monograph. 1884, 1899.
Spring's immortality and other poems. 1893, 1895, 1896.
Pictures of travel and other poems. 1898.
Christina Rossetti: a biographical and critical study. 1898.
The taking of the flag and other recitations. 1900. Introd by J. J. Nesbitt.
'John Clifford': a poem. [1908].
The heart's summer and other poems. [1913].
Holy quietude and other poems. [1913].
Lyrics of consolation. [1913].
Poetical pictures of the Great War. 4 sers 1917.
Half hours with representative novelists of the nineteenth century. 3 vols 1927.
Bell also edited some Pre-Raphaelites and contributed to Miles.

ARTHUR CHRISTOPHER BENSON
1862-1925

See col. 1420, below.

ROBERT LAURENCE BINYON
1869-1943

Collections

Selected poems. 1926.
A Binyon anthology. 1927.
Collected poems. 2 vols 1931.

§1

Four poems. In Primavera: poems by Binyon, S. Phillips, M. Ghose and A. S. Cripps, 1890.
Lyric poems. 1894.
Poems. Oxford 1895.
Dutch etchers of the seventeenth century. 1895.
London visions. 1896 (bk 1), 1896 (12 poems, of which 5 rptd from Pall Mall Gazette and Poems 1895), 1899 (bk 2), 1908 (collected edn, rptd from Poems 1895, above, and from Porphyrion and other poems, below, adding new poems).
The praise of life: poems. 1896.
The supper: a lyrical scene. 1897 (priv ptd).
John Crone and John Sell Cotman. 1897.
Porphyrion and other poems. 1898.
Western Flanders: a medley of things seen, considered and imagined. 1899.
Thomas Girtin: his life and works: an essay. 1900.
Odes. 1901, 1913 (rearranged and rev).
The death of Adam and other poems. 1903.
Dream come true. 1905.
Penthesilea: a poem. 1905.
Paris and Œnone. 1906.
Attila: a tragedy. 1907.
England and other poems. 1909.
Augeries. 1913.
The winnowing-fan: poems on the great war. 1914.
Bombastes in the shades: a play in one act. In Oxford pamphlets 1914-5, 1915.
The anvil and other poems. 1916.

The cause: poems of war. [1917?].
The new world: poems. 1918.
English poetry in its relation to painting and the other arts. 1918 (Br Acad).
Poetry and modern life. 1918.
The four years: war poems collected and newly augmented. 1919.
Six poems on Bruges. 1919. With 6 colour prints by F. Brangwyn.
The secret: sixty poems. 1920.
The English ode. Trans Royal Soc of Lit 2 1922.
Arthur: a tragedy. 1923.
Ayuli: a play in three acts and an epilogue. Oxford 1923.
The sirens: an ode. 1924, 1925.
Little poems from the Japanese, rendered into English verse. Leeds 1925 (priv ptd).
Tradition and re-action in modern poetry. 1926 (Eng Assoc).
The wonder night. 1927.
Boadicea: a play in eight scenes. 1927.
Sophro the wise: a play for children. 1927.
The idols: an ode. 1928.
Three short plays: Godstow nunnery, Love in the desert, Memnon. 1930. In verse.
Landscape in English art and poetry. Tokyo 1930, 1931.
Akbar. 1932, 1939.
English water-colours. 1933, 1944.
The Inferno of Dante, translated into English verse. 1933.
Three poems. Derby 1934.
The case of Christopher Smart. 1934 (Eng Assoc).
The young king. 1935.
The English romantic revival in art and poetry: a reconsideration. 1935 (Rickman Godlee lecture).
Brief candles. 1938.
The Purgatorio of Dante, translated into English triple rhyme. 1938.
Note on Milton's imagery and rhythm. In Seventeenth-century studies presented to Sir H. Grierson, Oxford 1938.
Art and freedom. Oxford 1939 (Romanes lecture).
The north start and other poems. 1941.
The ruins. Horizon 6 1942. Early versions of poems included in The burning of the leaves.
The Paradiso of Dante, translated into English triple rhyme. 1943.
British Museum diversion: a play for puppets. Horizon 10 1944.
The burning of the leaves and other poems. Ed C. M. Binyon 1944.
The madness of Merlin. Ed G. Bottomley 1947.
Binyon also pbd several works on oriental art.

§2

Streatfield, R. A. Two poets of the new century, Stephen Phillips and Binyon: a critical appreciation. 1901.
Archer, W. In his Poets of the younger generation, 1902.
William, H. H. Binyon and his contemporaries. In his Modern English writers, 1918.
Maynard, T. In his Our best poets: English and American, 1924.
Twitchett, E. G. The poetry of Binyon. London Mercury Sept 1930.
Thouless, P. Binyon and John Masefield. In her Modern poetic drama, Oxford 1934.
Southworth, J. G. Binyon. Sewanee Rev 43 1935; rptd in his Sowing the spring, 1940.
Edwardian poets. TLS 20 March 1953.
Sayers, D. L. Binyon's death, TLS 27 March 1953.

WILFRID SCAWEN BLUNT

1840–1922

Bibliographies

Reinehr, Sr M. J. In the writings of Blunt: an introduction and study, Milwaukee 1941.

Collections

The poetry of Blunt, selected and arranged by W. E. Henley and G. Wyndham. 1898.
Love poems. 1902.
Poetical works. 2 vols 1914.
Poems. 1923. Selected by F. Dell.

§1

Sonnets and songs by Proteus. 1875.
Proteus and Amadeus: a correspondence. Ed A. de Vere 1878. Between Blunt and W. Meynell on religion and philosophy.
The love sonnets of Proteus. 1880.
The future of Islam. 1882. Essays rptd from Fortnightly Rev.
The wind and the whirlwind. 1883. Poem on Britain in Egypt.
Ideas about India. 1885.
In vinculis. 1889.
A new pilgrimage and other poems. 1889.
The celebrated romance of the stealing of the mare. 1892, 1930. Tr from Arabic by A. Blunt, done into verse by Blunt.
Esther, love lyrics and Natalia's resurrection. 1892, Boston 1895 (as Esther and The love sonnets of Proteus).
The love lyrics and songs of Proteus. 1892 (Kelmscott Press). Rptd from 1875 and 1880 edns, above, but in full texts with additional sonnets.
Griselda. 1893.
Satan absolved, a Victorian mystery: a poem. 1899.
Mu'allaakāt: the seven golden odes. 1903. Done into English verse.
Atrocities of justice under British rule in Egypt. 1906, 1907 (with new preface).
The secret history of the English occupation of Egypt: being a personal narrative of events. 1907, 1907 (with special appendices).
India under Ripon. a private diary: 1909.
Gordon of Khartoum: being a personal narrative of events. 1911.
The land war in Ireland. 1912.
My diaries. 2 vols 1919–20, 1922 (with preface by Lady Gregory).

§2

Le Gallienne, R. Blunt. Miles 6.
'Ouida' (M. L. de la Ramée). In his Critical studies, 1900.
Schuster, G. N. In his Catholic spirit in modern English literature, New York 1922.
Cunninghame Graham, R. B. Blunt. Eng Rev Dec 1922.
Symons, A. In his The Café Royale, 1923.
Lytton, N. S. In his The English country gentleman, 1925.
MacCarthy, D. In his Portraits, 1931.
—— Shooting with Blunt. London Mercury May 1937.
Evans, B. I. In his English poetry in the later nineteenth century, 1933, 1966 (rev).
Forster, E. M. In his Abinger harvest, 1936.
Leslie, S. In his Men were different, 1937.
Finch, E. Blunt 1840–1922. 1938.
Blunt's band. TLS 24 Aug 1940.
Reinehr, Sr M. J. The writings of Blunt: an introduction and study. Milwaukee 1941.
White, W. A. E. Housman on Blunt and Kipling. N & Q 29 Nov 1941.
Croft-Cooke, R. Squire of Crabbet park. Listener 25 Sept 1947. *See* S. Cockerell, 2 and 16 Oct 1947 and R. Croft-Cooke, 9 Oct 1947.
Cockerell, S. Blunt's burial. TLS 28 May 1954.
Deux lettres inédites de Blunt à Gobineau. Revue de Littérature Comparée 30 1956.
Adams, W. S. In his Edwardian portraits, 1957.

Going, W. T. Oscar Wilde and Blunt: ironic notes on prison, prose and poetry. Victorian Newsletter no 13 1958.
— Blunt: Victorian sonneteer. Victorian Poetry 2 1964.
Scott, K. W. Blunt's sonnets and another poem to skittles. Victorian Poetry 3 1965.

FRANCIS WILLIAM BOURDILLON
1852–1921

§1

Among the flowers and other poems. 1878.
Aucassin and Nicolette: a love story. 1887 (tr with Old French text, introd, notes and bibliography), 1897 (rev), 1913 (trn only, rev and freer).
Young maids and old China. 1888.
Where lilies live and waters wind away. 1889.
Ailes d'alouette. 2 sers Oxford 1890–1902 (priv ptd).
A lost god. 1891.
Sursum corda: poems. 1893.
Nephelé. 1896. A tale.
Minuscula: lyrics of nature, art and love. 1897.
Through the gateway. 1900.
The early editions of the Roman de la rose. 1906 (Bibl Soc).
Preludes and romances. 1908.
Ode in defence of the Matterhorn against the proposed railway to its summit. 1910.
Moth-wings. 1913. Selected from Ailes d'alouette, above, with addns.
Christmas roses for nineteen hundred and fourteen. 1914.
Easter lilies for nineteen hundred and fifteen. 1915.
Russia re-born: poems. 1917.
Gerard and Isabel. 1921. A romance.

§2

Obituary. Times 14 Jan 1921.

OLIVER MADOX BROWN
1855–74

See col 1041, below.

ROBERT WILLIAMS BUCHANAN
1841–1901

Bibliographies

Jay, H. In her Buchanan, 1903.

Collections

Poetical works. 3 vols 1874.
Selected poems. 1882.
A poet's sketch book: selections from the prose writings of Buchanan. 1883.
Poetical works. 1844, 2 vols 1901 (enlarged as Complete poetical works).
The Buchanan ballads, old and new. 1892. Vol 1 in Buchanan's Poems for the people, selected from his ballad books with addns.

§1

Undertones. 1863.
Idylls and legends of Inverburn. 1865.
London poems. 1866.
Ballad stories of the sffections. 1867. Adopted into English verse from Scandinavian.
North coast and other poems. 1868.
David Gray and other essays, chiefly on poetry. 1868.
The book of Orm: a prelude to the epic. 1870.
Napoleon fallen: a lyrical drama. 1871.
The drama of kings. 1871.
The land of Lorne, including The cruise of the 'Tern' to the Outer Hebrides. 2 vols 1871, 1883 (as The Hebrid Isles).
The fleshly school of poetry and other phenomena of the day. 1872. Rptd from Contemporary Rev.
Saint Abe and his seven lovers. 1872, 1896 (with bibl note on the poem).
White rose and red: a love story. 1873.
Master-spirits. 1873. Essays.
The shadow of the sword. 3 vols 1876, 3 vols 1883 (adds preface), Liverpool 1919. A novel.
Balder the beautiful: a song of divine death. 1877.
A child of nature: a romance. 3 vols 1881.
God and the man. 1881.
Foxglove manor: a novel. 3 vols 1881.
The martyrdom of Madeline: a novel. 3 vols 1882.
Ballads of life, love and humour. 1882.
Love me for ever: a romance. 1883.
Annan water: a romance. 3 vols 1883.
The new Abelard: a romance. 3 vols 1884.
The master of the mine: a novel. 2 vols 1885.
Malt: a story of a caravan. 1885.
Stormy waters: a story of to-day. 3 vols 1885.
The earthquake; or six days and a sabbath. 1885.
That winter night; or love's victory. 1886, 1887 (rev and enlarged).
A look round literature. 1887. Essays.
The city of dream: an epic poem. 1888.
The heir of Linne: a novel. 2 vols 1888.
On descending into hell: a letter to the Home Secretary concerning the proposed suppression of literature. 1889.
The moment after: a tale of the unseen. 1890.
Come, live with me and be my love: a novel. 2 vols 1891.
The coming terror and other essays and letters. 1891. Includes On descending into hell.
The outcast: a rhyme for the time. 1891.
The piper of Hamelin: a fantastic opera in two acts. 1893.
The Wandering Jew: a Christmas carol. 1893.
Woman and the man: a story. 2 vols 1893.
Red and white heather. 1894. Prose tales and ballads.
Rachel Dene: a tale of the Deepdale mills. 2 vols 1894.
Lady Kilpatrick: a novel. 1895.
Diana's hunting: a novel. 1895.
A marriage by capture: a romance of to-day. 1896.
Effie Hetherington: a novel. 1896.
The devil's case: a bank holiday interlude. 1896. A poem.
The ballad of Mary the Mother: a Christmas carol. 1897. Includes other poems.
The Rev Annabel Lee: a tale of to-morrow. 1898.
Father Anthony: a romance of to-day. 1898.
The new Rome: poems and ballads of our Empire. 1899.
Andromeda: an idyll of the great river. 1900.
Sweet Nancy: a comedy in three acts. 1914.

§2

Rossetti, D. G. The stealthy school of criticism. Athenaeum 16 Dec 1871. Reply to Buchanan's attack.
Smith, G. B. In his Poets and novelists, 1875.
Stedman, E. C. Latter-day British poets. Scribner's Mag Feb 1875.
Walkley, A. B. In his Playhouse impressions, 1892.
Noble, J. A. Buchanan. Miles 6.
Obituary. Athenaeum 15 June 1901.
Murray, H. Buchanan: a critical appreciation. 1901.
Walker, A. S. Buchanan, the poet of modern revolt: an introduction to his poetry. 1901.
Jay, H. Buchanan. 1903.
Symons, A. In his Studies in verse and prose, 1904.
Hearn, L. In his Appreciation of poetry, ed J. Erskine, New York 1916.

Letters from D. G. Rossetti to A. C. Swinburne regarding the attacks made upon both Buchanan. 1921 (priv ptd).
Blodgett, H. Whitman and Buchanan. Amer Lit 2 1930.
Evans, B. I. In his English poetry in the later nineteenth century, 1933, 1966 (rev).
Cassidy, J. A. Buchanan and the fleshly controversy. PMLA 67 1952.
—— The original source of Hardy's Dynasts. PMLA 69 1954.
Fairchild, H. N. The immediate source of the Dynasts [The drama of kings]. PMLA 67 1952.
Storey, G. G. Buchanan's critical principles. PMLA 68 1953.

ARTHUR HENRY BULLEN
1857–1920

See col 1640, below.

CHARLES STUART CALVERLEY, earlier BLAYDS
1831–84

Bibliographies

In his Complete works, 1901.
King, H. D. A descriptive catalogue of the Calverley material in the Toronto University Library. N & Q Oct-Dec 1954.

Collections

Complete works, with a biographical notice by W. J Sendall. 1901.
Verses, translations and fly leaves. 1904.
Verses and translations. Ed O. Seaman 1905.

§1

Verses and translations. 1862, 1865 (3rd edn rev), 1871 (4th edn rev).
Translations into English and Latin. Cambridge 1866, 1885 (rev).
Theocritus translated into English verse. Cambridge 1869, 1883 (rev).
Fly leaves. Cambridge 1872, 1885 (as Verses and fly leaves).
The literary remains of Calverley, with a memoir by W. J. Sendall. 1885.
The eclogues of Virgil, translated into English verse. Ed M. Hadas, New York 1960.

§2

Whyte, W. Calverley. Miles 9 (10).
Thompson, F. Calverley. Academy 13 July 1901; rptd in his Literary criticism, ed T. L. Connolly, New York 1948.
Babington, P. L. Browning and Calverley, or poem and parody: a elucidation. 1925.
Ince, R. B. Calverley and some Cambridge wits of the nineteenth century. 1929.
A Cambridge poet. Spectator 9 Jan 1932. *See* A. Waugh, 16 Jan and reply 23 Jan 1932.
Evans, B. I. In his English poetry and the later nineteenth century, 1933, 1966 (rev).
Preston, A. W. Calverley of Cambridge. Queen's Quart 54 1947.
R., V. Calverley: myrtle and tamarisk. N & Q 15 March 1952.
King, H. D. Calverley and Jean Ingelow. N & Q 30 Aug 1952.
—— Words in the poems of Calverley. N & Q Aug 1953.
—— Calverley. N & Q 22 Nov 1952.

WILLIAM CANTON
1845–1926

Collections

Nineteen poems. 1925.
Poems. Ed G. D. Canton 1927. With bibliographical sketch.

§1

A lost epic and other poems. 1887.
The invisible playmate: a story of the unseen. 1894, 1912 (EL).
W. V. her book and various verses. 1896.
A child's book of saints. 1898, 1906 (EL).
In memory of W.V. 1901.
The comrades: poems, old and new. 1902.
A history of the British and Foreign Bible Society. 5 vols 1904–10.

§2

Noble, J. A. Canton. Miles 8 (7).
de M., S. The poetry of Canton. Contemporary Rev May 1927.

EDWARD CARPENTER
1844–1929

See col 1423, below.

'LEWIS CARROLL'
1832–98

See col 977, below.

MARY ELIZABETH COLERIDGE
1861–1907

Collections

Poems. Ed H. Newbolt 1908.
Gathered leaves from the prose of Mary E. Coleridge, with a memoir by E. Sichel. 1910. Includes 6 unpbd poems; Appendix A consists of Notes on the table talk of William Cory.
The collected poems. Ed T. Whistler 1954.

§1

The seven sleepers of Ephesus. 1893. A novel.
Fancy's following. Oxford 1896. Pbd under pseudonym Ἄνοδος.
The King with two faces. 1897. An historical romance.
Fancy's guerdon, by Anodos. 1897. Rptd partly from Fancy's following, above, with addns.
Non sequitur. 1900. Essays.
The fiery dawn. 1901. A novel.
The shadow on the wall. 1904. A romance.
The lady on the drawingroom floor. 1906. A novel.
Holman Hunt. 1908.

§2

Binyon, L. In The English poets, ed T. H. Ward vol 5, 1918.
Bridges, R. In his Collected essays vol 5, 1931. Rptd from Cornhill Mag.
Evans, B. I. In his English poetry in the later nineteenth century, 1933, 1966 (rev).
Reilly, J. J. In praise of Mary Coleridge. In his Of books and men, 1942.
Cecil, E. Mary Coleridge. Spectator 12 Nov 1943.

Chitty, J. E. Charlotte Yonge and Mary Coleridge. TLS 25 March 1944. *See* F. Algar and G. Battiscombe, 8 April and J. E. Chitty, 22 April 1944.
White, B. Mary Coleridge: an appreciation. E & S 31 1945.

WILLIAM JOHN COURTHOPE
1842–1917

See col 1426, below.

THOMAS WILLIAM HODGSON CROSLAND
1865–1924

Collections

Collected poems. 1917.
Last poems. 1928.

§1

The pink book: being verses good, bad and indifferent. Brighton 1894.
Literary parables. 1898.
Fifty fables. 1899.
Other people's wings. 1899. Parodies and verses.
The absent-minded male and other occasional verses. 1899.
The finer spirit and other poems. 1900.
Pleasant odes. 1900.
Outlook odes. 1902.
The unspeakable Scot. 1902. A satire.
The egregious English. 1903, 1925. First pbd under pseudonym 'Angus McNeill'.
The five notions. 1903. Parody of Kipling's The five nations.
The truth about Japan. 1904.
The lord of creation. 1904, 1925 (with appreciation by H. Savage).
Lovely woman. 1904. A satire.
Wisdom for the holidays. 1905. A satire.
The suburbans. 1905. A satire.
The wild Irishman. 1905. A satire.
The wicked life. 1905. A satire.
The red rose: a poem. 1905.
The country life. 1906. A satire.
The beautiful teetotaller. 1907. A satire.
Who goes racing? 1907. A satire.
Little stories. 1907.
Taffy was a Welshman. 1912. A satire.
The first stone. 1912. Satire on Wilde's De profundis.
Sonnets. 1912.
A chant of affection and other war verses. 1915.
Find the angels; The showman; A legend of the war. 1915. Parody of Machen.
War poems by X. 1916.
The English sonnet. 1917.
The fine old Hebrew gentleman. 1922. A satire.
Pop goes the weasel. 1924. Sequel to The unspeakable Scot.
The rogue. 1926. A satirical novel.

§2

Brown, W. S. The life and genius of Crosland. 1928.

JOHN DAVIDSON
1857–1909

Bibliographies

Stonehill, C. A. and H. W. In their Bibliographies of modern authors: second series, 1925.

Townsend, J. B. The quest for Davidson. Princeton Univ Lib Chron 13 1952. *See* David and Arthur Symons, 15 1954.
Lester, J. A., jr. Davidson: a Grub street bibliography. Charlottesville 1958.

Collections

Selected poems. 1905.
Poems and ballads. Ed R. Macleod 1959.
A selection of his poems. Ed M. Lindsay, preface by T. S. Eliot, with an essay by H. McDiarmid 1961.

§1

Diabolus amans: a dramatic poem. Glasgow 1885.
The north wall. Glasgow 1885. A novel.
Bruce. Glasgow 1886. A verse play.
Smith: a tragedy. Glasgow 1888.
Plays. Greenock 1889 (An unhistorical pastoral, A romantic farce, Scaramouch in Naxos), 1894 (adds Bruce and Smith, frontispiece by A. Beardsley).
Perpervid: the career of Ninian Jamieson. 1890.
The great men and a practical novelist. 1891. Collection of tales.
Laura Ruthven's widowhood: a novel. 1892. With C. J. Wills.
Persian letters. 1892. Trn of Montesquieu.
Fleet street eclogues. 2 sers 1893–6.
Sentences and paragraphs. 1893. Essays and epigrams.
Ballads and songs. 1894.
A random itinerary. 1894.
Baptist lake: a novel. 1894.
A full and true account of the wonderful mission of Earl Lavender. 1895. A satirical novel.
St George's day: a Fleet street eclogue. New York 1895. Included in Fleet street eclogues ser 2, above.
Miss Armstrong's and other circumstances. 1896. A collection of tales.
For the crown. 1896. Trn of Coppée.
New ballads. 1897.
Godfrida. 1898. A dramatic work.
The last ballad and other poems. 1899.
Self's the man: a tragi-comedy. 1901.
The testament of a vivisector. 1901.
The testament of a man forbid. 1901.
The testament of an empire-builder. 1902.
A rosary. 1903. Essays.
The knight of the maypole. 1903. A comedy in prose and verse.
A rosary. 1903. A play.
The testament of a Prime Minister. 1904.
A queen's romance. 1904. Trn of Hugo, Ruy Blas.
The theatrocrat: a tragic play of church and state. 1905.
Holiday and other poems, with a note on poetry. 1906.
God and Mammon. 1907. Pt 1 The triumph of Mammon, pt 2 Mammon and his message, pt 3 not completed.
The testament of John Davidson. 1908.
Fleet street and other poems. 1909.
Seventeen poems. 1925.

§2

Thompson, F. A thesis in verse. Daily Chron 29 June 1901. Review of The testament of a vivisector, rptd in his Literary criticisms, ed T. L. Connolly, New York 1948.
Archer, W. In his Poets of the younger generation, 1902.
Jackson, H. In his Eighteen nineties, 1913.
Fineman, H. Davidson: a study of the relation of his ideas to his poetry. Philadelphia 1916.
Johnson, L. In his Reviews and critical papers, ed R. Shafer 1921.
Petzold, G. von. Davidson und sein geistiges Werden unter dem Einfluss Nietzsches. Leipzig 1928.

Bett, H. In his Studies in literature, 1929.
Evans, B. I. In his English poetry in the later nineteenth century 1933, 1966 (rev).
Thouless, P. In his Modern poetic drama, Oxford 1934.
Lock, D. R. Davidson and the poetry and the 'nineties. London Quart 161 1936.
Weygandt, C. Henley, Stevenson and Davidson. In his Time of Yeats, New York 1937.
Applejoy, P. A view of Davidson against a 'nineties background. Catholic World Feb 1942.
Turner, P. Davidson: the novels of a poet. Cambridge Jnl 5 1952.
Lester, J. A., jr. Two notes on Davidson. N & Q March 1954.
— Prose-poetry transmutation in the poetry of Davidson. MP 1958.
Macleod, R. D. Davidson: a study in personality. 1957.
Townsend, J. B. Davidson: poet of Armageddon. New Haven 1961.
Reijnders, K. Tweemaal: non in een landschap. Forum der Letteren 3 1962.

RICHARD WATSON DIXON

1833–1900

Bibliographies

Nowell-Smith, S. Some uncollected authors, 29: Dixon. Book Collector 10 1961.

Selections

Poems: a selection, with a memoir by R. Bridges. 1909.

§1

The close of the tenth century of the Christian era. Oxford 1858. Prize essay.
Christ's company and other poems. 1861.
Historical odes and other poems. 1864.
Essay on the maintenance of the Church of England as an established church. 1874.
The life of James Dixon. DD, 1874.
The history of the Church of England from the abolition of the Roman jurisdiction. 6 vols 1878–1902. Memoir of Dixon by H. Gee, vol 5 1900.
The monastic comperta, so far as they regard the religious houses of Cumberland and Westmorland. Kendal 1879.
Mano: a poetical history in four books. 1883, 1891 (rev). A narrative poem.
Odes and eclogues. Oxford 1884 (priv ptd).
Lyrical poems. Oxford 1887 (priv ptd).
The story of Eudocia and her brothers. Oxford 1888 (priv ptd). With preface on five-beat couplet verse.
Songs and odes. Ed R. Bridges 1896.
Mackail, J. W. The life of William Morris. Vol. 1 1899. Dixon contributed reminiscences.
The last poems of Dixon. Ed R. Bridges 1905. With preface by Mary Coleridge.

Letters

The correspondence of Gerard Manley Hopkins and Dixon. Ed C. C. Abbott, Oxford 1935.

§2

Miles, A. H. Dixon. Miles 5.
Coleridge, Mary. The last hermit of Warksworth. In her Non sequitur, 1900.
Lahey, G. F. In his Gerard Manley Hopkins, 1930.
Bridges, R. Three friends: memoirs of Dolben, Dixon and Bradley. Oxford 1932.
Evans, B. I. In his English poetry in the later nineteenth century, 1933, 1966 (rev).

Kent, M. Dixon. Bookman (London) May 1933.
Hanson, W. G. Gerard Manley Hopkins and Dixon. London Quart 169 1944.
Sambrook, J. A poet hidden: the life of Dixon. 1962.
Soden, G. A poet hidden. TLS 30 March 1962.

AUSTIN DOBSON

1840–1921

See col 1427, below.

DIGBY MACKWORTH DOLBEN

1848–67

§1

Poems. Ed R. Bridges 1911 (with memoir and letters), 1915 (rev and enlarged). Memoir rptd in Three friends: memoirs of Dolben, Dixon and Bradley, Oxford 1932.

§2

Evans, B. I. In his English poetry in the later nineteenth century, 1933, 1966 (rev).
Watkin, Dom A. Dolben and the Catholic Church: some fresh evidence. Dublin Rev 225 1951.

CHARLES MONTAGU DOUGHTY

1843–1926

§1

On the Jöstedal-Brai glaciers in Norway. 1866. A geological paper.
Documents épigraphiques recueillis dans le nord de l'Arabie. Paris 1884. Introd by E. Renan.
Travels in Arabia deserta. 2 vols Cambridge 1888, London 1921 (new preface and introd by T. E. Lawrence). Abridged as Wanderings, below.
Under arms. 1900.
The dawn in Britain. 6 vols 1906; ed B. Fairley 1935 (selected passages); 1943.
Adam cast forth. 1908. Sacred drama in 5 songs.
Wanderings in Arabia. Ed E. Garnett 2 vols 1908. Abridgement of Travels in Arabia deserta, above.
The cliffs. 1909. A verse play.
The clouds. 1912. Poetic drama.
The titans. 1916.
Mansoul: or the riddle of the world. 1920, 1922 (rev).
Hogarth's Arabia. 1922 (priv ptd). Rptd from Observer.
Passages from Arabia deserta. Ed E. Garnett 1931.

§2

Burton, R. Academy 28 July 1888. On Arabia deserta.
Edinburgh Rev 207 1908. On Wanderings in Arabia and The dawn in Britain.
Chew, S. C. The poetry of Doughty. North Amer Rev Dec 1925.
Doughty. TLS 11 Feb 1926.
Armstrong, M. The works of Doughty. Fortnightly Rev Jan 1926.
Freeman, J. Doughty. Bookman (London) March 1926, London Mercury Aug 1926.
Fairly, B. Doughty: a critical study. 1927.
— Doughty and modern poetry. London Mercury June 1935.
— Doughty 1843–1926. Europäische Revue 12 1936.
— Doughty. UTQ 13 1943.
— The dawn in Britain after fifty years. UTQ 26 1957.
Hogarth, D. G. The life of Doughty. 1928.
Dibben, E. Doughty the man. Cornhill Mag May 1932.
Hanson, W. G. Nasrany in Arabia. London Quart 158 1933.

Attwater, D. Doughty and a Maronite monastery. Dublin Rev 194 1934.
Treneer, A. Doughty: a study of his prose and verse. 1935.
Doughty as an influence today: an over-simple creed. TLS 9 Nov 1935.
Taylor, W. Doughty's English. SPE 1939.
Brie, F. Doughty und sein Epos The dawn in Britain. Anglia 64 1940.
Cartwright, J. Doughty and Travels in Arabia deserta. Papers of Manchester Lit Club 64 1940.
Zwemer, S. M. Islam in Arabia deserta. Moslem World 33 1943.
The wandering Nazarene. TLS 21 Aug 1943.
Davis, H. Doughty. New York 1945 (Bergen lecture).
Storrs, R. Doughty and T. E. Lawrence. Listener 25 Dec 1947.
Brittain, M. Z. Doughty's mirror of Arabia. Moslem World 37 1947.
Cockerell, S. Doughty's Arabia deserta. TLS 6 May 1949.
Holloway, J. Poetry and plain language: the verse of Doughty. EC 4 1954.
Rope, H. E. G. A note on Doughty's Dawn in Britain. Nine 4 1956.
Bishop, J. The heroic ideal in Doughty's Arabia deserta. MLQ 21 1960.
Assad, T. J. Three Victorian travellers: Burton, Blunt, Doughty. 1964.

LORD ALFRED DOUGLAS
1870–1945

Bibliographies

Braybrooke, P. In his Douglas: his life and work. 1931.

Collections

Collected poems. 1919.
Select poems. 1926.
Collected satires. 1926.
Complete poems, including the light verse. 1928.

§1

Salome. 1894. Trn from Wilde's French.
Poems (Poèmes). Paris 1896. In French and English.
Tails with a twist. 1898.
The city of the soul. 1899.
The Duke of Berwick. 1899, 1925.
The placid pug and other rhymes. 1906.
The Pongo papers and the Duke of Berwick. 1907. Rhymes in Pongo papers rptd from Vanity Fair.
Sonnets. 1909, 1935, 1943 (with addns).
Oscar Wilde and myself. 1914.
The Rossiad. Galashiels [1916?]. A lampoon.
In excelsis. 1924. Sonnet sequence.
Nine poems. 1926 (priv ptd).
The autobiography of Douglas. 1929.
The true history of Shakespeare's sonnets. 1933.
Lyrics. 1935.
Without apology. 1938.
Oscar Wilde: a summing up. 1940; ed D. Hudson.
The principles of peotry: an address delivered before the Royal Society of Literature 1943.

§2

Brown, W. S. Douglas: the man and the poet. 1918.
Ellis, S. M. An authentic poet: Douglas. In his Mainly Victorian, 1925.
Braybrooke, P. Douglas: his life and work. 1931.
Sherard, R. H. A letter from Douglas on André Gide's lies about himself and Oscar Wilde. In his Si le grain ne meurt, Calvi Corsica 1933.
'Winwar, Frances' (F. Grebanier). Oscar Wilde and the yellow nineties. 1941. Foreword by Douglas.
Douglas: a poet of distinction. Times 21 March 1945. Obituary.
Douglas, F. A. K. Marquess of Queensberry: Oscar Wilde and the black Douglas. 1948.
Freeman, W. The life of Douglas. 1948.
Stopes, M. C. Douglas: his poetry and personality. 1949.
Oscar Wilde after fifty years. TLS 24 Nov 1950.
Benkovitz, M. J. Notes toward a chapter of biography: Douglas and Roland Firbank. BNYPL March 1963.

EDWARD DOWDEN
1843–1913

See col 1428, below.

ERNEST CHRISTOPHER DOWSON
1867–1900

Bibliographies

Stonehill, C. A. and H. W. In their Bibliographies of modern authors ser 2, 1925.
Harrison, H. G. In V. Plarr, Dowson 1888–1897, 1914.

Collections

Longaker, M. In his Dowson, Philadelphia 1944.
Poems, with a memoir by A. Symons. 1905.
Complete poems. New York 1929.
Poems and prose. New York 1932. With memoirs by A. Symons.
The poetical works. Ed D. Flower 1934. Includes 40 unpbd poems.
Poems. 1946. Includes Verses, Decorations and The Pierrot of the minute.
Poems. Ed M. Longaker, Philadelphia 1962.

§1

The book of the Rhymers' Club. 1892. Contains 6 poems by Dowson; The second book 1894 contains 6 more poems.
A comedy of masks: a novel. 3 vols 1893, 1896. With A. Moore.
Couperus, Majesty. 1894. With A. Texeira de Mattos. Trn.
Dilemmas: stories and studies in sentiment. 1895.
Zola, La terre. 2 vols 1895 (priv ptd). Trn.
Balzac, La fille aux yeux d'or. 1896. Trn.
Verses. 1896.
The Pierrot of the minute: a dramatic phantasy in one act. 1897, 1923 (Grolier Club).
Laclos, Les liaisons dangereuses. 2 vols 1898 (priv ptd). Trn.
Memoirs of Cardinal Dubois. 2 vols 1899. Trn.
Voltaire, La pucelle. 2 vols 1899. Trn.
Adrian Rome. 1899. With A. Moore.
Decorations in verse and prose. 1899.
Goncourt, E. de, The confidantes of a king: the mistresses of Louis XV. 2 vols 1907. Trn.
The story of beauty and the beast. 1908. Trn.
Stories. Ed M. Longaker, Philadelphia 1947.

§2

Sherard, R. H. Obituary. Author May 1900.
Jepson, E. The real Dowson. Academy Nov 1907.
Plarr, V. Dowson 1888–1897: reminiscences, unpublished letters and marginalia. 1914.
Huxley, A. Dowson. In The English poets, ed T. H. Ward vol 5, 1918.
Orage, A. R. In his Readers and writers, 1922.

Wheatley, K. Dowson's Extreme unction. MLN 38 1923.
Brégy, K. M. C. Dowson: an interpretation. In her Poets and pilgrims, 1925.
Thomas, W. R. Dowson at Oxford. Nineteenth Century April 1928.
Evans, B. I. In his English poetry in the later nineteenth century, 1933, 1966 (rev).
Jepson, E. In his Memories of a Victorian, 1933.
Plarr, M. Cynara: the story of Dowson and Adelaide: a novel. 1933.
Roberts, M. A critical note. John O'London's Weekly 30 Sept 1933.
Weygandt, C. Dowson and Arthur Symons. In his The time of Yeats, New York 1937.
'Gawsworth, John' (T. I. F. Armstrong). The Dowson legend. Essays by Divers Hands new ser 17 1938.
Wright, E. C. Eight poems by Dowson. BM Quart 12 1938.
Tillotson, G. In his Essays in criticism and research, Cambridge 1942.
Morrisette, B. A. The 'untraced quotation' of Dowson's dedication [from Flaubert's l'éducation sentimentale]. MLN 58 1943.
Longaker, M. Dowson. Philadelphia 1944.
— Dowson's Non sum qualis eram bonae sub regno Cynarae. Explicator 9 1951.
Dowson, TLS 31 March 1945.
Hackett, F. Poet Dowson. In his On judging books, 1947.
Thompson, F. Poems of Dowson. In his Literary criticism, ed T. L. Connolly, New York 1948.
Whittington-Egan, R. Dowson fifty years later. Poetry Rev 41 1950.
Marshall, L. B. A note on Dowson. RES new ser 3 1952. With text of poem Beata solitudo.
Raina, T. Dowson. Visva-Bharati Quart 19 1953.
Fletcher, I. Some unpublished letters of Dowson to Herbert Horne. N & Q March 1962.
Kermode, F. Amateur of grief. New Statesman 7 June 1963.
Goldfarb, R. M. The Dowson legend today. Stud in Eng Lit 1500–1900 (Rice Univ) 4 1964.
Munro, J. M. A previously unpublished letter from Dowson to Arthur Symons. Études Anglaises 17 1964.
Swann, T. B. Dowson. New York 1964.

GEORGE DU MAURIER

1834–96

See col 1049, below.

'VIOLET FANE' MARY MONTGOMERIE LAMB later SINGLETON, later LADY CURRIE

1843–1905

Collections

Collected verses. 1880.
Poems. 2 vols 1892. With critical introd.
Collected essays. 1902.

§1

From dawn to noon: poems. 1872.
Denzil place: a story in verse. 1875.
The queen of the fairies and other poems. 1876.
Anthony Bebington. 1877. Play in prose and verse.
Edwin and Angelina papers. 1878. Essays by 'V' rptd from the World.
Sophy, or the adventures of a savage. 3 vols 1881.
Thro' love and war. 3 vols 1886.
The story of Helen Davenant. 3 vols 1889.
Autumn songs. 1889.
Under cross and crescent: poems. 1896.
Betwixt two seas: poems and ballads written at Constantinople and Therapia. 1900.
Two moods of a man, with other papers and short stories. 1901.

§2

Japp, A. H. Mary M. Singleton. Miles 7 (9).
Obituary. Times 16 Oct 1905.

'MICHAEL FIELD', KATHERINE HARRIS BRADLEY

1846–1913

and

EDITH EMMA COOPER

1862–1914

Bibliographies

Sturgeon, M. In her Michael Field, 1922.

Selections

Selections. Ed T. Sturge Moore 1923.

§1

The new Minnesinger and other poems, by Arran Leigh. 1875.
Bellerophon and other poems, by Arran and Isla Leigh. 1881.
Callirrhoë, Fair Rosamund. [1884], 1897 (Fair Rosamund ptd separately). Plays.
The father's tragedy, William Rufus, Loyalty or love. [1885]. Plays.
Brutus Ultor: a play in verse. [1886].
Canute the great, The cup of water. [1887]. Plays.
Long ago. 1889. Based on fragments of Sappho.
The tragic Mary. 1890. Play.
Stephania: a trialogue. 1892.
Sight and song. 1892.
Underneath the bough: a book of verses. 1893, 1893 (rev and reduced edn), Portland Maine 1898 (adds new poems and restores some deleted from 2nd edn).
A question of memory: a play in four acts. 1893.
Attila, my Attila: a play in verse. 1896.
The world at auction: a drama in verse. 1898.
Noontime branches. Oxford 1899 (priv ptd). Play.
Anna Ruina: a drama in verse. 1899.
The race of leaves. 1901. Play.
Julia Domna: a drama in verse. 1903.
Brogia: a period play. 1905.
Queen Mariamne: a play. 1908.
Wild honey from various thyme: poems. 1908.
The tragedy of pardon, Diane. 1911. Plays.
The accuser, Tristran de Léonois, A messiah. 1911. 3 plays.
Poems of adoration. 1912.
Mystic trees. 1913.
Dedicated: an early work of Michael Field. 1914.
Whym Chow, flame of love. 1914 (priv ptd).
Deirdre; A question of memory; Ras Byzance. 1918. Plays.
In the name of time: a tragedy. 1919.
The Wattlefold: unpublished poems. Ed E. C. Fortey, Oxford 1930.
Works and days: extracts from the journals of Field. Ed T. and D. C. Sturge Moore 1934.

§2

Johnson, L. Michael Field. Miles 8 (9).
Sturgeon, M. In her Studies of contemporary poets, 1920 (rev).

— Michael Field. 1922.
Symons, A. Michael Field. Forum 69 1923.
Smith, L. P. Michael Field. Dial 78 1925; rptd in his Reperusals and recollections, 1936.
Boas, F. S. Two unpublished poems by Field. London Mercury July 1925.
Evans, B. I. In his English poetry in the later nineteenth century, 1933, 1966 (rev).
Alexander, C. In his Catholic literary revival, Milwaukee 1935.
Around my shelves. Poetry Rev 41 1950. With unpbd poem.

NORMAN ROWLAND GALE
1862–1942

Collections

Country lyrics, selected from A country muse and Orchard songs [1913].
Collected poems. 1914.

§1

Cricket song and other trifling verses. Rugby 1890. Anon.
A June romance. Rugby 1892 (priv ptd), 1894.
Here be the blue and white violets. Rugby nd.
A country muse. 2 sers 1892–3, 1894, 1895.
Orchard songs. 1893.
A verdant county. In A. Hayes, A fellowship in song, 1893.
Cricket songs. 1894.
On two strings. Rugby 1894 (priv ptd). With R. K. Leather.
Songs for little people. 1896.
Barty's star. [1903].
More cricket songs. 1905.
A book of quatrains. Rugby [1909].
Song in September. 1912.
Solitude. 1913.
A merry-go-round of song. 1919.
Verse in bloom. [1924].
A flight of fancies. [1926].
Messrs Bat and Ball. 1930.
Close of play. Rugby 1936.
Brackenham church. Oxford 1938 (priv ptd).

§2

Tomson, G. R. A country muse. Academy 3 Sept 1892.
Noble, J. A. Gale. Miles 8 (7).

RICHARD GARNETT
1835–1906

See col 1431, below.

SIR WILLIAM SCHWENCK GILBERT
1836–1911

See col 1159, below.

SIR EDMUND GOSSE
1849–1928

See col 1432, below.

DAVID GRAY
1838–61

Collections

The luggie and other poems, with a memoir by J. Hedderwick and a prefatory notice by R. M. Milnes. Cambridge 1862, 1874 (enlarged).

§2

Gray. Cornhill Mag 1863.
Buchanan, R. W. In his Gray and other essays, 1868.
Noble, J. A. Gray. Miles 6.
Russell, G. W. E. In his Selected essays, 1914.
Evans, B. I. In his English poetry in the later nineteenth century, 1933, 1966 (rev).
Gray: born 1838. TLS 29 Jan 1938.
Tusiani, J. Gray and Sergio Corazzina: a parallel. Eng Miscellany (Rome) 9 1958.
Stuart, A. V. Gray 1838–1861: a study of ms material and poetry. Poetry Rev 54 1963.

JOHN GRAY
1866–1934

§1

Silverpoints. 1893.
The blue calendar. 3 pts 1895–7 (priv ptd). Carols.
Spiritual poems, chiefly done out of several languages. 1896.
Ad matrem: poems. 1904.
The long road. Oxford 1926.
Sound: a poem. 1926 (priv ptd).
Poems. 1931.
Park: a fantastic story. 1932.
Gray also pbd trns from Bourget, Couperus, Goethe and Nietzsche, edns of Campion, Constable, Drayton and Sidney, devotional works and anthologies.

§2

Obituary. Times 19 June 1934.
Around my shelves. Poetry Rev 41 1950. Contains an unpbd poem.
Sewell, B. (ed). Two friends: Gray and André Raffalovich. Aylesford 1963. *See* TLS 31 May, 17 June 1963.

ALEXANDER BALLOCH GROSART
1835–99

See col 1650, below.

PHILIP GILBERT HAMERTON
1834–94

See col 1436, below.

THOMAS HARDY
1840–1928

See col 980, below.

FRANCES RIDLEY HAVERGAL
1836–79

Bibliographies

List of works by Havergal. [1873?].

Selections

Ivy leaves: selections from the poems of Havergal. [Ed F. A. Shaw] 1884.
Gems from Havergal: poetry, selected by F. A. Shaw. [1912].
Gems from Havergal: prose, selected by B. H. Shaw. [1912].
Darlow, T. H. In his Havergal, a saint of God: a new memoir, 1927.

§1

The ministry of song. 1869.
Under the surface. 1874.
Loyal responses or daily melodies for the King's minstrels. 1878. Hymns.
Life echoes. 1883.

§2

Havergal: a biographical sketch. [1881].
Miles, A. H. Havergal. Miles 10 (12).
Bullock, C. Near the throne: Havergal, the sweet singer and royal writer. [1902].
Chappell, J. Women who have worked and won: the life story of Havergal etc. [1904].
Enock, E. E. Havergal. [1929].
Darlow, T. H. Havergal, a saint of God: a new memoir, with a selection of extracts from her prose and verse. 1927.

ALFRED HAYES
1857–1936

§1

The last crusade and other poems. Birmingham 1887.
Welcome to the queen. Birmingham 1887.
David Westren. Birmingham 1888.
The march of man and other poems. 1891.
A fellowship in song: Hayes, Richard Le Gallienne, Norman Gale. 3 pts Rugby 1893.
The vale of Arden and other poems. 1895, Birmingham 1897.
The cup of quietness. 1911.
Simon de Montfort: an historical drama in five acts. 1918.
Boris Goduno, by Pushkin, rendered into English verse. [1918].
The Mayflower. 1920. With W. E. Sterling.
Czar Feodor Ionnovich, by Tolstoi, rendered into English verse. 1924.
The death of Ivan the terrible, by Tolstoi, rendered into English verse. 1926.

§2

Noble, J. A. Hayes. Miles 8 (7).

WILLIAM ERNEST HENLEY
1849–1903

Bibliographies

Chesterton, G. K. Henley. Eng Illustr Mag Aug 1903.
'Connell, John' (J. H. Robertson). In his Henley, 1949.
Sadleir, M. Some uncollected authors 10: Henley. Book Collector 5 1956.

Collections

Collected plays. 1892 (3 plays), 1896 (complete edn).
Works. 7 vols 1908, 5 vols 1921.
Henley. 1931. Selected poems.

§1

Deacon Brodie. 1880 (priv ptd), 1888 (finished version). A play, with R. L. Stevenson.
Admiral Guinea. 1884. A play, with R. L. Stevenson.
Beau Austin. 1884. A play, with R. L. Stevenson.
Macaire. 1885. A play, with R. L. Stevenson.
Mephisto: a new and original travestie by Byron M'Guiness. 1887.
A book of verses. 1888.
Pictures at play by two art-critics. 1888. With Andrew Lang.
Catalogue of pictures by the French and Dutch romanticists of this century, with an introduction and biographical notes of artists. 1889.
Views and reviews: essays in appreciation: literature. 1890.
The song of the sword and other verses. 1892.
London voluntaries and other verses. 1893.
Dictionary of slang and its analogues. 1894–1904. With J. S. Farmer.
Burns: life, genius, achievement: an essay. Edinburgh 1898. Rptd from The poetry of Burns, ed Henley and T. F. Henderson, Edinburgh 1896.
London types. 1898. Quatorzains, illustr W. Nicholson.
Poems. 1898.
Hawthorn and lavender: songs and madrigals. 1899, 1901 (with other verses).
For England's sake: verses and songs in time of war. 1900.
Views and reviews: essays in appreciation: art. 1902.
A song of speed. 1903. Rptd from The world's work.
Twenty-five new poems: a centenary discovery. Ed W. M. Parker, Poetry Rev 40 1949.
Henley also edited anthologies of verse and prose, and works of Blunt, Burns, Byron, Fielding, Shakespeare and Smollett.

Letters

Some letters of Henley. Ed V. Payen-Payne 1933.
Some early letters and verses of Henley. Ed J. H. Hallam, Blackwood's Mag Sept 1943.

§2

Meynell, A. Henley's poems. Merry England 11 1888.
Noble, J. A. Henley. Miles 8 (7).
Archer, W. In his Study and stage, 1899.
—— Henley. Pall Mall Mag Sept 1903.
Thompson, F. Henley. Academy 18 July 1903.
Cornford, L. C. Henley. 1913.
Noyes, A. In his Some aspects of modern poetry, 1924.
Symons, A. Modernity in verse. In his Studies in two literatures, 1924.
Lucas, E. V. In his The Colvins and their friends, 1928.
Williamson, K. Henley: a memoir. 1930.
Schappes, M. U. Henley's principles of criticism. PMLA 46 1931.
Pennell, E. R. Henley: lover of the art of book-making. Colophon 5 1931.
Welby, T. E. Aspects of Henley. In his Second impressions, 1933.
Gregory, H. Henley and his henchmen. Saturday Rev of Lit 15 July 1933.
—— On Henley's editorial career. In his Shield of Achilles, New York 1944.
Evans, B. I. In his English poetry in the later nineteenth century, 1933, 1966 (rev).
Niven, F. Henley. Lib Rev no 27 1934.
McCarthy, M. In her Handicaps: six studies, 1936.
Buckley, J. H. Henley. 1945.
—— and J. G. Fletcher. Who was Henley? Sewanee Rev 54 1946.
Purcell, J. M. Henley's Invictus. Explicator 5 1944. *See* H. M. McLuhan, 3 1944.

'Connell, John' (J. H. Robertson). Henley. 1949.
— Unpublished letters. Nat & Eng Rev 136 1951. To Henley from Henry James, Leslie Stephen, Meredith, Hardy et al.
— New light on George Wyndham: a selection of unpublished letters to Henley. Nat & Eng Rev 136 1951.
Looker, S. J. Shelley, Trelawny and Henley: a study of three Titans. Worthing 1950.
Armstrong, R. L. Henley's The way of death. Explicator 14 1956.
Braunlich, A. F. Some sources of Henley's Echoes. MLN 72 1957.
Herman, G. Henley's Space and dread of the dark. Explicator 22 1963.
Thompson, K. F. Beckford, Byron and Henley. Etudes Anglaises 14 1961. With a note by A. Parreaux.
San Juan, E. The question of values in Victorian activism. Personalist 45 1964.

EMILY HENRIETTA HICKEY

1845–1924

Selections

Selections. In E. M. Dinnis, Emily Hickey: poet, essayist, pilgrim: a memoir, [1927].

§1

A sculptor and other poems. 1881.
Browning, R. Strafford, with notes by Hickey. 1884.
Verse-tales, lyrics and translations. 1889.
Michael Villiers, idealist: and other poems. 1891.
Noel, R. B. W. Livingstone in Africa, with preface by Hickey. 1895.
Poems. 1896.
Ancilla domini: thoughts in verse on the life of the Blessed Virgin Mary. 1898 (priv ptd).
Our Lady of May and other poems. 1902.
Havelock the Dane: an old English romance rendered into later English. 1902.
Our Catholic heritage in English literature. 1910.
Later poems. 1913.
Devotional poems. 1922.
Jesukin and other Christmastide poems. 1924.

§2

Miles, A. H. Hickey. Miles 8 (9).
Dinnis, E. M. Emily Hickey: poet, essayist, pilgrim: a memoir. [1927].

EDMOND GORE ALEXANDER HOLMES

1850–1936

Selections

Sonnets and poems, selected and arranged by T. J. Cobden-Sanderson. 1920.

§1

Poems. 1876.
Poems: second series. 1879.
The silence of love. 1899, 1901.
What is poetry? 1900.
Walt Whitman's poetry: a study and a selection. 1902.
The triumph of love. 1903. Sonnets.
The creed of my heart and other poems. 1912.
Sonnets to the universe. 1918.
In quest of an ideal: an autobiography. 1920.
Holmes also wrote on education and philosophy.

LAURENCE HOUSMAN

1865–1959

Bibliographies

Housman, L. Book list. In his Back words and fore words, 1945.

Collections

Selected poems. 1908.
Little plays of St Francis. 3 vols 1935. Complete edn.
Collected poems. 1937.
The golden sovereign. 1937. Collection of plays.
Happy and glorious: a dramatic biography. 1945. Selection of Queen Victoria plays.
Back words and fore words: an author's year-book 1893–1945: a selection in chronological order from the plays, poems and prose writings. 1945.

§1

A farm in fairyland. 1894.
The house of joy. [1895]. Fairy tales.
Green arras. 1895. Poems.
All-fellows: seven legends of lower redemption, with insets in verse. 1896.
God and their makers. 1897.
The field of clover. 1898. Tales.
Spikenard: a book of devotional love-poems. 1898.
The story of the seven young goslings. [1899].
Rue. 1899. Poems.
The little land, with songs from its four rivers. 1899.
An Englishwoman's love-letters. 1900.
The love concealed. 1928.
Four plays of St Clare. 1934.
Victoria Regina: a dramatic biography. 1934.
The unexpected years. 1937, New York 1936. Autobiography.
A.E.H.: some poems, some letters and a personal memoir. 1937.
Hop-o'-me-heart: a grown-up fairy tale. Flansham 1938.
What next? provocative tales of faith and morals. 1938.
The preparation of peace. 1940.
Gracious majesty. 1941.
Palestine plays. 1942.
Samuel the king-maker: a play in four acts. 1944.
Cynthia. 1947. Poems.
Strange ends and discoveries: tales of this world and the next. 1948.
Old testament plays. 1950.
The family honour: a comedy in four acts. 1950.
The kind and the foolish: short tales of myth, magic and miracle. 1952.
Housman pbd more plays, dramatic dialogues, poems, fairy tales etc. See also under A. E. Housman, col 601, above.

§2

Archer, W. In his Poets of the younger generation, 1902.
Rudolf, A. Die Dichtung von Housman. Breslau 1930.
Repplier, A. The brothers Housman. Atlantic Monthly Jan 1940.

DOUGLAS HYDE

1860–1949

See col 1909, below.

SELWYN IMAGE

1849–1930

§1

Poems and carols. 1894.

[Collected] poems. Ed A. H. Mackmurdo 1932.
Image's letters were pbd 1932; he has also pbd lectures and introds.

§2

Miles, A. H. Image. Miles 10 (12).
Obituary. Times 22 Aug 1930.

LIONEL PIGOT JOHNSON

1867–1902

Collections

Twenty-one poems, selected by W. B. Yeats. Dundrum 1904.
Selections from the poems, including some now collected for the first time, with a prefatory memoir [by C. K. Shorter]. 1908.
Some poems, selected with an introduction by L. I. Guiney. 1912.
Poetical works, with an introduction by Ezra Pound. 1915.
The religious poems, selected by G. F. Engelbach, with a preface by W. Meynell. 1916.
A new selection from the poems, compiled by H. V. Marrot. 1927.
Select poems. 1931.
Selected poems. 1934.
The complete poems. Ed I. Fletcher 1953. More than 50 uncollected poems.

§1

Sir Walter Raleigh in the Tower: a prize poem. Chester 1885.
The fools of Shakespeare: an essay. In Noctes Shakesperianae, Winchester College Shakspere Soc 1887.
The book of the Rhymers' Club. 1892. Contains 6 poems by Johnson; Second book, 1894 contains 6 more.
The Gordon riots. 1893 (Catholic Truth Soc).
Bits of old Chelsea. 1894. Etchings by W. W. Burgess, descriptions by Johnson and R. Le Gallienne.
The art of Thomas Hardy. 1894 (with bibliography by J. Lane), 1923 (with ch on Hardy's poetry by J. E. Barton).
Poems. 1895.
Ireland and other poems. 1897.
James Clarence Mangan. In A treasury of Irish poetry, ed S. A. Brooke and T. W. Rolleston 1900. Not the same as review from Post liminium, in Mangan's prose writings.
Poetry and Ireland: [2] essays by W. B. Yeats and Johnson. Dundrum 1908. Preliminary note by E. C. Yeats (?) is on Johnson.
Post liminium: essays and critical papers. Ed T. Whittemore 1911.
Some Winchester letters. 1919.
Reviews and critical papers. Ed R. Shafer 1921.
Matthew Arnold: poetry and prose, with Sir William Watson's poem and essays by Johnson and H. W. Garrod. Ed E. K. Chambers, Oxford 1940.
Seven new poems. Ed I. Fletcher, Poetry Rev 41 1950.
Fifteen new poems. Poetry Rev 43 1952.

§2

Obituary. Athenaeum 18 Oct 1902.
Guiney, L. I. Obituary. Atlantic Monthly Dec 1902.
Waugh, A. In his Tradition and change, 1919.
TLS 7 July 1921.
Tynan, K. In her Memories, 1924.
Weygandt, C. In his Tuesdays at ten, Philadelphia 1928.
Pinto, V. de S. Johnson: an appreciation. Wessex 2 1932.
Evans, B. I. In his English poetry in the later nineteenth century, 1933, 1966 (rev).
Welby, T. E. Johnson. In his Second impressions, 1933.
Alexander, C. In his Catholic literary revival, Milwaukee 1955.
Shacksnovis, A. A poem by Johnson. TLS 15 Feb 1936.
Patrick, A. W. Johnson (1867–1902): poète et critique. Paris 1939.
Pick, J. Divergent disciples of Walter Pater. Thought 23 1948.
Feldman, A. B. The art of Johnson. Poet Lore 57 1953.
Palmer, H. Johnson. Spectator 17 April 1953.
Fletcher, I. Johnson's The dark angel. In Interpretations: essays on twelve English poets, ed J. Wain 1955.
Brophy, L. Laureate of the cross. Irish Digest Feb 1962.
Charlesworth, B. The gray world of Johnson. Carrell (Miami) 4 1963.

HARRIET ELEANOR HAMILTON KING

1840–1920

§1

Aspromonte and other poems. 1869.
The disciples. 1873.
A book of dreams. 1883.
Ballads of the north and other poems. 1889.
The prophecy of Westminster. 1895.
The hours of passion. 1902.
Letters and recollections of Mazzini. Ed G. M. Trevelyan 1912.

§2

Robertson, E. S. In his English poetesses, 1883.
Hickey, E. H. Hamilton-King. Miles 7 (9)
—— Two Catholic poetesses. Dublin Rev Jan 1921.

RUDYARD KIPLING

1865–1936

See col 1019, below.

ANDREW LANG

1844–1912

See col 1440, below.

FRANCIS BURDETT THOMAS COUTTS-NEVILL, 5th BARON LATYMER

1852–1923

Selections

Selected poems. 1923.

§1

The girls of England: a battle call. 1882.
Poems. 1896. Includes An essay in a brief model.
The training of the instinct of love, with a preface by E. Thring. 1885.
Two heirs presumptive: a tale. 1894.
The Alhambra and other poems. 1898.
The revelation of St Love the Divine: a poem. 1898.
The mystery of godliness. 1900.
The nut brown maid. 1901. New version of the old ballad.
The poet's charter, or the book of Job. 1903.
Musa verticordia. 1905.
The song of songs. 1906. The song of Solomon rearranged in dramatic form.
The heresy of Job. 1907. With Blake's engravings.

The romance of King Arthur. 1907. Uther Pendragon: a poem, Merlin: a play, Launcelot du Lake: a drama, The death of Launcelot: a poem.
Egypt and other poems. 1912.
Psyche: a poem. 1912.
A ballad of the war. 1915.
The royal marines. 1915.
Ventures in thought. 1915. Essays.
The spacious times, and others. 1920. Poems.
Well. 1922. A Yorkshire village, with F. Redmayne.
Latymer also ed Flowers of Parnassus. 27 vols 1900–6.

§2

Archer, W. In his Poets of the younger generation, 1902.
Obituary. Times 9 June 1923.

EMILY LAWLESS
1945–1913

See col 1907, below.

EUGENE JACOB LEE-HAMILTON
1845–1907

Bibliographies

Lyon, H. T. A publishing history of the writings of Lee-Hamilton. PBSA 51 1957.

Selections

Dramatic sonnets, poems and ballads: selections from the poems. Ed W. Sharp 1903.

§1

Poems and transcripts. 1878.
Gods, saints and men. 1880.
The new Medusa and other poems. 1882.
Apollo and Marsyas and other poems. 1884.
Imaginary sonnets. 1888.
The fountain of youth: a fantastic tragedy. 1891.
Sonnets of the wingless hours. 1894.
Forest notes. 1899. With Mrs Lee-Hamilton.
The lord of the dark red star. 1903. Fiction.
The romance of the fountain. 1905. Fiction.
Minima bella, with a preface by A. E. Lee-Hamilton. 1909.

§2

Symonds, J. A. Lee-Hamilton. Miles 8 (7).
Obituary. Times 11 Sept 1907.
Evans, B. I. In his English poetry in the later nineteenth century, 1933, 1966 (rev).
[Weber, C. J.] From Florence to Colby by way of Kansas. Colby Lib Quart 3 1954.
MacBeth, G. Lee-Hamilton and the romantic agony. CQ 4 1962.
Pantazzi, S. Lee-Hamilton. PBSA 57 1963.

EDWARD CRACROFT LEFROY
1855–91

Bibliographies

Smith, T. D'A. Some uncollected authors 30: Lefroy. Book Collector 10 1961.

Selections

Lefroy: his life and poems. Ed W. A. Gill, with critical estimate of sonnets by J. A. Symonds 1897. Selected poems and 30 new sonnets.

§1

Undergraduate Oxford. Oxford 1878. Rptd from Oxford & Cambridge Undergraduates' Jnl.
Lefroy also pbd sermons and addresses.

§2

Miles, A. H. Lefroy. Miles 8 (7).

RICHARD LE GALLIENNE
1866–1947

See col 1063, below.

SIR ALFRED COMYNS LYALL
1835–1911

§1

Asiatic studies, religious and social. 1882, 2 vols 1899 (one essay omitted, essay on history and fable added).
Warren Hastings: a biography. 1889.
Verses written in India. 1889, 1907 (rev and enlarged as Poems).
The rise of the British dominion in India. 1893, 1910 (5th edn corrected and enlarged).
Tennyson. 1902 (EML).
The life of the Marquis of Dufferin and Ava. 2 vols 1905.
Some aspects of Asiatic history. 1910.
Studies in literature and history. Ed J. O. Miller 1915.

§2

Miles, A. H. Lyall. Miles 5.
Prothero, G. W. Commemorative address. 1912. In Commemorative addresses of the academic committee, 1912 (Royal Soc of Lit).
Ubert, C. P. Lyall. Proc Br Acad 5 1912.
Durand, H. M. The life of Lyall. Edinburgh 1913.

EDWARD ROBERT BULWER LYTTON, 1st EARL OF LYTTON, 'OWEN MEREDITH'
1831–91

Bibliographies

Harlan, A. B. In his Owen Meredith: a critical biography, New York 1946.

Collections

Poetical works. 2 vols 1867.
Poems. 2 vols Boston 1869.
The imperial bouquet of pretty flowers. Ed N. A. Chick, Calcutta 1877. Selection of poems and public speeches in India, with critique on his poetry rptd from Pioneer.
Poems, selected by M. Bethem-Edwards. 1890.
Selected poems, with an introduction by Lady [B.] Balfour. 1894.

§1

Clytemnestra, the Earl's return, the artist and other poems. 1855.
The wanderer. 1857, 1893 (rev, adds preface, discards pseudonym).
Lucile. 1860, 1893 (3rd edn, adds preface). A novel in verse.
Tannhäuser: or the battle of the bards, by Neville Temple and Edward Trevor. 1861. Really by Julian Fane and Lytton.

Serbski pesme or national songs of Servia. 1861; ed G. H. Powell 1918. Free versions of Serbian songs and ballads.
The ring of Amasis, from the papers of a German physician (Dr N—). 2 vols 1863, 1890 (shortened and recast in form of a novel).
Chronicles and characters. 2 vols 1868. 'An attempt at a poetic history of the education of man.'
Orval: or the fool of time and other imitations and paraphrases. 1869. Founded on the Infernal comedy by Krazinski. Many Serbski pesme rptd in appendix.
Julian Fane: a memoir. 1871.
Memoir of Edward Lord Lytton. In Speeches of Edward Lord Lytton. 1874.
Fables in song. 2 vols Edinburgh 1874; tr French, 1191.
King Poppy: a story without end. 1875 (priv ptd), 1892 (rev). A narrative poem.
The life, letters and literary remains of Edward Bulwer, Lord Lytton. 2 vols 1883. On his nove ist father.
Glenaveril, or the metamorphoses: a poem in six books. 2 vols 1885; tr French, 1888.
Baldine and other tales. 2 vols 1886. Tr from the German of K. E. Elder.
After paradise: or legends of exile with other poems. 1887.
Marah. 1892. Preface by E. L. [Edith Lady Lytton].

Letters

Personal and literary letters. Ed Lady B. Balfour 2 vols 1906.
Letters of Owen Meredith to Robert and Elizabeth Barrett Browning. Ed A. B. and J. L. Harlan, Waco Texas
Letters of Edward Bulwer-Lytton, Baron Lytton, to 1937. Richard Bentley 1829–73, and of his son Lord Lytton to George Bentley 1873–87. Bodleian Lib Record 2 1948.

§2

Obituary. Times 25–6 Nov 1891.
'Owen Meredith'. Athenaeum 28 Jan 1893.
Whyte, W. Robert Earl of Lytton. Miles 5.
Balfour, Lady B. The history of Lord Lytton's Indian administration 1876–80. 1899.
Sadleir, M. Bulwer and his wife: a panorama 1803–36. 1931.
Strachey, G. L. The first Earl of Lytton. Independent Rev March 1907. Review of Personal and literary letters, rptd in his Characters and commentaries, 1933.
Lytton, Earl of. The poetry of Owen Meredith. In The eighteen-eighties, ed W. de la Mare, Cambridge 1930.
Evans, B. I. In his English poetry in the later nineteenth century, 1933, 1966 (rev).
Harlan, A. B. Not by Elizabeth Barrett Browning. PMLA 57 1942.
— Owen Meredith: a critical biography. New York 1946.

WILLIAM HURRELL MALLOCK

1849–1923

See col 1066, below.

PHILIP BOURKE MARSTON

1850–87

Collections

Collected poems, with biographical sketch by L. C. Moulton. 1892.

§1

Song-tide and other poems. 1871; ed W. Sharp 1888 (enlarged with memoir).
All in all: poems and sonnets. 1875.
Wind-voices. 1883.
For a song's sake and other stories. Ed W. Sharp, with memoir 1887. Memoir rptd in Song-tide, 1888.
Garden secrets. Ed L. C. Moulton, Boston 1887.
A last harvest: lyrics and sonnets from The book of love. 1891. Biographical sketch by L. C. Moulton.

§2

Swinburne, A. C. Fortnightly Rev Jan 1891.
Kernahan, C. Marston. Miles 8 (7).
— In his Celebrities, 1923.
Drinkwater, J. Marston. In The English poets, ed T. H. Ward vol 5, 1918.
Osborne, C. C. Marston. 1926 (priv ptd).
Evans, B. I. In his English poetry in the later nineteenth century, 1933, 1966 (rev).

HERMAN CHARLES MERIVALE

1839–1906

See col 1194, below.

ALICE MEYNELL, née THOMPSON

1847–1922

Bibliographies

Tuell, A. K. In her Mrs Meynell and her literary generation, New York 1925.
Stonehill, C. A. and H. W. In their Bibliographies of modern authors ser 2, 1925.
Meynell, F. Alice Meynell 1847–1922: catalogue of the centenary exhibition of books, manuscripts, letters and portraits. 1947.

Collections

Poems: collected edition. 1913.
Essays. 1914.
The poems: complete edition. 1923; ed F. Page 1940, Oxford 1940 (OSA).
Selected essays. 1926.
Selected poems and prose. Ed A. A. Cock 1928.
Wayfaring: selected essays and poems. 1929.
Selected poems. Ed W. M[eynell] 1930.
The poems: centenary edition. Ed F. Meynell 1947.
Essays: centenary edition. Ed F. Meynell 1947.
Prose and poetry: centenary vol. Ed F. Page, V. Meynell, O. Sowerby and F. Maynell, with an introduction by V. Sackville-West. 1947.

§1

Preludes, by A. C. Thompson. 1875. Pbd before marriage.
C. H. Boughton ARA. 1883; J. L. E. Meissonier, 1883. In Some modern artists and their work, ed W. Meynell 1883.
The poor sisters of Nazareth: an illustrated record of life at Nazareth House Hammersmith. 1889.
The life and work of Holman Hunt. 1893. With W. Farrar.
Rhythm of life and other essays. 1893.
Poems. 1893.
The colour of life and other essays. 1896.
Other poems. 1896 (priv ptd).
Letters of Elizabeth Barrett Browning. Pall Mall Gazette 11 March 1897, N & Q 16 Dec 1944 (rev).
The children. 1897. Essays.
London impressions. 1898.
The spirit of place and other essays. 1899.
John Ruskin: a biography. 1900.
Later poems. 1902, 1914 (as Shepherdess and other poems 2 poems omitted).
Children of old masters. 1903.
The red letter poets. 12 vols 1903. Introds to 10 of the vols.
Ceres' runaway and other essays. 1909.

Mary, the mother of Jesus: an essay. 1912.
Francis Thompson, by E. Meynell. 1913. Contains letters and articles by Alice Meynell.
Childhood 1913.
Ten poems 1913–5. 1915.
Poems on the war. 1916.
A father of women and other poems. 1917.
Hearts of controversy. [1917].
Aenigma Christi. In O. R. Vassall-Phillips, The mother of Christ, 1920.
Second person singular and other essays. Oxford 1921.
Last poems. 1923.
Page, F. Alice Meynell: an uncollected poem. N & Q 19 Dec 1942.
Memorabilia. N & Q 24 April 1943. A note on Ruskin.
Price, F. Alice Meynell: some uncollected verse. N & Q 30 Dec 1944.
The wares of Autolycus: selected literary essays. Ed P. M. Fraser, Oxford 1965. Largely from Pall Mall Gazette 1895–8.
Mrs Meynell also translated D. Barbé, Lourdes yesterday, to-day and to-morrow, 1894; A. Venturi, The madonna, 1901; *and* R. Bazin, The nun, 1908.

§2

Noble, J. A. Alice Meynell. Miles 9.
Thompson, F. Mrs Meynell's poems. Tablet 21 Jan 1893; rptd in his Literary criticisms, ed T. L. Connolly, New York 1948.
Archer, W. In his Poets of the younger generation, 1902.
The letters of George Meredith to Alice Meynell 1896–1907. Annotated, reprinting Meredith's article on her prose.
Chesterton, G. K. Alice Meynell. Dublin Rev 172 1923, 441 1947.
Noyes, A. In his Some aspects of modern poetry, 1924.
— Alice Meynell. In his Pageant of letters, 1940.
Burdett, O. Poems of Alice Meynell. In his Critical essays, 1925.
Tuell, A. K. Mrs Meynell and her literary generation. New York 1925.
Newbolt, H. In his Studies green and gray, 1926.
Meynell, V. Alice Meynell: a memoir. 1929, 1948.
Galland, R. Alice Meynell. Revue Anglo-américaine 7 1930.
Hall, W. C. Alice Meynell. Papers of Manchester Literary Club 56 1930.
Tynan, K. A shrine to Alice Meynell. Commonweal 21–8 Jan 1931.
Braybrooke, P. Alice Meynell and her poetry. In his Some Victorians and Georgian Catholics, 1932.
Evans, B. I. In his English poetry of the later nineteenth century, 1933, 1966 (rev).
Moore, V. Alice Meynell. In her Distinguished woman writers, 1934.
Michalik, K. Alice Meynell: her life and her works. Cracow 1934.
Chambers, E. K. Alice Meynell's Rhythm of life. In his A sheaf of studies, Oxford 1942.
Price, F. N & Q 27 March, 10 April, 18 Dec 1943, 30 Dec 1944, 4 Oct 1947, 8 July 1950.
Paraclita, Sr M. Aubrey de Vere, Tennyson and Alice Meynell. Thought 21 1946.
Hamilton, G. R. Alice Meynell. Poetry Rev 38 1947.
Meynell, V. A personal note. Ibid.
Meynell, F. Alice Meynell: an address for the Alice Meynell centenary. Poetry Rev 38 1947.
An idyll of life and letters. TLS 18 Oct 1947.
Connolly, T. L. Alice Meynell centenary tribute. 1947.

SIR LEWIS MORRIS

1833–1907

Collections

Poetical works. 3 vols 1882, 1907 (rev and enlarged). Songs unsung, 1883, and Songs of Britain (4th edn) sometimes vols 4 and 5 of 1st edn of Poetical works.
Selections. 1897.
Poems. 1904. Authorized selection.

§1

Songs of two worlds. 3 sers 1871–5, 1878.
The epic of Hades. 1876 (bk 2 only), 1877 (bks 1–2), 1877 (complete).
Gwen: a drama in monologue. 1879.
The ode of life. 1880.
Songs unsung. 1883.
Gycia: a tragedy. 1886. Mostly verse.
Songs of Britain. 1887.
A vision of saints. 1890.
Odatis: an old love-tale: a poem. 1892.
Love and sleep and other poems. 1893.
Ode on the marriage of HRH the Duke of York and HSH Princess Victoria Mary of Teck. 1893.
Meliora: a poem. 1894.
Songs without notes. 1894.
Idylls and lyrics. 1896.
The diamond jubilee: an ode. 1897. Rptd from Times.
Harvest-tide. 1901.
The life and death of Leo the Armenian (Emperor of Rome): a tragedy. 1904.
The new rambler: from desk to platform. 1905. Essays.

§2

Rees, J. R. Morris. Miles 5.
Obituary. Times 13 Nov, 24 Dec 1907; Athenaeum 16 Nov 1907.
Evans, B. I. In his English poetry in the later nineteenth century, 1933, 1966 (rev).
B., E. M. Lewis Morris. Nat Rev Feb 1934.

ROBERT FULLER MURRAY

1863–94

The scarlet gown: being verses by a St Andrew's man. 1891, 1909 (new poems, with introd by A. Lang); ed J. H. Baxter 1932.
Murray: his poems, with a memoir by A. Lang. 1894.

ERNEST JAMES MYERS

1844–1921

Collections

Gathered poems. 1904.
Selected poems. 1931.

§1

The Puritans. 1869. One-act play.
Poems. 1877.
The defence of Rome and other poems. 1880.
Aeschylus: an essay. 1880. In Hellenica, ed E. Abbott 1880.
The Iliad of Homer done into English prose. 1883. With A. Lang and W. Leaf.
The judgment of Prometheus and other poems. 1886.
Lord Althorp: a biography. 1890.

§2

Miles, A. H. Myers. Miles 8 (7).
Obituary. Times 28 Nov 1921.

FREDERIC WILLIAM HENRY MYERS

1843–1901

Collections

Collected poems, with autobiographical and critical fragments. Ed E. Myers 1921.

§1

[Burns centenary poem.] In The Burns centenary poems, ed G. Anderson and J. Finlay 1859.
The distress in Lancashire: Chancellor's medal poem. Cambridge 1863.
Saint Paul. 1867.
Poems. 1870.
Greek oracles. In Hellenica, ed E. Abbott 1880.
Wordsworth. 1881 (EML).
The renewal of youth and other poems. 1882.
Essays classical and modern. 2 vols 1883.
Phantasms of the living. 1886. With E. Gurney and F. Podmore.
Science and a future life, with other essays. 1893.
Human personality and its survival of bodily death. 2 vols 1903.
Fragments of prose and poetry. Ed E. Myers 1904.
Saint John the Baptist. [1927].

§2

Morshead, E. D. A. The renewal of youth, and other poems. Academy 18 Nov 1882.
Anderson, M. B. Myers. Dial 4 1884.
Symonds, J. A. Myers. Miles 8 (7).
Mallock, W. H. The gospel of Myers. Nineteenth Century April 1903.
Muirhead, J. H. The survival of the soul: Human personality and its surival of bodily death. Contem porary Rev July 1903.
Sidgwick, A. The posthumous works of Myers. Independent Rev 5 1904.
Benson, A. C. In his Leaves of the tree: studies in biography, 1911.
Lodge, O. J. In his Conviction of survival, 1930.
The road to immortality: being a description of the after life purporting to be communicated by the late F. W. H. Myers through Geraldine Cummins. 1932, 1935 (as Beyond human personality).
Evans, B. I. In his English poetry in the later nineteenth century, 1933, 1966 (rev).
MacArthur, J. S. Believer in the future life. Hibbert Jnl 41 1943.
—— Nineteenth-century prophet on France. Church Quart Rev 138 1944.

EDITH NESBIT, afterwards BLAND

1858–1924

§1

Lays and legends. 2 sers 1886–92.
The lily and the cross. [1887].
Leaves of life. 1888.
Corals, sea songs etc. [1889].
Life's sunny side. 1890. With others.
Songs of two seasons. [1890].
Sweet lavender. [1892].
Our friends and all about them. [1893].
The star of Bethlehem. [1894].
Doggy tales. [1895]. Fiction.
A pomander of verse. 1895.
Rose leaves. [1895].
Songs of love and empire. 1898.
The red house: a novel. 1902.
The phoenix and the carpet. [1904]. Fiction.
The rainbow and the rose. 1905.
The incomplete amorist: a novel. 1906.
Ballads and lyrics of Socialism 1883–1908. 1908.
Jesus in London, with seven pictures by S. Pryse. [1908].
Harding's luck. 1909. Fiction.
Ballads and verses of the spiritual life. 1911.
The magic world. 1912. Tales.
Many voices: poems [1922].
To the adventurous. [1923]. Fiction.
The complete history of the Bastable family. 1928.
E. Nesbit wrote many other novels and tales, mainly for children; see col 1097, below.

§2

Japp, A. H. E. Nesbit. Miles 9.
Moore, D. L. E. Nesbit: a biography. 1933, 1967 (rev).
Streatfeild, N. Magic and magician: E. Nesbit and her children's books. 1958.
1958 marks the centenary of the birth of E. Nesbit. Publisher's Weekly 13 Oct 1958.

SIR HENRY JOHN NEWBOLT

1862–1937

Collections

Collected poems 1897–1907. 1910.
Prose and poetry, selected by the author. 1920.
Selected poems. Ed J. Betjeman 1940.

§1

A fair death. 1882. Anon.
Taken from the enemy: a novel. 1892.
Mordred: a tragedy. 1895.
Admirals all and other verses. 1897 etc, New York 1898.
The island race. 1898. Poems.
The sailing of the long ships and other poems. 1902.
The year of Trafalgar. 1905. Prose.
The old country: a romance. 1906.
Clifton chapel and other school poems. 1908.
Songs of memory and hope. 1909.
The new June. 1909. Fiction.
The Twymans: a tale of youth. Edinburgh 1911.
Poems new and old. 1912.
Drake's drum and other songs of the sea. 1914.
Aladore. Edinburgh 1914. Fiction.
The book of the blue sea. 1914. Prose.
The story of the Oxfordshire and Buckingham light infantry, the old 43rd and 52nd regiments. 1915.
The war and the nations. 1915. Rptd from Fortnightly Rev.
The book of the thin red line. 1915.
Tales of the great war. 1916.
A new study of English poetry. 1917.
The book of the happy warrior. 1917. Prose.
St George's day and other poems. 1918.
Submarine and anti-submarine. 1918. Prose.
The book of the long trail. 1919. Prose.
Poetry and time. 1919 (Warton lecture).
The book of good hunting. 1920. Prose.
A naval history of the war 1914–18. 5 vols 1920–31.
The book of the Grenvilles. 1921.
Days to remember. 1923. On the European war, with J. Buchan.
Studies green and gray. 1926. Criticism.
The linnet's nest. 1927. Poetry.

The building of Britain. 1927. On paintings.
The idea of an English association. 1928 (English Assoc).
A child is born. 1931. Poetry.
My world as in my time. 1932. Prose.
A perpetual memory and other poems, with brief memoirs by W. de la Mare and F. Furse. 1939.
The later life and letters of Newbolt. Ed M. Newbolt 1942. Vol 2 of My world as in my time.
Newbolt also edited and contributed to the Teaching of English ser, 1925–32.

§2

Archer, W. In his Poets of the younger generation, 1902.
Bridges, R. Newbolt. Miles 7.
Kernahan, C. In his Six famous living poets, 1922.
Palmer, H. Watson and Newbolt. In his Post-Victorian poetry, 1938.
The lyrics of Newbolt. Times 23 April 1938.
Betjeman, J. Newbolt after a hundred years. Listener 28 June 1962.

ARTHUR O'SHAUGHNESSY
1844–81

See col 1906, below.

JOHN PAYNE
1842–1916

Bibliographies

Wright, T. In his Life of Payne, 1919.

Collections

The poetical works. 2 vols 1902.
Selections from the poetry of Payne, made by T. and L. Robinson. New York 1906.

§1

The masque of shadows and other poems. 1870.
Intaglios. 1871.
Songs of life and death. 1872.
Lautrec. 1878.
New poems. 1880.
The descent of the dove. 1902.
Vigil and vision. 1903; Supplement, 12 Sonnets de combat, 1903 (priv ptd).
Songs of consolation. 1904. Includes Descent of the dove, above.
Hamid the luckless and other tales in verse. 1904. Rptd from Flowers from Syrian gardens (Poetical works, vol 1), with Hamid the luckless in place of The scavenger of Baghdad.
Sir Winfrith and other poems. Olney 1905.
Verses for the Newton-Cowper centenary. 1907.
The quatrains of Ibn El-Tefrid. 1908 (priv ptd), 1909 (with omissions); ed T. Wright 1921.
Carol and cadence. 1908.
Flower o' the thorn. 1909.
Humoristica. 3 sers 1909–[10] (priv ptd).
The way of the winepress. Olney 1920.
Nature and her lover and other poems. Ed T. Wright, Olney 1922. Rptd from Carol and cadence, above.
The autobiography of Payne, with preface and annotations by T. Wright. 1926.
Payne also translated Villon, 1878; The book of a thousand nights and one night, 1882–4; Tales from the Arabic, 1884–5; Decameron, 1886; Matteo Bandello, 1890; Omar Kheyyam of Nisha Pour, 1898; Shemseddin Mohammed Hafiz, 1901; Tales from the Arabian Nights, 1906; Flowers of France, 1906, 1907, 1913, 1914; Heine, 1911.

§2

Forman, H. B. In his Our living poets, 1871.
Garnett, R. Payne. Miles 8 (7).
Wright, T. The life of Payne. 1919.
Evans, B. I. In his English poetry in the later nineteenth century, 1933, 1966 (rev).
Lhombréaud, R. Une lettre inédite de Mallarmé en anglais. Revue de Littérature Comparée 26 1952.
Ryan, M. Payne et Mallarmé: une longue amitié. Revue de Littérature Comparée 32 1958.

STEPHEN PHILLIPS
1864–1915

See col 1194, below.

VICTOR GUSTAVE PLARR
1863–1929

Scenes from the Alcestis of Euripides. 1886 (priv ptd).
The book of the Rhymers' Club. 1892 (contains 6 pieces by Plarr), 1894 (bk 2, contains 6 more poems).
In the Dorian mood: verses. 1896.
Nine poems. In The garland of new poetry by various writers, 1899.
Literary etiquette. 1903. Prose.
The tragedy of Asgard. 1905.
Ernest Dowson 1888–97: reminiscences, unpublished letters and marginalia. 1914.
Plarr's Lives of the Fellows of the Royal College of Surgeons of England. Rev D'A. Power, W. G. Spencer and G. E. Gask. 2 vols 1930. Includes memoir of Plarr.

SIR FREDERICK POLLOCK
1845–1947

§1

Leading cases done into English, by an apprentice of Lincoln's Inn. 1876 (2nd edn).
Spinoza: his life and philosophy. 1880.
Essays in jurisprudence and ethics. 1882.
An introduction to the history of the science of politics. 1890.
Oxford lectures and other discourses. 1890. Prose.
Leading cases done into English and other diversions. 1892.
Outside the law: diversions partly serious. 1927. Prose and verse.
For my grandson: remembrances of an ancient Victorian. 1933.
Holmes-Pollock letters: the correspondence of Mr Justice Holmes and Pollock 1874–1932. Ed M. de W. Howe 2 vols Cambridge 1942.
Pollock also wrote on legal subjects.

§2

Wright, R. A. W. In memoriam Pollock. In his Legal essays and addresses, 1940.
Shientag, B. L. Pollock: legal scholar and teacher. In his Moulders of legal thought, 1943.

SIR ARTHUR QUILLER-COUCH
1863–1944

See col 1071, below.

ERNEST RADFORD

Translations from Heine and other verses. 1882.
Measured steps. 1884.
Syllabus of a course of 12 lectures upon the method of art study. 1885–6. [1885].
Chambers twain. 1890.
The book of the Rhymers' Club. 1892 (contains 5 pieces by Radford), 1894 (bk 2, with 8 more pieces).
Old and new: a collection of poems. 1895.
Dante Gabriel Rossetti. [1905].
A collection of poems. 1906.
Johnson and the literary club. [1907].
Songs in the whirlwind. 1918. With A. Radford.

SIR WALTER RALEIGH
1861–1922

See col 1449, below.

HARDWICK DRUMMOND RAWNSLEY
1850–1920

§1

A book of Bristol sonnets. 1877.
The miners' rescue, Troedyrhin colliery, Rhondda Vale, Glamorganshire, April 20 1877: a poem. 1877.
Sonnets at the English lakes. 1881.
Sonnets round the coast. 1887.
Poems, ballads and bucolics. 1890.
Notes for the Nile, together with a metrical rendering of the hymns of ancient Egypt and of the precepts of Ptah-Hotep: the oldest book in the world. 1892.
The undoing of De Harcla: a ballad of Cumberland. 1892.
Tennyson and other memorial poems. Glasgow 1893.
Idylls and lyrics of the Nile. 1894.
Ballads of brave deeds, with a frontispiece and preface by G. F. Watts. 1896.
Sonnets in Switzerland and Italy. 1899.
Ballads of the war. 1900.
A sonnet chronicle 1900–6. Glasgow 1906.
Poems at home and abroad. Glasgow 1909.
The European war 1914–5: poems. [1915].
Rawnsley also pbd 12 books on the English lake country, all but the first in Glasgow : A coach drive, Keswick 1890; Literary associations, 1894; Life and nature, 1899; Ruskin, 1901; A rambler's notebook, 1902; Lake country sketches, 1903; Months at the lake, 1906; Wordsworth, Tennyson, 1906; Round the lake country, 1909; By fell and dale, 1911; Chapters, 1913; Past and present, 1916.

He also pbd sermons, biographies etc.

§2

Noble, J. A. Rawnsley. Miles 8 (7).
Rawnsley, E. F. Canon Rawnsley: an account of his life. Glasgow 1923.

JAMES RHOADES
1841–1923

Collections

Collected poems. Ed L. N. P[arker] 1925.

§1

Poems. 1970.
Timoleon: a dramatic poem. 1875.
The Georgics of Virgil, translated into English verse. 1881.
Dux Redux, or a forest tangle: a comedy. 1887.
The Aeneid of Virgil books 1–6, translated into English verse. 1893.
Teresa (a tragedy in one act) and other poems. 1893.
The little flowers of St Francis of Assisi, rendered into English verse. 1904, Oxford 1925 (WC).
Out of the silence. 1907.
The Aenid of Virgil, translated into English verse. 1907.
The training of the imagination. 1908. Prose.
O soul of mine! 1912.
The city of the fire gates. 1913.
Words by the wayside. 1915.
The poems of Virgil, translated into English verse. Oxford 1921 (WC).

§2

Layard, G. S. Rhoades (1841–1923). Bookman (London) May 1923.

JAMES LOGIE ROBERTSON
1846–1922

§1

Poems. Dundee 1878.
Orellana and other poems. Edinburgh 1881.
Our holiday among the hills. Edinburgh 1882. With Janet L. Robertson.
Horace in homespun, by Hugh Haliburton. Edinburgh 1886, 1925 (signed, adding new poems and memoir by Janet L. Robertson).
The white angel of the Polly Ann and other stories. Edinburgh 1886.
'For puir auld Scotland's sake', by Hugh Haliburton. Edinburgh 1887. Essays.
New songs of innocence. Edinburgh 1889.
In Scottish fields, by Hugh Haliburton. Edinburgh 1890. Essays.
Ochil idylls and other poems, by Hugh Haliburton. 1891.
A history of English literature for secondary schools. Edinburgh 1894.
Furth in field, by Hugh Haliburton. 1895. Essays.
Outlines of English literature for young scholars. Edinbugh 1897.
Nature in books: a literary introd to natural science. 1914.
Petition to the Deil and other war verses. Paisley 1917.
Robertson also edited Burns's letters and poems.

§2

Robertson, J. L. In J. L. Robertson, Horace in homespun, Edinburgh 1925.

AGNES MARY FRANCES ROBINSON, later DARMESTETER, later DUCLAUX
1857–1944

Collections

Lyrics selected from the works. 1891.
Collected poems, lyrical and narrative, with a preface. 1902.

§ 1

A handful of honeysuckle. 1878.
The crowned Hippolytus of Euripides, with new poems. 1881.
The new Arcadia and other poems. 1884.
An Italian garden: a book of songs. 1886.
Songs, ballads and a garden play. 1888.
Poésies, traduites de l'anglais par J. Darmesteter. 1888.
The end of the Middle Ages: essays and questions of history. [1888].
Retrospect and other poems. 1893.
Grands écrivains d'outre-manche: les Brontë—Thackeray—les Brownings—Rossetti. [1901].
The return to nature: songs and symbols. 1904.
Images and meditations: poems. 1923.
Mme Duclaux also wrote books on Margaret of Angoulême, Queen of Navarre, Marguerite du temps passé *(tales), Froissart, Renan, French sociology, writers, history, Pascal, Hugo, Racine; introds to edns of Browning (in French), Mrs Browning, Madame de Sévigné, Renan, Marie Lenéru, and to books by her husband James Darmesteter, whose* Nouvelles études anglaises *she translated.*

§ 2

Robertson, E. S. In his English poetesses, 1883.
Watson, W. Lyrics selected from the works of A. Mary F. Robinson (Madame Darmesteter). Academy 21 Feb 1891.
Symons, A. A. M. F. Darmesteter. Miles 8 (7).
Lynch, H. A. Mary F. Robinson. Fortnightly Rev Feb 1902.
Marandon, S. Qui fut Mary Robinson? Les Langues Modernes 54 1960.

JAMES RENNELL RODD, 1st BARON RENNELL

1858–1941

§ 1

Newdigate prize poem: Raleigh. [1880].
Songs in the south. 1881.
Rose leaf and apple leaf. Philadelphia 1882.
Poems in many lands. 1883, 1886.
Feda with other poems, chiefly lyrical. 1886.
The unknown madonna and other poems. 1888.
Sir Walter Raleigh. 1889. Prose.
The violet crown and songs of England. 1891, 1913 (with new poems).
Ballads of the fleet and other poems. 1897, 1901 (with additional pieces).
Myrtle and oak. 1902.
Love, worship and death: some renderings from the Greek Anthology. 1916.
Social and diplomatic memories. 3 sers 1922–5. Prose.
Trentaremi and other moods. 1923.
Diplomacy. 1929. Prose.
War poems with some others. 1940.
Lord Rennell also pbd books on Frederick, Crown Prince and Emperor, modern Greece, Greece of the Middle Ages, Homer's Ithaca, Rome, and several pamphlets and introds.

§ 2

Williams, F. H. The poems of Rennell Rodd. American 5 1882.
Miles, A. H. Rennell Rodd. Miles 8 (7).

GEORGE RUSSELL

1867–1935

See col 1912, below.

WILLIAM SHARP

1855–1905

See col 1064, below.

DORA SIGERSON SHORTER

1866–1918

See col 1911, below.

GEORGE AUGUSTUS SIMCOX

1841–1905

§ 1

Prometheus unbound: a tragedy. 1867.
Poems and romances. 1869.
Recollections of a rambler. 1874.
Simcox also pbd a history of Latin literature and edited the Greek Testament, Demosthenes, Juvenal and Thucydides.

§ 2

Miles, A. H. Simcox. Miles 8 (7).
Haber, T. B. The poetic antecedents of Housman's Hell gate. PQ 31 1952. *See* J. Sparrow 33 1954.

JOSEPH SKIPSEY

1832–1903

Collections

Songs and lyrics, collected and revised. 1892.

§ 1

Poems, songs and ballads. 1862.
The collier lad and other lyrics. 1864 (priv ptd).
Poems. 1871.
A book of miscellaneous lyrics. Bedlington 1878, 1881 (rev as A book of lyrics, including Songs, ballads and chants).
Carols from the coal-fields and other songs and ballads. 1886. With biographical note by R. S. Watson.
Skipsey also edited 6 vols of the Canterbury poets.

§ 2

Watts [-Dunton], T. Skipsey's Miscellaneous lyrics. Athenaeum 16 Nov 1878.
Lewin, W. Songs and lyrics. Academy 20 April 1892.
Watson, R. S. Skipsey: his life and work. [1908].
Runciman, J. F. Skipsey: poet of the Northumbrian pits. Living Age 262 1909.
Miles, A. H. Skipsey. Miles 5.
Evans, B. I. In his English poetry in the later nineteenth century, 1933, 1966 (rev).

DOUGLAS BROOKE WHEELTON SLADEN

1856–1933

§ 1

Frithjof and Ingebjorg and other poems. 1882.
Australian lyrics. Melbourne 1883.
A poetry of exiles and other poems. 1884, 1885 (rev).
A summer Christmas and a sonnet upon the S.S. Ballaarat. 1884.
In Cornwall and across the sea, with poems written in Devonshire. 1885.

Edward the Black Prince: an epic drama. 1887.
A ballad for the tercentenary of the Spanish Armada. Penzance 1888.
Lestee the loyalist: a romance of the founding of Canada. Tokyo 1890.

§2

Gordon, A. L. The life and best poems of the poet of Australia. 1934 (Westminster Abbey memorial volume).
Sladen also pbd novels, biographies, books of travel and Twenty years of my life, 1915, *and* My long life, 1939.

JAMES KENNETH STEPHEN
1859–92

Collections

Select poems. 1926.

§1

Lapsus calami. Cambridge 1891, 1891 (3rd edn, with omissions and addns).
Quo musa tendis? Cambridge 1891.
Lapsus calami and other verses, with introduction by H. Stephen. 1896.
Stephen also pbd books on international law and a defence of compulsory Greek.

§2

Miles, A. H. Stephen. Miles 9 (10).
J. K. S. Academy 19 Aug 1905.
Benson, A. C. In his Leaves of the tree: studies in biography, 1911.
Evans, B. I. In his English poetry in the later nineteenth century, 1933, 1966 (rev).
Master of light verse: in memory of J.K.S. TLS 31 Jan 1941.

ROBERT LOUIS STEVENSON
1850–94

See col 1004, below.

ARTHUR SYMONS
1865–1945

Bibliographies

Danielson, H. In his Bibliographies of modern authors, 1921.
Welby, T. E. In his Symons, 1925.
Symons' personal papers. Princeton Lib Chron 14 1952.

Collections

Poems. 2 vols 1902.
Poésies. Bruges 1907. Collected and tr, with an essay, by L. Thomas.
Works. 9 vols 1924. Incomplete.
Amoris victima. 1940 (priv ptd). Selection of verse and prose, some unpbd.

§1

An introduction to the study of Browning. 1886, 1906 (rev and enlarged).
Days and nights. 1889, 1924 (with original notice by William Pater).
Silhouettes. 1892, 1896 (rev).
London nights. 1895, 1897 (rev).
Amoris victima. 1897.
Studies in two literatures. 1897.
Aubrey Beardsley. 1898, 1905 (rev), 1948.
The symbolist movement in literature. 1899.
Images of good and evil. 1899.
The loom of dreams. 1901 (priv ptd).
Cities. 1903. Prose.
Plays, acting and music. 1903, 1909 (rev). Prose.
Studies in prose and verse. 1904. Rptd partly from Studies in two literatures, above.
Spiritual adventures. 1905. Prose sketches.
A book of twenty songs. 1905.
The fool of the world and other poems. 1906.
Studies in seven arts. 1906. Prose.
Cities of Italy. 1907.
Great acting in English. 1907 (priv ptd).
William Blake. 1907.
London: a book of aspects. 1909 (priv ptd). Prose.
The romantic movement in English poetry. 1909.
Dante Gabriel Rossetti. 1910.
Knave of hearts 1894–1908. 1913.
Figures of seven centuries. 1916. Prose.
Tragedies. 1916. The death of Agrippa, Cleopatra in Judaea, The harvesters.
Tristran and Iseult. 1917. Play.
Cities and sea-coasts and islands. 1917. Prose.
Colour studies in Paris. 1918. Prose.
The toy cart. 1919. Play.
Cesare Borgia, Iseult of Brittany, The toy cart. New York 1920. Plays.
Charles Baudelaire. 1920. Prose.
Studies in Elizabethan drama. 1920. Rptd with addns from Studies in two literatures, above.
Lesbia and other poems. New York 1920.
Love's cruelty. 1923.
Carlo Goldoni: an essay. In The good-humoured ladies, tr R. Aldington, 1923.
Dramatis personae. Indianapolis 1923, 1925 (corrected). Prose.
The Café Royal and other essays. 1923.
From Catallus, chiefly concerning Lesbia. 1924. Latin and English poems.
Notes on Joseph Conrad with some unpublished letters. 1925.
Studies in modern painters. New York 1925.
Eleonora Dusa. 1926. Distinct from essay in The Café Royal. above,
Parisian nights. 1926. Essays.
A study of Thomas Hardy. 1927.
Studies in strange souls. 1929. Rossetti and Swinburne.
From Toulouse-Lautrec to Rodin with some personal impressions. 1929.
Confessions: a study in pathology. New York 1930.
A study of Oscar Wilde. 1930.
Mes souvenirs. Chapelle-Réanville 1931. In English prose.
Wanderings. 1931. Prose.
Jezebel Mort and other poems. 1931.
Notes on two mss. Eng Rev May 1932.
A study of Walter Pater. 1932.

Translations

Zola, L'assommoir. 1894 (included in Zola's works), 1928 (separately, with introd).
Verhaeren, The dawn. 1898, 1916 (in Verhaeren's plays).
d'Annunzio, The child of pleasure. 1898. Verses only, tr Symons.
— The dead city. 1900.
— Gioconda. 1901.
— Francesca da Rimini. 1902.
Baudelaire, Poems in prose. 1905, 1925 (included in Les fleurs du mal, below).
— Les fleurs du mal, Petits poèmes en prose, Les paradis artificiels. 1925.
— The letters of Charles Baudelaire to his mother. 1928.
Pignata, The adventures of Giuseppe Pignata. 1930.
Louys, The woman and the puppet. 1935.
Symons also pbd edns and anthologies of English poets.

§2

Thompson, F. Symons. Academy 7 Jan 1905. Review of Studies in prose and verse, rptd in his Literary criticisms, ed T. L. Connolly, New York 1948.
Urban, W. M. Symons and impressionism. Atlantic Monthly Sept 1914.
Waugh, A. In his Tradition and change, 1919.
Welby, T. E. Symons. 1925.
Yeats, W. B. In his Autobiographies, 1926.
Wildi, M. Symons also Kritiker der Literatur. Heidelberg 1929.
Evans, B. I. In his English poetry in the later nineteenth century, 1933, 1966 (rev).
Thouless, P. In her Modern poetic drama, Oxford 1934.
Weygandt, C. Ernest Dowson and Symons. In his Time of Yeats, New York 1937.
Symons. TLS 3 Feb 1945. Obituary; *see* 24 Feb, 10 March 1945.
Jennings, R. Symons: poet, dramatist, impressionist, traveller. New Statesman 17 Feb 1945.
Pick, J. Divergent disciples of Walter Pater. Thought 23 1948.
Sklare, A. B. Symons: an appreciation of the critic of literature. Jnl of Aesthetics 9 1951.
Duffy, C. A Symons annotation. N & Q 10 Dec 1949.
Orel, H. The forgotten ambassadors: Russian fiction in Victorian England. Amer Slavic & East European Rev 12 1953.
Garbáty, T. J. An appraisal of Symons by Pater and Mallarmé. N & Q May 1960.
Peters, R. L. The Salome of Symons and Aubrey Beardsley. Criticism 2 1960.
Witt, M. A note on Yeats and Symons. N & Q Dec 1960.
Lhombréaud, R. Symons: his life and letters. 1962.
—— Symons: a critical biography. 1963.
Harris, W. Innocent decadence: the poetry of the Savoy. PMLA 77 1962.
Goldfarb, R. M. Symons' decadent poetry. Victorian Poetry 1 1963.
Baugh, E. Symons, poet: a centenary tribute. REL 6 1965.
Munro, J. M. Symons as poet: theory and practice. Eng Lit in Transition 6 1963.
Stanford, D. Symons as a literary critic. Contemporary Rev Oct-Nov 1965.

JOHN TODHUNTER
1839–1916

See col 1906, below.

HENRY DUFF TRAILL
1842–1912

See col 1454, below.

HERBERT TRENCH
1865–1923

See col 1911, below.

KATHARINE TYNAN
1861–1931

See col 1910, below.

ARTHUR EDWARD WAITE
1857–1942

Collections

Collected poems. 2 vols 1914.

§1

Israfel: letters, visions and poems. 1886.
A soul's comedy. 1887.
Lucasta: parables and poems. 1889.
A book of mystery and vision. 1902.
Strange houses of sleep. 1906.
The book of the holy grail. 1921. Poems.
The holy grail: its legends and symbolism. 1933.
Shadows of life and thought: a retrospective review in the form of memoirs. 1938.
Waite also wrote on alchemy, freemasonry, the Rosicrucians etc.

FREDERICK WILLIAM ORDE WARD
1843–1922

Collections

Selected poems. Ed C. O. O. Ward and R. Markland 1924.

§1

The cry of the woman-child. 1886. By Harald Williams, pseudonym for his first 6 books.
Women must weep. 1886.
'Twixt kiss and lip, or under the sword. 1890.
Confessions of a poet. 1894.
Matin bells and scarlet and gold. 1897.
English roses. 1899.
New century hymns for the Christian year. [1901].
The prisoner of love. 1904.
The last crusade: patriotic poems. [1917].
Songs for sufferers, from a sick-room. [1917].
Ward also pbd theological works and a paper on Shelley.

§2

Miles, A. H. Ward. Miles 12.
TLS 18 Dec 1924. Review of Selected poems.

JOHN BYRNE LEICESTER WARREN, 3rd BARON DE TABLEY
1835–95

Collections

Poems, dramatic and lyrical. 2 sers 1893–5.
Collected poems. 1903.
Select poems. Ed J. Drinkwater 1924.

§1

Poems. 1859. With G. Fortescue.
Ballads and metrical sketches. 1860.
The threshold of Atrides. 1861.
Glimpses of antiquity. 1862.
Praeterita. 1863.
An essay on Greek federal coinage. 1863.
On some coins of Lycia under the Rhodian domination, and of the Lycian league. 1863.
Eclogues and monodramas. 1864.
Studies in verse. 1865.
Philoctetes: a metrical drama. 1866.
Orestes: Orestes: a metrical drama. 1867.
A screw loose: a novel. 1868.
Ropes of sand: a novel. 1869.
Rehearsals: a book of verses. 1870.
Searching the net: a book of verses. 1873.
The soldier of fortune: a tragedy. 1876.
A guide to the study of book plates. 1880.
The flora of Cheshire. Ed S. Moore 1899. Includes letters and memoir by M. G. Duff.

Orpheus in Thrace and other poems. Ed E., Lady Leighton-Warren 1901.

§2

Le Gallienne, R. The poetry of Lord de Tabley. Nineteenth Century May 1893.
Miles, A. H. Lord de Tabley. Miles 6.
Monkhouse, C. Poems dramatic and lyrical, by Lord de Tabley. Academy 6 April 1895.
Watts [-Dunton], T. Lord de Tabley. Athenaeum 30 Nov 1895; rptd in his Old familiar faces, 1916.
Gosse, E. Lord de Tabley: a portrait. Contemporary Rev Jan 1896; rptd in his Critical kit-kats, 1896.
Walker, H. Warren. 1903.
Hearn, L. In his Life and literature, New York 1917.
Bridges, R. Lord de Tabley's poems. In his Collected essays vol 7, Oxford 1931.
Evans, B. I. In his English poetry in the later nineteenth century, 1933, 1966 (rev).
Lord de Tabley. TLS 25 April 1935.
Taplin, G. B. The life, works and literary reputation of Lord de Tabley. Cambridge Mass 1946.
Pitts, G. Lord de Tabley: poet of frustration. West Virginia Univ Philological Papers 14 1963.

SIR THOMAS HERBERT WARREN
1853–1930

§1

By Severn sea and other poems. Oxford 1897, 1898.

§2

Magnus, L. Warren of Magdalen. 1932.

SIR WILLIAM WATSON
1858–1935

Autograph letters and mss of Watson are in Bodley.

Bibliographies

Watson, W. In his Heralds of the dawn, 1912.
Swayze, W. E. The Watson collection. Yale Univ Lib Gazette 27 1952.
Woolf, C. Some uncollected authors 12: Watson. Book Collector 5 1956. *See* N. Colbeck, 6 1957, W. E. Swayze, ibid.

Collections

Collected poems. 1898.
Selected poems. 1903.
[Collected] Poems. Ed J. A. Spender 2 vols 1905.
A hundred poems selected from various volumes. 1922.
Poems selected with notes by the author. 1928.
The poems of Watson 1878–1935. 1936.
I was an English poet: poems selected by Lady Watson. Ashville 1941.

§1

The prince's quest and other poems. 1880, 1892.
Epigrams of art, life and nature. Liverpool 1884. With note on epigrams.
Wordsworth's grave and other poems. 1890, 1892 (as Poems, adds 26 poems).
Lachrymae musarum. 1892 (priv ptd), 1892 (adds poems). Verses on the death of Tennyson.
Shelley's centenary. 1892 (priv ptd).
The eloping angels: a caprice. 1893.
Excursions in criticism: being some prose recreations of a rhymer. 1893.
Odes and other poems. 1894.
The father of the forest and other poems. 1895.
Ode for the centenary of the death of Burns. 1895.
The purple east: a series of sonnets on England's desertion of Armenia. 1896.
The lost Eden. New York 1897.
The year of shame, with an introduction by the Bishop of Hereford. 1897.
The hope of the world and other poems. 1898.
New poems. Greenfield Mass 1902, 1909.
Ode on the day of the coronation of King Edward VII. 1902.
For England: poems written during estrangement. 1904.
Sable and purple with other poems. 1910.
The heralds of the dawn. 1912. A play.
The muse in exile. 1913. With address on the poet's place in life.
The man who saw and other poems arising out of the war. 1917.
Retrogression and other poems. 1917.
Pencraft: a plea for the older ways. 1917. Prose.
The superhuman antagonists and other poems. 1919.
Ireland arisen. 1921.
Ireland unfreed. 1921.
Poems brief and new. 1925.

§2

Noble, J. A. Watson. Miles 8 (7).
Archer, W. In his Poets of the younger generation, 1902.
Macfie, R. C. Watson's poems. Bookman (London) March 1923.
Kernahan, C. In his Five more famous living poets, 1928.
Harper, G. M. In his Literary appreciations, Indianapolis 1937.
Wolf, H. Watson. Spectator 8 Nov 1930.
Wood, W. F. The poetry of Watson. Poetry Rev 23 1932.
Yeats, W. B. Scholar poet. In his Letters to the new island, ed H. Reynolds, Cambridge Mass 1934.
Watson: a distinguished poet. Times 14 Aug 1935. Leader and obituary.
Nichols, W. B. The chord of iron: an elegy of Watson. 1935.
Scott-James, R. A. Editorial notes. London Mercury Sept 1935.
May, J. L. In his John Lane and the 'nineties, 1936.
Bett, H. K. The poetry of Watson. London Quart 161 1936.
Hall, W. C. Watson. Papers of Manchester Literary Club 62 1937.
Weygandt, C. The old main line. In his Time of Yeats, New York 1937.
Palmer, H. Watson and Newbolt. In his Post-Victorian poetry, 1938.
Shackford, M. H. Shelley's centenary by Watson. In her Studies of certain nineteenth-century poets, Natick Mass 1946.
Nelson, J. G. William Watson. New York 1966.

THEODORE WATTS-DUNTON
1836–1914

See col 1456, below.

OSCAR WILDE
1854–1900

See col 1182, below.

JAMES CHAPMAN WOODS

A child of the people and other poems. 1879.
A pageant of poets and other poems. 1931.
Woods also pbd guide-books, travel books etc.

MARGARET LOUISA WOODS
1856–1945

See col 1083, below.

THEODORE WRATISLAW
1871–1933

Collections

Selected poems. Ed J. Gawsworth 1955. With biographical note.

§1

Love's memorial. Rugby 1892. Anon.
Some verses. Rugby 1892. Anon.
Caprices: poems. 1893.
The pity of love: a tragedy. 1895.
Orchids: poems. 1896.
Swinburne. 1900.
Love in a mist, adapted as a comedietta by Mrs F. Ward. Worcester 1903.
Two ballads transcribed from the French of Master François Villon. Rugby 1933.

§2

Ellis, S. M. A poet of the nineties: Wratislaw. In his Mainly Victorian, 1925.
Around my shelves. Poetry Rev 41 1950. Contains unpd epitaph.

WILLIAM BUTLER YEATS
1865–1939

See col 1915, below.

W. W.

3. THE NOVEL

I. GENERAL WORKS

(1) BIBLIOGRAPHIES ETC

Wedgwood, F. J. Contemporary records: fiction 1–10. Contemporary Rev July 1883–Dec 1886.
Chandler, F. W. In his Literature of roguery, 2 vols Boston 1907.
Baker, E. A. and J. Packman. A guide to the best fiction in English. 1913, 1932 (rev and enlarged).
Nield, J. Guide to historical novels. 1913.
Parrish, M. L. In his Victorian lady novelists, 1933. On George Eliot, Mrs Gaskell, the Brontës.
Blakey, D. The Minerva Press 1790–1820. 1939.
Ehrsam, T. G. and R. H. Deily. Bibliographies of twelve Victorian authors. New York 1936. Includes Kipling, Hardy, R. L. Stevenson; supplement by J. G. Fucilla, MP 37 1939.
Block, A. The English novel 1740–1850: a catalogue. 1939, 1961 (rev). Includes prose romances, short stories and trns of foreign fiction.
Summers, M. A Gothic bibliography. [1941].
Queen, E. The detective short story: a bibliography. Boston 1943.
Henkin, L. J. Problems and digressions in the Victorian novel 1860–1900. Bull of Bibliography 18–20 1943–50.
Carter, J. and M. Sadleir. Victorian fiction. Cambridge 1947.
Victorian fiction. Princeton 1947. A Princeton exhibition.
Bleiler, E. F. Checklist of fantastic literature. Chicago 1948.
Rouse, H. B. A selective and critical bibliography of studies in prose fiction. JEGP 49–52 1950–2.
Sadleir, M. XIX century fiction: a bibliographical record. 2 vols 1951.
Leclaire, L. A general analytical bibliography of the regional novelists of the British Isles 1800–1950. Paris 1954.
Cook, D. E. and I. S. Monro. Short story index. New York 1955.
Roger, D. Fantastic novels: a check-list. Perth 1957.
Henderson, J. The Gothic novel in Wales 1790–1820, with a checklist of novels connected with Wales. Nat Lib of Wales Jnl 1960.
Maison, M. In her Search your soul, Eustace: a survey of the religious novel in the Victorian age. 1961.
Stevenson, L. In his English novel: a panorama, 1961.
— (ed). Victorian fiction: a guide to research. Cambridge Mass 1964.
Ray, G. N. Nineteenth-century English fiction. Los Angeles 1964. A lecture.
Carter, J. Victorian detective fiction: a catalogue of the collection made by Dorothy Glover and Graham Greene. 1966.

(2) HISTORIES AND STUDIES

Taylor, H. Novels of fashionable life. Quart Rev 48 1832.
Oliphant, M. O. Modern novelists—great and small. Blackwood's Mag May 1855.
— Sensation novels. Blackwood's Mag May 1962.
— Novels. Blackwood's Mag Aug 1863, Sept 1867.
— New novels. Blackwood's Mag Sept 1880.
— Recent novels. Blackwood's Mag March 1882.
— Three young novelists. Blackwood's Mag Sept 1884. On F. M. Crawford, 'F. Anstey', J. F. Fargus.
— Novels. Blackwood's Mag Dec 1886. On Children of Gibeon, Princess Casamassima, Sir Percival, A bachelor's blunder.
Smith, W. M. The novel and the drama: some advice to an author. Blackwood's Mag June 1845.
Patmore, C. K. D. Popular serial literature. North Br Rev 7 1847.
Smith, I. G. Recent works of fiction. North Br Rev 15 1851.
Stephen, J. F. The relation of novels to life. In Cambridge essays contributed by members of the University, 1855.
Sellar, W. Y. Religious novels. North Br Rev 26 1856.
Jeaffreson, J. C. Novels and novelists. 2 vols 1858.
Mansel, H. L. Sensation novels. Quart Rev 113 1863.
Smith, A. Novels and novelists of the day. North Br Rev 38 1863.
Senior, N. W. Essays on fiction. 1864. On Scott, Lytton, Thackeray.
Arnold, T. Recent novel writing. Macmillan's Mag Jan 1866.
Japp, A. H. Children and children's books. Contemporary Rev May 1869.
Mozley, A. On fiction as an educator. Blackwood's Mag Oct 1870.
Pollock, J. Novels of their times, I. Macmillan's Mag Aug–Sept 1872.
Brandes, G. Hovedstrømninger i det 19 aarhundredes litteratur. Copenhagen 1875; tr 6 vols 1901–2.
Shard, A. I. Recent Scotch novels. Edinburgh Rev 143 1876.
— The new Scottish novelists. Edinburgh Rev 184 1826.
Watt, J. C. Great novelists: Scott, Thackeray, Dickens, Lytton. Edinburgh 1880.
Lanier, W. S. The English novel. New York 1883.
Besant, W. The art of fiction. 1884. Reply by James, below.
Hildebrand, K. About old and new novels. Contemporary Rev March 1884.
Morris, M. W. Some thoughts about novels. Macmillan's Mag March 1887.
— Candour in English fiction. Macmillan's Mag Feb 1890.
James, H. The art of fiction. In his Partial portraits, 1888; rptd in his House of fiction, ed L. Edel 1957.
— The new novel. In his Notes on novelists, 1914; rptd in James and H. G. Wells, ed L. Edel and G. N. Ray 1958.
Hitchman, F. Penny fiction. Quart Rev 171 1890.
Howells, W. D. Criticism and fiction. Boston 1891.
MacColl, M. Morality in fiction. Contemporary Rev Aug 1891.
Saintsbury, G. Names in fiction. Macmillan's Mag Dec 1888.
— The present state of the English novel. In his Miscellaneous essays, 1892.
— The historical novel. Macmillan's Mag Aug–Oct 1894; rptd in his Essays, 1895.
— A history of nineteenth-century literature. 1896.
— Novels of university life. Macmillan's Mag March 1898.
— The English novel. 1913.

Wedgwood, F. J. Fiction and faith. Contemporary Rev Aug 1892.
Crawford, F. M. The novel. 1893.
Gosse, E. Questions at issue. 1893. Includes The tyranny of the novel, The limits of realism in fiction.
Edwards, A. A. B. The art of the novelist. Contemporary Rev Aug 1894.
Minto, W. The literature of the Georgian era. 1894. Includes novelists from Mrs Radcliffe to Bulwer-Lytton.
On the art of writing fiction. [1894]. Essays by Baring-Gould, 'Lance Falconer', L. T. Meade et al.
My first book. Ed J. K. Jerome 1894. Essays by Besant, Payn, Russell, Allen, Hall Caine, Ballantyne, Kipling, Stevenson, Marie Corelli and other novelists.
Bridges, R. Novels that everybody read. In his Suppressed chapters and other bookishness, New York 1895.
Harrison, F. Studies in early Victorian literature. 1895. On Disraeli, Thackeray, Dickens, C. Brontë, C. Kingsley, Trollope, George Eliot.
Lilly, W. S. Four English humourists of the nineteenth century. 1895. On Dickens, Thackeray, George Eliot, Carlyle.
Noble, J. A. The fiction of sexuality. Contemporary Rev April 1895.
Douglas, G. The Blackwood group. 1897.
Gregg, H. C. The Indian Mutiny in fiction. Blackwood's Mag May 1897.
— Early Victorian fiction.
— The medical woman in fiction. Blackwood's Mag July 1898.
Murray, D. C. My contemporaries in fiction. 1897. Dickens to George Moore.
Traill, H. D. The new fiction. 1897. Rptd essays, mainly on 19th-century fiction.
Women novelists of Queen Victoria's reign. 1897. Appreciation by A. Sergeant, C. M. Yonge et al.
Scudder, V. D. Social ideals in English letters. New York 1898.
Cross, W. L. The development of the English novel. New York 1899.
Lyall, A. C. The Anglo-Indian novelist. Edinburgh Rev 190 1899; rptd in his Asiatic studies, 1907.
— Novels of adventure and manners. Edinburgh Rev 192 1900.
Oliphant, J. Victorian novelists. 1899.
Gwynn, S. L. Some recent novels of manners. Edinburgh Rev 192 1900.
Beers, H. A. A history of English romanticism in the nineteenth century. New York 1901.
Brownell, W. C. Victorian prose masters. New York 1901.
Machen, A. Hieroglyphics. 1902.
Möbius, H. The Gothic romance. Leipzig 1902.
— Die englischen Rosenkreuzerromane und ihre Vorlaüfer, während des 18 und 19 Jahrhunderts. Hamburg 1911.
Cazamian, L. Le roman social en Angleterre 1830–50. Paris 1904. On Dickens, Disraeli, Mrs Gaskell, Charles Kingsley.
— L'influence de la science 1860–90. Strasbourg 1923.
— L'anti-intellectualisme et l'esthéticisme 1880–1900. Paris 1935.
— Les doctrines d'action et l'aventure 1880–1914. Paris 1955.
Courtney, W. L. The feminine note in fiction. 1904.
Dawson, W. J. Makers of English fiction. 1905.
Stevenson, R. L. Essays in the art of writing. 1905.
'Melville, Lewis' (L. S. Benjamin). Victorian novelists. 1906.
Baker, E. A. History in fiction. 2 vols 1907.
— The history of the English novel. 9 vols 1924–38 (vols 5–9).
Chandler, F. W. The literature of roguery. 2 vols Boston 1907.

Courtney, W. P. The secrets of our national literature. 1908. Anon and pseudonymous fiction.
Jackson, H. Great English novelists. [1908].
— The eighteen-nineties: a review of art and ideas at the close of the nineteenth century. 1913.
Canby, H. S. The short story in English. New York 1909.
Zeidler, K. J. Beckford, Hope und Morier als Vertreter des orientalischen Romans. Leipzig 1909.
Dibelius, W. Englische Romankunst. 2 vols Berlin 1910.
Phelps, W. L. Essays on modern novelists. New York 1910.
— The advance of the English novel. New York 1916.
Williams, H. Two centuries of the English novel. 1911.
— Modern English writers. 1918, 1925 (rev).
Johnson, R. B. Famous reviews. 1914.
— Women novelists. 1918.
— Novelists on novels. 1928.
Gregory, A. The French revolution and the English novel. New York 1915.
Waugh, A. Fiction in the nineteenth century. In his Reticence in literature and other papers, 1915.
— Tradition and change. 1919.
Hearn, L. Interpretations of literature. 2 vols 1916. 2 chs in vol 1 on English fiction in the 19th century.
Scarborough, D. The supernatural in modern English fiction. New York 1917.
Whiteford, R. N. Motives in English fiction. 1918.
Phillips, W. C. Dickens, Reade and Collins—sensation novelists: a study in the conditions and theories of novel writing in Victorian England. New York 1919.
Russell, F. T. Satire in the Victorian novel. New York 1920.
Birkhead, E. The tale of terror: a study of the Gothic romance. 1921.
Chevalley, A. Le roman anglais de notre temps. Oxford 1921.
Ditchfield, P. H. The parson in literature. Trans Royal Soc of Lit 1 1921.
Lubbock, P. The craft of fiction. 1921.
Villard, L. La femme anglaise au dix-neuvième siècle et son évolution d'après le roman anglais contemporain. Paris 1921.
Oster, E. Das Verhältnis von Mutter und Kind im englischen Roman von 1700–1860. Bonn 1923.
Gutermuth, E. Das Kind im englischen Roman von Richardson bis Dickens. Giessener Beiträge 2 1924.
Killen, A. M. Le roman terrifiant ou roman noir. Paris 1924.
Speare, M. E. The political novel. New York 1924.
Priestley, J. B. The English comic characters. 1925.
— The English novel. 1927.
Weygandt, C. A century of the English novel. New York 1925.
Burdett, O. The Beardsley period: an essay in perspective. 1925.
Ellis, S. M. Mainly Victorian. [1925]. Short essays on minor Victorian novelists.
— Wilkie Collins, Le Fanu and others. 1931.
Frierson, W. C. L'influence du naturalisme français sur les romanciers anglais de 1885 à 1900. Paris [1925].
— The English controversy over realism in fiction 1885–95. PMLA 43 1928.
— The English novel in transition 1885–1940. Norman Oklahoma 1942.
Quiller-Couch, A. T. Dickens and other Victorians. Cambridge 1925. On Dickens, Thackeray, Disraeli, Mrs Gaskell, Trollope.
Walpole, H. The English novel. 1925.
Wharton, E. The writing of fiction. 1925.
Drew, E. The modern novel. 1926.
Jansonius, H. Some aspects of business life in early Victorian fiction. Amsterdam 1926.
Williams, O. Some great English novels. 1926.

de Vooys, S. The psychological element in the English sociological novel of the 19th century. Amsterdam 1927.
Forster, E. M. Aspects of the novel. 1927 (Clark lectures).
Myers, W. L. The later realism: a study of characterization in the British novel. Chicago 1927.
Prothero, R. E. The light reading of our ancestors: chapters on the growth of the English novel [to Scott]. 1927.
Railo, E. The haunted castle: a study of the elements of English romanticism. 1927.
Wortham, H. E. 'The constant nymph' and the musical novel. Nineteenth Century Feb 1927.
Brauchli, J. Der englischen Schauerroman um 1800. Weida 1928.
Collins, A. S. The profession of letters 1780–1832. 1928.
Heidler, J. B. The history from 1700 of English criticism of prose fiction. Urbana 1928.
Muir, E. The structure of the novel. 1928.
Taylor, H. W. Some 19th-century critics of realism. Texas Univ Bull 8 July 1928.
Wild, F. Die englische Literatur der Gegenwart seit 1870: Drama und Roman. Wiesbaden 1928.
de la Mare, W. Some women novelists of the seventies. In The eighteen-seventies, ed H. G. Barker 1929 (Royal Soc of Lit).
Devonshire, M. G. The English novel in France 1830–70. 1929.
Proper, C. B. A. Social elements in English prose fiction between 1700 and 1832. Amsterdam 1929.
Rotter, A. Der Arbeiterroman in England seit 1880. Reichenburg 1929.
Somervell, D. C. English thought in the 19th century. 1929. Discusses 19th-century novelists.
Cruse, A. The Englishman and his books in the early 19th century. 1930.
— The Victorians and their books. 1935.
— After the Victorians. 1938.
Ford, F. M. The English novel. 1930.
Howe, S. Wilhelm Meister and his English kinsmen. New York 1930.
— Novels of Empire. New York 1950.
Reid, F. Minor fiction in the eighties. In The eighteen-eighties, ed W. de la Mare 1930 (Royal Soc of Lit).
Gibson, B. H. History from 1800–32 of English criticism of prose fiction. Urbana 1931.
Rogers, W. H. Portraits of romantic poets in contemporary minor fiction. Western Research Univ Bull 34 1931.
— The reaction against melodramatic sentimentality in the English novel 1796–1830. PMLA 49 1934.
Sadleir, M. In his Bulwer: a panaroma, 1931.
— Things past. 1944. Essays on the Gothic novel, George Eliot, Trollope, Rhoda Broughton.
Collins, N. Facts of fiction. 1932.
Darton, F. J. H. Children's books in England. Cambridge 1932, 1958 (rev).
Leavis, Q. D. Fiction and the reading public. 1932.
Baker, J. E. The novel and the Oxford movement. Princeton 1932.
Lovett, R. M. and H. S. Hughes. The history of the novel in England. Boston 1932.
Tompkins, J. M. S. The popular novel in England 1770–1800. 1932.
Watt, W. W. Shilling shockers of the Gothic school: a study of chapbook Gothic romances. Cambridge Mass 1932.
The great Victorians. Ed H. J. and H. Massingham 1932.
Edgar, P. The art of the novel. New York 1933.
Singer, G. F. The epistolary novel. Philadelphia 1933.
Cecil, D. Early Victorian novelists. 1934, 1964 (rev).
— The early Victorian novelists as they look to the reader. Eng Literary & Educational Rev 9 1939.
Elwin, M. Victorian wallflowers. 1934. 'Christopher North' to 'Ouida'.
— Old gods falling. 1939. On Moore, Stevenson, Lang, Haggard et al.

Smith, W. H. Architecture in English fiction. New Haven 1934.
Neuschaffer, W. Dostojewskijs Einfluss auf den englischen Roman. Heidelberg 1935.
Crewe, Marquess of. Novels not by novelists. Essays by Divers Hands 15 1936.
Ernst, G. Die Rolle des Geldes im englischen Roman des neunzehnten Jahrhunderts. Villingen 1936.
Rosa, M. W. The silver-fork school: novels of fashion preceding Vanity Fair. New York 1936.
Shepperson, A. B. The novel in motley: a history of the burlesque novel in English. Cambridge Mass 1936.
Verschoyle, D. (ed). The English novelists. 1936.
Delafield, E. M. Ladies and gentlemen in Victorian fiction. 1937.
König, G. Der viktorianische Schulroman. Berlin 1937.
Lukács, G. Der historische Roman. Berlin 1937; tr 1962.
Muller, H. J. Modern fiction: a study of values. New York 1937.
Stevenson, L. The novelist as fortune hunter. Virginia Quart Rev 13 1937.
— The second birth of the English novel. UTQ 14 1945.
— The intellectual novel in the nineteenth century. Personalist 31 1950.
— Darwin and the novel. Nineteenth-Century Fiction 15 1961.
— The modern values of Victorian fiction. College Lang Assoc Jnl 4 1960.
— The English novel: a panorama. 1961.
— (ed). Victorian fiction: a guide to research. Cambridge Mass 1964.
Utter, R. P. and G. B. Needham. Pamela's daughters. New York 1937.
Wright, W. F. Sensibility in English prose fiction 1760–1814. Urbana 1937.
Types of popular fiction 1837–1937. TLS 1 May 1937.
Brown, W. C. Prose fiction and English interest in the Near East 1775–1925. PMLA 53 1938.
Summers, M. The Gothic quest. 1938.
Swinnerton, F. Variations of form in the novel. E & S 33 1938.
Anson, H. The Church in 19th-century fiction. Listener 4–11, 25 May 1939.
Johnson, D. D. Fear of death in Victorian fiction. West Virginia Bull of Philology 3 1939.
— 'Without benefit of clergy' in Victorian fiction. Ibid 4 1943.
Daiches, D. The novel and the modern world. 1940, 1960 (rev).
Gallaway, W. F. The conservative attitude toward fiction 1770–1830. PMLA 54 1940.
Henkin, L. Darwinism in the English novel 1860–1910. New York 1940.
Marriott, J. English history in English fiction. 1940.
Pritchett, V. S. Zola and the English novel. New Statesman 22 Feb 1941.
— Politics in Victorian novels. New Statesman 7 July 1945.
— The living novel. 1946. On Scott, Disraeli, Dickens, George Eliot, Butler, Conrad.
— Books in general. 1953. On Henry James, Collins, Dickens, Meredith, Gissing, 'Ouida'.
— The working novelist. 1965. On Conrad, Maria Edgeworth, Kipling, Ada Leverson, Trollope, Edith Wharton et al.
Wilson, E. The wound and the bow. Boston 1941. On Dickens, Kipling.
Bentley, P. The English regional novel. 1942.
Gerould, G. H. The patterns of English and American fiction. Boston 1942.
Haycroft, H. Murder for pleasure: the life and times of the detective story. 1942.
Maly-Schatter, F. The puritan element in Victorian fiction. Zürich 1942.

Mayo, R. D. The Gothic short story in the magazines. MLR 37 1942.
— How long was Gothic fiction in vogue? MLN 58 1943.
— Gothic romance in the magazines. PMLA 65 1950.
Taylor, J. T. Early opposition to the English novel: the popular reaction from 1760 to 1830. New York 1943.
Wagenknecht, E. Cavalcade of the English novel. New York 1943, 1954 (rev).
Wells, J. M. The artist in the English novel 1850–1919. West Virginia Bull of Philology 4 1943.
Bowen, E. Post-Victorian. Cornhill Mag 161 1944.
Eaker, J. G. Emergent modernism in late Victorian fiction. South Atlantic Quart 44 1945.
Fox, R. The novel and the people. New York 1945.
Hinkley, L. L. Ladies of literature. New York 1946.
McCullough, B. Representative English novelists. New York 1946.
Stebbins, L. P. A Victorian album: some lady novelists of the period. New York 1946.
The Trollopian. Ed B. A. Booth, Los Angeles 1946–. Title changed in 1949 to Nineteenth-Century Fiction.
Bailey, J. O. Pilgrims through space and time. New York 1947. On scientific and Utopian fiction.
Gooch, G. P. Historical novels. Essays by Divers Hands 23 1947.
MacCarthy, B. A. The later women novelists 1744–1818. Cork 1947.
Leavis, F. R. The great tradition. 1948. On George Eliot, Henry James, Conrad, Dickens.
Parkinson, C. N. Portsmouth Point: the British navy in fiction. Liverpool 1948.
Simon, I. Formes du roman anglais de Dickens à Joyce. Liège 1949.
Booth, B. A. Form and technique in the novel. In The reinterpretation of Victorian literature, ed J. Baker, Princeton 1950.
Brown, E. K. Rhythm in the novel. Toronto 1950.
Drummond, A. L. The Churches in English fiction. Leicester 1950.
Frye, N. The four forms of fiction. Hudson Rev 2 1950.
McHugh, V. A primer of the novel. New York 1950.
Phelps, G. Russian realism and English fiction. Cambridge Jnl Feb 1950.
— The Russian novel in English fiction. 1956.
Church, R. The growth of the English novel. 1951.
Davis, R. G. The sense of the real in English fiction. Comparative Lit 3 1951.
Troughton, M. Elections in English fiction. Contemporary Rev Nov 1951.
Kettle, A. Introduction to the English novel. 2 vols 1951–3.
— The early Victorian social-problem novel. In From Dickens to Hardy, ed B. Ford, 1958 (Pelican).
Neill, S. D. A short history of the English novel. 1951.
Mendilow, A. A. Time and the novel. 1951.
Praz, M. La crisi dell' eroe nel romanzo vittoriano. Florence 1952; tr 1956.
Schubel, F. Die 'fashionable novels'. Upsala 1952.
Watt, I. Realism and the novel. EC 2 1952.
Penzoldt, P. The supernatural in fiction. 1953. British short stories only.
Van Ghent, D. The English novel: form and function. New York 1953.
Allen, W. The English novel; a short critical history. 1954.
Leclaire, L. Le roman régionaliste dans les Iles Britanniques 1800–1950. Paris 1954.
Tillotson, K. Novels of the eighteen-forties. Oxford 1954.
— The tale and the teller. In her Mid-Victorian studies, 1965.
Burns, W. The genuine and the counterfeit: a study in Victorian and modern fiction. College Eng Dec 1956. Reply by D. T. Torchiana, Dec 1958.
'O'Connor, Frank' (M. F. O'Donovan). The mirror in the roadway. 1956.
Thomson, P. The Victorian heroine. 1956.
Dalziel, M. Popular fiction a hundred years ago. 1957.
Proctor, M. R. The English university novel. Berkeley 1957.
Taylor, W. A. Historical fiction. Cambridge 1957. Introd by A. Duggen.
Altick, R. D. The English common reader. Chicago 1957.
Varma, D. P. The Gothic flame. 1957.
Stevenson, W. B. Detective fiction. Cambridge 1958.
Tillyard, E. M. W. The epic strain in the English novel. 1958.
From Jane Austen to Joseph Conrad. Ed R. C. Rathburn and M. Steinmann, Minneapolis 1958.
Allott, M. (ed). Novelists on the novel. 1959.
Brightfield, M. F. America and the Americans 1840–60 as depicted in English novels of the period. Amer Lit 31 1959.
— The medical profession in early Victorian England as depicted in the novels of the period 1840–70. Bull of History of Medicine 35 1961.
— The coming of the railroad to early Victorian England as viewed by novels of the period 1840–70. Technology & Culture 3 1962.
Flanagan, T. The Irish novelists 1800–50. New York 1959.
Martin, H. C. Style in prose fiction. New York 1959.
Stang, R. The theory of the novel in England 1850–70. New York 1959.
Boggs, W. A. Looking backward at the Utopian novel 1888–1900. BNYPL June 1960.
Lockhead, M. Clio junior: historical novels for children. Quart Rev 299 1961.
Bland, D. S. Endangering the reader's neck: background description in the novel. Criticism 3 1961.
Blunden, E. On Regency fiction: a fragment. E & S new ser 14 1961.
Maison, M. Search your soul, Eustace; a survey of the religious novel in the Victorian age. 1961.
Rosenberg, E. From Shylock to Svengali: Jewish criminal and paragon in the English novel 1795–1895. Stanford 1961.
Tomlinson, T. B. Literature and history: the novel. Melbourne Critical Rev 4 1961.
Buckley, J. H. The fourth dimension of Victorianism. Victorian Newsletter no 21 1962.
Bicarnic, S. Writing for the magazines. Studia Romanica et Anglica 13–14 1962. On novelists in Cornhill Mag 1860–8.
Shain, C. E. The English novelists in the American Civil War. Amer Quart 14 1962.
Tanner, T. Mountains and depths: an approach to 19th-century dualism. REL 3 1962.
Harris, W. V. Identifying the decadent fiction of the eighteen-nineties. Eng Fiction in Transition 5 1962.
Jelly, O. Fiction and illness. REL 3 1962.
Johnson, W. S. Victorian self-consciousness. Victorian Newsletter no 21 1962.
Bostrom, I. The novel and Catholic emancipation. Stud in Romanticism 2 1963.
Hardin, E. F. The American girl in British fiction. HLQ 26 1963.
Hollingsworth, K. The Newgate novel 1830–47. Detroit 1963. On Bulwer, Ainsworth, Dickens, Thackeray.
Hulin, J. P. Exotisme et littérature sociale au début de l'ère Victorienne. Etudes Anglaises 16 1963.
James, L. Fiction for the working man 1830–50. 1963.
Blanke, G. H. Aristokratie und Gentleman im englischen und amerikanischen Roman des 19 und 20 Jahrhunderts. Germanische-romanische Monatsschrift 7 1963.
Montgomery, M. Fiction's use of history. Georgia Rev 17 1963.
Smith, D. J. Music in the Victorian novel. Kenyon Rev 25 1963.
Hobsbaum, P. University life in English fiction. Twentieth Century 173 1964.

Freeman, W. Dictionary of fictional characters. 1965.
Gillie, C. Character in English literature. 1965.
Graham, K. English criticism of the novel 1865–1900. Oxford 1965.
Hardy, B. The appropriate form: an essay on the novel. 1965.
Harvey, W. J. Character and the novel. 1965.
Karl, F. R. An age of fiction: the nineteenth-century British novel. New York 1965.
Schnieder, R. M. Loss and gain?: the theme of conversion in later Victorian fiction. Victorian Stud 9 1965.
Schneewind, J. B. Moral problems and moral philosophy in the Victorian period. Victorian Stud 9 1965. On Charlotte Yonge, Mrs Gaskell, Hale White, George Eliot.
Seymour Smith, M. A cupful of tears: sixteen Victorian novelettes. 1965.
Tillotson, G. and K. Mid-Victorian studies. 1965. On Charlotte Yonge, Trollope, George Eliot et al.
Carrier, E. J. Fiction in public libraries 1876–1900. New York 1965.
Donovan, R. A. The shaping vision: imagination in the English novel from Defoe to Dickens. New York 1966.
Griest, G. L. A Victorian Leviathan: Mudie's Select Library. Nineteenth-Century Fiction 20 1966.
Howard, D. et al. Tradition and tolerance in nineteenth-century fiction: critical essays on some English and American novels. 1966.
Lodge, D. Language of fiction: essays in criticism and verbal analysis of the English novel. 1966. On key words in Jane Eyre, Hard times, Tess of the d'Urbervilles.
Madden, W. A. The search for forgiveness in some nineteenth-century English novels. Comparative Lit Stud 3 1966. On Heart of Midlothian, Vanity Fair, Wuthering Heights, Middlemarch, Tess of the d'Urbervilles, Lord Jim.
Marcus, S. The other Victorians: a study of sexuality and pornography in mid-nineteenth-century England. New York 1966.
Miller, J. H. Some implications of form in Victorian fiction. Comparative Lit Stud 3 1966.
Waller, J. O. A composite Anglo-Catholic concept of the novel 1841–68. BNYPL June 1966.
Craig, D. Fiction and the rising industrial class. EC 7 1967.

M. A.

II. THE EARLY NINETEENTH-CENTURY NOVEL

MARIA EDGEWORTH
1767–1849

Bibliographies

Slade, B. C. Maria Edgeworth 1767–1849: a bibliographical tribute. 1937.

Collections

[Works]. 13 vols Boston etc 1822–5, 20 vols in 10 New York 1835–6 (Harper's Stenotype Lib).
Tales and miscellaneous pieces. 14 vols 1825.
Tales and novels. 18 vols 1832–3, 1848, 1857, 10 vols 1893, 12 vols 1893.
Classic tales (a selection), with a biographical sketch by G. A. Oliver. Boston 1883.
Tales. Ed A. Dobson 1903. Children's stories.
Tales that never die. Ed C. Welsh, with introd by C. E. Norton, New York 1908.
Selections from the works. Ed G. Griffin, with introd by M. C. Seton [1918].

§1

Almost all new London edns (including collected edns) pbd in her lifetime have considerable revisions and corrections; see especially Belinda, Patronage, *below. Only complete works are listed here; numerous edns of single stories, as well as selections, have been omitted. With the exception of* Harrington and Ormond, *French trns of part or all of every book up to* 1821 *were first pbd in the periodical* Bibliothèque Britannique (*from* 1816, Bibliothèque Universelle), Geneva.

Adelaide and Theodore. Dublin 1783. Tr from Mme de Genlis, Adèle et Théodore. Only 1 vol ptd, recalled before pbn; probably anon. No known copy.
Letters for literary ladies, to which is added An essay on the noble science of self-justification. 1795 (anon), 1799 (signed), 1805, Georgetown 1810, London 1814.
The parent's assistant: or stories for children. 3 vols 1795 (anon; no known copy; contains The little dog Trusty, The orange man, Tarlton, Lazy Lawrence, The false key, The purple jar, The bracelets, Mademoiselle Panache, The birthday present, Old Poz, The mimic), 1796 (adds Barring out), 6 vols 1800 (signed; adds 8 new stories and omits 3 transferred to Early lessons), illustr 1800, Cork 1800 (vol 1 of London edn only), Drogheda 1802 (selected), London 1804, 3 vols Georgetown 1809, Boston [181?], 6 vols 1813, 3 vols Boston 1813, Boston, Philadelphia and New York [1814], 6 vols 1817, 2 vols New York 1820, 6 vols 1822, 1824, 6 vols Paris 1827, 3 vols Dublin 1829, London 1831, 3 vols Paris 1836, London 1848; ed A. T. Ritchie 1897. One or more stories often rptd and combined with stories from her other books in England and USA; tr French, nd (before 1817); one or more stories often rptd and combined with stories from her other books in France and Germany; tr Irish (Forgive and forget, with Rosanna; *see* Popular Tales, below), 1833 (Ulster Gaelic Soc).
Practical education. 2 vols 1798, 3 vols 1801, 2 vols New York 1801, London 1808, 1811 (as Essays on practical education), 1815, Providence and Boston 1815, Boston 1823, New York 1835; tr French, 1800; tr German, 1803. With her father R. L. Edgeworth.
Castle Rackrent, an Hibernian tale: taken from facts, and from the manners of the Irish squires, before the year 1782. 1800, 1800, Dublin 1800 (all anon), London 1801 (signed), Dublin 1802 (3rd edn), Newbern NC [*c.* 1802] (no known copy), London 1804, 1810, Boston 1814, London 1815, Paris 1841; ed Henry Morley 1886 (Morley's Universal Lib); ed A. T. Ritchie 1895; ed B. Mathews 1910 (EL) (all 3 with Absentee, below); ed A. M. Jeffares, Edinburgh 1953; ed G. Watson, Oxford 1964; tr German, 1802.
[Early lessons]. Harry and Lucy, part i: being the first part of Early lessons, by the author of the Parent's assistant. 1801 (by R. L. Edgeworth and Mrs Honora Edgeworth; substantially a reprint of Practical education: or the history of Harry and Lucy, vol 2 (anon), ptd but never (?) pbd 1780); pt ii, 1801 (by R. L. Edgeworth); Rosamond, pt i, 1801 (containing The purple jar from Parent's assistant and 2 other stories); pt ii, 1801 (3 stories); pt iii, 1801 (The rabbit); Frank,

pts i–iv, 1801; The little dog Trusty, The orange man, and The cherry orchard: being the tenth part of Early lessons [first 2 stories from Parent's assistant], 1801–2 (2 issues); [complete work] 10 vols 1803 (no known copies of pts i, ii, iv–vi), 7 vols Philadelphia 1804–8, 10 vols 1809, 2 vols 1813, 6? vols Boston 1813, 2 vols 1815, 17 London edns to 1848, 3 vols Paris 1836; ed L. Valentine 1875; several American edns of separate sections of work; tr German, 1801; French, 1803; Italian, 1830; Dutch, 1810 (Rosamond).

Moral tales for young people (including Mademoiselle Panache transferred from Parent's assistant). 5 vols 1801, 3 vols 1802, 1806, 1809 (5th edn), Philadelphia 1810, Georgetown 1811, London 1813, 1817, New York 1818, 1819, London 1821, 2 vols 1826, Paris 1827, 1830, 3 vols 1833, Paris 1834, 1839, 1 vol 1846, Philadelphia 1846; ed L. Valentine 1874; tr French, 1804 (one story); German, nd. Tales often rptd singly and in selections, sometimes combined with stories from Parent's assistant, both in France and USA.

Belinda. 3 vols 1801, 2 vols Dublin 1801, 3 vols 1802, 2 vols Dublin 1802; ed A. L. Barbauld 1810 (Br Novelist ser) (with Modern Griselda, below; major alterations in latter part of story), 3 vols 1811, 2 vols Boston and New York 1814, 1820 (Br Novelist ser) (with Modern Griselda), Paris 1842; ed A. T. Ritchie 1896; tr French, 1802; German, 1803.

The mental thermometer. 1801 (Juvenile Lib, vol 2) (signed), 1815 (Irish Farmers' Jnl 15–22 July) (anon), 1825 (in Friendship's offering) (signed).

Essay on Irish bulls. 1802, 1803, Philadelphia 1803, New York 1803 (2 edns), London 1808. Essay on Irish humour; with R. L. Edgeworth.

Popular tales. 3 vols 1804, 2 vols Philadelphia 1804, 3 vols 1805, 1807, 1811, 2 vols Poughkeepsie 1813, 3 vols 1814, 1817, 2 vols Philadelphia 1819, Paris 1827, 3 vols Paris 1837; ed A. T. Ritchie 1895; tr French, 1813 (selection); German, 1807; Bengali (Encyclopaedia Bengalensis), 1849 (Lame Jervas). Tales often tr and rptd singly and in selections.

The modern Griselda: a tale. 1805, 1805; ed A. L. Barbauld 1810 (Br Novelist ser) (with Belinda), Georgetown 1810, London 1813, 1819, 1820 (Br Novelist ser) (with Belinda), Paris 1843; tr French, 1813.

Leonora. 2 vols 1806, New York 1806, London 1815; tr French, 1807; German, 1809.

Review of the Stranger in Ireland: or a tour in the southern and western parts of that country in the year 1805 by J. Carr esq. Edinburgh Rev 10 1807. Anon.

Essays on professional education, by R. L. (and Maria) Edgeworth. 1809, 1812.

Tales of fashionable life. Vols 1–3 (Ennui, Almeria, Madame de Fleury, The dun, Manoeuvring), 1809 (3 edns), 2 vols Georgetown 1809, Boston 1810, 3 vols 1813, 1 vol Paris 1813, 3 vols 1815, 1824; tr French, 1811. Vols 4–6 (Vivian, Emilie de Coulanges, The absentee), 1812 (3 edns), Boston 1812, London 1814, 1818, 6 vols in 3 Paris 1831; tr French, 1813; Swedish, 1837 (Vivian); numerous selections and edns of single tales.

Cottage dialogues among the Irish peasantry, by Mary Leadbeater, with notes and a preface by Maria Edgeworth. 1811, Philadelphia 1811. Irish and later edns omit Maria Edgeworth's preface and notes.

Patronage. 4 vols 1814, 1814, 3 vols Philadelphia 1814, 4 vols 1815 (in the 1825 collected edn, above, there were substantial alterations, including rewriting of the last vol), 2 vols Paris 1841 (with Comic dramas, below); tr French, 1816.

Continuation of Early lessons. 2 vols 1814, 1815, Boston 1815, London 1816, 10 edns to 1845. From 1821 pbd as vols 3–4 of Early lessons, above; tr French, 1839–44. Continuation of Harry and Lucy, Frank, Rosamond, the first with R. L. Edgeworth.

On French oaths. Irish Farmers' Jnl 1–8 July 1815 (anon), Amulet or Christian & Literary Remembrancer 1827 (signed).

Readings on poetry. 1816, 1816, New York 1816, Boston 1816. With R. L. Edgeworth; preface and last ch by Maria Edgeworth.

Comic dramas, in three acts. 1817, 1817, Philadelphia 1817, Boston 1817, 2 vols Paris 1841 (with Patronage). Love and law, The two guardians, The rose, the thistle and the shamrock; The two guardians omitted from collected edns of 1825, 1832–3.

Harrington: a tale; and Ormond: a tale. 3 vols 1817, 1817, New York 1817, Philadelphia 1817, 1 vol Paris 1841; ed A. T. Ritchie 1895; ed A. H. Johnson 1900 (Gresham's Lib of Standard Authors); tr French, 1817.

Review and analysis of Théorie des peines et des récompenses, par J. Bentham; redigée en françois d'après les manuscrits, par E. Dumont. Philanthropist 7 1819 (1st instalment), Inquirer 1 1822 (1st–2nd instalments) (anon; incomplete; complete ms in Bibliothèque Publique et Universitaire, Geneva).

Memoirs of Richard Lovell Edgeworth esq. 2 vols 1820, 1821, 1 vol 1844 (abridged); ed B. L. Tollemache 1896 (selection). Vol 1 by R. L. Edgeworth, vol 2 by Maria Edgeworth.

Rosamond: a sequel to Early lessons. 2 vols 1821, Philadelphia 1821, London 1822, 1830, 1 vol Paris 1836, 2 vols 1842, 1 vol Paris 1846; tr German, 1827; French, 1839–44; Italian, 1846.

Frank: a sequel to Frank in Early lessons. 3 vols 1822, 2 vols New York 1822, Cambridge Mass 1822, 3 vols 1825, 6 London edns to 1848, 1 vol Paris 1835, 1836, 1846; tr German, 1827; French, 1831; Italian, 1839.

Harry and Lucy concluded: being the last part of Early lessons. 4 vols 1825, Boston 1825, London 1827, 1 vol Paris 1836, 3 vols 1837, 1840, 1 vol Paris 1846; tr French, 1826.

Thoughts on bores. Janus (Edinburgh) 1826. Anon; first acknowledged in collected edn 1832–3, vol 17.

Little plays for children: The grinding organ; Dumb Andy; The dame school holiday. 1827, Philadelphia 1827, New York 1827. Vol 7 of Parent's assistant.

Garry Owen: or the snow-woman. 1829 (The Christmas box, ed C. Croker), 1832 (with Poor Bob the chimney sweeper, 1819?; no known copy?), Paris 1835 (Poor Bob), 1844 (Garry Owen), Edinburgh 1848 (Garry Owen), 1849 (Poor Bob) (both in Chamber's Lib for Young People); tr French, 1835.

Helen: a tale. 3 vols 1834, 1834, 2 vols Philadelphia 1834, 1 vol Paris 1834, 1837, London 1838 (Bentley's Standard Novelists), Paris 1846, 1846; ed A. T. Ritchie 1896; tr French, 1834; Swedish, 1836–7; Danish, 1870.

Orlandino. Edinburgh 1848 (Chambers's Lib for Young People), Boston 1848, Paris 1849, Edinburgh 1853 (with 3 stories by other hands).

The most unfortunate day of my life: being a hitherto unpublished story, together with the Purple jar and other stories. 1931.

Letters and Papers

Many unpbd letters are now in the National Library of Ireland, Dublin. Letters to Swiss correspondents are in the Bibliothèque Publique et Universitaire, Geneva.

Memoirs of Mrs Inchbald, including her familiar correspondence. Ed J. Boaden 2 vols 1833.

Davy, J. Fragmentary remains of Sir Humphry Davy. 1858.

A memoir of Maria Edgeworth, with a selection from her letters by the late Mrs [Frances] Edgeworth. 3 vols 1867 (priv ptd).

Constable, T. Archibald Constable and his literary correspondents. 3 vols Edinburgh 1873.

Le Breton, A. L. A memoir of Mrs Barbauld, including letters and notices of her family and friends. 1874.

Graves, R. P. Life of Sir W. R. Hamilton, including selections from his poems, correspondence and miscellaneous writings. 3 vols Dublin 1882–91.

Hare, A. J. C. The life and letters of Maria Edgeworth. 2 vols 1894.
Hill, C. Some unpublished letters of Maria Edgeworth. Hampstead Annual 1897.
Correspondence of Ricardo with Maria Edgeworth. Economic Jnl 17 1907.
Grey, R. Maria Edgeworth and Etienne Dumont. Dublin Rev 145 1909.
Butler, H. J. and H. E. The black book of Edgeworthstown and other Edgeworth memories 1585–1817. 1927.
— Sir Walter Scott and Maria Edgeworth: some unpublished letters. MLR 23 1928.
Partington, W. (ed). The private letter-books of Sir Walter Scott. 1930.
— Sir Walter's post-bag. 1932.
Chosen letters. Ed F. V. Barry 1931. Includes 8 unpbd letters.
Waller, R. D. Letters addressed to Mrs Gaskell by celebrated contemporaries. Bull John Rylands Lib 19 1935.
Romilly, S. H. Romilly-Edgeworth letters 1813–18. 1936.
— The lost letters of Maria Edgeworth. Quart Rev 268 1937.
Hone, J. The Moores of Moore Hall. 1939. Includes some of her letters to the Moore family.
Tour in Connemara, and the Martins of Ballinahinch. Ed H. E. Butler 1950.
Haüsermann, H. W. The Genevese background. 1952. First pbn of a number of her letters preserved in or near Geneva.
Butler, R. F. Maria Edgeworth and Sir Walter Scott: unpublished letters 1823. RES new ser 9 1958.
Donner, H. W. Echoes of Beddoesian rambles. Studia Neophilologica 33 1961. Includes some of her letters about Thomas Lovell Beddoes.
Colvin, C. Two unpublished mss by Maria Edgeworth. REL 8 1967.

§2

[Pictet, C.] Practical education. Bibliothèque Britannique 12 1799. Critical comments by translators following twelfth and final extract.
Castle Rackrent. Monthly Rev May 1800; Br Critic Nov 1800.
Belinda. Monthly Rev April 1802.
Pictet, M.-A. In his Voyage de trois mois en Angleterre, en Ecosse et en Irlande. Geneva 1802.
[Jeffrey, F.] Popular tales. Edinburgh Rev 4 1804.
— Leonora. Edinburgh Rev 8 1806.
— Tales of fashionable life, vols 1–3. Edinburgh Rev 14 1809.
— Tales of fashionable life, vols 4–6. Edinburgh Rev 20 1812.
— Harrington and Ormond. Edinburgh Rev 28 1817.
— Memoirs of Richard Lovell Edgeworth. Edinburgh Rev 34 1820.
[Stephen, H. J. and W. Gifford] Tales of fashionable life, vols 1–3. Quart Rev 2 1809.
[Croker, J. W.] Tales of fashionable life, vols 4–6. Quart Rev 7 1812.
— Memoirs of Richard Lovell Edgeworth. Quart Rev 23 1820.
Foster, J. Tales of fashionable life, vols 4–6. Eclectic Rev 8 1812.
[Smith, S.] Patronage. Edinburgh Rev 22 1814.
[Ward, J., later first Earl of Dudley]. Patronage. Quart Rev 10 1814.
Harrington and Ormond. Blackwood's Mag Aug–Sept 1817.
Memoirs of Richard Lovell Edgeworth. London Mag May 1820.
Miss Edgeworth's tales and novels. Fraser's Mag Nov 1832.
[Lockhart, J. G.] Helen. Quart Rev 51 1834.
—In his Memoirs of the life of Sir Walter Scott, 7 vols Edinburgh 1837–8, 10 vols Edinburgh 1839.
[Peabody, Rev. W. B. O.] Helen. North Amer Rev 39 1834.
Hall, Mrs S. C. Edgeworthstown: memories of Maria Edgeworth. Art Jnl 11 1849, 28 1866.
Hayward, A. Miss Edgeworth. Edinburgh Rev 126 1867; rptd in his Biographical and critical essays, 5 vols 1858–74.
Hillard, G. S. In his Life, letters and journals of George Ticknor, 1876.
Oliver, G. A. A study of Maria Edgeworth, with notices of her father and friends. Boston 1882.
Ritchie, A. T. In her Book of sybils, 1883.
Zimmern, H. Maria Edgeworth. 1883.
Krans, H. S. In his Irish life in Irish fiction, New York 1903.
Lawless, E. Maria Edgeworth. 1904 (EML).
Ward, W. Moral fiction a hundred years ago. Dublin Rev 144 1909.
Hill, C. Maria Edgeworth and her circle in the days of Buonaparte and Bourbon. 1910.
Paterson, A. The Edgeworths: a study of later eighteenth century education. 1914.
Colum, P. Maria Edgeworth and Ivan Turgenev. Br Rev 11 1915.
Michael, E. F. Die irischen Romane von Maria Edgeworth. Dresden 1918.
Woolf, V. The lives of the obscure: the Taylors and the Edgeworths. In her Common reader, 1925.
Scott, W. Letters. Ed H. J. C. Grierson 12 vols 1932–7.
Baker, E. A. In his History of the English novel vol 6, 1935.
Gwynn, S. In his Irish literature and drama, 1936.
McHugh, R. J. Maria Edgeworth's Irish novels. Studies 27 1938.
Millhauser, M. Maria Edgeworth as a social novelist. N & Q 17 Sept 1938.
Palfrey, T. R. Maria Edgeworth and Louise Swanton Belloc. N & Q 25 March 1939.
Longford, C. Maria Edgeworth and her circle. Irish Writing 6 1948.
Armytage, W. H. G. Little woman. Queen's Quart 56 1949.
Humours and moralities. TLS 20 May 1949.
Clarke, I. C. Maria Edgeworth: her family and friends. 1950.
Newby, P. H. Maria Edgeworth. 1950.
Davie, D. A. Miss Edgeworth and Miss Austen: the Absentee. Irish Writing 29 1954.
— In his Heyday of Sir Walter Scott, 1961.
Flanagan, T. In his Irish novelists 1800–50, New York 1959.
Inglis-Jones, E. The great Maria. 1959.
Colvin, C. A visit to Abbotsford. REL 5 1964.
Newcomer, J. Maria Edgeworth the novelist: a bicentenary study. Fort Worth 1967.

M. S. B. and C. E. C.

SIR WALTER SCOTT
1771–1832

Almost all mss by or relating to Scott are now in public libraries. The Pierpont Morgan Library, New York, has the largest single collection of Scott's own works, including the Journal, Lady of the lake, Rokeby, Bridal of Triermain, Lord of the Isles, Guy Mannering, Antiquary, Old Mortality, Black dwarf, Ivanhoe, Monastery, Peveril of the Peak, Quentin Durward, St Ronan's Well, Woodstock, Anne of Geierstein, *the first ser of* Tales of a grandfather, *the* Life of Napoleon *and* Doom of Devorgoil. *The National Library of Scotland, Edinburgh, owns* Marmion, Heart of Midlothian, Redgauntlet *and minor works.* Harold the Dauntless *is in the Huntington Library. The BM has* Kenilworth *and* Tapestried chamber. Fortunes of Nigel *and* Count Robert of Paris *are in King's School, Canter-*

bury. Bride of Lammermoor, *and memoirs of* Goldsmith, Johnson *and part of* Sterne *are in the Signet Library, Edinburgh. The unpbd* Siege of Malta *is in the New York Public Library. Harvard has the* Life of Swift. *The largest collection of mss relating to Scott is in the National Library of Scotland. It contains the Abbotsford Collection acquired in 1931–2 and the Walpole Collection of about 6,000 letters to Scott purchased from Abbotsford by Sir Hugh Walpole in 1921 and bequeathed by him to the library. Scott's interleaved copy of the novels, with his ms corrections (used for the Magnum opus edn and by Messrs A. & C. Black for their rev texts) is now in private hands in the USA.*

Bibliographies

Anderson, J. P. In C. D. Yonge, Life of Scott, 1888.

Ball, M. In her Scott as a critic of literature, New York 1907.

Worthington, G. Bibliography of the Waverley novels. 1930. First edns only.

Ruff, W. A bibliography of the poetical works of Scott 1796–1832. Trans Edinburgh Bibl Soc 1 1938.

National Library of Scotland. Catalogue of manuscripts vol 1. Edinburgh 1938.

Corson, J. C. A bibliography of Scott: a classified and annotated list of books and articles relating to his life and works 1797–1940. Edinburgh 1943.

Dyson, G. The manuscripts and proof sheets of Scott's Waverley novels. Trans Edinburgh Bibl Soc 4 1960.

Collections

Poems

Works. 6 vols Edinburgh 1806–8. Lay, Marmion, Minstrelsy, Sir Tristrem.

Works. 8 vols Edinburgh 1812. Various edns of the Minstrelsy, Lay, Marmion, Sir Tristrem, Lady of the lake, Don Roderick and Ballads and lyrical pieces, with covering title-pages.

Poetical works. 12 vols Edinburgh 1820, 10 vols Edinburgh 1821, 8 vols Edinburgh 1822, 10 vols Edinburgh 1823, 10 vols Edinburgh 1825, 11 vols Edinburgh 1830. 1830 contains the dramas, new essays on ballad poetry and new introds to the Lay, Marmion, etc, and was issued in 8vo and 18mo, vol 11 being sold separately to complete the edns of 1821, 1823 and 1825.

Poetical works. [Ed by J. G. Lockhart] 12 vols Edinburgh 1833–4, often rptd in 12 and 1 vol edns; ed G. Gilfillan 3 vols Edinburgh 1857; ed F. T. Palgrave 1866 etc (Globe); ed W. M. Rossetti 1870; ed W. B. Scott 1883; ed W. Minto 2 vols Edinburgh 1887–8; ed J. Dennis 5 vols 1892 (Aldine); ed J. L. Robertson, Oxford, 1894 etc; ed A. Lang 1895 (Dryburgh).

Novels

The first collected edns of the novels were issued at Edinburgh in 3 formats between 1819 and 1833, in 41, 53 and 41 vols, as follows:

Novels and tales (Waverley–Montrose). 8vo 12 vols 1820 (for 1819), 12mo 16 vols 1821, new edn 1825 (for 1824), 18mo 12 vols 1823.

Historical romances (Ivanhoe–Kenilworth). 8vo 6 vols 1822; 12mo 8 vols 1822; 18mo 6 vols 1824.

Novels and romances (Pirate–Quentin Durward). 8vo 7 vols 1824 (for 1823), 12mo 9 vols 1824, 18mo 7 vols 1825 (for 1824).

Tales and romances (St Ronan's Well–Woodstock). 8vo 7 vols 1827 new edn 7 vols 1834, 12mo 9 vols 1827, 18mo 7 vols 1827.

Tales and romances (Chronicles of the Canongate; Tales of my landlord, fourth series). 8vo 7 vols 1833, 12mo 8 vols 1833, 18mo 6 vols 1833.

Introductions, and notes and illustrations. 8vo 2 vols 1833, 12mo 3 vols 1833, 18mo 3 vols 1833.

Waverley novels. 48 vols Edinburgh 1829–33 (author's last revision with notes, known as the 'Magnum opus' edn), 48 vols Edinburgh 1830–4. Edns followed at average rate of one every 2 years, the best known being: Fisher's edition, 48 vols 1836–9; Cabinet edition, 25 vols Edinburgh 1841–3; Abbotsford edition, 12 vols Edinburgh 1842–7; Library edition, 25 vols Edinburgh 1852–3; Centenary edition (text rev with notes by D. Laing), 25 vols Edinburgh 1870–1; Dryburgh edition (text again rev), 25 vols 1892–4; Border edition (unrev text but with notes by A. Lang), 48 vols Edinburgh 1892–4; Standard edition, 25 vols 1895–7; Victoria edition 25 vols 1897; Edinburgh Waverley, 48 vols Edinburgh 1901–3; Soho edition, 25 vols 1904; Fine Art Scott 25 vols (illustr) [1910]; Oxford Scott, 24 vols 1912, etc; New Crown edition, 25 vols 1932.

Selections

Tales from Scott. Ed E. Sullivan 1894; Scottish selections from the Waverley novels, ed J. K. Craigie, Oxford 1916; The week-end Scott, ed J. T. Christie 1931; The Waverley pageant, ed H. Walpole 1932; Short stories, ed D. Cecil, Oxford 1934 (WC); Selections from the prose, ed J. C. Trewin 1952; One crowded hour, ed J. Sutherland 1963.

§ 1

For single short poems (priv ptd) and contributions to miscellanies, song-books etc, see W. Ruff, Bibliography, *above.*

The chase, and William and Helen: two ballads from the German of Gottfried Augustus Bürger. Edinburgh 1796. A few of the original sheets reissued with new title-page, London 1807.

Goetz of Berlichingen, with the iron hand: a tragedy, translated from the German of Goethé. 1799 (a few copies having 'By William Scott'), Paris 1826.

The eve of Saint John: a Border ballad. Kelso 1800.

The lay of the last minstrel. 1805, 1805, 1806 (3 edns), 1807, 1808, 1808, 1809, 1810, 1811, 1812, 1816, 1823, Philadelphia 1806, Boston 1807, New York 1811, Baltimore 1812, Paris 1821; tr German, 1820; French, 1821; Polish, 1822; Russian, 1826; Dutch, 1840; Spanish, 1843.

Ballads and lyrical pieces. Edinburgh 1806, 1806, 1810, 1812, 1819, 1820, Boston 1807, New York 1811.

Marmion: a tale of Flodden Field. Edinburgh 1808 (4 edns), 1810, 1810, 1811, 1811, 1815, 1821, 1825, 1830, Baltimore 1812, Paris 1821; tr French, 1820; Danish, 1824; Russian, 1828; Italian, 1832.

The lady of the lake: a poem. Edinburgh 1810 (8 edns), 1811, 1814, 1816, 1819, 1825, Baltimore 1811, Paris 1821; tr French, 1813; German, 1819, 1819; Italian, 1821; Polish, 1822; Russian, 1827; Czech, 1828; Swedish, 1828; Spanish, 1830; Portuguese, 1842.

The vision of Don Roderick: a poem. Edinburgh 1811 (priv ptd), 1811, 1811, 1815, Boston 1811, Philadelphia 1811, Paris 1821; tr French, 1821; Spanish, 1829.

Rokeby: a poem. Edinburgh 1813 (5 edns), 1815, 1821, Baltimore 1813, Paris 1821; tr French, 1820; Spanish, 1829.

The bridal of Triermain: or the vale of St John, in three cantos. Edinburgh 1813 (3 edns), 1814, 1817, Philadelphia 1813, Paris 1821; tr French, 1821; Spanish, 1830. Anon.

Waverley: or 'tis sixty years since. 3 vols Edinburgh 1814 (4 edns), 1815, 1816, 1817, 1821, Boston 1815, New York 1815, 1819, 1822, Paris 1822; tr French, 1818; German, 1822; Hungarian, 1823; Swedish, 1824–6; Russian, 1827; Italian, 1830; Spanish, 1835; Portuguese, 1844; The first of the novels, all anon.

Guy Mannering: or the astrologer, by the author of Waverley. 3 vols Edinburgh 1815, 1815, 1817, 1820 (6th edn), Boston 1815, Paris 1822; tr French, 1816;

German, 1817; Danish, 1823; Russian, 1824; Dutch, 1824–5; Spanish, 1835; Portuguese, 1842–3.
The Lord of the Isles: a poem. Edinburgh 1815 (5 edns), Boston 1815, Philadelphia 1815, Paris 1821; tr French, 1821; German, 1822; Spanish, 1830; Portuguese, 1839; Italian, 1884.
The field of Waterloo: a poem. Edinburgh 1815 (3 edns), Boston 1815, New York 1815, Paris 1815, Philadelphia 1815, Lexington 1816; tr French, 1821; German, 1825.
The antiquary, by the author of Waverley. 3 vols Edinburgh 1816, 1816, 1818 (5th edn), 1821, New York 1816, Paris 1821, Berlin 1822; tr French, 1817; Dutch, 1825; Swedish, 1827; Polish, 1828; Spanish, 1831–2; Danish, 1856–7.
Tales of my landlord, collected and arranged by Jedediah Cleishbotham [The black dwarf; Old Mortality]. 4 vols Edinburgh 1816, 1817, 1817, 1818, 1819, 1819, New York 1817, Paris 1821; tr French, 1817; Russian, 1824; Spanish, 1826; Portuguese, 1838.
The black dwarf, tr Swedish, 1825.
Old Mortality, tr Dutch, 1824; German, 1824; Danish, 1834.
Harold the dauntless: a poem. Edinburgh 1817, New York 1817, Paris 1826; tr French, 1820. Anon.
Rob Roy, by the author of Waverley. 3 vols Edinburgh 1818 (for 1817), 1818 (3 edns), New York 1818, Philadelphia 1818, 1818, Paris 1822; tr French, 1818, 1818, 1818; German, 1819; Swedish, 1824–5; Spanish, 1828; Russian, 1829; Italian, 1830; Danish, 1856.
Tales of my landlord: second series [The Heart of Mid-Lothian]. 4 vols Edinburgh 1818 (4 edns), Philadelphia 1818, Paris 1821; tr French, 1818; Danish, 1822; Italian, 1824; Dutch, 1825; Russian, 1825; Spanish, 1831.
Tales of my landlord: third series [The bride of Lammermoor and A legend of Montrose]. 4 vols Edinburgh 1819 (3 edns), Philadelphia 1819, Paris 1821.
The bride of Lammermoor, tr French, 1819; Russian, 1824; Spanish, 1828; Portuguese, 1836.
A legend of Montrose, tr French, 1819; Italian, 1822; Spanish, 1827; Portuguese, 1837.
Ivanhoe: a romance, by the author of Waverley. 3 vols Edinburgh 1820 (for 1819), 1820, 1821, Philadelphia 1820, Paris 1821; tr French, 1820; German, 1820; Dutch, 1824; Spanish, 1825; Russian, 1826; Portuguese, 1838.
The monastery: a romance, by the author of Waverley. 3 vols Edinburgh 1820, 1820, Philadelphia 1820, Paris 1821; tr French, 1820; Russian, 1829; Spanish, 1840.
The abbot, by the author of Waverley. 3 vols Edinburgh 1820, Paris 1820, Philadelphia 1820; tr French, 1820; Spanish, 1845.
Kenilworth: a romance, by the author of Waverley. 3 vols Edinburgh 1821, 1821, Paris 1821, Philadelphia 1821, 1821; tr French, 1821 (3 edns); Italian, 1821; Spanish, 1831.
The pirate, by the author of Waverley. 3 vols Edinburgh 1822 (for 1821), 1822, Boston 1822, Paris 1822, Philadelphia 1822; tr French, 1822; Dutch, 1825; Spanish, 1830.
The fortunes of Nigel, by the author of Waverley. 3 vols Edinburgh 1822 (3 edns), New York 1822, Paris 1822, Philadelphia 1822; tr French, 1822; Swedish, 1827; Russian, 1829; Spanish, 1836.
Halidon Hill: a dramatic sketch. Edinburgh 1822, 1822, New York 1822, Paris 1822, Philadelphia 1822; tr French, 1822; German, 1823.
Peveril of the Peak, by the author of Waverley. 4 vols Edinburgh 1822 (for 1823), 1823, Paris 1823, Philadelphia 1823; tr French, 1823–4; Swedish, 1825–6; Russian, 1830; Spanish, 1836.
MacDuff's Cross: a drama. In A collection of poems, chiefly manuscript, ed Joanna Baillie 1823; tr German, 1824.

Quentin Durward, by the author of Waverley. 3 vols Edinburgh 1823, 1823, Paris 1823, Philadelphia 1823; tr French, 1823–4; Dutch, 1824; Russian, 1826; Spanish, 1827.
St Ronan's Well, by the author of Waverley. 3 vols Edinburgh 1824 (for 1823), 1824, Boston 1824, Paris 1824; tr French, 1824; Russian, 1828; Spanish, 1841.
Redgauntlet: a tale of the eighteenth century, by the author of Waverley. 3 vols Edinburgh 1824, Paris 1824, Philadelphia 1824; tr French, 1824; Spanish, 1833–4.
Tales of the Crusaders, by the author of Waverley [The betrothed; The talisman]. 4 vols Edinburgh 1825, Paris 1825, Philadelphia 1825; tr French, 1825; Italian, 1826.
The betrothed, tr Spanish, 1840.
The talisman, tr Spanish, 1825; German, 1826.
Woodstock: or the cavalier, by the author of Waverley. 3 vols Edinburgh 1826, New York 1826, Paris 1826, Philadelphia 1826; tr French, 1826; Russian, 1829; Spanish, 1831.
Chronicles of the Canongate [first series: Croftangry's introds; The Highland widow; The two drovers; The surgeon's daughter]. 2 vols Edinburgh 1827, 1828, Paris 1827, Philadelphia 1827; tr French, 1827; Dutch, 1828; Russian, 1830.
Chronicles of the Canongate, second series, by the author of Waverley [Croftangry's introd; The fair maid of Perth]. 3 vols Edinburgh 1828, 1828, Paris 1828, Philadelphia 1828, Zwickau 1828; tr French, 1828–9; Russian, 1829; Spanish, 1835.
My aunt Margaret's mirror, The tapestried chamber, Death of the laird's Jock, A scene at Abbotsford. Keepsake 1829.
My aunt Margaret's mirror, The tapestried chamber, tr French, 1829; Spanish, 1830.
Anne of Geierstein: or the maiden of the mist, by the author of Waverley. 3 vols Edinburgh 1829, New York 1829, Paris 1829, Philadelphia 1829; tr French, 1829; Spanish, 1831.
The house of Aspen; a tragedy. Keepsake 1830 Pbd separately, Paris 1830, tr in Le Keepsake français, Paris 1830.
The doom of Devorgoil: a melo-drama; Auchindrane: or the Ayrshire tragedy. Edinburgh 1830, New York 1830, Paris 1830.
Tales of my landlord, fourth series [Count Robert of Paris and Castle Dangerous]. 4 vols Edinburgh 1832 (for 1831), Paris 1831, 1831, New York 1832, Philadelphia 1832.
Count Robert, tr French, 1831; Spanish, 1834.
Castle Dangerous, tr French, 1831; Spanish, 1840; Portuguese, 1842.

Miscellaneous Prose Works

Miscellaneous prose works. 6 vols Edinburgh 1827.
Miscellaneous prose works. Ed J. G. Lockhart 28 vols Edinburgh 1834–6. Cited below as MPW.
Southey's Amadis de Gaul. Edinburgh Rev 3 1804. MPW 18.
Sibbald's Chronicle of Scotish poetry. Edinburgh Rev 3 1804. Not rptd.
Godwin's Life of Chaucer. Edinburgh Rev 3 1804. MPW 17.
Ellis's Specimens of early English poetry. Edinburgh Rev 4 1804. MPW 17.
Chatterton's Works by Southey and Cottle. Edinburgh Rev 4 1804. MPW 17.
Johnes's Translation of Froissart. Edinburgh Rev 5 1805. MPW 19.
Colonel Thornton's Sporting tour. Edinburgh Rev 5 1805. MPW 15.
Godwin's Fleetwood: a novel. Edinburgh Rev 6 1805. MPW 18.

The new practice of cookery. Edinburgh Rev 6 1805. MPW 19.
Report of the Highland Society upon Ossian. Edinburgh Rev 6 1805. Not rptd.
Todd's edition of Spenser. Edinburgh Rev 7 1806. MPW 17.
Ellis's Specimens of English romance; Ritson's Metrical romances. Edinburgh Rev 7 1806. MPW 17.
Beresford's Miseries of human life. Edinburgh Rev 9 1807. MPW 19.
Herbert's Miscellaneous poetry. Edinburgh Rev 9 1807. MPW 17.
Cromek's Reliques of Robert Burns. Quart Rev 1 1809. MPW 17.
Southey's Chronicle of the Cid. Quart Rev 1 1809. MPW 18.
Barrett's Life of Swift. Quart Rev 1 1809. Not rtpd.
Carr's Caledonian sketches. Quart Rev 1 1809. MPW 19
Campbell's Gertrude of Wyoming. Quart Rev 1 1809. MPW 17.
Cumberland's John of Lancaster. Quart Rev 1 1809. MPW 18.
Memoir of the life of Sir Ralph Sadler. In Clifford's edn of The state papers of Sir Ralph Sadler, 2 and 3 vols Edinburgh 1809. MPW 4.
Croker's The battle of Talavera. Quart Rev 2 1809. MPW 17.
Maturin's Fatal revenge: or the family of Montorio. Quart Rev 3 1810. MPW 18.
Evans's Old ballads and Aikin on song writing. Quart Rev 3 1810. MPW 17.
View of the changes in the administration of justice in Scotland. Edinburgh Annual Register 1808 1 1810. Not rptd.
Southey's Curse of Kehama. Quart Rev 5 1811. MPW 17.
Cursory remarks upon the French order of battle, particularly in the campaigns of Buonaparte. Edinburgh Annual Register 1809 2 1811. Not rptd.
The inferno of Altisidora. Edinburgh Annual Register 1809 1 1811. Not rptd.
Account of the poems of Patrick Carey. Edinburgh Annual Register 1810 3 1812. Not rptd.
Biographical memoir of John Leyden MD. Edinburgh Annual Register 1811 4 1813. MPW 4.
Abstract of the Eyrbiggia-saga. In Illustrations of northern antiquities, Edinburgh 1814. MPW 5.
Paul's letters to his kinsfolk. Edinburgh 1816 (3 edns), 1819, Philadelphia 1816; tr French, 1822; Swedish, 1826.
Jane Austen's Emma. Quart Rev 14 1816. Not rptd.
Culloden papers. Quart Rev 14 1816. MPW 20.
History of Europe, 1814. Edinburgh Annual Register 1814 7 1816. Not rptd.
Childe Harold, canto III and other poems. Quart Rev 16 1817. Not rptd.
Tales of my landlord. Quart Rev 16 1817. MPW 19.
History of Europe, 1815. Edinburgh Annual Register 1815 8 1817. Not rptd.
Introduction. In Border antiquities of England and Scotland [ed J. Greig] vol 2, 1817. MPW 7.
Alarming increase of depravity among animals. Blackwood's Mag Oct 1817. Not rptd.
Chivalry. In Encyclopaedia Britannica, suppl to 4th–6th edns, vol 3, pt 1, 1818. MPW 6.
Remarks on Frankenstein: or the modern Prometheus: a novel by Mrs Shelley. Blackwood's Mag Mar 1818. MPW 18.
Maturin's Women: or pour et contre. Edinburgh Rev 30 1818. MPW 18.
Douglas on the passage of rivers. Quart Rev 18 1818. Not rptd.
Kirkton's History of the Church of Scotland. Quart Rev 18 1818. MPW 19.
Hon Horace Walpole's letters to Mr Montagu. Quart Rev 19 1818. Not rptd.

Childe Harold—Canto IV. Quart Rev 19 1818. MPW 17.
Remarks on General Gourgaud's account of the campaign of 1815. Blackwood's Edinburgh Mag Nov 1818. Not rptd.
Drama. In Encyclopaedia Britannica, suppl to 4th–6th edns, vol 3, pt 2, 1819. MPW 6.
The late Duke of Buccleuch and Queensberry. Edinburgh Weekly Jnl 12 May 1819. MPW 4.
The late Lord Somerville. Edinburgh Weekly Jnl 27 Oct 1819. MPW 4.
Description of the regalia of Scotland. Edinburgh 1819.
The visionary. (Signed 'Somnambulus'). Edinburgh Weekly Jnl 1–15 Dec 1819. Rptd as The visionary, nos I–III, Edinburgh 1819.
King George III. Edinburgh Weekly Jnl 9 Feb 1820. MPW 4.
Account of the coronation of George IV. Edinburgh Weekly Jnl 25 July 1821. Rptd in Lockhart, Life of Scott.
Alexander Campbell. Edinburgh Weekly Jnl 19 May 1824. Not rptd.
Romance. In Encyclopaedia Britannica, suppl to 4th–6th edns, vol 6, pt 1, 1824. MPW 6.
Lord Byron. Edinburgh Weekly Jnl 1824. MPW 4.
Correspondence of Lady Suffolk. Quart Rev 30 1824. MPW 19.
Lives of the novelists. 2 vols Paris 1825. Pirated from Ballantyne's novelist's library. *See* Edited works, below.
Galt's The omen. Blackwood's Mag July 1826. MPW 18.
Provincial antiquities of Scotland. 2 vols Edinburgh 1826. Issued in 10 pts 1819–26. Rptd (not illustr) in MPW 7.
Pepys's Memoirs. Quart Rev 33 1826. MPW 20.
Life of John Philip Kemble. Quart Rev 34 1826. MPW 20.
The currency [signed 'Malachi Malagrowther']. Edinburgh Weekly Jnl 22 Feb, 1–8 March 1826. Rptd as A letter to the editor of the Edinburgh Weekly Jnl, from Malachi Malagrowther, on the proposed change of currency, Edinburgh 1826 (3 edns); A second letter etc Edinburgh 1826 (3 edns); A third letter etc, Edinburgh 1826 (3 edns). The first edn of the first letter entitled Thoughts on the proposed change of currency. MPW 21.
The Duke of York. Edinburgh Weekly Jnl 10 Jan 1827. MPW 4.
Works of John Home esq. Quart Rev 36 1827. MPW 19.
On the supernatural in fictitious composition: works of Hoffmann. Foreign Quart Rev 1 1827. MPW 18.
On planting waste lands. Quart Rev 36 1827. Review of Monteath's The forester's guide. MPW 21.
The life of Napoleon Buonaparte. 9 vols Edinburgh 1827, 1827, New York 1827, Paris 1827, Philadelphia 1827; tr French, 1827; German, 1827–8; Spanish, 1827; Italian, 1827–8; Danish, 1829; Russian, 1833.
Life of Napoleon. Edinburgh Weekly Jnl 19 Sept 1827. In reply to Gourgaud. Rptd in Lockhart, Life of Scott.
Tales of a grandfather: being stories taken from Scottish history. 3 vols Edinburgh 1828 (for 1827), 1828 (4 edns), 1829, 1829, Paris 1827; tr French, 1828.
Molière. Foreign Quart Rev 2 1828. MPW 17.
Religious discourses by a layman. 1828, 1828, New York 1828, Paris 1828, Philadelphia 1828; tr French, 1828; German, 1828.
On ornamental plantations and landscape gardening. Quart Rev 37 1828. Review of Steuart's The planter's guide. MPW 21.
Davy's Salmonia: or days of fly-fishing. Quart Rev 38 1828. MPW 20.
Tales of a grandfather, being stories taken from Scottish history: second series. 3 vols Edinburgh 1829 (for 1828), 1829, Paris 1828, Boston 1829; tr French, 1828.
Pitsligo's Thoughts concerning man's condition. Blackwood's Mag May 1829. Not rptd in MPW.
Morier's Hajji Baba in England. Quart Rev 39 1829. MPW 18.

Ancient history of Scotland. Quart Rev 41 1829. Review of Ritson's Annals of the Caledonians, Picts and Scots. MPW 20.
Revolutions of Naples in 1647 and 1648; Masaniello and the Duke of Guise. Foreign Quart Rev 4 1829. Not rptd.
Tytler's History of Scotland. Quart Rev 41 1829. MPW 21.
Tales of a grandfather, being stories taken from the history of Scotland: third series. 3 vols Edinburgh 1830 (for 1829), Boston 1829, Paris 1830; tr French, 1830.
The history of Scotland. 2 vols 1830 (for 1829–30), Cambridge Mass 1830, Paris 1830, Philadelphia 1830; tr French, 1833–4.
Letters on demonology and witchcraft. 1830, 1831, New York 1830, Paris 1830; tr French, 1832; Italian, 1839.
Southey's Life of John Bunyan. Quart Rev 43 1830. MPW 18.
Tales of a grandfather, being stories taken from the history of France: fourth series. 3 vols 1831 (for 1830), Paris 1831, Philadelphia 1831; tr French, 1831.
Pitcairn's Ancient criminal trials of Scotland. Quart Rev 44 1831. MPW 21.
Reliquiae Trottcosienses. Harper's Monthly Mag April 1889 (in part); Nineteenth Century Oct 1905 (in part).
Private letters of the seventeenth century. Scribner's Mag 14 1893 (in part); ed D. Grant, Oxford 1948 (complete).

Letters and Journal

Letters of Scott addressed to the Rev R. Polwhele, D. Gilbert, F. Douce. 1832.
Letters between James Ellis and Scott. Newcastle 1850.
Journal 1825–32. Ed D. Douglas 2 vols Edinburgh 1890, 1891, 1910, 1927, New York 1890; rev J. G. Tait 3 vols Edinburgh 1939–46, 1 vol Edinburgh 1950.
Familiar letters. Ed D. Douglas 2 vols Edinburgh 1894, Boston 1894.
The letters of Scott and Charles Kirkpatrick Sharpe to Robert Chambers 1821–45. Edinburgh 1904 (for 1903).
Cook, D. Lockhart's treatment of Scott's letters. Nineteenth Century Sept 1937.
Butler, H. J. and H. E. Scott and Maria Edgeworth: some unpublished letters. MLR 23 1928.
Partington, W. The private letter-books of Scott. 1930, New York 1930.
—— Sir Walter's postbag: more stories and sidelights from his unpublished letter-books. 1932.
Some unpublished letters of Scott from the collection in the Brotherton Library. Ed J. A. Symington, Oxford 1932.
The letters of Scott. Ed H. J. C. Grierson 12 vols 1932–7. No index.
Tait, J. G. The missing tenth of Scott's journal. Edinburgh 1936.
—— Scott's journal and its editor. Edinburgh 1938.
The correspondence of Scott and Charles Robert Maturin. Ed F. E. Ratchford and W. H. McCarthy, Austin 1937.
Lambert, M. and J. T. Hillhouse. The Scott letters in the Huntington Library. HLQ 2 1939.
Harman, R. N. An unpublished letter of Scott. Yale Univ Lib Gazette 14 1940.
Jones, W. P. Three unpublished letters of Scott to Dibdin. HLQ 3 1940.
Struve, G. Scott letters discovered in Russia. Bull John Rylands Lib 28 1944.
—— Russian friends and correspondents of Scott. Comparative Lit 2 1950.
Aspinall, A. Scott's baronetcy: some new letters. TLS 25 Oct 1947.
—— Some new Scott letters. TLS 27 March, 10 and 24 April 1948.
Häusermann, H. W. A new Scott letter. RES 25 1949.
Scott, D. F. S. Some English correspondents of Goethe. 1949. One letter from Scott.
Downs, N. Two unpublished letters of Scott. MLN 69 1954.
Adams, R. M. A letter of Scott. MP 54 1956.
Guthke, K. S. Die erste Nachwirkung von Herders Volksliedern in England. Archiv 193 1957. 10 letters from M. G. Lewis to Scott.
—— Some unpublished letters of M. G. Lewis. N & Q May 1957. One letter to Scott.
Maxwell, J. C. An uncollected Scott letter. RES new ser 9 1958.
Enkvist, N. E. Scott, Lord Bloomfield and Bernadotte. Studia Neophilologica 32 1960.
Green, D. B. New letters of Scott 1813–31. N & Q Jan–March 1961.
McDonald, W. U. A letter of Scott to William Scott on the Jeffrey–Swift controversy. RES new ser 12 1961.
Kies, P. P. An unpublished letter of Scott. Research Stud Washington State Univ 30 1962.
Russell, N. H. New letters of Scott. RES new ser 14 1963.
Wood, G. A. M. Letters between Scott and the Marquis of Lothian. N & Q Oct–Dec 1964.

Edited Works

An apology for Tales of terror. Kelso 1799. Priv ptd in 12 copies, of which one has variant title: Tales of terror.
Minstrelsy of the Scottish Border. 2 vols Kelso 1802, 3 vols Edinburgh 1803, 1806, 1810, 1812; tr French, 1826; ed T. F. Henderson 4 vols Edinburgh 1902, 1932.
Sir Tristrem: a metrical romance by Thomas of Ercildoune. Edinburgh 1804, 1806, 1811, 1819, Paris 1837.
Original memoirs of Sir H. Slingsby and of Captain Hodgson. Edinburgh 1806.
The works of John Dryden. 18 vols 1808, 1821; rev G. Saintsbury 18 vols Edinburgh 1882–93.
Memoirs of Capt George Carleton. Edinburgh 1808, 1809 (4th edn).
Queenhoo-Hall: a romance, by Joseph Strutt. 4 vols Edinburgh 1808.
Memoirs of Robert Cary, Earl of Monmouth and Fragmenta regalia by Sir Robert Naunton. Edinburgh 1808.
The life of Edward Lord Herbert of Cherbury, written by himself. Edinburgh 1809. Attributed to Scott.
A collection of scarce and valuable tracts. 13 vols 1809–15. 'Somers tracts.'
English minstrelsy. 2 vols Edinburgh 1810.
The poetical works of Anna Seward. 3 vols Edinburgh 1810.
The ancient British drama. 3 vols 1810. Attributed to Scott.
Memoirs of Count Grammont, by Anthony Hamilton. 2 vols 1811.
The Castle of Otranto, by Horace Walpole. Edinburgh 1811.
Secret history of the court of King James the First. 2 vols Edinburgh 1811.
The modern British drama. 5 vols 1811. Attributed to Scott.
Memoirs of the reign of King Charles the First, by Sir Philip Warwick. Edinburgh 1813. Attributed to Scott.
The works of Jonathan Swift. 19 vols Edinburgh 1814, 1824.
The letting of humours blood in the head vaine, by S. Rowlands. Edinburgh 1814, 1815.
Memorie of the Somervilles. 2 vols Edinburgh 1815.
The history of Donald the Hammerer. In E. Burt, Letters from a gentleman in the north of Scotland, 5th edn vol 1 1818, 1822, Glasgow 1876.
Trivial poems and triolets, by Patrick Carey. 1820.
Memorials of the Haliburtons. 1820, 1824.
Northern memoirs writ in the year 1658 by Richard Franck. Edinburgh 1821.
Ballantyne's novelist's library. 10 vols 1821–4.
Chronological notes of Scottish affairs from the diary of Lord Fountainhall. Edinburgh 1822.

Military memoirs of the great civil war, being the military memoirs of John Gwynne. Edinburgh 1822.
Lays of the Lindsays. Edinburgh 1824. Suppressed; copy at Abbotsford.
Auld Robin Gray: a ballad, by Lady Anne Barnard. Edinburgh 1825 (Bannatyne Club).
The Bannatyne miscellany, vol. 1. Edinburgh 1827 (Bannatyne Club). Ed with D. Laing.
Memoirs of the Marchioness de la Rochejaquelein. Edinburgh 1827.
Proceedings in the court-martial held upon John, Master of Sinclair, 1708. Edinburgh 1828 (Roxburghe Club).
Memorials of George Bannatyne, 1545–1608. Edinburgh 1829 (Bannatyne Club).
Trial of Duncan Terig and Alexander Bane Macdonald, 1754. Edinburgh 1831 (Bannatyne Club).
Memoirs of the insurrection in Scotland in 1715, by John, Master of Sinclair, with notes and introductory notice by Scott. Edinburgh 1858 (Abbotsford Club).

§2

[Jeffrey, F.] Scott's Lay of the last minstrel. Edinburgh Rev 6 1805; rptd in his Contributions to the Edinburgh Review vol 2, 1844.
— Scott's Marmion. Edinburgh Rev 12 1808.
— Scott's Lady of the lake. Edinburgh Rev 16 1810; rptd ibid vol 2.
— Scott's Vision of Don Roderick. Edinburgh Rev 18 1811.
— Scott's Lord of the Isles. Edinburgh Rev 24 1815.
— Waverley. Edinburgh Rev 24 1815; rptd ibid vol 3.
— Scott's edition of Swift. Edinburgh Rev 27 1816; rptd ibid vol 1.
— Tales of my landlord. Edinburgh Rev 28 1817; rptd ibid vol 3.
— Rob Roy. Edinburgh Rev 29 1818; rptd ibid vol 3.
— Ivanhoe. Edinburgh Rev 33 1820; rptd ibid vol 3.
— Nigel. Edinburgh Rev 37 1822; rptd ibid vol 3.
[Ellis, G.] Scott's Lady of the lake. Quart Rev 3 1810.
— The bridal of Triermain. Quart Rev 9 1813.
[Grahame, J.] Vindication of the Scotish Presbyterians and Covenanters against the aspersions of the author of Tales of my landlord. Glasgow 1817.
[McCrie, T.] Review of Tales of my landlord. Edinburgh Christian Instructor 14 1817; rptd in his Miscellaneous writings, Edinburgh 1841.
[Chambers, W.] The life and anecdotes of the Black Dwarf. Edinburgh 1820.
[Scott, J.] Living authors no 1: The author of the Scotch novels. London Mag Jan 1820.
[Talfourd, T. N.] On the living novelists no II: the author of Waverley. New Monthly Mag May 1820; rptd in his Critical and miscellaneous writings, Philadelphia 1842 etc.
Touchstone, T. A letter to the author of Waverley on the moral tendency of those popular works. 1820.
[Adolphus, J. L.] Letters to Richard Heber containing critical remarks on the series beginning with Waverley. 1821, 1822.
Aiton, W. A history of the rencounter at Drumclog with an account of what is correct and what is fictitious in the Tales of my landlord. Hamilton 1821.
[Chambers, R.] Illustrations of the author of Waverley: being notices and anecdotes of real characters etc presumed to be described in his works. Edinburgh 1822, 1825, 1884.
— Life of Scott, with Abbotsford notanda by R. Carruthers. 1871.
[Hazlitt, W.] The pirate. London Mag Jan 1822; rptd in his Works vol 11, 1904.
— Peveril of the Peak. London Mag Feb 1823; rptd in his Works vol 11, 1904.
— In his Spirit of the age, 1825.
[Senior, N. W.] Novels of the author of Waverley. Quart Rev 26 1822; rptd in his Essays on fiction, 1864.
— The pirate. Quart Rev 26 1822; rptd in his Essays on fiction, 1864.
— Peveril of the Peak, Quentin Durward, St Ronan's Well, Redgauntlet, Tales of the Crusaders, Woodstock, Chronicles of the Canongate. London Rev 1 1830; rptd in his Essays on fiction, 1864.
Warner, R. Illustrations of the novels of the author of Waverley. 3 vols 1823–4.
[Mudie, R.] The Scottish novelist. In his Attic fragments, 1825.
Pichot, A. Voyage historique et littéraire en Angleterre et en Ecosse. Paris 1825; tr 1825.
[Croker, J. W.] Two letters on Scottish affairs to Malachi Malagrowther. 1826.
[Caze, J. F.] Réfutation de la vie de Napoléon de Scott. Paris 1827.
[Gourgaud, G.] Réfutation de la vie de Napoléon par Scott. Paris 1827.
Jacob, C. G. Scott: ein biographisch-literarischer Versuch. Cologne 1827.
Bonaparte, L. Réponse à Scott sur son Histoire de Napoléon. Stuttgart 1828.
Withers, W. A letter to Scott exposing certain fundamental errors in his late Essay on planting. 1828.
Skene, J. A series of sketches of the existing localities alluded to in the Waverley novels. Edinburgh 1829.
— Memories of Scott. Ed B. Thomson 1909.
[Peabody, W. B. O.] Waverley Novels. North Amer Rev 32 1831.
— Sir Walter Scott. North Amer Rev 36 1833.
[Cunningham, A.] Abbotsford. Athenaeum 13–20 Aug 1831.
[Fox, W. J.] On the intellectual character of Scott. Monthly Repository Nov 1832.
[Lauder, T. D.] Funeral of Scott, by an eyewitness. Tait's Mag Nov 1832.
Martineau, H. Characteristics of the genius of Scott. Tait's Mag Dec 1832; rptd in her Miscellanies vol 1, Boston 1836.
— The achievements of the genius of Scott. Tait's Mag Jan 1833; rptd ibid.
Vedder, D. Memoir of Scott. Dundee 1832.
Madden, R. R. In his Infirmities of genius vol 2, 1833.
Nayler, B. S. Memoir of the life and writings of Scott. Amsterdam 1833.
The Waverley anecdotes, illustrative of the incidents, characters, and scenery described in the novels. 2 vols 1833 etc.
Allan, G. Life of Scott. Edinburgh 1834 (for 1832–4).
Hogg, J. Familiar anecdotes of Scott. New York 1834; rptd as Domestic manners and private life of Scott, Glasgow 1834, 1838, Edinburgh 1846, 1882, Stirling 1909.
Mézières, L. In his Histoire critique de la littérature anglaise vol 3, Paris 1834.
Irving, W. Abbotsford and Newstead Abbey. Philadelphia 1835.
Gillies, R. P. Recollections of Scott. 1837 (for 1836).
Hall, B. The Countess [Purgstall] and Scott. In his Schloss Hainfeld, Edinburgh 1836.
Lockhart, J. G. Memoirs of the life of Scott. 7 vols Edinburgh 1837–8, 10 vols Edinburgh 1839 etc; ed A. W. Pollard 5 vols 1900 (adds material from the Narrative, below); ed S. M. Francis 5 vols Boston 1902. Abridged as Narrative, 2 vols Edinburgh 1848, 1 vol 1853 etc.
— The Ballantyne-humbug handled. Edinburgh 1839.
Ballantyne Trustees. Refutation of the mistatements and calumnies contained in Mr Lockhart's Life of Scott respecting the Messrs Ballantyne. 1838 (3 edns), 1839, Boston 1838.
— Reply to Mr Lockhart's pamphlet entitled the Ballantyne-humbug handled. 1839.
[Carlyle, T.] Memoirs of the life of Scott. Westminster Rev 28 1838.

Cochrane, J. G. Catalogue of the library at Abbotsford. Edinburgh 1838.

[Keble, J.] Life and writings of Scott. Br Critic 24 1838; rptd in his Occasional papers, Oxford 1877.

McDonald, G. Life of Scott. 1838.

[Prescott, W. H.] Memoir of Scott. North Amer Rev 46 1838; rptd in his Biographical and critical miscellanies, 1845.

Dickens, C. The Ballantyne humbug handled. Examiner 31 March, 29 Sept 1839; rptd in his To be read at dusk, 1898, and Miscellaneous papers vol 1, 1911.

The Lockhart and Ballantyne controversy. Tait's Mag Oct 1839.

Scott, J. Journal of a tour to Waterloo and Paris with Scott in 1815. 1842.

Browne, J. A free examination of Scott's opinions respecting 'Popery'. Edinburgh 1845.

Grant, G. Life of Scott. 1849.

Bartlett, A. D. Historical account of Cumnor Place Berks, followed by some remarks on the statements in Kenilworth. Oxford 1850.

Macleod, D. Life of Scott. 1852.

[Matthews, G. K.] Abbotsford and Scott. 1853.

French, G. J. Parallel passages from two tales elucidating the origin of the plot of Guy Mannering. Manchester 1855.

— An inquiry into the origin of the authorship of some of the earlier Waverley novels. Bolton 1856.

Fitzpatrick, W. J. Who wrote the earlier Waverley novels? 1856 (2nd edn).

Patterson, J. Memoir of Joseph Train, the antiquarian correspondent of Scott. Glasgow 1857.

[Bagehot, W.] The Waverley novels. Nat Rev 6 1858; rptd in his Literary studies, 1879.

Jefferson, J. C. In his Novels and novelists from Elizabeth to Victoria vol 2, 1858.

White, J. Robert Burns and Scott: two lives. 1858.

Eberty, F. Scott: ein Lebensbild. 2 vols Breslau 1860.

Leland, C. G. The skeptics of the Waverley novels. Continental Monthly April 1863.

Elze, K. Sir Walter Scott. Dresden 1864.

[Harkom, J. M.] Scott: the character of his genius and the moral influence his works are fitted to exercise. 1867.

Jellett, J. H. The poetry of Scott. In his Afternoon lectures 5th ser, Dublin 1869.

Gilfillan, G. Life of Scott. Edinburgh 1870, 1871, 1884.

Ballantyne & Co. The history of the Ballantyne Press and its connection with Scott. Edinburgh 1871.

Cornish, S. W. The Waverley manual: a handbook of the chief characters. Edinburgh 1871.

Gibson, J. Reminiscences of Scott. Edinburgh 1871.

Gleig, G. R. The life of Scott. Edinburgh 1871.

Hunnewell, J. F. The lands of Scott. Edinburgh 1871.

Lockhart, C. S. M. The centenary memorial of Scott. 1871.

Mackenzie, R. S. Scott: the story of his life. Boston 1871.

Sproat, G. M. Scott as a poet. Edinburgh 1871.

[Stephen, L.] Some words about Scott. Cornhill Mag Sept 1871; rptd in his Hours in a library 1st ser, 1874.

— The story of Scott's ruin. Cornhill Mag April 1897; rptd in his Studies of a biographer vol 2, 1898.

[Forman, H. B.] Scott: a centenary tribute. London Quart Rev 38 1872.

The Scott Exhibition 1871: catalogue. Edinburgh 1872.

Airy, G. B. On the topography of the Lady of the lake. 1873; rptd in Lady of the lake, ed A. Lang 1904.

Constable, T. Archibald Constable and his literary correspondents. 3 vols Edinburgh 1873.

Ferrier, S. E. Recollections of visits to Ashistiel and Abbotsford. Temple Bar Feb 1874.

Doyle, F. H. In his Lectures on poetry delivered at Oxford, 1877.

Rogers, C. Genealogical memoirs of the family of Sir Walter Scott. 1877.

Hutton, R. H. Sir Walter Scott. 1878 (EML).

Veitch, J. The history and poetry of the Scottish Border. Glasgow 1878, Edinburgh 1893.

— In his Feeling for nature in Scottish poetry vol 2, Edinburgh 1887.

— The Vale of the Manor and the Black Dwarf. Blackwood's Mag Sept 1890; rptd in his Border essays, Edinburgh 1896.

Wedgwood, J. Scott and the romantic reaction. Contemporary Rev Oct 1878.

Canning, A. S. G. The philosophy of the Waverley novels. 1879.

— History in fact and fiction. 1897.

— History in Scott's novels. 1905.

— Scott studied in eight novels. 1910.

Rogers, M. The Waverley dictionary. Chicago 1879.

Sir Walter Scott. Church Quart Rev 8 1879.

Watt, J. C. Scott, Thackeray, Dickens, Lytton. Edinburgh 1880.

Colston, J. History of the Scott Monument, Edinburgh. Edinburgh 1881.

Grey, H. Key to the Waverley novels. 1881.

Kerr, J. B. On supposed unpublished verses by Scott. History of Berwickshire Nat Club 9 1881.

Shairp, J. C. The Homeric spirit in Scott. In his Aspects of poetry, Oxford 1881.

Jackson, J. E. Amye Robsart. Nineteenth Century March 1882.

Stevenson, R. L. A gossip on romance. Longman's Mag Nov 1882; rptd in his Memories and portraits, 1887.

Dickson, N. The Bible in Waverley: or Scott's use of the sacred Scriptures. Edinburgh 1884.

Natorp, O. Zu Scotts Lay of the last minstrel. Archiv 72 1884.

Krummacher, M. Zu Scotts Lady of the lake. Archiv 76–7 1886–7.

Wood, J. The life of Scott. Edinburgh 1886.

Yonge, C. D. Life of Scott. 1888.

Mann, M. F. Quentin Durward. Anglia 12 1889.

Woodruff, E. H. Scott at work. Scribner's Mag Feb 1889.

Canning, T. Catholicism in the Waverley novels. Dublin Rev 109 1891.

Smiles, S. A publisher and his friends: memoir and correspondence of John Murray. 2 vols 1891.

Swinburne, A. C. The journal of Scott 1825–32. Fortnightly Rev May 1891; rptd in his Studies in prose and poetry, 1894.

R., E. Constable and Scott. Temple Bar Dec 1892.

Smith, W. Ruskin and Carlyle on Scott. Igdrasil 3 1892.

Collyer, J. M. 'The catastrophe' in St Ronan's Well. Athenaeum 4 Feb 1893.

Maxwell-Scott, M. M. Abbotsford: the personal relics and antiquarian treasures of Scott. 1893.

Stevenson, R. Scott's voyage in the Lighthouse yacht. Scribner's Mag Oct 1893.

Walker, H. In his Three centuries of Scottish literature vol 2, Glasgow 1893.

The ethics of Scott. London Quart Rev 82 1894.

Minto, W. In his Literature of the Georgian era, Edinburgh 1894.

Saintsbury, G. Scott and Dumas. Macmillan's Mag Sept 1894; rptd in his Essays in English literature: second series, 1895.

— Sir Walter Scott. Edinburgh 1897.

Burgess, S. The law in Scott. In The lawyer, ed W. Andrews 1896.

Johnstone, G. P. The first book printed by James Ballantyne: being An apology for Tales of terror. Pbns Edinburgh Bibl Soc 1 1896, 9 1913.

Quiller-Couch, A. T. Scott and Burns. In his Adventures in criticism, 1896.

— The memory of Scott. In his Studies in literature: third series, Cambridge 1929.

Scott, A. The story of Scott's first love. Edinburgh 1896.

Jack, A. A. Essays on the novel as illustrated by Scott and Miss Austen. 1897.

Napier, G. G. The homes and haunts of Scott. Glasgow 1897.
Oliphant, M. O. Annals of a publishing house: William Blackwood and his sons. 2 vols Edinburgh 1897.
Franke, E. Quellen des Lay of the last minstrel. Archiv 101 1898.
Maigron, L. Le roman historique à l'époque romantique: essai sur l'influence de Scott. Paris 1898, 1912.
Novels and novelists: chapters on the Waverley novels. 1898.
Hay, J. Sir Walter Scott. 1899.
Oliphant, J. In his Victorian novelists, 1899.
Hertel, H. Die Naturschilderungen in Scotts Versdichtungen. Leipzig 1900.
MacRitchie, D. The proof-sheets of Redgauntlet. Longman's Mag March 1900.
—— Waverley in France. Dunedin Mag 2 1914.
Gaebel, K. Beiträge zur Technik der Erzählung in den Romanen Scotts. Marburger Studien zur Englischen Philologie 2 1901.
Hudson, W. H. Sir Walter Scott. 1901.
Roesel, L. K. Die litterarischen und persönlichen Beziehungen Scotts zu Goethe. Leipzig 1901.
Schüler, M. Quellenforschung zu Scotts Rob Roy. Leipzig 1901.
Sidney, P. Who killed Amy Robsart? being some account of her life and death; with remarks on Scott's Kenilworth. 1901.
Chesterton, G. K. The position of Scott. In his Twelve types, 1902.
Crockett, W. S. The Scott country. 1902, 1930 (rev).
—— The footsteps of Scott. Edinburgh 1908.
—— The Scott originals. Edinburgh 1912 (for 1911), 1932 (rev).
—— The centenary of Waverley. Records Glasgow Bibl Soc 4 1915.
—— Scott's Shakespeare. Bookman (London) Dec 1921.
—— The religion of Scott. Hibbert Jnl 27 1929.
Cross, W. L. An earlier Waverley. MLN 17 1902.
Freye, W. The influence of Gothic literature on Scott. Rostock 1902.
Siebert, A. Untersuchungen zu Waverley. Berlin [1902].
Abramczyk, R. Über die Quellen zu Ivanhoe. Halle 1903.
Carruth, W. H. The relation of Hauff's Lichtenstein to Scott's Waverley. PMLA 18 1903.
Crockett, W. S. and J. L. Caw. Sir Walter Scott. 1903.
Millar, J. H. In his Literary history of Scotland, 1903.
Wolf, M. Scott's Kenilworth. Leipzig, 1903.
Bouchier, J. Local and personal proverbs in the Waverley Novels. N & Q 14–21 May 1904.
Gärdes, J. Scott als Charakterzeichner in The Heart of Midlothian. Vegesack 1904.
Hughes, M. A. Letters and recollections of Scott. Ed H. G. Hutchinson 1904.
Symons, A. Was Scott a poet? Atlantic Monthly Nov 1904. Reply by G. Smith, March 1905.
Ainger, A. In his Lectures and essays vol 1, 1905.
Laidlaw, W. Recollections of Scott 1802–4. Ed J. Sinton, Trans Hawick Archaeological Soc 1905.
Letters of Scott's family to their old governess. Ed F. A. W. Henderson 1905.
Macartney, M. H. H. Scott's use of the preface. Longman's Mag Aug 1905.
O'Donoghue, D. J. Scott's tour in Ireland in 1825. Glasgow 1905.
Wenger, K. Historische Romane deutscher Romantiker: Untersuchungen über den Einfluss Walter Scotts. Berne 1905.
Elliot, W. F. The trustworthiness of Border ballads. Edinburgh 1906.
—— Further essays on Border ballads. Edinburgh 1910.
François, V. E. Scott and Alfred de Vigny. MLN 21 1906.
Fyfe, W. T. Edinburgh under Scott. 1906.
Gest, J. M. The law and lawyers of Scott. Amer Law Register 54 1906; rptd in his Lawyer in literature, 1913.
Lang, A. Sir Walter Scott. 1906.
—— Scott and the Border minstrelsy. 1910.
Norgate, G. Le G. The life of Scott. 1906.
[Bailey, J. C.] The Waverley novels. TLS 5 April 1907; rptd in his Poets and poetry, Oxford 1911.
—— Scott's poetry. TLS 19 Aug 1909; rptd in his Poets and poetry, Oxford 1911.
Ball, M. Scott as a critic of literature. New York 1907.
Brooke, S. A. In his Studies in poetry, 1907.
Kerlin, R. T. Ivanhoe and Sydney's Arcadia. MLN 22 1907.
Korff, H. A. Scott und Alexis. Heidelberg 1907.
Young, C. A. The Waverley novels: an appreciation. Glasgow 1907.
Jackson, H. In his Great English novelists, [1908].
Ballantyne, Hanson & Co. The Ballantyne Press and its founders 1796–1908. Edinburgh 1909.
Franke, P. W. Der Stil in den epischen Dichtungen Scotts. Berlin 1909.
Hofer, E. Scotts Einfluss auf Ph. J. v. Rehfues' Roman Scipio Cicala. Mähr. Weisskirchen 1909.
MacCunn, F. A. Scott's friends. Edinburgh 1909.
Husband, M. F. A. Dictionary of characters in the Waverley novels. 1910.
Verrall, A. W. The prose of Scott. Quart Rev 213 1910; rptd in his Collected literary essays, 1913.
Neilson, G. Roderick Dhu: his poetical pedigree. Scott Historical Rev 8 1911.
Streissle, A. Personifikation und poetische Beseelung bei Scott und Burns. Heidelberg 1911.
Thompson, G. W. William Hauff's specific relation to Scott. PMLA 26 1911.
Watson, J. Waverley novels. In F. Watson, From a northern window, 1911.
Elton, O. In his Survey of English literature 1780–1830 vol 1, 1912. Chs on Scott rev and pbd separately, 1924.
Forsythe, R. S. Two debts of Scott to Le morte d'Arthur. MLN 27 1912.
Lorenzen, H. L. Peveril of the Peak: ein Beitrag. Berlin 1912.
Morgan, A. E. Scott and his poetry. 1912.
Ripari, R. Romantic and non-romantic elements in the works of Scott. Castello 1912.
Watt, L. M. In his Scottish life and poetry, 1912.
Dickins, L. Scott's masterpiece. Englishwoman 19 1913. On The Highland widow.
Hofmann, G. Entstehungsgeschichte von Scotts Marmion. Königsberg 1913.
Knothe, F. Untersuchungen zu Redgauntlet. Görlitz 1913.
Olcott, C. S. Country of Scott. Boston 1913.
Steiger, O. Die Verwendung des schottischen Dialekts in Scotts Romanen. Darmstadt 1913.
Kent, W. H. Scott and the Catholic revival. Catholic World Nov 1914.
Macleod, K. Scott's doctors and quacks. Caledonian Medical Jnl 9 1914.
—— Scott's madfolk. Ibid.
Reinert, M. Untersuchungen zu Der Abt. Erlangen 1914.
Watson, G. Literary blunders of the author of Waverley. Trans Hawick Archaeological Soc 1914.
Emerson, O. F. The earliest English translations of Bürger's Lenore. Cleveland 1915.
—— Scott's early translations from Bürger. JEGP 14 1915.
—— The early literary life of Scott. JEGP 23 1924.
Erskine, J. Walter Scott. Columbia Univ Quart 17 1915; rptd in his Delight of great books, 1928.
Symon, J. D. Marischal's most martial alumnus. Aberdeen Univ Rev 3 1916. On A legend of Montrose.
Anstice, R. H. The poetical heroes of Scott. Aberdeen 1917.
Chisholm, J. Scott as a judge. Edinburgh 1918.

Devonshire, J. M. The 'decline' of Scott in France. French Quart 1 1919.
Ker, W. P. Sir Walter Scott. Anglo-French Rev 2 1919; rptd in his Collected essays vol 1, 1925.
— Scott's Scotland. [1922]; rptd in his Collected essays vol 1, 1925.
— In his On modern literature, Oxford 1955.
Dobie, W. G. M. Law and lawyers in the Waverley novels. Juridical Rev 32 1920.
Lieder, P. R. Scott and Scandinavian literature. Northampton Mass 1920.
Withington, R. Scott's contribution to pageantic development. SP 17 1920.
Stalker, A. The intimate life of Scott. 1921.
Churchman, P. H. and E. A. Peers. A survey of the influence of Scott in Spain. Revue Hispanique 55 1922.
Shears, L. A. The influence of Scott on the novels of Theodor Fontane. New York 1922.
Vissink, H. Scott and his influence on Dutch literature. Zwolle 1922.
Yolland, A. Scott's influence on Jósika. Oxford Hungarian Rev 1 1922.
Cole, O. B. A last memory of Scott. Cornhill Mag Sept 1923.
Croce, B. Walter Scott. Critica 20 Jan 1923; rev and tr in his European literature in the nineteenth century, 1924.
Draper, F. W. M. The rise and fall of the French romantic drama with special reference to Scott. 1923.
Buchan, J. Some notes on Scott. 1924; rptd in his Homilies and recreations, [1926].
— The man and the book: Scott. 1925.
— Sir Walter Scott. 1932.
Jones, H. In his Essays on literature and education, [1924].
Newbolt, H. J. Peacock, Scott and Robin Hood. Essays by Divers Hands new ser 4 1924; rptd in his Studies green and grey, 1926.
Randall, V. Scott and the Waverley novels. Nineteenth Century Oct 1924.
Brewer, W. Shakespeare's influence on Scott. Boston 1925.
Fletcher, C. R. L. Sir Walter Scott. Quart Rev 244 1925.
Lindström, E. Scott och den historiska romanen och novellen i Sverige intill 1850. Gothenburg 1925.
Low, D. H. The first link between English and Serbo-Croat literature. Slavonic Rev 3 1925. Asan Aga.
Macintosh, W. Scott and Goethe. Galashiels [1925].
Sommerkamp, F. Scotts Kenntnis und Ansicht von deutscher Literatur. Archiv 148 1925.
Brinton, C. C. In his Political ideas of the English romanticists, Oxford 1926.
Cornford, L. C. The making of Sir Walter. In his Interpretations, 1926.
Fiske, C. F. Scott of Buccleugh clan: a study in non-romantic temperament. Poet Lore 37 1926.
— Epic suggestion in the imagery of the Waverley novels. New Haven 1940.
Garnard, H. J. The influence of Scott on the works of Balzac. New York 1926.
Graham, W. Scott's dilemma. MLN 41 1926. On Scott's own review of Tales of my landlord.
Maynadier, G. H. Ivanhoe and its literary consequences. In Essays in memory of B. Wendell, Cambridge Mass 1926.
Peers, E. A. Studies in the influence of Scott in Spain. Revue Hispanique 68 1926.
[Wood, A.]. A Scott centenary. Blackwood's Mag Feb 1926.
— Scott's man Friday. Blackwood's Mag Nov 1930. On John Ballantyne.
Baikie, J. The charm of the Scott country. 1927.
Baldensperger, F. La grande communion romantique de 1827: sous le signe de Scott. Revue de Littérature Comparée 7 1927.

Cook, D. Murray's mysterious contributor. Nineteenth Century April 1927. On Greenfield, recommended by Scott as a contributor to Quart Rev.
— Additions to Scott's poems. TLS 15–22 Nov 1941. Reply by W. M. Parker 13 Dec 1941.
Koch, J. Scotts Beziehungen zu Deutschland. Germanisch-romanische Monatsschrift 15 1927.
Scudder, H. H. A Queen at chesse. MLN 42 1927. Kenilworth.
White, H. A. Scott's novels on the stage. New Haven 1927.
Sir Walter Scott Quarterly. Vol 1 nos 1–4.
[Gordon, G. S.] The chronicles of the Canongate. TLS 12 April 1928; rptd in Scott centenary articles, 1932; rptd in his Lives of authors, 1950 (rev).
Gordon, R. K. Scott and the Comédie humaine. MLR 23 1928.
— Dryden and the Waverley novels. MLR 34 1939.
— Shakespeare and some scenes in the Waverley novels. Queen's Quart 45 1939.
— Le voyage d'Abbotsford. Trans Royal Soc of Canada 34 1940.
— Shakespeare's Henry IV and the Waverley novels. MLR 37 1942.
— Scott and Wordsworth's Lyrical ballads. Trans Royal Soc of Canada 3rd ser 37 1943.
— Scott and Shakespeare's tragedies. Trans Royal Soc of Canada 3rd ser 39 1945.
— Scott's prose. Trans Royal Soc of Canada 3rd ser 45 1951.
Grierson, H. J. C. Scott and Carlyle. E & S 13 1928; rptd in his Essays and addresses, 1940.
— Sir Walter Scott Bart: a new life. 1938.
— Sir Walter Scott. Univ of Edinburgh Jnl 11 1942; rptd in Edinburgh University: Scott lectures, Edinburgh 1950.
Hartland, R. W. Scott et le roman frénétique: contribution à l'étude de leur fortune en France. Paris 1928.
Jordan, J. C. The Eve of St Agnes and the Lay of the last minstrel. MLN 43 1928.
Reitzel, W. Scott's review of Jane Austen's Emma. PMLA 43 1928.
Roe, F. C. Scott and France. Scots Mag Oct 1928.
Batho, E. C. Scott and the sagas. MLR 24 1929.
Boas, L. S. A great rich man: the romance of Scott. New York 1929.
Krappe, E. S. A Scandinavian source for Tony Foster's death in Kenilworth. MP 26 1929.
Milligan, J. Scott's heroic struggle. Eng Rev Feb 1929. Reply by H. G. L. King, March 1929.
Carswell, D. Sir Walter: a four-part study in biography. 1930, Garden City NY 1930 (as Scott and his circle).
— The legend of Abbotsford. Nineteenth Century Sept 1932.
— Sir Walter's secret: a literary inquest. Scots Mag Dec 1933. On order in which novels were written.
Dickson, W. K. Scott and the Parliament House. Juridical Rev 42 1930.
Gray, W. F. Some forgotten writings of Scott. Quart Rev 255 1930.
— Scott in sunshine and shadow: the tribute of his friends. 1931.
— The religion of Scott. Hibbert Jnl 31 1933.
Gwynn, S. The life of Scott. 1930.
Haber, T. B. The chapter-tags in the Waverley novels. PMLA 45 1930.
Koskimies, R. Raunioiden romantiikka keskiaika Ludwig Tieckin, Walter Scottin ja Victor Hugon teoksissa. Porvoo 1930.
— Scottin mesterivuodet 1814–19. Porvoo 1931.
— Walter Scott novellistina. Valvoja-Aika Sept 1932.
[Marshall, D.] Scott and Scots Law. Scottish Law Rev 46–50 1930–4; rptd in his Scott and Scots law, 1932 (in part; *see below*).

Marshall, J. R. Walter Scott, quartermaster. Blackwood's Mag April 1930.
Pierce, F. E. Scott and Hoffmann. MLN 45 1930. On influence of Das Gelübde on Surgeon's daughter.
Richmond, D. A. Scott's trust for creditors. Accountants' Mag 34 1930.
Cook, E. T. Sir Walter's dogs. Edinburgh 1931.
Falconer, J. A. Two manuscripts at Abbotsford. Archiv 160 1931. Trns of German plays.
Johnston, C. N. (Lord Sands). Scott's congé. 1931 (3rd edn).
Kelley, M. W. Jock of Hazeldean and Childe 293 E. MLN 46 1931.
Ker, J. I. The land of Scott. 1931.
Lightwood, J. T. In his Music and literature, 1931.
Weekly, E. Scott and the English language. Atlantic Monthly Nov 1931.
Zellars, G. G. Influencia de Scott en España. Revista de Filologia Española 18 1931.
Blunden, E. The poetry of Scott. Queen's Quart 39 1932.
Bos, K. Religious creeds and philosophies as represented by characters in Scott's works and biography. Amsterdam 1932.
Collins, N. In his Facts of fiction, 1932.
Mackenzie, A. M. The survival of Scott. London Mercury Jan 1932.
MacNalty, A. S. The Great Unknown. Epsom 1932.
Marshall, D. Scott and Scots law. Edinburgh 1932.
Miller, J. Through a Scottish layman's eyes. Queen's Quart 39 1932.
Mudie, P. L. K. Scott and the lure of the road. 1932.
Orians, G. H. Romance ferment after Waverley. Amer Lit 3 1932.
— Scott and Hawthorn's Fanshawe. New England Quart 11 1938.
— Scott, Mark Twain and the Civil War. South Atlantic Quart 40 1941.
Patten, J. A. Scott: a character study. 1932.
Pope-Hennessy, U. The Laird of Abbotsford. 1932.
— Sir Walter Scott. Quart Rev 259 1932. On portraits of Scott.
— Scott in his works. Essays by Divers Hands new ser 12 1933.
— Sir Walter Scott. 1948.
Scott centenary articles: essays from the Times Literary Supplement. Oxford 1932.
Shortreed, R. The making of the Minstrelsy. Ed W. E. Wilson, Cornhill Mag Sept 1932.
Scott to-day. Ed H. J. C. Grierson 1932.
Smith, M. O. Scott and his modern rivals. Queen's Quart 39 1932.
Van Antwerp, W. C. A collector's comment on his first editions of the works of Scott. San Francisco 1932.
— A note on Old Mortality. Book-Collector's Quart 9 1933.
Wright, S. F. The life of Scott. [1932].
Boatright, M. C. Witchcraft in the novels of Scott. SE 13 1933.
— Demonology in the novels of Scott. SE 14 1934.
— Scott's theory and practice concerning the use of the supernatural in prose fiction in relation to the chronology of the Waverley novels. PMLA 50 1935.
Cecil, D. Sir Walter Scott. 1933.
— Scott's vision of life. Listener 9 Feb 1950.
Clark, A. M. Scott and the University. Univ of Edinburgh Jnl 5 1933.
Jack, J. W. Scott's view from the Wicks of Baiglie. Perth 1933.
Keller, W. Scott: eine Rektoratsrede. Münster 1933.
Parsons, C. O. Association of the White Lady with wells. Folklore 4 1933.
— Demonological background of Donnerhugel's narrative and Wandering Willie's tale. SP 30 1933.
— Scott's experiences in haunted chambers. MP 30 1933.
— Two notes on Scott. N & Q 4 Feb 1933.
— Character names in the Waverley novels. PMLA 49 1934.
— The Highland feasts of Fergus MacIvor and Lord Lovat. MLN 49 1934.
— Scott's translations of Bürger's Das Lied von Treue. JEGP 33 1934.
— Journalistic anecdotage about Scott. N & Q 5 Dec 1942.
— Scott's Letters on demonology and witchcraft: outside contributors. N & Q 21–8 March 1942. Replies by C. L'E. Ewen 18 April 1942, and by J. Seton-Anderson 9 May 1942.
— The Bodach Glas in Waverley. N & Q 13 Feb 1943.
— The Dalrymple legend in the Bride of Lammermoor. RES 19 1943.
— The interest of Scott's public in the supernatural. N & Q 14 Aug 1943. Reply by M. Summers, 11 Sept 1943.
— Minor spirits and superstitions in the Waverley novels. N & Q 19 June, 3 July 1943.
— The original of the Black Dwarf. SP 60 1943.
— Scott's fellow demonologists. MLQ 4 1943.
— Sir John Sinclair's Raspe and Scott's Dousterswivel. N & Q 30 Jan 1943. Reply by M. W. Brockwell 13 March 1943.
— Scott in Pandemonium. MLR 38 1943.
— The deaths of Glossin and Hatteraick in Guy Mannering. PQ 24 1945.
— The influence of Grillparzer on the Heart of Midlothian. N & Q 15 Dec 1945.
— The supernatural in Scott's poetry. N & Q 13, 27 Jan, 24 Feb, 10 March 1945.
— Scott's prior version of the Tapestried chamber. N & Q Nov 1962.
— Witchcraft and demonology in Scott's fiction. Edinburgh 1964.
— Chapbook versions of the Waverley novels. Stud in Scottish Lit 3 1966.
Struve, P. Scott and Russia. Slavonic Rev 11 1933.
Dargan, E. P. Scott and the French romantics. PMLA 49 1934.
Freeman, D. Scott's villains. Dublin Rev 195 1934.
Hawkes, C. P. In his Authors-at-arms, 1934.
Krzyzanowski, J. Scott in Poland. Slavonic Rev 12 1934.
Paul, A. Der Einfluss Scotts auf die epische Technik Theodor Fontanes. Breslau 1934.
Stuart, D. M. Scott: some centenary reflections. 1934.
Genévrier, P. Scott, historien français: ou roman tourangeau de Quentin Durward. Tours 1935.
H., O.E. Scott and Douce. Bodleian Quart Record 7 1935.
Randall, D. A. Waverley in America. Colophon new ser 1 1935.
Ruff, W. Scott and the Erl-king. E Studien 69 1935.
— An uncollected preface by Scott. N & Q Nov 1954.
— Cancels in Scott's Life of Napoleon. Trans Edinburgh Bibl Soc 3 1957.
Schumacher, D. F. Der Volksaberglaube in den Waverley Novels. Göttingen 1935.
Stenzel, E. Religiöse Charaktertypen der englischen und schottischen Kirchengeschichte in den Romanen Scotts. Breslau 1935.
Buck, G. In Fortsetzung Bagehots: die Waverley-Romane. Hamburg 1936.
Burr, A. Scott: an index placing the short poems in his novels and in his long poems and dramas. Cambridge Mass 1936.
Hillhouse, J. T. The Waverley novels and their critics. Minneapolis 1936.
— Sir Walter's last long poem. HLQ 16 1953.
Möller, J. Die romantische Landschaft bei Scott. Emsdetten 1936.
Muir, E. Scott and Scotland. 1936.
— In The English novelists, ed D. Verschoyle 1936.
— In From Anne to Victoria, ed B. Dobrée 1937.

— Scott. Univ of Edinburgh Jnl 13 1945; rptd in his Essays on literature and society, 1949, 1965, and in Edinburgh University: Sir Walter Scott lectures, 1950.
Strout, A. L. James Hogg's Familiar anecdotes of Scott. SP 33 1936.
— An unpublished ballad-translation by Scott: The battle of Killiecrankie. MLN 54 1939. Reply by J. C. Corson, ibid.
— Hogg's Domestic manners. N & Q 26 Sept 1942.
Walker, J. F. Scott as a popularizer of history. Aberdeen Univ Rev 23 1936.
Korn, M. Scott und die Geschichte. Anglia 61 1937.
Landis, P. N. The Waverley novels: or a hundred years after. PMLA 52 1937.
Parker, W. M. Lockhart's Life of Scott: a plea for revision. TLS 20 March 1937.
— The origin of Scott's Nigel. MLR 34 1939.
— Suggestions for Scott's Muse. TLS 23 March 1940.
— Scott's book marginalia. TLS 21–28 Sept 1940.
— Scott's prologue to Helga. TLS 4 Jan 1941.
— More Scott marginalia. TLS 3–17 May 1941.
— Scott as amicus curiae. Juridical Rev 55 1943.
— Scott's knowledge of Shakespeare. Quart Rev 290 1952.
— Correcting Scott's text. TLS 9 Dec 1955.
Weir, J. L. Thoughts on the Minstrelsy of the Scottish Border. N & Q 11 Sept 1937.
Larsen, T. The classical element in Scott's poetry. Trans Royal Soc of Canada 32 1938.
Mennie, D. M. A MS variant of Scott's Battle of Sempach. Anglia Beiblatt 49 1938.
— Scott's unpublished translations of German plays. MLR 33 1938.
Rossi, J. Scott and Carducci. MLN 53 1938.
Smith, J. C. Scott and Shakespeare. E & S 24 1938.
Van Patten, N. A newly discovered issue of Scott's The vision of Don Roderick. Library 4th ser 18 1938.
Munroe, D. Scott and the development of historical study. Queen's Quart 45 1939.
Dobie, M. R. The development of Scott's Minstrelsy. Trans Edinburgh Bibl Soc 2 1940.
Knickerbocker, W. S. Border and bar: revised interpretations of Scott. Sewanee Rev 48 1940.
Osborn, J. M. In his John Dryden: some biographical facts and problems, New York 1940.
McDavid, R. I. Ivanhoe and Simms' Vasconselos. MLN 56 1941.
Moore, J. R. Defoe and Scott. PMLA 56 1941.
— Scott and Henry Esmond. N & Q 17 June 1944.
— Scott's Antiquary and Defoe's History of apparitions. MLN 59 1944.
— Poe's reading of Anne of Geierstein. Amer Lit 22 1951.
K., H.G.L. The siege of Malta. N & Q 17 Jan 1942. Reply by J. C. Corson 21 Feb 1942.
Birrell, J. H. Scott's debt to Burns. Burns Chron 2nd ser 18 1943.
Brightfield, M. F. Scott, Hazlitt and Napoleon. California Univ Pbns in Eng 14 1943.
Chapman, R. W. Cancels in Scott's Minstrelsy. Library 4th ser 23 1943.
— Scott's Antiquary. RES 19 1943.
Swaen, A. E. H. Sir Walter's tooverstaf. Neophilologus 28 1943.
Dixon, W. M. In his Apology for the arts, 1944.
Fremantle, A. F. A plea for the Waverley novels. Contemporary Rev May 1944.
Kern, J. D. An unidentified review possibly by Scott. MLQ 6 1945. Tytler's Petrarch, Quart Rev 8 1812.
Pottle, F. A. The power of memory in Boswell and Scott. In Essays on the eighteenth century presented to D. Nichol Smith, Oxford 1945.
Aspinall, A. Scott's baronetcy. RES 22 1946.
Bushnell, G. H. On the Notices of the Christians in Peveril of the Peak. Scots Mag Sept 1946; rptd in his From bricks to books, 1949.

Lamborn, E. A. G. Scott's heraldry. N & Q 18 May, 1 June 1946.
— The heraldry of Scott's poems. N & Q 20 Aug 1949.
Pritchett, V. S. In his Living novel, 1946.
Sells, A. L. The return of Cleveland: some observations on the Pirate. Durham Univ Jnl 38 1947.
Mayo, R. D. The chronology of the Waverley novels: the evidence of the manuscripts. PMLA 63 1948.
Shand, J. The good-natured genius. Nineteenth Century Oct 1948.
Klančar, A. J. Scott in Yugoslavia. Slavonic Rev 27 1949.
Roberts, S. C. The Scott lectures for 1948. Univ of Edinburgh Jnl 14 1949; rptd in Edinburgh University: Sir Walter Scott lectures, 1950.
Trevelyan, G. M. Influence of Scott on history. In his Autobiography and other essays, 1949.
Cowley, J. Scott's The lawyer and the Bishop. Juridical Rev 62 1950.
— Lockhart and the publication of Marmion. PQ 32 1953.
Edinburgh University. H. J. C. Grierson, Edwin Muir, G. M. Young, S. C. Roberts, Scott lectures 1940–8. Edinburgh 1950.
Johnston, G. B. Scott and Jonson. N & Q 25 Nov 1950.
McDonald, T. P. Scott's fee book. Juridical Rev 62 1950.
Needler, G. H. Goethe and Scott. Toronto 1950.
Smith, R. M. Chaucer allusions in the letters of Scott. MLN 65 1950.
— Scott and the Pictish question. MLN 66 1951.
Young, G. M. Scott and history. In Edinburgh University, Sir Walter Scott lectures, Edinburgh 1950; *also* Essays by Divers Hands new ser 25 1950.
Booth, B. A. Trollope on Scott: some unpublished notes. Nineteenth-Century Fiction 5 1951.
Gordon, S. S. Waverley and the 'unified design'. ELH 18 1951.
Pearsall, R. B. Scott and Ritson on Allan Ramsay. MLN 66 1951.
Smith, D. N. The poetry of Scott. Univ of Edinburgh Jnl 15 1951.
Thomas, L. H. C. Walladmor: a pseudo-translation of Scott. MLR 46 1951.
Todd, W. B. Twin titles in Scott's Woodstock 1826. PBSA 45 1951.
— The early editions and issues of Scott's Border antiquities. SB 9 1957.
Daiches, D. Scott's achievement as a novelist. Nineteenth-Century Fiction 6 1952; rptd in his Literary essays, Edinburgh 1956.
— Scott's Redgauntlet. In From Jane Austen to Joseph Conrad, ed R. C. Rathburn and M. Steinmann, Minneapolis 1958.
The disinherited baronet. TLS 20 June 1952.
Holman, C. H. The influence of Scott and Cooper on Simms. Amer Lit 23 1952.
Kirk, R. Scott and Bentham. Fortnightly Rev Dec 1952; rptd in his Conservative mind, Chicago 1953 (rev).
Lane, L. Dickens and Scott: an unusual borrowing. Nineteenth-Century Fiction 6 1952. Replies by K. J. Fielding 7 1953; L. Lane 8 1954.
Noyes, A. The poetry of Scott. Quart Rev 290 1952.
Pettet, E. C. Echoes of the Lay of the last minstrel in the Eve of St Agnes. RES new ser 3 1952.
Heist, W. W. The collars of Gurth and Wamba. RES new ser 4 1953.
Roberts, P. Scott's contributions to the English vocabulary. PMLA 68 1953.
Alciatore, J. C. Stendhal et Scott: le comte de Nerwinde et Sir Piercy Shafton. Symposium 8 1954.
Forbes, D. The rationalism of Scott. Cambridge Jnl April 1954.
Pearson, H. Scott: his life and personality. 1954.
Allen, W. In his Six great novelists, 1955.
Duncan, J. E. The anti-romantic in Ivanhoe. Nineteenth-Century Fiction 9 1955.

Berkeley, D. S. Scott and Restoration 'préciosité'. Nineteenth-Century Fiction 10 1956.
Corson, J. C. The Border antiquities. Bibliotheck 1 1956; A supplementary note, 3 [1960].
— Scott studies 1–2. Univ of Edinburgh Jnl 18 1957.
Fisher, P. F. Providence, fate and the historical imagination in the Heart of Midlothian. Nineteenth-Century Fiction 10 1956.
Hennig, J. Goethe's translation of Scott's criticism of Hoffmann. MLR 51 1956.
Mayhead, R. The Heart of Midlothian: Scott as artist. EC 6 1956. Replies by J. H. Pittock 7 1957; D. Craig 8 1958.
Montgomerie, W. Scott as ballad editor. RES new ser 7 1956.
— William Macmath and the Scott ballad manuscripts. Stud in Scottish Lit 1 1964.
Benjamin, E. B. A borrowing from the Faerie Queene in Old Mortality. N & Q Dec 1957.
Gell, W. Reminiscences of Scott's residence in Italy 1832. Ed J. C. Corson 1957.
Goldstone, H. The question of Scott. Eng Jnl 46 1957.
Gordon, R. C. A Victorian anticipation of recent Scott criticism. PQ 36 1957.
— The bride of Lammermoor: a novel of Tory pessimism. Nineteenth-Century Fiction 12 1958.
Green, F. C. Scott's French correspondence. MLR 52 1957.
Hanford, J. H. The manuscript of the Pirate. Princeton Univ Lib Chron 18 1957.
Kaser, D. Waverley in America. PBSA 51 1957.
Meiklejohn, M. F. M. Scott and Alessandro Manzoni. Italian Stud 12 1957.
Bramley, J. A. The genius of Scott. Contemporary Rev March 1958.
— The journal of Scott. Contemporary Rev March 1965.
Butler, R. F. Maria Edgeworth and Scott: unpublished letters 1823. RES new ser 9 1958.
Jack, I. Sir Walter Scott. 1958 (Br Council pamphlet).
Tillyard, E. M. W. Scott's linguistic vagaries. Etudes Anglaises 11 1958; rptd in his Essays literary and educational, 1962.
McDonald, W. U. Scott's conception of Don Quixote. Midwest Rev March 1959.
— Scottish phrenologists and Scott's novels. N & Q Nov 1962.
Shannon, E. F., jr. Locksley Hall and Ivanhoe. N & Q June 1959.
Lynskey, W. The drama of the elect and the reprobate in Scott's Heart of Midlothian. Boston Univ Stud in Eng 4 1960.
Rinsler, N. Gérald de Nerval and Scott's Antiquary. Revue de Littérature Comparée 34 1960.
Biggins, D. Measure for measure and the Heart of Midlothian. Etudes Anglaises 14 1961.
Davie, D. A. The heyday of Scott. 1961.
— The poetry of Scott. Proc Br Acad 47 1961.
Hart, F. R. Proofreading Lockhart's Scott: the dynamics of biographical reticence. SB 14 1961.
— The Fair Maid, Manzoni's Betrothed and the grounds of Waverley criticism. Nineteenth-Century Fiction 18 1964.
— Scott's novels. Charlottesville 1966.
Simeone, W. E. The Robin Hood of Ivanhoe. Jnl of Amer Folklore 74 1961.
Marshall, W. H. Point of view and structure in the Heart of Midlothian. Nineteenth-Century Fiction 16 1962.
Massey, I. Mary Shelley, Scott and 'Maga'. N & Q Nov 1962.
Devlin, D. D. Scott and Redgauntlet. REL 4 1963.
Lauber, J. Scott on the art of fiction. Stud in Eng Lit 1500–1900 3 1963.
Welsh, A. The hero of the Waverley novels. New Haven 1963.
Bushnell, N. S. Scott's advent as novelist of manners. Stud in Scottish Lit 1 1964.
— Scott's mature achievement as novelist of manners. Stud in Scottish Lit 3 1966.
Johnson, E. Sceptred kings and laureled conquerors: Scott in London and Paris 1815. Nineteenth-Century Fiction 18 1964.
Johnston, A. In his Enchanted ground, 1964. On Scott's edn of Sir Tristrem.
Keith, C. The author of Waverley: a study in the personality of Scott. 1964.
Ogden, J. Isaac D'Israeli and Scott. N & Q May 1964.
Raleigh, J. H. What Scott meant to the Victorians. Victorian Stud 7 1964.
Chandler, A. Scott and the medieval revival. Nineteenth-Century Fiction 19 1965.
Crawford, T. Scott. Edinburgh 1965 (Writers & Critics).
French, R. The religion of Scott. Stud in Scottish Lit 2 1965.
Greene, M. Pushkin and Scott. Forum for Modern Lang Stud 1 1965.
Ostrowski, W. Scott in Poland. Stud in Scottish Lit 2 1965.
Ochojski, P. M. Scott's continuous interest in Germany. Stud in Scottish Lit 3 1966.
Macintyre, D. C. Scott and the Waverley novels. REL 7 1966.
Pike, B. A. Scott as pessimist: a view of St Ronan's Well. Ibid.

J. C. C.

JANE AUSTEN
1775–1817

Details and locations of literary mss are in Chapman and Southam (see Bibliographies, *below), and of the letters in Chapman (see* Letters, *below). Many letters were destroyed after Jane Austen's death, some were mutilated, and there are probably some to be located.*

Bibliographies

Edmonds, J. L. Jane Austen: a bibliography. Bull of Bibliography 12 1925.
Keynes, G. L. Jane Austen: a bibliography. 1929.
Chapman, R. W. Jane Austen: a critical bibliography. Oxford 1953, 1955 (corrected).
Southam, B. C. Jane Austen's literary manuscripts. Oxford 1964.

Collections

Novels by Miss Jane Austen. 5 vols (vol i: Sense and sensibility, with a memoir by Henry Austen dated 5 Oct 1832; ii: Pride and prejudice; iii: Emma; iv: Mansfield Park; v: Northanger Abbey and Persuasion), 1833, 1837, 1856, 1866, 1869, 6 vols (vol vi: the 1871 Memoir) 1878–9; 2 vols Philadelphia 1838; Steventon edition, 6 vols 1882, 1886; Routledge sixpenny novels, 1883; ed R. B. Johnson 10 vols 1892, 1898; 12 vols Boston 1892; Winchester edition, 10 vols 1898, 1906; Temple edition, 10 vols 1899; Hampshire edition, ed R. B. Johnson 6 vols 1902; ed R. B. Johnson 10 vols 1908, 1909, 6 vols 1922; 5 vols 1922; Adelphi edition, 7 vols 1923.

Oxford edition. Ed R. W. Chapman 5 vols Oxford 1923, 1926, 1933, 1943, 1946, 1948, 1952, 6 vols (vol vi: Minor works) 1954; Georgian edition, 5 vols 1927; Chawton edition, 6 vols 1948.

§1

Volume the first. Ed R. W. Chapman, Oxford 1933.

Love and freindship. Ed G. K. Chesterton 1922; ed B. C. Southam, Oxford 1963 (as Volume the second, Jane Austen's title).

Volume the third. Ed R. W. Chapman, Oxford 1951.

The 3 ms notebooks contain transcripts of virtually all the uvenilia c. 1787–93, entered and corrected until c. 1809.

Charades written a hundred years ago by Jane Austen and her family. [Ed M. A. Austen-Leigh] 1895. 3 of the 22 by Jane Austen.

Lady Susan. Ed J. E. Austen-Leigh 1871 (in Memoir); ed R. W. Chapman, Oxford 1925; ed R. B. Johnson 1931; ed R. B. Johnson 1934 (with The Watsons and Sanditon); ed J. Bailey 1939 (with The Watsons); ed Q. D. Leavis 1958 (with Sense and sensibility and The Watsons). Composed *c.* 1793–4, with addn probably *c.* 1805.

The Watsons. Ed J. E. Austen-Leigh 1871 (in Memoir); ed A. B. Walkley 1923; completed by L. Oulton 1923; ed R. W. Chapman, Oxford 1927; completed by E. and F. Brown 1927; ed R. B. Johnson 1934 (with Lady Susan and Sanditon); ed J. Bailey 1939 (with Lady Susan); ed Q. D. Leavis 1958 (with Sense and sensibility and Lady Susan); completed by J. Coates 1958. Fragment of *c.* 17,500 words, written *c.* 1804–5.

Minor works. Ed R. W. Chapman, Oxford 1954, 1968. Vol vi of Works; collected edn of juvenilia, early works, verse and the ms fragments (rev B.C. Southam).

Sense and sensibility. 3 vols 1811, 1813 (corrected), Bentley's standard novels 23 1833, 2 vols Philadelphia 1833, 1 vol 1844, 1846, 1847, 1849, 1851, 1851 (with Pride and prejudice), 1852, 1856, 1857, New York 1857 (with Persuasion), Leipzig 1864 (Tauchnitz), London 1870, 1877, New York 1880, London 1883, 1884, 1887, Boston 1892; ed A. Dobson 1896; 1899; ed R. B. Johnson 1906; ed D. Cecil, Oxford 1931 (WC); ed P. Quennell 1933; ed Q. D. Leavis 1958 (with Lady Susan and The Watsons); ed I. Watt, New York 1961; ed M. M. Lascelles 1962; tr French, 1815; Danish, 1855–6; German, 1939; Portuguese, 1943; Italian, 1945; Finnish, 1952. Originally written in letters c. 1795 as Elinor and Marianne; re-writing as Sense and sensibility begun Nov 1797, rev 1809–10, pbd anon c. Nov 1811.

Pride and prejudice. 3 vols 1813, 1813, 2 vols 1817, Philadelphia 1832 (as Elizabeth Bennet), Bentley's standard novels 30 1833, 1 vol 1839, 1844, 1846, Boston 1848, London 1851, 1851 (with Sense and sensibility), 1852, 1856, New York 1859 (with Northanger Abbey), London 1870, Leipzig 1870 (Tauchnitz), London 1877, New York 1880, London 1883, 1884, 1886, Boston 1892, Philadelphia 1893; ed G. Saintsbury 1894; ed A. Dobson 1895; 1896, 1897, 1899; ed E. V. Lucas 1900; ed R. B. Johnson 1906; ed K. M. Metcalfe, Oxford 1912; ed W. D. Howells, New York 1918; ed R. W. Chapman, Oxford 1929 (WC); Moscow 1961; ed B. A. Booth, New York 1963; ed M. M. Lascelles 1963; tr French, 1822; Finnish, 1922; Spanish, 1924; Italian, 1935; Portuguese, 1941; Icelandic, 1956. Originally written, perhaps in letters, Oct 1796 to Aug 1797 as First impressions, rev 1809–10, 1811, 1812, pbd anon Jan 1813, 2nd edn Nov 1813.

Mansfield Park. 3 vols 1814 1816 (corrected), 2 vols Philadelphia 1832, Bentley's standard novels 27 1833, 1 vol Belfast 1846, London 1851, 1856, 1857, New York 1857, Leipzig 1867 (Tauchnitz), London 1870, 1875, 1876, 1877, 1883, 1884, 1889, Boston 1892; ed A. Dobson 1897; 1898, 1899; ed R. B. Johnson 1906; ed M. M. Lascelles, Oxford 1929 (WC); ed Q. D. Leavis 1957; ed M. M. Lascelles 1963; tr French, 1816; Finnish, 1954. Written Feb 1811 to June 1813, pbd anon May 1814, 2nd edn Feb 1816.

Emma. 3 vols 1816, Philadelphia 1816, Bentley's standard novels 30 1833, 2 vols Philadelphia 1833, 1 vol 1841, 1849, 1851, 1856, 1857, New York 1857, London 1870, 1877, Leipzig 1877 (Tauchnitz), London 1881, 1883; ed A. Dobson 1896; 1898, 1899; ed R. B. Johnson 1906; ed E. V. Lucas, Oxford 1907 (WC); ed M. M. Lascelles 1964; tr French, 1816; Italian, 1945; German, 1956. Written 21 Jan 1814 to March 1815, pbd anon Dec 1815.

Northanger Abbey and Persuasion. 4 vols 1818, Bentley's standard novels 28 1833, 1 vol 1848, 1850, 1856, 1857, 1870, Leipzig 1871 (Tauchnitz), London 1877, 1883, 1895; ed A. Dobson 1897, 1899; ed R. B. Johnson 1906; ed M. M. Lascelles 1962. Pbd Dec 1817 with a biographical notice by Henry Austen.

Northanger Abbey. 2 vols Philadelphia 1833, 1 vol 1848, New York 1859 (with Pride and prejudice), New York 1881, Boston 1892, London 1895; ed E. V. Lucas 1901; ed K. M. Metcalfe, Oxford 1923; ed M. Sadleir, Oxford 1930 (WC); ed M. Elwin 1961; tr French, 1824; Spanish, 1921; Portuguese, 1943; German, 1948; Finnish, 1951. Originally written c. 1798–9 as Susan, re-written by 1803, rev as Catherine 1816–17.

Persuasion. 2 vols Philadelphia 1832, New York 1857 (with Sense and sensibility); Boston 1892, London 1909, 1928; ed F. Reid, Oxford 1930 (WC); ed D. W. Harding 1965 (with Memoir); tr French, 1821; German, 1822; Spanish, 1919; German, 1948; Finnish, 1951. Written 8 Aug 1815 to Aug 1816.

Two chapters of Persuasion. Ed R. W. Chapman, Oxford 1926 (250 copies with ms facs). First draft of chs 10 and 11 in vol 2, written 8 to 16 July 1816. Ch 10 first ptd in 1871 Memoir.

Plan of a novel according to hints from various quarters. Ed J. E. Austen-Leigh 1871 (in Memoir, altered and reduced); ed R. W. Chapman, Oxford 1926. Probably written early 1816. The 1926 edn includes Jane Austen's transcript of opinions of Mansfield Park and Emma, and notes on dates of composition and profits from several of the novels.

Sanditon. Ed J. E. Austen-Leigh 1871 (in Memoir, extracts amounting to one-sixth); ed R. W. Chapman, Oxford 1925 (250 copies with ms facs); ed R. B. Johnson 1934 (with Lady Susan and The Watsons). A fragment of c. 24,000 words written 17 Jan to 18 March 1817.

Three evening prayers. Ed W. M. Roth, San Francisco 1940. Of unknown date.

Shorter works. Ed R. Church 1963. Selection.

Letters

Austen-Leigh, J. E. A memoir of Jane Austen. 1870, 1871 (enlarged with extracts from letters).

Letters of Jane Austen. Ed Edward Lord Brabourne 2 vols 1884.

Letters of Jane Austen selected from the compilation of Lord Brabourne by S. C. Woolsey. Boston 1892.

Hubback, J. H. and E. C. Jane Austen's sailor brothers. 1906. Includes unpbd letters to Francis Austen.

Austen-Leigh, W. and R. A. Jane Austen: her life and letters. 1913. Includes extensive quotations from unpbd letters.

Five letters from Jane Austen to her niece Fanny Knight. Ed R. W. Chapman, Oxford 1924 (facs).

The letters of Jane Austen. Ed R. B. Johnson 1925. Selection.

Jane Austen's letters. Ed R. W. Chapman 2 vols or 1 Oxford 1932, 1 vol Oxford 1952 (with corrections and addns, including notes and indexes to the literary works).

Letters of Jane Austen 1796–1817. Ed R. W. Chapman, Oxford 1955 (WC). Selection.

§2

Further titles in J. P. Anderson's bibliography appended to G. Smith, Life of Jane Austen, 1891; *in the bibliographies of Chapman and Keynes above; and in* C. B. Hogan, Jane Austen and her early public, RES new ser 1 1950.

Critical Rev Feb 1812; Br Critic May 1812. Reviews of Sense and sensibility.

Br Critic Feb 1813; Critical Rev March 1813. Reviews of Pride and prejudice.

[Scott, W.] Quart Rev 14 1815. Review of Emma.

Br Critic July 1816; Monthly Rev July 1816; GM Sept 1816; Literary Panorama June 1816. Reviews of Emma.

Br Critic March 1818; GM July 1818; Edinburgh Mag new ser 2 1818. Reviews of Northanger Abbey and Persuasion.
[Whately, R.] Quart Rev 24 1821. Review of Northanger Abbey and Persuasion.
Retrospective Rev 7 1823. In a review of Life and adventures of Peter Wilkins.
Edinburgh Mag 16 1824. In a review of Inheritance.
[Lister, T. H.] Edinburgh Rev 53 1830. In a review of Women as they are.
Elwood, A. K. In her Memoirs of the literary ladies of England, 1843.
Macaulay, T. B. The diary and letters of Mme D'Arblay. Edinburgh Rev 76 1843.
[Lewes, G. H.] Recent novels. Fraser's Mag Dec 1847.
— The lady novelists. Westminster Rev 58 1852.
— The novels of Jane Austen. Blackwood's Mag July 1859.
[Kirk, J. F.] Thackeray as a novelist. North Amer Rev July 1853.
[Pollock, W. F.] British novelists. Fraser's Mag Jan 1860.
Kavanagh, J. In her English women of letters, Leipzig 1862.
[Simpson, R.] Jane Austen. North Br Rev 52 1870.
Austen-Leigh, J. E. A memoir of Jane Austen. 1870, 1871 (enlarged), Boston 1892 (as Lady Susan, The Watsons); ed R. W. Chapman, Oxford 1926 (text of 1871, omitting extracts from juvenilia, minor works and fragments); ed D. W. Harding 1965 (1871 text, omitting extracts etc, with Persuasion).
Smith, G. Jane Austen. Nation (New York) 1870.
Forsyth, W. In his Novels and novelists of the eighteenth century, 1871.
Ritchie, A. T. In her Toilers and spinners, 1874; in her Book of sibyls, 1883 (rev).
'Tytler, S.' (H. Keddie). Jane Austen and her works. [1880].
W., M.A. Style and Miss Austen. Macmillan's Mag Dec 1884.
Oliphant, M. O. In his Literary history of England, 1882.
[Lefroy, F. C.] Is it just? and a Bundle of letters. Temple Bar Feb 1883. By a grandniece of Jane Austen.
Pellew, W. G. Jane Austen's novels. Boston 1883.
Lang, A. In his Letters to dead authors, 1886.
Adams, O. F. Chapters from Jane Austen. Boston 1888.
— The story of Jane Austen's life. Chicago 1891, Boston 1897 (rev).
Cone, H. G. and J. L. Gilder. In their Pen-portraits of literary women, [1888].
Higginson, T. W. In his Women and men, New York 1888.
Dodge, R. E. N. The note of provinciality in Miss Austen's novels. Harvard Monthly June 1889.
Fawcett, H. In her Some eminent women of our time, 1889.
Malden, S. F. Jane Austen. 1889.
Jack, A. A. Essays on the novel as illustrated by Scott and Miss Austen. 1897.
Pollock, W. H. Jane Austen, her contemporaries and herself. 1899.
Howells, W. D. In his Heroines of fiction, New York 1901.
— Introduction to Pride and prejudice. 1918.
Bonnell, H. H. Charlotte Brontë, George Eliot, Jane Austen. New York 1902.
Hill, C. Jane Austen, her homes and her friends. 1902, 1923. Quotes extensively from family mss otherwise unknown.
James, H. In his Question of our speech, New York 1905.
Mitton, G. E. Jane Austen and her times. [1905].
Austen-Leigh, W. In his Augustus Austen-Leigh, 1906.
— and R. A. Jane Austen: her life and letters. 1913.
Hubback, J. H. and E. C. Jane Austen's sailor brothers. 1906.
— Pen-portraits in Jane Austen's novels. Cornhill Mag July 1928.
Phelps, W. L. Introduction to Jane Austen's novels. 1906.
Helm, W. H. Jane Austen and her country-house comedy. 1909.
— and M. G. Knight. In their Chawton Manor and its owners, 1911.
Austen-Leigh, M. A. In her James Edward Austen-Leigh: a memoir, 1911.
— Personal aspects of Jane Austen. 1920.
Bradley, A. C. Jane Austen. E & S 2 1911; rptd in his A miscellany, 1929.
Benson, A. C. Jane Austen at Lyme Regis. Cornhill Mag May 1909.
— Realism in fiction. Cornhill Mag May 1912.
Fitzgerald, P. Jane Austen: a criticism and appreciation. 1912.
Sackville, M. Jane Austen. 1912.
Brinton, S. G. Old friends and new fancies: an imaginary sequel to the novels of Jane Austen. [1913].
Cornish, F. W. Jane Austen. 1913.
Bassi, E. Medaglione letterari la vita e le opera di Jane Austen e George Eliot. Rome 1914.
Rague, K. and P. Jane Austen. Paris 1914.
Villard, L. Jane Austen: sa vie et son oeuvre. Paris 1915; tr 1924 (in part).
Farrer, R. Jane Austen. Quart Rev 228 1917.
Johnson, R. B. In his Women novelists, [1918].
— A new study of Jane Austen. In L. Villard, Jane Austen, 1924.
— Jane Austen. 1925.
— Jane Austen. [1927].
— Jane Austen: her life, her work, her family and her critics. [1930].
Moore, G. In his Avowals, 1919.
Firkins, O. W. Jane Austen. New York 1920.
Lubbock, P. In his Craft of fiction, 1921.
Meynell, A. In her Second person singular, 1921.
Murry, J. M. In his Problem of style, 1921.
Walkley, A. B. In his Pastiche and prejudice, 1921; More prejudices, 1923; Still more prejudices, 1925.
The novels of Jane Austen. Edinburgh Rev 239 1924.
[Chapman, R. W.] Jane Austen's methods. TLS 9 Feb 1922.
Chapman, R. W. Jane Austen and her publishers. London Mercury Aug 1930.
— Jane Austen: a reply to Mr Garrod. Trans Royal Soc of Lit 10 1931.
— Jane Austen's library. Book Collectors' Quart 11 1933.
— Jane Austen's text. TLS 13 Feb 1937.
— Jane Austen: facts and problems. Oxford 1948, 1950 (corrected).
— Northanger Abbey. TLS 13 Oct 1949.
— Jane Austen's friend Mrs. Barrett. Nineteenth-Century Fiction 4 1950.
Bald, A. M. In her Women writers of the nineteenth century, 1923.
Birrell, A. In his More obiter dicta, 1924.
Hopkins, A. B. Love and friendship. South Atlantic Quart 24 1925.
— Jane Austen the critic. PMLA 40 1925.
MacKinnon, F. D. Topography and travel in Jane Austen's novels. Cornhill Mag Aug 1925.
Priestley, J. B. In his English comic characters, 1925.
Rowland-Brown, L. Jane Austen abroad. Nineteenth Century Nov 1925.
Woolf, V. In her Common reader, 1925.
— In her Granite and rainbow, 1958.
Sadleir, M. The Northanger novels. Oxford 1927.
Garrod, H. W. Jane Austen: a depreciation. Trans Royal Soc of Lit new ser 8 1928.
Bailey, J. C. Introductions to Jane Austen. 1931.
Canby, H. S. Emma and Mr Knightley. New York 1931.
Apperson, G. L. A Jane Austen dictionary. 1932.
MacCarthy, D. In his Criticism, 1932.
Reitzel, W. Mansfield Park and Lovers vows. RES 9 1933.

Lascelles, M. Miss Austen and some books. London Mercury April 1934.
— Some characteristics of Jane Austen's style. E & S 22 1937.
— Jane Austen and her art. Oxford, 1939, 1941 (corrected).
Rawlence, G. Jane Austen. 1934.
Cecil, D. Jane Austen. 1935.
— In his Fine art of writing, 1957.
— Jane Austen's lesser works. 1964 (Jane Austen Soc).
Bowen, E. In English novelists, ed D. Verschoyle 1936.
Forster, E. M. In his Abinger harvest, 1936.
Smith, L. P. In his Re-perusals and re-collections, 1936.
Austen-Leigh, E. Jane Austen and Steventon. 1937.
— Jane Austen and Bath. 1939.
— Jane Austen and Lyme Regis. 1940.
— Jane Austen and Southampton. 1949.
Seymour, B. K. Jane Austen. 1937.
Turpin, A. R. Jane Austen. Eng Rev 69 1937.
Jenkins, E. Jane Austen. 1938.
Ragg, L. M. Jane Austen in Bath. 1938.
Wilson, M. Jane Austen and some contemporaries. 1938.
Anson, H. The Church in nineteenth-century fiction, i: Jane Austen. Listener 20 April 1939.
Alexander, S. In his Philosophical and literary pieces, 1939.
Austen-Leigh, R. A. Pedigree of Austen. 1940 (priv ptd).
— Austen papers 1704–1856. 1942 (priv ptd). With addns and corrections to the Memoir and Life and letters.
— Jane Austen and Lyme Regis. 1946.
— Jane Austen and Southampton. 1949.
Harding, D. W. Regulated hatred: an aspect of the work of Jane Austen. Scrutiny 8 1940.
Jane Austen society: annual report, 1940– . Contains annual address, occasional historical notes.
Tompkins, J. M. S. Elinor and Marianne. RES 16 1940.
Gorer, G. The myth in Jane Austen. Amer Image 2 1941.
—Poor honey. London Mag Aug 1957.
Leavis, Q. D. A critical theory of Jane Austen's writings. Scrutiny 10 1942, 12 1944.
Woolf, L. The economic determinism of Jane Austen. New Statesman 18 July 1942.
Kaye-Smith, S. and G. B. Stern. Talking of Jane Austen. 1944.
— More talk of Jane Austen. 1950.
Brower, R. A. The controlling hand: Jane Austen and Pride and prejudice. Scrutiny 13 1945.
— In his Fields of light, New York 1951.
Kliger, S. Jane Austen's Pride and prejudice in the eighteenth-century mode. UTQ 16 1947.
[Knight, Fanny]. Letter by a niece of Jane Austen. Cornhill Mag 163 1948.
Daiches, D. Jane Austen, Karl Marx and the aristocratic dance. Amer Scholar 17 1948.
Maugham, W. S. Pride and prejudice. Atlantic Monthly May 1948.
Ashton, H. Parson Austen's daughter. 1949.
Jane Austen and Jane Austen's house. 1949 (Jane Austen Memorial Trust).
Muir, E. In his Essays on literature and society, 1949.
Jane Austen and the sense of evil. New York Times Book Rev 28 Aug 1949.
Schorer, M. Fiction and the 'matrix of analogy'. Kenyon Rev 11 1949.
— Pride unprejudiced. Kenyon Rev 18 1956.
— The humiliation of Emma Woodhouse. Literary Rev 2 1959.
Collins, B. B. Jane Austen's Victorian novel. Nineteenth-Century Fiction 4 1950.
Emden, C. S. Northanger Abbey re-dated? N & Q Sept 1950.
Hayes, E. N. Emma: a dissenting opinion. Nineteenth-Century Fiction 4 1950.
Hogan, C. B. Jane Austen and her early public. RES new ser 1 1950.
Kennedy. M. Jane Austen. 1950.
— 'How ought a novelist?' Fortnightly Rev Nov 1952.
Wilson, E. A long talk about Jane Austen. In his Classics and commercials, New York 1950.
Bradbrook, F. W. Style and judgment in Jane Austen's novels. Cambridge Jnl June 1951.
— Letters of Jane Austen. Ibid.
— Lord Chesterfield and Jane Austen. N & Q Feb 1958.
— Sources of Jane Austen's ideas about nature in Mansfield Park. N & Q June 1961.
— Jane Austen: Emma. 1961.
— Lydia Languish, Lydia Bennet and Dr Fordyce's sermons. N & Q Nov 1964.
— Jane Austen and her predecessors. 1966.
Duncan-Jones, E. E. (E. E. Phare). Notes on Jane Austen. N & Q Jan 1951.
— Jane Austen and Clarissa. N & Q Sept 1963.
— Lydia Languish, Lydia Bennet and Dr Fordyce's Sermons. N & Q May 1964. Reply by F. W. Bradbrook, Nov 1964.
McKillop, A. D. Allusions to prose fiction in Volume the third. N & Q Sept 1951.
— The context of Sense and sensibility. Rice Inst Pamphlets 44 1958.
Parks, E. W. Jane Austen's art of rudeness. UTQ 20 1951.
— Exegesis in Jane Austen's novels. South Atlantic Quart 51 1952.
— Jane Austen's lure of the next chapter. Nineteenth-Century Fiction 7 1953.
— A human failing in Pride and prejudice. Nineteenth-Century Fiction 10 1956.
Warner, S. T. Jane Austen. 1951, 1964 (rev).
Austen, C. My aunt Jane Austen. 1952. Recollections written in 1867.
Becker, M. L. Presenting Jane Austen. New York 1952.
Mudrick, M. Jane Austen: irony as defense and discovery. Princeton 1952.
Tucker, A. E. H. Religion in Jane Austen's novels. Theology 55 1952.
Greene, D. J. Jane Austen and the peerage. PMLA 68 1953.
Trilling, L. A portrait of Western man. Listener 11 June 1953.
— Mansfield Park. Partisan Rev 21 1954; rptd in his Opposing self, New York 1955; rev as Jane Austen and Mansfield Park in Pelican guide to English literature, ed B. Ford vol 5, 1957.
— Emma. Encounter June 1957.
Van Ghent, D. In her English novel, New York 1953.
Wright, A. H. Jane Austen's novels: a study in structure. 1953, 1964 (rev).
Cohen, L. D. Insight, the essence of Jane Austen's artistry. Nineteenth-Century Fiction 8 1954.
Duffy, J. M. Emma: the awakening from innocence. ELH 21 1954.
— Structure and idea in Persuasion. Nineteenth-Century Fiction 8 1954.
Paul, D. The gay apprentice. Twentieth Century Dec 1954.
Burchell, S. C. Jane Austen: the theme of isolation. Nineteenth-century Fiction 10 1956.
Bush, D. Mrs Bennet and the dark gods. Sewanee Rev 64 1956.
Freeman, K. T'other Miss Austen. 1956.
Shannon, E. F. Emma: character and construction. PMLA 71 1956.
Bowen, E. Persuasion. London Mag April 1957.
Mathison, J. K. Northanger Abbey and Jane Austen's conception of the value of fiction. ELH 24 1957.
'O'Connor, Frank.' In his Mirror in the roadway, 1957.
Murrah, C. The background of Mansfield Park. In From Jane Austen to Joseph Conrad, ed R. C. Rathburn and M. Steinmann, Minneapolis 1958.

Rawson, C. J. The sentimental hero in fiction and life. N & Q June 1958.
— Nice and sentimental. N & Q May 1964.
Gillie, C. Sense and sensibility: an assessment. EC 9 1959.
Southam, B. C. Jane Austen: an early comment on Mansfield Park. N & Q Nov 1959.
— The text of Sanditon. N & Q Jan 1961.
— Jane Austen: a broken romance? N & Q Dec 1961.
— Interpolations to Jane Austen's Volume the third. N & Q May 1962.
— The manuscript of Volume the first. Library 5th ser 17 1962.
— Mrs Leavis and Miss Austen: the 'critical theory' reconsidered. Nineteenth-Century Fiction 17 1963.
— A note on Volume the first. N & Q Nov 1962.
— Northanger Abbey. TLS 12 Oct 1963. Reply by A. H. Burke 9 Nov 1963.
— Jane Austen. TLS 30 Nov 1962. Replies by S. G. Brade-Birks 21 Dec 1962, C. B. Hogan 11 Jan 1963, B. C. Southam 25 Jan 1963, A. H. Burke 8 Feb 1963.
— Jane Austen and Clarissa. N & Q May 1963.
— Jane Austen's juvenilia: the question of completeness. N & Q May 1964.
— Jane Austen's literary manuscripts. Oxford 1964.
— (ed). Jane Austen: critical essays. 1968.
Hubback, J. The parents in Jane Austen's novels. [1960] (priv ptd).
Martin, W. R. Emma: a definition of virtue. Eng Stud in Africa 3 1960.
— Sensibility and sense: a reading of Persuasion. Ibid.
Booth, W. C. In his Rhetoric of fiction, Chicago 1961. On Emma.
Heath, W. W. Discussions of Jane Austen. Boston 1961.
Halliday, E. M. Narrative perspective in Pride and prejudice. Nineteenth-Century Fiction 15 1961.
Jack, I. The epistolary element in Jane Austen. Eng Stud Today 2 1961.
Levine, J. A. Lady Susan: Jane Austen's character of the merry widow. Stud in Eng Lit 1500–1900 1 1961.
Litz, A. W. The loiterer: a reflection on Jane Austen's early environment. RES new ser 12 1961.
— The chronology of Mansfield Park. N & Q June 1961.
— Jane Austen: a study of her artistic development. 1965.
Watson, W. Jane Austen in London. 1961.
Babb, H. S. Jane Austen's novels: the fabric of dialogue. Columbus 1962.
Bradbury, M. Jane Austen's Emma. CQ 4 1962.
Ebiike, S. Jane Austen. Tokyo 1962.
— Persuasion: symptoms of romanticism. Stud in Eng Lit (Tokyo) 2 1962.
— Pride and prejudice and first impressions. Stud in Eng Lit (Tokyo) 5 1965.
Hughes, R. E. The education of Emma Woodhouse. Nineteenth-Century Fiction 16 1962.
Rosenfeld, S. Jane Austen and private theatricals. E & S new ser 15 1962.
Simon, I. Jane Austen and the art of the novel. E Studies 43 1962.
Cady, J. and I. Watt. Jane Austen's critics. CQ 5 1963.
Griffin, C. The development of realism in Jane Austen's early novels. ELH new ser 14 1963.
Liddell, R. The novels of Jane Austen. 1963.
Lodge, D. A question of judgment: the theatricals at Mansfield Park. Nineteenth-Century Fiction 17 1963.
Sparrow, J. Jane Austen and Sydney Smith. In his Independent essays, 1963.
Jane Austen: a collection of critical essays. Ed I. Watt, Englewood Cliffs NJ 1963.
ten Harmsel, H. Jane Austen: a study in fictional conventions. Hague 1964.
White, E. M. Emma and the parodic point of view. Nineteenth-Century Fiction 18 1964.
Craik, W. A. Jane Austen: the six novels. 1965.
Kearful, F. J. Satire and the form of the novel. ELH 32 1965.
McCann, C. J. Setting and character in Pride and prejudice. Nineteenth-Century Fiction 19 1965.
Wiltshire, J. Mansfield Park. Critical Rev 8 1965.
Zietlow, P. N. Luck and fortuitous circumstance in Persuasion. ELH Ibid.
Donohue, J. W. Ordination and the divided house at Mansfield Park. Nineteenth-Century Fiction 20 1966.
Edwards, T. R. The difficult beauty of Mansfield Park. Ibid.
Ryle, G. Jane Austen and the moralists. Oxford Rev 1 1966.
Sherry, N. Jane Austen. 1966.
Crane, R. S. Persuasion. In his Idea of the humanities vol 2, Chicago 1967.
Lerner, L. The truthtellers: Jane Austen, George Eliot, D. H. Lawrence. 1967.
Poirier, R. In his A world elsewhere, New York 1967.
Fleishman, A. A reading of Mansfield Park. Minneapolis 1967.

B. C. S.

THOMAS LOVE PEACOCK
1785–1866

Bibliographies

Brett-Smith, H. F. B. and C. E. Jones. In Works: Halliford edition, below. Index bibliography in vol 1, 1934, with Peacockiana to 1933; indexes to verse in vol 7.
Sadleir, M. In his XIX century fiction: a bibliographical record, 2 vols 1951. Lists novels and pieces in Bentley's Miscellany.
Read, B. Peacock: an enumerative bibliography. Bull of Bibliography 24 1964.
Ward, W. S. Contemporary reviews of Peacock: a supplementary list for the years 1805–20. Bull of Bibliography 25 1967.

Collections

Headlong Hall, Nightmare Abbey, Maid Marian and Crotchet Castle. Vol 57 of Bentley's Standard novel ser 1837, 1849. All rev, with new preface.
[Works]. Ed H. Cole 3 vols 1875. With preface by Baron Houghton, biographical notice by Edith Nicolls.
[Works]. Ed R. Garnett, illustr H. Railton 10 vols 1891.
[Novels and Rhododaphne]. 5 vols 1895–7. Introds to each vol by G. Saintsbury; illustr F. H. Townsend, except vol 2 (Headlong Hall, Nightmare Abbey), illustr H. R. Millar.
Novels. 1903.
[Works]. Ed R. B. Johnson 3 vols 1905–6.
Plays. Ed A. B. Young 1910.
Selections. Ed W. H. Helm 1911.
[Works]. The Halliford edition. Ed H. F. B. Brett-Smith and C. E. Jones 10 vols 1924–34. Biographical introd in vol 1 not yet superseded; bibliographical notes follow each major work, full collations with binding notes and publishing history; letters; appendix of lost and doubtful works; indexes in vol 1, 1934.
Selections. Ed H. F. B. Brett-Smith 1928.
Pleasures of Peacock. Ed B. R. Redman 1947.
Novels. Ed D. Garnett 1948, 2 vols 1963 (corrected).
A selection. Ed H. L. B. Moody 1966.

§ 1

For contributions to periodicals, see Works, Halliford edn vol 1, pp. 179–81; *for posthumous works including fragments, see* Contents of vols 7–8; *for critical reviews and occasional journalism, see* Contents of vols 9–10.

Answer to the question, Is history or biography the more improving study? Juvenile library (later Juvenile encyclopaedia), pt 1 (Feb 1800) issued in pts 1800–3; rptd 6 vols 1803.
The monks of St Mark. 1804 (priv ptd).

Palmyra and other poems. 1806, 1812 (below, extensively rev), 1817.

The genius of the Thames: a lyrical poem in two parts. 1810, 1812 (below, rev), 1817.

The genius of the Thames, Palmyra and other poems. 1812, 1817 (reissued as 'second edition' in 1817, title and contents pages only reset).

The philosophy of melancholy: a poem in four parts, with a mythological ode. 1812.

Sir Hornbook, or Childe Launcelot's expedition: a grammatico-allegorical ballad. [1813], 1814, 1815, 1815, [1817?] (no known copy), 1818; ed H. Cole ('Felix Summerly') 1843, 1845, 1855 (illustr H. Corbould, redrawn for Home Treasury ser). Anon.

Sir Proteus: a satirical ballad, by P. M. O'Donovan esq. 1814. Anon.

Headlong Hall. 1816 (anon), Philadelphia 1816, London 1816 (rev), 1823 (rev), 1837 (slightly rev) (Bentley's Standard Novels), 1849, New York 1845 (with Nightmare Abbey as no 7, Wiley and Putnam's Library of Choice Reading), 1850 (Putnam's Choice Library), London 1856 (first signed edn), New York 1887 (first signed US edn), 1888, 1895; ed R. Garnett 1908 (EL); Oxford 1929 (WC); ed J. Mair 1940 (with Nightmare Abbey and Crotchet Castle); ed J. Tamagnan, Paris 1958 (abridged); ed P. Yarker 1961 (EL). All edns 1850–1929 include Nightmare Abbey, below.

Melincourt, by the author of Headlong Hall. 3 vols 1817, 2 vols Philadelphia 1817, 1 vol 1856 (with new preface); tr French, 2 vols 1818.

The Round Table: or King Arthur's Feast, embellished with eighteen engravings. [1817?]. Announced as By the author of Sir Hornbook in Edinburgh Rev 29 1817. Only known copy at Chapin Library, Williamstown Mass.

Rhododaphne, or the Thessalian spell: a poem. 1818, Philadelphia 1818; Southern Literary Messenger (Richmond Virginia) 9 1843 (attributed to Richard Dabney; attribution later withdrawn). Anon.

Nightmare Abbey, by the author of Headlong Hall. 1818, Philadelphia 1819, ed C. E. Jones 1923; 1837 (Bentley's Standard Novels) (rev; all subsequent edns except 1923 follow rev text), 1849, New York 1845, 1850 (with Headlong Hall), London 1856, New York 1887, 1888, 1895; ed R. Garnett 1908 (EL); Oxford 1929 (WC); ed J. Mair 1940 (with Headlong Hall and Crotchet Castle); ed A. Hodge, introd by J. B. Priestley 1947 (with Crotchet Castle), tr Italian, 1958; ed J.-J. Mayoux, Paris 1936 (with Misfortunes of Elphin) (with French trn); New York and Toronto 1964; ed C. Connolly 1953; ed P. Yarker 1961 (EL); tr German, 1913; Italian, 1952; Portuguese, 1958; dramatized by A. Sharp 1953; by H. Nicholson 1954 (for BBC Third Programme Dec 1949). All edns in English 1850–1929 include Headlong Hall, above.

The four ages of poetry. Ollier's Literary Miscellany no 1 (only issue) 1820 (anon), [Belfast 1863] (priv ptd) (anon); ed R. Garnett 1891 (with Calidore etc); ed A. S. Cook, Boston 1891 (with Shelley's Defence); ed H. F. B. Brett-Smith 1921 (with Shelley's Defence and Browning's Essay on Shelley), 1923 (corrected); ed J. E. Jordan, Indianapolis 1965 (with Shelley's Defence).

Maid Marian, by the author of Headlong Hall. 1822; 1837 (Bentley's Standard Novels) (rev), 1849, 1856 (with Crotchet Castle); ed G. Saintsbury, illustr F. H. Townsend 1959 (with Crotchet Castle); tr German, 1823; French, 1826; 1855; Serbo-Croat, 1957; operatic adaptation by J. R. Planché, music by H. Bishop 1822?, New York 1823; concert adaptation by C. LeFleming [c. 1939].

The misfortunes of Elphin, by the author of Headlong Hall. 1829; illustr H. W. Bray, Newtown Montgomeryshire 1928; ed R. W. Chapman, Oxford 1924 (WC) (with Crotchet Castle); Paris 1936 (with Nightmare Abbey, above) (with French trn); War Song of Dinas Vawr, tr Welsh, E. Roberts set to music by C. Harper [Wrexham 1933]; Seithenyn episodes rptd in J. B. Priestley, Fools and philosophers, 1925.

Crotchet Castle, by the author of Headlong Hall. 1831; 1837 (Bentley's Standard Novels) (rev), 1849; 1856 (with Maid Marian); ed H. Morley 1887; ed R. W. Chapman, Oxford 1924 (WC) (with Misfortunes of Elphin); ed J. Mair 1940 (with Headlong Hall, Nightmare Abbey); ed A. Hodge, introd by J. B. Priestley 1947 (with Nightmare Abbey), tr Italian, 1958; ed K. Hopkins, illustr P. Reddick 1964.

Report from the select committee on steam navigation to India: appendix. 1834.

Review of Report from the Select Committee of the House of Commons on Steam Navigation to India. Edinburgh Rev 60 1835. *See also* Halliford edn of Works vol 1, p. clxvi.

Paper money lyrics, and other poems. 1837 (priv ptd).

A whitebait dinner at Lovegrove's at Blackwall. 1851 (priv ptd). Greek and Latin versions by Peacock (englished by John Cam Hobhouse, texts and details in Halliford edn of Works vol 7).

Memoirs of Percy Bysshe Shelley. Fraser's Mag June 1858–March 1862; ed H. F. B. Brett-Smith 1909; ed B. H. Clark, New York 1928 (in Great short biographies of the world); ed H. Wolfe 2 vols 1933 (in The life of P. B. Shelley, as comprised in the Life by T. J. Hogg, the Recollections by E. J. Trelawny, and Memoirs by Peacock).

Unpublished letters of Percy Bysshe Shelley from Italy 1818–22. Fraser's Mag March, May 1860; ed H. F. B. Brett-Smith 1909 (with Memoirs of Shelley).

Gryll Grange, by the author of Headlong Hall. Fraser's Mag April–Dec 1860; 1861 (rev), 1947 (Penguin).

Gl'ingannati, the deceived: a comedy performed at Siena in 1531, and Aelia Laelia Crispis. 1862; ed H. H. Furness 1901 (in New variorum edition of Shakespeare, Twelfe Night, vol 13).

A bill for the better promotion of oppression on the Sabbath day. Illustr L. Fraser, Plaistow 1926 (priv ptd).

Letters and Papers

Peacock's books and letters from Shelley were sold at Sotheby's, June 1866; his granddaughter, Edith Nicolls Clarke, sold the literary mss to BM in 1903, pbd variously by Garnett and Young, complete by Brett-Smith and Jones; her daughters sold letters and miscellaneous mss at Sotheby's, Nov 1949. The Whitton papers, including Peacock's letters etc as executor for Shelley, were sold at Sotheby's July 1918, and the Hogg family papers, including Peacock's letters, at Sotheby's July 1922 and June–July 1948; see price catalogues in BM.

Letters to Edward Hookham and Percy B. Shelley, with fragments of unpublished manuscripts. Ed R. Garnett, Boston 1910.

Halliford edition vol 8. Ed H. F. B. Brett-Smith and C. E. Jones 1934. Includes some letters to Peacock, correspondence other than Shelley and Hogg.

New Shelley letters. Ed W. S. Scott 1948. Combines 3 vols of letters by and to Shelley, 1943–4, including Peacock's: The Athenians, Shelley at Oxford, Harriet and Mary.

Two letters of Peacock. Ed D. B. Green. PQ 40 1961.

§2

For a fuller account of early reviews see B. Read *and* W. S. Ward *under* Bibliographies, *above.*

[Hodgson, F.] The genius of the Thames. Monthly Rev Feb 1811.

Rhododaphne. La Belle Assemblée April 1818. Extensive quotation of about one-sixth of whole; rptd in Athe-

naeum or Spirit of the English Magazines (Boston) July 1818.
Rhododaphne. Virginia Evangelical & Literary Mag (Richmond) May 1819. Ascribes authorship to Dabney for first time.
[Fonblanque, A.] Crotchet Castle. Westminster Rev 15 1831.
[Spedding, J.] Headlong Hall [etc]. Edinburgh Rev 68 1839. A review of Bentley Standard Novels, rptd as preface to Wiley and Putnam edn of 1845 etc; rptd in Spedding, Reviews and discussions, 1879.
Langley, H. Headlong Hall and Nightmare Abbey. United States Mag & Democratic Rev 16 1845.
Garnett, R. Shelley, Harriet Shelley and Mr Peacock. In his Relics of Shelley, 1862. An attack, part of controversy between Peacock and Lady Shelley.
[Hannay, J.] Recent humourists: Aytoun, Peacock, Prout. North Br Rev 45 1866; rptd Living Age (Boston) 2 Oct 1866.
Smith, G. B. Thomas Love Peacock. Fortnightly Rev Aug 1873; rptd in his Poets and novelists, 1875.
[Cole, H.] Peacock: biographical notes from 1785 to 1862. [1874?] (priv ptd, copy in BM).
[Gosse, E.] Thomas Love Peacock. London Soc June 1875.
Shelley, P. B. On Rhododaphne. In his Notes on sculpture, ed H. B. Forman 1879. Written 1818.
Buchanan, R. Peacock: a personal reminiscence. New Quart Mag 4 1875; rptd in his A look round literature, 1887.
Saintsbury, G. Thomas Love Peacock. Macmillan's Mag April 1886; rptd in his Essays in English literature 1780–1860, 1890.
Strachey, E. Nonsense as a fine art. Quart Rev 167 1888.
—— Recollections of Peacock. In Calidore and miscellanea, ed R. Garnett 1891.
Stoddard, R. H. In his Under the evening lamp, New York 1892.
Garnett, R. In his Essays of an ex-librarian, 1901. Rptd from his edn of Peacock, 1891.
Axon, W. E. A. The juvenile library. Library new ser 2 1901. Identifies Peacock's first pbd work; reprints the verses which won the Extra prize.
Young, A. B. The life and novels of Peacock; inaugural dissertation University of Freiburg. Norwich 1904 (priv ptd).
—— Peacock and the Overland route. N & Q 17 Aug 1907. Bibliographical data on Peacock's India House career, evidence before Select committees etc. Augmented by further references, chiefly to Marine records etc in Halliford edn vol 1, pp. 165–7.
Freeman, A. M. Peacock: a critical study. 1911.
Van Doren, C. The life of Peacock. 1911.
Hartley, L. C. Thomas Love Peacock. Manchester Quart 34 1915.
Foster, W. The East India House: its history and associations. 1924. Chs 14–15 discuss the Examiner's department, including James Mill, Peacock, Strachey et al.
Newbolt, H. Peacock, Scott and Robin Hood. Trans Royal Soc of Lit 4 1924; rptd in his Studies green and gray, 1926.
Priestley, J. B. In his English comic characters, 1925. On Prince Seithenyn in Misfortunes of Elphin.
—— Thomas Love Peacock. 1927 (EML), 1966 (with preface by J. I. M. Stewart).
Wright, H. The associations of Peacock with Wales. E & S 12 1926.
Digeon, A. A. Peacock, ami de Shelley. Revue Anglo-américaine 5 1928.
Dannenberg, F. Peacock in seinem Verhältnis zu Shelley. Germanisch-romanische Monatsschrift 20 1932.
Mayoux, J.-J. Un épicurien anglais: Peacock. Paris 1932.
Able, A. H. George Meredith and Peacock: a study in literary influence. Philadelphia 1933.
Brett-Smith, H. F. B. The l'Estrange-Peacock correspondence. E & S 18 1933.
Nesbitt, G. L. In his Benthamite reviewing: the first twelve years of the Westminster review 1824–36, New York 1934.
Fedden, H. R. In the English novelists, ed D. Verschoyle 1936.
Cellini, B. Thomas Love Peacock. Rome 1937.
White, N. I. In his Unextinguished hearth: Shelley and his contemporary critics, Durham NC 1938. Reprints burlesque perhaps by Peacock entitled Dinner by the amateurs of vegetable diet.
Mason, R. Notes for an estimate of Peacock. Horizon April 1944.
Steuert, H. Two Augustan studies: Thomas Gray and Peacock. Dublin Rev Jan 1945.
Mackerness, E. E. Peacock's musical criticism. Wind & Rain 4 1948.
Notopoulos, J. A. In his Platonism of Shelley, Durham NC 1949.
House, H. The works of Peacock. Listener 8 Dec 1949.
Jones, F. L. Macaulay's theory of poetry in Milton. MLQ 13 1952.
Campbell, O. W. Thomas Love Peacock. 1953.
Robinson, E. Peacock: critic of scientific progress. Annals of Science 10 1954.
Manganelli, G. T. L. Peacock. Paragone (Florence) 5 1954.
Salz, P. J. Peacock's use of music in his novels. JEGP 54 1955.
Wimsatt, W. K. jr and C. Brooks. Peacock vs Shelley: rhapsodic didacticism. In their Literary criticism, New York 1957.
Black, S. The Peacockian essence. Boston Univ Stud in Eng 3 1957.
Stěpaník, K. A source of Keats's La belle dame sans merci. Philologica Pragensia 1 1958.
Bernstein, H. T. In his Steamboats on the Ganges, Bombay 1960.
Nicholes, E. L. In Shelley and his circle vol i, Cambridge Mass 1961. Introd and commentary in letters and papers 1792–1809.
Tillyard, E. M. W. In his Essays literary and educational, 1962.
Beyer, W. W. The case of Peacock's Rhododaphne. In his Enchanted forest, New York 1963.
Stewart, J. I. M. Thomas Love Peacock. 1963 (Br Council pamphlet).
Fain, J. T. Peacock on the spirit of the age 1809–60. In Essays in honor of C. A. Robertson, Gainesville 1965.
Baker, J. E. Shelley's Platonic answer to a Platonic attack on poetry. Iowa City 1965.
Chandler, A. The quarrel of the Ancients and the Moderns: Peacock and the medieval revival. Bucknell Rev 13 1965.
Harrold, W. Keats's Lamia and Peacock's Rhododaphne. MLR 61 1966.
Kennedy, W. Peacock's economists: some mistaken identities. Nineteenth-Century Fiction 21 1967.

E. L. N.

FREDERICK MARRYAT

1792–1848

Bibliographies

Sadleir, M. In his Excursions in Victorian bibliography, 1922.
—— In his XIX century fiction: a bibliographical record, 2 vols 1951.

Collections

Works. 2 vols Philadelphia 1836, 14 vols Leipzig 1839–42.
Novels: the King's own edition. Ed W. L. Courtney 24 vols 1896–9.

Novels. Ed R. B. Johnson 24 vols 1896–8, 26 vols 1929–30.
Sämmtliche Werke. 42 vols Brunswick 1835–9, 26 vols Stuttgart 1843–6.
Œuvres complètes. 26 vols Paris 1836–8, 60 vols 1838–41.

§ 1

A code of signals for the use of vessels employed in the merchant service. 1817, 1837 (rev), 1841 (last edn rev Marryat).
A suggestion for the abolition of the present system of impressment in the naval service. 1822.
The naval officer: or scenes and adventures in the life of Frank Mildmay. 3 vols 1829, 1 vol 1836, 1839 etc, Paris 1840, London [1873] (with memoir by Florence Marryat); illustr H. R. Millar, ed D. Hannay 1897; tr German, 1835; French, 1838, 1838.
The King's own. 3 vols 1830, 1 vol Paris 1834, 3 vols 1836, 1 vol 1838 etc; 1874 (with memoir by Florence Marryat); illustr F. H. Townsend, ed D. Hannay 1896; ed W. C. Russell 1906; ed R. B. Johnson 1912; tr German, 1835; French, 1837.
Newton Forster: or the merchant service. 3 vols 1832, 1 vol Paris 1834, London 1838 etc; illustr E. J. Sullivan, ed D. Hannay 1897; tr German, 1836; French, 2 vols 1837.
Peter Simple. 3 vols Philadelphia 1833–4, London 1834, 1 vol Paris 1834; illustr R. W. Buss 3 vols 1837, 1 vol 1838 etc; illustr J. A. Symington, ed D. Hannay 1895; ed W. C. Russell 1904; ed R. B. Johnson 1907; ed M. Sadleir 2 vols 1929 (with Buss's illustrations); tr French, 1834; German, 1835. Serialized to end of ch 42 in Metropolitan Mag June 1832–Sept 1833.
Jacob Faithful. 3 vols Philadelphia 1834, London 1834, 1834, 1 vol Paris 1834, 3 vols 1835; illustr R. W. Buss 3 vols 1837, 1 vol 1838, Leipzig 1842 etc; illustr H. M. Brock, ed D. Hannay 1895; ed R. B. Johnson 1912; ed G. Saintsbury 2 vols 1928 (with 12 plates by Buss); ed D. Veale 1936; tr French and German, 1836. Serialized in Metropolitan Mag Sept 1833–Oct 1934.
The floral telegraph: a new mode of communication by floral signals, with plates. 1836 (anon), 1850 (reissued with Marryat's name on title page). Attributed to Marryat.
The Pacha of many tales. 3 vols 1835, 1835, 1 vol 1838, Paris 1840; tr German, 1835; French, 1837. The stories appeared intermittently in Metropolitan Mag June 1831–May 1835.
The diary of a blasé. Philadelphia 1836. Appeared in part in Metropolitan Mag 1836, subsequently as Diary on the continent in Olla podrida, below.
The pirate and the Three cutters, with illustrations by C. Stanfield. 1836, New York 1836 (as Stories of the sea), 2 vols Philadelphia 1836, 1 vol Paris 1836, 15 pts 1845, 1861 (with a memoir) etc; illustr E. J. Sullivan with introd by D. Hannay 1897; tr German, 1836; French, 1837.
Japhet in search of a father. 4 pts New York 1835–6, 3 vols 1836, 1836, 1 vol Paris 1836, London 1838 etc; illustr H. M. Brock with introd by D. Hannay 1895; tr French and German, 1836. Serialized in Metropolitan Mag Nov 1834–Jan 1836.
Mr Midshipman Easy. 3 vols 1836, 1 vol Paris 1836, London 1838 etc; illustr F. Pegram, ed D. Hannay 1896; ed W. C. Russell 1904; ed R. B. Johnson 1906; ed O. Warner 1954; tr German, 1836; French, 1837. The first 4 chs appeared in Metropolitan Mag Aug 1836.
Snarleyyow: or the dog fiend. 3 vols 1837, 1 vol Philadelphia 1837, Paris 1837, London 1847 (as The dog fiend) etc; illustr H. R. Millar, ed D. Hannay 1897. Serialized in Metropolitan Mag Jan 1836–July 1837.
The phantom ship. 3 vols 1839, 1 vol Paris 1839, London 1847 etc; illustr H. R. Millar, ed D. Hannay 1896; ed W. C. Russell 1906; ed M. W. Disher 1948; tr French and German, 1839. Serialized in New Monthly Mag March 1837–Aug 1839.
A diary in America, with remarks on its institutions. 2 pts 6 vols 1839, Philadelphia 1839–40; ed J. Zanger 1960 (with bibliography); ed S. W. Jackman, New York 1963 (abridged).
Poor Jack. 12 monthly pts illustr C. Stanfield 1840, 1 vol 1840, Paris 1841 etc; ed D. Hannay 1897; tr German, 1840; French, 1841.
Olla podrida. 3 vols 1840, 1 vol Paris 1840, 3 vols 1842, 1 vol 1849 etc. Diary on the Continent first appeared in Metropolitan Mag 1836 as Diary of a blasé, the shorter pieces partly in the same jnl, partly in New Monthly Mag, and Moonshine in Keepsake and in Stories of the sea, New York 1836.
Masterman Ready: or the wreck of the Pacific, written for young people. 3 vols 1841–2, 1 vol Paris 1842, London 1845 etc; ed D. Hannay, illustr F. Pegram 1901; tr German, 1843.
Joseph Rushbrook: or the poacher. 3 vols 1841, 1 vol Paris 1841, London 1846 (as The poacher) etc. Serialized weekly in Era Dec 1840–May 1841.
Percival Keene. 3 vols 1842, 1 vol Paris 1842, London 1848, 1857 (with memoir) etc; tr French, 1843; German, 1843.
Narrative of the travels and adventures of Monsieur Violet in California, Sonora and Western Texas. 3 vols 1843, 1 vol 1843 (as Travels and romantic adventures of Monsieur Violet among the Snake Indians), 1849 etc.
The settlers in Canada, written for young people. 2 vols 1844 etc; ed O. Warner 1956; tr French, 1852.
The mission: or scenes in Africa. 2 vols 1845; illustr J. Gilbert 1860; tr German, 1851; French, 1853.
The privateer's-man one hundred years ago. 2 vols 1846, 1 vol Paris 1846. Serialized in New Monthly Mag Aug 1845–June 1846.
The children of the New Forest. 2 vols 1847; illustr Frank Marryat 1849, 1850 etc; tr French, 1854. Planned for part-issue. Pt 1 only issued April 1847.
The little savage. 2 vols 1848–9 (pbd posthumously by Frank S. Marryat who completed the work from ch 3 of vol 2), 1853; illustr A. W. Cooper and J. Gilbert 1893 etc.
Valerie: an autobiography. 2 vols 1849 etc; tr German, 1850. Serialized to the end of vol 2 ch 3 in New Monthly Mag 1846–7. Finished by another hand and pbd posthumously.

There were many pirateed edns of Marryat's books pbd in America; see M. Sadleir, XIX century fiction, *above.*

Marryat owned and edited Metropolitan Mag *1832–6 and contributed 2 papers on* Novels and novel writing, Nov 1832, Oct 1834. *In 1836 he sponsored an anon novel by his sub-editor Edward Howard,* Rattlin the reefer. *This and Howard's other novels,* The old Commodore, Outward bound, Jack ashore, Sir Henry Morgan the buccaneer, *were often attributed to Marryat.*

§ 2

Neale, W. J. Will Watch vol 3, appendix 1834. Neale's account of his quarrel with Marryat.
Marryat's Snarleyyow. Dublin Univ Mag Sept 1837.
Marryat's novels. Fraser's Mag May 1838.
Lockhart, J. G. Quart Rev 64 1839. Review of Diary in America.
Empson, W. Marryat's Diary in America. Edinburgh Rev 70 1839.
Horne, R. H. In his A new spirit of the age vol 1, 1844.
Whitehead, C. Marryat. Bentley's Miscellany May 1848.
Marryat's sea stories. Dublin Univ Mag March 1856.
[Norris, E., née Marryat]. Captain Marryat at Langham. Cornhill Mag Aug 1867.
Marryat, Florence. Life and letters of Marryat. 2 vols 1872.

[Hannay, J.] Sea novels: Captain Marryat. Cornhill Mag Feb 1873.
Escott, T. H. S. Land and sea. London Soc Jan 1873. Comparison with Lever.
Poe, E. A. Francis Marryatt [sic]. In his Works, ed J. H. Ingram vol 4, 1875. A review of Joseph Rushbrook.
Hannay, D. Life of Frederick Marryat. 1889.
Conrad, J. Tales of the sea. Outlook 1898; rptd in his Notes on life and letters, 1924.
Walters, J. C. Dickens and Captain Marryat. Dickensian 14 1918.
Iddesleigh, S. H. Marryat as novelist. Monthly Rev Sept 1904.
Biron, H. C. In his Pious opinions, 1923.
Ley, J. W. T. Captain Marryat and Dickens. Dickensian 22 1926.
McGrath, M. A. A century of Marryat. Nineteenth Century Oct 1929.
Meyerstein, E. H. W. TLS 11 Nov 1933. On the sources of Peter Simple. *See also* W. L. Rowbotham 31 May 1934.
— Captain Marryat and the Ariadne. Mariner's Mirror 21 1935.
— A note on Masterman Ready. English 3 1941.
Bader, A. L. Captain Marryat and the American pirates. Library 4th ser 16 1935.
— The gallant captain and Brother Jonathan. Colophon 2 1936.
— Marryat's The Ocean Wolf. PQ 16 1937.
— Captain Marryat the man. N & Q 29 Jan 1938.
Walcutt, C. C. Captain Marryat and Boswell's Life of Johnson. N & Q 8 Jan 1938.
Lloyd, C. Captain Marryat and the old navy. 1939.
Woolf, V. The captain's death bed. In her Captain's death bed and other essays, 1950.
Warner, O. Captain Marryat: a rediscovery. 1953.
— Mr Golding and Marryat's Little savage. REL 5 1954.
Bowers, R. H. Some Marryat letters. N & Q Nov 1954.
Scott, K. W. TLS 1 Oct 1954. On the sources of M. Violet.
Zanger, J. Marryat, M. Violet and Edward La Salle. Nineteenth-Century Fiction 12 1958.
Ganzel, D. Samuel Clemens and Captain Marryat. Anglia 80 1963.
Schuhmann, K. Phrenologie und Ideologie: Marryats Mr Midshipman Easy. Die Neueren Sprachen 13 1964.
Doubleday, N. F. Jack Easy and Billy Budd. Eng Lang Notes 2 1965.

A. P. H.

III. MINOR FICTION 1800–1835

This section has been restricted, with few exceptions, to writers born between 1760 and 1800.

JOHN BANIM 1798–1842 and MICHAEL BANIM 1796–1874

The pseudonym 'the O'Hara family' was used for work in which both brothers collaborated but which was mostly planned, written or extensively revised by John Banim.

Bibliographies

Sadleir, M. In his XIX century fiction: a bibliographical record, 2 vols 1951.

§1

The Celt's paradise, in four duans by John Banim. 1821. A poem.
Damon and Pythias: a tragedy in five acts by John Banim. 1821, [1825?] (in J. Duncombe, British theatre vol 61), 1865 (in British Theatre vol 3), [1883] (in J. Dicks, Standard plays). By J. Banim; R. L. Sheil had a small share in this play.
A letter to the committee appointed to appropriate a fund for a national testimonial commemorative of His Majesty's first visit to Ireland. Dublin 1822. By J. Banim.
Revelations of the dead alive. 1824 (anon), 1845 (as London and its eccentricities in the year 2023: or revelations of the dead alive, by the author of Boyne Water). Essays by J. Banim.
Tales by the O'Hara family [ser 1] containing Crohoore of the billhook; The Fetches; John Doe. 3 vols 1825; ser 2 comprising The Nowlans and Peter of the Castle, 3 vols 1826, 1827.
  Sers 1–2 (as vols 1, 7 and 11 of the Parlour novelist) 3 vols London and Belfast 1846.
  Peter of the Castle and The Nowlans. 3 vols 1833.
  The Nowlans. 3 vols 1833, 1 vol 1853.
  Crohoore of the bill-hook and The Fetches 1838, 1848; Crohoore tr German, 1828; French, 1829.
  John Doe. 1842, 1853.
  The Peep o'day: or John Doe and Crohoore of the billhook. Ed M. Banim, Dublin 1865, London 1870, 1876.
  The Peep o'day: or Captain John Doe, the last of the guerillas. New York 1877, 1897.
  Peter of the Castle and The Fetches. Ed M. Banim, Dublin 1866.
The Boyne Water: a tale by the O'Hara family. 3 vols 1826, 1836; ed M. Banim, Dublin 1865, New York 1880; tr French, 1829.
The Anglo-Irish of the nineteenth century: a novel. 3 vols 1828, 1 vol Dublin 1865 (as Lord Clangore). By J. Banim.
The Croppy: a tale of 1798 by the authors of the O'Hara tales etc. 3 vols 1828, 2 vols Philadelphia 1839, 1 vol Dublin 1865; tr French, 4 vols 1833.
The denounced: or the last baron of Crana by the authors of Tales of the O'Hara family [and The conformists]. 3 vols 1830, New York 1830; ed M. Banim, Dublin 1866.
The smuggler: a tale by the authors of Tales of the O'Hara family. 3 vols 1831, 1 vol 1833, 1849, 1856.
The chaunt of the cholera: songs for Ireland by the authors of the O'Hara tales etc. 1831.
The ghost hunter and his family, by the O'Hara family. 1833, Philadelphia 1833, 1851. 1863, [1870] (as Joe Wilson's ghost), [1913]; tr French, 2 vols 1833.
The Mayor of Wind-gap and Canvassing, by the O'Hara family. 3 vols 1835, New York 1835; ed M. Banim, Dublin 1865. Canvassing is by Miss Martin of Ballynahinch.
The bit o'writin' and other tales by the O'Hara family. 3 vols 1838, 2 vols Philadelphia 1838; ed M. Banim, Dublin 1865.
Father Connell by the O'Hara family. 3 vols 1842, New York 1842, 1 vol 1849, Dublin 1858 (with introd and notes).

The loaded dice, by John Banim. In The omnibus of modern romance, New York 1844.
Clough Fion by M. Banim. Dublin Univ Mag Sept 1852.
The town of the cascades, by M. Banim. 2 vols 1864.
John Banim also wrote the following plays: The prodigal: a tragedy (*all trace lost*); Turgesius; The moorish wife; Sylla (*adapted from M. Jouy*); *and the novel*, The dwarf bride, 1829–31 (*ms lost*). Crohoore of the bill-hook *was dramatized by W. Mitchell*, Newcastle-on-Tyne 1828.

§2

[Lister, T. H.] Novels descriptive of Irish life. Edinburgh Rev 52 1831.
Griffin, D. The life of Gerald Griffin. 1843. Chs 7–8.
Horne, R. H. In his A new spirit of the age vol 2, 1844.
Irish Quart Rev 4–6 1854–6. Papers on John Banim.
Murray, P. J. The life of John Banim. 1857.
Steger, M. A. John Banim: ein Nachahmer Walter Scotts. Erlangen 1935.
Flanagan, T. In his Irish novelists 1800–50, Berkeley 1959. Chs 11–12.

RICHARD HARRIS BARHAM
1788–1845

See col 365, above.

EATON STANNARD BARRETT
1786–1820

Bibliographies

Summers, M. In his A Gothic bibliography, [1941].

§1

The rising sun: a serio-comic satiric romance by Cervantes Hogg, FSM. 2 vols 1807.
The second Titan war against heaven: a satirical poem by the author of the Rising sun. 1807.
All the talents: a satirical poem in three dialogues by Polypus. 1807 (at least 19 edns).
All the talents' garland, including Elijah's mantle and other poems. 1807, 1807.
The comet, by the author of All the talents. 1808.
The Miss-led general: a serio-comic, satiric, mock-heroic romance, by the author of the Rising sun. 1808, 1808.
The setting sun: or Devil amongst the placemen [and] a parody on the Beggar's opera, by Cervantes Hogg. 3 vols 1809.
The tarantula: or the dance of fools. 2 vols 1809.
Woman: a poem. 1810, 1818, 1819, 1822, 1841.
The metropolis: or a cure for gaming interspersed with anecdotes of living characters in high life by Cervantes Hogg. 3 vols 1811.
The heroine: or adventures of a fair romance reader. 3 vols 1813, 1814 (rev and sub-titled Adventures of Cherubina), 1815, 2 vols Philadelphia 1815, 3 vols 1816; ed W. Raleigh 1909; ed M. Sadleir 1927, New York 1928.
My wife! what wife? a comedy in three acts. 1815.
The talents run mad: or 1816, a satirical poem. 1816.
Six weeks at Long's, by a late resident. 3 vols 1817, 1817.

§2

McKillop, A. D. MLN 53 1938. On The hero: or the adventures of a night, incorrectly attributed to Barrett.
Mendenhall, J. C. Univ of Pennsylvania General Mag 30 1927. Barrett's letters to his bookseller.

THOMAS HAYNES BAYLY
1797–1839

See col 366, above.

ANNA MARIA BENNETT
c. 1750–1808

§1

Anna: or memoirs of a Welch heiress, interspersed with anecdotes of a Nabob. 4 vols 1785 (anon), 1786, 1796, 2 vols Dublin 1804, 1 vol 1854; tr French, 1788.
Juvenile indiscretions: a novel by the author of Anna, or the Welch heiress. 5 vols 1786, 1805; tr French, 1788.
Agnes de Courci: a domestic tale. 4 vols Bath 1789; tr French, 1789.
Ellen, Countess of Castle Howell: a novel. 4 vols 1794, 2 vols Dublin 1794, 4 vols 1805; tr French, 1822.
Henry Bennett and Julia Johnson. [1794?]; tr French, 1794.
The beggar girl and her benefactors: a novel. 7 vols 1797, 3 vols Dublin 1798, 5 vols 1799, 1 vol Philadelphia 1801, 5 vols 1813.
De Valcourt: a novel. 2 vols 1800, Philadelphia 1801.
Vicissitudes abroad: or the ghost of my father. 6 vols 1806; tr French, 1809.
Faith and fiction: or shining lights in a dark generation, a novel by Elizabeth [or rather A.M.] Bennett. 5 vols 1816; tr French, 1816.
Emily: or the wife's first error; and Beauty and ugliness: or the father's prayer and the mother's prophecy—two tales by Elizabeth [or rather A. M.] Bennett. 4 vols 1819.
These last 2 titles are doubtfully attributed to A. M. Bennett in BM catalogue, which also adopts the DNB's erroneous form of name, Agnes Maria Bennett.

§2

Lewes, C. L. In his Memoirs vol 4, 1805.
Fuller, J. F. A curious genealogical medley. In Miscellanea genealogica et heraldica, 1913. On A. M. Bennett and her relations.

MARGUERITE, COUNTESS OF BLESSINGTON, née POWER
1789–1949

Bibliographies

Sadleir, M. In his XIX century fiction: a bibliographical record, 2 vols 1951.

§1

Sketches and fragments. 1822, 1823. Anon.
The magic lantern: or sketches and scenes in the metropolis, by the author of Sketches and fragments. 1822, 1823.
Journal of a tour through the Netherlands to Paris in 1821 by the author of Sketches and fragments etc. 1822.
Rambles in Waltham Forest: a stranger's contribution to the triennial sale for the benefit of the Wanstead Lying-in charity. 1827. Verse, illustr C. M. H.
The repealers. 3 vols 1833, 1834 (as Grace Cassidy: or the repealers).
Conversations of Lord Byron with the Countess of Blessington. 1834, 1850, Boston 1859 (as A journal of conversations with Lord Byron) (with a memoir of the author), 1893; tr French, 1933. Serialized in New Monthly Mag 1832–3.
The two friends. 3 vols 1835.

The confessions of an elderly gentleman. Illustr E. T. Parris 1836, 1847; tr German, 1837.
The victims of society. 3 vols 1837, Paris 1837.
The works of Lady Blessington. 2 vols Philadelphia 1838. For contents *see* Sadleir, above.
The confessions of an elderly lady. Illustr E. T. Parris 1838.
The governess. 2 vols 1839, Paris 1840.
The idler in Italy. 2 vols 1839, 3 vols 1839, Paris and Philadelphia 1839.
Desultory thoughts and reflections. 1839, 1839, New York and Paris 1839.
The belle of a season. Illustr A. E. Chalon 1840. Verse.
The idler in France. 2 vols 1841, Paris 1841.
The lottery of life. 3 vols 1842, 1844, [1857], Paris 1842. Tales.
Meredith. 3 vols 1843.
Strathern: or life at home and abroad. 4 vols 1845.
The memoirs of a femme de chambre. 3 vols 1846, Leipzig 1846, Philadelphia [1850] (as Ella Stratford: or the orphan child).
Marmaduke Herbert. 3 vols 1847, 2 vols Leipzig 1847.
Country quarters, with a memoir by Miss [M. A.] Power. 3 vols 1850, 2 vols Leipzig 1850, 1 vol 1852 (2nd edn).
Lady Blessington edited various gift books and was for many years editor and principal contributor to The Book of Beauty *and* Keepsake. *She also edited* Lionel Deerhurst: or fashionable life under the Regency, by Barbara Hemphill, 3 vols 1846.

§2

Madden, R. R. The literary life and correspondence of the Countess of Blessington. 3 vols 1855.
Maginn, W. In his A gallery of illustrious literary characters, 1873.
The Blessington papers. In Collection of autograph letters formed by A. Morrison ser 2, 1895. Chiefly letters written to Lady Blessington.
Sadleir, M. Blessington-D'Orsay. 1933, 1947.
Rosa, M. W. The silver fork school: novels of fashion preceding Vanity Fair. New York 1936. Ch 8.

CAROLINE ANNE BOWLES, later SOUTHEY
1786–1854

See col 365, above.

ANNA ELIZA BRAY, née KEMPE, first married name STOTHARD
1790–1883

Collections

Novels and romances. 10 vols 1845–6, 12 vols 1884 (rev).

§1

Letters written during a tour through Normandy, Britanny and other parts of France in 1818; with engravings after drawings by C. Stothard. 1820.
Memoirs, including original journals, letters, papers and antiquarian tracts of the late C. A. Stothard; and some account of a journey in the Netherlands. 1823.
De Foix: or sketches of the manners and customs of the fourteenth century, an historical romance. 3 vols 1826.
The White Hoods: an historical romance. 3 vols 1828; tr French, 1828.
The Protestant: a tale of the reign of Queen Mary, by the author of De Foix, The White Hoods etc. 3 vols 1828, 1833.
Fitz of Fitz-ford: a legend of Devon. 3 vols 1830.
The Talba, or Moor of Portugal: a romance. 3 vols 1830, 2 vols New York 1831.
Trials of domestic life. 3 vols 1834, 1848.
Warleigh, or the fatal oak: a legend of Devon. 3 vols 1834.
A description of the part of Devonshire bordering on the Tamar and the Tavy in a series of letters to Robert Southey esq. 3 vols 1836, 1838 (as Traditions, legends, superstitions and sketches of Devonshire), 2 vols 1879 (as The borders of the Tamar and the Tavy).
Trelawney of Trelawne, or the prophecy: a legend of Cornwall. 3 vols 1837, 1845.
Trials of the heart. 3 vols 1839.
The mountains and lakes of Switzerland; with descriptive sketches of other parts of the Continent. 3 vols 1841.
Henry de Pomeroy, or the eve of St John: a legend of Cornwall and Devon. 3 vols 1842, 1 vol 1846 (with The white rose: a domestic tale).
Courtenay of Walreddon: a romance of the west. 3 vols 1844.
The father's curse and The daughter's sacrifice: two tales. 3 vols 1848.
The life of Thomas Stothard; with personal reminiscences. 1851.
A peep at the pixies: or legends of the west, with illustrations by H. K. Browne. 1854.
Handel: his life, personal and professional, with thoughts on sacred music. 1857.
The good St Louis and his times. 1870.
The revolt of the Protestants of the Cevennes; with some account of the Huguenots in the seventeenth century. 1870.
Hartland Forest: a legend of North Devon. 1871.
Roseteague: or the heir of Treville Crewse. 2 vols 1874.
Joan of Arc and the times of Charles VII, King of France. 1874.
Silver linings: or light and shade. 1880.
Autobiography of Anna Eliza Bray [to 1843]. Ed J. A. Kempe 1884.
Mrs Bray edited the Poetical remains *of her husband, Rev E. A. Bray, and* A selection from sermons, 2 vols 1860; *also* M. M. Colling, Fables and other pieces in verse, 1831.

§2

Boase, G. C. Anna Eliza Bray and her writings. Lib Chron 1 1884.

MARY BRUNTON, née BALFOUR
1778–1818

Collections

Works. 7 vols Edinburgh 1820.

§1

Self control. 3 vols Edinburgh 1811, 1811, 1811, 1 vol Edinburgh 1839, London 1849 etc.
Discipline, by the author of Self control. 3 vols Edinburgh 1814, 3 vols 1815, 1832 (to which is prefixed a memoir of 1819 of the life and writings of the author, including extracts from her correspondence [by her husband Alexander Brunton]), 1849, 1852 etc.
Emmeline; with some other pieces to which is prefixed a memoir of her life including some extracts from her correspondence [by her husband Alexander Brunton]. Edinburgh 1819.

SIR SAMUEL EGERTON BRYDGES
1762–1837

See col 1269, below.

LADY CHARLOTTE SUSAN MARIA BURY, née CAMPBELL

1775–1861

Bibliographies

Sadleir, M. In his XIX century fiction: a bibliographical record, 2 vols 1951.

§1

Poems on several occasions, by a lady. Edinburgh 1797. Anon.

Self indulgence: a tale of the nineteenth century. 2 vols Edinburgh 1812, Philadelphia 1812.

Conduct is fate. 3 vols Edinburgh 1822. Anon.

Suspirium sanctorum, or holy breathings: a series of prayers. 1826. Anon.

Alla giornata: or to the day. 3 vols 1826. Anon.

Flirtation: a novel. 3 vols 1827 (anon), 1828, 1828.

The exclusives. 3 vols 1830.

The three great sanctuaries of Tuscany: Valombrosa, Camaldoli, Laverna, a poem illustrated by E. Bury. 1833.

Journal of the heart, edited by the authoress of Flirtation. 1830; ser 2, 1835.

The separation, by the authoress of Flirtation. 3 vols 1830, 2 vols New York 1830.

The disinherited; and the Ensnared, by the authoress of Flirtation. 3 vols 1834.

The devoted, by the authoress of the Disinherited etc. 3 vols 1836.

The divorced. 2 vols 1837, 1 vol 1858.

Love, by the authoress of Flirtation. 3 vols 1837, 2 vols Philadelphia 1838, 1 vol London and New York 1860.

Diary illustrative of the times of George the Fourth interspersed with original letters from the late Queen Caroline and from other distinguished persons. 2 vols 1838 (anon), 4 vols 1838 (expanded, vols 3–4 ed J. Galt; BM copy contains suppressed pages), Philadelphia 1838–9, 2 vols 1896 (as The Court of England under George the Fourth); ed A. F. Steuart 2 vols 1908 (as The diary of a lady in waiting).

The history of a flirt, related by herself. 3 vols 1840. Anon.

Family records: or the two sisters. 3 vols 1841.

The wilfulness of woman, by the authoress of the History of a flirt. 3 vols 1844.

The manœuvring mother, by the author of the History of a flirt. 3 vols 1842, 1 vol 1858.

The roses, by the author of the History of a flirt. 3 vols 1853.

The lady of fashion, by the author of the History of a flirt. 3 vols 1856.

The two baronets: a novel of fashionable life. 1864.

Lady Charlotte also edited Mrs C. F. Gore, Memoirs of a peeress: or the days of Fox, 1837, *and* Caroline Lucy, Lady Scott, A marriage in high life, 1828, 1857; tr French, 1832; German, 1837.

§2

Lady Charlotte Bury. New Monthly Mag March 1837.

Rosa, M. W. The silver fork school: novels of fashion preceding Vanity Fair. New York 1936. Ch 7.

Prucher, A. Figure europee del primo '800 nel Diary di Lady Bury. Florence 1961.

WILLIAM CARLETON

1794–1869

Bibliographies

Sadleir, M. In his XIX century fiction: a bibliographical record, 2 vols 1951.

Selections

Popular tales and legends of the Irish peasantry [by Carleton, Denis O'Donoho, Mrs S. C. Hall etc]. Illustr S. Lover, Dublin 1834. Contains 2 stories by Carleton.

The battle of the factions and other tales of Ireland. Philadelphia 1845.

Characteristic sketches of Ireland and the Irish [by Carleton, Lover and Mrs Hall]. Dublin 1845, Halifax 1846, 1849, 1852 (as Tales and stories of Ireland). Contains 5 tales by Carleton.

Alley Sheridan and other stories. Dublin 1857. Serialized in Nat Mag 1857.

The poor scholar; Frank Martin and the fairies; The country dancing master and other Irish tales. 1869.

Works. New York 1882.

Amusing Irish tales. Ser 1, London and Glasgow 1889; ser 2, 1890.

Stories from Carleton. Ed W. B. Yeats [1889], New York 1889.

Stories from Carleton. Ed T. Hopkins [1905].

Carleton's stories of Irish life. Ed D. Figgis, Dublin 1919, New York 1920.

Tubber Derg or the red well; Party fight and funeral; Dandy Kehoe's christening and other Irish tales. nd.

§1

Father Butler; The Lough Dearg pilgrim: being sketches of Irish manners. Dublin 1829, Philadelphia 1835, London and Dublin 1839. Anon; first pbd in Christian Examiner 1828 and Church of Ireland Mag respectively.

Traits and stories of the Irish peasantry. Illustr W. H. Brooke. Ser 1, 2 vols Dublin 1830, 1832, 1834, 1835; ser 2, 3 vols Dublin 1833, 1834; sers 1–2 5 vols Dublin 1836; in monthly parts illustr Phiz et al 1842; with autobiographical introd 2 vols 1843; illustr Phiz 5 vols 1853, 2 vols 1856, 1 vol 1860 (as Irish life and character), illustr W. Harvey et al 2 vols 1864, 1 vol 1872, 1875, 2 vols 1876, 1 vol 1877, 2 vols 1881 (with author's last corrections), 10 pts New York 1886, 1 vol 1893; ed D. J. O'Donoghue 4 vols 1896; ed F. A. Niccolls, Boston 1911; tr German, 1837; 3 tales tr French, 1861.

Tales of Ireland. Illustr W. H. Brooke, Dublin and London 1834, 1848. First pbd in the Christian Examiner 1831.

Fardorougha the miser: or the convicts of Lisnamona. Dublin, London and Edinburgh 1839, Dublin 1846, London 1848 (with introd), 1857, 1871 etc. First pbd in the Dublin Univ Mag 1837–8; tr Irish, 1933.

The fawn of Spring-vale; The clarionet and other tales. 3 vols Dublin and London 1841; re-issued as Jane Sinclair or the fawn of Spring-vale etc, 3 vols Dublin and London 1843; and as The clarionet; the dead boxer; and Barney Branagan, 1850.

Parra Sastha: or the history of Paddy Go-Easy and his wife Nancy. Dublin 1845, 1846.

Rody the rover: or the Ribbonman. Dublin 1845, Philadelphia [186–].

Valentine M'Clutchy, the Irish agent: or the chronicles of the Castle Cumber property, with the pious aspirations of Solomon M'Slime. 3 vols Dublin 1845, illustr Phiz 1 vol Dublin 1847, 1859, London 1860; tr French, serialized in L'Univers 1845.

Tales and sketches illustrating the character, usages etc of the Irish peasantry. Dublin 1845; illustr Phiz 1846, 1849, 1851, 1855 (as Irish life and character). Some of these stories were rptd from the Irish Penny Jnl.

Denis O'Shaughnessy going to Maynooth. Illustr W. H. Brooke 1845. First pbd in Traits and stories ser 2, 1833.

The black prophet: a tale of Irish famine. Belfast and London 1847; illustr W. Harvey, London and Belfast

1847, 1862; ed D. J. O'Donoghue, illustr J. B. Yeats 1899; tr Irish, 1940. First pbd in Dublin Univ Mag 1846.

Art Maguire: or the broken pledge. Dublin 1845, London and Dublin 1847.

The emigrants of Ahadarra: a tale of Irish life. 1848, 1857, 1871.

The Irishman at home: characteristic sketches of the Irish peasantry. Dublin 1849. First pbd in part in the Dublin Penny Jnl.

The tithe proctor: being a tale of the tithe rebellion in Ireland. 1849, 1857.

Red hall: or the baronet's daughter. 3 vols 1852, 1 vol Dublin 1853, 3 vols 1854, 1 vol Dublin 1858 (as The black baronet: or the Chronicles of Ballytrain), 1875.

The Squanders of Castle Squander. 2 vols 1852, 1 vol 1876. First pbd in Illustr London Mag 1851–2.

Willy Reilly and his dear Cooleen Bawn: a tale founded upon fact. 3 vols 1855, 1 vol Dublin 1857, Philadelphia 1883, London 1896; ed E. A. Baker 1904, Dublin 1909.

The evil eye: or the black spectre. Illustr E. Fitzpatrick, Dublin 1860, 1864.

Redmond Count O'Hanlon, the Irish rapparee: an historical tale. Dublin 1862. First pbd in Hibernian Mag 1861.

The double prophecy: or trials of the heart. 2 vols Dublin 1862. Serialized in Hibernian Mag and Irish Amer 1861.

The silver acre and other tales. 1862. Serialized in Illustr London Mag 1853–4, illustr Phiz.

The fair of Emyvale, and the Master and scholar. 1870. Serialized in the Illustr London Mag July–Sept 1853 (illustr Phiz).

The red haired man's wife. Dublin and London, 1889. Serialized in Carlow College Mag 1870.

The life of William Carleton: being his autobiography [continued] by D. J. O'Donoghue. 2 vols 1896; ed P. Kavanagh 1968.

The courtship of Phelim O'Toole. Ed A. Cronin 1962. First pbd in Traits and stories ser 2, 1833.

According to O'Donoghue, above, vol 2 pp. 309 and 344, Carleton left the ms of a 3-vol novel, Anne Cosgrave: or the chronicles of Silver Burn, *which seems never to have been pbd.*

§2

Our portrait gallery, 15: Carleton. Dublin Univ Mag Jan 1841.

Davis, T. O. Nation (London) 12 July 1845; rptd in his Essays literary and historical, 1914.

Murray, P. A. Edinburgh Rev 196 1852.

Shaw, R. Carleton's country. Dublin and Cork 1930.

McHugh, R. Carleton: a portrait of the artist as propagandist. Studies 27 1938.

Kiely, B. Poor scholar: a study of the works and days of Carleton. 1947.

Flanagan, T. In his Irish novelists 1800–50, New York 1959. Chs 16–18.

Bell, S. H. Carleton and his neighbours. Ulster Folklife no 7 1961.

Morrison, R. A note on Carleton. Universities Rev 31 1965.

FREDERICK CHAMIER
1796–1870

§1

The life of a sailor, by a Captain in the Navy. 3 vols 1832, 2 vols Philadelphia 1833, London 1850, 1856, [1873?]. Pbd in part in Metropolitan Mag 1831.

The unfortunate man. 3 vols 1835, 2 vols New York 1835.

Ben Brace, the last of Nelson's Agamemnons. 3 vols 1836, 2 vols Philadelphia 1836, 1 vol 1839 (rev), 1840, 1856 etc.

The Arethusa. 3 vols 1837, 1 vol 1860 (as The saucy Arethusa), 1867 etc.

Walsingham the gamester. 3 vols 1837, 1 vol Philadelphia 1838.

Jack Adams the mutineer. 3 vols 1838, 1 vol 1861 (subtitled The mutiny of the Bounty).

The spitfire: a tale of the sea. 3 vols 1840, 2 vols Philadelphia 1840, 1 vol [1860].

Tom Bowling: a tale of the sea. 3 vols 1841, 1 vol 1883 etc.

Passion and principle: a novel. 3 vols 1842.

The perils of beauty. 3 vols 1843.

Ben Bradshawe: the man without a head. 3 vols 1843, 1 vol 1859. Anon.

The mysterious man: a novel by the author of Ben Bradshawe. 3 vols 1844.

Count Königsmark: an historical romance. 3 vols 1845.

Jack Malcolm's log. 3 vols 1846.

Review of the French revolution of 1848. 2 vols 1849, 1852 (as France and the French).

My travels: or an unsentimental journey through France, Switzerland and Italy. 3 vols 1855.

Chamier revised W. James, Naval history of Great Britain *and continued it with an account of the Burmese war and the battle of Navarino*, 6 vols 1837. *He also tr* Zagoskin, Young Muscovite, or the Poles in Russia: a novel, 3 vols 1834, 2 vols New York 1834.

§2

Soane, J. Memoirs of Mr and Mrs J. Soane, Miss Soane and Captain Chamier from 1800 to 1835. [1835?] (priv ptd).

Memoir of Chamier. New Monthly Mag April 1838.

Times 2 Nov 1870.

Danilewicz, M. L. Chamier's anecdotes of Russia [pbd in the New Monthly Mag 1829–30]. Slavonic & East European Rev 40 1961.

MARY CHARLTON

Bibliographies

Blakey, D. In her Minerva Press, 1939.

Summers, M. In his A Gothic bibliography, [1941].

§1

The Parisian: or genuine anecdotes of distinguished and noble personages. 2 vols 1794. Anon.

Andronica, or the fugitive bride: a novel. 2 vols 1797.

Phedora: or the forest of Minski. 4 vols 1798.

Ammorvin and Zallida. 2 vols 1798.

Rosella, or modern occurrences: a novel. 4 vols 1799, 2 vols Dublin 1800.

The pirate of Naples: a novel. 3 vols 1801.

The wife and the mistress: a novel. 4 vols 1802, 1803.

The homicide: a novel taken from the Comedie di Goldoni. 2 vols 1805, 1813 (as Rosaura di Viralva: or the homicide).

Pathetic poetry for youth. 1815.

Grandeur and meanness, or domestic persecution: a novel. 3 vols 1824.

Past events, or the treacherous guide: a romance. 3 vols 1830.

Mary Charlton also translated The reprobate, 2 vols 1802, *and* The rake and the misanthrope, 2 vols 1804, *both from the German of Augustus La Fontaine; and* The philosophic kidnapper, 3 vols 1803, *from the French.*

RICHARD COBBOLD
1797–1877

Bibliographies

Sadleir, M. In his XIX century fiction: a bibliographical record, 2 vols 1951.

§ 1

Original, serious and religious poetry. Ipswich 1827.
Valentine verses: or lines of truth, love and virtue, with illustrations [by Cobbold]. Ipswich 1827.
The spirit of the litany of the Church of England. Eye 1833. Poem.
Men and women. 1843. Anon.
The history of Margaret Catchpole, a Suffolk girl, with illustrations [by Cobbold himself]. 3 vols 1845, 2 vols 1845, 1 vol 1847, 1852, [1856], [1858] (enlarged), [1878]; ed C. Shorter, Oxford 1907 (WC), 1930. Dramatized by E. Stirling, 1858.
Mary Ann Wellington: the soldier's daughter, wife and widow, with illustrations [by Cobbold]. 3 vols 1846, 1 vol 1853 ('improved'), [1875].
Zenon the Martyr: a record of the piety, patience and persecution of the early Christian nobles. 3 vols 1847, 1855, [1874].
The young man's home, or the penitent returned: a narrative of the present day. 3 vols 1848.
The bottle, or Cruikshank illustrated: a poem. 1848.
The character of woman: a lecture delivered April 1848. Diss nd.
Freston Tower: or the early days of Cardinal Wolsey, with illustrations [by Cobbold]. 3 vols 1850, 1 vol 1856, [1880], 1913.
Courtland: a novel, by the daughter of Mary Ann Wellington. 3 vols 1852.
John H. Steggall: a real history of a Suffolk man, narrated by himself, edited by the author of Margaret Catchpole. 1857, 1859, nd (in picture boards, as The Suffolk gipsy).
Geoffrey Gambado: or a simple remedy for hypochondriacism and melancholy splenetic humours. [1865] (priv ptd).
Cobbold left a novel in ms, Jack Rattler: or the horrors of transportation, *now in the Sadleir collection. He also pbd sermons and devotional works.*

GEORGE CROLY
1780–1860

See col 375, above.

ALLAN CUNNINGHAM
1784–1842

§ 1

The magic bridle. nd.
Songs, chiefly in the rural language of Scotland. 1813.
Sir Marmaduke Maxwell: a dramatic poem; The mermaid of Galloway; The legend of Richard Faulder etc. 1822. The mermaid of Galloway rptd 1845.
Traditional tales of the English and Scottish peasantry. 2 vols 1822; ed H. Morley 1887.
The songs of Scotland, ancient and modern, with introduction and notes. 4 vols 1825.
Paul Jones: a romance. 3 vols Edinburgh 1826; tr German, 5 vols 1842.
Sir Michael Scott: a romance. 3 vols 1828.
Lives of the most eminent British painters, sculptors and architects. 6 vols 1829–33, 1830–7, 3 vols New York 1839, 5 vols New York 1844; ed W. Sharp 1886 (selection), [1893]; ed R. Davies and C. A. Hunt 1908 (selection).

Some account of the life and works of Sir Walter Scott. Boston 1832.
The Maid of Elvar: a poem in twelve parts. 1833.
The cabinet gallery of pictures, selected from the collections of art, public and private, which adorn Great Britain, with biographical and critical descriptions. 2 vols 1833–4, 1836.
Biographical and critical history of the British literature of the last fifty years. Paris 1834.
Lord Roldan: a romance. 3 vols 1836, 2 vols New York 1836.
The life and correspondence of Robert Burns. 1836.
The life and land of Burns with contributions by T. Campbell [and] an essay by T. Carlyle. New York 1841.
The life of Sir David Wilkie. Ed P. Cunningham 3 vols 1843.
Poems and songs. Ed P. Cunningham 1847, 1875.
Select songs. In C. Rogers, The modern Scottish minstrel vol 3, 1856.
Cunningham also contributed a tale, Gowden Gibbie, *to* A. Picken's Club Book, 1831, *and wrote memoirs of Burns, Byron and Thomson for his edns of their works. He edited* M. Pilkington, General dictionary of painters, 1840, *and* The anniversary 1829. *He contributed 12 papers of* Recollections *to* Blackwood's Mag Nov 1819–Jan 1821, *and was a frequent contributor to the* London Mag 1820–5.

§ 2

Gilfillan, G. In his Galleries of literary portraits vol 1, Edinburgh 1856.
Hall, S. C. Allan Cunningham. Art Jnl 18 1866.
Maginn, W. In his A gallery of Illustrious literary characters, ed W. Bates 1873.
Hogg, D. The life of Cunningham, with selections from his works and correspondence. Dumfries 1875.
Drinkwater, J. Cunningham to Robert Southey. In his Book for bookmen, 1926. A letter.
Allan Cunningham. TLS 31 Oct 1942.
Sikes, H. M. Hazlitt, the London Magazine and the 'anonymous reviewer' [of Cunningham's Sir Marmaduke Maxwell]. BNYPL March 1961.
Süsskand, P. Cunninghams Seemannslied und die Gedichtinterpretation in der Oberstufe. Die Neueren Sprachen new ser 12 1963.

CHARLOTTE DACRE, afterwards BYRNE
1782–*c.* 1841

§ 1

The confessions of the nun of St Omer: a tale by Rosa Matilda. 3 vols 1805.
Hours of solitude: a collection of original poems by Charlotte Dacre, better known by the name of Rosa Matilda. 2 vols 1805.
Zofloya, or the Moor: a romance of the fifteenth century by Charlotte Dacre, better known as Rosa Matilda. 3 vols 1806; ed M. Summers 1928; tr French, 4 vols 1812.
The libertine, by Charlotte Dacre, better known as Rosa Matilda. 4 vols 1807, 1807; tr French, 3 vols 1816.
The passions, by Rosa Matilda. 4 vols 1811.
George the Fourth: a poem by the author of Hours of solitude [and] lyrics designed for various melodies. 1822.

§ 2

Summers, M. Byron's 'lovely Rosa'. In his Essays in petto, 1928.

ROBERT CHARLES DALLAS

1754–1824

Collections

Miscellaneous works and novels. 7 vols 1813.

§ 1

Miscellaneous writings, consisting of Poems; Lucretia: a tragedy; and Moral essays; with a vocabulary of the passions. 1797.
Percival, or nature vindicated: a novel. 4 vols 1801.
Elements of self-knowledge: an anatomical display of the human frame and an enquiry into the genuine nature of the passions. 1802, 1805 (rev).
The history of the Maroons, from their origin to the establishment of their chief tribe at Sierra Leone. 2 vols 1803; tr German, 1805.
Aubrey: a novel. 4 vols 1804.
The Morlands: tales illustrative of the simple and surprising. 4 vols 1805.
The Knights: tales illustrative of the marvellous. 3 vols 1808.
Not at home: a dramatic entertainment. 1809, New York 1811.
The new conspiracy against the Jesuits detected and exposed. 1815; tr French, 1816; German, 1820; Italian, 1835.
A letter to C. Butler esq relative to the new conspiracy against the Jesuits. 1817.
Felix Alvarez: or manners in Spain containing accounts of the late Peninsular War, interspersed with poetry. 3 vols 1818.
Ode to the Duke of Wellington, and other poems. 1819.
Sir Francis Darrell, or the vortex: a novel. 4 vols 1820.
Adrastus: a tragedy; Amabel or the Cornish lovers; and other poems. 1823.
Recollections of the life of Lord Byron from the year 1808 to the end of 1814. Ed A. R. C. Dallas 1824, Philadelphia 1825.
Dallas also edited some of Byron's letters (1824 and 1825) and made a number of trns from the French, including The siege of Rochelle: or the Christian heroine, by Madame de Genlis, 3 vols 1808.

SELINA DAVENPORT

The sons of the viscount and the daughters of the Earl: a novel depicting recent scenes in fashionable life. 4 vols 1813.
The hypocrite, or the modern Janus: a novel. 5 vols 1814.
Donald Monteith, the handsomest man of the age: a novel. 5 vols 1815, 1832.
The original of the miniature: a novel. 4 vols 1816.
Leap Year, or Woman's privilege: a novel. 5 vols 1817.
An angel's form and a devil's heart: a novel. 4 vols 1818.
Preference: a novel. 2 vols 1824.
Italian vengeance and English forbearance: a romance. 3 vols 1828.
The Queen's page: a romance. 3 vols 1831.
The unchanged: a novel. 3 vols 1832.
Personation: a novel. 3 vols 1834.

ISAAC D'ISRAELI

1766–1848

See col 1277, below.

EMILY EDEN

1797–1869

§ 1

Portraits of the princes and peoples of India. 1844.
The semi-detached house. Ed Lady T. Lewis 1859 (anon), 1860, Boston 1860, London 1872; ed A. Eden 1928, illustr S. Suba, Boston 1948.
The semi-attached couple, by E. E., the author of the Semi-detached house. 2 vols 1860, Boston 1861, London 1865; ed J. Gore 1927, 1934; ed A. Eden, illustr S. Suba, Boston 1947; illustr D. Braby 1955.
Up the country: letters from the upper provinces of India. 2 vols 1866, 1867; ed E. Thompson 1930.
Letters from India. Ed E. Eden 2 vols 1872.
Letters. Ed V. Dickinson 1919.

§ 2

Dunbar, J. Golden interlude: the Edens in India. 1955.

PIERCE EGAN

1772–1849

See col 1279, below.

SUSAN EDMONSTONE FERRIER

1782–1854

Bibliographies

Leclaire, L. In his A general analytical bibliography of the regional novelists of the British Isles 1800–1950, Paris 1954.

Collections

Miss Ferrier's novels. 2 vols London and New York 1873–4.
Miss Ferrier's novels. London and Edinburgh 6 vols 1882.
Novels. Ed R. B. Johnson, illustr N. Erichsen 6 vols 1894.
Works. Ed Lady M. Sackville 4 vols 1928. Vol 4 consists of Doyle's Memoir, below.

§ 1

Marriage: a novel. 3 vols 1818 (anon), 1819, 2 vols Edinburgh 1826, 1 vol 1831, 1841, 1847, 1856 (rev), [1873], [1878], New York 1882, 2 vols Boston 1893; ed Earl of Iddesleigh (with biographical preface by A. Goodrich-Freer) 2 vols 1902; ed R. B. Johnson 1928 (EL), 1953; tr French, 4 vols 1825.
The inheritance, by the author of Marriage. 3 vols 1824, 1825, 1 vol 1831, 1841, 1847, 1857 (rev), [1873], [1878], 2 vols Boston 1893; ed Earl of Iddesleigh (with biographical preface by A. Goodrich-Freer) 2 vols 1903.
Destiny: or the chief's daughter, by the author of Marriage and the Inheritance. 3 vols Edinburgh 1831, 1 vol 1841 (rev), 1856, [1873], [1878], 2 vols Boston 1893.

§ 2

Lockhart, J. G. Noctes ambrosianae 58. Blackwood's Mag Sept 1831.
[Moir, G.] Susan Ferrier's novels. Edinburgh Rev 74 1842.
Miss Ferrier's novels. Temple Bar Oct 1878.
Hamilton, C. J. In her Women writers ser 1, 1892. Ch 14.
Douglas, G. In his Blackwood group, [1897].
Memoir and correspondence of Susan Ferrier 1782–1854. Ed J. A. Doyle 1898, 1929.
Gwynn, S. Miss Ferrier. Macmillan's Mag April 1899.
Johnson, R. B. In his Women novelists, [1918].

Saintsbury, G. In his Collected essays and papers vol 1, 1923.
Birrell, A. In his More obiter dicta, 1924.
Grant, A. Susan Ferrier of Edinburgh: a biography. Denver 1957.
Parker, W. M. Susan Ferrier and John Galt. 1965.

JAMES BAILLIE FRASER
1783–1856
Bibliographies

Sadleir, M. In his XIX century fiction: a bibliographical record, 2 vols 1951.

§1

Journal of a tour through part of the Himālā mountains and to the sources of Jumna and Ganges. 1820.
Narrative of a journey into Khorasan 1821–2 including accounts of countries NE of Persia. 1825.
Travels and adventures in the Persian provinces on the south banks of the Caspian Sea, with notices on the geology and commerce of Persia. 1826.
The Kuzzilbash: a tale of Khorasan. 3 vols 1828. Anon.
The Persian adventurer: being the sequel to the Kuzzilbash. 3 vols 1830.
The Highland smugglers, by the author of Adventures of a Kuzzilbash. 3 vols 1832.
Tales of the Caravanserai: the Khan's tale. 1833, Philadelphia 1833, London 1850.
An historical and descriptive account of Persia including descriptions of Afghanistan and Beloochistan. 1834, New York 1836, 1842, London 1843.
Narrative of the residence of the Persian princes in London 1835–6, their journey from Persia and subsequent adventures. 2 vols 1838, 1838.
A winter's journey (Tâtar) from Constantinople to Teheran, with travels through various parts of Persia. 2 vols 1838.
Travels in Koordistan, Mesopotamia etc. 2 vols 1840.
Mesopotamia and Assyria. 1842, New York 1842, 1845, Edinburgh 1846.
Allee Neemro, the Buchtiaree adventurer. 3 vols 1842.
The dark falcon. 4 vols 1844.
A military memoir of Colonel James Skinner and several personages in the service of the native powers in India. 2 vols 1851.
Fraser was a regular contributor to Blackwood's Mag 1829–38.

JOHN GALT
1779–1839
Bibliographies

Lumsden, H. The bibliography of Galt. Records of Glasgow Bibl Soc 9 1931.
Booth, B. A. A bibliography of Galt. Bull of Bibliography 16 1936.

Collections

Works. Ed D. S. Meldrum and S. R. Crockett, illustr J. Wallace 10 vols Edinburgh and Boston 1895.
Novels. Ed Δ [D. M. Moir] 4 vols 1907.
Works. Ed D. S. Meldrum and W. Roughead, illustr C. E. Brock 8 vols Edinburgh 1936.

§1

The battle of Largs: a Gothic poem with several miscellaneous pieces. 1804. Anon.
Cursory reflections on political and commercial topics as connected with the Regent's accession to royal authority. 1812.
Voyages and travels in the years 1809, 1810 and 1811, containing statistical, commercial and miscellaneous observations on Gibraltar, Sardinia, Sicily, Malta, Serigo and Turkey. 1812.
The life and administration of Cardinal Wolsey. 1812, 1817, Edinburg 1824; ed W. Hazlitt 1846.
The tragedies of Maddelen, Agamemnon, Lady Macbeth, Antonia and Clytemnestra. 1812, 1812.
Letters from the Levant: containing views of the state of society, manners, opinions and commerce in Greece and the archipelago. 1813.
Naval history of Great Britain, by Dr John Campbell. 8 vols 1813. Galt contributed the anon lives of Hawke, Byron and Rodney, vols 5–6.
The new British theatre, edited by John Galt. 4 vols 1814–15. Contains several of Galt's own dramas, including The witness, afterwards performed and ptd at Edinburgh as The appeal.
The Majolo: a tale. 2 vols 1816. Anon.
Life and studies of Benjamin West. 2 pts 1816–20, 1 vol Philadelphia 1816, 1817, London 1817, 1820; abridged Boston 1831, 1832 (as The progress of Genius: or authentic memoirs of the early life of West); ed N. Wright, Gainesville 1960.
The crusade: a poem. 1816.
The earthquake: a tale. 3 vols Edinburgh 1820 (anon), 2 vols New York 1821.
The wandering Jew: or the travels and observations of Hareach the prolonged, by the Rev T. Clark [J. Galt]. 1820, [1820] (rev as The travels and observations of Hareach, the wandering Jew).
All the voyages round the world, by Samuel Prior. 1820, New York 1843. 'Samuel Prior' was another of Galt's pseudonyms.
A tour of Europe and Asia, by Rev T. Clark [Galt]. 2 vols 1820.
George the Third, his Court and family. 2 vols 1820, 1824.
Pictures historical and biographical, drawn from English, Scottish and Irish history. 2 vols 1821, 1824.
The Ayrshire legatees: or the Pringle family. Edinburgh 1821 (anon), Edinburgh 1823 (with Gathering of the West, below), New York 1823, Edinburgh 1841 (with Annals of the parish, below) and a memoir by Δ [D. M. Moir], 1844 etc; ed J. I. Watson (with Annals of the parish, below) Glasgow 1877; ed A. Ainger (with Annals) 1895, 1896, 1903; ed G. B. Macdonald 1910; abridged, Glasgow [1922]; ed F. Beaumont [1930]. First pbd in Blackwood's Mag 1820–1, rptd in Portfolio (Philadelphia) 1821–2.
Annals of the parish: or the chronicle of Dalmailing during the ministry of the Rev Micah Balwhidder. Edinburgh 1821 (anon), Philadelphia 1821, Edinburgh 1822, 1841 (with Ayrshire legatees, above), 1844 etc; ed J. I. Watson (with The Ayrshire legatees) Glasgow 1877; ed S. R. Crockett 1895; ed A. Ainger 1895; ed G. S. Gordon 1908; ed J. MacInnes [1908]; abridged by G. C. Pringle (as The minister of Dalmailing) 1909; ed G. B. Macdonald 1910 (EL); illustr H. W. Kerr 1910, 1928; ed W. M. Parker 1952; ed J. Kinsley, Oxford 1967; tr French, 3 vols 1824.
Sir Andrew Wylie, of that ilk. 3 vols Edinburgh 1822, 1822, 2 vols New York 1822, London 1841, 1850, 1854, 1868 etc, 2 vols Boston 1895.
The Provost. Edinburgh 1822 (anon), 1822, New York 1822, Edinburgh 1842 (with The steamboat and The omen), 1850, 1869, 2 vols Boston 1896; illustr J. M. Aitken 1913; tr French, 3 vols 1824 (with Annals).
The steamboat. Edinburgh 1822, New York 1823; rptd with Provost and Omen, Edinburgh 1842, 1850, 1869. First pbd in Blackwood's Mag Feb–Sept 1821.
The gathering of the West: or We've come to see the King. Edinburgh 1823 (anon, with Ayrshire legatees); ed B. A. Booth, Baltimore 1939. First pbd in Blackwood's Mag.
The entail: or the lairds of Grippy. 3 vols Edinburgh 1823, ed Δ [D. M. Moir]. New York 1823, London 1842, 1850, 2 vols Boston 1896; ed J. Ayscough, Oxford 1913 (WC).
Ringan Gilhaize: or the Covenanters. 3 vols Edinburgh 1823 (anon), 2 vols New York 1823, Glasgow [1870]; ed G. Douglas 1899, 1902.

Glenfell: or Macdonalds and Campbells. Edinburgh [1823]; tr French, 1823.
Modern geography and history, by the Rev T. Clark [i.e. J. Galt]. 1823.
The spaewife: a tale of the Scottish chronicles. 3 vols Edinburgh 1823, 2 vols Philadelphia 1824, 1 vol [1880?].
Rothelan: a romance of the English histories. 3 vols Edinburgh 1824, 2 vols New York 1825.
The bachelor's wife: a selection of curious and interesting extracts. Edinburgh 1824. Essays.
The omen. Edinburgh 1825 (anon); rptd with Provost and Steamboat, 1842, New York 1844 (in The omnibus of modern romance), 1850, 1869.
The last of the lairds: or the life and opinions of Malachi Mailings esq of Auldbiggings. Edinburgh 1826, New York 1827; illustr H. W. Kerr 1926. The final chs were written by D. M. Moir.
Lawrie Todd: or the settlers in the woods. 3 vols 1830, 1830, 2 vols New York 1830, 1832; ed G. Thorburn 1845, 1849 (rev), [1880?].
Southennan. 3 vols 1830, 2 vols New York 1830.
The life of Lord Byron. 1830, 1830, New York and Philadelphia 1830, 1831, 1832, New York 1835, 1841, 1845, [1908]; tr French, 1836.
The lives of the players. 2 vols 1831, Boston 1831, 1 vol 1886.
Bogle Corbet: or the emigrants. 3 vols [1831].
The member: an autobiography. 1832, 1833 (with The Radical, below, as The reform).
The Radical: an autobiography. 1832, 1833 (with The member, above, as The reform).
The Canadas as they at present commend themselves to the enterprise of emigrants, colonists and capitalists, compiled and condensed from original documents furnished by John Galt, by Andrew Picken. 1832.
Stanley Buxton: or the schoolfellows. 3 vols 1832, 2 vols Philadelphia 1833, Boston 1833.
Poems. 1833.
Eben Erskine: or the traveller. 3 vols 1833, 2 vols Philadelphia 1933.
The stolen child: a tale of the town. 1833, Philadelphia 1833.
Stories of the study. 3 vols 1833.
The Ouranoulogos: or the celestial volume. Illustr J. Martin 1833.
Autobiography. 2 vols Edinburgh 1833 (Bibliography vol 2, pp. 410–2), Boston 1834, Philadelphia 1834.
The literary life and miscellanies. 3 vols 1834.
Efforts, by an invalid. Greenock 1835, London 1835. Verse.
A contribution to the Greenock calamity fund. Greenock 1835. Verse.
The demon of destiny and other poems. Greenock 1839.
The Howdie and other tales. Ed W. Roughead, Edinburgh 1923.
A rich man and other stories. Ed W. Roughead 1925.
Poems. Ed G. H. Needler, Toronto 1954.
Galt contributed 5 stories—The book of life, The fatal whisper, Haddad-Ben-Ahab, The painter, The unguarded hour—*to* A. Picken, The book club 3 vols 1831, *all rptd in* W. Hazlitt, Romancist's and novelist's library, 1841. *9 of his plays*—The apostate, Hector, Love honour and interest, The masquerade, The mermaid, Orpheus, The prophetess, The watch house, The witness (rptd Edinburgh 1818 as The appeal)—*were included in* New British Theatre, 4 vols 1814–15, *which he edited. Vols 3–4 of* Lady C. Bury, Diary illustrative of the times of George IV, *were ed Galt, and he contributed a* Life of John Wilson *to* Scottish descriptive poems, 1803, *and a preface to* A. Graydon, Memoirs, 1822. *He was a frequent contributor, under a variety of pseudonyms, to Fraser's and Blackwood's Mags 1829–36.*

§2

Quart Rev 25 1821. Review of Annals of the parish.
Jeffrey, F. Secondary Scottish novels. Edinburgh Rev 39 1823.
Maginn, W. In his A gallery of illustrious literary characters, 1873.
Millar, J. H. The novels of Galt. Ed W. Bates [1873].
Edinburgh Rev 143 1876, 184 1896.
[Meldrum, D. S.] The novels of Galt. Blackwood's Mag June 1896.
Douglas, G. In his Blackwood group, Edinburgh [1897].
Gordon, R. K. John Galt. Toronto 1920. With bibliography.
Roughead, W. A gossip on a novel of Galt's. In his Fatal countess, Edinburgh 1924.
—— 'The last of the lairds': a centenary tribute. In his Malice domestic, Edinburgh 1928.
Lumsden, H. Memoir. Prefixed to his Bibliography of Galt, 1931.
Kitchin, G. In his Edinburgh essays on Scots literature, 1933.
Aberdein, J. W. John Galt. Oxford 1936.
MacCurdy, E. A literary enigma. Stirling 1936. Galt's part in the Canadian boat song.
Booth, B. A. Galt's Lives of the Admirals. N & Q 29 Oct 1938.
Innis, M. Q. A Galt centenary. Dalhousie Rev 29 1940.
Lyell, F. H. A study of the novels of Galt. Princeton 1942.
Parker, W. M. New Galt letters. TLS 6 June 1942.
—— Susan Ferrier and Galt. 1965.
Needler, G. H. Galt's dramas. 1945.
Pritchett, V. S. A Scottish documentary. In his Living novel, 1946.
Hamilton, T. W. John Galt. 1947.
Brownlie, W. M. Galt: social historian. 1952.
Dickinson, W. C. Galt, The Provost and the Burgh. Greenock 1954.
Frykman, E. Galt and eighteenth-century Scottish philosophy: some notes on the intellectual background of Galt's Scottish stories. Upsala 1954.
—— Galt's Scottish stories 1820–3. Upsala 1959.
Skain, C. E. Galt's America. Amer Quart 8 1956.
Klinck, C. F. Galt's Canadian novels. Ontario History 49 1957.
Cogswell, F. Scott-Byron: an unpublished Galt ms. Stud in Scottish Lit 1 1964.
Harriet Pigott left ms material for a life of Galt, now in Bodley.

THOMAS GASPEY

1788–1871

The mystery, or forty years ago: a novel. 3 vols 1820; tr French, 4 vols 1821.
Calthorpe, or fallen fortunes: a novel. 3 vols 1821, 2 vols Philadelphia 1821; tr French, 4 vols 1821.
Takings, or the life of a collegian: a poem. Illustr R. Dagley 1821.
The Lollards: a tale. 3 vols 1822.
Other times: or the monks of Leadenhall. 3 vols 1823.
The witch finder, or the wisdom of our ancestors: a romance. 3 vols 1824.
Richmond: or scenes in the life of a Bow Street officer, drawn up from his private memoranda. 3 vols 1827. Anon. Also attributed to T. S. Surr.
The history of George Godfrey, written by himself. 3 vols 1828. Anon.
The self condemned: a romance, by the author of the Lollards. 3 vols 1836, New York 1836.
'Many coloured life': or tales of woe and touches of mirth, by the author of the Lollards etc. 1842.
Laurence Stark: a family picture. Translated [from J. J. Engel] by Gaspey. Heidelberg 1843.
The life and times of the good Lord Cobham. 2 vols 1843.
The pictorial history of France. 1843.
Glory: a tale of morals drawn from history. 1844.

The dream of human life, by the author of the Lollards. 2 vols 1849.
The history of Smithfield. 1852.
The history of England under the reign of George III, George IV, William IV and Queen Victoria [to 1852]. 4 vols 1855–9. Continued to 1859 by H. Tyrrell.
Gaspey also wrote philological works and guide books.

WILLIAM NUGENT GLASCOCK
1787?–1847

Bibliographies

Sadleir, M. In his XIX century fiction: a bibliographical record, 2 vols 1951.

§1

The naval sketch book: or the service afloat and ashore, with characteristic reminiscences, fragments and opinions, by an officer of rank. 2 sers 4 vols 1826–34, 2 vols 1843. Ser 2 by the author of Tales of a tar.
Sailors and saints: or matrimonial manœuvres. 3 vols 1829, 1829. 2 vols New York 1829.
Tales of a tar. 1830.
The naval service: or officers' manual for every grade in His Majesty's ships. 2 vols 1836, 1 vol 1848; ed J. Allen with ch on the steam engine by R. Roughton 1854, 1859.
Land sharks and sea gulls. 3 vols 1838.

GEORGE ROBERT GLEIG
1796–1888

§1

Narrative of the campaigns at Washington and New Orleans 1814–15. 1821, Philadelphia 1821, 1826, 1827, 1836, 1847; tr German, 1832.
The subaltern. Edinburgh 1825, New York 1825, Edinburgh 1826, 1826, 1845, 1872 (rev), London 1915 (EL). Serialized in Blackwood's Mag March–Sept 1825.
Tales of a voyage to the Arctic ocean. 3 vols 1826.
The subaltern's log book including anecdotes of well known military characters. 2 vols 1828.
Sermons doctrinal and practical. 1829.
The Chelsea pensioners. 3 vols 1829, 1833, 1 vol 1841.
The country curate. 2 vols 1830, 1 vol 1834, 1846 (rev), 1856. Chs 1–9 serialized in Blackwood's Mag Nov 1825–May 1826.
The life of Sir T. Munro. 3 vols 1830, 1 vol 1849 (rev).
The history of the Bible. 2 vols 1830–1, New York 1831, 1844; ed S. Stall, Philadelphia 1915.
Lives of the most eminent British military commanders. 3 vols 1831–2.
The history of the British Empire in India. 4 vols 1830–5.
Allan Breck: a novel. 3 vols 1834.
The chronicles of Waltham. 3 vols 1835, 1861 (as Waltham: or chronicles of a country village).
The hussar. 2 vols 1837, 1 vol [1857].
Chelsea Hospital and its traditions. 3 vols 1838, 1 vol 1839.
Germany, Bohemia, Hungary. 3 vols 1839.
The life of Oliver Cromwell. Sandbornton NH 1840.
Memoirs of the life of Warren Hastings. 3 vols 1841.
A memoir of Major General Craufurd, with an account of his funeral. 1842.
The veterans of Chelsea Hospital. 3 vols 1844, 1 vol 1857.
The light dragoon. 2 vols 1844, 1 vol 1853.
A sketch of the military history of Great Britain. 1845.
Sale's brigade in Afghanistan. 1846, 1879.
The story of the battle of Waterloo. 1847, 1907.
The life of Robert, first Lord Clive. 1848, 1907.
The Leipsic campaign. 1852.
India and its army. 1857. Rptd from Edinburgh Rev 1857.
Essays biographical, historical and miscellaneous, contributed chiefly to the Edinburgh and Quarterly Reviews. 2 vols 1858.
The life of the Duke of Wellington. 1862, 1909 (EL).
The life of Sir Walter Scott. Edinburgh 1871. Rptd from Quart Rev.
The history of the reign of George III to the battle of Waterloo. 1873.
The great problem: can it be solved? 1876.
With the Harrises seventy years ago. 1889.
Personal reminiscences of the first Duke of Wellington. Ed M. E. Gleig, Edinburgh 1904.
Gleig edited The only daughter, 1859, *and* Katherine Randolph: or self-devotion, [1859], by [Harriette Campbell]. A subaltern in America, *of which 21 chs appeared in* Blackwood's Mag March–Sept 1827, *appears never to have been completed. He pbd sermons and devotional works and engaged in controversies on military and Church matters.*

§2

Maginn, W. In his A gallery of illustrious literary characters, ed W. Bates [1873]. Rptd from Fraser's Mag.
Hamley, E. B. Death of Mr Gleig. Blackwood's Mag Aug 1888.

CATHERINE GRACE FRANCES GORE, née MOODY
1799–1861

Bibliographies

Sadleir, M. In his XIX century fiction: a bibliographical record, 2 vols 1951.

§1

Theresa Marchmont, or the maid of honour: a tale. 1824; rptd in vol 1 of Edinburgh tales, 1845.
The bond: a dramatic poem. 1824.
Richelieu: or the broken heart. 1826. Attributed to Mrs Gore.
The lettre de cachet: a tale; The reign of terror: a tale. 1827.
Hungarian tales, by the author of the Lettre de cachet. 3 vols 1829. Selection rptd in Edinburgh tales, 1845.
Romances of real life, by the author of Hungarian tales. 3 vols 1829, 1 vol 1859.
Women as they are: or the manners of the day. 3 vols 1830, 1830.
The historical traveller, comprising narratives connected with European history. 2 vols 1831.
Pin-money: a novel, by the authoress of the Manners of the day. 3 vols 1831, 1854, 2 vols Philadelphia 1834.
The Tuileries: a tale, by the authoress of Hungarian tales. 3 vols 1831, 2 vols New York 1831, 1841 (as The soldier of Lyons).
Mothers and daughters: a tale of the year 1830. 3 vols 1831, 1 vol 1834 (anon), 1849.
The opera: a novel, by the authoress of Mothers and daughters. 3 vols 1832.
The fair of Mayfair. 3 vols 1832 (anon), 2 vols Philadelphia 1834 (as The miseries of marriage: or the fair of Mayfair).
The sketch book of fashion, by the authoress of Mothers and daughters. 3 vols 1833.
Polish tales, by the authoress of Hungarian tales. 3 vols 1833.
The Hamiltons: or the new era. 3 vols 1834, 1 vol 1850 (sub-titled Official life in 1830).
The diary of a désennuyée. 2 vols 1836. Anon.
Mrs Armytage: or female domination, by the authoress of Mothers and daughters. 3 vols 1836.

Memoirs of a peeress: or the days of Fox. Ed Lady C. Bury 3 vols 1837, 2 vols Philadelphia 1837, 1859 (rev).
Stokeshill Place: or the man of business. 3 vols 1837.
The heir of Selwood: or three epochs of a life. 3 vols 1838, 2 vols Philadelphia 1838, 1 vol 1855.
The rose fancier's manual. 1838.
Mary Raymond and other tales. 3 vols 1838, 2 vols Philadelphia 1838.
The woman of the world, by the authoress of the Diary of a désennuyée. 3 vols 1838, 1 vol [1861].
The Cabinet Minister, by the authoress of Mothers and daughters. 3 vols 1839.
The courtier of the days of Charles II, with other tales. 3 vols 1839, 2 vols New York 1839, 1 vol Paris 1839, London 1847.
Dacre of the South: or the olden time, a drama. 1840.
The dowager: or the new school for scandal. 3 vols 1840, 2 vols Philadelphia 1841, 1 vol 1854, [1876].
Preferment: or my uncle the Earl. 3 vols 1840, 1 vol 1857.
The abbey and other tales. 2 vols Philadelphia 1840.
Greville: or a season in Paris. 3 vols 1841, 1 vol Paris 1841, 3 vols 1844, 1 vol [1858].
Cecil, or the adventures of a coxcomb: a novel. 3 vols 1841 (anon), 1 vol 1845, 1860.
Cecil a peer: a sequel to Cecil or the adventures of a coxcomb, by the same author. 3 vols 1841, 1842 (as Ormington: or Cecil, a peer, with a word from the author).
Paris in 1841. 1842 (with engravings after T. Allom).
Fascination, and other tales. Ed Mrs Gore 3 vols 1842, 1 vol [1862].
The man of fortune and other tales. 3 vols [1842], 2 vols Philadelphia 1842.
The ambassador's wife. 3 vols 1842, 1863.
The money-lender. 3 vols 1843, 1 vol New York (as Abednego the money-lender), London 1854.
Modern chivalry: or a new Orlando furioso. Illustr G. Cruikshank 2 vols 1843. Anon.
The banker's wife, or court and city: a novel. 3 vols 1843, 1 vol 1859.
Agathonia, a romance. 1844. Anon.
Marrying for money. In Omnibus of modern romance, New York 1844.
The birthright and other tales. 3 vols 1844.
Quid pro quo: or the day of the dupes. [1844]. Comedy.
The popular member, The wheel of fortune [etc]. 3 vols 1844.
Self, by the author of Cecil. 3 vols 1845, 1856.
The story of a royal favourite. 3 vols 1845.
The snow storm: a Christmas story, with illustrations by George Cruikshank. [1845], 1895.
Peers and parvenus: a novel. 3 vols 1846, 1859.
New Year's day: a winter's tale, with illustrations by George Cruikshank. [1846], [1846].
Men of capital. 3 vols 1846, 1 vol 1857.
The débutante: or the London season. 3 vols 1846, 1 vol 1861.
Sketches of English character. 2 vols 1846, 1 vol 1852.
Castles in the air: a novel. 3 vols 1847, 1 vol Leipzig 1856, London 1857.
Temptation and atonement, and other tales. 3 vols 1847, [1860?].
The inundation, or pardon and peace: a Christmas story. Illustr G. Cruikshank [1847].
The diamond and the pearl: a novel. 3 vols 1849, [1859] (rev).
Adventures in Borneo. 1849.
The Dean's daughter: or the days we live in. 3 vols 1853, 2 vols Leipzig 1853, 1 vol New York 1883.
The lost son: a winter's tale. [1854].
Progress and prejudice. 3 vols 1854, 2 vols Leipzig 1854, 1 vol New York 1854.
Mammon: or the hardships of an heiress. 3 vols 1855, 2 vols Leipzig 1855.
A life's lessons: a novel. 3 vols 1856, 2 vols Leipzig 1857.
The two aristocracies: a novel. 3 vols 1857, 2 vols Leipzig 1857.
Heckington: a novel. 3 vols 1858, 2 vols Leipzig 1858, 1 vol 1864.
Mrs Gore contributed to Tales of all nations, 1827, *and to* The tale book, Königsberg 1859. *She also wrote the following plays:* The maid of Croissey, King O'Neil, The Queen's champion (*all pbd in* Webster's acting national drama) *and* A good night's rest (*in* Duncombe's British theatre); *and she edited the following trns:* Picciola: or captivity captive, 1837 (*from the French*); Charles de Bernard, The lover and the husband [etc] 3 vols 1841; Modern French life, 3 vols 1842 (*tales from the French*); *and* T. C. Heiberg, The Queen of Denmark, 3 vols 1846 (*from the Danish*).

§2

Lister, T. H. Edinburgh Rev 51 1830. Review of Women as they are.
Catherine Frances Gore. New Monthly Mag March 1837.
[Hayward, A.] Edinburgh Rev 73 1841. Review of Cecil.
Horne, R. H. In his A new spirit of the age vol 1, 1844.
Female novelists no 2: Mrs Gore. New Monthly Mag June 1852.
Athenaeum 9–23 Feb 1861. Obituary etc.
Rosa, M. W. The silver fork school: novels of fashion preceding Vanity Fair. New York 1936. Ch 6.

THOMAS COLLEY GRATTAN
1792–1864

Bibliographies

Sadleir, M. In his XIX century fiction: a bibliographical record, 2 vols 1951.

§1

Philibert: a poetical romance. 1819. 6 cantos with notes.
Highways and byways: or tales of the roadside, picked up in the French provinces by a walking gentleman. Ser 1, 1823; ser 2, 3 vols 1825, 2 vols Philadelphia 1825; ser 3, 3 vols 1827; sers 1–2 rptd 1847, 1848; tr French, 3 vols 1825.
The history of Switzerland. 1825, New York 1913 (with History of Netherlands, below). An abridgement of Planta, History of the Helvetic confederacy.
Ben Nazir the Saracen: a tragedy. 1827.
Traits of travel: or tales of men and cities. 3 vols 1829.
The heiress of Bruges: a tale of the year 1600. 4 vols 1830, 3 vols Brussels 1830, London 1831, 1 vol 1834, 1853; tr French, 6 vols 1831.
History of the Netherlands. 1830, New York 1855, 1899 (as Holland: the history of the Netherlands [continued] by J. Hawthorne), Philadelphia 1907 (as Holland and Belgium, ed W. H. Claflin; Switzerland, ed C. Dandliker, rev E. J. Benton), New York 1913, 1916, 1928, 1932 etc.
Jacqueline of Holland: a historical tale. 3 vols 1831, 1843 (rev), 1857, [1884].
Legends of the Rhine and of the Low Countries. 1832, Frankfurt 1836 (with Planché, Lays and legends of the Rhine), Philadelphia 1843, London 1849.
Agnes de Mansfeldt: a historical tale. 3 vols 1836, 1 vol Brussels 1846, London 1847, 1847.
The boundary question revised, and Dr Franklin's red line shown to be the right one, by a British subject. New York 1843; rptd in his Civilised America, 1859, below.
The master passion and other tales and sketches. 2 vols 1845.
The Cagot's hut; and The conscript's bride. 1852.
The forfeit hand and other tales. 1857.
The curse of the black lady and other tales. 1857.

Civilised America. 2 vols 1859.
England and the disrupted states of America. 1861, 1861, 1862.
Beaten paths and those who trod them. 2 vols 1862. Reminiscences.

SARAH GREEN

Bibliographies

Blakey, D. In her Minerva press, 1939.
Summers, M. In his A Gothic bibliography, [1941].

§1

Charles Henly: or the fugitive restored. 2 vols 1790.
Mental improvement for a young lady on her entrance into the world, addressed to a favourite niece. 1793.
A letter to the publisher of Brother's prophecies. 1795.
Court intrigue: or the victim of constancy. 1799.
The history of the Tankerville family. 3 vols 1806.
The private history of the Court of England. 1808, 1808.
Tales of the manor. 2 vols 1809.
The festival of St Jago: a Spanish romance. 2 vols 1810.
The reformist!!! a serio-comic-political novel. 2 vols 1810, 1816 (as Percival Ellingford: or the reformist).
Romance readers and romance writers. 3 vols 1810. Prefaced by a critical Literary retrospection, partly rptd in R. B. Johnson, Novelists on novels, 1928.
The royal exile: or victims of human passions. 4 vols 1810, 1811.
Good men of modern date: a satirical tale. 3 vols 1812.
Deception: a fashionable novel. 3 vols 1813.
The fugitive: or family incidents. 3 vols 1814.
The Carthusian friar: or the mysteries of Montanville. 1814.
Who is the bridegroom? or nuptial discoveries. 3 vols 1822.
Gretna-Green marriages: or the nieces. 3 vols 1823.
Scotch novel reading, or modern quackery: a novel really founded on facts, by a Cockney. 3 vols 1824.
Parents and wives: or inconsistency and mistakes. 3 vols 1825.
Sarah Green also translated Raphael: or a peaceful life, from the German of A. Lafontaine, 2 vols 1812.

BASIL HALL

1788–1844

See col 1282, below.

ELIZABETH HAMILTON

1758–1816

§1

Translation of the letters of a Hindoo Rajah, with a preliminary dissertation on the history of the Hindoos. 2 vols 1796, Dublin 1797, London 1801, 1811, Boston 1819. Essays in fictional form.
Memoirs of modern philosophers: a novel. 3 vols Bath 1800, London 1800, 1801, 2 vols Dublin 1801; tr French, 4 vols 1802 (as Bridgetina: ou les philosophes modernes).
Letters on the elementary principles of education. 2 vols Bath 1801, 1802, 1803, Alexandria Virginia 1803, London 1810, 1818, Boston 1825, London 1837.
Memoirs of the life of Agrippina, the wife of Germanicus. 3 vols Bath 1804, London 1804, 2 vols 1811.
Letters addressed to the daughter of a nobleman on the formation of the religious and the moral principle. 2 vols 1806, 1814.
Exercises in religious knowledge. Edinburgh 1809, 1810.
The cottagers of Glenburnie. Edinburgh 1808, 1808, 1822, London 1837 etc, Edinburgh 1851 (with memoir); ed J. L. Watson, Glasgow [188–].
A series of popular essays illustrative of principles connected with the improvement of the understanding, the imagination and the heart. 3 vols Edinburgh 1813.
Hints addressed to patrons and directors of schools; to which are subjoined examples of questions calculated to excite and exercise the minds of the young. 1815. The appendix was rptd separately, Salem 1829.

§2

[Jeffrey, F.] Edinburgh Rev 12 1808. Review of Cottages of Glenburnie.
Benger, E. O. Memoirs of Mrs Elizabeth Hamilton with selections from her correspondence and unpublished writings. 1818.

THOMAS HAMILTON

1789–1842

Bibliographies

Sadleir, M. In his XIX century fiction: a bibliographical record, 2 vols 1951.

§1

The youth and manhood of Cyril Thornton. 3 vols 1827, 2 vols New York 1827, 3 vols Edinburgh 1827, 1829, 1830, 1 vol 1842, 1868, 1880 (as Cyril Thornton: his youth and manhood).
Annals of the Peninsular campaigns 1808–14. 3 vols 1829, Philadelphia 1831; rev F. Hardman 1849.
Men and manners in America. 2 vols Edinburgh 1833, Philadelphia 1834, 1 vol 1834 (augmented).
Hamilton contributed freely to Blackwood's Mag 1826–38.

§2

[Wilson, J.] Blackwood's Mag July 1827. Review of Cyril Thornton.
Douglas, G. In his Blackwood group, 1897.

ELIZABETH HELME

d. 1813

Bibliographies

Blakey, D. In her Minerva Press, 1939.
Summers, M. In his A Gothic bibliography, [1941].

§1

Louisa: or the cottage on the moor. 2 vols 1787, Wilmington 1795 (as The history of Louisa the lovely orphan), 1840 (in pts).
Clara and Emmeline: or the maternal benediction. 2 vols 1788; tr French, 1788.
Duncan and Peggy: a Scottish tale. 2 vols 1794, 1815.
The farmer of Inglewood forest: a novel. 4 vols 1796, 1811, 1825 (7th edn), 1841, 1842, 1878; tr French, 4 vols 1818.
Instructive rambles in London and the adjacent villages. 2 vols 1798, 1800, 1806, 1808, 1812, New York 1814.
Albert: or the wilds of Strathnavern. 4 vols 1799, 1821.
James Manners, little John and their little dog Bluff. 1799, 1813 (4th edn), 1818.
St Margaret's cave, or the nun's story: an ancient legend. 4 vols 1801.

Maternal instruction: or family conversations on moral and entertaining subjects. 2 vols 1802, 1810, 1815.
St Clair of the Isles, or the outlaws of Barra: a Scottish tradition. 4 vols 1803, 1 vol 1840, 1841, 1867, [1889].
The pilgrim of the cross: or the chronicles of Christabelle de Mowbray. 4 vols Brentford 1805.
The history of England related in familiar conversations by a father to his children. 2 vols 1805.
The history of Scotland related in familiar conversations by a father to his children. 2 vols Brentford 1806.
The fruits of reflection: or moral remembrances on various subjects. 2 vols Brentford 1809.
Magdalen, or the penitent of Godstow: an historical novel. 3 vols 1812, Boston 1813.
Modern times, or the age we live in: a posthumous novel. 3 vols Brentford 1814, 1817.
A preparatory exercise on the road leading to the land of learning. Brentford 1816.
Elizabeth Helme pbd an abridgement of Plutarch's Lives, 1795, *trns of* Cortez, 1799, Columbus, 1800 *and* Pizarro, 1800 *from the German of J. H. Campe, and of* Travels from the Cape of Good Hope, 1790, *from the French of F. Le Vaillant.*

WILLIAM BROWNE HOCKLEY
1792–1860

Pandurang Hari: or memoirs of a Hindoo. 3 vols 1826, 2 vols 1873 (with introd by H. B. E. Frere). Written by Cyrus Redding from Hockley's notes.
The Zenana: or a Nawab's leisure hours, by the author of Pandurang Hari. 3 vols 1827; ed Lord Stanley of Alderley 2 vols 1874.
The English in India. 3 vols 1828.
The Vizier's son. 3 vols 1831.
The memoirs of a Brahmin: or the fatal jewels. 3 vols 1843.

BARBARA HOFLAND

See Barbara Hoole, below.

JAMES HOGG
1770–1835

See col 267, above.

JAMES HOOK
1771–1828

Pen Owen: a novel. 3 vols Edinburgh 1822 (anon), 2 vols New York 1822, 1 vol 1842, 1849, 1869.
Percy Mallory. 3 vols Edinburgh 1824, 2 vols Philadelphia 1824.
James Hook also pbd pamphlets and sermons.

THEODORE EDWARD HOOK
1788–1841

Bibliographies

Sadleir, M. In his XIX century fiction: a bibliographical record, 2 vols 1951.

Collections

Ausgewählte Romane, aus dem Englischen von E. A. Moriarty und J. Seybt. 16 pts Leipzig 1842–3.
Choice humorous works, with a new life of the author, portraits by Maclise and D'Orsay, caricatures and facsimiles, [1873], 1902.
Bon-mots of Samuel Foote and Theodore Hook. Ed W. Jerrold 1894.

§1

The soldier's return: or what can beauty do? a comic opera. 1805 (anon), Philadelphia 1807.
Catch him who can: a musical farce. 1806, 1829.
The invisible girl: a piece in one act. 1806, 1826.
Tekeli, or the siege of Montgatz: a melodrama in three acts. 1806, 1807, New York 1807, 1808, 1815, Philadelphia 1823, New York 1825.
The fortress: a melo-drama, from the French. 1807.
Music-mad: a dramatic sketch. 1808, New York 1812.
The man of sorrow, by Alfred Allendale. 3 vols 1808, 1 vol 1842 (as Ned Musgrave: or the most unfortunate man in the world), 1854, New York 1854, Philadelphia nd.
Killing no murder: a farce in two acts. 1809 (2nd edn, together with a preface and the scene suppressed by the Lord Chamberlain), 1809, 1809, 1809, New York 1809, London 1810, 1811; ed G. Daniel 1833.
Safe and sound: an opera in three acts. 1809, New York 1810.
Darkness visible: a farce. 1811, 1811, New York 1812, London 1817.
The trial by jury: a comic piece in two acts. 1811, New York 1811.
Facts illustrative of the treatment of Napoleon Buonaparte in Saint Helena. 1819 (anon), 1910 (in C. K. Shorter, Napoleon in his own defence).
Exchange no robbery, or the diamond ring: a comedy. 1820, 1829; ed G. Daniel 1887.
Tentamen: or an essay towards the history of Whittington, by Vicesimus Blinkinsop. 1820, 1821. A satire on Sir Matthew Wood, the partisan of Queen Caroline.
Sayings and doings: a series of sketches from life. 3 sers 9 vols 1824–8. Ser 1 rptd 1824 (anon), Andover [183–] (rev), London 1836, 1872; ser 2, 2 vols Philadelphia 1825, 1 vol 1838, 1872; ser 3, 1839; sers 1–3, 3 vols 1836, 1838; tr French, 1828.
Maxwell, by the author of Sayings and doings. 3 vols 1830, 1 vol 1849, 1854 (rev), [1878].
Life of General Sir David Baird. 2 vols 1832.
Love and pride, by the author of Sayings and doings. 3 vols 1833, Philadelphia 1834, 1842 (as The widow and the Marquess: or love and pride), 1868.
The parson's daughter, by the author of Sayings and doings. 3 vols 1833, Philadelphia 1833, 1835 (rev and corrected), 1847, 1867, 1872.
Gilbert Gurney, by the author of Sayings and doings. 3 vols 1836, Paris 1836, London 1841, 1850; tr French, 1861. Serialized in New Monthly Mag 1834–5.
Jack Brag, by the author of Sayings and doings. 3 vols 1837, Paris 1837, London 1839, 1847, 1850, 1872, 1884.
Gurney married: a sequel to Gilbert Gurney, by the author of Sayings and doings. 3 vols 1838, 1839, Paris and Philadelphia 1839, London 1842, [1863]. Serialized in New Monthly Mag 1837–8.
Births, deaths and marriages, by the author of Sayings and doings. 3 vols 1839, 2 vols Philadelphia 1839, London 1842 (as All in the wrong: or births, deaths and marriages), [1863] (as All in the wrong).
Precepts and practice. Illustr Phiz 3 vols 1840, 1857, [1863]. A collection of pieces first pbd in New Monthly Mag.
Fathers and sons: a novel. 3 vols 1842, Philadelphia 1842, London 1847, [1860], 1872. Serialized in New Monthly Mag 1840–1.
Peregrine Bunce, or settled at last: a novel. 3 vols 1842, 1 vol 1857.
Ned Musgrave, or the most unfortunate man in the world: a comic novel. Nd, 1854. First pbd as The man of sorrow, 1808.
The Ramsbottom letters. 1872, [1874] (as The Ramsbottom papers, complete and unabridged).
Hook also edited Reminiscences of Michael Kelly, 1826, *and* J. A. Bernard, The French stage and the French people,

1841, *as well as the following novels:* A. Dumas, Pascal Bruno, 1837; J. T. J. Hewlett, Peter Priggins, 3 vols 1841; The Parish Clerk, 3 vols 1841; *and* H. M. G. Smythies, Cousin Geoffrey: the old bachelor, 3 vols 1840. *He was editor of* John Bull *from 1820 to 1841*, *and of* New Monthly Mag & Humourist *from vol 49 to 62.*

§2

Maginn, W. Blackwood's Mag March 1824. Review of Sayings and doings.
— In his A gallery of illustrious literary characters, ed W. Bates [1873].
Lockhart, J. G. Blackwood's Mag Feb 1825. Review of Sayings and doings.
[Lockhart, J. G.] Peregrine Bunce. Quart Rev 72 1843.
— Hook: a sketch. 1852 (3 edns), 1853.
Memoir. New Monthly Mag Oct 1841. With portrait.
Theodore Edward Hook. Fraser's Mag Nov 1841.
Horne, R. H. In his A new spirit of the age vol 2, 1844.
Theodore Edward Hook. Chambers's Jnl 7 Feb 1846.
A graybeard's gossip about his literary acquaintance no 6. New Monthly Mag Aug 1847.
Barham, R. H. D. The life and remains of Hook. 2 vols 1849, 1853 (rev and corrected), 1877 (rev).
Hall, A. M. and S. C. Memories of authors: Hook and his friends. Atlantic Monthly April 1865.
Saintsbury, G. Theodore Hook. Macmillan's Mag Nov 1893.
— Three humorists. Hook, Barham, Maginn. Macmillan's Mag Dec 1895; rptd in his Collected essays vol 2, 1923.
Hook, satirist and novelist. Temple Bar Nov 1894.
St Cyres, S. H. N. Theodore Hook. Cornhill Mag Jan 1904.
Brightfield, M. F. Hook and his novels. Cambridge Mass 1928.
Repplier, A. The laugh that failed. Atlantic Monthly Aug 1936.
Hoaxer and wit: Hook. TLS 23 Aug 1941.
Shuman, R. B. Structure and style in the novels of Hook. N & Q Aug 1958.
— Hook as a legal critic. Ibid.

BARBARA HOOLE, afterwards HOFLAND, née WREAKS 1770–1844

§1

Poems. Sheffield [1805].
The history of an officer's widow and her young family. 1809 (anon), 1814, Philadelphia 1815, London 1834.
Little dramas for young people on subjects taken from English history. 1810.
A season at Harrogate in a series of poetical epistles from Benjamin Blunderhead esquire to his mother. Knaresborough 1812, Harrogate 1838 (rev).
The history of a clergyman's widow and her young family. 1812 (anon), 1825, [1866].
The son of a genius: a tale for the use of youth. 1812, New York 1814, London 1816, New York 1818, London 1819, 1821, 1822, 1827 (rev), 1832, 1841 etc; tr French, 1817.
Says she to her neighbour, What? by an old-fashioned Englishman. 4 vols 1812.
Patience and perseverance: or the modern Griselda, by the author of Says she to her neighbour, What? 4 vols 1813.
The panorama of Europe: or a new game of geography. 1813, 1824, 1828, 1840 etc.
Iwanowna: or the maid of Moscow. 1813, 2 vols 1816. Anon.
A visit to London: or Emily and her friends. 4 vols 1814.
The merchant's widow and her family. 1814 (anon), 1823 (as The history of a merchant's widow and her young family), 1826, 1857, 1867; tr French, 1831.
A father as he should be: a novel. 4 vols 1815.
Theodore, or the Crusaders: a tale for youth. 1815, 1824, 1826, 1833, [1879].
The affectionate brothers: a tale. 2 vols 1816, 1829, [1835?], 1863.
Matilda, or the Barbadoes girl: a tale. 1816 (anon), 1819, [1825?] (5th edn), 1866.
The good grandmother and her offspring: a tale. 1817, 1828, 1850.
The blind farmer and his children. 1819 (2nd edn), [1830?] (6th edn), New York 1831.
Ellen the teacher. 2 vols 1815, 1819, 1822, 1825, 1833, [1879].
A descriptive account of the mansions and gardens of White Knights; with twenty-three engravings from pictures by T. J. Hofland. [1819] (priv ptd).
Tales of the Priory. 4 vols 1820.
The young cadet: or Henry Delamere's voyage to India. 1821, 1827, New York 1828, 1836 (rev).
Tales of the manor. 4 vols 1822.
Adelaide, or the intrepid daughter: a tale. 1823 (anon), [1825?] (3rd edn).
The daughter of a genius: a tale for youth. 1823, 1823, 1848, [1879].
Integrity: a tale. 1823, Philadelphida 1828, London 1836, 1840, 1868.
Decision: a tale. 1824, 1867.
Patience: a tale. 1824, 1838.
Alfred Campbell, the young pilgrim: containing travels in Egypt and the Holy Land. 1825, 1841.
Moderation: a tale. 1825, 1826.
The young Northern traveller: being a series of letters from Frederic to Charles. 1825.
Reflection: a tale. 1826, 1838, 1868.
The young pilgrim: or Alfred Campbell's return to the East. 1826.
William and his Uncle Ben: a tale. 1826, [1865].
Self-denial: a tale. 1827, [1830?].
Katharine: a tale. 1828.
Africa described, in its ancient and present state. 1828, 1834.
Beatrice: a tale founded on facts. 3 vols 1829.
The daughter-in-law, her father and famiy. 1829.
Elizabeth and her three beggar boys. [1830?], New York 1838.
The sisters: a domestic tale. 1828, [1830?], 1866, Philadelphia [187–]; tr French, 1832.
The stolen boy: an Indian tale. [1830?], Cincinnati [1844?].
The captives in India: a tale; and A widow and a will. 3 vols 1834. The captives [alone], Washington 1835.
The young Northern traveller: or the invalid restored. [1830?] (rev); tr French, 1834.
Richmond and the surrounding scenery. Illustr J. D. Harding et al 1832.
Fortitude: a tale. 1835.
Rich boys and poor boys, and other tales. [1836?], [1840].
Humility: a tale. 1837, 1868.
Energy: a tale. 1838.
The illustrated alphabet, with poetry. 1839.
Farewell tales. 1840.
The young Crusoe: a tale. [1840?]; ed A. Gardiner, Manchester [1894].
Alicia and her aunt: or think before you speak. 1841 (rev), [1860?].
The Czarina: an historical romance of the Court of Russia. 3 vols 1842.
The godmother's tales. 1842.
The King's son: a romance of English history. 3 vols 1843.
Emily's reward: or the holiday trip to Paris. 1844.
The unloved: a domestic story. 3 vols 1844, New York 1844, 1 vol 1860.

Daniel Dennison; and the Cumberland statesman. 3 vols 1846.
Popular description of Sir John Soane's house, museum and library. Ed A. T. Bolton 1919.

§2

Ramsay, T. The life and literary remains of Barbara Hofland. 1849.
L'Estrange, A. G. K. In his Friendships of Mary Russell Mitford, 1882.

THOMAS HOPE
1770–1831

§1

Observations on the plans by James Wyatt for Downing College. 1804.
Household furniture and interior decoration. 1807, 1937, 1946.
The costume of the Ancients. 2 vols 1809, 1812 (enlarged), New York [1962] (as Costumes of the Greeks and Romans).
Designs of modern costumes. 1812.
Anastasius: or memoirs of a modern Greek, written at the close of the eighteenth century. 3 vols 1819 (anon), 1820, 1820, 2 vols New York 1821, 1832, London 1836.
An essay on the origins and prospects of man. 3 vols 1831.
An historical essay on architecture. 2 vols 1835, 1835, 1840; tr French, 1839; index by E. Cresy, 1836.

§2

[Smith, S.]. Edinburgh Rev 35 1821. Review of Anastasius.
Zeidler, K. J. Beckford, Hope und Morier als Vertreter des orientalischen Romans. Leipzig 1909.
Baumgarten, S. Le crépuscule néo-classique: Hope. Paris 1958.
Moussa-Mahmoud, F. Orientals in picaresque (Hope, Morier, Meadows Taylor). Cairo Stud in Eng 1962.

EDWARD HOWARD
1792?–1841

Bibliographies

Sadleir, M. In his Excursions in Victorian bibliography, 1922.
— In his XIX century fiction: a bibliographical record, 2 vols 1951.
Howard in both works is wrongly identified as the Hon Edward Granville Howard.

§1

Rattlin the reefer, edited by the author of Peter Simple. Illustr A. Hervieu 3 vols 1836, 1836, 1 vol Paris 1836, 3 vols 1837, 1 vol Leipzig 1837, London 1838, 1850 etc; ed W. L. Courtney, illustr E. F. Wheeler, London and Boston 1897, 1903; ed G. Pocock 1930 (EL); tr French, 1837; German, 1837. The first 58 chs were serialized in Metropolitan Mag Sept 1834–Feb 1836. Dramatized by J. T. Haines, 1836.
The old Commodore, by the author of Rattlin the reefer. 3 vols 1837, 1 vol 1837, Paris 1837, London 1855; tr French, 1838; German, 1838.
Outward bound: or a merchant's adventures. 3 vols 1838, 2 vols Philadelphia 1838, 1 vol 1860, 1875; tr French, 1838; German, 1838. Serialized in Metropolitan Mag 1836–7.
Memoirs of Admiral Sir Sidney Smith. 3 vols 1839; tr German, 1840.
Jack ashore. 3 vols 1840, 1 vol Paris 1840, 1848 etc; tr French, 1840; German, 1844.
Sir Henry Morgan the buccaneer. 3 vols 1842, 1 vol Paris 1842, New York 1847, London 1857 etc; tr German, 1844.
Howard was sub-editor, and from 1837 to 1839? editor, of Metropolitan Mag. *He contributed stories and sketches to it and to* New Monthly Mag *etc.*

§2

Marryat, F. Metropolitan Mag Aug 1836. On the pbn of Rattlin the reefer.
Memoir of Edward Howard, with portrait by Osgood. New Monthly Mag Dec 1838.
Athenaeum 8 Jan 1842; Annual Register 1842. Obituaries.
Bentley, G. N & Q 22 June, 20 July 1889, 19 Nov, 17 Dec 1892. On the authorship of Rattlin the reefer.

MARY HOWITT, née BOTHAM
1799–1888

See col 1286, below.

WILLIAM HOWITT
1792–1879

See col 1286, below.

CATHERINE HUTTON
1756–1846

See col 1288, below.

GEORGE PAYNE RAINSFORD JAMES
1799–1860

Bibliographies

Sadleir, M. In his XIX century fiction: a bibliographical record, 2 vols 1951.

Collections

Works, revised and corrected by the author, with an introductory preface. 21 vols 1844–9.
Novels and tales. 43 vols [c. 1860].

§1

The ruined city: a poem. 1828 (priv ptd), 1829 (with Adra: or the Peruvians).
Adra, or the Peruvians: the ruined city etc. 1829.
Richelieu: a tale of France. 3 vols 1829, 1831, 1 vol 1839, 1856, 1874, 2 vols New York 1895; ed R. Dircks 1909 (EL).
Darnley: or the field of the cloth of gold. 3 vols 1830, 1 vol 1836, 1850, 1853, 1874.
De l'Orme, by the author of Richelieu and Darnley. 3 vols 1830, 1 vol 1836, 1837 (rev), 1854, 1856.
The history of chivalry. 1830, New York 1839, London 1857.
Philip Augustus: or the brothers in arms, by the author of Darnley, De l'Orme etc. 3 vols 1831, 1 vol 1837, 1850, 1851, 1854.
Memoirs of great commanders. 3 vols 1832, 2 vols Boston 1835; illustr Phiz [or rather E. Corbould] 1858.
Henry Masterton: or the adventures of a young cavalier, by the author of Richelieu, Darnley etc. 3 vols 1832, 1837, 1 vol Leipzig 1840, London 1851.

The string of pearls, by the author of Darnley etc. 2 vols 1832, 1 vol 1849. Tales.
France in the lives of her great men: the history of Charlemagne. 1832, New York 1845, London 1847 (2nd edn, as The history of Charlemagne, with a sketch of the history of France).
Delaware, or the ruined family: a tale. 3 vols Edinburgh 1833, 1 vol 1848 (as Thirty years since: or the ruined family), 1855, 1865.
Mary of Burgundy: or the revolt of Ghent, by the author of Darnley. 3 vols 1833, 2 vols 1837, 3 vols 1844, 1 vol 1850, 1854, 1877.
The life and adventures of John Marston Hall, by the author of Darnley. 3 vols 1834, 1 vol 1851.
The gipsey: a tale, by the author of Richelieu. 3 vols 1835, 1 vol 1850, 1854, 2 vols New York 1855, 1 vol 1879.
On the educational institutions of Germany. 1835.
My aunt Pontypool. 3 vols 1835, 1 vol 1857.
One in a thousand: or the days of Henri Quatre, by the author of the Gipsey. 3 vols 1835, 2 vols New York 1836, 1 vol 1845, 1850.
The desultory man, by the author of Richelieu. 3 vols 1836.
A history of the life of Edward the Black Prince and of various events connected therewith. 2 vols 1836.
Attila: a romance, by the author of the Gipsey. 3 vols 1837, 2 vols New York 1837, 3 vols 1845, 1 vol 1853, [1879].
Memoirs of celebrated women. 2 vols 1837, Philadelphia 1839. Ed James.
The life and times of Louis the Fourteenth. 4 vols 1848, 2 vols 1851, 1 vol 1874, 2 vols 1890–1.
The robber: a tale by the author of Richelieu. 3 vols 1838, 1 vol 1850, 2 vols New York 1855.
Henry of Guise: or the states of Blois. 3 vols 1839, 2 vols New York 1840, 1 vol 1854.
A brief history of the United States boundary question, drawn up from official papers. 1839.
The Huguenot: a tale of the French Protestants, by the author of the Gipsey. 3 vols 1839, 1 vol 1853, 1865, [1881].
A book of the passions, with sixteen engravings. 1839, Paris 1939.
Charles Tyrrell: or the bitter blood. 2 vols 1839, New York 1839, 1 vol 1852, 1865.
Blanche of Navarre: a play. 1839, New York 1839.
The gentleman of the old school: a tale. 3 vols 1839, 1 vol 1852.
The King's highway: a novel. 3 vols 1840, 2 vols New York 1840, 3 vols 1844, 1 vol 1851, 1854, New York 1880.
The man at arms, or Henry de Cerons: a romance. 1840, 2 vols New York 1840, 1 vol 1842, 1844, 1857, New York 1879.
Corse de Leon, or the brigand: a romance. 3 vols 1841, 1 vol 1851, 1882.
Letters illustrative of the reign of William III from 1696 to 1708 now first published. 3 vols 1841.
Bertrand de la Croix: or the siege of Rhodes. 1841. First pbd in The Club book 1831; rptd in Eva St Clair and other tales, 1843.
The ancient regime: a tale. 3 vols 1841, 1 vol 1850 (as Castlenau).
The Jacquerie, or the lady and the page: an historical romance. 3 vols 1841, 1 vol Paris 1842, London 1852.
The life of Henry the Fourth, King of France and Navarre. 3 vols 1847, 2 vols New York 1847.
Morley Ernstein: or the tenants of the heart. 3 vols 1842, 1 vol Brussels 1842, 3 vols 1843, 1 vol 1850, 1853; tr Swedish, 1844.
Some remarks on the Corn laws, with suggestions for an alteration in the sliding scale. 1841.
A history of the life of Richard Cœur de Lion, King of England. 4 vols 1842–9, 2 vols 1854.
The commissioner: or de lunatico inquirendo. Illustr Phiz 1843 (anon), Dublin 1843.
Forest days: a romance of old times. 3 vols 1843, 1 vol 1852; tr Hungarian, 1873, abridged 1911.
The false heir. 3 vols 1843, 1 vol 1853.
Eva St Clair and other collected tales. 2 vols 1843, 1 vol 1855.
Agincourt: a romance. 3 vols 1844, 1 vol Leipzig 1844, New York 1844, London 1852.
Arabella Stuart: a romance from English history. 3 vols 1844, 1 vol 1853.
Rose d'Albret: or troublous times. 3 vols 1844, 1 vol 1856.
Arrah Neil: or times of old. 3 vols 1845, 1 vol 1853, 1887.
The smuggler: a tale. 3 vols 1845, 1 vol Paris 1845, London 1851, New York 1880, London 1887, 1908.
Beauchamp: or the error. 3 vols 1848. Serialized in New Monthly Mag 1845–6.
The stepmother: or evil doings. 1845 (priv ptd), 3 vols 1846, 1 vol 1855.
Heidelberg: a romance. 3 vols 1846, 1 vol Paris 1846, Leipzig 1846, London 1852.
The castle of Ehrenstein, its lords spiritual and temporal, its inhabitants earthly and unearthly. 3 vols 1847, 1 vol New York 1847, 3 vols 1849, 1 vol 1854, New York 1879. Chs 1–6 ptd in Novel Times 1845; chs 1–13 illustr Phiz in Ainsworth's Mag 1845.
A whim and its consequences. 3 vols 1847 (anon), 1850, 1 vol 1853.
The convict: a tale. 3 vols 1847, 1 vol New York 1847, 3 vols 1849, 1 vol 1851, 1854, 1890.
Russell: a tale of the reign of Charles II. 3 vols 1847, New York 1847, London 1849, 1 vol 1854.
Margaret Graham: a tale founded on facts. 2 vols 1848, 1 vol 1857, New York 1878 (sub-titled The reverses of fortune). Serialized in New Monthly Mag 1847.
The last of the fairies. Illustr J. Gilbert 1848, 1863, New York 1879.
Sir Theodore Broughton: or laurel water. 3 vols 1848, 1 vol 1853.
Camaralzaman: a fairy drama. 1848.
Gowrie: or the King's plot. 1848 (as vol 17 of the Collected works), 1851.
An investigation of the circumstances attending the murder of John, Earl of Gowrie and Alexander Ruthven. 1849.
Rizzio: or scenes in Europe during the sixteenth century, by W. H. Ireland. 3 vols 1849. Ed James.
Dark scenes of history. 3 vols 1849, 1 vol 1852.
The forgery: or best intentions. 3 vols 1849, 1 vol 1853.
John Jones's tales for little John Joneses. 2 vols 1849.
The woodman: a romance of the times of Richard III. 3 vols 1849, 1849, 1 vol 1857.
The old oak chest: a tale of domestic life. 3 vols 1850, 1 vol New York 1880.
Henry Smeaton: a Jacobite story of the reign of George I. 3 vols 1851.
The fate: a tale of stirring times. 3 vols 1851.
Remorse and other tales. New York 1852.
Revenge: a novel. 3 vols 1852.
Adrian, or the clouds of the mind: a romance. 2 vols 1852, 1 vol New York 1852. With M. B. Field.
Pequinillo: a tale. 3 vols 1852, 1 vol New York 1852.
The bride of Landeck. New York 1858. First pbd in Harper's New Monthly Mag June–Nov 1852.
Agnes Sorel: an historical romance. 3 vols 1853, 1 vol New York 1853, 1884, 1889.
A life of vicissitudes: a story of revolutionary times. New York 1852, 3 vols 1853 (as The vicissitudes of a life: a novel).
An oration on the character and services of the late Duke of Wellington. Boston 1853.
Ticonderoga, or the black eagle: a tale of times not long past. 3 vols 1854, 1 vol New York 1854, London 1859 (as The black eagle: or Ticonderoga).
Prince Life: a story for my boy. 1856.
The old dominion, or the Southampton massacre: a novel. 3 vols 1856, 1 vol New York 1856, London 1858.

Leonora d'Orco: a historical romance. 3 vols 1857, 1 vol 1858; tr French, 1858.

Lord Montagu's page: a historical romance. 3 vols 1858, 1 vol Philadelphia 1858.

The cavalier: an historical novel. Philadelphia 1859, 2 vols 1854 (as Bernard Marsh: a novel).

The man in black: an historical novel of the days of Queen Anne. Philadelphia 1860.

James contributed to Seven tales by seven authors, ed F. E. Smedley 1849, 1860, *and wrote lives of eminent foreign statesmen for vols 2–5 of* Lardner's cabinet cyclopaedia, 1836, 2 vols Philadelphia 1836.

§2

The novels of James. Dublin Univ Mag March 1842.

Horne, R. H. In his A new spirit of the age vol 1, 1844.

Recollections of James. Bentley's Miscellany Feb 1861.

Frost, W. A. The novels and short stories of James. N & Q 26 Aug 1916. Annotated list.

Ellis, S. M. The solitary horseman: or the life and adventures of James. 1927. With bibliography.

Duffy, C. Letter from G. P. R. J. to B. Taylor. N & Q 19 June 1943.

CHRISTIAN ISOBEL JOHNSTONE
1781–1857

Clan-Albin: a national tale. 4 vols London, Edinburgh and Dublin 1815, 1853 (as Clan Albyn).

The cook and housewife's manual, containing the most approved modern receipts for making soups, gravies, sauces, by Margaret Dods. Edinburgh 1826 (10 edns, by 1854).

The students: or biography of Grecian philosophers. 1827.

Elizabeth de Bruce: a novel. 3 vols Edinburgh and London 1827.

The diversions of Hollycot: or the mother's art of thinking. 1828, Edinburgh 1876.

Scenes of industry displayed in the beehive and the ant-hill. [1829?], 1830.

Nights of the round table: or stories of Aunt Jane and her friends. 2 pts Edinburgh 1832.

Lives and voyages of Drake, Cavendish and Dampier with a view of the earlier discoveries in the South sea and the history of the bucaniers. New York 1832, 1842, 1844.

The wars of the Jews, adapted to young persons. 1832, New York, Boston 1853 (as Stories from the history of the Jews).

True tales of the Irish peasantry, as related by themselves, selected from the Report of the Poor-Law Commissioners. 1836.

Rational reading lessons. 1842.

The Edinburgh tales. 3 vols Edinburgh and Dublin 1845, 1850. Ed Mrs Johnstone. Includes 15 tales by Mrs Johnstone first pbd in Inverness Courier, Edinburgh Weekly Chron and Johnstone's Mag, later merged with Tait's Mag, which she and her husband owned and edited.

Mrs Johnstone also edited the Poems of Robert Nicoll, 1842.

ISABELLA KELLY, later HEDGELAND

§1

Madeleine, or the Castle of Montgomery: a novel. 4 vols 1794 (anon), 1799.

A collection of poems and fables. 1794.

The Abbey of St Asaph: a novel by the author of Madeleine. 3 vols 1795.

The ruins of Avondale Priory: a novel. 3 vols 1796.

Joscelina, or the rewards of benevolence: a novel. 2 vols 1797.

Eva: a novel. 3 vols 1799; tr French, 1803.

Ruthinglenne, or the critical moment: a novel. 3 vols 1801.

The Baron's daughter: a Gothic romance. 4 vols 1802.

Poems. 1802.

A modern incident in domestic life. 2 vols Brentford 1803.

The secret: a novel. 4 vols Brentford 1805.

Poems and fables on several occasions. 1805, Chelsea 1807.

Literary information consisting of anecdotes, explanations and derivations. 1811.

Jane de Dunstanville, or characters as they are: a novel. 4 vols 1813.

Isabella Kelly also pbd some educational works.

§2

Loomis, R. E. The problem of the Gothic novel in Wales. Nat Lib of Wales Jnl 13 1964.

JAMES SHERIDAN KNOWLES
1784–1862

See col 1132, below.

LADY CAROLINE LAMB, née PONSONBY
1785–1828

§1

Glenarvon. 3 vols 1816 (anon), 1816 (with important new preface), 1816, 1817, 1 vol [1865] (as The fatal passion).

Verses from Glenarvon; to which is prefixed the original introduction not published with the early editions of that work. 1816.

A new canto. 1819. Anon.

Graham Hamilton. 2 vols 1822 (anon), Philadelphia 1822, London 1823.

Ada Reis: a tale. 3 vols 1823 (anon), 2 vols Paris 1824.

Fugitive pieces and reminiscences of Lord Byron with some original poetry, letters and recollections of Lady Caroline Lamb. Ed I. Nathan 1829.

§2

Mayer, S. R. T. Lady Caroline Lamb. Temple Bar June 1878.

Green, A. J. Did Byron write the poem to Lady Caroline Lamb? PQ 7 1928.

Jenkins, E. Lady Caroline Lamb. 1932.

Cecil, D. The young Melbourne and the story of his marriage with Caroline Lamb. 1939, 1948.

FRANCIS LATHOM
1777–1832

The castle of Ollada. 2 vols [1794?].

The midnight bell: a German story founded on incidents in real life. 3 vols 1798 (anon), 1825; tr French, [1799].

Orlando and Seraphina, or the funeral pile: a drama. 1799. Based on Tasso, Gerusalemme liberata.

Men and manners: a novel. 4 vols 1799, 1800.

Mystery: a novel. 2 vols 1800; tr French, nd; German, nd.

All in a bustle: a comedy by the author of the Castle of Ollada. Norwich 1795, 1800.

The dash of the day: a comedy. Norwich 1800, 1800, 1800.

Holiday time, or the school boy's frolic: a farce. Norwich 1800.

Curiosity: a comedy. 1801. Adapted from the French of Madame de Genlis.

The wife of a million: a comedy. Norwich [1802?].

Astonishment!!! a romance of a century ago. 2 vols 1802.

Very strange but very true, or the history of an old man's young wife: a novel. 4 vols 1803.
Ernestine: a tale from the French. 2 vols 1803.
The impenetrable secret: find it out! 2 vols 1805.
The mysterious freebooter, or the days of Queen Bess: a romance. 4 vols 1806.
Human beings: a novel. 3 vols 1807.
The fatal vow, or St Michael's Monastery: a romance. 2 vols 1807.
The unknown: or the northern gallery. 3 vols 1808; tr French, 1810.
London: or truth without treason. 4 vols 1809.
The romance of the Hebrides: or wonders never cease! 3 vols 1809.
Italian mysteries, or more secrets than one: a romance. 3 vols 1820; tr French, 1823.
The one pound note and other tales. 2 vols 1820.
Puzzled and pleased: or the two old soldiers and other tales. 3 vols 1822.
Live and learn, or the first John Brown, his friends, enemies and acquaintances, in town and country: a novel. 4 vols 1823.
The Polish bandit: or who is my bride? and other tales. 3 vols 1824.
Young John Bull: or born abroad and bred at home. 3 vols 1828.
Fashionable mysteries: or the rival Duchesses and other tales. 3 vols 1829.
Mystic events, or the vision of the tapestry: a romantic legend of the days of Anne Boleyn. 4 vols 1830.

THOMAS PIKE LATHY

Reparation, or the school for libertines: a dramatic piece in three acts. Boston 1800.
Usurpation, or the inflexible uncle: a novel. 3 vols 1805.
The paraclete: a novel. 5 vols 1805.
The invisible enemy, or the mines of Wielitska: a Polish legendary romance. 4 vols 1806.
Gabriel Forrester: or the deserted son. 4 vols 1807.
Love, hatred and revenge: a Swiss romance. 3 vols 1809.
The angler: a poem in ten cantos, with proper instructions in the art, rules to choose fishing rods, lines, hooks etc. 1819, 1820. Almost entirely plagiarized from The anglers, by Thomas Scott of Ipswich, 1758.
Memoirs of the Court of Louis XIV, comprising biography and anecdotes of the most celebrated characters of that period. 3 vols 1819.

SIR THOMAS DICK LAUDER
1784–1848

Lochandhu: a tale of the eighteenth century. Ed C. M. Montgomery 3 vols Edinburgh 1825, Elgin 1891; tr French, 1828.
The Wolfe of Badenoch: an historical romance. 1827, 1870, 1886, Stirling 1930.
An account of the great floods of 1829 in the province of Moray and adjoining districts. Edinburgh 1830; ed G. Gordon, Elgin 1873.
Highland rambles and long legends to shorten the way. 2 vols Edinburgh 1837, London 1880.
Legendary tales of the Highlands. 3 vols 1841, 1 vol 1881.
The Edinburgh tales. Ed C. I. Johnstone 3 vols 1845–6. Lauder contributed The story of Farquharson of Inverey to vol 1, and Donald Lamont, the Braemar drover, to vol 3.
Memorial of the royal progress in Scotland. 1843.
Directions for taking and curing herrings; and for curing cod, ling, tusk and hake, with Gaelic translations by A. Macgregor. Edinburgh 1846, Dublin 1846.
The mill of Dalveney (chiefly drawn from the Account of the great floods etc). 1872.
Lauder edited Sir U. Price, Essays on the picturesque, *to which he contributed an essay* On the origin of taste, *and* Gilpin's Forest scenery. *With Thomas Brown and William Rhind he issued the* Miscellany of natural history, 2 vols 1833–4. *He also pbd some topographical works.*

HARRIET LEE
1757–1851

§1

The errors of innocence. 5 vols 1786.
The new peerage, or our eyes may deceive us: a comedy. 1787, Dublin 1788.
The Canterbury tales. 5 vols 1797–1805, 1799 (vols 1–2), 2 vols 1826, 1832 (rev and with new Preface), 1842, Boston and New York 1886. In 1st edn Harriet Lee's name appears alone on title-page of vols 1, 4–5; not at all on vol 2; jointly with Sophia Lee's on vol 3. Sophia Lee wrote only the introd, The two Emilys (separately pbd 2 vols [1800?]; tr French, 1800) and Pembroke. Vol 3 was rptd separately Dublin 1799, as The officer's tale and clergyman's tale; vol 4 was also often rptd separately (5th edn 1823) as Kruitzner: or the German's tale. The latter was dramatized by Byron in 1822 as Werner.
The mysterious marriage, or the heirship of Roselva: a drama. 1798, Dublin 1798.
The three strangers. 1826. A dramatization of Kruitzner.

§2

Obituary. Bristol Jnl 9 Aug 1851.
Mrs Harriet Lee. Littell's Living Age 31 1851.

SOPHIA LEE
1750–1824

The chapter of accidents: a comedy. 1780, 1780, Dublin 1781 etc; tr German, 1782, 1788. Based on Diderot, Père de famille.
The recess: or a tale of other times. 3 vols 1785, 1786, Portsea 1800, London 1804, [1825?]; tr French, 1787; Portuguese, 1806.
A hermit's tale, recorded by his own hand and found in his cell, by the author of the Recess. 1787 (anon), Dublin 1787.
Almeyda, Queen of Granada: a tragedy. 1796, Dublin 1796. Partly from Shirley, The Cardinal.
The Canterbury tales. 5 vols 1797–1805, 2 vols 1826, 1831. Mainly by Harriet Lee. Sophia contributed 2 tales to vols 2–3, and the introd to vol 1.
The life of a lover, in a series of letters. 6 vols 1804; tr French, 5 vols 1808 (as Savinia Rivers).
Ormond: or the debauchee. 3 vols 1810.
Sophia Lee translated Varbeck, *one of Baculard d'Arnaud's* Nouvelles historiques, *as* Warbeck: a pathetic tale, 1786.

MATTHEW GREGORY LEWIS
1775–1818

Bibliographies

Summers, M. In his A Gothic bibliography, [1941].

§1

The effusions of sensibility: an unfinished burlesque novel [1791]. In Mrs Baron-Wilson, Life and correspondence of Lewis vol 2, 1839.
The monk: a romance. 3 vols 1796, 1796, 2 vols Dublin 1796, Waterford '1796' (watermarked 1818), 3 vols

1797, 2 vols Dublin 1797, 3 vols 1798 (expurgated as Ambrosio: or the monk, rptd New York 1830), 3 vols Paris 1807, 1 vol [1820?], 1846, Philadelphia [185–], [1884]; ed R. F. Stalham 3 vols 1906, 1924; ed E. A. Baker 1907; ed L. F. Peck, New York 1952, 1959, London 1960; tr French, 1803; Spanish, 1822. Dramatized as Aurelio and Miranda, 1799; adapted as Raymond and Agnes: or the bleeding nun of the Castle of Lindenberg, 1820, New York 1821, London 1823, New York 1828, London 1841; dramatized under that title, 1829, [1877?]. Dramatized in French, 1798; tr French (abridged), [1884?] (as Le moine incestueux).

Village virtues: a dramatic satire. 1796.

The minister: a tragedy translated from the German of Schiller. 1797.

The Castle spectre: a drama. 1798 (7 edns), Dublin 1798, London 1799, 1803 etc.

Rolla, or the Peruvian hero: a tragedy translated from the German of Kotzebue. 1799 (4 edns).

Tales of terror. Kelso 1799 (reissued as An apology for tales of terror). Includes 4 ballads by Lewis with others by Scott and Southey.

The love of gain: a poem imitated from Juvenal. 1799. With Latin text.

Alonzo the brave and fair Imogine: a ballad [from Monk]. 1797 (in Poetry original and selected vol 2), Glasgow [1800?] (anon), [1810?] etc.

The East Indian: a comedy. 1800, 1800, Dublin 1800 (as Rivers: or the East Indian). Adapted as an opera, 1818, 1886.

Adelmorn the outlaw: a romantic drama. 1801, 1801, Dublin 1801, New York 1805, 1815; tr German, 1829.

Songs in Adelmorn the outlaw. 1801.

Alfonso, King of Castile: a tragedy. 1801, 1802, Philadelphia 1802, 1810, New York 1811.

Tales of wonder, written and collected by M. G. Lewis. 2 vols 1801, Dublin 1801, 1805, Vienna 1805, 1 vol 1836, [1869]. With contributions by Scott and Southey.

Tales of terror and wonder. Ed H. Morley 1887.

Tales in verse of terror and wonder. Ed L. E. Smith, Girard Kansas [1925].

The wild wreath. Ed M. E. Robinson 1804. Contains 4 poems by Lewis.

The bravo of Venice: a romance translated from the German [of J. H. D. Zschokke]. 1805, 1807, 1809, 1830, 1834, [1844], 1856 etc. Abridged as Rugantino: the bravo of Venice, 1805, 1810, 1823, 1834, 1837 etc.

Adelgirtha, or the fruits of a single error: a tragedy. 1806 (4 edns), New York 1812, London 1817, Boston [1858].

Feudal tyrants, or the Counts of Carlsheim and Sargans: a romance, taken from the German. 4 vols 1806, 1807.

Romantic tales. 4 vols 1808, 1838, 1848. Separate tales often rptd.

Venoni, or the novice of St Mark's: a drama. 1809. Philadelphia 1810, London 1829.

Monody on the death of Sir John Moore. 1809.

Timour the tartar: a grand romantic melodrama. 1811, 1829, 1868.

One o'clock or the Knight and the wood demon: a grand musical romance. [1811], New York 1813, London 1824 etc.

Poems. 1812.

The harper's daughter, or love and ambition: a tragedy. Philadelphia 1813.

The isle of devils: a historical tale [in verse] founded on an anecdote in the annals of Portugal. Kingston Jamaica 1827, 1912.

Crazy Jane [by Lewis, with other songs]. Waterford [1830?] (anon), Manchester [1835?].

Journal of a West India proprietor kept during a residence in the island of Jamaica. 1834, 1845 (as Journal of a residence among the negroes in the West Indies), 1861; ed M. Wilson 1929.

Tales of mystery. Ed G. Saintsbury 1891. Selections from Mrs Radcliffe, Lewis and Maturin.

Lewis also translated, with others, Anthony Hamilton, Fairy tales and romances, 1849. *In 1899 appeared an edn of his trn of* Hamilton, Les quatres Facardins, *with continuations by Lewis and the Duc de Lévis.* Les mystères de la Tour Saint-Jean, 4 vols Paris 1819, *is described on title-page as* 'par Lewis, auteur du Moine', *but cannot be identified as a trn of any known work of his.* Tales of terror [in verse], with an introductory dialogue, 1801, Dublin 1808, *is generally but wrongly attributed to Lewis. Summers lists various other spurious attributions, imitations, parodies and plagiarisms.*

§2

Impartial strictures on the poem called the Pursuits of literature [by T. J. Mathias] and particularly a vindication of the romance of the Monk. 1798.

[Baron-Wilson, M.] The life and correspondence of Lewis, with many pieces never before published. 2 vols 1839.

Bortone, G. Fra il voto e l'amore: note critiche sul Monaco del Lewis. Naples 1908.

Church, E. A bibliographical myth. MP 19 1922. On Tales of terror, 1801.

Taylor, A. The three sins of the hermit. MP 20 1923. On the ultimate sources of the Monk.

Emerson, O. F. Monk Lewis and the Tales of terror. MLN 38 1923.

Schneider, R. Der Mönch in der englischen Literatur bis auf Lewis's Monk 1795. Berlin 1927.

Coykendall, F. A note on the Monk. Colophon new ser no 1 1935. Detailed bibliographical analysis.

Moss W. Lewis and Mme de Staël. E Studies 34 1953.

Guthke, K. S. Some bibliographical errors concerning the romantic age. PBSA 51 1957. On Lewis's sources and authorship.

—— Some unpublished letters of Lewis. N & Q May, Sept 1957.

—— Die erste Nachwirkung von Herders Volksliedern in England. Brunswick 1957.

—— Some unidentified early English translations from Herder's Volkslieder. MLN 73 1958.

—— Englische Vorromantik und deutscher Sturm und Drang: Lewis's Stellung. Göttingen 1958.

—— Lewis' The twins: text and commentary. HLQ 25 1962.

—— F. L. Schröder, J. F. Regnard and Lewis. HLQ 27 1963.

Parreaux, A. The publication of the Monk. Paris 1960.

Adelsperger, W. Aspects of staging in Adelgirtha. Ohio State Univ Theatre Collection Bull no 7 1960.

Peck, L. F. A life of Lewis. Cambridge Mass 1961.

—— An early copy of the Monk. PBSA 57 1963.

—— On the date of the Tales of wonder. Eng Lang Notes 2 1964.

—— New poems by Lewis. Archiv 153 1966.

Lévy, M. Le manuscrit du Moine. Caliban 3 1965.

Thomas, W. They called him Monk. Personalist 47 1966.

JOHN GIBSON LOCKHART

1794–1854

See col 1291, below.

SAMUEL LOVER

1797–1868

Collections

Characteristic sketches of Ireland and the Irish, by Carleton, Lover and Mrs Hall. Dublin 1845, Halifax 1846, 1849, 1852 (as Tales and stories of Ireland). Lover's contributions are Paddy Mullonney's travels in France; A legend of Clanmacnoise; Ballads and ballad singers.

Poetical works. [1880].
Collected writings: treasure trove edition. Ed J. J. Roche 10 vols Boston 1901–13.
Works: new library edition. Ed J. J. Roche 6 vols Boston 1902.

§1

The parson's horn-book. 2 pts Dublin 1831 (anon), 1831. Satires on the Established Church in Ireland by Lover et al.
Legends and stories of Ireland. Illustr W. Harvey and Lover 2 sers 1831–4 (ser 1 rptd Dublin 1832), 1844, 2 vols 1860 etc; ed D. J. O'Donoghue 1899.
Popular tales and legends of the Irish peasantry. Dublin 1834, 1837. Ed and illustr Lover.
Rory O'More: a national romance. Illustr Lover 3 vols 1837, 1839 (rev), [1879], New York 1886, London 1893; ed D. J. O'Donoghue 1898, Boston 1901. A dramatization was pbd 1837 (Webster's Acting national drama vol 3), 1883 (Dicks's Standard plays).
The white horse of the peppers: a comic drama in two acts. 1838 (in Webster's Acting national drama vol 7).
The hall porter: a comic drama in two acts. 1839 (in Webster's Acting national drama vol 7), 1884 (in Dicks's Standard plays).
The happy man: an extravaganza in one act. 1839 (in Webster's Acting national drama vol 7), Boston [1858], New York [1883].
Songs and ballads. 1839, New York 1847, Philadelphia 1847, London 1858.
The Greek boy: a musical drama in two acts. [1840] (in Webster's Acting national drama vol 9).
Il Paddy Whack in Italia: an operetta in one act. [1842?] (in J. Duncombe's British theatre vol 44).
Handy Andy: a tale of Irish life. 1842, 1849, 1855, 1862, 1869, New York 1877, London 1884, 1884; ed C. Whibley 1896; ed D. J. O'Donoghue 1898, Boston 1901, London 1904 (with 24 illustrations by Lover), New York 1906; ed E. Rhys 1907 (EL); ed S. O'Faoláin 1945 (abridged).
Treasure trove: the first of a series of accounts of Irish heirs, a romantic tale of the last century. Illustr Lover 1844, New York 1844, London [1856] (as He would be a gentleman: or treasure trove, rptd New York 1877, London 1893), [1862], New York 1862 (as Irish heirs), 1890; ed D. J. O'Donoghue 1899.
The low back car etc. [1855?]. Illustr W. Magrath, Philadelphia 1890, 1892. Songs.
The lyrics of Ireland, edited and annotated by Lover. 1858, 1884 (as Poems of Ireland, to which is added Lover's Metrical tales).
Rival rhymes in honour of Burns; with curious illustrative matter, collected and edited by Ben Trovato [Lover]. 1859.
Metrical tales and other poems. 1860, 1884 (with Poems of Ireland).
Original songs for the rifle volunteers. 1861. With C. Mackay and T. Miller.
MacCarthy More, or possession nine points of the law: a comic drama in two acts. [1861] (in T. H. Lacy's Acting edition of plays vol 51).
Tom Crosbie and his friends. New York 1878.
Barney the Baron: a farce in one act; [and] The happy man: an extravaganza in one act. [1883] (J. Dicks's Standard plays).
Further stories of Ireland. Ed D. J. O'Donoghue 1899.

§2

Samuel Lover. Dublin Univ Mag Feb 1851.
The life, genius and writings of Lover. Temple Bar Aug 1868.
Bernard, W. B. The life of Lover, artistic, literary and musical, with selections from his unpublished papers and correspondence. 2 vols 1874.
Symington, A. J. Lover: a biographical sketch, with selections from his writings and correspondence. 1880.
—— In Poets and the poetry of the century, ed A. H. Miles vol 9 1894. With a selection from Lover's poems.
Layard, G. S. Lover as a graphic humourist. Mag of Art 19 1896.
Schmid, F. Samuel Lover. Century Mag 3 1897.

WILLIAM MAGINN
1793–1842

See col 1293, below.

CHARLES ROBERT MATURIN
1782–1824

Bibliographies

Summers, M. In his A Gothic bibliography, [1941].
Sadleir, M. In his XIX century fiction: a bibliographical record, 2 vols 1951.

Selections

Tales of mystery. Ed G. Saintsbury 1891. Selections from Mrs Radcliffe, Lewis and Maturin.

§1

Fatal revenge: or the family of Montorio, by Dennis Jasper Murphy. 3 vols 1807, 4 vols 1824, 1 vol 1841.
The wild Irish boy, by the author of Montorio. 3 vols 1808, 2 vols New York 1808, 1814, 1839.
The Milesian chief: a romance by the author of Montorio and the Wild Irish boy. 4 vols 1812, 2 vols Philadelphia and New York 1812; tr French, 1828.
Lines on the battle of Waterloo: prize poem. Dublin 1816.
Bertram, or the Castle of St Aldobrand: a tragedy. 1816 (7 edns), 1817, 1817, 1827, 1829, New York 1847, 1848, London 1865, 1884, 1956; tr French, 1821.
Manuel: a tragedy in five acts by the author of Bertram. 1817, 1817. Unpbd extracts in New Monthly Mag 1819.
Women, or pour et contre: a tale by the author of Bertram etc. 3 vols Edinburgh 1818, 2 vols Philadelphia 1818; tr French, 1818.
Fredolfo: a tragedy in five acts. 1819.
Sermons. 1819, 1821.
Melmoth the wanderer: a tale by the author of Bertram. 4 vols Edinburgh 1820, 1821, 3 vols 1892 (with memoir and bibliography); ed W. F. Axton, Lincoln Nebraska 1961, London 1966; tr French, 1821, 1965. Dramatized by B. West, [1823], [1830?].
The Albigenses: a romance by the author of Bertram etc. 4 vols 1824, 3 vols Philadelphia 1824.
Five sermons on the errors of the Roman Catholic Church. 1824, 1826.
Leixlip Castle. 3 vols 1825.
The universe: a poem, 1821, *which bears Maturin's name, was really by James Wills.*

§2

Edinburgh Rev 35 1821. A review of Melmoth, partly rptd in Famous reviews, ed R. B. Johnson 1914.
The writings of Maturin. London Mag May 1821.
The conversations of Maturin. New Monthly Mag May–June 1827.
Maturin and the novel of terror. TLS 26 Aug 1920.
Idman, N. Maturin: his life and works. Helsinki 1923.
Scholten, W. Maturin: the terror-novelist. Amsterdam 1933.
Buchan, A. M. Maturin's birth date. N & Q 8 July 1950.
Reboul, P. Villiers de l'Isle-Adam et le Melmoth de Maturin. Revue de Littérature Comparée 25 1951.

Hammond, M. E. Maturin and Melmoth the wanderer. English 11 1956.
Piper, H. W. and A. N. Jeffares. Maturin the innovator. HLQ 21 1958.

WILLIAM HAMILTON MAXWELL
1792–1850

Bibliographies

Sadleir, M. In his XIX century fiction: a bibliographical record, 2 vols 1951.

§1

O'Hara: or 1798. 2 vols 1825. Anon.
Stories of Waterloo and other tales. 3 vols 1829, 1 vol 1833, 1834, 1850 etc.
Wild sports of the West, with legendary tales and local sketches. 2 vols 1832, 1833, New York 1833, 1 vol 1847, 1849; illustr F. Gillett [1915]; ed Earl of Dunraven 1915; tr Irish, 1933.
The Hamilton wedding: a humorous poem. 1833.
The field-book: or sports and pastimes of the United Kingdom. 1833.
The dark lady of Doona. 1834, 1846, [1854?], 1862, 1913; tr French, 1834.
My life, by the author of Stories of Waterloo. 3 vols 1835, 2 vols New York 1835, 1 vol 1838 (as The adventures of Captain Blake: or my life), 3 vols 1846, 1 vol 1849 etc.
The bivouac: or stories of the Peninsular War. 3 vols 1837, 1 vol 1839, 1880.
The victories of the British armies. 2 vols 1839, 1 vol 1868 (as The victories of Wellington and the British armies), 1885, 1891.
Life of the Duke of Wellington. 3 vols 1839–41, 1845–6, 1 vol 1852 (abridged); tr German, 1840.
Rambling recollections of a soldier of fortune. Dublin 1842, 1848; illustr Phiz 1850, 1857 (as Flood and field: or the recollections of a soldier of fortune).
Memoirs of Sir Robert Peel. 2 vols 1842.
The fortunes of Hector O'Halloran and his man Mark Anthony O'Toole. 13 pts illustr [R. Doyle] and J. Leech 1842–3, 1851, 1853, [1882] etc.
Wanderings in the Highlands and Islands, with sketches taken on the Scottish border: being a sequel to Wild sports in the West. 2 vols 1844, 1 vol 1853 (as Sports and adventures in the Highlands etc).
Hints to a soldier on service. 2 vols 1845.
History of the Irish rebellion in 1798, with memoirs of the Union and Emmett's insurrection in 1803. 1845; illustr G. Cruikshank 1864, 1887.
Peninsular sketches, by actors on the scene. 2 vols 1845, [1860?] (as Stories of the Peninsular war: or Peninsular sketches).
Captain O'Sullivan: or adventures, civil, military and matrimonial of a gentleman on half-pay. 3 vols 1846, 1 vol New York 1846, London 1858 (as Adventures of Captain O'Sullivan).
Hillside and Border sketches, with legends of the Cheviots and the Lammermuir. 2 vols 1847, 1 vol New York, Philadelphia 1847, 2 vols 1849 (as Legends of the Cheviots and the Lammermuir: a companion to Wild sports of the West), 1 vol 1852 (as Border tales and legends etc).
The Irish movements: their rise, progress and certain termination, with a few broad hints to patriots and pikemen. 1848.
Brian O'Linn: or luck is everything. 3 vols 1848, 1 vol 1856 (as Luck is everything: or the adventures of Brian O'Linn).
Erin-Go-Bragh: or Irish life pictures. 2 vols 1859 (with a memoir of Maxwell by W. Maginn), 1 vol 1860.
Terence O'Shaughnessy's first attempt to get married. In Tales from Bentley vol 1, 1859.

Maxwell contributed to Nimrod's Sporting, 1838, and to Pic-Nic Papers pt 1 1870.

§2

Maginn, W. W. H. Maxwell. Bentley's Miscellany April 1840. Prefixed to Erin-Go-Bragh 2 vols 1859.
Dublin Univ Mag Aug 1841.
Times 16 Jan 1851. Obituary.

MARY MEEKE
d. 1816?

Bibliographies

Blakey, D. In her Minerva Press, 1939.
Summers, M. In his A Gothic bibliography, [1941].

§1

Count St Blancard, or the prejudiced judge: a novel. 3 vols 1795.
The Abbey of Clugny. 3 vols 1795.
The mysterious wife, by Gabrielli. 4 vols 1797.
Palmira and Ermance. 3 vols 1797.
Ellesmere: a novel. 4 vols 1799.
The Sicilian. 4 vols 1799.
Harcourt, by Gabrielli. 4 vols 1799.
Anecdotes of the Altamont family, by the author of the Sicilian etc. 4 vols 1800.
Which is the man? a novel. 4 vols 1801.
What shall be, shall be: a novel. 4 vols 1801, 1823.
The mysterious husband, by Gabrielli. 4 vols 1801.
Independence, by Gabrielli. 4 vols 1802.
Midnight weddings: a novel. 3 vols 1802, 1814; tr French, 1820.
Amazement! 3 vols 1804.
The old wife and the young husband. 3 vols 1804.
Murray House. 3 vols 1804. Also attributed to Eliza Parsons.
The nine days' wonder. 3 vols 1804.
Something odd, by Gabrielli. 3 vols 1804.
The wonder of the village. 3 vols 1805.
Something strange, by Gabrielli. 4 vols 1806.
Ellen, heiress of the Castle. 3 vols 1807.
Julian: or my father's house. 4 vols 1807. Listed in Biographical dictionary of living authors, 1816, but no copy located.
'There's a secret: find it out': a novel. 4 vols 1808.
Laughton Priory, by Gabrielli. 4 vols 1809.
Matrimony the height of bliss or extreme of misery. 4 vols 1811.
Stratagems defeated: a novel, by Gabrielli. 4 vols 1811.
Conscience: a novel. 4 vols 1814.
The Spanish campaign, or the Jew: a novel. 3 vols 1815.
The veiled protectress: or the mysterious mother. 5 vols 1819.
Mrs Meeke also translated a number of works from French and German, including several novels, Mme du Deffand's Unpublished correspondence, 1810, *and the completion of Mrs Collyer's trn of* Klopstock's Messias, 1811.

MARY RUSSELL MITFORD
1787–1855

Bibliographies

Sadleir, M. In his XIX century fiction: a bibliographical record, 2 vols 1951.

Collections

Works, prose and verse. Philadelphia 1841.
Dramatic works. 2 vols 1854.

§1

Poems. 1810, 1811 (with addns).
Christina, the maid of the South Seas: a poem. 1811.
Blanche of Castile. 1812.
Watlington Hill: a poem. 1812.
Narrative poems on the female character. Vol 1, 1813. No more pbd.
Julian: a tragedy in five acts. 1823, 1823, 1823, 1829.
Our village: sketches of rural character and scenery. 5 vols 1824–32 (vol 1 rptd 1825), 3 vols 1836, 2 vols Paris 1839, 2 vols 1852, 1 vol 1862 (as Children of the village), 1881 (as Village tales and sketches; illustr F. Barnard et al 1889 (selection); ed E. Rhys 1891 (selection); ed A. T. Ritchie, illustr H. Thomson 1893 (selection); ed E. Gollancz 1900 (selection); ed A. T. Ritchie, illustr H. Thomson 1902, 1910 (with additional illustrations by A. Rawlings); illustr C. E. Brock 1904 (as Sketches of English life and character) (selection); illustr S. A. Forbes 1909, Chicago 1910, London 1928; 1936 (EL); illustr J. Hassall 1947. First pbd in Lady's Mag 1819.
Foscari: a tragedy. 1826, 1827 etc.
Foscari and Julian: tragedies. 1827.
Dramatic scenes, sonnets and other poems. 1827.
Rienzi: a tragedy. 1828, 1828, 1828 etc.
Mary, Queen of Scots: a scene in English verse. 1831.
Lights and shadows of American life. 3 vols 1832. Ed Miss Mitford.
Charles the First: an historical tragedy in five acts. 1834, [1885].
Sadak and Kalasrade, or the waters of oblivion: a romantic opera. [1836].
Belford Regis: or sketches of a country town. 3 vols 1835, 1 vol 1846, 1849; ed L. S. Jast 1942.
Country stories 1837, 1850; illustr G. Morrow 1895.
Recollections of a literary life: or books, places and people. 3 vols 1852, 1859, 1 vol 1883 (as Recollections and selections from my favourite poets and prose writers).
Atherton and other tales. 3 vols 1854, 1 vol Boston 1854.
The life of Mary Russell Mitford in a selection from her letters. Ed A. G. L'Estrange 3 vols 1870, 1870, 2 vols New York 1870, 5 vols 1870–2.
Letters to C. Boner. 1871, 1876.
The letters of Mary Russell Mitford: second series. Ed H. F. Chorley 2 vols 1872; ed R. B. Johnson [1925].
The friendships of Mary Russell Mitford in letters from her literary correspondents. Ed A. G. L'Estrange 2 vols 1882, 1 vol New York 1882.
Correspondence with C. Boner and J. Ruskin. Ed E. Lee [1914], Chicago [1915].
Stories of village and town life: or word pictures of old England. Ed J. P. Briscoe and E. M. P. Knight 1915. A collection of stories first pbd in various annuals.
Miss Mitford contributed 4 tales to Mrs C. Johnstone, Edinburgh Tales, 3 vols 1845–6, *and edited* Finden's Tableaux of the affections: paintings by W. Perring, 1839. *She also edited* Stories of American life by American writers, 3 vols 1830, *and selections of American children's stories as* Tales for young people, 3 vols 1835, *and* Tales and stories, 1866. *In the BM copy of* Literary Pocket Book for 1819 *are a sonnet and a diary for 1819–23 in her hand.*

§2

Croker, T. C. My village versus Our village. 1833.
Collas, A. In his Authors of England with illustrative notices, 1838.
[Smith, W. H.] Miss Mitford's Recollections. Blackwood's Mag March 1852.
Oliphant, M. O. Mary Russell Mitford. Blackwood's Mag June 1854.
— Miss Austen and Miss Mitford. Blackwood's Mag March 1870.
Manning, A. M. R. Mitford. Macmillan's Mag Feb 1870.
Kettle, R. M. Memoirs and letters with letters of Mary Russell Mitford to him during ten years. 2 vols 1871.
Maginn, W. A. In his A gallery of illustrious literary characters, ed W. Bates [1873].
Martineau, H. In her Biographical sketches 1852–75, 1877.
Roberts, W. J. Mary Russell Mitford: the tragedy of a blue-stocking. 1913.
Hill, C. Mary Russell Mitford and her surroundings. 1920.
Gosse, E. In his Books on the table, 1921.
Woolf, V. In her Common reader, 1925.
Astin, M. Mary Russell Mitford: her circle and her books. 1930.
Kent, M. Mary Mitford's letters. Cornhill Mag June 1936.
Bond, W. L. Incomparable old maid: letters of M. R. Mitford. English 2 1939.
Agate, J. In English wits, ed L. Russell 1940.
Horne, R. H. Miss Mitford after forty years. N & Q 9 March 1946.
Watson, V. G. M. R. Mitford. 1949.
Dodds, M. H. M. R. Mitford and Jane Austen. N & Q 29 April 1950.
Duncan-Jones, C. M. Miss Mitford and Mr Harness: records of a friendship. 1954.
Miller, B. (ed). Elizabeth Barrett to Miss Mitford: unpublished letters. 1954.
Coles, W. A. M. R. Mitford: the inauguration of a literary career. Bull John Rylands Lib 40 1957.
— Magazine and other contributions by M. R. Mitford and Thomas Noon Talfourd. SB 12 1958.
Lauterbach, C. E. Let the printer do it. N & Q Jan 1963. On Miss Mitford's typographical devices.
Lewis, J. M. R. Mitford letters. BM Quart 29 1965.

DAVID MACBETH MOIR

1798–1851

Collections

Poetical works. Ed T. Aird 2 vols 1852 (with memoir).

§1

The bombardment of Algiers and other poems. Edinburgh 1816. Anon.
The legend of Geneviève with other tales and poems by Delta. Edinburgh 1824.
The life of Mansie Wauch, taylor in Dalkeith, written by himself. Edinburgh 1828 (anon); illustr G. Cruikshank 1839 (rev and enlarged), 1853, 1880; ed T. F. Henderson [1902]; illustr C. M. Hardie 1911. First pbd in Blackwood's Mag Oct 1824–Dec 1828.
The bridal of Borthwick. In The Club book, ed A. Picken 3 vols 1831; ed W. Hazlitt 1841.
Outlines of the ancient history of medicine. 1831, [1931].
Memoir of Galt, 1841. Prefixed to Annals of the parish in Blackwood's Standard Novels series.
Domestic verses by Delta. Edinburgh 1843 (priv ptd), 1843, 1871.
Sketches of the poetical literature of the past half-century. Edinburgh 1851, 1852, 1856.
The Roman antiquities of Inveresk. Edinburgh 1860. First pbd in Statistical account of Scotland, 1845.
Moir also wrote several medical works, the final chs of John Galt, The last of the Lairds, *nearly 400 contributions to Blackwood's Mag, and various memoirs and periodical articles. The Blackwood Collection in the National Libary of Scotland includes over 500 letters from Moir to the Blackwood family.*

§2

[Maginn, W.] Gallery of literary characters no 11: Dr Moir. Fraser's Mag Sept 1833; rptd in his A gallery of illustrious literary characters, ed W. Bates [1873].
Obituary. Blackwood's Mag Aug 1851.
[Review of Poetical works]. Eclectic Rev 96 1852.
Gilfillan, G. In his Galleries of literary portraits vol 2, Edinburgh 1856.
Douglas, G. The Blackwood group. [1897].
MacCurdy, E. A literary enigma: the Canadian boat song. Stirling 1936. Attributes to Moir and Lockhart.
Robson, E. H. A. Preparation for a study of metropolitan Scots of the first half of the nineteenth century as exemplified in Mansie Wauch. 1937.
Needler, G. H. The lone shieling: origins and authorship of the Blackwood Canadian boat song. Toronto 1941. Attributed to Moir.
Nolte, E. Moir as Morgan Odoherty. PMLA 72 1957.
—— A letter from Morgan Odoherty. Stud in Scottish Lit 2 1965.
Little, G. L. Christabess, by S. T. Colebritche esq [a parody by Moir in Blackwood's Mag June 1819]. MLR 56 1961.

SYDNEY, LADY MORGAN

See under Owenson, below.

JAMES JUSTINIAN MORIER
1780–1849

Bibliographies

Sadleir, M. In his XIX century fiction: a bibliographical record, 2 vols 1951.

§1

Journey through Persia, Armenia and Asia Minor to Constantinople 1808–9, including an account of the mission under Sir Harford Jones to the Shah of Persia. 1812; tr German, 1815.
Second journey through Persia, Armenia and Asia Minor to Constantinople 1810–16, with a voyage by the Brazils and Bombay to the Persian Gulf and an account of the Embassy under Sir G. Ouseley. 1818; tr German, 1820.
The adventures of Hajji Baba of Ispahan. 3 vols 1824, 1824 (with preface), 1 vol 1835 (rev), Philadelphia 1855, London 1856, 1863, Philadelphia [1880?], Manchester 1892; ed G. Curzon 1895, 2 vols Chicago 1895; ed E. G. Browne 2 vols 1895; ed C. J. Wills 1897; ed C. E. Beckett 1900, 1924; illustr H. R. Millar 1904, 1914 (EL); ed C. W. Stewart, Oxford 1923 (WC); illustr C. Le R. Baldridge 1937; illustr H. Guilbeau 2 vols New York 1947; ed R. Jennings 1949; ed R. D. Altick, New York [1954]; tr German, 1824; Czech, 1877; Persian, 1905.
The adventures of Hajji Baba of Ispahan in England. 2 vols 1828, 1 vol 1835 (rev), 1850; ed L. S. Jast 1942.
Zohrab the hostage, by the author of Hajji Baba. 3 vols 1832, 1832, 1833 (rev with notes), 1 vol 1836, 1864.
Ayesha: the maid of Kars, by the author of Zohrab. 3 vols 1834, 1834, 1 vol Paris 1843, London 1846; tr Swedish, 1836.
Abel Allnutt: a novel. 3 vols 1837, 2 vols Philadelphia 1837.
An oriental tale, by the author of Hajji Baba. [1839].
The adventures of Tom Spicer, who advertised for a wife: a poem. 1840 (priv ptd).
The Mirza. 3 vols 1841.
Literary contributions by various authors in aid of the funds of the hospital for consumption and diseases of the chest, edited by Mrs Leicester Stanhope. 1846. Contains contributions by Morier.
Misselmah: a Persian tale. Brighton 1847.
Martin Toutrond: a Frenchman in London in 1831. 1849 (anon), 1849 (signed), 1852. Written in French by Morier and translated by himself.
Morier also 'edited' with a preface W. Hauff, The banished, 3 vols 1839, *and* St Roche: a romance from the German, 3 vols 1847.

§2

[Thomson, H.] Quart Rev 30 1824. Review of Hajji Baba.
A letter on Hajji Baba, by a friend of the author of Anastasius. Blackwood's Mag Jan 1824.
[Scott, W.] Quart Rev 39 1829. Review of Hajji Baba.
[Lockhart, J. G.] Quart Rev 48 1832. Review of Zohrab the hostage.
James Morier. Fraser's Mag Feb 1833.
Maginn, W. In his A gallery of illustrious literary characters, ed W. Bates [1873].
Zeidler, K. J. Beckford, Hope und Morier als Vertreter des orientalischen Romans. Leipzig 1909.
The sun and the pen. TLS 22 July 1949.
Moussa-Mahmoud, F. Orientals in picaresque (Hope, Morier, Meadows Taylor). Cairo Stud in Eng 1962.

WILLIAM MUDFORD
1782–1848

§1

A critical enquiry into the moral writings of Dr Samuel Johnson. 1802 (anon), 1803.
Augustus and Mary, or the maid of Buttermere: a domestic tale. 1803.
Nubilia in search of a husband, including sketches of modern society, and interspersed with moral and literary disquisitions. 1809 (anon), 1809 (4th edn, containing 2 additional chs).
The contemplatist: or a series of essays upon morals and literature. 1811.
The life and adventures of Paul Plaintive esq, an author, compiled from original documents, and interspersed with specimens of his genius, in prose and poetry, by Martin Gribaldus Swammerdam (his nephew and executor). 2 vols 1811.
A critical examination of the writings of Richard Cumberland esq. 2 vols 1812, 1812, 1 vol 1812 (as The life of Richard Cumberland esq, embracing a critical examination of his various writings), 2 vols 1814.
The historical account of the battle of Waterloo: comprehending a circumstantial narrative of the whole events of the war of 1815. Part 1, 1816, 1817 (as An historical account of the campaign in the Netherlands in 1815).
The five nights of St Albans. 3 vols Edinburgh 1829 (anon), 2 vols Philadelphia 1833, 1 vol [1878].
The Premier. 3 vols 1831.
Stephen Dugard: a novel, by the author of Five knights of St Albans. 3 vols [1840] (anon), [1860].
The iron shroud: or Italian revenge. [1840?] (anon), rptd in Tales from Blackwood, below, vol 1.
Tales and trifles from Blackwood's and other popular magazines. 2 vols 1849.
Arthur Wilson: a study. 3 vols 1872. Anon.
Mudford also prefixed a life of James Beattie to Beauties from the writings of Beattie, 1809, *and a critique of Goldsmith to his edn of the* Essays, 1804. *He translated several works from the French, including* Helvétius, De l'esprit, *edited several papers at different times and was a frequent contributor to Blackwood's Mag. For details of his edn of the* British novelists, 1810–17, *see also* M. Sadleir, XIX century fiction: a bibliographical record vol 2, pp. 141–2.

§2

[Lockhart, J. G.] Blackwood's Mag Oct 1829. Review of Five nights of St Albans.
Guthke, K. S. Georg Büchner und Mudford. Archiv 198 1961.

AMELIA OPIE, née ALDERSON
1769–1853

Collections

Works. 2 vols New York 1835.
Works. 3 vols Philadelphia [1841] (with biographical sketch), 1848.
Miscellaneous tales. 12 vols 1845–7.

§1

The dangers of coquetry: a novel. 2 vols [1790] (anon). Only known copy is in Harvard College Lib.
The father and daughter: a tale in prose, with an epistle from the maid of Corinth to her lover, and other poetical pieces. 1801 (2nd edn), 1804 (4th edn), Georgetown 1812, London 1819 (8th edn), 1844 (10th edn).
Poems. 1802, 1803, 1804, 1806, 1808, 1811.
An elegy to the memory of the late Duke of Bedford, written on the evening of his interment. 1802.
Adeline Mowbray, or the mother and daughter: a tale. 3 vols 1804, 1805, 2 vols Georgetown 1808, London 1810, 1844 (with The welcome home and The Quaker and The young man of the world).
Simple tales. 4 vols 1806, 1806, 1815 (4th edn).
The warrior's return and other poems. 1808, Philadelphia 1808.
Temper, or domestic scenes: a tale. 3 vols 1812, 4 vols 1813 (3rd edn); tr French, 1813 (as Emma et Saint-Aubin).
Tales of real life. 3 vols 1813, 1816 (3rd edn); tr French, 1814 (as Conseils à mon fils).
Valentine's Eve. 3 vols 1816, 1816; tr French, 1816 (as Catherine Shirley).
New tales. 4 vols 1818, 1819 (3rd edn); tr French, 1818.
Tales of the heart. 4 vols 1820.
Madeline: a tale. 2 vols 1822.
Illustrations of lying, in all its branches. 2 vols 1825, Boston 1826, New York 1827, Exeter NH 1832, Hartford 1833; ed T. O. Summers, Nashville 1882.
Tales of the Pemberton family, for the use of children. 1825, 1826.
The black man's lament: or how to make sugar. 1826. Verse.
Detraction displayed. 1828. A manual showing how to defeat calumny.
A wife's duty: a tale. 1828, 1847.
Happy faces: or benevolence and selfishness; and The revenge. 1830. Tales.
Lays for the dead. 1834, 1840.
The ruffian boy; and After the ball: or the two Sir Williams. 1858.
Murder will out. In The omnibus of modern romance, New York 1844.
Mrs Opie also contributed a memoir to Lectures on painting, 1809, *by her husband,* John Opie. *She pbd a number of tales, poems etc in* Friendship's Offering, European Mag *and other periodicals between 1795 and 1841. To* Mrs Margaret Roberts, Duty: a novel, 1814, *she contributed a character of the author.*

§2

Brightwell, C. L. Memorials of the life of Amelia Opie, from her letters, diaries and other manuscripts. Norwich 1854, 1854.
— Memoir of Amelia Opie. 1855.
Mrs Opie. Leisure Hour 3 1854.
Hall, Mrs A. M. Memoirs of Mrs Opie. Art Jnl 6 1854.
— Retrospect of a long life. 2 vols 1883.
Kavanagh, J. In her English women of letters vol 2, 1863.
Martineau, H. In her Biographical sketches 1852–75, 1877.
Hall, S. C. Retrospect of a long life. 2 vols 1883.
[Ritchie, Lady]. Mrs Opie. Cornhill Mag Oct 1883; rptd in her A book of sibyls, 1883.
Robertson, E. S. In her English poetesses, 1883.
Ross, J. A. In her Three generations of Englishwomen: memoirs and correspondence of Mrs John Taylor, Mrs Sarah Austin and Lady Duff Gordon, 2 vols 1888.
Amelia Opie. Temple Bar Aug 1893.
Earland, A. John Opie and his circle. 1911.
Macgregor, M. E. Amelia Alderson Opie, worldling and Friend. Northampton Mass 1933. With a bibliography.
Menzies-Wilson, J. and H. Lloyd. Amelia: the tale of a plain Friend. Oxford 1937.
Bond, W. L. Amelia Opie, novelist and Quaker. English 3 1940.

SYDNEY OWENSON, afterwards LADY MORGAN
1776–1859

Bibliographies

Sadleir, M. In his XIX century fiction: a bibliographical record, 2 vols 1951.

§1

Poems. Dublin 1801.
St Clair: or the heiress of Desmond, by S. O. Dublin 1803, Philadelphia 1807, 2 vols Stockdale 1812 (corrected and greatly enlarged); tr Dutch, 1816.
Twelve original Hibernian melodies. [1805].
The novice of St Dominick. 4 vols 1805, 1806, 1808, 1823.
The wild Irish girl. 3 vols 1806, 1 vol Philadelphia 1807, 3 vols 1813, 1815, 1 vol 1846, New York 1855, London 1856, 1879, New York 1883.
The lay of an Irish harp: or metrical fragments. 1807, New York 1808, Philadelphia [181–].
Patriotic sketches of Ireland written in Connaught. 2 vols 1807, 1 vol Baltimore 1809.
Woman: or Ida of Athens. 4 vols 1809, 2 vols Philadelphia, New York and Baltimore 1809.
The missionary: an Indian tale. 3 vols 1811 (4 edns), New York 1811, 1859 (extensively rev as Luxima, the prophetess: a tale of India).
O'Donnel: a national tale. 3 vols 1814, 1814, 1815, New York 1816, London 1835, 1 vol 1835 (rev), 1836, 1850, 1895.
France. 2 vols 1817, 1817, Philadelphia 1817, 1817, London 1818 (with additional notes); tr French, 1817.
Florence Macarthy: an Irish tale. 4 vols 1818, 1818, 1819, 1 vol 1839, 1856; tr French, 1819.
Italy. 2 vols 1821, 3 vols 1821 (text differs in part from that of the 2 vols edn), 2 vols New York 1821; tr French, 1821; Italian, 1821. Notes on law, statistics and literary disputes, with appendix on the state of medicine by Sir Thomas Charles Morgan.
Letters to the reviewers of Italy. 1821.
The life and times of the Salvator Rosa. 2 vols 1824, Paris 1824, 1 vol 1846, 1855; tr French, 1824.
Absenteeism. 1825.
The O'Briens and the O'Flahertys: a national tale. 4 vols 1827, 1827, 1827, 1828, Philadelphia 1828, 1 vol 1838, 1856; ed R. S. Mackenzie 2 vols New York 1856, 1869; tr French, 1828.
The book of the boudoir. 2 vols 1829, 1829, New York 1829, London 1836. Autobiographical sketches.
France in 1829–30. 2 vols 1830.

Dramatic scenes from real life. 2 vols 1833, New York 1833.
The book without a name. 2 vols 1841. With Sir T. C. Morgan.
The Princess: or the Beguine. 3 vols 1835, Paris 1835; tr French, 1835; German, 1835.
Woman and her master. 2 vols 1840, Philadelphia 1840.
Letter to Cardinal Wiseman. 1851.
Passages in my autobiography. 1859, New York 1859.
Memoirs: autobiography, diaries and correspondence. Ed W. H. Dixon 2 vols 1862, 1863, 1 vol 1863.
Both France *and* Italy *aroused considerable controversy, to which Lady Morgan replied.*

§2

Fitzpatrick, W. J. The friends, foes and adventures of Lady Morgan. Dublin 1859, 1860 (enlarged as Lady Morgan: her career literary and personal etc). First pbd in the Irish Quart Rev July 1859.
Gleig, G. R. Blackwood's Mag Feb 1863. Review of the Memoirs.
Kavanagh, J. In her English women of letters vol 2, 1863.
Maginn, W. In his A gallery of illustrious literary characters, ed W. Bates [1873].
Temple Bar Feb 1893.
Stevenson, L. The wild Irish girl: the life of Sydney Owenson, Lady Morgan. 1936.
Moraud, M. I. Une irlandaise libérale en France sous la Restauration: Lady Morgan. Paris 1954.
Flanagan, T. In his Irish novelists, New York 1959.
Bolster, R. French romanticism and the Irish myth. Hermathena 99 1964.

ELIZA PARSONS
1748–1811

Bibliographies

Summers, M. In his A Gothic bibliography, [1941].

§1

The history of Miss Meridith. 2 vols 1790.
The errors of education. 3 vols 1791, 2 vols Dublin 1792.
The intrigues of a morning. 1792. A play.
Woman as she should be: or memoirs of Mrs Menville. 4 vols 1793.
Ellen and Julia. 2 vols 1793.
The Castle of Wolfenbach: a German story. 2 vols 1793, 1 vol 1835; ed D. P. Varma 1968.
Lucy: a novel. 3 vols 1794.
The voluntary exile. 5 vols 1795.
The mysterious warning: a German tale. 4 vols 1796; ed D. P. Varma 1968.
Women as they are. 4 vols 1796.
The girl of the mountains. 4 vols 1797.
An old friend with a new face. 3 vols 1797.
Anecdotes of two well-known families, written by a descendant and prepared for the press by Mrs Parsons. 3 vols 1798.
The peasant of Ardenne forest. 4 vols 1799.
The valley of St Gothard: a novel. 3 vols Brentford 1799.
The miser and his family. 4 vols 1800.
The mysterious visit: a novel founded on facts. 4 vols Brentford and Norbury 1802.
Murray House: a plain unvarnished tale. 3 vols Brentford 1804.
The convict or Navy Lieutenant: a novel. Brentford 1807.
In 1804 she pbd 6 tales from La Fontaine as Love and gratitude.

CONSTANTINE HENRY PHIPPS, MARQUIS OF NORMANBY
1797–1863

The English in Italy: a novel. 3 vols 1825. Anon. A collection of romances.
Matilda: a tale of the day. 1825 (3 edns), 4 vols Paris 1826.
Historiettes: or tales of Continental life. 3 vols 1827.
The English in France. 3 vols 1828.
Yes and no: a tale of the day, by the author of Matilda. 2 vols 1828.
Clorinda, or the necklace of pearls: the tale of a bystander. Keepsake 1829; tr Spanish, 1830.
The English at home. 3 vols 1830.
The contrast, by the author of Matilda, Yes and no etc. 3 vols 1832.
A year of revolution, from a journal kept in Paris 1848. 2 vols 1857, Paris 1858.
The Congress and the Cabinet. 1859, Paris 1860; tr French, 1860.
An historical sketch of Louise de Bourbon, Duchess Regent of Parma. 1861.
A vindication of the Duke of Modena from the charges of Mr Gladstone, from official documents. 1861.
Several of the Marquis of Normanby's speeches were also pbd.

ANDREW PICKEN
1788–1833

§1

Tales and sketches of the West of Scotland, by Christopher Keelivine. 1824. Mary Ogilvie rptd from above, 1840 (6th edn), illustr R. Cruikshank.
The sectarian: or the Church and the Meeting-house. 3 vols 1829.
The dominie's legacy: a series of tales illustrative of the scenery and manners of Scotland. 3 vols 1830, 1831, 2 vols Philadelphia 1833.
Travels and researches of eminent English missionaries, including an historical sketch of the progress of Protestant missions of late years. 1830, 1831.
The Club book, edited by the author of the Dominie's legacy. 3 vols 1831, 2 vols New York 1836. Picken contributed The deer-stalker, Eisenbach, The three Kearneys, all of which were rptd in the Romancist and Novelist's Lib 1840–1. The other contributors included Galt, Hogg, Cunningham, James, Jerdan and Moir.
Waltham: a novel. 1832.
The Canadas as they at present commend themselves to the enterprise of emigrants, colonists and capitalists, compiled and condensed from original documents furnished by John Galt. 1832, 1836.
Traditionary stories of old families and legendary illustrations of family history, with historical and biographical notes. 2 vols 1833, 1 vol Philadelphia 1833.
The Black Watch. 3 vols 1834.
Picken also wrote A life of John Wesley, *tales for* Fraser's Mag *and a narrative entitled* Experience of life, *which remain unpbd.*

§2

Brown, R. Memoirs of Ebenezer Picken, poet, and of Andrew Picken, novelist. In Paisley Burns Club publications, 1878.

JOHN WILLIAM POLIDORI
1795–1821

§1

On the punishment of death. Pamphleteer 8 1816.
An essay upon the source of positive pleasure. 1818.

Ximenes, the wreath and other poems. 1819.
The vampyre: a tale. 1819, 1830; illustr F. Gilbert 1884; tr Italian, 1829. First pbd in New Monthly Mag April 1819, and wrongly attributed to Byron.
Ernestus Berchtold, or the modern Oedipus: a tale. 1819. Anon.
The diary of J. W. Polidori 1816, relating to Byron, Shelley etc. Ed W. M. Rossetti 1911.

§2

Rieger, J. Polidori and the genesis of Frankenstein. Stud in Eng Lit 1500–1900 3 1963.

ROBERT POLLOK
1798–1838

See col 395 above.

JOHN POOLE
1786?–1872

See col 1137, below.

ANNA MARIA PORTER
1780–1832

§1

Artless tales. 2 vols 1793–5. Anon.
Walsh Colville: or a young man's first entrance into life. 1797, 1833, 1840.
Octavia. 3 vols 1798, 1833; tr French, [1799?].
The lake of Killarney: a novel. 3 vols 1804, 1 vol 1853, 1856 (as Rose de Blaquière: or the lake of Killarney).
A sailor's friendship; and A soldier's love. 2 vols 1805.
The Hungarian brothers. 3 vols 1807, 1808, 1819, 2 vols Exeter NH 1825, 1 vol 1832 (rev); rptd in The novel newspaper vol 2, 1839; tr French, 1818.
Don Sebastian, or the house of Braganza: an historical romance. 4 vols 1809, 1835; rptd in The novel newspaper vol 2, 1839; tr French, 1820.
Ballad, romances and other poems, 1811, Philadelphia 1816.
The recluse of Norway. 4 vols 1814, 1815, 1 vol 1852; tr French, 1815.
Tales of pity on fishing, shooting and hunting, intended to inculcate in the mind of youth sentiments of humanity toward the brute creation. 1814.
The Knight of St John: a romance. 3 vols 1817, 1817, 1 vol 1852; tr French, 1818.
The fast of St Magdalen: a romance. 3 vols 1818, 1819; tr French, 1819.
The village of Mariendorpt: a tale. 4 vols 1821; tr French, 1821.
Roche-Blanche, or the hunters of the Pyrenees: a romance. 3 vols 1822; tr French, 1822.
O'Hara: or 1798. 2 vols 1825.
Honor O'Hara: a novel. 3 vols 1826; tr French, 1827.
Tales round a winter hearth, by Jane and Anna Maria Porter. 2 vols 1826. Anna Maria contributed Glenawan, Lord Howth, Jeanie Halliday.
Coming out, by Jane and Anna Maria Porter. 3 vols 1828.
The Barony. 3 vols 1830.

§2

Elwood, A. K. In her Memoirs of the literary ladies of England vol 2, 1843.
De La Mare, W. In his Material of fiction, 1933.

JANE PORTER
1776–1850

§1

A defence of the profession of an actor. 1800.
Thaddeus of Warsaw. 4 vols 1803, 1806, 1809, 1812, 1816 etc, 2 vols Exeter NH 1829, 1832, 1 vol 1831 (rev), 1845, 1849, 1854, New York 1860 etc, Philadelphia 1868.
Sketch of the campaign of Count A. Suwarrow Ryminski. 1804.
Aphorisms of Sir Philip Sidney. 2 vols 1807.
The Scottish chiefs: a romance. 5 vols 1810, 1811, 1816, 1820, 2 vols 1831 (rev), Chicago 1899; ed K. D. Wiggin and N. A. Smith 1921; ed R. M. Smith, New York 1927; tr French, 1814; Irish, 1937.
The pastor's fireside. 3 vols 1815, 4 vols 1817, 2 vols 1832 (with new introd), [1846] (rev with appendix), 1849, 1856, 1880; abridged S. S. Wilkinson 1822; tr French, 1817.
Duke Christian of Luneberg: or traditions from the Hartz. 3 vols 1824, 1824; tr French, 1824.
Tales round a winter hearth, by Jane and Anna Maria Porter. 2 vols 1826.
Coming out, by Jane and Anna Maria Porter. 3 vols 1828.
The field of the forty footsteps. 3 vols 1828.
Sir Edward Seaward's narrative of his shipwreck and consequent discovery of certain islands in the Caribbean Sea; with a detail of many extraordinary and highly interesting events of his life from 1733 to 1749 as written in his own diary, edited by Jane Porter. 3 vols 1831, New York 1831, 1 vol 1852 (abridged); ed W. H. G. Kingston 1879. Written by Jane Porter.
Young hearts, by a recluse; preface by Jane Porter. 1834.

§2

[Barrow, J.] Quart Rev 48 1832. Review of Sir Edward Seaward's narrative.
Miss Jane Porter. Fraser's Mag April 1835.
Hall, A. M. Memoirs of Jane Porter. Art Jnl 2 1850.
Maginn, W. In his A gallery of illustrious literary characters, ed W. Bates [1873].
Wilson, M. A romantic novelist. In her These were Muses, 1924.

ANN RADCLIFFE, née WARD
1764–1823

Bibliographies

Summers, M. In his A Gothic bibliography, [1941].

Collections

Poems. 1815, 1816, 1845. A collection of the poetical pieces in the novels.
Novels, with memoir by Scott. 1824.
Poetical works. 2 vols 1834.
Novels. [1877].
Tales of mystery. Ed G. Saintsbury 1891. Selections from Mrs Radcliffe, Lewis and Maturin.

§1

The Castles of Athlin and Dunbayne: a Highland story. 1789, 1793, 1793, Philadelphia 1796, Boston 1797, London 1811, 1821, 1824, 1827, 1836 etc; tr French, 1819.
A Sicilian romance. 2 vols 1790, 1792, 1796, 1809, 1818, 1821, 1 vol 1826, 1830 etc; tr German, 1792; French, 1798 etc; Spanish, 1819; Russian, 1819; Italian, 1883, 1889.
The romance of the forest, interspersed with some pieces of poetry. 3 vols 1791 (anon), 1792, 2 vols Dublin 1792, 3 vols 1794, 1795, 1796, 2 vols Dublin 1801,

London 1806, 1 vol 1810, 1816, 3 vols 1820, 1824, 1825, 2 vols Boston 1835, 1 vol 1846, Philadelphia 1872; ed D. M. Rose 1904; tr German, 1793; French, 1800 etc, 1869; Italian, 1871.

The mysteries of Udolpho: a romance, interspersed with some pieces of poetry. 4 vols 1794, 1794, 3 vols Dublin 1794, 4 vols 1795, Boston 1795, Worcester Mass 1795, 3 vols Dublin 1800, 4 vols 1803, 1806 etc, 1824 (with a memoir), 1844, 3 vols Philadelphia 1828; ed D. M. Rose 2 vols 1903; ed R. A. Freeman [1931] (EL); ed B. Dobrée, Oxford 1966; tr German, 1795; French, 1797, 1808 etc, 1864, 1869.

A journey made in the summer of 1794 through Holland and the western frontier of Germany. 1795, Dublin 1795; tr French, 1795.

The Italian, or the confessional of the black penitents: a romance. 3 vols 1797, 1797, 2 vols New York 1797, Dublin 1797, 3 vols 1811 etc; illustr P. Ross 1956 (as The confessional of the black penitents); ed F. Garber, Oxford 1968; tr French, 1794 etc; German, 1797, 1801; Italian, [1944].

Gaston de Blondeville, or the Court of Henry III keeping festival in Ardenne: a romance; St Alban's abbey: a metrical tale; with some poetical pieces, [and] a memoir of the author [by W. Radcliffe?] with extracts from her journals. 4 vols 1826, 2 vols 1834, 1839. Vols 3–4 of the first edn have the half-title: Posthumous works of Mrs Radcliffe, and were rptd (in part) as Poetical works 2 vols 1834; tr French, 1826.

Summers lists many spurious attributions, adaptations etc.

§2

Lefèvre-Deumier, J. Célébrités anglaises: Ann Radcliffe. Paris 1895.

Lang, A. Mrs Radcliffe's novels. In his Adventures among books, 1905. First pbd in Cornhill Mag July 1900.

Summers, M. A great mistress of romance: Ann Radcliffe. Trans Royal Soc of Lit [1917]; rptd in his Essays in petto, 1928.

MacIntyre, C. F. Ann Radcliffe in relation to her time. New Haven 1920.

Birkhead, E. In her Tale of terror, 1921.

Killen, A. M. Le roman terrifiant ou roman noir, de Walpole à Ann Radcliffe, et son influence sur la littérature francaise jusqu'en 1840. Paris 1923.

Wieten, A. S. S. Mrs Radcliffe: her relation towards romanticism. Amsterdam 1926. Appendix on false attributions.

Tompkins, J. M. S. In her Popular novel in England 1770–1800, 1932. Ch 8 and Appendix 3 (Mrs Radcliffe's sources).

Mayo, R. D. Ann Radcliffe and Ducray-Duminil. MLR 36 1941.

Sypher, W. Social ambiguity in a Gothic novel. Partisan Rev 12 1945.

Ruff, W. Ann Radcliffe: or the hand of taste. In The age of Johnson: essays presented to C. B. Tinker, New Haven 1949.

Havens, R. D. Ann Radcliffe's nature descriptions. MLN 66 1951.

Grant, A. Ann Radcliffe. Denver 1952.

Humphrey, G. Victor: ou l'enfant de la forêt, et le roman terrifiant. French Rev 33 1959.

Ware, M. Mrs Radcliffe's 'picturesque embellishment'. Tennessee Stud in Lit 5 1960.

—— Sublimity in the novels of Ann Radcliffe: a study of the influence of Burke's Enquiry. Copenhagen 1963.

Bradbrook, F. W. Sources [in Udolpho] of Jane Austen's ideas about nature in Mansfield Park. N & Q June 1961.

Coolidge, A. C. Charles Dickens and Mrs Radcliffe: a farewell to Wilkie Collins. Dickensian 58 1962.

Beaty, F. L. Mrs Radcliffe's fading gleam. PQ 42 1963.

Lévy, M. Une nouvelle source d'Ann Radcliffe: les Mémoires du Comte de Comminge. Caliban 1 1964.

Decottignies, J. Un domaine maudit dans les lettres françaises aux environs de 1800. Revue des Sciences Humaines 116 1964.

Thomas, D. The first poetess of romantic fiction: Ann Radcliffe. English 15 1964.

Allen, M. L. The black veil: three versions of a symbol. E Studies 47 1966.

Arnaud, P. Un document inédit: le contrat des Mysteries of Udolpho. Etudes Anglaises 20 1967.

REGINA MARIA ROCHE, née DALTON
1764?–1845

Bibliographies

Summers, M. In his A Gothic bibliography, [1941].

§1

The Vicar of Lansdowne: or country quarters. 2 vols 1789, 1800; tr French, 1789.

The maid of the hamlet. 2 vols 1793, Dublin 1802.

The children of the Abbey: a tale. 4 vols 1796, 1797, 1800 (4th edn), 1810 (6th edn), 2 vols Hartford 1822, 4 vols 1825 (10th edn), 1 vol 1862; tr Spanish, 1868.

Clermont: a tale. 4 vols 1798, Philadelphia 1802; ed D. P. Varma 1968.

The nocturnal visit. 4 vols 1800; tr French, 1801.

Alvondown Vicarage: a novel. 2 vols 1807. (Anon).

The discarded son: or the haunt of the banditti. 5 vols 1807.

The houses of Osma and Almeria: or the Convent of St Ildefonso. 3 vols 1810.

The Monastery of St Colomba. 5 vols 1812.

Trecothiek Bower: or the lady of the West Country. 3 vols 1813.

London tales. 2 vols 1814. Anon.

Anna, or Edinburgh: a novel. 3 vols 1814.

The Munster cottage boy. 4 vols 1819, 1820.

The bridal of Dunamore and Lost and won: two tales. 3 vols 1823.

The tradition of the Castle: or scenes in the Emerald Isle. 4 vols 1824.

The Castle chapel. 3 vols 1825; tr French, 1825.

Contrast. 3 vols 1828.

The nun's picture. 3 vols 1834, 1836.

WILLIAM PITT SCARGILL
1787–1836

Essays on various subjects. 1815.

Moral discourses principally intended for young people. 1816.

Elizabeth Evanshaw, the sequel of Truth: a novel. 3 vols 1827. Truth was not by Scargill.

Blue-stocking Hall. 3 vols 1827, 2 vols New York 1828.

Truckleborough Hall: a novel. 3 vols 1827.

Penelope, or love's labour lost: a novel. 3 vols 1828.

Rank and talent: a novel, by the author of Truckleborough Hall. 3 vols 1829, 1 vol 1856.

Tales of my time, by the author of Blue-stocking Hall. 3 vols 1829.

Tales of a briefless barrister. 3 vols 1829.

The peace of the county: a letter to the Freeholders of Suffolk. 1830.

Atherton: a tale of the last century, by the author of Rank and talent. 3 vols 1831.

The usurer's daughter, by a contributor to Blackwood's Magazine. 3 vols 1832, 1 vol 1853.

The autobiography of a Dissenting Minister. 1832, 1835, 1835.

A reformer's reasons for voting for Earl Jermyn. [1832].

The Puritan's grave, by the author of the Usurer's daughter. 3 vols 1833.

Provincial sketches, by the author of the Usurer's daughter. 1835.

The widow's offering: a selection of tales and essays. Ed M. A. Scargill 2 vols 1837, 1856 (unauthorized, as The English sketch book), 1857 (authorized 2nd edn, as Essays and sketches).

MICHAEL SCOTT
1789–1835

§1

Tom Cringle's log. 2 vols 1833, 1834, 1 vol Paris 1836, Edinburgh 1842 etc, New York [1883]; ed M. Morris, illustr J. A. Symington 1895; illustr H. Edwards, New York 1899; ed E. Rhys [1915?] (EL); ed W. McFee, illustr M. Schaeffer, New York 1927; ed J. Webber 1956 (abridged). First pbd in Blackwood's Mag 1829–33 (anon).

The cruise of the Midge, by the author of Tom Cringle's log. 2 vols Edinburgh 1836, 1 vol Paris 1836, Edinburgh 1842, London 1878; illustr F. Brangwyn 1894. First pbd in Blackwood's Mag 1834–5 (anon).

§2

Douglas, G. In his Blackwood group, 1897.

SIR MARTIN ARCHER SHEE
1769–1850

See col 1138, below.

MARY WOLLSTONECRAFT SHELLEY, née GODWIN
1797–1851

Bibliographies

Wise, T. J. In his A Shelley library, 1924.

Collections

Tales and stories [from Keepsake]. Ed R. Garnett 1891.

§1

History of a six weeks' tour through a part of France, Switzerland, Germany and Holland. 1817. Anon. With her husband Percy Bysshe Shelley.

Frankenstein: or the modern Prometheus. 3 vols 1818 (anon), 2 vols 1823, 1 vol 1831 (rev), rptd 1849, New York 1845, London [1856] etc; ed H. R. Haweis 1886; ed E. Rhys 1912 (EL); illustr N. Carbe, New York [1932, 1949]; illustr L. Ward, New York 1934; ed E. L. Pearson, illustr E. Henry, New York 1934; ed H. Bloom, New York 1965; tr Italian, [1944], 1952; French, [1946], 1947; Spanish, 1945, 1947, 1959; German, 1948; Portuguese, 1957; Bengali, 1958; Polish, 1958; Swedish, 1959; Arabic, 1959; Japanese, 1959; Malayalam, 1959; Yugoslav, 1960; Urdu, 1960; Russian, 1965; Czech, 1966.

Valperga: or the life and adventures of Castruccio Prince of Lucca, by the author of Frankenstein. 3 vols 1823.

The last man, by the author of Frankenstein. 3 vols 1826, 1826; ed H. J. Luke, Lincoln Nebraska 1965.

The fortunes of Perkin Warbeck: a romance, by the author of Frankenstein. 3 vols 1830, 1830 ('revised, corrected and illustrated with a new introduction by the author'), 1857.

Lodore, by the author of Frankenstein. 3 vols 1835, 1 vol New York 1835.

Falkner: a novel, by the author of Frankenstein. 3 vols 1837, 1 vol New York 1837.

Lives of the most eminent literary and scientific men of France. In D. Lardner's Cabinet Cyclopaedia, 1838. With others.

Lives of the most eminent literary and scientific men of Italy, Spain and Portugal. In D. Lardner's Cabinet Cyclopaedia, 3 vols 1835–7. By J. Montgomery, Mary Shelley et al.

Rambles in Germany and Italy in 1840, 1842 and 1843. 2 vols 1844.

The Swiss peasant. 1859. In The tale book, by C. A. Bowles, J. S. Knowles and M. W. Shelley, Königsberg 1859.

The choice: a poem on Shelley's death. Ed H. B. Forman 1876 (priv ptd).

The heir of Mandolfo [a tale]. Appleton's Jnl Jan 1877; ed R. D. Spector, New York 1963 (in Seven masterpieces of Gothic horror).

Shelley and Mary: a collection of letters and documents of a biographical character in the possession of Sir Percy and Lady Shelley. 3 vols 1882 (priv ptd).

The romance of Mary W. Shelley, John Howard Payne and Washington Irving. Boston 1907. The Payne-Shelley letters, with remarks by F. B. Sanborn.

Letters, mostly unpublished. Ed H. H. Harper, Boston 1918.

Proserpine and Midas: mythological dramas. Ed A. Koszul 1922.

Harriet and Mary: being the relations between P. B., Harriet and Mary Shelley and T. J. Hogg as shown in letters between them. Ed W. S. Scott 1944.

Letters. Ed F. L. Jones 2 vols Norman Oklahoma 1944.

Journal. Ed F. L. Jones, Norman Oklahoma 1947.

Unpublished fragments by Shelley and Mary. SP 45 1948.

Two Mary Shelley letters. Ed C. L. Cline, N & Q 28 Oct 1950.

Letters. Ed E. Nitchie, Keats-Shelley Memorial Bull 3 1950.

Eight letters. Ed E. Nitchie, ibid.

My best Mary: selected letters. Ed M. Spark and D. Stanford 1953.

Mary Shelley to Maria Gisborne: new letters 1818–22. Ed F. L. Jones, SP 52 1955.

Mathilda. Ed E. Nitchie, Chapel Hill 1959.

The last man. Ed H. J. Luke, Lincoln Nebraska 1965.

Mary Shelley edited Shelley's Poems, 1830. *In 1824 she brought out his* Posthumous poems *and in 1840 his* Essays, letters from abroad, translations and fragments. *In 1886 the Shelley Soc pbd an edn of* Hellas *with notes by Mary Shelley et al.*

§2

Gilfillan, G. In his Galleries of literary portraits vol 1, Edinburgh 1856.

[Reeve, H.] Edinburgh Rev 156 1882. Review of Lady Shelley's Shelley and Mary.

Moore, H. Mary Wollstonecraft Shelley. Philadelphia 1886.

Marshall, F. A. The life and letters of Mary Wollstonecraft Shelley. 2 vols 1889.

Rossetti, L. M. Mrs Shelley. 1890.

Eimer, M. Die persönlichen Beziehungen zwischen Byron und den Shelleys. Heidelberg 1901.

Godwin, W. The elopement of P. B. Shelley and M. W. Godwin as narrated [in a letter of 27 Aug 1814 to John Taylor]. Ed H. B. Forman, [Boston?] 1911 (priv ptd).

Vohl, M. Die Erzählungen der Mary Shelley und ihre Urbilder. Heidelberg 1912.

Gosse, E. Shelley's widow. In his Silhouettes, 1925. A study of The last man.

Church, R. Mary Shelley. 1928.

Dodd, C. I. Eagle-feather. 1933. A biography of Mary Shelley.
Jones, F. L. Letters of Mary W. Shelley in the Bodleian Library. Bodleian Quart Record 8 1937.
Booth, B. A. The pole: a story by Claire Clairmont? ELH 5 1938.
'Grylls, R. G.' (Lady Mander). Mary Shelley. 1938.
Norman, S. Mary Shelley, novelist and dramatist. In her On Shelley, 1938.
— Mary Shelley 1797–1851. Fortnightly Rev Feb 1951.
Nitchie, E. The stage history of Frankenstein. South Atlantic Quart 41 1942.
— Mary Shelley's Mathilda: an unpublished story and its biographical significance. SP 40 1943.
— Mary Shelley: author of Frankenstein. New Brunswick 1953.
— Shelley at Eton: Mary Shelley versus Jefferson Hogg. Keats–Shelley Memorial Bull 11 1960.
— Mary Shelley, traveler. Keats–Shelley Jnl 10 1961.
Jones, F. L. Mary Shelley and Claire Clairmont. South Atlantic Quart 42 1943.
Ehrsam, T. G. Mary Shelley in her letters. MLQ 7 1946.
Mary Shelley and G. H. Lewes. TLS 12 Jan 1946.
Milhauser, M. The noble savage in Mary Shelley's Frankenstein. N & Q 15 June 1946.
Maanen, W. van. Mary Shelley en haar 'thriller' Frankenstein. Gids 4 1949.
Spark, M. Child of light: a reassessment of Mary Shelley. 1951.
— Mary Shelley: a prophetic novelist. Listener 22 Feb 1951.
Mary Shelley. TLS 2 Feb 1951.
Awad, L. The alchemist in English literature, I: Frankenstein. Bull Faculty of Arts, Fuad I Univ May 1951.
Lovell, E. J. Byron and the Byronic hero in the novels of Mary Shelley. SE 30 1951.
— Byron and Mary Shelley. Keats–Shelley Jnl 2 1953.
— Byron, Mary Shelley and Mme de Staël. Keats–Shelley Jnl 14 1965.
Gérard, A. Prométhée à l'envers: ou le mythe de Frankenstein. Synthèses Jan 1953.
Sencourt, R. M. W. Shelley. Contemporary Rev Oct 1957.
Bloom, H. A letter of consolation to Mary Shelley. Yale Lib Gazette 33 1958.
— Frankenstein: or the new Prometheus. Partisan Rev 32 1965.
Blunden, E. Mary Shelley's romances. In English studies in Japan: essays and studies presented to Dr Y. Yamato, 1958.
Preu, J. A. The tale of terror. Eng Jnl 47 1958.
Bigland, E. Mary Shelley. 1959.
Goldberg, M. A. Moral and myth in Frankenstein. Keats–Shelley Jnl 8 1959.
Moore, D. L. Byron, Leigh Hunt and the Shelleys. Keats–Shelley Memorial Bull 10 1959.
McKenney, J. L. Nietzsche and the Frankenstein creature. Dalhousie Rev 41 1960.
Palmer, D. J. and R. E. Dowse. Frankenstein: a moral fable. Listener 23 Aug 1962.
Massey, M. I. Mary Shelley, Walter Scott and Maga. N & Q Nov 1962.
Moeckli, G. Un Genevois méconnu: Frankenstein. Musées de Genève 3 1962.
Lund, M. G. Mary Shelley and the monster. Univ of Kansas City Rev 28 1962.
— Shelley as Frankenstein. Forum 4 1963.
Harper, G. M. Mary Shelley's residence with Thomas Taylor the Platonist. N & Q Dec 1962.
Palacio, J. de. Shelley's library catalogue: an unpublished document [in Mary's hand]. Revue de Littérature Comparée 36 1962.
— Mary Shelley's Latin studies: her translation of Apuleius. Revue de Littérature Comparée 38 1964.
Pollin, B. R. Philosophical and literary sources of Frankenstein. Comparative Lit 17 1965.

Rieger, J. Dr Polidori and the genesis of Frankenstein. Stud in Eng Lit 1500–1900 3 1963.
Nelson, L. Night thoughts on the Gothic novel. Yale Rev 52 1963.
Peter, M. A portrait of Mary W. Godwin by John Opie in the Tate Gallery. Keats–Shelley Memorial Bull 14 1963.
Dunleavy, G. W. Two new Mary Shelley letters and the 'Irish' chapters of Perkin Warbeck. Keats–Shelley Jnl 31 1964.
Luke, H. J. The last man: Mary Shelley's myth of the solitary. Prairie Schooner 39 1965.

MARY MARTHA SHERWOOD, née BUTT
1775–1851

Collections

Works. 7 vols New York 1834, 16 vols 1855.
[Stories]: Lily series. 6 vols 1871.
Mrs Sherwood's juvenile library. 3 vols 1880; illustr M. Sibree 1891 (selection).

§1

The traditions: a legendary tale, written by a young lady. 2 vols 1795.
Margarita, by the author of the Traditions. 4 vols 1799.
The history of Susan Gray. 1802, 1815, Wellington 1825, Philadelphia 1825, London 1830, Lowell 1836.
The history of little Henry and his bearer. Wellington 1814, Boston 1818, London 1826 (23rd edn), 1832 etc; French, 1820; German, [1850?]; tr Assamese, 1853; Portuguese [nd?].
The history of Lucy Clare. Wellington 1815, 1824 (14th edn), London 1853 etc.
The lady and her ayah: an Indian story. Dublin 1816, Boston and New York 1822 (as The ayah and lady), Madras 1902.
Memoirs of Sergeant Dale, his daughter and the orphan Mary. 1816, 1830 etc.
The Indian pilgrim: or the progress of the pilgrim Nazarene. Wellington 1818, 1818, 1820, 1826, 1832 etc.
The history of the Fairchild family, or the child's manual: being a collection of stories calculated to show the importance and effects of a religious education. 3 pts 1818–47 (pt 3 with Streeten Butt), 1818, 1819, 1822 etc, 1875 (with some account of the authoress by J. M.); ed M. E. Palgrave, illustr F. M. Rudland 1902; ed [and abridged] by Lady Strachey, illustr S. Tawse 1913; tr French, 1839; German, 1839.
The history of Theophilus and Sophia. Wellington 1811, 1822 (6th edn), New York [1828?], London [1830?] (as The shepherd of the Pyrenees), 1836 etc.
The errand boy. Wellington 1819, Boston 1821, London 1830 (rev).
The hedge of thorns. 1819, Philadelphia 1827.
A drive in a coach through the streets of London: a story founded on fact. Wellington 1819 (4th edn).
The golden clue. 1820.
The governess: or the little female academy. Wellington 1820, London 1832 (5th edn). An adaptation of Sarah Fielding's work of that title.
The iron cage. [1820?].
Dudley Castle: a tale. 1820, [1834].
The Lambourne bell. [1820?], [1824?].
The may-bee. New York [1820?], Wellington 1825.
The Welsh cottage. Wellington 1820.
The wishing cap etc. New York [1820?], Wellington 1822, 1827, London [1871?].
Procrastination: or the evil of putting that off till tomorrow which ought to be done today. [1820?].
The nurse-maid's diary. [1820?].
The young mother. [1820?].

The history of Emily and her mother. Wellington [1820?], Philadelphia 1820; tr French, 1825. An extract from The governess, above.
Mary Anne. [1820?], [1823?], [1825?].
The recaptured negro. Wellington 1821 (2nd edn), Newburyport Mass 1822 (as Dazee: or the recaptured negro).
The history of George Esmond, founded on facts which occurred in the East Indies, and now published as a useful caution to young men going out to that country. 1821.
The infant's progress from the valley of destruction to everlasting glory. Wellington 1821, 1825, 1830, 1835 etc.
The potter's common. 4 pts Wellington 1822–3.
The orphans of Normandy: or Florentin and Lucie. 1822 (2nd edn), 1825.
Stories explanatory of the Church catechism. Wellington 1822 (9th edn), Baltimore 1823, London 1835, 1855.
The history of Henry Milner, a little boy who was not brought up according to the fashions of this world. 4 pts 1822–37.
The little beggars. 1824, 1830, Philadelphia [1830] (rev as The children of the Hartz Mountains: or the little beggars).
Père la Chaise. Wellington 1823, 1827, 1834.
The history of Mrs Catherine Crawley. Wellington 1824.
Waste not, want not. 4 pts 1824, 1825, 1879.
The blessed family. 1824 (4th edn), [1830?].
The penny tract. 1824, [1830?].
The blind man and little George. [1824?], [1830?].
The lady of the manor: conversations on the subject of confirmation. 7 vols Wellington 1825, 1829, London 1842, 5 vols 1860.
Juliana Oakley. 1825 (4th edn), New York 1825, 1833, London 1827, 1837.
The history of Little Lucy and her Dhaye. Wellington 1825 (2nd edn).
My three uncles; and the Swiss cottage. [1825?].
The fountain of living waters: a vision. [1825].
The gipsy babes. Wellington 1826, 1827, Concord NH 1829.
My uncle Timothy: an interesting tale for young persons. 1825.
The infant's grave. Wellington 1825 (2nd edn).
The two dolls. Wellington 1826.
Little Arthur. Wellington 1826 (6th edn).
The two sisters. 1827.
Clara Stephens: or the white rose. Philadelphia 1827 (rev).
The lady in the arbour. Wellington 1827, 1828.
Mary Grant: or the secret fault. Philadelphia 1827.
The rose: a fairy tale. Wellington 1827 (8th edn).
Religious fashion: or the history of Anna. Philadelphia 1827.
The pulpit and the desk. Wellington 1827.
The dry ground. Wellington 1827, 1828.
The wish: or little Charles. Philadelphia 1827 (rev), 1832.
Ermina: or the second part of Juliana Oakley. Philadelphia 1827.
The thunder-storm. Wellington 1828.
Southstone's rock. Wellington 1828.
Soffrona and her cat Muff. Wellington 1828, 1838.
The rosebuds. Wellington 1828.
Poor Burruff. Wellington 1828 (2nd edn).
My aunt Kate. Wellington 1828.
The rainbow. Wellington 1828.
The little Sunday-school child's reward. Wellington 1828 (15th edn).
Little Robert and the owl. Wellington 1828 (8th edn).
The idiot boy. Wellington 1828.
Home: a tale. Wellington 1828, New Haven 1833.
The history of little George and his penny. Wellington 1828 (14th edn).
The hills. Wellington 1828.
The fawns. Wellington 1828.
Arzoomund. Wellington 1829 (2nd edn).
Emancipation. Wellington 1829.
The little orphan. 1829.
Little Sally. 1829.
The orange grove. Wellington 1829, [1860?].
Susannah: or the three guardians. Philadelphia 1829 (rev).
The bitter sweet. 2 pts Wellington [1830?].
Charles Lorraine: or the young soldier. [1830?], [1866], [1887].
Do what you can. [1830?].
Do your own work. [1830?].
The flowers of the forest. 1830, 1834, 1839; tr Portuguese, 1835.
The golden chain. Illustr R. E. Bewick, Berwick 1830.
The history of Mary Saunders. [1830?].
The hop picking. 2 pts [1830?].
Obedience. Berwick 1830, 1831.
The Oddingley murders. 1830; sequel, 1830.
Old times. 2 pts [c. 1830].
The poor man of colour: or the sufferings, privations and death of Thomas Wilson in the suburbs of the British metropolis. [1830?].
Roxobel. 3 vols 1830–1, New York [187–].
The young forester. 4 pts [1830?].
Hard times. 1831.
The mail coach; and The old lady's complaint. [1830?].
The broken hyacinth: or Ellen and Sophia. Philadelphia 1832 (rev).
The latter days. 1833.
The little Momiere. 1833.
The nun. 1833, 1836, 1856 etc.
Victoria. 1833.
The convent of St Clair. Berwick 1833.
The father's eye. [1833].
Intimate friends. 1834 (2nd edn).
It is not my business. [1835?].
Social tales for the young. [1835?], [1841].
Sabbaths on the Continent. 1835.
The red book. 1836 (4th edn), [1845?].
The parson's case of jewels. Berwick 1837.
The monk of Cimiés. [1837?], Ipswich [1855].
Sea-side stories. [1838?].
The Christmas carol. [1839].
The druids of Britain. [1840?].
Joys and sorrows of childhood. [1844].
Shanty the blacksmith: a tale of other times. [1844].
The history of John Marten: a sequel to the Life of Henry Milner. 1844.
Caroline Mordaunt: or the governess. [1845?], [1853].
Duty is safety: or troublesome Tom. 1841 (in Holiday Keepsake), Philadelphia and New York 1847, London 1864, 1877.
The infirmary. 1846 (19th edn).
The De Cliffords: an historical tale. 1847, 1847. With Sophia Kelly.
The fairy knoll. 1848.
The story book of wonders. 1849.
The golden garland of inestimable delights. 1849. With Sophia Kelly.
The mirror of maidens in the days of Queen Bess. 1851. With Sophia Kelly.
The two Knights, or Delancey Castle: a tale of the Civil Wars. [1851].
Boys will be boys: or the difficulties of a schoolboy's life. 1854. With Sophia Kelly.
The life of Mrs Sherwood, chiefly autobiographical, with extracts from Mr Sherwood's journal during his imprisonment in France and residence in India; ed S. Kelly 1854; ed I. Gilchrist 1907 (abridged); ed F. J. H. Darton 1910 (enlarged).
Joan: or the trustworthy. 2 pts 1860.
In 1877 the Book Society pbd the following from Holiday Keepsake, Juvenile Forget-me-not *and other annuals:* Duty is safety, The fall of pride, Frank Beauchamp: or the sailor's family, Grandmamma Parker, Jack the sailor boy, The lost trunk and the Good nurse, Martin and The

rose and nightingale, Think before you act, The traveller, Uncle Manners, The white pigeon.
Mrs Sherwood also pbd educational and devotional works.

§2

Tabor, M. E. Mrs Sherwood. In Pioneer women ser 3, 1925.
Wilson, M. In her Jane Austen and some contemporaries, 1938.
Smith, N. G. R. The state of mind of Mrs Sherwood. 1946.
Mrs Sherwood's doctrine. TLS 18 Jan 1947.
Who made the burnt child fear the fire? TLS 15 June 1951.
Keith, S. Gruesome examples for children: the real purpose of Mr Fairchild. N & Q May 1965.

HORATIO (HORACE) SMITH

1779–1849

Bibliographies

Sadleir, M. In his XIX century fiction: a bibliographical record, 2 vols 1951.

Collections

Poetical works. 2 vols 1846, 1 vol 1851.
Poetical works of Horace and James Smith. Ed E. Sargent, New York 1857.

§1

The runaway: or the seat of benevolence. 4 vols 1800.
Trevanion: or matrimonial errors. 4 vols 1801.
Horatio: or memoirs of the Davenport family. 1807.
First impressions, or trade in the West: a comedy. 1813, 1813, 1816.
Amarynthus the nympholept: a pastoral drama, with other poems. 1821.
Gaieties and gravities: a series of essays, comic tales and fugitive vagaries. 3 vols 1825, 2 vols Philadelphia and New York 1825, 3 vols 1826, New York 1852. Mainly rptd from the London Mag and New Monthly Mag.
The Tor hill. 3 vols 1826, Paris 1827, 1835; tr French, 1827.
Brambletye House: or cavaliers and roundheads. 3 vols 1826, 1826, 1826, 1833, 2 vols 1839 etc.
Reuben Apsley. 3 vols 1827.
Zillah: a tale of the Holy City. 4 vols 1828, 3 vols 1828; tr French, 1829.
The New Forest: a novel. 3 vols 1829, 1830.
The midsummer medley for 1830: a series of comic tales. 2 vols 1830.
Walter Colyton: a tale of 1688. 3 vols 1830, 1830.
Festivals, games and amusements, ancient and modern. 1831, New York 1831 (with addns by S. Woodworth), 1832, 1833, 1841.
Tales of the early ages. 3 vols 1832.
Gale Middleton: a story of the present day. 3 vols 1833.
The involuntary prophet: a tale of the early ages. 1835.
The tin trumpet: or heads and tales, for the wise and waggish, to which are added poetical selections by the late Paul Chatfield MD, edited by Jefferson Saunders esq. 2 vols 1836 (anon), New York 1859, London 1875, 1890.
Jane Lomax: or a mother's crime. 3 vols 1838.
Oliver Cromwell: an historical romance. 3 vols 1840.
The moneyed man: or the lesson of a life. 3 vols 1841, 1843.
Massaniello: a historical romance. 3 vols 1842.
Adam Brown: the merchant. 3 vols 1843.
Arthur Arundel: a tale of the English revolution. 3 vols 1844.
Love and Mesmerism. 3 vols 1845.

For Horace and James Smith's parodies, see col 400, above.
Horace edited his brother's Memoirs, letters and comic miscellanies in prose and verse, 2 vols 1840, 1841.

§2

Sargent, E. Memoir of Horace Smith. Prefixed to Rejected addresses, New York 1871.
Beavan, A. H. James and Horace Smith. 1899.
Parker, W. M. The stockbroker author. Quart Rev 290 1952.

GEORGE SOANE

1790–1860

See col 1139, below.

LOUISA SIDNEY STANHOPE

Bibliographies

Blakey, D. In her Minerva Press, 1939.
Summers, M. In his A Gothic bibliography, [1941].

§1

Montbrasil Abbey: or maternal trials. 2 vols 1806.
The bandit's bride, or the maid of Saxony: a romance. 4 vols 1807, 1818.
Striking likenesses, or the votaries of fashion: a novel. 4 vols 1808.
The age we live in: a novel. 3 vols 1809.
Di Montranzo, or the novice of Corpus Domini: a romance. 4 vols 1810.
The confessional of Valombre: a romance. 4 vols 1812.
Madelina: a novel. 4 vols 1813, 1814.
Treachery, or the grave of Antoinette: a romance. 4 vols 1815.
The nun of Santa Maria di Tindaro: a tale. 3 vols 1818.
The Crusaders: an historical romance of the twelfth century. 5 vols 1820.
The festival of Mora: an historical romance. 4 vols 1821.
The siege of Kenilworth: an historical romance. 4 vols 1824.
Runnemede: an ancient legend. 3 vols 1825.
The seer of Tiviotdale: a romance. 4 vols 1827.
The Corsair's bride: a legend of the sixteenth century. 3 vols 1830.
Sydney Beresford: a tale, by the author of the Bandit's bride. 3 vols 1835.

AGNES STRICKLAND

1796–1874

See col 1090, below.

THOMAS SKINNER SURR

1770–1847

Consequences: a novel. 3 vols 1796.
Christ's Hospital: a poem. 1797.
George Barnwell: a novel. 3 vols 1798, Dublin 1798, 1834 (6th edn); tr French, [1799].
Splendid misery. 3 vols 1801, 1802, 1807.
A winter in London, or sketches of fashion: a novel. 3 vols 1806 (8 edns), 1824 (14th edn); tr French, 1810.
The magic of wealth: a novel. 3 vols 1815.
Richmond: or scenes in the life of a Bow Street Officer. 3 vols 1827 (anon), 2 vols New York 1827. Also attributed to T. Gaspey.
The reign of fashion. 3 vols 1830.
Surr pbd 3 pamphlets on banking.

EDWARD JOHN TRELAWNY

1792–1881

See col 1307, below.

FRANCES TROLLOPE, née MILTON

1780–1863

Bibliographies

Sadleir, M. In his XIX century fiction: a bibliographical record, 2 vols 1951.

§1

Domestic manners of the Americans. Illustr A. Hervieu 2 vols 1832 (4 edns), 1 vol New York 1832, London 1839, New York 1904; ed M. Sadleir 1927; ed D. Smalley, illustr Hervieu, New York 1949, 1960; tr Spanish, 1835; French, 1841 (3rd edn).

The refugee in America: a novel. 3 vols 1832, 2 vols New York 1833.

The Abbess: a romance. 3 vols 1833.

The mother's manual, or illustrations of matrimonial economy: an essay in verse. 1833. Anon.

Belgium and Western Germany in 1833. 2 vols 1834, Paris 1834.

Tremordyn cliff. 3 vols 1835.

Paris and the Parisians in 1835. 2 vols 1836, 1 vol New York 1836; tr French, [1911].

The life and adventures of Jonathan Jefferson Whitlaw: or scenes on the Mississippi. Illustr A. Hervieu 3 vols 1836, 1836, 1 vol Paris 1836, London [1857] (as Lynch law).

The vicar of Wrexhill. Illustr A. Hervieu 3 vols 1837, 1 vol 1840, 1860.

A romance of Vienna. 3 vols 1838, 2 vols Philadelphia 1838.

Vienna and the Austrians, with some account of a journey through Swabia, Bavaria, the Tyrol and the Salzbourg. Illustr A. Hervieu 2 vols Paris 1838.

The widow Barnaby. 3 vols 1839, 1 vol 1840, 1856, [1860], [1881]; tr French, 1877.

The life and adventures of Michael Armstrong, the factory boy. 3 vols 1840, 2 vols New York 1840. First pbd in 12 monthly nos 1839–40.

One fault: a novel. 3 vols 1840, 1858.

The widow married: a sequel to the Widow Barnaby. Illustr R. W. Buss 3 vols 1840.

Charles Chesterfield: or the adventures of a youth of genius. Illustr Phiz 3 vols 1841, 1846.

The ward of Thorpe Combe. 3 vols 1842, 1 vol Paris 1842, London 1857; tr French, 1858.

The blue belles of England. 3 vols 1842.

A visit to Italy. 2 vols 1842.

The Barnabys in America: or adventures of the widow wedded. Illustr Leech 3 vols 1843, [1859] (as Adventures of the Barnabys in America).

Hargrave: or the adventures of a man of fashion. 3 vols 1843.

Jessie Phillips: a tale of the present day. Illustr Leech 3 vols 1843, 1844. First pbd in 11 monthly pts 1842–3.

The Laurringtons: or superior people. 3 vols 1844.

Young love: a novel. 3 vols 1844.

The attractive man: a novel. 3 vols 1846.

The Robertses on their travels. 3 vols 1846.

Travels and travellers: a series of sketches. 2 vols 1846, 1 vol Paris 1846.

Father Eustace: a tale of the Jesuits. 3 vols 1847.

The three cousins: a novel. 3 vols 1847, [1858].

Town and country: a novel. 3 vols 1848, [1857] (as The days of the Regency).

The young Countess: or love and jealousy. 3 vols 1848, 1 vol 1860 (as Love and jealousy).

The lottery of marriage: a novel. 3 vols 1849, 1 vol [1860].

The old world and the new: a novel. 3 vols 1849.

Petticoat government: a novel. 3 vols 1850, 1 vol New York 1850, London 1857.

Mrs Mathews, or family mysteries: a novel. 3 vols 1851, 1 vol 1864.

Second love, or beauty and intellect: a novel. 3 vols 1851.

Uncle Walter: a novel. 3 vols 1852.

The young heiress: a novel. 3 vols 1853, 1864.

The life and adventures of a clever woman, illustrated with occasional extracts from her diary. 3 vols 1854.

Gertrude: or family pride. 3 vols 1855, 1864.

Fashionable life: or Paris and London. 3 vols 1856.

Valentine to Cincinnati. Ed M. W. Fligor, Bull Historical & Philosophical Soc of Ohio 18 1960.

Mrs Trollope also edited T. A. Trollope, A summer in Brittany, 2 vols 1840, *and his* A summer in Western France, 2 vols 1841.

§2

Hamilton, T. Domestic manners of the Americans. Blackwood's Mag May 1832.

[Lockhart, J. G.] Domestic manners of the Americans. Quart Rev 47 1832.

Novels for Christmas 1837. Fraser's Mag Jan 1838. Contains a review of The vicar of Wrexhill, rptd in Famous reviews, ed R. B. Johnson 1914.

Frances Trollope. New Monthly Mag March 1839.

Horne, R. H. In his A new spirit of the age vol 1, 1844.

Trollope, F. E. Frances Trollope: her life and literary works from George III to Victoria. 2 vols 1895.

Wilson, M. In her These were Muses, 1924.

Sadleir, M. Trollope: a commentary. 1927. Appendix contains a calendar of events in the life of Frances Trollope and a bibliography.

Pope-Hennessy, U. In her Three English women in America, 1929. On F. Trollope: F. Kemble, H. Martineau.

Stebbins, L. P. and R. P. The Trollopes: the chronicle of a writing family. 1946.

McCourt, E. A. Mrs Trollope among the savages. Dalhousie Rev 28 1948.

Hudleston, C. R. Anthony Trollope's mother. N & Q 28 May 1949.

Bigland, E. The indomitable Mrs Trollope. 1953.

Vaillant, P. A propos d'une récente acquisition de la bibliothèque de Grenoble: une relation anglaise, annotée par Stendhal, sur les mœurs américaines vers 1830 [i.e. Mrs Trollope's Domestic manners of the Americans]. Grenoble 1957.

Chaloner, W. H. Mrs Trollope and the early factory system. Victorian Stud 4 1960.

GEORGE WALKER

1772–1847

Bibliographies

Summers, M. In his A Gothic bibliography, [1941].

§1

The romance of the cavern: or the history of Fitz-Henry and James. 2 vols 1792.

The haunted castle: a Norman romance. 2 vols 1794. Anon.

The house of Tynian: a novel. 4 vols 1795. Anon.

Theodore Cyphon, or the benevolent Jew: a novel. 3 vols 1796, 2 vols Philadelphia 1796, 3 vols 1823.

Cinthelia: or a woman of ten thousand. 4 vols 1797; tr French, [1798–9?].

The vagabond: a novel. 2 vols 1799, 1799, 1799, Boston 1800 and Harrisonburg 1814 (as The vagabond: or practical infidelity); tr French, 1807.
The three Spaniards: a romance. 3 vols 1800, New York [1882]; tr French, 1805.
Poems on various subjects. 1801, Philadelphia 1804.
Don Raphael: a romance. 3 vols 1803.
Two girls of eighteen. 2 vols 1806.
The adventures of Timothy Thoughtless: or the misfortunes of a little boy who ran away from boarding school. 1813.
The travels of Sylvester Tramper. 1813. Anon.
The battle of Waterloo: a poem. 1815.
The midnight bell. 3 vols 1824.

ROBERT WARD, afterwards PLUMER WARD
1765–1846

§1

An inquiry into the foundation and history of the law of nations in Europe from the time of the Greeks and Romans to the age of Grotius. 2 vols 1795, Dublin 1795.
A treatise of the relative rights and duties of belligerents and neutral powers in maritime affairs, in which the principles of the armed neutralities and the opinions of Hübner and Schlegel are fully discussed. 1801, 1875.
An essay on contraband: being a continuation of the treatise of the relative rights and duties. 1801.
A view of the relative situations of Mr Pitt and Mr Addington previous to and on the night of Mr Patten's motion. 1803.
An enquiry into the manner in which the different wars of Europe have commenced during the last two centuries. 1804.
Tremaine: or the man of refinement. 3 vols 1825 (anon), 1825, 1825, 1827, 1835 etc; tr French, 1830.
De Vere: or the man of independence. 4 vols 1827, 1827, 1827, 3 vols 1833.
Illustrations of human life. 3 vols 1837, 1843. Contains Atticus, St Laurence, Fielding or society.
An historical essay on the real character and amount of the precedent of the Revolution of 1688, in which the opinions of Mackintosh, Price, Hallam and Locke are initially considered. 2 vols 1838.
The reviewer reviewed. 1838. Anon. An answer to a review of An historical essay, above, in Edinburgh Rev.
Pictures of the world at home and abroad. 3 vols 1839, 1843. Contains Sterling, Penruddock, The enthusiasts.
De Clifford: or the constant man. 4 vols 1841, 3 vols Philadelphia 1841.
Ward also edited P. G. Patmore, Chatsworth: or the romance of a week, 1844.

§2

[Rose, W. S.] Novels of fashionable life [including Tremaine]. Quart Rev 33 1826.
[Lockhart, J. G.] Quart Rev 36 1827. Review of De Vere.
Phipps, E. Memoirs of the political and literary life of Ward, with selections from his correspondence, diaries and unpublished literary remains. 2 vols 1850.
Robert Plumer Ward. Bentley's Miscellany Sept 1850.
Patmore, P. G. My friends and acquaintances. 3 vols 1855. Contains a number of Ward's letters.
Rosa, M. W. The silver fork school: novels of fashion preceding Vanity Fair. New York 1936.

JANE WEST
1758–1852

Bibliographies

Summers, M. In his A Gothic bibliography, [1941].

§1

Miscellaneous poems, translations and imitations. 1780.
Miscellaneous poetry, written at an early period of life. 1786.
The humours of Brighthelmstone. 1788. A poem.
Edmund: a tragedy. 1791.
Miscellaneous poems and a tragedy [Edmund surnamed Ironside]. York 1791, 1797, 1804.
The advantage of education, or the history of Maria Williams: a tale for very young ladies (by Mrs Prudentia Homespun). 2 vols 1793, 1803.
A gossip's story, and a legendary tale, by the author of the Advantages of education. 2 vols 1796, 1797, 1797, 1 vol Cork 1799, London 1804.
An elegy on the death of Edmund Burke. 1797.
A tale of the times. 3 vols 1799, 1799, 2 vols Dublin 1799, Alexandria Virginia 1801, 3 vols 1803.
Poems and plays. 4 vols 1799–1805. Contains Adela, The minstrel, How will it end?
Letters addressed to a young man on his first entrance into life. 3 vols 1801, 1802, 2 vols Charlestown 1803, London 1806, 1 vol New York 1806, London 1818.
The infidel father. 3 vols 1802.
Letters to a young lady in which the duties and character of women are considered. 3 vols 1806, 1806, 1811.
The mother: a poem in five books. 1809, 1810.
The refusal. 3 vols 1810, 2 vols Philadelphia 1810.
The loyalists: an historical novel. 3 vols 1812, 2 vols Boston 1813.
Alicia de Lacy: an historical romance. 4 vols 1814.
Ringrove: or old fashioned notions. 2 vols 1827.
Mrs West also pbd a devotional work and translated a selection from the works of Massillon.

JOHN WILSON
1785–1854

See also col 1308, below.

A. P. H.

IV. THE MID-NINETEENTH-CENTURY NOVEL

BENJAMIN DISRAELI, 1st EARL OF BEACONSFIELD
1804–81

Bibliographies

Contributions to a bibliography of Disraeli. N & Q 29 April–8 July 1893.
Aronstein, P. In his Disraelis Leben und dichterische Werke, Anglia 17 1895.
Sadleir, M. In his Excursions in Victorian bibliography, 1922.
—— In his XIX century fiction, 2 vols 1951.
Dahl, C. In Victorian fiction: a guide to research, ed L. Stevenson, Cambridge Mass 1964.

Collections

Novels and tales. 10 vols 1870–1. With preface by Disraeli.
Novels and tales. 10 vols 1871–81.
Novels and tales: Hughenden edition. 11 vols 1881. With portrait and biographical sketch.
Works: Empire and Earls edition. Ed E. Gosse with biographical preface by R. Arnot 20 vols 1904–5.
Novels and tales: Bradenham edition. Ed P. Guedella 12 vols 1926–7.
Tales and sketches. Ed J. L. Robertson 1891.
Young England. Ed B. N. Langdon Davies, illustr Byam Shaw 4 vols 1904. Vivian Grey, Coningsby, Sybil, Tancred.

§1

Rumpel Stiltskin: a dramatic spectacle, by 'B. D.' and 'W. G. M.' [Disraeli, W. G. Meredith]. 1823 (priv ptd); ed M. Sadleir, Glasgow 1952.
The modern Aesop. 2 weekly pts Star Chamber 24–31 May 1826; ed M. Sadleir 1928 (with the Dunciad of to-day, here attributed to Disraeli, 2 weekly pts, from Star Chamber 10–17 May 1826).
Vivian Grey. Vols 1–2 1826, vols 3–5 1827; 1 vol 1853 (with preface); ed W. S. Northcote [1888]; ed L. Woolf 2 vols 1904. Key to Vivian Grey, 1827 (10th edn). On pamphlet Key to Vivian Grey (1827) in Bodley, probably by Disraeli, *see also* M. Fido, N & Q Nov 1965.
The voyage of Captain Popanilla, by the author of Vivian Grey. 1828; ed W. S. Northcote 1906.
Contarini Fleming: a psychological autobiography. 4 vols 1832, 1834, 3 vols 1846, 1 vol 1853, 1888; ed W. S. Northcote 1905; tr German, 1909.
The wondrous tales of Alroy and the Rise of Iskander. 4 vols 1832, 1834, 3 vols 1846, 1853, [1888]; ed W. S. Northcote 1906. Alroy rptd separately, 1888; tr German, 1855. Dramatized by P. P. Gruenfeld, 1896.
The revolutionary epick. 2 vols 1834, 1864 (rev); ed W. D. Adams 1904.
Henrietta Temple: a love story. 3 vols 1837, 1 vol 1853, [1888]; ed W. S. Northcote 1906; tr Swedish, 1859.
Venetia: or the poet's daughter. 3 vols 1837, 1853, 2 vols 1858, [1888]; ed W. S. Northcote 1905.
The tragedy of Count Alarcos, by the author of Vivian Grey. 1839, 1853 (with Ixion); ed W. S. Northcote 1906 (with Alroy, above).
Coningsby: or the new generation. 3 vols 1844, 1844, 2 vols Paris 1846, 1 vol [1888]; ed F. Hitchman 1888–9; 1891; ed B. N. Langdon-Davies [1911], 1959 (EL); ed 'André Maurois', Oxford 1931 (WC); ed W. Allen 1948; tr French, 1846. Anti-Coningsby: or the new generation grown old, by an embryo MP, 1844; Strictures on Coningsby, with remarks on the present state of parties and the character of the age, 1844; A key to the characters in Coningsby, 1844; A new key to the characters in Coningsby, [1845].
Sybil: or the two nations. 3 vols 1845, 1 vol Paris 1845, London 1853, 1882, [1888]; ed H. D. Traill 1895 (illustr F. Pegram); ed W. S. Northcote 1905; ed W. Sichel, Oxford 1925 (WC); ed V. Cohen 1934 (illustr F. Pegram); tr French, 1859; Dutch, 1889.
Tancred: or the new crusade. 3 vols 1847; ed W. S. Northcote 1905; tr German, 1914 (postscript by Oscar Levy).
Ixion in Heaven; The infernal marriage; Popanilla; Count Alarcos. 1853; ed W. S. Northcote 1906. Ixion 2 monthly pts New Monthly Mag Dec 1832–Jan 1833; rptd separately 1925, 1927 (with W. E. Aytoun, Endymion); Infernal marriage 2 monthly pts New Monthly Mag July–Aug 1834; rptd separately, 1929; Popanilla (*see above*); Count Alarcos (*see above*).
Lothair. 3 vols 1870 (7 edns), New York 1870, Leipzig 1870, London 1877, 1908; tr French, 1872; German, 1874; Hungarian, 1878. Lothaw: or the adventures of a young gentleman in search of a religion, by Mr Benjamins (F. Bret Harte), [1871]; Lothair, the critics and the Rt Hon Benjamin Disraeli's general preface to all his works, by E. W., [1872]; Lothair: its beauties and blemishes, by G. E., 1873; Lothair's children, by H. R. H. (Campbell MacKellar), 1890.
Endymion, by the author of Lothair. 3 vols 1880, 1 vol New York 1880, London 1881, New York 1881 (with key to the characters); tr German, 1881. Parodied by H. F. Lester in his Ben D'Ymion and other parodies, 1887.
Tales and sketches. Ed J. L. Robertson 1891. Collects from periodicals for the first time True story, Carrier pigeon, Consul's daughter, Walstein, Speaking Harlequin, Midland ocean, Ibrahim pacha, Court of Egypt, Valley of Thebes, Egyptian Thebes, Shoubra, Bosphorus, Interview with a great Turk, Munich.
Unfinished novel [no title]. 3 pts Times 20–3 Jan 1905; rptd in W. F. Monypenny and G. E. Buckle, The life of Disraeli, 6 vols 1910–20, below.

Political Writings and Speeches

An inquiry into the plans, progress and policy of American mining companies. 1825.
Lawyers and legislators: or notes on the American mining companies. 1825.
The present stage of Mexico, as detailed in a report presented to the General Congress by the Secretary of State for the Home Department and Foreign Affairs at the opening of the Session in 1825. 1825.
England and France: or a cure for the ministerial Gallomania. 1832.
What is he? 1833, 1833 (rev); ed F. Hitchman [1884] (with Vindication of the English Constitution).
The crisis examined. 1834.
Vindication of the English Constitution in a letter to a noble and learned lord. 1835; ed F. Hitchman [1884] (with What is he?); ed F. A. Hyndman [1895].
The letters of Runnymede, The spirit of Whiggism. 1836; ed F. Bickley 1923; ed W. Hutcheon 1913. Letters of Runnymede first pbd in Times Jan–May 1836; 1836 (priv ptd); ed F. Hitchman 1885.
Speech in the House of Commons, Friday 15 May 1846. 1846.
England and Denmark: speech in the House of Commons 19 April 1848. 1848.
The Parliament and the Government: speech on the labours of the Session, August 30 1848. 1848.
The new Parliamentary reform: speech in the House of Commons, Tuesday June 20 1848. 1848.
Financial policy: speech in the House of Commons, June 30 1851. 1851.
Address delivered to the members of the Manchester Athenaeum on the 23 October 1844 on the importance of literature to men of business. 1852.
Lord George Bentinck: a political biography. 1852 (4 edns), 1858, 1872 (8th edn rev); ed C. Whibley 1905.
Parliamentary reform, House of Commons 25 March 1852. 1852.
Mr Disraeli to Colonel Rathbone. [1858]. Letters on the annexation of Oude.
Parliamentary reform, House of Commons February 28 1859. 1859.
Public expenditure: speech in the House of Commons June 3 1862. 1862.
Mr Gladstone's finance 1853–62. 1862. Speeches in the House of Commons 24 February 1860, 8 April 1862.
Church policy: speech to the Oxford Diocesan Society, October 30 1862. 1862.
Speech at a public meeting of the Oxford Diocesan Society for the augmentation of small livings in the Sheldonian Theatre November 25 1864. 1864.

'Church and Queen': five speeches 1860–4, edited with a preface by a member of the University of Oxford. 1865.

Two speeches in the City of Edinburgh on 29 and 30 October 1867. 1867.

Speeches on Parliamentary reform 1848–66. Ed M. Corry 1867.

The Prime Minister on Church and State: speech at the Hall of the Merchant Taylors Company, June 17 1868. [1868].

Speeches on the Conservative policy of the last thirty years. Ed J. F. Bulley [1870].

Speech at the banquet of the National Union of Conservative and Constitutional Associations at the Crystal Palace, Monday June 24 1872. 1872.

Speech at Free Trade Hall Manchester, April 3 1872. [1872]; rptd in Representative British orations, ed C. Adams vol 3, 1884.

Mr Osborne Morgan's Burials Bill: speech by Disraeli moving the rejection, House of Commons, March 26 1873. 1873.

Inaugural address delivered to the University of Glasgow, November 19 1873. 1873.

Speech at Aylesbury, 20 September 1876. 1876. On the Eastern question.

Selected speeches. Ed T. E. Kebbel 2 vols 1882.

Whigs and Whiggism: political writings. Ed W. Hutcheon 1913. Contains What is he?, Crisis examined, Vindication of the English constitution, Letters of Runnymede, Spirit of Whiggism, and various unrptd articles from Times 1837–41, Morning Post 1835, Press 1853, Fraser's Mag 1835–6.

The radical Tory: Disraeli's political development illustrated from his original writings and speeches. Ed H. W. J. Edwards 1937.

Editions

The life of Paul Jones, from original documents in the possession of John Henry Sherburne, Register of the Navy of the United States. 1825. Preface by Disraeli.

The works of Isaac Disraeli. 9 vols 1849–59.

Letters

Home letters 1830–1. Ed R. Disraeli 1885, 1885, 1887 (below).

Correspondence with his sister. Ed R. Disraeli 1886; rptd with above, 1887 (as Lord Beaconsfield's letters 1830–52); ed A. Birrell 1928.

A new sheaf of Disraeli letters: hitherto unpublished correspondence with his sister Sarah. Ed C. I. Freed, Amer Hebrew 15 April 1927.

Letters of Disraeli to Lady Bradford and Lady Chesterfield. Ed Marquis of Zetland 2 vols 1929.

Some early letters of Lord Beaconsfield. Ed E. T. Cook, Saturday Rev 21–8 May 1932.

Letters to Frances Anne, Marchioness of Londonderry 1837–61. 1938.

Disraeli's letters to Robert Carter. Ed H. H. Hoeltje, PQ 31 1952.

Disraeli's fan mail. Ed B. R. Jerman, Nineteenth-Century Fiction 9 1955.

§2

Thackeray, W. M. Coningsby. Morning Chron 13 May 1844.

— Coningsby. Pictorial Times 25 May 1844.

— Sybil. Morning Chron 13 May 1845.

— Codlingsby, by D. Shrewsberry esq. Punch Jan–June 1847; rptd in Novels by eminent hands, 1856. Parody of Coningsby.

Forçade, E. De la jeune Angleterre. Revue des Deux Mondes 1 Aug 1844.

[Lewes, G. H.] Coningsby. Br Quart Rev 10 1849.

Lowell, J. R. Tancred. North Amer Rev 63 1846; rptd in his Round table, [1913].

Milnes, R. M. Mr Disraeli's Tancred: the emancipation of the Jews. Edinburgh Rev 86 1847.

— Disraeli's Lothair. Edinburgh Rev 132 1870.

Francis, G. H. Disraeli: a critical biography. 1852.

Hayward, A. Mr Disraeli: his character and career. Edinburgh Rev 97 1853.

— Lothair. Macmillan's Mag June 1870.

Aytoun, W. E. Disraeli: a biography. Blackwood's Mag March 1854.

Macknight, T. Disraeli: a literary and political biography. 1854.

Gilfillan, G. In his Galleries of literary portraits vol 2, Edinburgh 1856.

Gleig, G. R. The Right Honourable Benjamin Disraeli. Blackwood's Mag Aug–Oct 1858.

MacGilchrist, J. Life of Disraeli. [1868].

Challemel-Lacour, P. Le roman politique en Angleterre. Revue des Deux Mondes 15 July 1870. Reviews Lothair.

Hanley, E. B. Lothair. Blackwood's Mag June 1870.

Simpson, R. Lothair. North Br Rev 52 1870.

Stephen, L. Disraeli's novels. In his Hours in a Library ser 2, 1876.

O'Connor, T. P. and A. Foggo. Disraeli: a biography. 2 vols 1878–81.

Brandes, G. Disraeli. Berlin 1878; tr 1880.

Hitchman, F. The public life of Beaconsfield. 1879.

Collins, M. In his Pen sketches vol 1, 1879.

Cucheval-Clarigny, A. Lord Beaconsfield et son temps. 1880.

MacColl, M. Lord Beaconsfield. Contemporary Rev June 1881.

Manners, J. (Duchess of Rutland). Some personal recollections of the later years of the Earl of Beaconsfield. 1881.

Sichel, W. S. The wit and humour of Lord Beaconsfield. Macmillan's Mag June 1881.

— Disraeli as a landscape painter. Time 18 1885.

— Disraeli and the colonies. Blackwood's Mag April 1900.

— Disraeli. 1904.

Skelton, J. A last word on Disraeli. Contemporary Rev June 1881.

Greg, W. R. In his Miscellaneous essays vol 1, 1882.

Bauer, B. Disraelis romantischer und Bismarcks socialistischer Imperialismus. Chemnitz 1882.

Walpole, S. Lord Beaconsfield's speeches. Edinburgh Rev 155 1882.

Ewald, A. C. Disraeli and his times. 2 vols 1883.

O'Connor, T. P. Lord Beaconsfield. 1884.

Harrison, F. In his Choice of books, 1886.

— In his Studies in early Victorian literature, 1895.

Saintsbury, G. Disraeli. Mag of Art 9 1886.

Kebbel, T. E. The life of Lord Beaconsfield. 1888.

— Lord Beaconsfield and other Tory memories. 1907.

Philipson, D. In his Jew in English fiction, 1889.

Froude, J. A. In Prime Ministers of Queen Victoria, ed S. J. Reid 1890.

Brewster, F. C. Disraeli in outline. 1890. Biography, with abridgements of the novels.

Fraser, W. A. Disraeli and his day. 1891.

Lake, H. Personal reminiscences of Beaconsfield. [1891].

Aronstein, P. Disraelis Leben und Jugendschriften. Offenbach 1892.

— Disraelis Leben und dichterische Werke. Anglia 17 1895.

Shelton, J. The table talk of Shirley. 1895. Includes reminiscences of Disraeli.

Greenwood, F. Characteristics of Lord Beaconsfield. Cornhill Mag Nov 1896.

Traill, H. D. The political novel. In his New fiction, 1897.

Whibley, C. Disraeli the younger. In his Pageantry of life, 1900.

Garnett, R. Shelley and Lord Beaconsfield. In his Essays of an ex-librarian, 1901.

de Vogüé, E-M. La littérature impérialiste: Disraeli et Rudyard Kipling. Revue des Deux Mondes 1 May 1901.
Muret, M. In his L'esprit juif, Paris 1901.
Bryce, J. In his Studies in contemporary biography, 1903.
Meynell, W. Disraeli: an unconventional biography. 1903, 1927 (rev).
Mendes, H. P. Key to Vivian Grey. 1904.
Cazamian, L. In his Le roman social en Angleterre 1830–50, Paris 1904.
'Melville, Lewis' (L. S. Benjamin). The novels of Disraeli. Fortnightly Rev Nov 1904; rptd in his Victorian novelists, 1906.
Samuel, H. B. Two Dandy novels. Academy & Lit 67 1904. On Vivian Grey and Bulwer-Lytton's Pelham.
Howes, R. W. Key to Vivian Grey. 1907.
Monypenny, W. F. and G. E. Buckle. The life of Disraeli. 6 vols 1910–20, 2 vols 1929 (rev). The standard life.
Ward, A. D. The political and social novel. CHEL vol 13 1907.
Baring, E. Disraeli. 1912.
Cecil, A. Disraeli: the first two phases. Quart Rev 218 1913.
Schmitz, O. A. H. Die Kunst der Politik: Lord Beaconsfield. Berlin 1911.
More, P. E. Disraeli and Conservatism. Atlantic Monthly Sept 1915.
Sherman, S. P. The Disraelian irony. In his Points of view, New York 1921.
Russell, G. W. E. In his Portraits of the seventies, 1916. On Lothair.
George, R. E. G. The novels of Disraeli. Nineteenth Century Nov 1924.
Speare, M. E. The political novel. New York 1924.
'Raymond, E. T.' (E. R. Thompson). Disraeli: the alien patriot. 1925.
Somervell, D. C. Disraeli and Gladstone. 1925.
Brandl, A. Zur Quelle von Disraelis Alroy. Archiv 98 1925.
Hever, E. Entstehungsgeschichte von Disraelis Vivian Grey. Berlin 1925.
Quiller-Couch, A. T. In his Charles Dickens and other Victorians, Cambridge 1925.
Clarke, E. G. Disraeli. 1926.
'Maurois, André' (E. S. W. Herzog). La vie de Disraeli. Paris 1927; tr 1928.
Bjerre, B. Den tredje Markisen av Hertford i Coningsby. Edda 25 1927.
Swinnerton, F. Disraeli as a novelist. Bookman (London) April 1927, London Mercury Jan 1928, Yale Rev 17 1928.
Murray, D. L. Disraeli. 1927.
Caspar, M. Disraelis Vivian Grey II als politischer Schlüssel-roman. Archiv 153 1928.
Grey, R. Disraeli in Fancy Street. Cornhill Mag Jan 1929. On self-portraiture in Endymion.
Stevenson, L. Stepfathers of Victorianism. Victorian Quart 3 1930. On Disraeli and Bulwer-Lytton.
Lovat-Fraser, J. A. With Disraeli in Italy. Contemporary Rev Aug 1930.
Segalowitsch, B. Disraelis Orientalismus. Berlin 1930.
Howe, S. Wilhelm Meister and his English kinsmen. 1930. On German influences on Disraeli.
Jean-Aubry, G. Disraeli et le solitaire de Bath. Figaro 5 Dec 1931. Beckford's marginal notes on Alroy.
Baumann, A. A. Benjamin Disraeli. In Great Victorians, ed H. J. and H. Massingham 1932.
'Paston, George' (E. M. Symonds). The young Disraeli and his adventures in journalism. Cornhill Mag Oct 1932.
Modder, F. M. Young Disraeli in Scotland. London Quart 1932.
— The alien patriot in Disraeli's novels. Quart Rev 159 1934.
Somerville, H. Disraeli and Catholicism. Month Feb 1932.
Seibat, H. Die Romankunst Disraelis. Jena 1933.
Rühl, H. Disraelis Imperialismus und die Kolonialpolitik seiner Zeit. Leipzig 1935.
Beeley, H. Disraeli. 1936.
Thane, E. Young Mr Disraeli. New York 1936.
Clive, C. L. Disraeli's only venture in dramatic composition. SE 16 1936.
Rosa, M. W. The Silver Fork school: novels of fashion preceding Vanity Fair. New York 1936.
Thomas, W. Deux chefs-d'œuvre de raillerie sociale et politique. Revue de l'Enseignement des Langues Vivantes Aug–Nov 1936.
Hudson, R. L. Poe and Disraeli. Amer Lit 8 1937.
Gilbert, F. The Germany of Contarini Fleming. Contemporary Rev Jan 1936.
Cline, C. L. Disraeli on the grotesque in literature. RES 16 1940.
— The failure of Disraeli's Contarini Fleming. N & Q Aug 1942.
— Disraeli and Thackeray. RES 19 1943.
— The unfinished diary of Disraeli's journey to Flanders and the Rhineland 1824. SE 1943.
— Coningsby and three Victorian novelists. N & Q Jan 1944.
Pritchett, V. S. In his Living novel, 1946.
Arnold, C. C. The speech style of Disraeli. Quart Jnl of Speech 33 1947.
James, S. B. The tragedy of Disraeli. Ibid.
Disraeli's patron. TLS 25 Sept 1948. On W. G. F. C. Bentinck.
Aldington, R. In his Four English portraits 1801–51, 1948.
Hamilton, R. Disraeli and the two nations. Quart Rev 288 1950.
Forbes-Boyd, E. Disraeli the novelist. E & S new ser 3 1950.
Holloway, J. Disraeli's 'view of life' in the novels. EC 2 1952.
— In his Victorian sage, 1953.
Roth, C. Disraeli. 1952.
Masefield, M. Peacocks and primroses: a survey of Disraeli's novels. 1953.
Jerman, B. R. Disraeli's fan mail. Nineteenth-Century Fiction 9 1955.
— The young Disraeli. Princeton 1960.
— The production of Disraeli's trilogy. PBSA 58 1964. On cost sheets for pbn of Coningsby, Sybil, Tancred.
Edelman, M. A political novel: Disraeli sets a lively pace. TLS 7 Aug 1959. On Coningsby.
Frietzshe, A. H. Disraeli's religion: the treatment of religion in Disraeli's novels. Utah 1959.
— The monstrous clever young man: the novelist Disraeli and his heroes. 1959.
— Action is not for me: Disraeli's Sidonia and the dream of power. Proc Utah Acad of Sciences, Arts & Letters 1959–60.
Maxwell, J. C. 'Jingler', 'Man John': two words from Disraeli. N & Q Oct 1960.
— Words from Vivian Grey. N & Q June 1961.
— Words from Popanilla. N & Q Sept 1961.
— Words from the Young Duke. N & Q Jan 1964.
Panting, D. E. 'Juvenile delinquency' and 'Bonansic': Young England coinage. N & Q Dec 1960.
— Thackeray v. Disraeli. Quart Rev 302 1966.
— Disraeli and the Roman Catholic Church. Quart Rev 304 1966.
Stewart, R. W. The publication and reception of Disraeli's Vivian Grey. Quart Rev 298 1960.
D'Avigdor-Goldsmid, H. J. Disraeli's novels. London Mag Oct 1960.
Moers, E. In her Brummel to Beerbohm, 1960.
Graubard, R. Disraeli, the romantic egoist. In his Burke, Disraeli, Churchill: the politics of perseverance, Cambridge Mass 1961.
Bloomfield, P. Disraeli. 1961.
Faber, R. Beaconsfield and Bolingbroke. 1961.

Greene, D. J. Becky Sharpe and Lord Steyne—Thackeray or Disraeli? Nineteenth-Century Fiction 16 1962.

Smith, S. M. Willenhall and Wodgate: Disraeli's use of Blue Book evidence. RES new ser 13 1962.

—— An unpublished letter from Dickens to Disraeli. N & Q June 1964.

—— Mr Disraeli's readers: letters written to Disraeli and his wife by nineteenth-century readers of Sybil. Nottingham 1966.

Rucker, A. Disraeli and the national aristocracy. Canadian Jnl of Economics 1962.

Lewis, C. J. Disraeli's conception of divine order. Jewish Social Stud 24 1962.

Hulin, J.-P. Exotisme et littérature sociale au début de l'ère victorienne. Etudes Anglaises 16 1963.

Dahl, C. Disraeli and Edward Bulwer-Lytton. Victorian Fiction 27 1964.

Duerksen, R. A. Disraeli's use of Shelley. Victorian Newsletter no 26 1964. On Venetia.

Fido, M. The key to Vivian Grey of 1827. N & Q Nov 1965. Probably by Disraeli.

Merritt, J. D. Disraeli as a Byronic poet. Victorian Stud 3 1965. Disraeli's poem in Alroy.

Blake, R. Disraeli. 1966.

—— Disraeli's political novels. History Today 16 1966.

—— Disraeli: the problems of a biographer. Cornhill Mag 175 1966.

Feldman, B. The imperial dreams of Disraeli. Psychological Rev 54 1966.

Tulein, D. W. Disraeli and R. Shelton Mackenzie: unpublished letters. Victorian Newsletter no 31 1967.

Levine, R. A. Disraeli's Tancred and the Great Arian Mystery. Nineteenth-Century Fiction 22 1968.

M. A.

CHARLES DICKENS
1812–70

Most of the mss of Dickens's works are in the Forster Collection at the Victoria and Albert Museum, London; a small quantity, including a few leaves of Pickwick, *in BM; the ms of* Great Expectations *in Wisbech Museum; and that of* Our mutual friend *in Pierpont Morgan Library, New York; others in various libraries or in private hands. The Forster Collection includes corrected proof-sheets and similar matter. A considerable number of letters, many still unpbd, are in private collections. See ms survey by A. Nisbet in* Victorian fiction: a guide to research, *below. For a convenient summary of the chief miscellaneous documents in private hands, see* B. Currie, Fishers of books, Boston 1931. *Dickens's private life, which entered largely into his work, is illustrated in various museums connected with his name, notably Dickens House (48 Doughty St, London WC1), the Birthplace Museum, Portsmouth and Eastgate House, Rochester. The sale catalogues of his effects have been ptd and annotated.*

Bibliographies etc

Items dealing with single works or special subjects are included in the appropriate sections below. Many biographical and critical works under §2, below, contain valuable bibliographies.

Catalogue of the beautiful collection of modern pictures, water-colour drawings and objects of art of Dickens, which will be sold by auction by Messrs Christie, Manson & Woods. [1870]; rptd in Dickens memento, 1884, and in Stonehouse catalogue, 1935, below.

Gad's Hill Place, Higham, by Rochester: catalogue of the household furniture, linen, about 200 dozen of superior wines and liquors, china, glass, horse, carriages, greenhouse plants, and other effects of the late Charles Dickens, which will be sold by auction by Messrs Thomas & Homan. Rochester [1870]. BM copy has buyers' names and prices in ms.

Pierce, G. A. The Dickens dictionary: a key to the characters and principal incidents in the tales of Dickens. Boston 1872; rptd with preface by C. Dickens jr 1878; 1880, 1894 (with addns by W. A. Wheeler), 1926, New York 1965 (rev).

De Fontaine, F. G. A cyclopaedia of the best thoughts of Dickens. 1873, 1883 (enlarged as The Fireside Dickens).

Forster, J. In his Life of Dickens vol 3, 1874.

Cook, J. Bibliography of the writings of Dickens. 1879.

[Shepherd, R. H.] The bibliography of Dickens. Manchester [1880]; rev and enlarged edns in Shepherd, Speeches of Dickens, 1884; and in his Plays and poems of Dickens vol 2, 1885.

Dickens memento: catalogue with purchasers' names and prices realised of the pictures, drawings and objects of art of the late Charles Dickens. Introd by F. Phillimore, Hints to collectors by J. F. Dexter [1884].

Johnson, C. P. Hints to collectors of original editions of the works of Dickens. 1885. *See* J. H. Slater's entries on Dickens in his Early editions, 1894.

Kitton, F. G. Dickensiana: a bibliography of the literature relating to Dickens and his writings. 1886. *See* C. F. Carty, Some addenda to Kitton's Dickensiana, Library Collector 5 1903.

—— The novels of Dickens: a bibliography and sketch. 1897.

—— The minor writings of Dickens: a bibliography and sketch. 1900. *See* bibliography of Kitton's writings on Dickens, Dickensian 1 1905.

Victoria and Albert Museum, South Kensington. A catalogue of the printed books bequeathed by John Forster. 1888.

—— A catalogue of the paintings, manuscripts, autograph letters, pamphlets etc, bequeathed by Forster. 1893.

—— The Dickens exhibition, March to October 1912. 1912, 1912 (not illustr).

Chapman & Hall Ltd. The works of Dickens and Thomas Carlyle, with full particulars of each edition and biographical introductions. [1900]. *See* B. W. Matz, Two great Victorian writers (Dickens and Carlyle). 1905. Describes the Chapman & Hall collected edns.

Eaton, S. (ed.). Dickens rare print collection. Philadelphia [1900] (priv ptd).

Dickens Fellowship, London. Dickens exhibition held at the Memorial Hall London, opened by P. Fitzgerald: catalogue of exhibits. Ed F. G. Kitton 1903.

—— The second Dickens exhibition at the New Dudley Gallery: catalogue with an introduction by J. W. T. Ley and P. Fitzgerald. 1908.

—— Catalogue of the third Dickens exhibition at the New Dudley Gallery, with an introduction by P. Fitzgerald. 1909.

Thomson, J. C. Bibliography of the writings of Dickens. Warwick 1904.

The Dickensian. 1905 —. In progress. Index 1905–34, 1935; 1935–60, 1961.

Williams, M. The Dickens concordance. 1907.

Philip, A. J. A Dickens dictionary. 1909, Gravesend 1928 (rev and enlarged by W. L. Gadd).

Hammerton, J. A. The Dickens companion: a book of anecdote and reference. [1910]. Vol 18 of Charles Dickens Library.

Wilkins, W. G. First and early American editions of the works of Dickens. Cedar Rapids Iowa 1910 (priv ptd). *See* I. R. Brussel, Anglo-American first editions 1826–1900: east to west, 1935.

—— Early foreign translations of Dickens. Dickensian 7 1911.

Brooklyn Public Library, New York. Dickens: a list of books and of references to periodicals in the Brooklyn Public Library. Brooklyn 1912.

Franklin Club of St Louis. An exhibition of books, prints, drawings, manuscripts and letters commemorative of the centenary of Dickens. [St Louis 1912].

Fyfe, T. A. Who's who in Dickens: a complete Dickens repertory in Dickens' own words. [1912].

Pugh, E. W. The Dickens originals. 1912.

Eckel, J. C. The first editions of the writings of Dickens: a bibliography. 1913. 1932 (rev and enlarged). For criticism *see* TLS 26 Jan 1933; Dickensian 29 1933; Publisher's Weekly 31 March 1934; and A new Dickens bibliography, Dickensian 39–41 1943–5.

Grolier Club, New York. Catalogue of an exhibition of the works of Dickens. New York 1913 (with introd by R. Cortissoz).

Dibelius, W. Dickens. Leipzig 1916, 1926 (rev). Extensive bibliography.

Anderson galleries, New York. Dickens collection, Thackeray collection etc from the library of E. W. Coggeshall of New York. 2 vols New York 1916. A collection of autograph letters; Lib of Congress copy has prices in ms.

—— The Dickens collection formed by the late R. T. Jupp of London. New York 1922. *See* Sotheran's catalogue, Picadilly ser 68 [1920]: the Dickens collection formed by R. T. Jupp, and relics of Mrs Winter.

—— The Dickens collection of the late W. G. Wilkins of Pittsburgh Pa. New York 1922.

Miller, W. and T. W. Hill, Dickens's manuscripts, Dickensian 13 1917. Their locations listed.

Rosenbach, A. S. W. (ed). A catalogue of the writings of Dickens in the library of Harry Elkins Widener. Philadelphia 1918 (priv ptd). With texts of many letters and publisher's agreements; collection now at Harvard. *See* E. Wolf and J. Fleming, Rosenbach: a biography, 1961.

American Art Association. The renowned collection of Dickens and Thackeray formed by George Barr McCutcheon. New York [1920].

—— The renowned collection of the works of Dickens formed by Thomas Hatton of Leicester, England. New York 1927. *See* Sotheby catalogue of the Hatton collection, [1931].

—— The renowned collection of the works of Dickens formed by Mr and Mrs Edward C. Daoust. New York 1929.

—— A Dickens collection of superlative merit: the library of Frederick W. Lehmann, St Louis. New York 1930.

Newton, A. E. The amenities of book collecting, 1920.

Cowan, R. E. and W. A. Clark jr (ed). The library of William Andrews Clark jr: vols 10–11, Cruikshank and Dickens. San Francisco 1921–3.

Sargent, G. H. Dickensiana in America. Bookman's Jnl Apr 1922.

Spencer, W. T. Dickensiana. In his Forty years in my bookshop, 1923.

Hopkins, A. A. and F. R. Newbury. A Dickens atlas. 1923.

Arnold, W. H. Ventures in book collecting. New York 1923.

Hayward, A. L. The Dickens encyclopaedia. 1924.

Suzannet, A. de. Oeuvres de Dickens. Vol 1 of his Catalogue d'un choix de livres imprimés et manuscrits. 4 vols Biarritz 1925 (priv ptd).

—— Catalogue of a further portion of the library of the Comte de Suzannet: the celebrated collection of materials concerning Dickens. [1938] (Sotheby & Co). For descriptions *see* Dickensian 30 1934, TLS 23 July 1938.

British Museum. Dickens: an excerpt from the general catalogue. 1926, 1960 (enlarged to 1955).

Delattre, F. Dickens et la France. Paris 1927.

Edgar, H. L. and R. W. G. Vail. Early American editions of the works of Dickens. BNYPL 33 1929; rptd with C. W. Cavanaugh, Charles Dickens, New York 1929.

Stevens, J. S. Quotations and references in Dickens. Boston 1929.

Currie, B. John Forster and the Dickens manuscripts. In his Fishers of Books, Boston 1931.

Hatton, T. and A. H. Cleaver. A bibliography of the periodical works of Dickens, bibliographical, analytical and statistical. 1933. Illustr, with facs.

Rubens, C. The dummy library of Dickens at Gad's Hill Place; recollections of a pilgrimage as narrated to J. C. Bay. Chicago 1934 (priv ptd). *See* L. C. Staples, Dickensian 54 1958.

Unique items in famous Dickens collections. Dickensian 30–2 1934–6.

Stonehouse, J. H. (ed). Catalogue of the library of Dickens from Gadshill, reprinted from Sotheran's Price current of literature. 1935. Valuable for listing of annotated public-reading copies; see Stonehouse's bibliography of reading edns in his Sikes and Nancy, 1921.

Pierce, D. Special bibliography: the stage versions of Dickens's novels. Bull of Bibliog 16 1936.

Sawyer, C. J. A Dickens library: exhibition catalogue of the Sawyer collection. [Letchworth 1936] (priv ptd). *See* Sawyer's sales catalogues of 1931, 1936 and 1938; and collations in Sawyer and F. J. H. Darton, English books: a signpost for collectors, 1927.

Parrish, M. L. List of writings of Dickens compiled from the collection at Dormy House, Pine Valley, New Jersey, Philadelphia 1938. *See* G. H. Gerould, Princeton Univ Lib Chron 8 1946, and Additions to the Dickens collection at Princeton, 21 1959.

Gummer, E. N. Dickens's works in Germany 1837–1937. Oxford 1940.

Wilson, R. A. Translations of Dickens. BM Quart 14 1940.

Hill, T. W. A unique collection of music: a catalogue of the Miller collection of Dickens music at the Dickens House. Dickensian 37 1941.

Houtchens, L. H. and C. W. Three early works (wrongly) attributed to Dickens. PMLA 59 1944.

Free Library of Philadelphia. The life and works of Dickens: an exhibition from the collection of William M. Elkins of Philadelphia. Philadelphia 1946. *See* L. Stevenson, Victorian Newsletter no 3 1953.

Fridlender, I. V. Charles Dickens 1838–1945. Leningrad 1946. A bibliography of trns, reviews, books and articles in Russian.

—— and I. M. Katarsky. Dickens: bibliografiya russkikh 1838–1960. Moscow 1962. Expanded edn of the above.

Miller, W. The Dickens student and collector: a list of writings relating to Dickens and his works 1836–1945. Cambridge Mass 1946; supplement, Brighton 1947 (priv ptd); supplement, Hove 1953 (priv ptd). *See* commentary and corrections in P. Calhoun and H. J. Heaney, Dickensiana in the rough, PBSA 41 1947; New York 1947 (separately).

Parke-Bernet Galleries. The distinguished collection of first editions, autographs etc by and relating to Dickens formed by Lewis A. Hird, Englewood NJ. New York 1953.

Fielding, K. J. Dickens: a survey. 1953, 1960 (rev), 1963 (rev) (Br Council pamphlet).

—— Dickens: a guide to research materials. Victorian Newsletter no 14 1958.

Collins, P. A. W. Dickens's periodicals: articles on education—an annotated bibliography. [Leicester] 1957.

Finlay, I. F. Dickens in the cinema. Dickensian 54 1958. Lists films of Dickens's writings 1902–58. Note by E. Wagenknecht, ibid.

Gordan, J. D. Reading for profit: the other career of Dickens—an exhibition from the Berg Collection. New York 1958. Annotated chronological listing of reading edns, letters, prompt books etc dealing with the public readings.

Prades, J. Los libros de Dickens en España. Libro Español 1 1958.

Dickson, S. A. The Arents collection of books in parts and associated literature. New York 1958.

Stange, G. R. Reprints of nineteenth-century British fiction. College Eng Dec 1959.

Carr, Sister M. C. (ed). Catalogue of the Dickens collection at the University of Texas. Austin 1961.

Dawson's Book Shop, Los Angeles. Books from the library of Dickens together with autograph letters etc from the Langstroth collections. Los Angeles [1961].

Ford, G. H. and L. Lane jr (ed.). The Dickens critics. Ithaca 1961. Bibliography includes Checklist of Dickens criticism 1840–1960.

Dutu, A. and S. Alexandrescu. Dickens in Rumania; a bibliography for the 150th anniversary. Bucharest 1962 (UNESCO).

Gimbel, R. An exhibition of manuscripts and first editions selected and described. Yale Univ Lib Gazette 37 1962.

Nisbet, A. In Victorian fiction: a guide to research, ed L. Stevenson, Cambridge Mass 1964.

Dickens studies: a journal of modern research and criticism. Boston 1965 —. In progress.

Hardwick, M. and M. The Dickens companion. 1965.

McPherson, B. (ed). Dickens: catalogue, Alfred and Isabel Reed Dickens collection, Dunedin Public Library, New Zealand. Wellington [1965]. With J. S. Ryan, Dickens and New Zealand: a colonial image, selected from the periodical publications of Dickens with historical and biographical notes by A. W. Reed.

Editing Dickens. TLS 6 April 1967.

Collections

During Dickens's lifetime and the duration of the chief copyrights, the only authorized collected edns issued in England were pbd by Chapman & Hall. These edns were expanded from time to time, and in due course furnished with introductory or critical matter. After Dickens's death, similarly annotated edns were issued by other firms, and new artists were procured for the illustrations; only the more important of these edns are given here. The authorized edns are not all included, because some varied merely in title, price and other technical details. Reprints not containing new material are omitted.

Editions published by Chapman & Hall

The works of Charles Dickens. 17 vols 1847–67; 1st ser 1847–52 also issued in weekly and monthly pts. The first systematic re-issue, known as the 'first cheap edition'. Frontispiece illustrations only. Contains some new prefaces; general Address to the reader about this edn in Pickwick Papers 1847. *See* S. Nowell-Smith, The cheap edition of Dickens's works (first series) 1847–52, Library 5th ser 22 1967.

Library edition. 22 vols 1858–9. Frontispiece illustrations only. Includes Reprinted pieces 1858, from Household Words. Dedicated to John Forster. Re-issued in 30 vols (including later works) 1861–74, with new title-pages and illustrations, including the original ones and addns by Marcus Stone, John Leech, Clarkson Stanfield et al.

The People's edition. 25 vols 1865–7. A re-issue of the Cheap edition, excluding prefaces etc.

Charles Dickens edition. 21 vols 1867–[75]. Mainly rptd from foregoing, with slight addns and revisions by Dickens, including the addn of running headlines and some new prefaces. This is the text most often rptd in later edns.

Household edition. 22 vols [1871–9]; issued in monthly pts. With new illustrations by F. Barnard, J. Mahoney et al. Includes Forster's Life of Dickens.

Illustrated library edition. 30 vols 1873–6.

Gadshill edition. Introds, general essay and notes by A. Lang 36 vols 1897–[1908]. Contains all the original illustrations, with many additional ones by Charles Green, Harry Furniss, Maurice Greiffenhagen et al. Vols 35–6, Miscellaneous papers (not previously collected), ed B. W. Matz 1908. Rptd in edn de luxe 38 vols 1903–[8], with Forster's Life of Dickens, 2 vols, added.

The authentic edition. 22 vols 1901–[6]. With the original illustrations and additional illustrations from the Gadshill edn.

Oxford India paper Dickens. 17 vols 1901–2. With Henry Frowde (afterwards Humphrey Milford). Copyright text, on thin paper, with the original illustrations. Forster's Life added 1907.

Biographical edition. Ed A. Waugh 19 vols 1902–3. With the original illustrations. Includes Collected papers (prefaces and minor works). Miscellaneous papers, ed B. W. Matz, as additional volume 1908.

Fireside Dickens. 23 vols 1903–7. Includes Forster's Life.

The national edition. Ed B. W. Matz 40 vols 1906–8. Includes Miscellaneous papers, letters, speeches, plays and poems, and Forster's Life, together with the original illustrations, and portraits, facs and drawings.

Centenary edition. 36 vols 1910–11. With original illustrations. A re-issue of the Gadshill edn, with Dickens's prefaces substituted for Lang's introds. Includes Miscellaneous papers.

Universal edition. 22 vols [1912].

Other Editions

New illustrated library edition. Introds by E. P. Whipple 29 vols New York 1876–7.

The works of Charles Dickens. 21 vols 1892–1925. Usually known as Macmillan edn. Rptd from 1st edns, with biographical and bibliographical introds by C. Dickens jr. Includes Letters, ed G. Hogarth and M. Dickens 1893.

Temple edition. Ed W. Jerrold 35 vols 1899–1903. Incomplete. Illustrations by W. C. Cooke et al.

Rochester edition. 11 vols (all pbd) 1899–1901. Introds by George Gissing and notes by F. G. Kitton.

Imperial edition. 16 vols 1901–3. Incomplete; includes A critical study by George Gissing and topographical illustrations by F. G. Kitton.

London edition. 13 vols Edinburgh 1901–2. Topographical notes by F. G. Kitton. Includes Kitton's Dickens: his life, writings and personality, 2 vols [1902].

Autograph edition. Ed F. G. Kitton 15 vols 1903–8. Only 6 works pbd. Original and later illustrations, introds by Gissing, Saintsbury, Dowden et al; annotations, bibliography and topography by Kitton.

Everyman's library. 22 vols [1906–21]. Introds to Barnaby Rudge and A tale of two cities by W. Jerrold, to remainder by G. K. Chesterton.

Charles Dickens library. Ed J. A. Hammerton 18 vols [1910]. 1200 illustrations in all, including the original ones and 500 specially drawn by Harry Furniss. Vol 17, The Dickens picture book (a compendium of information about illustrators of Dickens); vol 18, The Dickens companion (a biographical narrative with extracts, list of authorities, short-title bibliography etc).

Waverley edition. 30 vols 1913–18. With character-study illustrations by Charles Pears and coloured versions of F. Barnard's illustrations. Introds by G. B. Shaw, W. de Morgan, J. Galsworthy, A. C. Benson, H. Caine et al.

The Nonesuch Dickens. Ed A. Waugh, H. Walpole, W. Dexter and T. Hatton. 23 vols 1937–8. Text from Charles Dickens edn, 1867–75. Illustrations from original plates and blocks (over 800) bought from Chapman & Hall. Each work complete in one vol. Fullest collection of letters, 3 vols, ed Dexter. Includes The life of our Lord and other minor items not in other edns; also Miscellaneous papers as Collected papers 2 vols. *See* Nonesuch Dickensiana: the Nonesuch Dickens: retrospectus and prospectus [by A. Waugh, T. Hatton et al], 1937.

The New Oxford illustrated Dickens. 21 vols Oxford 1947–58. With illustrations remade from the original drawings. Introds by the following: Sketches by Boz, T. Holme; Pickwick, B. Darwin; Oliver Twist, H. House; Nickleby, S. Thorndike; Old curiosity shop, Earl of Wicklow; Barnaby Rudge, K. Tillotson; Chuzzlewit, G. Russell; Dombey, H. W. Garrod; Copperfield,

R. H. Malden; Bleak House, O. Sitwell; Hard times, D. Foot; Little Dorrit, L. Trilling; Tale of two cities, J. Shuckburgh; Great expectations, F. Page; Our mutual friend, E. S. Davies; Edwin Drood, S. C. Roberts; Christmas books, E. Farjeon; Christmas stories, M. Lane; American notes and Pictures from Italy, S. Sitwell; Master Humphrey's clock and A child's history of England, D. Hudson; Uncommercial traveller and Reprinted pieces, L. C. Staples. Apart from the last-named items, the edn excludes Dickens's minor and non-fictional writings.

The Clarendon Dickens. Ed. J. Butt and K. Tillotson, Oxford 1966– . In progress. The first edn based on a collation of texts, with textual variants and bibliographies. *See* J. Butt, Editing a nineteenth-century novelist: proposals for an edition of Dickens, in English studies today: second series, Berne 1961.

Selections

For fuller lists, see Dickens: an excerpt from the British Museum general catalogue, *above, and* W. Miller, The Dickens student and collector, ch 9. *Titles listed here are edited by people associated with Dickens or otherwise of special interest. Selections from particular kinds of his writing, e.g. his public readings, minor works, are listed in the appropriate sections below.*

'Ich' (ed). Immortelles from Dickens. 1856. With commentary.

Higginson, T. W. (ed). Child-pictures from Dickens, with a prefatory note by Dickens and illustrations by S. Eytinge. Boston 1868, London 1885.

De Fontaine, F. G. (ed). A cyclopaedia of the best thoughts of Dickens. 1873, 1883 (enlarged as The fireside Dickens).

Dickens, M. (ed). The Charles Dickens birthday book, compiled by his eldest daughter, with illustrations by his youngest daughter (K. Perugini). 1882.

Kent, W. C. M. (ed). The humour and pathos of Dickens, with illustrations of his mastery of the terrible and the picturesque. 1884.

— Introd to Wellerisms, ed C. F. Rideal 1886.

Mackenzie, C. H. (ed). The religious sentiments of Dickens. 1884. With commentary.

Perugini, K. (ed). The comedy of Dickens: extracts taken by his daughter Kate. 1906.

— Introd to Character sketches from Dickens, ed B. W. Matz 1924.

Williams, B. Character sketches from Dickens specially adapted for recitation by Bransby Williams. 1910.

— Second book of character sketches from Dickens. nd.

— My sketches from Dickens. 1913.

Woollcott, A. Mr Dickens goes to the play. 1922.

Leacock, S. (ed). The greatest pages of Dickens. Garden City NY 1934.

Straus, R. (ed). Dickens: the man and the book. 1936.

Wagenknecht, E. (ed). Introduction to Dickens. Chicago 1952.

Williams, E. (ed). Readings from Dickens, introd B. Darwin 1953, 1954.

Schilling, B. (ed). Comic scenes from Dickens. 1955.

Zabel, M. D. (ed). Dickens's best stories. New York 1959.

Johnson, E. and E. (ed). The Dickens theatrical reader. 1964.

§ I

Almost all the first edns of Dickens's works, major and minor, contain small textual discrepancies or technical variations in production which determine, whenever they can be established with final certainty, priority of pbn as between one copy or set of copies and another. For some causes, see under Pickwick papers *below. These minutiae are of importance to book-collectors, but affect the material state of the various works rather than the contents, and there is still considerable disagreement between experts about points of detail. Such points cannot be enumerated here in full. They are dealt with in* J. C. Eckel, The first editions of Dickens, 1932, The Dickensian *etc. The following entries do not include either reprints of separate works pbd after Dickens's death (unless they contain critical or introductory matter or illustrations of recognized value), or selections, abridgments, trns and school edns. Sequels, imitations and dramatizations are included up to 1900 only if they utilized Dickens's own scenes and characters or very close imitations of them, and were clearly meant to share the popularity of the original work, or to adapt it legitimately. Dickens's own 'reading versions' are given.*

All Dickens's novels were first pbd serially; and reviews, imitations, parodies, dramatizations etc often appeared before the work was complete.

Sketches by Boz

Sketches by 'Boz' illustrative of every-day life and every-day people. Illustr George Cruikshank 2 vols 1836; The second series, 1836. The ptd title-page of ser 2 is dated 1837, the engraved 1836. It was actually pbd on 17 Dec 1836 (the preface being dated the same day). There are variants in both sers. The Sketches appeared originally at intervals in Monthly Mag, Bell's Weekly Mag, Morning Chron, Evening Chron, Bell's Life in London (signed 'Tibbs'), Library of Fiction and Carlton Chron. For detailed list, *see* Appendix F, Letters of Dickens, ed M. House and G. Storey vol i, Oxford 1965. The earliest—Dickens's first appearance in print as an author—was A dinner at Poplar Walk (called Mr Minns and his cousin in ser 2) in Monthly Mag Dec 1833. Many items were substantially revised before republication: *see* J. Butt and K. Tillotson, Dickens at work, 1957, ch 2. After the first edn Dickens persuaded Chapman & Hall to purchase the copyright of both sers from John Macrone.

Sketches by 'Boz' [both sers]. 20 monthly pts Nov 1837–June 1839 (variants) with 40 illustrations by Cruikshank, 13 of them new; 1839, with new preface (the monthly pts in 1 vol; known as the first 8vo edn; variants), 2 vols Philadelphia 1836 (ser 1 only, as Watkins Tottle and other sketches, illustrative of every-day life and every-day people; variants), Calcutta 1837 (20 sketches from ser 2, as The new series of sketches by Boz); cheap edn 1850 (and in 20 weekly pts, and 5 monthly pts, July–Nov 1850; with new preface and frontispiece by Cruikshank).

'Bos' [Thomas Peckett Prest]. The sketch book, embellished with seventeen elegant engravings. [1837?]. Ostensibly, and partly in fact, a close imitation of Sketches by Boz, but from internal evidence written when Pickwick was advanced in monthly pbn and Oliver Twist begun.

[Grant, J.] Sketches in London. 1837–8. In shilling numbers, similar to Pickwick.

A dinner at Poplar Walk: being [Dickens's] first effusion 'in all the glory of print', reproduced in facsimile from the Monthly Magazine, December 1833. 1933 (priv ptd). With facs of page of 1847 Pickwick preface corrected by Dickens.

Darton, F. J. H. Dickens: positively the first appearance—a centenary review with a bibliography of Sketches by 'Boz' by J. E. S. Sawyer and F. J. H. Darton. 1933. Includes original text of A dinner at Poplar Walk.

Scenes of London life, from Sketches by Boz. Ed J. B. Priestley 1947 (selection).

[Hogarth, G.] Morning Chron 11 Feb 1836.

Literary Gazette 13 Feb 1836, 24 Dec 1836.

Satirist 14 Feb 1836.

Sun 15 Feb 1836.

Athenaeum 20 Feb 1836, 31 Dec 1836.

Court Jnl 20 Feb 1836, 31 Dec 1836.

Spectator 20 Feb 1836, 26 Dec 1836.

Atlas 21 Feb 1836.
Sunday Herald 21 Feb 1836.
Sunday Times 21 Feb 1836.
[Forster, J.] Examiner 28 Feb 1836.
Weekly Despatch 28 Feb 1836.
Metropolitan Mag March 1836.
Monthly Rev March 1836, Feb 1837.
Morning Post 12 March 1836.
Chambers's Edinburgh Jnl 9 April 1836.
[Buller, C.] Westminster Rev 27 1837.
[Haywood, A.?] Quart Rev 59 1837.
[Lewes, G. H.] Nat Mag Dec 1837.
[Lister, T. H.] Edinburgh Rev 68 1838.

Studies

Benignus, S. Studien über die Anfänge von Dickens. Esslingen 1895.
Matz, B. W. A bibliographical note. Dickensian 1 1905.
Dexter, W. The genesis of Sketches by Boz. Dickensian 30 1934.
—— Contemporary opinion on Dickens's earliest work. Dickensian 31 1935.
—— The reception of Dickens's first book. Dickensian 32 1936. *See also* 33 1937.
—— The Library of Fiction. Ibid. Reviews of The Tuggs's at Ramsgate.
Nielsen, H. Some observations on Sketches by Boz. Dickensian 34 1938. Bibliographical.
Boll, E. The Sketches by Boz. Dickensian 36 1940.
Hill, T. W. Notes on Sketches by Boz. Dickensian 46–8 1950–2.
Carlton, W. J. 'The old lady' in Sketches by Boz. Dickensian 49 1953.
—— Portraits in A parliamentary sketch. Dickensian 50 1954.
—— The third man at Newgate. RES new ser 8 1957.
—— Captain Holland identified. Dickensian 57 1961.
Tillotson, K. Dickens and a story by John Poole. Dickensian 52 1956. On origins of Mr Minns and his cousin.
Cox, C. B. Comic viewpoints in Sketches by Boz. English 12 1959.
Browning, R. In Dickens and the twentieth century, ed J. Gross and G. Pearson 1962.
Morley, M. Private theatres and Boz. Dickensian 59 1963.

Pickwick Papers

Bibliographies

Fitzgerald, P. H. The history of Pickwick, an account of its characters, localities, allusions and illustrations; with a bibliography. 1891.
Dickens Fellowship, London. The Pickwick exhibition held at the New Dudley Gallery: catalogue of exhibits ed B. W. Matz and J. W. T. Ley. 1907. Illustrated.
Davis, G. W. The posthumous papers of the Pickwick Club: some new bibliographical discoveries. 1928.
Eckel, J. C. Prime Pickwicks in parts: census with complete collation, comparison and comment; foreword by A. Edward Newton, 11 plates. New York 1928.
The English editions of Pickwick; Books about Pickwick. Dickensian 32 1936.
The Lombard Street edition of Dickens: the Pickwick papers, with [biographical and bibliographical] introduction by J. H. Stonehouse. 1931–2 (monthly pts). A reprint of the original text, with plates and wrappers (except date and imprint) in facs, including the suppressed plates; modern advertisements inserted in the same style as in the original pts.
Miller, W. and E. H. Strange. A centenary bibliography of the Pickwick papers. 1936. Reprints from early reviews.

Principal Separate Editions

The posthumous papers of the Pickwick Club containing a faithful record of the perambulations, perils, travels, adventures and sporting transactions of the corresponding members, edited by Boz. 20 (as 19) monthly pts, April 1836 to Nov 1837 except June 1837; illustr Robert Seymour, d. April 1836 (pts 1–2); Robert W. Buss (pt 3); Hablot Knight Browne ('Phiz') for remainder; 1 vol 1837 (Buss's illustrations omitted).

There are innumerable variants in the earliest copies, and the exact bibliographical details are still undecided, owing to (i) inequality of demand for each pt in the early stages, and consequent use of material in various states of production; (ii) textual and pictorial changes made in the course of serial issue, though the main body was unaltered; (iii) insertion in bound-up copies of discarded or extra plates; (iv) *the binding-up or improvization of 'perfect' copies out of different-state but genuine monthly pts. See* Eckel, *above.*

The posthumous papers of the Pickwick Club, with illustrations after Phiz. Launceston Tasmania 1838, Philadelphia 1838 ('with illustrations by Sam Weller jr [T. H. Onwhyn] and Alfred Crowquill' [Alfred Henry Forrester]), cheap edn London 1847 (and in 31 weekly pts, 8 monthly pts, April–Sept 1847; frontispiece by C. R. Leslie and preface describing origin of Pickwick and Dickens's relations with Robert Seymour), 1867 (Charles Dickens edn).
The posthumous papers of the Pickwick Club. Ed C. Dickens jr 2 vols 1886 (Jubilee edn, with valuable notes); ed C. P. Johnson; 2 vols 1887 (with facs of original illustrations, including Buss's, and additional drawings by J. Leech); ed C. Van Noorden, B. W. Matz and C. P. Johnson 2 vols 1909 (original illustrations and prefaces, 223 additional pictures, introd, notes etc); ed C. Fadiman, New York 1949; ed S. Marcus, New York 1964.
Bardell and Pickwick; Mr Chops, the dwarf [from Going into Society]; Mr Bob Sawyer's party: three readings, each in one chapter. nd (priv ptd). Both Pickwick items rptd Boston 1868 and in collections 1868, 1883, 1907.

Extra Illustrations

[Onwhyn, T., possibly aided by others]. Thirty-two illustrations by Mr Samuel Weller. 1837 (8 pts).
Heath, W. [20] Pickwickian illustrations. 1837.
'Crowquill, Alfred' (A. H. Forrester). Pictures picked from the Pickwick papers. 1837. Issued in pts.
Sibson, T. Racy sketches of expeditions from the Pickwick Club. 1838. Wrapper title, Sibson's racy sketches.
Plates to illustrate the cheap edition, from original designs by John Gilbert. [1847]. 32 plates.
Six original illustrations engaved on wood, by Phiz [H. K. Browne]. [1847], 1847. The above 2 pbns were apparently recognized by Dickens and his publishers.
Pickwick pictures. [1847]. Pbd by W. Strange; issued in 4 pts.
Onwhyn, T. Twelve illustrations to the Pickwick Club. Executed in 1847, but not pbd till 1894.
Dulcken, A. Scenes from the Pickwick papers, designed and drawn on stone. [1861]. 4 large oblong folio plates and a decorated title-page, produced as a book.
Pailthorpe, F. W. Illustrations to the Pickwick Club. 1882. 24, including engraved title-page.
Grego, J. (ed). Pictorial Pickwickiana: Dickens and his illustrators. 2 vols 1899. 350 reproductions, with notes and commentary. Includes supposititious productions.
Brock, C. E. Twelve extra illustrations to the Pickwick papers. Leamington Spa 1921.
Paget, H. M. Pickwick pictures: a series of character sketches. nd. Reading Versions by Dickens.

Imitations and Sequels

The Pickwick gazette, illustrated by Robert Cruikshank. 1837. 2 issues only, June–July.

Sam Weller's Pickwick jest book. Penny nos from 1 Nov 1837.
Sam Weller's sentiments on the Poor Law. Cleave's London Satirist 16 Dec 1837.
Posthumous papers of the Cadgers' club. 1837–8.
The beauties of Pickwick, by Sam Weller. 1838, 1883 (facs, with introd on original of Sam Weller, note on piracies, and other comments, 'by a lover of Dickens's works'). Partly quotation, partly invention.
'Poz'. The posthumous papers of the wonderful discovery club. [1838].
Mr Pickwick's collection of songs. [c. 1838].
Pickwick's mirthful almanac for 1839.
Reynolds, G. W. M. Pickwick abroad: or the tour in France, illustrated. 1839, 1864, 1905. Appeared serially Dec 1837–June 1838 in Monthly Mag, of which Reynolds was then editor. Also issued in monthly pts from Jan 1839. The book issue contains a long preface defending the imitation. 41 steel engravings by 'Alfred Crowquill' (A. H. Forrester) and J. Phillips, and 33 woodcuts by G. W. Bonner (views of Paris). *See* W. Miller, G. W. M. Reynolds and Dickens, Dickensian 13 1917.
— Noctes Pickwickianae. Teetotaler 27 June–8 Aug 1840.
— Pickwick married. Teetotaler 23 Jan–19 June 1841. Rptd and rev as The marriage of Mr Pickwick in his Master Timothy's book case, 1842. A tale occupying one-sixth of a long work.
'Bos' [T. P. Prest?]. The post-humourous notes of the Pickwickian Club. 2 vols [1839?]. Issued weekly, May 1837 to July 1839, 112 nos at 1d as The penny Pickwick, and 4d monthly; illustrated. *See* F. C. Roe, Dickensian 22 1926.
— Pickwick in America! 44 pts 1838–9. *See* F. C. Roe, Connoisseur 107 1941.
Pickwick in India. Madras 1839–40.
Dickens, C. Master Humphrey's clock nos 5–88 (2 May 1840–27 Nov 1841) passim. Pickwick and the Wellers revived.
The Pickwickian treasury of wit: or Joe Miller's jest book. 1846.
Viles, E. Marmaduke Midge, the Pickwickian legatee. [c. 1852].
[Besant, W. and J. Rice.] The death of Samuel Pickwick. In The case of Mr Lucraft and other tales, 2 vols 1876.
Miller, W. Imitations of Pickwick. Dickensian 32 1936.

Dramatizations etc

Rede, W. L. The peregrinations of Pickwick: or Boz-i-a-na. In Duncombe, British theatre, nd. Produced 3 April 1837.
Stirling, E. The Pickwick Club: a burletta in three acts. In Duncombe, British theatre, [1837]. Produced 27 March 1837.
'Moncrieff, William Thomas' (W. T. Thomas). Sam Weller, or the Pickwickians: a drama in three acts. 1837. Adapted for Lacy's acting edn of plays as The Pickwickians: or the peregrinations of Sam Weller, [1872]. Produced 10 July 1837.
The Pickwick songster. [1838].
Russell, H. The ivy green. [1844], 1846 etc. Song from ch 6 arranged for the piano. Also arranged for other instruments and for use as an air for quadrilles.
Emson, F. E. The Weller family: a comedy. 1878.
Gem, T. H. Bardell versus Pickwick, versified. Leamington [1881]. With music by F. Spinney.
The great Pickwick case, arranged as a comic opera; songs by Robert Pollitt. Manchester [1884].
Burnand, F. C. Pickwick: a dramatic cantata. [1889].
Parker, J. M. An evening with Pickwick: a literary and musical Dickens entertainment. New York 1889.
Hollingshead, J. Bardell versus Pickwick, dramatized by permission of the late Charles Dickens from his private reading-copy. [1907].

Athenaeum 26 March 1836 (advertisement), 3 Dec 1836.
Bath Herald 9 April 1836, 11 June 1836, 9 July 1836, 6 Aug 1836.
Bell's life in London 10 April 1836, 1 May 1836, 3 July 1836.
Court Jnl April 1836.
Lit Gazette 9 April 1836, and many subsequent articles; *see* particularly 13 Aug 1836 [by W. Jerdan].
News and Sunday Herald 10 April 1836.
Spectator 16 April 1836.
Fraser's Lit Chron 9 April 1836.
Lincoln Gazette 19 April 1836, 13 Sept 1836.
Satirist 30 April 1836, 11 Dec 1836.
Metropolitan Mag May 1836, and many subsequent articles.
Sun 2 May 1836.
Morning Post 11 May 1836.
John Bull 12 June 1836, 11 Sept 1836.
Sunday Times 12 June 1836.
Brighton Guardian 15 June 1836, 10 Aug 1836.
Examiner 4 Sept 1836, and many subsequent articles; *see* particularly [J. Forster], 2 July 1837; and 5 Nov 1837.
New Monthly Mag Sept 1836; *see* [W. MacKay], July 1870 (obituary).
[Poe, E. A.] Southern Lit Messenger Nov 1836, Sept 1837.
Monthly Rev Feb 1837.
Chambers's Jnl 29 April 1837.
Eclectic Rev April 1837.
[Buller, C.] Westminster Rev 27 1837.
[Haywood, A.?] Quart Rev 59 1837.
Star 7 Oct 1837.
Torch 14 Oct 1837.
[Lewes, G. H.?] Nat Mag Dec 1837.
Chasles, P. Journal des Débats 13 Oct 1838.
[Lister, T. H.] Edinburgh Rev 68 1838.
[Russell, C. W.] Dublin Rev 8 1840.
Fraser's Mag April 1840.
[Patmore, C.?] North Br Rev 7 1847.
[Whipple, E. P.] North Amer Rev 69 1849.
[Hamley, E. B.] Blackwood's Mag April 1857.
Saturday Rev 23 Feb 1861.

Studies

Calverley, C. S. An examination paper [on Pickwick papers]. [1857]; rptd in his Fly-leaves, 2nd edn Cambridge 1872. *See* W. Besant, Dickensian 32 1936.
Seymour, Mrs [Robert]. An account of the origin of the Pickwick papers. [1854] (priv ptd and apparently not circulated); ed. F. G. Kitton, St Albans 1901 (priv ptd).
Dickens, C. The history of Pickwick. Athenaeum 31 March 1866; correction, 7 April 1866. On the Seymour claims.
Hassard, J. R. G. A Pickwickian pilgrimage. Boston 1881. Chiefly on London scenes.
Lockwood, F. The law and lawyers of Pickwick. [1894], [1896].
Fitzgerald, P. H. Pickwickian manners and customs. [1897].
— Pickwickian studies. 1899.
— Bardell v. Pickwick, with notes and commentaries. 1902.
— The Pickwickian dictionary and cyclopaedia. [1903].
— Pickwick riddles and perplexities. 1912.
Neale, C. M. An index to Pickwick. 1897. Addenda, Dickensian 4 1908.
Hall, H. Mr Pickwick's Kent. 1899.
Machen, A. In his Hieroglyphics, 1902.
The Eatanswill gazette: official organ of the Eatanswill Club, Sudbury Suffolk—a journal devoted to Eatans-

willian, Pickwickian and Dickensian humour and research. 4 nos Sudbury 1907–8. Founded chiefly to defend the theory that Eatanswill in the Pickwick papers represents Sudbury, but contains other minutiae.

Dibelius, W. Zu den Pickwick papers. Anglia 35 1912.

Matz, B. W. The inns and taverns of Pickwick. [1921].

Huse, W. W. Pickle and Pickwick. Washington Univ Stud 10 1922.

Bennett, A. C. Chronology of Pickwick. Dickensian 19 1923. *See* F. D. MacKinnon, Cornhill Mag May 1926.

Lambert, S. W. When Mr Pickwick went fishing. New York 1925. On Seymour's claim to origin of Pickwick. *See* Dickensian 21 1925.

Dexter, W. Mr Pickwick's pilgrimages. 1926.

—— and J. W. T. Ley. The origin of Pickwick: new facts. 1936.

Bradley, T. J. How Dickens wrote his description of Bath. Dickensian 23 1927.

Matz, W. Pickwick Papers in the Dickensian 1905–29. Dickensian 26 1930.

Ley, J. W. T. Dickens and Surtees. Dickensian 27 1931.

—— Fair play for Buss. Dickensian 28 1932.

Suzannet, A. de. The original manuscript of Pickwick Papers. Ibid.

A Pickwick portrait gallery from the pens of divers admirers, friends and enemies. 1936.

Bay, J. C. The Pickwick papers: some bibliographical remarks. Chicago 1936, 1938 (rev); rptd in his Fortune of books, Chicago 1941.

Clendening, L. A handbook to Pickwick papers. New York 1936.

Dickensian: centenary numbers 32–3 1936–7.

Davis, E. R. Dickens and the evolution of caricature. PMLA 55 1940.

Roe, F. G. Pickwick in America. Connoisseur 107 1941. On plagiarisms of Pickwick.

Morley, M. Pickwick makes his stage debut. Dickensian 42 1946. *See* Dickensian 60 1964.

Hill, T. W. Notes on the Pickwick papers. Dickensian 44–5 1948–9.

Maclean, H. N. Mr Pickwick and the seven deadly sins. Nineteenth-Century Fiction 8 1954.

Carlton, W. J. A Pickwick lawsuit in 1837. Dickensian 52 1956.

Bovill, E. W. Tony Weller's trade. N & Q Aug 1956–Dec 1957.

Tillotson, K. Dickens's Count Smorltork. TLS 22 Nov 1957.

—— Pickwick and Edward Jesse. TLS 1 April 1960.

Auden, W. H. Dingley Dell and the Fleet. In his Dyer's hand, 1962.

Bevington, D. M. Seasonal relevance in the Pickwick papers. Nineteenth-Century Fiction 16 1962.

Killham, J. In Dickens and the twentieth century, ed J. Gross and G. Pearson 1962.

Axton, W. Unity and coherence in the Pickwick papers. Stud in Eng Lit 1500–1900 5 1965.

Patten, R. L. The interpolated tales in Pickwick papers. Dickens Stud 1 1965. Reply by H. M. Levy and W. Ruff 3 1967. *See also* ELH 34 1967.

Brophy, B. et al. In their Fifty works of English literature we could do without, 1967.

Colwell, M. Organisation in Pickwick papers. Dickens Stud 3 1967.

Hardy, B. The triumph of Dingley Dell. London Rev no 2 1967.

Oliver Twist

Oliver Twist; or, the parish boy's progress, by 'Boz'. 3 vols 1838, 1838 (by Charles Dickens), 1839 (by Charles Dickens, 2nd edn), 1840 (by 'Boz'), 1841 (by Charles Dickens, 3rd edn, with author's introd). All illustr G. Cruikshank. In 24 monthly instalments, Bentley's Miscellany Feb 1837–April 1839 (except June and Oct 1837 and Sept 1838). 2 vols Philadelphia 1839 [1838] unillustr, 1 vol 1839 (illustr G. Cruikshank): these Philadelphia edns are unique texts, partly based on proofs of Bentley's Miscellany before Dickens's corrections.

The adventures of Oliver Twist: or the parish boy's progress. New edition, revised and corrected. In 10 monthly pts and 1 vol 1846 (illustr and new cover by G. Cruikshank); cheap edn 1850 (and in 19 weekly pts, 5 monthly pts, Dec 1849–April 1850; with new preface by Dickens and frontispiece by G. Cruikshank); Charles Dickens edn 1867 (with rev preface); 1895 (with 26 water-colour drawings by G. Cruikshank); [ed J. Grego] [1903] (selections). Coloured drawings done specially by Cruikshank for a friend, F. W. Cosens, in 1866, though similar in design to the earlier line engravings. The 1903 edn contains Cruikshank's claim to have invented the substance of the novel. The 2 edns differ widely in colour reproduction. Ed E. Johnson New York 1957; ed and tr S. Monod, Paris 1957; ed J. H. Miller, New York 1962; ed P. Fairclough, introd A. Wilson 1966; ed K. Tillotson, Oxford 1966.

Sikes and Nancy: a reading from Oliver Twist. (Not pbd). [1868?]; rev as a Reading by Charles Dickens [1870?] (priv ptd). The [1870?] text rptd, with introd by J. H. Stonehouse, 1921. *See* W. C. M. Kent, Dickens as a reader, 1872, ch 18, and Oliver Twist, ed K. Tillotson, Oxford 1966, Appendix D.

Almar, G. Oliver Twist: a serio-comic burletta. [1839] (in B. N. Webster, Acting national drama, with engravings by Pierce Egan jr), Leipzig 1842 (in L. Hilsenberg's Modern English comic theatre), 1844 (in Dicks, Standard plays). Produced 19 Nov 1838.

'Poz'. Oliver Twiss. [1838].

'Bos' [T. P. Prest?]. The life and adventures of Oliver Twiss, the workhouse boy. 79 pts 1838–9, 1 vol [1839].

Barnett, C. Z. Oliver Twist or the parish boy's progress: a domestic drama. nd (in Duncombe's British theatre). Produced 21 May 1838.

Oliver Twist or the parish boy's progress: a drama. [1858]; nd (in T. H. Lacy's Acting edition of plays).

Emson, F. E. Bumble's courtship: a comic interlude. [1874] (in T. H. Lacy, Acting edition of plays).

For comprehensive list of reviews, see K. Tillotson's edn, Appendix F.

[Forster, J.] Examiner 12 March, 10 Sept, 19 Nov 1837, 18–25 Nov 1838, 25 Sept 1841.

Southern Literary Messenger May 1837.

[Buller, C.] Westminster Rev 27 1837.

[Hayward, A.] Quart Rev 59 1837.

[Lewes, G. H.] Nat Mag & Monthly Critic Dec 1837.

Torch 6 Jan 1838.

[Lister, T. H.] Edinburgh Rev 68 1838.

Athenaeum 17 Nov 1838, 26 Oct 1839.

Literary Gazette 24 Nov 1838.

Spectator 24 Nov 1838.

Dublin Univ Mag Dec 1838.

Monthly Rev Jan 1839.

[Thackeray, W. M.] Catherine. Fraser's Mag May 1839–May 1840.

—— Going to see a man hanged. Fraser's Mag Aug 1840.

Christian Examiner Nov 1839.

[Cleghorn, T.?] North Br Rev 3 1845.

Whipple, E. P. Atlantic Monthly Oct 1876.

Studies

Cruikshank, G. The artist and the author. 1872. Cruikshank's claim to have originated Oliver Twist; *see* Forster, Life of Dickens vol 2, 1873.

Law, M. H. The indebtedness of Oliver Twist to Defoe's History of the Devil. PMLA 40 1925.

Boll, E. Dickens in Oliver Twist. Psychoanalytic Rev 27 1940.

Grubb, G. G. On the serial publication of Oliver Twist. MLN 56 1941.

Morley, M. Early dramas of Oliver Twist. Dickensian 43 1947.
Brogan, C. Oliver Twist re-examined. Listener 26 Aug 1948.
Hill, T. W. Notes on Oliver Twist. Dickensian 46 1950.
Johnson, E. Dickens, Fagin and Mr Riah. Commentary 9 1950.
Fielding, K. J. Sir Francis Burdett and Oliver Twist. RES new ser 2 1951.
Greene, G. The young Dickens. In his Lost childhood, 1951, rptd from his edn, 1950.
Lane, L. Oliver Twist: a revision. TLS 20 July 1951.
— The Devil in Oliver Twist. Dickensian 52 1956.
— Dickens's archetypal Jew. PMLA 73 1958.
Kettle, A. In his Introduction to the English novel vol 1, 1952.
Auden, W. H. Huck and Oliver. Listener 1 Oct 1953.
Pritchett, V. S. In his Books in general, 1953.
Lucas, A. Oliver Twist and the Newgate novel. Dalhousie Rev 34 1954.
House, H. An introduction to Oliver Twist. In his All in due time, 1955.
Eoff, S. Oliver Twist and the Spanish picaresque novel. SP 54 1957.
Bishop, J. The hero-villain of Oliver Twist. Victorian Newsletter no 15 1959.
Stone, H. Dickens and the Jews. Victorian Stud 2 1959.
Tillotson, K. Oliver Twist. E & S new ser 12 1959.
— Oliver Twist in three volumes. Library 5th ser 18 1963.
Rosenberg, E. From Shylock to Svengali: Jewish stereotypes in English fiction. Stanford 1960.
Bayley, J. In Dickens and the twentieth century, ed J. Gross and G. Pearson 1962.
Marcus, S. Who is Fagin? Commentary 34 1962.
Hollingsworth, K. The Newgate novel 1830–47. Detroit 1963.
Robb, B. Cruikshank's etchings for Oliver Twist. Listener 22 July 1965.
Frederick, K. C. The cold, cold hearth: domestic strife in Oliver Twist. College Eng March 1966.

Nicholas Nickleby

Principal Editions

The life and adventures of Nicholas Nickleby, containing a faithful account of the fortunes, misfortunes, uprisings, downfallings and complete career of the Nickleby family, edited by 'Boz', with illustrations by 'Phiz'. Title on wrapper. On title-page, The life and adventures of Nicholas Nickleby, by Charles Dickens. 20 (as 19) monthly pts (with variants) April 1838 to Oct 1839; 1 vol Oct 1839 (with preface, and portrait of Dickens by Daniel Maclise, as The life and adventures of Nicholas Nickleby), Philadelphia 1839, cheap edn 1848 (and in 30 weekly pts, 8 monthly pts, Oct 1847–May 1848; with new preface, and frontispiece from painting by T. Webster), 1867 (Charles Dickens edn); ed A. Waugh 1953.
Nicholas Nickleby at the Yorkshire School: a reading in four chapters. [1861?] (priv ptd), nd (rev and 'in three chapters'), both rptd ('in four chapters').

Imitations, Dramatizations etc

'Bos' [T. P. Prest?]. Nickelas Nickelbery: containing the adventures of the family of Nickelbery, embellished with forty-two engravings. [1838?]. In weekly and monthly pts.
Onwhyn, T. Thirty-two illustrations to Nicholas Nickleby. [1838–9].
'Guess'. Scenes from the life of Nickleby married, with 22 plates by Quiz. 1840.
Stirling, E. Nicholas Nickleby: a farce. [1838] (in B. N. Webster, Acting drama), Leipzig 1841 (in L. Hilsenberg, Modern English comic theatre). Produced 19 Nov 1838. The ptd text contains a preface and dedication to Dickens.
— The fortunes of Smike: or a sequel to Nicholas Nickleby. nd (in B. N. Webster, Acting drama), Leipzig 1841 (in L. Hilsenberg, Modern English comic theatre). Produced 2 March 1840.
Simms, H. Nicholas Nickleby: a drama in four acts. [1883] (in Dicks, Standard plays).
Athenaeum 31 March 1838.
[Forster, J.] Examiner 1 April 1838, then irregularly until 27 Oct 1839; 23 Sept 1838.
Literary Gazette 7 April 1838.
[Cooke, J.?] Actors by Daylight 9 Feb 1839.
Odd Fellow 9 Feb 1839.
Town 7 Sept 1839.
Fraser's Mag April 1840.
Christian Remembrancer Dec 1842.
[Croker, J. W.] Quart Rev 71 1843.
[Cleghorn, T.?] North Br Rev 3 1845.

Studies

Thackeray, W. M. Dickens in France. Fraser's Mag March 1842. On a Parisian stage version of Nickleby. Illustr Thackeray.
Elliot, W. H. The country and church of the Cheeryble brothers. Selkirk 1893.
— The story of the 'Cheeryble' Grants. Manchester 1906.
Suddaby, J. The dramatic piracy of Nicholas Nickleby. Dickensian 7 1911.
— The Shaw Academy trials. Dickensian 11 1915.
Pascoe, C. E. Dickens in Yorkshire [1912].
Mulgrew, F. A real Dotheboys Hall. Cornhill Mag Dec 1914.
Darton, F. J. H. Vincent Crummles: his theatre and his times. 1926. Illustrated.
Morley, M. Nicholas Nickleby on the boards. Dickensian 43 1947.
— Where Crummles played. Dickensian 58–9 1962–3.
Suzannet, A. de. The original manuscript of Nicholas Nickleby. Dickensian 43 1947.
Hill, T. W. Notes on Nicholas Nickleby. Dickensian 45–6 1949–50.
Clinton-Baddeley, V. C. Benevolent teachers of youth. Cornhill Mag 169 1957.
— Snevellicci. Dickensian 57 1961.
Bergonzi, B. In Dickens and the twentieth century, ed J. Gross and G. Pearson 1962.
Alderson, B. R. Nicholas Nickleby illustrated. Genealogists' Mag 14 1962. Introd by K. J. Fielding.

Master Humphrey's Clock, Old Curiosity Shop, Barnaby Rudge

Master Humphrey's clock, by 'Boz', with illustrations by G. Cattermole and H. K. Browne. 88 weekly pts and 20 monthly nos from 4 April 1840; 3 vols 1840–1 ('by Charles Dickens') with preface to each vol, that to vol 3 being the preface to Barnaby Rudge; ed F. T. Marzials [1891] (with other early pieces). The Old Curiosity Shop pbd 25 April 1840 to 6 Feb 1841; Barnaby Rudge 13 Feb to 27 Nov 1841. Some variants in the periodical issues. Addresses to the reader, April 1840, Sept 1841, Nov 1841. The 'Clock' setting was not retained when the 2 long stories were pbd as separate works, and in most modern collected edns is usually included in a 'miscellany' vol.
'Bos' [*not* T. P. Prest]. Mister Humfries' clock: 'Bos', maker—a miscellany of striking interest. 1840.
'Brush'. Sketches of characters, from Master Humphrey's clock. [c. 1840].
Reynolds, G. W. M. Master Timothy's book-case. 1842, 1847, 1886.
Cooper, F. F. Master Humphrey's clock: a domestic drama. nd (in Duncombe, British theatre), [1886] (Dicks, Standard plays). Produced 26 May 1840.

Sibson, J. Fourteen extra illustrations to The old curiosity shop and Barnaby Rudge. 1841.

Stevens, J. 'Woodcuts dropped into the text'. SB 20 1967.

The old curiosity shop. 1841 (with the original illustrations; first separate edn; ptd from the stereotype plates of the Clock, vols 1–2, and retaining their pagination, but adding some matter on short pages), 4 extra illustrations by H. K. Browne issued separately; cheap edn 1848 (and in 20 weekly pts, 5 monthly pts June–Oct 1848; with new preface and Frontispiece by G. Cattermole).

Stirling, E. The old curiosity shop: a drama. nd (in T. H. Lacy, Acting edition of plays). Produced 9 Nov 1840.

Lander, G. The old curiosity shop: a drama. [1885] (in Dicks, Standard plays).

Monthly Rev May 1840.

Reynolds, G. W. M. Teetotaler 4 July 1840.

[Hood, T.] Athenaeum 7 Nov 1840.

Metropolitan Mag Dec 1840, March 1841.

Bristol Mag & Western Lit Jnl 23 Jan 1841.

Literaturnaiia gazeta 22 Feb 1841.

[Poe, E. A.) Graham's Mag May 1841.

[Forster, J.] Examiner 4 Dec 1841.

[Peabody, A. P.] Christian Examiner March 1842.

Christian Remembrancer Dec 1842.

Studies

FitzGerald, E. Little Nell's wanderings (1846). In A FitzGerald medley, ed G. Ganz 1933.

Harte, F. B. Dickens in camp. In his Poems, Boston 1871.

Dexter, W. Little Nell's journey. Dickensian 20 1924.

Huxley, A. In his Vulgarity in literature. 1930.

'Rutherford, Mark' (W. H. White). Little Nell. In his More pages from a journal, Oxford 1930.

Partington, W. The blacking laureate: the identity of Mr Slum. Dickensian 34 1938.

Bennett, W. C. The mystery of the Marchioness. Dickensian 36 1940. *See* G. G. Grubb, Dickens's Marchioness identified, MLN 68 1953.

Hill, T. W. ('T. K. Brumleigh'). On the road with the Trents. Dickensian 37–8 1941–2.

—— Notes on The old curiosity shop. Dickensian 49 1953.

Morley, M. Plays in Master Humphrey's Clock. Dickensian 43 1947.

Staples, L. C. Shavings from Dickens's workshop iv. Dickensian 50 1954. Cancelled passages from the proofs.

Cockshut, A. O. J. Sentimentality in fiction. Twentieth Century April 1957.

Spilka, M. Little Nell revisited. Papers of Michigan Acad of Sciences, Arts & Letters 45 1959.

Pearson, G. In Dickens and the twentieth century, ed J. Gross and G. Pearson 1962.

Reid, J. C. In his Hidden world of Dickens, Auckland 1962.

Gibson, J. W. The critical allegory. Dickensian 60 1964.

Dyson, A. E. Innocence and the grotesque. CQ 8 1966.

Steig, M. Phiz's Marchioness. Dickens Stud 2 1966.

Senelick, L. Little Nell and the prurience of sentimentality. Dickens Stud 3 1967.

Winters, W. A consummation devoutly to be wished. Dickensian 63 1967.

Barnaby Rudge: a tale of the riots of 'eighty. 1841 (with the original illustrations; first separate edn; ptd from the stereotype plates of the Clock, vols 2–3, and retaining their pagination), cheap edn 1849 (and in 24 weekly pts, 6 monthly pts, Nov 1848–April 1849; 4 extra illustrations by H. K. Browne issued separately).

Selby, C. and C. Melville. Barnaby Rudge: a domestic drama. [1841] (in Duncombe, British theatre), Leipzig 1841 (in L. Hilsenberg, Modern English comic theatre), London [1875], [1883?] (Dicks, Standard plays). Produced 28 June 1841.

'Bos'. Barnaby Rudge, illustrated by Phis. 9 pts 1841.

Higgie, T. H. Barnaby Rudge, or the murder at the Warren: a drama. [1854].

[Poe, E. A.] Philadelphia Saturday Evening Post 1 May 1841.

—— Graham's Mag Feb 1842.

Cooke, J. Actors' Note Book 26 May 1841.

Metropolitan Mag June 1841.

[Forster, J.] Examiner 4 Dec 1841.

[Hood, T.] Athenaeum 22 Jan 1842.

Christian Remembrancer Dec 1842.

[Cleghorn, T.?] North Br Rev 3 1845.

[Murray, P. A.] Dublin Rev 21 1846.

Studies

The King's Head, Chigwell. A short account of the historic 'Maypole' in Barnaby Rudge [1912].

Ulrich, A. Studien zu Dickens' Roman Barnaby Rudge. Jena 1931.

Gray, W. F. The prototype of Gashford. Dickensian 29 1933.

Brush, L. M. A psychological study of Barnaby Rudge. Dickensian 31 1935.

Morley, M. Plays in Master Humphrey's clock. Dickensian 43 1947.

Lukács, G. In his Historical novel, New York 1950 (tr).

Lane, L. Dickens and Scott: an unusual borrowing. Nineteenth-Century Fiction 6 1952. Queried by K. J. Fielding, 7 1953.

Hill, T. W. Notes on Barnaby Rudge. Dickensian 50–3 1954–7.

Ziegler, A. U. A Barnaby Rudge source. Dickensian 54 1958.

Folland, H. F. The doer and the deed: theme and pattern in Barnaby Rudge. PMLA 74 1959.

Gibson, F. A. A note on George Gordon. Dickensian 57 1961.

Gottshall, J. K. Devils abroad. Nineteenth-Century Fiction 16 1962.

Lindsay, J. In Dickens and the twentieth century, ed J. Gross and G. Pearson 1962.

Monod, S. Rebel with a cause: Hugh of the Maypole. Dickens Stud 1 1965.

Dyson, A. E. The genesis of violence. CQ 9 1967.

Martin Chuzzlewit

The life and adventures of Martin Chuzzlewit, his relatives, friends and enemies: comprising all his wills and his ways, with an historical record of what he did, and what he didn't; showing, moreover, who inherited the family plate, who came in for the silver spoons, and who for the wooden ladles: the whole forming a complete key to the House of Chuzzlewit, edited by 'Boz', with illustrations by 'Phiz'. [Title on wrapper. On title-page and for vol issue, The life and adventures of Martin Chuzzlewit, by Charles Dickens.] 20 (as 19) monthly pts, Jan 1843 to July 1844 (with variants); 1 vol 1844 (with preface), cheap edn 1849 (and in 32 weekly pts, 8 monthly pts, May–Nov 1849; with new preface, and frontispiece by F. Stone), 1867 (Charles Dickens edn, with rev preface); ed K. Hayens 1953; ed M. Mudrick, New York 1965.

Mrs Gamp [a reading]. 1858 (priv ptd, with The poor traveller), Boston 1868 (Mrs Gamp only), New York 1956 (facs of the author's prompt-copy, ed J. D. Gordan).

An account of a late expedition into the North, for an amateur theatrical benefit, written by Mrs Gamp. Fragment composed for use on theatrical tour on behalf of Leigh Hunt 1847. Not pbd in Dickens's lifetime, but included in Forster's Life, bk 6 ch 1; priv ptd from ms as Mrs Gamp with the strolling players: an unfinished sketch by Charles Dickens, New York 1899; as A new

Piljians Projiss, nd (facs of ms, illustr J. Leech, F. Barnard and F. W. Pailthorpe).
'Bos'. Life and adventures of Martin Puzzlewhit. Lloyd's Penny Sunday Times from 15 Jan 1843.
Stirling, E. Martin Chuzzlewit: a drama. [1844?] (in Duncombe, British theatre), nd (in T. H. Lacy, Acting edition of plays). Produced 9 July 1844.
— Mrs Harris: a farce. nd (in Duncombe, British theatre).
'Syr' [S. A. Allen]. My home and fireside: the speculations of Martin Chuzzlewit & Co among the 'Wenom of the Walley of Eden'. Philadelphia 1846.
Webster, B. Mrs Sarah Gamp's tea and turn out: a Bozzian sketch. nd. Produced 26 Oct 1846.
Higgie, T. and T. H. Lacy. Martin Chuzzlewit, or his wills and his ways: a drama. [1872] (in T. H. Lacy, Acting edition of plays). Produced 29 July 1844.
Dilley, J. J. and L. Clifton. Tom Pinch: a domestic comedy. [1884]. Produced 10 March 1881.
Christian Remembrancer Oct 1843.
[Hickson, W. E.?] Westminster Rev 40 1843.
[Blanchard, S. L.?] Ainsworth's Mag Jan 1844.
Critic Jan 1844.
Dublin Univ Mag March 1844.
[Chorley, H. F.] Athenaeum 20 July 1844.
Knickerbocker Sept 1844.
Monthly Rev Sept 1844.
[Forster, J.] Examiner 26 Oct 1844.
[Cleghorn, T.?] North Br Rev 3 1845.
Eng Rev Dec 1848.
Ecclesiastic & Theologian Oct 1855.
Nat Rev 13 1861.

Studies

Butler, Samuel. A translation, attempted in consequence of a challenge. Cambridge [1894]. Rptd from Eagle. A trn of an utterance of Mrs Gamp's (ch 19 of Martin Chuzzlewit) into Greek Homeric hexameters.
Osborne, C. C. Mr Pecksniff and his prototype. Independent Rev Sept 1906.
— The genesis of Mrs Gamp. Dickensian 23 1927.
Older, M. The mysterious Mrs Harris. Dickensian 29 1933.
Churchill, R. C. Dickens, drama and tradition. Scrutiny 10 1942.
Dickens in America: Martin Chuzzlewit centenary. TLS 9 Jan 1943.
Hill, T. W. Notes on Martin Chuzzlewit. Dickensian 42–3 1946–7.
Heilman, R. B. The New World in Dickens's writings. Trollopian 1 1947.
Pound, L. The American dialect of Dickens. Amer Speech 22 1947.
Nisbet, A. B. The mystery of Martin Chuzzlewit. In Essays dedicated to L. B. Campbell, Berkeley 1950.
Van Ghent, D. The Dickens world: a view from Todgers's. Sewanee Rev 58 1950.
Grubb, G. G. Dickens's Western tour and the Cairo legend. SP 48 1951.
Morley, M. Martin Chuzzlewit in the theatre. Dickensian 47 1951.
Fielding, K. J. Martin Chuzzlewit and the Liberator. N & Q June 1953.
Benjamin, E. B. The structure of Martin Chuzzlewit. PQ 34 1955.
Stone, H. Dickens's use of his American experiences in Martin Chuzzlewit. PMLA 72 1957.
Baetzhold, H. G. The model for Martin Chuzzlewit's Eden. Dickensian 55 1959.
Brogunier, J. The dreams of Montague Tigg and Jonas Chuzzlewit. Dickensian 58 1962.
Hardy, B. In Dickens and the twentieth century, ed J. Gross and G. Pearson 1962.
Whitley, J. S. The two hells of Martin Chuzzlewit. Papers of Michigan Acad of Science, Arts & Letters 50 1965.
Dyson, A. E. Howls the sublime. CQ 9 1967.

Dombey and Son

Dealings with the firm of Dombey and Son wholesale, retail and for exportation, with illustrations by H. K. Browne. [Title on wrapper. On title-page and for vol issue, Dombey and Son.] 20 (as 19) monthly pts, Oct 1846 to April 1848 (with variants), 1 vol 1848 (with preface), New York 1847 [1846–8], Philadelphia 1848, 1858 (cheap edn), 2 vols 1865 (with new frontispiece), 1867 (Charles Dickens edn, with new preface); ed A. Pryce-Jones, New York 1964. After Martin Chuzzlewit, Dickens for a time transferred his new works from Chapman & Hall to Bradbury & Evans. But Chapman & Hall pbd 12 separate extra illustrations to Dombey and Son, by 'Phiz' 2 pts 1848.
The story of little Dombey [a reading]. [1858] (priv ptd), 1858, 1862, nd, Boston 1868.
Inquest on the late Master Paul Dombey. The Man in the Moon, ed A. Smith and A. B. Reach, March 1847.
Dombey and Son finished: part the best and last. The Man in the Moon Feb 1848.
Nicholson, R. Dombey and Daughter: a moral fiction [1847]. In penny nos.
Brougham, J. Dombey and Son. [1885] (in Dicks, Standard plays). Produced New York 1848.
— Captain Cuttle: a few more scenes from the moral of Dombey and Son. [1884] (in Dicks, Standard plays). Produced New York 14 Jan 1850.
Dombey and Son: or Good Mrs Brown the child stealer. nd. Produced Royal Strand Theatre, London.
Carpenter, J. E. What are the wild waves saying? Vocal duet, music by Stephen Glover. [c. 1850]. *See* A voice from the waves: a vocal duet, words by R. Ryan, music by Stephen Glover [c. 1850].
'Buz'. Dolby and Father. New York 1868. Parody, in part, of Dombey and Son, with characters from other works by Dickens and some serious attacks upon him.
[Kent, W. C. M.] Sun 2 Oct 1846 and frequently thereafter; 13 April 1848.
Economist 10 Oct, 7 Nov, 12 Dec 1846.
Chambers's Jnl 24 Oct 1846.
Athenaeum 31 Oct 1846.
[Warren, S.] Blackwood's Mag Nov 1846.
[Hickson, W. E.?] Westminster Rev 47 1847.
[Patmore, C.?] North Br Rev 7 1847.
Christian Remembrancer Oct 1847.
[Aytoun, W. E.] Blackwood's Mag Oct 1848.
Rambler Jan 1848.
Dudley, A. Revue des Deux Mondes March 1848.
Sharpe's London Mag May 1848.
[Forster, J.] Examiner 28 Oct 1848.
Eng Rev Dec 1848.
People's Jnl 22 April 1848.
[Whipple, E. P.] North Amer Rev 69 1849.
Williams, S. F. Rose, Shamrock & Thistle June 1863.
'Nathaniel, Sir'. New Monthly Mag June 1864.

Studies

Sterry, S. The wooden midshipman. All the Year Round 29 Oct 1881.
'Bromhill, K.' (T. W. Hill). Phiz's illustrations to Dombey and Son. Dickensian 38–9 1942–3.
'Brumleigh, T. K.' (T. W. Hill). Notes on Dombey and Son. Ibid.
Butt, J. and K. Tillotson. Dickens at work on Dombey and Son. E & S new ser 4 1951.

Tillotson, K. A lost sentence in Dombey and Son. Dickensian 47 1951. *See* D. S. Bland 52 1956.
— In her Novels of the eighteen-forties, Oxford 1954.
Morley, M. Enter Dombey and Son. Dickensian 48 1952. Stage versions.
Staples, L. C. Shavings from Dickens's workshop ii. Dickensian 49 1953. Cancelled passages from the proofs.
Atthill, R. Dickens and the railway. English 13 1961.
Leavis, F. R. Sewanee Rev 70 1962.
Moynahan, J. In Dickens and the twentieth century, ed J. Gross and G. Pearson 1962.
Axton, W. Tonal unity in Dombey and Son. PMLA 78 1963.
— Dombey and Son; from stereotype to archetype. ELH 31 1964.
Stone, H. Dickens and Leitmotif: music-staircase imagery in Dombey and Son. College Eng Dec 1963.
— The novel as fairytale: Dombey and Son. E Studies 47 1966.
Lucas, J. Dickens and Dombey and Son: past and present imperfect. In D. Howard et al, Tradition and tolerance in nineteenth-century fiction, 1966.
Collins, P. Dombey and Son then and now. Dickensian 63 1967.

David Copperfield

The personal history, adventures, experiences and observations of David Copperfield the younger, of Blunderstone Rookery, (which he never meant to be published on any account), with illustrations by H. K. Browne. [Title on wrapper. On title-page and for vol issue, The personal history of David Copperfield.] 20 (as 19) monthly pts, May 1849 to Nov 1850 (with variants); 1 vol 1850 (with preface), 2 vols New York 1850, 1 vol 1858 (Cheap edn, with new preface), 1867 (Charles Dickens edn, with rev preface); ed E. Kibblewhite, Oxford 1916; ed F. M. Ford, A. Meynell et al, Bath 1922; ed H. S. Hughes 2 vols Garden City NY 1936; ed and abridged W. S. Maugham, Philadelphia 1948; ed E. K. Brown, New York 1950; ed and tr S. Monod 2 vols Paris 1956; ed G. H. Ford, Boston 1958; ed E. Johnson, New York 1962; ed T. Blount 1966.
David Copperfield: a reading in five chapters. nd (priv ptd), Boston 1868, 1921 (reprint of first edn, with a note by J. H. Stonehouse summarizing the Maria Beadnell correspondence and the relation between David Copperfield and Dickens's own life).
Halliday, A. Little Emily ('David Copperfield'): a drama. New York nd. Produced 9 Oct 1869.
Brougham, J. David Copperfield: a drama. [1885] (in Dicks, Standard plays). Produced New York 6 Jan 1851.
Graves, R. The real David Copperfield. 1933. Dickens's text rev at full length to 'sort what is true from what is false', with critical introd by way of justification.
[Hervey, T. K.] Athenaeum 5 May 1849.
Family Herald 28 July 1849.
Rambler Sept 1849.
[Chorley, H. F.] Athenaeum 23 Nov 1850.
Spectator 23 Nov 1850.
[Forster, J.?] Examiner 14 Dec 1850.
Fraser's Mag Dec 1850.
[Masson, D.] North Br Rev 15 1851.
[Stowe, W. H.] Times 11 June 1851.
Prospective Rev 7 1851.
Southern Literary Messenger Aug 1851.
[Oliphant, M.] Blackwood's Mag April 1855.

Studies

Arnold, M. The incompatibles. Nineteenth Century April 1881; rptd in his Irish essays ,1882.
Bluhm, R. Autobiographisches in David Copperfield, Reichenbach 1891.
Joyce, J. Ulysses. Paris 1922. Parody in Oxen of the Sun episode.
Kitchen, P. C. Holcroft, Dickens and David Copperfield. In Schelling anniversary papers, New York 1923.
Woolf, V. David Copperfield. Nation (London) 22 Aug 1925; rptd in her Moment and other essays, 1947.
Carden, P. T. Doctors' Commons. Dickensian 27 1931.
Dexter, W. The London of David Copperfield. Ibid.
Davis, E. The creation of Dickens's David Copperfield. Univ of Wichita Bull 16 1941.
Hill, T. W. Notes on David Copperfield. Dickensian 39–40 1943–4.
'Bromhill, K.' (T. W. Hill). Phiz's illustrations to David Copperfield. Dickensian 40 1944.
Mason, L. Jane Eyre and David Copperfield. Ibid.
Brown, E. K. Yale Rev 37 1948.
David Copperfield centenary number. Dickensian 45 1949.
[Fielding, K. J.] David Copperfield and dialect. TLS 30 April 1949.
— The making of David Copperfield. Listener 19 July 1951.
Strong, L. A. G. Dickensian 45 1949.
Oppel, H. Interpretation des David Copperfield. In his Die Kunst des Erzählens im englischen Roman des 19 Jahrhunderts, Bielefeld 1950.
Adrian, A. A. David Copperfield: a century of critical and popular acclaim. MLQ 11 1950.
Carlton, W. J. The 'deed' in David Copperfield. Dickensian 48 1952.
Staples, L. C. Shavings from Dickens's workshop i. Dickensian 48–9 1952–3. Cancelled passages from proofs.
Manheim, L. F. The personal history of David Copperfield. Amer Imago 9 1953.
Morley, M. Stage appearances of Copperfield. Dickensian 49 1953.
Needham, G. B. The undisciplined heart of David Copperfield. Nineteenth-Century Fiction 9 1955.
Spilka, M. David Copperfield as psychological fiction. CQ 1 1959.
Cardwell, M. Rosa Dartle and Mrs Brown. Dickensian 56 1960.
Marshall, W. H. The image of Steerforth and the structure of David Copperfield. Tennessee Stud in Lit 5 1960.
Collins, P. A. W. The Middlesex magistrate in David Copperfield. N & Q March 1961.
— David Copperfield and East Anglia. Dickensian 61 1965.
Kettle, A. REL 2 1961.
Jones, J. In Dickens and the twentieth century, ed J. Gross and G. Pearson 1962.
Monod, S. Une curiosité dans l'histoire de la traduction: Le neveu de ma tante, d'Amédée Pichot. Etudes Anglaises 14 1962.
Beebe, M. In his Ivory towers and sacred founts: the artist as hero in fiction. New York 1964.
Stone, H. Fairy-tales and ogres. Criticism 6 1964.
Gard, R. EC 15 1965.
Schilling, B. N. Mr Micawber's difficulties; Mr Micawber's abilities. In his Comic spirit, Detroit 1965.
Kincaid, J. R. The structure of David Copperfield. Dickens Stud 2 1966.
Oddie, W. Mr Micawber and the redefinition of experience. Dickensian 63 1967.

Bleak House

Bleak House, with illustrations by H. K. Browne. 20 (as 19) monthly pts, March 1852 to Sept 1853 (slight variants); 1 vol 1853 (with preface), 1858 (Cheap edn), 1868 (Charles Dickens edn, with rev preface); ed R. B Johnson 1953; ed M. D. Zabel, Boston 1956; ed G. Tillotson, New York 1964.

Simpson, J. P. Lady Dedlock's secret. [1885] (in French, Acting edition of plays). Produced 1874.
Lander, G. Bleak House, or Poor Jo: a drama. [1885] (in Dicks, Standard plays). Produced 1876.
[Chorley, H. F.] Athenaeum 6 March 1852, 17 Sept 1853.
Eng Rev July 1852.
Leader 5 Feb 1853.
Illustr London News 24 Sept 1853.
United States Mag & Democratic Rev Sept 1853.
Bentley's Monthly Rev Oct 1853.
Bentley's Miscellany Oct 1853.
[Sargent, W.] North Amer Rev 77 1853.
[Riggs, C. F.] Putnam's Monthly Mag Nov 1853.
Eclectic Rev Dec 1853.
[Stothert, J. A.] Rambler Jan 1854.
Ecclesiastic & Theologian Oct 1855.
'Nathaniel, Sir'. New Monthly Mag June 1864.

Studies

Denman, T. Uncle Tom's cabin, Bleak House, slavery and slave trade: six articles reprinted from Standard. 1853. *See* H. Stone, Dickens and Harriet Beecher Stowe, Nineteenth-Century Fiction 12 1958.
C., W. A Bleak House narrative in real life: a suit in the Irish Court of Chancery 1826–51. 1856.
Brimley, G. In his Essays, Cambridge 1858. Rptd from Spectator 24 Sept 1853.
Brewer, L. A. Leigh Hunt and Dickens: the Skimpole caricature. Cedar Rapids Iowa 1930 (priv ptd).
Gadd, W. L. The topography of Bleak House. Dickensian 26 1930.
Dexter, W. London places in Bleak House. Dickensian 26–7 1930–1.
Hill, T. W. Notes on Bleak House. Dickensian 40 1944.
— Hunt-Skimpole. Ibid.
'Bromhill, K.' (T. W. Hill). Phiz's illustrations to Bleak House. Ibid.
Stevenson, L. Who was Mr Turveydrop? Dickensian 44 1948.
Fogle, S. F. Skimpole once more. Nineteenth-Century Fiction 7 1953.
Morley, M. Bleak House scene. Dickensian 49 1953. Stage versions.
Staples, L. C. Shavings from Dickens's workshop v. Dickensian 50 1954. Cancelled passages from proofs.
Fielding, K. J. Skimpole and Leigh Hunt again. N & Q April 1955.
Manheim, L. F. The law as 'Father'. Amer Imago 12 1955.
Craig, G. A. Jane Eyre and Bleak House. In Society and the self in the novel, ed M. Schorer, New York 1956.
Grenander, M. E. The mystery and the moral: point of view in Bleak House. Nineteenth-Century Fiction 10 1956.
Haight, G. S. Dickens and Lewes on spontaneous combustion. Ibid.
Friedman, N. The shadow and the sun. Boston Univ Stud in Eng 3 1957.
Zabel, M. D. The undivided imagination. In his Craft and character in modern fiction, New York 1957.
Broderick, J. H. and J. E. Grant. The identity of Esther Summerson. MP 55 1958.
Crompton, L. Satire and symbolism in Bleak House. Nineteenth-Century Fiction 12 1958.
Ford, G. H. Self-help and the helpless in Bleak House. In From Jane Austen to Joseph Conrad, ed R. C. Rathburn and M. Steinmann, Minneapolis 1958.
Butt, J. Bleak House once more. CQ 1 1959.
Cox, C. B. A Dickens landscape. CQ 2 1960.
Krieger, M. The world of law as pasteboard mask. In his Tragic vision, Chicago 1960.
Deen, L. W. Style and unity in Bleak House. Criticism 3 1961.
Kettle, A. Dickens and the popular tradition. Zeitschrift für Anglistik und Amerikanistik 9 1961. Also in Carleton Miscellany 3 1961.
Worth, G. J. The genesis of Jo the crossing-sweeper. JEGP 60 1961.
Donovan, R. A. Structure and idea in Bleak House. ELH 29 1962.
Harvey, W. J. In Dickens and the twentieth century, ed J. Gross and G. Pearson 1962.
Blount, T. The graveyard satire of Bleak House in the context of 1850. RES new ser 14 1963.
— The Chadbands and Dickens's view of Dissenters. MLQ 25 1964.
— Dickens's slum satire in Bleak House. MLR 60 1965.
— The importance of place in Bleak House. Dickensian 61 1965.
— The ironmaster and the new acquisitiveness. EC 15 1965.
— Chancery as evil and challenge. Dickens Stud 1 1965.
— Poor Jo, education and the problem of juvenile delinquency. MP 62 1965.
— Sir Leicester Dedlock and 'Deportment' Turveydrop. Nineteenth-Century Fiction 21 1967.
Axton, W. The trouble with Esther. MLQ 26 1965.
— Esther's nicknames. Dickensian 62 1966.
Steig, M. The whitewashing of Inspector Bucket. Papers of Michigan Acad of Science, Arts & Letters 50 1965.
Sucksmith, H. P. Dickens at work on Bleak House: his memoranda and number plans. Renaissance & Modern Stud 9 1965.
Fradin, J. I. Will and society in Bleak House. PMLA 81 1966.
Collins, P. Dickens and Punch. Dickens Stud 3 1967.
Wilkinson, A. Y. Bleak House: from Faraday to Judgment Day. ELH 34 1967.

Hard Times

Hard times, for these times. 1854. No illustrations. Not issued in pts, but pbd weekly in Household Words 1 April to 12 Aug 1854. 1862 (illustr F. Walker), 1865 (Cheap edn), 1868 (Charles Dickens edn). Ed G. B. Shaw 1912; ed J. Richardson 1954 (EL); ed W. W. Watt, New York 1958; ed J. H. Middendor, New York 1960; ed C. Shapiro, New York 1961; ed R. D. Spector, New York 1964; ed G. H. Ford and S. Monod, New York 1966; ed R. Williams, New York 1966.
Cooper, F. F. Hard times: a domestic drama, 1854; [1886] (in Dicks, Standard plays). Produced 14 Aug 1854.
Nation, W. H. C. Under the earth: or the sons of toil. 1871 (in Dicks, Standard plays). Produced 22 April 1867.
[Dixon, W. H.] Athenaeum 12 Aug 1854.
[Forster, J.] Examiner 9 Sept 1854.
[Simpson, R.?] Rambler Oct 1854.
[Sinnett, J.?] Westminster Rev new ser 6 1854.
Br Quart Rev 20 1854.
[Oliphant, M.] Blackwood's Mag April 1855.

Studies

Hodgson, W. B. On the importance of the study of economic science. In Lectures on education delivered at the Royal Institution 1855. *See* GM Sept 1854.
Yates, E. H. and R. B. Brough. Hard times (refinished), by Charles Diggins. In Our miscellany, 1857. Parody.
Ruskin, J. In his Unto this last. Cornhill Mag Aug 1860.
Whipple, E. P. Atlantic Monthly March 1877.
Stumpf, W. Der Dickenssche Roman Hard times: seine Entstehung und seine Tendenzen. Freienwalde 1910.
Leavis, F. R. Hard times: an analytic note. In his Great tradition, 1948. Replies by A. J. A. Waldock, The status of Hard times, Southerly 9 1948; and D. H. Hirsch, Criticism 6 1964.

Hill, T. W. Notes on Hard times. Dickensian 48 1952.
Fielding, K. J. Dickens and the Department of practical art. MLR 48 1953.
— The battle for Preston. Dickensian 50 1954.
— Mill and Gradgrind. Nineteenth-Century Fiction 11 1957.
Boulton, J. T. Charles Knight and Hard times. Dickensian 50 1954.
Morley, M. Hard times on the stage. Dickensian 50 1954.
Williams, R. In his Culture and society 1780–1950, 1958.
Crockett, J. Theme and metaphor in Hard times. Spectrum 6 1962.
Holloway, J. In Dickens and the twentieth century, ed J. Gross and G. Pearson 1962.
Atkinson, F. G. Hard times: themes and motifs. Use of Eng 14 1963.
Carnall, G. D. Dickens, Mrs Gaskell and the Preston strike. Victorian Stud 8 1964.
Lodge, D. The rhetoric of Hard times. In his Language of fiction, 1966.

Little Dorrit

Little Dorrit, with illustrations by H. K. Browne. 20 (as 19) monthly pts, Dec 1855 to June 1857 (variants); 1 vol 1857 (with preface), 1861 (Cheap edn), 1868 (Charles Dickens edn, with rev preface).
Cooper, F. F. Little Dorrit. nd (in Penny Pictorial Plays). Produced 10 Nov 1856.
[Dixon, W. H.] Athenaeum 1 Dec 1855.
Illustr Times 8 Dec 1855.
Monthly Rev of Lit, Science & Art Jan 1856.
[Hanley, E. B.] Blackwood's Mag April 1857.
[Forster, J.] Examiner 13 June 1857.
Leader 27 June 1857.
[Stephen, J. F.] Edinburgh Rev 106 1857. Reply by Dickens, Household Words 1 Aug 1857.
[Stephen, J. F.?] Saturday Rev 4, 18 July 1857. Reply in Leader 11–18 July 1857.
Knickerbocker Aug 1857.
Hollingshead, J. Train Aug 1857.
Eclectic Rev Oct 1861.

Studies

Shaw, G. B. Dickens and Little Dorrit. Dickensian 4 1908.
Hill, T. W. Notes on Little Dorrit. Dickensian 41–2 1945–6.
Booth, B. A. Trollope and Little Dorrit. Trollopian 2 1948.
Burn, W. L. The neo-Barnacles. Nineteenth Century Feb 1948.
Staples, L. C. Shavings from Dickens's workshop iii. Dickensian 49 1953. Cancelled passages from proofs.
Trilling, L. Kenyon Rev 15 1953; also introd to New Oxford illustrated edn 1953, and in his Opposing self, New York 1955.
Morley, M. Little Dorrit, on and off. Dickensian 50 1954. Stage versions.
Leavis, Q. D. A note on literary indebtedness: Dickens, George Eliot, Henry James. Hudson Rev 8 1955.
Manheim, L. F. The law as 'father': an aspect of the Dickens pattern. Amer Imago 12 1955.
Bergler, E. Little Dorrit and Dickens' intuitive knowledge of psychic masochism. Amer Imago 14 1957.
Butt, J. The topicality of Little Dorrit. UTQ 29 1959.
Sherif, N. The Victorian Sunday in Little Dorrit and Thyrza. Cairo Stud in Eng 1960.
McMaster, R. D. Little Dorrit: experience and design. Queen's Quart 67 1961; rptd with annotations in Thought, Toronto 1961.
Wain, J. In Dickens and the twentieth century, ed J. Gross and G. Pearson 1962.
Jump, J. D. Clennam at the Circumlocution Office. Critical Survey 1 1963.
Wilde, A. Mr F's aunt and the analogical structure of Little Dorrit. Nineteenth-Century Fiction 19 1965.

Bell, V. M. Mrs General as Victorian England. Nineteenth-Century Fiction 20 1966.
Hewitt, D. An embarrassment of symbolic riches. London Rev 1 1966.
Herring, P. D. Dickens's monthly number plans for Little Dorrit. MP 64 1966.
Meckier, J. 'Sundry curious variations on the same tune'. Dickens Stud 3 1967.
Reid, J. C. Dickens: Little Dorrit. 1967.

A Tale of Two Cities

A tale of two cities, with illustrations by H. K. Browne. Appeared simultaneously in All the Year Round 30 April to 26 Nov 1859, and in 8 (as 7) monthly pts, June to Dec 1859. 1 vol 1859 (with preface). Variants. Philadelphia [1859] from advance proofs. 1864 (Cheap edn), 1868 (Charles Dickens edn). For full collation of 1859 pts, *see* C. J. Sawyer and F. J. H. Darton, English books vol 2, 1927. Ed E. Wagenknecht, New York 1950; ed E. Johnson, New York 1957; ed M. D. Zabel, New York 1958; ed S. Marcus, New York 1962; ed P. Pickrel, Boston 1962.
The Bastille prisoner: a reading. [1861?] (priv ptd). Arranged by Dickens, but never used. Not rptd.
Taylor, T. A tale of two cities: a drama. [1860] (in Lacy, Acting edition of plays). Dickens assisted in and contributed to this dramatization. Produced 16 Feb 1860.
Rivers, H. J. The tale of two cities: a drama. [1862].
Cooper, F. F. The tale of two cities: or the incarcerated victim of the Bastille. [1886] (in Dicks, Standard plays). Produced 7 July 1860. On authorship of this and Rivers's play, *see* F. R. Cooper, Nothing extenuate: the life of Frederick Fox Cooper, 1964.
[Kent, W. M. C.] Sun 11 Aug 1859.
[Forster, J.] Examiner 10 Dec 1859.
[Stephen, J. F.] Saturday Rev 17 Dec 1859.
Dublin Univ Mag Feb 1860.
Eclectic Rev Oct 1861.
Wills, F. and F. Langbridge. The only way: a dramatic version of A tale of two cities (1899). 1942. *See* J. Martin-Harvey, The story of The only way, Dickensian 23 1927.
Coleman, J. The truth about The dead heart and A tale of two cities. New Rev 1 1889. *See* E. W. Phillips, Watts Phillips: artist and playwright, 1891, and C.R. Dolmetsch, Dickens and The dead heart, Dickensian 55 1959.
Böttger, C. Dickens' historischer Roman A tale of two cities und seine Quellen. Königsberg 1913.
Falconer, J. A. The sources of A tale of two cities. MLN 36 1921.
Milley, H. J. W. Wilkie Collins and A tale of two cities. MLR 34 1939.
Hill, T. W. Notes on A tale of two cities. Dickensian 41 1945.
Morley, M. The stage story of A tale of two cities. Dickensian 51 1955.
Reinhold, H. A tale of two cities und das Publikum. Germanisch-romansche Monatsschrift 36 1955.
Stange, G. R. Dickens and the fiery past. Eng Jnl 46 1957.
Zabel, M. D. The revolutionary fate. In his Craft and character in modern fiction, New York 1957.
Blair, W. The French Revolution and Huckleberry Finn. MP 55 1958. Compares Dickens's treatment.
Manheim, L. A tale of two cities: a study in psychoanalytic criticism. Eng Rev Spring 1959.
Gross, J. In Dickens and the twentieth century, ed J. Gross and G. Pearson 1962.
Davis, E. In his Flint and the flame, Columbia Missouri 1963.
Gregory, M. Old Bailey speech in A tale of two cities. REL 6 1965.
Elliott, R. W. V. Dickens: A tale of two cities. 1966.

Great Expectations

Great expectations. Pbd weekly in All the Year Round 1 Dec 1860 to 3 Aug 1861. 3 vols 1861 (variants). No issue in pts, no illustrations. New York [1860], Philadelphia [1861], from advance proofs. 1862 (illustr M. Stone), 1863 (Cheap edn), 1868 (Charles Dickens edn). Ed G. B. Shaw 1937 (limited edn), 1947; ed E. Davis, New York 1948; ed K. Hayens 1953; ed and tr S. Monod, Paris 1959; ed A. Wilson, New York 1963; ed L. Crompton, Indianapolis 1964; ed A. Calder 1965; ed R. D. McMaster, Toronto 1965. *See* Forster's Life, bk 9 ch 3, for original ending.

Great expectations: a drama, in three stages. Founded on, and compiled from, the story of that name, by Charles Dickens. 1861 (priv ptd). A copyrighting device.

Great expectations: a reading, in three stages. [1861?] (priv ptd). Arranged by Dickens, but never used. Not rptd.

Gilbert, W. S. Great expectations: a drama. Produced 29 May 1871; not pbd. Typescript in BM.

Scott, S. My unknown friend; being a dramatized version of Great expectations. [1883?] (in Dicks, Standard plays). Produced 1872, New York.

[Chorley, H. F.] Athenaeum 13 July 1861.

[Forster, J.] Examiner 20 July 1861.

Saturday Rev 20 July 1861.

[Whipple, E. P.] Atlantic Monthly Sept 1861, Sept 1877.

[Dallas, E. S.] Times 17 Oct 1861.

Eclectic Rev Oct 1861.

[Trotter, L. J.] Dublin Univ Mag Dec 1861.

Br Quart Rev 35 1862.

[Capes, J. M. and J. E. E. D. Acton]. Rambler Jan 1862.

[Oliphant, M.] Blackwood's Mag May 1862, June 1871.

Studies

Gadd, W. L. The Great expectations country. [1929].

Shaw, G. B. Introduction (1937); rptd in A book of prefaces, ed Van Wyck Brooks et al, New York 1949; and in Majority 1931–52, ed H. Hamilton 1952.

Butt, J. Dickens's plan for the conclusion of Great expectations. Dickensian 45 1949.

Carter, J. New Colophon 2 1949. On Court of appeal.

Randall, D. A. Great expectations: its scarcity. Ibid.

Van Ghent, D. In her English novel: form and function, New York 1953. Replies by R. M. V. Kieft and G. Levine, Nineteenth-Century Fiction 15 1965, 18 1964.

Friedman, N. Versions of form in fiction: Great expectations and the Great Gatsby. Accent 14 1954. *See* E. Vasta, Dickensian 60 1964.

Hagan, J. H. Structural patterns in Great expectations. ELH 21 1954.

—— The poor labyrinth: the theme of social injustice in Great expectations. Nineteenth-Century Fiction 9 1955.

Jones, H. M. On rereading Great expectations. Southwest Rev 39 1954.

Stange, G. R. Expectations well lost: Dickens's fable for his time. College Eng Oct 1954.

Connolly, T. E. Technique in Great expectations. PQ 34 1955.

House, H. GBS on Great expectations. In his All in due time, 1955.

Morley, M. Stages of Great expectations. Dickensian 51 1955. Stage versions.

Drew, A. Structure in Great expectations. Dickensian 52 1956.

Hill, T. W. Notes to Great expectations. Dickensian 53–6 1957–60. *See* D. P. Deneau 60 1964.

Edminson, M. The date of the action in Great expectations. Nineteenth-Century Fiction 13 1959.

Nisbet, A. The autobiographical matrix of Great expectations. Victorian Newsletter no 15 1959.

Monod, S. Great expectations a hundred years after. Dickensian 56 1960.

Moynahan, J. The hero's guilt. EC 10 1960. *See* 11 1961.

Clinton-Baddeley, V.C. Wopsle. Dickensian 57 1961.

Fielding, K. J. The critical autonomy of Great expectations. REL 2 1961.

Forker, C. R. The language of hands in Great expectations. Texas Stud in Lit & Lang 3 1961.

Lindberg, J. Individual conscience and social injustice in Great expectations. College Eng Nov 1961.

Partlow, R. B. The moving I: point of view in Great expectations. Ibid.

Ricks, C. In Dickens and the twentieth century, ed J. Gross and G. Pearson 1962.

Stone, H. Fire, hand and gate. Kenyon Rev 24 1962.

Drew, E. In her Novel: a modern guide to fifteen English masterpieces, New York 1963.

Hardy, B. Food and ceremony in Great expectations. EC 13 1963.

Hynes, J. A. Image and symbol in Great expectations. ELH 30 1963.

Killy, W. Der Roman als Märchen. In his Wirklichkeit und Kunstcharakter, Munich 1963.

Lettis, R. and W. E. Morris (ed). Assessing Great expectations. San Francisco [1963]. Anthology of criticism, with bibliography.

Roll-Hansen, D. Characters and contrasts in Great expectations. In M.-S. Røstvig et al, The hidden sense and other essays, Oslo 1963.

Thomas, R. G. Dickens: Great expectations. 1964.

Bell, V. M. Parents and children in Great expectations. Victorian Newsletter no 27 1965.

Gillie, C. In his Character in English literature, 1965.

Meisel, M. The ending of Great expectations. EC 15 1965.

—— Miss Havisham brought to book. PMLA 81 1966.

Peyrouton, N. C. John Wemmick: enigma? Dickens Stud 1 1965.

Barnes, J. Dickens: Great expectations. 1966.

Marcus, P. L. Theme and suspense in Great expectations. Dickens Stud 2 1966.

Ridland, J. M. Huck, Pip and plot. Nineteenth-Century Fiction 20 1966.

Wentersdorf, K. P. Mirror-images in Great expectations. Nineteenth-Century Fiction 21 1967.

Our Mutual Friend

Our mutual friend. With illustrations by Marcus Stone. 20 (as 19) monthly pts, May 1864 to Nov 1865; 2 vols Feb and Nov 1865 (with 'Postscript in lieu of a preface'), 1 vol 1865; 1867 (Cheap edn), 1868 (Charles Dickens edn). Ed M. Engel, New York 1960; ed J. H. Miller, New York 1964.

[Chorley, H. F.] Athenaeum 28 Oct 1865.

[Forster, J.] Examiner 28 Oct 1865.

Eclectic Rev Nov 1865.

Saturday Rev 11 Nov 1865.

[Dallas, E. S.] Times 29 Nov 1865.

Christian Spectator Dec 1865.

Young Englishwoman 9 Dec 1865.

[James, H.] Nation (New York) 21 Dec 1865.

Annual Register for 1865.

Westminster Rev new ser 29 1866.

Studies

Field, K. Our mutual friend in manuscript. Scribner's Monthly Aug 1874.

Boll, E. The plotting of Our mutual friend. MP 42 1944. Prints Dickens's number-plans.

Hill, T. W. Notes on Our mutual friend. Dickensian 43 1947.

Morse, R. Partisan Rev 16 1949.

Quennell, P. C. In his Singular preference, 1952.

Morley, M. Enter Our mutual friend. Dickensian 52 1956. Stage versions.
Monod, S. L'expression dans Our mutual friend: manière ou maniérisme? Etudes Anglaises 10 1957.
Rérat, A. Le romanesque dans L'ami commun. Les Langues Modernes 52 1958.
Stone, H. Dickens and the Jews. Victorian Stud 2 1959.
McMaster, R. D. Birds of prey. Dalhousie Rev 40 1960.
Rosenberg, E. From Shylock to Svengali: Jewish stereotypes in English. Stanford 1960.
Bernard, R. The choral symphony in Our mutual friend. REL 2 1961.
Sharp, Sr M. C. The archetypal feminine. Univ of Kansas City Rev 27–8 1961.
LeVot, A. E. Our mutual friend and the Great Gatsby. Fitzgerald Newsletter 1962.
Kettle, A. In Dickens and the twentieth century, ed J. Gross and G. Pearson 1962.
Oppel, H. Our mutual friend. Die Neueren Sprachen Oct 1962; rptd in Der moderne englische Roman; Interpretationen, ed H. Oppel, Berlin 1965.
Hobsbaum, P. The critics and Our mutual friend. EC 13 1963.
Lanham, R. A. The birds of prey. Victorian Newsletter no 24 1963.
Miyoshi, M. Resolution of identity in Our mutual friend. Victorian Newsletter no 26 1964.
Muir, K. Image and structure in Our mutual friend. E & S 19 1966.
Nelson, H. S. Our mutual friend and Mayhew's London labour and the London poor. Nineteenth-Century Fiction 20 1966.
Shea, F. X. No change of intention in Our mutual friend. Dickensian 63 1967.

The Mystery of Edwin Drood

The mystery of Edwin Drood. With twelve illustrations by S. L. Fildes, and a portrait. In 6 monthly pts, April–Sept 1870 (Dickens's death in June 1870 having cut short the announced 12 pts); 1 vol 1870; Boston 1870 (from advance proofs); [1875] (Charles Dickens edn). Ed V. Starrett, New York 1941; ed 'Michael Innes' (J. I. M. Stewart) 1952; ed C. D. Lewis 1957; ed J. Wright, New York 1961. Forster prints a cancelled ch, How Mr Sapsea ceased to be a member of the Eight Club (Life, bk 11 ch 2). The ch-order in the pts seen through the press by Forster has been criticised by some commentators, as departing from Dickens's intentions.

Stephens, W. Lost: a drama. [1871?]. Rptd as The mystery of Edwin Drood: a drama. nd. Produced 4 Nov 1871.
Dickens, Charles jr, and J. Hatton. The mystery of Edwin Drood: a drama. nd (priv ptd). Written 1880; not produced. *See* letter from Charles Dickens jr, May 1871 in J. F. Daly, Life of Augustin Daly, New York 1917.
Athenaeum 2 April, 17 Sept 1870.
[Broome, F. N.] Times 2 April 1870.
Graphic 9 April 1870.
Every Saturday 7 May 1870.
Academy 14 May 1870.
Saturday Rev 17 Sept 1870.
Guardian 28 Sept 1870.
Spectator 1 Oct 1870.
Lawrenny, H. Academy 22 Oct 1870.
New Monthly Mag 22 Oct 1870.
[Woods, G. B.] Old & New Nov 1870.
Annual Register for 1870.
Dublin Rev new ser 16 1871.
[Oliphant, M.] Blackwood's Mag June 1871.

Studies

The complete Edwin Drood: full text with the history, continuations and solutions 1870–1912, by J. Cuming Walters, with a portrait, illustrations by Sir Luke Fildes R.A., F. G. Kitton, facsimiles and a bibliography. 1912.
Kerr, O. C. The cloven foot: being an adaptation [of Edwin Drood] to American scenes, characters, customs and nomenclature. New York 1870; rev, Piccadilly Annual 1870. Complete adaptation with conclusion and critical introd.
[Morford, H. et al]. John Jasper's secret: a sequel to Dickens' unfinished novel. Philadelphia 1871–2 (in pts), 1871, London 1872; rptd as by W. Collins and C. Dickens jr, New York 1901.
'Vase, Gillan' (Mrs Richard Newton). A great mystery solved: being a sequel to the Mystery of Edwin Drood. 3 vols 1878, 1 vol [1914].
Meynell, A. How Edwin Drood was illustrated. Century Mag Feb 1884.
[Edwards, H. S.] The mystery of Edwin Drood: suggestions for a conclusion. Cornhill Mag March 1884.
Proctor, R. A. Watched by the dead: a loving study of Dickens' half-told tale. 1887.
Lang, A. The puzzle of Dickens' last plot. 1905.
Walters, J. C. Clues to Dickens' Mystery of Edwin Drood. 1905.
Fildes, L. The mysteries of Edwin Drood. Times 3 Nov 1905. Replies by A. Lang and J. W. T. Ley 10, 21 Nov 1905.
Perugini, K. (née Dickens). Edwin Drood and Dickens's last days. Pall Mall Mag June 1906.
Charles, E. Keys to the Drood mystery. 1908, 1915.
J[ackson], H. About Edwin Drood. Cambridge 1911.
Nicoll, W. R. The problem of Edwin Drood. 1912. With bibliography by B. W. Matz, rev from Dickensian 1911.
Fennell, C. A. M. 'The opium-woman' and 'Datchery' in the Mystery of Edwin Drood. Cambridge 1913.
C[risp], W. E. The mystery of Edwin Drood completed. Ed M. L. C. Grant [1914]. 21 additional chs.
Trial of John Jasper for the murder of Edwin Drood: verbatim report of the proceedings by J. W. T. Ley. 1914. Report of a mock trial, G. K. Chesterton as judge, G. B. Shaw as juryman.
Saunders, M. The mystery in the Drood family. Cambridge 1914.
Kavanagh, M. A new solution of the Mystery of Edwin Drood. 1919, 1922 (with Dickens's text).
Edwin Drood number (March). Dickensian 15 1919.
Carden, P. T. The murder of Edwin Drood: an attempted solution. 1920.
Squire, J. C. The great unfinished. In his Life and letters, 1920.
Boyd, A. A new angle on the Drood mystery. Washington Univ Stud Humanistic Ser 9 1921.
Dickens' Mystery of Edwin Drood, completed by a loyal Dickensian. 1927.
Matz, W. A bibliography of Edwin Drood 1911–28. Dickensian 24–5 1928–9.
Dexter, W. New light on Edwin Drood (the illustrations). Sphere 9 Feb 1929.
Lehmann-Haupt, C. F. New facts concerning Edwin Drood. Dickensian 25 1929.
—— Studies on Edwin Drood. Dickensian 31–3 1935–7.
Duffield, H. John Jasper, strangler. Amer Bookman Feb 1930.
—— The Macbeth motif in Edwin Drood. Dickensian 30 1934.
Harris, E. John Jasper's gatehouse: a sequel. Rochester 1931.
Hopkins, A. A. A notable Drood collection. Dickensian 28 1932.
Graeme, B. Epilogue. 1933. A novel treating the Drood mystery as the basis of a detective story.

Roe, F. G. The Edwin Drood mystery: an American gift to London. Connoisseur 104 1939.
Wilson, E. The Mystery of Edwin Drood. New Republic 8 April 1940; rev in his Wound and the bow, Boston 1941.
Hill, T. W. Drood time in Cloisterham. Dickensian 40 1941.
—— Notes on Edwin Drood. Ibid.
Pritchett, V. S. In his Living novel, 1946.
Mills, W. W. Historical and critical notes on Edwin Drood. [1947].
MacVicar, H. M. The Datchery assumption: expostulation. Nineteenth-Century Fiction 4 1950. Reply by R. M. Baker, ibid.
Baker, R. M. The Drood murder case. Berkeley 1951.
Ford, G. H. Dickens's notebook and Edwin Drood. Nineteenth-Century Fiction 6 1952. *See* F. Aylmer and P. Pakenham, Dickensian 51 1955.
Fielding, K. J. The dramatization of Edwin Drood. Theatre Notebook 7 1953. Reply by E. Jones-Evans 8 1954.
—— Edwin Drood and Governor Eyre. Listener 25 Dec 1953.
Bleifuss, W. W. A re-examination of Edwin Drood. Dickensian 50–1 1954–5.
Morley, M. Stage solutions to the Mystery. Dickensian 53 1957.
Stelzmann, R. Ein neuer Lösungsversuch. Archiv 193 1957.
Cockshut, A. O. J. In Dickens and the twentieth century, ed J. Gross and G. Pearson 1962.
Cox, A. J. The morals of Edwin Drood. Dickensian 58 1962.
—— The Drood remains (the manuscript). Dickens Stud 2 1966.
—— 'If I hide my watch—'. Dickens Stud 3 1967.
Aylmer, F. The Drood case. 1964.
Collins, P. Inspector Bucket visits the Princess Puffer. Dickensian 60 1964.
Mitchell, C. The mystery of Edwin Drood: the interior and exterior of self. ELH 33 1966.
Cohen, J. B. Artists and artistry in Edwin Drood. Dickens Stud 3 1967.

Christmas Books

Christmas books. 1852 (Cheap edn of Works: in 17 weekly pts, 4 monthly pts, June–Sept 1852). Frontispiece by J. Leech. Collects the 5 books, with a preface. 1859 (Library edn); 1868 (Charles Dickens edn, with rev preface); 1878; ed C. Shorter, illustr C. Green and L. Rossi, 5 pts [1912]. First collected New York 1849 (without Haunted man).
A Christmas carol, in prose: being a ghost story of Christmas, with illustrations by John Leech. 1843. The variants of the title-page and end-papers of the 'first issue' are a matter of controversy. *See* J. C. Eckel, The first editions of Charles Dickens, 1932; C. J. Sawyer and F. J. H. Darton, English books vol 2, 1927, ch 7; Bookman (London) Dec 1931; TLS 14, 28 Jan 1932.
A Christmas carol. Ed facs (from original ms) F. G. Kitton 1890, 1897 (without introd), 1906; ed facs (from original edn) G. K. Chesterton and B. W. Matz 1922; E. Johnson, New York 1956. Principal later illustr edns: S. Eytinge, Boston 1869; Charles Pears [1905]; John Leech and F. Barnard (from Household edn of Works) 1907 (introd by W. P. Treloar).
A Christmas carol: reading edition. 1858, nd, rev Boston 1868.
[Hewitt, H.] A Christmas ghost story. 1844 (Peter Parley's Library). Plagiarization.
Barnett, C. Z. A Christmas carol: or the miser's warning. [1844] (in Duncombe, Acting edition), [1872] (in T. H. Lacy, Acting edition of plays), [1886] (in Dicks, Standard plays). Produced 5 Feb 1844.
Stirling, E. A Christmas carol: or past, present and future. [1844?]. Produced 4 Feb 1844.
Morning Chron 9 Dec 1843.
Athenaeum 23 Dec 1843.
Britannia 23 Dec 1843.
[Forster, J.] Examiner 23 Dec 1843.
Illustr London News 23 Dec 1843.
Bell's Weekly Messenger 30 Dec 1843.
[Russell, C. W.] Dublin Rev 15 1843.
[Blanchard, S. L.?] Ainsworth's Mag Jan 1844.
[Hood, T.] Hood's Mag Jan 1844.
[Thackeray, W. M.] Fraser's Mag Feb 1844.
GM Feb 1844.
Illustr Mag Feb 1844.
Tait's Mag Feb 1844.
[Starkey, D. P.] Dublin Univ Mag April 1844.
Westminster Rev 41 1844 (review of R. H. Horne).
Jaques, E. T. Charles Dickens in Chancery: his proceedings in respect of the Christmas carol. 1914.
Fiedler, F. Dickens' Gebrauch der rhythmischen Prosa im Christmas carol. Archiv 139 1919.
—— Wie Dickens das Christmas carol feite. Archiv 144 1922.
Newton, A. E. The greatest book in the world and other papers. Boston [1925]. Facs and criticism.
—— Rare books, mss etc collected by the late A. Edward Newton. Parke-Bernet Galleries, 3 vols New York 1941. Proof-sheets of A Christmas carol in vol 1.
Osborne, E. A. The facts about A Christmas carol. 1937 (priv ptd). Bibliographical.
Legal documents relating to the piracy of A Christmas carol. Dickensian 34 1938.
Calhoun, P. and H. J. Heaney. Dickens's Christmas carol after a hundred years: a study in bibliographical evidence. PBSA 39 1945.
Brown, J. M. Ghouls and holly. In his Seeing more things, 1948.
Morley, M. Curtain up on A Christmas carol. Dickensian 47 1951. Stage versions.
Butt, J. A Christmas carol: its origin and design. Dickensian 51 1955.
Gimbel, R. The earliest state of the first edition of Dickens' A Christmas carol. Princeton Univ Lib Chron 19 1958.
Todd, W. B. A Christmas carol. Book Collector 10 1961. Bibliographical.
Morris, W. E. The conversion of Scrooge. Stud in Short Fiction 3 1965.

The chimes: a goblin story of some bells that rang an old year out and a new year in. 1845 (for 1844). Illustr Daniel Maclise, John Leech, Richard Doyle and Clarkson Stanfield. Slight variants. Illustr John Leech and F. Barnard, New York 1887; illustr Arthur Rackham, introd E. Wagenknecht 1931 (priv ptd).
The chimes: reading edition. 1858, [1868?] (rev and priv ptd with Sikes and Nancy, from Oliver Twist).
Lemon, M. and G. A. à Beckett. The chimes: a goblin drama in four quarters. [1845] (in B. N. Webster, Acting national drama); [1887] (in Dicks, Standard plays). Produced 19 Dec 1844; authorized by Dickens.
Stirling, E. The chimes; in three peals. nd. Produced 26 Dec 1844.
[Planché, M. A.] Old Jolliffe: not a goblin story, by the spirit of a little bell awakened by The chimes. 1845.
—— The sequel to Old Jolliffe, written in the same spirit, by the same spirit. 1849.
The wedding bells: an echo of The chimes. 1846 (for 1845).
Morning Chron 17 Dec 1844.

[Chorley, H. F.] Athenaeum 21 Dec 1844.
[Russell, C. W.] Dublin Rev Dec 1844.
[Hunt, L. and J. Forster] Examiner 21 Dec 1844.
Illustr London News 21 Dec 1844.
Literary Gazette 21–8 Dec 1844.
Mirror of Lit 21 Dec 1844.
Bell's Life in London 22 Dec 1844.
Northern Star 21, 28 Dec 1844.
Spectator 21 Dec 1844.
Tablet 21 Dec 1844.
Times 25 Dec 1844.
Christian Remembrancer Jan 1845.
Douglas Jerrold's Shilling Mag Jan 1845.
Eclectic Rev Jan 1845.
Economist 18 Jan 1845.
[Forster, J.] Edinburgh Rev 81 1845.
[Hood, T.] Hood's Mag Jan 1845.
Tait's Mag Jan 1845.
Parker's London Mag Feb 1845.
'Bon Gautier' (Martin, T.) Tait's Mag April 1845.
[Cleghorn, T. ?] North Br Rev 3 1845.
Morley, M. Ring up the Chimes. Dickensian 47 1951. Stage versions.
Wagenknecht, E. In his Mr Dickens and the scandal-mongers, Norman Oklahoma 1965.

The cricket on the hearth: a fairy tale of home. 1846 (for 1845). Illustr Daniel Maclise, John Leech, Richard Doyle, Clarkson Stanfield and Edwin Landseer. Rptd from stereotype plates, 1887; illustr John Leech and Frederick Barnard 1887; introd Henry Morley 1887, 1904; illustr Hugh Thomson, introd W. de la Mare 1933 (priv ptd).
The cricket on the hearth: reading edition. 1858 nd.
Smith, A. R. The cricket on the hearth: a drama, in three acts, by the express permission of the author. [1845], [1855] (in Dicks, Standard plays); nd (in S. French, American edn). Produced 20 Dec 1845.
Stirling, E. The cricket on the hearth, a fairy tale of home. [1847] (in B. N. Webster, Acting national drama). Produced 31 Dec 1845.
Townsend, W. T. The cricket on the hearth: a fairy tale of home in three chirps. [1846] (Duncombe, Acting edition); nd (in T. H. Lacy, Acting edition of plays). Produced 5 Jan 1846.
Athenaeum 20 Dec 1845.
[Thackeray, W. M.] Morning Chron 24 Dec 1845.
[Forster, J.] Examiner 27 Dec 1845.
John Bull 27 Dec 1845.
Literary Gazette 27 Dec 1845.
Pictorial Times 27 Dec 1845.
Spectator 27 Dec 1845.
Times 27 Dec 1845.
Chambers's Jnl 17 Jan 1845.
Oxford & Cambridge Rev Jan 1846.
Macphail's Edinburgh Ecclesiastical Jnl Feb 1846.
Union Mag Feb 1846.
The critic on the art (of humbug) v. The cricket on the hearth. Mephystopheles 27 Dec 1845, 10, 17, 24, 31 Jan 1846.
Morley, M. The cricket on the stage. Dickensian 48 1952.
Fielding, K. J. The manuscript of The cricket on the hearth. N & Q July 1952.

The battle of life: a love story. 1846. Dickens's name on ptd title-page, not on engraved. Illustr Daniel Maclise, John Leech, Richard Doyle and Clarkson Stanfield. Variants.
Smith, A.[R.] The battle of life, dramatised from early proofs of the work, by the express permission of the author. [1846], [1888] (in Dicks, Standard plays), [1890]. Produced 21 Dec 1846.
Stirling, E. The battle of life: a drama. [1847 ?] (in Duncombe, Acting edition). Produced Jan 1847.
Morning Chron 24 Dec 1846.
[Marston, J. W.] Athenaeum 26 Dec 1846.
Daily News 26 Dec 1846.
[Forster, J.] Examiner 26 Dec 1846.
Literary Gazette 26 Dec 1846.
Spectator 26 Dec 1846.
Dublin Univ Mag Jan 1847.
Tait's Mag Jan 1847.
Times 2 Jan 1847.
[Patmore, C. ?] North Br Rev 7 1847.
Morley, M. The battle of life in the theatre. Dickensian 48 1952.
Gibson. F. A. A reconsideration of A battle of life. Dickensian 58 1962.
Todd, W. B. The battle of life: round six. Book Collector 15 1966. Bibliographical.

The haunted man and the ghost's bargain: a fancy for Christmas time. 1848. Illustr John Leech, Clarkson Stanfield, John Tenniel and F. Stone. Variant. W. C. M. Kent, Dickens as a reader, 1872, and Sotheran (Jan 1879) record a copy of the 1848 edn prepared by Dickens as a reading; but this reading was never used or pbd.
Times 21 Dec 1848.
[Marston, J. W.] Athenaeum 23 Dec 1848.
[Forster, J.] Examiner 23 Dec 1848.
Literary Gazette 23 Dec 1848.
Spectator 23 Dec 1848.
Daily News 25 Dec 1848.
Morning Chron 25 Dec 1848.
Macphail's Edinburgh Ecclesiastical Jnl Jan 1849.
Man in the Moon Jan 1849.
Sharpe's London Mag Jan 1849.
Tait's Mag Jan 1849.
Harte, F. B. The haunted man: a Christmas story, by Ch-r- -s D-c-k-n-s. In his Condensed novels, New York 1870.
Morley, M. Pepper and The haunted man. Dickensian 48 1952. Stage versions.
Stone, H. Dickens's artistry and The haunted man. South Atlantic Quart 61 1962.

Christmas Stories

The items collected under the title Christmas Stories *in most edns of the* Collected works *appeared in* Household Words 21 Dec 1850, *the* Extra Christmas Numbers *of* Household Words 1851–8 (*'containing the amount of one regular number and a half'*), *and the* Extra Christmas Numbers *of* All the Year Round 1859–67 (*'containing the amount of two ordinary numbers'*). *All these* Numbers *contained contributions by other authors also. Dickens's contributions to the 1850, 1852 and 1853 nos were rptd in* Reprinted pieces 1858, *and many edns of the* Christmas stories *exclude these (and his 1851 contribution) or exclude his 1850 contribution (as an essay, not a story). His contributions have frequently been rptd singly or in groups of two or three.*

Christmas stories from Household Words (1850–8). 9 pts [1859], 1 vol [1860].
Household Words Christmas stories 1851–58. 1868, 9 vols 1906.
Christmas stories from All the Year Round. 9 pts [1868?], 1 vol 1868, 9 vols [1907].
Christmas stories from Household Words and All the Year Round. 5 vols 1898. This and all the above items arc reprints of the complete Extra Christmas nos.
Christmas stories from Household Words and All the Year Round (1854–67). 1874 (Charles Dickens edn of Works, with 8 illustrations), 1876 (Illustrated Library edn of Works, with 14 illustrations).
Morley, M. Plays from the Christmas Numbers of Household Words. Dickensian 51 1955.
—— All the Year Round plays. Dickensian 52 1956.

Household Words
1850. A Christmas tree. The whole issue is called simply Christmas number.
1851. What Christmas is as we grow older. Whole issue called Extra number for Christmas.
1852. The poor relation's story; The child's story. In A round of stories by the Christmas fire.
1853. The schoolboy's story; Nobody's story. In Another round of stories by the Christmas fire.
1854. The first poor traveller; The road. In The seven poor travellers. *See Readings, below.*
Cooper, F. F. The seven poor travellers, or Heart-strings and purse-strings. 1855. Produced 12 March 1855.
Harris, E. Richard Watts's charity. Rochester 1906.
1855. The guest; The boots; The bill. In The Holly-Tree Inn. *See Readings, below.*
Webster, B. Holly tree inn: a drama. nd (in Dicks, Standard plays). Produced 31 Dec 1855.
1856. The wreck of the Golden Mary. The Wreck, excluding John Steadiman's account. *See Poems, doubtful and supposititious, below.*
1857. The perils of certain English prisoners, and their treasure in women, children, silver and jewels. Chs 1, 3 by Dickens, ch 2 by Wilkie Collins.
[Lucas, S.] Times 4 Dec 1857.
Saturday Rev 26 Dec 1857.
1858. Going into society; Let at last (in collaboration with Wilkie Collins). In A house to let. *See Readings, below* (Mr Chops the dwarf).
Saturday Rev 25 Dec 1858.

All the Year Round
1859. The mortals in the house; The guest in Master B.'s room; The ghost in the corner room; connecting links. In The haunted house.
1860. A message from the sea. Ch 1 and opening of ch 3 by Dickens, chs 2 and 5 by Dickens and Wilkie Collins.
A message from the sea: a drama in three acts; an outline of the plot. By Charles Dickens and Wilkie Collins. 1861 (for 1860). Persons of the drama and outline of the plot only. Pbd for copyright purposes. *See* M. Morley, above.
Brougham, J. A message from the sea (a drama founded on Charles Dickens's tale). [1883] (in Dicks, Standard plays). Not produced.
Carlton, W. J. Captain Morgan—alias Jorgan. Dickensian 53–4 1957–8.
1861. Tom Tiddler's ground. Chs 1, 6, 7.
1862. Somebody's luggage. 1, His leaving it till called for; 2, His boots; 7, His brown-paper parcel; 10, His wonderful end.
1863. Mrs Lirriper's lodgings. Chs 1, 7. A reading was priv ptd nd but never used or rptd.
[Dallas, E. S.] Times 3 Dec 1863.
Saturday Rev 12 Dec 1863.
1864. Mrs Lirriper's legacy. Chs 1, 7.
[Dallas, E. S.] Times 2 Dec 1864.
Saturday Rev 10 Dec 1864.
1865. Doctor Marigold's Prescriptions. Chs 1, 7. Doctor Marigold: a reading in two parts. nd (priv ptd), Boston 1868 etc.
[Dallas, E. S.] Times 6 Dec 1864.
Saturday Rev 16 Dec 1864.
1866. Mugby Junction. Barbox Brothers; Barbox Brothers & Co; Main line, The boy at Mugby; No 1 Branch line, The signal man. *See Readings, below.*
'Lyulph'. A girl at a railway junction's reply. [1867].
Astle, J. The gal at Mugby. Cheltenham 1867 (priv ptd).
1867. No thoroughfare. By Charles Dickens and Wilkie Collins. Overture and Act iii entirely by Dickens, Act ii entirely by Collins. Other acts in collaboration. *See Plays, below.*
Slow thoroughfare. By Warles Chickens and Chilky Dollins. Banter 23 Dec 1867.
No thoroughfare: the book in eight acts. Mask Feb 1868. Parody.
No throughfare. By C—s D—s, Bellamy Brownjohn and Domby. Boston 1868. A parody with reference also to Dickens's readings and American notes.
Lequel, L. Identity, or no thoroughfare: a drama. New York nd. Produced New York 6 Jan 1868.
Times 27 Dec 1867.

Readings

For reading-texts of individual items, see under Novels, Christmas books, Christmas stories, above.

The poor traveller; Boots at the Holly-tree inn; and Mrs Gamp. 1858 (priv ptd), 1858, nd.
Barbox brothers; The boy at Mugby; and The signalman: three readings, each in one chapter. [1866] (priv ptd).
Bardell and Pickwick; Mr Chops the dwarf; Mr Bob Sawyer's party: three readings, each in one chapter. nd (priv ptd).
The readings of Dickens, as condensed by himself. Boston 1868, London 1883, 1907. 10 readings. Items also issued separately Boston 1867–8.
Readings from the works of Dickens as arranged and read by himself. Ed J. Hollingshead. 1907. 10 readings.
Times 2 Jan 1854, 8 Jan 1869.
Leader 4 July 1857.
Saturday Rev 19 June 1858, 9 May 1868.
[Hollingshead, J.] Critic 4 Sept 1858; rptd in his Today vol 2, 1865 and his Miscellanies vol 3, 1874; also as Introd, above.
Manchester Guardian 1861–7; Dickensian 34 1938.
Harper's Weekly 28 Dec 1867.
Yates, E. Tinsley's Mag Feb 1869.
Graphic 12 Feb 1870.
Illustr London News 19 March 1870.
Field, K. Pen photographs of Dickens's readings. Boston [1868], 1871 (rev and enlarged). *See* her diary in L. Whiting, Kate Field: a record, 1899.
Kent, W. C. M. Dickens as a reader. 1872.
Dolby, G. Dickens as I knew him: the story of the reading tours 1866–70. 1885, 1912. *See* J. G. Ollé, Dickens and Dolby, Dickensian 54 1958.
Murray, D. C. Recollections. 1908. Ch 4.
Stonehouse, J. H. A first bibliography of the reading editions of Dickens's works. In his edn of Sikes and Nancy, 1921.
Dexter, W. For one night only: an account of the famous readings. Dickensian 37–8 1941–2.
— The readings in America. Dickensian 38 1942.
— ('L. A. Kennethe'). The unique reading books. Dickensian 39 1943.
Murphy, T. and R. Dickens as a professional reader. Quart Jnl of Speech 33 1947.
Fielding, K. J. Dickens and Thomas C. Evans. N & Q March 1951. *See* G. G. Grubb, Dickensian 48 1952.
Williams, E. Readings from Dickens. Introd B. Darwin 1953 (limited edn), 1954. Williams's Notes on the adaptations compare his versions with Dickens's.
Murphy, T. Interpretation in the Dickens period. Quart Jnl of Speech 41 1955.
Gordan, J. D. (ed). Mrs Gamp: a facsimile of the author's prompt copy. New York 1956. Discusses Dickens's methods.
— Reading for profit: the other career of Dickens. BNYPL Sept 1958. Also pbd separately.

Plays and Poems

Collections

The plays and poems of Dickens. with a few miscellanies in prose now first collected. Ed R. H. Shepherd 2 vols 1885. An earlier edn, 2 vols 1882, containing No thoroughfare, was withdrawn through copyright difficulties.

Poems and verses. Ed F. G. Kitton 1903.

Plays and poems. In Collected papers vol 2, 1937 (Nonesuch). The fullest collection.

Plays

O'Thello: an operatic burlesque (unpbd). Performed privately by Dickens's family and friends, 1833. Facs of fragments, Dickensian 13 1917, 26 1930. Included in Nonesuch, Collected papers, above.

The village coquettes: a comic opera in two acts, the music by John Hullah. 1836, Leipzig 1845 (in L. Hilsenberg, Modern English comic theatre), Amsterdam [1868?] (in Modern English comedies and farces no 1); rptd [1878] (facs), 1883 (in Dicks, Standard plays). First production, 6 Dec 1836, St James's Theatre.

Songs, choruses and concerted pieces in the operatic burletta of the village coquettes. 1837.

The following songs were pbd separately (Hullah's music, Dickens's words): The child and the old man 1836, Some folks who have grown old 1836, How beautiful at eventide 1836, No light bound of stag 1836, My fair home 1851, The cares of the day 1858, Autumn leaves 1871.

Reviews in Dickensian 30 1934.

The strange gentleman: a comic burletta, in two acts, by 'Boz', first performed at the St James's Theatre on Thursday September 29 1836. 1837 (with frontispiece by 'Phiz'), 1871 (without frontispiece). Variants; in some copies extra frontispiece by F. W. Pailthorpe. J. C. Eckel, The first editions of Dickens, 1932, mentions another reprint but gives no data.

The strange gentleman. [1883] (in Dicks, Standard plays), 2 pts 1904, 1928 (priv ptd, illustr with reproductions from original drawings by John Leech, John Orlando Parry et al). Dickens's first publicly produced play; a version as a short story, The great Winglebury duel, appeared in Sketches by Boz 1st ser 1836.

Adrian, A. A. The demise of the strange gentleman. Dickensian 51 1955. On the 1873 revival.

Hill, T. W. Dickens and his ugly duckling. Dickensian 37 1941.

Is she his wife? or something singular: a comic burletta in one act. [1872?]. The only known 1st edn. A unique copy of the real 1st edn—nd, presumably about 1837–was destroyed by fire in 1879. A reprint of the text had been made from it and was issued at Boston in 1877. Play produced at St James's Theatre London 6 March 1837. *See* R. H. Shepherd, A lost work of Dickens, Pen Oct 1880, and J. C. Eckel, The first editions of Dickens, 1932.

The lamplighter: a farce by Charles Dickens (1838) now first printed from a manuscript in the Forster Collection at the South Kensington Museum. 1879; ed W. L. Phelps, New York 1926 (with The lamplighter's story). Discovered and ptd by R. H. Shepherd. Never produced or ptd in Dickens's lifetime. Written as a farce for Macready (*see* his Diaries), but withdrawn. The substance was turned into a tale and included in The Pic Nic Papers as The lamplighter's story.

Mr Nightingale's diary: a farce in one act, by — [Dickens and Mark Lemon]. 1851 (priv ptd), Boston 1877 (some copies with frontispiece by F. W. Pailthorpe). Produced at Devonshire House 16 May 1851, both authors in the cast.

Horne, R. H. Bygone celebrities, II: Mr Nightingale's diary. GM May 1871.

Collins, W. Wilkie. The lighthouse. Not pbd? Acted at Dickens's Tavistock House Theatre, 19 June 1856. Prologue and Song of the wreck by Dickens; text of play rev by him during rehearsal. Ms (incomplete) in Berg Collection, New York Public Library.

The frozen deep: a drama, in three acts, by Wilkie Collins; not published. 1866. 'Not published' is part of title-page. The play was produced at Dickens's house, 6 Jan 1857; in supervising rehearsals he rewrote much of the play himself. *See* introd to Collins's version as a story-reading, Readings and writings in America 2 vols 1874.

Berger, F. Letter about The frozen deep. Dickensian 10 1914.

Brannan, R. L. (ed). Under the management of Mr Charles Dickens: his production of The frozen deep. Ithaca 1966. Prints the 1857 ms prompt-copy, shows the extent of Dickens's contributions, and gives details of the production, reviews etc.

No thoroughfare: a drama in five acts (altered from the Christmas story for performance on the stage), by Charles Dickens and Wilkie Collins [with the collaboration of C. S. Fechter]. 1867. Produced 26 Dec 1867. Possibly variants. *See Christmas Numbers 1867, above.*

Fitzgerald, S. J. A. Dickens and the St James's Theatre. Dickensian 16 1920.

Dexter, W. Dickens's early dramatic productions (from The strange gentleman to The lamplighter). Dickensian 33–4 1937–8.

Morley, M. Plays and sketches by Boz. Dickensian 52 1956.

Rosenberg, M. The dramatist in Dickens. JEGP 59 1960.

Harvey, P. D. A. Dickens as playwright. BM Quart 24 1961.

The Lord Chamberlain's copies of Dickens's plays. Appendix G, Letters of Dickens, ed M. House and G. Storey, vol 1 Oxford 1965.

See below (Biographies; Special periods and aspects), for studies of Dickens and the stage by T. E. Pemberton, S. J. A. Fitzgerald, A. Woolcott, J. B. van Amerongen, K. König and F. D. Fawcett.

Poems

Dexter, W. The love romance of Dickens, told in his letters to Maria Beadnell. 1936. Includes 4 poems written in Maria Beadnell's album 1829–31, and The bill of fare (1831).

Suzannet, A. de. Maria Beadnell's album. Dickensian 31 1935.

A fable (not a Gay one). Lines written in Ellen Beard's album 1834. Dickensian 28 1932. *See* Letters to Thomas Beard, below.

Song of the month no viii (Of all the months in the twelve that fly). Bentley's Miscellany Aug 1837. Unsigned. *See* W. Dexter, The song of August, Dickensian 35 1939, and W. J. Carlton, The death of Mary Hogarth, Dickensian 63 1967.

To Ariel. 1838. Written in Priscilla Horton's album 26 Oct 1838. Ariel was one of her stage-rôles. *See* Dickensian 30 1934.

The loving ballad of Lord Bateman. Illustrated by George Cruikshank. 1839, 1841, 1870 (rev, by Dickens?). On authorship, *see* A. L. Haight, Dickens tries to remain anonymous, Colophon new graphic ser no 1 1939. Dickens wrote the preface and notes and adapted at least part of the text, based on a traditional ballad.

Examiner 1841. The fine old English gentleman (7 Aug), The quack doctor's prescription (14 Aug), Subjects for painters: after Peter Pindar (21 Aug). Signed W. *See* Forster, Life bk 2 ch 12.

Prologue to The patrician's daughter: a tragedy in five acts by J. Westland Marston. Produced 10 Dec 1842, Drury Lane; pbd 1841 without the Prologue. Prologue in Sunday Times 11 Dec 1842 (and other jnls); another version in Letters vol 1, 1880.

A word in season. In Keepsake, ed Countess of Blessington 1844. Signed Charles Dickens.

Prologue to The elder brother, by Fletcher and Massinger, spoken by Miss Kelly at a benefit performance at her theatre by Dickens's company, 3 Jan 1846.

Daily News 1846. The British lion: a new song but an old story (24 Jan, signed Catnach). The hymn of the Wiltshire labourers (14 Feb, signed Charles Dickens). The Hymn rptd in Gems from the spirit mine, pbd by the League of Universal Brotherhood, 1850.

Elegy written in a country churchyard. [1849?]. Parody. *See* Dickensian 16 1920 (facs).

Starr, H. W. Dickens's parody of Gray's Elegy. Dickensian 51 1955.

New song. Signed T. Sparkler. In letter to Mark Lemon, 25 June 1849.

Prologue ('Prologues and epilogues, in good old days'), hitherto unpublished. Dickensian 37 1941. To Jerrold's The housekeeper?

Doubtful or Supposititious Play and Poems

The stratagems of Rozanza: a Venetian comedietta by C. J. H. Dickens. 1828. The existence of this ms, not in Dickens's handwriting, has been reported; apparently unpbd, its authenticity not established. Probably a trn of a Goldoni play. *See* Dickensian 22 1926 and J. W. T. Ley, note to his edn (1928) of Forster's Life, bk 1 ch 4.

Household Words 1850–1. Hiram Power's Greek slave (26 Oct 1850); Aspire! (25 Jan 1851). These poems, often attributed to Dickens through a misunderstanding of the Household Words contributors' book, are by E. B. Browning and another. *See* A. Lohrli, Greek slave mystery, N & Q Feb 1966.

The blacksmith. All the Year Round 30 April 1859. Attributed to Dickens on the evidence of Rev T. B. Lawes (Forster's Life bk 8 ch 5), but challenged by F. G. Kitton, Literature 15 Sept 1900, referring to the 'office' set of All the Year Round (now lost). *See* W. Miller and J. Suddaby, Dickensian 11 1915.

Child's hymn. In The wreck of The Golden Mary, Household Words Christmas no 1856. Attributed to Dickens on evidence of a letter to Rev R. H. Davies (Forster's Life bk 11 ch 3), probably misunderstood. *See* B. W. Matz, Dickensian 12 1916.

Periodicals Edited by Dickens

Dickens contributed many items to his periodicals and, particularly over his weeklies (in which almost all contributions were unsigned), accepted responsibility for the tenor as well as the quality of whatever he published; so he often silently rewrote or otherwise amended his colleagues' work. Many stories and essays by other contributors were rptd, especially in America, as his work. See B. W. Matz, Writings wrongly attributed to Dickens, Chambers's Jnl 16 Aug 1924, *rptd in* Dickensian 21 1925, *though Matz's list is incomplete.*

Bentley's Miscellany. Monthly from Jan 1837. Dickens was its first editor and resigned Feb 1839. Contents included Oliver Twist and sundry shorter items, mostly signed.

Prospectus for Bentley's Miscellany. Ptd from Dickens's ms. Appendix D: Letters of Dickens, ed M. House and G. Storey vol 1, Oxford 1965.

Extraordinary Gazette. Speech of his Mightiness on opening the second number of Bentley's Miscellany. 1837. Pamphlet, illustr H. K. Browne. Rptd with illustration, Dickensian 26 1930, 34 1938.

Daily News. From 21 Jan 1846. Dickens was its first editor and resigned 9 Feb 1846. Contents included his Travelling letters, rptd as Pictures from Italy, also other contributions, mostly signed. Facs of opening no pbd with Jubilee no, 21 Jan 1896. Dummy issue 19 Jan 1846 (rare) with contributions by Dickens.

Household Words. Weekly, 30 March 1850 to 28 May 1859, when it was incorporated into All the Year Round. Also in monthly pts and 19 half-yearly vols. Cheap edn, 19 vols 1868–73. Charles Dickens jr revived the magazine and its title 1881. Contents included A child's history of England, Hard times, Christmas stories and numerous unsigned essays.

The Household Narrative of Current Events. Monthly, April 1850 to Dec 1855; nos for Jan-March 1850 pbd retrospectively. Bound, 6 vols. A news supplement to Household Words.

The Household Words Almanac. Annually, 1856, 1857.

All the Year Round. Weekly from 30 April 1859. Also in monthly pts and half-yearly vols. Edited by Dickens until his death, and by Charles Dickens jr thereafter; incorporated 1895 in the revived Household Words. Bound, 20 vols 1859–68 (with General index, 1868); new ser 1868–88. Contents included A tale of two cities, The uncommercial traveller, Great expectations, Christmas stories and some unsigned essays.

Novels and tales reprinted from Household Words, conducted by Charles Dickens. 11 vols Leipzig 1856–9 (Tauchnitz).

New weekly illustrated periodical, Once a Week. 1859. Prospectus by Bradbury & Evans, with a statement, Mr Charles Dickens and his late publishers, about their differences with him.

Wills, W. H. Old leaves gleaned from Household Words. 1860. Dedication acknowledges Dickens's helpful revisions. One essay, A plated article, appears both here and in Dickens' Reprinted pieces, 1858.

Studies

Grant, J. The newspaper press. 2 vols 1871. Vol 2 ch 3, The Daily News.

Dickens, Charles jr. Dickens as an editor. Eng Illustr Mag Aug 1889.

Fitzgerald, P. H. Memoirs of an author. 2 vols 1894. Vol 1 ch 1, Dickens and Household Words. *See* Fitzgerald in Biographies, below.

—— Household Words memories. Household Words 28 March 1903.

—— Some memories of Dickens and Household Words. In The Dickens souvenir, ed D. C. Calthrop and M. Pemberton 1912.

Crowe, J. Reminiscences of thirty-five years. 1895. On the Daily News.

McCarthy, J. and J. R. Robinson. The Daily News jubilee. 1896. Chs 1–2.

Hollingshead, J. Fifty years of Household Words. Household Words Jubilee no 26 May 1900. *See* Hollingshead in Personal recollections, below.

Thomas, W. M. An old Household Words man. Household Words 28 March 1903.

Robinson, J. R. Fifty years of Fleet Street. 1904.

Lehmann, R. C. (ed). Dickens as editor: letters written by him to W. H. Wills, his sub-editor. 1912.

Escott, T. H. S. Literature and journalism. Fortnightly Rev Jan 1912.

Quail, J. Dickens and the Daily News. Nineteenth Century Oct 1920.

Van Dyke, C. A talk with Dickens's office-boy. Bookman (New York) March 1921.

Dexter, W. Bentley's Miscellany. Dickensian 33 1937.

— Dickens's contributions to Household Words. Dickensian 35 1939. Articles of which Dickens was part-author.

Rust, S. J. The first number of the Daily News. Dickensian 34 1938.

Grubb, G. G. Dickens's editorial methods. SP 40 1943.

— The editorial policies of Dickens. PMLA 58 1943.

— Dickens's influence as an editor. SP 42 1945.

— Dickens and the Daily News: the origin of the idea. In Booker memorial studies, ed H. Shine, Chapel Hill 1950.

— Dickens and the Daily News. Nineteenth-Century Fiction 6–7 1952–3.

— The American edition of All the Year Round. PBSA 47 1953.

— Dickens rejects. Dickensian 52 1956.

Buckler, W. E. Dickens's success with Household Words. Dickensian 46 1950.

— Household Words in America. PBSA 45 1951.

— Dickens the paymaster. PMLA 66 1951. *See* G. G. Grubb, Dickensian 51 1955.

Collins, P. A. W. 'Keep Household Words imaginative!' Dickensian 52 1956.

— Dickens's periodicals: articles on education. [Leicester] 1957.

— Dickens as editor: some uncollected fragments. Dickensian 56 1960.

— The significance of Dickens's periodicals. REL 2 1961.

— 'Inky fishing-nets': Dickens as editor. Dickensian 61 1965. His revision of contributors' work.

Adrian, A. A. Dickens as verse editor. MP 58 1960.

Lohrli, A. Household Words on American English. Amer Speech 37 1962.

— Household Words and its office book. Princeton Univ Lib Chron 26 1965.

Easson, A. Dickens, Household words, and a double standard. Dickensian 60 1964.

Ryan, J. S. (ed). Dickens and New Zealand. Wellington 1965. Articles from Household Words and All the Year Round.

Stone, H. Dickens and composite writing (in Household Words). Dickens Stud 3 1967.

— Dickens and the idea of a periodical. Western Humanities Rev 21 1967.

— New writings by Dickens. Dalhousie Rev 47 1967.

Other Minor Works and Papers

Most of the shorter items have been listed in the bibliographies by Shepherd, Kitton, Hammerton and Eckel (see above, Bibliographies), *and have been collected in the vols listed below. Only separate reprints issued in Dickens's lifetime, or subsequently pbd with comment or other supplementary matter, or items identified since the most generally available collection of his papers* (ed Matz 1908), *are included here. See* 'T. Kent Brumleigh' (T. W. Hill), Journalistics [*a list of Dickens's journalistic works*], Dickensian 48 1952.

Collections

Reprinted pieces. 1858. Vol 8 of the Library edn of the Works. 31 anon contributions to Household Words 1850–6.

The uncommercial traveller. 1861. 17 articles in All the Year Round 1860. 2nd ser 1868, in Charles Dickens edn of the Works (11 further contributions, first pbd 1863). 8 further contributions, first pbd 1863–9, added in Uncommercial traveller, 1875 (Illustrated Library edn of the Works). One more, first pbd 1869, added in Gadshill edn of the Works, 1908.

[Stephen, J. F.?] Saturday Rev 23 Feb 1861.

The plays and poems of Charles Dickens with a few miscellanies in prose now first collected. Ed R. H. Shepherd 2 vols 1885. *See* above, Plays and poems.

The Mudfog papers etc by Charles Dickens, now first collected. 1880. Introd by George Bentley. From Bentley's Miscellany 1837–8. Now usually included in Works in vol containing Sketches by Boz.

To be read at dusk, and other stories, sketches and essays by Charles Dickens, now first collected. 1898. Introd by F. G. Kitton, claiming that 24 of the 46 items had not been included in any previous bibliography. Items from Bentley's Miscellany, Examiner and Household Words. Includes one item (By rail to Parnassus) not by Dickens but by Henry Morley. Kitton had compiled Old lamps for new ones, New York 1897.

Collected papers. Ed A. Waugh 1903. In the Biographical edn of the Works. Contains Sketches of young gentlemen, Sketches of young couples, items from Bentley's Miscellany etc, and the Prefaces, Addresses to the reader, Editorial announcements etc from successive edns of the novels and from the periodicals.

Miscellaneous papers. Ed B. W. Matz 2 vols 1908. In Gadshill edn of the Works 1908, National edn 1908, Biographical edn (1 vol) 1908, Centenary edn 1911, Universal edn (1 vol) 1914. Also rptd separately. 140 items, mostly newly rptd, from Morning Chron, Examiner, Household Words, All the Year Round etc. One item (Lear on the stage) not by Dickens: *see* W. J. Carlton, below. Miscellaneous papers is not included in most subsequent edns of Works, but some use this title to describe items usually collected as 'Reprinted pieces', sometimes with other miscellaneous works.

Collected papers. 2 vols 1937. In the Nonesuch edn of the Works. Editorial note signed by all 4 editors. Adds 16 items not in Matz's Miscellaneous papers. One item not by Dickens: *see* K. J. Fielding, Women in the home: an article Dickens did *not* write, Dickensian 47 1951. The fullest collection.

Contributions to Morning Chronicle 1834–42

Dickens's first contribution to the Morning Chronicle [17–18 Sept 1834] now identified and republished for the first time. Dickensian 31 1935.

A new contribution to the Monthly Magazine [Nov 1834] and an early dramatic criticism in the Morning Chronicle [14 Oct 1834]. Ed W. Dexter, Dickensian 30 1934.

The story without a beginning: an unrecorded contribution by Boz to the Morning Chronicle [18 Dec 1834]. Ed W. J. Carlton, Dickensian 47 1951. Political satire.

Carlton, W. J. Dickens: dramatic critic. Dickensian 56 1960. Identifies and reprints 14 critiques, certainly or probably by Dickens. *See* W. J. Carlton, Dickens: shorthand writer, 1926, and annotation to Letters, ed M. House and G. Storey vol 1, Oxford 1965, for evidence of further dramatic critiques and news reports in the Chronicle.

A review and other writings by Dickens, edited from the original manuscripts by M. Tyson. Bull John Rylands Lib 18 1934. Review of Lord Londonderry's Letter to Lord Ashley on the Mines and Collieries Bill, Morning Chron 20 Oct 1842; here ptd from ms.

Sunday under three heads: as it is; as Sabbath Bills would make it; as it might be made. By Timothy Sparks. 1836 (illustr H. K. Browne); 1884 (facs, with introd); Manchester [1884] (facs, with introd).

Contemporary reviews. Dickensian 32 1936.

Johnson, E. Dickens and the bluenose legislator. Amer Scholar 17 1948.

A newly discovered Dickens fragment. Ed G. Seawim, Dickensian 54 1958. Theatrical Advertisement, Extraordinary, in Bentley's Miscellany Feb 1837. *See note by* M. Morley, Dickensian 57 1961.

Sketches of young gentlemen, dedicated to the young ladies, with six illustrations by Phiz. 1838. Anon. *See* below, Sketches of young couples.

Memoirs of Joseph Grimaldi, edited by 'Boz', with illustrations by George Cruikshank. 2 vols 1838 (variants); rev C. Whitehead 1846, 1853, 1866, 1884; ed. P. Fitzgerald 1903; ed R. Findlater 1968. Dickens wrote a preface and rewrote Grimaldi's ms; 'he has not swelled the quantity of matter, but materially abridged it' (preface).

The suppressed letter respecting Grimaldi. Dickensian 34 1938. A suppressed prefatory note, ptd in part in Forster, Life bk 2 ch 2.

Stott, R. T. Boz's Memoirs of Grimaldi. Book Collector 15 1966. Bibliographical.

Contributions to Examiner 1838–49

Theatrical critiques, 3 and 17 Dec 1837. *See* Letters, ed M. House and G. Storey vol 1, Oxford 1965, pp. 336, 344 and notes.

The coronation, 1 July 1838. *See* Letters, p. 408 and n.

Scott and his publishers, 2 Sept 1838. Ed K. J. Fielding, Dickensian 46 1950.

Reviews of books, 28 Jan 1838, 2 Sept 1838, 3 Feb 1839, 7 April 1839. *See* Letters, pp 356, 360, 428, 505, 536 and notes.

Review of Catherine Crowe's The night side of nature, 26 Feb 1848. Ed P. Collins, Dickensian 59 1963.

Ignorance and its victims, 29 April 1848. Ed A. W. C. Brice, Dickensian 63 1967.

Address issued by the committee of the Italian Refugee fund, 8 Sept 1849. Rptd Dickensian 10 1914.

Macready as King Lear, 27 Oct 1849. Ed L. C. Staples, Dickensian 44 1948. *See* W. J. Carlton, Dickens or Forster? Dickensian 59 1963, confirming Dickens's authorship of this, and showing that Forster wrote an earlier critique of Macready's Lear, formerly attributed to Dickens.

Sketches of young couples, with an urgent remonstrance to the gentlemen of England (being bachelors or widowers) on the present alarming crisis, by the author of Sketches of young gentlemen, with six illustrations by Phiz. 1840. Anon.

Sketches of young couples and young gentlemen, by Boz. 1846.

Sketches of young couples, young ladies, young gentlemen, by Quiz. Illustrated by Phiz. [1869]. Quiz (Edward Caswall?) was the author of Sketches of young ladies, 1837, to which Dickens's Sketches of young gentlemen, 1838, was a riposte.

The Pic Nic papers, by various hands. Edited by Charles Dickens, with illustrations by George Cruikshank, Phiz etc. 3 vols 1841. Variants. Introduction (in vol 2) and The lamplighter's story (in vol 1) by Dickens; the latter adapted from the farce, The lamplighter (*see above*, Plays). The farce and the story rptd, ed W. L. Phelps, New York 1926.

Grubb, G. G. and L. Mason. Dickens and J. C. Neal's Charcoal sketches. Dickensian 46 1950.

American notes for general circulation. 2 vols 1842 (variants); cheap edn 1850 (and in 12 weekly pts, 3 monthly pts, May-July 1850; with preface, and frontispiece by C. Stanfield); Charles Dickens edn 1868 (with rev preface and a postscript). A suppressed chapter, Introductory and necessary to be read, is given in Forster, Life bk 3 ch 8. The 1868 postscript, 'to be added to all future editions', was pbd in All the Year Round 6 June 1868 as A debt of honour.

Athenaeum 22, 29 Oct 1842.
Examiner 22–9 Oct 1842.
Literary Gazette 22 Oct 1842.
Mirror 28 Oct 1842.
[Payne, G. P.] Ainsworth's Mag Nov 1842.
Dublin Monthly Mag Nov 1842.
Fraser's Mag Nov 1842.
Monthly Rev Nov 1842.
[Hood, T.] New Monthly Mag Nov 1842.
Tait's Mag Nov 1842.
Chambers's Jnl 19–26 Nov 1842.
[Warren, S.] Blackwood's Mag Dec 1842.
Christian Remembrancer Dec 1842.
S., J. London Univ Mag 1 1842.
[Spedding, J.] Edinburgh Rev 76 1843; enlarged in his Reviews and Discussions, 1879. Reply by Dickens, Times 16 Jan 1843.
[Thompson, J. T.] New Englander Jan 1843.
[Felton, C.] North Amer Rev 56 1843.
Southern Literary Messenger Jan 1843.
[Wiseman, N.] Dublin Rev 15 1843.
[Hickson, W. E.?] Westminster Rev 40 1843.
[Croker, J. W.] Quart Rev 71 1843.
Whipple, E. P. Atlantic Monthly April 1877.

'Quickens, Quarles'. English notes, intended for very extensive circulation! Boston 1842; ed J. Jackson and G. H. Sargent, New York 1920. A parody and retort to American notes. Not by E. A. Poe, as often conjectured.

'Buz'. Current American notes. nd. A close parody; includes material transcribed from American notes.

[Cary, T. G.] Letter to a lady in France with answers to enquiries concerning the books of Capt Marryat and Mr Dickens. Boston 1843, 1844.

[Wood, Henry.] Change for American notes: in letters from London to New York, by an American lady. 1843.

Adshead, J. The fictions of Dickens on solitary confinement. In his Prisons and prisoners, 1845. On American notes, ch 7.

Tellkampf, J. L. Remarks on American notes. In his Essays on law reform, 1859.

Some notes on America to be rewritten: suggested, with respect, to Charles Dickens esq. Philadelphia 1868.

[Tallack, W.] Dickens's prison fiction. 1894. Issued by the Howard Assoc.

Wilkins, W. G. American parodies on American notes. Dickensian 4 1908. *See* his Dickens and America, 1911.

Dickensian special numbers on Dickens and America: Aug 1909, Aug 1910, Sept 1916, April 1926, Dec 1941.

Jackson, J. Dickens in Philadelphia. Philadelphia 1912 (priv ptd).

Johnson, L. H. The source of the chapter on American slavery in Dickens's American notes. Amer Lit 14 1943.

Teeters, N. K. and J. D. Shearer. Dickens and his Cherry Hill prisoners. In their Prison at Philadelphia: Cherry Hill, New York 1957.

Fielding, K. J. American notes and some English reviewers. MLR 59 1964.

International copyright. Letter in Times 16 Jan 1843. Rptd in Collected papers (Nonesuch edn).

Overs, John. Evenings of a working man, with a preface relative to the author by Charles Dickens. 1844. *See* G. G. Grubb, Dickensian 49 1953.

Address to the reader, Daily News 21 Jan 1846. Rptd in G. G. Grubb, Dickens and the Daily News: the early issues, Nineteenth-Century Fiction 6 1952.

Letter to the Editor, signed A Constant Reader, Daily News 22 Jan 1846. With reply by Dickens as editor. About misprints in opening number.

Letters on social questions. Capital punishment. 3 letters in this ser (pbd in the Daily News 9, 13 and 16 March 1846) have been rptd in the Collections above; also as a pamphlet 1849. 2 further letters have been rptd later: 23 Feb 1846, in TLS 12 Aug 1965, ed K. Tillotson; 28 Feb 1846, in The law as literature, ed L. Blom-Cooper 1961.

Pictures from Italy, the vignette illustrations on wood by Samuel Palmer. 1846, 1865 (Cheap edn), 1868 (Charles Dickens edn). Appeared in part in Daily News 21 Jan—11 March 1846, as Travelling letters—written on the road, by Charles Dickens.

Athenaeum 23 May 1846.
Times 1 June 1846.
Chambers's Jnl 20 June 1846.
London Jnl 20 June 1846.
GM July 1846.
Tait's Mag July 1846.
Literary Gazette 18 July 1846.
[Murray, P. A.] Dublin Rev 21 1846.
Macphail's Edinburgh Ecclesiastical Jnl Sept 1846.
'Savonarolo, Don Jeremy' [F. S. Mahony]. Facts and figures from Italy, addressed to Charles Dickens. 1847. Prefatory note by Dickens.
Cannavò, F. Nuova Antologia 1 Aug 1918.
Massoul, H. Trois voyages d'Italie: Charles de Brosses, Charles Dickens, Maurice Maeterlinck. Mercure de France 1 July 1924.
Brunner, K. Dickens und Mark Twain in Italien. In Festschrift für Walther Fischer, Heidelberg 1959.
Jannattoni, L. Byron e Dickens agli 'spettacoli' di Maestro Titta. Eng Miscellany (Rome) 10 1959.

The Early Closing Movement. Letter to the Committee of the Metropolitan Drapers' Association 28 March 1844. Pbd in the Student and Young Man's Advocate, Jan 1845. Rptd in Collected papers (Nonesuch edn).

Autobiographical fragment. Written c. 1845–6; not pbd by Dickens. In Forster, Life bk 1 ch 2.

The proposed benefit for Leigh Hunt: an unpublished pamphlet by Dickens [1847?]. Dickensian 36 1940.

An appeal to fallen women. Pamphlet [1847], written in connection with Miss Coutts's Home for fallen women. Rptd in Collected papers (Nonesuch edn) and in the collections of Letters to Miss Coutts ed Payne and Harper 1929, Osborne 1931 and Johnson 1952 (below).

[Charles Dickens]. (Proof.) [Private and Confidential]. Brackets thus on title-page. A pamphlet denouncing the forgeries of Thomas Powell, prepared by Dickens 1849 (priv ptd) and sent to various English and American newspapers. *See* W. Partington, Should a biographer tell? Atlantic Monthly Aug 1947; rptd with addns, Dickensian 43 1947 (reply by W. J. Carlton, ibid).

Dreadful hardships endured by the shipwrecked crew of The London, chiefly for want of water. Contribution sent to Punch [1849?] but not pbd. Facs in M. H. Spielmann, The history of Punch, 1895.

Public executions, Letters to the Times, 14 and 19 Jan 1849. Rptd as pamphlet, 1849.

The life of our Lord, written expressly for his own children, 1849. 1934. Not intended for pbn; probably written 1846. *See* Dickensian 30 1934.

Peyrouton, N. C. Some notes of explication. Dickensian 59 1963.

Prayer at night. Written for his children, c. 1849. Pbd by J. Suddaby, Dickensian 5 1909, and in Mr and Mrs Charles Dickens, ed W. Dexter 1935.

Contributions to his own Weeklies 1850–70

See above, *Periodicals*.

Dickens as editor: some uncollected fragments, ed P. Collins. Dickensian 56 1960.

A child's dream of a star, with illustrations by Hammett Billings. Boston 1871. From Household Words 6 April 1850.

Ecclesiastical registries. Pbd from ms, Collected papers (Nonesuch edn). Rev as The doom of English wills, Household Words 28 Sept, 5 Oct, 2, 23 Nov 1850, in collaboration with W. H. Wills.

A child's history of England, with a frontispiece by F. W. Topham [in each vol]. Vol 1, 1852, vol 2, 1853, vol 3, 1854; 1 vol 1863. Slight variants. Originally appeared intermittently in Household Words 25 Jan 1851–10 Dec 1853. Illustr Marcus Stone 1873.

Topham's illustration to A child's history of England. Dickensian 3 1907.
Birch, D. A forgotten book. Dickensian 51 1955.

One man in a dockyard. In collaboration with R. H. Horne, Household Words 6 Sept 1851. Ed P. Collins, Dickensian 59 1963.

A curious dance round a curious tree. [1860?]. Main text has title preceded by '1852'; the article is followed by an extract from Times headed 1860 and an appeal for St Luke's Hospital headed Contrast between 1852 and 1860. The paper, written by Dickens and W. H. Wills, originally appeared in Household Words 17 Jan 1852. Rptd in Wills, Old leaves, 1860.

Post Office money orders. Rptd 1852 (in part, anon) in Methods of employment (as Remarks by Charles Dickens esq), 1860 (in W. H. Wills, Old leaves). The paper, written by Dickens and Wills, originally appeared in Household Words 20 March 1852.

Gone astray, with illustrations by Ruth Cobb, from old prints and from photographs by T. W. Tyrell, and introduction and notes by B. W. Matz. 1912. Originally in Household Words 13 Aug 1853.

The late Mr Justice Talfourd. [1854]. Private pre-print of the article in Household Words 25 March 1854.

Pavilionstone, with an introduction by P. Fitzgerald. [1902]. Dickens's Out of town (Household Words 29 Sept 1855) with biographical preface describing Folkestone and the writing of Little Dorrit.

The lazy tour of two idle apprentices. In collaboration with Wilkie Collins. Originally appeared in Household Words 3–31 Oct 1857. Rptd [1875] (in part in Joseph Sly, King's Arms and Royal Hotel, Lancaster), 1890 (illustr), with No thoroughfare and The perils of certain English prisoners (*see Christmas Numbers, above*).

Personal. Household Words 12 June 1858; rptd in many contemporary newspapers and jnls. Dickens's statement about his marital difficulties. Rptd in Mr and Mrs Charles Dickens, ed W. Dexter 1935. Not in Collected papers (Nonesuch edn).

East London Hospital for Children, reprinted by permission of Charles Dickens esq from All the Year Round Dec 19th 1868. nd. Original magazine title, New uncommercial samples: A small star in the east.

Robert Keeley. In collaboration with Herman Merivale. All the Year Round 10 April 1869. Ed P. Collins, Dickensian, 60 1964.

To be read at dusk. In Keepsake for 1852, ed M. Power. Rptd 1852 (priv ptd); ed F. G. Kitton 1898 (with other stories, etc, above). The 1852 edn is probably a forgery; *see* J. Carter and H. G. Pollard, An enquiry into the nature of certain nineteenth-century pamphlets, 1934, and J. Carter, TLS 26 July 1934.

Manuscript notebook 1855– [1870?]. Described in Forster, Life bk 9 ch 7; excerpts in Mrs J. Comyns Carr's Reminiscences, ed E. Adam 1926, and in Letters, ed W. Dexter 1938, Appendix. Ms in Berg Collection, New York Public Library, to be edited by K. J. Fielding.

Smith, H. B. How Dickens wrote his books. Harper's Mag Dec 1924, rptd Strand Mag Feb 1925. Facs.
Ford, G. H. Dickens's notebook and Edwin Drood. Nineteenth-Century Fiction 6 1952.
Aylmer, F. John Forster and Dickens's memorandum book. Dickensian 51 1955. Reply by P. Pakenham, ibid.

Address of the English author to the French public, 17 January 1857. Prefixed to P. Lorain's authorized trn of Nicholas Nickleby, 2 vols Paris 1857. Rptd in Collected papers (Nonesuch).

The case of the reformers in the [Royal] Literary Fund; stated by Charles W. Dilke, Charles Dickens and John Forster. [1858] (priv ptd). Followed by A summary of facts in answer to allegations . . . [1858] (priv ptd by the Committee), and The Answer to the Committee's summary of 'facts' [1858] (priv ptd). *For Dickens's substantial authorship of the reformers' pamphlets, see* Speeches, ed K. J. Fielding, Oxford 1960.

Hunted down: a story, with an account of Thomas Griffiths Wainewright the poisoner. [1870]. Originally in New York Ledger 7–20 Aug, 3 Sept 1859; also in All the Year Round 4–11 April 1860; Leipzig 1860 (Tauchnitz, with Uncommercial traveller), Philadelphia [1861] (with Lamplighter and other novellettes). The account of Wainewright is by John Camden Hotten.

Curling, J. Janus Weathercock: the life of Thomas Griffiths Wainewright. 1938. Ch 7, As Dickens saw him.

The Gad's Hill gazette. [1860–6]. A family magazine mainly ed H. F. Dickens, to which Dickens contributed. Produced partly in ms and partly on a small private press, for domestic use only. *See* Dickensian July 1910 (facs) and P. Fitzgerald, Recreations of a literary man vol 1, 1882 (facs). Not rptd; incomplete runs in some libraries, notably New York Public Library and Yale Univ Library.

Dickens, H. F. The history of the Gad's Hill Gazette. Dickensian 25 1929.

Dramatic rights in fiction. Letter to the editor, Times 12 Jan 1861. Rptd in Collected papers (Nonesuch).

The election for Finsbury. Letter to the editor, Daily News 23 Nov 1861. Denying that he was a candidate. Rptd in Letters (Nonesuch edn).

The earthquake shock in England. Letter to the editor, Times 8 Oct 1863. Rptd in Collected papers (Nonesuch).

Procter, A. A. Legends and lyrics, with an introduction by Charles Dickens. New edn, with addns, illustr 1866. Introd included in later edns and in the Complete works, 1905.

Letter to the editor. Times 4 Sept 1867. Denying rumours about his state of health. Rptd in Letters (Nonesuch edn).

George Silverman's explanation. Atlantic Monthly Jan–March 1867; rptd in All the Year Round 1, 15, 29 Feb 1868; [1875] (Charles Dickens edn, with Drood).

Bradby, M. K. The explanation of George Silverman's explanation. Dickensian 36 1940.

Stone, H. Dickens's tragic universe: George Silverman's explanation. SP 55 1958.

Holiday romance. Our Young Folks (Boston) Jan, March–May 1868; rptd in All the Year Round 25 Jan, 8 Feb, 14 March, 4 April 1868; [1875] (Charles Dickens edn). Rptd with decorations by D. M. Palmer, 1920; pt 1 (The trial of William Tinkling) with illustrations by S. B. Pearce [1912]; pt 2 (The magic fishbone) with illustrations by S. B. Pearce [1911], by F. D. Bedford [1921], by Phyllis Bray, Oxford 1939.

Religious opinions of the late Reverend Chauncey Hare Townshend, published as directed in his will, by his literary executor [Charles Dickens]. 1869. Explanatory introd by Dickens.

On Mr Fechter's acting. Atlantic Monthly Aug 1869. Rptd Leeds [1872].

Letters and Speeches

Letters pbd separately or in small collections are not listed here if they have been rptd in the collected edns, unless they appeared in volume-form or with useful ancillary material. Those dealing with particular works or themes are entered under the appropriate works above. K. J. Fielding's edn of the Speeches *(Oxford 1960) contains particulars of earlier pbn of individual speeches in pamphlet-form etc, and these are not given here.*

Collections

Speeches literary and social by Dickens, now first collected, with chapters on Dickens as a letter writer, poet and public reader. [Ed R. H. Shepherd] 1870; rev and with a bibliography as The speeches of Dickens 1841–70, 1884; with introd by B. Darwin [1937]. On the origins and method of Shepherd's collection, *see* K. J. Fielding, Textual introd to his edition of Speeches. 2 further speeches added to National edn 1908, 7 further to Nonesuch edn of Collected papers 1937.

Speeches, letters and sayings of Dickens, to which is added a sketch of the author by George Augustus Sala, and Dean Stanley's sermon. New York 1870. Text of speeches from Shepherd's 1870 edn. Contains also some of the poems, a note on the readings and a biographical introd.

The letters of Dickens. edited by his sister-in-law [Georgina Hogarth] and his eldest daughter [Mamie (Mary) Dickens]. 3 vols 1880–2, 2 vols 1882, 1 vol 1893; with Letters to Wilkie Collins, 2 vols 1908 (National edn of Works). Much revision and re-arrangement between edns; *see* A. A. Adrian, Georgina Hogarth and the Dickens circle, Oxford 1957, ch 13, and preface to Pilgrim edn of the letters, vol 1 Oxford 1965. Contains Dickens's diary 1837–41 (incompletely and inaccurately): so does Nonesuch edn of the letters, vol 1. Complete transcript for 1838–9 in Pilgrim edn, vol 1. Only one other Dickens diary has survived, for 1867 (unpbd). *See* W. J. Carlton, The Dickens diaries, Dickensian 55 1959.

Athenaeum 29 Nov 1879.
Spectator 29 Nov, 6 Dec 1879.
Brownell, W. C. Nation 4 Dec 1879.
Saturday Rev 6 Dec 1879.
Literary World 12 Dec 1879, 18 Nov 1881.
Times 27 Dec 1879.
Minto, W. Fortnightly Rev Dec 1879.
'Browne, Matthew' (W. B. Rands). Contemporary Rev Jan 1880.
Scribner's Monthly Mag Jan 1880.
Atlantic Monthly Feb 1880.
Didier, E. L. North Amer Rev March 1880.
[Cullen, P.?] Dublin Rev 3rd ser 3 1880.
Temple Bar April 1880.
Westminster Rev new ser 58 1880.

The letters of Dickens. Ed W. Dexter 3 vols 1938 (Nonesuch). Fullest collection.

The speeches of Dickens. Ed K. J. Fielding, Oxford 1960. The standard edn.

Miller, M. H. Dickens at the English charity dinner. Quart Jnl of Speech 47 1961. The conventions of oratory on such occasions.

The Pilgrim edition of the letters of Dickens. Ed M. House and G. Storey, Oxford 1965–. First complete edn.

Heaphy, T. A wonderful ghost story: being Mr H's own narrative, reprinted from All The Year Round; with [3] letters hitherto unpublished of Charles Dickens respecting it. 1882. Dickens prefaced the article in All the Year Round 6 Oct 1861 with an editorial note.

Hans Christian Andersen's correspondence. Ed F. Crawford [1891]. Letters to and from Dickens. *See* E. Munksgaard, H. C. Andersen's visits to Dickens, Copenhagen 1937 (6 letters in facs), and E. Bredsdorff (below, Biographies).

Letters of Dickens to Wilkie Collins 1851–70, selected by Miss G. Hogarth. Ed L. Hutton 1892.

Furniss, H. A. Shakespeare birthday and a reminiscence of Dickens. Pall Mall Mag April 1906. His speech about Shakespeare at the Garrick Club 1854; not collected.

Dickens and Maria Beadnell. Ed G. P. Baker 1908 (Boston Bibliophile Soc) (with notes by J. H. Stonehouse); St Louis 1908 (priv ptd for W. K. Bixby, owner of the ms letters). *See* Piccadilly notes (Henry Sotheran) no iv 1933 for history of the letters and their discovery by J. H. Stonehouse. *See* also Dickensian 29 1933.

The Dickens-Kolle letters, supplemental to the letters from Dickens to Maria Beadnell. Ed H. B. Smith and H. H. Harper 1910 (Boston Bibliophile Soc).

Payne, E. F. and H. H. Harper. The romance of Dickens and Maria Beadnell Winter. 1929 (Boston Bibliophile Soc). A commentary on the foregoing and other newly discovered material.

Otto, K. Der Verlag Bernhard Tauchnitz 1837–1912. Leipzig 1912. Letters to his German publisher.

Dickens as editor: letters written by him to William Henry Wills, his sub-editor. Ed R. C. Lehmann 1912.

Letters to Mark Lemon. Ed T. J. Wise 1917 (priv ptd).

The unpublished letters of Dickens to Mark Lemon. Ed W. Dexter 1927.

Clark, C. Dickens and his Jewish characters. 1918. Letters, with commentary.

—— The story of a great friendship: Dickens and Clarkson Stanfield, with seven unpublished letters. 1918.

—— Dickens and Talfourd, with three unpublished letters [on copyright]. 1919.

—— Dickens and the begging-letter writer; with a letter. 1923.

An account of the first performance of Lytton's comedy Not so bad as we seem, with other matters of interest. 1919 (priv ptd). A letter from Dickens to R. H. Horne, dated 1853, with postscript by W. H. Wills.

Notes and comments on certain writings in prose and verse by Richard Henry Horne. 1920 (priv ptd). 6 letters.

Payne, E. F. and H. H. Harper. The charity of Charles Dickens. 1929 (Boston Bibliophile Soc). Narrative embodying some correspondence and the pamphlet by Dickens about the foundation, with the aid of Miss Burdett Coutts, of a Home for fallen women.

The letters of Dickens to the Baroness Burdett-Coutts. Ed C. C. Osborne 1931. Selection with narrative.

Dickens to his oldest friend: some unpublished letters to Thomas Beard, with a foreword by Sir Henry Fielding Dickens. 1931 (priv pbd). 5 pbd letters, one unpbd facs and A fable (facs), with brief comment.

Dickens to his oldest friend: the letters of a lifetime. Ed W. Dexter 1932. The whole available correspondence with notes, introd and facs. *See* B. Darwin (ed), Dickens and his oldest friend, Bookman (New York) Oct 1931–Jan 1932.

Dickens's letters to Charles Lever. Ed F. V. Livingston, introd by H. E. Rollins, Cambridge Mass 1933.

Mabbott, T. O. Correspondence of John Tomlin. N & Q 6 Jan 1934.

Mr and Mrs Charles Dickens: his letters to her. Ed W. Dexter 1934.

The love romance of Dickens, told in his letters to Maria Beadnell (Mrs Winter). Ed W. Dexter 1936.

Rolfe, F. P. The Dickens letters in the Huntington Library. HLQ 1 1938.

—— Additions to the Nonesuch edition of Dickens's letters. HLQ 5 1942.

—— More letters to the Watsons. Dickensian 38 1942.

[Dexter, W.] Unpublished letters to Lady Holland. Dickensian 36 1940.

—— A new Dickens letter (to Madame de la Rue 27 Sept 1845). Ibid.

—— Adventures among Dickens's letters. Dickensian 39 1943.

Lucas, J. P. To John Landseer, esquire. South Atlantic Quart 39 1940.

Altick, R. D. Dickens and America: some unpublished letters. Pennsylvania Mag of History 73 1949.

Whitley, A. Hood and Dickens: some new letters. HLQ 14 1950.

Miller, C. W. Letters from Thomas White of Virginia to Scott and Dickens. In English studies in honor of J. S. Wilson, Charlottesville 1951.

House, H. A new edition of Dickens's letters. Listener 18 Oct 1951; rptd in his All in due time, 1955.

—— A Dickens letter: copy or forgery? Dickensian 49 1953.

Fielding, K. J. Dickens, Thackeray and W. A. Chatto. Dickensian 48 1952.

—— and G. G. Grubb. New letters [1837–41] from Dickens to Forster. Boston Univ Stud in Eng 2 1956.

Johnson, E. The heart of Dickens. New York 1952, London 1953 as Letters from Dickens to Angela Burdett Coutts 1841–65.

Grubb, G. G. Dickens's quarrel with John Overs. Dickensian 49 1953.

—— Some unpublished correspondence of Dickens and Chapman & Hall. Boston Univ Stud in Eng 1 1955.

Dickens in Italy: a letter to Thomas Mitton [11 Aug 1844] now published for the first time. New York 1956 (Pierpont Morgan Library).

Rust, J. D. Dickens and the Americans: an unnoticed letter. Nineteenth-Century Fiction 11 1957.

Griffith, B. W. Dickens the philanthropist: an unpublished letter. Nineteenth-Century Fiction 12 1958.

Stone, H. Dickens and Harriet Beecher Stowe. Ibid. Letter to Mrs Cropper, Lord Denman's daughter.

Monod, S. Une amitié française de Dickens: lettres inédites à Philoclès Régnier. Etudes Anglaises 11 1958.

—— Misères et splendeurs d'une carrière littéraire. Les Lettres Françaises 27 Sept 1962. 19 unpbd letters.

Selected letters. Ed F. W. Dupee, New York 1960. Introd pbd as The other Dickens, Partisan Rev 27 1960.

Letters of English authors from the collection of Robert H. Taylor: a catalogue. Princeton 1960.

Nathan, A. Costumes by Nathan. 1960.

Carr, Sr M. C. Catalogue of the Dickens collection at the University of Texas. Austin 1961. Particulars of 146 letters, many unpbd, with quotations.

Grylls, R. G. Dickens and Holman Hunt. Texas Stud in Lit & Lang 6 1964. 3 unpbd letters.

Mistler, J. Un grand éditeur [Louis Hachette] et ses auteurs. Revue des Deux Mondes 15 July 1964.

Smith, S. M. An unpublished letter from Dickens to Disraeli. N & Q June 1964.

§2

Biographies

Dickens: a critical biography. 1858 (Our contemporaries, no 1).

[Taverner, H. T. and J. C. Hotten]. Dickens: the story of his life, by the author of the Life of Thackeray. [1870]; with Speeches by Dickens, [1873].

Sala, G. A. H. Charles Dickens. [1870]; with Speeches, letters and sayings of Dickens, New York [1870]. Enlarged from Daily Telegraph 10 June 1870.

Mackenzie, R. S. Life of Dickens, with personal recollections and anecdotes. Philadelphia [1870].

Perkins, F. B. Dickens: a sketch of his life and work. New York 1870.

Watkins, W. Dickens, with anecdotes and recollections of his life. [1870].

Hanaford, P. A. Life and writings of Dickens: a woman's memorial volume. Boston 1871.

Jerrold, W. B. The best of all good company: a [monthly] series. 1871–2. Pt 1, A day with Dickens, June 1871. Includes short life, personal appreciation, account of friendships and facs of handwriting. *See* GM July 1870.

Forster, J. The life of Dickens. 3 vols 1872–4 (revisions in successive edns of each vol), 2 vols 1876 (Library edn), 1879 (illustr); rev and abridged G. Gissing 1903; Memorial edn, ed B. W. Matz 2 vols 1911 (500 portraits, facs etc); ed G. K. Chesterton 2 vols 1927 (EL)

(rev); ed A. J. Hoppé 2 vols 1966; ed J. W. T. Ley 1928 (notes embody much new matter).
Wilson, H. Examiner 9 Dec 1871.
Literary World 15–22 Dec 1871, 22 Nov 1872.
Saturday Rev 9 Dec 1871.
Times 26 Dec 1871.
Payn, J. Chambers's Jnl 13–20 Jan 1872, 1 Feb 1873, 21 March 1874.
Fraser's Mag Jan 1872.
[Elwin, W.] Quart Rev 132 1872.
Stack, J. H. Fortnightly Rev Jan 1872.
Atlantic Monthly Feb 1872.
Buchanan, R. St Paul's Mag Feb 1872.
Guardian 6 March 1872, 22 Jan 1873.
Sheldon, F. North Amer Rev April 1872.
Athenaeum 16 Nov 1872.
Examiner 16 Nov 1872, 14 Feb 1874.
Br Quart Rev 57 1873, 59 1874.
Atlantic Monthly Feb 1873.
Temple Bar May 1873.
[Hutton, R. H.] Spectator 7 Feb 1874.
Lang, A. Academy 21 Feb 1874.
Carlton W. J. Postscripts to Forster. Dickensian 58 1962. Letters to Forster from readers of Life.
Monod, S. Forster's Life of Dickens and literary criticism. In English studies today 4th ser, Rome 1966.

Stoddard, R. H. Anecdote biographies of Thackeray and Dickens. New York 1874.
Langton, R. Dickens and Rochester. 1880. Rptd with addns from Papers of Manchester Literary Club. Partly incorporated in following.
—— The childhood and youth of Dickens, with retrospective notes and elucidations, from his books and letters. Manchester 1883 (priv ptd), 1891 (enlarged and rev), 1912. Supplements and controverts Forster.
Jones, C. H. A short life of Dickens, with selections from his letters. New York 1880.
Ward, A. W. Charles Dickens. 1882 (EML). *See* his Dickens (a lecture), in Science lectures 2nd ser, Manchester 1870.
Dickens, M. Charles Dickens, by his eldest daughter. 1885, 1911.
—— My father as I recall him. [1897].
Marzials, F. T. Life of Dickens. 1887. Contains bibliography by J. P. Anderson.
Du Pontavice de Heussey, R.Y.M. Un maître du roman contemporain: l'inimitable Boz. Paris 1889.
Kitton, F. G. Dickens by pen and pencil, including anecdotes and reminiscences collected by his friends and companions. 1890. Supplement 1890; additional illustrations 1891.
—— Dickens: his life, writings and personality. 2 vols Edinburgh [1902], 1 vol nd. *See* Bibliography of F. G. Kitton, Dickensian 1 1905.
Matz, B. W. Dickens: the story of his life and writings. [1902]. Rptd from Household Words 14 June 1902. *See* Bibliography of B. W. Matz, Dickensian 21 1925.
Shore, W. T. Dickens. 1904.
—— Dickens and his friends. 1909.
—— Charles Dickens. 1910.
Fitzgerald, P. H. The life of Dickens as revealed in his writings. 2 vols 1905.
—— Memories of Dickens, with an account of Household Words and All the Year Round and of the contributors thereto. Bristol 1913.
Ellison, O. Charles Dickens, novelist. [1908].
Moses, B. Charles Dickens. 1912.
Dibelius, W. Dickens. Leipzig 1916, 1926 (rev). Extensive bibliography. *See* his Englische Romanskunst, Berlin 1910, 1922 (rev.)
Dark, S. Charles Dickens. 1919.
Nicoll, W. R. Dickens's own story: sidelights on his life and personality. 1923.
Dexter, W. Dickens: the story of the life of the world's favourite author. 1927.
Dickens, H. F. Memories of my father. 1928. *See Personal Recollections, below*.
Straus, R. Dickens: a portrait in pencil. 1928, 1938 (as A portrait of Dickens).
'Ephesian' (C. E. B. Roberts). This side idolatry. 1928. A biography in the form of a novel.
Wagenknecht, E. The man Dickens: a Victorian portrait. Cambridge Mass 1929, Norman Oklahoma 1965 (rev).
—— Dickens and the scandal-mongers. Norman Oklahoma 1965.
Stonehouse, J. H. Green leaves: new chapters in the life of Dickens. 1930–1 (priv ptd), 1931 (rev and enlarged).
Dent, H. C. The life and characters of Dickens. 1933.
Darwin, B. Charles Dickens. 1933.
Leacock, S. Dickens: his life and work. 1933.
'Kingsmill, Hugh' (H. K. Lunn). The sentimental journey: a life of Dickens. 1934.
Wright, T. The life of Dickens. 1935. *See* his Autobiography, 1936: ch 14 on Dickens and Ellen Ternan.
Dybowski, R. Dickens. Warsaw 1936. With bibliography of Polish trns.
Pope-Hennessy, U. Dickens. 1945.
Lemonnier, L. Dickens. Paris 1946; tr Paris 1947.
Pearson, H. Dickens: his character, comedy and career. 1949.
Lindsay, J. Dickens: a biographical and critical study. 1950.
Symons, J. Dickens. 1951.
Johnson, E. Dickens: his tragedy and triumph. 2 vols New York 1952.
Fielding, K. J. Dickens: a survey. 1953, 1960 (rev), 1963 (rev) (Br Council pamphlet).
—— Dickens: a critical introduction. 1958, 1965 (rev and enlarged).
Harrison, M. Dickens: a sentimental journey in search of an unvarnished portrait. 1953.
Bowen, W. H. Dickens and his family. Cambridge 1956 (priv ptd).
Katarsky, I. M. Dickens. Moscow 1960.
Priestley, J. B. Dickens: a pictorial biography. 1961.
Hibbert, C. The making of Dickens. 1967.

Special Periods and Aspects

Lester, C. E. Dickens. In his Glory and shame of England vol 2, New York 1841, 1866 (rev).
Report of the dinner given to Dickens in Boston, 1 February 1842. Boston 1842.
The reception of Dickens. United States Mag April 1842.
Literary lions: Dickens. Pictorial Times 20 April 1844.
Howitt, W. The people's portrait gallery: Dickens. People's Jnl 3 June 1846.
'Morna' (T. M. O'Keefe). The battle of London life: or Boz and his secretary, with six [five] designs on stone by George Sala. 1849.
Powell, T. The living authors of England, New York 1849, London 1851 (rev as Pictures of the living authors of Britain). *See above*, *Minor Works*, Proof: private and confidential 1849.
—— Leaves from my life. Frank Leslie's Sunday Mag Feb 1887.
Yates, E. Mr Thackeray, Mr Yates and the Garrick Club: the correspondence and facts. 1859 (priv ptd). *See* Garrick Club: correspondence, 1858 (priv ptd), and Garrick Club: report of the committee, 1858 (priv ptd).
Clark, L. G. Letters from Dickens. Harper's Mag Aug 1862.
—— Appleton's Jnl 6 Aug 1870.
Reeve, L. A. Portraits of men of eminence, with biographical memoirs, vol 4. 1867.
Sherwood, J. D. Visits to the homes of authors: Dickens. Hours at Home July 1867.
The Charles Dickens Dinner: an authentic record of the public banquet on Nov 2nd 1867 prior to his departure for the United States, with a report of the speeches;

with a preface by W[illiam] C[harles] [Mark] K[ent]. 1867. Speeches by Dickens, Lytton, Trollope et al.
[Putnam, G. W.] Four months with Dickens, during his first visit to America. Atlantic Monthly Oct–Nov 1870.
Grant, J. The newspaper press, 2 vols 1871. Vol 1 ch 12, The morning chronicle; vol 2 ch 3, The daily news.
The parents of Dickens. Lippincott's Mag June 1874.
Kent, W. C. M. Dickens as a journalist. Time Dec 1881.
Fitzgerald, P. H. Recreations of a literary man. 2 vols 1882. Vol 1, Dickens as an editor; Dickens at home.
—— John Forster, by one of his friends. 1903.
Payn, J. The youth and middle age of Dickens. 1883. Rptd from Chambers's Jnl.
—— Some literary recollections. 1884.
Du Pontavice de Heussey, R.Y.M. Dickens à Paris 1853–6. Le Livre 10 April 1886.
Pemberton, T. E. Dickens and the stage. 1888.
Hone, P. Diary, ed B. Tuckerman 2 vols New York 1889. Vol 2, Dickens's reception in USA 1842.
Axon, W. E. A. Dickens and shorthand. Manchester [1892]. Dickens as a reporter.
Aronstein, P. Dickens und Carlyle. Anglia 18 1896.
Williamson, E. S. Glimpses of Dickens. Toronto 1898.
Wilson, F. W. Dickens in seinen Beziehungen zu den Humoristen Fielding und Smollett. Leipzig 1899.
Winter, A. Joseph Addison als Humorist in seinen Einfluss auf Dickens' Jugendwerke. Leipzig 1899.
McCarthy, J. Portraits of the sixties. 1903. Ch 2.
Robinson, J. R. Dickens and the Guild of Literature and Art. Cornhill Mag Jan 1904.
Bowes, C. C. The associations of Dickens with Liverpool. Liverpool 1905. Introd by E. A. Browne.
Wells, G. The tale of Dickens, told by a local man to local people. Rochester 1906.
Furniss, H. A Shakespeare birthday: a reminiscence of Dickens. Pall Mall Mag April 1906.
—— Dickens. In Some Victorian men, 1924. Mainly Dickens as actor, reader and speaker.
Welch, D. Dickens in Switzerland. Harper's Monthly Mag April 1906.
—— Dickens in Genoa. Harper's Monthly Mag August 1906.
Benham, W. Dickens in Kent. In his Memorials of old Kent, 1907.
Matz, B. W. Dickens as a journalist. Fortnightly Rev May 1908.
Beazell, W. P. (ed). Account of the Boz Ball in New York 14 February 1842, reprinted from the New York Aurora-Extra. Cedar Rapids, Iowa 1909 (priv ptd). *See* A. Nisbet, The Boz Ball, Amer Heritage 9 1957.
Tull, E. M. Dickens and Reading. Reading [1909].
Frieser, W. Die Schulen bei Dickens auf ihre geschichtliche Wahrheit geprüft. Leipzig 1909.
Winter, W. Old friends: literary recollections. New York 1909.
FitzGerald, S. J. A. Dickens and the drama. 1910.
Dibelius, W. Pierce Egan und Dickens. Archiv 124 1910.
—— Dickens und Shakespeare. Shakespeare-Jahrbuch 52 1916.
Fehr, B. Dickens und Malthus. Germanisch-romanische Monatsschrift 2 1910.
Snyder, J. F. Dickens in Illinois. Jnl of Illinois State Historical Soc 3 1910.
Wilkins, W. G. Dickens and America. 1911.
—— Dickens in cartoon and caricature. Introd by B. W. Matz. 1924 (Boston Bibliophile Soc) (facs with notes and comment).
Lightwood, J. T. Dickens and music. 1912.
Renton, R. John Forster and his friendships. 1912. Chs 4–5.
Calthrop, D. C. and M. Pemberton (ed). The Dickens souvenir of 1912. 1912.
Ley, J. W. T. The Dickens circle: a narrative of the novelist's friendships. 1918.
—— Captain Marryat and Dickens. Dickensian 22 1926.
—— Songs that Dickens knew. Dickensian 26–9 1930–3.
Fiedler, F. Dickens' Belesenheit. Archiv new ser 40 1920.
Langstaff, J. B. David Copperfield's library. 1924. Dickens's residence in boyhood at 13 Johnson Street, Camden Town, now used as a children's library.
Smith, H. B. How Dickens wrote his books. Harper's Mag 150 1924.
Humphreys, A. L. Dickens and his first schoolmaster [i.e. William Giles of Chatham]. Manchester 1926.
Van Amerongen, J. B. The actor in Dickens. 1926.
Carlton, W. J. Dickens, shorthand writer. 1926.
—— Some reporting adventures of Dickens. IPS Jnl 11 1948.
—— An echo of the Copperfield days. Dickensian 45 1949.
—— The Barrows of Bristol. Ibid.
—— Dickens and the two Tennysons. Dickensian 47 1951.
—— Mr Blackmore engages an office boy. Dickensian 48 1952.
—— When the cholera raged at Chatham. Dickensian 49 1953.
—— A companion of the Copperfield days. Dickensian 50 1954.
—— Dickens and the Ross family. Dickensian 51 1955.
—— Who was Dickens's French employer? Ibid.
—— John Dickens, journalist. Dickensian 53 1957.
—— Fanny Dickens. Ibid.
—— The third man at Newgate. RES new ser 8 1957. Dickens's visit in 1835.
—— Mr and Mrs Dickens: the Thomson-Stark letter. N & Q April 1960.
—— More about the Dickens ancestry. Dickensian 57 1961.
—— Dickens studies French. Dickensian 59 1963.
—— Dickens through French eyes in 1843. Ibid.
—— In the blacking warehouse. Dickensian 60 1964.
—— Dickens studies Italian. Dickensian 61 1965.
—— Dickens's forgotten retreat in France. Dickensian 62 1966.
—— The death of Mary Hogarth—before and after. Dickensian 63 1967.
—— Dickens and the Royal Society of Arts. Ibid.
Delattre, F. Dickens et la France. Paris 1927.
Payne, E. F. Dickens days in Boston: a record of daily events. Boston 1927.
Gray, W. F. The Edinburgh relatives and friends of Dickens. [1927]. Rptd from Dickensian.
Brightfield, M. F. Theodore Hook and his novels. Cambridge Mass 1928.
Darwin, B. The Dickens advertiser: a collection of the advertisements in the original parts of novels by Dickens. 1930. A narrative and criticism with facs. *See* W. Dexter and 'K. Bromhill' (T. W. Hill), The David Copperfield advertiser, Dickensian 41 1945.
S[awyer], C. J. and F. J. H. D[arton]. Dickens v. Barabbas. 1930.
Waugh, A. A hundred years of publishing: being the story of Chapman & Hall. 1930.
König, K. Dickens und das Theater. Stettin 1932.
Fabre, E. Dickens in France. Dickensian 28 1932.
Partington, W. Dickens, Thackeray and Yates. Saturday Rev 11 March 1933. *See* Bookman (London) 76 1933.
Winterich, J. T. An American friend of Dickens. New York 1933.
Buzzichini, M. Dickens, buon cristiano. Pan 2 1934.
Fantham, H. B. Dickens: a biological study of his personality. Character & Personality 2 1934.
Dexter, W. Dickens, journalist. Nineteenth Century June 1934.
—— Dickens and the Morning Chronicle. Fortnightly Rev Nov 1934.
—— For one night only: Dickens's appearances as an amateur actor. Dickensian 35–7 1939–41.
—— Provincial towns visited by Dickens and his amateur company. Dickensian 37 1941.
—— ('L. A. Kennethe'). Memorials of friendship. Ibid. Dickens's dedications of his books.

— The Dickens Fellowship in retrospect. Dickensian 40 1944. *See* A. W. Edwards and J. Greaves, Dickensian 47–8 1951–2. *See bibliography of Dexter's writings on Dickens*, Dickensian 40 1944.

Squires, P. C. The case of Dickens as viewed by biology and psychology. Jnl of Abnormal Psychology 30 1936.

— Dickens as criminologist. Jnl of Criminal Law & Criminology 29 1939.

Ilchester, Earl of. Chronicles of Holland House. 1937.

Connell, J. M. The religion of Dickens. Hibbert Jnl 36 1938.

Dean, F. R. Dickens and Manchester. Dickensian 34 1938.

Gummer, E. N. Dickens and Germany. MLR 33 1938.

— Dickens's works in Germany 1837–1937. Oxford 1940.

Pike, J. S. Dickens, Carlyle and Tennyson. Ed H. Davis, Atlantic Monthly Dec 1939.

Rand, F. H. Les adaptations théâtrales des romans de Dickens en Angleterre 1837–1870. Paris 1939.

Russev, R. From Lamb to Dickens. Annual of Sofia Univ Faculty of History & Philology 44 1948.

Storey, Gladys. Dickens and daughter. 1939. *See* G. B. Shaw, Dickens and Mrs Perugini, TLS 29 July 1939, in support of her contentions; also his letter about Mrs Perugini (Kate Dickens) and her parents, Time & Tide 27 July 1935.

Mason, L. A tale of three authors [Dickens, Ainsworth and Poe]. 1940. Rptd from Dickensian 36 1940. *See* his further essays on Dickens and Poe, Dickensian 36 1940, 39 1943, 42 1946, 47 1951. *See* G. G. Grubb and A. B. Nisbet below, and H. W. Webb, Nineteenth-Century Fiction 15 1961.

— The Dickensian: a tale of fifty years. Dickensian 51 1955. *See* TLS 15 Feb 1968.

Grubb, G. G. Dickens's first experience as a parliamentary reporter. Dickensian 36 1940.

— The personal and literary relationships of Dickens and Poe. Nineteenth-Century Fiction 5 1951.

— Personal and business relationships of Dickens and T. C. Evans. Dickensian 48 1952.

— Dickens's quarrel with John A. Overs. Dickensian 49 1953.

— Dickens and his brother Fred. Dickensian 50 1954.

Pattee, F. L. The shadow of Dickens [on American fiction of the 1850s]. In his Feminine fifties, New York 1940.

Shaskolskaya, T. Dickens and Carlyle. Trans of Herzen State Pedagogical Inst in Leningrad 29 1940.

Houtchens, L. H. Dickens and international copyright. Amer Lit 13 1942. *See* K. J. Fielding, Bull of Br Assoc for Amer Stud Aug 1962, and A. J. Clark, below.

— The spirit of the times and a 'New work by Boz'. PMLA 67 1952. A hoax.

— and C. W. Houtchens. Contributions of early American journals to the study of Dickens. MLQ 6 1945.

Dickensian (American no): centenary of Dickens's first visit. Dickensian 38 1942. *See* earlier American nos, Aug 1908, Aug 1909, Aug 1910, Sept 1916, April 1926.

Hill, T. W. The Staplehurst railway accident. Dickensian 38 1942.

— Books that Dickens read. Dickensian 45 1949.

— Dickensian biography from Forster to the present day. Dickensian 47 1951.

— Light on the Guild of Literature and Art and the Jerrold Fund. Ibid.

McNulty, J. H. Concerning Dickens and other literary characters. 1942.

Dana, H. W. L. Longfellow and Dickens. Cambridge [Mass] Historical Soc Pbns 28 1943.

Davis, E. R. Dickens and Wilkie Collins. Univ of Wichita Stud no 16 1945. *See* R. P. Ashley, below.

Boll, E. Dickens and Washington Irving. MLQ 5 1944. Reply by C. Wegelin 7 1946. *See* W. C. D. Pacey, Amer Lit 16 1945.

— The infusion of Dickens in Trollope. Trollopian 1 1946.

Pope-Hennessy, U. Dinner with Mr and Mrs Dickens; Dickens and his wine cellar. Wine & Food nos 44–5 1945. *See* M. Lane, Purely for pleasure, 1966.

— The Gad's Hill library. Dickensian 41 1945.

Kiddle, M. Caroline Chisholm and Dickens. Historical Stud of Australia & New Zealand 3 1945. *See* her Caroline Chisholm, Melbourne 1950, ch 5.

Randall, D. A. Dickens and Richard Bentley. TLS 12 Oct 1946. *See* 5–12 Jan, 2, 23 March, 2 Nov 1946, and R. A. Gettman, A Victorian publisher: a study of the Bentley papers, Cambridge 1960.

Christian, M. G. Carlyle's influence upon the social theory of Dickens. Trollopian 1–2 1946–7.

Cruikshank, R. J. In his Roaring century 1846–1946, 1946.

Hopkins, A. B. Dickens and Mrs Gaskell. HLQ 9 1946.

— Dickens: North and south and the difficulties of serial publication. In her Elizabeth Gaskell, 1952.

Staples, L. C. Dickens and Australian emigration. Dickensian 42 1946.

— The Dickens ancestry: some new discoveries. Dickensian 45 1949; 1951 (with addns).

— Sidelight on a great friendship. Dickensian 47 1951. Extracts from unpbd diary of Hon Mrs R. Watson.

— New letters of Mary Hogarth and her sister Catherine. Dickensian 63 1967.

Candiver, E. P. Dickens's knowledge of Shakespeare. Shakespeare Assoc Bull 21 1946.

Hamilton, R. Dickens in his characters. Nineteenth Century July 1947.

— Dickens triumphant. Quart Rev 149 1954.

Atkins, S. A possible Dickens influence in Zola. MLQ 8 1947.

Gibson, F. Dickens and Germany. Dickensian 43 1947.

Miller, W. Dickens's reading at the British Museum. Ibid.

Pound, L. The American dialect of Dickens. Amer Speech 22 1947.

Ford, G. H. The Governor Eyre case in England. UTQ 17 1948.

O'Sullivan, D. Dickens and Thomas Moore. Studies 37 1948.

Katkov, G. Steerforth and Stavrogin: on the sources of The possessed. Slavonic & East European Rev 27 1949. *See* M. A. Futrell and A. Wexler, below.

Ashley, R. P. Wilkie Collins reconsidered [in relation to Dickens]. Nineteenth-Century Fiction 4 1950.

— Collins and the Dickensians. Dickensian 49 1953. Reply by K. J. Fielding, ibid. *See* H. Stone, 53 1957, and A. A. Adrian, HLQ 16 1953.

Rolfe, F. P. Dickens and the Ternans. Nineteenth-Century Fiction 4 1950. *See* A. B. Nisbet below, and M. Morley, The theatrical Ternans, Dickensian 54–7 1958–61.

Vivian, C. H. Dickens, the True Sun and Samuel Laman Blanchard. Nineteenth-Century Fiction 4 1950.

Bredsdorff, E. H. C. Andersen og Dickens. Copenhagen 1951; rev and tr Cambridge 1956 and in Anglistica 8 1956.

Fielding, K. J. Dickens to Miss Burdett Coutts. TLS 2–9 March 1951. Letters.

— Women in the home: an article Dickens did *not* write. Dickensian 47 1951.

— Dickens and R. H. Horne. English 9 1952.

— J. H. Barrow and the Royal Literary Fund. Dickensian 48 1952.

— Charles Whitehead and Dickens. RES new ser 3 1952.

— Dickens and Colin Rae Brown. Nineteenth-Century Fiction 7 1953.

— A great friendship (Miss Burdett Coutts). Dickensian 49 1953. Further articles on Dickens and Miss Coutts, ibid; Nineteenth-Century Fiction 8 1954; Dickensian 51 1955, 57 1961, 61 1965. *See* C. B. Patterson, below.

— Dickens since Forster. TLS 9 Oct 1953.
— Dickens and The ruffian. English 10 1954.
— Dickens and the Royal Literary Fund 1855. TLS 15-22 Oct 1954.
— Dickens and the Royal Literary Fund 1858. RES new ser 6 1955.
— Dickens in 1858. Dickensian 52 1956.
— Dickens and the Hogarth scandal. Nineteenth-Century Fiction 10 1956.
— Dickens and his wife: fact or forgery? Etudes Anglaises 8 1955.
— Charles Reade and Dickens: a fight against piracy. Theatre Notebook July 1956.
— The monthly serialisation of Dickens's novels. Dickensian 54 1958. Reply by H. M. Levy 63 1967.
— The weekly serialisation of Dickens's novels. Ibid.
Hudson, R. B. The Dickens affair again. College Eng Nov 1951.
Nisbet, A. B. Dickens loses an election. Princeton Univ Lib Chron 11 1951.
— New light on the Dickens-Poe relationship. Nineteenth-Century Fiction 5 1951.
— Dickens and Ellen Ternan. Berkeley 1952.
Robinson, K. The Dickens circle. In his Wilkie Collins, 1951. *See* N. P. Davis, wife of Wilkie Collins, Urbana 1956.
Adrian, A. A. Dickens on American slavery: a Carlylean slant. PMLA 67 1952.
— A note on the Dickens-Collins friendship. HLQ 16 1953.
— Georgina Hogarth and the Dickens circle. Oxford 1957.
Fawcett, F. D. Dickens the dramatist: on stage, screen and radio. 1952.
Patterson, C. B. Angela Burdett-Coutts and the Victorians. 1953. Ch 5, Friendship with Dickens.
Monod, S. Du nouveau sur Dickens? Etudes Anglaises 7 1954.
Ray, G. N. Dickens versus Thackeray: the Garrick Club affair. PMLA 69 1954. Reply by E. Johnson 71 1956.
Brown, T. J. English literary autographs: Dickens. Book Collector 4 1955. Analysis of his handwriting.
Collins, P. A. W. Bruce Castle: a school Dickens admired. Dickensian 51 1955.
— Dickens and Froebel. Nat Froebel Foundation Bull no 94 1955.
— Dickens and Ragged schools. Dickensian 55 1959.
— Dickens and the prison governor. Dickensian 57 1961.
— Dickens and adult education. Leicester 1962.
— Dickens in conversation. Dickensian 59 1963.
— Dickens and the Edinburgh Review. RES new ser 14 1963.
— Dickens's reading. Dickensian 60 1964.
— Dickens and popular amusements. Dickensian 61 1965.
— Dickens and Punch. Dickens Stud 3 1967.
Futrell, M. A. Gogol and Dickens. Slavonic & East European Rev 34 1956.
— Dickens and Dostoevsky. Eng Miscellany (Rome) 7 1956.
Manning, J. Dickens and the Glasgow System. School & Soc 83 1956.
— Dickens and the Oswego System. JHI 18 1957.
Haight, G. S. Dickens and Lewes. PMLA 71 1956.
Hunter, R. A. and I. Macalpine. A note on Dickens's psychiatric reading. Dickensian 53 1957.
— Dickens and Conolly. TLS 11 Aug 1961. Reply by P. Collins 18 Aug 1961.
Stone, H. Dickens's knowledge of Thackeray's writings. Dickensian 53 1957.
— Dickens and Harriet Beecher Stowe. Nineteenth-Century Fiction 12 1958.
— Dickens and the Jews. Victorian Stud 2 1959. *See* 3 1960.
— Dark corners of the mind: Dickens's childhood reading. Horn Book Mag 39 1963; rptd in J. Warriner, English grammar and composition, New York 1964.
— Dickens, Browning and the mysterious letter. Pacific Coast Philology 1 1965.
Altick, R. D. In his English common reader: a social history of the mass reading public 1800–1900, Chicago 1957.
Peyrouton, N. C. Rapping the rappers. Dickensian 55 1959. Dickens and spiritualism.
— Dickens and the Christian socialists. Dickensian 58 1962.
— Some Boston abolitionists on Boz. Dickensian 60 1964.
— Dickens and the Chartists. Ibid.
Aylmer, F. Dickens incognito. 1959. *See* Sunday Times 13 Dec 1959, when G. Storey presented new evidence and Aylmer retracted part of his case about Dickens and Ellen Ternan.
Clark, A. J. The movement for international copyright in nineteenth-century America. Washington 1960.
Tillotson, K. A letter from Mary Hogarth. TLS 23 Dec 1960.
Rees, R. Dickens: or the intelligence of the heart. In his For love or money 1960.
Moers, E. The dandy: Brummell to Beerbohm. New York 1960. Ch 10.
Korg, J. (ed). London in Dickens's day: a book of primary source materials. Englewood Cliffs NJ 1960.
Cuza, J. A. Dickens in Philadelphia. Philadelphia History 4 1960.
Mackaness, G. A Dickens link with America. Amer Book Collector 11 1960.
— A Dickens link with Australia. Royal Australian Historical Soc Jnl 48 1962.
Waller, J. D. Dickens and the American Civil War. SP 57 1960.
Wagenknecht, E. Mrs Hawthorne on Dickens. Boston Public Lib Quart 12 1960.
Du Cann, C. G. L. The love-lives of Dickens. 1961.
Gilenson, B. Dickens in Russia. Dickensian 57 1961.
Calhoun, P. Dickens in Maine. Colby Lib Quart ser 6 1962.
Klinke, G. A. Dickens découvre l'Amérique. Revue de l'Université Laval 16 1962.
Lincoln, V. Charles: a novel inspired by certain events in the life of Mr Charles Dickens. New York 1962. His relations with women.
Wexler, A. Dickens und Dostojewski. Deutsche Rundschau 88 1962.
Elsna, H. Unwanted wife: a defence of Mrs Charles Dickens. 1963.
James, L. Fiction for the working man 1830–50. Oxford 1963. Ch 4, Plagiarisms of Dickens.
Chaudhry, G. A. Dickens and Hawthorne. Essex Inst Historical Collections, special Hawthorne no 1964.
Darroll, G. M. H. Dickens and Maria Beadnell. Eng Stud in Africa 7 1964.
Fanger, D. Dostoevsky and romantic realism: a study of Dostoevsky in relation to Balzac, Dickens and Gogol. Cambridge Mass 1965.
Fleissner, R. F. Dickens and Shakespeare. New York 1965.
Hutchings, R. J. Dickens at Bonchurch. Dickensian 61 1965.
Senelick, L. Charl'z Dikkens and the Russian encyclopaedias. Dickens Stud 1 1965.
Carrow, G. D. An informal call upon Dickens in 1867. University: a Princeton Quart no 27 1966; rptd in Dickensian 63 1967.
Carter, J. A. Memories of 'Charley Wag'. Dickensian 62 1966. Reprints J. H. Stocqueler's reminiscences of the young Dickens, pbd 1875.
Katarsky, I. M. Dikkens v. Rossii: seredina XIX veka. Moscow 1966.

Lansbury, C. Dickens and his Australia. Royal Australian Historical Soc Jnl 52 1966.
Bell, A. D. London in the age of Dickens. Norman Oklahoma 1967.

Personal Recollections and Memoirs

References to Dickens occur in numerous contemporary biographies and vols of reminiscence. They can be traced through his more intimate friendships, for which see J. W. T. Ley, The Dickens circle, 1918, *and* W. T. Shore, Dickens and his friends, 1909. *A number of extracts are given in* J. A. Hammerton, The Dickens companion, 1910, *and in* Peeps at Dickens: pen pictures from contemporary sources, Dickensian *passim. The following select and alphabetical list includes only writers not previously mentioned whose personal contacts with Dickens have more than casual interest.*

Ainger, A. Mr Dickens's amateur theatricals. Macmillan's Mag Jan 1871; rptd in his Lectures and essays vol 2, 1905.
Ainsworth, W. H. William Harrison Ainsworth and his friends, by S. M. Ellis. 2 vols 1911.
Andersen, H. C. In his Pictures of travel, New York 1871. Pp. 267–93, A visit at Dickens's house. *See* R. N. Bain's Life of Andersen 1895, and H. C. Andersen's correspondence (*above, Letters*).
Anderson, J. R. An actor's life. 1902.
[Beard, N.] Some recollections of yesterday. Temple Bar July 1894. By the son of Dickens's lifelong friend, Thomas Beard.
Berger, F. Reminiscences, impressions and anecdotes. [1913]. Ch 3.
—— Memories of Dickens. Living Age 332 1927.
—— 97. [1932]. Ch 1.
Boyle, Mary: her book. Ed C. Boyle 1901.
Browning, R. Life and letters, ed Mrs S. Orr 1908 (rev).
Carlyle, T. Thomas Carlyle: a history of his life in London 1838–81, by J. A. Froude. 2 vols 1884. *See* Carlyle's letters, ed C. R. Sanders, Bull John Rylands Lib 38 1956.
Chorley, H. F. Autobiography; with memoir and letters. Ed H. G. Hewlett 2 vols 1873. *See his* Charles Dickens, Athenaeum 18 June 1870.
C[hristian], E. E. Reminiscences of Dickens, from a young lady's diary. Englishwoman's Domestic Mag June 1871; rev and enlarged as Recollections of Dickens, his family and friends, Temple Bar April 1888. *See* J. C. Maxwell, Mrs Christian's reminiscences of Dickens, RES new ser 2 1951, and W. J. Carlton, Who was the lady? Dickensian 60 1964.
Clarke, C. and M. C. Recollections of writers. 1878. *See* Mary Cowden Clarke, My long life, 1896.
Cole, H. Fifty years of the public life of Sir Henry Cole. 2 vols 1884.
Collier, J. P. An old man's diary, forty years ago. 4 pts 1871–2 (priv ptd).
Collins, W. W.: about Dickens, from a marked copy of Forster's Life. Pall Mall Gazette 20 Jan 1890. *See* N. P. Davis, Life of Wilkie Collins, Urbana 1956.
Compton, H., Memoir by C. and E. Compton. 1879.
Cross, C. Dickens, a memory. New Liberal Rev 2 1901.
Dickens, A. T. Reminiscences of Dickens. Great Thoughts 12 Nov 1910.
—— My father and his friends. Nash's Mag Sept 1911.
—— New chapters from the life of Dickens. Cosmopolitan Mag 52 1912.
Dickens, Charles jr. Introds to Works, Macmillan edn, 21 vols 1892–1925.
—— Glimpses of Dickens. North Amer Rev May-June 1895.
—— Reminiscences of my father. Windsor Mag Christmas suppl 1934.

Dickens, H. F. Dickens at work. Lloyd's Weekly News 6 Feb 1910.
—— Chat about Dickens. Harper's Mag July 1914.
—— Memories of my father. 1928.
—— Recollections. 1934.
Dickens, K. *See* K. Perugini, below.
Dickens, M. Dickens at home. Cornhill Mag Jan 1885. *See Biographies, above.*
—— My father in his home life. Ladies' Home Jnl 29 1912.
Dickens, M. A. A child's memories of Gad's Hill. Strand Mag Jan 1897.
—— My grandfather as I knew him. Nash's Mag Oct 1911.
Drew, E. Dickens as I knew him. Tit-Bits 10 Feb 1912.
'Eliot, George'. Letters, ed G. S. Haight, 7 vols Oxford 1954–6.
Fields, Mrs A. A. Diaries, in Memories of a hostess, ed M. A. de W. Howe, Boston 1922. Ch 5, With Dickens in America. *See* unpbd diaries, ed L. C. Staples, Dickensian 47 1951.
Fields, J. T. Some memoirs of Dickens. Atlantic Monthly Aug 1870; rev and enlarged in his Yesterdays with authors, 1872; rptd as In and out of doors with Dickens, Boston 1876. *See* J. T. Fields: biographical notes and personal sketches, Boston 1881.
Frith, W. P. My autobiography and reminiscences. 3 vols 1887–8. *See* his daughter Mrs E. M. Ward's Memories of ninety years, [1924].
Hall, S. C. A book of memories of great men and women of the age, from personal acquaintance. 1870.
—— Retrospect of a long life, from 1815 to 1883. 2 vols 1883.
H[elps], A. In memoriam. Macmillan's Mag July 1870.
Hodder, G. Memories of my time. 1870.
Hogarth, G. How Dickens wrote. Evening News 10 Nov 1909.
Hollingshead, J. My lifetime. 2 vols 1895. *See* F. A. Gibson, Dickensian 62 1966.
—— In his According to my lights, 1900.
Hood, T. Thomas Hood: his life and times, by Walter Jerrold. 1907. *See* J. C. Reid, Thomas Hood, 1963.
Horne, R. H. Byegone celebrities: I, The guild of literature and art at Chatsworth; II, Mr Nightingale's Diary. GM Feb, May 1871; rptd with addns in Letters of E. B. Browning to R. H. Horne vol 2, 1887. *See* K. J. Fielding, Dickens and R. H. Horne, English 9 1952.
—— John Forster: his early life and friendships. Temple Bar April 1876.
Houghton, Baron (R. M. Milnes). Life, letters and friendships, by T. W. Reid. 2 vols 1890.
Hughes, J. L. Personal reminiscences relating to Dickens. Jnl of Education 101 1925.
Hullah, J. Life, by his wife. 1886.
Jeaffreson, J. C. A book of recollections. 2 vols 1894.
Jeffrey, F. Life of Lord Jeffrey, with a selection from his correspondence, by Lord Cockburn. 2 vols Edinburgh 1852.
Jerrold, D. Douglas Jerrold, dramatist and wit, by Walter Jerrold. [1918].
Jerdan, W. Autobiography. 4 vols 1852–3.
—— Personal reminiscences. Ed R. H. Stoddard 1874.
Knight, C. Passages of a working life. 3 vols 1864–5.
Latimer, E. W. A girl's recollection of Dickens. Lippincott's Mag Sept 1893.
Lehmann, R. C. Memories of half a century. 1908. Ch 7. *See* J. Lehmann, Ancestors and friends, 1962.
Lever, C. J. Life, by W. J. Fitzpatrick. 2 vols 1879.
Linton, E. (Mrs Lynn Linton). My literary life. 1899.
Locker-Lampson, F. My confidences. 1896.
Mackay, C. Forty years' recollections 1830–70. 2 vols 1877.
—— Through the long day: memorials of a literary life. 2 vols 1887.
Macready, W. C. Reminiscences and selections from his diaries and letters. Ed F. Pollock 2 vols 1875.

— Diaries. Ed W. Toynbee 2 vols 1912. *See* P. Collins, Macready and Dickens: some family recollections, Dickens Stud 2 1966.
Marryat, F. Life and letters, by Florence Marryat. 2 vols 1872.
Martin, T. Memories of Dickens. Great Thoughts 28 Sept 1907.
Martineau, H. Autobiography. 3 vols 1877.
Mason, E. T. Personal traits of British authors, vol 3. New York 1885.
Morley, H. Life, by H. S. Solly. 1898. Chs 10–11.
Norton, C. E. English friends, from his letters and journals, ed S. Norton and M. A. de W. Howe, Scribner's Mag 53 1913.
Perugini, K. [née Dickens]. Dickens as a lover of art and artists. Mag of Art Jan–Feb 1903.
— Edwin Drood and the last days of Dickens. Pall Mall Mag June 1906.
— Thackeray and my father. Pall Mall Mag Aug 1911.
— My father's love for children. Dickensian 7 1911.
— Foreword to Mr and Mrs Charles Dickens: his letters to her, ed W. Dexter 1935. *See* Gladys Storey, Dickens and daughter, 1939.
Pollock, F. Personal reminiscences. 2 vols 1887.
Priestley, Lady [Eliza]. The story of a lifetime. 1904. Includes letters etc from her uncle, W. H. Wills.
Ritchie, Lady [A. T., née Thackeray]. Chapters from some memories. 1894.
— Dickens as I remember him. Pall Mall Mag March 1912; rev in her From the porch, 1913.
Rogers, S. Samuel Rogers and his contemporaries, by P. W. Clayden. 2 vols 1889.
Russell, W. H. Life, by J. B. Atkins. 2 vols 1911.
Sala, G. A. H. Things I have seen and people I have known. 2 vols 1894. Vol 1 chs 2–3.
— Life and adventures. 2 vols 1895. Vol 1 chs 6–8, 25–8.
'Schoolfellow and friend.' Recollections of Dickens. Dickensian 7 1911.
Smith, S. Letters, ed N. C. Smith. 2 vols Oxford 1953.
Stone, M. Some recollections of Dickens. Dickensian 6 1910, 8 1912.
Thackeray, W. M. Letters and private papers, ed G. N. Ray 4 vols Oxford 1945–6. Also many allusions and criticisms in essays; *see* especially Jerome Paturot 1843, Charity and humour (English humourists, 1853), and above under Novels. *See* also K. Perugini, above; C. R. Williams, The personal relations of Dickens and Thackeray, Dickensian 35 1939; C. Mauskopf, Thackeray's attitude to Dickens's writing, Nineteenth-Century Fiction 21 1967.
Toole, J. L. Reminiscences, ed J. Hatton 1888. *See* 'Cuthbert Bede', Dickens and Toole, London Figaro 15 April 1874, rptd in Dickensian 28 1932.
Trollope, T. A. What I remember. 2 vols 1887. Vol 2 ch 7.
Wiggin, K. D. A child's journey with Dickens. Boston 1912.
Willis, N. P. Dashes at life. New York 1845.
Yates, E. Recollections and experiences. 2 vols 1884. Vol 1 ch 9, vol 2 ch 11.
Young, C. M., tragedian: memoir by J. C. Young. 2 vols 1871.

Critical Studies

Schmidt, J. Dickens: eine Charakteristik. Leipzig 1852.
Canning, A. S. G. Philosophy of Dickens. 1880.
— Dickens and Thackeray studied in three novels [Pickwick, Nickleby, Vanity Fair]. 1911.
— Dickens studied in six novels. 1912.
Gissing, G. Dickens: a critical study. 1898, 1903 (rev, in Imperial edn of the Works).
— Dickens. In Homes and haunts of English authors, 1906.
— Critical studies of the works of Dickens, ed T. Scott, New York 1924. 9 introds from works ed Gissing. The same introds ed B. W. Matz as The immortal Dickens, 1925. *See* P. Coustillas, Gissing's writings on Dickens, Dickensian 61 1965.
Hughes, J. L. Dickens as an educator. New York 1900.
Chesterton, G. K. and F. G. Kitton. Charles Dickens. 1903.
Baillie-Saunders, M. The philosophy of Dickens: a study of his life and teaching as a social reformer. 1905.
Chesterton, G. K. Charles Dickens. 1906; rptd as Dickens: a critical study, New York 1911 and as Dickens: the last of the great men, introd by A. Woollcott, New York 1942.
— Appreciations and criticisms of the works of Dickens. 1911; rptd as Criticisms and appreciations of the works of Dickens, 1933. Collects introds to EL.
— In The great Victorians, ed H. J. and H. Massingham 1932; rptd in his Handful of authors, 1953.
Leffmann, H. About Dickens: being a few essays on themes suggested by the novels. Philadelphia 1908 (priv ptd).
Munro, W. A. Dickens et Daudet, romanciers de l'enfant et des humbles. Toulouse 1908. *See* J. Garrett (ed), Dickens and Daudet, 1930.
Pugh, E. W. Dickens: the apostle of the people. 1908.
— The Dickens originals. 1912.
Smith, M. S. C. (ed). Studies in Dickens. New York 1910. Reviews, appreciations etc.
Fyfe, T. A. Dickens and the law. Edinburgh 1910.
Moses, B. Dickens and his girl heroines. 1911.
Spaventa-Filippi, S. Dickens. Rome 1911, 1924 (rev); rptd in his L'umorismo e gli umoristi, Milan 1932.
Walters, J. C. Phases of Dickens: the man, his message and his mission. 1911.
Charles Dickens: a Bookman (London) extra number. 1912. By various writers; chiefly reprints of prefaces, essays etc. Numerous illustrations previously pbd in other forms. Rptd 1914.
Jügler, R. Über die Technik der Charakterisierung in den Jugendwerken von Dickens. Halle 1912.
Lightwood, W. R. In Dickens street. 1912. Studies in Dickens characters.
Whipple, E. P. Dickens: the man and his work. 2 vols Boston 1912.
Swinburne, A. C. Charles Dickens, ed T. Watts-Dunton 1913. Rptd with addns, especially on Oliver Twist, from Quart Rev 1902.
Crotch, W. W. Dickens, social reformer. 1913.
— The pageant of Dickens. 1915, 1916 (rev).
— The soul of Dickens. 1916.
— The secret of Dickens. 1919.
— The touchstone of Dickens. 1920.
Gordon, E. H. The naming of characters in the works of Dickens. Lincoln Nebraska 1917.
Burton, R. E. Dickens: how to know him. Indianapolis 1919.
Phillips, W. C. Dickens, Reade and Collins, sensation novelists. New York 1919.
Hayward, A. L. The days of Dickens. [1926].
Heuer, H. Romaneske Elemente im Realismus von Dickens. Marburg 1927.
Cor, R. Un romancier de la vertu et un peintre du vice: Dickens-Proust. Paris 1928.
Holdsworth, W. S. Dickens as a legal historian. New Haven 1928.
Wierstra, F. D. Smollett and Dickens. Amsterdam 1928.
Clark, C. Dickens and democracy, and other studies. 1930.
Kent, W. R. G. Dickens and religion. 1930.
Procter, W. C. Christian teaching in the novels of Dickens. [1930].
Chancellor, E. B. Dickens and his times. 1932.
Sitwell, O. Dickens. 1932.
Wickhardt, W. Die Forman der Perspektive in Dickens Romanen. Berlin 1933.

Sennewald, C. Die Namengebung bei Dickens: eine Studie über Lautsymbolik. Leipzig 1936.
Jackson, T. A. Dickens: the progress of a radical. 1937.
Christie, O. F. Dickens and his age. 1939.
House, H. The Dickens world. Oxford 1941, 1942 (corrected).
Oehlbaum, I. Das pathologische Element bei Dickens. Siebnen 1944.
Rantavaara, I. Dickens in the light of English criticism. Helsinki 1944.
'Alain' (E. Chartier). En lisant Dickens. Paris 1945.
Lamm, M. Dickens och hans romaner. Stockholm 1947.
Schütze, J. Dickens' Frauenideal und das Biedermeier. Bremen-Blumenthal 1948.
Cruikshank, R. J. Dickens and early Victorian England. 1949.
Yamamoto, T. Growth and system of the language of Dickens: an introduction to a Dickens lexicon. Osaka 1950; 1952 (rev, containing Index by C. Higashida and M. Masui, also pbd separately, Osaka 1952).
— Dickens's style. Tokyo 1960.
Monod, S. Dickens romancier. Paris 1953; tr and rev Norman Oklahoma 1968.
— Dickens. Paris 1958. Includes Filmographie et discographie.
Ford, G. H. Dickens and his readers: aspects of novel-criticism since 1836. Princeton 1955.
Thalmann, L. Dickens in seinen Beziehungen zum Ausland. Zürich 1956.
Butt, J. and K. Tillotson. Dickens at work. 1957.
Miller, J. H. Dickens: the world of his novels. Cambridge Mass 1958.
Silman, T. I. Dickens. Moscow 1958.
Engel, M. The maturity of Dickens. Cambridge Mass 1959.
Manning, J. Dickens on education. Toronto 1959.
Miyazaki, K. Dickens's novels. Tokyo 1959.
Sükösd, M. Dickens. Budapest 1960.
Clark, W. R. (ed). Discussions of Dickens. Boston 1961.
Cockshut, A. O. J. The imagination of Dickens. 1961.
Ford, G. H. and L. Lane jr (ed). The Dickens critics. Ithaca 1961. Anthology with introd and bibliography.
Seehase, G. Dickens: zu einer Besonderheit seines Realismus. Halle 1961.
Collins, P. Dickens and crime. 1962, 1963 (rev).
— Dickens and education. 1963, 1964 (rev).
Gross, J. and G. Pearson (ed). Dickens and the twentieth century. 1962.
Peyrouton, N. C. (ed). Dickens criticism: a symposium. Cambridge Mass 1962.
Reid, J. C. The hidden world of Dickens. Auckland 1962.
Brown, I. Dickens in his time. 1963.
Davis, E. The flint and the flame: the artistry of Dickens. Columbia Missouri 1963.
Spilka, M. Dickens and Kafka. Bloomington 1963.
Marcus, S. Dickens: from Pickwick to Dombey. New York 1964.
Garis, R. The Dickens theatre: a reassessment of the novels. Oxford 1965.
Stoehr, T. Dickens: the dreamer's stance. Ithaca 1965.
Axton, W. F. Circle of fire: Dickens's vision and style and the popular Victorian theatre. Lexington Kentucky 1966.
Coolidge, A. C. Dickens as a serial novelist. Ames Iowa 1967.
Dabney, R. H. Love and property in the novels of Dickens. Berkeley 1967.
Jarmuth, S. L. Dickens's use of women in his novels. New York 1967.

Shorter Studies

Special chs in general histories of English literature are not included. The Dickensian *has recorded these as they have appeared from 1905 onwards, and has also rptd earlier pieces from time to time.*

Some thoughts on arch-waggery and, in especial, on the genius of Boz. Court Mag April 1837. Rptd in Dickensian 4 1908.
[Lister, T.] Dickens's tales. Edinburgh Rev 68 1838.
Dickens and his works. Fraser's Mag April 1840.
Wilson, J. ('Christopher North'). Speech at Edinburgh banquet for Dickens, 25 June 1841. Rptd in Dickensian 12 1916 from Edinburgh Advertiser 29 June 1841.
Rymer, J. M. Popular writing. Queen's Mag 1 1842.
S., J. Dickens's works. London Univ Mag 1 1842.
Whitman, W. Boz and democracy. Brother Jonathan 26 Feb 1842. Rptd in his Rivulets of prose, New York 1928.
Horne, R. H. In his A new spirit of the age vol 1, 1844. *See* E. B. Browning's 2 letters to Horne, 1844, priv ptd 1919 as Dickens and other spirits of the age.
Boz versus Dickens. Parker's London Mag Feb 1845.
Danzel, W. Über Dickens' Romane. Blätter für Literarische Unterhaltung 9–13 Aug 1845.
[Cleghorn, T.?]. Writings of Dickens. North Br Rev 3 1845.
[Eagles, J.] A few words about novels. Blackwood's Mag 64 1848.
[Whipple, E. P.] North Amer Rev 69 1849; rptd in his Literature and life, 1851.
— The genius of Dickens. Atlantic Monthly May 1867.
Skelton, F. W. On the genius of Dickens. Knickerbocker May 1852.
The genius and characters of Dickens. Working Man's Friend & Family Instructor 21 Aug 1852.
Cruikshank, G. A letter from Hop-o'-my-thumb to Charles Dickens esq. [1854]. Rptd from George Cruikshank's Mag Feb 1854.
[Oliphant, M.] Blackwood's Mag April 1855, June 1871.
Talbot, G. F. The genius of Dickens. Putnam's Monthly Mag March 1855.
Trollope, A. The warden. 1855. Dickens as Mr Popular Sentiment, ch 15. *See* L. Stevenson, Dickens and the origin of The warden, Trollopian 2 1947.
— St Paul's Mag July 1870.
— Autobiography. 1883. Ch 13.
Dickens. Ecclesiastic & Theologian 17 1855.
Taine, H. Dickens: son talent et ses oeuvres. Revue des Deux Mondes 1 Feb 1856; rptd in his Histoire de la littérature anglaise vol 5, Paris 1863–4; tr Edinburgh 1871.
[Hamley, E. B.] Remonstrance with Dickens. Blackwood's Mag April 1857.
[Stephen, J. F.] Mr Dickens as a politician; light literature and the Saturday Review. Saturday Rev 3 Jan, 11 July 1857. Replies in Leader 18 July 1857, and by J. Hollingshead, Dickens and his critics, Train Aug 1857; rptd in his Essays vol 2, 1865 and his Miscellanies vol 3, 1874. *See* above, Novels (Little Dorrit).
Jeaffreson, J. C. In his Novels and novelists vol 2, 1858.
Bagehot, W. Nat Rev 7 1858; rptd in his Literary studies vol 2, 1879.
Masson, D. British novelists and their styles. 1859. Ch 4. Enlarged from North Br Rev 15 1851.
[Turner, G.] Dickens and his reviewers. Welcome Guest 1 1860.
Galloway, A. H. A critical dissertation on some of the writings of Dickens. Liverpool [1862?].
Williams, S. F. Dickens: a series of criticisms. Rose, Shamrock & Thistle 3–4 1863–4.
Fitzgerald, P. H. Two English essayists: Lamb and Dickens. In Afternoon lectures on literature and art. 1864.
[McCarthy, J.] Westminster Rev new ser 26 1864; rptd in his Con amore, 1868.
Gourdault, J. Les privilégiés et les pauvres gens dans les romans de Dickens. Revue des Cours Littéraires 2 1865.
[Norton, C. E.] North Amer Rev April 1868.

Sala, G. A. H. Sensationalism in literature. Belgravia Feb 1868.
Stott, G. Contemporary Rev Jan 1869.
Dickens's moral services to literature. Spectator 17 April 1869.
Dickens's use of the Bible. Temple Bar Sept 1869.
Austin, A. Temple Bar July 1870.
Buchner, A. Revue des Cours Littéraires 7 1870.
[Fraser, G.] Saturday Rev 11 June 1870.
Fraser's Mag July 1870.
Ham, J. P. Parables of fiction: a memorial discourse on Dickens. 1870.
[Hutton, R. H.] The genius of Dickens. Spectator 18 June 1870; rptd in his Brief literary criticisms, 1906.
—— The dispute about Dickens. Spectator 7 Feb 1874. Rptd in his Criticisms of contemporary thought and thinkers, vol 1 1894.
Jowett, B. Sermon in Westminster Abbey 19 June 1870. 1870. Rptd in his Sermons biographical and miscellaneous, 1899.
Stanley, A. P. Sermon preached in Westminster Abbey June 19, 1870. 1870; rptd in his Sermons on special occasions, 1882.
Times, 10 June 1870 (leading article); rptd with obituary of Dickens (11 June 1870) in Eminent persons: biographies reprinted from the Times 1870–9, 1880.
Harte, F. B. Dickens in camp. In his Poetical works, Boston 1871.
Two English novelists: Dickens and Thackeray. Dublin Rev April 1871.
London Quart Rev 35 1871.
Buchanan, R. W. The good genie of fiction. St Paul's Mag Feb 1872.
Lewes, G. H. Dickens in relation to criticism. Fortnightly Rev Feb 1872. *See* G. S. Haight, Dickens and Lewes, PMLA 71 1956.
Peacock, W. F. Dickens's nomenclature. Belgravia April–May 1873.
Davey, S. Darwin, Carlyle and Dickens. 1875.
Bulwer and Dickens: a contrast. Temple Bar Jan 1875.
Dilthey, W. Dickens und das Genie des erzählenden Dichters. Westermanns Monatshefte 41 1877. Scattered references in later books and essays. *See* A. Zech, Wilhelm Dilthey's analysis of Dickens, in Stanford studies in language and literature, ed H. Craig, Stanford 1941.
'Browne, Matthew' (W. B. Rands). The letters of Dickens. Contemporary Rev Jan 1880.
[Cullen, P.] The letters of Dickens. Dublin Rev April 1880.
Ruskin, J. Fiction, fair and foul. Nineteenth Century June 1880–Oct 1881; rptd in On the old road vol 2, 1885. Numerous brief references to Dickens throughout Ruskin's career; *see* Index to Works, ed E. T. Cook and A. D. O. Wedderburn, 1902–12.
Watt, J. C. Great novelists: Scott, Thackeray, Dickens, Lytton. Edinburgh 1880.
Morris, M. Fortnightly Rev Dec 1882.
Cook, D. Dickens as a dramatic critic. Longman's Mag May 1883.
Hennequin, E. Dickens: étude analytique. Nouvelle Revue 49 1887.
Howells, W. D. Dickens's Christmas books. In his Criticism and fiction, New York 1891.
—— In his My literary passions, New York 1895.
—— In his Heroines of fiction vol 1, New York 1901.
Lang, A. Dickens. In his Essays in little, 1891. *See* list of Lang's writings on Dickens, Dickensian 41 1945; and R. L. Green, Andrew Lang: real reader of Dickens, Dickensian 57 1961.
Harrison, F. Dickens's place in literature. [1894]; rptd in his Studies in early Victorian literature, 1895.
Lilly, W. S. Four English humorists of the nineteenth century 1895. Dickens, Thackeray, George Eliot and Carlyle.

Saintsbury, G. In his Corrected impressions, 1895. 2 papers on Dickens rev in his Collected essays vol 2, 1923.
Aronstein, P. Dickens-studien. Anglia 18 1896.
—— Dickens und Carlyle. Ibid.
—— Die sozialen und politischen Strömungen in England im zweiten Drittel unseres Jahrhunderts. Archiv 100 1898.
Rideal, C. F. Dickens' heroines and women-folk. [1896] (rev).
Murray, D. C. First the critics, and then a word on Dickens. In his My contemporaries in fiction, 1897.
Henley, W. E. Some notes on Dickens. Pall Mall Mag Aug 1899.
—— In his Views and reviews, 1909.
Meynell, A. Dickens as a writer. Pall Mall Gazette 11–18 Jan 1899.
—— Dickens as a man of letters. Atlantic Monthly Jan 1903.
—— Notes of a reader of Dickens. Dublin Rev April 1912. Rptd as Dickens as a man of letters in her Hearts of controversy, 1917.
Jerome, J. K. My favourite novelist and his best book. Munsey's Mag April 1900.
—— Dickens. Pall Mall Gazette 7 Feb 1912.
[Thompson, F.] Mrs Boythorn and her canary. Academy 19 July 1902.
Cazamian, L. Le roman social en Angleterre 1830–50. 2 vols Paris 1903, 1934 (rev).
Lord, W. F. Dickens. Nineteenth Century Nov 1903.
Johnson, R. B. Dickens as artist. Book Monthly Jan 1906.
Sibbald, W. A. Dickens revisited. Westminster Rev Jan 1907.
More, P. E. The praise of Dickens. In his Shelbourne essays 5th ser, New York 1908.
Barlow, G. The genius of Dickens. [1909].
Christian, E. B. V. Leaves of the lower branch: the attorney in life and letters. 1909.
Spielmann, M. H. How Dickens improved his style. Graphic 12 March 1910. Facs of ms.
Beerbohm, M. Dickens, by G—rge M—re. In A Christmas garland, 1912. A parody of George Moore which is also an oblique criticism of Dickens.
Escott, T. H. S. Dickens: his work, age and influence. London Quart Rev 117 1912.
Nabokoff, V. Dickens: a Russian appreciation. Dickensian 8 1912. Trd from Retch 25 Jan 1912.
Shaw, G. B. On Dickens. Dickensian 10 1914. Numerous references to Dickens in Prefaces, etc; introds to Hard times, 1912, Great expectations, 1937 1947. *See* A. Henderson, Bernard Shaw, New York 1956, ch 55; and H. F. and J. R. Brooks, Dickens in Shaw, Dickensian 59 1963.
Powys, J. C. In his Visions and revisions, 1915.
—— In his Pleasures of literature, 1938.
Leacock, S. Fiction and reality: a study of the art of Dickens. In his Essays and literary studies, 1916.
—— Two humorists: Dickens and Mark Twain. Yale Rev 24 1934.
Laski, E. de. The psychological attitude of Dickens towards surnames. Amer Jnl of Psychology 29 1918.
Crotch, W. W. The decline [in Dickens's reputation]—and after! Dickensian 15 1919.
[Woolf, V.] Dickens by a disciple. TLS 27 March 1919.
Darwin, F. In his Springtime and other essays, 1920.
Zweig, S. Drei Meister: Balzac, Dickens, Dostojewski. Leipzig 1920; tr 1930. Incorporated into his Die Baumeister der Welt vol 1, 1920, tr 1939. Essay on Dickens tr in Dial Jan 1923.
Santayana, G. Dickens. Dial Nov 1921; rptd in his Soliloquies in England 1922, and his Essays in literary criticism, New York 1957.
Westendorpf, K. Das Prinzip der Verwendung des Slang bei Dickens. Greifswald 1923.

Whibley, C. A study of Dickens. Dickensian 19 1923. *See* Empire Mag March 1923.
Elton, O. Dickens and Thackeray. 1924. Separate issue of chs from A survey of English literature 1830–80, 2 vols 1920, with some addns.
Smith, H. B. How Dickens wrote his books. Harper's Mag Dec 1924; rptd Strand Mag Feb 1925.
Priestley, J. B. The secret of Dickens. Saturday Rev 26 Sept 1925.
—— The English comic characters. 1925. The two Wellers, Dick Swiveller, Mr Micawber.
—— English humour. 1929.
—— New judgment. Dickensian 40 1944.
Quiller-Couch, A. T. Dickens and other Victorians. Cambridge 1925.
Stevens, J. S. Dickens's use of the English Bible. Dickensian 21 1925.
Apostolai, N. Tolstoy and Dickens. In his Family views of Tolstoy ed Aylmer Maude, 1926.
Belloc, H. Dickens revisited. New Statesman 22 Jan 1927.
Eliot, T. S. Wilkie Collins and Dickens. TLS 4 Aug 1927; rptd in his Selected essays, 1932.
'Maurois, André' (E. S. W. Herzog). Un essai sur Dickens. Paris 1927; rptd in his Etudes anglaises, Paris 1927; rev, enlarged and tr as Dickens, 1934.
Devonshire, M. G. The English novel in France 1830–70. 1929.
Walpole, H. In The eighteen-seventies, ed H. Granville-Barker 1929.
Lemonnier, L. L'actualité de Dickens. Mercure de France 15 Nov 1936.
—— Génie de Dickens. French Rev 11 1938.
Saxe, J. L. Bernard Shaw's phonetics: a comparative study in Cockney sound-changes. Copenhagen 1936. Compares Dickens's dialect usages.
Compton-Rickett, A. Dickens once again. In his Portraits and personalities, 1937.
Young, G. M. In his Daylight and champaign, 1937.
Brussel, J. A. Dickens, child psychologist and sociologist. Psychiatric Quart Suppl 1938.
Crabb Robinson, H. On books and their authors. Ed E. J. Morley 3 vols 1938. Many references to Dickens 1837–64.
Matthews, W. Cockney past and present. 1938.
Sitwell, O. Dickens and the modern novel. In his Trio, 1938.
Lucas, A. Some Dickens women. Yale Rev 29 1940.
Maly-Schatter, F. The Puritan element in Victorian fiction, with especial reference to George Eliot, Dickens and Thackeray. Zürich 1940.
'Orwell, George' (E. Blair). In his Inside the whale, 1940; rptd in his Critical essays, 1946.
Wilson, E. Dickens: the two Scrooges. In his Wound and the bow, Boston 1941. *See* Foreword to his Triple thinkers, 1952.
Churchill, R. C. Dickens, drama and tradition. Scrutiny 10 1942.
Grubb, G. G. Dickens's pattern of weekly serialisation. ELH 9 1942.
Stoll, E. E. Heroes and villains: Shakespeare, Middleton, Byron, Dickens. RES 18 1942; rptd in his From Shakespeare to Joyce, New York 1944.
Stevenson, L. Dickens's dark novels. Sewanee Rev 51 1943.
Simpson, E. Jonson and Dickens: a study in the comic genius of London. E & S 29 1944.
'Cranfield, Lionel' (E. Sackville-West). Books in general. New Statesman 10 Feb, 3 Nov 1945; rptd 1949 (rev, as Dickens and the world of childhood, in his Inclinations).
Laird, J. Philosophy in the works of Dickens. In his Philosophical incursions into English literature, Cambridge 1946.
Shettle, G. T. Dickens and the church, and other essays. 1946.

Warner, R. On reading Dickens. In his Cult of power, 1946.
Heilman, R. B. The New World in Dickens's writings. Trollopian 1–2 1946–7.
House, H. Two aspects of Dickens. Listener 23 Jan 1947.
—— The macabre Dickens; The Dickens story. Both in his All in due time, 1955.
Wenger, J. Character-types of Scott, Balzac, Dickens and Zola. PMLA 62 1947.
Aldington, R. The underworld of young Dickens. In his Four English portraits, 1948.
Aydelotte, W. O. The England of Marx and Mill as reflected in fiction. Tasks of Economic History 7 1948.
Winters, W. Dickens and the psychology of dreams. PMLA 63 1948.
—— Dickens: the pursuers and the pursued. Victorian Newsletter no 23 1963.
—— The death hug in Dickens. Lit & Psychology 16 1966.
Highet, G. Dickens as a dramatist. In his People, places and books, New York 1949.
Eisenstein, S. Dickens, Griffith and the film today. In his Film form, New York 1949.
Petersen, E. L. Searcher after truth. In If by your art, ed E. L. Petersen, Pittsburgh 1949.
Allen, W. The world of Dickens's imagination. Listener 16 Feb 1950.
Boege, F. Point of view in Dickens. PMLA 65 1950.
—— Recent criticism of Dickens. Nineteenth-Century Fiction 8 1954.
Roland-Holst, H. Romanskunst als Levensschool (Tolstoi, Balzac en Dickens). Arnhem 1954.
Johnson, E. Dickens, Fagin and Mr Riah. Commentary 9 1950.
—— The present state of Dickensian studies. Victorian Newsletter no 7 1955.
—— Dickens and Shaw: critics of society. Virginia Quart Rev 33 1957.
Lukács, G. The historical novel, tr H. and S. Mitchell New York 1950.
Oppel, H. Die Kunst des Erzählens im englische Roman des 19 Jahrhunderts. Bielefeld 1950.
Van Ghent, D. The Dickens world: a view from Todgers's. Sewanee Rev 58 1950.
Wilson, A. Dickens and the divided conscience. Month May 1950.
—— Dickens: a haunting. CQ 2 1960.
—— The heroes and heroines of Dickens. REL 2 1961.
Rooke, E. Fathers and sons in Dickens. E & S new ser 4 1951.
Praz, M. La crisi dell'eroe nel romanze vittoriano. Florence 1952; tr as The hero in eclipse in Victorian fiction, 1956. Pt 2.
Gibson, P. Dickens's use of animism. Nineteenth-Century Fiction 7 1953.
Grazhdanskaia, Z. T. Uchenye zapiski Moskovskogo Oblastnogo Pedagogischeskogo Instituta 26 1953.
Lindsay, J. Dickens and women. Twentieth Century Nov 1953.
Izzo, C. Autobiografismo di Dickens. Venice 1954.
——Cultura e Scuola 1 1961.
Pritchett, V. S. The humour of Dickens. Listener 3 June 1954; rev as The comic world of Dickens in The Avon book of modern writing no 2, New York 1955.
—— The great reformist. New Statesman 1 Oct 1960.
Trilling, L. Introduction to Little Dorrit. In his Opposing self, New York 1955.
—— The Dickens of our day. In his Gathering of fugitives, Boston 1956.
Clark, W. R. The rationale of Dickens's death-rate. Boston Univ Stud in English 2 1956.
—— The hungry Mr Dickens. Dalhousie Rev 36 1956.
'O'Connor, Frank' (M. O'Donovan). Dickens: the intrusion of the audience. In his Mirror in the roadway, New York 1956.

Pascal, R. Dickens and Kafka. Listener 26 April 1956.
Plichet, A. and P. Dickens et ses observations neuro-psychiatriques. La Presse Medicale 25 Dec 1956.
Borinski, L. Dickens' Spätstil. Die Neueren Sprachen Sept 1957.
— Meister des modernen englischen Romans. Heidelberg 1963.
Coveney, P. The child in Dickens. In his Poor monkey: the child in literature, 1957, 1967 (rev as The image of childhood).
Dalziel, M. In her Popular fiction 100 years ago, 1957.
James, G. I. Dickens: an essay in Christian evaluation. Blackfriars Mag Nov 1957.
Milner, I. The nature of the hero in Dickens and the eighteenth-century tradition. Philologica 9 1957.
Pearson, G. Dickens and his readers. Universities & Left Rev 1 1957.
— Dickens: the present position. In Dickens and the twentieth century, ed J. Gross and G. Pearson 1962.
Zabel, M. D. The reputation revised. In his Craft and character in modern fiction, New York 1957.
Bush, D. A note on Dickens's humour. In From Jane Austen to Joseph Conrad, ed R. C. Rathburn and M. Steinmann, Minneapolis 1958. Also in his Engaged and disengaged, Cambridge Mass 1966.
Cox, C. B. In defence of Dickens. E & S new ser 11 1958.
Lane, L. jr. Dickens's archetypal Jew. PMLA 73 1958.
— Dickens and the double. Dickensian 54 1958.
McMaster, R. D. Dickens and the horrific. Dalhousie Rev 38 1958. The influence of his childhood reading.
Mitchell, R. J. and M. D. R. Leys. Dickens's London. In their History of London life, 1958.
Perez de Alaya, R. Cervantes en Dickens. In his Principios y fináles de la novela, Madrid 1958.
Reinhold, H. Kritik an der religiösen und moralischen Anschauungen in Dickens' Werken im 19 Jahrhundert. Anglia 76 1958.
Stone, H. Dickens and interior monologue. SP 55 1958.
Harder, K. B. Dickens names his characters. Names 7 1959.
Horsman, E. A. Dickens and the structure of the novel. Dunedin 1959.
Quirk, R. Dickens and appropriate language. Durham 1959.
— The language of Dickens. In Langue et littérature, Paris 1961.
— Some observations on the language of Dickens. REL 2 1961.
Raleigh, J. H. Dickens and the sense of time. Nineteenth-Century Fiction 13 1959.
Smith, S. M. Anti-mechanism and the comic in Dickens. Renaissance & Modern Stud 3 1959.
Stang, R. The theory of the novel in England 1850–70. 1959. Ch 1.
Viebrock, H. Die Leistung der Syntax für den Stil, dargestellt an Dickens' Prosa. In Sprache und Literatur Englands und Amerikas, ed G. Müller-Schwefe and H. Metzger vol 3, Tübingen 1959.
— The knocker: a motif in Hoffman and Dickens. E Studies 43 1962.
Wilson, A. H. The great theme in Dickens. Susquehanna Univ Stud 6 1959.
Brain, R. Dickens, neuro-psychiatrist; Dickensian diagnoses. Both in his Some reflections on genius, 1960.
Coolidge, A. C. Dickens's humour. Victorian Newsletter no 18 1960.
— Dickens and the heart as hope for heaven. Victorian Newsletter no 20 1961.
— Dickens and the philosophic basis of melodrama. Ibid.
— Dickens's complex plots. Dickensian 57 1961.
— Dickens's use of character as novelty. South Atlantic Quart 61 1962.
Fiedler, L. A. In his No! in thunder, Boston 1960.
Rosenberg, M. The dramatist in Dickens. JEGP 59 1960.
Bauer, H. In his Seasoned to taste, Seattle 1961.
Butt, J. Editing a nineteenth-century novelist: proposals for an edition of Dickens. In English studies today 2nd ser, Berne 1961.
— (ed). Dickens number. REL 2 1961.
— Dickens's manuscripts. Yale Univ Lib Gazette 36 1962.
Collins, P. A. W. Queen Mab's chariot among the steam engines: Dickens and 'fancy'. E Studies 42 1961.
Hardy, B. The change of heart in Dickens's novels. Victorian Stud 5 1961.
Kettle, A. Dickens and the popular tradition. Zeitschrift für Anglistik und Amerikanistik 9 1961; rptd in Carleton Miscellany 3 1961 (reply by J. O. Perry, and by Kettle 4 1962).
Stone, A. E. The innocent eye: childhood in Mark Twain's imagination. New Haven 1961. Compares Dickens.
Beaumont, G. Pour l'amour de Dickens. Nouvelles Littéraires 15 Feb 1962.
Fielding, K. J. Dickens's novels and the discovery of the soul. Aryan Path 33 1962.
Beaumont, G. Pour l'amour de Dickens. Nouvelles Littéraires 15 Feb 1962.
Fielding, K. J. Dickens's novels and the discovery of the soul. Aryan Path 33 1962.
Gross, J. Dickens: some recent approaches. In Dickens and the twentieth century, ed J. Gross and G. Pearson 1962.
Empson, W. The symbolism of Dickens. Ibid.
Kaverin, V. O Dikkense. Inostrannaja Literatura 8 1962.
Monod, S. Misères et splendeurs d'une carrière littéraire. Les Lettres Françaises 27 Sept 1962.
Perry, J. O. The popular tradition of melodrama in Dickens. Carleton Miscellany 4 1962.
Seehase, G. and I. Bemerkungen zur neuesten sowjetischen Dickensforschung. Zeitschrift für Anglistik und Amerikanistik 10 1962.
Cross, B. M. Comedy and drama in Dickens. Western Humanities Rev 17 1963.
Ward, W. A. Language and Dickens. Listener 23 May 1963.
Bodelsen, C. A. Symbolism in Dickens; Dickens the social critic; The physiognonomy of the name. All in Essays and papers presented to C. A. Bodelsen, Copenhagen 1964.
Bryner, C. Gogol, Dickens and the realistic novel. Etudes Slaves et Est-Européennes 8 1963.
Williams, R. Social criticism in Dickens. CQ 6 1964.
Brook, G. L. The language of Dickens. Bull John Rylands Lib 47 1965.
— Dickens as a literary craftsman. Bull John Rylands Lib 49 1967.
Davie, D. A. (ed). Russian literature and modern English fiction. Chicago 1965. Includes V. G. Korolenko, My first encounter with Dickens, 1912, and A Russian correspondent, Dickens in Russia: a moral educator, TLS 7 Sept 1940.
Harvey, W. J. In his Character and the novel, 1965.
Hill, A. G. The real world of Dickens, CQ 7 1965.
Holloway, J. Dickens's vision of society. Listener 25 Feb 1965; rptd in The novelist as innovator, ed W. Allen 1965.
Storey, G. Dickens, a forradalmár regényiró. Különlenyomat a Filológiai Közlöny, Budapest 1965.
Wall, S. Dickens's plot of fortune. REL 6 1965.

Topographical Studies

Pemberton, T. E. Dickens's London. Guildford 1876.
Frost, T. In Kent with Dickens. 1880.
Langton, R. Dickens and Rochester. 1880.
Rimmer, A. About England with Dickens. 1883, 1899.
Allbut, R. London rambles 'en zigzag' with Dickens. [1886].

— Rambles in Dickens's land. 1899, 1903 (rev).
Hughes, W. R. A week's tramp in Dickens-land, together with personal reminiscences of the Inimitable Boz. 1891.
Dickens, Charles jr. Disappearing Dickensland. North Amer Rev June 1893.
— Notes on some Dickens places and people. Pall Mall Mag July 1896.
Fitzgerald, P. H. Bozland: Dickens' places and people. 1895.
— Boz and Bath. Bath 1905.
Trumble, A. In jail with Dickens. 1896. A study of the prisons described by Dickens.
'Miltoun, Francis' (F. M. Milburg). Dickens' London, with many illustrations and plans. 1904.
Ward, H. S. and C. W. B. The real Dickens land, with an outline of Dickens's life. 1904.
Kitton, F. G. The Dickens country. 1905, 1911, 1925.
Harris, E. Gad's Hill Place and Dickens. Rochester 1910.
— Dickensian Chatham. Rochester 1911.
Nicklin, J. A. Dickens-land, pictured by E. W. Haslehurst. 1911.
Smith, F. H. In Dickens' London: twenty-two photogravure proofs reproducing charcoal drawings. New York 1914, 1916.
Matz, B. W. Dickensian inns and taverns. 1922, 1923 (rev). For further topographical items, *see* Bibliography of B. W. Matz, Dickensian 21 1925.
Hopkins, A. A. and N. F. Read. A Dickens atlas. New York 1923.
Miller, L. References in the works of Dickens to Rochester, Chatham and neighbourhood and to persons resident therein. Bath [1923] (priv ptd).
Clark, C. Dickens' London: a lecture. 1923.
Dexter, W. The London of Dickens. 1923, 1930.
— The Kent of Dickens. 1924.
— The England of Dickens. 1925.
— The London Dickens knew. Dickensian 25–6 1929–30. With maps.
— Days in Dickensland. 1933. Chiefly London and Kent; incorporates material from the above.
Cooper, T. P. With Dickens in Yorkshire, with an introduction by B. W. Matz. York 1923, 1924 (rev).
Chancellor, E. B. The London of Dickens. 1924.
Kent, W. R. G. With Dickens in the Borough. [1926].
— The George Inn, Southwark. [1932].
— London for Dickens-lovers. 1935.
Moreland, A. Dickens in London: 47 drawings with descriptive notes. 1928.
— Dickens landmarks in London. 1931.
Wilson, S. G. F. Canterbury and Dickens. Canterbury [1928].
Barnes, A. W. A Dickens guide. 1929.
Leacock, S. Dickens and Canada. Queen's Quart 46 1939.
Arnold, R. Great expectations. Nineteenth Century Oct 1946.
Elling, C. Man laeser Dickens. Copenhagen 1949.
Hamilton, L. Dickens in Canada. Dalhousie Rev 30 1950.
Green, F. London homes of Dickens. 1951.
Addison, W. In the steps of Dickens. 1955.
Anderson, D. D. Dickens on Lake Eyrie. Inland Seas 17 1961.
Guildhall Art Gallery, London. Dickens and his London: an exhibition. 1962.
Denton, C. R. Dickens's Lakeland excursion. Country Life 19 Sept 1963.
Hutchings, R. J. Dickens at Winterbourne. Shanklin 1964; rev in Dickensian 61 1965.

Dickens's Illustrators and Illustrations

For extra illustrations to particular works, see under Novels and Minor Works, above. The following entries include only (1) general collections of illustrations or commentaries on them; (2) works dealing with an illustrator's relations with Dickens; not general biographies of the artists.

Barnard, F. A series of character sketches from Dickens. [1879]. Lithographed. 6 plates. Re-issued in photogravure in 1887 uniformly with 2 further sers (6 plates each) pbd in 1884 and 1885 respectively. All the 18 plates in photogravure were reissued later in 6 sections for subscribers, with letterpress by T. Archer.
Archer, T. Dickens: a gossip about his life, works and characters, with eighteen full-page character sketches (reproduced in photogravure) by Frederick Barnard, and other illustrations by well-known artists, in six sections for subscribers only. [1895?], [1902].
'Kyd' (J. C. Clarke). The characters of Dickens portrayed in original water colour sketches. [c. 1887].
Gibson, C. D. People of Dickens. New York 1897. 6 plates.
Grego, J. Pictorial Pickwickiana: Dickens and his illustrators, with 350 drawings and engravings [by various artists who illustrated original or early edns of Dickens]. 2 vols 1899. Commentary and bibliographical notes are not confined to the Pickwick papers.
Kitton, F. G. Dickens and his illustrators. 1899. All the recognized illustrators, with 22 portraits and 70 unpbd illustrations, and bibliography.
— 'Phiz' (Hablot Knight Browne): a memoir. 1882.
— (ed). Dickens illustrations: facsimiles of the original drawings, sketches and studies for illustrations by Cruikshank, Browne, Leech, Stone and Fildes. 1900.
Eaton, S. Dickens rare print collection. Philadelphia [1900] (priv ptd).
Fraser, W. A. The illustrators of Dickens. Dickensian 2 1906.
Layard, G. S. Suppressed plates, wood engravings etc. 1907.
Scenes and characters from the works of Dickens: being 866 drawings by various artists printed from the original woodblocks engraved for 'The household edition' 1908. With an introductory note.
Hammerton, J. A. The Dickens picture-book: a record of the Dickens illustrators. [1910]. Vol 17 of The Charles Dickens Library. *See* above, Collected works.
Ley, J. W. T. Robert William Buss. Dickensian 6 1910.
Crowdy, W. L. Famous Dickens pictures. 1912. Reproduction of 12 illustrations by Charles Green, with brief introd.
Lewin, F. G. Characters from Dickens: a portfolio of 20 Vandyck gravures from the drawings of F.G.L., with introd by B. W. Matz. 1912.
Browne, E. A. Phiz and Dickens. 1913. By the artist's son.
Cohn, A. M. A bibliographical catalogue of the printed works illustrated by George Cruikshank. 1914.
— George Cruikshank: a catalogue raisonné. 1924.
Fraser, C. L. Characters from Dickens. [1924]. 18 coloured plates and decorations. Foreword by H. Macfall.
Reynolds, F. The Buchanan portfolio of characters from Dickens. Glasgow [1925]. 14 coloured plates.
Nonesuch Dickensiana. 1937. 1, A. Waugh, Dickens and his illustrators; 2, T. Hatton, A bibliographical list of the original illustrations to the works of Dickens.
Millican, J. N. B. Phiz without sparkle. Dickensian 41 1945.
Dickens illustrations. TLS 19 May 1945. *See* 7 April–19 May 1945.
Yarre, D'A. P. Dickens without Phiz? Dickensian 42 1946.
Weitenkampf, F. American illustrators of Dickens. Boston Public Lib Quart 5 1953.
Johannsen, A. (ed). Phiz illustrations from the novels of Dickens. Chicago 1956. 516 etchings from 7 novels.

P. A. W. C.

GEORGE HENRY BORROW
1803–81

Borrow's mss are chiefly in Norwich Public Library and in the Romany Collection of the Brotherton Library at Leeds University.

Bibliographies

Knapp, W. I. In his Life, writings and correspondence of Borrow, 2 vols 1899.
Thomas, E. In his George Borrow, 1912.
Black, G. F. In Gypsy Lore Soc Monographs 1 1914.
Wise, T. J. A bibliography of the writings in prose and verse of Borrow. 1914.
Stephen, G. A. In his Borrow House Museum: a brief account of the life of Borrow and his Norwich home, Norwich 1927.
Fréchet, R. In his George Borrow, Paris 1956.

Collections

The works. 4 vols 1900–2. Includes Lavengro, Bible in Spain, Romany Rye, Zincali.
The works: definitive edition. 5 vols [1906]. Contains Zincali, Bible in Spain, Lavengro, Romany Rye, Wild Wales, Romano Lavo-Lil; completed 1928 with Celtic bards, chiefs and kings, ed H. G. Wright.
The works: Norwich edition. Ed C. K. Shorter 16 vols 1923–4. Includes unpbd ms material.
Isopel Berners, extracted from Lavengro and the Romany Rye. Ed T. Seccombe 1901.
Gypsy stories from Borrow's Bible in Spain. Ed W. H. Rouse 1905.
The pocket Borrow: selection from the works. Ed E. Thomas 1912.
Selections from the works. 1913.
Selections from the works. Ed S. A. Richards 1921.
Selections from the works; with essays by Richard Ford, Leslie Stephen and George Sainsbury. Ed H. S. Milford, Oxford 1924.
Selections from the works. Ed W. E. Williams 1927.

§1

The Zincali: or an account of the gypsies of Spain, with an original collection of their songs and poetry, and a copious dictionary of their language. 2 vols 1841, 1843, 1843, 1846, 1870, 1882, 1888, 1893, 1901 (definitive edn); ed H. Walpole, illustr B. Freedman 1936; ed W. Starkie 1961 (EL); Italian epitome, 1878; tr Spanish, 1932.
The Bible in Spain: or the journeys, adventures and imprisonments of an Englishman, in an attempt to circulate the Scriptures in the Peninsula. 3 vols 1843 (6 edns), 1896 (18th edn) etc; ed E. Thomas 1906 (EL); Oxford 1906 (WC); tr German, 1844; Spanish, [1921]. For supplementary ch, *see* below.
Lavengro: the scholar, the gypsy, the priest. 3 vols 1851, 1872, 1888, 1896; ed T. Watts[-Dunton] 1893; ed W. I. Knapp 1900; ed F. H. Groome 2 vols 1901; 1904 (WC); ed I. Seccombe 1906 (EL); ed W. Starkie 1961 (EL); tr French, 1862, 1892, 1941.
The Romany Rye: a sequel to Lavengro. 2 vols 1857, 1858, 1872, 1888, 1896; ed T. Watts[-Dunton] [1900]; [ed W. I. Knapp] 1900; ed J. Sampson 1903; 1906 (EL); 1906 (WC); ed W. Starkie 1949.
The Welsh and their literature. Quart Rev 109 1861.
Wild Wales: its people, language and scenery. 3 vols 1862, 1865, 1888, 1896, 1901 (authoritative edn); 1906 (EL); Oxford 1920 (WC).
Romano Lavo-Lil: word-book of the Romany, or English gypsy language; with many pieces in gypsy, illustrative of the way of speaking and thinking of the English gypsies; with specimens of their poetry and an account of certain gypsies or places inhabited by them, and of various things relating to gypsy life in England. 1874, 1888, 1905, 1907, 1908, 1919.
Letters to the British and Foreign Bible Society. Ed T. H. Darlow 1911.
Letters to his wife Mary Borrow. 1913 (priv ptd).
Letters to his mother Ann Borrow, and to other correspondents. 1913 (priv ptd).
A supplementary chapter to the Bible in Spain, inspired by Ford's Hand-book for travellers in Spain. 1913 (priv ptd).
Wild Wales: suppressed chapters. Ed H. G. Wright, Welsh Outlook 9–10 1922–3.
Celtic bards, chiefs and kings. Ed H. G. Wright 1928. Probably written 1857–60.

Editions

Celebrated trials and remarkable cases of criminal jurisprudence, from the earliest records to the year 1825. 6 vols 1825; in The complete New Gate calendar, ed J. L. Rayner 1925–6 (priv ptd) (Navarre Soc); ed E. H. Bierstadt 1928 (rev).
Mousei echen Isus Gheristos i tuta puha itche ghese. St Petersburg 1835.
El Nuevo Testamento, traducido al español. Madrid 1837.
Evangelioa San Lucasen Guissan: el Evangelio segun S Lucas, traducido al Vascuence. Madrid 1838.

Translations in Verse and Prose

Faustus: his life, death and descent into Hell, translated from the German [of F. M. von Klinger]. 1825. Anon.
Romantic ballads, translated from the Danish, and miscellaneous pieces. Norwich 1826, 1826, 1913, London 1926.
Targum: or metrical translations from thirty languages and dialects. St Petersburg 1835; in Targum and the Talisman with other pieces, [1892] (facs).
The Talisman, from the Russian of Alexander Pushkin, with other pieces. St Petersburg 1835; in Targum and the Talisman, [1892] (facs).
Embeo e Majaró Lucas: brotoboro randado andre la chipe griega, acana chibado andré o Romano, o chipe es Zincales de Sesé; El evangelio segun S Lucas, traducido al Romani, o dialecto de los gitanos de España. [Madrid] 1837, 1871, 1872.
The sleeping bard: or visions of the world, death and hell, by Elis Wyn, translated from the Cambrian British. 1860. Reviewed anon by Borrow, Quart Rev 109 1861.
The Turkish jester: or the pleasantries of Cogia Nasr Eddin Effendi, translated from the Turkish. Ipswich 1884.
The death of Balder, from the Danish of Johannes Ewald (1773). 1889.
Welsh poems and ballads. Ed E. Rhys 1915.
Ballads of all nations, translated by Borrow: a selection. Ed R. B. Johnson 1927.

The following are ballads, poems and tales priv ptd for T. J. Wise 1913, 1914 and rptd in Norwich edn 1923–4:

Marsk Stig: a ballad. 1913.
The serpent knight and other ballads. 1913.
The King's wake and other ballads. 1913.
The Dalby bear and other ballads. 1913.
The mermaid's prophecy and other songs relating to Queen Dagmar. 1913.
Hafbur and Signe: a ballad. 1913.
The story of Yvashka with the bear's ear, translated from the Russian. 1913.
The Verner raven, The Count of Vendel's daughter and other ballads. 1913.
The return of the dead and other ballads. 1913.
Axel Thordson and Fair Valborg: a ballad. 1913.
King Hacon's death and Bran and the black dog: two ballads. 1913.

Marsk Stig's daughters and other songs and ballads. 1913.
The tale of Brynild and King Valdemar and his Sister: two ballads. 1913.
Proud Signild and other ballads. 1913.
Ulf Van Yern and other ballads. 1913.
Ellen of Villenskov and other ballads. 1913.
The songs of Ranild. 1913.
Niels Ebbesen and Germand Gladenswayne: two ballads. 1913.
Child Maidelvold and other ballads. 1913.
Ermeline: a ballad. 1913.
The giant of Bern and Orm Ungerswayne: a ballad. 1913.
Little Engel: a ballad; with a series of epigrams from the Persian. 1913.
Alf the Freebooter, Little Danneved and Swayne Trost, and other ballads. 1913.
King Diderik and the fight between the lion and dragon and other ballads. 1913.
The nightingale, the Valkyrie and raven, and other ballads. 1913.
Grimmer and Kamper, The end of Sivard Snaren-Swayne and other ballads. 1913.
The fountain of Maribo and other ballads. 1913.
Queen Berngerd, the bard and the dreams and other ballads. 1913.
Finnish arts: or Sir Thor and Damsel Thure, a ballad. 1913.
Brown William, The power of the harp and other ballads. 1913.
The song of Deirdra, King Byrge and his brothers, and other ballads. 1913.
Signelil: a tale from the Cornish and other ballads. 1913.
Young Swaigder or the force of runes and other ballads. 1913.
Emelian the fool: a tale translated from the Russian. 1913.
The story of Tim, translated from the Russian. 1913.
Mollie Charane and other ballads. 1913.
Grimhild's vengeance: three ballads. Ed E. Gosse 1913.
The brother avenged and other ballads. 1913.
The gold horns, translated from the Danish of Adam Gottlob Oehlenschläger. Ed E. Gosse 1913.
Tord of Hafsborough and other ballads. 1914.
The expedition to Birting's Land and other ballads. 1914.

§2

For further titles see G. A. Stephen and R. Fréchet under Bibliographies, above.

Chasles, P. The Zincali. Revue des Deux Mondes 1 Aug 1841.
— The Bible in Spain. Revue des Deux Mondes 1 May 1843.
[Lockhart, J. G.] The Bible in Spain. Quart Rev 71 1842.
[Ford, R.] The Bible in Spain. Edinburgh Rev 64 1843.
Aytoun, W. E. Lavengro. Blackwood's Mag March 1851.
Montégut, E. The Romany Rye. Revue des Deux Mondes 1 Sept 1857; rptd in his Ecrivains modernes de l'Angleterre: deuxième série, Paris 1889.
— The sleeping bard. Revue des Deux Mondes 15 Feb 1862.
Elwin, W. Roving life in England. Quart Rev 10 1857. Reviews Lavengro, Romany Rye.
— Mr Borrow. Athenaeum 6 Aug 1881. Obituary.
Hake, A. E. Recollections of Borrow. Athenaeum 13 Aug 1881.
— George Borrow. Macmillan's Mag Nov 1881.
Stephen, L. In his Hours in a Library: third series, 1881.
Tal-a-Hen. Borrow in Wales. Red Dragon 3 1883.
Watts [-Dunton], T. Reminiscences of Borrow. Athenaeum 3–10 Sept 1881; rptd in his Old familiar faces, 1916.
Saintsbury, G. George Borrow. Macmillan's Mag Jan 1886; rptd in his Essays in English literature 1780–1860, 1890.
Birrell, A. The office of literature. In his Obiter dicta ser 2, 1887.
— In his Res judicatae, 1892.
— Borrow and his works. Quart Rev 189 1899.
Henley, W. E. In his Views and reviews, 1890.
Harvey, E. Borrow: personal recollections. Eastern Daily Press 1 Oct 1892.
Monkhouse, A. In his Books and plays, 1894.
Dutt, W. A. Borrow in East Anglia. 1896.
Knapp, W. I. Life, writings and correspondence of Borrow, derived from official and other authentic sources. 2 vols 1899.
Findlater, J. H. George Borrow. Cornhill Mag Nov 1899.
Johnson, L. O rare George Borrow. Outlook 1 April 1899; rptd in his Post liminium, 1911.
Whibley, C. George Borrow. Blackwood's Mag April 1899.
Herzfeld, G. George Borrow. Archiv 107 1901.
Seccombe, T. Borrow: his homes and haunts. Bookman (London) Feb 1902.
— George Borrow. TLS 10 July 1903.
Euren, H. F. Norwich notables 8: Borrow. Norwich Mercury 18 July 1903.
Shorthouse, J. H. The successor of Monsieur Lesage. In his Life, letters and literary remains vol 2, 1905.
Conan Doyle, A. Through the magic door. 1907.
— Borrowed scenes. In his Danger and other stories, 1918. Parodies of Borrow.
Walling, R. A. J. Borrow: the man and his work. 1908.
Blaesing, B. George Borrow. Berlin 1910.
Jenkins, H. Borrow in Russia. Nat Rev 54 1910.
Cantrill, T. C. and J. Pringle. Borrow's second tour in Wales. Y Cymmrodor 22 1910; 1911 (separately).
Thomas, E. Borrow: the man and his books. 1912.
— In his Literary pilgrim in England, 1917.
Jenkins, H. Life of Borrow, compiled from unpublished official documents, his works, correspondence etc. 1912.
More, P. E. George Borrow. Nation (New York) 1912; rptd in his Demon of the absolute, Princeton 1928.
Shorter, C. K. Borrow and his circle: wherein may be found many hitherto unpublished letters of Borrow and his friends. 1913.
— The life of Borrow. [1920].
— Borrow in Scotland. Fortnightly Rev April 1913.
Adams, M. In the footsteps of Borrow and FitzGerald, [1914].
Shane, L. Borrow in Spain. Dublin Rev 155 1914.
Howells, W. D. The editor's easy chair. Harper's Monthly Mag May 1914.
Ralli, A. The works of Borrow. Fortnightly Rev Oct 1915.
— In his Critiques, 1927.
Rhys, E. Unpublished prose miscellanies of Borrow. Y Cymmrodor 25 1915.
Walker, H. In CHEL vol 14, 1916.
Schevill, R. Borrow: an English humourist in Spain. Univ of California Chron 18 1916; 1916 (separately).
Elton, O. In his Survey of English literature 1830–80 vol 1, 1920.
Hearn, L. In his Life and literature, New York 1917.
Wright, H. G. The forsaken merman: source. MLR 13 1918.
— Borrow's Celtic bards, chiefs and kings. Quart Rev 479 1924.
— Was Borrow ever in Denmark? MLR 23 1928.
— Borrow and Grundtvig. TLS 12 June 1930.
— Influence of Borrow in Norway and Sweden. MLR 29 1934.
Jerrold, W. Borrow's Joseph Sell. Cornhill Mag Jan 1921.
Hopkins, R. J. Borrow, lord of the open road. [1922].
Hustvedt, S. B. Borrow and his Danish ballads. JEGP 22 1923.

Rye, W. The inaccuracies of Borrow. History Teachers' Miscellany 2 1924.
TLS 28 Aug 1924. Leading article.
Moore, G. In his Avowals, 1924.
Speck, W. A. Borrow and Goethe's Faust. PMLA 41 1926.
Boyle, A. Portraiture in Lavengro. Cornhill Mag Sept 1928.
Elam, S. M. George Borrow. New York 1929.
Quennell, P. C. Celtic bards, chiefs and kings. New Statesman 5 Jan 1929.
— The real and the imaginery in Lavengro. New Statesman 15 Nov 1941.
— In his Singular preference, 1952.
Colton, A. George Borrow. Atlantic Monthly May 1931.
Parks, E. W. Portrait of Lavengro. In his Segments of southern thought, Athens Georgia 1938.
Dearden, S. The gypsy gentleman. 1939.
Holst, O. Engelske oversaettelser af danske folkeviser. Danske Studier (Copenhagen) 38 1941.
Tilford, J. E. Contemporary criticism of Lavengro: a re-examination. SP 41 1944.
— The critical approach to Lavengro-Romany Rye. SP 46 1949.
— The formal artistry of Lavengro-Romany Rye. PMLA 64 1949.
— A note on Borrow's bookish dialogue. In Studies for Sturgis E. Leavitt, Washington 1953.
Reed, E. L. Borrow's translation of the Walpurgisnacht. JEGP 44 1945.
Toldberg, H. Grundtvig og den engelske antikvarer. Orbis Litterarum 5 1947. With summary in English.
Marchand, L. The Symington collection. Jnl Rutgers Univ Lib 12 1948.
Armstrong, M. D. George Borrow. 1950.
Boyle, A. Portraiture in Lavengro. N & Q 12 May, 18 Aug, 15 Sept, 13–27 Oct, 8 Dec 1951; 19 Jan–2 Feb, 1 March, 13 Sept 1952.
Bigland, E. In the steps of George Borrow. 1951.
Vesey-Fitzgerald, B. Gypsy Borrow. 1953.
Hepworth, P. Original manuscripts acquired by Norwich Public Libraries. Jnl Gypsy Lore Soc 1954.
Fréchet, R. Borrow devant la critique. Etudes Anglaises 7 1954.
— Borrow: vagabond, polyglotte, agent biblique, écrivain. Paris 1956.
— Borrow and the Celts. Hon Soc of Cymmrodorion 1960.
Alden, J. T. J. Wise and Tales of the wild and wonderful. Book Collector 8 1959. On Borrow's authorship of the Tales (1825). Reply by J. Rubinstein, ibid.
Francis, H. J. Borroviana. Jnl of Gypsy Lore Soc 1961.
Bartle, G. E. Borrow's Old Radical. N & Q July 1963.
Meyers, R. R. George Borrow. New York 1966.
Wade, R. A. R. A gypsy's views on Lavengro. Jnl of Gypsy Lore Soc 45 1966.

M. A.

WILLIAM MAKEPEACE THACKERAY
1811–63

Bibliographies

Shepherd, R. H. The bibliography of Thackeray: the published writings in prose and verse and the sketches and drawings from 1829 to 1880. 1881, 1887 (rev and enlarged in his edn of Sultan Stork and other stories).
Johnson, C. P. Hints to collectors of original editions of the works of Thackeray, 1885.
— The earlier writings of Thackeray. 1888.
Anderson, J. P. In H. C. Merivale and F. T. Marzials, Life of Thackeray, 1891.
Spielmann, M. H. Thackeray's hitherto unidentified contributions to Punch: with a complete bibliography from 1845 to 1848. 1899.
Williams, W. J. In Works of Thackeray: biographical edition vol 13, 1899.
Dickson, F. S. Bibliography of Thackeray in the United States. In J. G. Wilson, Thackeray in the United States vol 2, 1904.
'Melville, Lewis' (L. S. Benjamin). In his William Makepeace Thackeray vol 2, 1910. Supersedes the bibliography in his Life of Thackeray, 1899.
Van Duzer, H. S. A Thackeray library: first editions and first publications, portraits, water colours, etchings drawings and manuscripts. New York 1919.
Parrish, M. L. Catalogue of an exhibition of the works of Thackeray. Philadelphia 1940.
Ray, G. N. Articles newly identified as Thackeray's. In his edn of Letters and private papers of Thackeray vol 2, Cambridge Mass 1945.
— Thackeray and Punch: 44 newly identified contributions. TLS 1 Jan 1949.
Gordan, J. D. Thackeray. BNYPL May 1947. Catalogue of Berg collection.
Randall, D. A. Notes towards a correct collation of the first editions of Vanity Fair. PBSA 42 1948.
Stevenson, L. In Victorian fiction: a guide to research, ed Stevenson, Cambridge Mass 1964.

Collections

Works. Library edition 22 vols 1867–9 (2 more vols 1885–6); Cheaper illustrated edition 24 vols 1877–9; De luxe edition 26 vols 1878–86 (with memoir by L. Stephen); Standard edition 26 vols 1883–6; Pocket edition 27 vols 1887–93; ed H. E. Scudder 22 vols Boston 1889 (fuller than preceding English edns); Biographical edition 13 vols 1898–9 (with introds by A. T. Ritchie and biographical sketch by L. Stephen rptd from DNB); New century library 14 vols 1899–1900.
Prose works. Ed W. Jerrold 30 vols 1901–3.
Works. Ed 'Lewis Melville' (from vol 8) 20 vols 1901–7, 1911 (rptd from first edns and including much new matter); London edition 13 vols 1903 (topographical introds by J. McVicar in vols 1–12; vol 13 is Melville's Life of Thackeray, first pbd 2 vols 1899); Oxford edition 17 vols 1908 (introds by G. Saintsbury; much new matter); Centenary biographical edition 26 vols 1910–1 (enlarged from Biographical edition, above).

§1

Flore et Zéphyr: ballet mythologique par Théophile Wagstaff. 1836. 9 lithographed plates; no text.
The Yellowplush correspondence. Fraser's Mag Nov 1837–July 1838; Philadelphia 1838, New York 1852 (as The Yellowplush papers).
Some passages in the life of Major Gahagan. New Monthly Mag Feb 1838–Feb 1839; Philadelphia 1839 (as Reminiscences of Major Gahagan).
An essay on the genius of George Cruikshank. Westminster Rev June 1840; 1840; ed W. E. Church 1884.
The Paris sketch book, by Mr Titmarsh. 2 vols 1840, New York 1852. Several of the sketches rptd from Fraser's Mag, New Monthly Mag, National Standard, Corsair (New York).
Comic tales and sketches, edited and illustrated by Mr Michael Angelo Titmarsh. 2 vols 1841. Vol 1 contains The Yellowplush papers; vol 2 Some passages in the life of Major Gahagan, The professor (from Bentley's Miscellany Sept 1837), The Bedford Row conspiracy (from New Monthly Mag Jan–April 1840), Stubbs's calendar (from Comic Almanac 1839), 1848.
The second funeral of Napoleon, in three letters to Miss Smith of London; and The chronicle of the drum, by Mr M. A. Titmarsh. 1841.

The Irish sketch-book, by Mr M. A. Titmarsh. 2 vols 1843, 1 vol New York [1843], 2 vols 1845, 1 vol 1857.

The luck of Barry Lyndon: a romance of the last century. Fraser's Mag Jan-Dec 1844; 2 vols New York 1852–3, 1 vol 1856 (rev, with admissions, as The memoirs of Barry Lyndon Esq).

Jeames's diary. Punch 2 Aug 1845–7 Feb 1846; New York 1846.

Notes of a journey from Cornhill to Grand Cairo, by way of Lisbon, Athens, Constantinople and Jerusalem, performed in the steamers of the Peninsular and Oriental Company, by Mr M. A. Titmarsh. 1846, 1846 (with postscript signed W. M. T.), New York 1846.

The snobs of England, by one of themselves. Punch 28 Feb 1846–27 Feb 1847; 1848 (as The book of snobs, omitting chs 17–23), New York 1852 (complete), London 1855; ed G. K. Chesterton 1911.

Vanity Fair: pen and pencil sketches of English society. 20 monthly pts Jan 1847–July 1848; Vanity Fair: a novel without a hero, 1848, 1848, 2 pts New York 1848, 3 vols Leipzig 1849, 1 vol 1853 (rev), 1863 (rev); ed J. E. Wells 2 vols New York 1828; ed P. E. More 2 vols Garden City NY 1935; ed J. W. Beach, New York 1950; ed G. H. Ford, New York 1958; ed G. and K. Tillotson 1963.

Mrs Perkins's ball, by Mr M. A. Titmarsh. 1847 (3 edns), 1898 (facs).

The history of Samuel Titmarsh and the great Hoggarty diamond. Frasers's Mag Sept-Dec 1841; New York 1848 (as The great Hoggarty diamond), London 1849 (with original title), 1857.

'Our street', by Mr M. A. Titmarsh. 1848, 1848.

The history of Pendennis: his fortunes and misfortunes, his friends and his greatest enemy. 24 monthly pts Nov 1848–Dec 1850; 2 vols 1849–50, 3 vols Leipzig 1849–50, 2 vols New York 1850, London 1850, 1 vol 1856, 1863 (rev).

Doctor Birch and his young friends, by Mr M. A. Titmarsh. 1849, New York 1853.

Miscellanies: prose and verse. 2 vols Leipzig 1849–51. Vol 1 contains The great Hoggarty diamond, The book of snobs; vol 2 The Kickleburys abroad, A legend of the Rhine, Rebecca and Rowena, The second funeral of Napoleon, The chronicle of the drum.

The Kickleburys on the Rhine, by Mr M. A. Titmarsh. 1850, 1851 (with Preface being an essay on thunder and small beer), Frankfurt 1851, New York 1851, London 1866.

Stubbs's calendar: or the fatal boots. New York 1850.

Rebecca and Rowena: a romance upon romance, by Mr M. A. Titmarsh. 1850, Paris 1850. Revision of Proposals for a continuation of Ivanhoe, Fraser's Mag Aug-Sept 1846.

The history of Henry Esmond esq, a colonel in the service of Her Majesty Q. Anne, written by himself. 3 vols 1852, 2 vols Leipzig 1852, 1 vol New York 1852, 3 vols 1853, 1 vol 1858 (rev); ed G. N. Ray, New York 1950.

The confessions of Fitz-Boodle; and some passages in the life of Major Gahagan. New York 1852.

A shabby genteel story and other tales. New York 1852, 1853, 1853 (enlarged). Contains also The professor, The Bedford Row conspiracy, A little at Timmins's (from Punch 27 May–29 July 1848).

Men's wives. Fraser's Mag March–Nov 1843; New York 1852.

Jeames's diary, A legend of the Rhine and Rebecca and Rowena. New York 1853.

Mr Brown's letters to a young man about town; with the Proser and other papers. Punch 1845, 1848–51; New York 1853.

Punch's prize novelists, The fat contributor and Travels in London. Punch 1844–5, 1847–8, 1850; New York 1853. Contains also Going to see a man hanged, from Fraser's Mag Aug 1840.

The English humourists of the eighteenth century: a series of lectures delivered in England, Scotland and the United States of America. 1853, 1853 (rev), Leipzig 1853, New York 1853, London 1858; ed E. Regel 6 vols Halle 1885–91; ed W. L. Phelps, New York 1900. Notes by G. Hodder.

The Newcomes: memoirs of a most respectable family, edited by Arthur Pendennis esqre. 24 monthly pts Oct 1853–Aug 1855; Harper's Mag Nov 1853–Oct 1855; 2 vols 1854–5, 4 vols Leipzig 1854–5, 2 vols New York 1855, 1 vol 1860, 1863 (rev).

The rose and the ring, or the history of Prince Giglio and Prince Bulbo: a fireside pantomime for great and small children, by Mr M. A. Titmarsh. 1855 (for 1854), 1855, 1855, New York 1855, London 1866; ed G. N. Ray, New York 1947 (ms facs).

Miscellanies: prose and verse. 4 vols 1855–7, 1861, 1865. Vol 1 (4 pts) 1855 contains Ballads, The book of snobs, The fatal boots (i.e. Stubbs's calendar) and Cox's diary (i.e. Barber Cox from Comic almanac 1840), The tremendous adventures of Major Gahagan (i.e. Some passages in the life of Major Gahagan); vol 2 (3 pts) 1856 contains: The memoirs of Mr Charles J. Yellowplush and the diary of C. Jeames de la Pluche esq, Sketches and travels in London (including Mr Brown's letters to a young man), Novels by eminent hands (i.e. Punch's prize novelists), Character sketches (from Heads of the people 1840–1); vol 3 (3 pts) 1856 contains The Memoirs of Barry Lyndon esq, Burlesques (A legend of the Rhine, Rebecca and Rowena), A little dinner at Timmins's, The Bedford Row conspiracy; vol 4 (3 pts) 1857 contains The Fitz-Boodle papers, Men's wives (omitting The ——'s wife), A shabby genteel story, The history of Samuel Titmarsh, The great Hoggarty diamond.

Ballads. Boston 1856.

Christmas books. 1857. Contains Mrs Perkins's ball, 'Our street', Doctor Birch and his young friends.

The Virginians: a tale of the last century. 24 monthly pts Nov 1857–Sept 1859; Harper's Mag Dec 1857–Nov 1859; 2 vols 1858–9, 4 vols Leipzig 1858–9, 1 vol New York 1859, London 1863 (rev); ed G. Saintsbury and J. L. Robertson 1911.

The four Georges: sketches of manners, morals, court and town life. Cornhill Mag July–Oct 1860; Harper's Mag Aug-Nov 1860; New York 1860, 1860, London 1861, Leipzig 1861; ed G. Meredith and T. Bayne 1903.

Lovel the widower. Cornhill Mag Jan–June 1860; Harper's Mag Feb–July 1860; New York 1860, London 1861 (rev).

The adventures of Philip on his way through the world, shewing who robbed him, who helped him, and who passed him by. Cornhill Mag Jan 1861–Aug 1862; Harper's Mag Feb 1861–Sept 1862; 3 vols 1862, 2 vols Leipzig 1862, 1 vol New York 1862.

Roundabout papers. Cornhill Mag Jan 1860–Feb 1863; 1863, New York 1863; ed J. E. Wells, New York 1925 (from ms).

Miscellanies. 6 vols New York 1864. Rptd from New York edns of 1852–3.

Denis Duval. Cornhill Mag March–June 1864; Harper's Mag April–Aug 1864; New York 1864, London 1867, Leipzig 1867.

Early and late papers hitherto uncollected. Ed J. T. Fields, Boston 1867. From Fraser's Mag, Quart Rev, Cornhill Mag etc 1841–63.

Miscellanies vol 5. Boston 1870. Contains Catherine (from Fraser's Mag May 1839–Feb 1840), Christmas books, Ballads etc.

The students' quarter: or Paris five and thirty years since. [1874?]. From Corsair (New York) 24 Aug 1839–18 Jan 1840. All except More aspects of Paris life rev and rptd in The Paris sketch book, 1840.

The orphan of Pimlico: and other sketches, fragments and drawings. 1876. Notes by A. I. Thackeray.

Sultan Stork and other stories and sketches (1829–44), now first collected [by R. H. Shepherd]. 1887. From Snob 1829, Fraser's Mag 1829, 1842, National Standard 1833–4, Times 1837, Ainsworth's Mag 1842 etc.

Reading a poem. 1891 (priv ptd). From Britannia 1, 8 May 1841.

Loose sketches, an eastern adventure etc. 1894. Loose sketches by M. A. Titmarsh from Britannia 1 May–5 July 1841; An eastern adventure of the fat contributor from Punch's pocket-book 1847; Preface to Sketches after English landscape painters by L. Marvy 1850.

The hitherto unidentified contributions of W. M. Thackeray to Punch, with a complete authoritative bibliography from 1845 to 1848. Ed M. H. Spielmann 1899.

Mr Thackeray's writings in the National Standard and the Constitutional. Ed W. T. Spencer 1899.

Stray papers: being stories, reviews, verses, and sketches 1821–47. Ed 'Lewis Melville' 1901. Subtitle should read 1829–51.

The new sketch book: being essays now first collected from the Foreign Quarterly Review. Ed R. S. Garnett 1906.

The knights of Borsellen: a hitherto unpublished romance. Harper's Mag July 1911. Notes by Lady Ritchie.

Thackeray's contributions to the Morning Chronicle. Ed G. N. Ray, Urbana 1955. *See* E. M. White, SB 19 1966.

Letters from a club arm-chair. Ed H. Summerfield, Nineteenth-Century Fiction 18 1964.

Letters

A collection of letters of Thackeray 1847–55. Ed J. O. Brookfield, Scribner's Mag April–Oct 1887; 1887.

Thackeray's letters to an American family. Ed L. W. Baxter, Century Mag Nov 1903–March 1904; 1904.

Some family letters of Thackeray, together with recollections by his kinswoman B. W. Cornish. 1911.

Unpublished letters. Ed C. K. Shorter 1916 (priv ptd).

Thackeray and Edward FitzGerald, a literary friendship: unpublished letters and verses by Thackeray. Ed C. K. Shorter 1916 (priv ptd). Introd by Lady Ritchie.

Letters of Anne Thackeray Ritchie, with forty-two additional letters from her father. Ed H. Ritchie 1924.

The letters and private papers of Thackeray. Ed G. N. Ray 4 vols Cambridge Mass 1945–6.

§2

[Rigby, E. (later Lady Eastlake).] Quart Rev 84 1848. Review of Vanity Fair and Jane Eyre, rptd in Famous reviews, ed R. B. Johnson 1914.

Charlotte Brontë and Thackeray. Oxford & Cambridge Mag 1 1856.

Gilfillan, G. In his Galleries of literary portraits vol 2, Edinburgh 1856.

Yates, E. Mr Thackeray, Mr Yates, and the Garrick Club: the correspondence and facts. 1859 (priv ptd), 1895.

Bagehot, W. Sterne and Thackeray. Nat Rev April 1864; rptd in his Literary studies, 1879.

Brown, J. Thackeray. North Br Rev 40 1864; rptd as Thackeray's death in his Horae subsecivae vol 3, 1882.

Dickens, C. In memoriam W. M. T. Cornhill Mag Feb 1864.

Hannay, J. A brief memoir of the late Mr Thackeray. Edinburgh 1864.

—— Studies on Thackeray. 1869.

Reed, W. B. Haud immemor: a few personal recollections of Mr Thackeray in Philadelphia. Philadelphia 1864 (priv ptd).

Senior, N. W. In his Essays on fiction, 1864.

Taylor, B. Thackeray. Atlantic Monthly March 1864.

'Taylor, Theodore'. Thackeray: the humourist and the man of letters. 1864, New York 1864 (enlarged).

The style of Balzac and Thackeray. Dublin Univ Mag Dec 1864.

Boyes, J. F. A memorial of Thackeray's schooldays. Cornhill Mag Jan 1865.

Bedingfield, R. Recollections of Thackeray. Cassell's Mag April, Sept 1870.

Fields, J. T. In his Yesterdays with authors, Boston 1872.

[Grego, J.] Thackerayana: notes and anecdotes illustrated by nearly 600 sketches by Thackeray. 1875, 1901.

Lunt, G. Recollections of Thackeray. Harper's Mag Jan 1877.

Pryme, A. T. and A. Bayne. Memorials of the Thackeray family. 1879.

Trollope, A. Thackeray. 1879 (EML).

Church, W. E. Thackeray as an artist and art critic. [1880?] (priv ptd).

Conrad, W. Thackeray: ein Pessimist als Dichter. Berlin 1887.

D., D. Some few Thackerayana. Nat Rev Aug 1889.

Lang, A. Thackeray's London. In his Lost leaders, 1889.

—— In his Essays in little, 1891.

Ritchie, A. T. The boyhood of Thackeray. St Nicholas Dec 1889. By the novelist's daughter.

—— Chapters from some unwritten memoirs. 1894.

—— The first number of the Cornhill. Cornhill Mag July 1896; rptd in her From the porch, 1913.

—— Blackstick papers. 1908.

Merivale, H. C. and F. T. Marzials. Life of Thackeray. 1891.

Davies, G. S. Thackeray as Carthusian. Grey Friars 2 1892.

Crowe, E. With Thackeray in America. 1893.

—— Thackeray's haunts and homes. 1897.

Irvine, J. W. A study for Colonel Newcome. Nineteenth Century Oct 1893.

Thackeray, F. St J. Reminiscences of Thackeray. Temple Bar July 1893.

Harrison, F. Thackeray's place in literature. Forum Nov 1894; rptd in his Studies in early Victorian literature, 1895.

Howells, W. D. In his My literary passions, New York 1895.

Jack, A. A. Thackeray: a study. 1895.

Saintsbury, G. In his Corrected impressions, 1895, 1898 (rev).

—— A consideration of Thackeray. Oxford 1931. Introds rptd from Oxford edn of Thackeray's works.

Spielmann, M. H. In his History of Punch, 1895.

Hunter, W. W. The Thackerays in India. 1897.

Vulpius, W. Thackeray in Weimar. Century Mag April 1897.

—— Thackerays Lehrlingszeit in Weimar. Neuphilologische Monatsschrift 9 1938.

'Melville, Lewis' (L. S. Benjamin). The life of Thackeray. 2 vols 1899.

—— The Thackeray country. 1905.

—— Thackeray: a biography. 2 vols 1910, 1 vol 1927 (without bibliography).

—— Some aspects of Thackeray. 1911.

—— On an unreprinted article by Thackeray. New Criterion Oct 1926.

Merrill, K. Characterization at the beginning of Pendennis. PMLA 15 1900.

Brownell, W. C. In his Victorian prose masters, New York 1901.

Smith, G. M. Our birth and parentage. Cornhill Mag Jan 1901. On Thackeray and the Cornhill Mag.

Lord, W. F. The apostle of mediocrity. Nineteenth Century March 1902; rptd in his Mirror of the century, 1906.

Whibley, C. William Makepeace Thackeray. 1903.

Elwin, W. Thackeray's boyhood; Thackeray at Cambridge; Thackeray in search of a profession. Monthly Rev June, Sept–Oct 1904.

Wilson, J. G. Thackeray in the United States 1852–3, 1855–6. 2 vols 1904.
Brookfield, C. and F. Mrs Brookfield and her circle. 2 vols 1905.
Thackeray as a sub-editor. GM Nov 1906.
Werner, R. M. Der Einfluss der deutschen Literatur auf Thackeray. Teplitz-Schönau 1907.
Carr, J. C. In his Some eminent Victorians, 1908.
Frisa, H. Deutsche Kulturverhältnisse in der Auffassung Thackerays. Vienna 1908.
Walter, E. Entstehungsgeschichte von Vanity Fair. Berlin 1908.
Cleghorn, S. N. Contemporary opinions of Thackeray. Atlantic Monthly Aug 1910.
Mudge, I. G. and M. E. Sears. A Thackeray dictionary. 1910.
Romilly, A. J. Thackeray studies. 1912.
Dickson, F. S. Thackeray and Fielding. North Amer Rev April 1913.
Smith, F. H. In Thackeray's London. New York 1913.
Stephenson, N. W. The spiritual drama in the life of Thackeray. New York 1913.
Lafleur, P. T. Sainte-Beuve, Balzac and Thackeray. MLR 9 1914.
Frodsham, G. H. The humour of Thackeray. Cornhill Mag Dec 1915.
Ely, C. B. The psychology of Becky Sharp. MLN 35 1920.
Vogel, G. Thackeray als historischer Romanschriftsteller. Leipzig 1920.
Matthews, B. Thackeray and the theatre. Scribner's Mag April 1921.
Gibson, E. C. S. Thackeray and Charterhouse. Cornhill Mag June 1922.
Sandwith, Mrs H. Becky Sharp and Emma Bovary. Nineteenth Century Jan 1922.
Sutcliffe, E. G. Thackeray's romanticism. South Atlantic Quart 21 1922.
Bailey, J. Thackeray and the English novel. In his Continuity of letters, Oxford 1923.
Chancellor, E. B. The London of Thackeray. 1923.
Knaphe, W. Die Geschichte der Ermordung der Karoline von Braunschweig-Wolfenbüttel. Anglia Beiblatt 34 1923. On Barry Lyndon.
Buttler, P. Die Ausländer in den Romanen Thackerays. Giessener Beiträge 1 1924.
Elton, O. Dickens and Thackeray. 1924; rptd with addns from his Survey of English literature 1830–80, 2 vols 1920.
Patterson, J. M. Thackeray's diary. Bookman (New York) Dec 1924.
Schild, B. Die Personencharakterisierung bei Thackeray. Giessener Beiträge 2 1924.
Weill, M. Thackeray et la société anglaise du xviiie siècle. Revue Anglo-américaine 2 1924.
Quiller-Couch, A. T. In his Charles Dickens and other Victorians, Cambridge 1925.
Hubbell, J. B. Thackeray and Virginia. Virginia Quart Rev 3 1927.
Krishnaswami, P. R. Some Thackeray originals: I Who was Colonel Newcome?; II James Binnie; III Rummun Loll; IV The Rev Charles Honeyman. Cornhill Mag Dec 1927–March 1928; rptd with addns in his In Thackeray's workshop, Madras 1956.
Forsythe, R. S. A noble rake: the life of Charles, Lord Mohun. Cambridge Mass 1928. On Henry Esmond.
—— Thackeray, critic of his times. North Dakota Univ Quart Jnl 22 1932.
Minchin, H. C. Thackeray in the Temple. Cornhill Mag Sept 1928.
Hirst, W. A. The chronology in Thackeray's novels. Cornhill Mag Nov 1929.
Wells, C. W. Thackeray and the Victorian compromise. In Essays in criticism by members of the Department of English, University of California, Berkeley 1929.
Clapp, E. R. Critic on horseback. Sewanee Rev 38 1930.
Enzinger, P. Thackeray, critic of literature. North Dakota Univ Quart Jnl 20–1 1930–1.
Simpson, W. A. Thackeray's last heroine. Cornhill Mag May 1930.
Steuerwald, C. Die Londoner Vulgärsprache in Thackerays Yellowplush papers. Leipzig 1930.
Whitton, F. E. Thackeray and the army. Nineteenth Century Nov 1931.
Barbeau, A. Sur un passage des Newcomes. Revue Anglo-américaine 9 1932.
Bauke, L. Die Erzählkunst in Vanity Fair. Hamburg 1932.
Digeon, A. Sur un chapitre des Newcomes. Revue Anglo-américaine 9 1932.
Elwin, M. Thackeray: a personality. 1932.
Las Vergnas, R. Thackeray: l'homme, le penseur, le romancier. Paris 1932.
Swinnerton, F. In Great Victorians, ed H. J. and H. Massingham 1932.
Behmenberg, W. Der Snobbismus bei Thackeray. Düsseldorf 1933.
Ellis, G. U. Thackeray. 1933.
Kurrelmeyer, W. Thackeray and Friedrich von Heyden. MLN 48 1933.
Smith, S. N. In defence of Thackeray. Nineteenth Century July 1933.
Stevenson, L. Vanity Fair and Lady Morgan. PMLA 48 1933.
—— The showman of Vanity Fair. 1947.
Wells, J. E. On a sheet of Thackeray's manuscript. Cornhill Mag Jan 1933.
Cecil, D. In his Early Victorian novelists, 1934, 1964 (rev).
Gulliver, H. S. Thackeray's literary apprenticeship: a study of the early newspaper and magazine work. Valdosta 1934 (priv ptd).
Thackeray, C. B. Thackeray and the melancholy humorist: the gentle art of 'debunking'. Cornhill Mag Aug 1935.
Hurst, H. Ironischer und sentimentaler Realismus bei Thackeray. Hamburg 1938.
Kohl-Bramstedt, E. Marriage and misalliance in Thackeray and Fontane. German Life & Letters 9 1938.
Wethered, H. N. The art of Thackeray. 1938.
Goodell, M. M. Three satirists of snobbery: Thackeray, Meredith, Proust. Britannica 17 1939.
Dodds, J. W. Thackeray in the Victorian frame. Sewanee Rev 48 1940.
—— Thackeray as a satirist previous to Vanity Fair. MLQ 2 1941.
—— Thackeray: a critical portrait. New York 1941.
Pacey, W. C. D. Balzac and Thackeray. MLR 36 1941.
—— A probable addition to the Thackeray canon. PMLA 60 1945.
Pritchett, V. S. The great flunkey. New Statesman 22 March 1941; rptd in his In my good books, 1942.
—— Master of ceremonies. New Statesman 27 Dec 1963.
Boll, E. The author of Elizabeth Brownrigge: a review of Thackeray's technique. SP 39 1942.
Scudder, H. H. Thackeray and N. P. Willis. PMLA 57 1942.
—— Thackeray and Sir Martin Archer Shee. PMLA 61 1946.
Cline, C. L. Disraeli and Thackeray. RES 19 1943.
Moore, J. R. Scott and Henry Esmond. N & Q 17 June 1944.
—— Thackeray's William Dobbin. N & Q 29 Oct 1949.
Brogan, H. O. Rachel Esmond and the dilemma of the Victorian ideal of womanhood. ELH 13 1946.
Touster, E. B. The literary relationship of Thackeray and Fielding. JEGP 46 1947.
Winegarner, L. Thackeray's contributions to the British and Foreign Review. JEGP 47 1948.
Ray, G. N. The 'unwritten part' of Pendennis and Henry Esmond. Listener 4 Aug 1949.

— Vanity Fair: one version of the novelist's responsibility. Essays by Divers Hands 25 1950.
— The buried life: a study of the relation between Thackeray's fiction and his personal history. Oxford 1952.
— Dickens versus Thackeray: the Garrick club affair. PMLA 69 1954. Replies by E. Johnson and Ray, 71 1956.
— Thackeray: the uses of adversity 1811–46. New York 1955; The age of wisdom 1847–63, New York 1958.
— Thackeray's Book of Snobs. Nineteenth-Century Fiction 10 1956.
Ennis, L. Thackeray: the sentimental cynic. Evanston 1950.
Fraser, R. A. Sentimentality in the Newcomes. Nineteenth-Century Fiction 4 1950.
— Pernicious casuistry: a study of character in Vanity Fair. Nineteenth-Century Fiction 12 1958.
Greig, J. Y. T. Thackeray: a reconsideration. Oxford 1950.
— Thackeray: a novelist by accident. In From Jane Austen to Joseph Conrad, ed R. C. Rathburn and M. Steinmann, Minneapolis 1958.
Maitre, E. Balzac, Thackeray et Charles de Bernard. Revue de la Littérature Comparée 24 1950.
— Nouvelles sources françaises de Thackeray. Études Anglaises 17 1964.
Young, G. M. In his Last essays, 1950.
Fuller, H. and V. Hammersley. Thackeray's daughter: some recollections of Anne Thackeray. Dublin 1951.
MacCarthy, B. G. Thackeray in Ireland. Studies 11 1951.
Tilford, J. E. The 'unsavoury plot' of Henry Esmond. Nineteenth-Century Fiction 6 1952.
— The love theme of Henry Esmond. PMLA 67 1952.
— The untimely death of Rachel Esmond. Nineteenth-Century Fiction 12 1958.
— The degradation of Becky Sharp. South Atlantic Quart 58 1959.
Some letters of Whitwell Elwin. TLS 18–25 Sept 1953.
Lester, J. A. Thackeray's narrative technique. PMLA 69 1954.
Tillotson, G. Thackeray the novelist. Cambridge 1954.
Tillotson, K. Vanity Fair. In her Novels of the eighteen-forties, Oxford 1954.
Tobias, R. C. American criticism of Thackeray. Nineteenth-Century Fiction 8 1954.
Baker, J. E. Vanity Fair and the celestial city. Nineteenth-Century Fiction 10 1956.
— Thackeray's recantation. PMLA 76 1962.
Sherbo, A. A note on Thackeray's Amelia. Nineteenth-Century Fiction 10 1956.
Rader, R. W. Thackeray's injustice to Fielding. JEGP 56 1957.
Ivashova, V. Thackeray the satirist. Moscow 1958.
Brander, L. Thackeray. 1959 (Br Council pamphlet).
Craig, G. A. On the style of Vanity Fair. In Style in prose fiction, ed H. C. Martin, New York 1959.
Schübel, F. Thackeray's Begriffe 'gentleman' und 'snob'. In Festschrift für Walther Fischer, Heidelberg 1959.
Taube, M. The character of Amelia in the meaning of Vanity Fair. Victorian Newsletter no 18 1960.
— Contrast as a principle of structure in Vanity Fair. Nineteenth-Century Fiction 18 1964.
— Thackeray and the reminiscential vision. Ibid.
— Thackeray at work. Ibid.
— The race for money in the structure of Vanity Fair. Victorian Newsletter no 24 1963.
— The George-Amelia-Dobbin triangle in the structure of Vanity Fair. Victorian Newsletter no 29 1966.
Pantučkova, L. Thackeray's literary criticism in the Morning Chronicle. Brno Stud in Eng 2 1960.
— The relationship of Thackeray to Fielding. Sbornik Praci Filosofické Fakulty Brnenské Univ 11 1962.
Taylor, A. C. Balzac et Thackeray. Revue de la Littérature Comparée 34 1960.
Davies, P. G. The miscegenation theme in the works of Thackeray. MLN 76 1962.
Johnson, E. D. H. Vanity Fair and Amelia. MP 59 1961.
Marshall, W. H. Dramatic irony in Henry Esmond. Revue des Langues Vivantes 27 1961.
Worth, G. J. The unity of Henry Esmond. Nineteenth-Century Fiction 15 1961.
Green, D. J. Becky Sharp and Lord Steyne: Thackeray or Disraeli? Nineteenth-Century Fiction 16 1962.
Sharp, M. C. Sympathetic mockery: a study of the narrator's character in Vanity Fair. ELH 29 1962.
Talon, H. A. Time and memory in Henry Esmond. RES new ser 13 1962.
— Thackeray's Vanity Fair revisited: fiction as truth. In Of books and humankind, ed J. Butt 1964.
Alexandrov, B. Thackeray in Russia. Soviet Lit Dec 1963.
Stewart, D. H. Thackeray's modern detractors. Papers of Michigan Acad of Science, Arts & Letters 48 1963.
— Vanity Fair: life in the void. College Eng Dec 1963.
Mathison, J. K. The German sections of Vanity Fair. Nineteenth-Century Fiction 18 1964. Reply by G. J. Worth 19 1965.
von Henry, A. Misunderstandings about Becky's characterization in Vanity Fair. Nineteenth-Century Fiction 18 1964.
Dyson, A. E. Vanity Fair: an irony against heroes. CQ 6 1964; rptd in his Crazy fabric, 1965.
Fido, M. The history of Pendennis: a reconsideration. EC 14 1964.
Loofbourow, J. Thackeray and the form of fiction. Princeton 1964.
Stevens, J. A note on photography: the ms of Vanity Fair. AUMLA no 21 1964.
— The use of illustration in Vanity Fair. REL 6 1965.
Harden, E. F. The fields of Mars in Vanity Fair. Tennessee Stud in Lit 10 1965.
Tennyson, C. W. M. Thackeray. Essays by Divers Hands 33 1965.
White, E. M. Thackeray, Dolly Duster and Lady Charlotte Campbell Bury. RES new ser 16 1965.
— Thackeray's contributions to Fraser's Magazine. SB 19 1966.
Wilkinson, A. Y. The Thomeavesian way of knowing the world: technique and meaning in Vanity Fair. ELH 32 1965.

L. S.

THE BRONTËS

Bibliographies

Anderson, J. P. In A. Birrell, Life of Charlotte Brontë, 1887.
Wood, B. A bibliography of the works of the Brontë family. 1895 (Brontë Soc); Supplement, 1897.
— Some bibliographical notes on the Brontë literature. 1910 (Brontë Soc).
Catalogue of the Gleave Brontë collection at the Moss Side Free Library. Manchester 1905.
Wise, T. J. A bibliography of the writings in prose and verse of the Brontë family. 1917 (priv ptd).
— A Brontë library: a catalogue of printed books, manuscripts and autograph letters by the members of the Brontë family. 1929 (priv ptd).
[Hatfield, C. W.] Catalogue of the Bonnell collection in the Brontë Parsonage Museum. 1932 (Brontë Soc).
Ruff, W. First American editions of Brontë novels. Brontë Soc Trans 8 1934.
Christian, M. G. A census of Brontë manuscripts in the United States. Trollopian 2–3 1947–8.
— In Victorian fiction: a guide to research, ed L. Stevenson, Cambridge Mass 1964.
Marchand, L. A. An addition to the census of Brontë manuscripts. Nineteenth-Century Fiction 4 1950.

Collections and Composite Works

Poems by Currer, Ellis and Acton Bell. 1846, 1848, Philadelphia 1848, London 1860 (with the Professor, Emma).
The life [by Mrs Gaskell] and works of Charlotte Brontë and her sisters. 7 vols 1872–3.
The works of Charlotte, Emily and Anne Brontë: Temple edition. 12 vols 1893, 1901; ed M. Sinclair 1905, 1938.
The life [by Mrs Gaskell] and works of Charlotte Brontë and her sisters: Haworth edition. Ed Mrs H. Ward and C. K. Shorter 7 vols 1899–1900.
The novels of the sisters Brontë: Thornton edition. Ed T. Scott 12 vols 1901. Includes Mrs Gaskell's Life of Charlotte Brontë, ed T. Scott and B. W. Willett.
The novels and poems of Charlotte, Emily and Anne Brontë. 7 vols 1901–7 (WC). General introd by T. Watts-Dunton prefixed to the Professor.
Poems by Charlotte, Emily and Anne Brontë now for the first time printed. New York 1902.
Brontë poems: selections from the poetry of Charlotte, Emily, Anne and Branwell Brontë. Ed A. C. Benson 1915.
The orphans and other poems by Charlotte, Emily and Branwell Brontë. 1917 (priv ptd).
The Shakespeare Head Brontë. Ed T. J. Wise and J. A. Symington 19 vols Oxford 1932–8. Novels in 11 vols; life and letters in 4 vols; miscellaneous and unpbd writings in 2 vols; poems in 2 vols.
Unpublished manuscripts. Brontë Soc Trans 8 1933.
The works of the Brontë sisters: Heather edition. Ed P. Bentley 6 vols 1949.
Hopewell, D. New treasures at Haworth. Brontë Soc Trans 12 1951.
New acquisitions: letters from Emily, Anne and Patrick. Ibid.

§1

CHARLOTTE BRONTË, later NICHOLLS

1816–55

Jane Eyre: an autobiography, edited by Currer Bell. 3 vols 1847, 1848 (with dedication and preface), 1848, 1 vol New York 1848, London 1850, 2 vols Leipzig 1850, 1 vol 1857, 1858 etc; ed C. K. Shorter [1889]; ed W. R. Nicoll 1902 (with The Moores); ed M. Sinclair [1908] (EL); ed M. Lane [1957] (EL); ed M. Schorer, Boston 1959.
Shirley: a tale, by Currer Bell. 3 vols 1849, 2 vols Leipzig 1849, 1 vol New York 1850, London 1852, 1857, 1860, 1862 etc; ed M. Sinclair [1908] (EL).
Villette, by Currer Bell. 3 vols 1853, 1 vol Leipzig 1853, New York 1853, London 1855, 1857, 1858, 1860, 1861, 1866, 1867 etc; ed M. Sinclair [1908] (EL); ed M. Lane [1957] (EL).
The professor: a tale, by Currer Bell. 2 vols 1857 (with preface by A. B. Nicholls), 1 vol New York 1857, London 1860 (with Emma and poems by Currer, Ellis and Acton Bell), 1860, 1862 etc; ed M. Sinclair [1910] (EL).
Emma. Cornhill Mag April 1860; 1860 (with Professor). Fragment.
Unpublished letters of Charlotte Brontë. Hours at Home 2 1870. Letters to Ellen Nussey.
The story of the Brontës, their home, haunts, friends and works: part second—Charlotte's letters. Bradford 1889. Letters to Ellen Nussey; ptd but not pbd.
The adventures of Ernest Alembert: a fairy tale. Ed T. J. Wise 1896 (priv ptd); rptd in Literary anecdotes of the nineteenth century, ed W. R. Nicoll and T. J. Wise vol 2, 1896.
The Moores. Ed W. R. Nicoll 1902 (with Jane Eyre). Fragment.
Richard Cœur de Lion and Blondel: a poem. Ed C. K. Shorter 1912 (priv ptd).

The love letters of Charlotte Brontë to Constantin Heger. Ed M. H. Spielmann, Times 29 July 1913; 1914 (priv ptd).
Letters recounting the deaths of Emily, Anne and Branwell Brontë by Charlotte Brontë; to which are added letters signed 'Currer Bell' and 'C. B. Nicholls.' 1913 (priv ptd).
Saul and other poems. 1913 (priv ptd).
Lament befitting these times of night. Ed G. E. MacLean, Cornhill Mag Aug 1916; 1916 (priv ptd).
Unpublished essays in novel writing by Charlotte Brontë. Ed G. E. MacLean 1916.
The violet: a poem written at the age of fourteen. Ed C. K. Shorter [1916] (priv ptd).
The Red Cross Knight and other poems. 1917 (priv ptd).
The Swiss emigrant's return and other poems. 1917 (priv ptd).
The four wishes: a fairy tale. Ed C. K. Shorter 1918 (priv ptd).
Latest gleanings: being a series of unpublished poems from early manuscripts. Ed C. K. Shorter 1918 (priv ptd).
Napoleon and the spectre: a ghost story. 1919 (priv ptd).
Thackeray and Charlotte Brontë: being some hitherto unpublished letters by Charlotte Brontë. 1919 (priv ptd).
Darius Codomannus: a poem written at the age of eighteen years. 1920 (priv ptd).
The complete poems of Charlotte Brontë. Ed C. K. Shorter and C. W. Hatfield 1923.
An early essay by Charlotte Brontë. Ed M. H. Spielmann, Brontë Soc Trans 6 1924.
Conversations. Ed D. Cook, Bookman (London) Dec 1925. Playlet in prose and verse.
The twelve adventurers and other stories. [Ed C. W. Hatfield 1925].
Miniature magazines of Charlotte Brontë, with unpublished poems. Ed D. Cook, Bookman (London) Dec 1926.
An account of her honeymoon in a letter to Miss Catherine Winkworth. Leeds 1930 (priv ptd).
The spell: an extravaganza. Ed G. E. MacLean, Oxford 1931.
Two unpublished poems by Charlotte Brontë, transcribed by C. W. Hatfield. Brontë Soc Trans 7 1931.
Two unpublished manuscripts foreshadowing Villette. Ibid.
Legends of Angria: compiled from the early writings of Charlotte Brontë. Ed F. E. Ratchford and W. C. De Vane, New Haven 1933.
Review at Gazemba: lines previously unpublished by Charlotte Brontë. Brontë Soc Trans 8 1934.
The story of Willie Ellin: fragments of an unpublished novel. Brontë Soc Trans 9 1936.
Letters of 'K.T.' to Charlotte Brontë [with rough drafts of 2 replies]. Brontë Soc Trans 9 1937.
Charlotte Brontë and Hartley Coleridge, 1840. Ed C. W. Hatfield, Brontë Soc Trans 10 1940.
Edgerley, C. M. A Charlotte Brontë manuscript. Ibid.
A Frenchman's journal: a Charlotte Brontë manuscript transcribed by C. M. Edgerley. Ibid.
Four essays by Charlotte Brontë. Brontë Soc Trans 12 1952.
Two letters from Charlotte Brontë to Mrs Gaskell. Ibid.

EMILY JANE BRONTË

1818–48

Wuthering Heights: a novel, by Ellis Bell. 2 vols 1847 (with vol 3, Agnes Grey: a novel by Acton Bell, i.e. Anne Brontë), 1 vol New York 1848, London 1850 (with Agnes Grey; rev edn with biographical notice of the authors, a selection from their literary remains and a preface by Currer Bell), 1851, Leipzig 1851, London 1858 etc; ed E. Rhys [1907] (EL); ed R. Macaulay 1926;

ed H. W. Garrod, Oxford 1930 (WC); ed R. A. Gettmann, New York 1950; ed V. S. Pritchett, Boston [1956]; ed T. C. Moser, New York 1962; ed W. M. Sale, New York 1963.
Poems of Emily Brontë. Ed A. Symons 1906.
The complete works of Emily Brontë. Ed C. K. Shorter and W. R. Nicoll 2 vols 1910–11.
The complete poems of Emily Jane Brontë. Ed C. K. Shorter and C. W. Hatfield 1924.
An unpublished verse by Emily Jane Brontë. Brontë Soc Trans 8 1934.
Two poems: Love's rebuke, Remembrance. Ed F. E. Ratchford, Austin 1934 (priv ptd).
The Gondal saga. Ed H. Brown and J. Mott, Brontë Soc Trans 8 1934.
Gondal poems, now first published from the manuscript in the British Museum. Ed H. Brown and J. Mott, Oxford 1938.
The complete poems. Ed C. W. Hatfield, New York 1941.
Cornish, D. H. The Brontës' study of French. Brontë Soc Trans 11 1947. 2 compositions by Emily written in French in 1842.
Five essays written in French by Emily Jane Brontë. Tr L. W. Nagel, ed F. E. Ratchford, Austin 1948.
The complete poems. Ed P. Henderson 1951.
A diary paper. Brontë Soc Trans 12 1951.
Gondal's Queen: a novel in verse. Ed F. E. Ratchford, Austin 1955.

ANNE BRONTË

1820–49

Agnes Grey. [*See* Emily Brontë, above]; Philadelphia 1850, London 1858 (with Wuthering Heights), 1860, 1862, 1889 etc.
The tenant of Wildfell Hall, by Acton Bell. 3 vols 1848 (reissued as 2nd edn with new preface), 1 vol New York 1848, London 1854, 1859, 1867 etc; ed M. Sinclair [1914] (EL)
Self-communion: a poem. Ed T. J. Wise 1900 (priv ptd).
Dreams and other poems. 1917 (priv ptd).
The complete poems of Anne Brontë. Ed C. K. Shorter and C. W. Hatfield 1923.

§2

Dobell, S. Athenaeum 4 July 1846. Review of Poems by Currer, Ellis and Acton Bell.
— Currer Bell. Palladium Sept 1850; rptd in his Life and letters vol 1, 1878. On Wuthering Heights.
[Lewes, G. H.] Fraser's Mag Dec 1847. On Jane Eyre.
— Edinburgh Rev 91 1850. On Shirley.
[Rigby, E. (later Lady Eastlake)]. Quart Rev 84 1848; rptd in Famous reviews, ed R. B. Johnson 1914. Review of Vanity Fair and Jane Eyre.
Forcade, E. Revue des Deux Mondes 1 Nov 1848. On Jane Eyre.
— Revue des Deux Mondes 15 Nov 1849. On Shirley.
Charlotte Brontë and Thackeray. Oxford & Cambridge Mag 1 1856.
P., W.P. Jottings on Currer, Ellis and Acton Bell. 1856.
Gaskell, E. C. The life of Charlotte Brontë. 2 vols 1857. *See* col. 865, above.
Shepheard, H. A vindication of the clergy daughters' school from the remarks in the Life of Charlotte Brontë. Kirkby Lonsdale 1857.
Skelton, J. Charlotte Brontë. Fraser's Mag May 1857; rptd in his Essays in history and biography, Edinburgh 1883.
Roscoe, W. C. The Miss Brontës. In his Poems and essays vol 2, 1860.

'Selden, Camille'. Charlotte Brontë et la vie morale en Angleterre. In his L'esprit des femmes de notre temps, Paris 1865.
Martineau, H. In her Biographical sketches, 1869. From Daily News April 1855.
'E' (Ellen Nussey). Reminiscences of Charlotte Brontë. Scribner's Monthly May 1871.
Smith, G. B. The Brontës. Cornhill Mag July 1873; rptd in his Poets and novelists, 1875.
Reid, T. W. Charlotte Brontë: a monograph. 1877.
Stephen, L. Charlotte Brontë. Cornhill Mag Dec 1877; rptd in his Hours in a library ser 3, 1879.
Swinburne, A. C. A note on Charlotte Brontë. 1877.
— Emily Brontë. In his Miscellanies, 1886.
Grundy, F. H. Patrick Branwell Brontë. In his Pictures of the past, 1879.
Turner, J. H. Haworth past and present. Brighouse 1879.
— Brontëana: the Rev Patrick Brontë, his collected works and life. 1898.
Robinson, A. M. F. Emily Brontë. 1883.
Scruton, W. The birthplace of Charlotte Brontë. 1884.
— Thornton and the Brontës. 1898.
Montégut, E. Charlotte Brontë. In his Ecrivains modernes de l'Angleterre ser 1, Paris 1885.
Leyland, F. A. The Brontë family with special reference to Patrick Branwell Brontë. 2 vols 1886.
Birrell, A. Life of Charlotte Brontë. 1887.
Holroyd, A. Currer Bell. [1887]. Rptd from Bradford Advertiser 1855.
Candy, F. H. Some reminiscences of the author of Jane Eyre. GM Oct 1889.
Lang, A. Charlotte Brontë. Good Words April 1889.
Wright, W. The Brontës in Ireland. 1893.
Richardson, F. (later Macdonald). The Brontës at Brussels. Woman at Home July 1894.
— The secret of Charlotte Brontë; followed by some reminiscences of the real Monsieur and Madame Heger. 1914.
Transactions & publications of the Brontë Society. Bradford [later Haworth] 1895. Separate items not listed in this section.
Harrison, F. Charlotte Brontë's place in literature. Forum March 1895; rptd in his Studies in early Victorian literature, 1895.
Saintsbury, G. Three mid-century novelists. In his Corrected impressions, 1895.
Shorter, C. K. Charlotte Brontë and her circle. 1896, [1914] (rev as The Brontës and their circle).
— Charlotte Brontë and her sisters. 1905.
— The Brontës: life and letters. 2 vols 1908.
Mackay, A. M. The Brontës: fact and fiction. 1897.
— The Brontës at Cowan Bridge. Bookman (London) Oct 1904.
Oliphant, M. O. The sisters Brontë. In A. Sergeant et al, Women novelists of Queen Victoria's reign, 1897.
Yates, W. W. The father of the Brontës, with a chapter on Currer Bell. 1897.
Howells, W. D. Jane Eyre. Harper's Bazaar Dec 1900; rptd in his Heroines of fiction, New York 1901.
Bonnell, H. H. Charlotte Brontë, George Eliot, Jane Austen: studies in their works. New York 1902.
Gosse, E. The challenge of the Brontës. 1903 (priv ptd); rptd in his Selected essays ser 2, 1928.
Lord, W. F. The Brontë novels. Nineteenth Century March 1903; rptd in his Mirror of the century, 1906.
Smith, G. C. M. The Brontës at Thornton. Bookman (London) Oct 1904.
Hobson, E. Shirley land. Westminster Rev 166 1906.
Dimnet, E. Les sœurs Brontë. Paris 1910; tr 1927.
Meynell, A. Charlotte and Emily Brontë. Dublin Rev April 1911; rev in her Hearts of controversy, [1917].
Harper, J. Charlotte Brontë and the Heger family. Blackwood's Mag April 1912.
Junge, H. Der Stil in den Romanen Charlotte Brontës. Halle 1912.

Masson, F. The Brontës. 1912.
Sinclair, M. The three Brontës. 1912, 1914 (rev).
Ralli, A. Self-expression in Charlotte Brontë's books. Fortnightly Rev Sept 1913; rptd in his Critiques, 1927.
— Emily Brontë: the problem of personality. North Amer Rev March 1925; rptd in his Critiques, 1927.
Chadwick, E. A. In the footsteps of the Brontës. 1914.
— Patrick Branwell Brontë: a vindication. Nineteenth Century Aug 1918.
Smith, J. C. Emily Brontë: a reconsideration. E & S 5 1914.
Brown, L. R. Charlotte Brontë and Belgium. Nineteenth Century April 1916.
Spielmann, M. H. Charlotte Brontë in Brussels. TLS 13 April 1916.
— The inner history of the Brontë-Heger letters. 1919.
Charlotte Brontë 1816–1916: a centenary memorial prepared by the Brontë Society; foreword by Mrs H. Ward. 1917.
Crichton-Browne, J. Patrick Branwell Brontë: an extenuation. Fortnightly Rev July 1918.
Symons, A. Emily Brontë. Nation (London) 24 Aug 1918; rptd in his Dramatis personae, 1923.
Masson, J. The Brontës as seen through French eyes. London Quart Rev 131 1919.
Dooley, L. Psycho-analysis of Charlotte Brontë as a type of the woman of genius. Amer Jnl of Psychology 31 1920.
Kavanagh, C. The symbolism of Wuthering Heights. [1920].
Sandwith, M. T. E. Jane Eyre and Eugénie Grandet. Nineteenth Century Aug 1922.
Bald, M. A. Women writers of the nineteenth century. Cambridge 1923.
Dodds, M. H. Gondaliand. MLR 18 1923. On Emily Brontë's poems.
— A second visit to Gondaliand. MLR 21–2 1926–7.
— Heathcliff's country. MLR 39 1944.
Mirsky, D. S. Emily Brontë. London Mercury Jan 1923.
Law, A. Emily Brontë and the authorship of Wuthering Heights. Altham 1925.
— Patrick Branwell Brontë. [1924].
Read, H. Charlotte and Emily Brontë. Yale Rev 14 1925; rptd in his Reason and romanticism, 1926.
Woolf, V. Jane Eyre and Wuthering Heights. In her Common reader, 1925.
Cook, D. Emily Brontë's poems: textual corrections and unpublished verses. Nineteenth Century Aug 1926.
Green, J. Charlotte Brontë et ses sœurs. Revue Hebdomadaire 17 July 1926; tr Virginia Quart Rev 5 1929.
Kuhlman, R. Natur-paganismus in der Weltanschauung von Emily Brontë. Schloppe 1926.
S[anger], C. P. The structure of Wuthering Heights. 1926.
Bell, H. K. Charlotte Brontë's husband. Cornhill Mag Jan 1927.
Tompkins, J. M. S. Jane Eyre's 'iron shroud'. MLR 22 1927.
Ratchford, F. E. Charlotte Brontë's Angrian cycle of stories. PMLA 43 1928.
— The Brontës' web of dreams. Yale Rev 21 1931.
— The Brontës' web of childhood. New York 1941.
— War in Gondal: Emily Brontë's last poem. Trollopian 2 1947.
— Brontë cousins in America. Texas Univ Lib Chron 4 1952.
Spens, J. Charlotte Brontë. E & S 14 1928.
Wilson, R. All alone: the life and private history of Emily Jane Brontë. 1928.
Hale, W. T. Anne Brontë: her life and writings. Bloomington 1929.
Langbridge, R. Charlotte Brontë: a psychological study. 1929.
Simpson, C. Emily Brontë: 1929.
Sugden, K. A. R. A short history of the Brontës. Oxford 1929.
Romieu, E. and G. La vie des sœurs Brontë. Paris 1930; tr 1931.
Benson, E. F. Charlotte Brontë. 1932.
Bradby, G. F. The Brontës and other essays. Oxford 1932.
Edgar, P. Judgments on appeal, 2: the Brontës. Queen's Quart 39 1932; rptd in his Art of the novel, 1933.
Haldane, E. S. The Brontës and their biographers. Nineteenth Century Dec 1932.
Morgan, C. Emily Brontë. In Great Victorians, ed H. J. and H. Massingham 1932; rptd in his Reflections in a mirror, 1944.
West, R. Charlotte Brontë. In Great Victorians, ed H. J. and H. Massingham, 1932 and in Saturday Rev of Lit 5 Nov 1932.
Wise, T. J. and J. A. Symington. The Brontës: their lives, friendships and correspondence. 4 vols Oxford 1932 (Shakespeare Head Brontë).
Bradner, L. The growth of Wuthering Heights. PMLA 48 1933.
Charlier, G. The Brussels life in Villette. Contemporary Rev Nov 1933; tr French in his Passages, Brussels 1947.
O'Byrne, C. The Gaelic source of the Brontë genius. 1933.
Willis, I. C. The Brontës. 1933.
— The authorship of Wuthering Heights. 1936. Summarized in Trollopian 2 1947.
Cecil, D. In his Early Victorian novelists, 1934, 1964 (rev).
The Brontës: their lives recorded by their contemporaries. Ed E. M. Delafield 1935.
Newton, A. E. The Brontë country. In his Derby day and other adventures, Boston 1935.
Gary, F. Charlotte Brontë and George Henry Lewes. PMLA 51 1936.
Hatfield, C. W. Emily Brontë's 'lost love'. TLS 29 Aug 1936.
Moore, V. The life and eager death of Emily Brontë. 1936.
Schulte, C. Genie im Schatten: das Leben der Charlotte Brontë. Dresden 1936.
Dry, F. S. The sources of Wuthering Heights. Cambridge 1937.
— The sources of Jane Eyre. Cambridge 1940.
Harrison, G. E. Haworth Parsonage: a study of Wesley and the Brontës. 1937.
— The clue to the Brontës. 1948.
Maurer, K. W. The poetry of Emily Brontë. Anglia 49 1937.
Wells, A. L. Les sœurs Brontë et l'étranger. Paris 1937.
White, W. B. The miracle of Haworth. 1937.
Johnson, M. The Brontës in Ireland. Cornhill Mag July 1938.
Ocampo, V. Emily Brontë: terra incognita. Buenos Aires 1938.
Traz, R. de. La famille Brontë. Paris 1938.
Brown, H. The influence of Byron on Emily Brontë. MLR 34 1939.
Ford, B. Wuthering Heights. Scrutiny 7 1939.
Kinsey, E. Pattern for genius. New York 1939.
Cornish, D. H. These were the Brontës. 1940.
Turnell, M. Wuthering Heights. Dublin Rev 206 1940.
Escombe, L. Emily Brontë et ses démons. Paris 1941.
Moore, T. S. Beyond east and west. Asiatic Rev 37 1941. On Emily Brontë.
Brash, W. B. The Brontës of Haworth: through trial to triumph. London Quart Rev 167 1942.
Hinkley, L. L. Charlotte and Emily: the Brontës. New York 1945.
Jones, W. S. H. Jane and Charlotte. London Quart Rev 170 1945.
Jaloux, E. D'Eschyle à Giraudoux. Fribourg 1946.
Lewis, N. Tenant of Wildfell Hall. New Statesman 17 Aug 1946.
Willy, M. Emily Brontë: poet and mystic. English 6 1946.
Bentley, P. The significance of Haworth. Trollopian 2 1947.

— The Brontës. 1947.
— The Brontë sisters. 1950 (Br Council pamphlet).
Chase, R. The Brontës: or myth domesticated. Kenyon Rev 9 1947; rptd in Forms of modern fiction, ed W. V. O'Connor, Minneapolis 1948.
Klingopulos, G. D. The novel as dramatic poem, 2: Wuthering Heights. Scrutiny 14 1947.
Mason, L. Charlotte Brontë and Charles Dickens. Dickensian 43 1947.
— Jane Eyre and David Copperfield. Ibid.
Evans, M. Byron and Emily Brontë. Life & Letters June 1948.
Maugham, W. S. Wuthering Heights. In his Great novelists and their novels, Philadelphia 1948, London 1955 (rev as Ten novels and their authors).
Raymond, E. In the steps of the Brontës. 1948.
— The Brontë legend: its causes and treatment. Essays by Divers Hands 26 1953.
Tillotson, K. 'Rugby chapel' and Jane Eyre. N & Q 16 Oct 1948.
— Jane Eyre. In her Novels of the eighteen-forties, Oxford 1954.
Tinker, C. B. The poetry of the Brontës. In his Essays in retrospect, New Haven 1948.
Watson, M. R. Wuthering Heights and the critics. Trollopian 3 1948.
— Tempest in the soul: the theme and structure of Wuthering Heights. Nineteenth-Century Fiction 4 1950.
Egg, I. Die Bestimmung des Frauenbildes im viktorianischen Roman Charlotte Brontë und George Eliot. Zürich 1949.
Hanson, L. and E. M. The four Brontës. 1949, Hamden Conn 1967 (rev).
Schorer, M. Fiction and the matrix of analogy. Kenyon Rev 11 1949. On Wuthering Heights.
Steen, E. Problemet Emily Brontë. Edda 49 1949.
Traversi, D. A. Wuthering Heights after a hundred years. Dublin Rev 222 1949.
Braithwaite, W. S. The bewitched parsonage. New York 1950.
Debû-Bridel, J. Le secret d'Emily Brontë. Paris 1950.
Lane, M. Mr Nicholls. Cornhill Mag 164 1950.
— The Brontë story: a reconsideration of Mrs Gaskell's Life of Charlotte Brontë. 1953.
Morgan, E. Women and poetry. Cambridge Jnl Aug 1950.
Scargill, M. H. All passion spent: a revaluation of Jane Eyre. UTQ 19 1950.
Edgerley, C. M. Brontë papers. Shipley 1951. Rptd from Brontë Soc Trans 1931–46.
MacCarthy, B. G. Emily Brontë. Studies 39 1951.
Michell, H. Haworth. Dalhousie Rev 31 1951.
Bontoft, G. T. Maria and Elizabeth Brontë. Contemporary Rev Jan 1952.
Buckler, W. E. Chapter vii of Wuthering Heights: a key to interpretation. Nineteenth-Century Fiction 7 1953.
Martin, R. B. Charlotte Brontë and Harriet Martineau. Ibid.
Van Ghent, D. The window figure and the two-children figure in Wuthering Heights. Ibid; rptd in her English novel: form and function, New York 1953.
Dupont, V. Trois notes sur les Brontë. Etudes Anglaises 6 1953.
Quievreux, L. Bruxelles, les Brontës et la famille Heger. Brussels 1953.
Senseman, W. M. Charlotte Brontë's use of physiognomy and phrenology. Papers of Mich Acad of Science, Arts & Letters 38 1953.
Spark, M. and D. Stanford. Emily Brontë: her life and work. 1953.
Lewis, C. D. Emily Brontë. In his Notable images of virtue, Toronto 1954.
Bates, M. C. Charlotte Brontë and the Kay-Shuttleworths. Harvard Lib Bull 9 1955.
Crompton, M. Passionate search: a life of Charlotte Brontë. 1955.

Duthie, E. L. Charlotte Brontë and Constantin Heger. Contemporary Rev March 1955.
Lehman, B. H. Of material, subject and form: Wuthering Heights. In his Image of the work: essays in criticism, Berkeley 1955.
Poli, S. La fortuna di Charlotte Brontë. Eng Miscellany (Rome) 6 1955.
Blondel, J. Emily Brontë: expérience spirituelle et création poétique. Paris 1956.
— Emily Brontë: récentes explorations. Etudes Anglaises 11 1958.
Burns, W. The critical relevance of Freudianism. Western Rev 20 1956.
Shannon, E. F., jr. The present tense in Jane Eyre. Nineteenth-Century Fiction 10 1956.
— Lockwood's dreams and the exegesis of Wuthering Heights. Nineteenth-Century Fiction 14 1960.
Girdler, L. Shirley and Scott's The black dwarf. MLN 71 1957.
Mathison, J. K. Nelly Dean and the power of Wuthering Heights. Nineteenth-Century Fiction 11 1957.
Bataille, G. Emily Brontë et le mal. Critique Feb 1957; rptd in his Littérature et le mal, Paris 1957.
Crandall, N. Emily Brontë: a psychological portrait. Rindge NH 1957.
Korg, J. The problem of unity in Shirley. Nineteenth-Century Fiction 12 1958.
Woodring, C. R. The narrators of Wuthering Heights. Ibid.
Heilman, R. B. Charlotte Brontë's new Gothic. In From Jane Austen to Joseph Conrad, ed R. C. Rathburn and M. Steinmann, Minneapolis 1958.
— Charlotte Brontë, reason and the moon. Nineteenth-Century Fiction 14 1960.
Hopkins, A. B. The father of the Brontës. Baltimore 1958.
Paden, W. D. An investigation of Gondal. New York 1958.
Visick, M. The genesis of Wuthering Heights. Hong Kong 1958.
Worth, G. J. Emily Brontë's Mr Lockwood. Nineteenth-Century Fiction 12 1958.
Adams, R. M. Wuthering Heights: the land east of Eden. Nineteenth-Century Fiction 13 1959.
Brick, A. R. Wuthering Heights: narrative, audience and message. College Eng Nov 1959.
— Lewes's review of Wuthering Heights. Nineteenth-Century Fiction 14 1960.
Gérin, W. Anne Brontë. 1959.
— Branwell Brontë. 1961.
Goldstone, H. Wuthering Heights revisited. Eng Jnl April 1959.
Hafley, J. The villain in Wuthering Heights. Nineteenth-Century Fiction 13 1959.
Harrison, A. and D. Stanford. Anne Brontë: her life and work. 1959.
Brammer, M. M. The manuscript of the Professor. RES new ser 11 1960.
Colby, R. A. Villette and the life of the mind. PMLA 75 1960.
Collard, M. Wuthering Heights: the revelation. [1960].
Dean, C. Joseph's speech in Wuthering Heights. N & Q Feb 1960.
Du Maurier, D. The infernal world of Branwell Brontë. 1960.
Dunbar, G. S. Proper names in Villette. Nineteenth-Century Fiction 14 1960.
Justus, J. Beyond Gothicism: Wuthering Heights and an American tradition. Tennessee Stud in Lit 5 1960.
Prescott, J. Jane Eyre: a romantic exemplum with a difference. In Twelve original essays on great English novels, ed C. Shapiro, Detroit 1960.
Solomon, E. The incest theme in Wuthering Heights. Nineteenth-Century Fiction 14 1960.
— Jane Eyre: fire and water. College Eng Dec 1963.

McKibbin, R. C. The image of the book in Wuthering Heights. Nineteenth-Century Fiction 15 1961.
Marshall, W. H. The self, the world, and the structure of Jane Eyre. Revue des Langues Vivantes 27 1961.
Livermore, A. L. Byron and Emily Brontë. Quart Rev 300 1962.
Moody, P. The challenge to maturity in Wuthering Heights. Melbourne Critical Rev no 5 1962.
Bell, V. Wuthering Heights and the unforgivable sin. Nineteenth-Century Fiction 17 1963.
—— Wuthering Heights as epos. College Eng Dec 1963.
Moser, T. What is the matter with Emily Jane? conflicting impulses in Wuthering Heights. Nineteenth-Century Fiction 17 1963.
Sharps, J. C. Charlotte Brontë and the mysterious Miss H. English 14 1963.
Thompson, W. Infanticide and sadism in Wuthering Heights. PMLA 781 1963.
Drew, P. Charlotte Brontë as a critic of Wuthering Heights. Nineteenth-Century Fiction 18 1964.
Hughes, R. E. Jane Eyre: the unbaptized Dionysos. Ibid.
Monod, S. L'imprécision dans Jane Eyre. Études Anglaises 17 1964.
Lock, J. and W. T. Dixon. A man of sorrows. 1965. On Rev Patrick Brontë.
Momberger, P. Self and world in the works of Charlotte Brontë. ELH 32 1965.
Ewbank, I. S. Their proper sphere: a study of the Brontë sisters as early Victorian female novelists. 1966.
Fraser, J. The name of action: Nelly Dean and Wuthering Heights. Nineteenth-Century Fiction 20 1966.
Knies, E. A. The 'I' of Jane Eyre. College Eng April 1966.
Martin, R. B. The accents of persuasion: Charlotte Brontë's novels. 1966.
Moser, L. E. From portrait to person: a note on the surrealistic in Jane Eyre. Nineteenth-Century Fiction 20 1966.
Pearsall, R. B. The presiding tropes of Emily Brontë. College Eng Jan 1966.

L. S.

ELIZABETH CLEGHORN GASKELL, née STEVENSON

1810–65

Mrs Gaskell's mss are gathered chiefly in Leeds in the Brotherton Library of the University; in Manchester in the Arts Library of the University, the John Rylands Library and the Manchester Central Library; in London in the archives of John Murray Ltd; in USA in the Parrish Collection at Princeton University, the Symington Collection at Rutgers University and the Berg Collection in New York Public Library. Some 60 letters by Mrs Gaskell are in the possession of her great-grand-daughter, Mrs Trevor Jones.

Bibliographies

Green, J. A. A bibliographical guide to the Gaskell collection in Moss Side Library. Manchester 1911.
Sadleir, M. In his Excursions in Victorian bibliography, 1922.
Northup, C. S. In G. de W. Sanders, Elizabeth Gaskell, New Haven 1929.
Whitfield, A. S. In his Mrs Gaskell: her life and work, 1929.
Parrish, M. L. In his Victorian lady novelists, New York 1933. First edns in Parrish's collection, now in Princeton Univ Library.
Hopkins, A. B. In her Elizabeth Gaskell: her life and work, 1952. Includes collections of short stories with lists of their contents.
Allott, M. In her Elizabeth Gaskell, 1960 (Br Council pamphlet).

Barry, J. D. In Victorian fiction: a guide to research, ed L. Stevenson, Cambridge Mass 1964.

Collections

The works. 15 vols Leipzig 1849–57. Includes Life of Charlotte Brontë.
The novels and tales. Illustr G. du Maurier 8 vols 1872–3.
The works. 8 vols 1897.
The works: Knutsford edition. Ed A. W. Ward 8 vols 1906. Biographical and critical essays by Ward; omits Life of Charlotte Brontë and the poems.
The novels and tales. Ed C. K. Shorter 11 vols Oxford 1906–19 (WC). Includes Life of Charlotte Brontë, the poems, sequel to Cranford and various prefaces by Mrs Gaskell.
Selections from the works. Ed E. A. Chadwick [1911].
Cranford, with Right at last, The Manchester marriage, The crooked branch, The cage at Cranford. 1946.

§1

Sketches among the poor, no 1: Poem written with her husband. Blackwood's Mag Jan 1837; rptd in Knutsford edn vol 1, WC edn vol 10, above.
Account of Clopton Hall, Warwickshire. In W. Howitt, Visits to remarkable places, 1840; rptd WC edn vol 10, above.
Life in Manchester, by Cotton Mather Mills esq. 2 pts W. Howitt's Jnl of Lit & Popular Progress 1, 3 1847; 8 Manchester 1848. Contains Libbie Marsh's three eras, rptd 1850, 1855, tr French, 1854; The sexton's hero rptd 1865, tr French, 1867; Christmas storms and sunshine, rptd 1865, tr French, 1864.
Mary Barton: a tale of Manchester life. 2 vols 1848 (anon), 1849, 1849, Leipzig 1849, 1 vol 1854 (includes 2 lectures by W. Gaskell on the Lancashire dialect), 1861, New York 1864, London 1865, 1866, 1867, 1869 etc; ed T. Seccombe 1911 (EL); ed L. Cooper 1947; ed M. F. Brightfield 1958; tr French, 1849, 1865; Russian, 1861, 1936; Hungarian, 1875; Spanish, 1879. Dramatized by D. Boucicault as The long strike, 1867.
The moorland cottage, by the author of Mary Barton. 1850 (illustr Birket Foster), New York 1868, London 1898 (with Cranford).
Bran: poem. Household Words 22 Oct 1853; rptd WC edn vol 10, above.
The scholar's story. Household Words 25 Dec 1853; rptd WC edn vol 10, above. W. Gaskell's trn of the Breton ballad of the Vicomte de la Villemarque, with introd by Mrs Gaskell.
Ruth: a novel, by the author of Mary Barton. 3 vols 1853, Leipzig 1853, London 1855, Boston [1855], 2 vols [1857], 1 vol [1861], 1867 (8th edn), [1895]; tr French, 1856, 1954.
Cranford, by the author of Mary Barton, Ruth etc. 22 weekly pts Household Words 13 Dec–21 May 1853; 1853, New York 1853, London 1855, 1858, 1858, 1864 (illustr); ed A. T. Ritchie 1891 (illustr H. Thomson); 1896 (illustr T. H. Robinson); ed W. R. Nicoll 1898 (with The moorland cottage, above); 1898 (illustr H. M. Brock); ed B. Herford 1898; ed E. V. Lucas 1899 etc; ed E. Rhys 1906 (EL); ed G. A. Payne 1914; ed A. Thirkell 1951; ed D. Ascoli 1952, 1954 (EL); tr French, 1856; German, [1857?]; Hungarian, 1884; Portuguese, 1943. Dramatized by S. M. Du Pré, 1902; B. Hatch, 1902; M. F. Hutchinson, 1906; M. Coleman, 1952.
Lizzie Leigh and other tales. 1855, 1865, 1871, 1871 etc. Contains Lizzie Leigh, 3 weekly pts Household Words 30 March–13 April 1850, tr French, 1882; Well of Pen-Morfa, 2 weekly pts Household Words 16–23 Nov 1851; Heart of John Middleton, Household Words 28 Dec 1850; Old nurse's story, Household Words Xmas no 1852; Traits and stories of the Huguenots, Household Words 10 Dec 1853; Morton Hall, 2 weekly pts Household Words 19–26 Nov 1853; My French master, 2

weekly pts Household Words 17–24 Dec 1853; Squire's story, Household Words Xmas no 1853; Libbie Marsh's three eras (*see* Life in Manchester, above); Christmas storms and sunshine (*see* Life in Manchester); Hand and heart, Sunday School Parish Mag (Manchester) July 1849, rptd 1855; Bessy's troubles at home, Sunday School Parish Mag Jan 1852, rptd 1855, 1865; Disappearances, Household Words June 7 1851, rptd 1865.

Hand and heart and Bessy's troubles at home, by the author of Mary Barton. 1855. *See* Lizzie Leigh and other tales, above.

North and South, by the author of Mary Barton, Ruth, Cranford etc. 21 weekly pts Household Words 2 Sept 1854–27 Jan 1855; 2 vols 1855, 1 vol 1855, Leipzig, New York 1855, London 1859 (4th edn), New York 1864, 1865, 1867, 1869, 1870 etc; ed E. A. Chadwick 1914 (EL); ed E. Bowen 1951; tr French, 1859.

A Christmas carol: poem. Household Words 27 Dec 1856.

The life of Charlotte Brontë. 2 vols 1857, 1857, 1857 (rev and corrected), New York 1857, London 1858, New York 1858, London 1859, 1 vol 1860, 1862, 1872 etc; ed C. K. Shorter 1900; ed T. Scott and B. Willett 1901, [1905]; ed M. Sinclair 1908 (EL); 1914 (Haworth edn); ed M. Lane 1947; tr German, 1859; French, 1877.

Maria Vaughan, by the author of the Lamplighter (Maria S. Cummins). Preface by Mrs Haskell. 1857; tr German, 1857.

My Lady Ludlow. 14 weekly pts Household Words 19 June–25 Sept 1858; New York 1859, 1861. *See* Round the sofa, below.

Round the sofa. 1859, 1859, 1861 (as My Lady Ludlow and other tales included in Round the sofa), 1866; tr French, 1860. Contains My Lady Ludlow, above, An accursed race, Household Words 25 Aug 1855; Doom of the Griffiths, Harper's Mag Jan 1858, rptd Leipzig 1861; Half a lifetime ago, 2 weekly pts 6–20 Oct 1855; The poor Clare, 2 weekly pts 13–27 Dec 1855; The half-brothers, Dublin Univ Mag Nov 1858, rptd Leipzig 1861.

Right at last and other tales. 1860, New York 1860, London 1867. Contains Right at last, Household Words 27 Nov 1858 (as The sin of a father); A Manchester marriage, Household Words Xmas no 1858, tr French, 1867; Lois the witch, 3 weekly pts All the Year Round Oct 8–22 1859, rptd Leipzig 1861; Crooked branch, All the Year Round Xmas no 1859 (as The ghost in the garden room), rptd Leipzig 1861.

Lois the witch and other tales. Leipzig 1861. Reprints Lois the witch (*see* Right at last, above); Doom of the Griffiths (*see* Round the sofa); Crooked branch (*see* Right at last); Half-brothers (*see* Round the sofa); Grey woman, 3 weekly pts All the Year Round 5–19 Jan 1861, rptd Leipzig 1861.

Garibaldi at Caprera by Colonel [C. A. Vecchj], translated from the Italian by L. and M. Ellis. Preface by Mrs Gaskell. Cambridge 1862.

A dark night's work. 9 weekly pts All the Year Round 24 Jan–21 March 1863; 1863 (illustr G. du Maurier), New York 1863, Leipzig 1863, London 1864; tr German, 1865; French, 1867.

Sylvia's lovers. 3 vols 1863 (illustr G. du Maurier), 2 vols Leipzig 1863, New York 1863, London 1870, 1 vol 1904 etc; ed T. Seccombe 1910, 1914 (EL); ed A. Pollard 1964; tr German, 1863–4; French, 1865.

The cage at Cranford. All the Year Round 28 Nov 1863; rptd WC edn, above.

Robert Gould Shaw. Macmillan's Mag Dec 1863.

Cousin Phillis: a tale. 4 monthly pts Cornhill Mag Nov 1863–Feb 1864; New York 1864, London 1865 (*see* below); tr French, 1866, 1867 (with A dark night's work and Sexton's hero).

Cousin Phillis and other tales. 1865 (illustr G. du Maurier), Leipzig 1867, London 1870; ed T. Seccombe 1908, 1912 (EL). Reprints Cousin Phillis, above, Company manners, Household Words 20 May 1854; Mr Harrison's confessions, Ladies Companion Feb–April 1851, tr French, 1866; Sexton's hero (*see* Life in Manchester, above).

The grey woman and other tales. 1865 (illustr G. du Maurier), 1871, 1871. Reprints Grey woman (*see* Lois the witch and other tales); Curious if true, Cornhill Mag Feb 1860; Six weeks at Heppenheim, Cornhill Mag May 1862, tr French, 1868; Libbie Marsh's three eras (*see* Life in Manchester, above); Christmas storms and sunshine (*see* Life in Manchester); Hand and heart (*see* Lizzie Leigh, above); Bessy's troubles at home (*see* Lizzie Leigh); Disappearances (*see* Lizzie Leigh).

Wives and daughters: an every-day story. 18 monthly pts Cornhill Mag Aug 1864–Jan 1866 (last pt completed by F. Greenwood); 2 vols 1866 (illustr G. du Maurier), Leipzig 1866, New York 1866, London 1869, 1870 etc; ed T. Seccombe 1912; ed R. Lehmann 1948; tr German, 1867; French, 1868. Dramatized by M. Macnamara, 1947.

Two fragments of ghost stories. Knutsford edn vol 7 1906, above.

Letters and Diaries

Letters on Charlotte Brontë. 1916 (priv ptd).

'My diary': the early years of my daughter Marianne. 1923 (priv ptd). Written 10 March 1835–28 Oct 1838.

Letters of Mrs Gaskell and C. E. Norton 1855–65. Ed J. Whitehill, Oxford 1932.

Letters. Ed R. D. Waller, Bull John Rylands Lib 19 1935.

Letters. Ed J. A. V. Chappie and A. Pollard, Manchester 1966.

§2

Greg, W. R. Mary Barton. Edinburgh Rev 89 1849; rptd in his Mistaken aims, 1876.

Montégut, E. Mary Barton, Ruth. Revue des Deux Mondes April–June 1853; rptd in his Ecrivains modernes de l'Angleterre: deuxième série, Paris 1889.

— North and South. Revue des Deux Mondes Oct-Dec 1855; rptd ibid.

Landor, W. S. Last fruit off an old tree. 1853. Epistle 268: To the author of Mary Barton.

Hédouin, A. Ruth. Athenaeum Français 31 May 1856.

Green, H. In his Knutsford: its traditions and history, 1859.

de Mouy, C. Mrs Gaskell. Revue Européenne 18 1861.

Dicey, E. Mrs Gaskell. Nation (London) 7 Dec 1865.

Masson, D. Mrs Gaskell. Macmillan's Mag Dec 1865.

Milnes, R. M. Mrs Gaskell. Pall Mall Gazette 14 Nov 1865.

Greenwood, F. Obituary. Cornhill Mag Jan 1866.

James, H. Wives and daughters. Nation (New York) 2 1866; rptd in his Notes and reviews, 1921.

Smith, G. B. Mrs Gaskell and her novels. Cornhill Mag Feb 1874.

Minto, W. Mrs Gaskell's novels. Fortnightly Rev Sept 1878.

Dickens, C. In his Letters, ed G. Hogarth and M. E. Dickens 3 vols 1880–2.

— In his Letters to Wilkie Collins, ed L. Hutton 1892.

Howitt, M. In her Mary Howitt: an autobiography, 2 vols 1889.

— Stray notes about Mrs Gaskell. Good Words Sept 1895.

Shorter, C. K. In his Charlotte Brontë and her circle, 1896.

Lyall, E. (A. E. Bayly). In A. Sergeant et al, Women novelists of Queen Victoria's reign, 1897.

Payne, G. A. Mrs Gaskell and Knutsford. 1900.

— Mrs Gaskell: a brief biography. 1929.

Ritchie, A. T. The author of Cranford. Cornhill Mag Dec 1906; rptd in her Blackstick papers, 1908.

More, P. E. In his Shelburne essays: series 5, New York 1908.

Coleridge, M. E. In her Gathered leaves, 1910.
Herford, C. H. Mrs Gaskell. Manchester Guardian 29 Sept 1910.
'Melville, Lewis'. The centenary of Mrs Gaskell. Nineteenth Century Sept 1910.
Sargisson, C. S. Mrs Gaskell's early surroundings and their influence on her writings. Bookman (London) Sept 1910.
Seccombe, T. Elizabeth Cleghorn Gaskell. Ibid.
Ward, A. W. Disraeli, Charles Kingsley, Mrs Gaskell, George Eliot. CHEL 13 1916.
Cazamian, L. In his Le roman social en Angleterre 1830–50, Paris 1904.
Shaen, M. J. In her Memorials of two sisters, Susanna and Catherine Winkworth. 1908.
Chadwick, E. H. Mrs Gaskell: haunts, homes and stories. 1910, 1913 (rev).
Bald, M. E. In her Women writers of the nineteenth century, 1923.
Quiller-Couch, A. T. In his Charles Dickens and other Victorians, 1925.
Johnston, J. The sociological significance of the novels of Mrs Gaskell. Jnl of Social Forces 1928.
Whitfield, A. S. Mrs Gaskell: her life and work. 1929.
Sanders, G. de W. Elizabeth Gaskell. New Haven 1929. *See* under Bibliographies, above.
Haldane, E. Mrs Gaskell and her friends. 1930.
Brockbank, J. In Papers of the Manchester Literary Club, Manchester 1932.
Eliot, T. S. Letters of Mrs Gaskell and C. E. Norton, edited by Jane Whitehill. New England Quart 6 1933. A review.
Cecil, D. Mrs Gaskell. In his Early Victorian novelists, 1934, 1964 (rev).
Walker, R. D. TLS 25 July 1935. Letters on Cranford and the Last generation in England.
Hopkins, A. B. Mrs Gaskell in France 1849–50. PMLA 53 1938.
—— Dickens and Mrs Gaskell. HLQ 9 1946.
—— Mary Barton: a Victorian best-seller. Trollopian 3 1948.
—— Elizabeth Gaskell: her life and work. 1952. *See* under Bibliographies, above.
Pritchett, V. S. New Statesman 21 June 1941. On North and south.
Wagenknecht, G. In his Cavalcade of the English novel, 1943.
Stebbins, L. P. In her A Victorian album, 1946.
Mary Barton. TLS 30 Aug 1947.
Lehmann, R. A neglected Victorian classic. Penguin New Writing 32 1948; also pbd as introd to Wives and daughters, 1948.
ffrench, Y. Mrs Gaskell. 1949.
—— In From Jane Austen to Joseph Conrad, ed R. C. Rathburn and M. Steinmann, Minneapolis 1958.
Bland, D. S. Mary Barton and historical accuracy. RES new ser 1 1950.
Rubenius, A. The woman question in Mrs Gaskell's life and works. Upsala [1950], Copenhagen and Cambridge Mass 1951.
Johnson, E. In his Charles Dickens: his tragedy and triumph, 2 vols New York 1952. On Mrs Gaskell's contributions to periodicals etc.
Collins, H. P. The naked sensibility. EC 3 1953.
Lane, M. In her Brontë story, 1953.
Tillotson, K. Mary Barton. In her Novels of the eighteen-forties, Oxford 1954.
Lewis, N. In her A visit to Mrs Wilcox, 1957.
Kovalev, Y. V. In his Literature of Chartism, Moscow 1956; tr Victorian Stud 2 1958.
Williams, R. The industrial novels. In his Culture and society 1780–1950, 1958, 1961 (Pelican), 1963 (with addn). On Mary Barton.
Shusterman, D. W. R. Greg and Mrs Gaskell. PQ 36 1957.

Kettle, A. The early Victorian social-problem novel. In From Dickens to Hardy, ed B. Ford 1958 (Pelican).
Grossman, L. Mrs Gaskell's influence on Dostoevsky. Voprosi Literaturi 4 1959; tr Anglo-Soviet Jnl 21 1960. Includes comment by Karl Marx, The English middle class, New York Tribune 1 Aug 1854.
Allott, M. Elizabeth Gaskell. 1960 (Br Council pamphlet).
—— The old nurse's story: a link between Wuthering Heights and the Turn of the screw. N & Q March 1961.
Altick, R. D. Dion Boucicault stages Mary Barton. Nineteenth-Century Fiction 14 1960.
Laski, M. Words from Mrs Gaskell. N & Q Sept, Dec 1961. Continued by B. L. Heilbron, Jan 1962.
Pollard, A. Mrs Gaskell. Bull John Rylands Lib 43 1961.
—— Mrs Gaskell: novelist and biographer. Manchester 1965.
—— 'Sooty Manchester' and the social-reform novel 1845–55. Br Jnl of Industrial Medicine 18 1961.
—— Mrs Gaskell's short stories. Cambridge Rev 8 May 1965.
—— Mrs Gaskell's Life of Charlotte Brontë. Bull John Rylands Lib 47 1965. With appendix on some new Gaskell letters by A. H. Preston.
Shain, C. E. English novelists and the American Civil War. Amer Quart 14 1962.
Dodsworth, M. Women without men at Cranford. EC 13 1963.
Barry, J. D. Elizabeth Cleghorn Gaskell and Charles Kingsley. Victorian Fiction 27 1964.
Carnall, G. D. Dickens, Mrs Gaskell and the Preston Strike. Victorian Stud 8 1964.
Julin, J.-P. Les débuts littéraires de Mrs Gaskell: réflexions sur un poème oublié. Etudes Anglaises 17 1964.
Chapple, J. A. V. The letters of Mrs Gaskell. Manuscripts 16 1964.
—— Gaskell letters. TLS 25 Aug 1966.
Gross, J. Mrs Gaskell. Listener 11 March 1965; rptd in The novelist as innovator, ed W. Allen 1965.
Handley, G. The chronology of Sylvia's lovers. N & Q Aug 1965.
Sharps, J. G. Mrs Gaskell's observation and intention. Fontwell 1965.
—— Articles by Mrs Gaskell in the Pall Mall Gazette (1865). N & Q Aug 1965.
Schneewind, J. B. Moral problems and moral philosophy in the Victorian period. Victorian Stud 9 1965.
Wright, E. Mrs Gaskell: the basis for reassessment. Oxford 1965.
—— Mrs Gaskell and the world of Cranford. REL 6 1965.
Johnson, C. A. Russian Gaskelliana. REL 7 1966. On her influence on Dostoevsky.

M. A.

CHARLES READE
1814–84

Bibliographies

Sadleir, M. In his Excursions in Victorian bibliography, 1922.
Elwin, M. In his Reade: a biography, 1930.
Parrish, M. L. Wilkie Collins and Reade. 1940.
Rives, L. In her Reade: sa vie, ses romans, Toulouse 1940.
Burns, W. In Victorian fiction: a guide to research, ed L. Stevenson, Cambridge Mass 1964.

Collections

Uniform library edition. 17 vols 1895.

§1

Peregrine Pickle. [1851] (priv ptd).
The ladies' battle, or un duel en amour: a comedy in three acts. [1851], Boston [1855], London 1877 (rev).
Angelo: a tragedy in four acts. [1851].
The lost husband: a drama in four acts. [1852], 1872.
Gold! a drama in five acts. [1853], 1899.
Peg Woffington: a novel. 1853, Boston 1855, London 1857, 1868, [1872], 1899, [1901] etc.
Christie Johnstone: a novel. 1853, 1854, Boston 1855, London 1857, 1868, 1872 etc.
The courier of Lyons, or the attack upon the mail: a drama in four acts. 1854, Cambridge 1895 (as The Lyons mail).
The King's rival: a drama in five acts by Tom Taylor and Reade. 1854.
Masks and faces, or before and behind the curtain: a comedy in two acts by Tom Taylor and Reade. 1854, Boston 1855.
Two loves and a life: a drama in four acts by Tom Taylor and Reade. 1854.
Clouds and sunshine. Bentley's Miscellany June-Sept 1854; Art: a dramatic tale, ibid Dec 1853–Jan 1854, Boston 1855.
It is never too late to mend: a matter of fact romance. 3 vols 1856, 1856, 2 vols Boston 1856, Leipzig 1856, 1 vol 1857, 1868, [1872], 1893, 1900 etc.
Poverty and pride: a drama in five acts. 1856.
The course of true love never did run smooth. 1857, 1868, [1873]. Contains The bloomer; Art: a dramatic tale; Clouds and sunshine, above.
The hypochondriac: adapted to the English stage from the Malade imaginaire of Molière. 1857.
Propria quae maribus: a jeu d'esprit; and The box tunnel: a fact. Bentley's Miscellany Nov 1853, Boston 1857. Propria pro maribus is the same story as The bloomer, above.
White lies: a story. London Jnl 11 July–5 Dec 1857, 3 vols 1857, 1 vol Boston 1858, London 1868 1872 (as Double marriage: or white lies).
Cream. 1858, [1873]. Contains Jack of all trades: a matter-of-fact romance (Harper's Mag Dec 1857–May 1858), The autobiography of a thief.
A good fight and other tales. New York 1859; A good fight, ed A. Lang 1910. A good fight, Once a Week 2 July–1 Oct 1859, was expanded into The cloister and the hearth, below.
It is never too late to mend: proofs of its prison revelations. 1859. Pamphlet.
Le faubourg Saint-Germain: pièce en deux actes. Paris 1859.
'Love me little, love me long'. 2 vols 1859, New York 1859, Leipzig 1859, London 1868, [1873].
The eighth commandment. 1860.
Monopoly versus property. 1860. Pamphlet.
The cloister and the hearth: a tale of the Middle Ages. 4 vols 1861, 1861 (rev), 1 vol New York 1861, London 1862, 2 vols Leipzig 1864, 1868, 1873; ed W. Besant 4 vols 1894, 1 vol 1900, 1901, 1902, 1903; ed A. C. Swinburne 1905 (EL); ed C. B. Wheeler 1915 etc.
Hard cash: a matter-of-fact romance. All the Year Round 28 March–26 Dec 1863 (as Very hard cash), 3 vols 1863, 1864, 1 vol New York 1864, 3 vols Leipzig 1864, 1 vol 1868, [1872], 1898, [1906], 1909.
It's never too late to mend: a drama in four acts. [1865], [1873]; ed L. Rives, Toulouse 1940.
Griffith Gaunt: or jealousy. Argosy Dec 1865–Nov 1866, 3 vols 1866, 1 vol Boston 1866, 3 vols 1867, 1868 (5th edn), 1869, [1872].
Dora: a pastoral drama in three acts. [1867].
The double marriage: a drama in five acts by August Maquet and Reade. [1867].
Foul play, by Dion Boucicault and Reade. Once a Week 4 Jan–20 June 1868, 3 vols 1868, 1 vol Boston 1868, London 1869, [1873], 1927.
Put yourself in his place. Cornhill Mag March 1869–July 1870, 3 vols 1870, 1 vol New York 1870, London 1871, 1876.
Foul play: a drama in four acts by Dion Boucicault and Reade. [1871?], 1883 (rev as Foul play: a drama in a prologue and five acts by Reade).
Rachel the reaper: a rustic drama in three acts. 1871.
A terrible temptation: a story of the day. Cassell's Mag April–Sept 1871, 3 vols 1871, 1 vol Boston 1871, London [1882].
To the editor of the Daily Globe, Toronto: a reply to criticism. 1871. Pamphlet.
Kate Peyton, or jealousy: a drama in a prologue and four acts. 1872, 1883 (rev).
The legal vocabulary. 1872. Pamphlet.
The wandering heir. Graphic Dec 1872, Toronto 1872, Boston, New York, 1873, London, 1882, 1905, 1924.
Cremona violins: four letters reprinted from the Pall Mall Gazette [19–31 Aug 1872]. Gloucester 1873.
A simpleton: a story of the day. London Soc Aug 1872–Sept 1873, 3 vols 1873, 1 vol New York 1873.
A hero and a martyr: a true and accurate account of the heroic feats and sad calamity of James Lambert. 1874, New York 1875.
Trade malice: a personal narrative; and The wandering heir: a matter of fact romance. 1875.
The jilt: a novel. Belgravia March–June 1877, New York 1877.
A woman hater. Blackwood's Mag June 1876–June 1877, 3 vols 1877, 1 vol New York 1877.
Golden crowns: Sunday stories. Manchester [1877].
The coming man: letters contributed to Harper's Weekly. New York 1878.
Dora: or the history of a play. 1878. Pamphlet.
The well-born workman: or a man of the day. 1878. Play adapted from Put yourself in his place, above.
Single heart and double face: a matter-of-fact romance. Life 8 June–7 Sept 1882, New York 1882, London 1884.
The countess and the dancer, or high life in Vienna: a comedy drama in four acts. 1883.
Love and money: an original drama in prologue and four acts by Reade and Henry Pettitt. 1883.
Readiana: comments on current events. 1883, New York 1884.
Good stories of man and other animals. 1884, New York 1884.
The jilt and other stories. 1884.
A perilous secret. Temple Bar Sept 1884–May 1885, 2 vols 1884, 1 vol New York 1884, London 1885, 1891.
Nance Oldfield: a comedy in one act. [1884?] (priv ptd).
The picture. Harper's Mag March–April 1884, New York 1884.
Bible characters. 1888.
Androgynism: or woman playing at man. English Rev Aug–Sept 1911. From an unpbd ms.

§2

Reade's novels. Blackwood's Mag Oct 1869.
Archer, W. In his English dramatists, 1882.
Besant, W. The novels of Reade. GM April 1882.
'Ouida' (M. L. de la Ramée). Reade. GM April 1882.
Buchanan, R. Personal recollections of Reade. Pall Mall Gazette 16 April 1884; rptd in his Look round literature, 1887.
Courtney, W. L. Reade's novels. Fortnightly Rev Oct 1884; rptd in his Studies new and old, 1889.
Fields, A. An acquaintance with Reade. Century Mag Nov 1884.
Littledale, R. F. Reade. Academy 19 April 1884.
Swinburne, A. C. Reade. Nineteenth Century Oct 1884; rptd in his Miscellanies, [1886].
Reade, C. L. and C. Reade, dramatist, novelist, journalist: a memoir compiled chiefly from his literary remains. 2 vols 1887.

Howells, W. D. My literary passions. New York 1895.
Quiller-Couch, A. T. In his Adventures in criticism, 1896.
Coleman, J. Reade as I knew him. 1903.
Lord, W. F. Reade's novels. Nineteenth Century Aug 1903; rptd in his Mirror of the century, 1906.
Ahlers, E. Reades Romane und ihr Verhältnis zu ihren literarischen Vorbildern. Münster 1914.
Phillips, W. C. Dickens, Reade and Collins: sensation novelists. New York 1919.
Allen, P. Mrs Stirling, Reade and Mlle Rachel. Anglo-French Rev July 1920.
Hornung, E. W. Reade. London Mercury June 1921.
Turner, A. M. Another source for the Cloister and the hearth. PMLA 40 1925. *See* O. E. Kuehne, Classical Weekly 25 April 1932.
— Reade and Montaigne. MP 30 1933.
— The making of the Cloister and the hearth. Chicago 1938.
Hruby, A. Zur Darstellungstechnik der englishcen Romanen: die Personen in Reades 'matter of fact' Romanen. Vienna 1928.
Sutcliffe, E. G. Reade's notebooks. SP 27 1930.
— The stage in Reade's novels. SP 27 1930.
— Fœmina vera in Reade's novels. PMLA 46 1931.
— Plotting in Reade's novels. PMLA 47 1932.
— Psychological presentation in Reade's novels. SP 38 1941.
— Fact, realism and morality in Reade's fiction. SP 41 1944.
— Unique and repeated situations and themes in Reade's fiction. PMLA 60 1945.
— Reade in his heroes. Trollopian 1 1946.
Elwin, M. Reade: a biography. 1931.
'Orwell, George'. Books in general. New Statesman 17 Aug 1940.
Rives, L. Reade: sa vie, ses romans. Toulouse 1940.
Tolles, W. Tom Taylor and the Victorian drama. New York 1940.
Haines, L. F. Reade, Mill and Zola: a study of the character and intention of Reade's realistic method. SP 40 1943.
Burns, W. More Reade notebooks. SP 42 1945.
— Pre-raphaelitism in Reade's early fiction. PMLA 60 1945.
— and E. G. Sutcliffe. 'Uncle Tom' and Reade. Amer Lit 17 1946.
— Reade and the Collinses. MLN 62 1947.
— The cloister and the hearth: a classic reconsidered. Trollopian 2 1947.
— The Sheffield flood: a critical study of Reade's fiction. PMLA 63 1948.
— Reade: a study in Victorian authorship. New York 1961.
McMahon, D. H. The composition and early history of Masks and faces. Washington State College Research Stud 14 1946.
Booth, B. A. Trollope, Reade and Shilly-shally. Trollopian 1–2 1946–7.
Bond, W. H. Nance Oldfield: an unrecorded printed play by Reade. Harvard Lib Bull 1 1947.
Woodring, C. R. Reade's debt to William Howitt. Nineteenth-Century Fiction 5 1951.
Gettmann, R. A. The serialization of A good fight. Nineteenth-Century Fiction 6 1952.
Bowers, R. H. The cancelled 'Song of Solomon' passage in Hard cash. Ibid.
Price, J. B. Reade and Charles Kingsley. Contemporary Rev March 1953.
Fielding, K. J. Reade and Dickens: a fight against piracy. Theatre Notebook 10 1956.
Martin, R. B. The Reade collection. Princeton Univ Lib Chron 17 1956.
— Manuscripts and correspondence of Reade. Princeton Univ Lib Chron 19 1958.
Smith, S. M. Realism in the drama of Reade. English 12 1958.
— Propaganda and hard facts in Reade's didactic novels. Nottingham Renaissance & Modern Stud 4 1960.

L. S.

ANTHONY TROLLOPE

1815–82

Bibliographies etc

Lavington, M. In T. H. S. Escott, Anthony Trollope, 1913.
Sadleir, M. In his Excursions in Victorian bibliography, 1922.
— Trollope: a bibliography. 1928, 1934 (rev), 1964.
— In his XIX century fiction: a bibliographical record, 1951.
Irwin, M. L. Trollope: a bibliography. New York 1926.
Gerould, W. G. and J. T. A guide to Trollope. Princeton 1948.
Smalley, D. In Victorian fiction: a guide to research, ed L. Stevenson, Cambridge 1964.

Collections

Chronicles of Barsetshire. 8 vols 1878; The Barsetshire novels, ed F. Harrison 8 vols 1906, 1923, 1928; The Barchester novels: Shakespeare head edition, ed M. Sadleir 14 vols Oxford 1929; The Oxford illustrated Trollope, ed M. Sadleir and F. Page 15 vols Oxford 1948–54 (unfinished). 36 of the works have been issued Oxford 1907–. (WC).

§1

The Macdermotts of Ballycloran. 3 vols 1847, 1848, 1 vol 1859, 1865, 1866, Philadelphia [1871?], London [1905].
The Kellys and the O'Kellys, or landlords and tenants: a tale of Irish life. 3 vols 1848, 1 vol 1859, 1865 (5th edn), 1866, Oxford 1929 (WC), New York 1937.
La Vendée: an historical romance. 3 vols 1850, 1 vol [1875].
The Warden. 1855, 1858, 1859, Leipzig 1859, New York 1862, London 1866, 1870, 1886, 1902, Oxford 1918 (WC).
Barchester Towers. 3 vols 1857, 1 vol 1858, 2 vols Leipzig 1859, New York [1860], 1 vol 1866, 1870, 1886, 1902, 1903, [1906], Oxford 1918 (WC).
The three clerks: a novel. 3 vols 1858, 1 vol 1859, 1860, New York 1860, London 1865, 1878, 1884, 1891, 1900, 1903, 1904, 1907 (WC).
Doctor Thorne: a novel. 3 vols 1858, 1858, 2 vols Leipzig 1858, 1 vol 1859, New York 1859, London 1865, [1901], 1906, Oxford 1926 (WC).
The Bertrams: a novel. 3 vols 1859, 2 vols Leipzig 1859, 1 vol New York 1859, London 1860, 1861, 1866, [1904].
The West Indies and the Spanish Main. 1859, Leipzig 1860, New York 1860, London 1860, 1861, 1862, 1869.
Castle Richmond: a novel. 3 vols 1860, 2 vols Leipzig 1860, 1 vol New York 1860, London 1860, 1866, [1905].
Framley Parsonage. Cornhill Mag Jan 1860–April 1861; 3 vols 1861, 2 vols Leipzig 1861, 1 vol New York 1861 London 1861, 1869, 1872, 1879, 1886, 1890, 1903, [1904], 1906 [1907], Oxford 1926 (WC).
The Civil Service as a profession. 1861 (priv ptd). A lecture.
Tales of all countries. 1861; second series, 1863; [both sers] 1864, 1866, Oxford 1931 (WC).
Orley Farm. 20 monthly pts March 1861–Oct 1862; 2 vols 1862, 3 vols Leipzig 1862, 1 vol New York 1862, London 1868, 1871, 1906, Oxford 1935 (WC), New York 1950.
The struggles of Brown, Jones and Robinson, by one of the firm. Cornhill Mag Aug 1861–March 1862; New York 1862, London 1870.

North America. 2 vols 1862, 3 vols Leipzig 1862, 2 vols New York 1862, London 1864, 1 vol 1866; ed D. Smalley and B. A. Booth, New York 1951.
The present condition of the northern states of the American Union. [1862?] (priv ptd). A lecture.
Rachel Ray: a novel. 2 vols 1863, Leipzig 1863, 1 vol New York 1863, London 1864, 1866, Oxford 1924 (WC).
The small house at Allington. Cornhill Mag Sept 1862–April 1864; 2 vols 1864, 3 vols Leipzig 1864, 1 vol New York 1864, London 1864, 1869, 1872, 1877, 1879, 1903, 1906, [1909], 1914, Oxford 1938 (WC).
Can you forgive her? 20 monthly pts Jan 1864–Aug 1865; 2 vols 1864, 1865, 3 vols Leipzig 1865, 1 vol New York 1865, London 1866, 1868, 1869, 1871, 1873, 1889, [1907], Oxford 1938 (WC).
Hunting sketches. Pall Mall Gazette 9 Feb–20 March 1865; 1865, 1866; ed J. Boyd 1934; ed L. Edwards 1952.
Miss Mackenzie. 2 vols 1865, 1 vol New York 1865, London 1866, [1876], Oxford 1924 (WC).
The Belton estate. Fortnightly Rev 15 May 1865–1 Jan 1866; 3 vols 1866 (3 edns), 2 vols Leipzig 1866, 1 vol New York 1866, London 1866, 1868, Oxford 1923 (WC).
Travelling sketches. Pall Mall Gazette 3 Aug–6 Sept 1865; 1866.
Clergymen of the Church of England. Pall Mall Gazette 20 Nov 1865–25 Jan 1866; 1866.
The Claverings. Cornhill Mag Feb 1866—May 1867; New York 1866 (?), 2 vols 1867, Leipzig 1867, 1 vol 1871, 1872, Oxford 1924 (WC).
Nina Balatka: the story of a maiden of Prague. Blackwood's Mag July 1866–Jan 1867 (anon); 2 vols 1867, 1 vol Leipzig 1867, London 1879, Oxford 1946 (WC) (with Linda Tressel).
The last chronicle of Barset. 32 weekly pts 1 Dec–6 July 1867; 2 vols 1867, 3 vols Leipzig 1867, 1 vol New York 1867, London 1869, 1872, 1879, 1906, [1909], 1910, 1914, Oxford 1932 (WC).
Lotta Schmidt and other stories. 1867, 1870, 1882.
Linda Tressel. Blackwood's Mag Oct 1867–May 1868 (anon); 2 vols 1868, 1879, Oxford 1946 (WC) (with Nina Balatka).
Higher education for women. [1868] (priv ptd). A lecture.
Phineas Finn: the Irish Member. St Paul's Mag Oct 1867–May 1869; 2 vols 1869, 3 vols Leipzig 1869, 1 vol New York 1869, London 1870, 1871, 1911, Oxford 1937 (WC).
He knew he was right. 32 weekly pts 17 Oct 1868–22 May 1869; 2 vols 1869, 3 vols Leipzig 1869, 1 vol New York 1870, London 1870, 1871, Oxford 1948 (WC).
Did he steal it? a comedy in three acts. 1869 (priv ptd); ed R. H. Taylor, Princeton 1952.
The vicar of Bullhampton. 11 monthly pts July 1869–May 1870; 1870, 2 vols Leipzig 1870, 1 vol New York 1870, London 1871, 1875, Oxford 1924 (WC).
An editor's tales. St Paul's Mag Oct 1869–May 1870; 1870, 1971, 1873, 1876.
On English prose fiction as a rational amusement. [1870] (priv ptd). A lecture.
The commentaries of Caesar. 1870, New York 1872.
Sir Harry Hotspur of Humblethwaite. Macmillan's Mag May–Dec 1870; 1871, Leipzig 1871, New York 1871, Oxford 1928 (WC).
Ralph the heir. 19 monthly pts Jan 1870–July 1871 (supplement to St Paul's Mag); 3 vols 1871, 2 vols Leipzig 1871, 1 vol New York 1871, London 1871, 1872, 1878, Oxford 1939 (WC).
The Golden Lion of Granpere. Good Words Jan–Aug 1872; 1872, Leipzig 1872, New York 1872, London 1873, 1873, 1885, Oxford 1947 (WC).
The Eustace diamonds. Fortnightly Rev July 1871–Feb 1873; New York 1872, 3 vols 1873 (for 1872), 2 vols Leipzig 1873, 1 vol 1875, Oxford 1930 (WC).
Australia and New Zealand. 2 vols 1873, 7 pts Melbourne 1873, 3 vols Leipzig 1873, 4 pts 1874, 2 vols 1876.

Lady Anna. Fortnightly Rev April 1873–April 1874; 2 vols Leipzig 1873, London 1874, 1 vol New York 1874, London 1875, Oxford 1936 (WC).
Phineas redux. Graphic 19 July 1873–10 Jan 1874; 2 vols 1874, 3 vols Leipzig [1874], 1 vol New York 1874, London 1874, 1875, 1913, Oxford 1937 (WC).
Harry Heathcote of Gangoil: a tale of Australian bush life. Graphic 25 Dec 1873; 1874, 1874, Leipzig 1874, New York 1874, 1883, London 1963.
The way we live now. 20 monthly pts Feb 1874–Sept 1875; 2 vols 1875, 4 vols Leipzig 1875, 1 vol New York 1875, 2 vols 1876, 1 vol 1879, Oxford 1941 (WC), New York 1950.
The Prime Minister. 8 monthly pts Nov 1875–June 1876; 4 vols 1876, Leipzig 1876, 1 vol New York 1876, Toronto 1876, London 1877, 1878, Oxford 1938 (WC).
The American Senator. Temple Bar May 1876–July 1877; 3 vols 1877, Leipzig 1877, 1 vol New York 1877, London 1877, 1878, 1886, Oxford 1931 (WC), New York 1940.
Christmas at Thompson Hall. Graphic 25 Dec 1876; New York 1877, London 1885.
Is he Popenjoy? a novel. All the Year Round 13 Oct 1877–13 July 1878; 3 vols 1878, Leipzig 1878, 1 vol New York 1878, London 1879, Oxford 1944 (WC).
Iceland. Fortnightly Rev Aug 1878; 1878 (priv ptd).
How the 'mastiffs' went to Iceland. 1878 (priv ptd).
South Africa. 2 vols 1878, Leipzig 1878, 1 vol 1879 (rev and abridged); ed P. Haworth 1938 (abridged).
The lady of Launay. Light 6 April–11 May 1878; New York 1878.
An eye for an eye. Whitehall Rev 24 Aug 1878–1 Feb 1879; 2 vols 1879, 1 vol Leipzig 1879, New York 1879, London 1879 (rev).
John Caldigate. Blackwood's Mag April 1878–June 1879; 3 vols 1879, Leipzig 1879, 1 vol New York 1879, London 1880, 1885, Oxford 1946 (WC).
Cousin Henry: a novel. Manchester Weekly Times Suppl 8 March–24 May 1879; 2 vols 1879, 1 vol Leipzig 1879, New York 1879, London 1880, Oxford 1929 (WC).
Thackeray. 1879, New York 1879 (EML).
The Duke's children: a novel. All the Year Round 4 Oct 1879–24 July 1880; 3 vols 1880, Leipzig 1880, 1 vol New York 1880, London 1880, Oxford 1938 (WC).
The life of Cicero. 2 vols 1880, New York 1880.
Dr Wortle's school: a novel. Blackwood's Mag May–Dec 1880; 2 vols 1881, 1 vol 1881, Leipzig 1881, New York 1881, Oxford 1928 (WC).
Ayala's angel. 3 vols 1881, Leipzig 1881, 1 vol New York 1881, London 1882, 1884, Oxford 1929 (WC).
Why Frau Frohmann raised her prices, and other stories. 1882. New York 1882, Leipzig 1883 (omits Alice Dugdale).
The fixed period: a novel. Blackwood's Mag Oct 1881–March 1882; 2 vols 1882, 1 vol Leipzig 1882, New York 1882.
Lord Palmerston. 1882, 1883 (Eng Political Leaders ser).
Marion Fay: a novel. Graphic 3 Dec 1881–3 June 1882; 3 vols 1882, 2 vols Leipzig 1882, 1 vol New York 1882, London 1884.
Kept in the dark: a novel. Good Words May–Dec 1882; 2 vols 1882, 1 vol Leipzig 1882, New York 1882, London 1883.
Not if I know it. Life Dec 1882; New York 1883.
The two heroines of Plumplington. Good Words Dec 1882; New York 1882; ed J. Hampden 1953.
Mr Scarborough's family. All the Year Round 27 May 1882–16 June 1883; 3 vols 1883, Leipzig 1883, 1 vol New York 1883, London 1883, Oxford 1947 (WC).
The Landleaguers. Life 16 Nov 1882–4 Oct 1883; 3 vols 1883, 1 vol New York 1883, London 1884.
An autobiography. 2 vols 1883, 1 vol Leipzig 1883, New York 1883; ed M. Sadleir Oxford 1923 (WC); ed C. Morgan 1946; ed B. A. Booth, Berkeley 1947; ed F. Page, Oxford 1950; ed J. B. Priestley 1962.

Alice Dugdale and other stories. Leipzig 1883.
La mère bauche and other stories. Leipzig 1883.
The mistletoe bough and other stories. Leipzig 1883.
An old man's love. 2 vols Edinburgh 1884, 1 vol Leipzig 1884, New York 1884, Oxford 1936 (WC).
The noble jilt: a comedy. Ed M. Sadleir 1923 (500 copies).
London tradesmen. Pall Mall Gazette 10 July–7 Sept 1880; ed M. Sadleir 1927.
Four lectures. Ed M. L. Parrish 1938.
The tireless traveller: twenty letters to the Liverpool Mercury 1875. Ed B. A. Booth, Cambridge 1941.
Novels and tales. Ed J. Hampden 1946. Contains Barchester Towers, Dr Wortle's school, 4 short stories.
The parson's daughter and other stories. Ed J. Hampden 1949.
The spotted dog and other stories. 1950.
Mary Gresley and other stories. Ed J. Hampden 1951.
Letters to the Examiner. Ed H. G. King, Princeton Univ Lib Chron 26 1965.

Letters

Letters. Ed B. A. Booth, Oxford 1951.

Unreprinted Contributions to Periodicals

My tour in Holland. Cornhill Mag Nov 1862.
W. M. Thackeray. Cornhill Mag Feb 1864.
On anonymous literature. Fortnightly Rev 1 July 1865.
The Irish church. Fortnightly Rev 15 Aug 1865.
Public schools. Fortnightly Rev 1 Oct 1865.
The Civil Service. Fortnightly Rev 15 Oct 1865.
An essay on Carlylism. St Paul's Mag Dec 1867.
Mr Freeman on the morality of hunting. Fortnightly Rev 1 Dec 1869.
Charles Dickens. St Paul's Mag July 1870.
Christmas Day at Kirkby cottage. Routledge's Xmas Annual 1870.
Cicero as a politician. Fortnightly Rev 1 April 1877.
Cicero as a man of letters. Fortnightly Rev 1 Sept 1877.
Whist at our club. Blackwood's Mag May 1878.
Catherine Carmichael: or three years running. Masonic Mag Dec 1878.
George Henry Lewes. Fortnightly Rev 1 Jan 1879.
Novel reading. Nineteenth Century Jan 1879.
In the hunting field. Good Words Feb 1879.
A walk in a wood. Good Words Sept 1879.
The genius of Hawthorne. North Amer Rev Sept 1879.
Longfellow. North Amer Rev April 1881.

§2

For an incomplete list of contemporary reviews see M. L. Irwin, Bibliography, *above*.
[Hutton, R. H.] Spectator 11 Oct 1862. Review of Orley Farm.
— Spectator 9 April 1864. Review of Small house at Allington.
— Spectator 12 June 1869. Review of He knew what he wanted.
Friswell, J. H. In his Modern men of letters, 1870.
The novels of Trollope. Dublin Rev 72 1872.
[Shand, A. I.] Mr Trollope's novels. Edinburgh Rev 146 1877.
Freeman, E. A. Anthony Trollope. Macmillan's Mag Jan 1883.
Pollock, W. H. Anthony Trollope. Harper's Mag May 1883.
James, H. Anthony Trollope. Century Mag July 1883; rptd in his Partial portraits, 1888, and in his House of fiction, ed L. Edel 1957.
— In his Notes and reviews, Cambridge Mass 1921.
Anthony Trollope. Westminster Rev 121 1883.
Austin, A. Last reminiscences of Trollope. Temple Bar Jan 1884.

English character and manners as portrayed by Trollope. Westminster Rev 123 1884.
Hawthorne, J. Confessions. Boston 1887.
Harrison, F. In his Studies in early Victorian literature, 1895.
Saintsbury, G. In his Corrected impressions, 1895.
— Trollope revisited. E & S 6 1920.
Lord, W. F. The novels of Trollope. Nineteenth Century May 1900; rptd in his Mirror of the century, 1906.
Stephen, L. In his Studies of a biographer vol 4, 1902.
Street, G. S. In his Book of essays, 1902.
Bryce, J. In his Studies in contemporary biography, 1903.
Bettany, F. G. In praise of the novels of Trollope. Fortnightly Rev June 1905.
Escott, T. H. S. An appreciation and reminiscence of Trollope. Fortnightly Rev Dec 1906.
— Trollope: his work, associates and literary originals. 1913.
Trollope's political novel. Spectator 3 May 1913.
Newton, A. E. A great Victorian. In his Amenities of book collecting, 1920.
Randell, W. L. Trollope and his work. Fortnightly Rev Sept 1920.
Knox, R. A. A ramble in Barsetshire. London Mercury Feb 1922.
— In his Literary distractions, 1958.
Sadleir, M. A guide to Trollope. Nineteenth Century April 1922.
— A Trollope love-story: Mary Thorne. Nineteenth Century Sept 1924.
— Trollope and his publishers. Library 4th ser 5 1924.
— The Victorian woman as Trollope knew her. Bermondsey Book March 1925.
— Trollope: a commentary. 1927, 1945 (rev).
— A conundrum for Trollopians. TLS 19 Oct 1940, 20 Dec 1941. Replies by S. Nowell-Smith 26 Oct 1940, M. Oliphant 22 Nov 1941; *see* 20 Dec 1941, 3 Jan 1942.
— A new Trollopian item. TLS 25 July 1942; *see* 8 Aug, 29 Aug 1942.
— An addendum to Enemies of books. New Colophon 1 1948.
Whibley, C. Trollope's autobiography. Eng Rev July 1923.
Newbolt, F. Reg. versus Mason. Nineteenth Century Feb 1924. On Orley Farm.
Nichols, S. van B. The significance of Trollope. New York 1925.
Payne, G. H. Belles lettres in ballot boxes: a forgotten statesman. Forum Feb 1925. On Palliser.
Quiller-Couch, A. T. In his Charles Dickens and other Victorians, Cambridge 1925.
Grey, R. Trollope and his mother. Cornhill Mag Nov 1926.
Gwynn, S. Trollope and Ireland. Contemporary Rev Jan 1926.
Ellis, S. M. Trollope and mid-Victorianism. Fortnightly Rev Sept 1927.
Priestley, J. B. In Barsetshire. Saturday Rev 12 Nov 1927.
Walpole, H. Anthony Trollope. 1928 (EML).
— Anthony Trollope. In The great Victorians, ed H. J. and H. Massingham 1932.
More, P. E. My debt to Trollope. In his Demon of the absolute, Princeton 1929.
MacCarthy, D. In his Portraits, 1931.
Belloc, H. Anthony Trollope. London Mercury Dec 1932.
Huxley, L. Trollope and the Cornhill. Cornhill Mag Dec 1932.
Waugh, A. Trollope after fifty years. Fortnightly Rev Dec 1932.
Koets, C. C. Female characters in the works of Trollope. Amsterdam 1933.
Cecil, D. In his Early Victorian novelists, 1934, 1964 (rev).

Brown, C. R. They were giants. 1935.
Pavey, L. A. In The English novelists, ed D. Verschoyle 1936.
Sampson, A. Trollope in the twentieth century. London Mercury Feb 1937.
Trollope's House of Commons. TLS 20 March 1937.
Milley, J. H. W. The Eustace diamonds and the Moonstone. SP 36 1939.
Booth, B. A. Trollope in California. HLQ 3 1940.
— Trollope and the Pall Mall Gazette. Nineteenth-Century Fiction 4 1950.
— Trollope on Scott. Nineteenth-Century Fiction 5 1951.
— Trollope on the novel. In Essays dedicated to L. B. Campbell, Berkeley 1950.
— Trollope and the Royal Literary Fund. Nineteenth-Century Fiction 7 1953.
— Trollope: aspects of his life and work. Bloomington 1958.
— Orley Farm: artistry manqué. In From Jane Austen to Joseph Conrad, ed R. C. Rathburn and M. Steinmann, Minneapolis 1958.
— Author to publisher: Trollope and William Isbister. Princeton Univ Lib Chron 23 1962.
Wildman, J. H. Trollope's England. Providence 1940.
— Trollope today. College Eng April 1946.
— Trollope illustrates the distinction. Nineteenth-Century Fiction 4 1950.
Piper, M. Trollope. New Statesman 17 Feb 1940.
Chapman, R. W. The text of Trollope. TLS 25 Jan, 22 March 1941.
— Trollope's American Senator. TLS 21 June 1941.
— Trollopian criticism. TLS 5, 26 July 1941.
— Trollope's autobiography. N & Q 1 Nov 1941.
— The text of Trollope's autobiography. RES 17 1941.
— The text of Trollope's novels. Ibid.
— The text of Phineas redux. RES 17–8 1941–2. Replies by G. Bone 17 1941, C. B. Tinker 18 1942.
— A correction in Trollope. TLS 7 March 1942.
— The text of Ayala's angel. MP 39 1942.
— The text of Phineas Finn. TLS 25 March 1944. Replies by S. Nowell-Smith 15 April, R. L. Purdy 29 July 1944.
— The text of Barchester Towers. TLS 30 Aug 1947. Reply by B. H. P. Fisher 4 Oct 1947.
— Personal names in Trollope's political novels. In Essays presented to Sir Humphrey Milford, Oxford 1948.
— Trollope on Emma and the Monk: unpublished notes. Nineteenth-Century Fiction 4 1950.
Wade, A. The text of Trollope. TLS 10 Jan 1942. Reply by H. E. Allen 4 April 1942.
Edwards, R. Trollope on Church affairs. TLS 21 Oct 1944.
Greenberg, A. A Victorian novel. Partisan Rev 11 1944; rptd in his Art and culture, Boston 1961.
Jones, F. P. Trollope on the classics. Classical Weekly 15 May 1944.
Parker, W. M. Trollope and 'Maga'. Blackwood's Mag Jan 1945.
Stebbins, L. P. and R. P. The Trollopes: the chronicle of a writing family. 1945.
The Trollopian. Ed B. A. Booth, Los Angeles 1945–49. Title changed in 1949 to Nineteenth-Century Fiction.
Brash, W. B. The triumph of Trollope. London Quart 170 1945.
Vincent, C. J. Trollope: a Victorian Augustan. Queen's Quart 52 1945.
Bowen, E. Trollope: a new judgment. Oxford 1946.
Latymer, Lord. The lost children. TLS 19 Jan 1946. Replies 26 Jan 1946.
Mason, L. Dickens, Trollope and Joe Whelks. Dickensian 42 1946.
Pritchett, V. S. Trollope. New Statesman 8 June 1946.
Burn, W. L. Surtees and Trollope. Blackwood's Mag April 1947.
— Trollope's politics. Nineteenth Century March 1948.
Taylor, R. H. The manuscript of Trollope's American Senator. PBSA 41 1947.
Tinker, C. B. Trollope. Yale Rev new ser 36 1947; rptd in his Essays in retrospect, New York 1948.
Child, H. Anthony Trollope. In his Essays and reflections, ed S. C. Roberts, Cambridge 1948; rptd from TLS 20 Jan 1927.
Myers, W. C. Again that dear county. In If by your art: testament to Percival Hunt, Pittsburgh 1948.
Sherman, J. A. The financial motif in the Barchester novels. College Eng May 1948.
Muir, M. Trollope in Australia. Adelaide 1949.
Brown, B. C. Anthony Trollope. 1950.
Drinker, H. S. The lawyers of Trollope; W. Thorp, Trollope's America. New York 1950 (Grolier Club).
Skinner, E. L. Mr Trollope's young ladies. Nineteenth-Century Fiction 4 1950.
Bloomfield, M. W. Trollope's use of Canadian history in Phineas Finn. Nineteenth-Century Fiction 5 1951.
Stryker, D. The significance of Trollope's American Senator. Ibid.
Tingay, L. O. Trollope and the Beverley election. Ibid.
— The reception of Trollope's first novel. Nineteenth-Century Fiction 6 1952.
— The publication of Trollope's first novel. TLS 30 March 1956. Replies by S. Norman 6 April, J. Hagan 4 May 1957.
— Trollope's popularity: a statistical approach. Nineteenth-Century Fiction 11 1957.
Tracy, G.-M. L'œuvre de Trollope: ou le paradis perdu. Mercure de France March 1950.
Robbins, F. E. Chronology and history in Trollope's Barset and parliamentary novels. Nineteenth-Century Fiction 5 1951.
Coyle, W. Trollope and the bi-columned Shakespeare. Nineteenth-Century Fiction 6 1952.
— Trollope as social anthropologist. College Eng April 1956.
Fraser, R. A. Trollope's younger characters. Nineteenth-Century Fiction 6 1952.
Briggs, A. Trollope, Bagehot and the English constitution. Cambridge Jnl March 1952; rptd in his Victorian people, 1954.
Robinson, C. F. Trollope's jury trials. Nineteenth-Century Fiction 6 1952.
Parks, E. W. Trollope and the defence of exegesis. Nineteenth-Century Fiction 7 1953.
Adams, R. M. Orley Farm and real fiction. Nineteenth-Century Fiction 8 1954.
Adams, R. M. Miss Dunstable and Miss Coutts. Nineteenth-Century Fiction 9 1955.
Baker, J. E. Trollope's third dimension. College Eng Jan 1955.
Cockshut, A. O. J. Trollope: a critical study. 1955.
Houston, M. C. Structure and plot in the Warden. SE 34 1955.
Maxwell, C. Trollope and Ireland. Dublin Mag 31 1955.
Donovan, R. A. Trollope's 'prentice work. MP 53 1956.
Hackett, F. The Trollope problem. New Republic 8 Oct 1956.
Helling, R. A century of Trollope criticism. Helsinki 1956.
Windolph, F. L. Trollope and the law. In his Reflections of the law in literature, Philadelphia 1956.
Gragg, W. B. Trollope and Carlyle. Nineteenth-Century Fiction 13 1959.
Hagan, J. H. The Duke's children: Trollope's psychological masterpiece. Ibid.
— The divided mind of Trollope. Nineteenth-Century Fiction 14 1960.
Maxwell, J. C. Cockshut on Dr Wortle's school. Nineteenth-Century Fiction 13 1959.

Mizener, A. Trollope: the Palliser novels. In From Jane Austen to Joseph Conrad, ed R. C. Rathburn and M. Steinmann, Minneapolis 1958.
Davies, H. S. Trollope. 1960 (Br Council pamphlet).
—— Trollope and his style. REL 1 1960.
Laski, A. L. Myths of character. Nineteenth-Century Fiction 15 1961.
Thale, J. The problem of structure in Trollope. Ibid.
Arnold, R. The Whiston matter. 1961. On the Warden.
Best, G. F. A. The road to Hiram's hospital. Victorian Stud 5 1961.
Brace, G. W. The world of Trollope. Texas Quart 4 1961.
Lundeen, T. B. Trollope and the mid-Victorian episcopate. Historical Mag of Protestant Episcopal Church 30 1961.
Mohan, R. Trollope's political novels. Indian Jnl of Eng Stud 1 1961.
Dustin, J. E. Thematic alternation in Trollope. PMLA 77 1962.
Hawkins, S. Mr Harding's church music. ELH 29 1962.
Park, C. C. Trollope and the modern reader. Mass Rev 3 1962.
Borinski, L. Trollope's Palliser novels. Die Neueren Sprachen Aug 1963.
Cadbury, W. Shape and theme: determinants of Trollope's forms. PMLA 78 1963.
—— The uses of the village: form and theme in the Vicar of Bullhampton. Nineteenth-Century Fiction 18 1964.
Goldberg, M. A. Trollope's The Warden. Nineteenth-Century Fiction 17 1963.
Hewitt, M. Trollope: historian and sociologist. Br Jnl of Sociology 14 1963. On the place of women.
Hornback, B. G. Trollope and the calendar of 1872. N & Q Dec 1963.
Shaw, W. D. Moral drama in Barchester Towers. Nineteenth-Century Fiction 19 1965.
Tillotson, G. Trollope's style. In his Mid-Victorian studies, 1965.
Kenney, B. G. Trollope's ideal statesman: Plantagenet Palliser and Lord John Russell. Nineteenth-Century Fiction 20 1966.
Aitken, D. 'A kind of felicity': some notes about Trollope's style. Ibid.
Polhemus, R. M. Cousin Henry: Trollope's note from underground. Ibid.

L. S.

GEORGE MEREDITH
1828–1909

Bibliographies

Lane, J. Meredith and his reviewers 1849–90. In R. Le Gallienne, George Meredith, 1890, 1900 (bibliography continued to 1899).
Esdaile, A. J. K. Bibliography of the writings in prose and verse of Meredith. 1907.
—— A chronological list of Meredith's publications 1849–1911. 1914.
Livingston, L. S. First editions of Meredith including manuscript agreements with his publishers and the original manuscript of the Tragic comedians. [1912].
Forman, M. B. A bibliography of the writings in prose and verse of Meredith. 1922.
—— Meredithiana: being a supplement to the bibliography of Meredith. 1924.
Coolidge, B. A catalogue of the Altschul collection of Meredith in the Yale University Library. New Haven 1931 (priv ptd).
Hudson, R. B. The Altschul collection of Meredith seventeen years later. Yale Univ Lib Gazette 22 1948.
Sawin, H. L. Meredith: a bibliography of Meredithiana 1920–53. Bull of Bibliography 21 1955.
Stevenson, L. In Victorian poets: a guide to research, ed F. E. Faverty, Cambridge Mass 1956, 1968 (rev).

Cline, C. L. In Victorian fiction: a guide to research, ed L. Stevenson, Cambridge Mass 1964.

Collections

Novels

Collected edition. 12 vols 1885–95. Omits Tragic comedians, Short stories, Amazing marriage.
Library edition, Revised edition [or] New Popular edition. 18 vols 1897–8. Celt and Saxon added 1910; texts rev Meredith.
Edition de luxe. 39 vols 1896–1912. Includes Miscellaneous prose, bibliography by A. Esdaile, and variant readings.
Pocket edition. 15 vols 1901–6.
Memorial edition. 27 vols 1909–11, New York 1909–12.
Standard edition. 15 vols 1914–20.
Mickleham edition. 18 vols 1922–4.

Poems

Poetical works. Ed G. M. Trevelyan 1912.
Selected poems. Ed G. Hough, Oxford 1962.

§ 1

Poems. 1851, New York 1898, London 1909, New York 1909 (adds Poems from Modern love, Scattered poems).
The shaving of Shagpat: an Arabian entertainment. 1856 (for 1855), 1865, 1872, 1912; ed F. M. Meynell, illustr H. Guilbeau, New York 1955; tr French, 1921.
Farina: a legend of Cologne. 1857, 1865, 1868, 1898 (with Short stories).
The ordeal of Richard Feverel: a history of father and son. 3 vols 1859, 2 vols 1875, 1 vol 1878 (rev), Leipzig 1875, Boston 1888, London 1890, 1899, 1901, New York 1906, London 1910; ed F. W. Chandler, New York 1917; ed R. Sencourt 1935; ed N. Kelvin, New York 1961; tr French, Revue des Deux Mondes 1865; Italian, 1873; Czech, 1902; German, 1904; Hungarian, 1930?; Russian, 1932.
Evan Harrington: or he would be a gentleman. New York 1860 (mag version), 3 vols 1861, 1 vol 1866, 1885, Melbourne and Sydney 1888, London 1889, [1911]; ed G. F. Reynolds, New York 1922; tr French, 1910.
Modern love, and Poems of the English roadside, with Poems and ballads. 1862; ed E. Cavazza, Portland Maine 1891, Boston 1892 (rev), London 1892 (adds The sage enamoured, The honest lady), 1894, 1895, Portland Maine 1898; ed R. le Gallienne, New York 1909; ed C. Day Lewis 1948; tr French, 1910.
The cruise of the Alabama and the Sumter: from the private journals and other papers of Commander R. Semmes. 1864. Introductory and concluding chs by Meredith.
Emilia in England. 3 vols 1864, 1 vol 1886 (as Sandra Belloni); tr French, 1866.
Rhoda Fleming: a story. 3 vols 1865, 2 vols New York 1888, 1 vol Melbourne and Sydney 1889, London 1890, 1901.
Vittoria. 3 vols 1867 (for 1866), Boston 1888, 1 vol 1890.
The adventures of Harry Richmond. 3 vols 1871, 1871, 1 vol 1886, Boston 1886, Melbourne and Sydney 1887, London 1889, 1901, 1912; tr German, [1904]; French, 1948.
Beauchamp's career. 3 vols 1876 (for 1875), 2 vols 1876, 1 vol Leipzig 1876, London 1889; ed G. M. Young, Oxford 1950; tr French, 1928.
The house on the beach: a realistic tale. New York 1877, 1878, London 1894 (adds The tale of Chloe, The case of General Ople and Lady Camper), 1898 (rev in Short stories); tr French, 1929.
The egoist: a comedy in narrative. 3 vols 1879, New York 1879, 1 vol 1880, 1880, 2 vols New York [1888], 1 vol 1890; ed W. C. Brownell, New York 1901, Leipzig 1910, London 1912; The egoist arranged for the stage, ed A. Sutro 1920 (priv ptd); The egoist, ed Lord Dunsany,

Oxford 1947 (WC); ed L. Stevenson, Boston 1958; ed A. Wilson, New York 1963; tr Russian, 1894; French, 1904; German, 1905; Italian, [1922].

The tragic comedians: a study in a well-known story, enlarged from the Fortnightly Review. 2 vols 1880, 1881, 1 vol 1881, 1881, New York 1881, Leipzig 1881; ed C. K. Shorter 1891 (rev), 1892, Boston 1892, [1914], 1946 (Penguin); tr French, 1909; German, 1909.

Poems and lyrics of the joy of earth. 1883, 1883, 1894, 1895.

Diana of the crossways: a novel, considerably enlarged from the Fortnightly Review. 3 vols 1885, 1885, 1885, 1 vol New York 1885 (incomplete mag version), New York 1885, 1885, Melbourne and Sydney 1887, London 1890, New York 1891, London 1901, 1909; ed A. Symons, New York [1930?]; tr German, 1886; Italian, 1909; French, 2 vols 1931. 26 chs only ptd in Fortnightly Rev 1884.

Ballads and poems of tragic life. 1887, Boston 1887, London 1894, 1897.

A reading of earth. 1888, Boston 1888, London 1895, New York and London 1901.

Jump-to-glory Jane: a poem. 1889 (priv ptd); illustr L. Housman 1892.

The case of General Ople and Lady Camper. New York 1890, 1891, 1894 (adds The tale of Chloe, The house on the beach), 1900; tr French, 1931; Italian, 1944. First pbd 1877 in New Quart Mag.

The tale of Chloe: an episode in the history of Beau Beamish. New York 1890, 1891, London 1894 (adds The house on the beach, The case of General Ople and Lady Camper), New York 1898 (in Short stories, below), Portland Maine 1899, London 1900; tr French, Mercure de France 1908; tr Italian, 1944. First pbd in New Quart Mag 1879.

One of our conquerors. 3 vols 1891 (3 edns), 2 vols Leipzig 1891, 1 vol Melbourne and Sydney 1891, Boston 1891, London 1892.

Poems: The empty purse, with Odes to the comic spirit, to youth in memory and verses. 1892, 1895.

Lord Ormont and his Aminta: a novel. 3 vols 1894, 1 vol New York 1894, London 1895, Leipzig 1895.

The tale of Chloe and other stories. 1894, 1895.

The amazing marriage. 2 vols 1895, New York 1895, London 1896, 1896, 1 vol 1896 (rev), Leipzig 1897; tr Dutch (De Gids, condensed), 1896; French, 1939.

On the idea of comedy and the uses of the comic spirit: a lecture delivered at the London Institute, February 1st 1877. 1897, New York 1897; ed L. Cooper, Ithaca 1956; tr French, 1898; German, 1910. First pbd in New Quart Mag 1877.

Selected poems. 1897, New York 1897. Meredith's selection.

Odes in contribution to the song of French history. 1898, New York 1898; tr French, 1916.

Poems. 2 vols New York and London 1898. A collection.

Short stories: The tale of Chloe. The house on the beach, Farina, The case of General Ople and Lady Camper. New York 1898.

A reading of life, with other poems. 1901.

Twenty poems. 1909. Collected from Household Words, some repudiated by Meredith's son.

Last poems. 1909.

Poems written in early youth (published in 1851), Poems from Modern love (first edition) and Scattered poems. 1909, New York 1909.

Milton 1909. A poem on the tercentenary of Milton's birth.

Celt and Saxon. 1910, New York 1910.

Periodical Contributions and Prefaces

Many of the occasional works are collected in Miscellaneous prose, *vol 23 of the* Memorial edition, *above. Items in that vol are marked* 'Mem' *below. For serial pbns of fiction and poems, which are not listed below, see* Memorial edition vol 27.

Sorrows and joys. Household Words 24 Aug 1850; Two blackbirds (with R. H. Horne), 9 Nov 1850; New Year's Eve, 28 Dec 1850; Time (with W. H. Wills), 24 May 1851; Force and his master, 13 Sept 1851; Gentleness of death, 4 Oct 1851; A word from the cannon's mouth, 25 Oct 1851; Queen Zuleima, 1 Nov 1851; Britain, 22 Nov 1851; Familiar things, 6 Dec 1851; The Glastonbury thorn, 20 Dec 1851; Wassail bowl, 3 Jan 1852; The linnet hawker, 10 Jan 1852; A new way of manufacturing glory, 7 Feb 1852; War (with R. H. Horne), 21 Feb 1852; The first-born, 10 July 1852; Holidays, 24 Dec 1853; Motley, 4 Feb 1854; Rhineland, 19 July 1856. Identified from the contributor's book in Princeton Univ Lib.

Austrian poets. Fraser's Mag Aug 1852. Review and trn.

Songs from the dramatists. Fraser's Mag Nov 1854.

Belles lettres. Westminster Rev new ser 11–13 1857–8.

A story-telling party. Once a Week 24 Dec 1859.

Correspondence from the seat of war in Italy. Morning Post 22 June–24 July 1866 (Mem).

La maison forestière, par M. Erckmann-Chatrian. Fortnightly Rev Jan 1867. Review (Mem).

Training in theory and practice, by Archibald Maclaren. Fortnightly Rev March 1867. Review (Mem).

Notes in South Germany. Fortnightly Rev Aug 1867.

Saint Paul: a poem, by Frederic H. Myers. Fortnightly Rev Jan 1868. Review (Mem).

Reminiscences of a septuagenarian from 1802 to 1815, by Emma Sophia, Countess Brownlow. Fortnightly Rev Feb 1868. Review (Mem).

Chronicles and characters, by the Hon R. Lytton. Fortnightly Rev June 1868. Review (Mem).

The anecdotalist. Pall Mall Gazette 2 March 1868; The cynic of society, 28 March 1868; The consummate epicure, 25 April 1868; A working Frenchwoman, 30 April 1868; The third-class carriage, 23 May 1868; English country inns, 27 June 1868. Literary essays.

Mistral's Mirèio, tr H. Crichton. Pall Mall Gazette 27 March 1869. Review and trn.

Homer's Iliad in English rhymed verse, by Charles Merivale. Fortnightly Rev May 1869. Review (Mem).

A pause in the strife. Pall Mall Gazette 9 July 1886. Article (Mem).

Concession to the Celt. Fortnightly Rev Oct 1886. Article (Mem).

Fine passages in prose and verse. Fortnightly Rev Aug 1887 (Mem).

Mrs Meynell's two books of essays. Nat Rev Aug 1896. Review (Mem).

Introduction. In Thackeray, The four Georges, 1903 (Mem).

Leslie Stephen. Author April 1904 (Mem).

Introduction. In Lady Duff Gordon, Letters from Egypt, 1904 (Mem).

Introduction. In The Japanese spirit by Yoshimaburo Okakura, 1905 (Mem).

Introduction. In Collected poems of Dora Sigerson Shorter, 1907 (Mem).

Up to midnight: a series of dialogues contributed to the Graphic, now reprinted for the first time. Boston 1913. First pbd in Graphic 1872–3; the reprint is incomplete.

The contributions of Meredith to the Monthly Observer, January–July 1849. Ed M. B. Forman 1928 (priv ptd).

Letters

Letters, collected and edited by his son [W. M. Meredith]. 2 vols 1912.

Letters to E. Clodd and C. K. Shorter. 1913 (priv ptd).

Letters to R. H. Horne. Cape Town 1919 (priv ptd).

Letters to A. C. Swinburne and T. Watts-Dunton. Cape Town 1922 (priv ptd).

Letters to Alice Meynell, with annotations thereto. 1923.

Letters to various correspondents. Pretoria 1924 (priv ptd).
George, R. E. G. Unpublished letters of Meredith. Nineteenth Century Feb 1928.
— On some hitherto unpublished letters of Meredith. Bookman (New York) Feb 1928.
Letters. Ed C. L. Cline 3 vols Oxford 1968.
See also Symons, Cline, Baylen, below.

§2

McCarthy, J. In his Con amore: or critical studies, 1868.
Hutton, R. H. The adventures of Harry Richmond. Spectator 20 Jan 1872.
Shore, A. The novels of Meredith. British Quart Rev 69 1879.
Courtney, W. L. Meredith's novels. Fortnightly Rev June 1886.
Watson, W. Fiction—plethoric and anaemic. Nat Rev Oct 1889.
— In his Excursions in criticism, 1898.
Wilde, O. The decay of lying: a dialogue. Nineteenth Century Jan 1889; rptd in his Intentions, 1891.
— The critic as artist. In his Intentions, 1891.
— The soul of man under Socialism. Fortnightly Rev Feb 1891.
Bainton, G. In his Art of authorship, 1890. Quotes Meredith's advice on novel writing.
Henley, W. E. In his Views and reviews, 1890.
Ross, J. In her Early days recalled, 1891.
— In her Fourth generation, 1912.
Gosse, E. In his Gossip in a library, 1891.
Lynch, H. Meredith: a study. 1891.
Dolman, F. Meredith as a journalist. New Rev 8 1893.
Bridges, R. In his Overheard in Arcady, 1894.
Dowden, E. Meredith's poetry. In his New studies in literature, 1895.
Mr Meredith's novels. Edinburgh Rev 181 1895.
Schwob, M. In his Spicilège, Paris 1896.
Smith, G. The women of Meredith. Fortnightly Rev May 1896.
Robertson, J. M. Concerning preciosity. Yellow Book 13 1897.
Shaw, G. B. Meredith on comedy. Saturday Rev 27 March 1897.
Wilson, S. L. In his Theology of modern literature, 1899.
Brownell, W. C. In his Victorian prose masters, New York 1901.
Legras, C. In his Chez nos contemporains d'Angleterre, Paris 1901.
Leonard, R. M. Politics in Meredith's novels. New Liberal Rev 2 1901.
Jerrold, W. C. Meredith: an essay towards appreciation. 1902.
Samuel Richardson and Meredith. Macmillan's Mag March 1902.
O., H. (Harold Owen). Mr Meredith on the future of Liberalism, Home Rule and Imperialism, education and the use of votes. Manchester Guardian 2 Feb 1903.
Burnand, F. C. In his Records and reminiscences, 2 vols 1904.
Sharp, W. In his Literary geography, 1904.
Stead, W. T. Character sketch: Meredith. Rev of Reviews 29 1904.
Legouis, E. L'égoïste de Meredith. Revue Germanique 1 1905.
Moffat, J. Mr Meredith on religion. Hibbert Jnl 3 1905
— Meredith: a primer to the novels. 1909.
— Dickens and Meredith. Hibbert Jnl 21 1922.
More, P. E. The novels of Meredith. In his Shelburne essays ser 2, New York 1905.
Pigou, A. C. The optimism of Browning and Meredith. Independent Rev 6 1905.
Stevenson, R. L. Books which have influenced me. In his Essays in the art of writing, 1905.
Trevelyan, G. M. Optimism and Mr Meredith: a reply. Independent Rev 6 1905.
— The poetry and philosophy of Meredith. 1906.
— In his Clio: a muse, and other essays, 1913.
— Englishmen and Italians. Proc Br Acad 9 1919.
Cordelet, H. La femme dans l'œuvre de Meredith. Revue Germanique 2 1906.
de Selincourt, B. Meredith's hymn to colour. Independent Rev 11 1906.
Henderson, M. S. (later Gretton). Some thoughts underlying Meredith's poems. International Jnl of Ethics 16 1906.
— Meredith: novelist, poet, reformer. 1907. B. de Selincourt on the poems, chs 14–17.
— The writings and life of Meredith: a centenary study. Oxford 1926.
S[idgwick], A. S. and E. M. In their Henry Sidgwick: a memoir, 1906.
Magnus, L. The succession of Mr Meredith. Fortnightly Rev Dec 1907.
Quiller-Couch, A. T. Meredith's poetry. In his From Cornish window, 1906.
— The poetry of Meredith. In his Studies in literature, Cambridge 1918.
Greene, H. C. George Meredith. Atlantic Monthly June 1907.
Short, T. S. On some of the characteristics of Meredith's prose-writing. 1907.
Curle, R. H. P. Aspects of Meredith. 1908.
Meredith and the Jews. Jewish Chron 14 Feb 1908.
Barrie, J. M. George Meredith. 1909.
Chesterton, G. K. The moral philosophy of Meredith. Contemporary Rev July 1909.
— In his Victorian age in literature, 1913.
Clodd, E. Meredith: some recollections. Fortnightly Rev July 1909.
Davray, H. D. Meredith: souvenirs et reflexions. Revue Hebdomadaire 5 June 1909.
Forman, M. B. Meredith: some early appreciations. 1909.
— Meredith and the Monthly Observer. 1911.
Hammerton, J. A. Meredith in anecdote and criticism. 1909, Edinburgh 1911 (rev). Quotes many contemporary reviews not rptd elsewhere.
Matz, B. W. Meredith as publisher's reader. Fortnightly Rev Aug 1909.
Thomson, J. James Thomson 'B.V.' on Meredith. 1909.
Bailey, E. B. The novels of Meredith. New York 1910.
Dick, E. Meredith: drei Versuche. Berlin 1910.
Elmer, J. The novels of Meredith. 1910.
Frey, E. Die Dichtungen Merediths. Zürich 1910.
— Die Romane Merediths: ein Versuch. Winterthur 1913.
Lubbock, P. The collected works of Meredith. Quart Rev 212 1910.
MacKechnie, J. Meredith's allegory the Shaving of Shagpat re-interpreted. 1910.
Watson, F. Meredith and education. Nineteenth Century Feb 1910.
Beach, J. W. The comic spirit of Meredith. 1911.
— In his Twentieth-century novel: studies in technique, New York 1932.
— In his Concept of nature in nineteenth-century English poetry, New York 1956.
Henderson, A. In his Interpreters of life and the modern spirit, 1911.
Hyndman, H. M. In his Record of an adventurous life, New York 1911.
Jack, A. A. Meredith–intellectual poetry. In his Poetry and prose: being essays on modern English poetry, 1911.
Brendel, A. Die Technik des Romans bei Meredith. Munich 1912.
Collins, J. P. Conversations with Meredith. Pall Mall Mag 50 1912.
Figgis, D. Meredith: the philosopher in the artist. In his Studies and appreciations, 1912.

Jones, D. M. English writers and the making of Italy. London Quart Rev 118 1912.
Benedetti, A. Meredith: poeta. Palermo 1913.
Foote, G. W. Meredith: freethinker. Eng Rev 13 1913.
Torretta, L. Meredith: romanziere, poeta, pensatore. Naples 1913.
Verrall, A. W. In his Collected literary essays, Cambridge 1913.
Bedford, H. The heroines of Meredith. 1914.
Hartog, W. G. Meredith, France and the French. Fortnightly Rev Oct 1914.
Harris, F. In his Contemporary portraits, New York 1915.
Photiadès, C. Meredith: sa vie–son imagination–son art–sa doctrine. Paris 1910; tr 1916.
Symons, A. Meredith as a poet. In his Figures of several centuries, 1916.
— Meredith: with some unpublished letters. Fortnightly Rev Jan 1923.
Lee, J. Meredith's literary relations with Germany. MLR 12 1917.
Morley, J. In his Recollections, 2 vols 1917. Vol i ch 4 on Meredith.
Thomas, E. In his Literary pilgrim in England, 1917.
Campbell, O. J. Some influences of Meredith's philosophy upon his fiction. Wisconsin Stud in Lang & Lit 2 1918.
Crees, J. H. E. Meredith: a study of his works and personality. Oxford 1918.
— Meredith revisited. [1921].
MacCarthy, D. Meredith's method. In his Remnants, 1918.
— In his Portraits, 1931.
Sully, J. In his My life and friends, 1918.
Butcher, A. M. Memories of Meredith. 1919.
Ellis, S. M. Meredith: his life and friends. 1919.
Watson, A. F. Meredith and Italy. Fortnightly Rev Feb 1919.
Dimond, C. Music in the novels of Meredith. Nineteenth Century May 1920.
'H.C.H.' The idea of comedy. New Statesman 14 Jan 1920.
Raymond, E. In his Portraits of the nineties, 1921.
Strong, A. T. In his Three studies in Shelley, and an essay on nature in Wordsworth and Meredith, 1921.
Galland, R. Meredith and British criticism. 1923.
— Meredith: les cinquante premières années. Paris 1923.
— Meredith et l'Allemagne: quelques traductions inconnues. Revue de Littérature Comparée 3 1923.
— Meredith et Galsworthy. Revue Anglo-américaine 12 1934.
'Lee, Vernon'. In her Handling of words, 1923.
Sherman, S. P. In his On contemporary literature, 1923.
Wolff, L. Meredith: poète et romancier. Paris 1924.
Brewer, E. V. Unpublished aphorisms by Meredith. Yale Rev 14 1925.
— The influence of Jean Paul Richter on Meredith's conception of the comic. JEGP 29 1930.
Burdett, O. In his Critical essays, 1925.
Chislett, W. Meredith: a study and an appraisal. [1925].
Milnes, G. R. [later Turquet-Milnes]. Meredith and the cosmic spirit. 1925.
Priestley, J. B. George Meredith. 1926 (EML).
Fernandez, R. In his Messages, 1927.
Forster, E. M. In his Aspects of the novel, 1927.
Gamper, F. Die Sprache Merediths. Mulhouse 1927.
Erskine, J. In his Delight of great books, 1928.
Gretton, R. H. George Meredith. Contemporary Rev March 1928.
Hardy, T. GM: a reminiscence. Nineteenth Century Feb 1928.
Senft, O. Meredith als Pädagog Langensalza 1928.
Woolf, V. The novels of Meredith. In her Common reader: second series, 1928.
— Meredith revisited. In her Granite and rainbow, 1958.
Granville-Barker, H. Tennyson, Swinburne, Meredith and the theatre. In Eighteen-seventies: essays by Fellows of the Royal Society of Literature, 1929.
Sencourt, R. E. The life of Meredith. 1929.
Lowes, J. L. In his Of reading books, 1930.
Waugh, A. In his Hundred years of publishing: the story of Chapman and Hall 1830–1930, 1930.
Alberts-Arndt, B. Die englische Gesellschaft im Spiegel der Romane von Meredith. Karlsruhe 1931.
Fiedler, H. G. Notes by Meredith on Grillparzer's Ahnfrau. MLR 26 1931.
Peel, R. The creed of a Victorian pagan. Cambridge Mass 1931.
Tenney, C. D. 'Rose pink and dirty drab': Meredith as a critic. Sewanee Rev 39 1931.
Dobrée, B. Some novels of Meredith. Nat Rev Feb 1932.
'Field, Michael'. Meredith and Michael Field. Cornhill Mag March 1932.
Roberts, M. Meetings with some men of letters. Queen's Quart 39 1932.
Roberts, W. W. Music in Meredith. Music & Letters 13 1932.
Tuell, A. K. In her Victorian at bay, 1932.
Able, A. H. Meredith and Thomas Love Peacock: a study in literary influence. Philadelphia 1933.
Wharton, E. In her Backward glance, 1934.
Bierig, E. Frauengestalten bei Meredith. Cologne 1936.
Mainland, W. F. A German source for the Shaving of Shagpat. MLR 31 1936.
Bush, D. In his Mythology and the romantic tradition in English poetry, Cambridge Mass 1937.
Mackay, M. E. Meredith et la France. Paris 1937.
Woods, A. Meredith as champion of women and of progressive education. Oxford 1937.
Littmann, H. Das dichterische Bild in der Lyrik Merediths und Thomas Hardys im Zusammenhang mit ihrer Weltanschauung. Berne 1839, Zürich [1938] (as Die Metapher in Merediths und Hardys Lyrik).
Robinson, E. A. Meredith's literary theory and science: realism vs the comic spirit. PMLA 53 1938.
Zipf, G. K. New facts in the early life of Meredith. Harvard Stud 20 1938.
Everett, E. M. In his Party of humanity: the Fortnightly Review and its contributors 1865–74, Chapel Hill 1939.
Goodell, M. Three satirists of snobbery: Thackeray, Meredith, Proust. Hamburg 1939.
Petter, G. Meredith and his German critics. 1939. Trns and summaries of German articles.
Ramsay, A. A. W. The crisis in the Cabinet 1845. Cornhill Mag Aug 1939. On the scandal used in Diana of the Crossways.
Milner, V. A talk about Meredith. Nat Rev Nov 1940.
— Talks with Meredith. Nat Rev Nov 1948.
Chambers, E. K. Meredith's Modern love; Meredith's nature poetry. In his Sheaf of studies, Oxford 1942.
Mayo, R. D. The Egoist and the willow pattern. ELH 9 1942.
Hewitt-Thayer, H. W. Ferdinand Lassalle in the novels of Spielhagen and Meredith. Germanic Rev 19 1944.
Hudson, R. B. The Egoist as a play. MLN 59 1944.
— The meaning of egoism in the Egoist. Trollopian 3 1948.
— Meredith's early life. TLS 4 Dec 1948.
— The publishing of Rhoda Fleming. SB 6 1954.
— Meredith's Autobiography and the Adventures of Harry Richmond. Nineteenth-Century Fiction 9 1955.
Mayer, F. P. Meredith: an osbcure comedian. In If by your art: testament to Percival Hunt, Pittsburgh 1948.
Sassoon, S. George Meredith. 1948.
Sitwell, O. The novels of Meredith and some notes on the English novel. Oxford 1948.
Tinker, C. B. Meredith's poetry. In his Essays in retrospect, New Haven 1948.
Gettmann, R. A. Meredith as publisher's reader. JEGP 48 1949.

— Serialization and Evan Harrington. PMLA 64 1949.
Brooks, C. and R. P. Warren. Lucifer in starlight. In their Understanding poetry, New York 1950 (rev).
Eaker, J. G. Meredith's human comedy. Nineteenth-Century Fiction 5 1951.
Mueller, W. R. Theological dualism and the 'system' in Richard Feverel. ELH 18 1951.
Stone, J. Meredith and Goethe. UTQ 21 1952.
Buckler, W. E. The artistic unity of Richard Feverel chapter xxxiii. Nineteenth-Century Fiction 7 1953.
Hill, C. J. Meredith's 'Plain story'. Ibid.
— The portrait of the author in Beauchamp's Career. JEGP 52 1953.
— Theme and image in the Egoist. Univ of Kansas City Rev 20 1954.
Curtin, F. D. Adrian Harley: the limits of Meredith's comedy. Nineteenth-Century Fiction 7 1953.
Brunner, B. A. Meredith's symbolism: Lord Ormont and his Aminta. Nineteenth-Century Fiction 8 1954.
Pritchett, V. S. In his Books in general, 1953.
— Books in general. New Statesman, 25 Sept, 23 Oct 1954.
Wright, W. F. Art and substance in Meredith: a study in narrative. Lincoln Nebraska 1953.
Stevenson, L. Meredith and the interviewers. MP 51 1953.
— The ordeal of Meredith. 1954.
— Meredith's atypical novel: a study of Rhoda Fleming. In B. H. Lehman et al, Image of the work: essays in criticism, Berkeley 1955.
— Meredith and the problem of style in the novel. Zeitschrift für Anglistik und Amerikanistik 6 1958.
— Darwin and the novel. Nineteenth-Century Fiction 15 1961.
Day Lewis, C. Meredith and responsibility. In his Notable images of virtue, Toronto 1954.
Bynner, W. A young visit with Meredith. Virginia Quart Rev 32 1956.
Kessler, J. Meredith's spiritual laughter. Western Humanities Rev 10 1956.
Landis, J. C. Meredith's comedy. Boston Univ Stud in Eng 2 1956.
Lindsay, J. Meredith: his life and work. 1956.
Austin, D. S. Meredith on the nature of metaphor. UTQ 27 1957.
Bartlett, P. Meredith: early manuscript poems in the Berg Collection. BNYPL Aug 1957.
— Meredith's lost 'Cleopatra'. Yale Univ Lib Gazette 33 1958.
— Richard Feverel, knight-errant. BNYPL July 1959.
— The novels of Meredith. REL 3 1962.
— Meredith on Mistral's Mirèio. Yale Univ Lib Gazette 38 1963.
— George Meredith. 1963 (Br Council pamphlet).
— A manuscript of Meredith's Modern love. Yale Univ Lib Gazette 15 1966.
Beerbohm, M. Hethway speaking. In his Mainly on the air, 1957 (enlarged). Meredith's conversation reported by a Chelsea neighbour.
Cline, C. L. The letters of Meredith. Univ of Texas Lib Chron 6 1957.
— The betrothal of Meredith to Marie Vulliamy. Nineteenth-Century Fiction 16 1962.
— The missing Meredith letters. Book Collector 14 1965.
Friedman, N. The jangled harp: symbolic structure in Modern love. MLQ 18 1957.
Watson, R. Sandra Belloni: the philosopher upon the sentimentalists. ELH 24 1957.
Bailey, D. D. American criticism of Meredith's novels 1860–95. Trans Wisconsin Acad of Sciences, Arts & Letters 47 1958.
Clark, A. P. The manuscript collections of the Princeton University Library. Princeton Univ Lib Chron 19 1958.

Haight, G. S. Meredith and the Westminster Review. MLR 53 1958.
Gudas, F. Meredith's One of our conquerors. In From Jane Austen to Conrad: essays collected in memory of James T. Hillhouse, ed R. C. Rathburn and M. Steinmann, Minneapolis 1958.
Wright, E. C. The significance of the image patterns in Meredith's Modern love. Victorian Newsletter no 13 1958.
Green, D. B. Meredith's Austrian poets: a newly identified review essay with translations. MLR 54 1959.
Huzzard, J. A. Meredith and the Risorgimento. Italica 36 1959.
Peterson, V. A. The entitlement of Love in the valley. Victorian Newsletter no 15 1959.
Rossi, S. George Meredith. Milan 1959.
— Meredith cinquant' anni dopo. Aevum 33 1959.
Stang, R. In his Theory of the novel in England 1850–70, 1959.
Weil-Nordon, P. Meredith vu par Sir Arthur Conan Doyle. Etudes Anglaises 12 1959.
Baylen, J. O. Meredith and W. T. Stead: three unpublished letters. HLQ 24 1960.
— Meredith and W. T. Stead: two unpublished letters. Texas Stud in Lit & Lang 4 1962.
— and P. G. Hogan. W. T. Stead's interview with Meredith: an unpublished version. Tennessee Stud in Lit 8 1963.
Fanger, D. Joyce and Meredith: a question of influence and tradition. Modern Fiction Stud 6 1960.
— Meredith as novelist. Nineteenth-Century Fiction 16 1962.
Marshall, W. H. Richard Feverel, the original man. Victorian Newsletter no 18 1960.
Tompkins, J. M. S. Meredith's Periander. RES new ser 11 1960.
Hardy, B. 'A way to your hearts through fire or water': the structure of imagery in Harry Richmond. EC 10 1960; rptd in her Appropriate form, 1964.
Auchinloss, L. In his Reflections of a Jacobite, Boston 1961.
Buchen, I. H. The importance of the minor characters in the Ordeal of Richard Feveral. Boston Univ Stud in Eng 5 1961.
— The Ordeal of Richard Feverel: science versus nature. ELH 29 1962.
— Science, society and individuality: the Egoist. Univ of Kansas City Rev 30 1964.
— The egoists in the Egoist: the sensualists and the ascetics. Nineteenth-Century Fiction 19 1965.
Field, G. W. Herman Hesse as critic of English and American literature. Monatshefte 53 1961. Extensive quotations from Hesse's review of Egoist.
Thomson, F. C. Stylistic revisions in One of our conquerors. Yale Univ Lib Gazette 36 1961.
— The design of One of our conquerors. Stud in Eng Lit 1500–1900 2 1962.
Kelvin, N. A troubled Eden: nature and society in the works of Meredith. Edinburgh 1961.
Morris, J. W. Beauchamp's career: Meredith's acknowledgment of his debt to Carlyle. In Studies in honor of John C. Hodges and Alwin Thaler, Knoxville 1961.
— The germ of Meredith's Lucifer in starlight. Victorian Poetry 1 1963.
— Inherent principles of order in Richard Feverel. PMLA 78 1963.
Prichard, K. S. Contrasts: Meredith and Marchesi. Meanjin 20 1961.
Karl, F. C. Beachamp's career: an English ordeal. Nineteenth-Century Fiction 16 1962.
Kerpneck, H. A shorn Shagpat. Book Collector 11 1962.
— Meredith, sun-worshipper and Diana's Redworth. Nineteenth-Century Fiction 18 1964.
Beer, G. Meredith's revisions of the Tragic comedians. RES new ser 14 1963.

— Some compositor's misreadings of the Tragic comedians. N & Q 11 June 1964.
— Meredith and the Satirist. RES new ser 15 1964. Account of unpbd play by Meredith.
— The amazing marriage: a study in contraries. REL 7 1966.
— Meredith's contributions to the Pall Mall Gazette. MLR 60 1965.
— Meredith's idea of comedy 1876–80. Nineteenth-Century Fiction 20 1966.
d'Ardenne, S. R. T. O. Troilus and Criseyde and the Tragic comedians. E Studies 44 1963.
Collins, A. N. Meredith's ataxia: a corrective note. Eng Lang Notes 2 1964.
Hergenhan, L. T. A note on some of Meredith's contemporary reviewers. N & Q 11 June 1964.
— Meredith's revisions of Harry Richmond. RES new ser 14 1963.
— Meredith's attempts to win popularity: contemporary reactions. Stud in Eng Lit 1500–1900 4 1964.
— Meredith's use of revision: a consideration of the revisions of Richard Feverel and Evan Harrington. MLR 59 1964.
— The reception of Meredith's early novels. Nineteenth-Century Fiction 19 1965.
Ketcham, C. H. Meredith and the Wilis. Victorian Poetry 1 1963.
Sudrann, J. 'The linked eye and mind': a concept of action in the novels of Meredith. Stud in Eng Lit 1500–1900 4 1964.
Talon, H. A. Le comique, le tragique et le romanesque dans The ordeal of Richard Feverel. Etudes Anglaises 17 1964.
Kruppa, J. E. Meredith's late novels: suggestions for a critical approach. Nineteenth-Century Fiction 19 1965.
— Meredith at work: the Tale of Chloe. Nineteenth-Century Fiction 20 1966.
Lees, F. N. Meredith and Othello. N & Q March 1965.
Poston, L. Dramatic reference and structure in the Ordeal of Richard Feverel. Stud in Eng Lit 1500–1900 6 1966.
Williams, I. M. The organic structure of the Ordeal of Richard Feverel. RES new ser 18 1967.

G. B.

'GEORGE ELIOT', MARY ANN EVANS, later CROSS

1819–80

The ms Scenes of clerical life *is in the Pierpont Morgan Library, New York; the mss of all other major works are in the BM. The largest collection of letters is in Yale Univ Library; other collections are to be found in the BM, the National Library of Scotland, Princeton Univ Library, the Berg Collection in the New York Public Library, the Huntington Library and Coventry Public Library. George Eliot's diary for 1879 is in the Berg Collection; other journals and diaries are at Yale. Yale also has several notebooks, including the 'Quarry' for* Felix Holt; *the Quarry for* Romola *is at Princeton; Harvard has the main* Middlemarch *Quarry, though 2 other* Middlemarch *notebooks are in the Folger Library.*

Bibliographies etc

Sutton, C. W. George Eliot: a bibliography. Papers of Manchester Literary Club 1881.
Anderson, J. P. In O. Browning, Life of George Eliot, 1890.
Waldo, F. and G. A. Turkington. In M. Blind, George Eliot, 1904.
Mudge, I. G. and M. E. Sears. A George Eliot dictionary. New York 1924.
Muir, P. H. A bibliography of the first editions of George Eliot. Bookman's Jnl suppl 1927–8.
Parrish, M. L. In her Victorian lady novelists: first editions in the library at Dormy House, New Jersey, 1933.
Barry, J. D. The literary reputation of George Eliot's fiction. Bull of Bibliography 22 1959.
Harvey, W. J. In Victorian fiction, ed L. Stevenson, Cambridge Mass 1964.

Collections

Novels: illustrated edition. 6 vols 1867–[78].
Wise, witty and tender sayings. Ed A. Main, Edinburgh 1872.
Novels. 9 vols New York 1876.
The George Eliot birthday book. Ed A. Main, Edinburgh 1878.
Works: cabinet edition. 24 vols 1878–[85].
Novels: cheap edition. 6 vols 1881.
Works: fireside edition. 12 vols New York 1885.
Works. 8 vols Chicago 1886.
Works: edition de luxe. 12 vols Boston 1886–7.
Complete poems. New York 1888.
Complete poems. Ed M. Browne, Boston 1889.
Works: Rosehill edition. 24 vols Boston 1893–5.
Works: standard edition. 21 vols Edinburgh 1895.
Works. 24 vols New York 1895.
Works: Foleshill edition. 12 vols Boston 1900, Toronto 1902.
Works: Nuneaton edition. 20 vols Boston 1900.
Works: library edition. 10 vols 1901.
Works: Warwick edition. 14 vols Edinburgh 1901.
Works: new popular edition. 10 vols 1906.
Works: Riverside edition. 22 vols Boston and New York 1907.
Works: large paper edition. 25 vols Boston and New York 1908.
Works: illustrated copyright edition. 21 vols 1908–11.
Works: new cabinet edition. 17 vols 1913.
Works: national library edition. 10 vols New York 1926.

§ 1

The life of Jesus critically examined, by David Friedrich Strauss, translated from the fourth German edition. 3 vols 1846, 1 vol 1892, New York 1855. Begun by Mrs Charles Hennell and completed anon by Eliot.
The essence of Christianity, by Ludwig Feuerbach, translated from the second German edition by Marian Evans. 1854, New York 1857, 1957.
Scenes of clerical life. 2 vols Edinburgh 1858, 1859, 1860, 1863 (with Silas Marner), 1868 etc, New York 1858, Leipzig 1859; ed A. Mattheson, Oxford 1909 (WC); ed W. W. Fowler and E. Limouzin 1916; ed A. M. Macmillan 1924; tr French, 1884; German, 1885. First pbd in Blackwood's Mag: The sad fortunes of the Rev Amos Barton, Jan–Feb 1857; Mr Gilfil's love story, March–June 1857; Janet's repentance, July–Nov 1857.
[Lucas, S.] Times 2 Jan 1858.
Literary Gazette 23 Jan 1858.
John Bull's Weekly 8 Feb 1858.
Saturday Rev 29 May 1858.
Nat Rev 7 1858.
Atlantic Monthly May 1858.
Edinburgh Rev 110 1859.
Tomlinson, M. The beginning of George Eliot's art. Sewanee Rev 27 1919.
Laski, M. Some words from Scenes of clerical life. N & Q 9 Aug 1962.
Noble, T. A. George Eliot's Scenes of clerical life. New Haven 1965.
Adam Bede. 3 vols Edinburgh 1859 (7 edns), 1862 (10th edn), New York 1859, 2 vols Leipzig 1859; ed L. J. Wylie, New York 1915; ed S. W. Paterson, New York 1923; ed G. S. Haight, New York 1949; ed G. Bullett 1953; ed M. H. Goldberg, New York 1956; tr German, 1860; French, 1861; Dutch, 1870; Hungarian, 1888.

[Jewsbury, G.] Athenaeum 26 Feb 1859.
Saturday Rev 26 Feb 1859.
Literary Gazette 26 Feb 1859.
[Dallas, E. S.] Times 12 April 1859.
Atlantic Monthly Oct 1859.
[Mozley, A.] Bentley's Quart Rev 1 1859.
[Collins, W. L.] Blackwood's Mag April 1859.
Edinburgh Rev 110 1859.
North Br Rev 30 1859.
Westminster Rev new ser 15 1859.
Dublin Rev 47 1859.
Mottram, W. The story of George Eliot in relation to Adam Bede. 1905.
Williams, O. In his Some great English novels, 1926.
Diekhoff, J. J. The happy ending of Adam Bede. ELH 3 1936.
Van Ghent, D. In her English novel: form and function, New York 1953.
Fyfe, A. J. The interpretation of Adam Bede. Nineteenth-Century Fiction 9 1955.
Jones, W. M. From abstract to concrete in Adam Bede. College Eng Nov 1955.
Thale, J. Adam Bede: Arthur Donnithorne and Zeluco. MLN 70 1955.
Creager, G. R. An interpretation of Adam Bede. ELH 23 1956.
Hussey, M. Structure and imagery in Adam Bede. Nineteenth-Century Fiction 10 1956.
Harvey, W. J. The treatment of time in Adam Bede. Anglia 75 1957.
Foakes, R. A. Adam Bede reconsidered. English 12 1959.
Deneau, D. P. Inconsistencies and inaccuracies in Adam Bede. Nineteenth-Century Fiction 14 1960.
Casson, A. The Scarlet letter and Adam Bede. Victorian Newsletter no 20 1961.
Adam, I. W. A new look at Hetty Sorrel. Victorian Newsletter no 22 1962.
Gregor, I. The two worlds of Adam Bede. In Gregor and B. Nicholas, The moral and the story, 1962.
Ryals, C. de L. The thorn imagery in Adam Bede. Victorian Newsletter no 22 1962.
Selig, R. L. The red haired lady orator: parallel passages in the Bostonians and Adam Bede. Nineteenth-Century Fiction 16 1962.
Buchen, I. H. Arthur Donnithorne and Zeluco. Victorian Newsletter no 23 1963.
Colby, R. A. Miss Evans, Miss Mulock and Hetty Sorel. Eng Lang Notes 2 1965.

The mill on the Floss. 3 vols Edinburgh 1860, 2 vols Edinburgh 1860, 1 vol Edinburgh 1861 (corrected), 1862 (5th edn), New York 1860, Boston 1860; ed I. Austerman, New York 1913; ed R. O. Morris 1913; ed J. M. Dorey, Boston 1914; ed H. T. Eaton, Boston 1928; ed M. E. Clark, Chicago 1929; ed M. Herzberg, Boston 1929; ed G. Bullett 1953; ed M. H. Goldberg, New York 1956; ed G. S. Haight, Boston 1961; tr German, 1861; French, 1863; Dutch, 1870.

[Jewsbury, G.] Athenaeum 7 April 1860.
Saturday Rev 14 April 1860.
[Dallas, E. S.] Times 19 May 1860.
Atlantic Monthly June 1860.
[Collins, W. L.] Blackwood's Mag May 1860.
Nat Rev 11 1860. With review of Scenes of clerical life and Adam Bede.
North Br Rev 33 1860.
Quart Rev 108 1860. With review of Scenes of clerical life and Adam Bede.
Tait's Mag May 1860.
Dublin Univ Mag 57 1861.
Isenbarth, N. Die Psychologie der Charactere in Mill on the Floss. Die Neueren Sprachen 21 1913.
Tomlinson, M. Dodsons and Tullivers. Sewanee Rev 26 1918.
Luskey, A. E. The Mill on the Floss and Storm's Immensee. Modern Lang Jnl 10 1926.
Steinhoff, W. R. Intention and fulfillment in the ending of the Mill on the Floss in the imagery of the work. Ed B. Evans and J. Miles, Berkeley 1955.
Paris, B. J. Towards a revaluation of the Mill on the Floss. Nineteenth-Century Fiction 11 1957.
Rubin, L. River imagery as a means of foreshadowing in the Mill on the Floss. MLN 71 1956.
Welsh, A. George Eliot and the romance. Nineteenth-Century Fiction 14 1960.
Casson, A. The mill on the Floss and Keller's Romeo und Julia auf dem Dorfe. MLN 75 1960.
Brown, K. The ending of the Mill on the Floss. N & Q 11 June 1964.
Drew, E. In her Novel: a modern guide to fifteen English masterpieces, New York 1964.
Lee, R. H. The unity of the Mill on the Floss. Eng Stud in Africa 7 1964.
Bolton, F. Le manuscrit du Mill on the Floss. Etudes Anglaises 18 1965.
Levine, G. Intelligence as deception: the Mill on the Floss. PMLA 80 1965.

Silas Marner: the weaver of Raveloe. Edinburgh 1861 (7 edns), 1864 (with Scenes of clerical life), 1868 etc; ed B. Carmen, Boston 1895; ed R. Herrick, New York 1895; ed E. L. Gulick 1899; ed R. Garnett 1905; ed J. R. Colby, New York 1906; ed F. T. Baker, New York 1911; ed E. Harrington, New York 1930; ed K. M. Lobb 1958; tr German, 1861; French, 1862; Hungarian, 1885.

[Jewsbury, G.] Athenaeum 6 April 1861.
Literary Gazette 6 April 1861.
Saturday Rev 13 April 1861.
[Dallas, E. S.] Times 29 April 1861.
Ludlow, J. M. Elsie Veneer and Silas Marner. Macmillan's Mag Aug 1861.
Englishwoman's Domestic Mag new ser 3 1861.
London Rev 2 1861.
Dublin Univ Mag 59 1862.
North Br Rev 38 1863.
Fairlay, E. The art of George Eliot in Silas Marner. Eng Jnl 2 1913.
Parsons, C. O. Background material illustrative of Silas Marner. N & Q 28 Dec 1946.
Heilman, R. B. Return to Raveloe. Eng Jnl 46 1957.
Thomson, F. C. The theme of alienation in Silas Marner. Nineteenth-Century Fiction 20 1966.

Romola. 3 vols 1863, 1865 (illustr), 2 vols 1880 etc, 1 vol New York 1863, 2 vols Leipzig 1863; ed G. Biagi 2 vols 1907; ed C. B. Wheeler 1916; ed V. Meynell, Oxford 1929 (WC); tr German, 1864; Dutch, 1864; French, 1887. First pbd, illustr Leighton, Cornhill Mag July 1862–Aug 1863.

Athenaeum 11 July 1863.
Saturday Rev 25 July 1863.
Br Quart Rev 38 1863.
London Rev 7 1863.
Westminster Rev 80 1863.
Oliphant, Two cities: two books. Blackwood's Mag July 1874.
Davidson, H. A. The study of Romola. Boston 1902.
Stowell, R. S. A study of Romola. Boston 1903.
Tosello, M. Le fonti italiane della Romola. 1956.
Huzzard, J. A. The treatment of Florence and Florentine characters in Romola. Italica 1956.
Robinson, C. Romola: a reading of the novel. Victorian Stud 6 1962.
Poston, L. Romola and T. Trollope's Filippo Strozzi. Victorian Newsletter no 25 1964.

Brother Jacob. Cornhill Mag July 1864; rptd with Silas Marner in Works, 1878, above; tr Italian, 1880.

Felix Holt the radical. 3 vols Edinburgh 1866, 2 vols Edinburgh 1866, Leipzig 1867; ed V. Meynell, Oxford 1913 (WC); tr German, 1867; Dutch, 1867; Hungarian, 1874.

[Morley, J.] Saturday Rev 16 June 1866.
Athenaeum 23 June 1866.
[Dallas, E. J.] Times 26 June 1866.
[James, H.] Nation (New York) 16 Aug 1866.
[Collins, W.] Blackwood's Mag July 1866.
Chambers's Jnl 11 Aug 1866.
Contemporary Rev Sept 1866.
Edinburgh Rev 124 1866.
London Rev 12 1866.
London Quart Rev 27 1866.
[Sedgwick, A. G.?] North Amer Rev 103 1866.
Speare, M. E. George Eliot and radicalism. In his Political novel, New York 1925.
Milner, I. Felix Holt and realism in George Eliot. Casopsis pro Moderni Filologii 37 1955.
Williams, R. In his Culture and society, 1958, 1961 (Pelican), 1963 (with addn).
Thomson, F. C. The genesis of Felix Holt. PMLA 74 1959.
— Felix Holt as classical tragedy. Nineteenth-Century Fiction 16 1962.
Carroll, D. R. Felix Holt: society as protagonist. Nineteenth-Century Fiction 17 1963.
Address to working men, by Felix Holt. Blackwood's Mag Jan 1868.
The Spanish gypsy: a poem. Edinburgh 1868 (3 edns), 1875 (5th edn), Boston 1868.
[Hamely, E. B.] Blackwood's Mag June 1868.
Br Quart Rev 48 1868.
Edinburgh Rev 128 1868.
Fraser's Mag Oct 1868.
London Quart Rev 31 1868.
London Rev 16 1868.
[Morley, J.] Macmillan's Mag July 1868.
[James, H.]—North Amer Rev 107 1868.
Nation (New York) 2 July 1868.
St James Mag new ser 1 1868.
St Paul's Mag new ser 2 1868.
Saturday Rev 4 July 1868.
Agatha. 1869 (priv ptd). First pbd in Atlantic Monthly 1869. 2nd edn a forgery? *See* J. Carter and H. G. Pollard, An enquiry into the nature of certain nineteenth-century pamphlets, 1934.
Brother and sister: sonnets by Marian Lewes. 1869 (priv ptd). A forgery? *See* Agatha, above.
How Lisa loved the King. Boston 1869, 1883. First pbd in Blackwood's Mag May 1869.
Amgart. Macmillan's Mag July 1871.
Middlemarch: a study of provincial life. 4 vols Edinburgh 1872, 1873, 1 vol 1874 (corrected), 2 vols Berlin 1872, New York 1872; ed W. F. Neff, New York 1926; ed G. Bullett 1930; ed R. M. Hewit, Oxford 1947 (WC); ed G. S. Haight, Boston 1956; ed Q. Anderson 1963; ed F. Kermode 1964; ed W. J. Harvey 1965 (Penguin); tr German 1872–3; Dutch, 1873; Hungarian, 1874–5. First pbd in 8 bks, Dec 1871–Dec 1872.
Athenaeum 2 Dec 1871, 3 Feb, 30 March, 1 June, 27 July, 7 Dec 1872.
Examiner 2 Dec 1871, 3 Feb, 30 March, 8 June, 27 July, 5 Oct, 7 Dec 1872.
Spectator 16 Dec 1871, 3 Feb, 30 March, 5 Oct, 7 Dec 1872.
Saturday Rev 7, 21 Dec 1872.
[Collins, W. L.] Blackwood's Mag Dec 1872.
[Simcox, E.] Academy 1 Jan 1873.
Atlantic Monthly April 1873.
[Hutton, R. H.] Br Quart Rev 57 1873.
[McCarthy, J.] The story of two worlds. Catholic World Sept 1873.
[Houghton, Lord]. Edinburgh Rev 137 1873.
[Colvin, S.] Fortnightly Rev Jan 1873.
[James, H.] Galaxy 15 1873; rptd in his House of fiction, ed L. Edel 1957.
London Quart Rev 40 1873.
[Parry, T. S.?] North Amer Rev 116 1873.
[Laing, R.] Quart Rev 134 1873.
[Smith, G. B.] St Paul's Mag 12 1873.
Tomlinson, M. Rosamund and Lydgate. South Atlantic Quart 17 1918.
Sackville-West, E. Books in general. New Statesman 23 Nov 1940.
Annan, N. Books in general. New Statesman 27 Nov 1943.
Debanke, C. Week-end with Middlemarch. Queen's Quart 52 1945.
Halstead, F. G. George Eliot: medical digressions in Middlemarch. Bull History of Medicine 20 1946.
Briggs, A. Middlemarch and the doctors. Cambridge Jnl Sept 1948.
Schorer, M. Fiction and the matrix of analogy. Kenyon Rev 11 1949.
Kitchel, A. Quarry for Middlemarch. Nineteenth-Century Fiction 4 (suppl) 1950.
Kettle, A. In his Introduction to the English novel vol 1, 1951.
Steiner, F. G. A preface to Middlemarch. Nineteenth-Century Fiction 9 1955.
Beaty, J. History by indirection; the era of reform in Middlemarch. Victorian Stud 1 1957.
— The forgotten past of Will Ladislaw. Nineteenth-Century Fiction 12 1958.
— Middlemarch from notebook to novel. Urbana 1960.
Anderson, Q. George Eliot in Middlemarch. In From Dickens to Hardy, ed B. Ford 1958 (Pelican).
Ferris, S. J. Middlemarch: George Eliot's masterpiece. In From Jane Austen to Joseph Conrad, ed R. C. Rathburn and M. Steinmann, Minneapolis 1958.
Carroll, D. R. Unity through analogy; the art of Middlemarch. Victorian Stud 3 1959.
Monod, S. George Eliot et les personnages de Middlemarch. Etudes Anglaises 12 1959.
Lerner, L. D. The cool gaze and the warm heart. Listener 29 Sept 1960.
Prest, J. The industrial revolution in Coventry. 1960.
Stallknecht, N. P. Resolution and independence; a reading of Middlemarch. In Twelve original essays on great English novels, ed C. Shapiro, Detroit 1960.
Greenberg, R. A. The heritage of Will Ladislaw. Nineteenth-Century Fiction 15 1961.
Hagan, J. Middlemarch: narrative unity in the story of Dorothea Brooke. Nineteenth-Century Fiction 16 1962.
Hoggart, R. A Victorian masterpiece. Listener 8 March 1962.
Daiches, D. George Eliot: Middlemarch. 1963.
Pinney, T. Another note on the forgotten past of Will Ladislaw. Nineteenth-Century Fiction 17 1963.
Ferguson, S. C. Mme Laure and operative irony in Middlemarch. Stud in Eng Lit 1500–1900 3 1963.
Fernando, L. George Eliot, feminism and Dorothea Brooke. REL 4 1963.
Hastings, R. Dorothea Brooke: the struggle for existence in Middlemarch. Thoth 4 1963.
Tomlinson, T. B. Middlemarch and modern society. Melbourne Critical Rev 6 1963.
Adam, I. A Huxley echo in Middlemarch. N & Q 11 June 1964.
Gillespie, H. R. George Eliot's Tertius Lydgate and Charles Kingsley's Tom Thurnall. N & Q 11 June 1964.
Goldfarb, R. M. Caleb Garth of Middlemarch. Victorian Newsletter no 26 1964.
Hardy, B. In her Appropriate form, 1964.
Isaacs, N. D. Middlemarch, crescendo of obligatory drama. Nineteenth-Century Fiction 18 1964.

Luecke, J. M. Ladislaw and the Middlemarch vision. Nineteenth-Century Fiction 19 1965.

The legend of Jubal and other poems. Edinburgh 1874, Boston 1874, Toronto 1874; tr Dutch, 1888. The legend of Jubal first pbd Macmillan's Mag May 1870.

[Sincox, G. A.] Academy May 1874.

[Minto, W.] Examiner 16 May 1874.

[James, H.] North Amer Rev 119 1874.

Saturday Rev 13 June 1874.

Daniel Deronda. 4 vols Edinburgh 1876, 1877, 1 vol 1877, New York 1876; ed F. R. Leavis, New York 1961; ed E. L. Jones 2 vols 1964 (EL); tr German, 1876; Swedish, 1878; Italian, 1882–3; Hebrew, 1892. First pbd in 8 bks Jan-Sept 1876.

Athenaeum 29 Jan, 4 March, 11, 24 April, 3 June, 1, 29 July, 2 Sept 1876.

Examiner 29 Jan, 4 March, 1 April, 3 June, 5 Aug, 2 Sept 1876.

Saturday Rev 16–23 Sept 1876.

[James, H.] Daniel Deronda: a conversation. Atlantic Monthly Dec 1876; rptd in F. R. Leavis, The great tradition, 1948.

—— Nation (New York) 24 Feb 1876.

Br Quart Rev 64 1876.

Edinburgh Rev 144 1876.

[Colvin, S.] Fortnightly Rev Nov 1876.

[Dicey, A. V.?] Nation (New York) 12–19 Oct 1876.

Church Quart Rev 5 1877.

[Whipple, E. P.] North Amer Rev 124 1877.

Kaufman, D. George Eliot and Judaism. 1877.

Scherer, W. George Eliot und das Judentum. In his Kleine Schriften vol 2, Berlin 1893.

Philipson, D. In his Jew in English fiction, Cincinnati 1911.

Modder, F. In his Jew in the literature of England, Philadelphia 1939.

Liptzin, S. Jewish Book Annual 10 1951.

Beebe, M. Visions are creators: the unity of Daniel Deronda. Boston Univ Stud in Eng 1 1955.

Goldberg, H. George Henry Lewes and Daniel Deronda. N & Q 10 Aug 1957.

Colby, R. A. An American sequel to Daniel Deronda. Nineteenth-Century Fiction 12 1958.

Beaty, J. Daniel Deronda and the question of unity in fiction. Victorian Newsletter no 15 1959.

Carroll, D. R. The unity of Daniel Deronda. EC 9 1959.

—— Mansfield Park, Daniel Deronda and ordination. SP 62 1965.

Peterson, V. A. Forgotten bastards: a note on Daniel Deronda. Victorian Newsletter no 15 1959.

Preyer, R. Beyond the liberal imagination: vision and unreality in Daniel Deronda. Victorian Stud 3 1960.

Rosenberg, E. In his From Shylock to Svengali, 1960.

Knoepflmacher, U. C. Daniel Deronda and William Shakespeare. Victorian Newsletter no 19 1961.

Steinhaff, W. R. The metaphorical texture of Daniel Deronda. Books Abroad 35 1961.

Lainoff, S. James and Eliot: the two Gwendolens. Victorian Newsletter no 21 1961.

Robinson, C. The severe angel: a study of Daniel Deronda. ELH 31 1964.

A college breakfast party. Macmillan's Mag July 1878.

Impressions of Theophrastus Such. Edinburgh 1879, New York 1879, Leipzig 1879; tr German, 1880 (in part).

[Saintsbury, G.] Academy June 1879.

Br Quart Rev 70 1879.

Edinburgh Rev 150 1879.

Examiner 7 June 1879.

[Allen, G.] Fortnightly Rev July 1879.

Fraser's Mag July 1879.

Nation (New York) 19 June 1879.

[Eggleston, E.] North Amer Rev 124 1879.

Essays and leaves from a note-book. Ed C. L. Lewes, Edinburgh 1884, New York 1884.

[Beeching, H. C.] Academy March 1884.

[Jacobs, J.] Athenaeum 23 Feb 1884.

Saturday Rev 8 March 1884.

Early essays. 1919 (priv ptd). Not rptd from mss, as the preface claims, but from cuttings of George Eliot's contributions to the Coventry Herald exhibited in 1919.

Essays. Ed T. Pinney 1963.

Letters

George Eliot's life as related in her letters and journals, arranged and edited by her husband J. W. Cross. 3 vols Edinburgh 1885.

Letters from George Eliot to Elma Stuart 1872–80. Ed R. Stuart 1909.

The letters of George Eliot, selected by R. B. Johnson. 1926.

George Eliot's family life and letters. Ed A. Paterson 1928.

The George Eliot letters. Ed G. S. Haight 7 vols New Haven 1954–6. First complete edn.

§2

Scherer, E. H. A. In his Etudes critiques sur la littérature contemporaine, 10 vols Paris 1863–95. Vols 1, 5 and 8 contain essays on George Eliot.

James, H. The novels of George Eliot. Atlantic Monthly Oct 1866.

—— The life of George Eliot. Atlantic Monthly May 1885.

[Lancaster, H. H.] George Eliot's novels. North Br Rev 45 1866.

Morley, J. George Eliot's novels. Macmillan's Mag Aug 1866.

—— The life of George Eliot. Macmillan's Mag April 1885.

George Eliot. Br Quart Rev 45 1867.

Browne, M. George Eliot as a poet. Contemporary Rev July 1868.

McCarthy, J. George Eliot and George Lewes. Galaxy 7 1869.

Hutton, R. H. In his Essays theological and literary, 2 vols 1871.

—— In his Essays on some of the modern guides of English thought in matters of faith, 1887.

—— In his Brief literary criticisms, ed E. M. Roscoe 1906.

Smith, G. B. George Eliot. St Paul's Mag 12 1873.

Carpenter, J. E. Religious influences in current literature: George Eliot. Unitarian Rev 3 1875.

'Roslyn, Guy' (J. Hatton). George Eliot in Derbyshire. 1876.

George Eliot and Comtism. London Quart Rev 47 1877.

Dowden, E. In his Studies in literature 1789–1877, 1878.

Brown, J. C. The ethics of George Eliot's works. Edinburgh 1879.

[Shand, A. I.] Contemporary literature: novelists. Blackwood's Mag March 1879.

Axon, W. E. A. George Eliot's use of dialect. Eng Dialect Soc Miscellany 1880.

Taylor, B. In his Critical essays and literary notes, New York 1880.

George Eliot. Church Quart Rev 12 1881.

George Eliot. London Quart Rev 57 1881.

Allardyce, A. George Eliot. Blackwood's Mag Feb 1881.

Barry, W. J. The genius of George Eliot. Dublin Rev 5 1881.

—— The religion of George Eliot. Dublin Rev 6 1881.

Boyce, J. George Eliot and Carlyle. Nation (New York) 3 March 1881.

Call, W. M. W. George Eliot: her life and writings. Westminster Rev 60 1881.

Kebbel, T. Village life according to George Eliot. Fraser's Mag Feb 1881.

—— Miss Austen and George Eliot. Nat Rev Oct 1883.

Paul, C. K. George Eliot. Harper's New Monthly Mag May 1881.

Sarson, G. George Eliot and Thomas Carlyle. Modern Rev 2 1881.

Simcox, E. George Eliot. Nineteenth Century May 1881.
Sully, J. George Eliot's art. Mind 6 1881.
Ward, R. Scepticism in George Eliot. Jnl of Science 18 1881.
[Wedgwood, J.] The moral influence of George Eliot. Contemporary Rev Feb 1881.
Russell, G. W. E. George Eliot: her genius and writings. 1882.
— George Eliot revisited. Contemporary Rev March 1896
[Bayne, P.] Shakespeare and George Eliot. Blackwood's Mag April 1883.
Blind, M. George Eliot. 1883, Boston 1904 (rev and enlarged).
Cooke, G. W. George Eliot: a critical study. 1883.
Myers, F. W. H. George Eliot. In his Essays modern, 2 vols 1883.
The life and letters of George Eliot. Edinburgh Rev 161 1885.
George Eliot's life. London Quart Rev 64 1885.
George Eliot. Br Quart Rev 81 1885.
Cleveland, R. E. George Eliot's poetry and other studies. 1885.
Draskowitz, H. In his Drei englische Dichterinnen, Berlin 1885.
Montégut, E. In his Écrivains modernes de l'Angleterre ser 1, Paris 1885.
Whipple, E. P. The private life of George Eliot. North Amer Rev 141 1885.
— In his Recollections of eminent men, Boston 1887.
Wolzogen, E. von. George Eliot: eine biographisch-kritische Studie. Leipzig 1885.
[Yonge, C. M.] George Eliot and her critics. Monthly Packet May 1885.
Dawson, W. J. In his Quest and vision, 1886.
— In his Makers of English fiction, New York 1905.
Harrison, F. The life of George Eliot. In his Choice of books and other literary pieces, 1886. Rptd from Fortnightly Rev.
— George Eliot's place in literature. Forum 20 1895.
Lonsdale, M. George Eliot: thoughts upon her life, her books and herself. 1886.
Woolson, A. G. George Eliot and her heroines. New York 1886.
Barine, A. In his Portraits des femmes, Paris 1887.
Conrad, H. George Eliot: ihr Leben und Schaffen dargestellt nach ihren Briefen und Tagebüchern. Berlin 1887.
Bell, J. George Eliot as a novelist. Aberdeen 1888.
Hamley, E. In his Shakespeare's funeral and other papers, Edinburgh 1889.
Browning, O. Life of George Eliot. 1890.
Jacobs, J. In his George Eliot, Matthew Arnold, Browning, Newman: essays and reviews from the Athenaeum, 1891.
Negri, G. George Eliot: la sua vita e suoi romanzi. 2 vols Milan 1891.
Whiting, M. B. George Eliot as a character artist. Westminster Rev 138 1892.
Bender, H. George Eliot: ein Lebensbild. Hamburg 1893.
Westermarck, H. George Eliot: och der engelska naturalistika romanen. Helsingfors 1894.
Lilly, W. S. In his Four English humourists of the nineteenth century, 1895.
Saintsbury, G. In his Collected impressions, 1895.
Newdegate, A. A. The Cheverels of Cheverel Manor. 1899.
Oliphant, J. In his Victorian novelists, 1899.
Rickett, A. In his Prophets of this century, 1899.
Howells, W. D. In his Heroines of fiction, 2 vols Boston 1901.
Thomson, C. L. George Eliot. 1901.
Brownell, W. C. In his Victorian prose masters, New York 1901.
Bonnell, H. H. In his Charlotte Brontë, George Eliot, Jane Austen: studies of their works, 1902.
Gould, G. M. Biographic clinics: the origin of the ill-health of De Quincey, Carlyle [et al]. 6 vols Philadelphia 1903–9. Vol 2 1904 is on George Eliot.
Stephen, L. George Eliot. 1902 (EML).
Barry, W. Heralds of revolt. In his Studies in modern literature and dogma, 1904.
Johnson, M. L. George Eliot and George Combe. Westminster Rev 156 1906.
Paul, H. In his Stray leaves, 1906.
Richter, H. George Eliot: fünf Aufsätze. Berlin 1907.
Olcott, C. S. George Eliot: scenes and people in her novels. New York 1910.
Gardner, C. The inner life of George Eliot. 1912.
— George Eliot. London Quart Rev 132 1919.
— George Eliot's 'quarries'. Atlantic Monthly Nov 1925.
Clifford, W. K. George Eliot: some personal recollections. Bookman (London) Oct 1927.
Deakin, M. H. The early life of George Eliot. Manchester 1913.
Rhotert, C. Die Frau bei George Eliot. Berlin 1915.
Berle, L. W. George Eliot and Thomas Hardy: a contrast. New York 1917.
Block, L. J. The poetry of George Eliot. Sewanee Rev 26 1918.
Zuber, E. Kind und Kindheit bei George Eliot. Frauenfeld 1919.
Cross, W. L. George Eliot in retrospect. Yale Rev 9 1920.
Royce, J. In his Fugitive essays, Cambridge Mass 1920.
Gosse, E. In his Aspects and impressions, 1922.
Wenley, R. M. Marian Evans and George Eliot. Washington Univ Stud 9 1922.
Bald, M. A. In his Women writers of the nineteenth century, Cambridge 1922.
J., A.C. Notes on the influence of Sir Walter Scott on George Eliot. Edinburgh 1923.
Cazamian, M. L. Le roman et les idées: l'influence de la science. Strasbourg 1923.
Pfeiffer, S. George Eliots Beziehungen zu Deutschland. Heidelberg 1925.
Woolf, V. In her Common reader, 1925.
Haldare, E. S. George Eliot and her times. 1927.
Pond, E. J. Idées morales et religieuses de George Eliot. Paris 1927.
Devonshire, M. G. In her English novel in France 1830–70, 1929.
Simon-Baumann, L. Die Darstellung der Charaktere in George Eliots Romanen. Leipzig 1929.
— George Eliot über Heinrich Heine. Anglia 55 1931.
Bassett, J. J. The purpose in George Eliot's art. Anglia 54 1930.
Kaboth, K. George Eliots Beziehungen zu Frankreich. Breslau 1930.
May, J. L. George Eliot. 1930.
Parlett, M. George Eliot and humanism. SP 27 1930.
— The influence of contemporary criticism on George Eliot. SP 30 1933.
Romieu, E. and G. La vie de George Eliot. Paris 1930; tr 1932.
Sparrow-Simpson, W. J. The religion of George Eliot. Church Quart Rev 112 1931.
Toyoda, M. Studies in the mental development of George Eliot. Tokyo 1931.
Macy, J. George Eliot: Victorian queen. Amer Bookman 75 1932.
Purdy, R. L. Journals and letters of George Eliot. Yale Univ Lib Gazette 7 1932.
Sackville-West, V. In Great Victorians, ed H. J. Massingham 1932.
Bourl'honne, P. George Eliot: essai de biographie intellectuelle et morale 1819–54. Paris 1933.
Fremantle, A. George Eliot. 1933.
Gary, F. In search of George Eliot: an approach through Marcel Proust. Symposium 4 1933.

Kitchel, A. T. George Lewes and George Eliot. New York 1933.
Cecil, D. In his Early Victorian novelists, 1934.
Masefield, M. In her Women novelists from Fanny Burney to George Eliot, 1934.
Berti, L. Considerazioni sui realismo morale di George Eliot. Florence 1935.
Clarke, I. C. In her Six portraits, 1935.
Williams, B. C. George Eliot and John Chapman. Colophon 1 1935.
—— George Eliot: a biography. New York 1936.
—— George Eliot: social pressures on the individual. Sewanee Rev 46 1938.
Davis, J. George Eliot and education. Education Forum 1 1937.
Murray, E. C. Samuel Lawrence's portrait of George Eliot. BM Quart 11 1937.
Bethell, S. L. The novels of George Eliot. Criterion 18 1938.
Anson, H. The church in nineteenth-century fiction: George Eliot. Listener 25 May 1939.
Dewes, S. Marian: the life of George Eliot. 1939.
Haight, G. S. George Eliot and John Chapman; with Chapman's diaries. New Haven 1940.
—— Cross's biography of George Eliot. Yale Univ Lib Gazette 25 1950.
—— The Tinker collection of George Eliot manuscripts. Yale Univ Lib Gazette 30 1955.
—— George Eliot's theory of fiction. Victorian Newsletter no 10 1956.
—— George Eliot's originals. In From Jane Austen to Joseph Conrad, ed R. C. Rathburn and M. Steinmann, Minneapolis 1958.
—— The George Eliot and G. H. Lewes collections. Yale Univ Lib Gazette 36 1961.
—— (ed). A century of George Eliot criticism. Boston 1965.
Maly-Schlatter, F. The Puritan element in Victorian fiction, with special reference to the works of George Eliot, Dickens and Thackeray. Zürich 1940.
Wright, W. F. George Eliot as industrial reformer. PMLA 56 1941.
Annan, N. George Eliot: books in general. New Statesman 27 Nov 1943.
Young, P. M. George Eliot and music. Music & Letters 24 1943.
Bisson, L. A. Proust, Bergson and George Eliot. MLR 40 1945.
Dodds, M. H. George Eliot and Charles Dickens. N & Q 6 April 1946.
Hinkley, L. In her Ladies of literature, New York 1946.
McCullough, B. In his Representative English novelists, Defoe to Conrad, New York 1946.
Pritchett, V. S. In his Living novel, 1946.
Stebbins, L. P. In her Victorian album, New York 1946.
Baily, F. E. In his Six great Victorian novelists, 1947.
Bullett, G. George Eliot: her life and books. 1947.
Rendall, V. George Eliot and the classics. N & Q 13, 27 Dec 1947, 3 April, 26 June 1948.
Bennett, J. George Eliot: her mind and art. 1948.
T., C. George Eliot in defence of George Lewes. More Books 23 1948.
Hough, G. George Eliot. Horizon Jan 1948.
Leavis, F. R. In his Great tradition, 1948.
Naumann, W. The architecture of George Eliot's novels. MLQ 9 1948.
Simon, I. In her Formes du roman anglais de Dickens à Joyce, Liège 1949.
—— Innocence in the novels of George Eliot. In English studies today, ed G. A. Bonnard, Berne 1961.
Willey, B. In his Nineteenth-century studies, Coleridge to Matthew Arnold, 1949.
Bissell, C. T. Social analysis in the novels of George Eliot. ELH 18 1951.
Cooper, L. George Eliot. 1951.
Arthos, J. George Eliot: the art of vision. Revista di Letterature Moderne 3 1952.
Hanson, L. and E. Marian Evans and George Eliot. 1952.
Holloway, J. In his Victorian sage, 1953.
Casey, W. George Eliot's theory of fiction. West Virginia Univ Bull 9 1953.
Speaight, R. George Eliot. 1954.
Svaglic, M. J. Religion in the novels of George Eliot. JEGP 53 1954.
West, A. The higher humbug. New Yorker 2 Oct 1954. Replies by G. S. Haight 6 Nov 1954, A. West 13 Nov 1954.
House, H. Qualities of George Eliot's unbelief. In his All in due time, 1955.
Kaminsky, A. R. George Eliot, G. H. Lewes and the novel. PMLA 70 1955.
Leavis, Q. D. A note on literary indebtedness: Dickens, George Eliot, Henry Sands. Hudson Rev 8 1955.
Murphy, H. R. The ethical revolt against Christian orthodoxy in early Victorian England. Amer Historical Rev 60 1955.
O'Brien, K. George Eliot: a moralizing fabulist. Essays by Divers Hands new ser 27 1955.
Rust, J. D. George Eliot on the Blithedale romance. Boston Public Lib Quart 7 1955.
—— The art of fiction in George Eliot's reviews. RES new ser 7 1956.
Praz, M. In his Hero in eclipse in Victorian fiction, 1956.
Stone, W. H. Hale White and George Eliot. UTQ 25 1956.
Beaty, J. George Eliot's notebook for an unwritten novel. Princeton Univ Lib Chron 18 1957.
Hardy, B. The image of the opiate in George Eliot's novels. N & Q 10 Nov 1957.
—— The novels of George Eliot. 1959.
Hyde, W. J. George Eliot and the climate of realism. PMLA 72 1957.
Owens, R. J. The effect of George Eliot's linguistic interests on her work. N & Q 10 July 1957.
Stang, R. The literary criticism of George Eliot. PMLA 72 1957.
—— Discussions of George Eliot. Boston 1960.
Walters, G. A memory of George Eliot. Listener 2 June 1957.
Maheu, P. G. La pensée religieuse et morale de George Eliot. Paris 1959.
Paris, B. J. George Eliot's unpublished poetry. SP 56 1959.
—— George Eliot, science fiction and fantasy. Extrapolation 5 1964.
—— Experiments in life: George Eliot's quest for values. Detroit 1965.
Stump, R. Movement and vision in George Eliot's novels. Seattle 1959.
Thale, J. The novels of George Eliot. New York 1959.
Carroll, D. R. An image of disenchantment in the novels of George Eliot. RES new ser 11 1960.
Crompton, M. George Eliot: the woman. 1960.
Allott, M. George Eliot in the 1860's. Victorian Stud 5 1961.
Auchincloss, L. In his Reflections of a Jacobite, New York 1961.
Harvey, W. J. The art of George Eliot. 1961.
McKenzie, K. A. Edith Simcox and George Eliot. 1961.
—— George Eliot and George Sand. Jnl of Australian Lang & Lit Assoc 1964.
Masters, D. C. George Eliot and the Evangelicals. Dalhousie Rev 41 1961.
Levine, G. Determinism and responsibility in the works of George Eliot. PMLA 77 1962.
—— Isabel, Gwendolen and Dorothea. ELH 30 1963.
Yuill, W. E. Character is fate: a note on Thomas Hardy, George Eliot and Novalis. MLR 57 1962.
Worth, G. J. The intruder motif in George Eliot's fiction. In Six studies in nineteenth-century English literature and thought, ed H. Orel and G. J. Worth, Lawrence Kansas 1962.

Cox, C. B. In his Free spirit, 1963.
Katona, A. Problems of adjustment in George Eliot's early novels. Acta Litteraria & Academica Scientiarum Hungaricae 6 1963.
McAuley, J. Edmund Spenser and George Eliot. Hobart 1963.
Milner, I. George Eliot and the limits of Victorian realism. Philologica Pragensia 6 1963.
Pinney, T. George Eliot's reading of Wordsworth. Victorian Newsletter no 24 1963.
Rubenstein, E. L. A forgotten tale by George Eliot. Nineteenth-Century Fiction 17 1963.
Sambrook, A. J. The natural historian of our social classes. English 14 1963.
Wade, R. George Eliot and her poetry. Contemporary Rev July 1963.
Allen, W. George Eliot. New York 1964.
Feltes, N. N. George Eliot and the unified sensibility. PMLA 79 1964.
Knoepflmacher, U. C. George Eliot, Feuerbach and the question of criticism. Victorian Stud 7 1964.
—— Religious humanism and the Victorian novel. Princeton 1965.
Ledger, M. A. George Eliot and Nathaniel Hawthorne. N & Q June 1964.
Merton, S. George Eliot and William Hale White. Victorian Newsletter no 25 1964.
Thomson, P. The three Georges. Nineteenth-Century Fiction 18 1964.
Mansell, D. Ruskin and George Eliot's realism. Criticism 7 1965.
—— George Eliot's conception of form. Stud in Eng Lit 1500–1900 5 1965.
Tillotson, G. and K. The George Eliot letters. In their Mid-Victorian studies, 1965.
Adam, I. Character and destiny in George Eliot's fiction. Nineteenth-Century Fiction 20 1966.

W. J. H.

V. MINOR FICTION 1835–1870

This section has been restricted, with one or two exceptions, to novelists born after 1799 and before 1831.

WILLIAM HARRISON AINSWORTH 1805–82

Bibliographies

Locke, H. A bibliographical catalogue of the published novels and ballads of Ainsworth. 1925.

Collections

Works. 14 vols 1850–1. With a memoir by S. L. Blanchard.
Collected works. 16 vols 1875, 31 vols 1878–80, 12 vols 1923.
There is no complete edn of Ainsworth's writings.

§1

Poems by Cheviot Tichburn. 1822.
Monody on the death of John Philip Kemble. Manchester 1823.
December tales. 1823.
The Boeotian. Manchester 1824.
The works of Cheviot Tichburn. Manchester 1825.
A summer evening tale. 1825.
Consideration on the best means of affording immediate relief to the operative classes in the manufacturing districts. 1826.
Letters from cockney lands. 1826, 1827.
Sir John Chiverton: a romance. 1826. Anon; in collaboration with J. P. Aston.
May fair, in four cantos. 1827.
Rookwood: a romance. 3 vols 1834 (anon), 1834, 1835, 1836, Paris 1836, 1837, Leipzig 1837, 1851, 1857, 1875 etc.
Crichton. 3 vols 1837, Paris 1837, 3 vols 1849 (rev), 1853, 1854 etc.
Jack Sheppard: a romance. 1839, 15 weekly pts 1840, 1 vol 1840, 1854, 1856, 1862, 1865, 1884 etc. First pbd in Bentley's Miscellany 1839–40.
The Tower of London. 13 monthly pts 1840; 1 vol 1840, 1842, 1842, 1843, 1844, 1845, 1853, 1854, 1878, 1882 etc.
Guy Fawkes, or the gunpowder treason: an historical romance. 3 vols 1841, 1857, 1878, 1884, 1891. First pbd in Bentley's Miscellany Jan 1840–Nov 1841.

Old Saint Paul's: a tale of the Plague and the Fire. 12 monthly pts 1841; 3 vols 1841, 1847, 1855, 1857, 1884, 1891 etc. First pbd in Sunday Times Jan-Dec 1841.
The miser's daughter: a tale. 3 vols 1842, 1843, 1848, 1855, 1879, 1886, 1892. First pbd in Ainsworth's Mag 1842.
Modern chivalry: or a new Orlando Furioso. 2 vols 1843. With Catherine Gore.
Windsor castle: an historical romance. 3 vols 1843, 1843, 11 pts 1843–4, 1 vol 1844, 1847, 1853, 1878, 1884, 1891 etc. First pbd in Ainsworth's Mag 1842–3.
Saint James's, or the Court of Queen Anne: an historical romance. 3 vols 1844, 1846, 1853, 1879, 1889. First pbd in Ainsworth's Mag 1884.
James the Second, or the revolution of 1688: an historical romance. 3 vols 1848, 1854, 1890.
The Lancashire witches: a novel. 1849 (priv ptd), 3 vols 1849 (as The Lancashire witches: a romance of Pendle forest), 1854, 1878, 1884. First pbd in Sunday Times 1848.
Life and adventures of Mervyn Clitheroe. 12 monthly pts Dec 1851–March 1852, Dec 1857–June 1858; 1 vol 1858 (as Mervyn Clitheroe).
The Star Chamber: an historical romance. 2 vols 1854, 1857, 1861, 1879, 1889, 1892. First pbd in Home Companion 1853.
The flitch of bacon: or the custom of Dunmow. 1854, 1855, 1874, 1879, 1889, 1892. First pbd in New Monthly Mag 1853–4.
Ballads: romantic, fantastical and humorous. 1855, [1872] (with memoir of Ainsworth by J. Crossley, and adding The combat of the thirty). Rptd from the novels.
The spendthrift: a tale. 1857, 1879, 1889, 1892. First pbd in Bentley's Miscellany 1855–7.
The combat of the thirty, from a Breton lay of the fourteenth century. 1859.
Ovingdean Grange: a tale of the South Downs. 1860, 1879, 1891. First pbd in Bentley's Miscellany 1859–60.
The Constable of the Tower: an historical romance. 3 vols 1861, 1880, 1906. First pbd in Bentley's Miscellany 1861.
The Lord Mayor of London: or city life in the last century. 3 vols 1862, 1880, 1906. First pbd in Bentley's Miscellany 1862.

Cardinal Pole or the days of Philip and Mary: an historical romance. 3 vols 1863, 1864, 1881 etc. First pbd in Bentley's Miscellany 1862–3.
John Law the projector. 3 vols 1864, 1866, 1881. First pbd in Bentley's Miscellany 1863–4.
The Spanish match: or Charles Stuart at Madrid. 3 vols 1865, 1865, 1880, 1894. First published in Bentley's Mag 1864–5 as The house of seven chimneys.
Auriol: or the elixir of life. 1865 (with The old London merchant, and A night's adventure in Rome–2 short stories), [1875], 1875, 1881, 1890, 1892. First pbd in Ainsworth's Mag and New Monthly Mag 1844–6.
The Constable de Bourbon. 3 vols 1866, 1880. First pbd in Bentley's Miscellany 1865–6.
Old Court: a novel. 3 vols 1867; 1880. First pbd in Bentley's Miscellany 1866–7.
Myddleton Pomfret: a novel. 3 vols 1868, 1881. First pbd in Bentley's Miscellany 1867–8.
Hilary St Ives: a novel. 3 vols 1870, 1881. First pbd in New Monthly Mag 1869.
The South Sea Bubble: a tale of the year 1720. [1871], 1902. First pbd in Bow Bells 1868.
Talbot Harland. 1871. First pbd in Bow Bells 1870.
Tower Hill. [1871]. First pbd in Bow Bells 1871.
Boscobel, or the Royal Oak: a tale of the year 1651. 3 vols 1872, 1874, 1875, 1879, 1889. First pbd in New Monthly Mag 1872.
The good old times: the story of the Manchester rebels of '45. 3 vols 1873, 1874 (as The Manchester rebels of the fatal '45), 1880, 1884, 1890, 1892, 1893.
Merry England: or nobles and serfs. 3 vols 1874, [1875]. First pbd in Bow Bells 1874.
The goldsmith's wife: a tale. 3 vols 1875, [1875]. First pbd in Bow Bells 1874.
Preston Fight, or the insurrection of 1715: a tale. 3 vols 1875, 1879.
Chetwynd Calverley: a tale. 3 vols 1876, [1877]. First pbd in Bow Bells 1876.
The leaguer of Lathom: a tale of the Civil War in Lancashire. 3 vols 1876, 1880.
The fall of Somerset. 3 vols 1877, [1878]. First pbd in Bow Bells 1877–8.
Beatrice Tyldesley. 3 vols 1878, [1879]. First pbd in Bow Bells 1878.
Beau Nash: or Bath in the eighteenth century. 3 vols [1879], 1880, 1881, 1889.
Stanley Brereton. 3 vols [1881], 1882, 1884. First pbd in Bolton Weekly Jnl 1881.
Ainsworth edited Bentley's Miscellany *from March 1840, and from 1842 began the pbn of* Ainsworth's Magazine *which lasted until 1853, when he bought* The New Monthly Magazine. *From 1821 to 1881 he contributed many stories and serials, with a few poems, to Arliss's Pocket Mag, Edinburgh Mag, European Mag, London Mag, Keepsake and other annuals, Fraser's Mag, Bentley's Miscellany, Sunday Times, Ainsworth's Mag, New Monthly Mag, Home Companion and Bow Bells.*

§2

Horne, R. H. In his A new spirit of the age vol 2, 1844.
Friswell, J. H. In his Modern men of letters, 1870.
Maginn, W. In his A gallery of illustrious characters 1830–8, ed W. Bates [1873].
Evans, J. The early life of Ainsworth. 1882.
Axon, W. E. A. Ainsworth: a memoir. 1902.
Gribble, F. Estimate of Ainsworth. Fortnightly Rev March 1905.
Shelley, H. C. Untrodden English ways. 1910.
Ellis, S. M. Ainsworth and his friends. 2 vols 1911. Includes bibliography.
Elwin, M. In his Victorian wallflowers, 1934.
Parsons, C. O. The friendship of Theodore Martin and Ainsworth. N & Q 23 June 1934.
—— Ainsworth's use of John Elwes in the Miser's daughter. N & Q 24 Aug 1946.
Mason, L. William Harrison Ainsworth. Dickensian 36 1939.
Weber, C. J. Ainsworth and Thomas Hardy. RES 17 1941.
Bevan, B. Harrison Ainsworth. Contemporary Rev Aug 1955.
Hollingsworth, K. In his Newgate novel 1830–47, Detroit 1963.

WILLIAM EDMONDSTOUNE AYTOUN
1813–65

See col 503, above.

'A. J. BARROWCLIFFE', ALBERT JULIUS MOTT

Amberhill: or guilty peace. 2 vols 1856, 1862.
Trust for trust. 3 vols 1859.
Normanton. 1862, 1865.

'CUTHBERT BEDE', EDWARD BRADLEY
1827–89

The adventures of Mr Verdant Green, an Oxford freshman; with numerous illustrations designed and drawn on the wood by the author: 'a college joke to cure the dumps'. 1853.
The further adventures of Mr Verdant Green, an Oxford undergraduate: being a continuation of the Adventures of Mr Verdant Green, an Oxford freshman, with illustrations by the author. 1854.
Mr Verdant Green married and done for: being the third and concluding part of the Adventures of Mr Verdant Green, an Oxford freshman. 1857. The 3 pts have been frequently rptd together as Mr Verdant Green, with illustrations by the author.
Motley: prose and verse, grave and gay, with illustrations by the author. 1855.
Love's provocations: being extracts taken in the most unmanly and unmannerly manner from the diary of Miss Polly C——; illustrations by the author. 1855.
Photographic pleasures popularly portrayed with pen and pencil. 1855.
Medley. [1856].
The shilling book of beauty, edited and illustrated by Cuthbert Bede. 1856.
Tales of college life. 1856, 1862 (as College life).
Nearer and dearer, a tale of out school: a novelette illustrated by the author. 1857.
Fairy fables, with illustrations by Alfred Crowquill. 1858.
Funny figures, by A. Funnyman. 1858. 'One shilling plain: two shillings coloured,' the latter with 24 coloured pictures.
Happy hours at Wynford Grange: a story for children, with coloured illustrations. 1859.
Glencreggan: or a highland home in Cantire, illustrated from the author's drawings. 2 vols 1861.
Our new rector: or the village of Norton, edited by Cuthbert Bede. 1861.
The curate of Cranston; with other prose and verse. 1862.
A tour in tartan-land. 1863.
The visitor's handbook to Rosslyn and Hawthornden. 1864.
The white wife; with other stories, supernatural, romantic, legendary, collected and illustrated by Cuthbert Bede. 1865.
The rook's garden: essays and sketches. 1865.

Mattins and muttons, or the Beauty of Brighton: a love story. 2 vols 1866.
Round the peat fire at Glenbrechy, with illustrations by the author. Xmas no of Once a Week 1869.
Little Mr Bouncer and his friend Verdant Green, with illustrations by the author. 1873.
'Cuthbert Bede' was a frequent contributor to Punch, All the Year Round, Field, GM, Once a Week, St James's Mag, London Rev, Quiver, Boy's Own Paper, Illustr London News and N & Q.

RICHARD DODDRIDGE BLACKMORE

1825–1900

Bibliographies

Keogh, A. In W. L. Phelps, Essays on modern novelists, New York 1910, pp. 265–7.
Dunn, W. H. In his R. D. Blackmore: the author of Lorna Doone, 1956. *See* also Bernbaum and Carter under §2, below.

§1

Poems by Melanter. 1854.
Epullia [and other poems], by the author of Poems by Melanter. 1854.
The bugle of the Black Sea: or the British in the East, by Melanter. 1855.
The fate of Franklin. 1860.
The farm and fruit of old: a translation in verse of the first and second Georgics of Virgil, by a market-gardener. 1862.
Clara Vaughan: a novel. 3 vols 1864, 1872 (rev).
Cradock Nowell: a tale of the New Forest. 3 vols 1866, 1873 (rev). First pbd in Macmillan's Mag May 1865–Aug 1866.
Lorna Doone: a romance of Exmoor. 3 vols 1869, 1873 (6th edn); ed H. S. Ward, New York 1908; ed H. Warren, Oxford 1914 (WC); ed R. O. Morris 1920.
The Georgics of Virgil, translated. 1871; ed R. S. Conway 1932.
The maid of Sker. 3 vols Edinburgh 1872, 1873. First pbd in Blackwood's Mag Aug 1871–July 1872.
Alice Lorraine; a tale of the South Downs. 3 vols 1875, 1876 (6th edn rev). First pbd in Blackwood's Mag March 1874–April 1875.
Cripps the carrier: a woodland tale. 3 vols 1876, 1877.
Erema: or my father's sin. 3 vols 1877, 1878. First pbd in Cornhill Mag Nov 1876–Nov 1877.
Figaro at Hastings, St Leonards, with illustrations by the author. 1877.
Mary Anerley: a Yorkshire tale. 3 vols 1880, 1881. First pbd in Fraser's Mag July 1879–Sept 1880.
Christowell: a Dartmoor tale. 3 vols 1882, 1882. First pbd in Good Words Jan–Dec 1881.
The remarkable history of Sir Thomas Upmore Bart MP, formerly known as 'Tommy Upmore'. 2 vols 1884, 1884, 1885.
Humour, wit and satire: containing i Book of beauty; ii Motley; iii Medley, with numerous illustrations by the author. 1885.
Fotheringay and Mary Queen of Scots: being an account, historical and descriptive, of Fotheringay Castle, the last prison of Mary Queen of Scots and the scene of her trial and execution, with illustrations by the author. 1886. First pbd in Leisure Hour 1865.
Springhaven: a tale of the great war. 3 vols 1887. First pbd in Harper's Mag April 1886–April 1887.
Betrothal ring of Mary Queen of Scots 1565: a description of the Darnley ring discovered in 1820 by a labourer, Robert Wyatt, when digging in the eastern mound on which stood the eastern keep of Fotheringay Castle; printed for the Tercentenary of Mary Queen of Scots Exhibition held at Peterborough. 1887.
Kit and Kitty: a story of west Middlesex. 3 vols 1890, New York [1890].
Perlycross: a tale of the western hills. 3 vols 1894, New York 1894, 1894.
Fringilla: a tale in verse. 1895.
Tales from the telling house. 1896.
Dariel: a romance of Surrey. 1897, New York 1897.
Argyll's highlands: or MacCailein Mor and the Lords of Lorne; with traditional tales. Ed J. Mackay, Glasgow 1902.

§2

For a fuller list see Q. G. Burris, Richard Doddridge Blackmore, Urbana 1930, pp. 212–16.
Smith, G. B. Mr Blackmore's novels. International Rev 7 1879.
The novels of Mr Blackmore. Blackwood's Mag Sept 1896.
Snell, F. J. The Blackmore country. 1906.
Phelps, W. L. Lorna Doone. In Essays on modern novelists, New York 1910.
Bernbaum, E. Blackmore and American cordiality. Southwest Rev 11 1925.
—— On Blackmore and Lorna Doone: a selected bibliography, with brief comments. Lib Jnl 15 June 1925.
Burris, Q. G. Blackmore: his life and novels. Urbana 1930.
Elwin, M. In his Victorian wallflowers, 1934.
Etherington, J. R. M. Blackmore and his illustrators. N & Q 24 March 1945.
—— Blackmore and a libel suit. N & Q 15 Dec 1945.
—— Blackmore. New Eng Rev 13 1946.
Gill, W. W. and M. Words in Lorna Doone. N & Q 19 Oct, 30 Nov 1946.
Seybolt, P. S. Blackmore's Poems by Melanter. New Colophon 2 1950.
Dunn, W. H. R. D. Blackmore. N & Q Nov 1953.
—— Blackmore: the author of Lorna Doone. 1956.
Hyde, W. J. Social propaganda in Blackmore. N & Q April 1954.
Buckler, W. E. Blackmore's novels before Lorna Doone. Nineteenth-Century Fiction 10 1956.
Budd, K. The last Victorian: Blackmore and his novels. 1960.
Carter, J. A. Supplement to Blackmore bibliography. N & Q Aug 1962.

ARCHIBALD BOYD

The Duchess, or woman's love and woman's hate: a romance. 3 vols 1850. Anon.
The Crown ward: a novel. 3 vols 1856.
The Cardinal: a romance. 3 vols 1858.

CHARLES WILLIAM SHIRLEY BROOKS

1816–74

See col 1147, below.

ROBERT BARNABAS BROUGH

1828–60

See col 1147, below.

FRANCES BROWNE

1816–79

The star of Attéghéi; the vision of Schwartz; and other poems. 1844.
Lyrics and miscellaneous poems. Edinburgh 1848.
The Ericksons; the clever boy: or consider one another. Edinburgh 1852.
Pictures and songs of home. [1856].
Granny's wonderful chair and its tales of fairy times. 1857 (for 1856); ed R. L. Green 1963.
Our uncle the traveller: stories. 1859.
The young foresters. [1860].
The orphans of Elfholm. 1860.
My share of the world, an autobiography [a novel]. 3 vols 1861.
The Castleford case. 3 vols 1862.
The hidden sin: a novel. 3 vols 1866. Anon.
The exile's trust: a tale of the French Revolution, and other stories. [1869].
The nearest neighbour and other stories. [1875].
The dangerous guest: a story of 1745. [1886].
The foundling of the fens: a story of a flood. [1886].
The first of the African diamonds. [1887].

EDWARD GEORGE EARLE LYTTON BULWER-LYTTON, 1st BARON LYTTON

1802–73

Bibliographies

Dahl, C. In Victorian fiction, ed L. Stevenson, Cambridge Mass 1964.

Collections

Novels. 10 vols 1840.
Dramatic works. 1841, 1859, 1863, 1873, [1887], [1890]. Includes (in addn to The Duchess de la Vallière, The lady of Lyons, Richelieu, Money) odes on Elizabeth, Cromwell, Nelson.
Critical and miscellaneous works. 2 vols Philadelphia 1841.
Poems, collected and arranged by C. D. Macleod. New York 1845.
Poetic and dramatic works. 5 vols 1848, 1852–4.
Novels. 41 vols 1859–62, 22 vols 1877–8 (Library edn).
Poetical works. 1859, 1865, 1873.
Novels and romances. 43 vols 1864, 23 vols 1867, 11 vols 1868.
Miscellaneous prose works. 3 vols 1868.
Speeches, with memoir by his son. 2 vols 1874.
Works. 38 vols 1874, 26 vols 1877–8 (Knebworth edn).
Novels. 29 vols 1895–8 (New Knebworth edn).

§1

Ismael: an oriental tale, with other poems. 1820.
Delmour: or the tale of sylphid, and other peoms. 1823. Anon.
Sculpture: a poem which obtained the Chancellor's Medal, July 1825. Cambridge 1825.
Weeds and wild flowers, by E.G.L.B. Paris 1826 (priv ptd).
Falkland. 1827, 2 vols Paris 1833, [1876] etc.
O'Neill: or the rebel. 1827, Paris 1829.
Pelham: or the adventures of a gentleman. 3 vols 1828, 1839, 1854, 1860, 1873, Paris 1874, 1877 etc.
The disowned. 4 vols 1828, 3 vols 1829, 1831, 2 vols 1835, 1852, 1855, Paris 1858, 1874 etc.
Devereux: a tale. 3 vols 1829, 1831, 1836, 1839, 1841, 1852, 1855, Paris 1859, 1861, 1874, 1879 etc.
Paul Clifford. 3 vols 1830, 1835, Stockholm 1835, 1854, 2 vols Paris 1858, 1860, 1861, 1874, 1878, [1879], 1880 etc.
The Siamese twins: a satirical tale of the times. 1831.
Eugene Aram. 3 vols 1832, 2 vols Paris 1832, 1849, 1854, 1861, [1873], Paris 1873, 1877, 1878, 1879, [1881] etc.
Asmodens at large. 1833, Philadelphia 1833.
England and the English. 2 vols 1833, Paris 1833, 1834 (3rd edn with new preface), 1840, 1874, [1887].
Godolphin. 3 vols 1833 (anon), 1850, 1854, 1860, 1862, 1874, 1879 etc.
A letter to a late Cabinet Minister on the crisis. [1834] (20 edns).
The last days of Pompeii. 3 vols 1834, 1835 ('revised and corrected'), 2 vols Brussels 1837, 1839, 1850, 1854, 1856, 1861, 1872, 1873, [1879], 1880, [1881], [1883], [1884] etc; ed E. Johnson, New York 1956.
The pilgrims of the Rhine. 1834, Frankfurt 1838, London 1840, 1850, 1854, 1860, 1861, 1865 etc.
Rienzi, the last of the Roman Tribunes. 3 vols 1835, 2 vols Milan 1836, 1837, 1854, 2 vols Paris 1859, London 1861, 1874, 1878, [1879], [1883], [1885] etc.
The student: a series of papers. 2 vols 1835, 1840.
Literary remains of William Hazlitt, with thoughts on his genius and writings. 2 vols 1836.
The Duchess de la Vallière. 1836.
Athens: its rise and fall. 2 vols 1837, 1874, 2 vols nd.
Ernest Maltravers, 3 vols 1837, 1851, 1854, Paris 1859, London 1861, 1873, 1876, 1877, 1879, 1880 etc.
Leila: or the siege of Granada. Berlin 1837, London 1838, 1847, 9 pts 1850 (as Leila and Calderon the courtier), 1855, 1862, 1878 (with original title), 1879.
Alice: or the mysteries. 3 vols 1838, 1852, 1854, 1860, 1873, 1875, [1879], 1880 etc.
Richelieu: or the conspiracy. 1839, 1850, 1873, [1881], [1885], Paris 1897.
The sea captain, or the birthright: a drama. 1839, Paris 1840, [1885].
Money: a comedy. 1840, 1848, 1851, 1873, 1874, [1883], [1885] etc.
Night and morning. 3 vols 1841, 1851, 1854, 2 vols 1876, 1878, Paris 1879, [1880], [1889] etc.
Eva, the ill-omened marriage and other poems. 1842.
Zanoni. 3 vols 1842, 1853, 1856, Paris 1858, London 1860, 1862, [1880], [1892] etc.
The last of the Barons. 3 vols 1843, 1850, 1854, 1860, 1874, 1878, 1884, [1888] etc; ed F. C. Romilly 1913.
Poems of Schiller. 2 vols 1844, 1852, 1859, 1870, 1877, [1887], [1889].
Confessions of a water patient, in a letter to W. Harrison Ainsworth. 1846.
Lucretia: or children of the night. 3 vols 1846, 2 vols Leipzig 1846, 1 vol 1847, 1853, 1855, 1860, 2 vols 1863, 1874, 1877, 1889.
The new Timon. 1846.
The works of Laman Blanchard; sketches from life. 3 vols 1846. With long introd by Lytton.
A word to the public. 1847.
Harold, the last of the Saxons. 3 vols 1848, 1848, 1853, 1855, 1866, 1874, 1892 etc; ed G. L. Gomme [1906].
King Arthur: an epic poem. 3 pts 1848–9, 2 vols 1849, 1870 (rev), [1888].
The Caxtons: a family picture. 3 vols 1849, 2 vols 1849, 1853, 1854, 1855, 1874, 1890, 1892, 1896, [1898], [1899] etc. First pbd anon in Blackwood's Mag.
Letters to John Bull esquire. 1851.
Not so bad as we seem, or many sides to a character: a comedy. 1851, 1853.

Outlines of the early history of the East: a lecture, delivered at the Royston Mechanics' Institute. Royston 1852.
'My novel', by Pisistratus Caxton: or varieties in English life. Paris 1852, 4 vols 1853, 1854, 1856, 1861, 2 vols Paris [1861], London 1892. First pbd in Blackwood's Mag.
Address to the associated societies of the University of Edinburgh on his installation as their honorary president and his speech at the public dinner, January 20th 1854. Edinburgh 1854.
Speech delivered at the Leeds Mechanics' Institution. 1854.
The haunted and the haunters. 1857, 1905 etc.
Speech on the representation of the people bill, delivered in the House of Commons, March 22nd 1859. 1859.
What will he do with it? by Pisistratus Caxton. 4 vols 1859, 1860, 2 vols Paris 1860, 1864, 1875, 1892, 1902. First pbd in Blackwood's Mag.
St Stephen's: a poem. 1860. First pbd in Blackwood's Mag.
The new Reform Bill: speech delivered in the House of Commons, revised and corrected by the author. 1860.
A strange story. 2 vols 1862 (3 edns), 1863 (rev), 1864, 1865, 1875, 1886, Madrid 1893, 1928. First pbd in Blackwood's Mag.
Caxtoniana. 2 vols 1863, 1875.
The boatman by Pisistratus Caxton. 1864. First pbd in Blackwood's Mag.
Lost tales of Miletus. 1866, 1870.
The Princess Alexandra gift book. Ed J. Sherer 1868. Contains contributions by Lytton.
The rightful heir. 1868, Leipzig 1869.
The odes and epodes of Horace: a metrical translation into English. 1869, 1872, [1887], 1894.
Walpole: or every man has his price. 1869.
The coming race. 1871 (anon), 1872, 1873, 1874, 1875, 1886, Madrid 1893, 1928. First pbd in Blackwood's Mag.
Kenelm Chillingly: his adventures and opinions. 3 vols 1873, 1874, 1875, [1876], 1878, 1892, 1904 etc.
The Parisians. 4 vols 1873, Edinburgh [1873], 2 vols 1876, 1878, [1890], 1892. First pbd in Blackwood's Mag.
Pamphlets and sketches. 1875.
Quarterly essays. 1875.
Parisanias the Spartan. 1876. An unfinished historical romance ed Lytton's son.
Letter of Bulwer-Lytton to Macready 1836–66. Hasark NJ 1911 (Carteret Book Club).
Lytton also pbd the following poems in Knight's Quart Mag under the pseudonym 'Edmund Bruce': Poems to Zoe (June 1823); The first songstresses in town (Oct 1823); Narenor: a tale, I, sonnet to A.T. on her birthday (April 1824); Madame Catalani, sonnet written on the first leaf of Keats' poems, Despair, Song, To M . . . (Jan 1824); II (Aug 1824).
New Monthly Mag 33–48 *was ed Lytton and contains many articles, poems and sketches from his pen. For a list see appendix to* M. Sadleir, Bulwer: a panorama, 1931.

§2

'North, Christopher' (J. Wilson). Noctes ambrosianae. Blackwood's Mag March 1829.
[Landon, L. E.] Bulwer as a man and a novelist. New Monthly Mag May 1831.
Bulwer. Quart Rev 48 1832. An attack.
Laube, H. Bulwer und der Saint-Simonismus. In Moderne Charackteristiken, 2 vols Mannheim 1835.
Carlyle, T. The dandiacal body. In Sartor Resartus, Boston 1836. First pbd in Fraser's Mag Aug 1834.
Planché, G. In his Portraits littéraires vol i, Paris 1836.
Chorley, H. F. In his Authors of England, 1838.
'Yellowplush, C. J.' (W. M. Thackeray). Epistle to Sir Edward Lytton Bulwer Bart. Fraser's Mag Jan 1840; rptd in Thackeray's Works in the Yellowplush correspondence.
Horne, R. H. In his A new spirit of the age vol 2, 1844.
Lowell, J. R. The new Timon. North Amer Rev 64 1847.
Powell, T. In his Pictures of the living authors of England, 1851.
Oliphant, M. O. Bulwer. Blackwood's Mag Feb 1855.
Gilfillan, G. In his Galleries of literary portraits vol 2, Edinburgh 1856.
'Rochester, Mark' (C. Kent). The Derby Ministry: a series of Cabinet pictures. 1858.
Senior, N. W. In his Essays on fiction, 1864.
Friswell, J. H. In his Modern men of letters, 1870.
Böddeker, K. Über Bulwers Übersetzungen Schillerischer Gedichte. Archiv 49 1872.
Reid, T. W. In his Cabinet portraits, 1872.
Cooper, T. Lord Lytton: a biography. 1873.
Frost, W. A. Lord Lytton: the man and the author. 1873.
—— Bulwer Lytton: errors of his biographers. 1913.
Jowett, B. Lord Lytton: the man and the author; to which is attached a biography by M. Marsden. 1873.
Tawle, G. M. Reminiscences of Lytton. Appleton's Jnl 9 1873.
Ten Brink, J. E. G. Bulwer-Lytton: biografie en kritick. Haarlem 1873.
Maginn, W. A. In his A gallery of illustrious characters 1830–8, ed W. Bates [1873].
Heywood, J. C. How they strike me. Philadelphia 1877.
'Lytton, Lady'. A blighted life. 1880. Authorship denied by Rosina Bulwer-Lytton.
Lennox, W. P. Plays and players. 2 vols 1881.
The life, letters and literary remains, edited by his son. 2 vols 1883.
Letters of the late Edward Bulwer, Lord Lytton, to his wife, published in vindication of her memory. Ed L. Devey 1884.
Walsh, W. S. In his Pen pictures of Victorian authors, New York 1884.
Watt, J. C. In his Great novelists, [1885].
Devey, L. The life of Rosina Lady Lytton. 1887.
Griswold, H. T. In his Home life of great authors, Chicago 1887.
Matthews, W. In his Men, places and things, Chicago 1887.
Jeaffreson, J. C. In his Novels and novelists, 2 vols 1888.
Cooke, P. J. Bulwer-Lytton's plays. [1894].
Saintsbury, G. The poetry of Lytton. Forum 22 1896.
Howells, W. D. Nydia. Harper's Bazaar 25 Aug 1900.
Lord, W. F. The novels of Lytton. Nineteenth Century Sept 1901.
—— The wand of Prospero. Nineteenth Century Jan 1924.
A sketch from memory. Macmillan's Mag March 1901.
The last days of Pompeii: contemporary criticism. Bookman (New York) July 1903.
Cazamian, L. In his Le roman social en Angleterre 1830–50, Paris 1903.
McCarthy, J. In his Portraits of the sixties, 1903.
Wilstack, P. Dramatizations of Lytton. Bookman (New York) July 1903.
A visit to Bulwer-Lytton at Knebworth in 1857. Blackwood's Mag Jan 1905.
'Melville, Lewis' (L. S. Benjamin). In his Victorian novelists, 1906.
Escott, T. H. S. Edward Bulwer, first Baron Lytton of Knebworth. 1910.
Lytton, V. A. G. R. B. The life of Lytton, by his grandson. 2 vols 1913.
—— Bulwer-Lytton. 1948.
Gosse, E. The life of Bulwer. Fortnightly Rev Dec 1913.
Bell, E. G. An introduction to the prose romances, plays and comedies of Bulwer. Chicago 1914.
The unpublished letters of Lady Bulwer Lytton to A. E. Chalon. Ed S. M. Ellis 1914.
Messac, R. Bulwer-Lytton et Dostoievski: de Paul Clifford à Raskolnikof. Revue de Littérature Comparée 6 1926.

Qualia, C. B. French dramatic sources of Bulwer-Lytton's Richelieu. PMLA 42 1927.
Stewart, C. N. Bulwer-Lytton as an Occultist. 1927.
'Maurois, André' (E. S. W. Herzog). Les derniers jours de Pompéi. Paris 1928; tr Southwest Rev 16 1930. A study of Lytton and his wife.
Liljegren, S. B. Quelques romans anglais: source partielle d'une religion nouvelle. In Mélanges Baldensperger vol 2, Paris 1930. On Lytton and theosophy.
—— Bulwer-Lytton's novels and Isis unveiled. Upsala 1957.
Sheppard, A. T. In his Art and practice of historical fiction, 1930.
Stevenson, L. Stepfathers of Victorianism. Virginia Quart 6 1930.
Sadleir, M. Bulwer, a panorama: i, Edward and Rosina 1803–36. 1931.
Bangs, A. R. Mephistophiles in England: or the confessions of a Prime Minister. PMLA 47 1932. Here attributed to Lytton.
R., V. The Athenaeum and Bulwer Lytton. N & Q 23 Feb 1935.
Seifert, H. Bulwers Verhältnis zur Geschichte. Leipzig 1935 (priv ptd).
Watts, H. H. Lytton's theories of prose fiction. PMLA 50 1935.
Rosa, M. W. The Silver Fork School: novels of fashion preceding Vanity Fair. New York 1936.
Pritchett, V. S. Books in general. New Statesman 15 April 1944.
Dickson, S. The Bulwer-Lytton Collection. Princeton Lib Chron 8 1946.
Gillen, F. Letters by Bulwer-Lytton. More Books 22 1947.
Letters of Bulwer-Lytton to Richard Bentley 1829–73. Bodleian Lib Record 2 1948.
Hollingsworth, K. Who suggested the plan for Bulwer's Paul Clifford? MLN 63 1948.
—— Bulwer's Paul Clifford again. MLN 66 1951.
—— In his Newgate novel 1830–47, Detroit 1963.
Shattuck, C. H. Bulwer and Victorian censorship. Quart Jnl of Speech 34 1948.
—— Bulwer and Macready: a chronicle of the early Victorian theatre. Urbana 1958.
Cordasco, F. Notes on Bulwer-Lytton's classical scholarship. N & Q 28 April, 9 June 1951.
Dahl, C. Bulwer-Lytton and the School of catastrophe. PQ 32 1953.
—— Recreators of Pompeii. Archaeology 9 1956.
—— History on the hustings: Bulwer-Lytton's historical novels of politics. In From Jane Austen to Joseph Conrad, ed R. C. Rathburn and M. Steinmann, Minneapolis 1958.
Lloyd, M. Bulwer-Lytton and the Idealist principle. Eng Miscellany (Rome) 1 1956.
Ganzel, D. Bulwer and his Lady. MP 58 1960.
—— Patent wrongs and patent theatres. PMLA 76 1961.
Barr, D. J. A misquotation in Lytton. N & Q Dec 1961.
Fredin, J. I. The absorbing tyranny of everyday life: Bulwer-Lytton's A strange story. Nineteenth-Century Fiction 16 1962.

ROSINA, LADY BULWER-LYTTON, née WHEELER
1804–82

§1

Cheveley: or the man of honour. 3 vols 1839 (3 edns).
The budget of the Bubble family. 3 vols 1840.
The Prince-Duke and the page: an historical novel. 3 vols 1841.
Bianca Cappello: an historical romance. 3 vols 1843.
Memoirs of a Muscovite. 3 vols 1844.
The peer's daughters: a novel. 3 vols 1849.
Miriam Sedley, or the tares and the wheat: a tale of real life. 3 vols 1851.
The school for husbands: or Molière's life and times. 3 vols 1852.
Behind the scenes: a novel. 3 vols 1854.
Very successful! 3 vols 1856, [1859].
Lady Bulwer-Lytton's appeal to the justice and charity of the English public. [1857].
The world and his wife, or a person of consequence: a photographic novel. 3 vols 1858.
The household fairy [etc]. 1870.
Shells from the sands of time. 1876. Essays.
Rosina Bulwer-Lytton did not write A blighted life, *which was pbd in her name in 1880.*

§2

Devey, L. Life of Rosina, Lady Lytton. 1887.
Sadleir, M. Bulwer, a panorama: i, Edward and Rosina 1803–36. 1931.
Philip, I. G. Winwood Reade and Lady Bulwer Lytton. Bodleian Lib Record 1 1939.

HENRY FOTHERGILL CHORLEY
1808–82

See col 1374 below.

CHARLES CLARKE

Charlie Thornhill, or the dunce of the family: a novel. 3 vols 1863.
A box for the season: a sporting sketch. 2 vols 1864.
Which is the winner? or the first gentleman of his family. 3 vols 1864.
Crumbs from a sportsman's table. 2 vols 1865, [1869].
The flying scud: a sporting novel. 2 vols 1867 (anon), 1868 (3rd edn).
Tom Crackenthorpe: hunting and steeplechasing. 1867.
The Beauclercs, father and son: a novel. 3 vols 1867.
Lord Falconberg's heir: a novel. 2 vols 1868.
A forecastle frolic: being a round of stories for Christmas, conducted by Charles Clarke. [1868].
Myra Gray, or sown in tears, reaped in joy: a novel. 3 vols 1870.
Calcraft's Confessions: or coward-conscience. 1870.
Chips from an old block. [1871].

MARY COWDEN CLARKE
1809–98

See col 1375, below.

CAROLINE CLIVE, née MEYSEY-WIGLEY
1801–73

§1

IX poems by V. 1840, 1841 (enlarged); ed E. Partridge 1928 (with biographical introd).
I watched the heavens: a poem by V. 1842.
Saint Oldooman: a myth of the nineteenth century. 1845 (anon). A satire on Newman's Lives of the English saints.
The Queen's ball: a poem by V. 1847.
The valley of the Rea: a poem. 1851.
The Morlas: a poem by V. 1853.

Paul Ferroll: a tale, by the author of IX poems by V. 1855, 1929.
Poems by the author of Paul Ferroll. 1856, 1872; ed A. Greathed 1890.
Year after year: a tale. 1858.
Why Paul Ferroll killed his wife. 1860.
John Greswold. 2 vols 1864.

§2

[Coleridge, H. N.] Quart Rev 66 1840. Review of IX poems by V.
Brown, J. Henry Vaughan. In Horae subsecivae ser 1, Edinburgh 1822. The essay includes an appreciation of IX poems by V.
Sergeant, A. Mrs Archer Clive. In Women novelists of Queen Victoria's reign, 1897.

HENRY COCKTON
1807–53

The life and adventures of Valentine Vox, the ventriloquist. 1840, 1853 (rev).
Stanley Thorn. 3 vols 1841.
George St George Julian, the Prince of Swindlers. 1841, 1844.
Sylvester Sound the somnambulist. 1844.
The love match. 1845.
The steward: a romance of real life. 1850.
The sisters: or the fatal marriage. 1851.
Lady Felicia: a novel. 1852.
Percy Effingham: or the germ of the world's esteem. 3 vols 1853.

CHARLES ALSTON COLLINS
1828–73

A new sentimental journey. 1859. First pbd in All the Year Round June–July 1859.
The eyewitness: his evidence about many wonderful things. 1860. First pbd in All the Year Round 1859–60.
A cruise upon wheels: the chronicles of some autumn wanderings among the deserted post roads of France. 2 vols 1862, 1863, 1926.
The bar sinister: a tale. 2 vols 1864.
Strathcairn: a novel. 2 vols 1864.
At the bar: a tale. 2 vols 1866.

MORTIMER COLLINS
1827–76

§1

Idyls and rhymes. Dublin 1855.
Summer songs. 1860.
Who is the heir? a novel. 3 vols 1865.
Sweet Anne Page. 3 vols 1868.
The ivory gate. 2 vols 1869.
A letter to the Right Honourable Benjamin Disraeli MP. 1869.
The Vivian romance. 3 vols 1870.
Marquis and merchant. 3 vols 1871.
The inn of strange meetings and other poems. 1871.
The secret of long life. 1871. Essays.
The British birds: a communication from the ghost of Aristophanes. 1872.
The Princess Clarice: a story of 1871. 2 vols 1872.
Two plunges for a pearl. 3 vols 1872. First pbd in London Soc Jan–Nov 1871.
Squire Silchester's whim. 3 vols 1873.
Miranda: a midsummer madness. 3 vols 1873.

Mr Carington: a tale of love and constancy. 3 vols 1873. Pbd as by Robert Turner Cotton.
Transmigration. 3 vols 1874.
Frances. 3 vols 1874.
Sweet and twenty. 3 vols 1875.
Blacksmith and scholar and From midnight to midnight. 3 vols 1876. From midnight to midnight rptd separately, 1883.
A fight with fortune. 3 vols 1876.
You play me false: a novel, by Mortimer and Frances Collins. 3 vols 1878.
The village comedy, by Mortimer and Frances Collins. 3 vols 1878.
Pen sketches from a vanished hand, from the papers of the late Mortimer Collins, edited by Tom Taylor, with notes by the editor and Mrs Mortimer Collins. 2 vols 1879.
Thoughts in my garden, edited by Edmund Yates, with notes by the editor and Mrs Mortimer Collins. 2 vols 1880.
Selections from the poetical works. Ed F. P. Cotton 1886.

§2

Collins, Frances. Mortimer Collins: his letters and friendships, with some account of his life. 2 vols 1877.
Ellis, S. M. In his Wilkie Collins, Le Fanu and others, 1931.

WILLIAM WILKIE COLLINS
1824–89

Bibliographies

Sadleir, M. In his Excursions in Victorian bibliography, 1922.
Parrish, M. L. Wilkie Collins and Charles Reade. 1940.
Cordasco, F. and K. Scott. Wilkie Collins and Charles Reade: a bibliography of critical notices and studies. New York 1949.
Andrew, A. W. A Wilkie Collins check-list. Eng Stud in Africa 3 1960.
Ashley, R. In Victorian fiction, ed L. Stevenson, Cambridge Mass 1964.

§1

Memoirs of the life of William Collins RA; with selections from his journals and correspondence. 2 vols 1848.
Antonina, or the fall of Rome: a romance of the fifth century. 3 vols 1850.
Rambles beyond railways: or notes in Cornwall taken a-foot. 1851, 1961 (adds The cruise of the Tomtit, first pbd in Household Words 1855).
Mr Wray's cash box, or the mask and the mystery: a Christmas sketch. 1852.
Basil: a story of modern life. 3 vols 1852, 1862 (preface and text much rev).
Hide and seek. 3 vols 1854.
After dark. 2 vols 1856. 6 stories with connecting narrative: A terribly strange bed; A stolen letter; Sister Rose; The lady of Glenwith Grange; Gabriel's marriage; The yellow mask. All originally pbd in Household Words 1953–5.
The dead secret. 2 vols 1857. First pbd in Household Words from 3 Jan 1857.
The Queen of Hearts. 3 vols 1859. 11 stories with connecting narrative: The black cottage; The family secret (first pbd in Nat Mag 1857 as Uncle George: or the family mystery; The dream-woman (first pbd in Household Words 1855); The hollytree inn (first pbd ibid as The ostler; *see* also The frozen deep, below); Mad Monkton; The dead hand (first pbd in Household Words 1857 in The lazy tour; *see* below); The biter bit; The parson's scruple; A plot in private life; Fauntleroy (first

pbd in Household Words 1858); Anne Rodway (first pbd in Household Words 1856). 5 stories from The Queen of Hearts rptd as A plot in private life and other tales, Leipzig 1859.

The woman in white. 3 vols 1860, 1861 (contains correction of all dates in latter part of Marion Halcombe's diary in consequence of criticism in Times). First pbd in All the Year Round from 26 Nov 1859.

A message from the sea: a drama in three acts. 1861. With Dickens.

No name. 3 vols 1862. First pbd in All the Year Round from 15 March 1862.

No name: a drama in five acts. 1863. *See* below.

My miscellanies. 2 vols 1863. Various articles and sketches, all first pbd in Household Words.

Armadale. 2 vols 1866. First pbd in Cornhill Mag and Harper's Mag 1864–5.

Armadale: a drama in three acts. 1866.

The frozen deep: a drama in three acts. 1866 (ptd, never pbd).

No thoroughfare: a drama in five acts. 1867. With Dickens. Also issued 1867 with a different text from Act iv scene 3 to end.

The moonstone: a romance. 3 vols 1868. First pbd in All the Year Round from 4 Jan 1868.

Black and white: a love story in three acts. 1869. With Charles Fechter.

Man and wife: a novel. 3 vols 1870.

No name: a drama in four acts. 1870. A different text from that pbd in 1863, above.

The woman in white: a drama in prologue and four acts. 1871.

Poor Miss Finch: a novel. 3 vols 1872. First pbd in Cassell's Mag 1871.

The new Magdalen: a dramatic story in a prologue and three acts. 1873.

Miss or Mrs? and other stories in outline. 1873. Miss or Mrs? (first pbd in Graphic); Blow up with the Brig! (first pbd in All the Year Round Xmas no 1859); The haunted house (as The ghost in the cupboard room); The fatal cradle (first pbd in All the Year Round Xmas no 1861); Tom Tiddler's ground (as Picking up waifs at sea).

The frozen deep and other stories: readings and writings in America. 2 vols 1874. The frozen deep (story version of play, first pbd in Temple Bar); The dream woman (story from The Queen of Hearts, transferred from the first person into the third and with a conclusion added for public reading); John Hago's ghost (first pbd in Home Jnl). For dramatic text of Frozen deep, *see* Under the management of Mr Charles Dickens, ed R. L. Brannan, Ithaca 1966.

The law and the lady: a novel. 3 vols 1875.

Miss Gwilt: a drama in five acts. 1875 (ptd, never pbd).

The two destinies: a romance. 2 vols 1876.

The moonstone: a dramatic story in three acts. 1877 (priv ptd).

The haunted hotel: a mystery of modern Venice, to which is added My Lady's money. 2 vols 1879. First pbd in Belgravia 1875.

A rogue's life: from his birth to his marriage. 1879. First pbd in Household Words from 1 March 1856; text slightly rev.

The fallen leaves: first series. 3 vols 1879. Not successful; sequel never written. First pbd in Canadian Monthly 1878.

Considerations on the copyright question addressed to an American friend. 1880.

Jezebel's daughter. 3 vols 1880. Book version of play, The red vial.

The black robe. 3 vols 1881. First pbd in Canadian Monthly 1880.

Heart and science: a story of the present time. 3 vols 1883. First pbd in Belgravia 1882.

I say no. 3 vols 1884.

The evil genius: a domestic story. 3 vols 1886. Ch i also pbd separately under same title, Bolton 1885.

The guilty river. 1886 (Arrowsmith's Annual).

Little novels. 3 vols 1887. Mrs Zant and the ghost; Miss Morris and the stranger; Mr Cosway and the landlady; Mr Medhurst and the Princess; Mr Lismore and the widow; Miss Jeromette and the clergyman; Miss Minor and the groom; Mr Lepel and the housekeeper; Mr Captain and the Nymph; Mr Marmaduke and the minister; Mr Percy and the prophet; Miss Bertha and the Yankee; Miss Dulane and My Lord; Mr Policeman and the cook. Most or all were originally pbd in various periodicals under different titles: Mrs Zant and the ghost was pbd with My Lady's money as The ghost's touch, Leipzig 1879; Miss Minor and the groom as A shocking story, New York 1878; Miss Morris and the stranger originally appeared as Why I married him.

The legacy of Cain. 3 vols 1889.

Blind love. 3 vols 1890. Preface by Sir Walter Besant. First pbd in Illustr London Mag 1889. By Collins up to the end of the 18th weekly pt, when the onset of his last illness obliged him to hand it over to Besant to complete. Besant's work begins at ch 49 and is based throughout on a complete synopsis drawn up by Collins.

The lazy tour of two idle apprentices; No thoroughfare; The perils of certain English prisoners. 1890. With Dickens. The lazy tour was first pbd in Household Words 1857 in 5 pts, of which Collins wrote pt i (top of p. 316, col 2 to end), pt 2 (beginning to break in p. 340, col 2), pt 3 (reflections of Mr Idle, pp. 363–5), whole of pt 5. No thoroughfare was first pbd in All the Year Round Xmas no 1867, Collins writing whole of Act 2 and contributing to Acts 1 and 4. Perils was first pbd in Household Words Xmas no 1857, Collins writing all except pts 1–2.

The following magazine stories by Collins have not been rptd in book form: The Chief Mate's story, The deliverance (Household Words Xmas no 1856), Over the way, Trottles' report, Let at last (with Dickens) (Household Words Xmas no 1858); A new mind (Household Words New Year extra no 1859); ch 4 and portions of chs 2, 5 of A message from the sea (All the Year Round Xmas no 1860); The Devil's spectacles (unidentified, 1879); Fie! fie! or the fair physician (Pictorial World Xmas Suppl 23 Dec 1882).

The following articles have not been rptd in book form:

Illuminated Mag: The last stage-coachman (Aug 1843).

Household Words: The National Gallery and the Old Masters (25 Dec 1856); A fair penitent (18 July 1857); The debtor's best friend (19 Sept 1857); A deep design on society (2 Jan 1858); The little Huguenot (9 Jan 1858); Thanks to Doctor Livingstone (23 Jan 1858); Strike! (6 Feb 1858); A sermon for Sepoys (27 Feb 1858); Dramatic Grub Street (6 March 1858); A shy scheme (20 March 1858); Awful warning to bachelors (27 March 1858); Sea-breezes with a London smack (4 Sept 1858); Highly proper! (2 Oct 1858); A clause for the new Reform Bill (with Dickens) (9 Oct 1858); Dr Dulcamara MP (with Dickens) (18 Dec 1858); Pity a poor prince (15 Jan 1859); Burns viewed as a hat-peg (12 Feb 1859); A column to Burns (26 Feb 1859); A breach of British privilege (19 March 1859); A dramatic author (28 May 1859).

All the Year Round: Sure to be healthy, wealthy and wise (30 April 1859); The Royal Academy in red (28 May 1859); My advisers(?) (18 June 1859); A new view of society (20 Aug 1859); Cooks at college (?) (29 Oct 1859); The Tattlesnivel bleater (?) (21 Dec 1859); My boys (?) (28 Jan 1860); My girls (?) (17 Feb 1860); Boxing-Day (22 Dec 1860); A night in the jungle (certainly by Collins) (3 Aug 1961); An unreported speech (16 Nov 1861); A trial at Toulouse (?) (15 Feb 1862); Notes of interrogation (?) (10 May 1862); Suggestions from a maniac (13 Feb 1864); To let (18 June 1864); Going into housekeeping (8 July 1865).

The office-book of All the Year Round appears to be no longer in existence. Although it is certain that Collins contributed largely to the earlier nos, his work can only be identified by internal evidence, and the above attributions are advanced with the utmost caution. My advisers, My boys, and My girls are attributed to Collins by analogy with My spinsters, which he contributed to Household Words and rptd in My miscellanies.

Pall Mall Gazette: Books necessary for a liberal education (11 Feb 1886).

Universal Review: Reminiscences of a story-teller (1888, p. 182).

§2

Forster, J. In his Life of Charles Dickens, 3 vols 1872–4; ed J.W.T. Ley 1928.

Dickens, C. In his Letters, ed G. Hogarth and M. Dickens 3 vols 1880–2; Pilgrim edition, ed M. House and G. Storey, Oxford 1965– .

— Letters to Wilkie Collins 1851–70. Ed G. Hogarth 1892.

Wolzogen, E. von. Wilkie Collins: ein biographisch-kritischer Versuch. Leipzig 1885.

Lang, A. Contemporary Rev Jan 1890. Obituary.

Swinburne, A. C. Fortnightly Rev Nov 1890. Obituary.

— In his Studies in prose and poetry, 1894.

Y[ates], E. Temple Bar Aug 1890. Obituary.

Quilter, H. Preferences in art, life and literature. 1892.

Beard, N. Some recollections of yesterday. Temple Bar July 1894.

Reeve, W. Recollections of Wilkie Collins. Chambers's Jnl 16 June 1906.

Winter, W. Old friends. New York 1907.

Caine, T. H. In his My story, 1908.

Lehmann, R. C. In his Memories of half a century, 1908.

— In his Charles Dickens as editor, 1912.

Shore, W. T. In his Charles Dickens and his friends, 1909.

Phillips, W. C. Dickens, Reade and Collins: sensation novelists. New York 1919.

Ellis, S. M. Wilkie Collins, Le Fanu and others. 1931.

Sehlbach, H. Untersuchungen über die Romankunst von Wilkie Collins. Jena 1931.

de la Mare, W. The early novels of Wilkie Collins. In The eighteen-sixties, 1932 (Royal Soc of Lit).

Eliot, T. S. Wilkie Collins and Dickens. In his Selected essays, 1932.

Flower, D. Authors and copyright in the nineteenth century, with unpublished letters from Wilkie Collins. Book-Collector's Quart 7 1932.

Elwin, M. In his Victorian wallflowers, 1934.

Hardy, J. T. In his Books on the shelf, 1934.

Hyder, C. K. Collins and the Woman in white. PMLA 54 1939.

— Collins in America. In Studies in English in honor of R. D. O'Leary and S. L. Whitcomb, Lawrence Kansas 1940.

Milley, H. J. W. The Eustace diamonds and the Moonstone. SP 36 1939.

— Collins and A tale of two cities. MLR 34 1939.

Davis, E. Charles Dickens and Wilkie Collins. Univ of Wichita Stud 2 1945.

McCleary, G. F. A Victorian classic. Fortnightly Rev Aug 1946.

Ashley, R. P. Collins and a Vermont murder trial. New England Quart 21 1948.

— Wilkie Collins's first short story. More Books 23 1948.

— Wilkie Collins reconsidered. Nineteenth-Century Fiction 4 1950.

— Wilkie Collins and the detective story. Nineteenth-Century Fiction 6 1952.

— Wilkie Collins. 1952.

— Wilkie Collins and the American theatre. Nineteenth-Century Fiction 8 1954.

— The Wilkie Collins collection. Princeton Univ Lib Chron 17 1956.

MacEachan, D. B. Collins and British law. Nineteenth-Century Fiction 5 1951.

Booth, B. A. Collins and the art of fiction. Nineteenth-Century Fiction 6 1952.

Robinson, K. Wilkie Collins: a biography. 1951.

Hill, T. The enigma of Wilkie Collins. Dickensian 48 1952.

— The late Wilkie Collins. Ibid.

Pritchett, V. S. The roots of detection. In his Books in general, 1953.

Davis, N. P. The life of Wilkie Collins. Urbana 1956.

Hart, F. R. Wilkie Collins and the problem of biographical evidence. Victorian Newsletter no 12 1957.

— Manuscripts of Wilkie Collins. Princeton Univ Lib Chron 18 1957.

Corrigan, B. Antonio Fogazzari and Wilkie Collins. Comparative Lit 18 1961.

Lawson, L. A. Wilkie Collins and the Moonstone. Amer Imago 20 1963.

THOMAS COOPER

1805–92

See col 516, above.

CATHERINE CROWE, née STEVENS

1800?–76

§1

Aristodemus: a tragedy. 1838.

Adventures of Susan Hopley: or the adventures of a maid servant. 3 vols 1841.

Men and women: or manorial rights. 3 vols 1844.

The Seeress of Prevorst. 1845. From the German of A. J. C. Kerner.

The story of Martha Ginnis and her son. In The Edinburgh tales, ed C. I. Johnstone vol i, 1845.

The story of Lily Dawson. 3 vols 1847.

Pippie's warning: or mind your temper. 1848.

The night side of nature: or ghosts and ghost seers. 2 vols 1848.

Light and darkness: or mysteries of life. 3 vols 1850.

Adventures of a beauty. 3 vols 1852.

Uncle Tom's Cabin adapted for young persons. 1853. From the novel by Harriet Beecher Stowe.

The cruel kindness: a romantic play. 1853.

Linny Lockwood: a novel. 2 vols 1854.

Ghosts and family legends: a volume for Christmas. 1859.

Spiritualism and the age we live in. 1859.

The story of Arthur Hunter and his first shilling; with other tales. [1861].

The adventures of a monkey. 1862.

§2

Sergeant, A. In his Women novelists of Queen Victoria's reign, 1897.

Clapton, G. T. Baudelaire and Catherine Crowe. MLR 25 1930.

Hughes, R. Une étape de l'esthétique de Baudelaire: Catherine Crowe. Revue de Littérature Comparée 17 1937.

SARAH ELLIS, née STICKNEY

1810?–72

Pictures of private life. 3 sers 1833–7.

The poetry of life. 2 vols 1835.

Home, or the iron rule: a domestic story. 3 vols 1836.
The women of England, their social duties and domestic habits. [1839].
The sons of the soil: poem. [1840].
Look to the end: or the Bennets abroad. 2 vols [1845].
Temper and temperament: or varieties of character. 2 vols [1846].
The island Queen: a poem. 1846.
Prevention better than cure: or the moral wants of the world we live in. [1847].
Social distinction: or hearts and homes. 3 vols [1848–9].
Fireside tales for the young. 4 vols [1849?].
Pique: a novel. 3 vols 1850, [1869].
The mother's mistake: a tale. [1856].
Friends at their own firesides: or pictures of the private life of the people called Quakers. 2 vols 1858.
The widow Green and the three nieces. 1859.
Janet, one of many: a story in verse. 1862.
The Brewer's family. [1863].
William and Mary: or the fatal blow. [1865].
Share and share alike: or the grand principle. 1865.
Northern Roses: a Yorkshire story. 3 vols 1868.
The brewer's son: a story. [1881].
The home life and letters of Mrs Ellis, compiled by her nieces. [1893].

LADY GEORGINA CHARLOTTE FULLERTON
1812–85

§1

Ellen Middleton: a tale. 3 vols 1844.
Grantley Manor: a tale. 3 vols 1847.
The old Highlander and other verses. 1849 (priv ptd).
Lady-Bird: a tale. 3 vols 1852.
The life of St Frances of Rome. 1855.
La Comtesse de Bonneval: her life and letters. 2 vols 1857.
Our Lady's little books. 4 nos 1860–1. Ed Lady Georgiana Fullerton.
Laurentia: a tale of Japan. 1861.
Rose Leblanc. 1862.
Too strange not to be true. 3 vols 1864.
Constance Sherwood: an autobiography of the sixteenth century. 3 vols 1865.
A stormy life. 3 vols 1867.
The helpers of the holy souls. 1868.
Mrs Gerald's niece: a novel. 3 vols 1869.
The gold-digger and other verses. Edinburgh 1872.
Dramas from the lives of the saints: Germaine Cousin, the shepherdess of Pibrac. [1872].
Life of Luisa de Carvajal. 1873.
Seven stories. 1873.
A sketch of the life of the late Father H. Young. 1874.
The life of Mère Marie de la Providence. 1875.
The miraculous medal: life and visions of Catherine Labouré. 1880.
A will and a way. 3 vols 1881.
The fire of London: a play. [1882].
The life of Elisabeth Lady Falkland 1585–1639. 1883.

§2

Craven, A. The life of Lady Georgiana Fullerton, translated from the French by H. J. Coleridge. 1888.
Yonge, C. M. In A. Sergeant et al, Women novelists of Queen Victoria's reign, 1897.
Taylor, F. M. The inner life of Lady Georgiana Fullerton, with notes of retreat and diary. [1899].
Lockhead, M. Two minor Victorian novelists: Lady Georgiana Fullerton and Mrs Norton. Quart Rev 293 1955.

MARGARET GATTY, née SCOTT
1809–73

§1

The fairy godmothers and other tales. 1851.
Parables from nature. 5 sers 1855–71. Frequently rptd, especially the earlier sers, and tr German, Swedish, French, Danish, Russian and Italian, 1856–80. Sers 1–2 rptd 1885 with memoir by J. H. Ewing.
'Worlds not realized'. 1856, 1869 (with next item).
Proverbs illustrated. 1857, 1869 (with preceding item).
The poor incumbent: a tale. 1858.
Legendary tales. 1858.
Aunt Judy's tales. 1859.
The human face divine and other tales. 1860.
Aunt Judy's letters. 1862.
British seaweeds, drawn from Professor Harvey's Phycologia britannica. 1863, 2 vols 1872.
Domestic pictures and tales. 1866.
Waifs and strays of natural history. 1871.
A book of emblems, with interpretations thereof. 1872.
The book of sundials. 1872.
Mrs Gatty also founded and contributed constantly to Aunt Judy's Mag for Children, *from May 1866.*

§2

Maxwell, C. Mrs Gatty and Mrs Ewing. 1949.

JAMES GRANT
1822–87

§1

Sketches in London. 1838. Illustr Phiz et al.
The romance of war: or the Highlanders in Spain [France and Belgium]. 4 vols 1846–7.
Adventures of an aide-de-camp: or a campaign in Calabria. 3 vols 1848.
Memoirs and adventures of Sir William Kirkaldy of Grange. Edinburgh 1849.
The Scottish Cavalier: an historical romance. 3 vols 1850.
Memorials of the Castle of Edinburgh. 1850, Edinburgh 1862.
Memoirs and adventures of Sir John Hepburn. 1851.
Jane Seton, or the King's Advocate: a Scottish historical romance. 3 vols 1853.
Bothwell: or the days of Mary Queen of Scots. [1854].
Philip Rollo: or the Scottish musketeers. 2 vols 1854.
Frank Hilton: or the Queen's Own. 1855.
The yellow frigate: or the three sisters. [1855].
Harry Ogilvie, or the Black Dragoons: new edition. 1856.
The phantom regiment: or stories of 'ours'. [1856], [1964].
The Highlanders of Glen Ora. 1857, 1862 (as Laura Everingham: or the Highlanders of Glen Ora).
Memoirs of James Marquis of Montrose. 1858.
Arthur Blane: or the hundred cuirassiers. [1858].
Hollywood Hall: a tale of 1715. 1859, 1861 (as Lucy Arden: or Hollywood Hall).
Legends of the Black Watch or Forty-Second Highlanders. 1859.
The Cavaliers of fortune: or British heroes in foreign lands. 1859.
Mary of Lorraine: an historical romance. 1860.
Oliver Ellis: or the Fusiliers. 1861.
Jack Manly: his adventures by sea and land. 1861.
Dick Rodney: or the adventures of an Eton boy. [1862].
The Captain of the Guard. 1862.
Letty Hyde's lovers: or the Household Brigade. 1863.
Second to none: a military romance. 3 vols 1864.

Adventures of Rob Roy. 1864.
The King's Own Borderers: a military romance. 3 vols 1865.
The Constable of France and other military historiettes. 1866.
The white cockade: or faith and fortitude. 3 vols 1867.
First love and last love: a tale of the Indian Mutiny. 3 vols 1868.
The girl he married: a novel. 3 vols 1869.
The secret dispatch: or the adventures of Captain Balgonie 1869.
Lady Wedderburn's wish: a tale of the Crimean War. 3 vols 1870.
Only an ensign: the retreat from Cabul. 3 vols 1871.
Under the Red Dragon. 3 vols 1872.
British battles on land and sea. 3 vols [1873–5], 4 vols [1884–8], [1896–7].
Fairer than a fairy: a novel. 3 vols 1874.
Shall I win her? the story of a wanderer. 3 vols 1874.
The Queen's cadet and other tales. 1874.
One of the six hundred: a novel. 3 vols 1875.
Did she love him? a novel. 3 vols 1876.
Morley Ashton: a story of the sea. 3 vols 1876.
Cassell's illustrated history of India. 2 vols [1876–7].
Six years ago: a novel. 2 vols 1877.
Vere of Ours, the Eighth or King's: a novel. 3 vols 1878.
The Ross-shire Buffs: a novel. [1878].
The Lord Hermitage: a novel. 3 vols 1878.
The Royal Regiment and other novelettes. 1879.
The Duke of Albany's Own Highlanders: a novel. 3 vols 1880.
Cassell's old and new Edinburgh. 3 vols [1880–3].
Lady Glendonwyn: a novel. 3 vols 1881.
Derval Hampton: a story of the sea. 2 vols 1881.
The Cameronians: a novel. 3 vols 1881.
Violet Jermyn: or tender and true. 1882.
The Scot's Brigade and other tales. 1882.
Jack Chaloner: or the Fighting Forty-Third. [1883].
The dead tryst, and a haunted life. [1883].
Miss Cheyne of Essilmont: a novel. 3 vols 1883.
The Master of Aberfeldie: a novel. 3 vols 1884.
Colville of the Guards. 3 vols 1885.
The Royal Highlanders, or the Black Watch in Egypt: a novel. [1885].
Cassell's history of the war in the Soudan. 6 vols [1885–6].
Dulcie Carlyon: a novel. 3 vols 1886.
The tartans of the clans of Scotland. 1886.
Playing with fire: a story of the Soudan war. 3 vols 1887.
Love's labour lost: a novel. 3 vols 1888, 1889.

§2

Ellis, S. M. In his Mainly Victorian, [1925].

GERALD GRIFFIN

1803–40

Collections

Works. 8 vols 1842–3. Vol 1, Life; vol 2, The Collegians; vol 3, Card drawing; vol 4, Holland-tide; vol 5, Tales of the Munster festivals; vol 6, The Duke of Monmouth; vol 7, Talis qualis: or tales of the jury room; vol 8, Poetical works.

§1

Holland-tide: or Munster popular tales. 1827, 1857.
Tales of the Munster festivals. 3 vols 1827.
The Collegians, or the colleen Bawn: a tale of Garryowen. 3 vols 1829, 1861, 1887; ed P. Colum 1918. For the dramatization by Dion Boucicault, *see* p. 600, below.
The rivals: Tracy's ambition. 3 vols 1830.
The Christian physiologist: tales illustrative of the five senses. 1830, Dublin 1854 (as The offering of friendship: or tales of the five senses).
The invasion. 4 vols 1832.
Tales of my neighbourhood. 3 vols 1835.
The Duke of Monmouth. 1836.
Gisippus: a play. 1842.
Poetical works. 1851.
The Kelp-Gatherer: an Irish tale. Dublin 1854.
The beautiful Queen of Leix, or the self-consumed: an Irish tale. Dublin 1854.
A story of Psyche. Dublin 1854.
The day of trial: an Irish tale. Dublin 1854.
Card-drawing, the half sir, and Suil Dhur the coiner. Dublin 1857.
Poetical works. Dublin 1926. Includes Gisippus, above.

§2

Griffin, D. The life of Gerald Griffin. 1843.
Mannin, E. Two studies in integrity: Griffin and the Reverend Francis Mahony. 1954.

ANNA MARIA HALL, née FIELDING

1800–81

§1

Sketches of Irish character. 3 vols 1829; ser 2, 1831.
Chronicles of a schoolroom. 1830.
The buccaneer. 3 vols 1832. Anon.
The outlaw: an historical romance. 1835.
Tales of a woman's trials. 1835.
Uncle Horace. 1837. Anon.
Lights and shadows of Irish life. 3 vols 1838. First pbd in New Monthly Mag.
The Hartopp jubilee: or profit from play. [1840?].
Marian: or a young maid's fortunes. 3 vols 1840.
Number one: a tale. 1844.
Little Chatterbox: a tale. 1844.
Characteristic sketches of Ireland and the Irish, by Carleton, Lover and Mrs S. C. Hall. 1845.
The whiteboy: Ireland in 1822. 2 vols 1845.
The forlorn hope: a story of Old Chelsea. [1846].
Uncle Sam's money box. 1848 etc.
Grandmamma's pockets. 1848.
Midsummer Eve: a fairy tale of love. 1848, 1870. First pbd in Art Jnl.
The whisperer. 1848 etc.
Seven tales, by seven authors. Ed F. E. Smedley 1849, 1860. Contains The last in the lease by Mrs Hall.
The swan's egg: a tale. 1850.
Stories of the Irish peasantry. 1851. First pbd in Chambers's Jnl.
Stories of the governess. 1852.
The worn thimble: a story of woman's duty and woman's influence. 1853.
The drunkard's Bible. 1854.
Popular tales and sketches. 1856.
The two friends: a temperance sketch. [1856].
A woman's story. 3 vols 1857.
The lucky penny and other tales. 1857.
Turns of fortune: a tale. 1858.
There is no hurry and Deeds not words: tales. 1858.
The unjust judge. 1858.
All is not gold that glitters: a tale. 1858.
Cleverness: a tale. 1858.
The governess: a tale. 1858.
Wives and husbands: a tale. 1858.
The tale book. Königsberg 1859. Contains The dispensation by Mrs Hall.
Daddy Dacre's school: a story for the young. 1859.

Mamma Milly: a story. [1860].
Fanny's fancies. [1860].
The golden casket, by M. Howitt. [1861]. Contains William and his teacher by Mrs Hall.
Can wrong be right? a tale. 2 vols 1862.
Building a house with a teacup. [1863].
The village garland: tales and sketches. 1863.
Nelly Nawlan and other stories. 1865.
Ronald's reason: or the little cripple. [1865].
The cabman's cat. [1865].
The playfellow and other illustrated stories. 1866.
The way of the world and other stories. 1866.
The Prince of the fairy family: a fairy tale. [1867].
Alice Stanley and other stories. 1868.
The fight of faith: a story. 2 vols 1869.
The rift in the rock: a tale. [1871].
Digging a grave with a wine glass. 1871.
Chronicles of a cosy nook. 1875.
Boons and blessings: stories and sketches to illustrate the advantages of temperance. 1875.
Ann Leslie and other stories. 1877.
Mrs Hall also conducted St James's Mag, 1861, *and* Sharpe's London Mag *from 1845. In addn to her novels and tales she pbd plays and miscellaneous hack-work as well as several books of travel with her husband S. C. Hall.*

§2

Maginn, W. In his A gallery of illustrious literary characters, ed W. Bates [1873].
Hall, S. C. Retrospect of a long life. 1883.

JAMES HANNAY
1827–73

See col 1386, below.

SIR ARTHUR HELPS
1813–75

See col 1388, below.

THOMAS HUGHES
1822–96

Bibliographies

Parrish, M. L. and B. K. Mann. Charles Kingsley and Hughes: first editions in the library at Dormy House. 1936.

§1

History of the Working Tailor's Association. [1850]. Tracts on Christian Socialism 11.
A lecture on the shop system, especially as it bears upon the females engaged in it, delivered at Reading. 1852.
Tom Brown's school days, by an old boy. Cambridge 1857 (3 edns), 1861, 1868, 1869, 1871, 1882, 1896, 1897, 1903, 1903, [1904]; ed V. Rendall 1904, 1905, 1905, 1906, 1907 etc; ed F. Sidgwick 1913.
The scouring of the white horse: or the long vacation ramble of a London clerk, illustrated by Richard Doyle. 1859, 1859, 1889 (with The ashen faggot; a tale for Christmas) etc.
Account of the lock-out of engineers 1851–2, prepared for the National Association for the Promotion of Social Science. Cambridge 1860.
Tom Brown at Oxford, by the author of Tom Brown's schooldays. 3 vols Cambridge 1861, 1864, 1865, 1869, 1871, 1872, 1874, 1875, 1877, 1877, 1879, 1880, 1883, 1886, 1889, 1905 etc.
Tracts for priests and people, no 1: Religio laici. Cambridge 1861 (4 edns). Afterwards included in Tracts for priests and people, ser i.
The struggle for Kansas. Appended to J. M. Ludlow, A sketch of the history of the United States, Cambridge 1862.
The cause of freedom: which is its champion in America, the North or the South? [1863].
A layman's faith. 1868.
Alfred the Great. 3 pts 1869, [1871], 1873, 1874, 1877, 1881, 1887, 1898 etc.
Memoir of a brother. 1873, 1873.
Lecture on the history and objects of co-operation, delivered at Manchester. Manchester 1878.
The old Church: what shall we do with it? 1878.
The manliness of Christ. 1879, 1880, 1907.
Rugby, Tennessee: being some account of the settlement founded on the Cumberland plateau by the Board of Aid to Land Ownership. 1881.
Memoir of Daniel MacMillan. 1882, 1882 (corrected), 1883.
Address by Thos Hughes on the occasion of the presentation of a testimonial of his services to the cause of co-operation, 6th December 1884. Manchester 1885.
Life and times of Peter Cooper. 1886 (priv ptd).
James Fraser, second Bishop of Manchester: a memoir 1818–35. 1887, 1888, 1889.
Co-operative production: an address delivered at the Annual Co-operative Congress, Carlisle. Manchester [1887].
Church reform and defence: an address delivered in Wadham College Hall, Oxford. 1887.
David Livingstone. 1889, 1889.
Co-operative faith and practice: an address. [1890].
Vacation rambles. 1895.
Early memories for the children. 1899 (priv ptd).
Fragments of autobiography. Ed H. C. Shelley, Cornhill Mag March–May 1925.
Hughes also wrote introds to James Lowell, Biglow Papers, 1859; J. F. D. Maurice, Christian Socialism, 1898 *etc.*
Some letters of Hughes. Economic Rev 24 1914.

§2

Ritchie, J. E. In his British Senators, 1869.
Cooper, T. In his Men of mark, 6 vols 1876–82.
Hinton, R. J. In his English radical leaders, New York 1887.
Ludlow, J. M. Hughes and Septimus Hansard. Economic Rev 6 1896.
Thomas Hughes. Macmillan's Mag May 1896. Obituary.
Tollemache, L. A. In his Essays and mock essays and character sketches, 1898.
Selfe, S. Chapters from the history of Rugby School, together with notes on the characters and incidents depicted in Tom Brown's schooldays. 1910.
Hamer, M. B. Hughes and his American Rugby. [1928].
Harrison, E. The Englishry of Tom Brown. Queen's Quart 50 1943.
Mack, E. C. and W. H. G. Armytage. Hughes: the life of the author of Tom Brown's school days. 1953.
Davison, W. W. Tom Brown's school days. Georgia Rev 9 1955.
Osborne, R. A re-reading of Tom Brown. Spectator 17 Aug 1956.
Maison, M. M. Tom Brown and company: scholastic novels of the 1850's. English 12 1958.
Winn, W. E. Tom Brown's schooldays and the development of muscular Christianity. Church History 29 1960.

JEAN INGELOW
1820–97

See col 527, above.

DOUGLAS WILLIAM JERROLD
1803–57

See col 1149, below.

GERALDINE ENSOR JEWSBURY
1812–80

§1

Zoe: the history of two lives. 3 vols 1845.
The half-sisters: a tale. 2 vols 1848.
Marian Withers. 3 vols 1851.
The history of an adopted child. 1853.
Constance Herbert. 3 vols 1855.
The sorrows of gentility. 2 vols 1856.
Angelo: or the pine forest in the Alps. 1856.
A selection from the letters of Geraldine Jewsbury to Jane Welsh Carlyle. Ed Mrs A. Ireland 1892.

§2

[Woolf, V.] Geraldine and Jane. TLS 28 Feb 1929. *See* also subsequent correspondence.
Howe, S. Geraldine Jewsbury: her life and errors. 1935.

JULIA KAVANAGH
1824–77

§1

The Montyon prizes. [1846].
The three paths: a story for young people. 1848.
Madeleine: a tale of Auvergne. 1848.
Nathalie: a tale. 3 vols 1850.
Woman in France during the eighteenth century. 2 vols 1850.
Women of Christianity exemplary for acts of piety and charity. 1852.
Daisy Burns: a tale. 3 vols 1853.
Grace Lee: a tale. 3 vols 1855.
Rachel Gray: a tale founded on fact. 1856.
Adèle: a tale. 3 vols 1858.
A summer and winter in the Two Sicilies. 2 vols 1858.
Seven years and other tales. 3 vols 1860.
French women of letters: biographical sketches. 2 vols 1862.
English women of letters: biographical sketches. 2 vols 1863.
Queen Mab: a novel. 3 vols 1863.
Beatrice: a novel. 3 vols 1865.
Sybil's second love: a novel. 3 vols 1867.
Dora: a novel. 3 vols 1868.
Silvia. 1870.
Bessie: a novel. 3 vols 1872.
John Dorrien: a novel. 3 vols 1875.
The pearl fountain and other fairy tales. 1876.
Two lilies: a novel. 3 vols 1877.
Forget-me-nots. 3 vols 1878. Short stories.

§2

Macquoid, K. S. In A. Sergeant et al, Women novelists of Queen Victoria's reign, 1897.

CHARLES KINGSLEY
1819–75

Bibliographies

Parrish, M. L. and B. K. Mann. Charles Kingsley and Thomas Hughes: first editions in the library at Dormy House. 1936.
Barry, J. D. In Victorian fiction: a guide to research, ed L. Stevenson, Cambridge Mass 1964.
See M. F. Thorp *under* §2, *below*.

Collections

Works. 28 vols 1880–5, 1888–9.
Works. Ed M. Kingsley 7 vols 1898–9.
Novels, poems and memories. 14 vols 1899.
The life and works. 19 vols 1901–3.

§1

The saint's tragedy, with a preface by Professor Maurice. 1848, 1859, 1861.
On English composition; On English literature. In Introductory lectures delivered at Queen's College London, 1849.
Twenty-five village sermons. 1849, 1857, 1861 (with other sermons, as Town and country sermons), 1867, 1868, 1872, 1877, 1880 etc.
Alton Locke, tailor and poet: an autobiography. 2 vols 1850 (anon), 1852, 1856 (with preface addressed to the working men of Great Britain), 1862 (with a new preface To the undergraduates of Cambridge), 1875, 1876 (with a prefatory memoir by Thomas Hughes), 1877, 1879, 2 vols 1881 (with Hughes's memoir), 1889, 1892, [1893] etc.
Cheap clothes and nasty, by Parson Lot. 1850, 1851.
The application of associative principles and methods to agriculture: a lecture. 1851.
Yeast: a problem. 1851 (anon), 1859 (4th edn, with a new preface), 1867, 1875, 1877, 1879, 1881, 1888, 1893, 1895 etc. First pbd Fraser's Mag July–Dec 1848.
Who are the friends of order? 1852.
Phaethon: or loose thoughts for loose thinkers. Cambridge 1852, 1854, 1859.
Sermons on national subjects. 1852, 1872 (as The King of the Earth, and other sermons preached in a village church), 1873.
Hypatia: or new foes with an old face. 2 vols 1853, 1 vol 1856, 1863, 1874, 1876, 1879, 2 vols 1881, 1889, 1895, 1897, 1899, 1903 etc. First pbd in Fraser's Mag Jan 1852–April 1853.
Alexandria and her schools. Cambridge 1854.
Sermons on national subjects: second series. 1854, 2 vols 1872, 1880.
Who causes pestilence? 1854.
Glaucus: or the wonders of the shore. Cambridge 1855, 1856 (3rd edn, corrected and enlarged), 1859 (enlarged), 1862, 1873, 1879, 1886, 1904. First pbd in North Br Rev Nov 1854.
Sermons for the times. 1855, 1858, 1872, 1878.
Sermons for sailors. [1855], 1885 (as Sea sermons).
The country parish: a lecture. In Lectures to ladies on practical subjects, Cambridge 1855, 1857.
Westward Ho! or the voyages and adventures of Sir Amyas Leigh, Knight, of Burrough in the County of Devon, in the reign of her most Glorious Majesty Queen Elizabeth, rendered into modern English by Charles Kingsley. 3 vols Cambridge 1855, 1855, 1861, 1865, 1869, 1873, 1876, 1879, 2 vols 1881, 1894, 1896, 1898; ed W. K. Leask 1899, [1900], [1901]; 2 vols 1901, 1902, [1903], 1904, 1905; ed J. T. Winterich, New York 1947; ed L. A. G. Strong 1953; ed J. A. Williamson 1955.
The heroes: or Greek fairy tales for my children, with 8 illustrations by the author. Cambridge 1856, 1862, 1864, 1868, 1873, 1875, 1879, 1885, 1887, 1889, 1899, 1900, 1902, 1903, 1904, 1905, 1906 etc.
Two years ago: a novel. 3 vols Cambridge 1857, 1859, 1877, 1879, 2 vols 1881, 1889, 1902, 1903, [1904] etc.
Andromeda and other poems. 1858, 1862.
Miscellanies reprinted chiefly from Fraser's Magazine and the North British Review. 2 vols 1859.

The good news of God: sermons. 1859, 1866, 1872, 1878, 1881 etc.
The massacre of the innocents: an address. [1859].
The limits of exact science as applied to history: inaugural lecture. Cambridge 1860.
Ode performed in the Senate-House Cambridge, composed for the installation of his Grace the Duke of Devonshire, Chancellor of the University. Cambridge 1862.
Speech of Lord Dundreary on the Great Hippocampus Question. Cambridge 1862.
The Gospel of the Pentateuch: a set of parish sermons. 1863, 1864, 1872, 1878, 1881.
The water-babies: a fairy tale for a land-baby with two illustrations by J. Noel Paton. 1863, 1869, 1871, 1872, 1878, 1879, 1885 (with 100 illustrations by Linley Sambourne), 1889, 1903, 1904, 1905, [1905], 1906, [1907], [1908], 1908, 1909 (3 edns), 1912, 1913 etc.
Hints to stammerers, by a minute philosopher. 1864. Also issued as The irrationale of speech.
The Roman and the Teuton: a series of lectures delivered before the University of Cambridge. Cambridge 1864; ed F. M. Müller 1875, 1879.
Mr Kingsley and Dr Newman: a correspondence on the question whether Dr Newman teaches that truth is no virtue. 1864.
'What, then, does Dr Newman mean?': a reply to a pamphlet lately published by Dr Newman. 1864; ed W. Ward, Oxford 1913 (with Newman's Apologia).
David: four sermons delivered before the University of Cambridge. 1865, 1874 (5 sermons).
American notes: letters from a lecture tour 1874. Ed R. B. Martin, Princeton 1958.
Hereward the Wake: 'last of the English'. 2 vols 1866, 1867, 1877, 1879, 1881, 1908, [1909], 1911 (with introd and notes), 1912, 1914; ed L. A. G. Strong 1954. First pbd in Good Words Jan–Dec 1865.
Three lectures delivered at the Royal Institution on the Ancien Régime before the French Revolution. 1867.
The water of life and other sermons. 1868, 1872, 1881.
Discipline and other sermons. 1868, 1872, 1881.
The hermits. 3 pts [1868], 1 vol 1878, 1880.
Madam How and Lady Why: or first lessons in earth-lore for children. 1870, 1872, 1880, 1889, 1897 etc. First pbd in Good Words for the Young Nov 1868–Oct 1869.
At last: a Christmas in the West Indies, with illustrations. 2 vols 1871, 1872, 1880, 1889, 1910.
Poems: collected edition. 1872, 1878 (enlarged), 1879, 1880 (enlarged as vol i of Works), 2 vols 1884 (enlarged), 1889, 1913, 1927.
Town geology. 1872, 1879.
Plays and Puritans, and other historical essays. 1873, 1880.
Prose idylls, new and old. 1873, 1880, 1889.
Westminster sermons. 1874, 1877.
Health and education. 1874.
Lectures delivered in America in 1874. 1875.
Letters to young men on betting and gambling. 1877.
True words for brave men. 1878, 1879, 1914.
All Saints Day and other sermons. Ed W. Harrison 1878.
Historical lectures and essays. 1880 (Works vol 17), 1889.
Sanitary and social lectures and essays. 1880 (Works vol 17), 1889.
Literary and general lectures and essays. 1880 (Works vol 20).
Scientific lectures and essays. 1885 (Works vol 19).
From death to life: fragments of teaching to a village congregation, with letters on the life after death, edited by his wife. 1887.
Words of advice to schoolboys, collected from hitherto unpublished notes and letters. Ed E. F. Johns 1912.
The tutor's story, by the late Charles Kingsley, revised and completed by his daughter 'Lucas Malet'. 1916, 1920. This story, of which c. 150 foolscap pages were left in ms by Kingsley, seems to have been written about 1863.

American notes: letters from a lecture tour 1874. Ed R. B. Martin, Princeton 1958.
Kingsley also contributed prefaces etc to the following: C. B. Mansfield, Paraguay, Brazil and the Plate, edited with a sketch of the author's life, 1856; The history and life of J. Tauler with 25 of his sermons, 1857; H. Brooke, The fool of quality, 1859; The pilgrim's progress, 1860. *Separately ptd sermons and short tracts have been omitted here. These, and Kingsley's articles in periodicals, are listed in full in M. F. Thorp's biography (1937) below.*

§2

Kingsley as a lyric poet. Chambers's Jnl 16 June 1854.
Brimley, G. In his Essays, 1858.
Masson, D. In his British novelists and their styles, Cambridge 1859.
Greg, W. R. In his Literary and social judgments, 1868.
Friswell, J. H. In his Modern men of letters, 1870.
Phillips, S. In his Essays from the Times, 2 vols 1871.
Helps, A. Charles Kingsley. Macmillan's Mag Feb 1874. Obituary.
Recollections of Kingsley. Good Words 16 1875.
James, H. Life and letters of Charles Kingsley. Nation (New York) 24 1876.
Page, H. A. The Chartism of Kingsley. Good Words 17 1876.
Charles Kingsley: his letters and memories of his life, edited by his wife. 2 vols 1877 etc. Rptd as vols 1–4 of Life and works, 1901–2. Abridged 2 vols 1879 (for 1878).
Boyd, A. K. H. Charles Kingsley. Fraser's Mag Feb 1877.
Stephen, L. In his Hours in a library ser 3, 1879.
Henley, W. E. In The English poets, ed T. H. Ward vol 4, 1880.
Rigg, J. H. Modern Anglican theology. 1880 (3rd edn). Includes Memoir of Kingsley.
Stanley, A. P. Sermons at Westminster. 1882.
Müller, M. In his Biographical essays, 1884.
Davies, G. J. In his Successful preachers, 1884.
Tulloch, J. In his Movements of religious thought in the nineteenth century, 1885.
Nielsen, F. Charles Kingsley og den Kristelige Socialisme i England. Copenhagen 1888.
Mallock, M. M. Charles Kingsley. Dublin Rev 24 1890.
Martineau, J. In his Essays, 4 vols 1890–1.
Lang, A. In his Essays in little, 1891.
Kaufmann, M. Charles Kingsley, Christian Socialist and social reformer. 1892.
Marriott, J. A. R. Charles Kingsley, novelist. 1892.
Groser, H. G. Charles Kingsley. Prefixed to a selection from the poems in The poets and the poetry of the century, ed A. H. Miles vol 5, 1893 etc.
Groth, E. Charles Kingsley als Dichter und Sozialreformer. Leipzig 1893.
Harrison, F. In his Studies in early Victorian literature, 1895.
Stubbs, C. W. Charles Kingsley and the Christian Social Movement. 1899.
Cazamian, L. Le roman social en Angleterre 1830–50. Paris 1903.
Lord, W. F. Kingsley's novels. Nineteenth Century June 1904.
Benson, A. C. The leaves of the tree. In his Studies in biography, 1911.
Keller, L. Charles Kingsley und die religiös-sozialen Kämpfe in England im 19 Jahrhundert. Berlin [1911].
Chape, R. P. The historical basis of Kingsley's Westward Ho. [1912].
Vulliamy, C. E. Charles Kingsley and Christian Socialism. 1914.
Jacobson, A. Charles Kingsleys Beziehungen zu Deutschland. Heidelberg 1917.
Courtney, J. E. Charles Kingsley. Fortnightly Rev June 1919.

'Melville, Lewis' (L. S. Benjamin). The centenary of Charles Kingsley. Contemporary Rev June 1919.
Williams, S. T. Yeast: a Victorian heresy. North Amer Rev 212 1920.
Brunner, K. Charles Kingsley als christlichsozialer Dichter. Anglia 46–7 1922–3.
Brown, W. H. Charles Kingsley: the work and influence of Parson Lot. Manchester 1924.
Brown, W. H. Maurice, Kingsley and Hughes. Manchester Quart 51 1925.
Juhnke, E. Charles Kingsley als sozialreformatorischer Schriftsteller. Anglia 49 1925.
Geffcken, J. Kingsleys Hypatia und ihr geschichtlicher Hintergrund. Neue Jahrbücher für Wissenschaft- und Jugendbildung 2 1926.
Sedgwick, J. H. A mid-Victorian Nordic. North Amer Rev 225 1928.
Partington, W. Westward Ho! with Charles Kingsley. Colophon 3 1933.
Baldwin, S. E. Charles Kingsley. Ithaca 1934. With bibliography.
Hanawalt, M. Charles Kingsley and Science. SP 34 1937.
Nicol, A. Kingsley und die Geschichte. Würzburg 1937.
Marmo, M. The social novel of Kingsley. Salerno 1937.
Thorp, M. F. Charles Kingsley. Princeton 1937. With bibliography.
— The Kingsley collection. Princeton Univ Lib Chron 8 1946.
Conacher, W. M. Kingsley. Queen's Quart 45 1938.
Matthews, R. E. Three articles from the pen of Kingsley. In Stanford studies in language and literature, ed H. Craig, Stanford 1941.
Houghton, W. E. The issue between Kingsley and Newman. Theology Today 4 1947.
Kendall, G. Kingsley and his ideas. 1947.
Pope-Hennessy, U. Canon Charles Kingsley. 1948.
— Kingsley as a children's writer. TLS 15 June 1951.
Adrian, A. A. Charles Kingsley visits Boston. HLQ 20 1950.
Martin, R. B. Kingsley. Princeton Univ Lib Chron 13 1952.
— The dust of combat: a life of Charles Kingsley. 1960.
— Manuscript sermons of Charles Kingsley. Princeton Univ Lib Chron 23 1962.
Price, J. B. Reade and Kingsley. Contemporary Rev March 1953.
Robertson, T. L. The Kingsley-Newman controversy and the Apologia. MLN 69 1954.
Williams, R. Alton Locke. In his Culture and society 1780–1950, 1958, 1961 (Pelican).
Blinderman, C. S. Huxley and Kingsley. Victorian Newsletter no 20 1961.
Waller, J. O. Charles Kingsley and the American Civil War. SP 60 1963.

HENRY KINGSLEY
1830–76

Bibliographies

Ellis, S. M. Henry Kingsley. 1931. With Kingsley's contributions to magazines.

Collections

Novels. 7 vols 1872, 1885.
Novels. Ed C. K. Shorter 8 vols 1894–5.

§1

The recollections of Geoffrey Hamlyn. 3 vols 1859, 1860, 1872, 1885, [1891] (with memoir by C. K. Shorter), 1909 etc, Oxford 1924 (WC).
Ravenshoe. 3 vols 1861, 1862, 1864, 1872, 1875, 1885, 1903, 1906, 1909, 1910 etc, Oxford 1925 (WC).
Austin Elliott. 2 vols 1863 (3 edns), 1866, 1872, 1885, Oxford 1932 (WC).
The Hillyars and the Burtons: a story of two families. 3 vols 1865, 1866, 1870, 1895 (with a note on Old Chelsea Church by C. K. Shorter).
Leighton Court: a country house story. 2 vols 1866, 1867.
Silcote of Silcotes. 3 vols 1867, 1869.
Mademoiselle Mathilde. 3 vols 1868, 1870, 1885. First pbd in GM.
Stretton. 3 vols 1869, 1870, 1879, 1885.
Tales of old travel re-narrated. 1869, 1871.
The boy in grey and other stories and sketches. 1871.
Hetty and other stories. 1871, 1885.
The lost child. 1871.
Old Margaret and other stories. 2 vols 1871, 1872, 1885, 1895.
Valentin: a French boy's story of Sedan. 2 vols 1872, [1874] (rev), 1885.
Hornby Mills and other stories. 2 vols 1872, 1873, 1885.
Oakshott Castle, by Mr Granby Dixon, edited by Henry Kingsley. 3 vols 1873, 1878. 'Granby Dixon' was Kingley's pseudonym.
Reginald Hetherege. 3 vols 1874, 1875.
Number seventeen. 2 vols 1875, 1876, 1879.
Fireside studies. 2 vols 1876.
The Grange garden: a romance. 3 vols 1876.
The mystery of the island. 1877.

§2

Geoffrey Hamlyn. North Br Rev 31 1859.
The Hillyars and the Burtons. North Amer Rev 101 1865.
Quiller-Couch, A. T. In his Adventures in criticism, 1896.
'Melville, Lewis' (L. S. Benjamin). In his Victorian novelists, 1906.
Russell, G. W. E. In his Selected essays, 1914.
Henry Kingsley. TLS 2 Jan 1930.
Ellis, S. M. Henry Kingsley 1830–76: towards a vindication. 1931.
Sadleir, M. In his Things past, 1944.
Thirkell, A. Henry Kingsley. Nineteenth-Century Fiction 5 1951.
— The works of Henry Kingsley. Ibid.
Buckler, W. E. Henry Kingsley and the Gentleman's Magazine. JEGP 50 1951.
Wolff, R. L. Henry Kingsley. Harvard Lib Bull 13 1959.

WILLIAM HENRY GILES KINGSTON
1814–80

§1

The Circassian chief: a romance of Russia. 3 vols 1843.
The Prime Minister: an historical romance. 3 vols 1845.
The albatross, or voices from the ocean: a tale of the sea. 3 vols 1851.
The pirate of the Mediterranean: a tale of the sea. 3 vols 1851.
Peter the whaler: his early life and adventures in the Arctic regions. 1851 etc.
Manco, the Peruvian chief: or an Englishman's adventures in the country of the Incas. 1853.
The emigrant's home, or how to settle: a story of Australian life. 1856.
Digby Heathcote: or the early days of a country gentleman's son and heir. 1860.
Ernest Bracebridge: or schooldays. 1860, [1871].
Will Weatherhelm: or the yarn of an old sailor about his early life and adventures. 1860, 1879 (enlarged).
The fire-ships: a tale of the last naval war. 3 vols 1862, 1867, [1871].
Count Ulrich von Lindburg: a tale of the Reformation in Germany. [1868].
The royal merchant: or events in the days of Sir Thomas Gresham, as narrated in the diary of E. Verner, whilom

his page and secretary during the reigns of Queens Mary and Elizabeth. 1870, [1880] (as The golden grasshopper).
Millicent Courtenay's diary: or the experiences of a young lady at home and abroad. [1873].
Eldol the Druid: or the dawn of Christianity in Britain. [1874].
Jovinian, or the early days of Papal Rome: a tale. 1877.
The rival Crusoes. 1879.
The ferryman of Brill, and other stories. [1880].
The above is a representative selection from Kingston's 100 or more stories, mainly for boys and of the sea. He also translated Jules Verne and edited the following periodicals: Colonist; Colonial Mag & East India Rev; Kingston's Annual for Boys; Union Jack.

§2

Kingsford, M. R. The life, work and influence of Kingston. Toronto 1947.
Willey, M. M. Peter the whaler, plagiarist. New Colophon 2 1949.

LAETITIA ELIZABETH LANDON
1802–38

See col 531, above.

GEORGE ALFRED LAWRENCE
1827–76

§1

The marriage of Marie Antoinette with the Dauphin: a prize poem recited in Rugby School, June 20 1845. Rugby 1845.
Songs of feast, field and fray, by Δ. 1853.
Guy Livingstone: or thorough. 1857 (anon), 1863 (6th edn); ed S. Kaye-Smith 1928.
Sword and gown. 1859. First pbd in Fraser's Mag.
Barren honour: a tale. 2 vols 1862. First pbd in Fraser's Mag.
Border and Bastille. 1863, New York 1866. Includes Songs of feast, field and fray, above.
A bundle of ballads. 1864.
Maurice Dering, or the quadrilateral: a novel. 2 vols 1864, Leipzig 1864.
Sans merci: or kestrels and falcons. 3 vols 1866, 1866.
Brakespeare: or the fortunes of a free lance. 3 vols 1868.
Breaking a butterfly: or Blanche Ellerslie's ending. 3 vols 1869.
Anteros: a novel. 3 vols 1873.
Silverland. 1873.
Hagarene. 3 vols 1874.

§2

Edinburgh Rev 108 1858. Review of Guy Livingstone.
Montégut, E. In his Écrivains modernes de l'Angleterre ser i, Paris 1885.
Roberts, W. G. A. Lawrence's Songs of feast, field and fray. TLS 4, 18 July 1935.
Fleming, G. H. Lawrence and the Victorian sensation novel. Tucson 1952.

'HOLME LEE', HARRIET PARR
1828–1900

Maude Talbot. 3 vols 1854.
Thorney Hall: a story of an old family. 1855.

Gilbert Massenger. 1855.
Kathie Brande: a fireside history of a quiet life. 2 vols 1856.
Sylvan Holt's daughter. 3 vols 1858.
Against wind and tide. 3 vols 1859.
Hawksview: a family history. 1859.
Legends from Fairyland, narrating the history of Prince Glee and Princess Trill, [and] the cruel persecutions of Aunt Spite. 1860.
The Wortlebank diary and some old stories from Kathie Brande's portfolio. 3 vols 1860.
The wonderful adventures of Tuflongbo and his elfin company, in their journey of little content through the enchanted forest. 1861.
Warp and woof: or the reminiscences of Doris Fletcher. 3 vols 1861.
Tuflongbo's journey in search of ogres, with some account of his early life. 1862.
Annie Warleigh's fortunes. 3 vols 1863.
The true pathetic history of Poor Match. 1863, [1863] (as Poor Match: his life, adventures and death).
In the silver age: essays—that is, dispersed meditations. 2 vols 1864.
Life and death of Jeanne d'Arc. 2 vols 1866.
Mrs Wynward's ward. 2 vols 1867.
Basil Godfrey's caprice. 3 vols 1868.
Contrast: or the schoolfellows. 1868.
For richer, for poorer. 3 vols 1870.
Maurice and Eugénie Guérin: a monograph. 1870.
Her title of honour. 1871.
The beautiful Miss Barrington. 3 vols 1871.
Echoes of a famous year. 1872.
Country stories, old and new, in prose and verse. 2 vols 1872.
Katherine's trial. 1873.
The vicissitudes of Bessie Fairfax. 3 vols 1874.
This work-a-day world. 3 vols 1875.
Ben Milner's wooing. 1876.
Straightforward. 3 vols 1878.
Mrs Denys of Cote. 3 vols 1880.
A poor squire. 2 vols 1882.
Loving and serving. 3 vols 1883.

JOSEPH SHERIDAN LE FANU
1814–73

§1

The cook and anchor: being a chronicle of old Dublin city. 3 vols Dublin 1845 (anon), 1873 (as Morley Court); ed B. S. Le Fanu [1895].
The fortunes of Colonel Torlogh O'Brien. Dublin 1847 (anon), 1855, nd, 1896.
Ghost stories and tales of mystery. Dublin 1851.
The house by the church-yard. 3 vols 1863, 1866, [1870], Dublin 1904.
Wylder's hand: a novel. 3 vols 1864, [1870], [1903].
Uncle Silas: a tale of Bartram-Haugh. 3 vols 1864, 1865, 1 vol 1865, 2 vols Leipzig 1865, [1871], Dublin 1904, [1913]; ed E. Bowen 1946.
Guy Deverell. 3 vols 1865, 2 vols Leipzig 1865, 1 vol 1866, [1869].
All in the dark. 2 vols 1866, [1869].
The tenants of Malory: a novel. 3 vols 1867, [1872].
A lost name. 3 vols 1868.
Haunted lives: a novel. 3 vols 1868.
The Wyvern mystery: a novel. 3 vols 1869, 1889, [1904].
Checkmate. 3 vols 1871.
The rose and the key. 3 vols 1871.
Chronicles of Golden Friars. 3 vols 1871.
In a glass darkly. 3 vols 1872, 1884, 1923, 1929.
Willing to die. 3 vols 1873, [1895?].
The Purcell papers, with a memoir by Alfred Perceval Graves. 3 vols 1880.

The watcher and other weird stories. [1894].
The evil guest. [1895].
Poems. Ed A. P. Graves 1896.
Madam Crowl's ghost and other tales of mystery. Ed M. R. James 1923.
Le Fanu joined the staff of the Dublin Univ Mag in 1837 and many of his tales and novels were originally pbd there. He was editor and proprietor 1869–72.

§2

Kenton, E. A forgotten creator of ghosts. Bookman (New York) July 1929.
Benson, E. F. Sheridan Le Fanu. Spectator 21 Feb 1931.
Ellis, S. M. Wilkie Collins, Le Fanu and others. 1931. With bibliography, including partial list of Le Fanu's contributions to periodicals.
Pritchett, V. S. An Irish ghost. In his Living novel, 1946.
—— Aristophanes and Le Fanu. New Statesman 4 Jan 1958.
Dagg, T. S. C. Le Fanu: a memorial discourse. Dublin 1949.
Browne, N. Sheridan Le Fanu. 1951.

CHARLES JAMES LEVER
1806–72

Collections

The military novels, illustrated by George Cruikshank and 'Phiz'. 9 vols nd.
Works. 34 vols 1876–8. Harry Lorrequer edn.
Novels, edited by his daughter [Julia Kate Neville]. 37 vols 1897–9.

§1

The confessions of Harry Lorrequer. Dublin 1839, 1845, 1882, 1884; ed 'Lewis Melville' (L. S. Benjamin) [1907] (EL).
Diary and notes of Horace Templeton, late Secretary of Legation. Philadelphia [1840?], 2 vols 1848, [1878].
Charles O'Malley, the Irish dragoon, edited by Harry Lorrequer. 2 vols Dublin 1841, London 1842, 1845, 3 vols Leipzig 1848, 2 vols 1857, 1876.
Our Mess. 3 vols Dublin 1843–4, 1857, 1876, 1885. Vol i, Jack Hinton; vols 2–3, Tom Burke of 'Ours'.
Arthur O'Leary: his wanderings and ponderings in many lands. 3 vols 1844, 1845, 1 vol 1856 (as Adventures of Arthur O'Leary), 1877, 1886.
St Patrick's Eve. 1845, 1871 (with A rent in the cloud etc).
Nuts and nutcrackers. 1845.
Tales of the trains. 1845.
The O'Donoghue: a tale of Ireland fifty years ago. Dublin 1845, 1858, 1868, 1876.
The Knight of Gwynne: a tale of the time of the Union. 1847, 1858, 1867, 1877, 1889.
The Martins of Gro' Martin. 1847, 1856, 1856, 1878.
Confessions of Con Cregan, the Irish Gil Blas. 2 vols [1849], 1854, 1876, 1891.
Roland Cashel. 1850, 1858, 1864.
The Daltons: or three roads in life. 2 vols 1850–2, 1859, 1876.
Maurice Tiernay: the soldier of fortune. 1852, [1855], 2 vols 1861, 1878.
The Dodd family abroad. 2 vols 1852–4, 1859, 1877.
Sir Jasper Carew: his life and experiences. [1855], 1878.
The fortunes of Glencore. 3 vols 1857, 1878.
Davenport Dunn: or the man of the day. 1859.
One of them. 1861, 1877.
A day's ride. 2 vols 1863, 1878.
Barrington. 1863, 2 vols Leipzig 1863, 1 vol 1878.
Cornelius O'Dowd upon men, women and other things in general. 3 sers 1864–5, 1 vol 1874. First pbd in Blackwood's Mag.

Luttrell of Arran. 1865, 1877.
A rent in a cloud. [1865], 1878 (with St Patrick's Eve etc).
Tony Butler. 3 vols Edinburgh 1865, 1878.
Sir Brook Fossbrooke. 3 vols 1866, 1867, 1878.
The Bramleighs of Bishop's Folly. 3 vols 1868, 1877.
Paul Gosslett's confessions in law and the Civil Service. 1868, 1924. First pbd in Saint Paul's Mag.
That boy of Norcott's. 1869, 1878 (with A rent in a cloud, above, etc).
Lord Kilgobbin: a tale of Ireland in our own time. 3 vols 1872, 1877, 1906.
Gerald Fitzgerald the Chevalier. 1899. First pbd in Dublin Univ Mag; rptd 27 years after Lever's death.
Lever edited Dublin Univ Mag 1835–72 and from 1835 was also a regular contributer to Blackwood's Mag.

§2

The works of Lever. Blackwood's Mag April 1862.
Friswell, J. H. In his Modern men of letters, 1870.
Fitzpatrick, W. J. Life of Lever. 2 vols 1879.
Downey, E. Lever: life in his letters. 2 vols 1906.
Rolfe, F. P. Letters of Lever to his wife and daughter. Huntington Lib Bull no 10 1936.
Stevenson, L. Dr Quicksilver. 1939.
McHugh, R. Charles Lever. Studies 27 1938.
Genn, F. Books in general. New Statesman 5 Sept 1942.
Hennig, J. Lever and Rodolphe Toepffer. MLR 43 1948.

GEORGE HENRY LEWES
1817–78

See col 1542, below.

ELIZA LYNN LINTON,
née LYNN
1822–98

§1

Azeth the Egyptian. 3 vols [1846].
Amymone: a romance of the days of Pericles. 3 vols 1848.
Realities: a tale. 3 vols 1851.
Witch stories. 1861. First pbd in All the Year Round.
The Lake country, illustrated by W. J. Linton. 1864.
Grasp your nettle: a novel. 3 vols 1865.
Lizzie Norton of Greygrigg: a novel. 3 vols 1866.
Sowing the wind. 3 vols 1867.
Ourselves: essays on women. 1869, 1870, 1884.
The true history of Joshua Davidson. 1872, 1873.
Patricia Kemball: a novel. 3 vols 1874.
The mad Willoughbys and other tales. 1875.
The atonement of Leam Dundas: a novel. 3 vols 1877.
The world well lost. 2 vols 1877.
At night in a hospital. 1879. Rptd from Belgravia.
Under which lord? a novel. 1879.
The rebel of the family. 3 vols 1880.
With a silken thread and other stories. 3 vols 1880.
My love: a novel. 3 vols 1881.
Jane: a novel. 1883.
The girl of the period and other essays from the Saturday Review. 2 vols 1883.
The autobiography of Christopher Kirkland. 3 vols 1885.
Stabbed in the dark: a tale. [1885].
The rift in the lute: a tale. Glasgow [1885].
Paston Carew, millionaire and miser: a novel. 3 vols 1886.
Through the long night. 3 vols 1888.
About Ireland. 1890.
An octave of friends; with other silhouettes and stories. 1891.
About Ulster. 1892.
The one too many. 3 vols 1894.
In haste and at leisure. 3 vols 1895.

Dulcie Everton. 2 vols 1896.
Twixt cup and lip [etc]. 1896. Short stories.
My literary life; with a prefatory note by Beatrice Harraden. 1899.
The second youth of Theodora Desanges, with an introduction by G. S. Layard. 1900.

§2

Tweedie, Mrs A. A chat with Mrs Lynn Linton. Temple Bar July 1894.
Linton, W. J. Autobiographical memories. 1895. By the husband.
Layard, G. S. Eliza Lynn Linton: her life, letters and opinions. 1901.
D., C. Mrs Lynn Linton and Dickens. N & Q 10 April 1943.
G., E. B. Mrs Lynn Linton and Thornton Hunt. N & Q 9, 23 Oct 1943.

THOMAS HENRY LISTER
1800–42

§1

Granby: a novel. 3 vols 1826 (3 edns), 1838.
Herbert Lacy. 3 vols 1828.
Epicharis: an historical tragedy. 1829.
Arlington: a novel. 3 vols [1832].
Flirtation. 3 vols [1833?].
Romance of real life. 3 vols [1833?].
Yes and no. 2 vols 1834.
Anne Grey: a novel, by Harriet Lister, edited by the author of Granby. 3 vols 1834.
The life and administration of Edward first Earl of Clarendon; with original correspondence and authentic papers never before published. 3 vols 1837–8.
An answer to the misrepresentations contained in an article [by J. W. Croker] on the life of Clarendon in no 124 of the Quarterly Review. 1839.
Hulse House. 1860.

§2

Moers, E. In her Dandy, 1961.

GEORGE MacDONALD
1824–1905

Collections

Works of fancy and imagination. 10 vols 1871.
MacDonald: an anthology. Ed C. S. Lewis 1946.

§1

Within and without: a poem. 1855.
Poems. 1857.
Phantastes: a faerie romance for men and women. 1858.
David Elginbrod. 3 vols 1863.
Adela Cathcart. 3 vols 1864.
The portent: a story of the inner vision of the Highlanders commonly called the second sight. 1864. First pbd in Cornhill Mag 1860.
Alec Forbes of Howglen. 3 vols 1865.
Annals of a quiet neighbourhood. 3 vols 1867. First pbd anon in Sunday Mag 1866.
Dealings with the fairies. 1867.
The disciple and other poems. 1867.
Unspoken sermons. 3 sers 1867–89.
Guild Court. 3 vols 1868. First pbd in Good Words 1867.
Robert Falconer. 3 vols 1868. First pbd in Argosy 1867.
The seaboard parish. 3 vols 1868.
The miracles of Our Lord. 1870.
At the back of the north wind. 1871 (for 1870). First pbd in Good Words for the Young.
Ranald Bannerman's boyhood. 1871. First pbd in Good Words for the Young.
The Princess and the goblin. 1872 (for 1871).
The Vicar's daughter. 3 vols 1872.
Wilfred Cumbermede. 3 vols 1872.
Gutta Percha Willie: the working genius. 1873.
England's Antiphon. 1874.
Malcolm. 3 vols 1875.
The wise woman: a parable. 1875, 1895 (as The lost Princess: or the wise woman); ed E. Yates 1965.
Exotics: a translation of the spiritual songs of Novalis, the Hymn Book of Luther and other poems from the German and Italian. 1876. Verse.
Thomas Wingfold, curate. 3 vols 1876.
St George and St Michael. 3 vols 1876.
The Marquis of Lossie. 3 vols 1877.
Sir Gibbie. 3 vols 1879.
Paul Faber, surgeon. 3 vols 1879.
A book of strife, in the form of the diary of an old soul. 1880, 1909, 1913.
Mary Marston. 3 vols 1881.
Castle Warlock: a homely romance. 3 vols 1882.
Orts. 1882, 1893 (enlarged as A dish of orts).
Weighed and wanting. 3 vols 1882.
The gifts of the child Christ and other tales. 2 vols 1882. Later pbd as Stephen Archer and other tales, nd.
A threefold cord: poems by three friends. 1883 (priv ptd). Ed MacDonald.
Donal Grant. 3 vols 1883.
The Princess and Curdie. 1883 (for 1882).
The tragedie of Hamlet, with a study of the text of the folio of 1623. 1885.
What's mine's mine. 3 vols 1886.
Cross purposes, and The shadows: two fairy stories. 1886. Rptd from Dealings with the fairies.
Home again: a tale. 1887.
The elect lady. 1888.
A rough shaking: a tale. 1890.
The light Princess and other fairy stories. 1890.
A cabinet of gems, cut and polished by Sir Philip Sidney, now for their more radiance presented without their setting by George MacDonald. 1891.
There and back. 3 vols 1891.
The flight of the shadow. 1891.
The hope of the Gospel. 1892.
Heather and snow. 2 vols 1893.
Poetical works. 2 vols 1893.
Lilith: a romance. 1895.
Rampolli: growths from a long-planted root, being translations chiefly from the German, along with a year's diary of an old soul. 1897. Poems.
Salted with fire: a tale. 1897.

§2

Geddes, W. D. MacDonald as a poet. Blackwood's Mag March 1891.
Johnson, J. MacDonald: a biography and critical appreciation. 1906.
MacDonald, R. In his Essays from a northern window, [1911]. By his son.
MacDonald, G. MacDonald and his wife, with an introduction by G. K. Chesterton. 1924.
Evans, B. I. In his English poetry in the later nineteenth century, 1933, 1966 (rev).
Menander's mirror: Princess and goblins. TLS 26 Dec 1942.
Parsons, C. O. MacDonald and Henry More. N & Q 5 May 1945.
— The progenitors of Black Beauty in humanitarian literature. N & Q 19 April–31 May 1947.

Fremantle, A. The visionary novels of MacDonald. New York 1954.
Ragg, L. M. MacDonald and his household. English 11 1956.
Wolff, R. L. The golden key: a study of the fiction of MacDonald. New Haven 1961.

ANNE MANNING
1807–79

§1

A sister's gift: conversations on sacred subjects. 1826.
Stories from the history of Italy, from the invasion of Alaric to the present time. 1831.
Village bells. 3 vols 1838, 1859.
The maiden and married life of Mary Powell, afterwards Mistress Milton. 1849; 1855, 1859 (with Deborah's diary), 1860, 1866, 1874. First pbd in Sharpe's Mag 1849. *See* Deborah's diary, below.
The household of Sir Thomas More. 1851, 1860, 1870, 1887, 1896 etc. First pbd in Sharpe's Mag.
Queen Philippa's golden rule. 1851.
The colloquies of Edward Osborne, citizen and cloth worker of London. 1852.
The drawing room table book. 1852.
Cherry and violet: a tale of the Plague. 1853.
The provocations of Madame Palissy. 1853.
Chronicles of Merry England. 1854.
Claude the Colpasteur. 1854.
Jack and the tanner of Wymondham. 1854.
The hill side: illustrations of some of the simplest terms used in logic. 1854.
Some account of Mrs Clarida Singlehart. 1855.
Stories from the history of the Caliph Haroun al Raschid. 1855.
A Sabbath at home. 1855.
The Old Chelsea Bun House: a tale. 1855.
Tasso and Leonora: the commentaries of Ser Pantaleone degli Gambacorti. 1856.
The week of darkness: a short manual for the use and comfort of mourners. 1856.
Helen and Olga: a Russian story. 1857.
Lives of good servants. 1857.
The good old times: a tale of Auvergne. 1857.
An English girl's account of a Moravian settlement. 1858. Ed Anne Manning.
Deborah's diary. 1858. Sequel to Mary Powell, above.
The year nine: a tale of the Tyrol. 1858.
The ladies of Bever Hollow. 2 vols 1858.
Poplar House Academy. 2 vols 1859.
Autobiography of Valentine Duval. 1860.
Town and forest. 1860.
The day of small things. 1860.
Chronicle of Ethelfled. 1861.
Family pictures. 1861.
The cottage history of England. 1861.
A noble purpose nobly won. 2 vols 1862. On Joan of Arc.
Bessy's Money: a tale. 1863.
Meadowleigh. 1863.
The Duchess of Trajetto. 1863.
An interrupted wedding. 1864.
Belfast: a tale. 1865.
Selvaggio: a tale of Italian country life. Edinburgh 1865.
Miss Biddy Frobisher: a saltwater story. 1866.
The Lincolnshire tragedy: passages in the life of the Faire Gospeller, Mistress Anne Askewe, recounted by Nicholas Moldwarp. 1866.
The masque at Ludlow and other romanesques. 1866.
Diana's crescent. 2 vols 1868.
Jacques Bonneval. 1868.
The Spanish barber: a tale. 1869.
Margaret More's Tagebuch. 1870.
One trip more. 1870.
Compton Friars. 1872.
The lady of limited income. 2 vols 1872.
Lord Harry Bellair. 2 vols 1874.
Monk's Norton. 2 vols 1874.
Heroes of the desert: the story of the lives of Moffat and Livingstone. 1875.
An idyll of the Alps. 1876.
Anne Manning contributed articles and stories to Golden Hours 1868–76, a mag ed Dr Whittemore. The following serials, not rptd, were pbd there: Madame Prosni and Madame Bleay, 1868; Rosita, 1869; On the Grand Tour, 1870; Octavia Solaro, 1871; Illusions dispelled, 1871. *The only book pbd under her own name was* Stories from the history of Italy, 1831.

§2

Yonge, C. M. In A. Sergeant et al, Women novelists of Queen Victoria's reign, 1897.

ANNE MARSH, later MARSH-CALDWELL, née CALDWELL
1791–1874

Two old men's tales: The deformed and The Admiral's daughter. 2 vols 1834, 1834.
Tales of the woods and fields: a second series of Two old men's tales. 3 vols 1836, 1846, 1850.
The triumphs of time. 1844, 1849.
Mount Sorel: or the heiress of the de Veres. 2 vols 1845, [1856].
Emilia Wyndham. 3 vols 1846, 1848, 2 vols Leipzig 1852.
Father Darcy. 2 vols 1846, [1857].
Norman's Bridge: or the modern Midas. 1847, 1850, [1855].
The Protestant Reformation in France: or the history of the Hugonots. 1847.
Angela: a novel. 3 vols 1848, [1855], [1875].
Mordaunt Hall: or a September night. 3 vols 1849, 1853.
Tales of the first French Revolution. 1849.
Lettice Arnold: a tale. 1850, [1856], [1876].
The Wilmingtons. 3 vols 1850, 1852.
Ravenscliffe. 3 vols 1851, 2 vols Leipzig 1852, [1855].
Time the avenger. 3 vols 1851, 1853.
Castle Avon. 3 vols 1852, 2 vols Leipzig 1852, [1855].
The Longwoods of the Grange. 1853, 1862.
Aubrey. 3 vols 1854, 2 vols Leipzig 1854, 1 vol [1857], [1875].
The heiress of Houghton: or the mother's secret. 3 vols 1855, 2 vols Leipzig 1855, [1858].
Woman's devotion: a novel. 3 vols 1855.
Evelyn Marston. 3 vols 1856, 2 vols Leipzig 1856, [1860].
Margaret and her bridesmaids. 1856, [1860].
The rose of Ashurst. 3 vols 1857, 2 vols Leipzig 1857, 1 vol 1859.
Mr and Mrs Asheton. 3 vols 1860, 1864.
The ladies of Lovel-Leigh. 3 vols 1862.
Chronicles of Dartmoor. 3 vols 1866.
Lords and ladies. 1866.

JOHN WESTLAND MARSTON
1819–90

See col 1152, below.

HARRIET MARTINEAU
1802–76

Bibliographies

Rivlin, J. B. Harriet Martineau: a bibliography of the separately printed books. BNYPL May-July, Oct 1946–Jan 1947.

§1

Devotional exercises for the use of young persons. 1823, 1832 (enlarged as Devotional exercises, to which is added a guide to the study of the scriptures.
Addresses with prayers and original hymns for the use of families, by a lady. 1826.
Traditions of Palestine. 1830. Ed Harriet Martineau.
Essential faith of the universal Church deduced from the sacred records. 1831.
Five years of youth: or sense and sentiment. 1831.
Illustrations of political economy. 9 vols 1832–4. Includes Life in the wilds; Ellin of Gavreloch; A Manchester strike; Cousin Marshall; The loom and the lugger; Sowers not reapers etc.
The Faith as unfolded by many prophets: an essay addressed to the disciples of Mohammed. 1832.
Providence as manifested through Israel. 1832.
Poor laws and paupers illustrated, 1: The parish: a tale; 2: The hamlets: a tale; 3: The town: a tale; 4: The land's end: a tale. 4 pts 1833–4.
Illustrations of taxation. 1834. Includes The park and the paddock; The scholars of Arneside.
Miscellanies. 2 vols [Boston] 1836.
Society in America. 3 vols 1837.
A retrospect of western travel. 3 vols 1838.
Deerbrook: a novel. 3 vols 1839.
Guides to service. [1839?].
The martyr age of the United States of America. 1840.
The hour and the man: an historical romance. 3 vols 1841.
The playfellow: a series of tales. 4 vols 1841. The settlers at home (rptd separately 1856); The peasant and the Prince (rptd separately 1856); Feats on the Fiord (rptd separately 1844, 1856, 1883 etc); The Crofton boys (rptd separately 1856).
The rioters. nd; 1842 (unauthorized). A short story.
Life in the sick-room: or essays by an invalid. 1844.
Dawn Island: a tale. Manchester 1845. Pbd on behalf of the Anti-Corn Law League.
Forest and game-law tales. 3 vols 1845–6.
Letters on Mesmerism. 1845.
The billow and the rock. 1846.
The land we live in. 1847. With Charles Knight.
Eastern life, past and present. 3 vols 1848.
Household education. 1849.
History of England during the Thirty Years' Peace 1816–46. 2 vols 1849–50, 1855 (rev as History of the peace 1816–46), 4 vols [1877–8].
Two letters on cow-keeping. [1850?].
Letters on the laws of man's nature and development. 1851. With H. G. Atkinson.
Introduction to the history of the peace from 1800 to 1815. 1851, 1878.
Half a century of the British Empire: a history of the Kingdom and the people from 1800 to 1850. Pt 1 (all pbd), [1851].
Merdhen, the manor and the eyrie, and old landmarks and old laws. 1852.
Letters from Ireland. 1853. Rptd from Daily News.
The positive philosophy of August Comte freely translated and condensed. 2 vols 1853.
Complete guides to the Lakes. 1854.
Guide to Windermere, with tours to the neighbouring lakes and other interesting places. Windermere [1854], [1854], [1856].
The factory controversy: a warning against meddling legislation. Manchester 1855.
A history of the American compromises. 1856. Rptd in part from Daily News.
Corporate traditions and national rights: local dues on shipping. [1857].
Guide to Keswick and its environs. Windermere [1857].
Suggestions towards the future government of India. 1858.
Endowed schools of Ireland. 1859. Rptd from Daily News.
England and her soldiers. 1859.
Survey of the Lake District. 1860.
Health, husbandry and handicraft. 1861.
Biographical sketches. 1869, 1877 (enlarged and with autobiographical sketch). Rptd from Daily News.
Harriet Martineau's autobiography, with memorials by Maria Weston Chapman. 3 vols 1877.
The Hampdens: an historiette. 1880 (illustr J. E. Millais).
Harriet Martineau also wrote over 1,600 articles for Daily News 1851–66, as well as contributing to Edinburgh Rev from 1859.

§2

[Lockhart, J. G.] Illustrations of political economy nos 1–12. Quart Rev 49 1833. An attack.
Horne, R. H. In his A new spirit of the age vol 2, 1844.
Maginn, W. In his A gallery of illustrious literary characters, ed W. Bates [1873].
Oliphant, M. O. Harriet Martineau. Blackwood's Mag April 1877.
Miller, Mrs Fenwick. Harriet Martineau. 1884.
Payn, J. In his Literary recollections, 1884.
Hamilton, C. J. Harriet Martineau. 1884.
Escher, E. Harriet Martineaus sozialpolitische Novellen. Zürich 1925.
Bosanquet, T. Harriet Martineau. 1927.
Marvin, F. S. Harriet Martineau: triumph and tragedy. Hibbert Jnl 25 1927.
Pope-Hennessy, U. Three English women in America [Fanny Trollope, Fanny Kemble, Harriet Martineau]. 1929.
Fay, C. R. Economics in a novel. Dalhousie Rev 13 1932.
Calkins, E. E. Harriet Martineau: deaf bluestocking. Colophon 14 1933.
Ruenberg, N. E. Harriet Martineau: an example of Victorian conflict. Philadelphia 1933.
Stearns, B.-M. Miss Sedgwick observes Harriet Martineau. New England Quart 7 1934.
Bloore, S. Miss Martineau speaks out. New England Quart 9 1936.
Boyle, E. In his Biographical essays 1790–1890, Oxford 1936.
Ratcliffe, S. K. Eccentric Englishwomen: Harriet Martineau. Spectator 21 May 1937.
Nevill, J. C. Harriet Martineau. 1943.
Martin, R. B. Charlotte Brontë and Harriet Martineau. Nineteenth-Century Fiction 7 1953.
Wheatley, V. The life and work of Harriet Martineau. 1957.
Webb, R. K. Harriet Martineau: a radical Victorian. 1960.

AUGUSTUS SEPTIMUS MAYHEW
1826–75

The greatest plague of life: adventures of a lady in search of a good servant, illustrated by George Cruikshank. [1847]. With his brother Henry Mayhew.
The good genius that turned everything into gold, or the Queen Bee and the magic dress: a Christmas fairytale. 1847. With Henry Mayhew.
Whom to marry and how to get married, illustrated by George Cruikshank. [1848]. With Henry Mayhew.

The image of his father: or one boy is more trouble than a dozen girls, illustrated by 'Phiz'. 1848. With Henry Mayhew.
The magic of kindness: or the wondrous story of the good Huan, illustrated by George Cruikshank and Kenny Meadows. [1849], [1869] (illust Walter Crane). With Henry Mayhew.
Living for appearances: a tale. 1855. With Henry Mayhew.
Kitty Lamere or a dark page in London life: a tale. 1855.
Paved with gold, or the romance and reality of London streets: an unfashionable novel, illustrated by H. K. Browne. 1858.
The finest girl in Bloomsbury: a serio-comic tale of ambitious love. 1861.
Blow hot—blow cold: a love story. 1862.
Faces for fortunes. 3 vols 1865.
The comic almanack. 1870 etc. With Henry Mayhew.

JOHN MILLS
d. c. 1885

The old English gentleman: or the fields and the woods. 3 vols 1841, 1841, 1854.
The stage coach: or the road of life. 3 vols 1843.
D'Horsay: or the follies of the day, by a man of fashion. 1844; ed J. Grego 1902 (with introd, sketch of D'Orsay's career, key to the characters mentioned in the satire and bibliography of works written by Mills).
The English fireside: a tale of the past. 3 vols 1844.
The days of old. In The Edinburgh tales vol 2, 1845.
The old hall: or our hearth and homestead. 3 vols 1845.
The sportsman's library. Edinburgh 1845.
Christmas in the olden time: or the wassail bowl. [1846].
The life of a foxhound. 1848, 1849, 1861, 1892, [1910], 1921.
A capful of moonshine: or 'tis not all gold that glitters. 1849.
Our county. 3 vols 1850.
The belle of the village. 3 vols 1852.
The life of a race-horse. 1854, 1861.
The wheel of life. 1855.
The flyers of the hunt, illustrated by J. Leech. 1859, 1865.
Stable secrets: or Puffy Doddles, his sayings and sympathies. 1863.
Too fast to last. 3 vols 1881, [1882].
On the spur of the moment. 3 vols 1884.
Jack Cherton of Sydney. [1906].

DINAH MARIA MULOCK, later CRAIK
1826–87

§1

The Ogilvies: a novel. 3 vols 1849, 1875.
Cola Monti: or the story of a genius. [1849], [1866] (rev), [1883].
Olive. 3 vols 1850.
The head of the family. 3 vols 1851.
Alice Learmont: a fairy tale. 1852, 1884 (rev).
Bread upon the waters: a governess's life. 1852.
Avillion and other tales. 3 vols 1853.
Agatha's husband: a novel. 3 vols 1853.
A hero: Philip's book. 1853.
John Halifax, gentleman. 3 vols 1856, 2 vols Leipzig 1857, 1 vol 1859, [1897], [1898], 2 vols [1900], 1903 etc.
Nothing new: tales. 1857.
A woman's thoughts about women. 1858.
A life for a life. 3 vols 1859.
Poems. [1859].
Romantic tales. 1859.
Domestic stories. [1859?].
Our year: a child's book. 1860.
Studies from life. 1861.
Mistress and maid. 2 vols 1863.
The fairy book: the best popular fairy stories selected and rendered anew. 1863.
Christian's mistake. 1865.
A New Year's gift for sick children. 1865.
Home thoughts and home scenes. 1865.
A noble life. 2 vols 1866.
How to win love, or Rhoda's lesson: a story for the young. [1866?].
Two marriages. 2 vols 1867.
The woman's kingdom. 3 vols 1869.
A brave lady. 3 vols 1870.
The unkind word and other stories. 2 vols 1870.
Fair France: impressions of a traveller. 1871.
Little Sunshine's holiday. 1871.
Hannah. 2 vols 1872.
Is it true? tales curious and wonderful. 1872.
The adventures of a Brownie. 1872.
My mother and I. 1874.
Sermons out of church. 1875.
The little lame Prince. 1875.
Will Denbigh, nobleman. 1877.
The laurel bush. 1877.
Young Mrs Jardine. 3 vols 1879.
Children's poetry. 1881.
His little mother and other tales. 1881.
Thirty years: poems new and old. 1881, 1888 (as Poems by the author of John Halifax, gentleman).
Plain speaking. 1882.
An unsentimental journey through Cornwall. 1884.
Miss Tommy. 1884.
About money and other things. 1886.
King Arthur—not a love story. 1886.
Work for the idle hands [in Ireland]. 1886.
An unknown country. 1887.
Fifty golden years: incidents in the Queen's reign. [1887].
Concerning men and other papers. 1888.
Mrs Craik also edited various works as well as publishing trns from the French.

§2

Miles, A. H. In The poets and poetry of the century vols 7–8, 1893–1906.
Parr, [Louisa]. In A. Sergeant et al, Women novelists of Queen Victoria's reign, 1897.
—— The author of John Halifax, gentleman: a memoir. 1898.
Reade, A. L. The Mellards and their descendants; with memoirs of Dinah Maria Mulock. 1915.
—— The author of John Halifax, gentleman. N & Q 9 June 1951.
Johnson, R. B. In his Women novelists, [1918].

SIR CHARLES AUGUSTUS MURRAY
1806–95

§1

Travels in North America during the years 1834, 1835 and 1836, including a summer residence with the Pannee tribe of Indians and a visit to Cuba and the Azore Islands. 2 vols 1839, 1854 (rev).
The prairie-bird. 3 vols 1844, 1 vol 1845, 1857, [1874].
Hassan, or the child of the Pyramid: an Egyptian tale. 2 vols 1857, 1901.
Nom-ed-dyn, or the light of the faith: an Eastern fairy tale. [1883].
A short memoir of Mohammed Ali, founder of the Vice-Royalty of Egypt. Ed H. Maxwell 1898.

§2

Maxwell, H. The Hon Sir Charles Murray KCB: a memoir. 1898.

JOHN MASON NEALE

1818–66

See col 541, above.

WILLIAM JOHNSON NEALE

1812–93

Cavendish: or the patrician at sea. 1831.
The lauread: a satire. 1833.
The Port Admiral: a tale of the war. 3 vols 1833.
Will-Watch, from the auto-biography of a British officer. 3 vols 1834.
The Priors of Prague. 3 vols 1836.
Gentleman Jack: a naval story. 1837.
The flying Dutchman: a legend of the High Seas. 3 vols 1839.
The law of parliamentary elections. 1839.
Paul Periwinkle: or the pressgang. 1841 (illustr 'Phiz').
The naval surgeon. 3 vols 1841.
History of the mutiny at Spithead and the Nore. 1842.
The Captain's wife. 3 vols 1842.
The lost ship: or the Atlantic steamer. 3 vols 1843.
A letter to the Attorney General Sir W. W. Follett, suggesting some amendments in the proposed new County Courts Bill. 1844.
Scapegrace at sea. 3 vols 1863 (2nd edn).

JOHN HENRY NEWMAN

1801–90

See col 1311, below.

CAROLINE NORTON

1808–77

See col 544, above.

LAURENCE OLIPHANT

1829–88

§1

A journey to Katmandu with the camp of Jung Bahadoor, including a sketch of the Nepaulese Ambassador at home. 1852.
The Russian shores of the Black Sea in the autumn of 1852, with a voyage down the Volga, and a tour through the country of the Don Cossacks. Edinburgh 1853, 1853 (enlarged), 1854.
The coming campaign. Edinburgh 1855.
Minnesota and the Far West. Edinburgh 1855.
The Trans-Caucasian provinces the proper field of operation for a Christian army. Edinburgh 1855.
The Trans-Caucasian campaign of the Turkish army under Omar Pasha: a personal narrative. Edinburgh 1856.
Narrative of the Earl of Elgin's mission to China and Japan in the years 1857, 58, 59. 2 vols Edinburgh 1859.
Patriots and filibusters: incidents of political and exploratory travel, reprinted from Blackwood's Magazine with corrections and additions. Edinburgh 1860.
Universal suffrage and Napoleon the Third. 1860.
On the present state of political parties in America. Edinburgh 1866.
Piccadilly: a fragment of contemporary biography. 1866, Edinburgh 1870, 1874; ed M. Sadleir 1928. First pbd in Blackwood's Mag 1865.
The land of Gilead, with excursions in the Lebanon. Edinburgh 1880.
The land of Khemi: up and down the Middle Nile. Edinburgh 1882.
Traits and travesties, social and political. Edinburgh 1882. Largely rptd from Blackwood's Mag. Includes The autobiography of a joint-stock company, The adventures of a war correspondent etc.
Altiora Peto. 2 vols Edinburgh 1883.
A trip to the north-east of Lake Tiberias in Jaulan. 1885.
Haifa: or life in modern Palestine. 1885, Edinburgh 1887.
Sympneumata: or evolutionary forces now active in man. Edinburgh 1885.
Masollam. A problem of the period. 3 vols Edinburgh 1886.
Episodes in a life of adventure: or moss from a rolling stone. Edinburgh 1887. Rptd from Blackwood's Mag.
Fashionable philosophy and other sketches. Edinburgh 1887. Rptd from Nineteenth Century and Blackwood's Mag. Dramatic sketches and stories, mainly satirical.
The star in the east. 1887. A pamphlet written for Mohammedans.
Scientific religion: or higher possibilities of life and practice through the operation of natural forces, with an appendix by a clergyman of the Church of England [Haskett Smith]. 1888.

§2

Liesching, L. F. Personal reminiscences of Oliphant. [1891].
Oliphant, M. O. Memoir of Oliphant and of Alice Oliphant his wife. 2 vols Edinburgh 1891.
Scott, C. N. Oliphant: supplementary contributions to his biography. 1895.
Owen, R. D. My perilous life in Palestine. 1928. By Oliphant's second wife.
Kent, M. An errant genius. Cornhill Mag Nov 1936.
Henderson, P. The life of Oliphant. 1956.
Dearden, S. Laurence Oliphant. Cornhill Mag 169 1956.
Ryan, A. P. Laurence Oliphant. Listener 31 May 1956.

MARGARET OLIPHANT OLIPHANT, née WILSON

1828–97

§1

Passages in the life of Mrs Margaret Maitland. 3 vols 1849. *See* Lilliesleaf, below.
Caleb Field. 1851.
Merkland: a story of Scottish life. 3 vols 1851.
Memoirs and resolutions of Adam Graeme of Mossgray. 3 vols 1852.
Katie Stewart. 1853.
Harry Muir: a story of Scottish life. 3 vols 1853.
Quiet heart: a story. 1854.
Magdalen Hepburn: a story of the Scottish Reformation. 1854.
Lilliesleaf: conclusion of Margaret Maitland. 3 vols 1855.
Zaidee: a romance. 3 vols 1856.
The Athelings: or the three gifts. 3 vols 1857.
The days of my life. 1857.
Sundays. 1858.
The Laird of Nordlaw. 3 vols 1858.
Orphans: a chapter in life. 1858.
Agnes Hopetoun's schools and holidays. 1859.
The house on the moor. 1861.
The last of the Mortimers. 1862.
The life of Edward Irving. 2 vols 1862.
The rector and the doctor's family. 3 vols 1863 (Chronicles of Carlingford). Anon.
Salem Chapel. 2 vols 1863 (Chronicles of Carlingford). Anon.

Heart and cross. 1863.
The perpetual curate. 3 vols 1864 (Chronicles of Carlingford). Anon.
Agnes. 3 vols 1866.
Miss Marjoribanks. 3 vols 1866 (Chronicles of Carlingford). Anon.
A son of the soil. 1866.
Madonna Mary. 3 vols 1867.
Francis of Assisi. 1868.
The Brownlows. 3 vols 1868.
Historical sketches of the reign of George II. 2 vols 1869.
The minister's wife. 1869.
John: a love story. 2 vols 1870.
The three brothers. 3 vols 1870.
Squire Arden. 3 vols 1871.
At his gates. 3 vols 1872.
Memoirs of the Count de Montalembert: a chapter of recent French history. 1872.
Ombra [etc]. 3 vols 1872.
May. 3 vols 1873.
Innocent: a tale of modern life. 1873.
A rose in June. 2 vols 1874.
For love and life. 3 vols 1874.
The story of Valentine and his brother. 3 vols 1875.
Whiteladies. 3 vols 1875.
Dress. 1876.
Phoebe junior: a last chronicle of Carlingford. 3 vols 1876. Anon.
The curate in charge. 2 vols 1876.
The makers of Florence: Dante, Giotto, Savonarola and their city. 1876.
Carita. 3 vols 1877.
Dante. 1877.
Mrs Arthur. 3 vols 1877.
Young Musgrave. 3 vols 1877.
The primrose path: a chapter in the annals of the Kingdom of Fife. 3 vols 1878.
Molière. 1879. With F. Tarver.
Within the precincts. 3 vols 1879.
The two Mrs Scudamores. 1879. Tales from Blackwood's Mag.
The greatest heiress in England. 3 vols 1879.
A beleaguered city. 1880.
Cervantes. 1880.
He that will not when he may. 3 vols 1880.
Harry Joscelyn. 3 vols 1881.
A little pilgrim in the unseen. 1882.
In trust: a story of a lady and her lover. 3 vols 1882.
Literary history of England in the end of the eighteenth and beginning of the nineteenth century. 3 vols 1882.
Hester: a story of a contemporary life. 3 vols 1883.
It was a lover and his lass. 3 vols 1883.
Sheridan. 1883 (EML).
The ladies Lindores. 3 vols 1883.
Sir Tom. 3 vols 1884.
The wizard's son. 3 vols 1884.
Two stories of the seen and unseen. 1885.
Madam. 3 vols 1885.
Oliver's bride: a true story. 1886.
A country gentleman and his family. 3 vols 1886.
Effie Ogilvie. 2 vols 1886.
A house divided against itself. 3 vols 1886.
The son of his father. 3 vols 1887.
The makers of Venice: Doges, conquerors, painters and men of letters. 1887.
Memoir of the life of John Tulloch. 1888.
The land of darkness, along with some further chapters in the experience of the little pilgrims. 1888.
Joyce. 3 vols 1888.
The second son. 3 vols 1888.
Cousin Mary. 1888.
Neighbours on the green: a collection of stories. 1889.
A poor gentleman. 3 vols 1889.
Lady Car: the sequel of a life. 1889.
Kirsteen: a story of a Scottish family seventy years ago. 1890.
Royal Edinburgh: her saints, kings, prophets and poets. 1890.
The Duke's daughter and the fugitives. 3 vols 1890.
Sons and daughters. 1890.
The mystery of Mrs Blencarrow. 1890.
Janet. 3 vols 1891.
Jerusalem: its history and hope. 1891.
Memoirs of the life of Laurence Oliphant and Alice Oliphant his wife. 1891.
The railway man and his children. 3 vols 1891.
Diana Trelawny: the story of a great mistake. 2 vols 1892.
The cuckoo in the nest. 3 vols 1892.
The heir presumptive and the heir apparent. 3 vols 1892.
The marriage of Elinor. 3 vols 1892.
The Victorian age of English literature. 2 vols 1892. With F. R. Oliphant.
Lady William. 3 vols 1893.
The sorceress. 3 vols 1893.
Thomas Chalmers, preacher, philosopher and statesman. 1893.
A house in Bloomsbury. 2 vols 1894.
Historical sketches of the reign of Queen Anne. 1894.
The prodigals and their inheritance. 2 vols 1894.
Who was lost and is found. 1894.
A child's history of Scotland. 1895.
Sir Robert's fortune: a story of a Scotch moor. 1895.
The makers of modern Rome. 1895.
Two strangers. 1895.
Jeanne d'Arc: her life and death. 1896.
Old Mr Tredgold. 1896.
The two Marys. 1896.
The unjust steward: or the minister's debt. 1896.
Annals of a publishing house: William Blackwood and his sons, their Magazine and friends. 2 vols 1897.
The lady's walk. 1897.
The sisters Brontë. 1897.
The ways of life: two stories. 1897.
A widow's tale and other stories. 1898.
That little cutty; and two other stories. 1898.
Mrs Oliphant also wrote more than 200 articles and stories for Blackwood's Mag between July 1852 and June 1897 (*see* Coghill, below), *as well as introds to several books.*

§2

Coghill, A. L. The autobiography and letters of Mrs Oliphant. 1899 (3 edns). Includes (except in 3rd edn) a complete list of Mrs Oliphant's contributions to Blackwood's Mag.
'Melville, Lewis' (L. S. Benjamin). In his Victorian novelists, 1906.
Ritchie, A. T. From the porch. 1913.
Johnson, R. B. In his Women novelists, [1918].
Clarke, I. C. In her Six portraits, 1935.
Stebbins, L. In her A Victorian album, New York 1946.
Keith, S. Margaret Oliphant. N & Q March 1955. On the attribution of novels to Mrs Oliphant. *See* V. Colby, Feb 1966.
Moore, K. A valiant Victorian. Blackwood's Mag March 1958.
Lockhead, M. Margaret Oliphant. Quart Rev 299 1961.
Colby, R. and V. A beleaguered city: a fable for the Victorian age. Nineteenth-Century Fiction 16 1962.

FRANCIS EDWARD PAGET

1806–82

See col 1633, below.

JAMES PAYN
1830–98

§1

Stories from Boccaccio. 1852.
Poems. Cambridge 1853.
Stories and sketches. 1857.
Leaves from Lakeland. [1858].
Furness Abbey and its neighbourhood. Windermere [1858].
A handbook to the English lakes. [1858].
The foster brothers. 1859.
The Bateman household. 1860. Rptd from Chambers's Jnl.
Richard Arbour: or the family scapegrace. Edinburgh 1861, [1869] (as The family scapegrace: or Richard Arbour).
Meliboeus in London. Cambridge 1862.
Lost Sir Massingbird: a romance of real life. 2 vols 1864. First pbd in Chambers's Jnl.
Married beneath him. 3 vols 1865.
People, places and things. 1865.
Mirk Abbey. 1866.
The Clyffards of Clyffe. 3 vols 1866.
The Lakes in sunshine: being photographic and other pictures of the Lake District of Westmoreland and North Lancashire with descriptive letterpress by James Payn. 2 vols Windermere 1867–70.
Lights and shadows of London life. 1867.
Carlyon's year. 2 vols 1868.
Blondel Parva. 2 vols 1868.
Bentinck's tutor, one of the family: a novel. 1868.
Maxims by a man of the world. 1869.
A perfect treasure: an incident in the early life of Marmaduke Drake esq. 1869.
A county family: a novel. 3 vols 1869.
Not wooed but won: a novel. 1871.
Like father, like son: a novel. 1871.
A woman's vengeance. 1872.
Gwendoline's harvest: a novel. 3 vols 1872.
Cecil's trust: a novel. 3 vols 1872.
Murphy's master and other stories. 2 vols 1873.
The best of husbands. 3 vols 1874.
At her mercy. 3 vols 1874.
Walter's word: a novel. 3 vols 1875.
Halves: a novel; and other tales. 3 vols 1876.
Fallen fortunes. 3 vols 1876.
What he cost her. 3 vols 1877.
By proxy: a novel. 2 vols 1878.
Less black than we're painted: a novel. 3 vols 1878.
Under one roof: an episode in a family history. 3 vols 1879.
High spirits: being certain stories written in them. 3 vols 1879.
A confidential agent. 3 vols 1880.
From exile: a novel. 3 vols 1881.
A grape from a thorn: a novel. 3 vols 1881.
Some private views: being essays from the Nineteenth Century review with some occasional articles from the Times. 1881.
For cash only: a novel. 3 vols [1882].
Thicker than water: a novel. 3 vols 1883.
Kit: a memory. 3 vols 1883.
The canon's ward: a novel. 3 vols 1884.
Some literary recollections. 1884, 1885.
The talk of the town: a novel. 2 vols 1885.
The luck of the Darrells: a novel. 3 vols 1885.
In peril and privation: stories of marine disaster retold. 1885.
The heir of the ages: a novel. 3 vols 1886.
Glow-worm tales. 3 vols 1887.
Holiday tasks: being essays written in vacation time. 1887.
The eavesdropper: an unparalleled experience. 1888.

A Prince of the blood: a novel. 3 vols 1888.
The mystery of Mirbridge. 3 vols 1888.
Notes from the [Illustrated London] News. 1890.
The word and the will: a novel. 3 vols 1890.
The burnt million: a novel. 3 vols 1890.
Sunny stories and some shady ones. 1891.
A stumble on the threshold. a novel: 2 vols 1892.
A modern Dick Whittington: or a patron of letters. 2 vols 1892.
A trying patient. 1893. Short stories.
Gleams of memory with some reflections. 1894.
In Market Overt: a novel. 1895.
The disappearance of George Driffell. 1896.
Another's burden. 1897.
The backwater of life: or essays of a literary veteran, with a biographical introduction by Sir Leslie Stephen. 1899.
Payn was editor of Chambers's Jnl 1859–74 and of Cornhill Mag 1882–96.

§2

'Melville, Lewis' (L. S. Benjamin). In his Victorian novelists, 1906.
Russell, G. W. E. In his Selected essays, 1914.

SAMUEL PHILLIPS
1814–54

Caleb Stukely: a novel. 3 vols Edinburgh 1844, 1854, 1862.
Letters from the Orient, by Countess Hahn-Hahn, translated by the author of Caleb Stukely. 1845.
The literature of the rail. 1851.
Essays from the Times: being a selection from the literary papers which have appeared in that journal. 1851; ser 2, 1854. Both sers, 2 vols 1871.
Memoirs of the Duke of Wellington. 1852 (anon), 1856. Usually attributed to Phillips.
Guide to the Crystal Palace and park. 1854.
The Portrait Gallery of the Crystal Palace. 1854.
We're all low people there. 1854.
Phillips was also editor of the Literary Gazette; for his career see obituary Times, 17 Oct 1854.

WATTS PHILLIPS
1825–74

See col 1154, below.

THOMAS MAYNE REID
1818–83

§1

The Rifle Rangers: or adventures of an officer in southern Mexico. 2 vols 1850, 1853, [1857], [1871], 1891 etc.
The scalp hunters: or romantic adventures in northern Mexico. 3 vols 1851, 1852, [1886], 1892 etc.
English Family Robinson. 1851.
The desert home: or the adventures of a lost family in the wilderness. 1852, [1884].
The boy hunters: or adventures in search of a white buffalo. 1852, [1884], [1892].
The young voyageurs: or the boy hunters in the north. [1853], [1884], Paris [1877].
The forest exiles: or the perils of a Peruvian family amid the wilds of the Amazon. [1854].
The white chief: a legend of northern Mexico. 3 vols 1855, [1871].
The hunter's feast: or conversations around the camp fire. [1855], [1860], [1871].

The quadroon: or a lover's adventures in Louisiana. 3 vols 1856, Paris 1858.
The bush boys: or the adventures of a Cape farmer and his family in the wild karoos of southern Africa. 1856, [1884].
The young jägers: or a narrative of hunting adventures in southern Africa. 1857, 1884, Paris 1859.
The plant hunters: or adventures among the Himalaya mountains. 1857, Paris 1859, [1884], [1892].
The war trail: or the hunt of the wild horse. 1857, Paris 1861.
Ran away to sea. 1858, 1884.
Oceola the Seminole. New York 1858, 3 vols 1859, [1861], Paris 1873, [1890].
The boy tar: or a voyage in the dark. 1859, Paris 1861, [1884].
Bruin: or the great bear hunt. 1860, Paris 1863, [1884].
Odd people: being a popular description of singular races of men. 1860, Paris 1862, [1884].
Quadrupeds, what they are, and where found: a book of zoology for boys. [1860], 1867.
The wild huntress. 3 vols 1861, 1865, 1871, Paris [1875], [1890].
The maroon: a novel. 3 vols 1862, [1864], Paris [1874], [1891].
Croquet. 1863, 1865, 1866, New York 1869.
The tiger hunter. 1863.
Garibaldi rebuked by one of his best friends: being a letter addressed to him by Captain Mayne Reid. 1864.
The cliff climbers: or the lone home in the Himalayas. [1864], Paris 1865, [1872], [1888].
Ocean waifs. 1864, [1871]; tr French, [1869?].
The white gauntlet: a romance. 3 vols [1864], [1865], Paris 1865, [1872].
Lost Lenore. 3 vols 1864, 1865, [1872], [1888], [1908]. Pbd under the pseudonym 'Charles Beach'.
The boy slaves. [1865], Paris [1869], London [1872].
The headless horseman: a strange tale of Texas. 2 vols 1866, [1868], [1874], [1888].
Afloat in the forest. 1866, [1868].
The bandolero: or a marriage among the mountains. 1866, [1867] (as The mountain marriage: or the Bandolero), [1873].
The guerilla chief and other tales. 1867, [1871], [1891].
The giraffe hunters. 3 vols 1867, [1868], Paris [1869].
The child wife: a tale of the two worlds. 3 vols 1868, 1888.
The fatal cord: a tale of backwood retribution. [1869], [1872] (with The falcon rover).
The yellow chief: a romance of the Rocky Mountains. [1870].
The castaways: a story of adventure in the wilds of Borneo. 1870, Paris [1872].
The white squaw and the yellow chief. 2 pts [1871].
The lone ranche: a tale of the Staked Plain. 2 vols 1871.
A zigzag journey through Mexico. [1872].
The finger of fate: a romance. 2 vols 1872, Paris 1873.
The death shot: a romance of forest and prairie. 3 vols 1873, 1884.
Gaspar the gaucho: a tale of the Gran Chaco. Paris [1874], [1879], [1884].
The half blood. 1875.
The flag of distress: a story of the South Sea. 3 vols 1876, 1879.
Gwen Wynn: a romance of the Wye. 3 vols 1877, 1889.
The Queen of the lakes: a romance of the Mexican valley. 1879.
The free lances: a romance of the Mexican valley. 3 vols 1881, [1888].
The chase of Leviathan: or adventures in the ocean. Paris 1882, 1885.
Love's martyr: a tragedy. Perth [1884].
The lost mountain: a tale of Sonora. Paris [1883], 1884.
The land of fire: a tale of adventure. [1884], Paris 1885.
The Vee Boers: a tale of adventure in Southern Africa. Paris [1884], London [1885], [1907].

The pierced heart and other stories. [1885].
The Star of Empire: a romance. 1886, [1888].
No quarter. 3 vols 1888.
The naturalist in Siluria. 1889.
Stories of bold deeds and brave men, by Mayne Reid and others. Beeton's Annual [1893].
A dashing dragoon: the Murat of the American army (Philip Kearny). New York 1913 (Mag of History extra no 22).
Mayne Reid also translated 2 novels from the French of L. de Bellemare and edited Frederick Whittaker, The Cadet Button.

§2

Reid, E. Mayne Reid: a memoir of his life. 1890.
—— Captain Mayne Reid: his life and adventures. 1900.

GEORGE WILLIAM McARTHUR REYNOLDS

1814–79

§1

The youthful imposter. 3 vols Paris 1835.
Songs of twilight, by Victor Hugo. 1836. From the French.
Grace Darling, or the heroine of the Fern Islands: a tale founded on recent facts. 1839.
The appointment: a tale. Isis 1 1839.
Pickwick abroad: or the tour in France. 1939.
Modern literature of France. 2 vols 1839, 1841.
The last day of a condemned, by Victor Hugo. 1840. From the French.
Alfred: or the adventures of a French gentleman. [1840], 1846.
Robert Macaire in England, illustrated by 'Phiz'. 3 vols 1840.
Sister Anne: a novel by Paul de Kock. 1840. From the French.
The drunkard's progress: a tale. 1841.
Master Timothy's bookcase. 1842.
The steam-packet: a tale of the river and the ocean. 1844.
Sequel to Don Juan. [1843], 1845.
Alfred de Rosanne. 1846.
The French self instructor. 1846.
Faust: a romance of the Second Empire. [1847].
The parricide: or the youth's career of crime. 1847.
Mysteries of London. 2 vols 1847; ser 2, 2 vols nd.
The mysteries of the Court of London. 8 vols 1849–56.
Mary Price. 2 vols 1852.
Soldier's wife. 1853.
Joseph Wilmot: or the memoirs of a man servant. 2 vols 1854.
Rosa Lambert. 1854.
Ciprina: or the secrets of the picture gallery. Philadelphia [1855].
Loves of the harem. 1855, 1871.
Agnes: or beauty and pleasure. 2 vols 1857, 1858.
Ellen Percy: or the memoirs of an actress. 2 vols 1857.
Wagner the werewolf. 1857, 1872.
The Empress Eugenie's boudoir. 1857.
Canonbury House: or the Queen's prophecy. 1870.
Bronze statue: or the virgin's kiss. 1872.
The bibliography of Reynolds is extremely obscure. It is impossible to trace the dates of pbn in many cases. His books were often issued in cheap edns of which no records are available. Undated fiction includes Agnes Evelyn; The banker's daughter: Caroline of Brunswick; Catherine Volman or a father's revenge; Coral Island or the hereditary curse; Count Chrisoval; The Countess of Lascelles; The days of Hogarth or the mysteries of old London; The Duke of Marchmont; Edgar Montrose; Eustace Quentin; Gipsy chief; Isabella Vincent; Karaman or the bandit chief; Kenneth: a romance of

the Highlands; Leila; Life in Paris; Lord Saxondale; Margaret or the discarded Queen; Mary Middleton; Massacre of Glencoe; The necromancer; Omar Pasha or the Vizier's daughter; Pope Joan or the female Pontiff; Robert Bruce; Rose Foster; The Rye House plot; The seamstress; The soldier's wife; Venetian Trelawny; Vivian Bertram; Wallace, the hero of Scotland; The white lady: a romance of love and war; The young Duchess.

Also undated are Mysteries of the Court of Naples; Mary Stuart, Queen of Scots.

Reynolds edited Reynolds' Miscellany, 1847 *and* Reynolds' Political Instructor, 1849–50.

§2

Mischievous literature. Bookseller July 1868. A long article dealing with Reynolds and including an incomplete list of his works, without dates.
Reynolds and penny fiction. TLS 24 Jan 1924.
Pollard, H. G. Novels in newspapers. RES 18 1942.
Hunter, J. V. Reynolds: sensational novelist and agitator. Book Handbook 4 1947.
Dalziel, M. In her Popular fiction a hundred years ago, 1958.
James, L. In his Fiction for the working man, 1963.

LEITCH RITCHIE
1800?–65

Friendship's offering. 1824–44. Ed Ritchie 1842–4.
Head-pieces and tale-pieces by a travelling artist. 1826. Short stories.
Tales and confessions. 1829.
The game of life. 2 vols 1830.
The romance of history: France. 3 vols 1831, [1872] (illustr T. Landseer).
Schinderhannes, the robber of the Rhine. 1833, 1878 (as The robber of the Rhine).
The library of romance. 15 vols 1833–5. Ed Ritchie.
Wanderings by the Seine. [1835?] (illustr J. M. W. Turner).
The magician. 3 vols 1836.
Beauty's costume: a series of female figures in the dresses of all the times and nations with descriptions by Leitch Ritchie. 1838.
The poetical works of Thomas Pringle with a sketch of his life by Leitch Ritchie. 1838.
The Wye and its associations: a picturesque ramble. 1839.
A view of the opium trade, historical, moral and commercial. 1843.
The British world in the East. 2 vols 1846.
Wearyfoot Common: a tale. 1855.
The new shilling. 1857.
Winter evenings. 2 vols 1859.
The midnight journey [by Ritchie] and other tales [by Mrs Crowe] reprinted from Chambers's Journal. 1871.

Ritchie also contributed The Cheatrice Packman *to* The Club-Book, ed A. Picken 3 vols 1831, *and* The storm lights of Anzasia *to* The tale book, Königsberg 1859, *as well as the letterpress to 9 of Heath's Picturesque Annuals 1832–40.*

EMMA ROBINSON
1814–90

§1

Richelieu in love. 1844.
Whitefriars: or the days of Charles II. 3 vols [1844].
Whitehall: or the days of Charles I. 3 vols 1845.
Caesar Borgia: an historical romance. 3 vols 1846.
Owen Tudor: an historical romance. 3 vols 1846.
The Maid of Orleans. 1849.
The gold worshipper, or the days we live in: a future historical novel. 3 vols 1851.
Westminster Abbey: or the days of the Reformation. 3 vols 1854.
The city banker: or love and money. 3 vols 1856.
Mauleverer's divorce. 1858.
Which wins, love or money? 1862.
Cynthia Thorold. 3 vols 1862.
Epithalamium in honour of the marriage of their Royal Highnesses the Prince and Princess of Wales. 1863.
Madeleine Graham. 3 vols 1864.
Christmas at Old Court. 3 vols 1864.
Dorothy Firebrace: or the armourer's daughter of Birmingham. 3 vols 1865.
The matrimonial Vanity Fair. 1868.

§2

Latham, E. and A. Algar. Emma Robinson. N & Q 6 May, 3 June 1944.

GEORGE HERBERT BUONAPARTE RODWELL
1800–52

See col 1155, below.

'JOHN RUFFINI', GIOVANNI DOMENICO RUFFINI
1807–81

§1

Lorenzo Benoni: or passages from the life of an Italian, edited by a friend. 1853.
Doctor Antonio: a tale. 1855.
The Paragreens on a visit to the Paris Universal Exhibition. 1856. Illustr John Leech.
Lavinia. 3 vols 1860.
Vincenzo: or sunken rocks. 3 vols 1863.
A quiet nook in the Jura. 1867.
Carlino. 1870.

§2

Linaker, A. Ruffini. 1882.
Nota, A. Ruffini. 1899.

GEORGE AUGUSTUS HENRY SALA
1828–96

§1

The Great Exhibition. 1850.
A journey due north: being notes of a residence in Russia in the summer of 1856. 1858. First pbd in Household Words.
Grand national, historical and chivalric pantomime, ye belle alliance: or harlequin good humour and ye Field of ye Clothe of Golde. [1856]. Verse.
How I tamed Mrs Cruiser, by Benedict Cruiser, illustrated by 'Phiz'. 1858.
Gaslight and daylight; with some London scenes they shine upon. 1859.
Twice round the clock: or the hours of the day and night in London. [1859]. First pbd in H. Vizetelly, The welcome guest.
Lady Chesterfield's letters to her daughter. 1860.
Looking at life: or thoughts and things. 1860.
Make your game, or the adventures of the stout gentleman, the slim gentleman and the man with the iron chest: a narrative of the Rhine and thereabouts. 1860.

The Baddington peerage, who won and who wore it: a story of the best and worst society, illustrated by 'Phiz'. 3 vols 1860. First pbd in H. Vizetelly, Illustr Times.
Dutch pictures, with some sketches in the Flemish manner. 1861, 1883 (with Pictures done with a quill).
Accepted addresses. 1862.
The seven sons of Mammon. 3 vols 1862. First pbd in Temple Bar.
The ship chandler and other tales. 1862.
The two prima donnas; the dumb door porter. 1862.
Breakfast in bed, or philosophy between the sheets: a series of indigestible discourses. 1863.
The perfidy of Captain Slyboots and other tales. 1863.
The strange adventures of Captain Dangerous. 3 vols 1863.
After breakfast: or pictures done with a quill. 2 vols 1864. First pbd in All the Year Round and Household Words.
Quite alone. 3 vols 1864. Finished by another hand; first pbd in All the Year Round.
Robson [the actor]: a sketch. 1864.
My diary in America in the midst of war. 2 vols 1865. First pbd in Daily Telegraph.
A trip to Barbary by a roundabout route. 1866.
William Hogarth: essays on the man, the work and the time. 1866. First pbd in Cornhill Mag.
From Waterloo to the Peninsula: four months' hard labour in Belgium, Holland, Germany, Spain. 2 vols 1867.
Banter. 1868.
The complete correspondence and works of Charles Lamb, with an essay on his life and genius by Sala. Vol 1 (all pbd), 1868.
The battle of the safes: or British invincibles versus Yankee ironclads. 1868.
Notes and sketches of the Paris Exhibition. 1868.
Rome and Venice; with other wanderings in Italy 1866–7. 1869.
Wat Tyler MP. 1869. An 'operatic extravaganza'.
Charles Dickens: an essay. [1870].
The late MD—and other tales. [1870].
Papers humorous and pathetic: being selections from the works of Sala, revised and abridged by the author for public reading. 1872.
Under the sun: essays mainly written in hot countries. 1872.
The story of the Count de Chambord: a trilogy. 1873.
India and the Prince of Wales. [1875].
Paris herself again in 1878–9. 2 vols 1879.
The hats of humanity historically, humorously and aesthetically considered. [1880].
America revisited. 2 vols 1882.
Living London: echoes re-echoed. 1883.
Stories with a vengeance. [1883]. With others.
Dead men tell no tales, but live men do: nine stories. [1884].
Echoes of the year 1883. [1884].
A journey due south. 1885. First pbd in Daily Telegraph.
Mrs General Mucklestrap's four tall daughters. [1887].
Right round the world. [1887]. First pbd in Daily Telegraph.
Dublin Whiskey: an essay. [1888].
Not a friend in the world and other stories. [1890].
London up to date. 1894.
Things I have seen and people I have known. 2 vols 1894.
Brighton as I have known it. 1895.
The life and adventures of Sala. 2 vols 1895.
The thorough good cook: a series of chats on the culinary art and nine hundred recipes. [1895].
Margaret Foster: a dream within a dream. 1897.
Paris herself again. Ed P. H. P. Perry 1948.
Sala also edited Temple Bar 1860–6.

§2

Friswell, J. H. In his Modern men of letters, 1870.
Straus, R. Sala: the portrait of an eminent Victorian. 1942.
Mabbott, T. O. Dickens, Sala and S. C. Hall. N & Q 4 Dec 1943.
— Sala's notebooks. N & Q 24 May 1952.

MARMION W. SAVAGE
1803–72

The Falcon family: or young Ireland. 1845, 1854.
The bachelor of the Albany. 1848; ed B. Dobrée 1927.
My uncle the curate: a novel. 3 vols 1849.
Reuben Medlicott: or the coming man. 3 vols 1852.
Sketches, legal and political, by the Rt Hon R. L. Sheil. 1855. Ed Savage.
Clover Cottage. 1856. Tom Taylor's Comedietta, Nine points of the law, was founded on this.
The woman of business, or the lady and the lawyer: a novel. 3 vols 1870.

ELIZABETH MISSING SEWELL
1815–1906

Amy Herbert, by a lady. 1844. Ed W. Sewell.
Gertrude. 1846.
Laneton Parsonage: a tale for children on the practical use of a portion of the Church Catechism. 3 pts 1846–8.
Margaret Percival. 1847.
The sketches: three tales. 1848.
The child's first history of Rome. 1849.
Was it a dream? 1849.
Margaret Percival in America: a tale. 1850.
The Earl's daughter. 1850. Ed W. Sewell.
Stories illustrative of the Lord's Prayer. 1851.
A journal kept during a summer tour. 1852.
A first history of Greece. 1852.
The experience of life. 1853.
Katharine Ashton. 1854.
Cleve Hall. 1855.
Ivors. 1856.
Ursula: a tale. 1858.
Tales by the author of Amy Herbert. 1858.
History of the early Church from the first preaching of the Gospel to the Council of Nicea. 1859.
Impressions of Rome, Florence and Turin. 1862.
Ancient history of Egypt, Assyria and Babylonia. 1862.
A glimpse of the world. 1863.
The principles of education drawn from nature and revelation and applied to female education in the upper classes. 2 vols 1865; rev Mrs G. J. Chitty and L. H. M. Soulsby 1914.
The journal of a home life. 1867.
After life. 1868. A sequel to the preceding. The 2 vols were pbd together in 1891 as Home and after life.
Uncle Peter's fairy tale for the nineteenth century. 1869. Ed E. M. Sewell.
Thoughts for the age. 1870.
The giant, edited by the author of Amy Herbert. 1871.
What can be done for our young servants? [1873].
Some questions of the day. 1875.
Popular history of France to the death of Louis XIV. 1876.
Notebooks of an elderly lady. 1881. Rptd from Monthly Packet.
Letters on daily life. 1885. Rptd from Monthly Packet.
Outline history of Italy from the fall of the Western Empire. 1895 (preface by L. H. M. Soulsby).
Conversations between youth and age. 1896.
The autobiography of Elizabeth M. Sewell, edited by her niece Eleanor L. Sewell. 1907.
Elizabeth Sewell also pbd devotional works and textbooks.

ELIZABETH SARA SHEPPARD

1830–62

Charles Auchester: a memorial. 3 vols 1853.
Counterparts: or the cross of love. 3 vols 1854.
The double coronet. 2 vols 1856.
Rumour. 3 vols 1858.
Almost a heroine. 3 vols 1859.
Elizabeth Sheppard also edited Beatrice Reynolds, My first season, 1855.

JOHN PALGRAVE SIMPSON

1807–87

See col 1156, below.

CATHERINE SINCLAIR

1800–64

Modern accomplishments: or the march of intellect. 1836.
Modern society, or the march of intellect: conclusion of Modern accomplishments. 1837.
Hill and valley: or hours in England and Wales. Edinburgh 1838.
Holiday house: a series of tales. Edinburgh 1839, [1856] (as Holiday house: a book for the young) etc.
Shetland and the Shetlanders: or the northern circuit. 1840.
Scotland and the Scotch: or the western circuit. 2 pts 1840, 1859 (rev).
Modern flirtations: or a month at Harrowgate. 3 vols Edinburgh 1841.
Scotch courtiers and the Court. Edinburgh 1842. A poem of Victoria's visit to Scotland.
Jane Bouverie: or prosperity and adversity. Edinburgh 1846, 1855 (as Jane Bouverie and how she became an old maid).
The journey of life. 1847.
The lives of Caesars: or the juvenile Plutarch. [1847], [1862] (abbreviated as Anecdotes of the Caesars).
The business of life. 2 vols 1848.
Sir Edward Graham: or railway speculators. 3 vols 1849, 1854 (as The mysterious marriage: or Sir Edward Graham).
Lord and Lady Harcourt: or country hospitalities. 1850, [1856] (as Country hospitalities: or Lord and Lady Harcourt).
The kaleidoscope of anecdotes and aphorisms. 1851.
Beatrice: or the unknown relatives. 3 vols 1852. Preface also rptd separately as a tract, Modern superstition, 1857.
A letter on the principles of the Christian faith, by Hannah Sinclair. 1852. Ed Catherine Sinclair.
Popish legends: or Bible truths. 1852.
Frank Vansittart: or the model schoolboys. 1853.
Lady Mary Pierrepoint. 1853.
London homes: including The murder hole, The drowning dragon, The priest and the curate, Lady Mary Pierrepoint and Frank Vansittart. 6 pts 1853.
The priest and the curate: or the two diaries. 1853.
Cross purposes: a novel. 3 vols 1855, [1857] (as Porchester Abbey, or cross purposes: a tale).
The cabman's holiday: a tale. 1855.
Charlie Seymour: or the good and bad choice. 1856 (4th edn).
Memoirs of the English Bible. [1858].
Sketches and stories of Wales and the Welsh. [1860] (3 edns).
Letters for children with pictures. 6 nos Edinburgh 1863–4. 'Hieroglyphic' stories in letter-form.
The first of April picture letter. Edinburgh 1864.

FRANCIS EDWARD SMEDLEY

1818–64

§1

Seven tales by seven authors. 1849, 1850. Ed Smedley; includes his Mysteries of Redgrave Court.
Frank Fairleigh: or scenes from the life of a private pupil. 1850 (illustr by G. Cruikshank), 1854, 1866, 1878, 1892, 1904.
Lewis Arundel: or the railroad of life, illustrated by 'Phiz'. 1852, [1855], 2 vols 1892, 1898.
The fortunes of the Colville family: a Christmas story. 1853.
Harry Coverdale's courtship and all that came of it, illustrated by 'Phiz'. 1855.
Mirth and metre. 1855. With E. H. Yates.
Gathered leaves: being a collection of the poetical writings of the late F. E. Smedley, with a memorial preface by Edmund Yates. 1865.
Last leaves from Beechwood. Ed W. Brailsford, Enfield 1867. Poems.
The 'wicked Lady Ferrers': a legend of Markyate Cell in Flamstead, being the poem of F. E. Smedley entitled Maude Allinghame, extracted from Mirth and metre, with an introductory note, forming an attempt to solve the mystery of 'The lady highwayman' by W. B. Gerish. Bishop's Stortford 1911.
Smedley also edited George Cruikshank's Mag 1854.

§2

Ellis, S. M. In his Mainly Victorian, 1925.

MENELLA BUTE SMEDLEY

1820–77

See col 549, above.

ALBERT RICHARD SMITH

1816–60

§1

Beauty and the Beast, illustrated by Alfred Crowquill. [1843?].
The wassail bowl. 2 vols 1843. Comic sketches from the Wassail bowl, 1848.
The adventures of Mr Ledbury and his friend Jack Johnson. 3 vols 1844, 1847.
The adventures of Jack Holyday; with something about his sister. 1844.
The fortunes of the Scattergood family. 3 vols 1845, 1853.
The Marchioness of Brinwilliers, the poisoner of the seventeenth century: a romance of old Paris; etchings by John Leech. 1846, 1856, 1860, 1886.
The physiology of evening parties. [1846?], 1849 (as The natural history of evening parties), 1872.
The man in the moon. 5 vols 1847–9.
The natural history of stuck-up people. 1847, 1872.
The natural history of the ballet girl. 1847, 1872.
The natural history of the gent. 1847, 1872.
The natural history of the flirt. 1848, 1872.
The natural history of the idler upon town. 1848, 1872.
The struggles and adventures of Christopher Tadpole at home and abroad, illustrated by John Leech. 1848, 1853, 1864, 1897.
A bowl of punch. 1848.
A pottle of strawberries to beguile a short journey or a long half-hour. 1848.
The Pottleton legacy: a story of town and country life. 1849 (illustr H. K. Browne).

Gavarni in London: sketches of life and character; with illustrative essays by popular writers, edited by Albert Smith. 1849, 1859 (as Sketches of London life and character).
A month at Constantinople. 1850.
Comic tales and sketches. 1852.
Pictures of life at home and abroad. 1852.
The momentous question: a lay in three fyttes. 1852 (priv ptd).
The story of Mont Blanc. 1853, 1854 (enlarged), 1860 (with a life by E. H. Yates).
The English hotel nuisance. 1855.
To China and back: being a diary kept out and home. [1859].
Wild oats and dead leaves. 1860.
The London medical student, edited by Albert Smith. 1861.

§2

Thorington, J. M. Mont Blanc sideshow: the life and times of Albert Smith. Philadelphia 1933.

ALEXANDER SMITH

1829–67

See col 550, above.

JOHN STERLING

1806–44

See col 1306, below.

ROBERT SMITH SURTEES

1803–64

Collections

Sporting novels: with all the coloured plates from the original editions. 6 vols nd (priv ptd), [1926].
Novels. 10 vols 1930.

§1

The horseman's manual: being a treatise on soundness, the law of warranty and generally on the laws relating to horses. 1831.
Jorrocks' jaunts and jollities: or the hunting, racing, driving, sailing, eating, eccentric and extravagant exploits of that renowned sporting citizen, Mr John Jorrocks of St Botolph Lane and Great Coram Street; with illustrations by Phiz. 1838, 1839, 1843, 1869 (rev and enlarged; illustr Henry Alken), 1874 etc. First pbd in New Sporting Mag July 1831–Sept 1834.
Handley Cross, or the spa hunt: a sporting tale. 3 vols 1843 (no illustrations), 17 monthly pts March 1853–Oct 1854; expanded as Handley Cross: or Mr Jorrocks's hunt; illustr John Leech 1854, 1888 (new illustrations), 1891, 1892 etc.
Hillingdon Hall, or the cockney squire: a tale of country life. 3 vols 1845, 1888 (with coloured illustrations) etc. Portions first pbd in New Sporting Mag.
The analysis of the hunting field: being a series of sketches of the principal characters that compose one; the whole forming a slight souvenir of the season 1845–6. 1845 (anon; illustr Henry Alken), 1869 etc.
Hawbuck Grange: or the sporting adventures of Thomas Scott esq. 1847 (illustr 'Phiz'), [1888], 1891, 1892 etc. First pbd in Bell's Life 1846–7.
Mr Sponge's sporting tour. 13 monthly pts 1853 (illustr John Leech), 1853, [1888], 1892, 1893 (as Soapey Sponge's sporting tour) etc.
Ask Mamma: or the richest commoner in England. 13 monthly pts 1858 (illustr John Leech), 1858, [1888], 1892, 1903, 1904 etc.
Plain or ringlets? 13 monthly pts 1860 (illustr John Leech), 1860, [1888], 1892, 1900 etc.
Mr Romford's hounds. 12 monthly pts 1865 (illustr John Leech and 'Phiz'), 1865 (as Mr Facey Romford's hounds), 1892, 1911.
Surtees also helped to found New Sporting Magazine, which he edited 1831–6.

§2

Frith, W. P. In his John Leech, 1891.
'O'Neill, M.' (N. Higginson, afterwards Skrine). Novels by Surtees. Blackwood's Mag April 1913.
—— The author of Jorrocks. Blackwood's Mag June 1924.
Ellis, S. M. R. S. Surtees. Bookman (London) Dec 1922.
—— In his Mainly Victorian, 1925.
—— Dickens and Surtees. Dickensian 26 1930.
Cuming, E. D. Handley Cross behind the scenes. Blackwood's Mag Oct 1924.
—— Surtees: creator of Jorrocks. 1924.
Rivers, W. C. The place of Surtees. London Mercury Oct 1924.
Surtees, H. C. and H. R. Leighton. The family of Surtees. Newcastle 1925.
—— Robert Smith Surtees. TLS 27 March 1930.
Dobrée, B. In his Essays of the year, 1930.
Somerville, E. A. O. Certes a classic. New Statesman 15 March 1930.
Tidey, G. Surtees on fishing. 1931.
Renwick, W. L. Jorrocks: a conversation. E & S 17 1932.
Steel, A. Jorrocks's England. 1932.
Newton, A. E. Jack Jorrocks. In his End papers, Boston 1933.
Watson, F. Surtees: a critical study. 1933.
—— Sporting heroes: Jorrocks and madcap Mytton. TLS 26 March 1938.
Bell, Q. Surtees. New Statesman 9 March 1940.
Pope-Hennessy, U. Hamsterby and Jorrocks. In her Durham company, 1941.
R., G. The sporting novels of Surtees. More Books 19 1944.
Shand, J. Squire Surtees. Atlantic Monthly Jan 1945.
Burn, W. L. Surtees and Trollope. Blackwood's Mag April 1947.
Collison, R. L. Surtees: satirist and sociologist. Nineteenth-Century Fiction 7 1953.
—— A Jorrocks handbook. 1964.

JEMIMA, BARONESS TAUTPHOEUS née MONTGOMERY

1807–93

§1

The initials: a novel. 3 vols 1850, 1853, 2 vols. Leipzig 1854, 1858, 1863 (6th edn).
Cyrilla: a tale. 3 vols 1853, 2 vols Leipzig 1853, 1872; tr German, 1854.
Quits: a novel. 3 vols 1857, 2 vols Leipzig 1858, 1860, 1864; tr German [1863].
At odds: a novel. 2 vols 1863, Leipzig 1863, 1 vol 1873.

§2

Thorpe, L. Baroness Tautphoeus, an early Victorian novelist. Eng Miscellany (Rome) 13 1962.

PHILIP MEADOWS TAYLOR

1808–76

§1

Sketches in the Deccan. 1837.
Confessions of a Thug. 3 vols 1839, 1858, 1873 etc, Oxford 1917 (WC).
Tippoo Sultaun: a tale of the Mysore War. 3 vols 1840, 1880.
Letters from Meadows Taylor esq during the Indian Rebellion 1857. 1857 (priv ptd).
Tara: a Mahratta tale. 3 vols 1863, 1874, 1881.
Ralph Darnell. 3 vols 1865, 1879.
The people of India. 6 vols 1868–72.
A student's manual of the history of India from the earliest period to the present. 1870, 1871, 1896.
Seeta. 3 vols 1872, 1880, 1890.
The story of my life, edited by his daughter. Edinburgh 1877, 1878, 1920 (with introd and notes).
A noble Queen: a romance of Indian history. 3 vols 1878, 1880, 1890.

§2

Singh, B. Meadows Taylor and other predecessors of Kipling. In his A survey of Anglo-Indian fiction, Oxford 1934.
Pritchett, V. S. Books in general. New Statesman 8 Nov 1941.
Edwardes, M. The articulate hero: Philip Meadows Taylor. Twentieth Century Sept 1953.

THOMAS ADOLPHUS TROLLOPE

1810–92

§1

A summer in Brittany. Ed F. Trollope 2 vols 1840.
A summer in Western France. Ed F. Trollope 2 vols 1841.
Impressions of a wanderer in Italy, Switzerland, France, Spain. 1850.
The girlhood of Catherine de Medici. 1856.
A decade of Italian women. 2 vols 1859.
Tuscany in 1849 and in 1859. 1859.
Filippo Strozzi: a history of the last days of the old Italian liberty. 1860.
La Beata: a Tuscan Romeo and Juliet. 2 vols 1861.
Paul the Pope [Paul V] and Paul the Friar [Paolo Sarpi]: a story of an interdict. 1861.
A Lenten journey in Umbria and the Marches. 1862.
Marietta: a novel. 2 vols 1862.
Giulio Malatesta: a novel. 3 vols 1863.
Beppo the conscript: a novel. 2 vols 1864.
Lindisfarne Chase: a novel. 3 vols 1864.
History of the Commonwealth of Florence to 1531. 4 vols 1865.
Gemma: a novel. 3 vols 1866.
Artingale Castle. 3 vols 1867.
Leonora Casaloni: a novel. 2 vols 1868.
The dream numbers: a novel. 3 vols 1868.
The Garstangs of Garstang Grange. 3 vols 1869.
A siren. 3 vols 1870.
Durnton Abbey: a novel. 3 vols 1871.
The Stilwinches of Combe Mavis: a novel. 3 vols 1872.
Diamond cut diamond: a story of Tuscan life and other stories. 2 vols 1875.
The Papal Conclaves as they were and as they are. 1876.
A family party in the Piazza of St Peter and other stories. 3 vols 1877.
A peep behind the scenes at Rome. 1877. First pbd in part in Standard.
Story of the life of Pius IX. 2 vols 1877.
Sketches from French history. 1878. First pbd in St Paul's Mag.
Homes and haunts of Italian poets. By F. E. Trollope and T. A. Trollope 1881.
What I remember. 3 vols 1887–9.
The General Election: a working man's advice. 1892.

§2

Mahoney, J. L. T. A. Trollope: a Victorian man of letters. Univ of Rochester Lib Bull 15 1960.

ELIOT WARBURTON

1810–52

See col 1404, below.

SAMUEL WARREN

1807–77

Collections

Works. 5 vols 1854–5.

§1

Passages from the diary of a late physician, with notes and illustrations by the editor. 2 vols New York 1831 (pirated), 2 vols 1832 (anon; vol 3, signed, 1838), 1841, 1842, 1848, 1853, 1864, [1884]. First pbd in Blackwood's Mag 1830–7.
A popular and practical introduction to law studies. 1835, 1845 (rewritten and enlarged), 2 vols 1863 (rewritten and enlarged).
Select extracts from Blackstone's commentaries. 1837.
Adventures of an attorney in search of practice. 1839.
The opium question. 1840.
Ten thousand a year. 3 vols 1841, 1845, 1849, 1854, 1855, [1884], [1887], 1899. First pbd in Blackwood's Mag; dramatized by R. B. Peake [1886].
Now and then. 1847.
The moral, social and professional duties of attorneys and solicitors. 1848.
Letter to the Queen on a late court martial (Captain G. Douglas). 1850.
The lily and the bee: an apologue of the Crystal Palace. 1851, 1854 (rev).
The Queen or the Pope? Edinburgh 1851 (6 edns).
A manual of the Parliamentary Election Law. 1852.
The intellectual and moral development of the present age. Edinburgh 1853 (2nd edn).
The law and practice of election committees. 1853.
Miscellanies, critical, imaginative and juridical, contributed to Blackwood's Magazine. 2 vols 1855.
An abridgement of Blackstone's Commentaries. 1855, 1856.
Labour: its rights, difficulties, dignity and consolations. 1856.

EDWIN WAUGH

1817–90

See col 558, above.

CHARLES WHITEHEAD

1804–62

See col 560, above.

GEORGE JOHN WHYTE-MELVILLE

1821–78

Bibliographies

Freeman, J. C. Whyte-Melville: a bibliography. Bull of Bibliography 19 1949.

Collections

Works. Ed H. Maxwell 24 vols 1898–1902.
Works. 25 vols nd (Library edn).

§1

Horace translated into English verse. 1850.
Captain Digby Grand: an autobiography. 2 vols 1853.
Tilbury Nego: or passages in the life of an unsuccessful man. 1854.
General Bounce: or the lady and the locusts. 2 vols 1855.
Kate Coventry: an autobiography. 1856.
The Arab's ride to Cairo: a legend of the desert. Edinburgh. [1857?]. Verse.
The interpreter: a tale of the war. 1858.
Holmby House. 2 vols 1860.
Market Harborough: or how Mr Sawyer went to the shires. 1861.
Good for nothing: or all down hill. 2 vols 1861.
The Queen's Maries. 2 vols 1862.
The gladiators: a tale of Rome and Judea. 3 vols 1863.
The Brookes of Bridlemere. 3 vols 1864.
Cerise: a tale of the last century. 3 vols 1866.
'Bones and I': or the skeleton at home. 1868.
The white rose. 3 vols 1868.
M. or N. 2 vols 1869.
Songs and verses. 1869, 1924.
Contraband: or a losing hazard. 2 vols 1871.
Sarchedon: a tale of the great Queen. 3 vols 1871.
Satanella: a story of Punchestown. 2 vols 1872.
The true cross: a legend of the Church. 1873. Verse.
Uncle John. 3 vols 1874.
Katerfelto: a story of Exmoor. 1875.
Sister Louise: or the story of a woman's repentance. 1876.
Rosine. 1877.
Riding recollections. 1878.
Roy's wife: a novel. 2 vols 1878.
Black but comely: or the adventures of Jane Lee. 3 vols 1879.
The bones at Rothwell: a lecture. [Rothwell 1903].
Hunting poems. 1911.

§2

'Melville, Lewis' (L. S. Benjamin). In his Victorian novelists, 1906.
Ellis, S. M. In his Mainly Victorian, [1925].
Fortescue, J. In The eighteen-sixties, 1932 (Royal Soc of Lit).
Freeman, J. C. Whyte-Melville and Galsworthy's Bright beings. Nineteenth-Century Fiction 5 1951.

WILLIAM GORMAN WILLS

1828–91

See col 1159, below.

MRS HENRY WOOD, née ELLEN PRICE

1814–87

§1

Danesbury House. Glasgow 1860.
East Lynne. 3 vols 1861, 1862, 1888, 1895, 1903, [1906], 1907 etc.
The golden casket. Ed M. Howitt [1961]. Contains The Elchester college boys by Mrs Henry Wood.
Mrs Halliburton's troubles. 3 vols 1862.
The Channings. 3 vols 1862. *See* Roland Yorke, below.
The shadow of Ashlydyat. 3 vols 1863.
The foggy night at Offord: a Christmas gift for the Lancashire fund. 1863.
Verner's pride. 3 vols 1863.
William Allair: or running away to sea. 1864.
Lord Oakburn's daughters. 3 vols 1864.
Oswald Cray. 3 vols Edinburgh 1864.
Trevlyn Hold: or Squire Trevlyn's heir. 3 vols 1864.
Mildred Arkell: a novel. 3 vols 1865.
St Martin's Eve: a novel. 3 vols 1866.
Elster's folly: a novel. 1866.
Lady Adelaide's oath. 3 vols 1867, 1889 (as Lady Adelaide).
A life's secret. 2 vols 1867.
Orville College: a story. 2 vols 1867.
Mixed sweets from Routledge's annual, by Mrs Henry Wood and others. [1867]. Prose and verse.
Castle Wafer: or the plain gold ring. New York [1868?].
The Red Court farm: a novel. 3 vols 1868.
Anne Hereford: a novel. 3 vols 1868.
Roland Yorke: a novel. 3 vols 1869. A sequel to The Channings, above.
Bessy Rane: a novel. 3 vols 1870.
George Canterbury's will: a novel. 3 vols 1870.
Dene Hollow: a novel. 3 vols 1871.
Within the maze: a novel. 3 vols 1872.
The master of Greylands. 3 vols 1873.
Johnny Ludlow. 6 sers (12 vols) 1874–89.
Told in the twilight. 3 vols 1875. Contains Parkwater and 9 shorter stories.
Bessy Wells. 1875.
Adam Grainger: a tale. 1876.
Edina: a novel. 3 vols 1876.
Parkwater; with four other tales. 1876. First pbd in Told in the twilight, 1875.
Our children. 1876.
Pomeroy Abbey: a romance. 3 vols 1878.
Court Netherleigh: a novel. 3 vols 1881.
About ourselves. 1883.
Lady Grace and other stories. 3 vols 1887.
The story of Charles Strange: a novel. 3 vols 1888.
Featherston's story. 1889.
The unholy wish and other stories. 1890.
Edward Burton. Boston 1890.
Summer stories from the Argosy, by Mrs Henry Wood and other authors. 2 pts 1890.
The house of Halliwell: a novel. 3 vols 1890.
Ashley and other stories. 1897.

§2

Wood, C. W. Memorials of Mrs Henry Wood. 1894.
Sergeant, A. In his Women novelists of Queen Victoria's reign, 1897.
Elwin, M. In his Victorian wallflowers, 1934.

CHARLOTTE MARY YONGE

1823–1901

Bibliographies

Laski, M. and K. Tillotson. In A chaplet for Charlotte Yonge, ed G. Battiscombe and M. Laski 1965.

Collections

Novels and tales: new edition. 40 vols 1879–99.

§1

Le Château de Melville: ou recréations du cabinet d'étude. 1838.
Abbey Church: or self-control and self-conceit. 1844, 1872.
Scenes and characters: or eighteen months at Beechcroft. 1847.
Kings of England: a history for young children. 1848.
Henrietta's wish: or domineering a tale. 1850.
Kenneth: or the rearguard of the Grand Army. 1850.
Langley School. 1850.
Landmarks of history. 3 vols 1852–7.
The two guardians: or home in this world. 1852, 1861.
The heir of Redclyffe. 1853, 1854, 1868 (17th edn); ed A. Meynell 1909 (EL); ed C. Haldane 1965.
The herb of the field. 1853, 1887.
The castle builders: or the deferred confirmation. 1854, 1859.
Heartsease: or the brother's wife. 1854, 1862.
The little Duke: or Richard the fearless. 1854, 1857, 1891; ed E. Mason 1910 (EL).
The history of the life and death of the good Knight Sir Thomas Thumb. 1855, 1859.
The Lances of Lynwood. 1855, 1857, 1894 (abridged); ed L. M. Crump 1911 (EL).
The railroad children. 1855.
Bed Sylvester's word. 1856.
The daisy chain. 2 vols 1856, 1868 (9th edn) etc.
Harriet and her sister. [1856?].
Leonard the Lionheart. 1856.
Dynevor Terrace: or the clue of life. 2 vols 1857, 1858, 1860.
The instructive picture book: lessons from the vegetable world. 1857.
The Christmas mummers. 1858.
Friarswood post office. 1860.
Hopes and fears: or scenes from the life of a spinster. 2 vols 1860, 1861.
The mice at play. 1860.
The strayed falcon. 1860.
Pigeon pie. 1860, 1861.
The Stokesley secret. 1861, 1862, 1892 (with Countess Kate).
The young stepmother: or a chronicle of mistakes. 1861.
Biographies of good women. 2 sers 1862–5.
The Chosen People: a compendium of sacred and Church history for school children. 1862.
Countess Kate. 1862.
Sea spleenwort and other stories. 1862.
A history of Christian names. 2 vols 1863, 1884.
The apple of discord: a play. 1864.
A book of golden deeds of all times and all lands. 1864, 1871 etc.
Historical dramas. 1864.
Readings from standard authors. 1864.
The trial: more links of the daisy chain 1864, 1868 (4th edn), 2 vols 1870.
The Wars of Wapsburgh. 1864.
The clever woman of the family. 2 vols 1865, 1867.
The dove in the eagle's nest. 2 vols 1866, 1 vol 1870; ed E. Hall 1908 (EL).
The Prince and the page: a story of the last Crusade. 1866.
The Danvers papers: an invention. 1867.
A shilling's book of golden deeds. 1867.
The six cushions. 1867.
Cameos from English history. 9 vols 1868–99.
The chaplet of pearls: or the white and black Ribaumont. 1868.
Historical selections: a series of readings in English and European history. 2 vols 1868–70. With E. Sewell.
New ground: Kaffirland. 1868.
The pupils of St John the Divine. 1868.
A book of worthies, gathered from the old histories and now written out anew. 1869.
Keynotes of the first lessons for every day in the year. 1869.
The seal: or the inward spiritual grace of confirmation. 1869.
The caged lion. 1870.
A storehouse of stories. 2 sers 1870–2. Ed C. M. Yonge.
Little Lucy's wonderful glove. 1871.
Musings over the Christian year and Lyra innocentium, together with a few gleanings of recollections of the Rev J. Keble, gathered by several friends. 1871.
A parallel history of France and England, consisting of outlines and dates. 1871.
Pioneers and founders: or recent works in the mission field. 1871.
Scripture readings for schools, with comments. 5 vols 1871–9.
A history of France. In an Historical course for schools, ed E. A. Freeman 1872.
In memoriam Bishop Patterson. 1872.
P's and Q's: the question of putting upon. 1872.
Questions on the Prayer-book. 1872.
Aunt Charlotte's stories of English history for the little ones. 1873.
Life of John Coleridge Patterson, missionary Bishop to the Melanesian Islands. 2 vols 1873, 1878 (6th edn).
The pillars of the house: under wode, under rode. 4 vols 1873, 2 vols 1875.
Aunt Charlotte's stories of French history for the little ones. 1874.
Lady Hester: or Ursula's narrative. 1874.
Questions on the collects. 1874.
Questions on the epistles. 1874.
Questions on the gospels. 1874.
Aunt Charlotte's stories of Bible history for the little ones. 1875.
My young Alcides: a faded photograph. 1875.
Aunt Charlotte's stories of Greek history for the little ones. 1876.
Eighteen centuries of beginnings of Church history. 1876.
The three brides. 1876.
Aunt Charlotte's stories of German history for the little ones. 1877.
Aunt Charlotte's stories of Roman history for the little ones. 1877.
The disturbing element: or chronicles of the Bluebell Society. 1878.
A history of France. In History primers, ed J. R. Green 1878.
The story of the Christians and Moors of Spain. 1878.
Burnt out: a story for mothers' meetings. 1879, 1880.
Magnum bonum: or Mother Carey's brood. 1879.
Short English grammar for use in schools. 1879.
Bye-words: a collection of tales new and old. 1880.
Love and life: an old story in eighteenth-century costume. 1880.
Nelly and Margaret: or good for evil. [1880?].
Verses on the gospel for Sundays and holy days. 1880.
Aunt Charlotte's evenings at home with the poets. 1881.
Cheap Jack. 1881.
Frank's debt. 1881, 1882.
How to teach the New Testament. 1881.
Lads and lasses of Langley. 1881.
Practical work in Sunday schools. 1881.
Questions on the Psalms. 1881.
Wolf. 1881.
Given to hospitality. 1882.
Historical ballads. 1882.
Langley little ones: six stories. 1882.
Pickle and his page boy, or unlooked for: a story. 1882.
Sowing and sewing: a Sexagesima story. 1882.
Talks about the laws we live under: or at Langley night-school. 1882.
Unknown to history: a story of the captivity of Mary of Scotland. 2 vols 1882, 1884.
Aunt Charlotte's stories of American history. 1883. With J. H. Hastings Weld.

English Church history, adapted for use in day and Sunday schools. 1883.
Landmarks of recent history 1770–1883. 1883.
Langley adventures. 1883.
The miz maze, or the Winkworth puzzle: a story in letters by nine authors. 1883. With F. Awdry, M. Bramston, C. R. Coleridge, F. M. Peard et al.
Shakespeare's plays for schools, abridged and annotated. 1883.
Stray pearls: memoirs of Margaret de Ritanmont, Viscountess of Bellaise. 1883.
The armourer's 'prentices. 1884.
The daisy chain birthday book. 1885.
Higher reading-book for schools, colleges and general use. 1885.
Nuttie's father. 1885.
Pixie lawn. In Please tell me a tale: short original stories for children, 1885.
The two sides of the shield. 1885.
Astray: a tale of a country town. 1886. With M. Bramston, C. Coleridge and E. Stuart.
Chantry house. 2 vols 1886, 1887.
Just one tale more. 1886. With others.
The little rick-burners. 1886.
A modern Telemachus. 1886.
Teachings on the catechism: for the little ones. 1886.
Victorian half-century: a jubilee book. 1886.
Under the storm: or steadfast's charge. 1887.
What books to lend and what to give. 1887.
Womankind. 1887.
Beechcroft at Rochstone. 1888.
Conversations on the Prayer Book. 1888.
Deacon's book of dates: a manual of the world's chief historical landmarks, and an outline of universal history. 1888.
Hannah More. 1888.
Nurse's memories. 1888.
Our new mistress: or changes at Brookfield Earl. 1888.
Preparation of prayer-book lessons. 1888.
The cunning woman's grandson: a tale of Cheddar a hundred years ago. 1889.
Neighbour's fare. 1889.
The parent's power: address to the conference of the Mother's Union. 1889.
A reputed changeling: or three seventh years two centuries ago. 1889.
Life of HRH the Prince Consort. 1890.
More bywords. 1890.
The slaves of Sabinns: Jew and Gentile. 1890.
The constable's tower: or the times of Magna Charta. 1891.
Old times at Otterbourne. 1891.
Seven heroines of Christendom. 1891 (6th edn).
Simple stories relating to English history. 1891.
Twelve stories from early English history. 1891.
Twenty stories and biographies from 1066 to 1485. 1891.
Two penniless princesses. 1891.
Westminster historical reading books. 2 vols 1891–2.
The cross roads: or a choice in life. 1892.
The Hanovarian period, with biographies of leading persons. 1892.
The Stuart period, with biographies of leading persons. 1892.
That stick. 1892.
The Tudor period, with biographies of leading persons. 1892.
Chimes for the mothers: a reading for each week in the year. 1893.
The girl's little book. 1893.
Grisly Grisell, or the laidly lady of Whitburn: a tale of the Wars of the Roses. 1893.
The strolling players: a harmony of contrasts. 1893. With C. Coleridge.
The treasure in the marches. 1893.
The cook and the captive: or Attalus the hostage. 1894.
The rubies of St Lo. 1894.
The story of Easter. 1894.
The Carbonels. 1895.
The long vacation. 1895.
The release: or Caroline's French kindred. 1896.
The wardship of Steepcombe. 1896.
The pilgrimage of the Ben Beriah. 1897.
Founded on paper: or uphill and downhill between the two jubilees. 1898.
John Keble's parishes: a history of Hursley and Otterbourne. 1898.
The patriots of Palestine: a story of the Maccabees. 1898.
Scenes with Kenneth etc. 1899.
The herd boy and his hermit. 1900.
The making of a missionary: or day dreams in earnest. 1900.
Modern broods: or developments unlooked for. 1900.
Reasons why I am a Catholic, and not a Roman Catholic. 1901.

C. M. Yonge edited and contributed to three journals: Monthly Packet 1851–94; Monthly Paper of Sunday Teaching 1860–75; *and* Mothers in Council 1890–1900. *Much of her work was first serialized in* Monthly Packet, Churchman's Companion *and* Mag for the Young.

§2

Coleridge, C. R. Charlotte Mary Yonge: her life and letters. 1903. With bibliography.
Charlotte Mary Yonge. Church Quart Rev 57 1904.
Romanes, E. Charlotte Mary Yonge: an appreciation. 1908.
Bailey, S. Charlotte Mary Yonge. Cornhill Mag Aug 1934.
Cruse, A. The world of C. Yonge. In her Victorians and their books. 1935.
Battiscombe, G. Charlotte Mary Yonge: the story of an uneventful life. 1943.
Battiscombe, G. and M. Laski (ed). A chaplet from Charlotte Yonge. 1965. Contains essays by G. Battiscombe, K. Briggs, L. Cooper, A. Fairfax-Lucy, A. Gillie, R. Harris, E. Jenkins, M. Kennedy, M. Laski, V. Powell, C. Storr, K. Tillotson.
Chapman, H. W. Books in general. New Statesman 21 Aug 1943.
Leavis, Q. D. Charlotte Yonge and Christian discrimination. Scrutiny 12 1944.
Mare, M. and A. C. Percival. Victorian best-seller: the world of Charlotte Yonge. 1947.
Dodds, M. H. Jane Austen and Charlotte Yonge. N & Q 30 Oct 1948.
Avery, G. In her Nineteenth-century children, 1965.
Tillotson, K. The heir of Redclyffe. In her Mid-Victorian studies, 1965.

W. J. H.

VI. THE LATE-NINETEENTH-CENTURY NOVEL

'LEWIS CARROLL', CHARLES LUTWIDGE DODGSON 1832–98

Bibliographies

Collingwood, S. D. The life and letters of Carroll. 1898.
Williams, S. H. A bibliography of the writings of Carroll. 1924.
Parrish, M. L. List of the writings of Carroll collected by Morris L. Parrish. Pine Valley NJ 1829 (priv ptd); Supplementary list, Pine Valley NJ 1933 (priv ptd).
Williams, S. H. and F. Madan. A handbook of the literature of the Rev C. L. Dodgson. Oxford 1931. Addns by F. Madan, Oxford 1935; *see* Green, below.
Catalogue of an exhibition at Columbia University. New York 1932.
Livingston, F. V. The Harcourt Amory collection of Carroll in Harvard College Library. Cambridge Mass 1932.
Madan, F. and H. Hartley. Carroll centenary exhibition catalogue. 1932.
Black, D. Discovery of Carroll documents. N & Q Feb 1953.
Weaver, W. The mathematical manuscripts of Carroll. Princeton Univ Lib Chron 6 1954.
Green, R. L. Carroll's periodical publications. N & Q March 1954.
—— The Carroll handbook. Oxford 1962. Based on Williams and Madan, above.

Collections

No collection is absolutely complete, mathematical works and various juvenilia being excluded.

Collected verse. Ed J. F. McDermott, New York 1929.
Complete works. Ed A. Woollcott, New York 1939.
Works. Ed R. L. Green 1965.

§1

The following books and pamphlets, generally accepted as by Dodgson, bear his name, his pseudonym or other pseudonyms, or are anon. For ascriptions, and for ephemera, offprints etc omitted from the following list, see Green, Carroll handbook, 1962.

The fifth book of Euclid treated algebraically. Oxford 1858, 1868 (rev).
Rules for court circular. Oxford 1860, 1862.
A syllabus of plane algebraical geometry, part I. Oxford 1860.
Notes on the first two books of Euclid. Oxford 1860.
The formulae of plane trigonometry. Oxford 1861.
Notes on the first part of algebra. Oxford 1861.
Endowment of the Greek professorship. Oxford 1861.
An index to In memoriam. 1862.
The enunciations of the propositions of Euclid, bks I and II. Oxford 1863, 1873 (rev).
Croquet castles for five players. [Oxford 1863].
Examination statute. [Oxford 1864].
A guide to the mathematical student, part I. Oxford 1864.
American telegrams. [Oxford] 1865.
The new method of evaluation as applied to π. [Oxford] 1865.
The dynamics of a parti-cle. Oxford 1865.
Alice's adventures in Wonderland. 1865, New York 1866, London 1866, 1886, 1897 (both rev); ed M. Gardner, New York 1960.
Castle-croquet for four players. [Oxford] 1866.
The elections to the Hebdomadal Council. Oxford 1866.
Condensation of determinants. 1866.
The deserted Parks. Oxford 1867.
An elementary treatise on determinants. 1867.
Bruno's revenge. Aunt Judy's Mag 4 1867; ed J. Drinkwater 1924.
The offer of the Clarendon trustees. Oxford 1868.
Phantasmagoria and other poems. 1869.
The Guildford gazette extraordinary. [Guildford] 1869.
Songs from Alice's adventures in Wonderland 1870. With addns.
To all child readers of Alice's adventures in Wonderland. [Oxford] 1871.
Through the looking-glass, and what Alice found there. 1872 (for 1871), 1897 (rev).
The new belfry of Christ Church, Oxford. Oxford 1872.
The vision of the three T's. Oxford 1873.
A discussion of the various methods of procedure in conducting elections. Oxford 1873.
The blank cheque: a fable. Oxford 1874.
Notes by an Oxford chiel. Oxford 1874.
Suggestions as to the best method of taking votes. Oxford 1874.
Euclid, book V, proved algebraically. Oxford 1874.
Vivisection as a sign of the times. Pall Mall Gazette 12 Feb 1875; nd (no known copy).
Some popular fallacies about vivisection. Oxford 1875 (priv ptd).
Euclid books I, II edited. Oxford 1875, 1882 (rev).
Song for Puss in boots. Brighton 1876 (no known copy).
A method of taking votes on more than two issues. [Oxford] 1876.
The hunting of the snark: an agony in eight fits. 1876.
An Easter greeting to every child who loves Alice. [Oxford] 1876.
Fame's penny-trumpet. [Oxford] 1876.
Word-links: a game for two players. Oxford 1878.
Euclid and his modern rivals. 1879, 1885 (rev); Supplement, 1885.
Doublets: a word-puzzle. 1879, 1880.
Lanrick: a game for two players. Oxford 1881.
Dreamland. [Oxford 1882].
Mischmasch: a word-game. [Oxford] 1882.
Lawn tennis tournaments: the true method of assigning prizes. 1883.
Rhyme? and reason? 1883.
Christmas greetings: from a fairy to a child. [1884].
Twelve months in a curatorship. Oxford 1884; Supplement, Postscript, Oxford 1884.
The principles of parliamentary representation. 1884; Supplement, 1885.
The profits of authorship. 1884 (no known copy).
A tangled tale. 1885.
Three years in a curatorship. Oxford 1886.
Suggestions at to the elections of proctors. Oxford 1886.
The game of logic. 1886, 1887.
Alice's adventures underground. 1886; ed M. Gardner, New York 1965.
Curiosa mathematica, part I: a new theory of parallels. 1888.
The nursery Alice. 1889; ed M. Gardner, New York 1966.
Sylvie and Bruno. 1889.
Circular billiards, for two players. [Oxford 1890].
Eight or nine wise words about letter-writing. Oxford 1890.
A postal problem. [Oxford?] 1891; Supplement, 1891.
Curiosissima curatoria. Oxford 1892.
Syzygies and Lanrick: a word-puzzle and a game. 1893.
Curiosa mathematica, part II: pillow-problems. 1893.

Sylvie and Bruno concluded. 1893.
A disputed point in logic. [Oxford] 1894. 5 papers.
What the tortoise said to Achilles. 1894.
Symbolic logic, part 1: elementary. 1896.
Resident women-students. Oxford 1896.
Three sunsets and other poems. 1898.
The Lewis Carroll picture book. 1899, New York 1961 (as Diversions and digressions).
The story of Sylvie and Bruno. Ed E. H. Dodgson 1904.
Feeding the mind. 1907.
Some rare Carrolliana. 1924 (priv ptd).
Novelty and romancement. Boston 1925. Rptd from Train 2 1856.
Further nonsense verse and prose. Ed L. Reed 1926.
A Christmas Carroll. Edinburgh 1930 (priv ptd).
To M.A.B. Edinburgh 1931 (priv ptd).
For the Train. Ed H. J. Schonfield 1932. Contributions to Train 1856–7.
The rectory umbrella and Mischmasch. Ed F. Milner 1932.
How the boots got left behind. 1943 (priv ptd).
Fugitive pieces by Carroll. Ed R. L. Green, TLS 31 July 1953.
Useful and instructive poetry [1845]. Ed D. Hudson 1956.
Mathematical recreations of Carroll. New York 1958.

Letters, Diaries etc

The life and letters of Carroll by S. D. Collingwood. 1898.
The Carroll picture book. Ed S. D. Collingwood 1899.
Six letters by Carroll. Ed W. Partington 1924 (priv ptd).
Tour in 1867. Philadelphia 1928; ed J. F. McDermott, New York 1935 (as The Russian journal).
Two letters to Marion. Bristol 1932 (priv ptd).
A selection from the letters of Carroll to his child-friends. Ed E. M. Hatch 1933.
Diaries. Ed R. L. Green 2 vols 1953.

§2

Hatch, B. Lewis Carroll. Strand Mag 15 1898.
Collingwood, S. D. The life and letters of Carroll. 1898.
Bowman, I. The story of Carroll. 1899.
Maitland, E. A. Childish memories of Carroll. Quiver 34 1899.
Powell, F. Y. In O. Elton, Frederick York Powell, 1906.
Furniss, H. Recollections of Carroll. Strand Mag 35 1908.
Moses, B. Carroll in Wonderland and at home. New York 1910.
Cammaerts, E. The poetry of nonsense. 1925.
Arnold, E. M. Reminiscences of Carroll. Atlantic Monthly Dec 1929.
de la Mare, W. In the Eighteen-eighties, ed de la Mare 1930; 1932 (separately).
Reed, L. The life of Carroll. 1932.
Chesterton, G. K. Lewis Carroll. New York Times 1932; in his A handful of authors, 1953.
Strong, T. B. Lewis Carroll. Times 27 Jan 1932.
De Sausmarez, F. B. Theatricals at Oxford; with prologues by Carroll. Nineteenth Century Feb 1932.
Hargreaves, A. and C. Alice's recollections of Carrollian days. Cornhill Mag July 1932.
Leslie, S. Carroll and the Oxford movement. London Mercury July 1933.
Empson, W. In his Some versions of pastoral, 1935.
Ayres, H. M. Carroll's Alice. New York 1936.
Weaver, W. Carroll correspondence numbers. New York 1940.
— Lewis Carroll: mathematician. Scientific Amer 194 1956.
— Alice in many tongues. Madison 1964.
Rowell, E. M. 'To me he was Mr Dodgson'. Harper's Mag Feb 1943.
Lennon, F. B. Victoria through the looking-glass: the life of Carroll. New York 1945, 1962 (rev).
Green, R. L. Carroll and the St James's Gazette. N & Q 7 April 1945.
— The story of Carroll. 1949.
— Carroll and stage children. Stage 21 Oct 1954.
— The griffin and the jabberwock. TLS 1 March 1957.
— Lewis Carroll. 1960.
Atkinson, G. Memories of Carroll. Hampshire Chron 13 March 1948.
Gernsheim, H. Lewis Carroll, photographer. 1949, 1951 (rev).
Alexander, P. Logic and the humour of Carroll. Proc Leeds Philosophical Soc 6 1951.
Dodgson, V. Lewis Carroll. London Calling 28 June 1951.
Wilson, E. Lewis Carroll: an estimate. In his Shores of light, New York 1952.
Sewell, E. In her Field of nonsense, 1952.
Parisot, H. Carroll: une étude. Paris 1952.
Taylor, A. L. The white knight: a study of C. L. Dodgson. Edinburgh 1952.
Shawyer, E. Lewis Carroll. Observer 14 Feb 1964.
Schöne, A. M. Humor and Komik in Carrols Nonsense-traummärchen. Deutsches Vierteljahrsschrift 28 1954.
Hudson, D. Lewis Carroll. 1954.
— Lewis Carroll. 1958 (Br Council pamphlet).
Greenacre, P. Swift and Carroll: a psychoanalytic study of two lives. New York 1955.
Bond, W. H. The publication of Alice's adventures in Wonderland. Harvard Lib Bull 10 1956.
Hatch, E. Recollections of Carroll. Listener 30 Jan 1958.
Godman, S. Carroll's final corrections to Alice. TLS 2 May 1958.
Black, D. The theory of committees and elections. Cambridge 1958.
Gardner, M. The games and puzzles of Carroll. Scientific Amer March 1960.
— The annotated Alice. New York 1960.
— The annotated Snark. New York 1962.
Kirk, D. F. Charles Lutwidge Dodgson, semeiotician. Gainesville 1962.
O'Brien, H. Alice in Wonderland: the French lesson-book. N & Q Dec 1963.
Leach, W. Alice in Wonderland in perspective. Victorian Newsletter no 25 1964.
Ettleson, A. Carroll's Through the looking-glass decoded. New York 1966.
Rackin, D. Alice's journey to the end of night. PMLA 81 1966.

R. L. G.

THOMAS HARDY
1840–1928

Bibliographies etc

Hodgson & Co. A catalogue of the library of Hardy. 1938.
Wilson, C. A. A descriptive catalogue of the Grolier Club Hardy exhibition. Portland Maine 1940.
Weber, C. J. The first hundred years of Hardy 1840–1940; a centenary bibliography of Hardiana. Waterville Maine 1942, New York 1965. For many notes and short articles *see* indices to Colby Lib Quart and Colby Mercury.
Purdy, R. L. Hardy: a bibliographical study. Oxford 1954, 1968 (rev).
Stevenson, L. In The Victorian poets: a guide to research, ed F. E. Faverty, Cambridge Mass 1956, 1968 (rev).
Beebe, M., B. Culotta, E. Marcus. Criticism of Hardy: a selected checklist [mainly since 1940]. Modern Fiction Stud 6 1960.

Fayen, G. S. In Victorian fiction: a guide to research, ed L. Stevenson, Cambridge Mass 1964.
Bunnosuke, Y. Bibliography of Hardy in Japan. Tokyo 1957.

Collections

Wessex novels. 16 vols 1895–6.
[Works]: Wessex edition. 24 vols 1912–31; rptd in part as Autograph edition, 20 vols New York 1915; Anniversary edition, 21 vols 1920.
[Works]: Mellstock edition [de luxe]. 37 vols 1919–20.
Selected poems. 1916, 1921, 1929 (rev and enlarged as Chosen poems).
Collected poems. 1919, 1923, 1928, 1930.
Short stories. 1928.
Selected poems. Ed G. M. Young 1940.
Hardy's love poems. Ed C. J. Weber 1963.

§1

For single short poems, priv ptd or uncollected contributions to books, periodicals and newspapers, and dramatizations by the Hardy players, see R. L. Purdy, Bibliographical study, above.

Desperate remedies: a novel. 3 vols 1871 (anon), 1 vol New York 1874 (rev), London 1889 ('new edition' with Prefatory note), 1892 ('popular edition'), 1896 (rev, with addn to Prefatory note), 1912 (rev, with further addn to Prefatory note), 1920.

Under the greenwood tree: a rural painting of the Dutch school. 2 vols 1872, 1 vol 1873, New York 1873, London 1876 (illustr R. Knight), 1878, 1891, 1896 (rev, with preface), 1912 (rev, with further preface), 1920; tr French, 1910, 1923, 1924; Swedish, 1937; German, 1949; Polish, 1958.

A pair of blue eyes: a novel. 3 vols 1873, 1 vol New York 1873, London 1877, 1895 (rev, with preface), 1912 (rev, with Postscript), 1920 (rev); tr French, 1913, 1933; Spanish, 1919, 1929; Polish, 1929; Finnish, 1961. First pbd Tinsleys' Mag Sept 1872–July 1873, Semi-weekly New York Tribune 26 Sept–16 Dec 1873.

Far from the madding crowd. 2 vols 1874 (illustr H. Paterson [Allingham]), 1 vol New York 1874, 2 vols 1875 (rev), 1 vol 1877, 1895 (with preface), 1902 (rev), 1912, 1919; tr French, 1891, 1901, 1953; Swedish, 1920; Spanish, 1922; Polish, 1931, 1958; Russian, 1937; Italian, 1955; Hindi, 1956; Yugoslav, 1959. First pbd anon in Cornhill Mag Jan–Dec 1874, Every Saturday 31 Jan–24 Oct 1874, Littell's Living Age 31 Jan 1874–9 Jan 1875, Eclectic Mag March 1874–Feb 1875, Semi-weekly New York Tribune 26 June–15 Dec 1874 Dramatization (by Hardy and J. Comyns Carr), Prince of Wales Theatre Liverpool, 27 Feb 1882.

The hand of Ethelberta: a comedy in chapters. 2 vols 1876 (illustr G. Du Maurier), 1 vol New York 1876, London 1877, 1895 (rev, with preface), 1912 (rev, with Postscript), 1920. First pbd Cornhill Mag July 1875–May 1876, New York Times 20 June 1875–9 April 1876.

The return of the native. 3 vols 1878, 1 vol New York 1878, London 1880, 1884, 1895 (rev, with preface), 1912 (rev, with Postscript), 1920; tr Hungarian, 1898; Swedish, 1921; French, 1923, 1932, 1933; Czech, 1924; Chinese, 1936, 1953, 1964; Italian, 1948; German, 1949, 1956; Japanese, 1953, 1956; Yugoslav, 1959; Korean, 1962. First pbd Belgravia Jan–Dec 1878 (illustr A. Hopkins), Harper's New Monthly Mag Feb 1878–Jan 1879.

Fellow-townsmen. New York 1880, London 1888 (rev for Wessex tales). First pbd New Quart Mag new ser 2 1880, Harper's Weekly 17 April–15 May 1880.

The trumpet-major: a tale. 3 vols 1880, 1 vol New York 1880, London 1881, 1895 (rev, with preface), 1912, 1920; tr French, 1881, 1882, 1958; Russian, 1960, 1961; Arabic, 1963. First pbd Good Words Jan–Dec 1880, Demorest's Monthly Mag Jan 1880–Jan 1881.

A Laodicean: a novel. New York 1881, 3 vols 1881 (rev), 1 vol 1882, 1896 (rev, with preface), 1912 (rev, with Postscript), 1920. First pbd Harper's New Monthly Mag (European edn) Dec 1880–Dec 1881 (illustr G. Du Maurier) and in Amer edn Jan 1881–Jan 1882.

Two on a tower: a romance. 3 vols 1882, 1 vol New York 1882, 3 vols 1883 (rev), 1 vol 1883 (rev), 1895 (rev, with preface), 1912 (rev, with addn to preface), 1920. First pbd Atlantic Monthly May–Dec 1882.

The romantic adventures of a milkmaid: a novel. New York [1883], London 1913 (rev for A changed man). First pbd Graphic 25 June 1883, Harper's Weekly 23 June–4 Aug 1883.

The Mayor of Casterbridge: the life and death of a man of character. 2 vols 1886, 1 vol New York 1886, London 1895 (rev, with preface), 1912 (rev, with addn to preface), 1920; ed R. B. Heilman, Boston 1962; tr French, 1922; Norwegian, 1948; Finnish, 1956; Hindi, 1958; Polish, 1960. First pbd Graphic and Harper's Weekly 2 Jan–15 May 1886.

The woodlanders. 3 vols 1887, 1 vol New York 1887, London 1887, 1895 (rev, with preface), 1912 (rev, with Postscript), 1920; tr French, 1932; Norwegian, 1949. First pbd Macmillan's Mag May 1886–April 1887, Harper's Bazar 15 May 1886–9 April 1887.

Wessex tales: strange, lively, and commonplace. 2 vols 1888, 1 vol New York 1888, London 1889, 1896 (with preface; adds An imaginative woman), 1912 (with addn to preface; omits An imaginative woman), 1920 (with addn to preface). Includes The three strangers (first pbd Longman's Mag March 1883, Harper's Weekly 3–10 March 1883); The withered arm (Blackwood's Mag Jan 1888); Fellow-townsmen (*see* above, 1880); Interlopers at the Knap (Eng Illustr Mag May 1884); The distracted preacher (New Quart Mag new ser 1 1879 and Harper's Weekly 19 April–17 May 1879). An imaginative woman, tr French, 1912, 1918, 1947; Japanese, 1923, 1951, 1956, 1961 (Pall Mall Mag April 1894).

A group of noble dames. 1891, New York 1891, London 1896 (with preface), 1912, 1920. Includes The first Countess of Wessex (Harper's New Monthly Mag Dec 1889); Barbara of the house of Grebe; The Marchioness of Stonehenge; Lady Mattisfont; The Lady Kenway; Squire Patrick's lady; Anna, Lady Baxby (these 6 bowdlerized in Graphic 1 Dec 1890, Harper's Weekly 29 Nov–20 Dec 1890); The Lady Penelope (Longman's Mag Jan 1890); The Duchess of Hamptonshire as The impulsive lady of Groome Castle (Light 6–13 April 1878; Harper's Weekly 11–18 May 1878), as Emmeline: or passion versus principle (Independent New York 7 Feb 1884); The Honourable Laura as Benighted travellers (Bolton Weekly Jnl 17 Dec 1881, Harper's Weekly 10–17 Dec 1881).

Tess of the d'Urbervilles: a pure woman faithfully presented. 3 vols 1891, 1892 (rev), 1 vol New York 1892 (illustr), London 1892 (with preface), 1895 (rev, with additional preface), 1912 (rev, note to prefaces, 'General preface to the novels and poems'), 1919, 1926; ed W. E. Buckler, Boston 1960; ed S. Elledge New York 1965 (with critical essays); tr Russian, 1893, 1931, 1937, 1955, 1957, 1961, 1964; Italian, 1894, 1930, 1933, 1950; German, 1895, 1925, 1936, 1950, 1951, 1953, 1961, 1964; Swedish, 1900, 1931, 1960; French, 1901, 1924, 1957; Danish, 1924; Spanish, 1924; Polish, 1929, 1956, 1957, 1961; Dutch, 1934; Lettish, 1935; Chinese, 1936; Czech, 1937, 1948, 1949; Norwegian, 1948; Japanese, 1951, 1952, 1956, 1961; Yugoslav, 1952, 1953, 1956, 1958, 1962; Hindi, 1954, 1956, 1960; Hungarian, 1956, 1959, 1964; Korean, 1959–1964; Bulgarian, 1961; Rumanian, 1963. First pbd, omitting some chs, in Graphic 4 July–26 Dec 1891 (illustr H. von Herkomer et al) (chs 10–11 ptd Nat Observer (Edinburgh) 14 Nov 1891, ch 14 in Fortnightly Rev May 1891), in Harper's Bazar 18 July–26 Dec 1891 (ch 4 in Eclectic Mag June 1891); rptd complete in John O'London's Weekly 24 Oct 1895–10 July 1926; dramatized 1894–5, produced New York 2 March 1897 (rev L. Stoddard); produced Dorchester 1924, London 1925, 1929 (rev Hardy). *See* M. Roberts, below.

The three wayfarers: a pastoral play in one act. New York 1893, New York and London 1930 (rev, illustr), Dorchester 1935, New York 1943 (facs). Dramatized from The three strangers, Wessex tales; produced Terry's 3 June 1893.

Life's little ironies: a set of tales with some colloquial sketches entitled A few crusted characters. 1894, New York 1894, London 1896 (with preface), 1912 (rev, omits preface, adds Prefatory note), 1920. Includes The son's veto (first pbd in Illustr London News 1 Dec 1891). For conscience' sake (Fortnightly Rev March 1891); A tragedy of two ambitions (Universal Rev Dec 1888); On the western circuit (bowdlerized in Eng Illustr Mag Dec 1891); To please his wife (Black & White 27 June 1891); The melancholy hussar of the German legion (Bristol Times & Mirror 4, 11 June 1890 etc); The fiddler of the reels (Scribner's Mag May 1893); A tradition of eighteen hundred and four (Harper's Xmas Dec 1882); A few crusted characters as Wessex folk (Harper's New Monthly Mag March–June 1891); tr German, 1904, 1924 (in part); French, 1920, 1922; Japanese, 1929; Arabic, 1948; Italian, 1949, 1953; Hungarian, 1962; Chinese, nd.

The spectre of the real, by Hardy and Florence Henniker. To-day 17 Nov 1894; rptd in Scarlet and grey: stories of soldiers and others by Florence Henniker, 1896.

Jude the obscure. 1896 (for 1895) (with preface), New York 1896 (for 1895), 1912 (rev, with Postscript), 1920; ed A. Alvarez, New York 1961 (in Guerard 1963, below); ed I. Howe, Boston 1965; tr German, 1897, 1957; Swedish, 1900; French, 1901, 1903, 1913, 1927, 1931, 1950, 1953, 1956, 1957; Japanese, 1925, 1928, 1956; Danish, 1926; Czech, 1927, 1957, 1964; Italian, 1929, 1933, 1946, 1961; Russian, 1933, 1963; Norwegian, 1948; tr Yugoslav, 1953, 1956, 1964; Chinese, 1959; Portuguese, 1959, 1962; Hungarian, 1960; Yiddish, 1961; Polish, 1964. First pbd abridged and modified as The simpletons, then as Hearts insurgent in Harper's New Monthly Mag Dec 1894–Nov 1895 (illustr W. Hatherell).

The well-beloved: a sketch of a temperament. 1897 (with preface), New York 1897, London 1912 (rev), 1920; tr French, 1909, 1929; Spanish, 1921, 1938; Portuguese, 1952. First pbd as The pursuit of the well-beloved in Illustr London News and Harper's Bazar 1 Oct–17 Dec 1892.

Wessex poems and other verses, with thirty illustrations by the author. 1898, New York 1899, London 1912, 1920.

Poems of the past and the present. 1902 (for 1901), 1902 (rev), 1912, 1920.

The dynasts: a drama of the Napoleonic wars. Pt 1, 1903 (for 1904), 1904 (rev); pt 2, 1905 (for 1906); pt 3, 1908, 1910; The dynasts, 1 vol 1910, 1913, 1920, 3 vols 1927; ed J. Wain 1965; Prologue and epilogue, 1914; tr Chinese, 1937. Abridged version produced by H. Granville-Barker 25 Nov 1914–30 Jan 1915.

Select poems of William Barnes, chosen and edited with a preface and glossorial notes. 1908, 1922 (for 1921), 1933.

Time's laughingstocks and other verses. 1909, 1910, 1913, 1915, 1920.

A changed man, The waiting supper and other tales. 1913, 1920. Includes A changed man (first pbd Sphere 21–28 April 1900); The waiting supper (Murray's Mag Jan–Feb 1888 and Harper's Weekly 31 Dec 1887–7 Jan 1888); Alicia's diary (Manchester Weekly Times 15–22 Oct 1887); The grave by the handpost (St James's Budget 30 Nov 1897); Enter a dragoon (Harper's Monthly Mag Dec 1900); A tryst at an ancient earthwork (Detroit Post 15 March 1885); What the shepherd saw (Illustr London News 5 Dec 1881); A committee-man of the Terror (ibid 22 Nov 1896); Master John Horseleigh, Knight (ibid 12 June 1893); The Duke's reappearance (Saturday Rev 14 Dec 1896); A mere interlude (Bolton Weekly Jnl 17–24 Oct 1885); The romantic adventures of a milkmaid (1883, above).

Satires of circumstance: lyrics and reveries with miscellaneous pieces. 1914, 1915, 1919, 1920.

Moments of vision and miscellaneous verses. 1917, 1919, 1920.

The play of Saint George. Cambridge 1921 (priv ptd), New York 1928 (with modernized version by R. S. Loomis).

Late lyrics and earlier with many other verses. 1922, 1926.

The famous tragedy of the Queen of Cornwall. 1923, 1924 (rev), 1926.

Human shows, far phantasies: songs and trifles. 1925, New York 1925, 1931.

Life and art: essays, notes and letters. Ed E. Brennecke, New York 1925 (unauthorized). *See* Hardy's personal writings, below.

Winter words in various moods and metres. 1928, New York 1928, 1931. Partially serialized Daily Telegraph 19 March–26 Sept 1928.

Hardy, F. E. The early life of Hardy 1840–91. 1928, New York 1928; The later years of Hardy 1892–1928, 1930, New York 1930. Collected 1962, New York 1962. Both mainly by Hardy, and dictated to his second wife.

An indiscretion in the life of an heiress. 1934 (priv ptd); ed C. J. Weber, Baltimore 1935. First pbd Harper's Weekly 29 June–27 July 1878, New Quart Mag 1878 (rev); a reworking of The poor man and the lady, Hardy's first novel, now lost. *See* R. L. Purdy, above.

Our exploits at West Poley. Ed R. L. Purdy, Oxford 1952. First pbd Household (Boston) Nov 1892–April 1893.

Hardy, E. Some unpublished poems of Hardy. London Mag Jan 1956.

—— Hardy: plots for five unpublished stories. London Mag Nov 1958.

—— An unpublished poem by Hardy. TLS 2 June 1966. Facs of A Victorian rehearsal.

Hardy's drawings for a child. TLS 19 July 1957.

Hardy's personal writings: prefaces, literary opinions, reminiscences. Ed H. Orel, Lawrence Kansas 1966. Includes prefaces to Wessex edn of novels and poetry and to works by others; also How I built myself a house (Chambers's Jnl 18 March 1865); The Dorsetshire labourer (Longman's Mag July 1883) rptd as The Dorset farm labourer, Dorchester 1884; The Rev William Barnes BD (Atheneaum 16 Oct 1886), rptd in L. Johnson, The art of Hardy, below; The profitable reading of fiction (Forum March 1888); Candour in English fiction (New Rev Jan 1890); The science of fiction (ibid April 1891); The tree of knowledge (ibid 1894); Memories of church restoration (Society for the Protection of Ancient Buildings: General Meeting, London 1906), rptd Cornhill Mag Aug 1906 (rev) [all in Life and art, above]; Dorset in London (The society of Dorset men in London, 1908); Maumbury ring (Times 9 Oct 1908); The ancient cottages of England (The preservation of ancient cottages, 1927).

Letters and Notebooks

For a fuller list of collections of correspondence containing Hardy letters, see G. S. Fayen under Bibliographies, above.

Letters of Hardy [at Colby]. Ed C. J. Weber, Waterville Maine 1954.

Hardy's notebooks and some letters from Julia Augusta Martin. Ed E. Hardy 1955.

Forty years in an author's life: a dozen letters (1876–1915) from Hardy. Colby Lib Quart 4 1956.
Bowden, A. The Hardy collection. Lib Chron of Univ of Texas 7 1962.
Parker, W. M. Hardy's letters to Sir George Douglas. English 14 1963.
'Dearest Emmie': Hardy's letters to his first wife. Ed C. J. Weber, New York 1963.
The architectural notebook. Ed C. Beatty, Dorchester 1966. Foreword by J. Summerson.

§2

For further reviews etc see C. J. Weber, First hundred years, *under Bibliographies, above.*
Boucher, L. Le roman pastoral en Angleterre. Revue des Deux Mondes 15 Dec 1875.
Mr Hardy's novels. New Quart Mag 2 1879.
Mr Hardy's novels. Br Quart Rev 73 1881.
Ellis, H. Hardy's novels. Westminster Rev 120 1883; rptd and expanded (1896 and 1928) in his From Marlowe to Shaw, ed J. Gawsworth 1950.
— Concerning Jude the obscure. Savoy 6 1896; rptd 1931.
Johnson, L. The art of Hardy. 1894, 1923 (with ch on the poetry by J. E. Barton).
Barrie, J. M. Hardy: the historian of Wessex. Contemporary Rev July 1889.
Trent, W. P. The novels of Hardy. Sewanee Rev 1 1893.
— Hardy as a novelist. Citizen 1 1896.
Macdonell, A. Thomas Hardy. 1894, New York 1895.
Butler, A. J. Mr Hardy as a decadent. Nat Mag 27 1896.
Gosse, E. Mr Hardy's new novel. Cosmopolis 1 1896.
— The lyrical poetry of Hardy. In his Some diversions of a man of letters, New York 1919 and Selected essays, 1928.
Kendall, M. Pessimism in the poems of Hardy. London Quart Rev 91 1899.
Archer, W. Thomas Hardy. Pall Mall Mag 23 1901; rptd in his Real conversations, 1904.
Howells, W. D. In his Heroines of fiction, New York 1901.
Beerbohm, M. The dynasts. Saturday Rev 30 Jan 1904.
— Hardy as a panoramatist. Littell's Living Age 240 1904.
— A sequelula to the Dynasts: a Christmas garland. 1922.
Garwood, H. Hardy: an illustration of the philosophy of Schopenhaeur. Philadelphia 1911.
Hedgcock, F. A. Essai de critique: Hardy, penseur et artiste. Paris 1911.
Saxelby, F. O. A Hardy dictionary. 1911.
Abercrombie, L. Hardy: a critical study. 1912, New York 1927 (abridged).
Lea, H. Hardy's Wessex. 1913.
Strachey, L. Mr Hardy's new poems. New Statesman 19 Dec 1914; rptd in his Literary essays, New York 1949.
Child, H. Thomas Hardy. 1916.
Duffin, H. C. Hardy: a study of the Wessex novels. 1916, 1921 (with appendix on the poems and Dynasts), 1937 (rev).
Berle, L. W. George Eliot and Hardy: a contrast. 1917.
Quiller-Couch, A. T. The poetry of Hardy. In his Studies in literature vol 1, 1918.
Fairley, B. Notes on the form of the Dynasts. PMLA 34 1919.
Symons, A. Thomas Hardy. Dial 68 1920.
— A study of Hardy. 1927.
Beach, J. W. Bowdlerized versions of Hardy. PMLA 36 1921.
— The technique of Hardy. Chicago 1922.
— In his Concept of nature in nineteenth-century English poetry, New York 1936.
Chew, S. C. Hardy, poet and novelist. Bryn Mawr 1921, New York 1928 (rev).

Grey, R. Certain women of Hardy. Fortnightly Rev Oct 1922.
— Women in the poetry of Hardy. Fortnightly Rev Jan 1926.
'Vernon Lee' (V. Paget). In her Handling of words, 1923.
Aldington, R. Conrad and Hardy. Literary Rev 5 1924.
Brennecke, E. Hardy's universe: a study of a poet's mind. 1924.
— The life of Hardy. New York 1925.
Fletcher, J. G. The spirit of Hardy. Yale Rev 13 1924.
Grimsditch, H. B. Character and environment in the novels of Hardy. 1925.
Lowes, J. L. Two readings of earth [by Hardy and Meredith]. Yale Rev 15 1926; rptd in his Essays in appreciation, Boston 1936.
Richards, I. A. In his Science and poetry, 1926, 1935 (rev).
Valakis, A. The moira of Aeschylus and the immanent will of Hardy. Classical Jnl March 1926.
Chase, M. E. Hardy from serial to novel. Minneapolis 1927.
Mayoux, J. J. La fatalité intérieure dans les romans de Hardy. Revue Anglo-américaine 4 1927.
— L'amour dans les romans de Hardy. Revue Anglo-américaine 5 1928.
Boughton, R. A musical association with Hardy. Musical News Feb 1928.
Braybrooke, P. Hardy and his philosophy. 1928.
Collins, V. H. Talks with Hardy at Max Gate 1920–2. New York 1928.
— The love poetry of Hardy. E & S 28 1942.
Ellis, S. M. Hardy: some personal recollections. Fortnightly Rev March 1928.
Elliott, G. R. Spectral etching in the poetry of Hardy. PMLA 43 1928; rptd in his Cycle of modern poetry, Princton 1929.
— Hardy's poetry and the ghostly moving-picture. South Atlantic Quart 27 1928.
'D'Exideuil, P.' (G. Lasselin). Le couple humain dans l'oeuvre de Hardy. Paris 1928; tr 1930 (rev).
Hommage à Hardy. Revue Nouvelle 1928. Special no with some trns, short bibliography, James Joyce letter; J. M. Murry, La suprématie de Hardy; E. Jaloux, Le pessimisme de Hardy; J. Schlumberger, Hardy, poète tragique; J.-L. Vandoyer, Souvenirs d'une lecture; R. Fernandez, Le romancier; G. d'Hangest, Méditation avec Hardy sur la dignité humaine; P. d'Exideuil, La vision des Dynasts; F. Hellens, Actualité de Hardy; C. du Bos, Quelques traits du visage de Hardy.
West, R. Two kinds of memory and The long chain of criticism. In her Strange necessity, 1928.
Zachrisson, R. E. Hardy as man, writer and philosopher: an appreciation, with a Swedish Hardy bibliography. Stockholm 1928.
Dobrée, B. In his Lamp and the lute, Oxford 1929.
Gardner, W. H. Some thoughts on the Mayor of Casterbridge. Oxford 1930.
Lucas, F. L. In his Eight Victorian poets, Cambridge 1930, 1940 (as Ten Victorian poets), 1948 (rev).
Williams, C. In his Poetry at present, Oxford 1930.
Firor, R. A. Folk-ways in Hardy. Philadelphia 1931.
Hickson, E. C. The versification of Hardy. Philadelphia 1931.
de Ridder-Barzin, L. Le pessimisme de Hardy. Brussels 1932.
Stevenson, L. In his Darwin among the poets, Chicago 1932.
Woolf, V. The novels of Hardy. In her Common reader ser 2, 1932; rptd in Victorian literature: modern essays in criticism, ed A. Wright, New York 1961.
— Half of Hardy. In her Captain's death bed and other essays, 1950.
Budke, W. Die Darstellung der Frau bei Hardy unter besonderer Berüchsichtigung Schopenhauers. Münster 1933.

Chapman, F. Hardy the novelist. Scrutiny 3 1934.
Smith, W. H. In his Architecture in English fiction, New Haven 1934.
Wilmsen, G. Hardy als impressionistischer Landschaftsmaler. Düsseldorf 1934.
Lillard, R. G. Irony in Hardy and Conrad. PMLA 50 1935.
Behr, A. von. Der Typen-konflikt in Hardys Romanen. Marburg 1936.
Ford, F. M. Thomas Hardy. American Mercury 38 1936; rptd in his Portraits from life, New York 1937.
Schumacher, M. Biologische Probleme in Hardys Werk. Bonn 1936.
Lawrence, D. H. Study of Hardy. In his Phoenix, 1936. Six novels and the real tragedy (ch 3) first pbd Book Collector's Quart 2 1932, John O'London's Weekly 12–19 March 1932.
Weber, C. J. Chronology in Hardy's novels. PMLA 53 1938. Replies by Emery, Murphree and Strauch, below.
— Hardy of Wessex: his life and literary career. New York 1940, Hamden Conn 1962, 1965 (rev).
— Ainsworth and Hardy. RES 17 1941.
— The manuscript of Hardy's Two on a tower. PBSA 40 1946. Reply by R. C. Schweik 60 1966.
— Hardy in America: a study of Hardy and his American readers. Waterville Maine 1946.
— The tragedy of Little Hintock: new light on the Woodlanders. In Booker memorial studies, ed H. Shine, Chapel Hill 1950.
— Hardy and the lady from Madison Square. Waterville Maine 1952.
— Hardy's copy of Schopenhauer. Colby Lib Quart 4 1957.
Chakravarty, A. C. The Dynasts and the post-war age in poetry. 1938.
Lang, V. Crabbe and Tess of the d'Urbervilles. MLN 53 1938.
Littmann, H. Das dichterische Bild in der Lyrik George Merediths und Hardys im Zusammenhang mit ihrer Weltanschauung. Berlin 1938.
Pound, E. Happy days; The promised land. In his Culture, Norfolk Conn 1938.
Powys, J. C. In his Enjoyment of literature, New York 1938.
Rutland, W. R. Hardy: a study of his writings and their background. Oxford 1938.
— Thomas Hardy. 1938 (Order of Merit ser).
Anderson, M. L. Hardy's debt to Webster in the Return of the native. MLN 54 1939.
Emery, J. P. Chronology in the Return of the native. PMLA 54 1939.
Forster, E. M. Woodlanders on Devi. New Statesman 6 May 1939.
Hicks, G. The pessimism of Hardy. In his Figures of transition, New York 1939.
Murphree, A. A. and C. F. Strauch. The chronology of the Return of the native. MLN 54 1939.
Daiches, D. In his Poetry and the modern world, Chicago 1940.
Grew, E. Hardy as musician. Music & Letters 21 1940.
Leishman, J. B. Hardy's burning veracity. RES 16 1940.
John O'London's Weekly 7 June 1940. Includes S. Sassoon, Hardy as I knew him; H. M. Tomlinson, The Wessex novels; A. T. Quiller-Couch, The dynasts.
Sherman, E. Music in Hardy's life and work. Musical Quart 26 1940.
— Hardy: lyricist, symphonist. Music & Letters 21 1940.
Southern Rev 6 1940. Hardy centennial issue, including W. H. Auden, A literary transference; H. Baker, Hardy's poetic certitude; J. Barzun, Truth and poetry in Hardy, (rev in his Energies of art, New York 1956); R. P. Blackmur, The shorter poems of Hardy (rptd in his Expense of greatness, New York 1940 and Language as gesture, New York 1952); D. Davidson, The traditional basis of Hardy's fiction (rptd in his Still rebels, still yankees and other essays, Baton Rouge 1957); B. Dobrée, The dynasts; F. R. Leavis, Hardy the poet; A. Mizener, Jude the obscure as a tragedy (rptd in his Sense of life in the modern novel, Boston 1964 and Modern British fiction, ed M. Schorer, New York 1961); K. A. Porter, Notes on a criticism of Hardy (rptd in her Days before, New York 1952); D. Schwartz, Poetry and belief in Hardy; A. Tate, Hardy's philosophic metaphors (rptd in his Reason in madness, New York 1941); M. D. Zabel, Hardy in defense of his art: the aesthetic of incongruity (rev in his Craft and character in modern fiction, New York 1957). For Auden, Davidson, Schwartz, Zabel, *see* Guerard 1963, below.
Aliesch, P. Studien zu Hardys Prosastil. Berne 1941.
Blunden, E. Thomas Hardy. 1942.
Purdy, R. L. Hardy and Jowett. TLS 3 Oct 1942, 2 Jan 1943.
— Source for Hardy's A committee-man of the terror: the journal of Mary Frampton. MLN 58 1943.
— Hardy and Florence Henniker: the writing of the Spectre of the real. Colby Lib Quart 1 1944.
— The authorship of Hardy's biography. TLS 30 Dec 1960.
Cecil, D. Hardy the novelist. 1943.
Hardy's method. TLS 10 April 1943.
Leavis, Q. D. Hardy and criticism. Scrutiny 11 1943.
Roberts, M. The dramatic elements in Hardy's poetry. Queen's Quart 51 1944.
— Tess in the theatre: two dramatizations of Tess of the d'Urbervilles, one by Lorimer Stoddard. Toronto 1950.
— Hardy's poetic drama and the theatre. New York 1965.
Bailey, J. O. Hardy's imbedded fossil. SP 42 1945.
— Hardy's Mephistophelian visitants. PMLA 61 1946.
— Hardy and the cosmic mind: a new reading of the Dynasts. Chapel Hill 1956.
— Hardy's vision of the self. SP 56 1959.
— Temperament as motive in the Return of the native. Eng Fiction in Transition 5 1962.
— Evolutionary meliorism in the poetry of Hardy. SP 60 1963.
Hopkins, A. B. The Dynasts and the course of history. South Atlantic Quart 44 1945.
Laird, J. The dynasts. In his Philosophic incursions into English literature, 1946.
Bowra, C. M. The lyrical poetry of Hardy. Nottingham 1947; rptd in his Inspiration and poetry, Cambridge 1951.
Muchnic, H. Thomas Mann and Hardy. In The stature of Thomas Mann, ed C. Neider, New York 1947.
Sherman, G. W. Hardy and the Reform League. N & Q 6 Sept 1947.
— The influence of London on the Dynasts. PMLA 63 1948.
— The wheel and the beast: the influence of London on Hardy. Nineteenth-Century Fiction 4 1950.
— Hardy and the agricultural labourer. Nineteenth-Century Fiction 7 1953.
Southworth, J. G. The poetry of Hardy. New York 1947.
Stallman, R. W. Hardy's hour-glass novel. Sewanee Rev 55 1947; rptd in his Houses that James built, Ann Arbor 1961.
Webster, H. C. On a darkling plain: the art and thought of Hardy. Chicago 1947.
Bebbington, W. G. The original manuscript of the Trumpet-major. Windsor 1948.
Guerard, A. J. Hardy: the novels and stories. Cambridge Mass 1949; rptd New York 1964, adding The illusion of simplicity: the poetry of Hardy, Sewanee Rev 72 1964.
Stewart, J. I. M. The integrity of Hardy. E & S new ser 1 1948.
— In his Eight modern writers, Oxford 1963 (OHEL).

Horsman, E. A. The language of the Dynasts. Durham Univ Jnl 41 1949.
Richards, M. C. Hardy's ironic vision. Nineteenth-Century Fiction 4 1950.
Bisson, L. Proust and Hardy: incidence or coincidence? In Studies in French language, literature and history, ed C. F. Mackenzie, New York 1950.
Brogan, H. O. Visible essences in the Mayor of Casterbridge. ELH 17 1950.
—— Science and narrative structure in Austen, Hardy and Woolf. Nineteenth-Century Fiction 11 1957.
Brown, E. K. In his Rhythm of the novel, Toronto 1950.
Bush, D. In his Science and English poetry, New York 1950.
Fiedler, L. A. The third Hardy. Nation (New York) 2 Sept 1950.
Flower, N. In his Just as it happened, 1950.
Grigson, G. Exasperating pessimist. Listener 2 March 1950.
Hawkins, D. Thomas Hardy. 1950.
Books from Hardy's Max Gate library. Colby Lib Quart 2 1950.
Kettle, A. In his Introduction to the English novel vol 2, 1951. On Tess.
Lewis, C. D. The lyrical poetry of Hardy. Proc Br Acad 37 1951.
Newton, W. Chance as employed by Hardy and the naturalists. PQ 30 1951.
—— Hardy and the naturalists: their use of physiology. MP 49 1951.
de Sola Pinto, V. Hardy and Housman. In his Crisis in English poetry 1880–1940, 1951.
Dike, D. A. A modern Oedipus: the Mayor of Casterbridge. EC 2 1952.
Fairchild, H. N. The immediate source of the Dynasts. PMLA 67 1952.
Holloway, J. In his Victorian sage, 1953.
—— Hardy's major fiction. In From Jane Austen to Joseph Conrad, ed R. Rathburn and M. Steinmann, Minneapolis 1958; rptd in his Charted mirror, 1960, and in Guerard 1963, below.
—— Tess and the awkward age. In his Charted mirror, 1960.
van Ghent, D. On Tess of the d'Urbervilles. In her English novel: form and function, New York 1953; rptd in Modern British fiction, ed M. Schorer, New York 1961 and in Guerard 1963, below.
Brown, D. Thomas Hardy. 1954, 1961 (rev).
—— The Mayor of Casterbridge. 1962.
Cassidy, J. A. The original source of Hardy's Dynasts. PMLA 69 1954.
Clifford, E. The child, the circus and Jude the obscure. Cambridge Jnl June 1954.
—— War and peace in the Dynasts. MP 54 1956.
—— The trumpet-major notebook and the Dynasts. RES new ser 8 1957.
—— Hardy and the historians. SP 56 1959.
—— The impressionistic view of history in the Dynasts. MLQ 22 1961.
Hardy, E. Hardy: a critical biography. 1954.
—— Emma Hardy's diaries: some foreshadowings of the Dynasts. English 14 1962.
Korg, J. Hardy's The dynasts: a prophecy. South Atlantic Quart 53 1954.
Hardy after fifty years. TLS 15 Jan 1954.
Andersen, C. R. Time, space and perspective in Hardy. Nineteenth-Century Fiction 9 1955.
Bartlett, P. Seraph of heaven: a Shelleyan dream in Hardy's fiction. PMLA 70 1955.
—— Hardy's Shelley. Keats-Shelley Jnl 4 1955.
Holland, N. Jude the obscure: Hardy's symbolic indictment of Christianity. Nineteenth-Century Fiction 9 1955.
Matchett, W. H. The woodlanders: or realism in sheep's clothing. Ibid.
Moynahan, J. The Mayor of Casterbridge and the Old Testament's first book of Samuel: a study of some literary relationships. PMLA 71 1956.
Starr, W. T. Romain Rolland and Hardy. MLQ 17 1956.
Davidson, D. Futurism and archaism in Toynbee and Hardy. In his Still rebels, still yankees and other essays, Baton Rouge 1957.
Goldberg, M. A. Hardy's double-visioned universe. EC 7 1957.
Roppen, G. Darwin and Hardy's universe. In his Evolution and poetic belief, Oslo 1957.
Slack, R. The text of Hardy's Jude the obscure. Nineteenth-Century Fiction 11 1957.
Goodheart, E. Hardy and the lyrical novel. Nineteenth-Century Fiction 12 1958.
Hoopes, K. R. Illusion and reality in Jude the obscure. Ibid.
Hyde, W. J. Hardy's view of realism: a key to the rustic characters. Victorian Stud 2 1958.
—— Hardy's response to the critics of Jude. Victorian Newsletter no 19 1961.
Johnson, S. F. Hardy and Burke's 'sublime'. In Style in prose fiction, 1958 (Eng Inst Essays).
O'Connor, W. V. Cosmic irony in Hardy's The three strangers. Eng Jnl 47 1958.
Raleigh, J. H. Victorian morals and the modern novel. Partisan Rev 25 1958.
Reinhard-Stocker, A. Charakterdarstellung und Schicksalsgestaltung in den Romanen Hardys. Winterthur 1958.
Walcutt, C. C. Character and coincidence in the Return of the native. In Twelve original essays in great English novels, ed C. Shapiro, Detroit 1958.
Collie, M. J. Social security in literary criticism. EC 9 1959. On Woodlanders.
Danby, J. F. Under the greenwood tree. CQ 1 1959.
Short, C. In defense of Ethelberta, Nineteenth-Century Fiction 13 1959.
Drake, R. Y. A Laodicean: a note on a minor novel. PQ 40 1961.
Hurley, R. A note on some emendations in Jude the obscure. Victorian Newsletter no 15 1959.
Hynes, S. Hardy and Barnes: notes on literary influence. South Atlantic Quart 58 1959.
—— The pattern of Hardy's poetry. Chapel Hill 1961. *See* Guerard 1963, below.
Paterson, J. The Mayor of Casterbridge as tragedy. Victorian Stud 2 1959. Reply by H. C. Webster 4 1960. Rptd in Guerard 1963, below.
—— The return of the native as antichristian document. Nineteenth-Century Fiction 14 1960.
—— The making of the Return of the native. Berkeley 1960.
—— The genesis of Jude the obscure. SP 57 1960.
—— Hardy, Faulkner and the prosaics of tragedy. Centennial Rev of Arts & Sciences 5 1962.
—— The latest gossip: Hardy and the Toucan press monographs. Victorian Stud 9 1965.
Perkins, D. Hardy and the poetry of isolation. ELH 1959; rptd in Guerard 1963, below.
Stanford, R. Hardy and Lawrence's The white peacock. Modern Fiction Stud 5 1959.
Wheeler, O. B. Four versions of the Return of the native. Nineteenth-Century Fiction 14 1960.
Carpenter, R. C. Hardy's 'gurgoyles'. Modern Fiction Stud 6 1960.
—— Hardy and the old masters. Boston Univ Stud in Eng 6 1961.
—— Thomas Hardy. New York 1964.
Harkness, B. Bibliography and the novelistic fallacy. SB 12 1960.
Karl, F. R. The Mayor of Casterbridge: a new fiction defined. Modern Fiction Stud 6 1960; rptd in Modern British fiction, ed M. Schorer, New York 1961; rev for his An age of fiction, New York 1964.

May, D. The novelist as moralist and the moralist as critic. EC 10 1960. On Mayor of Casterbridge.
McDowell, F. P. Hardy's 'seemings or personal impressions': the symbolical use of image and contrast in Jude the obscure. Modern Fiction Stud 6 1960.
— In defense of Arabella: a note on Jude the obscure. Eng Lang Notes 1 1964.
Deen, L. W. Heroism and pathos in Hardy's Return of the native. Nineteenth-Century Fiction 15 1961.
Elsbree, L. Tess and the local cerealia. PQ 40 1961.
Fayen, G. S. Hardy's The woodlanders: inwardness and memory. Stud in Eng Lit 1500–1900 1 1961.
Hagan, J. A. A note on the significance of Diggory Venn. Nineteenth-Century Fiction 16 1962.
Hardy, E. Some recollections, together with some relevant poems by Hardy. Ed E. Hardy and R. Gittings, Oxford 1961.
McCann, E. Blind will or blind hero: philosophy and myth in Hardy's Return of the native. Criticism 3 1961.
Smart, A. Pictorial imagery in the novels of Hardy. RES new ser 12 1961.
Deacon, L. Tryphena and Hardy. Beaminster 1962. The first Toucan press monographs; *see* Paterson, above.
— and T. Coleman. Providence and Mr Hardy. 1966.
Felkin, E. Days with Hardy, from a 1918–9 diary. Encounter April 1962.
Gregor, I. and B. Nicholas. The novel as moral protest: Tess of the d'Urbervilles. In their Moral and the story, 1962.
Griffin, E. G. Hardy and the growing consciousness of the immanent will: a study in the relationship of philosophy to literary form. Cairo Stud in Eng 1 1962.
King, R. W. Verse and prose parallels in the works of Hardy. RES new ser 13 1962.
Schweik, R. C. Moral perspective in Tess of the d'Urbervilles. College Eng Oct 1962.
— Theme, character and perspective in Hardy's The return of the native. PQ 41 1962.
— Character and fate in Hardy's The Mayor of Casterbridge. Nineteenth-Century Fiction 21 1967.
Sixt, E. Zur Strucktur des Romans bei Hardy. Munich 1962.
Wing, G. Tess and the romantic milkmaid. REL 3 1962.
— Thomas Hardy. 1963.
Beckman, R. A character typology for Hardy's novels. ELH 30 1963.
Brick, A. Paradise and consciousness in Hardy's Tess. Nineteenth-Century Fiction 17 1963.
Gerber, H. Hardy's The well-beloved as a comment on the well-despised. Eng Language Notes 1 1963.
Gose, E. B., jr. Psychic evolution: Darwinism and initiation in Tess of the d'Urbervilles. Nineteenth-Century Fiction 18 1964.
Hardy: a collection of critical essays. Ed A. J. Guerard, New York 1963. Contains essays and excerpts from studies above by Alvarez, Auden, Davidson, van Ghent, Guerard, Holloway, Hynes, Lawrence, Paterson, Perkins, Schwartz, Zabel.
Heilman, R. B. Hardy's Mayor and the problem of intention. Criticism 5 1963.
— Hardy's Mayor: notes on style. Nineteenth-Century Fiction 18 1964.
— Hardy's Sue Bridehead. Nineteenth-Century Fiction 20 1966.
Heywood, C. Miss Braddon's The doctor's wife: an intermediary between Madame Bovary and the Return of the native. Revue de Littérature Comparée 38 1964.
Morcos, L. The overworld: a projection of Hardy's personality. Cairo Stud in Eng 2 1963.
Morrell, R. The Dynasts reconsidered. MLR 58 1963.
— Hardy: the will and the way. Kuala Lumpur 1965.
Hardy, B. In her Appropriate form, 1964.
Marshall, W. H. Motivation in Tess of the d'Urbervilles. Revue des Langues Vivantes 29 1964.
Parrish, J. Hardy on the evidence of things unseen. Victorian Poetry 2 1964.
Riesner, D. Kunstprosa in der Werkstatt: Hardys The Mayor of Casterbridge 1884–1912. In Festschrift für Walter Hübner, Berlin 1964.
Singh, G. Hardy and Leopardi: a study in affinity and contrast. Rivista di Letterature Moderne e Comparate 17 1964.
Fernando, L. Hardy's rhetoric of painting. REL 6 1965.
Hildick, W. In his Word for word: a study of authors' alterations, 1965. On Tess.
Howe, I. Hardy as a 'modern novelist'. New Republic 26 June 1965. On Jude.
— Note on Hardy's stories. Hudson Rev 19 1966.
— Thomas Hardy. 1967.
Jones, L. O. Desperate remedies and the Victorian sensation novel. Nineteenth-Century Fiction 20 1966.
Minakawa, S. Appreciation of Hardy's works in Japan. Beaminster 1965.
Sankey, B. The major novels of Hardy. Denver 1965.
Friedman, A. Hardy: Weddings be funerals. In his Turn of the novel, New York 1966.
Gifford, H. Hardy and Emma. E & S new ser 19 1966.
Gregor, I. What kind of fiction did Hardy write? EC 16 1966.
Lodge, D. Tess, nature and the voices of Hardy. In his Language of fiction, 1966.
Kramer, D. Two 'new' texts of Hardy's The woodlanders. SB 20 1967.
Williams, R. Thomas Hardy. CQ 6 1964.

G. S. F.

HENRY JAMES
1843–1916

Bibliographies

Phillips, L. A bibliography of the writings of James. Boston 1906, New York 1930 (rev).
Richardson, L. N. [Table of biographical and critical studies]. In his James: representative selections, New York 1941; rptd in The question of Henry James, ed F. W. Dupee, New York 1945.
[Catalogue of exhibition 24 Oct–8 Dec 1946]. Gazette of Grolier Club 2 1947.
Hamilton, E. C. Biographical and critical studies of James 1941–8. Amer Lit 20 1949; V. R. Dunbar, Addenda, 22 1950.
Leary, L. Articles on American literature 1900–50. Durham NC 1954.
Spiller, R. E. In Eight American authors: a review of research and criticism, ed F. Stovall, New York 1956.
Beebe, M. and W. T. Stafford. Criticism of James: a selected checklist. Modern Fiction Stud 3 1957.
Edel, L. and D. H. Laurence. A bibliography of James. 1957, 1961 (rev) (Soho Bibliographies).
Birch, B. James: some bibliographical and textual matters. Library 5th ser 20 1965.
Blanck, J. In his Bibliography of American literature vol 5, New Haven 1968.

Collections

[Novels and tales]. 14 vols 1883, 1886–7.
Novels and tales: New York edition. 26 vols New York 1907–18, 1961–5, 24 vols 1908–9, 1913.
Uniform tales. 14 vols 1915–20, 7 vols Boston 1917–18.
Novels and stories. Ed P. Lubbock 35 vols 1921–3.
The art of the novel: critical prefaces [to New York edn, above]. Ed R. P. Blackmur, New York 1934.
American novels and stories. Ed F. O. Matthiessen, New York 1947.
Complete plays. Ed L. Edel, Philadelphia 1949, London 1949.

Ghostly tales. Ed L. Edel, New Brunswick 1948 (for 1949).
Complete tales. Ed L. Edel 12 vols 1962–5, Philadelphia 1962–5.

§1

James was an inveterate reviser, freely revising not only from serial to book, but from one edn to the next, and even from one impression to the next within a single edn. For serial pbn of separate tales, see Edel and Laurence, Bibliography, *above. Modern reprints, unless of special interest, have not been included below.*

A passionate pilgrim, and other tales. Boston 1875. A passionate pilgrim; The last of the Valerii; Eugene Pickering; The madonna of the future; The romance of certain old clothes; Madame de Mauves.
Transatlantic sketches. Boston 1875, Leipzig 1883 (rev as Foreign parts).
Roderick Hudson. Boston 1876 (for 1875), 3 vols 1879 (rev), 1 vol 1880, Boston 1882 (rev), London 1888; ed L. Edel, New York 1960; tr Italian, 1960. First pbd in Atlantic Monthly Jan–Dec 1875.
The American. Boston 1877, London [1877] (unauthorized), 1879, [*c.* 1888], 1894 (unauthorized); tr German, 1877 (2 versions), 1878 (3rd version); Polish, 2 vols 1879; Russian, 1880 (Weekly Novoye Vremya); French, 2 vols 1884; Swedish, 1884, 1944, 1960 (3 versions); Italian, 1934; Serbian, 1956; Korean, 1957; Japanese, 1958, 1959 (2 versions). First pbd in Atlantic Monthly June 1876–May 1877. Dramatic version, 1891 (2 impressions, privptd); acted at Opera Comique, London, 26 Sept 1891.
French poets and novelists. 1878, Leipzig 1883 (rev), London 1884 (rev); ed L. Edel, New York 1964.
Watch and ward. Boston 1878; ed L. Edel 1960. First pbd in Atlantic Monthly Aug–Dec 1871.
The Europeans. 2 vols 1878, Boston 1879 (for 1878), London 1879; ed E. Sackville-West 1952; ed L. Edel 1967 (with Washington Square, below). First pbd in Atlantic Monthly July–Oct 1878.
Daisy Miller. New York 1879 (for 1878), 2 vols 1879 (with An international episode and Four meetings), 1 vol 1880, New York 1883 (with An international episode, The diary of a man of fifty and A bundle of letters), London 1888, New York 1892 (with An international episode), 1900; tr French, 1883 (Revue Britannique), 1886; Russian, 1898 (Zhivopisnoye obozreniye), 1946; Danish, 1920; Italian, 1930; Japanese, 1941; Bengali, 1956; Korean, 1957; Croatian, 1958; German, 1958; Spanish, 1958; Polish, 1961; Turkish, 1963. First pbd in Cornhill Mag June–July 1878. Dramatic version, 1882 (priv ptd), Boston 1883. First pbd in Atlantic Monthly April–June 1883.
An international episode. New York 1879, 2 vols 1879 (with Daisy Miller and Four meetings), 1 vol 1880, New York 1883 (with Daisy Miller, The diary of a man of fifty, and A bundle of letters), New York 1892 (with Daisy Miller), New York 1902; tr French, 1886; Japanese, 1915, 1956 (2 versions); Danish, 1920. First pbd in Cornhill Mag Dec 1878–Jan 1879.
The madonna of the future and other tales. 2 vols 1879, 1 vol 1880, 1888. Vol 1: The madonna of the future; Longstaff's marriage; Madame de Mauves; vol 2: Eugene Pickering; The diary of a man of fifty; Benvolio.
Confidence. 2 vols 1880 (for 1879), Boston 1880, 1 vol 1880, 1881, 1882, Boston 1891; ed H. Ruhm, New York 1962 (from ms); tr Italian, 1946. First pbd in Scribner's Monthly Aug 1879–Jan 1880.
Hawthorne. 1879, New York 1880, London 1883, 1887, 1902 (EML); ed W. M. Sale jr, Ithaca 1956.
A bundle of letters. Boston [1880], New York [1880], (both unauthorized), New York 1880 (with The diary of a man of fifty), 1883 (with Daisy Miller, An international episode, and The diary of a man of fifty). First pbd in Parisian 18 Dec 1879.

Washington Square. New York 1881 (for 1880), 2 vols 1881, 1 vol 1881, 1889; ed L. Edel 1967 (with Europeans, above); tr Russian, 1881 (Zagranichnyi vestnik); Italian, 1950 (2 versions); Japanese, 1950; Spanish, 1951, 1952, 1958 (3 versions); Hebrew, 1952; Croatian, 1953; French, 1953; Greek, c. 1953; German, 1956; Portuguese, c. 1956; Korean, 1960. First pbd in Cornhill Mag June–Nov 1880 and in Harper's New Monthly Mag July–Dec 1880.
The portrait of a lady. 3 vols 1881, Boston 1882 (for 1881), 1 vol 1882; ed G. Greene, Oxford 1947 (WC); ed L. Edel, Boston 1956; tr French, 1933; Italian, 1943, 1963 (2 versions); Portuguese, 1944; Spanish, 1944, 1958 (2 versions); Swedish, 1947; German, 1950; Finnish, 1955; Urdu, 1958. First pbd in Macmillan's Mag Oct 1880–Nov 1881 and in Atlantic Monthly Nov 1880–Dec 1881.
The point of view. 1882 (priv ptd).
The siege of London, The pension Beaurepas, and The point of view. Boston 1883, Leipzig 1884 (rev). A passionate pilgrim replaced The pension Beaurepas in the Leipzig edn.
Portraits of places. 1883, Boston 1884, Leipzig 1884 (truncated).
Notes on a collection of drawings by Mr George du Maurier. 1884. Catalogue of Fine Art Society's exhibition.
A little tour in France. Boston 1885 (for 1884), 1900, London 1900, Boston 1907, 1914. First pbd as En province in Atlantic Monthly July–Nov 1883, Feb, April–May 1884.
Tales of three cities. Boston 1884, London 1884. The impressions of a cousin; Lady Barberina; A New England winter.
The art of fiction. Boston 1885 (for 1884), 1887 (for 1888?), 1889. Pbd with Walter Besant's essay of same title; rptd in The house of fiction, ed L. Edel 1957.
The author of Beltraffio. Boston 1885. The author of Beltraffio; Pandora; Georgina's reasons; The path of duty; Four meetings.
Stories revived. 3 vols 1885, 2 vols 1885. Vol 1: The author of 'Beltraffio'; Pandora; The path of duty; A day of days; A light man; vol 2: Georgina's reasons; A passionate pilgrim; A landscape-painter; Rose-Agathe; vol 3: Poor Richard; The last of the Valerii; Master Eustace; The romance of certain old clothes; A most extraordinary case.
The Bostonians. 3 vols 1886, New York 1886, 1 vol 1886; ed P. Rahv, New York 1945; ed L. Trilling 1952; ed I. Howe, New York 1956 (Modern Lib); ed L. Edel 1967; tr French, 1955; German, 1964. First pbd in Century Mag Feb 1885–Feb 1886.
The Princess Casamassima. 3 vols 1886, New York 1886, 1 vol 1887, 1888; ed L. Trilling 2 vols New York 1948; tr Danish, 1887; German, 1954; Croatian, 1958. First pbd in Atlantic Monthly Sept 1885–Oct 1886.
Partial portraits. 1888, New York 1888, London 1894.
The reverberator. 2 vols 1888, New York 1888, 1 vol 1888; ed S. Nowell-Smith 1949. First pbd in Macmillan's Mag Feb–July 1888.
The Aspern papers; Louisa Pallant; The modern warning. 2 vols 1888, New York 1888, 1 vol 1890; Aspern papers tr French, 1920 (Journal des Débats), 1929; Italian, 1944, 1946 (2 versions); Spanish, 1944 (for 1946), 1949, 1950 (3 versions); Swedish, 1951; German, 1953; Czech, 1959; Flemish, 1959. Aspern papers first pbd in Atlantic Monthly March–May 1888.
A London life; The Patagonia; The liar; Mrs Temperly. 2 vols 1889, New York 1889, 1 vol 1889, Leipzig 1891 (Patagonia omitted).
The tragic muse. 2 vols Boston 1890, 3 vols 1890, 1 vol 1891; ed L. Edel, New York 1960; ed R. P. Blackmur, New York 1961. First pbd in Atlantic Monthly Jan 1889–May 1890.

Daudet, A., Port Tarascon. New York 1891 (for 1890), London 1891 (for 1890). Tr James. First pbd in Harper's New Monthly Mag June–Nov 1890.

The lesson of the master; The marriages; The pupil; Brooksmith; The solution; Sir Edmund Orme. New York 1892, London 1892.

The real thing, and other tales. New York 1893, London 1893. The real thing; Sir Dominick Ferrand; Nona Vincent; The Chaperon; Greville Fane.

Picture and text. New York 1893.

The private life; The wheel of time; Lord Beaupré; The visits; Collaboration; Owen Wingrave. 1893, 2 vols New York 1893. The private life (including Lord Beaupré and The visits) and The wheel of time (including Collaboration and Owen Wingrave).

Essays in London and elsewhere. 1893, New York 1893.

Theatricals. New York 1894, London 1895. Tenants; Disengaged (acted Hudson Theatre, New York, 11 March 1909).

Guy Domville. 1894 (priv ptd). Acted St James's Theatre, 5 Jan 1895.

Theatricals: second series. 1894, New York 1894. The album; The reprobate (acted Royal Court Theatre, 14 Dec 1919).

Terminations. 1895, New York 1895. The death of the lion; The Coxon fund; The middle years; The altar of the dead.

Embarrassments. 1896, New York 1896, London 1897. The figure in the carpet; Glasses; The next time; The way it came.

The other house. 2 vols 1896, New York 1896, 1 vol 1897; ed L. Edel 1948. First pbd in Illustr London News 4 July–26 Sept 1896.

The spoils of Poynton. 1897, New York 1897; ed L. Edel 1967; tr French, 1928 (Revue de Paris), 1929; Croatian, 1959. First pbd as The old things in Atlantic Monthly April–Oct 1896.

What Maisie knew. 1898 (for 1897), Chicago 1897; tr Danish, 1919; French, 1947; German, 1955. First pbd in Chapbook 15 Jan–1 Aug 1897 and in New Rev Feb–Sept 1897 (rev and abridged).

John Delavoy. New York 1897 (priv ptd).

In the cage. 1898, Chicago 1898, New York 1906; ed M. D. Zabel 1958; tr French, 1929; Italian, 1933.

The two magics: The turn of the screw; Covering end. 1898, New York 1898; Turn of the screw tr French, 1929; Italian, 1932, 1934, 1960 (3 versions); Portuguese, 1943; Spanish, 1945, 1946 (2 versions); Danish, 1950; Dutch, 1951; Swedish, 1951; German, 1953, 1954, 1962 (3 versions); Korean, 1957; Arabic, 1958; Japanese, 1958, 1962 (2 versions); Polish, 1959; Croatian, 1960. Turn of the screw first pbd in Collier's Weekly 26 Jan–2 April 1898.

The awkward age. 1899, New York 1899; ed L. Edel 1967; tr French, 1956. First pbd in Harper's Weekly 1 Oct 1898–7 Jan 1899.

The soft side. 1900, New York 1900. The great good place; 'Europe'; Paste; The real right thing; The great condition; The tree of knowledge; The abasement of the Northmores; The given case; John Delavoy; The third person; Maud-Evelyn; Miss Gunton of Poughkeepsie.

The sacred fount. New York 1901, London 1901; ed L. Edel, New York 1953, London 1959 (rev).

The wings of the dove. 2 vols New York 1902, London 1902; ed H. Read 1948; ed R. P. Blackmur, New York 1958; tr French, 1953; German, 1962.

The better sort. 1903, New York 1903. Broken wings; The Beldonald Holbein; The two faces; The tone of time; The special type; Mrs Medwin; Flickerbridge; The story in it; The beast in the jungle; The birthplace; The papers.

The ambassadors. 1903, New York 1903; ed L. Edel, Boston 1960; ed S. P. Rosenbaum, New York 1966; tr French, 1950; Croatian, 1955; German, 1956; Polish, 1960. First pbd in North Amer Rev Jan–Dec 1903.

William Wetmore Story and his friends. 2 vols Edinburgh 1903, 2 vols Boston 1903.

The golden bowl. 2 vols New York 1904, London [1905]; ed R. P. Blackmur, New York 1952; tr French, 1954; Croatian, 1960; German, 1964.

The question of our speech; The lesson of Balzac. Boston 1905. 2 lectures.

English hours. 1905, Boston 1905, 1914.

The American scene. 1907, New York 1907; ed W. H. Auden, New York 1946.

Views and reviews. Ed L. Phillips, Boston 1908.

Julia Bride. New York 1909.

Italian hours. 1909, Boston 1909.

The finer grain. New York 1910, London 1910. The velvet glove; Mora Montravers; A round of visits; Crapy Cornelia; The bench of desolation.

The James year book. Ed E. G. Smalley, Boston [1911], London [1912]. With introds by James and W. D. Howells.

The outcry. [1911], New York 1911.

A small boy and others. New York 1913, London 1913. An autobiography continued in Notes of a son and brother and Middle years, below; collected as Autobiography, ed F. W. Dupee 1956.

The American volunteer motor-ambulance corps in France. 1914.

Notes of a son and brother. New York 1914, London 1914.

Notes on novelists. 1914, New York 1914.

The question of the mind. [1915].

Pictures and other passages from James. Ed R. Head 1916, New York [1917].

The ivory tower. [1917], New York 1917; Notes for the Ivory tower, New York [1947].

The sense of the past. [1917], New York 1917.

The middle years. [Ed P. Lubbock] [1917], New York 1917.

Gabrielle de Bergerac. New York 1918.

Within the rim. [1919].

Travelling companions. New York 1919. Travelling companions; The sweetheart of M. Briseux; Professor Fargo; At Isella; Guest's confession; Adina; De Grey: a romance.

A landscape painter. New York 1919 (for 1920). A landscape painter; Poor Richard; A day of days; A most extraordinary case.

Refugees in Chelsea. [1920] (priv ptd).

Master Eustace. New York 1920. Master Eustace; Longstaff's marriage; Théodolinde; A light man; Benvolio.

Notes and reviews. Ed P. de Chaignon La Rose, Cambridge Mass 1921.

The scenic art. Ed A. Wade, New Brunswick 1948.

Eight uncollected tales. Ed E. Kenton, New Brunswick 1950. The story of a year; My friend Bingham; The story of a masterpiece; A problem; Osborne's revenge; Gabrielle de Bergerac; Crawford's consistency; The ghostly rental.

Daumier, caricaturist. [1954].

The American essays. Ed L. Edel, New York 1956.

The future of the novel: essays on the art of fiction. Ed L. Edel, New York 1956, London 1957 (with variations, as The house of fiction).

The painter's eye: notes and essays on the pictorial arts. Ed J. L. Sweeney 1956.

Parisian sketches. Ed L. Edel and I. D. Lind, New York 1957.

Literary reviews and essays on American, English and French literature. Ed A. Mordell, New York [1957].

French writers and American women. Ed P. Buitenhuis, Branford Conn 1960.

Letters and Papers

See also Section C, Published letters, in Edel and Laurence, Bibliography, *above.*

Letters to an editor [Clement Shorter]. 1916 (priv ptd).
Letters. Ed P. Lubbock 2 vols 1920, New York 1920.
'A most unholy trade': being letters on the drama. Cambridge Mass 1923 (priv ptd).
Three letters to Joseph Conrad. 1926 (priv ptd).
Letters to Walter Berry. Paris 1928 (priv ptd).
Letters to A. C. Benson and Auguste Monod. 1930.
Theatre and friendship: commentary by Elizabeth Robins. 1932.
Perry, R. B. The thought and character of William James. 2 vols Boston 1935.
Notebooks. Ed F. O. Matthiessen and K. B. Murdock, New York 1947; tr French, 1954.
James and Robert Louis Stevenson: a record of friendship and criticism. Ed J. A. Smith 1948.
Harlow, V. Thomas Sergeant Perry. Durham NC 1950.
Selected letters. Ed L. Edel, New York 1955.
James and the Bazar letters. Ed L. Edel and L. H. Powers, BNYPL Feb 1958; rptd in Howells and James: a double billing, New York 1958.
James and H. G. Wells: a record of their friendship. Ed L. Edel and G. N. Ray 1958.

§2

Howells, W. D. James's Passionate pilgrim and other tales. Atlantic Monthly April 1875; Henry James jr, Century Nov 1882; Editor's study, Harper's New Monthly Mag Oct 1888; Mr Henry James's later work, North Amer Rev Jan 1903. All rptd in Discovery of a genius, ed A. Mordell, New York 1961.
Newburgh, M. L. H. Mr Henry James jr and his critics. Literary World 14 Jan 1882.
Brownell, W. C. James's Portrait of a lady. Nation (New York) 2 Feb 1882.
—— In his American prose masters, New York 1909.
Tilley, A. The new school of fiction. Nat Rev April 1883.
Fawcett, E. Henry James's novels. Princeton Rev new ser 14 1884.
Scudder, H. E. James, Crawford and Howells. Atlantic Monthly June 1886.
Conrad, J. James: an appreciation. North Amer Rev Jan 1905; rptd in his Notes on life and letters, 1921.
Cary, E. L. The novels of James. New York 1905.
Fullerton, M. The art of James. Quart Rev 212 1910.
Paget, V. The handling of words. Eng Rev June 1910.
Hueffer, F. M. James: a critical study. 1913.
'West, Rebecca' (C. I. Andrews). Henry James. 1916.
Freeman, J. In his Moderns, 1916.
Lubbock, P. Henry James. Quart Rev 226 1916.
—— In his Craft of fiction, 1921.
Powys, J. C. In his Suspended judgments, New York 1916.
Scott, D. In his Men of letters, 1916.
Sherman, S. P. The aesthetic idealism of James. Nation (New York) 5 April 1917; rptd in his On contemporary literature, New York 1917.
Beach, J. W. The method of James. New Haven 1918, Philadelphia 1954 (enlarged).
Cairns, W. B. Character-portrayal in the work of James. Univ of Wisconsin Stud in Lang & Lit no 2 1918.
[James number]. Little Rev Aug 1918.
Liljegren, S. B. American and European in the works of James. Lund 1919.
Pound, E. In his Instigations, New York 1920; rptd in his Make it new, New Haven 1935.
Gosse, E. In his Aspects and impressions, 1922.
Perry, B. Commemorative tribute to James. [Amer Acad of Arts & Letters] Notes & Monographs 1922.
Bradford, G. In his American portraits 1875–1900, Boston 1922.
Bosanquet, T. James at work. 1924. By his secretary.
Phelps, W. L. In his Howells, James, Bryant and other essays, New York 1924.
Brooks, V. W. The pilgrimage of James. New York 1925.
—— New England: Indian summer. New York 1940.
Hughes, H. L. Theory and practice in James. Ann Arbor 1926.
Edgar, P. James: man and author. 1927.
Garnier, M. R. James et la France. Paris 1927.
Chislett, W., jr. In his Moderns and near-moderns, New York 1928.
Borchers, L. Frauengestalten und Frauenprobleme bei James. Berlin 1929.
Roberts, M. James's criticism. Cambridge Mass 1929.
Gide, A. Henry James. Yale Rev 19 1930.
Kelley, C. P. The early development of James. Urbana 1930, 1965 (rev).
Edel, L. James: les années dramatiques. Paris 1931.
—— The prefaces of James. Paris 1931.
—— James: the untried years 1843–70. 1953; The conquest of London 1870–81, 1962; The middle years 1882–95, Philadelphia 1962.
—— Henry James. Minneapolis 1960 (Univ of Minnesota pamphlets). *See* 1963, below.
Grattan, C. H. The three Jameses: a family of minds. New York 1932.
Greene, G. In his Contemporary essays, 1933; rptd with addns in his Lost childhood, 1951.
Alice James: her brothers, her journal. Ed A. R. Burr, New York 1934; ed L. Edel, New York 1964 (enlarged).
[James number]. Hound & Horn 7 1934.
Warren, A. In his Elder Henry James, New York 1934.
Snell, E. M. The modern fables of James. Cambridge Mass 1935.
Spender, S. In his Destructive element, 1935.
Waldock, A. J. A. In his James, Joyce and others, 1937.
Winters, Y. In his Maule's curse, Norfolk Conn 1938; rptd in his In defense of reason, New York 1947.
Diffené, P. I. James: Versuch einer Würdigung seiner Eigenart. Bochum 1939 (priv ptd).
Matthiessen, F. O. In his American renaissance, New York 1941.
—— James: the major phase. New York 1944.
—— The James family. New York 1947.
Nuhn, F. In his Wind blew from the east, New York 1942.
[Henry James centenary numbers]. New Republic 13 Feb 1943; Mark Twain Quart 5 1943; Kenyon Rev 5 1943.
Foley, R. N. Criticism in American periodicals of the works of James 1866–1916. Washington 1944.
Le Clair, R. C. In his Three American travellers in England, Philadelphia 1945 (priv ptd).
—— Young Henry James 1843–1870. New York 1955.
Dupee, F. W. (ed). The question of James: a collection of critical essays. New York 1945.
—— Henry James. New York 1951, Garden City NY 1956 (rev and enlarged).
Nowell-Smith, S. (ed). The legend of the master. 1947.
Stein, G. In her Four in America, New Haven 1947.
Andreas, O. James and the expanding horizon. Seattle 1948.
Leavis, F. R. In his Great tradition, 1948.
Milano, P. James: o il proscritto volontario. Milan 1948.
Stevenson, E. The crooked corridor. New York 1949.
Swan, M. Henry James. 1950 (Br Council pamphlet).
—— Henry James. 1952.
Canby, H. S. Turn west, turn east: Mark Twain and James. Boston 1951.
Bewley, M. In his Complex fate, 1952.
Baumgärtel, G. James im Spiegel moderner britischer Literaturkritik. Tübingen 1954.
Bowden, E. T. The themes of James: a system of observation through the visual arts. New Haven 1956.
[James numbers]. Modern Fiction Stud 3 1957; Nineteenth-Century Fiction 12 1958.
Anderson, Q. The American James. New Brunswick 1957.
Crews, F. C. The tragedy of manners: moral drama in the later novels of James. New Haven 1957.

Hoffmann, C. G. The short novels of James. New York 1957.
Levy, L. B. Versions of melodrama: a study of the fiction and drama of James 1865–97. Berkeley 1957.
Markow Totevy, G. Henry James. Paris 1958. Introd by André Maurois.
McCarthy, H. T. James: the creative process. New York 1958.
Wegelin, C. The image of Europe in James. Dallas 1958.
Holder-Barell, A. The development of imagery and its functional significance in James's novels. Berne 1959.
Horne, H. Basic ideas of James' aesthetics as expressed in the short stories concerning artists and writers. Marburg 1960.
Jefferson, D. W. Henry James. Edinburgh 1960 (Writers & Critics).
—— James and the modern reader. Edinburgh 1964.
Marks, R. W. James's later novels: an interpretation. New York 1960.
Poirier, R. The comic sense of James: a study of the early novels. 1960.
Willen, G. (ed). A casebook on James's The turn of the screw. New York 1960. 15 critical essays and text.
Cargill, O. The novels of James. New York 1961.
—— In his Toward a pluralistic criticism, Carbondale 1965.
Sanford, C. L. In his Quest for paradise: Europe and the American moral imagination, Urbana 1961.
Stallman, R. W. The houses that James built. East Lansing 1961.
Tilley, W. H. The background of the Princess Casamassima. Gainesville 1961.
Ward, J. A. The imagination of disaster: evil in the fiction of James. Lincoln 1961.
Cornwell, E. F. In her 'Still point', New Brunswick 1962.
Krook, D. The ordeal of consciousness in James. Cambridge 1962.
Putt, S. G. In his Scholars of the heart, 1962.
—— A reader's guide to James. 1966.
Wright, W. F. The madness of art. Lincoln 1962.
Cox, C. B. In his Free spirit, Oxford 1963.
James: a collection of critical essays. Ed L. Edel, Englewood Cliffs NJ 1963.
Geismar, M. James and the Jacobites. Boston 1963, London 1964 (as James and his cult).
Sharp, St M. C. The confidante in James. Notre Dame Ind 1963.
Stafford, W. T. (ed). James's Daisy Miller: the story, the play, the critics. New York 1963. Texts and critical commentary.
Stewart, J. I. M. In his Eight modern writers, Oxford 1963 (OHEL vol 12).
Wiesenfarth, J. James and the dramatic analogy: a study of the major novels of the middle period. New York 1963.
Gale, R. L. The caught image: figurative language in the fiction of James. Chapel Hill 1964.
—— Plots and characters in the fiction of James. Hamden Conn 1965.
Gastón, N. V. Introducción a James. San Juan, Puerto Rico 1964.
Holland, L. B. The expense of vision: essays on the craft of James. Princeton 1964.
Lowery, B. Marcel Proust et James: une confrontation. Paris 1964.
Sayre, R. F. The examined self: Benjamin Franklin, Henry Adams, James. Princeton 1964.
Stone, E. The battle and the books: some aspects of James. Athens Ohio 1964.
Vaid, K. B. Technique in the tales of James. Cambridge Mass 1964.
West, M. A stormy night with the Turn of the screw. Phoenix 1964.
Bell, M. Edith Wharton and James. New York 1965.
Blackall, J. F. Jamesian ambiguity and the Sacred fount. Ithaca 1965 (for 1966).
Clair, J. A. The ironic dimension in the fiction of James. Pittsburgh 1965.
Cranfill, T. M. and R. L. Clark jr. An anatomy of the Turn of the screw. Austin 1965.
Lebowitz, N. The imagination of loving: James's legacy to the novel. Detroit 1965.
McElderry, B. R. Henry James. New York 1965.
Monteiro, G. James and John Hay. Providence 1965.
Holder, A. Three voyagers in search of Europe. Philadelphia 1966.

D. H. L.

GEORGE ROBERT GISSING
1857–1903

The main sources of material are the Huntington Library, which possesses the mss of Born in exile, The crown of life, Denzil Quarrier, Eve's ransom, In the year of jubilee, The nether world, Thyrza, The whirlpool; *the Berg Collection, New York Public Library, which has the mss of* Demos, The emancipated, New Grub Street, Will Warburton, *as well as Gissing's diary, commonplace book and letters, particularly those to Gabrielle Fleury Gissing; the Yale Library, which contains the letters to Bertz and much family correspondence; the Carl H. Pforzheimer Library, which has a miscellaneous collection; and the Univ of Texas, which holds the ms of* Workers in the dawn. *Many items of current interest will be found in the Gissing Newsletter 1965–.*

Bibliographies

Scott, T. In his edn of Gissing, Critical studies of the works of Charles Dickens, New York 1924.
Donnelly, M. C. In her Gissing: grave comedian, Cambridge Mass 1954.
Gordan, J. D. Gissing 1857–1903: an exhibition from the Berg Collection. New York 1954.
Korg, J. Gissing: an annotated bibliography of writings about him [since 1940]. Eng Lit in Transition 1 1958.
—— In Victorian fiction: a guide to research, ed L. Stevenson, Cambridge Mass 1964.
Ward, A. C. In his George Gissing, 1959.
Wolff, J. J. Gissing: an annotated bibliography of writings about him: supplement I [before 1940]. Eng Lit in Transition 3 1960; supplement III, 7 1964.
Coustillas, P. Gissing's short stories: a bibliography. Ibid.
—— and P. Goetsch. Gissing: an annotated bibliography of writings about him—foreign journals, supplement II. Ibid.

§ 1

Notes on Social Democracy. Pall Mall Gazette 9, 11 Sept 1880; The new censorship of literature, 15 Dec 1884; Why I don't write plays, 10 Sept 1892.
Workers in the dawn: a novel. 3 vols 1880; ed R. Shafer 2 vols New York 1935.
The unclassed: a novel. 3 vols 1884, 1895 (rev), New York 1896, London 1905, 1911, 1930.
Isabel Clarendon. 2 vols 1886.
Demos: a story. 1886, 1890, 1897, 1914, New York 1886, London 1915, 1928, 1936; tr Russian, 1891.
Thyrza: a tale. 3 vols 1887, 1895, 1927; tr Russian, 1893; Italian, 1939.
A life's morning. 3 vols 1888, New York 1888, London 1914, 1928, 1938; ed W. Plomer 1947; tr Russian, 1890.
The nether world: a novel. 3 vols 1889, New York 1889, London 1928, 1929.
The emancipated: a novel. 3 vols 1890, 1893, New York 1895, London 1911.

New Grub Street: a novel. 3 vols 1891, 1892, 1907, 1927, 1938, New York 1904, 1905, 1926; ed G. W. Stonier 1959; ed I. Howe 1963; tr Russian, 1891.
Denzil Quarrier: a novel. 3 vols 1892, 1911, New York 1892.
Born in exile: a novel. 3 vols 1892, 1907; tr French, 1932; Italian, 1955.
The odd women. 3 vols 1893, New York 1893, London 1907.
In the year of jubilee. 3 vols 1894, New York 1895, London 1911, 1947.
Eve's ransom. 1895, New York 1895, London 1912, 1929; tr Dutch, 1904.
The paying guest. 1895, New York 1895.
Sleeping fires. 1895, New York 1895, London 1927.
The whirlpool. 1897, New York 1897, London 1911.
Human odds and ends: stories and sketches. 1898.
The town traveller. 1898, New York 1898, Toronto 1899.
Charles Dickens: a critical study. 1898, 1902 (with topographical notes by F. G. Kitton), 1926, New York 1898, 1924.
The crown of life. 1899, 1927, New York 1899, Toronto 1899.
The Rochester edition of the works of Charles Dickens. 9 vols (all pbd) 1900–1. Introds by Gissing, notes by F. G. Kitton.
By the Ionian sea: notes of a ramble in southern Italy. 1901, 1905, 1917; ed V. Woolf 1933; tr Japanese, 1947; Italian, 1957.
Our friend the charlatan. 1901, New York 1901.
Forster's life of Dickens, abridged and revised. 1903.
The private papers of Henry Ryecroft. 1903, 1908, 1912, 1914, 1929, 1939, 1953, New York 1903, 1915, 1918, 1927, 1961; tr Dutch, 1920; Japanese, 1924; Swedish, 1929; Chinese, c. 1950; Korean, 1960; French, 1966.
Veranilda: a romance. 1904, 1905, Oxford 1929 (WC). Preface by F. Harrison.
Will Warburton: a romance of real life. 1905, 1908, New York 1916, Oxford 1929 (WC).
Dickens. In Homes and haunts of famous authors, 1906.
The house of cobwebs and other stories. 1906, New York 1915 (preface by T. Seccombe), London 1931; tr Japanese, 1930; Chinese, 1951.
An heiress on condition. Philadelphia 1923.
Sins of the fathers and other tales. Chicago 1924. 4 short stories.
Critical studies of the works of Charles Dickens. Ed T. Scott, New York 1924. Introds to the Rochester edn, including 3 unpbd.
The immortal Dickens. 1925.
A victim of circumstance and other stories. 1927, Boston and New York 1927, London 1932.
A Yorkshire lass. New York 1928 (priv ptd).
Selections, autobiographical and imaginative, from the works of Gissing, with biographical and critical notes by his son [A. C. Gissing]. Ed V. Woolf 1929.
Hope in vain. [Winchester] 1930 (priv ptd). A poem.
Autobiographical notes, with comments on Tennyson and Huxley. In Three letters to Edward Clodd, Edinburgh 1930 (priv ptd).
Brownie, now first reprinted from the Chicago Tribune, together with six other stories attributed to [Gissing]. Ed G. E. Hastings, V. Starrett and T. O. Mabbott, New York 1931.
Stories and sketches published for the first time in book form. Ed A. C. Gissing 1938.
My first rehearsal. Eng Lit in Transition 9 1966. An unpbd short story.

Letters and Papers

Letters to Edward Clodd. 1914 (priv ptd).
Letters to an editor [C. K. Shorter]. 1915 (priv ptd).
Letters to members of his family. Ed A. and E. Gissing 1927.
Steiner, J. Gissing to his sister: letters of Gissing. More Books 22 1947.
The letters of Gissing to Eduard Bertz 1887–1903. Ed A. C. Young, New Brunswick 1961.
Gissing and H. G. Wells; their friendship and correspondence. Ed R. A. Gettmann, Urbana 1961.
Gissing's commonplace book. Ed J. Korg, New York 1962.
The letters of Gissing to Gabrielle Fleury Gissing. Ed P. Coustillas, New York 1965.

§2

Sichel, E. Two philanthropic novelists: Mr Walter Besant and Mr Gissing. Murray's Mag 3 1888.
Wells, H. G. The novels of Mr Gissing. Contemporary Rev Aug 1897.
—— Gissing: an impression. Monthly Rev Oct 1897.
Dolman, F. The novels of Gissing. Nat Rev Oct 1897.
White, G. George Gissing. Sewanee Rev 6 1898.
Bennett, A. Mr Gissing: an inquiry. Academy 16 Dec 1899.
Findlater, J. H. The spokesman of despair. Nat Rev Nov 1904.
Waugh, A. George Gissing. Nineteenth Century Sept 1904.
Wedd, N. George Gissing. Independent Rev 2 1904.
Harrison, A. George Gissing. Nineteenth Century Sept 1906.
Seccombe, T. The work of Gissing: an introductory survey. Prefixed to Gissing, House of cobwebs, 1906.
More, P. E. In his Shelburne essays ser 5, New York 1908.
Roberts, M. The private life of Henry Maitland. 1912, 1923 (rev); ed 'Morchard Bishop' 1958. Biography disguised as a novel.
—— George Gissing. Queen's Quart 37 1930.
—— The letters of Gissing. Virginia Quart 7 1931.
Swinnerton, F. Gissing: a critical study. 1912.
Björkman, E. In his Voices of to-morrow, New York 1914.
James, H. The English novel and the work of Gissing. In his Notes on novelists, 1914.
Clodd, E. In his Memories, 1916.
Follett, H. T. and W. In their Some modern novelists New York 1918.
Alden, S. Gissing: humanist. North Amer Rev 216 1922.
Yates, M. Gissing: an appreciation. Manchester 1922.
Cazamian, M. L. Le roman et les idées: l'influence de la science. Strasbourg 1923.
Gissing, E. Gissing: a character sketch. Nineteenth Century Sept 1927.
—— Some personal recollections of Gissing. Blackwood's Mag May 1929.
Gosse, E. In his Leaves and fruit, 1927.
Gissing, A. C. Gissing: some aspects of his life and work. Nat Rev Aug 1929.
—— Gissing's unfinished romance. Nat Rev Jan 1937.
Brewster, D. and A. Burrell. Gissing: release through fiction? In their Adventure or experience: four essays, New York 1930.
Rotter, A. Frank Swinnerton und Gissing: eine kritische Studie. Brünn 1930.
Woolf, V. In her Common reader ser 2, 1932.
Stadler, C. F. Die Rolle der Antike bei Gissing. Quackenbrück 1932 (priv ptd).
Oda, M. George Gissing. Tokyo 1933.
Weber, A. Gissing und die soziale Frage. Beitrag zur Englischen Philologie 20 1932.
McKay, R. C. Gissing and his critic Frank Swinnerton. Philadelphia 1933.
Heriot, E. Un Julien Sorel anglais. Revue Bleue 71 1933.
Van Maanen, W. Gissing's life from his letters. Neophilologus 18 1933.
Burrell, A. In Modern fiction, ed D. Brewster and A. Burrell 1934.
Wells, H. G. In his Experiment in autobiography, 2 vols 1934.
Shafer, R. The vitality of Gissing. Amer Rev Sept 1935.

Gapp, S. V. Gissing, classicist. Philadelphia 1936.
Muller, H. J. In his Modern fiction: a study of values, New York 1937.
Sieper, H. Psychologische Studien zu den Romanen Gissings. Munich 1937.
Haasler, G. Die Darstellung der Frau bei Gissing. Greifswald 1938.
Leavis, Q. D. Gissing and the English novel. Scrutiny 7 1938.
Niebling, R. F. The Adams Gissing collection. Yale Univ Lib Gazette 16 1942.
Daley, N. L. Some reflections on the scholarship of Gissing. Classical Jnl Oct 1942.
Webster, H. T. Possible influences of Gissing's Workers of the dawn on Maugham's Of human bondage. MLQ 7 1946.
Henry Ryecroft's question. In Menander's mirror, TLS 16 Jan 1943.
The permanent stranger. TLS 14 Feb 1948.
Kirk, R. Who knows Gissing? Western Humanities Rev 4 1950.
Korg, J. Gissing's outcast intellectuals. Amer Scholar 19 1950.
—— Division of purpose in Gissing. PMLA 7 1955.
—— The spiritual theme of Gissing's Born in exile. In From Jane Austen to Joseph Conrad, ed R. C. Rathburn and M. Steinmann, Minneapolis 1958.
—— Gissing: a critical biography. Seattle 1963.
Price, J. B. George Robert Gissing. Contemporary Rev Aug 1953.
Pritchett, V. S. Poor Gissing. In his Books in general, 1953.
Thomas, J. D. The public purposes of Gissing. Nineteenth-century Fiction 8 1954.
Wolff, J. J. Gissing's revision of the Unclassed. Ibid.
Donnelly, M. C. Gissing: grave comedian. Cambridge Mass 1954.
Pettoello, D. Nato in esilio. Turin 1955. Introd to trn of Born in exile.
Adams, R. M. Gissing and Clara Collet. Nineteenth-Century Fiction 11 1957.
Cope, J. I. Definition as structure in Gissing's Ryecroft papers. Modern Fiction Stud 3 1957.
Gettmann, R. A. Bentley and Gissing. Nineteenth-Century Fiction 11 1957.
—— In his A Victorian publisher, Cambridge 1960.
Bergonzi, B. The novelist as hero. Twentieth Century Nov 1958.
'Maurois, André' (E. S. W. Herzog). George Gissing. Revue de Paris 65 1958.
Bruny, S. Gissing, peintre des bas-fonds Londoniens et humaniste accompli. Synthèse 14 1959.
Kocmanová, J. The revolt of workers in the novels of Gissing, James and Conrad. Brno Stud in Eng 1 1959.
Murry, J. M. In his Katherine Mansfield and other literary studies, 1959.
Ward, A. C. Gissing. 1959.
Young, A. C. Gissing's friendship with Eduard Bertz. Nineteenth-Century Fiction 13 1959.
—— The death of Gissing: a fourth report. In Essays in literary history, ed R. Kirk and C. F. Main, New Brunswick 1961.
'Orwell, George' (E. Blair). George Gissing. London Mag June 1960.
Francis, C. J. Gissing and Schopenhauer. Nineteenth-Century Fiction 15 1961.
Mitchell, J. M. Notes on Gissing's stories. Stud in Eng Lit (Tokyo) 1962.
Coustillas, P. Gissing à Manchester. Études Anglaises 16 1963.
—— Gissing's feminine portraiture. English Lit in Transition 6 1963.
—— Gissing's writings on Dickens. Dickensian 61 1965.
—— Some unpublished letters from Gissing to Hardy. English Lit in Transition 9 1966.

—— Henry Hick's recollections of Gissing. HLQ 29 1966.
Howe, I. Gissing: poet of fatigue. In his A world more attractive, New York 1963.
Koike, S. Gissing in Japan. BNYPL Nov 1963.
—— The education of Gissing. Stud in Eng Lit (Tokyo) 42 1966.
Preble, H. E. Gissing's articles for Vyestnik evropy. Victorian Newsletter no 23 1963.
Harris, W. V. An approach to Gissing's short stories. Stud in Short Fiction 2 1965.
Davis, O. H. Gissing: a study in literary leanings. 1966.

B. A. B.

ROBERT LOUIS STEVENSON
1850–94

The great depository of Stevenson material is the Edwin J. Beinecke Collection at Yale, which contains 1,000 letters by Stevenson and 2,000 to and about him, as well as a large group of mss, including the Amateur emigrant, *most of* Catriona, Ebb tide, Wrong box, Records of a family of engineers, Body snatcher, *and part of* An inland voyage, St Ives *and* Weir of Hermiston. *The Huntington Library possesses most of* Kidnapped, Beach of Falesá, St Ives, *the* Silverado squatters *diary, the South Seas journal, and the Cévennes journal. The Pierpont Morgan Library has* Dr Jekyll and Mr Hyde *and a draft of* Weir of Hermiston; *the Widener Library at Harvard has a late version of* Catriona; *and the Princeton Library has a draft of* St Ives. *The Mitchell Library at Sydney has* In the South Seas. *2 important groups of letters, to Mrs Sitwell and to W. E. Henley, are held by the National Library of Scotland.*

Bibliographies

Prideaux, W. F. A bibliography of the works of Stevenson. 1903, 1917 (rev F. V. Livingston).
Slater, J. H. A bibliography of RLS. 1914.
First editions of the works of Stevenson 1850–94, with other Stevensoniana exhibited Nov 5–28 1914. New York 1914 (Grolier Club).
Ehrsam, T. G. and R. H. Deily. In their Bibliographies of twelve Victorian authors, New York 1936.
Stevenson 1850–94: catalogue of the Stevenson collection, Edinburgh Public Library. Edinburgh 1950.
McKay, G. L. The Stevenson library of E. J. Beinecke. 6 vols New Haven 1951–64.

Collections

Edinburgh edition. Ed S. Colvin 28 vols 1894–8.
Thistle edition. 26 vols New York 1902.
Household edition. 10 vols New York 1906.
Pentland edition. Ed E. Gosse 20 vols 1906–7.
Swanston edition. 25 vols 1911–12. Introd by A. Lang.
Vailima edition. Ed L. Osbourne and F. Van de G. Stevenson 26 vols 1922–3.
Skerryvore edition. 30 vols 1924–6.
Tusitala edition. 35 vols 1923–4.
South Seas edition. 32 vols 1925.

§ 1

No attempt is made to record early essays and other ephemera, including uncollected contributions to books and periodicals.

The Pentland rising. Edinburgh 1866 (priv ptd), [1925].
The charity bazaar. Edinburgh [not before 1871] (priv ptd); Westport Conn 1929.
An appeal to the clergy. Edinburgh 1875.
An inland voyage. 1878, 1881, 1887, Boston 1883; tr French, 1919.
Edinburgh: picturesque notes, with etchings. 1879, 1888, 1896, 1903, 1912, 1923, New York 1889, 1896. First pbd in Portfolio June–Dec 1878.

Travels with a donkey in the Cévennes. 1879, 1887, Boston 1879; tr French, 1901; Irish, 1937; Czech, 1948.

Deacon Brodie, or the double life: a melodrama founded on facts in four acts and ten tableaux. Edinburgh 1880 (priv ptd), 1888 (rev, priv ptd). With W. E. Henley.

Virginibus puerisque and other papers. 1881, 1887; tr Danish, 1950. 12 essays, all (except Some portraits by Raeburn) rptd from Cornhill Mag, Macmillan's Mag and London Mag.

Familiar studies of men and books. 1882, 1888, 1901, New York 1882, 1887, 1902, 1905. 9 essays rptd from Cornhill Mag and other periodicals.

New Arabian nights. 2 vols 1882, New York 1882, 1882, 1886, 1886, 1903, 1905; tr French, 1885; German, 1896; Finnish, 1898; Dutch, 1898–1900; Norwegian, 1901; Russian, 1901; Hungarian, 1902; Japanese, 1910; Chinese, 1914; Italian, 1920; Danish, 1921; Czech, 1922; Swedish, 1929; Yugoslav, 1954; Spanish, 1958; Korean, 1960. Vol i: The suicide club, The rajah's diamond; vol ii: The pavilion on the links, The Sire de Malétroit's door, Providence and the guitar. The stories of vol i originally appeared in London, 8 June–26 Oct 1878, as Latter-day Arabian nights; those in vol ii were rptd from Cornhill Mag, Temple Bar and London Mag.

The story of a lie. 1882. A forgery? *See* J. Carter and H. G. Pollard, An enquiry into the nature of certain nineteenth-century pamphlets, 1934. First pbd in New Quart Mag Oct 1879; tr German, 1924; Czech, 1927.

The Silverado squatters: sketches from a Californian mountain. 1883, 1895, New York 1884, 1888, 1888, 1904, 1923, Boston 1884. First pbd in Century Mag Nov–Dec 1883.

Treasure Island. 1883, 1884, 1885, Boston 1884, 1885, New York 1886 (3 edns), Leipzig 1884; tr French, 1885; Dutch, 1885; Italian, 1886; Swedish, 1887; Hungarian, 1887; Danish, 1887; Spanish, 1889; German, 1897; Finnish, 1899; Norwegian, 1900; Russian, 1901; Czech, 1902; Icelandic, 1906; Catalan, 1915; Arabic, 1921; Latin, 1922; Polish, 1925; Afrikaans, 1925; Hebrew, 1926; Yiddish, 1927; Japanese, 1928; Chinese, c. 1928; Swahili, 1929; Roumanian, 1935; Azerbaijani, 1936; Armenian, 1937; Todzhik, 1940; Portuguese, 1940; Turkmen, 1941; Yakutsk, 1941; Esthonian, 1949; Bulgarian, 1950; Kazakh, 1950; Moldavian, 1950; Flemish, 1950; Yugoslav, 1950; Lithuanian, 1951; Luganda, 1951; Hindi, 1959; Turkish, 1959; Kirghiz, 1960; Vietnamese, 1960; Malayalam, 1960; Georgian, 1960; Korean, 1961; Tamil, 1962; First pbd in slightly different form in Young Folks 1 Oct 1881–22 Jan 1882, as by 'Captain George North'.

Admiral Guinea: a melodrama in four acts. Edinburgh 1884 (priv ptd). With W. E. Henley.

Beau Austin: a play in four acts. Edinburgh 1884 (priv ptd). With W. E. Henley.

A child's garden of verses. 1885, 1895, New York 1885, 1895; tr Latin, 1922. 39 of the 64 poems priv ptd in 1883 as Penny whistles, including 9 poems omitted from A child's garden; these 9 poems were priv ptd by L. S. Livingston in 1912 as Verses by RLS.

More new Arabian nights: the dynamiter. 1885, 1895, 1907, New York 1887, 1905. Except for Zero's tale of the explosive bomb, largely the work of Fanny Stevenson.

Prince Otto: a romance. 1885, 1908, New York 1886 (4 edns), 1902, 1905; tr French, 1897; Polish, 1897; Hungarian, 1898; Swedish, 1945; Japanese, 1948; Spanish, 1958. First pbd in Longman's Mag April–Oct 1885.

Macaire: a melodramatic farce in three acts. Edinburgh 1885 (priv ptd). With W. E. Henley.

Strange case of Dr Jekyll and Mr Hyde. 1886, New York 1886, 1887, 1888; tr German, 1887; Danish, 1889; French, 1890; Finnish, 1897; Swedish, 1897; Hungarian, 1899; Czech, 1900; Russian, 1901; Italian, 1905; Dutch, 1909; Norwegian, 1917; Polish, 1924; Arabic, 1927; Hebrew, 1928; Japanese, 1928; Irish, 1929; Greek, 1948; Afrikaans, 1949; Thai, 1949; Portuguese, 1956; Chinese, 1957; Hindi, 1959; Gujarati, 1962.

Kidnapped: being memoirs of the adventures of David Balfour in the year 1751; how he was kidnapped and castaway; his sufferings in a desert isle; his journey in the wild highlands; his acquaintance with Alan Breck Stewart and other notorious Highland Jacobites; with all that he suffered at the hands of his uncle, Ebenezer Balfour of Shaws, falsely so-called: written by himself and now set forth by Robert Louis Stevenson. 1886, 1887, 1891, 1895, New York 1886 (4 edns); tr German, c. 1889; Dutch, 1892; Spanish, 1898; Danish, 1900; Norwegian, 1900; Russian, 1901; French, 1905; Italian, 1906; Finnish, 1910; Swedish, 1921; Czech, 1922; Japanese, 1926; Hungarian, 1927; Polish, 1927; Icelandic, 1934; Greek, 1950; Flemish, 1954; Yugoslav, 1954; Roumanian, 1960; Chinese, 1961; Gujarati, 1961; Hindi, 1962.

Some college memories. Edinburgh 1886. A forgery? *See* Carter and Pollard. First pbd in the New Amphion: being the book of the Edinburgh University Union Fancy Fair, Edinburgh 1886.

The merry men and other tales and fables. 1887, New York 1887 (4 edns); tr Dutch, 1905; French, 1920; Danish, 1921; German, 1925; Czech, 1928. Includes The merry men, Will o' the mill, Markheim, Thrawn Janet, Olalla, The treasure of Franchard, collected from Cornhill Mag and other periodicals.

Underwoods. 1887, New York 1887, 1905. 38 poems in English, 16 in Scots.

Memoirs and portraits. 1887, New York 1887, 1905. 16 essays, including Some college memories and Thomas Stevenson, mainly rptd from Cornhill Mag and Longman's Mag.

Thomas Stevenson, civil engineer. 1887 (priv ptd). Also pbd in Contemporary Rev June 1887.

Ticonderoga. Edinburgh 1887 (priv ptd). First pbd in Scribner's Mag Dec 1887; rptd in Ballads, 1890.

The hanging judge: a drama in three acts and six tableaux. Edinburgh 1887 (priv ptd); ed E. Gosse 1914 (priv ptd). With Fanny Stevenson.

The misadventures of John Nicholson: a Christmas story. New York 1887, 1887, 1893; tr Swedish, 1897; Czech, 1919; French, 1921; Hungarian, 1921; Finnish, 1933; Spanish, 1955. Piratically rptd from Yule-Tide: Cassell's Christmas annual for 1887.

The papers of H. Fleeming Jenkin; with a memoir by R. L. Stevenson. 2 vols 1887. Memoir rptd alone, New York 1887, London 1912.

The black arrow: a tale of the two roses. 1888, 1891, 1900, 1904, 1906, New York 1888, 1905, 1914, 1916; tr French, 1901; Norwegian, 1903; Swedish, 1905; Danish, 1911; Finnish, 1913; German, 1922; Italian, 1924; Polish, 1928; Dutch, 1934; Spanish, 1949; Japanese, 1950; Yugoslav, 1951; Hebrew, 1953; Portuguese, 1953; Flemish, 1954; Czech, 1957; Esthonian, 1957; Ukrainian, 1958; Bulgarian, 1959; Lithuanian, 1960; Russian, 1960; Albanian, 1961; Hindi, 1961; Roumanian, 1961; Vietnamese, 1961; Latvian, 1964; Burmese, nd; Arabic, nd. First pbd in Young Folks 30 June–20 Oct 1883 as The black arrow: a tale of Tunstall Forest, by Captain George North.

The master of Ballantrae: a winter's tale. 1889, 1899, New York 1889, 1895, 1904, 1905, 1907, Leipzig 1889; tr Swedish, 1890; Russian, 1901; Danish, 1908; German, 1911; French, 1920; Finnish, 1921; Czech, 1925; Dutch, 1929; Italian, 1929; Hungarian, 1930; Irish, 1938; Japanese, 1940; Norwegian, 1949; Polish, 1949; Spanish, 1953; Flemish, 1954; Chinese, 1954; Yugoslav, 1954; Portuguese, 1956; Lithuanian, 1959. This edn was preceded by a small priv ptd edn in 1888 to establish copyright. The novel was first pbd in Scribner's Mag Nov 1888–Oct 1889.

The wrong box. 1889, 1892, 1895, New York 1889, 1890, 1905; tr Dutch, 1900; French, 1905; Norwegian, 1926; Czech, 1928; Danish, 1946; Yugoslav, 1955. With Lloyd Osbourne.

Ballads. 1890, New York 1890. Includes The song of Rahéro, The feast of famine, Ticonderoga, Heather ale, Christmas at sea—each, except the last, with notes.

Father Damien: an open letter to the Reverend Dr Hyde of Honolulu. 1890, 1901, 1909, 1910, Sydney 1890, Boston 1900. This edn was preceded by a priv ptd edn at Sydney and a second at Edinburgh. The letter was first pbd in Scots Observer 3, 10 May 1890.

Across the plains, with other memories and essays. 1892, 1925, New York 1892, 1905, Leipzig 1892. 12 essays mainly rptd from Scribner's Mag.

A footnote to history: eight years of trouble in Samoa. 1892, New York 1892.

Three plays: Deacon Brodie, Beau Austin, Admiral Guinea. 1892, New York 1892.

The wrecker. 1892, 1899, New York 1892, 1905; tr Swedish, 1893; Czech, 1905; French, 1906; Italian, 1920; Norwegian, 1949; Portuguese, 1960; Russian, 1960; Lithuanian, 1964; German, nd. First pbd in Scribner's Mag Aug 1891–July 1892. With Lloyd Osbourne.

Island nights entertainments: consisting of The beach of Falesá, The bottle imp, The isle of voices. 1893, 1902, 1904, New York 1893, 1905, Leipzig 1893; tr Danish, 1900; Russian, 1901; Finnish, 1917; French, 1920; German, 1926; Hungarian, 1926; Czech, 1927; Chinese, c. 1935; Italian, 1939; Norwegian, 1949; Polish, 1949; Japanese, 1955. First pbd, respectively, in Illustr London News 2 July–6 Aug 1892; Black & White 28 March–4 April 1891; Nat Observer 4–25 Feb 1893.

War in Samoa. 1893 (priv ptd). First pbd in Pall Mall Gazette 4 Sept 1893.

Catriona: a sequel to Kidnapped, being memoirs of the further adventures of David Balfour at home and abroad in which are set forth his misfortunes anent the Appin murder; his troubles with Lord Advocate Grant; captivity on the Bass Rock; journey into Holland and France; and singular relations with James More Drummond or MacGregor, a son of the notorious Rob Roy, and his daughter Catriona, written by himself, and now set forth by Robert Louis Stevenson. 1893, 1895, 1899, New York 1893, 1895, 1905; tr Russian, 1901; French, 1907; Norwegian, 1917; Swedish, 1917; Danish, 1921; German, 1926; Czech, 1927; Italian, 1929; Irish, 1933; Spanish, 1950; Yugoslav, 1953; Flemish, 1954; Finnish, 1955; Portuguese, 1955; Dutch, 1957; Hungarian, 1958; Polish, 1958. First pbd in Atalanta Dec 1892–Sept 1893, as David Balfour: memoirs of his adventures at home and abroad.

The ebb-tide: a trio and a quartette. Chicago 1894, London 1894, 1909, 1912, New York 1905; tr Swedish, 1898; French, 1905; Czech, 1927; Polish, 1930; Italian, 1930; Danish, 1946; Norwegian, 1949; Portuguese, 1956; Spanish, 1957. First pbd in Today 11 Nov 1893–3 Feb 1894. With Lloyd Osbourne.

The body-snatcher. New York 1895. First pbd in Pall Mall Xmas no 1884.

The amateur emigrant from the Clyde to Sandy Hook. Chicago 1895, New York 1902, 1905; tr Danish, 1911; Finnish, 1931. First pbd in Edinburgh edn of Works vol 3, 1895.

The strange case of Dr Jekyll and Mr Hyde, with other fables. 1896. The fables were first pbd in Longman's Mag Aug–Sept 1895.

Weir of Hermiston: an unfinished romance. 1896, New York 1896, 1905, Leipzig 1896; tr French, 1912; German, c. 1925. The first printing in book form is that of a copyright edn, Chicago 1896. The novel was originally pbd in Cosmopolis Jan–April 1896.

A mountain town in France: a fragment. New York 1896.

Songs of travel and other verses. 1896. First pbd in Edinburgh edn of Works vol 14, 1895.

St Ives: being the adventures of a French prisoner in England. 1897, 1899, New York 1895, 1895, Leipzig 1898; tr Swedish, 1898; Dutch, 1904; French, 1904; Danish, 1909; Italian, 1929; Polish, 1929; German, 1930; Czech, 1948; Norwegian, 1949; Flemish, 1952; Portuguese, 1961. 30 chs by Stevenson, the remainder by A. T. Quiller-Couch. First pbd in Pall Mall Mag Nov 1896–Nov 1897.

Three short poems. 1898 (priv ptd), Chicago 1902.

RLS Teuila. New York 1899 (priv ptd). 20 poems.

In the South Seas. New York 1896, 1908, London 1900; tr French 1920; Czech, 1921; Italian, 1929; German, 1948; Spanish, 1959. 15 of the 35 letters priv ptd in 1890 as The South Seas: a record of three cruises; the letters first pbd in the Sun (New York) 1891.

The morality of the profession of letters. New York 1899. First pbd in Fortnightly Rev April 1881.

A Stevenson medley. Ed S. Colvin 1899. Includes the Davos-Platz booklets, mainly ptd from the original blocks.

Essays and criticisms. Boston 1903.

Prayers written at Vailima, with an introduction by Mrs Stevenson. 1905. First pbd in Edinburgh edn of Works vol 21, 1896.

Tales and fantasies. 1905. Includes The misadventures of John Nicholson, The body-snatcher, The story of a lie.

Essays of travel. 1905.

Essays in the art of writing. 1905.

Essays. Ed W. L. Phelps, New York 1906. A selection.

Lay morals and other papers. 1911. 10 essays.

Records of a family of engineers. 1912.

Memoirs of himself. Philadelphia 1912 (priv ptd).

The poems and ballads of Stevenson: complete edition. New York 1913.

Political fragments. [1915] (priv ptd).

The waif woman. 1916. First pbd in Scribner's Mag Dec 1914.

On the choice of a profession. 1916. First pbd in Scribner's Mag Jan 1915.

An ode of Horace: book ii, ode iii—experiments in three metres. [1916] (priv ptd).

Poems hitherto unpublished. Ed G. S. Hellman 2 vols Boston 1916 (Bibliophile Soc).

New poems and variant readings. 1918.

Poems hitherto unpublished. Ed G. S. Hellman and W. P. Trent, Boston 1921 (Bibliophile Soc).

Hitherto unpublished prose writings. Ed H. H. Harper, Boston 1921 (Bibliophile Soc).

Stevenson's workshop. Ed W. P. Trent, Boston 1921 (Bibliophile Soc). With variant ms readings of poems.

When the devil was well. Ed W. P. Trent, Boston 1921 (Bibliophile Soc).

Confessions of a unionist: an unpublished talk on things current, written in 1888. Ed F. V. L[ivingston], Cambridge Mass 1921.

The best thing in Edinburgh: an address to the Speculative Society of Edinburgh in March 1873. Ed K. D. Osbourne, San Francisco 1923.

Selected essays. Ed H. G. Rawlinson 1923.

The castaways of Soledad: a manuscript by Stevenson hitherto unpublished. Ed G. S. Hellman, Buffalo 1928 (priv ptd).

Monmouth: a tragedy. Ed C. Vale, New York 1928.

The manuscripts of Stevenson's Records of a family of engineers: the unfinished chapters. Chicago 1930.

Essays. Ed M. Elwin 1950.

Salute to RLS. Ed F. Holland, Edinburgh 1950.

Tales and essays. Ed G. B. Stern 1950.

Silverado journal. Ed J. E. Jordan, San Francisco 1954.

From Scotland to Silverado. Ed J. D. Hart, Cambridge Mass 1966. First complete texts of Amateur emigrant and Silverado squatters, with unpbd essay, Simoneau's at Monterey.

Letters and Papers

Vailima letters: being correspondence addressed by Stevenson to Sidney Colvin, November 1890–October 1894. 1895.
The letters of Stevenson to his family and friends, selected. Ed S. Colvin 2 vols 1899, 4 vols 1911 (enlarged).
Some letters by Stevenson. Ed H. Townsend, New York 1902. 5 letters to A. T. Haddon 1879–84.
Familiar epistle in verse and prose. 1896 (priv ptd). Written in 1872 to Charles Baxter.
Three letters. 1902 (priv ptd). To Mrs Sitwell.
Letters to an editor. [1914] (priv ptd). To C. K. Shorter.
Letters to Charles Baxter. [1914] (priv ptd).
Some letters of Stevenson. Ed L. Osbourne 1914.
New letters. Ed S. Colvin, Scribner's Mag June–Aug 1923.
Henry James and Stevenson: a record of friendship and criticism. Ed J. A. Smith 1948. Chiefly letters.
RLS: Stevenson's letters to Charles Baxter. Ed De Lancey Ferguson and M. Waingrow, New Haven 1956.

§2

Archer, W. RLS: his style and thought. Time Nov 1885.
— RLS at Skerryvore. Critic 5 Nov 1887.
— In memoriam RLS. New Rev Jan 1895.
Droppers, G. Robert Louis Stevenson. Harvard Monthly March 1887.
James, H. In his Partial portraits, 1888.
— In his Notes on novelists, 1914.
Doyle, A. C. Mr Stevenson's methods in fiction. Nat Rev Jan 1890.
Lang, A. In his Essays in little, 1891.
— In his Adventures among books, 1905.
Lowe, C. Stevenson: a reminiscence. Bookman (London) Nov 1891.
Walkley, A. B. In his Playhouse impressions, 1892. On the plays.
Crockett, S. R. The apprenticeship of Stevenson. Bookman (London) March 1893.
Gosse, E. In his Questions at issue, 1893.
— In his Critical kit-kats, 1896.
— Stevenson's relations with children. Chambers's Jnl 17 June 1899.
Gwynn, S. Stevenson: a critical study. Fortnightly Rev Dec 1894.
— The posthumous works of Stevenson. Fortnightly Rev April 1898.
— Stevenson. 1939.
With Stevenson in Samoa. Cornhill Mag July 1894.
Armour, M. The home and early haunts of Stevenson. 1895.
[Brown, A.] Robert Louis Stevenson by A.B., with a prelude and a postlude by L[ouisa] I[mogen] G[uiney]. Boston 1895 (priv ptd).
Fraser, M. In Stevenson's Samoa. 1895.
Raleigh, W. Robert Louis Stevenson. 1895.
Quiller-Couch, A. T. In his Adventures in criticism, 1896.
Symons, A. In his Studies in two literatures, 1897.
— In his Studies in prose and verse, [1894].
Black, M. M. Robert Louis Stevenson. [1898].
Burton, R. In his Literary likings, Boston 1898.
Geddie, J. The home life of Stevenson. 1898.
Simpson, E. B. RLS's Edinburgh days. 1898.
— Robert Louis Stevenson. 1906.
— The RLS originals. 1912.
Cornford, L. C. Robert Louis Stevenson. 1899.
Primrose, A. P. (Earl of Rosebery). In his Appreciations and addresses, 1899.
Stevenson, by two of his cousins. Eng Illustr Mag May 1899.
Le Gallienne, R. The dethroning of Stevenson. In his Sleeping beauty and other prose fancies, 1900.

Baildon, H. B. Stevenson. 1901.
Balfour, G. The life of Stevenson. 2 vols 1901.
Gotch, T. C. Stevenson from a painter's point of view. St George April 1902.
Bonet-Maury, G. Stevenson: voyageur et romancier. Revue des Deux Mondes 1 Sept 1902.
Colvin, S. Stevenson at Hampstead. Hampstead Annual Dec 1902.
— In his Memories and notes of persons and places, 1921.
— et al. Stevenson: his work and personality. 1924.
Lennox, C. In his James Chalmers of New Guinea, 1902.
Muirhead, J. H. Stevenson's philosophy of life. In his Philosophy and life, 1902.
Stephen, L. In his Studies of a biographer vol 4, New York 1902.
Hammerton, J. A. Stevensoniana. 1903, 1907, 1910 (rev).
Marriott Watson, H. B. Stevenson: an appreciation. Fortnightly Rev Sept 1903.
Pinero, A. W. Stevenson the dramatist: a lecture. 1903; ed C. Hamilton, New York 1914.
Strong, I. and L. Osbourne. Memories of Vailima. 1903.
Japp, A. H. Stevenson: an estimate. 1905.
Johnstone, A. Recollections of Stevenson in the Pacific. 1905.
Nevinson, H. W. From Leith to Samoa. 1905.
Compton-Rickett, A. In his Vagabond in literature, 1906.
Stevenson, M. I. Letters from Samoa. 1906.
— Stevenson's baby book: being a record of the sayings and doings of RLS. San Francisco 1922.
Torrey, B. In his Friends on the shelf, Boston 1906.
Chapman, J. J. In his Emerson and other essays, New York 1909.
Moors, H. J. With Stevenson in Samoa. 1910.
Phelps, W. L. In his Essays on modern novelists, New York 1910. Bibliographies by A. Keogh.
Beach, J. W. The sources of Stevenson's Bottle imp. MLN 25 1910.
Strong, I. Robert Louis Stevenson. 1911.
Webster, A. RLS and Henry Drummond. 1912.
Aydelotte, F. Stevenson's darkening counsel. Eng Jnl June 1912.
Dawson, N. P. RLS and the Fontainebleau trait. Bookman (New York) Nov 1912.
Robert Louis Stevenson. Bookman (New York) (extra no) 1913.
Watt, F. RLS. 1913.
Masson, R. O. Robert Louis Stevenson. 1914.
— The life of Stevenson. 1923.
Swinnerton, F. Stevenson: a critical study. 1914.
Cruse, A. Robert Louis Stevenson. 1915.
Chalmers, S. The penny piper of Saranac: an episode in Stevenson's life. 1916.
Clayton, H. On the trail of Stevenson. [1916].
Knowlton, E. C. A Russian influence on Stevenson. MP 14 1916.
Rice, R. A. Stevenson: how to know him. Indianapolis 1916.
Harrison, B. With Stevenson at Grez. Century Dec 1916.
Daplyn, A. J. Stevenson at Barbizon. Chambers's Jnl 14 July 1917.
Lansing, R. R. Stevenson's French reading as shown in his correspondence. Poet Lore March 1918.
Brown, G. E. A book of RLS: works, travels, friends and commentators. [1919].
Bay, J. C. Echoes of Stevenson. Chicago 1920.
Fletcher, C. B. Stevenson's Germany: the case against Germany in the Pacific. 1920.
Guthrie, C. J. Stevenson: some personal recollections. Edinburgh 1920.
Harper, H. H. Stevenson: an appreciation. Boston [1920].
'Schwob, Marcel' (M. A. Marcel). RLS. Portland Maine 1920.
Cowell, H. J. Stevenson and missions. Holborn Rev new ser 11 1920.

— Stevenson: an Englishman's re-study. [1946].
— Maggie Stevenson: mother of Stevenson. London Quart 173 1948.
— RLS and Father Damien. London Quart 175 1950.
Snyder, A. D. Paradox and antithesis in Stevenson's essays. JEGP 19 1920.
— Stevenson's conception of the fable. JEGP 21 1922.
Eaton, C. Stevenson at Manasquan. Chicago 1921.
Trent, W. P. Stevenson's workshop. Boston 1921.
Delebecque, J. A propos du roman d'aventures: notes sur quelques ouvrages de Stevenson. Mercure de France 1 Jan 1921.
Robertson, S. Sir Thomas Browne and Stevenson. JEGP 20 1921.
Low, W. H. Stevenson and Margarita. New York 1922.
Clarke, W. E. Stevenson in Samoa. Yale Rev 10 1921.
I can remember Stevenson. Ed R. Masson 1922.
Claxton, A. E. Stevenson as I knew him in Samoa. Chambers's Jnl 2 Sept 1922.
Freeman, J. Robert Louis Stevenson. London Mercury April 1922.
'Lee, Vernon' (Violet Paget). In her Handling of words, 1923.
Pears, E. R. Some recollections of Stevenson. Scribner's Mag Jan 1923.
Horne, J. Stevenson in Wick. Chambers's Jnl 20 Oct 1923.
Jaen, R. Notes on Stevenson's Olalla. Univ of Cal Chron July 1923.
Adcock, A. St J. et al. Stevenson: his work and personality. 1924.
Noyes, A. In his Some aspects of modern poetry, 1924.
Osbourne, L. An intimate portrait of RLS. New York 1924.
Sarolea, C. Stevenson and France. 1924.
Steuart, J. A. Stevenson: man and writer. 2 vols [1924].
Clark, E. M. The kinship of Hazlitt and Stevenson. SE 4 1924.
Hellman, G. S. The true Stevenson: a study in clarification. Boston 1925.
A cadger's creel. Ed G. B. Douglas, Edinburgh 1925.
Benson, E. F. The myth of Stevenson. London Mercury July–Aug 1925.
Burriss, E. E. The classical culture of Stevenson. Classical Jnl Feb 1925.
Fraser, J. A. L. Stevenson and the Jacobite tradition. [1925].
— Scott and Stevenson: a lecture. [1929].
Torossian, A. Stevenson as a literary critic. Univ of Cal Chron 27 1925.
Boodle, A. A. RLS and his sine qua non: flashlights from Skerryvore. 1926.
Champion, P. Marcel Schwob et Stevenson. Revue Universelle 1 Dec 1926.
Cunningham, A. Cummy's diary: a diary kept by Stevenson's nurse on the Continent during 1863. Ed R. T. Skinner 1926.
Sherman, S. P. RLS encounters the 'modern' writers on their own ground. In his Critical woodcuts, New York 1926.
— Who made the Stevenson myth?; What is biographical truth? In his Emotional discovery of America, New York 1932.
Stewart, G. R. jr. The real treasure island. Univ of Cal Chron 28 1926.
Chesterton, G. K. Robert Louis Stevenson. 1927.
MacCulloch, J. A. Stevenson and the Bridge of Allan, with other Stevenson essays. 1927.
Masson, R. O. RLS at Pitlochry. Cornhill Mag March 1927.
Bonnerot, L. Quelques notes sur l'exotisme de Stevenson. Revue Anglo-américaine 5 1928.
Garrod, H. W. The poetry of Stevenson. In his Profession of poetry, Oxford 1929.
— The poetry of Stevenson. In Essays presented to Sir Humphrey Milford, Oxford 1948.
Morris, D. B. Stevenson and the Scottish Highlanders. Stirling 1929.
Carré, J. M. La vie de Stevenson. Paris 1929; tr New York 1930.
— Stevenson et la France. In Mélanges Baldensperger vol i, Paris 1930.
Chrétien, L. E. La vocation de Stevenson. Paris 1930.
MacPherson, H. D. Stevenson: a study in French influence. New York 1930.
Dark, S. Robert Louis Stevenson. 1931.
Muir, E. Robert Louis Stevenson. Bookman (New York) Sept 1931.
Fabre, F. Stevenson dans le Velay. Revue d'Auvergne 46 1932.
Richards, H. Stevenson and his poetry. London Quart Rev 157 1932.
Tomlinson, H. M. In Great Victorians, ed H. J. and H. Massingham 1932.
Evans, B. I. In his English poetry in the later nineteenth century, 1933, 1966 (rev).
Ewing, J. A. The Fleeming Jenkins. In his An engineer's outlook, 1933.
Galsworthy, J. Four more novelists in profile. In his Candelabra, New York 1933.
Heanley, K. The mystery of Lettermore. Cornhill Mag May 1933.
Lockett, W. G. Stevenson at Davos. 1934.
Delattre, F. Un dilettante de l'aventure: Stevenson. Revue d'Histoire de la Philosophie new ser 2 1934.
Colquhoun, G. Stevenson and the French language. Modern Languages 16 1935.
Mackaness, G. Stevenson: his associations with Australia. Jnl & Proc Royal Australian Historical Soc 21 1935.
MacCarthy, M. In his Handicaps: six studies, New York 1936.
MacLean, C. La France dans l'oeuvre de Stevenson. Paris 1936.
Smith, J. A. Henry James and Stevenson. London Mercury Sept 1936.
— R. L. Stevenson. 1937.
— Books in general. New Statesman 18 Nov 1950.
Dalglish, D. N. Presbyterian pirate: a portrait of Stevenson. Oxford 1937.
Field, I. This life I've loved. 1937.
Sagara, J. Stevenson. Tokyo 1938.
Carter, J. The hanging judge acquitted. Colophon new ser 3 1938.
Stevenson after fifty years: a recovery of reputation. TLS 30 April 1938.
'Bermann, R. A.' (A. Höllriegel). Home from the sea: Stevenson in Samoa. Indianapolis 1939.
Issler, A. R. Stevenson at Silverado. Caldwell Idaho 1939.
— Happier for his presence: San Francisco and Stevenson. Stanford [1949].
— Our mountain hermitage: Silverado and Stevenson. Stanford [1950].
Vandiver, E. P. Stevenson and Shakespeare. Shakespeare Assoc Bull 14 1939.
Moorman, L. J. In his Tuberculosis and genius, Chicago 1940.
Snyder, E. D. A note on RLS. MLN 55 1940. Juvenilia.
Ashe, M. J. Stevenson's Catholic learning. Catholic World Nov 1942.
— Stevenson after fifty years. Catholic World Dec 1944.
Moore, J. R. Stevenson's Catriona. N & Q 18 July 1942.
— DeFoe, Stevenson and the pirates. ELH 10 1943.
— Stevenson's source for the Merry men. PQ 23 1944.
V., R. and E. D. Stevenson: the wrong box. N & Q 4 April, 14 Aug, 21 Nov 1942.
Haber, T. B. Stevenson and Israel Hands. Eng Jnl June 1943.
P., A. E. Stevenson and Poe. N & Q 18 Dec 1943.
Pritchett, V. S. Books in general. New Statesman 24 March 1945.

Daiches, D. Stevenson. New York 1946.
— Weir of Hermiston. Scottish Periodical 1 1947.
— Stevenson and the art of fiction. New York 1951.
— Which RLS? Nineteenth-Century Fiction 6 1952.
Fisher, A. B. No more a stranger. Stanford 1946. A fictional account of Stevenson in Monterey.
Parsons, C. O. Stevenson's use of witchcraft in Thrawn Janet. SP 43 1946.
Scott, J. D. Stevenson and G. D. Brown: the myth of Lord Bratfield. Horizon May 1946.
Cooper, L. Stevenson. 1947.
Child, H. Stevenson after fifty years. In his Essays and reflections, Cambridge 1948.
Stern, G. B. No son of mine. New York 1948. Fiction.
Wilsey, M. Kidnapped in manuscript. Amer Scholar 18 1948.
McCleary, G. F. Stevenson in young folks. Fortnightly Rev Feb 1949.
— Stevenson's early writings. Fortnightly Rev Nov 1950.
Michel, A. Stevenson: sein Verhältnis zum Bösen. Berne 1949.
Elwin, M. The strange case of Stevenson. 1950.
Hinkley, L. L. The Stevensons: Louis and Fanny. New York 1950.
McGaw, Sr M. M. Stevenson in Hawaii. Honolulu 1950.
McLaren, M. Stevenson and Edinburgh: a centenary study. 1950.
Balfour, M. L. G. In defense of the Hanging judge. New Colophon 3 1950.
Green, R. L. The Stevenson centenary. Contemporary Rev Nov 1950.
— Stevenson in search of a madonna. E & S new ser 3 1950.
Keith, C. Stevenson today. Queen's Quart 57 1950.
Randall, D. A. Ticonderoga. New Colophon 3 1950. On its authenticity.
Furnas, J. C. Voyage to windward: the life of Stevenson. New York 1951.
Brown, J. M. RLS and Dr Jekyll. Saturday Rev of Lit 1, 8 Dec 1951.
Greene, G. From feathers to iron. In his Lost childhood and other essays, 1951.
Hayes-McCoy, G. A. Stevenson and the Irish question. Studies 39 1951.
— The centenary of Stevenson. Ibid.
Ferguson, J. The Appin murder case. Scottish Historical Rev 31 1952.
Ellison, J. W. Tusitala of the South Seas. New York 1953.
Abel, D. RLS and Prufrock. N & Q Jan 1953.
Sharp, R. L. Stevenson and James's childhood. Nineteenth-Century Fiction 8 1954.
Cameron, J. The Appin murder—a summing up. Scottish Historical Rev 33 1954.
Miallon, G. La critique Stevensonienne du centenaire. Etudes Anglaises 7 1954.
Paluka, F. J. Technique in four Stevenson stories. Florida State Univ Stud 40 1954.
Stevenson, Fanny. Our Samoan adventure. Ed C. Neider, New York 1955. A diary.
McArthur, W. P. The Appin murder. Scottish Historical Rev 34 1955.
Mulder, E. Stevenson: fantasia y conciencia de escritor. Cuadernos Hispano-americanos 83 1956.
Aldington, R. Portrait of a rebel: the life and work of Stevenson. 1957.
Chamson, A. Stevenson et les Cévennes. Revue des Deux Mondes April 1957.
Stevenson, R. Stevenson's musical interests. PMLA 72 1957.
Young, A. C. Edmund Gosse visits Stevenson. Jnl of Rutgers Univ Lib 20 1957.
La Guardia, E. The sire de Malétroit's door. Amer Imago 15 1958.
McKay, G. L. Some notes on Stevenson, his finances, and his agents and publishers. New Haven 1958.
— Note on Stevenson's Requiem. Yale Univ Lib Gazette 36 1962.
Marshall, G. Stevenson and the lepers. Blackfriars July–Aug 1958.
Poston, L. Markheim and Chesterton's The hammer of God. Nineteenth-Century Fiction 12 1958.
Baker, R. S. The RLS factor. Nation (New York) 14 Nov 1959. On Child's garden of verses.
Bromley, J. A. The courage of Stevenson. Hibbert Jnl 57 1959.
Caldwell, E. N. Last witness for Stevenson. Norman Oklahoma 1960.
Fiedler, L. In his No! in thunder, Boston 1960. On Master of Ballantrae.
Zabel, M. D. Stevenson: the two major novels. New York 1960.
Aring, C. D. The case becomes less strange. Amer Scholar 30 1960. On dreams and Jekyll and Hyde.
Bevington, M. M. Locke and Stevenson on comparative morality. N & Q Feb 1960.
Gossmann, A. On the knocking at the gate in Markheim. Nineteenth-Century Fiction 17 1963.
Grundy, J. O. RLS in Greenwich Village. BNYPL March 1963.
Nakajima, A. Light, wind and dreams: an interpretation of the life and mind of Stevenson. Tokyo 1963.
Kiely, R. Stevenson and the fiction of adventure. Cambridge Mass 1964.
Bonds, R. E. The mystery of the Master of Ballantrae. English Lit in Transition 7 1964. Reply by E. M. Eigner, ibid.
Thomas, D. The beach of Falesá. 1964. Film scenario based on Stevenson's life.
Faurot, R. M. From records to romance: Stevenson's The black arrow and the Paston letters. Stud in Eng Lit 1500–1900 5 1965.
Issler, A. R. Stevenson in Monterey. Pacific Historical Rev 34 1965.
Egan, J. J. Markheim: a drama of moral psychology. Nineteenth-Century Fiction 20 1966.
— The relationship of theme and art in the Strange case of Dr Jekyll and Mr Hyde. English Lit in Transition 9 1966.
Eigner, E. M. Stevenson and romantic tradition. Princeton 1966.
Miyoshi, M. Dr Jekyll and the emergence of Mr Hyde. College Eng March 1966.
Strouse, N. The Silverado episode. Quart News Letter Book Club of Cal 31 1966.
Saposnik, I. S. Markheim: a fictional Christmas sermon. Nineteenth-Century Fiction 21 1967.
Booth, B. A. The Vailima letters of Stevenson. Harvard Lib Bull 15 1967.

B. A. B.

GEORGE MOORE
1852–1933

Letters and other mss are to be found in the National Library Dublin, Berg Collection of the New York Public Library, Univ of Texas, Univ of Washington, Univ of Kansas and Yale Univ; smaller collections may be found at Harvard, Princeton, Duke, the Univ of Indiana and London Univ.

Bibliographies

Williams, I. A. Bibliographies of modern authors no 3: George Moore. 1921.
Danielson, H. Moore: a bibliography 1878–1921. In J. Freeman, A portrait of Moore, 1922.
Collet, G.-P. In his Moore et la France, Geneva and Paris 1957. Lists uncollected articles and prefaces.
Gerber, H. E. Moore: an annotated bibliography of writings about him. Eng Lit in Transition 2 1959. Supplemented in succeeding issues.

Korg, J. In Victorian fiction: a guide to research, ed L. Stevenson, Cambridge Mass 1964.

Collections

Works: Carra edition. 21 vols 1922–4; Uniform edition, 20 vols 1924–33; Ebury edition, 20 vols 1936–8.

§1

No attempt is made to cite uncollected contributions to periodicals or prefaces to works by such other writers as Zola and Dostoevsky; see Collet, above.

Worldliness: a comedy in three acts. c. 1874. 'The author believes and hopes, that no copy of this, his first published work, now exists' (*see* I. A. Williams, above); no known copy.

Flowers of passion. 1878 (for 1877). Poems.

Martin Luther: a tragedy in five acts. 1879. Verse; with Bernard Lopez.

Pagan poems. 1881.

A modern lover. 3 vols 1883, 1 vol 1885 (rev), New York 1890. Rewritten in 1917 as Lewis Seymour and some women.

A mummer's wife. 1885 (for 1884), 1886 (for 1885) (rev), 1918 (rev), New York 1889 (as An actor's wife), 1903, 1917 (rev); tr French, 1888; Dutch, c. 1895.

Literature at nurse: or circulating morals. 1885. Pamphlet on the selection of books at Mudie's Library.

A drama in muslin: a realistic novel. 1886, 1915 (largely rewritten as Muslin), New York 1915; tr Russian, 1887; Dutch, 1888.

A mere accident. 1887, 1895 (rewritten as John Norton in Celibates); tr French, 1887; Norwegian, nd.

Parnell and his island. 1887; tr French, 1887. Sketches.

Confessions of a young man. 1888, 1889 (rev), 1904 (rev), 1917 (rev), 1926 (expanded), New York 1888, 1917 (rev); tr French, 1888; Czech, 1910; Italian, 1929; Japanese, 1952.

Spring days: a realistic novel—a prelude to Don Juan. 1888, 1912 (rev with preface), New York 1891 (as Shifting love), 1912.

Mike Fletcher: a novel. 1889, New York 1890.

Impressions and opinions. 1891, 1913 (rev), New York 1891, 1913.

Vain fortune. [1891], 1895 (rev), New York 1892, 1892 (rev); tr French, 1893; Dutch, 1895.

Modern painting. 1893, 1897 (for 1896) (enlarged), New York 1893, 1898 (enlarged), 1923 (with article from Impressions and opinions); tr Czech, 1909.

The strike at Arlingford: a play in three acts. 1893, New York 1894.

Esther Waters: a novel. 1894, 1899 (rev), 1920 (rev), 1926 (rev), Chicago 1894, 1899 (rev), New York 1894, 1899, 1901, 1917, 1921 (rev), 1932; tr Danish, 1895; Russian, 1895; Swedish, 1899; German, 1904; French, 1907; Italian, 1934. Dramatized 1913, Boston 1913.

The Royal Academy. 1895. New budget extra, no 1.

Celibates. 1895, New York 1895, 1915. Includes Mildred Lawson, John Norton, Agnes Lahens; tr Czech, 1905 (with other stories).

Evelyn Innes. 1898, 1898 (rev), 1901 (rev), 1908 (rev), New York 1898; tr German, 1905.

The bending of the bough: a comedy in five acts. 1900, 1900 (rev), New York 1900.

Sister Theresa. 1901, 1909 (rev), [1928] (entirely rewritten), New York 1901, 1918, Philadelphia 1901, Leipzig 1901 (rev); tr German, 1905.

The untilled field. 1903, 1914 (rev), 1926 (rev), 1931 (rev), New York 1903, Leipzig 1903 (rev), Philadelphia 1903; tr Irish, 1902 (in part). Short stories.

The lake. 1905, 1905 (rev), 1921 (rev), New York 1906, Leipzig 1906 (rev); tr French, 1923; Italian, 1933.

Memoirs of my dead life. 1906, 1907, 1915 (expanded), 1921 (rev and enlarged), Leipzig 1906 (rev), New York 1907 (for 1906), 1920 (rev) ; tr French, 1922; Chinese, c. 1935.

Reminiscences of the impressionist painters. Dublin 1906; tr German, 1908.

The apostle: a drama in three acts. Dublin 1911, Boston 1911, London 1923; tr German, 1911. Rewritten as The passing of the Essenes, 1930.

'Hail and farewell': a trilogy. London and New York 3 vols 1911–14, 2 vols 1925. Pt 1, Ave; Pt 2, Salve; Pt 3, Vale.

Elizabeth Cooper: a comedy in three acts. Dublin 1913, Boston 1913; tr French as Clara Florise by Edouard Dujardin, 1914. Rewritten as The coming of Gabrielle, 1920.

The brook Kerith: a Syrian story. 1916, 1916 (rev), 1921 (rev), 1927, 1929, 1952, New York 1916, 1916 (rev), 1923 (rev); tr French, 1927.

Lewis Seymour and some women. 1917, New York 1917, 1922. A rewriting of A modern lover, above.

A story-teller's holiday. London and New York 1918 (priv ptd), 2 vols 1928 (rev with additional tales).

Avowals. 1919 (priv ptd), 1921 (rev), New York 1919 (priv ptd).

The coming of Gabrielle: a comedy. 1920 (priv ptd), New York 1921 (priv ptd), Leipzig 1922 (rev).

Héloïse and Abélard. 2 vols 1921 (priv ptd), 1 vol 1925, New York 1921, 1923 (rev), 1932. Some 'fragments' i.e. addns and corrections, were priv ptd New York 1921 and later edns.

In single strictness. 1922 (priv ptd), 1927 (as Celibate lives), New York 1922, 1923 (rev), 1927 (as Celibate lives).

Conversations in Ebury Street. 1924, 1930 (rev), New York 1924.

Peronnik the fool. New York 1924 (with Daphnis and Chloe), Mt Vernon NY 1926 (separately), Chapelle-Réanville France 1928 (rev), London 1933, 1933 (with Daphnis and Chloe).

The pastoral lives of Daphnis and Chloe, done into English from Longus. 1924, 1927, 1933 (with Peronnik, above), 1954, New York 1924 (with Peronnik), 1934.

Pure poetry: an anthology. 1924, New York 1924.

Ulick and Soracha. 1926, New York 1926. Incorporated in A story-teller's holiday, 1928.

The making of an immortal: a play in one act. New York 1927; tr French, Revue des Deux Mondes 15 Jan 1915.

A flood. New York 1930.

The passing of the Essenes: a drama in three acts. 1930, 1931 (rev), New York 1930. A revision of The apostle, above.

Aphrodite in Aulis. 1930, 1931 (rev), New York 1930, 1931 (rev).

The talking pine. Paris 1931, Tempe Arizona 1948.

A communication to my friends. 1933 (used as new preface for Uniform and subsequent editions of A mummer's wife).

Letters

Moore versus Harris. Detroit 1921, Chicago 1925.

Letters to Edouard Dujardin 1866–1922. New York 1929. From the French, tr 'John Eglinton' (W. K. Magee).

Letters from Moore: the Greek background of Aphrodite in Aulis. Ed P. J. Dixon, London Mercury Nov 1934.

Crawford, V. M. Moore: letters of his last years. London Mercury Dec 1936.

Letters to John Eglinton. Bournemouth 1942.

Ross, M. Robert Ross: friend of friends. 1952. Contains 18 letters.

Letters to Lady Cunard 1895–1933. Ed R. Hart-Davis 1957.

§2

Howells, W. D. Review of Celibates. Harper's Weekly 27 July 1895.

Quiller-Couch, A. T. In his Adventures in criticism, 1896.
Murray, D. C. My contemporaries in fiction. 1897.
Peck, H. T. In his Personal equation, New York 1898.
Bennett, A. In his Fame and fiction, 1901.
Huneker, J. G. Literary men who loved music. In his Overtones: a book of temperaments, New York 1904.
—— The later George Moore. In his Pathos of distance, New York 1913.
Reid, F. The novels of Moore. Westminster Rev Aug 1909.
Archer, W. Conversation with Mr Moore. Critic July 1901; rptd in his Real conversations, 1904.
Boyd, E. A. In his Ireland's literary renaissance, Dublin 1916.
Mitchell, S. L. George Moore. 1916.
Lucas, E. V. His fatal beauty: or the Moore of Chelsea. 1917 (priv ptd). Dramatic satire, played at Chelsea Palace, 20 March 1917.
Beerbohm, M. In his Christmas garland, 1912. A parody.
—— In his Mainly on the air, 1957 (enlarged). A broadcast of 1950, first pbd in Atlantic Monthly Dec 1950.
Sherman, S. P. The aesthetic naturalism of Moore. In his On contemporary literature, New York 1917.
—— Moore: an Irish epicure. In his Main stream, New York 1927.
Harris, F. Moore and Jesus. In his Contemporary portraits ser 2, New York 1919.
Freeman, J. A portrait of Moore in a study of his work. 1922.
Ervine, St J. In his Some impressions of my elders, 1923.
Gillet, L. Moore l'aventureux. Revue des Deux Mondes 15 Oct 1923.
—— George Moore. Revue des Deux Mondes 1 April 1933.
Jean-Aubry, G. Moore and Emile Zola. Bookman's Jnl Dec 1924.
Jaloux, E. In his Figures étrangères ser 1, Paris 1925.
Ransom, J. C. A man without a country. Sewanee Rev 33 1925.
—— In his World's body, New York 1938.
Blanche, J. E. George Moore. Nouvelles Littéraires 16, 23 June 1928. Recollections.
—— In his Portraits of a lifetime, 1937.
Clutton-Brock, A. In his Essays on literature and life, 1926.
Read, H. Pure poetry. In his Reason and romanticism, 1926.
Goodwin, G. Conversations with Moore. 1929.
—— Call back yesterday, 1935. Fiction.
Rascoe, B. Moore: the man of letters. In his Titans of literature, New York 1932.
'Mansfield, Katherine'. Esther Waters revisited. In her Novels and novelists, 1930.
Bock, H. The brook Kerith: eine kritische Studie. Die Neueren Sprachen June 1931.
Farmer, A. J. Moore et les influences françaises. In his Mouvement esthéthique et 'décadent' en Angleterre 1873–1900, Paris 1931.
MacCarthy, D. In his Portraits, 1931.
—— A critic's day book. Life & Letters March, June 1933.
Sechler, R. P. Moore: 'a disciple of Walter Pater.' Philadelphia 1931.
Wolfe, H. George Moore. 1931.
—— In his Post Victorians, 1933.
—— The three interviews of Moore. In his Portraits by inference, 1934.
Weferling, H. Das Religiöse bei Moore. Bottrop 1932.
Bowra, C. M. George Moore. New Oxford Outlook 1 1933.
Burdett, O. George Moore. London Mercury March 1933.
Davray, H. D. George Moore. Mercure de France 15 March 1933.
Duclaux, M. Souvenirs sur Moore. Revue de Paris March 1933.
'Eglinton, John' (W. K. Magee). Moore at St Winifred's Well. Life & Letters March 1933; rptd with Recollections of Moore in his Irish literary portraits, 1935.
Ford, F. M. Contrasts: memories of John Galsworthy and Moore. Atlantic Monthly May 1933; rptd in his It was a nightingale, Philadelphia 1933.
Gilomen, W. Moore: Jugendwerk, Naturalismus und Abkehr. Zürich 1933.
—— Moore and his friendship with W. B. Yeats. E Studies 19 1937.
Gogarty, O. St J. Moore: a conversation in Ebury Street. Saturday Rev of Lit 28 Jan 1933.
Paul-Dubois, L. George Moore, irlandais. Correspondant 10 Oct 1933.
Whitall, G. George Moore. Bookman (New York) March 1933.
—— In his English years, New York 1935.
Swinnerton, F. In his Georgian scene, New York 1934.
Ferguson, W. D. The influence of Flaubert on Moore. Philadelphia 1934.
Steward, S. M. J.-K. Huysmans and Moore. Romanic Rev 25 1934.
Krüger, F. Moore und die irische Renaissance. Neuphilologische Monatsschrift July–Aug 1935.
Morgan, C. Epitaph on Moore. 1935.
—— Moore: a centenary appreciation. Listener 28 Feb 1952.
Hone, J. M. The life of Moore. 1936.
—— Moore and some correspondents. Dublin Mag 22 1947.
—— Moore: the making of a writer. TLS 29 Feb 1952.
O'Faoláin, S. Pater and Moore. London Mercury Aug 1936.
Yeats, W. B. In his Dramatis personae, 1936.
Hoare, D. M. Moore and Joyce: contrast. In her Some studies in the modern novel, 1938.
Elwin, M. Moore: the comedy of a card; Moore: tragedy or farce? In his Old gods falling, 1939.
Edgar, P. Moore and George Russell. Canadian Poetry Mag July 1939.
Hicks, G. The miracle of Esther Waters. In his Figures of transition, New York 1939.
Auriant. Un disciple anglais d'Emile Zola—Moore: documents inédits. Mercure de France May 1940.
Woolf, V. In her Death of the moth, 1942.
Gregory, H. On Moore and regionalism in realistic fiction. In his Shield of Achilles, New York 1944.
Gettmann, R. A. Moore's revisions of The lake, The wild goose and Esther Waters. PMLA 59 1944.
'O'Sullivan, Seumas' (James Starkey). In his Essays on recollections, Dublin 1944.
McCullough, B. Esther Waters. In his Representative English novelists, New York 1946.
Cordasco, F. Moore and Edouard Dujardin. MLN 62 1947.
Frierson, W. C. Moore compromised with the Victorians. Trollopian 1 1947.
Niess, R. J. Moore and Paul Alexis: the death of La Pellegrin. Romanic Rev 38 1947.
Fitzpatrick, K. A plea for Evelyn Innes. Southerly 9 1948.
Clark, B. H. Moore: at home in Paris. In his Intimate portraits, New York 1951.
Battock, M. George Moore. Dublin Mag 27 1952.
Nejdefors-Frisk, S. Moore's naturalistic prose. Upsala 1952.
Collet, G.-P. Moore et la France. Geneva 1957.
Temple, R. Z. In her Critic's alchemy, New York 1953.
Schwab, A. T. Irish author and American critic: Moore and James Huneker. Nineteenth-Century Fiction 8–9 1954–5.

Shumaker, W. The narrative mode: Moore's Hail and farewell. In his English autobiography, Berkeley 1954.
Chaiken, M. The composition of Moore's A modern lover. Comparative Lit 7 1955.
— Balzac, Zola and Moore's A drama in muslin. Revue de Littérature Comparée 29 1955.
— Moore's A mummer's wife and Zola. Revue de Littérature Comparée 31 1957.
Brown, M. J. Moore: a reconsideration. Seattle 1955.
— Introduction. In his edn of Esther Waters, New York 1958.
Cunard, N. GM: memories of Moore. 1957.
Noel, J. C. Moore et Mallarmé. Revue de Littérature Comparée 32 1958.
— Moore: l'homme et l'oeuvre. Paris 1966.
Brown, C. S. Balzac as a source of Moore's Sister Theresa. Comparative Lit 11 1959.
Howarth, H. In his Irish writers 1880–1940, New York 1959.
O'Sullivan, V. In his Opinions, 1959.
Heywood, C. Flaubert, Miss Braddon and Moore. Comparative Lit 12 1960.
— D. H. Lawrence's The lost girl and its antecedents by Moore and Bennett. E Studies 47 1966.
Hough, G. Moore and the novel. REL 1 1960; rptd in his Image and experience, 1960.
— Moore and the nineties. In Edwardians and late Victorians, ed R. Ellmann, New York 1960; rptd in his Image and experience, 1960.
Blissett, W. F. Moore and literary Wagnerism. Comparative Lit 13 1961.
Burkhart, C. B. Moore and Father and son. Nineteenth-Century Fiction 15 1961.
Gregor, I. and B. Nicholas. The case of Esther Waters. In their Moral and the story, 1962.
Watson, S. R. Moore and the Dolmetches. Eng Lit in Transition 6 1963. Reply by J. W. Weaver, ibid.
Michie, D. M. A man of genius and a man of talent. Texas Stud in Lit & Lang 6 1964. On his collaboration with Yeats.
Lyons, F. S. L. Moore and Edward Martyn. Hermathena 97 1964.
Jeffares, A. N. A drama in muslin. In Essays presented to Amy G. Stock, Jaipur 1965.
Uslenghi, R. M. Una prospettiva di unità nell'arte di Moore. Eng Miscellany (Rome) 15 1965.
Weaver, J. W. Stage management in the Irish theatre: an unknown article by Moore? Eng Lit in Transition 9 1966.
Bartlett, L. C. Maggie: a new source for Esther Waters. Ibid.

B. A. B.

RUDYARD KIPLING
1865–1936

Bibliographies

Livingston, L. S. The works of Kipling. New York 1901.
Martindell, E. W. A bibliography of the works of Kipling. 1922, 1923 (enlarged).
Livingston, F. V. Bibliography of the works of Kipling. New York 1927; Supplement, 1938.
Chandler, L. H. A summary of the works of Kipling, including items ascribed to him. New York 1930.
Catalogue of the works of Kipling exhibited at the Grolier Club 1929. New York 1930.
Ballard, E. A. Catalogue intimate and descriptive of my Kipling collection: books manuscripts and letters. Philadelphia 1935 (priv ptd).
Ehrsam, T. G. and R. H. Deily. In their Bibliographies of twelve Victorian authors, New York 1936; Supplement, MP 37 1939.
Stewart, J. McG. Kipling: a bibliographical catalogue. Ed A. W. Yeats, Toronto 1959.
Gerber, H. E. and E. Lauterbach. Kipling: an annotated bibliography of writings about him. Eng Fiction in Transition 3 1960; Supplement 8 1965.

Collections

Collected Works

Lovell's authorized edition. 11 vols New York 1890–1.
Tauchnitz edition. 19 vols Leipzig 1890–1926.
Outward bound edition. 36 vols New York 1897–1937.
Edition de luxe. 38 vols 1897–1938.
Trade edition. 31 vols New York 1898–1932.
Brushwood edition. 15 vols New York 1898–9.
Manuscript edition. 33 vols New York 1898–1932.
Swastika edition. 15 vols New York 1899.
Uniform edition. 29 vols 1899–1938.
Uniform pocket edition. 37 vols 1907–38.
Bombay edition. 31 vols 1913–38.
Seven seas edition. 27 vols New York 1914–26.
Service Kipling. 17 in 32 vols 1914–15.
New world edition. 28 in 13 vols New York 1923.
Mandalay edition. 26 vols New York 1925–6.
Compact edition. 16 in 6 vols New York 1936.
Sussex edition. 35 vols 1937–39.
Burwash edition. 28 vols 1941.
Sussex and Burwash are the only edns containing all acknowledged and authorized works, and are identical in contents. Cited as SBE, below.
Library edition. 24 vols 1949–51.
Centenary edition. 23 vols 1965.

Selections

Soldier tales. 1896, New York 1896 (as Soldier stories).
The Kipling reader. 1900, 1901 (rev), 1908, 1925 (as Selected stories).
Kipling stories and poems every child should know. New York 1909. 14 stories, 26 poems.
Selected stories. Ed W. L. Phelps, New York 1921.
A Kipling anthology: prose. 1922.
The one volume Kipling. New York 1928. Contains The light that failed, The city of dreadful night, The story of the Gadsbys, 77 poems and 87 stories already collected, and 4 stories collected (with Kipling's authority) for the first time: The last relief, For one night only, The legs of Sister Ursula, The lamentable comedy of willow wood.
Humorous tales. 1931. 20 stories, 9 poems.
Animal stories from Rudyard Kipling. 1932. 11 stories and 8 poems.
All the Mowgli stories. 1933. 9 stories, 9 poems, How to say the names in this book.
Collected dog stories. 1934. 8 stories, 5 poems, and first pbn of A sea dog.
A Kipling pageant. New York 1935. 37 stories, 52 poems, new Foreword.
More selected stories. 1940.
A Kipling treasury. 1940. 8 stories, 10 poems.
Twenty-one tales. 1946.
Ten stories. 1947.
A choice of Kipling's prose. Ed W. S. Maugham 1952.
Kipling: a selection of his stories and poems. Ed J. Beacroft 2 vols New York 1956.
Kipling: short stories selected. Ed E. Parone, New York 1960.
The fifty best short stories. Ed R. Jarrell, New York 1961.
The Kipling sampler: selections from a great story-teller's best. Ed A. Greendale, Greenwich Conn 1962.
In the vernacular—the English in India: short stories by Kipling. Ed R. Jarrell, New York 1963.
The English in England: short stories by Kipling. Ed R. Jarrell, New York 1963.

Verse

The Cornhill booklet: occasional poems. Boston 1900 (unauthorized).

Collected verse. New York 1907 (first pbn of The fires), London 1912 (omits The sacrifice of Er-Heb).

Twenty poems. 1819. 3 first rptd here from periodicals.

Kipling's verse: inclusive edition 1885–1918. 3 vols 1919, New York 1919 (omits Mowgli's song at the Council Rock), 1921 (adds Philadelphia, When 'Omer smote 'is bloomin' lyre), London 1921 (omits Great heart, adds 12 poems rptd from periodicals), 1927 (adds verses from Debits and credits, 7 rptd from periodicals and A song of the desert), 3 vols 1929 (adds 6 poems to The muse among the motors), 1933 (adds verses from Brazilian sketches, Limits and renewals, and 10 rptd from periodicals etc).

Uncollected verse: inclusive edition 1881–1922 (priv ptd and without permission, for E. W. Martindell and E. A. Ballard in 1922 in edn of 12 copies, containing many poems uncollected elsewhere, some not by Kipling).

A Kipling anthology: verse. 1922, New York 1922.

Songs of youth. 1924, New York 1925.

A choice of songs. 1925 (with one unpbd poem).

Sea and Sussex. 1925 (with one unpbd poem), New York 1926.

Songs of the sea. 1927 (with one poem rptd from periodical), New York 1927.

Selected poems. 1931.

East of Suez: being a selection of eastern verses. 1931.

Kipling: sixty poems. 1939.

Kipling's verse: definitive edition. 1940, New York 1940. Omits early and miscellaneous verse rptd only in SBE.

So shall ye reap: poems for these days. 1941.

A choice of Kipling's verse. Ed T. S. Eliot 1941.

A Kipling anthology. Ed W. G. Bebbington 1964.

§ 1

Schoolboy lyrics. Lahore 1881 (c. 50 copies priv ptd). Rptd in SBE except The night before.

Echoes, by two writers. Lahore 1884. 32 poems by Kipling, 7 by his sister.

Quartette, by four Anglo-Indian writers. Lahore 1885. Prose and verse by Kipling, his sister and parents. 2 stories by Kipling subsequently rptd; for 2 stories and 5 poems, no authorized reprint.

Departmental ditties and other verses. Lahore 1886, Calcutta 1886 (with 5 new poems), Calcutta 1888 (with 10 new poems), 1890 (10 new poems), 1891 (with glossary), 1898 (Edition de luxe), New York 1899 (rev) etc.

Plain tales from the hills. Calcutta 1888 (40 stories, 32 rptd from Civil & Military Gazette), 1890 (rev), New York 1890 (with letter from Kipling), New York 1899 (pirated, adds The last relief, only collected in SBE), New York 1899 (adds Bitters neat and Haunted subalterns, also collected in SBE with biographical introd by C. E. Norton), 1899 (rev).

Soldiers three. Allahabad 1888, 1890 (rev). 7 stories, 6 rptd from Week's News.

The story of the Gadsbys. Allahabad 1888, 1890 (rev). 8 scenes, 6 rptd from Week's News.

In black and white. Allahabad 1888, 1890 (rev). 8 stories, 7 rptd from Week's News.

Under the deodars. Allahabad 1888, 1890 (rev). 6 stories, 5 rptd from Week's News.

The phantom rickshaw and other tales. Allahabad 1888, 1890 (rev). 4 stories rptd from Quartette and Week's News.

Wee Willie Winkie and other child stories. Allahabad 1888 (for 1889), 1890 (rev). 4 stories, 3 rptd from Week's News.

Departmental ditties, barrack-room ballads and other verses. New York 1890. Ballads and other verses rptd from Scots Observer and Eng Illustr Mag.

The courting of Dinah Shadd and other stories. New York 1890, 1890. With essay by A. Lang. 6 stories rptd from magazines; 2nd edn substitutes Badalia Herodsfoot for Krishna Mulvaney.

The light that failed. New York 1890 (with happy ending as ptd in Lippincott's Mag, 12 chs), New York 1890 (unhappy ending, 14 chs), 1891 (15 chs, dedicatory poem and preface), 1898 (rev).

The city of dreadful night and other sketches. Allahabad 1890 (suppressed). 18 stories and sketches from Civil & Military Gazette and Pioneer; 4 not in SBE.

The city of dreadful night and other places. Allahabad 1891 (suppressed), 1891. 11 sketches rptd from Pioneer.

The Smith administration. Allahabad 1891 (suppressed). 20 articles rptd from Civil & Military Gazette and Pioneer.

Letters of marque. Allahabad 1891 (suppressed), 1891 (vol 1 suppressed). 19 articles rptd from Pioneer.

American notes. New York 1891. Piratical reprint from Pioneer.

Mine own people. New York 1891. With essay by H. James. 12 stories, 6 rptd from Courting of Dinah Shadd.

Life's handicap: being stories of mine own people. 1891, New York 1891. All stories from Mine own people except A conference of the powers, plus 17 stories, all but 3 rptd from periodicals.

The Naulahka: a story of West and East. 1892, New York 1892. Rptd from Century Mag. In collaboration with Wolcott Balestier.

Barrack-room ballads and other verses. 1892 (all but 8 poems rptd from books and periodicals), New York 1892, 1893 (as Ballads and barrack-room ballads, with 4 new poems from periodicals).

Many inventions. 1893. 14 stories (9 rptd from periodicals) and 2 poems.

The jungle book 1894 (7 stories rptd from periodicals, 7 poems), New York 1894 (with variants), London 1899 (rev).

The second jungle book. 1895 (8 stories rptd from periodicals, and 8 poems), New York 1895 (textual variants), London 1895 (rev). The two jungle books, 1924, stories rearranged; New York 1948 with foreword by N. Doubleday.

Out of India. New York 1895. City of dreadful night and other places, Letters of marque, rptd without authority.

Soldiers three; The story of the Gadsbys; In black and white. New York 1895. Rev, 2 new stories from Civil and Military Gazette, not in English edn of 1895 or until SBE.

Wee Willie Winkie; Under the deodars; The phantom 'rickshaw. New York 1895. Rev, 2 new stories from Civil & Military Gazette, not in English edn of 1895 or until SBE.

The seven seas. 1896. 47 poems, 13 here first pbd.

The Kipling birthday book. 1896. Many quotations from verses in Civil & Military Gazette not otherwise rptd.

'Captains courageous': a story of the Grand Banks. 1897 (serialized in McClure's Mag and Pearson's Mag), New York 1897 (slight textual variants); ed J. de L. Ferguson, New York 1959.

An almanac of twelve sports. 1898. Verses to drawings by W. Nicholson.

The day's work. 1898. 12 stories rptd from periodicals; The brushwood boy rptd separately New York 1899, 1907, London 1907; The Maltese cat, London, and New York 1936.

A fleet in being: notes of two trips with the Channel Squadron. 1898 (rptd from Times, Morning Post, World).

Recessional and other poems. 1899. Unauthorized reprint of 4 poems from periodicals.

Stalky & Co. 1899 (9 stories rptd from magazines; The complete Stalky & Co., 1929, adds 5 stories, 4 previously collected in other vols, one from magazine); ed S. Marcus, New York 1962.

From sea to sea. New York 1899, 1900. Rev versions of Letters of marque, City of dreadful night, Smith administration, American notes etc.

With number three; Surgical and medical, and new poems. Santiago 1900. Unauthorized collection from periodicals etc; all items in SBE.

Kim. 1901 (serialized in McClure's Mag and Cassell's Mag), New York 1962 (preface by J. I. M. Stewart), New York 1962 (preface by C. E. Carrington), New York 1962 (preface by A. L. Rowse).

Just so stories for little children. 1902 (12 stories, 11 rptd from periodicals, and 9 poems); [Just so song book 1903, music by E. German]; New York 1903 (Outward bound edition vol 20, includes The tabu tale rptd from periodicals otherwise only collected in SBE); The Just so stories painting books, 1922–3.

The five nations. 1903. 54 poems, 28 of them unpbd.

Traffics and discoveries. 1904. 11 stories rptd from periodicals, 11 poems.

Puck of Pook's Hill. 1906 (11 stories rptd from Strand Mag; 16 poems), New York 1906 (small textual variants); All the Puck stories [with Rewards and fairies], 1935.

Letters to the family: notes on a recent trip to Canada. Toronto 1908. 8 articles rptd from newspapers, later included in Letters of travel; 7 poems later included in Songs from books and Verse.

Actions and reactions. 1909 (8 stories rptd from periodicals; 8 poems), New York 1909 (slight textual variants).

Abaft the funnel. New York 1909 (pirated), New York 1909 (authorized). 30 stories and sketches and one poem from Indian newspapers. No English edn until SBE.

Rewards and fairies. 1910, New York 1910 (textual variants), London 1926 (school edn, rev). 11 stories, (9 from periodicals), 23 poems.

A history of England. 1911, 1930 (rev). By C. R. L. Fletcher; 23 poems by Kipling, rptd in various verse collections and SBE.

Songs from books. New York 1912, Toronto 1912, London 1913 (with many addns). Poems from prose vols, many expanded.

The new army in training. 1915. 6 articles rptd, much rev, from Daily Telegraph.

France at war. 1915. 6 articles rptd from newspapers.

Fringes of the Fleet. 1915. 6 articles rptd from newspapers, and 6 poems.

Tales of 'the trade'. 1916. 3 articles rptd from Times.

Sea warfare. 1916. Fringes of the Fleet, Tales of 'the trade', Destroyers at Jutland, rptd from newspapers; one poem.

The war in the mountains. 1917, New York 1917; tr Italian, 1917. 5 newspaper articles. In SBE.

A diversity of creatures. 1917. 14 stories (12 rptd from periodicals), 14 poems.

The eyes of Asia. New York 1918. 4 articles rptd from newspapers. No English edn until SBE.

To fighting Americans. Paris [1918]. 2 speeches rptd from newspapers. Not in SBE.

The graves of the fallen. 1919, 1928 (rev as War graves of the Empire). Much is by Kipling; only one epitaph from it in SBE.

The years between. 1919 (46 poems, 12 new, rest rptd from periodicals etc), 1919. Bombay, Seven seas edns vol 25 add The muse among the motors, 20 parodies all in SBE.

Letters of travel (1892–1913). 1920. From tideway to tideway, Letters to the family, Egypt of the magicians rptd from periodicals), 1938 (Sussex edn vol 24 adds Brazilian sketches, 7 articles rptd from Morning Post pbd separately New York 1940).

The Irish Guards in the Great War. 2 vols 1923, New York 1923. Only rptd in SBE.

Land and sea tales for Scouts and Guides. 1923. One story, 8 poems new; 10 stories rptd from periodicals etc.

Debits and credits. 1926. 14 stories rptd from magazines, 21 poems, 2 of them rptd.

A book of words. 1928. 31 speeches; 6 added in SBE.

Thy servant a dog. 1930 (3 stories, 2 rptd from Cassell's Mag), 1938 (as Thy servant a dog and other dog stories; adds 2 stories and 2 poems not previously collected).

Limits and renewals. 1932. 14 stories (11 rptd from magazines), 19 poems (one rptd).

Souvenirs of France. 1933. Sketches rptd from newspapers.

Something of myself for my friends known and unknown. 1937. Serialized in Morning Post, New York Times, Civil & Military Gazette.

Stories, Poems and Speeches published separately

This list does not include over 120 items ptd separately for copyright purposes, or the hundreds of pirated edns.

The seven nights of creation. Calcutta 1886. Poem of 145 lines, 80 only in SBE.

One word more. [Allahabad 1888].

My great and only. Allahabad 1890.

'Cleared'. Edinburgh 1890.

The record of Badalia Herodsfoot. [1890].

My lord the elephant. Boston 1892.

His Excellency. Rutlam Canada 1895, Bombay 1899. Not in SBE.

Rudyard Kipling's regrets. New Haven 1896. Poem Mulvaney's regrets from Yale Lit Mag. Not in SBE.

Recessional. 1897, 1914.

The vampire. New York 1898 (priv ptd), Boston 1898 etc.

Mandalay. New York 1898.

The man who would be king. New York 1899.

The drums of the Fore and Aft. New York 1899.

The brushwood boy. New York 1899, 1907.

Ballad of East and West. New York 1899.

The betrothed. New York 1899.

Black Jack. New York 1899. Unrevised story from Soldiers three.

The absent-minded beggar. 1899 etc.

Kipling masterpieces. New York 1899. 5 stories ptd as separate booklets.

The sin of witchcraft. 1901. Letter rptd from Times; not in SBE.

The science of rebellion: a tract for the times. 1901.

The settler. 1903.

The Gipsy trail. Boston 1904 etc. Rptd from Century Mag Dec 1892.

They. 1905, New York 1906.

The army of a dream. 1905.

Letter on a possible source of the Tempest. Providence 1906 (priv ptd), New York 1916. Rptd from Spectator 1898.

South Africa. New York 1906. Copyright issue, rptd from Standard 1906. Not in SBE.

Doctors: an address. 1908.

With the night mail: a story of 2000 A.D. New York 1909.

A song of the English. 1909, 1915.

A patrol song. 1909.

If-. New York 1910, London 1914, 1915, 1935 etc.

The glory of the garden. Manchester nd, [New York 1923] (priv ptd). First pbd in A history of England, 1911.

Why snow falls at Vernet. Mansfield 1911 (in Pages from the Merrythought), 1923 (priv ptd), 1963 (priv ptd). Not in SBE.

The female of the species. New York 1912.

Ulster: a poem. Belfast 1912, Ely 1914 (priv ptd).

The secret bargain and the Ulster plot: a speech. 1914. Not in SBE.

The children's song. 1914, 1918.

Hymn before action. 1914, 1915.

A call to the nation. 1915. Speech; not in SBE.

National bands. 1915. In SBE as The soul of a battalion.

The holy war. 1917, 1918.

Kipling's message. 1918. Speech; not in SBE.

The Irish Guards. 1918. Poem.
Justice. 1918.
The feet of the young men. New York 1920.
England and the English. 1920, New York 1921 (as The mind of the English).
Some notes on a bill. Little Rock 1920 (priv ptd). Poem rptd from Author (Boston) 1891; not in SBE.
The first assault upon the Sorbonne [in English and French]. New York 1922 (limited edn; rptd in SBE).
The King's pilgrimage. 1922.
Independence. 1923, New York 1924.
The potted princess. New York 1925 (priv ptd).
Collah-wallah and the poison stick. New York 1925 (priv ptd).
On dry-cow fishing as a fine art. Cleveland 1926 (priv ptd).
The art of fiction. 1926.
St Andrews: two poems. 1926.
The legs of Sister Ursula. San Francisco 1927.
A tour of inspection. New York 1928 (priv ptd).
The lamentable comedy of willow wood. San Francisco 1929.
Supplication of the black Aberdeen. 1929.
The benefactors. New York 1930.
His apologies. 1932.
Selections from the freer verse Horace. New York 1932 (copyright edn, rptd from Magdalene College Mag 1932), Liverpool 1965 (priv ptd). Not in SBE.
The fox meditates. 1933.
Two forewords. New York 1935.
Hymn of breaking strain. 1935.
Ham and the porcupine: a just so story. 1935 (in The Princess Elizabeth gift book), New York 1935 (copyright pamphlet), Kipling Jnl 25 1958. Not in SBE.
The Maltese cat. 1936.
Toomai of the elephants. 1937.
Teem: a treasure-hunter. New York 1938.
Tommy. 1943.
For uncollected items, unauthorized edns, poems set to music, copyright and miscellaneous reprints see J. McG. Stewart Bibliographical catalogue, Toronto 1959.

Contributions to Books not reprinted elsewhere

Lister, R. J. A catalogue of a portion of the library of Edmund Gosse. 1893, 1924 (in E. H. Cox, Library of Edmund Gosse). Poem.
Ralph, J. War's brighter side. 1901. Prose and verse.
Landon, P. (ed). Helio-tropes: or new posies for sundials. 1904. Poem.
Baden-Powell, R. S. S. Sketches in Mafeking. 1907. Verses.
Rice, W. and F. The little book of limericks. 1910. Rptd from periodicals.
Lowther, H. C. From pillar to post. 1911. Poem.
The King's book of Quebec. Ottawa 1911. Article.
The Kipling reader. New York 1912 (How to bring up a lion, rptd from Ladies' Home Jnl 1902), New York 1962 (in Everyman's ark, ed S. P. Johnson).
Newton, W. D. War. 1914. Introd.
Chevrillon, A. Britain and the War. 1917. Preface.
Q. Horati Flacci carmen liber quintus. Oxford 1920, 1920 (rev), 1922 (rev). 3 poems, collected; 2nd and subsequent edns also contain uncollected prose version.
Bland-Sutton, J. The story of a surgeon. 1929. Introd.
Tusser, T. Five hundred points of good husbandry. Ed E. V. Lucas 1931. Benediction.
Cave, E. et al. Ant antics. 1933. Limerick.
Atholl, Duchess of, and J. C. French. India and the report of the joint select committee. [1934]. Prose message affixed.
Also uncollected prose and verse in bibliographical, biographical and critical studies, catalogues and Kipling Jnl 1927– (in progress). *See also the unauthorized pamphlets ptd privately (a few copies only) for E. W. Martindell and A. E. Ballard, of which bound vols are in Bodley with the titles* Flies in amber, More flies in amber, Still more flies in amber—*128 prose items, many not by Kipling. Most are drawn from the Indian papers and from* United Services College Chron *and* St James's Gazette.

Letters

Kipling's letters have not been collected. Books containing more than 2 or 3 are:
Letters from Kipling to Guy Paget 1919–36. 1936 (12 copies, priv ptd).
Carrington, C. E. Rudyard Kipling. 1955. Authorized biography.
Cohen, M. N. Kipling to Rider Haggard: the record of a friendship. 1965.
About 20 uncollected letters may be found in Kipling Jnl, *and usually not more than one in each of the following:*
Year boke of the sette of odd volumes. 1892.
Letters to A. P. Watt. 1892 (letter), 1893 (2), 1902 (3), 1924 (4).
Wilson, B. The tenth island. 1897.
The school budget: no 13. Horsmonden 1898 (rptd in Academy, Critic etc).
Bullen, F. T. The cruise of the 'Cachalot'. 1898.
Clemens, A. M. A ken of Kipling. New York 1899.
Knowles, F. W. A Kipling primer. Boston 1899.
Lawrence, A. Sir Arthur Sullivan. 1899.
Pond, J. H. Eccentricities of genius. New York 1900.
Joline, A. H. Meditations of an autograph collector. New York 1902.
Young, A. B. F. The complete motorist. 1904.
D'Humières, R. Through Isle and Empire. 1905. Rptd from newspapers.
The Times and the publishers. 1906 (priv ptd).
The surplus 1909 (Salvation Army pbn); 1913 (in Census surplus and Empire); 1924 (in The Salvation Army: British Empire exhibition handbook).
Stedman, L. and G. M. Gould. Life and letters of Edmund Clarence Stedman. New York 1910.
Harris, J. C. The life and letters of Joel Chandler Harris. New York 1918.
Bordeaux, H. Guynemer, knight of the air. 1918.
The Americanization of Edward Bok. New York 1920.
Proc Amer Acad of Arts & Letters 11 1921.
Maitland, E. M. The log of HMA R 34. 1921.
Johnson, R. U. Remembered yesterdays. 1923.
Leslie, S. Mark Sykes: his life and letters. 1923.
Trevelyan, J. P. The life of Mrs Humphry Ward. 1923.
Cushing, H. The life of William Osler. 1925.
Cook, T. A. The sunlit hours. New York 1925.
A letter from Kipling to Joseph Conrad. 1926.
Haggard, H. R. The days of my life. 1926.
Hall, A. V. South Africa and other poems. 1926.
Howells, M. Life and letters of William Dean Howells. New York 1928.
Lawrence, W. R. The India we served. 1928.
Lemperley, P. Among my books. Cleveland 1929.
Jones, D. A. The life and letters of Henry Arthur Jones. 1930.
Wise, T. J. The Ashley library vol 10. 1930. Letters to E. W. Gosse.
Trowbridge, U. and A. Marshall. John Lord Montagu of Beaulieu. 1930.
Phelps, W. L. Letters of James Whitcomb Riley. Indianapolis 1930.
Carpenter, W. M. (ed). A few significant and important Kipling items. Chicago 1930.
Catalogue of the works of Kipling exhibited at the Grolier Club. New York 1930.
Lucas, E. V. Postbag diversions. 1934.
Rice, H. C. Kipling in New England. Brattleboro 1936, 1951 (rev).

Letter to R. D. Bloomfield. Daily Express 18 Jan 1936.
Hillman, A. and W. W. Skeat. Salem the mouse-deer: wonder stories of the Malayan forest. 1938.
Catalogue of the William Inglis Morse collection. Dalhousie Univ Lib 1938.
Letter to G. B. Burgin. Daily Telegraph 4 Jan 1940; Kipling Jnl 53 1940.
Connell, J. Henley. 1949.
Carr, J. D. The life of Sir Arthur Conan Doyle. 1949.
Haggard, L. R. The cloak that I left. 1951.
Green, R. L. A. E. W. Mason. 1952.
Hovelaque, B. Lettres de guerre à André Chevrillon. Revue des Deux Mondes 15 Sept 1959.
Cohen, M. N. Rider Haggard: his life and works. 1960.

§2

For a fuller list see H. E. Gerber and E. S. Lauterbach, Kipling: an annotated bibliography of writings about him, English Fiction in Transition 3 1960 (*with* Supplement, 8 1965); *also the quarterly* Kipling Jnl 1927– (*in progress*) (*ed W. A Young 1927–31; B. M. Bazley 1932–9; E. D. W. Chaplin 1939–57; R. L. Green 1957–*).
Lang, A. [Three reviews 1886–9]; rptd Kipling Jnl 32 1965.
—— Mr Kipling's stories. In his Essays in little, 1891; rptd in Gilbert, below, 1965.
Barrie, J. M. Mr Kipling's stories. Contemporary Rev March 1891.
Gosse, E. W. Rudyard Kipling. Century Mag Oct 1891; rptd in his Questions at issue, 1893.
—— Wolcott Balestier. Century Mag April 1892; rptd in his Portraits and sketches, 1912.
James, H. [Introduction]. In Mine own people, New York 1891; rptd in his Views and reviews, 1908 and in Gilbert, below, 1965.
Lynd, R. The works of Kipling. Bookman (London) Oct 1891.
—— Traffics and mafficks: the strange case of Mr Kipling. Bookman Nov 1904.
Cope, G. The books of Kipling. GM Aug 1892.
Meynell, A. The soldier's poet. Merry England April 1893.
Crockett, S. R. On some tales of Mr Kipling's. Bookman (London) Feb 1895.
Robinson, E. K. Kipling in India. McClure's Mag 7 1896.
—— Rudyard Kipling as journalist. Literature 4 1899.
Howells, D. The laureate of the larger England. McClure's Mag 8 1897.
Murray, D. C. In his My contemporaries in fiction, 1897.
Forster's notebook of Kipling. Birmingham 1898.
Graz, F. Beiträge zu einer Kritik Kiplings. Leipzig 1898.
The works of Mr Kipling. Blackwood's Mag Oct 1898.
Clemens, W. M. A ken of Kipling. New York 1899.
Mansfield, M. F. and A. Wessels. Kiplingiana. New York 1899.
Lawton, W. C. Kipling the artist. New York 1899.
Livingston, L. S. Kipling's first book. New York 1899.
'Monkshood, G. F.' (W. J. Clarke). Kipling: an attempt at appreciation. 1899, 1913 (rev as Kipling: his life and work).
—— The less familiar Kipling and Kiplingiana. 1917, 1922 (rev), 1936 (rev).
Norton, C. E. Kipling: a biographical sketch. New York 1899.
Parker, W. B. The religion of Mr. Kipling. New York 1899.
Roberton, W. The Kipling guide book. Birmingham 1899.
Walker, A. H. Mr Kipling's schoolmasters and schoolboys. Bookman (London) June 1899.
Kinnosuké, A. A Japanese view of Kipling. Arena 21 1899.
Johnston, C. Rudyard Kipling. Calcutta Rev 109 1899.
Adams, F. W. L. In his Essays in modernity, 1899.
Knowles, F. L. A Kipling primer. Boston 1899.
Le Gallienne, R. Kipling: a criticism. 1900.
—— et al. Around the world with Kipling. 1926.
Dawborn, R. H. M. Opium in India: a medical interview with Kipling. Therapeutic Gazette (Detroit) 15 Nov 1900.
Dowden, E. The poetry of Mr Kipling. New Liberal Rev Feb 1901.
Russell, C. E. Are there two Kiplings? Cosmopolitan (New York) 31 1901.
de Vogüé, E. M. La littérature impérialiste: Disraeli et Kipling. Revue des Deux Mondes 1 May 1901.
Archer, W. In his Poets of the younger generation, 1902.
Powell, F. Y. Rudyard Kipling [with bibliography]. Eng Illustr Mag 30 1903.
Beerbohm, M. Kipling's entire. Saturday Rev 14 Feb 1903; rptd in his Around theatres, 1953.
Gwynn, S. Mr Kipling as poet and prophet. Pilot 8 1903.
Freeman, L. R. The inimitable cruelty of Kipling. Overland Monthly (San Francisco) April 1904.
Dalrymple, C. M. Kiplings Prosa. Marburg 1905.
Chesterton, G. K. In his Heretics, 1905.
Stoddard, C. W. Kipling at Naulahka. Nat Mag 22 1905.
Marcosson, I. F. Rudyard Kipling. Book News Monthly Dec 1906.
Millard, F. B. How Kipling discovered America. Bookman (New York) Jan 1908.
Leeb-Lundberg, W. Word-formation in Kipling. Lund 1909, Cambridge 1909.
London, J. 'These bones shall rise again'. In his Revolution and other essays, New York 1910.
Charles, C. Kipling: his life and works. 1911.
Young, W. A. A dictionary of the characters and scenes in the stories and poems of Kipling 1886–1911. 1911, 1921 (rev); rev J. H. McGrivring 1967 (as A Kipling dictionary).
Hooker, W. B. The later works of Mr Kipling. North Amer Rev May 1911.
Forbes, E. A. Across India with Kim. World's Work (Chicago) 24 1912.
Durand, R. A handbook to the poetry of Kipling. 1914.
Sarath-Roy, A. R. Kipling seen through Hindu eyes. North Amer Rev Feb 1914.
Falls, C. Kipling: a critical study. 1915.
Munson, A. Kipling's India. New York 1915.
Palmer, J. L. Rudyard Kipling, 1915.
Hopkins, R. T. Kipling: a literary appreciation. 1915.
—— Kipling: a character study: life, writings and literary landmarks. 1915, 1921 (rev).
—— Kipling's Sussex. 1921, 1924 (rev as The Kipling country).
—— Kipling's Sussex revisited. 1929.
—— Kipling: the story of a genius. 1930.
Matthews, B. These many years. New York 1917.
Harris, F. Rudyard Kipling. Pearson's Mag 37 1917; rptd in his Contemporary portraits, New York 1919 (priv ptd).
Hart, W. M. Kipling the story teller. Berkeley 1918.
Hutton, M. Kipling. McGill Univ Mag 17 1918; rptd in his Many minds, New York 1928.
Gerould, K. F. The remarkable rightness of Kipling. Atlantic Monthly Jan 1918.
—— The man who made Mulvaney. Harper's Mag April 1936.
Sherwood, J. B. Kipling's women. Fine Arts Jnl (Chicago) 37 1919.
Chevrillon, A. La poésie de Kipling. Revue des Deux Mondes 15 April 1920; rptd in his Three studies in English literature, 1923.
—— Rudyard Kipling. Paris 1936.
Worster, W. J. A. Merlin's isle: a study of Kipling's England. [1921].

Waterhouse, F. A. The literary fortunes of Kipling. Yale Rev 10 1921; rptd (rev) in his Random studies in the romantic chaos, New York 1923.
Legouis, E. Kipling: revue politique et littéraire. Revue Bleue 9 1921.
Johnson, L. In his Reviews and critical papers, 1921. 3 reviews.
Gilmer, H. W. The classical element in the poems of Kipling. Classical Weekly 25 April 1921.
Ferguson, J. de L. Kipling's revisions of his published works. Urbana 1923.
—— The education of Kipling. Education 44 1924.
—— 'The pen took charge'. New Colophon 1 1948.
Kinsella, E. P. Impressions of Kipling. Strand Mag 65 1923.
Braybrooke, P. Kipling and his soldiers. 1925.
Cooper, A. P. Rudyard Kipling. New York 1926.
Dobrée, B. Rudyard Kipling. Criterion 6 1927; rptd in his Lamp and the lute, Oxford 1929 and in Gilbert, below, 1965.
—— Rudyard Kipling. 1951.
—— Kipling: realist and fabulist. 1967.
Dunsterville, L. C. Stalky's reminiscences. 1928.
Carpenter, W. M. Kipling's college. Evanston 1929.
Brion, M. Rudyard Kipling. Paris [1929].
Williams, C. In his Poetry at present, Oxford 1930.
Garland, H. Roadside meetings. New York 1930.
Marquardt, H. Kipling und Indien. Breslau 1931.
Thirkell, A. Three houses. Oxford 1931.
Weynants-Ronday, M. Kipling et l'Egypte. Chronique d'Egypte (Brussels) 6 1931.
Stevenson, L. The ideas in Kipling's poetry. UTQ 1 1932.
Green, H. M. Kipling as a journalist. Australian Quart 13 1932.
—— Kipling as a verse maker. Australian Quart 16 1932.
Brulé, A. Une leçon de style: les variantes du Livre de la jungle. Revue Anglo-américaine June 1932.
MacMunn, G. Kipling's women. 1933.
—— Kipling: craftsman. 1937.
Nazari, E. Kipling: saggio critico. Palermo 1933.
Tapp, H. A. United Services College 1874–1911. Aldershot 1933; supplement, Cheshunt 1960.
Berlage, H. Über das englische Soldatenlied, mit besonderer Berücksichtigung der Soldatenlieder Kiplings. Emsdetten 1933.
Keiseritsky, H. von. Englische Tierdichtung: eine Untersuchung über Kipling, Charles G. D. Roberts und Ernest Thompson Setôn. Jena 1935.
Thibault-Chambault. Kipling et les animaux sauvages. Saint-Lô 1935.
Maurois, A. Kipling. Revue Hebdomadaire 9 Feb 1935.
Beresford, G. C. Schooldays with Kipling. 1936.
Rice, H. C. Kipling in New England. Brattleboro 1936, 1951 (rev).
—— Into the hold of remembrance: notes on Kipling material in the Doubleday collection. Princeton Univ Lib Chron 22 1961; rptd Kipling Jnl 28 1961.
Rosati, S. Kipling. Nuova Anthologia 383 1936.
'Kingsmill, Hugh' (H. K. Lunn). Rudyard Kipling. Eng Rev Feb 1936.
Hooper, C. F. Kipling's younger days. Saturday Rev 7 March 1936.
Hill, E. T. The young Kipling. Atlantic Monthly April 1936.
—— My friend Kipling. Classmate 45 1938.
Gillet, L. Rudyard Kipling. Revue des Deux Mondes 1 Feb 1936.
Fechter, P. Imperialismus und Dichtung: zum Tode Kiplings. Deutsche Rundschau 246 1936.
Colvin, I. Rudyard Kipling. Nat Rev Feb 1936.
Charnwood, Lord. Rudyard Kipling. Eng Rev March 1936.
Chaigne, L. R. Kipling parmi les hommes. Etudes May 1936.
Mason, J. S. A Yale footnote to Kipling. New Haven 1937.
Van de Water, F. Kipling's Vermont feud. Weston Vermont 1937.
Voltan, C. The allegorical world of beast in Kipling. Teramana 1937.
Rowbotham, A. H. Kipling and France. French Rev 10 1937.
Collins, J. P. Kipling at Lahore. Nineteenth Century Jan 1937.
Mehrota, K. Kipling and 'the bubble reputation'. Essays & Stud (Allahabad) 1938.
Weygandt, A. M. Kipling's reading and its influence on his poetry. Philadelphia 1939.
—— A study of Kipling's use of historical material in Brother Square-toes and A priest in spite of himself. Delaware Notes 27 1955; rptd in Kipling Jnl 22–3 1955–6.
Feilhauer, L. Das Gentlemanideal bei Kipling. Marburg 1939.
Lemonnier, L. Kipling. Paris 1939.
Fleming, A. M. Some childhood memories of Kipling by his sister. Chambers's Jnl March 1939.
—— More childhood memories of Kipling. Chambers's Jnl July 1939.
Haward, E. Kipling myths and traditions in India. Nineteenth Century Feb 1939.
Merther, E. Das Prosawerk Kiplings. Berlin 1940.
Shanks, E. Kipling: a study in literature and political ideas. 1940.
Milner, V. Mrs Rudyard Kipling. Nat Rev Feb 1940.
Mabbott, T. O. Kipling at Gloucester Mass. N & Q April 1940.
Renwick, W. L. Re-reading Kipling. Durham Univ Jnl 32 1940; rptd in Rutherford, below, 1964.
Braddy, N. Kipling, son of empire. New York 1941.
Wilson, E. The Kipling that nobody read. Atlantic Monthly Feb 1941; rptd in his Wound and the bow, Boston 1941, in Rutherford 1964 and in Gilbert 1965, below.
Clemens, C. A chat with Kipling. Dalhousie Rev 21 1941.
Ponton, D. Kipling at home. 1942, 1953 (rev as Kipling at home and at work).
Carpenter, L. R. Kipling: a friendly profile. Chicago 1942.
'Orwell George', (E. Blair). Rudyard Kipling. Horizon Feb 1942; rptd in his Critical essays, 1946, and in Rutherford 1964 and in Gilbert 1965, below.
Ford, B. A case for Kipling? Scrutiny 11 1942; rptd in Gilbert, below, 1965.
Cookson, G. T. S. Eliot on Kipling. English 4 1942.
Wells, H. W. Kipling's barrack-room language. Amer Speech 18 1943.
Trilling, L. Mr Eliot's Kipling. Nation (New York) 16 Oct 1943; rptd in Rutherford 1964 and Gilbert 1965, below.
Morgan, C. Communication with Keats; Menander's mirror. TLS 24 April 1943.
—— The house of Macmillan. 1944.
Auden, W. H. The poet of encirclement. New Republic 25 Oct 1943.
Kernahan, C. 'Nothing quite like Kipling had happened before'. 1944.
McLuhan, H. M. Kipling and Forster. Sewanee Rev 52 1944.
Brown, H. Kipling: a new appreciation. 1945.
Croft-Cooke, R. Rudyard Kipling. 1948.
Lewis, C. S. Kipling's world. In Literature and life, 1948 (Eng Assoc), Kipling Jnl 25 1958; rptd in his They asked for a paper, 1962 and in Gilbert, below, 1965.
D., A. A note on Rider Haggard and Kipling. N & Q 12 Nov 1949.
Connell, J. Rudyard Kipling. Nat Rev 135 1950.

Penzoldt, P. In his Supernatural in fiction, 1952.
Hill, D. L. Kipling in Vermont. Nineteenth-Century Fiction 7 1953; Kipling Jnl 30 1963.
Trevelyan, G. M. In his Layman's love of letters, 1954; rptd Kipling Jnl 19 1954 (in part).
MacCarthy, D. In his Memories, 1953.
Edwardes, M. Kipling and the imperial imagination. Twentieth Century June 1953.
Carrington, C. E. Kipling: his life and work. 1955. The authorized biography.
Escarpit, R. Kipling: servitudes et grandeurs impériales. Paris 1955.
Birkenhead, Earl of. The young Kipling. Trans Royal Soc of Lit 27 1955.
—— Kipling and the Vermont feud. Trans Royal Soc of Lit 30 1961.
Miller, B. Kipling's first novel. Cornhill Mag 168 1956.
Yeats, A. W. Kipling twenty years after. Dalhousie Rev 36 1956.
MacKendrick, P. Kipling and the nature of the classical. Classical Jnl Nov 1956.
Léaud, F. Du nouveau sur Kipling. Etudes Anglais 9 1956.
—— La poétique de Kipling. Paris 1958.
Hollis, C. Kim and the apolitical man. Spectator 6 July 1956; rptd Kipling Jnl 23 1956.
Eliot, T. S. In praise of Kipling. In his On poetry and poets, 1957. Rev preface to A choice of Kipling's verse, 1941.
—— Rudyard Kipling. Mercure de France Jan 1959; rev in Kipling Jnl 26 1959, rptd Gilbert, below, 1965.
Chaudhuri, N. C. The finest story about India in English. Encounter April 1957; rptd in Kipling Jnl 28 1961.
Bushnell, N. S. Kipling's ken of India. UTQ 27 1957.
Tompkins, J. M. S. The art of Kipling. 1959, 1965 (rev).
Kaplan, I. Kipling's first visit to America. Dalhousie Rev 39 1959.
Baldwin, A. W. The Macdonald sisters. 1960.
Sutcliff, R. Rudyard Kipling. 1960.
Annan, N. Kipling's place in the history of ideas. Victorian Stud 3 1960; rptd in Rutherford, below, 1964.
Crouch, M. Puck country. Junior Bookshelf 24 1960.
Harbord, R. E. et al. The reader's guide to Kipling's work. 5 vols 1961–7 (priv ptd).
Pearson, H. Caroline Balestier. In his Pilgrim daughters, 1961.
Gilbert, E. L. What happens in Mrs Bathurst. PMLA 77 1962; rptd in Kipling Jnl 30 1963.
—— The aesthetics of violence. Eng Lit in Transition 7 1964.
Solomon, E. The light that failed as a war novel. Eng Lit in Transition 5 1962.
Jarrell, R. On preparing to read Kipling. Amer Scholar 31 1962.
Bateman's, Sussex. 1963. Anon.
Stewart, J. I. M. In his Eight modern writers, Oxford 1963 (OHEL vol 12).
—— Rudyard Kipling. New York 1966, London 1967.
Deutsch, K. W. and N. Wiener. The lonely nationalism of Kipling. Yale Rev 52 1963.
Bodelsen, C. A. Aspects of Kipling's art. Manchester 1964.
—— Wireless and Kaspar's song: a Kipling problem. E Studies 46 1965.
Rutherford, A. (ed). Kipling's mind and art. Edinburgh 1964. 5 rptd essays of 1940–60, and 6 new.
Munro, J. Kipling's Kim and co-existence. Ibid.
Bauer, H. C. The centenary of Masonry's cherished verbalist Kipling. Masonic Papers (Seattle) 3 1964.
Husain, S. S. Kipling and India. Dacca 1964.
Manley, S. Kipling: creative adventurer. New York 1965.
Cohen, M. N. Kipling to Rider Haggard: the record of a friendship. 1965.
Gilbert, E. L. (ed). Kipling and the critics. New York 1965, London 1965. 14 rptd essays of 1891–1962, one new.
Green, R. L. Kipling and the children. 1965.
—— (ed). Kipling Jnl: centenary no Dec 1965. Contributions by E. Blunden, R. Sutcliff, C. E. Carrington, B. Dobrée, J. M. S. Tompkins, G. C. Carter, M. N. Cohen, E. L. Gilbert, N. Coghill et al.
Potter, P. Kipling: a re-assessment. Listener 8 April 1965.
Dunman, J. Kipling re-estimated. Marxism Today Aug 1965–Feb 1966.
Rowse, A. L. Blowing Kipling's trumpet. Sunday Telegraph 19 Dec 1965.
Lloyd, R. Kipling. Church Times 31 Dec 1965.
Cornell, L. L. Kipling in India. 1966.
Faber, R. The vision and the need: late Victorian imperialist aims. 1967.
Rao, K. B. Kipling's India. Norman Oklahoma 1967.
Sandison, A. The wheel of Empire. 1967.
Trewin, J. C. Kipling and the theatre. E & S new ser 18 1967.

R. L. G.

VII. MINOR FICTION 1870–1900

This section has been restricted to writers born between 1830 and 1865 whose more important works were written before 1900.

GRANT ALLEN, i.e. CHARLES GRANT BLAIRFINDIE ALLEN

1848–99

§1

Physiological aesthetics. 1877.
The colour-sense: its origin and development. 1879.
Early Britain: Anglo-Saxon Britain. [1881].
The evolutionist at large. 1881.
Vignettes from nature. 1881.
The colours of flowers, as illustrated in the British flora. 1882.
Colin Clout's calendar, April–October. 1883.
Flowers and their pedigrees. 1883.
Nature studies. [1883]. With Andrew Wilson, Thomas Foster, Edward Clodd and R. A. Proctor.
Biographies of working men. 1884.
Philistia. 3 vols 1884. Pbd under the pseudonym 'Cecil Power'.
Strange stories. 1884.
Babylon. 3 vols 1885. Pbd under the pseudonym 'Cecil Power'.
Darwin. 1885.
The miscellaneous and posthumous works of H. T. Buckle. [1885]. Ed Allen.
Kalee's shrine. Bristol 1886. With May Cotes.
In all shades. 3 vols 1886.

The sole trustee. [1886].
For Maimie's sake: a tale of love and dynamite. 1886.
The beckoning hand and other stories. 1887.
A terrible inheritance. [1887].
Commonsense science. Boston 1887.
Force and energy: a theory of dynamics. 1888.
This mortal coil: a novel. 3 vols 1888.
The white man's foot. 1888.
The devil's die: a novel. 3 vols 1888.
Falling in love, with other essays. 1889.
The tents of Shem: a novel. 3 vols 1889. Contains 16 stories first pbd in Cornhill Mag, Longman's Mag and Belgravia, under the pseudonym 'J. Arbuthnot Wilson'.
Dr Palliser's patient. 1889.
The jaws of death. [1889].
A living apparition. [1889].
The great taboo. 1890.
Recalled to life. Bristol [1891].
What's bred in the bone. 1891.
Dumaresq's daughter: a novel. 3 vols 1891.
The Duchess of Powysland: a novel. 3 vols 1892.
Science in Arcady. 1892.
The tidal Thames. 1892.
The Attis of Caius Valerius Catullus, translated into English verse. 1892.
The scallywag. 3 vols 1893.
Michael's Cray. 1893.
Ivan Greet's masterpiece and other stories. 1893.
Blood Royal: a novel. 1893.
An army doctor's romance. [1893].
At market value. 2 vols 1894.
The lower slopes. 1894. Poems.
Post-prandial philosophy. 1894. First pbd in Westminster Gazette.
In memoriam G. P. Macdonell. 1895.
The British barbarians: a hill-top novel. 1895.
The story of the plants. 1895.
The woman who did. 1895.
Under sealed orders: a novel. 3 vols 1895.
Moorland idylls. 1896.
A splendid sin. 1896.
An African millionaire. 1897.
The evolution of the idea of God. 1897.
Cities of Belgium. 1897.
Florence. 1897.
Paris. 1897.
Tom unlimited: a story for children. 1897. Pbd under the pseudonym 'Martin Leach Warborough'.
The type-writer girl. 1897. Pbd under the pseudonym 'Olive Pratt Rayner'.
Linnet: a romance. 1898.
The incidental Bishop. [1898].
Venice. 1898.
The European tour: a handbook for Americans and colonists. 1899.
Flashlights on nature. 1899.
Rosalba: the story of her development. 1899. Pbd under the pseudonym 'Olive Pratt Rayner'.
Miss Cayley's adventures. 1899.
Twelve tales: selected stories. 1899.
Hilda Wade. 1900. First pbd in Strand Mag.
The natural history of Selborne, by Gilbert White. 1900. Ed Allen.
Sir Theodore's guest and other stories. Bristol 1902.
The desire of the eyes and other stories. nd.
Evolution in Italian art. 1908.

§2

Harrison, F. Grant Allen. 1899.
Clodd, E. Grant Allen: a memoir, with a list of writings. 1900.
Le Gallienne, R. In his Attitudes and avowals, 1910.

'F. ANSTEY', THOMAS ANSTEY GUTHRIE

1856–1934

Bibliographies

Turner, M. J. A bibliography of the works of F. Anstey (Thomas Anstey Guthrie). 1931 (priv ptd).

Collections

Humour and fantasy. 1931. Includes Vice versa; The tinted Venus; A fallen idol; The brass bottle; The talking horse; Salted almonds.

§1

Vice versa: or a lesson to fathers. 1882, 1883 (rev), 1894 (with addns).
The giant's robe. 1884.
The black poodle and other tales. 1884.
The tinted Venus. Bristol 1885.
A fallen idol. 1886.
Burglar Bill and other pieces. [1888], [1892] (enlarged as The young reciter); ed C. L. Graves 1931 (with Mr Punch's model music-hall songs and dramas, below).
The parish. 3 vols 1889.
Voces populi. 2 sers 1890–2. From Punch.
Tourmalin's time cheques. Bristol 1891, 1905 (as The time bargain: or Tourmalin's time cheques).
The travelling companions. 1892, 1908 (rev).
Mr Punch's model music-hall songs and dramas. 1892.
The talking horse and other tales. 1892.
Mr Punch's pocket Ibsen. 1893, 1895 (enlarged).
The man from Blankley's and other sketches, 1893. From Punch.
Under the rose: a story in scenes [from Punch]. [1894].
Lyre and lancet: a story in scenes. 1895.
Puppets at large: scenes and subjects from Mr Punch's show. 1897.
Baboo Jabberjee BA. 1897. From Punch.
Love among the lions. 1898. From Idler Mag.
Paleface and Redskin, and other stories for boys and girls. [1898].
The brass bottle. 1900. From Strand Mag.
A Bayard from Bengal. 1902. From Punch.
Only toys! 1903. From Strand Mag.
Salted almonds and other tales. 1906.
In brief authority. 1915.
Percy and others: sketches, mainly reproduced from Punch. 1915.
The last load: stories and essays. 1925.
Four Molière comedies, freely adapted. 1931.
Three Molière plays, freely adapted. 1933.
A long retrospect. Oxford 1936.

SABINE BARING-GOULD

1834–1924

§1

The path of the just: tales of holy men and children. 1857.
Iceland: its scenes and sagas. 1863.
The book of were wolves: being an account of a terrible superstition. 1865.
Post-mediaeval preachers. 1865.
Curious myths of the Middle Ages. 2 sers 1866–8.
The silver store, collected from mediaeval, Christian and Jewish mines. 1868, 1887 (with addns), 1898 (with addns). Poems.
Through flood and flame: a novel. 3 vols 1868.
Curiosities of the olden times. [1869].
Origin and development of religious belief. 2 pts 1869–70.
In exitu Israel: an historical novel. 2 vols 1870.

The lives of the saints. 17 vols 1872–89, 16 vols 1897–8 (rev).
Yorkshire oddities, incidents and strange events. 2 vols 1874.
Some modern difficulties. 1875.
The Vicar of Morwenstow: life of R. S. Hawker. 1876, 1876 (rev), 1899 (rev).
Ernestine: a novel, by Wilhelmine von Hillern. 1879. Tr from the German by Baring-Gould.
Germany past and present. 2 vols 1879.
Mehalah: a story of the salt marshes. 2 vols 1880.
John Herring: a West of England romance. 3 vols 1883, 1884.
Please tell me a tale: a collection of short original stories for children. 1885. Baring-Gould contributed Gottlob's picture.
Just one more tale: a second collection of stories for children, being a companion volume to Please tell me a tale. 1886. Baring-Gould contributed Wow Wow.
Court Royal. 3 vols 1886.
Germany. 1886, [1905] (rev), 1921 (rev and enlarged by J. MacCabe).
Little Tu'penny. 1887.
Jack Frost's little prisoners. 1887. With other stories.
Red spider. 2 vols 1887.
The Gaverocks: a tale of the Cornish coast. 3 vols 1887.
Richard Cable the lightshipman. 3 vols 1888.
Eve: a novel. 2 vols 1888.
The Pennycomequicks: a novel. 3 vols 1889.
Grettir the outlaw: a story of Iceland. 1889.
Historic oddities and strange events. [Freaks of Fanaticism and other strange events]. 2 vols 1889–91.
Arminell: a social romance. 3 vols 1890.
Jacquetta and other stories. 1890.
My Prague pig and other stories for children. 1890.
Old country life. 1890.
In troubadour land: Provence and Languedoc. 1891.
Urith: a tale of Dartmoor. 3 vols 1891.
Margery of Quether and other stories. 1891.
In the roar of the sea: a tale of the Cornish coast. 3 vols 1892.
Strange survivals. 1892.
Through all the changing scenes of life: a tale. [1892].
The tragedy of the Caesars. 2 vols 1892.
Mrs Curgenven of Curgenven: a novel. 3 vols 1893.
Cheap Jack Zita. 3 vols 1893.
A book of fairy tales retold. 1894.
Colour in composition. In On the art of writing fiction, [1894].
The deserts of southern France. 2 vols 1894.
The Icelander's sword, or the story of Oraefadal. 1894.
Kitty alone: a story of three fires. 3 vols 1894.
The Queen of love: a novel. 3 vols 1894.
English minstrelsie. 1895–9.
A book of nursery songs and rhymes. [1895]. Ed Baring-Gould.
A garland of country song: English folk song. 1895.
Fairy tales from Grimm. 1895. Introd by Baring-Gould.
Noemi. 1895.
Dartmoor idylls. 1896.
The broom squire. 1896.
Perpetua: a story of Nimes in AD 213. 1897.
Guasvas the tinner. 1897.
Bladys of the Stewponey. 1897.
Life of Napoleon. 1897.
A study of St Paul. 1897.
Domitia: a tale. 1898.
An old English home and its dependencies. 1898.
A book of the West: introduction to Devon and Cornwall. 2 vols 1899.
Pabo the priest. 1899.
The crock of gold. [1899]. Fairy tales.
Furze bloom: tales of the western moors. 1899.
A book of Dartmoor. 1900.
Winefred: a story of the chalk cliffs. 1900.

In a quiet village: tales. 1900.
A book of Brittany. 1901.
Bath waters, by Preston King, with an historical sketch by S. Baring-Gould. [1901].
The Frobishers: a story of the Staffordshire potteries. 1901.
Royal Georgie. 1901.
Brittany. 1902.
Nebo the nailer. 1902.
Miss Quillet: a novel. 1902.
Chris of all sorts. 1903.
Amazing adventures, drawn by H. B. Neilson and written by S. Baring-Gould. [1903].
A book of North Wales. 1903.
A book of ghosts. 1904.
Siegfried: a romance. 1904. Founded on Wagner's operas.
In Dewisland: a novel. 1904.
A book of South Wales. 1905.
A book of the Riviera. 1905.
Monsieur Pichelmère and other stories. 1905.
A book of the Rhine. 1906.
Lives of the British saints. 1907. [With J. Fisher].
A book of the Cevennes. 1907.
A book of the Pyrenees. 1907.
Devonshire characters and strange events. 1908.
Cornish characters and strange events. 1909.
A history of Sarawak under its two white Rajahs 1839–1908. 1909.
Family names and their story. 1910.
The land of Teck and its neighbourhood. 1911.
Cliff castles and cave dwellings of Europe. 1911.
Sheepstor. [Plymouth] 1912.
A book of folk lore. [1913].
Early reminiscences 1834–64. 1923.
Further reminiscences 1864–94. 1925.
Baring-Gould also wrote a number of devotional and theological works, and contributed introds to several books on folk-lore and theology. A few ephemeral works are unrecorded here.

§2

Ellis, S. M. In his Mainly Victorian, [1925].
Powys, L. A Devonshire gentleman. North Amer Rev 121 1925.
Purcell, W. Onward Christian soldier: a life of Sabine Baring-Gould. 1957.
Reeves, J. The everlasting circle. 1960.
Hyde, W. J. The stature of Baring-Gould as a novelist. Nineteenth-Century Fiction 15 1961.

SIR JAMES MATTHEW BARRIE
1860–1937

See col 1188, below.

ARTHUR CHRISTOPHER BENSON
1862–1925

See col 1420, below.

SIR WALTER BESANT
1836–1901

§1

Studies in early French poetry. 1868.
Jerusalem: the city of Herod and Saladin. 1871. With E. H. Palmer.
The French humourists. 1873.

The literary remains of C. F. T. Drake. 1877. Ed Besant, with a memoir.
Constantinople. 1879. With W. J. Brodribb.
Gaspard de Coligny. 1879.
Rabelais. 1879.
The survey of western Palestine. By C. R. Condor 1881. Ed E. H. Palmer and Besant.
The revolt of man. 1882.
All sorts and conditions of men. 3 vols 1882.
All in a garden fair. 3 vols 1883.
The captain's room. 3 vols 1883.
The life and achievements of E. H. Palmer. 1883.
Life in an hospital: an East End chapter. [1883].
Readings in Rabelais. 1883.
The art of fiction: a lecture. 1884.
Dorothy Forster. 3 vols 1884.
Uncle Jack [etc]. 1885. 5 tales.
Children of Gibeon. 3 vols 1886.
Twenty-one years' work 1865–86. 1886 (Palestine Exploration Fund), 1895 (with addns).
Katherine Regina. Bristol [1887].
The world went very well then. 3 vols 1887.
Herr Paulus. 3 vols 1888.
The inner house. Bristol 1888.
The eulogy of Richard Jefferies. 1888.
Fifty years ago. 1888.
The doubts of Dives. Bristol [1889]; rptd in Verbena camellia stephanotis, below, 1892.
The bell of St Paul's. 3 vols 1889.
For faith and freedom. 3 vols 1889.
To call her mine, etc. 1889.
Armorel of Lyonesse. 3 vols 1890.
Captain Cook. 1890.
The demoniac. Bristol [1890].
The holy rose, etc. 1890.
St Katherine's by the Tower. 3 vols 1891.
Verbena camellia stephanotis etc. 1892. The doubts of Dives and 2 short stories.
The ivory gate. 3 vols 1892.
London. 1892.
The history of London. 1893.
The Society of Authors. 1893.
The rebel Queen. 3 vols 1893.
Beyond the dreams of avarice. 1895.
In deacon's orders, etc. 1895.
Westminster. 1895.
The charm and other drawing room plays. 1896. With W. Pollock.
The city of refuge. 3 vols 1896.
The master craftsman. 2 vols 1896.
A fountain sealed. 1897.
The rise of the Empire. [1897].
Alfred: a lecture. 1898.
The changeling. 1898.
The orange girl. 1899.
The pen and the book. 1899.
South London. 1899.
The fourth generation. 1900.
East London. 1901.
The Lady of Lynn. 1901.
The story of King Alfred. 1901.
Autobiography. 1902.
A five year's tryst and other stories. 1902.
London in the eighteenth century. 1902.
The fascination of London series. 11 vols 1902–6. Ed Besant, who collaborated with G. E. Mitton for the Strand, Westminster and Holborn-Bloomsbury vols.
No other way. 1902.
The survey of London. 10 vols 1902–12. Ed Besant.
London in the time of the Stuarts. 1903.
As we are and as we may be. 1903. Essays.
Essays and historiettes. 1903.
The Thames. 1903.
London in the time of the Tudors. 1904.
Mediaeval London. 2 vols 1906.
Early London: Prehistoric, Roman, Saxon and Norman. 1908.
London in the nineteenth century. 1909.
London south of the Thames. 1912.

Fiction (in collaboration with James Rice)

Ready-money Mortiboy. 3 vols 1872. Dramatic version, as Ready money, by Rice and W. Maurice, was produced at the Court Theatre, 12 March 1874.
My little girl. 3 vols 1873.
The golden butterfly. 3 vols 1876.
The case of Mr Lucraft and other tales. 2 vols 1876.
This son of Vulcan. 3 vols 1876.
With harp and crown. 1877.
Such a good man. 1877.
The monks of Thelema. 3 vols 1878. First pbd in World.
By Celia's arbour. 3 vols 1878. First pbd in Graphic.
'Twas in Trafalgar Bay and other stories. 1879.
The seamy side. 3 vols 1880. First pbd in Time.
The chaplain of the fleet. 3 vols 1881.
Sir Richard Whittington. 1881.
The ten years' tenant and other stories. 3 vols 1881.
Besant also contributed introds to works by Charles Reade, Defoe, J. H. Round et al.

§2

Vollenweider, J. Besants soziales Fühlen und Denken. Tubenthal 1927.
Boege, F. W. Besant, novelist. Nineteenth-Century Fiction 10–11 1956–7.
Boll, E. Besant on the art of the novel. Eng Fiction in Transition 2 1959.

WILLIAM BLACK
1841–98

Collections

New and revised edition of the novels. 28 vols 1892–8.

§1

Love or marriage. 3 vols 1868.
In silk attire. 3 vols 1869.
Kilmeny. 3 vols 1870.
The monarch of Mincing Lane. 3 vols 1871.
A daughter of Heth. 3 vols 1871.
Mr Pisistratus Brown MP in the Highlands. 1871. Rptd from Daily News with addns.
The strange adventures of a phaeton. 2 vols 1872.
A Princess of Thule. 3 vols 1874.
The maid of Killeena and other stories. 1874, 1892 (as The maid of Killeena and the marriage of Moira Fergus).
Three feathers. 3 vols 1875.
Madcap Violet. 3 vols 1876.
Lady Silverdale's sweetheart and other stories. 1876.
Green pastures and Piccadilly. 3 vols 1877.
Macleod of Dare. 3 vols 1878.
Oliver Goldsmith. 1878 (EML).
White wings. 3 vols 1880.
Sunrise. 3 vols 1881.
The beautiful wretch; The four Macnicols; The pupil of Aurelius. 3 vols 1881.
Yolande. 3 vols 1883.
Adventures in Thule: three stories for boys. 1883.
Shandon Bells. 3 vols 1883.
Judith Shakespere. 3 vols 1884.
White heather. 3 vols 1885.
The wise women of Inverness and other miscellanies. 1885.
Sabine Zembra. 3 vols 1887.

In far Lochaber. 3 vols 1888.
Strange adventures of a house-boat. 3 vols 1888.
The penance of John Logan and two other stories. 1889.
Nanciebel: a tale of Stratford-on-Avon. New York 1889.
The new Prince Fortunatus. 3 vols 1890.
Stand fast, Craig Royston! 3 vols 1890.
Donald Ross of Heimra. 3 vols 1891.
Wolfenburg. 3 vols 1892.
The magic inkstand and other tales. 1892.
The handsome Humes. 3 vols 1893.
Highland cousins. 3 vols 1894.
Briseis. 1896.
Wild Eelin. 1898.
With the eyes of youth, and other sketches. 1903.

§2

Reid, T. W. William Black, novelist: a biography. 1902.
'Melville, Lewis' (L. S. Benjamin). In his Victorian novelists, 1906.
Scene and sentiment: Black reaches his centenary. TLS 8 Nov 1941.

MARY ELIZABETH BRADDON, later MAXWELL
1837–1915

§1

Garibaldi and other poems. 1861.
Three times dead: or the secret of the heath. [1854], 1861 (as The trail of the serpent: or the secret of the heath). First ptd in penny pts, undated.
Lady Lisle. 1861.
Captain of the Vulture. 1862.
Lady Audley's secret. 3 vols 1862. First ptd in Robin Goodfellow and Sixpenny Mag.
Ralph the bailiff and other tales. [1862].
Eleanor's victory. 3 vols 1863.
Aurora Floyd. 3 vols 1863.
John Marchmont's legacy. 3 vols 1863.
The doctor's wife. 3 vols 1864.
Henry Dunbar: the story of an outcast. 2 vols 1864.
Only a clod. 3 vols 1865.
Sir Jasper's tenant. 3 vols 1865.
The lady's mile. 3 vols 1866.
Birds of prey. 3 vols 1867.
Rupert Godwin. 3 vols 1867.
Dead Sea fruit. 3 vols 1868.
Charlotte's inheritance. 3 vols 1868.
Run to earth. 3 vols 1868.
Fenton's quest: a novel. 3 vols 1871.
The Lovels of Arden. 3 vols 1871.
The summer tourist: a book for long and short journeys. 1871. Ed Miss Braddon.
Robert Ainsleigh. 3 vols 1872.
To the bitter end. 3 vols 1872.
Lucius Davoren, or publicans and sinners: a novel. 3 vols 1873.
Milly Darrell and other tales. 3 vols 1873.
Strangers and pilgrims. 3 vols 1873.
Taken at the flood: a novel. 3 vols 1874.
Lost for love: a novel. 3 vols 1874.
Hostages to fortune. 3 vols 1875.
A strange world. 3 vols 1875.
Dead men's shoes. 3 vols 1876.
Put to the test. 1876. Ed Miss Braddon.
Joshua Haggard's daughter. 3 vols 1876.
Weavers and weft, and other tales. 3 vols 1877.
Only a woman. 1878. Ed Miss Braddon.
An open verdict. 3 vols 1878.
The cloven foot: a novel. 3 vols 1879.
Vixen: a novel. 3 vols 1879.
Aladdin: or the wonderful lamp. [1880]. Rev Miss Braddon.
Just as I am: a novel. 3 vols [1880].
The missing witness: an original drama in four acts. [1880].
The story of Barbara: a novel. 3 vols [1880].
Asphodel. 3 vols 1881.
Dross, or the root of evil: a comedy in four acts. [1882].
Married beneath him: a comedy in four acts. [1882].
Marjorie Daw: a household idyl in two acts. [1882].
Mount Royal: a novel. 3 vols 1882.
Phantom fortune. 3 vols 1883.
Married in haste. [1883].
The golden calf: a novel. 3 vols 1883.
Under the red flag. 1884.
Ishmael. 3 vols [1884].
Wyllard's weird. 3 vols [1885].
One thing needful: a novel. 3 vols 1886.
Cut by the county. 1886.
Mohawks. 3 vols [1886].
Like and unlike. 3 vols 1887.
The fatal three. 3 vols [1888].
The day will come. 3 vols [1889].
One life, one love. 3 vols 1890.
Gerard, or the world, the flesh and the devil: a novel. 3 vols 1891.
The Venetians. 3 vols 1892.
All along the river: a novel. 3 vols 1893.
Thou art the man. 3 vols [1894].
Sons of fire. 3 vols [1896].
London pride: or when the world was younger. [1896].
Under love's rule. 1897.
Rough justice. [1898].
In high places. 1898.
His darling sin. [1899].
The infidel: a story of the great revival. [1900].
The conflict. 1903.
A lost Eden. 1904.
The rose of life. 1905.
The white house. 1906.
Her convict. 1907.
Dead love has chains. 1907.
During Her Majesty's pleasure. 1908.
Our adversary. 1909.
Beyond these voices. 1910.
The green curtain. 1911.
Miranda. 1913.
Mary. 1916.
Flower and weed, and other tales. Nd.
Miss Braddon also edited Belgravia *from 1866, the* Belgravia Annual *from 1867, and* Mistletoe Bough *from 1878.*

§2

Maxwell, M. B. Time gathered. 1938.
Sadleir, M. Mary Elizabeth Braddon. TLS 2 Oct 1937.
— Notes on Lady Audley's secret. TLS 11 May 1940.
— Miss Braddon. TLS 10 Oct 1942.
— In his Things past, 1944.
Summers, M. Miss Braddon. TLS 29 Aug 1942.
— Miss Braddon's black band. TLS 24 April 1943.
— The black band scandal. TLS 17 Feb 1945.
Miss Braddon. TLS 15 April, 16 Sept, 10–24 Oct 1944.
Heywood, C. Flanbert, Miss Braddon and George Moore. Comparative Lit 12 1960.
— The return of the native and Miss Braddon's The doctor's wife: a probable source. Nineteenth-Century Fiction 18 1964.
— Miss Braddon's The doctor's wife: an intermediary between Madame Bovary and the Return of the native. Revue de Littérature Comparée 38 1964.

RHODA BROUGHTON

1840–1920

§1

Not wisely, but too well. 3 vols 1867.
Cometh up as a flower. 2 vols 1867.
Red as a rose is she. 3 vols 1870.
'Goodbye, sweetheart': a tale. 3 vols 1872.
Nancy: a novel. 3 vols 1873.
Tales for Christmas Eve. 1873, 1879 (as Twilight stories).
Joan: a tale. 3 vols 1876.
Second thoughts. 2 vols 1880.
Belinda. 3 vols 1883.
Doctor Cupid: a novel. 3 vols 1886.
Alas!: a novel. 3 vols 1890.
A widower indeed. 1891. With E. Bisland.
Mrs Bligh: a novel. 1892.
A beginner. 1894.
Scylla or Charybdis?: a novel. 1895.
Dear Faustina. 1897.
The game and the candle. 1899.
Foes in law. 1900.
Lavinia. 1902.
A waif's progress. 1905.
Mamma. 1908.
Thr Devil and the deep sea. 1910.
Between two stools. [1912].
Concerning a vow. [1914].
A thorn in the flesh. 1917 (3rd edn).
A fool in her folly. [1920]. With an appreciation by Mrs Belloc Lowndes.

§2

Rhoda Broughton's secret. TLS 30 Nov 1940.
Sadleir, M. In his Things past, 1944.
MacColl, D. S. Rhoda Broughton and Emilia Pattison. Nineteenth Century Jan 1945.
Harris, R. J. Emilia Francis Strong: portraits of a lady. Nineteenth-Century Fiction 8 1954.
Ketcham, C. H. A woman's arm: George Eliot and Rhoda Broughton. N & Q March 1954.

OLIVER MADOX BROWN

1855–1874

§1

Gabriel Denver: a novel. 1873.
The Dwale Bluth, Hebditch's legacy and other literary remains, with a memoir of the author. Ed W. M. Rossetti and F. Hueffer 2 vols 1876. Prefixed is a Lament by P. B. Marston. Contains the original version of Gabriel Denver, as The black swan. Vol 2 contains 13 lyrics.

§2

Marston, P. B. Oliver Madox Brown. Scribner's Mag July 1876.
Ingram, J. H. Oliver Madox Brown: a biographical sketch. 1883.
—— In the poets and poetry of the century, ed A. H. Miles vol 8, 1893 etc.

ROBERT BUCHANAN

1841–1901

See col 615, above.

SAMUEL BUTLER

1835–1902

See col 1406, below.

SIR THOMAS HENRY HALL CAINE

1853–1931

Bibliographies

Gibbon, W. C. In his Bibliographical account of works relating to the Isle of Man vol 2, 1939.

§1

Richard III and Macbeth: a dramatic study. 1877.
Recollections of D. G. Rossetti. 1882, 1929 (rev).
Sonnets of three centuries. 1882. Ed Hall Caine.
Cobwebs of criticism. 1883.
The shadow of a crime. 3 vols 1885.
The Deemster. 3 vols 1887.
A son of Hagar. 3 vols 1887.
Life of Coleridge. 1887.
The bondman: a new saga. 3 vols 1890.
The little Manx nation. 1891.
The scapegoat. 2 vols 1891.
Capt'n Davy's honeymoon and other stories. 1893.
The Manxman. 1894.
The Christian. 1897.
The Eternal City. 1901.
The prodigal son. 1904.
My story. 1908.
The white prophet. 2 vols 1909.
King Edward: a prince and a great man. Rptd from Daily Telegraph 1910.
The woman thou gavest me. 1913.
King Albert's book. 1914. Ed Hall Caine.
The drama of 365 days: scenes in the Great War. 1915. Rptd from Daily Telegraph.
Our girls: their work for the war. 1916.
The master of man. 1921.
The woman of Knockaloe. 1923.
Life of Christ. 1938.

§2

Kenyon, C. F. Hall Caine: the man and the novelist. 1901.
MacCarthy, D. In his Portraits, 1931.

MARY CHOLMONDELEY

1859–1925

§1

The Danvers jewels. [1887].
Sir Charles Danvers: a novel. 2 vols 1889.
Diana Tempest. 3 vols 1893.
The devotee: an episode in the life of a butterfly. 1897.
Red pottage. 1899.
Moth and rust: together with Geoffrey's wife and the Pitfall. 1902.
Prisoners (fast bound in misery and iron). 1906.
The lowest rung, with the Hand on the latch, St Luke's summer and the Understudy. 1908.
Notwithstanding. 1913.
Under one roof: a family record. [1918].
The romance of his life, and other romances. 1921.

§2

Lubbock, P. Mary Cholmondeley: a sketch. 1928.
Kent, M. A novelist of yesterday. Cornhill Mag Feb 1935.

MARY COLERIDGE
1861–1907

See col 618, above.

'HUGH CONWAY', FREDERICK JOHN FARGUS
1847–85

Called back. Bristol [1883], 1885 (with life of the author).
Bound together: tales. 2 vols 1884.
Chewton Abbot and other tales. [1884].
Dark days. Bristol 1884.
Slings and arrows. Bristol 1885.
At what cost and other stories. [1885].
A family affair. 3 vols 1885.
A cardinal sin. 3 vols 1886.
Carriston's gift; A fresh start; Julian Vanneck; and A dead man's face. Bristol 1886.
'Somebody's story': an exact reproduction of Conway's original ms. [1886].
Living or dead. [1886].
A life's idylls and other poems. Bristol 1887.

MARIE CORELLI
1864–1924

§1

A romance of two worlds. 2 vols 1886.
Vendetta, or the story of one forgotten: a novel. 3 vols 1886.
Thelma: a society novel. 3 vols 1887.
Ardath: the story of a dead self. 3 vols 1889.
My wonderful wife: a study in smoke. 1889.
Wormwood: a drama of Paris. 3 vols 1890.
The silver domino. 1892. Anon.
The soul of Lilith. 3 vols 1892.
Barabbas: a dream of the world's tragedy. 3 vols [1893].
The sorrows of Satan, or the strange experiences of one Geoffrey Tempest, millionaire: a romance. 1895.
The murder of Delicia. 1896.
The mighty atom. 1896.
Cameos: short stories. 1896.
Zisha: the problem of a wicked soul. 1897.
Jane: a social incident. 1897.
Boy: a sketch. 1900.
The master Christian. 1900.
A Christmas greeting of various thoughts, verses and fancies. 1901.
'Temporal Power': a study in supremacy. 1902.
The vanishing gift: an address on the decay of the imagination, delivered before the Philosophical Institution, Edinburgh. [1902].
The plain truth of the Stratford-on-Avon controversy, concerning the fully-intended demolition of old houses in Henley Street and the changes proposed to be effected on the national ground of Shakespeare's birthplace. 1903.
God's good man: a simple love story. 1904.
The strange visitation of Josiah McNason: a Christmas ghost story. 1904.
Free opinions freely expressed on certain phases of modern social life and conduct. 1905.
The treasure of heaven: a romance of riches. 1906.
Woman or suffragette? a question of national choice. 1907.
Holy orders. 1908.
The devil's motor. 1910.
The life everlasting: a reality of romance. 1911.
Innocent, her fancy and his fact: a novel. 1914.
Eyes of the sea. 1917.
The young Diana: an experience of the future. 1918.
My little bit. 1919.
The love of long ago, and other stories. 1920.
The secret power. 1921.
Love and the philosopher. 1923.
Open confession to a man from a woman. 1925.
Poems. Ed B. Vyver 1925.

§2

Carr, K. Miss Marie Corelli. 1901.
Murray, H. In his Robert Buchanan and other essays, 1901.
Coates, T. F. G. and R. S. W. Bell. Marie Corelli: the writer and the woman. 1903.
Vyver, B. Memoirs of Marie Corelli, with an epilogue by J. Cuming Walters. [1930].
Elwin, M. Nine best sellers. In his Old gods falling, 1939.
Bullock, G. Marie Corelli: the life and death of a best-seller. 1940.
—— The Corelli wonder. Life & Letters 41 1944.
Jaggard, W. Marie Corelli. N & Q 13 March, 24 April 1943.
Sadleir, M. The camel's back: or the last tribulation of a Victorian publisher. In Essays presented to Sir Humphrey Milford, Oxford 1948.
Bigland, E. Marie Corelli: the woman and the legend. 1953.
Scott, W. S. Marie Corelli: the story of a friendship. 1955.

HUBERT MONTAGUE CRACKANTHORPE
1870–96

Bibliographies

Harris, W. A bibliography of writings about Crackanthorpe. Eng Fiction in Transition 6 1963.

§1

Wreckage: seven studies. 1893.
Sentimental studies and a set of village tales. 1895.
Vignettes: a miniature journal of whim and sentiment. 1896.
Last studies. 1897.

§2

Frierson, W. C. Crackanthorpe: analyst of the affections. Sewanee Rev 36 1928.
Worth, G. J. The English Maupassant School of the 1890's. MLN 1957.
Harris, W. Crackanthorpe as realist. Eng Fiction in Transition 6 1963.

SAMUEL RUTHERFORD CROCKETT
1860–1914

§1

Dulce cor: being the poems of Ford Berêton. 1886. 'Ford Berêton' was Crockett's pseudonym.
The Stickit minister and some common men. 1893. Stories.
The play-actress. 1894.
The lilac sunbonnet. 1894.
Mad Sir Uchtred of the hills. 1894.
The raiders. 1894.
Bog-myrtle and peat: tales, chiefly of Galloway. 1895.

The men of the Moss Hags. 1895.
Sweetheart travellers. 1895.
The grey man. 1896.
The smugglers of the Clone. 1896.
Cleg Kelly, arab of the city. 1896.
The surprising adventures of Sir Toady Lion with those of General Napoleon Smith. 1897.
Lad's love: tales. 1897.
Lochinvar. 1897.
The standard bearer. 1898.
The red axe. 1898.
The black Douglas. 1899.
Kit Kennedy. 1899.
Ione March. 1899.
Joan of the sword hand. 1900.
The Stickit minister's wooing. 1900.
Little Anna mark. 1900.
Love idylls. 1901.
The silver skull. 1901.
Cinderella. 1901.
The firebrand. 1901.
The dark o' the moon; being certain further histories of folk called 'raiders'. 1902.
Flower o'-the-corn. 1902.
The adventurer in Spain. 1903.
The banner of blue. 1903.
The loves of Miss Anne. 1904.
Raiderland: all about grey Galloway. 1904.
Red cap tales. 2 vols 1904–8. Abbreviated versions of some of Scott's novels.
Strong Mac. 1904.
The cherry riband. 1905.
Sir Toady Crusoe. 1905.
Maid Margaret of Galloway. 1905.
Kid McGhie. 1906.
Fishers of men. 1906.
The white plumes of Navarre. 1906.
Me and myn. 1907.
Little Esson. 1907.
Vida: or the Iron Lord of Kirktown. 1907.
Deep Moat Grange. 1908.
Princess Penniless. 1908.
The bloom o' the heather. 1908.
The men of the mountain. 1909, 1910.
Rose of the wilderness. 1909.
The seven wise men. 1909.
Dew of their youth. 1910.
Young Nick and old Nick. [1910].
The lady of the hundred dresses. 1911.
Love in Pernicketty Town. [1911].
The smugglers: chronicles of the last raiders of Solway. [1911].
Anne of the barricades. [1912].
The Moss Troopers. 1912.
Sweethearts at home. [1912].
Sandy's love affair. 1913.
A tatter of scarlet. 1913.
Silver sand. 1914.
Hal o' the Ironsides. 1915.
The azure hand. [1917].
The white Pope. 1920.
Rogue's Island. 1926.
Crockett also wrote forewords to Carlyle's Montaigne and other essays, 1897 etc.

§2

Dudgeon, F. Glossaries to Crockett's The Stickit minister, The raiders, The lilac sunbonnet. 1895.
Harper, M. M. Crockett and grey Galloway: the novelist and his works. [1907].

JOHN DAVIDSON

1857–1909

See col 619, above.

'GEORGE DOUGLAS', GEORGE DOUGLAS BROWN

1869–1902

§1

Love and a sword. 1899. Pbd under the pseudonym 'Kennedy King'.
The house with the green shutters. 1901.

§2

Lennox, C. Brown: a memoir, and reminiscences of Brown by Andrew Melrose. 1903.
Muir, E. In his Latitudes, 1924.

ERNEST DOWSON

1867–1900

See col 624, above.

SIR ARTHUR CONAN DOYLE

1859–1930

Bibliographies

Locke, H. A bibliographical catalogue of the writings of Conan Doyle 1879–1928. 1928. Incomplete.

Collections

Works: the author's edition. 12 vols 1903. Incomplete.
The principal works of fiction. 20 vols 1913.
Tales of adventure and medical life: a selection. 1922.
Tales of terror and mystery: a selection. 1922.
Tales of twilight and the unseen: a selection. 1922.
Tales of long ago: a selection. 1922.
Tales of pirates and blue water: a selection. 1922.
Tales of the ring and the camp: a selection. 1922.
Collected poems. 1922.
The Conan Doyle historical romances. 2 vols 1931–2.

§1

A study in scarlet. In Beeton's Christmas annual: twenty-eighth season, [1887].
The mystery of Cloomber. 1889.
Micah Clarke. 1889.
Mysteries and adventures. 1889, 1893 (as The gully of Bluemansdyke and other stories).
The sign of four. 1890. First pbd in Lippincott's Mag Feb 1890.
The captain of the polestar and other tales. 1890.
The firm of Girdlestone. 1890.
The white company. 3 vols 1891. First pbd in Cornhill Mag Jan–Dec 1891.
The doings of Raffles Haw. 1892.
The great shadow. 1892.
Beyond the city. 1892.
The adventures of Sherlock Holmes. 1892. First pbd in Strand Mag July 1891–June 1892.
The refugees. 3 vols 1893. First pbd in Harper's Mag 1893.
Jane Annie. 1893. A comic opera, with J. M. Barrie.
The memoirs of Sherlock Holmes. 1894. First pbd in Strand Mag Dec 1892–Dec 1893.
Round the red lamp: being facts and fancies of medical life. 1894.

The parasite. 1894.
The Stark Munro letters. 1895. First pbd in Idler Mag 1894–5.
The exploits of Brigadier Gerard. 1896. First pbd in Strand Mag 1894–5.
Rodney Stone. 1896. First pbd in Strand Mag 1896.
Uncle Bernac: a memory of the Empire. 1897.
Songs of action. 1898.
The tragedy of the Korosko. 1898. First pbd in Strand Mag May–Dec 1897.
A duet with an occasional chorus. 1899.
The great Boer War. 1900.
The green flag and other stories of war and sport. 1900. The Croxley Master was first pbd in Strand Mag 1900, and was later rptd separately, New York 1907.
The hound of the Baskervilles. 1902. First pbd in Strand Mag 1901–2.
The war in South Africa: its cause and conduct. 1902.
Adventures of Gerard. 1903. The separate stories were all first pbd in Strand Mag 1900–3, but some under different titles from those in 1st edn.
The return of Sherlock Holmes. 1905. First pbd in Strand Mag Oct 1903–Dec 1904.
Sir Nigel. 1906. First pbd in Strand Mag July 1905–Dec 1906.
Through the magic door. 1907. First pbd in Cassell's Mag Nov 1906–Oct 1907.
Round the fire stories. 1908.
The crime of the Congo. 1909.
The last galley. 1911.
Songs of the road. 1911.
The lost world. 1912. First pbd in Strand Mag 1912.
The poison belt. 1913. First pbd in Strand Mag 1913.
The German war: sidelights and reflections. 1914.
The valley of fear. 1915. First pbd in Strand Mag 1914–5.
The British campaign in France and Flanders. 6 vols 1916–9.
A visit to three fronts. 1916.
His last bow. 1917. The separate stories were all first pbd in Strand Mag 1893–1917.
Danger! and other stories. 1918.
The new revelation: or what is spiritualism? 1918.
The Guards came through, and other poems. 1919.
The vital message. 1919.
The wanderings of a spiritualist. 1921.
The case for spirit photography. 1922.
The coming of the fairies. 1922.
Our American adventure. 1923.
Three of them. 1923.
Memories and adventures. 1924.
The mystery of Joan of Arc. 1924. From the French of Léon Denis.
Our second American adventure. 1924.
The spiritualist's reader. 1924.
The history of spiritualism. 2 vols 1926.
The land of mist. 1926.
The case-book of Sherlock Holmes. 1927. The separate stories were all first pbd in Strand Mag.
Pheneas speaks. 1927.
The Maracot Deep and other stories. 1929.
Our African winter. 1929.
The adventure of the blue carbuncle. Ed E. W. Smith, New York 1948.
Great stories of Conan Doyle: a centenary volume. Ed J. D. Carr 1959.

§2

Blathwayt, R. An interview with Dr Conan Doyle. Bookman (London) May 1892.
Hodder-Williams, J. E. Sir Arthur Conan Doyle. Bookman (London) April 1902.
[Prothero, G.] The novels of Conan Doyle. Quart Rev 200 1904.
Adcock, A. St-J. Sir Arthur Conan Doyle. Bookman (London) Nov 1912.
Knox, R. In his Essays in satire, 1928.
Messac, R. Le 'detective novel' et l'influence de la pensée scientifique. Paris 1929.
Lamond, J. Conan Doyle: a memoir. 1931.
Roberts, S. C. Doctor Watson. 1931.
—— Holmes and Watson: a miscellany. Oxford 1953.
Bell, H. W. Sherlock Holmes and Dr Watson. 1932.
Blakeney, T. S. Sherlock Holmes: fact or fiction? 1932.
Ernest, B. M. and H. Carrington. Hondini and Conan Doyle: the story of a strange friendship. New York 1932.
Baker Street studies. Ed H. W. Bell 1934.
Kernahan, C. Personal memories of Sherlock Holmes. London Quart 159 1934.
Starret, V. The private life of Sherlock Holmes. 1934, Chicago 1960 (rev and enlarged).
221B: studies in Sherlock Holmes by various hands. Ed V. Starrett, New York 1940.
Smith, E. W. Appointment in Baker St. New York 1938.
Adrian, M. C. The true Conan Doyle. 1943.
Pearson, H. Conan Doyle: his life and art. 1943, 1961 (rev).
The misadventures of Sherlock Holmes. Ed E. Queen, Boston 1944.
Profile by gaslight: an irregular reader about the private life of Sherlock Holmes. Ed E. W. Smith, New York 1944.
Doyle, A. C. The true Conan Doyle. 1945.
Clutton-Brock, A. T. S. Eliot and Conan Doyle. TLS 19 Jan 1951. *See* subsequent correspondence.
Sherlock Holmes journal. 1952–.
Sayers, D. In her Unpopular opinions, 1946.
The Baker Street journal: an irregular quarterly of Sherlockiana. Ed E. W. Smith, New York 1946–.
Christ, J. F. An irregular guide to Sherlock Holmes. New York 1947.
Warrack, G. Sherlock Holmes and music. 1947.
Carr, J. D. The life of Conan Doyle. 1948.
Knox, E. V. The passing of Sherlock Holmes. Strand Mag Dec 1948.
Crocker, S. F. Sherlock Holmes's appreciation of nature. West Virginia Univ Philological Papers 6 1949.
Grazebrook, O. F. Studies in Sherlock Holmes, 5: Dr Watson and Rudyard Kipling. 1949.
Kenner, H. Baker Street to Eccles Street: the Odyssey of a myth. Hudson Rev 1 1949.
Brend, G. My dear Holmes: a study in Sherlock. 1951.
Moore, J. R. Conan Doyle, Tennyson and Rasselas. Nineteenth-Century Fiction 7 1953.
Stern, M. B. Sherlock Holmes: rare book collector. PBSA 47 1953.
Holroyd, J. E. Homage to Holmes. New Statesman 23 Jan 1954.
—— Baker Street by-ways. 1959.
Ridley, M. R. Sherlock Holmes and the detective story. Listener 14 Jan 1954.
Krogman, W. M. Sherlock Holmes as an anthropologist. Scientific Monthly March 1955.
Watson, J. G. The religion of Sherlock Holmes. Literary Guide 70 1955.
Weil-Nordon, P. Conan Doyle et la France. Etudes Anglaises 10 1957.
—— George Meredith V par Conan Doyle. Etudes Anglaises 12 1959.
—— Conan Doyle centenary 1859–1959. 1959.
—— Conan Doyle: l'homme et l'oeuvre. Paris 1964.
Bayley, J. O. A letter from Conan Doyle on the novelist-journalist. 12 1958.
Harrison, M. In the footsteps of Sherlock Holmes. 1958.
Preston, P. A note on T. S. Eliot and Sherlock Holmes. MLR 54 1959.
Van Lierre, E. J. A doctor enjoys Sherlock Holmes. New York 1959.
Jejeune, A. Age of the great detectives. TLS 23 June 1961.

Baring-Gould, W. S. Sherlock Holmes. 1962.
Hardwick, J. M. and M. The Sherlock Holmes companion. 1962.
—— Four Sherlock Holmes plays. 1964.
—— The man who was Sherlock Holmes. 1964.
Klinefeeter, W. Sherlock Holmes in portrait and profile. Syracuse NY 1963.
Kissane, J. and J. M. Sherlock Holmes and the ritual of reason. Nineteenth-Century Fiction 17 1963.
Isherwood, C. In his Exhumations, 1966.

GEORGE LOUIS PALMELLA BUSSON DU MAURIER
1834–96

§1

English society at home. 1880.
Peter Ibbetson. 2 vols 1892. First pbd in Harper's Mag.
Trilby. 3 vols 1894. First pbd in Harper's Mag.
The Martian: a novel. 1897.
Social pictorial satire. 1898.
A legend of Camelot. 1898.

Letters

The young Du Maurier: a selection of his letters 1860–7. Ed D. du Maurier 1951.

§2

Gilder, J. L. and J. B. Trilbyana. The rise and progress of a popular novel. 1895.
Armstrong, T. Reminiscences of Du Maurier. 1912.
Wood, T. M. Du Maurier, the satirist of the Victorians: a review of his art and personality. 1913.
Lucas, E. V. George du Maurier at thirty-three. Cornhill Mag Oct 1934; rptd in his All of a piece, 1937.
Du Maurier, D. The Du Mauriers. 1937.
Feipel, L. N. The American issues of Trilby. Colophon 2 1937.
Lanoire, M. Un anglo-français, Du Maurier. Revue de Paris 15 March 1940.
Trilby reappears. TLS 3 April 1948.
Whitely, D. P. Du Maurier: his life and work. 1948.
Stevenson, L. Du Maurier and the romantic novel. Essays by Divers Hands 30 1960.

JULIANA HORATIA EWING, née GATTY
1841–85

Collections

Uniform edition. 18 vols 1894–6. Complete; vol 17, Miscellanea (later called Tales of the Khoja), consists of uncollected articles, tales and trns from Aunt Judy's Mag, London Soc etc. Vol 18 is H. K. F. Eden's life, below.
Jackanapes, Daddy Darwin's dovecot, and the Story of a short life. 1916 (EL).
Mrs Overtheway's remembrances and other stories. 1916 (EL).

§1

Melchior's dream and other tales. 1862. Ed Mrs Gatty. First pbd in Monthly Packet 1861.
Mrs Overtheway remembrances. 1869. First pbd in Aunt Judy's Mag 1866–8.
The Brownies and other tales. 1870. First pbd in Aunt Judy's Mag 1865–70, and Little Folks.
A flat iron for a farthing. 1872. First pbd in Aunt Judy's Mag 1870–1.
Lob-lie-by-the-fire: or the luck of Lingborough and other tales. 1874. 4 of the 5 stories were first pbd in Aunt Judy's Mag; Lob had not appeared before.
Six to sixteen. 1875. First pbd in Aunt Judy's Mag 1872.
Jan of the windmill. 1876. First pbd in Aunt Judy's Mag 1872–3 as The miller's thumb.
A great emergency and other tales. 1877. First pbd in Aunt Judy's Mag 1873–5.
We and the world. 1880. First pbd in Aunt Judy's Mag 1877–9.
Old fashioned fairy tales. 1882. First pbd in Aunt Judy's Mag 1870–6.
Brothers of pity and other tales. 1882. First pbd in Aunt Judy's Mag 1876–9.
Blue and red. 1883. First pbd in Aunt Judy's Mag 1881.
Jackanapes. 1884. First pbd in Aunt Judy's Mag Oct 1879.
Daddy Darwin's dovecot. 1884. First pbd in Aunt Judy's Mag 1881.
The story of a short life. 1885. First pbd in Aunt Judy's Mag as Laetus sorte mea.
Mary's meadow. 1886. First pbd in Aunt Judy's Mag 1883–4.
Dandelion clocks and other tales. 1887. First pbd in Monthly Packet 1871, and Aunt Judy's Mag 1875–7.
The peace egg: a Christmas mumming play. 1887. First pbd in Aunt Judy's Mag 1884.
Snapdragon and old Father Christmas. 1888. Snapdragon was first pbd in Monthly Packet 1870; Old Father Christmas, first pbd in Little Folks, had already been collected in The Brownies and other tales.
Verses for children. 3 vols 1888. The blue bells on the lea—Mother's birthday review and A soldier's children was first pbd in Aunt Judy's Mag 1880–3. The verses were originally issued 1883–5 in 24 quarto vols with coloured illustrations.
Mrs Ewing also assisted in editing Aunt Judy's Mag 1874–6, *and contributed a memoir of Mrs Gatty to the latter's* Parables from Nature, sers 1–2 1885.

§2

Gatty (later Eden), H. K. F. Juliana Horatia Ewing and her books. 1885 (in Uniform edition, above).
Marshall, E. In A. Sargeant et al, Women novelists of Queen Victoria's reign, 1897.
Juliana Ewing's world: morality with fun. TLS 9 Aug 1941.
Maxwell, C. Mrs Gatty and Mrs Ewing. 1949.
Laski, M. Mrs Ewing, Mrs Molesworth and Mrs Hodgson Burnett. 1951.
Avery, G. Mrs Ewing. 1961.

'MICHAEL FAIRLESS', MARGARET FAIRLESS BARBER
1869–1901

§1

The gathering of Brother Bilarius. 1901.
The roadmender and other papers. 1902; ed N. E. Dowson 1926 (with addns). First pbd in Pilot.
The child king: four Christmas writings. 1902.
The grey brethren and other fragments in prose and verse. 1905.
Stories told to children. Ed 'M. E. Dowson' (W. S. Palmer) 1914.

§2

'Dowson, M. E.' (W. S. Palmer) and A. M. Haggard. Michael Fairless: her life and writings. 1913.

'LANOE FALCONER', MARY ELIZABETH HAWKER
1848–1908

§1

Mademoiselle Ixe. 1891 (for 1890).
Cecilia de Noël. 1891.
The Hôtel d'Angleterre and other stories. 1891.
Shoulder to shoulder: a tale of love and friendship. [1891].
The wrong prescription. In Tavistock tales by Gilbert Parker etc, 1893.
Old Hampshire vignettes. 1907.
'*Lanoe Falconer' also contributed* The short story *to* On the art of writing fiction, 1894.

§2

Phillipps, E. M. Lanoe Falconer. Cornhill Mag Feb 1912.
—— Lanoe Falconer (author of Mademoiselle Ixe). 1915.

JOHN MEADE FALKNER
Bibliographies

Pollard, H. G. Some uncollected authors: J. M. Falkner. Book Collector 9 1960.

§1

Handbook for travellers in Oxfordshire. 1894.
The lost Stradivarius. 1895, Oxford 1954 (WC).
Moonfleet. 1898.
A history of Oxfordshire. 1899.
Handbook for Berkshire. 1902.
The nebuly coat. 1903, Oxford 1954 (WC).
Bath in history and social tradition. 1918.
Poems. 1933.

§2

Pritchett, V. S. In his Living novel, 1946.

'VIOLET FANE'
1843–1905

See col 625, above.

BENJAMIN LEOPOLD FARJEON
1843–1903

§1

Grif: a story of Australian life. Dunedin NZ 1866, 2 vols 1870.
Shadows on the snow: a Christmas story. Dunedin NZ 1866, [1904].
Joshua Marvel. 3 vols 1871.
London's heart. 3 vols 1873.
Christmas stories: Blade o'grass; Golden grain; and Bread and cheese and kisses. 3 pts 1874.
Jessie Trim: a novel. 3 vols 1874.
Love's victory: a novel. 2 vols 1875.
At the sign of the silver flagon. 3 vols 1876.
The Duchess of Rosemary Lane: a novel. 3 vols 1876.
The house of white shadows: a novel. 3 vols 1884.
The shield of love. 1884 (Arrowsmith's Christmas Annual).
Christmas angel. [1885].
Great Porter Square: a mystery. 3 vols 1885.
The sacred nugget: a novel. 3 vols 1885.
Self-doomed. [1885].
The golden land: or links from shore to shore. 1886.
In a silver sea. 1886.
The nine of hearts. [1886].
A secret inheritance. 3 vols 1887.
The tragedy of Featherstone: a novel. 3 vols 1887.
Devlin the barber. 1888.
Miser Farebrother: a novel. 3 vols 1888.
Toilers of Babylon. 3 vols 1888.
The blood white rose. [1889].
Doctor Glennie's daughter: a story of real life. 1889.
A strange enchantment. 1889.
A young girl's life: a novel. 3 vols 1889.
Basil and Annette: a novel. 3 vols 1890.
The mystery of M. Felix: a novel. 3 vols 1890.
The peril of Richard Pardon: a novel. 1890.
A very young couple: a novel. 1890.
For the defence: a realistic story. 1891.
The march of fate: a novel. 3 vols 1893.
The last tenant. [1893].
Something occurred. 1893.
Aaron the Jew: a novel. 3 vols 1894.
The betrayal of John Fordham. 1896.
Miriam Rozella. 1898.
Samuel Boyd of Catchpole Square: a mystery. 1899.
The mesmerists. 1900.
The pride of race, in five panels. 1901.
The mystery of the Royal Mail. 1902.
The amblers. 1904.
The clairvoyante. 1905.
Mrs Dimmock's worries. 1906.
Stories by Farjeon also appeared in the following collections: In Australian wilds, ed P. Mennell 1889; Seven Xmas eves, 1894, *and* Fifty-two stories of the British Empire, ed A. H. Miles 1900.

§2

B. L. Farjeon. Victoria Mag 32 1879.
Bok, E. W. B. L. Farjeon. Author (Boston) 3 1891.

FREDERIC WILLIAM FARRAR
1831–1903

§1

Eric, or little by little: a tale of Roslyn School. Edinburgh 1858.
Julian Home: a tale of college life. Edinburgh 1859.
St Winifred's: or the world of school. 1862.
The three Homes: a tale for fathers and sons. 1873 (under the pseudonym 'F.T.L.'), 1896 (signed).
Darkness and dawn, or scenes in the days of Nero: an historic tale. 2 vols 1891.
Gathering clouds: a tale of the days of St Chrysostom. 2 vols 1895.
Allegories. 1898.
Farrar also pbd many sermons and theological works, the more important of which are listed col 1606, below.

§2

Farrar, R. The life of Frederick William Farrar. 1904.
Russell, G. W. E. Sketches and snapshots. 1910.
'Kingsmill, Hugh' (H. K. Lunn). After Puritanism 1850–1900. 1929.

PERCY HETHERINGTON FITZGERALD
1834–1925

Roman candles. 1861.
Words for the wordly. [1861].
The night mail: its passengers, and how they fared at Christmas. 1862.
Two English essayists: Charles Lamb and Charles Dickens. 1863.
Bella Donna, or the cross before the name: a romance. 2 vols 1864. Pbd under the pseudonym 'Gilbert Dyce'.
The life of Laurence Sterne. 2 vols 1864.
Fairy Alice. 2 vols 1865.
A famous forgery: the story of Dr Dodd. 1865.
Never forgotten: a novel. 3 vols 1865.
Charles Lamb: his friends, his haunts and his books. 1866.
Charles Townshend: wit and statesman. 1866.
Jenny Bell: a story. 3 vols 1866.
The second Mrs Tillotson: a story, reprinted from All the Year Round. 3 vols 1866.
School days at Saxonhurst, illustrated by 'Phiz'. 1867.
Seventy-five Brooke Street: a story. 3 vols 1867.
The dear girl. 3 vols 1868.
Diana Gay: or the history of a young lady. 3 vols 1868. First pbd in Belgravia.
The life of David Garrick from original family papers. 2 vols 1868, 1899 (rev).
Proverbs or comediettas written for private representation. 1869.
Beauty Talbot. 3 vols 1870.
Principles of comedy and dramatic effect. 1870.
The Rev Alfred Hoblush and his curacies. [1870].
The Kembles: an account of the Kemble family. 2 vols [1871].
Two fair daughters. 3 vols 1871.
Life and adventures of Alexander Dumas. 2 vols 1873.
Kings and Queens of an hour: records of love, romance, oddity and adventure. 2 vols 1873.
The middle-aged lover: a story. 2 vols 1873.
The romance of the English stage. 2 vols 1874.
The life of Samuel Johnson [by Boswell], edited with new notes. 3 vols 1874, 1888.
The life, letters and writings of Charles Lamb, edited with notes. 1876.
The parvenu family: or Phoebe, girl and wife. 3 vols 1876.
Little Dorinda: who won and who lost her! [1878].
Croker's Boswell and Boswell: studies in the life of Johnson. 1880.
A little life. 1880.
The life of George IV. 2 vols 1881.
The world behind the scenes. 1881.
Young Coelebs: a novel. 3 vols 1881.
The life and writings of Charles Lamb. 4 vols 1882.
A new history of the English stage. 2 vols 1882.
The Royal Dukes and Duchesses of the family of George III: a view of their life and manners for seventy years 1760–1830. 2 vols 1882.
Recreations of a literary man: or does writing pay? 2 vols 1882.
The life and times of William IV. 2 vols 1884.
Puppets: a romance. 3 vols 1884.
The art of the stage as set out in Lamb's dramatic essays, with a commentary. 1885.
Fatal zero. 1886.
Lives of the Sheridans. 2 vols 1886.
The book fancier. 1886.
A day's tour. 1887.
Chronicles of Bow Street. 2 vols 1888.
The life of John Wilkes. 2 vols 1888.

Life of Mrs Catherine Clive. 1888.
Music hall land. [1890].
King Theodore of Corsica. 1890.
The story of 'Bradshaw's' Guide. [1890].
Life of James Boswell. 2 vols 1891.
Editing à la mode: an examination [of G. Birkbeck Hill's Boswell]. [1891].
History of Pickwick. 1891.
Three weeks at Mopetown. 1891.
The art of acting. 1892.
The bachelor's dilemma. 1892.
Henry Irving. 1893, 1895 (rev).
Memoirs of an author. 2 vols 1894.
The Savoy Opera. 1894.
Bozland. 1895.
Pickwickian manners and customs. [1897].
A critical examination of Dr G. Birkbeck Hill's 'Johnsonian' edition. 1898.
The good Queen Charlotte. 1899.
John Forster. 1903.
The Pickwickian dictionary. [1903].
Lightning tours. 1903.
Pickwickian wit and humour. 1903.
The Garrick Club. 1904.
Lady Jean. 1904.
Robert Adam. 1904.
The life of Charles Dickens, traced in his works. 2 vols 1905.
Sir Henry Irving: a biography. 1906.
Josephine's troubles: a story. [1907].
Shakespearian representation. 1908.
Samuel Foote. 1910.
Jane Austen. 1912.
Pickwick riddles and perplexities. 1912.
Memories of Charles Dickens. 1913.
Worldlyman: a modern morality of our day. [1913].
Fitzgerald also wrote a number of books on Roman Catholicism, London etc.

RICHARD GARNETT
1835–1906

See col 1431, below.

SIR EDMUND GOSSE
1845–1928

See col 1432, below.

'SARAH GRAND', FRANCES ELIZABETH McFALL, née CLARKE
1862–1943

§1

Ideala: a study from life. 1888. Anon.
A domestic experiment, by the author of Ideala. 1891.
The heavenly twins. 3 vols 1893.
Singularly deluded, by the author of Ideala. 1893.
Our manifold nature. 1894. Stories.
The Beth book. 1898.
The modern man and maid. 1898.
The human quest: being some thoughts in contribution to the subject of the art of happiness. 1900.
Babs the impossible. 1901.

Emotional moments. 1908. Stories.
Adnam's orchard: a prologue. 1912.
The winged victory. 1916.
Variety. 1922. Stories.
Mrs MacFall also wrote a preface to 'Bartholomew's' As they are, 1908, *and a personal sketch of Matilda B. B. Edwards prefixed to her* Mid-Victorian memories, 1919.

§2

Sarah Grand. Critic (New York) 23 1893.
Cotton, J. J. Madame Grand. Macmillan's Mag Sept 1900.
Foerster, E. Die Frauenfragen in den Romanen englischer Schriftstellerinnen der Gegenwart (George Egerton, Mona Caird, Sarah Grand). Marburg 1907.

SIR HENRY RIDER HAGGARD
1856–1925

Bibliography

McKay, G. L. A bibliography of the writings of Rider Haggard. 1930.
Scott, J. E. A bibliography of the works of Rider Haggard. 1947.

§1

Cetywayo and his white neighbours. 1882, 1888 (with addns).
Dawn. 3 vols 1884.
The witch's head. 3 vols 1885.
King Solomon's mines. 1885; ed R. L. Green 1955.
She. 1887. First pbd in Graphic 1886–7.
Jess. 1887. First pbd in Cornhill Mag 1886–7.
Allan Quatermain. 1887. First pbd in Longman's Mag 1887.
A tale of three lions. New York 1887. First pbd in Atalanta 1887.
Mr Meeson's will. 1888. First pbd in Illustr London News summer 1888.
Maiwa's revenge: or the war of the little hand. 1888.
My fellow laborer and the Wreck of the 'Copeland'. New York 1888. First pbd in Collier's Once a Week 1888.
Colonel Quaritch VC. 3 vols 1888.
Cleopatra. 1889. First pbd in Illustr London News 1889.
Allan's wife and other tales. 1889.
Beatrice. 1890.
The world's desire. 1890. With Andrew Lang; first pbd in New Rev 1890.
Eric Brighteyes. 1891.
Nada the lily. 1892.
Montezuma's daughter. 1893.
The people of the mist. 1894.
Church and State. 1895.
Joan Haste. 1895.
Heart of the world. New York 1895, London 1896.
The wizard. Bristol 1896.
Dr Therne. 1898.
A farmer's year. 1899. First pbd in Longman's Mag 1898–9.
The last Boer War. 1899.
Swallow. 1899.
Black heart and white heart, and other stories. 1900.
Lysbeth. 1901.
A winter pilgrimage. 1901. First pbd in Queen 1901.
Rural England. 2 vols 1902.
Pearl Maiden. 1903.
Stella Fregelius. 1904.
The brethren. 1904.
Ayesha: the return of She. 1905.
A gardener's year. 1905. First pbd in Queen 1904.
Report on Salvation Army colonies. 1905, 1905 (rev as The poor and the land).
The way of the spirit. 1906.
Benita. 1906.
Fair Margaret. 1907.
The ghost kings. 1908.
The yellow god. New York 1908, London 1909.
The lady of Blossholme. 1909.
Morning star. 1910.
Queen Sheba's ring. 1910.
Regeneration: an account of the social work of the Salvation Army. 1910.
The Mahatma and the hare. 1911.
Red eve. 1911.
Rural Denmark. 1911.
Marie. 1912.
Child of storm. 1913.
A call to arms. 1914 (priv ptd).
The wanderer's necklace. 1914.
The holy flower. 1915.
The after-war settlement and employment of ex-service men. 1916.
The ivory child. 1916.
Finished. 1917.
Love eternal. 1918.
Moon of Israel. 1918.
When the world shook. 1919.
The ancient Allan. 1920.
Smith and the Pharaohs, and other tales. Bristol 1920.
She and Allan. 1921.
The virgin of the sun. 1922.
Wisdom's daughter. 1923.
Heu-Heu. 1924.
Queen of the dawn. 1925.
The days of my life. 2 vols 1926. First pbd in Strand Mag 1926, but expanded in book form.
Treasure of the lake. 1926.
Allan and the ice gods. 1927.
Mary of Marion Isle. 1929.
Belshazzar. 1930.

§2

Elwin, M. In his Old gods falling, 1939.
Green, R. L. He, She and It. TLS 27 May, 17 June, 1 July 1944.
—— In his Tellers of tales, Leicester 1965.
Gibbons, S. Voyage of rediscovery. Fortnightly Rev Dec 1945.
Scott, J. E. Hatchers-out of tales. New Colophon 1 1948.
Greene, G. Books in general. New Statesman 14 July 1951.
Haggard, L. R. The cloak that I left: a biography. 1951.
—— A born story teller. Listener 22 June 1961.
Miller, H. In his Books in my life, 1952.
Rider Haggard. TLS 22 June 1956.
Baker, G. A great Rider Haggard accession. Princeton Univ Lib Chron 17 1956.
Ellis, H. F. The niceties of plagiarism. Atlantic Monthly Jan 1959.
Cohen, M. Rider Haggard: his life and works. 1960.
—— Rudyard Kipling to Rider Haggard: the record of a friendship. 1965.

PHILIP GILBERT HAMERTON
1834–1894

See col 1436, below.

BEATRICE HARRADEN
1864–1936

Things will take a turn. 1889, 1915 (rev).
Master Roley. 1889.

Ships that pass in the night. 1893.
In varying moods: short stories. 1894.
Untold tales of the past. 1897.
A new book of the fairies. 1897.
The fowler. 1899.
The scholar's daughter. 1906.
Hilda Strafford and the remittance man. 1906.
Interplay. 1908.
Out of the wreck I rise. 1912.
The guiding thread. 1916.
Where your treasure is. 1918.
Spring shall plant. 1920.
Thirteen all told: tales. 1921.
Patuppa. 1923.
Youth calling. 1924.
Rachel. 1926.
Katherine Frensham. 1927.
Search will find it out. 1928.

JOSEPH HATTON

1841–1907

Provincial papers: being a collection of tales and sketches. 1861.
Bitter sweets: a love story. 3 vols 1865. Dramatized as Two May days, 1871.
Against the stream. 3 vols 1866.
The Tallants of Barton: a tale of fortune and finance. 3 vols 1867.
Not in society: a posthumous story by Vaughan Morgan edited by Joseph Hatton. 1868, [1877] (rptd with other tales by Hatton).
Pippins and cheese. 1868.
Christopher Kenrick. 2 vols 1869.
Behind a mask: a romance of real life. 1870.
With a show in the north: reminiscences of Mark Lemon, with Lemon's revised text of Falstaff. 1871.
Kites and pigeons: a novelette. [1872]. Dramatized as Birds of a feather: a serio-comic play, [1872].
The valley of poppies. 2 vols 1872.
In the lap of fortune: a story 'stranger than fiction'. 3 vols 1873.
Clytie: a novel of modern life. 3 vols 1874. Dramatized, [1874].
Romantic Caroline: a comedy founded upon the comedy of Barrière and Thiboust. [1874].
The Queen of Bohemia: a novel. 2 vols 1877.
Cruel London: a novel. 3 vols 1878.
Liz: a drama. [1879].
Much too clever: a comedy. [1879]. With J. Oxenford.
Three recruits and the girls they left behind them. 3 vols 1880.
Today in America. 2 vols 1881.
'The new Ceylon': British North Borneo. 1881.
Journalistic London. 1882.
The dove's nest. 1883.
A modern Ulysses: a novel. 3 vols 1883.
Henry Irving's impressions of America. 2 vols 1884.
John Needham's double: a story founded upon fact. [1885].
The old house at Sandwich. 2 vols 1887.
The Park Lane mystery. Bristol [1887].
The gay world. 3 vols 1887.
Captured by Cannibals. 1888.
By order of the Czar. 3 vols 1890 (2nd edn).
Club-land, London and provincial. 1890.
Old lamps and new. [1890].
The Princess Mazaroff: a romance. 2 vols 1891.
Cigarette papers for after-dinner smoking. 1892. Essays and sketches.
The fate of Fenella, by twenty-four authors. 1892.
In jest and earnest: a book of gossip. 1893.
Under the Great Seal. 3 vols 1893.
Tom Chester's sweetheart: a tale of the press. [1895].
When Greek meets Greek. 1895.
The banishment of Jessop Blythe. 1895.
A world afloat. [1897].
The dagger and the cross: a novel. 1897.
The Vicar: a novel. 1898.
The white King of Manoa: an Anglo-Spanish romance. 1899.
When rogues fall out. 1899.
In male attire. 1900.
A vision of beauty. 1902.
The life and work of Alfred Gilbert. 1903.
Hatton also wrote works on cocoa, tobacco, etc, and edited E. W. Streeter, Great diamonds, 1882, *and* J. L. Toole, Reminiscences, 1889.

'JOHN OLIVER HOBBES', PEARL MARY TERESA CRAIGIE

1867–1906

§1

Some emotions and a moral. 1891.
The sinner's comedy. 1892.
A bundle of life. 1893.
A study in temptations. 1893.
The gods, some mortals and Lord Wickenham. 1895.
The tales of John Oliver Hobbes. [1895].
The herb moon. 1896.
The school for saints. 1897.
The ambassador: a comedy in three acts. 1898.
Osbern and Ursyne: a drama in three acts. 1900.
Robert Orange. 1900. Sequel to School for saints, above.
The serious wooing. 1901.
The wisdom of the wise. 1901. A comedy.
Love and the soul hunters. 1902.
Tales about temperaments. 1902.
Imperial India: letters from the East. 1903.
The artist's life. 1904. Critical essays.
Letters from a silent study. 1904.
The vineyard. 1904.
The flute of Pan. [1905]. Originally written as a play and on its failure converted into a novel.
The dream and the business. 1906.

§2

Archer, W. In his Real conversations, 1904.
Courtney, W. L. In his Feminine note in fiction, 1904.
Richards, J. M. The life of Hobbes. 1911.
Clarke, I. C. In her Six portraits, 1935.

'ANTHONY HOPE', SIR ANTHONY HOPE HAWKINS

1863–1933

§1

A man of mark. 1890.
Father Stafford. 1891.
Mr Witt's widow. 1892.
A change of air. 1893.
Half a hero. 2 vols 1893.
Sport Royal and other stories. 1893.
The Dolly dialogues. 1894.
The god in the car. 2 vols 1894.
The indiscretion of the Duchess. 1894.
The prisoner of Zenda. 1894; ed R. L. Green 1966 (EL) (with Rupert, below).
The chronicle of Count Antonio. 1895.
Comedies of courtship. 1896.
The heart of Princess Osra and other stories. 1896.

Phroso. 1897.
Rupert of Hentzau: being a sequel to a story by the same writer entitled the Prisoner of Zenda. Bristol [1898].
Simon Dale. 1898.
The King's mirror. 1899.
Quisanté. 1900.
Tristram of Blent. 1901.
The intrusions of Peggy. 1902.
Double harness. 1904.
A servant of the public. 1905.
Sophy of Kravonia. 1906.
Tales of two people. 1907.
The great Miss Driver. 1908.
Dialogue. 1909 (Eng Assoc lecture).
Second string. 1910.
Mrs Maxon protests. 1911.
The new (German) Testament: some texts and a commentary. [1914].
Militarism, German and British. 1915.
A young man's year. 1915.
Why Italy is with the Allies. 1917.
Captain Dieppe. 1918.
Beaumaroy home from the wars. 1919.
Lucinda. 1920.
Little tiger. 1925.
Memories and notes. [1927].

§2

Mallet, C. Anthony Hope and his books: being the authorized life of Sir Anthony Hope Hawkins. 1935.
Putt, S. G. The prisoner of the prisoner of Zenda: Hope and the novel of society. EC 6 1956.

WILLIAM HENRY HUDSON
1841–1922

Bibliographies

Wilson, G. F. A bibliography of the writings of Hudson. 1922.

Collections

Collected works. 24 vols 1922–3.
A Hudson anthology, arranged by Edward Garnett. 1924.
Hudson's South American romances: The purple land; Green mansions; El Ombú [etc]. 1930.
Birds of wing and other wild things: selections from the works of Hudson by H. F. B. Fox. 1930.
The best of Hudson. Ed O. Shepard, New York 1949.
Works: uniform edition. 1951–.

§1

The purple land that England lost: travels and adventures in the Banda Oriental, South America. 2 vols 1885.
A crystal age. 1887 (anon), 1906 (with signed preface).
Ralph Herne. Youth 12 1888. Hudson's first story; not separately rptd, but included in Collected works, 1922–3, above.
Fan: the story of a young girl's life. 3 vols 1892. Pbd under the pseudonym 'Henry Harford'.
The naturalist in La Plata. 1892.
Birds in a village. 1893, [1920] (with Poems of birds by various writers).
Idle days in Patagonia. 1893.
British birds, with a chapter on structure and classification by Frank E. Beddard. 1895.
Birds in London. 1898.
Nature in Downland. 1900.
Birds and man. 1901.
El Ombú [and other tales]. 1902, 1909 (as South American sketches).
Hampshire days. 1903.
Green mansions: a romance of the tropical forest. 1904.
A little boy lost. 1905.
The land's end: a naturalist's impressions in West Cornwall. 1908.
Afoot in England. 1909.
A shepherd's life: impressions of the South Wiltshire downs. 1910.
Adventures among birds. 1913.
Far away and long ago: a history of my early life. 1918, 1931 (rev).
Birds in town and village. 1919.
The book of a naturalist. [1919].
Birds of La Plata. 2 vols 1920.
Dead man's plack, and An old thorn. 1920.
A traveller in little things. 1921.
A hind in Richmond Park. Ed M. Roberts 1922.
Rare, vanishing and lost British birds. 1923. Compiled from Hudson's notes by L. Gardiner.
153 letters. Ed E. Garnett 1923, 1925 (as Letters from W. H. Hudson to Edward Garnett).
Men, books and birds, with notes, some letters, and an introduction by Morley Roberts. 1925.
Hudson also contributed notes to P. L. Sclater, Argentine Ornithology, 2 vols 1888–9, *and a preface to* P. Fountain, The great deserts and forests of North America, 1901; *he pbd a few periodical articles, and a number of pamphlets, the latter mostly for the Society for the Protection of Birds.*

§2

R., E. The work of Hudson. Eng Rev April 1909.
Rhys, E. Hudson, rare traveller. Nineteenth Century July 1920.
Curle, R. W. H. Hudson. Fortnightly Rev Oct 1922.
Massingham, H. J. Untrodden ways: adventures on English coasts, heaths and marshes and also among the works of Hudson, Crabbe and other country writers. 1923.
Hughes, M. Y. A great skeptic: Hudson. Univ of California Chron 26 1924.
Roberts, M. Hudson: a portrait. 1924.
Nicholson, E. M. Hudson's Birds in a village. Cornhill Mag July 1925.
Salt, H. S. Hudson as I saw him. Fortnightly Rev Feb 1926.
Harper, G. M. In his Spirit of delight, 1928.
Fletcher, J. V. The creator of Rima, Hudson: a belated romantic. Sewanee Rev 41 1933.
Charles, R. H. The writings of Hudson. E & S 20 1935.
Ford, F. M. W. H. Hudson. Amer Mercury 37 1936.
Hamilton, E. The spirit of Hudson: an evaluation. Quart Rev 275 1940.
—— W. H. Hudson. 1946.
Baker, C. The source book for Hudson's Green mansions. PMLA 61 1946.
Liandrat, F. Hudson, naturaliste: sa vie et son oeuvre. Lyons 1946.
West, H. F. Hudson's reading. 1947.
Fairchild, H. N. Rima's mother. PMLA 68 1953.
Haymaker, R. E. From pampas to hedgerows and downs: a study of Hudson. New York 1954.
Dewar, D. R. Hudson's first days in England. N & Q Feb 1959.
—— Hudson's visit to Ireland. N & Q May 1960.

RICHARD JEFFERIES
1848–87

Collections

Out-of-doors with Jefferies: an anthology. Ed E. F. D[aglish] 1935.
Jefferies: selections of his work. Ed H. Williamson 1937.

Jefferies' England: nature essays by Jefferies. Ed S. J. Looker 1937.
The essential Jefferies. Ed M. Elwin 1948.
The Jefferies companion. Ed S. J. Looker 1948.
Works: uniform edition. Ed H. C. Warren 6 vols 1948–9.

§1

Jack Bass, Emperor of England. Swindon 1873.
Reporting, editing and authorship. Swindon [1873].
A memoir of the Goddards of North Wilts. Swindon [1873].
The scarlet shawl: a novel. 1874.
Restless human hearts. 3 vols 1875.
Suez-cide!! or how Miss Britannia bought a dirty puddle and lost her sugarplums. 1876.
The world's end. 3 vols 1877.
The gamekeeper at home: sketches of natural history and rural life. 1878.
Wild life in a southern county. 1879.
The amateur poacher. 1879.
Green Ferne Farm. 1880.
Hodge and his masters. 2 vols 1880.
Round about a great estate. 1880.
Wood magic: a fable. 2 vols 1880.
Bevis: the story of a boy. 3 vols 1882; ed E. V. Lucas 1904.
Nature near London. 1883.
The story of my heart: my autobiography. 1883.
The dewy morn: a novel. 2 vols 1884.
The life of the fields. 1884.
Red deer. 1884.
After London: or wild England, I: The relapse into barbarism; II: Wild England. 2 pts 1885.
The open air. 1885.
Amaryllis at the fair: a novel. 1887.
Field and hedgerow: being the last essays of Jefferies, collected by his widow. 1889.
The toilers of the field. 1892.
The early fiction of Jefferies. Ed G. Toplis 1896.
T. T. T. Wells. 1896. An early romance rptd from North Wilts Herald.
The hills and the vale. Ed E. Thomas 1909.
Hodge and his masters. Ed H. Williamson 1937.
The nature diaries and notebooks of Jefferies. Ed S. J. Looker, Billericay 1941.
Jefferies' countryside: nature essays. Ed S. J. Looker 1944.
Chronicles of the hedges and other essays. Ed S. J. Looker 1948.
Field and hedgerow. Ed S. J. Looker 1948.
The gamekeeper at home. Ed C. H. Warren 1948.
Field and farm: essays now first collected. Ed S. J. Looker 1957.

§2

Besant, W. The eulogy of Jefferies. 1888.
Salt, H. S. Jefferies: a study. 1894.
— The faith of Jefferies. 1906. Pamphlet.
Symons, A. In his Studies in two literatures, 1897.
Thomas, E. Jefferies: his life and work. 1909.
Masseck, C. J. Jefferies: étude d'une personnalité. Paris 1913; tr St Louis 1914. With bibliography.
Thom, A. F. The life worship of Jefferies. [1920].
Arkell, R. Richard Jefferies. 1933.
— Jefferies and his countryside: biography of a countryman. 1947.
Williamson, H. Jefferies. Atlantic Monthly June 1937.
— Report on the Jefferies centenary. Adelphi new ser 25 1948.
— Some nature writers and civilisation. Essays by Divers Hands 30 1960.
Looker, S. J. Jefferies. TLS 27 Nov 1938.
— Richard Jefferies. N & Q 19 June 1943.
— Jefferies. N & Q 12 Feb, 7 Oct 1944.
— (ed). Jefferies: a tribute. Worthing 1946.
Thomas, E. Jefferies. 1938.
Church, L. F. The centenary of Jefferies. London Quart 173 1948.
Marshall, D. E. Jefferies 1848–1948. Contemporary Rev Nov 1948.
Warren, C. H. Jefferies. Fortnightly Rev Nov 1948.
Mercer, W. C. G. M. Hopkins and Jefferies. N & Q 10 May 1952.
Blench, J. W. The novels of Jefferies. Cambridge Jnl March 1954.
Williamson, G. The eye of Jefferies. Literary Guide 70 1955.
Hyde, W. J. Jefferies and the naturalistic peasant. Nineteenth-Century Fiction 11 1957.
Keith, W. J. Jefferies: a critical study. 1966.

JEROME KLAPKA JEROME
1859–1927

§1

Idle thoughts of an idle fellow. 1886.
On the stage and off. 1888.
Stageland. 1889.
Three men in a boat (to say nothing of the dog). Bristol 1889.
Diary of a pilgrimage (and six essays). Bristol 1891.
Told after supper. 1891.
Novel notes. 1893. Rptd from Idler.
John Ingerfield and other stories. 1894.
Sketches in lavender, blue and green. 1897.
The second thoughts of an idle fellow. 1898.
Three men on the bummel. 1900.
The observations of Henry. 1901.
Paul Kelver. 1902.
Tea-table talk. 1903.
Tommy and Co. 1904.
Idle ideas in 1905. 1905.
The passing of the third floor back, and other stories 1907. Dramatized, 1910.
The angel and the author and others. 1908.
They and I. 1909.
Malvina of Brittany. 1916.
All roads lead to Calvary. 1919.
Anthony John. 1923.
A miscellany of sense and nonsense from the writings of Jerome, selected by the author. 1923.
My life and times. 1926.

§2

Walkley, A. B. In his Playhouse impressions, 1892.
Moss, A. Jerome: his life and works. 1929.

ANDREW LANG
1844–1912

See col 1440, below.

EMILY LAWLESS
1845–1913

See col 1907, below.

'VERNON LEE'

1856–1935

See col 1444, below.

RICHARD LE GALLIENNE

1866–1947

§1

My lady's sonnets. [Liverpool] 1887 (priv ptd).
Volumes in folio. 1889. Poems.
George Meredith: some characteristics. 1890.
The student and the body-snatcher. [1890]. With R. K. Leather.
The book-bills of Narcissus: an account rendered. [Derby] 1891, 1895 (3rd edn, rev).
English poems. 1892.
A fellowship in song. [Rugby 1893]. With Alfred Hayes and Norman Gale.
The religion of a literary man. 1893.
Young lives. 1893.
Limited editions: a prose fancy; together with Confessio Amantis: a sonnet. 1893 (priv ptd).
Bits of old Chelsea. 1894. With Lionel Johnson.
Prose fancies. 2 sers 1894–6.
Robert Louis Stevenson and other poems. 1895.
The quest of the golden girl. 1896.
Retrospective reviews. 2 vols 1896.
If I were God. 1897.
Rubáiyát of Omar Khayyám: a paraphrase. 1897.
The romance of Zion Chapel. 1898.
The worshipper of the image. 1899.
Sleeping beauty and other prose fancies. 1900.
The beautiful lie of Rome. 1900.
Rudyard Kipling: a criticism. 1900.
Travles in England. 1900.
The life romantic. 1901.
Perseus and Andromeda: the story retold. New York 1903.
Odes from the Divan of Hafiz freely rendered. 1903.
An old country house. 1903.
The burial of Romeo and Juliet. 1904.
How to get the best out of books. 1904.
Romances of old France. New York 1905.
Omar repentant. 1908. Poems.
Painted shadows. 1908.
Little dinners with the Sphinx and other prose fancies. 1909.
Attitudes and avowals, with some retrospective reviews. 1910.
New poems. 1910.
Orestes: a tragedy. New York 1910.
The loves of the poets. New York 1911.
October vagabonds. 1911.
The maker of rainbows, and other fairy-tales and fables. 1912.
The lonely dancer and other poems. 1914.
The highway to happiness. 1914.
Vanishing roads and other essays. 1915.
The silk-hat soldier and other poems. 1915.
Pieces of eight. 1918.
The junk man and other poems. New York 1920.
A jongleur strayed. New York 1922.
Old love stories retold. 1924.
The romantic Nineties. 1926; ed H. M. Hyde 1952.
There was a ship. [New York] 1930.
Le Gallienne also edited Hazlitt's Liber Amoris, 1893, *A. H. Hallam's* Poems, 1893, *and Walton's* Compleat angler, 1896, *and tr Wagner's* Tristan *into verse*, 1909.

§2

Archer, W. In his Poets of the younger generation, 1902.
Johnson, L. In his Reviews and critical papers, ed R. Shafer 1921.
Mead, H. R. Le Gallienne's Perseus and Andromeda. PBSA 43 1949.
Whittington-Egan, R. and G. Smerdon. The quest of the golden boy: the life and letters of le Gallienne. 1960.

'EDNA LYALL', ADA ELLEN BAYLY

1857–1903

§1

Won by waiting: a story of home life in France and England. 1879, 1886 (rev).
Donovan: a novel. 3 vols 1882.
We two: a novel. 3 vols 1884.
In the golden days: a novel. 3 vols 1885.
Autobiography of a slander. 1887.
Knight-errant: a novel. 3 vols 1887.
Their happiest Christmas. 1889.
Derrick Vaughan, novelist. 1889.
A hardy Norseman: a novel. 3 vols 1890.
Max Hereford's dream: a tale. 1891.
To right the wrong. 3 vols 1894.
Doreen: the story of a singer. 1894.
How the children raised the wind: a tale. 1896.
The autobiography of a truth. 1896.
Mrs Gaskell. In A. Sergeant et al, Women novelists of Queen Victoria's reign, 1897.
Wayfaring men: a novel. 1897.
Hope the hermit: a novel. 1898.
In spite of all: a novel. 1901.
The Burges letters: a record of child life in the Sixties. 1902. Autobiography.
The hinderers: a story of the present time. 1902.

§2

Payne, G. A. Edna Lyall: an appreciation, with biographical and critical notes. [1903].
Escreet, J. M. The life of Edna Lyall (Ada Ellen Bayly). 1904.

'FIONA MacLEOD', WILLIAM SHARP

1855–1905

Collections

Writings: uniform edition, arranged by Mrs William Sharp. 7 vols 1909–10.
Selected writings, arranged by Mrs. William Sharp. 5 vols 1912.
Writings: pocket edition. 8 vols 1927.

§1

Writings published under the pseudonym 'Fiona MacLeod'

Pharais: a romance of the Isles. Derby 1894.
The mountain lovers. 1895.
The sin eater and other tales. Edinburgh 1895.
The washer of the ford and other legendary moralities. Edinburgh 1896.
Green fire: a romance. 1896.
From the hills of dream: mountain songs and island runes. 1896. Edinburgh [1897]. Poems.

The laughter of Peterkin: a retelling of old tales of the Celtic wonderland. 1897.
The shorter stories of Fiona MacLeod, rearranged, with additional tales. 3 vols Edinburgh [1897].
The dominion of dreams. 1899.
The divine adventure; Iona; By sundown shores: studies in spiritual history. 1900.
The house of Usna: a drama. 1903.
The winged destiny: studies in the spiritual history of the Gael. 1904.
Where the forest murmurs: nature essays. 1906.
From the hills of dream: threnodies and songs, and later poems. 1907.
The immortal hour: a drama. 1908.
A little book of nature, selected from the writings of Fiona MacLeod by Mrs William Sharp. 1909.

Writings published under the name William Sharp

The human inheritance, the new hope, motherhood. 1882.
D. G. Rossetti: a record and a study. 1882.
Earth's voices, transcripts from Nature, Sospitra, and other poems. 1884.
Euphrenia, or the test of love: a poem. 1884.
Jack Noel's legacy: a story for boys. Young Folks 1886. A serial.
Life of P. B. Shelley. 1887.
Under the banner of St James: a romance of the discovery of the Pacific. Young Folks 1887. A serial.
Life of Heinrich Heine. 1888.
Romantic ballads and poems of phantasy. 1888, 1889 (with 2 addns).
The secret of the seven fountains: a story for boys. Young Folks 1888. A serial.
The sport of chance: a novel. 3 vols 1888. First pbd in People's Friend (Dundee) 1887 as A deathless hate.
Children of to-morrow: a romance. 1889.
Life of Robert Browning. 1890.
Sospiri di Roma. 1891.
A fellowe and his wife. 1892. With B. W. Howard.
The life and letters of Joseph Severn. 1892.
The Pagan Review. Ed W. H. Brooks. No 1 (all pbd) Aug 1892. Written entirely by Sharp under various pseudonyms.
The red rider: a romance of the Garibaldian campaign in the Two Sicilies. Weekly Budget 1892. A serial.
The last of the Vikings, being the adventures in the East and West of Sigurd, the Boy King of Norway. Old & Young 1893. A serial.
Fair women in painting and poetry. 1894. Vistas. Derby 1894.
Ecce puella and other prose imaginings. 1896.
Madgeo' the Pool, the Gypsy Christ and other tales. 1897.
Wives in exile: a comedy in romance. 1898.
Silence farm: a novel. 1899.
Literary geography. 1904.
Songs and poems, old and new. 1909.
From May 1879 to Dec 1905 Sharp contributed articles, sketches and poems to Fortnightly Rev, Nineteenth Century, Examiner, Chambers's Jnl, Good Words, Athenaeum, Academy, Portfolio, Art Jnl, Nat Rev, Atlantic Monthly, Literature, Harper's Mag, Century Mag, Quart Rev, Pall Mall Mag, Evergreen, Savoy, Dome, Eng Illustr Mag, Contemporary Rev, Country Life, and North Amer Rev, both under his own name and (1895–1905) as 'Fiona MacLeod'. He also edited several vols in the Canterbury Poets Ser and 3 anthologies.

§2

Rhys, E. The new mysticism. Fortnightly Rev June 1900.
Yeats, W. B. The later work of Fiona MacLeod. North Amer Rev 175 1902.
Noyes, A. Fiona MacLeod. Bookman (London) Jan 1906.
Tynan, K. Fiona MacLeod. Fortnightly Rev March 1906.
Sharp, E. A. William Sharp (Fiona MacLeod): a memoir compiled by his wife. 1910, 2 vols 1912. With a list of Sharp's writings.
More, P. E. In his Shelburne essays ser 8, New York 1913.
Evans, B. I. In his English poetry in the later nineteenth century, 1933.
Fiechter, S. Von William Sharp zu Fiona MacLeod. Tübingen 1936.
Waugh, A. Fiona MacLeod: a forgotten mystery. Spectator 14 Aug 1936.
Iorio, J. J. A Victorian controversy: William Sharp's Letters on motherhood. Colby Literary Quart 4 1957.
Garbaty, T. J. Fiona MacLeod: defence of her views and her identity. N & Q Dec 1960.

'LUCAS MALET', MARY ST LEGER KINGSLEY, later HARRISON

1852–1931

§1

Mrs Lorimer. 2 vols 1882.
Colonel Enderby's wife. 3 vols 1885.
A counsel of perfection. 1888.
Little Peter. 1888.
The wages of sin: a novel. 3 vols 1891.
The Carissima. 1896.
The gateless barrier. 1900.
The history of Sir Richard Calmady: a romance. 2 vols 1901.
The far horizon. 1906.
The score. 1909.
Adrian Savage. 1911.
The tutor's story: an unpublished novel by Charles Kingsley, revised and completed by Lucas Malet. 1916.
Damaris. 1916.
Deadham Hard. 1919.
The tall villa. 1920.
Da Silva's widow and other stories. 1922.
The survivors. 1923.
The dogs of want. 1924.
The private life of Mr Justice Syme. 1932. Left unfinished at her death and completed by Gabrielle Vallings.

§2

Archer, W. In his Real conversations, 1904.
Courtney, W. L. In his Feminine note in fiction, 1904.

WILLIAM HURRELL MALLOCK

1849–1923

Bibliographies

Nickerson, C. C. A bibliography of the novels of Mallock. Eng Fiction in Transition 6 1963.

§1

Poems. 1867 (priv ptd).
The parting of the ways: a poetic epistle. 1867.
Newdigate Prize poem: The Isthmus of Suez. Oxford 1871.
Everyman his own poet: or the inspired singer's recipe book. Oxford 1872. Anon.
The new republic: or culture, faith and philosophy in an English country house. 2 vols 1877; ed J. M. Patrick, Gainesville 1950.
Lucretius. 1878.

The new Paul and Virginia: or Positivism on an island. 1878.
Is life worth living? 1879.
Poems. 1880.
A romance of the nineteenth century. 2 vols 1881.
Social equality: a short study in a missing science. 1882.
Atheism and the value of life: five studies in contemporary literature. 1884.
Property and progress: or a brief enquiry into contemporary social agitation in England. 1884. A reply to H. George, Progress and poverty.
The landlords and the national income: a chart showing the proportion borne by the rental of the landlords to to the gross income of the people. 1884.
The old order changes: a novel. 3 vols 1886.
In an enchanted island: or a winter retreat in Cyprus. 1889.
A human document: a novel. 3 vols 1892.
Labour and the popular welfare. 1893, 1894 (with Appendix).
Verses. 1893. Partly rptd from the 1880 collection, above.
The heart of life: a novel. 3 vols 1895.
Studies of contemporary superstition. 1895.
Classes and masses, or wealth, wages and welfare in the United Kingdom: a handbook of social facts for political thinkers and speakers. 1896.
Aristocracy and evolution: a study of the rights, the origin and the social functions of the wealthier classes. 1898.
The individualist: a novel. 1899.
Doctrine and doctrinal disruption: being an examination of the intellectual position of the Church of England. 1900.
Lucretius on life and death. 1900. A very free adaptation of Lucretius in the metre of FitzGerald, Omar Khayyám.
The fiscal dispute made easy: or a key to the principles involved in the opposite policies. 1903.
Religion as a credible doctrine. 1903.
The veil of the temple: or from night to twilight. 1904.
The reconstruction of belief. 1905.
A critical examination of Socialism. New York 1907.
An immortal soul. 1908.
The nation as a business firm: an attempt to cut a path through jungle. 1910.
Social reform as related to realities and delusions: an examination of the increase and distribution of wealth from 1801 to 1910. 1914.
The limits of pure democracy. 1918, 1924 (abridged as Democracy, with an introd by the Duke of Northumberland).
Capital, war and wages: three questions in outline. 1918.
Memoirs of life and literature. 1920.

§2

Shaw, G. B. Socialism and superior brains: a reply to Mr Mallock. 1909.
Adams, A. B. The novels of Mallock. Orono 1934.
Woodring, C. R. Mallock: a neglected wit. More Books 22 1947.
—— Notes on Mallock's The new republic. Nineteenth-Century Fiction 6 1952.
Yarker, P. Shaw and Mallock. TLS 24 Nov 1950.
—— Voltaire among the Positivists: a study of Mallock's The new Paul and Virginia. E & S 8 1955.
—— Mallock's other novels. Nineteenth-Century Fiction 14 1960.
Nickerson, C. C. Mallock's contributions to the Miscellany. Victorian Stud 6 1962.
—— Mallock's pseudonyms. N & Q Dec 1963.
—— The novels of Mallock. Eng Fiction in Transition 6 1963.
Tucker, A. V. Mallock and late Victorian Conservatism. UTQ 31 1962.

HELEN BUCKINGHAM MATHERS, later REEVES

1853–1920

Comin' thro' the rye: a novel. 1875. Anon.
The token of the silver lily. 1877. A poem.
As he comes up the stair, by the author of Comin' thro' the rye. 1878.
Cherry ripe! a romance, by the author of Comin' thro' the rye. 3 vols 1878.
Land o' the leal. 1878. Anon.
My Lady Green Sleeves, by the author of Comin' thro' the rye. 3 vols 1879.
Story of a sin, by the author of Comin' thro' the rye. 1882.
Sam's sweetheart. 3 vols 1883.
Eyre's acquittal: a sequel to Story of a sin. 3 vols 1884.
Jock o' Hazelgreen. 1884.
Found out, by the author of Comin' thro' the rye. [1885].
Murder or manslaughter? a novel. [1885].
The fashion of this world. [1886].
Blind justice: a story. 1890.
The mystery of no 13: a novel. 1891.
My Jo, John: a novel. 1891.
The fate of Fenella. 1892.
T'other dear charmer: a novel. [1892].
A study of a woman, or Venus Victrix: a novel. 1893.
What the glass told: a novel. 1893.
A man of to-day: a novel. 3 vols 1894.
The lovely Malincourt: a novel. 1895.
The juggler and the soul. 1896.
The sin of Hagar. 1896.
David Lyall's love story, by the author of the Land o' the leal. 1897.
Bam Wildfire: a character sketch. 1898.
Becky. 1900.
Cinders: a novel. 1901.
'Honey'. 1902.
Venus Victrix and other stories. 1902.
Dahlia and other stories. 1903.
Dimples. 1903.
The face in the mirror and other stories. 1903.
Griff of Griffithscourt. 1903.
The new Lady Teazle and other stories. 1903.
'Side-shows'. 1904.
The ferryman. 1905.
Tally ho! 1906.
Pigskin and petticoat. 1907.
The pirouette and other stories. 1907 (2nd edn).
Gay Lawless. 1908.
Love the thief. 1909.
Man is fire: woman is tow, and other stories. [1912].

LEONARD MERRICK, originally MILLER

1864–1938

Collections

Works. 12 vols 1918–19. Introd to each vol by M. Hewlett, W. D. Howells, N. Munro, H. G. Wells et al.

§1

Mr Bazalgette's legacy. 1888.
Violet Moses. 3 vols 1891.
The man who was good. 2 vols 1892.
This stage of fools. 1896.
Cynthia: a daughter of the Philistines. 2 vols 1896, 1897.
One man's view. 1897.
The actor manager. 1898.
The worldlings. 1900.

When love flies out of the window. 1902.
Conrad in quest of his youth. 1903.
Quaint companions. 1903.
Whispers about women. 1906.
The house of Lynch. 1907.
The man who understood women, and other stories. [1908].
All the world wondered, and other stories. 1911.
The position of Peggy Harper. 1911.
While Paris laughed. 1914.
The chair on the boulevard: short stories. 1919.
To tell you the truth. [1922].
The call from the past, and other stories. 1924.
Four stories. 1925.

'HENRY SETON MERRIMAN', HUGH STOWELL SCOTT
1862–1903

Collections

Works. 14 vols 1909–10.

§1

Young Mistley. 2 vols 1888. Anon.
The phantom future. 2 vols 1888.
Suspense. 3 vols 1890.
Prisoners and captives. 3 vols 1891.
The slave of the lamp. 2 vols 1892.
From one generation to another. 2 vols 1892.
With edged tools. 3 vols 1894.
The grey lady. 1895.
Flotsam: the study of a life. 1896.
The money-spinner and other character notes. 1896. With S. G. Tallentyre.
The sowers. 1896.
In Kedar's tents. 1897.
Roden's corner. 1898.
Dross. 1899.
The isle of unrest. 1900.
The velvet glove. 1901.
The vultures. 1902.
Barlasch of the Guard. 1903.
The last hope. 1904.
Tomaso's fortune and other stories. 1904.

WILLIAM MINTO
1845–93

See col 1446, below.

EDITH NESBIT
1858–1924

See col 641, above.

ARTHUR MORRISON
1863–1945

§1

The shadows around us. 1891.
Martin Hewitt: investigator. 1894.
Tales of mean streets. 1894.
Chronicles of Martin Hewitt. 1895.
Zig-zags at the zoo. 1895.
A child of the Jago. 1896.
Hewitt: third series. 1896.
The Dorrington deed box. 1897.
To London town. 1899.
Cunning Murrell. 1900.
The hole in the wall. 1902.
The red triangle. 1903.
The green eye of Goona. 1904.
Divers vanities. 1905.
Green ginger. 1909.
The painters of Japan. 2 vols 1911.
Guide to an exhibition of Japanese and Chinese paintings. 1914.
Short stories of to-day and yesterday. 1929.
Fiddle O'Dreams. 1933.
Morrison also wrote, in collaboration, several unpbd plays.

§2

Wells, H. G. A slum novel. Saturday Rev 28 Nov 1896.
Findlater, J. H. The slum movement in fiction. Nat Rev 35 1900.
Pritchett, V. S. In his Living novel, 1947.
Bell, J. A study of Morrison. E & S 5 1952.
Brome, V. In his Four realist novelists, 1965.

LADY AUGUSTA NOEL
1838–1902

Effie's friends: or chronicles of the woods and shore. 1865. Anon.
The story of wandering Willie. 1870.
The life and times of Conrad the squirrel: a story for children. 1872.
Owen Gwynne's great work. 2 vols 1875.
From generation to generation: a novel. 2 vols 1879; ed J. Gore 1929.
Faith and unfaith. In In a good cause: a collection of stories, 1885.
Hithersea Mere. 3 vols 1887.
The wise man of Sterncross. 1901.

'OUIDA', MARIE LOUISE de la RAMÉE
1839–1908

§1

Held in bondage. 3 vols 1863. First pbd in New Monthly Mag as Granville de Vigne: a tale of the day, Jan 1861–June 1863.
Strathmore. 3 vols 1865. First pbd in New Monthly Mag.
Chandos. 1866.
Under two flags. 3 vols 1867.
Cecil Castlemaine's gage and other novelettes. 1867. First ptd in Bentley's Miscellany.
Idalia. 3 vols 1867. First pbd in New Monthly Mag March 1865–Feb 1867.
Tricotrin. 2 vols 1869.
Puck. 3 vols 1870.
Folle Farine. 3 vols 1871.
A dog of Flanders and other stories. 1872. First pbd in Lippincott's Mag.
Pascarel. 3 vols 1873.
Two little wooden shoes. 1874.
Signa. 3 vols 1875.
In a winter city. 1876.
Ariadne: the story of a dream. 3 vols 1877.
Friendship. 3 vols 1878.
Moths. 3 vols 1880.
Pipistrello and other stories. 1880.
A village commune. 2 vols 1881.
In Maremma. 3 vols 1882.
Bimbi: stories for children. 1882.
Frescoes: dramatic sketches. 1883.
Wanda. 3 vols 1883.
Princess Napraxine. 3 vols 1884.

A rainy June. [1885].
Othmar. 3 vols 1885.
Don Gesualdo. 1886.
A house party. 1887.
Guilderoy. 3 vols 1889.
Ruffino etc. 1890. Contains Ruffino; An orchard; Trottolino; The bullfinch.
Syrlin. 3 vols 1890.
Santa Barbara. 1891. Tales.
The tower of Taddeo. 3 vols 1892.
The new priesthood: a protest against vivisection. 1893.
Two offenders and other tales. 1894.
The silver Christ, and A lemon tree. 1894.
Toxin. 1895.
Views and opinions. 1895. Essays.
Le Selve and other tales. 1896.
An altruist. 1897.
The Massarenes. 1897.
La Strega and other stories. 1899.
Critical studies. 1900.
The waters of Edera. 1900.
Street dust and other stories. 1901.
Helianthus. 1908. Unfinished.

Ouida contributed various articles from 1897 onwards to Fortnightly Rev, Nineteenth Century, North Amer Rev and other journals. She also wrote several articles in Italian for Nuova Antologia.

§2

Burnand, F. C. Strapmore! a romance by Weeder. 1878. First pbd in Punch 1878.
Street, G. S. An appreciation of Ouida. In his Quales ego, 1896.
Beerbohm, M. In his More, 1899.
Lee, E. Ouida: a memoir. 1914.
Elwin, M. In his Victorian wallflowers 1934.
Macaulay, R. Eccentric Englishwomen: Ouida. Spectator 7 May 1937.
ffrench, Y. Ouida. 1938.
Bigland, E. Ouida: the passionate Victorian. 1950.
Stirling, La dernière romancière. Revue de Paris 62 1955.
— The fire and the wicked: the life and times of Ouida. 1957.
Tappe, E. D. Ouida's Idalia: the source of its Moldavian scenes. N & Q July–Aug 1959.

WALTER PATER
1839–94

See col 1412, below.

'Q', SIR ARTHUR THOMAS QUILLER-COUCH
1863–1944

Collections

Selected stories by Q chosen by the author. [1921].
The Duchy edition of tales and romances by Q. 30 vols 1928.
Collected poems. 1929.
'Q' anthology. Ed F. Brittain 1948.

§1

Athens: a poem. [Bodmin] 1881.
Dead man's rock. 1887.
The astonishing history of Troy Town. 1888.
The splendid spur. 1889.
Noughts and crosses: stories. 1891.
A blot of ink, by René Bazin. 1892. Tr from the French by Quiller-Couch and P. M. Francke.
I saw three ships, and other winter's tales. 1892.
The blue pavillions. 1892.
The Warwickshire Avon. 1892.
The delectable Duchy: stories. 1893.
Green bays: verses and parodies. 1893.
Fairy tales, far and near. 1895.
Wandering heath: stories. 1895.
Adventures in criticism. 1896.
Ia. 1896.
Poems and ballads. 1896.
St Ives, by Robert Louis Stevenson. 1898. Completed from ch 31 by Quiller-Couch.
The ship of stars. 1899.
Old fires and profitable ghosts: stories. 1900.
The laird's luck and other fireside tales. 1901.
The Westcotes. 1902.
The white wolf and other fireside tales. 1902.
The adventures of Harry Revel. 1903.
Two sides of the face: tales. 1903.
The collaborators: or the comedy that wrote itself. 1903.
Hetty Wesley. 1903.
Fort Amity. 1904.
Shakespeare's Christmas and other stories. 1905.
Shining ferry. 1905.
From a Cornish window. 1906.
Sir John Constantine. 1906.
The Mayor of Troy. 1906.
Major Vigoureux. 1907.
Poison Island. 1907.
Merry-garden and other stories. 1907.
True Tilda. 1909.
Corporal Sam and other stories. 1910.
Lady Good for Nothing. 1910.
The sleeping beauty and other tales from the Old French, illustrated by Edmund Dulac. [1911].
Brother Copas. 1911.
Hocken and Hunken. 1912.
The vigil of Venus and other poems. 1912.
In powder and crinoline: old fairy tales retold. [1913].
News from the Duchy. 1913.
Poetry. 1914.
Nicky-Nan, reservist. 1915.
On the art of writing. Cambridge 1916.
Memoir of A. J. Butler. 1917.
Mortallone and Aunt Trinidad: tales of the Spanish Main. 1917.
Foe-Farrell. 1918.
Shakespeare's workmanship. 1918.
Studies in literature. 3 sers Cambridge 1918–29.
On the art of reading. Cambridge 1920.
Charles Dickens and other Victorians. Cambridge 1925.
Honourable men—Livingstone; Lincoln; Gordon. 1925. Rptd from Roll call of honour, below.
Victors of peace—Florence Nightingale; Pasteur; Father Damien. [1926]. Rptd from Roll call of honour, below.
The age of Chaucer. 1926.
A lecture on lectures. 1927.
The poet as citizen and other papers. Cambridge 1934.
Memories and opinions: an unfinished autobiography. Ed S. C. Roberts, Cambridge 1944.

Editions

The golden pomp: lyrics from Surrey to Shirley. 1895.
The story of the sea. 2 vols 1895–6.
Historical tales from Shakespeare. 1899, 1905.
The Oxford book of English verse 1250–1900. Oxford 1900.
The world of adventure: a collection of stirring scenes. 6 vols 1904.
The pilgrim's way: a little book of good counsel for travellers. 1906.
Select English classics. 1908–.
The Oxford book of ballads. Oxford 1910.
The roll call of honour. 1912.

The Oxford book of Victorian verse. Oxford 1912.
The King's treasuries of literature. 1920–.
The works of Shakespeare. Cambridge 1921—(New Cambridge edn). The comedies were edited by Quiller-Couch and J. D. Wilson, the tragedies and histories by Wilson alone.
The Oxford book of English prose. Oxford 1925.

§2

Archer, W. In his Poets of the younger generation, 1902.
Brittain, F. Quiller-Couch: a biographical study of 'Q'. Cambridge 1947.

JAMES RICE
1843–82

See under Sir Walter Besant, col 1038, above.

MRS J. H. RIDDELL, i.e. CHARLOTTE ELIZABETH LAWSON COWAN
1832–1906

§1

Zuriel's grandchild. [1855?], 1873 (as Joy after sorrow).
The ruling passion. 3 vols 1857, 1896. Pbd under the pseudonym 'Rainey Hawthorne'.
The moors and the fens. 3 vols 1858. Pbd under the pseudonym 'F. G. Trafford'.
The rich husband. 3 vols [1858?]. Anon.
Too much alone, by F. G. Trafford. 3 vols 1860.
City and suburb, by F. G. Trafford. 3 vols 1861.
The world in the Church, by F. G. Trafford. 3 vols 1863 (2nd edn).
George Geith of Fen Court: a novel by F. G. Trafford. 3 vols 1864.
Maxwell Drewitt: a novel by F. G. Trafford. 3 vols 1865.
Phemie Keller: a novel by F. G. Trafford. 3 vols 1866.
The race for wealth: a novel. 3 vols 1866. First pbd in Once a Week.
Far above rubies: a novel. 3 vols 1867 (2nd edn).
The miseries of Christmas. In Routledge's Christmas Annual, 1867.
Austin Friars: a novel. 3 vols 1870.
A life's assize: a novel. 3 vols 1871. First pbd in St James's Mag April 1868–Feb 1870.
The Earl's promise: a novel. 3 vols 1873.
Home, sweet home: a novel. 3 vols 1873.
Mortomley's estate: a novel. 3 vols 1874.
Frank Sinclair's wife and other stories. 3 vols 1874.
The uninhabited house. In Routledge's Christmas Annual, 1875.
Above suspicion: a novel. 3 vols 1876.
Her mother's darling: a novel. 3 vols 1877.
The haunted river: a Christmas story. In Routledge's Christmas Annual, 1877.
Fairy water: a Christmas story. 1878. First pbd as Routledge's Christmas annual, 1873.
The disappearance of Mr Jeremiah Redworth. Routledge's Christmas Annual, 1878.
The mystery in Palace Gardens: a novel. 3 vols 1880. First pbd in London Soc.
The curate of Lawood: or every man has his golden chance. [1882].
Daisies and buttercups: a novel. 3 vols 1882.
The Prince of Wales's garden party and other stories. 1882.
Idle tales. 1882.
A struggle for fame. 3 vols 1883.
Susan Drummond: a novel. 3 vols 1884. First pbd in London Soc 1883, as Three wizards and a witch.
Weird stories. 1884.
Berna Boyle: a love story of the County Down. 3 vols 1884.
Mitre Court: a tale of the great city. 3 vols 1885. First pbd in Temple Bar.
For Dick's sake. 1886.
Miss Gascoigne: a novel. 1887.
The nun's curse. 3 vols 1888.
Princess Sunshine and other stories. 2 vols 1889.
The head of the firm: a novel. 3 vols 1892.
The rusty sword: or thereby hangs a tale. 1894. First pbd in Dawn of day, 1893.
A silent tragedy: a novel. 1893.
The banshee's warning and other tales. 1894.
Did he deserve it? 1897.
A rich man's daughter. 1897.
Handsome Phil and other stories. 1899.
The footfall of fate. 1900.
Poor fellow. 1902.
Mrs Riddell also collaborated with A. H. Norway in The Government official, 3 vols 1887. *She revised Sir C. P. Roney's* How to spend a month in Ireland, 1874, *and wrote* A mad tour: or a journey undertaken in an insane moment through Central Europe on foot, 1891.

§2

Black, H. C. In her Notable women authors of the day, 1893.
Ellis, S. M. In his Wilkie Collins and others, 1931.

WILLIAM CLARK RUSSELL
1844–1911

The hunchback's charge: a romance. 3 vols 1867.
The book of authors. [1871].
Is she a wife? 3 vols 1871. Pbd under the pseudonym 'Sydney Mostyn'.
Memoirs of Mrs Laetitia Boothby. 1872.
Perplexity. 3 vols 1872. Pbd under the pseudonym 'Sydney Mostyn'.
Representative actors. [1872].
The surgeon's secret, by Sydney Mostyn. 1872.
Which sister? by Sydney Mostyn. 2 vols 1873.
Kitty's rival, by Sydney Mostyn. 3 vols 1873.
The book of table talk: selections from the conversations of poets, philosophers, statesmen and divines; notes and memoirs by Clark Russell. 1874.
John Holdsworth, Chief Mate. 3 vols 1875.
Is he the man? 3 vols 1876.
Captain Fanny. 3 vols 1876.
The Lady Maud. 3 vols 1876.
The wreck of the 'Grosvenor'. 3 vols 1877.
The frozen pirate. 2 vols 1877.
Auld lang syne. 2 vols 1878.
The little Loo, by Sydney Mostyn. 3 vols 1878, 1883 (as Little Loo). 'Little Loo' is the name both of a ship and of a personage; hence the slight change of title in 2nd edn.
A sailor's sweetheart: the wreck of the Waldershare. 3 vols 1880.
An ocean tragedy. 3 vols 1881.
An ocean free-lance. 3 vols 1881.
My watch below: yarns. 1882. First pbd in Daily Telegraph.
Sailor's language: a collection of sea-terms and their definitions. 1883.
A sea queen. 3 vols 1883.
Round the galley fire: stories. 1883. First pbd in Daily Telegraph.

On the fo'c'sle head. 1884.
Jack's courtship: a sailor's yarn of love and shipwreck. 3 vols 1884.
A strange voyage. 3 vols 1885.
In the middle watch. 1885.
A voyage to the Cape. 1886.
A book for the hammock. 1887. Tales.
The golden hope. 3 vols 1887.
The death ship. 3 vols 1888.
The mystery of the ocean star: a collection of maritime sketches. 1888.
Betwixt the Forelands: historical essays. [1899].
Marooned. 3 vols 1889.
William Dampier. 1889.
Nelson and the naval supremacy of England. 1890. With W. H. Jacques.
Nelson's words and deeds. 1890. Ed Russell.
My shipmate Louise. 3 vols 1890.
The romance of Jenny Harlowe; and sketches of maritime life. 1890.
Collingwood. 1891.
Master Rockafellar's voyage. 1891.
My Danish sweetheart: a novel. 3 vols 1891.
A marriage at sea. 2 vols 1891.
A strange elopement. 1892.
Alone on a wide wide sea. 3 vols 1892.
The British seas: picturesque notes. 1892. By Russell et al.
The emigrant ship. 3 vols 1893.
List, ye landsmen! 3 vols 1893.
The tragedy of Ida Noble. 1893.
The good ship Mohock. 2 vols 1894.
Miss Parson's adventure. 1894. Stories by Russell et al.
The convict ship. 3 vols 1895.
Heart of oak. 3 vols 1895.
The phantom death and other stories. 1895.
The honour of the flag and other stories. 1896.
The tale of the ten. 3 vols 1896.
What cheer! 1896.
A noble haul. 1897.
Pictures from the life of Nelson. 1897.
The two captains. 1897.
The last entry. 1897.
A tale of two tunnels. 1897.
Romance of a midshipman. 1898.
The ship: her story. 1899.
The pretty Polly. 1900.
Rose island. 1900.
A voyage at anchor. 1900.
The sequel. 1901.
The ship's adventure. 1901.
Overdue. 1903.
Abandoned. 1904.
Wrong side out. 1904.
An Atlantic tragedy and other stories. 1905.
His island Princess. 1905.
The life of Nelson in a series of episodes. 1905.
The yarn of old harbour town. 1905.
The turnpike sailor: or rhymes on the road. 1907.
The father of the sea and other verses. 1911.

'MARK RUTHERFORD', WILLIAM HALE WHITE

1831–1913

Bibliographies

Nowell-Smith, S. Mark Rutherford: a bibliography of the first editions. 1930.

§1

Works Published Pseudonymously

The following appeared as 'by Mark Rutherford', the first 6 being 'edited by his friend Reuben Shapcott'.

The autobiography of Mark Rutherford, dissenting minister. 1881. A novel.
Mark Rutherford's deliverance: being the second part of his autobiography. 1885, 1888 (rev and expanded with the Autobiography, above).
The revolution in Tanner's Lane. 1887.
Miriam's schooling and other papers. 1890.
Catharine Furze. 2 vols 1893.
Clara Hopgood. 1896.
Pages from a journal, with other papers. 1900, 1910 (expanded), Oxford 1930 (WC).
More pages from a journal. 1910.
Last pages from a journal. Ed D. V. White 1915.

Other Writings

An argument for an extension of the franchise: letter to G. J. Holyoake. 1866.
Benedict de Spinoza, Ethic. 1883. Tr White.
A dream of two dimensions. 1884. Anon and priv ptd. Later included in Last pages from a journal, above.
Benedict de Spinoza, Tractatus de intellectus emendatione: translation [by White] revised by Amelia H. Stirling. 1895.
The inner life of the House of Commons, by William White; preface by Justin McCarthy; introduction by the author's son [i.e. White]. 2 vols 1897.
A description of the Wordsworth and Coleridge mss in the possession of Mr T. Norton Longman. 1897.
An examination of the charge of apostasy against Wordsworth. 1898.
Coleridge's poems: a facsimile reproduction of the proofs and mss of some of the poems; edited by the late James Dykes Campbell, with preface and notes by W. Hale White. 1899.
John Bunyan, by the author of 'Mark Rutherford'. 1905.
Selections from Dr Johnson's Rambler. 1907. Ed White.
The life of John Sterling, by Thomas Carlyle. Oxford 1907 (WC). Ed White.
The early life of Mark Rutherford (W. Hale White), by himself. 1913. Preface by White's son. An autobiography.
Letters to three friends. Ed D. V. White 1924.

§2

Selby, T. G. In his Theology of modern fiction, 1896.
Low, F. H. Mark Rutherford: an appreciation. Fortnightly Rev Sept 1908.
Sperry, W. L. Mark Rutherford. Harvard Theological Rev 7 1914.
Taylor, A. E. The novels of Mark Rutherford. E & S 5 1914.
Taylor, W. D. Mark Rutherford. Queen's Quart 25 1917.
Massingham, H. W. Memorial introduction. In Autobiography of Mark Rutherford, 1923.
Murry, J. M. The religion of Mark Rutherford. In his To the unknown God, 1924.
Nicoll, W. R. Introduction to the novels of Mark Rutherford. [1924]. Pamphlet.
—— Memories of Mark Rutherford. 1924.
White, D. V. The Groombridge diary. 1924.
Klinke, H. William Hale White. Frankfurt 1931. In German.
Garnett, D. Books in general. New Statesman 8 Aug 1936, 2 Jan 1937.
Harrison, A. W. Rutherford and J. A. Froude. London Quart 164 1939.
Praz, M. The autobiography of Mark Rutherford. Anglica 1 1946.
Buchman, U. C. Willima Hale White: the problem of self-adjustment in a world of changing values. Zürich 1950.
Merton, E. S. The autobiographical novels of Mark Rutherford. Nineteenth-Century Fiction 5 1951.

— The personality of Mark Rutherford. Nineteenth-Century Fiction 6 1952.
— Mark Rutherford: the world of his novels. BNYPL Sept 1963.
Stock, I. André Gide, White and the Protestant tradition. Accent 12 1952.
— William Hale White (Mark Rutherford). 1956.
Stone, W. H. Browning and Mark Rutherford. RES new ser 4 1953.
— The confessional fiction of Mark Rutherford. UTQ 23 1953.
— Religion and art of White. Stanford 1954.
Beresford, R. Mark Rutherford and hero-worship. RES new ser 6 1955.
Low, F. B. Walks and talks with Mark Rutherford. Contemporary Rev June 1955.
MacLean, C. M. Mark Rutherford: a biography of W. H. White. 1955.
Michie, J. A. The wisdom of Mark Rutherford. London Quart 184 1959.
Thomson, P. The novels of Mark Rutherford. EC 14 1964.

OLIVE SCHREINER
1865–1920

§1

The story of an African farm: a novel. 2 vols 1883. First pbd under the pseudonym 'Ralph Iron'.
Dreams. 1891.
Dream life and real life: tales by Ralph Iron. 1893.
The political situation in Cape Colony. 1896. With S. C. Schreiner.
Trooper Peter Halket of Mashonaland. 1897.
An English-South African's view of the situation: words in season. 1899.
Closer union: a letter on the South African Union and the principles of government. 1909.
Woman and labour. 1911.
Thoughts on South Africa. 1923.
The letters of Olive Schreiner. Ed S. C. Schreiner 1924.
From man to man: or perhaps only. 1926. With introd by S. C. Schreiner.
Undine. 1928. With introd by S. C. Schreiner.

§2

Schreiner, S. C. The life of Olive Schreiner. 1924.
Chapin, A. le B. Their trackless way. 1931. Contains memories of Olive Schreiner.
Cazamian, M. L. In his Le roman et les idées en Angleterre vol 3, Paris 1955.
Davidson, B. In memory of Olive Schreiner. New Statesman 26 March 1955.
Hobman, D. L. Olive Schreiner: her friends and times. 1955.
Plomer, W. Olive Schreiner: her life and ideals. Listener 24 March 1955.
Renier, D. A South African rebel. Listener 7 April 1955.
Gregg, L. Memories of Olive Schreiner. 1957.
Kindilien, C. T. Stephen Crane and the savage philosophy of Olive Schreiner. Boston Univ Stud in Eng 3 1957.

GEORGE BERNARD SHAW
1856–1950

See col 1169, below.

JOSEPH HENRY SHORTHOUSE
1834–1903

Collections

Collected edition of the novels. 6 vols 1891–4.

§1

John Inglesant: a romance. Birmingham 1880 (priv ptd), 2 vols 1881, 1881, 1882 (10 edns), 1 vol 1883 (3 edns) etc; ed M. Ramsey 1961 (abridged as John Inglesant in England).
The little schoolmaster Mark: a spiritual romance. 2 pts 1883–4.
Sir Percival: a story of the past and present. 1886.
A teacher of the violin and other tales. 1888.
The Countess Eve. 1888.
Blanche, Lady Falaise: a tale. 1891.
The life and letters of Shorthouse, edited by his wife [Sarah], with an introduction by John Hunter Smith. 2 vols 1905. Contains Literary remains.
Shorthouse also pbd a paper On the Platonism of Wordsworth, 1882, *and wrote introds to* George Herbert, The Temple *and to several devotional works.*

§2

Gardiner, S. R. John Inglesant. Fraser's Mag May 1882.
John Inglesant. Dublin Rev April 1882.
'Lee, Vernon'. The little schoolmaster Mark. Academy 29 Dec 1883.
West, H. E. John Inglesant and Sartor resartus: two phases of religion. [1884].
Wilson, H. S. The philosophy of John Inglesant. Modern Rev 5 1884.
Sir Percival. Blackwood's Mag Dec 1886.
Linnell, C. The true story of John Inglesant. Athenaeum 27 July, 17 Aug 1901.
Hutton, E. Shorthouse. Blackwood's Mag April 1903.
Montgomery, J. D. Personal recollections of Shorthouse. Temple Bar June 1903.
Acton, J. E. D. C., Baron. In his Letters to Mary Gladstone, 1904. Contains a discussion of Shorthouse's historical point of view.
Durham, J. Marius the Epicurean and John Inglesant. [1905].
More, P. E. In his Shelburne essays ser 3, New York 1906.
Gosse, E. In his Portraits and sketches, 1912.
Coats, R. H. Birmingham mystics of the mid-Victorian era. Hibbert Jnl 16 1918.
Fleming, W. K. Some truths about John Inglesant. Quart Rev 245 1925.
Polak, M. The historical, philosophical and religious aspects of John Inglesant. Oxford 1934.
Thurmann, E. Der Niederschlag der evangelischen Bewegung in der englischen Literatur. Emsdetten 1938.
Anson, H. The Church in nineteenth-century fiction: Shorthouse. Listener 4 May 1939.
Hough, G. Books in general. New Statesman 3 Aug 1946.
Bishop, M. John Inglesant and its author. Essays by Divers Hands. 1958.

HENRY HAWLEY SMART
1833–93

§1

Breezie Langton: a story of fifty-two to fifty-five. 3 vols 1869.
Bitter is the rind. 3 vols 1870, [1909] (as Bit and bridal).
A race for a wife: a novel. 1870.

Cecile: or modern idolaters. 3 vols 1871.
False cards. 3 vols 1873.
Broken bonds. 3 vols 1874.
Two kisses. 3 vols 1875.
Courtship in seventeen hundred and twenty, in eighteen hundred and sixty. 2 vols 1876.
Bound to win: a tale of the turf. 3 vols 1877.
Play or pay: a novelette. 1878.
Sunshine and snow: a novel. 3 vols 1878.
Social sinners: a novel. 3 vols 1880.
Belles and ringers: a novelette. 1880.
The great Tontine: a novel. 3 vols 1881.
At fault. 3 vols 1883.
Hard lines: a novel. 3 vols 1883.
From post to finish: a novel. 3 vols 1884.
Salvage: a collection of stories. [1884].
Tie and trick: a melodramatic story. 3 vols 1885.
Lightly lost. 1885.
Struck down: 'a tale of Devon'. 1886.
Plucked: a tale of a trap; [with] other contributions by Annie Thomas. [1886].
Bad to beat: a novel. [1886].
The outsider: a novel. 2 vols 1886.
A false start: a novel. 3 vols 1887.
Cleverly won: a romance of the Grand National—a novelette. 1887.
The pride of the paddock. 1888.
The master of Rathkelly: a novel. 2 vols 1888.
Saddle and sabre: a novel. 3 vols 1888.
The last coup: a novelette. 1889.
Long odds: a novel. 3 vols 1889.
A black business: a novelette. [1890].
Without love or licence: a tale of South Devon. 3 vols 1890.
Thrice past the post: a novel. 1891.
Beatrice and Benedick: a romance of the Crimea. 2 vols 1891.
'The plunger': a turf tragedy of five-and-twenty years ago. 2 vols 1891.
A member of Tattersall's: a novel. 1892.
Vanity's daughter: a novel. 1893.
A racing rubber: a novel. 1895.

ANNE ISABELLA THACKERAY, later LADY RITCHIE
1837–1923

§1

The story of Elizabeth. 1863, 1895 (with Two hours and From an island).
The village on the cliff. 1867.
Five old friends; and a young prince. 1868.
To Esther and other sketches. 1869.
Old Kensington. 1873.
Bluebeard's keys and other stories. 1874.
Toilers and spinsters and other essays. 1874.
Madame de Sévigné. 1881.
Miss Angel. 1875.
Miss Williamson's divagations. 1881.
A book of sibyls: Mrs Barbauld, Mrs Opie, Miss Edgeworth, Miss Austen. 1883.
Mrs Dymond. 1885.
Jack Frost's little prisoners. 1887.
Records of Tennyson, Ruskin and Robert and Elizabeth Browning. 1892.
Lord Tennyson and his friends. 1893.
Lord Amherst and the advance to Burma. 1894. With R. Evans.
Chapters from some memoirs. 1894.
Blackstick papers. 1908.
A discourse on modern sibyls. 1913 (Eng Assoc lecture).
From the porch. 1913. Essays.
W. M. Thackeray and Edward FitzGerald, a literary friendship: unpublished letters and verses by W. M. Thackeray, with an introduction by Lady Ritchie. 1916.
From friend to friend, edited by Emily Ritchie. 1919. Reminiscences and a short story, Binnie.
Letters of Anne Thackeray Ritchie. Ed H. Ritchie 1924.
Lady Ritchie also edited or contributed introds to works by Thackeray, Mary Russell Mitford, Mrs Gaskell, Maria Edgeworth etc.

§2

Earl, E. The author of the Story of Elizabeth: Anne Thackeray Ritchie. Cornhill Mag March 1927.
Kent, M. Anne Thackeray Ritchie. Cornhill Mag June 1937.
Woolf, V. The enchanted organ: Anne Thackeray. In her Moment and other essays, 1948.
Fuller, H. T. and V. Hammersley. Thackeray's daughter: some reminiscences of Anne Thackeray Ritchie. 1952.

HENRY DUFF TRAILL
1842–1900

See col 1454, below.

KATHARINE TYNAN
1861–1931

See col 1910, below.

ETHEL LILIAN VOYNICH
1864–1960

§1

Stories from Garshin. 1893. A trn.
The humour of Russia. 1895. A trn.
Nihilism as it is. 1895. A trn.
The gadfly. 1897.
Jack Raymond. 1901.
Olive Latham. 1904.
An interrupted friendship. 1910.
Chopin's letters translated, with preface and editorial notes. 1931.
Put off thy shoes. 1945.

§2

Courtney, W. L. In his Feminine note in fiction, 1904.
Kettle, A. E. L. Voynich: a forgotten English novelist. EC 7 1957.

THEODORE WATTS-DUNTON
1832–1914

See col 1456, below.

SIR FREDERICK WEDMORE
1844–1921

See col 1456, below.

MRS HUMPHRY WARD, i.e. MARY AUGUSTA WARD, née ARNOLD

1851–1920

Collections

Writings, with introductions by the author. 16 vols 1911–12 (Westmorland edn).

§1

Milly and Olly: or a holiday among the mountains. 1881.
Miss Bretherton. 1884.
Amiel's Journal in time, translated with introduction and notes. 2 vols 1885.
Robert Elsmere. 3 vols 1888 (3 edns) etc; tr German, [1890].
University Hall: opening address. 1891.
The history of David Grieve. 3 vols 1892 (6 edns, the 6th with a prefatory letter answering criticisms).
Marcella. 3 vols 1894.
Unitarians and the future: the Essex Hall lecture 1894. 1894.
The story of Bessie Costrell. 1895. First pbd in Cornhill Mag May–July 1895.
Sir George Tressady. 1896. First pbd in Century Mag Nov 1895–Oct 1896.
Helbeck of Bannisdale. 1898.
Eleanor. 1900. First pbd in Harper's Mag Jan–Dec 1900.
Lady Rose's daughter. 1903. First pbd in Harper's Mag May 1902–April 1903.
The marriage of William Ashe. 1905. First pbd in Harper's Mag June 1904–May 1905.
Fenwick's career. 1906.
Play-time of the poor. 1906. Rptd from Times.
William Thomas Arnold, journalist and historian. Manchester 1907. With C. E. Montague. Originally pbd as preface to W. T. Arnold, Fragmentary studies on Roman imperialism, 1907.
Diana Mallory. 1908. First pbd in Harper's Mag Nov 1907–Oct 1908 as The testing of Diana Mallory.
Daphne: or marriage à la mode. 1909. First pbd in McClure's Mag Jan–June 1909.
Canadian born. 1910.
Letters to my neighbours on the present election. 1910.
The case of Richard Meynell. 1911.
The mating of Lydia. 1913.
The Coryston family. 1913.
Delia Blanchflower. 1915.
Eltham House. 1915.
England's effort, with a preface by the Earl of Rosebery. 1916.
A great success. 1916.
Lady Connie. 1916.
'Missing'. 1917.
Towards the goal, with an introduction by Theodore Roosevelt. 1917.
The war and Elizabeth. 1918.
A writer's recollections. 1918.
Cousin Philip. 1919.
Fields of victory: the journey through the battlefields of France. 1919.
Harvest. 1920, 1929 (as Love's harvest).

§2

Courtney, W. L. In his Feminine note in fiction, 1904.
Phelps, W. L. In his Essays on modern novelists, New York 1910. Includes a bibliography of Mrs Ward's writings by A. Keogh.
Walters, J. S. Mrs Humphry Ward: her work and influence. 1912.
Gwynn, S. L. Mrs Humphry Ward. 1917.
Johnson, L. In his Reviews and critical papers, ed R. Shafer 1921.
Trevelyan, J. P. Life of Mrs Humphry Ward. 1923.
Beccard, M. Religiöse Fragen in den Romanen von Mrs Humphry Ward. Münster 1935.
Thurmann, E. Der Niederschlag der evangelischen Bewegung in der englischen Literatur. Emsdetten 1938.
Marvin, F. S. Robert Elsmere: fifty years after. Contemporary Rev Aug 1939.
Lewis, N. Books in general. New Statesman 23 Aug 1947.
Lederer, C. Mary Arnold Ward and the Victorian ideal. Nineteenth-Century Fiction 6 1951.
Trevelyan, J. Mrs Humphry Ward and Robert Elsmere. Spectator 8 June 1952.
Mrs Humphry Ward. TLS 15 June 1951.
Fife, H. M. A letter from Mrs Humphry Ward to Vernon Lee. Colby Literary Quart 3 1954.
Cazamian, M. L. In his Le roman et les idées en Angleterre vol 3, Paris 1955.
Sackow, R. Robert Elsmere. Georgian Rev 9 1955.
Willey, B. How Robert Elsmere struck some contemporaries. E & S new ser 10 1957.
Knoepflmacher, U. C. The rival ladies; Mrs Ward's Lady Connie and Lawrence's Lady Chatterley's lover. Victorian Stud 4 1960.
Laski, M. Words from Robert Elsmere. N & Q June 1961. Addns by R. L. Green, Oct 1961.

STANLEY JOHN WEYMAN

1855–1928

Collections

The novels in thin paper and arranged chronologically, with an introduction in the first volume by the author. 21 vols 1911, 1922.

§1

The house of the wolf. 1890.
The new Rector. 2 vols 1891.
The story of Francis Cludde. 1891.
A gentleman of France: being the memoirs of Gaston de Bonne, Sieur de Marsac. 3 vols 1893.
The man in black. 1894.
My Lady Rotha. 1894.
Under the red robe. 2 vols 1894.
From the memoirs of a Minister of France. 1895.
The red cockade. 1895.
A little wizard. New York 1895
The Castle Inn. 1898.
Shrewsbury: a romance. 1898.
Sophia. 1900.
Count Hannibal. 1901.
In King's byways. 1902. Short stories.
The long night. 1903.
The Abbess of Vlaye. 1904.
Starvecrow Farm. 1905.
Chippinge. 1906.
Laid up in lavender. 1907. Stories.
The wild geese. [1908].
The great house. 1919.
Ovington's bank. 1922.
The traveller in the fur cloak. 1924.
Queen's folly. 1925.
The lively Peggy. 1928.

OSCAR WILDE

1854–1900

See col 1182, below.

EMMA CAROLINE WOOD, LADY WOOD

1802–79

Rosewarn: a novel. 3 vols 1866. Pbd under the pseudonym 'C. Sylvester'.

Sorrow on the sea: a novel. 3 vols 1868.
Sabina: a novel. 3 vols 1868.
On credit. 2 vols 1870.
Seadrift: a novel. 3 vols 1871.
Cloth of frieze: a novel. 3 vols 1872.
Wild weather: a novel. 2 vols 1873.
Up hill: a novel. 3 vols 1873.
Ruling the roast: a novel. 3 vols 1874.
Below the salt: a novel. 3 vols 1876.
Through fire and water: a novel. 2 vols 1876.
Sheen's foreman: a novel. 3 vols 1877.
Youth on the prow: a novel. 3 vols 1879.
Lady Wood also pbd an anthology, Leaves from the poet's laurels, 1869.

MARGARET LOUISA WOODS, née BRADLEY

1856–1945

§1

A village tragedy. 1887.
Lyrics and ballads. 1889.
Esther Vanhomrigh. 3 vols 1891.
The vagabonds. 1894.
Songs. Oxford 1896 (priv ptd).
Aëromancy and other poems. 1896.
Wild justice. 1896.
Weeping ferry and other stories. 1898.
Sons of the sword: a romance of the Peninsular War. 1901.
The Princess of Hanover. 1902.
The King's revoke. 1905.
The invader. 1907.
Poems old and new. 1907.
Pastels under the southern cross. 1911. Essays of travel.
Collected poems. 1914.
Come unto these yellow sands. [1915].
A poet's youth. 1923.
The Spanish lady. 1927.

§2

Courtney, W. L. In his Feminine note in fiction, 1904.

EDMUND HODGSON YATES

1831–94

§1

My haunts and their frequenters. 1854.
Mirth and metre. 1855. With F. E. Smedley.
Our miscellany: containing contributions by W. H. Painsworth, G. P. R. Jacobus, T. B. Macawley and other eminent authors. 1857. Ed Yates and R. B. Brough.
Mr Thackeray, Mr Yates and the Garrick Club: the correspondence and facts, stated by Edmund Yates. 1859 (priv ptd).
The life and correspondence of Charles Matthews the Elder, comedian, by Mrs Matthews, abridged and condensed by Edmund H. Yates. 1860.
After office hours. [1861].
Broken to harness: a story of English domestic life. 3 vols 1864.
For better, for worse: a romance of the affections. 2 vols 1864.
The business of pleasure. 2 vols 1865. Essays.
Pages in waiting. 1865. Rptd from Temple Bar.
Running the gauntlet: a novel. 3 vols 1865.
Kissing the rod: a novel. 3 vols 1866.
Land at last: a novel in three books. 3 vols 1866.
Black sheep: a novel. 3 vols 1867.
The rock ahead: a novel. 3 vols 1868.
Wrecked in port: a novel. 3 vols 1869.
A righted wrong: a novel. 3 vols 1870.
Dr Wainwright's patient. 3 vols 1871.
Castaway: a novel. 3 vols 1872.
The yellow flag: a novel. 3 vols Dublin 1872.
A waiting race: a novel. 3 vols 1872.
Nobody's fortune: a novel. 3 vols 1872.
The impending sword. 3 vols 1874.
Two by tricks: a novel. 2 vols 1874.
A silent witness: a novel. 3 vols 1875.
Celebrities at home. Sers 1–3 (all pbd), 1877–9. Rptd from World.
Yates: his recollections and experiences. 2 vols 1884.
Yates also contributed a memoir of Albert Smith to that writer's Mont Blanc, 1860, *and of F. E. Smedley to* Gathered leaves, 1865; *he edited* M. Collins, Thoughts in my garden, 1880, *and was successively editor of* Temple Bar *from 1860*, Tinsley's Mag *from 1867*, Time *from 1879, and* World.

§2

The last days of Edmund Yates. Temple Bar July 1894.

ISRAEL ZANGWILL

1864–1926

Bibliographies

Peterson, A. Zangwill: a selected bibliography. Bull of Bibliography 23 1961.

Collections

Works. 14 vols 1925.

§1

The Premier and the painter. 1888. With Louis Cowen.
The bachelor's club. 1891.
The big bow mystery. 1892.
Children of the Ghetto. 3 vols 1892.
The old maid's club. 1892.
Ghetto tragedies. 1893.
Merely Mary Ann. 1893.
The King of Schnorrers: grotesques and fantasies. 1894.
Joseph the dreamer. 1895.
The master. 1895.
Without prejudice: reprinted articles. 1896.
The celibates' club. 1898.
Dreamers of the ghetto. 1898.
'They that walk in darkness'. 1899.
The mantle of Elijah. 1900.
Blind children. 1903. Poems.
The grey wig: stories and novelettes. 1903.
Ghetto comedies. 1907.
Italian fantasies. 1910.
The war god: a tragedy. 1911.
The next religion. 1912. A play.
The melting pot: a drama. 1914.
The war for the world. 1916.
The principles of nationalities. 1917 (Conway Memorial lecture).
Chosen peoples: Hebraic ideal versus the Teutonic, with a foreword by H. Samuel. 1918 (Davis Memorial lecture).
Hands off Russia: a speech delivered at the Royal Albert Hall, February 8th 1919. 1919.
Jinny the carrier. 1919.
The voice of Jerusalem. 1920.

§2

Wells, H. G. Mr Zangwill's Master. Saturday Rev 18 May 1895.
—— Mr Zangwill's egoists. Saturday Rev 2 Jan 1897.
Oliphant, J. In his Victorian novelists, 1899.
Baron, A. and I. Finestein. The case of Zangwill. Jewish Quart 5 1957.
Feftwich, J. Zangwill: a biography. New York 1957.
Wohlgelernter, M. Zangwill: a study. 1964.

W. J. H.

VIII. CHILDREN'S BOOKS

The following are not included: (i) alphabets as such; (ii) didactic works of all kinds, including those meant merely to convey knowledge in a domestic or familiar way; (iii) works in which pictures purposely predominate over text; (iv) anthologies, with a few special exceptions, particularly in respect of fairy tales. The more voluminous writers are represented only by a typical selection.

(1) GENERAL WORKS

Trimmer, S. The guardian of education. 5 vols 1802–4.

[Kendrew, J. (publisher of York).] A collection of the publications of J. Kendrew. nd.

'Titmarsh, Michael Angelo' (W. M. Thackeray). On some illustrated children's books. Fraser's Mag April 1846.

Yonge, C. M. Children's literature of the last century [1769–1869]. Macmillan's Mag July–Sept 1869.

—— A storehouse of stories. 2 vols 1870–2. Selections from 18th and 19th centuries, with historical introduction.

—— What books to lend and what to give. [1887].

Mackarness, Mrs H. Children of the olden time. 1874.

'Tytler, Sarah' (H. Keddie). Childhood a hundred years ago. 1877.

Tuer, A. W. 1,000 quaint cuts from books of other days. [1886].

—— Pages and pictures from forgotten children's books. 1898–9.

—— Stories from old fashioned children's books. 1899–1900.

Welsh, C. On coloured books for children. 1887. No 12 of priv ptd Opuscula of the sette of odd volumes.

Molesworth, Mrs M. L. The best books for children. Pall Mall Gazette 29 Oct 1887.

—— On the art of writing fiction for children. Atalanta 6 1893.

—— Story-reading and story-writing. Chambers's Jnl 5 Nov 1898.

Hewins, C. The history of children's books [early English and American]. Atlantic Monthly Jan 1888.

Salmon, E. Juvenile literature as it is. 1888.

Pearson, E. Banbury chapbooks and nursery toy book literature of the eighteenth and early nineteenth centuries. 1890 (priv ptd).

Field, Mrs E. M. The child and his book. 1891.

Anon. Children yesterday and today. Quart Rev 183 1896.

White, G. Children's books and their illustrators. Studio special no 1897–8.

'Tallentyre, S. G.' (E. B. Hall). The road to knowledge a hundred years ago. Cornhill Mag Dec 1900.

Lucas, E. V. Old fashioned tales. 1905. Selections with introd.

—— Forgotten tales of long ago. 1906. Selections with introd.

Dodd, C. I. Some aspects of children's books. Nat Rev Jan 1905.

Moses, M. J. Children's books and reading. New York 1907.

H.M. Stationery Office. Catalogue of the British section of the international exhibition of the book industry and graphic arts, Leipzig. 1914. Special section devoted to children's books; introd by A. Rackham and F. J. H. Darton.

Barry, F. V. A century of children's books. 1922.

The Horn Book Magazine. Boston 1924–. In progress.

Andreae, G. The dawn of juvenile literature in England. Amsterdam 1925.

[Gumuchian et Cie.] Les livres de l'enfance du XVe au XIXe siècle. Préface de Paul Gavault. Paris [1930]. A bookseller's catalogue, virtually a bibliography.

Fulham Public Libraries. Catalogue of an exhibition of children's books of long ago; foreword by F. E. Hansford. [1931].

Sayers, W. C. B. A manual of children's libraries. 1932

Darton, F. J. H. Children's books in England: five centuries of social life. Cambridge 1932; ed K. M. Lines, Cambridge 1958 (rev).

Ridding, L. E. A nursery library seventy-five years ago. Contemporary Rev Sept 1932.

Hazard, P. Les livres, les enfants et les hommes. Paris 1932; tr Boston 1944.

Rosenbach, A. S. W. Early American children's books. Portland Maine 1933 (priv ptd).

James, P. Children's books of yesterday. Studio special no 1933.

Maxe, M. Children's books ancient and modern. Nat Rev Dec 1933.

Junior Bookshelf. Huddersfield 1936–. In progress.

König, G. Der viktorianische Schulroman. Berlin 1937.

Smith, E. S. The history of children's literature: a syllabus with selected bibliographies. Chicago 1937.

Osborne, E. Children's books in the nineteenth century. Junior Bookshelf 2 1937.

—— From morality and instruction to Beatrix Potter. Eastbourne 1949.

Barnes, W. Children's literature past and present. Educational Forum 3 1939.

Moore, A. C. My roads to childhood. New York 1939.

Lines, K. M. Four to fourteen: a library of books for children. Cambridge 1940, 1950 (rev), 1956 (rev).

Morgan, P. E. Reward books. N & Q 31 July 1943.

—— A few notes on the production of children's books to 1860. N & Q 9–23 March 1943.

Green, R. L. Tellers of tales. Leicester 1946, 1953 (rev), London 1965 (rewritten and expanded). A survey of children's books 1800–1964, with bibliographies.

—— (ed). Modern fairy stories. 1955; Tales of make-believe, 1960. Selected nineteenth-century stories.

Mahony, B. E. et al. Illustrators of children's books 1744–1945. Boston 1947.

Smith, J. A. Children's illustrated books. 1948.

Milne, A. A. Books for children. Cambridge 1948.

Muir, P. H. Children's books of yesterday. 1948. Catalogue of Nat Book League exhibition.

—— English children's books 1600–1900. 1954.

Trease, G. Tales out of school. 1948, 1964 (rev).

Jordan, A. M. From Rollo to Tom Sawyer, and other papers. Boston 1948.

Turner, E. S. Boys will be boys. 1948. Penny dreadfuls etc.

Partridge, C. Evangelical children's books 1828–59. N & Q 4 Feb 1950.

Opie, I. and P. The Oxford dictionary of nursery rhymes. Oxford 1951, 1952 (corrected).

—— The lore and language of school-children. Oxford 1959.

St John, J. The Osborne collection of early children's books 1566–1910. Toronto 1958, 1966 (corrected).

Egoff, S. A. Children's periodicals of the nineteenth century. 1951 (Lib Assoc pamphlet).

Lewis, C. S. On three ways of writing for children. Proc of Annual Conference, Lib Assoc 1952; rptd in his Of other worlds, 1966.

Smith, L. H. The unreluctant years: a critical approach to children's literature. Chicago 1953.
Meigs, C. et al. A critical history of children's literature. New York 1953.
Hürlimann, B. Europäische Kinderbücher in drei Jahrhunderten. Zürich 1959, 1963 (rev); tr Oxford 1967.
Ford, B. (ed). Young writers, young readers. 1960. Articles by various authors from Jnl of Education, etc.
Fisher, M. Intent upon reading. Leicester 1961, 1964 (rev).
— Growing point. Northampton 1962–. In progress.
Crouch, M. Treasure seekers and borrowers. 1962.
Thwaite, M. F. From primer to pleasure: children's books in England to 1900. 1963.
Avery, G. and A. Bull. Nineteenth-century children. 1965.
De Vries, L. (ed). Flowers of delight [1765–1830]. 1965.
Ellis, A. How to find out about children's literature. Oxford 1966, 1968 (rev).

(2) PRINCIPAL WRITERS

Edgeworth, Maria (1767–1849). The parent's assistant: or stories for children. 3 vols 1795.
— [Early lessons] Harry and Lucy part 1. 1801 etc.
— Moral tales for young people. 5 vols 1801. *For full bibliography see col 665, above.*
Taylor, Isaac ('of Ongar') (1759–1829). Scenes in Europe. 1819.
— Bunyan explained to a child. 2 pts 1824, 1825.
— The biography of a brown loaf. 1829.
— The ship. 1830.
Taylor, Ann, neé Martin (1757–1830). The family mansion: a tale. 1819.
Taylor, Ann (neé Martin), and Jane. Correspondence between a mother and her daughter at school. 1817.
Taylor, Ann, afterwards Gilbert (1782–1866). The wedding among the flowers. 1808.
For Ann Taylor *see* Autobiography and other memorials of Mrs Gilbert ed J. Gilbert 2 vols 1874.
Taylor, Jane (1783–1824). Display: a tale for young people. 1815.
— Contributions of Q. Q. 2 vols 1824.
For Jane Taylor *see* Memoirs and poetical remains, with extracts from correspondence, ed I. Taylor 2 vols 1825; Mrs H. C. Knight, Jane Taylor: her life and letters, 1880; L. B. Walford, Four biographies from Blackwood, 1888.
Taylor, Ann, afterwards Gilbert, and Jane. Original poems for infant minds, by several young persons [i.e. Ann and Jane Taylor, Isaac Taylor their father, Isaac Taylor their brother, Bernard Barton, and Adelaide O'Keeffe (*see* below)]. 2 vols 1804–5, 1875 (complete edn finally rev Mrs Gilbert); ed E. V. Lucas [1903] with Rhymes for the nursery etc. Many selections under various titles, e.g. Little Ann and other poems, illustr Kate Greenaway [1883]; Meddlesome Mattie and other poems for infant minds, ed E. Sitwell 1925.
Taylor, Ann, afterwards Gilbert, and Jane. Rhymes for the nursery. 1806, 1835 (27th edn).
— Hymns for infant minds. 1808, 1844 (with addns), 1868 (47th edn).
— Signor Topsy-turvy's wonderful magic lantern: or the world turned upside down. 1810.
Taylor, Jefferys (1792–1853). Harry's holiday. 1818 (with preface by Jane Taylor).
— Ralph Richards, the miser. 1821.
— Aesop in rhyme. 1822.
The Taylors of Ongar. The family pen: memorials, biographical and literary, of the Taylor family of Ongar, by [Canon] Isaac Taylor. 2 vols 1867. Contains recollections by editor's father, memoir of Jane Taylor, short pieces by various members of the family not all pbd elsewhere, and lists of works by them all. *See also* Sir Francis Galton, Hereditary genius, 1869; D. M. Armitage, The Taylors of Ongar, Cambridge 1938.
[Roscoe, William (1753–1831)]. The butterfly's ball and the grasshopper's feast. GM Nov 1806; 1807; ed C. Welsh 1883.
— The butterfly's birthday. 1809.
[Dorset, Catherine Ann, née Turner (1750?–1817?)] The peacock At Home: a sequel to the Butterfly's ball. 1807; ed C. Welsh 1883.
— The lion's masquerade. 1807.
The butterfly's ball produced many imitations besides those by Mrs Dorset, such as The elephant's ball by W.B., 1807; The lion's parliament, [1808?]; The rose's breakfast, 1808; The horse's levée, 1808; The fishes grand gala by Mrs Cockle, 1808; The tyger's theatre by Samuel James Arnold (1774–1852), 1808; Flora's gala, 1808; The feast of the fishes by 'Theresa Tyro', 1808; The ape's concert by 'A. Tabby', 1808; The council of dogs, 1808; The wedding among the flowers by Ann Taylor, 1808; The lobster's voyage, 1808; Le fête de la rose by B. Hoole, Mrs Hofland, [1809?]. *See* A. W. Tuer, Pages and pictures from forgotten children's books, 1898–9.
Turner, Elizabeth (d. 1846). The daisy: or cautionary stories in verse, adapted to the ideas of children, from four to eight years old. 1806; ed C. Welsh 1883, 1900.
— The cowslip. 1811; ed C. Welsh 1883.
— The pink. 1811; ed M. Howitt 1835 (with addns).
— The crocus. [c. 1820?].
— The rose. nd.
— The blue-bell: or tales and fables. 1838.
— Short poems for young children. 1859 (not first edn?).
Selections are Mrs Turner's cautionary stories, ed E. V. Lucas 1897; Grandmamma's book of rhymes, ed G. K. Chesterton 1927. *For examples by her and other nineteenth century verse-writers, see* The book of verse for children, ed R. L. Green 1962.
Hofland, Mrs, née Wreaks (1770–1844). Son of a genius. 1812.
— Adelaide: or the massacre of St Bartholomew. 1822.
— The young Crusoe. 1828.
See col 733, above.
Lamb, Charles (1775–1834). The king and queen of hearts. 1805; ed E. V. Lucas 1902.
— The adventures of Ulysses. 1808; ed A. Lang 1890.
— Prince Dorus. 1811 (anon); ed A. W. Tuer 1889.
— Beauty and the beast. [1811?] (anon); ed A. Lang 1887.
Lamb, Charles and Mary Ann (1764–1847). Tales from Shakespear designed for the use of young persons. 2 vols 1807 (for 1806); ed A. Lang 1899; ed F. J. Furnivall 2 vols 1901; ed J. C. Trewin 1965.
— Mrs Leicester's school: or the history of several young ladies, related by themselves. 1807 (anon); ed A. Ainger 1885.
— Poetry for children, entirely original, by the author of Mrs Leicester's school. 1809 (anon); ed R. H. Shepherd 1872.
See col 1291, below.
Sherwood, Mrs Mary Martha, née Butt (1775–1851). The history of the Fairchild family: or the child's manual, being a collection of stories calculated to show the importance and effects of a religious education. 3 pts 1818–47; ed M. E. Palgrave 1902. *See* 'F. Anstey' (T. Anstey Guthrie), On an old-fashioned children's book, in his Last load, 1925.
— The history of Henry Milner. 4 pts 1822–37. *See* 'F. Anstey', Mrs Sherwood's notion of a model Youth, in his Last load, 1925.

— Little Henry and his bearer Boosy. 1832. *See col 764, above.*

Hack, Maria, née Barton (1777–1844). Winter evenings: or tales of travellers. 4 vols 1818–59, 1853 (rev).

— English stories. 3 sers 1820–5; ser 1–2 rev D. M. Smith 1872.

— Harry Beaufoy: or the pupil of nature. 1821.

Penrose, Elizabeth, née Cartwright (1780–1837). Mrs Markham's history of England. 1823.

— Mrs Markham's history of France. 1828.

Elliott, Mary, née Belson. Precept and example: or midsummer holidays. 1812 (2nd edn).

— The orphan boy: or a journey to Bath. [1814].

— Simple truths in verse. 1816.

— The modern Goody Two-shoes, exemplifying the good consequences of early attention to learning and virtue. 1819.

— Rural employment: or a peep into village concerns. 1820.

Hughes, Mary, née Robson. Aunt Mary's tales for the enlightenment and improvement of little girls. 1813.

— The ornaments discovered. 1815.

— The alchemist. 1818.

— The metamorphoses. 1818.

— The orphan girl: a moral tale. 1819.

Cameron, Lucy Littleton, née Butt (1781–1858). The history of Margaret Whyte. nd. Written 1798 but not pbd till later.

— The polite little children. 1822 (6th edn).

— The two lambs. 1821.

See Life, ed C. Cameron 1862, [1873] (rev G. T. Cameron).

Mrs Cameron was the sister of Mrs Sherwood, above.

Callcott, Maria, née Dundass (1785–1842). Little Arthur's history of England. 1835.

Howitt, William (1792–1879). The boy's country book: being the real life of a country boy, written by himself. 1839.

— A boy's adventures in the wilds of Australia. 1854.

See col 1286, below.

Marryat, Frederick (1792–1848). Masterman Ready: or the wreck of the Pacific, written for young people. 3 vols 1841–2.

— The settlers in Canada, written for young people. 2 vols 1844.

— The children of the New Forest. 2 vols [1847].

— The little savage. 2 parts 1848–9. Ed F. S. Marryat; of pt 2 Frederick Marryat only wrote 2 chs.

See O. Warner, Captain Marryat: a rediscovery 1953, *and col 704, above.*

'Parley, Peter'. The inventor of this pseudonym was an American, Samuel Goodrich (1793–1860), but the name was at once adopted by English writers and publishers. Goodrich claimed in his Recollections of a lifetime, 1857, to have compiled 116 'Parley' books (*see* his List), but their titles also were used, and their text often freely adapted, in English edns by rivals. For summary of the books and authors, *see* F. J. H. Darton, Children's books in England, Cambridge 1932, and Peter Parley and the battle of the children's books, Cornhill Mag Nov 1932. Goodrich's first 'Parley' book was Tales of Peter Parley about America, Boston 1827. The writers who can be certainly identified as having produced original work under this pseudonym are:

Mogridge, George (1787–1854), also as 'Alan Gray', 'Aunt Mary', 'Aunt Newbury', 'Aunt Upton', 'Grandfather Gregory', 'Grandmamma Gilbert', 'Ephraim Holding', 'Old Humphrey', 'The Traveller', 'Uncle Adam', 'Uncle Newbury'. The juvenile moralists. 1829; The juvenile culprits, 1829.

See C. Williams, Life, character and writings, 1856; A. R. Buckland in Mogridge, John Strong the boaster, 1904.

Martin, William (1801–67). The parlour book. [1835?].

— The book of sports. [1837?].

— The hatchups of me and my schoolfellows. 1858.

— Holiday tales. 1860.

Clark, Samuel (1810–75). Peter Parley's wonders of earth, sea and sky. [1837].

See his Memorials from journals and letters, ed his wife 1878.

Howard, Edward (1792?–1841). Rattlin the reefer. Ed and rev F. Marryat 3 vols 1836. *See col 735, above.*

Strickland, Agnes (1796–1874). The moss-house. 1822. Anon.

— The rival Crusoes. 1826.

Corner, Julia (1798–1875). The village school; with the history and what became of some of the scholars. [1848].

— The child's own Sunday book. 1850.

— The cow boy: or the reward of honesty. [1854].

— Little plays for little actors. [1854].

[Jerram, Jane Elizabeth]. The child's own story book. 1837.

Howitt, Mary, née Botham (1799–1888). Sketches of natural history. 1834. This contains first pbn of The spider and the fly.

— Tales in prose for young people. [1836].

— The children's year. 1847.

— Our cousins in Ohio. 1849.

— Tales for all seasons. [1881].

See col 1286, below.

Hall, Anna Maria, née Fielding (1800–81). The Hartopp jubilee. [1840?]. *See col 932, above.*

Sinclair, Catherine (1800–64). Holiday House: a series of tales. Edinburgh 1839.

— Frank Vansittart: or the model schoolboys. 1853.

— Charlie Seymour: or the good and bad choice. 1856 (4th edn).

— The first of April picture letter. Edinburgh 1864.

See E. V. Lucas, Introd to Old fashioned tales, 1905, *and col 965, above.*

[Bevan, Favell Lee, afterwards Mortimer (1802–1878)]. The peep of day. 1833.

See E. Bevan, A law-giver in the nursery, Times 27 June 1933.

Martineau, Harriet (1802–76). The playfellow. 1841. 4 pts frequently issued separately, viz The settlers at home, 1856; The peasant and the Prince, 1856; Feats on the fiord, 1844; The Crofton boys, 1856.

See V. Wheatley, The life and work of Harriet Martineau, 1957, *and col 949, above.*

Mozley, Harriet, née Newman (1803–52). The fairy bower. 1841.

— The lost brooch. 1841.

— Louisa. 1842.

— Family adventures. 1852.

See C. R. Coleridge, C. M. Yonge, 1903; K. Tillotson, Novels of the eighteen-forties, Oxford 1954.

Paget, Francis Edward (1806–82). Tales of the village children. 2 sers 1844–5.

— The hope of the Katzekopfs. 1844 (by 'William Churne of Staffordshire'), 1846 (with new preface).

— Luke Sharp. 1845.

See col 1633, below.

Gatty, Margaret, née Scott (1809–73). The fairy godmothers and other tales. 1851.

— Parables from nature. 5 sers 1855–71; sers 1–2 ed J. H. Ewing 1885 (with memoir).

— Aunt Judy's tales. 1859.

See C. Maxwell, Mrs Gatty and Mrs Ewing, 1949.

Mrs Gatty founded, edited and contributed to Aunt Judy's Mag; *see col 930, above.*

Lemon, Mark (1809–70). The enchanted doll: a fairy tale for little people. 1849.

— Fairy tales. 1868.

— Tinykin's transformations: a child's story. 1869. *See col 1150, below.*

Thackeray, William Makepeace (1811–63). The rose and the ring, or the history of Prince Giglio and Prince Bulbo: a fireside pantomime for great and small children, by Mr M. A. Titmarsh. 1855 (for 1854). *See col 858, above.*

Dickens, Charles (1812–70). Holiday romance. All the Year Round Jan–March 1868. 4 stories, 3 often rptd separately as Captain Boldheart, The magic fishbone, Mrs Orange and Mrs Alicumpaine. *See col 858, above.*

Lear, Edward (1812–88). A book of nonsense. 1846 (anon), 1861 (enlarged), 1863 (enlarged), 1870.

— A book of nonsense and more nonsense. 1862.

— Nonsense songs, stories, botany and alphabets. 1871.

— More nonsense, pictures, rhymes, botany etc. 1872.

— Laughable lyrics: a fresh book of nonsense poems, songs, botany, music etc. 1877.

— Queery Leary nonsense. 1911. Compiled by Lady Strachey, with introd by the Earl of Cromer and some new material.

— Teapots and quails, and other new nonsenses. Ed A. Davidson and P. Hofer 1953 (unpbd fragments).

Lear also pbd books of travel, and several of his travel diaries have been edited. His letters were edited by Lady Strachey in 1907, with a further selection in 1911. For detailed bibliography see W. B. O. Field, Lear on my shelves, New York 1933; A. Davidson, Edward Lear, 1938; S. A. Nock, Lear of the nonsense verses, Sewanee Rev 49 1941; J. Anderson, Lear and the origin of nonsense, E Studies 31 1950; E. Sewell, The field of nonsense, 1952; B. Reade, Lear: an exhibition [catalogue with introduction and notes], 1958. *See col 1680, below.*

Macleod, Norman (1812–72). The gold thread. 1861; ed D. Macleod 1907.

Smiles, Samuel (1812–1904). Self-help, with illustrations of character and conduct. 1859.

Kingston, William Henry Giles (1814–80). The Circassian chief: a romance of Russia. 3 vols 1843. Kingston wrote over 100 books; *see col 940, above.*

Browne, Frances (1816–79). Granny's wonderful chair and its tales of fairy times. 1857 (for 1856); ed D. Radford 1906 (EL); ed R. L. Green 1963.

— Our uncle the traveller. 1859.

— The young foresters. [1860].

See D. Radford, Introd to Granny's wonderful chair, 1906 (EL). *See col 917, above.*

[Hawkshaw, Mrs]. Aunt Effie's rhymes for little children. [1852].

— Aunt Effie's gift to the nursery. 1854.

[Charlesworth, Maria Louisa (1819–80).] Ministering children. 1854; [sequel], 1862.

Kingsley, Charles (1819–75). Glaucus: or the wonders of the shore. Cambridge 1855.

— Westward Ho! or the voyages and adventures of Sir Amyas Leigh [etc]. 3 vols Cambridge 1855.

— The heroes: or Greek fairy tales for my children. Cambridge 1856.

— The water-babies: a fairy tale for a land-baby. 1863.

— Hereward the Wake: 'last of the English'. 2 vols 1866.

— Madam How and Lady Why: or first lessons in earth-lore for children. 1870.

See col 935, above.

Ruskin, John (1819–1900). The King of the Golden River: or the black brothers—a legend of Styria. 1851.

Ingelow, Jean (1820–97). Tales of Orris. Bath 1860, London 1865 (as Stories told to a child).

— Mopsa the fairy. 1869, 1964.

— The little wonder-horn. 1872.

See col 527, above.

Rossetti, Christina (1830–94). Sing-song: a nursery rhyme book. 1872, 1893 (with addns).

— Speaking likenesses. 1874.

— Maude: a story for girls. 1897. Introd by W. M. Rossetti.

See Not all roses in the Victorian nursery, TLS 29 May 1959; *and col 496, above.*

Sewell, Anna (1820–78). Black Beauty: the autobiography of a horse. 1877.

See W. J. F. Jarrold, Appreciation and life of author, in 1922 edn; C. O. Parsons, The progenitors of Black Beauty in humanitarian literature, N & Q 19 April, 3–31 May 1947.

St John, Percy Bolingbroke (1821–89). The Arctic Crusoe. [1854].

— The coral reef. [1868].

— The sailor Crusoe. [1876].

Hughes, Thomas (1822–96). Tom Brown's school days, by an old boy. Cambridge 1857; ed V. Rendall 1904; ed F. Sidgwick, 1913.

See E. C. Mack and W. H. G. Armytage, Thomas Hughes, 1952; *see col 933, above.*

Hart, Elizabeth Anna, née Smedley (b. 1822). Poems written for a child. 1868. With M. B. Smedley.

— Child-world. 1869. With M. B. Smedley.

— Child-nature. 1869.

— The runaway. 1872; ed G. Raverat 1936.

— Poor Nelly. 1880.

— Two fourpenny bits. 1880.

— May Cunningham's trial. 1883.

— The mystery of Shoncliff School. 1888.

All anon; also other children's books, novels and poems. See R. L. Green, Mrs Hart, author of the Runaway, TLS 23 Nov 1956.

Yonge, Charlotte Mary (1823–1901). The little Duke. 1854.

— The Lances of Lynwood. 1855.

— The daisy chain, or aspirations: a family chronicle. 2 vols 1856.

— A book of golden deeds. 1864.

— The dove in the eagle's nest. 2 vols 1866.

— Unknown to history: a story of the captivity of Mary of Scotland. 2 vols 1882.

Over 100 other books; see col 972, above.

Rands, William Brighty (1823–82). Lilliput levee. 1864.

— Lilliput lectures. 1871.

— Lilliput revels. 1871.

— Lilliput legends. 1872.

— Lilliput lyrics. Ed R. B. Johnson 1899.

See col 548, above.

MacDonald, George (1824–1905). Dealings with the fairies. 1867.

— At the back of the north wind. 1871 (for 1870).

— Ranald Bannerman's boyhood. 1871.

— The Princess and the goblin. 1872 (for 1871).

— The wise woman: a parable. 1875, New York 1876 (as A double story), 1895 (as The lost Princess); ed E. Yates 1965.

— The Princess and Curdie. 1883 (for 1882).

— The light princess and other fairy tales [with special preface by MacDonald]. 1893.

— The [complete short] fairy tales of MacDonald. Ed G. MacDonald 1920; The light princess and other tales of fantasy, ed R. L. Green 1961.

See G. MacDonald, MacDonald and his wife, 1924; J. M. Bullock, A centennial bibliography of MacDonald, Aberdeen 1925; C. S. Lewis, MacDonald: an anthology, 1946; R. L. Wolff, The golden key: a study of the fiction of MacDonald, New Haven 1961, *and col 945, above.*

Palgrave, Francis Turner (1824–97). The five days' entertainments at Wentworth Grange. 1868.

— The children's treasury of English song. 2 pts 1875. *See col 545, above.*

Ballantyne, Robert Michael (1825–94). Snowflakes and sunbeams: or the young fur traders. 1856.

— The robber kitten. 1858.
— Ungava: a tale of Esquimeaux-land. 1858.
— Martin Rattler: or a boy's adventures in the forests of Brazil. 1858.
— The coral island. 1858; ed E. Rhys 1907; ed J. M. Barrie 1913.
— The world of ice. 1860.
— The dog Crusoe and his master. 1861.
— The gorilla hunters. 1861.
— The wild man of the West. 1863.
— The lifeboat. 1864.
— The lighthouse. 1865.
— Fighting the flames. 1867.
— Deep down: a tale of the Cornish mines. 1868.
— Erling the bold: a tale of the Norse sea-kings. 1869.
— The iron horse: or life on the line. 1871.
— Post haste. 1880.
Ballantyne wrote over 100 books. See E. S. Quayle, Ballantyne the brave, 1967; Personal reminiscences in book-making, 1893; Hudson's Bay: or everyday life in the wilds of North America, Edinburgh 1848 (priv ptd).
Keary, Annie (1825–79). The heroes of Asgard. 1857. With Eliza Keary.
— Little Wanderlin and other fairy tales. 1865.
— Sidney Grey: or a year from home. 1876.
— Father Phim. 1879; ed G. Avery 1962.
See Memoir of Annie Keary by her sister, 1882, *and* Letters, 1883 (selected).
'A.L.O.E.', 'A Lady of England' (Charlotte Maria Tucker) (1825–93). The Claremont tales: or illustrations of the Beatitudes. [1854].
— Wings and strings: a tale for the young. 1855.
— Upwards and downwards, or the sluggard and the diligent: a story for boys. 1856.
— The rambles of a rat. 1857.
— The story of a needle. 1858.
— Fairy Know-a-bit. 1866.
— The little maid. [1874].
— Life in the eagle's nest: a tale of Afghanistan. [1833].
For over 140 other works see A. Giberne, A Lady of England: the life and letters of Charlotte Maria Tucker, 1895.
Craik, Dinah Maria, née Mulock (1826–87). Alice Learmont: a fairy tale. 1852, 1884 (rev).
— A hero: Philip's book. 1853.
— Our year: a child's book. 1860.
— The fairy book: the best popular fairy stories selected and rendered anew. 1863.
— Little Sunshine's holiday: a picture from life. 1871.
— The adventures of a Brownie as told to my child. 1872.
— The little lame Prince and his travelling cloak: a parable for young and old. 1875.
See col 951, above.
Mackarness, Matilda Anne, née Planché (1826–81). Old Joliffe. 1845.
— A trap to catch a sunbeam. 1849.
— The golden rule. 1859.
'Holme Lee', Harriet Parr (1828–1900). Legends from Fairyland. 1860.
— The wonderful adventures of Tuflongbo. 1861.
— Tuflongbo's journey in search of ogres. 1862.
See col 941, above.
Church, Alfred John (1829–1910). Stories from Homer. 1878.
— The chantry priest of Barnet: a tale of the Two Roses.
— The count of the Saxon shore: a tale of the departure of the Romans from Britain. 1887.
Many other retellings of classical authors etc; see his Memories of men and books, 1908.
Kingsley, Henry (1830–76). The boy in grey. 1871.
— The lost child. 1871.
— Valentin: a French boy's story of Sedan. 2 vols 1872.
See S. M. Ellis, Henry Kingsley: towards a vindication, 1931, *and col 939, above.*
Marshall, Emma, née Martin (1830–99). Happy days at Fernbank. 1861.
— Life's aftermath. 1876.
— Bristol diamonds. 1888.
— Under Salisbury's spire. 1890.
See B. Marshall, Emma Marshall: a biographical sketch, 1900.
Farrar, Frederic William (1831–1903). Eric, or little by little: a tale of Roslyn School. Edinburgh 1858.
— St Winifred's: or the world of school. 1862.
See R. Farrar, Life of Farrar, 1904, *and col 1052, above.*
Fenn, George Manville (1831–1909). Hollowdell Grange: or holiday hours in a country house. 1866.
— Nat the naturalist. 1882.
— Bunyip land. 1884.
— The silver canon. 1884.
— Brownsmith's boy. 1886.
— Mother Carey's chicken. 1888.
— The Queen's scarlet. 1895.
— Marcus: the young centurion. [1904].
Also over 100 novels and boys' stories, and numerous short tales.
'Lewis Carroll' (Charles Lutwidge Dodgson) (1832–98). Alice's adventures in Wonderland. 1865, 1886 (rev), 1897 (rev); ed E. Graham 1946; ed M. Gardner, New York 1960; ed R. L. Green 1965 (EL).
— Through the looking-glass, and what Alice found there. 1872 (for 1871), 1897 (rev).
— The hunting of the Snark. 1876; ed M. Gardner, New York 1962.
— Sylvie and Bruno. 1889; Sylvie and Bruno concluded, 1893.
For full bibliography see col 977, above.
Henty, George Alfred (1832–1902). Out on the Pampas: or the young settlers. 1871 (for 1870).
— The young franc-tireurs. 1872.
— Facing death. 1883.
— Under Drake's flag. 1883.
— With Clive in India. 1884.
— True to the old flag. 1885.
— With Wolfe in Canada. 1887.
— The cat of Bubastes. 1889.
— Redskin and cowboy. 1892.
— In Greek waters. 1893.
— Beric the Briton. 1893.
— On the Irrawaddy. 1897.
— With Buller in Natal. 1901.
— With Roberts to Pretoria. 1902.
— With Kitchener in the Sudan. 1903.
— With the Allies to Pekin. 1904.
Also over 75 others; see G. M. Fenn, Henty: the story of an active life, 1907; L. Coffin, Henty: a bibliographical study, Bull of Bibliography 19 1949, *and typescript bibliographies in Lilly Library Indiana and in BM.*
'Hesba Stretton', formerly Sarah Smith (1832–1911). Jessica's first prayer. 1867.
— Little Meg's children. 1868.
— Alone in London. 1869.
— The King's servants. 1873.
— Lost Gip. 1873.
— The Wonderful Life [of Christ]. 1875.
— The sweet story of old. [1884].
Also many others; see DNB.
Hood, Thomas ('Tom') (1835–1874). Fairy realm. 1865.
— Petsetilla's posy: a fairy tale for young and old. [1870].
— From nowhere to the North Pole: a Noah's ark-aeological narrative. 1875 (for 1874).
See Henry W. Lucy, GM Jan 1875.
Molesworth, Mary Louisa, née Stewart (1839–1921). Tell me a story. 1875.

— Carrots: just a little boy. 1876.
— The cuckoo clock. 1877.
— The tapestry room. 1879.
— A Christmas child. 1880.
— The adventures of Herr Baby. 1881.
— Hoodie. 1882.
— Two little waifs. 1883.
— Christmas tree land. 1884.
— Us: an old fashioned story. 1885.
— Four winds farm. 1887 (for 1886).
— The children of the castle. 1890.
— Nurse Heatherdale's story. 1891.
— The carved lions. 1895; ed G. Avery 1960; ed R. L. Green 1964.
— The house that grew. 1900.
— Peterkin. 1902.
— The story of a year. 1910.
— Fairies afield. 1911.
— Fairy stories. Ed R. L. Green 1957.
With many more; see R. L. Green, Mrs Molesworth, 1961.

'Ouida', Louise de la Ramée (1839–1908). A dog of Flanders, and other stories. 1872.
— Bimbi: stories for children. 1882.
With many novels; see col 1070, above.

Hardy, Thomas (1840–1928). Our exploits at West Poley. Household Nov 1892–April 1893; 1952; in Tales of make-believe, ed R. L. Green 1960. *See col 980, above.*

'Ismay Thorn' (Edith Caroline Pollock). A six-years' darling: or Trix in town. [1880].
— Over the wall. [1881].
— Sister Sue. 1884.
— Quite unexpected. [1889].
— Geoff and Jim. 1894.
— Courage. 1899.

Stables, William Gordon (1840–1910). Aileen Aroon: a memoir [of a dog]. [1884].
— 'Twixt school and college. 1891.
— A fight for freedom. 1897.
— In quest of the giant sloth. 1902.
— Leaves from the log of a sailor. 1906.

Ewing, Juliana Horatia, neé Gatty (1841–85). Melchior's dream and other tales. 1862.
— Mrs Overtheway's remembrances. 1869.
— The Brownies and other tales. 1870.
— A flat iron for a farthing. 1872.
— Lob-lie-by-the-fire: or the luck of Lingborough. 1874.
— Six to sixteen. 1875.
— Jan of the windmill. 1876.
— A great emergency and other tales. 1877.
— We and the world. 1880.
— Old fashioned fairy tales. 1882.
— Brothers of pity and other tales. 1882.
— Jackanapes. 1884 (for 1883).
— Daddy Darwin's dovecot. 1884.
— The story of a short life. 1885.
— Mary's meadow. 1886.
Also a few small volumes of verse and prose. See H. K. F. Gatty (later Eden), Juliana Horatia Ewing and her books, 1885; C. Maxwell, Mrs Gatty and Mrs Ewing, 1949; G. Avery, Mrs Ewing, 1961, *and col 1049, above.*

Ker, David (1842–1914). On the road to Khiva. 1874.
— The boy slave in Bokhara. 1875.
— The wild horseman of the Pampas. 1876.
— Lost among white Africans. 1886.
— Vanished! or the strange adventures of Arthur Hawksleigh. 1895.
— O'er Tartar deserts. 1898.

Montgomery, Florence (1843–1923). A very simple story. 1867.
— Misunderstood. 1869.
— Moral tales for children. 1886 (new edn).
— Behind the scenes in a schoolroom. 1914.

Lang, Andrew (1844–1912). The black thief: a new and original drama. 1882 (priv ptd).
— The Princess Nobody: a tale of Fairyland. 1884, 1955 (in Modern fairy stories, ed R. L. Green).
— The gold of Fairnilee. 1888; ed G. Avery 1967 (as The gold of Fairnilee and other stories) (with Princess Nobody, above, and Tales of a fairy court, below).
— Prince Prigio. 1889; ed R. L. Green 1961 (with Prince Ricardo, below).
— Prince Ricardo of Pantouflia. 1893.
— The story of the Golden Fleece. 1903.
— The story of Joan of Arc. 1906.
— Tales of a fairy court. 1906.
— Tales of Troy and Greece. 1907.
See R. L. Green, Andrew Lang, 1962; *col 1440, below, and below under Fairy Tales.*

Greenaway, Catherine ('Kate') (1846–1901). Under the window: pictures and rhymes for children. [1878].
— Marigold garden: pictures and rhymes. 1885.
See M. H. Spielmann and G. S. Layard, Kate Greenaway, 1905; A. C. Moore, A century of Kate Greenaway, New York 1946; C. Newcomb, The secret door: the story of Kate Greenaway, New York 1946.

'Ascott Hope', A. R. Hope-Moncrieff (1846–1927). A book about boys. 1868.
— A pack of troubles. [1874].
— The Pampas: a story of adventure. 1876.
— The wigwam and the warpath. 1884.
— Ups and downs. 1895.

Jefferies, Richard (1848–87). Bevis: the story of a boy. 3 vols 1882; ed E. V. Lucas 1904, 1932. *See col 1060, above.*

Burnett, Frances Hodgson, née Hodgson (1849–1924). Little Lord Fauntleroy. 1886.
— Sara Crewe: or what happened at Miss Minchin's. 1888.
— Little St Elizabeth, and other stories. 1890.
— The one I knew best of all. 1893.
— The captain's youngest, and other stories. 1894.
— Two little pilgrims' progress. 1895.
— A little Princess: being the whole story of Sara Crewe now told for the first time. 1905.
— Racketty Packetty house. 1907.
— The secret garden. 1911.
Also other stories, novels etc. See V. Burnett, The romantic lady, 1928, *and* M. Laski, Mrs Ewing, Mrs Molesworth and Mrs Hodgson Burnett, 1950.

De Morgan, Mary (1850–1907). On a pincushion and other tales. 1877.
— The necklace of Princess Fiorimonde and other stories. 1880.
— The wind fairies and other tales. 1900.
See introd by R. L. Green to the Necklace of Princess Fiorimonde and other stories: being the complete fairy tales of Mary De Morgan, 1963.

Stevenson, Robert Louis (1850–94). Treasure Island. 1883.
— A child's garden of verses. 1885.
— Kidnapped: being memoirs of the adventures of David Balfour. 1886.
— The black arrow: a tale of the two roses. 1888.
— Catriona: a sequel to Kidnapped. 1893.
Also other romances, novels etc. For a full bibliography see col 1004, above.

Shaw, Flora Louise, later Lady Lugard (1852–1929). Castle Blair: a story of youthful days. 1878.
— Hector: a story for young people. 1883.
— A sea change. 1886 (for 1885).
See E. H. C. M. Bell, Flora Shaw, 1947.

Corkran, Alice (1852–1916). Bessie Lang. 1876.
— The adventures of Mrs Wishing-to-be and other stories. 1883.
— Down the snow stairs: or from goodnight to good-morning. 1887.

— Margery Merton's girlhood. 1888.
— Joan's adventures at the North Pole. 1889.
Reed, Talbot Baines (1852–93). The adventures of a three-guinea watch. 1883.
— The fifth form at St Dominics. 1887.
— The cockhouse at Fellsgarth. 1893.
— The master of the shell. 1894.
— Kilgorman. 1895. With memoir by J. Sime.
— A book of short stories. 1897. With sketch of author by C. A. Hutchison.
Clifford, Lucy, Mrs W. K. Clifford, née Lane (1853?–1929). Anyhow stories, moral and otherwise. 1882, 1899 (enlarged).
'L. T. Meade', Elizabeth Thomasina Meade, later Mrs Toulmin Smith (1854–1914). The children's pilgrimage. 1883.
— The autocrat of the nursery. 1884.
— A world of girls: the story of a school. 1886.
— A sweet girl graduate. 1891.
— Beyond the blue mountains. 1893.
Also over 250 other stories for girls.
Wilde, Oscar Fingall O'Flahertie Wills (1854–1900). The happy Prince and other tales. 1888.
— A house of pomegranates. 1891. *See col 1182, below.*
'F. Anstey', Thomas Anstey Guthrie (1856–1934). Vice versa: or a lesson to fathers. 1882.
— Paleface and Redskin, and other stories for boys and girls. 1898.
— Only toys! 1903.
— In brief authority. 1915.
See col 1034, above.
Haggard, Henry Rider (1856–1925). King Solomon's Mines. 1885; ed R. L. Green 1955.
See col 1055, above for his romances and novels.
'Edna Lyall', Ada Ellen Bayly (1857–1903). How the children raised the wind. 1896. *See col 1064, above.*
'E. Nesbit', Edith Nesbit, afterwards Bland and Tucker (1858–1924).
— The story of the treasure seekers. 1899; ed E. Graham 1958.
— The book of dragons. 1900.
— Nine unlikely tales for children. 1901.
— The would-be-goods. 1901.
— Five children—and it. 1902; ed R. L. Green 1959.
— The phoenix and the carpet. [1904].
— The new treasure seekers. 1904.
— Oswald Bastable—and others. 1905.
— The story of the amulet. 1906.
— The railway children. 1906.
— The enchanted castle. 1907.
— The house of Arden. 1908.
— Harding's luck. 1909.
— The magic city. 1910.
— The wonderful garden: or the three C's. 1911.
— The magic world. 1912.
— Wet magic. 1913.
— Five of us—and Madeline [stories linked by Rosamund Sharp]. 1925.
See her My schooldays, Girl's Own Paper 18 1897; ed N. Streatfeild 1965 (as Long ago when I was young); D. L. Moore, E. Nesbit: a biography, 1933 (with bibliography), 1967 (rev); N. Streatfeild, Magic and the magician, 1958; A. Bell, E. Nesbit, 1960, *and col 641, above.*
Grahame, Kenneth (1859–1932). Pagan papers. 1894, 1898 (rev).
— The golden age. 1895.
— The headswoman. 1898.
— Dream days. 1899 (for 1898).
— The wind in the willows. 1908; ed A. A. Milne 1951.
— Bertie's escapade. 1949. Rptd from Chalmers, below.
See P. R. Chalmers, Life, letters and unpublished writings of Grahame, 1933; Mrs[Elspeth] Grahame, First whisper of the Wind in the willows, 1944; P. Green, Kenneth Grahame: a biography, 1959; E. Graham, Kenneth Grahame, 1963; and for bibliography, R. L. Green, Kenneth Grahame, TLS 9 June 1945.
Barrie, James Matthew (1860–1937). The boy castaways of Black Lake island. 1901 (priv ptd). The only extant copy is in Beinecke Collection, Yale.
— Peter Pan in Kensington Gardens [from The little white bird, 1902]. 1906.
— Peter Pan: or the boy who wouldn't grow up. 1928. A play first produced in 1904.
— Peter and Wendy. 1911, 1921 (as Peter Pan and Wendy).
See R. L. Green, Fifty years of Peter Pan, 1954 *and col 1188, below.*
Crockett, Samuel Rutherford (1860–1914). Sweetheart travellers. 1895.
— The surprising adventures of Sir Toady Lion. 1897.
— Sir Toady Crusoe. 1905.
— Sweethearts at home. [1912].
See col 1044, above for his romances, novels and stories.
Seton, Ernest Thompson (1860–1946). Wild animals I have known. 1898.
— The trail of the Sandhill stag. 1899; ed R. L. Green 1966 (with other stories).
— The lives of the hunted. 1901.
— Two little savages. 1903.
— Wood myth and fable. 1905.
— Rolf in the woods. 1911.
See his autobiography, The trail of an artist-naturalist, 1951.
Phillpotts, Eden (1862–1960). The human boy. 1899.
— The human boy again. 1908.
— From the angle of seventeen. 1912.
— The human boy's diary. 1922.
See his From the angle of eighty-eight, 1951.
'Q', Arthur Thomas Quiller-Couch (1863–1944). Dead man's rock. 1887.
See col 1071, above, for his novels and other works.
Bannerman, Helen (1863–1946). The story of little black Sambo. 1899.
— The story of little black Mingo. 1901.
— The story of little black Quibba. 1902.
Housman, Laurence (1865–1959). A farm in Fairyland. 1894.
— The house of joy. [1895].
— The story of the seven young goslings. [1899].
See col 632, above.
Kipling, Rudyard (1865–1936). The jungle book. 1894.
— The second jungle book. 1895.
— 'Captains Courageous': a story of the Grand Banks. 1897.
— Stalky & Co. 1899.
— Kim. 1901; ed C. E. Carrington, New York 1960; ed J. I. M. Stewart, New York 1962.
— Just so stories for little children. 1902.
— Puck of Pook's Hill. 1906.
— Rewards and fairies. 1910.
— Land and sea tales for Scouts and Guides. 1923.
See C. E. Carrington, Rudyard Kipling, 1955; R. L. Green, Kipling and the children, 1965; *and col 1019, above.*
Crompton, Frances Eliza, later Walsh (1866–1952). Friday's child. 1889.
— Master Bartlemy. 1892.
— The gentle heritage. 1893, 1964.
— Messire, and other tales. 1894.
— The green garland. 1896.
— The voyage of the 'Mary Adair'. 1899.
— The rose carnation. 1900.
— The little swan maidens. 1903.
Potter, Helen Beatrix (1866–1943). The tale of Peter Rabbit. 1900 (priv ptd), 1902.
— The tailor of Gloucester. 1902 (priv ptd), 1903.
— The pie and the patty-pan. 1905.

— The tale of Tom Kitten. 1907.
— The roly-poly pudding. 1908.
— Ginger and Pickles. 1909.
— The tale of Mr Tod. 1912.
— The tale of Pigling Bland. 1913.
— The fairy caravan. 1929 (priv ptd), Philadelphia 1929, London 1952.
With many others; see M. Lane, The tale of Beatrix Potter, 1946; L. Linder and W. A. Herring, The art of Beatrix Potter, 1955; M. Crouch, Beatrix Potter, 1960; Journals 1881–97, ed L. Linder 1966.

Lucas, Edward Verrall (1868–1938). A book of verse for children. 1897. Ed Lucas.
— The Flamp, The Ameliorator and the Schoolboy's apprentice. 1897.
— Anne's terrible good nature and other stories. 1908.
— The slowcoach. 1910.
— Playtime and company: a book for children. 1925.
See his Reading, writing and remembering, 1932; *and* A. Lucas, A memoir of E. V. Lucas, 1938.

Sharp, Evelyn (1869–1955). The making of a school girl. 1897.
— Wymps and other fairy tales. 1897.
— All the way to Fairyland. 1898.
— The youngest girl in the school. 1901.
See Fairytales as they are, as they were and as they should be, Brighton [1899]; *and* Unfinished adventure: selected reminiscences, 1933.

Upton, Bertha and Florence (d. 1922). The adventures of two Dutch dolls and a golliwogg. [1895], 1966.
— The golliwogg's bicycle club. [1896].
— The golliwogg at the seaside. [1897].
— The Vege-man's revenge. [1901].
— The golliwogg's Christmas. [1907].
With 10 others. See E. Osborne, The birth of the golliwogg, Junior Bookshelf 12 1948.

Belloc, Hilaire (1870–1953). The bad child's book of beasts. 1896.
— More beasts for worse children. 1897.
— The moral alphabet. 1899.
— Cautionary tales for children. 1907.
— More cautionary tales. 1930.

Buchan, John (1875–1940). Sir Quixote of the moors. 1895.
— John Burnet of Barns. 1897.
— Prester John. 1910.
— The thirty-nine steps. 1915.
— The magic walking-stick. 1932.
See his Memory hold-the-door, 1940; J. A. Smith, John Buchan, 1965.

(3) MINOR WRITERS

Porter, Jane (1776–1850). The two princes of Persia, addressed to youth. 1801.
See col 758, above.

Somerville, Elizabeth, née Townsend? (c. 1776–1832). The village maid: or dame Burton's moral stories. 1801.
— My birthday: or moral dialogues and stories. 1802.
— Aurora and Maria: or the advantages of adversity. 1809.

Aikin, Lucy (1781–1864). Poetry for children. 1803.
— An English lesson book. 1828; rptd as Holiday stories for young readers, 1858.

Barton, Bernard (1784–1849). Bible letters for children [by Lucy Barton], with introductory verses by B. Barton. 1831.
— Fisher's juvenile scrapbook. 1836.
See also under Jane and Ann Taylor *and col 365, above.*

Hurry, Mrs Ives, née Mitchell. Tales of instruction and amusement. [c. 1803].
— The faithful contrast: or virtue and vice accurately delineated in a series of moral and instructive tales. 1803.
— National amusements for leisure hours. 1804.
— Moral tales. 1807.

Bingley, William (1774–1823). Animal biography. 3 vols 1804, 4 vols 1820.
— Useful knowledge. 3 vols 1816.
— Travels in Africa. 1819.

Taylor, Joseph. The general character of the dog, illustrated by a variety of anecdotes. 1804.
— The wonders of the horse, recorded in anecdotes. 1813, New York 1836.
— Tales of the robin, and other small birds. 1815.

'Edward Baldwin' (William Godwin) (1756–1836). Fables ancient and modern adapted for the use of children. 1805. *See also vol 2 above.*

Fenwick, Eliza. A visit to the juvenile library [i.e. B. Tabart's bookshop]. 1805.
— Infantine stories. 1810.
— Lessons for children: or rudiments of good manners, morals and humanity. nd; The bad family and other stories, ed E. V. Lucas 1898 (selection).

Monget, M. Moral playthings: or tales for children. 1806.

Ventum, Harriet. Tales for domestic instruction. 1806.
— Charles Leeson: or the soldier. 1810.

Cockle, Mary. The juvenile journal: or tales of truth. 1807.

Day, Isaac. Scenes for the young. 1807.

Carey, John (1756–1826). Learning better than house or land, as exemplified in the history of Harry Johnson and Dick Hobson. 1808, 1813 (3rd edn improved), 1864 (omits some characteristic passages).

O'Keeffe, Adelaide (1776–1855). Original poems calculated to improve the mind of youth and allure it to virtue. 1808.
— Zenobia, Queen of Palmyra. 1814.
— National characters exhibited in 40 geographical poems. 1818.
— Poems for young children. [1849?].
See also under Ann and Jane Taylor, *col 1087, above.*

Parkinson, James (1755–1824). Dangerous sports: a tale addressed to children. 1808 (2nd edn).

Richardson, Mrs. Original poems intended for the use of young persons, on a plan recommended by the Rev Dr Isaac Watts. 1808.

Argus, Arabella (pseudonym?). The juvenile spectator. 1810.
— The adventures of a donkey. 1813.
— Ostentation and liberality: a tale. 1821. Possibly pbd earlier.

Mant, Alicia Catherine. Ellen: or the young godmother. 1812.
— The canary bird. 1817.
— The cottage in the chalk-pit. 1822.
— Tales for Ellen. 1825.

Barnard, Caroline. The parent's offering: or tales for children. 2 vols 1813.
— The prize: or the lace makers of Missenden. 1817.

[Peacock, Thomas Love (1785–1866)]. Sir Hornbook, or Childe Launcelot's expedition: a grammatico-allegorical ballad. [1813]. *For full bibliography see col 700, above.*

Cecil, Sabina (pseudonym?). Little John: or the picture book. 1815. Also, uniform, nd or various dates up to 1822, Little Ann, Charles, Charlotte, Edward, Eliza, George, Henry, James, Jane, Mary, Sally, Thomas, William.

Leonard, Eliza Lucy. The ruby ring: or the transformations. 1815.

— The miller and his golden dream. Wellington 1822.
Vaux, Frances Bowyer. Henry: a story for little boys and girls. 2 pts 1815–16.
— Domestic pleasures: or the happy fireside. 1816.
— The dew-drop: or the summer morning's walk. 1818.
Mister, Mary. The adventures of a doll. 1816.
— Mungo: or the little traveller. Dublin 1817.
— Little anecdotes for little people. 1817.
Sullivan, William Francis. The history of Mr Rightaway and his pupils. 1816.
— Pleasant stories: or the history of Ben the sailor and Ned the soldier. [1818].
— Young Wilfred: or the punishment of falsehood. 1821.
Bloomfield, Robert (1766–1823). The history of little Davy's new hat. 1815. *See col 367, above.*
Clark, Emily. Tales at the fireside: or a father and mother's stories. 3 vols Brentford 1817.
Crichton, A. The festival of Flora: a poem, with botanical notes. 1818 (2nd edn).
Marshall, Mrs. Henwick tales: designed to amuse the mind of youth. 1818 (3rd edn).
— Ida, or living for others: a story for the young. [1865].
— Grannie's wardrobe: or the lost key. [1867].
'Martha Blackford', Isabella Stoddart. The Eskdale herdboy: a Scottish tale. 1819.
— The Scottish orphans: a moral tale, being a continuation of the Scottish orphans. 1823.
Hedge, Mary Ann. Affection's gift to a beloved God-child. 1819.
— Samboe: or the African boy. 1823.
— Radama: or the enlightened African. 1824.
Barton, R. C. Chrysallina, or the butterfly's gala: an entertaining poem addressed to children. 1820.
Upton, W. The school girl; The school boy. 1820.
White, E. Gertrude: or thoughtlessness and inattention corrected. 1823.
[Benson, Edward White]. Education at home, or a father's instruction: miscellaneous pieces for the young. 1824.
Copley, Esther, née Hewlett (living in 1859). The old man's head: or youthful recollections. [1824].
— The young reviewers: or the poems dissected. [c. 1830].
For other works, especially on domestic economy, see incomplete list at end of My mother's stories, 1838.
Baker, M. Emily and her cousins: a tale of real life for little girls. 1828.
Taylor, Emily (1795–1872). Tales of the Saxons. 1832.
— The boy and the birds. 1835.
For other works see Sir F. Galton, Hereditary genius, 1869 *and* DNB (Edgar Taylor).
Barwell, Louisa Mary (1800–85). The value of time: a tale for children. 1834.
— Good in everything: or the early history of Gilbert Harland. 1852.
Coleridge, Sara (1802–52). Pretty lessons in verse for good children. 1834. *See col 515, above.*
Bruce, Carlton. The boy's friend: or the maxims of a cheerful old man. 1835.
Tytler, Margaret Fraser. Tales of the great and brave. 1838.
— Tales of many lands. 1839.
— The wonder-seeker. 1846.
— Little Fanny's journal. 1855.
Webb, Mrs J. B. The travels and adventures of Charles Durand. 1839.
— A tale of the Vaudois. 1841.
— Naomi: or the last days of Jerusalem. 1841.
Tytler, Ann Fraser. May and Florence: or grave and gay. nd.
— Leila: or the island. 1839.
Barth, C. G. Winter evening stories. [c. 1840].
Bingley, Thomas. Tales about travellers. 1840.
— Tales about birds. 1840 (2nd edn).
Kelty, Mary Ann (1789–1873). Mamma and Mary, discoursing upon good and evil. 1840.
— Gentle Gertrude: a tale for youth. [1843?].
Richmond, Legh (1772–1827). The young cottager and other tales. [c. 1840].
Wilberforce, Samuel (1805–73). Agathos and other Sunday stories. 1840; ed A. J. Mason, Cambridge 1908.
Gresley, William (1801–1886). Hymns for the young. 2 pts 1843.
Sewell, Elizabeth Missing (1815–1906). Amy Herbert, by a lady. 1844.
— Laneton Parsonage: a tale for children on the practical use of a portion of the Church Catechism. 3 pts 1846–8.
— Stories illustrative of the Lord's Prayer. 1851.
See col 964, above.
Jesse, Edward (1780–1868). Anecdotes of dogs. 1846.
'Harriet' (Lydia Falconer Miller, née Fraser) (1811?–76).
— Little Amy's birthday, and other tales: a story-book for autumn. 1846.
— Home and its pleasures: simple stories for young people. 1852.
— The ocean child, or showers and sunshine: a tale of girlhood. 1857.
Bunbury, Selina. The triumph of truth: or Henry and his sister. [1847?].
— The blind clergyman and his little guide. 1850.
de Chatelain, Clara. The silver swan: a fairy tale. 1847.
— Merry tales for little folk. 1851.
— The Lilliputian library: new series. Guben [1861?].
James, George Payne Rainsford (1799–1860). The last of the fairies. 1848.
See col 736, above for his novels etc.
Mayhew, Augustus Septimus (1826–75) and Henry (1812–77). The good genius that turned everything into gold, or the Queen Bee and the magic dress: a Christmas fairy tale. 1847.
— The magic of kindness: or the wondrous story of the good Huan. [1849].
See col 950, above.
Burden, Mrs. The three baskets: or how Henry, Richard and Charles were occupied while papa was away. [c. 1850].
— The favourite dog and the idle cat. [1854].
— Little Miss Fanny and her visit to the sea shore. [1854].
— The stray child. [1854].
— The faithful dog. [1857].
Clarke, Mary Victoria Cowden (1809–98). The girlhood of Shakespeare's heroines. 3 vols 1851–2. *See col 1375, below.*
Crewdson, Jane. Aunt Jane's verses for children. 1851, 1871 (3rd edn with addns).
B[oyle], Eleanor Vere. Child's play. [1852].
Crompton, Sarah. Tales that are true. 1853.
— Fairy tales and fables in short words. [1872].
Maitland, Julia Charlotte. The doll and her friends. 1854.
— Cat and dog: or memoirs of puss and the captain. 1854.
Bishop, James. The painted picture play-book. [1855]; ser 2, 1856.
Bowman, Anne. Charade dramas for the drawing room. 1855.
— The castaways. 1857.
— The boy voyagers: or the pirates of the East. 1859.
— Among the Tartar tents. 1861.
— The boy foresters. [1868].
Landells, E. Home pastime: or the child's own toy-maker. 2 pts [1858].
Betham-Edwards, Matilda Barbara (d. 1919). Charles and Ernest, or play and work: a story of Hazlehurst School. Edinburgh 1859.
[Leathely, Mrs.] Chick-seed without chickweed. nd, 1860.

Balfour, Clara Lucas. Passages in the history of a shilling. [1862].
— Lame Dick's lantern: a story for children. 1874.
Bethell, Augusta. Maud Latimer: a tale for young people. 1863.
— Among the fairies. [1883].
Greenwood, James (1832–1929). The adventures of Ruben Davidger. 1863.
— King Lion. Beeton's Boys Own 1864 (serialized); ed G. A. Henty 1891.
— The hatchet throwers. 1866.
— Legends of savage life. 1867.
— The purgatory of Peter the cruel. 1868.
— The bear king. 1868.
See J. W. Robertson Scott, The story of the Pall Mall Gazette, 1950.
Lushington, Henrietta, Lady, née Prescott (d. 1875). The happy home: or the children at the red house. 1864.
— Hacco the dwarf, and other tales. 1865.
Greene, the Hon Mrs, née Louisa Lilias Plunket (d. 1891). Cushions and corners: or holidays at Old Orchard. 1864.
— The little castle maiden: simple stories for young children. [1871].
— Gilbert's shadow: or the magic beads. 1875.
— The schoolboy baronet. 1870.
— Dora's doll's house: a story for the young. [1880].
— Bound by a spell: or the hunted witch of the forest. 1885.
[Noel, Lady Augusta (1838–1902)]. Effie's friends: or chronicles of the woods and shore. 1865. *See col 1070, above.*
'Roland Quiz' (Richard M. H. Quittenton). Juvenile rhymes and little stories. [1865].
Gilbert, William (1804–90). The magic mirror: a round of tales for young and old. 1866.
— King George's middy. 1869.
'Sarah Tytler' (Henrietta Keddie). Girlhood and womanhood: a story of some fortunes and misfortunes. 1868.
— A houseful of girls. 1889.
[Tuckett, Elizabeth]. Our children's story, by one of their gossips. 1870.
— The children's journey and other stories. 1872.
[Stephenson, Elizabeth, née Tabor]. When I was a little girl. 1871.
— Nine years old. 1872 (for 1871).
— Aunt Mary's bran pie. 1875.
— Pansie's flour bin. 1880.
— 'At the Hollies': or staying with Auntie. 1889.
Cobb, James Francis. Silent Jim: a Cornish story. [1871].
— The watchers on the longships. 1878.
— Off to California. [1885].
Knatchbull-Hugessen, Edward Hugessen, Baron Brabourne (1829–93). Stories for my children. 1869.
— Tales at tea-time. 1872.
— Whispers from fairyland. 1875.
— Higgledy-piggledy. 1877.
— The mountain sprite's kingdom. 1881.
— Friends and foes from fairyland. 1886.
Thompson, D'Arcy Wentworth (1829–1902). Nursery nonsense: or rhymes without reason. 1864.
— Fun and earnest: or rhymes with reason. 1865.
See col 1727, below.
Havergal, Frances Ridley (1836–1879). Brucy: a little worker for Christ. 1873 (2nd edn).
See col 628, above.
Stebbing, Beatrice, later Batty. Effie and her ayah: or the faithful monkey and his little white mistress. [1873].
— Stories of my pets. 1886.
— The life and adventures of a very little monkey. 1888.
Giberne, Agnes. Drusie's own story. 1874.
— The hillside children. 1878.
— A modern Puck: a fairy story for children. 1898.
Austin, Stella. Stumps: a story for children. 1873.
— Somebody. 1875.
— Rags and tatters. 1876.
— Pat. 1880.
— Great grandmother's shoes. 1882.
— Tom the hero. 1887.
— Tib and Sib. 1892.
Crake, Augustine David. The first chronicle of Æscendune: a tale of the days of St Dunstan. 1874, 1880 (as Edwy the fair).
— Alfgar the Dane, or the second chronicle of Æscendune: a tale of the days of Edmund Ironside. 1875.
— The rival heirs: being the third and last chronicle of Æscendune. 1882.
— The last Abbot of Glastonbury: a tale of the dissolution of the monasteries. [1884].
— The doomed city, or the last days of Durocina: a tale of the Anglo-Saxon conquest of Britain and the mission of Saint Augustine. [1885].
'Brenda', Mrs G. Castle Smith. Froggy's little brother. [1875].
— A Saturday's bairn. [1877].
— The shepherd's darling. [1888].
— A little brown tea-pot. [1902], 1927 (as Rosamund's home: or a little brown tea-pot).
— More about Froggy: a sequel to Froggy's little brother. [1914].
Potter, Frederick Scarlett. Erling: or the days of St Olaf. [1876].
— Cousin Flo. [1877].
— Princess Myra and her adventures among the fairy-folk. [1880].
— A venturesome voyage. [1898].
'Edward Garrett' (Isabella Fyvie, later Mayo). Doing and dreaming: a tale for the young. 1877.
— The magic flower-pot, and other stories. [1878].
'Esmé Stuart' (Miss Leroy). The little brown girl. 1877.
— The unwelcome guest: a story for girls. 1886.
— Harum Scarum: a poor relation. 1896.
[Sue Chesnutwood Perkins?]. Honor Bright: or the four-leaved shamrock. [1879].
— Robin and Linnet. [1880].
— Peas-blossom. 1883.
— One of a covey. nd.
— Tom's opinion. nd.
Hocking, Silas Kitto. Her Benny: a tale of street life. [1879].
— Poor Mike: the story of a waif. [1882].
— Dick's fairy: a tale of the streets, and other stories. [1883].
— Smugglers' keep. 1913.
Locker, Hannah Jane, née Lampson. The pedlar of Capthorne Common, and other stories. 1879.
— Shaw's farm. [1880].
— What the blackbird said: a story in four chirps. 1881.
Barker, Lady Mary Anne, later Broome. Holiday stories for boys and girls. 1873.
— The white rat and some other stories. [1880].
Walton, Catherine Augusta (Mrs O.F.). A peep behind the scenes. [1877].
— Christie's old organ: or home, sweet home. [1882].
— Nobody loves me. 1883.
— Christie the King's servant: a sequel to Christie's old organ. [1898].
Coleridge, Christabel Rose. The girls of Flaxby. 1882.
— The green girls of Greythorpe. [1890].
— A pair of old shoes. [1892].
— Minstrel Dick: a tale of the XIVth century. 1896.
Allingham, William (1824–89). In fairyland: a series of pictures from the elf world by Richard Doyle, with a poem by William Allingham [A forest in fairyland]. 1870 (for 1869).
— The fairies: a child's song. 1883. Rptd from Day and night songs, 1854.
— Rhymes for the young folk. [1887].
See col 502, above.
[Whitaker, Evelyn (1857–1903)]. Laddie. 1880 (for 1879).
— Tip cat. 1884.

— Lil. 1889.
— Pris. 1892.
Overton, Robert (1859–1924). Me and Bill. 1883.
— The King's pardon! 1895.
— Far from home. 1896.
Everett-Green, Evelyn (1856–1932). His mother's book. 1883.
— Uncle Roger: or a summer of surprises. [1885].
— The head of the house. [1886].
— Dulcie's little brother. 1887.
— Molly Melville: a tale for girls. 1897.
— The family next door. 1908.
— General John: a story for Boy Scouts. 1910.
— The imprudence of Carol Carew. 1933.
Also over 100 others.
Adams, William Henry Davenport (1828–91). Sunshine and shadow: or stories from Cragford, for the young folk. 1888.
See col 1110, below.
Field, Louise Frances, Mrs E. M. Field. Bryda: a tale of the Indian Mutiny. [1890].
— Master Magnus: or the Prince, the Princess and the dragon. [1895].
Baring-Gould, Sabine (1834–1924). Grettir the outlaw: a story of Iceland. 1889.
— A book of fairy tales retold. 1894.
— The crock of gold. [1899]. Fairy tales.
See col 1034, above.
Hueffer, Ford Hermann Madox, afterwards Ford (1873–1939). The brown owl. 1892.
— The feather. 1892.
— The Queen who flew. 1894.
Lindsay, Caroline Blanche Elizabeth Fitzroy, Lady (d. 1912). A string of beads. 1892.
— The flower seller. 1896.
— A Christmas posy. 1902.
Pickering, Wilhelmina, Mrs A. M. W. Stirling (1865–1965). The adventures of Prince Almero: a tale of the wind-spirit. [1890].
— The Queen of the goblins. 1892.
Penrose, Ethel Charlotte, née Coghill (d. 1938). The fairy cobbler's gold. 1890.
— Clear as the noon-day. [1893].
— Darby and Joan: being the adventures of two children. [1894].
Hyne, Charles John Cutliffe Wright (1865–1944). The captured cruiser. 1893.
— The adventures of Captain Kettle. 1898. With several sequels.
See his My joyful life, 1935.
Landor, Owen. Whither bound? a story of two lost boys. [1894].
Marchant, Bessie, afterwards Comfort (b. 1862). The old house by the water. [1894].
— Weasel Tim. [1896].
— The Rajah's daughter: or the half-moon girl. 1899.
— Winning his way: a story for boys. [1899].
Meredith, Hal, author of the Sexton Blake series of penny dreadfuls (1894 and later). *See below, under Periodicals,*
— The Union Jack library of high class fiction. Meredith also contributed to the Halfpenny Marvel Library.
'Maggie Brown' (Margaret Hamer, later Mrs Andrewes). Wanted–a King: or how Merle set the nursery rhymes to rights. 1890.
— The surprising adventures of Tuppy and Tue. 1897.
— The book of Betty Barber. 1910.
Edwardes, Charles. The new house-master: a school story. [1895].
Farrow, George Edward (1862–c. 1920). The Wallypug of Why. [1895]. With 6 sequels.
— The missing Prince. 1896.
— The little Panjandrum's Dodo. 1899.
— The mandarin's kite. 1900.
— The cinematograph train and other stories. 1904.
— The mysterious Shin Shira. 1914.
See C. Scott-Sutherland, The great Panjandrum, Junior Bookshelf 29 1965.
'A. Nobody' (Gordon Frederick Browne) (1858–1932). Nonsense for somebody, anybody or everybody: written and illustrated by A. Nobody. [1895].
— Some more nonsense. 1896.
— A. Nobody's scrapbook. 1900.
O'Grady, Standish James (1846–1928). The chain of gold, or in crannied rocks: a boy's tale of adventure. 1895.
See col 1892, below.
Parry, Sir Edward Abbott (1863–1943). Katawampus: its treatment and cure. 1895.
— Butterscotia: or a cheap trip to fairyland. 1896.
— The first book of Krab. 1897.
— Gamble gold. 1907.
Debenham, Mary H. Two maiden aunts. [1895].
Whishaw, Frederick J. Boris the bear-hunter. 1895.
— Gubbins minor, and some other fellows: a story of school life. [1897].
— The adventures of a stowaway. [1897].
Höhler, Mrs Edwin, née Agnes Venetia Goring (1870–1933). The picture on the stairs. 1897.
— For Peggy's sake. 1898.
— The green toby jug, and the Princess who lived opposite. 1898, [1920] (as The green toby jug and other stories).
— The bravest of them all. 1899.
Haverfield, Eleanor Louisa (b. 1870). The doctor's little Dot. 1898.
— Our vow: a story for children. 1899.
— Blind loyalty. 1900. A sequel to Our vow.
Le Feuvre, Amy. A puzzling pair. [1898].
— His big opportunity. [1898].
— Bunny's friends. [1899].
Kearton, Richard (1862–1928). Our bird friends: a book for all boys and girls. 1900.

(4) ANONYMOUS WORKS

including those under unidentified pseudonyms

Summer rambles: or conversations instructive and amusing, for the use of children, by a Lady. 1801.
A cup of sweets, that can never cloy: or delightful tales for good children, by a London Lady. 1804.
A true history of a little old woman who found a silver penny. 1805.
W., S. A visit to a farm-house. 1805 (2nd edn).
— A visit to London. 1808, 1820 ('with additions and improvements by T.H.').
— The Warren family: or scenes at home. 1813.
Rhyme and picture books 1806–8. *Many ephemeral works much alike in scope and design appeared during these years; only a few have had a long life. The chief are:*
Cobbler, stick to your last: or the adventures of Joe Dobson. nd.
The talking bird: or Dame Trudge and her parrot. nd.
Whimsical incidents, or the power of music. nd.
Dame Trot and her comical cat. 1803.
The comic adventures of Old Mother Hubbard and her dog. 1805. Partly, and perhaps wholly, by Sarah Catherine Martin (1768–1826). *See* I. and P. Opie, Oxford dictionary of nursery rhymes, 1951, 1952 (corrected).
Dame Partlet's farm: containing an account of the great riches she obtained by industry, the good life she led, and alas, good reader! her sudden death. 1806.

T., B.A. The history of Mother Twaddle, and the marvellous achievements of her son Jack, by B.A.T. 1807. A rhymed version of Jack and the beanstalk.

The book of trades: or the library of the useful arts. 1807. Many edns in various forms, with valuable illustrations.

The adventures of the little girl in the wood. 1808. With coloured plates.

The history of little Henry, exemplified in a series of figures. 1810. Verses; coloured illustrations with movable heads. Similar works issued at the same time: The young Roscius; Frank Feignwell; Little Fanny; Lauretta the little Savoyard. *See* Paper dolls and other cut-out toys (description of collection of W. M. Stone), Newark Pa 1931 (priv ptd).

Felissa: or the life and opinions of a kitten of sentiment. 1811, 1903.

My real friend: or incidents in life, founded on truth. 1812.

Verses for little children, written by a young lady for the amusement of her junior brothers and sisters. 1813.

Buds of genius: or some account of the lives of celebrated characters. 1816, 1818.

The little warbler of the cottage and her dog Constant, by a lover of children. 1816.

H., M. The winter scene, to amuse and instruct the rising generation.

Motherless Mary: a tale, shewing that goodness even in poverty is sure of meeting its proper reward. 1818. *The same author also wrote* Arthur and Alice: or the little wanderers; Whim and contradiction: or the party of pleasure; Walter and Hubert, nd, *all 1816 or earlier.*

Nursery morals, chiefly in monosyllables. 1818.

Rhyme and picture books. 1821–3. *Many appeared at this time, following a fashion; few had long life. The chief are:*

The history of sixteen wonderful old women. 1821. Supposed first use of limerick metre. Also, uniform but nd, Anecdotes and adventures of fifteen gentlemen.

Aldiborontiphoskyphorniostikos: a round game for merry parties. [c. 1822]. A nonsense story for reading aloud.

Deborah Dent and her donkey. 1823; ed A. W. Tuer 1887.

The Dame and her donkeys five. 1823; ed A. W. Tuer 1888.

[Sharpe, R. S. and Mrs Pearson?]. Dame Wiggins of Lee and her seven wonderful cats: a humorous tale, written principally by a lady of ninety. 1823 (illustr R. Stennet?); ed J. Ruskin 1885 (with addns); extra-illustr Kate Greenaway; ed A. W. Tuer 1887 (facs).

Always happy! or anecdotes of Felix and his sister Serena. 1823 (5th edn).

The tell-tale: an original collection of moral and amusing stories. 1823.

Town and country tales, intended for the amusement and moral instruction of youth. 1824.

The milkmaid, a fable: by a Lady. [1825?].

Interesting walks of Henry and his tutor. 1827.

Edith Vernon's life work. [1864].

Little songs for me to sing. 1865; Songs for Little Folks, 1865. By various writers. Illustr Sir J. E. Millais, with music by Henry Leslie. Editor unidentified.

(5) FAIRY TALES AND LEGENDS

The stories already accumulated—traditional tales like Jack the giant-killer *and* Dick Whittington *existing in chap-book form, and the semi-traditional tales tr from Perrault, d'Aulnoy and the* Cabinet des fées *authors (see vol 2, above)—became a common repertory which editors and publishers varied and used at will. The chief collections made before fresh matter appeared with the impetus given to the study of Märchen by the brothers Grimm were* Temple of the fairies, 2 vols 1804 (anon); Popular stories for the nursery, by Benjamin Tabart [4 vols?] 1809, [1818] (as Popular fairy tales: or a Liliputian library); *one or more tales were issued separately at various dates. A great increase in the common stock was made by trns of Grimm, Andersen and others (see under Translations, below), by wider investigation of folk-lore, by the use of Edwin Lane's version of the Arabian Nights, and by the invention of new tales. Only the principal general collections are included here.*

Temple of the fairies. 2 vols 1804, 1823 (rev as The Court of Oberon: or temple of the fairies). Anon.

'Catherine Calico'. Fairy tales. 1826. From the Cabinet des fées.

Croker, Thomas Crofton. Fairy legends and traditions of the south of Ireland. 3 pts 1825–8; ed T. Wright 1882.

Chambers, Robert. The popular rhymes of Scotland. 1826, 1842 (rev with addns).

Keightley, Thomas. Fairy mythology. 1828, 1847 (enlarged).

Southey, Robert. The three bears. 1835. In The doctor. Previously thought to be Southey's own invention, but a version in verse by Eleanor Mure, written 1831, apparently not pbd, was discovered about 1950. *See* Times 7, 9 Aug 1951; TLS 23 Nov 1951. Included in The book of verse for children, ed R. L. Green 1962.

'Felix Summerly' (Sir Henry Cole). The home treasury. 1841–9. Original edn 12 vols, afterwards regrouped into 5; included ballads and other matter. *For contents see* F. J. H. Darton, Children's books in England, Cambridge 1932, ch 13.

'Ambrose Merton' (William John Thoms). Gammer Gurton's famous histories, newly revised and amended. [1846]. Guy of Warwick and other romances.

—— Gammer Gurton's famous stories, newly revised and amended. [1846]. A miscellany of fairy tales and ballads.

Montalba, Anthony. Fairy tales of all nations. 1849.

[Cundall, Joseph]. A treasury of pleasure books for young and old. 1849.

Burkhardt, C. B. Fairy tales and legends of many nations. Dublin 1849.

Halliwell, James Orchard. Popular rhymes and nursery tales of England. 1849.

Palmer, F. P. Old tales for the young, as newly retold. 1855.

Kingsley, Charles. The heroes: or Greek fairy tales for my children. 1856.

Keary, Annie and Eliza. The heroes of Asgard, and the giants of Jotenheim. 1857.

Planché, James Robinson. Four and twenty [French] fairy tales. 1858.

Cox, Sir George. Tales of ancient Greece. 1861.

Knowles, Sir James. The story of King Arthur and his knights of the Round Table. 1862.

Mulock, Dinah Maria, later Mrs Craik. The fairy book: the best popular fairy stories selected and rendered anew. 1863.

Church, Alfred John. Stories from Homer. 1878.

Mason, J. The old fairy tales: collected and edited. [1873].

Lang, Andrew. The blue fairy book. 1889. Special introd in larger paper edn only.

Further collections under colours: Red, 1890; Green, 1892; Yellow, 1894; Pink, 1897; Grey, 1900; Violet, 1901; Crimson, 1903; Brown, 1904; Orange, 1906; Olive, 1907; Lilac, 1910. *All rptd with illustrations,* New York 1966–7. *Selections include* Old friends among the fairies, 1926; The rose fairy book, 1951; *and* Fifty favourite fairy

tales, ed K. M. Lines 1963; More favourite fairy tales, ed Lines 1967.
— The Arabian nights entertainments. 1898.
— The book of romance. 1902.
— The red romance book. 1905.
Jacobs, Joseph. English fairy tales. 1890; [sequel], 1894.
— Celtic fairy tales. 1891.
— Indian fairy tales. 1892.
— The book of wonder voyages. 1896.
Yeats, William Butler. Irish fairy tales. 1892.
Molesworth, Mary Louisa, née Stewart. Stories of the saints for children. 1892.
Macleod, Mary. Stories from the Faerie Queene. 1897.
— The book of King Arthur and his noble knights. 1900.
Canton, William. A child's book of saints. 1898.
Newbolt, Sir Henry. Stories from Froissart. 1899.

(6) TRANSLATIONS

Andersen, Hans Christian. Eventyr og historier. 5 sers 1835–72. Select tales tr Mary Howitt, 1846; Charles Boner, 1846; Caroline Peachey, 1846; Catherine de Chatelain, 1852; H. W. Dulcken, 1866; Plesner and S. Rugeley-Powers, 1867; Mrs H. B. Paull, 1867; A. Wehnert, 1869; H. L. D. Ward and A. Plesner, 1872; Mrs E. Lucas, 1899; H. L. Braekstad, ed E. Gosse 1900.

Arabian nights entertainments. *See vol 2.* From E. W. Lane's version 3 vols 1839–41 derive the Dalziel edn 1863–5, and one 'revised and emendated throughout' by H. W. Dulcken, nd; A. Lang, 1898, translated from A. Galland's French version 12 vols 1704–17.

Asbjörnsen, Peter Christian and Joergen Moe. Norske folkeeventyr. 2 sers 1842–71. Tr Sir George Webbe Dasent as Popular tales from the Norse, 1859, and Tales from the Fjeld, 1874; also by H. L. Braekstad in Round the Yule log, 1881. Dasent also translated, from the Icelandic, The saga of burnt Njal, 1861.

d'Aulnoy, Marie Catherine la Mothe, Countess. Les contes des fées. [1700?]. For eighteenth-century trns *see vol 2.* Besides many miscellaneous fairy tale collections that include one or more of her stories, *see* Fairy tales and novels by the Countess D'Anois, 2 vols 1817 (anon); J. R. Planché, 1855; A. Macdonal and Miss Lee, 1892 (with introd by A. T. Ritchie).

Bechstein, Ludwig. Deutsches Märchenbuch . 1845. Tr in part as The old story-teller, 1854.

Brentano, Clemens. Geschichte vom braven Kasperl und dem schönen Annerl. 1838. Also other stories, such as Gockel, Hinkel und Gackeleia, tr K. Freiligrath-Kroeker as Fairy tales from Brentano, 1884, and New fairy tales from Brentano, 1887.

Chamisso, Adelbert von. Peter Schlemihl. 1813. Various trns, usually as The shadowless man, by William Howitt (c. 1850) and others anon and nd.

'C. Collodi' (Carlo Lorenzini). Pinocchio: la storia di un burratino. 1881. First tr as The story of a puppet, 1891 (anon).

Cottin, Sophie. Élizabeth: ou les exilés de Sibérie. 1806. Tr (anon, attributed to Fanny Burney) as Elizabeth: or the exiles of Siberia, 1807; tr Mary Meeke 1817.

Fouqué, Friedrich Heinrich Karl de la Motte, Baron. Aslauga's knight, tr T. Carlyle 1827; Sintram and his companions, tr J. C. Hare 1820; with Undine, 1896, introd by C. M. Yonge; Undine, tr G. Soane 1818; T. Tracy 1841; E. Gosse 1896.

Grimm, Jakob Ludwig and Wilhelm Carl. Kinder und Hausmärchen. 3 vols 1819–22. Anon trns by Edgar Taylor, 2 vols 1823–6, 1839 (2nd edn as Gammer Grethel); ed J. Ruskin 1869, 1876 (as Grimm's goblins); tr Mrs H. B. Paull [1872]; L. Crane 1882; M. Hunt 1884 (introd by A. Lang); Mrs E. Lucas 1884; B. Marshall 1900.

Hoffmann, E. T. A. Nussknacker und Mausekönig. 1816. Tr Mrs St Simon, New York 1853. Adapted by Alexandre Dumas as Les aventures d'un casse-noisette, 1845; tr C. Bertall 1875; included in the anon A picture story book [1880?]. Version from Hoffman as Nutcracker and mouse-king, 1893.

Hoffmann, Heinrich. Lustige Geschichten und drollige Bilder. 1845. Tr (J. R. Planché?) as The English Struwwelpeter: or pretty stories and funny pictures for little children, Leipzig 1848; *see* I. and P. Opie, TLS 25 Nov 1955.

König Nussknacker und der arme Reinhold. 1851. Tr J. R. Planché as King Nut-cracker: or the dream of poor Reinhold—a fairy tale for children, Leipzig 1853; 'A.H.' as King Nutcracker and the poor boy, 1854; anon as The wondrous tale of King Nutcracker and poor Richard, 1860.

Lossius, Caspar Freidrich. Gumal und Lina. Tr from a French version by S. B. Moens as Gumal and Lina: or the African children, 1817.

Musset, Paul de. Monsieur le Vent et Madame la Pluie. 1846. Tr Emily Makepeace as Mr Wind and Madame Rain, 1864.

Schmid, Christoph von. Die Ostereier. 1816; Das Blumenkörbchen, 1825. Tr 'G.T.B.' as The basket of flowers, and other tales [Lewis, the little emigrant; Christmas eve; The diamond ring; The gold snuff-box], Halifax 1857. Many edns of these and other stories in separate vols preceded it, from the same publisher.

Spyri, Johanna. Heidi. 1880; tr 1884.

Verne, Jules. Cinq semaines en ballon. 1863; tr 1870 (anon).
— Voyage au centre de la terre. 1864. Tr J. V. 1872; F. A. Malleson 1876.
— De la terre à la lune. 1865; with sequel, Autour de la lune, 1870. Tr Q. Mercier and E. G. King as From the earth to the moon, and a trip round it, 1873.
— Vingt milles lieues sous les mers. 1870. Tr anon 1873; H. Frith 1876.
— Le tour du monde en quatre-vingts jours. 1873. Tr G. M. Towle and N. D'Anvers 1874; H. Frith 1879.
— L'île mystérieuse. 1875. Tr W. H. G. Kingston 1875.
— Les Indes noires. 1877. Tr W. H. G. Kingston as The child of the cavern, 1875.
— Hector Servadoc. 1877. Tr E. Frewer 1878.

Also many others. See K. Allott, Jules Verne, 1940, *and the list of trns in EL edns of* Five weeks in a balloon *etc.*

Wyss, Johann David Rudolf. Der schweizerische Robinson. 2 pts 1812–13. English versions: The family Robinson Crusoe, chiefly from the French trns by Mme de Montholieu (1814), who expanded the original, anon 1814 (apparently 2 issues, 1 vol and 2 vols, containing Wyss's 1st pt only); complete version 1816 (anon). Tr, with revisions and abridgements, W. H. Davenport Adams 1869–70; W. H. G. Kingston 1879; A. Clark 1957.

(7) PERIODICALS

Over 300 periodicals for children that began pbn before 1900 are listed and, in many cases, described in S. A. Egoff, Children's periodicals of the nineteenth century, 1951 (Lib Assoc pamphlet no 8).

R. L. G.

4. DRAMA

I. GENERAL INTRODUCTION

Mss of plays submitted to the Lord Chamberlain in the first quarter of the century are in the Larpent Collection in the Huntington Library; those of plays submitted during the second quarter of the century have now been deposited by the Lord Chamberlain in the BM. See below, D. MacMillan (1939) *and* British Museum (1964).

(1) BIBLIOGRAPHIES ETC

Baker, D. E., I. Reed and S. Jones. Biographia dramatica. 3 vols in 4 1812.
[Genest, J.] Some account of the English stage from 1660 to 1830. 10 vols Bath 1832.
Lowe, R. W. A bibliographical account of English theatrical literature. 1888.
Cameron, J. A bibliography of Scottish theatrical literature. Trans Edinburgh Bibl Soc 1 1896; Supplement, ibid.
Adams, W. D. A dictionary of the drama. Vol 1 (A–G), 1904.
'Clarence, Reginald' (H. J. Eldridge). 'The stage' cyclopaedia: a bibliography of plays. 1909. An alphabetical list of plays, with theatres and dates of first London productions.
Parker, J. Who's who in the theatre. 1912, 1967 (rev F. Gaye). Contains lists of casts and long 'runs' and much other valuable information.
O'Neill, J. J. A bibliographical account of Irish theatrical literature. Dublin 1920.
Firkins, I. T. E. Index to plays 1800–1926. New York 1927; Supplement to Index to plays 1800–1926, New York 1935.
Gilder, R. and G. Freedley. Theatre collections in libraries and museums: an international hand book. New York 1936.
Sper, F. The periodical press of London: theatrical and literary, excluding the daily newspaper 1800–30. Boston 1938.
MacMillan, D. Catalogue of the Larpent plays in the Huntington Library. San Marino 1939. Corrections and addns by E. Pearce, HLQ 6 1943.
Ewing, M. The authorship of some nineteenth-century plays. MLN 57 1942.
—— Notes on Nicoll's handlist for 1800–50. MLN 58 1943.
Tobin, J. E. Early nineteenth-century drama. N & Q 21 April, 5 May 1945.
Stone, M. W. Unrecorded plays published by William West. Theatre Notebook 1 1946.
Forsyth, G. Notes on pantomime with a list of Drury Lane pantomimes 1879–1914. Theatre Notebook 2 1947.
Loewenberg, A. A bibliography of the theatre of the British Isles excluding London. 1950.
Nicoll, A. A history of English drama 1660–1900. Vol IV: Early nineteenth-century drama 1800–1850, 1955; vol V: Late nineteenth-century drama 1850–1900, 1959 (2nd edn).
Stratman, C. J. Additions to Allardyce Nicoll's handlist of plays 1800–18. N & Q June 1961.
—— A bibliography of British dramatic periodicals. New York 1962.
—— English tragedy 1819–23. PQ 41 1962.
British Museum. Plays submitted to the Lord Chamberlain 1824–51: catalogue of additions to the manuscripts. 1964.
Arnott, J. F. and J. W. Robinson. English theatrical literature 1559–1900: a bibliography. 1969.

(2) GENERAL HISTORIES

Arthur, G. From Phelps to Gielgud: reminiscences of the stage through sixty-five years. 1936.
Bergholz, H. Die Neugestaltung des modernen englischen Theaters 1870–1930. Berlin 1933.
Block, A. The changing world in plays and theatre. Boston 1939.
Booth, M. R. English melodrama. 1964.
Broadbent, R. J. A history of pantomime. [1901].
—— Stage whispers. [1901].
Brook, D. The romance of the English theatre. 1945.
Bunn, A. The stage. 3 vols 1840, Philadelphia 1840.
Child, H. Nineteenth-century drama. CHEL vol 13 1916.
Coleman, J. Players and playwrights I have known. 2 vols 1888, 1889, Philadelphia 1890.
Cunliffe, J. W. Modern English playwrights: a short history of the English drama from 1825. New York 1927.
Dickens, C. The amusements of the people. Household Words 30 March, 30 April 1850. A vivid picture of the early Victorian cheap theatres in London; *see* Great expectations chs 31, 47 and, for its provincial parallel, Nicholas Nickleby chs 20–5, 29, 48.
—— The guild of literature and art. Household Words 10 May 1851.
—— Gaslight fairies. Household Words 10 Feb 1855. All 3 articles rptd in Miscellaneous papers in the Gadshill edn of the Works.
Disher, M. W. Clowns and pantomimes. 1925.
—— Winkles and champagne. 1938. A history of the 19th-century music halls.
—— Blood and thunder: Mid-Victorian melodrama and its origins. 1949.
Doran, J. 'Their Majesties' servants': annals of the English stage, from Betterton to Kean. 2 vols 1864, 1865, New York 1865; ed R. H. Stoddard 1880; rev R. W. Lowe 3 vols 1888.
—— In and about Drury Lane and other papers. 2 vols 1881, Boston [19–?].
Downer, A. S. Players and painted-stage: nineteenth-century acting. PMLA 61 1946.
Ebers, J. Seven years of the King's Theatre. 1823.
The eighteen-seventies. 1929 (Royal Soc of Lit). Includes Sir A. Pinero, The theatre in the 'seventies; and H. Granville-Barker, Tennyson, Swinburne, Meredith and the theatre.
Elton, O. A survey of English literature 1780–1830. Vol 2, 1912.
Filon, A. The English stage: an account of the Victorian drama. 1897.

Fitzball, E. Thirty-five years of a dramatic author's life. 2 vols 1859.
Fitzgerald, P. H. The book of theatrical anecdotes. 2 vols 1874.
— The romance of the English stage. 2 vols 1874.
— The world behind the scenes. 1881.
— A new history of the English stage [1660–1842]. 2 vols 1882.
Frenz, H. Die Entwicklung des sozialen Dramas in England vor Galsworthy. Bleicherode-am-Harz 1941.
[Frere, B.] The adventures of a dramatist on a journey to the London managers. 2 vols 1813, 1813, 1832.
Fricker, R. Das historische Drama in England von der Romantik bis zur Gegenwart. Berne 1940.
Frohman, D. Memories of a manager: reminiscences of the old Lyceum and of some players of the last quarter century. 1911.
G., G.M. The stage censor: an historical sketch 1544–1907. 1908.
The genuine rejected addresses, presented to the committee of management for Drury Lane Theatre; preceded by that written by Lord Byron. 1812, 1812, 1929.
Glick, C. William Poel: his theories and influence. Shakespeare Quart 15 1964.
Godwin, George. On the desirability of obtaining a national theatre. 1878.
Hanley, P. Random recollections of the stage. [1883] (priv ptd), [1884], 1887 (as A jubilee of playgoing).
Hanratty, J. Melodrama—then and now. REL 4 1963.
Harris, A. Five years at old Drury Lane. 1884.
Headlam, S. D. The function of the stage. 1889.
Hodson, H. A letter from Miss Henrietta Hodson, an actress, to the members of the dramatic profession. [1877].
Hogarth, G. Memoirs of the musical drama. 1838, [1851] (as Memoirs of the opera).
Holbrook, A. C. The dramatist: or memoirs of the stage. Birmingham 1809.
Holcroft, T. Memoirs of the late Thomas Holcroft, written by himself and continued to the time of his death [by William Hazlitt]. 3 vols 1816, 1852; ed Elbridge Colby 1925.
Hollingshead, J. My lifetime. 2 vols 1895, 1895.
— Theatrical licenses. 1875.
Hudson, L. The English stage 1850–1950. 1951.
Jackson, H. The eighteen-nineties. 1923.
Jerome, J. K. On the stage—and off. 1885, nd (15th edn), [1891].
— Stage-land: curious habits and customs of its inhabitants. 1889, 1890, New York 1891, London 1892.
Klemm, W. Die englische Farce im 19 Jahrhundert. Berne 1946.
Knight, J. The history of the English stage during the reign of Victoria. 1901.
Lawrence, J. Dramatic emancipation. 1813.
Lawrence, W. J. Old theatre days and ways. 1935.
Lee, Henry. Memoirs of a manager. 2 vols Taunton 1830.
Lennox, Lord W. P. Plays, players and playhouses. 2 vols 1881.
Mantzius, K. In Skuespilkunstens historie. 5 vols. Copenhagen 1897–1907; tr 6 vols 1903–21.
Meeks, L. H. Sheridan Knowles and the theatre of his time. Bloomington 1933.
Meisel, M. Political extravaganza: a phase of nineteenth-century British theatre. Theatre Survey 3 1962.
— Shaw and the nineteenth-century theater. Princeton 1963.
Miller, A. I. The independent theatre in Europe. 1931.
Molloy, J. F. The romance of the Irish stage. 2 vols 1897, 1897, New York 1897.
Morgan, A. E. Tendencies of modern English drama. 1923.
Nicholson, W. The struggle for a free stage. 1906.
Nicoll, A. British drama. 1925.
— The English theatre: a short history. 1936.
— A history of the English drama. *See Bibliographies, above.*
Odell, G. C. D. Shakespeare from Betterton to Irving. 2 vols New York 1920, 1964.
An old stager (Matthew Mackintosh). Stage reminiscences: being recollections chiefly personal. Glasgow 1866, 1870.
Oliver, D. E. The English stage: its origins and modern developments. [1912].
Palmer, J. The censor and the theatres. 1913.
'Paterson, Peter' (J. C. Bertram). Behind the scenes: being the confessions of a strolling player. 1852, Edinburgh 1858, 1864 (enlarged).
Pellizzi, C. Il teatro inglese. Milan 1934; tr 1935 (as English drama: the last great phase). Vol 3 of Il teatro del Novecento.
Perugini, M. E. The omnibus book: being digressions on social and theatrical life 1830–50. 1933.
Poel, W. William Poel and his stage productions. 1933 (priv ptd).
Pulling, C. They were singing. 1952.
Reade, C. The eighth commandment. 1860.
Rede, L. T. The road to the stage: or the performer's preceptor. 1827, 1835; ed W. L. Rede 1836, 1868, 1871, New York 1863.
Report from the Select Committee on dramatic literature. 1832.
Reynolds, E. Early Victorian drama 1830–70. Cambridge 1936, New York 1965.
Rice, C. The London theatre in the eighteen-thirties. Ed A. C. Sprague and B. Shuttleworth 1950.
Rowell, G. The Victorian theatre: a survey. Oxford 1956.
Rosenfeld, S. Pictorial records of provincial theatres. Theatre Notebook 2 1948.
— Theatrical history: bills of the play. N & Q 21 July 1951.
Rubinstein, H. F. The English drama. 1928.
Ryan, R. Dramatic table talk. 3 vols 1825–30.
Ryley, S. W. The itinerant. 9 vols 1808–27, [1860] (abridged), 1880; 1817 (vols 1–3 of original edn only).
Schelling, F. E. English drama. 1914.
Sharp, R. F. A short history of the English stage to 1908. 1909.
Short, E. Theatrical cavalcade. 1942.
— Fifty years of vaudeville. 1946.
— Sixty years of theatre. 1951.
— The British drama grows up. Quart Rev 295 1957.
Speaight, G. (ed). Professional and literary memoirs of George Dibdin the younger. 1956.
— Pantomime. Theatre Notebook 5 1951.
Stahl, E. Das englische Theater im 19 Jahrhundert. Munich 1914.
Thackeray, T. J. On theatrical emancipation and the rights of dramatic authors. 1832.
[Winston, James]. The theatric tourist. 1805.
Thorndike, A. H. English comedy. New York 1929.
Troubridge, St V. Fitzball and Elliston: or how to submit a play in 1820. Theatre Notebook 7 1953.
Watson, E. B. Sheridan to Robertson. Cambridge Mass 1926, New York 1964.
West, E. J. From a player's to a playwright's theatre: the London stage 1870–90. Quart Jnl of Speech 28 1942.
Wilson, A. E. Pantomime pageant. 1945.
— The story of pantomime. 1949.
Wynne, A. The growth of English drama. Oxford 1914.

(3) HISTORIES OF INDIVIDUAL THEATRES

Angus, J. K. A Scotch playhouse: being the historical records of the old Theatre Royal, Marischal Street Aberdeen. Aberdeen 1878, 1878.

Baily, L. J. R. The Royal West London Theatre in the nineteenth century. N & Q 21 Oct 1944. Further note by G. Morice 16 June 1945.

Baker, H. B. History of the London stage 1576–1903. 1904.

Baker, W. T. The Manchester stage 1800–1900. 1903.

Baynham, W. The Glasgow stage. [1892].

Board, M. E. The story of the Bristol stage 1490–1925. Bristol 1925.

Brereton, A. The Lyceum and Henry Irving. 1903.

Broadbent, R. J. Annals of the Liverpool stage. Liverpool 1908.

Burley, T. L. G. Playhouses and players of East Anglia. Norwich 1928.

Chapman, J. K. A complete history of theatrical entertainments, dramas, masques and triumphs, at the English Court. [1849], [1849] (as The Court Theatre and royal dramatic record).

Cotton, W. The story of the drama in Exeter. Exeter 1887.

Delderfield, E. R. Cavalcade by candlelight: the story of Exeter's five theatres 1725–1950. Exmouth 1950.

Dibdin, C. History and illustrations of the London theatres. 1826.

Dibdin, J. C. The annals of the Edinburgh stage. 1888.

Disher, M. W. Greatest show on earth: Astley's. 1937.

F[letcher], I. K. The Royal Marylebone Theatre. Theatre Notebook 17 1962.

Hamilton, C. and L. Baylis. The Old Vic. 1926.

Hannam-Clark, T. Drama in Gloucestershire. 1928.

Harcourt, B. The Theatre Royal, Norwich. 1903.

Hinton, P. The dramatic library of the old Theatre Royal, Birmingham. Theatre Notebook 1 1945.

Hollingshead, J. Gaiety chronicles. 1890.

King, R. North Shields theatres. Gateshead 1948.

Lawson, R. The story of the Scottish stage. Glasgow 1917.

Leacroft, R. Remains of the theatres at Ashby de la Zouch and Loughborough. Theatre Notebook 4 1950.

—— Remains of the Fisher theatres at Beccles, Bungay, Lowestoft and North Walsham. Theatre Notebook 5 1951.

Levey, R. M. and J. O'Rorke. Annals of the Theatre Royal, Dublin. Dublin 1880.

Lingwood, H. R. Ipswich playhouse: chapters of local theatrical history. [Ipswich 1936].

Macqueen-Pope, W. J. Theatre Royal, Drury Lane. 1945.

—— Haymarket: theatre of perfection. 1948.

—— Gaiety: theatre of enchantment. 1949.

—— St James', theatre of distinction. 1957.

The Manchester stage 1880–1900. [1900]. Criticisms rptd from Manchester Guardian.

Maude, C. The Haymarket Theatre. 1903.

Morley, M. The first Strand Theatre. Theatre Notebook 18 1964.

Morice, G. A record of some nineteenth-century London theatres. N & Q 9 Oct 1934, 26 Feb 1944, 30 March 1945. Notes by H. Harting 8 April 1944, C. D. Williams 22 April 1944.

Odell, M. T. The Old Theatre, Worthing, 1807–55. Aylesbury 1938.

—— Mr Trotter of Worthing and the Brighton Theatre. 1944.

—— More about the Old Theatre, Worthing. Worthing 1945.

Oswald, H. The Theatres Royal in Newcastle upon Tyne. Newcastle 1936.

Pemberton, T. E. The Birmingham theatres [1862–79]. Birmingham [1889].

—— The Theatre Royal, Birmingham 1774–1901. Birmingham 1901.

Penley, B. S. The Bath stage. 1892.

Porter, H. C. A history of the theatres of Brighton from 1774 to 1855. Brighton 1886.

Powell, G. R. The Bristol stage. 1919.

Rhodes, R. C. The Theatre Royal, Birmingham 1774–1924. 1924.

Sandoe, J. Private theatricals and private theatres. Colorado-Wyoming Jnl of Letters 1939.

Senior, W. The old Wakefield Theatre. Wakefield 1894.

Shawe-Taylor, D. Covent Garden. 1948.

Sheppard, T. Evolution of the drama in Hull and district. Hull 1917.

Sheridan, P. Late and early joys at the Players' Theatre. 1953.

Sherson, E. London's lost theatres of the nineteenth century. 1925.

Stirling, E. Old Drury Lane: fifty years' recollections. 2 vols 1881.

Troubridge, St V. Minor Victorian playhouses. N & Q 17 Aug 1940. Note by G. Morice 14 Sept 1940.

—— Adelphi advertising in 1862. Theatre Notebook 7 1953.

Watts, G. T. Theatrical Bristol. Bristol 1915.

Webster, B. The series of dramatic entertainments performed by Royal Command at Windsor Castle 1848–9. [1849].

Williams, M. Some London theatres past and present. 1883.

Wilson, A. E. The Lyceum. 1952.

Winslow, D. F. Daly's: the biography of a theatre. 1944.

Wyndham, H. S. The annals of Covent Garden theatre 1732–1897. 2 vols 1906.

(4) CRITICISM

Agate, J. (ed). These were actors: extracts from a newspaper cutting book 1811–33. 1943.

—— Those were the nights. [1946].

Archer, C. William Archer: life, work and friendships. [1931].

Archer, W. English dramatists of today. 1882.

—— About the theatre. 1886.

—— The theatrical 'World'. 5 vols 1893–7.

—— Study and stage: a yearbook of criticism. 1899.

—— Play-making. 1912, 1913, 1926, 1930.

—— The old drama and the new. 1923.

Arnold, M. Letters of an old playgoer. Ed B. Matthews, New York 1919.

Baylen, J. O. A note on William Archer and the Pall Mall Gazette. 1888. Univ of Mississippi Stud in Eng 4 1963.

—— William Archer, W. T. Stead and the theatre; some unpublished letters. Univ of Mississippi Stud in Eng 5 1964.

Beerbohm, M. Around theatres. 2 vols 1924, New York 1930, London 1953.

Borsa, M. Il teatro inglese contemporaneo. Milan 1906; tr 1908.

Brereton, A. Some famous Hamlets. 1884.

Carter, H. The new spirit in drama and art. 1912.

Chandler, F. W. Aspects of modern drama. New York 1914.

Clapp, H. A. Reminiscences of a dramatic critic; with an essay on the art of Henry Irving. 1902.

Cook, D. A book of the play. 2 vols 1876, 1876, 1881, 1882.

—— Hours with the players. 2 vols 1881.

—— Nights at the play. 2 vols 1883.

—— On the stage. 2 vols 1883.

Cooke, J. The stage. [1840].

Courtney, W. L. The idea of tragedy in ancient and modern drama, with a prefatory note by Sir A. W. Pinero. 1900.

Craig, E. G. The art of the theatre. Edinburgh 1905.

— On the art of the theatre. 1911, Chicago [1911].

Davies, R. In A voice from the attic, Toronto 1960.

Desultory thoughts on the national drama, past and present, by an old playgoer. 1850.

Dickinson, T. H. The contemporary drama of England. 1920.

Dimmick, R. C. Our theatres today and yesterday. 1913.

A new drama: or we faint!!! decline of the drama!!! review of the actors!!! reprinted from Bentley's Monthly Review. 1853.

'Dramaticus'. An impartial view of the stage. 1816.

— The stage as it is. 1847.

Dukes, A. Modern dramatists. [1911].

Ellehauge, M. Striking figures amongst modern English dramatists. Copenhagen 1931.

Ervine, St J. The Victorian theatre. Fortnightly Rev Nov 1946.

Fitzgerald, P. H. Principles of comedy and dramatic effect. Bungay 1870.

Fornelli, G. Tendenze e motivi nel dramma inglese moderno e contemporaneo. Florence [1930].

Forster, J. S. and G. H. Lewes. Dramatic essays with notes and an introduction by W Archer and R. W. Lowe. 1896.

Hastings, C. Le théâtre français et anglais. Paris 1900; tr 1901.

Goldman, E. The social significance of modern drama. 1914.

Grau, R. Forty years' observation of music and drama. 1909.

Grein, J. T. Dramatic criticism. 5 vols 1899–1905.

Hadow, W. H. The use of comic episodes in tragedy. 1915.

Hale, E. E. Dramatists of today. 1906.

Hamilton, C. The theory of the theatre. 1910.

Hazlitt, W. A view of the English stage. 1818, 1821, 1851, 1854, 1895; ed W. Archer and R. W. Lowe 1906, 1957, and in Collected works, 1902–4, 1936.

Henderson, A. The changing drama. 1914.

Hobson, H. Verdict at midnight: sixty years of dramatic criticism. 1952.

Horne, R. H. A new spirit of the age. 2 vols 1844.

Howe, P. P. Dramatic portraits. 1913.

Huneker, J. G. Iconoclasts: a book of dramatists. 1905.

Hunt, Leigh. Critical essays on the performers of the London theatres. 1807.

— Dramatic essays. Ed W. Archer and R. W. Lowe 1894.

— Dramatic criticism 1803–31. Ed L. H. and C. W, Houtchens 1950.

Jones, F. M. On the causes of the decline in the drama. 1834.

Jones, H. A. The renascence of the English drama. 1895.

Kendal, Madge. The drama. [1884] (4 edns).

— Dramatic opinions. 1890.

Knight, J. Theatrical notes. 1893.

Lamb, C. The art of the stage. Ed P. Fitzgerald 1885.

— Dramatic essays. Ed B. Matthews 1891, New York 1893.

Lewes, G. H. On actors and the art of acting. 1875, 1875.

Martin, Sir T. Essays on the drama: first series. 1874; second series, 1889.

Meredith, G. On the idea of comedy and the uses of the comic spirit. 1897. First pbd 1877 in New Quart Rev.

Morley, H. The journal of a London playgoer 1851–86. 1866, 1891.

Morris, M. Essays in theatrical criticism. 1882.

Nag, U. C. The English theatre of the Romantic Revival. Nineteenth Century Sept 1928.

Neville, H. The stage: its past and present in relation to fine art. 1871, 1875.

Pascoe, C. E. Dramatic notes. 1870.

[Purnell, T.] Dramatists of the present day, by 'Q'. 1871.

Quinlan, M. A. Poetic justice in the drama: the history of an ethical principle in literary criticism. Notre Dame Indiana 1912.

Russell, E. R. The theatre and things said about it. Liverpool 1911.

Schmid, H. The dramatic criticism of William Archer. Berne 1964.

Schoonderwoerd, N. H. G. J. T. Grein: ambassador of the theatre 1862–1935. Assen 1963.

Scott, C. W. Thirty years at the play, and dramatic table talk. [1892].

— From The bells to King Arthur: a critical record of first-night productions at the Lyceum Theatre from 1871 to 1895. 1896, 1897.

— The drama of yesterday and to-day. 2 vols 1899.

— Some notable Hamlets of the present time. 1900, 1905.

Shaw, G. B. The quintessence of Ibsenism. 1891, 1913 (rev).

— Dramatic opinions and essays. 2 vols 1907.

— Our theatres in the nineties. 3 vols 1932.

Spence, E. F. Our stage and its critics. 1910.

Syles, L. D. Essays in dramatic criticism. 1898.

Taylor, T. The theatre in England. 1871.

Thouless, P. Modern poetic drama. Oxford 1934.

Tomlins, F. G. A brief view of the English drama. 1840.

Walbrook, H. M. Nights at the play. 1911.

Walkley, A. B. Playhouse impressions. 1892.

— Frames of mind. 1899.

— Drama and life. 1907.

Wilson, M. G. jr. George Henry Lewes as critic of Charles Kean's acting. Educational Theatre Jnl 16 1964.

(5) ACTORS AND ACTING

'Archer, Frank' (F. B. Arnold). An actor's note-books. [1912].

Archer, W. Henry Irving, actor and manager: a critical study. 1883, 1883, [1884].

— William Charles Macready. 1890.

Armstrong, C. F. A century of great actors 1750–1850. 1912.

Armstrong, M. Fanny Kemble: a passionate Victorian. New York 1938.

Baker, H. B. Our old actors. 1881.

Bancroft, Lady (M. E.) and Sir S. Mr and Mrs Bancroft on and off the stage, written by themselves. 2 vols 1888 (6 edns), 1889, 1891.

— The Bancrofts: recollections of sixty years. 1909.

Barnes, E. Anna Cora: the life and theatre of Anna Cora Mowatt. 1954.

Barnes, J. H. Forty years on the stage. 1914.

Bedford, P. J. Recollections and wanderings. 1864.

Beerbohm, M. Herbert Beerbohm Tree. 1921.

Boaden, J. Memoirs of the life of John Philip Kemble. 2 vols 1825, Philadelphia and New York 1825.

— Memoirs of Mrs Siddons. 2 vols 1827, Philadelphia 1827, London 1831, 1893.

— Life of Mrs Jordan. 2 vols 1831 (3 edns).

Bond, J. and E. Macgeorge. Life and reminiscences of Jessie Bond. 1930.

Brereton, A. Henry Irving. 1883, 1884, 1885.

— The life of Henry Irving. 1905, 1908.

Brook, D. A pageant of English actors. [1950].

Calvert, A. H. Sixty-eight years on the stage. 1911.

Calvert, W. Sir Henry Irving and Miss Ellen Terry. 1897. Rptd from Souvenir of Sir Henry Irving, [1895] and Souvenir of Miss Ellen Terry, [1897].

Campbell, T. Life of Mrs Siddons. 2 vols 1834, New York 1834, London 1839.
Campbell, Mrs P. My life and some letters. 1922.
Child, H. A poor player: the story of a failure. Cambridge 1939.
Clapp, H. A. Reminiscences of a dramatic critic, with an essay on the art of Henry Irving. 1902.
Clarke, A. B. The unlocked book: a memoir of John Wilkes Booth. 1938.
Cole, J. W. The life and theatrical times of Charles Kean. 2 vols 1859, 1859.
Cole, T. and H. K. Chinoy (ed). Actors on acting. New York 1949.
Coleman, J. Memoir of Samuel Phelps. 1886.
Compton, C. and E. Memoir of Henry Compton. 1879.
'Cornwall, Barry' (B. W. Procter). The life of Edmund Kean. 2 vols 1835.
Craig, E. G. Henry Irving, Ellen Terry: a book of portraits. [Chicago 1899].
— Henry Irving. 1930.
— Henry Irving 1838–1938. London Mercury Feb 1938.
Darlington, W. A. The actor and his audience. 1949.
Dawson, J. The autobiography of James Dawson. Truro 1865.
Day, W. C. Behind the footlights. 1885.
[Ellerslie, A.] The diary of an actress. 1885.
'Boz' (Charles Dickens). Memoirs of Joseph Grimaldi, with illustrations by G. Cruikshank. 2 vols 1838; ed C. Whitehead 1846; ed P. Fitzgerald 1903.
— Macready as Benedict. Examiner 4 March 1843.
— On Mr Fechter's acting. Atlantic Monthly Aug 1869.
Both articals are rptd in Miscellaneous papers *in the Gadshill edn of the* Works.
Dickens, C. jr (ed). The life of Charles J. Mathews. 2 vols 1879, New York 1879.
Disher, M. W. The last romantic: the authorized biography of Sir John Martin-Harvey. 1848.
— Mad genius: a biography of Edmund Kean. 1950.
Donaldson, W. A. Recollections of an actor. 1865; rptd as Fifty years of green-room gossip, [1881].
Downer, A. S. The eminent tragedian: William Charles Macready. Cambridge Mass 1966.
[Ballantyne, J.] Dramatic characters of Mrs Siddons. Edinburgh 1812.
Driver, L. S. Fanny Kemble. Chapel Hill 1933.
Dunkel, W. D. Kean's portrayal of Cardinal Wolsey. Theatre Notebook 6 1952.
Dunlap, W. Memoirs of George Frederick Cooke. 2 vols 1813, New York 1813, London 1815.
Dyer, R. Nine years of an actor's life. 1833.
Ellis, S. M. The life of Michael Kelly: musician, actor and bon viveur 1762–1826. 1930.
[Archer, W. and R. W. Lowe]. The fashionable tragedian. Edinburgh 1877, 1877 (with postscript). On Irving.
Field, K. Adelaide Ristori: a biography. 1867.
Letters of Edward FitzGerald to Fanny Kemble 1871–83. Ed W. A. Wright 1895, New York 1895.
Fitzgerald, P. H. The Kembles. 2 vols [1871].
— Henry Irving: a record of twenty years at the Lyceum. 1893, 1895 (rev).
— Sir Henry Irving. 1906, Philadelphia 1906.
Fothergill, B. Mrs Jordan. 1965.
Francis, B. Fanny Kelly of Drury Lane. New York 1950.
Frenz, H. and L. W. Campbell. William Gillette on the London stage. Queen's Quart 3 1945.
Fyvie, J. Tragedy queens of the Georgian era. 1903.
— Comedy queens of the Georgian era. 1906.
Galt, J. The lives of the players. 2 vols 1831, Boston 1831, London 1886.
Gibbs, H. Affectionately yours, Fanny: Fanny Kemble and the theatre. 1947.
Glover, J. M. Jimmy Glover his book. 1911.
— Jimmy Glover and his friends. 1913.
Goddard, A. Players of the period: a series of anecdotal, biographical and critical monographs of the leading English actors of the day. 2 vols 1891.
Goodman, W. The Keeleys: on stage and at home. 1895.
Hansford, F. E. From Dorchester to Drury Lane: the story of Edmund Kean 1787–1833. Dorset Year Book 1963–4.
Harley, G. D. An authentic biographical sketch of William Henry West Betty, the celebrated young Roscius. 1804, 1804, 1805.
Hatton, J. Reminiscences of Mark Lemon. 1872.
Hawkins, F. W. The life of Edmund Kean. 2 vols 1869.
Hiatt, C. Ellen Terry and her impersonations. 1898, 1900.
— Henry Irving: a record and a review. 1899.
Hillebrand, H. N. Edmund Kean. New York 1933.
Hingston, E. P. The Siddons of modern Italy: Adelaide Ristori. 1856.
Holman, L. E. Lamb's 'Barbara S-': the life of Frances Maria Kelly, actress. 1935.
Hook, T. Reminiscences of Michael Kelly. 2 vols 1826, 1826, New York 1826.
Irving, Sir H. The stage. 1878.
— The stage as it is. [1881].
— English actors. Oxford 1886.
— The art of acting. Chicago [1887] (authorized edn), Edinburgh 1891.
— The drama: addresses. New York [1892], London 1893, 1893, New York 1893.
— The theatre in its relation to the stage. Boston 1898.
— A speech delivered at Sunderland. [1900] (priv ptd).
Irving, L. Henry Irving: the actor and his world. 1951.
Jackson, J. Strictures upon the merits of young Roscius. Glasgow 1804, London 1804, 1804.
Kemble, F. A. Record of a girlhood. 3 vols 1878, 1878, New York 1879.
— Notes upon some of Shakespeare's plays. 1882.
— Further records 1843–83. 2 vols 1890, New York 1891.
Kendal, M. Dame Madge Kendal, by herself. 1933.
Kennard, Mrs A. Mrs Siddons. 1887.
Lawrence, W. J. Barry Sullivan: a biographical sketch. 1893.
— The life of Gustavus Vaughan Brooke. Belfast 1892.
Macready, W. C. Reminiscences. Ed Sir F. Pollock 2 vols 1875, 1876, 1912.
Marston, J. W. Our recent actors. 2 vols 1888, Boston 1888, 1 vol 1890.
Martin, T. Helen Faucit Lady Martin. 1900, 1900.
Mason, A. E. W. Sir George Alexander and the St James's Theatre. 1935.
Mathews, Mrs. Memoirs of Charles Mathews. 4 vols 1838–9, 1839, Philadelphia 1839.
Matthews, J. B. and L. Hutton. Actors and actresses of Great Britain and the United States. 5 vols New York [1886].
Meisel, M. Perspectives on Victorian and other acting: the actor's last call, or no curtain like the shroud. Victorian Stud 6 1963.
Molloy, J. F. The life and adventures of Edmund Kean. 2 vols 1888, 1897.
Mosely, B. L. Miss Alma Murray as Beatrice Cenci. 1887.
Munden, T. S. Memoirs of Joseph Shepherd Munden, by his son. 1844, 1846.
Oliver, E. S. Melville's Goneril [in The confidence-man] and Fanny Kemble. New England Quart 18 1945.
Oxberry, W. Oxberry's dramatic biography. 7 vols 1825–7.
Pascoe, C. E. The dramatic list. 1879, 1880 (rev and enlarged).
Paulus, G. Beerbohm Tree and 'the new drama'. UTQ 27 1957.
Peake, R. B. Memoirs of the Colman family. 2 vols 1841.
Pearce, C. E. Madame Vestris and her times. 1923.
Pearson, H. The last actor managers. 1950.
— Beerbohm Tree: his life and laughter. 1955.
Pemberton, T. E. A memoir of Edward Askew Sothern. 1889, 1889, 1890.

—— John Hare, comedian 1865–95. 1895.
—— The Kendals. 1900.
—— Ellen Terry and her sisters. 1902.
Percy, E. Remember Ellen Terry and Edith Craig. 1948.
Phelps, W. M. and J. Forbes-Robertson. The life and life-work of Samuel Phelps. 1886.
Playfair, G. W. Kean. 1939.
Raymond, G. Memoirs of R. W. Elliston. 2 vols 1842–3, 1 vol 1844, 1845, 2 vols 1846, 1851, 1857.
Reed, J. W. jr. Browning and Macready: the final quarrel. PMLA 75 1960.
Robins, E. Both sides of the curtain. 1940.
Rosenfeld, S. An Irving collection. Theatre Notebook 4 1950.
Russell, E. R. Irving as Hamlet. 1875, 1875.
Russell, W. C. Representative actors. [1872], 1875, 1883, 1888.
St Clare Byrne, M. Charles Kean and the Meininger myth. Theatre Research (Recherches Théâtrales) 6 1964.
St John, C. (ed). Ellen Terry and Bernard Shaw: a correspondence. [1949].
Saintsbury, H. A. and C. Palmer (ed). We saw him act: a symposium on the art of Sir Henry Irving. 1939.
Salvini, T. Leaves from the autobiography of Tommaso Salvini. 1893.
Scott, C. Ellen Terry. New York 1900 (rev).
Shattuck, C. H. The dramatic collaborations of William Charles Macready. Urbana 1938.
—— (ed). Bulwer and Macready: a chronicle of the early Victorian theatre. Urbana 1958.
—— Macready prompt-books. Theatre Notebook 4 1961.
—— Mr Macready produces As you like it: a prompt-book study. Urbana 1962.
—— (ed). William Charles Macready's King John: a facsimile prompt-book. Urbana 1963.
Shuttleworth, B. Irving's Macbeth. Theatre Notebook 5 1951.
Sillard, R. S. Barry Sullivan and his contemporaries. 1901.
Simpson, H. and Mrs C. Brown. A century of famous actresses 1750–1850. [1913].
Smythe, A. J. The life of William Terriss. 1898.
Sprague, A. C. Shakespeare and the actors: the stage business in his plays 1660–1905. Cambridge Mass 1944.
—— Shakespearian players and performances. Cambridge Mass 1953.
Steen, M. A pride of Terrys: family saga. [1962].
Terry, Ellen. The story of my life. 1908.
—— Memoirs, with additional chapters by E. Craig and C. St John. 1933.
Thomas, J. B. Charley's aunt's father: a life of Brandon Thomas. 1955.
Toole, J. L. Reminiscences of J. L. Toole, related by himself and chronicled by J. Hatton. 2 vols 1889 (3 edns), 1890, 1892 (abbreviated).
Tree, Herbert Beerbohm. Thoughts and afterthoughts 1913, 1915.
Trewin, J. C. Mr Macready: a nineteenth-century tragedian and his theatre. [1955].
—— Benson and the Bensonians. 1960.
Vandenhoff, G. Leaves from an actor's notebook. New York 1860; tr German, 1860; London 1860 (as Dramatic reminiscences), 1865 (as An actor's notebook).
Waitzkin, L. The witch of Wych Street: a study of the theatrical reforms of Madame Vestris. Cambridge Mass 1933.
Walbrook, H. M. Henry Irving. Fortnightly Rev Feb 1938.
Ward, G. Genevieve Ward: a biographical sketch. [1881].
West, E. T. The London stage 1870–90: a study in the conflict of the old and new schools of acting. Univ of Colorado Stud ser B 2 1943.
—— Henry Irving 1870–90. In Studies in speech and drama in honor of A. M. Drummond, Ithaca 1944.
Young, C. M. A memoir of Charles Mayne Young. 2 vols 1891, 1891.

(6) DESIGN

Campbell, L. B. A history of costuming on the English stage between 1660 and 1823. Wisconsin Univ Stud 2 1918.
Hunter, J. W. Some research problems in a study of the Corsican brothers. Ohio State Univ Theatre Bull 9 1962.
Jackson, A. S. and J. C. Morrow. Aqua scenes at Sadler's Wells Theatre. Ibid.
Nicoll, A. The development of the theatre. 1927, 1937 (rev).
S[charf], G. Recollections of the scenic effects of Covent Garden Theatre during the season 1838–9. 1839.
Southern, R. Trickwork in the English nineteenth-century theatre. Life & Letters May 1939.
—— Benwell on Victorian scene-painting. Theatre Notebook 1 1946.
—— Théodore de Banville and the Hanlon Lees troupe. Theatre Notebook 2 1948.
—— The picture-frame proscenium of 1880. Theatre Notebook 5 1951.
—— Changeable scenery: its origins and development in the British theatre. 1952.

(7) SPECIAL STUDIES

Armstrong, W. A. The nineteenth-century matinée. Theatre Notebook 14 1959.
Bancroft, S. and W. Archer. Byron on the stage. In Byron the poet, ed W. A. Briscoe 1924.
Booth, M. R. The drunkard's progress: nineteenth-century temperance drama. Dalhousie Rev 44 1964.
Bowley, V. E. A. English versions of Victor Hugo's plays. French Quart 10 1928.
Byrne, M. St C. 'Stalls and places in the orchestra'. TLS 24 Nov 1932.
—— Supplement to the Playbill. TLS 29 June 1933.
—— Charles Kean and the Meininger myth. Theatre Research: Recherches Théâtrales 6 1964.
Carré, J. M. Goethe en Angleterre. Paris 1920.
Chew, S. C. The relation of Lord Byron to the drama of the romantic period. Baltimore 1914.
Cooke, W. M. Schiller's Robbers in England. MLR 11 1916.
Disher, M. W. The century of juvenile drama. TLS 26 Feb–11 March 1944.
Dubois, A. E. Shakespeare and 19th-century drama. ELH 1 1934.
—— Beginnings of tragic comedy in the drama of the nineteenth century. Baltimore 1944.
Ellehauge, M. The initial stages in the development of the English problem play. E Studien 66 1932.
Enkvist, N. E. Caricatures of Americans on the English stage prior to 1870. Copenhagen 1951.
Fairfax, W. Robert Browning and the drama. 1891.
Faulkner, S. The Octoroon war. Educational Theatre Jnl 14 1962.
—— The great train scene robbery. Quart Jnl of Speech 50 1964.
Fitzgerald, P. H. The Garrick Club. 1904.
Frank, M. A. Ibsen in England. 1919.
Ganzel, D. Patent wrongs and patent theatres: drama and law in the early nineteenth century. PMLA 76 1961.
Gillet, J. E. A forgotten German creditor of the English stage. Nineteenth Century April 1912.
Gosse, E. The revival of poetic drama. Atlantic Monthly Aug 1902.
Huber, R. Ibsens Bedeutung für das englische Drama. Marburg 1914.

Mander, R. and J. Mitchenson. Maria Marten—an early version. Theatre Notebook 2 1948.
Pallette, D. B. The English actor's fight for respectability. Theatre Annual 7 1949.
Pemberton, T. E. Charles Dickens and the stage. 1888.
Price, C. The regulations of a nineteenth-century theatrical booth. Theatre Notebook 4 1950.
Rea, T. Schiller's poems and dramas in England. 1906.
Schaal, D. The rehearsal situation at Daly's theatre. Educational Theatre Jnl 14 1962.
Scott, H. The early doors: origins of the music hall. 1946.
Sellier, W. Kotzebue in England. Leipzig 1901.
Sharp, R. F. Travesties of Shakespeare's plays. Library 4th ser 1 1920.
Speaight, G. The juvenile drama. [1946].
—— Pope in the toy theatre: 'The silver palace'. Theatre Notebook 7 1953.
Stokoe, F. W. German influence in the English romantic period 1788–1818. Cambridge 1926.
Stone, M. W. William Blake and the juvenile drama. Theatre Notebook 1 1945.
Thompson, L. F. Kotzebue: a survey of his progress in England and France. Paris 1928.
Thorp, W. The stage adventures of some Gothic novels. PMLA 63 1928.
Wells, S. Burlesques of Charles Kean's Winter's tale. Theatre Notebook 16 1962.
White, H. A. Sir Walter Scott's novels on the stage. New Haven 1927.
Wilson, A. E. Penny plain, two pence coloured: a history of the juvenile drama. 1932.
Wray, E. English adaptations of French drama between 1780 and 1815. MLN 43 1928.

8) THEATRICAL PERIODICALS

The Covent-Garden theatrical gazette. Nos 1–148 1816–7. Daily.
The British stage and literary cabinet. Vols 1–6 1817–22. Monthly.
The drama: or theatrical pocket magazine. Vols 1–7 1821–5; new ser vols 1–2 1825–6. Monthly.
The theatrical observer. Vols 1–16 Dublin 1821–3. Daily. From vol 9 called Nolan's theatrical observer, the longest lived of several competing periodicals of this title.
The independent theatrical observer. Vols 10–11 Dublin 1822. Daily. This was intended as continuation of The original theatrical observer, which was in fact continued.
The era. Vols 1–103 1838–1939. Weekly.
The Glasgow dramatic review. Nos 1–54 Glasgow 1844–8. Fortnightly.
The Manchester dramatic and musical review. Nos 1–43 Manchester 1846–7. Weekly.
The era almanack. 1868–1919. Annually; from 1914 called Era annual.
The London entr'acte. Nos 1–137 1870–2. Weekly. Continued as Entr'acte nos 138–1,974 1872–1907.
The theatre. 4 sers 1877–97. Monthly. Ed Clement Scott 1880–91.
Dramatic notes. 1879–93. Annually. Ed A. Brereton 1882–7.
The stage directory. Nos 1–14 1880–1. Monthly. Continued weekly as The stage since 1881.
For further titles to this summary list see C. J. Stratman, A bibliography of British dramatic periodicals, 1962; *and* J. F. Arnott and J. W. Robinson, English theatrical literature 1559–1900: a bibliography, 1969.

(9) COLLECTIONS OF PLAYS

The following list is largely based on 2 articles by R. C. Rhodes, Library 4th ser 16 1935.
The London theatre: a collection of the most celebrated dramatic pieces. Ed T. J. Dibdin 26 vols 1815–8.
The new English drama. Ed W. Oxberry 20 vols 1818–23. Contains 100 plays, each with separate title-page. *Oxberry.*
[John] Duncombe's new acting drama. 12 nos [one play each] 1821–5.
[Thomas] Dolby's British theatre. 12 vols 1823–5. Contains 84 plays, each with separate title-page. Continued as Cumberland, below. *Dolby.*
The British drama: a collection of the most esteemed tragedies, comedies, operas and farces in the English language. 2 vols 1824–6, Philadelphia 1837–8. *BD.*
The London stage: a collection of the most reputed tragedies, comedies, operas, melo-dramas, farces and interludes. 4 vols [1824–7]. *L.St.*
[John] Duncombe's British theatre. 67 vols [1828–52]. *Duncombe.*
[John] Cumberland's British theatre; with remarks biographical and critical [by 'D.G.', George Daniel]. 48 vols 1826–[61]. Contains 398 plays, each with separate title-page, but including several originally issued in Cumberland Minor. *Cumberland.*
[Thomas] Richardson's new minor drama; with remarks biographical and critical by W. T. Moncrieff. 4 vols 1828–31. *Richardson.*
[John] Cumberland's minor theatre; with remarks biographical and critical [by 'D.G.', George Daniel]. 17 vols 1828–43. *Cumberland Minor.*
The acting drama. 1834.
[John Duncombe's] minor British drama. 24 nos [one play each] [1834]. *Duncombe Minor.*
The acting national drama. Ed B. N. Webster 18 vols 1837–[59] (Dramatic Authors' Soc). *Webster.*
The London acting drama. 31 nos (or more) [one play each] 1837–8.
Pattie's play: or weekly acting drama. at least 45 nos [often several to each play] [1838–9].
[James] Pattie's universal stage: or theatrical prompt book. 100 nos [one play each] [1839–45]. From no 32 onwards pbd by William Barth.
The modern English comic theatre. Ed L. Hilsenberg, J. A. Diezemann and C. Albrecht 6 sers Leipzig 1843–[90?]. With notes in German. *Mod Eng Com Th.*
The new British theatre. [c. 1860]. *New BT.*
[T.H.] Lacy's acting edition of plays, dramas, extravaganzas, farces etc. 165 vols [1849–1917]. In progress; pbd as single plays. In 1872 bought by French, who also pbd 2 sers in New York. For contents *see* Lacy, List of plays wholly or partially the property of T. H. Lacy, 1864, and Samuel French, Descriptive catalogue of plays and dramatic works, from c. 1891. *Lacy; French; French NY; French Minor NY.*
The British drama, illustrated. 12 vols 1864–72.
[John Dicks]. The British drama. 12 vols [each containing 14–20 plays] [1866–?]. *Dicks' BD.*
De Witt's acting plays. New York [1868–84]. *De Witt.*
[John] Dicks' standard plays. [1875–1908]. *Dicks.*
Moses, M. J. (ed). Representative British drama, Victorian and modern. Boston 1918. *Moses; Boston.*
Rowell, G. (ed). Nineteenth-century plays. Oxford 1953 (WC). *Rowell.*
Brings, L. M. (ed). Gay nineties melodramas. Minneapolis 1963.
Booth, M. (ed). Hiss the villain: six English and American melodramas. 1964.

II. THE EARLY NINETEENTH-CENTURY DRAMA 1800–35

This section has been restricted, with a few exceptions, to writers born between 1760 and 1800. Moreover here, and in the following sections, cross-references have not usually been included to the unacted poetic dramas of the period, which will be found under Poetry, col 159f., above. Plays are listed in order of production, not of pbn and, for the most part, unpbd plays are not included.

The following abbreviations have been adopted:

Ba burletta, Bal ballet, Bsq burlesque, C comedy, CO comic opera, D drama, Ext extravaganza, F farce, MD melodrama, MF musical farce, O opera, Oa operetta, P pantomime, Spec spectacle, T tragedy; *and for theatres, the word 'theatre' being omitted:* Adel Adelphi, CG Covent Garden, CL Royal City of London, Cob Royal Coburg, Com Comedy, Crit Criterion, DL Drury Lane, D of Y Duke of York's, EOH English Opera House, Gai Gaiety, Gar Garrick, Glo Globe, H Haymarket, K Kings, Lyc Lyceum, NT New Theatre, OH Opera House, Olym Olympic, P'cess Princess's, PW Prince of Wales's, RA Royal Amphitheatre, RC Royal Circus, Sav Savoy, St J St James's, Str Strand, Sur Surrey, SW Sadler's Wells, TR Theatre Royal, Vic Victoria. Cumberland, Dicks *etc refer to their collections of plays (listed in full col 1123–4, above), and references to vols 4 and 5 of* A. Nicoll, A history of English drama, Cambridge 1955, 1959, *have been abbreviated as* Nicoll.

SAMUEL JAMES ARNOLD
1774–1852

Auld Robin Gray: a pastoral entertainment. (H 29 July 1794). 1794.

The shipwreck: a comic opera. (DL 19 Dec 1796). 1796, 1797, New York 1805, London 1807; Oxberry 9.

The Creole: or the haunted island. 3 vols 1796. A novel.

The veteran tar, or a chip of the old block: a comic opera. (DL 29 Jan 1801). 1801.

'Foul deeds will rise': a musical drama. (H 18 July 1804). 1804.

Man and wife: or more secrets than one. C. (DL 5 Jan 1809). 1809 (8 edns), New York 1809, Boston 1855; Dicks 575.

The devil's bridge: an opera. (Lyc 6 May 1812). Dublin 1820, [1825?]; Cumberland 42.

The woodman's hut: a melodramatic romance. (DL 12 April 1814). 1814; Oxberry 4; [1822], [1859]; Dicks 935.

The maid and the magpye: or which is the thief? MD. (Lyc 28 Aug 1815). 1815. From Caigniez, La pie voleuse.

Free and easy: a musical farce. (EOH 16 Sept 1816); Cumberland 42.

A letter to all the proprietors of Drury-Lane Theatre, excepting Peter Moore esq. 1818.

Forgotten facts in the Memoirs of Charles Mathews, comedian, recalled in a letter to Mrs Mathews, his biographer. [1839].

See also Nicoll 3, pp. 234, 377; 4, pp. 255–6, 569.

JOANNA BAILLIE
1762–1851

See col 363, above.

EDWARD BALL, later FITZBALL
1792–1873

§1

The innkeeper of Abbeville: or the ostler and the robber. MD (Norwich Theatre 6 March 1822; Sur 1822). 1822.

Peveril of the Peak. D. (Sur 6 Feb 1823). [1823]. From Scott. Dicks 950; Cumberland Minor 3; Lacy 90.

The floating beacon: or the Norwegian wreckers. MD. (Sur 19 April 1824). Cumberland Minor 2; Lacy 75.

The pilot: or a tale of the sea. Ba. (Adel 31 Oct 1825). 1825. Dicks 347, Dicks BD [1867]. From Fenimore Cooper.

The Flying Dutchman: or the phantom ship. MD. (Adel 1 Jan 1827). Cumberland Minor 2; Lacy 71.

Jonathan Bradford: or the murder at the roadside inn. MD. (Sur 12 June 1833). Lacy 55; Dicks 370; Duncombe 12.

Zazezizozu. Bsq. (CG 4 April 1836). Duncombe 21. From the French.

The miller of Derwent Water. D. (Olym 2 May 1853). Lacy 12.

See also Nicoll 4, pp. 312–17, 584; 5, pp. 367–8, 792.

Thirty-five years of a dramatic author's life. 2 vols 1859.

Fitzball was one of the most prolific writers the English stage has seen. He adapted many novels, especially Scott's, to the stage, and wrote a large number of songs of which the most famous is 'The bloom is on the rye' (My pretty Jane'), and the libretti for well known operas such as The daughter of the regiment *and* Maritana.

JOHN BANIM
1798–1842

See col 707, above.

WILLIAM BARRYMORE
d. 1845

§1

The dog of Montargis: or the Forest of Bondy. D. (CG 30 Sept 1814). Dicks 163. From Pixérécourt, Le chien de Montargis.

Trial by battle: or Heaven defend the right. Spec. (Cob 11 May 1818). Duncombe 8; [1854]; New BT 62.

Wallace, the hero of Scotland. MD. (RA 6 Oct 1817). Duncombe Minor 1; Boston [1856?]; Lacy 73; Dicks 953.

El Hyder, the chief of the Ghaut Mountains. MD. (Cob 7 Dec 1818). Lacy 6; Dicks 140.

Gilderoy: or the bonnie boy. MD. (Cob 25 June 1822). Richardson 2; Cumberland Minor 8.

The secret. Ba. (RA 11 May 1824). [1854]; Lacy 48; New BT 478.

The two sisters. D. Duncombe 66.

The fatal snowstorm. D. (Astley's). Cumberland Minor 13; Richardson 4.

See also Nicoll, 4, pp. 261–2, 570.

THOMAS HAYNES BAYLY

1797–1839

See col 366, above.

SAMUEL BEAZLEY

1786–1851

The boarding-house: or five hours at Brighton. MF. (Lyc 26 Aug 1811). 1811 (3 edns), 1816; Cumberland Minor 15.
Is he jealous? Oa. (EOH 2 July 1816). 1816; Oxberry 3; Dicks 774; New BT 72.
My uncle. Oa. (EOH 23 June 1817). 1817.
Jealous on all sides: or the landlord in jeopardy. CO. (EOH 19 Aug 1818). 1818.
The steward: or fashion and feeling. C. (CG 15 Sept 1819). 1819; Dicks 539.
Love's dream. O. (EOH 5 July 1821). From Scribe, La somnambule. Duncombe, 8.
The lottery ticket: or the lawyer's clerk. F. (DL 13 Dec 1826). 1827; Lacy 68; Dicks 226.
The roué. 3 vols 1828. A novel.
The Oxonians: a glance at society. 3 vols 1830. A novel.
You know what. F. (SW 28 Nov 1842). Dicks 653.
See also Nicoll, 4, pp. 263–4, 571.

JAMES BOADEN

1762–1839

Songs and choruses in Osmyn and Daraxa: a musical romance. (K 7 March 1793).
Fontainville Forest. D. (CG 25 March 1794). 1794, 1794. From Ann Radcliffe, The romance of the forest.
The secret tribunal. D. (CG 3 June 1795). 1795.
A letter to George Steevens: containing a critical examination of the papers of Shakespeare [forged by W. H. Ireland and] published by Samuel Ireland; to which are added Extracts from Vortigern. 1796.
The Italian monk. D. (H 15 Aug 1797). 1797, 1797. From Ann Radcliffe, The Italian.
Cambro-Britons: an historical play. (H 21 July 1798). 1798.
Aurelio and Miranda (original title, The monk). D. (DL 29 Dec 1798). 1798, 1799. From M. G. Lewis, The monk.
The voice of nature. D. (H 31 July 1802). 1803. From Caigniez, Le jugement de Salomon.
The maid of Bristol. D. (H 24 Aug 1803). 1803.
An inquiry into the authenticity of various pictures and prints which have been offered to the publick as portraits of Shakspeare. 1824.
Memoirs of the life of John Philip Kemble, including a history of the stage from the time of Garrick to the present period. 2 vols 1825.
Memoirs of Mrs Siddons, interspersed with anecdotes of authors and actors. 2 vols 1827.
The man of two lives. 2 vols 1828. A novel.
The life of Mrs Jordan, including original, private correspondence and numerous anecdotes of her contemporaries. 2 vols 1831.
Memoirs of Mrs Inchbald; including her familiar correspondence with the most distinguished persons of her time; to which are added The massacre and A case of conscience, now first published from her autograph copies. 2 vols 1833.
The doom of Giallo: or the vision of judgment. 2 vols 1835. A novel.
On the sonnets of Shakespeare: identifying the persons to whom they are addressed, and elucidating several points in the poet's history. 1837.

ALFRED BUNN

1796–1860

Poems. 1816.
Tancred: a tale, and other poems. 1819. Anon.
Kenilworth: an historical drama. (CG 8 March 1831). [1821]; Duncombe 10; Lacy 98. Adapted from T. J. Dibdin's dramatization of Scott.
A letter to the Rev J. A. James, with notes critical, religious and moral. Birmingham 1824.
My neighbour's wife. F. (CG 7 Oct 1833). Lacy, 18; Dicks, 316.
The minister and the mercer. C. (DL 8 Feb 1824). 1834. From Scribe, Bertrand et Raton.
Songs, duets etc. In the opera The bronze horse, adapted from Scribe's drama Le cheval de bronze, [1836].
The stage: both before and behind the curtain. 3 vols 1840.
The Bohemian girl. O. (DL 27 Nov 1843). 1872. From St Georges, La gipsy; music by M. W. Balfe.
The daughter of St Mark. O. (DL 27 Nov 1844). [1845]. Tr Bunn; music by Balfe.
The enchantress. O. (DL 14 May 1845). [1845]. Tr Bunn; music by Balfe.
The bondman. O. (DL 11 Dec 1846). [1847]. Tr Bunn; music by Balfe.
A word with Punch. No 1 (all pbd) [1847]. A satire upon G. A. À Beckett, D. W. Jerrold and M. Lemon, with extracts from their writings.
Old England and New England, in a series of views taken on the spot. 2 vols 1853.
See also Nicoll 4, pp. 276, 575; 5, pp. 287.

JOHN C. CROSS

d. 1810

Collections

Circusiana: or a collection of the most favourite ballets, spectacles, melodrames etc performed at the Royal Circus, St George's Fields. 2 vols 1809, 1812 (as The dramatic works of Cross).

§1

The insolvent debtor: a simple pathetic tale [in verse], founded on facts; to which is added a small collection of miscellaneous poetry. Salisbury 1793.
The purse: or benevolent tar: a musical drama. (H 8 Feb 1794). 1794, 1794, Dublin 1794, 1797.
The apparition! a musical dramatic romance. (CG 29 April 1794). 1794; Songs and choruses, 1794.
Parnassian bagatelles: being a miscellaneous collection of poetical attempts. 1796. Contains 2 plays, both acted 1796.
The raft, or both sides of the water: a musical drama. (CG 17 March 1798). 1798; Songs, 1798.
The songs in the new splendid serious spectacle called Cora: or the virgin of the sun. (RC July 1799). [1799].
The enchanted harp: or harlequin for Ireland. P. (RC 22 April 1802). 1802.
The rival statues: or harlequin humourist. P. (RC 11 April 1803). 1803.
John Bull and Buonaparte: or a meeting at Dover. Spec. (RC 8 Aug 1803).
Pedlar's acre: or harlequin mendicant. P. (RC 2 July 1804). 1804.
The false friend: or assassin of the rocks. MD. (RC 25 Aug 1806).
See also Nicoll 3, pp. 249–51, 380; 4, pp. 286–7, 578.

CHARLES DANCE
1794–1863

A match in the dark. F. (Olym 21 Feb 1833). 1836; Dicks 852.
The Beulah spa. C. (Olym 18 Nov 1833). 1833; Dicks 446.
Pleasant dreams. F. (CG 24 May 1834). 1834; Lacy 80; Dicks 590.
The Bengal tiger. Ba. (Olym 18 Dec 1837). Mod. Eng. Com. Th. 1; Dicks 336.
Naval engagements. Ba. (Olym 3 May 1838). Webster 4; Dicks 351.
Delicate ground: or Paris in 1793. C. (Lyc 27 Nov 1849). Dicks 1008.
A morning call. C. (DL 17 March 1851). [1847]; Lacy 22.
Marriage a lottery. F. (Str 20 May 1858); Lacy 36.
See also Nicoll 4, pp. 288–9, 578–9; 5, pp. 335.

CHARLES ISAAC MUNGO DIBDIN known as CHARLES DIBDIN
1768–1833

§1

Wizard's wake: or harlequin's regeneration. P. (SW 23 Aug 1802). [1803].
The little gipsies. O. (SW 2 April 1804). [1804].
Harlequin and the water kelpe. P. (SW 14 April 1806). 1806.
Mirth and metre: consisting of poems, serious, humorous and satirical. 1807.
The wild man: or the water pageant. O. (SW 22 May 1809). 1809, 1814; Cumberland Minor, 96.
The council of ten: or the lake of the grotto. MD. (SW 3 June 1811). 1811.
The farmer's wife. CO. (CG 1 Feb 1814). 1814; Dicks 110; Dibdin's London Theatre 17.
My spouse and I. CO. (DL 7 Dec 1815). 1815, 1816; Cumberland 41; Dicks 180.
Young Arthur, or the child of mystery: a metrical romance. 1819.
Life in London: or the day and night adventures of Logic, Tom and Jerry. Ext. (Olym 12 Nov 1821). 1821.
Comic tales and lyrical fancies: including the Chessiad, a mock heroic in five cantos; and the wreath of love in four cantos. 1825.
History and illustrations of the London theatres: comprising an account of the origin and progress of the drama in England. 1826.
Dibdin was enormously productive. Most of his pieces were pantomimes, operatic farces and melodramas, and only a few were ever pbd. See also Nicoll 4, pp. 290–6, 580.

§2

Memoirs of Charles Dibdin the younger. Ed G. Speaight 1955.

THOMAS JOHN DIBDIN
1771–1841

§1

The mouth of the Nile, or the glorious first of August: a musical entertainment. (CG 25 Oct 1798). 1798.
The Jew and the doctor. F. (CG 23 Nov 1798). 1800, 1809 (in Mrs Inchbald's Collection of farces, vol 2). Cumberland 34.
Il Bondocani: or the caliph robber. CO. (CG 15 Nov 1800). 1801, 1801 (songs and choruses).
Valentine and Orson. MD. (CG 3 April 1804). 1804; Cumberland 27.
The cabinet. O. (CG 9 Feb 1802). Dublin 1802 (pirated), 1805, New York 1809, 1810, 1811; 1802, 1803 (songs and duets); Cumberland 21.
Two faces under a hood. O. (CG 17 Nov 1807). [1807], 1807 (songs and duets).
Harlequin harper: or a jump from Japan. P. (DL 27 Dec 1813). 1813.
A metrical history of England: or recollections in rhyme of some of the most prominent features in our national chronology. 2 vols 1813.
Ivanhoe: or the Jew's daughter. D. (Sur 20 Jan 1820). 1820; Cumberland Minor 2; Lacy 92. From Scott.
The fate of Calais. D. (Sur 3 April 1820). 1820, nd; Cumberland Minor 8.
The reminiscences of Thomas Dibdin. 2 vols 1827, 1837.
Thomas Dibdin's penny trumpet. 1832. A periodical of which only 4 nos appeared.
Bunyan's Pilgrim's progress metrically condensed. 1834.
Dibdin also wrote many songs, and several collections were pbd. For numerous other works, see Nicoll 3, pp. 256, 382–3 *and* 4, pp. 296–305, 580–581. *They include dramatic versions of several of Scott's novels.*

§2

Sandoe, J. Some notes on the plays of Dibdin. Univ of Colorado Stud 8th ser 1 1940.
Master of melodrama. TLS 20 Sept 1941.

WILLIAM DIMOND
1780?–1836?

The sea-side story. CO. (CG 12 May 1801). 1801, 1806, 1801 (airs, duets and trios).
The hero of the north. MD. (DL 19 Feb 1803). 1803 (7 edns), 1803 (songs and choruses).
The hunter of the alps. MD. (H 3 July 1804). 1804 (3 edns); Cumberland 39; Lacy 91; Dicks 961.
The foundling of the forest. MD. (H 10 July 1809). 1809, Philadelphia 1810, London 1814, Dublin 1818; Cumberland 40; Lacy 99; Dicks 74.
Gustavus Vasa. O. (CG 29 Nov 1810). 1811. From his own melodrama, The hero of the north, above.
Brother and sister. CO. (CG 1 Feb 1815). 1829; Lacy 46.
The lady and the devil. CO. (DL 3 May 1820). 1820; Cumberland 46; Lacy 90; Dicks 435. From Calderón, La dame duende.
The nymph of the grotto: or a daughter's vow. O. (CG 15 Jan 1829). 1829.
Stage struck. F. (EOH 12 Nov 1835). Lacy 10; Dicks 324.
Nicoll 4, pp. 306–7, 581, *notes further pieces by Dimond, mainly comic operas produced at Drury Lane and Covent Garden.*

JOHN THOMAS HAINES
1799?–1843

The idiot witness: or a tale of blood. MD. (Cob 6 Oct 1823). Duncombe 5; Lacy 46.
Jacob faithful, the lighter boy: a tale of the Thames. D. (Vic 16 Dec 1834). Duncombe 16; Dicks 507.
My Poll and my partner Joe. MD. (Sur 31 Aug 1835). Lacy 71; Dicks 500; French 1058; Cumberland Minor 9.
The ocean of life: or every inch a sailor. D. (Sur 4 April 1836). Lacy 69; Dicks 634; Cumberland Minor 11.

Richard Plantagenet: or a legend of Walworth. D. (Vic 1 Dec 1836). Dicks 449; Cumberland Minor 14.
Angeline de Lis. D. (St J 29 Sept 1837). Webster 3; Dicks 669.
The Rye House plot: or the maltster's daughter. D. (SW 4 June 1828) Dicks 426.
Jack Sheppard. MD. (Sur 21 Oct 1839). 1839. From Ainsworth.
Ruth: or the lass that loves a sailor. MD. (Vic 23 Jan 1843). Lacy 44; Dicks, 925.
See also Nicoll 4, pp. 322–3, 586–7.

JAMES HAYNES
1788–1851

§1

Conscience: or the bridal night. T. (DL 21 Feb 1821). 1821, New York 1821. First produced as Lorenzo 10 Feb 1821.
Durazzo. T. (CG Nov 1838). 1823, New York 1823.
Mary Stuart. T. (DL 22 Jan 1840). 1840; Dicks 749.

§2

James Haynes's Conscience: or the bridal night. London Mag March 1821.

CHARLES KEMBLE
1775–1854

The point of honour. D. (H 15 July 1800). 1800, 1801, 1805; Cumberland 28; Dicks 791. From Mercier, Le déserteur.
The wanderer: or the rights of hospitality. D. (CG 12 Jan 1808). 1808, [1809]. From Kotzebue, Eduard in Schottland. Rev as The royal fugitive (CG 26 Nov 1829).
Plot and counterplot: or the portrait of Michael Cervantes. F. (H 30 June 1808). 1808, 1812; Cumberland 31; Lacy 90; Dicks 803. From Dieulafoi, Le portrait de Michel Cervantes.
For unpbd plays see Nicoll 4, pp. 334, 591.
Kemble (afterwards Butler), F. A. Record of a girlhood: an autobiography. 3 vols 1878.
—— Records of later life. 3 vols 1882.

JAMES KENNEY
1780–1849

§1

Society: a poem in two parts; with other poems. 1803.
Raising the wind. F. (CG 5 Nov 1803). 1803, 1804, 1805, 1810; Dicks 208; Lacy, suppl 2; Cumberland 19.
Matrimony. CO. (DL 20 Nov 1804). 1804 (3 edns); Dicks 906; Cumberland 26; Lacy 37. From Marsollier, Adolphe et Clare.
False alarms: or my cousin. CO. (DL 12 Jan 1807). 1807, 1807, 1807 (airs, duets and trios).
Ella Rosenberg. MD. (DL 19 Nov 1807). 1807; Dicks 216; Cumberland 27.
The blind boy. MD. (CG 1 Dec 1807). 1807; Dicks 753; Cumberland 25; Lacy 58.
The world. C. (DL 31 March 1808). 1808.
Turn him out. CO. (Lyc 7 March 1812). 1812, 1812. First performed as The tyrant and the parasite (Lyc 25 Jan 1812).
Valdi, or the libertine's son: a poem. 1820.

Love, law and physic. F. (CG 20 Nov 1812). Dublin 1921; Dicks, 673; Cumberland 24; Lacy, suppl 1.
The portfolio: or the family of Anglade. MD. (CG 1 Feb 1816). 1816.
Sweethearts and wives. CO. (H 7 July 1823). 1823; Webster 15; Dicks 228; 1823 (songs, duets, choruses).
Spring and autumn: or th ebride at fifty. F. (H 6 Sept 1827). Lacy 24; Dicks 708.
The Sicilian vespers. T. (Sur 21 Sept 1840). From Delavigne, Les vêpres siciliennes.
See also Nicoll, 4, pp. 336–8, 591–2.

§2

Clayden, P. W. Rogers and his contemporaries. 2 vols 1889.

JAMES SHERIDAN KNOWLES
1784–1862

Collections

The dramatic works of Knowles, with a memoir by R. Shelton Mackenzie. Baltimore 1835, Calcutta 1838.
Plays: The hunchback, The wife, The beggar of Bethnal Green, The daughter. 1838. Separate plays bound together, with a general title.
The dramatic works. 3 vols 1841, 2 vols 1856, [1883].
Various dramatic works of Knowles. 2 vols 1874 (priv ptd).

§1

The Welch harper: a ballad. 1796.
Fugitive pieces. 1810.
Brian Boroihme: or the maid of Erin. D. (Belfast 2 March 1812; CG 20 April 1837). Webster 8; French 109; Dicks 670. From D. O'Meara.
Caius Gracchus. T. (Belfast 13 Feb 1815; DL 18 Nov 1823). Glasgow 1823; Cumberland 6; Dicks 298.
The elocutionist: a collection of pieces in prose and verse, peculiarly adapted to display the art of reading. Belfast [1823]?, 1831 (7th edn), New York 1844, [1883] (28th edn).
Virginius: or the liberation of Rome. T. (TR Glasgow 1820; CG 17 May 1820). 1820, 1820, 1823 (5th edn); Dolby 12; Cumberland 6; Dicks 246; Moses, Boston 1918.
William Tell. D. (DL 11 May 1825). 1825; Cumberland 22; Lacy 83; Dicks 238.
The beggar's daughter of Bethnal Green. C. (DL 22 Nov 1828). 1828; Dicks 695. Rev as The beggar of Bethnal Green (Vic 1834), 1834.
The hunchback. D. (CG 5 April 1832). 1832, 1832, 1836 (9th edn); Lacy 67; Dicks 206; Cumberland 13; New York [1876?]; tr German, 1838.
The wife: a tale of Mantua. (CG 24 April 1833). 1833 (6 edns); French 109; Dicks 288. Charles Lamb wrote a prologue and an epilogue to the play.
The love-chase. C. (H 9 Oct 1837). 1837; Cumberland 41; Lacy 68; Dicks 322.
Fortescue: a novel. 1846 (priv ptd), 3 vols 1847.
George Lovell: a novel. 3 vols 1847.
The rock of Rome: or the arch heresy. 1849.
The idol demolished by its own priest: an answer to Cardinal Wiseman's lectures on transubstantiation. Edinburgh 1851.
The gospel attributed to Matthew is the record of the whole original apostlehood. 1855.
Old adventures. In The tale book by Knowles et al, Königsberg 1859.
Lectures on dramatic literature etc: lectures on oratory, gesture and poetry; to which is added a correspondence with four clergymen in defence of the stage. Ed S. W. Abbott and F. Harvey 2 vols 1873 (priv ptd).
Lectures on dramatic literature: Macbeth. 1875.

Tales and novelettes. Rev and ed F. Harvey 1874 (priv ptd).
For other plays see Nicoll 4, pp. 338–9; 5, pp. 445.

§2

Hazlitt, W. In his Spirit of the age, 1825.
Horne, R. H. In his A new spirit of the age vol 2, 1844.
Knowles. Blackwood's Mag Oct 1863.
Knowles, R. B. The life of Knowles. Rev and ed F. Harvey 1872 (priv ptd).
Maginn, W. A gallery of illustrious characters. Ed W. Bates [1873], 1883. Essay on Knowles first pbd, with drawing by Maclise, in Fraser's Mag Sept 1836.
Hasberg, L. Knowles Leben und dramatische Werke. Lingen 1883.
Klapp, W. Knowles Virginius und sein angebliches französisches Gegenstück. Rostock 1904.
Meeks, L. H. Knowles and the theatre of his time. Bloomington 1933. With bibliography.

MICHAEL ROPHINO LACY
1795–1867

Love and reason. C. (CG 22 May 1827). 1827. From Scribe, Bertrand et Suzette.
The two friends. C. (H 11 July 1828). Cumberland 37; Dicks 679. From Scribe, Rodolphe.
The maid of Judah: or the Knights Templars. O. (CG 7 March 1829). Cumberland 25. From Scott, Ivanhoe.
Robert the devil: or the fiend father. O. (CG 2 Feb 1830). Lacy 31. From A. E. Scribe and G. Delavigne.
Cinderella: or the fairy-queen and the glass slipper. CO. (CG 13 April 1830). 1830, 1840 (songs and duets); Lacy 18; Dicks 1060.
Fra Diavolo: or the inn of Terracina. O. (CG 3 Nov 1831). 1831, 1833. From Scribe, Fra Diavolo, with music by Auber.
Doing for the best. D. (SW 13 Nov 1861). Lacy 55.
Doing my uncle. F. (Sur 8 Sept 1866). Lacy 72.
See also Nicoll 4, pp. 340, 592; 5, pp. 446, 801. *According to DNB he provided the first English adaptations of* Semiramide, Cinderella, William Tell, Fra Diavolo, *and others less famous. He wrote an oratorio,* The Israelites in Egypt, *for music by Handel and Rossini, and collaborated in Schälcher's* Life of Handel.

MATTHEW GREGORY LEWIS
1775–1818

See col 742, above.

SAMUEL LOVER
1797–1868

See col 744, above.

CHARLES ROBERT MATURIN
1782–1824

See col 746, above.

HENRY M. MILNER

Barmecide: or the fatal offspring. D. (DL 3 Nov 1818). 1818.
The bandit of the blind mine. D. (Cob 15 Oct 1821). [1821].
Frankenstein: or the demon of Switzerland. MD. (Cob 18 Aug 1823). Duncombe 2; Lacy 75. From Mrs Shelley.
Alonzo the brave and the fair Imogene: or the spectre bride. MD. (Cob 19 June 1826). Duncombe 2.
The gambler's fate: or a lapse of twenty years. MD. (DL 15 Oct 1827). 1827; Dicks 308. From V. Ducange, Trente ans.
Mazeppa: or the wild horse of Tartary. D. (RA 4 April 1831). Philadelphia nd, New York nd; Cumberland Minor 5; Dicks 620. From Byron.
Gustavus of Sweden: or the masked ball. D. (Vic 8 Nov 1833). Duncombe 13; Dicks 630.
Dick Turpin's ride to York. D. (Sur 30 Aug 1841). Dicks 632.
See also Nicoll 4, pp. 356–7, 599.

MARY RUSSELL MITFORD
1787–1855

See col 748, above.

'WILLIAM THOMAS MONCRIEFF', WILLIAM THOMAS THOMAS
1794–1857

Collections

Selections from the dramatic works. 3 vols 1851.

§1

All at Coventry: or love and laugh. Ba. (Olym 8 Jan 1816). [1816]; Richardson Minor 2; Lacy 59.
Giovanni in London: or the libertine reclaimed. CO. (Olym 26 Dec 1817). 1825, 1818 (songs, duets, choruses); L.St 3; Cumberland 17; B.D. 3; Dicks 104.
Wanted a wife: or a cheque on my banker's. C. (DL 3 May 1819). 1819.
The Lear of private life. D. (Cob 27 April 1820). Dicks 924; Richardson Minor 1; Cumberland Minor 7. From Mrs Opie, Father and daughter.
Prison-thoughts: elegy written in the King's Bench, in imitation of Gray. 1821.
The spectre bridegroom: or a ghost in spite of himself. F. (DL 2 July 1821). 1821, New York 1821; Cumberland 16; Lacy 35; Dicks 353.
Tom and Jerry: or life in London. Ba. (Adel 26 Nov 1821). 1826; Cumberland 33; Lacy 88; Dicks 82; French Minor NY. From Egan, Life in London.
The cataract of the Ganges: or the Rajah's daughter. MD. (DL 27 Oct 1823). 1823; Richardson 3; Cumberland 33; French NY.
The new guide to the Spa of Leamington Priors; to which is added historical notices of Warwick and its Castle. 1822, 1824.
Excursion to Stratford upon Avon; with a compendious life of Shakespeare, account of the Jubilee, catalogue of the Shakespeare relics. Leamington 1824.
Songs, duets and glees sung at the Royal Gardens Vauxhall. [1827].
The somnambulist: or the phantom of the village. MD. (CG 19 Feb 1828). 1828; Cumberland 18; Lacy 86; Dicks 224. From Scribe, La somnambule.
Poems. 1829 (priv ptd at the author's press).
The march of intellect: a comic poem. 1830.
Old Booty: serio-comic sailor's tale. 1830. In verse.

The triumph of reform: a comic poem with six plates by R. Seymour. [1832].
Eugene Aram: or St Robert's cave. MD. (Sur 8 Feb 1832). Cumberland Minor 10; Lacy 103; Dicks 312.
The scamps of London: or the cross roads of life. D. (SW 13 Nov 1843). 1851; Lacy 81; Dicks 472; French 1213.
An original collection of songs, sung at the Theatres Royal etc. [1850].
Moncrieff also edited Richardson's new minor drama 4 vols 1828–31.
For other plays see Nicoll 4, pp. 358–61, 600.

RICHARD BRINSLEY PEAKE
1792–1847

French characteristic costumes. 1816.
Amateurs and actors. F. (EOH 29 Aug 1818). 1818. Cumberland 16; Dicks 962.
The duel: or my two nephews. F. (CG 18 Feb 1823). 1823; Cumberland 22. First produced as My two nephews.
Jonathan in England. F. (EOH 3 Sept 1824). Dicks 589 (as Americans abroad).
The Middle Temple: or which is my son? Oa. (EOH 27 June 1829). Webster 1; Dicks 692.
In the wrong box. F. (Olym 3 Feb 1834). 1834; Dicks 737.
The chain of gold: or a daughter's devotion. Ba. (Adel 29 Sept 1834). Dicks 694.
Snobson's seasons: being annals of Cockney sports. [1838?].
Memoirs of the Colman family, including their correspondence with the most distinguished personages of their time. 2 vols 1841.
Cartouche, the celebrated French robber. 3 vols 1844.
Ten thousand a year. D. (Adel 29 March 1844). Cumberland Minor 16; Dicks 445.
The title deeds. C. (Adel 21 June 1847). [1847]; Webster 14; Dicks 1013.
For other plays see Nicoll 4 pp. 369–71, 603.

JAMES ROBINSON PLANCHÉ
1796–1880

Collections

The extravaganzas of Planché 1825–71. Ed T. F. D. Croker and S. Tucker 5 vols 1879.

§1

The vampyre: or the bride of the Isles. MD. (EOH 9 Aug 1820). 1820; Cumberland 27; Lacy 107; Dicks 875. From Le vampire.
Maid Marian: or the huntress of Arlingford. O. (CG 3 Dec 1822). [1822]. From Peacock.
Costumes of Shakespeare's King John [etc] selected from the best authorities with biographical, critical and explanatory notices by J. R. Planché. 5 pts 1823–5.
Shere Afkun, the first husband of Nourmahal: a legend of Hindoostan. 2 pts 1823. A poem.
A woman never vext: or the widow of Cornhill. C. (CG 9 Nov 1824). Dicks 880; Cumberland 8; Dolby. From Rowley.
Descent of the Danube from Ratisbon to Vienna, during the autumn of 1827; with anecdotes and recollections, historical and legendary. 1828.
The Jenkinses: or boarded and done for. F. (DL 9 Dec 1830). Lacy 8; Dicks 889.
Olympic revels: or Prometheus and Pandora. (Olym 3 Jan 1831). 1834; Lacy 41. With C. Dance.

Olympic devils: or Orpheus and Eurydice. Ba. (Olym 26 Dec 1831). 1836; Lacy 41. With C. Dance.
History of British costume. 1834, 1847, 1874.
Court favour: or private and confidential. Ba. (Olym 29 Sept 1836). Webster 2; Dicks 883.
Riquet with the tuft. Ba. (Olym 26 Dec 1836). Webster 1. With C. Dance, from Riquet à la houppe.
Regal records: or a chronicle of the coronation of the Queens Regnant of England. 1838.
The captain of the watch. D. (CG 25 Feb 1841). [1841]; Lacy 18; Dicks 293; French 270. From Lockroy, Le chevalier du guet.
The king of the peacocks. Ext. (Lyc 26 Dec 1848). [1849]; Lacy 19.
The Pursuivant of Arms: or heraldry founded upon facts. 1852, [1859] (rev), [1874].
The recollections and reflections of Planché: a professional autobiography. 2 vols 1872.
William with the ring: a romance in rhyme. 1873.
The conqueror and his companions. 2 vols 1874.
A cyclopaedia of costume: or dictionary of dress; including notices of contemporaneous fashions on the Continent and a general chronological history of the costumes of the principal countries of Europe. 2 vols 1876–9.
Suggestions for establishing an English art theatre. 1879.
Planché also wrote several other works on armoury, archaeology and cognate subjects, and translated or edited French and German fairy-tales, books on heraldry etc. For numerous other dramatic pieces see Nicoll 4, pp. 376–83, 604–5; 5, pp. 527–8.

§2

Obituary. Athenaeum 5 June 1880.
Obituary. Jnl of Br Archaeological Assoc 36 1880.
Simpson, J. P. J. R. Planché. Theatre Aug 1880.
MacMillan, D. Planché's early classical burlesques. SP 25 1928.
—— Burlesques with a purpose 1830–70. PQ 8 1929.
Rhodes, R. C. Library 16 1935.
Troubridge, St V. Gilbert and Planché. N & Q 22 March, 12 July 1941.

ISAAC POCOCK
1782–1835

Hit or miss! O. (Lyc 26 Feb 1810). 1810 (3 edns), 1811, 1816 (Dibdin's London Theatre 6), 1818; Cumberland, 34.
The miller and his men. MD. (CG 21 Oct 1813). 1813, 1816, 1820; Cumberland 26; Dicks 28; Dicks BD; Lacy, suppl 1; Boston 1856.
The magpie or the maid? MD. (CG 15 Sept 1815). [1815], 1816; Cumberland 28; Lacy 87; Dicks 948. First produced as The daughter (DL 7 Sept 1815). From Caigniez, La pie voleuse.
Robinson Crusoe: or the bold bucaniers. MD. (CG 7 April 1817). 1817; Cumberland 28; Lacy 89; [1871]; Dicks 214. From Pixérécourt, Robinson Crusoë.
Rob Roy Macgregor: or auld lang syne! MD. (CG 12 March 1818). 1818, 1818; Oxberry 10; Lacy 3; Dicks 70; BD 2; Dicks BD [1867]; Waverley dramas [1845]. From Scott.
Montrose: or the children of the mist. MD. (CG 14 Feb 1822). 1822, Baltimore 1822. From Scott, The legend of Montrose.
Nigel: or the crown jewels. MD. (CG 28 Jan 1823). 1923. From Scott, The fortunes of Nigel.
The robber's bride. MD. (CG 22 Oct 1829). Cumberland Minor 11; Boston 1856; Dicks 362; Cumberland 28; Lacy 69.
See also Nicoll 4, pp. 383–5, 606.

JOHN POOLE

1786–1872

§1

Byzantium: a dramatic poem. nd.
Hamlet travestie. Bsq. (NT 24 Jan 1811). 1810, 1811 (2nd–3rd edns), 1814 (5th edn), 1817; Lacy 10; New York 1866.
The hole in the wall. F. (DL 23 June 1813). 1813, New York 1813.
A short reign and a merry one. F. (CG 19 Nov 1819). 1819.
Simpson and Co. C. (DL 5 Dec 1822). New York 1823, 1827; Cumberland 43; Lacy 74; Dicks 336.
'Twould puzzle a conjuror. F. (H 11 Sept 1824). Lacy 14; Dicks 648.
Paul Pry. C. (H 13 Sept 1825). Duncombe 1; New York 1826; Lacy 15; Dicks 321; tr German, 1854; Hungarian, 1882.
Lodgings for single gentlemen. F. (H 15 June 1829). Lacy 115; Dicks 403; Duncombe 54.
Patrician and parvenu: or confusion worse confounded. C. (DL 21 March 1835). 1835.
Crotchets in the air: or an [un]scientific account of a balloon-trip in a familiar letter to a friend. 1838, 1838.
Little Pedlington and the Pedlingtonians. 2 vols 1839, 1860.
Phineas Quiddy: or sheer industry. 3 vols 1843.
Christmas festivities: tales, sketches and characters, with beauties of the modern drama in four specimens. 4 vols 1845–8.
The comic miscellany for 1845. 1845. Ed Poole.
The comic sketch-book or sketches and recollections. 1859 ('new edn').
For other dramatic pieces, see Nicoll 4, pp. 386–7, 606.

§2

Fitzgerald, P. The author of Paul Pry. GM Sept 1874.

RICHARD JOHN RAYMOND

The castle of Paluzzi: or the extorted oath. MD. (CG 27 May 1818). 1818.
Cherry bounce. F. (SW 27 Aug 1821). Lacy 69; Dicks 360; Duncombe 9.
Robert the devil: or the wizard's ring. MD. (Cob 21 June 1830). 1830; Cumberland 33.
The deuce is in her. F. (Adel 28 Aug 1830). Duncombe 7; Dicks 993.
The farmer's daughter of the Severnside: or the broken heart. D. (Cob 11 April 1831); Lacy 26.
The old oak tree. MD. (EOH 24 Aug 1835); Duncombe 18.
Mrs White. Oa. (EOH 23 June 1836). Duncombe 22; Lacy 55; Dicks 360.
The discarded daughter. (Sur 5 April 1847). Duncombe 59.
See also Nicoll 4, pp. 388–9, 606.

WILLIAM BARNES RHODES

1772–1826

§1

The satires of Juvenal translated into English verse. 1801.
Epigrams, in two books. 1803.
Eccentric tales in verse, by Cornelius Crambo. 1808.
Bombastes furioso: a burlesque tragic opera. (H 7 Aug 1810). [Dublin] 1813, London 1822 (pirated), 1822 (first authorized edn), 1830; Duncombe 48; Cumberland 43; Lacy 3; Dicks 222.

§2

Bibliotheca dramatica: a catalogue of the dramatic library of W. B. Rhodes esq, which will be sold by auction by Mr Sotheby. [1825].
Obituary. GM Nov 1826.

LORD JOHN RUSSELL, 1st EARL RUSSELL

1792–1878

Don Carlos: or persecution. D. (Sur 8 June 1848). 1822 (6 edns). From Schiller.
Caius Gracchus. [1830]. From Monti.
For Russell's other writings, biographical, political, historical and miscellaneous (including the suppressed story The nun of Arouca *1822), see* S. Walpole, The life of Lord John Russell, 2 vols 1889.

THOMAS JAMES SERLE

Rafaelle Cimaro. T. (unacted). 1819.
The man in the iron mask: or the secrets of the Bastille. D. (Cob 16 Jan 1832). Duncombe Minor 22; Dicks 428.
The merchant of London. D. (DL 26 April 1832). 1832; Dicks 1033.
The gamester of Milan. D. (Vic 21 April 1834). Duncombe 14.
The ghost story. D. (Adel 4 Jan 1836). 1836.
The parole of honour. D. (CG 4 Nov 1837). 1837; Duncombe 24; Dicks 1032.
Joan of Arc, the Maid of Orleans. D. (CG 28 Nov 1837). 1837; Duncombe 34; Dicks 1029.
Master Clarke. D. (H 26 Sept 1840). [1840]; Dicks 1031.
Joan of Arc, the Maid of Orleans. 3 vols 1841.
The players: or the stage of life. 3 vols 1847.
For other dramatic pieces see Nicoll 4, pp. 399–410, 610; 5, p. 561.

SIR MARTIN ARCHER SHEE

1769–1850

§1

Rhymes on art: or the remonstrance of a painter; with notes and a preface, including strictures on the state of the arts, criticism, patronage and public taste. 1805, 1805 (with additional preface and notes).
Elements of art: a poem in six cantos, with notes and a preface; including strictures on the state of the arts, criticism, patronage and public taste. 1809.
The commemoration of Reynolds, in two parts, with notes and other poems. 1814.
Alasco, T. (Sur 5 April 1824). 1824.
Oldcourt. 1829. A novel.
Cecil Hyde. 1834. A novel.

§2

Shee, M. A. The life of Shee, President of the Royal Academy. 2 vols 1860.

RICHARD LALOR SHEIL

1791–1851

§1

Adelaide: or the emigrants. T. (Crow Street, Dublin 19 Feb 1814). Dublin 1814, 1816.
The apostate. T. (CG 3 May 1817). 1817 (4 edns), 1818.

Bellamira: or the fall of Tunis. T. (CG 22 April 1818). 1818 (3 edns).

Evadne: or the statue. T. (CG 10 Feb 1819). 1819 (5 edns); Dicks 25; Oxberry 14; Lacy 24; BD 4. From Shirley, The traitor.

Damon and Pythias. T. (CG 28 May 1821). 1821; Dicks 19; Duncombe 61; BD 3. By Banim, altered and rev for the stage by Sheil.

The speeches of the Right Honourable Richard Lalor Sheil MP, with a memoir. Ed T. MacNevin, Dublin 1845.

Sketches of the Irish Bar, with memoir and notes by R. S. Mackenzie. 2 vols New York 1854–6. W. H. Curran was joint-author of these. Sheil's own contributions, with other papers, were later rptd as Sketches, legal and political, ed M. W. Savage 2 vols 1855.

Sheil also wrote 2 unpbd plays, Montoni: or the phantom (CG 3 May 1820), *and* The Huguenot (CG 11 Dec 1822). *In 1824 he adapted* Massinger, Fatal dowry, *for Drury Lane.*

§2

[Maturin, C. and W. Gifford]. The tragic drama: The apostate. Quart Rev 17 1817.

Sheil. Fraser's Mag June 1846.

MacCullagh, W.T., afterwards MacCullagh Torrens. Memoirs of Sheil. 1855.

GEORGE SOANE
1790–1860

§1

Knight Damon and a robber chief. 1812.

The eve of St Marco. 1813. A novel.

The innkeeper's daughter. MD. (DL 7 April 1817). 1817; Duncombe 43; Lacy 114.

The falls of Clyde. MD. (DL 29 Oct 1817). 1817, 1818; French 1894; Cumberland 31.

Self-sacrifice: or the maid of the cottage. D. (EOH 19 July 1819). 1819.

The Hebrew. D. (DL 2 March 1820). 1820. From Scott, Ivanhoe.

Faustus. MD. (DL 16 May 1825). 1825; Cumberland 33.

Specimens of German romance, selected and translated from various authors. 1826.

Pride shall have a fall: or the ladder of life. MD. (Cob 30 July 1832). 1824.

The frolics of Puck. 1834.

Zarah. MD. (Queen's 7 Sept 1835). Cumberland 35; Lacy 92; Dicks 357.

Life of the Duke of Wellington, compiled from his Grace's despatches, and other authentic records and original documents. 2 vols 1839–40.

The last ball, and other tales. 3 vols 1843.

The syren. CO. (P'cess 14 Oct 1844). [1844]. From Scribe, La sirène.

January Eve: a tale of the times. 1847.

New curiosities of literature, and book of the months. 2 vols 1847.

Haydée: or the secret. O. (Str 3 April 1848). 1848. From Scribe, Haydée.

For other dramatic works see Nicoll 4, pp. 403–4, 612.

§2

Bowman, W. P. Some plays by Soane. MLN 54 1939.

CHARLES A. SOMERSET

Crazy Jane. MD. (Sur 19 June 1827). Cumberland Minor 2.

The roebuck: or guilty and not guilty. D. (Sur 1 Oct 1827). Duncombe 2; Dicks 544. From Kotzebue.

A day after the fair: or the roadside cottage. F. (Olym 5 Jan 1829). Cumberland Minor 3; New York 1828 (for 1829?); Lacy 76; Dicks 415.

Home sweet home!: or the ranz des vaches. MD. (CG 19 March 1829); 1829; Duncombe 3; Dicks 296. Adapted from the German.

Shakespeare's early days. Ba. (CG 29 Oct 1829). Cumberland 28; Lacy 93; Dicks 792. First called The life of William Shakespeare.

The female Mascaroni: or the fair brigands. Oa. (Sur 12 Feb 1821). Cumberland Minor 13.

The mistletoe bough: or the fatal chest. (Garrick's Subscription Theatre 1834). Cumberland Minor 12 (as The mistletoe bough: or young Lovel's bride); Lacy 100.

The sea. D. (Queen's 1834). Cumberland Minor 7; Lacy 105.

See Nicoll 4, pp. 404–5, 612; 5, pp. 574, 817.

SIR THOMAS NOON TALFOURD
1795–1854

Collections

Tragedies; to which are added a few sonnets and verses. 1844, 1852 (11th edn).

§1

Poems on various subjects, including a poem on the education of the poor; an Indian tale; and the offering of Isaac: a sacred drama. 1811.

The Athenian captive. T. (4 Aug 1835). 1838, New York 1838; Dicks 327.

Ion. T. (CG 26 May 1836). [1835] (priv ptd), [1835] (priv ptd, with a few sonnets), 1836 (3 edns), 1837 (4 edns), New York 1837; Dicks 319.

The letters of Charles Lamb, with a sketch of his life by T. N. Talfourd. 1837.

Speech delivered in the House of Commons on moving for leave to bring in a Bill to consolidate the law relating to copyright and to extend the term of its duration. 1837.

Glencoe: or the fate of the Macdonalds. T. (H 23 May 1840). 1839 (priv ptd), 1840; Dicks 323.

Three speeches in favour of a measure for an extension of copyright. 1840.

Speech for the defendant in the prosecution of the Queen v. Moxon for the publication of Shelley's works. 1841.

Recollections of a first visit to the Alps, in August and September 1841. [1842?] (priv ptd).

Vacation rambles and thoughts. 2 vols 1845, 1851 (3rd edn).

Supplement to Vacation rambles, consisting of recollections of a tour through France to Italy, and homewards by Switzerland, in the vacation of 1846. 1854.

Final memorials of Charles Lamb, consisting chiefly of his letters not before published. 1848, 1850.

Encyclopaedia metropolitana. Ed E. Smedley. Contributions to the history of Greece and of Rome, and on early Greek poetry, c. 1848–50.

The importance of literature to men of business: an address delivered to members of the Manchester Athenaeum. 1852.

The Castilian. T. (unacted?). 1853.

Talfourd also contributed important reviews and critical essays to Pamphleteer, New Monthly Mag *and* Retrospective Rev *1816–25, and later to other periodicals.*

§2

Horne, R. H. In his A new spirit of the age vol i, 1844.

Dickens, C. The late Mr Justice Talfourd. Household Words 25 March 1854.

A memoir of the late Mr Justice Talfourd, by a member of the Oxford Circuit. 1854.

Brain, J. A. An evening with Talfourd. Reading [1889]. A lecture.

Merriam, H. G. Edward Moxon: publisher of poets. New York 1939.

Newdick, R. S. A Victorian Demosthenes. Quart Jnl of Speech 25 1939.

Harrocks, S. H. Talfourd. N & Q 25 June 1949. Further notes by F. Taylor 6 Aug 1949 and J.M.T. 7 Jan 1950.

McCormick, J. P. An early champion of Wordsworth: Talfourd. PMLA 68 1953.

BENJAMIN THOMPSON
1776?–1816

Collections

The German theatre. 6 vols 1800, 1801, 1811 (4th edn). Contains trns of 19 plays, by Kotzebue, Goethe, Schiller et al.

§1

The stranger. D. (DL 24 March 1798). 1798, 1801 etc; Lacy 22; Dicks 12. From Kotzebue, Menschenhass und Reue.

Ignes de Castro. T. (unacted) 1800. From Quita.

The Florentines: or secret memoirs of the noble family D.C. 1808.

An account of the introduction of merino sheep into the different states of Europe and at the Cape of Good Hope. 1810.

Oberon's oath: or the paladin and the princess. MD. (DL 21 May 1816). 1816 (with a memoir of Thompson).

Thompson translated several other dramas of Kotzebue besides those included in The German theatre, *above. His own opera,* Godolphin, *was put on at Drury Lane 12 Oct 1813. See* Nicoll 3, pp. 311, 397.

JOHN TOBIN
1770–1804

§1

The honey moon. C. (DL 31 Jan 1805). 1805, 1807; Lacy 16; Cumberland 13; Dicks 14.

The curfew. D. (DL 19 Feb 1807). 1807 (7 edns); Cumberland 43; Dicks 102; BD 4.

The school for authors. C. (CG 5 Dec 1808). 1808.

The faro table: or the guardians. C. (DL 5 Nov 1816). 1816.

The farce All's fair in love *(CG 29 April 1803) is unpbd. The operatic farce* Yours or mine? *(CG 23 Sept 1816) was pbd with Benger's* Memoirs, *below. See also* Nicoll 4, pp. 413, 614.

§2

Benger, E. O. Memoirs of Tobin, with a selection from his unpublished writings. 1820.

BENJAMIN NOTTINGHAM WEBSTER
1797–1882

High ways and by ways. F. (DL 15 March 1831). Cumberland 28. From Monsieur Rigaud and Partie et revanche.

Paul Clifford, the highwayman of 1770: or crime and ambition. D. (Cob 12 March 1832). Cumberland Minor 6. From Lytton.

The modern Orpheus: or music the food of love. F. (CG 15 April 1837). Webster 1.

The village doctor: or the hind's disease. C. (H 24 July 1839). Webster 7.

Caught in a trap. F. (H 25 Nov 1843). Webster 10.

Pierrot (the married man) and Polichinello (the gay single fellow). Ba (Adel 27 Dec 1847). Webster 14.

Belphegor, the mountebank: or pride of Bath. D. (Adel 13 Jan 1851). Webster 17.

The man of law. D. (H 9 Dec 1851). Webster 17.

Webster wrote, adapted or translated about a hundred plays. See Nicoll 4, pp. 417–8, 616; 5, pp. 618, 823. *A memoir will be found in his* Acting national drama vol 4, 1838.

III. THE MID-NINETEENTH-CENTURY DRAMA

THOMAS WILLIAM ROBERTSON
1829–1871

Collections

Principal dramatic works, with a memoir by his son [T. W. S. Robertson]. 2 vols 1889.

§1

The Chevalier de St George. D. (P'cess 20 May 1845). [1870?]; Lacy 25. From the French of M. Mélesville and R. de Beauvoir.

Noémie. D. (P'cess 14 April 1846). Lacy 23; New York nd. Played as Ernestine. From the French of A. D'Ennery and Clément.

The ladies' battle. C. (H 18 Nov 1851). Boston [1856?]; Lacy, suppl 1. From the French of A. E. Scribe and Legouvé.

Faust and Marguerite. D. (P'cess April 1854). Lacy 15. From the French of M. Carré.

My wife's diary, adapted from Les mémoires de deux jeunes mariées of A. D'Ennery and Clairville. F. (Olym 18 Dec 1854). Lacy 18. Played as A wife's journal.

The star of the north. D. (SW 5 March 1855, as The northern star). Lacy 93. From the French.

Peace at any price. F. (Str 13 Feb 1856). Lacy 95.

The half caste: or the poisoned pearl. D. (Sur 8 Sept 1856). Lacy 97.

Two gay deceivers: or black, white and grey. F. (Str 1858). Lacy 23. With T. H. Lacy. From E. M. Labiche, Deux profonds scélérats.

The cantab. F. (Str 14 Feb 1861). Lacy 50.

David Garrick. From the French of 'M. Mélesville' (A. H. J. Duveyrier), Sullivan. C. (PW Birmingham April 1864; H 30 April 1864). De Witt; French 117; Philadelphia 1903.

Society. C. (PW Liverpool 1865; PW 11 Nov 1865). Lacy 71.

Robinson Crusoe. B. (unacted?). [1865?]. After A. E. Scribe, Un verre d'eau.

David Garrick: a love story. 1865. A novel.
The ring. In A bunch of keys, ed T. Hood 1865.
Ours. C. (PW Liverpool 23 Aug 1866; PW 16 Sept 1866). De Witt; French 132.
The poor-rate. In Rates and taxes, ed T. Hood 1866.
Caste. C. (PW 6 April 1867). De Witt; French 131; ed M. J. Moses, Boston 1918; ed M. Slater 1951; Rowell.
Play. C. (PW 15 Feb 1868). French 132.
Exceptional experiences. In A. Halliday, Savage Club papers for 1868.
Home. C. (H 14 Jan 1869). New York [1879]; French 131; De Witt. Founded on G. V. E. Augier, L'aventurière.
School. C. (PW 16 Jan 1869). De Witt; French 133; Philadelphia 1903.
My Lady Clara. D. (Alexandra, Liverpool 22 Feb 1869; Gai 27 March 1869, as Dreams). New York [1875?]; French 131 (as Dreams).
A breach of promise. C. (Glo 10 April 1869). French 128.
Progress. C. (Glo 18 Sept 1869). French 133. Founded on V. Sardou, Les Ganaches.
The nightingale. D. (Adel 15 Jan 1870). French 132.
M.P. C. (PW 23 April 1870). French 132.
Birth. C. (New TR Bristol 5 Oct 1870). French 131.
War. D. (St J. 16 Jan 1871). French 133.
Birds of prey: or a duel in the dark. D. (unacted?). Lacy 93.
Not at all jealous. F. (Court 29 May 1871). Lacy 91.
A row in the house. F. (Toole's 30 Aug 1883). French 128.
Dazzled not blinded. nd. A novel.
Stephen Caldrick. nd. A novel.

§2

The comedies of Robertson. Broadway 6 1870.
Friswell, J. H. In his Modern men of letters, 1870.
Robertson and the modern theatre. Temple Bar June 1875.
Jones, W. W. Robertson as a dramatist. Theatre 1 1879.
Pemberton, T. E. The life and writings of Robertson. 1893.
Hawkins, F. Academy 3 June 1893. Review of preceding.
Shaw, G. B. Robertson's Caste. Saturday Rev June 1897.
Grein, K. Robertson 1829–71: ein Beitrag zur Geschichte des neueren englischen Dramas. Marburg 1911.
Armstrong, C. F. Shakespeare to Shaw: studies in the life's work of six dramatists of the English stage. 1913.
Harrison, D. Tom Robertson: a century of criticism. Contemporary Rev April 1929.
Rahill, F. A mid-Victorian regisseur. Theatre Arts Nov 1929.
Bulloch, J. M. Dame Madge Kendal's Robertson ancestors. N & Q 3–17 Dec 1932.
Savin, M. Robertson: his plays and stagecraft. Providence 1950.

OTHER DRAMATISTS 1835–70

GILBERT ABBOT À BECKETT
1811–56

§1

The man with the carpet bag. F. (?Vic 29 Sept 1834; Str 1835). Cumberland Minor 13; Dicks 959; Mod. Eng Com Th 3; Lacy 68.
The postillion. Ba. (St J 13 March 1837). Cumberland 43.
Don Caesar de Bazan. D. (P'cess 8 Oct 1844). Lacy 12; Dicks 800. With M. Lemon; based on the play by Dumanois and Dennery.
Scenes from the rejected comedies, by some of the competitors for the prize of £500 offered by Mr B. Webster. 1844.
The comic Blackstone. 1844, 1846 (illustr G. Cruikshank).
The chimes: or a goblin tale. D. (Adel 19 Feb 1844). Webster 11. From Dickens's novel; in collaboration with M. Lemon.
St George and the dragon. Bsq. (Adel 24 March 1845). Webster 11. With M. Lemon.
Peter Wilkins: or the loadstone rock and the flying Indians. D. (Adel 9 April 1846). Webster 12. With M. Lemon.
The quizziology of the British drama. 1846.
The comic history of England, with coloured etchings and woodcuts by John Leech. 2 vols 1847–8, 1894, [1897?].
The castle of Otranto. (H 24 April 1848). Webster 14. In verse.
The comic history of Rome, illustrated by John Leech. 1852, [1897].
À Beckett is supposed to have written '50 or 60' pieces. Nicoll *lists* 55 (4, pp. 249–51 *and* 567; 5, p. 233), *mainly burlesques and farces.*

§2

À Beckett, A. W. The à Becketts of Punch: memories of father and sons. 1903.

GEORGE ALMAR

The rover's bride: or the bittern's swamp. MD. (Sur 30 Aug 1830). Cumberland Minor 11.
Pedlar's acre: or the wife of seven husbands. D. (Sur 22 Aug 1831). Cumberland Minor 5; Lacy 84; Dicks 280.
The tower of Nesle. MD. (Sur 17 Sept 1832). Cumberland Minor 6; Lacy 91; Dicks 234.
The knights of St John: or the fire banner. MD. (SW 26 Aug 1833). Duncombe 12; Lacy 56.
The clerk of Clerkenwell: or the three black bottles. MD. (SW 27 Jan 1834). Cumberland Minor 7.
The bull-fighter: or the bridal ring. MD. (Sur 8 Oct 1838). Cumberland Minor 14.
Oliver Twist: or the parish boy's progress. D. (Sur 19 Nov 1838). Webster 6; Dicks 293; Mod. Eng. Com. Th. 1. From Dickens.
Jane of the Hatchet: or the siege of Beauvais. Spec. (Sur 20 July 1840). Duncombe 41.
See also Nicoll 4, pp. 252–3, 568; 5, pp. 239–40, 777.

MORRIS BARNETT
1800–56

The bold dragoons. Ba. (Adel 9 Feb 1820). Lacy 19; Dicks 509.
Tact: or the wrong box. F. (Queen's 21 Feb 1831). Duncombe 13.

Mrs G. of the golden pippin: a musical entertainment. (Queen's 14 March 1831). Duncombe 8.
The spirit of the Rhine. D. (Queen's 22 Sept 1835). Duncombe 29.
The yellow kids. Ba. (Adel 19 Oct 1835). Duncombe 18; Dicks 967.
Monsieur Jacques. Ba. (St J 13 Jan 1836). Lacy 28; Dicks 503. From Cogniard, Le pauvre Jacques.
The serious family. F. (H 30 Oct 1849). Dicks 1007. From Le mari à la campagne.
Sarah Blange. D. (Olym 27 Oct 1852). Lacy 31 (as Sarah the Creole).
See also Nicoll 4, pp. 261, 510; 5, pp. 249–50.

THOMAS LOVELL BEDDOES
1803–49

See col 409, above.

WILLIAM BAYLE BERNARD
1807–75

The four sisters. F. (Str 3 May 1832). Lacy 23; Dicks 411.
The conquering game. C. (Olym 28 Nov 1832). Dicks 676; Duncombe 36.
Lucille: or the story of a heart. D. (EOH 4 April 1836). 1836; Dicks 410; Lacy 28. From Lytton, Pilgrims of the Rhine.
St Mary's Eve: or a story of the Solway. Ba. (Adel 1 Jan 1838). Dicks 382; Lacy 33.
Marie Ducange. D. (Lyc 29 May 1841). Lacy 32; Dicks 475.
The round of wrong: or a fireside story. D. (H 19 Dec 1846). Dicks 1000; Webster 13.
The passing cloud. D. (DL 8 April 1850). Lacy 1.
The evil genius. C. (H 8 March 1856). Lacy 26.
A life's trial. D. (H 19 March 1857). Lacy 30.
The tide of time. C. (H 13 Dec 1858). Lacy 38.
The life of Samuel Lover, artistic, literary and musical, with selections from his unpublished papers and correspondence. 2 vols 1874.
See also Nicoll 4, pp. 266–7, 572; 5, pp. 259, 778.

EDWARD LITT LEMAN (LAMAN) BLANCHARD
1820–89

§1

The artful dodge. F. (Olym 21 Feb 1842). Lacy 42.
Pork chops. Ext. (Olym 13 Feb 1843). Lacy 45 (as Pork chops: or a dream at home).
Faith, hope and charity: or chance and change. D. (Sur 7 July 1845). Duncombe 54.
Adam's illustrated descriptive guide to the watering-places of England and companion to the coast. 2 vols 1848.
Adam Buff: or the man without a shirt. F. (Sur 4 March 1850). Duncombe 65.
The stranger's and visitor's conductor through London. 1851, 1857 (as Bradshaw's guide through London and its environs).
Cherry and fair star: or the singing apple, the talking bird and the dancing waters. P. (SW 26 Dec 1861). [1862].
A handy book on dinners: dinners and diners at home and abroad: with piquant plates and choice cuts. 1860.
Harlequin and the house that Jack built. P. (DL 26 Dec 1861). [1862].
Riquet with the tuft: or harlequin and old mother Shipton. P. (P'cess 26 Dec 1862). [1863].
An induction; The three temptations. In drawing-room plays, ed C. Scott 1870.
Blanchard also wrote many other pieces, mainly DL pantomimes: Nicoll 4, pp. 268–9, 573; 5, pp. 262–5, 779.

§2

Scott, C. and C. Howard. The life and reminiscences of Blanchard. 2 vols 1891.

DIONYSIUS LARDNER BOUCICAULT
1822–90

Collections

Forbidden fruit and other plays. Ed A. Nicoll and F. T. Clark, Princeton 1940.
Krause, D. (ed). The Dolmen Boucicault; with an essay by the editor on the theatre of Dion Boucicault and the complete authentic texts of Boucicault's three Irish plays. 1964.

§1

London assurance. C. (CG 4 March 1841). 1841, 1841; Lacy 34; Dicks 1044; Moses, Boston 1918.
The old guard. D. (P'cess 9 Oct 1843). Dicks 1056.
Old heads and young hearts. C. (H 18 Nov 1844). [1845], [1845]; Webster 13; Mod Eng Com Th, 3.
The knight of Arva. C. (H 22 Nov 1848). New York [1868?].
The queen of spades. D. (DL 29 March 1851). Lacy 24. From Scribe, La dame de pique.
The Corsican brothers. D. (P'cess 24 Feb 1852). [1852]; Lacy. From Dumas *père*.
The colleen bawn: or the brides of Garryowen. D. (New York 28 March 1860; Adel 10 Sept 1860). Lacy 63; Dicks 389; Rowell. From Griffin, The collegians.
The octoroon: or life in Louisiana. (New York 6 Dec 1859; Adel 18 Nov 1861). Lacy 65; Dicks 391.
Arragh-na-Pogue: or the Wicklow wedding. (TR, Dublin 7 Nov 1864; P'cess 22 March 1865). [1865], Chicago nd; French [1919].
The shaughraun. D. (New York 14 Nov 1874; DL 4 Sept 1875). Lacy 123; Dicks 390; Webster; New York [1885?].
The art of acting. New York 1926.
For other dramatic works see Nicoll 4, pp. 267–70, 573; 5, pp. 267–9, 779.

§2

Dion Boucicault on himself. Theatre Nov 1879.
Dion Boucicault as a dramatist. Saturday Rev 1 May 1886.
Dion Boucicault. Critic (New York) 9 1886.
Leaves from the diary of Dion Boucicault. North Amer Rev 149 1889.
Obituary. Athenaeum 27 Sept 1890.
Walsh, T. The career of Dion Boucicault. [1915].
Duggan, G. C. The stage Irishman. Dublin 1937.
Downer, A. S. The case of Mr Lee Moreton. Theatre Notebook 4 1950.
Ritchie, H. M. The influence of melodrama on the early plays of Sean O'Casey. Modern Drama 5 1962.
Hunter, J. W. Some research problems in a study of the Corsican brothers. Ohio State Univ Theatre Bull 9 1962.
Faulkner, S. The Octoroon war. Educational Theatre Jnl 14 1962.
— The great train scene robbery. Quart Jnl of Speech 50 1964.

CHARLES WILLIAM SHIRLEY BROOKS

1816–74

§1

The wigwam. Ba. (Lyc 25 Jan 1847). Dicks 1004.
The Creole: or love's fetters. MD. (Lyc 8 April 1847). Lacy 1; Dicks 1009.
Anything for a change. F. (Lyc 7 June 1848). Lacy 4; [1872?]; French 43; De Witt.
The opera; The coulisses; Foreign gentlemen in London. In A. R. Smith, Gavarni in London, 1849.
The daughter of the stars. D. (Str 5 Aug 1850). Lacy 2.
The exposition: a Scandinavian sketch. Ext. (Str 28 April 1851). Lacy 3.
The Russians of the south. 1854.
Aspen court: a story of our own time. 3 vols 1855, 1857 (rev).
The Gordian knot: a story of good and evil; with illustrations by J. Tenniel. 1860. First pbd in pts [1858–9].
Timour the Tartar: or the iron master of Samarkand-by-Oxus. Ext. (Olym 26 Dec 1860). Lacy, 49. With J. Oxenford.
The silver cord: a story. 3 vols 1861.
Sooner or later, with illustrations by G. du Maurier. 2 vols 1868.
The Naggletons, and Miss Violet and her 'offers'. 1875.
Wit and humour: poems from Punch. 1875. Ed Brooks.
Brooks also contributed regularly to Punch from 1851, becoming editor in 1870. For other dramatic works, see Nicoll 4, pp. 271, 574; 5, p. 277.

§2

Jerrold, B. Shirley Brooks. GM May 1874.
Layard, G. S. A great Punch editor: being the life, letters and diaries of Shirley Brooks. 1907.

ROBERT BARNABAS BROUGH

1828–60

§1

The enchanted isle, or 'raising the wind' on the most approved principles: a drama without the smallest claim to legitimacy, consistency, probability, or anything else but absurdity, in which will be found much that is unaccountably coincident with Shakespeare's Tempest. (Amphitheatre, Liverpool 1848; Adel 20 Nov 1848). [1848]; Webster 14. With W. Brough.
Camaralzaman and Badoura: or the peri who loved the Prince. Ext. (H 26 Dec 1848). Webster 15. With W. Brough.
The sphinx. Ext. (H 9 April 1849). Webster 15. With W. Brough.
The second calendar: extravaganza. (H 26 Dec 1850). Webster 15. With W. Brough.
A cracker bon-bon for Christmas parties. 1852. Includes 3 short plays (unacted) and Christmas miscellanies in prose and verse.
The Alain family: a tale. 1853. Tr by Brough from the French of J. B. A. Karr.
Songs of the governing classes and other lyrics. 1855, 1890.
Béranger's songs translated into English verse. 1856.
The life of Sir John Falstaff; with a biography of the knight, from authentic sources. 1858. First pbd in 10 pts 1857–8. Illustr George Cruikshank.
The siege of Troy: a burlesque. (Lyc 27 Dec 1858). 1858.
Alfred the Great: or the minstrel king. Ext. (Olym 26 Dec 1859). Lacy 43. With W. Brough.
Alf the minstrel, or the Princess Diamonducky and the hazel fairy: a dragon story for Christmas. 1859.
Miss Brown: a romance; and other tales in prose and verse. 1860. Rptd from Welcome Guest, a periodical briefly ed Brough.
Which is which?: or Miles Cassidy's contract. 2 vols 1860.
Marston Lynch: a personal biography; with a memoir of the author by G. A. Sala. 1860. First pbd in Train 1856–7.
Shadow and substance, by C. H. Bennett and R. B. Brough. 1860.
Character sketches by C. H. Bennett and R. B. Brough. [1872].
Other extravaganzas by the brothers Brough will be found in Lacy 6, 14, 15, 27, 29, 32, 52, 88 *and* Suppl 2. *See also* Nicoll 4, p. 271; 5, pp. 277–8.

§2

Archer, W. In Poets and the poetry of the century, ed A. H. Miles vol 5, 1893.

JOHN BALDWIN BUCKSTONE

1802–79

§1

Luke the labourer: or the lost son. D. (Adel 17 Oct 1826). 1826; Cumberland Minor 2; Lacy 69; Dicks 830; ed A. E. Morgan 1935 (in English plays 1660–1820).
The may queen: or Sampson the serjeant. Ba. (Adel 9 Oct 1828). 1834; Dicks 818.
Ellen Wareham. D. (H 24 April 1833). Dicks 837.
Agnes de Vere. D. (Adel 10 Nov 1834). 1836; Lacy 106; Dicks 805; Boston 1885.
Isabelle: or a woman's life. D. (Adel 27 Jan 1834). 1835; Dicks 817; Act Nat Drama 8. Also called Thirty years of a woman's life.
Jack Sheppard. D. (Adel 28 Oct 1839). Webster 7.
The green bushes: or a hundred years ago. D. (Adel 27 Jan 1845). Webster 11; Boston [1857?]; Dicks 827.
The flowers of the forest: a gipsy story. MD. (Adel 11 March 1847). Webster 13; Boston [1857?]; Dicks 1002.
Nine too many. Ba. (Adel 11 March 1847). Dicks 1004.
An alarming sacrifice. F. (H 12 July 1849). Boston [1885?]; Dicks 1012.
See also Nicoll 4, pp. 272–5, 574–5; 5, pp. 286–7, 781.

§2

John Baldwin Buckstone. Once a Week Nov 1872.
Maginn, W. A. In his Gallery of illustrious characters, ed W. Bates [1873], 1883. The essay on Buckstone was first pbd, with a drawing by Maclise, in Fraser's Mag Dec 1836.
Taylor, T. Impressions of Buckstone. Theatre Dec 1879.

JOSEPH STIRLING COYNE

1803–68

The queer subject. F. (Adel 28 Nov 1836). Webster 1; Dicks 782.
Valsha: or the slave queen. Ba. (Adel 30 Oct 1837). Webster 2; Dicks 702. From La guerre des servantes.
How to settle accounts with your laundress. F. (Adel 26 July 1847). Webster 14; Dicks 1006.
The barmaid; The potato can. In A. R. Smith, Gavarni in London, 1849.

The hope of the family. C. (H 3 Dec 1853). Lacy 13.
The secret agent. C. (H 10 March 1855). Lacy 18. Partly from the German.
The man of many friends. C. (H 1 Sept 1855). Lacy 23; New York 1855.
Pippins and pies: or sketches out of school. 1855.
The love-knot. C. (DL 8 March 1858). Lacy 35; Boston [1858?].
The woman in red. D. (Vic 28 March 1864). Lacy 92. From La tireuse des cartes.
Sam Spangles: or the history of a harlequin. 1866.
'Oil is better for a wig than vinegar': a dramatic proverb. In Mixed sweets from Routledge's annual, [1867].
For other dramatic works, see Nicoll 4, pp. 284–5, 578; 5, pp. 327–8, 786.

'HENRY THORNTON CRAVEN', HENRY THORNTON

1818–1905

Done Brown. F. (Adel, Edinburgh 1845). Duncombe 56; Lacy 81.
Bletchington House: or the surrender. D. (CL 20 April 1846). Duncombe 56.
The village nightingale. Ba. (Str 23 June 1851). French 108.
Bowl'd out: or a bit of brummagem. F. (P'cess 9 July 1860). Lacy 47.
The chimney corner. D. (Olym 21 Feb 1861). Lacy 50.
Miriam's crime. D. (Str 9 Oct 1863). Lacy 60.
Milky white: a serio-comic drama. (PW, Liverpool 20 June 1864; Str 28 Sept 1864). Lacy 85.
Meg's diversion. C. (Roy 17 Oct 1866). Lacy 73.
See also Nicoll 4, pp. 285; 5, pp. 328–9, 786.

CHARLES DICKENS

1812–70

See col 779, above.

RICHARD HENGIST HORNE

1803–84

See col 524, above.

DOUGLAS WILLIAM JERROLD

1803–57

Collections

Writings. 8 vols 1851–4.
Works, with an introductory memoir by his son W. B. Jerrold. 4 vols 1863–4.
Tales, now first collected. Ed J. L. Robertson 1891.
The whimsical tales of Jerrold. Allentown Pa 1949.

§1

Paul Pry. F. (Cob 27 Nov 1827). Lacy 47; Dicks 982; Mod Eng Com Th. 67.
Fifteen years of a drunkard's life. MD. (Cob 24 Nov 1828). Duncombe 3; Dicks 220.
Black-eyed Susan: or all in the Downs. MD. (Sur 8 June 1829). Duncombe 4; Lacy 23; Boston [1857?]; Dicks 230; Moses, Boston 1918; Rowell.
The mutiny at the Nore: or British sailors in 1797. MD. (Royal Pavilion 7 June 1830). Lacy 78; Dicks 795; Cumberland Minor 5.
The bride of Ludgate. C. (DL 8 Dec 1831). Cumberland 30; Lacy 93; Dicks 530.
The rent day. D. (DL 25 Jan 1832). 1832; Lacy 15; Dicks 210; Duncombe 25.
Beau Nash, the king of Bath. C. (H 16 July 1834). 1834; Dicks 554.
Men of character. 3 vols 1838.
Heads of the people, drawn by Kenny Meadows, described by Douglas Jerrold [et al]. 2 vols 1840–1.
Punch's letters to his son. 1843.
The story of a feather. 1844.
Time works wonders. C. (H 26 April 1845). 1845; Lacy 92; Dicks 851; Mod Eng Com Th ser 3.
Punch's complete letter writer. 1845.
The chronicles of Clovernook; with some account of the hermit of Bellyfulle. 1846.
Mrs Caudle's curtain lectures. 1846 etc.; ed W. Jerrold 1907 (WC); tr Hungarian, 1860; French, 1865; German, 1869; Swedish, 1872; Italian, 1885.
A man made of money. 1849.
Cakes and ale. 1852. Tales and essays.
The Brownrigg papers. Ed B. Jerrold 1860.
Other times: being Liberal leaders contributed to Lloyd's Weekly Newspaper by Douglas and Blanchard Jerrold. 1868.
The barber's chair: and the hedgehog letters. Ed B. Jerrold 1874. Rptd from Douglas Jerrold's Weekly Newspaper.
For other dramatic works see Nicoll 4, pp. 331–3, 590; 5, pp. 436, 800.

§2

Horne, R. H. In his A new spirit of the age vol i, 1844.
Powell, T. In his Pictures of the living authors of Britain, 1851.
Hannay, J. Douglas Jerrold. Atlantic Monthly Nov 1858.
Jerrold, W. B. The life and remains of Jerrold. 1859.
Phillips, G. S. Douglas Jerrold. North Amer Rev 59 1859.
Stirling, J. H. Jerrold, Tennyson and Macaulay. Edinburgh 1868.
Bedford, H. Douglas Jerrold. Month May 1870.
Copping, E. Douglas Jerrold. New Rev Sept 1892.
Fyvie, J. Douglas Jerrold. Macmillan's Mag March 1903.
Jerrold, W. Jerrold and Punch. 1910.
—— Jerrold: dramatist and wit. 2 vols [1914].

MARK LEMON

1809–70

§1

P.L.: or 30 Strand. MF. (Str 25 April 1836). Duncombe 22; Dicks 977.
Arnold of Winkelreid: or the Flight of the Sempach. D. (Sur 25 July 1836). Duncombe 22.
The MP for the rotten borough. MF. (EOH 27 July 1838). Dicks 719.
A familiar friend. Ba. (Olym 8 Feb 1840). [1840]; Dicks 981.
The gentleman in black: or the loves of the devils. (Olym 9 Dec 1840). [1840?]; Dicks 776.
What will the world say? (CG 25 Sept 1841). 1841.
Grandfather Whitehead. C. (H 31 Sept 1842). Webster 10; Dicks 505.
Hearts are trumps. F. (Str 30 July 1849). [1863]; Dicks 1058.
The enchanted doll: a fairy tale for little people; the illustrations by R. Doyle. 1849.
Prose and verse. 1852.
The railway belle. F. (Adel 20 Nov 1854). Lacy 17.
A Christmas hamper. 1860. Tales.
Wait for the end: a story. 3 vols 1863.

Legends of number nip. 1864. From the German of J. C. A. Musaeus.
The jest book: the choicest anecdotes and sayings, selected and arranged by Mark Lemon. Cambridge 1864.
Loved at last: a story. 3 vols 1864.
Tom Moody's tales, edited [or rather written] by Mark Lemon; illustrated by H. K. Browne. 1864.
Falkner Lyle: or the story of two wives. 3 vols 1866.
Leyton Hall and other tales. 3 vols 1867.
Golden fetters. 3 vols 1867. A novel.
Up and down the London streets. 1867. Historical and descriptive lectures.
Fairy tales; with illustrations by R. Doyle and C. H. Bennett. 1868.
Tinykin's transformations: a child's story. 1869.
The small house over the water, and other stories; with portrait and illustrations by G. Cruikshank. 1888.
Lemon, with Henry Mayhew, founded Punch, *the first number of which appeared on 17 July 1841. He remained editor until his death.*
For other dramatic works see Nicoll 4, pp. 343–5, 594–5; 5, pp. 455, 803.

§2

Friswell, J. H. In his Modern men of letters, 1870.
Hatton, J. Reminiscences of Lemon. GM July–Dec 1870.
— The true story of Punch. London Soc 28, 30 1875–6.
Spielmann, M. H. The history of Punch. 1895.
Adrian, A. A. Lemon: first editor of Punch. 1966.

LEOPOLD DAVID LEWIS
1828–90

The mask: a humorous and fantastic review, edited by Lewis and Alfred Thompson [and entirely written by them]. Feb–Dec 1868.
The bells. D. (Lyc 25 Nov 1871). Lacy 97; New York 1872. From Erckmann-Chatrian, Le juif polonais.
A peal of merry bells, 3 vols [1880]. A novel.
For other dramatic works see Nicoll 5, p. 459.

GEORGE WILLIAM LOVELL
1804–78

§1

The provost of Bruges. T. (DL 10 Feb 1836). 1837; Dicks 681. From Leitch Ritchie, The serf, in his Romance of history.
Love's sacrifice: or the rival merchants. D. (CG 12 Sept 1842). Lacy 67; Dicks 650.
The wife's secret. D. (Park Theatre, New York 12 Oct 1846; H 17 Jan 1848). Lacy 82; Dicks 1005.
Look before you leap: or wooings and weddings. C. (H 29 Oct 1846). Webster 13; Dicks 998.
See also Nicoll 4, pp. 347, 596; 5, p. 463.

§2

Dunkel, W. D. The career of Lovell. Theatre Notebook 5 1951.

E. G. E. L. BULWER-LYTTON, 1st BARON LYTTON
1803–73

See col 917, above.

W. R. S. MARKWELL

Louis XI: an historical drama. (DL 14 Feb 1835). Lacy 9. From Delavigne.
The prophet's curse. D. (unacted?). 1862.
See also Nicoll 5, p. 477.

JOHN WESTLAND MARSTON
1819–90

Collections

Dramatic and poetical works. 2 vols 1876. Includes all the plays, below (some, e.g. Strathmore, much rev), except The heart and the world (fragments only) and Trevanion.

§1

Poetry as an universal nature: a lecture; to which is added The poet: an ode. 1838.
Poetic culture: an appeal to those interested in human destiny. 1839.
The patrician's daughter. T. (DL 10 Dec 1842). 1841, 1842 (3 edns), Boston 1856; Lacy 43.
Gerald: a dramatic poem, and other poems. 1842.
Borough politics. F. (H 27 June 1846). Webster 12.
The heart and the world. D. (H 4 Oct 1847). 1847.
Strathmore. T. (H 20 June 1849). 1849; Lacy 56. From Scott, Old Mortality.
Philip of France and Marie de Méranie. T. (Olym 4 Nov 1850). 1850.
Anne Blake. D. (P'cess 28 Oct 1852). 1852, Boston [1856?]; Lacy 49.
The death-ride: a tale of the light brigade. 1855.
A life's ransom. D. (Lyc 16 Feb 1857). Lacy 54; Boston [1861?].
A hard struggle. D. (Lyc 1 Feb 1858). Lacy 48; Boston [1860?].
A lady in her own right: a novel. 1860.
The wife's portrait: a household picture under two lights. D. (H 10 March 1862). Lacy 54.
The family credit and other tales. 1862.
Pure gold. D. (SW 9 Nov 1863). Lacy 61.
Donna Diana. C. (P'cess 2 Jan 1864).
The favourite of fortune. C. (H 2 April 1866).
Life for life. D. (Lyc 6 March 1869).
Our recent actors: being recollections of late distinguished performers, with some incidental notices of living actors. 2 vols 1888.
Marston also edited National Magazine, *with J. Saunders, 1857–64 For other dramatic works see* Nicoll 4, p. 353; 5, pp. 478–9.

§2

Horne, R. H. In his A new spirit of the age vol 2, 1844.
Powell, T. In his Pictures of the living authors of Britain, 1851.
Obituary. Athenaeum 11 Jan 1890.
Clarke, H. E. In The poets and the poetry of the century, ed A. H. Miles vol 4 [1891].

CHARLES JAMES MATHEWS
1803–78

§1

My wife's mother. C. (H 3 July 1833). Lacy 23; Dicks 659.
Truth: or a glass too much. Ba. (Adel 10 March 1834). Webster 3.
The hump-backed lover. F. (Olym 7 Dec 1835). Cumberland Minor 12; Dicks 660.

Why did you die? Ba. (Olym 20 Nov 1837). Webster 2; Dicks 662.
The black domino. B. (Olym 18 Jan 1838). Webster 3. From Scribe, Le domino noir.
Patter versus clatter. F. (Olym 21 May 1838). Lacy 118; Dicks 660.
Lettre aux auteurs dramatiques de la France. 1852; tr Mathews 1852.
Married for money. F. (DL 10 Oct 1815). French 117.
My awful dad. C. (Ga 13 Sept 1875). French 117.
The life of Mathews [chiefly autobiographical]. Ed C. Dickens 2 vols 1879.
For other dramatic works see Nicoll 4, pp. 353–4, 597–8; 5, pp. 480, 806.

§2

Mathews, A. Memoirs of Charles Mathews, comedian. 4 vols 1838–9; abridged E. Yates 1860. On early years.
Biographical sketch. Webster 3 [1838].

JOHN MADDISON MORTON

1811–91

Collections

Comediettas and farces. New York 1886.

§1

My husband's ghost. F. (H 26 April 1836). Boston [1857?]; Cumberland 35; Lacy 93.
Chaos is come again: or the race-ball. F. (CG 19 Nov 1838). Webster 6.
The thumping legacy. F. (DL 11 Feb 1843). [1843]; Lacy 5.
The mother and child are doing well. F. (Adel 24 Feb 1845). Webster 11.
Lend me five shillings. F. (H 19 Feb 1846). Lacy 30; Duncombe 4.
Done on both sides. F. (Lyc 24 Feb 1847). Duncombe 61; Lacy 26.
Box and Cox. F. (Lyc 1 Nov 1847). Lacy 5; Dicks 1059; Duncombe 74; Mod Eng Com Th 4. From Une chambre à deux lits.
John Dobbs: or a dab at anything. F. (Str 23 April 1849). Duncombe 64; Lacy 7.
Where there's a will there's a way. F. (Str 6 Sept 1840). Duncombe 64; Lacy 19.
See also Nicoll 4, pp. 361–3, 600–1; 5, pp. 495–7, 807.

§2

Scott, C. John Maddison Morton. London Soc 49 [1886].

JOHN OXENFORD

1812–77

My fellow clerk. MF. (EOH 20 April 1835). 1835; Dicks 558.
The dice of death. MD. (EOH 14 Sept 1835). Duncombe 28; French 110; Dicks 592.
Twice killed. Ba. (Olym 26 Nov 1835). Duncombe 21; Lacy 24; Dicks 531.
A day well spent: or three adventures. MF. (EOH 4 April 1836). Duncombe 31; Lacy 34; Dicks 531.
A quiet day. Ba. (Unacted). Duncombe 34; Dicks 987; Mod Eng Com Th 2.
No followers. Ba. (Str 4 Sept 1837). Duncombe 34; Dicks 978; Mod Eng Com Th 1.
Doctor Dilworth. F. (Olym 15 April 1839). Webster 7; Boston [1857?]; Dicks 558.
The autobiography of Goethe. 1848, 1888. Tr Oxenford.
The reigning favourite. D. (Str 9 Oct 1849). Lacy new ser 1.
Eckermann, J. P. Conversations of Goethe with Eckermann and Soret. 1850, 1874. Tr Oxenford, with the following works.
Callery, J. M. and M. Yvan, History of the insurrection in China; with a supplementary chapter. 1853.
Molière, Tartuffe. Webster 17 [1853].
Burger, G. A., Lenora. 1855.
The illustrated book of French songs from the sixteenth to the nineteenth century. 1855.
Jacobs, F. C. W., Hellas: or the home, history, literature and art of the Greeks. 1855.
Fischer, Kuno, Francis Bacon of Verulam. 1857.
Cormon, E. and M. Carré, Lara: an opera. [1865].
Wagner Festival, Royal Albert Hall, May 1877. Selections from the German texts of Der Ring des Nibelungen, Rienzi etc; with English versions by Dr Hueffer and Oxenford. 1877.
According to DNB Oxenford also translated Calderón, Vida es sueño, *and a large portion of* Boiardo, Orlando innamorato. *For other dramatic works see* Nicoll 4, pp. 367, 602–3; 5, pp. 509–11, 809.

WATTS PHILLIPS

1825–74

§1

The model republic: or Cato Potts in Paris. [1848?]. Etchings.
Showing how the Honourable Mr Teddington Locke MP was not returned for the incorruptible borough of Bubengrub; drawn and etched by Watts Phillips, from notions by Edward Grant. [1850?].
The wild tribes of London. 1855. On the slums.
The dead heart. D. (Adel 10 Nov 1859). Lacy 82. This play had considerable renown, and was revived by Irving at the Lyceum in 1889. 2 novels were founded on it: C. Gibbon, The dead heart: a tale of the Bastille, 1865; and A. R. Phillips, Love in death, 1889.
The hooded snake: a story of the secret police. [1860].
Amos Clark, or the poor dependent: a story of country life in the seventeenth century. 1862.
Canary bird, a story of town life in the seventeenth century: a sequel to Amos Clark. 1862.
His last victory. D. (St J 21 June 1862). Lacy 59.
Camilla's husband. D. (Olym 22 Nov 1862). Lacy 59.
Paul's return. C. (P'cess 15 Feb 1864). Lacy 62.
Theodora, actress and empress. T. (New Sur 9 April 1866). Lacy 74.
Lost in London. D. (Adel 16 March 1867). Lacy 80.
Maud's peril. D. (Adel 23 Oct 1867). Lacy 80.
Not guilty. D. (Queen's 13 Feb 1869). Lacy 84.
Who will save her? a novel. 3 vols 1874.
For other dramatic works see Nicoll 5, p. 523.

§2

Phillips, E. W. Phillips: artist and playwright. 1891.

GEORGE DIBDIN PITT

1799–1855

The last man: or the miser of Eltham Green. D. (Sur 22 July 1833). Duncombe 24.
The monster of the Eddystone: or the lighthouse keepers. MD. (SW 7 April 1834). Cumberland Minor 10; Lacy 69.
The Jersey girl: or the red robbers. MD. (Sur 9 Feb 1835). Lacy 26; Dicks 512.

The twins, Paul and Philip. Ba. (Queen's 21 Jan 1836). Dicks 419.
Simon Lee: or the murder of the Five Fields Copse. D. (CL 1 April 1839). Lacy 78.
Susan Hopley: or the vicissitudes of a servant girl. (Vic 31 May 1841). Lacy 69; Cumberland Minor 145.
The beggar's petition: or a father's love and a mother's care. D. (CL 18 Oct 1841). Lacy 97; Dicks 514.
Marianne, the child of charity: or the head of a lawyer. (Vic 30 Dec 1844). French 119; Dicks 825.
See also Nicoll 4, pp. 372–6, 604; 5, pp. 526, 810.

CHARLES READE
1814–84

See col 878, above.

WILLIAM LEMAN REDE
1802–47

§1

The rake's progress. MD. (City 28 Jan 1833). Duncombe 12; New York [1856?]; Lacy 32; Dicks 240.
An affair of honour. F. (Olym 12 March 1835). 1835; Cumberland 44; Lacy 78; Dicks 517.
Come to town: or next door neighbours. Ba. (Str 25 April 1836). Duncombe 21.
The flight to America: or twelve hours in New York. D. (Adel 7 Nov 1836). Duncombe 24; New York [1840?].
The peregrinations of Pickwick: or Boz-i-a-na. F. (Sur Oct 1836). 1837. Duncombe 33.
Jack in the water: or the ladder of life. D. (Olym 25 April 1842). Cumberland Minor 16; Dicks 574.
The royal rake [George IV], and the adventures of Alfred Chesterton. 1842 (priv ptd). A satirical romance.
Our village: or lost and found. D. (Olym 17 April 1843). Lacy 88; Dicks 711.
La somnambula: or the somnambulist. CO. (CG 1848). [1848].
Rede started July *in 1842 as a rival to* Punch, *but only 2 issues appeared. For other dramatic works see* Nicoll 4, pp. 389–91, 607.

§2

Obituary. Era 11 April 1847.
Recollections of Rede. New Monthly Mag May 1847.

GEORGE HERBERT BUONAPARTE RODWELL
1800–52

Where shall I dine? F. (Olym 12 Feb 1819). [1819]; Dicks 973.
Freaks and follies: or a match for the old one. F. (Adel 5 Nov 1827). Dicks 988.
Teddy the tiler. F. (CG 8 Feb 1830). Cumberland 25; Dicks 784. From Pierre le couvreur.
Was I to blame? Ba. (Adel 13 Dec 1830). Lacy 32.
I'll be your second. F. (Olym 10 Oct 1831). Lacy 3.
The first rudiments of harmony. 1831.
A letter to the musicians of Great Britain, containing a prospectus of proposed plans for the better encouragement of native musical talent, and for the erection and management of a grand national opera in London. 1833.
A catechism of music. [1840?] (21st edn).
A catechism on harmony. [1841?].
My wife's out. F. (CG 2 Oct 1843). Lacy 45; Dicks 699.
The picnic: or husbands, wives and lovers. F. (Adel 4 Dec 1843). Dicks 561.
Memoirs of an umbrella. [1845]. A novel.
Woman's love: a romance of smiles and tears. [1846].
The seven maids of Munich: or the ghost's tower. MD. (P'cess 19 Dec 1846). 1846 (songs, duets, choruses only).
Old London bridge: a romance of the sixteenth century. [1848–9].
The devil's ring, or fire, water, earth and air: a grand musical fairy romance in three acts and four elements. [1850]. In verse.
For other dramatic works see Nicoll 4, pp. 395, 608.

CHARLES SELBY
1801–63

Collections

Farces and melodramas. 1835.

§1

A day in Paris. MF. (Str 18 July 1832). Duncombe 16; Dicks 425.
The married rake. C. (Queen's 9 Feb 1835). Duncombe 16; Lacy 71; Dicks 676.
The two murderers: or the auberge des Adrets! MD. (CG 1834). Duncombe 16. (Stuttgart 1842; Duncombe [1845], Lacy 30; Dicks 325; French [1845?] as Robert Macaire: or the two murderers). From Benjamin, Saint-Amand and Polyanthe, L'auberge des Adrets.
Little sins and pretty sinners. Ba. (Queen's 12 Jan 1836). Duncombe 30; Dicks 957.
The loves of Lord Bateman and the fair Sophia. Bsq. (Str 3 July 1839). Duncombe 37.
Maximums and speciments of William Muggins, natural philosopher and citizen of the world. 1841, 1859.
The boots at the Swan. F. (Str 8 June 1842). Duncombe 45; Dicks 564; Lacy 503.
The mysterious stranger. D. (Adel 30 Oct 1844). Webster 10; Boston 1855 (as Satan in Paris: or the mysterious stranger); Dicks 798.
Taken in and done for. F. (Str 10 May 1849). Lacy 3.
Events to be remembered in the history of England; forming a series of interesting narratives of the most remarkable occurrences in each reign. 1851, 1891 (28th edn).
The dinner question, by Tabitha Tickletooth. 1860.
For other dramatic works see Nicoll 4, pp. 397–9, 610; 5, pp. 560, 815.

JOHN PALGRAVE SIMPSON
1807–87

Second love and other tales from the notebook of a traveller. 3 vols 1846.
Gisella. 1847.
Pictures from revolutionary Paris, sketched during the first phases of the revolution of 1848. Edinburgh 1848.
The lily of Paris: or the king's nurse. 3 vols 1849.
Second love. C. (H 23 July 1856). Lacy 28; Boston [1856].
Daddy Hardacre. D. (Olym 26 March 1857). Lacy 100.
World and stage. C. (H 12 March 1859). Lacy 97.
A school for coquettes. C. (Str 4 July 1859). Lacy 41.
A scrap of paper. C. (St J 22 April 1861). Lacy 51. From Sardou, Pattes de mouche.
Court cards. C. (Olym 25 Nov 1861). Lacy 53. From Barbier Carré, La fileuse.
Sybilla: or step by step. C. (Olym 29 Oct 1864). Lacy 64.

The road-side inn (Lyc 21 Jan 1865). A version of Selby, Robert Macaire, prepared for Fechter and also used by Irving.
Alone, C. (Court 25 Oct 1873). French 103. In collaboration with H. C. Merivale.
Carl Maria von Weber: the life of an artist; from the German by J. P. Simpson. 2 vols 1865.
For ever and never: a novel. 2 vols 1884.
For other dramatic works see Nicoll 5, pp. 567–8, 816.

Letters

Letters from the Danube. 1847.

EDWARD STIRLING

1807–94

The Pickwick Club: or the age we live in. Ba. (CL 27 March 1837). Duncombe 26. From Dickens.
The wreck at sea: or the Fern light. D. (Adel 3 Dec 1838). Webster 6 (as Grace Darling); French 106.
The little back parlour. F. (EOH 17 Aug 1839). Duncombe 38; French 111.
The serpent of the Nile. Ba. (Adel 20 April 1840). Duncombe 41.
The Bohemians: or the rogues of Paris. D. (Adel 6 Nov 1843). [1870?]. BD 10; Dicks 98. From Sue, Les mystères de Paris.
Lestelle: or the wrecker's bride. D. (Sur 21 Aug 1845). Duncombe 54.
The jockey club. Ext. (Adel 19 Oct 1846). Webster 13.
The bould soger boy. F. (Olym 6 Nov 1848). French 111.
See also Nicoll 4, pp. 406–9, 612–3; 5, pp. 584, 818.

SIR HENRY TAYLOR

1800–86

See col 553, above.

TOM TAYLOR

1817–80

There is a large collection of Taylor mss in the British Theatre Museum.

§1

A trip to Kissingen. F. (Lyc 14 Nov 1844). Dicks 881.
Masks and faces: or before and behind the curtain. C. (H 20 Nov 1852). 1854; Dicks; Lacy; Rowell. With C. Reade. Played also as Peg Woffington.
Plot and passion. D. (Olym 17 Oct 1853). Lacy 13; Dicks 1048; New York [1869?]. With J. Lang.
Still waters run deep. C. (Olym 14 May 1855). Lacy 22; Dicks 1049; Boston [1856?].
Going to the bad. C. (Olym 5 June 1858). Lacy 37.
Our American cousin. C. (Laura Keene's, New York 18 Oct 1858; H 11 Nov 1861). 1869; Lacy.
The fool's revenge. D. (SW 18 Oct 1859). Lacy 43; New York [1863?]. From Victor Hugo, Le roi s'amuse.
Up at the hills. C. (St J 29 Oct 1860). Lacy 50.
Handbook of the pictures in the International Exhibition of 1862. 1862.
The railway station, painted by W. P. Frith, described by Tom Taylor. 1862.
The ticket-of-leave man. D. (Olym 27 May 1863). Lacy 59, Rowell. From Brisebane and Nus, Le retour du Melun.
Birket Foster's pictures of English landscape; with pictures in words by Tom Taylor. 1863 (for 1862).
A marriage memorial: verse and prose, commemorative of the wedding of the Prince and Princess of Wales, March 10 1863. [1863].
Life and times of Sir Joshua Reynolds, commenced by C. R. Leslie, continued by Tom Taylor. 2 vols 1865.
English painters of the present day: essays by J. B. Atkinson [etc] and Tom Taylor. 1871.
The theatre in England: some of its shortcomings and possibilities. 1871.
English artists of the present day: essays by J. B. Atkinson [et al] and Tom Taylor. 1872.
Leicester Square: its associations and its worthies; with a sketch of Hunter's scientific character and works by Richard Owen. 1874.
Storm at midnight, and other poems. Ed J. H. Burn, Mintlaw 1893.
Taylor edited Punch *from 1874 until his death in 1880. Besides the above works, he edited* C. R. Leslie, Autobiographical recollections, 1860; B. R. Haydon, Life, 1853; *and* Mortimer Collins, Pen sketches by a vanished hand, 2 vols 1879. *For other dramatic works see* Nicoll 4, pp. 411, 614; 5, pp. 592–9, 820.

§2

Sheehan, J. Tom Taylor. Dublin Univ Mag Aug 1877.
Hughes, T. In memoriam Tom Taylor. Macmillan's Mag Aug 1880.
Tolles, W. Taylor and the Victorian Drama. New York 1940.

ALFRED, BARON TENNYSON

1809–92

See col 412, above.

CHARLES WHITEHEAD

1804–62

See col 560, above.

ALFRED SYDNEY WIGAN

1814–78

A model of a wife. F. (Lyc 27 Jan 1845). Lacy 61; Dicks 1008.
The loan of a wife. F. (Lyc 7 July 1846). Duncombe 56. From the French.
Five hundred pounds reward. F. (Lyc 28 Jan 1847). Duncombe 58; Dicks 1003. From Le capitaine de voleurs.
Tit for tat. F. (Olym 22 Jan 1855). Lacy 17. With F. Talfourd.
See also Nicoll 4, pp. 419, 617; 5, p. 621.

THOMAS EGERTON WILKS

1812–54

The wolf and the lamb. C. (H 23 June 1832). Duncombe 32; Dicks 968.
The seven clerks: or the three thieves and the dreamer. D. (Sur 3 Nov 1834). Duncombe 15; Lacy 40; Dicks 923.
The King's wager: or the camp, the cottage and the Court. Ba. (Vic 5 Dec 1837). [1837]; Duncombe 34; Lacy 62; Dicks 501.
The wren boys. F. (CL 8 Oct 1838). Duncombe 32; Lacy 52; Dicks 404.
Ben the boatswain: or sailors' sweethearts! D. (Sur 19 Aug 1839). Duncombe 38; Lacy 28.

Bamboozling. F. (Olym 16 May 1842). Duncombe 41; Lacy 28; Dicks 627.
Sixteen string Jack: or the knaves of knaves' acre. MD. (SW 28 Nov 1842). Duncombe 63; French 105.
Kennyngton Crosse: or the old farm house on the common. D. (Sur 12 June 1848). Lacy 75.
See also Nicoll 4, pp. 420–1, 617.

WILLIAM GORMAN WILLS
1828–91

§1

Old times: a novel, with illustrations by the author. 1857. First pbd in pts Waterford [1856]–7.
Life's foreshadowings: a novel. 3 vols 1859.
Notice to quit. 3 vols 1861.
The wife's evidence. 3 vols 1864, 1 vol 1876.
David Chantry. 3 vols 1865, 1 vol 1877.
The three watches. 3 vols 1865.
The love that kills: a novel. 3 vols 1867.
Charles the First. T. (Lyc 28 Sept 1872). Edinburgh 1873. In verse.
Drawing room dramas. Edinburgh 1873. In verse; with the Hon Mrs Greene.
Eugene Aram. D. (Lyc 19 April 1873).
Olivia. D. (Court 28 March 1878). 1878 (priv ptd) From The Vicar of Wakefield.
Faust. D. (Lyc 16 Dec 1885). [1886], 1887.
Melchior. 1885. A poem in blank verse.
For other dramatic works see Nicoll 5, pp. 627–8, 824.

§2

Archer, W. In his English dramatists of to-day, 1882.
Wills, F. W. G. Wills: dramatist and painter. 1898.

IV. THE LATE NINETEENTH-CENTURY DRAMA

SIR WILLIAM SCHWENCK GILBERT
1836–1911

Bibliographies etc

Searle, T. A bibliography of Gilbert, with bibliographical adventures in the Gilbert and Sullivan operas; introduction by R. E. Swartwout. [1931] (priv ptd), 1931 (as Gilbert: a topsy-turvy adventure).
Halton, F. J. Gilbert and Sullivan operas: a concordance. New York 1935.
Dunn, G. E. A Gilbert and Sullivan dictionary. 1936.
Allen, R. Gilbert: an anniversary survey and exhibition checklist. Charlottesville 1946.

Collections

Original plays. Ser 1, 1876; ser 2, [1881] etc; ser 3, 1895; ser 4, 1911, 1920 (enlarged).
The Gilbert and Sullivan birthday book, compiled by A. Watson. 1888.
Original comic operas; containing The sorcerer; Patience; HMS Pinafore; Princess Ida; The pirates of Penzance; The Mikado; Iolanthe; Trial by jury. [1890].
The Gilbert and Sullivan birthday souvenir, arranged and compiled by Kitty Lofting. [1895?].
Original comic operas, second series: containing The gondoliers, The Grand Duke; The Yeomen of the Guard; His Excellency; Utopia limited; Ruddigore; The mountebanks; Haste to the wedding. [1896?].
The Savoy operas: being the complete text of the Gilbert and Sullivan operas. 1926.
Selected operas. 2 sers 1928.
Scenes and songs from the Savoy operas, and some Bab ballads, selected by J. Compton. 1930.
Complete plays of Gilbert and Sullivan. New York 1936.
A treasury of Gilbert and Sullivan: the words and music of one hundred and two songs from eleven operettas. New York 1941.

§1

The key of the strong room. In T. Hood, A bunch of keys, 1865.
The income-tax. In T. Hood, Rates and taxes, 1866.
Ruy Blas: a burlesque. (unacted?) In Warne's Christmas annual 1866, illustr Gilbert.
A new and original extravaganza entitled Dulcamara: or the little duck and the great quack. (St J 29 Dec 1866). 1866.
La vivandière, or true to the corps: an operatic extravaganza. (St James's Hall, Liverpool 15 June 1867; Queen's 22 Jan 1868). Liverpool 1867, 1868. From Donizetti, La figlia del regimento.
Harlequin, cock-robin and jenny wren, or Fortunatus and the water of life, the three bears, the three gifts, the three wishes and the little man who woo'd the little maid: grand comic Christmas pantomime. (Lyc 26 Dec 1867). 1867.
The merry zingara, or the tipsy gipsy and the pipsy wipsy: a whimsical parody on the 'Bohemian girl'. (Roy 21 March 1868). 1868.
Robert the devil, or the nun, the dun and the son of a gun: an operatic extravaganza. (Gai 21 Dec 1868). (1868).
No cards: a musical piece in one act for four characters; music by L. Elliott. (Gallery of Illustration 29 March 1869). (1901).
The pretty druidess; or the mother, the maid and the mistletoe bough: an extravaganza. (Charing Cross 19 June 1869). [1869].
An old score: an original comedy drama. (Gai 19 July 1869). Lacy 85; French 1610.
Ages ago: opera in one act. Music by F. Clay. (Gallery of illustration 22 Nov 1869). 1869 (vocal score), (1895) (libretto). Later expanded into Ruddigore, below.
The 'Bab' ballads: much sound and little sense, with illustrations by the author. 1869, 1870.
The Princess: a whimsical allegory: being a respectful perversion of Mr Tennyson's poem. Bsq. (Olym 8 Jan 1870). Lacy 87.
The gentleman in black: an original musical legend; music by F. Clay. (Charing Cross 26 May 1870). Lacy 88.
The palace of truth: a fairy comedy. (H 19 Nov 1870). Lacy 88.
A medical man: a comedietta. (Unacted?). In C. W. Scott, Drawing-room plays and parlour pantomimes, 1870.
Randall's thumb: an original comedy. (Court 25 Jan 1871). Lacy 91.
A sensation novel, in three volumes. Oa. Music by F. Pascal. (Gallery of Illustration 30 Jan 1871). 1912.
Creatures of impulse: a musical fairy tale; music by A. Randegger. (Court 15 April 1871). Lacy 91.
On guard: an entirely original comedy. (Court 28 Oct 1872). Lacy 98.
Pygmalion and Galatea: an entirely original mythological comedy. (H 9 Dec 1871). French 103.
Thespis, or the Gods grown old: a grotesque opera.

(Gai 23 Dec 1871). 1871. Full musical score never pbd. With Arthur Sullivan.

Happy Arcadia. Oa. Music by F. Clay. (Gallery of Illustration 28 Oct 1872). 1872; 1896.

The wicked world: an entirely original fairy comedy. (H 4 Jan 1873). [1873] (priv ptd); French 126. First pbd in Tom Hood's Annual 1871.

The happy land: a burlesque version of the Wicked world, by F. Tomline [i.e. W. S. Gilbert] and G. A. à Beckett. (Court 3 March 1873; prohibited by the Lord Chamberlain 7 March 1873). 1873.

The wedding march [Le chapeau de paille d'Italie]: an eccentricity. (Court 15 Nov 1873). French 114.

More 'Bab' ballads; with illustrations by the author. (1873).

A stage play, with introduction by W. Archer. (unacted?). New York 1916. First pbd in Tom Hood's Comic Annual 1873.

Charity. D. (H 3 Jan 1874; denounced as immoral, and withdrawn). French 123.

Topsy-Turvydom: original extravaganza. (Crit 21 March 1874). Oxford 1931.

Sweethearts: an original dramatic contrast. (PW 7 Nov 1874). French 111.

The 'Bab' ballads and more 'Bab' ballads: much sound and little sense; with illustrations by the author. (1874). Complete.

Trial by jury: a novel original dramatic cantata. (Roy 23 March 1875). 1875, 1888 (full score), (1898) (with Sorcerer). With Arthur Sullivan.

Tom Cobb, or fortune's toy: an entirely original comedy. (St J 24 April 1875). French 117.

Eyes and no eyes: or the art of seeing. CO. Music by F. Pascal. (St George's Hall 5 July 1875). 1896. From Hans Andersen, The emperor's new clothes.

Broken hearts: an entirely original fairy play. D. (Court 17 Dec 1875). French 118.

Dan'l Druce, blacksmith: a new and original drama. (H 11 Sept 1876). French 118.

Princess Toto: comic opera; music by F. Clay. (Str 2 Oct 1876). [1876?].

Fifty 'Bab' ballads. 1876 etc.

On bail: a farcical comedy. (Crit 2 Feb 1877). French 117. From Meilhac and Halévy, Le levallon. A re-written version of Committed for trial, played Globe 24 Jan 1874 as by 'F. L. Tomline', condemned as 'unfit for public presentation', and never pbd.

Engaged: an entirely original farcical comedy. (H 3 Oct 1877). French 118.

The sorcerer: an entirely original modern comic opera. (Opéra Comique 17 Nov 1877). [1877], [1884?]. (Sav 11 Oct 1884 with addns and alterations). [1898] (with Trial by jury).

The ne'er-do-well. D. (Olym 25 Feb 1878). [1878] (priv ptd).

HMS Pinafore, or the lass that loved a sailor: an entirely original nautical comic opera. (Opéra Comique 25 May 1878). [1878], New York 1879. With Arthur Sullivan.

Gretchen. C. (Olym 24 May 1879). 1879.

The pirates of Penzance, or the slave of duty: an entirely original comic opera. (Fifth Avenue, New York 31 Dec 1879; Opéra Comique 3 April 1880). [1887?]. With Arthur Sullivan.

An entirely new and original aesthetic opera, in two acts, entitled Patience: or Bunthorne's bride! (Opéra Comique 23 April 1881). [1881]. With Arthur Sullivan.

Foggerty's fairy: a comedy (Crit 5 Dec 1881). 1881 (priv ptd), 1890.

An entirely original fairy opera in two acts, entitled Iolanthe: or the peer and the peri. (Sav 25 Nov 1882). [1885]. With Arthur Sullivan.

A respectful operatic per-version of Tennyson's Princess in two acts, entitled Princess Ida: or Castle Adamant. (Sav 5 Jan 1884). [1884]. With Arthur Sullivan.

Comedy and tragedy: an original drama. (Lyc 26 Jan 1884). French 139.

An entirely new and original Japanese opera in two acts, entitled the Mikado: or the town of Titipu. (Sav 14 March 1885). [1885]; tr Danish, 1887; German, [1887]. With Arthur Sullivan.

An entirely original supernatural opera in two acts, entitled Ruddygore: or the witch's curse! (St J 22 Jan 1887). [1887]. Spelling of title altered to Ruddigore 4 days after production because of objections. With Arthur Sullivan.

A new and original opera in two acts, entitled the Yeomen of the Guard: or the merryman and his maid. (Sav 31 Oct 1888). [1888]. With Arthur Sullivan.

An entirely new and original drama in four acts, entitled Brantinghame Hall. (St J 29 Nov 1888). 1888 (priv ptd).

Les brigands: opéra bouffe en trois actes, par H. Meilhac et L. Halévy; musique de J. Offenbach; l'adaptation anglaise par Gilbert. (TR, Plymouth 2 Sept 1889; Ave 16 Sept 1889). 1871; [1884], [1899], 1914. Text in French and English.

An entirely original comic opera in two acts, entitled the Gondoliers: or the King of Barataria. (Sav 7 Dec 1889). [1889]. With Arthur Sullivan.

Songs of a Savoyard, illustrated by the author. 1890. Lyrics from the operas performed at the Savoy Theatre.

Foggerty's fairy and other tales. 1890.

Rosencrantz and Guildenstern: a tragic episode in three tableaux, founded on an old Danish legend. (Vaudeville 3 June 1891). French 133.

An entirely original comic opera in two acts, entitled the Mountebanks; [music] by A. Cellier. (Lyric 4 Jan 1892). 1892.

A musical version of Le chapeau de paille d'Italie in three acts, entitled Haste to the wedding; music by G. Grossmith. (Crit 27 July 1892). 1892.

His Excellency: an entirely original comic opera in two acts; music by O. Carr. (Sav 7 Oct 1894). 1894.

The Grand Duke, or the statutory duel: a comic opera. (Sav 7 March 1896). 1896.

The fortune hunter. C. (Birmingham 27 Sept 1897, Queen's OH, Crouch End 18 Oct 1897). [1897] (priv ptd).

The Bab ballads, with which are included Songs of a Savoyard; with 350 illustrations by the author. 1898.

The fairy's dilemma: a domestic pantomime. (Gar 3 May 1904). [1904] (priv ptd).

The Pinafore picture book: the story of HMS Pinafore. 1908.

Rutland Barrington, by himself; with a preface by W. S. Gilbert. 1908.

An original opera in two acts, entitled Fallen fairies: or the wicked world; [music] by [Sir] E. German. (Gar 11 Dec 1909). 1909.

The hooligan. F. (Coliseum 27 Feb 1911). Pbd in Century Illustr Mag Nov 1911.

A colossal idea: an original farce; with introduction and decorations by T. Searle. 1932. Written 1873; unacted.

Lost Bab ballads: collected and illustrated by T. Searle. 1932.

Searle's bibliography also lists the following plays and pantomimes, which have not been ptd: Robinson Crusoe, 1867 (with H. J. Byron, T. Hood, H. S. Leigh and A. Sketchley); Allow me to explain, 1867; Highly improbable, 1867; Great expectations, 1871; The realm of joy, 1873; Ought we to visit her?, 1874 (with Mrs A. Edwards); Committed for trial, 1874; Ali Baba and the forty thieves, 1878 (with H. J. Byron, F. C. Burnand and R. Reece). *Various songs were also pbd separately. Gilbert illustrated several books by other authors.*

§2

Adams, W. D. Mr Gilbert as a dramatist. Belgravia Oct 1881.

Archer, W. In his English dramatists of today, 1882.
—— In his Real conversations, 1904.
Gilbert: an autobiography. Theatre April 1883.
Marshall, A. F. The spirit of Gilbert's comedies. Month Oct 1885.
Grossmith, G. A society clown. 1888.
W. S. Gilbert at home. Critic (New York) 19 1891.
Fitzgerald, P. H. The Savoy opera and the Savoyards. 1894.
Bulloch, J. M. The work of Gilbert. Book Buyer 17 1898.
—— The anatomy of the 'Bab' ballads. N & Q 14, 28 Nov 1936, 22 May 1937.
—— Gilbert's father. N & Q 19 Dec 1936.
Beerbohm, M. Gilbert as humorist. Saturday Rev 14 May 1904.
Browne, A. In J. T. Grein, Stars of the stage, 1907.
Sichel, W. The English Aristophanes. Fortnightly Rev Oct 1911.
Goldberg, A. Gilbert, a study in modern satire: handbook on Gilbert and the Gilbert and Sullivan operas. Boston [1913].
—— The story of Gilbert and Sullivan. 1929.
Cellier, F. A. and C. Bridgeman. Gilbert, Sullivan and D'Oyly Carte: reminiscences of the Savoy and the Savoyards. 1914, 1927.
Newman, E. The Gilbert and Sullivan operas. Littell's Living Age 303 1919.
Baring, M. Gilbert and Sullivan. Fortnightly Rev Sept 1922.
Rowland-Brown, H. The Gilbertian idea. Cornhill Mag April 1922.
Wilkinson, C. Gilbert and Sullivan. London Mercury March 1922.
Dark, S. and R. Grey. Gilbert: his life and letters. 1923.
Fitzgerald, S. J. A. The story of the Savoy opera. 1924.
Wilson, A. C. Gilbert. Manchester Quart 51 1925.
Godwin, A. H. Gilbert and Sullivan: a critical appreciation of the Savoy operas; with an introduction by G. K. Chesterton. 1926.
Hamilton, E. Gilbert: a mid-Victorian Aristophanes. Theatre Arts Monthly Nov 1927.
Lytton, H. A. Secrets of a Savoyard. [1927].
Perry, H. T. E. The Victorianism of Gilbert. Sewanee Rev 36 1928.
Du Bois, A. E. Gilbert, practical classicist. Sewanee Rev 37 1929.
—— Additions to the bibliography of Gilbert's contributions to magazines. MLN 47 1932.
Quiller-Couch, A. T. In his Studies in literature ser 3, Cambridge 1929.
Lambton, G. Gilbertian characters, and a discourse on Gilbert's philosophy in the Savoy operas. 1931.
Granville-Barker, H. Exit Planché, enter Gilbert. London Mercury March–April 1932.
Ellehauge, M. Initial stages in the development of the English problem-play: the Savoy opera. E Studien 66 1932.
Kendal, M. Gilbert. Cornhill Mag Sept 1933.
Pearson, H. Gilbert and Sullivan: a biography. 1935, 1947 (rev).
—— Gilbert: his life and strife. 1957.
Two Victorian humorists: Burnand and the mask of Gilbert. TLS 21 Nov 1936.
Bulloch, J. M. et al. The Bab ballads by titles. N & Q 22 May, 27 Nov 1937.
Vandiver, E. P. Gilbert and Shakespear. Shakespeare Assoc Bull 12 1938.
Troubridge, St V. Gilbert and Planché. N & Q 22 March, 12 July 1941.
—— Gilbert's sources. N & Q 29 March 1941.
Parrott, I. Arthur Sullivan. Music & Letters 23 July 1942.
Leyburn, J. G. Words by Gilbert. Yale Univ Lib Gazette 17 1943.
Boas, G. The Gilbertian world and the world of today. English 7 1948.
Darlington, W. A. The world of Gilbert and Sullivan. New York 1950.
Baily, L. The Gilbert and Sullivan book. 1952.
Williamson, A. Gilbert and Sullivan opera. 1953.
Hughes, G. The music of Arthur Sullivan. 1960.
Allen, R. Gilbert: an anniversary survey. Theatre Notebook 15 1961.
Mander, R. and J. Mitchenson. A picture history of Gilbert and Sullivan. 1962.
Moore, F. L. (ed). The handbook of Gilbert and Sullivan. 1962.

HENRY ARTHUR JONES
1851–1929

Bibliographies

Jones, D. A. Appendices A-B of her Life and letters of Jones, 1930.

Collections

Representative plays. Ed C. Hamilton (with historical, biographical and critical introd) 4 vols 1926. Vol 1, The silver king, The middleman, Judah, The dancing girl; vol 2, The crusaders, The tempter, The masqueraders, The case of rebellious Susan; vol 3, Michael and his lost angel, The liars, Mrs Dane's defence, The hypocrites; vol 4, Dolly reforming herself, The divine gift, Mary goes first, The goal, Grace Mary.

There is a uniform (but not complete) demy 8vo edn of 24 of Jones's plays pbd by Samuel French, nd.

§ 1

Hearts of oak: a domestic drama. (TR Exeter, 29 May 1879). Lacy 122. Rewritten with fuller dialogue as Honour bright, 1879, but unacted in this form. Both versions priv ptd Ilfracombe 1879.
Harmony: a domestic drama. (Grand, Leeds 13 Aug 1879 as Harmony restored; TR Exeter 11 Dec 1879 as It's only round the corner; Str 14 June 1884 as Harmony). Lacy 119. Performed as The organist, Lyc, New York May 1892; Royalty 25 Sept 1895.
Elopement: a comedy. (TR, Oxford 19 Aug 1879). Lacy 122; [Ilfracombe] 1879 (priv ptd).
A clerical error: a comedy. (Court 16 Oct 1879). [Ilfracombe] 1879 (priv ptd); Lacy 152.
A drive in June. D. (unacted). [Ilfracombe] 1879 (priv ptd).
An old master: a comedy. (P'cess 6 Nov 1880). Lacy 119; Ilfracombe 1880 (priv ptd).
A garden party. C. (unacted). [Ilfracombe] 1880 (priv ptd).
Humbug. C. (unacted). [Ilfracombe] 1881 (priv ptd).
Lady Caprice: a comedy. (unacted). [Ilfracombe] 1880 (priv ptd).
A bed of roses: a comedy. (Glo 26 Jan 1882). Lacy 119; Ilfracombe 1882 (priv ptd).
The silver king. D. (P'cess 16 Nov 1882). [1907]; French 1675. With H. A. Herman.
The wedding guest. C. (unacted). [Ilfracombe] 1882 (priv ptd).
Breaking a butterfly. D. (Prince's 3 March 1884). [1884] (priv ptd). With H. A. Herman. Founded on Ibsen, A doll's house.
Saints and sinners. D. (PW, Greenwich 17 Sept 1884, Vaudeville 25 Sept 1884). 1891.
Sweet Will: a comedy. (New Club, CG 5 March 1887, Shaftesbury 27 July 1893). Lacy 131.
The middleman. D. (Shaftesbury 27 Aug 1889). [1907].
Judah. D. (Shaftesbury 21 May 1890). New York 1894 (with a preface by Joseph Knight).
The deacon: a comedy sketch. (Shaftesbury 27 Aug 1890). Lacy 133.

The dancing girl: a drama. (H 15 Jan 1891). [1907].
The crusaders: an original comedy of modern London life. (Avenue 2 Nov 1891). 1893 (with a preface by W. Archer.)
The bauble shop. D. (Crit 26 Jan 1893). [1893].
The tempter: a tragedy in verse. (H 30 Sept 1893). [1893] (priv ptd), 1898.
The masqueraders. C. (St J 28 April 1894). [1894] (priv ptd), 1899.
The case of rebellious Susan. C. (Crit 3 Oct 1894). 1894 (priv ptd), 1897.
The triumph of the Philistines: a comedy. (St J 11 May 1895). 1895 (priv ptd), 1899.
Grace Mary. T. (Unacted). [1895] (priv ptd); rptd in The theatre of ideas, 1915.
The renascence of the English drama: essays, lectures and fragments relating to the modern English stage 1883–94. 1895.
Michael and his lost angel. D. (Lyc 15 Jan 1896). [1896] (priv ptd), 1896 (with preface by Joseph Knight).
The rogue's comedy. D. (Gar 21 April 1896). [1896] (priv ptd), 1898.
The physician. D. (Crit 26 March 1897). [1897] (priv ptd), 1899.
The liars: an original comedy. (Crit 6 Oct 1897). [1897] (priv ptd), New York 1901; French 2519.
The manoeuvres of Jane: an original comedy. (H 29 Oct 1898). [1898] (priv ptd), 1904.
Carnac Sahib. D. (Her Majesty's 12 April 1899). 1899 (priv ptd), 1899.
The lackey's carnival. D. (D of Y 26 Sept 1900). 1900 (priv ptd).
Mrs Dane's defence. D. (Wyndham's 9 Oct 1900). [1900] (priv ptd), 1905.
The Princess's nose: a comedy. (D of Y 11 March 1902). [1902] (priv ptd).
Chance the idol. D. (Wyndham's 9 Sept 1902). [1902] (priv ptd).
James the fogey. D. (Unacted). [1902] (priv ptd).
Whitewashing Julia: a comedy. (Gar 2 March 1903). [1903] (priv ptd), 1905.
Joseph entangled: a comedy. (H 19 Jan 1904). [1904] (priv ptd), [1906].
The chevaleer: a comedy. (Gar 27 Aug 1904). [1904] priv ptd), [1905?].
Chrysold. D. (Unacted). [1904] (priv ptd).
The sword of Gideon. D. (Unacted). [1905?] (priv ptd).
The heroic Stubbs: a comedy. (Terry's 24 Jan 1906). [1906] (priv ptd).
The hypocrites. D. (Hudson, New York 30 Aug 1906; Hicks's, London 27 Aug 1907). [1907] (priv ptd), [1908].
The evangelist: a tragi-comedy. (Knickerbocker, New York 30 Sept 1907). [1908?] (as The Galilean's victory).
Dolly reforming herself: a comedy (H 3 Nov 1908). [1908] (priv ptd), [1913]. Samuel French & Co also pbd in New York a one-act version called Dolly's little bills.
The knife. D. (Palace 20 Dec 1909). [New York 1909?].
Fall in, rookies. D. (Alhambra 24 Oct 1910). [1910] (priv ptd).
We can't be as bad as all that. D. (Nazimova's 39th Street, New York 30 Dec 1910; Croydon Hippodrome 4 Sept 1916). New York 1910 (priv ptd).
The ogre. D. (St J 11 Sept 1911). [1911?].
Lydia Gilmore. D. (Lyc, New York 11 Feb 1912). [1912?].
Mary goes first: a comedy. (Playhouse 18 Sept 1913). 1913.
The divine gift. D. (Unacted). 1913.
The foundations of a national drama: a collection of lectures, essays and speeches, delivered and written in the years 1896–1912, revised and corrected, with additions. 1913.
The goal. D. (P'cess, New York 26 Oct 1914; Palace, London 20 May 1919). [1919?] (priv ptd). In The theatre of ideas, 1915.

The lie. D. (Harris, New York 24 Dec 1914; New, London 13 Oct 1923). New York 1915, London 1923.
The theatre of ideas: a burlesque allegory; and three one-act plays: The goal; Her tongue; Grace Mary. 1915.
The pacifists: a parable. (St J 4 Sept 1917). [1917?] (priv ptd).
Patriotism and popular education. 1919, 1919.
My dear Wells: a manual for the haters of England; being a series of letters upon Bolshevism, collectivism, internationalism and the distribution of wealth, addressed to Mr H. G. Wells. 1921, 1922, New York 1921, 1921.
What is capital? an inquiry into the meaning of the words 'capital' and 'labour'. 1925.

D. A. Jones's bibliography, above, also records unpbd plays and 4 film scenarios, written in 1920, which were neither used nor ptd.

Jones also produced some pamphlets, including one of some length on the question of dramatic censorship, and was a frequent contributor to the periodical press, usually on aspects of the drama.

§2

Walkley, A. B. In his Playhouse impressions, 1892.
—— In his Drama and life, 1907.
Bettany, W. A. L. Jones and modern English drama. Theatre 31 1893.
Blathwayt, R. Jones. Idler Aug 1893.
Hamilton, J. A. Jones. Munsey's Mag 9 1894.
Newton, H. C. Jones. Theatre March 1896.
Bulloch, J. M. Jones; with bibliography of his plays. Book Buyer 16 1898.
Beerbohm, M. The popular success of Jones. Saturday Rev 13 Oct 1900.
Tarpey, W. K. Jones's work as a dramatist. Critic 37 1900.
Grein, J. T. In his Dramatic criticism vol 3, 1902.
Matthews, J. B. A study of the drama. Boston 1910.
Grossmith, W. From studio to stage. 1913.
Howe, P. P. In his Dramatic portraits, 1913.
Winter, W. In his Wallet of time vol 2, 1913.
Chandler, F. W. In his Aspects of modern drama, New York 1914.
Dickinson, T. H. Jones and the dramatic renascence. North Amer Rev Nov 1915.
Wauchope, G. A. Jones and the new social drama. Sewanee Rev 29 1921.
Archer, W. In his Old drama and the new, 1923.
Jones, dramatist, self-revealed: a conversation on the art of writing plays with Archibald Henderson. Nation (London) 5–12 Dec 1925.
Shorey, P. Jones. New York 1925.
Allen, P. Jones. Fortnightly Rev May 1929.
Obituary. London Mercury Feb 1929.
Shelley, H. C. Jones. Bookman (London) Feb 1929.
Jones, D. A. The life and letters of Jones. 1930.
Cordell, R. A. Jones and the modern drama. 1932.
Ellehauge, M. Initial stages in the development of the English problem-play. E Studien 66 1932.
Northend, M. Jones and the development of the modern English drama. RES 18 1942.
Baily, J. O. Science in the dramas of Jones. In Booker memorial studies, ed H. Shine, Chapel Hill 1950.
Weales, G. In his Religion in modern English drama, Philadelphia 1961.

SIR ARTHUR WING PINERO
1855–1934

Collections

The social plays of Pinero. Ed C. Hamilton (with general introd and critical preface to each play) 4 vols New

York 1917–22. Vol 1, The second Mrs Tanqueray, The notorious Mrs Ebbsmith; vol 2, The gay Lord Quex, Iris; vol 3, Letty, His house in order; vol 4, The thunderbolt, Mid-channel.

§1

Many of the plays were priv ptd before production for use as prompt books etc.

*The plays marked * constitute a uniform (but not complete) edn in 29 vols, the first 11 with introductory notes by M. C. Salaman.*

Hester's mystery: a comedy. (Folly 5 June 1880). Lacy 136.

The money spinner: an original comedy. (Prince's, Manchester 5 Nov 1880; St J 8 Jan 1881). Lacy 146.

The squire: an original comedy. (St J 29 Dec 1881). [1905].

The rocket: an original comedy. (PW, Liverpool 30 July 1883; Gai 10 Dec 1883). [1905].

In chancery: an original fantastic comedy. (Lyc, Edinburgh 19 Sept 1884; Gai 24 Dec 1884). [1905].

*The magistrate: a farce. (Court 23 Jan 1885). 1892.

*The schoolmistress: a farce. (Court 27 March 1886). 1894.

*The hobby-horse: a comedy. (St J 23 Oct 1886). 1892.

*Dandy Dick: a farce. (Court 27 Jan 1887). 1893.

*Sweet Lavender: a domestic drama. (Terry's 21 March 1888). 1893.

*The weaker sex: a comedy. (Court 16 March 1889). 1894.

*The profligate. D. (Gar 24 April 1889). 1892.

*The Cabinet Minister: a farce. (Court 23 April 1890). 1892.

*Lady Bountiful: a story of years. D. (Gar 7 March 1891). 1892.

*The Times: a comedy. (Terry's 24 Oct 1891). 1891.

*The Amazons: a farcical romance. (Court 7 March 1893). 1895.

*The second Mrs Tanqueray. D. (St J 27 May 1893). 1895.

*The notorious Mrs Ebbsmith: a drama. (Gar 13 March 1895). 1895.

*The benefit of the doubt: a comedy. (Com 16 Oct 1895). 1896.

*The Princess and the butterfly, or the fantastics: a comedy. (St J 29 March 1897). 1898.

*Trelawny of the 'Wells': a comedietta. (Court 20 Jan 1898). New York 1898, London 1899.

The beauty stone: an original romantic musical drama. (Sav 28 May 1898). With J. C. Carr, music by Arthur Sullivan.

*The gay Lord Quex. C. (Glo 8 April 1899). 1900.

*Iris. D. (Gar 21 Sept 1901). 1902.

Preface. In W. L. Courtney, Idea of tragedy, 1900.

Robert Louis Stevenson the dramatist: a lecture. 1903, 1909 (in Critic 42), New York 1914 (with introd and biographical appendix by C. Hamilton).

*Letty. D. (D of Y 8 Oct 1903). 1904.

*A wife without a smile: a comedy in disguise. (Wyndham's 9 Oct 1904). 1905.

*His house in order. C. (St J 1 Feb 1906). 1909.

*The thunderbolt. C. (St J 9 May 1908). 1909.

*Mid-channel. D. (St J 2 Sept 1909). 1910.

*Preserving Mr Panmure: a comic play. (Com 19 Jan 1911). 1912.

*The 'mind the paint' girl: a comedy. (D of Y 17 Feb 1912). 1913.

The widow of Wasdale Head: a fantasy. (D of Y 14 Oct 1912).

Browning as a dramatist. Trans Royal Soc of Lit 31 1912.

Playgoers: a domestic episode. (St J 31 March 1913). French 2507.

*The big drum: a comedy. (St J 1 Sept 1915). 1915.

*The freaks, an idyll of suburbia: a comedy. (New 14 Feb 1918). 1922.

A seat in the park. C. (Winter Garden 21 Feb 1922). French 2618.

*The enchanted cottage: a fable. (D of Y 1 March 1922). 1922.

A private room. D. (Little 14 May 1928). French 852.

*Dr Harmer's holidays: a contrast in nine scenes. (Shubert-Belasco, Washington 16 March 1931). 1930. Pbd with Child man: a sedate farce (unacted) in Two plays, 1930 (with preface).

The following were also produced but remain unpbd: Lords and Commons. C. (H 24 Nov 1883); Low water, C. (Glo 12 Jan 1884); A cold June. C. (Duchess 20 May 1932).

§2

Archer, W. In his English dramatists of to-day, 1882.

—— In his Theatrical 'World', 5 vols 1893–7.

—— In his Study and stage, 1899.

—— In his Real conversations, 1904.

—— In his Old drama and the new, 1923.

Cook, D. Plays, plagiarisms and Mr Pinero. Theatre Jan 1882.

—— The case of Mr Pinero. Theatre Feb–April 1882.

Sharp, R. F. Pinero and farce. Theatre Oct 1892.

Walkley, A. B. In his Playhouse impressions, 1892.

—— In his Frames of mind, 1899.

—— In his Drama and life, 1908.

Mr Pinero and the literary drama. Theatre July 1893.

Hamilton, J. A. Pinero. Munsey's Mag July 1894.

Fyfe, H. H. Mr Pinero's plays as literature. Theatre June 1895.

—— Pinero, playwright: a study. 1902. With casts.

—— Pinero's plays and players. 1930.

Wilson, H. S. The notorious Mrs Ebbsmith. 1895.

Courtney, W. L. The idea of comedy and Mr Pinero's new play [The Princess and the butterfly]. Fortnightly Rev May 1897.

—— Realistic drama. Fortnightly Rev June 1913.

Frohman, D. In his Memories of a manager, 1899.

Kobbé, G. The plays of Pinero. Forum 26 1899.

Hamelius, J. P. Pinero und das englische Drama der Jetztzeit. Brussels 1900.

Tarpey, W. K. English dramatists of to-day: Pinero. Critic 37 1900.

Beers, H. A. The English drama of to-day. North Amer Rev 180 1905.

Hale, E. E. In his Dramatists of to-day, New York 1905.

Pinero's skill as a dramatist. Nation (New York) 6 Sept 1906.

Rideing, W. H. Some women of Pinero's. North Amer Rev July 1908.

Stocker, W. Pineros Dramen. Marburg 1911.

Walbrook, H. H. In his Nights at the play, 1911.

Armstrong, C. F. In his Shakespeare to Shaw, 1913.

Howe, P. P. In his Dramatic portraits, 1913.

Moore, G. In his Impressions and opinions, 1913.

Chandler, F. W. In his Aspects of modern drama, New York 1914.

Pinero as a playwright. New Republic 13 1917.

Phelps, W. L. Pinero. Bookman (New York) April 1918.

Dickinson, T. H. In his Contemporary drama of England, 1920.

Krutch, J. W. Pinero the timid. Nation (New York) 19 Nov 1924.

Wilson, E. Sixty-five years of realism. New Republic 43 1925.

Cunliffe, J. W. In his Modern English playwrights, New York 1927.

Holt, E. A dramatist's jubilee. Fortnightly Rev March 1928.

Ellehauge, M. Initial stages in the development of the English problem-play. E Studien 66 1932.

Mason, A. E. W. Sir George Alexander and the St James's Theatre. 1935.
Boas, F. S. Pinero: dramatist and stage chronicler. In his From Richardson to Pinero, 1936.
Küther, H. Pinero und sein Verhältnis zu Henrik Ibsen. Münster 1937.
Weber, C. J. Plagiarism and Thomas Hardy. New Colophon 2 1937.
Dunkel, W. D. Pinero: a critical biography with letters. Chicago [1941], London 1943.
Stoakes, J. P. The reception of The second Mrs Tanqueray. Florida State Univ Stud 1953.
Pearson, H. Pinero and Barrie: a backstage view. Theatre Arts July 1958.
Davies, C. W. Pinero: the drama of reputation. English 14 1962.

GEORGE BERNARD SHAW
1856–1950
Bibliographies etc

Wells, G. H. A bibliography of the books and pamphlets of Shaw, with occasional notes by Shaw. 1925. Suppl to Bookman's Jnl Feb–April 1925; rev and enlarged in Bookman's Jnl July–Aug, Sept 1928.
Broad, C. L. and V. M. Dictionary to the plays and novels of Shaw, with bibliography of his works and of the literature concerning him; with a record of the principal Shavian play productions. 1929.
Holmes, M. Some bibliographical notes on the novels of Shaw; with some comments by Shaw. [1929].
Catalogue of an exhibition at 7 Albemarle St London to celebrate his ninetieth birthday. 1946.
Loewenstein, F. E. The history of a famous novel [An unsocial Socialist]. 1946 (priv ptd).
— The rehearsal copies of Shaw's plays: a bibliographical study. 1950, New York 1950.
Mander, R. and J. Mitchenson. Theatrical companion to Shaw. [1954], New York 1955.
Levidova, Y. Shaw. Moscow 1956.
Farley, E. and M. Carlson. Shaw: a selected bibliography 1945–55. Modern Drama 2 1959.
Keough, L. C. Shaw 1946–55: a selected bibliography. Bull of Bibliography 22–3 1959–60.
A Continuing checklist of Shaviana *has been running in the* Shaw Rev *since its inception as the* Shaw Bull *in 1951*.

Collections

Plays pleasant and unpleasant. 2 vols 1898. Vol 1, Plays unpleasant: Widowers' houses (rev), Mrs Warren's profession, The philanderer; vol 2, Plays pleasant: Arms and the man, Candida, The man of destiny, You never can tell.
Three plays for Puritans: The Devil's disciple, Caesar and Cleopatra and Captain Brassbound's conversion. 1901.
Dramatic opinions and essays, with an apology; containing as well a word on the dramatic opinions and essays of Shaw by James Huneker. 2 vols New York 1906, 1906 (with preface), London 1907. Selected from Saturday Rev 5 Jan 1895–21 May 1898.
Selected passages from the works of Shaw chosen by Charlotte F. Shaw. 1912, New York 1913 (as The wisdom of Shaw).
Cabinet collection of the plays. 13 vols 1926–32.
The Socialism of Shaw. Ed J. Fuchs, New York 1926.
Works. 33 vols 1930–8. First 30 vols issued as Ayot St Lawrence edn, New York 1930–2. (Limited collected edn).
Standard edition. 34 vols 1931–51.
Complete plays. 1931, 1934, 1938, 1950, 1952, 1965.
Prefaces. 1934. Includes the prefaces, with any added notes made by the author, up to 1934, the more important prefaces being: Getting married (Getting married); Parents and children (Misalliance); Epistle dedicatory, The revolutionist's handbook, Maxims for revolutionists (Man and superman); [On prostitution and censorship of plays] (Mrs Warren's profession); On doctors (The doctor's dilemma); Imprisonment (S. and B. Webb, English local government); The infidel half century (Back to Methuselah); On the prospects of Christianity (Androcles and the lion); Saint Joan (Saint Joan); Mainly about myself (Plays unpleasant); 1938 (includes prefaces later than 1934 and additional early items), 1965.
London music in 1888–89 as heard by Corno di Bassetto (later known as Bernard Shaw); with some further autobiographical particulars, 1937 (in Standard edn, above), New York 1937, 1963.
Shaw gives himself away: an autobiographical miscellany. Newtown 1939.
[Works]. 10 vols 1946. Selection pbd by Penguin Books in commemoration of Shaw's 90th birthday.
Shaw on vivisection. Ed G. H. Bowker 1949, Chicago 1951.
The quintessence of GBS. Ed S. Winsten 1949, New York 1949, 1962 (as Wit and wisdom of Shaw).
Plays and players: selected essays. Ed A. C. Ward 1952.
Selected prose. Ed D. Russell, New York 1952.
Selected plays and other writings. Ed W. Irvine, New York 1956.
Shaw on theatre. Ed E. J. West, New York 1958, 1959 (rev by D. H. Laurence), London 1959.
Dramatic criticism 1895–8. Ed J. F. Mathews, New York 1959.
Shaw: a prose anthology. Ed H. M. Burton 1959. Preface by A. C. Ward.
How to become a musical critic. Ed D. H. Laurence 1960, New York 1961.
Platform and pulpit. Ed D. H. Laurence, New York 1961, London 1962.
Shaw on Shakespeare. Ed E. Wilson, New York 1961, London [1962].
The theatre of Shaw: ten plays chosen and discussed. Ed A. S. Downer 2 vols New York 1961.
Complete plays with prefaces. 6 vols New York 1962.
GBS on music. 1962.
The matter with Ireland. Ed D. H. Laurence and D. H. Greene 1962, New York 1962.
Shaw on language. Ed A. Tauber, New York [1963], London 1965.
Religious speeches. Ed W. S. Smith, University Park Pa 1964.
Selected non-dramatic writings of Shaw. Ed D. H. Laurence, Boston [1965].
Shaw's ready reckoner: a guide to civilization. Ed N. H. Leigh-Taylor, New York 1965, London 1966.
Shaw: selections of his wit and wisdom. Ed C. T. Harnsberger, Chicago [1965].
Shaw on religion. Ed W. S. Smith 1967.

§1

Copyright performances are preceded by an asterisk.

Cashel Byron's profession: a novel. 1886, [1889] (rev), 1901 (newly rev as Novels of his nonage, no 4). First pbd in To-day 1885–6; dramatized as The admirable Bashville.
An unsocial Socialist. 1887. First pbd in To-day 1884.
Fabian essays in Socialism. 1889. Ed Shaw.
The quintessence of Ibsenism. 1891, 1913 (completed to the death of Ibsen).
Widowers' houses. (Independent Theatre Soc, Royalty 9 Dec 1892). 1893, 1898 (rev in Plays pleasant and unpleasant).
Arms and the man. (Avenue 21 April 1894). 1898 (in Plays pleasant); tr German, 1903.
Candida. (*TR, South Shields 30 March 1895; Her Majesty's, Aberdeen 30 July 1897; Str 1 July 1900). 1898 (in Plays pleasant); tr German, 1903.
On going to church. New York 1896, Boston 1905, London 1957. First pbd in Savoy Jan 1896.

The Devil's disciple. (*Bijou 17 April 1897; Hermanus Bleecker Hall, Albany NY; Savoy 14 Oct 1907). 1901 (in Three plays for Puritans); tr German, 1903.
The man of destiny. (Grant Theatre, Croydon 1 July 1897; Com 29 March 1901). 1898 (in Plays pleasant).
The perfect Wagnerite: a commentary on the Ring of the Niblungs. 1898, 1902 (with new preface), Berlin 1908 [1907] (new preface and ch), New York 1909, London 1913 (new preface), 1923 (new preface).
The gadfly: or the son of the Cardinal. (Victoria Hall, Bayswater 23 March 1898).
Mrs Warren's profession. (*Bijou 30 March 1898; Stage Soc, New Lyric Club 5 Jan 1902). 1898 (in Plays unpleasant), 1903 (Stage Soc edn with author's apology; apology alone, with introd by J. Corbin, The tyranny of police and press, New York 1905).
The philanderer. (*Bijou 30 March 1898; New Stage Club, Cripplegate Institute 20 Feb 1905). 1898 (in Plays unpleasant).
Caesar and Cleopatra. (*TR, Newcastle 15 March 1899; tr German, Neues Theater, Berlin 31 March 1906; New Amsterdam, New York 30 Oct 1906; Leeds 16 Sept 1907, Sav 25 Nov 1907). 1901 (in Three plays for Puritans).
Fabianism and the Empire: a manifesto. 1900. Ed Shaw.
Love among the artists. Chicago 1900, London 1914. First pbd in Our Corner 1887–8.
The admirable Bashville: or constancy rewarded. (*Bijou 3 March 1901; Pharos Club, Covent Garden 14 Dec 1902). From Cashel Byron's profession, 1901 (with Cashel Byron's profession, rev).
Man and superman: a comedy and a philosophy. (*Bijou 29 June 1903; Stage Soc, Court 21 May 1905). 1903 (includes Epistle dedicatory, The revolutionist's handbook, and Maxims for revolutionists), New York 1904 (with textual variations), London 1911 (with new foreword).
The common sense of municipal trading. 1904, 1908 (with new preface).
How he lied to her husband. (*Bijou 1904; Berkeley Lyceum, New York 26 Sept 1904; Court 28 Feb 1905). 1907 (with John Bull's other island); tr German 1906.
John Bull's other island. (Court 1 Nov 1904). 1907 (with Major Barbara, and How he lied to her husband), 1912 (with new prefatory material).
Passion, poison and petrification, or the fatal gazogene: a tragedy. Bsq. (Theatrical Garden Party, Regent's Park 14 July 1905). [1905]. First pbd in Harry Furniss's Christmas Annual 1905, 1926 (in Translations and tomfooleries).
The irrational knot: being the second novel of his nonage. 1905. First pbd in Our Corner 1885–7.
Major Barbara. (Court 28 Nov 1905). 1907 (with John Bull's other island), 1945 (film version).
The doctor's dilemma. (Court 20 Nov 1906). 1911 (with Getting married and The shewing-up of Blanco Posnet); tr German, 1909.
Interlude at the Playhouse. (Playhouse 28 Jan 1907). Daily Mail 29 Jan 1897; rptd in Cyril Maude, Behind the scenes with Cyril Maude, 1927, New York 1928 (as Lest we forget).
The sanity of art: an exposure of the current nonsense about artists being degenerate. 1908. A criticism of Max Nordau, Entartung; rev and rptd from Liberty, New York 1895.
Getting married. (H 12 May 1908). 1911 (with The doctor's dilemma); tr German, 1910.
Socialism and superior brains: a reply to Mr [W. H.] Mallock. 1909. From Fortnightly Rev 1894.
Press cuttings: a topical sketch compiled from the editorial and correspondence columns of the daily papers. (Civic and Dramatic Guild, Court 9 July 1909). 1909.
The shewing-up of Blanco Posnet. (Abbey Theatre, Dublin 25 Aug 1909; Aldwych 5 Dec 1909). 1909, 1911 (with The doctor's dilemma).

Misalliance. (D of Y 23 Feb 1910). 1914 (with A treatise on parents and children, The dark lady of the sonnets, and Fanny's first play); tr German, 1910 (for 1911?).
The dark lady of the sonnets. (H 24 Nov 1910). 1914 (in Misalliance). Originally pbd in Eng Rev Jan 1911.
Fanny's first play. (Little 19 April 1911). 1914 (in Misalliance); tr German, 1911.
Overruled. (D of Y 14 Oct 1912). 1916 (in Androcles and the lion). Originally pbd in Eng Rev May 1913.
Androcles and the lion. (St J 1 Sept 1913). 1916 (with Over-ruled and Pygmalion), [1962] (Shaw alphabet edn); tr German, 1913. Originally pbd in Everybody's Sept 1914.
Great Catherine. (Vaudeville 18 Nov 1913). 1919 (in Heartbreak House).
The music cure. (Little 28 Jan 1914). 1926 (in Translations and tomfooleries).
Common sense about the War. Suppl to New Statesman 14 Nov 1914, 1931 (in What I really wrote about the War).
The Inca of Perusalem. (Birmingham Rep 7 Oct 1916; Crit 16 Dec 1917). 1919 (in Heartbreak House).
Augustus does his bit. (Stage Soc, Court 21 Jan 1917). 1919 (in Heartbreak House).
O'Flaherty VC. (40th Squadron, RFC, Treziennes, Belgium 17 Feb 1917; 39th St Theatre, New York, 21 June 1920; Stage Soc, Lyric 19 Dec 1920). 1919 (in Heartbreak House); tr French, 1956.
How to settle the Irish question. Dublin 1917.
Annajanska, the Bolshevik Empress. (Coliseum 21 Jan 1918). 1919 (in Heartbreak House).
Peace Conference hints. 1919.
Heartbreak House. (Garrick Theatre, New York, 10 Nov 1920; Court 18 Oct 1921). 1919 (with Great Catherine and Playlets of the war: O'Flaherty VC; The Inca of Perusalem; Augustus does his bit; and Annajanska, the Bolshevik Empress).
Ruskin's politics. 1921.
Back to Methuselah: a metabiological pentateuch. (Garrick Theatre, New York 27 Feb 1922; Birmingham Rep 9 Oct 1923; Court 18 Feb 1924). 1921 (with preface on Creative evolution as the creed of the twentieth century), 1945 (rev with a postscript).
Jitta's atonement, adapted from the German of S. Trebitsch. (Shubert-Garrick Theatre, Washington 8 Jan 1923; Grand, Fulham 26 Jan 1925). 1926 (in Translations and tomfooleries).
Saint Joan: a chronicle play in six scenes and an epilogue. (Garrick Theatre, New York 28 Dec 1923; New 26 March 1924). 1924; tr German, 1924.
Imprisonment. New York [1925]. The preface to English prisons under local government by Beatrice and Sidney Webb, 1922, Chislehurst 1944.
Table-talk of GBS: conversations on things in general between Shaw and his biographer, by Archibald Henderson. 1925.
The glimpse of reality. (Fellowship Hall, Glasgow 8 Oct 1927; Arts 20 Nov 1927). 1926 (in Translations and tomfooleries).
Do we agree? a debate between G. K. Chesterton and Shaw with Hilaire Belloc in the chair. [1928].
The intelligent woman's guide to Socialism and Capitalism. 1928, 1929 (with new introd); tr Hebrew, 1931 (with new preface); 1937 (with two new chapters on Fascism and Sovietism).
The apple cart: a political extravaganza. (Teatr Polski, Warsaw 14 June 1929; Malvern Festival 19 Aug 1929; Queen's 17 Sept 1929). 1930; tr German, 1929.
Bernard Shaw and Karl Marx: a symposium 1884–9. New York 1930. Articles on Marx by Shaw and controversy between Shaw and P. H. Wicksteed, ed R. W. Ellis.
Immaturity. 1930 (in Limited collected edn), 1931 (in Standard edn).
Doctors' delusions. 1931 (in Limited collected edn), 1932 (rev in Standard edn).

What I really wrote about the War. 1931.

The adventures of the black girl in her search for God. 1932.

Short stories, scraps and shavings, 1932 (in Limited collected edn). Includes various short stories rptd from periodicals 1885–1916, some unpbd dramatic fragments etc, 1934 (in Standard edn, with Adventures of the black girl).

Too true to be good. (National Theatre, Boston 29 Feb 1932; Malvern Festival 6 Aug 1932; New 17 Sept 1932). 1934 (with Village wooing and On the rocks); tr German, 1932.

The future of political science in America: a lecture. New York 1933, London 1933 (as The political madhouse in America and nearer home).

On the rocks. (Winter Garden Theatre 25 Nov 1933). 1934 (in Too true to be good); tr German, 1934.

Village wooing. (Little Theatre, Dallas, Texas 16 April 1934; Tunbridge Wells Rep 1 May 1934). 1934 (in Too true to be good); tr German, 1934.

The six of Calais. (Regent's Park 17 July 1934). 1936; tr German, 1935.

The simpleton of the Unexpected Isles. (Guild Theatre, New York 18 Feb 1935; Malvern Festival 29 July 1935; Arts 7 March 1945). 1935, 1936 (in Standard edn); tr German, 1935.

William Morris as I knew him. New York 1936. First pbd as preface to M. Morris, William Morris: artist, writer, Socialist, 1936.

The millionairess. (Akademie Theater, Vienna 4 Jan 1936; De la Warr Pavilion, Bexhill 17 Nov 1936; New 27 June 1952). 1936; tr German, 1936.

Cymbeline refinished. (Embassy 16 Nov 1937). 1946 (in Geneva, below).

Geneva. (Malvern Festival 1 Aug 1938; Saville 22 Nov 1938). 1939, 1946 (in Standard edn, with Cymbeline refinished and Good King Charles).

In good King Charles's golden days. (Malvern Festival 12 Aug 1939; New 9 May 1940). 1939, 1946 (in Geneva, above).

Everybody's political what's what? 1944.

Buoyant billions. (Schauspielhaus, Zürich 21 Oct 1948; Malvern Festival 13 Aug 1949; Princes 10 Oct, 19 Oct 1949). 1949, 1950 (in Standard edn, with Farfetched fables and Shakes versus Shaw); tr German, 1948.

Shakes versus Shav. (Littleton Hall, Malvern 9 Aug 1949; Riverside Theatre, Federal Gardens, Battersea 10 June 1951). A puppet play written for Waldo Lanchester Marionette Theatre. 1950 (with Buoyant billions). Originally pbd in Arts Council Bull Sept 1949.

Sixteen self sketches. 1949 (in Standard edn).

Farfetched fables. (Watergate Theatre 6 Sept 1950). 1950 (with Buoyant billions).

Rhyming picture guide to Ayot Saint Lawrence. Luton 1950.

My dear Dorothea: a practical system of moral education for females; with a note by Stephen Winsten. 1956.

An unfinished novel. Ed S. Weintraub 1958.

The rationalization of Russia. Ed H. M. Geduld, Bloomington [1964].

For Pen portraits and reviews *see* Limited collected edition, 1931, Standard edition 1932; *for* Music in London 1890–94 3 vols *and* Our theatres in the Nineties 3 vols, *see* Standard edition 1932; *all under* Collections, *above. Shaw also pbd many pamphlets (especially for Fabian Soc), lectures, and periodical articles; and edited or introduced numerous works by other authors; for selections see under* Collections, *above. Works by Shaw have been widely translated. His general practice after 1908 (affected by the two wars), was to publish his plays first in German.*

Letters

Letters to Miss Alma Murray. Edinburgh 1927; More letters to Miss Alma Murray, Edinburgh 1932.

Ellen Terry and Shaw: a correspondence. 1931.

Florence Farr, Shaw and W. B. Yeats letters. Ed C. Bax, Dublin 1941, New York 1942, London 1946.

Correspondence between Shaw and Mrs Patrick Campbell. Ed A. Dent 1952.

Advice to a young critic and other letters [to R. Golding Bright]. Ed E. J. West, New York [1955], London [1956] (without West's notes).

A letter from Shaw to J. C. Williamson. Cremorne NSW 1955 (priv ptd). Preface by W. W. Stone.

Letters to Granville-Barker. Ed C. B. Purdom, New York 1957, London 1957.

Lowe, R. L. Two Shaw letters. MLR 53 1958.

To a young actress: the letters of Shaw to Molly Tompkins. Ed P. Tompkins, New York [1960], London [1961].

Kilty, J. (adaptor). Dear Liar; a comedy of letters adapted from the correspondence of Shaw and Mrs Patrick Campbell. 1960.

Hogan, P. G. jr and J. D. Baylen. An unpbd letter from Shaw to Archer. N & Q July 1963.

Collected letters 1874–97. Ed D. H. Laurence [1965].

Staud, G. Shaw's letters to Sándor Hevesi. Theatre Research: Recherches Théâtrales 8 1967.

§2

Mallock, W. H. A Socialist in a corner. Fortnightly Rev May 1894.

Walkley, A. B. In his Frames of mind, 1899.

Street, G. S. Shaw and Sheridan. Blackwood's Mag June 1900.

Hale, E. E. In his Dramatists of to-day, New York 1905.

Mencken, H. L. Shaw: his plays. Boston 1905.

—— An American reaction to Shaw's forty-letter alfabet. Quart Jnl of Speech 24 1948.

Castren, G. G. Shaw. Helsinki 1906.

Huneker, J. G. Iconoclasts: a book of dramatists. [1906].

Boynton, H. W. Shaw as critic. Atlantic Monthly April 1907.

Hankin, St J. Shaw as critic. Fortnightly Rev June 1907.

Jackson, H. Shaw. 1907.

Chesterton, G. K. Shaw. 1909, New York 1909, 1935 (with new ch), New York 1950.

Bab, J. Shaw. Berlin 1910, 1926 (rewritten).

Deacon, R. M. Shaw as artist-philosopher. 1910.

Dukes, A. In his Modern dramatists, 1911.

—— In his Youngest drama, 1924.

—— A doll's house and the open door, with two letters from Shaw. Theatre Arts Jan 1928.

Montague, C. E. In his Dramatic values, 1911, 1925 (rev).

Henderson, A. Shaw: his life and works. 1911, Cincinnati 1911.

—— In his European dramatists, 1914.

—— Is Shaw a dramatist? New York 1929.

—— Shaw, playboy and prophet. New York 1932, 1956. The official biography.

—— Shaw's stature. Queen's Quart 58 1951.

—— Shaw: man of the century. New York 1956.

—— Shaw and America: the end of a century. Modern Drama 2 1959.

Caro, J. Shaw and Shakespeare. Frankfurt 1912.

Cestre, C. Shaw et son oeuvre. Paris 1912.

Hamon, A. F. A. The technique of Shaw's plays. Tr F. Maurice 1912.

—— Le Molière du xxe siècle: Shaw. Paris 1913; tr 1916.

—— and H. Hamon. Considérations sur l'art dramatique à propos de la comédie de Shaw. Paris 1913.

Armstrong, C. F. In his Shakespeare to Shaw, 1913.

Norwood, G. Euripides and Shaw: an address to the Newport (Mon) Literary Society. 1913, 1921 (in his Euripides and Shaw, with other essays).

Richter, H. Die Quintessenz des Shawismus. E. Studien 46 1913.

Hevesi, S. Shaw—breviarum. Budapest 1914.
McCabe, J. Shaw: a critical study. 1914.
Howe, P. P. Shaw: a critical study. 1915.
Palmer, J. Shaw: harlequin or patriot? New York 1915, London 1915 (as Shaw: an epitaph).
Owen, H. Common sense about the Shaw. 1915.
Parker, D. C. Shaw as a musical critic. Opera Mag (New York) June 1915.
Rehbach, W. Shaw als Dramatiker. Leipzig 1915.
Burton, R. Shaw: the man and the mask. New York 1916.
Scott, D. In his Men of letters, 1916.
Fischer, F. Shaw als Dramatiker und sein Verhältnis zu Henrik Ibsen. Weimar 1917.
Slosson, E. E. In his Six major prophets, 1917.
Skimpole, H. Shaw. 1918.
Harris, F. In his Contemporary portraits, New York 1919.
—— Frank Harris on Shaw: an unauthorised biography based on first hand information, with a postscript by Shaw. 1931.
Duffin, H. C. The quintessence of Shaw. 1920, 1939 (expanded).
Engel, F. Shaw und seine besten Bühnenwerke. Berlin 1921.
Lord, D. A. Shaw. 1921.
—— Martyrs according to Shaw. 1921.
Phelps, W. L. In his Essays on modern dramatists, 1921.
Pearson, H. In his Modern men and mummers, New York 1922, 1938 (in his Thinking it over).
—— Shaw: his life and personality. 1942, 1961.
—— GBS: a postscript. New York 1950, London 1951.
—— The origin of Androcles and the lion. Listener 13 Nov 1952.
—— A Pygmalion pickle: Beerbohm Tree, Mrs Pat and GBS. Theatre Arts Dec 1956.
—— Shaw as producer. Listener 16 Aug 1956.
—— My uninvited collaborator: GBS. Horizon 1 1958.
Jones, H. A. Shaw as a thinker. Eng Rev 36–7 1923.
—— In his Mr Mayor of Shakespeare's town, 1925 (priv ptd).
Nicolaysen, L. Shaw. Munich 1923.
Guedalla, P. In his A gallery, 1924.
Shanks, E. Shaw. 1924.
Collis, J. S. Shaw. 1925, New York 1926. With annotations by Shaw.
Eulenberg, H. Gegen Shaw: eine Streitschrift, mit einer Shaw-Parodie des Verfassers. Dresden 1925.
Whitehead, G. Shaw explained: a critical exposition of the Shavian religion. [1925].
Aas, L. Shaw og Hans Verker. Oslo 1926.
Braybrooke, P. The genius of Shaw. [1926].
—— The subtlety of Shaw. [1930].
Cammaerts, E. Molière and Shaw. Nineteenth Century Sept 1926.
Gardiner, A. G. Certain people of importance. 1926.
Grein, J. T. Notes about Shaw. Illustr London News 7 Aug 1926.
Robertson, J. M. Mr Shaw and the Maid. 1926.
Cohn, E. Eltern und Kinder bei Shaw. Leipzig 1927.
Groos, R. In his Esquisses, Paris 1928.
D'Angelo, E. Shaw's theory of stage representation. Quart Jnl of Speech 15 1929.
Rider, D. Adventures with Shaw. [1929].
Tetauer, F. Shaw: ideologie a dramatika. Prague 1929.
Wagenknecht, E. A guide to Shaw. New York 1929.
Colbourne, M. The real Shaw. Toronto 1930, London 1939 (rev), 1949 (rev), New York 1949.
De Casseres, B. Mencken and Shaw. New York [1930].
Wainger, B. M. Henry Sweet—Shaw's Pygmalion. SP 37 1930.
Brinser, A. The respectability of Shaw. Cambridge Mass 1931.
Craig, E. G. In his Ellen Terry and her secret self, [1931].
—— Reflections on the Irving-Shaw controversy. Listener 17 July 1952.
Crouch, A. P. Shaw: a sketch (strictly unauthorised). Bath [1931–2].
Ellehauge, M. The position of Shaw in European drama and philosophy. Copenhagen 1931.
Vallese, T. Il teatro di Shaw. Rome 1931.
Welby, T. E. Frank Harris—Shaw: an antithesis. Fortnightly Rev 1 Jan 1932.
Burdett, O. A critical stroll through Shaw. London Mercury June 1933.
Hollis, C. Mr Shaw's St Joan. [1933].
Lengnick, P. Ehe und Familie bei Shaw. Königsberg 1933.
Moore, M. Shaw et la France. Paris 1933.
Ubugata, K. Shô o kataru. Tokyo 1933.
Heuser, H. Die Eigenart des Sozialismus Shaws. Frankfurt 1934.
Lehmann, F. W. A. Shaws Verhältnis zu Romantik und Idealismus. Bonn 1934.
Rattray, R. F. Shaw: a chronicle and an introduction. 1934.
—— Shaw: a chronicle. 1951, New York 1951.
'Maurois, André' (E. S. W. Herzog). Shaw. Revue Hebdomadaire March 1935.
—— Shaw par Shaw. Revue de Paris 57 1950.
Gupta, S. C. S. The art of Shaw. 1936.
Heydet, X. Shaw—Kompendium: Verzeichnis und Analyse seiner Werke. Paris 1936.
Knowlton, T. A. Economic theory of Shaw. Orono 1936.
Saxe, J. Shaw's phonetics. Copenhagen 1936.
Sobia, A. Les femmes dans le théâtre de Shaw. Revue de l'Ensignement des Langues Vivantes 1936.
Timmler, M. Die Anschauungen Shaws über die Aufgabe des Theaters auf Grund seiner Theorie und Praxis. Breslau 1936.
Zeller, H. Die Frauengestalten in Shaws dramatischen Werken. Tübingen 1936.
Hackett, J. P. Shaw, George versus Bernard. 1937.
—— Shaw and Yeats. Studies 32 1943.
Ehrmann, R. E. H. Shaw und der Viktorianische Sozialismus. Antwerp 1937.
Lorenz, R. Shaws Auseinandersetzung mit der Tragik des Daseins. Essen 1937.
Sherard, R. H. Shaw, Frank Harris and Oscar Wilde. 1937.
Caudwell, C. In his Studies in a dying culture, 1938.
Wilson, E. Shaw at eighty. In his Triple thinkers, New York 1938, 1948 (rev).
—— Shaw on Shakespeare. 1962.
Shaw, C. M. Bernard's brethren; with comments by Shaw. [1939], New York [1939].
Esdaile, F. Show me Shaw. 1941.
—— Shaw's postscript to fame. [1942].
Smith, W. Shaw and his critics 1892–1938. Poet Lore 47 1941.
Sörensen, E. Shaws Puritanismus. Hamburg 1941.
Dunkel, W. O. Shaw. Sewanee Rev 50 1942.
—— The essence of Shaw's dramaturgy. College Eng March 1949.
Isaacs, E. J. R. The playwright as critic: GBS. Theatre Arts 36 1942.
Pilger, E. Shaw in Deutschland. Münster 1942.
Strauss, E. Shaw: art and Socialism. 1942.
—— Shaw. 1950.
Barzun, J. Shaw in twilight. Kenyon Rev 5 1943.
Cohen, A. D. The religion of GBS. Adelphi 20 1943.
Nathan, G. J. Shaw. Amer Mercury 58 1944, 70 1950.
—— Kid Hepburn vs Rocky Shaw. Theatre Arts Nov 1952.
Shaw birthday issue. Saturday Rev of Lit July 1944.
Robson, E. W. and M. M. Shaw among the innocents. [1945].
Titterton, W. R. So this is Shaw. [1945].
West, E. J. GBS: music and Shakespearean blank verse. In Elizabethan studies in honor of G. F. Reynolds, Boulder 1945.

— An epitaph for Shaw. Western Humanities Rev 5 1951.
— Shaw and his critics 1946–51. Quart Jnl of Speech 38 1952.
— 'Arma virumque': Shaw did not sing. Colorado Quart 1 1953.
— Shaw's criticism of Ibsen: a reconsideration. Boulder 1953.
— Saint Joan: a modern classic reconsidered. Quart Jnl of Speech 40 1954.
— GBS and the rival queens: Duse and Bernhardt. Quart Jnl of Speech 43 1957.
Bentley, E. R. The playwright as thinker: a study of drama in modern times. New York 1946.
— Shaw's politics. Kenyon Rev 8 1946.
— Shaw: a reconsideration. New York 1947, Norfolk Conn 1957 (amended), London 1967.
— Shaw dead. Theatre Arts Jan 1951.
— My fair lady. Modern Drama 1 1958.
— The making of a dramatist 1892–1903. Tulane Drama Rev 1960.
Currall I. L. Shavio Phoenetica: a system of phonetic English based on Shaw's instructions. 1946 (priv ptd).
— To GBS from ILC: an open letter. [1946] (priv ptd).
Ellgar, H. Shaw: ett liv-ett Geni. Stockholm 1946.
Irvine, W. Shaw's musical criticism. Musical Quart 32 1946.
— Man and superman: a step in Shavian disillusionment. HLQ 10 1947.
— Shaw's early novels. Trollopian 2 1947.
— Shaw and Chesterton. Virginia Quart Rev 23 1947.
— Shaw, the Fabians and the Utilitarians. JHI 7 1947.
— Shaw's Quintessence of Ibsenism. South Atlantic Quart 67 1947.
— The universe of GBS. New York 1949.
— Shaw and America. Modern Drama 2 1959.
Jennings, R. 'Nearly Methuselah' and 'Shaw v. Shakespeare'. Nineteenth Century Aug 1946.
Loewenstein, F. E. Mr Shaw regrets—. Amer Mercury 63 1946.
— Do you remember, Mr Shaw? Adam 14 1946.
— The autograph manuscripts of Shaw. Book Handbook 2 1947.
— Shaw through the camera. 1948.
Peacock, R. In his Poet in the theatre, 1946.
Trebitsch, S. Shaw dem Neunzigjähringe. Zürich 1946.
— In his Chronicle of a life, 1953.
Wherly, E. S. Shaw for the millions. [Belfast] [1946].
Winsten, S. (ed). GBS 90: aspects of Shaw's life and work. 1946, New York 1946 (without Winsten's introd.)
— Days with Shaw. 1949, New York 1949.
— Shaw's corner. 1952, New York 1953.
— Jesting apostle: the private life of Shaw. 1956, New York 1957.
Evans, H. M. and D. A. A visit with GBS. Berkeley 1947.
Hobsbawm, E. J. Shaw's Socialism. Science & Soc 11 1947.
Nethercot, A. H. The quintessence of idealism. PMLA 62 1947.
— The truth about Candida. PMLA 64 1947.
— The schizophrenia of Shaw. Amer Scholar 21 1952.
— Shaw, philosopher. PMLA 69 1954.
— Men and supermen: the Shavian portrait gallery. Cambridge Mass 1954.
— Shaw, ladies and gentlemen. Modern Drama 2 1959.
— Shaw's feud with higher education. Jnl of General Education 16 1964.
Clarke, W. Shaw: an appreciation and interpretation. Altrincham 1948.
Glicksberg, C. I. Shaw versus science. Dalhousie Rev 28 1948.
— The criticism of Shaw. South Atlantic Quart 50 1951.
— Shaw the novelist. Prairie Schooner 25 1951.
Rebora, P. Shaw: comico e tragico. Florence 1948.
Fergusson, F. The theatricality of Shaw and Pirandello. Partisan Rev 16 1949.
Joad, C. E. M. Shaw. 1949.
— (ed). Shaw and society: an anthology and a symposium. 1953.
Jones, W. S. H. One of our conquerors. London Quart Jan, April 1949.
Laing, A. M. (ed). In praise of Shaw: an anthology for old and young. [1949].
Bridie, J. Shaw as playwright. New Statesman 11 Nov 1950.
Dickmann, E. El mensaje de Shaw al cumplir 94 años. Buenos Aires [1950].
Fuller, E. Shaw: critic of Western morals. New York 1950.
Gilkes, A. M. GBS, GKC and paradox. Fortnightly Rev Oct 1950.
Höffinghoff, G. Shaw als Publizist. Münster 1950.
Jaffe, G. Shaws opplatning av dramatisk diktkunst sammenlighnet med Shakespeares. Edda 50 1950.
Pettis, A. GBS: in tune with the infinitesimal. Catholic World 1950.
Philipp, G. Shaws Stellung zu Demokratie und Faschismus. Münster 1950.
Smith, J. P. GBS on the theatre. Tamarack Rev 15 1950.
Stoppel, H. Das Bild Menschlicher Grösse bei Shaw. Kiel 1950.
Ward, A. C. Shaw. 1950, 1951, 1957, 1960 (all rev).
— Shaw. 1951.
West, A. A good man fallen among Fabians. 1950.
Baiwir, A. The legacy of Shaw. Revue des Langues Vivantes 17 1951.
— Nouvelle lumière sur Shaw. Ibid.
Baldi, S. Per l'arte di Shaw. Revue des Lettres Modernes June 1951.
Boas, F. S. Joan of Arc in Shakespeare, Schiller and Shaw. Shakespeare Quart 2 1951.
Casson, L. GBS and the Court Theatre. Listener 12 July 1951.
Clemens, C. Shaw and Mark Twain. N & Q March 1951.
Crane, M. Pygmalion: Shaw's dramatic theory and practice. PMLA 66 1951.
Ervine, St J. The mind of Shaw. Listener 15 Nov 1951.
— Portrait of Shaw. Listener 18 Aug 1955.
— Shaw: his life, work and friends. 1956.
— GBS in the theatre. Listener 12 July 1956.
Fechter, P. Shaw. Gütersloh 1951.
Filipovic, R. Shaw. Linguistitia Republika 7 1951.
Gassner, J. Shaw as drama critic. Theatre Arts May 1951.
— When Shaw boils the pot. Theatre Arts July 1953.
— In his Theatre in our times, New York 1954.
— Shaw and the making of the modern mind. College Eng 1962.
— In his Ideas in the drama, New York 1964.
Hackett, F. Shaw—and Wells. Atlantic Monthly May 1951.
Harvey, C. J. D. Shaw. Ons Eie Boek 17 1951.
Johnson, A. E. Encounters with GBS. Dalhousie Rev 31 1951.
Kawatake, S. Shaw in Japan. Rising Generation 97 1951.
Kochanowski, E. Evolution und Übermensch bei Shaw im Anschluss an das Denken des 19 Jahrhunderts. Kiel 1951.
Kropotkin, A. Pleasant memories of Shaw. Amer Quart 72 1951.
Langner, L. Shaw and 'Back to Methuselah'. Theatre Arts Nov 1951.
— In his Magic curtain, New York 1951.
— GBS and the lunatic. New York 1963.
MacCarthy, D. Shaw. 1951, New York 1951 (as Shaw's plays in review).
Mann, T. GBS—mankind's friend. Yale Rev 40 1951; Listener 18 Jan 1951.

Morgan, L. H. Shaw the playwright. Books Abroad 25 1951.
Patch, B. Thirty years with GBS. 1951, New York 1951.
Predan, J. Shaw. Hladinska Revija 6 1951.
Russell, B. Shaw. Virginia Quart Rev 27 1951.
— Shaw, the admirable iconoclast. Listener 3 Sept 1953.
Sheean, V. My last visit with Shaw. Atlantic Monthly Jan 1951.
Torbarnia, J. Shaw: Cetiri drame. Matica Hrvatska 1951.
Ussher, A. Shaw's 'feast of reason'. Listener 9 Aug 1951.
— Three great Irishmen: Shaw, Yeats, Joyce. 1952.
Vandewalle, G. Shaw en het Britse socialisme. Ghent 1951.
Vidan, I. Uz izdanje četiriju drama Shawa. Hrvatska Kolo 4, April 1951.
Weber, C. J. A talk with Shaw. Colby Lib Quart 3 1951.
D'Agostino, N. Shaw (ritratti critici contemporanei). Belfragor 7 1952.
Besenbruch, M. Shaw als Historiker. Erlangen 1952.
Elliott, R. C. Shaw's Captain Bluntschli: a latter-day Falstaff. MLN 67 1952.
Hirai, H. Shaw and Oscar Wilde. Eibungaku-kenkyu 28 1952.
Jacobson, S. Androcles in Hollywood. Theatre Arts Dec 1952.
Kirchner, G. Shaws Pygmalion und Smolletts Peregrine Pickle. Die Neueren Sprachen 56 1952.
Krutch, J. W. GBS enters heaven (?). Saturday Rev 24 May 1952.
Lutter, T. Shaw. Budapest 1952.
Molnar, J. Shaw's four kinds of women. Theatre Arts Dec 1952.
Smith, J. P. Superman versus man: Shaw on Shakespeare. Yale Rev 42 1952.
— The unrepentant pilgrim: a study in the development of Shaw. Boston 1965, London 1966.
Holberg, S. M. The economic rogue in the plays of Shaw. Buffalo 1953.
Kronenberger, L. (ed). Shaw: a critical survey. Cleveland [1953].
McDowell, F. P. W. Technique, symbol and theme in Heartbreak House. PMLA 68 1953.
— 'The eternal against the expedient': structure and theme in Shaw's The apple cart. Modern Drama 2 1959.
— Spiritual and political reality: Shaw's The simpleton of the Unexpected Isles. Modern Drama 3 1960.
— Another look at Shaw: a reassessment of his dramatic theory, his practice and his achievement. Drama Survey 1 1961.
— Crisis and unreason: Shaw's On the rocks. Educational Theatre Jnl Oct 1961.
— Protean wit and wisdom: Shaw's uncollected essays and speeches. Modern Drama 5 1962.
— More GBS. Drama Survey 1 1962.
— Heaven, hell and turn-of-the-century London: reflections on Shaw's Man and superman. Drama Survey 2 1963.
— Shaw's increasing stature. Drama Survey 3 1964.
Mehta, L. S. Shaw: the successor to Shakespeare. Modern Rev 94 1953.
Shiras, M. GBS: a profile. Chicago Rev 7 1953.
Morilia, R. Shaw o dell'amor platonico. Letterature Moderne 5 1954.
Cecchi, E. L'eclisse di Shaw. Moyen Age June 1955.
Drew, A. P. Pygmalion and Pickwick. N & Q May 1955.
Gatch, K. H. The last plays of Shaw: dialectic and despair. In English stage comedy, ed W. K. Wimsatt, New York 1955.
Krabbe, H. Shaw on Shakespeare and English Shakespearian acting. Aarhus and Copenhagen 1955.
Lüdeke, H. Some remarks on Shaw's history plays. E Studies 36 1955.
McCarthy, M. Shaw at the Phoenix. Partisan Rev 22 1955.
Mullik, B. R. Shaw. Delhi 1955, 1957, 1960, 1964 (rev and enlarged).
Percy, E. Shaw: a personal memory. Listener 26 May 1955.
Perruchot, H. La haine des masques: Montherlant, Camus, Shaw. Paris 1955.
Schirmer-Imhoff, R. Saint Joan: die Quelle und ihre Bearbeitung. Anglia 74 1955.
Shattuck, C. H. Shaw's 'bad quarto'. JEGP 54 1955.
Stoppel, H. Shaw and sainthood. E Studies 36 1955.
Albert, S. Shaw: the artist as philosopher. Jnl of Aesthetics 14 1956.
The nun and the dramatist: Shaw to the Abbess of Stanbrook. Atlantic Monthly July–Aug 1956, Cornhill July 1956. An extract from In a great tradition: tribute to Dame Laurentia McLachlan by the Benedictines of Stanbrook, 1956.
Bibesco, M. Memories of Shaw. Listener 26 April 1956.
Borinski, L. Shaw und die Stilexperimente des frühen 20 Jahrhunderts. Die Neueren Sprachen 60 1956.
Clurman, R. 'GBS 100'. New York Herald Tribune Book Rev 22 July 1956.
Couchman, G. W. Shaw, Caesar and the critics. Speech Monograph 23 1956.
— Here was a Caesar: Shaw's comedy today. PMLA 72 1957.
— Antony and Cleopatra and the subjective convention. PMLA 76 1961.
Frank, J. Major Barbara—Shaw's Divine Comedy. PMLA 71 1956.
Hanley, T. I. The strange triangle of GBS. Boston [1956].
Laurence, D. H. The facts about Why she would not. Theatre Arts Aug 1956.
— Genesis of a dramatic critic. Modern Drama 2 1959.
Oppel, H. Shaw—Versuch einer Characterskizze. Die Neueren Sprachen 60 1956.
Papajewski, H. Shaw's chronicle play St Joan. Germanisch-romanische Monatsschrift 37 1956.
Papers of the Shaw Festival. Ed M. W. Steinberg, Vancouver 1956.
Richardson, H. B. The Pygmalion reaction. Psychoanalytic Rev 63 1956.
Schindler, B. Shaw: seine Kritik an der englischen Lebensform in seinen sozialkritischen Dramen. Halle 1956.
Sion, G. Shaw, le paladin du monde occidentale. Revue Générale Belge (Brussels) Aug 1956.
Smith, W. S. Shaw's bout with Christianity. Nation (New York) 28 July 1956.
Stokes, S. Conversation with Shaw. Listener 6 Sept 1956.
Tippett, M. An Irish Basset-Horn. Listener 26 July 1956.
Valency, M. Shaw: the durable dramatist. Theatre Arts July 1956.
Arnot, R. P. Shaw and William Morris: a lecture. 1957.
Balutowa, B. Dramat Bernarda Shaw. Lodz 1957.
Barber, G. S. Shaw's contributions to music criticism. PMLA 72 1957.
Casserley, C. J. Living at Shaw's Corner. Listener Oct 1957.
Collins, P. A. W. Shaw on Shakespeare. Shakespeare Quart 8 1957.
Debnicki, A. and R. Górski. Shaw no scenach polskich. Okres pierwszy 1903–13. Pt 2.2. 1957.
Fremantle, A. Shaw and religion. Commonweal 67 1957.
Fried, V. Tecka za Shawem? Svetová Literatura 6 1957.
Galinsky, H. Shaw als Gegenstand der Kritik und als Quelle dramatischer Anregung für T. S. Eliot. Germanisch-romanische Monatsschrift 38 1957.
Gordan, J. D. Shaw 1856–1950: an exhibition from the Berg Collection. BNYPL March–May 1957.

Harrison, R. and S. McKenna. Shaw and the actor. Theatre Arts March 1957.
Helsztyński, S. Shaw w setna rocznice urodzin 1856–1956. Kwartalnik Neolilogiczny 1957.
Johnson, E. Dickens and Shaw: critics of society. Virginia Quart Rev 33 1957.
Jones, H. M. Shaw as Victorian. Victorian Stud 1 1957.
Melchinger, S. Drama zwischen Shaw und Brecht. Bremen 1957.
O'Donnell, N. F. Shaw, Bunyan and Puritanism. PMLA 72 1957.
—— The conflict of wills in Shaw's tragicomedy. Modern Drama 4 1962.
Batson, E. J. GBS: the orator and the man. English 14 1962.
—— The religion of Shaw. Aryan Path 34 1963.
Cheny, D. R. The Fabianism of Shaw. Queen's Quart 69 1962.
Dupler, D. An analytic study of the use of rhetorical devices in three selected plays of Shaw: Saint Joan, Androcles and the lion, and Candida. Speech Monographs 29 1962.
Eaton, P. Shaw and Shaviana. Book Collector 11 1962.
Jones, A. R. In Contemporary theatre, ed J. R. Brown and B. Harris 1962.
Meyer, H. Der Dramatiker Shaw. Neue Deutsche Hefte 89 1962.
Nucete Sardi, J. Shaw: su teatro y su mejor personaje. Revista Nacional de Cultura (Caracas) 153 1962.
Ohmann, R. M. Shaw: the style and the man. Middletown Conn 1962.
Perdeck, A. Bernard Shaw. Hague 1962.
Pesch, L. In his Die romantische Rebellion in der modernen Literatur und Kunst, Munich 1962.
Shenfield, M. Shaw: a pictorial biography. 1962.
Soper, P. GBS as play director. In Studies in honor of John C. Hodges and Alwin Thaler, ed R. B. Davies and J. L. Lievsay 1962.
Styan, J. L. In his Dark comedy: the development of modern comic tragedy, 1962.
Benedek, M. G. B. Shaw. Budapest 1963.
Brooks, H. F. and J. R. Dickens in Shaw. Dickensian 59 1963.
Crompton, L. Shaw's challenge to Liberalism. Prairie Schooner 37 1963.
Demaray, J. G. Shaw and C. E. M. Joad: the adventures of two Puritans in their search for God. PMLA 78 1963.
Du Cann, C. G. L. The loves of Shaw. 1963.
Duerksen, R. A. Shelley and Shaw. PMLA 78 1963.
Dukore, B. F. Shaw improves Shaw. Modern Drama 6 1963.
Dunbar, J. Mrs GBS: a biographical portrait of Charlotte Shaw. 1963.
Mandell, O. (ed). The theatre of Don Juan: a collection of plays and views 1630–1963. 1963.
Meisel, M. Shaw and the nineteenth-century theatre. Princeton 1963.
Nichols, M. H. Rhetoric and criticism. Baton Rouge 1963. On Kenneth Burke, I. A. Richards, Shaw.
Purdom, C. B. A guide to the plays of Shaw. 1963.
Quinn, M. Form and intention: a negative view of Arms and the man. CQ 5 1963.
Williamson, A. Shaw: man and artist. New York 1963.
Woodbridge, H. E. Shaw: creative artist. Carbondale 1963.
Armstrong, W. A. Shaw and Forbes-Robertson's Hamlet. Shakespeare Quart 15 1964.
Brown, T. J. Shaw 1856–1950. Book Collector 13 1964.
Cavallini, G. Ibsen, Shaw, Pirandello: analia della funzione sociopedagogica del teatro. Milan 1964.
Cohn, R. Hell on the twentieth-century stage. Wisconsin Stud in Contemporary Lit 5 1964.
Gollin, R. M. Beerbohm, Wilde, Shaw and the Good-natured critic. BNYPL Feb 1964.
Rosset, B. C. ('Ozy'). The war against Shaw. New York 1957.
—— Shaw of Dublin: the formative years. University Park Pa 1964.
Mayne, F. Types and contrasts in Shaw. Eng Stud in Africa 7 1964.
Roy, R. M. Shaw's philosophy of life. Calcutta 1964.
Solomon, S. J. The ending of Pygmalion: a structural view. Educational Theatre Jnl 16 1964.
—— Saint Joan as epic tragedy. Modern Drama 6 1964.
Watson, B. B. A Shavian guide to the intelligent woman. 1964.
Abbott, A. S. Shaw and Christianity. New York [1965].
Brown, I. Shaw in his time. [1965].
Costello, D. P. The serpent's eye: Shaw and the cinema. Notre Dame [1965].
Kaufmann, R. J. (ed). Shaw: a collection of critical essays. Englewood Cliffs NJ [1965].
O'Donovan, J. Shaw and the charlatan genius. Dublin [1965].
Pilecki, G. A. Shaw's Geneva. Hague 1965.
Romm, A. S. Dzhordzh Shou 1856–1950. Leningrad 1965.
Adam, R. What Shaw *really* said. [1966].
Hughes, E. Bernard Shaw. Moscow 1966.
See also Shaw Soc Bull nos 1–50 1946–53, *later* Shavian no 1– 1953–; Shaw Soc of America Bull I nos 1–2 New York 1951, *later* Shaw Bull 1 no 3– 1952–; Shaw Rev I no 1 [1959]–; Independent Shavian I no 1– 1962–. Modern Drama 2 Sept 1959 *was completely devoted to critical works on Shaw.*

OSCAR FINGALL O'FLAHERTIE WILLS WILDE

1854–1900

Bibliographies

'Mason, Stuart' (C. S. Millard). A bibliography of the poems of Wilde. 1907, 1914, 1967.
—— Bibliography of Wilde. 1908 (priv ptd), [1914]; ed T. d'A. Smith 1967.
Cowan, R. E. and W. A. Clark. The library of W. A. Clark: Wilde and Wildeana. San Francisco 1922.
Finzi, J. C. Wilde and his literary circle: a catalogue of manuscripts and letters in William Andrews Clark Memorial Library. 1957.

Collections

Oscariana: epigrams. 1895, 1895, 1910 (a new selection taken from Sebastian Melmoth, below), 1912. All priv ptd.
Sebastian Melmoth. 1904, 1905, 1908, 1911.
The best of Wilde: being a collection of the best poems and prose extracts of the writer, collected by Oscar Hermann. Ed W. W. Massee, New York [1905].
Epigrams and aphorisms. Boston 1905.
Poems. 2 vols New York 1906.
The wisdom of Wilde, selected with introduction and index by Temple Scott. New York 1906, 1908.
[Works]. 14 vols 1908. 13 vols pbd by Methuen, London: the remaining vol, The picture of Dorian Gray, pbd by Charles Carrington, Paris.
[Works. Ed R. B. Ross]. 12 vols (with 2 suppl vols). 1908, 1909, 14 vols Boston 1910, 1911.
The Wilde calendar, with some unrecorded sayings selected by Stuart Mason. 1910, 1911 (rev), 1914 (rev).
Selected poems, including the Ballad of Reading Gaol. 1911 (4 edns), 1925 (13th edn). Selected by R. B. Ross.
Charmides, and other poems. 1913, 1914.
Aphorisms, selected and arranged by G. N. Sutton. 1914.
Selected prose. 1914. With preface by R. B. Ross.
Werke. Ed A. Zweig 2 vols Berlin [1930].

Works, with drawings by Donia Nachshen. [1931].
Complete works. 4 vols Paris 1936.
Obras completas; prefacio, traducción y notas de Julio Gómez de la Serna. Madrid 1943.
Selected works with twelve unpublished letters. Ed R. Aldington 1946.
Castle Press edition of works. 1948–.
Essays. Ed H. Pearson 1950.
Five famous plays. Ed A. Harris 1952.
Plays, prose writings and poems etc. Ed H. Pearson 1955. A reissue of The picture of Dorian Gray, The importance of being earnest, The ballad of Reading Gaol and other works, 1930.
Selected writings. Ed R. Ellmann, Oxford 1961.
Complete works. Ed P. Drake, introd by V. Holland 1966. A rev edn of works ed G. F. Maine 1948, including the 4-act version of Importance of being earnest.

§1

Newdigate prize poem: Ravenna, recited in the Theatre, Oxford 26 June 1878. Oxford 1878.
Poems. 1881 (3 edns); 1882 (4th–5th edns), 1892 (priv ptd), Boston 1881, 1882.
Vera, or the nihilists: a drama. (New York, Union Square 20 Aug 1883). 1880 (priv ptd), 1882 (priv ptd), 1902 (priv ptd).
The happy Prince and other tales, illustrated by Walter Crane and Jacomb Hood. 1888, 1888, 1889, 1902, Boston 1888; tr Spanish, 1922.
The Duchess of Padua: a tragedy of the xvi century, written in Paris in the xix century. (New York, Broadway 26 Jan 1891 as Guido Ferranti). [New York 1883] (priv ptd), 1907 (prefatory letter by R. B. Ross).
The picture of Dorian Gray. [1891], 1895, Paris 1901 etc; tr Czech, [1905]; Danish, 1905; Dutch, [1893]; Finnish, 1906; French, 1895; German, [1901]; Greek, [1912]; Hungarian, 1907; Italian, [1906]; Polish, 1906; Russian, [1905]; Swedish, [1905]; Yiddish [1912]. First pbd in Lippincott's Mag July 1890 in a version lacking 6 chs.
Intentions. 1891, 1894; tr French, 1905; Spanish, [1926].
Lord Arthur Savile's crime, and other stories. 1891, New York 1891; tr Spanish, [1922].
A house of pomegranates; the design and decoration by C. Ricketts and C. H. Shannon. 1891; tr Spanish, [1922]; German, 1914.
Lady Windermere's fan: a play about a good woman. (St J 20 Feb 1892). 1893, 1893, nd; tr Italian, 1912; Spanish, 1920; French adaptation, 1956.
A woman of no importance. C. (H 19 April 1893). 1894, New York 1894.
The sphinx, with decorations by Charles Ricketts. 1894, 1910 (with notes by R. B. Ross).
An ideal husband. D. (H 3 Jan 1895). 1899, [1914]. With preface signed by R. B. Ross.
The importance of being earnest: a trivial comedy for serious people (St J 14 Feb 1895). 1899, nd, New York nd; ed V. Holland 2 vols New York 1957 (original and longest version, from ms); tr Spanish, 1920.
The soul of man. 1895 (priv ptd), 1912 (as The soul of man under Socialism; with preface by R. B. Ross). Originally pbd under longer title in Fortnightly Rev Feb 1891 and included under shorter title in Sebastian Melmoth, 1891.
Salomé: drame en un acte. (Paris, Théâtre de l'Œuvre 11 Feb 1896; London, New Stage Club, Bijou theatre 10 Feb 1905). Paris 1893; tr Lord Alfred B. Douglas 1894 (illustr Aubrey Beardsley), 1906, 1912; 1906, 1908, 1911 (without illustrations); tr Dutch, 1918; Spanish, 1919.
The ballad of Reading Gaol, by C.3.3. 1898 (6 edns), 1899, 1910, 1910; tr French, 1898; German, [1907]; Hungarian, 1912; Norwegian, [1915]; Russian, 1919; Swedish, 1907.
The portrait of Mr W. H. Portland Maine 1901; ed V. Holland 1958. First pbd in Blackwood's Mag July 1889; later rptd with Lord Arthur Savile's crime, above.
De profundis. 1905 (with preface by R. B. Ross), 1907 etc, New York 1908, [1909] (with 80 pp. of new matter); ed V. Holland 1949; tr German, 1905; French, 1905; Spanish, [1925].
—— The suppressed portion of De profundis now for the first time published by his literary executor, Robert Ross. New York 1913 (priv ptd). Fuller text of whole work in Letters, ed Hart-Davis, 1962, below.
A Florentine tragedy. (Literary Theatre Society 10 June 1906). Written 1893–4; ms lost; first pbd in first collected edn of the works, 1908, with opening scene by T. Sturge Moore, replacing one lost. Rptd in subsequent collected edns.
To M[argaret] B[urne] J[ones]. [1920] (priv ptd). With note by 'Stuart Mason' (C. S. Millard).
For love of the King: a Burmese masque. [1922].

Letters

Four letters [to Robert Ross]—not included in the English edition of De profundis. 1906 (priv ptd).
Wilde v. Whistler: being an acrimonious correspondence on art between Wilde and James A. McNeill Whistler. 1906 (priv ptd).
Resurgam: unpublished letters. [Ed C. K. Shorter] 1917 (priv ptd).
After Reading: letters to Robert Ross. 1921.
After Berneval: letters to Robert Ross. 1922.
Letters to the Sphinx (Ada Leverson); with reminiscences of the author by Ada Leverson. 1930.
Letters. Ed R. Hart-Davis 1962.
Gollin, R. M. Beerbohm, Wilde, Shaw and 'the good-natured critic': some new letters. BNYPL Feb 1964.

§2

Gómez Carillo, E. Esquisses: siluetas de escritores y artistas. Madrid 1892.
Archer, W. In his Theatrical 'World', 5 vols 1893–7.
'Y.T.O.', L. C. M. S. Amery, F. W. Hirst and H. A. A. Cruso. Aristophanes at Oxford. Oxford 1894. A satire, in verse.
Young, D. Apologia pro Wilde. [1895].
Grein, J. T. In his Dramatic criticism vol 3, 1902.
Sherard, R. H. Wilde: the story of an unhappy friendship. 1902 (priv ptd), 1905.
—— The life of Wilde, with a full reprint of the famous revolutionary article Jacta alea est, by Jane Francesca Elgee, mother of Wilde. 1906. Supplemented by The real Wilde [1917].
—— Wilde twice defended. Chicago 1934.
—— Bernard Shaw, Frank Harris and Wilde. 1937.
Gide, A. Wilde. In his Prétextes: réflexions critiques sur quelques points de littérature et de morale, Paris 1903, 1910 (as Wilde: In memoriam (souvenirs), le De profundis); tr 'Stuart Mason' (C. S. Millard) 1905 (with introd, notes and bibliography).
—— Wilde. 1951. Tr with addns.
Hagemann, C. Wilde: Studien zur modernen Weltliteratur. Minden 1904.
Blei, F. In memoriam Wilde. Leipzig 1905.
La Jeunesse, E., A. Gide and F. Blei. Recollections of Wilde by E. La Jeunesse. Greenwich Conn 1905.
Young, J. M. S. Osrac the self-sufficient and other poems, with a memoir of the late Wilde. 1905.
Glaenzer, R. B. Decorative art in America: a lecture by Wilde; together with letters, reviews and interviews. New York 1906.
The trial of Wilde, from the shorthand reports. 1906.
Leadman, W. M. The literary position of Wilde. Westminster Rev Aug 1906.

Ingleby, L. C. Wilde. 1907.
—— Wilde: some reminiscences. 1912.
Hankin, St J. The collected plays of Wilde. Fortnightly Rev May 1908.
Weisz, E. Psychologische Streifzüge über Wilde. Leipzig 1908. With introd by R. Foerster.
Woodbridge, H. E. Wilde as a poet. Poet Lore 19 1908.
Balen, C. L. van. Manner en vrouwen van beteekenis in onze dagen. Haarlem 1910.
Esdaile, A. J. K. The new Hellenism. Fortnightly Rev Nov 1910.
Brémont, A. de Wilde and his mother: a memoir. 1911.
Henderson, A. In his Interpreters of life and the modern spirit, 1911.
Crosland, T. W. H. The first stone: on reading the unpublished parts of the De profundis. 1912 (priv ptd).
Kenilworth, W. W. A study of Wilde. New York 1912.
Ransome, A. Wilde: a critical study. 1912, [1913].
Wilde, three times tried. 1912.
Bock, E. J. Walter Paters Einfluss auf Wilde. Bonn 1913.
Hopkins, R. T. Wilde: a study of the man and his work, with introduction by T. M. Williams. 1913.
Howe, P. P. In his Dramatic portraits, 1913.
Bendz, E. The influence of Pater and Matthew Arnold in the prose writings of Wilde. Gothenberg 1914.
—— Wilde: a retrospect. Vienna 1921.
Birnbaum, M. Wilde: fragments and memories. 1914.
Douglas, Lord A. Wilde and myself. 1914.
—— Wilde: a summing-up. 1940, 1962.
'Mason, Stuart' (C. S. Millard). Wilde: art and morality—a defence of the Picture of Dorian Gray. 1915. With the correspondence called forth by the book, and bibliography.
—— Wilde and the aesthetic movement. Dublin 1920.
—— Who wrote For love of the King? Birmingham 1926.
Wood, A. I. P. Wilde as a critic. North Amer Rev Dec 1915.
Fehr, B. Studien zu Wildes Gedichten. Berlin 1918.
—— Das gelbe Buch in Wildes Dorian Gray. E Studien 55 1921.
Harris, F. Wilde: his life and confessions: together with memories of Wilde, by Bernard Shaw. 2 vols New York 1918; ed G. B. Shaw 1938, East Lansing Michigan 1959 (4th edn). *See* also Harris, Contemporary portraits vol 1, 1915.
Richter, H. Wildes Persönlichkeit in seinen Gedichten. E Studien 54 1920.
Le Gallienne, R. Wilde and Willie Hughes. Bookman (New York) Oct 1921.
Engel, F. Wilde und sein besten Bühnenwerke: eine Einführung. Berlin 1922.
Duthuit, G. Le rose et le noir: de Walter Pater à Wilde. Paris 1923.
Housman, L. Echo de Paris: a study from life. 1923. Recollections of a conversation between the author, Wilde et al.
Jackson, H. In his Eighteen nineties, 1923.
Powys, J. C. In his Suspended judgments, New York 1923.
Lintot, B. Wilde as a letter-writer. Littell's Living Age 320 1924.
Shanks, E. Wilde. London Mercury July 1924.
González-Ruano, C. Notas sobre Wilde. Madrid 1925.
Choisy, L. F. Wilde. Paris 1927.
'Maurois, André' (E. S. W. Herzog). In his Etudes anglaises: Dickens, Walpole, Ruskin et Wilde, Paris 1927.
Rudwin, M. Wilde et Barbey d'Aurévilly. Revue Anglo-américaine 6 1927.
Cook, H. Lucius: French sources of Wilde's Picture of Dorian Gray. Romanic Rev 19 1928.
Davray, H. D. Wilde: la tragédie finale; suivi d'épisodes et souvenirs et des apocryphes. Paris 1928.
Temborius, H. Neuromantische Wesenzüge bei Wilde. Zeitschrift für Französischen und Englischen Unterricht 27 1928.
Atkinson, G. T. Wilde at Oxford. Cornhill Mag May 1929.
Braybrooke, P. Wilde: a study. 1930.
Herzog, A. Die Märchen Wildes. Mulhouse 1930.
Symons, A. A study of Wilde. 1930.
Thompson, V. The two deaths of Wilde. San Francisco 1930.
Lemonnier, L. La vie de Wilde. Paris 1931.
Cooper-Prichard, A. H. Conversations with Wilde. 1931.
Eichbaum, G. Die persönlichen und literarischen Beziehungen zwischen Wilde und James MacNeill Whistler. Bibliographie für Englische Studien 65 1931.
Ricketts, C. S. Wilde: recollections by Jean Paul Raymond and Charles Ricketts. 1932.
Ellehauge, M. Initial stages in the development of the English problem-play. E Studien 66 1932.
Herbert Spencer and Wilde: from Works and days, the dairy of Michael Field. Ed T. S. Moore, Cornhill Mag May 1932.
Evans, B. I. In his English poetry in the later nineteenth century, 1933, 1966 (rev).
Renier, G. J. Wilde. 1933.
Zanco, A. Wilde. Genoa 1934.
Silver, R. G. Oscar makes a call [on Whitman]. Colophon 20 1935.
Lavrin, J. In his Aspects of modernism from Wilde to Pirandello, 1936.
Lewis, L. and H. J. Smith. Wilde discovers America. New York 1936.
O'Sullivan, V. Aspects of Wilde. 1936.
Flanagan, J. T. Wilde's twin city appearances. Minnesota History 17 1936.
Snider, R. Satire in the comedies of Congreve, Sheridan, Wilde and Noel Coward. Orono Maine 1937.
—— Wilde's progress down east. New England Quart 13 1940.
Saix, G. de. Wilde et le théâtre. Mercure de France 279 1937.
—— La femme couverte de joyaux: version française inédite établie. L'Age Nouveau June 1938.
—— Une tragédie de femme par Wilde. Mercure de France 286 1938.
—— Le cinquième évangile selon Saint Oscar Wilde: dix-neuf contes inédits. Mercure de France 296 1940.
Brasol, B. Wilde. 1938.
Ullmann, S. von. Synästhesien in den dichterischen Werken von Oscar Wilde. E Studien 72 1938.
'Kingsmill, Hugh' (H. K. Lunn). The intelligent man's guide to Wilde. Fortnightly Rev Sept 1938.
Franzero, C. M. Vita di Wilde. Florence 1938.
Hicks, G. In his Figures of transition, New York 1939.
Perry, H. T. E. In his Masters of dramatic comedy and their social themes, Cambridge Mass 1939.
Smithers, J. The early life and vicissitudes of Jack Smithers [Wilde's publisher]. 1939.
'Winwar, Frances' (Frances Grebanier). Wilde and the yellow nineties. New York 1940.
Kernahan, C. Wilde and Heine. Dublin Mag Jan–March 1940.
Wilson, T. G. Victorian doctor, Sir W. Wilde. 1942. On Wilde's father.
Wyndham, H. A Chelsea Récamier: Wilde's mother. Catholic World May 1943.
—— 'Speranza' (Lady Wilde) and her first editor. English 6 1946.
—— When Wilde was editor. Life & Letters 55 1947.
—— 'Edited by Wilde'. Lib Rev 17 1949.
Nethercot, A. H. Wilde and the devil's advocate. PMLA 59 1944.
—— Wilde on subdividing himself. PMLA 60 1944.
Bentley, E. R. In his Playwright as thinker: a study of drama in modern times, New York 1946.
Pearson, H. The life of Wilde. 1946.

Roditi, E. Wilde's poetry as art history. Poetry 69 1946.
— Wilde. Norfolk Conn 1947.
— Wilde and Henry James. Kansas Univ City Rev 1948.
Wilson, E. 'One must always seek what is most tragic'. New Yorker 29 June 1946.
Agate, J. Wilde and the theatre. Masque 3 1947.
— An unwise forgery. Princeton Univ Lib Chron 8 1947.
Maurer, O. A Philistine source for Dorian Gray. PQ 26 1947.
Wimberley, L. Wilde meets Woodberry. Prairie Schooner 12 1947.
Merle, R. Wilde. 1948.
— Wilde on la 'destinée' de l'homosexuel. Paris 1955.
Pick, J. Divergent disciples of Walter Pater. Thought 23 1948.
Oswald, V. A. Wilde, Stefan George, Heliogabalus. MLQ 10 1949.
Thomas, J. D. The composition of 'The harlot's house'. MLN 65 1950.
Woodcock, G. The paradox of Wilde. 1950.
Ervine, St J. Wilde. 1951.
Wyndham, H. Speranza: a biography of Lady Wilde. 1952.
Byrne, P. The Wildes of Merrion Square. Tallahassee Fla 1952.
Broad, L. The friendships and follies of Wilde. 1954.
Ebermayer, E. Das ungewöhnliche Leben des Wilde. 1954.
Holland, V. Son of Wilde. 1954.
— Wilde: a pictorial biography. Oxford 1960.
Ojala, A. Aestheticism and Wilde. 2 vols Helsinki 1954–5.
Mercier, V. The fate of Wilde. 1955.
Vortriede, W. A dramatic device in Faust and the Importance of being earnest. MLN 70 1955.
Bergler, E. Salome: the turning point in the life of Wilde. Psychoanalytic Rev 43 1956.
Foster, R. Wilde as parodist. College Eng Oct 1956.
Furnell, J. The stringed lute: an invocation in dialogue of Wilde. 1956. Introd by G. Wilson Knight.
Hyde, H. M. (ed). The three trials of Wilde. New York 1956, London 1962.
— New light on the Wilde tragedy. Waterloo Rev 2 1959.
— Wilde: the aftermath. 1963.
Peckham, M. What did Lady Windermere learn? College Eng Oct 1956.
Reinert, O. Satiric strategy in the Importance of being earnest. Ibid.
— The courtship dance in the Importance of being earnest. Modern Drama 1 1959.
Finzi, J. C. (ed). Wilde and his literary circle: a catalogue of manuscripts and letters in William Andrews Clark Memorial Library. Los Angeles 1957.
Szerer, M. Dramat Wilde'a. Fragm. Prawo in Zycie 13–14 1957.
Yü, M. M. S. Two masters of irony: Wilde and Strachey. 1957.
Dianotti Cerutti, M. T. Wilde e il suo problema religioso. Modena 1958.
Ryals, C. de L. Wilde's Salome. N & Q Feb 1959.
Washington, L. S. Wilde. Southern Univ Bull 46 1959.
Woodward, A. G. Wilde. English Stud in Africa 2 1959.
Ganz, A. The divided self in the society comedies of Wilde. Modern Drama 3 1960.
— The meaning of the Importance of being earnest. Modern Drama 6 1963.
Zagona, H. G. The legend of Salome and the principle of art for art's sake. Geneva 1960.
Burke, E. C. P. Wilde: the final scene. London Mag May 1961.
— Wilde and his actors. Theatre Arts Feb 1961.
Leslie, S. Wilde and Catholicism. Month Oct 1962.
Rhynehart, J. G. Wilde's comments on early works of W. B. Yeats. Irish Book 1 1962.
Auden, W. H. An improbable life. New Yorker 9 March 1963. On Letters, ed Hart-Davis, 1962.
Charlsworth, B. The solitary prison of Wilde. Spectrum 6 1963.
Croft-Cooke, R. Bosie: the story of Lord Alfred Douglas, his friends and enemies. 1963.
Ellmann, R. Romantic pantomime in Wilde. Partisan Rev 30 1963.
Toliver, H. E. Wilde and the importance of 'sincere and studied triviality'. Modern Drama 5 1963.
Freedman, M. The modern tragicomedy of Wilde and O'Casey. College Eng April 1964.
Wilson, H. Epistolary autobiography: the letters of Wilde. PMLA 63 1964.

SIR JAMES MATTHEW BARRIE

1860–1937

Bibliographies

Garland, H. A bibliography of the writings of Barrie. 1928.
Cutler, B. D. Barrie: a bibliography, with full collations of the American unauthorised editions. [1931].
Block, A. Barrie: his first editions, points and values. 1933.
Wynne, M. G. The Barrie collection. Yale Univ Lib Gazette 23 1949.
Beinecke, W. jr. Barrie in the Parrish collection. Princeton Univ Lib Chron 17 1956.
— Beinecke Collection of Barrie. Yale Univ Lib Gazette 1965.

Collections

Novels, tales and sketches. 12 vols New York 1896–1902. Thistle edn.
The Kirriemuir edition of the works. 10 vols 1913, 1922.
Uniform edition of the works. 11 vols 1913–32.
Half hours. [1914], New York 1914, 1919 (with Der Tag). Contains the following plays, all produced at D of Y; Pantaloon (5 April 1905); The twelve-pound look (1 March 1910); Rosalind (14 Oct 1912); The will (4 Sept 1913).
Uniform edition of the plays. 12 vols 1918–38. Includes the following 1st edns: What every woman knowns (D of Y 3 Sept 1908), 1918; Alice sit-by-the-fire (D of Y 5 April 1905), 1919; A kiss for Cinderella (Wyndham's 3 March 1916), 1920; Dear Brutus (Wyndham's 17 Oct 1917), 1922; Mary Rose (H 22 April 1920), 1924; Peter Pan: or the boy who would not grow up (D of Y 27 Dec 1904), 1928; The boy David (His Majesty's Dec 1936), 1938 (preface by H. G[ranville]-B[arker]).
Works. 10 vols New York 1918.
Echoes of the war. [1918], New York [1918]. Contains The old lady shows her medals (7 April 1917); The new word (22 March 1915); Barbara's wedding (Apollo 23 Aug 1927); A well-remembered voice (28 June 1918).
Representative plays. Ed W. L. Phelps, New York 1926.
Plays. 1928. Includes first pbn of Old friends (D of Y 1 March 1910), Half an hour (Hippodrome 29 Sept 1913); Seven women (NT 7 April 1917), being the first act of The adored one with altered ending.
Selections from the plays. 1929.
Selections from the prose works. 1929.
Works: Peter Pan edition. 14 vols New York 1929–31.
McConnachie and JMB: speeches by Barrie with a preface by Hugh Walpole. 1938.
Plays. Ed A. E. Wilson 1942. Definitive edn with first pbn of The professor's love story (Star, New York 19 Dec 1892, Com 25 June 1894); Little Mary (Wynd-

ham's 24 Sept 1903) a dramatic version of The little minister.
Plays and stories. Ed R. L. Green 1962.

§1

There were numerous American pirated edns of many of the works of fiction; as a rule these are not noted.
Caught napping. D. (Unacted). 1883 (priv ptd).
Better dead. 1888 (for 1887), 1888, New York [1890] (with My Lady Nicotine, below), New York 1891, London 1891 (3 edns), 1896, 1903, 1925.
Auld licht idylls. 1888, 1895, 1898 (11th edn), New York 1897. Based on articles first pbd in St James's Gazette and in Home Chimes 1884–5.
When a man's single: a tale of literary life. 1888, New York 1896.
An Edinburgh eleven: pencil portraits from college life. 1889, New York 1892. First pbd in Br Weekly 1888.
A window in Thrums. 1889, 1892, 1898 (16th edn), New York 1897. Ch i separately rptd as The sabbath day, 1895.
Richard Savage. D. (Crit 16 April 1890), 1891 (priv ptd). With H. B. Marriott Watson.
My Lady Nicotine. 1890, New York 1896.
Ibsen's ghost: or Toole up-to-date. (Toole's 30 May 1891). 1939 (priv ptd).
The little minister. 3 vols 1891, 1891, New York 1891, 1891, 2 vols Leipzig 1891, London 1892, New York 1892, London 1897, 1898, 1903, 1905, 1907. First pbd in Good Words Jan–Dec 1891; dramatic version (H 6 Nov 1897); 1942 (in Plays, above).
Walker, London: a farcical comedy. (Toole's 25 Feb 1892). 1907.
A holiday in bed, and other sketches; with a short biographical sketch of the author. New York 1892. Unauthorized collection of contributions to periodicals.
Jane Annie, or the good conduct prize: a new and original English comic opera. (Sav 13 May 1893). 1893. With A. Conan Doyle.
A lady's shoe. New York [1893] (unauthorized 1st edn, with The inconsiderate waiter), London 1894 (in Miss Parson's adventure by W. C. Russell, and other stories by other writers), New York 1898.
Two of them. New York [1893]. Unauthorized collection of contributions to periodicals.
An Auld Licht manse, and other sketches. New York [1893]. Unauthorized collection of contributions to periodicals.
A Tillyloss scandal. New York [1893], [1893], 1894, 1915? Unauthorized collection of contributions to periodicals.
A powerful drug; and other stories. New York [1893]. Unauthorized collection of contributions to periodicals.
Allahakbarries C[ricket] C[lub]. 1893 (priv ptd), 1950.
Scotland's lament: a poem on the death of Robert Louis Stevenson, December 3rd 1894. 1895 (priv ptd), 1918 (priv ptd). First pbd in Bookman (London) Jan 1895.
Margaret Ogilvy; by her son J. M. Barrie, 1896, 1896, New York 1896.
Sentimental Tommy: the story of his boyhood. 1896, 1896, 1897, New York 1897, 1900, 1909; tr Czech, 1902.
Jess. Boston [1898]. Unauthorized collection of the first 16 stories in A window in Thrums.
The Allahakbarrie book of Broadway cricket for 1899. 1899 (priv ptd), 1950.
Life in a country manse. New York 1899. Unauthorized; first pbd in Br Weekly July–Aug 1891; rptd in A holiday in bed and other sketches, 1892, and A Tillyloss scandal, [1893].
The wedding guest. C. (Gar 27 Sept 1900). 1900 (pbd as a supplement to Fortnightly Rev), New York 1900.
Tommy and Grizel. 1900, New York [1900], Toronto 1900. First pbd in Scribner's Mag Jan–Nov 1900.
Quality Street. C. (Vaudeville 17 Sept 1902). 1913, 1913, New York 1918.
The Admirable Crichton. (Duke of York's 4 Nov 1914). 1914, New York 1918; tr French, 1920.
The little white bird. 1902, New York 1902, Toronto 1902. First pbd in Scribner's Mag Aug–Nov 1902.
Peter Pan in Kensington Gardens; from The little white bird; with drawings by Arthur Rackham. 1906, New York 1906, 1921; tr French, 1917.
When Wendy grew up: an afterthought. D of Y 3 Sept 1908). 1957.
George Meredith. 1909, Chicago 1910 (as Neither Dorking nor the Abbey), Portland Maine 1911, 1912, 1914 (all 4 pirated). First pbd in Westminster Gazette 26 May 1909 as Neither Dorking nor the Abbey.
Peter and Wendy. 1911, New York 1911, London 1915, 1921 (as Peter Pan and Wendy), New York 1921; tr Spanish, 1925. Many adaptations of Peter Pan for young children pbd.
Der Tag. D (Coliseum 21 Dec 1914). [1914], New York 1914, 1919 (with Half hours).
Shakespear's legacy. F. (14 April 1916). [1916] (priv ptd).
Who was Sarah Findlay? by Mark Twain; with a suggested solution of the mystery by Barrie. 1917 (priv ptd).
The truth about the Russian dancers (Coliseum 16 March 1920). New York 1962.
Shall we join the ladies? (Royal Dramatic Academy's Theatre 27 March 1921). In The black mask, ed C. Asquith 1927.
Courage: the Rectorial Address delivered at St Andrews University, May 3rd 1922. [1922], [1922], New York 1922. First pbd in St Andrews Univ Mag 17 1922.
Neil and Tintinnabulum. In The flying carpet, ed C. Asquith 1925.
The entrancing life: speech at Edinburgh. October 28th 1930. 1930.
The Greenwood hat. 1930 (priv ptd), 1937.
Farewell, Miss Julie Logan. 1932 (in uniform edn). First pbd in Christmas suppl to Times 24 Dec 1931.
For Dear Brutus, Mary Rose, Peter Pan, The boy David, What every woman knows, *and other plays first pbd in uniform edn*; *for* Pantaloon, The twelve-pound look, Rosalind, *and* The will, *first pbd in* Half hours; *for* The old lady shows her medals, *first pbd in* Echoes of the War; *for* Old friends, Half an hour *and* Seven women *first pbd in* Plays, 1928; *for* The professor's love story *and* Little Mary *first pbd in* Plays, 1942; *see under collections. The following have not been pbd:* The adored one (D of Y 4 Sept 1913) *as* Legend of Leonora (Empire, New York 5 Jan 1914); Rosy rapture: or the pride of the beauty chorus (D of Y 22 March 1915). *For other dramatic works, see* Nicoll 5, pp. 251, 778 and R. L. Green, Barrie, 1960.
For the numerous contributions to periodicals, see Garland, Bibliography. *Barrie contributed prefaces to various books, including* R. M. Ballantyne, The coral island, 1913; Daisy Ashford, The young visiters, 1919.
For American pirated edns of the works of fiction, as a rule not noted here, see Cutler, Barrie: a bibliography.

Letters

Letters. Ed V. Meynell 1942.
Malany, M. H. Letters by Barrie to the Duchess of Sutherland. Boston Public Lib Quart 5 1953.

§2

Hammerton, J. A. Barrie and his books: biographical and critical studies. 1900.
—— Barrie: the story of a genius. 1929.
Beerbohm, M. The child Barrie. Saturday Rev 7 Jan 1905.

Browne, E. A. Barrie's dramatic and social outlook. Fortnightly Rev May 1906.
Bookman autumn double number. 1910; Special Xmas number, 1920.
Howe, P. P. In his Dramatic portraits, 1913.
Marcosson, I. F. and D. Frohman. Charles Frohman: manager and man. 1916.
Scott, D. In his Men of letters, 1916.
Parker, W. M. In his Modern Scottish writers, Edinburgh 1917.
Herford, O. The question of the moment: did Barrie write the Young visiters? Bookman (New York) Oct 1919.
Hind, C. L. In his Authors and I, 1921.
Phelps, W. L. In his Essays on modern dramatists, New York 1921.
Walbrook, H. M. Barrie and the theatre. 1922.
Braybrooke, P. Barrie: a study in fairies and mortals. [1924].
Vernon, F. In his Twentieth century theatre, 1924.
Frith, J. C. How Barrie 'commenced author'. Bookman's Jnl 11 1925.
Goitein, P. L. A new approach to an analysis of Mary Rose. [1926].
Moult, T. Barrie. 1929.
Darton, F. J. H. Barrie. 1929.
Délavénay, E. Mary Rose et le problème de la personnalité chez Barrie. Revue Anglo-américaine 6 1929.
Eshenauer, W. Barrie als Dramatiker. Würzburg 1930.
Kennedy, J. Thrums and the Barrie country. 1930.
Kaplan, I. B. A Scot in America. Colophon 1 1936.
Roy, J. A. Barrie. 1937.
Chalmers, P. R. The Barrie inspiration. 1938.
Darlington, W. A. Barrie. 1938.
Mackail, D. The story of JMB. 1941. The authorized biography.
Asquith, C. In her Haply I may remember, 1950.
— Portrait of Barrie. 1954.
Blake, G. Barrie and the Kailyard School. [1951].
Green, R. L. Fifty years of Peter Pan. 1954. Includes Scenario for a silent film of Peter Pan.
— Barrie. 1960.
Karpe, M. The origins of Peter Pan. Psychoanalytic Rev 43 1955.
Brockett, L. and O. G. Barrie and the journalist at his elbow. Quart Jnl of Speech 44 1958.
Pearson, H. Pinero and Barrie: a backstage view. Theatre Arts July 1958.
McGraw, W. R. Barrie's concept of dramatic action. Modern Drama 5 1962.

OTHER DRAMATISTS 1870–1900

For Synge, Yeats and the other Anglo-Irish dramatists of the Nineties and after, see col 1915, below; for an explanation of the abbreviations, see under Early Nineteenth-Century Drama, *col 1125, above.*

JAMES ALBERY

1838–99

Collections

Dramatic works. Ed W. Albery 2 vols 1939. Includes memoir, chronological table, correspondence and newspaper reports in full.

§1

Two roses. C. (Vaudeville 4 June 1870). French 118; Rowell.
The pink dominos. C. (Crit 31 March 1877). [1878]. From Hennequin and Delacour.
Our boys. C. (Vaudeville 16 Jan 1875). Lacy 116.
Married in haste. C. (H 2 Oct 1875). French 115.
£20 a year—all found. F. (Folly 17 April 1876). Lacy 116.
See also Nicoll 5, pp. 237–8, 777.
See also Nicoll 5, pp. 295–9, 782.

§2

Wrey, P. Byron. London Soc Aug 1874.
Archer, W. In his Dramatists of to-day, 1882.
Obituary. Era 19 April 1884.

ROBERT BUCHANAN

1841–1901

See col 615, above.

HENRY JAMES BYRON

1834–84

§1

George de Barnwell. Bsq. (Adel 26 Dec 1862). Lacy 57.
War to the knife. C. (PW 10 June 1865). Lacy 67.
Paid in full. 3 vols 1865. First pbd in Temple Bar.
Cyril's success. C. (Glo 28 Nov 1868). Lacy 89.
Partners for life. C. (Glo 7 Oct 1871). Lacy 108.
Old soldiers. C. (Str 25 Jan 1873). Lacy 113.
Weak woman. C. (Str 6 May 1875). Lacy 112.

'HENRY VERNON ESMOND', HENRY VERNON JACK

1869–1922

In and out of a punt. C. (St J 9 May 1896). French 148.
One summer's day. C. (Com 16 Sept 1897). New York [1901?].
The wilderness. C. (St J 11 April 1901). New York 1901.
When we were twenty-one. C. (Com 2 Sept 1901). New York 1901.
Billy's little love affair. C. (Crit 2 Sept 1903). [1904?].
Her vote. C. (Playhouse 18 May 1909). French 158.
Eliza comes to stay. F. (Crit 12 Feb 1913). French 2510.
The law divine. C. (Wyndham's 29 Aug 1918). French 1035.
For earlier plays, see Nicoll 5, pp. 359, 790.

'MICHAEL FIELD'

See col 626, above.

SYDNEY GRUNDY
1848–1914

§1

The snowball. F. (Str 2 Feb 1879). French 131.
In honour bound. C. (PW 25 Sept 1880). French 123. From Scribe, Une chaîne.
The silver shield. C. (Str 19 May 1885). French 142.
A fool's paradise. C. (PW, Greenwich 7 Oct 1887 as The mousetrap). French 142.
A pair of spectacles. C. (Gar 22 Feb 1890). French 142; Rowell. From Labiche and Delacour, Les petits oiseaux.
Haddon Hall. O. (Sav 24 Sept 1892). 1892.
Sowing the wind. C. (Com 30 Sept 1893). 1893 (priv ptd); French 148.
A bunch of violets. C. (H 25 April 1894). French 142. From Geuillet, Montjoye.
The days of his vanity: a passage in the life of a young man. 1894.
The play of the future, by a playwright of the past: a glance at the Future of the theatre by John Palmer. 1914.
See also Nicoll 5, pp. 396–7, 795.

§2

Watson, W. Grundy and the critics. Theatre Oct 1894.
Beerbohm, M. Degenerates. Saturday Rev 4 Nov 1899.

'JOHN OLIVER HOBBES'
1867–1906

See col 1058, above.

'PAUL MERRITT', R. MAETZGER
1848–1895

§1

Glin Gath: or the man in the cleft. D. (Grecian 1 April 1872). French 99.
Thad: or linked by love. C. (Grecian 29 July 1872). French 128.
'British born'. D. (Grecian 17 Oct 1872). French 109. With H. Pettitt.
Chopsticks and spikins. F. (Grecian 25 Sept 1873). French 109.
Velvet and rags: a Spanish romance of the present day. D. (Grecian 6 April 1874). French 112. With G. Conquest.
Hand and glove. D. (Grecian 25 May 1874). French 109. With G. Conquest.
The word of honour. D. (Grecian 22 Oct 1874). French 113.
The golden plough. MD. (Adel 11 Aug 1877). French 111. Rev from his Grace royal (P'cess, Edinburgh 31 May 1876).
New Babylon: or daughters of Eve, by Merritt and W. H. Poole. 3 vols 1882.
Pleasure: by Merritt and A. Harris. Theatre Oct 1887.
Loaded dice: a story of modern life. Round Table Annual 1891.
See also Nicoll 5, pp. 485–7, 806.

§2

Archer, W. In his English dramatists of today, 1882.

HERMAN CHARLES MERIVALE, 'FELIX DALE'
1839–1906

§1

A son of the soil. D. (Court 4 Sept 1872). Lacy 97. From Ponsard, Lion amoureux.
A husband in clover. F. (Lyc 26 Dec 1873). French 100.
The white pilgrim. T. (Court 14 Feb 1874). 1874 (priv ptd), 1883 (with other poems). French 113. From the legend by G. A. à Beckett.
Peacock's holiday. F. (Court 16 April 1874). French 115.
The lady of Lyons married and settled. F. (Gai 5 Oct 1878). French 115.
Faucit of Balliol: a story in two parts. 3 vols 1882.
Florien: a tragedy in five acts and other poems. (unacted?). 1884.
Binko's blues: a tale for children of all growths. 1884.
Life of W. M. Thackeray. 1891. Completed by Sir F. T. Marzials.
Bar, stage and platform: autobiographic memories. 1902.
See also Nicoll 5, pp. 487, 806.

§2

Adams, W. D. Merivale. Theatre May 1890.
Bancroft, S. B. and E. The Bancrofts: recollections of sixty years. 1909.

T. A. PALMER
1838–1905

Too late to save: or doomed to die. D. (TR, Exeter 1861). 1878.
Among the relics. C. (TR, Plymouth 22 Nov 1869). French 108.
Rely on my discretion. F. (Roy 17 Jan 1870). French 106.
Insured at Lloyd's. D. (New Queen's, Manchester 5 Nov 1870). French 110.
A dodge for a dinner. F. (Str 28 Dec 1872). French 100.
The last life. D. (Greenwich 9 Feb 1874). French 103. From Mrs S. C. Hall, Stories of Irish life.
East Lynne. D. (Nottingham 19 Nov 1874). French 103. From Mrs Henry Wood.
Woman's rights. Ca. (Grand, Douglas Aug 1882). French 121.

STEPHEN PHILLIPS
1864–1915

§1

Orestes and other poems. 1884 (priv ptd).
Primavera: poems by four authors. Oxford 1890. 16 poems, 4 by Phillips.
Eremus: a poem. 1894.
Christ in Hades. 1896; ed C. L. Hind 1917.
Poems. 1897, 1898 (enlarged and rev).
Herod. T. (Her Majesty's 31 Oct 1900). 1901.
Marpessa: a poem. 1900, 1928.
Ulysses. D. (His Majesty's 1 Feb 1902). 1902.
Paolo and Francesca. T. (St J 6 March 1902). 1900.
The sin of David. D. (Stadttheater, Düsseldorf 30 Sept 1905; Sav July 1914). 1904, 1912 (rev).
Nero. T. (His Majesty's 25 Jan 1906). Part omitted appears as one-act play, Nero's mother, in Lyrics and dramas, 1913.
Faust. T. (His Majesty's 5 Sept 1908). 1908. With J. Comyns Carr.

Iole. D. (Cosmopolis June 1913). 1908 (in New poems, below).
New poems. 1908.
Pietro of Siena. D. (Studio 10 Oct 1911). 1910.
The new Inferno. 1911.
The King. D. (unacted). 1912, 1913 (in Lyrics and dramas, below).
Lyrics and dramas. 1913.
Armageddon: a modern epic drama. (NT 1 Jan 1915). Rptd from Lyrics and dramas, 1913. Partly in verse and partly in prose.
Panama and other poems, narrative and occasional. 1915.
Harold: a chronicle play. (Unacted). Poetry Rev Jan, March 1916; ed A. Symons 1927.
The last heir, *also called* The bride of Lammermoor, *though acted was never pbd.* The adversary, *included in* Lyrics and dramas, 1913 *was never acted.*

§2

Academy 1 Jan 1898. Review of Poems 1897.
Farrer, R. J. Herod through the opera glass. 1901. A parody of Phillips's Herod.
Streatfeild, R. A. Two poets of the new century: Phillips and Laurence Binyon. 1901. Rptd from Monthly Rev.
Archer, W. In his Poets of the younger generation, 1902.
Real conversations. 1904.
Hale, E. E. In his Dramatists of to-day, 1906.
Kyle, G. Edited by Phillips. Poetry Rev Jan–Feb 1916.
Meynell, A. Phillips. Poetry Rev Jan–Feb 1916.
Waugh, A. Phillips. Fortnightly Rev Jan 1916, rptd in his Tradition and change, 1919.
Kernahan, C. In good company. 1917.
Celebrities. 1923.
Colvin, S. In English poets, ed T. H. Ward vol 5, 1918.
Liljegren, S. B. Die Dichtung Phillips. E Studien 52 1923.
Weygandt, C. Tuesdays at ten. Philadelphia 1928.

ROBERT REECE
1838–91

§1

Prometheus: or the man on the rock. Ext. (Roy 23 Dec 1865). Lacy 68.
Whittington, Junior and his sensation cat. Bsq. (Roy 23 Nov 1870). Lacy 89.
Dora's device. C. (Roy 11 Jan 1871). Lacy 90.
Paquita: or love in a frame. C.O. (Roy 21 Oct 1871). Lacy 94.
The very last days of Pompeii. B. (Vaudeville 13 Feb 1872). Lacy 95.
May: or Dolly's delusion. D. (Str 4 April 1874). French 126.
Green old age. O. (Vaudeville 31 Oct 1874). French 103.
Valentine and Orson. Bsq. (Gai 23 Dec 1882). 1882.
See also Nicoll 5, pp. 537–9, 812.

§2

Archer, W. In his English dramatists of today, 1882.
Obituary. Era 11 July 1891.

ROBERT LOUIS STEVENSON
1850–94

See col 1004, above.

J. F. A.

5. PROSE

I. GENERAL WORKS

For bibliographies of prose, see Introduction, *col 1, above; and for historical studies which include accounts of nineteenth-century prose, see* Literary Histories and Surveys, *col 3, above.*

PROSE SELECTIONS

Restricted to non-dramatic prose, although some mixed anthologies are listed. For anthologies of nineteenth-century verse and drama, see Poetry, Drama, above.

'Shepard, W.' (W. S. Walsh). Enchiridion of criticism: the best criticisms on the best authors of the nineteenth century. Philadelphia 1885.

Mason, E. T. British letters illustrative of character and social life. 3 vols New York 1888.

Stevenson, E. Early reviews of great writers 1786–1832. [1890].

Craik, H. English prose: selections, with critical introductions by various writers and general introductions to each period. Vol 5, 1896.

Haney, J. L. Early reviews of English poets 1757–1885. 1904.

Dawson, W. J. and C. W. The great English letter-writers. 2 vols 1908.

—— The great English essayists. New York 1909.

Dickinson, T. H. and F. W. Roe. Nineteenth-century English prose: critical essays. New York [1908].

Van Tieghem, P. Le mouvement romantique (Angleterre-Allemagne-Italie-France): textes choisis, commentés et annotés. Paris 1912.

Johnson, R. B. Famous reviews. 1914. Reviews of Jane Austen, Tennyson, Charlotte Brontë, Thackeray, George Eliot, Macaulay, Maturin.

Walker, Mrs H. A book of Victorian poetry and prose. Cambridge 1915.

Bryan, W. F. and R. S. Crane. The English familiar essay. Boston [1916].

Jones, E. D. Nineteenth-century English critical essays. Oxford 1916 (WC).

Woods, G. B. English poetry and prose of the romantic movement. New York 1916, 1929 (with supplementary bibliography).

Alden, R. M. Readings in English prose of the nineteenth century. New York 1917.

—— Critical essays of the early nineteenth century. New York 1921.

Rees, B. J. Nineteenth-century letters. New York [1919].

Peacock, W. English prose. 5 vols Oxford 1921–2 (WC). Vols 3–5.

Rhys, E. Modern English essays 1870 to 1920. 5 vols 1923 (EL).

Roe, F. W. Nineteenth-century English prose: early essayists: Lamb, Hazlitt, Hunt, De Quincey, Macaulay. New York 1923.

Campbell, O. J. and S. F. Gingerich. Critical essays on poetry, drama and fiction. Ann Arbor 1924.

Opdycke, J. B. The literature of letters: famous literary letters as related to life, to the history of literature and to the art of composition. Chicago [1925].

Mordell, A. Notorious literary attacks. New York 1926.

Bell, M. Half hours with representative novelists of the nineteenth century: being passages from their works with brief biographies and introductions and a critical essay. 3 vols 1927.

Grabo, C. H. Romantic prose of the early nineteenth century. New York [1927].

Lieder, P. R., R. M. Lovett and R. K. Root. British poetry and prose, a book of readings part two: Wordsworth to Yeats. Boston 1928.

Cofer, B. D. Nineteenth-century essays, from Coleridge to Pater. New York 1929.

Craig, H. and J. M. Thomas. English prose of the nineteenth century. New York 1929.

King, R. W. England from Wordsworth to Dickens. [1929].

Sampson, G. Nineteenth-century essays. Cambridge 1929.

Reed, A. G. English literature: the romantic period. New York [1929].

Bernbaum, E. Earlier Victorian period. New York 1930.

—— Later Victorian literature. New York 1930.

—— Anthology of romanticism and guide through the romantic movement. 5 vols New York 1930.

—— The romantic period. New York 1930.

Collins, V. H. From Goldsmith to Landor: essays and conversations, 1930.

Foster, F. M. K. and H. C. White. Victorian prose. New York 1930.

Miller, G. M. English literature: the Victorian period. New York 1930.

Reilly, J. J. Masters of nineteenth-century prose. New York 1930.

Routh, H. V. England under Victoria. [1930].

Wellesley, D. The annual: a selection from the Forget-Me-Nots, Keepsakes and other annuals of the nineteenth century. 1930. With introd by V. Sackville-West.

Barton, M. and O. Sitwell. Victoriana: a symposium of Victorian wisdom, compiled from many original sources. 1931.

Watson, E. H. L. Contemporary comments: writers of the early nineteenth century as they appeared to each other. 1931.

Bald, R. C. Literary friendships in the age of Wordsworth: an anthology. Cambridge 1932.

Boas, G. A Punch anthology. 1932.

—— Prose of yesterday: Dickens to Galsworthy. 1937.

Campbell, O. J., J. F. A. Pyre and B. Weaver. Poetry and criticism of the romantic movement. New York 1932.

Smith, J. H. and E. W. Parks. The great critics: an anthology of literary criticism. New York 1932, 1939 (rev).

Patterson, R. F. Six centuries of English literature. 6 vols 1933. Vol 5, Wordsworth to Trollope (introd by E. Legouis); vol 6, Meredith to Rupert Brooke (introd by G. K. Chesterton).

Withington, R. Essays and characters, Lamb to Thompson. New York 1933.

—— and C. Van Winkle. Eminent British writers of the nineteenth century: prose. 1934.

Ffrench, Y. News from the past 1805–77. 1934. Extracts from English newspapers.

Mayer, F. P. Victorian prose. New York 1935.

Delafield, E. M. Ladies and gentlemen in Victorian fiction. 1937.

Hayward, J. Silver tongues: famous speeches from Burke to Baldwin. 1937.

Marchant, J. History through the Times: a collection of leading articles on important events 1800–1937. 1937.
Postgate, R. and A. Vallance. Those foreigners. 1937. Foreign affairs in English newspapers 1815–1937.
Bowyer, J. W. and J. L. Brooks. The Victorian age: prose, poetry and drama. New York 1938.
Harrold, C. F. and W. D. Templeman. English prose of the Victorian era. New York 1938.
MacIntyre, C. F. and M. Ewing. English prose of the romantic period. 1938.
Booth, B. A. A cabinet of gems: short stories from the English annuals. Berkeley 1938.
Strong, L. A. G. English domestic life during the past 200 years: an anthology selected from the novelists. 1942.
Grigson, G. The Romantics. 1943.
—— The Victorians. 1950.
Secker, M. The eighteen-nineties: a period anthology in prose and verse. 1948.
Walbank, F. A. England yesterday and today in the work of the novelists, 1837 to 1938. 1949.
Aldington, R. The religion of beauty: selections from the aesthetes. 1950.
Goodwin, M. Nineteenth-century opinion. 1952 (Pelican). From the monthly Nineteenth Century.
Wain, J. Contemporary reviews of romantic poetry. 1953.
White, R. J. Political tracts of Wordsworth, Coleridge and Shelley. Cambridge 1953.
Bullock, A. and M. Shock. The liberal tradition from Fox to Keynes. 1956.
James, E. An anthology of English prose 1400–1900. Cambridge 1956.
Noyes, R. English romantic poetry and prose. New York 1956.
Hugo, H. E. The romantic reader. New York 1957.
Kovalev, Y. K. An anthology of Chartist literature. 1958.
Buckler, W. E. Prose of the Victorian period. Boston 1958.
—— Novels in the making. Boston 1961. On Dickens, George Eliot, Conrad.
Orel, H. The world of Victorian humor. New York 1961.
Peters, R. L. Victorians on literature and art. New York 1961.
Rosenbaum, R. A. Earnest Victorians: six great Victorians as portrayed in their own words and those of their contemporaries. New York 1961.
Woodring, C. Prose of the romantic period. Boston 1961.
Hoffman, D. G. and S. Hynes. English literary criticism, romantic and Victorian. New York 1963.
Johnson, E. D. H. The world of the Victorians. New York 1964.

R. L. C.

II. EARLY NINETEENTH-CENTURY PROSE

WILLIAM COBBETT
1763–1835

Cobbett's mss and correspondence are widely scattered both in Britain and the USA. The notable collection in Nuffield College Oxford, listed by M. L. Pearl in typescripts in the possession of Nuffield and Bodley, includes many mss of pbd articles written for his periodicals and numerous items of unpbd material such as correspondence, fragments of diaries and family papers. Cobbett's works appeared in widely different forms: he was an active translator and editor of the writings of others, a publisher who frequently added his own 'dedications' and introds, a compiler of works of instruction and reference, and above all, a prolific journalist and periodical-owner. From this last source, supplemented by ephemeral reports of his lectures, a great variety of pamphlet reprints of articles was derived. His pbd 'letters' too are usually part of his political journalism. Selections from his early writings intended to discredit his tergiversation, and spurious pbns under his name, add to the complexity of the canon.

Bibliographies

Smith, E. In his Cobbett: a biography, 2 vols 1878.
Carlyle, E. I. In his Cobbett: a study of his life, 1904.
Clark, M. A. In his Peter Porcupine in America 1792–1800, Philadelphia 1939.
Muirhead, A. M. An introduction to a bibliography of Cobbett. Library 4th ser 20 1939.
Pearl, M. L. Cobbett: a bibliographical account of his life and times. Oxford 1953.

Collections
including selections by hostile editors

The works of Peter Porcupine. Philadelphia 1795, 1796; also as Porcupine's works, 2 vols Philadelphia [1795–97], 1 and 2 vols [1796–7] (variously collected.)
Porcupine's works. 12 vols 1801. Hostile selections, 1807–32: Cobbett against himself, 1807; The cameleon, 1807; Elements of reform, 1809, (rev as Parliamentary reform, Manchester and Bolton 1816); The friend of the people, [1816–17]; The beauties of Cobbett, 3 pts [1819–20], Dublin 1820, rev as Politics for the people, Birmingham [1819–20] (2 edns); Cobbett's reflections on religion, no 1; on politics, no 2, Sunderland [1819], Manchester, no 2, 1832; and Life of Thomas Paine, Durham 1819; The book of wonders, 2 pts [selections: Cobbett versus Wright], 1821; Cobbett's gridiron 1822, Manchester 1832 (rev as Cobbett's cardinal virtues); Cobbett's book of the Roman Catholic Church, 1825; The political mountebank, 11 nos Preston 1826; The poor man's friend, 1826; Cobbett's penny trash, 3 nos 1831 (no 1 also as Cobbett's genuine penny trash).
Porcupine revived. New York 1813. 'By William Cobbett'; anon editor.
Selections from Cobbett's political works. Ed J. M. and J. P. Cobbett, weekly pts and 6 vols 1835–7. Selections from Porcupine's works and Political register.
The beauties of Cobbett. [Ed J. Oldfield] monthly pts and 1 vol, 1836. Selections from Porcupine.
The last of the Saxons. Ed E. P. Hood 1854. Autobiographical selections.
Mr Cobbett's remarks on our Indian empire. 1857. Selections from Political register 1804–22; perhaps ed J. M. Cobbett.
The days of good Queen Bess; Social aspects of the Reformation; The suppression of the English monasteries. 1917. 3 booklet selections by the Catholic Truth Society from History of the Protestant Reformation 1917; tr Polish, 1947.
A history of the last hundred days of English freedom. Ed J. L. Hammond 1921. Selections from Political register 1817.
Selections, with Hazlitt's essay. Ed A. M. D. Hughes, Oxford 1923.
Life and adventures of Peter Porcupine. Ed G. D. H. Cole 1927. Autobiographical selections to 1800.

The progress of a ploughboy. Ed W. Reitzel 1933, 1947 (rev as The autobiography of Cobbett). Autobiographical selections to 1835.

The opinions of Cobbett. Ed G. D. H. and M. Cole 1944. Selections from Political register 1802–35.

Cobbett and Lamb. Ed W. V. Aughterson, Melbourne 1958.

§1

The soldier's friend. 1792, 1793 ('by a subaltern'). Anon; written with Cobbett?

Impeachment of Mr Lafayette. Philadelphia 1793, Hagerstown 1794. Tr Cobbett.

Observations on the emigration of Dr Priestley. Philadelphia 1794, 1794 (author and publisher anon), New York 1794, London 1794 (3 edns), [Liverpool?] 1794, Birmingham 1794, Philadelphia 1795 ('3rd edn' naming publisher with Story of a farmer's bull, Address), 1795, 1796 ('4th edn' naming Peter Porcupine as author), 1796, London 1798, Philadelphia 1798.

A bone to gnaw for the Democrats, part 1. Philadelphia 1795 (3 edns; anon in 1st), 1796 ('4th edn' by 'Peter Porcupine'), 1797 ('3rd edn' pbd by Cobbett); part 2, 1795, 1795, 1797, 1797; pts 1–2, 1797 (with A rod for the backs of the critics by 'Humphrey Hedgehog') [J. Gifford]).

A kick for a bite, by Peter Porcupine. Philadelphia 1795, 1796.

Le tuteur anglais. Philadelphia 1795, Paris 1801 ('Le Maître d'anglais') ('2ème' edn), 1803 ('3ème' edn), Philadelphia 1805 ('2nd edn'), Paris 1810, 1815, 1816, 1817, 1819, 1823, 1827, 1830, 1832, 1850, 1854, and 1861 ('35ème' edn); also numerous pirated edns.

A little plain English, by Peter Porcupine. Philadelphia 1795, Boston 1795, London 1795, Philadelphia 1796.

Summary of the law of nations. Philadelphia 1795, London 1802 (as A compendium of the law of nations), 1829 ('4th edn'). By G. F. von Martens; tr Cobbett.

A description of St Domingo. Philadelphia 1796. By M. L. E. Moreau de St Mery; tr Cobbett.

A new year's gift to the Democrats, by Peter Porcupine. Philadelphia 1796, 1796, 1798.

A prospect from the Congress gallery, by Peter Porcupine. Philadelphia 1796, 1796. Continued as monthly periodical The political censor 1796–7.

The bloody buoy, by Peter Porcupine. Philadelphia 1796, 1796, Reading Pa 1797 (German trn as Die Blut-Fahne); (facs and English trans of extracts of this trn, Description of an old book, ed J. A. Donahoe, Wilmington [c. 1958]); London [1796], Cambridge 1797 (as Annals of blood by an American), London 1798 ('4th', '7th', '10th', '11th' edns), Paradise Pa 1823 ('2nd' edn), Philadelphia 1823 ('3rd' edn).

The political censor. Philadelphia 1796–7. A monthly periodical, ed Cobbett, nos 2–9, a continuation of A prospect from the Congress gallery and continued as Porcupine's gazette.

The scare-crow, by Peter Porcupine. Philadelphia 1796, 1797. Rptd from Political censor, 1796, above.

The life and adventures of Peter Porcupine, by Peter Porcupine. Philadelphia 1796, 1796, 1797, London 1797, Glasgow 1797, 1798, London 1809 ('2nd edn'), rev as The life of William Cobbett, 1809, 1816 ('2nd', '7th', '8th', '9th' edns); ed G. D. H. Cole 1927 ('with other records of his early career').

An answer to Paine's Rights of man. Philadelphia 1796. By H. Mackenzie, above. Ed Cobbett with A letter to John Swanwick.

The life of Thomas Paine, by 'Peter Porcupine'. [1796?], 1797, 1797 (as Cobbett's review of the life). Hostile edns, Sunderland 1819, Durham 1819 (rptd from the Political censor, 1796, above, ed Cobbett from lives of Paine by H. Mackenzie and 'F. Oldys' [G. Chalmers]).

The gros mousqueton diplomatique: or diplomatic blunderbuss. Philadelphia 1796. By P. A. Adet, tr and ed Cobbett, rptd from Political censor, 1796, above.

The history of Jacobinism. 2 vols Philadelphia 1796 (with appendix), 1796 (as History of the American Jacobins), Edinburgh 1797, London 1798 (with appendix). By W. Playfair, ed Cobbett with his own appendix, History of the American Jacobins.

A letter to the infamous Tom Paine, by Peter Porcupine. Philadelphia 1796, London 1797, Glasgow 1797, Edinburgh 1797, [1798?]. Rptd from Political censor, 1796, above.

A letter from Edmund Burke. Philadelphia 1796. By Burke; ed Cobbett, with preface.

Observations on the debates of the American Congress by Peter Porcupine. [Philadelphia 1797?], London 1797. Rptd from Political censor, 1796, above.

Porcupine's gazette and United States daily advertiser (daily evening periodical, ed Cobbett, Philadelphia, 4 March 1797–28 Aug 1799, title changed to Porcupine's gazette 24 April 1799; weekly, Bustleton, 6 Sept 1799–11 Oct 1799 and 19–26 Oct 1799; New York, final no, 13 Jan 1800; another tri-weekly edn, Philadelphia, 3 March 1798–28 Aug 1799, title changed to The country porcupine 30 April 1798). Porcupine's gazette inspired a Pennsylvanian German imitation and partial trn: Der deutsche Porcupein und Lancaster Anzeigs Nachrichten, (weekly) Lancaster, 3 March 1798–25 Dec 1799, later Der Americanische Staatsbothe.

A view of the war with France. Philadelphia 1797. By T. Erskine et al, ed Cobbett as 'Peter Porcupine', with 'dedication' and 'appendix'.

The anti-Gallican. Philadelphia 1797. By 'A citizen of New England', 'Leonidas', 'Philo-Leonidas', 'Ascanius', 'Impartial'; brief dedication by Cobbett and pbd by him.

An answer to Paine's letter to Washington. Philadelphia 1798. By P. Kennedy; brief 'advertisement' by 'P.P.' (Cobbett) and pbd by him.

The democratic judge, by 'Peter Porcupine'. Philadelphia 1798; pbd in England as The republican judge, 1798 (3 edns).

Observations on the dispute between the United States and France. Philadelphia 1798. By R. G. Harper et al, ed Cobbett with 'preface' and appendix; '3rd' American edn pbd and ed Cobbett.

Detection of a conspiracy, by 'Peter Porcupine'. Philadelphia 1798, London 1799, Dublin 1799.

Detection of Bache, by 'Peter Porcupine'. Philadelphia 1798. Broadside, rptd from Porcupine's Gazette 20 June 1798, above.

French arrogance, by 'Peter Porcupine'. Philadelphia 1798, New York 1915 (in Magazine of History, no 44).

Remarks on the insidious letter [The antidote], by Peter Porcupine. Philadelphia 1798. Broadside, rptd from Porcupine's Gazette July 1798, above.

Democratic principles illustrated by example, by Peter Porcupine. 2 pts (pt 1 extracted from pt 2 of A bone to gnaw 1795, pt 2 extracted from The bloody buoy, 1796), Dublin [1797–]1798, London 1798 ('2nd'–'11th' edns), Aberdeen 1798 ('7th' edn), Edinburgh 1798 ('7th' edn), Birmingham [1798] (shortened [unauthorized?] rev pt 1 as Read and reflect: a faint picture of the horrors).

The cannibal's progress. 1798, Philadelphia 1798 (as Introductory address to the people of America) [numerous edns of this and other trns from the German pbd Albany, Amherst, Boston, Charleston, Hartford, Newburyport, New Haven, Northampton, Portsmouth, Savannah, Vergennes, Walpole 1798; Cobbett inspired many of these American edns including German edns Der Fortgang der Menschenfresser]; 1798 (rev as A warning to Britons), 1801 (as The cannibal's progress, with an introductory address to the subjects of the

British Empire), 1803. Tr A. Aufrere, ed Cobbett with 'introductory addresss'.

Remarks on the explanation by Dr Priestley, by Peter Porcupine. 1799 (rptd from Porcupine's Gazette Sept 1798–Jan 1799); tr French 1798 (ed Cobbett as Lettres au Docteur Priestley).

The trial of republicanism. Philadelphia 1799 (no known copy), London 1801 (with postscript).

Proposals for publishing Porcupine's works. [Philadelphia] 1799.

The rush-light. Fortnightly periodical, ed 'Peter Porcupine'; New York 15 Feb–30 April 1800 nos 1–5; London, 30 Aug 1800 no 6–repbd as An address to the people of England [Philadelphia? 1800?]; nos 1–4 repbd as The American rush-light, 1800. The republican rush-light 30 Aug 1800 no 7 is a forgery.

History of the campaigns of Suworow. New York 1800. Tr J. F. Anthing, ed and pbd Cobbett with additional trn, A history of his Italian campaign, by Cobbett.

Cobbett's advice. [1800]. Broadside, rev and repbd as Prospectus of the Porcupine, 1800.

The porcupine. Daily periodical, ed Cobbett, 30 Oct 1800–31 Dec 1801, nos 1–3 (another edn); from no 299 as The porcupine and anti-Gallican monitor; from 1 Jan 1802 absorbed by True Briton.

A collection of facts, including letters to Lord Hawkesbury. 1801, Philadelphia 1802. Rptd mainly from Porcupine, 1801, above.

Letters to Addington 1802.

Letters to Lord Hawkesbury and Addington. 1802, 1802. Rptd mainly from A collection of facts, 1801, and from Letters to Addington, 1802, above.

Cobbett's political register. Weekly periodical, ed Cobbett as Cobbett's annual register, Jan 1802–Dec 1803; as Cobbett's weekly political register 7 Jan 1804–5 April 1817 (none issued in England 12 April–5 July 1817, but twice weekly edn 12 Sept 1810–22 June 1811); Cobbett's weekly political pamphlet, July–Dec 1817; Cobbett's weekly political register Jan 1818–7 April 1821 (none issued 21 March, 2 May, 27 June–15 Aug, 17 Oct–14 Nov 1818, 29 May–7 Aug, 16 Oct, 20–27 Nov 1819, or 26 Feb–18 March 1820); as Cobbett's weekly register, 14 April–Dec 1827; Cobbett's weekly political register, Jan 1828–12 Sept 1835 (no 11); extracts 1830–2 pbd as Cobbett's two-penny trash, 1831, 1832; [from 20 June 1835 (no 12) ed W. Cobbett jr]; as Renewal of Cobbett's Register, Jan 1836 (unnumbered) and 20 Feb 1836 ('no 2'). Many pamphlet reprints of articles in Political register were issued, particularly after 1810; periodicals borrowing largely from it, or derived from it, or influenced by it, are: Le Mercure Anglais (ed Cobbett, monthly French trn of a part, 16 Feb–?May 1803, no known copies); cheap weekly edns 12 Oct 1816 (first no pbd 2 Nov)–6 Jan 1820 (none pbd in England 12 April–5 July 1817), unstamped twopenny edns pbd mainly alongside the stamped); Cobbett's American political register, New York 6 Jan–29 June 1816, May 1817–Jan 1818; Ulster register, Belfast ?1817 (pbd J. Lawless with Cobbett's agreement, no known copy); Weekly register, Dublin (unauthorized imitation 1822–4, no known copy); hostile imitations pbd 1816–17 with Government aid at Romsey (Romsey political register, c. Nov 1816); Detector c. Jan 1817; Friend of the people, Dec 1816–Jan 1817; Anti-Cobbett, March–April 1817); Norwich, (Brunswick weekly political register, Feb–March 1817); Oxford; and other places (see Home Office Papers 41/1/490, 42/158/160).

Letter to Lord Auckland on the Post Office. 1802. Rptd from Political Register 27 Nov 1802.

A treatise on fruit trees (by W. Forsyth, ed Cobbett with introd and notes, 'adapting . . . the treatise to . . . America'), Philadelphia 1802, New York, 1802 Albany 1803, Philadelphia 1803 (by 'an American farmer', as An epitome of Mr Forsyth's treatise).

Narrative of the taking of the invincible standard. 1803. Rptd from Political Register 25 Dec 1802.

The empire of Germany. 1803. By J. G. Peltier, tr Cobbett with a trn of a memoir by Peltier rptd from Political Register 1802.

Four letters to the Chancellor of the Exchequer. 1803. Rptd from Political Register 9, 16, 23, 30 April 1803.

Important considerations for the people of this Kingdom. 1803 etc. Anon. Rptd from Political Register 30 July 1803.

The political Proteus: R. B. Sheridan. 1804. Rptd largely from Political Register 1803.

Cobbett's parliamentary debates. 1804–. Ed Cobbett with J. Wright till 1811; then by Wright only. From 1813 (vol 24) as The parliamentary debates; supplemented by Cobbett's parliamentary history, similarly edited, 36 vols 1806–20, which also passed out of his hands in 1812 and is entitled The parliamentary history from vol 13. The parliamentary debates became Hansard's parliamentary debates in 1818 and eventually the present Hansard.

Cobbett's spirit of the public journals. Weekly periodical ed Cobbett 2 Jan–26 Dec 1804; 1 vol 1805.

Cobbett's complete collection of state trials. 33 vols 1800–26. Cobbett with J. Wright and T. B. Howell until 1811; then by T. B. Howell; from 1812 dissociated from Cobbett as Howell's state trials.

Cobbett's remarks on Burdett's letter. 1809. Rptd from Political Register 24 March 1810.

An essay on sheep. 1811, New Haven 1813. By R. R. Livingston, ed Cobbett from first edn, New York 1809 with his preface and notes.

Three letters to the electors of Bristol. Bath 1812. Rptd from Political Register 4 July, 1, 15 Aug 1812.

Letters to the Prince Regent. 1812. No known copy. Rptd from Political Register 1812.

Letter to the inhabitants of Southampton on the Corn Bill. 1814. Rptd from Political Register 4 June 1814.

Five letters to Lord Sheffield. 1815. Rptd from Political Register 26 Aug 1815.

Letters on the late war between the United States and Great Britain. New York 1815. One letter rptd as An address to the clergy of Massachusetts, Boston 1815, 1815, taken from Political Register 10 Dec 1814. Rptd, except for one letter, from Political Register 1811–15.

Paper against gold. 2 vols 1815, 15 pts 1817 (24 Feb–29 March) and 1 vol, 1821 and 1822 ('4th' edn) (accompanied by separately pbd Preliminary part of Paper against gold, 1821), 1828 (omits last 3 of a total of 32 articles or 'letters'), New York 1834, Manchester 1841 ('condensed' by M. Chappelsmith), London 1841 (no known copy), New York 1846. Paper against gold rptd from Political Register 1810–5; Preliminary part of Paper against gold rptd from Political Register 1803–6.

Cobbett's American political register 1816–7. *See* Cobbett's Political Register, above.

[Address] To the journeymen and labourers. Manchester 1816. Rptd from Political Register 2 Nov 1816 and also issued as unstamped Political Register by Cobbett in London.

A letter addressed to Mr Jabet of Birmingham. Coventry 1816. Rptd from Political Register 9 Nov 1816.

Our anti-neutral conduct reviewed. [New York 1817]. Rptd mainly from American Political Register 1817.

Cobbett's new year's gift to old George Rose. Nottingham 1817. Rptd from Political Register 4 Jan 1817.

Mr Cobbett's taking leave of his countrymen. 1817. Rptd from Political Register 5 April 1817.

Cobbett's address to the Americans. [1817].

Mr Cobbett's address to his countrymen. [1817].

[Long Island prophecies] Cobbett's too long petition: Letter to Tierney; Letter to the Regent. 1822 (5 issues including caption title Long Island prophecies). Rptd from Political Register 7 Feb, 1 July 1818, 30 Oct 1819.

A year's residence in the United States of America. New York 1818–19, London 1818–19, 1818–19, Belfast 1818–19, London 1822 ('3rd' edn), 1822, 1828 (another '3rd' edn), Paris 1834 (partial trn in French as De la culture des betteraves), London 1922, Carbondale and Fontwell [1964].

A grammar of the English language. New York 1818, London '1819' (for 1818), 1819 (3 edns), 1820 ('4th' edn), 1823 (with additional 'six lessons'), Madras 1823 (no known copy), London 1824, Berlin 1824, Jena 1825, London 1826, 1829, 1831, 1832, New York 1832, 1833, London 1833, 1836, New York 1837, London 1840, 1842, 1844, New York 1846, London 1847, 1850, 1852, Philadelphia 1852, London 1860 (as An abridgement), 1863, 1863, 1865, 1866 (2 edns, one with ch on pronunciation by J. P. Cobbett), 1868, 1870, [1880], 1882 (as Grammar for the million); ed R. Waters, New York 1883 as (How to get on in the world), 1884, London 1889, 1906, 1923 (as Cobbett's easy grammar), [c. 1940]; tr German, 1839.

The trial of Miss Tocker. New York 1818, Boston 1818. Ed Cobbett with 'letter' and 'address'.

Correspondence between Cobbett, Tipper and Burdett. 1819.

A full report of a public meeting [with a speech by Cobbett]. 1819.

Cobbett's evening post. Daily periodical, ed Cobbett, 29 Jan–1 April 1820.

Cobbett's parliamentary register. Weekly periodical, ed Cobbett, 6 May–Dec 1820.

A ptd circular letter inviting subscriptions in support of Cobbett's candidature at Coventry, 25 Feb 1820, beginning 'Sir, You have already heard that I am a candidate . . .'

A letter from the Queen to the King [by 'Queen Caroline', actually by Cobbett]. 1820, Philadelphia 1821 ('5th edn') etc. Rptd from Political Register 19 Aug 1820.

An answer to the speech of the Attoney-General against the Queen. 1820. Rptd from Political Register 26 Aug 1820.

The Queen's answer to the letter from the King. 1821, Philadelphia 1821. Rptd from Political Register 27 Jan 1821.

Cobbett's sermons. 12 monthly pts 1821–2 (nos 1–3 as Cobbett's monthly religious tracts, nos 4–12 as Cobbett's monthly sermons), 1822 ('stereotype' edn), 1823, France and Italy 1822 (no known copies), London (Andover ptd) as Twelve Sermons 1828, New York (as Thirteen sermons with 'address', an additional sermon, and Good Friday, which was also pbd separately, London 1830), 1834, Philadelphia [183?], New York 1846.

Preliminary part of Paper against gold. *See* Paper against gold, 1815, above.

The American gardener. 1821, Baltimore 1823, 1829 (rev as The English gardener), New York 1835, 1841, Concord 1842, New York 1844, 1846, Philadelphia 1851, New York 1856, [188?], Claremont [1850–8?]; tr Italian, 1826.

Cottage economy. 7 monthly pts Aug 1821–March 1822 etc; 1822, 1823 ('new' edn), 1824 ('6th' edn), New York 1824, London 1826, 1828, Frome 1829 (as Cottage domestic economy [extracts from Cobbett et al ed 'I.B.'–Marchioness of Bath]), London 1831, New York 1833 (with The poor man's friend), London 1835, 1838 ('15th' edn), 1843 ('16th' edn), ('17th' edn) 1850, Hartford 1854, London [1865] ('19th' edn); ed G. K. Chesterton 1926; tr Greek, 1829 (no known copy).

The farmer's friend. 1822. Rptd from Political Register 15 Dec 1821, 5 Jan 1822.

[Proceedings at the dinner:] Cobbett's warnings to Norfolk farmers. 1822. Rptd from Political Register 29 Dec 1821, 5 Jan 1822.

American slave trade. 1822. By J. Torrey jr, ed Cobbett with preface from 1st Amer edn, Portraiture of domestic slavery, Philadelphia 1822.

The farmer's wife's friend. 1822. Rptd from Political Register 23 March 1822.

The statesman. Daily evening periodical 1806–24, incorporated in the Globe and traveller, 1824, part owned by Cobbett March 1822–May 1823, when he wrote articles for it, some rptd in Cobbett's collective commentaries 1822, below.

The horse hoeing husbandry. 1822, 1829. Ed Cobbett with introd from A specimen etc by J. Tull, 1731.

Reduction no robbery. 1822. Rptd from Political Register 22 June 1822.

Cobbett's collective commentaries. 1822. Mainly rptd from Statesman 1822, above.

Mr Cobbett's publications. A descriptive catalogue frequently rptd from Political Register and advertisements in Cobbett's books 1822–4; later versions as List of Mr Cobbett's publications, c. 1824; List of Mr Cobbett's books 1828–32, 1834, 1842; and The Cobbett library, 1830, 1835.

Narrative. London? 1823 (no known copy). Rptd from Political Register 11 Jan 1823.

The Norfolk yeoman's gazette. Weekly periodical, ed Cobbett, Norwich 8 Feb–3 May 1823.

To Lord Suffield. 1823. Rptd from Political Register 1 Feb 1823.

A French grammar. 1824, Paris 1825, London 1829, New York 1832, 1837, 1841, London 1840, 1842, ('9th' edn) 1844, New York 1848, London 1849, ('10th' edn), 1851 ('11th' edn), 1861 ('11th edn' rev J. P. Cobbett), [1862?] ('15th' edn), [1882] ('new' edn), New York 1884, London [1875?]; J. P. Cobbett, Practical exercises, 1834.

A history of the Protestant Reformation in England and Ireland. 16 nos 1824–6, many nos rptd and bound together; nos 1–3 tr French in pts, nos 1–16 ('17') tr Italian in pts.

[pt 1]. 1824, 1824 (for 1826), Baltimore 1824 (for 1826), London 1825 (for 1826), New York 1825 (2nd Amer edn), [1926], Pittsburgh 1825 (3rd Amer edn) (for 1826), Philadelphia 1825 (for 1826), Baltimore 1826 ('4th American 'edn); tr Spanish, 1826; French, 1826; Philadelphia 1826 (as A history of the Reformation), Paris 1826, 1826, 1827, Baltimore 1827; tr Italian, 1827; [Portugal, Spain, Holland (no known copies) 1828]; London 1829, Aschaffenberg 1832, 1833, 1839, New York 1832, Naples 1841, Sydney 1844, 1846, London 1850, Philadelphia [1850?], 1853, Dublin 1868, 1869, [186?–7?], [189?]; ed F. A. Gasquet 1896; [189?], New York 1897, [1905], London 1917 (3 booklet extracts), New York [193?]; tr Polish, 1947 (abstract) [pt 2]. A list of the abbeys confiscated, 1827, 1829, 1868.

[pts 1–2]. 2 vols 1827; tr German, 1827–8; French, 1827, 1829; tr Spanish, 1830; New York 1832, 1832–4; Hungarian, 1834; French, 1836, 1836 ('6ème' edn), 1841; New York 1849, London [1853–7], New York 1961, Dublin 1867, London 1868, New York [186?], [1886], London 1905.

Gold for ever. 1825; rptd in Political Register 10 Sept 1825.

Big O and Sir Glory. 1825. Rptd from Political Register 24 Sept 1825.

Cobbett at the King's cottage [1826]. Rptd from Political Register 5 Aug 1826.

Cobbett's poor man's friend. 4 nos Aug–Nov 1826. Hostile imitation; The poor man's friend, 1826. No 5 Oct 1827, nos 2–4, pbd as 'new' edn Oct 1830, 1833 (rev as Cobbett's poor man's friend) (in Cottage economy, below), 1826, 1829, [1830], ('new' edn), [1832], [1836–184?].

Catalogue of American trees. 1827. Rptd from Political Register 8 Dec 1827.

Elements of the Roman history. 1828, 1829 (rev as An abridged history of the Emperors, 1829). By J. H. Sievrac, tr Cobbett.

The woodlands. 7 nos Dec 1825–March 1828, 1 vol 1825 (for 1828).

Noble nonsense. [1828]. Rptd from Political Register 3 May 1828.

The English gardener. 1829 (for 1828) (2 edns), 1833, 1838, 1845. Rev from American gardener, above.

Usury. 1828, 1834, 1856. By J. O'Callaghan, ed Cobbett from 1st edn New York 1824, with dedication.

Facts for the men of Kent. [1828]. Rptd from Political Register 25 Oct 1828.

A letter to the Pope. 1828. Rptd from Political Register 15 Nov 1828.

A treatise on Cobbett's corn. 1828, 1831 ('with an addition').

Letter to Mr Huskisson. [London? 1828] (no known copy) [Philadelphia 1828]. Rptd from Political Register 2 Aug 1828.

Englishmen, hear me. 1829. A placard; no known copy. Rptd from Political Register 21 Feb 1829.

The emigrant's guide. 1829, 1830, 1830.

Mr Cobbett's lecture. 5 pts 1829–30. 5 lectures; third lecture also pbd Birmingham [1830] as broadside, A summary report.

Report of lecture-speech, Halifax. Halifax 1830, 1830.

Three lectures, Sheffield. Sheffield 1830.

Mr Cobbett's address to the tax-payers. [1830]. Rptd from Political Register 10 April 1830, with addns.

Good Friday. 1830; rptd in Thirteen sermons, New York 1834, below, and in Political Register 9 March 1833.

Rural rides. 1830, 1830. Rptd from Political Register 1821–6; later edns from Political Register 1821–34; rptd 1833 (as Cobbett's tour in Scotland and the northern counties of England in 1832); ed J. P. Cobbett 1853, 1885, 1886, 1908, 1908, [1910], [1912], [1914], 1923, 1926; ed G. D. H. and M. Cole 1930 (with addns not previously rptd from Political Register), 1932, 1934, 1948, 1950, 1953, 1957, 1958.

Cobbett's exposure of the pretended friends of the blacks. 1830. Rptd from Political Register 26 June 1830.

French Revolution: an address to the people of Paris. Birmingham 1830. Rptd from Political Register 21 Aug 1830.

Tableau de l'Angleterre. 3 nos. French trn from Political Register 14–21 Aug 1830.

Advice to young men. 14 pts June 1829–Sept 1830; 1 vol London ('Andover' ptd '1829') (for 1830) (2 edns), 'London 1829' (for 1830), Paris 1830 (no known copy), New York 1831, 1833, Claremont [183?], London 1837, Huntsville 1840, London 1842, New York 1844, 1846, [1847] (extract, as Advice to lovers), Philadelphia 1851, London 1861, 1868, [1874], [1876], Philadelphia 1881, London 1885, 1886, 1887, [1892], [London 1900?], 1906, New York 1911, Allahabad 1914 (extract, as Advice to a youth), London 1926, 1930, 1937 (extract, as Advice to a lover); tr French, 1842, 1889.

Eleven lectures on the French and Belgian revolutions. 11 pts Sept–Oct 1830; 1 vol 1830.

A letter to the king. [1830].

History of George the Fourth. ? pts 1830–4; 2 vols 1830–4, 2 vols 1834; rptd in Political Register 1830–4.

A Talleyrand Perigord [Paris? 1830] (no known copy). Tr French, from Political Register 16 Oct 1830.

Aux braves ouvriers de Paris. [Paris? 1830] (no known copy). Tr French, from Political Register 30 Oct 1830.

Cobbett's plan of parliamentary reform. 1830. Rptd from Political Register 30 Oct 1930.

Surplus population. [1831?], [1835?]. A play, rptd from Political Register 28 May 1831 and Cobbett's twopenny trash June 1831.

A report of the trial of William Cobbett. 1831 (5 edns), New York 1831. Ed anon; not by Cobbett.

Cobbett's twopenny trash. 24 pts July 1830–July 1832; 2 vols 1831–2, 1832. One pt (Tithes) tr Welsh, 1831 (no known copy). Rptd from Political Register 1830–2, except for vol 1 nos 1–6 and vol 2 nos 4, 10; Cobbett's penny trash, nos 1–3; no 1 also issued as Cobbett's genuine twopenny trash, is a hostile imitation.

A spelling book. 1831, 1831, 1832, 1834, 1845 ('9th' edn).

Cobbett's letter on the abolition of tithes. Dublin [1831?]. Rptd from Political Register 10 Sept 1831. Rptd as Mr Cobbett's propositions, Manchester 1831.

Cobbett's Manchester lectures. 1832.

A geographical dictionary. 1832. Ed Cobbett et al.

Mansell & Co's report of the important discussion held in Birmingham. Birmingham [1832], [1832]. Ed anon, not by Cobbett.

Extracts from Cobbett's register, and Mr Cobbett's remarks. Birmingham [1832].

Mr Cobbett's answer to Mr Stanley's manifesto. [1833], [1833]. Rptd from Political Register 29 Dec 1832.

Cobbett's poor man's friend. [1833]. Rev from Poor man's friend, 1826–7, above; rptd from Political Register 5 Jan 1833.

The speeches of W. Cobbett MP. 2 nos 1833. Rptd from True Sun 1833.

The flash in the pan. 1833. Rptd from Political Register 18–25 May 1833.

Cobbett's magazine. Monthly periodical Feb 1833–March 1834; title changed to Saturday magazine, April 1834. Ed J. M. and J. P. Cobbett with some articles by Cobbett.

Disgraceful squandering of the public money. Glasgow 1833. Rptd from Political Register 15 June 1831.

The curse of paper money. 1833. By W. M. Gouge, ed Cobbett with preface and introd rptd from Political Register 20 July 1833, the rest from Philadelphia 1823 edn.

A new French and English dictionary. 1833.

Popay the police spy. 1833. Rptd from Political Register 17 Aug 1833.

Four letters to Worsley. 1834. Rptd from Political Register 31 Aug–19 Oct 1833.

Rights of industry 1833. By Cobbett and J. Fielden. Rptd from Political Register 14 Dec 1833.

Mr Cobbett's speech for an abolition of the malt tax. 1834. Rptd from Political Register 22 March 1834.

Life of Andrew Jackson. 1834, New York 1834, 1834, Baltimore 1834, [another Amer edn 1834], New York [1837?]. Ed Cobbett from the Life by J. H. Eaton, Philadelphia 1824.

Get gold! get gold! Leeds 1834. Rptd from Political Register 16 Aug 1834.

[Five] Letters to the Earl of Radnor. 1834. Rptd from Political Register 9, 23 Aug, 20 Sept, 18, 25 Oct 1834.

Three lectures on Ireland. Dublin 1834. First lecture in another version in Political Register 4 Oct 1834.

Cobbett's legacy to labourers. 1834 (for 1835), 1835, 1835, New York 1835, 1844, London 1872. Dedication rptd as A letter to Peel, 1836, below.

The malt tax. 1835. Rptd from Political Register 24 March 1835.

Cobbett's legacy to parsons. 1835 (6 edns), New York 1835, 1844, 1860, London 1868, 1869, Croydon 1876 (as There being no gospel for tithes), London 1947; tr Welsh, 1833.

Cobbett's legacy to Peel. 1836. Rptd from Political Register 24 Jan–18 April 1835.

Doom of the tithes. 1836. Introd by Cobbett to a trn from a Spanish work Historia y origen di las rentas Iglesia, 1793.

Cobbett's reasons for war against Russia. 1854. Ed anon; extracts rptd from Political Register 1822, 1826, 1829, 1833, 1834.

Mr Cobbett's remarks on our Indian empire. 1857. By Cobbett and J. Fielden, ed anon; extracts rptd from Political Register 1804–22.

A history of the last hundred days of English freedom. 1921. By Cobbett, ed J. L. Hammond; rptd from Political Register 26 July–18 Oct 1817.

Letters

Cobbett's 'letters' were mostly part of his polemical and political writings, not always despatched to those to whom they were 'addressed' but ptd for the first time in his periodicals, above. The following are collections of letters in the conventional sense, or commentaries upon letters or mss.

'Melville, Lewis' (L. S. Benjamin). In his Life and letters of Cobbett, 2 vols 1913.
Countryman 4 1931, 6 1932, 10–11 1935, 12 1936, 16 1938.
Cole ,G. D. H. Letters from Cobbett to Edward Thornton 1797–1800. Oxford 1937.
Pearl, M. L. Cobbett at Botley, Cobbett and his men, Cobbett and his family, Cobbett and the 'Chop-sticks'. Countryman 153–4 1951, 157 1953.
Davis, C. R. Cobbett letters in the library. Jnl Rutgers Univ Lib 17 1954.
Fontinelles, A. Un inédit de Cobbett: lettre à Thomas Hulme. Etudes Anglaises 15 1962.

§2

Hazlitt, W. Character of Cobbett. In his Table talk vol i, 1821 and Spirit of the age, 1825 (2nd edn).
—— Mr Cobbett and the Quakers. Atlas 21 Dec 1828. Unsigned.
Carlile, R. Life of Cobbett. Republican 12 May 1826.
French, D. French versus Cobbett. 1829.
The life of Cobbett. 1835.
The life, dedicated to his sons. 1835.
Memoirs. Leeds 1835.
Huish, R. Memoirs. 1836.
Gilfillan, G. In his A second gallery of literary portraits, Edinburgh 1852, and in his Portraits in prose, ed H. Macdonald, New Haven 1947.
Sievrac, J. H. Fraser's Mag Feb 1862.
Bulwer, H. L. In his Historical characters, 1867.
Sala, G. A. H. Cobbett's comedy. Belgravia Feb 1875.
Stephen, L. William Cobbett. New Rev Oct–Nov 1893.
Stephen, J. F. In his Horae sabbaticae ser 3, 1894.
Hudson, W. H. Through Cobbett's country. Saturday Rev 28 Dec 1901.
Carlyle, E. I. Cobbett: a study of his life. 1904.
Cole, G. D. H. The life of Cobbett. 1924, 1927, 1947 (rev).
Chesterton, G. K. William Cobbett. [1925].
'Bowen, Marjorie' (H. G. Long). Peter Porcupine. 1935.
Reitzel, W. Cobbett and Philadelphia journalism. Pennsylvania Mag of History & Biography 59 1935.
Higgins, C. Cobbett in Wiltshire. Country Life 30 July 1938, 26 Aug 1939.
Muirhead, A. M. Rural rides. Bibl N & Q 2 1939.
Clark, M. E. Peter Porcupine in America. Philadelphia 1939.
Cameron, K. N. Shelley, Cobbett and the National Debt. JEGP 63 1943.
Baker, E. Cobbett and Quakers. Friends Quart new ser 2 1948.
Pemberton, W. B. William Cobbett. 1949.
Birchfield, J. Ringing voice. Land 1950.
Ausubel, H. Cobbett and Malthusianism. JHI 13 1952. *See* Kegel, below.
Davis, C. R. Cobbett: Philadelphia bookseller and publisher. Jnl Rutgers Univ Lib 16 1952.
—— Cobbett and Gillray. Jnl Rutgers Univ Lib 19 1955.
Vallins, G. H. Cobbett's 'Grammar'. English 10 1954.
Ford, E. H. and E. Emery. Cobbett and Philadelphia journalism. In their Highlights in the history of the American press, Minneapolis 1954.
Chaloner, W. H. Cobbett and Manchester: the first election address. Manchester Guardian 16 May 1955.
Postlethwaite, F. A. Cobbett on Dickens. Dickensian 52 1956.
Hussey, M. Cobbett's advice. Jnl of Education Feb 1957.
Neilson, W. and F. In their Verdict for the doctor: the case of Benjamin Rush. 1958.
Lange, H. Cobbett: Leben und Wirken des englischen politischen Reformers und Schriftstellers. Zeitschrift für Anglistik und Americanistik 6 1958.
Bressler, L. A. Peter Porcupine and the bones of Thomas Paine. Pennsylvania Mag of History & Biography 82 1958.
Kegel, C. H. Cobbett and Malthusianism. JHI 19 1958.
Renker, A. Cobbett and his cornstalk paper. Papermaker (Wilmington Del) 28 1959; tr German in Amor Librorum 1958.
Martin, E. W. Cobbett and the making of modern England. History Today Jan 1960.
Potter, J. Cobbett in North America. Bull of Br Assoc for Amer Stud new ser no 2 1961.

M. L. P.

WALTER SAVAGE LANDOR
1775–1864

Bibliographies

Forster collection, South Kensington Museum: catalogue of the printed books. 1888; Catalogue of the paintings, manuscripts, autograph letters, pamphlets etc, 1893.
The Browning collections: catalogue of autograph letters and manuscripts, [and] books, the property of R. W. Barrett Browning, sold by Sotheby. 1–8 May 1913.
Wise, T. J. and S. Wheeler. A bibliography of the writings in prose and verse of Landor. 1919.
Wise, T. J. A Landor library. 1928 (priv ptd).
Super, R. H. The publication of Landor's early works. PMLA 63 1948; rptd in his Publication of Landor's works, below.
—— Notes on some obscure Landor editions. PBSA 46 1952.
—— Landor's unrecorded contributions to periodicals. N & Q 8 Nov 1952.
—— Landor's American publications. MLQ 14 1953.
—— The publication of Landor's works. 1954.
—— In The English romantic poets and essayists: a review of research and criticism, ed C. W. and L. H. Houtchens, New York 1957, 1966 (rev).
Karlson, M. The Landor collection. Yale Univ Lib Gazette 27 1953.
Brumbaugh, T. B. On collecting Landor. Emory Univ Quart 12 1956.
—— A Landor collection. Lib Chron 8 1966.
Metzdorf, R. F. The Tinker library. New Haven 1959.
Lyde, R. G. A Landor gift. BM Quart 22 1960.
Nowell-Smith, S. Gebir: a poem (1798). Library 5th ser 17 1962.
Lohrli, A. The first publication of Landor's Diana de Poictiers. N & Q Jan 1963.

Collections

Gebir, Count Julian and other poems. 1831.
The works of Landor. 2 vols 1846, 1853, 1868, 1895.
Poemata et inscriptiones. 1847.
Selections from the [prose] writings. Ed G. S. Hillard, Boston 1856.
Cameos selected from the works of Landor by E. C. Stedman and T. B. Aldrich. Boston 1874.
The works and life of Landor. Ed J. Forster 8 vols 1876. Vol 1 is an abridgement of Forster's Landor, 1869.
Selections from the writings of Landor. Ed S. Colvin 1882.
Poems. Ed E. Radford [1889].
Imaginary conversations. Ed C. G. Crump 6 vols; Poems, dialogues in verse and epigrams, 2 vols; Longer prose works, 2 vols 1891–3.
Aphorisms. Ed R. B. Johnson 1897.
Selections. Ed W. B. S. Clymer, Boston 1898.

Love poems. Ed 'F.C.' 1901.
Shorter works. 1904.
A day-book. Ed J. Bailey, Oxford 1919.
The complete works: prose. Ed T. E. Welby 12 vols 1927–31; Poetry, ed S. Wheeler 4 vols 1933–6; 3 vols Oxford 1937.
Imaginary conversations and poems. Ed H. Ellis 1933 (EL).
Poetry and prose, with Swinburne's poem and essays by E. de Selincourt, W. Raleigh and O. Elton. Ed E. K. Chambers, Oxford 1946.
Shorter poems. Ed J. B. Sidgwick, Cambridge 1946.
Brevities, epigrammi. Tr and ed A. Obertello, Florence [1946].
The sculptured garland: a selection from the lyrical poems. Ed R. Buxton 1948.
Poems. Ed G. Grigson 1964.

§1

Poems. 1795.
Moral epistle respectfully dedicated to Earl Stanhope. 1795.
To the burgesses of Warwick. [Warwick 1797]; ed R. H. Super, Oxford 1949 (Luttrell Soc).
Gebir: a poem in seven books. 1798, Oxford 1803; Gebirus poema, Oxford 1803 (Latin trn by Landor); Gebir and Count Julian, ed H. Morley 1887.
Poems from the Arabic and Persian with notes by the author of Gebir. Warwick 1800 (first issue, with French preface); Warwick and London 1800 (second issue), 1927 (facs).
Poetry by the author of Gebir. Warwick 1800 (first issue, with An address to the fellows of Trinity College Oxford, Postscript to Gebir etc), 1802 (second issue).
Iambi incerto auctore. [Oxford? 1802?].
Simonidea. Bath [1806].
Three letters written in Spain to D. Francisco Riguelme [Riquelme]. 1809.
Ode ad Gustavum regem; ode ad Gustavum exulem. 1810.
Count Julian: a tragedy. 1812.
Commentary on memoirs of Mr Fox. 1812 (ptd but not pbd); rptd as Charles James Fox: a commentary on his life and character, ed S. Wheeler 1907.
Letters addressed to Lord Liverpool and the Parliament on the preliminaries of peace by Calvus. 1814.
Letter from Mr Landor to Mr Jervis. Bath 1814, Gloucester Jnl 23 May 1814.
Idyllia nova quinque heroum atque heroidum. Oxford 1815.
Sponsalia Polyxenae. Pistoia 1819.
Idyllia heroica decem librum phaleuciorum unum. Pisa 1820.
Poche osservazioni sullo stato attuale di que' popoli che vogliono governarsi per mezzo delle rappresentanze. [Naples?] 1821.
Imaginary conversations of literary men and statesmen. Vols 1–2 1824, 1826; vol 3 1828; vols 4–5 1829; 5 vols Boston 1882, London 1883; [selections] ed H. Ellis 1886, [1895]; ed A. G. Newcomer, New York 1899; Classical (imaginary) conversations Greek, Roman, modern, ed G. M. Adam, Washington [1901]; ed J. P. Mahaffy [1910, 1925]; ed F. A. Cavenagh, Oxford 1914; ed E. de Selincourt, Oxford 1915 (WC); ed T. E. Welby, Oxford 1934 (introd by C. Williams, notes by F. A. Cavenagh and A. C. Ward); ed R. H. Boothroyd 1936 (Limited Edns Club); tr German, 1878, 1919, 1923, Süddeutsche Monatshefte Sept 1932.
Citation and examination of William Shakspeare before the worshipful Sir Thomas Lucy Knight touching deer stealing, to which is added a conference of Master Edmund Spenser, a gentleman of note, with the Earl of Essex touching the state of Ireland. 1834, 1891; ed H. W. Mabie, New York [1891].
Pericles and Aspasia. 2 vols 1836, Philadelphia 1839, 1 vol Boston 1871; ed C. G. Crump 2 vols 1890 (Temple Lib); ed H. Ellis [1892]; ed G. R. Dennis 1903.
The letters of a conservative, in which are shown the only means of saving what is left of the English Church. 1836.
Terry Hogan: an eclogue. 1836. Anon, probably Landor's.
A satire on satirists and admonition to detractors. 1836.
Literary hours by various friends. Ed J. Ablett, Liverpool 1837 (priv ptd). Contains prose and verse by Landor.
The pentameron and pentalogia. 1837, Boston 1888 (with Citation and examination of Shakspeare, minor prose pieces and criticisms); ed H. Ellis 1889; ed D. Pettoello, Turin 1954.
High and low life in Italy. Monthly Repository Aug 1837–April 1838; tr French 1911, (fragment rptd from Nouvelle Revue Française 1 June 1911).
Andrea of Hungary and Giovanna of Naples. 1839.
Fra Rupert. 1840.
To Robert Browning. [1845]. Rptd from Morning Chron 22 Nov 1845.
The hellenics enlarged and completed. 1847; The hellenics, comprising heroic idyls &c, Edinburgh 1859 (enlarged); The hellenics and Gebir, ed A. Symons 1907 (Temple Classics); tr Italian, 1908; French, 1916.
The Italics of Landor. 1848.
Savagius Landor Lamartino. [Bath? 1848].
Imaginary conversation of King Carlo-Alberto and the Duchess Belgioioso on the affairs and prospects of Italy. [1848].
Carmen ad heroinam. [Bath? 1848].
Epistola ad Pium IX pontificem. [Bath? 1849].
Epistola ad Romanos. [Bath? 1849].
Ad Cossuthum et Bemum. [Bath? 1849].
Statement of occurrences at Llanbedr. Bath [1849].
Popery, British and foreign. 1851, Boston 1851.
On Kossuth's voyage to America. [Birmingham? 1851].
Tyrannicide, published for the benefit of the Hungarians in America. [Bath 1851].
Imaginary conversations of Greeks and Romans. 1853; Epicurus Leontion and Ternissa [1896].
The last fruit off an old tree. 1853.
Letters of an American mainly on Russia and revolution. 1854.
Antony and Octavius: scenes for the study. 1856.
Letter from Landor to R. W. Emerson. Bath [1856]; rptd with Emerson's paper on Landor from Dial, ed S. A. Jones, Cleveland 1895.
Landor and the Honorable Mrs Yescombe. [Bath 1857].
Mr Landor threatened. Bath [1857], [1857].
Dry sticks fagoted by Landor. Edinburgh 1858.
Mr Landor's remarks on a suit preferred against him at the summer assizes in Taunton 1858. 1859.
Savonarola e il priore di San Marco. Florence 1860.
Heroic idyls with additional poems. 1863.
An address to the Fellows of Trinity College Oxford on the alarm of invasion. 1917 (priv ptd).
Garibaldi and the President of the Sicilian Senate (an Imaginary conversation). 1917 (priv ptd).
A modern Greek idyl. 1917 (priv ptd).
To Elizabeth Barrett Browning and other verses. 1917 (priv ptd).
See vols ed S. Wheeler and H. C. Minchin under Letters, below.
Two anon works sometimes attributed to Landor, The dun cow (1808) *and* A reply from the den (after 1858) *are probably not his.*

Letters and Papers

Lowell, J. R. Some letters of Landor. Century Mag Feb 1888. To Mary Boyle.
Morrison, A. Collection of autograph letters and historical documents: the Blessington papers. 1895 (priv ptd). 90 letters and mss of Landor.
Wheeler, S. Letters and other unpublished writings of Landor. 1897.
— Letters of Landor private and public. 1899.

Tatham, E. H. R. Some unpublished letters of Landor. Fortnightly Rev Feb 1910. To Walter Birch.
Boselli, A. Una lettera di Landor a Margherita Bodoni; Landor e G. B. Bodoni. Aurea Parma 2 1913.
Blakeney, E. H. A letter believed to be hitherto unpublished. Winchester 1929 (priv ptd). To Caroline Southey.
Mason, A. H. Landor and Lady Blessington. Howard College Bull 87 1929.
Armstrong, A. J. Unpublished letters of Landor. Baylor Bull 35 1932.
Minchin, H. C. Landor: last days, letters and conversations. 1934. Not quite a duplicate of the preceding.
Bagnall, A. G. Some Landor letters to J. E. Fitzgerald. Turnbull Lib Record 2 1940.
Pfeiffer, K. G. Landor's critique of the Cenci. SP 39 1942. Letter to Leigh Hunt. Reply by R. H. Super, 40 1943.
Hubbell, J. B. Some new letters of Landor. Virginia Mag of history & biography 51 1943. To G. P. R. James.
Super, R. H. Landor's letters to Wordsworth and Coleridge. MP 55 1958.
Brumbaugh, T. B. A Landor letter. N & Q Jan 1963. To Lady Blessington.

§2

[Southey, R.] Critical Rev Sept 1799. Review of Gebir.
— Annual Rev 1 1803. Review of Poetry 1802.
— Quart Rev 8 1812. Review of Count Julian.
H[are], J. C. On Landor's Imaginary conversations. London Mag May 1824.
[Taylor, H.] Quart Rev 30 1824. Review of Imaginery conversations.
[Forster, J.] Evidences of genius for dramatic poetry: Landor. New Monthly Mag Oct 1836.
— Edinburgh Rev 83 1846; rptd in Eclectic Mag June 1846. Review of Works.
— Landor: a biography. 2 vols. 1869, 1 vol Boston 1869; London 1876 (abridged), 1895.
Emerson, R. W. Walter Savage Landor. Dial Oct 1841.
Quillinan, E. Imaginary conversation between Mr Landor and the editor of Blackwood's Magazine. Blackwood's Mag April 1843; rptd in Eclectic Museum 2 1843.
Horne, R. H. Landor. In his New spirit of the age, 1844. Written chiefly by Elizabeth Barrett.
[De Quincey, T.] On Goethe and Landor. Westmorland Gazette 8 May 1819.
— Notes on Landor. Tait's Mag Jan–Feb 1847.
— Orthographic mutineers (with special reference to the Works of Landor). Tait's Mag March 1847.
— Milton versus Southey and Landor. Tait's Mag April 1847. The last three rptd in his Collected writings, ed D. Masson, Edinburgh 1890.
[De Vere, A.] Edinburgh Rev 91 1850; rptd in his Essays chiefly on poetry, 1887. Review of Works etc.
[Spender, E.] Life and opinions of Landor. London Quart Rev 24 1865.
Field, K. Last days of Landor. Atlantic Monthly April–June 1866.
[Houghton, Baron (R. M. Milnes).] Forster's Life of Landor. Edinburgh Rev 130 1869; rptd in Living Age 4 Sept 1869 and in his Monographs personal and social, 1873.
[Linton, E. L.] Walter Savage Landor. North Br Rev 50 1869; rptd in Living Age 21 Aug 1869.
— Walter Savage Landor. Broadway Aug 1869.
— Reminiscences of Landor. Fraser's Mag July 1870.
— An unpublished fragment by Landor. Athenaeum 23 Nov 1889.
— The autobiography of Christopher Kirkland. 1885. Deals with her friendship with Landor.
— Landor, Dickens, Thackeray. Bookman (New York) April 1896; rptd in her My literary life, 1899.
[Dickens, C.] Landor's life. All the Year Round 24 July 1869; rptd in Every Saturday 14 Aug 1869.
Trollope, T. A. Some recollections of Landor. Lippincott's Mag April 1874.
— What I remember. 1887.
Stephen, L. Landor's Imaginary conversations. Cornhill Mag Dec 1878; rptd in Living Age 4 Jan 1879 and in his Hours in a library, 1879.
Colvin, S. Landor. 1881 (EML).
Lytton, R. Lady. Reminiscences of Landor. Tinsleys' Mag June 1883; rptd in Living Age 21 July 1883.
Sarrazin, G. In his Poètes modernes de l'Angleterre, Paris 1885.
Swinburne, A. C. Landor. Encyclopaedia britannica 1882 (9th edn); rptd in his Miscellanies, 1886.
Crosse, Mrs A. Walter Savage Landor. Temple Bar June 1891; rptd in Living Age 11 July 1891.
Evans, E. W. Landor: a critical study. New York 1892.
Benson, A. C. Llanthony Abbey and two of its priors. Nat Rev 28 1896; rptd in Eclectic Mag Feb 1897.
Thompson, F. Walter Savage Landor. Academy 27 Feb 1897.
Holyoake, M. Q. The last writings of Landor. GM Jan 1899.
White, W. H. The editing of a classic. Athenaeum 22 Dec 1900.
Wall, G. E. Stray words from Landor. Critic March 1901.
Duke, R. E. H. Notes on the family of Savage of Warwickshire. Miscellanea Genealogica et Heraldica 3rd ser 4–5 1901–2.
— A pedigree of the paternal ancestry of Landor. Miscellanea Genealogica et Heraldica 4th ser 5 1912.
Auer, J. Landor in seinen Beziehungen zu den Dichtern des Trecento: Dante, Boccaccio, Petrarca. Rheydt 1903.
Betham, E. The Llanthony maze. In his House of letters: being excerpts from the correspondence of Matilda Betham, 1905.
Thompson, E. N. S. Dante and Landor. MLN 20 1905.
Schwichtenberg, O. E. Southeys Roderick the last of the Goths und Landors Count Julian. Königsberg 1906.
Symons, A. The poetry of Landor. Atlantic Monthly June 1906; rptd in his Romantic movement in English poetry, 1909.
Tatham, E. H. R. Unpublished Latin verse by Landor. Athenaeum 22 June 1907.
Schlaak, R. Entstehungs- und Textgeschichte von Gebir. Halle 1909.
Beckh, G. F. Landor und die englische Literatur von 1798–1836. Marburg 1911.
Carré, J. M. Two unpublished poems of Landor. MLR 7 1912.
Cory, H. E. Landor and the academic attitude in poetry. Univ of California Chron 14 1912.
Bradley, W. A. The early poems of Landor: a study of his development and debt to Milton. 1914.
Peruzzi de' Medici, E. Walter Savage Landor. Cornhill Mag April 1915; rptd in Living age 29 May 1915.
Borenius, T. Pictures by the old masters in the library of Christ Church Oxford. Oxford 1916. The Landor-Duke bequest.
Wheeler, S. Landor: his early life and lost writings. Bookman (London) July 1916.
— Landor's Llanthony. Nineteenth Century March 1921.
— Landor: the man and the poet. Nineteenth Century Feb 1922.
Goldmark, R. I. The influence of Greek literature on Landor. In her Studies in the influence of the classics on English literature, New York 1918.
Henderson, W. B. D. Swinburne and Landor: a study of their spiritual relationship and its effect on Swinburne's moral and poetic development. 1918.
Nitchie, E. The classicism of Landor. Classical Jnl Dec 1919.

Browning, R. Some records of Landor. Ed by T. J. Wise 1919 (priv ptd). 3 letters to I. Blagden.
Williams, S. T. Echoes of Landor. Texas Rev 7 1922; rptd in his Studies in Victorian literature, New York 1923.
— The story of Gebir. PMLA 36 1921.
— Landor as a critic of literature. PMLA 38 1923.
— Landor's criticism in poetry. MLN 40 1925.
Dolson, G. B. Southey and Landor and the Consolation of philosophy of Boethius. Amer Jnl of Philology 43 1922.
Aldington, R. Landor's Hellenics. In his Literary studies and reviews, 1924.
Mason, A. H. Landor, poète lyrique. Paris 1924.
Flasdieck, H. M. Landor und seine Imaginary conversations. E Studien 58 1924.
Bailey, J. C. Some notes on the unpopularity of Landor. Essays by Divers Hands new ser 5 1925.
Raleigh, W. A. In his On writing and writers, 1926.
Herzfeld, G. Fouqué und Landor: ein merkwürdiges literarisches Motiv. Archiv Aug 1926.
Richter, H. Landor: Persönlichkeit, Dichtung, die Phantasiegespräche. Anglia 50–1 1926–7.
Mabbott, T. O. Landor on Chatterton and Wordsworth: marginal notes. N & Q 9 March 1929.
Fornelli, G. Landor e l'Italia. Forlì 1930.
Ashley-Montagu, M. F. Three unpublished Imaginary conversations by Landor. Nineteenth Century June 1930; rptd Living Age Oct 1930.
— Another unpublished Imaginary conversation by Landor. Nineteenth Century Sept 1931.
— Some Landor waifs. RES 8 1932.
— Three unknown portraits of Landor. Colophon new ser 2 1937.
— An unpublished poem by Landor. Nineteenth Century Jan 1939.
Mukherjee, K. Landor, Rose Aylmer and their association with Calcutta. Calcutta Rev Oct 1930.
de Selincourt, E. Classicism and romanticism in the poetry of Landor. In England und die Antike, ed F. Saxl, Berlin 1932.
— Landor's prose. In his Wordsworthian and other studies, Oxford 1947. Introd to WC edn of Imaginary conversations.
Anderson, M. B. The fate of Virgil as conceived by Dante: a dialogue of the dead and the living between Landor and Willard Fiske. San Francisco 1931.
Ferrando, G. Una visita di Emerson a Landor. Illustrazione Toscana Nov 1931.
Hawkes, C. P. The Spanish adventure of Landor. Cornhill Mag May 1933; rptd in his Authors-at-arms, 1934.
Richards, I. A. Fifteen lines from Landor. Criterion 12 1933; rptd in his Speculative instruments, 1955. Reply by C. Mauron 12 1933.
Elkin, F. Landor's studies of Italian life and literature. Philadelphia 1934.
Erich, E. Southey und Landor. Göttingen 1934.
Phelps, W. L. Landor and Browning. ELH 1 1934.
Super, R. H. Forster as Landor's literary executor. MLN 52 1937.
— An unknown child of Landor's. MLN 53 1938.
— Extraordinary action for libel: Yescombe v. Landor. PMLA 56 1941. Addn by R. F. Metzdorf, ibid.
— Landor's 'dear daughter' Eliza Lynn Linton. PMLA 59 1944.
— Landor's Rose Aylmer. Explicator Feb 1945.
— When Landor left home. MLQ 6 1945.
— Landor and the 'Satanic school'. SP 42 1945.
— The authorship of Guy's porridge pot and The dun cow. Library 5th ser 5 1950. Reply by R. Czerwinski 16 1961, Manuscripts 16 1964.
— A grain of truth about Wordsworth and Browning, Landor and Swinburne. MLN 67 1952. Reply by L. Kerr, TLS 31 July 1959.
— 'None was worth my strife': Landor and the Italian police. PBSA 47 1953.
— Landor: a biography. New York 1954, London 1957.
— 'The fire of life'. Cambridge Rev 16 Jan 1965.
Becker, G. J. Landor's political purpose. SP 35 1938.
Bradner, L. In his Musae anglicanae: a history of Anglo-Latin poetry 1500–1925, New York 1940.
Elwin, M. Savage Landor. New York 1941, 1958 (rev and enlarged as Landor: a replevin).
Peterson, D. E. A note on a probable source of Landor's Metellus and Marius. SP 39 1942.
Leavis, F. R. Landor and the seasoned epicure. Scrutiny 11 1943.
Craig, M. J. Landor and Ireland. Dublin Mag new ser 18 1943.
Chambers, E. K. Some notes on Landor. RES 20 1944.
Beach, L. B. Hellenism and the modern spirit. Books Abroad 20 1946.
Bald, R. C. Landor's Sponsalia Polyxenae. Library 5th ser 4 1949.
Davie, D. A. The shorter poems of Landor. EC 1 1951; rptd in his Purity of diction in English verse, 1952. Replies by W. J. Harvey and Davie 2 1952.
— Landor as poet. Shenandoah 4 1953.
Artom Treves, G. Io sono Landor. In her Anglo-Fiorentini di cento anni fa, Florence 1953; tr as The golden ring by S. Sprigge, 1956.
Gossman, A. Landor and the 'higher fountains'. Classical Jnl April 1955. Addn by D. M. Robinson, Oct 1956.
Oppel, H. Landor's Iphigeneia. Die Neueren Sprachen June 1955.
Keys, A. C. Landor's marginalia to the Dictionnaire philosophique. AUMLA no 5 1956.
Brumbaugh, T. B. Landor and Garibaldi. N & Q Oct 1958.
Hamilton, G. R. Walter Savage Landor. 1960.
Zall, P. M. Landor's marginalia on a volume of Cowper's poems. BNYPL Jan 1960.
Mahmoud, F. M. The Arabian original of Landor's Gebir (1798). Cairo Stud in Eng 1960.
Paden, W. D. Twenty new poems attributed to Tennyson, Praed and Landor. Victorian Stud 4 1961. Reply by R. H. Super, ibid.
Owens, R. J. Palgrave's marginalia on Landor's Works. N & Q June 1961.
Litzinger, B. A. The prior's niece in Fra Lippo Lippi. N & Q Sept 1961.
Grigson, G. 'I strove with none'. Listener 30 May 1963; rptd in his edn of Poems, above.
Vitoux, P. L'oeuvre de Landor. Paris 1964.
Perrine, L. Landor and immortality. Victorian Poetry 2 1964.
Nowell-Smith, S. Landor echoes Crabbe. TLS 2 April 1964.
Mercier, V. The future of Landor criticism. In Some British Romantics, ed J. V. Logan, J. E. Jordan and N. Frye, Columbus 1966.
Megally, S. H. Landor's dramatic dialogues. Cairo Stud in Eng 1963–6.
Prasher, A. L. The censorship of Landor's Imaginary conversations. Bull John Rylands Lib 49 1967.

R. H. S.

LEIGH HUNT

1784–1859

The most noteworthy collection of Hunt mss is the Brewer Collection at the State Univ of Iowa, Iowa City: over 100 literary mss and more than 650 letters from Hunt. Bodleian MS Eng Poet e 38 is a notebook containing unptd draft poems by Hunt. Other mss can be found at the Pierpont Morgan Library, New York, and in the Berg Collection at the New York Public Library (see TLS 22 Nov 1957). Letters are widely scattered, but over 100 can be found in the Brotherton Library at the Univ of Leeds; significant smaller groups can be found at Princeton Univ and Library of Congress. For further details, see Commentary, Book Collector 3 1954.

Bibliographies

Ireland, A. List of the writings of William Hazlitt and Hunt. 1868.

Swann, J. H. Catalogue of the Alexander Ireland collection in the Free Reference Library. Manchester 1898.

Mitchell, A. A bibliography of the writings of Hunt. Bookman's Jnl (London) 15 1927; rptd in Bibliographies of modern authors, 3rd ser, 1931.

Brewer, L. A. My Hunt library: first editions. Iowa City 1932.

Bay, J. C. The Hunt collection of Luther Albertus Brewer. Cedar Rapids Iowa 1933.

Landré, L. In his Leigh Hunt vol 2, Paris 1936.

Bernbaum, E. Keats, Shelley, Byron, Hunt: a critical sketch of important books and articles concerning them published in 1940–1950. Keats-Shelley Jnl 1 1952.

Hanlin, F. S. The Brewer-Leigh Hunt collection at the State University of Iowa. Keats-Shelley Jnl 8 1959.

Green, D. B. and E. G. Wilson (ed). Keats, Shelley, Byron, Hunt and their circles: a bibliography July 1 1950–June 30 1962. Lincoln Nebraska 1964.

Collections

Poetical works. 3 vols 1819. 5 separate pbns bound together with collective title-pages.

Poetical works. 1832. A cautious selection.

Poetical works. 1844, 1846. Another selective edn.

Poetical works. Ed his son Thornton Hunt. 1860. Collected and arranged with 'his own final judgment'.

Poetical works. Ed S. Adams Lee 2 vols Boston 1866.

In 1870 Smith, Elder pbd a uniform reprint in 7 vols of some of Hunt's prose works. There has been no full collected edn of the prose, though substantial parts have been completed.

A tale for a chimney corner and other essays. Ed E. Ollier [1869].

Favorite poems. Cambridge Mass 1877.

Essays. Ed A. Symons 1887.

Hunt as poet and essayist. Ed C. Kent 1889.

Poetical works of Hunt and Hood. Ed J. H. Panting [1889]. A selection.

Essays and poems. Ed R. B. Johnson 2 vols 1891.

Tales. Ed W. Knight 1891.

Dramatic essays. Ed W. Archer and R. W. Lowe 1894.

Essays and sketches. Ed R. B. Johnson, Oxford [1906] (WC).

Selections in prose and verse. Ed J. H. Lobban 1909.

Leigh Hunt. Ed E. Storer [1911].

Poetical works. Ed H. S. Milford, Oxford 1923. The definitive edn; a few pieces remain uncollected; to some Milford provides references; he omits juvenilia and the trn Amyntas.

Prefaces, mainly to his periodicals. Ed R. B. Johnson 1927.

Essays. Ed J. B. Priestley 1929 (EL). A selection.

Dramatic criticism 1808–31. Ed L. H. and C. W. Houtchens, New York 1950.

Literary criticism. Ed L. H. and C. W. Houtchens, with an essay, Leigh Hunt as man of letters, by C. D. Thorpe, New York 1956.

Political and occasional essays. Ed L. H. and C. W. Houtchens, with an essay, Leigh Hunt as political essayist, by C. R. Woodring, New York 1962.

§1

Juvenilia written between the ages of twelve and sixteen. 1801, 1801, 1802, 1803.

Critical essays on the performers of the London theatres. 1807.

An attempt to shew the folly and danger of Methodism. 1809.

The reformist's answer to the article entitled State of parties in the last Edinburgh Review (no 30). 1810.

The Prince of Wales v the Examiner: a full report of the trial of John and Leigh Hunt, to which are added observations on the trial by the editor of the Examiner. 1812.

The feast of the poets with notes, and other pieces. 1814 (2 issues, different imprints), 1815 ('amended and enlarged').

The descent of liberty: a mask. 1815, 1816.

The story of Rimini. 1816, 1817, 1819, Boston 1844.

Musical copyright: Whitaker versus Hume; to which are subjoined observations on the defence made by Sergeant Joy, by Leigh Hunt. 1816.

The round table: a collection of essays. 1817. The round table in Examiner was principally by Hazlitt: but of the 52 papers collected in vol form 10 are by Hunt.

Foliage: or poems original and translated. 1818.

Hero and Leander, and Bacchus and Ariadne. 1819.

Amyntas: a tale of the woods. 1820. Tr from Tasso; dedicated to Keats.

The months descriptive of the successive beauties of the year. 1821; ed W. Andrews 1897; ed R. H. Bath 1929. Founded on articles in the Literary pocket-book.

Ultra-Crepidarius: a satire on William Gifford. 1823.

Bacchus in Tuscany, translated from the Italian of F. Redi. 1825.

The keepsake for 1828. 1827. Hunt contributed anon Dreams on the borders of the land of poetry and Pocket books and keepsakes.

Lord Byron and some of his contemporaries. 1828, 2 vols 1828, 3 vols Paris 1828 (with addns). The Autobiography, 1850, below, was partly a reconstruction of this work.

Sir Ralph Esher: or adventures of a gentleman of the Court of Charles II. 3 vols 1832 (anon), 1850 (4th edn, with preface). A novel; some copies dated 1830.

Christianism: or belief and unbelief reconciled. 1832. Expanded for general circulation into The religion of the heart, 1853, below.

The indicator and the companion: a miscellany for the fields and the fireside. 2 vols 1834, 1840, 1845. Hunt's selections from the periodicals named.

Captain sword and captain pen. 1835, 1839, 1849 (with new preface).

A legend of Florence: a play. 1840, 1840 (with added preface); rptd in G. H. Lewes, Modern British dramatists, 1867.

The seer: or common-places refreshed. 2 pts 1840–1, 1850.

Heads of the people drawn by Kenny Meadows, with original essays. 1840. Hunt's contributions are The monthly nurse and The omnibus conductor.

Notice of the late Mr Egerton Webbe. 1840. Rptd from Morning Chron.

The poems of Geoffrey Chaucer modernized. 1841. Ed R. H. Horne and Hunt, who modernized the Tales of the Squire and the Friar.

The palfrey: a love-story of old times. 1842.

Imagination and fancy; with an essay in answer to the question What is poetry? 1844, 1845, 1846, 1852, 1883; ed E. Gosse 1907.

Wit and humour, with an illustrative essay. 1846, 1846.

Stories from the Italian poets. 2 vols 1846, 1854. An excerpt entitled Dante's Divine comedy: the book and its story, 1903.

Men, women and books. 2 vols 1847, 1852.

A jar of honey from Mount Hybla. 1848, 1852.

The town: its memorable characters and events. 2 vols 1848, 1859; ed A. Dobson, Oxford 1907 (WC).

The autobiography. 3 vols 1850, 1860 ('revised by the author; with further revision, and introduction by his eldest son'); ed R. Ingpen 2 vols New York 1903; ed E. Blunden, Oxford 1928 (WC); ed J. E. Morpurgo 1949; ed from the ms in the Brewer Collection by S. F. Fogle as Leigh Hunt's Autobiography: the earliest sketches, Gainesville 1959.

Table talk. 1851.

The religion of the heart. 1853. *See* Christianism, *above*.
The old court suburb: or memorials of Kensington. 2 vols 1855, 1855 (enlarged), 1860; ed A. Dobson 2 vols 1902.
Stories in verse now first collected. 1855.
A saunter through the West End. 1861.
A day by the fire; and other papers hitherto uncollected. Ed J. E. Babson 1870.
The wishing-cap papers, now first collected [by J. E. Babson]. Boston 1873.
Ballads of Robin Hood. Ed L. A. Brewer, Cedar Rapids Iowa 1922.
The love of books. Ed L. A. and E. T. Brewer, Cedar Rapids Iowa 1923. Rptd from Hunt's My books.
Marginalia. Ed L. A. Brewer, Cedar Rapids Iowa 1926.
Musical evenings or selections, vocal and instrumental. Ed D. R. Cheney, Columbia Missouri 1964.
Hunt on eight sonnets of Dante. Ed D. Rhodes, Iowa City 1965.

Periodicals

No register has yet been made of Hunt's very numerous and often anon contributions to periodicals other than those which he edited. The following references may be found useful so far as uncollected writings are concerned: papers signed 'Mr Town, Junior' *in* Traveller (before 1805); *theatre articles in* News (1805–7); *papers in* Statesman (1806); *notices of plays in* Times (Aug 1807); *essays and verses in* New Monthly Mag (particularly 1825–6, and occasionally until 1850), Atlas (c. 1828–30), True Sun, *and* Weekly True Sun (*c.* 1833–4), Spectator 1858–9); Morning Chronicle *at intervals throughout his life. See also the article in DNB, which points out some of Hunt's contributions to musical criticism.*
The examiner: a Sunday paper. 1808–21. Hunt's editorial work ended in 1821, but he contributed until 1825.
The reflector: a quarterly magazine. 1810–11. Re-issued as Reflector: a collection of essays, 2 vols 1812.
The literary pocket-book: or companion for the lover of nature and art. 1818–22 (for 1819–23).
The indicator. 76 nos Wednesday 13 Oct 1819–21 March 1821; 2 vols in 1 1822. Other Indicators appeared in Literary Examiner 1823; no 89 and last in New Monthly Mag May 1832.
The liberal: verse and prose from the south. 1822–3 (4 nos, 2 vols); rptd New York 1967.
The literary examiner. 1823. Probably ed John Hunt.
The companion. 9 Jan 1828–23 July 1828 (nos 1–28); rptd New York 1967.
The chat of the week. 28 June 1930–28 Aug 1830.
The tatler: a daily journal of literature and the stage. 4 Sept 1830–13 Feb 1832.
Leigh Hunt's London journal. 2 vols 2 April 1834–26 Dec 1835; rptd New York 1967.
The monthly repository. July 1837–April 1838. Ed F. E. Mineka as The dissidence of dissent, Chapel Hill 1944.
Leigh Hunt's journal. 7 Dec 1850–29 March 1851. Weekly.

Anthologies etc

Classic tales, serious and lively; with critical essays. 5 vols 1806–7, 1895. Critical papers by Hunt on Henry Mackenzie, Goldsmith, Henry Brooke, Voltaire and Dr Johnson.
The masque of anarchy, a poem by Percy Bysshe Shelley: now first published, with a preface by Hunt. 1832.
The dramatic works of R. B. Sheridan. 1840, 1846, 1851.
The dramatic works of Wycherley, Congreve, Vanbrugh and Farquhar. 1840, 1851.
One hundred romances of real life. 1843, 1888.
The foster brother: a tale of the wars of Chiozza. 3 vols 1845. By Thornton Hunt; ed Leigh Hunt.
Readings for railways. 1849; ser 2, 1853 (with J. B. Syme).
A book for a corner. 2 vols 1849, 1858.
Beaumont and Fletcher. 1855. A selection.
The book of the sonnet. Ed Hunt and S. Adams Lee 2 vols Boston 1867. Includes Hunt's essay on the sonnet.

Letters

Correspondence. Ed his eldest son 2 vols 1862.
Selections from Hunt's correspondence with B. R. Haydon, Charles Ollier and Southwood Smith. Ed S. R. T. Mayer, St James's Mag 1874–5.
Mayer, S. R. T. Hunt and Lord Brougham; with original letters. Temple Bar June 1876.
Six letters addressed to W. W. Story 1850–6. 1913.
Letter on Hogg's Life of Shelley. Ed L. A. Brewer, Cedar Rapids Iowa 1927.
My Hunt library: the holograph letters. Ed L. A. Brewer, Iowa City 1938. 900 letters and ms scraps, most unpbd.
Gates, P. G. A Hunt-Byron letter. Keats-Shelley Jnl 2 1953.
Kaser, D. E. Two new Hunt letters. N & Q March 1955.
Barnett, G. L. Hunt revises a letter. HLQ 20 1957.
Marshall, W. H. Hunt on Walt Whitman: a new letter. N & Q Sept 1957.
—— Three new Hunt letters. Keats-Shelley Jnl 9 1960.
Green, D. B. Some new Hunt letters. N & Q Aug 1958.
Sanders, C. R. The correspondence and friendship of Carlyle and Hunt: the early years. Bull John Rylands Lib 45 1963.
—— The correspondence and friendship of Carlyle and Hunt: the later years. Bull John Rylands Lib 46 1963.
Enkvist, N. E. In his British and American literary letters in Scandinavian public collections, Abo 1964.
Barnes, W. Hunt's letters in the Luther Brewer collections: plans for a new edition. Books at Iowa no 3 1965.

Dubious Ascriptions

Among the pbns sometimes attributed to Hunt, Reminiscences of Michael Kelly the singer 2 vols 1826 *should not stand: it was prepared by Theodore Hook.* The rebellion of the beasts: or the ass is dead! Long live the ass!, 1825 *by* 'a late Fellow of St John's College, Cambridge' *may or may not be Hunt's; it is nowhere mentioned in his available letters.* Dictionary of anonymous and pseudonymous English literature, ed J. Kennedy, W. A. Smith and A. F. Johnson, *describes* Florentine tales, 1847, as '*largely by Thomas Powell, but after his death* by J. H. Leigh Hunt'. *Powell, however, was sufficiently alive in 1849 to emigrate to New York, pursued by the execrations of Browning. A poem in* Ollier's Literary Miscellany 1820–The universal Pan–*signed L., is more the fault of* '*Barry Cornwall*' *than of Hunt.*

Marshall, W. H. An early misattribution to Byron: Hunt's The feast of the poets. N & Q May 1962.

§2

Numerous references to Hunt will also be found in the standard edns of the works and in letters of Byron, Hazlitt, Keats and Shelley.
Hunt, Leigh. Autobiographical paper. Monthly Mirror April 1810.
Keats, J. In his Poems, 1817.
'Z'. The cockney school of poetry. Blackwood's Mag Oct 1817–Jan 1818.
'A'. Mr Hunt's Hero and Leander. London Mag July 1820.
Shelley, P. B. The Cenci. 1821. Dedication.
—— Letters to Hunt. Ed T. J. Wise 2 vols 1894.

Lamb, C. Letter of Elia to Robert Southey esq. London Mag Oct 1823.
[Kent, E.] Flora domestica. 1823.
— Sylvan sketches. 1825.
Hazlitt, W. In his Spirit of the age, 1825.
[Lytton, E. B.] Sir Ralph Esher. New Monthly Mag March 1832.
Brougham, H. P. (Baron Brougham and Vaux). In his Speeches, 4 vols 1837.
Hall, S. C. In his Book of gems, 1838. A notice of Hunt; also memoranda by Hunt on Shelley, Keats and Tennyson.
— In his A book of memoirs, [1876].
[Macaulay, T. B.] Comic dramatists of the Restoration. Edinburgh Rev 72 1841.
Horne, R. H. In his A new spirit of the age vol 1, 1844.
— (ed). Letters of E. B. Browning. 2 vols 1877.
Howitt, W. In his Homes and haunts of the British poets, 2 vols 1847.
[Ireland, A.] The genius and writings of Hunt. Manchester Examiner July 1847.
Haydon, B. R. In his Autobiography and journals, 3 vols 1853.
Dickens, C. In his Bleak house. 1853. The character Harold Skimpole.
[—] Hunt: a remonstrance. All the Year Round 24 Dec 1859.
— In his Letters 3 vols 1880–2.
Moore, T. In his Memoirs, journals and correspondence vol 8, 1856.
[Ollier, E.] The occasional. Spectator 3 Sept 1859.
— Correspondence of Hunt. Spectator 22 March 1862.
— A literary life. All the Year Round 12 April 1862.
[Hunt, T. L.] A man of letters of the last generation. Cornhill Mag Jan 1860.
[Carlyle, T.] Memoranda concerning Mr Leigh Hunt. Macmillan's Mag July 1862.
Collier, J. P. The late Duke of Devonshire and Hunt. Athenaeum 8 March 1862.
Hawthorne, N. In his Our old home, 1863.
Kent, C. Footprints on the road. 1864.
Bates, W. (ed). A gallery of illustrious literary characters 1830–8 drawn by the late Daniel Maclise RA and accompanied by notices chiefly by the late William Maginn LL D. [1876].
Procter, B. W. An autobiographical fragment. 1877.
Cowden Clarke, C. and M. In their Recollections of writers, 1878.
Dowden, E. In his Life of Shelley 2 vols 1886.
Saintsbury, G. In his Essays in English literature 1780–1860, 1890.
Monkhouse, W. C. Life of Hunt. 1896.
Johnson, R. B. Leigh Hunt. 1896.
— Shelley-Leigh Hunt. 1928.
Punchard, C. D. Helps to the study of Hunt's essays. 1899.
Allingham, W. Diary. 1907, 1967.
Adams, M. Some Hampstead memories. Illustr F. Adcock 1909.
Miller, B. Hunt's relations with Byron, Shelley and Keats. 1910.
Moebus, O. Hunts Kritik der Entwicklung der englischen Literatur bis zum Ende des 18 Jahrhundert. Strasbourg 1916.
Howe, P. P. In his Life of William Hazlitt, 1922, 1928 (rev).
Gosse, E. In his More books on the table, 1923.
Brewer, L. A. Some Lamb and Browning letters to Hunt. Cedar Rapids Iowa 1924.
— The joys and sorrows of a book collector. Cedar Rapids Iowa 1928.
— Some letters from my Hunt portfolios. Cedar Rapids Iowa 1929.
Forman, M. B. Hunt: some unfamiliar apologists. London Mercury June 1926.
Blunden, E. Hunt's Examiner examined. 1928.
— Hunt: a biography. 1930, New York 1930 (as Hunt and his circle).
— Hunt's London Journal. Eibungaku Kenkyu 28 1952.
— Critics who have influenced taste, 9: Hunt. Times 30 May 1963.
— and E. C.-J. Most sincerely yours. Medical Bull 2 1954.
Law, M. H. The English familiar essay as exemplified in the writings of Hunt. Philadelphia 1934.
Munby, A. N. L. Letters to Hunt from his son Vincent. 1934.
Roberts, M. Hunt's place in the reform movement 1808–10. RES 11 1935.
Fisher, E. Hunt und die italienische Literatur. Freiburg 1936.
Kishimoto, I. Hunt's marginalia on Shakespeare. Stud in Eng Lit (Tokyo) 1936.
Brawner, J. P. Hunt and his wife Marianne. West Virginia Univ Stud 3 1937.
Strout, A. L. Hunt, Hazlitt and 'Maga'. ELH 4 1937.
Landré, L. In his Contribution à l'histoire du romantisme anglais, 2 vols Paris 1936.
Watson, M. R. The Spectator tradition and the development of the familiar essay. ELH 13 1946.
— Magazine serials and the essay tradition 1746–1820. Baton Rouge 1956.
Gates, P. G. Hunt's review of Shelley's posthumous poems. PBSA 42 1948.
— Hunt and his autobiography. Charles Lamb Soc Bull 16 1950.
Stout, G. D. The political history of Hunt's Examiner. St Louis 1949.
— Hunt's Shakespeare. In Studies in memory of F. M. Webster, St Louis 1951.
Cohen, B. B. Haydon, Hunt and 6 sonnets (1816) by Wordsworth. PQ 29 1950.
Counihan, D. Hunt and Dickens. TLS 5 Oct 1951.
Fitzgerald, M. Hunt, Landor and Dickens. TLS 26 Oct 1951.
Ristine, F. H. Hunt's Horace. MLN 66 1951.
Fogle, S. F. Skimpole once more. Nineteenth-Century Fiction 7 1953.
— Hunt and the Laureateship. SP 55 1958.
— Hunt's lost brother and the American legacy. Keats-Shelley Jnl 8 1959.
— Hunt, Thomas Powell and the Florentine tales. Keats-Shelley Jnl 14 1965.
Narita, S. Poet's house by Hunt. Eng Teachers' Mag no 1 1952.
Walton, C. C. Hunt: the spirit of an age. Amateur Book Collector 3 1952.
MacCarthy, D. In his Humanities, 1953.
Norman, S. Hunt, Moore and Byron. TLS 2 Jan 1953.
Stuart, D. N. In his Portrait of the Prince Regent, 1953.
— The Prince Regent and the poets. Essays by Divers Hands 27 1955.
Boas, G. Great Englishmen at school. E & S new ser 7 1954.
Fielding, K. J. Skimpole and Hunt again. N & Q April 1955.
Fleece, J. Hunt's Shakespearean criticism. In Essays in honor of Walter Clyde Curry, Nashville 1955.
Mackerness, E. D. Hunt's musical journalism. Monthly Musical Record Nov–Dec 1956.
Wallace, I. In his Fabulous originals: lives of extraordinary people who inspired memorable characters in fiction, New York 1956.
Blumenthal, W. H. Barbs and bludgeons. Amateur Book Collector 7 1957.
Houtchens, L. H. and C. W. In English romantic poets and essayists, ed Houtchens, New York 1957, 1966 (rev).
Kaser, D. Hunt and his Pennsylvania editor. Pennsylvania Mag of History 81 1957.

Crompton, L. Satire and symbolism in Bleak House. Nineteenth-Century Fiction 12 1958.
Emerson, F. W. The Spenser-followers in Hunt's Chaucer. N & Q July 1958.
Green, D. B. The first publication of Hunt's Love letters made of flowers. PBSA 52 1958.
— Hunt's hand in Samuel Carter Hall's Book of gems. Keats-Shelley Jnl 8 1959.
— The publication of Hunt's imagination and fancy. SB 12 1959.
— Hunt an honorary citizen of Philadelphia. Keats-Shelley Jnl 9 1960.
Sanders, M. Literary Hampstead. Listener 7 Aug 1958.
Hunt's Examiner. Colby Lib Quart 4 1958.
Deschamps, J. Hunt et Stendhal. Stendhal Club 1 1959.
Landré, L. Hunt: a few remarks about the man. Keats-Shelley Memorial Bull 10 1959.
— Hunt: his contribution to English romanticism. Keats-Shelley Jnl 8 1959.
Moore, D. L. Byron, Hunt and the Shelleys: new light on certain old scandals. Keats-Shelley Memorial Bull 10 1959.
Pope, W. B. Hunt and his companions. Keats-Shelley Jnl 8 1959.
Richardson, J. Friend of genius. Listener 17 Sept 1959.
Russell, R. The portraiture of Hunt. Keats-Shelley Memorial Bull 10 1959.
Saunders, B. In his Portraits of genius, 1959.
Thorpe, C. D. The nymphs. Keats-Shelley Memorial Bull 10 1959.
Trewin, J. C. Hunt as a dramatic critic. Ibid.
Woodring, C. R. The Hunt trails: informations and manoeuvres. Ibid.
George Peabody and others. TLS 11 Dec 1959.
Hayward, J. Commentary. Book Collector 9 1960.
Marshall, W. H. Byron, Shelley, Hunt and the Liberal. Philadelphia 1960.
Wolfe, J. and L. An earlier version of Abou. N & Q March 1960.
A Hunt evening, Nov 20, 1959. Philadelphia 1960.
Cameron, K. N. In his Shelley and his circle 1773–1822 vol 1, Cambridge Mass 1961.
Cheney, D. R. Source wanted. N & Q Aug 1961. Reply by E. Morgan, Nov 1961.
— The original of a Hunt translation identified. N & Q May 1962.
Jones, D. L. Hazlitt and Hunt at the opera house. Symposium 16 1962.
Nowell-Smith, S. Hunt's The descent of liberty, 1815. Library 5th ser 17 1962.
Fisher, W. Hunt as friend and critic of Keats: 1816–59. Lock Haven Rev 1st ser no 5 1963.
Howell, A. C. Milton's mortal remains and their literary echoes. Ball State Teachers College Forum 4 1963.
Brewer, L. A. Hunt association books. Books at Iowa no 1 1964.

R. L. C.

CHARLES LAMB

1775–1834

Bibliographies

North, E. D. In B. E. Martin, In the footprints of Lamb, 1891.
Dodd, Mead and Co. Descriptions of a few books from Lamb's library, and of some presentation copies and first editions of his rarer books. New York [1899]. A sale catalogue.
Livingston, L. S. Some notes on three of Lamb's juveniles. Bibliographer 1 1902.
— A bibliography of the first editions in book form of the writings of C. and Mary Lamb, published prior to C. Lamb's death in 1834. New York 1903.
Hutchinson, T. In his Works in prose and verse of C. and Mary Lamb vol 1, Oxford [1908].
Thomson, J. C. Bibliography of the writings of C. and Mary Lamb. Hull 1908.
American Art Association. The literary treasures of W. T. Wallace. New York 1920. A sale catalogue, nos 755–804.
Wise, T. J. In his Ashley library: a catalogue vol 3, 1923. Describes more than 40 Lamb items.
Tregaskis, J. An important collection of some of the rarer works of Lamb, together with some 'Lambiana'. 1927. A bookseller's catalogue with facs.
Griffith, R. H. Lamb: an exhibition of books and manuscripts in the library of the University of Texas. Austin 1935.
Finch, J. S. The Scribner Lamb collection. Princeton Univ Lib Chron 7 1946.
Woodring, C. R. Lamb in the Harvard library. Harvard Lib Bull 10 1956.
Barnett, G. L. and S. M. Tave. In English romantic poets and essayists: a review of research and criticism, ed C. W. and L. H. Houtchens, New York 1957, 1966 (rev).

Collections

Works. 2 vols 1818.
Poetical works of Rogers, Lamb [et al]. Paris 1829. Unauthorized.
Prose works. 3 vols 1835.
Poetical works. 1836.
Works. [Ed T. N. Talfourd] 1840 (includes Letters with a sketch of his life), 2 vols New York 1852, 4 vols 1850 (vols 1–2 new edns of Letters and Final memorials).
Complete correspondence and works. Vol 1 (no more pbd), 1868. Introd by G. A. H. Sala.
Complete correspondence and works. Ed T. Purnell 4 vols 1870 (vol 1 reissue of incomplete 1868 edn).
Complete works. Ed R. H. Shepherd 1874.
Life, letters and writings. Ed P. Fitzgerald 6 vols 1875, 1924.
Works. Ed C. Kent [1876].
Works. Ed A. Ainger 7 vols 1883–8, 12 vols 1899–1900.
Works. Ed E. V. Lucas 7 vols 1903–5, 6 vols 1912 (includes rev edn of Letters in 2 vols but omits Dramatic specimens).
Works. Ed W. Macdonald 12 vols 1903.
Works. Ed T. Hutchinson 2 vols Oxford [1908] (OSA).

Selections

The best of Lamb. Ed E. V. Lucas 1914.
Lamb: prose and poetry. Ed G. S. Gordon, Oxford 1921.
Lamb's criticism: a selection. Ed E. M. W. Tillyard, Cambridge 1923.
Everybody's Lamb. Ed A. C. Ward 1933.
Essays and letters. Ed J. M. French, New York 1937.
Selections from Lamb and Hazlitt. Ed R. W. Jepson 1940.
The portable Lamb. Ed J. M. Brown, New York 1949.
Lamb and Elia. Ed J. E. Morpurgo 1949 (Pelican).
Selected essays, letters, poems. Ed J. L. May 1953.
Essays. Ed R. Vallance and J. Hampden 1963 (Folio Soc).
A Lamb selection. Ed F. B. Pinion 1965.

§ 1

Sentimental tablets of the good Pamphile by J. C. Gorjy. Tr P. S. Dupuy 1795. Rev for pbn by Lamb.
Original letters etc of Sir John Falstaff and his friends. 1796, 2 vols Philadelphia 1813; ed R. H. Shepherd 1877; ed I. Gollancz 1907. Lamb's assistance to the author J. White is purely conjectural.
Poems on the death of Priscilla Farmer by Charles Lloyd. Bristol 1796. Includes Lamb's The grandam.
Poems on various subjects by S. T. Coleridge. 1796. Includes 4 sonnets by Lamb.

[Sonnets by various authors. Ed S. T. Coleridge] Bristol 1796 (priv ptd). Includes 4 sonnets by Lamb.

Poems by S. T. Coleridge, second edition, to which are now added poems by Lamb and Charles Lloyd. Bristol 1797.

Blank verse by Charles Lloyd and Lamb. 1798.

A tale of Rosamund Gray and old blind Margaret. Birmingham 1798, London 1798, 1835 (with Recollections of Christ's Hospital); ed R. B. Johnson 1928 (Golden Cockerel Press).

John Woodvil: a tragedy; to which are added Fragments of Burton. 1802.

The king and queen of hearts. 1805 (anon), 1806, 1808, 1809; ed E. V. Lucas 1902 (facs). *See* Tregaskis catalogue, above.

Tales from Shakespear, designed for the use of young persons. 2 vols 1807, 1809, 1810, Philadelphia 1813 (unauthorized), London 1816, 1822, 1 vol 1831; ed F. J. Furnivall 2 vols 1901; 1906 (EL); ed G. Tillotson 1962 (EL); ed J. C. Trewin 1964 (Nonesuch Lib); tr German, 1842, 1843; French, 1847; Spanish, 1847, 1893; Swedish, 1851. Some of the tales were issued separately as well as in pairs and tetrads. Mary Lamb's name first appeared on the title-page in 1838 (6th edn).

Adventures of Ulysses. 1808, 1819, 1827; ed A. Lang 1890; ed E. A. Gardner, Cambridge 1921.

Specimens of English dramatic poets who lived about the time of Shakespeare, with notes. 1808, 1813, 2 vols 1835, 1 vol 1854 (with added extracts from the Garrick plays); ed I. Gollancz 2 vols 1893; ed J. D. Campbell 1907.

Mrs Leicester's school: or the history of several young ladies related by themselves. 1809 (anon), 1809, 1810, Georgetown DC 1811, London 1814, 1828 (10th edn). *See* Woodring bibliography, above.

Poetry for children, entirely original, by the author of Mrs Leicester's school. 2 vols 1809 (anon), 1 vol Boston 1812, New Haven 1820; ed R. H. Shepherd 1872; ed A. W. T[uer] 2 vols 1892 (facs).

Beauty and the beast, or a rough outside with a gentle heart: a poetical version of an ancient tale. [1811] (anon), 1813, 1825; ed R. H. Shepherd 1886; ed A. Lang [1887].

Prince Dorus, or flattery put out of countenance: a poetical version of an ancient tale. 1811 (anon), 1818; ed A. W. T[uer] 1889; ed J. P. Briscoe, [Nottingham] 1896.

Mr H: or beware a bad name. Philadelphia 1813, 1825.

The poetical recreations of the Champion. 1822. Ed and pbd by J. Thelwall with many contributions by Lamb.

Elia: essays which have appeared under that signature in the London Magazine. 1823 (anon), 1823. *See* endnote, below.

Elia: second series. Philadelphia 1828. Anon and unauthorized.

Album verses. 1830.

Satan in search of a wife, with the whole process of his courtship and marriage, and who danced at the wedding, by an eyewitness. 1831. Anon.

The last essays of Elia: being a sequel to essays published under that name. 1833. Anon.

Elia. 2 vols 1835. Moxon's first collected edn of both sers.

Essays of Elia [both sers]; to which are added Letters, and Rosamund: a tale. Paris 1835. Unauthorized.

Recollections of Christ's Hospital. 1835 (with Rosamund Gray and other pieces).

Eliana: being the hitherto uncollected writings. [Ed J. E. Babson] 1864.

Mary and C. Lamb: poems, letters and remains. Ed W. C. Hazlitt 1874.

The following later edns may be noted among the innumerable reprints of the essays of Elia: both sers ed N. L. Hallward and S. C. Hill 2 vols 1895–1900; 1901 (WC); 1906 (EL); ed A. H. Thompson 2 vols Cambridge 1913; ed W. Macdonald 2 vols 1929 (introd by R. Lynd); 2 vols Newtown 1929–30 (Gregynog Press); ed M. Elwin 1952. First ser ed O. C. Williams, Oxford 1911. Second ser ed F. Page, Oxford 1929 (introd by E. Blunden). A notable edn of a single essay is The old benchers of the Inner Temple, ed F. D. Mackinnon, Oxford 1927.

Letters and Papers

Most edns of Lamb's works, above, include his letters.

Letters of Lamb, with a sketch of his life. Ed T. N. Talfourd 2 vols 1837.

Final memorials of Lamb, consisting chiefly of his letters not before published, with sketches of some of his companions. Ed T. N. Talfourd 2 vols 1848.

Letters. Ed W. C. Hazlitt 2 vols 1886.

Hazlitt, W. C. The Lambs: their lives, their friends and their correspondence. 1897.

—— Lamb and Hazlitt: further letters and records. 1900.

Lucas, E. V. Lamb and the Lloyds. 1898.

—— An unpublished letter of Lamb. TLS 13 Feb 1937.

Letters. Ed H. H. Harper 5 vols Boston 1905 (priv ptd). Vol 1 contains facs.

Letters. Ed W. Macdonald 2 vols 1906 (EL); ed E. V. Lucas, selected and arranged by G. Pocock 2 vols 1945 (EL).

Some Lamb and Browning letters to Leigh Hunt. Ed L. A. Brewer, Cedar Rapids Iowa 1924. With facs.

Seven letters to Charles Ryle of the East India House 1828–32. Oxford 1931. With facs.

The letters of Lamb to which are added those of his sister Mary Lamb. Ed E. V. Lucas 3 vols 1935. Incorporates the projected edn by the late Mrs G. A. Anderson, unrestricted by former difficulties of copyright.

Howe, M. A. DeW. Lamb to Hazlitt: a new-found letter. Spectator 5 Aug 1938.

Finch, J. S. Lamb's Companionship . . . in almost solitude. Princeton Univ Lib Chron 6 1945.

Letters. Ed G. Woodcock 1950. A selection.

Barnett, G. L. Lamb to John Britton: an unpublished letter. MLQ 13 1952.

Selected letters. Ed T. S. Matthews, New York 1956.

Watson, V. T. N. Talfourd and his friends. TLS 20–7 April 1956.

Klingopulos, G. D. Lamb and John Chambers. TLS 5 Sept 1958.

Barker, J. R. Some early correspondence of Sarah Stoddart and the Lambs. HLQ 24 1960.

Woodring, C. R. Lamb takes a holiday. Harvard Lib Bull 14 1960.

Skeat, T. C. Letters of C. and Mary Lamb and Coleridge. BM Quart 26 1962.

Braekman, W. Two hitherto unpublished letters of C. and Mary Lamb to the Morgans. E Studies 44 1963.

Green, D. B. Three new letters of Lamb. HLQ 27 1963.

§2

Annual Rev 1 1802; Retrospective Rev 1 1820. Reviews of John Woodvil.

[Brown, T.] John Woodvil. Edinburgh Rev 2 1803.

Annual Rev 7 1808; Monthly Rev April 1809; Critical Rev May 1810. Reviews of Dramatic specimens.

[Wilson, J.] The works. Blackwood's Mag Aug 1818.

—— Manifesto. Blackwood's Mag Oct 1823.

[Hunt, L.] The works. Examiner 21–8 March 1819; Indicator 31 Jan–7 Feb 1821.

—— Lamb. Leigh Hunt's London Jnl 7 Jan 1835.

Br Critic Feb 1819; European Mag April 1819; Literary Gazette 14 Aug 1819; Monthly Rev Nov 1819. Reviews of Works.

[Talfourd, T. N.] Remarks on the writings of Lamb. New Monthly Mag Aug 1820.

[Coleridge, H. N.] On Lamb's poetry. Etonian March 1821.

—— Last essays of Elia. Quart Rev 54 1835.

Hazlitt, W. In his Table-talk 2 vols 1821–2; The spirit of the age, 1825; The plain speaker, 2 vols 1826. Rptd in Complete works, ed P. P. Howe vols 8, 11–12 1930–4.
[Lockhart, J. G.] Letter of Timothy Tickler to Christopher North. Blackwood's Mag Sept 1823.
Monthly Rev June 1823. Review of Essays of Elia.
[Jerdan, W.] Album verses. Literary Gazette 10 July 1830.
—— Literary Gazette 8 Dec 1832. Review of Tennyson's poems mocking the Baa-Lamb school.
—— Last essays of Elia. Literary Gazette 2 March 1833.
Br Mag Aug 1830; Monthly Rev Aug 1830. Reviews of Album verses.
[Dyer, G.] Memoir of Lamb. GM March 1835.
[Forster, J.] Lamb: his last words on Coleridge; Lamb: an autobiographic sketch. New Monthly Mag Feb, April 1835.
[Maginn, W.] Lamb. Fraser's Mag Feb 1835.
[Moxon, E.] Lamb. 1835 (priv ptd).
[Patmore, P. G.] Personal recollections of the late C. Lamb, with original letters. Court Mag March–April, Dec 1835.
—— My friends and acquaintance. 3 vols 1854.
[Procter, B. W.] Recollections of Lamb. Athenaeum 3, 24 Jan, 7 Feb 1835.
—— Lamb: a memoir. 1866.
Mirror 24 Jan 1835; Oxford Univ Mag 2 1835; Monthly Rev Feb 1836. Obituaries.
Monthly Rev Sept 1835. Review of Rosamund Gray.
[Field, B.] Lamb. Annual Biography & Obituary 20 1836.
Characteristics of Lamb. Amer Quart Rev 19 1836.
[Bulwer-Lytton, E. G.] Talfourd's Letters and life. Westminster Rev 27 1837.
—— Lamb and some of his companions. Quart Rev 122 1867.
Life and writings of Lamb. Amer Quart Rev 22 1837.
Br & Foreign Rev 5 1837 (attributed to Talfourd); Edinburgh Rev 66 1837 (attributed to W. Empson); Literary Gazette 8, 15 July 1837; Tait's Mag Sept 1837; Dublin Univ Mag Feb 1838. Reviews of Talfourd's edn of Letters.
[Felton, C. C.] The letters of Lamb. North Amer Rev 46 1838.
British artists and writers on art. Br & Foreign Rev 6 1838.
Hood, T. Hood's own. 1839. Rptd in Thomas Hood and Lamb: being the literary reminiscences of Hood, ed W. Jerrold 1930.
[Macaulay, T. B.] Comic dramatists of the Restoration. Edinburgh Rev 72 1841.
Chasles, P. Le dernier humoriste anglais. Revue des Deux Mondes 15 Nov 1842.
Gilfillan, G. Lamb. In his A gallery of literary portraits vol 1, Edinburgh 1845.
[Lewes, G. H.] Br Quart Rev 7 1848. Review of 1848 edn of Works.
—— Lamb and his friends. Br Quart Rev 8 1848.
Christian Remembrancer 16 1848; Eclectic Rev new ser 24 1848; Westminster Rev 50 1849. Reviews of Final memorials.
[Smith, W. H.] Final memorials. Blackwood's Mag Aug 1849.
Tuckerman, H. T. In his Characteristics of literature, New York 1849.
Fitzgerald, P. Lamb: his friends, his haunts and his books. 1866.
Craddock, T. Lamb. 1867.
[Hill, A. S.] Lamb and his biographers. North Amer Rev 104 1867.
Massey, G. Lamb. Fraser's Mag May 1867.
Ollier, E. A few reminiscences. [1867]. Prefixed to Essays of Elia ser 1.
Robinson, H. C. Diary, reminiscences and correspondence. Ed T. Sadler 3 vols 1869.
—— The correspondence of Robinson with the Wordsworth circle 1808–66. Ed E. J. Morley 2 vols Oxford 1927.
—— Robinson on books and their writers. Ed E. J. Morley 3 vols 1938.
C. and Mary Lamb: their editors and biographers. Westminster Rev new ser 45 1874.
Clarke, C. C. and M. C. Recollections of writers. 1878.
Russell, J. F. Lamb's notes on a metrical novel. N & Q 17 Sept, 5 Nov 1881.
Ainger, A. Lamb. 1882 (EML).
Gilchrist, A. Mary Lamb. 1883.
Swinburne, A. C. Lamb and George Wither. In his Miscellanies, 1886.
Birrell, A. In his Obiter dicta ser 2, 1887.
De Quincey, T. In his Collected writings, ed D. Masson vols 3, 5 Edinburgh 1889–90.
Pater, W. In his Appreciations, 1889.
Martin, B. E. In the footprints of Lamb. 1891.
Lucas, E. V. Bernard Barton and his friends. 1893.
—— The life of Lamb. 2 vols 1905, 1910 (5th edn), 1921 (rev). The standard life.
—— At the shrine of St Charles. 1934.
—— Recollections of Lamb [by Walter Wilson]. London Mercury Dec 1934.
[Welford, C.] A descriptive catalogue of the library of Lamb. New York 1897.
[Gosse, E.] Lamb. Quart Rev 192 1900.
Dobell, B. Sidelights on Lamb. 1903.
Lake, B. A general introduction to Lamb, together with a special study of his relation to Robert Burton. Leipzig 1903.
Rees, J. R. With Elia and his friends. 1903.
Derocquigny, J. Lamb: sa vie et ses œuvres. Lille 1904.
Jerrold, W. Lamb. 1905.
More, P. E. In his Shelburne essays ser 2, 1905; ser 4, 1906.
The letters of C. and Mary Lamb. Athenaeum 3 June 1905.
Irwin, S. T. Hazlitt and Lamb. Quart Rev 204 1906.
Bensusan, S. L. Lamb. 1910.
Williams, O. Lamb's friend the census-taker: life and letters of John Rickman. 1912.
—— Lamb. 1934.
Masson, F. Lamb. 1913.
Symons, A. In his Figures of several centuries, 1916.
Smith, H. B. Lamb's Album. Scribner's Mag Oct 1923.
Burriss, E. E. The classical culture of Lamb. Classical Weekly 6 Oct 1924.
Foster, W. Mr Lamb of the Accountant's Office. In his East India House, 1924.
Graveson, W. C. and Mary Lamb 'in hearty, homely, loving Hertfordshire'. Hertford 1925.
Manning, T. The letters of Thomas Manning to Lamb. Ed G. A. Anderson 1925.
Cambridge and Lamb. Ed G. E. Wherry, Cambridge 1925.
Blunden, E. Leigh Hunt's Examiner examined. 1928.
—— Lamb and his contemporaries. Cambridge 1933.
—— Lamb: his life recorded by his contemporaries. 1934.
—— Elia and Christ's Hospital. E & S 22 1936.
—— Lamb. 1954.
Birkhoff, B. As between friends: criticism of themselves and one another in the letters of Coleridge, Wordsworth and Lamb. Cambridge Mass 1930.
Hard, F. Lamb on Spenser. SP 28 1931.
—— Lamb and Spenser again. SP 30 1933.
The Elian miscellany. Ed S. M. Rich 1931.
Morley, F. V. Lamb before Elia. 1932.
Plesner, K. F. Elia og hans venner: Lamb, Hazlitt, De Quincey. Copenhagen 1933.
Evans, B. I. Lamb. Nineteenth Century Dec 1934.
French, J. M. Lamb and Milton. SP 31 1934.
—— A chip from Elia's workshop. SP 37 1940.
—— Elia. Jnl of Rutgers Univ Lib 11 1948.

May, J. L. Lamb: a study. 1934.
Thompson, D. Our debt to Lamb. In Determinations, ed F. R. Leavis 1934.
Tillett, N. S. Elia and the Indicator. South Atlantic Quart 33 1934.
—— Mary Lamb. South Atlantic Quart 47 1948.
Ward, A. C. The frolic and the gentle. 1934.
Holman, L. E. Lamb's 'Barbara S-': the life of Frances Maria Kelly, actress. 1935.
Johnson, E. C. Lamb always Elia. 1935.
—— Lamb and Coleridge. Amer Scholar 6 1937.
Newdick, R. S. The first Life and letters of Lamb: a study of T. N. Talfourd as editor and biographer. Ohio State Univ Contributions in Eng no 3 1935.
Orage, A. R. The danger of the whimsical. In his Selected essays and critical writings, ed H. Read and D. Saurat 1935.
The Charles Lamb Society. Monthly Bulletin May 1935–.
Gupta, H. M. Das. Elia and the Elizabethan revival. Calcutta Rev July 1937.
Iseman, J. S. A perfect sympathy: Lamb and Sir Thomas Browne. Cambridge Mass 1937.
Tilley, M. P. Lamb, Marston and Du Bartas. MLN 53 1938.
Cook, E. T. Justly dear: C. and Mary Lamb. 1939. A biographical novel.
'Bell, Neil' (S. Southwold). So perish the roses. 1940. A biographical novel.
Ross, E. C. The ordeal of Bridget Elia. Norman Oklahoma 1940.
B., E. G. Notes on the letters of C. and Mary Lamb. N & Q 10 May 1941.
Lang, V. The character in the Elia essays. MLN 56 1941.
McCusker, H. Lamb and his friends. More Books Dec 1941.
Daggett, G. H. Lamb's interest in dreams. College Eng Dec 1942.
Houghton, W. E. Lamb's criticism of Restoration comedy. ELH 10 1943.
Howe, W. D. Lamb and his friends. Indianapolis 1944.
Anthony, K. The Lambs: a study of pre-Victorian England. New York 1945.
Barnett, G. L. Dating Lamb's contributions to the Table book. PMLA 60 1945.
—— First American review of Lamb. PMLA 61 1946. Reply by S. A. Larrabee 74 1959.
—— A critical analysis of the Lucas edition of Lamb's letters. MLQ 9 1948.
—— Corrections in the text of Lamb's letters. HLQ 18 1955.
—— An unpublished review by Lamb. MLQ 17 1956.
—— Lamb's part in an edition of Hogarth. MLQ 20 1959.
—— A disquisition on Punch and Judy. HLQ 25 1962.
—— Lamb: the evolution of Elia. Indiana Univ Humanities ser no 53 1964.
—— The pronunciation of Elia. Stud in Romanticism 5 1965.
Dédéyan, C. In his Montaigne dans le romantisme anglo-saxon, Paris 1946.
McKechnie, S. Lamb of the India House. N & Q 2 Nov 1946–8 March 1947.
—— Six of Lamb's 'true works' discovered: audited accounts in India Office Library. Times 21 June 1955.
Young, P. M. A revised chapter on ears. Music & Letters 27 1946.
Finch, J. S. Lamb's copy of the History of Philip de Commines, with autograph notes by Lamb and Coleridge. Princeton Univ Lib Chron 9 1947.
Hine, R. L. Lamb and his Hertfordshire. 1949.
Turnbull, J. M. Two Lamb poems. TLS 5 Feb 1949.
Prance, C. A. A forgotten skit by Lamb. TLS 9 Feb 1951.
Legouis, P. et al. Lamb's latinity. TLS 20–7 June, 1 Aug 1952.
Patterson, C. I. Lamb's insight into the nature of the novel. PMLA 67 1952.
—— Lamb, Shakespeare and the stage reconsidered. Emory Univ Quart 20 1964.
Richardson, J. P. G. Patmore on Lamb and Hazlitt. TLS 19 June 1953.
Barnet, S. Lamb's contributions to the theory of dramatic illusion. PMLA 69 1954.
—— Lamb and the tragic Malvolio. PQ 33 1954.
Jessup, B. The mind of Elia. JHI 15 1954.
Powys, J. C. In his Visions and revisions: a book of literary devotions, 1955.
Morgan, P. F. On some letters of Lamb. N & Q Dec 1956.
—— Lamb and Hood: records of a friendship. Tennessee Stud in Lit 9 1964.
Foxon, D. The chapbook editions of the Lambs' Tales from Shakespear. Book Collector 6 1957.
Whalley, G. Coleridge's debt to Lamb. E & S new ser 11 1958.
Ades, J. I. Lamb: romantic criticism and the aesthetics of sympathy. Delta Epsilon Sigma Bull 6 1961.
—— Lamb's judgment of Byron and Shelley. Papers on Eng Lang & Lit 1 1965.
Nethery, W. Lamb in America 1849–66. Amer Book Collector Feb 1962.
—— Lamb in America to 1848. Worcester Mass 1963.
Fukuhara, R. The life of Lamb. Tokyo 1963.
Haven, R. The romantic art of Lamb. ELH 30 1963.
Mulcahy, D. J. Lamb: the antithetical manner and the two planes. Stud in Eng Lit 1500–1900 3 1963.
Webb, A. Lamb's use of the character. Southern Quart 1 1963.
Fréchet, R. Lamb's 'artificial comedy'. REL 5 1964.
Fukuda, T. A study of Lamb's Essays of Elia. Tokyo 1964.
Hashi, Y. Lamb's way of thinking. Kobe 1964.
Weber, H. Studien zur Form der Essays bei Lamb. Heidelberg 1964.
Meserole, H. T. Lamb's reputation and influence in America to 1835. Jnl of General Education 16 1965.
Reiman, D. H. Thematic unity in Lamb's familiar essays. JEGP 64 1965.
Tillotson, G. The historical importance of certain Essays of Elia. In Some British Romantics, ed J. V. Logan et al, Columbus Ohio 1966.

R. P.

WILLIAM HAZLITT

1778–1830

Bibliographies

Douady, J. Liste chronologique des oeuvres de Hazlitt. Paris 1906.
Keynes, G. L. Bibliography of Hazlitt. 1931.
Schneider, E. W. In English romantic poets and essayists: a review of research and criticism, ed C. W. and L. H. Houtchens, New York 1957, 1966 (rev)

Collections

The 12 vols ed Hazlitt's son 1838–58, under §1, below, were part of a projected collected edn that was to include all the ptd works with addns from ms and other sources. The 7 vols ed W. C. Hazlitt 1869–86, under §1, below, represent part of a similar project.

The collected works. Ed A. R. Waller and A. Glover 13 vols 1902–6. Introd by W. E. Henley.
The complete works. Ed P. P. Howe 21 vols 1930–4. Based on the edn of A. R. Waller and A. Glover, above, with additional notes, Life of Napoleon and other uncollected matter.

Selections

For a comprehensive list of selections pbd before 1930, see Keynes, Bibliography, above.

Hazlitt: essayist and critic. Ed A. Ireland 1889.

Hazlitt: essays on poetry. Ed D. Nichol Smith, Edinburgh 1901.

Selections. Ed W. D. Howe, Boston 1913.

Hazlitt on English literature. Ed J. Zeitlin, New York 1913.

Selected essays. Ed G. Sampson, Cambridge 1917.

Selected essays. Ed G. L. Keynes 1930 (Nonesuch Lib).

Essays and characters. Ed S. Williams 1937.

Selections from Lamb and Hazlitt. Ed R. W. Jepson 1940.

Selected essays. Ed R. Wilson 1942.

Hazlitt painted by himself. Ed C. M. Maclean 1948.

The essays: a selection. Ed C. M. Maclean 1949.

The Hazlitt sampler. Ed H. M. Sikes, Greenwich Conn 1962.

Essays. Ed R. Vallance and J. Hampden 1964 (Folio Soc).

§1

An essay on the principles of human action: being an argument in favour of the natural disinterestedness of the human mind, to which are added some remarks on the systems of Hartley and Helvetius. 1805 (anon); ed W. Hazlitt jun [1835–6] (with additional essay on abstract ideas).

Free thoughts on public affairs: or advice to a patriot in a letter addressed to a member of the old opposition. 1806 (anon); ed W. C. Hazlitt 1886 (with Spirit of the age, Letter to William Gifford).

An abridgement of the Light of nature pursued, by Abraham Tucker. 1807. Anon.

The eloquence of the British senate: or select specimens from the speeches of the most distinguished parliamentary speakers from the beginning of the reign of Charles I to the present time, with notes. 2 vols 1807 (anon), 1808, Brooklyn 1809–10, London 1812.

A reply to the Essay on population by the Rev T. R. Malthus, in a series of letters. 1807 (anon), New York 1967. Letters 1–3 first pbd in Cobbett's Political Register 14 March, 16–23 May 1807.

A new and improved grammar of the English tongue for the use of schools; to which is added a New guide to the English tongue [by Godwin]. 1810. Rptd only in Complete works, ed P. P. Howe, above. Outline of English grammar, 1810, is an abridgement by Godwin.

Memoirs of the late Thomas Holcroft, written by himself and continued to the time of his death [by Hazlitt]. 3 vols 1816, 1852 (abridged); ed E. Colby 2 vols 1925; Oxford 1926 (WC).

The round table: a collection of essays on literature, men and manners. 2 vols Edinburgh 1817 (includes 12 essays by Leigh Hunt); ed W. Hazlitt jun 1841 (retains Hunt's essays, omits 12 by Hazlitt, adds 3 uncollected essays from Liberal 1882–3); 1869 (omits Hunt's essays with one exception and a few of Hazlitt's); ed W. C. Hazlitt 1871 (Hazlitt's essays only, with Northcote's conversations, Characteristics); 1936 (EL) (with Characters of Shakespear's plays). Texts of these edns are identical with Waller and Glover, Collected works, above.

Characters of Shakespear's plays. 1817, 1818, Boston 1818; ed W. Hazlitt jun 1838, 1848, 1854; New York 1845; ed W. C. Hazlitt 1869 (with Lectures on the dramatic literature of the age of Elizabeth); 1903 (with Lectures on English poets); 1905; 1906 (EL) (with Round table, rptd 1936); ed J. H. Lobban, Cambridge 1908; Oxford 1916 (WC); ed C. Morgan 1948 (as Liber amoris and dramatic criticisms, introd rptd in his Writer and his world, 1960); tr German, 1838.

A view of the English stage: or a series of dramatic criticisms. 1818, 1821; ed W. Hazlitt jun 1851 (selection pbd as Criticisms and dramatic essays of the English stage); ed W. Archer and R. W. Lowe 1895 (as Dramatic essays), New York 1957 (as Hazlitt on theatre); ed W. S. Jackson 1906 (text from original articles, with 3 uncollected contributions from Examiner). Originally contributed to Morning Chron, Champion, Examiner and Times 1814–18.

Lectures on the English poets, delivered at the Surrey Institution. 1818, Philadelphia 1818, London 1819; ed W. Hazlitt jun 1841 (further matter in 4 appendixes); ed W. C. Hazlitt 1869 (with Lectures on English comic writers); 1903 (with Characters of Shakespear's plays); 1908; 1910 (EL) (with Spirit of the Age); Oxford 1924 (WC); Oxford 1929.

A letter to William Gifford esq. 1819, 1820; ed W. C. Hazlitt 1886 (with Spirit of the age, Free thoughts). First draft in Examiner 15 June 1818.

Lectures on the English comic writers, delivered at the Surry Institution. 1819, Philadelphia 1819; ed W. Hazlitt jun 1841 (expanded, mainly from prefaces originally contributed to Oxberry's New English drama 1818–9); ed W. C. Hazlitt 1869 (with Lectures on English poets); ed A. Dobson 1900; ed R. B. Johnson, Oxford 1907 (WC); ed W. E. Henley 1910 (EL) (with essays from New Monthly Mag and Monthly Mag); ed A. Johnson 1965 (EL).

Political essays, with sketches of public characters. 1819, 1822. Mainly rptd from articles in various periodicals 1813–8, but including extracts from the Eloquence of the British senate, Reply to Malthus.

Lectures chiefly on the dramatic literature of the age of Elizabeth, delivered at the Surry Institution. 1820, 1821; ed W. Hazlitt jun 1840; New York 1845; ed W. C. Hazlitt 1869 (with Characters of Shakespear's plays).

Table-talk: or original essays. 2 vols 1821–2, 1824, Paris 1825, New York 1845–6 (Hazlitt's selection from Table-talk 1821–2, with essays later collected in Plain speaker, below); ed W. Hazlitt jun 2 vols 1845–6 (based like all succeeding edns on first edn); ed W. C. Hazlitt 1869; 1901 (WC); 1908 (EL); 1909.

Liber amoris: or the new Pygmalion. 1823 (anon), 1884; ed R. Le Gallienne 1893; ed (with much additional matter) R. Le Gallienne [and W. C. Hazlitt] 1894 (priv ptd); 1907; Portland Maine 1908; ed C. Morgan 1948 (as Liber amoris and dramatic criticisms, i.e. Characters of Shakespear's plays etc, introd rptd in his Writer and his world, 1960).

Characteristics, in the manner of Rochefoucault's Maxims. 1823 (anon); ed R. H. Horne 1837, 1927; ed W. C. Hazlitt 1871 (with Round table, Northcote's conversations).

Sketches of the principal picture-galleries in England, with a criticism on Marriage à-la-mode. 1824 (anon); ed W. Hazlitt jun 1843 (as part of Criticisms on art ser 1). Originally contributed to London Mag 1822–3. Hogarth essay rptd from Round table 1817.

Select British poets: or new elegant extracts from Chaucer to the present time, with critical remarks. 1824 (withdrawn owing to infringements of copyright in the contemporary section), 1825 (omitting copyright matter, as Select poets of Great Britain).

The spirit of the age: or contemporary portraits. 1825, 1825 (anon) (2nd edn enlarges Coleridge, adds Cobbett from Table-talk), Paris 1825 (re-arranged, omitting Moore and Irving, adds Canning and Knowles); ed W. Hazlitt jun 1858; ed E. C. Hazlitt 1886 (with Letter to William Gifford, Free thoughts); [selection] ed R. B. Johnson 1893; Oxford 1904 (WC); 1910 (EL) (with Lectures on English poets). Partly rptd from London Mag and New Monthly Mag.

The plain speaker: opinions on books, men and things. 2 vols 1826 (anon); ed W. Hazlitt jun 2 vols 1851–2; ed W. C. Hazlitt 1870; 1928 (EL).

Notes of a journey through France and Italy. 1826, Philadelphia 1833.

The life of Napoleon Buonaparate. 4 vols 1828–30 (vols 1–2 re-issued 1830), 3 vols New York 1847–8; rev W. Hazlitt jun 4 vols 1852; 6 vols Paris and Boston 1895 (Napoleon Soc); 6 vols [1910] (Grolier Soc); tr German, 1835.

Conversations of James Northcote esq RA 1830; ed W. C. Hazlitt 1871 (with Round table, Characteristics); ed E. Gosse 1894; ed F. Swinnerton 1949. Rptd from New Monthly Mag Aug 1826–March 1827, London Weekly Rev 1829, Atlas March–Nov 1829, Court Jnl 1830.

Literary remains of the late William Hazlitt, with a notice of his life by his son, and thoughts on his genius and writings by E. L. Bulwer esq MP and Mr Sergeant Talfourd MP. 2 vols 1836, 1 vol New York 1836. 22 essays mainly rptd from periodicals.

Painting [by B. R. Haydon] and the fine arts [by Hazlitt]. Edinburgh 1838. Rptd from Encyclopaedia britannica 7th edn suppl vol 1 1816.

Sketches and essays, now first collected by his son. 1839, 1852 (as Men and manners); ed W. C. Hazlitt 1872 (with Winterslow); 1902 (WC). 18 essays rptd from periodicals.

Criticisms on art, and sketches of the picture galleries of England. Ed W. Hazlitt jun 2 sers 1843–4; ed W. C. Hazlitt 1873 (expanded as Essays on the fine arts).

Winterslow: essays and characters written there, collected by his son. 1850; ed W. C. Hazlitt 1872 (with Sketches and essays); 1902 (WC). Partly rptd from Literary remains, but mainly from periodicals.

A reply to Z. Ed C. Whibley 1923. Unpbd reply to article signed 'Z' in Blackwood's Mag Aug 1818.

New writings by Hazlitt. Ed P. P. Howe 2 sers 1925–7. Articles rptd from periodicals and Oxberry's New English drama 1818–9.

Hazlitt in the workshop: the manuscript of the Fight, transcribed with collation, notes and commentary. Ed S. C. Wilcox, Baltimore 1943.

Letters and Papers

Hazlitt, W. C. Memoirs of Hazlitt, with portions of his correspondence. 2 vols 1867.

— Lamb and Hazlitt: further letters and records. 1900.

Howe, P. P. Unpublished letters. Athenaeum 8–15 Aug 1919.

— New Hazlitt letters. London Mercury March 1923, May 1924, Aug 1925.

— Three Hazlitt letters. TLS 21 March 1936.

Bonner, W. H. The journals of Sarah and William Hazlitt 1822–31. Univ of Buffalo Stud 24 1959.

Barker, J. R. Some early correspondence of Sarah Stoddart and the Lambs. HLQ 24 1960.

Moyne, E. J. An unpublished letter of Hazlitt. PMLA 77 1962.

Jones, S. Hazlitt and John Bull: a neglected letter. RES new ser 17 1966.

— Nine new Hazlitt letters and some others. Etudes Anglaises 19 1966.

§2

Annual Rev 4 1805; Eclectic Rev 3 1807; Monthly Rev April 1807. Reviews of Essay on the principles of human action.

Annual Rev 6 1807; Monthly Rev June 1809. Reviews of the Eloquence of the British senate.

Annual Rev 6 1807; Monthly Rev May 1808; Edinburgh Rev 16 1810. Reviews of Reply to Essay on population.

[Hunt, L.] Characters of Shakespeare's plays. Examiner 26 Oct, 2 Nov, 23 Nov 1817.

— English comic writers. Examiner 18 April, 6 June 1819.

— Lectures on the dramatic literature of the age of Elizabeth. Examiner 19 March 1820.

— Plain speaker. Companion 12–19 March 1828.

— Mr Hazlitt and the utilitarians. Tatler 28 Sept 1830.

[Jeffrey, F.] Characters of Shakespeare's plays. Edinburgh Rev 28 1817.

Br Critic June 1817; Eclectic Rev new ser 7 1817; Edinburgh Mag Nov 1817 (with review of Characters of Shakespeare's plays); Literary Gazette 3, 17 May, 7 June 1817; Quart Rev 17 1817 (attributed to J. Russell). Reviews of Round table.

Champion 20–27 July 1817 (attributed to J. H. Reynolds); Br Critic Jan 1818; Quart Rev 18 1818 (attributed to J. Russell); Monthly Rev May 1820 (with reviews of Lectures on English poets and English comic writers). Reviews of Characters of Shakespeare's plays.

[Barrett, E. S.] Lectures on English poets. Quart Rev 19 1818.

[Patmore, P. G.] Lectures on English poets. Blackwood's Mag Feb–April 1818.

— My friends and acquaintance. 3 vols 1854.

Jeffrey and Hazlitt. Blackwood's Mag June 1818.

Hazlitt cross-questioned. Blackwood's Mag Aug 1818. Attributed to Lockhart or Wilson.

Br Critic Oct 1818. Review of View of English stage.

On the Cockney school of prose writers. New Monthly Mag Oct–Nov 1818.

Br Critic Dec 1818. Review of Lectures on English poets.

[Dana, R. H.] Lectures on English poets. North Amer Rev 8 1819.

[Reynolds, J. H.] Lectures on English comic writers. Edinburgh Mag Dec 1818–Feb 1819.

— Conversations of James Northcote. Athenaeum 2, 23 Oct 1830.

Br Rev 13 1819. Review of Hazlitt's essays, criticisms and lectures.

Quart Rev 22 1819 (attributed to Gifford); Edinburgh Monthly Rev March 1820; Monthly Rev Nov 1820. Reviews of Political essays.

[Scott, J.] Lectures on the dramatic literature of the age of Elizabeth. London Mag Feb 1820.

[Talfourd, T. N.] Lectures on the dramatic literature of the age of Elizabeth. Edinburgh Rev 34 1820.

— Table-talk. London Mag May 1821.

Monthly Rev Sept 1820. Review of Lectures on dramatic literature.

[Matthews, J.] Table-talk. Quart Rev 26 1821.

[Crowe, E. E.] Table-talk. Blackwood's Mag Aug 1822.

Br Critic June 1821, Aug 1822; New Edinburgh Rev 1 1821; Examiner 8 Sept 1822; Monthly Censor Dec 1822; London Mag June 1823 (attributed to J. H. Reynolds); Monthly Rev May 1823. Reviews of Table-talk.

Blackwood's Mag June 1823 (attributed to Lockhart). Review of Liber amoris.

[Forbes, W. H.] Hunt and Hazlitt. Blackwood's Mag July 1824.

Investigator 8 1824. Review of Characteristics.

[Wilson, J.] The spirit of the age. Blackwood's Mag March 1825.

Eclectic Rev new ser 23 1825; Edinburgh Rev 42 1825 (attributed to Jeffrey); Examiner 9 Jan 1825; London Mag June 1825 (attributed to H. Southern); Monthly Rev May 1825. Reviews of Spirit of the age.

Monthly Rev June 1826. Review of Plain speaker.

Monthly Rev Aug 1826. Review of Notes of a journey.

Literary Chron 26 Aug 1826. Memoir of Hazlitt.

Br Mag Oct 1830; Monthly Rev Oct 1830. Reviews of Conversations of Northcote.

[Procter, B. W.] My recollections of the late William Hazlitt. New Monthly Mag Nov 1830.

Amer Quart Rev 20 1836; Dublin Univ Mag Oct 1836; Tait's Mag Aug 1836. Reviews of Literary remains.

Tait's Mag Nov-Dec 1836. Writings of Hazlitt.

[Merivale, J. H.] Literary remains. Edinburgh Rev 64 1837.

Tait's Mag Oct 1837. Hazlitt as a critic of the drama and the fine arts.

[Darley, G.] Painting and the fine arts. Athenaeum 14–28 July 1838.

[Egerton, F.] Painting and the fine arts. Quart Rev 62 1838.

Br & Foreign Rev 6 1838. British artists and writers on art.

Medwin, T. Hazlitt in Switzerland. Fraser's Mag March 1839.

Tait's Mag April 1843. Review of Criticisms on art.

[Whipple, E. P.] The British critics. North Amer Rev 61 1845.

Gilfillan, G. Hazlitt; Hazlitt and Hallam. Both in his Galleries of literary portraits vol 2, Edinburgh 1857.

Stephen, L. In his Hours in a library ser 2, 1876.

Cross, L. Hazlitt. New Monthly Mag March 1880.

[Noble, J. A.] On Liber amoris. Temple Bar March 1881.

De Quincey, T. In his Collected writings, ed D. Masson vols 3, 5, 9, 11 Edinburgh 1889–90.

Saintsbury, G. In his Essays in English literature 1780–1860 ser 1, 1890.

Hazlitt, W. C. Four generations of a literary family. 2 vols 1897.

—— The Hazlitts: an account of their origin and descent, with autobiographical particulars of Hazlitt. 2 vols Edinburgh 1911–12 (priv ptd).

Birrell, A. Hazlitt. 1902 (EML).

More, P. E. The first complete edition of Hazlitt. In his Shelburne essays ser 2, 1905.

Irwin, S. T. Hazlitt and Lamb. Quart Rev 204 1906.

Wright, E. Hazlitt and Sainte-Beuve. Academy 25 Aug 1906.

Douady, J. Vie de Hazlitt. Paris 1907.

Sichel, W. Hazlitt: romantic and amorist. Fortnightly Rev Jan 1914.

Howe, P. P. Hazlitt and Liber amoris. Fortnightly Rev Feb 1916.

—— Hazlitt's second marriage. Fortnightly Rev Aug 1916.

—— Hazlitt and Blackwood's. Fortnightly Rev Oct 1919.

—— Life of Hazlitt. 1922, 1928 (rev); ed F. Swinnerton 1947.

Hayens, K. Heine, Hazlitt and Mrs Jameson. MLR 17 1922.

Chase, S. P. Hazlitt as a critic of art. PMLA 39 1924.

Clark, E. M. The kinship of Hazlitt and Stevenson. SE 4 1924.

Newdick, R. S. Coleridge on Hazlitt. Texas Rev 9 1924.

Carver, P. L. Hazlitt's contributions to the Edinburgh Review. RES 4 1928.

—— The authorship of a review of Christabel attributed to Hazlitt. JEGP 29 1930. By Brougham?

—— The influence of Maurice Morgann [on Hazlitt et al]. RES 6 1930.

Chandler, Z. E. An analysis of the stylistic technique of Addison, Johnson, Hazlitt and Pater. Univ of Iowa Humanistic Stud 4 1928.

Garrod, H. W. The place of Hazlitt in English criticism. In his Profession of poetry and other lectures, Oxford 1929.

Babcock, R. W. The direct influence of late 18th century Shakespeare criticism on Hazlitt and Coleridge. MLN 45 1930.

Stephenson, H. W. Hazlitt and Hackney College. 1930.

Praz, M. Is Hazlitt a great essayist? E Studies 13 1931.

Schnöckelborg, G. Schlegels Einfluss auf Hazlitt als Shakespeare-Kritiker. Münster 1931.

Baker, H. T. Hazlitt as a Shakespearean critic. PMLA 47 1932.

Woolf, V. In her Common reader ser 2, 1932.

Jantzen, A. Hazlitt und die bildende Kunst. Schramberg 1933.

Schneider, E. W. The aesthetics of Hazlitt. Philadelphia 1933, 1952.

—— The unknown reviewer of Christabel: Jeffrey, Hazlitt, Tom Moore. PMLA 70 1955. By Moore? Replies by H. H. Jordan, MP 54 1956 (by Hazlitt and Jeffrey?); E. W. Schneider, PMLA 77 1962 (by Moore?); K. Coburn, TLS 20 May 1965.

Pearson, H. The fool of love. 1934.

Sargeaunt, G. M. Hazlitt as a critic of painting. In his Classical spirit, 1936.

Strout, A. L. Hunt, Hazlitt and 'Maga'. ELH 4 1937.

Vigneron, R. Stendhal et Hazlitt. MP 35 1938.

Dechamps, J. Hazlitt et Napoléon. Revue des Etudes Napoléoniennes 1939.

Caldwell, J. R. Beauty is truth. Univ of California Pbns in Eng 8 1940. Keats' debt to Hazlitt.

Wilcox, S. C. Hazlitt and Northcote. ELH 7 1940.

—— Hazlitt's aphorisms. MLQ 9 1948.

Larrabee, S. A. Hazlitt's criticism and Greek sculpture. JHI 2 1941.

Niblett, W. R. Hazlitt's contribution to literary criticism. Durham Univ Jnl new ser 2 1941.

Wardle, R. M. Outwitting Hazlitt. MLN 57 1942.

Brightfield, M. F. Scott, Hazlitt and Napoleon. Univ of California Pbns in Eng 14 1943.

Maclean, C. M. Born under Saturn: a biography. 1943.

Reilly, J. J. Hazlitt, liberal and humanitarian. Catholic World Nov 1944.

Bullitt, J. M. Hazlitt and the romantic conception of the imagination. PQ 24 1945.

Dédéyan, C. In his Montaigne dans le romantisme anglo-saxon, Paris 1946.

Gates, P. G. Bacon, Keats and Hazlitt. South Atlantic Quart 46 1947.

Štěpaník, K. Hazlitt jako literární kritik. Spisy Filosofické Fakulty Masarykovy Univ (Brno) 46 1947. With English summary.

Thorpe, C. D. Keats and Hazlitt: a record of personal relationship and critical estimate. PMLA 62 1947.

Albrecht, W. P. Hazlitt's Principles of human action, and the improvement of society. In If by your art: testament to Percival Hunt, Pittsburgh 1948.

—— Hazlitt and the Malthusian controversy. Univ of New Mexico Pbns in Lang & Lit 4 1950.

—— Hazlitt's preference for tragedy. PMLA 71 1956. Replies by S. Barnet and W. P. Albrecht, 73 1958.

—— Hazlitt on the poetry of wit. PMLA 75 1960.

—— Liberalism and Hazlitt's tragic view. College Eng Nov 1961.

—— Hazlitt on Wordsworth: or the poetry of paradox. In Six studies in 19th-century English literature and thought, ed H. Orel and G. J. Worth, Univ of Kansas Humanistic Stud 35 1962.

—— Hazlitt and the creative imagination, Lawrence Kansas 1965.

Gordon, R. K. Hazlitt on some of his contemporaries. Trans Royal Soc of Canada 42 1948.

Cohen, B. B. Hazlitt: Bonapartist critic of the Excursion. MLQ 10 1949.

Maxwell, J. C. Some Hazlitt quotations. N & Q 15 Sept 1951. Replies and addns by S. C. Wilcox 10 May 1952; D. S. Bland 19 July 1952; F. V. Bernard, G. T. Fairclough and Maxwell, Jan 1964.

Muir, K. Keats and Hazlitt. Proc of Leeds Philosophical & Literary Soc 6 1951; rptd in John Keats: a reassessment, ed Muir, 1958.

Smith, K. In his Malthusian controversy, 1951.

Haddakin, L. Keats's Ode on a Grecian urn and Hazlitt's lecture On poetry in general. N & Q 29 March 1952.

Carnall, G. D. A Hazlitt contribution. TLS 19 June 1953. Identifies an article by Hazlitt on materialist philosophy in Monthly Rev 1809.

Fitzgerald, M. H. et al. The text of Hazlitt. TLS 27 Feb–8 May, 5–12 June 1953. A correspondence on the identity of the initials in the essay Of persons one would wish to have seen.

Patterson, C. I. Hazlitt as a critic of prose fiction. PMLA 68 1953.

Richardson, J. P. G. Patmore on Lamb and Hazlitt. TLS 19 June 1953.

Andrews, J. Bacon and the dissociation of sensibility. N & Q Nov 1954. On Hazlitt's anticipation of T. S. Eliot.

Brooks, E. L. Was Hazlitt a news reporter? N & Q Aug 1954.

Stallbaumer, V. R. Hazlitt's Life of Thomas Holcroft. Amer Benedictine Rev 5 1954.

Whitley, A. Hazlitt and the theatre. SE 34 1955.

Klingopulos, G. D. Hazlitt as critic. EC 6 1956.

Voisine, J. Un nouveau Jean-Jacques: Hazlitt. In his J.-J. Rousseau en Angleterre à l'époque romantique, Paris 1956.

Will, F. Two critics of the Elgin Marbles: Hazlitt and Quatremère de Quincy. Jnl of Aesthetics 14 1956.

Zall, P. M. Hazlitt's 'romantic acquaintance': Wordsworth and Charles Lloyd. MLN 71 1956.

Cecil, D. Hazlitt's occasional essays. In his Fine art of reading, 1957.

Davies, R. T. Keats and Hazlitt. Keats-Shelley Memorial Bull 8 1957.

Müller, R. Some problems concerning Keats and Hazlitt. Ibid.

Salter, C. H. The first English romantic art critics. Cambridge Rev 8 June 1957.

Adams, D. K. Swinburne and Hazlitt. N & Q Dec 1959.

Robinson, R. E. Hazlitt's Life of Napoleon Buonaparte: its sources and characteristics. Geneva and Paris 1959.

Sikes, H. M. The poetic theory and practice of Keats: the record of a debt to Hazlitt. PQ 38 1959.

—— Hazlitt, the London Magazine and the 'anonymous reviewer'. BNYPL March 1961.

—— 'The infernal Hazlitt', the New Monthly Magazine and the North Dakota Drama Critique 4 1961.

—— 'The infernal Hazlitt', the New Monthly Magazine and the Conversations of James Northcote RA. In Essays presented to Stanley Pargellis, ed H. Bluhm, Chicago 1965.

Mahoney, J. L. Hazlitt on the marks of genius. North Dakota Quart 28 1960.

—— The quest for objectivity in Hazlitt's dramatic criticism. Drama Critique 4 1961.

Priestley, J. B. Hazlitt. 1960.

Marshall, W. H. An addition to the Hazlitt canon. PBSA 55 1961.

Baker, H. Hazlitt. Cambridge Mass 1962.

Elliott, E. C. Reynolds and Hazlitt. Jnl of Aesthetics 21 1962.

Jones, D. L. Hazlitt and Hunt at the opera house. Symposium 16 1962.

Jones, S. Hazlitt as lecturer: three unnoticed contemporary accounts. Etudes Anglaises 15 1962.

—— Hazlitt in Edinburgh. Etudes Anglaises 17 1964.

Hummel, W. C. Liber amoris: Hazlitt's Napoleon. Kansas Mag 1963.

Kinnaird, J. The forgotten self. Partisan Rev 30 1963.

—— 'Philo' and Prudence: a new Hazlitt criticism of Malthus. BNYPL March 1965.

Noxon, J. Hazlitt as moral philosopher. Ethics 73 1963.

Trawick, L. M. Sources of Hazlitt's 'metaphysical discovery'. PQ 42 1963.

—— Hazlitt, Reynolds and the ideal. Stud in Romanticism 4 1965.

Garrett, W. Hazlitt's debt to C. W. Dilke. Keats-Shelley Memorial Bull 15 1964.

Sallé, J.-C. Hazlitt the associationist. RES new ser 15 1964.

Watson, T. C. Johnson and Hazlitt on the imagination in Milton. Southern Quart 2 1964.

Cain, R. E. David Hume and Adam Smith as sources of the concept of sympathy in Hazlitt. Papers on Eng Lang & Lit 1 1965.

Donohue, J. W. Hazlitt's sense of the dramatic actor as tragic character. Stud in Eng Lit 1500–1900 5 1965.

Coburn, K. Hazlitt on the disinterested imagination. In Some British Romantics, ed J. V. Logan et al, Columbus Ohio 1966.

De Villiers, A. Hazlitt and the pleasure of tragedy. Eng Stud in Africa 9 1966.

Milner, P. L. Hazlitt on the genius of Shakespeare. Southern Quart 5 1966.

O'Hara, J. D. Hazlitt and the functions of the imagination. PMLA 81 1966 RP. Replies 83 1968.

R. P.

THOMAS DE QUINCEY
1785–1859

Bibliographies

Masson, D. The collected writings of De Quincey, vol 14: appendix chronological and bibliographical. 1890.

Axon, W. E. A. The De Quincey collection at Moss Side. Lib Assoc Record 2 1900.

—— The canon of De Quincey's writings, with references to some of his unidentified articles. Trans Royal Soc of Lit 32 1914.

Green, J. A. De Quincey: a bibliography based upon the De Quincey collection in the Moss Side Library, Manchester. 1908.

Jones, C. E. Some De Quincey manuscripts. ELH 8 1941.

Byrns, R. H. Some unpublished works of De Quincey. PMLA 71 1956.

Jordan, J. E. In English romantic poets and essayists: a review of research and criticism, ed C. W. and L. H. Houtchens, New York 1957, 1966 (rev).

Moreux, F. In her Thomas De Quincey, Paris 1964.

Collections

De Quincey's writings. 24 vols Boston 1851–9, 22 vols in 11 Boston 1873. Ed J. T. Fields, with the consent of De Quincey; contents of early vols rptd directly from magazines.

Selections grave and gay, from writings, published and unpublished, of De Quincey, revised and arranged by himself. 14 vols Edinburgh 1853–60. Pbd under separate titles as follows: 1, Autobiographic sketches, 1853 (revision and enlargement of articles in Tait's Mag, Blackwood's Mag, Hogg's Instructor, with important new Preface); 2, Autobiographic sketches, 1854 (adds Laxton, Northamptonshire, The Priory Chester); 3, Miscellanies, 1854 (adds Postscript [to the System of the heavens] on the true relations of the Bible to merely human science); 4, Miscellanies, 1854 (adds Postscript [to On murder considered as one of the fine arts)]; 5, Confessions of an English opium eater, 1856 (much enlarged, and including The daughter of Lebanon); 6, Sketches, critical and biographic, 1857 (adds Notes to Whiggism in its relations to literature); 7, Studies on secret records, personal and historic, with other papers, 1858 (adds Supplementary note on the Essenes appended to the article on Secret societies); 8, Essays sceptical and anti-sceptical, on problems neglected or misconceived, 1858 (prefatory addns to some articles); 9, Leaders in literature, with a notice of traditional errors affecting them, 1858; 10, Classic records reviewed or deciphered, 1859; 11, Critical suggestions on style and rhetoric, with German tales and other narrative papers, 1859 (prefatory addn on Johnson's Life of Milton); 12–13, Speculations, literary and philosophic, with German tales and other narrative papers, 1859 (with appendix on Pope); 14, Letters to a young man whose education has been neglected, and other papers, 1860 (partly prepared before De Quincey's death, 8 Dec 1859, and pbd posthumously; includes Traditions of the Rabbins by George Croly, which had been ptd by J. T. Fields in the Boston edn and continued to be rptd as De Quincey's up to 2nd Amer edn of 1873 and 4th Edinburgh edn of 1878).

Works. 17 vols Edinburgh 1862–3 (to have been completed in 15 vols; 2 vols added in course of pbn), 16 vols Edinburgh 1871 (vols retain earlier dates, 1862–3; there are addns to last 4), 16 vols Edinburgh 1878 (all vols save 1st are dated 1862 or 1863; 3 essays added).

Works: Riverside edn. 11 vols Boston 1877 (3rd edn). With notes and general index; several times rptd.

Collected writings: new and enlarged edn by David Masson. 14 vols Edinburgh 1889–90. With introds and notes; considerable new material now first collected. Standard edn, several times rptd.

Uncollected writings, with preface and annotations by James Hogg. 2 vols 1890.

Posthumous works, edited from original mss with introductions and notes by A. H. Japp. 2 vols 1891–3. Vol 1: Suspiria de profundis, with other essays, critical, biographical, philosophical, imaginative and humorous; vol 2: Conversation and Coleridge, with other essays.

New essays: his contributions to the Edinburgh Saturday Post and the Edinburgh Evening Post 1827–8. Ed S. M. Tave, Princeton 1966.

Selections

Selected essays. Ed D. Masson 2 vols 1888.

Essays. Ed C. Whibley 1903.

Joan of Arc; The English mail-coach; and The Spanish military nun. Ed C. M. Newman 1905.

Literary criticism. Ed H. Darbishire, Oxford 1909.

The English mail-coach and other essays. 1914 (EL); ed J. E. Jordan 1961 (EL).

De Quincey selections. Ed M. R. Ridley, with essay by Francis Thompson 1927.

The ecstasies of De Quincey. Ed T. Burke 1928.

Selected writings of De Quincey. Ed P. Van D. Stern, New York 1937.

Thomas De Quincey. Ed B. Dobrée 1965.

Selected essays on rhetoric. Ed F. Burwick, Carbondale 1967.

§1

Translation from Horace, ode 22 lib 1 (third prize translation). Juvenile Lib 1 1800.

Concerning the relations of Great Britain, Spain and Portugal, as affected by the convention of Cintra, by Wordsworth, appendix on the letters of Sir J. Moore by De Quincey. 1809.

Close comments upon a straggling speech. 1818; rptd PMLA 55 1940.

Confessions of an English opium eater. London Mag Sept-Oct 1821, Sept 1822 (appendix); 1822, 1823, Edinburgh 1856 (greatly enlarged); ed R. Garnett 1885 (from 1st edn, with De Quincey's Conversations with R. Woodhouse, a note on De Quincey and Musset); ed D. Masson 1904; ed A. Beatty 1907 (rptd from London Mag); ed G. Douglas 1907 (EL); ed G. Saintsbury 1928 (from 1st edn); ed W. Bolitho with lithographs by Zhenya Gay, Oxford 1930; with wood engravings by B. Hughes-Stanton 1948, 1963; ed E. Sackville-West 1950 (from 1st edn with selections from Autobiography); ed M. Elwin 1956 (both edns with Suspiria); ed J. E. Jordan 1960 (EL); tr French, 1828 (adaptation by Musset), 1860 (in part by C. Baudelaire), 1890 ('première traduction intégrale'), 1962; German, 1888, 1928, 1947; Italian, 1889, 1956; Spanish, 1927, 1936; Swedish, 1869, 1926; Norwegian, 1878; Danish, 1921; Dutch, 1953; Japanese, 1950, 1951, 1952.

Popular tales and romances of the northern nations. 3 vols 1823. De Quincey contributed anon an unidentified trn from the German of J. A. Apel, The fatal marksman.

[Walladmor: a novel freely translated from the English of Sir Walter Scott, and now freely translated from the German into English. 2 vols 1825. A German forgery by G. W. H. Haering, freely adapted in English; *see* De Quincey's paper on Walladmor, 1838.]

Klosterheim: or the masque. Edinburgh 1832; ed S. Mackensie 1855; rptd in penny edn as The mystery of the masque, 1898.

The gallery of portraits. Ed A. T. Malkin 7 vols 1832–7. De Quincey contributed anon a Life of Milton to vol 1.

Encyclopaedia britannica. 7th edn 1827–42. Articles on Goethe, 1835; Pope, 1837–8; Schiller, 1838; Shakespeare, 1838.

The logic of political economy. Edinburgh 1844.

China. 1857. Rev from articles in Titan, with preface and addns.

The wider hope: essays on future punishment, with a paper on the supposed scriptural expression for eternity. 1890.

Dr Johnson and Lord Chesterfield. New York 1945 (priv ptd).

Recollections of the Lake poets. Ed E. Sackville-West 1948. Rev text supplemented from Tait's Mag 1839–40. *See* Reminiscences, below.

Niels Klim, by Ludvig Holberg. Tr De Quincey, ed S. Musgrove, Auckland Univ College Bull 42 1953.

Reminiscences of the English Lake poets. Ed J. E. Jordan 1961 (EL). Rev text with notes on 1839–40 mag text.

Letters and Papers

Gordon, M. In his Christopher North: a memoir of John Wilson, 2 vols Edinburgh 1862. One letter to Wilson.

Knight, C. In his Passages of a working life, 3 vols 1864–5. Quotes several letters to Knight.

Hill, R. and F. In their Recorder of Birmingham, 1878. One letter to M. D. Hill.

Japp, A. H. Some unconscious confessions of De Quincey. GM Aug 1886. Extracts from mss.

Archivist & Autograph Rev 1 June 1888. An essay on novels, facs.

New Rev 3 Dec 1890. 2 newly discovered papers: The dark interpreter; The loveliest sight for woman's eyes.

—— 4 Jan 1891. Further newly discovered papers: On miracles; Why the pagans could not invest their gods with any iota of grandeur; Great forgers: Chatterton, Walpole and Junius.

De Quincey memorials: being letters and other records here first published, with communications from Coleridge, the Wordsworths, Hannah More, Professor Wilson and others. Ed A. H. Japp 2 vols 1891.

Clowes, A. A. In his Charles Knight: a sketch, 1892.

Fields, Mrs J. T. In her A shelf of old books, 1894. Facs of letter to Fields.

Hill, G. B. In his Talks about autographs, Boston 1896. One letter to Mrs Hill.

Oliphant, M. O. W. and Mrs G. Porter. In their Annals of a publishing house: William Blackwood and his sons, 3 vols Edinburgh 1897–8. 6 letters to Blackwood.

Axon, W. E. A. De Quincey and J. F. Ferrier. Manchester Quart 17 1898. De Quincey's testimonial for Ferrier.

Priestley, E. In his Story of a lifetime, 1908. One letter to Chambers, extract of a letter to Mrs Chambers.

Lessons of the French Revolution: an unpublished paper. Independent 77 1914.

Fairbrother, E. H. Horatio De Quincey. N & Q 9 Oct 1915. One letter to War Office.

Armitt, M. L. In his Rydal, Kendal 1916. 5 letters to W. A. Duckworth.

Gray, W. F. De Quincey as Lady Nairne's tenant. Chambers's Jnl 20 Feb 1926. One letter to Lady Nairne's lawyers, one to J. H. Burton.

A diary of De Quincey 1803, here reproduced in replica as well as in print from the original manuscript in the possession of the Rev C. H. Steel. Ed H. A. Eaton [1927].

Moore, E. H. Some unpublished letters of De Quincey. RES 9 1933. 4 letters to rental agents.

Parsons, C. O. The woes of De Quincey. RES 10 1934. 3 letters.
De Quincey at work: as seen in one hundred and thirty new and newly edited letters. Ed W. H. Bonner, Buffalo 1936.
McCusker, H. De Quincey and the landlord. More Books Feb 1939.
De Quincey on French drama. Ibid. 7 fragments.
Brockway, W. and B. K. Winer. A second treasury of the world's great letters. New York 1941. One letter to William Tait.
Grantham, E. De Quincey to his publisher. More Books 20 Dec 1945. One letter to J. A. Hessey.
Unpublished letters of De Quincey and Elizabeth Barrett Browning. Ed S. Musgrove, Auckland Univ College Bull 44 1954. 7 letters, 2 to Southey.
Green, D. B. A De Quincey letter. N & Q Sept 1958.
De Quincey to Wordsworth: a biography of a relationship, with the letters of De Quincey to the Wordsworth family. Ed J. E. Jordan, Berkeley 1962.

Contributions to Periodicals

Westmorland Gazette. De Quincey was editor 11 July 1818–5 Nov 1819.
London Mag. De Quincey contributed some 45 articles irregularly 1821–5, notably: Confessions of an English opium eater, Sept–Oct 1821; On the knocking at the gate in Macbeth, Oct 1823.
Knight's Quart Mag 1824–5. 2 stories from the German: The incognito: or Count Fitz-Hum; and possibly The love charm of Tieck, which is more probably by Julius Hare.
Blackwood's Mag. The sport of fortune, 1821 (trn of Schiller); 6 articles 1826–8, notably: On murder considered as one of the fine arts, Feb 1827. 15 articles 1830–4, notably: Richard Bentley, 1830; Dr Parr and his contemporaries, 1831; The Caesars, 1832–4; also several political articles not rptd and only partly identifiable. 28 articles 1837–45, notably: Revolt of the Tartars, 1837; Casuistry, 1839–40; On murder considered as one of the fine arts, 2nd pt, 1839; On the Essenes, 1840; Style, 1840–1; Homer and the Homeridae, 1841; The pagan oracles, 1842; Coleridge and opium eating, 1845; Suspiria de profundis 1845; 2 articles, 1849: The English mailcoach; The vision of sudden death.
Edinburgh Saturday Post, Edinburgh Evening Post 1827–8. 39 articles, anon or signed 'X.Y.Z.'
Edinburgh Literary Gazette 1829. Sketch of Prof Wilson, 3 articles.
Tait's Mag. Some 40 articles 1833–41: Sketches of life and manners, from the Autobiography of an English opium eater (some 27 articles); Samuel Taylor Coleridge, 1834–5 (4 articles); Lake reminiscences, 1839 (5 articles); some 30 articles 1845–8: On Christianity as an organ of political movement, 1846; System of the heavens as revealed by Lord Rosse's telescopes, 1846; Joan of Arc, 1847; Secret societies, 1847; Conversation, 1847; 3 articles, 1851: Lord Carlisle on Pope.
Glasgow Athenaeum Album. 2 articles, 1848: Sortilege; Astrology.
North Br Rev. 3 articles, 1848: Reviews of Foster's Goldsmith; Roscoe's Pope; Talfourd's Final memorials of Charles Lamb.
Hogg's Instructor. 24 articles, 1850–3: Conversations (final pt), 1850; The Sphinx's riddle, 1850; A sketch from childhood, 1851–2; Judas Iscariot, 1853.
Titan. 6 articles, 1856–7.

§2

Montgomery, J. Confessions. Sheffield Iris 1821.
Confessions. Monthly Rev March 1823. Anon review.
Cottle, J. In his Early recollections, 2 vols 1837–9.

Gillies, R. P. In his Memoirs of a literary veteran, 3 vols 1851.
'Peregrine'. Lord Carlisle, Pope and Mr De Quincey. Tait's Mag Aug 1851.
[Brown, G. W.] North Amer Rev 74 1852. Review of Ticknor and Fields.
'Nathaniel, Sir' (F. Jacox). The humour of De Quincey. New Monthly Mag Oct 1852.
Thomas De Quincey. Eclectic Mag Dec 1852.
T., H. T. (H. Tuckerman). De Quincey's writings. Christian Examiner 4th ser 19 1853.
De Quincey's Miscellanies. New Monthly Mag July 1854.
De Quincey and his works. Westminster Rev 61 1854.
Life and adventures of an opium-eater. Dublin Univ Mag April, Sept 1854.
'Monkshood' (F. Jacox?). Thomas De Quincey. Bentley's Miscellany March 1855.
Masson, D. In his Essays biographical and critical, 1856.
— Dead men whom I have known. Macmillan's Mag May 1865.
— In his Wordsworth, Shelley, Keats and other essays, 1874.
— De Quincey. 1881 (EML).
Gilfillan, G. In his A gallery of literary portraits, 2 vols Edinburgh 1856–7.
Thomas De Quincey. GM Aug 1857.
Thomas De Quincey. London Quart Rev 8 1857.
Bayne, P. In his Essays in biography and criticism, 2 vols 1857–8.
[Phillips, G. S.] North Amer Rev 88 1859. Review of Fields.
Baudelaire, C. Les paradis artificiels: opium et hachisch. Paris 1860.
S., H. W. Life and writings of De Quincey. Fraser's Mag Dec 1860– Jan 1861.
[Kebbel, T. E.] Quart Rev 110 1861. Review of Selections grave and gay.
Landreth, P. In his Studies and sketches in modern literature, Edinburgh 1861.
Burton, J. H. The book-hunter. 1862.
Alden, H. M. Thomas De Quincey. Atlantic Monthly Sept 1863.
De Quincey. Christian Examiner Jan 1863.
The works of De Quincey. Br Quart Rev 38 1863.
De Quincey—grave and gay. North Br Rev 39 1863; rptd Eclectic Mag Dec 1863.
Spring, L. W. De Quincey and his writings. Continental Monthly June 1864.
'North, Christopher' (J. Wilson) et al. In their Noctes ambrosianae, 4 vols 1864.
Thomas De Quincey. Eclectic Mag Dec 1868.
[Day, H. B.) The opium habit. New York 1868.
Smith, J. F. The admission register of the Manchester school vol 2, 1868 (Chetham Soc vol 73).
Stirling, J. H. Jerrold, Tennyson and Macaulay. 1868.
Martineau, H. In her Biographical sketches, 1869.
Fields, J. T. In his Yesterdays with authors, 1872.
Minto, W. A. In his A manual of English prose literature, Edinburgh 1872, 1881 (rev).
Robinson, H. C. In his Diary, reminiscences and correspondence, ed T. Sadler 2 vols 1872.
— In his Correspondence with the Wordsworth circle 1808–66, ed E. J. Morley 2 vols Oxford 1927.
— In his Crabb Robinson on books and their writers, ed E. J. Morley 3 vols 1938.
Espinasse, F. In his Lancashire worthies, 2 vols 1874–7.
Stephen, L. In his Hours in a library, 1874.
Davey, S. Darwin, Carlyle and Dickens, with other essays. [1876].
Ingram, J. H. Thomas De Quincey. International Rev 4 1877.
Lathrop, G. P. Some aspects of De Quincey. Atlantic Monthly Nov 1877.

Mackay, C. Forty years' recollections of life, literature and public affairs. 2 vols 1877.
'Page, H. A.' (A. H. Japp). De Quincey: his life and writings; with unpublished correspondence. 2 vols 1877, 1 vol 1890 (rev with omissions and addns). With appendix by W. C. B. Eatwell, A medical view of Mr De Quincey's case.
— Early intercourse of the Wordsworths and De Quincey. Century Mag 41 1891.
Procter, B. W. ('Barry Cornwall'). An autobiographical fragment, and biographical notes. 1877.
Conway, M. D. In his English lakes and their genii, Harper's Mag Dec 1880–Feb 1881.
Carlyle, T. In his Reminiscences, ed. J. A. Froude 2 vols 1881.
— In his Letters 1826–36, ed C. E. Norton 2 vols 1888.
Hodgson, S. H. In his Outcast essays, and verse translations, 1881.
Troup, G. E. Life of George Troup, journalist. Edinburgh 1881.
Froude, J. A. In his Thomas Carlyle, 4 vols 1882–4.
Payn, J. In his Some literary recollections, 1884.
Mason, E. T. In his Personal traits of British authors, 4 vols 1885.
Woodhouse, R. Notes of conversations with De Quincey. In Confessions, ed R. Garnett 1885.
Brandl, A. In his Samuel Taylor Coleridge und die englische Romantik, Berlin 1886; tr 1887.
Cook, A. S. Native and foreign words in De Quincey. MLN 1 1886.
Findlay, J. R. Personal recollections of De Quincey. 1886.
Brown, J. In his Life of William B. Robertson DD, 1888.
Ingleby, C. M. In his Essays edited by his son, 1888.
Salt, H. S. In his Literary sketches, 1888.
— De Quincey. 1904.
— De Quincey the defaulter. Saturday Rev 30 May 1908.
— The depreciation of De Quincey. Nat Rev May 1928.
Sandford, Mrs H. In her Thomas Poole and his friends, 2 vols 1888.
Bourget, P. C. J. In his Etudes et portraits, Paris 1889.
Rae-Brown, C. A reminiscence of De Quincey. Universal Rev 5 1889.
Stuart, M. In Letters from the Lake poets, S. T. Coleridge, Wordsworth, Southey to Daniel Stuart. 1889 (priv ptd).
Bain, J. De Quincey and his supposed descent from the Earls of Winchester. Genealogist new ser 7 1890.
Pollitt, C. De Quincey's editorship of the Westmorland Gazette, with selections from his work on that journal from July 1818 to November 1819. 1890.
Saintsbury, G. In his Essays in English literature 1780–1860, 1890.
— In his A history of English prose rhythm, 1912.
Anderson, M. B. The style of De Quincey. Dial 12 Aug 1891.
Bayne, T. De Quincey and Charlotte Brontë. N & Q 9 Sept 1893.
Bertram, J. In his Some memories of books, authors and events, 1893.
Contades, G. de. La Jeanne d'Arc de De Quincey. Revue des Deux Mondes 15 Feb 1893.
Birrell, A. In his Essays about men, women and books, 1894.
L[andreth?], P. Emerson's meeting with De Quincey. Blackwood's Mag April 1894.
Dowden, E. How De Quincey worked. Saturday Rev 23 Feb 1895.
Chancellor, E. B. In his Literary types, 1895.
Hogg, J. De Quincey and his friends: personal recollections, souvenirs and anecdotes. 1895.
Wyzewa, T. de. In his Ecrivains étrangers, Paris 1896.
Lang, A. In his Life and letters of John Gibson Lockhart, 2 vols 1897.
Stansfield, A. In his Essays and sketches, Manchester 1897.
'Barine, Arvède' (C. Vincens). Névrosés: Hoffmann, Quincey, Edgar Poe, G. de Nerval. Paris 1898.
Christoph, F. Über den Einfluss Jean Paul Friedrich Richters auf De Quincey. Hof 1898–9.
Axon, W. E. A. De Quincey's highwayman. In his Echoes of old Lancashire, 1899.
— Thomas De Quincey. Bookman (London) Feb 1907.
— De Quincey and The stranger's grave. Nation (London) Dec 1907.
— De Quincey and T. F. Dibdin. Library 2nd ser 8 1907.
— Some De Quincey proof sheets. Scottish Rev 26 Nov 1908.
Dawson, W. J. In his Makers of modern prose, 1899.
Hitchcock, R. De Quincey: a study. 1899.
Dunn, W. A. De Quincey's relation to German literature and philosophy. Strasbourg 1900.
Cooper, L. Prose-poetry of De Quincey. Leipzig 1902.
Gould, G. M. Biographic clinics: the origin of the ill health of De Quincey, Carlyle, Darwin, Huxley and Browning. Philadelphia 1903.
Symons, A. In his Studies in prose and verse, 1904.
Sessions, F. In his Literary celebrities of the English Lake-district, 1905.
Jarvis, J. B. The neglect shown to De Quincey. Month Nov 1906.
Robinson, H. P. De Quincey and the 'grand style'. Academy 17 Feb 1906.
Compton-Rickett, A. In his Personal forces in modern literature, 1906.
— In his Vagabond in literature, 1906.
Durand, W. Y. De Quincey and Carlyle in their relation to the Germans. PMLA 22 1907.
Guerrier, P. Etude médico-psychologique sur De Quincey. Lyons 1907.
Rannie, D. W. In his Wordsworth and his circle, 1907.
Sellar, E. M. In his Recollections and impressions, 1907.
Winchester, C. T. In his A group of English essayists, New York 1910.
Stekel, W. Die Traüme der Dichter. Wiesbaden 1912.
Dupouy, R. In his Opiomanes, mangeurs, buveurs et fumeurs d'opium, Paris 1912.
Green, J. A. Notes on the portraits of De Quincey. Manchester Quart 32 1913.
Eaton, H. A. De Quincey's love of music. JEGP 13 1914.
— The letters of De Quincey to Wordsworth 1803–7. ELH 3 1936.
— De Quincey: a biography. Oxford 1936.
Walker, H. In his English essay and essayists, 1915.
Patterson, W. M. In his Rhythm of prose, New York 1916.
MacFarlane, C. In his Reminiscences of a literary life, 1917.
Leonard, L. P. De Quincey's Dream-fuge. Poet Lore Nov 1917.
Peltier, P. Musset et Baudelaire à propos des Confessions d'un mangeur d'opium. Mercure de France 16 Dec 1918.
Duckers, J. S. The De Quincey family. TLS 21 Oct 1920.
Hussey, D. De Quincey's mother. Athenaeum 12–19 March 1920; rptd in Living Age 1 May 1920.
Wells, J. E. The story of Wordsworth's Cintra. SP 18 1921.
— De Quincey's punctuation of Wordsworth's Cintra. TLS 3 Nov 1932.
— Wordsworth and De Quincey in Westmorland politics 1818. PMLA 55 1940. Addn by L. N. Broughton 56 1941.
— De Quincey and the Prelude in 1839. PQ 20 1941.
Elton, O. In his A sheaf of papers, 1922.
Fowler, J. H. De Quincey as literary critic. 1922 (Eng Assoc pamphlet).
Paull, H. M. De Quincey—and style. Fortnightly Rev July 1922.

Lalou, R. De Thomas de Quincey à Baudelaire. Revue Germanique April 1923.
'Lee, Vernon' (Violet Paget). The syntax of De Quincey. In her Handling of words, 1923.
Richter, H. Thomas de Quincey. E Studien 58 1924
Marks, J. In her Genius and disaster: studies in drugs and genius, New York 1925.
Hudson, H. H. De Quincey on rhetoric and public speaking. In Studies in rhetoric and public speaking in honor of James Albert Winans, New York 1925.
Scott, J. H. Rhythmic prose. Univ of Iowa Humanistic Stud 3 1925.
'Impassioned prose'. TLS 16 Sept 1926.
Powell [Dodds], A. E. In her Romantic theory of poetry, 1926.
Johnson, J. C. In his Biography: the literature of personality, 1927.
Meyer, G. Das Verhältnis De Quinceys zur Nationalökonomie. Freiburg 1927.
Richards, A. E. The day book and ledger of Wordsworth's carpenter. PQ 6 1927.
Bostock, J. K. Johanna d'Arc als Nationalistin und Protestantin. E Studien 62 1928.
Bragman, L. J. The medical wisdom of De Quincey. Annals of Medical History 10 1928.
Burke, T. De Quincey, the goblin. Nineteenth Century May 1928.
— The obsequies of Mr Williams: new light on De Quincey's famous tale of murder. Bookman (New York) Nov 1928.
Jan, E. von. Das literische Bild der Jeanne D'Arc 1429–1926. Halle 1928.
Cramer, M. De Quincey und John Wilson (Christopher North): ihre literarischen und persönlichen Beziehungen. Münster 1929.
Meyerstein, E. H. W. De Quincey's copy of Chatterton's Miscellanies. TLS 8 May 1930.
Brede, A. Theories of poetic diction. Michigan Acad of Science, Arts & Letters 14 1931.
Clapton, G. T. Baudelaire et De Quincey. Paris 1931.
Simmons, E. J. Gogol and English literature. MLR 26 1931.
Wellek, R. Immanuel Kant in England 1798–1838. Princeton 1931.
— De Quincey's status in the history of ideas. PQ 23 1944.
Griggs, E. L. Coleridge, De Quincey and nineteenth-century editing. MLN 47 1932.
Woolf, V. In her Common reader ser 2, 1932.
Plesner, K. F. Elia og hans venner: Lamb, Hazlitt, De Quincey. Copenhagen 1933.
Abrams, M. H. The milk of paradise: the effect of opium visions on the works of De Quincey, Crabbe, Francis Thompson and Coleridge. Cambridge Mass 1934.
Mann, K. Thomas De Quincey. Sammlung (Amsterdam) 1 1934.
Astre, G.-A. H. de Balzac et 'L'anglais mangeur d'opium'. Revue de Littérature Comparée 15 1935.
— De Quincey, mystique et symboliste. Revue Hebdomadaire Oct 1937.
Cabanès, A. Grands névropathes. Paris 1935.
Elwin, M. De Quincey. 1935.
Scott, C. A. De Quincey and Lamb. TLS 24 Jan 1935.
Sackville-West, E. A flame in sunlight: the life and work of De Quincey. 1936.
Sehrt, E. T. Geschichtliches und religiöses Denken bei De Quincey. Berlin 1936.
De Quincey's sanctuary. TLS 25 July 1936.
Super, R. H. De Quincey and a murderer's conscience. TLS 5 Dec 1936.
Forward, K. 'Libellous attack' on De Quincey. PMLA 52 1937.
— De Quincey's 'cessio bonorum'. PMLA 54 1939.
Galinsky, H. K. Is De Quincey author of the Love charm? MLN 52 1937.
Larrabee, S. A. Critical terms in the art of sculpture. N & Q 3 April 1937.
Paul-Marguerite, E. Thomas De Quincey. Revue Bleue March 1937.
Reilly, J. J. The vagaries of De Quincey. Catholic World July 1937.
Strout, A. L. De Quincey and Wordsworth, N. & Q 11 June 1938.
Brown, C. S., jr. The musical structure of De Quincey's Dream-fugue. Musical Quart 24 1938; rptd in his Music and literature: a comparison of the arts, Athens Georgia 1948.
— De Quincey and the participles in Mallarmé's Coup de dés. Comparative Lit 16 1964.
Hughes, R. Vers la contrée du rêve: Balzac, Gautier et Baudelaire, disciples de Quincey. Mercure de France 1 Aug 1939. Replies by G.-A. Astre 15 Sept 1939; J. Castier and J. Crépet 1 Nov 1939; rebuttal, 15 Sept and 1 April 1940; reply by Crépet 1 May 1940.
Kassner, R. Thomas De Quincey. Corona 9 1939.
— Transfiguration. Zürich [1946].
Seever, M. H. Drug addiction problems. Sigma Xi Quart 27 1939.
R., V. De Quincey: some objections and corrections. N & Q 17 June, 1, 15 July, 9 Sept 1939; 21 Sept, 14–21 Dec 1940.
Metcalf, J. C. De Quincey: a portrait. Cambridge Mass 1940.
— De Quincey's critical years. Virginia Quart Rev 16 1940.
Proctor, S. K. De Quincey's theory of literature. Ann Arbor 1943.
Hendricks, C. H. De Quincey, symptomatologist. PMLA 60 1945.
Schneider, E. The 'dream' of Kubla Khan. PMLA 60 1945.
— Coleridge, opium and Kubla Khan. Chicago 1953.
Prod'homme, J.-G. Berlioz, Musset and De Quincey. Musical Quart 32 1946.
Lindesmith, A. R. Opiate addiction. Bloomington 1947.
Hollinger, R. E. De Quincey's use of Americanisms. Amer Speech 23 1948.
Jordan, J. E. De Quincey's dramaturgic criticism. ELH 18 1951.
— De Quincey: literary critic. Berkeley 1952.
— De Quincey on Wordsworth's theory of diction. PMLA 68 1953.
— De Quincey to Wordsworth: a biography of a relationship. Berkeley 1962.
Musgrave, S. and J. A De Quincey manuscript. TLS 30 March 1951.
Bett, W. R. The infirmities of genius. 1952.
Poulet, G. Timelessness and romanticism. JHI 15 1954.
Wright, B. The cave of Trophonius: myth and reality in De Quincey. Nineteenth-Century Fiction 8 1954.
Michelsen, P. Der Traümer und die Ratio: zu Leben und Werk De Quinceys. Deutsche Universitäts-Zeitung 9 1954.
— De Quincey und Schiller. German Life & Letters new ser 9 1956.
— De Quincey und Goethe. Euphorion 50 1956.
— De Quinceys Lessing-Bild. Monatshefte für Deutschen Unterricht 50 1958.
— De Quincey und die Kantische Philosophie. Revue de Littérature Comparée 33 1959.
— De Quincey und Jean Paul. JEGP 61 1962.
— De Quincey als Versdichter: seine Übersetzung der Luise von J. H. Voss. Archiv 202 1965.
Alegria, F. Los sueños de Thomas De Quincey. Nueva Democracia 35 1955.
Patterson, C. I. De Quincey's conception of the novel as literature of power. PMLA 70 1955.
Rockwell, F. S. De Quincey and the ending of Moby-Dick. Nineteenth-Century Fiction 9 1955.

Byrns, R. H. De Quincey's first article in Blackwood's Magazine. BNYPL July 1956.
— De Quincey's revisions in the Dream-Fugue. PMLA 77 1962.
— A note on De Quincey's The vision of sudden death. N & Q May 1962.
Jamieson, P. F. Musset, De Quincey and Piranesi. MLN 71 1966.
Kobayashi, S. Rhythm in the prose of De Quincey. [Tokyo] 1956.
Praz, M. In his Hero in eclipse in Victorian fiction, 1956.
Zanco, A. Temi e psicologia di De Quincey. Rivista di Letterature Moderne e Comparate 9 1956.
Jack, I. De Quincey revises his Confessions. PMLA 72 1957.
Maxwell, J. C. 'Scarlet' and 'pink' in politics. N & Q Feb 1957.
Bilsland, J. W. On De Quincey's theory of literary power. UTQ 26 1957.
Appleman, P. D. H. Lawrence and the intrusive knock. Modern Fiction Stud 3 1958.
Hjorth-Moritzsen, A. De Quincey: en engelske klassiker. Copenhagen 1959.
Leistikow, K. U. Zu einem Gedanken De Quinceys. Antaios 1 1959.
Jacobsen, D. I was sacrificed. Spectator 18 Dec 1959.
Brown, T. J. English literary autographs XXXIV: De Quincey. Book Collector 9 1960.
Hussain, I. Beckford, Wainewright, De Quincey and oriental exoticism. Venture 1 1960.
Mayoux, J.-J. De Quincey et le sens du temps. Lettres Nouvelles new ser 36 1960.
Swinnerton, F. De Quincey: forgotten highbrow. Saturday Rev 17 Sept 1960.
Wolfe, R. H. De Quincey quotes himself. N & Q March 1960.
— De Quincey, Wordsworth and Hamlet. N & Q Jan 1961.
— De Quincey and Wordsworth: some affinities. Ball State Univ Forum 6 1965.
Carnall, G. D. De Quincey on the knocking at the gate. REL 2 1961.
Leech, C. De Quincey as literary critic. Ibid.
Mondor, H. Quincey, Dickens, Poe, Ruskin parmi bien d'autres: comme les voyait Mallarmé. Figaro Littéraire 18 Nov 1961.
Amer, H. Les Confessions de Thomas de Quincey. Nouvelle Revue Française 10 Oct 1962.
Gossman, A. On the knocking at the gate in Markheim. Nineteenth-Century Fiction 16 1962.
Miller, J. H. In his Disappearance of God, Cambridge Mass 1963.
Le Breton, G. De Quincey et Wordsworth. Mercure de France April 1964.
Davies, H. S. Thomas De Quincey. 1964 (Br Council pamphlet).
McFarland, G. F. Julius Charles Hare: Coleridge, De Quincey and German literature. Bull John Rylands Lib 47 1964.
Moreux, F. De Quincey: la vie-l'homme-l'œuvre. Paris 1964.
Goldman, A. The mine and the mint: sources for the writings of De Quincey. Carbondale 1965.
Grant, D. In Some British Romantics, ed D. Logan, J. E. Jordan and N. Frye, Columbus Ohio 1966.
Grieve, A. Menus faits pour un mangeur d'opium. Langues Modernes Jan-Feb 1966.
Rozenberg, P. Essais pédagogiques: carnet de travail 1, De Quincey. Ibid.

J. E. J.

THOMAS CARLYLE

1795–1881

Bibliographies

Anderson, J. P. Bibliography of Carlyle. In R. Garnett, Life of Carlyle, 1887.
Lane, W. C. The Carlyle collection: a catalogue of books on Oliver Cromwell and Frederick the Great bequeathed by Carlyle to Harvard College Library. Cambridge Mass 1888.
Wead, M. E. A catalogue of the Dr Samuel A. Jones Carlyle collection. Ann Arbor 1919.
Dyer, I. W. A bibliography of Carlyle's writings and ana. Portland Maine 1928.
Coffin, E. F. American first editions of Carlyle. Amer Book Collector 4 1933.
Thrall, M. M. H. Bibliography of Carlyle. In her Rebellious Frasers, New York 1934. Contributions to Fraser's Mag.
Clark, A. P. The ms collections of the Princeton University Library. Princeton Univ Lib Chron 1958.
Tennyson, G. B. Unnoted encyclopaedia articles by Carlyle. Eng Lang Notes 1 1963. Adds articles on Persia and Quakers.
— Carlyle's poetry to 1840: a checklist and discussion, a new attribution and six unpublished poems. Victorian Poetry 1 1963.
— Carlyle's earliest German translation. Amer N & Q 3 1964.
Moore, C. Carlyle: a critical bibliography. In English romantic poets and essayists, ed C. W. and L. H. Houtchens, New York 1966 (rev).

Collections

Collected works. 16 vols 1857–8; Library edition, 34 vols 1869–71; People's edition, 37 vols 1871–4; Edition de luxe, 20 vols Boston 1884; Sterling edition, 20 vols Boston 1885; People's edition, 20 vols in 10 Boston 1885; Ashburton edition, 17 vols with 3 suppl vols 1885–8; Collected works, 12 vols New York 1885; Collected works 20 vols in 10 New York [1887]; Copyright edition, 37 vols 1888, 20 vols 1894.
Centenary edition. Ed H. D. Traill 30 vols 1896–9, New York 1896–1901. The fullest collection.
Chelsea edition. 11 vols [1900], [1900?] ('cheap issue'); Edinburgh edition, 30 vols New York 1903, 15 vols 1903; Centennial edition, ed W. J. Rolfe 26 vols Boston [1904?]; Standard edition, 18 vols New York 1905.

Selections

Passages selected from the writings of Carlyle, with a biographical memoir by T. Ballantyne. 1855.
Ausgewählte Schriften. Ed A. Kretschmar 6 vols Leipzig 1855–6.
The Carlyle anthology. Ed E. Barrett, New York 1876.
Carlyle: ein Lebensbild, und Goldkörner aus seinen Werken. Leipzig 1882.
The socialism and unsocialism of Carlyle. 2 vols New York [1891].
Rescued essays. Ed P. Newberry [1892].
Readings from Carlyle. Ed W. K. Leask 1894.
Sozialpolitische Schriften. Ed P. Hensel, tr German E. von Pfannkuche 3 vols Göttingen 1894–8.
Thoughts on life. Ed R. Duncan 1895.
Outline of the doctrines of Carlyle. 1896.
Arbeiten und nicht verzweifeln: Auszüge aus Carlyles Werken. Tr German and ed A. Kretschmar and M. Kühn, Düsseldorf 1902.
Collectanea Carlyle 1821–55. Ed S. A. Jones 1903.
Zerstreute historische Aufsätze. Tr German and ed T. A. Fischer, Leipzig 1905.

Pages choisies des grands écrivains: Carlyle. Tr French and ed E. Masson, Paris 1905.
Arbeta och förtvifla icke: lefvande ord ur Thomas Carlyle. Tr Swedish and ed E. Ryding, Stockholm 1906.
Pen portraits. Ed R. B. Johnson 1906.
Essais choisis de critique et de morale. Tr French and ed E. Barthélemy, Paris 1907.
Short passages from the works of Carlyle. Ed Sarah Spencer 1908.
Pocket Carlyle. Ed R. Gardner 1908.
Masters of literature: Carlyle. Ed A. W. Evans 1909.
Selected essays. Ed A. S. Pringle-Pattison 1909.
Nouveaux essais choisis de critique et de morale du genre biographique. Tr French and ed E. Barthélemy, Paris 1909.
Lavora, non disperarti: brani scelti delle sue opera. Tr Italian and ed V. Morali, Turin 1910.
Carlyles skrifter. Tr Danish, 1916.
Carlyle a faithful friend of Germany: eine Auswahl. Ed J. Bube, Leipzig 1919.
Pagine scelte. Tr Italian and ed G. Valori, Milan 1920.
The best of Carlyle. Ed T. O. Glencross 1923.
Carlyle: an anthology. Ed G. M. Trevelyan 1953.
Selected works, reminiscences and letters. Ed J. Symons 1955 (Reynard Lib).
Selections. Ed A. M. D. Hughes, Oxford 1957.

§1

For poems by Thomas and his wife Jane Welsh Carlyle, see I. W. Dyer, Bibliography, *above*; Love letters of Carlyle and Jane Welsh, ed A. Carlyle vol 2 pp. 341–60; *and* G. B. Tennyson, Carlyle's poetry to 1840, *above.*

On the phenomenon of thunder. Dumfries & Galloway Courier 6, 20 June 1815. Signed 'Ichneretes'.
Examination of some compounds which depend on very weak affinities, by Jacob Berzelius. Edinburgh Philosophical Jnl 1 1819. Tr Carlyle.
Remarks upon Professor Hansteen's inquiries concerning the magnetism of the earth. Edinburgh Philosophical Jnl 3–4 1820–1.
Outlines of Professor Mohs' new system of crystallography and mineralogy. Ibid. Tr Carlyle.
[Articles in Brewster's Edinburgh encyclopaedia]. 14 1820: Montaigne; Lady Montagu; Montesquieu; Montfaucon; Montucla; Dr John Moore; Sir John Moore; Persia; Quakers; 15 1822: Necker; Nelson; Netherlands; Newfoundland; Pascal; William Pitt, Earl of Chatham; William Pitt the Younger; 17 1824: Sismondi, Political economy, tr Carlyle. Rptd, except for Persia, Quakers and Pascal, and trn of Sismondi, in Montaigne and other essays chiefly biographical, ed S. R. Crockett 1897.
Joanna Baillie's metrical legends. New Edinburgh Rev 1 1821.
Goethe's Faust. New Edinburgh Rev 2 1822; ed R. Garnett, Pbns of Eng Goethe Soc 4 1888.
Schiller's life and writings. London Mag Oct 1823, Jan, July-Sept 1824; rptd as The life of Schiller, 1825, 1845, Boston 1833; tr German, with introd by Goethe, Frankfurt 1830.
Elements of geometry and trigonometry with notes, translated from the French of A. M. Legendre, Edinburgh 1824. Trn and introductory ch on Proportion by Carlyle.
Wilhelm Meister's apprenticeship: a novel from the German of Goethe. 3 vols Edinburgh 1824 (anon), 1839, Philadelphia 1840, 1842, Boston 1851, London 1858, Boston 1865; ed E. Dowden 1890; ed N. H. Dole, Boston 1901.
Jean Paul Friedrich Richter. Edinburgh Rev 46 1827.
State of German literature. Ibid.
German romance: specimens of its chief authors with biographical and critical notices, by the translator of Wilhelm Meister, and the author of the life of Schiller. 4 vols Edinburgh 1827. Vol 1: Musaeus and Fouqué; vol 2: Tieck and Hoffman; vol 3: Richter; vol 4: Goethe. Rptd 2 vols 1874 as Tales by Musaeus, Tieck, Richter.
Life and writings of Werner. Foreign Rev 1 1828.
Goethe's Helena. Ibid.
Goethe. Foreign Rev 2 1828.
Life of Heyne. Ibid.
Burns. Edinburgh Rev 48 1828.
German playwrights. Foreign Rev 3 1829.
Voltaire. Ibid.
Signs of the times. Edinburgh Rev 49 1829.
Novalis. Foreign Rev 4 1829.
Jean Paul Friedrich Richter again. Foreign Rev 5 1830.
Jean Paul Richter's review of Madame de Staël's De l'Allemagne. Fraser's Mag Feb, May 1830.
Cui bono? and four fables by Pilpay Junior. Fraser's Mag Sept 1830.
Thoughts on history. Fraser's Mag Nov 1830.
Luther's Psalm. Fraser's Mag Jan 1831.
Cruthers and Jonson. Ibid.
Peter Nimmo: a rhapsody. Fraser's Mag Feb 1831.
The Beetle. Ibid.
Taylor's historic survey of German poetry. Edinburgh Rev 53 1831.
Schiller. Fraser's Mag March 1831.
The sower's song. Fraser's Mag April 1831.
The Niebelungenlied. Westminster Rev 15 1831.
Tragedy of the night-moth. Fraser's Mag Aug 1831.
German literature of the fourteenth and fifteenth centuries. Foreign Quart Rev 8 1831.
Characteristics. Edinburgh Rev 54 1831.
Faust's curse. Athenaeum 7 Jan 1832.
Schiller, Goethe and Madame de Staël, and Goethe's portrait. Fraser's Mag March 1832.
Biography. Fraser's Mag April 1832.
Boswell's Life of Johnson. Fraser's Mag May 1832.
Death of Goethe. New Monthly Mag June 1832.
Corn Law rhymes. Edinburgh Rev 55 1832.
Goethe's works. Foreign Quart Rev 10 1832.
The tale, by Goethe. Fraser's Mag Oct 1832.
Novelle, by Goethe. Fraser's Mag Nov 1832.
Diderot. Foreign Quart Rev 11 1833.
Quae cogitavit on history again. Fraser's Mag May 1833.
Count Cagliostro. Fraser's Mag July-Aug 1833.
Sartor resartus. Fraser's Mag Nov 1833–Aug 1834. Pbd separately with subtitle The life and opinions of Herr Teufelsdröckh in three books, with preface by R. W. Emerson, Boston 1836, London 1838, 1841, 1849; ed E. Dowden 1896; ed A. MacMechan, Boston 1896; ed J. A. S. Barrett 1897, 1905 (rev); ed J. Wood 1902; ed P. C. Parr 1913; ed C. S. Northup, New York 1921; ed A. Thorndike, New York [1921]; ed W. D. Johnson, Boston 1924; ed F. W. Roe, New York 1927; ed C. F. Harrold, New York 1937; tr Dutch, 1880; German, 1882; French, 1899. 58 sets from Fraser's Mag bound with new title-page, London 1834, for distribution to friends. *See* W. Sewell, Quart Rev 66 1840.
Death of Edward Irving. Fraser's Mag Jan 1835.
Mirabeau. Westminster Rev 26 1837.
The diamond necklace. Fraser's Mag Jan-Feb 1837.
Parliamentary history of the French Revolution. Westminster Rev 27 1837.
The French Revolution: a history. 3 vols 1837, 1839, 1848; ed C. R. L. Fletcher 3 vols 1902; ed J. H. Rose 3 vols 1902; ed C. F. Harrold, New York 1937; tr German, 1844; French, 1865, 1888. Reviewed by J. S. Mill, London & Westminster Rev 27 1837; W. M. Thackeray, Times 3 Aug 1837; P. Chasles, Revue des Deux Mondes Oct 1840; H. Merivale, Edinburgh Rev 71 1840. *See* R. T. Kerlen, Contemporary criticism of Carlyle's French Revolution, Sewanee Rev 20 1912.
Lectures on German literature. May 1837. Not pbd; *see* Spectator 6 May 1837 for concise report.

Sir Walter Scott. Westminster Rev 28 1838.

Varnhagen von Ense's memoirs. Westminster Rev 32 1828.

Critical and miscellaneous essays. 4 vols Boston 1838, New York 1839, London 1839, 5 vols 1840, 4 vols 1847, 1857. Contains most contributions to periodicals to 1838.

Appeal for London Library. Examiner 27 Jan 1839.

Petition on the Copyright Bill. Examiner 7 April 1839.

[Six lectures on revolutions in modern Europe. May 1839. Not pbd.]

On the sinking of the Vengeur. Fraser's Mag July 1839.

Chartism. 1840 (for 1839), Boston 1840, 1842.

On heroes, hero-worship, and the heroic in history: six lectures delivered in May 1840. 1841, 1842, 1846; ed A. MacMechan, Boston 1901; ed J. C. Adams, Boston 1907; ed P. C. Parr 1910; ed H. M. Buller 2 vols 1926; tr French, 1888; Spanish, 1893; German, 1895; Italian, 1897.

Preface to Emerson's essays. Boston 1841, London 1841, 1844, 1906.

Baillie the Covenanter. Westminster Rev 37 1842.

Dr Francia. Foreign Quart Rev 31 1843.

Past and present. 1843, Boston 1843, London 1845; ed O. Smeaton 1902 (Temple Classics); ed F. Harrison [1903]; ed E. Mims, New York 1918; ed A. M. D. Hughes, Oxford 1921; ed J. Paton, New York 1927; ed E. Rhys nd (with Emerson's review) (EL); ed R. D. Altick, Boston 1965. *See* R.B.E., Thoughts on Carlyle: or a commentary on Past and present, 1843; F. Schneider, Carlyle's Past and present und der Chronica Jocelini de Brakelonda, Halle 1911; Dial July 1843 (Emerson's review); W. H. Smith, Blackwood's Mag July 1843; S. T. Williams, South Atlantic Quart 21 1922; G. J. Calder, The writing of Past and present: a study of Carlyle's manuscripts, New Haven 1949.

On the opening of Mazzini's letters. Times 19 June 1844.

An election to the Long Parliament. Fraser's Mag Oct 1844.

Oliver Cromwell's letters and speeches, with elucidations. 2 vols 1845, New York 1845, 3 vols 1846 (enlarged), 4 vols 1850; ed S. C. Lomas 1904; ed W. A. Shaw [1907] (EL); ed E. Sanderson, New York [1924] (abridged). *See* C. Remusat, De Cromwell selon M. Carlyle et M. de Lamartine, Revue des Deux Mondes March 1854; J. B. Mozley, Essays historical and theological vol 1, Oxford 1878; H. Mazel, Le Cromwell de Carlyle, Mercure de France Nov 1911.

Thirty-five unpublished letters of Oliver Cromwell. Fraser's Mag Dec 1847.

Louis Philippe. Examiner 4 March 1848.

Repeal of the Union. Examiner 29 April 1848.

Legislation for Ireland. Examiner 13 May 1848.

Ireland and the British Chief Governor; Irish regiments of the new era. Spectator 13 May 1848.

Death of Charles Buller. Examiner 2 Dec 1848.

Indian meal. Fraser's Mag May 1849.

Ireland and Sir Robert Peel. Spectator 14 April 1849.

Trees of liberty, from Mr Bramble's unpublished Arboretum Hibernicum. Nation (Dublin) 1 Dec 1849.

Occasional discourse on the nigger question. Fraser's Mag Dec 1849; 1853 (separately).

Latter-day pamphlets. 1850, New York 1850, London 1855, 1858. 8 pamphlets: 1 (Feb) The present time; 2 (March) Model prisons; 3 (April) Downing street; 4 (April) The new Downing street; 5 (May) Stump-orator; 6 (June) Parliaments; 7 (July) Hudson's statue; 8 (Aug) Jesuitism. For reviews *see* Athenaeum 1850; Blackwood's Mag June 1850; J. Hanay, Blackwood v. Carlyle: a vindication by a Carlylian, 1850; Revue des Deux Mondes April 1850; Eclectic Rev 28 1850; D. Masson, North Br Rev 14 1850.

Two hundred and fifty years ago: a fragment about duels. Leigh Hunt's Jnl 7, 21 Dec 1850, 11 Jan 1851.

Life of John Sterling. 1851, 1852; ed W. H. White 1907 (WC). For reviews and critiques *see* Athenaeum 1851; Br Quart Rev 15 1852; Eclectic Rev 2 1851; North Br Rev 16 1852; Revue des Deux Mondes July 1852; Tait's Mag 18 1851; 'George Eliot', Westminster Rev 57 1852; S. T. Williams, South Atlantic Quart 19 1920.

The opera. Keepsake 1852.

The Prinzenraub. Westminster Rev 7 1855.

Suggestions for a national exhibition of Scottish portraits. Proc Soc of Antiquaries of Scotland 1 1855.

State and appeal for Miss Lowe and her sister. Times 1 Nov 1855.

The history of Friedrich II of Prussia, called Frederick the Great. 6 vols 1858–65, 13 vols Leipzig 1858–65, 6 vols New York 1858–64, 1863–71, 7 vols 1869, 10 vols 1872–3; ed C. Ransome, New York 1892 (abridged); ed E. Sanderson 1909 (abridged); ed A. M. D. Hughes, Oxford 1916 (abridged); tr German, 1858–69. For reviews and critiques *see* Athenaeum 1862, 1864, 1865; Atlantic Monthly Nov 1862; Blackwood's Mag Feb 1859, July 1865; Dublin Rev 47 1859, 51 1862; Eclectic Mag 62 1864; Eclectic Rev June 1862, June 1864, Oct 1865; Edinburgh Rev 110 1859; Fraser's Mag Dec 1858, May 1864, Dec 1865; Harper's New Monthly Mag Dec 1858, Sept 1862; Nat Rev Oct 1858; North Amer Rev April 1859, April 1866; North Br Rev 30 1859, 43 1865; Preussische Jahrbücher 2 1858; Quart Rev 105 1859, 118 1865; Revue des Deux Mondes Jan-Feb 1873; Westminster Rev 15 1859; H. H. Lancaster, Essays and reviews, Edinburgh 1876.

Inspector Braidwood. Times 2 July 1861.

Memoranda concerning Mr Leigh Hunt. Macmillan's Mag July 1862.

Ilias (Americana) in nuce: the American Iliad in a nutshell. Macmillan's Mag Aug 1863.

Inaugural address at Edinburgh, April 2nd 1866, on the choice of books, with a memoir of Carlyle by J. C. Hotten. 1866, 1869 ('with a new life of the author').

Shooting Niagara: and after? Macmillan's Mag Aug 1867.

Reminiscences of Sir William Hamilton. In Memoir of Sir William Hamilton, 1868.

On the French-German war. Times 18 Nov 1870.

Early Kings of Norway. Fraser's Mag Jan-March 1875; rptd with An essay on the portraits of John Knox, 1875. *See* J. Drummond, The portraits of John Knox and George Buchanan, Trans Antiquarian Soc of Edinburgh 1875.

On the Eastern question. Times 28 Nov 1876.

On the crisis. Times 5 May 1877. On Disraeli's foreign policy.

Last words of Carlyle on trades-unions, promoterism and the signs of the times. Ed J. C. Aitken, Edinburgh 1882.

Wotton Reinfred. New Rev Jan-March 1892; rptd in Last words, 1892, below. An unfinished philosophical novel.

Last words of Carlyle: Wotton Reinfred, a romance; Excursion (futile enough) to Paris; Letters. 1892, New York 1892 (with introd on Wotton Reinfred).

Lectures on the history of literature, delivered April to July 1838. Ed J. R. Greene 1892; ed R. P. Karkaria, Bombay 1892. *See* E. Dowden, Transcripts and studies, 1887; Spectator 30 July 1892.

Rescued essays of Carlyle. Ed Newberry [1892]. Contains Louis-Philippe; The repeal of the Union; Legislation for Ireland; Ireland for the British Chief Governor; Irish regiments of the new era; Trees of liberty; Death of Charles Buller.

Historical sketches of notable persons and events in the reigns of James I and Charles I. Ed A. Carlyle 1898. Written 1842–3.

Collectanea 1821–55. Ed S. A. Jones, Canton Pa 1903. Contains Metrical legends of exalted characters; Faustus; Faust's curse; Heintze's German translation of Burns; Indian meal; A letter to the editor of the London Times [concerning the Misses Lowe].

Carlyle's unfinished history of German literature. Ed H. Shine, Lexington Kentucky 1951.

Letters and Journals

About 6,000 letters by Thomas Carlyle and 3,000 by Jane Welsh Carlyle have been found; roughly one half have been pbd, many with omissions. About two-thirds of the ms letters are in the National Library of Scotland; other large holdings are owned by the Marquess of Northampton (Ashburton letters), the descendants of Alexander Carlyle in Canada, the Victoria and Albert Museum, the John Rylands Library, Harvard, Yale, the Henry E. Huntington Library, New York Public Library, Trinity College Cambridge, Carlyle's House Chelsea, the Pierpont Morgan Library, the Univ of Edinburgh, the BM, the Goethe-Schiller Archiv Weimar, and the Arched House Ecclefechan. Both Carlyles kept journals, from which Froude and other biographers have quoted, but which have not yet been completely pbd. See I. W. Dyer, Bibliography, above, pp 143–84, 271–7.

Reminiscences. Ed J. A. Froude 2 vols 1881; ed C. E. Norton 2 vols 1887, 1932 (EL); tr German, 1897. Reviews: Edinburgh Rev 153 1881; A. Hayward, Quart Rev 151 1881; H. Larkin, Br Quart Rev 74 1881; H. Taylor, Nineteenth Century June 1881; A. Lang, Fraser's Mag April 1881; Cornhill Mag March 1881; Fortnightly Rev April 1881; Inquirer March-April 1881; Blackwood's Mag July 1882. *See* I. W. Dyer, Carlyle bibliography pp 209–18.

Letters to Mrs B. Montagu and B. W. Procter. 1881, Lakeland Michigan 1907.

Conway, M. D. Thomas Carlyle. 1881. Contains many letters and excerpts from letters.

Shepherd, R. H. Memoirs of Carlyle. 2 vols 1881. Contains many letters.

Glasgow Herald. 16 Feb 1882. Letters to Henry Inglis.

Reminiscences of my Irish journey in 1849 by Carlyle. Century Mag May-July 1882; 1882 (with changes), New York 1882.

Letters and memorials of Jane Welsh Carlyle. Ed J. A. Froude 3 vols 1883.

Letters of William Maccall and Jane Welsh Carlyle. Pall Mall Gazette 26 Nov, 19 Dec 1884.

The correspondence of Carlyle and Ralph Waldo Emerson. Ed C. E. Norton, Boston 1883, 1883, Boston 1886 (with addns), 1888; ed J. Slater, New York 1964 (with addns and notes).

Early letters of Carlyle 1814–26. Ed C. E. Norton 2 vols 1886, 2 vols in 1 1886.

[Letters to Coventry Patmore]. Athenaeum 17 July 1886.

Correspondence between Goethe and Carlyle. Ed C. E. Norton 1887; ed H. Oldenberg, Berlin 1887; ed G. Hecht, Dachau [1913]. Reviews: F. Max Müller, Contemporary Rev June 1886; Eng Goethe Soc 1886; E. Flügel, Grentzboten 46 1887; H. Grimm, Deutsche Rundschau Oct 1887; H. H. Boyesen in his Essays on German literature, 1892; O. Baumgarten, Carlyle und Goethe, Tübingen 1906.

Early letters of Carlyle 1826–36. Ed C. E. Norton 2 vols 1888, 2 vols in 1 1889.

Early letters of Jane Welsh Carlyle. Ed D. G. Ritchie 1889.

Excursion (futile enough) to Paris, autumn 1851. New Rev Oct-Dec 1891; rptd in Last words, 1892, above.

Conversations with Carlyle. By C. G. Duffy 1892. Records much conversation, with many letters.

Briefe Carlyles an Varnhagen von Ense. Ed R. Preuss, Berlin 1892. Letters from Carlyle to Varnhagen von Ense in Last words, 1892, above.

Strachey, G. Reminiscences of Carlyle with some unpublished letters. New Rev July 1893.

Strachey, E. Some letters and conversations of Carlyle. Atlantic Monthly June 1894.

Two note books of Carlyle from 23 March 1822 to 16 May 1832. Ed C. E. Norton, New York 1898.

Letters of Carlyle to his youngest sister. Ed C. T. Copeland, Boston 1899.

Letters of Jane Welsh Carlyle to her housemaid. Ed R. Blunt, Cornhill Mag Oct 1901.

New letters and memorials of Jane Welsh Carlyle. Ed A. Carlyle 2 vols 1903. Vol 2 pp. 87–115 contains a part of the journal which she kept 21 Oct 1855–5 July 1856.

New letters of Carlyle. Ed A. Carlyle 2 vols 1904.

Unpublished letters of Carlyle. Ed F. Harrison 1907.

Pitollet, C. Quelques lettres inédites de Carlyle. Revue Germanique 4 1908.

Love letters of Carlyle and Jane Welsh. Ed A. Carlyle 2 vols 1909.

Letters from Carlyle to the Socialists of 1830. New Quart 2 1909.

[Letters to Ruskin]. In Works of John Ruskin, ed E. T. Cook and A. D. O. Wedderburn 36–37 1909; Carlyle's letters to Ruskin, ed C. R. Sanders, Bull John Rylands Lib 41 1958.

Letters to William Allingham. 1911.

Carré, J.-M. Quelques lettres inédites de William Taylor, Coleridge et Carlyle à Henry Crabb Robinson sur la littérature allemande. Revue Germanique 8 1912.

Eight new love letters of Jane Welsh. Ed A. Carlyle, Nineteenth Century Jan 1914.

Letters by Carlyle to a fellow student [John Fergusson]. Ed D. Gorrie, Fortnightly Rev April 1914, Oct 1921.

More new letters of Jane Welsh Carlyle. Ed A. Carlyle, Nineteenth Century July-Dec 1914.

Mrs Carlyle and her little Charlotte. Ed R. Blunt, Strand Mag March-April 1915.

Correspondence between Carlyle and Browning. Ed A. Carlyle, Cornhill Mag May 1915.

Carlyle's unpublished letters to Miss Wilson. Nineteenth Century May-June 1921.

Carlyle and Thomas Spedding. Cornhill Mag May-June 1921.

Blunt, R. Jane Welsh Carlyle's unpublished letters. Forum 66–67 1921–2.

Notes of a three-days' tour to the Netherlands, August 1842. Cornhill Mag Oct-Nov 1922.

Letters of Carlyle to John Stuart Mill, John Sterling and Robert Browning. Ed A. Carlyle 1923.

Jane Welsh Carlyle: letters to her family 1839–63. Ed L. Huxley 1924.

New letters of Carlyle to Eckermann. Ed W. A. Speck, Yale Rev 15 1926.

Letters from Jane Welsh Carlyle. Ed L. Huxley, Cornhill Mag Oct-Nov 1926.

Letters of Jane Welsh Carlyle to Joseph Neuberg 1848–62. Ed T. Scudder 1931.

Carlyle and John Forster: an unpublished correspondence. Ed W. F. Gray, Quart Rev 268 1937.

Roberts, W. W. English autograph letters in the John Rylands Library. Bull John Rylands Lib 25 1941.

Two old letters [Carlyle to his mother]. Ed D. Gallup, Yale Univ Lib Gazette 24 1949.

Jane Welsh Carlyle: a new selection of her letters. Ed T. Bliss 1950.

Letters of Carlyle to William Graham. Ed J. Graham jr, Princeton 1950.

Carlyle: letters to his wife. Ed T. Bliss 1953.

Four unpublished letters of Carlyle. Ed S. H. Nobbe, PMLA 70 1955. To Geraldine Jewsbury.

Carlyle's last letters to Froude. Ed W. H. Dunn, Twentieth Century Jan, March, June 1956.

[Carlyle's letters to Clough]. Correspondence of A. H. Clough. Ed F. L. Mulhauser 2 vols Oxford 1957.

Marrs, E. W. J. jr. Discovery of some new Carlyle letters. Thoth (Syracuse Univ NY) 3 1962. 245 letters written to the Canadian Carlyles.

Sanders, C. R. The correspondence and friendship of Carlyle and Leigh Hunt. Bull John Rylands Lib 45–6 1963.

— Editing the Carlyle letters. In Editing nineteenth-century texts, ed J. M. Robson, Toronto 1967.
— Some lost and unpublished Carlyle-Browning correspondence. JEGP 62 1963.

§2

Sterling, J. On the writings of Carlyle. Westminster Rev 33 1839; rptd in his Essays and tales, 1848.
Mazzini, J. On the History of the French Revolution. Morning Chron 1840; On the genius and tendency of the writings of Carlyle, Br & Foreign Rev 16 1844. Both rptd in Life and writings of Mazzini vol 4, 1867.
Grant, J. In his Portraits of public characters 2 vols 1841.
Horne, R. H. In his A new spirit of the age vol 2, 1844.
Gilfillan, G. Carlyle and Sterling. In his A gallery of literary portraits, Edinburgh 1845.
Lester, J. W. In his Criticisms, 1847.
Montégut, E. Carlyle: sa vie et ses écrits. Revue des Deux Mondes April 1849.
— Littérature américaine: du culte des héros, Carlyle et Emerson. Revue des Deux Mondes Sept 1850.
— Carlyle et John Sterling. Revue des Deux Mondes July 1852.
Ossoli, M. F. In his Memoirs, ed Clarke, Emerson and Channing 2 vols Boston 1852.
Ballantyne, T. Passages selected from the writings of Carlyle, with a biographical memoir. 1855. The memoir was written with Carlyle's knowledge and cooperation.
Schmidt, J. Übersicht der englischen Literatur des 19 Jahrhunderts. Leipzig 1856.
— Porträts aus dem neunzehnten Jahrhundert. Berlin 1878.
Brimley, G. [Carlyle's Life of Sterling]. In his Essays, Cambridge 1858.
Häusser, L. Macaulay's Friedrich der Grosse mit einem Nachtrag über Carlyle. Historische Zeitschrift 1 1859.
McNicoll, T. In his Essays on English literature, 1861.
Stephen, J. F. In his Essays from the Saturday Review, 1862.
— The late Mr Carlyle's papers. 1886.
Kebbel, T. E. Essays upon history and politics. 1864.
Taine, H. A. L'idéalisme anglais: étude sur Carlyle. Paris 1864.
— In his Histoire de la littérature anglaise, 4 vols Paris 1864; tr Edinburgh 1871.
Japp, A. H. In his Three great teachers of our own times: Carlyle, Tennyson and Ruskin, 1865.
Alexander, P. P. Mill and Carlyle: an examination of Mr John Stuart Mill's doctrine of causation in relation to moral freedom, with an occasional discourse on Sauerteig, by Smelfungus. Edinburgh 1866.
— Carlyle redivivus: being an occasional discourse on Sauerteig, by Smelfungus. Glasgow 1881.
Althaus, F. Carlyle: eine biographisch-literarische Characteristik. In his Unsere Zeit, 2 vols Leipzig 1866.
— Englische Characterbilder 1. Berlin 1869.
Thoreau, H. D. Carlyle and his works. In his Yankee in Canada, Boston 1866.
Smith, A. Last leaves: sketches and criticisms. Edinburgh 1868.
Greg, W. R. Kingsley and Carlyle. In Literary and social judgments, 1869 (2nd edn).
Lowell, J. R. In his My study windows, Boston 1871.
Morley, J. In his Critical miscellanies ser 1, 1871.
Mr Carlyle and Père Bouhours. Catholic World Sept 1871.
Sillem, J. A. De klaagliedern van Carlyle. De Gids (Amsterdam) Aug 1871.
— Carlyle's leerjaren. De Gids Sept 1881.
Clark, D. Pen photographs. Toronto 1873.
Hodge, D. Carlyle: the man and the teacher. Edinburgh [1873].
Stephen, L. [Review of Carlyle's essay on Scott]. In his Hours in a library ser 1, 1874.
— In his Historians and essayists, New York 1899.
— In his Studies of a biographer vol 3, 1902. On Froude.
— In his Some early impressions, 1924.
Hood, E. P. Carlyle: philosophic thinker, theologian, historian and poet. 1875.
McCrie, G. In his Religion of our literature: essays upon Carlyle, Browning, Tennyson, 1875.
Davey, S. In his Darwin, Carlyle and Dickens, [1876].
Dowden, E. Transcendental movement and literature. In his Studies in literature 1789–1877, 1878.
— Carlyle's lectures on periods of European culture. Nineteenth Century May 1881; rptd in his Transcripts and studies, 1888.
Bayne, P. In his Lessons from my masters: Carlyle, Tennyson and Ruskin, 1879.
Courtney, W. L. Carlyle's political doctrines. Fortnightly Rev Dec 1879.
Guernsey, A. H. Carlyle: his life, his books, his theories. 1879.
Crozier, J. B. In his Religion of the future, 1880.
— Civilization and progress. 1885.
— My inner life. 1898.
— The wheel of wealth. 1906.
Grant, C. Carlyle als Moralist. Deutsche Rundschau July-Sept 1880.
Boglietti, G. Tommaso Carlyle. Nuova Antologia April 1881.
Conway, M. D. Thomas Carlyle. 1881.
Francison, A. National lessons from the life and works of Carlyle. [1881].
Hamley, E. B. Carlyle: an essay from Blackwood's Magazine. Edinburgh 1881.
Higginson, T. W. Carlyle's laugh. Atlantic Monthly Oct 1881.
James, H. (the elder). Some personal recollections of Carlyle. Atlantic Monthly May 1881; rptd in his Literary remains, Boston 1885.
Knighton, W. Conversations with Carlyle. Contemporary Rev June 1881.
Larkin, H. Carlyle and Mrs Carlyle: a ten years' reminiscence. Br Quart Rev 74 1881.
— Carlyle and the open secret of his life. 1886.
Mead, E. D. The philosophy of Carlyle. Boston 1881.
Nicoll, H. J. Thomas Carlyle. Edinburgh 1881.
Oliphant, M. O. Thomas Carlyle. Macmillan's Mag April 1881. *See* her Life of Edward Irving 2 vols 1862 (2nd edn rev).
Reid, S. J. Carlyle, his work and worth, with some personal reminiscences: an address. Manchester [1881].
Saintsbury, G. Carlyle: his life and writings. Westminster Rev 59 1881. For Saintsbury's other writings on Carlyle, *see* I. W. Dyer, Bibliography, above, pp. 445–6.
— Froude and Carlyle. Bookman (London) April 1930.
Shairp, J. C. In his Aspects of poetry, Oxford 1881.
Shepherd, R. H. and C. N. Williamson. Memoirs of Carlyle with personal reminiscences and selections from his private letters. 2 vols 1881.
Stanley, A. P. Sermon on Carlyle, preached at Westminster Abbey, Feb 6 1881. 1881.
Symington, A. J. Some personal reminiscences of Carlyle. New York Independent May-June 1881; Paisley 1886.
'Valbert, G.' (C. V. Cherbuliez). Carlyle. Revue des Deux Mondes March-April 1881.
Wylie, W. H. Carlyle: the man and his books. 1881.
Fischer, T. A. Thomas Carlyle. Leipzig 1882.
Froude, J. A. Carlyle: a history of the first forty years of his life 1795–1835. 2 vols 1882.
— The early life of Carlyle. Nineteenth Century July 1881.
— Carlyle: a history of his life in London 1834–81. 2 vols 1884; all 4 vols tr German 1887. Reviews: Br Quart Rev 81 1885; Dublin Rev Jan 1885; Blackwood's Mag July 1882; Fortnightly Rev May 1883, Nov 1884; Macmillan's Mag Nov 1884; North Amer Rev 140 1885; Quart Rev 159 1885; Westminster Rev 128 1887. *See* J. Wedgewood, Mr Froude as a biographer, Contemporary Rev May 1881; D. A. Wilson, Mr Froude

and Carlyle, 1898; The truth about Carlyle, 1913; J. A. Froude, My relations with Carlyle, with a letter from Sir James Stephen, 1903; J. Crichton-Browne, Froude and Carlyle: the imputation considered medically, Br Medical Jnl 27 1903, 1903 (pamphlet); J. Crichton-Browne and A. Carlyle, The nemesis of Froude: a rejoinder to J. A. Froude's My relations with Carlyle 1903; W. H. Dunn, Froude and Carlyle, 1930; James Anthony Froude: a biography, 2 vols Oxford 1963.

Scherer, E. In his Etudes critiques de littérature, Paris 1882.

— In his Essays on English literature, tr G. Saintsbury 1891.

Smith, W. C. Reminiscences of Carlyle and Leigh Hunt: being extracts from the diary of the late John Hunter of Craigcrook. Good Words 23 1882.

Burroughs, J. Carlyle. Century Mag Aug 1883. For Burroughs' other writings on Carlyle, *see* I. W. Dyer, Bibliography, above, p. 306.

Harrison, F. Histories of the French Revolution. North Amer Rev 137 1883; rptd in his Choice of books, 1886.

— In his Studies in early Victorian literature, 1895.

— Carlyle and the London Library. 1906.

Krummacher, M. Notizen über den Sprachgebrauch Carlyles. E Studien 6 1883.

— Sprache und Stil in Carlyles Friedrich II. E Studien 11 1888.

Birrell, A. In his Obiter dicta, 1884.

Howells, J. Carlyle's holidays in Wales. Red Dragon Mag April–June 1884.

Sadler, T. Carlyle and Neuberg. Macmillan's Mag Aug 1884.

Breitinger, H. Carlyle: ein Nachahmer Jean Pauls? Gegenwart 28 1885.

Masson, D. Carlyle personally and in his writings: two lectures. 1885.

— In his Edinburgh sketches and memories, 1892.

— In his Memories of London in the 'forties, 1908.

Müller, F. M. Goethe and Carlyle: an inaugural address. Eng Goethe Soc 1886.

Norton, C. E. Recollections of Carlyle. New Princeton Rev July 1886.

— Letters, with biographical comment by his daughter. Ed S. Norton and M. A. de W. Howe, Boston 1913.

Garnett, R. Life of Carlyle. 1887.

Hutton, R. H. In his Essays on some of the modern guides to English thought in matters of faith, 1887.

— In his Criticisms on contemporary thought and thinkers, 1894.

Pollock, F. In his Personal remembrances, 2 vols 1887.

Arnold, A. S. The story of Carlyle. 1888.

Browning, O. Carlyle as an historian. Athenaeum Nov 1888.

Flügel, E. Carlyles religiöse und sittliche Entwicklung und Weltanschauung. Leipzig 1887; tr New York 1891.

— Letters, with biographical comment by his daughter. Ed S. Norton and M. A. de W. Howe, Boston 1913.

Conrad, H. Carlyle und Schiller. Vierteljahrschrift für Litteraturgeschichte 2 1889.

— Carlyle und Jean Paul. Gegenwart 39 1891.

James, L. G. Carlyle's philosophy of history. Westminster Rev 132 1889.

Robertson, J. M. In his Essays towards a critical method, 1889.

— Modern humanists: sociological studies of Carlyle. 1891.

— In his Modern humanists reconsidered, 1927.

Troye, V. Carlyle hans liv og hans vaerk. Bergen 1889.

Anderson, J. M. Humor: Carlyle and Browning. Poet-Lore Aug 1890.

Davidson, D. In his Memories of a long life, Edinburgh 1890. On Jane Carlyle, who grew up with Davidson in Haddington.

Dreer, F. J. In his A catalogue of the collections of autographs formed by Dreer, 2 vols Philadelphia 1890.

Dilthey, W. Thomas Carlyle. Archiv für Geschichte der Philosophie 4 1891.

Ireland, Mrs A. Life of Jane Welsh Carlyle. 1891.

Rose, H. In his The new political economy: the social teaching of Carlyle, 1891.

Boyeson, H. H. Carlyle and Goethe. In his Essays on German literature, New York 1892.

Caird, E. The genius of Carlyle. In his Essays on literature, Glasgow 1892.

Gibbins, H. de B. English social reformers. 1892.

Nichol, J. Thomas Carlyle. 1892 (EML).

Strachey, G. Carlyle and the 'Rose-goddess'. Nineteenth Century Sept 1892. Kitty Kirkpatrick as Blumine in Sartor resartus.

Collingwood, W. G. In his Life and work of John Ruskin, 1893.

Espinasse, F. In his Literary recollections and sketches, 1893.

Schulze-Gaevernitz, G. von. Carlyles Welt und Gesellschafts-anschauung. Dresden 1893.

Anderson, F. The mask of Cromwell. Eng Illustr Mag Nov 1895.

Blunt, R. The Carlyles' Chelsea home. 1895.

Lilly, W. S. In his Four English humorists of the nineteenth century, 1895.

Streuli, W. Carlyle als Vermittler deutscher Literatur und deutsches Geistes. Zürich 1895.

Aronstein, P. Dickens und Carlyle. Anglia 18 1896.

Kellner, L. Goethe und Carlyle. Nation (Berlin) 21–8 March 1896.

— Macht ist Recht. Nation 21 July 1906.

— In his Die englische Literatur im Zeitalter der Königen Viktoria, Leipzig 1909.

— In his Die englische Literatur der neuesten Zeit, Leipzig 1921.

Macpherson, H. C. Thomas Carlyle. Edinburgh [1896].

Schröder, R. Carlyles Abhandlung über den Goetheschen Faust. Archiv 96 1896.

Wilson, H. S. Carlyle and Taine on the French Revolution; Goethe and Carlyle. In his History and criticism, 1896.

Mackinnon, J. Carlyle and Goethe. In his Leisure hours in the study, 1897.

Schmidt, F. J. Thomas Carlyle. Preussische Jahrbücher July–Sept 1897.

Walker, H. In his Age of Tennyson, 1897.

— In his Literature of the Victorian era, Cambridge 1910.

— In his English essay and essayists, [1915].

Wilhelmi, J. H. Carlyle und Nietzsche: wie sie Gott suchten und was für einen Gott sie fanden. Göttingen 1897.

Gosse, E. Carlyle and Macaulay. Littell's Living Age April 1898.

Kraeger, H. Carlyles deutsche Studien und der Wotton Reinfred. Anglia Beiblatt 1898.

— Byron und Carlyle. In his Der Byronische Heldentypus, Munich 1898.

— Carlyles Stellung zur deutschen Sprache und Literatur. Anglia 22 1899.

— Zu Carlyles Sartor resartus. Anglia Beiblatt 10 1899.

Scudder, V. D. Social ideals in English letters. Boston 1898.

Traill, H. D. In his Social England, 6 vols 1898.

Wilson, P. Carlyle and Emerson. In Leaders in literature, Edinburgh 1898.

Maulsby, D. L. The growth of Sartor resartus. Malden Mass 1899.

Thayer, W. R. In his Throne makers, New York 1899.

Trevelyan, G. M. Carlyle as an historian. Nineteenth Century Sept 1899; Life & Letters Dec 1930.

Wells, J. T. Carlyle: his religious experiences as reflected in Sartor resartus. Edinburgh 1899.

Wilson, S. L. The theology of Carlyle. In his Theology of modern literature, Edinburgh 1899.

Barthélemy, E. Carlyle: essai biographique et critique. Paris 1900 (2nd edn).
Gildemeester, F. von. Thomas Carlyle. Nijkerk [1900].
Schmeding, O. Über Wortbildung bei Carlyle. Halle 1900.
Brownell, W. C. In his Victorian prose masters, New York 1901.
Hensel, P. Thomas Carlyle. Stuttgart 1901.
Ward, M. A. In his Prophets of the nineteenth century, Boston 1901.
'Bos, Charles du' (H. Boeuf). Le Kantisme de Carlyle. Archiv für Geschichte der Philosophie 15 1902.
Chesterton, G. K. In his Twelve types, 1902.
— In his Varied types, 1903.
— In his Victorian age in literature, [1913].
Matz, B. W. Carlyle: a brief account of his life and writings. 1902.
d'Eichthal, E. Carlyle et la Saint-Simonisme. Revue Historique 82 1903.
Gazeau, J. In his L'impérialisme anglais: son évolution–Carlyle-Seely-Chamberlain, Paris 1903.
Gould, G. M. In his Biographic clinics: the origin of the ill-health of De Quincey, Carlyle etc vol 1, Philadelphia 1903.
Kühler, F. Carlyle und Schiller. Anglia 26 1903.
Ravenna, G. La teoria dell'Eroe in Carlyle e Nietzsche. Nuova Antologia July 1903.
Wiecki, E. von. Carlyle's Helden und Emerson's Repräsentanten. Königsberg 1903.
Batt, M. Carlyle's Life of Schiller. MP 1 1904.
Cazamian, L. In his Le roman social en Angleterre 1830–50, Paris 1904.
— In his L'Angleterre moderne: son évolution, Paris 1911; tr 1912.
— Carlyle. Paris 1913; tr 1932.
— In his L'évolution psychologique et la littérature en Angleterre, Paris [1920].
— A propos de Carlyle. In his Essais en deux langues, Paris 1938.
'Lee, Vernon' (V. Paget). Carlyle and the present tense. Contemporary Rev March 1904.
Lincke, O. Über die Wortzusammensetzung in Sartor resartus. Berlin 1904.
Lyttleton, A. T. Carlyle's life and works. In his Modern poets of faith, doubt, and paganism and other essays, 1904.
Oswald, E. Carlyle noch einmal. Archiv 112 1904.
Pape, H. Jean Paul als Quelle von Carlyles Anschauung und Stil. Rostock 1904.
Sharp, W. The country of Carlyle. In his Literary geography, 1904.
Sloan, J. M. The Carlyle country, with a study of his life. 1904.
Warner, P. Carlyle: the man and his influence. 1904.
Fletcher, J. B. Newman and Carlyle. Atlantic Monthly May 1905.
Nevinson, H. W. Wedded genius: Carlyle's letters. In his Books and personalities, 1905.
— Carlyle and the London Library. New Statesman May 31 1941. *See* TLS May 3 1941.
More, P. E. The spirit of Carlyle. In Shelburne essays ser 1, New York 1905.
Baumgarten, O. Carlyle und Goethe. Tübingen 1906.
Shelley, H. C. In Carlyle's country. In his Literary by-paths in old England, Boston 1906.
Adler, E. Jane Welsh Carlyle. 1907.
Allingham, W. A diary. Ed H. Allingham and D. Radford 1907. Records many conversations with Carlyle.
Durand, W. Y. De Quincey and Carlyle in their relation to the Germans. PMLA 22 1907.
MacCunn, J. In his Six radical thinkers: Bentham, Mill, Cobden, Carlyle, Mazzini, T. H. Green, 1907.
Schmidt, W. In his Der Kampf um den Sinn des Lebens von Dante bis Ibsen vol 2, Berlin 1907.
Craig, R. S. The making of Carlyle: an experiment in biographical explication. 1908.
Goodwin, E. J. Ethics of Carlyle. International Jnl of Ethics 15 1908.
Emerson, R. W. Journals with annotations. 10 vols Boston 1909. For Emerson's other writings on Carlyle, *see* Dyer, Bibliography, above, p. 337.
Krauske, O. Macaulay and Carlyle. Berlin 1909.
Ströle, A. Carlyle's Anschauung vom Fortschritt in der Geschichte. Gütersloh 1909.
Wedgewood, J. A study of Carlyle. In his Nineteenth century teachers and other essays, 1909.
Archibald, R. C. Carlyle's first love: Margaret Gordon, Lady Bannerman. 1910.
Earland, A. In her Ruskin and his circle, 1910.
Lehmann, E. Die religion Carlyles. Deutsche Rundschau April–June 1910.
Luntowski, A. Menschen: Carlyle, Whitman etc. Leipzig 1910.
Roe, F. W. Carlyle as a critic of literature. New York 1910.
— Social philosophy of Carlyle and Ruskin. New York 1921.
Vaughan, C. E. Carlyle and his German masters. E & S 1 1910.
Cook, E. T. In his Life of Ruskin, 2 vols 1911.
Johnson, W. S. Carlyle: a study of his literary apprenticeship 1814–31. New Haven 1911.
McRobert, G. Thomas Carlyle. Border Mag Aug 1911.
Moisant, X. L'individualisme de Carlyle. Revue de Philosophie 19 1911.
— In his L'optimisme au xixe siècle, Beauchesne 1911.
Stawell, F. M. Goethe's influence on Carlyle. International Jnl of Ethics 21 1911.
Brandl, A. Chartisten, Sozialisten und Carlyle. Deutsche Rundschau April–June 1912.
Kure, J. Carlyle og hans hustru med en sammentraengt gennemgang af hans udvikling og livsanskuelse. Copenhagen 1912.
Cestre, C. La doctrine sociale de Carlyle. Revue du Mois Nov 1913.
Fehr, B. Der deutsche Idealismus in Carlyles Sartor resartus. Germanisch-romanische Monatsschrift 5 1913.
Gooch, G. P. Carlyle and Froude. In his History and historians in the nineteenth century, 1913, 1952 (rev).
— Some great English historians. Contemporary Rev Dec 1956.
Goudie, G. In his David Laing: a memoir, 1913.
Hildebrand, A. Carlyle und Schiller. Berlin 1913.
Lorenz, A. C. Diogenes Teufelsdröckh und Carlyle. Leipzig 1913.
Meyer, M. Carlyles Einfluss auf Kingsley in sozialpolitischer und religiös-ethischer Hinsicht. Weimar 1914.
Perry, B. Carlyle: how to know him. Indianapolis [1915].
Hearn, L. On the philosophy of Sartor resartus. In Interpretations of literature, ed J. Erskine vol 1 New York 1916.
Klein, A. Die Weltanschauung Carlyles. Neue Jahrbücher für das klassische Altertum 38 1916.
Morgan, W. Carlyle and German thought. Queen's Quart 23 1916.
Robertson, J. G. Carlyle. CHEL 13 1916.
Stewart, H. L. Carlyle's conception of history. Political Science Quart 32 1917.
— Carlyle's conception of religion. Amer Jnl of Theology 21 1917.
— Alleged Prussianism of Carlyle. International Jnl of Ethics 28 1918.
— Carlyle and his critics. Nineteenth Century Sept 1919.
— Carlyle's place in philosophy. Monist 29 1919.
— Declining fame of Carlyle. Royal Soc of Canada Proc 3 1920.
Kemper, E. Carlyle als Imperialist. Zeitschrift für Politik 11 1918.
Upham, A. H. Rabelaisianism in Carlyle. MLN 33 1918.

Besch, J. Sprecher Gottes in unserer Zeit: Schleiermacher, Carlyle, Tolstoi. Stuttgart 1919.
Carré, J. M. In his Goethe en Angleterre, Paris 1920.
Elton, O. In his A survey of English literature 1830–80, 2 vols 1920.
Ralli, A. Guide to Carlyle. 2 vols [1920].
— Carlyle and Shakespeare. In his Later critiques, 1933.
Hohlfeld, A. R. Poems in Carlyle's translation of Wilhelm Meister. MLN 36 1921.
Bruce, H. L. Blake, Carlyle and the French Revolution. In C. M. Gayley anniversary papers, Berkeley 1922.
Leopold, W. Die religiöse Wurzel von Carlyles literarischer Wirksamkeit: dargestellt an seinem Aufsatz State of German literature. Halle 1922.
— Carlyle and Franz Horn. JEGP 28 1929.
Morley, E. J. Carlyle in the Diary, reminiscences and correspondence of H. C. Robinson. London Mercury Oct 1922.
Davidson, M. A lady who deserves to be remembered [Carlyle's niece Mary A. Carlyle]. Sewanee Rev 31 1923.
— The record of a broken friendship. South Atlantic Quart 24 1925.
— Time and little Charlotte. Sewanee Rev 36 1928.
Williams, S. T. Carlyle's Past and present: a prophecy. In his Studies in Victorian literature, New York [1923].
Wilson, D. A. Life of Carlyle, vol 1: Carlyle till marriage 1795–1826, 1923; vol 2: Carlyle till the French Revolution 1826–37, 1924; vol 3: Carlyle on Cromwell and others 1837–47, 1925; vol 4: Carlyle at his zenith 1848–53, 1927; vol 5: Carlyle to three score-and-ten 1853–65, 1929; vol 6: Carlyle in old age [completed by D. W. MacArthur], 1934.
Neff, E. E. Carlyle and Mill: mystic and utilitarian. New York 1924.
— Carlyle. 1932.
Schanck, N. Die sozial-politischen Anschauungen Coleridges und sein Einfluss auf Carlyle. Bonn 1924.
Thrall, M. M. A phase of Carlyle's relation to Fraser's Magazine. PMLA 39 1924.
— Two articles attributed to Carlyle. MLN 46 1931.
Hagberg, K. Carlyle: romantik och puritanism i Sartor resartus. Stockholm 1925.
Liljegren, S. B. The origin of Sartor resartus. Anglica (Leipzig) 1925.
Marx, O. Carlyle's translation of Wilhelm Meister. Baltimore 1925.
Mott, F. L. Carlyle's American public. Philosophical Quart 4 1925.
Geissendoerfer, T. Carlyle and J. P. F. Richter. JEGP 25 1926.
— Carlyle und Jean Paul. Hesperus 16 1958.
Hamilton, M. A. Thomas Carlyle. [1926].
Hess, O. Carlyles Stellung zum Germantum. Freiburg 1926.
Willcocks, M. P. Between the old world and the new. New York 1926.
Blankenagel, J. C. Carlyle as a critic of Grillparzer. PMLA 42 1927.
Young, N. Carlyle: his rise and fall. [1927].
Brie, F. In his Imperialistische Strömungen in der englischen Literatur, Halle 1928.
— Helden und Heldenverehrung bei Carlyle. Heidelberg 1948.
Chamberlin, B. D. Carlyle as a portrait painter. Sewanee Rev 36 1928.
Drew, E. Jane Welsh and Jane Carlyle. New York 1928.
Grierson, H. J. C. Scott and Carlyle. E & S 13 1928.
— Carlyle and Hitler [1931]. In his Essays and addresses, 1940.
— Thomas Carlyle. Proc Br Acad 26 1940.
Harrold, C. F. Carlyle's interpretation of Kant. Philosophical Quart 7 1928.
— Two critics of democracy: Carlyle and H. L. Mencken. South Atlantic Quart 27 1928.
— Carlyle's general method in the French Revolution. PMLA 43 1928.
— The translated passages in Carlyle's French Revolution. JEGP 27 1928.
— Carlyle and Novalis. SP 27 1930.
— The mystical element in Carlyle. MP 29 1932.
— Carlyle and German thought 1819–34. New Haven 1934.
— Carlyle and the mystical tradition. Catholic World 142 1935.
— The nature of Carlyle's Calvinism. SP 33 1936.
— Remembering Carlyle: a visit with his nephew. South Atlantic Quart 36 1937.
Lehman, B. H. Carlyle's theory of the hero. Durham NC 1928.
Strachey, L. Carlyle. Nation (London) 28 Jan 1928; rptd in his Portraits in miniature, 1928.
— Some new Carlyle letters. Spectator 10 April 1909.
Fischer, W. Thomas und Jane Carlyle im Spiegel der Briefe Amely Böltes an Varnhagen von Ense 1844–53. E Studien 64 1929.
— Des Darmstädter Schriftstellers Johann Heinrich Künzel 1810–73 Beziehungen zu England mit ungedruckten (oder wenig bekannten) Briefen von Carlyle, Dickens etc. Giessen 1939.
Houseman, L. Fire-lighters: a dialogue on a burning topic. London Mercury Jan 1929.
Macy, J. Carlyle: from Ecclefechan to the world. Bookman (London) Aug 1929.
Murray, R. H. Carlyle the romantic radical. In his Studies in the English social and political thinkers of the 19th century, Cambridge 1929.
Stockley, V. In his German literature as known in England 1750–1830, 1929.
Storrs, M. The relation of Carlyle to Kant and Fichte. Bryn Mawr 1929.
Taylor, A. C. Carlyle: sa première fortune littéraire en France 1825–65. Paris 1929.
— Carlyle et la pensée latine. Paris 1937.
Wellek, R. Carlyle and German romanticism. In Zvláštní Otisk z Xenia Pragensia 1929.
— In his Kant in England, Princeton 1931.
— Carlyle and the philosophy of history. Philosophical Quart 23 1944.
Woolf, V. Geraldine and Jane. Bookman (London) Feb 1929.
Burdett, O. The two Carlyles. 1930.
Dunn, W. H. Froude and Carlyle: a study of the Froude-Carlyle controversy. 1930.
— Centennial of Sartor resartus. London Quart Rev 155 1931.
Howe, S. Carlyle and Wilhelm Meister. In Wilhelm Meister and his English kinsmen, New York 1930.
Quennell, P. C. Literary enigma. New Statesman 22 March 1930.
— Noble savage. Spectator 10 Feb 1956.
Sagar, S. Round by Repentance Tower: a study of Carlyle. 1930. A Roman Catholic study.
Barrett, J. A. S. Carlyle's debt to Goethe. Hibbert Jnl 30 1931.
Calder, G. J. Carlyle's Past and present. Yale Univ Lib Gazette 6 1931.
— The writing of Past and present: a study of Carlyle's manuscript. Yale Stud in Eng 112 1949.
— Carlyle and 'Irving's London circle'. PMLA 69 1954.
— Erasmus A. Darwin: friend of Thomas and Jane Carlyle. MLQ 20 1959.
Cofer, D. B. In his Saint Simonism in the radicalism of Carlyle, College Station Texas 1931.
Lotter, K. Carlyle und die deutsche Romantik. Nuremberg 1931.
MacKinnon, M. Carlyle's 'Impious queen of hearts': a Canadian. Queen's Quart 38 1931.
Muirhead, J. H. Carlyle's transcendental symbolism. In his Platonic tradition in Anglo-Saxon philosophy, 1931.
Sarolea, C. The tragedy of Carlyle. Eng Rev April 1931.

Huxley, L. Carlyle and Huxley: early influences. Cornhill Mag March 1932.
Irvine, L. In his Ten letter writers, 1932.
Keys, D. R. Bengough and Carlyle. UTQ 2 1932.
Lovett, R. M. In his Goethe in English literature, Open Court April 1932.
Mönch, W. Carlyles Welt und Geschichtsbild. Neuphilologische Monatsschrift 3 1932.
Morse, B. J. Crabb Robinson and Goethe in England. E Studies 67 1932.
Suzannet, A. de. Mérimée et Carlyle. Bulletin du Bibliophile Aug 1932.
Tilby, W. In The great Victorians, ed H. and H. J. Massingham 1932.
Carr, E. H. In his Romantic exiles, 1933. On Carlyle and Alexander Herzen.
Dyer, I. W. Carlyle reconsidered. Sewanee Rev 41 1933.
Ishida, K. Arnold on Carlyle. Stud in Eng Lit (Tokyo) 13 1933.
'Kingsmill, Hugh' (H. K. Lunn). Some modern lightbringers extinguished by Carlyle. Eng Rev Jan 1933. An imitation of Carlyle's style.
— The table of truth. Bookman (London) 1933.
Knickerbocker, K. L. Source of Swinburne's Les noyades. Philosophical Quart 12 1933.
Parsons, C. O. A Goethe poem and Carlyle's translation. Archiv 164 1933.
— Carlyle on Ramsay and Ferguson. MLR 29 1934.
— Carlyle's gropings about Montrose. E Studien 71 1937.
Brooks, R. Manuscripts pertaining to Carlyle's Frederick the Great. Yale Univ Lib Gazette 9 1934.
Haldane, E. Edward Irving. Quart Rev 263 1934.
Keller, W. Carlyle und der Führergedanke. Zeitschrift für Französischen und Englischen Unterricht 33 1934.
Klipstein, E. Carlyle: der Mensch. Deutsche Rundschau Dec 1934.
Lebendige Vergangenheit Chartism: Recht und Macht. 1934.
Lammond, D. Carlyle. 1934.
Leopold, W. F. Carlyle's handbooks on the history of German literature. In C. F. Harrold, Carlyle and German thought, New Haven 1934.
Armstrong, T. P. Carlyle und Uhland: parallel passages. N & Q 28 Sept 1935.
Borbein, H. Carlyle im Lichte des deutschen Schicksals. Neuphilologische Monatsschrift 6 1935.
Goldberg, M. H. Carlyle and Ruskin. TLS 16 May 1935.
— Jeffrey: mutilator of Carlyle's Burns. PMLA 56 1941.
— Carlyle, Pictet and Jeffrey. MLQ 7 1946.
Heinemann, G. Von Führertum, Helden und Heldenverehrung: eine Würdigung Carlyles. Die Deutsche Höhere Schule 2 1935.
Hicks, G. Literature and resolution. Eng Jnl March 1935.
Mämpel, A. Carlyle als Künstler. Bochum 1935.
Scudder, T. Carlyle receives a friend. Sat Rev of Lit 14 Sept 1935.
— In his Lonely wayfaring man: Emerson and some Englishmen, New York 1936.
— Jane Welsh Carlyle. New York 1939.
Shine, H. Carlyle and the German philosophy problem during the year 1826–7. PMLA 50 1935.
— Articles in Fraser's Magazine attributed to Carlyle. MLN 51 1936.
— Carlyle and Fraser's letter on the doctrine of St Simon. N & Q 24 Oct 1936.
— Carlyle's views on the relation between religion and poetry up to 1832. SP 33 1936.
— Carlyle's fusion of poetry, history and religion by 1834. Chapel Hill 1937.
— Carlyle and the St-Simonians: the concept of historical periodicity. Baltimore 1941.
— Carlyle's early writings and Herder's Ideen: the concept of history. In Booker memorial studies, Chapel Hill 1950.
— Carlyle's early reading to 1834, with an introductory essay on his intellectual development. Lexington Kentucky 1953.
— Thomas Carlyle. Victorian Newsletter no 13 1958.
Volbrath, W. Carlyle und Chamberlain: zwei Freunde Deutschlands. Munich 1935.
Wissman, P. Carlyles Buch über Helden und Heldenverehrung im Dienste nationalpolitischer Schulung. Zeitschrift für Neusprachlichen Unterricht 34 1935.
Woolf, L. Quack, quack! 1935.
Blackstone, B. Carlyle and Little Gidding. TLS 28 March 1936.
Dwyer, J. J. A French Catholic among eminent Victorians: François Rio. Catholic World Feb 1936.
Jost, T. Carlyle und das neue Deutschland. Die Deutsche Höhere Schule 3 1936.
Kummer, G. Anonymity and Carlyle's early reputation in America. Amer Lit 8 1936.
Murphy, E. M. Carlyle and the St-Simonians. SP 33 1936.
Smith, L. P. The Rembrandt of English prose. In his Reperusals and recollections, 1936. On Carlyle as an artist in portraiture and prose style.
Vance, W. S. Carlyle in America before Sartor resartus. Amer Lit 7 1936.
Aldag, P. Carlyle und die Juden. Hochschule und Ausland Feb 1937.
Carlyle on coronations. New Statesman 10 April 1937.
Drummond, A. L. In his Edward Irving and his circle, 1937.
Eckloff, L. Carlyle als Denker-dichter und Seher. Forschungen und Fortschritte 13 1937.
Gauger, H. Die Psychologie des Schweigens in England. Heidelberg 1937.
Grey, W. Carlyle und das Puritanertum. Würzburg 1937.
Klenze, C. von. Carlyle and German letters. In his C. T. Brooks: translator from the German, Boston 1937.
Richter, K. Carlyle-Nietzsche-Chamberlain. Deutschlands Erneuerung 21 1937.
Tronchon, H. In his Le jeune Edgar Quinet, Paris 1937.
Wipperman, W. Carlyle und das neue Deutschland. Neue Jahrbuch für Deutsche Wissenschaft 13 1937.
Basch, V. Carlyle. Paris 1938.
Hirst, W. A. The manuscript of Carlyle's French Revolution. Nineteenth Century Jan 1938.
Jervis, H. Carlyle and the Germ. TLS 20 Aug 1938.
Lippincott, B. E. In his Victorian critics of democracy, Minneapolis 1938.
Plagens, H. Carlyles Weg zu Goethe. Bottrop 1938.
Rubin, J. J. Whitman and Carlyle: 1846. MLN 53 1938.
— Carlyle on contemporary style. MLN 57 1942.
Seillière, E. L'amitié d'Emerson et de Carlyle. Journal Economiste 108 1938.
— L'actualité de Carlyle: un précurseur du Nationalsocialisme. Paris 1939.
Thornton-Cook, E. Carlylean courtship. Cornhill Mag Jan-April 1938.
Wittig, H. Das innere Gefüge der Gedankenwelt Carlyles. Historische Zeitschrift 159 1938.
Beatty, R. C. Macaulay and Carlyle. PQ 18 1939.
Fermi, L. Thomas Carlyle. Messina 1939.
Hartwig, G. H. An immortal friendship: Carlyle and Emerson. Hibbert Jnl 33 1939.
Paine, G. The literary relations of Whitman and Carlyle, with especial reference to their contrasting views on democracy. SP 36 1939.
Pike, J. S. Dickens, Carlyle and Tennyson. Ed H. Davis, Atlantic Monthly Dec 1939.
Tuell, A. K. Carlyle's marginalia in Sterling's Essays and tales. PMLA 54 1939.
— In her John Sterling, New York 1941.
Wagner, A. Goethe, Carlyle, Nietzsche and the German middle class. Monatshefte für Deutschen Unterricht 31 1939.

Young, L. M. Carlyle and the art of history. Philadelphia 1939.
Brooks, R. Carlyle: journey to Germany autumn 1858. New Haven 1940.
Fervacque, P. L'actualité de Carlyle. Revue de Littérature Comparée 20 1940.
Griggs, E. H. In his Moral leaders, New York 1940.
Kimball, L. R. E. Carlyle and Charles Butler of Wall Street. In Essays and studies in honor of Carleton Brown, New York 1940.
Moore, C. Carlyle and fiction 1822–34. In Nineteenth-century studies, ed H. Davis et al, Ithaca 1940.
— Carlyle's 'Diamond necklace' and poetic history. PMLA 58 1943.
— Sartor resartus and the problem of Carlye's 'conversion'. PMLA 70 1955.
— The persistence of Carlyle's 'Everlasting Yea'. MP 54 1957.
Rudman, H. W. Italian nationalism and English letters. New York 1940.
Smith, F. M. Whitman's poet-prophet and Carlyle's hero. PMLA 55 1940.
Virtue, J. Carlyle's 'Mr Symmons'. In Studies in English in honor of R. D. O'Leary and S. L. Whitcomb, Lawrence Kansas 1940.
Kavanagh, J. Tales of my grandfather. Asiatic Rev new ser 37 1941.
Lea, F. A. Carlyle and the French Revolution. Adelphi Nov-Dec 1941.
— Carlyle: prophet of today. 1943.
Pritchett, V. S. Books in general. New Statesman Dec 1941.
— The Carlyles. In his Books in general, 1953.
Elander, P. H. On Carlyle's religious crisis. In A philological miscellany presented to Eilert Ekwall, Upsala 1942.
McKeehan, I. P. Carlyle, Hitler and Emerson: a comparison of political theories. Univ of Colorado Stud in Humanities 2 1942.
Reilly, J. J. In his Of books and men, New York 1942. On Jane Welsh Carlyle.
— Jane Carlyle appraises her contemporaries. Catholic World Feb 1944.
Sanders, C. R. In his Coleridge and the Broad Church movement, Durham NC 1942.
— The Edward Stracheys, Carlyle and Kitty Kirkpatrick. In his Strachey family, Durham NC 1953.
— Carlyle's letters. Bull John Rylands Lib 38 1955.
— The question of Carlyle's conversion. Victorian Newsletter no 10 1956.
— The Victorian Rembrandt. Bull John Rylands Lib 39 1957.
— Carlyle, Browning and the nature of the poet. Emory Univ Quart 16 1960.
— Carlyle and Tennyson. PMLA 76 1961. Contains some letters.
— Retracing Carlyle's Irish journey of 1849. Studies 50 1961.
— Carlyle, poetry and the music of humanity. Western Humanities Rev 16 1962.
— The Byron closed in Sartor resartus. Stud in Romanticism 3 1964.
— Carlyle as editor and critic of literary letters. Emory Univ Quart 20 1964.
Thompson, J. W. and B. J. Holm. In their History of historical writing vol 2, New York 1942.
Fiedler, H. G. The friendship of Carlyle and Varnhagen von Ense with a letter hitherto unknown. MLR 38 1943.
Memorabilia. N & Q 31 July, 11 Sept, 25 Sept, 23 Oct, 18 Dec 1943. On Carlyle and Tennyson, R. H. Hutton, Emerson and Browning.
Page, F. Balder dead. E & S 28 1943. On Carlyle's influence on Arnold.
Price, F. Jowett on Carlyle. N & Q 17 July 1943.
Rowse, A. L. The message of Past and present. New Statesman 5–12 June 1943.
Salomon, R. Notes on Carlyle's Journey to Germany autumn 1858. MLN 58 1943.
Schreiber, C. F. Carlyle's Goethe mask. Yale Univ Lib Gazette 18 1943.
Stark, W. St-Simon as a realist. Jnl of Eng History 3 1943.
Bentley, E. R. Modern hero-worship: notes on Carlyle, Nietzsche and Stefan George. Sewanee Rev 52 1944.
— A century of hero-worship. Philadelphia 1944.
— The premature death of Carlyle. Amer Scholar 15 1945.
Deaton, M. B. Carlyle's use of metaphor. College Eng March 1944.
Holmberg, O. David Hume in Carlyle's Sartor resartus. Bulletin de la Société Royal des Lettres de Lund 1933–4, 1944.
G. F. Watts and Carlyle. N & Q 26 Feb 1944.
Ethlinger, L. Carlyle on portraits of Frederick the Great: an unpublished letter. MLR 40 1945.
G[rantham], E. A gift from Carlyle to Boston. More Books 20 1945. Prints a letter of 19 Dec 1854 to H. T. Wake.
Molony, J. C. Fall of an idol: effect on Carlyle's fame of his Reminiscences and the Froude biography. Blackwood's Mag June 1945.
Schapiro, J. S. Carlyle: prophet of Fascism. Jnl of Modern History 17 1945.
Cassirer, E. The preparation: Carlyle. In his Myth of the state, New Haven 1946.
Kippenberg, A. Carlyles Weg zu Goethe. Bremen 1946.
Kirby, T. A. Carlyle and Irving. ELH 13 1946.
— Carlyle on Chaucer. MLN 61 1946.
— Carlyle, FitzGerald and the Naseby project. MLQ 8 1947.
Schilling, B. N. Human dignity and the great Victorians. New York 1946.
Blackburn, W. Carlyle and the composition of the Life of Sterling. SP 44 1947.
Christian, M. G. Carlyle's influence on the social theory of Dickens. Trollopian 1–2 1947.
Brown, T. W. Froude's Life of Carlyle. In his If by your art: testament to Percival Hunt, Pittsburgh 1948.
Carlyle and Pickwick. N & Q 24 Jan 1948.
Ford, G. H. The Governor Eyre case in England. UTQ 17 1948.
Jackson, H. Introduction: Carlyle. In his Dreamers of dreams: the rise and fall of 19th-century idealism, 1948.
Obertello, A. Carlyle's critical theories: their origin and practice. Genoa 1948.
Halliday, J. L. Mr Carlyle: my patient. 1949. A psychiatric analysis.
Pope-Hennessy, J. In his Monckton Milnes, 1949.
Willey, B. In his Nineteenth-century studies, 1949.
Irvine, W. Carlyle and T.H. Huxley. In Booker memorial studies, ed H. Shine, Chapel Hill 1950.
Templeman, W. D. Tennyson's Locksley Hall and Carlyle. Ibid.
Origo, I. The Carlyles and the Ashburtons: a Victorian friendship. Cornhill Mag 164 1950.
— A measure of love. 1957.
Warren, A. H. The hero as poet: Dante, Shakespeare. In his English poetic theory 1825–65, Princeton 1950.
Buckley, J. H. In his Victorian temper, Cambridge Mass 1951.
Lloyd, J. E. Victorian writers and the Great Exhibition. N & Q 22 Dec 1951.
Short, C. Edward FitzGerald on some fellow Victorians. Western Humanities Rev 5 1951.
Adrian, A. A. Dickens on American slavery: a Carlylean slant. PMLA 67 1952.

— Dean Stanley's report of conversations with Carlyle. Victorian Stud 1 1957.
Bett, W. R. In his Infirmities of genius, New York 1952.
Burtis, M. E. In his Moncure Conway 1832–1907, New Brunswick 1952.
Filler, L. Carrington and Carlyle: cross-currents in history and Belles-lettres. Antioch Rev 12 1952.
Gascoyne, D. Thomas Carlyle. 1952 (Br Council pamphlet).
Hanson, L. and E. Necessary evil: the life of Jane Welsh Carlyle. 1952.
Martin, R. B. Coventry Patmore. Princeton Univ Lib Chron 14 1952. Patmore letters acquired by Princeton, including some from Carlyle.
Rogers, W. H. A study in contrasts: Carlyle and Macaulay as book reviewers. Florida State Univ Stud 5 1952.
Slater, J. George Ripley and Carlyle. PMLA 67 1952.
— Goethe, Carlyle and the open secret. Anglia 76 1958.
Stebbins, L. P. Friendship and love: Jane Welsh, Carlyle and Edward Irving. In her London ladies, New York 1952.
Symons, J. Carlyle: the life and ideas of a prophet. 1952.
Brooks, E. L. B. W. Procter and the genesis of Carlyle's Frederick the Great. Harvard Lib Bull 7 1953.
Holloway, J. In his Victorian sage, 1953.
LeRoy, G. C. In his Perplexed prophets: six 19th-century British authors, Philadelphia 1953.
Majut, R. Georg Büchner and some English thinkers. MLR 48 1953.
Williams, R. The idea of culture. EC 3 1953.
— In his Culture and society 1780–1950, 1958, 1961.
Eidson, J. O. C. S. Wheeler: Emerson's 'Good Grecian'. New England Quart 27 1954. Wheeler helped Emerson to edit Carlyle's works for pbn in USA.
Evans, J. In her John Ruskin, 1954.
Fielding, K. J. Carlyle, Charles Dickens and William Maccall. N & Q Nov 1954.
King, M. P. 'Illudo Chartis': an initial study in Carlyle's mode of composition. MLR 49 1954. The first version of Sartor resartus.
Strout, A. L. Writers on German literature in Blackwood's Magazine, with a footnote on Carlyle. Library 5th ser 9 1954.
Tillotson, K. In her Novels of the eighteen-forties, Oxford 1954.
— Matthew Arnold and Carlyle. Proc Br Acad 42 1956.
Fain, J. T. Word echoes in Past and present. Victorian Newsletter no 8 1955.
Parker, W. M. Dean Milman and the Quarterly Review. Quart Rev 293 1955. Contains excerpts from unpbd letters of Milman and Carlyle.
Simpson, D. J. Carlyle and natural law. History of Ideas Newsletter no 1 1955.
Watt, W. M. Carlyle on Muhammad. Hibbert Jnl 53 1955.
Carlylean vision. TLS 3 Feb 1956.
Duckett, M. Carlyle, 'Columbus' and Joaquin Miller. PQ 35 1956.
Kegel, C. H. An uncertain biographical fact. Victorian Newsletter no 10 1956. On the date of first meeting between Carlyle and Ruskin.
— Lord John Manners and the young English movement: romanticism in politics. Western Political Quart 14 1961.
— Carlyle and Ruskin. Brigham Young Univ Stud 5 1964.
Pearsall, R. Carlyle and Emerson: horses and revolutions. South Atlantic Quart 55 1956.
Taylor, A. J. P. In his Englishmen and others, 1956.
Blair, W. The French Revolution and Huckleberry Finn. MP 55 1957.
Burd, V. A. Ruskin's antidote for Carlyle's purges. Boston Univ Stud in Eng 3 1957.
Dickins, L. G. The friendship of Dickens and Carlyle. Dickensian 53 1957.
Gordon, R. C. A Victorian anticipation of recent Scott criticism. PQ 36 1957. Julia Wedgwood's refutation of Carlyle's view of Scott.
Pankhurst, R. K. P. The St-Simonians, Mill and Carlyle. 1957.
Roellinger, F. X., jr. The early development of Carlyle's style. PMLA 72 1957.
Straka, G. M. The spirit of Carlyle in the old South. Historian 20 1957.
Sutherland, J. R. In his On English prose, Toronto 1957.
Cooke, A. L. Whitman as a critic: democratic vistas with special reference to Carlyle. Walt Whitman Newsletter no 4 1958.
Cooper, B. A comparison of Quintus Fixlein and Sartor resartus. Trans of Wisconsin Acad of Sciences, Arts & Letters 48 1958.
Fraser, R. A. Shooting in Niagara in the novels of Thackeray and Trollope. MLQ 19 1958.
Kaye, J. B. In his Bernard Shaw and the 19th-century tradition, Norman Oklahoma 1958.
Mackerness, E. D. The voice of prophecy: Carlyle and Ruskin. In Pelican Guide to English literature, ed B. Ford vol 6, 1958.
Pennington, D. H. Cromwell and the historians. History Today Sept 1958.
Rollins, H. E. C. E. Norton and Froude. JEGP 57 1958. On Froude's biography of Carlyle.
Saponaro, M. Una donna tra due poeti. Nuova Antologia 93 1958. On Mazzini and Carlyle.
Welsh, A. A Melville debt to Carlyle. MLN 73 1958.
Altick, R. D. Browning's Transcendentalism. JEGP 58 1959. On Carlyle's relation to Browning's poem.
Ericson, E. E. An American indebtedness to Carlyle. N & Q Dec 1959. On Marietta Holley.
Gragg, W. B. Trollope and Carlyle. Nineteenth-Century Fiction 13 1959.
Jacobs, W. D. Carlyle and Mill. CEA Critic 21 1959.
Saunders, B. In her Portraits of a genius, 1959.
Taylor, A. C. Carlyle interprète de Dante. Etudes Anglaises 12 1959.
Witte, W. In his Schiller and Burns and other essays, Oxford 1959.
— Carlyle's conversion. In his Era of Goethe, 1960. On Carlyle's conversion to Goethe.
Deneau, D. P. Relationship of style and device in Sartor resartus. Victorian Newsletter no 17 1960.
Hart, F. R. Boswell and the Romantics: a chapter in the history of biographical theory. ELH 27 1960.
Jones, J. Carlyle, Whitman and the democratic dilemma. Eng Stud in Africa 3 1960.
Lindberg, J. The artistic unity of Sartor resartus. Victorian Newsletter no 17 1960.
— The decadence of style: symbolic structure in Carlyle's later prose. Stud in Scottish Lit 1 1964.
Lockhead, M. Jane Welsh Carlyle. Quart Rev 298 1960.
Peters, R. L. Some illustrations of Carlyle's symbolist imagery. Victorian Newsletter no 16 1960.
Malin, J. C. Carlyle's philosophy of clothes and Swedenborg's. Scandinavian Stud 33 1961.
Metzger, L. Sartor resartus: a Victorian Faust. Comparative Lit 16 1961.
Morris, J. W. Beauchamp's career: Meredith's acknowledgement of his debt to Carlyle. In Studies in honor of J. C. Hodges and A. Thaler, Knoxville 1961.
Ota, S. Carlyle's relation with modern Japanese literature. Stud in Eng Lit (Tokyo) 1961.
Smeed, J. W. Carlyles Jean-Paul Übersetzungen. Deutsche Vierteljahrsschrift fur Literaturwissenschaft und Geistesgeschichte 35 1961.
— Carlyle and Jean Paul Richter. Comparative Lit 16 1964.
Kim, S. A comparative study of Emerson and Carlyle. Eng Lang & Lit (Korea) no 11 1962.
West, P. Carlyle's creative disregard. Melbourne Critical Rev no 5 1962.

Berger, H. L. Emerson and Carlyle: stylists at odds. Emerson Soc Quart no 33 1963.
Brown, T. J. English literary autographs 47: Carlyle. Book Collector 12 1963.
Carter, R. C. Margaret Fuller and the two sages. Colby Lib Quart 6 1963.
Cobban, A. Carlyle's French Revolution. History 48 1963.
Deen, L. W. Irrational form in Sartor resartus. Texas Stud in Lang & Lit 5 1963.
Johnson, W. S. Swinburne and Carlyle. Eng Lang Notes 1 1963.
Ludwig, H. Die Self-komposite bei Carlyle, Matthew Arnold und Hopkins. Tübingen 1963.
Miller, J. H. In his Disappearance of God, Cambridge Mass 1963.
Peyre, H. In his Literature and sincerity, New Haven 1963.
Ryan, A. S. The attitude towards the reader in Sartor resartus. Victorian Newsletter no 23 1963.
—— Carlyle, Jeffrey and the 'Helotage' chapter of Sartor resartus. Victorian Newsletter no 27 1965.
DeLaura, D. Arnold and Carlyle. PMLA 79 1964.
Earle, P. G. Unamuno and the theme of history. Hispanic Rev 32 1964.
Crossman, R. H. S. Carlyle and Froude. New Statesman 17 Jan 1964.
Hertz, R. N. Victory and the consciousness of battle: Emerson and Carlyle. Personalist 45 1964.
Levine, G. Sartor resartus and the balance of fiction. Victorian Stud 8 1964.
Levine, R. A. Carlyle as poet: the Phoenix image in 'organic filaments'. Victorian Newsletter no 25 1964.
Pouilliart, R. Maurice Maeterlinck et Carlyle. Revue de Littérature Comparée 38 1964.
Watkins, C. C. Browning's 'Red cotton night-cap country' and Carlyle. Victorian Stud 7 1964.
Holme, T. The Carlyles at home. Oxford 1965.
Krohn, M. Carlyle: Friedrich der Grosse-Schlesien. Jahrbuch der Schlesischen Friedrich-Wilhelm-Universität zu Breslau 10 1965.
Martin, P. E. Carlyle and Mill: the anti-self-consciousness theory. Thoth 6 1965.
Tennyson, G. B. Sartor called Resartus. Princeton 1965.
Waller, J. O. Carlyle and his nutshell Iliad. BNYPL Jan 69 1965.
Sharrock, R. Carlyle and the sense of history. E & S 19 1966.

C. R. S.

III. MINOR PROSE 1800–35

This section has been restricted, with one or two exceptions, to critics, essayists and miscellaneous writers born between 1765 and 1800. Cross-references have been included to critical writings appearing elsewhere, but not to essays and miscellaneous writings. No cross-references have been given to the section on English Studies (cols 1635–68 below). Studies and anthologies of 19th-century essays and criticism are listed cols 6, 1197 above.

JOHN ANSTER

1793–1867

See col 363, above.

JAMES BOADEN

1762–1839

See col 1127, above.

SIR JOHN BOWRING

1792–1872

See col 369, above.

SIR SAMUEL EGERTON BRYDGES

1762–1837

Bibliographies

Woodworth, M. K. The literary career of Brydges. Oxford 1935. Bibliography, pp. 167–88, includes mss, books written or edited by Brydges, some of his contributions to periodicals, and books about Brydges. Some minor addns in TLS 16 Nov 1935.

§1

Sonnets and other poems, with a versification of the six bards of Ossian. 1785 (anon), 1785 (signed and expanded), 1795, 1807 (further expanded as Poems).
The topographer: containing a variety of original articles, illustrative of the local history and antiquities of England. 4 vols 1789–91. With Lawrence Stebbing Shaw.
Topographical miscellanies. 1792.
Mary de Clifford: a story; interspersed with many poems. 1792 (anon), 1800.
Verses on the late unanimous resolutions to support the Constitution [with] some other poems. Canterbury 1794.
Arthur Fitz Albini: a novel. 2 vols 1798, 1799, 1810.
Le Forester: a novel. 3 vols 1802.
Censura literaria: containing titles, abstracts and opinions of old English books, with original disquisitions, articles of biography and other literary antiquities. 10 vols 1805–9, 1815 (articles re-arranged chronologically).
The British bibliographer. 4 vols 1810–4.
The sylvan wanderer: consisting of a series of moral, sentimental and critical essays. 4 pts Lee Priory 1813–21 (priv ptd).
The ruminator: containing a series of moral, critical and sentimental essays. 2 vols 1813.
Occasional poems, written in the year 1811. Lee Priory 1814 (priv ptd).
Select poems. Lee Priory 1814 (priv ptd).
Bertram: a poetical tale. Lee Priory 1814 (priv ptd), 1816.
Restituta: or titles, extracts and characters of old books in English literature revived. 4 vols 1814–16.
Excerpta Tudoriana: or extracts from Elizabethan literature, with a critical preface. 2 vols Lee Priory 1814–18 (priv ptd).
Archaica: containing a reprint of scarce old English tracts, with prefaces, critical and biographical. 2 vols 1815 (priv ptd).
Desultoria: or comments of a South-Briton on books and men. Lee Priory 1815 (priv ptd).

Lord Brokenhurst: or a fragment of winter leaves. Geneva 1819; rptd in his Tragic tales, 1820.
Coningsby. Paris 1819; rptd in his Tragic tales, 1820.
Sir Ralph Willoughby: an historical tale of the sixteenth century. Florence 1820.
Res literariae: bibliographical and critical. 3 nos Naples, Rome, Geneva 1820–2.
The hall of Hellingsley: a tale. 3 vols 1821.
Odo, Count of Lingen: a poetical tale in six cantos. Geneva 1824, Paris 1826.
Gnomica: detached thoughts, sententious, axiomatic, moral and critical. Geneva 1824.
Letters on the character and poetical genius of Lord Byron. 1824.
An impartial portrait of Lord Byron as a poet and a man. Paris 1825.
Recollections of foreign travel on life, literature and self-knowledge. 2 vols 1825.
Modern aristocracy: or the bard's reception. Geneva 1831. Poem on Byron.
The lake of Geneva: a poem moral and descriptive. 2 vols Geneva 1832.
Imaginative biography. 2 vols 1834.
The autobiography, times, opinions and contemporaries of Sir Egerton Brydges. 2 vols 1834.
Moral axioms in single couplets for the use of the young. 1837.
Human fate, and an address to the poets Wordsworth and Southey: poems. Great Totham 1846 (priv ptd).
*Also a large number of genealogical works. Brydges edited (with matter included in the above) one or more works by the following: Edward Phillips (*Theatrum poetarum anglicanorum*), Duchess of Newcastle, Greene, Ralegh, Thomas Stanley, Breton, Drayton, Henry Wotton, William Browne, Wither, Brathwait, William Hammond, John Hall (of Durham), Chapman, William Collins, Milton, several minor 17th-century poets and some Latin and Italian writers; also a number of books on economic and social questions (summarized by M. K. Woodworth, above, Appendix) and numerous pamphlets.*

§2

Woodworth, M. K. The literary career of Brydges. Oxford 1935.
Sadleir, M. Archdeacon Francis Wrangham: a supplement. Library 4th ser 19 1939.
Jones, W. P. Brydges on Lord Byron. HLQ 13 1950.
— New light on Brydges. Harvard Lib Bull 11 1957.

CHARLES BUCKE
1781–1846

§1

The philosophy of nature: or the influence of scenery on the mind and heart. 2 vols 1813, 4 vols 1821 (as On the beauties, harmonies and sublimities of nature; with occasional remarks on the laws, customs, manners and opinions of various nations), 3 vols 1837 (enlarged), New York 1843 (with notes, commentaries and illustrations, selected and rev W. P. Page).
Amusements in retirement. 1816.
The fall of the leaf, and other poems. 1819.
The Italians, or the fatal accusation: a tragedy. 1819 (7 edns), 1820 (with the prefaces to the 1st, 3rd, 6th, 7th and 8th edns). Produced Drury Lane, 3 April 1819.
A classical grammar of the English language; with a short history of its origin and formation. 1829.
Julio Romano, or the force of the passions: an epic drama in six books. 1830.
On the life, writings and genius of Akenside; with some account of his friends. 1832.
The book of human character. 2 vols 1837.
A letter intended (one day) as a supplement to Lockhart's Life of Sir Walter Scott. 1838 (priv ptd). On Scott's mention of Bucke's dispute with Kean.
The life of John, Duke of Marlborough. 1839.
Ruins of ancient cities: with general and particular accounts of their rise, fall and present condition. 2 vols 1840, New York 1845.

§2

The assailant assailed: being a vindication of Mr Kean. 1819. On his conduct in connection with The Italians.
A defence of Edmund Kean Esq: being a reply to Mr Buck's preface, and remarks on his tragedy of The Italians. [1819].
Bucke's Julio Romano. Monthly Rev May 1830.

THOMAS CAMPBELL
1777–1844

See col 261, above.

RICHARD CARLILE
1790–1843

§1

The order for the administration of the loaves and fishes: or the communion of corruption's host, to be read at the Treasury the day preceding all Cabinet dinners. 1817.
Life of Thomas Paine. In Political and miscellaneous writings of Paine vol 1, 1819; 1821 (separately).
The deist: or moral philosopher. 2 vols 1819–20. Selections from writers ancient and modern.
An address to men of science, calling upon them to stand forward and vindicate the truth from the foul grasp and persecution of superstition. 1821.
To the reformers of Great Britain. 6 pts [1821]. Letters from Dorchester Gaol.
Observations on Letters to a friend on the evidences, doctrines and duties of the Christian religion, by Olinthus Gregory. 1821.
Every man's book: or what is God? 1826.
Richard Carlile's first sermon upon the mount: a sermon upon the subject of deity. 1827.
The gospel according to Richard Carlile, shewing the true parentage, birth and life of our allegorical Lord and Saviour Jesus Christ. 1827.
A new view of insanity: in which is set forth the mismanagement of public and private madhouses. 1831.
Church reform: the only means to that end, stated in a letter to Sir Robert Peel. 1835.
Carlile also edited various periodicals including The Republican, 1820; The Lion, 1828; The Prompter, 1831; The Gauntlet, 1834;

§2

Vice versus reason: a copy of the bill of indictment against Carlile for publishing Paine's Age of reason. 1819.
Holyoake, G. J. The life and character of Carlile. 1870.
Campbell, T. C. The battle of the press. 1899.
Aldred, G. A. Carlile, agitator: his life and times. 1923.

ROBERT CARRUTHERS
1799–1878

§1

The history of Huntingdon. 1824.
The poetry of Milton's prose: selected from his various writings, with notes and an introductory essay. 1827.

The Highland note-book: or sketches and anecdotes. Edinburgh 1843.
Chambers's cyclopaedia of English literature. [1857], [1876] (rev Carruthers).
The life of Alexander Pope; including extracts from his correspondence. 1857 (rev and enlarged from memoir in edn of Pope's Poetical works, 1853).
Carruthers edited the following: Pope, Poetical works, 4 vols 1853, 1853–4, 1858 (rev); Boswell, Tour to the Hebrides, 1851; Falconer, Shipwreck, 1858; James Montgomery, Poetical Works, 1860; Chambers Household edition of Shakespeare, 1861–3 (with W. Chambers); R. Chambers, Life of Sir W. Scott, 1871; Gray's Select poems, 1876.

§2

Obituary. Scotsman 28 May 1878.

HENRY FRANCIS CARY
1772–1844

See col 371, above.

CHARLES COWDEN CLARKE
1787–1877

§1

Readings in natural philosophy: or a popular display of the wonders of nature etc. 1828.
Tales from Chaucer in prose: designed chiefly for the use of young persons. 1833, 1870 (carefully rev).
Adam the gardener. 1834. A boys' book.
The riches of Chaucer. 1835, 1870.
Carmina minima. 1859.
Shakespeare characters: chiefly those subordinate. 1863.
Molière-characters. Edinburgh 1865.
On the comic writers of England. GM April-Dec 1871. On Chaucer; Jonson; Beaumont and Fletcher; Butler; Addison and Steele; Swift; Burlesque writers; English satirists; Wycherley and Congreve.
Cowden Clarke also edited Nyren, Young cricketers' tutor 1833, *and the text of most of the vols in Gilfillan's Library Edition of the British Poets. For his collaborations with his wife Mary Cowden Clarke and for her biographical sketch of him, see col 1375, below.*

§2

Altick, R. D. The Cowden Clarkes. New York 1948. Contains a list of writings of Charles and Mary Cowden Clarke.
Blunden, E. Letters from Charles and Mary Cowden Clarke to Alexander Main 1864–86. Keats-Shelley Memorial Bull 3 1951.

HARTLEY COLERIDGE
1796–1849

See col 372, above.

HENRY NELSON COLERIDGE
1798–1843

Six months in the West Indies in 1825. 1826 (anon), 1832, 1841 (both with addns); tr Dutch, 1826.
Introductions to the study of the Greek classic poets. Pt 1 (all pbd), 1830, 1834. On Homer.
Specimens of the table-talk of the late Samuel Taylor Coleridge. 2 vols 1835, 1836 (with slight alterations), 1851 etc.
For H. N. Coleridge's edns of his uncle's Literary remains, Aids to reflection, Confessions of an inquiring spirit, Biographia literaria *etc, see under S. T. Coleridge, col 211, above. His pseudonymous and anon critical essays and reviews in Etonian, Br Critic and Quart Rev are summarized in* W. Graham, Henry Nelson Coleridge: expositor of romantic criticism, PQ 4 1925.

EDWARD COPLESTON
1776–1849

§1

Advice to a young reviewer, with a specimen of the art. Oxford 1807 (anon); ed J. C. Collins 1903 (in Critical essays and literary fragments); ed G. S. Gordon 1927 (in Three Oxford ironies; with bibliographical notes) (with note on the author by V.M.D.).
The Examiner examined: or logic vindicated. 1809 (anon).
A reply to the calumnies of the Edinburgh Review against Oxford: containing an account of the studies pursued in that university. Oxford 1810; A second reply, Oxford 1810; A third reply, Oxford 1811.
Praelectiones academicae Oxonii habitae. Oxford 1813. 35 Latin lectures on poetry.
Remains of the late Edward Copleston, with an introduction containing some reminiscences of his life. Ed R. Whately 1854.
Copleston also pbd An inquiry into the doctrines of necessity and pre-destination, in four discourses, 1821, *and a number of sermons, charges and pamphlets.*

§2

Copleston, W. J. Memoir of Copleston with selections from his diary and correspondence. 1851. Includes bibliography.
Tuckwell, W. In his Pre-Tractarian Oxford: a reminiscence of the Oriel Noetics, 1909.

GEORGE LILLIE CRAIK
1798–1866

The New Zealanders. 1830. Anon.
The pursuit of knowledge under difficulties, illustrated by anecdotes. 2 vols 1830–1 (anon), 1844, 3 vols 1845, 2 vols 1858 (rev and enlarged), 1 vol 1865 (rev and enlarged), Edinburgh 1881, 1906 (rev and enlarged).
Paris and its historical scenes. 2 vols 1831–2. Anon.
The pictorial history of England: being a history of the people as well as a history of the Kingdom. 4 vols 1837–41 (to the accession of George III), 1841–4 (during the reign of George III), 9 vols 1850 (vol 9 with index by H. C. Hamilton). With C. MacFarlane
The history of British commerce from the earliest times. 3 vols 1844. Rptd from The pictorial history of England by Craik and MacFarlane.
Sketches of the history of literature and learning in England from the Norman Conquest. 6 vols 1844–5, 2 vols 1861 (much enlarged, as A compendious history of English literature and language from the Conquest), 1 vol 1862 (abridged); ed H. Craik [1883] (abridged edn, with ch on recent literature by Craik, as A manual of English literature and of the history of the English language).
Spenser and his poetry. 3 vols 1845.
Bacon: his writings and his philosophy. 3 vols 1846–7, 1 vol 1860 ('corrected').
The pursuit of knowledge under difficulties, illustrated by female examples. 1847. A suppl to the first work of the same title.

The romance of the peerage: or curiosities of family history. 4 vols 1848–50.
Paris and its historical buildings. 1849.
Outlines of the history of the English language for the use of junior classes. 1851, 1864 (5th edn, rev and improved).
The English of Shakespeare illustrated by a philological commentary on Julius Caesar. 1857.

JOHN WILSON CROKER
1780–1857

Bibliographies

Brightfield, M. F. In his Croker, Berkeley 1940.

Selections

The Croker papers 1808–57. Ed B. Pool 1967.

§1

Familiar epistles on the state of the Irish stage. Dublin 1804 (anon), 1804 (with addn); ed W. Donaldson 1875. Letters in verse addressed to F. Jones.
An intercepted letter from Canton. Dublin 1804. A satire on Dublin society.
The amazoniad, or figure and fashion: a scuffle in high life. 2 pts Dublin 1806. Anon; a satirical poem.
A sketch of the state of Ireland. 1808. Anon.
The battles of Talavera. Dublin 1809, 1812 (9th edn, as Talavera; to which are added other poems).
A key to the orders in council. 1812. Anon.
The letters on the subject of the naval war with America. 1813.
A letter on the fittest style and situation for the Wellington testimonial about to be erected in Dublin. 1815.
Stories for children from the history of England. 1817.
Keats's Endymion. Quart Rev 19 1818.
Substance of the speech in the House of Commons on the Roman Catholic question. 1819.
An answer to O'Meara's Napoleon in exile. New York 1823. Rptd from Quart Rev.
Royal memoirs on the French Revolution, with historical and biographical illustrations. 1823. Trns of 2 memoirs by Madame Royale, Duchess of Angoulême, and the Narrative of journey to Brussels and Coblenz by Louis XVIII.
Progressive geography for children. 1828.
Poems by Alfred Tennyson. Quart Rev 49 1833.
The life of Samuel Johnson LlD by James Boswell. 5 vols 1831, 1835, 1848 ('thoroughly revised with much additional matter').
Speech on the reform question. 1831.
Speech on the question that 'The reform bill do pass'. 1831.
Resolutions moved by Mr Croker on the report of the reform bill. 1832.
Johnsoniana: or supplement to Boswell. 2 vols 1835, 1859 (with much new material).
Memoirs of the reign of George the second by John, Lord Hervey. 2 vols 1848.
Robespierre. 1835. Rptd from Quart Rev 54 1835.
Macaulay's History of England. Quart Rev 84 1849.
History of the guillotine. 1853. Rev from Quart Rev.
Correspondence with the Right Honourable Lord John Russell on some passages of Moore's diary; with a postscript by Mr Croker explanatory of Mr Moore's acquaintance and correspondence with him. 1854.
Essays on the early period of the French Revolution. 1857. Rptd with addns and corrections from Quart Rev.
An essay towards a new edition of Pope's works. 1871 (priv ptd).
The Croker papers: the correspondence and diaries of Croker. Ed L. J. Jennings 3 vols 1884 (with memoir), 1885 (rev).

Only the principal reviews are listed. A full list is given in Brightfield's study, above.

§2

Macaulay, T. B. The life of Johnson. Edinburgh Rev 54 1831; rptd in his Critical and historical essays contributed to the Edinburgh Review, 3 vols 1843.
Answers to Mr Macaulay's criticism on Mr Croker's edition of Boswell's Life of Johnson. 1856. Selected from Blackwood's Mag.
Maginn, W. A gallery of illustrious characters. Ed W. Bates [1873].
Quart Rev 158 1884.
Brightfield, M. F. Croker. Berkeley 1940.
Strout, A. L. Croker and the Noctes ambrosianae. TLS 9 March 1940.
—— Croker and Tennyson again. N & Q 26 July, 15 Nov 1947.
Lucas, F. L. Croker and Tennyson. TLS 30 Nov 1946. Further correspondence by J. Murray 14 Dec 1946, 18 Jan 1947; and C. P. Hsu 21 Dec 1946.
Staniforth, J. H. M. Croker's pettifoggery. TLS 25 Aug 1950.
de Beer, E. S. Macaulay and Croker: the reviewer of Croker's Boswell. RES 10 1959.
See under John Gibson Lockhart, below.

ALLAN CUNNINGHAM
1785–1842

See col 717, above.

GEORGE DANIEL
1789–1864

§1

Stanzas on Lord Nelson's death and victory, by G. D. and E[dwin] B[entley]. 1806.
The times: or the prophecy. 1811 (anon), 1813 (enlarged).
Miscellaneous poems. 1812. Includes Woman, and other poems rptd from Ackermann's Mag, mostly satirical.
R-y-l stripes, or a kick from Yar-th to Wa-s: a poem by P- P-, poet laureate. 1812. Suppressed and bought up by order of the Prince Regent. Only 6 copies known to exist.
The ghost of R-L stripes: a poem by P- P-, poet laureate. 1812.
Sophia's letters to the B-r-n Ger-b: or Whiskers in the dumps, by P- P-, poet laureate. 1812.
The r-l first born, by P- P-, poet laureate. 1812.
Suppressed evidence on r-l intriguing. 1813. By P- P-, poet laureate.
Virgil in London. 1814. Anon.
The modern dunciad: a satire; with notes biographical and critical. 1814 (anon), 1816, 1835 (with Virgil in London, and other poems).
London and Dublin: an heroic epistle to Counsellor Phillips, the celebrated Irish orator. 1817. Anon; probably by Daniel.
Doctor Bolus: a serio-comick-bombastick-operatick interlude. 1818. Anon.
Cumberland's British theatre; with remarks biographical and critical by D.G. 48 vols 1826–[61]. Daniel contributed a critical preface to each play.
Cumberland's minor theatre: with remarks biographical and critical by D.G. 17 vols 1828–43. Daniel contributed a critical preface to each farce etc.
Garrick in the green room. 1829. A biographical and critical analysis of a picture painted by Hogarth and engraved by W. Ward.

The disagreeable surprise: a farce. In Cumberland's British theatre vol 14, 1829.
Ophelia Keen! a dramatic legendary tale. 1829. Anon; an attack on Charles Kean's private life, suppressed.
Sworn at Highgate: a farce. In Cumberland's minor theatre vol 6, [1833].
Merrie England in the olden time. 2 vols 1842, [1873]. Illustr Leech and Cruikshank; rptd from Bentley's Miscellany.
The missionary: a religious poem. 1847.
Democritus in London: with the mad pranks and comical conceits of Motley and Robin Good-Fellow, to which are added notes festivous [etc]. 1852. A verse continuation of Merrie England, above, with The stranger guest: a religious poem.
An Elizabethan garland: a descriptive catalogue of seventy black-letter ballads printed between 1559 and 1597. 1856 (priv ptd).
Love's last labour not lost. 1863. Includes Recollections of Charles Lamb, Robert Cruikshank, a Reply to Macaulay's essay on Dr Johnson and other essays in prose and verse.
Recollections of Charles Lamb. 1927. Rptd from Love's last labour not lost.
Daniel also pbd a novel, The adventures of Dick Distich, 3 vols 1812 (anon).

§2

Obituary. Athenaeum 9 April 1864.
Catalogue of the most valuable, interesting and highly important library of the late George Daniel esq. 1864.

GEORGE DARLEY
1795–1846

See col 376, above.

CHARLES WENTWORTH DILKE
1789–1864

Old English plays: being a selection from the early dramatic writers. 6 vols 1814–15. Ed Dilke to supplement Dodsley's collection.
The papers of a critic: selected from the writings of Dilke, with a biographical sketch by his grandson, Sir Charles Wentworth Dilke. 2 vols 1875. Essays on Pope, Lady M. W. Montagu, 'Junius', Wilkes, 'Peter Pindar' et al, rptd from Athenaeum.
Dilke was for many years editor of Athenaeum *and contributed regularly 1848–64; his best earlier writing was for* Retrospective Rev 1820–5.

ISAAC D'ISRAELI
1766–1848

Collections

Miscellanies of literature. 1840, [1882–3] (monthly pts), [1884], [1886]. Includes Miscellanies of literature; Quarrels of authors; Calamities of authors; The literary character; Character of James I; Literary miscellanies (not the same as earlier work of this title); Goldsmith and Johnson; Molière; Racine; Sterne; Hume etc.
Works. Ed B. Disraeli 7 vols 1858–9 (with memoir), 1863, 1866, [1881].

§1

A defence of poetry. 1790, 1791.
Curiosities of literature: consisting of anecdotes, characters, sketches and dissertations literary, critical and historical. Ser 1, 1791, 3 vols 1793–1817 (with addns), 5 vols 1823; ser 2, 3 vols 1834 (containing the Secret histories); both sers 6 vols 1834, 3 vols 1849 (with memoir by B. Disraeli), 1858, 1866, 1881; ed E. V. Mitchell 1932 (abridged); ed E. Bleiler 1964 (abridged).
A dissertation on anecdotes. 1793, 1801 (with Literary miscellanies).
Domestic anecdotes of the French nation. 1794, 1800.
An essay on the manners and genius of the literary character. 1795, 1818 (rev and enlarged as The literary character), 2 vols 1822 (rev and enlarged), 1828 (rev and enlarged), 1 vol 1840 (rev as part of Miscellanies of literature); ed B. Disraeli 1927.
Miscellanies: or literary recreations. 1796, 1801 (as Literary miscellanies; adds The dissertation on anecdotes).
Vaurien: or sketches of the times. 2 vols 1797.
Mejnoun and Leila: the Arabian Petrarch and Laura. 1797, 1799 (adds Love and humility, The lovers, and a Poetical essay on romance), 1801 (adds The daughter).
Romances. 1799 (Mejnoun and Leila, Love and humility, The lovers), 1801 (adds The daughter), 1803, 1807 (omits The daughter).
The loves of Mejnoun and Leila. 1800; tr German, 1803.
Narrative poems. 1803.
Flim-flams! or the life and errors of my uncle, and the amours of my aunt! with an illuminating index! 3 vols 1805, 1806 (rev and enlarged).
Despotism: or the fall of the Jesuits. 2 vols 1811.
Calamities of authors: including some inquiries respecting their moral and literary characters. 2 vols 1812; ed B. Disraeli 1859, [1881].
Quarrels of authors: or some memoirs for our literary history. 3 vols 1814; ed B. Disraeli [1881] (with Calamities of authors). Includes Warburton; Pope and Curll; Pope and Cibber; Addison; Lintot's account book; Boyle; Bentley; Jonson; Dekker etc.
Inquiry into the literary and political character of James I. 1816.
Psyche. [1823?].
Commentaries on the life and reign of Charles the First, King of England. 5 vols 1828–31; ed B. Disraeli 2 vols 1851 (rev).
Eliot, Hampden and Pym. 1832.
Genius of Judaism. 1833; tr German, 1836.
Amenities of literature: consisting of sketches and characters of English literature. 2 vols 1841, 1 vol 1842, [1884]. A history of English literature from the beginnings to Bacon, with some chapters on contemporary literary affairs.

§2

Biographical sketch of D'Israeli. Monthly Mirror Dec 1796.
Corney, B. Curiosities of literature. 1837, 1838 (rev 'and acuminated', adding Ideas on controversy deduced from the practice of a veteran). An attack on D'Israeli.
Taylor, W. C. The late Isaac D'Israeli, Esq and the genius of Judaism. Bentley's Miscellany 23 1848.
Disraeli, B. The life and writings of Mr Disraeli by his son. Prefixed to Curiosities of literature, 1849.
Maginn, W. In his A gallery of illustrious characters, ed W. Bates [1873].
Axon, W. E. A. D'Israeli the novelist. GM Aug 1889.
Monypenny, W. F. and G. E. Buckle. The life of Benjamin Disraeli. 2 vols 1929 (rev). Vol 1 has a ch on Isaac D'Israeli.
Kopstein, S. D'Israeli. Jerusalem 1939.
Cline, C. L. The correspondence of Robert Southey and D'Israeli. RES 17 1941.
—— Unpublished notes on romantic poets by D'Israeli. SE 1941.
Anderson, G. K. D'Israeli's Amenities of literature: a centennial review. PQ 22 1943.
Samuel, W. S. D'Israeli: first published writings. N & Q 30 April 1949.

West, M. Poe's Ligeia and D'Israeli. Comparative Lit 16 1964.
Ogden, J. D'Israeli and Scott. N & Q May 1964, Nov 1965.
— D'Israeli and Judaism. Hebrew Union College Annual 37 1966.

NATHAN DRAKE
1766–1836

The speculator. 26 nos 27 March–22 June 1790; 1791, Dublin 1791. By Drake and an unidentified collaborator.
Literary hours: or sketches critical and narrative. Sudbury 1798, 2 vols Sudbury 1800 (enlarged), 3 vols 1804, 1820.
The old abbey tale. In Canterbury tales, by C. F. Barrett, Drake and others, 1802.
Essays biographical, critical and historical; illustrative of the Tatler, Spectator and Guardian. 3 vols 1805, 1814.
The gleaner: a series of periodical essays, selected and arranged from scarce and neglected volumes. 4 vols 1811.
Shakespeare and his times. 2 vols 1817, 1 vol Paris 1843.
Winter nights: or fire-side lucubrations. 2 vols 1820.
Evenings in autumn: a series of essays. 2 vols 1822.
Noontide leisure: or sketches in summer, including a tale of the days of Shakespeare. 2 vols 1824.
Mornings in spring: or retrospections biographical, critical and historical. 2 vols 1828.
Memorials of Shakespeare: or sketches of his character and genius by various writers. 1828.
The harp of Judah: or songs of Sion, being a metrical translation of the Psalms. 1837.

JOHN COLIN DUNLOP
d. 1842

The history of fiction: being a critical account of the most celebrated prose works of fiction from the earliest Greek romances to the novels of the present age. 3 vols 1814, Edinburgh 1816, London 1845; ed H. Wilson 2 vols 1888 (rev); tr German, 1851. Reviewed by Hazlitt, Edinburgh Rev 24 1814.
History of Roman literature from its earliest period to the Augustan age. 3 vols 1823–8.
Memoirs of Spain during the reigns of Philip IV and Charles II from 1621 to 1700. 2 vols Edinburgh 1834.
Selections from the Latin anthology translated into English verse. Edinburgh 1838.

GEORGE DYER
1775–1841

See col 378, above.

PIERCE EGAN
1772–1849

§1

The mistress of royalty: or the loves of Florizel and Perdita. 1814. Anon; attack on the Prince Regent and Mrs Robinson.
Boxiana: or sketches of ancient and modern pugilism. 4 vols 1818–24.
Sporting anecdotes, original and select. 1820.
Life in London: or the day and night scenes of Jerry Hawthorn esq and Corinthian Tom; with thirty-six scenes from real life, designed and etched by I. R. and G. Cruikshank. 1821, 1823. There were many imitations and parodies and several dramatic versions; Egan's own stage adaptation was produced at Sadler's Wells in 1822.
Account of the trial of J. Thurtell and J. Hunt; with an appendix; with portraits and many other illustrative engravings. 1824.
The life of an actor. 1825.
Anecdotes of the turf, the chase, the ring and the stage, embellished with thirteen coloured plates by T. Lane. 1827.
Finish to the adventures of Tom, Jerry and Logic in their pursuits through life in and out of London; with coloured illustrations by R. Cruikshank. [1828]; ed J. C. Hotten [1871].
The show folks, with nine designs on wood by Mr Theodore Lane; to which is added a sketch of the life of Mr Theodore Lane. 1831. A poem.
Matthews's comic annual: or the snuff-box and the leetel bird, an original humorous poem. 1831.
Pierce Egan's book of sports and mirror of life. 1832.
The pilgrims of the Thames in search of the National! illustrations on wood by Pierce Egan the younger. 1838.
Egan also wrote several other accounts of trials, a few guidebooks, some slang terms for F. Grose's Classical dictionary of the vulgar tongue, 1823, *etc.*

§2

Kolb, E. Pierce Egan. TLS 27 Aug 1938.

THOMAS ERSKINE, 1st BARON ERSKINE
1750–1823

Collections

The speeches (at length) of the Rt Hon C. J. Fox, T. Erskine [etc]. 1797.
Speeches of J. P. Curran; with the speeches of Grattan, Erskine and Burke. 2 vols New York 1809.
The speeches of the Hon Thomas Erskine, when at the bar, on subjects connected with the liberty of the press, and against constructive treasons; collected by J. Ridgway. 4 vols 1810, 1812, Georgetown 1813, 4 vols 1813–16, 1847 (with prefatory memoir by Lord Brougham), 2 vols 1870 (with memoir by E. Walford).
The modern orator: the most celebrated speeches of the Earl of Chatham, R. B. Sheridan, Lord Erskine and Edmund Burke. 1847.
The beauties of Erskine: consisting of selections from his prose and poetry, by A. Howard. [1834?].

§1

Plain thoughts of a plain man addressed to the common sense of the people of Great Britain. 1797.
A view of the causes and consequences of the present war with France. 1797 (35 edns); tr French, [1797] (23 edns at least).
Cruelty to animals: the speech of Lord Erskine in the House of Peers on the second reading of the bill for preventing malicious and wanton cruelty to animals. 1809, 1824.
Armata: a fragment. 1817 (anon, 4 edns); The second part of Armata, 1817 (3 edns). A political romance.
A short defence of the Whigs against the imputations attempted to be cast upon them during the late election for Westminster. 1819, 1819.
A letter to An elector of Westminster, author of A reply to the short defence of the Whigs. 1819.
The defences of the Whigs. 1819. Rptd from 2 preceding.
The farmer's vision, by E. 1819 (priv ptd).
A letter to the Earl of Liverpool on the subject of the Greeks. 1822 (2nd edn).

The poetical works; with a biographical memoir. 1823.
Age of reason: Erskine's defence of the cause of Newton, Boyle, Locke, Hale and Milton, versus T. Paine. [1831].
Erskine's opinion of Paine's Age of reason. [1831].
The speeches above constitute only a representative selection from a considerable body of pbd speeches and pamphlets.

§2

A sketch of the character of Erskine. Pamphleteer 23 1823.
Campbell, J. In his Lives of the Lord Chancellors ser 3, 6 1847.
Duméril, H. Erskine: étude sur le barreau anglais à la fin du XVIIIe siècle. Paris 1883.
Fraser, J. A. L. Erskine. Cambridge 1932.

JOHN FOSTER
1770–1843

§1

Essays in a series of letters to a friend. 2 vols 1805, 1806 (rev), 1806, 1 vol 1830 (9th edn, embodying final revisions); ed J. M. 1876 (as Decision of character and other essays). On a Man's writing memoirs of himself; On decision of character; On the application of the epithet romantic; On some of the causes by which evangelical religion has been rendered less acceptable to persons of cultivated taste.
Discourse on missions. 1818.
An essay on the evils of popular ignorance. 1820, 1821 (with a Discourse on the communication of Christianity to the people of Hindoostan), 1846 (rev and enlarged).
Contributions biographical, literary and philosophical to the Eclectic Review. 2 vols 1844; ed J. E. Ryland 1856.
Lectures delivered at Broadmead Chapel, Bristol. Ed J. E. Ryland 2 sers 1844–7, 2 vols 1853 (with addns).
The life and correspondence of John Foster. Ed J. E. Ryland, with notices of Mr Foster as a preacher and a companion by John Sheppard 2 vols 1846.
A brief memoir of Miss Sarah Saunders, with nine letters addressed to her during her last illness. [1847].
Fosteriana: consisting of thoughts, reflections and criticisms of John Foster, selected from periodical papers not hitherto published in a collected form. Ed H. G. Bohn 1858.
An essay on the improvement of time and other literary remains; with a preface by John Sheppard. Ed J. E. Ryland 1863, 1886 (with Notes of sermons and other pieces).
Letters from Foster to Thomas Coles MA, now first published with an appendix by Henry Coles. 1864.
An important introductory essay by Foster is prefixed to the 1825 and later edns of Doddridge, The rise and progress of religion. *Foster also pbd various sermons, religious discourses and controversial works. He was a regular contributor to the Eclectic Rev 1806–39.*

§2

Hall, R. Reviews. 1825. Includes a review of Foster's Essays, above.
Gilfillan, G. In his Galleries of literary portraits vol 2, Edinburgh 1856.
Whately, E. Life and writings of Foster the essayist. In his Afternoon lectures on English literature, Dublin 1863.
Everts, W. W. Life and thoughts of Foster. 1868.
Bayne, P. In his Six Christian biographies, 1887.
Kaufman, P. Foster's pioneer interpretation of the romantic. MLN 38 1923.

BASIL HALL
1788–1844

Account of a voyage of discovery to the west coast of Corea and the Great Loo-Choo Island; with an appendix and a vocabulary of the Loo-Choo language by H. I. Clifford. 1818, 1820 (with plates), Edinburgh 1826, 1840 (with an interview with Napoleon Bonaparte at St Helena).
Extracts from a journal written on the coasts of Chili, Peru and Mexico, in the years 1820, 1821, 1822. 2 vols 1823, Edinburgh 1824, 1825 (4th edn); tr Portuguese, 1906; Spanish, 1920.
Hall's voyages. 4 vols Edinburgh 1826–7.
Travels in North America in the years 1827 and 1828. 3 vols Edinburgh 1829, 2 vols Philadelphia 1829; tr French, [1841?].
Fragments of voyages and travels. Ser 1, 3 vols 1831; ser 2, 3 vols Edinburgh 1832; ser 3, 3 vols Edinburgh 1833, 1834; tr French, 1858. Autobiographical sketches from this work were separately pbd as The midshipman and The lieutenant and commander, 1862.
Schloss Hainfeld: or a winter in Lower Styria. Edinburgh 1836, 1836.
Patchwork. 3 vols 1841.
Voyages and travels. 1895. With biographical preface.
Travels in India, Ceylon and Borneo, selected and edited with biographical introduction by H. G. Rawlinson. 1931.

HENRY HALLAM
1777–1859

See col 1459, below.

JULIUS CHARLES HARE
1795–1855

Bibliographies

GM April 1855. Incomplete but accurate bibliography with much information unobtainable elsewhere.

§1

La Motte Fouqué's Sintram and his companions. 1820.
Guesses at truth, by two brothers. Ser 1, 1827, 1838 (with addns), 1840 (rev); ser 2, 1848 (title-page states '2nd edn with large addns', but preface explains that '2nd edn' means that part of ser 1 is included); both sers, 1866, 1871 (with memoir of J. C. Hare by E. H. Plumptre), 1905. With A. W. Hare, until his death; essays, epigrams etc.
Niebuhr's The History of Rome. 3 vols 1828–42. Vols 1–2 by Hare and Connop Thirlwall. Vol 3 by W. Smith and L. Schmitz; a 2nd edn of vols 1–2, rev and re-arranged by Hare, appeared 1829–32.
A vindication of Niebuhr's History of Rome. Cambridge 1829.
The old man of the mountain; The lovecharm; and Pietro of Abano: tales from the German of Tieck. 1831.
The victory of faith and other sermons. Cambridge 1840; ed E. H. Plumptre 1874 (introductory notices by J. F. D. Maurice and A. P. Stanley, the latter rptd from Quart Rev 97 1855).
The mission of the Comforter and other sermons, with notes. 2 vols 1846, Cambridge 1850 (rev); ed E. H. Plumptre 1876. Vindication of Luther ptd separately, 1855.
Schiller's poems. 1847. Tr with some poems by Goethe into English hexameters.
Memoir of John Sterling. Prefixed to Essays and tales of John Sterling, collected and ed Hare 2 vols 1848.

Thou shalt not bear false witness against thy neighbour: a letter to the editor of the English Review, with a letter from Professor Maurice to the author. 1849.
The life of Luther in forty-eight historical engravings by G. Koenig. 1855. Text by Hare, continued by S. Winkworth.
Charges to the clergy of the archdeaconry of Lewes 1840–54, with notes on events affecting the Church during that period; with a memoir of the author by F. D. Maurice. 3 vols 1856.
Fragments of two essays in English philology. Ed J. E. B. Mayor 1873.
Hare also pbd a number of sermons, charges and tracts on ecclesiastical subjects.

§2

Rigg, J. H. Modern Anglican theology. 1857.
Hare, A. J. C. Memorials of a quiet life. 1872.
Galinsky, H. K. Is Thomas De Quincey the author of The love-charm? MLN 52 1937. By Hare?
Sanders, C. R. Coleridge and the Broad Church movement. Durham NC 1942.

BENJAMIN ROBERT HAYDON

1786–1846

§1

The judgment of connoisseurs upon works of art compared with that of professional men, in reference more particularly to the Elgin Marbles. 1816.
New churches considered with respect to the opportunities they afford for the encouragement of painting. 1818.
Some enquiry into the causes which have obstructed the advance of historical painting for the last seventy years in England. 1829.
On academies of art (more particularly the Royal Academy) and their pernicious effect on the genius of Europe: lecture xiii. 1839.
Thoughts on the relative value of fresco and oil painting, as applied to the architectural decorations of the Houses of Parliament. 1842.

Letters, Diaries etc

The life of Haydon, from his autobiography and journals. Ed T. Taylor 3 vols 1853, 1853 (with additional appendix and index by W. R. S. Ralston); ed A. Huxley 2 vols 1926; ed A. P. D. Penrose 1927; ed E. Blunden, Oxford 1927 (WC); ed M. Elwin 1950.
Correspondence and table-talk: with a memoir by his son F. W. Haydon; with fascimile illustrations from his journals. 2 vols 1876.
The diary of Haydon. Ed W. B. Pope 5 vols Cambridge Mass 1960–3.

§2

Haydon and Wilkie. Fraser's Mag July 1847.
The autobiography of Haydon. Fraser's Mag Sept 1853.
The life of Haydon. Edinburgh Rev 98 1853.
Taylor's life of Haydon. Quart Rev 93 1853.
Haydon. Temple Bar Feb, April 1891.
'Paston, George' (E. M. Symonds). Little memoirs of the nineteenth century. 1902.
Haydon and his friends. 1905.
Forman, H. B. Keats and Haydon. Athenaeum 21 May 1904.
Sargant, F. W. Haydon, forerunner. Nineteenth Century Feb 1923.
Woolf, V. The genius of Haydon. Nation 18 Dec 1926; rptd in her Moment and other essays, 1947.
Walker, F. R. The diary of a defeated painter. Independent 118 1927.
Blunden, E. Haydon outside his autobiography. Nation 7 April 1928.
Wagner, I. Das literarische Werk des Malers Haydon. Göttingen 1934.
Sewter, A. C. A revaluation of Haydon. Art Quart 5 1942.
Lang, V. Haydon. PQ 26 1947.
George, E. The life and death of Haydon. Oxford 1948.
Cohen, B. B. Haydon, Hunt, Scott and Six sonnets (1816) by Wordsworth. PQ 29 1950.
Olney, C. Haydon: historical painter. Athens Georgia 1953.
Gray, D. and V. W. Walker. Haydon on Byron and others. Keats-Shelley Memorial Bull 7 1956.
Brooks, E. L. An unidentified article by Haydon. Keats-Shelley Jnl 6 1957.
Gaunt, W. A book of drawings by Haydon. Connoisseur June 1963.
Hayter, A. In her Sultry month, 1964.

JOHN ABRAHAM HERAUD

1799–1887

See col 384, above.

WILLIAM HONE

1780–1842

Bibliographies

Jerrold, W. B. Life of G. Cruikshank. 2 vols 1882. Includes list of Hone's works illustr Cruikshank.
Stephens, F. G. Memoir of G. Cruikshank. 1891. Also includes list of Hone's works illustr Cruikshank.

Collections

Facetiae and miscellanies with one hundred and twenty engravings drawn by George Cruikshank. 1827 (2nd edn). 12 of Hone's most successful political pamphlets including The political house that Jack built, The queen's matrimonial ladder, The political showman.

§1

The rules and regulations of an institution called tranquillity commenced as an economical bank. 1807.
The King's statue at Guildhall. 1815. A broadside.
Report of the coroner's inquest on Jane Watson. 1815.
The case of Elizabeth Fenning. 1815.
Appearance of an apparition to James Sympson commanding him to do strange things in Pall Mall, and what he did: with coloured illustrations by G. Cruikshank. 1816.
View of the Regent's bomb, now uncovered in St James's Park. 1816. A broadside.
An authentic account of the royal marriage, containing memoirs of Prince Leopold and Princess Charlotte. 1816.
Four trials at Kingston, with 13 questions to Mr Espinasse respecting Elizabeth Fenning. 1816.
An account of Christian slavery in Algiers. 1816.
An account of the riots in London, Dec 2 1816. 3 pts [1816].
The reformists' register and weekly commentary. Issued from 1 Feb 1816 to 25 Oct 1817; ed and owned by Hone, who was the largest contributor.
The life of William Cobbett, written by himself. 1816. Cobbett indignantly denied authorship; little doubt that Hone was responsible.
Another ministerial defeat: the trial of the dog for biting the noble lord [Castlereagh]. 1817. With woodcut by G. Cruikshank.
Official account of the noble lord's bite! and his dangerous condition. 1817. With woodcut by G. Cruikshank.
Bag Nodle's feast: or the partition and re-union of Turkey. 1817. A ballad on the alleged meanness of Lord and Lady Eldon.

The late John Wilkes's catechism. 1817.
The bullet Te Deum with the canticle on stone. 1817.
The political litany. 1817. For this and the 2 following parodies Hone was prosecuted, but defended himself successfully and was acquitted; *see* The trials of William Hone, below.
The sinecurist's creed. 1817.
A political catechism, dedicated without permission to His Most Serene Highness Omar, Bashan Day etc, etc of Algiers, by an Englishman. 1817.
The political house that Jack built. 1819. With 13 cuts by George Cruikshank.
The radical house that Jack built. 1819.
Dance in chains. 1819.
The Englishman's mentor: a picture of the Palais Royal. [1819?]
The Queen's matrimonial ladder: a national toy. 1819. With 14 'stepscenes' and illustrations in verse, with 18 other cuts by G. Cruikshank.
The Queen's budget opened. 1820.
The man in the moon. 1820. With 15 illustrations by Cruikshank.
The midnight intruder: or Old Nick at Carlton House. 3 pts 1820. A poem.
'Non mi ricordo'. 1820 (30 edns). Satire on George IV.
A political lecture on heads. 1820.
A political Christmas carol. 1820.
The form of prayer, with thanksgiving to Almighty God, to be used daily for the happy deliverance of Queen Caroline from the late most traitorous conspiracy. 1820.
The bank-restriction barometer. 1820. Originally ptd as a large open half-sheet, as an envelope for Cruikshank's 'Banknote not to be imitated'.
The apocryphal New Testament: being all the gospels, epistles and other pieces now extant, attributed in the first four centuries to Jesus Christ, his apostles and companions, and not included in the New Testament. 1820. Fiercely attacked in Quart Rev and furiously defended by Hone.
The political showman—at home! [1821].
The right divine of kings to govern wrong. 1821. An adaptation, with addns and alterations, of Defoe's Jure divino, 1706, with a preface by Hone and 2 woodcuts by G. Cruikshank.
An imaginary interview between W. Hone and a lady. 1822.
A slap at Slop and the Bridge St gang. 1821. A burlesque on Stoddart's New Times, illustr Cruikshank, who inspired it.
Ancient mysteries described. 1823. Old English miracle plays and other early dramas found by Hone in ms in BM and pbd with notes and illustrations, the latter by G. Cruikshank.
The every-day book: or everlasting calendar of popular amusements; with four hundred and ninety engravings [by G. Cruikshank and others]. 2 vols 1826–7.
The table book. 2 vols 1827–8. With 116 engravings by Cruikshank and others.
Full annals of the revolution in France. 1830.
The year-book of daily recreation and information concerning remarkable men and manners, times and seasons. 1832. Illustr George Cruikshank and others.
The early life and conversion of Willian Hone by himself, edited by his son. 1841.
Some account of the conversion of the late W. Hone, with further particulars of his life and extracts from his correspondence. 1853.

§2

The three trials of Hone, for publishing three parodies. 1818; ed W. Tegg 1876. The Trials were pbd separately in 1817.
Hackwood, F. W. Hone: his life and times. 1912.
Herd, H. In his Seven editors, 1955.

Sikes, H. M. Hone: Regency patriot, parodist and pamphleteer. Newberry Lib Bull 5 1961.

MARY HOWITT, née BOTHAM

1799–1888

For works written in collaboration with her husband see William Howitt, below.

Bibliographies

Woodring, C. R. William and Mary Howitt: bibliographical notes. Harvard Lib Bull 5 1951.

§1

Sketches of natural history. 1834, [1851] (7th edn, enlarged), [1864], [1872].
Wood Leighton: or a year in the country. 3 vols 1836.
Hymns and fireside verses. 1839.
Hope on, hope ever! 1840.
Strive and thrive: a tale. 1840.
Sowing and reaping: or what will come of it? 1841, 1841.
Work and wages: or life in service. [1842].
Little coin, much care. 1842.
Love and money: an every day tale. [1843].
No sense like common sense: or some passages in the life of Charles Middleton. 1843. Probably by William Howitt.
Fireside verses. [1845].
Ballads and other poems. 1847.
The children's year. 1847.
The heir of Wast-Waylan. 1847.
Our cousins in Ohio. 1849.
The picture book for the young. 1855.
Birds and flowers and other country things. [1855].
Marion's pilgrimage: a fire-side story; and other poems. [1859].
A popular history of the United States of America, from the discovery of the American continent to the present time. 2 vols 1859.
Lillieslea: or lost and found. 1861.
The cost of Caergwyn. 3 vols 1864.
Stories of Stapleford. 2 pts [1864].
Tales in prose for young people. [1864].
Tales in verse for young people. [1865].
Our four-footed friends. [1867].
Vignettes of American history. [1869], [1876].
Birds and their nests. [1872].
Tales for all seasons. [1881].
Mrs Howitt wrote, edited and translated some 110 works. Among her more notable trns are various tales from the Danish of Hans Andersen, and the novels of Fredrika Bremer from the Swedish in 18 vols.

§2

[Wilson, J.] Noctes ambrosianae. Blackwood's Mag Nov 1828, April 1831.
Mary Howitt: an autobiography. Ed Margaret Howitt 1889, [1891].
Britten, J. Mary Howitt. [1890]. A biography.
Woodring, C. R. Victorian samplers: William and Mary Howitt. Lawrence Kansas 1952.
Lee, A. Laurels and rosemary: the life of William and Mary Howitt. Oxford 1955.

WILLIAM HOWITT

1792–1879

Bibliographies

Woodring, C. R. William and Mary Howitt: bibliographical notes. Harvard Lib Bull 5 1951.

§ 1

A poet's thoughts at the interment of Lord Byron. 1824.
The book of the seasons: or the calendar of nature. 1831.
A popular history of priestcraft in all ages and nations. 1833, 1834 (4th edn, enlarged), [1834] (abridged).
Pantika: or traditions of the most ancient times. 2 vols 1835.
Colonization and Christianity: a popular history of the treatment of the natives by the Europeans in all their colonies. 1838.
The rural life of England. 2 vols 1838.
The boy's country-book: being the real life of a country boy. 1839.
Visits to remarkable places, old halls, battlefields and scenes illustrative of striking passages in English history and poetry. 1840; ser 2 'chiefly in the counties of Durham and Northumberland', 1842.
The student-life of Germany, by Dr Cornelius. 1841.
The rural and domestic life of Germany; with characteristic sketches of its cities and scenery, collected in a general tour, and during a residence in the country in 1840, 41 and 42. 1842.
German experiences, addressed to the English, both stayers at home and goers abroad. 1844.
The life and adventures of Jack of the mill, commonly called Lord Othmill: a fire-side story. 2 vols 1844.
Homes and haunts of the eminent British poets. 2 vols 1847, 1857 (3rd edn).
The hall and the hamlet: or scenes and characters of country life. 2 vols 1848.
The year-book of the country: or the field, the forest and the fireside. 1850.
Madam Dorrington of the dene: the story of a life. 3 vols 1851.
A boy's adventures in the wilds of Australia: or Herbert's note-book. 1854.
Land, labour and gold: or two years in Victoria; with visits to Sydney and Van Diemen's Land. 2 vols 1855.
Cassell's illustrated history of England: the text to Edward I by J. F. Smith and [thence] by W. Howitt. 8 vols [1856]–64.
Tallangetta, the squatter's home: a story of Australian life. 2 vols 1857.
The man of the people. 3 vols 1860.
The history of the supernatural in all ages and nations, and in all churches, christian and pagan, demonstrating a universal faith. 2 vols 1863.
The history of discovery in Australia, Tasmania and New Zealand from the earliest date to the present day. 1865.
Woodburn Grange: a story of English country life. 3 vols 1867.
The northern heights of London: or historical associations of Hampstead, Highgate, Muswell Hill, Hornsey and Islington. 1869.
The mad war-planet and other poems. 1871.
The religion of Rome described by a Roman. 1873.

Works written with Mary Howitt

The forest minstrel and other poems. 1823. With notes.
The desolation of Eyam, the emigrant: a tale of the American woods; and other poems. 1827.
Howitt's journal of literature and popular progress. 1847–9.
The literature and romance of Northern Europe: constituting a complete history of the literature of Sweden, Denmark, Norway and Iceland. 2 vols 1852.
Stories of English and foreign life. 1849.
Ruined abbeys and castles of Great Britain. 2 sers 1862–4. Separate extracts from the above were brought out—Yorkshire, 1863; the Wye, 1863; the Border, 1865.
Howitt also pbd some shorter tales and a number of trns, including von Chamisso de Boncourt, History of Peter Schlemihl, 1843, *and* J. Ennemoser, History of magic, 1854; *he wrote a number of minor works and many contributions to periodicals, including about 100 articles on spiritualism in Spiritual Mag.*

§ 2

Horne, R. H. William and Mary Howitt. In his A new spirit of the age vol 1, 1844.
Brown, Cornelius. The worthies of Nottinghamshire. 1883.
Hall, S. C. Retrospect of a long life. 2 vols 1883.
Howitt (later Watts), A. M. The pioneers of the spiritual reformation: life and works of D. J. Kerner; Howitt and his work for spiritualism: biographical sketches. 1883.
Mary Howitt: an autobiography. Ed Margaret Howitt 1889. With ch describing his youth by W. Howitt.
Woodring, C. R. Charles Reade's debt to William Howitt. Nineteenth-Century Fiction 5 1951.
— Victorian samplers: William and Mary Howitt. Lawrence Kansas 1952.
Lee, A. Laurels and rosemary: the life of William and Mary Howitt. Oxford 1955.

CATHERINE HUTTON

1756–1846

§ 1

The miser married: a novel. 1813.
The life of William Hutton, by himself; conclusion by Catherine Hutton. 1816, 1817, 1841.
The Welsh mountaineer: a novel. 3 vols 1817.
The history of Birmingham by William Hutton; continued to the present time by Catherine Hutton. 1819.
Oakwood Hall: a novel. 3 vols 1819.
The tour of Africa: containing a concise account of all the countries in that quarter of the globe hitherto visited by Europeans, selected from the best authors and arranged by C[atherine] H[utton]. 3 vols 1819–21.

Letters

Reminiscences of a gentlewoman of the last century: letters of Catherine Hutton. Ed C. H. Beale, Birmingham 1891.
Catherine Hutton and her friends. Ed C. H. Beale, Birmingham 1895.

§ 2

Miss Catherine Hutton. GM April–May 1846.
Colvile, F. L. The worthies of Warwickshire who lived between 1500 and 1800. Warwick [1870].
Jewitt, Ll. The life of William Hutton. [1872].

ANNA BROWNELL JAMESON, née MURPHY

1794–1860

§ 1

A first or mother's dictionary for children: containing upwards of 3,800 words. [1825?].
A lady's diary. 1826, 1826 (as Diary of an ennuyée), Paris 1836 (with Diary of a désenuyée).
The loves of the poets. 1829.
Memoirs of celebrated female sovereigns. 2 vols 1831.
Characteristics of women, moral, poetical and historical, with etchings. 2 vols 1832, 1833 (corrected and enlarged). This work comprises Shakespeare's heroines, frequently rptd under that title.
Beauties of the court of King Charles the second: a series of portraits, illustrating the diaries of Pepys, Evelyn,

Clarendon and other contemporary writers, with memoirs biographical and critical; the portraits from copies made by Mr Murphy. 1833.

Visits and sketches at home and abroad, with tales and miscellanies now first collected, and a new edition of the diary of an ennuyée, 4 vols 1834.

The romance of biography: or memoirs of women loved and celebrated by the poets, from the days of the troubadours to the present age. 2 vols 1837 (3rd edn).

Sketches of Germany: art—literature—character. Frankfurt 1837.

Winter studies and summer rambles in Canada. 3 vols 1838.

A handbook to the public galleries of art in and near London. 2 pts 1842.

Companion to the most celebrated private galleries of art in London; with a prefatory essay on art, artists, collectors and connoisseurs. 1844.

Memoirs of the early Italian painters, and of the progress of painting in Italy, from Cimabue to Bassano. 2 vols 1845, 1 vol 1859 (much enlarged).

Memoirs and essays. illustrative of art, literature and social morals. 1846.

Sacred and legendary art. 2 vols 1848; ed E. M. Hurll 2 vols Boston 1896.

Legends of the monastic orders as represented in the fine arts: forming the second series of Sacred and legendary art. 1850, 1852 (enlarged).

Legends of the Madonna as represented in the fine arts: forming the third series of Sacred and legendary art, illustrated. 1852.

A commonplace book of thoughts, memories and fancies, original and selected. 1854.

Sisters of charity, Catholic and Protestant, abroad and at home. 1855.

The communion of labour: a second lecture on the social employments of women. 1856.

The history of our Lord as exemplified in works of art, commenced by Mrs Jameson, completed by Lady Eastlake. 2 vols 1864.

Several ephemeral handbooks etc are omitted.

Letters

Letters of Anna Jameson to Ottilie von Goethe. Ed G. H. Needler 1939.

§2

Horne, R. H. In his A new spirit of the age vol 2, 1844.

Kingsley, C. The poetry of sacred and legendary art. Fraser's Mag March 1849.

Powell, T. Pictures of the living authors of Britain. New York 1950.

The writings of Anna Jameson. New Monthly Mag Dec 1853.

Macpherson, G. Memoirs of the life of Anna Jameson, with postscript by Mrs O. M. Oliphant. 1878.

Anna Jameson. Blackwood's Mag Feb 1879.

Hamilton, C. J. In her Women writers vol 2, 1893.

Erskine, Mrs S. Anna Jameson: letters and friendships 1812–60. 1915.

FRANCIS, LORD JEFFREY
1773–1850

§1

Observations on Mr Thelwall's letter to the editor of the Edinburgh Review. 1804.

Wordsworth's Poems. Edinburgh Rev 11 1807.

A summary view of the rights and claims of the Roman Catholics of Ireland. Edinburgh 1808. Rptd from Edinburgh Rev 11 1807.

Byron's Childe Harold. Edinburgh Rev 19 1812; Scott's Waverley, 24 1814; Byron's poetry, 27 1816; Keats's Poems, 34 1820; Byron's tragedies, 36 1822.

Essay on beauty. Rptd from Edinburgh Rev with addns in Encyclopaedia Britannica supplement, 1824, 1841; rptd in Contributions to the Edinburgh Rev vol 1, 1844.

Combinations of workmen: a speech. Edinburgh 1825.

Corrected report of the speech of the Lord Advocate of Scotland upon the motion of Lord John Russell, in the House of Commons, for reform of Parliament. 1831.

Eulogium of James Watt. 1839. Rptd from Encyclopaedia Britannica and included in the Life of Watt by D. F. J. Arago, 1839.

Two inaugural addresses and a parting address delivered at Glasgow University. First 3 addresses in Inaugural addresses by Lords Rectors of the University of Glasgow, ed J. B. Hay, Glasgow 1839.

Contributions to the Edinburgh Review. 4 vols 1844, 3 vols 1846, Philadelphia 1848, 1 vol 1853.

Samuel Richardson. 1852. Pamphlet.

Jonathan Swift. 1853. Pamphlet.

Peter and his enemies. Edinburgh 1859 (2nd edn). A story exposing abuses in the law.

Jeffrey's literary criticism. Ed D. N. Smith 1910. With list of Jeffrey's articles in Edinburgh Rev.

Contemporary reviews of romantic poetry. Ed J. Wain 1953.

For full list of his contributions to Edinburgh Rev *see* Wellesley Index to Victorian periodicals vol 1, Toronto 1966.

Letters

The letters of Jeffrey to Ugo Foscolo. Ed J. Purves, Edinburgh 1934.

§2

Cockburn, H. T. Life of Jeffrey; with a selection from his correspondence. 2 vols Edinburgh 1852, 1852, 1872 (Works of Cockburn, vol 1). With list of Jeffrey's articles in Edinburgh Rev.

Gilfillan, G. In his Galleries of literary portraits vol 2, Edinburgh 1856.

Carlyle, T. In his Reminiscences, ed J. A. Froude 2 vols 1881.

Taylor, James. Jeffrey and Craigcrook. Edinburgh 1892. With a sketch of Jeffrey's character and Craigcrook life by Moncreif.

Gates, L. E. In his Three studies in literature, New York 1899.

Elsner, R. Jeffrey und seine kritischen Prinzipien. Berlin [1908].

Hughes, M. Y. The humanism of Jeffrey. MLR 16 1921.

Beatty, J. M. Jeffrey and Wordsworth. PMLA 38 1923.

Bald, R. C. Jeffrey as a literary critic. Nineteenth Century Feb 1925.

Charvat, W. Jeffrey in America. New Eng Quart 14 1941.

Goldberg, M. H. Jeffrey: mutilator of Carlyle's Burns. PMLA 56 1941.

—— Carlyle, Pictet and Jeffrey. MLQ 7 1946.

Noyes, R. Wordsworth and Jeffrey in controversy. Bloomington 1941.

Daniel, R. Jeffrey and Wordsworth: the shape of persecution. Sewanee Rev 50 1942.

Derby, R. The paradox of Jeffrey: reason versus sensibility. MLQ 7 1946.

Greig, J. A. Jeffrey of the Edinburgh Review. 1948.

Guyer, B. Jeffrey's Essay on beauty. HLQ 13 1950.

—— The philosophy of Jeffrey. MLQ 11 1950.

Schneider, E. The unknown reviewer of Christabel: Jeffrey, Hazlitt, Tom Moore. PMLA 70 1955. *See* under Hazlitt, col 1230, above.

Clive, J. Scotch reviewers: the Edinburgh Review 1802–15. Cambridge Mass 1957.

Albrecht, W. P. A letter by Jeffrey. N & Q 5 March 1958.

Dwyer, J. T. Check list of primary sources of the Byron-Jeffrey relationship. N & Q 7 July 1960.

Thomson, D. C. Jeffrey: Charles Dickens' friend and critic. REL 2 1961.

MARY ANN LAMB

1764–1847

Bibliographies

See L. S. Livingston 1903 and J. C. Thomson 1908, under Charles Lamb, col 1223, above.

§ 1

Helen. Poem, pbd with Charles Lamb, John Woodvil, 1802.

Tales from Shakespear, designed for the use of young persons. 2 vols 1807 (for 1806), 1809; ed F. J. Furnivall 2 vols 1901. With Charles Lamb; Mary's name did not appear on the title-page of 1st edn.

Mrs Leicester's school: or the history of several young ladies, related by themselves. 1807 (anon), 1809, 1825 (9th edn), 1827; ed A. Ainger 1885 (with other writings) With Charles Lamb.

In Miss Westwood's album. N & Q 4 June 1870. Verses dated Enfield Chase 17 May 1828.

§ 2

Hazlitt, W. C. Mary and Charles Lamb. 1874.

Gilchrist, A. Mary Lamb. 1883.

Anderson, G. A. Poems by a sister (1812), wrongly attributed to Mary Lamb. TLS 21 Aug 1924.

Frend, G. G. The Lambs, Fanny Kelly and some others. Bookman (London) Nov 1926.

Riddell, W. R. The tragedy of Mary Lamb. Trans Royal Soc of Canada 22 1928.

Ross, E. C. The ordeal of Bridget Elia. 1940.

Anthony, K. The Lambs: a story of pre-Victorian England. New York 1945.

Grant, D. Mary Lamb and penny ballads. TLS 20 Sept 1947.

Tillett, N. S. Mary Lamb. South Atlantic Quart Jan 1948.

See also under Charles Lamb, col 1223, above.

CHARLES LLOYD

1775–1839

See col 389, above.

JOHN GIBSON LOCKHART

1794–1854

§ 1

Peter's letters to his kinsfolk, by Peter Morris the odontist. 3 vols Edinburgh 1819, 1 vol 1952 (abridged). Assisted by 'Christopher North' (J. Wilson).

Valerius: a Roman story. 3 vols Edinburgh 1821 (anon), 1 vol 1842 (rev).

Some passages in the life of Mr Adam Blair, minister of the gospel at Cross Meikle: a novel. Edinburgh 1822 (anon), 1843 (with Matthew Wald); ed D. Craig, Edinburgh 1963.

Reginald Dalton: a story of English university life. 3 vols Edinburgh 1823, 1 vol 1842, [1880].

Ancient Spanish ballads, historical and romantics: translated with notes. Edinburgh 1823, 1841 (rev), New York 1856 (rev with memoir), 1870.

The history of Matthew Wald: a novel. Edinburgh 1824 (anon), 1843 (with Adam Blair).

Janus: or the Edinburgh literary almanack. Edinburgh 1826. With John Wilson.

Life of Robert Burns. Edinburgh 1828, 1828, 1830, New York 1831, London 1838, 1847, 1871, 1872 etc; ed W. S. Douglas 1882, 1890 (rev J. H. Ingram); ed E. Rhys 1907 (EL); ed J. Kinsley 1959 (EL).

The history of Napoleon Buonaparte. 1829 (anon), 2 vols New York 1843, London 1867, 1878 (abridged by W. Tegg), Edinburgh 1885 (abridged), London 1889, 1906 (EL); ed J. H. Rose, Oxford 1916.

The history of the late war: including sketches of Buonaparte, Nelson and Wellington: for children. 1832. Preface signed 'J.G.L.'.

Memoirs of the life of Sir Walter Scott Bart. 7 vols Edinburgh 1837–8, 4 vols Paris 1838, 10 vols Edinburgh 1839, 1902–3 (with addns from Narrative, below), 1 vol 1842, 1845, 2 vols 1848 (rev and abridged as Narrative of the life of Sir Walter Scott), 1 vol 1850, 1853, 1871 (abridged with letter by J. R. H. Scott), 5 vols 1900; ed J. M. Sloan 1904 (abridged), 1906 (EL); ed O. L. Reid 1914 (abridged); tr German, 1839–41.

The Ballantyne-humbug handled. Edinburgh 1839. Reply to criticisms of the Life of Scott made by James Ballantyne's trustees and son.

The noctes ambrosianae of Blackwood. 4 vols Philadelphia 1843, Edinburgh 1863; ed R. S. Mackenzie 5 vols New York 1866, 1 vol 1904 (abridged). First pbd in Blackwood's Mag 1822–35. Mainly by John Wilson; but Lockhart wrote several of the earlier papers.

Theodore Hook: a sketch. 1953. First pbd in Quart Rev 72 1843.

Lockhart's literary criticism: with introduction and bibliography by M. C. Hildyard. Oxford 1931.

John Bull's letter to Lord Byron (1821). Ed A. L. Strout, Norman Oklahoma 1947.

Lockhart also supplied copious notes and an essay on the life and writings of Cervantes to the reprint of Motteux's Don Quixote, 5 vols 1822. For a list of his contributions to Blackwood's Mag April 1817–May 1846, and Quart Rev (which he edited) March 1826–June 1852, see M. C. Hildyard's selection, above.

§ 2

Gleig, G. R. Quart Rev 116 1864.

Maginn, W. In his A gallery of illustrious characters, ed W. Bates [1873].

Croker, J. W. The Croker papers. Ed L. J. Jennings 3 vols 1884.

Smiles, S. A publisher and his friends. 2 vols 1891.

Lang, A. The life and letters of Lockhart. 2 vols [1897].

Birrell, A. The biographer of Sir Walter Scott. In his Et cetera: a collection, 1930.

Hildyard, M. C. Lockhart. Cornhill Mag Sept 1932.

Rait, R. Boswell and Lockhart. Essays by Divers Hands new ser 12 1933.

Ewen, F. Lockhart, propagandist of German literature. MLN 49 1934.

Swann, E. In his Christopher North (John Wilson), Edinburgh 1934.

Macbeth, G. Lockhart: a critical study. Urbana 1935. With bibliography.

MacCurdy, E. A literary enigma: the Canadian boatsong. Stirling 1936.

Strout, A. L. Lockhart's Valerius. TLS 17 Oct 1936.

— Lockhart. N & Q 15–29 Oct, 3 Dec 1938, 11, 25 Sept, 9 Oct 1943, 9, 23 Sept, 7, 21 Oct, 4, 18 Nov 1944, 30 June, 14, 28 July, 11, 25 Aug, 8, 22 Sept, 6, 20 Oct, 3 Nov 1945, 9, 23 March, 20 April, 4, 18 May, 1, 15 June 1946.

— Lockhart on Don Juan. TLS 30 Nov 1940.

— An unpublished letter of Lockhart. TLS 16 March 1940.

— Blackwood's Magazine, Lockhart and John Scott. N & Q 11 Jan 1941.

— Lockhart and Croker. TLS 30 Aug, 13 Sept 1941.

— Lockhart as gossip. TLS 17, 31 Oct 1942.

— Lockhart as ogre. N & Q 2 June 1945.

— Lockhart's quotations. N & Q 7 Sept 1946.

— Lockhart, champion of Shelley. TLS 12 Aug 1955.
Parker, W. M. Lockhart and Scott. TLS 1 Oct 1938.
— Peter's letters to his kinsfolk. TLS 22–29 June 1940. *See* 6–20 July 1940.
— Lockhart's obiter dicta. TLS 5–12 Feb 1944.
— Lockhart's notes on Paradise lost. English 12 1958.
Cline, C. L. D'Israeli and Lockhart. MLN 56 1941.
F., L. Lockhart's novels. N & Q 15 March, 5 April 1941.
Brightfield, M. F. Lockhart's Quarterly contributors. PMLA 59 1944.
Parsons, C. O. The possible origin of Lockhart's Adam Blair. N & Q 17 Nov 1945.
Gordon, G. S. Lockhart: commemorative address, delivered 1930. Glasgow 1944.
Woolf, V. Lockhart's criticism. In her Moment and other essays, 1947.
Cowley, J. Lockhart and the publication of Marmion. PQ 32 1953.
Lochhead, M. Lockhart. 1954.
Hart, F. R. Proofreading Lockhart's 'Scott': the dynamics of biographical reticence. SB 14 1961.
See also under Sir Walter Scott, *col 670, above.*

WILLIAM MAGINN
1793–1842

For a bibliography see Sadleir, below.

Collections

Miscellaneous writings. Ed R. S. Mackenzie 5 vols New York 1855–7. Vols 1–2, The Odoherty papers; vol 3, Shakespeare papers; vol 4, Homeric ballads and comedies of Lucian; vol 5, The Fraserian papers, with a life of the author.
Miscellanies, prose and verse. Ed R.W. Montagu [Johnson] 2 vols 1885. With memoir.
Ten tales. 1933. Preface signed W.B.

§1

Whitehall: or the days of George IV. [1827]. Anon.
The city of demons. In A. A. Watts, The literary souvenir, 1828.
Memoirs of Vidocq, translated from the French [of E. Morice and L. F. L'Héritier]. 4 vols 1828–9; Memoirs of Madame Du Barri: translated from the French [of E. L. de La Mothe Langon], by the translator of 'Vidocq'. 4 vols 1830–1. Respectively vols 25–8 and 29–32 of Autobiography: a collection of the most instructive and amusing lives ever published. Vol 4 of Memoirs of Vidocq has a Sequel appended (apparently by the translator) signed H.T.R. Both trns are conjecturally attributed to Maginn by Halkett and Laing; they have also been assigned to George Borrow.
Magazine miscellanies. [1841]. Tales, verses, maxims etc.
The noctes ambrosianae of Blackwood. 4 vols Philadelphia 1843; ed R. S. Mackenzie 5 vols New York 1866. First pbd in Blackwood's Mag 1822–35. Mainly by John Wilson, but some papers by Maginn, J. G. Lockhart, James Hogg et al.
John Manesty, the Liverpool merchant; with illustrations by George Cruikshank. 2 vols 1844.
Maxims of Sir Morgan O'Doherty. Edinburgh 1849. A parody of La Rochefoucauld.
Homeric ballads; with translations and notes. 1850.
Jochonan in the city of demons. In Light from the East, ed G. Measom 1856.
A story without a tail. 1858. In Tales from Blackwood vol 2; ed G. Saintsbury 1928. First pbd in Blackwood's Mag 1834.
Shakespeare papers: pictures grave and gay. 1859, 1860 (adds paper on Hamlet and a sketch of Maginn signed B.).
A gallery of illustrious literary characters (1830–8) drawn by Daniel Maclise and accompanied by notices, chiefly by William Maginn; republished from Fraser's Magazine. Ed W. Bates [1873].
Maginn also wrote a great deal in Blackwood's Mag, Fraser's Mag and other journals. The anon The military sketch book, 2 vols 1827, *and* Tales of military life by the author of the Military sketch book, 3 vols 1829, *have also been implausibly attributed to Maginn.*

§2

[Lockhart, J. G.] The doctor. Fraser's Mag Jan 1831; rptd in A gallery of illustrious characters, ed W. Bates [1873].
[Kenealy, E. V. and D. M. Moir.] William Maginn. Dublin Univ Mag Jan 1844.
Hall, S. C. A book of memories of great men and women of the age, from personal acquaintance. 1871.
Sadleir, M. Bulwer: a panorama 1803–36. 1931. Appendix 4 consists of a bibliography of Maginn.
Elwin, M. Victorian wallflowers. 1934.
Thrall, M. Rebellious Fraser's. New York 1934.
Tragedy of a writer: Maginn. TLS 22 Aug 1942.
Wardle, R. M. Outwitting Hazlitt. MLN 57 1942.
— 'Timothy Tickler's' Irish blood. RES 18 1942.
MacCarthy, B. G. Centenary of Maginn. Studies 32 1943.
Herd, H. In his Seven editors, 1955.
Strout, A. L. Maginn as gossip. N & Q 2 June 1955.
Cooke, A. K. Maginn on John Keats. N & Q 3 March 1956.

THOMAS ROBERT MALTHUS
1766–1834

Bibliographies

Malthus bibliography. Keizai Ronshu (Economic Rev of Kansai Univ, Osaka) 7 1957.

§1

An essay on the principle of population. 1798, 1803, 2 vols 1806, 1807, 3 vols 1817 (5th edn with addns), 2 vols 1826, 1 vol 1872; ed G. T. Bettany 1890, 2 vols [1914] (EL), 1926; tr French, 1823; German, 1807; Italian, 1867; Russian, 1895; Japanese, 1876.
An investigation of the cause of the present high price of provisions. 1800, 1800.
A letter to Samuel Whitbread on his proposed Bill for the Amendment of the Poor Laws. 1807, 1807.
Observations on the effect of the Corn Laws on the agriculture and general wealth of the country. 1814, 1814, 1815.
An inquiry into the nature and progress of rent. 1815; ed J. H. Hollander 1903.
The grounds of an opinion on the policy of restricting the importation of foreign corn. 1815.
Statements respecting the East India College. 1817.
Principles of political economy. 1820; ed E. Maltby 1836 (with addns), 1936, Oxford 1951.
Godwin on Malthus. Edinburgh Rev 35 1821.
The measure of value stated and illustrated, with an application of it to the alterations in the value of English currency since 1790. 1823.
Definitions in political economy. 1827, 1853 (with addns by J. Cazenove), New York 1954.

Letters and Diaries

For Malthus's correspondence with Nassau Senior see Senior, Two lectures on population, 1829; *and with Ricardo, see* Ricardo, Works vols 6–9, ed P. Sraffa, Cambridge 1952.
Travel diaries. Ed P. James, Cambridge 1966.

§2

Hazlitt, W. A reply to the Essay on population by Malthus. 1807; in his Collected works. ed P. P. Howe vol 1, 1930.
— An examination of Malthus's doctrines. In his Political essays, 1819; in his Collected works vol 7, 1932.
— In his Spirit of the age, 1825; in his Collected works vol 11, 1932.
Godwin, W. Of population: an answer to Malthus's Essay. 1820.
Cobbett, W. To Parson Malthus on the rights of the poor. Weekly Political Register 8 May 1819.
— To Parson Malthus on the population of England. Political Register April 1823.
De Quincey, T. Malthus on population. London Mag Oct 1823; in his Collected writings, ed D. Masson, vol 9 1897.
Bradlaugh, C. Jesus, Shelley and Malthus. 1877.
Bonar, J. Parson Malthus. 1881.
— Malthus and his work. 1885, 1924.
Drysdale, C. R. The life and writings of Malthus. 1887.
Stephen, L. In his English Utilitarians vol 2, 1900.
Howe, P. P. Malthus and the publishing world. 1913.
Ricardo, D. Notes on Malthus's Principles of political economy. Ed J. H. Hollander and T. E. Gregory, Baltimore 1928.
Keynes, J. M. In his Essays in biography, 1933.
Potter, G. R. Unpublished marginalia in Coleridge's copy of Malthus's Essay on population. PMLA 51 1936. *See* 54 1939, pp. 613–15.
Albrecht, W. P. Hazlitt and the Malthusian controversy. Albuquerque 1950.
Smith, K. The Malthusian controversy. 1951.
Pulos, C. E. Shelley and Malthus. PMLA 67 1952.
Glass, D. V. (ed). Introduction to Malthus. 1953.
MacCleary, G. F. The Malthusian population theory. 1953.
Meek, R. L. (ed). Marx and Engels on Malthus. 1953.
Boner, H. A. Hungry generations: the nineteenth-century case against Malthusianism. 1955.

JOHN MITFORD
1781–1859

See col 391, above.

JAMES MONTGOMERY
1771–1854

See col 392, above.

WILLIAM MUDFORD
1782–1848

See col 752, above.

ROBERT OWEN
1771–1858

Bibliographies

Bibliography of Owen. Aberystwyth 1914, 1925.

Collections

Addresses. 1830.
A new view of society and other writings. Ed G. D. H. Cole 1927 (EL).

§1

A statement regarding the New Lanark establishment. 1812.
A new view of society: or essays on the principle of the formation of human character. 1813, 1816, 1817, New York 1825, Edinburgh 1826; abridged L. D. Abbott 1946.
Observations on the effect of the manufacturing system. 1815, 1817, 1818.
An address to the inhabitants of New Lanark at the opening of the New Institution established for the formation of character. 1816 (2nd edn), 1817.
Peace on earth: development of the plan for the relief of the poor and the emancipation of mankind. [1817].
Two memorials on behalf of the working classes: the first presented to the governments of Europe and America, the second to the Allied Powers assembled at Aix-la-Chapelle. 1818.
Lectures on an entire new state of society: comprehending an analysis of British society relative to the production and distribution of wealth. [1820?].
Report to the county of Lanark of a plan for relieving public distress and removing discontent by giving employment to the poor and working classes. Glasgow 1821, London 1832.
An exploration of the cause of the distress which pervades the civilised parts of the world and of the means whereby it may be removed. 1823.
Discourses on a new system of society as delivered in the Hall of Representatives of the United States. Louisville 1825.
Address at a public meeting in Philadelphia, to which is added an exposition of the pecuniary transactions between [Owen] and W. McClure. Philadelphia 1827.
Memorial to the Mexican Republic. Philadelphia 1827.
Debate on the evidences of Christianity between Owen and A. Campbell. Ed A. Campbell 2 vols Bethany Va 1829, London 1839.
Six lectures on charity at New Lanark. 1833–4.
Lectures on the marriages of the priesthood of the old immoral world. Leeds 1835.
The book of the new moral world concerning the rational system of society. Pt 1, 1836, Glasgow 1837.
Public discussion between Owen and J. H. Roebuck. Manchester 1837, 1837.
A development of the origin and effects of moral good and of the principles and practices of moral good. Manchester 1838.
The marriage system of the new world. Leeds 1838.
Six lectures delivered in Manchester previously to the discussion between Owen and J. H. Roebuck. Manchester [1839].
The catechism of the new moral world. Manchester [1840?].
Manifesto of Owen. 1840, 1841 (8th edn).
An outline of the rational system of society. Manchester [1840?], : Leeds 1840 (6th edn).
Social hymns. 1840, 1841.
The social Bible, being an outline of the rational system of society. [1840?].
The signs of the times: or the approach of the millenium. 1841 (2nd edn).
An address to the Socialists on the present position of the rational system of society, May 1841. 1841.
Lectures on the rational system of society versus Socialism as explained by the Bishop of Exeter and others. 1841.
What is Socialism? discussion between Owen and J. Brindley. 1841.
A development of the principles and plans on which to establish home colonies. 1841.
Address to the ministers of all religions, 21 Dec 1845. Philadelphia 1845.
On the employment of children in manufactories. [New Lanark 1848].

The revolution in the mind and practice of the human race. 1849; A supplement to the Revolution in mind and practice of the human race, 1849.
Letters on education. 1849.
The future of the human race. 1853, 1854.
Address to the human race on his eighty-fourth birthday. 1854.
The new existence of man upon the earth. 8 pts 1854–5.
Address in St Martin's Hall on 1 Jan 1855. 1855.
Tracts on the coming millenium. 1855.
Papers sent to the National Association for Promoting Social Sciences at its first meeting, 1857. [1857].
Life written by himself; with selections from his writings and correspondence. Vol 1 (2 pts), 1857–8; ed M. Beer 1920.
Owen also edited the following periodicals: The economist, 1821; The crisis, 1832–4; The new moral world, 1835–45; Weekly letters to the human race, 1850; his Journal, 1851–2; The rational quarterly review, 1853; and his Millennial gazette, 1856–8.

§2

Reybaud, M. R. L. In his Etude sur les réformateurs contemporaires, Paris 1840.
Holyoake, G. J. Life and last days of Owen. 1859.
— History of co-operation in England. 2 vols 1875–9.
Sargent, W. L. Owen and his social philosophy. 1860.
Martineau, H. In her Biographical sketches, 1869.
Owen, R. D. Threading my way. 1874.
Seligman, E. R. A. Owen and the Christian Socialists. Boston 1886.
Jones, L. Life, times and labour of Owen. 2 vols 1889–90.
Dolléans, E. Owen 1771–1858. Paris 1905.
Simon, H. Owen: sein Leben und seine Bedeutung. Jena 1905.
Podmore, F. Owen: a biography. 1906.
Sadler, M. E. Owen, Lovett, Maurice and Toynbee. 1907.
Davies, R. E. Life of Owen. 1907.
Clayton, J. Owen, pioneer of social reforms. 1908.
Hutchins, B. L. Owen, social reformer. 1912.
Joad, C. E. M. Owen, idealist. 1917.
McCabe, J. Owen. 1920.
Cole, G. D. H. Owen. 1925.
— Life of Owen. 1930; ed M. Cole 1965 (3rd edn).
— Owen and Owenism. In his Persons and periods, 1938.
Himes, N. E. The place of J. S. Mill and Owen in the history of English neo-Malthusianism. Quart Jnl of Economics 42 1928.
Bonar, J. Owen: a dialogue. Economic History 3 1934.
Rennard, T. A. Owen. 1937.
Fraser, E. M. Owen in Manchester 1787–1800. 1938.
Gray, A. In his Socialist tradition, 1946.
Dorfman, J. In his Economic mind in American civilisation 1606–1865, New York 1946.
Davies, A. T. Owen 1771–1858: pioneer social reformer and philanthropist. 1948.
Roberts, R. O. Owen, y dre newydd. Aberystwyth 1948.
— Owen. Social service 26 1952.
Harvey, R. H. Owen: social idealist. Berkeley 1949.
Cole, M. In her Makers of the Labour Movement, 1948.
— Owen of New Lanark. 1953.
Chaloner, W. H. Owen, Peter Drinkwater and the early factory system in Manchester. Bull John Rylands Lib 37 1954.
House, H. New Lanark. In his All in due time, 1955.
Murphy, J. Owen in Liverpool. Historical Soc of Lancs & Cheshire 112 1960.
Thomas, B. Owen of Newtown. Trans Cymmrodorian Soc 1960.

ROBERT DALE OWEN

1801–77

§1

An outline of the system of education at New Lanark. Glasgow 1824.
Moral physiology: or a brief and plain treatise on the population question. 1831, 1833 (10th edn), [1870] (new edn).
Pocahontas: a historical drama. New York 1837.
Situations: lawyers, clergy, physicians, men and women. 1839.
Address on free inquiry: on fear as a motive of action. 1840.
Address on the hopes and destinies of the human species. [1840?].
An address on the influence of the clerical profession; to which is added a tract and a warning: Truth and error; On the fear of God. 1840, [1845?].
Darby and Susan: a tale of Old England. [1840?].
A sermon on loyalty; a remonstrance to God; and a sermon on free inquiry. [1840].
Wealth and misery. [1840?].
A lecture on consistency. 1841.
Popular tracts. 1841.
Prossimo's experience; On the study of theology; Safest to believe. [1841].
Annexation of Texas: speech delivered in the House of Representatives on the right and duty of the United States now to accept the offer made by Texas of annexation. [Washington 1844].
Occupation of Oregon: speech delivered in the House of Representatives. [Washington 1844].
Labour: its history and its progress. Cincinnati 1848.
Hints in public architecture. New York 1849.
A brief practical treatise on the construction and management of plank roads. New Albany 1850.
Footfalls on the boundary of another world. 1860.
The policy of emancipation: in three letters. Philadelphia 1862.
The future of the north-west: in connection with the scheme of reconstruction without New England. Philadelphia 1863.
The wrong of slavery, the right of emancipation and the future of the African race in the United States. Philadelphia 1864.
Beyond the breakers. New York 1870. A novel.
The debatable land between this world and the next. 1871.
Threading my way: twenty-seven years of autobiography. New York 1874.
Looking back across the war-gulf, originally printed in Old and New Boston, May 1870. In The magazine of history, New York 1915.
Owen collaborated in a Discussion on the existence of God and the authenticity of the Bible, 1832 *with Origen Bacheler, and in a correspondence on* Divorce 1860 *with H. Greeley: and edited* The crisis 1832 (*with Robert Owen*) *and* The new harmony gazette, 1825.

§2

Leopold, R. W. Owen: a biography. 1940.

HENRY JOHN TEMPLE, 3rd VISCOUNT PALMERSTON

1784–1865

§1

The new Whig guide. 1819, 1824. By Palmerston and others; edited by 'E'.

Speech in the House of Commons on 1 June 1829, upon the motion of Sir J. Macintosh respecting the relations of England with Portugal. [1829].

Speech in the House of Commons on 16 February 1842, on Lord John Russell's motion against a sliding scale of duties on the importation of foreign corn. 1842.

Speech to the electors of Tiverton 31 July 1847. 1847.

Speech in the House of Commons on 25 June 1850, on Mr Roebuck's motion on the foreign policy of the government. 1850; tr French, 1850.

Opinions and policy of Viscount Palmerston; with a memoir by G. H. Francis. 1852. Selections from speeches.

Many further speeches pbd.

Letters and Diaries

Selections from [Palmerston's] diaries and correspondence. In H. L. E. Bulwer, Life, 5 vols 1871–6; tr French, 1878–9.

Selection from private journals of tours in France in 1815 and 1818. 1871.

The Palmerston papers: Gladstone and Palmerston—being the correspondence of Lord Palmerston with Mr Gladstone 1851–65. Ed P. Guedalla 1928.

Regina v. Palmerston: the correspondence between Queen Victoria and her Prime Minister 1837–65. Ed B. Connell 1962.

§2

[Francis, G. H.] The oratory of Lord Palmerston. Fraser's Mag March 1846.

Bulwer, H. L. E. The life of Palmerston, with selections from his diaries and correspondence. 5 vols 1871–6. With A. E. M. Ashley, who wrote part of vol 3 and the whole of vols 4–5; the whole rev and abridged by A. E. M. Ashley 2 vols 1879.

Trollope, A. Lord Palmerston. 1882.

Bell, H. C. F. Lord Palmerston. 2 vols 1936.

Pemberton, N. W. B. Lord Palmerston. 1954.

PETER GEORGE PATMORE

1786–1855

§1

Letters on England by Victoire, Count de Soligny. 1823. By Patmore.

British galleries of art. 1824. Anon.

Mirror of the month. 1826. Anon; a novel.

Rejected articles. 1826, 1826 (both anon), 1844 (4th edn, as Imitations of celebrated authors, or imaginary rejected articles). Parodies.

Sir Thomas Lawrence's cabinet of gems; with biographical and descriptive memorials by Patmore. 1837.

Finden's gallery of beauty: or Court of Queen Victoria. Ed P. G. Patmore [1841].

Chatsworth: or the romance of a week. Ed R. P. Ward 1844. Anon.

Marriage in May Fair: a comedy in five acts. 1854 (2nd edn).

My friends and acquaintances: being memorials, mind-portraits and personal recollections of deceased celebrities of the nineteenth century. 3 vols 1854. Reviewed in New Quart Rev 3 1854.

Patmore edited New Monthly Mag, 1841–53.

§2

Richardson, J. Patmore on Lamb and Hazlitt. TLS 19 June 1953.

FRANCIS PLACE

1771–1854

§1

The mystery of the sinking fund explained. 1821.

Illustrations and proofs of the principle of population. 1822; ed N. E. Himes 1930.

On the law of libel. 1823.

Observations on Mr Huskisson's speech on the laws relating to combinations of workmen. [1825].

An essay on the state of the country in respect to the condition and conduct of the husbandry labourers and to the consequences likely to result therefrom. [1831].

A letter to a Minister of State respecting taxes on knowledge. [1831], 3rd ed 1835.

Improvement of the working people: drunkenness—education etc. 1834.

Observations on a pamphlet relating to the Corn Laws. [1840].

§2

Wallas, G. Place. 1898.

Ervine, St J. G. Place. 1912.

BRYAN WALLER PROCTER

1787–1874

See col 396, above.

DAVID RICARDO

1772–1823

Bibliographies

Franklin, B. and G. Legman. Ricardo and Ricardian theory: a bibliographical check-list. New York 1949.

Collections

Collected works. Ed J. R. McCulloch 1846; tr French, 1846; Russian, 1882.

Works and correspondence. Ed P. Sraffa and M. H. Dobb 11 vols Cambridge 1951–7. Letters in vols 5–9.

§1

Three letters on the price of gold, contributed to the Morning Chronicle. 1809; ed J. H. Hollander, Baltimore 1903.

The high price of bullion. 1810, 1810 (3rd edn) (with addns), 1811 (4th edn) (corrected).

Reply to Mr Bosanquet's Practical observations on the Report of the Bullion Committee. 1811.

An essay on the influence of a low price of corn on the profits of stock. 1815.

Proposals for an economical and secure currency. 1816, 1819 (3rd edn).

On the principles of political economy and taxation. 1817, Georgetown DC 1819; ed E. C. K. Gonner 1891, [1911] (EL); tr French, 1819; German, 1821; Italian, 1856; Russian, 1895.

On protection to agriculture. 1822.

Plan for the establishment of a national bank. 1824.

Letters to T. R. Malthus 1810–23. Ed J. Bonar, Oxford 1887.

Letters to J. R. McCulloch 1816–23. Ed J. H. Hollander, New York 1895. *See* the same editor's collection of McCulloch's letters to Ricardo, Baltimore 1931.

Letters to H. Trower and others 1811–23. Ed J. Bonar and J. H. Hollander, Oxford 1899.

Correspondence with Maria Edgeworth. Economic Jnl 17 1907.

Notes on Malthus's Principles of political economy. Ed J. H. Hollander and T. E. Gregory, Oxford 1928.
Minor papers on the currency question 1809–23. Ed J. H. Hollander, Baltimore 1932.
An unpublished letter of Ricardo to Malthus. Jnl Political Economy 41 1933.
Un manuscrit inédit de Ricardo sur le problème monétaire. Ed E. Silberner, Revue d'Histoire Economique et Sociale 25 1940.

§2

[Bailey, S.] A critical dissertation on the nature, measures and causes of value, chiefly in reference to the writings of Ricardo. 1825.
Brougham, H. Historical sketches of statesmen in the time of George III. 3 ser 1839–43.
Bagehot, W. In his Economic studies, ed R. H. Hutton 1880.
De Quincey, T. In his Collected writings, ed D. Masson vol 9, 1890.
Gonner, E. C. K. Ricardo and his critics. Quart Jnl of Economics 4 1890.
Ashley, W. J. The rehabilitation of Ricardo. Economic Jnl 1 1891.
Cannan, E. Ricardo in Parliament. Economic Jnl 4 1894.
Stephen, L. In his English Utilitarians vol 2, 1900.
Bell, S. Ricardo and Marx. Jnl of Political Economy 15 1907.
Hollander, J. H. Ricardo: a centenary estimate. Baltimore 1910.
Bonar, J. Where Ricardo succeeded and where he failed. Bull of Amer Economics Assoc 4th ser 1 1911.
Lowenthal, E. The Ricardian socialists. New York 1911.
McDonald, R. A. Ricardo's criticism of Adam Smith. Quart Jnl of Economics 26 1912.
Kinloch, T. F. In his Six English economists, 1928.
Keynes, J. M. In his Essays in biography, 1933.
Cassels, J. M. Re-interpretation of Ricardo on value. Quart Jnl of Economics 49 1935.
St Clair, O. A key to Ricardo. 1957.
Blaug, M. Ricardian economics: a historical study. New Haven 1958.
Sharp, C. S. Ricardo on taxation. New York 1960.
Adelman, I. G. Theories of economic growth and development. 1961.

HENRY CRABB ROBINSON
1775–1867

§1

Strictures [by T. Clarkson] on a Life of W. Wilberforce by the Rev W. Wilberforce and the Rev S. Wilberforce; with a correspondence between Lord Brougham and Mr Clarkson; also a supplement. 1838. Ed Robinson.
Exposure of misrepresentations contained in the preface to the correspondence of William Wilberforce. 1840.
The diary, reminiscences and correspondence of Crabb Robinson. Ed T. Sadler 3 vols 1869, 2 vols 1872 (with Augustus De Morgan's Recollections of Robinson).
Blake, Coleridge, Wordsworth etc: being selections from the remains of Crabb Robinson. Ed E. J. Morley, Manchester 1922.
The correspondence of Crabb Robinson with the Wordsworth circle 1808–66. Ed E. J. Morley 2 vols Oxford 1927.
Crabb Robinson in Germany 1800–5: extracts from his correspondence. Ed E. J. Morley, Oxford 1929.
Crabb Robinson on books and their writers. Ed E. J. Morley 3 vols 1938.

§2

Bagehot, W. In his Literary studies vol 2, 1879.
Wright, H. G. Crabb Robinson's Essay on Blake. MLR 22 1927.
King, R. W. Crabb Robinson's opinion of Shelley. RES 4 1928.
Larg, D. G. Mme de Staël et Crabb Robinson. Revue de Littérature Comparée 8 1928.
—— Crabb Robinson and Madame de Staël. RES 5 1929.
Norman, P. Crabb Robinson and Goethe. 2 pts Pbns of Eng Goethe Soc 1930–1.
Morse, B. J. Crabb Robinson and Goethe in England. E Studien 67 1932.
Morley, E. J. The life and times of Crabb Robinson. 1935.
Baker, J. M. Crabb Robinson of Bury, Jena, the Times and Russell Square. 1937.
Gilbert, M. E. Two little-known references to Crabb Robinson. MLR 33 1938.
Brown, E. A note on Crabb Robinson's reactions to J. P. Kemble and Edmund Kean. Theatre Notebook 13 1958.
Elliott, I. Index to the Crabb Robinson letters in Dr Williams's Library. 1960.

SAMUEL ROMILLY
1757–1818

§1

Thoughts on the probable influence of the French Revolution on Great Britain. 1790.
Observations on the criminal law of England as it relates to capital punishments. 1810, 1811, 1813.
Speeches in the House of Commons. 1820.
Memoirs of the life written by himself; with a selection of his correspondence edited by his sons. 1840.

§2

Collins, W. J. Life and work of Romilly. 1908.
Atkinson, C. M. Account of the life and principles of Romilly. 1920.
Phillipson, C. Three critical law reformers. 1923.
Oakes, C. G. Romilly. 1935.
Romilly, S. H. Romilly-Edgeworth letters 1813–18. 1936.
Shientag, B. L. Romilly. [1936].

THOMAS ROSCOE
1791–1871

Gonzalo the traitor: a tragedy in five acts. 1820. Verse.
Benvenuto Cellini, Memoirs; with the notes and observations of G. P. Carpani. 1822, 1847; ed L. Ricci 1904 (rev), [1906] (EL).
The king of the peak. 3 vols 1823. Anon.
J. C. L. Simonde de Sismondi, Historical view of the literature of the south of Europe, with notes. 4 vols 1823, 2 vols 1846.
The Italian novelists: selected from the most approved authors, from the earliest period down to the close of the eighteenth century, translated from the original Italian; accompanied with notes critical and biographical. 4 vols 1825, 1 vol 1880.
The German novelists: tales selected from ancient and modern authors in that language; translated with critical and biographical notices. 4 vols 1826, 1 vol [1880].
Owain Goch: a tale of the revolution. 3 vols 1827. Anon.
L. A. Lanzi, The history of painting in Italy. 6 vols 1828, 1 vol 1852.

L. J. A. de Potter, Memoirs of S. de Ricci. 2 vols 1829.
The tourist in Switzerland and Italy. 1830. The 1st pt of his Landscape annual, in which the following subsequently appeared: Italy, 1831–3; France, 1834; Spain, 3 vols 1835–7; Spain and Morocco, [1838].
The Spanish novelists: a series of tales, from the earliest period to the close of the seventeenth century, translated with critical and biographical notices. 3 vols 1832.
The life of Michael Angelo Buonaroti. In Lives of eminent persons, 1833.
Silvio Pellico, My imprisonments. 1833.
— The duties of men. 1834.
Wanderings and excursions in North Wales. 1836. 1853. Illustrations after Cox et al.
Wanderings and excursions in South Wales, including the scenery of the river Wye. [1837]. With L. A. Twamley, later Meredith; illustrations after Cox et al.
Windsor Castle and its environs; illustrated with historical sketches by Thomas Roscoe and engravings by J. Carter. Pt 1 (all pbd), 1838.
The London and Birmingham railway; with the home and country scenes on each side of the line; historical details by P. Lecount. [1839].
The book of the Grand Junction Railway: being a history and description of the line from Birmingham to Liverpool and Manchester. 1839. Later issued with the preceding as Illustrated history of the London and North-Western Railway.
M. Fernandez de Navarett, The life and writings of Miguel de Cervantes Saavedra. 1839.
Legends of Venice. 1841.
Belgium in a picturesque tour. 1841.
Summer tour to the Isle of Wight, including Portsmouth, Southampton, Winchester etc. 1843.
J. G. Kohl, Travels in England and Wales. 1845.
Lives of the kings of England, from the Norman Conquest. Vol 1 (all pbd), 1846. On William I.
The last of the Abencerages, and other poems. 1850.
Roscoe also revised his father William's Leo X and Lorenzo de' Medici, *and contributed memoirs of the following authors to edns of their works: Fielding, Hurtado de Mendoza, Cervantes, Swift. He edited* The Juvenile Keepsake 1828–30 *and* The novelists' library 12 vols 1831–2.

NASSAU WILLIAM SENIOR
1790–1864

§1

An introductory lecture on political economy delivered before the University of Oxford, 6 Dec 1826. 1827.
Three lectures on the transmission of the precious metals from country to country and the mercantile theory of wealth. 1828, [1931].
Two lectures on population; to which is added a correspondence between the author and the Rev T. R. Malthus. 1829.
Three lectures on the cost of obtaining money and on some effects of private and government paper money. 1830, [1931].
Three lectures on the rate of wages. 1830.
Three lectures on the value of money. 1830, 1931.
A letter to Lord Howick on a legal provision for the Irish poor: commutation of tithes and a provision for the Irish Roman Catholic clergy. 1831.
Statement of the provision for the poor and of the condition of the labouring classes in a considerable portion of America and Europe. 1835.
An outline of the science of political economy. 1836, 1938.
Letters on the Factory Act as it affects the cotton manufacture. 1837, 1844.

Remarks on the opposition to the Poor Law Amendment Bill. 1841.
Four introductory lectures on political economy delivered before the University of Oxford. 1852.
A journal kept in Turkey and Greece in the autumn of 1857 and the beginning of 1858. 1859.
Resolutions and heads of report [on elementary education]. 1860.
Suggestions on popular education. 1861.
American slavery: a reprint of an article on Uncle Tom's cabin. [1862].
Address on education. 1863.
Biographical sketches. 1863.
Essays on fiction. 1864.
Historical and philosophical essays. [Ed M. C. M. Senior] 1865.
Journals, conversations and essays relating to Ireland. 2 vols 1868.
Journals kept in France and Italy from 1848 to 1852. Ed M. C. M. Simpson, formerly Senior 2 vols 1871.
Conversations with Thiers, Guizot and other distinguished persons during the Second Empire. Ed M. C. M. Simpson 2 vols 1878.
Conversations with distinguished persons during the Second Empire from 1860 to 1863. Ed M. C. M. Simpson 2 vols 1880.
Conversations and journals in Egypt and Malta. Ed M. C. M. Simpson 2 vols 1882.
Industrial efficiency and social economy. Ed S. L. Levy [1929].

§2

Bowley, M. Senior and classical economics. 1937.
Levy, S. L. Senior, the prophet of modern capitalism. [1943].

SYDNEY SMITH
1771–1845

Collections

Works. 4 vols 1839–40, 1839–40, 3 vols 1840, New York 1844, London 1850, 3 vols 1854, 2 vols 1859, 1 vol 1869.
Sermons preached at St Paul's Cathedral, the Foundling Hospital, and several churches in London, together with others addressed to a country congregation. 1846.
Selections from the writings of Smith. 2 vols 1855.
Wit and wisdom of Smith; with a biographical memoir and notes by E. A. Duyckinck. New York 1858. Long extracts almost forming an abridgement of the works.
The wit and wisdom of Smith. 1860. A different selection from the American, above; short complete extracts.
Selections. Ed E. Rhys 1892.
Bon-mots of Smith and R. Brinsley Sheridan. Ed W. Jerrold 1893.
The letters of Peter Plymley, with other selected writings, sermons and speeches. Ed G. C. Heseltine 1929.
Bullett, G. Smith: a biography and a selection. 1951.
Selected writings. Ed W. H. Auden, New York 1956.
Selected letters. Ed N. C. Smith, Oxford 1956 (WC).

§1

Six sermons. Edinburgh 1800, 2 vols 1801 (enlarged).
Elementary sketches of moral philosophy. 1804, 1805, 1806 (priv ptd), 1850 (public issue). Lectures at the Royal Institution 1804–6.
The letters of Peter Plymley on the subject of the Catholics to my brother Abraham who lives in the country. 1807–8, 1808 (the 9 letters collected); ed H. Morley 1886 (with Selected essays); ed G. C. Heseltine 1929 (with other selected writings).

A sermon upon the conduct to be observed by the Established Church towards Catholics and other dissenters. 1807.
Extracts from the Edinburgh Review. [1810?]. On Methodism; Indian missions; Proceedings of the Society for the suppression of vice.
The lawyer that tempted Christ: a sermon. York [1824] (priv ptd).
Catholic claims: a speech. 1825.
A sermon on religious charity. York 1825.
A letter to the electors upon the Catholic question. York 1826.
Mr Dyson's speech to the freeholders on reform. 1831. 'Dyson' was Smith.
Speech at the Taunton reform meeting. [1831].
The new reign: the duties of Queen Victoria—a sermon. 1837.
A letter to Archdeacon Singleton on the ecclesiastical commission. 1837.
A letter to Lord John Russell on the Church bills. 1838.
Second letter to Archdeacon Singleton: being the third of the cathedral letters. 1838.
Third letter to Archdeacon Singleton. 1839.
Ballot. 1839. Against the secret ballot.
Letters on American debts. 1844 (2nd edn). Rptd from Morning Chron.
A fragment on the Irish Roman Catholic Church. 1845 (7 edns).
Essays 1802–[27]. 2 vols 1874–80. Rptd from Edinburgh Rev.
Essays social and political 1802–25. [1874], [1877] (adds Essays from Edinburgh Rev and Letters of Peter Plymley, with a brief memoir by S. O. Beeton). Necker; Suppression of Vice; Bentham; Education; English Public Schools; C. J. Fox; Poor-Laws; Prisons; Reviews etc.

Letters

Nine letters. Ed E. Cheney, Philobiblon Soc Miscellany 15 1877–84.
Letters. Ed N. C. Smith 2 vols Oxford 1953.

§2

Horne, R. H. In his A new spirit of the age vol 1, 1844.
Holland, S. A memoir of Smith by his daughter; with a selection from his letters. Ed Mrs Austin 1855. With list of his articles in Edinburgh Rev.
Gilfillan, G. In his Galleries of literary portraits vol 2, Edinburgh 1856.
Vaughan, R. A. In his Essays and remains, 2 vols 1858.
Maginn, W. In his A gallery of illustrious characters, ed W. Bates [1873].
Milnes, R. M. In his Monographs, 1873.
Hayward, A. In his Selected essays vol 1, 1878.
Reid, S. J. A sketch of the life and times of Smith. 1884.
Chevrillon, A. Smith et la renaissance des idées libérales en Angleterre au XIXe siècle. Paris 1894.
Russell, G. W. E. Sydney Smith. 1905 (EML).
St Clair, O. Smith: a biographical sketch. 1913.
Biron, H. C. A Victorian prophet. Fortnightly Rev Jan 1921.
Williams, S. T. The literary criticism of Smith. MLN 38 1923.
Burdett, O. The Rev Smith. 1934.
Pearson, H. The Smith of Smiths. 1934.
Murphy, J. Some plagiarisms of Smith. RES 14 1938.
The Smith of Smiths. TLS 24 Feb 1945.
Auden, W. H. Portrait of a Whig. Eng Miscellany 3 1952.
Smith, N. C. Letters of Smith. N & Q 1 Sept 1954.
Sparrow, J. Jane Austen and Smith. TLS 2 July 1954; *see* 16 July–6 Aug, 15 Oct 1954.
Lane, W. G. Additional letters of Smith. Harvard Lib Bull 9 1955.
Green, D. B. Letters to Samuel Rogers from Tom Moore and Smith. N & Q 2 Dec 1955.
Halpern, S. Smith in the Edinburgh Review. BNYPL Nov 1962.

JOHN STERLING
1806–44

Collections

Poetical works. Ed R. W. Griswold, Philadelphia 1842.

§1

Thoughts on the foreign policy of England by Jacob Sternwall. 1827.
FitzGeorge: a novel. 3 vols 1832. Anon.
Arthur Coningsby: a novel. 3 vols 1833. Anon.
Poems. 1839.
The election: a poem in seven books. 1841. Anon.
Strafford: a tragedy. 1843.
Essays and tales: collected and edited with a memoir of his life by Julius Charles Hare. 2 vols 1848. Vol 1, historical and critical essays (Christabel, Napier's War in the Peninsula, Montaigne, Carlyle, Tennyson etc); vol 2, aphorisms, apologues etc.

Letters

Letters to a friend [William Coningham]. Brighton [1848] (priv ptd), 1851 (as Twelve letters), Bath [1872].
A correspondence between Sterling and Ralph Waldo Emerson. Ed E. W. Emerson, Boston 1897.

§2

Gilfillan, G. In his Galleries of literary portraits vol 2, Edinburgh 1856.
Carlyle, T. The life of Sterling. 1851, 1852; ed W. H. White, Oxford 1907 (WC).
Ince, R. B. Calverley and some Cambridge wits of the nineteenth century. 1929. Includes a study of Sterling's career.
Tuell, A. K. Sterling: a representative Victorian. New York 1941.
Burchell, S. C. The approaching darkness: a Victorian father to his son. Yale Univ Lib Gazette 28 1953.

WILLIAM TAYLOR
1765–1836

§1

Lessing, Nathan the wise, written originally in German. Norwich 1791 (priv ptd), London 1805; ed H. Morley 1886.
Goethe, Iphigenia in Tauris: a tragedy. 1793 (priv ptd), 1794.
Wieland. Dialogues of the gods. 1795.
Bürger, Ellenore. 1796. Rptd with some alterations from Monthly Mag March 1796.
Select fairy tales from the German of Wieland. 1796.
Tales of yore. 3 vols 1810. From French and German.
A letter concerning the two first chapters of Luke. 1810. Anon.
English synonyms discriminated. 1813, 1850; tr German, 1851.
Some biographic particulars of the late Dr Sayers. Prefixed to Frank Sayers, Collective works, Norwich 1823.
Historic survey of German poetry: interspersed with various translations. 3 vols 1828–30.
A memoir of the late Philip Meadows Martineau, surgeon. 1831. With F. Elwin.
Taylor's 1,754 articles and reviews were largely pbd in Monthly Rev 1793–1824.

§2

Carlyle, T. Taylor's historic survey of German poetry. Edinburgh Rev 53 1831.
Robberds, J. W. A memoir of the life and writings of Taylor of Norwich, containing his correspondence. 2 vols 1843.
Herzfeld, G. Taylor von Norwich: eine Studie über den Einfluss der neueren deutschen Literatur in England. Halle 1897.
Christensen, M. A. Taylor of Norwich and the higher criticism. JHI 20 1959.

EDWARD JOHN TRELAWNY
1792–1881

§1

The adventures of a younger son. 3 vols 1831, 1 vol 1835, 1848; ed E. Garnett 1890; ed H. N. Brailsford 2 vols 1914; ed E. C. Mayne, Oxford 1925 (WC).
Recollections of the last days of Shelley and Byron. 1858, 2 vols 1878 (with addns, as Records of Shelley, Byron and the author); ed E. Dowden 1906; ed J. E. Morpurgo 1952.
The relations of Percy Bysshe Shelley with his two wives Harriet and Mary, and a comment on the character of Lady Byron. 1920 (priv ptd).

Letters

Letters. Ed H. Buxton Forman 1910.
The relations of Lord Byron and Augusta Leigh; with a comparison of the characters of Byron and Shelley, and a rebuke to Jane Clairmont on her hatred of the former. 1920 (priv ptd). 4 letters.

§2

Garnett, R. Shelley's last days. Fortnightly Rev June 1878.
Mathilde Blind. Whitehall Rev 10 Jan 1880. Record of conversation.
Rossetti, W. M. Talks with Trelawny 1879–80. Athenaeum 15, 29 July, 5 Aug 1882.
Edgcumbe, R. Trelawny: a biographical sketch. Plymouth 1882.
Sharp, W. The life and letters of Joseph Severn. 1892.
Miller, J. Trelawny with Shelley and Byron. 1922.
Massingham, H. J. The friend of Shelley: a memoir of Trelawny. 1930.
Armstrong, M. Trelawny: a man's life. New York 1940.
Grylls, R. G. Trelawny. 1950.

RICHARD WHATELY
1787–1863

Bibliographies

Kane, P. E. Whately in the United States: a partial bibliography. Bull of Bibliography 23 1961.

Selections

Detached thoughts and apophthegms, extracted from some of the writings of Archbishop Whately. Ser 1 1854.
Selections from the writings of Dr Whately. 1856 (for 1855).
Miscellaneous remains from the common-place book of Whately: being a collection of notes and essays made during the preparation of his various works. Ed E. J. Whately 1864, 1865 (with addns).

§1

Historic doubts relative to Napoleon Bonaparte. 1819 (anon), 1821 etc. A travesty of the higher criticism.
Essays on some of the peculiarities of the Christian religion. Oxford 1825, 1846 (5th edn rev).
Elements of logic: comprising the substance of the article in the Encyclopaedia metropolitana, with additions. 1826, 1832 (4th edn rev), 1836 (6th edn rev), 1840 (rev), 1844 (rev), 1848 (rev).
Elements of rhetoric. 1828, 1836 (5th edn rev), 1846 (7th edn rev); ed D. Ehninger, Carbondale 1963. Rptd from Encyclopaedia metropolitana.
Introductory lectures on political economy. 2 pts 1831–2, 1847 (3rd edn rev), 1855 (rev and enlarged).
Sermons on various subjects. 1835, 1849 (adds 4 sermons), 1854–62 (enlarged, as Sermons on the principal Christian festivals and other occasions).
The Kingdom of Christ delineated. 1841, 1842, 1877 (abridged as Apostolical succession considered).
Historic certainties respecting the early history of America, by Rev Aristarchus Newlight [i.e. Whately]. 1851.
Miscellaneous lectures and reviews. 1861.
Whately also edited Thomas Whately, Remarks on some of the characters of Shakespeare, 1839; E. Copleston, Remains, 1854; Francis Bacon, Essays, 1856; W. Paley, Moral philosophy, *and* Evidences, 1859. *For many other works see BM catalogue and col 1599, below.*

§2

Blanco (afterwards White), J. M. The life of the Rev Blanco White, written by himself; with portions of his correspondence. Ed J. H. Thom 3 vols 1845.
'An old Oxonian'. Recollections of Archbishop Whately. Christian Observer Nov 1863.
Fitzpatrick, W. J. Memoirs of Archbishop Whately of Dublin; with a glance at his contemporaries and times. 2 vols 1864.
Archbishop Whately. Eclectic Rev Sept 1864.
Memoirs of Whately. Blackwood's Mag Oct 1864.
Whately, E. J. Life and correspondence of Whately. 2 vols 1866, 1868, 1875 (enlarged).
Parrish, W. M. Whately and his rhetoric. Quart Jnl of Speech 15 1929.

JOHN WILSON, 'CHRISTOPHER NORTH'
1785–1854

Collections

The works of Professor Wilson of the University of Edinburgh. Ed his son-in-law Professor Ferrier 12 vols Edinburgh 1855–8. Vols 5–8: Essays critical and imaginative, rptd 4 vols Edinburgh 1866.

§1

A recommendation of the study of the remains of ancient Grecian and Roman architecture, sculpture and painting: a prize poem. Oxford 1807.
Lines sacred to the memory of the Rev James Grahame. Glasgow 1811.
The isle of palms and other poems. Edinburgh 1812.
The magic mirror, addressed to Walter Scott esq. Edinburgh 1812.
The city of the plague and other poems. Edinburgh 1816.
Translation from an ancient Chaldee manuscript, from no vii of Blackwood's Magazine. [Edinburgh 1817].
Lights and shadows of Scottish life: a selection from the papers of the late Arthur Austin. Edinburgh 1822, 1853; tr French, 1826.

Little Hannah Lee: a winter's story. 1823. From Lights and shadows, above.

The trials of Margaret Lyndsay, by the author of Lights and shadows of Scottish life. Edinburgh 1823, 1854, Glasgow [1879], [1886].

The foresters, by the author of Lights and shadows of Scottish life and the Trials of Margaret Lyndsay. Edinburgh 1825, 1852.

Poems: a new edition. 2 vols 1825.

Janus: or the Edinburgh literary almanack. Edinburgh 1826. With Lockhart.

Some illustrations of Mr McCullogh's Principles of political economy by Mordecai Mullion, private secretary to Christopher North. Edinburgh 1826.

The poetical works of Milman, Bowles, Wilson and Barry Cornwall. Paris 1829.

The land of Burns: a series of landscapes and portraits, illustrative of the life and writings of the Scottish poet. 2 vols Glasgow 1840. Illustr D. O. Hill with letterpress by Robert Chambers and Wilson.

Blind Allan: a tale. [?1840], [Falkirk? 1850?]. From Lights and shadows, above.

The recreations of Christopher North. 3 vols Edinburgh 1842, Philadelphia 1850, 2 vols 1864.

The Noctes ambrosianae of Blackwood. 4 vols Philadelphia 1843, Edinburgh 1863; ed R. S. Mackenzie 5 vols New York 1866 (best edn), 4 vols 1868, 1 vol 1904. Mainly by Wilson, but some papers by J. Hogg, J. G. Lockhart, W. Maginn et al; first pbd in Blackwood's Mag 1822–35. Selections: ed J. Skelton, Edinburgh 1876; ed J. S. Moncrieff and J. H. Millar 1904.

The works of Robert Burns; with Dr Currie's memoir of the poet, and an essay on his genius and character by Professor Wilson. Vol 1, Glasgow 1843. Wilson's essay was rptd separately New York 1845, Philadelphia 1854, New York 1861.

Scotland illustrated by John C. Brown and other Scottish artists; with letter-press descriptions and an essay on the scenery of the Highlands by Professor Wilson. 1845. Wilson's essay is rptd in A history of the Scottish highlands, ed J. S. Keltie vol 1, Edinburgh 1875.

Specimens of the British critics by Christopher North. Philadelphia 1846.

The poetical works of Professor Wilson. Edinburgh 1865, 1874.

Tales by Professor Wilson: Lights and shadows, Margaret Lyndsay, The foresters. Edinburgh 1865.

Essays critical and imaginative. 4 vols Edinburgh 1866.

Letters from the Lakes by Professor Wilson. Ambleside 1889.

Lakeland poems by Professor Wilson. Ed W. Bailey-Kempling, Ambleside 1902.

Contemporary reviews of romantic poetry. Ed J. Wain 1953.

For a list of Wilson's extensive contributions to Blackwood's Mag see also Wellesley index to Victorian periodicals vol i, Toronto 1966.

§2

Lockhart, J. G. Peter's letters to his kinsfolk. 3 vols Edinburgh 1819.

Professor Wilson: a memorial and estimate by one of his students. Edinburgh 1854.

Gilfillan, G. In his Galleries of literary portraits vol 2, Edinburgh 1856.

Heart-break: the trials of literary life, or recollections of Christopher North. 1859. A story introducing recollections of Wilson.

Gordon, Mary. Christopher North: a memoir of Wilson, compiled from family papers and other sources. 2 vols Edinburgh 1862.

Hannay, J. Professor Wilson. In his Characters and criticisms, Edinburgh 1865.

Maginn, W. In his A gallery of illustrious characters, ed W. Bates [1873].

Saintsbury, G. In his Essays in English literature 1780–1860, 1890.

Oliphant, M. O. W. In his Annals of a publishing house: William Blackwood and his sons, 3 vols 1897–8.

Douglas, G. In his Blackwood group, 1897.

Masson, D. In his Memories of two cities, Edinburgh 1911.

Struve, H. von. Wilson (Christopher North) als Kritiker. Leipzig 1922.

Elwin, M. In his Victorian wall-flowers, 1934.

Strout, A. L. Wilson, 'champion' of Wordsworth. MP 31 1934.

—— Purple patches in the Noctes ambrosianae. ELH 2 1935.

—— Concerning the Noctes ambrosianae. MLN 51 1935. *See also* RES 13 1937, pp. 46–63, 177–89.

—— Wilson as a Shakespeare critic: a study of Shakespeare and the English romantic movement. Sh Jb 72 1936.

—— Unidentified quotations in the Noctes ambrosianae. N & Q 25 Jan 1936. *See also* 8–15 Feb 1936.

—— Christopher North on Tennyson. RES 14 1938.

—— Wilson as a professor. N & Q 11 March 1939.

—— Wilson and the chair of modern philosophy at the University of Edinburgh. N & Q 1 April 1939.

—— Wilson and the Orphan-maid: some unpublished letters. PMLA 55 1940.

—— The recreations of Christopher North 1842. N & Q 6 June, 1 Aug 1942.

—— A study in periodical patchwork: Wilson's Recreations of Christopher North, 1842. MLR 38 1943.

—— The first twenty-three numbers of the Noctes ambrosianae: excerpts from the Blackwood papers in the National Library of Scotland. Library 5th ser 12 1957.

Swann, E. Christopher North (John Wilson). Edinburgh 1934. Includes, pp. 239–52, lists of Wilson's works and of books and articles about him.

Wardle, R. M. The authorship of the Noctes ambrosianae. MP 42 1944.

Aurnor, N. S. An unknown castigator of Christopher North. In If by your art: testament to Percival Hunt, Pittsburgh 1948.

Gravely, W. H. Christopher North and the genesis of the Raven. PMLA 66 1951.

DOROTHY WORDSWORTH
1771–1855

§1

George and Sarah Green: a narrative by Dorothy Wordsworth. Ed E. de Selincourt, Oxford 1936.

The poetry of Dorothy Wordsworth, edited from the journals by H. Eigerman. New York 1940.

Letters and Diaries

Recollections of a tour made in Scotland AD 1803. Ed J. C. Shairp, Edinburgh 1874, 1874, 1894.

Letters to Sir George and Lady Beaumont. In W. Knight, Memorials of Coleorton, 2 vols 1887.

Journals of Dorothy Wordsworth. Ed W. Knight 2 vols 1897; ed E. de Selincourt 2 vols Oxford 1941; ed H. Darbishire, Oxford 1958 (WC).

Letters of the Wordsworth family from 1787 to 1855, collected by W. Knight. 3 vols 1907.

The letters of William and Dorothy Wordsworth. Ed E. de Selincourt 6 vols Oxford 1935–8.

Home at Grasmere: extracts and poems. Ed C. Clark 1960 (Pelican).

§2

The section on William Wordsworth, col 188 above, should also be consulted.

Chambers, W. William and Dorothy Wordsworth. Chambers's Jnl 15 Aug 1874.

Lee, E. Dorothy Wordsworth. 1886.
Maclean, C. M. Dorothy and William Wordsworth. 1927.
— Dorothy Wordsworth: the early years. 1932. With a bibliography.
de Selincourt, E. Dorothy Wordsworth: a biography. Oxford 1933.
Ashton, H. R. and K. Davies. I had a sister: a study of Mary Lamb, Dorothy Wordsworth, Caroline Herschel, Cassandra Austen. 1937.
Mallaby, G. Dorothy Wordsworth: the perfect sister. Atlantic Monthly Dec 1950.
Beaty, F. L. Dorothy Wordsworth and the Coleridges: a new letter. MLR 51 1956.
Laski, M. Dorothy Wordsworth's journals. N & Q June–Aug 1962.
Nabholtz, J. R. Dorothy Wordsworth and the picturesque. Stud in Romanticism 3 1963.
Willy, M. In her Three women diarists, 1963.

A. P.

IV. MID-NINETEENTH-CENTURY PROSE

JOHN HENRY NEWMAN

1801–90

Bibliographies

List of works written and edited by Cardinal Newman in the library of Sir W. H. Cope Bart. Portsmouth [1885?] (priv ptd).
Gillow, J. In his A literary and biographical history: or bibliographical dictionary of the English Catholics vol 5, [1902].
Guibert, J. In his Le réveil du Catholicisme en Angleterre au xixe siècle, Paris 1907.
Delattre, F. In his La pensée de Newman, Paris 1914. Selective bibliography.
Guitton, J. M. P. In his La philosophie de Newman, Paris 1933. Includes classified bibliography.
Läpple, A. In Newman Studien vol 1, ed H. Fries and W. Becker, Nuremberg, Bamberg, Passau 1948. A conspectus of Newman's writings. The vol includes a chronology of trns of Newman by W. Becker and a list of works on Newman by Becker and H. Fries.
Sloane, C. E. Newman: an illustrated brochure of his first editions. Worcester Mass 1953. A photographic and descriptive account of one of the most complete exhibitions of Newman first edns.

Collections

[Collected works]. 36 vols 1868–81. The first systematic reissue, described as the 'Uniform edition of Dr Newman's works', began with the pbn of Parochial and plain sermons and closed with his trn of the Select treatises of St Athanasius against the Arians. Some vols contain specially written prefaces and notes by the author. This edn was issued by Rivingtons, Burns & Oates, Pickering, and Longmans, Green & Co. From 1886 all the vols were pbd by Longmans.
    37 vols 1870–7, 40 vols 1874–1921 (with index by J. Rickaby), 38 vols 1890–7, 34 vols 1898, 41 vols 1908–18 (the fullest uniform edn), 38 vols 1917.
Ausgewählte Werke. Ed M. Laros 8 vols Mainz 1922–40. Several of the vols have been rptd.
Gesammelte Werke. Ed D. Feuling, E. Przywara, P. Simon 2 vols Munich 1924–8. A projected edn of the collected works abandoned after the second vol.
A new edition of the [selected] works. Ed C. F. Harrold 9 vols New York 1947–9. Projected in 12 vols and halted by the death of the editor.
Werken. Ed A. Pompen 7 vols Bussum 1946–58.
Gesamtausgabe seiner Predigten. 11 vols Stuttgart 1950–.
Textes Newmaniens. Ed H. Tristram, L. Bouyer, M. Nédoncelle 3 vols Paris 1955–.

Selections

Miscellanies from the Oxford sermons and other writings. 1870.
Six selections from the writings by a late member of Oriel College, Oxford [W. S. Lilly]. 1874.
Characteristics from the writings: being selections, personal, historical, philosophical and religious, from his various works, arranged by W. S. Lilly. 1875, 1876, 1880, 1882 (6th edn), 1949 (as A Newman anthology).
Selection adapted to the seasons of the ecclesiatical year from the Parochial and plain sermons. Ed W. J. C[opeland] 1878.
Echoes from the oratory: selections from the poems. New York 1884.
Sayings of Cardinal Newman. [1890].
Select essays. Ed G. Sampson [1903].
Le chrétien: choix de discours extraits des sermons de Newman—traduction et préface par R. Saleilles. Paris 1906.
Cardinal Newman. Ed W. Meynell [1907].
Literary selections. Ed Sister of Notre Dame 1913.
The spirit of Cardinal Newman. Ed C. C. Martindale 1914.
Le pensée de Newman: extraits choisis et traduits par F. Delattre, avec une introduction, une bibliographie et le texte anglais correspondant. Paris [1920].
Readings from Newman. Ed G. O'Neill 1923.
A Newman synthesis, arranged by E. Przywara 1930, 1963 (as The heart of Newman). An abridgement, in the original English, of the German arrangement entitled Christentum: ein Aufbau, vol iv.
The fine gold of Newman. Ed J. J. Reilly, New York 1931.
According to Cardinal Newman: the life of Christ and the mission of his Church. Ed A. K. Maxwell, New York 1932.
Favorite Newman sermons. Ed D. M. O'Connell, Milwaukee 1932.
The Newman book of religion. Ed A. Ambruzzi 1937.
Heart to heart; Kindly light; And with the morn. Ed D. M. O'Connell, New York 1938–41 and Paterson NJ 1947. 3 Newman prayerbooks.
A Newman treasury: selections from the prose works. Ed C. F. Harrold, New York 1943.
Newman on university education. Ed R. J. McHugh, Dublin 1944.
Die Kirche: Übertragung und Einführung von O. Karrer. 2 vols Einsiedeln and Cologne 1946.
Essays and sketches. Ed C. F. Harrold 3 vols New York 1948.
The living thoughts of Cardinal Newman. Ed H. Tristram 1948.
Sermons and discourses 1825–39. Ed C. F. Harrold, New York 1949; Sermons and discourses 1839–57, ed Harrold, New York 1949.
The idea of a liberal education: a selection from the works. Ed H. Tristram 1952.
Newman 1845–52, the honeymoon years: an anthology. Ed J. Bradley, Bradford 1953.

The mystical rose: thoughts on the Blessed Virgin from the writings of Newman. Ed J. Regina [1955].
Pensées sur l'église, traduit par A. Roucou-Barthélémy. Paris 1956.
Prose and poetry. Ed G. Tillotson 1957 (Reynard Lib).
Realizations: Newman's selections of his Parochial and plain sermons. Ed V. F. Blehl 1964. Foreword by M. Spark.

§1

St Bartholomew's eve: a tale of the sixteenth century in two cantos. 1821. Anon. With J. W. Bowden. The copy in the BM contains ms notes by J. R. Bloxam, assigning the separate parts to their authors.
Parish of St Clement Oxon. Dec 1 1924. Oxford 1924. A letter, signed by Newman, calling a meeting in aid of a fund for building a new church at Littlemore. Copy in Bodleian.
The life of Apollonius Tyanaeus; with a comparison between the miracles of Scriptures and those elsewhere related, as regards their respective object, nature and evidence. 1824 and 1853 (in Encyclopaedia metropolitana), 1825, 1853 (separately). The Life only was rptd in Historical sketches vol i, 1872 etc, and the Miracles of Scripture in Two essays on Scripture miracles and on ecclesiastical, 1870 etc.
Suggestions respectfully offered to certain resident clergymen of the University in behalf of the Church Missionary Society, by a Master of Arts. Oxford 1830; rptd in The via media of the Anglican Church vol 2, 1877 etc.
Memorials of the past. Oxford 1832. Poems; prefatory verse signed J. H. N. Many are included in Verses on various occasions, below.
The Arians of the fourth century: their doctrine, temper and conduct, chiefly as exhibited in the councils of the Church, between AD 325 and AD 381. 1833; ed G. H. Forbes 1854; 1871 (rev), 1876 (rev), 1888, 1890, 1890, 1895, 1901, 1908, 1919.
Tracts for the times, by members of the University of Oxford. [Ed Newman] 6 vols 1833–41. 90 tracts were issued anon between 9 Sept 1833 (3 tracts) and 27 Feb 1841 (no 90). 5 lists of the tracts and their authors are extant: (1) appendix to H. P. Liddon, Life of Pusey vol 3, 1897, pp. 473–80; (2) Sir G. Prevost, Whitaker's Almanack, 1883; (3) F. H. Rivington [based on information supplied by Newman in 1869], John Bull Sept 1890; (4) J. R. Bloxam, ms at Magdalen College Oxford; (5) W. J. Copeland, revision of list in Whitaker's Almanack, 1883. In the case of 2 tracts, further evidence has come to light. The following are by Newman: vol 1 nos 1–3, 6–7, 8 (with R. H. Froude), 10–11, 15 (with Sir W. Palmer), 19–21, 31, 33–4, 38, 41, 45; vol 2 no 47; vol 3 nos 71, 73, 74 (with B. Harrison), 75–6; vol 4 nos 79, 82; vol 5 nos 83, 85, 88; vol 6 no 90 (remarks on certain passages in the Thirty-Nine Articles). Nos 83 and 85 were rptd in Discussions and arguments on various subjects, 1872 etc, below; no 73 was rptd in Essays, critical and historical vol 1, 1872 etc, below; and nos 38, 41, 71, 82 and 90 were rptd in The via media of the Anglican Church vol 2, 1877 etc, below. No 90 has been frequently rptd separately: ed J. J. Frew 1855; ed E. B. Pusey (with appendix by J. Keble) 1865, 1866, 1893; ed A. W. Evans 1933; tr German, 1844.
Parochial sermons. 3 vols 1834–6, 6 vols (2–3 are of the 2nd edn) 1834–42, 6 vols 1837–42, 1838–44; ed W. J. Copeland 8 vols 1868 (including Plain sermons by contributors to the Tracts for the times, vol 5, as Parochial and Plain sermons), 8 vols 1872–3, 1875–80, 1877, 1879, 1881–4, 1886, 1900–2, 1924. Selection from the First four volumes of parochial sermons, 1841. Selection adapted to the seasons of the ecclesiastical year from the Parochial and plain sermons, ed W. J. Copeland 1870, 1878, 1882, 1890 (5th edn), nd (7th edn), 1908, 1915 (10th edn); tr German, 1907. Twelve sermons selected from the Parochial and plain sermons [1908].
To my parishioners, on occasion of laying of the first stone of the church at Littlemore. Oxford 1835. A letter by Newman. Copy in Bodleian.
The restoration of suffragan bishops recommended, as a means of effecting a more equal distribution of episcopal duties, as contemplated by His Majesty's recent Ecclesiastical Commission. 1835; rptd in The via media of the Anglican Church vol 2, 1877 etc, below.
Elucidations of Dr Hampden's theological statements. Oxford 1836. Signed J. H. N.
Make ventures for Christ's sake: a sermon. Oxford 1836 (anon); 1839 etc (in Parochial sermons, vol 4, below).
Lectures on the prophetical office of the Church, viewed relatively to Romanism and popular Protestantism. 1837; rptd, with additional matter, in The via media of the Anglican Church vol 1, 1877 etc, below.
A letter to the Rev Godfrey Faussett DD, Margaret Professor of Divinity, on certain points of faith and practice. Oxford 1838; rptd in The via media of the Anglican Church vol 2, 1877 etc, below.
Lectures on justification. 1838, 1840, 1874 (as Lectures on the doctrine of justification), 1885, 1890, 1892, 1900, 1924.
The Church of the Fathers. Dublin [1839] (anon), London 1840 (anon), 1842, 1857, 1868, 1872 (in Historical sketches vol 3; material omitted from the 1857 and 1868 edns rptd rev in Historical sketches vol 2, below), 1900, 1908, 1931; tr French, 1908.
The Tamworth reading room: letters on an address delivered by Sir Robert Peel Bart MP on the establishment of a reading room at Tamworth, by Catholicus, originally published in the Times, and since revised and corrected by the author. 1841; rptd in Discussions and arguments, 1872, below; Washington 1946.
A letter addressed to the Rev R. W. Jelf DD, Canon of Christ Church, in explanation of no 90 in the series called the Tracts for the times, by the author. Oxford 1841 (3 edns), 1877 (in The via media of the Anglican Church vol 2, 1877 etc, below). Signed J. H. N.
A letter to the Right Reverend Father in God, Richard [Bagot], Lord Bishop of Oxford, on occasion of no 90 in the series called the Tracts for the times. 1841, 1877 (in The via media of the Anglican Church vol 2, below).
Mr Vice-Chancellor, I write this respectfully to inform you...Oxford 1841. Ptd broadside letter acknowledging the authorship of Tract 90. Copy in Library of Congress. Rptd in R. D. Middleton, Newman at Oxford, 1950.
An essay on the miracles recorded in the excclesiastical history of the early ages. In Fleury's Ecclesiastical history, 1842; Oxford 1843, 1870 (in Two essays on Scripture miracles and on ecclesiastical), 1870, 1873 (in Two essays on Biblical and ecclesiastical miracles), 1881, 1885, 1890, 1890, 1901, 1924.
Sermons, bearing on subjects of the day. 1843, 1844; ed W. J. Copeland 1869, 1873, 1879, 1885, 1902, 1902, 1917; tr German, 1925 (selection), 1958 (complete).
Sermons, chiefly on the theory of religious belief, preached before the University of Oxford. 1843, 1844, 1872 (as Fifteen sermons preached before the University of Oxford), 1880, 1884, 1890, 1900, 1906, 1918; tr French, 1850, 1905 (6 sermons only), 1955 (complete).
Plain sermons by contributors to the Tracts for the times. 1843 (vol 5 (anon) by Newman), 1868 etc (in Parochial and plain sermons).
The Cistercian saints of England, [continued as] Lives of the English saints. 4 vols 1–2 1844–5 ed Newman, who wrote the prose portions of St Bettelin, St Edilwald and St Gundleas; ed A. W. Hutton 6 vols 1900–1.
An essay on the development of Christian doctrine. [The Advertisement contains Newman's retraction of anti-Catholic statements]. 1845, 1846, 1878, 1885, 1890, 1894, 1903, 1920, 1927; ed C. F. Harrold, New York

1949 (with appendix on Newman's textual changes by O. I. Schreiber); ed G. Weigel 1960; 1960; tr French, 1846, 1848, 1905 (with trn of The theory of developments in Christian doctrine: a sermon by Newman); German, 1846, 1922; Dutch, 1957; Polish, 1957. Newman's Retraction was tr French in J. Gondon, Motifs de conversion de dix ministres anglicans, Paris 1847.

Dissertatiunculae quaedam critico-theologicae (ex nupera Oxoniensi Biblioteca Patrum maxima ex parte desumpta; Latine autem liberius reddita etc). Rome 1847, London 1874 etc (in Tracts theological and ecclesiastical).

Loss and gain. 1848 (anon), 1853 (signed; with subtitle The story of a convert), Dublin 1853, London 1858, 1874, 1881, 1891, 1896, 1903, 1904, 1919, 1934; ed M. Trevor 1962; tr Italian, 1857; French, 1859, 1945 (extracts), 1949 (complete); German, 1861, 1924. A novel.

Discourses addressed to mixed congregations. 1849, 1850, 1880, 1881, 1886, 1891, 1892, 1902, 1921; tr French, 1850, 1853; German, 1851, 1924 (selection); Dutch, 1947; Italian, 1955.

Lectures on certain difficulties felt by Anglicans in submitting to the Catholic Church. 1850, 1850, Dublin 1857 (rev), London 1872 (as Difficulties felt by Anglicans in Catholic teaching considered I, In twelve lectures addressed to the party of the religious movement in 1833; II, In a letter addressed to the Rev E. B. Pusey &c), 1876 (as Certain difficulties felt by Anglicans in Catholic teaching considered in a letter addressed to the Rev E. B. Pusey and in a letter addressed to the Duke of Norfolk &c), 2 vols 1876–9, 1885 (as Difficulties felt by Anglicans in Catholic teaching), 1891, 1894 (as Certain difficulties felt by Anglicans in Catholic teaching considered), 1897, 1901, 1918–20; tr French, 1851; German, 1949 (selection), 1951.

Christ upon the waters: a sermon preached on occasion of the establishment of the Catholic hierarchy in this country. Birmingham 1850 (3 edns) [1852], London 1857 etc (in Sermons preached on various occasions, below), Birmingham [1898].

Lectures on the present position of Catholics in England, addressed to the Brothers of the Oratory. 1851, 1851, Birmingham 1851 (as Lectures on Catholicism in England), Dublin nd (as Lectures on Catholicism in England), 1872, 1800, 1889, 1890 (pt 5 omitted), 1892 (Silver Lib, with subtitle Addressed to the Brothers of the Oratory in the summer of 1851), 1903, 1908, 1913, 1924; ed D. M. O'Connell, SJ, Chicago 1925 (school edn); ed J. J. Daly, Beirut 1942; tr German, 1853; Dutch, 1958.

Discourses on the scope and nature of university education, addressed to the Catholics of Dublin. Dublin 1852, London 1859 (rev and altered, and with new titles to several of the discourses, as The scope and nature of university education), 1873 (with some titles of discourses again altered, and with addn of 10 pieces pbd in 1859 as Lectures and essays on university subjects, as The idea of a university defined and illustrated, I: In nine discourses addressed to the Catholics of Dublin; II: In occasional lectures and essays addressed to the members of the Catholic University), 1875, 1885, 1889, 1891, 1893, 1896 (2 discourses only, in My campaign in Ireland), 1898 (as The idea of a university etc), 1902; ed A. R. Waller 1903 (Cloister Lib; as The scope and nature of university education); ed J. Norris 1908 (Longman's Pocket Lib; as University teaching considered in nine discourses: being the first part of The idea of a university defined and illustrated etc), 1910 (as The idea of a university defined and illustrated etc), 1912; ed W. Ward 1915 (EL; as On the scope and nature of university education), 1923 (as The idea of a university defined and illustrated etc); ed D. M. O'Connell SJ, Chicago 1927, 1929, 1931 (as University teaching considered in nine discourses: being the first part of The idea of a university defined and illustrated); ed M. Yardley, Cambridge 1931 (Landmarks in the History of Education: as Select discourses from The idea of a university); ed D. M. O'Connell, New York 1941 (as The idea of a university defined and illustrated); ed R. J. McHugh, Dublin 1944 (nos 5–6, 7, 9, with part of the preface to Discourses on the scope and nature of university education, with excerpts from the second part of The idea of a university defined and illustrated, as Newman on university education); ed C. F. Harrold, New York 1947 (as The idea of a university defined and illustrated); ed L. L. Ward, New York 1948 (as The uses of knowledge; selections from The idea of a university); 1955 (EL; as On the scope and nature of university education); ed M. Yardley, Cambridge 1956 (as Select discourses from The idea of a university); ed G. N. Shuster, New York 1959 (as The idea of a university); ed M. J. Svaglic, New York 1960 (as The idea of a university defined and illustrated); tr German, 1927 (selection), 1957 (selection); Dutch, 1946. Many of the discourses have been rptd separately at various dates.

The second spring: a sermon preached in the synod of Oscott, on Tuesday July 13th 1852. 1852, 1857 etc (in Sermons preached on various occasions, below); ed F. P. Donnolly, New York 1911.

Verses on religious subjects. Dublin 1853. Anon. Most of the poems in this collection are rptd in Verses on various occasions, 1868 etc, below.

Lectures on the history of the Turks in its relation to Christianity, by the author of Loss and gain. Dublin 1854 (anon), 1872 etc (in Historical sketches vol 2); tr German, 1854.

Callista: a sketch of the third century. 1856 (anon), Leipzig [c. 1865] (Tauchnitz), London 1873, 1876, 1881, 1889 (with subtitle A tale of the third century), 1890, 1898, 1901, 1904 (with subtitle A tale of the third century), 1910 (with subtitle A tale of the third century), 1923, 1928, 1934 (with subtitle A sketch of the third century); ed A. Duggan 1962; dramatized version by F. C. Husenbeth, entitled The convert martyr, 1857; tr German, 1856, 1860, 1862, 1885, 1890, 1893, 1895, 1900, 1903, 1908, 1910, [1920], [1926]; French, 1857, 1859; 1867, 1868, 1867 (for 1869), 1873, 1875, 1877, 1880, 1881, 1884, 1885, 1888, 1890, 1891, 1894, 1896, 1908; dramatized version in French, 1874; nd; Polish, 1858; Italian, 1859, 1928; Czech, 1887; Serbo-Croat, [1926]; Spanish, 1948. A novel.

The office and work of universities [articles rptd from Catholic Univ Gazette]. 1856, 1859, 1872 etc (as The rise and progress of universities, in Historical sketches vol 2); ed G. Sampson [1902] (as University sketches); ed C. F. Harrold 1948 (selection of 8 of the 20 articles, in Essays and sketches vol 2); ed M. Tierney, Dublin 1952 (as University sketches); ed Tierney, New York 1964; tr German, 1949, 1958.

Sermons preached on various occasions. 1857, 1870, 1874, 1881, 1887, 1891, 1900, 1921; tr French, 1860; German, 1924 (selection). The mission of St Philip Neri was rptd separately, Rome 1901, and tr German, below.

Lectures and essays on university subjects. 1859, 1873 etc (as pt 2 of The idea of a university defined and illustrated). *See also under* Discourses on the scope and nature of university education, above.

The tree beside the waters: a sermon preached in the chapel of St Mary's College Oscott on Friday November 11 1859, at the funeral of the Right Rev Henry Weedall DD [1859], 1870 etc (in Sermons preached on various occasions, above).

Mr Kingsley and Dr Newman: a correspondence on the question whether Dr Newman teaches that truth is no virtue? 1864, 1913, 1931 (both with Apologia pro vita sua); tr German, 1865.

Apologia pro vita sua: being a reply to a pamphlet [by Charles Kingsley] entitled What, then, does Dr Newman mean? 7 pts, with appendix issued on successive Thursdays 21 April to 2 June 1864; the appendix pbd a fortnight later. Pts 1–2 and appendix were omitted by Newman from later edns. 1864, 1865 (as History of my religious opinions), 1865 (as Apologia pro vita sua: being a reply to a pamphlet entitled What, then, does Dr Newman mean?), 1865, 1865, 1869 (as History of my religious opinions), 1873 (as Apologia pro vita sua: being a history of his religious opinions), 1878, 1879, 1882 (as A history of his religious opinions), 1885 (as Apologia pro vita sua: history of his religious opinions), 1887 (as Apologia pro vita sua: being a history of his religious opinions), 1890; ed A. H. Barton 1891, 1892, 1897, 1902; ed W. P. Neville 1904; 1907 (Longmans' Pocket Lib); ed W. Meynell [1907] (an abridgement entitled Newman: the story of his religious opinions, abstracted in his own words from the Apologia pro vita sua); [1907], 1908; ed C. Sarolea [1912] (EL); ed W. Ward, Oxford 1913 (the 2 versions of 1864 and 1865, preceded by Newman's and Kingsley's pamphlets); ed J. Gamble 2 vols [1913] (Scott Lib) (text of 1864 with supplementary matter included in 1865 and Newman's and Kingsley's pamphlets); 1920 (Longman's Pocket Lib); [1921] (EL); 1924; ed D. M. O'Connell SJ with foreword by H. Belloc, Chicago 1930 (text of 1865); ed A. B. G. Hart, New York 1931; ed W. Ward, Oxford 1931 (the two versions of 1864 and 1865, preceded by Newman's and Kingsley's pamphlets); arranged by M. R. Grennan, with introd by J. J. Reilly, New York 1934 (as The heart of Newman's Apologia); ed M. Ward 1946; ed C. F. Harrold, New York 1947; ed A. C. Pegis, New York 1950 (Modern Lib); ed S. Leslie 1955 (EL); ed P. Hughes, New York 1956; ed A. D. Culler, New York 1956; 1959 (Fontana); ed B. Willey, Oxford 1964 (WC); ed M. J. Svaglic, Oxford 1967; tr French, 1866, 1939, 1951; German, 1913, 1920, 1922, 1951; Spanish, 1934, 1961; Dutch, 1946, 1949, 1956; Polish, 1948; Italian, 1956; Swedish, 1960.

The dream of Gerontius. Month May–June 1865, 1866 (dedication signed J. H. N.), 1868 etc (in Verses on various occasions, below); 1886 (22nd edn), 1888, 1897 (30th edn), 1898, 1900, set to music by E. Elgar, 1900; 1903 (34th edn); ed M. F. Egan, 1903; ed Egan 1906; ed E. B. (L.) 1907 (illustr); illustr 'Ryl' 1907; illustr M. P. Webb 1907; ed E. Bellasis 1909 (with ms facs); illustr R. T. Rose 1910; illustr F. E. Hiley 1911; illustr R. T. Rose 1911; ed M. F. Egan 1912; Oxford 1914 (together with Verses on various occasions, below and some poems from Lyra apostolica not included in Verses, 1868); ed G. Tidy, illustr S. Langdale 1916; ed J. Gliebe, New York 1916 (college edn); ed J. J. Clifford, Chicago 1917 (school edn); ed W. F. P. Stockley 1923; ed with concordance and chronicle by 'Anglican' (A. F. Dauglish) 1928; ed H. Tristram [1933]; ed M. Sargent, illustr M. P. Webb 1937; tr French, 1869, 1869, 1882, 1889, 1912, 1926, 1944, 1960; German, 1885, 1923, 1923 (in Der Gral vol 17), 1925, 1939, 1939, [1946] (English and German), 1952, 1959, 1960; Dutch, 1947.

A letter to the Rev E. B. Pusey DD on his recent Eirenicon. 1866 (3 edns), 1872 etc (in Difficulties felt by Anglicans in Catholic teaching); tr German, 1866, 1911, 1953 (selection); French, 1867 (in J. Gondon, De la réunion de l'église d'Angleterre protestante à l'église catholique).

The Pope and the revolution: a sermon preached in the Oratory Church Birmingham on Sunday October 7 1866. 1866, 1870 etc (in Sermons preached on various occasions, below); tr French, 1867; German, 1867.

Verses on various occasions. 1868 (dedication signed J. H. N.), 1869, 1874, 1880, 1883, 1888, 1890, 1903, 1912 (Longmans' Pocket Lib), Oxford 1914 (in The dream of Gerontius and other poems), 1918.

An essay in aid of a grammar of assent. 1870, 1870, 1874, 1881, 1885, 1891, 1892, 1901, 1903, 1909, 1924, 1930; ed C. F. Harrold, New York 1947; ed D. Gilson 1955, 1958; tr French, 1907; German, 1921, 1936–40; Polish, 1956; Spanish, 1960.

Two essays on Scripture miracles and on ecclesiastical. 1870, 1873 (as Two essays on Biblical and on ecclesiastical miracles), 1881, 1885, 1890, 1890, 1901, 1924. Rptd respectively from the Encyclopaedia metropolitana, 1824 etc, and from Newman's trn of a portion of Fleury's Ecclesiastical history.

Essays critical and historical. 2 vols 1872, 1877, 1885, 1890, 1895, 1901, 1910, 1919. Essays and periodical articles rptd. Poetry with reference to Aristotle's Poetics was rptd separately, ed A. S. Cook, Boston 1891.

Historical sketches [i.e. The office and work of universities, 1856, rptd as The rise and progress of universities; Lectures on the history of the Turks, 1854; Personal and literary character of Cicero, 1824; Apollonius of Tyana, 1824; Primitive Christianity (from the 1840 and 1842 edns of The Church of the Fathers); The Church of the Fathers (text of 1857 and 1868 edns) and various shorter pieces]. 3 vols 1872–3, 1873, 1876, 1878–81, 1891, 1901–3, 1920; tr German, 1948 (selection), 1949 (selection). The mission of St Benedict and The Benedictine schools only were rptd in 1908, ed H. Bennett, as The mission of the Benedictine order, and in 1914, ed H. N. Birt, as Cardinal Newman on the Benedictine order; the same two essays were tr German 1926. The mission of St Benedict was tr French, 1909. St Crysostom and The trials of Theodoret were tr German, 1923.

Discussions and arguments on various subjects. 1872, 1873, 1878, 1899, 1907, 1924. The Tamworth reading room, 1841, nos 82 and 85 of the Tracts for the times, 1838, and various periodical articles rptd.

Prologue to the Andria of Terence. 1882 (ptd for priv circulation). Copy of this work, written in 1820, in BM.

Orate pro anima Jacobi Roberti Hope Scott [a sermon]. [1873] (advertisement and text signed J. H. N.), 1874 etc (as In the world but not of the world, in Sermons on various occasions, above).

The idea of a university. 1873 etc. *See also above*, Discourses on the scope and nature of university education.

Tracts theological and ecclesiastical. 1874, 1891, 1895, 1899, 1902, 1924. Collects Dissertatiunculae quaedam critico-theologicae, 1847, and other uncollected pieces.

A letter addressed to his Grace the Duke of Norfolk on occasion of Mr Gladstone's recent expostulations. 1875, 1875 (with Postscript on Mr Gladstone's Vaticanism), 1875 (4th edn, with Postscript), New York 1875, London 1876 etc (appended to Certain difficulties felt by Anglicans in Catholic teaching, above); ed A. S. Ryan, Notre Dame 1962 (as Letter to his Grace the Duke of Norfolk, in Newman and Gladstone); tr German, 1875.

The via media of the Anglican Church, illustrated in lectures, letters, and tracts written between 1830 and 1841; with a preface and notes. 2 vols 1877, 1885, 1891, 1891–8, 1891 (Silver Lib), 1901, 1918–23; tr German, 1938 (preface to Lectures on the prophetical office only, vol i), 1947. Reprints Lectures on the prophetical office of the Church, viewed relatively to Romanism and popular Protestantism, 1837; Suggestions in behalf of the Church Missionary Society, 1830; nos 38, 41, 71, 82 and 90 of the Tracts for the times, 1833–41; The restoration of suffragan bishops recommended, 1835; A letter addressed to the Rev Godfrey Faussett, 1838; A letter addressed to the Rev R. W. Jelf, 1841; A letter to the Bishop of Oxford, 1841; and Retraction of anti-Catholic statements, 1843.

Two sermons preached in the Church of S Aloysius, Oxford on Trinity Sunday 1880. [Oxford 1880] (priv ptd).

What is of obligation for a Catholic to believe concerning the inspiration of the canonical scriptures: being a postscript to an article in the February no of the Nineteenth Century Review in answer to Professor Healy. [1884], 1890 (as Further illustrations, in Stray essays on controversial points variously illustrated).

Stray essays on controversial points variously illustrated. Birmingham 1890 (priv ptd). Reprints What is of obligation for a Catholic to believe, 1884 and 2 other periodical articles.

Poetry, with reference to Aristotle's Poetics. Boston 1891. *See also* Essays, critical and historical, above.

Meditations and devotions of the late Cardinal Newman. Ed W. P. Neville 1893, 1903, 1908, 1914, 1923, 1932, 1953; ed M. Trevor 1964; tr French, 1906; Italian, 1906, 1907, 1926; German, 1919, 1922, 1930, [1939], 1946, 1949, 1952, 1953, 1954, 1960, 1960; Spanish, 1952; Dutch, 1955.

My campaign in Ireland, part I: Catholic University reports and other papers. Ed W. P. Neville, Aberdeen 1896 (priv ptd). Part 2, Note on Cardinal Newman's preaching and influence at Oxford, by J. C. Shairp.

The mission of St Philip Neri: an instruction delivered in substance in the Birmingham Oratory, January 1850, and at subsequent times. Rome 1901. *See also* Sermons preached on various occasions, above.

The mission of the Benedictine order. 1908 etc. *See also* Historical sketches, above.

Sermon notes 1849–78. Ed Fathers of the Birmingham Oratory 1913; tr French, 1914.

Autobiographical writings. Ed H. Tristram 1956; tr French, 1956 (with English text); German, 1959; Spanish, 1963.

Faith and prejudice and other unpublished sermons. Ed C. S. Dessain, New York 1956, London 1957 (as Catholic sermons); tr Spanish, 1959.

On consulting the faithful in matters of doctrine. Ed J. Coulson 1961; tr German, 1940. Originally pbd in Rambler July 1859, rptd 1871, with addns and amendments, as an appendix to the 3rd edn of The Arians of the fourth century.

Works Edited, Translated, or with Contributions by Newman

Newman edited Br Critic July 1838–July 1841 and in May and July 1859 2 nos of Rambler, both of which journals contain articles by him. He also contributed to the following periodicals: London Rev, Br Mag, Dublin Rev, Catholic Univ Gazette (Dublin), Atlantis, Month, Nineteenth Century; and in the Conservative Jnl Feb 1843 he pbd his Retraction of anti-Catholic statements.

Encyclopaedia metropolitana. Ed E. Smedley, Hugh J. Rose and Henry J. Rose 29 vols 1817–45, 40 vols 1848–58. Newman contributed articles on Cicero, 1824, Apollonius Tyanaeus, 1824 and the Miracles of scripture, 1826. The essay on Cicero was rptd in Historical sketches vol 1 1872, that on Apollonius Tyanaeus was rptd separately, 1828, and included in Historical sketches vol 1 1872, and the essay on Miracles was rptd as pt 1 of Two essays on Scripture miracles and on ecclesiastical, 1870.

Elements of logic, by R. Whately. 1826, 1827, 1832 (4th edn, rev), 1836 (6th edn, rev), 1840 (rev), 1844 (rev), 1848 (rev). Newman had a large share in the composition.

Tracts for the times, by members of the University of Oxford. 6 vols 1833–41. Ed Newman. For a list of tracts contributed by Newman, *see above.*

Lyra apostolica. Most of the poems by Newman, but not all, were included in Verses on various occasions, 1868 etc. The hymn known as Lead, kindly light was first pbd anon in Br Mag, 1 Feb 1834, under the title of Faith; it was rptd without title as no 25 in the Lyra apostolica, and later in Verses on various occasions as The pillar of the cloud. Probably one of the most popular English hymns, it has been frequently rptd both in separate form and in anthologies and hymnals. Poems originally pbd in Br Mag. Of the 179 pieces Newman wrote 109; his contributions are signed δ. Derby 1836, 1837, 1838, 1840, 1843 (6th edn), 1864 (13th edn), 1866, London 1879, 1897; ed H. S. Holland and H. C. Beeching [1901].

A library of the Fathers of the Holy Catholic Church, anterior to the division of the East and West. Ed J. Keble, Newman, E. B. Pusey and [1843–57] C. Marriott. 48 vols Oxford 1838–85. Newman translated and annotated Select treatises of S Athanasius in controversy with the Arians, 2 vols 1842–4, 1881; rptd in part in A select library of Nicene and post-Nicene Fathers of the Christian Church, 2nd ser vol IV ed A. Robinson, Oxford 1892. Newman also contributed prefaces to the following volumes in A library of the Fathers: S Cyril's Catechetical lectures, 1838; S Cyprian's treatises, 1839; S Chrysostom on Galatians and Ephesians, 1840; and S Athanasius's historical tracts, 1843.

Godly meditations upon the Lord's supper, by C. Sutton. Oxford 1838. Preface by Newman.

Hymni ecclesiae: excerpti e breviariis Romano, Sarisburiensi, Eboracensi et aliunde. Oxford 1838 (preface by Newman), 1865 (with Newman's edn of Hymni ecclesiae e breviario Parisiensi).

Hymni ecclesiae e breviario Parisiensi. Oxford 1838 (Preface by Newman) 1865 (with Newman's edn of Hymni excerpti e breviariis Romano, Sarisburiensi, Eboracensi et aliunde).

Remains of the late Rev R. H. Froude. 4 vols 1838–9. Ed Newman and J. Keble.

Disce vivere: learn to live, by C. Sutton. Oxford 1839. Preface by Newman.

A rationale upon the Book of Common Prayer of the Church of England, by A. Sparrow. Oxford 1839. Preface by Newman.

The rich man's duty to contribute liberally to the building, rebuilding, repairing, beautifying and adorning of churches: to which is added the journal of William Dowsing etc, by E. Wells. Oxford 1840. Preface by Newman.

The life of George Bull, Bishop of St Davids, by R. Nelson. Oxford 1840. Preface by Newman.

Sacra privata: the private meditations, devotions and prayers of the Right Rev T. Wilson, reprinted entire. Oxford 1840. Preface by Newman.

Catena aurea: commentary on the four Gospels. 1841. Preface by Newman.

The devotions of Bishop [Lancelot] Andrewes. 2 pts Oxford 1842–4. Pt i tr from the Greek and arranged by Newman; pt 2 tr from the Latin by J. M. Neale. Pt i had appeared in 1840 as no 88 of Tracts for the times, above. Rptd Oxford 1867; ed and rev E. Venables 1883, 1883; Newman's trn rptd verbatim, ed H. B. Swete 1920; New York 1897 (250 copies); Nashville 1950 (photo facs of 1897 edn).

The ecclesiastical history of M. l'Abbé [Claude] Fleury, from the second Ecumenical Council to the end of the fourth century: translated, with notes and an essay on the miracles of the period. Oxford 1842; The ecclesiastical history from AD 400 to AD 429, Oxford 1843; The ecclesiastical history from AD 429 to AD 456, Oxford 1844. Newman's introd to vol 1 was rptd separately as An essay on the miracles recorded in the ecclesiastical history of the early ages, 1843 and in 1870 as pt 2 of Two essays on Scripture miracles and on ecclesiastical.

The Cistercian saints of England [continued as Lives of the English saints. Newman, the projector and, in the case of the first 2 vols, the editor of the ser, was the author of the Lives of the hermit SS Gundleus, Edelwald and Bettelin (prose portion).] 14 vols 1844–5; ed A. W. Hutton 6 vols 1900–1.

Thoughts on the work of the six days of creation, by J. W. Bowden. Oxford 1845. Ed Newman.

Maxims of the kingdom of heaven. 1860, 1867, 1873 (enlarged and re-arranged), 1887. A collection of passages from the Scriptures with a preface by Newman.

P. Terentius Phormio, expurgatus in usum puerorum; with English notes and translations [by Newman]. 1864, 1883, 1889.
Pincerna ex Terentio [i.e. the Eunuchus], expurgatus in usum puerorum; with English notes and translations [by Newman]. 1866, 1880, 1883, 1887.
Aulularia Plauti, expurgatus in usum puerorum; with English notes and translations [by Newman]. 1866, 1883, 1888.
Andria Terentii, expurgatus in usum puerorum; with English notes and translations [by Newman]. 1870, 1883, 1889.
The Church and the empires, preceded by a memoir of the author by Newman, by H. W. Wilberforce. 1874.
The Anglican ministry, with a preface by Cardinal Newman, by A. W. Hutton. 1879.
Notes of a visit to the Russian Church in the years 1840, 1841, by W. Palmer, selected and arranged by Cardinal Newman. 1882.
Addresses to Cardinal Newman, with his replies etc. 1879–81. Ed W. P. Neville 1905.
The argument from conscience to the existence of God, according to Newman, by A. J. Boekraad and H. Tristram. Louvain 1961. Among the unpbd writings by Newman, the paper entitled Proof of theism.

Letters

Letters and correspondence of Newman during his life in the English Church; with a brief autobiography. Ed A. Mozley 2 vols 1891.
Ward, W. P. The life of Newman based on his private journals and correspondence. 2 vols 1912, 1913, 2 vols in 1 1927.
Correspondence of Newman with John Keble and others 1839–45. Ed at Birmingham Oratory [by J. Bacchus] 1917.
Selections from the correspondence of the first Lord Acton, vol i: Correspondence with Cardinal Newman, Lady Blennerhassett, W. E. Gladstone and others. Ed J. N. Figgis and R. V. Laurence 1917.
Cross, F. L. John Henry Newman. 1933. Contains a set of unpbd letters to Alfred Plummer.
Cardinal Newman and William Froude FRS: a correspondence. Ed G. H. Harper, Baltimore 1933.
Mossner, E. C. Newman on Bishop Butler: an unpublished letter. Theology 32 1936.
Stephenson, G. Edward Stuart Talbot 1844–1934. 1936.
The Acland family: letters 1829–1901. Bodleian Lib Record 1 1940.
De correspondentie tussen Newman en [Charles] Meynell over de Grammar of assent. In O. M. Zeno, Newman's leer over het menselijk denken: inleiding op Newman's Grammar of assent etc, Utrecht and Nijmegen 1943; tr Leyden 1957.
Newman's letters and poems from Malta 1832–3. Ed H. Galea [Malta 1945].
Letters of Newman. Bodleian Lib Record 2 1949.
Tristram, H. The correspondence between Newman and the Comte de Montalembert. Dublin Rev 232 1949.
McGrath, F. Newman's university: idea and reality. 1951.
Letters of Newman: a selection. Ed D. Stanford and M. Spark. 1957.
The letters and diaries of Newman. Ed C. S. Dessain. Vol 11, Littlemore to Rome, October 1845 to December 1846, 1961; vol 12, Rome to Birmingham, January 1847 to December 1848, 1962; vol 13, Birmingham and London, January 1849 to June 1850, 1963; vol 14, ed C. S. Dessain and V. F. Blehl, Papal aggression, July 1850 to December 1851, 1963; vol 15, ed Dessain and Blehl, The Achilli trial, January 1852 to December 1853, 1964; vol 16, ed Dessain, Founding of a university, January 1854 to September 1855, 1965.
Newman family letters. Ed D. Mozley 1962.

§2

Jager, J.-N. In his Le protestantisme aux prises avec la doctrine catholique: ou controverses avec plusieurs ministres anglicans, Paris 1836.
Maurice, P. In his Popery of Oxford confronted, disavowed and repudiated, 2 pts 1837–51.
Froude, R. H. In his Remains of the Rev R. Hurrell Froude, [ed J. H. Newman and J. Keble] 2 pts 1838–9.
Nevile, C. A review of Mr Newman's Lectures on Romanism; with general observations on the Oxford tracts and Dr Pusey's Letter to the Bishop of Oxford. 1839.
Bennett, J. Justification as revealed in Scripture: in opposition to the Council of Trent and Mr Newman's Lectures. 1840.
Golightly, C. P. Brief remarks upon no 90 [of Tracts for the times]. Oxford 1841.
Pusey, E. B. The articles treated on in Tract 90 reconsidered and their interpretation vindicated in a letter to R. W. Jelf. 1841.
—— In his Holy eucharist, a comfort to the penitent: a sermon, Oxford 1843.
—— First letter to Newman in explanation chiefly in regard to the reverential love due to the ever-blessed Theotokos, and the doctrine of her immaculate conception etc. 1869. Pt 2 of his Eirenicon 1865–70.
Ward, W. G. A few more words in support of no 90 of the Tracts for the times. 1841.
Abeken, H. In his Das englische Bistum in Jerusalem, Berlin 1842.
Harper, F. W. A few observations on the teaching of Mr Newman concerning justification. 1842.
Illustration of the actual state of Oxford and of the attempts of Mr Newman to unprotestantize the National Church. Oxford 1842.
Wiseman, N. P. S. A letter respectfully addressed to the Rev Newman upon some passages in his letter to the Rev Dr Jelf. 1842.
Buchanan, J. On the Tracts for the times. Edinburgh 1843.
Mestral, A. de. In his L'école théologique d'Oxford, Lausanne 1843.
Palmer, W. A narrative of events connected with the publication of the Tracts for the times. Oxford 1843.
—— The doctrine of development and conscience, considered in relation to the evidences of Christianity and of the Catholic system. 1846.
Petri, M. Zeitgemässe Traktate nr 90: Bemerkungen über gewisse Stellen in den 39 Artikeln. In his Beiträge zur bessern Würdigung des Wesens und der Bedeutung des Puseyismus, 2 pts Gottingen 1843–44.
Unden, H. F. In his Die Zustände der anglikanischen Kirche, Leipzig 1843.
Bricknell, W. S. Oxford: tract no 90 and Ward's Ideal of a Christian church: a practical suggestion respectfully submitted to members of Convocation; with an appendix containing the testimonies of twenty-four prelates against tract no 90, and a series of extracts from Ward's Ideal. Oxford 1844.
—— The judgment of the bishops upon tractarian theology: a complete analytical arrangement of the charges delivered by the prelates of the Anglican Church, from 1837 to 1842 inclusive, so far as they relate to the tractarian movement. Oxford 1845.
Gerlach, O. von. In his Über den religiösen Zustand der anglikanischen Kirche in ihren verschiedenen Gliederungen im Jahre 1842, Potsdam 1845.
Goode, W. Tract XC historically refuted: or a reply to a work by the Rev F. Oakeley entitled The subject of tract XC historically examined. 1845, 1866.
Rogers, F. A short appeal to the members of Convocation upon the proposed censure of tract 90. 1845.

Saint Oldooman: a myth of the nineteenth century, contained in a letter from the Bishop of Verulanum to the Lord Drayton. 1845. A satire on Newman's Lives of the English saints.

White, J. B. The life of the Rev Joseph Blanco White, written by himself, with portions of his correspondence. Ed J. H. Thom 3 vols 1845.

Barter, W. B. A postscript to The English church not in schism: containing a few words on Mr Newman's Essay on development. 1846.

Crosthwaite, J. C. Modern hagiology: an examination of the nature and tendency of some legendary and devotional works lately published under the sanction of the Rev J. H. Newman. 1846. On the Lives of the English saints.

[Brownson, O. A.?] An essay on the Development of Christian doctrine by Newman, by an English Churchman. Brownson's Quart Rev 3 1846.

— The fourfold difficulty of Anglicanism by J. Spencer Northcote. Brownson's Quart Rev new ser 1 1847.

Faber, G. S. Letters on tractarian secession to popery; with remarks on Mr Newman's principle of development etc. 1846.

A few words to the author of an Essay on the development of Christian doctrine. 1846.

Fry, H. P. Sermons on the nature and design of heresy: on the defection of the Rev Newman from the Church of England and on other subjects. Hobart 1846.

Gillis, J. Lectures on the Essay of development. Edinburgh 1846.

Gondon, J. Conversion de soixante ministres anglicans ou membres des universités anglaises et de cinquante personnes de distinction; avec une notice sur MM Newman, Ward et Oakley. Paris 1846, 1847 (as Conversion de cent-cinquante ministres anglicans, revue et augmentée).

— Motifs de conversion de dix ministres anglicans exposés par eux-mêmes, et rétraction du Rev Newman. Paris 1847.

— Notice biographique sur le R. P. Newman. Paris 1853.

— De la réunion de l'église d'Angleterre protestante à l'église catholique: programme du Dr E. B. Pusey; réponse du Dr Newman; introduction par Mgr Manning sur la réunion de la chrétienté. Paris 1867.

Irons, W. J. The theory of development examined with reference specially to Mr Newman's Essay. 1846.

Irvine, A. Romanism briefly considered, as represented by the Rev Newman. 1846.

Maurice, J. F. D. The Epistle to the Hebrews: with a preface containing a review of Mr Newman's Theory of development. 1846.

Mithridates: or Mr Newman's Essay on development its own confutation, by a quondam disciple. 1846.

Moberly, G. The sayings of the great forty days, with an examination of Mr Newman's theory of developments. 1846.

A review of Mr Newman's Essay on the development of Christian doctrine, by an English churchman. 1846.

[Harris, E. F. S.] From Oxford to Rome: and how it fared with some who lately made the journey, by a companion traveller. 1847.

Mozley, J. B. The theory of the development: a criticism of Dr Newman's Essay on the development of Christian doctrine. Christian Remembrancer Jan 1847; rptd 1878 (separately).

Newman, F. W. In his Phases of faith: or passages from the history of my creed, 1850.

— Contributions chiefly to the early history of Cardinal Newman. 1891.

Butler, W. A. Letters on the development of Christian doctrine, in reply to Mr Newman's Essay. Ed Rev T. Woodward, Dublin 1850.

Grant, B. Orations to the Oratorians: being a supplement to the Rev Dr Newman's lectures on Catholicism in England. Nos 1–4, 1851.

Minton, S. An exposure of the inconsistencies, fictions and fallacies of Dr Newman's lectures at Birmingham [on the Position of Catholics in England]. 1851.

— Facts and figures: three letters to Dr Newman, in reply to some of his lectures recently delivered at Birmingham. Liverpool [1851].

Achilli v. Newman: a full and authentic report of the prosecution for libel tried before Lord Campbell and a special jury, June 1852; with introductory remarks by the editor of the Confessional unmasked. [1852].

Hare, J. C. Vindication of Luther against his recent English assailants. 1855. Against the Lectures on justification.

Maguire, R. The Oxford movement: strictures on the personal reminiscences and revelations of Dr Newman, Mr Oakeley and others; with special reference to the Essay on development. 1855.

Oakeley, F. Personal reminiscences of the Oxford movement; with illustrations from Dr Newman's Loss and gain. In his Popular lectures [on Church questions], 1855.

[Martineau, J.] Personal influences on our present theology: Newman. Nat Rev 3 1856.

Davis, C. H. Romanism and romanizingism, revived galatianism and perverted judaism: a sermon with copious notes and appendices on Dr J. H. Newman's assertion of a better 'hope in death' of a profane and 'bad Catholic' than of 'the most virtuous of protestants' and discussional memoranda. [1860].

Du Boulay, J. English common sense versus foreign fallacies in questions of religion. 1864. Remarks on Renan's Vie de Jésus and Newman's Essay on the development of Christian doctrine etc.

Kingsley, C. Mr Kingsley and Dr Newman: a correspondence on the question whether Dr Newman teaches that truth is no virtue? 1864.

— 'What, then, does Dr Newman mean?' a reply to a pamphlet lately published by Dr Newman. 1864.

Meyrick, F. But isn't Kingsley right after all? a letter to Dr Newman. 1864.

— On Dr Newman's rejection of Ligouri's doctrine of equivocation. 1864. *See also* W. E. Gladstone, below.

[Renouf, P. le P.] University education for English Catholics: a letter to the Very Rev Dr Newman by a Catholic layman. 1864.

Dr Newman and Charles Kingsley. London Quart Rev 23 1865.

D[arby], J. N. Analysis of Dr Newman's Apologia pro vita sua. 1866.

Ryder, H. I. Idealism in theology: a review of Dr Ward's scheme of dogmatic theology. 1867.

Vaughan, E. T. Dr Newman as a preacher. Contemporary Rev Jan 1869.

Harper, T. N. Dr Newman's Essay in aid of a grammar of assent. 8 pts. Pts 1–7 in Month 1870; pt 8 ptd for private circulation, no place [1871?] as Difficulties touching certain philosophical theories propounded in Dr Newman's Grammar of assent.

Husband, E. What will Dr Newman do? a letter to Newman [on the question of papal infallibility etc]. 1870.

Milman, H. H. Newman on the development of Christian doctrine. In his Savonarola, Erasmus and other essays reprinted from the Quarterly Review, 1870.

The poems of Newman. Blackwood's Mag Sept 1870.

Froude, J. A. Father Newman on the Grammar of assent. In his Short studies on great subjects ser 2, 1871.

— In his Short studies on great subjects ser 4, 1883.

Capes, J. M. To Rome and back. 1873.

Gladstone, W. E. Vaticanism: an answer to replies and reproofs. 1875. Reply by F. Meyrick, Does Dr Newman deserve Mr Gladstone's praises or not?, 1875.

Madaune, J.-M. de. Newman et l'école d'Oxford en 1833. Paris [1875].

Pearson, S. Conscience and the Church in their relations to Christ and Caesar: thoughts suggested by Dr Newman's pamphlet on the Vatican decrees. 1875.

Ries, F. Gladstone und die Katholiken Englands. In Stimmen aus Maria-Laach March 1875.
Stephen, L. The theory of belief of Dr Newman. Fortnightly Rev Nov–Dec 1877.
Oliver, S. Dr Newman's apologies: being four letters to the Undergraduate's Journal. Oxford 1878.
Burgon, J. W. Lives of twelve good men. 2 vols 1880.
Connelly, P. Cardinal Newman versus the Apostles' Creed. 1880.
Buddenseig, R. Newman und sein Anteil an der Oxforder Bewegung. Zeitschrift für Kirchengeschichte 5 1881.
Dr Newman and Mr Froude. Month May 1881.
Shairp, J. C. In his Aspects of poetry, Oxford 1881.
Earle, J. C. Dr Newman as a man of letters. Amer Catholic Quart 7 1882.
Jennings, H. J. Cardinal Newman: the story of his life. Birmingham 1882.
Mozley, T. Reminiscences chiefly of Oriel College and the Oxford movement. 2 vols 1882.
Paul, C. K. In his Biographical sketches, 1883.
Pattison, M. In his Memoirs, 1885.
Bijvanck, W. G. C. Balzac en Newman. De Gids I 1887; rptd in his Poëzie en leven in de 19de eeuw, Haarlem 1889.
Hutton, R. H. In his Essays on some of the modern guides of English thought in matters of faith. 1887.
—— J. H. Newman. Expositor new ser 2 1890.
—— Cardinal Newman. 1891.
—— Pilgrims in the region of faith: Amiel, Tolstoy, Pater, Newman. 1906.
A study on Cardinal Newman's Grammar of assent. 1889.
Ward, W. P. William George Ward and the Oxford Movement. 1889.
—— In his William George Ward and the Catholic revival, 1893.
—— In his Witnesses to the unseen and other essays, 1893.
—— The life and times of Cardinal Newman. 2 vols 1897.
—— Newman and Sabatier. Fortnightly Rev May 1901.
—— In his Problems and persons, 1903.
—— In his Ten personal studies, 1908.
—— The life of Newman based on his private journals and correspondence. 2 vols 1912, 1913, 2 vols in 1 1927.
—— In his Men and matters, 1914.
—— In his Last lectures, 1918.
[Church, R. W.] Cardinal Newman's course. Guardian 13 Aug 1890.
—— Cardinal Newman's naturalness. Guardian 20 Aug 1890.
Church, R. W. The Oxford movement: twelve years 1833–45. 1891.
—— In his Occasional papers vol 2, 1897.
Clement, W. Newman, Sibthorp and Lockhart: converts to the church of Rome. 2 pts [1890?].
Fletcher, J. S. A short life of Cardinal Newman. 1890.
Groot, J. V. de. De geloofsphilosophie van Kardinaal Newman. De Katholiek 1890.
Meynell, W. Newman: the founder of modern Anglicanism and a Cardinal of the Roman Church. 1890, 1907 (rev).
Oldcastle, J. Cardinal Newman: a monograph. Merry England 15 1890.
Abbott, E. A. Philomythus: an antidote against credulity —a discussion of Cardinal Newman's Essay on ecclesiastical miracles. 1891.
—— The Anglican career of Cardinal Newman. 2 vols 1892.
Bellesheim, A. Newman als Anglikaner auf Grund seiner Briefsammlung. Katholik 71 1891.
Bibliographie von aus Anlasz seines Todes über Newman erschienenen Büchern und Zeitschriftenaufsätzen. Literarischer Handweiser 1891.
Capecelatro, A. Commemorazione del Cardinale Newman nei solenni funerali fattigli dai confratelli dell' oratorio di Napoli il 6 novembre 1890. Rome 1891.
Flóystrup, E. E. Den anglokatholske bevaegelse i det nittende aarhunrede. Copenhagen 1891.
Jacobs, J. George Eliot, Matthew Arnold, Browning, Newman: essays and reviews from the Athenaeum. 1891.
[Kraus, F. X.] Newman: in memoriam. Deutsche Rundschau 17 1891.
Lockhart, W. Cardinal Newman: reminiscences of fifty years since, 1891.
Pierson, A. In Mannen van beteekenis in onze dagen, ed E. D. Pijzel, Haarlem 1891.
Treacy, J. V. Newman as a preacher. Amer Catholic Quart Rev 16 1891.
Bellasis, E. Cardinal Newman as a musician. 1892.
—— Memorials of Mr Serjeant Bellasis 1800–73. 1893.
—— Coram cardinali. 1916.
Birrell, A. In his Res judicatae: papers and essays, 1892.
Preston, J. W. Cardinal Newman: or catholicity down to date. Lyme Regis 1892.
Sanday, W. England's debt to Newman. Oxford 1892.
What then did Dr Newman do? being an inquiry into his share in the Catholic revival. Oxford 1892.
Caird, E. The evolution of religion. 2 vols Glasgow 1893.
Grabinski, G. La renaissance catholique en Angleterre et le Cardinal Newman, d'après une étude du Cardinal Capecelatro. Lyon 1893.
—— La conversione di Newman e il rinascimento cattolico in Inghilterra. 1903.
Liddon, H. P. In his Life of E. B. Pusey, 4 vols 1893–7.
Overton, J. H. In his English Church in the nineteenth century 1800–33, 1894.
Purcell, E. S. In his Life of Cardinal Manning, 2 vols 1895.
Chiniquy, C. The perversion of Dr Newman to the Church of Rome. Montreal 1896.
Hort, A. F. In his Life and letters of Fenton John Anthony Hort, 2 vols 1896.
Joye, D. Théorie du Cardinal Newman sur le développement du dogme chrétien. Paris 1896.
Rivington, L. The conversion of Cardinal Newman. 1896.
Barry, W. F. Cardinal Newman and Renan. Nat Rev 29 1897.
—— Newman. 1904, [1927] (rev).
—— The Turks, Cardinal Newman and the Council of Ten. 1919, 1920.
Brémond, H. Les sermons de Newman. Etudes 72 1897.
—— Newman: essai de biographie psychologique. Paris [1906]; tr 1907.
—— Newman: le développement du dogme chrétien. Paris 1906.
—— Autour de Newman. Annales de Philosophie Chrétienne Jan 1908.
—— L'inquiétude religieuse: aubes et lendemains de conversion. 2 vols 1909.
—— La vision et la rêve. Etudes June 1936.
Hemmer, H. Manning, Newman et la question de l'éducation des catholiques à Oxford. Revue d'histoire et de Littérature Religieuse 2 1897.
Mignot, E.-I. L'évolutionnisme religieux. Correspondant 186 1897.
Vere, A. de. In his Recollections, 1897.
Walsh, W. The secret history of the Oxford movement. 1897.
—— History of the Romeward movement in the Church of England 1833–64. 1900.
Firmin, A. (A. Loisy). Le développement chrétien d'après le Cardinal Newman. Revue du Clergé Français 17 1898.
—— Les preuves et l'èconomie de la révélation. Revue du Clergé Français 21 1900.
MacRae, A. Die religiöse Gewissheit bei Newman. Jena 1898.
Fairbairn, A.M. Catholicism: Roman and Anglican. 1899.
Gates, L. E. Newman as a prose-writer. In his Three studies in literature, New York 1899.

Thureau-Dangin, P. La renaissance catholique en Angleterre au XIXe siècle. 3 vols Paris 1899–1906; tr 2 vols 1914.
— Newman catholique, d'après des documents nouveaux. Paris 1912.
Alleaume, C. Newman et les conversions anglaises. Rouen 1900.
Donaldson, A. B. Five great Oxford leaders: Keble, Newman, Pusey, Liddon and Church. 1900.
Ridder, A. de. La renaissance catholique en Angleterre. Louvain [1900?].
Carry, E. Les années anglicanes du Cardinal Newman: trois conférences. Geneva 1901.
Faure (afterwards Goyau), L. F. Newman: sa vie et ses œuvres. Paris 1901.
Waller, A. R. and G. H. S. Burrow. John Henry Cardinal Newman. [1901].
Whyte, A. Newman: an appreciation. 1901.
Grappe, G. Newman: essai de psychologie religieuse; préface de P. Bourget. Paris 1902.
Semeria, G. Il Cardinale Newman. Rome 1902.
Dimnet, E. Quelques aspects du Cardinal Newman. Revue du Clergé Français 34 1903.
— La pensée catholique dans l'Angleterre contemporaine. Paris 1906.
— Newman et l'intellectualisme. Annales de Philosophie Chrétienne June, Aug 1907.
Fletcher, G. The Month and Newman. Month Jan–April 1903.
Juillière, de la. Newman et la connaissance religieuse. Bulletin de Littérature Ecclésiastique 1903.
Newman et la connaissaince religieuse. Bulletin de Littérature de Toulouse June 1903.
Bayart, P. La conversion de Newman. Arras 1904.
Bellamy, J. La théologie catholique au XIX siècle. Paris 1904 (Bibliothèque de Théologie Historique).
Blennerhassett, C. J. Newman: ein Beitrag zur religiösen Entwicklungsgeschichte der Gegenwart. Berlin 1904.
Gout, R. Du Protestantisme au Catholicisme: Newman. Anduze 1904.
Guiney, L. I. Hurrell Froude: memoranda and comments. 1904.
Jörimann, A.-Pl. Exposé critique de la doctrine de Newman. Geneva 1904.
Lilly, W. S. Cardinal Newman and the new generation. Fortnightly Rev Aug 1904.
— A last word on Newman. Fortnightly Rev June 1918.
Mounier, J. L'essai sur le développement de la doctrine chrétienne de Newman. Paris 1904.
Aveling, F. Universals and the illative sense. Dublin Rev 137 1905.
Gerrard, T. J. The Grammar of assent and the Sure future. Ibid.
— Bergson, Newman and Aquinas. Catholic World March 1913.
Fletcher, J. B. Newman and Carlyle: an unrecognized affinity. Atlantic Monthly May 1905.
Neville, W. P. (ed). Addresses to Cardinal Newman, with his replies. 1905.
Cardinal Newman and creative theology. Dublin Rev 138 1906.
Dawson, W. J. In his Makers of English prose, New York 1906.
Gasquet, A. (ed). Lord Acton and his circle. 1906.
Grandmaison, L. de. Newman considéré comme maître. Études 109–10 1906–7.
— Le développement du dogme chrétien. Revue Pratique d'Apologétique 3 1906.
Lebreton, J. Le primat de la conscience d'après Newman. Ibid.
— Autour de Newman. Revue Pratique d'Apologétique 3 1907.
— Newman: son œuvre littéraire et religieuse. Etudes Sept 1938.
Toohey, J. J. An indexed synopsis of An essay in aid of a grammar of asset. 1906.
Williams, W. J. Newman, Pascal, Loisy and the Catholic Church. 1906.
Guibert, J. Le réveil du Catholicisme en Angleterre au XIX siècle: conférences prêchées dans l'église Saint-Sulpice 1901–6. Paris 1907.
Tyrrell, G. The condemnation of Newman. Guardian 20 Nov 1907.
— Die Oxfordbewegung und die Wiedergeburt des Katholizismus in England. Akademische Bonifatiuskorrespondenz 1912.
— Newman. Akademische Bonifatiuskorrespondenz 1917.
— In S. Merkle and B. Besz, Religiöse Erzieher der Katholischen Kirche, Leipzig [1920].
— Kardinal Newman. Mainz 1921.
— Autorität und Gewissen. Hochland Jan 1939.
— Laie und Lehramt in der Kirche. Hochland Nov 1939.
— Newman oks ökumenische gestalt. Neue Ordnung 1946.
— Newman: ein grosser Brückenbauer zwischen den Konfessionen. Begegnung 13 1958.
— Kardinal Newmans ökumenische Sendung. In Festgabe Joseph Lortz, ed E. Iserloch and P. Manns vol 1, Baden-Baden 1958.
Morley, J. In his Miscellanies ser 4, 1908.
O'Dwyer, E. T. Cardinal Newman and the encyclical Pascendi dominici gregis: an essay. 1908.
Pesch, C. Theologische Zeitfragen. Freiburg 1908.
Pius X, Pope. [Brief to Bishop O'Dwyer, of Limerick]. In Acta Sanctae Sedis vol 41, 1908.
Sarolea, C. Cardinal Newman and his influence on religious life and thought. Edinburgh 1908.
Castle, W. R. Newman and Coleridge. Sewanee Rev 17 1909.
Cecil, A. In his Six Oxford thinkers, 1909.
— Wycliffe, Wesley, Newman: a study in contrasts. Dublin Rev 160 1917.
Gougaud, L. Le prétendu modernisme de Newman. Revue du Clergé Français 57 1909.
Carey, W. H. The story of the Oxford Movement. 1910.
Cornish, F. W. In his English church in the nineteenth century, 2 pts 1910.
Groot, J. V. de. Denkers van onzen tijd. Amsterdam 1910.
Rickaby, J. Newman memorial sermons. 1910.
— Index to the works of Newman. 1914.
Stock, E. In his English church in the nineteenth century, 1910.
Bucaille, V. Newman: histoire d'une âme. Paris 1912.
Cardinal Newman. Edinburgh Rev 215 1912.
Corcoran, T. Newman's ideals and Irish realities. Studies March 1912.
— Liberal studies and moral aims: a critical study of Newman's position. Thought 1 1926.
— Newman's theory of liberal education. Dublin 1929.
More, P. E. In his Shelburne essays ser 8, New York 1913.
Storr, V. F. In his Development of English theology in the nineteenth century 1800–60, 1913.
Fecker, F. Kardinal Newman und sein Weg zur Kirche. Munich 1914.
Foster, A. E. M. In his Anglo-Catholicism, 1914.
Dinsmore, C. A. Newman and Bright. Contract Quart 1915.
Feuling, D. J. H. Kardinal Newman. Historisch-politische Blätter 155 1915.
Ollard, S. L. In his A short history of the Oxford Movement, 1915.
— Newman decides. TLS 19 Jan 1946.

Ryan, E. Brownson and Newman. Ecclesiastical Rev 52 1915.
— College handbook to Newman. Washington 1930.
Stoel, H. Kardinal Newman. Gröningen 1915.
Ward, B. In his Sequel to Catholic emancipation [1830–50], 2 vols 1915.
Bloss, W. E. 'Twixt the old and the new: a study in the life and times of Newman. 1916.
Cadman, S. P. The three religious leaders of Oxford and their movements. New York 1916.
Wilson, R. F. Newman's church in Dublin [the University Church]. Dublin 1916.
Chesterton, C. The art of controversy: Macaulay, Huxley and Newman. Catholic World 1917.
Figgis, J. N. and R. V. Laurence. In their Selections from the correspondence of the first Lord Acton vol 1, 1917.
Laski, H. J. In his Studies in the problem of sovereignty, New Haven 1917.
Brickel, A. G. Cardinal Newman's theory of knowledge. Amer Catholic Quart Rev 43 1918.
— The Newman revival in Germany. Catholic World 117 1923.
Strachey, L. Cardinal Manning. In his Eminent Victorians, 1918.
Kelly, H. An examination of Newman's literary method. Dublin 1919.
Bonnegent, C. La théorie de la certitude dans Newman [with special reference to his An essay in aid of a grammar of assent]. Paris 1920.
Williams, S. T. Newman's literary preferences. Sewanee Rev 28 1920.
Przywara, E. Newmans Seele. Seele March 1921.
— Zum Newmanschen Denktypus. Jahrbuch des Verbandes der Vereine Katholischen Akademiker (Augsburg) 1922.
— Der Newmansche Seelentypus in der Kontinuität katholischer Aszese und Mystik. Jahrbuch des Verbandes der Vereine Katholischen Akademiker (Augsburg) 1923.
— Religionsbegründung: Max Scheler-J. H. Newman. Freiburg 1923.
— Ringen der Gegenwart. In his Gesammelte aufsätze 1922–27 vol 2, Augsburg 1929.
— Wege zu Newman. In his In und gegen: Stellungnahmen zur Zeit, Nuremberg 1955.
— and O. Karrer. Christentum: ein Aufbau. 8 vols Freiburg 1922. Selections. Vol 4 by E. Przywara, Einführung in Newmans Wesen und Werk.
Bacchus, F. J. Newman's Oxford university sermons. Month July 1922.
— How to read the Grammar of assent. Month Feb 1924.
Shuster, G. N. In his Catholic spirit in modern English literature, New York 1922.
— Newman: prose and poetry. Chicago 1925.
Cauchie, A. Le Cardinal Newman. Brussels 1923.
Knox, W. L. In his Catholic movement in the Church of England, 1923.
Mathieson, W. L. In his English church reform 1815–40, 1923.
Reilly, J. J. Newman as a controversialist. Catholic World 117 1923.
— Newman as a man of letters. New York 1925.
— The present significance of Newman. Thought 20 1945.
Webb, C. C. J. In his A century of Anglican theology and other lectures, Oxford 1923.
— Religious thought in the Oxford movement. 1928.
— Two philosophers of the Oxford movement. Philosophy 8 1933.
Battistini, P. Newman dans le mouvement d'Oxford 1833–9. Paris 1924.
Döberl, A. Döllinger und Newman. Gelbe Hette 1 1924.
Gore, C. The reconstruction of belief vol 3: The Holy Spirit and the Church. 1924.
Lunn, A. H. M. In his Roman converts, 1924.
Marín-Sola, F. L'évolution homogène du dogme catholique. Fribourg 1924.
Brilioth, Y. T. In his Anglican revival: studies in the Oxford movement, 1925.
De Havilland, J. R. Newman 1801–90. Dijon 1927.
Hartill, I. Lead, kindly light: an exposition of Newman's hymn. Chicago [1925].
Newman, B. Cardinal Newman: a biographical and literary study. 1925.
Pompen, A. Newmans idee van een universiteit. Nijmegen 1925.
White, N. J. D. John Henry Newman. 1925.
Boosten, J. P. John Henry Kardinal Newman. Hertogenbosch 1926.
Butler, E. C. The life and times of Bishop Ullathorne 1806–89. 2 vols 1926.
Fernandez, R. Messages. Paris 1926; tr 1927.
Geiger, S. Der Intuitionsbegriff in der katholischen Religionsphilosophie der Gegenwart. Freiburger Theologische Studien 30 1926.
Mozley, J. F. Newman's opportunity. Quart Rev 246 1926.
Rivière, J. Newman apologiste. Revue des Sciences Religieuses 6 1926.
Folghera, J.-D. Newman apologiste. Paris 1927; tr [1929].
Chevalier, J. Trois conférences d'Oxford: Saint Thomas, Pascal, Newman. Paris 1928.
Friedel, F. J. The mariology of Cardinal Newman. New York 1928.
Hardt, G. Newman als Prediger. Münster 1928.
Janssens, A. Anglicaansche bekeerlingen. Antwerp 1928.
Juergens, S. P. Newman on the psychology of faith in the individual. 1928.
— What is Newman's deepest message? Ecclesiastical Rev Feb 1928.
Karrer, O. Newman: Gebetbuch aus seinen Schriften gesammelt. Munich 1928.
— Kardinal J. H. Newman: Christliches reifen: texte zur religiösen lebensgestaltung. Licht vom licht VI, [1946].
— Newman and the spiritual crisis of the occident. Rev of Politics 9 1947.
— Die begründung des Gottesglaubens bei Newman. Hochland 45 1952.
— Newmanwerke und Newmanliteratur. Theologische Revue 50 1954.
— Newmans Weg in die Kirche und sein Weg in der Kirche. In J. Daniélou and H. Vorgrimler, Sentire ecclesiam. Freiburg 1961.
Tristram, H. Cardinal Newman and the function of education. Blackfriars 1928.
— Two leaders: Newman and Carlyle. Cornhill Mag Sept 1928.
— Newman and the oratory at Oxford. Oratory Parish Mag April 1933.
— Lead, kindly light: June 16 1833. Dublin Rev 193 1933.
— Newman and his friends. Ed J. L. May 1933.
— Cardinal Newman and the church of the Birmingham Oratory: a history and a guide. Gloucester [1934].
— Two suppressed passages from Newman's autobiographical memoirs, now first published. Revue Anglo-américaine 11 1934.
— Mr Newman and Father Clement. Dublin Rev 196 1935.
— Cardinal Newman and the Dublin Review. Dublin Rev 198 1936.
— Cardinal Newman's theses de fide and his proposed introduction to the French translation of the university sermons. Gregorianum 18 1937.
— The correspondence between Newman and the Comte de Montalembert. Dublin Rev 212 1949.

Tristram, H. F. v. Hügel and Newman. In Der beständige Aufbruch: Festschrift für Erich Przywara, ed S. Behn, Nuremberg 1959.
Durkin, M. A. Introductory studies in Newman. New York 1929.
Gwynn, D. R. In his Cardinal Wiseman, 1929.
Kilburn, E. E. Catholic emancipation and the second spring: a century's record, from 1829 to 1929. [1929].
MacKenna, B. A. Our Lady as seen by Cardinal Newman. Ecclesiastical Rev May 1929.
May, J. L. Cardinal Newman. 1929.
— Newman once more: The idea of a university. Catholic World March 1941.
— Scenes from the life of Newman. 1945.
O'Connell, D. M. A Newman centenary. Ecclesiastical Rev April 1929.
— Newman. Chicago 1930.
— A centenary of sermons. Commonweal 10 May 1931.
Semper, J. J. Questions and exercises to accompany Newman's The idea of a university. Chicago 1929.
Stewart, H. L. A century of Anglo-catholicism. 1929.
Burgum, E. B. Cardinal Newman and the complexity of truth. Sewanee Rev 38 1930.
Hovre, F. de. Le Catholicisme, ses pédagogues, sa pédagogie. Brussels 1930.
Martindale, C. C. Sibyl and sphinx: Newman and Manning in the 80s. Contemporary Rev Oct 1930.
— Newman and the Month. Month Dec 1950.
Olivero, F. La teoria poetica del Newman. Milan 1930.
Atkins, G. G. Life of Cardinal Newman. New York 1931.
Heseltine, G. C. In his English cardinals, 1931.
Baker, J. E. In his Novel and the Oxford movement, Princeton 1932.
Elbert, J. A. Newman's conception of faith prior to 1845. Philadelphia 1932.
— Evolution of Newman's conception of faith prior to 1845. Philadelphia 1933.
Jones, H. W. Two Oxford movements: Wesley and Newman. Hibbert Jnl 31 1932.
Leslie, S. In his Studies in sublime failure, 1932.
— In his Oxford movement 1833 to 1933, 1933.
— In Great catholics, ed C. C. H. Williamson 1938.
Simpson, W. J. S. In his History of the Anglo-Catholic revival from 1845. 1932.
Boycott, D. L. M. The secret history of the Oxford Movement. 1933.
Cross, F. L. Newman: with a set of unpublished letters. 1933.
— Newman and the doctrine of development. Church Quart Rev 115 1933.
D'Arcy, M. C. In The English way, ed M. Ward 1933.
Dawson, C. The spirit of the Oxford Movement. 1933.
Dimond, S. G. The philosophy and theology of the Oxford Movement and Anglo-Catholicism. London Quart 158 1933.
Donald, G. Men who left the Movement. 1933.
Faber, G. C. In his Oxford apostles: a character study of the Oxford Movement, 1933.
Flood, J. M. Cardinal Newman and Oxford. 1933.
Gladen, C. Die Erkenntisphilosophie Newmans im Licht der thomistischen Erkenntnislehre beurteilt. Paderborn 1933.
Guitton, J. La philosophie de Newman: essai sur l'idée de développement. Paris 1933.
Gunning, J. H. Newman: een boek voer protestanten en Roomschkatholieken. Amsterdam 1933.
Jackson, F. Newman's Idea of a university. 1933.
Kiener, Sr M. A. Newman the romantic, the friend, the leader. Ed G. K. Chesterton, Boston 1933.
Knox, E. A. The Tractarian Movement 1833–45: a study of the Oxford Movement as a phase of the religious revival in western Europe in the second quarter of the nineteenth century. 1933.
Mackeau, W. H. The eucharistic doctrine of the Oxford Movement. 1933.
McCorkell, E. J. Cardinal Newman and the Christian philosophic tradition. Toronto 1933.
Newman's autobiographical memoir relating to his tutorship at Oriel College. Revue Anglo-américaine 11 1933.
Ross, J. E. Newman: Anglican minister, Catholic priest, Roman Cardinal. [1933].
Schäfer, P. Die katholische Wiedergeburt der englischen Kirche. Munich 1933.
Smith, F. Fears and faith of Newman. Homiletic Rev 106 1933.
Stockley, W. F. P. Newman, education and Ireland. [1933].
Strong, L. A. G. Was Newman a failure? Nineteenth Century 113 1933.
Thirlwall, J. C. Cardinal Newman's literary preferences. MLN 48 1933.
Baker, A. E. In his Prophets for an age of doubt, 1934.
Dark, S. Newman. 1934.
DuBos, C. Henri Brémond: historian of the man capable of god. Dublin Rev 195 1934.
Gorce, D. Newman et les pères: sources de sa conversion et de sa vie intérieure: à l'occasion du centenaire du mouvement d'Oxford, 1833. Juvisy [1934].
— L'assentiment dans Newman. Etudes Carmélitaines 22 1937.
— Marie médiatrice et le mouvement d'Oxford. 1946.
— Introduction à Newman. Paris 1949.
— Le martyre de Newman: à la lumière par la croix. Paris [1961].
Grennan, M. R. The heart of Newman's Apologia. Ed J. J. Reilly, Toronto 1934.
Lamm, W. R. The spiritual legacy of Newman. Milwaukee 1934.
Sobry, P. Newman en zijn Idea of a university. Louvain 1934.
Ward, M. The Wilfrid Wards and the transition, vol I: The nineteenth century. 1934.
— Young Mr Newman. 1948.
— Het tragische van Newman's roeping en bestaan. Dietsche warande en Belfort July–Aug 1935.
Cockburn, G. H. Almost a critic. Expository Times Aug 1935.
Cronin, J. F. Cardinal Newman: his theory of knowledge. Washington 1935.
D'Cruz, F. A. Cardinal Newman: his place in religion and in literature. Madras [1935].
Kreischer, J. Wanderung zu Newman. Schildgenossen 15 1935.
— Wanderung zu Newman. Schildgenossen 15 1936.
— Die geistige Gestalt Newmans (zu seinem 50 todestag). Oberrhein. Pastoralblatt 1940.
Simon, P. Glauben und Erkennen nach Kardinal Newman. In Christliche Verwirklichung: Festgabe für Romano Guardini, Rothfels 1935.
Bouyer, L. Newman et le platonisme de l'âme anglaise. Revue de Philosophie 36 1936.
— Great preachers XIII: John Henry Newman. Theology 55 1952.
— Newman: sa vie, sa spiritualité. Paris 1952; tr 1958.
— Newman and English Platonism. Monastic Stud 1 1963.
Drees, L. Newman und seine Idea of a university im Lichte der Stilforschung. Hochland 33 1936.
Loosen, M. Newman in neuer Schau. Katholische Gedanke 9 1936.
Noack, U. Katholizität und Geistesfreiheit: nach den Schriften von John Dalberg-Acton 1834–1902. Frankfurt 1936.
O'Brien, J. H. John Henry Newman. Ecclesiastical Rev 76 1936.
Olive, M. Le problème de la Grammaire de l'assentiment d'après la correspondence entre Newman et William Froude. Bulletin de Littérature Ecclésiastique 37 1936.

Overmans, J. Harnack und Newman. Stimmen der Zeit 67 1936.
Pol, W. H. van de. De kerk in het leven en denken van Newman. Nijkerk 1936.
Bayer, R. J. Newman's Apologia: an enduring monument. Reading & Collecting March 1937.
Byrne, J. J. The notion of doctrinal development in the Anglican writings of Newman. Louvain 1937.
Collin, W. E. Cardinal Newman and recent French thought. Trans Royal Soc of Canada 3rd ser 31 1937.
Donahue, G. H. J. H. Cardinal Newman. Boston 1937.
McAllister, J. B. Newman rests. Commonweal 25 1937.
Noordmans, O. Newman en de oecumenische beweging. Nieuwe Theologische Studien Nov 1937.
Tardivel, F. Newman, éducateur. Paris 1937.
Vogel, C. J. de. De eigentlijke strekking van Newman's gedachten over de rechtvaardiging. Onder eigen vaadel 1937.
— Newmans gedachten over de rechtvaardigung: hun zin en recht ten opzichte van Luther en het protestantsche christendom. Wagenningen 1939. On the Lectures on justification.
Wrighton, B. The actuality of Newman. Arena I 1937.
Young, G. M. In his Daylight and champagne, 1937.
— Newman again. In his Last essays, 1950.
— and W. Handcock (ed). In their English historical documents 1833–74 vol 12, 1956.
Blyton, W. J. Side-lights on Newman. Month April 1938.
Delattre, E. Newman, éducateur. Etudes Anglaises 2 1938.
Grosche, R. Newman und die kirchliche Autorität; Newmans Bedeutung für die Gegenwart. In his Pilgernde Kirche, Freiburg 1938.
— Newman: zu seinen kritischen Schriften. Christliche Sonntag 12 1960.
Johnson, H. J. T. In his Anglicanism in transition, 1938.
Seiterich, E. Wege der Glaubensbegründung nach der sogenannten Immanenzapologetik. Freiburg 1938.
Soulairol, J. Actualité de Newman. Nouvelles Littéraires 8 Oct 1938.
Ancelet-Hustache, J. Actualité de Newman. Nouvelles Littéraires 14 Oct 1939.
Becker, W. Das Harren des Christen (nach Predigten Newmans). Würzburg 1939.
— Oekumenische Aspekte der Katholizität Newmans. In Festgabe Joseph Lortz, ed E. Iserloh and P. Manns vol 1, Baden-Baden 1958.
— Realisierung und realizing bei Newman. Theologische Jahrbuch 4 1960.
Mariella, Sr. Newman's Anglican sermons. Catholic World Jan 1939.
Newcomb, C. Newman and nature. Catholic World June 1939.
Siegmund, G. Newman: ein zeichen ökumenischer verständigung. Ostdeutsches Pastoralblatt (Breslau) 1939.
Fischer, E. Zum 50: todestag des Kardinals Newman. In Kirche und Leben: Jahrbuch der katholischen Schweiz, Immensee 1940.
Harrold, C. F. Newman and the Alexandrian Platonists. MP 37 1940.
— Newman: an expository and critical study of his mind, thought and art. New York 1945.
Tynan, M. The approach to Newman. Irish Ecclesiastical Record March 1940.
Wildman, J. H. Newman's first Apologia. Ecclesiastical Rev 102 1940.
Döpfner, J. Das Verhältnis von Natur und Übernatur bei Newman. Rome 1941.
Karl, A. Die Glaubensphilosophie Newmans. Grenzfragen zwischen Theologie und Philosophie 19 1941.
Ullathorne, W. B. In his From cabin-boy to Archbishop: the autobiography of Archbishop Ullathorne, 1941.
Fries, H. Die Religionsphilosophie Newmans. Tübingen 1942.
— Newmans Bedeutung für die Theologie. Theologische Quartalschrift 126 1946.
— Der gläubige Mensch: ein Beitrag zur Anthropologie Newmans. Theologische Quartalschrift 127 1947.
— Newman als moderner Kirchenvater. Die Kirche in der Welt: ein Losenblatt-lexicon vol 2, 1949.
— Newmans Weg zur katholischen Kirche. Religiöse Quellenschriften 13 1956.
— Newmans Beitrag zum Verständnis der Tradition. In M. Schmaus, Die mündliche Überlieferung, Munich 1957.
— Franz Xaver Kraus und Newman. In Der beständige Aufbruch: Festschrift für Erich Przywara, ed S. Behn, Nuremberg [1959].
— Newman: ein Wegbereiter der christlichen Einheit. Catholica 15 1961.
Ryan, A. S. Newman's conception of literature. In Critical studies in Arnold, Emerson and Newman, ed J. E. Baker, Iowa City 1942.
— The development of Newman's political thought. Rev of Politics 7 1945.
Woodruff, D. On Newman, Chesterton and exorbitance. In For Hilaire Belloc: essays in honour of his 72nd birthday, ed D. Woodruff, New York 1942.
Bernard, Sr M. Newman: 'saint of sincerity'. Catholic World April 1943.
Griffith, G. O. Interpreters of man: a review of secular and religious thought from Hegel to Barth. 1943.
Miller, L. G. Newman on the function of literature. Catholic World Aug 1943.
Annan, N. Books in general. New Statesman 25 March 1944.
P., S. C. and G. Crosse. Newman and a prayer. N & Q 29 Jan, 26 Feb 1944.
Walgrave, J. H. Kardinal Newman's theorie over de ontwikkeling van het dogma. Antwerp 1944; tr French, Tournai and Paris 1957; tr English, 1960 (as Newman the theologian).
— Newman's verantwoording van het geloof in de kerk. Antwerp 1946.
— Newman: wijsgeer van de zekerheid. Kultuurleven 20 1953.
— Newman san de Leuvense alma mater. Kultuurleven 21 1954.
— Newman's leer over het geweten, beschouwingen bij twee recente publicaties. Tijdschrift voor Philosophie 18 1956.
— Newman an de idee der doctrinale ontwikkeling. Tijdschrift voor Philosophie 20 1958.
— Newman over geloof en intellect. Kultuurleven 28 1958.
Benard, E. D. A preface to Newman's theology. St Louis 1945.
Donovan, C. F. Newman: a light amid encircling gloom. Amer Eccl Rev 113 1945.
Gwynn, D. Dominic Barberi and Newman's conversion. Clergy Rev Feb 1945.
Houghton, W. E. The art of Newman's Apologia. New Haven 1945.
— The issue between Kingsley and Newman. Theology Today 4 1947.
Newman: centenary essays. 1945.
Julia of the Trinity, Sr. Self-revelation in Newman's sermons. Catholic World Oct 1945.
Lloyd, R. D. Newman's Rubicon. Spectator 5 Oct 1945.
Marshall, R. M. Newman decides. TLS 27 Oct 1945.
Molony, J. C. A later-day saint. Blackwood's Mag Dec 1945.
Moody, J. John Henry Newman. New York 1945.
Mozley, J. H. Cardinal Newman and his forebears. N & Q Nov 1945.
Newman and Littlemore: a centenary anthology and appeal. Cowley Oxford 1945.

Newman decides: 'into port after a rough sea'. TLS 6 Oct 1945.
Ong, W. J. Newman and the religious life. Rev for Religions 4 1945.
— Newman's Essay on development in its intellectual milieu. Theological Stud 7 1946.
Ryan, J. K. Newman as poet. Thought 20 1945.
— and E. D. Benard (ed). American essays for the Newman centennial. Washington 1947. Contains a list of pbns of the centennial years 1944–6. Only a small selection from this material is listed here.
Tierney, M. (ed). A tribute to Newman: essays on aspects of his life and thought. Dublin [1945].
— Newman's doctrine of university education. Studies 42 1953.
Wheeler, G. (ed). Homage to Newman 1845–1945: a collection of essays. 1945.
Wise, J. W. Newman and the liberal arts. Thought 20 1945.
Flanagan, P. Newman: faith and the believer. Westminster Maryland 1946.
Haecker, T. Über Kardinal Newmans Grammatik der Zustimmung: über das Prinzip der Analogie. In his Christentum und Kultur, Munich 1946.
Hoeffken, T. Newman on liberal education. Kirkwood Missouri 1946.
Horne, E., P. Cadell and E. MacLagan. 'Swerga'. TLS 11–18 May 1946.
Lamborn, E. A. G. Newman's church at Littlemore. N & Q 9 Feb 1946.
Müller, G. Newmans Weg zur Kirche. Mannheim 1946.
Nédoncelle, M. Newman bienfaiteur de deux églises. Strasbourg 1946.
— La philosophie religieuse de Newman. Strasbourg 1946.
— L'influence de Newman sur Les yeux de la foi de Rousselot. Revue des Sciences Religieuses de l'Université de Strasbourg 27 1953.
— La spiritualité de Newman d'après ses poésies. Revue des Sciences Religieuses 30 1956.
— Newman et le développement dogmatique. Revue des Sciences religieuses 32 1958.
Schneider, R. Newmans Entscheidung. Freiburg 1946 and in his Weltreich und Gottesreich, Munich 1946.
Schwarzenbach, J. Newman: Zwiesprache des Lebens: aus den Werken ausgewählt und übertragen. Zürich 1946.
Simon, P. Newman and German catholicism. Dublin Rev 219 1946.
Sohngen, G. Newman: sein Gottesgedanke und seine Denkergestalt. Bonn 1946.
Wilberforce, R. Newman: his prophetic sense. Catholic World Jan 1946.
Conacher, W. M. Newman and liberal education. Queen's Quart 54 1947.
Middleton, R. D. Newman and Bloxam: an Oxford friendship. Oxford 1947.
— Newman at Oxford: his religious development. Oxford 1950.
— Tract XC. Journal of Ecclesiastical History 2 1951.
Emden, C. S. Cardinal Newman 1801–90: last links with Oriel. In his Oriel papers, Oxford 1948.
Knox, R. A. Newman and Roman Catholicism. Listener 11 March 1948.
Lutz, J. A. Newman: ein Zeit und Lebensbild. Zürich 1948.
Ruggles, E. Journey into faith: the Anglican life of Newman. New York 1948.
Sencourt, R. The life of Newman. 1948.
Hermans, F. Newman est-il un philosophe? Nouvelle Revue Théologique Feb 1949.
— Le second printemps, prédit par Newman. Nouvelle Revue Théologique 91 1959.
Hope, N. V. The issue between Newman and Kingsley: a consideration and a rejoinder. Theology Today 6 1949.
Pese, E. R. B. A suggested background for Newman's Dream of Gerontius. MP 47 1949.
Puchinger, G. De les van Newman's overgang naar Rome vor het hedendagse Nederlandse Calvinisme. Polemios: oecumenisch-nationale publicaties op Calvinistische grondslag 17 Dec, 25 Feb 1950.
Theis, N. Newman in der Gegenwart. Academia 4 1949.
— Newmans Philosophie der höheren Bildung. Luxemburg 1954.
Zeno, P. De apologetische waarde van Newman's Essay on development. In Donum lustrale catholicae universitatis noviomagensis oblatum, Nijmegen 1949.
— Newman's inwendig leven tijdens zijn jongensjaren. Annalen van het Tijmgenootschap 37 1949.
— Newman's psychological discovery: the illative sense. Franciscan Stud 10–12 1950–2.
— Pinkstergedachten: Newman; ingeleid en vertaald door P. Zeno OFM Cap. Ons Gestelyk Leven 29 1952.
— The Newman–Meynell correspondence. Franciscan Stud 12 1952.
— Newman's inner life, as shown by some of his poems. Irish Ecclesiastical Record 5th ser 81 1954.
— Newmans zelf-ingenommenheid en zelf-deprecatie. Annalen van het Thijmgenotschap 43 1955.
— Newman als priester en geestlijke leidsman. In De geestelijke leiding: verslagboek van de studiedagen van ons gestelijk leven voor priesters te stein, 1956.
— The reliability of Newman's autobiographical writings. Irish Ecclesiastical Record 5th ser 86–7 1956–7.
— Onze weg naar de zekerheid volgens Newman. Streven 10 1957.
— Newman, our way to certitude: an introduction to Newman's psychological discovery, the illative sense, and his Grammar of assent. Leyden 1957.
— Newman: le développement du dogme. Studia Catholica 34 1959.
— Newman: zijn geestelijk leven. Hilversum 1960.
— Newman and St Francis. Franciscan Annals 82 1960.
— Newman und Aristoteles. Streven 15 1962.
Boekraad, A. J. Newmannia. Katholiek Archief 5 1950.
— Newman's godsbewijs uit het geweten. Bijdragen 12 1951.
— Newman en de H. Schrift. Streven 7 1954.
— The personal conquest of truth according to Newman. Louvain 1955.
— Newman's argument of the existence of God. Philosophical Stud 6 1956.
— and H. Tristram. The argument from conscience to the existence of God according to Newman. Louvain 1961.
Crawford, C. E. Newman's Callista and the Catholic popular library. MLR 45 1950.
— The novel that occasioned Newman's Loss and gain. MLN 65 1950.
Culler, A. D. Newman on the uses of knowledge. Jnl of General Education 4 1950.
— The imperial intellect: a study of Newman's educational ideal. New Haven 1955.
Tillotson, G. Newman's Essay on poetry: an exposition and comment. In Perspectives of criticism, ed H. T. Levin, Cambridge Mass 1950; rptd (slightly rev) in his Criticism and the nineteenth century, 1951.
— In his Mid-Victorian studies, 1965. 3 articles.
Warren, A. H. Poetry with reference to Aristotle's Poetics, 1829. In his English poetic theory 1825–65, Princeton 1950.
Bantock, G. H. Newman and education. Cambridge Jnl 4 1951.
Havens, R. D. A parallel that is not a borrowing. MLN 66 1951.
K., A. Cardinal Newman and his forebears. N & Q 14 April, 26 May 1951.
McGrath, F. Newman's university: idea and reality. 1951.
— The consecration of learning: lectures on Newman's Idea of a university. Dublin 1962.

Svaglic, M. J. The structure of Newman's Apologia. PMLA 66 1951.
— The revision of Newman's Apologia. MP 50 1952.
— Newman and the Oriel fellowship. PMLA 70 1955.
— Charles Newman and his brothers. PMLA 71 1956.
Aubert, A. Newman: une psychologie concrète de la foi et une apologétique existentielle. Malines 1952.
Beales, A. C. F. In Pioneers of English education, ed A. V. Judges 1952.
Butler, C. Newman and modern education. Downside Rev 70 1952.
— The significance of Newman today: the theory of development. Dublin Rev 233 1959.
Gundersen, B. Cardinal Newman and apologetics. Skrifter utgitt av det Nroske Videnskaps-akademi i Oslo, Oslo 1952.
Kirk, R. The conservative mind of Newman. Sewanee Rev 60 1952.
Läpple, A. Der Einzelne in der Kirche: Wesenszüge einer Theologie des Einzelnen nach Newman, pt 1. Munich 1952.
O'Faolain, S. Newman's way: the odyssey of Newman. New York 1952.
Colby, R. A. The structure of Newman's Apologia pro vita sua in relation to his theory of assent. Dublin Rev 227 1953.
— Newman on Aristotle's Poetics. MLN 71 1956.
Cranny, T. A study in contrasts: Newman and Faber. Ecclesiastical Rev 129 1953.
Doolin, W. Newman and his medical school: the fateful first lustrum 1855–60. Studies 42 1953.
Hogan, J. J. Newman and literature. Ibid.
Holloway, J. In his Victorian sage, 1953.
Horgan, J. D. Newman on faith and reason. Studies 42 1953.
Lawlis, M. E. Newman on the imagination. MLN 68 1953.
Parkinson, H. J. (ed). Centenary addresses on Newman's Idea of a university. 1953.
Sumner, W. L. Newman and science. Nature 172 1953.
Wheeler, T. S. Newman and science. Studies 42 1953.
Yanitelli, V. R. (ed). A Newman symposium: report on the tenth annual meeting of the Catholic Renascence Society at the College of the Holy Cross, Worcester Mass 1952. New York 1953.
Kerrigan, A. More about Cardinal Newman: an important contribution to the history of scriptural exegesis. Irish Ecclesiastical Record 5th ser 8 1954.
Schiavo, C. Le theoria del' assenso nel Newman e nel Rosmini. Estratto dall' Annuario 13 1954.
Allen, L. Une lettre à Newman de l'évêque de la Rochelle, Clément Villecourt. Revue d'Histoire de l'Eglise de France 41 1955.
Bartz, W. Die demonstratio catholica des Eusebius Amort und der Konvergenzbeweis Newmans. Trierer Theologische Zeitschrift 64 1955.
Bastable, J. D. Cardinal Newman's philosophy of belief. Irish Ecclesiastical Record 5th ser 83 1955.
— The germination of belief within probability, according to Newman. Philosophical Stud 11 1961.
Dibble, R. A. Newman: the concept of infallible doctrinal authority. Washington 1955.
Dinwiddy, H. Cardinal Newman: the literary aspect. Dublin Rev 229 1955.
Duval, A. Newman. Revue des Sciences Philosophiques et Théologiques 39 1955.
Gawlik, W. Newmanowska analiza poznania konkretnego i religijnego. Collectanea Theologica 26 1955.
Manoir, H. du. Marie, nouvelle Eve, dans l'œuvre de Newman. Études Mariales 3 1955.
Messner, J. Newman, Haecker, Hochland. Hochland 48 1955.
Strolz, W. Newman, Kirchenvater der Neuzeit. Wort und Wahrheit 10 1955.
— Platon, Newman, Kafka und die Musik. Grosse Entschluss 12 1956.
— Leben und Werk von Newman. Anzeiger für Katholische Geistlichkeit 70 1961.
— Newman als Prediger. Ibid.
Artz, J. Newman und die Intuition. Theologische Quartalschrift 136 1956; tr 1957 (in Philosophy today).
— Die Eigenstandigkeit der Erkenntnistheorie Newmans. Theologische Quartalschrift 139 1959.
— Newman's contribution to the theory of knowledge. Philosophy Today 4 1960.
Baum, P. F. The road to Palermo. South Atlantic Quart 55 1956. On Lead, kindly light.
Baus, K. Kardinal Newmans Bedeutung für die Gegenwart. Trierer Theologische Zeitschrift 65 1956.
Bussche, H. Newman en de bijbel. Collationes Brugenses et Gandavenses 2nd ser 3 1956.
Cameron, J. M. John Henry Newman. 1956 (Br Council pamphlet).
Davis, H. F. Newman: Christian or humanist. Blackfriars 37 1956.
— Newman on educational method: educating for real life. Dublin Rev 230 1956–7.
— Newman: the individual and the church. Blackfriars 39 1958.
— Is Newman's theory of development catholic? Ibid.
— Newman, servant of God: a characteristic of his spirituality. Oscotian 19 1958.
— Newman the prophet. Ave Maria 9 1958.
— The genius of Newman. Mermaid (Birmingham University) 25 1959.
— The part played respectively by hierarchy and laity in the church according to Newman. L'ecclésiologie au XIXe siècle 5 1959.
— The genius of Newman. Newman 4 1960.
— In English spiritual writers, ed C. Davis [1961].
— Newman on faith and personal certitude. Jnl of Theological Stud 12 1961.
— Newman: theologia of the word in Christian life. Blackfriars 42 1961.
Elliott-Binns, L. E. English thought 1860–1900: the theological aspect. 1956.
Schiffers, N. Die Einheit der Kirche nach Newman. Düsseldorf 1956.
— Schrift und Tradition bei Newman. In Schrift und Tradition, Deutsche Arbeitsgemeinschaft für Mariologie, Essen 1962.
Schweik, R. C. Bishop Blougram's miracles. MLN 71 1956. On Browning's mistaken attribution of Newman's ideas to Cardinal Wiseman.
Wolff, P. Das Akademische und die Theologie nach Newman. Katholische Gedanke 12 1956.
Brunner, A. Idee und Entwicklung bei Hegel und Newman. Scholastik 32 1957.
Chadwick, O. From Bossuet to Newman: the idea of doctrinal development. Cambridge 1957.
— In his Mind of the Oxford Movement, 1960.
Dessain, C. S. Cardinal Newman on the theory and practice of knowledge: the purpose of the Grammar of assent. Downside 75 1957.
— Newman's first conversion. Studies 46 1957.
— Cardinal Newman's papers. Dublin Rev 234 1960.
— A poem wrongly ascribed to Newman. Bodleian Lib Record 6 1960.
— Newman's spirituality and its value today. Clergy Rev May 1960.
— Cardinal Newman on the laity. Life of Spirit 16 1961.
— Newman's spirituality: its value today. In English spiritual writers, ed C. Davis [1961].
— Cardinal Newman and the doctrine of uncreated grace. Clergy Rev 40 1962.
Fenton, J. C. Some Newman autobiographical sketches and the Newman legend. American Ecclesiastical Rev 136 1957.

Fenton, J. C. Newman's complaints examined in the light of priestly spirituality. Amer Ecclesiastical Rev 138 1958.
— The Newman legend and Newman's complaints. Amer Ecclesiastical Rev 139 1958.
Hammel, W. Der Einzelne und das Gewissen: religionsphilosophische Gedanken im Auschluss an das Werk Newmans. Kirche in der Welt 9 1957.
— Newmans Stellung in der Geistesgeschichte des 19 Jahrhunderts. Ibid.
Kenny, T. P. The political thought of Newman. 1957.
Molitor, A. Newman et l'intelligence chrétienne. Revue Nouvelle 26 1957.
Nigg, W. In his Prophetische Denker, Zürich 1957.
Reardon, B. M. G. Newman and the psychology of belief. Church Quart Rev 158 1957.
Willam, F. M. Newman und die Lehre von der unbefleckten Empfängnis. In Virgo Immaculata: acta congressus mariologici-mariani Romae anno MCMLIV, 14 1957.
— Newman, der grosse Kerygmatiker. Theologie und Glaube 5 1957.
— Newman und die kirchliche Lehrtradition. Orientierung 22 1958.
— Aristotelische Erkenntnislehre bei Whately und Newman. Freiburg 1960.
— Cardinalis Newman theses de doctrina et devotione Mariana et motus oecumenicus. In De Mariologia et oecumenismo, Rome 1962.
Biemer, G. The Anglican response to Newman? Philosophical Stud 8 1958.
— Die doppelte Suffizienz der Glaubensquellen nach Kardinal Newman. Theologische Quartalschrift 140 1960.
— Newman an das Vaticanum: Newmans Entwicklung der christlichen Lehre für heute. Wort und Wahrheit 16 1961.
— Überlieferung und Offenbarung: die Lehre von der Tradition nach Newman. In Überlieferung in der neueren Theologie, ed J. R. Geiselmann vol 4, Freiburg 1961.
— Kardinal Newman und die Selbstreform der Kirche. Oberrheinisches Pastoralblatt 64 1963.
— Traditio et scriptura iuxta anglicanos et Cardinalem Newman. In De scriptura et traditione, Rome 1963.
Blehl, V. The holiness of Newman. Month June 1958.
— Newman's delation. Dublin Rev 234 1960.
— Newman and the missing miter. Thought 35 1960.
— Newman on Latin prose style. Classical Folia 15 1961.
— Newman on trial: the Achilli trial. Month Feb 1962.
Brooke, O. Some reflections on Newman and the problem of contemporary theology. Pax 48 1958.
Butts, D. Newman's influence on Matthew Arnold's theory of poetry. N & Q June 1958.
The cause of Newman. Tablet 7, 21 June 1958, 24 Oct 1959, 21 Jan 1961.
Greaves, R. W. Golightly and Newman 1834–45. Jnl of Ecclesiastical History 9 1958.
Jazwisuka, M. R. Cardinal Newman and devotion to Our Lady. Unitas 10 1958.
Kaiser, F. J. The concept of conscience according to Newman. Washington 1958.
McManus, L. Newman and the Newman legend. Amer Ecclesiastical Rev 139 1958.
Renz, W. Newmans Idee einer Universität: Probleme höherer Bildung. Fribourg 1958.
— Um das Verständnis von Newmans Beitrag zur Theologie. Freiburger Zeitschrift für Philosophie und Theologie 6 1959.
Reynolds, E. E. Three cardinals: Newman, Wiseman, Manning. 1958.
Robinson, J. Newman's use of Butler's arguments. Downside Rev 76 1958.
Smith, B. A. Dean Church: the Anglican response to Newman. 1958.
Albert, Fr de l'Annonciation. Douce lumière de la nuit: Newman en marche vers la terre promise. Carmel 3–4 1959.
Beckmann, J. F. Another view of Newman. Amer Ecclesiastical Rev 138 1959.
Bohlen, H. Newmans Idee einer Universität. Theologische Revue 55 1959.
Bokenkotter, T. S. Cardinal Newman as an historian. Louvain 1959.
Brose, O. J. Church and Parliament: the reshaping of the Church of England 1828–60. Stanford 1959.
Cockshut, A. O. J. In his Anglican attitudes: a study of Victorian religious controversies, 1959.
Farge, J. L. Cardinal Newman and Bishop Stensen. Stenionana Catholica 5 1959.
Gill, J. M. Newman's dialectic in the Idea of a university. Quart Jnl of Speech 45 1959.
Hamer, J. Les maîtres du XIX siècle: Mohler, Newman, Scheeben. Revue des Sciences Philosophiques et Théologiques 43 1959.
Rombold, G. Das Wagnis des Glaubens: Newmans Grundlegung einer Philosophie der Person. Wort und Wahrheit 14 1959.
Barmann, L. F. Newman and the theory of doctrinal development. Amer Ecclesiastical Rev 143 1960.
— The spiritual teaching of Newman's early sermons. Downside Rev July 1962.
Dautzenburg, G. Newmans Kritik am Gentleman-ideal. Theologie und Glaube 50 1960.
Dupuis, B. De l'ombre à la lumière: introduction aux écrits spirituels de Newman. Vie Spirituelle 42 1960.
Hiemerer, M. Kardinal Newman und die Einheit der Kirche. In Das Alle eins seien, ed E. M. Heufelderer, Recklinghausen 1960.
Martin, A. Autobiography in Newman's novels. Month May 1960.
Novak, M. Newman on Nicea. Theological Stud 21 1960.
Whyte, J. H. Newman in Dublin: fresh light from the archives of propaganda. Dublin Rev 234 1960.
Browne, R. K. Newman and von Hügel: a record of an early meeting. Month July 1961. Reply by M. Hanbury, Oct 1961.
Dupuy, B. D. Bulletin d'histoire des doctrines: Newman. Revue des Sciences Philosophiques et Théologiques 45 1961.
Herrick, F. H. Gladstone, Newman and Ireland in 1881: correspondence. Catholic Historical Rev 47 1961.
Jordan, M. L. Question of aims: Newman and Pius XI on education. Catholic Educator 31 1961.
Lawler, J. G. Newman: biography or psychography? Renascence 14 1961.
Altholtz, J. L. In his Liberal Catholic movement in England: the Rambler and its contributors 1848–64. 1962.
Deen, L. W. Rhetoric of Newman's Apologia. ELH 29 1962.
MacDougall, H. A. The Acton–Newman relations: the dilemma of Christian liberalism. New York 1962.
Trevor, M. Newman: light in winter. 1962; Newman: the pillar of the cloud, 1962. A biography.
Springer, H. Quelques aspects des rapports entre les sciences et la foi dans l'œuvre du Cardinal Newman. Nouvelle Revue Théologique 85 1963.
Stern, J. Traditions apostoliques et magistères selon Newman. Revue des Sciences Philosophiques et Théologiques 47 1963.
Tracy, G.-M. Le Cardinal Newman. Paris [1963].

C. W.

JOHN RUSKIN

1819–1900

The works of Ruskin pbd before 1868 went out of copyright in 1907, and all edns since then, except those issued by Ruskin's publisher, George Allen (or by arrangement with him, as WC and Tauchnitz edns) are based on the early and in many cases unrevised text. There were no copyright edns of Ruskin pbd in America before the Brantwood edn of the Collected works 1891, *except the New York edn of the* Lectures on art 1870. *An attempt has been made to list here all non-copyright edns to 1900; it is, however, certain that many have been overlooked.*

Bibliographies

Allibone, S. A. A critical dictionary of English literature, and British and American authors, vol 2, Philadelphia 1870, pp. 1894–6. Useful for contemporary reviews and American edns.

[Shepherd, R. H.] The bibliography of Ruskin from 1834 to the present time. [1878], 1881 (5th edn).

Axon, W. E. A. Ruskin: a bibliographical biography. Manchester 1879, 1881 (enlarged). Rptd from Papers of Manchester Library Club vol 5.

Kennedy, W. S. A bibliography of Ruskin. Literary World (Boston) 13 June 1885.

Wise, T. J. and J. P. Smart. A bibliography of the writings in prose and verse of Ruskin. 19 pts 1889–93 (priv ptd), 2 vols 1964. The most minute account of the various early edns, listing some of the more important early reviews.

Jameson, M. E. A bibliographical contribution to the study of Ruskin. Cambridge Mass 1901. The fullest list of American edns, but at second hand and careless.

Copyright and copy-wrong: the authentic and the unauthentic Ruskin. 1907. Not a bibliography, but a summary of the controversy that arose when those of Ruskin's works that were ptd before 1865 went out of copyright in 1907, and were rptd in large numbers in their unrevised form.

Cook, E. T. and A. D. O. Wedderburn. The works of Ruskin: library edition, vol 38: Bibliography. 1912. Much the most comprehensive and reliable bibliography, including references to the detailed bibliographies prefixed to each work separately in the earlier vols of the set.

Carter, J. and H. G. Pollard. An enquiry into the nature of certain nineteenth-century pamphlets. 1934. 8 of the pamphlets discussed are by Ruskin.

Collections

Collected works. 15 vols New York 1861–3, 13 vols New York 1861–3.

Collected works. 11 vols 1871–80. Vol 1: Sesame and lilies, 1871; vol 2: Munera pulveris, Keston 1872; vol 3: Aratra Pentelici, Keston 1872; vol 4: The eagle's nest, Keston. 1872; vol. 5: Time and tide, Keston 1872; vol. 6: The crown of wild olive, Orpington 1873; vol 7: Ariadne Florentina, Orpington 1876; vol 8: Val d'Arno, Orpington 1874; vol 9: The queen of the air, Orpington 1874; vol 10: The two paths, Orpington 1878; vol 11: A joy for ever, Orpington 1880.

Collected works. 30 vols New York 1876, 20 vols New York 1876, 25 vols New York 1884 (Library edn), 12 vols New York 1885 (New edn), 19 vols New York 1886 (Popular edn), 18 vols New York 1886, 26 vols New York 1897 (New popular edn), 13 vols (including life by J. A. Hobson), New York 1899 (St Mark's edn), Albany [c 1900], 26 vols Boston 1900, 1900 (both illustr), 13 vols Boston 1900, 1900 (both illustr).

Selected works. 8 vols New York 1885, 4 vols Chicago 1900.

Collected works: Brantwood edition, with introductions by C. E. Norton. 22 vols New York 1891–2. First authorized American edn.

The poems of Ruskin: now first collected from original manuscript and printed sources, and edited in chronological order, with notes, biographical and critical, by W. G. Collingwood. 2 vols Orpington 1891.

Poems, collected and edited by James Osborne Wright. New York [1894?].

Ausgewählte Werke von Ruskin. Ed C. Broicher and W. Scholermann 15 vols Leipzig 1900–4.

The works of Ruskin: library edition. Ed E. T. Cook and A. D. O. Wedderburn 39 vols 1902–12. The only complete edn, reprinting almost every word Ruskin is known to have written and edited with meticulous care. The following works were first ptd here: Reply to Blackwood's criticism of Turner, 1836—the first draft of Modern painters; Letters on painted glass, 1844; Notes on the Louvre, 1844, 1849, 1854; An essay on baptism, 1850–1; Letters on politics, 1852; Notes on German galleries, 1859; The Rede Lecture at Cambridge, 1867; The aesthetic and mathematical schools of art in Florence, 1874; Studies in the discourses of Sir Josua Reynolds, 1875; Final lectures at Oxford, 1884; The grammar of Silica, nd; Letters to his father (various dates). Important addns or projected continuations to the following works were also included: Modern painters; The seven lamps of architecture; The stones of Venice; The queen of the air; Fors clavigera; Aratra pentelici; Love's Meinie; Mornings in Florence; Proserpina; Deucalion; Bibliotheca pastorum; Fiction, fair and foul; 'Our fathers have told us' (pt iii, Ara coeli); The pleasures of England; Praeterita; Dilecta.

Poems, with an essay on the author by G. K. Chesterton. 1906 (ML).

Collected works: Routledge's new universal edition. 15 vols 1907. Non-copyright; works as pbd before 1865.

The Ruskin House edition. 4 vols 1907 (WC).

A walk in Chamouni and other poems. [Ed J. R. Tutin] Hull 1908.

Selections and Extracts

The true and the beautiful in nature, art, morals and religion, selected from the writings of Ruskin with a notice of the author. Ed L. C. Tuthill, New York 1858 (2nd edn) etc.

Selections from the writings of Ruskin. [Ed W. S. Williams] 1861 etc.

Selections from the writings of Ruskin. Ed W. G. Collingwood 2 vols Orpington 1893 etc. Vol 1 is practically identical with the preceding item.

Ruskin on music. Ed A. M. Wakefield, Orpington 1894.

Ruskin on education. Ed W. Jolly, Orpington 1894 etc.

The Ruskin reader. [Ed W. G. Collingwood] Orpington 1895 etc.

Studies in both arts: being ten subjects drawn and described by Ruskin. [Ed W. G. Collingwood] Orpington 1895.

Was wir lieben und pflegen müssen: eine Sammlung Natur-Ansichten und Schilderungen aus den Werken des Ruskin. Ed J. Feis, Strasbourg 1895.

Turner and Ruskin: an exposition of Turner from the writings of Ruskin. Ed F. Wedmore 2 vols 1900.

Ruskin on pictures: a collection of criticisms by Ruskin not heretofore reprinted. Ed E. T. Cook 1902.

Obras escogidas. Ed E. Gonzalea-Blanco 2 vols Madrid [1906].

Ruskin: pages choisies, avec une introduction de Robert de la Sizeranne. Paris 1909 etc.

Readings from Ruskin. Ed S. Cunnington [1921].

Selections from Ruskin. Ed A. V. Benson, Cambridge 1923.

Selections from the prose. Ed C. I. Thomson [1925].

A book of Ruskin. Ed E. M. Hewetson 1927.

Ruskin as literary critic. Ed A. H. R. Ball, Cambridge 1928.

Selected writings. Ed P. C. Quennell 1952.

The lamp of beauty. Ed J. Evans 1959.

The genius of Ruskin. Ed J. D. Rosenberg 1963.

Ruskin today. Ed K. Clark 1964.

§ I

Ruskin's catalogues of drawings, minerals etc 1857–89, and his St George's Guild pbns 1878–85, have not been included. For them and for such Ruskiniana as catalogues of St George's Museum and pbns and magazines of Ruskin Societies, the bibliographies of T. J. Wise and J. P. Smart and of E. T. Cook and A. D. O. Wedderburn, above, should be consulted.

Salsette and Elephanta: a prize poem. Oxford 1839, Orpington 1789; rptd in Oxford prize poems, Oxford 1839, 1846.

The Scythian guest: a poem. 1849. A forgery executed between 1880 and 1890; *see also* Collected works, ed E. T. Cook and A. D. O. Wedderburn, vol 2 pp. 101–2; and J. Carter and G. Pollard, An enquiry into the nature of certain nineteenth-century pamphlets, 1934, pp. 225–6. The poem was first ptd in Friendship's offering, 1840, pp 52–60.

Modern painters: their superiority in the art of landscape painting to all the ancient masters proved by examples of the true, the beautiful, and the intellectual, from the works of modern artists, especially those of J. M. W. Turner, by a graduate of Oxford. 1843, 1844 (with new preface), 1846 (with new preface), New York 1847, London 1848, 1851 (with Ruskin's name for the first time), 1857, 1867; vol 2, 1846 (anon), 1848, 1851 (with Ruskin's name for the first time), 1856, 1869, 2 vols Orpington 1883 (rev and rearranged), New York 1883, Orpington 1885, 1888, 1891; vol 3, 1856, 1867; vol 4, 1856, 1868; vol 5, 1860; 5 vols New York 1865, London 1873 (Autograph edn), New York 1876, 1882, 2 vols New York 1884, 5 vols 1885, 5 vols Orpington 1888, 5 vols New York 1889, Orpington 1892, 2 vols Boston 1894, 5 vols New York 1894, Orpington 1897, 1898 etc; ed L. Cust 5 vols 1907 (EL; text from 1st edns); tr German, 1902–4.

Frondes agrestes: readings in Modern painters. Orpington 1875, New York 1876, 1876, Orpington 1876, 1878, 1879, 1880, New York 1880, Orpington 1883, 1884, 1886, 1889, 1890, 1891, 1893, 1895, 1895, 1896, 1898, 1899, New York 1899, 1900, London 1900, 1902.

Ruskin on painting, with a biographical sketch. New York 1879.

In montibus sanctis: studies of mountain form and of its visible causes, collected and completed out of Modern painters. 2 pts Orpington 1884–5. Rptd with Hortus inclusus, New York 1894.

Coeli enarrant: studies of cloud form and of its visible causes, collected and completed out of Modern painters. Pt 1 (all pbd) Orpington 1885. Rptd with Hortus inclusus, New York 1894.

Modern painters: a volume of selections. 1909.

Modern painters. Abridged and ed A. J. Finberg 1927.

Wedderburn, A. D. O. Modern painters: general index, bibliography and notes. Orpington 1888.

Mr Ruskin's Modern painters. Quart Rev 98 1856.

[Chorley, H. F.] Ruskinism. Edinburgh Rev 103 1856.

[Morris, W. and E. Burne-Jones. Ruskin and the Quarterly. Oxford & Cambridge Mag June 1856.

Pictures and picture criticism. Nat Rev 1856.

Literary style. Fraser's Mag April 1857.

Dolk, L. The reception of Modern painters. MLN 57 1942.

Burd, van A. Another light on the writing of Modern painters. PMLA 68 1953.

—— Ruskin's defence of Turner: the imitative phase. PQ 37 1958.

—— Background to Modern painters. PMLA 74 1959.

The seven lamps of architecture, with illustrations drawn and etched by the author. 1849, New York 1849, London 1855, New York 1876, Orpington 1880, New York 1880, Orpington 1883, New York 1884, 1885, 1885, Orpington 1886, New York 1889, Orpington 1890, 1891, 1894, 1895, 1897, 1898, 1899; ed R. Sturgie, New York 1899, 1900 (9 edns) etc; ed S. Image 1907 (text EL from 1st edn); ed A. Meynell 1910 (text from 1st edn); tr French, 1900; German, 1900. Index by A. D. O. Wedderburn, 1890 (priv ptd).

The King of the Golden River, or the black brothers: a legend of Styria. Illustr Richard Doyle 1851 (3 edns), 1856, Boston 1856 (in Curious stories), London 1859, New York 1860, London 1863, 1867, Boston 1875 (in Little Classics, ed. R. Johnson, vol 10), Boston 1876, New York 1876, Orpington 1882, New York 1882, London 1885, 1885, Boston 1885, Orpington 1886, 1888, New York 1888, 1888, Boston 1888, New York 1890, 1890, Orpington 1892, New York 1895, Boston 1895, 1899, New York 1899, 1900 etc. 1907 (EL); ed E. A. Noble, New York 1930; ed A. B. Allen 1946; ed M. L. Becker, Cleveland 1946; tr German, 1861, 1861; Italian, 1891; Welsh, 1909.

The stones of Venice, vol 1; The foundations, with illustrations drawn by the author. 1851, 1858; vol 2: The sea stories, with illustrations drawn by the author. 1853, 1867. Vol 3: The Fall, with illustrations drawn by the author. 1853, 1867. 3 vols New York 1865; London 1874; Orpington 1886, 1898, 1900 etc; ed L. M. Phillipps, 3 vols 1907 (EL); abridged by J. G. Links 1960; tr German, 1903; Hungarian, 1907.

Examples of the architecture of Venice, selected and drawn to measurement from the edifices by John Ruskin. 1851; 1887.

On the nature of Gothic: and herein the true functions of the workman in art. Being the greater part of the sixth chapter of the second volume of Mr Ruskin's Stones of Venice. 1854, 1854; 1892 (Kelmscott Press); Orpington 1899, 1900; tr French, 1907, 1908 (2 versions); Swedish [c. 1908]; Danish, 1917.

Notice of the paintings by Tintoretto, in the Scuola da San Rocco, at Venice. Extracted from Mr Ruskin's Stones of Venice, vol 3. Arundel Soc [1857].

The stones of Venice: introductory chapters and local indices for the use of travellers, while staying in Venice and Verona. 2 vols Orpington 1879–81, 1881–5, 1884–8, 1888–90, 1890. 1894, 1896, 1897, 1900, 1902, 1904, 1905; Leipzig 1906, 1907; tr French, 1905 (with preface, also ptd separately, by R. de la Sizeranne).

Selections from the Stones of Venice. Ed E. A. Parker 1925.

[Wedderburn, A. D. O.] The stones of Venice: index. 1886 (priv ptd).

Something on Ruskinism; with a 'vestibule' in rhyme. By an architect. 1851. Parody.

Notes on the construction of sheepfolds. 1851, 1851, Orpington 1875, New York 1876, Orpington 1879. Rptd in On the old road vol 2, 1885.

Dyce, W. Notes on shepherds and sheep. 1851.

A reply to Notes on the construction of sheepfolds by a graduate of the University of Cambridge. 1851.

Two letters concerning Notes on the construction of sheepfolds addressed to the Rev. F. D. Maurice by John Ruskin in 1851. Ed F. J. Furnivall 1890 (priv ptd).

Maurice, F. D. Three letters concerning Ruskin's Notes on the construction of sheepfolds. In Literary anecdotes of the nineteenth century, ed W. R. Nicoll and T. J. Wise vol 2 1896; also ptd separately.

Pre-Raphaelitism, by the author of Modern painters. 1851, 1862 (with Ruskin's name), New York 1876 (with other essays by Ruskin); 1891; ed W. M. Rossetti, Boston

1899; ed L. Binyon 1907 (EL) (with other essays by Ruskin). Also rptd in On the old road vol 1, 1885.

Rippingille, E. V. A reply to the author of Modern painters in his defence of Pre-Raphaelitism. 1852.

Young, Edward. Art, its constitution and capacities. Bristol 1854.

—— Pre-Raphaelitism: or a popular enquiry into some newly-asserted principles of art. 1857.

Ballantyne, John. What is Pre-Raphaelitism? Edinburgh 1856.

Thomas, W. C. Pre-Raphaelitism tested by the principles of Christianity. 1861.

National Gallery. Two letters to the Editor of the Times by the author of Modern painters. 1852. A forgery executed 1880–90; see Collected works, ed E. T. Cook and A. D. O. Wedderburn vol 12 p. 396, and J. Carter and H. G. Pollard, An enquiry into the nature of certain nineteenth-century pamphlets, 1934 pp. 227–9. The letters appeared in Times 4 Jan 1847, 29 Dec 1852, rptd in The arrows of the chace vol 1, 1880.

'Verax'. The abuses of the National Gallery. 1847. Includes Ruskin's first letter.

Moore, Morris. Revival of vandalism at the National Gallery: a reply to Messrs Ruskin, Heaphy and Wornum's letters in the Times. 1853.

Giotto and his works in Padua: being an explanatory notice of the series of woodcuts executed for the Arundel Society after the frescoes in the Arena Chapel. 1854. Really 3 pts 1853, 1854, 1860, bound up as 1 vol 1877, New York 1890, Orpington 1900, 1905.

Lectures on architecture and painting delivered at Edinburgh in November 1853, with illustrations drawn by the author. 1854, New York 1854, London 1855, New York 1885, Orpington 1891; ed C. E. Norton, New York 1892; Orpington 1899, London 1902 etc, 1907 (EL) (with other essays by Ruskin).

The opening of the Crystal Palace considered in some of its relations to the prospects of art. 1854. Rptd in On the old road vol 1, 1885.

Notes on some of the principal pictures exhibited in the rooms of the Royal Academy, 1855. 1855, 1855 (anon), 1855 (with suppl), 1907 (EL) (with other essays by Ruskin). Modern painters vol 2 (2nd edn) had included as Addenda: Notes on pictures exhibited in the Royal Academy, 1848. The later Notes, below, are all included in EL (1907), above.

Notes on some of the principal pictures exhibited in the rooms of the Royal Academy, and the Society of Painters in Water Colours, no 2, 1856. 1856, 1856, 1856 (adds Postscript; 4 edns).

Notes on some of the principal pictures exhibited in the rooms of the Royal Academy, and the Society of Painters in Water Colours, no 3, 1857. 1857, 1857.

Notes on some of the principal pictures exhibited in the rooms of the Royal Academy, the Old and New Societies of Painters in Water Colours, and the French Exhibition, no 4, 1858. 1858.

Notes on some of the principal pictures exhibited in the rooms of the Royal Academy, the Old and New Societies of Painters in Water Colours, the Society of British Artists, and the French Exhibition, no 5, 1859. 1859.

Notes on some of the principal pictures exhibited in the rooms of the Royal Academy, 1875. Orpington 1875 (4 edns).

Notes on so much of the catalogue of the present exhibition of the Royal Academy as relates to the works of the members. 1855 (priv ptd). A reply to Ruskin.

Hamley, Sir Edward. Mr Dusky's opinions on art. Blackwood's Mag July 1858. Rptd in his Shakespeare's funeral, 1889. A parody.

[Morgan, John.] [Index to Notes on the Royal Academy]. Aberdeen 1888 (priv ptd), 1890.

The harbours of England, engraved by Thomas Lupton, from original drawings made expressly for the work by J. M. W. Turner, with illustrative text by J. Ruskin. 1856, [1857?], [1859?], 1872, 1877; [ed T. J. Wise] Orpington 1895, London 1900 etc.

Notes on the Turner Gallery at Marlborough House, 1856. 1857 (5 edns, 4th adds Preface, 5th rev), [1907] (EL) (with other essays).

The elements of drawing in three letters to beginners, illustrated by the author. 1857, New York 1857, London 1857 (adds Appendix), 1859, 1860, 1861, New York 1876, London 1887, 1892, Orpington 1892, 1895, 1898, 1900 etc, London 1907 (EL) (with The elements of perspective); tr Italian, 1898; German, [1901] (abridged). Partly rptd in R. St J. Tyrwhitt, Our sketching club: letters and studies in landscape art with an authorised reproduction of the lessons and woodcuts in Professor Ruskin's Elements of drawing, 1874, 1875, 1882, 1886, Boston 1874.

The political economy of art: being the substance (with additions) of two lectures delivered at Manchester, July 10th and 13th 1857. 1857, 1867, 1868, New York 1876; ed O. Lodge 1907 (EL) (with Unto this last); ed C. F. G. Masterman 1907. Rptd with 2 supplementary papers, (1) Education in art (first pbd in Trans Nat Assoc for Promotion of Social Science, 1858, pp. 311–6); (2) Remarks addressed to the Mansfield art night class, Oct 14th [1873]; (3) Social policy must be based on the scientific principle of natural selection (read before Metaphysical Soc 11 May 1875; priv ptd 1875), in Collected works vol 11 Orpington 1880 as A joy for ever. Later rptd in this form: New York 1885, Orpington 1887, 1889, New York 1890, Orpington 1893, 1895, 1897, 1899, New York 1899, Orpington 1900 etc.

Cambridge School of Art: Mr Ruskin's inaugural address, delivered at Cambridge, Oct 29 1858. Cambridge 1858, Orpington 1879. Also ptd in Cambridge School of Art, inaugural soirée, Cambridge 1858.

The Oxford Museum, by Henry W. Acland and John Ruskin. 1859, 1860, 1866, (omitting Ruskin's contributions) 1867, 1893 (adds new Preface by Ruskin). Ruskin's original contributions are rptd in Arrows of the chace vol 1, 1880.

The unity of art, delivered at the annual meeting of the Manchester School of Art, Feb 22nd 1859. Manchester 1859. Largely rptd in The two paths, 1859, below.

The two paths: being lectures on art, and its application, to decoration and manufacture, delivered in 1858–9. 1859, Orpington 1884, 1887, New York 1889, London 1891, 1896, 1898, 1900 etc; ed G. Wallas 1907; ed O. Lodge 1907 (EL) (with other Ruskin essays).

The elements of perspective arranged for the use of schools, and intended to be read in connexion with the first three books of Euclid. 1859, 1876, 1907 (EL) (with The elements of drawing), 1910 (rev).

'Unto this last': four essays on the first principles of political economy. 1862, New York 1866, London 1876, Orpington 1877, 1882, 1884, New York 1855, Orpington 1887, 1888, 1890, 1892, 1893, 1895, 1896, 1898, 1899, 1900 etc; ed J. A. Hobson 1907; ed O. Lodge 1907 (EL) (with The political economy of art and Munera pulveris); ed J. D. C. Monfries and G. E. Hollingsworth 1931; tr French, 1902; German, 1902; Italian, 1902, 1946; Danish, 1917. First pbd in Cornhill Mag Aug–Nov 1860 and Harper's Mag Sept–Dec 1860.

The rights of labour according to John Ruskin, arranged by Thomas Barclay. Leicester [1887], [1888?], London 1889.

Papjewski, H. Zur Erkenntniss des Gehalts von Ruskins Unto this last. Breslau 1930.

Hendrick, G. The influence of Ruskin's Unto this last on Gandhi. Ball State Teachers College Forum 1 1960.

Sesame and lilies: two lectures delivered at Manchester in 1864: 1, Of kings' treasuries 2, Of queens' gardens. 1865, New York 1865, London 1865 (adds Preface), 1866, 1867, Orpington 1882 (with new Preface), 1884, New York 1884, 1885, Orpington 1886, 1887, 1888, New York 1888, Chicago 1889, Orpington 1889, 1890, 1891, New York 1891, 1892, Philadelphia 1892, Orpington 1892, London 1894, 1896, 1897, 1898, 1898, New York 1898, London 1900, 1900, New York 1900 (10 edns), Cambridge Mass 1900 etc; ed O. Lodge 1907 (EL) (with The two paths etc); ed T. Cartwright 1908; ed A. E. Roberts 1910; tr Swedish, 1900; German, 1900; French, 1906 (by Marcel Proust); Spanish, 1907; Italian, 1907; Hungarian, 1911. Also rev and enlarged with new Preface and a third lecture, The mystery of life and its arts as Collected works vol 1, Keston 1871; rptd in this form New York 1876, Orpington 1876, 1880, New York 1880, Orpington 1883, 1887, New York 1889, 1890, Orpington 1893, 1894, 1895, New York 1895, 1896, 1897, Toronto 1897, 1898, New York 1898, London 1898, 1898, 1899, 1900, New York 1900 (4 edns), Portland Maine 1900 etc; ed A. H. Bates, New York 1909; ed S. Wragge [1920]; ed J. W. Bartram 1925; ed G. E. Hollingsworth 1932.

Warren, P. W. T. Notes on Ruskin's Sesame and lilies. Cape Town 1898.

—— Reader's companion to Sesame and lilies. 1899.

Booth, J. B. Notes on Sesame and lilies. St George 4–5 1901–2.

Of kings' treasuries. New York 1899, London 1902; ed E. D. Jones 1907.

The queens' gardens: a lecture delivered at the Town Hall, Manchester on Wednesday Dec 14 1864. Manchester 1864. A forgery executed between 1880 and 1890, *see also* Collected works ed E. T. Cook and A. D. O. Wedderburn vol 18 pp 13–5, and J. Carter and H. G. Pollard, An enquiry into the nature of certain nineteenth-century pamphlets, 1934, pp. 232–5.

Of queens' gardens. New York 1899, London 1902.

The mystery of life and its arts. New York 1869. First pbd in The afternoon lectures on literature and art ser 5, Dublin 1869.

An inquiry into some of the conditions at present affecting the study of architecture in our schools. New York 1865, 1866, 1876. First pbd in The sessional papers of the Royal Institute of British Architects pt 3 1864–5; rptd in On the old road vol 1, 1885.

The ethics of the dust: ten lectures to little housewives on the elements of crystallisation. 1866, New York 1866, 1876, Orpington 1877 (with new Preface), 1883, New York 1885, Orpington 1886, 1888, New York 1889, 1890, Orpington 1890, New York 1891, Orpington 1892, Philadelphia 1893, Orpington 1894 (adds index), 1896, 1898, 1900 etc; ed G. Rhys 1908 (EL); ed R. O. Morris 1914.

The crown of wild olive: three lectures on work, traffic and war. 1866 (3 edns), New York 1866, 1876, Orpington 1882 (vol 6 of Collected works; rev and adding both a 4th lecture, The future of England and Notes on the political economy of Russia), New York 1885, Orpington 1886, 1889, New York 1889, 1890, 1890, Orpington 1890, New York 1891, Orpington 1892, 1894 (adds index), 1895, 1897; ed J. C. Saul and D. M. Duncan, Toronto 1897; London 1898, 1899, 1900, New York 1900 (14 edns), Boston 1900, Philadelphia 1900, Chicago 1900 etc; ed C. Bax 1907 (EL); ed W. F. Melton, New York 1919 (with The queen of the air); tr French, 1900; German, 1901.

War: a lecture delivered at the Royal Military Academy, Woolwich. 1866 (priv ptd).

[The future of England.] A paper read at the Royal Artillery Institution, Woolwich, Dec 14 1869. Woolwich 1869. This title appears on the wrapper; an unauthorized type facs without wrappers is discussed by J. Carter and H. G. Pollard, An enquiry into the ntaure of certain nineteenth-century pamphlets, 1934, pp. 238–9.

Time and tide by Weare and Tyne: twenty-five letters to a working man of Sunderland on the laws of work. 1867, 1867, New York 1868, 1876, 1884, 1885, Orpington 1886, 1891, New York 1891, London 1894 (with index), 1897, 1899, 1900 etc, 1910 (EL) (with other Ruskin essays); ed P. Kaufman, New York 1928; tr Swedish, 1903. First pbd in Leeds Mercury 1 March–4 May 1867, Manchester Daily Examiner & Times 1 March–7 May 1867; Letters i–ii, Scotsman 27 Feb, 4 March 1867; Letter v, Pall Mall Gazette 1 March 1867.

Leoni: a legend of Italy, by J. R. 1868. A forgery executed between 1880 and 1890; *see also* Collected works, ed E. T. Cook and A. D. O. Wedderburn vol 1, p. 288, and J. Carter and H. G. Pollard, An enquiry into the nature of certain nineteenth-century pamphlets, 1934, pp. 236–7. Originally pbd in Friendship's offering, 1837.

First notes on the general principles of employment for the destitute and criminal classes. 1868 (priv ptd), 1868 (enlarged with 'First' omitted from title). Rptd with further addns in The queen of the air, 1869. Portions of the 2nd version were ptd in Daily Telegraph 26 Dec 1868, together with a letter from Ruskin. These are rptd together with the complete text of the pamphlet in Arrows of the chace vol 2, 1880.

The queen of the air: being a study of the Greek myths of cloud and storm. 1869, 1869, New York 1869, 1876, 1885, 1885, Orpington 1887, New York 1889, London 1890, New York 1891, London 1892, 1895 (adds index), 1898, 1900, Chicago 1900 etc; tr German, 1905. Rptd in part from the preceding item and from passages in The Cestus of Aglaia, below. For a critical study *see also* R. W. Bond, St George 6 Jan 1903, pp. 46–74.

Samuel Prout. Oxford 1870 (priv ptd). A forgery? *See also* J. Carter and H. G. Pollard, An enquiry into the nature of certain nineteenth-century pamphlets, 1934, pp. 240–1. First pbd in Art March 1849, rptd in On the old road vol 1, 1885, and in Ruskin on painting, 1902.

Lectures on art delivered before the University of Oxford in Hilary Term 1870. Oxford 1870, New York 1870, Oxford 1875, New York 1876, Oxford 1880, New York 1885, Orpington 1887 (rev), New York 1889, Orpington 1890, New York 1891, Orpington 1891, 1894 (with index), 1898, 1900 etc; tr German, 1901.

The range of intellectual conception is proportioned to the rank in animated life. Metaphysical Soc Papers no 16 [1871] (priv ptd). Rptd in Contemporary Rev June 1871, and in On the old road vol 1, 1885.

Fors clavigera: letters to the workmen and labourers of Great Britain. 8 vols 1871–84, New York 1876 (vols 1–5); New York 1880, 1884 (vols 1–7); New York 1886 (vols 1–8); 3 vols New York 1890, 4 vols New York 1891, 8 vols New York 1899. Vols 1–7 appeared each year 1871–7, every vol being originally issued in 12 pts on the 1st or 2nd of each month; the 12 pts of vol 8 were issued irregularly Jan 1878–Xmas 1884. Most of the pts were rptd two or three times.

Letter to young girls. [Orpington 1876], [1890] (18th edn). Letters 65–6.

Fors clavigera: a new edition. Ed W. G. Collingwood 4 vols Orpington 1896, 1899–1902 etc. Though professing to omit only the letters to Ruskin, this abridgement actually omits some of Ruskin's own words.

Reading in Ruskin's Fors clavigera. [Ed C. A. Wurtzburg] Orpington 1899.

Faunthorpe, J. P. Index to Fors clavigera. Orpington 1887. Contains an Appendix not included in Fors. The indexes to vols 1, 2 and vols 3, 4 first appeared in 1873 and 1875 respectively, both rptd once.

Munera pulveris: six essays on the elements of political economy. Keston 1872 (= Collected works vol 2), New

York 1873, Orpington 1880, New York 1885, Orpington 1886, New York 1889, 1891, Orpington 1894, 1898, 1899 etc, 1907 (EL) (with The political economy of art and Unto this last); ed P. Kaufman, New York 1928 (with Time and tide); tr Spanish, 1907. First pbd in Fraser's Mag June 1862–April 1863.

Gold: a dialogue connected with the subject of Munera pulveris. Ed H. B. Forman 1891 (priv ptd). A reply to criticism by J. E. Cairnes, Macmillan's Mag Nov 1863.

Aratra pentelici: six lectures on the elements of sculpture. Keston 1872 (= Collected works, vol 3), New York 1876, 1876, Orpington 1879, New York 1885, Orpington 1890 (adds next item), New York 1891, 1892 etc; tr German, [1903] (5 lectures).

The relation between Michael Angelo and Tintoret: seventh of the course of lectures on sculpture delivered at Oxford 1870–1. Keston 1872, Orpington 1879, 1887. Rptd in 1890 and subsequent edns of Aratra pentelici.

The eagle's nest: ten lectures on the relation of natural science to art, given before the University of Oxford in Lent Term 1872. Keston 1872 (= Collected works, vol 4), New York 1876, Orpington 1880, New York 1885, 1886, Orpington 1887, 1891, New York 1891, 1892, Orpington 1894 (adds index), 1897, 1899, 1900 etc; tr German, [1902] (5 lectures).

The sepulchral monuments of Italy: monuments of the Cavalli family in the Church of Santa Anastasia, Verona. 1872 (Arundel Soc). Rptd in On the old road vol 1, 1885.

The nature and authority of miracle. Metaphysical Soc Papers no 32 1873 (priv ptd). Another edn dated 1873 is probably a forgery; *see* J. Carter and H. G. Pollard, An enquiry into the nature of certain nineteenth-century pamphlets, 1934, pp. 242–3. First pbd in Contemporary Rev March 1873; rptd in On the old road vol 2, 1885.

Love's meinie: lectures on Greek and English birds, given before the University of Oxford. Lecture 1: The robin, Keston 1873; Lecture 2: The swallow, Keston 1873; Lecture 3: The dabchicks, Orpington 1881. Lectures 1–2, New York 1876, Orpington 1883, 1892. Collected edns: Orpington 1881, New York 1885, Orpington 1893, 1897 (adds index) etc. Lecture 4 (The chough) first pbd in Collected works, ed E. T. Cook and A. D. O. Wedderburn, vol 25.

The poetry of architecture: or the architecture of the nations of Europe considered in its association with natural scenery and national character. New York 1873, 1876, 1890, Orpington 1893 (1st authorized edn), 1905 etc. First pbd in Architectural Mag Nov 1837–Dec 1838, and rptd in Crayon (New York) 1 1855.

Ariadne Florentina: six lectures on wood and metal engraving, with appendix, given before the University of Oxford in Michaelmas Term 1872. Orpington 1876 (= Collected works vol 7), New York 1876, Orpington 1890, New York 1891 etc. Originally issued in 7 pts: pts 1–2, 1873; pts 3–4, 1874; pts 5–7, 1875.

Val D'Arno: ten lectures on the Tuscan art directly antecedent to the Florentine Year of Victories, given before the University of Oxford in Michaelmas Term 1874. Orpington 1874 (= Collected works vol 8), 1882, New York 1885, 1886, Orpington 1890, New York 1891, London 1900 (with index) etc.

Mornings in Florence: being simple studies of Christian art, for English travellers. 6 pts Orpington 1876–7, 1881–3, 1889–92 (pt 1 rptd 1894), Orpington 1885, New York 1886, Orpington 1889, 1894 (adds index), 1899 etc; tr German, [1901]; French, 1906.

The shepherd's tower: a series of photographs of the sculptures of Giotto's tower, to illustrate part 7 of Mornings in Florence. 1881.

Proserpina: studies of wayside flowers, while the air was yet pure among the Alps, and in the Scotland and England which my father knew. Vol 1 (all collected): Orpington 1879, 1882, 1883, New York 1885, 1886. Originally issued in 6 pts. Pt 1 1875, New York 1876, Orpington 1878, 1883, 1884; pt 2 1875, New York 1876, Orpington 1879, 1886; pt 3 1876, New York 1876, Orpington 1879, 1889; pt 4 1876, New York 1877, Orpington 1880, 1899; pt 5 1878, New York 1878, Orpington 1881, 1896; pt 6 1879, New York 1879, Orpington 1882, 1897. Only 4 pts of vol 2 were pbd: pt 7 1882; pt 8 1882; pt 9 1885; pt 10 1886.

Deucalion: collected studies of the lapse of waves and life of stones. Vol 1 (all collected) Orpington 1879, 1882, New York 1885, 1886, 1889, Orpington 1891, Boston 1900. Originally issued in 6 pts. Pt 1 1875, New York 1876, Orpington 1883; pt 2 1875, New York 1876, Orpington 1883; pt 3 1876, New York 1877, Orpington 1883; pt 5 1878, 1888; pt 6 1879. Only 2 pts of vol 2 were pbd: pt 7 1880; pt 8 1883.

Yewdale and its streamlets: report of a lecture delivered in connection with the Kendal Literary and Scientific Institute. Kendal 1877. First pbd in Kendal Mercury 6 Oct 1877, and Kendal Times 6 Oct 1877. The lecture forms ch 12 in Deucalion pt 5.

Collingwood, W. G. The limestone Alps of Savoy. Orpington 1884. Supplements Deucalion.

Letters to the Times on the principal Pre-Raphaelite pictures in the Exhibition of 1854, from the author of Modern painters. 1876 (priv ptd). Originally pbd in Times 5, 25 May 1854; rptd in Arrows of the chace vol 1, 1880, and 'A. G. Crawford' (i.e. A. G. Wise), Notes on the pictures of Mr Holman Hunt exhibited at the rooms of the Fine Art Society, 1886.

Guide to the principal pictures in the Academy of Fine Arts at Venice, arranged for English travellers. 2 pts Venice 1877, Orpington 1882–3, London 1891 (rev); tr Italian, 1901; French, 1908.

Notes by Mr Ruskin on his drawings by the late J. M. W. Turner, exhibited at the Fine Arts Society's Galleries, March 1878; also an appendix containing a list of the engraved works of J. M. W. Turner exhibited at the same time. [1878], [1878], 1878 (with Addenda and Epilogue) (4 edns), 1878 (rev with appendix by W. Kingsley), 1878; 1878 (with 2nd pt On his own handiwork illustrative of Turner), 1878 (pt 2 rev) (4 edns). Rptd with Catalogue of the exhibition of the same drawings, 1900, and in Ruskin on pictures vol 1, 1902.

St Mark's rest: the history of Venice, written for the help of the few travellers who still care for her monuments. New York 1879, Orpington 1884 (1st complete and authorized collection), New York 1884, 1885, 1886, 1889, Orpington 1894, Chicago 1900, Boston 1900; tr Italian, 1901; French, 1908. Originally issued in 6 sections. Pt 1 1877, 1884, 1889, 1894; pt 2 1877, 1889. 1st Supplement 1877, 1887, 1889, 1894; tr Italian, 1885 (priv ptd). Pt 3 1879, 1887, 1889, 1894. 2nd Supplement 1879, 1889. Appendix 1884, 1894.

The laws of Fiesole: a familiar treatise on the elementary principles and practice of drawing and painting, as determined by the Tuscan masters, arranged for the use of schools. Vol 1 (all pbd), Orpington 1879, New York 1879, Orpington 1882, 1890, Boston 1900 etc.

Notes on Samuel Prout and William Hunt, illustrated by a loan collection of drawings, exhibited at the Fine Art Society's Galleries. 1789–80 (4 edns), 1880. Rptd in Ruskin on pictures vol 2, 1902.

Circular respecting memorial studies of St Mark's Venice, now in progress under Mr Ruskin's direction. 1879, 1879 (adds postscript), 1880.

Letters addressed by Prof Ruskin to the clergy on the Lord's Prayer and the Church. Ed F. A. Malleson 1879 (priv ptd), [1880] (adds Replies from clergy and laity, and an epilogue by Mr Ruskin), 1883, 1896 (rev and with additional letters), New York 1896. Also ptd in Contemporary Rev Dec 1879. Ruskin's letters rptd in On the old road vol 1, 1885, and separately from the holograph originals, ed T. J. Wise 1896 (priv ptd).

Sillar, W. C. A defence of the Church of England against the accusations contained in the letters of Mr Ruskin in the Contemporary Review. 1880.

Elements of English prosody for use in St George's schools, explanatory of the various terms used in Rock honeycomb. 1880.

Arrows of the chace: being a collection of scattered letters published chiefly in the daily newspapers 1840–1880, and now edited by an Oxford pupil [A. D. O. Wedderburn] with a preface by the author. 2 vols Orpington 1880, New York 1881, 1890. Vol 1, Letters on art and science; vol 2, Letters on politics, economy and miscellaneous matters.

'Our fathers have told us': sketches of the history of Christendom for boys and girls who have been held at its fonts. Orpington 1884, New York 1886 (3 edns), 1890, Orpington 1879 etc; tr French, 1903 (by Marcel Proust); Spanish, 1907. Originally issued in 5 pts: ch 1 1880, 1883, 1893; ch 2 1881, 1885; ch 3 1882, 1885; ch 4 1883, 1893. Ch 4 had been previously pbd in a Separate travellers' edition to serve as a guide to the Cathedral, Orpington 1881, 1886, 1897, 1898. Ruskin projected a 6th edn entitled Valle crucis, 2 chs of which were first pbd in Verona and other lectures, 1894. An intended 3rd edn, entitled Ara coeli, was first pbd in Collected works, ed E. T. Cook and A. D. O. Wedderburn, vol 33.

The art of England: lectures given in Oxford. Orpington 1884, New York 1883–4, 1885, 1885, 1886, Orpington 1887, New York 1889, 1892, Orpington 1898, 1898 (with The pleasures of England), 1900 etc. Originally issued in 7 pts; pt 1 1883, 1883, 1890; pt 2 1883, 1883, 1893; pt 3 1883, 1884, 1898; pt 4 1883, 1884, 1898; pt 5 1883, 1885; pt 6 1883, 1885; pt 7 1884, 1887, 1893.

The pleasures of England: lectures given in Oxford. Orpington 1884, New York 1885 (pts 1–3), 1885 (complete), Orpington 1898 (with The art of England), 1900 etc. Issued in 4 pts: pts 1–2 1884; pts 3–4 1885.

The storm cloud of the nineteenth century: two lectures delivered at the London Institution, Feb 4 & 11 1884. 2 pts Orpington 1884, New York 1884, London 1885. First lecture fully reported in Times 5 Feb 1884, Pall Mall Gazette 5 Feb 1884 (by E. T. Cook), and Art Jnl April 1884 (by A. D. O. Wedderburn).

On the old road: a collection of miscellaneous essays, pamphlets &c &c published 1834–85. [Ed A. D. O. Wedderburn] 2 vols Orpington 1885, 3 vols Orpington 1899 (rev) etc.

Praeterita: outlines of scenes and thoughts perhaps worthy of memory in my past life, volume 1. Orpington 1886, 1886, New York 1886, 1886, 1889, 3 vols New York 1890 (with vol 2), New York 1892, Orpington 1899, 1900; tr German, 1903, 1903. Largely from Fors clavigera, above. Originally issued in 12 pts: pts 1–7 1885, pts 8–12 1886, rptd New York 1885–6.

Praeterita: volume 2. Orpington 1887, New York 1889, 3 vols New York 1890 (with vol 1), 1892, Orpington 1899, 1900; tr German, 1903, 1903. Originally issued in 12 pts: pts 13–20 1886, pts 21–24 1887, New York 1886–7.

Praeterita: volume 3. 4 pts Orpington 1888–9, New York 1888–9, Orpington 1900 (with index and Dilecta, below), 1900. Pts 25–6 1888, pts 27–8 1889.

Praeterita. Ed K. Clark 1949. Abridged. *See also* S. E. Brown, The unpublished passages in the ms of Ruskin's autobiography, Victorian Newsletter no 16 1959.

Dilecta: correspondence, diary notes and extracts from books, illustrating Praeterita. 3 pts Orpington 1886–1900. Pt 2 1887, pt 3 first issued with reprint of pts 1–2 and Praeterita vol 3 1900.

Hortus inclusus: messages from the wood to the garden, sent in happy days to the sister ladies of the Thwaite, Coniston [Mary and Susie Beever]. [Ed A. Fleming] Orpington 1887, New York 1887, Orpington 1888, New York 1892 (with In montibus sanctis and Coeli enarrant) etc.

Ruskiniana, part 1: Letters published in, and collected from various sources, and mostly reprinted in Igdrasil, 1890. [Ed A. D. O. Wedderburn] 1890 (priv ptd).

Ruskiniana, part 2: lectures and addresses reported in the press, but not reprinted in collected works. [Ed A. D. O. Wedderburn] 1892 (priv ptd).

Verona and other lectures. [Ed W. G. Collingwood] Orpington 1894. The title lecture was delivered at the Royal Institution 4 Feb 1870; a partial report appeared in Pall Mall Gazette 5 Feb 1870; rptd in Igdrasil March 1892 vol 3, pp. 241–7. 2 of the other lectures were for an intended continuation of Our Fathers have told us, above.

Comments on Ruskin on the Divina commedia, compiled by G. P. Huntington, with an introduction by C. E. Norton. Boston 1903.

The Cestus of Aglaia. Orpington 1905; ed C. Bax 1907 (EL). Originally appeared in Art Jnl Jan–July 1865, Jan–Feb, April 1866. Chs 2, 6 were incorporated in The queen of the air, 1869; the rest was rptd in On the old road vol 1, 1885.

Contributions to Periodicals

Ruskin's longer contributions to periodicals were partly collected in On the old road, 2 vols 1885. *A complete list of those pbd in his lifetime is in* T. J. Wise and J. P. Smart, A bibliography of Ruskin vol 3, pp. 111–22. *A complete list of Ruskin's letters to newspapers is in* Collected works, ed E. T. Cook and A. D. O. Wedderburn, vol 38, pp. 48–55. *They were largely collected in* Arrows of the chace, 2 vols 1880, *and in* Ruskiniana pt 1, 1890. *Only those not rptd are listed here.*

On the convergence of perpendiculars. [Loudon's] Architectural Mag Feb 1838–Jan 1839.

On the propriety of combining works of art with the sublimity of nature considered. [Loudon's] Architectural Mag Jan 1839.

Notice respecting some artificial sections illustrating the geology of Chamouni, communicated in a letter to Prof Forbes. Proc Royal Soc of Edinburgh 4 1857–8. There is also a separate offprint.

Notes on the shape and structure of some parts of the Alps with reference to denudation. Geological Mag Feb, May 1865.

On banded and Brecciated concretions. Geological Mag Aug 1867–Jan 1870. There was also a separate offprint of each article.

Railways in Derbyshire. Manchester City News 2, 7, 13 April 1884.

The best hundred books. Pall Mall Gazette 19 Jan, 15, 23 Feb 1886.

Notes on Bewick's Birds. Art Jnl Oct, Dec 1886.

Arthur Burgess. Century Guild Hobby Horse April 1887.

Books which have influenced me. Br Weekly Extra 1887.

Books edited by Ruskin, or to which he supplied Prefaces, Notes or Appendices

Repton, Humphrey. Landscape gardening. 1840. Footnote on the proper shapes of pictures and engravings, pp. 32–8.

Handbook for travellers in Northern Italy. 1847 (3rd edn). Notes. Also in 4th (1852), 5th (1854) and 6th edns; incorporated in the text in subsequent edns.

The report of the National Gallery Site Commission. 1857. Evidence pp. 92–7. Rptd in Literary Gazette 22 Aug 1857, and in On the old road vol 1, 1885.

The report from the Select Committee [of the House of Commons] on Public Institutions, 1860. Evidence, pp. 113–23; rptd in On the old road vol 1, 1885.

The report of the Royal Academy Commission. 1863. Evidence, pp. 546–55; rptd in On the old road vol 1, 1885.

German popular stories. Ed E. Taylor 1868. Introd.

Tyrwhitt, St John. Christian art and symbolism. 1872. Preface; rptd in On the old road vol 1, 1885.

Catalogue of an exhibition of outlines by the late John Leech, at the Gallery, 9 Conduit Street. 1872. Preface. Rptd in Times 8 May 1872; in Percival Leigh, Portraits of children of the nobility illustrated by John Leech, 1875 (first pbd 1841); in Arrows of the chace vol 1, 1880.

Rendu, Louis. Theory of the glaciers of Savoy, translated by Alfred Wills. Ed G. Forbes 1874. Supplementary articles, pp. 199–200. Rptd in Arrows of the chace vol 1, 1880.

Corporation of Brighton. The exhibition of pictures lent by Prof Ruskin and the Arundel Society opened April 6 1876, the Royal Pavilion Gallery. [Brighton 1876]. Note on Botticelli's Zipporah.

Owen, A. C. The art schools of medieval Christendom. 1876. Preface and footnotes. Rptd in On the old road vol 1, 1885.

Somervell, Robert. A protest against the extension of railways in the Lake District. Windermere [1876]. Preface, and extracts from Fors clavigera. Rptd in On the old road vol 1, 1885.

Bibliotheca pastorum, edited by John Ruskin. Vol 1: The economist of Xenophon. Tr A. D. O. Wedderburn and W. G. Collingwood, Orpington 1876. Vol 2: Rock honeycomb: broken pieces of Sir Philip Sidney's Psalter, laid up in store for English homes. 2 pts Orpington 1877. [No vol 3]. Vol 4: A knight's faith: passages in the life of Sir Herbert Edwardes collated by John Ruskin. Orpington 1885.

The science of life: a pamphlet addressed to all members of the universities of Oxford and Cambridge, and all who are, or who will be, teachers, clergymen, fathers. 1877, 1878. 3 letters: 2–3 in 1st edn; 1, 3 in 2nd edn. Rptd in Arrows of the chace vol 2, 1885.

Zorzi, Alvise Piero. Osservazioni intorno ai ristauri interni ed esterni della Basilica di San Marco. Venice 1877. Letter, pp. 11–22. Rptd in Igdrasil May 1890, and Ruskiniana pt 1, 1890.

Swan, Henry, Collected notes on some of the pictures in the St George's Museum Sheffield. [Sheffield 1879]. Note on Fra Filippi and Carpaccio.

Notes on drawings by Mr Ruskin, places on exhibition by Prof Norton, Boston, Oct 1879. Cambridge Mass 1879. Notes on his own drawings.

Catalogue of the first exhibition of pictures and water colour drawings &c at Douglas Isle of Man, with original notes by Prof Ruskin. Douglas 1880.

The Ruskin cabinet at Whitelands College: notes on the sixty pictures by Prof Ruskin. [London] 1883.

[Alexander, Francesca]. The story of Ida: epitaph on a Etrurian tomb, by Francesca, edited with a preface by John Ruskin. Orpington 1883.

Smart, William. A disciple of Plato: a critical study of John Ruskin, with a note by Mr Ruskin. Glasgow 1883.

Horsfall, T. C. The study of beauty and art in large towns. 1883. Introd. Rptd in On the old road vol 1, 1885.

Collingwood, W. G. Deucalion—first supplement: the limestone Alps of Savoy, a study in physical geology. Orpington 1884. Preface.

The Bishop of Oxford and Prof Ruskin on vivisection. Victoria Soc for Protection of Animals from Vivisection, 1885.

Alexander, Francesca. Roadside songs of Tuscany, translated and illustrated by Francesca Alexander. Orpington 1885. Originally issued in 10 pts from April 1884–Aug 1885.

Chesneau, Ernest. The English school of painting, translated by L. N. Etherington. 1885. Introd.

Usury: its pernicious effects on English agriculture and commerce; an allegory dedicated, without permission, to the Bishops of Manchester, Peterborough and Rochester. [Ed R. G. Sillar] 1885. Introd. Rptd in On the old road vol 2, 1885.

Dame Wiggins of Lee and her seven wonderful cats, edited with additional verses by John Ruskin. Orpington 1885.

[Wise, A. G.] Notes on some of the principal pictures of Sir John Everett Millais at the Grosvenor Gallery by A. Gordon Crawford, with a preface and original and selected criticisms by John Ruskin. 1886.

A catalogue of the exhibition of water colour drawings by deceased masters of the British School at the Royal Institute. 1886. Appendix. Rptd in Ruskiniana pt 1, 1890.

Turner's rivers of France. 2 vols 1887. The introd consists of unauthorized extracts from Modern painters.

[Bitzius, Albert]. Ulric the Farm servant: a story of the Bernese Lowland, by Jeremias Gotthelf, translated into English by Julia Firth. Orpington 1888. Issued in 9 pts from July 1886–Oct 1888. Preface and notes.

Cook, Sir Edward Tyas. A popular handbook to the National Gallery including, by special permission, notes collected from the works of Mr Ruskin. 1888. Also Preface.

Alexander, Francesca. Christ's folk in the Apennine: reminiscences of her friends among the Tuscan peasantry. Orpington 1889. Issued in pts 1887–9. Preface etc.

White, William. The principles of art as illustrated in the Ruskin Museum Sheffield, with passages from the writings of John Ruskin. 1895.

Letters and Diaries

There is a long list of Ruskin's private letters and notebooks in Collected works, ed Cook and Wedderburn, vol 38, pp. 56–93. *See also:*

Sotheby & Co. Catalogue of the mss and remaining library of Ruskin, removed from his residence Brantwood. 24 July 1930; Final portion, 18 May 1931.

Thorpe, W. The Ruskin mss. Princeton Univ Lib Chron 1 1940.

Hogan, C. B. The Yale collection of the mss of Ruskin. Yale Lib Gazette 16 1942. *See also* 27 1952.

Skelton, R. Ruskin: the final years—a survey of the Ruskin correspondence in the John Rylands Library. Bull John Rylands Lib 37 1955.

Letters upon subjects of general interest from Ruskin to various correspondents. Ed T. J. Wise 1892 (priv ptd).

Stray letters from Prof Ruskin to a London bibliophile [F. S. Ellis]. Ed T. J. Wise 1892 (priv ptd).

Letters from Ruskin to William Ward. Ed T. J. Wise 2 vols 1892 (priv ptd), Boston 1922 (with a biography of Ward by William C. Ward, introd by A. M. Brook).

Letters to Ruskin to his secretary [C. A. Howell]. New Rev March 1892.

Three letters and an essay by Ruskin 1836–41 found in his tutor's [Canon Dale's] desk. [Ed H. P. Dale] Orpington 1893.

Letters on art and literature. Ed T. J. Wise 1894 (priv ptd).

Letters to Ernest Chesneau. Ed T. J. Wise 1894 (priv ptd).

Letters addressed to a college friend [Edward Clayton] 1840–5. Orpington 1894, New York 1894.

Letters to Rev F. J. Faunthorpe. Ed T. J. Wise 1894 (priv ptd).

Letters to Rev F. A. Malleson. Ed T. J. Wise 1896 (priv ptd).

Letters to F. J. Furnivall. Ed T. J. Wise 1897 (priv ptd).

[14 letters to Miss Adelaide Ironside]. Catholic Press (Sydney) 3 Feb 1900.

Letters to M G & H G [Mary and Hellen Gladstone]. Edinburgh 1903 (priv ptd), New York 1903; rptd in North Amer Rev July 1903.

The letters of Ruskin to C. E. Norton. [Ed C. E. Norton] 2 vols Boston 1903.

Spielman, M. H. and G. S. Layard. Kate Greenaway. 1905.
The letters of Dr John Brown. Ed his son and D. W. Forrest 1907.
Young, M. F. Letters of a noble woman [Mrs La Touche]. 1908.
An ill assorted marriage. Ed C. K. Shorter 1915 (priv ptd). Letter to F. J. Furnivall.
Ruskin to Rawdon Brown. Ed P. Kaufmann, North Amer Rev Sept–Dec 1925.
A girl's [Jessie Leete's] friendship with Ruskin. Ed L. Huxley, Cornhill Mag Dec 1926–Jan 1927; Atlantic Monthly Dec 1926–Jan 1927.
The Giustani memoirs. Ed P. Dearmer, London Mercury Oct 1927.
The solitary warrior. Ed J. H. Whitehouse 1929.
Letters to Francesca, and Memoirs of the Alexanders. Ed L. G. Swett, Boston 1931.
Macdonald, Greville. Reminiscences of a specialist. 1932. *See also* TLS 14 March 1935.
Letters to Bernard Quaritch 1867–88. Ed C. Q. Wrentmore 1938.
M., M. 22 Ruskin letters. More Books Nov 1939.
Ruskin at the Lyceum. Letter to Thornton Leigh Hunt. TLS 8 June 1946.
Friends of a lifetime: letters to S. C. C[ockerell]. Ed V. Meynell 1940.
James, W. The order of release. 1947.
[Letter to Sir J. T. Coleridge. 1866]. Jnl Rutgers Univ Lib 12 1938. On Swinburne.
Two unpublished letters. N & Q 12 Nov 1949.
Häusermann, H. W. The Genevese background. 1952.
Ferguson, O. W. Ruskin's continental letters to Mrs Severn. JEGP 51 1952.
The gulf of years: letters to Kathleen Olander. Ed R. Unwin [1953].
Letters of Ruskin. Bull John Rylands Lib 26 1953.
Ruskin's letters from Venice 1851–2. Ed J. L. Bradley, New Haven 1955.
The diaries of Ruskin. Ed J. Evans and J. H. Whitehouse 3 vols Oxford 1956–9.
An unpublished Ruskin letter. Ed J. L. Bradley, Burlington Mag 100 1958.
A Ruskin letter. Ed D. V. Rexford, Jnl Rutgers Univ Lib 2 1959.
Spence, M. E. Ruskin's correspondence with Miss Blanche Atkinson. Bull John Rylands Lib 42 1959.
Spence, M. E. Ruskin's friendship with Mrs Fanny Talbot. Ibid.
Spence, M. E. Ruskin's correspondence with his god-daughter, Constance Oldham. Bull John Rylands Lib 43 1961.
Ruskin's advice to an amateur artist, Louisa Marchioness of Waterford. Ed J. L. Bradley, Stud in Eng Lit 1500–1900 1 1961.
Two unpublished letters to Edward Clayton. Ed S. M. B. Coulling, HLQ 27 1963.
Three Ruskin letters [to E. L. Tarbuck]. Ed R. E. T. Williams, N & Q 10 Jan 1963.
Spence, M. Dearest Mama Talbot. 1966. Letters to Mrs Talbot 1874–89.

Ruskin Periodicals

The Ruskin reading guild journal. Arbroath Jan–Dec 1889. Monthly; originally, from Nov 1887 to Dec 1888, circulated in ms form, ed W. Marwick.
[Continued as] Igdrasil: journal of the Ruskin reading guild—a magazine of literature, art and social philosophy. Orpington vol 1 Jan–Sept 1890, vol 2 Oct–Dec 1890, vol 3 Edinburgh June 1891–March 1892. Monthly, ed W. Marwick and K. Parkes.
[Continued as] World-literature: the journal of the reading guild and kindred societies, and supplement to Igdrasil. Vol 1 15 Sept–March 1892, vol 2 Edinburgh May–Sept 1892. Monthly, ed W. Marwick.
Saint George: the journal of the Ruskin Society of Birmingham (The Society of the Rose). Birmingham vols 1–13 March 1898–May 1911. Quarterly, ed J. H. Whitehouse et al.
The Ruskin Union journal. No 1 March 1900. No other no issued; Saint George became thenceforth the organ of the Ruskin Union as well.

§2

Mr Ruskin's works. Blackwood's Mag Sept 1851.
[Patmore, C.] Sources of expression in architecture. Edinburgh Rev 94 1851; rptd as Architectural styles in principle in art, 1889.
[Oliphant, M. O.] Modern light literature: art. Blackwoods' Mag Dec 1855.
Leslie, C. R. A handbook for young painters. 1855.
Mitford, M. R. Recollections of a literary life vol 3, 1855.
— Letters. Ed H. F. Chorley 2 vols 1872.
— Correspondence with C. Boner and Ruskin. Ed E. Lee 1914.
B., A. Notes on some of the critics of Ruskin. 1856.
Gaskell, E. C. In her Life of Charlotte Brontë. 2 vols 1857.
Gladstone, W. E. In his Studies on Homer and the Homeric age vol 3, Oxford 1858.
Hamerton, P. G. A painter's camp and thoughts on art. 2 vols 1862.
— Etching and etchers. 1868.
— Landscape. 1885.
Thornbury, G. W. The life of J. M. W. Turner. 2 vols 1862.
Patterson, R. H. Essays in history and art. Edinburgh 1862.
[Lancaster, H. H.] The writings of Mr Ruskin. North British Rev 36 1862.
Ruskin's literary spirit. Boston Rev 2 1862.
Ruskin as a religious writer. Christian Observer 62 1862.
Marsh, G. P. Lectures on the English language. New York 1863 (4th edn).
Milsand, J. L'esthétique anglaise. Paris 1864, Lausanne 1906.
Arnold, M. In his Essays in criticism, 1865.
Japp, A. H. In his Three great teachers of our own time, 1865.
Noel, R. On the use of metaphor and 'pathetic fallacy' in poetry. Fortnightly Rev 1 Aug 1866; rptd in his Essays on poetry and poets, 1886.
Rossetti, W. M. Fine art, chiefly contemporary. 1867.
— Ruskin as a writer on art. Broadway 2 1869.
— Dante Gabriel Rossetti. 2 vols 1895.
— Ruskin, Rossetti and Pre-Raphaelitism. 1899.
— Pre-Raphaelite diaries and letters. 1900.
— Rossetti papers. 1903.
Green, B. H. Mr Ruskin: his opinions and comparisons of painters—a few remarks dedicated to the shades of Raphael, Correggio, and Murillo. 1869.
Cook, D. Art in England. 1869.
Doyle, F. H. Lectures delivered before the University of Oxford 1868. 1869.
Friswell, J. H. Modern men of letters honestly criticised. 1870.
Bedford, H. Mr Ruskin as an art-critic. Month July–Aug 1871.
Eastlake, C. L. A history of the Gothic Revival. 1872.
Taine, H. In his Notes sur l'Angleterre, Paris 1872; tr 1872.
Kidd, G. B. Mr Ruskin and political economy. Derby 1873.
Torrey, J. A theory of fine art. New York 1874.
The Royal Gold Medal. Royal Institute of British Architects, Sessional Papers 1874–5.
Saintsbury, G. In his Modern English prose, Fortnightly Rev Feb 1876.
— In his Corrected impressions, 1895.

Mallock, W. H. The new Republic. 1877. Ruskin as Mr Herbert.
Wedderburn, A. D. O. Professor Ruskin at Brantwood. World 29 1877; rptd in Celebrities at home, ed E. Yates vol 2, 1878.
— A lake-side home, Brantwood. Art Jnl Nov–Dec 1881.
Whistler v. Ruskin. Times 26 Nov 1878.
Whistler, J. A. M'N. Whistler v. Ruskin: art and art critics. 1878; rptd in his Gentle art of making enemies, 1890.
Walker, R. B. John Ruskin. Manchester 1879.
Bayne, P. Lessons from my masters, Carlyle, Tennyson and Ruskin. 1879.
Poynter, E. J. In his Lectures on art, 1879.
Nisbet, H. The practical in painting. Edinburgh 1880.
Smart, W. Ruskin: his life and work. Manchester 1880.
— A disciple of Plato: a critical study of Ruskin. Manchester 1883.
Watt, P. B. The educational value of art. Glasgow 1880.
The progress of taste. Quart Rev 149 1880.
Owen, J. A. Mr Ruskin's May-Day festival at Whitelands College. Girl's Own Paper 2 1881.
Hamilton, W. The aesthetic movement in England 1882.
Cassels, W. Wealth: definitions by Ruskin and Mill compared. Glasgow 1882.
— The social problem. Glasgow 1885. Anon.
Watt, F. Mr Ruskin and political economy. St James's Mag 42 1882.
Mather, J. M. Life and teaching of Ruskin. Manchester 1883.
'Lee, Vernon' (Violet Paget). Belcaro [1883].
Geddes, P. The Round Table series iii: Ruskin, economist. Edinburgh 1883.
Froude, J. A. (ed). Letters and Memorials of Jane Welsh Carlyle. 1883.
— Thomas Carlyle: a history of his life in London. 1885.
Wilson, D. M. Ruskin, economist. Unitarian Rev (Boston) 23 1885.
Bishop, M. C. A teacher among teachers. Merry England 5 1885.
St George's cloth. Pall Mall Gazette 8 Feb 1886.
Royce, G. M. Ruskin v. Gibbon and Grote. New Englander 43 1886.
Van Dyke, J. C. Principles of art. New York 1887.
Martin, W. Aspects of nature in relation to individual and national life. Glasgow 1887.
The American trade in 'Ruskins': an interview at Mr Wiley's, New York. Pall Mall Gazette 21 Dec 1887.
Stillman, W. J. John Ruskin. Century Mag 35 1888. Rptd in his Old Rome and the New, 1897.
— In his Autobiography of a journalist, 2 vols 1901.
The works of Mr Ruskin. Edinburgh Rev 147 1888.
Mr Ruskin and the Edinburgh Review. Spectator 28 Jan 1888.
Moreton, W. T. The religious teachings of Ruskin. Christian World Pulpit 18, 25 April, 2 May 1888.
Stimson, F. J. Ruskin as a political economist. Quart Jnl of Economics 2 1888.
Fleming, A. The revival of hand spinning and weaving in Westmoreland. Century Mag Feb 1889.
Dyer, H. The foundation of social politics. Glasgow 1889.
Clayden, P. W. Samuel Rogers and his contemporaries. 1889.
— John Ruskin. Temple Bar new ser 6 1906.
Collingwood, W. G. Ruskin: a biographical outline. 1889.
— The art teaching of Ruskin. 1891.
— The life and work of Ruskin. 2 vols 1893, 1900 (with biographical addns, as The life of Ruskin).
— Ruskin relics. 1903.
Cook, E. T. Studies in Ruskin. Orpington 1890.
— Mr Ruskin in relation to modern problems. Nat Rev 23 1894.
— Ruskin and modern business. Spectator 17 Feb 1900.
— Ruskin as an artist and art critic. Studio March 1900.
— Book wars! Ruskin as the father of the Net System. Book Monthly May 1907.
— The life of Ruskin. 1911.
— Homes and haunts of Ruskin. 1912.
Downes, R. P. Ruskin: a study. 1890.
Scudder, V. D. An introduction to the writings of Ruskin. Boston 1890.
— On journey. 1937.
Cowper-Temple, G. (Lady Mount-Temple). Memorials. 1890 (priv ptd).
Robertson, J. M. In his Modern humanists, 1891.
— In his Modern humanists reconsidered, 1927.
Rose, H. The new political economy: the social teaching of Carlyle, Ruskin and George. 1891.
Richardson, B. W. Thomas Sopwith, with excerpts from his diaries. 1891.
The Communism of Ruskin. New York 1891.
Fitzgerald, P. Mr Ruskin, artist and publisher. GM Feb 1890.
Symonds, J. A. A morning at San Rocco. Nat Observer 1 Aug 1891.
Smetham, J. Letters. Ed S. Smetham and W. Davies 1891, 1892 (rev).
Sharp, W. Life and letters of Joseph Severn. 1892.
Bosanquet, B. In his History of aesthetic, 1892.
Gibbins, H. de B. English social reformers. 1892.
Oliphant, M. O. and F. R. In their Victorian age of English literature, 1892.
Ritchie, A. Records of Tennyson, Ruskin and Browning. 1892.
Waldstein (later Walston). The work of Ruskin. New York 1893, London 1894.
Marks, H. S. Pen and pencil sketches. 2 vols 1894.
de Reul, P. L'esthétique en Angleterre. Brussels 1894.
Ruskin: a study in development. London Quart Rev 81 1894.
Oddie, J. W. Ruskin at Corpus. Pelican Record 2 1894.
Schooling, J. H. The handwriting of Ruskin 1828–84. Strand Mag Dec 1895.
Smith, C. E. Journals and correspondence of Lady Eastlake. 2 vols 1895.
Brewster, W. T. Studies in structure and style. New York 1896.
de la Sizeranne, R. Ruskin et la religion de la beauté. Paris 1897; tr Vera Monckton Milnes, Countess Galway, Orpington 1899 (with 2 appendixes by G. Allen).
Browning, E. B. Letters. Ed F. G. Kenyon 2 vols 1897.
Fowler, J. H. In his Nineteenth-Century prose, Edinburgh 1897.
Muir, R. J. Ruskin revised, and other papers on education. Edinburgh 1897.
Sulman, T. A memorable art class. Good Words Aug 1897.
Fechheimer, S. S. Ueber die Bedeutung Ruskins für das Leben und die Erziehung in England. Jena 1898.
Hobson, J. A. Ruskin, social reformer. 1898.
— Ruskin and democracy. Contemporary Rev Jan 1902.
Spurgeon, C. H. In his Autobiography, 3 vols 1898.
Max Muller, F. Auld Lang Syne. 2 vols 1898.
Signac, P. L'éducation de l'œil. Revue Blanche 1 July 1898.
Ruskin as an artist. Scribner's Mag Dec 1898.
Marius, G. H. Een inleiding tot zijn werken. Hague 1899.
Millais, J. G. The life of Sir J. E. Millais. 2 vols 1899.
Palgrave, G. F. Francis Turner Palgrave. 1899.
Thompson, H. L. Memoir of H. G. Liddell. 1899.
Shepstone, H. J. A modern utopia [on Ruskin, Tennessee]. World-Wide Mag June 1899.
Paetow, F. Die Ruskin Co-operative Association und deren Hochschule für Socialismus. Neue Zeit 17 1899.
Bardoux, J. Le mouvement idéaliste et social dans la littérature anglaise: Ruskin. [Paris 1900].

— Le culte du Beau dans la cité nouvelle. Paris 1931 (4th edn).
— Ruskin: poète, artiste, apôtre. Paris 1931.
Bookman. Ruskin memorial number. March 1900.
Hocart, J. Ruskin: le prophète du Beau. Brussels 1900.
H., G (George Harley?). Mr Ruskin's illness. Br Medical Jnl 27 Jan 1900.
Isaacs, A. A. The fountain of Siena: an episode in the life of Ruskin. 1900.
Tuckwell, W. Reminiscences of Oxford. 1900.
Meynell, A. John Ruskin. Edinburgh 1900.
Pengelly, R. E. Ruskin: a biographical sketch. 1900.
Scalinger, G. M. L'estetica di Ruskin. Naples 1900.
Spielmann, H. M. Ruskin: a sketch of his life, with personal reminiscences. 1900.
Champneys, B. In his Memoirs and correspondence of Coventry Patmore, 2 vols 1900.
Ward, M. A. Prophets of the nineteenth century: Carlyle, Ruskin, Tolstoi. 1900.
Atkinson, B. Ruskin's social experiment at Barmouth. 1900. Rptd from Leisure Hour March 1897.
Ruskin Exhibition, Coniston. Catalogue. Ed W. G. Collingwood, Ulverston 1900, 1906 (rev).
Bateman, M. G. John Ruskin. Black & White 27 Jan 1900.
Dodd, L. T. and J. A. Dale. The Ruskin Hall movement. Fortnightly Rev Feb 1900.
Chapman, C. Reminiscences. Sunday Mag March 1900.
John Ruskin. Quart Rev 191 1900.
M[ac Coll], D. S. Ruskin and his critics. Saturday Rev 13, 20 Oct 1900.
Morton, E. P. Ruskin's pathetic fallacy and Keats's treatment of nature. Poet-Lore 12 1900.
Clemen, P. John Ruskin. Zeitschrift für Bildende Kunst new ser 11 1900.
Shaw, W. H. Ruskin: ethical and religious teacher. Oxford 1901.
Ashbee, C. R. An endeavour towards the teaching of Ruskin and William Morris: being a brief account of the work of the Guild of Handicraft in East London. 1901.
Davis, W. G. The failure of the Ruskin colony. Gunton's Mag 21 1901.
Garnett, R. Sir Francis Palgrave as a precursor of Ruskin. Hampstead Annual 1901.
Rawnsley, H. D. Ruskin and the English Lakes. Glasgow 1902.
Brunhes, H. J. Ruskin et la Bible pour servir à l'histoire d'une pensée. Paris 1902.
Harrison, F. John Ruskin. 1902 (EML).
Sänger, S. Ruskin: sein Leben und Lebenswerk. Strasbourg 1902.
Broicher, C. Ruskin und sein Werk. 3 vols Leipzig 1902.
McDill, H. C. Why the Ruskin colony failed. Gunton's Mag 22 1902.
von Bunsen, M. Ruskin: sein Leben und seine Werke. Leipzig 1903.
Atlay, J. B. Henry Wentworth Acland: a memoir. 1903.
Gladden, W. Witnesses of the light. 1903.
Pollock, M. Light and water. 1903.
Braam, J. W. The Ruskin Co-operative Colony. Amer Jnl of Sociology 9 1803.
Farrar, F. W. Ruskin as a religious teacher. 1904.
Burne-Jones, E. In his Memorials, 2 vols 1904.
Kitchin, G. W. Ruskin in Oxford, and other studies. 1904.
Davies, J. Ll. The Working Man's College 1854–1904. 1904.
Sieper, E. Das Evangelium der Schönheit in der englischen Literatur und Kunst des xix Jahrhunderts. Dortmund [1904].
Powell, F. Y. Ruskin and thoughts on democracy. 1905.
Hunt, H. Pre-Raphaelitism and the Pre-Raphaelite Brotherhood. 2 vols 1905.
Ruskin Commemoration, Venice 21 September 1905.
Vitali, G. Le idee fondamentali di Ruskin. Rivista d'Italia Dec 1905.
Cherfils, C. Canon de Turner: essai de synthèse critique des théories picturales de Ruskin. Paris 1906.
Zorzi, A. Ruskin in Venice. Cornhill Mag Aug–Sept 1906.
Harker, L. A. Ruskin and girlhood. Scribner's Mag Nov 1906.
Stephen, L. In his Studies of a biographer, 3 vols 1907.
Herford, C. H. Ruskin and the Gothic Revival. Quart Rev 207 1907.
Goring, K. M. The friends of living creatures and Ruskin. Fortnightly Rev Sept–Oct 1907.
Ruskin Double Number. Bookman (London). Oct 1908.
Hall Caine, T. H. In his My story, 1908.
Emslie, J. P. Recollections of Ruskin. Working Men's College Jnl 10 1908.
Rainero, C. Il pensiero di Ruskin e sua influenza sui contemporanei. Turin 1909.
Chevrillon, A. La penseé de Ruskin. Paris 1909.
Catalogue of Ruskin Exhibition in memory of Charles Eliot Norton. Boston 1909.
Earland, A. Ruskin and his circle. 1910.
Guillon, C. Le christianisme de Ruskin. Cahors 1910.
Wingate, A. Life of Ruskin. 1910.
Durrant, W. S. From art to social reform: Ruskin's nature of Gothic. Nineteenth Century May 1910.
Benson, A. C. Ruskin: a study in personality. 1911.
Mollerup, A. Ruskin: hovedtanker i hans vaerker. Copenhagen 1911.
Poulton, E. B. John Viriamu Jones and other Oxford memories. 1911.
Symon, J. D. Ruskin: his homes and haunts. 1911.
Vetter, T. Ruskin und William Morris: Feinde und Förderer der Technik. Zürich 1912.
Danel, J. Les idées sociales de Ruskin. Paris 1913.
Maurice, F. D. In his Life of Octavia Hill, 1913.
Taber, A. E. Work for all: a co-operative commonwealth based on Ruskin's teaching. Leeds 1914.
Whitehouse, J. H. Ruskin in old age. Scribner's Mag 43 1917.
— (ed). Ruskin centenary addresses. 1919.
— Ruskin the prophet. 1920.
— (ed). To the memory of Ruskin. 1935.
— Ruskin and Brantwood: an account of the Exhibition Rooms. 1937 (Ruskin Soc).
— Ruskin the painter and his works at Bembridge. 1938.
— Ruskin's influence to-day. Oxford 1945. Rptd from Contemporary Rev Feb 1944.
— (ed). Ruskin: renascence. 1946.
— (ed). Ruskin, prophet of the good life. 1948.
— Vindication of Ruskin. 1950.
Morley, E. J. Ruskin and social ethics. 1917 (Fabian Soc).
[Burdon, J.] Reminiscences of Ruskin. 1919.
Mumm, A. L. Ruskin and the Alps. Alpine Jnl 32 1919.
Proust, M. Pastiches et mélanges. Paris 1919; tr Gerard Hopkins as Marcel Proust: a selection from his miscellaneous writings, 1948.
— Lettres à une amie. Ed M. Riefstahl, Manchester 1942; tr 1949.
Masefield, J. John Ruskin. Bembridge 1920.
Graham, J. W. The harvest of Ruskin. 1920.
Shaw, G. B. Ruskin's politics. 1921.
Dunglas Home, D. D. D. Home: his life and mission. 1921.
Parry, E. A. Whistler v. Ruskin. Cornhill Mag Jan 1921.
Collingwood, R. G. Ruskin's philosophy. 1922.
Beerbohm, M. In his Rossetti and his circle, 1922.
Roe, F. W. The social philosophy of Carlyle and Ruskin. New York 1922.
Marriott, J. A. R. Ruskin's economics. Cornhill Mag April 1923.
Scott, G. In his Architecture of humanism, 1924 (2nd edn).
Thomas, W. Ruskin. Paris 1925.

Luxmoore, H. E. The Guild of St George. 1925.
Chambers, R. W. Ruskin—and others—on Byron. 1925 (Eng Assoc); rptd in his Man's unconquerable mind, 1939.
Stirling, A. M. W. The Richmond papers. 1926.
Audra, E. L'influence de Ruskin en France. Revue des Cours et Conférences 15 Jan 1926.
Collet, C. E. The development of Ruskin's views in interest. Economic Jnl 1 1926.
Alexander, G. C. Francesca Alexander. Cambridge Mass 1927.
'Maurois, André' (E. S. W. Herzog). In his Etudes anglaises, Paris 1927.
— Proust et Ruskin. E & S 17 1932.
Murray, J. Marcel Proust as critic and disciple of Ruskin. Nineteenth Century April 1927.
Woolf, V. Praeterita. New Republic 28 Dec 1927.
— In her Captain's death bed and other essays, 1950.
Williams-Ellis, A. The tragedy of Ruskin. 1928.
Maurice, E. S. Octavia Hill: early ideals. 1928.
Lucas, E. V. The Colvins and their friends. 1928.
Ruskin as a Communist: comparison with Marx. Socialist Rev Feb 1928.
Gomez de la Serna, R. Efigies. Madrid. 1929.
Clark, K. The Gothic Revival. 1929.
— Ruskin at Oxford. Oxford 1947.
Kreemers, R. Ruskin: zijn leven en zijn werken. Oisterwijk 1930.
Roche, A. J. Proust as translator of Ruskin. PMLA 45 1930.
Scott, E. H. Ruskin's Guild of St George. 1931.
MacCarthy, D. In his Portraits, 1931.
Ladd, H. The Victorian morality of art: an analysis of Ruskin's aesthetic. New York 1932.
Larg, D. John Ruskin. 1932.
Dunn, W. H. Lectures on three eminent Victorians. Claremont Cal 1932.
Bentley, J. A. Ruskin and modern fiction. Queen's Quart 39 1932.
Wilenski, R. H. John Ruskin. 1933.
Gally, H. Ruskin et l'esthétique intuitive. Paris 1933.
Janes, G. M. The social ethics of Ruskin. Quart Jnl of Univ of N Dakota 23 1933.
Sturge Moore, T. and D. C. Works and days from the journal of Michael Field. 1933.
Nevinson, H. W. 'Ruskin at Sallanches'. Spectator 22 Sept 1933.
'Sencourt, Robert' (R. E. G. George). Ruskin. Catholic World March 1933.
— Turner and Ruskin. Contemporary Rev Jan 1952.
Schaub-Koch, E. Le souvenir de Ruskin. Revue Hebdomadaire 25 Aug 1934.
Dalhoff, R. Studien über die Religiosität Ruskins. Würzburg 1935.
Inge, W. R. Plato and Ruskin. Tran Royal Soc of Lit 14 1935.
Crow, G. Ruskin. 1936.
Beard, C. A. Ruskin and the babble of tongues. New Republic 3 Aug 1936.
Falk, B. Turner the painter: his hidden life. 1938.
Lippincott, B. E. In his Victorian critics of democracy, 1938.
Mackail, J. W. In his Studies in humanism, 1938.
Ericson, E. E. A Ruskin allusion. E Studien 72 1938.
O'Brien, M. C. The personalist element in the sociological ideas of Ruskin. Washington 1939.
Finberg, A. J. The life of J. M. W. Turner. Oxford 1939.
Jackson, H. The printing of books. New York 1939.
— Dreamers of dreams. 1948.
Keefe, H. J. A century in print: the story of Hazell's. 1939.
Cockburn, J. Octavia Hill. Quart Rev 272. 1939.
Curtin, F. D. Aesthetics in English social reform: Ruskin and his followers. In Nineteenth-century studies, ed H. Davis et al, Ithaca 1940.
— Ruskin in French criticism. PMLA 77 1962.
Gilbert, K. Ruskin's relation to Aristotle. Philosophical Rev 49 1940.
Logan, J. V. Wordsworth and the pathetic fallacy. MLN 55 1940.
Reilly, J. J. Ruskin and war. Catholic World Dec 1940.
— Ruskin on love and marriage. Catholic World Dec 1946.
Angus, D. R. The relationship of Wordsworth's Ode on the intimations of immortality to Ruskin's theory of the infinite in art. MLR 36 1941.
Hagstotz, H. B. The educational theories of Ruskin. Lincoln Nebraska 1942.
Miles, J. Pathetic fallacy in the nineteenth century. Berkeley 1942.
Bell, E. M. Octavia Hill: a biography. 1942.
König, E. G. Ruskin und die Schweiz. Berne 1943.
Ironside, R. The art criticism of Ruskin. Horizon June 1943.
Bisson, L. A. Proust and Ruskin reconsidered in the light of Lettres à une amie. MLR 39 1944.
[Ruskin on photography]. Br Jnl of Photography March–April 1944.
Spender, J. A. In his Last essays, 1944.
Livingstone, R. W. Ruskin. Proc Br Acad 31 1945.
Orsini, N. Il futuro volitivo in Wordsworth e Ruskin. Anglica June 1946.
Delattre, F. Ruskin et Bergson: de l'intuition esthéthique à l'intuition métaphysique. Oxford 1947.
Dawson, A. M. P. A Victorian prophet with a message for today. Hibbert Jnl 45 1947.
Lambert, R. S. For the time is at hand. 1947.
Steegman, J. Lord Lindsay: The history of Christian art. Jnl Warburg & Courtauld Inst 10 1947.
C., T. Mrs Gaskell to Ruskin. More Books June 1948.
Ford, G. H. The Governor Eyre case in England. UTQ 17 1948.
Grigson, G. James Smetham. Cornhill Mag 163 1948.
Jump, J. D. Ruskin's reputation in the 1850s: the evidence of the three principal weeklies. PMLA 63 1948.
Robertson, M. Ruskin on watercolour. More Books April 1948.
Scott, W. S. Ruskin's parents. Quart Rev 287 1948.
— Ruskin and Rosie La Touche. Ibid.
Leon, D. Ruskin: the great Victorian. 1949.
Quennell, P. C. Ruskin: the portrait of a prophet. 1949.
Hough, G. In his Last Romantics, 1949.
Patmore, D. Life and times of Coventry Patmore. 1949.
Doughty, O. In his A Victorian Romantic: D. G. Rossetti, 1949.
Angeli, H. R. D. G. Rossetti: his friends and enemies. 1949.
Shaffer, R. B. Ruskin, Norton and Memorial Hall. Harvard Lib Bull 3 1949.
Mikimoto, R. The trace of Ruskin. 1949 (Tokyo Ruskin Soc).
Aldington, R. (ed). The religion of beauty: selections from the Aesthetes. 1950.
Warren, A. H. English poetic theory 1825–65. Princeton 1950.
Banyard, G. Ruskin. Fortnightly Rev Feb 1950.
Lunn, A. John Ruskin. Dublin Rev 224 1950.
Roellinger, F. X. Ruskin on education. Jnl of General Education 5 1950.
Smallwood, O. T. In quest of a faith: Ruskin's theological searchings. Cresset 13 1950.
C., O. Ruskin, Acland and the Oxford Museum. Harlequin 2 June 1950.
Evans, J. Millais' drawings of 1853. Burlington Mag July 1950.
— John Ruskin. 1954.
— Ruskin as an artist. Apollo 66 1957.
Townsend, F. G. Ruskin and the landscape feeling: a critical analysis of his thought 1843–56. Urbana 1951.

— The American estimate of Ruskin 1847–60. PQ 32 1953.
Hamilton, K. M. The road back to Ruskin. Hibbert Jnl 50 1951.
Litzenberg, K. Controversy over Ruskin. JEGP 50 1951.
Carré, J.-M. L'Italie de Goethe, de Ruskin et de Taine. Revue de Littérature Comparée 25 1951.
Buckley, J. H. In his Victorian temper, Cambridge Mass 1951.
Strachan, L. R. M. Ruskin and the Great Exhibition. N & Q 2 Feb 1952.
LeRoy, G. C. In his Perplexed prophets, Philadelphia 1953.
Dougherty, C. T. Joyce and Ruskin. N & Q Feb 1953.
— John Ruskin. Victorian Newsletter no 14 1958.
Brodrick, J. C. An Emerson–Ruskin parallel. N & Q July 1954.
Lloyd, M. Hawthorne, Ruskin and the hostile tradition. Eng Miscellany (Rome) 6 1955.
Fain, J. T. Ruskin and the economists. Nashville 1956.
Autret, J. L'influence de Ruskin sur la vie, les idées et l'œuvre de Marcel Proust. Geneva 1956.
Burd, V. A. Ruskin's quest for a theory of imagination. MLQ 17 1956.
— Ruskin's antidotes for Carlyle's purges. Boston Univ Stud in Eng 3 1957.
Tillotson, G. Hopkins and Ruskin. TLS 6 Jan 1956.
Adams, R. P. Architecture and the romantic tradition. Amer Quart 9 1957.
Kegel, C. H. Ruskin's St George in America. Ibid.
Spence, M. E. The Guild of St George: Ruskin's attempts to translate his ideas into practice. Bull John Rylands Lib 40 1957.
Sanders, C. R. Carlyle's letters to Ruskin: a finding list with some unpublished letters. Bull John Rylands Lib 41 1958.
Maslenikov, O. A. Ruskin, Bely and the Solo'yovs. Slavonic & East European Rev 35 1958.
Edwards, R. Ruskin on English contemporary artists. Connoisseur 144 1959.
Hollander, B. The international law of art. 1959.
Rathmell, J. C. A. Hopkins, Ruskin and the Sidney Psalter. London Mag Sept 1959.
Sokolnicki, M. Wiara w piekno a cynizm zycia: Ruskin. Wiadomosci no 34/595 1 1959.
Morris, B. Ruskin on the moral imagination in architecture. Colorado Univ Stud in Lang & Lit Jan 1957.
Fontaney, P. Ruskin d'après des livres nouveaux. Etudes Anglaises 13 1960.
Kimborough, R. Calm between crises: pattern and direction in Ruskin's mature thought. Trans Wisconsin Acad of Sciences, Arts & Letters 49 1960.
Kolb, P. Proust et Ruskin: nouvelles perspectives. Cahiers de l'Association Internationale des Etudes Françaises 12 1960.
Drawings by Ruskin: exhibition catalogue 1960 (Arts Council).
McLelland, V. A. Ruskin's apologia. Downside Rev 79 1961.
Thomas, J. D. Poetic truth and pathetic fallacy. Texas Stud in Lit & Lang 3 1961.
Francastel, P. La Venise de Ruskin et les archéologues. In Venezia nelle litterature moderne, ed C. Pellegrini, Venice 1961.
Brown, T. J. English literary autographs: xxxviii. Book Collector 10 1961.
Templeman, W. D. Ruskin's ploughshare and Hopkins' The windhover. E Studies 43 1962.
Gridley, R. Walden and Ruskin's The white thorn blossom. Emerson Soc Quart no 26 1962.
Bell, Q. Ruskin. Edinburgh 1963 (Writers & Critics).
Le Breton, G. La folie de Ruskin. Mercure de France Nov 1963.
Fishman, S. The interpretation of art. Berkeley 1963.
Boas, G. The heaven of invention. Baltimore 1963.
Arthos, J. Ruskin and Tolstoy. Dalhousie Rev 43 1963.
Lutyens, M. Effie in Venice. 1965.
— Millais and the Ruskins. 1967.

H. G. P.

CHARLES ROBERT DARWIN
1809–82

The chief ms collection is in the Cambridge Univ Library, including the unpbd ms of Natural selection, *an abstract of which is* On the origin of species, *below. Important collections of unpbd letters are in the American Philosophical Association, Philadelphia and in BM.*

Bibliographies

Handlist of Darwin papers at the University Library Cambridge. Cambridge 1960.
Osborne, E. A. The first edition of On the origin of species. Book Collector 9 1960.
Todd, W. B. Variant issues of On the origin of species. Ibid.
Freeman, R. B. The works of Darwin: an annotated bibliographical handlist. 1965.

Collections

Gesammelte Werke, tr J. V. Carus 13 vols Stuttgart 1875–81.
Gesammelte kleinere Schriften, tr E. Krause 2 vols Leipzig 1885.
Darwinism stated by Darwin himself. Ed N. Sheppard, New York 1884.
The living thoughts of Darwin. Ed J. Huxley and U. Fisher 1939.
The Darwin reader. Ed M. Bates and P. S. Humphrey 1957.
Darwin for today: the essence of his works. Ed S. E. Hyman, Cambridge Mass 1963.
Bibliographies of contributions to scientific journals and to books by others are in The life and letters, ed F. Darwin; More letters, ed F. Darwin and A. C. Seward; *and* G. T. Bettany, Life of Darwin, *below.*

§ 1

The zoology of the voyage of HMS Beagle, under the command of Captain Fitzroy RN, during the years 1832 to 1836, edited and superintended by Charles Darwin. 5 pts 1838–43.
Journal of researches into the geology and natural history of the various countries visited by HMS Beagle. 1839 (issued separately, and as vol 3: Journal and remarks, of The narrative of the voyages of HM Ships Adventure and Beagle, ed R. Fitzroy), 1840, New York 1952; ed M. Silsom tr German, 1844; 1845 (rev as Journal of researches into the natural history and geology), 1847, 1852, 1860 (with addns), 1870, 1872, 1873, 1876, 1879, 1882 etc; New York 1846, 1855 etc; tr Italian, 1872; German, 1875; French, 1875; Danish, 1876.
The structure and distribution of coral reefs, being the first part of the geology of the voyage of the Beagle. 1842, New York 1896, Berkeley Cal 1962; tr German, 1876; French, 1878; Italian, 1888.
Geological observations on the volcanic islands, being the second part of the geology of the voyage of the Beagle. 1844, New York 1896 (with third part); tr German, 1876.
Geological observations on South America, being the third part of the geology of the voyage of the Beagle. 1846; tr German, 1878.
Geology. In A manual of scientific enquiry prepared for the use of Her Majesty's Navy and adapted for travellers in general, ed J. F. W. Herschel, 1849, 1851, 1859, 1871, 1886; rev and rptd separately as Geology, 1849; as Manual of geology, 1859.

A monograph of the sub-class cirripedia. 2 vols 1851–4, 1 vol 1965.
A monograph of the fossil lepadidae. 2 vols 1851–4.
On the tendency of species to form varieties, and on the perpetuation of varieties and species by natural means of selection, by Charles Darwin and Alfred Wallace, communicated by Sir Charles Lyell and J. D. Hooker. Jnl of Linnean Soc, Zoology 3 1858; 1858 (offprint); rptd in The Darwin–Wallace celebration, 1st July 1908, by the Linnean Society, 1908; in G. Sarton, Discovery of the theory of natural selection, Isis 14 1930; in The Darwin reader 1957, above; in Evolution by natural selection, ed G. de Beer, Cambridge 1958; in Darwin, Wallace and the theory of natural selection, ed B. J. Loewenberg, New Haven 1957.
On the origin of species by natural selection. 1859, 1901, 1902, 1906, 1910, 1950, Cambridge Mass 1964; 1860 (2nd edn rev), 1861 (3rd edn rev), 1866 (4th edn rev), 1869 (5th edn rev), 1872 (as The origin of species) (6th edn rev), 1873, 1875, 1876 (with slight changes), 1878, 1880, 1882 etc; New York 1860 (with notes not in 2nd English edn), 1868, 1870 etc; A variorum text, ed M. Peckham, Philadelphia 1959; tr German, 1860 (with first form of Historical sketch, rev and expanded in 3rd English edn); French, 1862; Russian, 1864; Italian, 1865; Swedish, 1869; Danish, 1872; Hungarian, 1873–4; Spanish, 1877.
On the various contrivances by which British and foreign orchids are fertilised by insects. 1862, 1877 (rev as The various contrivances), 1882 etc, New York 1877, 1884; tr German, 1862; French, 1870; Italian, 1883.
On the movements and habits of climbing plants. Jnl of Linnean Soc 9 1865, 1865 (offprint), 1875 (rev, much enlarged, and pbd separately), 1876, 1882 etc, New York 1876; tr German, 1876; French, 1877; Italian, 1878.
The variation of animals and plants under domestication. 2 vols 1868, 1875 (rev), 1882 etc, New York 1878, 1890; tr French, 1868; German, 1868; Russian, 1869; Italian, 1876.
The descent of man, and selection in relation to sex. 2 vols 1871, 1871 (3 rev issues), 1874 (2nd edn rev), 1875 (rev), 1877 (rev), 1879, 1881, 1882 etc, New York 1871, 1872 etc; tr Dutch, 1871; German, 1871–2; Italian, 1871; French, 1872; Swedish, 1872; Danish, 1874–5; Polish, 1874; Hungarian, 1884.
The expression of the emotions in man and animals. 1872, 1873, 1890 (with addns) etc, New York 1873, 1896, 1899; ed M. Mead, New York 1955; tr Dutch, 1873; French, 1874; German, 1874; Italian, 1892.
Insectivorous plants. 1875, 1876, 1888 (2nd edn rev by F. Darwin) etc, New York 1875 etc; tr German, 1876; French, 1877; Italian, 1878.
The effects of cross and self fertilisation in the vegetable kingdom. 1876, 1878 (2nd edn rev), 1891 etc, New York 1877, 1892; tr French, 1877; Italian, 1878.
The different forms of flowers on plants of the same species. 1877, 1880 etc, New York 1877, 1896; tr German, 1877; French, 1878.
The life of Erasmus Darwin. In E. Krause, Erasmus Darwin, tr from German by W. S. Dallas, 1879, 1887; tr German, 1880.
The power of movement in plants, assisted by Francis Darwin, 1880, 1882, New York 1881; tr German, 1881; Italian, 1884.
The formation of vegetable mould, through the action of worms with observations on their habits. 1881, 1881 (rev), 1882 (rev), 1883 (corrected by F. Darwin) etc, New York 1882 etc; tr French, 1882; Italian, 1882; German, 1884.
Essay on instinct. In G. J. Romanes, Mental evolution in animals, 1883, 1885, New York 1883; tr French, 1887. A ch from unpbd Natural selection, above.
The foundations of the Origin of species: two essays written in 1842 and 1844. Ed F. Darwin 1909; rptd in Evolution by natural selection, above.

Letters, Diaries, Notebooks and Autobiography

The life and letters of Darwin, including an autobiographical chapter. Ed F. Darwin 3 vols 1887, 1887 (3 rev edns), 1888, New York 1888, 1891; tr German, 1887; French, 1888.
Darwin: his life told in an autobiographical chapter, and in a selected series of his published letters. Ed F. Darwin 2 vols 1892, 1902 etc, New York 1888, 1896, 1958; tr German, 1893.
More letters. Ed F. Darwin and A. C. Seward 2 vols 1903.
Emma Darwin, wife of Charles Darwin; a century of family letters. Ed H. E. Litchfield 2 vols Cambridge 1904 (priv ptd), 1915 (rev).
The complete correspondence between Wallace and Darwin 1857–81. In Alfred Russell Wallace, Letters and reminiscences, ed J. Marchant 2 vols 1916.
The autobiography of Darwin. 1929, 1931, 1937; ed N. Barlow 1958 ('with original omissions restored').
Diary of the voyage of HMS Beagle. Ed N. Barlow, Cambridge 1933.
Darwin and the voyage of the Beagle. Ed N. Barlow 1945.
Dupree, A. H. Some letters from Darwin to Jeffries Wyman. Isis 42 1951.
Some unpublished letters of Darwin. Ed G. de Beer, Notes & Records of Royal Soc 14 1959; Further unpublished letters of Darwin, ed de Beer, Annals of Science 14 1960.
Darwin's journal. Bull of BM (Natural History) historical ser 2 1959.
Notebooks on transmutation of species. Ed G. de Beer, Bull of BM (Natural History) historical ser 2 1961.
Ornithological notes. Ed N. Barlow, Bull of BM (Natural History) historical ser 2 1963.

§2

[Owen, R.] Darwin on the origin of species. Edinburgh Rev 3 1860.
[Jenkin, F.] The origin of species. North Br Rev 46 1867.
Müller, N. Lectures on Mr Darwin's philosophy of language. Fraser's Mag May–June 1876.
Butler, S. Evolution old and new. 1879.
— Unconscious memory. 1880.
— Luck or cunning as the main means of organic modification? [1886].
Aveling, E. B. The religious views of Darwin. 1882.
Canello, U. A. Letteratura e Darwinismo. Padua 1882.
Allen, G. Charles Darwin. 1885.
Bettany, G. T. Life of Darwin. 1887.
Holder, C. T. Darwin: his life and work. New York 1891.
Huxley, T. H. Darwiniana. 1893. Collects reviews and essays. 1859–88.
Stirling, J. H. Darwinianism: workmen and work. Edinburgh 1894.
Tille, A. Von Darwin bis Nietzsche: ein Buch Entwicklungsethik. Leipzig 1895.
Johnston, W. W. Ill-health of Darwin: its nature and its relation to his work. Amer Anthropologist new ser 3 1901.
Gould, G. M. In his Biographic clinics: the origin of the ill health of De Quincey, Carlyle, Darwin, Huxley and the Brownings, Philadelphia 1903.
Baldwin, J. M. Darwin and the humanities. Baltimore 1909.
Bryce, J. B. Personal reminiscences of Darwin and of the reception of the Origin of species. Proc Amer Philosophical Soc 48 1909.
Judd, J. W. The coming of evolution. Cambridge 1912.
Huxley, L. Charles Darwin. 1921.
Osborn, H. F. A priceless Darwin letter. Science 64 1926.
Down House. 1928 (report of Br Assoc).
Darwin, M. Memories of Down House. Nineteenth Century July 1929.

Barlow, N. Robert Fitzroy and Darwin. Cornhill Mag April 1932.
Haas, Ludwig. Der Darwinismus bei Nietzsche. Giessen 1932.
Huxley, J. Charles Darwin. Contemporary Rev Oct 1932.
Jandásek, L. The founder of the sokols. Slavonic Rev 10 1932.
Stevenson, L. Darwin among the poets. Chicago 1932.
Barber, O. H. G. Wells Verhältnis über Darwinismus. Leipzig 1934.
'West, Geoffrey' (G. H. Wells). Darwin: the fragmentary man. 1937.
Gantz, K. F. The beginnings of Darwinian ethics. Austin 1939.
Henkin, L. J. Darwinism in the English novel 1860–1910. New York 1940.
Hofstadter, R. Social Darwinism in American thought 1860–1915. Philadelphia 1941.
Loewenberg, B. J. Darwinism comes to America. Mississippi Valley Historical Rev 28 1941.
Hubble, D. The evolution of Darwin. Horizon 14 1946.
Ashley-Montagu, M. F. Theognis, Darwin and social selection. Isis 37 1947.
— Darwin: competition and cooperation. New York 1952.
Eiseley, L. C. Was Darwin wrong about the human brain? Harper's Mag Nov 1955.
— Darwin's century: evolution and the men who discovered it. New York 1958.
— Darwin, Coleridge and the theory of unconscious creation. Daedalus 94 1965.
Keith, A. Darwin revalued. 1955.
Yonge, C. M. Darwin to Bikini. New Statesman 10 Sept 1955.
A century of Darwin. Ed S. A. Barnett 1958.
de Beer, G. Darwin: lecture on a master mind. Oxford 1958.
— Charles Darwin. Proc Br Acad 44 1959.
— Darwin: evolution by natural selection. 1963.
Ellegard, A. Darwin and the general reader: the reception of Darwin's theory of evolution in the British periodical press 1859–72. Stockholm 1958.
Huxley, J. S. et al. A book that shook the world: anniversary essays on Darwin's Origin of species. Pittsburgh 1958.
— and H. B. D. Kettlewell. Darwin and his world. 1965.
Mandelbaum, M. Darwin's religious view. JHI 19 1958.
Commemoration of the centennial of the publication of the Origin of species. Proc Amer Philosophical Soc 103 1959. A symposium.
Darwin's biological work: some aspects reconsidered. Ed P. R. Bell 1959.
Darlington, D. C. Darwin's place in history. Oxford 1959.
Darwin, evolution and creation. Ed P. Zimmerman, St Louis 1959. A symposium.
Darwin's vision and Christian perspectives. Ed W. J. Ong, New York 1959. A symposium.
Evolution and anthropology: a centennial appraisal. Washington 1959 (Anthropological Soc of Washington). A symposium.
Fleming, D. The centenary of the Origin of species. JHI 20 1959.
Forerunners of Darwin 1745–1959. Ed H. B. Glass, O. Temkin and W. L. Straus jr, Baltimore 1959. A symposium.
Goldman, I. Evolution and anthropology. Victorian Stud 3 1959.
Greene, J. C. The death of Adam. Ames Iowa 1959.
Huxley, F. Darwin: life and habit. Amer Scholar 28–9 1959.
The impact of Darwinian thought on American life and culture. Austin 1959. A symposium.
Kettlewell, H. B. D. Darwin's missing evidence. Scientific Amer 200 1959.
Loewenberg, B. J. Darwin scholarship in the Darwin year. Amer Quart 11 1959.
— The mosaic of Darwinian thought. Victorian Stud 3 1959.
Luire, E. Louis Agassiz and the idea of evolution. Ibid.
Man, race and Darwin. Ed P. Mason, Oxford 1959. A symposium.
Mayr, E. Agassiz, Darwin and evolution. Harvard Lib Bull 13 1959.
Nachtwey, R. Der Irrweg des Darwinismus. Berlin 1959.
Passmore, J. Darwin's impact on British metaphysics. Victorian Stud 3 1959.
Peckham, M. Darwinism and Darwinisticism. Ibid.
Boller, P. B. Darwin's American champion. Southwest Rev 45 1960.
Evolution after Darwin, vol 1: The evolution of life; vol 2: The evolution of man; vol 3: Issues in evolution. Ed S. Tax and C. Callender, Chicago 1960. A symposium.
Hardin, G. J. Nature and man's fate. 1960.
Willey, B. Darwin and Butler: two versions of evolution. 1960.
Darwinism and the study of society: a centenary symposium. Ed M. Banton 1961.
Fleming, D. Darwin, the anaesthetic man. Victorian Stud 4 1961.
Gates, E. J. Darwin and Benito Lynch's El inglés de los güesos. Hispania 44 1961.
Greene, J. C. Darwin and the modern world view. Baton Rouge 1961.
Stauffer, R. C. On the origin of species: an unpublished version. Science 130 1961.
Wichler, G. Darwin: the founder of the theory of evolution and natural selection. Oxford 1961.
Cannon, W. P. The bases of Darwin's achievement: a revaluation. Victorian Stud 5 1962.
Darwin, Marx and Wagner: a symposium. Ed H. L. Plaine, Columbus 1962.
The evolution of living organisms. Ed G. W. Leeper, Melbourne 1962. A symposium.
Gruber, H. E. and V. The eye of reason: Darwin's development during the Beagle voyage. Isis 103 1962.
Stevenson, R. S. In his Famous illnesses in history, 1962.
Greenacre, P. The quest for the father: a study of the Darwin–Butler controversy. New York 1963.
Nursall, J. R. The consequences of Darwinism. Dalhousie Rev 42 1963.
Vorzimmer, P. Darwin and blending inheritance. Isis 54 1963.
— Darwin's ecology and its influence upon his theory. Isis 56 1965.
Wilson, J. B. Darwin and the transcendentalists. JHI 24 1965.

M. P.

WALTER BAGEHOT
1826–77

Collections

The works, with memoirs by R. H. Hutton. Ed F. Morgan 5 vols Hartford Conn 1889.
The works and life. Ed E. I. Barrington 10 vols 1915.
Collected works. Ed N. St John-Stevas 8 vols 1965–.

§ 1

Estimates of some Englishmen and Scotchmen. 1858. Rptd from Nat Rev.
Parliamentary reform: an essay reprinted, with considerable additions, from the National Review. 1859.
The history of the unreformed Parliament and its lessons: an essay reprinted from the National Review. 1860.

Memoir of the Rt Hon J. Wilson 1861. Rptd from Economist.

Count your enemies and economise your expenditure. 1862.

The English constitution, reprinted from the Fortnightly Review. 1867, 1872 (adds one ch); ed A. J. Balfour, Oxford 1928 (WC); ed R. H. S. Crossman 1964 (with bibliography on government and politics).

A practical plan for assimilating the English and American money, reprinted from the Economist with additions. 1869.

Physics and politics: or thoughts on the application of the principles of 'natural selection' and 'inheritance' to political society. 1872; ed J. Barzun, New York 1948.

Lombard Street: a description of the money market. 1873; ed E. Johnstone 1892 (brought up to date); ed H. Withers 1910; ed A. W. Wright 1915 (notes rev); ed F. C. Genovese, Homewood Ill 1962.

Some articles on the depreciation of silver and on topics connected with it, reprinted from the Economist. 1877.

Literary studies. Ed R. H. Hutton 2 vols 1879 (with memoir), 3 vols 1895, 1906 (re-issue of vol 3 with addns); ed G. Sampson 2 vols 1906 (EL). Rptd in part from Estimates, above.

Economic studies. Ed R. H. Hutton 1880.

Biographical studies. Ed R. H. Hutton 1881, 1907 (adds index).

Essays on parliamentary reform. 1883.

The postulates of English political economy: student's edition with a preface by A. Marshall. 1885. Rptd from Economic studies, above.

Estimations in criticism. Ed C. Lennox 2 vols 1908. Rptd from Literary studies, above.

Letters

The love-letters of Bagehot and Eliza Wilson. Ed E. I. Barrington 1933.

§2

Bagehot: in memoriam. 1878 (priv ptd). A collection of obituary notices.

Hutton, R. H. In his Criticisms on contemporary thought and thinkers, 2 vols 1894.

Stephen, L. In his Studies of a biographer vol 3, 1902.

Barrington, E. I. Life of Bagehot. 1914, 1915 (as vol 10 of Works and life of Bagehot, above).

Birrell, A. In his Collected essays and addresses vol 2, 1922.

Sampson, G. Bagehot. Bookman (London) Feb 1926.

Marriott, J. A. R. Bagehot. Fortnightly Rev Feb 1926.

Read, H. In his Sense of glory, Cambridge 1929; rptd in his Collected essays in literary criticism, 1951.

Feiling, K. G. In his Sketches in nineteenth-century biography, 1930.

Brinton, C. G. In his English political thought in the nineteenth century, 1933.

Driver, C. H. Bagehot and the social psychologists. In The social and political ideas of some representative thinkers of the Victorian age, ed F. J. C. Hearnshaw 1933.

Irvine, W. Walter Bagehot. New York 1939.

Young, G. M. Victorian psychology. TLS 25 Jan 1936.

—— The greatest Victorian: the case for Bagehot. Spectator 18 June and 2 July 1937; rptd in his Today and yesterday, 1948. *See also* H. W. Rudman, Bagehot: the greatest Victorian? History of Ideas News Letter no 5 1960.

The economist 1843–1943: a centenary volume. 1943.

Pritchett, V. S. Books in general. New Statesman 29 July 1946.

Dexter, B. Bagehot and the fresh eye. Foreign Affairs Oct 1945.

Barzun, J. The critic as statesman. Atlantic Monthly Aug 1946.

—— Bagehot: or the human comedy. In his Energies of art, New York 1956.

Easton, D. Bagehot and liberal realism. Amer Political Science Rev Feb 1949.

Briggs, A. Trollope, Bagehot and the English constitution. Cambridge Jnl March 1952; rptd in his Victorian people, 1954.

Chapman, R. W. The text of Bagehot's Constitution. PQ 31 1952.

Cameron, J. M. Men and ideas: Bagehot. Encounter Oct 1954.

Pearson, J. G. The acute realism of Bagehot. Listener 10 March 1955.

Sayers, R. S. Central banking after Bagehot. Oxford 1957.

Halsted, J. B. Bagehot on toleration. JHI 19 1958.

Stanford, D. Bagehot and the monarchy. Modern Age 3 1959.

St John-Stevas, N. Walter Bagehot. 1959. With selected writings and bibliography.

—— Walter Bagehot. 1963 (Br Council pamphlet).

—— Bagehot as a writer. Wiseman Rev 237 1963.

Buchan, A. The spare Chancellor: the life of Bagehot. 1959.

Mackenzie, R. Bagehot and 'the rule of mere numbers'. Listener 19 Nov 1959.

Tener, R. H. Bagehot and Tennyson. TLS 21 Aug 1959.

Wain, J. An introduction to Bagehot. REL 1 1960.

A. P.

V. MINOR PROSE 1835–70

This section has normally been restricted to writers born after 1799 and before 1830. Only critical writings listed in other sections have been cross-referenced.

WILLIAM DAVENPORT ADAMS
1851–1904

Famous books: sketches in the highways and byeways of English literature. 1875.

Dictionary of English literature: being a comprehensive guide to English authors and their works. [1878], [1880] (rev).

The witty and humorous side of the English poets, by Arthur H. Elliott [i.e. Adams]. 1880.

By-ways in book-land: short essays on literary subjects. 1888.

Rambles in book-land: short essays on literary subjects. 1889.

A book of burlesque: sketches of English stage travestie and parody. 1891.

With poet and player: essays on literature and the stage. 1891.

A dictionary of the drama: a guide to the plays, play-wrights, players and play-houses of the United Kingdom and America, from the earliest times to the present. Vol 1 (all pbd) 1904.

Adams also compiled 9 anthologies of anecdote, epigram, verse etc, and edited A. C. Calmour, Practical play-writing, [1891] *and* Disraeli, The revolutionary epick, 1904.

JOHN STUART BLACKIE

1809–95

See col 509, above.

ANDREW KENNEDY HUTCHINSON BOYD

1825–99

Selections

A. K. H. B.: a volume of selections. Ed C. Boyd [1914].

§1

The recreations of a country parson. 3 sers 1859–78.
The commonplace philosopher in town and country. 1862.
Leisure hours in town. 1862.
Counsel and comfort spoken from a city pulpit. 1863.
The graver thoughts of a country parson. 3 sers 1863–76.
The autumn holidays of a country parson. 1864.
The critical essays of a country parson. 1865.
Sunday afternoons at the parish church of a university city. 1866.
Lessons of middle age. 1868.
Changed aspects of unchanged truths. 1869.
Present-day thoughts. 1871.
Seaside musings on Sundays and weekdays. 1872.
A Scotch communion Sunday. 1873.
Landscapes, churches and moralities. 1874.
From a quiet place: discourses. 1879.
East coast days and memories. 1881.
Our little life: essays consolatory. 2 sers 1882–4.
Towards the sunset: teachings after thirty years. 1883.
A young man, his home and friends. 1884.
What set him right; with other chapters to help. 1885–8.
Our homely comedy and tragedy. 1887.
The best last, with other papers. 1888.
To meet the day through the Christian year. 1889.
Twenty-five years of St Andrews, September 1865 to September 1890. 2 vols 1892.
St Andrews and elsewhere: glimpses of some gone and of things left. 1894.
Occasional and immemorial days. 1895. Sermons.
The last years of St Andrews, September 1890 to September 1895. 1896.
Sermons and stray papers: with a biographical sketch by W. W. Tulloch. 1907.
Boyd also pbd several lectures and sermons.

§2

Story, R. H. A. K. H. B. Guild Life & Work (Edinburgh) 13 May 1899.
The true significance of Boyd. Eclectic Mag 132 1899.

GEORGE BRIMLEY

1819–57

Essays. Ed W. G. Clark, Cambridge 1858 (with memoir), 1860, 1882, [1905].
For appreciations of Brimley *see* G. Saintsbury, A history of criticism vol 3 1904, pp. 504–8; S. T. Williams, A mid-Victorian critic, Sewanee Rev 30 1922.

JOHN BROWN

1810–82

§1

Horae subsecivae: Locke and Sydenham, with other occasional papers. Vol 1, Edinburgh 1858; vol 2, Edinburgh 1861. Vols 1–2, 2 vols 1862; ed A. Dobson, Oxford 1907 (WC); vol 3, Edinburgh 1882.
Rab and his friends. Edinburgh 1859, London 1901 ('and other papers'), [1905] (with Our dogs, and notes), 1906 (EL) (with other papers and essays, and bibliography), 1908 (with character sketches of the author by A. C. Brown and E. T. Maclaren), 1931. From Horae subsecivae, above.
'With brains, Sir'. Edinburgh 1860. An essay on education extracted from Horae subsecivae vol 1, above.
On the deaths of Rev John M'Gilchrist, John Brown and John Henderson. Edinburgh 1860.
Letter to Rev Dr Cairns. Edinburgh 1860, 1861 (in Horae subsecivae vol 2, above). Contains Domestic and personal details of the life of John Brown DD (the elder).
Health: five lay sermons to working people. Edinburgh 1862.
Our dogs. Edinburgh 1862. From Horae subsecivae vol 2, above.
Marjorie Fleming: a sketch. Edinburgh 1863. Rptd from North Br Rev; included in Horae subsecivae vol 3, above.
Jeems the doorkeeper: a lay sermon. Edinburgh 1864, 1912 ('and other stories', viz Her last half crown, Landseer's picture, In clear dream and solemn vision, The black dwarf's bones). Subsequently included in Horae subsecivae vol 3, above.
Minchmoor. Edinburgh 1864, 1912 (with Enterkin, Biggar and the house of Fleming). Included in Horae subsecivae vol 3, above.
Locke and Sydenham. Edinburgh 1866. Originally in Horae subsecivae vol 1, above, but not included in later edns.
Sir Henry Raeburn and his works. Edinburgh 1876 (priv ptd). Included in Horae subsecivae vol 3, above.
John Leech. Edinburgh 1877, 1882. In Horae subsecivae vol 3, above.
Thackeray: his literary career. Boston 1877.
Something about a well; with more of Our dogs. Edinburgh 1882.

Letters

Letters; with letters from Ruskin, Thackeray and others. Ed J. Brown and D. W. Forrest 1907.

§2

Lang, A. Rab's friend. Century Illustr Monthly Mag Feb 1883.
Maclaren, E. T. Brown and his sister Isabella. 1889, 1896 (as Brown and his sisters Isabella and Jane), 1901 (with introductory note by A. C. Brown).
Masson, D. In his Edinburgh sketches and memories, 1892.
Peddie, A. Recollections of Brown, with a selection from his correspondence. 1893.
Brown, J. T. Brown: a biography and a criticism. 1903.

ROBERT CHAMBERS

1802–71

Bibliographies

Chambers, C. E. S. A catalogue of some of the rarer books, also manuscripts and autograph letters in the collection of C. E. S. Chambers; with a bibliography of the works of William and Robert Chambers. Edinburgh 1891 (priv ptd).

Selections

Select writings. 7 vols Edinburgh 1847. Vols 1–2, Essays familiar and humorous; vol 3, Essays moral and economic; vol 4, Essays philosophical, sentimental and historical sketches; vol 5, History of the rebellion of 1745–6; vol 6, Traditions of Edinburgh; vol 7, Popular rhymes of Scotland.

Essays familiar and humorous. 2 vols [1866].

§1

Illustrations of the author of Waverley: being notices and anecdotes of real characters, scenes and incidents supposed to be described in his works. Edinburgh 1822, 1825 (enlarged).

Traditions of Edinburgh. 4 vols Edinburgh 1828, 1869 (rev); ed C. E. S. Chambers 1912.

Walks in Edinburgh. Edinburgh 1825, 1829 ('with an improved plan, and a view of the city'). A sequel to Traditions of Edinburgh, above.

Notices of the most remarkable fires in Edinburgh from 1385 to 1824. Edinburgh 1825.

Popular rhymes of Scotland; with illustrations, collected from tradition. Edinburgh 1826, 1840 (rev with addns).

History of the rebellion in Scotland in 1745, 1746. 2 vols Edinburgh 1827, 1840 (greatly enlarged), 1869 (with appendix).

The picture of Scotland. 2 vols Edinburgh 1827. A topographical account of Scotland.

History of the rebellions in Scotland under the Marquis of Montrose and others, from 1638 till 1660. 2 vols Edinburgh 1828.

History of the rebellions in Scotland, under the Viscount of Dundee and the Earl of Mar, in 1689 and 1715. Edinburgh 1829.

The life of King James the First. 2 vols Edinburgh 1830.

Life of Sir Walter Scott. Edinburgh 1832; rev W. Chambers 1871, 1894 (rev with addns).

A biographical dictionary of eminent Scotsmen. 4 vols Glasgow 1832–5, 5 vols Glasgow 1855 (rev with supplemental vol by T. Thomson), 3 vols 1870 (rev T. Thomson), 1875 (with suppl of biographies to date of pbn).

Reekiana: or minor antiquities of Edinburgh. Edinburgh 1833. Rptd in 1869 edn of Traditions of Edinburgh, above.

Poems. Edinburgh 1835 (priv ptd). Rptd with some omissions with Popular rhymes of Scotland, to form vol of the Select writings, above.

English language and literature. Edinburgh 1836.

The life of Robert Burns with a criticism of his writings. Edinburgh 1838. By James Currie. Expanded by Chambers.

The poetical works of Robert Burns; to which are now added notes illustrating historical, personal and local allusions. Edinburgh 1838.

The prose works of Robert Burns; with the notes of Currie and Cromek, and many by the present editor. Edinburgh 1839.

Vestiges of the natural history of Creation. 1844 (anon), 1884 (12th edn, introd by A. Ireland), 1887 (introd by H. Morley).

Cyclopaedia of English literature. 2 vols Edinburgh 1844.

Explanations: a sequel to Vestiges by the author of that work. 1845.

Ancient sea-margins, as memorials of changes in the relative level of sea and land. Edinburgh 1848.

The history of Scotland. 2 vols 1849.

Tracings of the North of Europe. 1851 (priv ptd). Rptd from Chambers's Edinburgh Jnl. An account of voyagings in the Baltic.

Life and works of Robert Burns. 4 vols 1851.

Tracings of Iceland and the Faröe Islands. 1856.

Domestic annals of Scotland from the Reformation to the Revolution. 2 vols Edinburgh 1858, 1 vol Edinburgh 1885 (abridged).

Edinburgh papers. 5 pts Edinburgh 1859–61, 1861.

Sketch of the history of the Edinburgh Theatre Royal. Edinburgh 1859 (priv ptd).

Domestic annals of Scotland from the Revolution to the Rebellion of 1745. 1861. Intended to form vol 3 to Domestic annals of Scotland from the Reformation to the Revolution.

The book of days: a miscellany of popular antiquities. 2 vols 1862–4.

Smollett: his life and a selection of his writings. 1867.

The Threiplands of Fingask: a family memoir. 1880. Written in 1852. Also contains Life in a Scottish country mansion; Two days on the moors of Perthshire.

§2

Chambers, W. Memoir of Robert Chambers with autobiographical reminiscences of William Chambers. Edinburgh 1872, 1884 (enlarged).

Mackay, C. Two literary breakfasts. Eclectic Mag June 1884.

Parsons, C. O. Serial publication of Traditions of Edinburgh. Library 4th ser 14 1934.

Turnbull, A. William and Robert Chambers. Edinburgh [1946], [1963] (rev).

Millhauser, M. The literary impact of Vestiges of Creation. MLQ 17 1956.

WILLIAM CHAPPELL

1809–88

A collection of national English airs: consisting of ancient song, ballad and dance tunes, interspersed with remarks and anecdote, and preceded by an essay on English minstrelsy. 2 pts 1838–40.

Popular music of the olden time: a collection of ancient songs, ballads and dance tunes, illustrative of the national music of England; with short introductions to the different reigns, and notices of the airs from writers of the sixteenth and seventeenth centuries; also a short account of the minstrels. 2 vols [1855–9]; rev H. E. Wooldridge 2 vols 1893.

The Roxburghe ballads; with short notes by William Chappell, and copies of the original woodcuts. 3 vols 1869–75 (Ballad Soc).

The history of music. Vol 1 (all pbd), [1874].

Chappell founded the Musical Antiquarian Society, 1841, and edited one of its pbns as well as several other works.

HENRY FOTHERGILL CHORLEY

1808–72

§1

Sketches of a sea port town. 3 vols 1834.

Conti the discarded; with other tales and fancies. 3 vols 1835.

Memorials of Mrs Hemans; with illustrations of her literary character from her private correspondence. 2 vols 1836.

The authors of England: a series of medallion portraits of modern literary characters, engraved from the works of British artists by A. Collas; with illustrative notices by H. F. Chorley. 1838; rev G. B. 1861.

The lion: a tale of the coteries. 3 vols 1839. Anon.

Music and manners in France and Germany: a series of travelling sketches of art and society. 3 vols 1841.

Pomfret: or public opinion and private judgment. 3 vols 1845.
Old love and new fortune: a play [in verse]. 1850.
Modern German music: recollections and criticisms. 2 vols 1854.
Duchess Eleanour: a tragedy by H. F. C[horley]. [1854].
The may-queen: a pastoral. [1858].
Roccabella: a tale of a woman's life by Paul Bell. 2 vols [1859].
The amber witch: a romantic opera, in four acts [and in verse]. [1861].
The prodigy: a tale of music. 3 vols 1866. Anon.
Thirty years' recollections. 2 vols 1862 ed E. Newman, New York 1926.
Mendelssohn's letters from Italy and Switzerland [with biographical sketch by Chorley]. 1864.
Life of F. Mendelssohn Bartholdy, by W. A. Lampadius; with supplementary sketches by H. F. Chorley. 1865.
The national music of the world. Ed H. G. Hewlett 1880.
Chorley also edited several works and arranged Scribe's Black domino *for the English stage.*

§2

Linley, G. Musical cynics of London: a satire. 1862.
Chorley: autobiography, memoir and letters compiled by H. G. Hewlett. 2 vols 1873.
Chorley and his contemporaries. Temple Bar Dec 1873.
Marshall, J. In G. Grove, Dictionary of music and musicians vol 1, 1879.

MARY VICTORIA COWDEN CLARKE, née NOVELLO
1809–98

§1

The complete concordance to Shakespeare: being a verbal index to all the passages in the dramatic works of the poet. 18 monthly pts 1844–5, 1845, 1847, [1855] (rev).
A book of stories for young people. [1847]. By Mrs Howitt, Mrs S. C. Hall and Mrs Clarke (2 stories).
Shakespeare proverbs: or the wise saws of our wisest poet. 1848; ed W. J. Rolfe, New York 1908.
Kit Bam's adventures: or the yarns of an old mariner. 1849.
The girlhood of Shakespeare's heroines in a series of fifteen tales. 3 vols 1851–2, 1 vol 1879 (condensed by S. Novello), 5 vols [1892] (with new preface), 3 vols [1906] (EL).
The iron cousin: or mutual influence. 2 vols 1854, 1 vol 1862.
The song of a drop o' wather, by Harry Wandsworth Shortfellow. 1856.
World-noted women: or types of womanly attributes. New York 1858.
The life and labours of Vincent Novello. [1864].
The trust and the remittance: two love stories. 1873.
Short stories in metrical prose. 1873.
A rambling story. 2 vols 1874.
An idyl of London streets. Rome 1875.
Recollections of writers. 1878. With Charles Cowden Clarke.
The Shakespeare key: unlocking the treasures of his style. 1879. Selections; with Charles Cowden Clarke.
Honey from the weed: verses. 1881; Verse-waifs: forming an appendix to Honey from the weed, 1883.
A score of sonnets to one object. 1884.
Uncle, Peep and I: a child's novel. 1886.
Centennial biographic sketch of Charles Cowden Clarke. 1887 (priv ptd).
Memorial sonnets. 1888.
My long life. 1896, 1896.

Letters

Letters to an enthusiast: being a series of letters addressed to Robert Balmanno esq of New York 1850–61. Ed A. U. Nettleton, Chicago 1902.
Mary Cowden Clarke also pbd several edns of Shakespeare, the most elaborate being Cassell's Illustrated Shakespeare, with Charles Cowden Clarke. She translated Berlioz, Treatise upon modern instrumentation, *and edited* The Musical Times 1853–6.

§2

Blos, H. Die Auffassung der Frauengestalten Shakespeares in dem Werke der Mrs Cowden Clarke The Girlhood of Shakespeare's heroines. Würzburg 1936.
Altick, R. D. The Cowden Clarkes. New York 1948.
B., E. Cowden Clarke and Chaucer. N & Q 6 Aug 1949.
Black, M. W. The Cowden Clarkes and the Furnesses. Univ of Pennsylvania Lib Chron 18 1952.
The Novello–Cowden Clarke collection. Leeds 1955.
Falk, D. V. Mary Cowden Clarke and her East End Injun. Jnl Rutgers Univ Lib 24 1961.

FRANCES POWER COBBE
1822–1904

§1

An essay on intuitive morals: being an attempt to popularise ethical science. 2 vols 1855, 1857.
Female education and how it would be affected by university examinations. 1862.
Essays on the pursuits of women. 1863.
Thanksgiving: a chapter of religious duty. 1863.
Broken lights: an inquiry into the present condition and future prospects of religious faith. 1864, 1865.
The cities of the past. 1864.
Italics: brief notes on politics, people and places in Italy in 1864. 1864.
Religious duty. 1864, Boston 1883, London 1894.
Studies new and old of ethical and social subjects. 1865.
Hours of work and play. 1867.
The confessions of a lost dog. 1867.
Dawning lights: an inquiry concerning the secular results of the new reformation. 1868, 1894.
Criminals, idiots, women and minors? is the classification sound? Manchester 1869. On married women's property laws.
Auricular confession in the Church of England. 1872, [1898] (4th edn rev).
Darwinism in morals and other essays. 1872.
Doomed to be saved. 1874.
The hopes of the human race hereafter and here. 1874, 1894.
Re-echoes. 1876.
False beasts and true: essays on natural and unnatural history. [1876].
The duties of women. 1881, Boston 1881, 1888 (8th Amer edn); ed B. Atkinson 1905.
The peak in Darien, with some other inquiries touching concerns of the soul and body. 1882, Boston 1882, London 1894.
A faithless world 1885, 1891, 1894 (with Health and holiness, below).
Rest in the Lord, and other small pieces. 1887 (priv ptd).
The scientific spirit of the age, and other pleas and discussions. 1888.
The friend of man; and his friends—the poets. 1889.
The modern rack: papers on vivisection. 1889.
Health and holiness. 1891.
Miss Cobbe also wrote a large number of pamphlets against vivisection.

§2

Life: by herself. 2 vols 1894, 1904 (with addns and introd by B. Atkinson).
Chappell, J. Women of worth. [1908].

JOHN CONINGTON
1825–69

See col 515, above.

ENEAS SWEETLAND DALLAS
1828–79

§1

Poetics: an essay on poetry. 1852.
Curren Bell. Blackwood's Mag July 1857; Blake, Macmillan's Mag July 1864.
The gay science. 2 vols 1866.
The Stowe–Byron controversy: a complete résumé of all that has been written and said upon the subject, together with an impartial review of the merits of the case. [1869].
Kettner's Book of the table: a manual of cookery. 1877.
Dallas also edited an abridgement of Richardson's Clarissa, *1868. He was editor of* Once a Week, *1868, and on the staff of the* Times.

§2

Drinkwater, J. In The eighteen-sixties, Cambridge 1932.
Roberts, M. The dream and the poet. TLS 18 Jan 1936.
Roellinger, F. X. A note on Kettner's Book of the table. MLN 54 1939.
—— Dallas in Trollope's Autobiography. MLN 55 1940.
—— Dallas: a mid-Victorian critic of individualism. PQ 20 1941.
—— Dallas on imagination. SP 38 1941.
Buckler, W. E. William Shenstone and Dallas: an identification. N & Q 18 March 1950.
—— Dallas's appointment as editor of Once a Week. N & Q 24 June 1950.
Warren, A. H. Poetics: an essay on poetry, 1852. In his English poetic theory 1825–65, Princeton 1950.
Forsyth, R. A. The onward march of thought and the poetic theory of Dallas. Br Jnl of Aesthetics 3 1963.

JAMES WILLIAM DAVISON
1813–85

Chopin. [1843].
Music during the Victorian era, from Mendelssohn to Wagner: being the memoirs of J. W. Davison, compiled by his son Henry Davison from memoranda and documents; with numerous portraits of musicians, and important letters (previously unpublished) of Mendelssohn, Berlioz, Gounod, Jullien, Macfarren, Sterndale Bennett etc. 1912.
Davison was editor of The Musical World *from about 1844 until his death. He became musical critic of the* Times *c. 1846.*

AUBREY THOMAS DE VERE
1814–1902

See col 1628, below.

JOHN DORAN
1807–78

§1

Sketches and reminiscences [from Paris]. 1828.
The history and antiquities of the town and borough of Reading. Reading 1835. Anon.
Filia dolorosa: memoirs of Marie Thérèse Charlotte, Duchess of Angoulême. 1852. The first 115 pp. by Mrs I. F. Romer; completed by Doran.
Habits and men; with remnants of record touching the makers of both. 1854.
Table traits; with something on them. 1854.
Lives of the queens of England of the house of Hanover. 2 vols 1855, 1874 (rev and enlarged).
Knights and their days. 1856.
Monarchs retired from business. 2 vols 1857.
The history of Court fools. 1858.
New pictures and old panels. 1859.
The book of the Princes of Wales, heirs to the Crown of England. 1860.
Memoir of Queen Adelaide, Consort of King William IV. 1861.
'Their Majesties' servants': annals of the English stage from Thomas Betterton to Edward Kean: actors—authors—audiences. 2 vols 1864, 1865 (rev and enlarged); rev R. W. Lowe 3 vols 1888.
Saints and sinners: or in church and about it. 2 vols 1868.
A lady of the last century (Mrs E. Montagu), illustrated in her unpublished letters; collected and arranged, with a biographical sketch and a chapter on Blue Stockings. 1873.
London in the Jacobite times. 2 vols 1877.
Memoirs of our great towns; with anecdotic gleanings concerning their worthies and their oddities 1860–77. 1878.
In and about Drury Lane and other papers, reprinted from Temple Bar etc. [Ed G. B., i.e. G. Bentley?] 2 vols 1881.
Doran also edited or wrote introds for 10 other works.

§2

Jeafferson, J. C. The life and writings of Doran. Temple Bar April 1878.
Jowitt, J. Some departed contributors and literary friends. Reliquary 18 1878.
Doran. London Soc July 1882.

SIR FRANCIS HASTINGS CHARLES DOYLE
1810–88

See col 518, above.

ELIZABETH, LADY EASTLAKE, née RIGBY
1809–93

§1

A residence on the shores of the Baltic. 2 vols 1841, 1842 (as Letters from the shores of the Baltic). Anon.
The Jewess: a tale from the shores of the Baltic. 1843.
Livonian tales. 1846. The disponent; The wolves; The Jewess.
Vanity Fair and Jane Eyre. Quart Rev 84 1848.
Music and the art of dress: two essays. 1852. Anon; rptd from Quart Rev.
Treasures of art in Great Britain. 4 vols 1845–7. Tr from G. F. Waagen.

The history of our Lord as exemplified in works of art. 1864. Begun by Mrs A. Jameson; completed by Lady Eastlake.

Fellowship: letters addressed to my sister mourners. 1868. 7 letters written on the death of her husband.

Memoir of Sir C. L. Eastlake. Prefixed to Sir C. L. Eastlake, Contributions to the literature of the fine arts ser 2, 1870.

Life of John Gibson RA. 1870.

The schools of painting in Italy. 2 pts 1874. Tr from F. T. Kugler. First pbd in 1842, with Sir Charles Eastlake as editor, and in charge of the translation. There were two new edns before this, which is entirely tr Lady Eastlake and rev and remodelled from the latest researches.

Mrs Grote: a sketch. 1880.

Five great painters. 2 vols 1883. Essays rptd from Edinburgh Rev and Quart Rev: Leonardo da Vinci, Michael Angelo, Titian, Raphael, Dürer.

S. T. Coleridge and the English romantic school. 1887. Tr from the German of A. Brandl.

Letters

Journals and correspondence of Lady Eastlake, edited by her nephew C. E. Smith. 2 vols 1895. Forms a memoir of Lady Eastlake.

§2

Kugler, F. T. The schools of painting in Italy, edited and in part rewritten by A. H. Layard. 2 vols 1887. The introd gives an account of Lady Eastlake.

Obituary. Times 3 Oct 1893.

WHITWELL ELWIN
1816–1900

§1

The complete works of Alexander Pope, vols 1, 2, 6, 8, 1871–2. Vols 3–5, 9, 10, ed W. J. Courthope 1881–9.

John Forster. Prefixed to the catalogue of the Dyce and Forster Library, 1888.

Some eighteenth century men of letters. Ed Warwick Elwin, 2 vols 1902. Rptd from Quart Rev: Cowper, Sterne, Fielding, Goldsmith, Boswell and Dr Johnson. Includes anon memoir.

For Elwin's contributions to Quart Rev see Wellesley index to Victorian periodicals vol 1, Toronto 1966.

§2

Williams, S. T. A critic of eighteenth-century literature. Texas Rev 8 1922.

Some letters of Elwin. TLS 18–25 Sept 1953.

JOHN FORSTER
1812–76

§1

The cabinet cyclopaedia. Ed D. Lardner. To the section Lives of eminent British statesmen Forster contibuted the following biographies: vol 2 1836, Sir John Eliot (rptd enlarged 2 vols 1864) and Thomas Wentworth, Earl of Strafford; vol 3 1837, John Pym and John Hampden; vol 4 1838, Sir Henry Vane and Henry Marten; vols 6–7 1839, Oliver Cromwell. Forster's contributions were rptd 5 vols 1840 as Statesmen of the Commonwealth.

A treatise on the popular progress in English history. Introd to Memoirs of statesmen of the Commonwealth, 1840.

The life and adventures of Oliver Goldsmith. 1848, 2 vols 1854 (enlarged as The life and times of Goldsmith); ed R. Ingpen 1903 (abridged).

Daniel De Foe and Charles Churchill. 2 vols 1855. Rptd from Edinburgh Rev; later included in Historical and biographical essays, vol 2, below.

Historical and biographical essays. 2 vols 1858, 1860 (with rev and enlarged edn of vol 2). Vol 1, The debates on the Grand Remonstrance; The Plantagenets and the Tudors; The Civil Wars and Oliver Cromwell; vol 2, Defoe, Steele, Churchill, Foote.

The arrest of the five members by Charles the First; a chapter of history re-written. 1860.

The debates on the Grand Remonstrance, November and December 1641; with an introductory essay on English freedom under the Plantagenet and Tudor sovereigns. 1860. Rptd with addns from Historical and biographical essays, vol 1, above.

Walter Savage Landor: a biography. 2 vols 1869, 1876 (rev and abridged as vol 1 of The works of Landor).

The life of Charles Dickens. 3 vols 1872–4; ed G. Gissing 1903 (rev and abridged); ed G. K. Chesterton 2 vols 1927 (EL); ed J. W. T. Ley [1928] (rev).

Alexander Dyce: a biographical sketch. Prefixed to vol 1 of catalogue of the Dyce collection in the South Kensington Museum, 1875.

The life of Jonathan Swift. Vol 1 (all pbd), 1875. Completed by Sir H. Craik.

Dramatic essays by John Forster and G. H. Lewes. Ed W. Archer and R. W. Lowe 1896. 11 essays by Forster rptd from Examiner, 6 on Macready as actor and as producer, 4 on Forster and one on Charles Kean as Hamlet.

§2

Powell, T. Pictures of the living authors of Britain. 1851.

Morley, H. Sketch of Forster. Prefixed to the Handbook of the Forster and Dyce collections, 1877.

Elwin, W. Biographical notice. Prefixed to catalogue of the Dyce and Forster Library, 1888.

Renton, R. Forster and his friendships. 1912.

S[awyer], C. J. and F. J. H. D[arton]. Dickens v. Barabbas, Forster intervening. 1930. A study of Dickens' relations with his publishers and with Forster.

Elwin, M. Forster. In his Victorian wallflowers, 1934.

Grubb, G. G. New letters from Dickens to Forster. Boston Univ Stud in Eng 2 1956.

WILLIAM FORSYTH
1812–99

Hortensius: or the advocate; an historical essay. 1849, 1874 (illustr).

Fides laici. 1850. Anon; a long religious poem.

The great fair of Nijni Novogorod and how we got there. 1850 (priv ptd). Later included in Essays critical and narrative, 1874.

History of trial by jury. 1852.

History of the captivity of Napoleon at St Helena, from the letters and journals of the late Lieut-Gen Sir H. Lowe, and official documents not before made public. 3 vols 1853.

The life of M. T. Cicero. 2 vols 1864, 1867.

Rome and its ruins. [1865].

Marie Antoinette in the Conciergerie: a lecture. [1867].

The novels and novelists of the eighteenth century, in illustration of the manners and morals of the age. 1871.

History of ancient manuscripts: a lecture. 1872.

Hannibal in Italy: an historical drama. 1872.

Essays critical and narrative. 1874. Literary style; William Cobbett; Eugénie de Guérin etc.

The rules of evidence as applicable to the credibility of history; with the discussion thereon from the Journal of the Victoria Institute. 1874.
The Slavonic provinces south of the Danube: a sketch of their history and present state in relation to the Ottoman Porte. 1876.
Forsyth also pbd several legal works.

SIR FRANCIS GALTON
1822–1911

§1

The telotype: a printing electric telegraph. 1850.
The narrative of an explorer in tropical South Africa. 1853, 1889 (with biographical introd).
The art of travel: or shifts and contrivances available in wild countries. 1855, 1856, 1860 (both rev and enlarged), 1867, 1872.
Meteorographica or methods of mapping the weather. 1863.
Hereditary genius: an enquiry into its laws and consequences. 1869, 1914, 1950.
English men of science: their nature and nurture. 1874.
Inquiries into human faculty and its development. 1883, [1907] (EL).
Life history album 1884, 1902 (re-arranged). Ed Galton.
Record of family faculties. 1884.
Natural inheritance. 1889.
Finger prints. 1892. Supplementary ch on decipherment pbd separately 1893.
Fingerprint directories. 1895.
Index to achievements of near kinsfolk of some Fellows of the Royal Society. [1904].
Eugenics: its definition, scope and aims. 1905, 1906.
Probability, the foundation of eugenics. Oxford 1907.
Galton also edited a ser of Vacation tourists and notes of travel, 1860–3.

§2

Memories of my life. 1908.
Pearson, K. Life, letters and labours of Galton. 1914.
Blacker, C. P. Eugenics: Galton and after. 1952.

GEORGE GILFILLAN
1813–78

§1

A gallery of literary portraits. Ser 1, Edinburgh 1845; ser 2, Edinburgh 1850; ser 3, Edinburgh 1854; 2 vols Edinburgh 1856–7 (complete); ed (in part) W. R. Nicoll [1909] (EL). Short essays on poets, French revolutionaries, novelists, critics etc.
The connection between science, literature and religion: a lecture. 1849.
The bards of the Bible. Edinburgh 1851.
Lord Byron: a lecture. 1852. In Lectures delivered before the Young Men's Christian Association in Exeter Hall 1851–2.
The martyrs, heroes and bards of the Scottish Covenant. 1852. Appendix on the Massacre of Glencoe, rptd enlarged, with D. Campbell and J. S. Blackie, as The Campbells of Glenlyon, Stirling 1912.
The influence of Burns on Scottish poetry and song; an essay. In The modern Scottish minstrel, ed C. Rogers vol 4 Edinburgh 1855.
Library edition of poets of Britain. 48 vols 1853–60. Ed Gilfillan, with short memoirs and notes.
The history of a man, edited [in fact written] by Gilfillan. 1856. Autobiography.
Christianity and our era: a book for the times. Edinburgh 1857.
Alpha and omega: or a series of scripture studies. 2 vols 1860.
Specimens, with memoirs, of the less-known British poets. 3 vols Edinburgh 1860. With a long introductory essay; the work amounts to a richly illustrated history of minor British poetry.
Remoter stars in the church sky: being a gallery of uncelebrated divines. 1867. W. Anderson, J. Everett, Samuel Gilfillan, G. Croley, J. Bruce, T. Spencer, J. Jamieson, G. Steward, H. Stewart, F. W. Robertson etc.
Night: a poem. 1867.
Modern Christian heroes: a gallery of protesting and reforming men. 1869. Cromwell, Milton, Owen and Howe, Baxter and Bunyan, Scottish Covenanters, Secession and Relief Churches in their cradles, Wesley, Whitfield, Liberty of conscience.
The life of Sir Walter Scott. Edinburgh 1870.
The life of the Rev W. Anderson. 1873.
Life of Burns. In the Works of Burns: national edition, 1878.
Sketches literary and theological. Ed F. Henderson, Edinburgh 1881. Selections from an unpbd ms, critical and religious.
Gilfillan also pbd numerous single sermons and lectures.

Letters

Watson, R. A. and E. S. Gilfillan: letters and journals, with memoir. 1892. Includes list of his contributions to periodicals and his introductory essays.

§2

Livingston, P. In Livingston's Poems and songs, Aberdeen 1855 (9th edn).
In memoriam. Dundee 1878. Rptd from Dundee Advertiser.
Macrae, D. Gilfillan: anecdotes and reminiscences. 1891.
Aubin, R. A. Three notes on 'graveyard' poetry. SP 32 1935.
Scudder, T. Emerson in Dundee. Amer Scholar 4 1935; rptd rev as A harmless stranger: son of genius, in his Lonely wayfaring man: Emerson and some Englishmen, New York 1936.

WILLIAM EWART GLADSTONE
1809–98

Bibliographies

The British Museum Catalogue of additions to the manuscripts: the Gladstone papers, additional manuscripts 44,086–835. 1935.
Contributions to a bibliography of Gladstone. N & Q 10 Dec 1892, 7, 21 Jan 1893. Addns 18 Feb, 18 March, 10 June 1893.

§1

The State in its relations with the Church. 1838, 1841 (rev and enlarged); tr German, 1843.
Church principles considered in their results. 1840.
A manual of prayers from the liturgy, arranged for family use. 1845.
Studies on Homer and the Homeric age. 3 vols Oxford 1858; tr German, 1863.
Speeches on parliamentary reform in 1866; with an appendix. 1866.
A chapter of autobiography. 1868.
Juventus mundi: the gods and men of the heroic age. 1869.
Speeches on great questions of the day. 1870.
Rome and the newest fashions in religion: three tracts—the Vatican decrees; Vaticanism; Speeches of the Pope. 1875; tr Danish, 1876; German, 1875–6. Vatican decrees, originally pbd alone 1874, was tr French, 1875.
Homeric synchronism: an enquiry into the time and place of Homer. 1876; tr German, 1877.

Bulgarian horrors and the question of the East. 1876; tr Dutch, 1876; Russian, 1876.
The Church of England and ritualism. [1876].
Gleanings of past years 1843–78. 7 vols 1879. Miscellaneous papers and reviews.
Speeches of the Rt Hon W. E. Gladstone; with a sketch of his life. Ed H. W. Lucy 1885.
Speeches on the Irish question in 1886; with an appendix containing the full text of the Government of Ireland and the Sale and Purchase of Land Bills of 1886. [Ed P. W. Clayden], Edinburgh 1886.
Landmarks of Homeric study; together with an essay on the points of contact between the Assyrian tablets and the Homeric text. 1890.
The impregnable rock of Holy Scripture. 1890, 1892 (rev).
The speeches and public addresses of the Right Hon W. E. Gladstone MP; with notes and introductions. Ed A. W. Hutton and H. J. Cohen 2 vols 1892. This edn was projected in 10 vols, but only 2 appeared.
The odes of Horace. 1894, 1895.
The psalter; with a concordance and other auxiliary matter. 1895.
On the condition of man in a future life. 3 pts 1896.
Studies subsidiary to the works of Bishop Butler: additional volume uniform with the works. 1896.
Later gleanings, theological and ecclesiastical. 1897.
Gladstone's speeches: descriptive index and bibliography by A. T. Bassett; with a preface by Viscount Bryce OM and introductions to the selected speeches by Herbert Paul. 1916.
Two hymns translated into Latin verse by Gladstone. Winchester 1951.
Essay on public speaking. Ed L. D. Reid, Quart Jnl of Speech 39 1953.
For Gladstone's reviews see Wellesley index to Victorian periodicals vol i, Toronto 1966.

Letters and Diaries

Correspondence on church and religion. Ed D. C. Lathbury 2 vols 1910.
The Queen and Mr Gladstone. Ed P. Guedalla 1933. A selection from their correspondence.
Gladstone to his wife. Ed A. T. Bassett 1936.
Brush, E. P. Seven letters from Gladstone to Guizot. Jnl of Modern History 11 1939.
Knaplund, P. Extracts from Gladstone's private political diary, touching Canadian questions in 1840. Canadian Historical Rev 20 1939.
— Gladstone–Gordon correspondence 1851–96: selections from the private correspondence of a British Prime Minister and a colonial governor. Philadelphia 1961.
The political correspondence of Mr Gladstone and Lord Granville 1868–76. Ed A. Ramm 1952.

§2

[Francis, G. H.] The oratory of Gladstone. Fraser's Mag Dec 1846.
Gladstone as a man of letters. Fraser's Mag Nov 1879.
Smith, G. B. The life of Gladstone. 1879.
Laing, S. Gladstone as a theologian. Fortnightly Rev July 1886.
von Bunsen, T. A German view of Gladstone. Nineteenth Century Sept 1887.
Russell, G. W. E. Gladstone. 1891, 1913 (EL).
Gladstone as reader and critic. Academy 28 May, 2–9 July 1898.
Hamilton, E. W. Mr Gladstone: a monograph. 1898.
Paul, H. W. The life of Gladstone. 1901.
Morley, J. The life of Gladstone. 3 vols 1903; ed C. F. G. Masterman [1927] (abridged).
Zumbini, B. Gladstone nelle sue relazioni con l'Italia. Bari 1914.
Burdett, O. Gladstone 1927.
Marjoribanks, E. In L. Abercrombie et al, Revaluations: studies in biography, 1931.
Birrell, F. Gladstone. 1933.
Wyld, H. C. The best English, with notes on Gladstone's pronunciation. 1934.
Garratt, G. T. The two Mr Gladstones. 1936.
Mallet, C. Mr Gladstone. Contemporary Rev Sept 1936.
Eyck, E. Gladstone. Zürich 1938; tr 1938.
— Bismarck and Gladstone. Contemporary Rev Dec 1946.
Hammond, J. L. Gladstone and the Irish nation. 1938.
Lyttleton, E. Mr Gladstone. Quart Rev 271 1938.
Knaplund, P. Gladstone on a proposal to buy Dutch New Guinea. Jnl of Modern History 11 1939.
Hiley, F. C. W. Gladstone and Gordon. N & Q 10 Aug 1940.
Medlicott, W. N. The Gladstone government and the Cyprus convention 1880–5. Jnl of Modern History 12 1940.
Rudman, H. W. Italian nationalism and English letters: figures of the Risorgimento and Victorian men of letters. New York 1940.
Arnold, J. B. Giants in dressing gowns. Chicago 1942.
Morgan, C. The house of Macmillan 1843–1943. 1943.
Spender, J. A. Memorable men. In his Last essays, 1944.
Young, G. M. Mr Gladstone. Oxford 1944 (Romanes Lecture); rptd in his Today and yesterday, 1948.
Vidler, A. R. The orb and the cross: a normative study in the relations of Church and State with reference to Gladstone's early writings. 1945.
Murray, G. Gladstone 1898–1948. Contemporary Rev Sept 1948.
Armytage, W. H. G. Arnold and Gladstone: some new letters. UTQ 18 1949.
Jones, T. Mr Gladstone and the spoken word. Llandyssul 1949.
Hammond, J. L. and M. R. D. Foot. Gladstone and Liberalism. 1952.
Simon, J. A. The stature of Mr Gladstone. Oxford 1953.
Magnus, P. Gladstone: a biography. 1954.
Jones, H. M. The generation of 1830. Harvard Lib Bull 13 1959.
Myres, J. L. Homer and his critics. Ed D. Gray 1958.

SIR GEORGE GROVE
1820–1900

§1

Beethoven's nine symphonies: analytical essays, with a preface by G. Henschel. Boston 1884, London 1896 (rev as Beethoven and his nine symphonies); tr German, [1906].
A dictionary of music and musicians AD 1450–1880, by eminent writers. Ed Grove 4 vols 1879–89; ed J. A. F. Maitland 4 vols 1900, 5 vols 1904–10; ed N. C. Colles 6 vols 1927–40; ed E. Blom 9 vols 1954; American supplement, ed W. S. Pratt and C. N. Boyd, Philadelphia 1920.
A short history of cheap music as exemplified in the records of the house of Novello, Ewer & Co, with especial reference to the first fifty years of the reign of Queen Victoria; with portraits, and a preface by Grove. 1887.
Beethoven, Schubert, Mendelssohn. Ed E. Blom 1951.
Grove's wide literary activities included the writing of a large portion of Sir William Smith's Dictionary of the Bible, 1860–3, *other biblical works and a primer of geography. He edited various works on music, and was for some years editor of Macmillan's Mag.*

§2

E[dwards], F. G. A biographical sketch of Grove. [1897].
Groves, C. L. The life and letters of Grove. 1903.

ARTHUR HENRY HALLAM

1811–33

Bibliographies

Motter, T. H. V. Hallam's centenary: a bibliographical note. Yale Univ Lib Gazette 8 1934.
— Hallam's Poems of 1830: a census of copies. PBSA 35 1941. *See also* M. V. Bowman, SB 1 1948.

Collections

Remains, in verse and prose. 1834 (priv ptd). Ed with a prefatory memoir by Henry Hallam.
Remains in verse and prose, originally printed in 1834. 1852. This edn was never issued.
Remains in verse and prose, originally printed in 1834. 1853 (priv ptd), 1862, 1863, Boston 1863, London 1869. *See also* Motter, above, for variations in contents.
Poems, together with his essay on the lyrical poems of Alfred Tennyson. Ed R. Le Gallienne 1893.
Poetical remains. Appendix to Temple Classics edn of In Memoriam, 1899.
Writings. Ed T. H. V. Motter, New York 1943.

§1

On names; Remarks on Gifford's Ford; Two letters to Bartholomew Bouverie Esq; The battle of the Boyne; The bride of the lake. Eton Miscellany 1 1827.
[Review of Tennyson's Timbuctoo.] Athenaeum 22 July 1829. Anon. By Hallam?
Timbuctoo. [Cambridge 1829] (priv ptd).
Adonais: an elegy on the death of John Keats, author of Endymion, Hyperion etc, by Percy B. Shelley. Cambridge 1829. Unsigned note p. iii by Hallam, who arranged pbn.
Poems by A. H. Hallam Esq. [1820] (priv ptd).
Stanzas. Englishman's Mag Aug 1831.
On some of the characteristics of modern poetry, and on the lyrical poems of Alfred Tennyson. Ibid.
Essay on the philosophical writings of Cicero. Cambridge 1832 (priv ptd).
Oration on the influence of Italian works of imagination on the same class of compositions in England, delivered in Trinity College Chapel, December 16 1831. Cambridge 1832 (priv ptd).
Remarks on Professor Rossetti's Disquisizioni sullo spirito antipapale. 1832.
[Unsigned review of Sorelli, Il paradiso perduto di Milton, 1832 (3rd edn).] Foreign Quart Rev Oct 1832.
[Biographical sketches of Voltaire, Petrarch and Burke.] The gallery of portraits; with memoirs. 5 vols 1833–5. First issued monthly from June 1832; rptd 7 vols 1833–7, 3 vols 1853.
On hearing Miss Emily — play. Metropolitan Mag Jan 1833. Anon. By Hallam?
Some unpublished poems. Ed C. Tennyson and F. T. Baker, Victorian Poetry 3 1965.

Letters

Gaskell, C. M. Records of an Eton schoolboy [James Milnes Gaskell]. 1883 (priv ptd), 1939 (as An Eton boy 1820–30).
[Trench, M.] Richard Chevenix Trench, Archbishop: letters and memorial. 2 vols 1888.
Nicoll, W. R. and T. J. Wise. In their Literary anecdotes of the nineteenth century, 1895.
Tennyson, H. Alfred Lord Tennyson: a memoir. 2 vols 1897.
Brookfield, A. M. Some letters from Hallam. Fortnightly Rev July 1903. 6 letters, 3 rptd in whole or in part in F. M. Brookfield, The Cambridge 'Apostles', 1906.
Zamick, M. Unpublished letters of Hallam from Eton, now in the John Rylands Library. Bull John Rylands Lib 18 1934.

§2

Brown, J. Hallam. North Br Rev Feb 1851; rptd in his Horae subsecivae, Edinburgh 1858; separately pbd Edinburgh 1862; rptd in Tennyson and his friends, ed Hallam Lord Tennyson 1911.
Gladstone, W. E. On Tennyson. Quart Rev 106 1859; rptd in his Gleanings of past years vol 2, 1879; separately pbd in Gladstone on Tennyson, Old South Leaflets no 193 [Boston 1908].
— Personal recollections of Hallam. Daily Telegraph 5 Jan 1898, Youth's Companion (Boston) 6 Jan 1898; separately pbd, Companion Classics (Boston) 1 [1898].
[Field, A.?] Memoir of Hallam. In In memoriam, Boston 1861.
[Alford, F.] Life, journals and letters of Henry Alford. 1873.
Ritchie, A. T. Tennyson. Harper's Mag Dec 1883; rptd in Complete poetical works of Tennyson, New York 1884.
Maurice, J. F. The life of Frederick Denison Maurice, chiefly told in his own letters. 2 vols 1884.
Reminiscences and opinions of Francis Hastings Doyle. New York 1887.
[C. J. C.] Hallam's Remains. N & Q 27 Sept 1890.
Weld, A. G. Glimpses of Tennyson and of some of his relations and friends. 1903.
Brookfield, C. and F. Mrs Brookfield and her circle. 2 vols 1905.
Brookfield, F. M. The Cambridge 'Apostles'. 1906.
[Collins, C. W.] The Cambridge Apostles. Blackwood's Mag March 1907.
Toynbee, P. J. Dante in English literature. 2 vols 1909. Vol 2, pp. 416–24.
Thwing, F. B. Hallam. North Amer Rev Feb 1911.
Lounsbury, T. R. The life and times of Tennyson. New Haven 1915.
Shorter, C. K. The love-story of In memoriam. 1916 (priv ptd).
Cornish, Mrs. W. Memories of Tennyson. London Mercury Dec 1921–Jan 1922.
Nicolson, H. Tennyson. 1923.
Bassett, A. T. (ed). The Gladstone papers. [1930].
[Madan, G.] Hallam: one who 'perish'd in the green'. Times 15 Sept 1933.
In memoriam: A. H. H. Poetry Rev Nov–Dec 1933.
Boas, F. S. Hallam. Queen's Quart 41 1934.
Motter, T. H. V. A 'lost' poem by Hallam. PMLA 50 1935.
— Hallam's suppressed allusion to Tennyson. PMLA 57 1942.
— When did Tennyson meet Hallam? MLN 57 1942.
Tennyson, C. Tennyson papers, 2: J. M. Heath's commonplace book. Cornhill Mag April 1936.
Smith, H. J. Hallam. South Atlantic Quart 47 1948.
Pearce, H. Homage to Hallam. In The image of the work: essays in criticism, ed B. H. Lehman, Berkeley 1955.

JAMES HANNAY

1827–73

Biscuits and grog: personal reminiscences and sketches by Percival Plug RN. 1848. Part autobiography, part sketches, in the form of a narrative.

A claret-cup: further reminiscences and sketches of Percival Plug RN. 1848.
King Dobbs: sketches in ultra-marine. 1849. A satirical adventure story.
Hearts are trumps: an amphibious story. 1849.
Singleton Fontenoy RN. 3 vols 1850, 1 vol 1850.
Blackwood v. Carlyle, by a Carlylian. 1850.
The life and genius of Edgar Allan Poe. Prefixed to Poe, Poetical works, 1853.
Satires and satirists: six lectures. 1854.
Sand and shells: nautical sketches. 1854. Short stories rptd from Household Words and from United Service Mag.
Eustace Conyers: a novel. 3 vols 1855, 1 vol 1857.
Essays from the Quarterly Review. 1861. Table-talk, English political satires, Horace and his translators, The minstrelsy of Scotland, Literary biography etc.
A brief memoir of Mr Thackeray. Edinburgh 1864. Rptd from Edinburgh Courant.
Characters and criticisms: a book of miscellanies. Edinburgh 1865. Plutarch, Thackeray, Lady Mary Wortley Montagu, Development of English poetry, H. T. Buckle, Prof Wilson etc.
A course of English literature. 1866.
Memoir of Charles Churchill. Prefixed to Churchill, Poetical works, 1866.
Hogarth as a satirist. Prefixed to The complete works of William Hogarth, with descriptive letterpress by J. Trusler and E. F. Roberts, 1868.
Studies on Thackeray. [1869].
For Hannay's reviews see Wellesley index to Victorian periodicals vol i, Toronto 1966.

Letters

Worth, G. J. Thackeray and James Hannay: three new letters. JEGP 55 1956.

ABRAHAM HAYWARD

1801–84

The statutes founded on the common law reports, with observations and notes. 1832.
Faust. 1833 (priv ptd), 1833, 1834 (adds summary of pt 2 and account of Faust story). A prose trn of Goethe's pt 1, with notes on former versions.
Some account of a journey across the Alps in a letter to a friend. [1834] (priv ptd); rptd in Selections from the correspondence of Abraham Hayward, 1886.
Verses of other days. 1847 (priv ptd) (anon), 1878 (enlarged).
The art of dining. 1852 (anon); ed with addns C. Sayle 1899. Based on 2 articles in Quart Rev.
Lord Chesterfield: his life, character and opinions; and George Selwyn: his life and times. 1854.
Juridical tracts. Pt I (all pbd) 1856.
Biographical and critical essays. 5 vols 1858–74. Sydney Smith, S. Rogers, J. Smith, Lord Melbourne, Stendhal, Lord Eldon, British field sports, Dumas, Maria Edgeworth, Canning, H. Holland etc.
The life and writings of Mrs Piozzi (Mrs Thrale). Prefixed to the Autobiography, letters and literary remains of Mrs Piozzi, ed Hayward, 2 vols 1861, 1861 (rearranged and expanded).
Mr Kinglake and the Quarterlys, by an old reviewer. 1863.
More about Junius: the Franciscan theory unsound. 1868. Rptd with addns from Fraser's Mag.
The second armada: a chapter of future history. 1871. Anon. Rptd with addns from Times. An account of an imaginary invasion of England by Germany.
John Stuart Mill. 1873 (priv ptd). Rptd from Times. An account of the life and work of Mill which became the subject of an acute controversy.
Goethe. 1877.
Selected essays. 2 vols 1878 (from Biographical and critical essays).
Short rules for modern whist. [1878].
Sketches of eminent statesmen and writers. 2 vols 1880. Rptd with addns from Quart Rev: Thiers, Bismarck, Cavour, Metternich, Montalembert, Melbourne, Wellesley, Sévigné, Byron, Tennyson, du Deffand etc.
Hayward translated F. C. von Savigny, On the vocation of our age for legislation, [1831] (priv ptd) *and also pbd other legal and controversial works. He also reviewed extensively for Edinburgh Rev and Quart Rev; see* Wellesley index to Victorian periodicals vol i, Toronto 1966.

Letters

A selection from the correspondence of Hayward from 1834 to 1884, with an account of his early life. Ed H. E. Carlisle 2 vols 1886.

SIR ARTHUR HELPS

1813–75

Selections

Essays and aphorisms. Ed E. A. Helps 1892.

§1

Thoughts in the cloister and the crowd. 1835 (anon), 1901. Aphorisms.
Essays written in the intervals of business. 1841 (anon); ed F. J. Rowe and W. T. Webb 1889.
King Henry the second: an historical drama. 1843. Anon.
Catherine Douglas: a tragedy. 1843. Anon.
The claims of labour: an essay on the duties of the employers to the employed. 1844 (anon), [1907].
Friends in council. 4 sers 1847–59 (anon); ser 1 ed E. A. Helps [1907]. Dialogues on social and intellectual subjects.
The conquerors of the new world and their bondsmen: the events which led to negro slavery. 2 vols 1848–52. Anon.
A letter from one of the special constables in London on the late occasion of their being called out to keep the peace. 1848. Anon.
On the responsibilities of employers. 1849.
Companions of my solitude. 1851 (anon); ed E. A. Helps [1907]. Chiefly on social questions.
A letter on Uncle Tom's Cabin. Cambridge 1852.
The Spanish conquest in America and its relation to the history of slavery. 4 vols 1855–61; ed M. Oppenheim 4 vols 1900–4 (with maps and introd).
Oulita the serf: a tragedy. 1858. Anon.
Organization in daily life: an essay. 1862. Anon.
The life of Las Casas: the apostle of the Indians. 1868. Rptd from Spanish conquest, above.
Realmah. 2 vols 1868. Serialized in Macmillan's Mag Nov 1867–Nov 1868.
The life of Columbus. 1869; ed E. A. Helps [1910] (EL). Rptd from Spanish conquest, above.
The life of Pizarro. 1869. Rptd from Spanish conquest, above.
Casimir Maremma. 2 vols 1870, 1873.
Brevia: short essays and aphorisms. 1871.
Conversations on war and general culture. 1871.
The life of Hernando Cortes. 2 vols 1871. Rptd from Spanish conquest, above.
The life and labours of Mr [Thomas] Brassey 1805–70. 1872, 1888 (7th edn). Helps also edited Brassey, On work and wages, 1872.
Thoughts upon government. 1872.
Some talk about animals and their masters. 1873. Dialogues.
Ivan de Biron: a Russian story. 3 vols 1874.

Social pressure. 1875.
Helps also edited the speeches of Prince Albert, 1862, and Queen Victoria, Leaves from the journal of our life in Highlands, 1868, *and her* Mountain, loch and glen, 1869.

Letters

Correspondence. Ed E. A. Helps 1917.

RICHARD HENRY HORNE
1803–84

See col 524, above.

RICHARD HOLT HUTTON
1826–97

Selections

Aspects of religious and scientific thought. Ed E. M. Roscoe 1899. Selection from contributions to Spectator.
Brief literary criticisms selected from the Spectator. Ed E. M. Roscoe 1906.

§1

The incarnation and principles of evidence. [1862].
The relative value of studies and accomplishments in the education of women. 1862.
Studies in parliament. 1866. Rptd from Pall Mall Gazette: Disraeli, Cobden, Palmerston, Bright, Earl Grey etc.
The political character of the working class. 1867.
Essays theological and literary. 2 vols 1871. Vol 1, theological; vol 2, Goethe, Wordsworth, Shelley, Browning, George Eliot, Clough, Hawthorne.
Sir Walter Scott. 1878 (EML).
Essays on some of the modern guides of English thought in matters of faith. 1887.
Cardinal Newman. 1891.
Criticisms on contemporary thought and thinkers. 2 vols 1894. Carlyle, Emerson, Poe, Longfellow, Dickens, Leslie Stephen, J. S. Mill, Arnold, Clough, Renan, Huxley, Bagehot, Ruskin, Wordsworth, Darwin etc.

§2

Watson, W. Excursions in criticism. [1893].
Wedgwood, J. Hutton. Contemporary Rev Oct 1897.
Escott, T. H. S. Hutton: an estimate of his life and work. Bookman (London) Oct 1897.
Hogben, J. Hutton of the Spectator. Edinburgh 1899.
Boas, F. S. Critics and criticism in the 'seventies. In The eighteen-seventies, 1929 (Royal Soc of Lit).
LeRoy, G. C. Hutton. PMLA 56 1941.
Thomas, G. N. Hutton. TLS 24 April 1948.
Colby, R. A. 'How it strikes a contemporary': the Spectator as critic. Nineteenth-Century Fiction 11 1957.
Mackerness, E. D. Hutton and the Victorian lay sermon. Dalhousie Rev 37 1957; rptd in his Heeded voice, Cambridge 1959.
Tener, R. H. Clough, Hutton and University Hall. N & Q Dec 1960.
—— Hutton's Essays theological and literary: a bibliographical note. N & Q May 1960.
—— More articles by Hutton. BNYPL Jan 1962.
—— Sources of Hutton's Modern Guides essay on Carlyle. N & Q Dec 1963.
—— Hutton and 'agnostic'. N & Q Nov 1964.

JOSEPH KNIGHT
1829–1907

§1

Life of D. G. Rossetti. 1887.
Theatrical notes. 1893.
David Garrick. 1894.
A history of the stage during the Victorian era. 1901.
Knight contributed more than 500 lives (mainly of dramatists) to DNB. In 1886 he wrote an historical preface to J. Downes, Roscius anglicanus; *and he wrote prefaces to plays by Sheridan and Henry Arthur Jones. From 1883 till his death he edited N & Q.*

§2

Francis, J. C. Notes by the way; with memoirs of Knight. 1909.
Rendall, V. H. Some reminiscences of Knight. Nineteenth Century Dec 1911.

PERCIVAL LEIGH
1813–89

§1

Stories and poems. In The fiddle-faddle fashion book, 1840.
The comic Latin grammar. 1840 (anon); ed C. E. Smith, New York 1930.
The comic English grammar. 1840. Anon.
Portraits of children of the nobility: with memoirs and characteristic sketches. 1841. Illustr J. Leech.
Jack the giant killer. [1843]. Anon; verse. Illustr J. Leech.
Ye manners and customs of ye Englyshe, drawn from ye quick by Rychard Doyle; to which be added some extracts from Mr Pips hys diary contrybuted by P[ercival] L[eigh]. [1849], 1876 (extended).
Paul Predergast: or the comic schoolmaster. 3 pts [1859] (anon). Illustr Leech, A. Crowquill et al. Contains the two comic grammars and The comic Cocker on arithmetic.

§2

Obituary. Athenaeum 2 Nov 1889.
Frith, W. P. John Leech. Vol 1, 1891.

GEORGE HENRY LEWES
1817–78

See col 1542, below.

JOHN FERGUSON McLENNAN
1827–81

Primitive marriage: an inquiry into the origin of the form of capture in marriage ceremonies. Edinburgh 1865, London 1876 (as Studies in ancient history), 1886; 2nd ser, ed E. A. McLennan 1896.
Memoir of Thomas Drummond. Edinburgh 1867.
The patriarchal theory. Ed D. McLennan 1885.

FRANCIS SYLVESTER MAHONY
1804–66

§1

The reliques of Father Prout, late P.P. of Watergrasshill in the county of Cork, collected and arranged by Oliver

Yorke esq. 2 vols 1836, 1 vol 1859. Illustr 'Alfred Croquis esq' (Daniel Maclise). Rptd from Fraser's Mag 1834–6.

Facts and figures from Italy by Don Jeremy Savonarola, Benedictine monk, addressed during the last two winters to Charles Dickens, being an appendix to his Pictures [from Italy]. 1847.

The final reliques of Father Prout. Ed D. Jerrold 1876.

The works of Father Prout. Ed C. Kent 1881 (with memoir).

Mahony was the Paris correspondent of the Globe 1858–66.

§2

Obituary. Athenaeum 26 May 1866.

Hannay, J. Aytoun, Peacock and Prout. North Br Rev Sept 1866.

Bates, W. The Maclise portrait-gallery. 1883.

Clemens, C. A neglected humorist: Father Prout. Catholic World Sept 1933.

McAleer, E. C. Understanding the Shandon bells. MLN 66 1951.

Mannin, E. Two studies in integrity. 1954.

DAVID MASSON
1822–1907

§1

College-education and self-education: a lecture. [1854].

Essays biographical and critical, chiefly on English poets. Cambridge 1856. Shakespeare and Goethe, Dryden, Swift, Chatterton, Wordsworth, Scottish influence on British literature, Theories of poetry, De Quincey, The three devils, Milton's youth.

British novelists and their styles: being a critical sketch of the history of British prose fiction. Cambridge 1859.

The life of John Milton, narrated in connexion with the political, ecclesiastical and literary history of his time. 7 vols 1859–94, 1881–96 (rev edn of vols 1–3).

Recent British philosophy. Cambridge 1865, London 1877 (adds ch). British Comtism, Bain and Herbert Spencer, Ferrier and a British Hegelian, J. S. Mill on Sir William Hamilton, Swedenborgianism and 'Spiritualism' etc.

The state of learning in Scotland: a lecture. Edinburgh 1866.

University teaching for women. Edinburgh 1868. In Introductory lectures of the second series of lectures in Shandwick Place, 1868.

Drummond of Hawthornden: the story of his life and writings. 1873.

Chatterton: a story of the year 1770. 1874, 1899 (rev and enlarged). Rptd from Essays biographical and critical, above.

The three devils: Luther's, Milton's and Goethe's. 1874. 5 essays rptd from Essays biographical and critical, above, with How literature may illustrate history.

Wordsworth, Shelley, Keats and other essays. 1874. 4 essays rptd from Essays biographical and critical, above, with Shelley and Keats.

De Quincey. 1881, 1885 (rev) (EML).

Oliver Goldsmith. Memoir prefixed to Vicar of Wakefield, 1883.

Carlyle personally and in his writings: two lectures. 1885.

Edinburgh sketches and memories. 1892. Sir Walter Scott, Allan Ramsay, Carlyle's Edinburgh life, C. K. Sharpe, J. H. Burton, Dr John Brown etc.

Milton. In In the footsteps of the poets, [1893].

James Melvin, rector of the grammar school of Aberdeen: a sketch. Aberdeen 1895.

Memories of London in the 'forties: arranged and annotated by Flora Masson. Edinburgh 1908.

Memories of two cities, Edinburgh and Aberdeen. Ed F. Masson, Edinburgh 1911. Papers rptd from Macmillan's Mag: Dr Chalmers, David Welsh, 'Christopher North', Hugh Miller, De Quincey, W. Hamilton etc.

Shakespeare personally. Ed R. Masson 1914. Lectures delivered 1865–95 at Edinburgh University.

To Chambers's Educational Course Masson contributed: Ancient history *and* History of Rome, 1848; Mediaeval history, 1855 *and* Modern history, 1856; *for the same publishers he wrote an account of the British Museum, 1848. He also edited the poetry of Milton, 1874, and the works of De Quincey, 1889–90, and contributed numerous reviews to Macmillan's Mag and North Br Rev; see also* Wellesley index to Victorian periodicals vol i, Toronto 1966.

Letters

Macmillan, A. Letters. 1908.

§2

Barrie, J. M. An Edinburgh eleven. 1889.

Obituary. Times 8 Oct 1907.

Masson, F. Masson. Cornhill Mag Nov 1910, June 1911.

JOHN FREDERICK DENISON MAURICE
1805–72

Bibliographies

Gray, G. J. Bibliography of the writings of Maurice. In J. F. Maurice, Life of Maurice vol 1, 1884.

§1

Eustace Conway, or the brother and sister: a novel. 1834. Anon.

The Kingdom of Christ: or hints on the principles, ordinances and constitution of the Catholic Church. 3 vols 1837. *See col 1608, below.*

Moral and metaphysical philosophy. 1845, 2 vols 1872. A section of Encyclopaedia metropolitana, ed E. Smedley. Later expanded into 4 separate works: Ancient philosophy, 1850; Philosophy of the first six centuries, 1853; Mediaeval philosophy, 1857; Modern philosophy, 1862.

The religions of the world, and their relation to Christianity. 1847 (Boyle Lectures).

Theological essays. Cambridge 1853, 1853 (with addns), London, 1871; ed E. F. Carpenter 1958.

Sermons. 6 vols [1857–9], 1860.

The workman and the franchise: chapters from English history on the representation and education of the people. 1866.

The conscience: lectures on casuistry. 1868, 1872.

Social morality: twenty-one lectures. 1869.

The friendship of books and other lectures. Ed T. Hughes 1874.

Maurice also pbd numerous sermons, tracts etc, as well as contributing prefaces to works by others. He edited, at different periods, Athenaeum, Christian Socialist *and* Educational Mag. *For his reviews see* Wellesley index to Victorian periodicals vol i, Toronto 1966.

§2

Maurice and his writings. London Quart Rev 3 1855.

Rigg, J. H. Modern Anglican theology: chapters on Coleridge, Maurice [et al]. 1857.

Kingsley, C. Memorial of Maurice. Macmillan's Mag May 1872.

Davies, J. L. Secularism and Mr Maurice's theology. Contemporary Rev June 1874.

Stephen, L. The theology of Maurice. Fortnightly Rev May 1874.

A modern prophet. Atlantic Monthly Aug 1884.
Maurice, J. F. The life of Maurice, chiefly told in his own letters. 2 vols 1884.
Hutton, R. H. Essays on some of the modern guides of English thought in matters of faith. 1887.
Dungern, H. von. Der Führer der christlichsozialen Bewegung Englands von 1848–66: Maurice. Göttingen 1900.
Masterman, C. F. G. Maurice. 1907.
Sanders, C. R. Coleridge, Maurice and the distinction between the reason and the understanding. PMLA 51 1936.
— Maurice as a commentator on Coleridge. PMLA 53 1938.
— Sir Leslie Stephen, Coleridge and two Coleridgeans. PMLA 55 1940.
— Coleridge, Maurice and the church universal. Jnl of Religion 21 1941.
— A major outlet: Maurice. In his Coleridge and the Broad Church movement, Durham NC 1942.
Jenkins, C. Maurice and the new reformation. 1938.
Gloyn, C. K. The Church in the social order: a study of Anglican social theory from Coleridge to Maurice. Forest Grove Oregon 1942.
Higham, F. Maurice. 1947.
Reckitt, M. B. Maurice to Temple: a century of the social movement in the Church of England. 1947.
Dring, T. Maurice: the greatest prophet of the nineteenth century. London Quart 173 1948.
— The philosophy of Maurice. London Quart 187 1962.
Grylls, R. G. Queen's College 1848–1948, founded by Maurice. 1948.
Vidler, A. R. Witness to the light: Maurice's message for today. New York 1948.
— The theology of Maurice. 1948.
— F. D. Maurice and company. 1967.
Wood, H. G. Maurice. 1950.
Ramsey, A. M. Maurice and the conflicts of modern theology. Cambridge 1951.
Ranson, G. H. The kingdom of God as the design of society. Church History 30 1961.

HENRY MAYHEW
1812–87

Selections

The street trader's lot. 1851; ed S. Rubenstein 1947 (with introd by M. D. George).
Mayhew's London. Ed P. C. Quennell 1949, 1951.
London's underworld. Ed P. C. Quennell 1950. Selections from London labour and the London poor vol 4.
Mayhew's characters. Ed P. C. Quennell 1951.

§ 1

The wandering minstrel. 1834?, Philadelphia 1836, London 1850, Boston 1856, [1880] (with Intrigue), [1897] (with The tradesman's ball). A one-act farce.
But, however–. 1838, 1843, [1883]. A one-act farce. With Henry Baylis.
What to teach and how to teach it. Pt 1 1842. No more pbd.
The Prince of Wales's library: no 1—the primer. 1844.
The greatest plague of life: or the adventures of a lady in search of a servant. Illustr G. Cruikshank [1847], [1892]. With his brother Augustus Mayhew.
The good genius. 1847, 1879, New York 1890. Fairy tale. With Augustus Mayhew.
Whom to marry. [1848], 1854, 1872. With Augustus Mayhew.
The image of his father. Illustr 'Phiz' 1848, 1850, 1859. With Augustus Mayhew.
The magic of kindness. Illustr G. Cruikshank and K. Meadows [1848], [1869], Manchester [1879]. With Augustus Mayhew.
Acting charades. [1850], [1852].
London labour and the London poor. Nos 1–63. Vol 1 and pts of vols 2–3, 1851; expanded as 4 vols 1861–2; 4th vol only 1864. Some of the material first appeared as Labour and the poor, Morning Chron 1849–50.
1851: or the adventures of Mr and Mrs Sandboys. 1851. With John Binny.
Home is home, be it never so homely. In Meliora, ed Earl of Shrewsbury 1852.
The story of the peasant-boy philosopher. 1854, 1855, New York 1856, London 1857.
Living for appearances. 1855. With Augustus Mayhew.
The wonders of science: or young Humphry Davy. 1855, 1856, New York 1856.
The Rhine and its picturesque scenery. Illustr B. Foster 1856. 1860 (as The lower Rhine).
The great world of London. Pts 1–9 [1856]. Completed by John Binny as The criminal prisons of London and scenes of prison life, 1862.
The upper Rhine. Illustr B. Foster 1858.
Young Benjamin Franklin: or the right road through life. 1861, New York 1862, London [1870].
The boyhood of Martin Luther. 1863, [1879].
German life and manners as seen in Saxony at the present day. 2 vols 1864, 1 vol 1865.
The shops and companies of London and the trades and manufactories of Great Britain. Pts 1–7 [1865].
London characters. Illustr W. S. Gilbert et al [1870], 1874, 1881. With others.
The comic almanack. 2 vols 1871. With Augustus Mayhew, Thackeray et al. Collection of earlier writings.
Report concerning the trade and hours of closing usual among the unlicensed victualling establishments at certain so-called 'Working Men's Clubs'. 1871.
Mont Blanc. 1874, 1874. For private circulation. A comedy, with Athol Mayhew.
Mayhew edited Figaro in London, 1831–9 (*with Gilbert à Beckett*) *and* The thief, 1832. *He was one of the originators in 1841 and for a short time joint editor of* Punch. *He also edited* Only once a year, 1871.

HORACE MAYHEW
1816–72

Change for a chilling. [1848]. Illustr H. G. Hine.
The comic almanac for 1848. 1848. Ed Mayhew.
Model men, modelled by Mayhew, sculptured by H. G. Hine. 1848.
Model women and children, modelled by Mayhew, sculptured by H. G. Hine. 1848.
Guy Faux: a squib manufactured by Mayhew and Percy Cruikshank. [1849].
The tooth-ache, imagined by Mayhew and realized by George Cruikshank. [1849].
Letters left at the pastrycook's: being the clandestine correspondence between Kitty Clover at school, and her 'dear, dear friend' in town. 1853.
In Dec 1847 Mayhew brought out a Plum pudding pantomime at the Olympic Theatre, apparently unpbd. See obituary, Athenaeum 4 May 1872.

JOHN STUART MILL
1806–73

See col 1551, below.

HUGH MILLER

1802–56

Selections

Selections. Ed W. M. Mackenzie, Paisley 1908.

§1

Letters on the herring fishery. Inverness 1829. Rptd from Inverness Courier.
Poems written in the leisure hours of a journeyman mason. Inverness 1829.
Scenes and legends of the north of Scotland: or the traditional history of Cromarty. 1835.
Memoir of William Forsyth. 1839.
The Whiggism of the old school. Edinburgh 1839.
A letter to Lord Brougham. Edinburgh 1839.
The two parties in the Church of Scotland exhibited as missionary and anti-missionary. Edinburgh 1841.
The old red sandstone: or new walks in an old field. Edinburgh 1841, Glasgow 1858 (adds a series of geological papers), London 1906 (EL). Rptd from Witness.
Sutherland as it was and is: or how a country may be ruined. 1843. Anon.
Words of warning to the people of Scotland on Sir Robert Peels' Scotch currency scheme. Edinburgh 1844.
First impressions of England and its people. 1847.
The Sites Bill and the Toleration Laws. Edinburgh 1848.
Geology of the Bass. In The Bass Rock: its civil and ecclesiastical history by T. MacCrie, 1848.
Footprints of the Creator: or the asterolepsis of Stromness. 1849 (anon); ed L. F. F. Miller, Edinburgh 1861 (with memoir by L. Agassiz). A reply to Vestiges of creation, 1844.
Thoughts on the educational question. 1850. Rptd from Witness.
My school and schoolmasters: or the story of my education. Edinburgh 1854; ed A. M. Mackenzie, Edinburgh 1905.
The fossiliferous deposits of Scotland. Edinburgh 1854.
The two records—mosaic and geological: a lecture. 1854.
Geology versus astronomy: a view of the modifying effects of geologic discovery on the old astronomic inferences respecting the plurality of inhabited worlds. Glasgow [1855].
Strange but true: incidents in the life of J. Kitto. Edinburgh 1856.
The testimony of the rocks. Edinburgh 1857.
Voices from the rocks: or proofs of the existence of man during the palaeozoic period. 1857.
The cruise of the Betsy: or a summer ramble among the fossiliferous deposits of the Hebrides; with rambles of a geologist. Ed W. S. Symonds, Edinburgh 1858.
Sketch-book of popular geology: a series of lectures; with a preface by Mrs Miller. Edinburgh 1859.
The headship of Christ and the rights of the Christian people; with a preface by P. Bayne. Edinburgh 1861.
Essays historical and biographical, political and social, literary and scientific. Ed P. Bayne, Edinburgh 1862. Rptd from Witness.
Tales and sketches. Ed L. F. F. Miller, Edinburgh 1863.
Edinburgh and its neighbourhood, geological and historical; with the geology of the Bass Rock. Ed L. F. F. Miller, Edinburgh 1864.
Leading articles on various subjects. Ed J. Davidson, Edinburgh 1870.
Geology of the country around Otterburn and Elsdon. 1887.

§2

Brown, T. N. Labour and triumph: the life and times of Miller. 1858.
Bingham, W. The life and writings of Miller: an oration. 1859.
The life of Miller: a sketch for working men. 1862. Rptd from Northern Daily Express.
Bayne, P. The life and letters of Miller. 1871.
Watson, T. L. Life of Miller. Edinburgh 1880.
Leask, W. K. Miller. Edinburgh [1896].
Allibone's Dictionary of authors vol 2. 1859–71. Includes biography, bibliography, references to and extracts from reviews and articles on Miller.
Mackenzie, W. M. Miller: a critical study. 1905.
Masson, D. Miller. In his Memories of two cities: Edinburgh and Aberdeen, 1911.

RICHARD MONCKTON MILNES, 1st BARON HOUGHTON

1809–85

See col 539, above.

HENRY MORLEY

1822–94

§1

The dream of the Lilybell: tales and poems, with translations of the Hymns to night from the German of Novalis and Jean Paul's Death of an angel. 1845.
A tract upon health for cottage circulation. 1847.
Sunrise in Italy. 1848. A poem.
How to make home unhealthy. 1850. Anon. Rptd from Examiner; afterwards included in Early papers and some memories, 1891.
A defence of ignorance. 1851. A satirical essay on education.
Palissy the potter. 2 vols 1852.
The life of Geronimo Cardano of Milan, physician. 2 vols 1854.
Cornelius Agrippa von Nettesheim. 2 vols 1856.
Gossip. 1857. Tales, papers and verses rptd from Household Words.
Memoirs of Bartholomew Fair. 1859.
Fables and fairy tales. 1860.
Oberon's horn: a book of fairy tales. 1861.
English writers. Vol 1, 1864 (subsequently divided into 2 half vols); vol 2, 1867 (half vol only; 2nd half never pbd, and all 3 half vols allowed to go out of print). Vols 1–11, 1887–1895. 20 vols intended, but Morley only lived to write 10, vol 11 being completed by W. Hall Griffin.
The journal of a London playgoer from 1851 to 1866. 1866.
Fairy tales. 1867, [1877] (as The chicken market and other fairy tales). Tales previously pbd in Fables and fairy tales and Oberon's horn, above.
Tables of English literature. 1870, 1870 (with index).
Clement Marot and other studies. 2 vols 1871. Marot, Vesalius, Gesner, Cyrano de Bergerac, Gabriel Harvey, Caedmon's Paraphrase, Influence of the Celt on English literature etc.
A first sketch of English literature. [1873], 1886 (enlarged).
Cassell's library of English literature. 5 vols 1875–1881. Extracts from and summaries of the greatest English classics, with notes and explanatory text by Morley.
University College London 1827–78: a lecture. 1878.
An account of the new north wing and recent additions to University College London. 1881. Anon.
Of English literature in the reign of Victoria, with a glance at the past. Leipzig 1881.
Morley's universal library. 6 vols 1883–1888. 1891. Every vol with critical and biographical introd, by Morley.
Candide, by F. A. M. de Voltaire. 1884; [1922]. Trn by Morley; originally ptd with Johnson's Rasselas as Morley's Universal Library vol 19, above.

Cassell's national library. 213 vols 1886–92. A wide selection from the English classics with introd to each vol by Morley.
The Carisbrooke library. 14 vols 1889–92. Ed Morley.
Memoir of Thomas Sadler. [1891].
Early papers and some memories. 1891. Short autobiographical ch followed by How to make home unhealthy, A defence of ignorance, Dream of the Lilybell, and 16 other papers, largely rptd from Household Words and All the Year Round.

§2

Solly, H. S. The life of Morley. 1898.

FRANCIS TURNER PALGRAVE
1824–97

See col 545, above.

MARK PATTISON
1813–84

§1

The lives of the English saints. Ed J. H. Newman 4 vols 1844–5; rev A. W. Hutton 6 vols 1901. Pattison contributed anon lives of Stephen Langton and St Edmund.
Oxford studies. In Oxford essays, 1855. On university reform.
Report on elementary education in Protestant Germany. 1859. Contained in the Report of the Assistant Commissioners on the state of popular education in Continental Europe vol 4, 1861.
Tendencies of religious thought in England 1688–1750. In Essays and reviews, 1860; enlarged in Essays, 1889, below. *See col 1606, below.*
Suggestions on academical organisation, with special reference to Oxford. Edinburgh 1868.
Isaac Casaubon 1559–1614. 1875; ed H. Nettleship, Oxford 1892 (with index).
Encyclopaedia britannica. 1875–89 (9th edn). Pattison wrote articles on Bentley, Erasmus, Grotius, Sir Thomas More, Lipsius and Lord Macaulay; the last is rptd prefixed to Macaulay's Life of Pitt, 1902.
Review of the situation. In Essays on the endowment of research, 1876.
Milton. 1879, 1880 (rev) (EML).
Memoirs. Ed Mrs Pattison 1885.
Essays. Ed H. Nettleship 2 vols Oxford 1889, London [1908] (5 essays omitted). The 1889 edn contains (with dated list of other essays appearing in periodicals) Muretus, Life of Scaliger, University history, Oxford studies, Pope and his editors, and (in this edn only) Montaigne, P. D. Huet, Calvin at Geneva etc.
The Estiennes: a biographical essay, illustrated with original leaves from books printed by the three greatest members of that distinguished family. San Francisco 1949.
Pattison also edited Pope, Essay on man, 1869 *and his* Satires and epistles, 1872, *with notes.*

Letters

Montague, F. C. Some early letters of Pattison. Bull John Rylands Lib 18 1934.
Letters of Pattison to Gertrude M. Tuckwell. BM Quart 11 1937.

§2

Nettleship, H. Obituary. Academy 9 Aug 1884.
Althaus, T. F. Recollections of Pattison. 1885. Rptd from Temple Bar.
Tollemache, L. A. Recollections of Pattison. 1885. Rptd with addns from Jnl of Education.
Morley, J. In his Critical miscellanies vol 3, 1886.
Badger, K. Pattison and the Victorian scholar. MLQ 4 1945.
Emden, C. S. Pattison (1813–84) and J. A. Froude (1818–94): an appropriate friendship. In his Oriel papers, Oxford 1948.
Strachan, L. R. M. The Cambridge history of English literature on Mark Pattison. N & Q 24 Jan 1948.
Green, V. H. H. Oxford common room: a study of Lincoln College and Pattison. 1957.
Sparrow, J. Pattison and the idea of a university. Cambridge 1967.

AUGUSTUS WELBY NORTHMORE PUGIN
1812–52

§1

Gothic furniture in the style of the 15th century, designed and etched by A. W. N. Pugin. 1835.
Contrasts: or a parallel between the noble edifices of the fourteenth and fifteenth centuries and similar buildings of the present day, shewing the present decay of taste. 1836.
An apology for a work entitled Contrasts: being a defence of the assertions advanced in that publication, against the various attacks lately made upon it. Birmingham 1837.
The true principles of pointed or Christian architecture. 1841; tr French, 1850.
An apology for the revival of Christian architecture in England. 1843.
The present state of ecclesiastical architecture in England, re-published from the Dublin Review. 1843.
Glossary of ecclesiastical ornament and costume compiled and illustrated from ancient authorities and examples. 1844; rev B. Smith 1868.
Some remarks on the articles which have recently appeared in the Rambler relative to ecclesiastical architecture and decoration. 1850.
A treatise on chancel screens and rood lofts, their antiquity, use and symbolic signification; illustrated with figures. 1851.
Pugin also pbd engravings and pamphlets on religious and ecclesiastical matters.

§2

Ferrey, B. Recollections of A. N. Welby Pugin and his father, Augustus Pugin; with notices of their works. 1861.
Sirr, H. Pugin: a sketch. [1918].
Clark, K. In his Gothic revival, 1929.
Lomax, M. T. Pugin: a mediaeval Victorian. 1932.
Rope, H. E. G. Pugin. 1935.
Gwynn, D. R. Lord Shrewsbury, Pugin and the Gothic revival. 1946.

ANGUS BETHUNE REACH
1821–56

§1

The natural history of 'bores'. 1847.
The natural history of humbugs. 1847.
The natural history of tuft-hunters and toadies. 1848.
The comic Bradshaw: or bubbles from the boiler. 1848.
The natural history of the 'hawk' tribe. 1848.
A romance of a mince-pie: an incident in the life of John Chirrup. 1848, [1850?]. Illustr 'Phiz'.
Clement Lorimer: or the book with the iron clasps: a romance. 1849, 1856. Illustr G. Cruikshank.

Leonard Lindsay: or the story of a buccaneer. 2 vols 1850.
Claret and olives, from the Garonne to the Rhone: or notes social, picturesque and legendary, by the way. 1852, New York 1852.
A story with a vengeance: or how many joints go to a tale? [1852], [1853] (rev). With C. W. S. Brooks.
Men of the hour. 1856.
Christmas cheer. 1856. With J. Hannay and Albert R. Smith.
Sketches of London life and character, 1858. With Albert R. Smith et al.
Reach was for some time on the staff of Punch and wrote many contributions to periodicals.

§2

Obituary. Athenaeum 29 Nov 1856.
Mackay, C. Forty years' recollections of life, literature and public affairs 1830–70. 2 vols 1877.
Spielmann, M. H. History of Punch. 1895.

WILLIAM WINWOOD READE
1838–75

Charlotte and Myra: a puzzle in six bits. 1859.
Liberty Hall, Oxon. 3 vols 1860.
The veil of Isis: or the mysteries of the druids. 1861.
Savage Africa: being the narrative of a tour. 1863.
See-saw: a novel, edited by Reade. 1865. Written by Reade.
The martyrdom of man 1872, 1877 (4th edn); ed F. Legge 1910.
The African sketch-book. 2 vols 1873.
The story of the Ashantee campaign. 1874.
The outcast. 1875, 1933.

WILLIAM MICHAEL ROSSETTI
1829–1919

§1

The germ: thoughts towards nature in poetry, literature and art. 4 nos 1850. Ed W. M. Rossetti; he pbd a facs, rptd in 1901.
Swinburne's poems and ballads: a criticism. 1866.
Fine art, chiefly contemporary: notices re-printed. 1867.
Notes on the Royal Academy exhibition. 1868. With A. C. Swinburne.
Lives of famous poets. 1878. Essays originally written as introd to edns of Milton, Pope, Byron etc in Moxon's Popular Poets ser.
Memoir of Percy Bysshe Shelley, with new preface. 1886. Rptd from Rossetti's edn of Shelley, 1870.
Life of John Keats. 1887.
Dante Gabriel Rossetti as designer and writer. 1889.
D. G. Rossetti: his family letters, with a memoir. 2 vols 1895.
Ruskin; Rossetti; Preraphaelitism; papers 1854 to 1862. 1899.
Preraphaelite diaries and letters. 1900.
Rossetti papers 1862–70. 1903.
Some reminiscences. 2 vols 1906.
Democratic sonnets. 2 vols 1907.
Dante and his convito: a study with translations. 1910.
In addn to the 15 English poets in Moxon's Popular Poets, W. M. Rossetti was responsible for important edns of Walt Whitman, Shelley, Blake, D. G. and Christina Rossetti, and for the Chaucer Soc and EETS. He contributed largely to Encyclopaedia britannica (9th edn) and Shelley Soc Papers, and pbd trns of Dante's Inferno and of the versified autobiography of his father Gabriele Rossetti.

Letters

Letters about Shelley interchanged by Edward Dowden, Richard Garnett and Wm Michael Rossetti. Ed R. S. Garnett 1917.
Letters of William Michael Rossetti concerning Whitman, Blake and Shelley to Anne and Herbert Gilchrist. Ed C. Gohdes and P. F. Baum, Durham NC 1934.
Three Rossettis: unpublished letters to and from Dante Gabriel, Christina, William. Ed J. C. Troxell, Cambridge Mass 1937.
The Rossetti–Macmillan letters. Ed L. M. Packer, Berkeley 1963.

§2

See also under D. G. Rossetti, *col 490, above.*
Swinburne, A. C. In his Miscellanies, 1886. Includes a review of Lives of famous poets, above.
Soskice, J. M. Chapters from childhood: reminiscences of an artist's grand-daughter. [1921].
Horn, K. Rossetti. Zeitschrift für Französischen und Englischen Unterricht 23 1924.
Waller, R. D. The Rossetti family 1824–54. Manchester 1932.
'Winwar, Frances' (F. Grebanier). Dante Gabriel's or William Michael's? (an attempt to establish the authorship of some Rossetti sonnets published by the Duke University Press). PMLA 48 1933.
Justus W. Rossetti im Kreise der Praeraphaeliten. Münster 1934.
Lang, C. Y. ALS: Swinburne to Rossetti. Jnl Rutgers Univ Lib 14 1951.
Chewning, H. Rossetti and the Shelley renaissance. Keats–Shelley Jnl 4 1955.
Thale, J. The third Rossetti. Western Humanities Rev 10 1956.
Packer, L. M. Rossetti and the Quilter controversy: the gospel of intensity. Victorian Stud 7 1963.

WILLIAM BELL SCOTT
1811–90

See col. 549, above.

JOHN CAMPBELL SHAIRP
1918–85

§1

Charles the twelfth: a prize poem recited in the Theatre, Oxford. Oxford 1842.
Kilmahoe: a highland pastoral, with other poems. 1864.
John Keble: an essay. Edinburgh 1866.
Studies in poetry and philosophy. Edinburgh 1868, 1886 (with preface by G. D. Boyle). Wordsworth, Coleridge, Keble, The moral dynamic.
A. H. Clough: a sketch. Included in the anon memoir prefixed to Poems and prose remains of A. H. Clough, 2 vols 1869.
Culture and religion. 1870.
The life and letters of J. D. Forbes. 1873. With P. G. Tait and A. A. Reilly.
Recollections of a tour made in Scotland, 1803, by Dorothy Wordsworth. 1874. Ed Shairp.
On poetic interpretation of nature. Edinburgh 1877.
Robert Burns. 1879 (EML).
Aspects of poetry: being lectures delivered at Oxford. Oxford 1881. Virgil, Burns, Shelley, Ossian, Duncan MacIntyre, Wordsworth, Scott, Carlyle, Newman, and Five essays on poetry.
Sketches in history and poetry: collected and edited by Professor Veitch. Edinburgh 1887. Henry Vaughan,

The Ettrick shepherd, Early poetry of Scotland, Songs of Scotland before Burns, Queen Margaret of Scotland etc.
Glen Desseray, and other poems. Ed F. T. Palgrave 1888.
Shairp also pbd The wants of Scottish universities and some of the remedies, Edinburgh 1856, *and an* Address on missions, Edinburgh 1874. *For his reviews see* Wellesley index to Victorian periodicals vol 1, Toronto 1966.

§2

Rodger, M. Shairp: an address. Edinburgh 1885.
Knight, W. A. Shairp and his friends. 1888.
Sellar, W. Y. Portraits of friends. Boston 1889.

JAMES SMETHAM
1821–89

See col 550, above.

GOLDWIN SMITH
1823–1910

See col 1496, below.

WILLIAM SPALDING
1809–59

§1

A letter on Shakespeare's authorship of the Two noble kinsmen: a drama. 1833, 1876 (New Shakespeare Soc) (with life of Spalding by J. H. Burton).
Italy and the Italian islands from the earliest ages to the present time. 3 vols Edinburgh 1841, New York 1843.
The history of English literature with an outline of the origin and growth of the English language. Edinburgh 1853, London 1870 (11th edn, continued to 1870), Edinburgh 1877 (continued to 1876); tr German, 1854.
The British Empire. Glasgow 1856. With 19 other contributors Spalding assisted in compiling an encyclopaedic vol on the British Empire. He wrote a large number of memoirs for the biographical section and helped to prepare the historical section.
An introduction to logical science. Edinburgh 1857. Rptd from Encyclopaedia Britannica (8th edn).

§2

Gilfillan, G. In his Galleries of literary portraits vol 2, Edinburgh 1857.
Obituary. Scotsman 19 Nov 1859.

JAMES SPEDDING
1808–81

Evenings with a reviewer, or a free and particular examination of Mr Macaulay's article on Lord Bacon, in a series of dialogues. 2 vols 1848 (priv ptd), 1881 (with prefatory notice by G. S. Venables).
Companion to the railway edition of Lord Campbell's Life of Bacon, by a railway reader. 1853. Rptd from Examiner.
The works of Francis Bacon. Ed Spedding, R. L. Ellis and D. D. Heath 7 vols 1857–9.
The letters and the life of Francis Bacon, set forth in chronological order, with a commentary. 7 vols 1861–72.
Publishers and authors. 1867.
A conference of pleasure, composed about 1592 by Francis Bacon. 1870. Ed Spedding.
An account of the life and times of Francis Bacon. 2 vols Boston 1878. An abridged version of the American edn of the Works of Bacon in 15 vols. Consists mainly of Spedding's original commentary and constitutes a complete short biography of Bacon.
Reviews and discussions, literary, political and historical, not relating to Bacon. 1879. Dickens, Tennyson, English hexameters, Twelfth Night etc.
Studies in English history by James Gairdner and James Spedding. Edinburgh 1881. Contains 2 historical essays by Spedding.
Charles Tennyson, afterwards Turner. In Turner's Collected sonnets, old and new, 1898.
For Spedding's reviews see Wellesley index to Victorian periodicals vol i, Toronto 1966.

SIR JAMES FITZJAMES STEPHEN
1829–94

See col 1499, below.

FREDERIC GEORGE STEPHENS
1828–1907

§1

William Holman Hunt and his works. 1860. Anon.
Normandy, its Gothic architecture and history: a sketch. 1865.
Flemish relics: architectural, legendary and pictorial. 1866.
English children as painted by Sir Joshua Reynolds: an essay on some of the characteristics of Reynolds as a painter. 1867.
Masterpieces of Mulready: memorials of William Mulready. 1867.
The early works of Sir Edwin Landseer: a brief sketch of the life of the artist. 1869 (anon), 1874 (as Memoirs of Landseer), 1880 (extended as Sir Edwin Landseer).
Catalogue of prints and drawings in the British Museum: division 1, political and personal satires prepared by F. G. Stephens, and containing many descriptions by E. Hawkins. 4 vols 1870–83. Vols 5–11 by M. D. George, 1954.
A history of Gibraltar and its sieges. 1870. Anon.
English artists of the present day: essays by J. B. Atkinson, Sidney Colvin, F. G. Stephens, T. Taylor and J. L. Tupper. 1872.
Flemish and French pictures, with notes concerning the painters and their works. 1875.
Notes on Thomas Bewick, illustrating a loan collection of his drawings and woodcuts. 1880.
Notes on a collection of drawings and woodcuts by Thomas Bewick exhibited at the Fine Art Society's rooms 1880; also a complete list of all works illustrated by T. and J. Bewick. 2 pts 1881.
Notes on a collection of drawings, paintings and etchings by Samuel Palmer; with an account of the Milton series of drawings by L. R. Valpy. 1881.
Artists at home: photographed by J. P. Mayall and reproduced in facsimile. Ed with biographical notices and descriptions by F. G. Stephens 6 pts 1884.
Catalogue of the works of Sir Joshua Reynolds exhibited at the Grosvenor Gallery 1883–4. 1884.
J. C. Hook. 1884, [1888].
Memorials of William Mulready. 1890.
A memoir of George Cruikshank by Stephens and an essay on the genius of George Cruikshank by W. M. Thackeray. 1891.
Dante Gabriel Rossetti. 1894, 1908.

Lawrence Alma Tadema RA: a sketch of his life and work. 1895.

Sir Frederic Leighton: an illustrated chronicle by E. Rhys, with prefatory essay by Stephens. 1895, 1898 (rev G. White as Frederic Lord Leighton).

Stephens also wrote Notes to the Grosvenor Gallery catalogues of works by Reynolds [1884], Gainsborough [1885], Millais [1886] and Van Dyck [1887]. He was art-critic to Athenaeum from 1861 to 1901, contributing to every issue but two in those 40 years. His articles on the private collections of England are important.

§2

Rossetti, W. M. Obituary. Athenaeum 16 March 1907.

Stephens and the Pre-Raphaelite brothers; with reproduction of twenty-four pictures from his collection, and notes by J. B. Manson. [1920] (priv ptd).

Grylls, R. G. The correspondence of F. G. Stephens. TLS 5–12 April 1957.

JAMES HUTCHISON STIRLING

1820–1909

See col 1593, below.

SIR HENRY TAYLOR

1800–86

See col 553, above.

TOM TAYLOR

1817–80

See col 1157, above.

WILLIAM THOMAS THORNTON

1813–80

Over-population and its remedy. 1846.

A plea for peasant proprietors. 1848, 1874.

The siege of Silistria. 1854. A poem.

Zohráb: or a midsummer day's dream; and other poems. 1854.

Modern Manicheism, Labour's Utopia and other poems. 1857.

On labour: its wrongful claims and rightful dues; its actual present and possible future. 1869, 1870.

Old-fashioned ethics and common-sense metaphysics. 1873.

Indian public works and cognate Indian topics. 1875.

RICHARD CHENEVIX TRENCH

1807–86

See col 556, above.

ROBERT ALFRED VAUGHAN

1823–57

The witch of Endor and other poems. 1844.

Hours with the mystics: a contribution to the history of religious opinion. 2 vols 1856; ed R. Vaughan 2 vols 1860; ed W. Vaughan 2 vols [1880].

Essays and remains. Ed R. Vaughan 2 vols 1858 (with memoir). Largely rptd from Br Quart Rev; the elder Vaughan's memoir was enlarged and pbd separately, 1864.

BARTHOLOMEW ELIOT GEORGE WARBURTON

1810–52

The crescent and the cross: or romance and realities of Eastern travel. 2 vols 1845.

Zoë: an episode of the Greek war. 1847.

Memoirs of Prince Rupert and the Cavaliers: including their private correspondence, now first published from the original manuscripts. 3 vols 1849; tr French, 1851.

Reginald Hastings: or a tale of the troubles in 164–. 3 vols 1850.

Darien: or the merchant prince, a historical romance. 3 vols 1852.

Warburton also edited G. D. Warburton, Hochelaga, 1846, *and* R. F. Williams, Memoirs of Horace Walpole and his contemporaries, 1851. *For appreciations see* The late Eliot Warburton, Dublin Univ Mag Feb 1852, *and* Works of Eliot Warburton, Eng Rev 17 1852.

ROBERT ELDRIDGE ARIS WILLMOTT

1809–63

Lives of sacred poets. 2 sers 1834–8.

Conversations at Cambridge. 1836. Anon.

Letters of eminent persons, selected and illustrated. 1839.

Parlour table book: extracts from various authors. 1840.

Pictures of Christian life. 1841.

Poems. 1841, 1848 (rev and expanded).

Bishop Jeremy Taylor: his predecessors, contemporaries and successors. 1847, 1848 (rev).

A journal of summer time in the country. 1849, 1858, 1864 (4th edn, with memoir by C. Willmott), 1928 (with biographical note by E. P[artridge]).

Precious stones, aids to reflection, from prose writers of the sixteenth, seventeenth and eighteenth centuries. 1850.

Pleasures, objects and advantages of literature. 1851, 1852, 1856, 1860 (5th edn, enlarged); ed C. Metcalfe 1906.

The poets of the nineteenth century. 1857.

English sacred poetry. 1862, 1883. An anthology.

In addn to numerous sermons (of some literary distinction) Willmott also produced edns of Gray, Herbert, Akenside, Fairfax's Tasso, Wordsworth, James Montgomery and other English poets, mainly in Routledge's British Poets ser.

CHRISTOPHER WORDSWORTH

1807–85

See col 563, above.

A. P.

VI. LATE NINETEENTH-CENTURY PROSE

SIR LESLIE STEPHEN

1832–1904

Collections

Men, books and mountains: essays. Ed S. O. A. Ullmann, Minneapolis 1956. With list, 'probably almost complete', of Stephen's contributions to monthlies, quarterlies and annuals, and of their subsequent inclusion in collections.

§1

The poll degree from a third point of view. 1863.
Sketches from Cambridge, by a don. 1865; ed G. M. Trevelyan, Oxford 1932. Rptd from Pall Mall Gazette.
The Times on the American war: an historical study by L. S. 1865.
The playground of Europe. 1871, 1894 (rev); ed H. E. G. Tyndale, Oxford 1936; tr French, 1935.
Essays on freethinking and plainspeaking. 1873, 1905 (with introductory essays by J. Bryce and H. Paul).
Hours in a library. 3 sers 1874–9, 1892 (with addns), 4 vols 1907 (with addns).
History of English thought in the eighteenth century. 2 vols 1876.
Samuel Johnson. 1878 (EML).
Alexander Pope. 1880 (EML).
The science of ethics. 1882.
Swift. 1882 (EML).
The dictionary of national biography. 21 vols 1885–1909. Editor 1882–91; contributed 378 articles.
Life of Henry Fawcett. 1885.
An agnostic's apology, and other essays. 1893.
The life of Sir James Fitzjames Stephen. 1895.
Social rights and duties. 2 vols 1896.
Studies of a biographer. 4 vols 1898–1902.
The English Utilitarians. 3 vols 1900, 1950 (rptd by London School of Economics).
George Eliot. 1902 (EML).
Robert Louis Stevenson: an essay. 1902.
English literature and society in the eighteenth century. 1904.
Hobbes. 1904 (EML).
Some early impressions. 1924. Rptd from Nat Rev.
Stephen edited Alpine Jnl 1868–72 *and* Cornhill Mag 1871–82, *and contributed regularly to Saturday Rev, Pall Mall Gazette, Nation (New York), Fraser's Mag, Fortnightly Rev and Nat Rev. He also contributed essays to edns of various writers including Fielding, Richardson and Thackeray. He edited J. R. Green's letters and, with F. Pollock, W. K. Clifford's lectures and essays. For letters, see Maitland, below.*

§2

Trevelyan, G. O. Macmillan's Mag May 1860.
Life and letters of J. R. Lowell. Ed C. E. Norton 2 vols 1894.
Symons, A. Leslie Stephen. Saturday Rev July 1898.
Gosse, E. Sir Leslie Stephen. Eng Illustr Mag Nov 1903. With bibliography.
Bryce, J. Alpine Jnl 22 1904.
Harrison, F. Cornhill Mag April 1904.
Lee, S. Times 23 Feb 1904. *See* Lee's article on Stephen in DNB 2nd suppl 1912.
Maitland, F. W. Life and letters of Stephen. 1906.
Meredith, G. In his Letters, 1912.
Thompson, F. Stephen as a biographer. 1915.
Courtney, J. E. In her Freethinkers of the nineteenth century, New York 1920.
Williams, S. T. Stephen twenty years later. London Mercury Oct 1923.
Birrell, A. Anti-humbug. In his More obiter dicta, 1924.
Woolf, V. Stephen: the philosopher at home. Times 28 Nov 1932.
—— In her Captain's death bed and other essays, 1950.
—— My father: Leslie Stephen. Atlantic Monthly March 1950.
Engel, C. E. Stephen's letters to some French friends. Alpine Jnl Nov 1935.
MacCarthy, D. Leslie Stephen. Cambridge 1937 (Leslie Stephen lecture).
Leavis, Q. D. Stephen: Cambridge critic. Scrutiny 7 1939.
Wilson, J. D. Stephen and Matthew Arnold as critics of Wordsworth. Cambridge 1939.
Sanders, C. R. Stephen, Coleridge and two Coleridgeans. PMLA 55 1940.
Burn, W. L. Three generations of individualists. Listener 21 Dec 1950.
Butt, J. The Stephen family: a tradition of scholarly journalism. Listener 28 Dec 1950.
Annan, N. G. Stephen: his thought and character in relation to his time. 1951.
—— The intellectual aristocracy. In Studies in social history: a tribute to G. M. Trevelyan, ed J. H. Plumb 1955.
Himmelfarb, G. Mr Stephen and Mr Ramsay: the Victorian as intellectual. Partisan Rev 19 1952, Twentieth Century Dec 1952.
Maurer, O. Stephen and the Cornhill Magazine 1871–82. SE 32 1953.
Baldanza, F. To the lighthouse again. PMLA 70 1955.
Appleman, P. Evolution and two critics of art and literature. Proc Third International Congress on Aesthetics 1957.
Wellek, R. Stephen's stature as a literary critic. Victorian Newsletter no 11 1957.
Sheen, E. D. Stephen and modern criticism. College Lang Assoc Jnl 2 1958.
Bicknell, J. W. Stephen's English thought in the eighteenth century: a tract for the times. Victorian Stud 6 1962.
Bateson, F. W. God-killer. New Statesman 21 June 1963.

F. G. T.

SAMUEL BUTLER

1835–1902

Bibliographies

Jones, H. F. In his Butler: a memoir, 2 vols 1919.
Hoppé, A. J. A bibliography of the writings of Butler and of writings about him, with some letters from Butler to F. G. Fleay now first published. [1925]. For addns *see* J. B. Fort, Samuel Butler, Bordeaux 1934.
Catalogue of the collection of Butler in the Chapin Library, Williams College Williamstown. Portland Maine 1945.
Harkness, S. B. The career of Butler: a bibliography. 1955.
Gerber, H. E. Bibliography [of Butler]. English Fiction in Transition 1 1957.
Howard, D. F. Butler manuscripts. Ibid.
Davies, D. The Butler collection of the Honnold Library. Claremont Quart 7 1960.

Collections

The Shrewsbury edition of the works. Ed H. F. Jones and A. T. Bartholomew 20 vols 1923–6.

The essential Butler. Ed G. D. H. Cole 1950, 1961 (rev).

§1

For music see A. J. Hoppé, Bibliography, *above*.

A first year in Canterbury settlement. 1863; ed R. A. Streatfeild 1914 (with other early essays).

The evidence for the resurrection of Jesus Christ, as given by the four evangelists, critically examined. 1865. Anon.

Erewhon: or over the range. 1872 (anon), 1872 (rev and corrected), 1901 (rev); ed F. N. Hackett, New York 1917; ed L. Mumford, New York 1927; ed H. M. Tomlinson, New York 1931; ed A. Huxley, New York 1934; ed D. McCarthy 1960; ed K. Amis, New York 1961; tr Dutch, 1873; German, 1879; French, 1920; Spanish, 1926; Italian, 1945.

The fair haven: a work in defence of the miraculous element in our Lord's ministry upon earth, both as against rationalistic impugners and certain orthodox defenders, by the late J. P. Owen, edited by W. B. Owen, with a memoir of the author. 1873; ed R. A. Streatfeild 1913; ed A. T. Bartholomew 1929; ed G. Bullett 1938.

Life and habit: an essay after a completer view of evolution. 1878; ed R. A. Streatfeild 1910 (with addns).

Evolution, old and new: or the theories of Buffon, Dr Erasmus Darwin and Lamarck, as compared with that of Mr Charles Darwin. 1879, 1882 (with appendix and index); ed R. A. Streatfeild 1911.

Unconscious memory: a comparison between the theory of Dr Ewald Hering, professor of physiology at Prague, and the philosophy of the unconscious of Dr Edward von Hartmann; with translations from these authors. 1880; [ed R. A. Streatfeild] 1910 (with introd by M. Hartog).

Alps and sanctuaries of Piedmont and the Canton Ticino. 1882; ed R. A. Streatfeild 1913 (with author's revisions and index, and introd).

Selections from previous works, with remarks on Mr G. J. Romanes' Mental evolution in animals, and A psalm of Montreal. 1884.

Luck or cunning as the main means of organic modification? an attempt to throw additional light upon the late Mr Charles Darwin's theory of natural selection. 1887; ed H. F. Jones 1920.

Ex voto: an account of the Sacro Monte or New Jerusalem at Varallo-Sesia, with some notice of Tabachetti's remaining work at the sanctuary of Crea. 1888, 1889 (rev and enlarged); tr Italian, 1894.

A lecture on the humour of Homer, January 30th 1892; reprinted with preface and additional matter from the Eagle. Cambridge 1892.

The life and letters of Dr Samuel Butler, headmaster of Shrewsbury School 1798–1836, and afterwards Bishop of Lichfield. 2 vols 1896.

The authoress of the Odyssey, where and when she wrote, who she was, the use she made of the Iliad, and how the poem grew under her hands. 1897; ed H. F. Jones 1922. Butler's theory about the Odyssey was first announced in several articles written by him in Sicilian and English papers.

The Iliad of Homer, rendered into English prose. 1898; ed L. R. Loomis, New York 1942.

Shakespeare's sonnets reconsidered, and in part rearranged, with introductory chapters by Butler. 1899.

The Odyssey, rendered into English prose. 1900; ed L. R. Loomis, New York 1942.

Erewhon revisited twenty years later, both by the original discoverer of the country and by his son. 1901; ed G. M. Acklom, New York 1920.

The way of all flesh. [Ed R. A. Streatfeild] 1903; ed W. L. Phelps, New York 1916; ed T. Dreiser, New York 1936; ed G. B. Shaw 1936; ed R. A. Gettmann, New York 1948; ed W. Y. Tindall, New York 1950; ed M. D. Zabel, New York 1950; ed G. M. Acklom, New York 1952; ed A. C. Ward 1953; ed L. B. Salomon, New York 1957; ed D. F. Howard, Boston 1964.

Essays on life, art and science. Ed R. A. Streatfeild 1904.

Seven sonnets and A psalm of Montreal. [Ed R. A. Streatfeild] Cambridge 1904 (priv ptd).

God the known and God the unknown. [Ed R. A. Streatfeild] 1909.

The humour of Homer, and other essays. Ed R. A. Streatfeild 1913. With a biographical sketch by H. F. Jones.

Hesiod's works and days: a translation. 1924.

Letters and Notebooks

Note-books: selections. Ed H. F. Jones 1912; Selections, ed A. T. Bartholomew 1930.

Butleriana. 1932 (Nonesuch). Compiled mainly from previously unpbd portions of the note-books by A. T. Bartholomew.

Further extracts from the note-books. Ed A. T. Bartholomew 1934.

Letters between Butler and Miss E. M. A. Savage. Ed G. L. Keynes and B. Hill 1935.

Butler's notebooks: selections. Ed G. L. Keynes and B. Hill 1951.

Correspondence of Butler with his sister May. Ed D. F. Howard, Berkeley 1962.

The family letters of Butler 1841–86. Ed A. Silver, Stanford 1962.

§2

Sugameli, P. Origine trapanese dell' Odissea secondo Butler. Trapani 1892.

Streatfeild, R. A. Butler: a critical study. 1902.

— Samuel Butler. Monthly Rev Sept 1902.

— Butler: records and memorials. 1903.

Jones, H. F. Diary of a journey through North Italy to Sicily for the purpose of leaving the MSS of three books by Butler at Varallo-Sesia, Aci-Reale and Trapani. 1904.

— Charles Darwin and Butler: a step towards reconciliation. 1911.

— Butler: a memoir. 2 vols 1919.

— Butler as a musical critic. Chesterton May 1920.

— and A. T. Bartholomew. The Butler collection at St John's College Cambridge. Cambridge 1921.

MacCarthy, D. Samuel Butler. Independent Rev 3 1904.

— Butler: an impression. In his Remnants, 1918.

— Samuel Butler. Life & Letters Oct 1931.

Shaw, G. B. John Bull's other island and Major Barbara. 1907. Preface to Major Barbara.

— Butler when I was a nobody. Saturday Rev of Lit 29 April 1950.

Blum, J. Samuel Butler. [1910].

— ('Jean Florence'). Le litre et l'amphore. Paris 1924.

Salter, W. H. Essays on two moderns: Euripides; Butler. 1911.

Kellogg, V. L. Butler and biological memory. Science (Garrison NY) 35 1912.

H[arris], J. F. Butler and his note-books. 1913.

— Butler, author of Erewhon: the man and his work. 1916.

Jourdain, P. E. B. Aspects of Butler. Open Court 27 1913.

Barry, W. Butler of Erewhon. Dublin Rev 155 1914.

Hartog, M. M. Butler and recent mnemic biological theories. 1914.

Pestalozzi, G. Butler der jüngere: Versuch einer Darstellung seiner Gedankenwelt. Zürich 1914.

Rattray, R. F. The philosophy of Butler. Mind 23 1914.

— Butler: a chronicle and an introduction. 1935.

Cannan, G. Butler: a critical study. 1915.

Heitland, W. E. A 'few earnest words' on Butler. [1916].

Russell, E. S. Butler and the memory theories of heredity. In his Form and function, 1916.
Stillman, C. G. The literary and scientific work of Butler. North Amer Rev 204 1916.
—— Butler: a mid-Victorian modern. 1932.
Sincalie, M. The pan-psychism of Butler. In her A defence of idealism, 1917.
Yeats, J. B. Recollections of Butler. In his Essays Irish and American, 1918.
Clutton-Brock, A. In his Essays on books, 1920. 2 essays on Butler.
Duffin, H. C. Of Samuel Butler. In his Quintessence of Bernard Shaw, 1920.
Larbaud, V. Samuel Butler: conférence. Paris 1920.
—— Butler (étude et fragments traduits d'Erewhon). Nouvelle Revue Française Jan 1920.
—— Samuel Butler. Revue de France 1 Oct 1923.
Bellessort, A. Butler et son voyage aux pays imaginaires. Revue Politique et Littéraire 59 1921.
Chevalley, A. Samuel Butler. In his Le roman anglais de notre temps, 1921.
Gillet, L. Butler: a memoir par H. F. Jones. Revue des Deux Mondes 15 Aug 1921.
'Lee, Vernon'. Back to Butler: a metabiological commentary on GBS. New Statesman 24 Sept 1921.
Cany, H. S. The satiric rage of Butler. In his Definitions, New York 1922.
Cavenagh, F. A. Butler and education. Monist 32 1922.
Gosse, E. In his Aspects and impressions, 1922.
Quiller-Couch, A. T. Who wrote the Odyssey? Observer 23 April 1922.
Cazamian, L. In his Le roman et les idées en Angleterre: l'influence de la science 1868–90, Strasbourg 1923. Ch 3.
Semon, R. In his Mnemic psychology, 1923. Pt 1.
Smith, P. J. On strange altars. 1923.
Joad, C. E. M. Samuel Butler. 1924.
—— The vindication of Butler. Spectator 20–27 Feb 1925.
Willcocks, M. P. Butler of the Way of all flesh. Eng Rev 39 1924.
Bekker, W. G. An historical and critical review of Butler's literary works. Rotterdam [1925].
Blom, E. Imitation Handel. In his Stepchildren of music, 1925.
Lange, P. J. de. Butler: critic and philosopher. Zutphen 1925.
Aronstein, P. Butler der jüngere. Germanisch-romanische Monatsschrift 14 1926.
Garnett, Mrs M. Butler and his family relations. 1926.
Peper, E. George Bernard Shaw's Beziehungen zu Butler dem jüngeren. Ang 50 1926.
Wolff, E. Samuel Butler. Zeitschrift für künstliche Kultur 3 1926.
Fort, J. B. Butler en voyage. Revue Anglo-américaine 4 1927.
—— Butler: étude d'un caractère et d'une intelligence. Bordeaux 1934.
—— Butler l'écrivain: étude d'un style. Bordeaux 1935.
—— Butler 1935: le bilan d'un anniversaire. Langues Modernes 34 1936.
—— Les idées de Butler. Revue Philosophique de la France 61 1937.
Arns, K. Butler der jüngere. Neue Jahrbücher für Wissenschaft 4 1928.
—— Butler und die englische Gegenwartsliteratur. Der Gral 12 1928.
Bonnet, P. L'humeur de Butler, auteur d'Erewhon. Revue de l'Enseignement des Langues Vivantes Jan–Feb 1928.
Farrington, B. Butler and the Odyssey. New Adelphi 1 1928.
—— Butler and the Odyssey. 1929.
Meissner, P. Butler und seine Utopie: Jenseits der Berge. Zeitschrift für Französischen und Englischen Unterricht 28 1929.
—— Die Überwindung des 19ten Jahrhunderts im Denken von Butler. Germanisch-romanische Monatsschrift 17 1929.
—— Butler der jüngere: ein Studie zur Kultur des ausgehenden Viktorianismus. Leipzig 1931.
Shewan, A. Butler and Homer once more. Classical Weekly 13 May 1929.
Stoff, R. Die Philosophie des Organischen bei Butler, mit einer biographischen Übersicht zusammengestellt von H. E. Herlitschka. Vienna 1929.
Lovett, R. M. The way of all flesh. In his Preface to fiction: a discussion of great modern novels, Chicago 1931.
Vaughan, H. M. In his From Anne to Victoria: fourteen biographical studies between 1702 and 1901, 1931.
Carlo, S. E. di. Un romanziere e biologo inglese, amico dell' Italia: Butler. Milan 1933.
Wilson, E. The satire of Butler. New Republic 24 May 1933.
Blackmur, R. P. In his Double agent, New York 1935.
Davis, H. Samuel Butler. UTQ 5 1935.
Ervine, St J. The centenary of Butler. Fortnightly Rev Dec 1935.
Jordan-Smith, P. Butler: the first century. Colophon new ser 1 1935.
Keynes, G. L. and B. Hill. Distribution of Butler's manuscripts: new gift to the British Museum. TLS 23 Nov 1935.
Butler: born December 4 1835. TLS 7 Dec 1935.
Steele, R. Butler and the Odyssey. TLS 21 Dec 1935.
Arens, F. Dem Jahrhundertgedenken Butlers. Europäische Revue 7 1936.
Carswell, C. In English novelists, ed D. Verschoyle 1936.
Delattre, F. Butler et le Bergsonisme. Revue Anglo-américaine 13 1936.
Hill, B. Butler in Canada. Dalhousie Rev 16 1936.
Krog, F. Butlers Erewhon: eine Utopie? Anglia 60 1936.
Muggeridge, M. The earnest atheist: a study of Butler. 1936.
—— The legacy of Butler. Saturday Rev of Lit 20 Feb 1937.
Cowie, D. Butler in New Zealand. London Mercury March 1937.
Davis, H. J. The duplicity of Samuel Butler. Canadian Forum March 1937.
Plesner, K. F. Bruddet med Victorianismen: Butler. Copenhagen 1938.
Eyrignoux, L. La dette de Shaw envers Butler: deux documents. Etudes Anglaises 3 1939.
Hicks, G. Butler, cautious rebel. In his Figures of transition, New York 1939.
Bissell, C. A study of the Way of all flesh. In Nineteenth-century studies, ed H. Davis et al, Ithaca 1940.
—— The Butlerian inheritance of G. B. Shaw. Dalhousie Rev 41 1961.
Dilworth, N. The second passing of Butler. South Atlantic Quart 40 1941.
Holt, L. E. Butler and his Victorian critics. ELH 8 1941.
—— Butler's rise to fame. PMLA 57 1942.
—— Butler's revisions of Erewhon. PBSA 38 1944.
—— The note-books of Butler. PMLA 60 1945.
—— E. M. Forster and Butler. PMLA 61 1946.
—— Butler up to date. Eng Fiction in Transition 3 1960.
—— Samuel Butler. New York 1964.
R., V. and H. G. L. K. Erewhon. N & Q 13 Feb, 13 March 1943.
Cline, C. L. Coningsby and three Victorian novelists. N & Q 15 Jan 1944.
Forster, E. M. Books in general. New Statesman 15 July 1944.
—— The legacy of Butler. Listener 12 June 1952.
Pritchett, V. S. A Victorian son. In his Living novel, 1946.

Butler at Williams College. TLS 18 May 1946.
Cole, G. D. H. Butler and the Way of all flesh. 1947.
Furbank, P. N. Samuel Butler. Cambridge 1948.
Miller, B. Miss Savage and Miss Bartram. Nineteenth Century Nov 1948.
— Two fathers and their sons. Nineteenth Century Oct 1949.
Myers, R. M. Butler, Handelian. Musical Quart 34 1948.
Opitz, E. A. Butler: author of Erewhon. Contemporary Rev June 1948.
Humphry, J. Butler: author of Erewhon. Colby Lib Quart ser 2 1949.
Ruyer, R. Marx et Butler: ou technologisme et finalisme. Revue de Métaphysique et de Morale 55 1950.
Greene, G. In his Lost childhood and other essays, 1951.
Pocock, L. G. Butler and the authoress of the Odyssey. Listener 5 March 1951.
Swarthout, G. The way of all flesh. TLS 3 Aug 1951.
Davidson, J. W. Butler in the Antipodes. Listener 3 July 1952.
Hough, G. The aura of the Victorian vicarage. Listener 19 June 1952.
Toynbee, P. A satirist in a world beyond satire. Listener 26 June 1952.
Henderson, P. Butler: the incarnate bachelor. 1953.
Linde, I. D. The way of all flesh and A portrait of the artist as a young man. Victorian Newsletter 1956.
Wilson, A. The revolt of Butler. Atlantic Monthly Nov 1957.
Zabel, M. D. Butler: the Victorian insolvency. In his Craft and character, New York 1957.
O'Connor, W. V. Butler and Bloomsbury. In From Jane Austen to Conrad, ed R. C. Rathburn and M. Steinmann, Minneapolis 1958.
Raleigh, J. H. Victorian morals and the modern novel. Partisan Rev 25 1958.
Jones, J. J. The cradle of Erewhon: Butler in New Zealand. Austin 1959.
Oldham, J. B. Shrewsbury school library. Library 5th ser 14 1959.
Howard, D. F. The critical significance of autobiography in the Way of all flesh. Victorian Newsletter no 17 1960.
Maling, P. B. Butler at Mesopotamia, together with Butler's Forest Creek manuscript and his letters to Tripp and Acland. Wellington NZ 1960.
Willey, B. Darwin and Butler: two versions of evolution. 1960.
Knoepflmacher, U. C. Ishmael or anti-hero? the division of self: The way of all flesh. Eng Fiction in Transition 4 1961. Reply by Sr M. B. Quinn 5 1962.
Schösser, A. Der viktorianische Gulliver: Betrachtungen über Butlers Erewhon und Erewhon revisited. Zeitschrift für Anglistik und Amerikanistik 9 1961.
Simpson, G. G. Lamarck, Darwin and Butler: three approaches to evolution. Amer Scholar 30 1961.
Currie, A. W. Butler's Canadian investment. UTQ 32 1962.
Giovanni, A. Butler in Sicily. REL 3 1962.
Marshall, W. H. The way of all flesh: the dual function of Edward Overton. Univ of Texas Stud in Lang & Lit 4 1962.
Noon, W. T. Three young men in rebellion. Thought 38 1963.
Vita-Finzi, C. Butler and Italy. Italian Stud 18 1963.
Carey, G. O. Butler's theory of evolution: a summary. Eng Lit in Transition 7 1964.
Daniels, R. B. The conscience of Butler. Forum 4 1964.
Shoenberg, R. E. The literal-mindedness of Butler. Stud in Eng Lit 1500–1900 4 1964.

F. G. T.

WALTER HORATIO PATER
1839–94

Bodley has the ms of Pascal; *King's School Canterbury has* Diaphaneitè, *and Mr John Sparrow the ms of the unpbd chs of* Gaston de Latour, *as well as the ms of* Demeter and Persephone. *There are many further mss at Harvard; the letters are scattered.*

Bibliographies

Stonehill, C. A. and H. W. In their Bibliographies of modern authors ser 2, 1925.
See also G. d'Hangest, Pater: l'homme et l'œuvre, 1961, below, for the most complete bibliography.

Collections

Works. 9 vols 1900–1.
Works: new library edition. 10 vols 1910.
Selections. Ed E. E. Hale jr, New York 1901.
Selected essays. Ed H. G. Rawlinson 1927.
Selected works. Ed R. Aldington 1948.
Selected prose. Ed D. Patmore 1949.

§ 1

Most of Pater's essays and some of his fiction appeared in periodical form before being collected as books. The journals in which Pater pbd include Academy, Athenaeum, Bookman (London), Contemporary Rev, Guardian, Harper's Monthly Mag, Littell's Living Age, Macmillan's Mag, Nineteenth Century, Pall Mall Gazette and Westminster Rev. These and other occasional pbns are listed in d'Hangest, Pater: l'homme et l'œuvre, *below.*

Studies in the history of the Renaissance. 1873, 1877 (rev, omitting Conclusion and including The school of Giorgione as The Renaissance: studies in art and poetry), 1888 (Conclusion restored with changes); ed K. Clark 1961; tr French, 1917.
Marius the Epicurean: his sensations and ideas. 2 vols 1885, 1888 (with changes), 1892 (with extensive changes); ed J. C. Squire 2 vols 1929; ed A. K. Tuell, New York 1929; ed E. A. Parker 1931 (abridged); ed O. Burdett 1934; ed J. Sagmaster, New York 1935; tr French, 1922.
Imaginary portraits. 1887; ed E. J. Brzenk, New York 1962 (including An English poet); tr French (introd by A. Symons), 1899, (introd by P. Neel), 1930; Italian, 1944.
Appreciations: with an essay on style. 1889, 1890 (Aesthetic poetry replaced by review of Feuillet, La morte).
Plato and Platonism: a series of lectures. 1893; tr French, 1923.
Note on F. W. Bussell. In Oxford characters vi, 1893. Never rptd.
An imaginary portrait (The child in the house). Oxford 1894. Pbd as separate vol after earlier appearance in Macmillan's Mag; rptd in Miscellaneous studies, below.
Greek studies: a series of essays, prepared for the press by C. L. Shadwell. 1895.
Miscellaneous studies: a series of essays, prepared for the press by C. L. Shadwell. 1895.
Gaston de Latour: an unfinished romance, prepared for the press by C. L. Shadwell. 1896.
Essays from the Guardian. 1896 (priv ptd); [ed T. B. Mosher?], Portland Maine 1897; 1901 (uniform with Works, above).
Uncollected essays. [Ed T. B. Mosher?], Portland Maine 1903.
Sketches and reviews. New York 1919.
The chant of the celestial sailors: an unpublished poem. [Winchester] 1928 (priv ptd by E. H. Blakeney).
An English poet. Ed M. Ottley, Fortnightly Rev April 1931.

§2

Many of Pater's pbns were reviewed on their appearance in the following journals: Academy, Athenaeum, Atlantic Monthly, Bookman, Catholic World, Classical Rev, Contemporary Rev, Cornhill Mag, Critic, Current Lit, Dial, Edinburgh Rev, Mind, Nation, Nineteenth Century, Outlook, Quart Rev, Realm, Saturday Rev, Spectator, Westminster Rev.

[Morley, J.] Mr Pater's essays. Fortnightly Rev April 1873. Review of Renaissance.

[Pattison, Mrs M.] Westminster Rev 43 1873. Review of Renaissance.

Symonds, J. A. Academy 15 March 1873. Review of Renaissance.

—— Is music the type and measure of all art? In his Essays speculative and suggestive, 1890.

Saintsbury, G. Modern English prose. Fortnightly Rev Feb 1876.

—— Walter Pater. Bookman (London) 1906; rptd in his Prefaces and essays, 1933.

—— In his History of English criticism, 1911.

—— In his History of English prose rhythms, 1912.

Mallock, W. H. In his New republic, 2 vols 1877, 1 vol 1878.

—— In his Memoirs, 1920.

Sharp, W. Athenaeum 28 Feb 1885. Review of Marius.

—— Some personal reminiscences of Pater. Atlantic Monthly Dec 1894. Both rptd in his Papers critical and reminiscent, 1912.

—— Realm 1 1895. Review of Greek studies.

See also E. Sharp, William Sharp: a memoir, 1910.

Ward, Mrs H. Macmillan's Mag June 1885. Review of Marius.

—— In her A writer's recollections, 1918.

See also T. H. Ward, Reminiscences: Brasenose 1864–72, in Brasenose College Quarterly Monographs, Oxford 1909.

Wilde, O. Pall Mall Gazette 11 June 1887. Review of Imaginary portraits.

—— Speaker 22 March 1890. Review of Appreciations. Both rptd in his Reviews, 1908, and in A critic in Pall Mall, 1919.

—— The true function and value of criticism. Nineteenth Century July, Sept 1890; rptd in his Intentions, 1891.

Bosanquet, B. In his A history of aesthetic, 1892.

Johnson, L. Mr Pater upon Plato. Westminster Gazette 2 March 1893.

—— The spirit of Plato. Speaker 28 Oct 1893.

—— The work of Mr Pater. Fortnightly Rev Sept 1894.

—— A note upon Mr Pater. Academy 16 Jan 1897.

—— For a little clan. Academy 13 Oct 1900. All rev and rptd in his Post liminium, 1911.

Symons, A. The decadent movement in literature. Harper's Monthly Mag Nov 1893.

—— In his Studies in two literatures, 1897; rptd in his Studies in prose and verse, 1904; rev as A study of Pater, 1932.

—— In his Figures of several centuries, 1906.

Bussell, F. W. In memoriam W. H. Pater. Oxford Mag 13 1894.

Gosse, E. Pater: a portrait. Contemporary Rev Dec 1894. Also in Littell's Living Age 204 1895; rptd in his Critical kit-kats, 1896.

Hofmannsthal, H. von. Walter Pater. Die Zeit (Vienna) 1894; rptd in his Gesammelte Werke in Einzelausgaben (Prosa 1), Frankfurt 1950.

Beerbohm, M. Be it cosiness. Pageant 1 Dec 1895; rptd as Diminuendo in his Works, 1908.

Escott, T. H. S. Some Oxford memories of the pre-aesthetic age. Nat Rev Oct 1895.

—— Pater and other memories. Bookman's Jnl 10 1924.

Lang, A. Illustr London News 9 March 1895. Review of Greek studies.

Le Gallienne, R. Retrospective reviews: a literary log. 2 vols 1896.

—— On re-reading Pater. North Amer Rev Feb 1912.

Newman, E. Pater on music. In Studies in music, ed R. Grey 1901.

Greenslet, F. Walter Pater. New York 1904.

Moore, G. Avowals vi: Pater. Pall Mag Mag Aug 1904. Also in Lippincott's Mag 73 1904; rptd with changes in his Avowals, 1919. *See also* his Confessions, 1904 (rev).

Durham, J. Marius the Epicurean and John Inglesant. 1905.

Benson, A. C. Walter Pater. 1906 (EML).

—— Walter Pater. 1906 (Royal Institution of Great Britain).

Hutton, J. A. Pilgrims in the region of faith: Amiel, Tolstoy, Pater, Newman. Edinburgh 1906.

Wright, T. The life of Pater. 2 vols 1907.

—— In his Autobiography, 1936.

Pater's aesthetic outlook. Edinburgh Rev 206 1907.

Buchan J. In Nine Brasenose worthies. Brasenose College Quarter-centenary Monographs, Oxford 1909.

Cecil, A. In his Six Oxford thinkers, 1909.

Ross, R. Mr Benson's Pater. In his Masques and phases, 1909.

[Bailey, J.] A modern Platonist. TLS 1 Sept 1910; rptd in Bailey's poets and poetry, Oxford 1911.

Dowden, E. In his Essays modern and Elizabethan, 1910.

More, P. E. Walter Pater. Nation (New York) April 1911; rptd with addns in his Drift of romanticism, Boston 1913.

Bock, E. J. Paters Einfluss auf Oscar Wilde. Bonn 1913.

Hunecker, J. Pater re-read. In his Pathos of distance, 1913.

Ransome, A. In his Portraits and speculations, 1913.

Thomas, E. Pater: a critical study. 1913.

Bendz, E. The influence of Pater and Matthew Arnold in the prose-writings of Oscar Wilde. Gothenburg 1914.

Chew, S. C. Pater's quotations. Nation (New York) Oct 1914.

Powys, J. C. In his Visions and revisions, New York 1915.

Fehr, B. Pater und Hegel. Studien 50 1916.

Jackson, W. W. Ingram Bywater: the memoir of an Oxford scholar. Oxford 1917.

Proesler, H. Pater und sein Verhältnis zur deutschen Literatur. Freiburg 1917.

Michaud, R. Mystiques et réalistes anglo-saxons. Paris 1918.

Harris, F. In his Contemporary portraits ser 2, 1919.

Lucas, St J. Pater and the army. Blackwood's Mag March 1921.

Shafer, R. Pater redivivus. In his Progress and science: essays in criticism, New Haven 1922.

Shuster, G. N. Ruskin, Pater and the Pre-Raphaelites. In his Catholic spirit in modern English literature, New York 1922.

Cazamian, M. L. In his Le roman et les idées en Angleterre, 2 vols Paris 1923.

Jaloux, E. Walter Pater. Les Nouvelles Littéraires 8 Sept 1923.

Duthuit, G. Le rose et le noir: de Pater à Oscar Wilde. La Nouvelle Revue Française 1 Feb 1924; rptd with additional material in his Messages, Paris 1926.

Harrison, J. S. Pater, Heine and the old gods of Greece. PMLA 39 1924.

Duclaux, M. Souvenirs sur Pater. Revue de Paris 15 Jan 1925.

Ralli, A. Pater the humanist. North Amer Rev Feb 1925: rptd in his Critiques, 1927.

Mourey, G. Marcel Proust, John Ruskin et Pater. Le Monde Nouveau Aug–Sept, Oct 1926.

Staub, F. Das imaginäre Porträt Paters. Zürich 1926.

Yeats, W. B. In his Autobiographies, 1926.

—— Introduction. In his Oxford book of modern verse, Oxford 1936.

Smith, L. P. On re-reading Pater. Dial 83 1927; rptd in his Reperusals and recollections, 1936.

Chandler, Z. E. An analysis of the stylistic technique of Addison, Johnson, Hazlitt and Pater. Iowa City 1928.

Scott-James, R. A. The making of literature: some principles of criticism. 1928, 1948 (with addns).
Du Bos, C. Sur Marius l'Epicurien de Pater. In his Approximations, Paris 1930.
Eliot, T. S. The place of Pater. In The eighteen-eighties, ed de la Mare, Cambridge 1930; rptd as Arnold and Pater, Bookman (New York) Sept 1930 and in his Selected essays, 1932. Rptd in part as Pater and Marius the Epicurean in his Points of view, 1947.
Grabowski, Z. Pater: zycie, dzielo, styl. Poznan 1930.
Beyer, A. Paters Beziehungen zur französischen Literatur und Kultur. Halle 1931.
Farmer, A. J. Pater as a critic of English literature: a study of Appreciations. Grenoble 1931.
Rosenblatt, L. L'idée de l'art pour l'art dans la littérature anglaise pendant la période victorienne. Paris 1931.
— Marius l'Épicurien de Pater et ses points de départ français. Revue de Littérature Comparée 15 1935.
— The genesis of Marius the Epicurean. Comparative Lit 14 1962.
Welby, T. E. In his Revaluations: studies in biography, Oxford 1931; rptd in his Second impressions, 1933.
Burgum, E. B. Pater and the good life. Sewanee Rev 40 1932.
Garvin, K. In Great Victorians, ed H. J. and H. Massingham 1932.
Newman, B. Pater: a revaluation. Nineteenth Century May 1932.
Stauffer, D. A. Monna melancholia: a study in Pater's sources. Sewanee Rev 40 1932.
Eaker, J. G. Pater: a study in methods and effects. Iowa City 1933.
'Field, Michael' (K. H. Bradley and E. E. Cooper). Works and days. 1933.
'Lee, Vernon' (V. Paget). The handling of words: a page of Pater. Life & Letters 9 1933.
Praz, M. The romantic agony. Oxford 1933.
— Introduction. In his Ritratti immaginari di Pater, Rome 1944; rptd in his La casa della fama, Milan and Naples 1952.
Young, H. H. The writings of Pater: a reflection of British philosophical opinion from 1860 to 1890. Lancaster Pa 1933.
Van de Put, A. Pater and the Rosenmold pedigree. Lingard Papers new ser 17 1934.
Green, Z. E. Pater's unhappy beginnings. Eng Jnl 24 1935.
Cattan, L. Essai sur Pater. Paris 1936.
Fletcher, G. B. A. A textual error in Pater. TLS 29 Aug 1936.
O'Faolain, S. Pater and Moore. London Mercury Aug 1936.
Minchin, H. C. Walter Horatio Pater. Fortnightly Rev Aug 1939.
Oliviero, F. Il pensiero religioso ed estetico de Pater. Turin 1939.
Peel, J. H. B. Pater and perfection. Poetry Rev 30 1939.
Wainwright, B. B. A centenary query: is Pater outmoded? Eng Jnl 28 1939.
Walter Pater. TLS 5 Aug 1939. Also Pater: a prose that stands the test of time. Replies by A. Douglas, Pater and Dorian Gray, 12 Aug 1939.
Child, R. C. The aesthetic of Pater. New York 1940.
Symons, A. J. A. Wilde at Oxford. Horizon April–May 1941.
Schoen, M. Pater on the place of music among the arts. Jnl of Aesthetics 6 1942.
Law, H. H. Pater's use of Greek quotations. MLN 58 1943.
Morgan, C. In his House of Macmillan 1843–1943, 1943.
Coll, E. Q and Pater. TLS 16 Dec 1944.
Ironside, R. Walter Pater. Cornhill Mag 161 1944.
Tillotson, G. Pater, Mr Rose and the Conclusion of the Renaissance. E & S 32 1946.
— Arnold and Pater: critics historical, aesthetic and otherwise. E & S new ser 3 1950. Both rptd with changes in his Criticism and the nineteenth century, 1951.
Eckhoff, L. Den estetiske bevelgese. Edda 47 1947.
Hough, G. Books in general. New Statesman 29 Nov 1947.
— In his Last Romantics, 1949.
Huppé, B. F. Pater on Plato's aesthetics. MLQ 9 1948.
O'Connor, W. V. The poet as esthetician. Quart Rev of Lit 4 1948.
Osawa, M. Woolf and Pater. New Eng & Amer Lit 1 1948.
Pick, J. Divergent disciples of Pater. Thought 23 1948.
Read, H. Walter Pater. World Rev Nov 1948; rptd in his Tenth muse, 1957.
Bertocci, A. P. Charles du Bos and English literature: a critic and his orientation. New York 1949.
Bowra, C. M. Walter Pater. Sewanee Rev 57 1949; rptd in his Inspiration and poetry, 1957.
Izumii, H. A. A portrait of Pater. Urn 1 1949.
Pater preaches. TLS 13 April 1949.
Brown, E. K. Pater's Appreciations: a bibliographical note. MLN 65 1950.
Buckley, J. H. Pater and the suppressed Conclusion. MLN 56 1950.
Peters, F. E. Pater's Lacedaemon. Classical Bull 27 1950.
Osbourn, R. V. Marius the Epicurean. EC 1 1951.
Vollrath, W. Verschwiegenes Oxford: Matthew Arnold, Goethe und Pater. Heidelberg 1951.
Allott, K. Pater and Arnold. EC 2 1952.
Blissett, W. Pater and Eliot. UTQ 22 1953.
Millhauser, M. Pater and the flux. Jnl of Aesthetics 12 1953.
Singer, I. The aesthetics of 'art for art's sake'. Ibid.
Johnson, R. V. Pater and the Victorian anti-Romantics. EC 4 1954.
— Pater as critic: his critical practices considered in relation to his theories of life and art. Melbourne 1962.
Stanford, D. Pater's ideal aesthetic type. Cambridge Jnl May 1954.
Cecil, D. Pater: the scholar-artist. 1955; rptd in his Fine art of reading, 1957.
Fletcher, I. Leda and St Anne. Listener 21 Feb 1957.
— Walter Pater. 1959 (Br Council pamphlet).
— Why not take Pater seriously? EC 9 1959.
Wellek, R. Pater's literary theory and criticism. Victorian Stud 1 1957; rptd in his A history of modern criticism 1750–1950 vol 3, 1958.
Brzenk, E. J. Pater and Apuelius. Comparative Lit 10 1958. Reply by P. Turner, Victorian Stud 3 1960. Reply by U. C. Knoepflmacher, Victorian Stud 4 1961.
— The unique fictional world of Pater. Nineteenth-Century Fiction 13 1959.
Chandler, E. Pater on style. Anglistica 20 1958.
Appleman, P. Darwin, Pater and a crisis in criticism. In 1859: entering a year of crisis, ed P. Appleman et al, Bloomington 1959.
Duffey, B. The religion of Pater's Marius. Texas Stud in Lit & Lang 2 1960.
Iser, W. Pater: die Autonomie des Aesthetischen. Tübingen 1960.
Temple, R. The ivory tower as lighthouse. In Edwardians and late Victorians, New York 1960.
d'Hangest, G. Pater: l'homme et l'œuvre. 2 vols Paris 1961. With bibliography.
Lenaghan, R. T. Pattern in Pater's fiction. SP 58 1961.
Inman, B. A. The organic structure of Marius the Epicurean. PQ 41 1962.
Fishman, S. The interpretation of art. Berkeley 1963.
Campos, C. In his View of France from Arnold to Bloomsbury, Oxford 1965.
Charlesworth, B. Dark passages: the decadent consciousness in Victorian literature. Madison 1965.
Knoepflmacher, U. C. Religious humanism and the Victorian novel. Princeton 1965.

J. S.

VII. MINOR PROSE 1870–1900

This section has been restricted to writers born after 1829 whose more important writings fall within the 19th century. Cross-references have been included only to critical writings in other sections.

ALFRED AINGER
1837–1904

§1

Sermons preached in the Temple Church. 1870.
Charles Lamb. 1882, 1888 (rev) (EML).
Crabbe. 1903 (EML).
The gospel and human life: sermons. Ed H. C. Beeching 1904.
Lectures and essays. Ed H. C. Beeching 2 vols 1905. Miscellaneous studies of English writers.
Ainger also edited the writings and letters of Charles and Mary Lamb 1879–99. He contributed articles on Lamb, Tennyson et al to DNB.

§2

The life and letters of Ainger. Ed E. Sichel 1906.

WILLIAM ARCHER
1856–1924

§1

The fashionable tragedian: a criticism. Edinburgh 1877. An essay on Henry Irving, with R. W. Lowe.
English analyses of the French plays represented at the Gaiety Theatre London, June and July 1879. 1879. Rptd from London Figaro.
English dramatists of today. 1882. Includes Playwrights of yesterday, F. W. Broughton, H. J. Byron, W. S. Gilbert, Paul Merritt, A. W. Pinero, Alfred Tennyson etc.
Henry Irving, actor and manager: a critical study. [1883].
About the theatre: essays and studies. 1886. Mainly rptd from Theatre.
The drama 1837–87. In The reign of Queen Victoria, ed T. H. Ward vol 2, 1887.
Masks or faces? a study in the psychology of acting. 1888.
William Charles Macready. 1890.
The theatrical 'world'. 5 vols 1893–7. Archer's dramatic criticism rptd from World, Pall Mall Budget, Sketch, Athenaeum etc. Vol 1, prefaced by Letter from Archer to R. W. Lowe; vol 2, with introd by G. B. Shaw; vol 3, with prefatory letter from A. W. Pinero; vol 4, prefaced by Archer's essay On the need for an endowed theatre; vol 5, with introduction by Sydney Grundy.
Study and stage: a year-book of criticism. 1899.
America to-day: observations and reflections. 1900.
Poets of the younger generation. 1902. On Binyon, Quiller-Couch, Davidson, Housman, Kipling, Alice Meynell, Newbolt, Yeats, Stephen Phillips, Francis Thompson et al.
Real conversations. 1904. Dialogues with Pinero, Hardy, Stephen Phillips, George Moore, Gilbert et al.
A national theatre: scheme and estimates. 1907. With Sir H. Granville-Barker.
Some common objections. 3 pts 1908–9. On simplified spelling.
Through Afro-America: an English reading of the race problem. 1910.
The life, trial and death of Francisco Ferrer. 1911.
The great analysis: a plea for a rational world-order, with an introd by Gilbert Murray. 1912. Anon.
Play-making: a manual of craftmanship. 1912.
Art and the commonweal: delivered at South Place Institute on February 23 1912. 1912.
The playhouse. In Shakespeare's England vol 2, Oxford 1916. With W. J. Lawrence.
God and Mr Wells: a critical examination of God, the invisible King. 1917.
War is war, or the Germans in Belgium: a drama of 1914. New York 1919.
The green goddess: a play in four acts. New York 1921.
The old drama and the new: an essay in re-valuation. 1923.
William Archer as rationalist: a collection of his heterodox writings. Ed J. M. Robertson 1925.
Three plays; with a personal note by Bernard Shaw. 1927. Includes Martha Washington, Beatriz Juana, Lidia.
Archer translated into prose all Ibsen's more important plays, occasionally in collaboration with Charles Archer or Edmund Gosse, 1888–1913, as well as plays by Hauptmann and Maeterlinck. He also translated essays etc by Brandes and other Scandinavian writers, and pbd lectures, pamphlets etc, mainly polemical.

Letters

Ibseniana: letters from Archer to Charles Archer [1881–3]. London Mercury Oct 1937.

§2

Aas, L. Archer. 1920. In Norwegian.
Granville-Barker, H. Archer. Drama, Nov 1926.
—— The coming of Ibsen. In The eighteen-eighties, 1930 (Royal Soc of Lit).
Archer, C. Archer. 1931. Includes list of Archer's books and contributions to periodicals.

SIR WALTER ARMSTRONG
1850–1918

Alfred Stevens: a biographical study. 1881.
Sir J. E. Millais: his life and work. [1885].
The Thames from its source to the sea; illustrated with engravings and etchings. 2 vols [1886–7].
Notes on the National Gallery. 1887.
Celebrated pictures exhibited at the Glasgow International Exhibition, Fine Arts Section: a series of engravings, with notes and criticisms. 1888.
Memoir of Peter De Wint. 1888.
Scottish painters: a critical study. 1888.
Briton Riviere: his life and work. [1891].
Thomas Gainsborough. 1894, 1905 (rev).
The art of W. Orchardson. 1895.
The art of Velasquez. 1896.
The life of Velasquez. 1896.
Gainsborough and his place in English art. 1898.
Sir Joshua Reynolds. 1900.
Sir Henry Raeburn; with an introduction by R. A. M. Stevenson and a bibliographical and descriptive catalogue by J. L. Caw. 1901.
Turner. 1902.
The Peel collection and the Dutch school of painting. 1904.
Art in Great Britain and Ireland. 1909.
Lawrence. 1913.

Armstrong also translated works on art and contributed introds to various collections of pictures etc. For biography and criticism see M. H. Spielmann, Armstrong, 1918 (*rptd from Fortnightly Rev*).

ALFRED AUSTIN
1835–1913

See col 608, above.

PETER BAYNE
1830–96

§1

The Christian life, social and individual. Edinburgh 1855.
Essays in biography. 2 sers Boston 1857–8.
Essays biographical, critical and miscellaneous. Edinburgh 1859.
The testimony of Christ to Christianity. 1862; ed G. C. Morgan, New York [1904].
English puritanism: its character and history. In G. Gould, Documents relating to the settlement of the Church of England by the Act of Uniformity of 1662, 1862.
The Church's curse and the nation's claim. 1868.
Life and letters of Hugh Miller. 2 vols 1871.
The days of Jezebel: an historical drama. 1872.
The national history of England. 1873. Vol 4 by Bayne.
The chief actors in the Puritan revolution. 1878.
Lessons from my masters: Carlyle, Tennyson and Ruskin. 1879.
Two great Englishwomen: Mrs Browning and Charlotte Brontë; with an essay on poetry illustrated from Wordsworth, Burns and Byron. 1881.
Martin Luther: his life and work. 2 vols 1887.
Six Christian biographies: J. Howard, W. Wilberforce, T. Chalmers, T. Arnold, S. Budgett, J. Foster. 1887.
The Free Church of Scotland: her origin, founders and testimony. Edinburgh 1893.
Bayne also pbd several theological pamphlets.

§2

[Brownell, W. C.] Bayne's Lessons from my masters. Nation (New York) 20 Nov 1879.
Bayne. Academy 15 Feb 1896.

HENRY CHARLES BEECHING
1859–1919

See col 611, above.

JOSEPH BENNETT
1831–1911

Letter from Bayreuth descriptive and critical of Wagner's Der Ring des Nibelungen, with an appendix. 1877.
The musical year 1883: a record of noteworthy musical events in the United Kingdom, with a reprint of criticisms on many of them. [1884].
Novello's primers of musical biography. 5 vols [1884–5].
A story of ten hundred concerts: being a short account of the origin and progress of Monday popular concerts, St James's Hall London. 1887.
A short history of cheap music, as exemplified in the records of the house of Novello, Ewer & Co. 1887. Anon; preface by G. Grove.
History of the Leeds musical festivals 1858–89, with portraits and fac-similes. 1892. With F. R. Spark.
Forty years of music 1865–1905. 1908. With portrait.
Bennett also adapted works by Burns and Scott for music, wrote critical notes or introds for various musical works, and revised and edited Berlioz, Treatise on modern instrumentation and orchestration.

ARTHUR CHRISTOPHER BENSON
1862–1925

§1

Memoirs of Arthur Hamilton BA of Trinity College Cambridge, by 'Christopher Carr'. 1886.
William Laud, sometime Archbishop of Canterbury: a study. 1887.
Men of might: studies of great characters. 1892, 1921. With H. F. W. Tatham.
Le cahier jaune. Eton 1892 (priv ptd).
Poems. 1893.
Lyrics. 1895.
The professor. Eton 1895 (priv ptd).
Thomas Gray. Eton 1895 (priv ptd).
Genealogy of the family of Benson, with biographical and illustrative notes. Eton 1895 (priv ptd).
Babylonica. Eton 1895.
Essays. 1896.
Monnow: an ode. Eton 1896.
Lord Vyet and other poems. 1897.
Ode in memory of the Rt Honble William Ewart Gladstone. Eton 1898 (priv ptd).
Fasti Etonenses: a biographical history of Eton selected from the lives of celebrated Etonians. Eton 1899.
The life of Edward White Benson, sometime Archbishop of Canterbury. 2 vols 1899, 1 vol 1901 (abridged).
The professor and other poems. 1900.
Coronation ode: set to music by E. Elgar: book of words, with analytical notes by Joseph Bennett. 1902.
Ode to Japan. 1902 (priv ptd).
The schoolmaster: a commentary upon the aims and methods of an assistant-master in a public school. 1902.
The myrtle bough: a vale. Eton 1903 (priv ptd).
The hill of trouble and other stories. 1903.
The house of quiet: an autobiography. 1904. Anon.
Alfred Tennyson. 1904.
Rossetti. 1904 (EML).
Edward FitzGerald. 1905 (EML).
The thread of gold, by the author of the House of quiet. 1905.
The isles of sunset. 1905. Stories.
Peace and other poems. 1905.
Walter Pater. 1906 (EML).
The Upton letters, by T. B. 1905, 1906 (with new preface)
From a college window. 1906.
The gate of death: a diary. 1906. Anon.
The altar fire. 1907.
Beside still waters. 1907.
At large. 1908.
Poems. 1909.
The silent isle. 1910.
The leaves of the tree: studies in biography. 1911.
Ruskin: a study in personality. 1911.
Paul the minstrel and other stories: reprinted from the Hill of trouble and the Isles of sunset. 1911.
The child of the dawn. 1912.
Thy rod and thy staff. 1912.
Along the road. 1913.
Joyous gard. 1913.
Watersprings. 1913.
Where no fear was: a book about fear. 1914.
The orchard pavilion. 1914.
Hugh: memoirs of a brother. 1915. On Robert Hugh Benson.

Escape and other essays. 1915.
Father Payne. 1915. Anon.
Life and letters of Maggie Benson. 1917.
Cambridge essays on education. Cambridge 1917. Ed Benson, his own contribution being The training of the imagination.
The reed of Pan: English renderings of Greek epigrams (from the Greek Anthology) and lyrics. 1922.
The trefoil: Wellington College, Lincoln and Truro. 1923. On the early life of Archbishop Benson.
Magdalene College Cambridge: a little view of its buildings and history. Cambridge 1923.
Memories and friends. 1924.
Chris Gascoyne: an experiment in solitude, from the diaries of John Trevor. 1924.
The house of Menerdue. 1925.
Basil Netherby. [1926].
The canon. 1926.
Rambles and reflections. 1926.
Cressage. 1927.
Benson also produced several works of pamphlet length. He contributed introds to books by Matthew Arnold, Dickens, Whittier et al, and edited Selections from Ruskin, 1923, *and (with Lord Esher)*, Letters of Queen Victoria, 1907.

Letters and Diaries

Meanwhile: a packet of war letters, by H. L. G. [A. C. Benson], with a foreword by K. W. 1916.
Extracts from the letters of Dr A. C. Benson to M. E. A[llen]. 1926.
Diary. Ed P. Lubbock [1926].

§2

Archer, W. In his Poets of the younger generation, 1902.
Weygandt, C. The poetry of Benson. Sewanee Rev 14 1906.
Benson as seen by some friends. 1925.
Collins, J. P. Benson. Bookman (London) Aug 1925.
Macnaghten, H. Benson. Spectator 27 June 1925.

AUGUSTINE BIRRELL
1850–1933

Collections

Collected essays. 2 vols 1899. Obiter dicta, 2 sers; Res judicatae; Essays about men, women and books.
Selected essays 1884–1907. [1909].
Self-selected essays: a second series. [1917].
Collected essays and addresses 1880–1920. 3 vols 1922. Includes 5 uncollected essays.

§1

Obiter dicta. Ser 1, 1884 (anon and priv ptd); ser 2, 1887; 2 sers, 1910. Ser 1 includes an essay on Falstaff by G. Radford.
The life of Charlotte Brontë. 1887.
Res judicatae. 1892.
Essays about men, women and books. 1894.
The Liberal Magazine. [1894]. Pamphlet.
The duties and liabilities of trustees: six lectures. 1896.
Four lectures on the law of employers' liability at home and abroad. 1897.
The ideal university: a lecture. [1898].
Sir Frank Lockwood: a biographical sketch. 1898.
Seven lectures on the law and history of copyright in books. 1899.
Miscellanies. 1901.
William Hazlitt. 1902 (EML).
Emerson: a lecture. 1903.
In the name of the Bodleian and other essays. 1905.
Andrew Marvell. 1905 (EML).
Mr Balfour's parliament: a speech. [1905].
The Lords and the Education Bill: a speech. 1906.
On a dictum of Mr Disraeli's and other matters: an address. 1912.
A rogue's memoirs. 1912.
John Wesley, his times and work. Ch 2 in Letters of John Wesley, ed G. Eayrs 1915.
Frederick Locker-Lampson. 1920.
More obiter dicta. 1924.
Some early recollections of Liverpool. Liverpool 1924.
Et cetera. 1930.
Things past redress. [1937]. Autobiographical.
Birrell also supplied introds to reprints of Shakespeare, Johnson, Boswell, Lamb and Browning, and collaborated in translating Victor Hugo.

§2

Gaines, C. H. The good taste of Birrell. North Amer Rev June 1923.
Kernahan, C. In his Celebrities, 1923.
Mallet, C. Macaulay. Contemporary Rev March 1938. On Obiter dicta.
Ryan, A. P. Birrell: a lucky mid-Victorian. Listener 17 Aug 1950.
Edwards, O. Mask and slippers. Times 14 July 1955.

STOPFORD AUGUSTUS BROOKE
1832–1916

§1

The life and letters of the Rev F. W. Robertson. 1865.
Theology in the English poets. 1874, [1910] (EL). On Cowper, Coleridge, Wordsworth and Burns.
English literature. 1876, 1896 (rev), 1901 (with chs on English literature 1832–92, and on American literature by G. R. Carpenter), 1924 (with new ch on Literature since 1832 by G. Sampson).
Milton. 1879.
Riquet of the tuft. 1880. A play.
Notes on the Liber studiorum of J. M. W. Turner, with illustrations. 1885.
The inaugural address to the Shelley Society. 1886 (priv ptd); rptd in Studies in poetry, 1907, below.
Old Paris: ten etchings by C. Méryon, reproduced in copper and accompanied with preface and notes by Brooke. 1887.
Poems. Edinburgh 1888.
Dove Cottage: Wordsworth's home from 1800–8. 1890.
The history of early English literature: being the history of English poetry from its beginning to the accession of King Alfred. 2 vols 1892.
The development of theology as illustrated in English poetry from 1780–1830. 1893.
The need and use of getting Irish literature into the English tongue: an address. 1893.
Tennyson: his art and relation to modern life. 1894.
English literature from the beginning to the Norman Conquest. New York 1898.
Religion in literature and religion in life: two lectures. 1900.
King Alfred as educator of his people and man of letters; with an appendix of passages from the writings of Alfred, selected and translated from the Old English by Kate M. Warren. 1901.
The poetry of Robert Browning. 1902.
On ten plays of Shakespeare. 1905.
The sea-charm of Venice. 1907.
Studies in poetry. 1907. Blake, Scott, The lyrics of Shelley, Epipsychidion, Keats.
A study of Clough, Arnold, Rossetti and Morris; with an introduction on the course of poetry from 1822 to 1852. 1908.

Ten more plays of Shakespeare. 1913.
Naturalism in English poetry. 1920. Dryden and Pope; Young and Thomson; Collins and Gray; Crabbe and Cowper; Burns, Wordsworth, Shelley, Byron.

§2

Jacks, L. P. Life and letters of Brooke. 2 vols 1917.

ROBERT WILLIAMS BUCHANAN
1841–1901

See col 615, above.

ARTHUR JOHN BUTLER
1844–1910

The purgatory of Dante. 1880.
The paradise of Dante. 1885.
The hell of Dante. 1892.
Dante: his times and his work. 1895.
Life and letters of W. J. Butler, Dean of Lincoln. 1897. Preface signed by A. J. B.
Calendar of state papers, foreign series, of Elizabeth 1577–83. 6 vols 1901–13. Vol 6 completed by S. C. Lomas.
The forerunners of Dante: a selection from Italian poetry before 1300. Oxford 1910.
Butler also pbd trns from French, Italian and German, including Sainte-Beuve, Select essays chiefly bearing on English literature, [1895], *and* Scartazzini, Companion to Dante, 1893, *together with edns of Dante's* Commedia *both in the original and in H. F. Cary's version. For his contributions to* The Cambridge modern history *etc see bibliography in* A. T. Quiller-Couch, Memoir of Butler, 1917.

EDWARD CARPENTER
1844–1929

Bibliographies

A bibliography of the writings of Carpenter. 1916. Apparently by Carpenter himself; forms appendix to My days and dreams, and also pbd separately.
A bibliography of Carpenter. Sheffield 1949. Anon.

§1

The religious influence of art. Cambridge 1870. Burney Prize essay for 1869.
Narcissus and other poems. 1873.
Moses: a drama in five acts. [1875], 1909, 1910 (rev as The promised land).
Towards democracy. Pt 1, Manchester 1883; 2 pts, Manchester 1885; 3 pts, London 1892; pt 4 (Who shall command the heart?) 1902; 4 pts, 1905; tr German, [1903]–9; Italian, 1912; French, 1914; Japanese, [1915]; Russian, nd.
England's ideal and other papers on social subjects. 1887; tr German, [1912].
Civilization: its cause and cure, and other essays. 1889, 1921 (enlarged).
From Adam's Peak to Elephanta: sketches in Ceylon and India. 1892, 1903 (enlarged), 1910 (rev), 1911 (4 chs pbd separately as A visit to a gnani).
Sex-love: and its place in a free society. Manchester 1894.
Woman and her place in a free society. Manchester 1894.
Marriage in a free society. Manchester 1894.
Homogenic love: and its place in a free society. Manchester 1894 (priv ptd).

St George and the dragon. Manchester 1895. A children's play.
Love's coming-of-age: a series of papers on the relations of the sexes. Manchester 1896, London 1902, 1906 (enlarged), [1914] (omits Note on preventive checks); tr German, 1902; Dutch, 1904; Italian, 1909; French, 1917.
An unknown people. 1897. On the intermediate sex.
Angels' wings: a series of essays on art and its relation to life. 1898.
The story of Eros and Psyche from Apuleius and the first book of the Iliad of Homer done into English verse. 1900, 1923 (as Eros and Psyche together with some early verses). Eros and Psyche is in prose. The early poems are rptd from Narcissus, 1873, above.
The art of creation: essays on the self and its powers. 1904, 1907 (enlarged); tr Italian, 1909; French, 1923.
Prisons, police and punishment: an inquiry into the causes and treatment of crime and criminals. 1905.
Days with Walt Whitman; with some notes on his life and work. 1906.
The intermediate sex: a study of some transitional types of men and women. 1908; tr German, 1907; Russian, 1915.
Sketches from life in town and country, and some verses. 1908.
The drama of love and death: a study of human evolution and transfiguration. 1912.
Intermediate types among primitive folk: a study in social evolution. 1914.
The healing of nations and the hidden sources of their strife. 1915.
My days and dreams: being autobiographical notes. 1916.
Towards industrial freedom. 1917.
Pagan and Christian creeds: their origin and meaning. 1920.
Some friends of Walt Whitman. 1924. Comments on the Calamus section in Leaves of grass, with account of Anne Gilchrist.
The psychology of the poet Shelley. 1925. With George Barnefield.
Several of Carpenter's essays were originally pbd separately as tracts.

§2

Crosby, E. H. Carpenter, poet and prophet. Philadelphia 1901.
Swan, T. Carpenter: the man and his message. Manchester 1901, 1922 (rev).
Ellis, E. M. O. In her Three modern seers, [1910]. On James Hinton, Nietzsche and Carpenter.
Senard, M. Carpenter et sa philosophie. Paris 1914.
Lewis, E. Carpenter: an exposition and an appreciation. 1915.
Sime, A. H. M. Carpenter: his idea and ideals. 1916.
Carpenter: in appreciation. Ed G. Beith 1931. Contributions by E. J. Dent, G. L. Dickinson, Havelock and Edith Ellis, L. Housman, H. W. Nevinson et al.
Poet of democracy: Carpenter: aeons of peace and progress. TLS 2 Sept 1944.
Vanson, F. Carpenter: the English Whitman. Contemporary Rev June 1958.

JOHN CHURTON COLLINS
1848–1908

§1

Sir Joshua Reynolds as a portrait painter. 1874.
Bolingbroke: a historical study; and Voltaire in England. 1886.
Illustrations of Tennyson. 1891.
The study of English literature: a plea for its recognition and organization at the universities. 1891.

Jonathan Swift: a biographical and critical study. 1893.
Essays and studies. 1895. John Dryden, The predecessors of Shakespeare, Lord Chesterfield's letters, The Porson of Shakespearian criticism, Menander.
Ephemera critica: or plain truths about current literature. 1901.
Studies in Shakespeare. 1904.
Studies in poetry and criticism. 1905.
Voltaire, Montesquieu and Rousseau in England. 1908.
Greek influence on English poetry. Ed M. Macmillan 1910.
Posthumous essays. Ed L. Churton Collins 1912. Shakespeare, Johnson, Burke, Arnold, Browning etc.
Collins also pbd edns of Sidney, Greene, Lord Herbert, Milton, Dryden, Pope, Tennyson, Arnold et al.

§2

Luce, M. E. Collins. 1908.
Letters from Algernon Charles Swinburne to Collins 1873–86. 1910 (priv ptd).
Collins, L. C. Life and memoirs of Collins. 1912.
Palmer, D. J. In his Rise of English studies, Hull 1965.

SIR SIDNEY COLVIN

1845–1927

§1

Florence. In A complete collection of the English poems which have obtained the Chancellor's Gold Medal in the University of Cambridge vol 2, 1894. Colvin's was the prize-winning poem in 1865.
Notes on the exhibitions of the Royal Academy and Old Water-Colour Society. 1896.
A word for Germany, from an English republican: being a letter to Professor Beesly. 1870. Written in reply to A word for France.
E. J. Poynter; Albert Moore; E. Burne-Jones; Simeon Solomon; Frederick Walker; Ford Madox Brown. In English painters of the present day, 1871.
Millais; George Mason; Thomas Armstrong; G. H. Boughton. In English artists of the present day, 1872.
Children in Italian and English design. 1872.
A selection from occasional writings on fine art. 1873 (priv ptd).
The life and genius of Flaxman. Prefixed to the Catalogue of Flaxman drawings in the gallery of University College London, 1876.
Landor. 1881 (EML).
Keats. 1887 (EML).
A guide to the historical collection of prints exhibited in the second Northern Gallery of the British Museum. 1887.
Guide to the exhibition of Chinese and Japanese paintings. 1888. Anon.
Guide to the exhibition of drawings and sketches by Continental and British masters in the Print and Drawing Gallery. 1891, 1892 (condensed).
Guide to an exhibition of drawings and engravings by the old masters, principally from the Malcolm Collection, and of engravings of the early German and Italian schools. 1894, 1895 (pt i).
A Florentine picture chronicle. 1898. Illustr N. Finiguerra.
Guide to an exhibition of drawings and etchings by Rembrandt. 1899.
Engravings and engravers in England 1545–1695: a critical and historical essay. 1905.
On concentration and suggestion in poetry. 1905 (Eng Assoc pamphlet).
John Keats: his life and poetry, his friends, critics and after-fame. 1917.
Memories and notes of persons and places. 1921.
Colvin also edited a Landor selection, various collections of R. L. Stevenson's writings and letters, and Keats's poems and letters. He contributed the article on Stevenson to DNB, and wrote the prefaces to a number of BM catalogues.

§2

Stevenson, R. L. In his Vailima letters, 1895. Letters written by Stevenson to Colvin, Nov 1890–Oct 1894.
Garvin, J. L. A perfect friend. Observer 15 May 1927.
Lucas, E. V. The Colvins and their friends. 1928.

WILLIAM JOHN COURTHOPE

1842–1917

Essay on chivalry. 1860 (priv ptd). Harrow Prize essay.
The tercentenary of Croydon: a bucolic drama in three acts by Novus Homo. Oxford 1864.
The three hundredth anniversary of Shakespeare's birth. Oxford 1864. Awarded the Newdigate Prize.
Poems by Novus Homo. Oxford 1865.
The genius of Spenser. 1868. Chancellor's Prize essay.
Ludibria lunae, or the wars of the women and the gods: an allegorical burlesque. 1869.
The paradise of birds: an old extravaganza in modern dress. Edinburgh 1870.
Joseph Addison. 1884 (EML).
The liberal movement in English literature. 1885. Conservatism of eighteenth century poetry; Wordsworth's theory of poetry; Revival of romance; Poetry, music and painting; Coleridge and Keats; The prospects of poetry.
The life of Pope. 1889. Vol 5 of The works of Pope, begun in 1871 by Whitwell Elwin, continued from 1881 and completed by Courthope.
A history of English poetry. 6 vols 1895–1910.
Liberty and authority in matters of taste: an inaugural lecture. 1896; rptd in Life in poetry: law in taste, 1901, below.
The longest reign: an ode on the completion of the sixtieth year of the reign of Her Majesty Queen Victoria. Oxford 1897.
Life in poetry: law in taste. 1901. Lectures delivered while Professor of Poetry at Oxford.
The revolution in English poetry and fiction. 1907. In The Cambridge Modern History vol 10, Cambridge 1902.
A consideration of Macaulay's comparison of Dante and Milton. Proc Br Acad 3 1908.
The poetry of Spenser. CHEL vol 3 1909.
The connexion between ancient and modern romance. [1911] (Br Acad lecture).
Selections from the epigrams of M. Valerius Martialis: translated or imitated in English verse. 1914.
The country town and other poems; with a memoir by A. O. Prickard. 1920.
Courthope also contributed an address on E. H. Pember to Commemorative addresses, 1912 (*Royal Soc of Lit*). *For an appreciation, see* J. W. Mackail, Proc Br Acad 9 1919.

SIR HENRY CRAIK

1846–1927

The English citizen. 30 vols 1881–1914. Ed Craik.
The life of Jonathan Swift, Dean of St Patrick's Dublin. 1882, 2 vols 1894.
The State in its relation to education. 1884, 1896 (rev).
English prose selections. 5 vols 1893–6. Ed Craik with numerous critical introds.
A century of Scottish history, from the days before the '45 to those within living memory. 2 vols Edinburgh 1901.
Impressions of India. 1908.
The life of Edward, Earl of Clarendon, Lord High Chancellor of England. 2 vols 1911.

HENRY AUSTIN DOBSON

1840–1921

Bibliographies

Murray, F. E. A bibliography of Dobson. Derby 1900.
Murdoch, W. G. B. Eng Illustr Mag Dec 1903–Jan 1904.
Dobson, A. T. A. A bibliography of the first editions of published and privately printed books and pamphlets by Dobson; with a preface by Sir E. Gosse. 1925.
— In his Dobson: some notes, 1928.
— Catalogue of the collection of the works of Dobson, London University Library. 1960.

Collections

Selected poems. 1892.
Collected poems. 1897, 1902 (adds selection from Carmina votiva, 1901), 1909 (enlarged), 1913 (adds 27 pieces), Oxford 1923 (Oxford Poets).
Poems (selected). 1905.
Eighteenth century studies. 1912. Selected essays.
An anthology of prose and verse; with a foreword by Edmund Gosse. Ed A. T. A. Dobson 1922, 1924 (rev).
Complete poetical works. Ed A. T. A. Dobson, Oxford 1923.
Selected poems. Oxford 1924 (WC).
What is virtually a collected edn of the essays is formed by the WC reprints, 9 vols Oxford 1923–6.

§1

Vignettes in rhyme. 1873, 1874 (with omissions and addns).
The civil service handbook of English literature. 1874, 1880 (rev and extended).
Proverbs in porcelain. 1877, 1878 (enlarged), 1893 (as Proverbs in porcelain, to which is added Au revoir, the latter rptd from At the sign of the lyre; only retains the 6 proverbs from 1877 edn).
Hogarth. 1879.
Vignettes in rhyme and other verses. New York 1880, London 1883 (with addns and omissions as Old world idylls), 1906 (with further notes). Contents mainly a selection from Vignettes in rhyme and Proverbs in porcelain.
Fielding. 1883 (EML).
Thomas Bewick and his pupils. 1884.
At the sign of the lyre. 1885, New York 1885 (with addns and omissions), London 1889 (with further addns and omissions).
Richard Steele. 1886.
Life of Oliver Goldsmith. 1888.
Poems on several occasions. 2 vols 1889, 1895 (rev and adds 12 poems). Contents mainly as in Old world idylls and At the sign of the lyre.
The sundial: a poem. New York 1890.
Four Frenchwomen. 1890, Oxford 1923 (WC).
Horace Walpole. 1890; rev P. Toynbee, Oxford 1927.
William Hogarth. 1891, 1898 (enlarged); ed W. Armstrong 1902, 1907 (enlarged).
Eighteenth century vignettes. Ser 1, 1892, 1897 (At Leicester Fields added); ser 2, 1894; ser 3, 1896.
The ballad of Beau Brocade and other poems of the xviiith century. 1892.
The story of Rosina and other verses. 1895.
Miscellanies. Ser 1, New York 1898, London 1899 (with addns, and omissions, as A paladin of philanthropy), Oxford 1925 (WC); ser 2, 1901.
A Whitehall eclogue. [1899] (priv ptd). Never rptd, but quoted in A. T. A. Dobson, A Dobson causerie, Cornhill Mag Jan 1925.
Carmina votiva and other occasional verses. 1901 (priv ptd).
Samuel Richardson. 1902 (EML).
Side-walk studies. 1902, Oxford 1924 (WC).
Fanny Burney. 1903 (EML).
De libris: prose and verse. 1908, 1911 (adds 2 essays).
Old Kensington Palace and other papers. 1910, Oxford 1926 (WC).
At Prior Park and other papers. 1912, Oxford 1925 (WC).
Rosalba's journal and other papers. 1915, Oxford 1926 (WC).
A bookman's budget. Oxford 1917. A collection of extracts from the works of English prose writers with numerous contributions from Dobson.
Later essays 1917–20. Oxford 1921.
Three unpublished poems. 1930 (priv ptd).
A few priv ptd essays and pamphlets have not been included. Dobson also supplied introds to reprints of Shakespeare, Evelyn, Defoe, Addison, Prior, Gay, Fielding, Goldsmith, Reynolds, Scott, Thackeray and other English and French writers. Many of Dobson's poems were originally priv ptd singly; those included in Complete poetical works, 1923, *are not recorded here.*

Letters

Dobson, A. T. A. Dobson: some letters from his friends. Cornhill Mag Aug–Oct 1927, May 1928.
— Dobson letter book. Cleveland 1935 (Rowfant Club).

§2

Watson, W. In his Excursions in criticism, 1893.
Ellis, S. M. Dobson. Fortnightly Rev Oct 1921; rptd in his Mainly Victorian, 1925.
Gosse, E. Dobson. Quart Rev 237 1922.
Dobson's library: notes on sales. TLS 23 March 1922.
Kernahan, C. In his Celebrities, 1923.
Noyes, A. The poems of Dobson. Bookman (London) April 1924.
Dobson, A. T. A. An Austin Dobson causerie. Cornhill Mag Feb 1925.
— Dobson: some notes; with chapters by Edmund Gosse and George Saintsbury. 1928.
Weygandt, C. Dobson, Augustan. In his Tuesdays at ten, Philadelphia 1928.
Lipscomb, H. C. Horace and the poetry of Dobson. Amer Jnl of Philology 50 1929.
Evans, B. I. In his English poetry in the later nineteenth century, 1933, 1966 (rev). Ch 11.
Hasenclever, E. Das 18 Jahrhundert in Dobsons Dichtung. Göttingen 1939.
Dobson: a poet of two worlds. TLS 13 Jan 1940.
Dobson, D. de B. Dobson: a note by his daughter. Poetry Rev 33 1942.
Robinson, J. K. Dobson and the rondeliers. MLQ 14 1953.
Rawson, C. J. Dobson. N & Q Dec 1960.

EDWARD DOWDEN

1843–1913

Bibliographies

Shorter, C. K. Eng Illustr Mag Feb 1903.
Bayard, E. J. Irish Book Lover June 1913.

§1

Mr Tennyson and Mr Browning. 1863.
Shakespeare: a critical study of his mind and art. 1875; tr German, 1879.
Poems. 1876; [ed E. D. Dowden] 2 vols 1914 (with addns).
Shakspere. 1877. One of Macmillan's history and literature primers, ed J. R. Green.
Studies in literature 1789–1877. 1878. The French Revolution; The transcendental movement; The

scientific movement and literature; Wordsworth; Landor; Tennyson; Browning; George Eliot; Hugo; Whitman etc.

Southey. 1879. (EML)

Spenser the poet and teacher. Vol 1 of Works of Spenser, 1882.

The life of Percy Bysshe Shelley. 2 vols 1886, 1 vol 1896.

Transcripts and studies. 1888. Carlyle, Shelley, Wordsworth, Spenser, Shakespeare, Marlowe, Milton, Browning (Sordello).

New studies in literature. 1895. Meredith, Bridges, Donne, Goethe, Coleridge, E. Scherer etc.

The French Revolution and English literature: lectures. 1897.

A history of French literature. 1897. Vol 2 of E. Gosse, Short histories.

Literary criticism in France. In Studies in European literature: being the Taylorian Lectures 1889–99, Oxford 1900.

Puritan and Anglican: studies in literature. 1900. Puritanism and English literature, Thomas Browne, Hooker, Herbert, Vaughan, Milton, Jeremy Taylor, Baxter, Bunyan, Butler, Transition to the eighteenth century.

The poetry of Kipling. New Liberal Rev Feb 1901.

William Shakespeare as a comic dramatist: a monograph. In Representative English comedies, ed C. M. Gayley vol 1, New York 1903.

Robert Browning. 1904; 1915 (EL).

Michel de Montaigne. 1905.

Milton in the eighteenth century 1701–50. Proc Br Acad 3 [1909].

Essays modern and Elizabethan. 1910. Pater, Ibsen, Heine, Goethe, Cowper and William Hayley, Shakespeare etc.

Dowden also pbd edns of Browning, Shelley, Spenser and other English poets. For his edns of Shakespeare see vol 1.

Letters

A woman's reliquary. Dundrum 1913.

Fragments from old letters: E. D. to E. D. W. 1869–92. 1914.

Letters of Dowden and his correspondents. [Ed E. D. and H. M. Dowden] 1914.

Letters about Shelley interchanged by Dowden, Robert Garnett and Wm Michael Rossetti. Ed R. S. Garnett 1917.

§2

The poems of Dowden. Irish Monthly Aug 1881.

Fiske, H. S. Recollections of Dowden. Nation (New York) 22 May 1913.

Bicknell, P. F. Dowden's mind and art. Dial 16 July 1914.

Gerothwohl, M. A. Dowden as a critic. Fortnightly Rev June 1914.

Marshall, Lily E. The letters and poems of Dowden. Pisa [1914].

'Eglinton, John' (W. K. Magee). Life & Letters Dec 1933; rptd in his Irish literary portraits, 1935.

White, H. M. O. Dowden. 1943.

HENRY HAVELOCK ELLIS
1859–1939

Collections

The art of life: gleanings from the works of Ellis, collected by Mrs S. Herbert. [1929].

Selected essays. 1936 (EL).

Poems, selected by 'John Gawsworth'. [1937].

§1

The new spirit. 1890, 1892 (with new preface). Essays.

The criminal. 1890, 1901 (rev and enlarged).

The nationalisation of health. 1892.

Man and woman: a study of human secondary sexual characters. 1894, 1904 (rev and enlarged), [1914] (rev), 1934 (rev).

Sexual inversion. 2 vols 1897–1924. Originally vol 1 of Studies in the psychology of sex, with an appendix by J. A. Symonds. Later issued as vol 2 of that series, without Symonds' contribution.

Affirmations. 1898, 1915 (with new preface). Critical essays.

The evolution of modesty. 1899. Later issued as vol 1 of Studies in the psychology of sex.

The nineteenth century: a dialogue in Utopia. 1900.

Analysis of the sexual impulse. Philadelphia 1903. Later issued as vol 3 of Studies in the psychology of sex.

A study of British genius. 1904, 1927 (rev and enlarged).

Studies in the psychology of sex. 7 vols Philadelphia 1905–28.

The soul of Spain. 1908, 1937 (with new preface).

The problems of race degeneration. 1911.

The world of dreams. 1911, 1926 (new edn).

The task of social hygiene. 1912.

Impressions and comments. 3 sers 1914–24, 1 vol Boston 1931 (as Fountain of life).

Essays in war-time. 1916.

The philosophy of conflict and other essays in war-time. 1919.

Little essays of love and virtue. 1922.

Kanga Creek: an Australian idyll. Waltham St Lawrence 1922, [New York] 1935.

The dance of life. 1923.

Sonnets, with folk songs from the Spanish. Waltham St Lawrence 1925.

More essays of love and virtue. 1931. The two vols of Essays of love and virtue, above, were combined and enlarged as On life and sex, Garden City NY 1937, London 1945.

Concerning Jude the Obscure. 1931; rptd from Savoy Oct 1896.

The colour-sense in literature. 1931.

The revaluation of obscenity. Paris 1931.

Views and reviews: a selection of uncollected articles 1884–1932. 2 vols 1932.

Psychology of sex: a manual for students. 1933.

Chapman, with illustrative passages. 1934.

My confessional: questions of our day. 1934.

From Rousseau to Proust. 1936.

Questions of our day. 1936.

My life: the autobiography of Havelock Ellis. Boston 1939.

From Marlowe to Shaw: studies 1576–1936. In English literature, ed 'John Gawsworth' 1950.

The genius of Europe. Ed F. Delisle 1950.

From 1887 to 1889 Ellis edited the Mermaid series of old dramatists, and from 1889 to 1914 the Contemporary science series. He also edited a number of literary texts, including Heine's prose, Ibsen's plays and Vasari's Lives of Italian painters. *He wrote numerous pamphlets, particularly on sexual psychology, and contributed introds to a number of miscellaneous works.*

§2

Goldberg, I. Ellis: a biographical and critical survey: with a supplementary chapter on Mrs Edith Ellis. [1926].

Peterson, H. Ellis, philosopher of love. 1928. With bibliography.

Ishill, J. (ed). Ellis: in appreciation. Berkeley Heights 1929. Articles by various authors.

Rascoe, B. Ellis and the sex conscious era. Amer Mercury Jan 1940.

Sleigh, B. Notes on the letters of Ellis to Bernard Sleigh 1916–39. 1940.

Delisle, F. Friendship's odyssey. 1946.

Lafitte-Cyon, F. Ellis and Edith Lees. TLS 10 April 1953; *see also* 8, 15 May 1953.
Calder-Marshall, A. Havelock Ellis. 1959.
Collis, J. S. An artist of life: a study of the life and work of Ellis. 1959.

PERCY HETHERINGTON FITZGERALD
1834–1925

See col 1053, above.

RICHARD GARNETT
1835–1906

Primula: a book of lyrics. 1858 (anon), 1859 (signed, as Io in Egypt and other poems), 1893 (rev with addns as Poems).
Poems from the German. 1862.
Idylls and epigrams, chiefly from the Greek anthology. 1869, 1892 (as A chaplet from the Greek anthology).
Richmond on the Thames. 1870.
Carlyle. 1887.
Literature 1837–87. In T. H. Ward, Reign of Queen Victoria vol 2, 1887.
Shelley and Lord Beaconsfield. 1887 (priv ptd).
Emerson. 1888.
The twilight of the gods and other tales. 1888, 1903 (augmented). Cynical apologues.
Milton. 1890.
Iphigenia in Delphi. 1890. A play: also includes Homer's Shield of Achilles and other trns from the Greek.
The soul and the stars, by A. G. Trent. 1893, 1903 (expanded). First pbd in a more primitive form in University Mag March 1880. Unorthodox theology; Trent is a pseudonym.
The age of Dryden. 1895.
William Blake: painter and poet. 1895.
One hundred and twenty-four sonnets from Dante, Petrarch and Camoens. 1896.
History of Italian literature. 1897. Vol 4 of E. Gosse, Short histories of the literatures of the world.
Edward Gibbon Wakefield. 1898.
Essays in librarianship and bibliography. 1899.
Essays of an ex-librarian. 1901.
The queen and other poems. 1901.
English literature: an illustrated record by Richard Garnett and Edmund Gosse. 4 vols 1903–4. Vols 1–2 by Garnett.
Tennyson. 1903. With G. K. Chesterton.
Coleridge. 1904.
William Shakespeare, pedagogue and poacher. 1905. A play.
De flagello myrteo. 1905. Anon; aphorisms.
William Johnson Fox. 1910. Completed by Edward Garnett.
Letters about Shelley interchanged by Edward Dowden, Garnett and Wm Michael Rossetti. Ed R. S. Garnett 1917.
Garnett also pbd several tracts on library problems; he was keeper of BM printed books 1890–9. He contributed many articles to DNB and other composite works as well as editing or introducing Shelley's poems and various Shelleyana, Coleridge's poems, Milton's prose, novels by George Eliot, Charles Reade, Goldsmith etc. He was general editor of the International library of famous literature 20 vols 1899.

SIR WILLIAM EDMUND GOSSE
1849–1928

Bibliographies

Garnett, R. Eng Illustr Mag Sept 1903. Includes articles by and on Gosse.
Gullick, N. In E. Charteris, The life and letters of Gosse, 1931.
A catalogue of the Gosse correspondence in the Brotherton collection consisting mainly of letters written to Gosse 1867–1928. Ed P. Gosse, Leeds 1950.

Collections

Collected poems. 1911.
Collected essays. 12 vols 1912–27.
Selected poems. [1926].
Selected essays. 2 vols 1928.

§ 1

Madrigals, songs and sonnets. 1870. 32 by Gosse and 30 by J. A. Blaikie.
On viol and flute. 1873, 1890 (33 poems from the original edn and 36 poems drawn from other vols including New poems, 1879).
The ethical condition of the early Scandinavian peoples. [1874].
King Erik. 1876, 1893 (with introductory essay by Theodore Watts [-Dunton]). A tragedy in verse.
The unknown lover. 1878. A play for private performance with an essay on the Chamber drama in England.
New poems. 1879.
Studies in the literature of Northern Europe. 1879.
Memoir on Samuel Rowlands. Prefixed to Works of Rowlands, 1880.
Memoir of Thomas Lodge. Prefixed to Works of Lodge, 1882.
Gray. 1882, 1889 (rev) (EML).
Cecil Lawson: a memoir. 1883.
Lawrence Alma Tadema. 1883.
Seventeenth-century studies: a contribution to the history of English poetry. 1883. Rptd for the most part from Cornhill Mag.
A critical essay on the life and works of George Tinworth. 1883.
Notes on the pictures and drawings of Mr Alfred W. Hunt. 1884.
An epistle to Dr Oliver Wendell Holmes on his seventy-fifth birthday, 1884. 1884 (priv ptd).
Firdausi in exile and other poems. 1885.
The masque of painters. 1885 (priv ptd).
From Shakespeare to Pope. Cambridge 1885.
Raleigh. 1886.
The life of William Congreve. 1888, 1924 (rev and enlarged).
A history of eighteenth-century literature 1660–1780. 1889.
Robert Browning: personalia. Boston 1890.
Heinemann's international library. 21 vols 1890–1894. With a special introd by Gosse to each vol.
The life of Philip Henry Gosse. 1890.
Northern studies. 1890.
Gossip in a library. 1891. Short essays rptd from Saturday Rev, St James's Gazette and Black & White.
The life and writings of Thomas Nash. Prefixed to Unfortunate traveller, 1892.
Shelley in 1892: centenary address at Horsham. 1892 (priv ptd).
Wolcott Balestier: a portrait sketch. 1892 (priv ptd). Rptd from Century Mag.
The secret of Narcisse: a romance. 1892.

The rose of Omar: inscription for the rose-tree brought from Omar's tomb and planted on the grave of Edward FitzGerald, 1893. [1893] (priv ptd).
Questions at issue. 1893.
In russet and silver. 1894.
The Jacobean poets. 1894.
Critical kit-kats. 1896.
Short histories of the literature of the world. 15 vols 1897–1915. Vol 3 on modern English literature entirely by Gosse, who was also general editor.
A short history of modern English literature. 1898, 1924 (with 2 further chs).
Henry Fielding: an essay. Introd to Works of Fielding, 1898–9.
The life and letters of John Donne. 2 vols 1899.
Hypolympia, or the gods in the island: an ironic fantasy. 1901.
Queen Victoria. New York 1901. Unauthorized reprint from Quart Rev.
English literature: an illustrated record. 4 vols 1903–4. Vol 1 by Richard Garnett; vol 2 by Garnett and Gosse; vols 3–4 by Gosse.
The challenge of the Brontës. 1903 (priv ptd). Also in Pbns of Brontë Soc Feb 1904.
Jeremy Taylor. 1903 (EML).
British portrait painters and engravers of the eighteenth century—Kneller to Reynolds; with an introductory essay and biographical notes. 2 vols 1905.
Coventry Patmore. 1905.
French profiles. 1905.
Sir Thomas Browne. 1905 (EML).
Father and son: a study of two temperaments. 1907.
Ibsen. 1907.
Scandinavia 1815–70; Dano-Norwegian literature 1815–65. 1908. In The Cambridge modern history vol 11, 1902.
Biographical notes on the writings of Robert Louis Stevenson. 1908 (priv ptd).
Catalogue of the library of the House of Lords. 1908 (priv ptd).
Swinburne: personal recollections. 1909 (priv ptd). Rptd from Fortnightly Rev.
A paradox on beauty. 1909. Priv ptd offprint from Fasciculus Joanni Willis Clark dicatus.
The autumn garden. 1909.
Two visits to Denmark, 1872, 1874. 1911.
Portraits and sketches. 1912.
Browning's centenary. 1912. Addresses by Gosse, Arthur Pinero and Henry James.
The future of English poetry. 1913.
Lady Dorothy Nevill: an open letter. 1913 (priv ptd).
Sir Alfred East. 1914.
Two pioneers of Romanticism: Joseph and Thomas Warton. [1915].
Catherine Trotter: the precursor of the Blue-stockings. 1916 (priv ptd).
Inter Arma: being essays written in time of war. 1916. Rptd from Edinburgh Rev.
Reims revisited. 1916 (priv ptd). Rptd from Fortnightly Rev.
The life of Algernon Charles Swinburne. 1917.
Lord Cromer as a man of letters. 1917 (priv ptd). Rptd from Fortnightly Rev.
The novels of Benjamin Disraeli. 1918 (priv ptd). Also in Trans Royal Soc Lit 36.
France et Angleterre: l'avenir de leurs relations intellectuelles. 1918. Rptd from Revue des Deux Mondes.
Three French moralists, and the gallantry of France. 1918. On La Rochefoucauld, La Bruyère, Vauvenargues.
A catalogue of the works of A. C. Swinburne in the library of Gosse. 1919 (priv ptd).
Some diversions of a man of letters. 1919.
The first draft of Swinburne's Anactoria. Cambridge [1919] (priv ptd). A short critical essay.
Some literary aspects of France in the war. 1919 (priv ptd).
Malherbe and the classical reaction in the seventeenth century. Oxford 1920. A lecture.
Books on the table. New York 1921; More books on the table, 1923. Miniature monographs on literary subjects rptd from Sunday Times.
The continuity of literature: an address. 1922.
Byways round Helicon. 1922.
Aspects and impressions. 1922.
Swinburne: an essay written in 1875 and now first printed. Edinburgh 1925 (priv ptd).
Tallement des Réaux or the art of miniature biography: the Zaharoff lecture. Oxford 1925.
Silhouettes. 1925. Reviews rptd from Sunday Times.
The earliest Charles Lamb dinner. In Cambridge and Charles Lamb, Cambridge 1925.
Leaves and fruit. 1927.
Austin Dobson. In A. T. A. Dobson, Austin Dobson: some notes, 1928.
A memoir of Thomas Lovell Beddoes. Prefixed to Complete works of Beddoes, 2 vols 1928.
Two unpublished poems. Winchester 1929 (priv ptd).
Gosse also contributed to many periodicals and composite works. He wrote the article on Swinburne in DNB. He translated Ibsen's Hedda Gabler, 1891, *and* The master builder, 1893 (*with William Archer*), *as well as La Motte Fouqué's* Undine, 1896.

§2

Lister, R. J. Catalogue of a portion of the library of Gosse. 1893 (priv ptd).
Williams, S. T. Two Victorian boyhoods. North Amer Rev June 1921.
Cox, E. H. M. The library of Gosse. 1924. With an introd by Gosse.
Freeman, J. In his English portraits and essays. 1924.
Braybrooke, P. Considerations on Gosse, with introduction by Gilbert Frankau. 1925.
Saintsbury, G. Some memories of Gosse. London Mercury July 1928.
Levinson, A. Gosse. Nouvelles littéraires 9 June 1928.
Williamson, G. C. Gosse as a boy: a reminiscence. London Mercury Oct 1928.
Bellows, W. Gosse: some memories. 1929.
Charteris, E. The life and letters of Gosse. 1931.
Drinkwater, J. Gosse. Quart Rev 257 1931.
Woolf, V. Gosse. Fortnightly Rev June 1931. Rptd in her Moment and other essays, 1948.
Collier, J. and I. Lang. Just the other day. 1932.
Evans, B. I. In his English poetry in the later nineteenth century. 1933.
Gaylord, H. and J. Carter. Gosse and the Reading sonnets. TLS 8–22 Nov 1934.
Aas, L. Gosse. Edda 38 1938.
Morrisette, B. A. Early English and American critics of French symbolism. In Studies in honor of F. W. Shipley, Washington 1942.
Blunden, E. Book forgeries: An enquiry re-read. TLS 28 Sept 1946.
Mortimer, R. Gosse, a centenary tribute. Sunday Times 18 Sept 1949.
Richards, M. L. Gide's letters to Gosse. Jnl Rutgers Univ Lib 13 1950.
Hagedorn, R. Gosse and the Sonnets from the Portuguese. PBSA 46 1952.
Temple, R. Z. The critic's alchemy: a study of the introduction of French symbolism into England. New York 1953.
Waugh, A. Gosse. Virginia Quart Rev 32 1956.
Kruger, P. (ed). Correspondence de Georg Brandes, vol 2, Copenhagen 1957.
Cecil, D. Great writers re-discovered: Gosse. Sunday Times 12 May 1957.
White, W. Gosse on Walt Whitman. Victorian Stud 1 1957

Young, A. C. Gosse visits R. L. Stevenson. Jnl Lib Rutgers Univ 20 1957.
Shuman, R. B. A new Gosse letter. N & Q Jan 1959.
Bredsdorff, E. (ed). Correspondence with Scandinavian writers: with an introduction on Gosse and Scandinavian literature and a bibliographical supplement. Copenhagen 1960.
Brugmans, L. F. (ed). André Gide and Gosse: correspondence 1904–28. 1960.
Burkhart. C. George Moore and Father and son. Nineteenth Century Fiction 15 1960.
Østredt, E. Henrik Ibsens pionér i England—Gosse. Samtiden 71 1962.
Hoy, P. C. From André Gide to Gosse. Amer N & Q 2 1963.
Maltheisen, P. F. More on Gosse and Gide. N & Q Oct 1963.

FRANCIS HINDES GROOME

1851–1902

In gipsy tents. Edinburgh 1880.
A short border history. Kelso 1887.
The gypsies. In E. Magnússon, National life and thought of the various nations throughout the world, 1891.
Ordnance gazetteer of Scotland. Ed F. H. Groome 6 vols Edinburgh 1882–95.
Two Suffolk friends. Edinburgh 1895. Recollections of R. H. Groome and Edward FitzGerald.
Kriegspiel: the war-game. 1896. A novel.
Chambers's biographical dictionary. 1897. With David Patrick.
Gypsy folk-tales. 1899.
For an appreciation see T. Watts-Dunton, The Tarno rye: (Groome), Athenaeum 22 Feb 1902.

EDMUND GURNEY

1847–88

On some disputed points in music. Fortnightly Rev July 1876.
The power of sound. 1880. On music.
Phantasms of the living. 2 vols 1886, 1 vol 1918 (abridged by Mrs H. Sidgwick). With F. W. H. Myers and F. Podmore.
Tertium quid: chapters on various disputed questions. 2 vols 1887.
Gurney also contributed to Mind and Jnl of Soc for Psychical Research. See F. W. H. Myers, The work of Gurney in experimental psychology, Proc Soc for Psychical Research 5 1888.

SIR WILLIAM HENRY HADOW

1859–1937

Studies in modern music: Hector Berlioz, Robert Schumann, Richard Wagner: [ser 2, Frederick Chopin, Antonin Dvořák, Johannes Brahms]. 2 sers 1893–5.
Sonata form. [1896].
A Croatian composer: notes towards the study of Joseph Haydn. 1897.
The Oxford history of music. 6 vols Oxford 1901–5, 1929–38. Ed Hadow who wrote vol 5 (The Viennese period).
Citizenship. Oxford 1923.
Music. [1924] (Home Univ Lib), Oxford 1946, 1949 (rev G. Dyson).
A comparison of poetry and music. Cambridge 1926.
Collected essays. Oxford 1928.
The place of music among the arts: the Romanes lecture. Oxford 1933.
Richard Wagner. 1934 (Home Univ Lib).
Hadow pbd a number of other books on music, literature, education etc.

PHILIP GILBERT HAMERTON

1834–94

Observations on heraldry. 1851.
The isles of Loch Awe and other poems of my youth. 1855.
A painter's camp in the Highlands and thoughts about art. 2 vols Cambridge 1862, London 1866 (rev). Thoughts about art rptd separately 1873.
Contemporary French painters. 1865.
Etching and etchers. 1868.
Painting in France after the decline of classicism: an essay. 1869.
Wenderholme: a story of Lancashire and Yorkshire. 3 vols 1869.
The unknown river: an etcher's voyage of discovery. 1871.
English landscape painters: an essay. In English painters of the present day, 1871.
The etcher's handbook. 1871.
The intellectual life. 1873, 1929.
Chapters on animals. 1874.
Examples of modern etching. 1875.
Harry Blount: passages in a boy's life on land and sea. 1875.
Round my house: notes of rural life in France in peace and war. 1876.
The sylvan year: leaves from the notebook of Raoul Dubois. 1876.
Modern Frenchmen. 1878.
Marmorne, by A. Segrave. 1878.
The life of J. M. W. Turner. 1879.
The graphic arts. 1882.
Human intercourse. 1884.
Paris in old and present times, with especial reference to changes in its architecture and topography. 1885.
Landscape. 1885.
Imagination in landscape painting. 1887.
The Sâone: a summer voyage. 1887.
French and English: a comparison. 1889.
Turner. 1889. Written in French and distinct from the English work, above.
Portfolio papers. 1889. Critical essays rptd from Portfolio.
The present state of the fine arts in France. 1892.
Drawing and engraving. 1892.
Man in art: studies in religious and historical art, portrait and genre. 1892.
The etchings of Rembrandt. 1894, 1905 (with catalogue of all Rembrandt's etchings, by Campbell Dodgson).
The mount: narrative of a visit to the site of a Gaulish city on Mont Beuvray; with a description of the neighbouring city of Autun. 1897. Ed Mrs Hamerton.
The quest of happiness. Ed M. R. F. Gilman, Boston 1897.
Philip Gilbert Hamerton: an autobiography 1834–58, and a memoir by his wife 1858–94. 1897.
Hamerton edited Portfolio *from its inception in 1869 to his death.*

AUGUSTUS JOHN CUTHBERT HARE

1834–1903

§1

A handbook for travellers in Berks, Bucks and Oxfordshire. 1860.
A winter in Mentone. [1862].

A handbook for travellers to Durham and Northumberland. 1864.
Walks in Rome. 2 vols 1871, 1 vol 1925 (22nd edn).
Memorials of a quiet life. 3 vols 1872–6. Memoir of Maria Hare.
Wanderings in Spain. 1873.
Days near Rome. 2 vols 1875.
Cities of Northern and Central Italy. 3 vols 1876.
Walks in London. 2 vols 1878.
Life and letters of Frances, Baroness Bunsen. 2 vols 1879.
Cities of Southern Italy and Sicily. 1883.
Florence. 1884, 1925 (9th edn).
Venice. 1884.
Cities of Central Italy. 2 vols 1884.
Cities of Northern Italy. 2 vols 1884.
Sketches in Holland and Scandinavia. 1885.
Studies in Russia. 1885.
Days near Paris. 1887.
Paris. 1887.
North eastern France. 1890.
South eastern France. 1890.
South western France. 1890.
The story of two noble lives: Charlotte Countess Canning and Louisa Marchioness of Waterford. 3 vols 1893.
The life and letters of Maria Edgeworth. 2 vols 1894.
Sussex. 1894.
Biographical sketches. 1895. A. P. Stanley, Henry Alford, Mrs Duncan Stewart, Paray Le Monial.
The Gurneys of Earlham. 2 vols 1895.
North western France. 1895.
The story of my life. 6 vols 1896–1900. Abridged below.
The Rivieras. 1896.
Shropshire. 1898.
The years with mother. Ed M. Barnes 1952. Abridged from vols 1–3 of Story of my life, above.
In my solitary life. Ed M. Barnes 1953. Abridged from vols 4–6 of The story of my life, above.
Hare also pbd a collection of Epitaphs for country churchyards, Oxford 1856.

§2

Leslie, S. Men were different. 1937.
Tuell, A. K. In his John Sterling, New York 1941.
Maugham, W. S. Augustus. Cornhill Mag 164 1950.

FREDERIC HARRISON
1831–1923

Bibliographies

Farquharson, S. Eng Illustr Mag Oct 1903.
Bibliography of Harrison. Hawkhurst 1908.

Collections

Collected essays. 4 pts 1907–8.
Selected essays, literary and historical. Ed A. Jha 1925.

§1

Order and progress. 2 pts 1875. Political essays.
The present and the future. 1880.
The choice of books and other literary pieces. 1886.
Oliver Cromwell. 1888.
Annals of an old manor house, Sutton Place, Guildford. 1893, 1899 (abridged).
The meaning of history and other historical pieces. 1894.
Studies in early Victorian literature. 1895.
William the Silent. 1897.
Tennyson, Ruskin, Mill and other literary estimates. 1899.
Byzantine history in the early Middle Ages. 1900.
George Washington and other American addresses. 1901.
John Ruskin. 1902 (EML).
Theophano: the crusade of the tenth century: a romantic monograph. 1904.
Chatham. 1905.
Memories and thoughts: men-books-cities-art. 1906.
Nicephorus: a tragedy of new Rome. 1906. A verse drama on the same subject as Theophano, above, but with other characters and incidents.
Carlyle and the London Library: account of its foundation. 1907.
The philosophy of common sense. 1907.
The creed of a layman: apologia pro fide mea. 1907.
National and social problems. 1908.
Realities and ideals social, political, literary and artistic. 1908.
My alpine jubilee 1851–1907. 1908.
Autobiographic memoirs. 2 vols 1911. Vol 2 includes a comprehensive list of Harrison's contributions to periodicals.
Among my books: centenaries, reviews, memoirs. 1912.
The positive evolution of religion. 1913.
The German peril. [1915].
On society. 1918.
Obiter scripta 1918. 1919.
On jurisprudence and the conflict of laws. 1919.
Novissima verba: last words 1920. 1921.
De senectute: more last words. 1923.

Letters

Letters to Eugen Oswald. Bodleian Lib Record 2 1941.

§2

Harris, M. Two Victorian portraits. North Amer Rev Sept 1920. Lord Morley and Harrison.
Luce, M. Harrison. Nineteenth Century March 1923.
Saintsbury, G. Harrison. Fortnightly Rev March 1923.
Harrison, A. Harrison: thoughts and memories. 1926.
Ricks, C. B. Harrison and Bergson. N & Q May 1959.
Marandon, S. Harrison. Etudes Anglaises 13 1960.
Vogeler, M. S. Matthew Arnold and Harrison. Studies in Eng Lit 1500–1900 2 1962.

WILLIAM ERNEST HENLEY
1849–1903

See col 629, above.

AUBERON EDWARD WILLIAM HERBERT
1838–1906

§1

The Danes in camp: letters from Sönderborg. 1864.
A politician in trouble about his soul. 1884.
Anti-force papers, nos 1–3 [1885].
The voluntaryist creed. 1908.
Taxation and anarchism. [1912]. Discussion with J. H. Levy.
Herbert also collaborated with H. Wager on Bad air and bad health, 1894, *and with J. H. Levy et al in* A symposium on the land question, 1890, *and edited a series of letters as* The sacrifice of education to examination, 1889.

§2

Harris, S. H. Herbert: crusader for liberty. 1943.

CHARLES HAROLD HERFORD

1853–1931

§1

The essential characteristics of the romantic and classical styles: with illustrations from English literature. Cambridge 1880.

The first quarto edition of Hamlet 1603: two essays, to which the Harness prize was awarded, I by C. H. Herford; II by W. H. Widgery. 1880.

A sketch of the history of the English drama in its social aspects: being the essay which obtained the Le Bas prize 1880. Cambridge 1881.

The stoics as teachers: the Hare prize essay for 1881. Cambridge 1882.

Studies in the literary relations of England and Germany in the sixteenth century. Cambridge 1886.

The age of Wordsworth. 1897.

Robert Browning. 1905.

A sketch of the history of Shakespeare's influence on the Continent. 1905.

Memoir of W. H. Herford. In The student's Froebel, 1911.

Goethe. 1912.

Shakespeare. 1912.

Shakespeare's treatment of love and marriage, and other essays. 1921.

A sketch of recent Shakespearean investigation 1893–1923. 1923.

Ben Jonson. Ed C. H. Herford and P. and E. Simpson 11 vols Oxford 1925–52. Vols 1–2, The man and his work, were by Herford.

English literature. 1927 (Benn's Sixpenny Lib).

The case of German South Tyrol against Italy. 1927. Tr and ed Herford.

The post-war mind of Germany, and other European studies. 1927.

Wordsworth. 1930.

Philip Henry Wicksteed: his life and work. 1931.

Herford also contributed largely to composite works and periodicals, 12 of his articles in Bull John Rylands Lib 1918–28, being rptd separately as pamphlets. He edited or contributed to several edns of Shakespeare and pbd rhyming versions of Ibsen's Brand, 1894, *and* Love's comedy, 1900.

§2

Hoops, J. Nachruf. E Studien 66 1931.

Obituary. Bull John Rylands Lib 15 1931.

Robertson, J. G. Herford. Proc Br Acad 17 1931.

Gardner, E. G. Professor Herford as an Italian scholar. 1932.

Abercrombie, L. Herford and international literature. Bull John Rylands Lib 19 1935.

LIONEL JOHNSON

1867–1902

See col 633, above.

DENHAM JORDAN
('A Son of the Marshes')

1836–1920

Woodland, moor and stream: being the notes of a naturalist. 1889.

Annals of a fishing village. Ed J. A. Owen 1891.

On Surrey hills. 1891.

Within an hour of London town among wild birds and their haunts. 1892.

Forest tithes, and other studies from nature. 1893.

With the woodlanders and by the tide. 1893.

From spring to fall: or when life stirs. [1894].

The wild-fowl and sea-fowl of Great Britain. 1895.

In the green leaf and the sere. 1896.

Drift from longshore. 1898.

For his reviews up to 1900, mainly in Blackwood's Mag and Cornhill Mag, see Wellesley index to Victorian periodicals vol i, Toronto 1966.

WILLIAM PATON KER

1855–1923

Bibliographies

Pafford, J. H. P. Ker 1855–1923: a bibliography. 1950.

§1

The philosophy of art. 1883. In Essays in philosophical criticism, ed A. Seth and R. B. Haldane 1883.

Epic and romance: essays on mediaeval literature. 1897, 1908.

The dark ages. Edinburgh 1904; ed B. I. Evans 1955.

Essays on mediaeval literature. 1905.

English literature: mediaeval. [1912] (Home Univ Lib).

The art of poetry: seven lectures 1920–2. Oxford 1923.

Collected essays. Ed C. Whibley 2 vols 1925. Uncollected essays rptd from single pamphlets, periodicals and composite works.

Form and style in poetry: lectures and notes. Ed R. W. Chambers 1928.

On modern literature: lectures and addresses. Ed T. Spencer and J. R. Sutherland, Oxford 1955.

Ker also edited Dryden's essays, Berners's Froissart, and some other English and French classics.

§2

[MacCunn, J. and F. A.] Recollections of Ker by two friends. Glasgow 1924.

Chambers, R. W. Ker. Proc Br Acad 11 [1925].

—— Philologists at University College London. In his Man's unconquerable mind, 1939.

Read, H. New Criterion April 1926.

Re, A. del. A modern English humanist: Ker. In his Secret of the Renaissance, Tokyo 1930.

Evans, B. I. Ker as a critic of literature. Glasgow 1955.

ANDREW LANG

1844–1912

Bibliographies

[Falconer, C. M.] Specimens of a bibliography of the works of Lang. Dundee 1889 (priv ptd).

—— Catalogue of a library, chiefly the writings of Lang. Dundee 1898 (priv ptd).

Courtney, W. L. Eng Illustr Mag March 1904.

Green, R. L. Descriptions from the Darlington collection of Lang. Indiana Univ Bookman 7 1965. A full bibliography.

Collections

Ballades and verses vain. New York 1884. Selected by A. Dobson.

Ballades and rhymes: from Ballades and rhymes à la mode. 1911.

Poetical works. Ed Mrs Lang 4 vols in 2 1923.

The Augustan books of modern poetry: Lang. [1926]. Selected poems.

Essays of to-day and yesterday: Lang. 1926. Selected essays.

Lang and St Andrews: a centenary anthology. Ed J. B. Salmond, St Andrews 1944.

§ I

Ballads and lyrics of old France; with other poems. 1872, 1907.
Mythology and fairy tales. Fortnightly Rev May 1873. 'The first full refutation of Max Müller's mythological system'.
Aristotle's politics. 1877. With W. E. Bolland.
The Odyssey of Homer, book vi. 1877 (priv ptd).
Specimens of a translation of Theocritus. 1879 (priv ptd).
The Odyssey of Homer, done into English prose by S. H. Butcher and Lang. 1879, 1887, 1924, 1930.
Oxford: brief historical and descriptive notes. 1880, 1890, 1906, 1916.
Theocritus, Bion and Moschus rendered into English prose, with an introductory essay. 1880, 1889, 1922.
xxii ballades in blue china. 1880.
xxii and x: xxxii ballades in blue china. 1881, 1888 (with addns).
The library. 1881, 1892.
Notes on a collection of pictures by J. E. Millais. 1881.
The black thief: a play. 1882 (priv ptd).
Helen of Troy. 1882, 1883, 1913.
The Iliad of Homer, done into English prose by Lang, Walter Leaf and Ernest Myers. 1883, 1914.
Custom and myth. 1884, 1885 (rev), 1893, 1898, 1904.
Much darker days, by 'A huge longway'. 1884, 1885 (rev). Parodies Hugh Conway, Dark days.
The princess Nobody: a tale of fairy land. [1884].
'That very Mab'. 1885 (anon). With May Kendall.
Rhymes à la mode. 1885.
Lines on the inaugural meeting of the Shelley Society. 1886 (priv ptd). Anon. First pbd in Saturday Rev 13 March 1886.
The politics of Aristotle: introductory essays. 1886.
In the wrong paradise, and other stories. 1886.
The mark of Cain. Bristol 1886.
Letters to dead authors. 1886, 1893 (with addns), 1906 (with addns).
Books and bookmen. 1886, New York 1886, London 1892, 1912.
Myth, ritual and religion. 2 vols 1887, 1899 (rev).
Deulin, Charles. Johnny Nut and the golden goose. 1887. Tr Lang.
Aucassin and Nicolete. 1887, 1896, 1898, 1902, 1904, 1905.
Cupid and Psyche. 1887.
Beauty and the beast. 1887.
He, by the authors of It, King Solomon's wives and Bess. 1887. With W. H. Pollock.
Grass of Parnassus: rhymes old and new. 1888, 1892 (with addns).
The gold of Fairnilee. Bristol 1888.
Pictures at play or dialogues of the galleries: by two art-critics. 1888. With W. E. Henley.
Prince Prigio. Bristol 1889.
Letters on literature. 1889, 1892.
Lost leaders. 1889. Rptd from Daily News.
The dead leman and other tales from the French. 1889, 1890. With P. Sylvester.
Old friends: essays in epistolary parody. 1890, 1892.
The world's desire. 1890, 1894, [1907], 1916. With Sir H. Rider Haggard.
How to fail in literature: a lecture. 1890.
Etudes traditionnistes. Paris 1890. Essays from Saturday Rev, tr H. Carnoy.
Life, letters and diaries of Sir Stafford Northcote, first Earl of Iddesleigh. 2 vols Edinburgh 1890.
History of golf. In H. G. Hutchinson, Golf, 1890 (Badminton Lib).
Angling sketches. 1891, 1895.
Famous golf links. 1891. With H. G. Hutchinson et al.
On Calais sands. 1891. Poem with music by J. More Smieton.
Essays in little. 1891.
Memoir of the author. In W. Y. Sellar, The Roman poets of the Augustan age, Oxford 1892, 1899.
Piccadilly. In Great streets of the world, 1892.
A batch of golfing papers. Ed R. Barclay [1892]. By Lang et al.
Prince Ricardo of Pantouflia. Bristol [1893], 1932 (with Prince Prigio as Chronicles of Pantouflia).
Kirk's secret commonwealth. 1893.
The tercentenary of Izaak Walton. 1893 (priv ptd).
Homer and the epic. 1893.
St Andrews. 1893; ed G. H. Bushnell, St Andrews 1951.
Ban and arrière ban: a rally of fugitive rhymes. 1894.
Robert F. Murray: his poems; with a memoir by Lang. 1894.
Cock Lane and common-sense. 1894, 1896.
The voices of Jeanne d'Arc. 1895 (priv ptd).
My own fairy book. Bristol 1895. Collected fairy tales.
A monk of Fife. 1896.
Classical sport. In H. Peek, The poetry of sport, 1896 (Badminton Lib).
The life and letters of J. G. Lockhart. 2 vols 1897.
Modern mythology: a reply to Max Müller. 1897.
The book of dreams and ghosts. 1897, 1899.
Pickle the spy: or the incognito of Prince Charles. 1897.
The miracles of Madame Saint Katherine of Fierbois, translated from the edition of the Abbé J. J. Bowrassé, Tours 1858. Chicago 1897.
Waiting on the Glesca train. 1898. Poem set to music by R. T. Boothby.
The making of religion. 1898, 1900.
The companions of Pickle. 1898.
Parson Kelly. New York 1899, London 1900. With A.E.W. Mason.
The Homeric hymns: a new prose translation and essays. 1899.
Prince Charles Edward. 1900.
A history of Scotland from the Roman occupation. 4 vols Edinburgh 1900–7.
Notes and names in books. Chicago 1900 (priv ptd).
The mystery of Mary Stuart. 1901, 1901, 1904 (rev).
Alfred Tennyson. Edinburgh 1901.
Psychical research of the century. In the 19th century: a review of progress, 1901.
Magic and religion. 1901.
Adventures among books. Cleveland 1901 (priv ptd).
The young Ruthven. 1902 (priv ptd ballad).
The disentanglers. 1902.
James VI and the Gowrie mystery. 1902.
Hugo, Victor, Notre-Dame of Paris, with a critical introduction. 1902, 1924.
Social origins, by Lang; Primal Law, by J. J. Atkinson. 1903.
The valet's tragedy, and other studies. 1903.
The story of the golden fleece. 1903.
Memoir of the author. In C. I. Elton, William Shakespeare, his family and friends, ed A. H. Thompson 1904.
Historical mysteries. 1904, [1911].
New collected rhymes. 1905.
The puzzle of Dickens's last plot. 1905.
The secret of the totem. 1905.
Adventures among books. 1905.
The Clyde mystery: a study in forgeries and folklore. Glasgow 1905.
John Knox and the reformation. 1905.
Homer and his age. 1906.
Scott. In Homes and haunts of famous authors, 1906.
Sir Walter Scott. 1906.
The story of Joan of Arc. [1906].
Portraits and jewels of Mary Stuart. 1906.
Tales of a fairy court. [1907].
Australian problems. In Anthropological essays presented to Edward Burnett Tylor, Oxford 1907. With notice of Tylor's work by Lang.
'The end of an auld sang': a romantic plot against the

Union. 2 pts in The Union of 1707; a survey of events, Glasgow 1907.
The King over the water. 1907. Mainly by A. Shield.
Homer and anthropology. In R. R. Marett, Anthropology and the classics, Oxford 1908.
The origins of religion and other essays. 1908. Reprints from earlier vols, with one new essay on Theories of the origins of religion.
The maid of France: the life and death of Jeanne d'Arc. 1908, 1913, 1922; tr French, [1911]. A reply to Anatole France, Vie de Jeanne d'Arc, 1908.
The origin of terms of human relationship. [1909]. From Proc Br Acad 3 1909.
La Jeanne d'Arc de M. Anatole France. Paris 1909.
Sir George Mackenzie, King's Advocate: his life and times. 1909.
The world of Homer. 1910.
Sir Walter Scott and the Border minstrelsy. 1910.
Method in the study of totemism. Glasgow 1911.
A short history of Scotland. Edinburgh 1911.
Ode on a distant memory of Jane Eyre. [1912].
Shakespeare, Bacon and the great unknown. 1912.
History of English literature from Beowulf to Swinburne. 1912, 1912 (rev), 1913.
The Annesley case. 1912.
In praise of frugality. 1912 [priv ptd]. Poem tr from Pope Leo XII.
Ode to the opening century. 1912 (priv ptd). Poem from Pope Leo XII.
Highways and byways in the Border. 1913. With J. Lang.
Bibliomania. 1914 (priv ptd).
The new Pygmalion. 1962 (priv ptd). Poems.
Lang edited and introduced many English and other classics. He also pbd a series of fairy books consisting of re-tellings of traditional tales. He was one of the founders of the Soc for Psychical Research. His contributions to the 11th edn of Encyclopaedia britannica 1910–11 (*some from 9th edn*) *consisted of articles on Apparitions, Ballads, Casket letters, Crystal gazing, Fairy, Family, Edmund Gurney, Hauntings, James de la Cloche, Molière, Mythology, Names, Poltergeist, Prometheus, Psychical Research, Scotland (History), Second sight, Tale and Totem. He also contributed articles on Burns and Scott to* Chambers' encyclopaedia *and on ballads to* Chambers' cyclopaedia of English literature, *and reviewed extensively.*

§2

Brown, R. Semitic influence in Hellenic mythology, with special reference to works of Max Müller and Lang. 1898.
Wanliss, T. D. Scotland and Presbyterianism vindicated: being a critical review of the third volume of Mr Lang's history. Edinburgh 1905.
— The muckrake in Scottish history: or Mr Lang re-criticised. Edinburgh 1906.
Saintsbury, G. Obituary. Oxford Mag 17 Oct 1912.
— Lang. Quart Rev 240 1923.
— Lang in the 'seventies—and after. In The eighteen-seventies, 1929 (Royal Soc of Lit).
Gordon, G. S. Obituary. TLS 5 Sept 1912 (anon); rptd in his Lives of authors, 1950.
— Lang: Lang lecture. Oxford 1928; rptd in his Discipline of letters, Oxford 1949.
Ker, W. P. Commemorative address. Proc Academic Committee, Royal Soc of Lit 1913.
Rait, R. S., G. Murray, S. Reinach and J. H. Millar. Quart Rev 218 1913. Commemorative article.
Greenwood, G. G. Is there a Shakespeare problem? with a reply to Mr. J. M. Robertson and Mr Lang. 1916.
Beerbohm, M. Two glimpses of Lang. Life & Letters June 1929.
Shewan, A. Lang's work for Homer: Lang lecture. Oxford 1929.
Rait, R. S. Lang as historian: Lang lecture. Oxford 1930.
Cazamian, L. Lang and the maid of France: Lang lecture. Oxford 1931.
Buchan, J. Lang and the Border: Lang lecture. Oxford 1933.
Mackie, J. D. Lang and the house of Stuart: Lang lecture. Oxford 1934.
— Lang: the man and the writer. Listener 13 April 1944.
Grierson, H. J. C. Lang, Lockhart and biography: Lang lecture. Oxford 1935.
Webster, A. B. Lang's poetry: Lang lecture. Oxford 1937.
Niven, F. Lang. Lib Rev 44 1937.
Reid, F. Lang and Longman's. London Mercury March 1938; rptd in his Retrospective adventures, 1941.
Elwin, M. Old gods falling. 1939.
Christie, E. and A. K. Stewart. Some recollections of Lang and his wife. In their A long look at life, [1940].
Ormerod, J. The poetry of Lang. Derby 1943.
Bushnell, G. H. Notes on Lang. TLS 5 June 1943.
— Lang at fifty. Scots Mag March 1944.
Green, R. L. More notes on Lang. TLS 17 July 1943.
— He, She and It. TLS 27 May, 1 July 1944.
— Lang: poet and romantic 1844–1912. English 5 1944.
— Lang and the fairy-tale. RES 20 1944.
— Lang, critic and Dickensian. Dickensian 41 1944.
— Dear Andrew and Dear Louis. Scots Mag Aug 1945.
— Lang: a critical biography with a short-title bibliography of the works of Lang. Leicester 1946.
— Lang and Gifted Hopkins. N & Q April 1954.
— Lang. 1962.
— Lang: 'the greatest bookman of his age'. Indiana Univ Bookman 7 1965.
Parker, W. M. Lang and Longman's. Scots Mag March 1944.
Thompson, D'A. Andrew and Pat. Scots Mag May 1944.
Tolkien, J. R. R. On fairy-stories. In Essays presented to Charles Williams, Oxford 1947. Lang lecture for 1938, expanded; rptd in his Tree and leaf, 1964.
S., J. Lang in Selkirk. More Books 23 1948.
Murray, G. Lang the poet. Oxford 1948. Lang lecture.
Weber, C. J. Some letters on Hardy's Tess. Jnl Rutgers Univ Lib 13 1949.
Macmillan, H. P. Law and custom. Edinburgh 1949. Lang lecture.
Webster, A. B. (ed). Concerning Lang: being the Lang lectures delivered before the University of St Andrews 1927–37. Oxford 1949.
Black, J. B. Lang and the casket letter controversy. Edinburgh 1951. Lang lecture.
Salmond, S. B. Andrew Lang and journalism. Edinburgh 1951. Lang lecture.
Coats of many colours. TLS 23 Nov 1951. On the fairy books.
Dickinson, W. C. Lang, John Knox and Scottish Presbyterianism. Edinburgh 1952. Lang lecture.
Maurer, O. Lang and Longman's Magazine 1882–1905. SE 34 1955.

'VERNON LEE', VIOLET PAGET

1856–1935

Collections

A Vernon Lee anthology. Ed I. C. Willis 1929.

§1

Studies of the eighteenth century in Italy. 1880.
Tuscan fairy tales. [1880]. Ed Vernon Lee.
Belcaro: being essays on sundry aesthetical questions. [1883].

The prince of the hundred soups: a puppet-show in narrative, edited [i.e. written] with an introduction by Vernon Lee. 1883. Illustr S. Birch.
Ottilie: an eighteenth-century idyl. 1883.
Miss Brown: a novel. 3 vols 1884.
The Countess of Albany. 1884.
Euphorion: being studies of the antique and the mediaeval in the Renaissance. 2 vols 1884, 1 vol 1885 (rev).
Baldwin: being dialogues on views and aspirations. 1886.
A phantom lover: a fantastic story. Edinburgh 1886.
Juvenilia: being a second series of essays on sundry aesthetical questions. 2 vols 1887.
Hauntings: fantastic stories. 1890.
Vanitas: polite stories. 1892, 1911 (adds A frivolous conversion).
Althea: a second book of dialogues on aspirations and duties. 1894.
Au pays de Vénus. Paris [1894]. Tales tr French, rptd from Les lettres et les arts.
Renaissance fancies and studies: being a sequel to Euphorion. 1895.
Limbo and other essays. 1897, 1908 (adds Ariadne in Mantua).
Genius loci: notes on places. 1899.
Le rôle de l'élément moteur dans la perception esthétique visuelle: mémoire et questionnaire soumis au quatrième Congrès de psychologie. Imola 1901. With C. A. Thomson.
Ariadne in Mantua: a romance in five acts. Oxford 1903.
Penelope Brandling: a tale of the Welsh coast in the eighteenth century. 1903.
Hortus vitae: essays on the gardening of life. 1904.
Pope Jacynth and other fantastic tales. 1904, 1956.
The enchanted woods and other essays on the genius of places. 1905.
The spirit of Rome: leaves from a diary. 1906.
Sister Benvenuta and the Christ child: an eighteenth century legend. 1906.
The sentimental traveller: notes on places. 1908.
Gospels of anarchy and other contemporary studies. 1908.
Laurus nobilis: chapters on art and life. 1909.
Vital lies: studies of some varieties of recent obscurantism. 2 vols 1912.
Beauty and ugliness, and other studies in psychological aesthetics. 1912. With C. A. Thomson.
The beautiful: an introduction to psychological aesthetics. 1913.
The tower of the mirrors and other essays on the spirit of places. 1914.
Louis Norbert: a two-fold romance. 1914.
The ballet of the nations: a present-day morality; with a pictorial commentary by M. Armfield. 1915.
Satan the waster: a philosophic war trilogy, with notes and introduction. 1920.
The handling of words and other studies in literary psychology. 1923.
The golden keys and other essays on the genius loci. 1925.
Proteus: or the future of intelligence. 1925.
The poet's eye. 1926.
For Maurice: five unlikely stories. 1927.
Music and its lovers: an empirical study of emotion and imaginative responses to music. [Ed I. C. Willis] 1932.
The snake lady and other stories. [Ed H. Gregory], New York 1954.
Supernatural tales: excursions into fantasy. [Ed I. C. Willis] 1955.
'*Vernon Lee' also wrote introds to* C. A. Thomson, Art and man; E. E. Charteris, John Sargent; R. W. Semon, Mnemic psychology *etc.*

Letters

Vernon Lee's letters. [Ed I. C. Willis] 1937.

§2

The literary life of Vernon Lee. Literary World (Boston) 1 Nov 1884.
Preston, H. W. Vernon Lee. Atlantic Monthly Feb 1885.
Brooks, Van Wyck. Notes on Vernon Lee. Forum April 1911.
Shaw, G. B. Satan the waster. Nation 18 Sept 1920.
MacCarthy, D. Vernon Lee. Bookman (London) Oct 1931.
Libbey, F. E. The Vernon Lee papers. Colby Lib Quart Ser 3 1952. Colby College possesses all her papers.
Gardner, B. Who was Vernon Lee? Ibid.
—— An apology for Henry James's Tiger-cat. PMLA 68 1953.
Sutherland, J. H. Letters from G. Lowes Dickinson to Vernon Lee. Colby Lib Quart 3 1953.
Fife, H. M. Letters from Edith Wharton to Vernon Lee. Ibid.
Edel, L. Henry James and Vernon Lee. PMLA 69 1954.
Leighton, P. M. 'To my friend, Karl Hillebrand': the dedication in Ottilie and its aftermath. Colby Lib Quart 3 1953.
Comparetti, A. P. 'A most exquisitely beautiful play' that failed to reach the stage. Ibid. On Ariadne in Mantua.
Comparetti, E. F. A note on the origin of Ariadne in Mantua. Ibid.
Smith, G. W. Letters from Paul Bourget to Vernon Lee. Ibid.
Biron, A. H. Paget in Paraÿs. Colby Lib Quart 5 1960.
Willis, I. C. Vernon Lee. Ibid.
Corrigan, B. Vernon Lee and the Old Yellow Book. Ibid.
Pantazzi, S. Carlo Placci and Vernon Lee: their letters and their friends. Eng Miscellany (Rome) 12 1961.
—— Giovanni Ruffini's letters to Vernon Lee 1875–1879. Eng Miscellany (Rome) 13 1962.
Gunn, P. Vernon Lee, Violet Paget 1856–1935. 1964.

RICHARD LE GALLIENNE

1866–1947

See col 1063, above.

SIR ALFRED COMYNS LYALL

1835–1911

See col 636, above.

ALICE MEYNELL

1847–1922

See col 638, above.

WILLIAM MINTO

1845–93

Manual of English prose literature, biographical and critical. Edinburgh 1872. Essay on style; Biographies of De Quincey, Macaulay and Carlyle; History of English prose writers.
Characteristics of English poets from Chaucer to Shirley. 1874.
Defoe. 1879 (EML).
The crack of doom: a novel. 3 vols Edinburgh 1886.
The mediation of Ralph Hardelot. 3 vols 1888. A novel.
Was she good or bad? a holiday episode. 1889.
Logic inductive and deductive. 1893.
Plain principles of prose composition. Edinburgh 1893.

The literature of the Georgian era. Ed W. Knight, Edinburgh 1894 (with memoir). Chaucer, Spenser, Renaissance, Shakespeare, Pope and the eighteenth century, The novel, Wordsworth, Coleridge, Shelley, Keats etc.

GEORGE MOORE

1857–1933

See col 1014, above.

JOHN MORLEY, VISCOUNT MORLEY

1838–1923

Bibliographies

Stead, W. T. Eng Illustr Mag Dec 1903.

Collections

Collected works. 15 vols 1921, 12 vols 1923.
Selected essays. Ed H. G. Rawlinson 1923 (with memoir).

§1

Modern characteristics. 1865. Anon; essays.
Studies in conduct. 1867. Anon; essays.
Edmund Burke: a historical study. 1867.
Critical miscellanies. 2 sers 1871–7; 3 vols 1886 (with addns and omissions); ser 4, 1908. Robespierre, Carlyle, Byron, Macaulay, Emerson, Vauvenargues, J. S. Mill, George Eliot, Harriet Martineau, W. R. Greg, Comte etc
Voltaire. 1872, 1872 (rev).
Rousseau. 2 vols 1873.
The struggle for national education. 1873.
On compromise. 1874, 1886.
Diderot and the encyclopaedists. 2 vols 1878.
Edmund Burke. 1879, 1923 (rev) (EML).
The life of Richard Cobden. 2 vols 1881, 1 vol 1882 (abridged).
Emerson: an essay. New York 1884.
Walpole. 1889.
Studies in literature. 1890. Wordsworth, Aphorisms, Maine, The ring and the book, Macvey Napier, Victor Hugo's Ninety-three.
Machiavelli: the Romanes lecture. 1897.
Oliver Cromwell. 1900.
The life of William Ewart Gladstone. 3 vols 1903, 1 vol 1927 (abridged, with preface by C. F. G. Masterman).
Free trade v protection. 1904.
Literary essays. 1906. Byron, Carlyle, Macaulay, Wordsworth, On the study of literature.
Speeches on Indian affairs: with an appreciation. Madras 1908, 1917 (rev and enlarged).
Indian speeches 1907–8. 1909.
Science and literature. [Oxford] 1911 (priv ptd).
Notes on politics and history: a university address. 1913.
Recollections. 2 vols 1917.
Memorandum on resignation—August 1914; with an introduction by F. W. Hirst. 1928.
Morley also pbd several lectures, tracts and single speeches. He was general editor of the original EML ser and of Fortnightly Rev 1867–82. For a list of his reviews up to 1900, mainly in Macmillan's Mag, see Wellesley index to Victorian periodicals vol i, Toronto 1966.

§2

Cecil, Algernon. In his Six Oxford thinkers, 1909.
Harper, G. M. In his Morley and other essays, Princeton 1920.
Morison, J. L. Morley: a study in Victorianism. Kingston Ontario 1920.
MacCallum, J. D. Morley's criticism of English poetry and prose. Princeton [1921].
Massingham, H. W. Morley the humanist. Fortnightly Rev Nov 1923.
Morgan, J. H. Morley: an appreciation and some reminiscences. 1924.
Braybrooke, P. Morley, writer and thinker; with an introduction by W. B. Maxwell. 1924.
Hirst, F. W. Early life and letters of Morley. 2 vols 1927.
—— Richard Cobden and Morley. 1941.
Lewisohn, L. In his Cities and men, 1929.
Spender, J. A. Morley. Fortnightly Rev Dec 1938.
Everett, E. M. The party of humanity: the Fortnightly Review and its contributors 1865–74. Chapel Hill 1939.
Knickerbocker, F. W. The legacy of Morley. Sewanee Rev 47 1939.
—— Free minds: Morley and his friends. Cambridge Mass 1943.
Staebler, W. The liberal mind of Morley. Princeton 1943.
Villiers, M. Nineteenth-century commentary. Quart Rev 282 1944.
White, W. Morley and A. E. Housman. TLS 22 March 1947.
Scott, J. W. R. The life and death of a newspaper: Morley, W. T. Stead and other editors of the Pall Mall Gazette. 1952.
Gooch, G. P. Two elder statesmen, i: Morley. Contemporary Rev Oct 1956.
Moore, D. E. Morley: critic of public address. Quart Jnl of Speech 44 1958.
Stelzner, H. G. The British orators, viii: Morley's speechmaking. Quart Jnl of Speech 45 1959.
Das, M. N. India under Morley and Minto. [1964].

SIR HENRY NEWBOLT

1862–1937

See col 642, above.

JOHN OWEN

1836–96

§1

Evenings with the skeptics: or free discussion on free thinkers. 2 vols 1881.
Verse-musings on nature, faith and freedom. 1889, 1894 (enlarged).
The skeptics of the French renaissance. 1893.
The skeptics of the Italian renaissance. 1893, 1908 (3rd edn).
The five great skeptical dramas of history. 1896. The Prometheus vinctus of Aeschylus; the Book of Job; Goethe's Faust; Shakespeare's Hamlet; El magico prodigioso.
Owen also contributed regularly to Edinburgh Rev and Academy.

§2

C[otton], J. S. Owen. Academy 15 Feb 1896.

SIR CHARLES HUBERT HASTINGS PARRY

1848–1918

§1

Studies of great composers. 1887.
The art of music. 1893.
Summary of the history and development of mediaeval and modern European music. [1893?].
The evolution of the art of music. 1896, 1897; rev H. C. Colles, New York 1930.
Style in musical art: an inaugural lecture delivered at Oxford on March 7 1900. Oxford 1900.
The music of the seventeenth century. In Sir W. H. Hadow, Oxford history of music vol 3, 1902; rev E. J. Dent 1938.
Johann Sebastian Bach: the story of the development of a great personality. New York 1909, 1921, 1934 (rev).
Style in musical art. 1911.
College addresses delivered to pupils of the Royal College of Music. Ed H. C. Colles 1920 (with memoir).

§2

Fuller-Maitland, J. A. The life and work of Parry. Musical Quart 5 1919.
— The music of Parry and Stanford. 1934.
Graves, C. L. Parry: his life and works. 1926.
Greene, G. Two witnesses: a personal recollection of Parry and Friedrich von Hügel. 1930.

SIR ARTHUR THOMAS QUILLER-COUCH

1863–1944

See col 1071, above.

SIR WALTER ALEXANDER RALEIGH

1861–1922

Bibliographies

Bibliography of Raleigh's works 1883–1922. Periodical 8 Sept 1922. A chronological list.

§1

The English novel: being a short sketch of its history from the earliest times to the appearance of Waverley. 1891.
Robert Louis Stevenson. 1895.
The riddle: a pleasant pastoral comedy adapted from the Wife of Bath's tale as it is set forth in the works of Master Geoffrey Chaucer, presented at Otterspool on Midsummers Eve 1895. Liverpool 1895.
Style. 1897.
Milton. 1900.
Wordsworth. 1903.
The English voyages of the sixteenth century. In Hakluyt's Voyages vol 12, 1905.
Shakespeare. 1907, 1950 (EML).
Six essays on Johnson. Oxford 1910.
Romance: two lectures. Princeton 1916.
Shakespeare's England: an account of the life and manners of his age. 2 vols Oxford 1916. Planned by Raleigh, and the section The age of Elizabeth written by him.
England and the war: being sundry addresses delivered during the war. 1918.
The war in the air: being the story of the part played in the Great War by the Royal Air Force. Vol 1 Oxford 1922.
Laughter from a cloud. 1923. Humorous sketches and poems.
Some authors: a collection of literary essays 1896–1916. 1923.
On writing and writers: being extracts from his note-books, selected and edited by George Gordon. 1926.
The letters of Raleigh 1789–1922. Ed Lady Raleigh 2 vols 1926, 1928 (enlarged).
A selection from the letters of Raleigh 1880–1922. Ed Lady Raleigh 1928. Including some letters not previously pbd.

Raleigh also pbd pamphlets and lectures, and edited various English classics.

§2

Raleigh. Academy 18 Dec 1897.
Chapman, R. W. Raleigh. London Mercury July 1922.
Gordon, G. S. Raleigh. TLS 8 June 1922; rptd in his Lives of authors, 1950.
— Raleigh in his letters. London Mercury 13 April 1926; rptd in his Discipline of letters, Oxford 1949.
Jones, H. A. Raleigh and the Air History. 1922.
Crum, V. Raleigh. 1923.
Legouis, E. Raleigh d'après ses lettres. Revue Anglo-américaine 4 1926.
Hart, H. L. A. The position of Raleigh among literary critics. Nineteenth Century Oct 1927.
Garrod, H. W. In his Profession of poetry, Oxford 1929.
MacCarthy, D. In his Portraits, 1931.
Woolf, V. In her Captain's death bed and other essays, 1950.
Palmer, D. J. In his Rise of English studies, Hull 1965.

JOHN MACKINNON ROBERTSON

1856–1933

§1

Walt Whitman, poet and democrat. Edinburgh 1884.
The religion of Shakespeare: two discourses. [1887].
Essays towards a critical method. 1889.
Modern humanists. 1891. Carlyle, Mill, Emerson, Arnold, Ruskin, Spencer.
Buckle and his critics: a study in sociology. 1895.
The Saxon and the Celt: a study in sociology. 1897.
New essays towards a critical method. 1897.
Montaigne and Shakespeare. 1897, 1909 (adds 2 essays on the Originality and Learning of Shakespeare).
The dynamics of religion: an essay in English culture history. 1897, 1926 (rev). Originally pbd under pseudonym of M. W. Wiseman.
Miscellanies. 1898.
Patriotism and empire. 1899.
A short history of free thought, ancient and modern. 1899, 2 vols 1906 (rewritten and greatly enlarged), 1915 (rev and expanded).
Christianity and mythology. 1900, 1910 (expanded).
Studies in religious fallacy. 1900.
Letters on reasoning. 1902, 1905 (rev), [1935] (abridged).
A short history of Christianity. 1902, 1913 (rev), 1931 (condensed).
Criticisms. 2 vols 1902–3.
Browning and Tennyson as teachers: two studies. 1903.
Essays in ethics. 1903.
Pagan christs: studies in comparative hierology. 1903, 1911 (rev and expanded).
Studies in practical politics. 1903.
Essays in sociology. 2 vols 1904.
What to read: suggestions for the better utilisation of public libraries. 1904.
Rudyard Kipling: a criticism. Madras [1905].
Did Shakespeare write Titus Andronicus? a study in Elizabethan literature. 1905, 1924 (rev and expanded as Introduction to the study of the Shakespeare canon).

Pioneer humanists. 1907. Machiavelli, Bacon, Hobbes, Spinoza, Shaftesbury, Mandeville, Gibbon, Mary Wollstonecraft.
The evolution of states: an introduction to English politics. 1912.
The meaning of Liberalism. 1912, 1925 (rev and enlarged).
Rationalism. 1912, 1945 (abridged).
The Baconian heresy: a confutation. 1913.
Elizabethan literature. 1914.
The historical Jesus: a survey of positions. 1916.
The Jesus problem: a re-statement of the myth theory. 1917.
Shakespeare and Chapman: a thesis of Chapman's authorship of A lover's complaint, and his origination of Timon of Athens, with indications of future problems. 1917.
The problem of the Merry wives of Windsor. [1918].
The economics of progress. 1918.
Bolingbroke and Walpole. 1919.
The problem of Hamlet. 1919.
Free trade. 1919.
A short history of morals. 1920.
Charles Bradlaugh. 1920. Based on the chs contributed to H. B. Bonner, Memoir of her father, 2 vols 1894.
Voltaire. 1922.
The Shakespeare canon. 5 vols 1922–32.
Croce as Shakespearean critic. 1922.
Hamlet once more. 1923.
Explorations. 1923.
Ernest Renan. 1924.
Gibbon. 1925.
Mr Shaw and the Maid. [1925].
Spoken essays. 1925.
The problems of the Shakespeare sonnets. 1926.
Modern humanists reconsidered. 1927.
Jesus and Judas: a textual and historical investigation. 1927.
A history of free thought in the nineteenth century. 1929, 2 vols 1936 (rev).
The genuine in Shakespeare: a conspectus. 1930.
Literary detection: a symposium on Macbeth. 1931.
The state of Shakespeare study: a critical conspectus. 1931.
Marlowe: a conspectus. 1931.
Electoral justice: a survey of the theory and practice of electoral representation. [1931].
Robertson also pbd many rationalist, sociological and political tracts and lectures.

§2

Conybeare, F. C. The historical Christ: or an investigation of the views of Mr Robertson. 1914.
Wood, H. G. Rationalism and historical criticism: studies in the writings of Robertson. 1919.
— Did Christ really live? 1938.

GEORGE EDWARD BATEMAN SAINTSBURY

1845–1933

Bibliographies

James, W. P. English Illustr Mag Oct 1903. Includes reviews and articles on and by Saintsbury.
Bibliographies of modern authors. London Mercury Dec 1919.
Leuba, W. Bibliography of Saintsbury. Book-Collector's Quart 12 1933.

§1

A primer of French literature. Oxford 1880, 1884 (rev), 1891 (rev), 1896 (rev), 1912 (rev), 1925 (with supplementary ch on The present day by T. B. Rudmose-Brown).
Dryden. 1881 (EML).
A short history of the life and writings of Alain René Le Sage. [1881] (priv ptd).
A short history of French literature. Oxford 1882, 1897 (rev).
French lyrics. 1882.
Specimens of French literature from Villon to Hugo. Oxford 1883.
Specimens of English prose style from Malory to Macaulay. 1885.
Marlborough. 1885.
A history of Elizabethan literature. 1887. From Wyatt and Surrey to the Restoration.
Manchester. 1887. A history.
Essays in English literature 1780–1860. 2 sers 1890–5.
Essays on French novelists. 1891.
The pocket library of English literature. 6 vols 1891–2.
The Earl of Derby. 1892.
Miscellaneous essays. 1892. English prose style, Chamfort and Rivarol, Renan, Saint-Evremond, Baudelaire, A paradox, On Quinet, Contrasts of French and English literature etc.
Inaugural address delivered at Edinburgh University 15 October 1895. Edinburgh 1895.
Corrected impressions. 1895. Thackeray, Tennyson, Carlyle, Swinburne, Macaulay, Browning, Dickens, Arnold, Morris, Ruskin, Three mid-century novelists.
A history of nineteenth-century literature 1780–1895. 1896.
The flourishing of romance and the rise of allegory. Edinburgh 1897 (Periods of European literature, ed G. Saintsbury vol 2).
Sir Walter Scott. [1897].
A short history of English literature. 1898.
Matthew Arnold. 1899.
The history of criticism and literary taste in Europe. 3 vols Edinburgh 1900–4.
The earlier Renaissance. Edinburgh 1901 (Periods of European literature vol 5).
Loci critici. Boston 1903. An anthology of criticism.
Minor poets of the Caroline period. 3 vols Oxford 1905–21.
A history of English prosody from the twelfth century to the present day. 3 vols 1906–10.
The later nineteenth century. Edinburgh 1907. (Periods of European literature vol 12).
A historical manual of English prosody. 1910.
A history of English criticism: being the English chapters of A history of criticism and literary taste in Europe, revised, adapted and supplemented. Edinburgh 1911, 1949.
A history of English prose rhythm. 1912.
The historical character of the English lyric. Proc Br Acad 5 1912.
The English novel. 1913.
The first book of English literature. 1914.
The peace of the Augustans. 1916, Oxford 1946 (WC).
A history of the French novel to the close of the nineteenth century. 2 vols 1917–9.
Some recent studies in English prosody. Proc Br Acad 9 1919.
Notes on a cellar-book. 1920.
A letter book. 1922.
A scrap book. 1922.
A second scrap book. 1923.
The collected essays and papers 1875–1920. 4 vols 1923–4.
A last scrap book. 1924.
A consideration of Thackeray. 1931.
Prefaces and essays. Ed O. Elton 1933.
Shakespeare. Cambridge 1934. Rptd from CHEL vol 5 1910.
Muir, A. et al (ed). Saintsbury: the memorial volume—a new collection of his essays and papers: memoir by

A. B. Webster; personal portraits by O. Elton, H. J. C. Grierson, J. W. Oliver and J. Purves. 1945. A last vintage: essays and papers. 1950.

Saintsbury also pbd edns of or introds to many English and several French classics, the most important being the works of Balzac, Dryden, Fielding, Sterne, Smollett, Peacock and Thackeray. He contributed to CHEL and other composite works and translated 5 books from the French. For a list of his reviews up to 1900, mainly in Macmillan's Mag, see Wellesley index to Victorian periodicals vol i, Toronto 1966.

§2

Watson, W. In his Excursions in criticism, 1893.
Waugh, A. Living critics, viii. Bookman (London) Aug 1896.
Duncanson, R. The Tory professor. Univ Mag & Free Rev June 1897.
Dobson, A. Old Kensington Palace. 1910.
Bennett, A. In his Books and persons, 1917.
Priestley, J. B. Saintsbury: an appreciation. London Mercury Sept 1922; rptd in his Figures in modern literature, 1924.
Hewlett, M. In his Extemporary essays, 1922.
Guedalla, P. In his Masters and men, 1923.
Lewisohn, L. Saintsbury. Nation (New York) 5 Dec 1923; rptd in his Cities and men, 1929.
Williams, O. Contemporary criticism of literature. [1924].
Roberts, R. E. Saintsbury. Bookman (London) Oct 1925.
Gosse, E. In his Silhouettes, 1925.
Chapman, J. A. Papers on Shelley, Wordsworth and others. 1929.
Ralli, A. In his A history of Shakespearian criticism vol 2, Oxford 1932.
Chrystal, G. Saintsbury. London Mercury March 1933.
Elton, O. Saintsbury 1845–1933. Proc Br Acad 19 1933.
Webster, A. B. Saintsbury. Edinburgh [1934].
Richardson, D. Saintsbury and art for art's sake in England. PMLA 59 1944.
Jennings, R. Books in general. New Statesman 25 Aug 1945.
Wellek, R. Saintsbury. Eng Miscellany 12 1961.
Robinson, J. K. A neglected phase of the aesthetic movement: English Parnassianism. PMLA 68 1953.
Ryan, A. P. (ed). Critics who have influenced taste. 1965.

GEORGE BERNARD SHAW
1856–1950

See col 1169, above.

SIR JOHN SKELTON
1831–97

Nugae criticae: occasional papers written at the seaside. Edinburgh 1862.
Thalatta! or the great commoner: a political romance. Edinburgh 1862.
John Dryden: 'in defence'. 1865. Rptd from Fraser's Mag.
A campaigner at home. 1865. A novel.
Spring songs, by a western Highlander. 1865.
The great Lord Bolingbroke, Henry St John. Edinburgh 1868.
Benjamin Disraeli: the past and the future. 1868.
The impeachment of Mary Stuart. Edinburgh 1876.
The boarding-out of pauper children in Scotland. Edinburgh 1876.
Essays in romance and studies from life. Edinburgh 1878. Sketches and short stories.
The crookit Meg: a story of the year one. 1880. Rptd from Fraser's Mag.
Essays of Shirley. Edinburgh 1882.
Essays in history and biography, including the defence of Mary Stuart. Edinburgh 1883. Blake, Macaulay, Thackeray, C. Brontë, Dryden, Disraeli, etc.
Maitland of Lethington and the Scotland of Mary Stuart. 2 vols Edinburgh 1887–8.
The Local Government (Scotland) Act in relation to public health. Edinburgh 1890.
The handbook of public health. Edinburgh 1890; supplement, Edinburgh 1891.
Mary Stuart. 1893.
The table talk of Shirley. Edinburgh 1895. Reminiscences of and letters from Froude, Thackeray, Disraeli, Browning, Rossetti, Kingsley, Baynes, Huxley, Tyndall et al.
Summers and winters at Balmawhapple. 2 vols Edinburgh 1896. Ser 2 of The table talk of Shirley, above.
Charles the first. Edinburgh 1898.

Skelton reviewed extensively, especially for Blackwood's Mag; see Wellesley index to Victorian periodicals vol i, Toronto 1966.

ROBERT ALAN MOWBRAY STEVENSON
1847–1900

The devils of Notre Dame. 1894. Illustr Joseph Pennell.
The art of Velasquez. 1895, 1899 (rev and expanded).
Peter Paul Rubens. 1898, 1909, 1939. Rptd with addns from Portfolio.
Essay on Raeburn. In Sir Henry Armstrong, Sir Henry Raeburn, 1901.

ROBERT LOUIS STEVENSON
1850–94

See col 1004, above.

ALGERNON CHARLES SWINBURNE
1837–1909

See col 571, above.

JOHN ADDINGTON SYMONDS
1840–93

See col 1501, below.

ARTHUR SYMONS
1865–1945

See col 649, above.

HENRY DUFF TRAILL
1842–1900

Glaucus: a tale of a fish—a new and original extravaganza, performed July 1865. [1865].
Present versus past, performed June 1869. [1869].
The battle of the professors, performed June 1874. [1874].
The Israelitish question and the comments of the Canaan journals thereon. 1876. Anon; burlesque of leading London newspapers.
Central government. 1881, 1908 (rev H. Craik). An account of the English constitution.
Sterne. 1882 (EML).

Re-captured rhymes: being a batch of political and other fugitives arrested and brought to book. Edinburgh 1882.
The new Lucian: dialogues of the dead. 1884, 1900 (adds Dedication and supplementary dialogues).
Coleridge. 1884 (EML).
Shaftesbury. 1886.
William III. 1888.
Strafford. 1889.
Saturday songs. [1890]. Satirical verses largely rptd from Saturday Rev.
The Marquis of Salisbury. 1891.
Number twenty: fables and fantasies. [1892]. Chiefly in prose, with some in verse.
Two proper prides. In Mrs W. K. Clifford. A grey romance, 1894.
The barbarous Britishers: a tip-top novel. [1896]. A parody of G. Allen, The British barbarians.
From Cairo to the Soudan frontier. 1896. Letters rptd from Daily Telegraph.
Life of Sir John Franklin. 1896.
The new fiction, and other essays on literary subjects. 1897.
Lord Cromer: a biography. 1897.
The medicine man, performed May 1898. [1898]. With Robert Hichens.
England, Egypt and the Sudan. 1900.
The baby of the future. [1911]. Rptd from Punch. Parodies of nursery rhymes.
Traill also pbd an edn of Disraeli's Sybil. He was general editor of Social England, 1893-7, *and of the periodical* Literature, 1897-1900. *For his reviews in Contemporary Rev and Macmillan's Mag, see* Wellesley index to Victorian periodicals vol i, Toronto 1966. *For an appreciation of Traill, see* H. C. Beeching, Conferences on books and men, 1900.

ARTHUR BINGHAM WALKLEY
1855-1926

§1

Playhouse impressions. 1892.
Frames of mind. 1899.
Dramatic criticism: three lectures. 1903.
Drama and life. 1907.
Pastiche and prejudice. 1921.
More prejudice. 1923.
Still more prejudice. 1925.

§2

Obituary. Times 9 Oct 1926.
Child, H. H. The post-Victorians. 1933.

THOMAS HUMPHRY WARD
1845-1926

The English poets: selections with critical introductions by various writers and a general introduction by Matthew Arnold. 4 vols 1880-1. Ed Ward.
Men of the reign: a biographical dictionary of eminent persons of British and colonial birth who have died during the reign of Queen Victoria. 1885. Ed Ward.
The reign of Queen Victoria. a survey of fifty years of progress. 2 vols 1887. Ed Ward.
English art in the public galleries of London, published under the direction of Ward, with the assistance of Walter Armstrong and others. 1888.
Oxford, illustrated by J. Fulleylove, with notes by Ward. 1889.
Romney: a biographical and critical essay, with a catalogue raissonné of his works. 2 vols 1904. With W. Roberts.
History of the Athenaeum [Club] 1824-1925, based on materials collected by the late H. R. Tedder. 1926.

THEODORE WATTS-DUNTON, earlier WATTS
1832-1914

Bibliographies

Truss, T. J. Watts-Dunton: a primary bibliography. Bull of Bibliography 23 1961.

§1

Jubilee greeting at Spithead to the men of Greater Britain. 1897.
The coming of love and other poems. 1898, 1899 (includes Rhona Boswell's story in title and adds long prefatory note), 1906 (rev and enlarged).
Aylwin: a novel. 1899, [1900] (adds further introd), 1901 (with 2 appendixes).
Charlotte Brontë. Introd to vol 6 of Novels and poems of Charlotte, Emily and Anne Brontë, 1901 (WC).
The Rhodes memorial at Oxford: the work of Cecil Rhodes—a sonnet sequence. [1907].
Rossetti and Charles Wells: a reminiscence of Kelmscott Manor. In Joseph and his brethren by Charles Wells, Oxford 1908 (WC).
Vesprie towers: a novel. 1916.
Old familiar faces. 1916. Sketches rptd from Athenaeum: Borrow, Rossetti, Tennyson, Christina Rossetti, Gordon Hake, de Tabley, Morris and F. H. Groome.
Poetry and the renascence of wonder: with a preface by Thomas Hake. 1916. Article on Poetry rptd from Encyclopaedia Britannica 1885 (9th edn), on Renascence of wonder from Chambers' cyclopaedia of English literature vol 3, 1901.
Watts-Dunton also contributed an introd to Borrow's Lavengro, 1893, *a defence of Borrow to* Romany Rye, 1900, *and an introd to* Wild Wales, 1906.

§2

Hamelius, J. P. Watts. 1899.
Douglas, J. Watts-Dunton: poet, critic, novelist. 1904.
Hake, T. St E. and A. Compton-Rickett. Life and letters of Watts-Dunton. 1916.
Kernahan, C. In good company. 1917.
Watts-Dunton, C. The home-life of Swinburne. 1922.
Benson, A. C. Watts-Dunton. Life & Letters 8 1932; rptd in English critical essays (twentieth century), Oxford 1933 (WC).
Wright, H. G. Unpublished letters from Watts-Dunton to Swinburne. RES 10 1934.
Curle, R. H. C. Caravansary and conversation. 1937.
Hart, L. In his Reminiscences and reflections, 1939.
Marchand, L. The Athenaeum: a mirror of Victorian culture. Chapel Hill 1941.
— Watts-Dunton letter books. Jnl of Rutgers Univ Lib 17 1953.
Angeli, H. R. Watts-Dunton and Swinburne. TLS 24 March 1950.

SIR FREDERICK WEDMORE
1844-1921

Collections

Pages assembled: a selection from the writings imaginative and critical of Wedmore. 1913.

§1

The two lives of Wilfrid Harris. 1868.
A snapt gold ring. 2 vols 1871.
Two girls. 2 vols 1873.
Studies of English art. 2 sers 1876–80.
Pastorals of France: a last love at Pornic; Yvonne of Croisic; the four bells of Chartres. 1877.
The masters of genre painting: being an introductory handbook to the study of genre painting. 1880.
Four masters of etching; with original etchings by Haden, Jacquemart, Whistler and Legros. 1883.
The pictures of the season. 1883 (2nd edn).
Life of Honoré de Balzac. 1890.
A selection from the Liber studiorum of J. M. W. Turner; with historical introduction by F. Wedmore. In Sir E. J. Poynter, South Kensington drawing-book, [1890].
Renunciations: A chemist in the suburbs; A confidence at the Savile; The north coast; and Eleanor. 1893.
Pastorals of France: Renunciations. 1893.
English episodes. 1894. The vicar of Pimlico; Justice Wilkinshaw's attentions; The fitting obsequies; Katherine in the Temple; The new Marienbad-elegy.
Rembrandt. [1894].
Etching in England. 1895.
Orgeas and Miradou, with other pieces: To Nancy; The poet on the wolds. 1896. Orgeas rptd 1905 as Dream of Provence.
Fine prints. 1897, 1910 (enlarged).
On books and arts. 1899.
Whistler's etchings: a study and a catalogue. 1899.
The collapse of the penitent. 1900.
Cameron's etchings: a study and a catalogue. 1903.
Constable; Lucas; with a descriptive catalogue of the prints they did between them. 1904.
Whistler and others. 1906.
Some of the moderns. 1909. William Nicholson, Théodore Roussel, P. Wilson Steer, Bertram Priestman, Walter Sickert, David Muirhead, Horace Mann Livens, Philip Connard, Muirhead Bone, William Orpen.
Etchings. 1911.
Memories. 1912.
Painters and painting. [1913] (Home Univ Lib).
Brenda walks on. 1916. A novel.
Certain comments, with introductory essays by Sir G. Douglas and G. C. Williamson. 1925.

CHARLES WHIBLEY

1859–1930

§1

The cathedrals of England and Wales. 1888.
A book of scoundrels. 1897.
Studies in frankness. 1898.
The pageantry of life. 1900. Essays.
Musings without method: a record of 1900–1 by Annalist. 1902.
William Makepeace Thackeray. 1903.
Literary portraits. 1904.
William Pitt. 1906.
American sketches. 1908.
The letters of an Englishman. 2 vols 1911–2.
Essays in biography. 1913.
Political portraits. 2 sers 1917–23.
Literary studies. 1919.
Lord John Manners and his friends. 2 vols 1925.
Whibley also edited or introduced some 30 English, French and Latin classics. He was general editor of Tudor translations ser 2 1924–30. *Under the heading* Musings without method, he *contributed a monthly* causerie, *mainly political, to Blackwood's Mag from Feb 1900 to March 1929.*

§2

Whibley. Academy 27 Nov 1897.
Whibley. Blackwood's Mag April 1930.
Obituary. London Mercury April 1930.
Eliot, T. S. Whibley: a memoir. 1931 (English Assoc); rptd in his Selected essays, 1932.
'Connell, John' (J. R. Robertson). In his W. E. Henley, 1949.

OSCAR WILDE

1854–1900

See col 1182, above.

WILLIAM BUTLER YEATS

1865–1939

See col 1915, below.

A. P.

VIII. HISTORY

GENERAL STUDIES

Fueter, E. Die Geschichte der neueren Historiographie. Munich 1911, 1925, 1936 (rev); tr French, 1914.
Gooch, G. P. History and historians in the nineteenth century. 1913, 1952 (rev, with introd).
— Modern historiography. In his Maria Theresa and other studies, 1951.
— Some great English historians. Contemporary Rev Dec 1956–Jan 1957.
Butterfield, H. The Whig interpretation of history. 1931.
— Man on his past: the study of the history of historical scholarship. Cambridge 1955.
Woodward, E. L. Historians of the nineteenth century. In his War and peace in Europe and other essays, 1931.
Peardon, T. P. The transition in English historical writing 1760–1830. New York 1933.
Barnes, H. E. A history of historical writing. Norman Oklahoma 1937, 1938.
Thompson, J. W. and B. J. Holm. A history of historical writing. 2 vols New York 1942.
Neff, E. E. The poetry of history: the contribution of literature and literary scholarship to the writing of history since Voltaire. New York 1947.
Dockhorn, K. Der deutsche Historismus in England: ein Beitrag zur englischen Geistesgeschichte des 19 Jahrhunderts. Ed G. P. Gooch, Göttingen and Baltimore 1950.
Some modern historians of Britain: essays in honor of R. L. Schuyler. Ed H. Ausubel et al, New York 1951.
Wedgwood, C. V. Literature and the historian. 1956.
English historians: selected passages. Ed B. Newman, Oxford 1957.
The evolution of British historiography from Bacon to Namier. Ed J. R. Hale, Cleveland 1964.
Buckley, J. H. The triumph of time: a study of the Victorian concepts of time, history, progress and decadence. Cambridge Mass 1966.

HENRY HALLAM
1777–1859

§1

View of the state of Europe during the Middle Ages. 2 vols 1818, 3 vols 1819, 4 vols Philadelphia 1821, 2 vols Paris 1835, 3 vols 1837 (7th edn), 2 vols Paris 1840, London 1846 (9th edn), 3 vols 1853, 1855; ed W. Smith, New York 1871, 1880; ed G. L. Burr 2 vols New York 1899; ed A. R. Marsh, New York 1900 (as History of Europe during the Middle Ages); tr French, 1820–2; Italian, 1874. Hallam's Supplemental notes, 1848, were incorporated in 1853 and later edns.

The constitutional history of England from the accession of Henry VII to the death of George I. 2 vols 1827, 3 vols 1829, Boston 1829, London 1832, 2 vols 1846 (5th edn), 3 vols 1854 (7th edn), 1855, 1866 (11th edn); ed W. Smith, New York 1896; ed J. H. Morgan 3 vols 1912, 1930 (EL).

Survey of the principal repositories of the public records: extracted from the proceedings of the commissioners on the public records. 1833. With R. H. Inglis.

Memoir of A. H. Hallam. In Remains in verse and prose of A. H. Hallam, 1834 (priv ptd), 1862, Boston 1863.

Introduction to the literature of Europe in the fifteenth, sixteenth and seventeenth centuries. 4 vols 1837–9, Paris 1839, 2 vols New York 1841, 3 vols 1854 (4th edn), 4 vols 1855, 3 vols 1882; tr French, 1839–40.

§2

Southey, R. Hallam's Europe during the Middle Ages. Quart Rev 30 1818; rptd in his Essays moral and political, 1832.

Macaulay, T. B. Hallam's Constitutional history. Edinburgh Rev 48 1828; rptd in his Critical and historical essays, 1843.

Wordsworth, C. King Charles the first the author of Icon Basilike: in reply to Mr Hallam. 1828.

[Spalding, W.] Hallam's History of literature. Edinburgh Rev 72 1840.

Hare, J. C. Reply to Mr Hallam's remarks on Luther. In his Vindication of Luther against his recent English assailants, 1855.

[Dallas, E. S.] Hallam. Times 24 Jan 1859.

[Smith, C. C.] Hallam as an historian. North Amer Rev 92 1861.

Mignet, F. A. M. In his Eloges historiques, Paris 1864.

Weston, C. C. In Some modern historians of Britain, ed H. Ausubel, New York 1951.

Gooch, G. P. In his Some great English historians, Contemporary Rev Dec 1956.

Bond, W. H. Henry Hallam, the Times newspaper and Halliwell case. Library 5th ser 18 1963.

HENRY HART MILMAN
1791–1868

§1

Fazio: a tragedy. Oxford 1815, 1816, London 1818 (4 edns), 1821 (with the Belvidere Apollo etc), Baltimore 1833, New York 1846, 1864.

Samor: lord of the bright city. 1818, 1818, New York 1818.

The fall of Jerusalem: a dramatic poem. 1820, 1820, New York 1820, London 1821, 1822, 1853.

The martyr of Antioch: a dramatic poem. 1822.

Belshazzar: a dramatic poem. 1822, Boston 1822.

Anne Boleyn: a dramatic poem. 1826.

The character and conduct of the apostles. Oxford 1827 (Bampton lectures).

The history of the Jews. 3 vols 1829 (anon), 1830, New York 1832, 1841, London 1843, 1863, New York 1864, London 1866 (4th edn); ed A. P. Hayes, Philadelphia 1871; 3 vols 1878, 1880, 1892; ed G. H. Jones 2 vols 1909, 1923, 1930 (EL).

Poetical works of Milman, Bowles, Wilson and Barry Cornwall. Paris 1829.

Nala and Damayanti and other poems, translated from the Sanscrit. Oxford 1835, 1860, 1914; Nala (only) rev M. Williams, Oxford 1879.

The history of the decline and fall of the Roman empire, by Edward Gibbon. 12 vols 1838–9. Ed Milman.

The life of Edward Gibbon with selections from his correspondence. 1839, 1840. Ed Milman.

The history of Christianity from the birth of Christ to the abolition of paganism in the Roman Empire. 3 vols 1840, New York 1841, London 1863 (rev), 1867, New York 1894.

The poetical works of Howitt, Milman and Keats. Philadelphia 1840.

History of Latin Christianity, including that of the Popes to Nicolas V. 6 vols 1854–5, 1857, 9 vols 1864, 1867, 4 vols New York 1889–92, 1903.

Life of Thomas à Becket. New York 1860.

Memoir of Lord Macaulay. 1862, 1862, 1862 (in Macaulay's History of England vol 8); rptd from Proc Royal Soc 11 1862.

The Agamemnon of Aeschylus and the Bacchanals of Euripides. 1865; Bacchanals (only), 1888, rptd in The plays of Euripides, ed V. R. Reynolds 2 vols 1906, 1911, 1934 (EL). Tr Milman.

Annals of St Paul's Cathedral. Ed A. Milman 1868, 1869.

Savonarola, Erasmus and other essays reprinted from the Quarterly Review. Ed A. Milman 1870.

§2

Newman, J. H. Milman's History of Christianity. Br Critic 60 1841; rptd in his Essays critical and historical, 1872.

[Smith, W. H.] Dean Milman. Blackwood's Mag Dec 1868.

Stanley, A. P. The late Dean of St Paul's. Macmillan's Mag Jan 1869.

Green, J. R. Milman's Annals of St Paul's. Saturday Rev 2 Jan 1869; rptd in his Stray studies 2nd ser, 1903.

Milman, A. Milman, Dean of St Paul's: a biographical sketch. 1900.

Lecky, W. E. H. In his Historical and political essays, 1908.

Smyth, C. H. E. Dean Milman. 1949.

Forbes, D. In his Liberal Anglican view of history, Cambridge 1952.

Parker, W. M. Milman and the Quarterly Review. Quart Rev 293 1955.

GEORGE GROTE
1794–1871

§1

Statement of the question of parliamentary reform. 1821.

Analysis of the influence of natural religion on the temporal happiness of mankind, by Philip Beauchamp. 1822, 1875; tr French, 1875. Based on notes by Jeremy Bentham.

Institutions of ancient Greece. Westminster Rev 5 1826. A critique of W. Mitford, History of Greece.

Essentials of parliamentary reform. 1831, 1873 (in Minor works).

Grecian legends and early history. Westminster Rev 39 1843. On B. G. Niebuhr, Griechische Herrengeschichten.

A history of Greece. 12 vols 1845–56, 1854–7 (4th edn), 8 vols 1862, 12 vols 1869, 10 vols 1872, 1888, 12 vols New York 1900; ed A. D. Lindsay 12 vols 1906, 1934 (EL); ed J. M. Mitchell and M. O. B. Caspari 1907 (condensed); tr German, 1850–5; French, 1864–7.
Seven letters on the recent politics of Switzerland. 1847, 1876 (with Letter to A. de Tocqueville).
Plato's doctrine respecting the rotation of the earth and Aristotle's comment upon that doctrine. 1860, 1873 (in Minor works).
Plato and the other companions of Sokrates. 3 vols 1865, 1867, 1874, 4 vols 1885, 1888.
Review of the work of Mr J. S. Mill entitled Examination of Sir William Hamilton's philosophy. 1868 (for 1867), 1873 (in Minor works). Rptd from Westminster Rev 85 1866.
Aristotle. Ed A. Bain and G. C. Robertson 2 vols 1872, 1880 (for 1879).
Poems 1815–23. [1872] (priv ptd).
The minor works of George Grote; with remarks on his intellectual character, writings and speeches by A. Bain. 1873.
Posthumous papers. 1874 (priv ptd).
Fragments on ethical subjects. Ed A. Bain 1876.

§2

Mill, J. S. Grote's History of Greece. Spectator 4 April 1846, 5 June 1847, 3 March 1849.
— Grote's History of Greece vols 1–2. Edinburgh Rev 84 1846.
— Grote's History of Greece vols 9–11. Edinburgh Rev 98 1853; rptd in his Dissertations and discussions, 1868.
— Grote's Aristotle. Fortnightly Rev Jan 1873.
[Milman, H. H.] Grote's History of Greece. Quart Rev 78 1846.
[Smith, W. H.] Grote's Greece. Blackwood's Mag Aug 1847.
[Stanley, A. P.] Grote's History of Greece vols 3–4. Quart Rev 86 1850.
— Grote's Greece vols 4–8. Quart Rev 88 1850.
Schoemann, G. F. Die Verfassungsgeschichte Athens nach Grotes History of Greece. Leipzig 1854.
[Smith, W.] Grote's History of Greece. Quart Rev 99 1856.
— George Grote. Quart Rev 135 1873.
Freeman, E. A. The Athenian democracy. North Br Rev 25 1856; rptd in his Historical essays 2nd ser, 1873.
— Alexander the Great. Edinburgh Rev 105 1857; rptd in his Historical essays 2nd ser, 1873.
Cope, E. M. Plato's Theaetetus and Grote's criticisms. Cambridge 1866.
Grote, H. The personal life of Grote. 1873; tr German, 1874.
Stephen, L. In his English Utilitarians, 1900.
Pringle-Pattison, A. S. In his Philosophical radicals, 1907.
Momigliano, A. Grote and the study of Greek history. 1952.
Clarke, M. L. Grote: a biography. 1962.

THOMAS ARNOLD
1795–1842

§1

Thirteen letters on our social condition. 1822.
Sermons. 3 vols 1829–34; rev J. A. Forster 6 vols 1878.
Thucydides, The history of the Peloponnesian war. 3 vols Oxford 1830–5, 1840–2, 4 vols Oxford 1847–54. Ed Arnold.
Principles of Church reform. 1833 (3 edns), 1833 (4th edn with postscript); ed A. P. Stanley 1845 (in Miscellaneous works, below); ed M. J. Jackson and J. Rogan 1962.
The Oxford malignants and Dr Hampden. Edinburgh Rev 63 1836.
History of Rome. 3 vols 1838–42, Philadelphia 1846, 2 vols New York 1851; vol 3 chs 42–7 ed W. T. Arnold 1886 (as The second Punic war).
Two sermons on the interpretation of prophecy. 1839.
The Christian life: its course, its hindrances and its helps. 1841; ed Jane Arnold Forster 1878 (as vol 4 of Sermons).
Introductory lectures on modern history; with the inaugural lecture. Oxford 1842, 1843, New York 1845, London 1849 (4th edn).
The Christian life: its hopes, its fears and its close. Ed M. Arnold 1842, 1845 (3rd edn); ed J. A. Forster 1878 (as vol 5 of Sermons).
Fragment on the Church. 1844.
Sermons chiefly on the interpretation of scripture. Ed M. Arnold 1845; ed J. A. Forster 1878 (as vol 6 of Sermons).
Sermons preached in the chapel of Rugby School; with an address before confirmation. 1845, New York 1846; ed J. A. Forster 1878 (as vol 2 of Sermons).
History of the later Roman commonwealth. 2 vols 1845, New York 1846, London 1857. Rptd from Encyclopaedia metropolitana, ed E. Smedley 1845.
Miscellaneous works. Ed A. P. Stanley 1845, New York 1845 (with 9 essays added), London 1858 (2nd edn).
Arnold's travelling journals, with extracts from the Life and letters. Ed A. P. Stanley 1852.

§2

[Ward, W. G.] Arnold's Sermons. Br Critic 30 1841.
Stanley, A. P. A sermon preached in the chapel of Rugby School on the death of the Rev Thomas Arnold. Rugby 1842.
— The life and correspondence of Thomas Arnold. 2 vols 1844 (3 edns), New York 1845, London 1852, 1877 (10th edn), 1881; ed J. Fitch 1901; tr German, 1847.
[Greg, W. R.] Arnold's Lectures on modern history. Westminster Rev 39 1843.
Mozley, J. B. In his Essays historical and theological, 1878.
Martineau, J. In his Essays, reviews and addresses, 1890.
[Hutton, R. H.] Dr Arnold after fifty years. Spectator 18 June 1892.
Fitch, J. Thomas and Matthew Arnold and their influence on English education. New York 1899.
Strachey, L. In his Eminent Victorians, 1918.
Campbell, R. J. Thomas Arnold. 1927.
Whitridge, A. Dr Arnold of Rugby. New York 1928.
Bradby, G. F. In his Brontës and other essays, Oxford 1932.
Raven, C. E. In Pillars of the English Church, ed A. C. Deane 1934.
Trilling, L. In his Matthew Arnold, New York 1939, 1955 (corrected).
Paton, J. L. The Thomas Arnold centenary. Contemporary Rev Aug 1942.
Sanders, C. R. Coleridge and the Broad Church movement: studies in Coleridge, Arnold, Hare, Carlyle and Maurice. Durham NC 1942.
Shipton, I. Arnold of Rugby 1842–1942. Nat Rev June 1942.
Willey, B. In his Nineteenth-century studies, 1949.
Forbes, D. In his Liberal Anglican view of history, Cambridge 1952.
Wymer, N. Dr Arnold of Rugby. 1953.
Woodward, F. The doctor's disciples: a study of four pupils of Arnold of Rugby. Oxford 1954.
Barksdale, R. K. Arnold's attitude toward race. Phylon Quart 18 1957.
Christensen, M. A. Arnold's debt to German theologians. MP 55 1957.
Bamford, T. W. Thomas Arnold. 1960.
Jackson, M. J. and J. Rogan. Thomas Arnold. Church Quart Rev 162 1961.

Williamson, E. L. Significant points of comparison between the biblical criticism of Thomas and Matthew Arnold. PMLA 76 1961.
— The liberalism of Arnold: a study of his religious and political writing. University Alabama 1964.
Waller, J. O. Matthew and Thomas Arnold: soteriology. Anglican Theological Rev 44 1962.
Henderson-Howat, G. M. D. Arnold and the teaching of history. Quart Rev 301 1964.
Kerpneck. H. The road to Rugby chapel. UTQ 34 1965.

THOMAS BABINGTON MACAULAY 1st BARON MACAULAY

1800–59

The mss of the diary etc are in the library of Trinity College Cambridge, with annotated edns of the classics and the corrected proofs of the Life of Pitt.

Bibliographies etc

Catalogue of a portion of the library of Macaulay. 1863 (Sotheby's). About 470 other vols, many annotated, are at Wallington Hall, Northumberland.
Bryant, A. Macaulay. 1932. *See* pp. 172–84.
The reader's Macaulay. Ed W. H. French and G. D. Sanders, New York 1936. *See* pp. 21–9.

Collections

Scenes and characters from the writings of Macaulay. New York 1846.
Selections from Macaulay's essays and speeches. 2 vols 1856.
Biographical and historical sketches. New York 1857.
The miscellaneous writings of Lord Macaulay. Ed T. F. Ellis 2 vols 1860, 1865, 1871 (with Speeches), 4 vols 1880 (with Poems), 1 vol 1910, 1958 (EL) (with Lays).
Biographies by Lord Macaulay contributed to the Encyclopaedia Britannica; with extracts from his letters and speeches. Edinburgh 1860.
Oeuvres: traduites par M. G. Guizot. 6 vols Paris 1862–85.
The works of Lord Macaulay, edited by his sister Lady Trevelyan. 8 vols 1866, 1897.
Speeches and poems, with the report and notes on the Indian Criminal Code. 2 vols Boston [1874].
Selections from the writings. Ed G. O. Trevelyan 1876.
Morceaux choisis de l'histoire d'Angleterre et des chants de l'ancienne Rome. Ed W. Battier, Paris 1892.
Works: Albany edition. 12 vols 1898; Whitehall edition, 20 vols New York 1898–1900.
Works. 9 vols 1905–7 (vols 4–8, The history of England, ed T. F. Henderson).
The reader's Macaulay. Ed W. H. French and G. D. Sanders, New York 1936.
Prose and poetry. Ed G. M. Young 1953 (Reynard Lib).

§1

Pompeii: a poem which obtained the Chancellor's Medal 1819. [Cambridge 1819].
Evening: a poem which obtained the Chancellor's Medal 1821. Cambridge 1821.
Ivry. Knight's Quart Mag 1 1823; rptd in Lays, below.
A speech in the House of Commons, March 2 1831, on a bill to amend the representation of the people in England and Wales. 1831.
The speech of T. B. Macaulay on the second reading of the third Reform Bill, 16 December 1831. 1831.
A speech on the second reading of the East India Bill, 10 July 1833. 1833.
The Armada. Friendship's Offering 1833; rptd in Lays, below.

A Penal Code prepared by the Indian Law Commissioners and published by command of the Governor General of India in Council. Calcutta 1837. Compiled by Macaulay with the assistance of C. H. Cameron, J. M. Macleod, G. W. Anderson and F. Millett.
Critical and miscellaneous essays. 3 vols Boston and Philadelphia 1840–1, 5 vols Philadelphia 1841–4. Unauthorized.
Lays of ancient Rome. 1842, 1846 (7th edn), 1847, 1848 (with Ivry and The Armada, above), Leipzig 1851, Philadelphia 1860, 1864, New York 1871, 1881, London 1882, 1884 (3 edns), 1886, 1887, 1888; ed W. J. Rolfe, New York 1888; Glasgow 1889, London 1902, Oxford 1903 (WC), London 1910 (EL); ed G. M. Trevelyan 1928; many school edns, London and New York 1899–1929; tr German, 1853; Italian, 1869, 1918; French, 1892.
Critical and historical essays contributed to the Edinburgh Review. 3 vols 1843, New York 1843, London 1848, 1849 (containing all the essays Macaulay wished to preserve), 1850, 5 vols Leipzig 1850, 3 vols 1853, 2 vols 1854, 5 vols New York 1857, 7 vols New York 1859–61, London 1872; ed G. T. Bettany 1892; 5 vols 1900; ed F. C. Montague 3 vols 1903; ed A. J. Grieve 2 vols 1907 (EL), 2 vols Oxford 1913; ed H. Trevor-Roper 1965; many school edns of one or more essays; tr Italian, 1859–66; French, 1860; Dutch, 1865; Spanish, 1880, 1886–1903; Hebrew, 1944.
Speech in the House of Commons, February 26 1845, on the proposed duties on sugar. Edinburgh 1845.
Speech in the House of Commons, July 9 1845, on the Bill for the abolition of Scottish university tests. Edinburgh 1845; Government plan of education: speech in the House of Commons, April 19 1847, [1847].
The history of England from the accession of James II. Vols 1–2, 1849, Philadelphia 1849, New York 1850; vols 3–4, 1855; vol 5 ed Lady Trevelyan 1861; 10 vols Leipzig 1849–61; 8 vols 1858–62 (with memoir by H. H. Milman); ed S. A. Allibone 5 vols Philadelphia 1875; ed H. D. Sedgwick 10 vols Boston 1899; ed D. Jerrold 3 vols 1906, 1934 (EL); ed C. H. Firth 6 vols 1913–5; ed T. F. Henderson 5 vols Oxford 1931 (WC); many school edns of ch 3; tr Dutch, 1851–3, 1868; Italian, 1852–3; Danish, 1852–8; Hungarian, 1853; Polish, 1854–61; French, 1857–61, 1858; Czech, 1862–5; German, 1863 (5th edn); Finnish, 1866; Greek, 1897–1902; Spanish, 1905–6.
Inaugural address delivered on his installation as Lord Rector of the University of Glasgow. Glasgow 1849, Edinburgh 1849.
Speeches, parliamentary and miscellaneous. 2 vols 1853, 2 vols New York 1853. Unauthorized.
Speeches corrected by himself. 1854, New York 1854, London 1866; ed W. E. Gladstone 1909, 1924 (EL); ed G. M. Young, Oxford 1935 (WC); tr German, 1854; Spanish, 1885–1902.
The Indian Civil Service. 1855. A report by Macaulay, Ashburton, Jowett et al.
The Indian education minutes of Lord Macaulay. Ed H. Woodrow, Calcutta 1862.
Hymn by Lord Macaulay: an effort of his early childhood. Ed L. Horton-Smith, Cambridge 1902.
Marginal notes. Ed G. O. Trevelyan 1907.
Essay and speech on Jewish disabilities. Ed I. Abrahams and S. Levy, Edinburgh 1910, 1920.
Lord Macaulay's legislative minutes. Ed C. D. Dharker, Madras 1946.

Letters

Were human sacrifices in use among the Romans? correspondence between Mr Macaulay, Sir Robert Peel and Lord Mahon. 1860 (priv ptd); in Earl Stanhope, Miscellanies, 2 vols 1863–72; ed T. Thayer 1878 (priv ptd) (as Some inquiries concerning human sacrifice among the Romans).

Correspondence between the Bishop of Exeter and Macaulay in January 1849 on certain statements respecting the Church of England. 1860.
Selection from the correspondence of Macvey Napier, edited by his son. 1879. Letters to the editor of the Edinburgh Rev.
What did Macaulay say about America? Ed H. M. Lydenberg, New York 1925. 4 letters to H. S. Randall.
See G. O. Trevelyan, 1876, below.

§2

[Croker, J. W.] Noctes ambrosianae. Blackwood's Mag Nov 1831. A defence of Croker's edn of Boswell against Macaulay, the material supplied by Croker.
— The French Revolution. Quart Rev 46 1832. An attack on Macaulay's speeches.
— Macaulay's History of England. Quart Rev 84 1849.
Mahon, Lord (later Earl Stanhope). Lord John Russell and Mr Macaulay on the French Revolution. 1833. Rptd from Quart Rev 49 1833.
Montagu, B. Letters to Macaulay upon the review of the life of Lord Bacon. 1841.
Wilson, J. Lays of ancient Rome. Blackwood's Mag Dec 1842; rptd in his Essays critical and imaginative, Edinburgh 1866.
[Mill, J. S.] Macaulay's Lays. Westminster Rev 39 1843.
Horne, R. H. In his A new spirit of the age, 1844.
Spedding, J. Evenings with a reviewer: or a free and particular examination of Mr Macaulay's article on Lord Bacon. 2 vols 1848 (priv ptd); ed G. S. Venables 2 vols 1881.
Babington, C. Macaulay's character of the clergy in the seventeenth century considered. Cambridge 1849.
Forster, W. E. William Penn and Macaulay. Philadelphia 1850. Originally pbd as preface to T. Clarkson, Memoirs of William Penn, 1849.
Fairbairn, H. A defence of William Penn from the charges contained in the History of England by Macaulay. 1849.
Alison, A. Macaulay's History of England. Blackwood's Mag April 1849; rptd in his Essays political, historical and miscellaneous, 1850.
Dixon, W. H. William Penn: an historical biography with an extra chapter on the Macaulay charges. 1851, 1856 (rev).
[Dallas, E. S.] Macaulay's History of England. Times 17–18 Dec 1855, 11 Jan 1856.
— Macaulay. Times 1 Sept 1856.
— The late Lord Macaulay. Times 31 Dec 1859.
Bagehot, W. Macaulay. Nat Rev 2 1856; rptd in his Literary studies, ed R. H. Hutton 1879.
Devon, F. Vindication of the first Lord Dartmouth from the charge of conspiracy or high treason revived by Macaulay. 1856.
Miller, Hugh. Macaulay on Scotland: a critique. 1857.
Letters of Hannah More to Zachary Macaulay containing notices of Lord Macaulay's youth. Ed A. Roberts 1860.
Lancaster, H. H. Macaulay's place in English literature. North Br Rev 33 1860; rptd in his Essays and reviews, 1876.
[Stephen, J. F.] Macaulay. Saturday Rev 7 Jan 1860.
Thackeray, W. M. Nil nisi bonum. Cornhill Mag Feb 1860; rptd in his Roundabout papers, 1863.
Maurice, F. D. Macaulay. Macmillan's Mag Feb 1860.
Paget, J. The new examen: or an inquiry into the evidence relating to certain passages in Macaulay's history. Edinburgh 1861, 1934; rptd in his Paradoxes and puzzles, Edinburgh 1874.
Rowntree, J. S. An inquiry into the truthfulness of Lord Macaulay's portraiture of George Fox, in two lectures. York 1861.
Milman, H. H. Memoir of Macaulay. 1862. First pbd in Proc Royal Soc 11 1862.
Arnold, F. The public life of Macaulay. 1862.
Mignet, F. A. M. In his Eloges historiques, Paris 1864.
Stirling, J. H. Jerrold, Tennyson and Macaulay; with other critical essays. Edinburgh 1868.
Martineau, H. In her Biographical sketches, 1869.
Trevelyan, G. O. The life and letters of Macaulay. 2 vols 1876, New York 1876 (with appendix, Macaulay on American institutions), Leipzig 1876, London 1877 (rev), New York 1877, London 1878, 1 vol 1881, 2 vols Chicago 1885, 1 vol 1889, 1908 ('enlarged'), 1913; ed G. M. Trevelyan 2 vols Oxford 1932 (WC); 1 vol 1959, 2 vols Oxford 1961; tr Spanish (in part), 1899; P. Clarke, Index to Trevelyan's Life and letters of Macaulay, 1881.
Morley, J. Macaulay. Fortnightly Rev April 1876; rptd in his Critical miscellanies, 1877.
Froude, J. A. Macaulay. Fraser's Mag June 1876.
Gladstone, W. E. Macaulay. Quart Rev 142 1876; rptd in his Gleanings of past years, 1879.
Freeman, E. A. Macaulay. International Rev 3 1876.
Punshon, W. M. Macaulay. 1876.
Stephen, L. In his Hours in a library ser 3, 1879.
Kinkel, J. G. Macaulay: sein Leben und sein Geschichtswerk. Basle 1879.
Jones, C. H. Macaulay. New York [1880], 1901.
Canning, A. S. G. Macaulay: essayist and historian. 1882, [1913] (rev).
Morison, J. C. Macaulay. 1882 (EML).
Barbey d'Aurevilly, J. In his Littérature étrangère, Paris 1891.
Harrison, F. Macaulay's place in literature. Forum Sept 1894; rptd in his Studies in early Victorian literature, 1895.
Saintsbury, G. In his Corrected impressions, 1895.
Sedgwick, H. D. The vitality of Macaulay. Atlantic Monthly Aug 1899; rptd in his Essays on great writers, Boston 1903.
Jebb, R. C. Macaulay: a lecture. Cambridge 1900; rptd in his Essays and addresses, Cambridge 1907.
Paul, H. Macaulay and his critics. Anglo-Saxon Rev 4 1900; rptd in his Men and letters, 1901.
Bülow, G. Macaulay: sein Leben und seine Werke. Schweidnitz 1901.
Brownell, W. C. In his Victorian prose masters, New York 1901.
Macgregor, D. H. Lord Macaulay. 1901.
[Dicey, A. V.] Macaulay and his critics. Nation (New York) 15 May 1902.
Dawson, W. J. In his Makers of English prose, New York 1906.
Strachey, L. Macaulay's marginalia. Spectator 16 Nov 1907; rptd in his Spectatorial essays, 1964.
— In his Portraits in miniature, 1931.
Courthope, W. J. A consideration of Macaulay's comparison of Dante and Milton. Proc Br Acad 3 1908.
Roome, H. D. Two historians of the eighteenth century. Fortnightly Rev Nov 1909. On Macaulay and Lecky.
Thayer, W. R. Macaulay fifty years after. North Amer Rev 190 1909.
Trevelyan, G. M. In his Clio: a muse, 1913.
— Macaulay and the sense of optimism. Listener 12 Feb 1948.
Kellett, E. E. Macaulay's lay figures. Br Rev May 1914; rptd in his Suggestions, Cambridge 1923.
— Macaulay and the Authorized Version. London Quart Rev 148 1927; rptd in his Reconsiderations, Cambridge 1928.
— Macaulay's History. London Quart Rev 163 1938.
Chesterton, C. The art of controversy: Macaulay, Huxley and Newman. Catholic World July 1917.
Hassard, A. R. A new light on Lord Macaulay. Toronto 1918.
Williams, S. T. Macaulay's reading and literary criticism. PQ 3 1924.
Sampson, G. Macaulay and Milton. Edinburgh Rev 242 1925.

Roberts, S. C. Macaulay: the pre-eminent Victorian. 1927 (Eng Assoc); rptd in his An eighteenth-century gentleman and other essays, 1930.
Alston, D. Some personal recollections of Macaulay. London Mercury May 1928. Reminiscences by Henry Thornton.
Wells, J. Macaulay as a man of letters. Fortnightly Rev Oct 1928.
Abbott, W. C. Macaulay and the new history. Yale Rev 18 1929.
— Macaulay, historian. In his Adventures in reputation, Cambridge 1935.
Carver, P. L. The sources of Macaulay's essay on Milton. RES 6 1930.
Fisher, H. A. L. The Whig historians. In his Pages from the past, Oxford 1931.
Walcha, G. Macaulay als Geschichtschreiber. Leipzig 1931.
Bryant, A. Macaulay. 1932.
Willoughby, D. In Great Victorians, ed H. J. and H. Massingham 1932.
Dobrée, B. Macaulay. Criterion 12 1933.
Rolfe, J. C. Macaulay's Lays of ancient Rome. Classical Jnl May 1934.
le Breton, M. Edgar Poe et Macaulay. Revue Anglo-américaine 13 1935.
Davies, H. S. Macaulay's marginalia to Lucretius. In Lucretius, De rerum natura, tr R. C. Trevelyan, Cambridge 1937.
Young, G. M. In his Daylight and champaign, 1937; rptd in his Victorian essays, 1962.
Firth, C. H. A commentary on Macaulay's History of England. Ed G. Davies 1938, 1964.
Beatty, R. C. Lord Macaulay: Victorian liberal. Norman Oklahoma 1938.
Davies, G. The treatment of constitutional history in Macaulay's History of England. HLQ 2 1939.
Monroe, D. Macaulay: the study of an historian. Queen's Quart 46 1939.
— Macaulay: the last of the Whigs. Dalhousie Rev 19 1940.
Clark, H. H. The vogue of Macaulay in America. Trans Wisconsin Acad of Sciences, Arts & Letters 24 1942.
Templeman, W. D. Arnold's The literary influence of academies, Macaulay and Espinasse. SP 43 1946.
Bandy, W. T. Macaulay and his Italian translator: Paolo Emiliani-Giudici. Italica 25 1948.
Horn, R. D. Addison's Campaign and Macaulay. PMLA 63 1948.
Schuyler, R. L. Macaulay and his History a hundred years after. Political Science Quart 63 1948.
Carleton, W. G. Macaulay and the trimmers. Amer Scholar 19 1949.
Jones, F. L. Macaulay's theory of poetry in his Milton. MLQ 13 1952.
Geyl, P. Macaulay in his essays. In his From Ranke to Toynbee, Northampton Mass 1952; rptd in his Debates with historians, New York 1955.
St Aubyn, G. Macaulay. 1952.
Cutts, E. H. The background of Macaulay's Minute. Amer Hist Rev 58 1953.
Gooch, G. P. In his Some great English historians, Contemporary Rev Dec 1956.
Plumb, J. H. Macaulay. UTQ 26 1956; rptd in his Men and places, 1963.
Taylor, A. J. P. Macaulay and Carlyle. In his Englishmen and others, 1956.
Trevor-Roper, H. R. Macaulay and the Glorious Revolution. In his Men and events, 1957.
— Macaulay. Listener 14 Oct 1965.
Williams, C. In his Image of the city, 1958.
Wood, M. Macaulay, parliamentary speaker: his leading ideas. Quart Jnl of Speech 5 1958.
Browning, A. Macaulay 1800–59. Hist Jnl 1 1959.

de Beer, E. S. Macaulay and Croker. RES new ser 10 1959.
Hartley, A. Macaulay 1800–59. Manchester Guardian Weekly 31 Dec 1959.
Luciani, F. Macaulay nel centenario del morte. Idea 17 1959.
Potter, G. R. Macaulay. 1959.
Stokes, E. In his English Utilitarians and India, Oxford 1959.
— Macaulay: the Indian years. REL 1 1960.
Thomson, M. A. Macaulay. 1959 (Historical Assoc).
Cranston, M. Macaulay after a hundred years. Listener 7 Jan 1960.
Knowles, D. Macaulay 1800–59. Cambridge 1960. A centenary lecture.
Fraser, G. S. Macaulay's style as an essayist. REL 1 1960.
Clive, J. Macaulay's historical imagination. Ibid.
Wedgwood, C. V. Macaulay's Lays. Ibid.
Angus-Butterworth, L. M. In his Ten master historians, Aberdeen 1961.
Lowenthal, D. Macaulay and the freedom of the press. Amer Political Science Rev 57 1963.
Strawson, J. M. Macaulay as a military historian. Army Quart & Defence Jnl 86 1963.
Yoder, A. M. Macaulay revisited. South Atlantic Quart 63 1964.
Griffin, J. R. The intellectual milieu of Macaulay. Ottawa 1964.
Lamont, W. M. Macaulay, the Archbishop and the Civil War. History Today Nov 1964.
Chamberlin, W. H. The magnificent middlebrow. Saturday Rev 9 Oct 1965.
Munby, A. N. L. Macaulay's library. Glasgow 1966 (Murray Lecture).
Valenti, J. Macaulay and his critics. Saturday Rev 30 April 1966.

JAMES ANTHONY FROUDE
1818–94

§1

St Neot. In Lives of the English saints, 4 vols 1844–5; ed A. W. Hutton 6 vols 1900–1. Ser suggested by J. H. Newman.
Shadows of the clouds, by Zeta. 1847.
A sermon preached at St Mary Church on the death of the Rev George May Coleridge. Torquay 1847.
The nemesis of faith. 1848, 1849, New York 1879, London 1892, 1903.
England's forgotten worthies. Westminster Rev 58 1852.
The book of Job. 1854. Rptd from Westminster Rev 60 1853.
Suggestions on the best means of teaching English history. In Oxford essays by members of the University, Oxford 1855.
History of England from the fall of Wolsey to the death of Elizabeth. 12 vols 1856–70 (vols 1–2 rev 1858; vols 1–4, 7–8 rev 1862–4), 2 vols New York 1867–8, 12 vols New York 1869–71, London 1870 (as History of England from the fall of Wolsey to the defeat of the Spanish Armada), New York 1870, 1872, London 1875, 1881, 1893, New York 1899; ed W. L. Williams 10 vols 1909–1912 (EL).
The Edinburgh Review and Mr Froude's History. Fraser's Mag Sept 1858.
The pilgrim: a dialogue on the life and actions of King Henry the eighth, by William Thomas. 1861. Ed Froude.
Short studies on great subjects. 2 vols 1867, New York 1868, London 1872; ed H. Belloc 1915 (EL); Oxford 1924 (WC); Second series, 1871, New York 1872; Third series, 1877, New York 1882; Fourth series, 1883, New York 1883. Collected 3 vols 1877 (with

preface), New York 1878, 4 vols 1883, New York 1883, 5 vols 1907.
Inaugural address delivered to the University of St Andrews 19 March 1869. 1869.
The cat's pilgrimage. Edinburgh 1870; ed O. Maurer, New Haven 1949.
Calvinism: an address delivered to the University of St Andrews 17 March 1871. 1871.
The English in Ireland in the eighteenth century. 3 vols 1872–4, New York 1873–4, London 1881, New York 1888.
The life and times of Thomas Becket. New York 1878. Rptd from Nineteenth Century June–Nov 1877.
Caesar: a sketch. 1879, New York 1879, London 1880, New York 1884, London 1894, New York 1895, London 1903, 1937; tr Czech, 1884.
Science and theology ancient and modern. Toronto 1879, New York 1880 (in Theological unrest: discussions in science and religion).
Bunyan. 1880 (EML), New York 1880, London 1884, New York 1887, London 1894, New York 1895, London 1905.
Two lectures on South Africa delivered before the Philosophical Institute. Edinburgh 1880; ed M. Froude 1900.
Thomas Carlyle, Reminiscences. 2 vols 1881. Ed Froude.
Thomas Carlyle: a history of the first forty years of his life 1795–1835. 2 vols 1882, 1882, New York 1882, 1 vol New York 1882, 2 vols 1890, 1891; tr German, 1886.
Luther: a short biography. 1883, 1884, New York 1884.
Memorials of Jane Welsh Carlyle, prepared for publication by Thomas Carlyle. 3 vols 1883. Ed Froude.
Historical and other sketches. Ed D. H. Wheeler, New York 1883.
Thomas Carlyle: a history of his life in London 1834–81. 2 vols 1884, 1884, New York 1884, London 1890; tr German, 1886.
Oceana: or England and her colonies. 1886, 1887, New York 1887.
The Knights Templars. New York 1886.
My relations with Carlyle: together with a letter from the late Sir James Stephen. 1886; ed A. A. Froude and M. Froude 1903, 1903, New York 1903.
The English in the West Indies: or the bow of Ulysses. 1888, 1900, New York 1900.
Liberty and property: an address to the Liberty and Property Defence. 1888.
The two chiefs of Dunboy: or an Irish romance of the last century. 1889, New York 1889.
Lord Beaconsfield. 1890, New York 1890, London 1905 (9th edn); 1906, 1931 (EL).
The divorce of Catherine of Aragon: being a supplement to the History of England. 1891, New York 1891.
The Spanish story of the Armada and other essays. 1892, New York 1892, London 1896.
Life and letters of Erasmus. 1893, 1894, New York 1894; tr Dutch, 1896.
Lectures on the Council of Trent. 1893, 1896, New York 1896.
English seamen in the sixteenth century. 1895, New York 1895, 1901; ed A. A. Froude 1923, 1925.
Selected essays. Ed H. G. Rawlinson 1900.
The dissolution of the monasteries and other essays. 1905.
A siding at a railway station: an allegory. 1905.
Letters of J. A. Froude. Ed R. M. Bennett, Jnl Rutgers Univ Lib 11–12 1947–8, 25–6 1961–2.

§2

[Kingsley, C.] Froude's History of England. North Br Rev 26 1856.
—— Froude's History. Macmillan's Mag Jan 1864.
Maurice, F. D. Froude's History. Macmillan's Mag Aug 1860.
[Dallas, E. S.] Froude's History. Times 31 Aug–1 Sept 1860.
[Freeman, E. A.] Saturday Rev 16–30 Jan 1864, 27 Oct, 3, 24 Nov, 1 Dec 1866, 22–9 Jan, 5–12 Feb 1870, 8, 29 Sept 1877. Attacks on Froude's History.
—— Mr Froude's Life and times of Thomas Becket. Contemporary Rev March–April, June 1878. Reply by Froude, A few words on Mr Freeman, Nineteenth Century April 1879. Rejoinder by Freeman, Last words on Mr Froude, Contemporary Rev May 1879.
[Oliphant, M. W.] Mr Froude and Queen Mary. Blackwood's Mag Jan 1870.
Thumping English lies: Froude's slanders on Ireland and Irishmen. New York 1872.
Meline, J. F. Mary Queen of Scots and her latest English historian. New York 1872.
Cairns, J. E. Froude's English in Ireland. Fortnightly Rev Aug 1874.
Harrison, F. Froude's Life of Carlyle. North Amer Rev 140 1885; rptd in his Choice of books and other essays, 1886.
—— The historical method of Froude. Nineteenth Century Sept 1898; rptd in his Tennyson, Ruskin, Mill and other literary estimates, 1899.
Strachey, St Loe. Mr Froude. Spectator 27 Oct 1894.
Smith, Goldwin. Froude. North Amer Rev 159 1894.
—— Froude as a historian. Atlantic Monthly May 1906.
Fisher, H. A. L. Modern historians and their methods. Fortnightly Rev Dec 1894.
Skelton, J. Reminiscences of Froude. Blackwood's Mag Dec 1894–Jan 1895; rptd in his Table talk of Shirley: reminiscences of and letters from Froude, Edinburgh 1895.
[Doyle, J. A.] Freeman, Froude and Seeley. Quart Rev 182 1895.
Wilson, D. A. Mr Froude and Carlyle. 1898.
—— The truth about Carlyle. 1913.
Stephen, L. In his Studies of a biographer, 1902.
Crichton-Browne, J. The nemesis of Froude. 1903. A reply to Froude's My relations with Carlyle, above.
Paul, H. The life of Froude. 1905.
McNeill, R. Froude and Freeman. Monthly Rev Feb 1906.
Dawson, W. J. In his Makers of English prose, New York 1906.
Cecil, A. In his Six Oxford thinkers,1909.
Hone, J. M. The imperialism of Froude. New Statesman 1 June 1918.
Stewart, H. L. Froude and Anglo-Catholicism. Amer Jnl of Theology 22 1918.
Birrell, A. In his Collected essays and addresses, 1922.
Dunn, W. H. Froude and Carlyle: a study of the Froude–Carlyle controversy. New York 1930.
—— Froude: a biography. 2 vols Oxford 1961–3.
Clarke, F. Froude. London Mercury Aug 1930.
Strachey, L. One of the Victorians. Saturday Rev of Lit 6 Dec 1930; rptd in his Characters and commentaries, 1933.
Fish, A. The reputation of Froude. Pacific Historical Rev 1 1932.
Krieger, H. Die Bedeutung des Organischen im englischen Volks- und Staatsbegriff (Burke, Freeman, Seeley, Froude). Die Neueren Sprachen Jan 1938.
Bolitho, H. and J. Mulgan. The emigrants: early travellers to the Antipodes. 1939.
Harrison, A. W. Mark Rutherford and Froude. London Quart Rev 164 1939.
Emden, C. S. Mark Pattison and Froude. In his Oriel papers, Oxford 1948.
Maurer, O. Froude and Fraser's Magazine 1860–74. SE 28 1949.
Reynolds, B. In Some modern historians of Britain, ed H. Ausubel, New York 1951.
Badger, K. The ordeal of Froude, Protestant historian. MLQ 13 1952.

Murphy, H. R. The ethical revolt against Christian orthodoxy in early Victorian England. Amer Historical Rev 60 1955.
Gooch, G. P. In his Some great English historians, Contemporary Rev Dec 1956.
Willey, B. In his More nineteenth-century studies, 1956.
Rollins, H. E. Charles Eliot Norton and Froude. JEGP 57 1958.
Angus-Butterworth, L. M. In his Ten master historians, Aberdeen 1961.

HENRY THOMAS BUCKLE
1821–62

§1

History of civilization in England. 2 vols 1857–61, 1858–64, New York 1860–2, 3 vols 1866, 1867, 1868, 1869, 1871, 1873, 2 vols New York 1876, 3 vols 1878, 2 vols New York 1883, 3 vols 1885, 2 vols New York 1897, 3 vols 1903–4, Oxford 1931 (WC); ed J. M. Robertson 1904, 1925; ed A. Brisbane 4 vols New York 1913; tr German, 1860; Russian, 1862–4, 1895; Spanish, 1862; French, 1865; Hungarian, 1873–5; Hebrew, 1901.
The influence of women on the progress of knowledge. Fraser's Mag April 1858; tr Dutch, 1872.
Mill on liberty. Fraser's Mag May 1859.
A letter to a gentleman respecting Pooley's case. 1859.
Essays; with a biographical sketch of the author. Leipzig 1867, New York 1877; tr Russian, 1867.
Miscellaneous and posthumous works. Ed H. Taylor 3 vols 1872, 2 vols New York 1873; ed G. Allen 2 vols 1885 (abridged); ed J. M. Robertson 1904.

§2

Droysen, J. G. Grundriss der Historik. Berlin 1857; tr 1895.
[Pattison, M.] Buckle's History. Westminster Rev 68 1857; rptd in his Essays, ed H. Nettleship 1889.
S[andars], T. C. Buckle's History. Fraser's Mag Oct 1857.
— Buckle's History. Saturday Rev 11 July 1857.
[Stephen, J. F.] Buckle's History. Edinburgh Rev 107 1858.
[Pollock, W. F.] Buckle's History. Quart Rev 104 1858.
[Smith, W. H.] Buckle's History. Blackwood's Mag Nov 1858.
Coleridge, J. D. Mr Buckle and Sir John Coleridge. Fraser's Mag June 1859.
[Dallas, E. S.] Buckle's new volume. Times 20, 22–3 Aug 1861.
L[ewes]. G. H. Mr Buckle's scientific errors. Blackwood's Mag Nov 1861.
Froude, J. A. The science of history. In his Short studies, 1867.
[Macdonell, J.] The natural history of morals. North Br Rev 47 1867.
Etienne, L. Le positivisme dans l'histoire. Revue des Deux Mondes 15 March 1868.
Stirling, J. H. Buckle: his problem and his metaphysics. North Amer Rev 115 1872.
— Mr Buckle and the Aufklärung. Jnl of Speculative Philosophy 9 1875.
[Dicey, A. V.] Buckle. Nation (New York) 17 April 1873.
[Wedgwood, J.] Buckle. Spectator 30 Oct 1875.
Huth, A. H. The life and writings of Buckle. 2 vols 1880, New York 1880.
Stephen, L. An attempted philosophy of history. Fortnightly Rev May 1880.
Simcox, G. A. Buckle. Fortnightly Rev Feb 1880.
Benn, A. W. Buckle and the economics of knowledge. Mind 6 1881.
Robertson, J. M. Buckle and his critics. 1895.
Clarke, J. F. In his Nineteenth-century questions, Boston 1900.
Fraenkel, F. Buckle und seine Geschichtsphilosophie. Berner Studien zur Philosophie 50 1906.
Helmecke, C. A. Buckle's influence on Strindberg. Philadelphia 1924.
Wells, G. A. The critics of Buckle. Past & Present no 9 1956.
St Aubyn, G. A Victorian eminence: the life and works of Buckle. 1958.

SIR HENRY JAMES SUMNER MAINE
1822–88

§1

Memoir of Henry Fitzmaurice Hallam. [1851], 1862 (in Remains in verse and prose of A. H. Hallam). With F. Lushington.
Roman law and legal education. 1856 (in Cambridge essays), 1876 (in Village-communities, 3rd edn).
Ancient law: its connection with the early history of society and its relation to modern ideas. 1861, New York 1864, 1885 (10th edn); ed T. W. Dwight, New York 1888; London 1894 (15th edn), 1897 (16th edn); ed F. Pollock 1906, 1907, 1930; ed J. H. Morgan 1917, 1930, 1960 (EL); ed C. K. Allen, Oxford 1931 (WC); tr Russian, 1873; Hungarian, 1875; Chinese, 1959.
Village-communities in the east and west. 1871, 1876 (3rd edn with lectures, addresses, essays), 1895 (7th edn).
The early history of the property of married women: a lecture. [1873].
Lectures on the early history of institutions. 1875, New York 1888, 1893 (6th edn), 1897 (7th edn).
The effects of observation of India on modern European thought (Rede lecture 1875). 1875, 1876 (in Village-communities, 3rd edn).
The King in his relation to early civil justice. Proc Royal Inst 9 1882.
Dissertations on early law and custom. 1883, 1890; tr French, 1884; Russian, 1884; Spanish, c. 1885.
Popular government: four essays. 1885, New York 1888, London 1909; tr Spanish, 1888.
India. In The reign of Queen Victoria, ed T. H. Ward 1887.
International law (Whewell lectures 1888). 1888, New York 1889, London 1894; tr French, 1890.
Minutes 1862–9: with a note on Indian codification. Calcutta 1892.

§2

Mill, J. S. Mr Maine on village communities. Fortnightly Rev May 1871.
Benn, A. W. Maine's Popular government. Academy 7 Nov 1885.
[Dicey, A. V.] Maine's Popular government. Nation (New York) 25 March–1 April 1886.
Morley, J. Maine on popular government. Fortnightly Rev Feb 1886; rptd in his Oracles on man and government, 1923.
[Stephen, J. F.] Sir Henry Maine. Saturday Rev 11 Feb 1888.
Pollock, F. Maine and his work. Contemporary Rev Feb 1889; rptd in his Oxford lectures, 1890.
Grant Duff, M. E. Maine: a brief memoir with some of his Indian speeches and minutes. Ed W. Stokes 1892.
[Lyall, A.] Sir Henry Maine. Quart Rev 176 1893.
Wilson, Woodrow. A lawyer with a style. Atlantic Monthly Sept 1898.
Vinogradoff, P. The teaching of Maine. 1904.
Holdsworth, W. S. In his Historians of Anglo-American law, New York 1928.

— In his Some makers of English law, Cambridge 1938.
Smellie, K. B. Sir Henry Maine. Economica 8 1928.
Lippincott, B. E. In his Victorian critics of democracy, Minneapolis 1938.
Redfield, R. Maine's Ancient law in the light of primitive societies. Western Political Quart 3 1950.
Thorner, D. In Some modern historians of Britain, ed H. Ausubel, New York 1951.
Roach, J. Liberalism and the Victorian intelligentsia. Cambridge Historical Jnl 13 1957.

EDWARD AUGUSTUS FREEMAN

1823–92

Bibliographies

Stephens, W. R. W. The life and letters of Freeman. 2 vols 1895. *See* vol 2 pp. 481–91.

§1

Principles of church restoration. 1846.
Thoughts on the study of history with reference to the proposed changes in the public examinations. Oxford 1849.
A history of architecture. 1849.
Poems: legendary and historical. 1850. With G. W. Cox.
Remarks on the architecture of Llandaff Cathedral, with an essay towards the history of the fabric. 1850.
An essay on the origin and development of window tracery in England. Oxford 1851.
The preservation and restoration of ancient monuments. Oxford 1852.
Suggestions with regard to certain proposed changes in the University and colleges of Oxford. Oxford 1854. With F. H. Dickinson.
The history and antiquities of St David's. 1856. With W. B. Jones.
The history and conquests of the Saracens: six lectures. Oxford 1856, 1876, 1876.
Ancient Greece and mediaeval Italy. In Oxford essays by members of the University, Oxford 1857.
The parish church and priory. In G. F. Townsend, The town and borough of Leominster, Leominster [1863].
History of federal government: general introduction; history of the Greek federations. 1863; ed J. B. Bury 1893 (as History of federal government in Greece and Italy).
Froude's History of England. Saturday Rev 16–30 Jan 1864, 27 Oct, 3, 24 Nov, 1 Dec 1866, 22–9 Jan, 5–12 Feb 1870, 8, 29 Sept 1877. Anon.
The history of the Norman Conquest of England; its causes and its results. 6 vols Oxford 1867–79, vols 1–3 1870–5 (2nd edn), 6 vols New York 1873–80, vols 1–2 Oxford 1877 (3rd edn).
Old English history for children. 1869, 1881, 1892 (9th edn), 1911 (EL).
History of the Cathedral Church of Wells. 1870.
Historical essays. 1871, 1896 (5th edn); Historical essays: second series, 1873, 1880, 1889; Historical essays: third series, 1879; Historical essays: fourth series, 1892.
The growth of the English constitution from the earliest times. 1872, 1894, 1898; tr French, 1877; Hungarian, 1893.
General sketch of European history. 1872, 1873 (3rd edn), New York 1874, London 1905 (5th edn), 1910; tr Spanish, 1885.
The unity of history (Rede lecture 1872). 1872, 1873 (with Comparative politics, below).
The cathedral churches of the old foundation. In Essays on cathedrals, ed J. S. Howson 1872.
Comparative politics. 1873 (with The unity of history, above), 1896.
Disestablishment and disendowment: what are they? 1874, 1885.
History of Europe. 1876, 1877, 1884, New York 1884; ed F. J. C. Hearnshaw 1926; tr French, 1929.
Historical and architectural sketches, chiefly Italian. 1876.
The eastern question in its historical bearings: an address. Manchester 1876.
The Ottoman power in Europe. 1877, New York 1877.
The Turks in Europe. 1877, New York 1877.
Mr Froude's Life and times of Thomas Becket. Contemporary Rev March–April, June 1878. Reply by Froude, A few words on Mr Freeman, Nineteenth Century April 1879; rejoinder by Freeman, Last words on Mr Froude, Contemporary Rev May 1879.
The origin of the English nation. New York 1879.
How the study of history is let and hindered: an address [1879].
A short history of the Norman Conquest of England. Oxford 1880, 1896, 1901.
Sketches from the subject and neighbour lands of Venice. 1881.
The historical geography of Europe. 2 vols 1881, 1882; ed J. B. Bury 2 vols 1903.
Lectures to American audiences. Philadelphia 1882.
The reign of William Rufus and the accession of Henry the first. 2 vols Oxford 1882.
Some impressions of the United States. 1883.
An introduction to American institutional history. Johns Hopkins Univ Stud in Historical & Political Science 1 1883.
English towns and districts: addresses and sketches. 1883.
Farren, R. Cathedral cities: Ely and Norwich. Cambridge 1883.
— Cathedral cities: York, Lincoln and Beverley. Cambridge 1896. Introds by Freeman.
The office of the historical professor: inaugural lecture. 1884, 1886 (with The methods of historical study).
The methods of historical study. 1886; tr Russian, 1893; Hungarian, 1895.
The chief periods of European history: six lectures with an essay on Greek cities under Roman rule. 1886.
Greater Greece and greater Britain; George Washington the expander of England: two lectures. 1886.
Exeter. 1887 (Historic Towns ser).
Four Oxford lectures 1887: Fifty years of European history; Teutonic conquest in Gaul and Britain. 1888.
William the Conqueror. 1888, 1894; ed H. Ketcham, New York 1902.
Sketches from French travel. Leipzig 1891.
The history of Sicily from the earliest times. 4 vols Oxford 1891–4; tr German, 1895–1901. Vol 4 ed A. J. Evans.
Sicily: Phoenician, Greek and Roman. 1892.
The physical and political bases of national unity. In Britannic federation, ed A. S. White 1892.
Studies of travel: Greece, Italy. 2 vols New York [1893].
Sketches of travel in Normandy and Maine. Ed W. H. Hutton 1897.
Western Europe in the fifth century: an aftermath. 1904.
Western Europe in the eighth century and onward: an aftermath. 1904.

§2

[Carnarvon, Lord]. Freeman's Norman Conquest. Quart Rev 123 1867.
Green, J. R. Freeman's Norman Conquest. Saturday Rev 13, 27 April 1867, 15–29 Aug 1868, 3–10 Feb 1872; rptd in his Historical studies, 1903.
[Norton, C. E.] Freeman's Norman Conquest. North Amer Rev 105 1867.
[Bryce, J.] The late Professor Freeman. Nation 5 May 1892.
— Freeman as a historian. Nation 12 May 1892.
Stephens, W. R. W. The life and letters of Freeman. 2 vols 1895.

[Doyle, J. A.] Freeman, Froude and Seeley. Quart Rev 182 1895.
Harrison, F. The historical method of Freeman. Nineteenth Century Nov 1898; rptd in his Tennyson, Ruskin, Mill and other literary estimates, 1899.
Fiske, J. In his A century of science and other essays, Boston 1899.
Bryce, J. In his Studies in contemporary biography, 1903.
Krieger, H. Die Bedeutung des Organischen in englischen Volks- und Staatsbegriff (Burke, Freeman, Seeley, Froude). Die Neueren Sprachen 46 1938.
Wilkinson, B. Freeman and the crisis of 1051. Bull John Rylands Lib 22 1938.
Bevington, M. M. In his Saturday Review 1855–68, New York 1941.
Freeman: a reputation after fifty years. TLS 21 March 1942.
Cronne, H. A. Freeman 1823–92. History 28 1943.

SAMUEL RAWSON GARDINER

1829–1902

Bibliographies

Shaw, W. A. A bibliography of the historical works of Dr Creighton, Dr Stubbs, Dr S. R. Gardiner and Lord Acton. 1903.

§1

History of England from the accession of James I to the disgrace of Chief-Justice Coke 1603–16. 2 vols 1863.
Prince Charles and the Spanish marriage 1617–23. 2 vols 1869.
A history of England under the Duke of Buckingham and Charles I 1624–28. 2 vols 1875.
The personal government of Charles I: a history of England from the assassination of the Duke of Buckingham to the declaration of the judges on ship-money 1628–37. 2 vols 1877.
The fall of the monarchy of Charles I 1637–49 [-42]. 2 vols 1882.
History of England from the accession of James I to the outbreak of the Civil War 1603–42. 10 vols 1883–4, 1883–6, 1894–6, 1900–8. A collected edn of the 5 works listed above.
The Thirty Years' War. 1874, 1886 (7th edn), New York 1889, London 1903 (13th edn).
The first two Stuarts and the Puritan revolution 1603–60. 1876, Boston 1876, New York 1886, London 1888 (8th edn), New York 1890, London 1902 (15th edn), 1928 (23rd edn), 1930.
English history for students. 1881, New York 1881. With J. B. Mullingar.
Introduction to the study of English history. 1881, 1882, 1894, 1903. With J. B. Mullingar.
Outline of English history. 2 vols 1881, 1896, 1901, 1912; ed D. Salmon 1919, 1927.
Illustrated English history. 3 vols 1883, vol 1 1887 (5th edn); vol 3 1902 (continued to 1901), 1912 (continued to 1910).
Historical biographies. 1884, 1906.
An easy history of England. 1887–8.
The constitutional documents of the Puritan revolution 1628–60. Oxford 1889, 1899, 1906, 1958 (3rd edn rev). Ed Gardiner.
A student's history of England from the earliest times to 1885. 3 vols 1890–1, 1892, 1897, 1898, 1899; vol 3 (with continuations) 1902, 1907, 1910, 1920, 1922; ed A. H. Shearer, New York 1906, 1913, 1938, 1939 (as England).
A school atlas of English history. 1892, 1895, 1899, 1905, 1922, 1928, 1936.
Strafford: a tragedy, by Robert Browning. 1892, 1915. Ed Gardiner.
The Tudor period. 1893.
The Stuart period. 1894.
History of the Commonwealth and Protectorate 1649–60. 3 vols 1894–1901, 4 vols 1894–1903. Unfinished at Gardiner's death; completed by C. H. Firth, The last years of the Protectorate, 2 vols 1909.
Cromwell's place in history (Ford lectures 1896). 1897, 1897 (3rd edn).
What Gunpowder Plot was. 1897.
Oliver Cromwell. 1899, 1901; ed M. Ashley, New York 1962; tr German, 1903.
Gardiner also edited 17th-century documents for the Camden Soc and contributed to DNB (21 articles) and Encyclopaedia britannica 9th edn (17 articles).

§2

Seeley, J. R. History of the great Civil War. Academy 21 May 1887.
[Dicey, A. V.] Gardiner's History. Nation (New York) 20 March 1890, 12–19 May 1892, 11 April 1895, 6–13 Jan 1898.
Beer, G. L. Gardiner: an appreciation. Critic June 1901.
Powell, F. Y. Gardiner. EHR 17 1902.
— Two Oxford historians. Quart Rev 195 1902. With C. H. Firth; on Gardiner and J. R. Green.
Learned, H. B. Gardiner. Yale Scientific Monthly June 1902.
Firth, C. H. Gardiner. Proc Br Acad 1 1904.
Rhodes, J. F. Gardiner. Atlantic Monthly June 1902; rptd in his Historical essays, New York 1909.
Usher, R. G. A critical study of the historical method of Gardiner. Washington Univ Stud 3 1915.
Hunt, E. M. In Some modern historians of Britain, ed H. Ausubel, New York 1951.
MacDougall, D. J. Oliver Cromwell and his biographers. Historical Bull 33 1955.

JOHN EMERICH EDWARD DALBERG ACTON, 1st BARON ACTON

1834–1902

Bibliographies

Shaw, W. A. A bibliography of the historical works of Dr Creighton, Dr Stubbs, Dr S. R. Gardiner and Lord Acton. 1903.

§1

Römische Briefe vom Concil, von Quirinus. Munich 1870; tr 1870 (as Letters from Rome on the Council). By Acton et al; rptd from Allgemeine Zeitung 1869.
Sendschreiben an einen deutschen Bischof des vaticanischen Concils. Nördlingen [1870].
Zur Geschichte des vaticanischen Concils. Munich 1871.
The war of 1870: a lecture. 1871.
The history of freedom in antiquity: an address. Bridgnorth [1877]; tr French, 1878.
The history of freedom in Christianity: an address. Bridgnorth [1877]; tr French, 1878.
A lecture on the study of history. 1895, 1896, 1905, 1906 (in Lectures on modern history), 1911; tr German, 1897. Acton's inaugural lecture at Cambridge.
Lectures on modern history. Ed J. N. Figgis and R. V. Laurence 1906, 1952, 1956, New York 1959; ed H. R. Trevor-Roper 1961; ed H. Kohn, New York 1961 (as Renaissance to revolution: the rise of the free state).
Historical essays and studies. Ed J. N. Figgis and R. V. Laurence 1907.
The history of freedom and other essays. Ed J. N. Figgis and R. V. Laurence 1907.
Lectures on the French revolution. Ed J. N. Figgis and R. V. Laurence 1910.
Essays on freedom and power. Ed G. Himmelfarb, Boston 1948.
Essays on church and state. Ed D. Woodruff 1952.

Letters

Letters of Lord Acton to Mary, daughter of W. E. Gladstone; with a memoir. Ed H. Paul 1904.
Gasquet, F. A. Lord Acton and his circle. 1906.
Selections from the correspondence of the first Lord Acton. Ed J. N. Figgis and R. V. Laurence 1917.
de Janösi, F. E. The correspondence between Acton and Bishop Creighton. Cambridge Historical Jnl 6 1940.
Knaplund, P. The Poet-Laureateship in 1892: some Acton–Gladstone letters. Quart Rev 288 1950.
Döllinger, I. von. Briefwechsel mit Lord Acton 1850–69. Ed V. Conzemius, Munich 1963.
— Briefwechsel mit Lord Acton 1869–70. Ed V. Conzemius, Munich 1966.

§2

Bryce, J. Lord Acton. Proc Br Acad 1 1904.
— In his Studies in contemporary biography, 1903.
Fisher, H. A. L. Acton's historical work. In his Studies in history and politics, Oxford 1920.
Drew, M. Acton, Gladstone and others. 1924.
Blennerhassett, W. L. Acton 1834–1902. Dublin Rev 194 1934.
Noack, U. Geschichtswissenschaft und Wahreit nach den Schriften von Acton. Frankfurt 1935.
— Katholizität und Geistesfreiheit nach den Schriften von Acton. Frankfurt 1936.
— Politik als Sicherung der Freiheit nach den Schriften von Acton. Frankfurt 1947.
Woodward, E. L. The place of Acton in the liberal movement of the nineteenth century. Politica 4 1939.
Clark, G. N. Origin of the Cambridge modern history. Cambridge Historical Jnl 8 1945.
Matthew, D. Acton: the formative years. 1946.
Butterfield, H. Journal of Lord Acton: Rome 1857. Cambridge Historical Jnl 8 1946.
— Lord Acton. 1948 (Historical Assoc).
— Gasquet and the Acton–Simpson correspondence. Cambridge Historical Jnl 10 1950. With A. Watkin.
— Acton and the massacre of St Bartholomew. Cambridge Historical Jnl 11 1953.
— Lord Acton. Cambridge Jnl May 1953.
— Acton: his training, methods and intellectual system. In Studies in diplomatic history in honour of G. P. Gooch, ed A. Sarkissian 1961.
Davies, W. W. The politics of Lord Acton. Hibbert Jnl 45 1946.
Gooch, G. P. Acton: apostle of liberty. Foreign Affairs 25 1947; rptd in his Maria Theresa and other studies, 1951.
— Acton. Contemporary Rev April 1956; rptd in his Under six reigns, 1958.
— In his Some great English historians. Contemporary Rev Jan 1957.
Ogg, D. In his Herbert Fisher 1865–1940: a short biography, 1947.
Finer, H. Acton as historian and political scientist. Jnl of Politics 10 1948.
Fasnacht, G. E. Acton on nationality and Socialism. Oxford 1949.
— Acton's political philosophy: an analysis. Ed H. Butler 1952.
— Acton's notes for a Romanes lecture [History in the twentieth century]. Contemporary Rev Dec 1952.
— Acton in perspective. Church Quart Rev 154 1953.
— Acton on books and reading. TLS 6 May 1955.
Himmelfarb, G. The American revolution in the political philosophy of Lord Acton. Jnl of Modern History 21 1949.
— Acton: a study in conscience and politics. Chicago 1952.
Kochan, L. Acton fifty years after. Contemporary Rev June 1952.
— Acton on history. 1954.
Cairns, J. C. Acton: a portrait. UTQ 22 1952.
Hill, R. Acton and the Catholic reviews. Blackfriars Dec 1955.
Tonsor, S. J. Acton on Döllinger's historical theology. JHI 20 1959.
Hohl, C. L. Acton's visit to America 1853. Records of Amer Catholic Historical Soc of Philadelphia 71 1960.
Nurser, J. S. The religious conscience in Acton's political thought. JHI 22 1961.
Acton, H. Lord Acton. Chicago Rev 15 1962.
Altholz, J. L. In his Liberal Catholic movement in England: the Rambler and its contributors, 1962.
MacDougall, H. A. The Acton–Newman relations. New York 1962.
Watt, E. D. Ethics and politics: the example of Acton. UTQ 33 1964.

JOHN RICHARD GREEN

1837–83

Bibliographies

Letters of J. R. Green. Ed L. Stephen 1901. *See* pp. 497–503.

§1

Oxford during the last century: being two series of papers published in the Oxford Chronicle and Bucks and Berks Gazette during 1859. Oxford 1859 (anon); ed C. L. Stainer 1901 (as Studies in Oxford history); ed Mrs J. R. Green and K. Norgate 1901 (Green's ser only, in Oxford studies). With G. Roberson.
A short history of the English people. 1874, 1875, 1876, New York 1876, London 1877, 1878, 1880, New York 1880, London 1881, 1881, 1882, 1884, 1885, 1886; ed Mrs J. R. Green (with memoir) 1888; 4 vols 1889–91 (with tables and analysis by C. W. A. Tait); ed Mrs J. R. Green and K. Norgate 4 vols 1892–4 (illustr edn), New York 1893–5, 1 vol 1894, 4 vols 1895, 1907–8; ed G. B. Adams 2 vols New York 1898; ed A. S. Cook 3 vols New York 1900; 1 vol 1911 (rev), New York 1911, London 1916 (with Epilogue 1815–1914 by Mrs J. R. Green), New York 1916, London 1921; ed L. C. Jane 2 vols 1915 (with survey 1815–1914 by R. F. Farley), 1916, 1940 (EL); 2 vols 1960 (with survey 1815–1960); tr Italian, 1884; French, 1888; German, 1889; Russian, 1891–2; Chinese, 1898.
Stray studies from England and Italy. 1876, New York 1876; Stray studies: second series, ed Mrs J. R. Green 1903.
History of the English people. 4 vols 1877–80, New York 1878–80, London 1881, 1882, 5 vols New York 1882, 4 vols 1886, 1890, 8 vols 1895–6 (Eversley edn); 4 vols New York 1898 (as England, with suppl by J. Hawthorne), 1902; 4 vols 1901–3, 8 vols 1905–8, 10 vols New York 1910.
Readings from English history. 1879, New York 1879, London 1880, 1883, 1898. Ed Green.
A short geography of the British islands. 1879, 1884, 1893, 1896 (rev). With Mrs J. R. Green.
Essays of Joseph Addison. 1880, 1882, 1892, 1899, 1956 (with notes by G. St Quintin). Ed Green.
The making of England. 1881, 1882, New York 1882, London 1885 (3rd edn), 2 vols 1897, 1900.
The conquest of England. 1883, New York 1883, London 1884, 2 vols 1899 (3rd edn).
Letters of J. R. Green. Ed L. Stephen 1901.
Oxford studies. Ed Mrs J. R. Green and K. Norgate 1901.
Historical studies. Ed Mrs J. R. Green 1903.

§2

Bryce, J. Green: in memoriam. Macmillan's Mag May 1883.
— In his Studies in contemporary biography, 1903.

Powell, F. Y. Two Oxford historians. Quart Rev 195 1902. With C. H. Firth; on Green and S. R. Gardiner.
Rhodes, J. F. In his Historical essays, New York 1909.
Addison, W. G. J. R. Green. 1946.
Schuyler, R. L. Green and his Short history. Political Science Quart 64 1949.
Dougherty, H. J. Green: historian of the middle class. London Quart 6th ser 22 1953.
Angus-Butterworth, L. M. In his Ten master historians, Aberdeen 1961.

WILLIAM EDWARD HARTPOLE LECKY
1838–1903

§1

Friendship and other poems, by Hibernicus. 1859.
The religious tendencies of the age. 1860. Anon.
The leaders of public opinion in Ireland. 1861 (anon), 1871 (rev, omitting Clerical influences), New York 1872, London 1882, 2 vols 1903 (omitting Life of Swift), 1912; tr German, 1873; Life of Swift rev as introd to Prose works of Jonathan Swift, ed T. Scott 1901; Clerical influences, ed W. E. G. Lloyd and F. C. O'Brien, Dublin 1911.
On the declining sense of the miraculous. Dublin 1863.
History of the rise and influence of the spirit of rationalism in Europe. 2 vols 1865, 1865, 1866, 1869 (4th edn), New York 1870, 1872, London 1872, 1873, 1875, 1877, 1880, 1882, New York 1882, London 1884, 1887, 1890, 1892, 1997, 1898, 1900, New York 1903, London 1904, 1910, 1914 (rev), 1925, New York 1925; ed C. W. Mills, New York 1955; tr German, 1868, 1873; Dutch, 1894.
History of European morals from Augustus to Charlemagne. 2 vols 1869, 1877 (3rd edn), 1886 (7th edn rev), New York 1887, 1903, 1905, London 1911, 1929, New York 1929; ed C. Wood, New York 1926 (abridged); ed C. W. Mills, New York 1955; tr German, 1870. Ch 1 ed W. A. Hirst 1903 (as A survey of English ethics).
A history of England in the eighteenth century. 8 vols 1878–90, New York 1878–90, London 1883–90 (vols 1–2 3rd edn, vols 3–4 2nd edn), 1891, New York 1891, 12 vols 1892 (as A history of England 7 vols, A history of Ireland 5 vols), New York 1892–3, London 1908–12; chs on The religious revival tr German 1880.
The American revolution: chapters and passages relating to America from History of England in the eighteenth century. Ed J. A. Woodburn, New York 1898.
The French Revolution: chapters from History of England during the eighteenth century. Ed H. E. Bourne, New York 1904, 1928.
Poems. 1891, New York 1891.
The political value of history. Birmingham 1892, London 1892 (rev), 1908 (in Historical and political essays).
The Empire, its value and its growth: an inaugural address. 1893, 1908 (in Historical and political essays).
Speeches and addresses of Edward Henry 16th Earl of Derby. Ed T. H. Sanderson and E. S. Roscoe 2 vols 1894. Memoir by Lecky.
Democracy and liberty. 2 vols 1896, 1896, New York 1896, London 1899 (rev), 1900.
The map of life: conduct and character. 1899, New York 1899, London 1901, New York 1901, London 1913.
Historical and political essays. 1908, New York 1908, London 1910.

§2

'Eliot, George'. The influence of rationalism. Fortnightly Rev 15 May 1865; rptd in her Essays and leaves from a notebook, Edinburgh 1884.
[Stephen, J. F.] Mr Lecky on rationalism. Fraser's Mag Nov 1865.
[Church, R. W.] Lecky's History of European morals. Saturday Rev 1 May 1869.
Morley, J. Mr Lecky's first chapter. Fortnightly Rev May 1869.
—— Lecky on democracy. Nineteenth Century May 1896; rptd in his Oracles on man and government, 1923.
[Stephen, L.] Lecky's History of European morals. Nation (New York) 17 June 1869.
Appleton, C. E. Lecky's History of morals. Contemporary Rev June 1869.
[Hayward, A.] Lecky's History of England in the eighteenth century. Quart Rev 147 1878.
[Dicey, A. V.] Lecky's History of England. Nation (New York) 18–25 April 1878.
Gladstone, W. E. Lecky's History. Nineteenth Century June 1887.
McCarthy, J. Mr Lecky's last volumes. Contemporary Rev Nov 1890.
Walpole, S. Mr Lecky. Proc Br Acad 1 1904.
Lecky, E. van D. A memoir of Lecky by his wife. 1909.
Rhodes, J. F. In his Historical essays, New York 1909.
Roome, H. D. Two historians of the eighteenth century. Fortnightly Rev Nov 1909. On Macaulay and Lecky.
Franqueville, A. C. Notice sur la vie et les travaux du très-honorable W. E. H. Lecky. Paris 1910.
Hirst, W. A. The centenary of Lecky. Nineteenth Century April 1938.
Lippincott, B. E. In his Victorian critics of democracy, Minneapolis 1938.
Phillips, W. A. Lecky. Dublin 1939.
Auchmuty, J. J. Lecky: a biographical and critical study. 1946.
—— The Lecky–Lea correspondence in the Henry Charles Lea Library of the University of Pennsylvania. Hermathena 92 1958.
Hyde, H. M. A Victorian historian: private letters of Lecky 1859–78. 1947.
Mullett, C. F. In Some modern historians of Britain, ed H. Ausubel, New York 1951.
Gooch, G. P. In his Some great English historians, Contemporary Rev Jan 1957.

MANDELL CREIGHTON
1843–1901

Bibliographies

Shaw, W. A. A bibliography of the historical works of Dr Creighton, Dr Stubbs, Dr S. R. Gardiner and Lord Acton. 1903.
Creighton, L. Life and letters of Creighton. 2 vols 1904. *See* vol 2 pp. 517–22.

§1

History of Rome. 1875, 1877 (3rd edn), 1884 (10th edn), Toronto 1899, London 1912; tr Spanish, 1881; French, 1885.
The Tudors and the Reformation. 1876, New York 1877.
The age of Elizabeth. 1876, Boston 1876, New York 1887, London 1890, 1892 (9th edn), 1899, New York 1928, London 1930.
Epochs of English history. 10 vols 1876–95. Ed Creighton.
Historical biographies. 9 vols 1876–94. Ed Creighton.
The shilling history of England: being an introductory volume to Epochs of English history. 1879, New York 1879 (as The half-hour history of England); ed L. Creighton 1904.
A history of the Papacy during the period of the Reformation. 5 vols 1882–94, 1887-94 (rev), 6 vols 1897 (as History of the Papacy from the Great Schism to the sack of Rome), New York 1902–4, London 1919.
Memoir of Sir George Grey. Newcastle-on-Tyne 1884 (priv ptd); ed E. Grey 1901.

Epochs of Church history. 16 vols 1886–98. Ed Creighton.
Cardinal Wolsey. 1888, 1904; ed H. Ketcham, New York 1903.
Carlisle. 1889, 1889 (Historic Towns ser).
Persecution and tolerance (Hulsean lectures 1893–4). 1895.
The early renaissance in England (Rede lecture 1895). Cambridge 1895.
Queen Elizabeth. 1896, Paris 1896, 1899, New York 1899, London 1920, 1927, Leipzig 1943.
The heritage of the spirit and other sermons. 1896, 1913.
The story of some English shires. 1897, 1898.
Lessons from the cross: addresses. 1898.
The abolition of the Roman jurisdiction. 1899, 1899, New York 1899.
The Church and the nation: charges and addresses. Ed L. Creighton 1901.
Counsels for churchpeople. Ed J. H. Burn 1901.
Historical essays and reviews. Ed L. Creighton 1902, 1902.
Thoughts on education: speeches and sermons. Ed L. Creighton 1902; ed E. A. Knox 1906 (abridged).
Historical lectures and addresses. Ed L. Creighton 1903.
University and other sermons. Ed L. Creighton 1903.
The mind of St Peter and other sermons. Ed L. Creighton 1904.
Counsel for the young: extracts from letters. Ed L. Creighton 1905.
Life of Simon de Montfort. 1905.
The claims of the common life: sermons preached in Merton College chapel 1871–4. 1905.

§2

Acton, Lord. A history of the Papacy vols 2–3. EHR 2 1887.
Creighton, L. Life and letters of Creighton. 2 vols 1904.
Creighton and Stubbs. Church Quart Rev 61 1905.
Paul, H. In his Stray leaves, 1906.
Strachey, L. In his Portraits in miniature, 1931.
de Janösi, F. E. Correspondence between Acton and Creighton. Cambridge Historical Jnl 6 1940.
Fallows, W. G. Creighton and the English Church. Oxford 1964.

FREDERIC WILLIAM MAITLAND
1850–1906

Bibliographies

Smith, A. L. Maitland: two lectures and a bibliography. Oxford 1908.
Cameron, J. R. Maitland and the history of English law. Norman Oklahoma 1961. *See* pp. 168–94.

§1

Justice and police. 1885.
Why the history of English law is not written: an inaugural lecture. Cambridge 1888.
The history of English law before the time of Edward I. 2 vols Cambridge 1895, Boston 1895, Cambridge 1898, Boston 1898, Cambridge 1911 (2nd edn), 1 vol Washington 1959. With F. Pollock.
Domesday book and beyond: three essays. Cambridge 1897, Boston 1897, Cambridge 1907; ed E. Miller 1960.
Roman canon law in the church of England: six essays. Cambridge 1898.
Township and borough: being the Ford lectures 1897 with notes relating to the history of Cambridge. Cambridge 1898, 1965.
Political theories of the middle age, by Otto Gierke. Cambridge 1900, 1913, 1922, 1951. Tr Maitland.
English law and the renaissance (Rede lecture 1901). Cambridge 1901.
Essays on the teaching of history. Ed W. A. J. Archbold, Cambridge 1901. With H. M. Gwatkin et al.
The life and letters of Leslie Stephen. 1906, New York 1906, London 1907, 1910.
The constitutional history of England. Ed H. A. L. Fisher, Cambridge 1908, 1909, 1920, 1948, 1961. Lectures delivered 1887–8.
Equity: also the forms of action at common law. Ed A. H. Chaytor and W. J. Whittaker, Cambridge 1909, 1916, 1929, 1932; Equity, ed J. Brunyate, Cambridge 1936, 1949; Forms of action, ed Chaytor and J. Whittaker, Cambridge 1936, 1941, 1958.
Collected papers. Ed H. A. L. Fisher 3 vols Cambridge 1911.
A sketch of English legal history. Ed J. F. Colby, New York [1915]. Rptd from Social England, ed H. D. Traill 6 vols 1893–7. With F. C. Montague.
Selected essays. Ed H. D. Hazeltine, G. Lapsley and P. H. Winfield, Cambridge 1936.
Selected historical essays. Ed H. M. Cam, Cambridge 1957.
F. W. Maitland, historian: selections from his writings. Ed R. L. Schuyler, Berkeley 1960.
The letters of F. W. Maitland. Ed C. H. S. Fifoot, Cambridge 1965.
Maitland also edited medieval legal documents (chiefly for the Selden Soc) 1884–1907.

§2

[Roscoe, E. S.] The early history of English law. Edinburgh Rev 183 1896.
Pollock, F. Maitland. Quart Rev 206 1907.
Vinogradoff, P. Maitland. EHR 22 1907.
Smith, A. L. Maitland: two lectures and a bibliography. Oxford 1908.
Fisher, H. A. L. Maitland: a biographical sketch. Cambridge 1910.
Liebermann, F. Maitland's collected papers. Historische Zeitschrift 3rd ser 18 1915.
Barker, E. Maitland as a sociologist. Sociological Rev 29 1937.
Beck, A. Maitland and the Anglican continuity. Clergy Rev 10 1935.
Young, G. M. In his Daylight and champaign, 1937.
Holdsworth, W. S. In his Historians of Anglo-American law, New York 1928.
—— In his Some makers of English law, Cambridge 1938.
White, R. J. Maitland 1850–1950. Cambridge Jnl 4 1950.
Schuyler, R. L. The historical spirit incarnate: Maitland. Amer Historical Rev 57 1952.
Poole, A. L. Maitland and R. Lane Poole. Cambridge Historical Jnl 10 1952.
Hollond, H. A. Maitland. 1953. A memorial address.
Maitland, E. Maitland: a child's eye view. 1957.
Gooch, G. P. In his Some great English historians, Contemporary Rev Jan 1957.
Cameron, J. R. Maitland and the history of English law. Norman Oklahoma 1961.
Bell, H. E. Maitland: a critical examination and assessment. 1965.

SIR JAMES GEORGE FRAZER
1854–1941

Bibliographies

Besterman, T. A bibliography of Frazer. 1934.

§1

C. Sallusti Crispi Catalina et Jugurtha. 1884. Ed Frazer.
Totemism. Edinburgh 1887; tr French, 1898.
The golden bough: a study in comparative religion. 2 vols 1890, New York 1890, 3 vols 1900 (rev), New York

1900, 12 vols 1911–15 (as The golden bough: a study in magic and religion; vols 1–2: The magic art and the evolution of kings, 1911; vol 3: Taboo and the perils of the soul, 1911; vol 4: The dying god, 1911; vols 5–6: Adonis, Attis, Osiris, 1914; vols 7–8: Spirits of the corn and the wild, 1912; vol 9: The scapegoat, 1913; vols 10–11: Balder the beautiful, 1913; vol 12: Bibliography and general index, 1915), 1914–17, 1925–30, New York 1935, London 1936–7, New York 1951, 13 vols 1955 (with Aftermath); 1 vol 1922 (abridged), New York 1922, London 1923, 1924, 1925, New York 1927, London 1929, 2 vols New York 1929, 1 vol 1932, 1940, New York 1951, London 1959; chs 1–7 ed G. M. Trevelyan 1944 (as Magic and religion); ed T. H. Gaster, New York 1959, 1965 (as The new Golden bough); tr French, 1903–11, 1923; Italian 1925; Swedish, 1925; German, 1928.

Leaves from the Golden bough culled by Lady Frazer. 1924, New York 1924; tr French, 1925.

Passages of the Bible chosen for their literary beauty and interest. 1895, 1909, 1927. Ed Frazer.

Pausanias, Description of Greece. 6 vols 1898. Tr and ed Frazer.

The origin of totemism. Fortnightly Rev April–May 1899. Reply by A. Lang, Mr Frazer's theory of totemism, June 1899.

Pausanias and other Greek sketches. 1900, 1917 (as Studies in Greek scenery, legend and history); tr French, 1922.

Lectures on the early history of the kingship. 1905, 1920 (as The magical origin of kings); tr French, 1920.

Adonis, Attis, Osiris: studies in the history of oriental religion. 1906, 1907, 1914 (as vols 5–6 of Golden bough, above), New York 1962; Adonis, 1932; tr French, 1921, 1926.

Questions on the customs, beliefs and languages of savages. Cambridge 1907.

The scope of social anthropology. 1908, 1927 (with The devil's advocate, below).

Psyche's task: a discourse concerning the influence of superstitions on the growth of institutions. 1909, 1913, 1920, 1927 (as The devil's advocate: a plea for superstition), 1928.

Totemism and exogamy: a treatise on certain early forms of superstition and society. 4 vols 1910; tr French, 1923.

The letters of William Cowper. 2 vols 1912. Ed Frazer.

The belief in immortality and the worship of the dead. Vol 1 (Gifford lectures 1911–12), 1913; vol 2, 1922; vol 3, 1924.

Essays of Joseph Addison. 2 vols 1915. Ed Frazer.

Folk-lore in the Old Testament: studies in comparative religion, legend and law. 3 vols 1918, 1919, 1919, 1 vol 1923 (abridged), New York 1923, London 1927, New York 1927; tr French, 1924; German, 1960.

Sir Roger de Coverley and other literary pieces. 1920, 1927 (as The gorgon's head); tr French, 1922.

Apollodorus, The library. 2 vols 1921 (Loeb Lib). Tr and ed Frazer.

Sur Ernest Renan. Paris 1923.

Frazer: selected passages from his works. Ed G. Roth, Paris 1924.

The worship of nature. 1926, New York 1926; tr French, 1927.

Man, god and immortality: passages chosen by Pierre Sayn from the writings of Frazer, revised and edited by the author. 1927, New York 1927; tr French, 1928; Dutch, 1929; German, 1932.

Publii Ovidii Nasonis Fastorum libri sex. 5 vols 1929, 1 vol 1931 (Loeb Lib).

Myths of the origin of fire. 1930, 1930, New York 1942; tr Spanish, 1942.

The growth of Plato's ideal theory. 1930.

Garnered sheaves: essays, addresses and reviews. 1931.

The fear of the dead in primitive religion. 3 vols 1933–6.

Condorcet on the progress of the human mind (Zaharoff lecture 1933). Oxford 1933.

Creation and evolution in primitive cosmogonies, and other pieces. 1935.

Aftermath: a supplement to the Golden bough. 1936, New York 1937, London 1951, 1955 (as vol 12 of Golden bough).

Totemica: a supplement to Totemism and exogamy. 1937.

Greece and Rome: a selection from the works of Frazer. Ed S. G. Owen 1937.

Pasha the pom: the story of a little dog. Philadelphia 1937. With Lady Frazer.

Anthologia anthropologica. Ed R. A. Downie 4 vols 1938, 1939.

§2

[Lyall, A.] The golden bough. Edinburgh Rev 172 1890.

[Marindin, G. E.] The golden bough. Quart Rev 172 1891.

Lang, A. The golden bough. Fortnightly Rev Feb 1901.

—— Mr Frazer's theory of the crucifixion. Fortnightly Rev April 1901.

Jevons, F. B. Magic and religion. Edinburgh Rev 194 1901.

Blau, A. Die Bibel als Quelle für Folkloristik. Hamburg 1926.

Downie, R. A. Frazer: the portrait of a scholar. 1940.

Marett, R. R. et al. Frazer. Nature 24 May 1941.

—— Frazer 1854–1941. 1941.

Malinowski, B. In his A scientific theory of culture and other essays, Chapel Hill 1944.

Gross, J. J. After Frazer: the ritualistic approach to myth. Western Humanities Rev 5 1951.

Hodgart, M. J. C. In the shade of the Golden bough. Twentieth Century Feb 1955.

Huxley, M. Frazer within the bloody wood. New Statesman 16 April 1960.

Hyman, S. E. The tangled bank: Darwin, Marx, Frazer and Freud as imaginative writers. New York 1962.

Vickery, J. B. Golden bough: impact and archetype. Virginia Quart Rev 39 1963.

HENRY PETER BROUGHAM, 1st BARON BROUGHAM AND VAUX 1778–1868

The Brougham papers are at Univ College, London.

Bibliographies

Thomas, R. Bibliography of Brougham's works. In Works of Brougham, below, vol 11, Edinburgh 1873.

Collections

Selections from the speeches and writings. 1832.

Opinions of Lord Brougham on politics, theology, law, science, education &c &c. 1837, 2 vols Philadelphia 1839, 1 vol Paris 1841.

Speeches upon questions relating to public rights. 4 vols Edinburgh 1898, 2 vols Philadelphia 1841.

The critical and miscellaneous writings. 2 vols Philadelphia 1841.

Works. 11 vols 1855–61, Edinburgh 1872–3.

Contributions to the Edinburgh Review. 3 vols 1856.

Brougham's acts and bills from 1811 to the present time now first collected. Ed J. E. Eardley-Wilmot 1857, 1860 (as Brougham's law reforms).

§1

An inquiry into the colonial policy of the European powers. 2 vols Edinburgh 1803.

An inquiry into the state of the nation at the commencement of the present administration. 1806, 1806 (6th edn), 1806 (7th edn rev).

Practical observations upon the education of the people. 1825, 1825 (11th edn), 1825 (17th edn), 1825 (20th edn), Boston 1826; tr German, 1827.
Inaugural discourse on being installed Lord Rector of the University of Glasgow. Glasgow 1825.
Thoughts upon the aristocracy of England, by Isaac Tomkins, Gent. 1835, 1835 (6th edn), 1835 (11th edn).
'We can't afford it!': being thoughts upon the aristocracy of England part 2, by Isaac Tomkins, Gent. 1835, 1835 (4th edn), 1835 (6th edn).
A discourse of natural theology. Brussels 1835, London 1835 (4th edn), Philadelphia 1835; tr French, 1835.
Dissertations on subjects of science connected with natural theology. 2 vols 1839.
Historical sketches of statesmen who flourished in the time of George III. 2 vols 1839, Philadelphia 1839; Second series, 2 vols 1839, Philadelphia 1839; Third series, 2 vols 1842, Philadelphia 1842; collected 3 vols 1845–53, 2 vols Philadelphia 1854, 3 vols 1855–6, 1856–8; tr French, 1847.
Sketches of public characters. 2 vols Philadelphia 1839.
Political philosophy. 3 vols 1842–3, 1 vol Paris 1845, 3 vols 1846, 1853, 1855, 1861.
The British constitution. 1844, 1861 (3 edns).
Dialogues on instinct. 1844, Philadelphia 1845.
Albert Lunel: or the chateau of Languedoc. 3 vols 1844 (anon), 1872. A novel.
Lives of men of letters and science in the time of George III. 2 vols 1845–6, 3 vols 1845–7.
Masters and workmen: a tale illustrative of the social and moral condition of the people, by Lord B——. 3 vols 1851. A novel attributed to Brougham.
History of England and France under the house of Lancaster. 1852 (anon), 1855, 1861.
Analytical view of Sir Isaac Newton's Principia. 1855. With E. J. Routh.
Addresses on popular literature. 1858.
Tracts: mathematical and physical. 1860.
The life and times of Lord Brougham written by himself. 3 vols Edinburgh 1871, 1872 (3rd edn).
Selections from the correspondence of Macvey Napier: edited by his son. 1879. Includes letters from Brougham to the editor of the Edinburgh Review.
Brougham and his early friends: letters to James Loch 1798–1809. Ed R. H. M. Buddle-Atkinson and G. A. Jackson, 3 vols Edinburgh 1908 (priv ptd).

§2

Gilfillan, G. In his A gallery of literary portraits, Edinburgh 1845.
Bagehot, W. Brougham. Nat Rev 5 1857; rptd in his Biographical studies, 1881.
Campbell, J. C. Lives of Lyndhurst and Brougham. 1869.
Mignet, F. A. M. In his Nouveaux éloges historiques, Paris 1877.
Retournay, H. Brougham et le centenaire. Paris 1878.
Atlay, J. B. In his Victorian Chancellors, 1906.
Gilbert, A. M. The work of Brougham for education in England. Chambersburg 1922.
Aspinall, A. Brougham and the Whig party. Manchester 1927.
—— Brougham's Life and times. EHR 59 1944.
—— Thomas Barnes and Brougham: from friends to foes. TLS 27 July 1946.
Garratt, G. T. Lord Brougham. 1935.
Strout, A. L. Wordsworth versus Brougham. N & Q 28 May 1938.
—— Thomas Clarkson as champion of Brougham in 1818. N & Q 4 June 1938.
Baer, G. F. A. Brougham: champion of popular education. History of Education Jnl 6 1954.
Gash, N. Brougham and the Yorkshire election of 1830. Proc Leeds Philosophical & Lit Soc 8 1956.
Watkins, L. I. Brougham's authorship of rhetorical articles in the Edinburgh Review. Quart Jnl of Speech 42 1956.
Hawes, F. Henry Brougham. 1957.
New, C. W. The life of Brougham to 1830. Oxford 1961.

JAMES BRYCE, 1st VISCOUNT BRYCE OF DECHMONT

1838–1922

§1

The flora of the island of Arran. 1859.
The Holy Roman Empire (Arnold prize essay 1864). Oxford 1864, London 1871 (3rd edn rev), 1886 (8th edn), New York 1886, London 1892, 1896, 1904 (rev), 1906, 1919, New York 1921, London 1922 (enlarged); ed H. Kohn, New York 1961; tr German, 1873; French, 1890; Russian, 1891.
Report on the condition of education in Lancashire. 1867.
The academic study of the civil law: an inaugural lecture delivered at Oxford. 1871.
Trans-Caucasia and Ararat: being notes of a vacation tour in the autumn of 1876. 1877, 1877, 1896 (4th edn rev).
The trade marks registration act. 1877.
The predictions of Hamilton and de Tocqueville. Baltimore 1887.
Handbook of home rule: being articles on the Irish question. 1887. Ed Bryce.
The American commonwealth. 3 vols 1888, 2 vols 1888, 1889 (2nd edn rev), 1891, 1893–5 (3rd edn rev), 1895–6, 1 vol New York 1896 (abridged), 2 vols 1899, 1 vol New York 1899, 1906, 1934, 1958; 2 vols New York 1908 (with chapter on the Tweed ring by R. R. Wilson), 2 vols New York 1910 (new edn rev), 1914–15, 1918–19, 1922–3, 1924, 1926–7, 1931–3; ed L. M. Hacker 2 vols New York 1959; tr Russian, 1889–90; French, 1900–2; Croatian, 1905–7; Spanish, 1912–14; Italian, 1913. Selections: Chautauqua 1891 (as Social institutions of the United States); ed M. G. Fulton, New York 1918 (as Bryce on American democracy); ed H. S. Commager, New York 1961 (as Reflections on American institutions).
The migrations of the races of men considered historically. 1893.
Legal studies in the University of Oxford: a valedictory lecture. 1893.
Impressions of South Africa. 1897, New York 1897, London 1898, 1900 (3rd edn); tr German, 1900.
William Ewart Gladstone: his characteristics as man and statesman. 1898, New York 1898.
Studies in history and jurisprudence. 2 vols Oxford 1901, New York 1901.
Studies in contemporary biography. 1903, 1911, 1927.
The relations between the advanced and the backward races of mankind. Oxford 1903.
Constitutions. New York 1905; tr Spanish, 1952.
Marriage and divorce. New York 1905.
The hindrances to good citizenship. New Haven 1909.
South America: observations and impressions. 1912, New York 1912, 1913, London 1914 (rev), Detroit 1914, London 1916, New York 1917; tr Spanish, 1914; Portuguese, 1920.
University and historical addresses delivered during a residence in the United States. New York 1913.
The ancient Roman Empire and the British Empire in India; the diffusion of Roman and English law throughout the world—two essays. Oxford 1914.
Neutral nations and the war. 1914; tr Spanish, 1914; German, 1914.
The attitude of Great Britain in the present war. 1916; tr French, 1916.
Proposals for the prevention of future wars. 1917.

Essays and addresses in war time. New York 1918.
Modern democracies. 2 vols 1921, New York 1921, London 1929, New York 1931; tr Czech, 1927.
Canada: an actual democracy. Toronto 1921.
The study of American history. Cambridge 1921, New York 1922.
International relations: eight lectures. New York 1922.
Memories of travel. Ed Lady Bryce 1923, New York 1923.

§2

[Freeman, E. A.] Bryce's Holy Roman Empire. Saturday Rev 29 Oct 1864.
— The Holy Roman Empire. North Br Rev 42 1865; rptd in his Historical essays, 1871.
McCarthy, J. In his British political portraits, 1903.
Morley, J. In his Recollections, 1917.
Fisher, H. A. L. Viscount Bryce. Proc Br Acad 12 1926.
— James Bryce. 2 vols 1927.
Bryce's American commonwealth: fiftieth anniversary. Ed R. C. Brooks, New York 1939. Includes reviews by Acton, Woodrow Wilson et al.
Hirst, F. W. Memories of great Victorians. Contemporary Rev Aug 1950.
Toynbee, A. J. In his Acquaintances, 1967.

THOMAS CLARKSON

1760–1846

Bibliographies

Griggs, E. L. Clarkson: the friend of slaves. 1936. *See* pp. 199–204.

§1

An essay on the slavery and commerce of the human species 1786, Philadelphia 1786, London 1788, Georgetown Kentucky 1816.
An essay on the impolicy of the African slave trade. 1788, 1788 (rev).
A portraiture of Quakerism, as taken from a view of the moral education, discipline, peculiar customs, religious principles, political and civil œconomy and character of the Society of Friends. 3 vols 1806, New York 1806, London 1807 (3rd edn), Philadelphia 1808; ed R. Smeal, Glasgow 1869 (as A portraiture of the Christian profession and practice of the Society of Friends); tr French, 1820.
The history of the rise, progress and accomplishment of the abolition of the African slave-trade. 2 vols 1808, Philadelphia 1808, 1 vol Wilmington 1816, 2 vols Augusta Maine 1830, New York 1836, London 1839.
Memoirs of the private and public life of William Penn. 2 vols 1813, Philadelphia 1813, 1814, Dover New Hampshire 1827; ed W. E. Forster 1849, New York 1849.
An essay on the doctrines and practice of the early Christians as they relate to war. 1817, 1818 (3rd edn), 1824 (7th edn), 1832, 1839, 1844; tr French, 1824.
The cries of Africa to the inhabitants of Europe. [1822]; tr French, 1822; Spanish, 1823; Portuguese, 1823.
Thoughts on the necessity for improving the condition of the slaves in the British colonies with a view to their ultimate emancipation. 1823, 1823 (rev), 1824 (4th edn).
Researches antediluvian, patriarchal and historical. 1836.
Strictures on a life of William Wilberforce; with a correspondence between Lord Brougham and Mr Clarkson. Ed H. C. Robinson 1838.
Henry Christophe and Clarkson: a correspondence. Ed E. L. Griggs and C. H. Prater, Berkeley 1952.

§2

[Coleridge, S. T.] Clarkson's Abolition of the slave-trade. Edinburgh Rev 12 1808.
Wilberforce, R. I. and S. In their Life of William Wilberforce, 1838.
— The correspondence of William Wilberforce. 1840.
Elmes, J. Clarkson: a monograph. 1854.
Griggs, E. L. Clarkson: the friend of slaves. 1936.
Strout, A. L. Clarkson as champion of Brougham in 1818. N & Q 4 June 1938.
Brown, F. K. In his Fathers of the Victorians, Cambridge 1961.

ALBERT VENN DICEY

1835–1922

§1

The Privy Council (Arnold prize essay 1860). Oxford 1860, London 1887.
A treatise on the rules for the selection of parties in an action. 1870; ed J. H. Truman, New York 1876; London, 1886; ed J. B. Moore, New York 1896.
The law of domicil. 1879; tr French, 1887–8.
Can English law be taught at the universities? an inaugural lecture (Oxford 1883). 1883.
Lectures introductory to the study of the law of the constitution. 1885, 1889 (3rd edn rev as Introduction to the study of the law of the constitution), 1893, 1897, 1902, 1908, 1915 (8th edn), 1923, 1931; ed C. S. Wade 1939, 1959 (10th edn), 1960; tr French, 1902; Russian, 1905–7; Chinese, 1930.
England's case against Home Rule. 1886, 1887 (3rd edn), 1887 (as Why England maintains the union).
Letters on unionist delusions. 1887.
The verdict: a tract on the political significance of the report of the Parnell Commission. 1890.
A leap in the dark: or our new constitution. 1893, 1911.
A digest of the laws of England with reference to the conflict of laws. 1896, Boston 1896, London 1908; ed A. B. Keith 1922 (3rd edn), 1927, 1932; ed J. H. C. Morris 1949 (6th edn as Conflict of laws), 1958.
Lectures on the relation between law and public opinion in England during the nineteenth century. 1905, 1914, 1920, 1924, 1930; ed E. C. S. Wade 1962; tr French, 1906.
Letters to a friend on votes for women. 1909, 1912.
A fool's paradise: being a constitutionalist's criticism of the Home Rule Bill of 1912. 1913.
The statesmanship of Wordsworth. Oxford 1917.
Thoughts on the union between England and Scotland. 1920. With R. S. Rait.

§2

Rait, R. S. Memorials of Dicey. 1925.
Holdsworth, W. S. In his Historians of Anglo-American law, New York 1928.
Lawson, F. H. Dicey revisited. Political Stud 7 1959.

GEORGE FINLAY

1799–1875

Bibliographies

Miller, W. The Finlay papers. EHR 39 1924.

§1

The Hellenic kingdom and the Greek nation. 1836; ed S. G. Howe, Boston 1837.
Remarks on the topography of Oropia and Diacria. Athens 1838; tr German, 1842.
Greece under the Romans. Edinburgh 1844, 1857; ed V. R. Reynolds 1907, 1927 (EL).
ΕΠΙΣΤΟΛΗ ΠΡΟΣ ΤΟΥΣ ΑΘΗΝΑΙΟΥΣ. Athens 1844.
On the site of the Holy Sepulchre. 1847.

The history of Greece from its conquest by the Crusaders to its conquest by the Turks, and of the empire of Trebizond 1204–1461. Edinburgh 1851.
History of the Byzantine and Greek empires 716–1453. 2 vols Edinburgh 1853–4, 1855, 1 vol Edinburgh 1856 (2nd edn: 716–1507); Byzantine empire, ed V. R. Reynolds 1906, 1935 (EL).
The history of Greece under Othoman and Venetian domination. Edinburgh 1856; tr Greek, 1958.
History of the Greek revolution. 2 vols Edinburgh 1861.
Objects found in Greece in the collection of G. Finlay. Athens 1869.
A history of Greece from its conquest by the Romans to the present time B.C. 146 to A.D. 1864. Ed H. F. Tozer 7 vols Oxford 1877. Includes Greece under the Romans, Byzantine and Greek empires, and Greece under Othoman and Venetian domination.
Finlay also contributed letters from Greece to the Times 1864–70.

§2

Freeman, E. A. Finlay on the Byzantine Empire. North Br Rev 21 1854; rptd in his Historical essays, 1879.
— The Greek people and the Greek kingdom. Edinburgh Rev 103 1856; rptd in his Historical essays, 1879.
— The later Greek nation. Br Quart Rev 68 1878.
Autobiography. In his History of Greece vol 1, ed H. F. Tozer, Oxford 1877.
Mahaffy, J. P. Modern Greece. Contemporary Rev March 1878.
Miller, W. Finlay as a journalist. EHR 39 1924.

ALEXANDER WILLIAM KINGLAKE
1809–91

§1

Eothen: or traces of travel brought home from the East. 1844 (anon), 1844, 1845, New York 1845, 1845, Leipzig 1846, London 1847 (5th edn), 1849, New York 1849, London 1850, 1856, 1859, New York 1859, London 1864, 1878, Edinburgh 1879, New York 1879, 1891; ed A. I. Shand, Edinburgh 1896; ed W. Tuckwell 1898; ed J. W. Redway, New York 1898; ed J. Bryce, New York 1900; ed W. H. D. Rouse 1901; ed J. C. Hogarth, Oxford 1906; ed A. T. Quiller-Couch 1907; ed H. Spender 1908, 1931, 1954 (EL); illustr F. Brangwyn 1913; ed H. G. Smith 1927; ed B. J. Hayes 1931; ed G. Boas 1932; ed R. W. Jepson 1935; ed C. H. Hopkins, Edinburgh 1935; ed J. W. Oliver, Edinburgh 1941; ed R. Fedden 1948; ed P. H. Newby 1949, 1952; ed F. Baker 1964.
The rights of women. Quart Rev 75 1845.
The French lake. Ibid.
Victor Hugo on the great French puzzle. Blackwood's Mag Dec 1862. On Hugo's account of Waterloo in Les misérables.
The invasion of the Crimea: its origin and an account of its progress down to the death of Lord Raglan. Vols 1–2 Edinburgh 1863 (4 edns), 2 vols New York 1863–8, 8 vols Edinburgh 1863–87, 7 vols Leipzig 1863–89, 9 vols Edinburgh 1877–8 (6th edn); ed G. S. Clarke, Edinburgh 1899 (abridged); tr French, 1864; Russian, 1890.
Life of Madame de Lafayette. Blackwood's Mag Sept 1872.

§2

[Warburton, E.] Eothen. Quart Rev 75 1845.
[Reeve, H.] Kinglake's Crimean War. Edinburgh Rev 117 1863.
[Layard, A. H.] Kinglake's Invasion of the Crimea. Quart Rev 113 1863.
Hayward, A. Mr Kinglake and the quarterlys, by an old reviewer. 1863 (3 edns).
[Hamley, E. B.] Kinglake's Crimea. Blackwood's Mag March 1863.
Gregory, I. Eothen and the Athenaeum Club. Blackwood's Mag Dec 1895.
Tuckwell, W. Kinglake: a biographical and literary study. 1902.
Ince, R. B. In his Calverley and some Cambridge wits of the nineteenth century, 1929.
Ellis, A. W. Kinglake: called Eothen. London Mercury Aug 1933.
From Kinglake to Lawrence. TLS. 25 July 1935.
Carrington, N. T. Kinglake: Eothen. 1939.
Wood, F. An English traveller of the nineteenth century. Anglica 1 1946.
Fedden, R. Towards the dawn and the sun-rising. Nineteenth Century Aug 1948.

JOHN LINGARD
1771–1851

Bibliographies

Gillow, J. Bibliographical dictionary of the English Catholics. 5 vols 1885–1902. *See* vol 4 pp. 254–78.
Haile, M. and E. Bonney. Life and letters of Lingard. 1911. *See* pp. 383–8.

§1

Catholic loyalty vindicated. 1805.
The antiquities of the Anglo-Saxon Church. 2 vols Newcastle 1806, 1810, Philadelphia 1841, 1845 (rev as The history and antiquities of the Anglo-Saxon Church), 1858 (4th edn); tr French, 1828; German, 1847.
Letters on Catholic loyalty. Newcastle 1807.
Observations on the laws and ordinances which exist in foreign states relative to the religious concerns of their Roman Catholic subjects. 1817, 1851.
The history of England from the first invasion by the Romans to the accession of Henry VIII. 3 vols 1819, 8 vols 1819–30 (as History of England from the first invasion by the Romans to the accession of William and Mary in 1688), 14 vols 1825 (3rd edn), 13 vols 1837–9 (rev), 10 vols 1849, 1854 (6th edn with memoir by M. A. Tierney), 1883, Dublin 1888, Edinburgh 1902, 11 vols 1912–15 (supplementary vol by H. Belloc); ed P. Sadler, Paris 1836 (abridged); ed J. Burke 1855 (abridged); ed M. J. Kerney, Baltimore 1855, 1875; ed H. Mensch, Berlin 1863; ed T. Young, Dublin 1867; ed H. N. Birt 1903, 1912; tr French, 1825–31, 1833–5; Italian, [1835].
A collection of tracts on several subjects connected with the civil and religious principles of Catholics. 1826.
A new version of the four Gospels with notes critical and explanatory, by a Catholic. 1836, 1846, 1851.
Did the Church of England reform herself? Dublin Rev 9 1840.
The ancient church of England and the liturgy of the Anglican Church. Dublin Rev 11 1841.
Lingard also pbd a number of pamphlets defending the Catholic position against Anglican attacks.

§2

[Allen, J.] Lingard's History. Edinburgh Rev 42 1825.
— The massacre of St Bartholomew. Edinburgh Rev 44 1826. Reply by Lingard, A vindication of certain passages in the fourth and fifth volumes of the History of England, 1826 (3 edns), 1827 (rev), 1827; tr French, 1827.
[Milman, H. H.] The Reformation in England. Quart Rev 33 1825.

Todd, H. J. A vindication of Cranmer against some of the allegations of Dr Lingard. 1826.
[Hallam, H.] Lingard's History of England. Edinburgh Rev 53 1831.
[Wiseman, N. P.] Dr Lingard. Dublin Rev 35 1854.
Tierney, M. A. Memoir of Lingard. 1855.
Haile, M. and E. Bonney. Life and letters of Lingard. 1911, St Louis 1911.
Fletcher, J. Lingard 1771–1851. 1925.
Lechmere, J. A great Catholic historian: John Cardinal [sic] Lingard. Ecclesiastical Rev 94 1938.
Hollis, C. Lingard. Historical Bull 11 1933.
—— In Great Catholics, ed C. C. H. Williamson 1938.
Coonan, T. L. In Some modern historians of Britain, ed H. Ausubel, New York 1951.

JUSTIN McCARTHY
1830–1912

§1

Con amore: or critical chapters. 1868.
The settlement of the Alabama question. 1871.
Modern leaders: biographical sketches. New York 1872.
Dear Lady Disdain. 1875, New York 1876, London 1878, 1887. A novel.
A history of our own times from the accession of Queen Victoria to the Berlin Congress. Vols 1–2 1879, vols 3–4 1880 (as History of our own times from the accession of Queen Victoria to the general election of 1880), 5 vols Leipzig 1879–80, 4 vols 1880, 2 vols New York 1880, 1 vol New York 1880, 4 vols Chicago 1887, 5 vols 1889–97 (with continuation to the Diamond jubilee), 7 vols 1897–1905 (with continuation to the accession of Edward VII), 5 vols New York 1897–1905, 7 vols 1908; ed G. M. Adam 2 vols New York 1900; tr German, 1881; French, 1885–7.
The epoch of reform 1830–50. 1882, New York 1882, 1888.
A history of the four Georges. 2 vols 1884, New York 1884, 1884, 4 vols 1901 (as A history of the four Georges and of William IV, vols 3–4 completed by J. H. McCarthy), 2 vols 1905.
A short history of our own times. New York 1884, London 1888, 2 vols New York 1893, 1 vol 1907, New York 1908. *See* English literature in the reign of Queen Victoria, below.
Ireland's cause in England's parliament. Ed J. B. O'Reilly, Boston 1888.
Charing Cross to St Paul's. Illustr J. Pennell 1891, 1893, New York 1893.
Sir Robert Peel. 1891, New York 1891, London 1906 (4th edn).
Pope Leo XIII. 1896, 1899, New York 1899.
The Daily News jubilee: a political and social retrospect. 1896. With J. R. Robinson.
The story of Mr Gladstone's life. 1897, 1898 (rev), 1898.
The inner life of the House of Commons, by W. White. 2 vols 1897. Ed McCarthy.
Modern England. 2 vols 1899, New York 1899 (as The story of the people of England in the nineteenth century).
Reminiscences. 2 vols 1899, New York 1899.
English literature in the reign of Queen Victoria. Ed R. Ackermann, Dresden 1899. Selected from History of our own times, above.
The reign of Queen Anne. 2 vols 1902, New York 1902, London 1905.
Portraits of the sixties. 1903, New York 1903.
Ireland and her story. 1903.
British political portraits. 1903.
Irish literature. 10 vols Chicago 1904. Ed McCarthy et al.
The story of an Irishman. 1904, New York 1904 (as An Irishman's story). Autobiography.
Irish recollections. 1911. New York 1912.
Our book of memories: letters of McCarthy to Mrs Campbell Praed. 1912.
McCarthy also pbd novels, many in collaboration with Mrs Campbell Praed.

§2

O'Connor, T. P. In his Parnell movement, 1889.
Times 26 April 1912.

SIR JAMES MACKINTOSH
1765–1832

§1

Vindiciae gallicae. Dublin 1791, London 1791 (rev), 1791 (3rd edn), Philadelphia 1792, London 1838; tr French, 1792. A reply to Burke's Reflections on the revolution in France.
A discourse on the study of the law of nature and of nations. 1799, Dublin 1799, London 1828, 1835, Edinburgh 1835; ed J. G. Marvin, Boston 1843; tr French, 1830.
Mélanges philosophiques. Paris 1829.
Dissertation on the progress of ethical philosophy chiefly during the seventeenth and eighteenth centuries. 1830 (as suppl to Encyclopaedia britannica 7th edn), Edinburgh 1830 (priv ptd), Philadelphia 1832, 1834; ed W. Whewell, Edinburgh 1836 (as A general view of the progress of ethical philosophy), 1862, 1872 (4th edn).
The history of England. 3 vols 1830–2 (in Cabinet cyclopaedia, ed D. Lardner 1830–40), 3 vols Philadelphia 1830–3, 10 vols 1850 (completed by W. Wallace and R. Bell); ed R. J. Mackintosh 2 vols 1853.
The life of Sir Thomas More. 1831 (in Cabinet cyclopaedia), 1844.
History of the revolution in England in 1688 completed to the settlement of the crown by the editor William Wallace. 1834 (with memoir), Philadelphia 1835; London 1835 (Mackintosh's portion only, as A view of the reign of James II).
Tracts and speeches. 5 pts Edinburgh 1840 (25 copies).
Miscellaneous works. Ed R. J. Mackintosh 3 vols 1846, Philadelphia 1848, 1 vol 1851, Boston 1854, 3 vols 1854, 1 vol New York 1871, 1878.

§2

Memoirs of the life of Mackintosh. Ed R. J. Mackintosh 2 vols 1835, Philadelphia 1835, London 1853, Boston 1853.
[Croker, J. W.] Life of Mackintosh. Quart Rev 54 1835.
Macaulay, T. B. Sir James Mackintosh. Edinburgh Rev 61 1835; rptd in his Critical and historical essays vol 2, 1843.
Mill, James. A fragment on Mackintosh. 1835.
De Quincey, T. A glance at the works of Mackintosh. Tait's Mag June 1846; rptd in his Works, ed D. Masson 1897.
[MacDowall, A.] Miscellaneous works of Mackintosh. North Br Rev 5 1846.
Bulwer, H. In his Historical characters, 1868.

SIR THOMAS ERSKINE MAY, 1st BARON FARNBOROUGH
1815–86

§1

The Imperial Parliament. 1840 (anon in Penny cyclopaedia vol 17), 1841 (in Knight's Store of knowledge for all readers).

A treatise on the law, privileges, proceedings and usage of Parliament. 1844, 1851 (rev), 1859 (4th edn), 1868 (6th edn), 1879 (8th edn), 1883; ed R. R. D. Palgrave and A. B. Carter 1893; ed T. L. Webster and W. E. Grey 1906, 1924 (13th edn); ed G. Campion and T. G. B. Cocks 1950 (15th edn); ed E. Fellowes and T. G. B. Cocks 1957 (16th edn); ed B. Cocks 1965 (17th edn); tr German, 1888; Italian, 1888; French, 1909.

Remarks and suggestions with a view to facilitating the dispatch of public business in Parliament. 1849, 1849 (2nd edn).

On the consolidation of the election laws. 1850.

The constitutional history of England since the accession of George III. 2 vols 1861–3, 1863–5, Boston 1862–3, 3 vols 1871, 2 vols New York 1876–7, 3 vols 1878 (6th edn), 1896 (11th edn); ed F. Holland 3 vols 1912; tr French, 1865–6; Spanish, 1883–4.

Democracy in Europe: a history. 2 vols 1877, New York 1878; tr French, 1879; Italian, 1883.

The machinery of parliamentary legislation. 1881. Rptd from Edinburgh Rev 99 1854.

§2

[Smith, C. C.] May's Constitutional history. North Amer Rev 97 1863.

Arnold, M. In his Equality, Fortnightly Rev March 1878; rptd in his Mixed essays, 1879.

Times 18, 25, 27 May 1886.

CHARLES MERIVALE

1808–93

§1

History of Rome under the Emperors: the Augustan age. 1843.

A history of the Romans under the Empire. 7 vols 1850–62, 1862, New York 1864–79, 8 vols 1865, 1890; tr Italian, 1865; French, 1865–7; German, 1866–72.

C. Sallustii Crispi Catilina et Jugurtha. 1852; Jugurtha, 1884; Catilina, 1888. Ed Merivale.

The fall of the Roman Republic: a short history of the last century of the commonwealth. 1853, 1853 (2nd edn). An abridgement of vols 1–3 of History of the Romans, above.

An account of the life and letters of Cicero, by B. R. Abeken. 1854. Tr Merivale.

Keatsii Hyperionis libri tres. Cambridge 1863, 1882 (rev). Tr Merivale.

The conversion of the Roman Empire (Boyle lectures 1864). 1865, 1865, New York 1865.

The conversion of the northern nations (Boyle lectures 1865). 1866, New York 1866.

Homer's Iliad in English rhymed verse. 2 vols 1869.

The contrast between pagan and Christian society: a lecture. 1872, 1880.

A general history of Rome from the foundation of the city to the fall of Augustulus B.C. 753–A.D. 476. 1875, 1875, 1876, 1877, New York 1877, London 1891; ed C. Puller 1877, New York 1878 (abridged); ed O. Smeaton 2 vols 1910 (as History of Rome to the reign of Trajan), 1928 (EL).

The Roman triumvirates. 1876, 1883 (3rd edn), 1887 (5th edn), New York 1889.

The heathen world and St Paul. 1877.

The continental Teutons. In The conversion of the west, 5 vols 1878–9.

Four lectures on some epochs of early church history. 1879.

Autobiography and letters. Ed J. A. Merivale, Oxford 1898 (priv ptd), London 1899 (as Autobiography of Merivale with selections from his correspondence).

§2

Times 28 Dec 1893.

Watkins, H. W. In his Churchmen, scholars and gentlemen, Quart Rev 191 1900.

SIR WILLIAM FRANCIS PATRICK NAPIER

1785–1860

§1

The art of war. Edinburgh Rev 35 1821.

History of the war in the Peninsula and the south of France from the year 1807 to the year 1814. 6 vols 1828–40, 4 vols Paris 1839–40, Philadelphia 1842, 6 vols 1851 (rev), 5 vols 1856, New York 1856, 3 vols 1876–82, 6 vols 1882, 1900; ed R. W. O'Byrne 1889; ed W. T. Dobson 1889; ed E. A. Arnold 1905; ed A. T. Quiller-Couch, Oxford 1908; ed M. Fanshawe 1911; ed H. Strang 1913; tr French, 1828–44. Abridged by Napier as English battles, below.

A reply to various opponents. 1832 (in History vol 1, 2nd edn), 1833, 1833.

Colonel Napier's justification of his third volume. 1833.

The conquest of Scinde; with some introductory passages in the life of Major-General Sir Charles James Napier. 1845, 1845 (2nd edn).

History of General Sir Charles James Napier's administration of Scinde and campaign in the Cutchee Hills. 1851, 1857, 1858 (3rd edn).

English battles and sieges in the Peninsula. 1852, 1855, 1866, 1904, 1910; ed W. H. D. Rouse 2 vols 1905. Abridgment by Napier of The war in the peninsula, above.

The life and opinions of General Sir Charles James Napier. 4 vols 1857, 1857 (2nd edn).

§2

[Murray, G.] Napier's Peninsular war. Quart Rev 56 1836 (2 articles). Reply by Napier, Westminster Rev 26 1837.

Outram, J. The conquest of Scinde: a commentary. 1846.

[Dallas, E. S.] General Sir Charles Napier. Times 8, 10 April, 25 May, 24 July 1857.

The life of Napier. Ed H. A. Bruce 2 vols 1964.

[Hamley, E. B.] Life of Napier. Blackwood's Mag June 1864.

Holmes, T. R. E. In his Four famous soldiers, 1889.

Gwynn, S. L. A brotherhood of heroes: being memorials of Charles, George and William Napier. 1910.

FREDERICK YORK POWELL

1850–1904

Bibliographies

Elton, O. Powell: his life and a selection from his letters. 2 vols Oxford 1906. *See* vol 2 pp. vii–xvi.

§1

Early England up to the Norman Conquest. 1876, New York 1877, London 1895 (11th edn).

An Icelandic prose reader. Oxford 1879. With G. Vigfússon.

Alfred the Great and William the Conqueror. 1881.

Old stories from British history. 1882, 1885 (3rd edn).

Corpus poeticum boreale: the poetry of the old northern tongues. 2 vols Oxford 1883. Ed and tr with G. Vigfússon.

History of England. 3 vols 1885–90, 1898–1900, 1 vol 1904. With J. M. Mackay and T. F. Tout.
English history by contemporary writers. 1887. Ed Powell.
Sketches from British history. 1888, 1889.
The first nine books of the Danish history of Saxo Grammaticus translated by Oliver Elton. 1894. Ed Powell.
Some words on allegory in England. 1895 (priv ptd); ed E. Clarke and J. Todhunter 1910.
The tale of Thrond of Gate: commonly called Faereyinga saga. 1896. Tr Powell.
XXIV quatrains from Omar. New York 1900. Tr Powell.
Two Oxford historians. Quart Rev 195 1902. With C. H. Firth; on S. R. Gardiner and J. R. Green.
John Ruskin and thoughts on democracy. 1905.
Origines Islandicae: a collection of the more important sagas. 2 vols Oxford 1905. Ed and tr with G. Vigfússon.
Collingwood, W. G. Scandinavian Britain; with chapters introductory to the subject by F. York Powell. 1908.

§2

Rait, R. S. F. York Powell. EHR 19 1904.
Watson, H. B. M. Professor Powell. Athenaeum 14 May 1904.
Cook, T. A. F. York Powell. Monthly Rev June 1904.
Elton, O. Powell: his life and a selection from his letters and occasional writings. 2 vols Oxford 1906.
Wilkins, B. T. Powell and Charles A. Beard: a study in Anglo-American historiography and social thought. Amer Quart 11 1959.

SIR JOHN ROBERT SEELEY
1834–95

§1

A parallel between Shakespeare's King Lear and the Oedipus in Colono of Sophocles. In Three essays on King Lear by pupils of the City of London School, 1851.
David and Samuel, with other poems, by John Robertson. 1859.
The student's guide to the University of Cambridge. Cambridge 1863, 1866; rev R. B. Somerset 1874. Ed Seeley.
Classical studies as an introduction to the moral sciences: an introductory lecture. 1864.
Ecce homo: a survey of the life and work of Jesus Christ. 1866 (for 1865) (anon), 1866 (5th edn), Boston 1866, 1867, London 1867, 1895, Boston 1903, London 1905, 1914; ed O. Lodge 1908, 1923 (EL); ed J. E. Odgers 1910; tr German, 1867; Danish, 1874; Italian, nd.
Lectures and essays. 1870; ed M. Seeley 1895.
Livy, book 1. Oxford 1871, 1881 (3rd edn). Ed Seeley.
English lessons for English people. 1871. With E. A. Abbott.
Life and times of Stein: or Germany and Prussia in the Napoleonic age. 3 vols Cambridge 1878, 2 vols Boston 1879; tr German, 1883–7.
Natural religion, by the author of Ecce homo. 1882, Boston 1882, 1891 (3rd edn), 1895.
The expansion of England. 1883, Boston 1883, Leipzig 1884, London 1888, 1895, 1898, Boston 1900, London 1911; abridged 1887 (as Our colonial expansion); tr French, 1885; Portuguese, 1891; Italian, 1897; German, 1954.
A short history of Napoleon the first. 1886, Boston 1886, London 1900, Boston 1901; tr French, 1887.
Roman imperialism and other lectures and essays. Boston 1889.
Goethe reviewed after sixty years. Boston 1893, London 1894, Leipzig 1894.
The growth of British policy: an historical essay. 2 vols Cambridge 1895, 1903, 1 vol Cambridge 1921, 1922. Memoir by G. W. Prothero.
Introduction to political science. Ed H. Sidgwick 1896, 1901.

§2

Sidgwick, H. Ecce homo. Westminster Rev 86 1866; rptd in his Miscellaneous essays and addresses, 1904.
Stanley, A. P. Ecce homo. Macmillan's Mag June 1866.
Newman, J. H. An internal argument for Christianity. Month June 1866; rptd in his Discussions and arguments, 1872.
[Stephen, J. F.] Ecce homo. Fraser's Mag June–July 1866.
[Parker, J.] Ecce deus. 1867, New York 1867, London 1868 (3rd edn).
Gladstone, W. E. Ecce homo. Good Words Jan–March 1868; rptd 1868.
Stedefeld, G. F. Über die naturalistische Auffassung der Engländer. Berlin 1869.
Myers, F. W. H. A new eirenicon. In his Essays modern, 1883.
Morley, J. The expansion of England. Macmillan's Mag Feb 1884; rptd in his Critical miscellanies, 1886.
Jacobs, J. In his Literary studies, 1895.
[Doyle, J. A.] Freeman, Froude and Seeley. Quart Rev 182 1895.
Gazeau, J. L'impérialisme anglais, son évolution: Carlyle, Seeley, Chamberlain. Paris 1903.
Benn, A. W. In his History of English rationalism in the nineteenth century, 1906.
Rein, A. Seeley: eine Studie über den Historiker. Langensalza 1912.
Rosenbluth, E. Seeley: sein historisches und politisches Weltbild. Berlin 1934.
Brettschneider, G. Der Humanismus Seeleys. Leipzig 1937.
Krieger, E. Die Bedeutung des Organischen in englischen Volks- und Staatsbegriff (Burke, Freeman, Seeley, Froude). Die Neueren Sprachen 46 1938.
Rosenberg, H. Seeleys The expansion of England in Rahmen des nationalpolitischen Unterrichts. Neuphilologische Monatsschrift 10 1939.
Gooch, G. P. In his Some great English historians, Contemporary Rev Jan 1957.
Powell, H. G. Ecce homo: the historical Jesus in 1865. London Quart 191 1966.

GOLDWIN SMITH
1823–1910

§1

The war passages in Maud. Saturday Rev 3 Nov 1855.
Oxford university reform. In Oxford essays by members of the University, Oxford 1858.
Lectures on modern history. Oxford 1861, 1865 (as Lectures on the study of history), New York 1866, Toronto 1873.
Irish history and Irish character. Oxford 1861, 1862.
Rational religion and the rationalistic objections of the Bampton lectures for 1858. Oxford 1861. On H. L. Mansel, Limits of religious thought.
Does the Bible sanction American slavery? Oxford 1863, Cambridge Mass 1863.
The Empire: a series of letters published in the Daily News. Oxford 1863.
England and America: a lecture. Atlantic Monthly Dec 1864; rptd Boston 1865, Manchester 1865.
A letter to a Whig member of the Southern Independence Association. Boston 1864.
A plea for the abolition of tests in the University of Oxford. Oxford 1864.

The civil war in America: an address. 1866.
Three English statesmen: a course of lectures. 1867, New York 1867. On Pym, Cromwell and Pitt.
The reorganization of the University of Oxford. 1868.
The political destiny of Canada. Toronto 1877, 1878, New York 1878.
Cowper. 1880, New York 1880, 1884, London 1888, 1898, 1904 (EML).
Lectures and essays. Toronto 1881 (priv ptd).
False hopes: or fallacies socialistic and semi-socialistic briefly answered. New York 1883, London 1886.
Life of Jane Austen. 1890.
Loyalty, aristocracy and jingoism: three lectures. Toronto 1891.
Canada and the Canadian question. 1891, Toronto 1891.
A trip to England. Toronto 1891, 1892, New York 1892, London 1895.
The moral crusader: William Lloyd Garrison. Toronto 1892, New York 1892.
The United States: an outline of political history 1492–1871. 1893, New York 1893, 1899.
Bay leaves: translations from the Latin poets. New York 1893.
Specimens of Greek tragedy. 2 vols New York 1893. Tr Smith.
Essays on questions of the day: political and social. New York 1893, 1894 (rev), Boston 1894.
Oxford and her colleges. 1894, New York 1895, 1906.
Guesses at the riddle of existence. New York 1897, 1898.
Shakespeare the man. Toronto 1899, New York 1900.
The United Kingdom: a political history. 2 vols 1899, Toronto 1899, New York 1899.
Commonwealth or empire? a bystander's view of the question. New York 1902.
In the court of history: an apology for Canadians who were opposed to the South African War. Toronto 1902.
The founder of Christendom. Boston 1903.
My memory of Gladstone. 1904, 1904, Toronto 1904.
Irish history and the Irish question. 1905, Toronto 1905, New York 1905.
In quest of light. New York 1906.
No refuge but in truth. Toronto 1908, London 1909, New York 1909.
Reminiscences. Ed A. Haultain, New York 1910, 1911.
A selection from Smith's correspondence. Ed A. Haultain 1913, New York 1913.

§2

Andrews, C. M. Goldwin Smith. Amer Historical Rev 5 1900.
McCarthy, J. In his Portraits of the sixties, 1903.
Haultain, A. Smith: his life and opinions. 1913.
Micklewright, F. H. A. Smith: a liberal teacher. Congregational Quart 20 1942.
Wallace, E. Smith and social reform. Canadian Historical Rev 29 1948.
—— Goldwin Smith: liberal. UTQ 23 1954.
—— Smith on England and America. Amer Historical Rev 59 1954.
—— Smith on history. Jnl of Modern History 26 1954.
—— Goldwin Smith: Victorian liberal. Toronto 1957.
Ausubel, H. In his Some modern historians of Britain, New York 1951.
Brown, R. C. Smith and anti-imperialism. Canadian Historical Rev 43 1962.

PHILIP HENRY STANHOPE, 5th EARL STANHOPE called Viscount Mahon 1821–55

1805–75

§1

The life of Belisarius. 1829, 1848.
History of the war of the succession in Spain. 1832–3, 1836.
Lord John Russell and Mr Macaulay on the French Revolution. 1833. Rptd from Quart Rev 49 1833.
Letters from the Earl of Peterborough to General Stanhope in Spain. 1834. Ed Stanhope.
History of England from the Peace of Utrecht to the Peace of Aix-la-Chapelle. 7 vols 1836–54, 1839–54 (as History of England from the Peace of Utrecht to the Peace of Versailles 1713–83); ed H. Reed 2 vols New York (as History of England from the Peace of Utrecht to the Peace of Paris); 7 vols 1853–4 (3rd edn rev), Boston 1853–4, 4 vols Leipzig 1853–4, 7 vols 1858 (5th edn rev). For extracts, *see* below.
The rise of our Indian Empire. 1838, 1876 (3rd edn). Extracted from History of England, above.
Spain under Charles the second: extracts from the correspondence of the honourable Alexander Stanhope. 1840. Ed Stanhope.
Essai sur la vie du grand Condé. 1842 (priv ptd); tr 1845 (as The life of Louis Prince of Condé), New York 1845.
Correspondence between William Pitt and Charles Duke of Rutland. 1842 (priv ptd), 1890. Ed Stanhope.
The decline of the last Stuarts: extracts from despatches. 1843. Ed Stanhope.
The letters of Philip Dormer Stanhope, Earl of Chesterfield. 5 vols 1845–53. Ed Stanhope.
Historical essays contributed to the Quarterly Review. 1849, 1861. *See* Joan of Arc, below.
The Forty-Five. 1851, 1851. Extracted from History of England, above.
Secret correspondence connected with Mr Pitt's return to office in 1804. 1852 (priv ptd). Ed Stanhope.
Joan of Arc. 1854. Rptd from Historical essays, above.
Lord Chatham at Chevening 1769. 1855, 1859.
Addresses delivered at Manchester, Leeds and Birmingham. 1856.
Memoirs of Sir Robert Peel. 2 vols 1856–7. Ed Stanhope and E. Cardwell.
Were human sacrifices in use among the Romans? Correspondence between Mr Macaulay, Sir Robert Peel and Lord Mahon. 1860 (priv ptd); ed T. Thayer 1878 (priv ptd) (as Some inquiries concerning human sacrifice among the Romans).
Life of William Pitt. 4 vols 1861–2, 1862, 1867 (3rd edn), 3 vols 1879; tr French, 1862–3; Italian, 1864.
Miscellanies. 1863, 1863 (rev); Second series, 1872.
History of England comprising the reign of Queen Anne until the Peace of Utrecht. 1870, 1870, Leipzig 1870, 2 vols 1872 (4th edn).
Notes of conversation with Louis-Philippe at Claremont. 1873 (priv ptd).
The French retreat from Moscow and other historical essays. 1876.
Notes of conversations with the Duke of Wellington. 1888, 1889 (3rd edn); ed P. Guedalla, Oxford 1938 (WC).

§2

Macaulay, T. B. Lord Mahon's War of the Succession. Edinburgh Rev 56 1833; rptd in his Critical and historical essays, 1843.
[Dallas, E. S.] Stanhope's Life of Pitt. Times 21 May 1861, 25 April 1862.
[Macpherson, W.] The Stanhope miscellanies. Quart Rev 113 1863.
Times 25 Dec 1875.

SIR JAMES STEPHEN
1789–1859
§1

Critical and miscellaneous essays. Philadelphia 1843, 1846, 1848, Boston 1854, 1856, New York 1873.
Essays in ecclesiastical biography. 2 vols 1849, 1853 (3rd edn); ed J. F. Stephen 1860, 1872, 1907.
Lectures on the history of France. 2 vols 1851, 1852, 1 vol New York 1852, 1855, 2 vols 1857 (3rd edn rev).
Letters: with biographical notes by his daughter C. E. Stephen. Gloucester 1906 (priv ptd).

§2

Stephen, J. F. Biographical notice. In Essays in ecclesiastical biography, above, 1860.
Stephen, L. In his Life of Sir James Fitzjames Stephen, 1895.
—— In his Some early impressions, 1924.
Maitland, F. W. In his Life and letters of Leslie Stephen, 1906.
Russell, G. W. E. In his Short history of the Evangelical Movement, 1915.
Foden, N. A. Stephen: architect of empire. Auckland 1938.
Kinchin, O. A. The Stephen–Russell reform in official tenure. Canadian Historical Rev 26 1945.
Annan, N. In his Leslie Stephen, 1951.
Knaplund, P. Stephen and the British colonial system. Madison 1953.
Hughes, E. Stephen and the anonymity of the civil servant. Public Administration 36 1958.
Ward, J. M. The retirement of a titan: Stephen 1847–50. Jnl Modern History 31 1959.
Young, D. M. In his Colonial Office in the early nineteenth century, 1961.
Brown, F. K. In his Fathers of the Victorians, Cambridge 1961.

SIR JAMES FITZJAMES STEPHEN
1829–94
Bibliographies

Stephen, L. The life of J. F. Stephen. 1895. *See* pp. 483–6.
Radzinowicz, L. Stephen and his contribution to the development of criminal law. 1957. A lecture with bibliographical appendix.

§1

The relation of novels to life. In Cambridge essays, 1855.
The characteristics of English criminal law. In Cambridge essays, 1857.
Matthew Arnold and the Italian question. Saturday Rev 13 Aug 1859; ed M. M. Bevington, Durham NC 1953 (with Arnold's England and the Italian question).
Essays by a barrister. 1862. Anon.
Defence of the Rev Rowland Williams. 1862.
A general view of the criminal law of England. 1863, 1890; tr Russian, 1865.
Matthew Arnold and his countrymen. Saturday Rev 3 Dec 1864. Reply by Arnold, My countrymen, Cornhill Mag Feb 1866.
The definition of murder considered. 1866.
The Indian Evidence Act of 1872. 1872, Calcutta 1904 (as Introduction to the Indian Evidence Act).
Liberty, equality, fraternity. 1873, New York 1873, London 1874.
A digest of the law of evidence. 1876, 1876, St Louis 1876, London 1877 (3rd edn); ed J. W. May, Boston 1877, 1886; St Louis 1879, London 1881 (4th edn); ed G. Chase, New York 1885, 1886, 1898, 1912; ed W. Reynolds, Chicago 1888, 1895; ed H. and H. L. Stephen 1899 (5th edn), 1904, 1914, 1922 (10th edn); ed G. E. Beers, Hartford 1901, 1902, 1903, 1904, 1907; ed H. L. Stephen and L. F. Sturge 1936 (12th edn), 1946, 1948; tr Russian, 1910.
A digest of the criminal law (crimes and punishments). 1877, St Louis 1877, London 1879, 1883 (3rd edn), 1887; ed H. and H. L. Stephen 1894 (4th edn), 1904, 1926 (7th edn); ed L. F. Sturge 1947 (8th edn), 1950.
A digest of the criminal procedure in indictable offences. 1883. With H. Stephen.
A history of the criminal law of England. 3 vols 1883.
Letters on the Ilbert Bill: reprinted from the Times. 1883.
The story of Nuncomar and the impeachment of Sir Elijah Impey. 2 vols 1885.
The late Mr Carlyle's papers. 1886 (priv ptd). Defends Froude's conduct as Carlyle's literary executor.
Horae sabbaticae. 3 sers 1892. Rptd from Saturday Rev.

§2

Harrison, F. The religion of inhumanity. Fortnightly Rev June 1873.
Morley, J. Mr Mill's doctrine of liberty. Fortnightly Rev Aug 1873.
Stephen, L. The life of J. F. Stephen. 1895.
[Roscoe, E. S.] Sir J. F. Stephen. Edinburgh Rev 182 1895.
Pollock, F. Sir J. F. Stephen. Nat Rev Nov 1895.
Lippincott, B. E. In his Victorian critics of democracy, Minneapolis 1938.
Bevington, M. M. In his The Saturday Review 1855–68, New York 1941.
The art of government: Stephen and liberal doctrine. TLS 27 Nov 1948.
Annan, N. In his Leslie Stephen, 1951.
Radzinovicz, L. In his History of English criminal law, 1956.
—— Stephen and his contribution to the development of criminal law. 1957.
Roach, J. Liberalism and the Victorian intelligentsia. Cambridge Historical Jnl 13 1957.
Cockshut, A. O. J. In his Anglican attitudes, 1959.
Carré, M. H. Stephenism. Hibbert Jnl 64 1966.

WILLIAM STUBBS
1825–1901
Bibliographies

Shaw, W. A. A bibliography of the historical works of Dr Creighton, Dr Stubbs, Dr S. R. Gardiner and Lord Acton. 1903.
Letters of Stubbs. Ed W. H. Hutton 1904. *See* pp. 409–15.

§1

Registrum sacrum anglicanum: an attempt to exhibit the course of episcopal succession in England. Oxford 1858; ed S. E. Holmes, Oxford 1897.
Select charters and other illustrations of English constitutional history. Oxford 1866, 1870, 1874, 1884 (6th edn), 1895 (8th edn), 1900; ed H. W. C. Davis, Oxford 1913 (9th edn), 1921, 1929.
An address delivered by way of inaugural lecture. 1867, Oxford 1867 (rev).
Memorials of St Dunstan. 1874. Ed Stubbs.
The historical works of Gervase of Canterbury. 2 vols 1870–80. Ed Stubbs.
The constitutional history of England in its origin and development. 3 vols Oxford 1874–8, 1877–80, 1896–7, 1926–9; preface, ed C. Morley, Madison NJ 1950 (as Kettel Hall Christmas 1873).

The early Plantagenets. 1876, Boston 1876, London 1886 (5th edn), New York 1887, London 1889, New York 1889, London 1901 (10th edn).
Two lectures on the present state and prospects of historical study. Oxford 1876 (priv ptd).
The mediaeval kingdoms of Cyprus and Armenia: two lectures. Oxford 1878.
Chronicles of the reigns of Edward I and Edward II. 2 vols 1882–3. Ed Stubbs.
Origines Celticae. 2 vols 1883. Ed Stubbs and C. Deedes.
An address delivered by way of a last statutory lecture. Oxford 1884.
Seventeen lectures on the study of mediaeval and modern history. Oxford 1886, 1887, 1900.
Wilhelmi Malmesbiriensis de gestis regum Anglorum. 1887. Ed Stubbs.
Ordination addresses. Ed E. E. Holmes 1901.
Historical introductions to the Rolls Series. Ed A. Hassall 1902.
Lectures on European history. Ed A. Hassall 1904.
Letters of Stubbs. Ed W. H. Hutton 1904, 1906 (abridged).
Visitation charges. Ed E. E. Holmes 1904.
Lectures on early English history. Ed A. Hassall 1906.
Germany in the early Middle Ages 476–1250. Ed A. Hassall 1908.
Germany in the later Middle Ages 1200–1500. Ed A. Hassall 1908.
Genealogical history of the family of Bishop Stubbs, compiled by himself. Ed F. Collins 1915.
On convocation. Ed W. H. Hutton 1917.

§2

[Adams, H.] Stubbs's Constitutional history of England. North Amer Rev 119 1874.
[Dicey, A. V.] Stubbs's Constitutional history. Nation (New York) 4 March 1875.
Maitland, F. W. Stubbs: Bishop of Oxford. EHR 16 1901; rptd in his Collected papers, ed H. A. L. Fisher 1911.
Green, J. R. Stubbs's inaugural lecture. In his Stray studies 2nd ser, 1903.
Paul, H. In his Stray leaves, 1906.
Petit-Dutaillis, C. Studies and notes supplementary to Stubbs's Constitutional history. 3 vols Manchester 1908–29. With G. Lefebvre.
Cam, H. Stubbs seventy years after. Cambridge Historical Jnl 9 1948.
Edwards, J. G. William Stubbs. 1952.
Williams, N. J. Stubbs's appointment as Regius Professor. Bull Inst Historical Research 33 1960.
Richardson, H. G. and G. O. Sayles. In their Government of mediaeval England from the Conquest to Magna Carta, Edinburgh 1963.

JOHN ADDINGTON SYMONDS
1840–93

Bibliographies

Brown, H. F. In his Symonds: a biography vol 2, 1895.
Babington, P. L. Bibliography of the writings of Symonds. 1925.

§1

The Escorial: a prize poem. Oxford 1860.
The Renaissance: an essay. Oxford 1863.
The ring and the book. Macmillan's Mag Jan 1869.
Miscellanies, by J. A. Symonds M.D. 1871. Ed Symonds.
An introduction to the study of Dante. 1872, Edinburgh 1890; ed H. F. Brown 1899 (4th edn).
The renaissance of modern Europe: a lecture. 1872.
Studies of the Greek poets. 2 vols 1873–6, New York 1880, London 1893 (3rd edn), 1902, 1920.
Sketches in Italy and Greece. 1874, 1879.
The Renaissance in Italy. Vol 1: The age of the despots, 1875, 1876, New York 1881, 1883, London 1884, New York 1918, London 1923, New York 1960; tr Italian, 1900; vol 2: The revival of learning, 1877, 1880, New York 1883, 1888, London 1906, New York 1908, 1960; vol 3: The fine arts, 1877, 1879, New York 1883, London 1901, New York 1961; tr Italian, 1879; vols 4–5: Italian literature, 1881, New York 1882, London 1888, New York 1888; vols 6–7: The Catholic reaction, 1886, New York 1887, London 1909; collected 7 vols 1875–86, New York 1881–7, 5 vols 1900; ed A. Pearson 2 vols 1893, New York 1893, London 1904, 1935 (as A short history of the Renaissance in Italy).
Shelley. 1878, New York 1879, London 1887, New York 1894, 1901, London 1902, New York 1902 (EML).
Many moods: a volume of verse. 1878.
The sonnets of Michelangelo Buonarroti and Tommaso Campanella. 1878; Michelangelo, New York and London 1950. Tr Symonds.
Sketches and studies in Italy. 1879; tr German, 1912.
New and old: a volume of verse. 1880, Boston 1880.
Sketches and studies in southern Europe. 2 vols New York 1880.
Animi figura. 1882.
Notes on Mr D. G. Rossetti's new poems. Macmillan's Mag Feb 1882.
Italian byways. 1883, New York 1883, Leipzig 1884 (as New Italian sketches).
A problem in Greek ethics. 1883, 1901, 1908 (all priv ptd), 1928 (in Studies in sexual inversion).
Fragilia labilia. 1884 (priv ptd), Portland Maine 1902.
Vagabunduli libellus. 1884.
Shakspere's predecessors in the English drama. 1884, 1900.
Wine, women and song: mediaeval Latin students' songs. 1884, Portland Maine 1899, 1918, London 1907, 1925, 1931, San Francisco 1928 (as Medieval Latin students' songs). Tr Symonds.
Life of Ben Jonson. 1886.
Sir Philip Sidney. 1886, New York 1887, 1894, 1901, 1902, London 1902, 1906 (EML).
The life of Benvenuto Cellini. 1888, 1889, 1896, 1901, New York 1942; ed J. Pope-Hennessy, New York 1949. Tr Symonds.
Webster and Tourneur. 1888 (Mermaid ser), 1903, New York 1948, 1956, London 1954, 1959. Ed Symonds.
Essays speculative and suggestive. 2 vols 1890, 1 vol 1894, New York 1894; ed H. F. Brown 1907 (3rd edn).
The memoirs of Count Carlo Gozzi. 2 vols 1890; ed P. Horne, Oxford 1962. Tr Symonds.
A problem in modern ethics. 1891 (priv ptd) (anon), 1896, 1897 (in Sexual inversion by H. Ellis and Symonds), 1928 (in Studies in sexual inversion).
Our life in the Swiss highlands. 1892, 1907. With M. Symonds.
Midnight at Baiae. 1893.
In the key of blue and other prose essays. 1893, 1896 (3rd edn).
The life of Michelangelo Buonarroti. 2 vols 1893, 1893, 1911 (3rd edn), 1925, 1 vol New York 1928, 1936; tr Italian, 1943; Spanish, 1943.
Walt Whitman: a study. 1893, 1893, 1896, 1906.
Blank verse. Ed H. F. Brown 1894, 1895, New York 1895.
Giovanni Boccaccio as man and author. 1895.
Sketches and studies in Italy and Greece. Ed H. F. Brown 3 vols 1898, 1900. Includes Sketches in Italy and Greece, Sketches and studies in Italy, Italian byways.
Last and first: two essays. New York 1919.
Letters and papers. Ed H. F. Brown 1923.

§2

[Strachey, E.] Symonds's Renaissance in Italy. Spectator 24 July 1875, 27 Oct, 3 Nov 1877.
— Symonds's Studies of the Greek poets. Spectator 29 July 1876.
Hueffer, F. Symonds's Renaissance in Italy. Times 7 April 1882; rptd in his Italian and other studies, 1883.
Brown, H. F. Symonds: a biography. 2 vols 1895, New York 1895, London 1903.
Harrison, F. J. A. Symonds. 1896.
— In his Tennyson, Ruskin, Mill and other literary estimates, 1899.
Symons, A. In his Studies in two literatures, 1897.
— A study of Symonds. Fortnightly Rev Feb 1924.
Symonds, M. Last days of Symonds. 1906.
— Out of the past. 1925.
Brooks, Van W. Symonds: a biographical study. 1914.
Bräm, E. M. Die italienische Renaissance in dem englischen Geistesleben des 19 Jahrhunderts bei Ruskin, Symonds und Vernon Lee. Brugg Switzerland 1932.
Symonds: the historian of the renaissance. TLS 5 Oct 1940. Reply by H. Harris, 12 Oct 1940.
Grantham, E. Letters from Symonds to Swinburne. More Books 21 1946.
Mack, J. D. Symonds's Renaissance in Italy. New Colophon 1 1948.
Hale, J. R. In his England and the Italian Renaissance, 1954.
Peters, R. L. Athens and Troy: notes on Symonds' aestheticism. English Fiction in Transition 5 1962.
Grosskurth, P. M. Swinburne and Symonds: an uneasy literary relationship. RES new ser 14 1963.
— The genesis of Symonds's Elizabethan criticism. MLR 59 1964.
— Symonds: a biography. 1964.
Orsini, G. N. G. Symonds and De Sanctis: a study in the historiography of the Renaissance. Stud in Renaissance 11 1964.

CONNOP THIRLWALL
1797–1875

§1

Primitiae: or essays and poems. 1809 (priv ptd).
A critical essay on the gospel of Luke, by Dr F. Schleiermacher. 1825. Tr and ed Thirlwall.
The history of Rome, by B. G. Niebuhr. 3 vols Cambridge 1828–42, 1847–51 (3rd edn). Vols 1–2 tr Thirlwall and J. C. Hare.
A vindication of Niebuhr's History of Rome from the charges of the Quarterly Review, by J. C. Hare. Cambridge 1829. Postscript by Thirlwall.
The irony of Sophocles. Philological Museum 2 1833; rptd in Remains, below, 1877.
A letter to the Rev T. Turton on the admission of Dissenters to academical degrees. Cambridge 1834, 1834 (rev).
A history of Greece. 8 vols 1835–44 (in Cabinet cyclopaedia, ed D. Lardner), 1839–44, 1845–52, 2 vols New York 1845, 1848–51; tr German (in part), 1839–40; French, 1852.
Schleiermacher on the worth of Socrates as a philosopher. In A life of Socrates by G. Wiggers, 1840. Tr Thirlwall.
The centre of unity: a sermon. 1850; ed J. E. B. Mayor, Cambridge 1901.
The present state of the relations between science and literature. 1867.
Remains, literary and theological. Ed J. J. S. Perowne 3 vols 1877, 1878.
Essays, speeches and sermons. 1880.
Letters literary and theological. Ed J. J. S. Perowne and L. Stokes 1881.
Letters to a friend. Ed A. P. Stanley 1881, 1882, Boston 1883.

§2

Freeman, E. A. Greece during the Macedonian period. North Br Rev 21 1854; rptd in his Historical essays, 1879.
[Dicey, A. V.] Bishop Thirlwall. Nation (London) 28 Feb 1878.
[Beard, C.] Thirlwall's Remains. Theological Rev 15 1878.
Clark, J. W. In his Old friends at Cambridge and elsewhere, 1900.
Thirlwall, J. C. Thirlwall: historian and theologian. 1936.
Forbes, D. In his Liberal Anglican view of history, 1952.

SIR GEORGE OTTO TREVELYAN
1838–1928

§1

The Cambridge Dionysia: a classic dream by the editor of the Bear. Cambridge 1858.
Horace at the University of Athens: a dramatic sketch. Cambridge 1861 (anon), 1862.
The Pope and his patron. 1862.
The dawk bungalow: or 'Is his appointment pucka?' by H. Broughton. 1863. A comedy.
Letters from a competition wallah. Macmillan's Mag May 1863–May 1864; rptd 1864 (as The competition wallah), 1866, 1895.
Cawnpore. 1865, 1866, 1886, 1894, 1910.
The ladies in Parliament and other pieces. Cambridge 1869, London 1888.
The life and letters of Lord Macaulay. 2 vols 1876, New York 1876 (with appendix, Macaulay on American institutions), Leipzig 1876, London 1877 (rev), New York 1877, London 1878, 1 vol 1881, 2 vols Chicago 1885, 1 vol 1889, 1908 ('enlarged'), 1913; ed G. M. Trevelyan 2 vols Oxford 1932 (WC); 1 vol 1959, 2 vols Oxford 1961; tr Spanish (in part), 1899.
Selections from the writings of Lord Macaulay. 1876. Ed Trevelyan.
The early history of Charles James Fox. 1880, 1880, New York 1880, London 1881 (3rd edn), New York 1881, 1900, London 1901, 1905, 1908, 1911.
The American Revolution. 4 vols London and New York 1899–1907, 1899–1913, 1905–12, 1917–18, 1926–9; ed R. B. Morris, New York 1964 (abridged), London 1966.
Interludes in verse and prose. 1905, 1924.
Marginal notes by Lord Macaulay. 1907. Ed Trevelyan.
George the third and Charles Fox: the concluding part of The American Revolution. 2 vols 1912–14, New York 1912–14, 1915–16, London 1921–7.

§2

[Dallas, E. S.] Cawnpore. Times 31 May 1865.
[Griffin, M. J.] Trevelyan as a historian. Blackwood's Mag March 1899.
[Elliot, A. R. D.] Trevelyan's American Revolution. Edinburgh Rev 189 1899.
[Walpole, S.] Trevelyan on the American Revolution. Edinburgh Rev 199 1904.
Fisher, H. A. L. The Whig historians. In his Pages from the past, Oxford 1931.
Trevelyan, G. M. Sir G. O. Trevelyan: a memoir by his son. 1932.
— In his Autobiography and other essays, 1949.
Hirst, F. W. In his Memories of great Victorians, Contemporary Rev Aug 1950.

Gordon, D. C. In Some modern historians of Britain, ed H. Ausubel, New York 1951.
Cowboys and kings: three great letters. Ed C. E. Morrison, Cambridge Mass 1954.
Bratcher, J. T. G. M. Trevelyan's copy of Horace at Athens. Univ of Texas Lib Chron 8 1966.

SIR SPENCER WALPOLE

1839–1907

§1

The life of Spencer Perceval by his grandson. 2 vols 1874.
A manual of the law of salmon fisheries in England and Wales. 1877.
A history of England from the conclusion of the great war in 1815. 3 vols 1879–80, 5 vols 1879–86 (2nd edn), 6 vols 1890 (rev), 1902–5, 1912.
The electorate and the legislature. 1881, 1892.
Foreign relations. 1882.
The British fish trade. 1883.
The life of Lord John Russell. 2 vols 1889, 1889, 1891.
On parliamentary government in England, by A. Todd. 2 vols 1892; tr French, 1900. Ed Walpole.
The land of home rule: an essay on the history and constitution of the Isle of Man. 1893.
Some unpublished letters of Horace Walpole. 1902. Ed Walpole.
The history of twenty-five years 1856–1880. 2 vols 1904, 4 vols 1904–8. Vols 3–4 completed by A. C. Lyall.
Studies in biography. 1907, 1907, New York 1907.
Essays political and biographical. Ed F. Holland 1908.

§2

[Dicey, A. V.] Walpole's History of England from 1815. Nation (New York) 30 Oct 1879.
Fyffe, C. A. Walpole's History of England. EHR 2 1887.
Gladstone, W. E. The Melbourne government. Nineteenth Century Jan 1890.
[Roscoe, E. S.] Walpole's Life of Russell. Edinburgh Rev 171 1890.
—— The land of home rule. Edinburgh Rev 178 1893.
Hutchinson, H. G. Sir Spencer Walpole. Cornhill Mag Sept 1907.
Holland, F. Memoir of Walpole. In Essays political and biographical, 1908.

THOMAS WRIGHT

1810–77

§1

The history and topography of the County of Essex. 2 vols 1836.
Coup-d'œil sur les progrès et sur l'état actuel de la littérature anglo-saxonne en Angleterre: traduction de [P.-F.] de Larenaudière. Paris 1836. For English version *see* Biographia britannica, below.
The history and antiquities of London, Westminster, Southwark and parts adjacent. 5 vols 1837. Vols 1–4 by T. Allen; vol 5 by Wright.
The universities: Le Keux's Memorials of Cambridge; with historical and descriptive accounts by Thomas Wright and H. Longueville Jones. 2 vols 1841–2; ed C. H. Cooper 2 vols Cambridge 1860, 3 vols Cambridge [1880].
The history of Ludlow and its neighbourhood. Ludlow 1852 (for 1841–52).
Biographia britannica literaria: or biography of literary characters of Great Britain and Ireland. Anglo-Saxon period. 1842. Anglo-Norman period, 1846; Introduction also separately pbd as An essay on the state of literature and learning under the Anglo-Saxons, introductory to the Biographia Britannica literaria, 1839.
St Patrick's purgatory: an essay on the legends of Purgatory, Hell and Paradise current during the Middle Ages. 1844.
Essays on subjects connected with the literature, popular superstitions and history of England in the Middle Ages. 2 vols 1846. Rptd from periodicals.
England under the House of Hanover: its history during the reigns of the three Georges, illustrated from the caricatures and satires of the day. 2 vols 1848, [1868], 1876 (as Caricature history of the Georges).
The history of Ireland. 3 vols [1848–52].
Narratives of sorcery and magic. 2 vols 1851.
Historical and descriptive account of the caricatures of James Gillray. 1851, [1873] (expanded as The works of James Gillray, with the history of his life and times). With R. H. Evans.
The Celt, the Roman and the Saxon: a history of the early inhabitants of Britain, down to the conversion of the Anglo-Saxons. 1852, 1861 (rev), 1875, 1885.
The history of Scotland. 3 vols [1852–5], [1873–4], 1888.
Wanderings of an antiquary, chiefly upon the traces of the Romans in Britain. 1854.
A lecture on the antiquities of the Anglo-Saxon cemeteries of the ages of paganism, illustrative of the Faussett collection. Liverpool 1854.
Guide to the Caterham railway, and to the country around it. 1856.
The history of France. 3 vols [1856–62], 3 vols [1871–2] (including A faithful account of the war with Germany by Lt-Col Williams).
Miscellanea graphica: representations of remains in the possession of Lord Londesborough. Drawn by F. W. Fairholt; the historical introduction by Thomas Wright. 1857.
Dictionary of obsolete and provincial English. 2 vols 1857.
Guide to the ruins of the Roman city of Uriconium at Wroxeter near Shrewsbury. Shrewsbury 1859, 1859 (as The ruins of the Roman city of Uriconium), 1860, 1868, 1877 (6th edn).
History and antiquities of Cumberland and Westmoreland. In W. Whellan, The history and topography of Cumberland and Westmorland, Pontefract 1860.
Essays on archaeological subjects and on various questions connected with the Middle Ages. 2 vols 1861.
A history of domestic manners and sentiments in England during the Middle Ages. 1862, 1871 (expanded as The homes of other days).
Historical and descriptive sketch of Ludlow Castle. [1862?], Ludlow 1869 (4th edn rev), 1909 (13th edn) etc.
A history of caricature and grotesque in literature and art. 1865; tr French, 1867.
Ludlow sketches: a series of papers. Ludlow 1867.
Historical cartoons. By Gustav Doré. With descriptive text by Wright. [1868].
Womankind in Western Europe from the earliest times to the seventeenth century. 1869.
Uriconium: a historical account of the ancient Roman city. 1872.
Historical sketch of Stokesay Castle, Salop. Ludlow 1921, 1924.

Editions

Early English poetry. 4 vols 1836. Anthology.
The tour of the French traveller, M. de la Boullaye le Gouz, in Ireland, A.D. 1644. Ed T. C. Croker 1837. With notes by Wright.
Anglo-Norman poem on the conquest of Ireland by Henry the Second. Ed F. Michel 1837. With an introductory essay on the conquest by Wright.

Galfridi de Monemuta Vita Merlini. Vie de Merlin, attribuée à Geoffroy de Monmouth. Paris 1837. With F. Michel.

Early mysteries, and other Latin poems of the twelfth and thirteenth centuries. 1838.

Alliterative poem on the deposition of King Richard II. 1838 (Camden Soc).

Queen Elizabeth and her times. A series of original letters, selected from the inedited private correspondence of Lord Burghley, the Earl of Leicester etc. 2 vols 1838.

The political songs of England, from John to Edward II. 1839 (Camden Soc), ed E. Goldsmid 4 vols 1884.

Relations des voyages de Guillaume de Rubruk, Jean de Plan Carpin, Bernard, Saewulf etc. Ed F. Michel and Wright, in Recueil de Voyages et de Mémoires, publié par la Société de Géographie 4 Paris 1839.

The history of English poetry. By Thomas Warton. 3 vols 1840. Corrections and addns by Wright et al.

Popular treatises on science written during the Middle Ages, in Anglo-Saxon, Anglo-Norman and English. 1841 (Historical Soc of Science).

The Latin poems attributed to Walter Mapes. 1841 (Camden Soc).

Political ballads published in England during the Commonwealth. 1841 (Percy Soc).

Specimens of old Christmas carols. 1841 (Percy Soc).

The Archaeologist and Journal of Antiquarian Science. Sept 1841–June 1842. Ed J. O. Halliwell and Wright.

Reliquiae antiquae. Scraps from ancient manuscripts, illustrating Early English literature and the English language. 2 vols 1841–3, 2 vols 1845. Ed J. O. Halliwell and Wright.

A dialogue concerning witches and witchcrafts. By G. Gifford. 1842 (Percy Soc).

Specimens of lyric poetry, composed in England in the reign of Edward the First. 1842 (Percy Soc).

A selection of Latin stories. A contribution to the history of fiction during the Middle Ages. 1842 (Percy Soc).

The autobiography of Joseph Lister, of Bradford in Yorkshire. 1842.

The vision and the creed of Piers Ploughman. 1842, 2 vols 1856. With introd, notes and glossary. Anon.

A contemporary narrative of the proceedings against Dame Alice Kyteler. 1843 (Camden Soc).

Three chapters of letters relating to the suppression of the monasteries. 1843 (Camden Soc).

The owl and the nightingale: attributed to Nicholas de Guildford, with some shorter poems. 1843 (Percy Soc).

The Chester Plays. 2 vols 1843–7 (Shakespeare Soc).

St Brandan. A medieval legend of the sea. 1844 (Percy Soc.)

Anecdota Literaria. A collection of short poems in English, Latin and French, illustrative of the literature and history of England in the thirteenth century. 1844.

The archaeological album, or Museum of national antiquities. 1845.

The pastime of pleasure. By Stephen Hawes. 1845 (Percy Soc).

The seven sages in English verse. 1845 (Percy Soc); introd 1846.

Songs and carols from a manuscript of the fifteenth century. 1847 (Percy Soc).

The Canterbury tales of Geoffrey Chaucer: a new text. 3 vols 1847–51 (Percy Soc), 1853.

Early travels in Palestine, comprising the narratives of Arculf, Willibald, Bernard etc. 1848.

A new general biographical dictionary, projected and partly arranged by H. J. Rose. 12 vols 1848. Vols 2–12 ed Wright.

The religious poems of William de Shoreham. 1849 (Percy Soc).

Gualteri Mapes De nugis curialium. 1850 (Camden Soc).

The Anglo-Norman metrical chronicle of Geoffrey Gaimar. 1850 (Caxton Soc).

The ancient laws of the fifteenth century, for King's College Cambridge and Eton College, collected by J. Heywood and Wright. 1850.

The life of King Alfred, by R. Pauli. 1852.

The universal pronouncing dictionary. Compiled under the direction of Thomas Wright. 6 vols 1852–6.

Cambridge University transactions during the Puritan controversies of the 16th and 17th centuries. Collected by J. Heywood and Wright. 2 vols 1854.

The travels of Marco Polo, the Venetian. The translation of Marsden revised. 1854, 1904.

The history of Fulke Fitz Warine, with an English translation and notes. 1855 (Warton Club).

Songs and carols from a manuscript of the fifteenth century. 1856 (Warton Club). Distinct from Percy Soc vol 1847.

Johannis de Garlandia De triumphis ecclesiæ. 1856 (Roxburghe Club).

A volume of vocabularies, illustrating the condition and manners of our forefathers, from the tenth century to the fifteenth. 2 vols 1857–73 (priv ptd) (J. Mayer's Library of National Antiquities); ed R. P. Wülcker 2 vols 1884.

Les cent nouvelles nouvelles, publiées d'après le seul manuscrit connu, avec introduction et notes. 2 vols Paris 1857–8.

La Morte d'Arthure: the history of King Arthur and of the Knights of the Round Table, compiled by Sir Thomas Malory. 3 vols 1858, 3 vols 1866 (rev), 1893. Ed from 1634 edn.

Manual of ethnology, by J. C. Prichard, revised by Wright and Monsieur d'Avezac, extracted from Admiralty Manual of scientific enquiry. 1859 (3rd edn).

A glossary by Robert Nares: a new edition by J. O. Halliwell and Wright. 2 vols 1859, 1888, 1905.

Political poems and songs relating to English history, composed during the period from the accession of Edw III to that of Ric III. 2 vols 1859–61 (Rerum Britannicarum Medii Ævi Scriptores).

Songs and ballads, with other short poems, chiefly of the reign of Philip and Mary. 1860 (Roxburghe Club).

Fairy legends and traditions of the South of Ireland, by T. C. Croker. [1862], [1870], [1882], 1902.

The Royal dictionary-cyclopaedia, compiled under the direction of Wright. 5 vols [1862–7].

Alexandri Neckam De naturis rerum. 1863 (Rerum Britannicarum Medii Ævi Scriptores).

The historical works of Giraldus Cambrensis. 1863. Tr T. Forester and Sir R. Colt Hoare.

The roll of arms of the princes, barons and knights who attended Edward I to the siege of Caerlaverock in 1300. 1864. With trn and notes.

Autobiography of Thomas Wright of Birkenshaw 1736–97. 1864.

History of Julius Caesar, by Napoleon III. 2 vols [1865–6]. Tr Wright.

The chronicle of Pierre de Langtoft. 2 vols 1866–8 (Rerum Britannicarum Medii Ævi Scriptores).

The book of the Knight of La Tour-Landry, translated from the French into English in the reign of Henry VI. 1868, 1906 (rev) (EETS).

Churchwardens' accounts of the town of Ludlow. 1869 (Camden Soc).

Feudal manuals of English history: a series of popular sketches of our national history, compiled from the thirteenth century to the fifteenth. 1872.

The Anglo-Latin satirical poets and epigrammatists of the twelfth century. 2 vols 1872 (Rerum Britannicarum Medii Ævi Scriptores).

The Decameron of Boccaccio. 1874.

Killarney legends, by T. C. Croker [1876].

§2

Academy 29 Dec 1877.
Athenaeum 29 Dec 1877.
Garnett, R. Antiquarian club books. Quart Rev 82 1878.
Jewitt, L. Some departed contributors and literary friends. Reliquary 18 1878.
Fitch, E. A. Historians of Essex: Wright. Essex Rev 9 1900.

O. M.

IX. PHILOSOPHY

BIBLIOGRAPHIES

Rand, B. Bibliography of philosophy, psychology and cognate subjects. In Dictionary of philosophy and psychology, ed J. M. Baldwin, vol 3 New York 1905, 1949.
Jnl of Philosophy 31–4 1934–7. For years 1933–6.
Bibliographie de la philosophie. Paris 1938–9, 1952–3 (books and articles), 1954– (books only).
Jessop, T. E. A bibliography of Hume and of Scottish philosophy from Hutcheson to Balfour. 1938.

GENERAL STUDIES

Deuchar, R. A brief review of ancient and modern philosophy. 1864.
Masson, D. Recent British philosophy. 1865.
Laurie, S. S. Notes on certain British theories of morals. 1868.
McCosh, J. The present state of moral philosophy in England. 1868.
— Scottish philosophy from Hutcheson to Hamilton. 1874.
Ribot, T. La psychologie anglaise contemporaine. Paris 1870; tr 1873.
Renouvier, C. B. De l'esprit de la philosophie anglaise contemporaine. In his La critique philosophique vol 1, Paris 1872.
Überweg, F. History of philosophy from Thales to the present time. Vol 2, tr New York 1874 (from 4th German edn).
Liard, L. Les logiciens anglais contemporains. Paris 1878.
Morris, G. S. British thought and thinkers. 1880.
Höffding, H. Die englische Philosophie unserer Zeit. Tr German (from Danish), Berlin 1889.
— A history of modern philosophy. Tr 2 vols 1900.
Hutton, R. H. Criticisms on contemporary thought and thinkers. 2 vols 1894.
Merz, J. T. A history of European thought in the nineteenth century. 4 vols Edinburgh 1896–1914.
Bigge, S. British moralists. 2 vols 1897.
Stephen, L. The English Utilitarians. 3 vols 1900.
Halévy, E. La formation du radicalisme philosophique. 3 vols Paris 1901–4; tr 1928, 1952.
Sturt, H. (ed). Personal idealism: philosophical essays by eight members of the University of Oxford. 1902.
Dicey, A. V. Lectures on the relation between law and public opinion in England during the nineteenth century. 1905.
Ladd, G. T. The development of philosophy in the nineteenth century. Philosophical Rev 14 1905.
Benn, A. W. English rationalism in the nineteenth century. 1906.
Forsyth, J. M. English philosophy. 1910.
Jones, H. (ed). The schools of philosophy. 1912, 1914.
Perry, R. B. Present philosophical tendencies. 1912.
Seth, J. English philosophers and schools of philosophy. 1912.
Thilly, F. A history of philosophy. New York 1914, 1957 (3rd edn rev).
Davidson, W. L. Political thought in England: the Utilitarians from Bentham to J. S. Mill. 1915 (Home Univ Lib).
Barker, E. Political thought in England 1848–1914. [1915] (Home Univ Lib).
Tufts, J. H. Ethics in the last twenty-five years. Philosophical Rev 26 1917.
Sorley, W. R. A history of English philosophy. Cambridge 1920.
— Fifty years of Mind. Mind new ser 35 1926.
Taylor, A. E. Philosophy. In Recent developments in European thought, ed F. S. Marvin 1920.
Muirhead, J. H. (ed). Contemporary British philosophy. 2 vols 1924–5.
Vaughan, C. E. Studies in the history of political philosophy before and after Rousseau. 2 vols 1925, 1959.
Catlin, G. E. G. The science and method of politics. 1927.
— A history of the political philosophers. New York 1939, London 1950.
Hicks, G. D. In Geschichte der Philosophie, ed F. Überweg and M. Heinze, pt 5 Berlin 1927.
— A century of philosophy at University College London. Jnl of Philosophical Stud 3 1928.
'Kingsmill, Hugh' (H. K. Lunn). After Puritanism 1850–1900. 1929.
Somervell, D. C. English thought in the nineteenth century. 1929, 1950.
Muirhead, J. R. The Platonic tradition in Anglo-Saxon philosophy. New York 1931.
Hearnshaw, F. J. C. (ed). The social and political ideas of some representative thinkers of the age of reaction and reconstruction 1815–65. 1932.
Brinton, C. English political thought in the nineteenth century. 1933, 1949.
— A history of Western morals. New York 1959.
Webb, C. C. J. A study in religious thought in England from 1850. Oxford 1933.
Cunningham, G. W. The idealist argument in recent British and American philosophy. New York 1934.
Segerstedt, T. T. Problem of knowledge in Scottish philosophy. Lund 1935.
Mead, G. H. Movements of thought in the nineteenth century. Chicago 1936.
Mure, G. R. G. Oxford and philosophy. Philosophy 12 1937.
Routh, H. V. Towards the twentieth century. Cambridge 1937.
Ellwood, C. A. A history of social philosophy. New York 1938.
Metz, R. A hundred years of British philosophy. Tr New York 1938.
Bertocci, P. A. The empirical argument for God in late British thought. Cambridge Mass 1939.
Wright, W. K. A history of modern philosophy. New York 1941.

Quillian, W. F. The moral theory of evolutionary naturalism. New Haven 1945.
Brown, A. W. The Metaphysical Society: Victorian minds in crisis 1869–80. New York 1947.
Carré, M. H. Phases of thought in England. Oxford 1949.
Neill, T. P. Makers of the modern mind. Milwaukee 1949.
Plamenatz, J. The English Utilitarians. Oxford 1949, 1958 (rev) (Home Univ Lib).
Buckley, J. M. The revolt from rationalism in the seventies. In Booker memorial studies, ed H. Shine, Chapel Hill 1950.
Hallowell, J. H. Main currents in modern political thought. New York 1950.
Sabine, G. H. A history of political theory. New York 1950.
Broad, C. D. Five types of ethical theory. 1951.
Ulam, A. B. Philosophical foundations of English Socialism. Cambridge Mass 1951.
Carritt, E. F. Morals and politics. Oxford 1952.
Houghton, W. E. Victorian anti-intellectualism. JHI 13 1952.
—— The Victorian frame of mind 1830–70. New Haven 1957.
Robbins, L. The theory of economic policy in English classical political economy. 1952.
Holloway, J. The Victorian sage: studies in argument. 1953.
Paul, L. The English philosophers. 1953.
Elliot-Binns, L. E. English thought 1860–1900: the theological aspect. 1955.
Pucelle, J. L'idéalisme en Angleterre de Coleridge à Bradley. Neuchâtel 1955.
Carter, G. S. A hundred years of evolution. 1957.
Ellegard, A. The Darwinian theory and nineteenth-century philosophies of science. JHI 18 1957.
Passmore, J. A hundred years of philosophy. 1957 (with bibliography), 1966 (rev, without bibliography).
Shklar, J. N. After Utopia: the decline of political faith. Princeton 1957.
Silberner, E. La guerre et la paix dans l'histoire des doctrines économiques. Paris 1957.
Quinton, A. The neglect of Victorian philosophy. Victorian Stud 1 1958.
Randall, J. H. The changing impact of Darwin on philosophy. JHI 22 1961.
Kneale, W. and M. The development of logic. Oxford 1962.
Milne, A. J. M. The social philosophy of English idealism. 1962.
Nichols, D. Positive liberty 1880–1914. Amer Political Science Rev 56 1962.
Le Chevalier, C. Ethique et idéalisme: le courant néo-Hegelian en Angleterre, Bosanquet et ses amis. Paris 1963.
Simon, W. M. European Positivism in the nineteenth century. Ithaca 1963.

THOMAS KINGSMILL ABBOTT

1829–1913

Sight and touch: an attempt to disprove the received (or Berkeleian) theory of vision. 1864.
Logic versus Murray's Logic. Dublin 1881.
Elements of Logic. Dublin 1883.
Also works on religion.

JOHN ABERCROMBIE

1780–1884

§1

Inquiries concerning the intellectual powers and the investigation of truth. Edinburgh 1830, 1854 (15th edn).
The philosophy of the moral feelings. Edinburgh 1833, 8836 (4th edn), London 1841 (6th edn).
Address on the occasion of his installation as Lord Rector of the University of Aberdeen. Aberdeen 1835.
Essays and tracts. Edinburgh 1847.
The culture and discipline of the mind. Edinburgh 1837, 1862 (enlarged).
Also works on religion.

§2

MacLagan, D. Sketch of the life and character of Dr Abercrombie. 1854.

ROBERT ADAMSON

1852–1902

§1

Roger Bacon: the philosophy of science in the Middle Ages. Manchester 1876.
On the philosophy of Kant. Edinburgh 1879; tr German, 1880.
Fichte. 1881.
Moral theory and moral practice. In Ethical democracy, ed S. Coit 1900.
The development of modern philosophy, with other lectures and essays. Ed W. R. Sorley 2 vols 1903, 1930 (vol i).
The development of Greek philosophy. Ed W. R. Sorley and R. P. Hardie 1908.
A short history of logic. Ed W. R. Sorley 1911.

§2

Jones, H. Adamson. Mind new ser 11 1902.
Hicks, G. D. Adamson's philosophical lectures. Mind new ser 13 1904.
Rees, D. A. Adamson. Philosophical Quart 2 1952.

GRANT ALLEN

1848–99

See col 1031, above.

GEORGE DOUGLAS CAMPBELL, 8th DUKE OF ARGYLL

1823–1900

§1

Address delivered to the members of the Glasgow Athenaeum. Glasgow 1852.
Inaugural address as Chancellor of the University of St Andrews. Edinburgh 1852.
Phrenology. North Br Rev 17 1852.
Inaugural address as Rector of the University of Glasgow. 1855.
Address of the Duke of Argyll, before the British Association for the Advancement of Science. Glasgow 1855.
Address to the Royal Society of Edinburgh. Edinburgh 1864.
The reign of law. 1867, 1890 (19th edn).
Primeval man. 1869.
Iona. 1870, Edinburgh 1889.
On variety as an aim in nature. 1871.
On Hibernicisms in philosophy. Contemporary Rev Jan 1872.
On animal instinct. Contemporary Rev July 1875.
Morality in politics. Contemporary Rev July 1877.
The unity of nature. 1884.
The prophet of San Francisco. 1884. Reply by Henry George in his The peer and the prophet, 1884.

Scotland as it was and as it is. 2 vols Edinburgh 1887.
The identity of thought and language. Contemporary Rev Dec 1888.
What is truth? Edinburgh 1889.
The Highland nurse: a tale. 1892.
The unseen foundations of society. 1893.
The application of the historical method to economic science. 1894.
The burdens of belief and other poems. 1894.
Lord Bacon versus Professor Huxley. Nineteenth Century Dec 1894.
The philosophy of belief: or law in Christian theology. 1896.
Organic evolution cross-examined. 1898.
What is science? Edinburgh 1898.
Autobiography and memoirs. Ed Dowager Duchess of Argyll 2 vols 1906.
Also works on economics, religious affairs, geology and current politics.

§2

English, W. W. An essay on moral philosophy. 1869.
Bacon, T. S. The reign of God not the Reign of law. 1878.
Bain, F. W. The unseen foundation of the Unseen foundations of society. 1893.
'Goth, Amos'. The reign of lust, by the Duke of Oatmeal. 1895.
Knox, H. V. Argyll on purpose in nature. Philosophical Rev 7 1898.

JOHN AUSTIN
1790–1859

§1

The province of jurisprudence determined. 1832.
Centralisation. Edinburgh Rev 85 1847.
A plea for the Constitution. 1859.
Lectures on jurisprudence: or the philosophy of positive law. Ed S. Austin 3 vols 1861–3, 1885 (5th edn); tr French, 1894. Also referred to as 2nd edn of The province of jurisprudence determined, above.
The province of jurisprudence determined, and The uses of the study of jurisprudence. Ed H. L. A. Hart 1954.

§2

Mill, J. S. Austin on jurisprudence. In his Dissertations and discussions vol 3, 1867.
Campbell, F. G. B. An analysis of Austin's Lectures on jurisprudence. 1877.
Clark, E. C. Practical jurisprudence. 1883.
Purnalingam, P. An epitome of Maine's Ancient law and Austin's Jurisprudence. 1915.
Eastwood, R. A. A brief introduction to Austin's theory of positive law and sovereignty. 1916.
—— and G. W. Keeton. The Austinian theories of law and sovereignty. 1929.
Hearnshaw, F. J. C. Austin and the analytical jurists. In his Social and political ideas of some representative thinkers of the age of reaction and reconstruction, 1932.
Smith, C. I. Locke and Austin on the idea of morality. JHI 23 1962.

SAMUEL BAILEY
1791–1870

Bibliographies

Ireland, A. Bailey of Sheffield. N & Q 9 March 1878. *See* 16 March, 27 April 1878, 21 June 1879.

§1

Essays on the formation and publication of opinions and on other subjects. 1821, 1826 (rev), 1837 (enlarged).
Questions in political economy, politics, morals, metaphysics, polite literature and other branches of knowledge. 1823.
A critical dissertation on the nature, measures and causes of value. 1825.
A letter to a political economist. 1826.
Essays on the pursuit of truth and on the progress of knowledge. 1829, 1844 (rev and enlarged).
A discussion of parliamentary reform. 1831.
Rationale of political representation. 1835.
Letters of an Egyptian Kaffir on a visit to England. 1839.
Review of Berkeley's Theory of vision. 1842.
A letter to a philosopher in reply to some recent attempts to vindicate Berkeley's Theory of vision. 1842.
Letters on the philosophy of the human mind. Ser 1, 1846; 3 vols 1855, 1858, 1862.
Theory of reasoning. 1851, 1852.
Discourses on various subjects. 1852.
On the received text of Shakespeare's dramatic writings. 2 vols 1862, 1866.

§2

Mill, James. The formation of opinions. Westminster Rev 6 1826.
Thompson, T. P. Essays on the pursuit of truth. Westminster Rev 11 1829.
Wardlaw, R. Four sermons, with an appendix on an article in the Westminster Review. 1830.
Empson, W. Principles of belief and expectation as applied to miracles. Edinburgh Rev 52 1831.
Mill, J. S. Rationale of representation. London Rev 1 1835.
—— Bailey on Berkeley's Theory of vision (1842). In his Dissertations and discussions vol 2, 1859.
—— Mr Bailey's reply to the Westminster Review. Westminster Rev 39 1843.
Ferrier, J. F. Berkeley's Theory of vision (1843). In his Lectures on Greek philosophy and other philosophical remains, Edinburgh 1866.
Ribot, T. A. La psychologie anglaise contemporaine. Paris 1870; tr 1873.
Amano, K. In his Bibliography of the classical economists vol 4 pt 5, Tokyo 1964.

ALEXANDER BAIN
1818–1903

§1

On the applications of science to human health and well-being. 1848.
The senses and the intellect. 1855, 1864 (rev and enlarged), 1868 (enlarged), 1894; tr French, 1873, 1889, 1895; Russian, 1887.
The emotions and the will. 1859, 1865 (rev), 1875 (rev), New York 1876, 1899 (with addns); tr French, 1885; Russian, 1887.
On the study of character, including an estimate of phrenology. 1861.
An English grammar. 1863, 1872 (rev as A higher English grammar), 1879 (rev), 1904 (rev and enlarged). Also A first English grammar, with key, 1872, 1882.
The methods of debate: an address delivered to the Aberdeen University Debating Society. Aberdeen 1863.
A letter to Westerton, chairman of Mill's [election] committee. [1865].

English composition and rhetoric. 1866, 1869, 2 vols 1887–8 (enlarged).
Mental and moral science. 1868, 2 vols 1872 (enlarged), New York 1880; tr Russian, 1881.
Logic: deductive and inductive. 2 vols 1870, 1873, 1879, New York 1887 (rev); tr French, 1875; Spanish, 1881.
Mind and body: the theories of their relation. 1873, 1910 (11th edn); tr French, 1874; German, 1874; Russian, 1880; Spanish, 1881.
Education as a science. 1879 (7 edns), New York 1879, 1884, 1897; tr French, 1879; German, 1879; Italian, 1885; Spanish, 1888.
Presidential address to the Society for the development of the science of education. 1879.
James Mill. 1882. Enlarged from Mind 1–2 1876–7.
John Stuart Mill. 1882. Rptd from Mind 4–5 1879–80.
Practical essays. 1884.
On teaching English, with an enquiry into the definition of poetry. 1887. Auxiliary to enlarged edn of English composition and rhetoric, above.
Dissertations on leading philosophical topics. 1903.
Autobiography. Ed W. L. Davidson 1904. With bibliography.

Articles

Many of Bain's articles are rptd in Practical essays, Dissertations on leading philosophical topics, *and* On the study of character, *above.*
Constitution of matter. Westminster Rev 36 1841.
On toys. Westminster Rev 37 1842.
Mill's Logic. Westminster Rev 39 1843.
Carlyle's Cromwell. Westminster Rev 46 1847.
On the abuse of language in science and in common life. Fraser's Mag Feb 1847.
Oken's physiophilosophy. Chambers's Jnl 5 Feb 1848.
The scholastic logic. Chambers's Jnl 11 March 1848.
Wit and humour. Westminster Rev 48 1848.
Of a liberal education in general. Westminster Rev 49 1848.
Sydney Smith's moral philosophy. Chambers's Jnl 15 June 1850.
Reichenbach's researches. Chambers's Jnl 20 July 1850.
Grote's Plato. Macmillan's Mag July, Oct 1865.
The feelings and the will physiologically considered. Fortnightly Rev 15 Jan 1866.
The intellect viewed physiologically. Fortnightly Rev 1 Feb 1866.
A historical view of the theories of the soul. Fortnightly Rev 15 May 1866.
On early philosophy. Macmillan's Mag June 1866.
On the correlation of force in its bearing on mind. Macmillan's Mag Sept 1867.
The retentive power of the mind in its bearing on education. Fortnightly Rev Sept 1868.
Memoir of Clark. Jnl of Chemical Soc of London new ser 6 1868.
Notes on Bastian's paper. Fortnightly Rev April 1869.
On teaching English. Fortnightly Rev Aug 1869.
Darwinism and religion. Macmillan's Mag May 1871.
On Sully's Essays. Fortnightly Rev July 1874.
Sidgwick's Methods of ethics. Mind 1 1876.
Alexander's Moral causation. Ibid.
Spencer's Principles of sociology. Ibid.
Lewes on the postulates of experience. Ibid.
The gratification derived from the infliction of pain. Ibid.
Education as a science. Mind 2–3 1877–8.
Sully's Pessimism. Mind 2 1877.
The growth of the will. Popular Science Monthly May 1879.
Spencer's Data of ethics. Mind 4 1879.
Ward on free-will. Mind 5 1880. Reply by W. G. Ward, ibid.
Galton's statistics of mental imagery. Ibid.
Spencer's psychological congruities. Mind 6 1881.
Mind and body. Mind 8 1883.
Biographical memoirs of Clark, Shier and Arnott. Trans Aberdeen Philosophical Soc 1 1884.
Ward's Psychology. Mind 11 1886.
On feeling as indifference. Mind 12, 14 1887, 1889.
On Ward's Psychological principles. Mind 12 1887.
The distinction between will and desire (Symposium). Proc Aristotelian Soc 1 1888.
The nature of force (Symposium). Ibid.
Is the distinction of feeling, cognition and conation valid as an ultimate distinction of the mental functions? (Symposium). Ibid.
Notes on volition. Mind 16 1891.
Biographical notice of Robertson. Mind new ser 2 1893.
Ethics from a purely practical standpoint. International Jnl of Ethics 10 1900.

§2

Mill, J. S. Bain's psychology. In his Dissertations and discussions vol 3, 1867.
Ribot, T. A. English psychology. 1873.
Hyde, T. A. How to study character, including a review of Bain's criticisms of the phrenological system. 1884.
'Psychosis'. Our modern philosophers, Darwin, Bain and Spencer: a rhyme. 1884.
Davidson, W. L. Bain's philosophy. Mind new ser 13 1904.
MacKenzie, W. L. Bain's Autobiography. Mind new ser 14 1905.
Schiller, F. C. S. Bradley, Bain and pragmatism. Jnl of Philosophy 14 1917.
Fisch, M. H. Bain and the genealogy of pragmatism. JHI 15 1954.
Rodgers, P. C. Bain and the rise of the organic paragraph. Quart Jnl of Speech 51 1965.

ARTHUR JAMES BALFOUR, 1st EARL OF BALFOUR
1848–1930

§1

A defence of philosophic doubt. 1879, 1921.
Handel. [1887?].
The pleasures of reading: inaugural address as Rector of St Andrews University. 1888.
The religion of humanity. Edinburgh 1888.
A fragment on progress: inaugural address as Rector of the University of Glasgow. Edinburgh 1892.
Essays and addresses. Edinburgh 1893, 1905 (3rd edn enlarged).
The foundations of belief. 1895, 1901 (8th edn); tr French, 1896; German, 1896; Italian, 1906.
The nineteenth century: inaugural address at Cambridge. Cambridge 1900.
Reflections suggested by the new theory of matter: presidential address to the British Association for the Advancement of Science. 1904; tr German, 1905.
Decadence. Cambridge 1908.
Questionings on criticism and beauty. 1909, Oxford 1910 (rev as Criticism and beauty).
Francis Bacon. 1913.
Theism and humanism: Gifford lectures. 1915.
Essays speculative and political. 1920.
Theism and thought. [1923].
Familiar beliefs and transcendent reason. 1927.
Chapters of autobiography. Ed Mrs E. Dugdale 1930.

Articles

The philosophy of ethics. Mind 3 1878.
Transcendentalism. Ibid. Replies by E. Caird, H. Sidgwick and Balfour, 4 1879; by Sidgwick and Caird, 5 1880.

Watson on transcendentalism. Mind 6 1881.
Green's metaphysics of knowledge. Mind 9 1884.
Naturalism and ethics. International Jnl of Ethics 4 1894.
Creative evolution and philosophic doubt. Hibbert Jnl 10 1912. Reply by A. Wolf, ibid.
Also works on current affairs.

§2

Beesley, E. S. Positivism before the Church Congress: a reply to Balfour. 1889.
Martineau, J. Balfour's Foundations of belief. Nineteenth Century April 1895.
Wallace, W. Balfour's Foundations of belief. Fortnightly Rev April 1895.
Shurman, J. G. The rebound from agnosticism. Forum May 1895.
Mivart, St G. Spencer versus Balfour. Nineteenth Century Aug 1895.
Pearson, K. Reaction: a criticism of Balfour's attacks on rationalism. 1895.
Daniels, W. M. Balfour's criticism of transcendental idealism. Philosophic Rev 5 1896. Reply by R. B. Johnson, ibid.
Nicholson, J. A. The immorality of naturalism. 1896.
Cecil, H. M. Pseudo-philosophy at the end of the nineteenth century. 1897.
Rey, J. La philosophie de Balfour. Paris [1897].
Alderson, B. Balfour: the man and his work. 1903.
Jones, H. Balfour as sophist. Hibbert Jnl 3 1905.
Brown, F. The doings of Arthur. 1905.
Lobley, J. L. Positive knowledge: a reply to the Cambridge address. [1905].
Lodge, O. Balfour and Bergson. Hibbert Jnl 10 1912.
Seth, A. Balfour's Theism and humanism. Hibbert Jnl 14, 1916.
'Raymond, E. T.' (E. R. Thompson). Balfour: a biography. 1920.
Giddings, F. H. The grounds of presumption. Jnl of Philosophy 19 1922.
Mostyn, J. The Earl of Balfour and our scientific beliefs. 1925.
Kenyon, F. G. Balfour. Proc Br Acad 16 1930.
Malcolm, I. Z. Balfour. 1930.
Strutt, R. J. Balfour in his relation to science. 1930.
Wolf, A. Balfour. Jnl of Philosophical Stud 5 1930.
Webb, C. C. J. Balfour. [1931].
Dugdale, B. E. C. Balfour. 1936.
Young, K. Balfour: the happy life of the politician, Prime Minister, statesman and philosopher. 1963.

ALFRED BARRATT
1844–81

Physical ethics: or the science of action. 1869.
Physical metempiric; with a memoir by Dorothea Barratt. 1883.

THOMAS SPENCER BAYNES
1823–87

§1

An essay on the new analytic of logical forms. Edinburgh 1850.
Sir William Hamilton. 1857.
The Song of Solomon in the Somerset dialect. [1860].
The Somerset dialect: its pronunciation. 1861.
Shakespeare studies and other essays; with biographical preface by Lewis Campbell. 1894, 1896.

§2

Skelton, J. In his Table-talk of Shirley: reminiscences of Froude, Baynes, Tyndall and others, 1895.

EDWARD SPENCER BEESLY
1831–1915

§1

The social future of the working class. 1869.
Letters to the working classes. [1870].
Cataline, Clodius and Tiberius (Necker and Calonne: an old story). 1878.
Some public aspects of positivism. 1881.
Comte as a moral type. 1885.
Positivism before the Church Congress: a reply to Mr Balfour. 1889.

§2

Harrison, R. In his Before the Socialists, 1965.

GEORGE BENTHAM
1800–84

§1

An outline of a new system of logic. 1827.
The classification of fictions. Psyche 33 1928.
Also works on botany.

§2

Liard, L. In his Les logiciens anglais, Paris 1878.
Jackson, B. D. George Bentham. 1906.

GEORGE BOOLE
1815–64

§1

Address on the genius and discoveries of Sir Isaac Newton. Lincoln 1835.
The mathematical analysis of logic. Cambridge 1847; tr Spanish, 1960.
The right use of leisure. 1847.
The claims of science, especially as founded in its relations to human nature. 1851.
An investigation of the laws of thought on which are founded the mathematical theories of logic and probabilities. 1854; ed P. E. B. Jourdain 1916 (as Boole's Collected logical works vol 2); New York 1961 (corrected).
Studies in logic and probability. Ed R. Rhees 1952.

§2

Jevons, W. S. Pure logic, with remarks on Boole's system. 1864.
Hughlings, I. P. The logic of names: an introduction to Boole's laws of thought. 1869.
Liard, L. In his Les logiciens anglais, Paris 1878.
Boole, M. E. The mathematical philosophy of Gratry and Boole. 1897.

BERNARD BOSANQUET
1848–1923
§ I

Knowledge and reality. 1885.
Introduction to Hegel's philosophy of the fine arts. 1886.
Logic: or the morphology of knowledge. 2 vols Oxford 1888, 1911.
Essays and addresses. 1889, 1899 (3rd edn).
'In darkest England': on the wrong track. 1891.
A history of aesthetic. 1892, 1917 (4th edn).
The civilisation of Christendom and other studies. 1893 1899 (2nd edn).
Aspects of the social problem. 1895. Ed Bosanquet.
The essentials of logic. 1895; tr Hebrew, 1952.
Companion to Plato's Republic. 1895.
Rousseau's Social contract. 1895.
Psychology of the moral self. 1897.
The philosophical theory of the state. 1899, 1923 (4th edn).
The communication of moral ideas as a function of an ethical society. 1900.
Education of the young in Plato. Cambridge 1900.
The social criterion. 1907.
Truth and coherence. St Andrews 1911.
The principle of individuality and value. 1912.
The value and destiny of the individual. 1913.
The distinction between mind and its objects. Manchester 1913.
Germany in the nineteenth century. Manchester 1915.
Three lectures on aesthetic. 1915, ed R. Ross, Indianapolis 1963.
Social and international ideals. 1917.
Some suggestions in ethics. 1918.
Implication and linear inference. 1920.
What religion is. 1920.
Meeting of extremes in contemporary philosophy. 1921.
Three chapters on the nature of mind. Ed H. Bosanquet 1923.
Science and philosophy and other essays. Ed J. H. Muirhead and R. C. Bosanquet 1927.

Articles

Logic as the science of knowledge. In A. Seth and R. B. Haldane, Essays in philosophical criticism, 1883.
Our right to regard evil as a mystery. Mind 8 1883. Reply to F. H. Bradley, ibid.
Bradley on fact and inference. Mind 10 1885.
Comparison in psychology and in logic. Mind 11 1886.
Is mind synonymous with consciousness? (symposium). Proc Aristotelian Soc 1 1888.
The philosophical importance of a true theory of identity. Mind 13 1888.
Hegel's Correspondence. Ibid.
The part played by aesthetic in the growth of modern philosophy. Proc Aristotelian Soc 1 1889.
What takes place in voluntary action? (symposium). Ibid.
The aesthetic theory of ugliness. Ibid.
The relation of the fine arts to one another (symposium). Ibid.
Booth's Labour and life of the people. International Jnl of Ethics 2 1891.
Origin of the perception of an external world (symposium). Proc Aristotelian Soc 2 1892.
The permanent meaning of the argument from design. Ibid.
Will and reason. Monist 2 1892.
The principles and chief dangers of the administration of charity. In Philanthropy and social progress, [1893].
On the nature of aesthetic emotion. Mind new ser 3 1894.
The reality of the general will. International Jnl of Ethics 4 1894.
On an essential distinction in theories of experience. Proc Aristotelian Soc 3 1895.
The evolution of religion. International Jnl of Ethics 5 1895.
Are character and circumstances co-ordinate factors in human life, or is either subordinate to the other? Proc Aristotelian Soc 3 1896.
Time and the absolute. Ibid.
Charity organisation. Contemporary Rev Jan 1897. With H. Bosanquet.
In what sense, if any, do past and future time exist? Mind new ser 6 1897. Replies by S. H. Hodgson and G. E. Moore, ibid.
The relation of sociology to philosophy. Ibid.
Hegel's theory of the political organism. Mind new ser 7 1898.
A moral from Athenian history. International Jnl of Ethics 9 1898.
Social automatism and the imitation theory. Mind new ser 8 1899.
'Ladies and Gentlemen'. International Jnl of Ethics 10 1900.
The meaning of social work. International Jnl of Ethics 11 1901.
Recent criticism of Green's ethics. Proc Aristotelian Soc new ser 2 1902.
The Dark Ages and the Renaissance. International Jnl of Ethics 12 1902.
Hedonism among idealists. Mind new ser 12 1903.
Imitation and selective thinking. Psychological Rev 10 1903.
Plato's conception of death. Hibbert Jnl 2 1904.
Xenophon's Memorabilia of Socrates. International Jnl of Ethics 15 1905.
Can logic abstract from the psychological conditions of thinking? Proc Aristotelian Soc new ser 6 1906.
The meaning of teleology. Proc Br Acad 2 1906.
Contradiction and reality. Mind new ser 15 1906.
The place of experts in democracy (symposium). Proc Aristotelian Soc new ser 9 1909.
Cause and ground. Jnl of Philosophy 7 1910. Reply to H. S. Shelton, ibid. Replies by Shelton and Bosanquet, 8 1911.
Charity organization and the majority report. International Jnl of Ethics 20 1910. Reply to T. Jones, ibid.
On a defect in the customary logical formulation of inductive reasoning. Proc Aristotelian Soc new ser 11 1911.
The place of leisure in life. International Jnl of Ethics 21 1911.
The prediction of human conduct: a study in Bergson. Ibid.
Purpose and mechanism (symposium). Proc Aristotelian Soc new ser 12 1912.
The analysis of categorical propositions. Mind new ser 23 1914.
Idealism and the reality of time. Ibid.
The import of propositions (symposium). Proc Aristotelian Soc new ser 15 1915.
Note on G. D. H. Cole's paper on Conflicting social obligations. Ibid.
Science and philosophy. Ibid.
Patriotism in the perfect state. In The international crisis in its ethical and psychological aspects, 1915.
Causality and implication. Mind new ser 25–6 1916–17. Reply by C. A. Mercier 26 1917.
The function of the state in promoting the unity of mankind. Proc Aristotelian Soc new ser 17 1917.
Realism and metaphysics. Philosophical Rev 26 1917.
The relation of coherence to immediacy and specific purpose. Ibid.
Do finite individuals possess a substantive or an adjectival mode of being? (symposium). Proc Aristotelian Soc new ser 18 1918; Supplement 1 1918.
Appearance and reality, and the solution of problems. Philosophical Rev 28 1919. Replies by W. P. Montague and K. E. Gilbert, ibid.

The basis of Bosanquet's logic'. Mind new ser 28 1919. Reply to L. J. Russell 27 1918.
The state and the individual. Mind new ser 28 1919. Reply to C. D. Broad 27 1918.
Croce's Aesthetic. Proc Br Acad 9 1920. Replies by H. W. Carr and Bosanquet, Mind new ser 29 1920.
Appearances and the absolute. Philosophical Rev 29 1920.
The notion of a general will. Mind new ser 29 1920. Reply to C. D. Broad, ibid.
Implication and linear inference. Jnl of Philosophy 19 1922.
7+5 = 12. Philosophical Rev 31 1922. Reply to G. W. Cunningham, ibid.
A word about 'coherence'. Mind new ser 31 1922.
Life and philosophy [of Bosanquet]. In J. H. Muirhead, Contemporary British philosophy, 1924. A self-evaluation, with bibliography of books.

§2

Johnson, W. E. Bosanquet's Logic. Mind 14 1889.
Ball, S. The moral aspects of Socialism. International Jnl of Ethics 6 1896. Replies by Bosanquet, ibid; by Ball and S. Webb, 7 1897; by Bosanquet, Ball, J. S. Mackenzie and F. Brocklehurst, ibid.
Robins, E. P. Bosanquet's theory of judgment. Philosophical Rev 7 1898.
Gibson, W. R. B. The relation of logic to psychology, with special reference to the views of Bosanquet. Proc Aristotelian Soc new ser 3 1903. Reply by Bosanquet, ibid.
Sabine, G. H. Bosanquet's logic and the concrete universal. Philosophical Rev 21 1912.
—— Liberty and the social system. Philosophical Rev 25 1916.
Bussey, G. C. Bosanquet's doctrine of freedom. Ibid. Replies by M. D. Crane and Bussey, ibid.
Cuming, A. Lotze, Bradley and Bosanquet. Mind new ser 26 1917.
Russell, L. J. The basis of Bosanquet's logic. Mind new ser 27 1918. Replies by Bosanquet, 28 1919; Russell, 29 1920; Bosanquet, 30 1921.
Turner, J. E. Bosanquet's theory of mental states. Mind new ser 27 1918.
Broad, C. D. Bosanquet's Implication and linear inference. Mind new ser 29 1920. Reply by Bosanquet, 31 1922.
Carroll, M. C. Method in the metaphysics of Bosanquet. Philosophical Rev 29 1920.
—— The nature of the absolute in the metaphysics of Bosanquet. Philosophical Rev 30 1921.
—— The principle of individuality in the metaphysics of Bosanquet. Ibid.
Tsanoff, R. A. The destiny of the self in Bosanquet's theory. Philosophical Rev 29 1920.
Hinman, E. L. Modern idealism and the logos teaching. Philosophical Rev 30 1921.
Gilbert, K. Humor and Bosanquet's theory of experience. Philosophical Rev 31 1922.
—— The principle of reason in the light of Bosanquet's philosophy. Philosophical Rev 32 1923.
Schiller, F. C. S. An idealist in extremis. Mind new ser 31 1922.
Bradley, A. C. and R. B. Haldane. Bosanquet. Proc Br Acad 10 1923.
Carr, H. W. Bosanquet. Proc Aristotelian Soc new ser 23 1923.
Cunningham, G. W. Bosanquet on teleology as a metaphysical category. Philosophical Rev 32 1923.
—— Bosanquet on philosophical method. Philosophical Rev 35 1926.
Hoernlé, R. F. A. Bosanquet's Idealism. Philosophical Rev 32 1923.
Leighton, J. A. An estimate of Bosanquet's philosophy. Ibid.
Lodge, R. C. Bosanquet and the future of logic. Ibid.
Sabine, H. Bosanquet's theory of the real will. Ibid.
Schaub, E. L. Bosanquet's interpretation of religious experience. Ibid.
Muirhead, J. H. Bosanquet. Mind new ser 32 1923.
—— Bosanquet as I knew him. Jnl of Philosophy 20 1923.
—— (ed). Bosanquet and his friends: letters illustrating sources and development of his philosophical opinions. 1935.
Webb, C. C. J. Bosanquet's philosophy of religion. Hibbert Jnl 22 1924.
Bradley, A. C. Bosanquet. [1924].
Dendy (later Bosanquet), H. Bosanquet. 1924.
Watson, J. Bosanquet on mind and the absolute. Philosophical Rev 34 1925.
Laski, H. J. Bosanquet's theory of the general will (symposium). Proc Aristotelian Soc Suppl 8 1928.
Lindsay, A. D. Bosanquet's theory of the general will (symposium). Ibid.
Stedman, R. E. Bosanquet's account of religion. Hibbert Jnl 29 1931. Reply by J. H. Muirhead, ibid.
—— An examination of Bosanquet's doctrine of self-transcendence. Mind new ser 40 1931.
—— Nature in the philosophy of Bosanquet. Mind new ser 43 1934.
Foster, M. B. The concrete universal: Cook Wilson and Bosanquet. Mind new ser 40 1931.
Hall, E. W. Bosanquet on the psychical and the logical idea. Monist 41 1931.
Carritt, E. F. In his Morals and politics, Oxford 1935.
Croce, B. Lettere di Bosanquet. Critica 34 1936.
Pfannenstill, B. Bosanquet's philosophy of the state. Lund 1936.
Dockhorn, K. In his Die Staatsphilosophie des englischen Idealismus: ihre Lehre und Wirkung, Bochum 1937.
Trott, A. von. Bosanquet und der Einfluss Hegels auf die englische Staatsphilosophie. Zeitschrift für Deutsche Kulturphilosophie 4 1937.
Ramsey, P. The idealistic view of moral evil: Royce and Bosanquet. Philosophy & Phenomenological Research 6 1946.
Milne, A. J. M. In his Social philosophy of English idealism, 1962.
Le Chevalier, C. Ethique et idéalisme: le courant néo-Hegelian en Angleterre, Bosanquet et ses amis. Paris 1963.

FRANCIS HERBERT BRADLEY
1846–1924

§1

The presuppositions of critical history. Oxford 1874.
Ethical studies. Oxford 1876, 1927 (rev), 1959; ed R. G. Ross, New York 1951.
Mr Sedgwick's hedonism. 1877.
The principles of logic. 1883, 1922 (rev edn with commentary and terminal essays), 1958.
Appearance and reality. 1893, 1897 (rev), Oxford 1959; tr Italian, 1947.
Essays on truth and reality. Oxford 1914, 1962.
Aphorisms. Oxford 1930.
Collected essays. 2 vols Oxford 1935.

Articles

Most of Bradley's many articles, including those listed with replies below, are rptd in his Appearance and reality, Essays on truth and reality *or* Collected essays *(with bibliography), above.*
Is self-sacrifice an enigma? Mind 8 1883. Reply by B. Bosanquet, ibid.
Is there such a thing as pure malevolence? Ibid. Reply by A. Bain, ibid.

Jones' Browning as a philosophical and religious teacher. International Jnl of Ethics 2 1892.
Consciousness and experience. Mind new ser 2 1893.
On Jones' doctrine of simple resemblance. Ibid. Reply by W. James, ibid.
A personal explanation. International Jnl of Ethics 4 1894. Reply to A. L. Hodder, 3 1892.
A reply to criticism by J. Ward. Mind new ser 3 1894. Reply by Ward, ibid.
Some remarks on punishment. International Jnl of Ethics 4 1894. Reply by H. Rashdall, 5 1895.
Rational hedonism. International Jnl of Ethics 5 1895. Reply to E. E. C. Jones and J. S. Mackenzie, ibid; reply by E. E. C. Jones, ibid.
Note. Mind new ser 14 1905. Reply to A. Sidgwick, 13 1904.
On truth and copying. Mind new ser 16 1907. Reply by H. Sturt, ibid.
On the ambiguity of pragmatism. Mind new ser 17 1908. Replies by A. Sidgwick and F. C. S. Schiller, ibid.
On appearance, error and contradiction. Mind new ser 19 1910. Reply by F. C. S. Schiller, ibid.

§2

Sidgwick, H. Bradley's Ethical studies. Mind 1 1876. Replies by Bradley and Sidgwick 2 1877.
Dyde, S. W. Bradley's Principles of logic. Jnl of Speculative Philosophy 18–19 1884–5.
Bosanquet, B. Knowledge and reality. 1885.
Ward, J. Bradley's analysis of mind. Mind 12 1887.
— Bradley's doctrine of experience. Mind new ser 34 1925.
Carr, H. W. Bradley's Appearance and reality. Proc Aristotelian Soc 2 1894.
— Bradley's theory of appearance. Proc Aristotelian Soc new ser 2 1902.
Mackenzie, J. L. Bradley's view of the self. Mind new ser 3 1894.
Sidgwick, A. Bradley and the sceptics. Ibid.
— Notes on a note. Mind new ser 18 1909.
Seth, A. A new theory of the absolute. Contemporary Rev Nov–Dec 1894.
— In his Man's place in the cosmos, 1902 (2nd edn).
Robins, E. P. Bradley's theory of judgment. Philosophic Rev 7 1898.
Stout, G. F. Alleged self-contradictions in the concept of relation: a criticism of Bradley. Proc Aristotelian Soc new ser 2 1902. Replies by H. W. Carr, S. H. Hodgson, J. Lindsay, ibid; by A. J. Finberg and Carr 3 1903.
— Bradley's theory of judgment. Proc Aristotelian Soc new ser 3 1903.
— Bradley on truth and falsity. Mind new ser 34 1925.
Knox, H. Bradley's 'absolute criterion'. Mind new ser 14 1905. Replies by Bradley, ibid; Knox 16 1907.
Schiller, F. C. S. Bradley's theory of truth. Mind new ser 16 1907.
— The new developments of Bradley's philosophy. Mind new ser 24 1915.
— Bradley, Bain and pragmatism. Jnl of Philosophy 14 1917.
— The origin of Bradley's scepticism. Mind new ser 34 1925.
James, W. Bradley or Bergson? Jnl of Philosophy 7 1910. Reply by Bradley, ibid.
Russell, B. Some explanations in reply to Bradley. Mind new ser 19 1910. Reply by Bradley 20 1911.
Rashdall, H. The metaphysics of Bradley. Proc Br Acad 5 1912.
Broad, C. D. Bradley on truth and reality. Mind new ser 23 1914.
Strange, E. H. Bradley's doctrine of knowledge. Ibid.
Eliot, T. S. Leibnitz's monads and Bradley's finite centers. Monist 26 1916.

— Knowledge and experience in the philosophy of Bradley. Ed A. Bolgan 1964. A Harvard PhD thesis, written 1916.
Cuming, A. Bradley, Lotze and Bosanquet. Mind new ser 26 1917.
Lazarus, S. C. In memoriam F. H. Bradley. Australasian Jnl of Psychology & Philosophy 2 1924.
Hicks, G. D. Bradley's treatment of nature. Mind new ser 34 1925.
— The metaphysical systems of Bradley and Ward. Philosophy 1 1926.
— Critical realism: studies in the philosophy of mind and nature. 1938.
Keeling, S. V. La nature de l'expérience chez Kant et chez Bradley. Montpellier 1925.
Muirhead, J. H. Bradley's place in philosophy. Mind new ser 34 1925.
— British idealism as represented by Bradley. Idealismus 1 1934.
Taylor, A. E. Bradley. Proc Br Acad 11 1925.
— Mind new ser 34 1925.
Swabey, W. C. The system of Bradley. Monist 37 1927.
Hall, E. W. Bradley on idea as image and meaning. Monist 40 1930.
Konvitz, M. R. Bradley's ideal morality and Fite's moral ideal. International Jnl of Ethics 41 1930.
Campbell, C. A. Scepticism and construction. Glasgow [1931].
— The metaphysics of Bradley. Church Quart Rev 150 1950.
Kagey, R. The growth of Bradley's logic. 1931. With bibliography.
— Reality and the real in Bradley. Monist 44 1934.
Goretti, C. Il valore della filosofia di Bradley. Rivista di Filosofia 24 1933.
Chappuis, A. Der theoretische Weg Bradleys. Paris and Basle 1934.
Das, D. Bradley's doctrine of immediate experience. Rev of Philosophy & Religion 5 1934.
Kimpel, B. F. A critique of the logic of contradiction. New Haven 1934.
Segerstedt, T. T. Value and reality in Bradley's philosophy. Lund 1934.
Church, R. W. On Ewing's neglect of Bradley's theory of internal relations. Jnl of Philosophy 32 1935. Reply by Ewing, ibid.
— Bradley on relations. Philosophical Rev 46 1937.
— Bradley's dialectic. Ithaca 1942.
— Bradley's theory of relations and the law of identity. Philosophical Rev 51 1942.
Dockhorn, K. In his Die Staatsphilosophie des englischen Idealismus: ihre Lehre und Wirkung, Bochum 1937.
Loomba, R. M. Bradley and Bergson. Lucknow 1937.
Ross, R. G. Scepticism and dogma. New York 1940.
Will, F. L. Internal relations and the principle of identity. Philosophical Rev 1940.
Mack, R. D. Appeal to immediate experience. New York 1945.
Lofthouse, W. F. Bradley. 1949.
Antonelli, M. T. La metafisica di Bradley. Milan 1953.
Wollheim, R. A. In The revolution in philosophy, ed A. J. Ayer 1956.
— Bradley. 1959 (Pelican).
Kulkarni, N. G. Bradley's anti-rational argument. Philosophical Quart 7 1957. Reply by C. A. Campbell 8 1958.
Pears, D. F. et al. Metaphysics. In The nature of metaphysics, ed D. F. Pears 1957.
Krook, D. In her Three traditions of moral thought, Cambridge 1959.
Rivano, J. Motivaciones para la filosofia de Bradley. Annales de la Universidad de Chile 1961.
Assaad, F. M. L'autre et l'absolu dans la philosophie de Bradley. Revue de Métaphysique et de Morale 67 1962.

Bollier, E. P. T. S. Eliot and Bradley: a question of influence. Tulane Stud in Eng 12 1962.
Milne, A. J. M. In his Social philosophy of English idealism, 1962.
Le Chevalier, C. In his Ethique et idéalisme: le courant néo-Hegelien en Angleterre, Bosanquet et ses amis, Paris 1963.
Maclachlan, D. L. C. Presuppositions in Bradley's philosophy. Dialogue 2 1963.
Kenna, J. C. Ten unpublished letters from W. James to Bradley. Mind new ser 75 1966.
Randall, J. H. Green: the development of English thought from Mill to Bradley. JHI 27 1966.

JOHN HENRY BRIDGES
1832–1906

§1

The unity of Comte's life and doctrine: a reply to J. S. Mill. 1866, 1910.
Religion and progress. 1879.
Five discourses on positive religion. 1882.
Comte: the successor to Aristotle and St Paul. 1883.
Positivism and the Bible. 1885.
Roger Bacon's Opus majus edited. 1897; ed H. G. Jones 1914 (as The life and work of Roger Bacon).
Some guiding principles in the philosophy of history. 1906.
Essays and addresses. Ed L. T. Hobhouse 1907.
Illustrations of positivism. Ed E. S. Beesly 1907; ed H. G. Jones 1915 (enlarged).

§2

Bridges, M. A. (ed). Recollections of J. H. Bridges [by various authors]. 1908.
Torlesse, F. H. Some account of Bridges and his family. 1912.
Liveing, S. A nineteenth-century teacher. 1926.

THOMAS BROWN
1778–1820

§1

Observations on the Zoonomia of Erasmus Darwin. Edinburgh 1798.
Observations on the nature and tendency of the doctrine of Hume concerning the relations of cause and effect. Edinburgh 1805, 1806 (enlarged), 1818 (enlarged as Inquiry into the relation of cause and effect), 1835 (4th edn).
An examination of some remarks in the reply of Inglis to Playfair. Edinburgh 1806.
Lectures on the philosophy of the human mind. 4 vols Edinburgh 1820, 1834 (8th edn with memoir by D. Welsh), 1860 (20th edn).
Poetical works. 4 vols Edinburgh 1820.
Sketch of a system of philosophy of the human mind, part 1. Edinburgh 1820. No more pbd.
Lectures on ethics. Edinburgh 1846, London 1860.

§2

Shepherd, M. An essay upon the relation of cause and effect, with observations upon the opinions of Brown. 1824.
Welsh, D. Account of the life and writings of Brown. Edinburgh 1825.
Payne, G. Elements of mental and moral science. 1828.
Crybbace, T. T. An essay on moral freedom; to which is attached a review of Brown's theory of causation and agency. Edinburgh 1829.
Mill, J. In his Analysis of the phenomena of the human mind, 1829.
Wainwright, L. A vindication of Paley's theory of morals from the principal objects of Stewart and Brown. 1830.
Reid, T. An examination of the article entitled Philosophy of perception—Reid and Brown. Edinburgh 1831.
Young, J. Lectures on intellectual philosophy. Glasgow 1835.
Upham, T. C. Elements of mental philosophy. Portland 1839.
Carson, A. History of providence as manifested in Scripture, and an examination of the philosophy of Brown. Edinburgh 1840.
Hamilton, W. In his Discussions, 1852.
Milsand, J. Brown, le médecin philosophe. Revue des Deux Mondes April 1858.
Réthoré, F. Critique de la philosophie de Brown. Paris 1863.
Bain, A. In his Senses and the intellect, 1865.
McCosh, J. In his Scottish philosophy, 1875.
Dobrzyńska-Rybicka, L. Die Ethik von Brown. Poznan 1909.
Landes, M. W. Brown: associationist. Philosophical Rev 35 1926.

SAMUEL BUTLER
1835–1902

See col 1406, above.

EDWARD CAIRD
1835–1908

§1

A critical account of the philosophy of Kant. Glasgow 1877.
The problem of philosophy at the present time. Glasgow 1881.
Hegel. Edinburgh 1883.
The social philosophy and religion of Comte. Glasgow 1885; tr French, 1907.
The critical philosophy of Kant. 2 vols Glasgow 1889, 1909.
Essays on literature and philosophy. 2 vols Glasgow 1892. Vol 1 rptd as Essays on literature, 1909.
The evolution of religion. 2 vols Glasgow 1893, 1899 (3rd edn).
Individualism and Socialism. Glasgow 1897.
The evolution of theology in the Greek philosophers. 2 vols Glasgow 1904, 1923.
Lay sermons and addresses. Glasgow 1907.

Articles

Reply to Stirling. Jnl of Speculative Philosop hy 13 1879.
Kant's deduction of the categories, with relation to the views of Stirling. Jnl of Speculative Philosophy 14 1880.
The problem of philosophy at the present time. Jnl of Speculative Philosophy 16 1882.
Green's last work. Mind 8 1883.
The modern conception of the science of religion. International Jnl of Ethics 1 1891.
Jowett. International Jnl of Ethics 8 1897.
Anselm's argument for the being of God. Jnl of Theological Stud 1 1899.
Idealism and the theory of knowledge. Proc Br Acad 1 1904.
St Paul and the idea of evolution. Hibbert Jnl 2 1904. Reply by H. G. Smith, ibid.

The influence of Kant on modern thought. Quart Rev 200 1904.

§2

Stirling, J. H. Caird on Kant. Jnl of Speculative Philosophy 16 1882.
Blakeney, E. H. Caird's Essays. [1893].
Bosanquet, B. Caird. Proc Br Acad 3 1908.
MacVannel, J. A. Caird. Jnl of Philosophy 5 1908.
Mackenzie, J. S. Caird. International Jnl of Ethics 19 1909.
—— Caird as a philosophical teacher. Mind new ser 18 1909.
Watson, J. The idealism of Caird. Philosophical Rev 18 1909.
Jones, H. and J. H. Muirhead. The life and philosophy of Caird. 1921.
Lindsay, A. D. The idealism of Caird and Jones. Philosophy 1 1926.
Warren, W. P. In his Pantheism in neo-Hegelian thought, New Haven 1933.

JOHN CAIRD

1820–98

The unity of the sciences. Glasgow 1874.
An introduction to the philosophy of religion. Glasgow 1880, 1901.
Spinoza. Edinburgh 1888.
University addresses. Glasgow 1898.
The fundamental ideas of Christianity. 2 vols Glasgow 1899. With memoir by E. Caird.
Also works on religion.

HENRY CALDERWOOD

1830–97

§1

The philosophy of the infinite. Edinburgh 1854, Cambridge 1861 (enlarged).
Moral philosophy as a science and as a discipline. Edinburgh 1868.
Handbook of moral philosophy. 1872, 1888 (14th edn, rewritten).
On teaching: its ends and means. Edinburgh 1874, 1881 (3rd edn).
The relations of mind and brain. 1877, 1884 (enlarged), 1892.
The relations of science and religion. New York 1881.
Evolution and man's place in nature. 1893, 1896.
The vocabulary of philosophy and student's book of reference. 1894.
Hume. Edinburgh 1898.
Also works on religion.

§2

Vera, A. An inquiry into speculative and experimental science, with special reference to Calderwood and Ferrier. 1856.
Calderwood, W. and D. Woodside. Life of Calderwood. 1900.

THOMAS CARLYLE

1795–1881

See col 1248, above.

WILLIAM BENJAMIN CARPENTER

1813–85

§1

Principles of mental physiology. 1874, 1896 (7th edn).
Is man an automaton? 1875.
Mesmerism and spiritualism. 1877.
Nature and man: essays scientific and philosophical. Ed J. E. Carpenter 1888 (with memoir).
Also works on science.

§2

Lingard, J. T. Carpenter's theory of attention. Mind 2 1872.
Gill, W. L. Evolution and progress, with a review of quasi opponents, as Le Conte and Carpenter. 1875.
Guthrie, M. The causational and free-will theories of volition: being a review of Carpenter's Mental physiology. 1877.

THOMAS CHALMERS

1780–1847

See col 1602, below.

STANTON COIT

1857–1944

Ethical culture as a religion for the people. 1888; tr French, 1891.
The ethical movement defined. [1898?]; rptd in The ethical movement, ed H. J. Bridges 1911.
Ethical democracy: essays in social dynamics. 1900.
Humanity and God. International Jnl of Ethics 16 1906.
Ethical mysticism. In Aspects of ethical religion: essays in honour of Felix Adler, 1926.
Spinoza's moral insight. In Spinoza: tercentenary addresses, ed I. Maltuck 1932.
Also works on religion and current events.

SAMUEL TAYLOR COLERIDGE

1772–1834

See col 211, above.

GEORGE COMBE

1788–1858

§1

Essays on phrenology. 1819, Edinburgh 1825 (as System of phrenology), 2 vols 1836 (4th edn), 1843 (5th edn), 1853 (rev).
Elements of phrenology. Edinburgh 1824, 1850 (7th edn enlarged).
Letter to Francis Jeffrey in answer to his criticism of phrenology in the Edinburgh Review. 1826.
The constitution of man considered in relation to external objects. Edinburgh 1828, 1840 (4th edn rev and enlarged).
Letter on the prejudices of the great in science and philosophy against phrenology. Edinburgh 1829.
Lectures on popular education. Edinburgh 1833, 1837 (enlarged), 1848 (enlarged).
Moral philosophy. Edinburgh 1840. Also pbd as Lectures on moral philosophy 1840, 1846 (3rd edn enlarged).

Notes on the United States of America. 3 vols Edinburgh 1841, 2 vols Philadelphia 1841.
Remarks on national education. Edinburgh 1847.
Phrenology as applied to painting and sculpture. 1855.
On the relation between religion and science. Edinburgh 1847, 1857 (4th edn enlarged), 1893 (as Science and religion).
Select works. 5 vols 1893–4.
Also works on phrenology.

§2

Gibbon, C. Life of Combe. 1878.
Capen, N. Reminiscences of Spurzheim and Combe. 1881.

RICHARD CONGREVE
1818–99

§1

Pilgrimage: a prize poem recited in Rugby School. 1837.
The new religion in its attitude to the old. 1859.
The propagation of the religion of humanity. 1860.
Religion de l'humanité. Paris 1864.
Two addresses: systematic policy, education. 1870.
Essays political, social and religious. 3 vols 1874, 1900.
Human catholicism. 2 nos 1876–7.
The religion of humanity [annual addresses]. 1878, 1881, 1882, 1894.
Also works on historical and contemporary questions.

§2

Thomas, P. Comte and Congreve. 1910.

THOMAS COOPER
1805–92

See col 516, above.

CAROLINE FRANCES CORNWALLIS
1786–1858

Pericles: a tale of Athens. 2 vols 1846.
Selections from the letters. Ed M. C. Power 1864.
Also 15 books on philosophy and science for the series Small books on great subjects, 1842–54.

THOMAS DAVIDSON
1840–1900

§1

A short account of the Niobe group. New York 1875.
Longfellow. Boston 1882.
The Parthenon frieze and other essays. 1882.
The philosophical system of Rosmini-Serbati. 1882.
The place of art in education. Boston 1885.
The moral aspects of the economic question. Boston 1886.
The conditions, divisions, and methods of complete education. Orange NJ 1887.
A handbook to Dante. 1887.
Prolegomena to In memoriam. Boston 1889.
Bruno's thought. In Giordano Bruno: two addresses by D. G. Brinton and T. Davidson, Philadelphia 1890.
The evolution of scripture. New York 1891.
Aristotle and ancient educational ideals. New York 1892.
The education of the Greek people. New York 1894.
Rousseau and education according to nature. New York 1898.
A history of education. New York 1900.
The education of the wage-earners. Ed C. M. Bakewell, Boston [1904].
The philosophy of Goethe's Faust. Ed C. M. Bakewell, Boston 1906.
Education as world-building. Ed E. Moore, Cambridge Mass 1925.

§2

Bakewell, C. M. A democratic philosopher and his work. International Jnl of Ethics 11 1901.
Knight, W. Memorials of Davidson. Boston 1907.
Blau, J. L. Rosmini, Domodossola, and Davidson. JHI 18 1958.
Lataner, A. Introduction to Davidson's Autobiographical sketch. Ibid.

AUGUSTUS DE MORGAN
1806–71

§1

The schoolmaster: essays on practical education. 1836.
Essay on probabilities. 1838, 1849.
First notions of logic. 1839.
The globes, celestial and terrestrial. 1845.
Formal logic: or the calculus of inference, necessary and probable. 1847; ed A. E. Taylor 1926.
Statement in answer to an assertion made by Hamilton. [1847].
On the syllogism [five papers with an appendix]. Trans Cambridge Philosophical Soc 8–10 1849–64.
On the difficulty of correct description of books. 1853, Chicago 1902.
Syllabus of a proposed system of logic. 1860.
A budget of paradoxes. Ed E. De Morgan 1872, 2 vols Chicago 1915, New York 1954.
Newton: his friend and his niece. Ed S. E. De Morgan and A. C. Ranyard 1885.
Essays on the life and work of Newton. Ed P. E. B. Jourdain 1914.
Also works on mathematics and education.

§2

Liard, L. In his Les logiciens anglais, Paris 1878.
De Morgan, S. E. Memoir. 1882.

CHARLES LUTWIDGE DODGSON, 'LEWIS CARROLL'
1832–98

§1

The game of logic. 1886.
A logical paradox. Mind new ser 3 1894. Replies by A. Sidgwick, W. E. Johnson, ibid; A. Sidgwick, 4 1895; E. E. C. Jones, 'W', 14 1905; A. W. Burks, I. M. Copi, 59 1950; and A. J. Baker, 64 1955.
What the tortoise said to Achilles. Mind new ser 4 1895. Replies by W. J. Rees, 60 1951; D. G. Brown, 63 1954.
Symbolic logic. 1897.

§2

Woolen, C. J. Lewis Carroll: philosopher. Hibbert Jnl 46 1948.
See also col 977, above.

ROBERT LESLIE ELLIS

1817–59

The philosophical works of Francis Bacon. 1857. Ed with J. Spedding.

Mathematical and other writings. Ed W. Walton, with memoir by H. Goodwin, Cambridge 1863.

JAMES FREDERICK FERRIER

1808–64

§1

Institutes of metaphysic: the theory of knowing and being. Edinburgh 1854, 1856.

Scottish philosophy: the old and the new. Edinburgh 1856.

Lectures on Greek philosophy and other philosophical remains. Ed A. Grant and E. L. Lushington 2 vols Edinburgh 1866.

Philosophical works. 3 vols Edinburgh 1875–88. Vol 1, Institutes of metaphysic (3rd edn); vols 2 and 3, Lectures on Greek philosophy and other philosophical remains (2nd edn).

§2

Cairns, J. An examination of Ferrier's theory of knowing and being. 1856.

—— The Scottish philosophy: a vindication and reply. Edinburgh 1856.

Fraser, A. C. In his Essays in philosophy, Edinburgh 1856.

—— Philosophical life of Ferrier. Macmillan's Mag Jan 1868.

Smith, J. An examination of Cairn's Examination. Edinburgh 1856.

Vera, A. An inquiry into speculative and experimental science, with special reference to Calderwood and Ferrier. 1856.

Deuchar, R. A brief review of ancient and modern philosophy, with refutations of Ferrier. Edinburgh 1864.

Grote, J. In his Exploratio philosophica, Cambridge 1865.

Tulloch, J. In his Theories in philosophy and religion, Edinburgh 1884

Haldane, E. Ferrier. Edinburgh 1894.

Segerstedt, T. T. In his Problem of knowledge in Scottish philosophy, Lund 1935.

Thomson, A. The philosophy of Ferrier. Philosophy 39 1964.

ROBERT FLINT

1838–1910

§1

The philosophy of history in France and Germany. Edinburgh 1874.

Theism: the Baird lecture for 1876. Edinburgh 1877, 1880 (3rd edn), London 1883, Edinburgh 1902 (10th edn).

Anti-theistic theories. Edinburgh 1879, 1885 (3rd edn).

Vico. Edinburgh 1884.

Historical philosophy in France, French Belgium and Switzerland. 1893.

Socialism. 1894, 1908 (rev).

Sermons and addresses. 1899.

Agnosticism. 1903.

Philosophy as scientia scientiarum. Edinburgh 1904.

On theological, Biblical and other subjects. Edinburgh 1905.

Also works on religion.

§2

MacLeod, N. Scottish divines. 1883.

Macmillan, D. Life of Flint. 1914.

THOMAS FOWLER

1832–1904

Elements of deductive logic. Oxford 1866. *See below.*

Elements of inductive logic. Oxford 1870, 2 pts Oxford 1895 (rev and combined with the previous as Logic, deductive and inductive, 10th rev edn of Elements of deductive logic, 6th rev edn of Elements of inductive logic).

Locke. 1880.

Bacon. 1881.

Shaftesbury and Hutcheson. 1882.

Progressive morality: an essay in ethics. 1884, 1895 (enlarged).

The principles of morals. 2 pts 1886–7. With J. M. Wilson.

Also works on Oxford.

ALEXANDER CAMPBELL FRASER

1819–1914

§1

Introductory lecture on logic and metaphysics. Edinburgh 1851.

Essays in philosophy. Edinburgh 1856.

Rational philosophy in history and in system. Edinburgh 1858.

Whately and the restoration of the study of logic. Cambridge [1863].

On mental philosophy. Edinburgh 1868.

Life and letters of Berkeley, and an account of his philosophy. Oxford 1871.

Berkeley. Edinburgh 1881.

Locke. Edinburgh 1890.

The philosophy of theism. 2 ser 1895–6, 1899 (rev).

Reid. 1898.

Biographia philosophica. Edinburgh 1904.

Locke as a factor in modern thought. Proc Br Acad 1 1904.

Berkeley and spiritual realism. 1908.

§2

Seth, A. Fraser. Proc Br Acad 6 1914.

—— Mind new ser 24 1915.

SIR FRANCIS GALTON

1822–1911

See col 1381, above.

WILLIAM GRAHAM

1839–1911

Idealism: an essay metaphysical and critical. 1872.

The creed of science, religious, moral and social. 1881, 1884 (rev).

The social problem. 1886.
Socialism, new and old. 1890, 1891.
English political philosophy from Hobbes to Maine. 1899.

THOMAS HILL GREEN
1836–82

§1

Liberal legislation and freedom of contract. Oxford 1881.
Prolegomena to ethics. Ed A. C. Bradley, Oxford 1883, 1907 (5th edn).
The witness of God, and faith: two lay sermons. Ed A. and C. Toynbee 1883.
Works. Ed R. L. Nettleship 3 vols 1885–8 (with memoir), 1889–90.
An essay of the value and influence of works of fiction. Ed F. N. Scott, Ann Arbor 1911.

§2

Hodgson, J. R. Green as a critic. Contemporary Rev Dec 1880. Replies by Green Jan 1881; and Spencer, Feb 1881.
Nettleship, R. L. and J. Bryce. Professor T. H. Green: In memoriam. Contemporary Rev May 1882.
Caird, E. Green's last work. Mind 8 1883.
Balfour, A. J. Green's metaphysics of knowledge. Mind 9 1884.
Sidgwick, H. Green's ethics. Ibid.
— Lectures on the ethics of Green, Spencer and Martineau. 1902.
Calderwood, H. Another view of Green's last work. Mind 10 1885.
Ritchie, D. G. Political philosophy of Green. Contemporary Rev June 1887.
— The principles of state interference: essays on Spencer, Mill and Green. 1891.
Seth, A. Hegelianism and personality. Edinburgh 1887, 1893.
Upton, C. B. Theological aspects of the philosophy of Green. New World 1 1892.
Chubb, P. The significance of Green's philosophical and religious teaching. Jnl of Speculative Philosophy 22 1888.
Chadwick, J. W. Green. Unitarian Rev 31 1889.
Conybeare, F. C. Political philosophy of Green. Nat Rev Aug 1889.
Dewey, J. Philosophy of Green. Andover Rev 11 1889.
— Green's theory of the moral motive. Philosophical Rev 1 1892.
— Self-realization as the moral ideal. Philosophical Rev 2 1893.
Oxford metaphysics and ethics adapted to a natural system. Edinburgh 1889.
Eastwood, A. On thought-relations. Mind 16 1891.
Fairbrother, W. H. Green and his critics. Proc Aristotelian Soc 2 1894.
— The philosophy of Green. 1896.
Haldar, H. Green and his critics. Philosophical Rev 3 1894.
James, G. F. Green und der Utilitarismus. Halle 1894.
Laurie, S. S. The metaphysics of Green. Philosophical Rev 6 1897.
Johnson, R. B. C. The metaphysics of knowledge: an examination of Green's theory of reality. Princeton 1900.
Knox, H. V. Green's refutation of empiricism. Mind new ser 9 1900.
— Has Green answered Locke? Mind new ser 23 1914.
McGilvary, E. B. 'The eternal consciousness'. Mind new ser 10 1901.
Bosanquet, B. Recent criticism of Green's ethics. Proc Aristotelian Soc new ser 2 1902. Replies by S. H. Hodgson, A. E. Taylor, and Bosanquet, ibid.
Bryce, J. In his Studies in contemporary biography, 1903.
Jones, E. E. C. Green's account of Aristotle's Ethics. Hibbert Jnl 1 1903.
Nettleship, R. L. Memoir of Green. 1906.
Barbour, G. F. Green and Sidgwick on the community of the good. Philosophical Rev 17 1908.
Muirhead, J. H. The service of the state: four lectures on the political teaching of Green. 1908.
MacCunn, J. In his Six radical thinkers, 1910.
Townsend, H. G. The principle of individuality in the philosophy of Green. Ithaca 1914.
Harkness, G. E. Green as a philosopher of religion. Personalist 5 1924.
Montagné, P. Bibliographie relative à Un radical religieux en Angleterre: ou la philosophie de Green. Toulouse 1927.
Selsam, H. Green: critic of empiricism. 1930.
Lamont, W. D. Introduction to Green's moral philosophy. 1934.
Bongioanni, F. M. I Prolegomena to ethics di Green. Rivista di Filosofia 27 1936.
Goretti, C. La metafisica della conoscenza in Green. Ibid.
Lewis, H. D. Was Green a hedonist? Mind new ser 45 1936.
— 'Self-satisfaction' and the 'true good' in Green's moral theory. Proc Aristotelian Soc new ser 42 1942.
— Does the good will define its own content? a study of Green's Prolegomena. Ethics 58 1948.
— Individualism and collectivism. Ethics 63 1952.
Tilgher, A. La filosofia religosa di Green. Religio 12 1936.
Borrelli, P. Contributi allo storia della filosofia. Alessandria 1937.
Dockhorn, K. Die Staatsphilosophie des englischen Idealismus: ihre Lehre und Wirkung. Bochum 1937.
Reimann, H. Bahnbrecher des Idealismus in der englischen Philosophie. Goetheanum 17 1938.
Routh, D. A. The philosophy of international relations: Green versus Hegel. Politica 3 1938.
Lindsay, A. D. Green and the idealists. In F. J. C. Hearnshaw, The social and political ideas of some representative thinkers of the Victorian age, New York 1950.
Munro, D. H. Green, Rousseau and the culture pattern. Philosophy 26 1951.
Monson, C. H. Prichard, Green and moral obligation. Philosophical Rev 63 1954.
Wayper, C. L. In his Political thought, New York 1954.
Robinson, D. S. In his Crucial issues in philosophy, Boston 1955.
Richter, M. Green and his audience: liberalism as a surrogate faith. Rev of Politics 18 1956.
— The politics of conscience: Green and his age. Cambridge Mass 1964.
Holloway, H. Mill and Green on the modern welfare state. Western Political Quart 12 1960.
Pucelle, J. La nature et l'esprit dans la philosophie de Green: la renaissance de l'idéalisme en Angleterre au XIXe siècle. Louvain 1961.
Milne, A. J. M. In his Social philosophy of English Idealism, 1962.
Sandelius, W. E. Liberalism in the political philosophy of Green. In Six studies in nineteenth-century English literature and thought, ed H. Orel and G. J. Worth, Lawrence Kansas 1962.
Le Chevalier, C. Ethique et idéalisme: le courant néo-Hegelian en Angleterre, Bosanquet et ses amis. Paris 1963.
Randall, J. H. Green: the development of English thought from Mill to Bradley. JHI 27 1966.

GEORGE GROTE

1794–1871

See col 1460, above.

JOHN GROTE

1813–66

§1

A few notes on a pamphlet by Mr Shilleto entitled Thucydides or Grote? 1851.
Old studies and new. Cambridge 1856.
Essays and reviews. Cambridge 1862.
Exploratio philosophica. 2 pts Cambridge 1865, 1900.
An examination of the Utilitarian philosophy. Ed J. P. Mayor, Cambridge 1870.
Sermons. Cambridge 1872.
A treatise on the moral ideals. Ed J. P. Mayor, Cambridge 1876.
Plato's utilitarianism: a dialogue by Grote and H. Sidgwick. Classical Rev 3 1889.

§2

Whitmore, C. E. The significance of John Grote. Philosophical Rev 36 1927.

SIR WILLIAM HAMILTON

1788–1856

§1

Works of Reid. 2 vols Edinburgh 1846, 1 vol Edinburgh 1852 (3rd edn), 2 vols Edinburgh 1863 (6th edn). Ed Hamilton.
Letter to De Morgan on his claim to an independent rediscovery of a new principle in the theory of syllogism. 1847.
Discussions on philosophy and literature, education and university reform. 1852, 1853 (enlarged), 1866.
Collected works of Stewart. 11 vols Edinburgh 1854–60. Ed Hamilton.
Lectures on metaphysics and logic. Ed H. L. Mansel and J. Veitch 4 vols Edinburgh 1859–60, London 1861–6 (rev).

Articles

On the philosophy of the unconditioned. Edinburgh Rev 50 1829.
Philosophy of perception. Edinburgh Rev 52 1830.
On logic: recent English treatises. Edinburgh Rev 56 1833.
On idealism: Collier. Edinburgh Rev 68 1839.

§2

Calderwood, H. Philosophy of the infinite. Edinburgh 1854, 1861 (enlarged).
Hare, J. C. Vindication of Luther against his recent English assailants. 1855 (2nd edn enlarged).
Ulrici, H. Englische Philosophie: Hamilton. Zeitschrift für Philosophie 27 1855.
Baynes, T. S. Spencer on Hamilton. In his Edinburgh essays, 1857.
McCosh, J. Hamilton's metaphysics. Dublin Univ Mag 54 1859.
—— Examination of Hamilton's logic. In his Philosophical papers, 1866.
—— In his Scottish philosophy, New York 1875.
Tyler, S. Philosophy of Hamilton. Biblical Repertory & Princeton Rev 31 1859.
Rémusat, C. de. Hamilton. Revue des Deux Mondes April 1859, March 1860.
Deuchar, R. A brief review of ancient and modern philosophy. Edinburgh 1864.
Jones, J. H. Know the truth: a critique on the Hamiltonian doctrine of limitation. New York 1865.
Masson, D. In his Recent British philosophy, 1865.
Mill, J. S. Examination of Hamilton's philosophy. 1865, 1865 (rev), 1867 (rev), 1872 (rev). *See col 1552, below.*
Stirling, J. H. Hamilton: being the philosophy of perception. 1865.
—— Was Hamilton a Berkeleian? Fortnightly Rev 1 Sept 1866.
Bolton, M. P. W. Inquisitio philosophica: an examination of the principles of Kant and Hamilton. 1866.
—— The Scoto-Oxonian philosophy. 1869.
'Inquirer'. The battle of the two philosophers, Hamilton and Mill. 1866.
Mansel, H. L. The philosophy of the conditioned. 1866.
Ryan, M. The celebrated theory of parallels; with appendix refuting Hamilton's philosophy of the unconditioned. Washington 1866.
Veitch, J. Memoir of Hamilton. Edinburgh 1869.
—— Hamilton. Edinburgh 1882.
—— Hamilton: the man and his philosophy. 1883.
Murray, J. C. Outline of Hamilton's philosophy. Boston 1870.
'An old student'. What do we know? 1872.
Billing, M. Kritik öfver Hamilton's lära om det obetingade. Lund 1877.
Liard, L. In his Les logiciens anglais, Paris 1878.
Fink, W. C. An analysis of Hamilton's Lectures on metaphysics. Calcutta 1880.
Morris, G. S. In his British thought and thinkers, 1880.
Monck, W. S. H. Hamilton. 1881.
Green, T. H. The logic of the formal logicians. In his Works vol 2, 1886.
Bourdillart, F. La réforme logique de Hamilton. Paris 1891.
Grote, J. Exploratio philosophica, pt 2. Cambridge 1900.
Rasmussen, S. V. Studier over Hamilton's filosofi. Copenhagen 1925.
Segerstedt, T. T. The problem of knowledge in Scottish philosophy. Lund 1935.
Bednarowski, W. Hamilton's quantification of the predicate. Proc Aristotelian Soc 56 1956.

THOMAS NORTON HARPER

1821–93

The metaphysics of the School. 3 vols 1879–84.

FREDERIC HARRISON

1831–1923

Order and progress. 2 pts 1875.
Science and humanity: a lay sermon. 1879.
The social factor in psychology. [1879].
The present and the future. 1880.
The ghost of religion. In 'E.L.Y.' (ed), The nature and reality of religion, 1885.
Politics and a human religion. 1885.
Moral and religious socialism. 1891.
The meaning of history and other historical pieces. 1894.
Tennyson, Ruskin, Mill and other literary estimates. 1900.
Positivism: its position, aims and ideals. 1901.
The religion of duty. Philadelphia 1901.
Herbert Spencer. Oxford 1905.
Collected essays. 4 pts 1907–8.
Bibliography of Harrison. Hawkhurst 1908. BM copy with ms notes.
Autobiographic memoirs. 2 vols 1911.
Among my books: centenaries, reviews, memoirs. 1912.

The positive evolution of religion. 1913.
On society. 1918.
See col 1437, above.

SIR JOHN FREDERICK WILLIAM HERSCHEL
1792–1871

A preliminary discourse on the study of natural philosophy. 1831, 1842, 1851; tr French, 1834; Italian, 1840; Polish, 1955.
The importance of literature to men of business. 1833, 1852.
Essays. 1857.
Familiar lectures on scientific subjects. 1866, 1871.
Also works on astronomy and mathematics.

JAMES HINTON
1822–1875

§1

Man and his dwelling place. 1859, 1872 (rev).
Life in nature. 1862; ed H. Ellis 1932.
The mystery of pain. 1866 (anon), 1874 etc; ed R. H. Hutton [1911].
Selections from manuscripts. 4 vols 1870–4.
Chapters on the art of thinking, and other essays. Ed C. H. Hinton 1879.
Others' needs. 1881.
Philosophy and religion. Ed C. Haddon 1881, 1884.
The lawbreaker and the coming of the law. Ed M. Hinton 1884.
Also works on medicine.

§2

Hopkins, J. E. Life and letters of Hinton. 1878, 1882 (4th edn).
Haddon, C. The larger life: studies in Hinton's ethics. 1886.
— A law of development. 1883. Based on Hinton's unpbd writings.
Ellis, E. M. O. In her Three modern seers, [1910].
— Hinton: a sketch. [1918].

SHADWORTH HOLLOWAY HODGSON
1832–1912

§1

Time and space. 1865.
The theory of practice. 2 vols 1870.
Five idols of the theatre. [1872].
The pre-suppositions of miracles. [1876].
Is monism tenable? [1878].
The philosophy of reflection. 2 vols 1878.
Philosophy in relation to its history. [1880].
Outcast essays and verse translations. 1881.
The practical bearing of speculative philosophy. 1881.
The method of philosophy. 1882.
The two senses of 'reality'. 1883.
The relation of philosophy to science. 1884.
Philosophy and experience. 1885.
The reorganisation of philosophy. 1886.
The unseen world. 1887.
The metaphysic of experience. 4 vols 1898.
Inter-relation of the academical sciences. [1906].
Some cardinal points in knowledge. [1911].

§2

Dauriac, L. La méthode et la doctrine de Hodgson. L'Année Philosophique 1899.
Carr, H. W. Hodgson. Mind new ser 21 1912.
Hicks, G. D. Hodgson. Proc Br Acad 6 1914.

THOMAS HENRY HUXLEY
1825–95

§1

On the educational value of the natural history sciences. 1854.
On races, species and their origin. 1860.
Evidence as to man's place in nature. Edinburgh 1863; tr French, 1868.
On the methods and results of ethnology. 1865.
Lay sermons, addresses and reviews. 1870, 1871 (2nd edn), 1887 (3rd edn).
Critiques and addresses. 1873.
The evidence of the miracle of resurrection. 1876.
American addresses. 1877.
Hume. 1878.
Science and culture, and other essays. 1881.
The advance of science in the last half-century. New York 1887.
Social diseases and worse remedies. 1891, 1891 (2nd edn).
Essays on some controverted questions. 1892.
Evolution and ethics. 1893, 1893, 1893. With Prolegomena (1894) in Collected essays vol 9, below.
Collected essays. 9 vols 1893–4; tr Italian, 1956 (in part).
Scientific memoirs. Ed M. Foster and E. R. Lankester 5 vols 1898–1903.
Religion without revelation. Ed J. Huxley 1957.

Articles

Almost all of Huxley's articles and some monographs are rptd in the vols of essays listed above.
Time and life. Macmillan's Mag Dec 1859.
Bishop Berkeley on the metaphysics of sensation. Macmillan's Mag June 1871.
Balfour's attack on agnosticism. Nineteenth Century March 1895.
Also wrote extensively on scientific subjects.

§2

Young, G. R. Modern scepticism, viewed in relation to modern science. 1865.
Morris, F. O. Difficulties of Darwinism. 1869.
Lillie, J. Letter to Huxley. 1871.
Maschi, L. Confutazione delle dottrine trasformistiche di Huxley, Darwin. Parma 1874.
Porter, J. L. Science and revelation: their distinctive provinces. 1874.
Professor Huxley in America. New York 1876.
Hall, A. W. The problem of human life. 1880.
Jordan, W. L. Huxley on the laws of motion. 1882.
Denison, E. B. A review of Hume and Huxley on miracles. 1883.
McCosh, J. Agnosticism of Hume and Huxley. 1884.
Savile, B. W. Gladstone and Huxley on the Mosaic cosmogony. 1886.
Tafel, R. L. Huxley and Swedenborg. 1889.
Garbett, E. L. Huxley's mendacity on the effects of Noah's flood. 1891.
— Facts of the Jesus-Huxley case, on Noah's flood. 1893.
Hahn, G. Huxley. 1895.
White, F. E. Huxley on the relation of the ethical to the cosmic process. International Jnl of Ethics 5 1895. Replies by J. Royce, ibid; J. M. Baldwin and White 6 1895.

Huxley, L. Life and letters of Huxley. 2 vols 1900, 1903. With bibliography.
— Huxley. 1920.
— Carlyle and Huxley: early influences. Cornhill Mag March 1932.
— An American student in Huxley's laboratory. Cornhill Mag June 1934.
Mitchell, P. C. Huxley. 1900, 1913.
Clodd, E. Huxley. 1902.
Wace, H. On agnosticism. 1902.
Clarke, W. N. Huxley and Brooks. 1903.
Thompson, W. H. Huxley and religion. 1905.
Davis, J. R. A. Huxley. 1907.
McGilvary, E. B. Huxley's epiphenomenalism. Jnl of Philosophy 7 1910.
Cadman, S. P. Darwin and other English thinkers. 1911.
Leighton, G. R. Huxley. 1912.
Huxley memorial lectures. Birmingham 1914.
Wenley, R. M. Huxley in his epoch. Monist 35 1925.
Gissing, G. R. Autobiographical notes, with comments on Tennyson and Huxley. 1930.
Ayres, C. E. Huxley. New York 1932.
Huxley, A. Huxley as a man of letters. 1932.
— The olive tree. 1937.
Huxley memorial lectures 1925–32. 1932.
Peterson, H. Huxley: prophet of science. New York 1932.
Armstrong, H. E. Our need to honour Huxley's will. 1933.
MacBride, E. W. Huxley. 1934.
Huxley, J. (ed). Huxley's Diary of the voyage of HMS Rattlesnake. 1935.
Chesterton, G. K. The Huxley heritage. Amer Rev 8 1937.
Grusendorf, A. A. Huxley on higher education. School & Soc 53 1941.
Foley, L. The Huxley tradition of language study. Modern Lang Jnl 26 1942.
Teller, J. D. Huxley's 'evil' influence. Scientific Monthly Feb 1943.
— Huxley on the aims of education. Educational Forum 8 1944.
Huxley, J. S. and D. Cleverdon. Julian Huxley on T. H. Huxley: a new judgment. 1945.
The Huxley papers: a descriptive catalogue. 1946.
Irving, J. A. Evolution and ethics. Queen's Quart 55 1948.
Houghton, W. E. The rhetoric of Huxley. UTQ 18 1949.
Irvine, W. Carlyle and Huxley. In Booker memorial studies, ed H. Shine, Chapel Hill 1950.
— Apes, angels and Victorians: the story of Darwin, Huxley and evolution. New York 1955.
— Huxley. 1960; rptd in British writers and their work, ed B. Dobrée, vol 2 Lincoln Nebraska 1964.
Armytage, W. H. G. Arnold and Huxley: some new letters 1870–80. RES new ser 4 1953.
Hallam, G. W. Source of the word 'agnostic'. MLN 70 1955.
Bibby, C. Huxley's idea of a university. Universities Quart 10 1956.
— The prince of controversialists. Twentieth Century March 1957.
— Huxley and the reception of the Origin. Victorian Stud 3 1959.
— Huxley: scientist, humanist and educator. 1959.
Blinderman, C. S. The Oxford debate and after. N & Q March 1957.
— Huxley. Scientific Monthly April 1957.
— Huxley and Kingsley. Victorian Newsletter no 20 1961.
— Semantic aspects of Huxley's literary style. Jnl of Communication 12 1962.
— Huxley's theory of aesthetics: unity in diversity. Jnl of Aesthetics 21 1962.
Stanley, O. Huxley's treatment of 'nature'. JHI 18 1957.
Armstrong, A. MacC. Wilberforce v. Huxley: a retrospect. Quart Rev 296 1958.
Crowe, M. B. Huxley and humanism. Studies 49 1960.
Krutch, J. W. If you don't mind my saying so. Amer Scholar 32 1963.
Cockshut, A. O. J. Huxley: the scientific sage. In his Unbelievers: English agnostic thought 1840–90, 1964.
Eisen, S. Huxley and the positivists. Victorian Stud 7 1964.
Noland, R. W. Huxley on culture. Personalist 45 1964.
Cherry, D. The two cultures of Arnold and Huxley. Wascona Rev 1 1966.

WILLIAM STANLEY JEVONS
1835–82

§ 1

Pure logic: or the science of quality apart from quantity. 1864.
The state in relation to labour. 1866.
The substitution of similars. 1869.
Elementary lessons in logic. 1870, 1884, 1891, 1905, 1957.
The mechanical performance of logical inference. Philosophical Trans 1870.
The theory of political economy. 1871, 1879 (enlarged), New York 1965 (with bibliography); tr French, 1879; Spanish, 1879; Italian, 1947.
Logic. 1872, 1876, 1880, 1889; tr Italian, 1878; Spanish, 1885, 1941.
The principles of science. 2 vols 1874, New York 1877 (rev); tr Polish, 1960.
Primer of logic. 1878.
Studies in deductive logic. 1880, 1896 (3rd edn).
Methods of social reform, and other papers. Ed H. A. Jevons 1883.
Letters and journal ed by his wife. 1886.
Pure logic and other minor works. Ed R. Adamson and H. A. Jevons 1890.
The principles of economics. Ed H. Higgs 1905.
Also works on specific economic questions.

§ 2

Liard, L. In his Les logiciens anglais, Paris 1878.
Cornelissen, C. Theorie der waarde; kritiek op de theorieën van Robertus, Marx, Jevons. Amsterdam 1903; tr French, 1926.
Keynes, J. M. Jevons. Royal Statistical Soc Jnl 99 1936.
Eckard, E. W. Economics of Jevons. Washington 1940.
Henry, D. P. and W. Mays. Jevons and logic. Mind new ser 62 1953.

SIR HENRY JONES
1852–1922

§ 1

Morality as freedom. 1888.
Browning as a philosophical and religious teacher. Glasgow 1891, 1899.
Is the order of nature opposed to the moral life? Glasgow 1894.
A critical account of the philosophy of Lotze. Glasgow 1895.
The immortality of the soul in the poems of Tennyson and Browning. 1905.
The philosophy of Martineau. 1905.
Social responsibilities. Glasgow 1905.
Tennyson. 1905.
Idealism as a practical creed. 1909.
The working faith of the social reformer, and other essays. 1910.
The immanence of God and the individaluity of man. Manchester 1912.

Social powers. Glasgow 1913.
Philosophical landmarks: being a survey of the recent gains and the present problems of reflective thought. Houston 1915.
The idealism of Jesus. 1919.
The obligations and privileges of citizenship: a plea for the study of social science. Houston 1919.
The principles of citizenship. 1919.
The life and philosophy of Edward Caird, with J. H. Muirhead. Glasgow 1921.
A faith that enquires. 1922.
Old memories: autobiography. Ed T. Jones [1923].
Essays on literature and education. Ed H. J. W. Hetherington [1924].

Articles

The nature and aims of philosophy. Mind new ser 2 1893.
Idealism and epistemology. Ibid.
The present attitude of reflective thought towards religion. Hibbert Jnl 1–2 1902–4.
Balfour as sophist. Hibbert Jnl 3 1905.
Divine immanence. Hibbert Jnl 5 1907.
Robert Browning and Elizabeth Browning. CHEL 13 1907.
The ethical demand of the political situation. Hibbert Jnl 8 1910.

§2

Muirhead, J. H. Jones. [1923].
—— Jones. International Jnl of Ethics 33 1923.
Hetherington, H. J. W. Life and letters of Jones. 1924.
Jones, H. M. Jones. 1953.

JOHN NEVILLE KEYNES

1852–1949

Studies and exercises in formal logic. 1884, 1887 (enlarged), 1894 (enlarged), 1906 (rewritten and enlarged).
The scope and method of political economy. 1891, 1897 (rev), 1904 (rev), New York 1955, 1963.

SIMON SOMERVILLE LAURIE

1829–1909

§1

On the philosophy of ethics. Edinburgh 1866.
Notes expository and critical on certain British theories of morals. Edinburgh 1868.
Life and educational works of Comenius. Cambridge 1881.
Metaphysica nova et vetusta: a return to dualism. 1884; tr French, 1901.
Ethica: or the ethics of reason. 1885, 1891 (rev and enlarged); tr French, 1902.
Institutes of education: introduction to rational psychology. Edinburgh 1892, 1899 (rev), 1909.
Studies in the history of educational opinion from the renaissance. Cambridge 1903.
Synthetica: meditations epistemological and ontological. 2 vols 1906.
Also works on education.

§2

Remacle, G. La philosophie de Laurie. Brussels 1909.

GEORGE HENRY LEWES

1817–78

§1

A biographical history of philosophy. 4 vols 1845–6, 1 vol 1857 (rev), 2 vols 1867 (as History of philosophy), 2 vols 1871 (rev), 2 vols 1880; tr German, 1871–6; Hungarian, 1876–8; Russian, 1889.
The Spanish drama: Lope de Vega and Calderón. 1846.
Ranthorpe. 1847. A novel.
Rose, Blanche and Violet. 3 vols 1848. A novel.
The life of Robespierre. 1849, 1899 (3rd edn).
The noble heart: a tragedy. 1850.
A certain age. 1851; The game of speculation, 1851; A chain of events, 1852; Taking by storm, 1852. Plays.
Comte's philosophy of the sciences. 1853, 1878, 1883, 1890.
The lawyers. 1853; Stay at home, 1853; Strange history in nine chapters, 1853; Buckstone's adventure with the Polish princess, 1855. Plays.
The life and works of Goethe. 2 vols 1855, 1864, 1873 (abridged), 1875 (3rd edn rev), 2 vols Leipzig 1882, 1890, [1906], 1908; tr German, 1857; Russian, 1860; French, 1866.
Sea-side studies at Ilfracombe, Tenby, the Scilly Isles and Jersey. Edinburgh 1858, 1860.
The physiology of common life. 2 vols 1859–60, Leipzig 1860.
Captain Bland. 1860. A play.
Selections from the modern British dramatists. Leipzig 1861, 2 vols Leipzig 1867 (new edn).
Studies in animal life. 1862.
Aristotle: a chapter from the history of science. 1864; tr German, 1864.
The foundations of a creed. 2 vols [1873], 1875 (in Problems of life and mind, 1st ser); vol 1 tr Russian, 1873.
Problems of life and mind. 5 vols [1873]–9.
On actors and the art of acting. 1875, New York 1957; tr German, [1875?].
The physical basis of mind. 1877 (in Problems of life and mind, 2nd ser).
The study of psychology. 2 vols 1879 (in Problems of life and mind, 3rd ser); tr French, [1879?]; Italian, 1907.
The principles of success in literature. Ed F. N. Scott 1891; ed T. S. Knowlson [1898].
Dramatic essays reprinted from the Examiner. Ed W. Archer and R. W. Lowe 1894.
Literary criticism. Ed A. R. Kaminsky, Lincoln Nebraska 1964.

Articles

GHL's literary receipts *are pbd for the first time from the ms in the Berg Collection, New York Public Library, in* The George Eliot letters vol 7, ed G. S. Haight, New Haven 1956, *and identify some anon articles.*

Hegel's aesthetics: philosophy of art. Br & Foreign Rev 13 1842.
Lesurques: or the victim of judicial error. Blackwood's Mag Jan 1843.
Character and works of Goethe. Br & Foreign Rev 14 1843.
Dramatic reform. Edinburgh Rev 78 1843.
The modern metaphysics and moral philosophy of France. Br & Foreign Rev 15 1843.
Balzac and George Sand. Foreign Quart Rev 33 1844.
State of criticism in France. Br & Foreign Rev 16 1844.
The state of historical science in France. Ibid.
Lessing. Edinburgh Rev 82 1845.
The three Fausts: Goethe, Marlowe, Calderón. Br & Foreign Rev 18 1845.
Algazzali's confessions: Arabian philosophy. Edinburgh Rev 85 1847.

The coming reformation. Douglas Jerrold's Shilling Mag May–Aug 1847.
Recent novels: French and English. Fraser's Mag Dec 1847.
The revolutionary firebrand. Douglas Jerrold's Shilling Mag April 1847.
The great tragedian. Blackwood's Mag Sept 1848.
Strauss's political pamphlet: Julian the Apostate and Frederick William IV. Edinburgh Rev 88 1848.
Macaulay's History of England. Br Quart Rev 9 1849.
Coningsby, by B. D'Israeli. Br Quart Rev 10 1849.
Shakespeare's critics: English and foreign. Edinburgh Rev 90 1849.
The apprenticeship of life. Leader March–June 1850.
Currer Bell's Shirley. Edinburgh Rev 91 1850.
Spencer's Social statics. Leader March–April 1851.
Herman Melville, Leader Nov 1851.
Metamorphoses, a tale. Blackwood's Mag May–June 1856.
The art of history: Macaulay. Br Quart Rev 23 1856.
Phrenology in France. Blackwood's Mag Dec 1857.
Hunger and thirst. Blackwood's Mag Jan 1858.
People I have never met. Blackwood's Mag Feb 1858.
Food and drink. Blackwood's Mag March–May 1858.
A pleasant French book. Blackwood's Mag Dec 1858.
Falsely accused, a criminal trial in Nürnberg 1790. Blackwood's Mag Feb 1859.
The novels of Jane Austen. Blackwood's Mag July 1859.
Voluntary and involuntary actions. Blackwood's Mag Sept 1859.
Another pleasant French book. Blackwood's Mag Dec 1859.
A word about Tom Jones. Blackwood's Mag March 1860.
Great wits, mad wits. Blackwood's Mag Sept 1860.
Seeing is believing. Blackwood's Mag Oct 1860.
Uncivilized man. Blackwood's Mag Jan 1861.
Spontaneous generation. Blackwood's Mag Feb 1861.
Spontaneous combustion. Blackwood's Mag April 1861.
Mrs Beauchamp's vengeance. Blackwood's Mag May 1861.
How the world treats discoverers. Blackwood's Mag Nov 1861.
Buckle's scientific errors. Ibid.
Fechter in Hamlet and Othello. Blackwood's Mag Dec 1861.
A box of books. Blackwood's Mag April 1862.
Hugo's last romance. Blackwood's Mag Aug 1862.
Foreign actors and the English drama. Cornhill Mag Aug 1863.
Miseries of a dramatic author. Cornhill Mag Oct 1863.
Unctuous memories. Cornhill Mag Nov 1863.
Publishers before the age of printing. Cornhill Mag Jan 1864.
The two aspects of history. Cornhill Mag March 1864.
Bookselling in the thirteenth century. Cornhill Mag April 1864.
Shakespeare in France. Cornhill Mag Jan 1865.
Comte. Fortnightly Rev Jan 1866.
Causeries. Fortnightly Rev Oct 1866.
Legrange and Hegel. Contemporary Rev Oct 1874.
The uniformity of nature. Mind 1 1876.
What is sensation? Ibid.
Consciousness and unconsciousness. Mind 2 1877.
The course of modern thought. In E. L. Burlingame, Current discussion vol 2, 1878.

2§

The new Phaedo. Blackwood's Mag Feb 1884.
Boyd, A. K. H. Recent metaphysical works: Lewes, Maurice, Fleming. Fraser's Mag Dec 1857. Review of Biographical history of philosophy.
Biltz, C. Die dramatische Frage der Gegenwart. 1859.
Sidgwick, H. Lewes's History of philosophy. Academy Nov 1871.
Henderson, J. S. Lewes on Schelling and Hegel. Contemporary Rev Sept 1872.
Ribot, T. In his English psychology, 1873.
Harrison, F. Lewes's Problems of life and mind. Fortnightly Rev July 1874.
Bain, A. Lewes on the postulates of experience. Mind 1 1876.
Carrau, L. La philosophie de Lewes. Revue Philosophique 2 1876.
Hodgson, S. H. In his Philosophy of reflection, 1878.
Hamilton, E. Lewes's doctrine of sensibility. Mind 4 1879.
Trollope, A. George Henry Lewes. Fortnightly Rev Jan 1879.
Sully, J. Lewes. New Quart Mag new ser 2 1879.
Read, C. Lewes's posthumous volumes. Mind 6 1881.
Bosanquet, B. A misquotation of Hegel by Lewes. Mind 7 1882.
Cross, J. W. In his Life of George Eliot, 2 vols 1885–6.
Green, T. H. Spencer and Lewes: their application of the doctrine of evolution to thought. In his Works, ed Nettleship vol 1, 1886.
Grassi Bertazzi, G. Esame critico della filosofia di Lewes, pt 1. Messina 1906. No more pbd.
Kitchel, A. T. Lewes and George Eliot: a review of records. New York [1933].
Gary, F. Charlotte Brontë and Lewes. PMLA 51 1936.
C., T. George Eliot in defense of Lewes. More Books 23 1948.
Greenhut, M. Lewes and the classical tradition in English criticism. RES 24 1948.
—— Lewes as a critic of the novel. SP 45 1948.
—— Lewes's criticism of the drama. PMLA 64 1949.
Kaminsky, J. The empirical metaphysics of Lewes. JHI 13 1952.
Hirshberg, E. W. Captain Bland on the New York stage. BNYPL Aug 1953.
The George Eliot letters. Ed G. S. Haight 7 vols New Haven 1954–6.
Kaminsky, A. R. George Eliot, Lewes and the novel. PMLA 70 1955.
Haight, G. S. Dickens and Lewes. PMLA 71 1956.
Brett, R. L. Lewes: dramatist, novelist and critic. E & S new ser 11 1958.

JAMES McCOSH

1811–94

Bibliographies

Dulles, J. H. McCosh bibliography. [Princeton 1895].

§1

Method of the divine government physical and moral. 1850, 1856 (rev), 1867 (9th edn), New York 1880.
On the method in which metaphysics should be prosecuted. Belfast 1852.
Typical forms and special ends in creation, with G. Dickie. Edinburgh 1855, 1862.
The imagination: its use and abuse. 1857.
The intuitions of the mind inductively investigated. 1860, 1865 (rev), New York 1869, 1872 (rev).
The association of ideas. Dublin 1861.
The supernatural in relation to the natural. Cambridge 1862.
An examination of Mill's philosophy. 1866, 1871, 1877, New York 1880.

Philosophical papers: 1, Examination of Hamilton's logic; 2, Reply to Mill's 3rd edition [of his Examination of Hamilton's philosophy]; 3, Present state of moral philosophy in Britain in relation to theology. 1868, New York 1869.
The laws of discursive thought. 1870, New York 1881 (rev), 1891 (rev).
Christianity and Positivism. New York 1871, 1875.
Questions of modern thought. Philadelphia 1871. With others.
Scottish philosophy from Hutcheson to Hamilton. 1874, New York 1875, 1880.
Ideas in nature overlooked by Tyndall in his Belfast address. New York 1875.
The development hypothesis: is it sufficient? New York 1876.
The emotions. New York 1880.
The conflicts of the age. New York 1881.
The nature of development. Boston 1881.
Realistic philosophy defended. 2 vols New York 1887. Reprint of 8 papers in Philosophical series, New York and London 1882–5.
Psychology: the cognitive powers. New York 1886, 1891.
Psychology: the motive powers, emotions, conscience, will. New York 1887.
The religious aspect of evolution. New York 1888, New York 1890 (enlarged).
First and fundamental truths: a treatise on metaphysics. New York 1889.
The tests of the various kinds of truth. New York 1889. Enlargement of 1st of Philosophical series, earlier rptd in Realistic philosophy defended, above.
The prevailing types of philosophy: can they reach reality logically? New York 1890.
Our moral nature. New York 1892.
The philosophy of reality: should it be favored by America? New York 1894.

Articles

Typical forms: Goethe, Owen, Fairbairn. North Br Rev 15 1851.
Scottish metaphysicians. North Br Rev 27 1857.
Hamilton's metaphysics. Dublin Univ Mag 54 1859.
Intuitionalism and the limits of religious thought. North Br Rev 30 1859.
Mill's reply to his critics. Br & Foreign Evangelical Rev 17 1868; rptd in Amer Presbyterian & Theological Rev new ser 6 1868.
Recent improvements in formal logic in Britain. Ibid.
Berkeley's philosophy. Presbyterian Quart & Princeton Rev new ser 2 1873.
Elements involved in emotions. Mind 2 1877.
Contemporary philosophy: historical. Princeton Rev 1 1878.
Contemporary philosophy: mind and brain. Ibid.
Final cause. Princeton Rev 3 1879.
Law and design in nature. North Amer Rev 128 1879.
Development and growth of conscience. Princeton Rev 6 1880.
On causation and development. Princeton Rev 7 1881; rptd in Br & Foreign Evangelical Rev 30 1881.
The Concord school of philosophy. Princeton Rev 9 1881.
The Scottish philosophy as contrasted with the German. Princeton Rev 10 1882; rptd in Br & Foreign Evangelical Rev 32 1883.
A study of the mind's imagery, with H. F. Osborn. Princeton Rev 13 1884.
What an American philosophy should be. New Princeton Rev 1 1886.
Realism: its place in the various philosophies. New Princeton Rev 2 1886.
Recent works on Kant. Presbyterian & Reformation Rev 1 1890.
The office of induction in fundamental philosophy. Mind 16 1891.
Reality: what place it should hold in philosophy. In Addresses and proceedings of the International Congress of education of the World's Columbian exposition, New York 1894.
Also works on religion and education.

§2

Sloane, W. M. (ed). Life of McCosh: a record chiefly autobiographical. New York 1896.
Volbeda, S. De intuitieve philosophie van McCosh. Amsterdam [1914].

SIR JAMES MACKINTOSH
1765–1832

§1

Disputatio physiologica inauguralis de actione musculari. Edinburgh 1787.
Vindiciae gallicae. Dublin 1791, London 1791 (rev), 1837 (new edn).
A discourse on the study of the law of nature and of nations. 1799, 1828, 1835 (enlarged); tr French, 1830.
Dissertation on the progress of ethical philosophy. Edinburgh 1830; ed W. Whewell, Edinburgh 1836, 1862, 1872.
History of England. 3 vols 1830–2, 10 vols 1850, 2 vols 1853.
History of the revolution in England in 1688, with life by Wallace. 1834.
Inaugural address as Rector of the University of Glasgow; Parting address. In Inaugural addresses, ed J. B. Hay 1839.
Tracts and speeches. 5 pts Edinburgh 1840 (25 copies).
Miscellaneous works. Ed R. J. Mackintosh 3 vols 1846, 1 vol 1851, 3 vols 1854.

§2

Hazlitt, W. In his Spirit of the age, 1825.
Everett, A. H. Mackintosh. North Amer Rev 35 1832.
De Quincey, T. Mackintosh's History of the revolution. Tait's Mag new ser 1 1834.
[Croker, J. W.] Life of Mackintosh. Quart Rev 54 1835.
Mackintosh, R. J. Memoirs of the life of Mackintosh. 2 vols 1835.
Mill, James. A fragment on Mackintosh. 1835.
Macaulay, T. B. In his Critical and historical essays vol 2, 1843.
Peabody, A. P. Mackintosh. North Amer Rev 66 1848.
Carmichael, R. Notes and observations in reply to Mackintosh. In J. Butler, Fifteen sermons, 1856.
[Ripley, G.] Ethical philosophy of Mackintosh. Christian Examiner 13 1833.
Meteyard, E. In his A group of eminent Englishmen, 1871.
See col 1492, above.

SIR HENRY JAMES SUMNER MAINE
1822–88

See col 1472, above.

HENRY LONGUEVILLE MANSEL
1820–71

§1

The demons of the wind and other poems. 1838.

Prolegomena logica: an inquiry into the psychological character of logical processes. Oxford 1851, 1860 (enlarged).
Artis logicae rudimenta, from the text of Aldrich, with notes and marginal references. 1852, 1856, 1862.
The limits of demonstrative science: a letter to Whewell. Oxford 1853.
Man's conception of eternity. Oxford 1854.
Psychology, the test of moral and metaphysical philosophy. Oxford 1855.
A lecture on the philosophy of Kant. Oxford 1856.
The limits of religious thought examined. 1858, 1867 (5th edn); tr Danish, 1888.
An examination of Maurice's strictures on the Bampton lectures of 1858. 1859.
Metaphysics, or the philosophy of consciousness. Edinburgh 1860, 1866.
A letter to Goldwin Smith concerning his postscript to his lectures on the study of history. Oxford 1861.
A second letter to Smith, with an examination of some passages in his Rational religion. Oxford 1862.
The philosophy of the conditioned. 1866.
Letters, lectures and reviews. Ed H. W. Chandler 1873.
The Gnostic heresies of the 1st and 2nd centuries. Ed J. B. Lightfoot 1875.
Also works on religion.
Maurice, J. F. D. In his Theological essays, 1852.
— What is revelation? 1859.
— Sequel to the inquiry, What is revelation? 1860.
Whewell, W. A letter to the author of the Prolegomena logica. Oxford 1852.
Calderwood, H. Philosophy of the infinite. Edinburgh 1854.
McCosh, J. In his Intuitions of the mind, 1860.
Young, J. In his Province of reason, 1860.
Smith, G. In his Rational religion, Oxford 1861.
Spencer, H. In his First principles, 1862.
Jones, J. H. Know the truth. New York 1865.
Mill, J. S. Examination of Sir William Hamilton's philosophy. 1865 (2nd edn).
Deuchar, R. Review of Mill's Examination of Hamilton. Edinburgh 1865.
Bolton, M. P. W. Examination of the principles of the Scoto-Oxonian philosophy. 1869.
Green, T. H. In his Works vol 2, 1886.
Burgon, J. W. In his Lives of twelve good men, 2 vols 1888–9.
Martineau, J. In his Essays, reviews and addresses vol 3, 1891.

HARRIET MARTINEAU

1802–76

See col 949, above.

JAMES MARTINEAU

1805–1900

§1

The rationale of religious inquiry. 1836, 1844, 1845, 1853, [1908] (as What is Christianity?).
The Christian view of moral evil. 1839.
Introductory lecture on mental and moral philosophy. 1841.
Endeavours after the Christian life. 2 vols 1843–7, 1 vol 1881 (6th edn); ed J. E. Carpenter 1907.
Miscellanies. Ed T. S. King, Boston 1852.
A plea for philosophic studies. 1854.
Essays philosophical and theological. Boston 1866, 2 vols 1868, New York 1879.
Is there any axiom of causality? Contemporary Rev Aug 1870.
The place of mind in nature, and intuition in man. 1872.
Religion as affected by modern materialism. 1874; tr German, 1878.
Modern materialism in its relations to religion and theology. 1876, New York 1877.
The supposed conflict between efficient and final causation. 1877.
Ideal substitutes for God considered. 1878, 1879 (3rd edn).
The relation between ethics and religion. 1881.
A study of Spinoza. 1882, 1883 (rev).
A study of religion, its sources and contents. 2 vols 1888, 1889 (rev), 1900.
Types of ethical theory. 2 vols Oxford 1885, 1886, 1889, 1891 (enlarged), 1898.
Essays, reviews and addresses. 4 vols 1890–1.
National duties, and other sermons and addresses. Ed G. and E. Martineau 1903.
Also specifically religious works; see col 1608, below.

§2

Tyndall, J. Materialism and its opponents. Fortnightly Rev Nov 1875.
Sidgwick, H. Martineau's defence of types of ethical theory. Mind 11 1886.
— Lectures on the ethics of Green, Spencer and Martineau. 1902.
Dyde, B. W. A basis for ethics. Mind 13 1888.
— Martineau's idiopsychological ethics. Jnl of Speculative Philosophy 22 1888.
Rashdall, H. Martineau and the theory of vocation. Mind 13 1888.
Moore, A. L. Science and faith. 1889.
Stephens, H. A complete analysis of Martineau's Type of ethical theory. [1890].
Spencer, H. Martineau on evolution. In his Essays, 1891.
Hertz, J. H. The ethical system of Martineau. New York 1894.
Wilkinson, J. J. Martineau's Ethik. Leipzig 1899.
Jackson, A. W. Martineau: a biography and study. 1900.
Mellone, S. H. Martineau as an ethical teacher. International Jnl of Ethics 10 1900.
— In his Leaders of religious thought in the nineteenth century, 1902.
Knight, W. A. Inter amicos: letters between Martineau and Knight. 1901.
Drummond, J. and C. B. Upton. Life and letters of Martineau. 2 vols 1902.
Crauford, A. H. G. Recollections of Martineau. 1903.
Seth, A. Martineau's philosophy. Hibbert Jnl 1 1903. Reply by G. Galloway, ibid.
Watson, J. Martineau: a saint of theism. Ibid.
Carpenter, J. E. Martineau: theologian and teacher. 1905.
Jones, H. The philosophy of Martineau in relation to the Idealism of the present day. 1905.
Upton, C. B. Martineau's philosophy. 1905.
Walker, L. J. Martineau and the humanists. Mind new ser 17 1908. Replies by F. C. S. Schiller and Walker, new ser 18 1901.
Cadman, S. P. In his Charles Darwin and other English thinkers, with reference to their religious and ethical value, [1911].
Mukerji, N. C. Martineau on the object and mode of moral judgment. International Jnl of Ethics 24 1913.
Bertocci, P. A. In his Empirical argument for God in late British thought, Cambridge Mass 1939.
Dewey, R. E. and D. Loftsgordan. Dante and Martineau: a report of changing values. Ethics 72 1961.
Short, H. L. Priestley and Martineau. Hibbert Jnl 60 1962.
The living tradition, 4: Worship and poetry: Martineau. Hibbert Jnl 61 1963.

Martineau studies: 1, His prayers, 2, His Christology. Ibid.
Paget, A. Young Mr Martineau. Hibbert Jnl 63 1965.

JOHN FREDERICK DENISON MAURICE
1805–72

See col 1392, above.

JAMES MILL
1773–1836

§1

An essay on the impolicy of a bounty on the exportation of grain. 1804.
Commerce defended. 1807, 1808; tr Japanese, 1959.
Schools for all, not schools for Churchmen only. 1812.
Proposals for establishing in the metropolis a day school for the application of the methods of Bell, Lancaster and others to the higher branches of education. 1815. With F. Place.
History of British India. 3 vols 1817, 1820, 6 vols 1826, 9 vols 1840–8 (with notes and continuation by H. H. Wilson), 1856, 10 vols 1858, 1872; tr German, 1839–40.
An account of the maison de force at Ghent. 1817.
Elements of political economy. 1821, 1824 (rev and enlarged), 1826 (rev and enlarged), 1844, New York 1963; tr French, 1823; German, 1824, 1921; Spanish, 1827; Italian, 1854; Japanese, 1923, 1940, 1948.
An essay on government. 1821, Cambridge 1937, New York 1955; tr Italian, 1848. *See* Essays on government etc, below.
Statement of the question of parliamentary reform. 1821.
Essays on government, jurisprudence, liberty of the press, prisons and prison discipline, colonies (separately issued 1820), law of nations and education. [1825] (50 copies), [1828]. Rptd from the suppl to 5th edn of Encyclopaedia britannica, to which he contributed other articles.
Analysis of the phenomena of the human mind. 2 vols 1829; ed J. S. Mill 1869.
On the ballot. 1830, [1830] (3rd edn).
A fragment on Mackintosh. 1835, 1870.
The principles of toleration. 1837.
Selected economic writings. Ed D. Winch, Edinburgh 1966.

Articles

Filangeri on the science of legislation. Edinburgh Rev 9 1807.
Smith on money and exchange. Edinburgh Rev 13 1808.
Leckie on the foreign policy of Great Britain. Ibid.
Emancipation of Spanish America. Edinburgh Rev 14 1809. With F. de Miranda.
De Guigne's Voyage à Péking. Ibid.
Jovellanos on agriculture and legislation. Ibid.
Molina's account of Chile. Ibid. With F. de Miranda.
Taylor's Plato. Ibid.
Bexon's Code de la législation pénale. Edinburgh Rev 15 1809.
Affairs of India. Edinburgh Rev 16 1810.
Religious toleration. Ibid.
Code d'instruction criminelle. Edinburgh Rev 17 1810.
Prince Eugene's Memoirs. Ibid.
Chas's Sur la souveraineté. Edinburgh Rev 17 1811.
Liberty of the press. Edinburgh Rev 18 1811.
Wilkes' History of Mysore. Ibid.
East India monopoly. Edinburgh Rev 20 1812.
Malcolm on India. Ibid.
Education of the poor. Edinburgh Rev 21 1813.
Malcolm's Sketch of the Sikhs. Ibid.
State of Ireland. Ibid.
Neild on prisons. Edinburgh Rev 22 1814.
Periodical literature: Edinburgh Review. Westminster Rev 1 1824.
Periodical literature: Quarterly Review. Westminster Rev 2 1824.
Observations sur les conditions nécessaires à la perfection d'un code pénal. In E. Livingston, Rapport sur le project d'un code pénal, fait à l'Assemblée Générale de l'Etat de la Louisiana, Paris 1825.
Southey's Book of the Church. Westminster Rev 3 1825.
Ecclesiastical establishments. Westminster Rev 5 1826.
The nature, measures and causes of value, by Bailey. Ibid.
The formation of opinions. Westminster Rev 6 1826.
State of the nation. Ibid.
Summary review of the conduct and measures of the seventh Imperial Parliament. In Parliamentary review for 1826, 1826.
The ballot. Westminster Rev 13 1830. Partly rptd in Objections to the ballot answered from the writings and speeches of Mill, Grote etc, 1837.
The ballot: a dialogue. London Rev 1 1835.
The Church and its reform. Ibid.
State of the nation. Ibid.
Law reform. London Rev 2 1836.
Aristocracy. Ibid.
Political economy: useful or not? a dialogue. Ibid.
Bribery and intimidation at elections. London & Westminster Rev 3 1836.
Theory and practice: a dialogue. Ibid.
For further attributions see bibliography in Selected economic writings, ed Winch, *above.*

§2

Spence, W. Agriculture the source of the wealth of Britain: a reply to the objections urged by Mill. 1808.
Thompson, T. P. An exposition of the fallacies on rent, tithes etc in the form of a review of Mill's Elements. 1826, 1832. Rptd from Pamphleteer 27 1823.
Smith, L. Remarks upon An essay on government by Mill. 1827.
Maurice, F. D. James Mill: sketches of contemporary authors, xiii. Athenaeum June 1828.
Macaulay, T. B. Mill's Essay on government. Edinburgh Rev 49 1829.
—— Bentham's defence of Mill. Ibid.
—— Utilitarian theory of government, and the greatest happiness principle. Edinburgh Rev 50 1829.
Cotterill, C. F. An examination of the doctrines of value, as set forth by Smith, Ricardo, McCulloch and Mill. 1831.
Mill, J. S. In E. L. Bulwer, England and the English vol 2, 1833. Altered by Bulwer.
—— Letter to the editor. Edinburgh Rev 79 1844.
—— In his Autobiography, 1873, New York 1924; ed J. Stillinger, Illinois 1961 (as Early draft of J. S. Mill's Autobiography).
Rumbold, E. A. A vindication of the character and administration of Rumbold from the misrepresentations of Mill. 1868.
Ribot, T. A. La psychologie anglaise. Paris 1870; tr 1873.
Bisset, A. In his Essays on historical truth, 1871.
Bower, G. S. Hartley and Mill. 1881.
Bain, A. James Mill. 1882.
Morley, J. Life of Mill. Fortnightly Rev April 1882.
Quesnel, L. Les deux Mill. Biblioth Univ 13 1882.
Stuart-Glennie, J. S. James and J. S. Mill. Macmillan's Mag April 1882.
McCosh, J. In his Scottish philosophy, New York 1885.
Marion, H. Mill d'après les recherches de Bain. Revue Philosophique 16 1886.
Stephen, L. James Mill. In his English Utilitarians vol 2, 1900.

Halévy, E. In his La formation du radicalisme philosophique, 3 vols Paris 1901–4; tr 1928, 1952.
Davidson, W. L. In his Political thought in England: the Utilitarians from Bentham to J. S. Mill, 1915.
Dickinson, Z. C. Utilitarian psychology: the two Mills and Bain. In his Economic motives: a study in the psychological foundation of economic theory, Cambridge Mass 1922.
Cavenagh, F. A. (ed). James and John Stuart Mill on education. Cambridge 1931.
Seikritt, W. Die dogmenhistorische Stellung von Mill in der englischen Volkswirtschaftlehre. Limburg 1936.
Catlin, G. The later Utilitarians: James and J. S. Mill. In his History of the political philosophers, New York 1939, London 1950.
Forbes, D. James Mill and India. Cambridge Jnl Oct 1951.
Sraffa, P. (ed). Works of David Ricardo, vols 6–9. Cambridge 1952.

Correspondence

Burston, W. H. James Mill on the aims of education. Cambridge Jnl 6 1952.
Judges, A. V. (ed). Pioneers of English education. 1954.
Albee, E. In his History of English Utilitarianism, 1959.
Cumming, I. James Mill on education. Auckland 1959.
—— Useful learning: Bentham's Chrestomathia with particular reference to the influence of James Mill on Bentham. Auckland 1961.
—— The second founder of association psychology. Auckland 1964.
Stokes, E. The English Utilitarians and India. Oxford 1959.
Rauner, R. M. S. Bailey and the classical theory of value. Cambridge Mass 1961.
Hamburger, J. James Mill on universal suffrage and the middle class. Jnl of Politics 24 1962.
—— James Mill and the art of revolution. New Haven 1963.
Ghosh, R. N. The colonization controversy: Wilmot-Horton and the classical economists. Economica 31 1964.
Robson, J. M. J. S. Mill and Bentham, with some observations on James Mill. In Essays in English literature from the Renaissance to the Victorian age, ed M. MacLure and F. W. Watt, Toronto 1964.

JOHN STUART MILL

1806–73

Bibliographies

MacMinn, N., J. R. Hainds and J. M. McCrimmon (ed). Bibliography of the published writings of Mill. Evanston 1945. *See* review by J. Viner, MP 43 1945.
Amano, K. Mill. Vol 3, pt 4 of his Bibliography of the classical economists, Tokyo 1964.
Hascall, D. and J. M. Robson. Bibliography of writings on Mill. Mill News Letter 1 1965–. In progress.

Collections

Gesammelte Werke. 12 vols Leipzig 1869–80.
Collected works. Ed F. E. L. Priestley, F. E. Mineka, J. M. Robson et al 25 vols Toronto 1963–. Vols 2–3, Principles of political economy, 1965; vols 4–5, Essays on economics and society, 1967; vols 12–3, Earlier letters, 1963.

§1

Jeremy Bentham, Rationale of judicial evidence, 5 vols 1827. Ed Mill, with notes and addns.
A system of logic, ratiocinative and inductive. 2 vols 1843, 1846 (rev; significant alterations also pbd separately as Two chapters of A system of logic), 1851 (rev), 1856 (rev), 1862 (rev), 1865 (rev), 1868 (rev), 1872 (rev), subsequent edns without textual authority; tr German, 1849, 1863, 1868, 1872–3, 1877, 1884–6; Russian, 1865–7; French, 1866, 1880, 1889, 1896, 1897 (bk 6); Hungarian, 1874–7; Spanish, 1897; Japanese 1949–59; Italian, 1957 (bks 2–3).
Essays on some unsettled questions of political economy. 1844, 1874, 1877, 1948; tr Italian, 1878; Japanese 1936.
Principles of political economy. 2 vols 1848, 1849 (rev), 1852 (rev), 1857 (rev), 1862 (rev), 1865 (rev), 1871 (rev); ed W. J. Ashley 1909; ed J. M. Robson, Toronto 1965 (vols 2–3 of Collected works, above); tr Italian, 1851, 1953; German, 1852, 1864, 1869–81, 1881–5, 1913–21; French, 1854, 1861, 1873; Russian, 1860, 1865, 1874, 1875, 1897; Dutch, 1876; Japanese, 1875, 1939, 1949, 1955; Spanish, 1943.
Remarks on Mr Fitzroy's Bill. 1853.
On liberty. 1859, 1859, 1864, 1869; many later edns without textual authority; tr Dutch, 1859, 1870; French, 1860, 1861, 1864, 1877, 1925; German, 1860, 1869, 1896, 1928, 1945, 1948; Czech, 1861; Russian, 1861, 1864, 1866–9, 1882; Italian, 1865, 1890, 1895, 1921, 1924, 1946; Japanese, 1871, 1877, 1895, 1914, 1925, 1928, 1929, 1933, 1935, 1946, 1948, 1950, 1952; Slovene, 1881; Icelandic, 1886; Swedish, 1889, 1917, 1948; Spanish, 1890, 1965; Chinese, 1905; Hebrew, 1909, 1946; Norwegian, 1947; Persian, 1959.
Thoughts on parliamentary reform. 1859, 1859 (with addns), 1867 (in Dissertations and discussions, below, vol 3).
Dissertations and discussions. 2 vols 1859, 3 vols 1867, 4 vols 1875, Boston 5 vols 1864–8, New York 5 vols 1874–82; tr Russian, 1864–5.
Considerations on representative government. 1861, 1861 (rev), 1865, subsequent edns without textual authority; tr French, 1862, 1865, 1877; German, 1862, 1873; Russian, 1863; Italian, 1865, 1886, 1946; Spanish, 1865, 1878, 1965; Danish, 1876; Japanese, 1871, 1890, 1921, 1955.
Utilitarianism. 1863, 1864 (rev), 1867 (rev), 1871 (rev); subsequent edns without textual authority; tr Italian, 1866, 1946; Russian, 1866–9, 1882; Japanese, 1877, 1880, 1923, 1928, 1935, 1946, 1954; French, 1883, 1889, 1903, 1906, 1919, 1922, 1925, 1964; Spanish, 1891, 1955; Hebrew, 1933; Polish, 1959.
Auguste Comte and Positivism. 1865, 1866 (rev); subsequent edns without textual authority; tr French, 1868, 1879, 1885, 1890, 1893, 1898, 1903; German, 1871, 1874; Italian, 1903; Japanese, 1923.
An examination of Hamilton's philosophy. 1865, 1865 (rev), 1867 (rev), 1872 (rev); subsequent edns without textual authority; tr French, 1869; German, 1908.
Inaugural address at St Andrews. 1867, 1867; tr German, 1869; Hungarian, 1874; Japanese, 1885, 1948.
England and Ireland. 1868 (5 edns); subsequent edns without textual authority.
James Mill, Analysis of the phenomena of the human mind. 2 vols 1869 (2nd edn). Ed Mill, with notes.
The subjection of women. 1869, 1869, 1870; subsequent edns without textual authority; tr French, 1869, 1876; German, 1869, 1872, 1880, 1891; Italian, 1870, 1883, 1926; Russian, 1869, 1870, 1871, 1896, 1906; Spanish, 1892, 1965; Japanese, 1878, 1921, 1923, 1928, 1929, 1948, 1950, 1957, 1959.
Chapters and speeches on the Irish land question. 1870, 1870.
Autobiography. 1873, 1873, 1874, 1874, 1879, 1908; ed H. J. Laski, Oxford (WC) 1924, (with appendix of speeches); ed R. Howson, New York 1924 (from holograph ms); 1926, 1944, 1957, 1960; tr Danish, 1874; French, 1874, 1885, 1894, 1907; German, 1874; Russian, 1874, 1896; Spanish, 1892, 1939; Italian, 2 vols 1921; Japanese, 1922, 1928, 1948, 1958; Polish, 1948; Chinese, nd. Early draft. Ed J. Stillinger, Urbana 1961.
Three essays on religion. Ed H. Taylor 1874, 1874 1885, 1904, 1923; tr French, 1875, 1884; German, 1875; Italian, 1946, 1958; Japanese, 1878, 1927.

Socialism. Chicago 1879; ed W. D. Porter, New York 1891; tr French, 1879; German, 1880; Italian, 1880, 1899. Rptd from Fortnightly Rev, ed H. Taylor. In vol 5 of Collected works, above.
Early essays. Ed J. W. M. Gibbs 1897.
Mill on the protection of infant industries. Ed J. Bonar 1911.
The spirit of the age. Ed F. A. von Hayek, Chicago 1942.
Four dialogues of Plato. Ed R. Borchard 1946.
Prefaces to liberty. Ed B. Wishy, Boston 1959.
Essays on economics and society. Ed J. M. Robson 2 vols Toronto 1967 (vols 4–5 of Collected works).
Mill also wrote on India and on botany.

Letters etc

Letter. In Report of the proceedings of a meeting for the purpose of hastening the removal of the trade restrictions on the commerce of literature, 1852.
Letter. In The opinions of certain authors on the bookselling question, 1852.
Correspondence inédite avec G. d'Eichthal. Ed E. d'Eichthal, Paris 1898.
Lettres inédites de Mill à Comte. Ed L. Lévy-Bruhl, Paris 1899.
Letters. Ed H. S. R. Elliot 2 vols 1910.
Carlyle, T. Letters to Mill, Sterling and Browning. Ed A. Carlyle 1923.
Two letters on the measure of value. Ed J. H. Hollander, Baltimore 1936.
Tocqueville, A. de. Oeuvres complètes vol 6. Ed J.-P. Mayer, Paris 1954. Includes letters from Mill.
Mill's boyhood visit to France 1820–1, a journal and notebook. Ed A. J. Mill, Toronto 1960.
Earlier letters. Ed F. E. Mineka 2 vols Toronto 1963 (vols 12–3 of Collected works).

Speeches

Speech on corruption at elections. In F. D. Maurice, Corruption at elections, 1864.
Speech on co-operation. Co-operator June 1864.
Speech upon the Reform Bill. 1866.
Speech. In Report of the various proceedings taken by the London Trades Council and the Conference of Amalgamated Trades in reference to the Royal Commission on trades unions, 1867.
Speech on the admission of women to the electoral franchise. 1867.
Personal representation. 1867.
Speech. In Proceedings at the public breakfast held in honour of W. L. Garrison, 1868.
Speech on the married women's property bill. In Bright, Lowe, Mill and Lefevre in the debate on the second reading of the Bill to amend the law with respect to the property of married women, Manchester 1868.
Speech at the National Education League. Birmingham 1870.
Speech on land tenure reform. 1871; rptd in Dissertations and discussions, above, vol 4, 1875.
Speech on the land question. In Land tenure reform association; report of the public meeting held March 18 1873, 1873; rptd in Dissertations and discussions, above vol 4, 1875.
A speech in the Music Hall Edinburgh. Edinburgh 1873. On women's suffrage.
Views on England's danger through the suppression of her maritime power. 1874.
Speech on the utility of knowledge. In his Autobiography, ed H. J. Laski, Oxford 1924 (WC).
Speech on the British constitution. Ibid.
Speech on perfectibility. Ibid.
Notes of my speech against Sterling. Ibid.
Speech on the Church. Ibid.
Speech on secular education. Ibid.
Speech on the present state of literature. Adelphi Jan 1924.
Speech on the influence of lawyers. Economica 5 1925.
Closing speech on the co-operative system. Archiv für Sozialwissenschaft und Sozialpolitik 62 1929. Erroneously entitled Further reply to the debate on population.
Speech on the influence of the aristocracy. Ibid.
Speech on the British constitution. Ibid.
Speech on the coalition ministry. Ibid.
Speech on the use of history. Bermondsey Book 6 1929.
Speech on population. Jnl of Adult Education 4 1929.
Speech on population: reply. Ibid.
Second speech on population. Ibid.
Speech on parliamentary reform (1823 or 1824). Realist 1 1929.

Articles

Mill wrote some 500 articles for newspapers.

Periodical literature: Edinburgh Review. Westminster Rev 1 1824.
War expenditure. Westminster Rev 2 1824.
Brodie's History of the British Empire. Ibid.
Quarterly Review: political economy. Westminster Rev 3 1825.
Law of libel and liberty of the press. Ibid.
Corn laws. Ibid.
Ireland. Parliamentary History & Rev for 1825, 1826.
Game Laws. Westminster Rev 5 1826.
The Silk Trade. Ibid.
Mignet's French revolution. Ibid.
Modern French historical works: age of chivalry. Westminster Rev 6 1826.
Paper Currency and commercial distress. Parliamentary History & Rev for 1826–7, 1828.
Foreign dependencies: trade with India. Ibid.
New corn laws. Westminster Rev 7 1827.
Intercourse between the United States and the British colonies in the West Indies. Parliamentary Rev for 1827, 1828.
The nature, origin and progress of rent. In Adam Smith, An inquiry into the nature and causes of the wealth of nations, ed J. R. McCulloch, vol 4 Edinburgh 1828.
Whately's Elements of logic. Westminster Rev 9 1828.
Scott's Life of Napoleon. Ibid. Also issued separately as A critical examination of the preliminary view of the French Revolution, prefixed to Scott's Life of Bonaparte, 1828.
Use and abuse of political terms. Tait's Mag 1 1832.
On genius. Monthly Repository Oct 1832.
Austin's Lectures on jurisprudence. Tait's Mag 2 1832.
What is poetry? Monthly Repository Jan 1833.
Corporation and Church property. Jurist 4 1833. Also issued separately as Corporation and Church property resumable by the State, 1833; rptd in Dissertations and discussions, above, vol 1, 1859; tr Italian, 1864.
Writings of Junius Redivivus. Monthly Repository April 1833.
Writings of Junius Redivivus. Tait's Mag 3 1833.
Remarks on Bentham's philosophy. In E. L. Bulwer, England and the English, 1833.
A few observations on Mr Mill. Ibid. Altered by Bulwer.
Views of the Pyrenees. Monthly Repository Sept 1833.
Blakey's History of moral science. Monthly Repository Oct 1833.
The two kinds of poetry. Monthly Repository Nov 1833.
Comparison of the tendencies of French and English intellect. Ibid.
On Miss Martineau's Summary of political economy. Monthly Repository May 1834.
Letter from an Englishman to a Frenchman. Monthly Repository June 1834.
Miss Austin's translation of Cousin's report on the state of public instruction in Prussia. Monthly Repository July 1834.
The close of the session. Monthly Repository Sept 1834.

On punishment. Monthly Repository Oct 1834.
Dr King's lecture on the study of anatomy. Monthly Repository Nov 1834.
Postscript. London Rev 1 1835.
The monster trial. Monthly Repository June 1835.
Rationale of political representation. London Rev 1 1835.
Tennyson's Poems. Ibid.
Parliamentary proceedings of the session. Ibid.
De Tocqueville on democracy in America. London Rev 2 1835.
The close of the session. Ibid.
State of society in America. Ibid.
Guizot's Lectures on European civilization. Ibid. Partly by Mill.
Commencement of the session: progress of reform. London & Westminster Rev 3 1836.
Walsh's Contemporary history: Tories, Whigs and Radicals. Ibid.
Aphorisms: thoughts in the cloister and the crowd. London & Westminster Rev 4 1837; partly rptd in Dissertations and discussions, above, vol 1, 1859.
Fonblanques's England under seven administrations. London & Westminster Rev 5 1837.
Taylor's Statesman. Ibid. With G. Grote.
Carlyle's French revolution. Ibid.
The Spanish question. Ibid. Partly by Mill.
Parties and the ministry. London & Westminster Rev 6 1837.
Letters from Palmyra. Ibid; partly rptd in Dissertations and discussions, above, vol 1, 1859.
Radical party in Canada. Ibid.
Bentham. London & Westminster Rev 7 1838. Also issued separately, 1838; rptd in Dissertations and discussions, above, vol 1, 1859; ed F. R. Leavis, Mill on Bentham and Coleridge, 1950; tr Japanese, 1939, 1954.
Milnes's Poems of many years. London & Westminster Rev 7 1838.
Penal code for India. Ibid.
Lord Durham and his assailants. Ibid (2nd edn).
Lord Durham's return. London & Westminster Rev 32 1838.
Reorganization of the reform party. Westminster Rev 32 1839.
Coleridge. London & Westminster Rev 33 1840; rptd in Dissertations and discussions, above, vol 2, 1859; ed F. R. Leavis, Mill on Bentham and Coleridge, 1950; tr Japanese, 1939.
Plato: the Apology, the Crito, and part of the Phaedo. Westminster Rev 34 1840.
Milnes's Poetry for the people. Ibid.
Essays on government. Ibid.
Smith's Remarks on law reform. Westminster Rev 35 1841.
Carpenter's Principles of physiology. Westminster Rev 37 1842.
Bailey on Berkeley's theory of vision. Westminster Rev 38 1842.
Macaulay's Lays of ancient Rome. Westminster Rev 39 1843.
Bailey's reply to the Westminster Review. Ibid.
Letter to the editor [concerning James Mill]. Edinburgh Rev 79 1844.
The currency question. Westminster Rev 41 1844.
De Quincey's Logic of political economy. Westminster Rev 43 1845.
Duveyrier's Political views of French affairs. Edinburgh Rev 83 1846.
The French revolution of 1848 and its assailants. Westminster Rev 51 1849. Also issued separately, 1849; rptd in Dissertations and discussions, above, vol 2, 1859; tr French, 1875, 1888.
The negro question. Fraser's Mag Jan 1850.
Letter. In Public agency v. trading companies, 1851.
Newman's Political economy. Westminster Rev 56 1851.
Centralization. Edinburgh Rev 115 1862.
The slave power. Westminster Rev 78 1862; rptd in Amer edn of Dissertations and discussions, above, vol 3.
Notes on Senior's political economy. Ed F. A. von Hayek, Economica new ser 12 1945.

§2

Bain, A. Mill's Logic. Westminster Rev 39 1843.
— A letter to Westerton, chairman of Mill's committee. [1865].
— In his James Mill: a biography, 1882.
— J. S. Mill: a criticism. 1882.
— Mill's theory of the syllogism. In his Dissertations on leading philosophical subjects, 1903.
— In his Autobiography, 1904.
Torrens, R. The budget, with an introduction applying Mill's deductive method. 1844.
— The principles and practical operation of Peel's bill of 1844. 1857 (2nd edn).
Whewell, W. Of induction, with especial reference to Mill's System of logic. 1849.
— Comte and positivism. Macmillan's Mag March 1866.
[Bagehot, W.] Mill. Prospective Rev 6 1850. Review of A system of logic.
Ballantyne, J. R. Oo the philosophy of induction. Allahabad 1851.
— The method of induction. Mirzapore 1852.
Gouraud, C. Tendences de l'économie politique en France et en Angleterre. Revue des Deux Mondes April 1852.
Reybaud, L. Mill et l'économie politique en Angleterre. Revue des Deux Mondes April 1855.
Lyall, A. In his Agonistes: or philosophical strictures, 1856.
Mill. Nat Rev 9 1859. By J. Martineau?
Mill on liberty. Bentley's Quart Rev 2 1859.
Mill on liberty. Universal Rev 1859.
Who is the reformer: Mill or Bright? 1859.
Lees, F. R. Law and liberty, with especial relation to the temperance question, the prohibition of the liquor traffic, and the objections of Mill. Leeds 1860.
— Relations of liberty to the temperance question. 1860.
Lorimer, J. Mill on representative government. North Br Rev 35 1861.
Taine, H. A. Mill et son Système de logique. Revue des Deux Mondes March 1861.
— In his Histoire de la littérature anglaise vol 4, Paris 1863–4; tr 2 vols Edinburgh 1871.
— Le positivisme anglais: étude sur Mill. Paris 1864; tr 1870.
Baudrillart, H. J. L. In his Publicistes modernes, Paris 1862.
Kirkman, T. P. On a so-called theory of causation, vide System of logic by Mill, bk 3 ch 5. Liverpool [1862].
Reybaud, M. R. L. In his Economistes modernes, Paris 1862.
Mills politische Schriften. Preussische Jahrbücher 10 1862.
True and false democracy. Boston 1862.
Cummings, C. A. The later writings of Mill. Christian Examiner 74 1863.
Napier, J. The miracles: Butler's argument on miracles, explained and defended, with observations on Hume, Baden Powell and Mill. Dublin 1863.
Schérer, E. H. A. In his Etudes critiques sur la littérature contemporaine vol 1, Paris 1863.
Stebbing, W. Analysis of Mill's System of logic. 1864.
Utilitarianism explained and exemplified in moral and political government. 1864.
Christie, W. D. Mill for Westminster. Macmillan's Mag May 1865.
— Mill and Hayward. 1873. Also as Reply to Hayward, 1873 (without correspondence).
Deuchar, R. Review of An examination of Hamiltonian philosophy by Mill. Edinburgh 1865, 1865.
Fothergill, S. Liberty, liquor, licence and prohibition, in answer to Mill. Swindon [1865].

Fraser, A. C. Mill's Examination of Hamilton's philosophy. North Br Rev new ser 4 1865.
Grote, J. In his Exploratio philosophica pt 1, Cambridge 1865.
—— An examination of the utilitarian philosophy. Cambridge 1870.
Masson, D. Recent British philosophy, including some comments on Mill's answer to Hamilton. 1865, 1877.
Parker, J. Mill on liberty: a critique. 1865.
Plummer, J. Remarkable men: Mill. Cassell's Illustr Family Paper Sept 1865.
—— Philosophical politicians: Mill. Working Man Aug 1866.
Schiel, J. Die Methode der inductiven Forschung als die Methode der Naturforschung in geträngter Darstellung, hauptsächlich nach Mill. Brunswick 1865.
Spencer, H. Mill verses Hamilton: the test of truth. Fortnightly Rev July 1865.
Stephen, J. F. Spencer on Mill. Saturday Rev Aug 1865.
—— Liberty, equality, fraternity. 1873.
Mill als Philosoph und Nationalökonom. Unsere Zeit 1 1865.
Mill's review of Hamilton. Christian Examiner 79 1865. By O. B. Frothingham?
Alexander, P. P. Mill and Carlyle: an examination of Mill's doctrine of causation in relation to moral freedom. Edinburgh 1866.
—— Moral causation: or notes on Mill's notes to the chapter on freedom in the 3rd edition of his Examination of Hamilton. Edinburgh 1868.
Bridges, J. H. The unity of Comte's life and doctrine: a reply to strictures on Comte's later writings, addressed to Mill. 1866.
Cairnes, J. E. University education in Ireland: a letter to Mill. 1866.
'G.R.' Logic and utility: the tests of truth and falsehood, and of right and wrong. 1866.
'Inquirer'. The battle of the two philosophies: Mill and Hamilton. 1866.
Lange, F. A. Mill's Ansichten über die sociale Frage und die angebliche Umwälzung der Socialwissenschaft durch Carey. Duisberg 1866.
Littré, E. Auguste Comte et Stuart Mill; G. Wyrouboff, Stuart Mill et la philosophie positive. Paris 1866.
Longe, F. D. A refutation of the wage-fund theory of modern political economy as enunciated by Mill and Fawcett. 1866.
—— A critical examination of George's Progress and poverty and Mill's theory of wages. [1883].
McCosh, J. An examination of Mill's philosophy, being a defence of fundamental truth. 1866, 1877 (rev).
—— Mill's reply to his critics. Br & Foreign Evangelical Rev 17 1868; rptd in Amer Presbyterian & Theological Rev new ser 6 1868.
Mansel, H. L. The philosophy of the conditioned: comprising some remarks on Hamilton's philosophy and on Mill's examination of that philosophy. 1866.
—— Supplementary remarks on Mill's criticism of Hamilton. Contemporary Rev Sept 1867.
O'Hanlon, H. F. A criticism of Mill's pure idealism, and an attempt to shew that, if logically carried out, it is pure nihilism. Oxford 1866.
Sangar, J. M. Episcopal vows: what do they mean? Letter to the Bishop of St David's on his recent endorsements of the alleged infidelity of Mill. 1866.
Shedden, T. On Hamilton and Mill. In his Three essays on philosophical subjects, 1866.
Smith, H. B. Mill's Examination of Hamilton's philosophy. Amer Theological Rev 1 1866.
Symonds, T. C. Hamilton versus Mill: a thorough discussion of each chapter in Mill's Examination of Hamilton. 2 pts Edinburgh 1866, 1868.
Ward, J. H. Mill. Boston Rev 6 1866.
—— Political writings of Mill. Ibid.
'W.G.D.' Mill and the inductive origin of first principles. Jnl of Sacred Lit new ser 9 1866.
Wyrouboff, G. Stuart Mill et la philosophie positive: E. Littré, Auguste Comte et Stuart Mill. Paris 1866.
McCosh on Mill and fundamental truth. Biblical Repertory & Princeton Rev 38 1866. By L. H. Atwater?
Stuart Mill on mind and matter [poem]. Blackwood's Mag Feb 1866. By Lord Neaves?
Stuart Mill again: or the examiner examined [poem]. Blackwood's Mag Aug 1866. By Lord Neaves?
'A retired constructor'. Odd bricks from a tumbledown private building. 1866. A dialogue on Mill and Hamilton.
Blakesley, G. H. A review of Mill's essay on liberty. Cambridge 1867.
Brewster, D. The radical party: its principles, objects and leaders—Cobden, Bright and Mill. Manchester 1867.
Hayes, W. Remarks, with reference to the land-laws of England, on some passages in Mill's Principles and Blanc's Letters on England. 1867.
'A liberal'. A review of Mill's essay on liberty. 1867.
Millet, J. An Millius veram mathematicorum axiomatum originem invenirit. Paris and London 1867.
Morley, J. Mill's inaugural address. Fortnightly Rev March 1867.
—— In his Critical miscellanies ser 2, 1877.
—— In his Critical miscellanies ser 4, 1908.
—— In his Recollections vol 1, 1917.
Purnell, T. In his Literature and its professors, 1867.
Romilly, H. Public responsibility and vote by ballot. 1867 (2nd edn).
Vasey, G. Individual liberty, legal, moral and licentious, in which the political fallacies of Mill's essay on liberty are pointed out. 1867, 1877. By 'Index'.
Beggs, T. The deterrent influence of capital punishment: a reply to the speech of Mill. 1868, 1868 (rev).
Blackwood, F. T. H. T. Mill's plan for the pacification of Ireland examined. 1868.
Haven, J. Mill versus Hamilton. Bibliotheca Sacra 25 1868.
Holyoake, G. J. A new defence of the ballot in consequence of Mill's objections to it. 1868.
—— Mill as some of the working classes knew him. 1873.
Laurie, S. S. In his Notes expository and critical on certain British theories of morals, Edinburgh 1868.
Mill. Br Quart Rev 48 1868.
The philosophy of Mill. Theological Eclectic 4 1868.
Bowen, F. Mill and his critics. Amer Presbyterian Rev 18 1869.
Eccarius, J. G. Eines Arbeiters Widerlegung der nationalökonomischen Lehren Mills. Berlin 1869.
English, W. W. An essay on moral philosophy. 1869.
Goggia, P. E. La mente di Mill: saggio di logica positiva applicata specialmente alla storia. Leghorn 1869.
Hazard, R. G. Two letters on causation and freedom in willing, addressed to Mill. Boston 1869.
Janet, P. Mill et Hamilton: le problème de l'existence des corps. Revue des Deux Mondes Oct 1869.
McCarthy, J. The English Positivists. Galaxy 7 1869.
'A Westminster elector'. Mill and the ballot: a criticism. 1869.
Gneist und Mill: alt-englische und neu-englische Staatsanschauungen. Berlin 1869.
The Grosvenor Papers no 1: an answer to Mill's Subjection of women. 1869.
Jordan, W. Die Zweideutigkeit der Copula bei Mill. Stuttgart 1870.
Killick, A. H. The student's handbook, synoptical and explanatory, of Mill's System of logic. 1870.
MacCaig, D. A reply to Mill on the subjection of women. Philadelphia 1870.
McLaren, C. B. B. Hamilton's natural dualism, Mill's psychological theory and Berkeley's spiritual realism. In his University lectures in metaphysics, moral philosophy and English composition, Edinburgh 1870.

Ribot, T. A. In his La psychologie anglaise contemporaine, Paris 1870; tr 1873.
Stirling, J. Mill on trades unions. In Recess studies, ed A. Grant, Edinburgh 1870; tr French, Jnl des Economistes 20 1870.
Stuart-Glennie, J. S. The principle of the conservation of force and Mill's System of logic. Nature April 1870.
— James and John Stuart Mill: traditional and personal memorials. Macmillan's Mag April 1882.
White, C. Ecce femina: an attempt to solve the women question, an examination of arguments in favour of female suffrage by Mill. Hanover NH 1870.
Mill. Appleton's Jnl 3 1870.
Mill's Subjection of woman from a woman's point of view. 1870.
Blackie, J. S. In his Four phases of morals, Edinburgh 1871.
Ward, W. G. Mill's denial of necessary truth. Dublin Rev new ser 17 1871.
— Mill on the foundation of morality. Dublin Rev new ser 18 1872.
— Mill's reply to the Dublin Review. Dublin Rev new ser 21 1873.
— Mill's denial of freewill. Dublin Rev new ser 22 1874.
— Mill's philosophical position. Ibid.
— Mill on causation. Dublin Rev new ser 27 1876.
— In his Essays on the philosophy of theism, 2 vols 1884.
An alphabetical list of the philosophers and discoverers of Mill's System of logic. Oxford 1871.
The rule and motive of certitude. Dublin Rev new ser 17 1871.
Buckle, T. H. Mill on liberty. In his Miscellaneous and posthumous works, ed H. Taylor, vol 1 1872. Also in his Essays, Leipzig 1867.
Greg, W. R. In his Enigmas of life, 1872.
Mill and his school. Quart Rev 133 1872.
Bourne, H. R. F. (ed). Mill: notices of his life and works. 1873. Also pbd in Popular Science Monthly 1873. Rptd from Examiner.
Conway, M. D. In memoriam J. S. Mill. [1873].
Courcelle-Seneuil, J.-G. L'oeuvre de Mill. Jnl des Economistes 31 1873.
Grote, G. Mill on the philosophy of Hamilton. In his Minor works, 1873. Separately issued, 1868.
Hayward, A. Mill. Times 10 May 1873. Obituary notice of special importance.
Holbeach, H. Mill's Autobiography and Stephen on liberty. Saint Paul's Mag Dec 1873.
Hooker, I. B. Correspondence with Mill. In her Womanhood, its sanctities and fidelities. Boston [1873], 1888.
Maccall, W. The newest materialism: sundry papers on the books of Mill, Comte, Bain, Spencer, Atkinson and Feuerbach. 1873.
Marston, M. Life of Mill, politician, philosopher, critic and metaphysician. [1873].
Murphy, J. J. Mill. Macmillan's Mag Aug 1873. A poem.
Pillon, F. L'origine de la justice selon Bentham et Mill. Critique Philosophique April 1873.
— Mill au point de vue religieux. Critique Philosophique June 1873.
— Mill, socialiste. Critique Philosophique June–July 1873.
— Polémique de Mahaffy contre l'école associationiste. Critique Philosophique Aug 1873.
— Polémique de Mahaffy contre Mill au sujet des jugements mathématiques. Ibid.
— La science de la morale selon Bentham et Mill. Critique Philosophique April 1874.
— La raison profonde de la crise mentale de Mill: contradiction entre l'éducation intellectuelle et l'éducation morale dans la doctrine associationniste. Critique Philosophique July 1875.
Renouvier, C. De l'esprit de la philosophie anglaise: Utilitarianism—Owen and Mill. Critique Philosophique Feb 1873.
— La mort de Mill. Critique Philosophique May 1873.
— Les rapports du criticisme avec la philosophie de Mill. Critique Philosophique June 1873.
— Le principe du socialisme d'après l'Autobiographie de Mill. Critique Philosophique Nov 1873.
— L'opinion de Mill sur la liberté et la nécessité des actes. Critique Philosophique May 1874.
Sidgwick, H. J. S. Mill. Academy 15 May 1873.
— Methods of ethics. 1901 (6th edn). Preface especially.
Simcox, E. The influence of Mill's writings. Contemporary Rev July 1873.
Sprague, A. P. Mill and Agassiz. Nat Quart Rev 28 1873.
Thornton, W. T. Old-fashioned ethics and common-sense metaphysics, with some of their applications. 1873.
Wright, C. Commemorative notice of Mill. Boston 1873.
— In his Philosophical discussions, New York 1877.
Mill. Quart Rev 135 1873.
L'éducation de Mill, d'après son Autobiographie. Critique Philosophique Dec 1873.
Mill and the land-laws. Nation Jan 1873.
Polémique de Mahaffy contre Mill au sujet des jugements mathématiques. Critique Philosophique Aug 1873.
Althaus, F. Mill. Unsere Zeit. 10 1874.
Becker, L. E. Liberty, equality, fraternity: a reply to Stephen's strictures on Mill's Subjection of women. Manchester 1874.
Birks, R. T. Modern Utilitarianism: or the systems of Paley, Bentham and Mill examined and compared. 1874.
Browne, W. R. The Autobiography of Mill. 1874.
Crane, C. B. Mill and Christianity. Baptist Quart 8 1874.
Fonblanque, E. B. de. Life and labours of Albany Fonblanque. 1874.
Grote, H. Posthumous papers of George Grote. 1874.
Hale, E. E. Mill. Old & New 9 1874.
— Mill's history of Rome. Ibid.
Henshaw, S. E. Mill and Mrs Taylor. Overland Monthly Dec 1874.
Hinsdale, B. A. A history of a great mind: a survey of the education and opinions of Mill. Cincinnati 1874.
Ierson, H. The religious views of Mill. Unitarian Rev 1 1874.
Musgrave, A. Capital: Mill's fundamental propositions. Contemporary Rev Oct 1874.
Reeves, H. Autobiography of Mill. Edinburgh Rev 139 1874.
Russell, E. R. On the Autobiography of Mill. Liverpool 1874.
Chernyshevski, N. L'économie politique jugée par la science, critique des Principes d'économie politique de Mill. Vol 1, tr from Russian, Brussels 1874.
The autobiography of an atheist. Scribner's Monthly March 1874.
Mill. Westminster Rev new ser 45 1874.
Goethe and Mill: a contrast. Westminster Rev new ser 46 1874.
Mill's Autobiography. Quart Rev 136 1874.
Mill's Autobiography. Br Quart Rev 59 1874.
La crise du développement mental de Mill d'après son Autobiographie. Critique Philosophique Jan 1874.
Mill, education and science. Popular Science Monthly Jan 1874.
'Antichrist'. The Jesus Christ of Mill. 1875.
Brown, J. A. The religious opinions of Mill. Lutheran Quart 5 1875.
Carrau, L. In his La morale utilitaire, Paris 1875.
— Le dualisme de Mill. Revue Philosophique 8 1879.
Irons, W. J. An examination of Mill's Three essays on religion. 1875.
Rickaby, J. Mill's essay on nature. Month Jan 1875.
— Mill on the utility of religion. Month April 1875.

— Free will and four English philosophers: Hobbes, Locke, Hume and Mill. 1906.
Seccombe, J. T. Science, theism and revelation considered in relation to Mill's essay on nature. 1875.
Upton, C. B. Mill's Essays on religion. Theological Rev 12 1875.
Ce qu'il y a de possible en fait d'attributs de la Divinité, selon Mill. Critique Philosophique April 1875.
Mill's Three essays on religion. Westminster Rev new ser 47 1875.
La personnalité divine et la création dans la pensée de Mill. Critique Philosophique April 1875.
La question de l'immortalité dans la philosophie de Mill. Ibid.
La révélation et les espérances chrétiennes dans la philosophie de Mill. Ibid.
Mill et Morley: note sur l'introduction des possibilités dans les analyses de Mill. Critique Philosophique June 1875.
Blachford, Lord. The reality of duty as illustrated by the Autobiography of Mill. Contemporary Rev Aug 1876.
Cannegieter, T. De nuttigheidsleer van Mill en van der Wijck. Groningen 1876.
Kaspary, J. In his Natural laws: or the infallible criterion, 1876.
Mahaffy, J. P. Anticipation of Mill's theory of the syllogism by Locke. Mind 1 1876. Reply by C. J. Munro, ibid.
'N.N.' Thirteen pages on intellectual property written with special reference to a doubtful doctrine of Mill. Manchester [1876].
Parker, J. In his Job's comforters: or scientific sympathy, New York 1876.
Leaving us an example: is it living—and why? an enquiry suggested by certain passages in Mill's Essays on religion. [1876], 1880 (2nd, 3rd and 4th edns as The gospel for the nineteenth century).
Adams, L. Mill. New Englander 36 1877.
Jevons, W. S. Mill's philosophy tested. Contemporary Rev Dec 1877–Nov 1879.
Paoli, A. Dei concetti direttivi di Mill nella logica e nella psicologia. Rome 1877.
Is theism immoral? an examination of Mill's arguments against Mansel's view of religion. Swansea 1877.
Edwards, T. The relativity, the unconditioned, belief and knowledge: some remarks on Mill's Examination of Hamilton. Calcutta 1878.
Moffatt, R. S. The principles of a time policy: containing a recriticism of the theories of Ricardo and Mill on rent, value and cost of production. 1878.
Adamson, R. Jevons on Mill's experimental methods. Mind 3 1878.
Robertson, G. C. Mill's philosophy tested by Jevons. Ibid. Replies by A. Strachey and W. S. Jevons, ibid.
Courtney, W. L. The metaphysics of Mill. 1879.
— Life of Mill. 1889.
Fontpertius, A. F. de. Un écrit posthume de Mill sur le socialisme. Jnl des Economistes 8 1879.
Funck-Brentano, T. In his Les sophistes grecs et les sophistes contemporains, Paris 1879.
Morris, G. S. In his British thought and thinkers, 1880.
Brochard, V. La logique de Mill. Revue Philosophique 12 1881.
Hodgson, S. H. De Quincey as political economist: or De Quincey and Mill on supply and demand. In his Outcast essays and verse translations, 1881.
Kohn, B. Untersuchungen über das Causalproblem auf dem Boden einer Kritik der einschlägigen Lehren Mills. Vienna 1881.
Laveleye, E. de. Les tendances nouvelles de l'économie politique en Angleterre. Revue des Deux Mondes April 1881.
Wägner, S. Mills Logiska system och dess kunskapsterriska forütsättninger. Lund 1881.
Blind, K. Mill über Irland. Die Gegenwart 21 1882.
Fox, C. Memories of old friends. Ed H. N. Pym 2 vols 1882 (2nd edn, with 14 Mill letters).
Gast, H. La religion dans Mill. Montauban 1882.
Quesnel, L. Les deux Mill. Bibliothèque Universitaire 13 1882.
'W.C.' Wealth: definitions by Ruskin and Mill compared. Glasgow [1882].
Carruthers, J. Communal and commercial economy, with an examination of the correlated theorems of the pseudo-science of wealth as taught by Ricardo and Mill. 1883.
Galasso, A. Della conciliazione dell'egoismo coll'altruismo secondo Mill. Naples 1883.
Green, T. H. In his Prolegomena to ethics, ed A. C. Bradley, Oxford 1883.
— The logic of Mill. In his Works vol 2, 1886.
Clough, J. S. On Mill's position as a moralist. Cambridge 1884.
Fouillée, A. Les études récentes sur la propriété. Revue des Deux Mondes March 1884.
Frege, G. In his Die Grundlagen der Arithmetik, Breslau 1884; tr J. L. Austin, Oxford 1950.
Olivier, S. Mill on Socialism. To-day new ser 2 1884.
Gizycki, G. von. Über den Utilitarismus. Vierteljahrsschrift für Wissenschaftliche Philosophie 8 1884.
Zuccante, G. Del determinismo di Mill. Filosofia delle Scuole Italiane 1884–5.
— Alcune idee del Comte e dello Mill, intorno alla psicologia. Tendiconti, Reale Instituto Lombardo di Scienze e Lettere 30 1897.
— Intorno all'utilitarismo dello Mill. Rivista Italiana de Filosofia 1898.
— Mill e l'utilitarismo. Florence 1922.
Horny, F. Mills Vorschläge zur Hebung der arbeitenden Klasse. Vierteljahrsschrift für Volkswirtschaft, Politik und Kulturgeschichte 88 1885.
Levin, T. W. Notes on inductive logic: an introduction to Mill's System of logic. Cambridge 1885.
Levy, J. H. Mill's propositions and inferences of mere existence. Mind 10 1885.
Löchen, A. Om Mills Logik. Christiania 1885.
Paepe, C. de. Mill, socialiste. Société Nouvelle 1 1885.
Brandes, G. M. C. In his Eminent authors of the nineteenth century, New York 1886, London 1924 (as Creative spirits of the nineteenth century).
Dunbar, C. F. The reaction in political economy. Quart Jnl of Economics 1 1886.
Lauret, H. Philosophie de Mill. Paris 1886.
Sutherland, J. An alleged gap in Mill's Utilitarianism. Mind 11 1886.
Foote, G. W. What was Christ? a reply to Mill. 1887.
Monck, W. H. S. Mill's doctrine of natural kinds. Mind 12 1887. Replies by M. H. Towley, ibid; F. and C. L. Franklin 13 1888.
Horton, S. D. The parity of moneys as regarded by Smith, Ricardo and Mill. 1888. By 'Amicus curiae'.
Jenks, E. Carlyle and Mill. Orpington 1888.
Michaëlis, C. T. Mills Zahlbegriff. Berlin 1888.
Bastable, C. F. On some applications of the theory of international trade. Quart Jnl of Economics 4 1889.
Donisthorpe, W. In his Individualism: a system of politics, 1889.
Gomperz, T. Mill: ein Nachruf. Vienna 1889.
— Zur Erinnerungen an Mill. In his Essays und Erinnerungen, Stuttgart 1905.
Hansen, S. Versuch einer Kritik des Mill'schen Subjectivismus. Vierteljahrsschrift für Wissenschaftliche Philosophie 13 1889.
Lilla, V. Critica della doctrina etica-giuridica di Mill. Naples 1889.

Störring, G. W. Mills Theorie über den psychologischen Ursprung des Vulgärglaubens an die Aussenwelt. Halle 1889.
Stout, G. F. The genesis of the cognition of physical reality. Mind 15 1890. Replies by J. Pikler and Stout, ibid; J. M. Baldwin, 16 1891.
—— Belief. Mind 16 1891.
Martineau, J. In his Essays, reviews and addresses vol 3, 1891.
Ritchie, D. G. In his Principles of state interference, 1891.
Ward, J. Mill's science of ethology. International Jnl of Ethics 1 1891.
Čáda, F. Mill: pojema a obor logiky. Prague 1892.
—— Noetická záhada u Herbata a Milla. Prague 1894; tr German, 1895.
Carus, P. Nature and morality: an examination of the ethical views of Mill. Open Court 6 1892.
Drysdale, C. R. The population question according to Malthus and Mill. 1892.
Ferri, F. L'utilitarismo di Mill. Milan 1892.
Towers, C. M. D. Mill and the London and Westminster Review. Atlantic Monthly Jan 1892.
Bonar, J. In his Philosophy and political economy, 1893.
—— The economics of Mill. Jnl of Political Economy 19 1911.
—— Mill, the reformer. Indian Jnl of Economics 10 1930.
—— In his Tables turned, 1931.
Cannan, E. In his History of the theories of production and distribution in English political economy from 1776 to 1848, 1893.
Laurie, H. Methods of inductive inquiry. Mind new ser 2 1893.
Pick, G. V. Digest of political economy: the Principles of Mill. 1893.
Henrici, J. Einführung in die Induktive Logik an Bacons Beispiel nach Mills Regeln (Festschrift). Heidelberg 1894.
Hutton, R. H. In his Criticisms on contemporary thought and thinkers, 2 vols 1894.
Douglas, C. Mill: a study of his philosophy. Edinburgh 1895.
—— The ethics of Mill. Edinburgh 1897.
Hoffding, H. In his Geschichte der neueren Philosophie vol 2, Leipzig 1895–6; tr 1900.
Michel, H. De Millii individualismo. Paris 1895.
Payot, J. Quid apud Millium Spencerumque de exteris rebus disserentes sit reprehendum. Orléans 1895.
Robertson, J. M. In his Modern humanists, 1895.
—— In his Modern humanists reconsidered, 1927.
Taylor, A. In his Memories of a student, 1895.
Watson, J. Comte, Mill and Spencer. Glasgow 1895.
Carlile, W. W. The humanist doctrine of causation. Philosophical Rev 5 1896.
Harrison, F. Mill. Nineteenth Century Sept 1896.
—— Mill. Revue occidentale 17 1898.
—— In his Tennyson, Ruskin, Mill and other literary estimates, 1899.
—— Comte and Mill. In his On society, 1918.
McKechnie, W. S. In his State and the individual, Glasgow 1896.
Sänger, S. Mill als Philosoph. Archiv für Geschichte der Philosophie 9 1896.
—— Mill's Theodizee. Archiv für Geschichte der Philosophie 13 1900.
—— Mill: sein Leben und Lebenswerk. Stuttgart 1901.
Taussig, F. W. Wages and capital. 1896.
Dilke, C. W. Mill. Cosmopolis March 1897.
Folghera, P. Le syllogisme: Mill et Rabier. Revue Thomiste 3 1897.
Kriegel, F. Mills Lehre vom Wert, Preis und der Bodenrente. Berlin 1897.
Leader, R. E. Life and letters of J. A. Roebuck. 1897. With Roebuck's unfinished autobiography.
Neatby, W. B. The existential import of propositions. Mind new ser 6 1897.
Pira, C. Framställning och kritik af Mills, Lotzes, och Sigwarts läror om begreppsbildingen i logiken. Stockholm 1897.
Seal, H. The individual always the unit. Westminster Rev 147 1897.
Betham-Edwards, M. In his Reminiscences, 1898.
Hibben, J. G. The heart and the will in belief: Romanes and Mill. North Amer Rev Jan 1898.
Lévy-Bruhl, L. Comte et Mill d'après leur correspondance. Revue Philosophique 23 1898.
Pringle, G. O. S. Mill's humanity. Westminster Rev 150 1898.
Ely, R. T. Mill. Progress 4 1899.
Faguet, E. Comte et Mill. Revue Bleue 14 1899.
Graham, W. In his English political philosophy from Hobbes to Maine, 1899.
Kent, C. B. R. The English radicals. 1899.
Balmforth, R. Mill and political education. In his Some social and political pioneers of the nineteenth century, 1900.
Bunge, N. K. Mill envisagé comme économiste. In Esquisses de littérature politico-économique, Geneva 1900 (tr from Russian).
Daniels, W. M. Letter to Mill. Atlantic Monthly Nov 1900.
Stephen, L. In his English Utilitarians vol 3, 1900.
McMahan, A. B. An interesting memorial of two great authors. Dial 31 1901. On Mill and Browning.
Albee, E. In his History of English Utilitarianism, 1902.
Lubac, J. Mill et le socialisme. Paris 1902.
Überweg, F. In his Grundriss der Geschichte der Philosophie vol 4, Berlin 1902.
Hanschmann, A. B. Palissy der Künstler, Naturforscher und Schriftsteller als Vater der induktiven Wissenschaftsmethode des Bacon, mit der Darstellung der Inductionstheorie Bacons und Mills. Leipzig 1903.
Lewels, M. Mill: die Stellung eines Empiristen zur Religion. Münster 1903.
Moore, G. E. In his Principia ethica, Cambridge 1903.
Reichel, H. Darstellung und Kritik von Mills Theorie der induktiven Methode. Zeitschrift für Philosophie und Philosophische Kritik 122–3 1903–4.
Simon, D. Mill und Pestalozzi. Vienna 1904.
Dicey, A. V. In his Lectures on the relations between law and public opinion in England during the nineteenth century, 1905.
Martinazzoli, A. La teorica dell'individualismo secondo Mill. Milan 1905.
Thouverez, E. Mill. Paris 1905.
Wellington, S. Mill, the saint of rationalism. Westminster Rev 163 1905.
Abb, E. Kritik des kantischen Apriorismus vom Standpunkte des reinen Empirismus aus, unter besonderer Berücksichtigung von Mill und Mach. Zürich 1906.
Barth, P. Zu Mills 100 Geburtstage. Vierteljahrsschrift für wissenschaftliche Philosophie 30 1906.
Becher, S. Erkenntnistheoretische Untersuchungen zu Mills Theorie der Kausalität. Halle 1906.
Benn, A. W. In his History of English rationalism in the nineteenth century vol 1, 1906.
Bicknell, P. F. An apostle of clear thinking. Dial 40 1906.
—— Mill. Popular Science Monthly Nov 1906.
Boyd, W. F. Mills Utilitarismus im Vergleich mit dem seiner Vorgänger. Leipzig 1906.
Ellis, M. A. Variations in the editions of Mill's Principles. Economic Jnl 16 1906.
Gribble, F. Mill. Fortnightly Rev Aug 1906.
Hubbard, E. Mill and Harriet Taylor: little journeys to homes of great lovers, 18. East Aurora NY 1906.
Moskowitz, H. Das moralische Beurteilungsvermögen in der englischen Ethik von Hobbes bis Mill. Erlangen 1906.

Renner, H. Mill. Philosophische Wochenschrift 2 1906.
Sidgwick, R. The library of Mill. Cornhill Mag Nov 1906.
Kantzer, E. M. La religion de Mill. Caen 1906.
Mill, Spencer and Socialism. Independent Aug 1906.
Mill als Politiker und Sozialist. Vorwärts May 1906.
Anoyaut, M. L'état progressif et l'état stationnaire de la richesse nationale chez Smith et Mill. Paris 1907.
MacCunn, J. In his Six radical thinkers, 1907.
Schatz, A. In his L'individualisme économique et social, Paris 1907.
Seth, A. The philosophical radicals. Edinburgh 1907.
Education, personally supervised. North Amer Rev 184 1907.
Davenport, H. J. In his Value and distribution, Chicago 1908.
Seth, J. The alleged fallacies in Mill's Utilitarianism. Philosophical Rev 17 1908.
—— In his English philosophers and schools of philosophy, 1912.
Steglich, A. Mills Logik der Daten. Leipzig 1908.
Whittaker, T. W. Comte and Mill. 1908; rptd in his Reason, Cambridge 1934.
Gide, C. L'apogée et le décline de l'école classique: Mill. In Gide and C. Rist, Histoire des doctrines économiques, Paris 1909; tr 1948.
Guskar, H. Der Utilitarismus bei Mill und Spencer in kritischer Beleuchtung. Archiv für Systematisch Philosophie 15 1909.
Tawney, G. A. Mill's theory of inductive logic. Cinncinnati 1909.
Winsløw, C. Mills Etik: et forsøg til en fremstilling og kritik. Copenhagen 1909.
Taylor, M. A note on the private life of Mill. In Letters of Mill, ed H. S. R. Elliot 2 vols 1910.
—— Mrs Mill: a vindication by her granddaughter. Nineteenth Century Feb 1912.
Thieme, E. Die Sozialethik Mills. Leipzig 1910.
Ward, W. P. Mill and the mandate of the people. Dublin Rev 147 1910.
—— In his Men and matters, 1914.
Musings without method. Blackwood's Mag June 1910.
The political faith of Mill. Current Lit 49 1910.
The testimony of Mill to mysticism. Outlook 95 1910.
Cadman, S. P. In his Darwin and other English thinkers, 1911.
Finkelstein, F. Die allgemeinen Gesetze bei Comte und Mill. Heidelberg 1911.
Haney, L. H. In his History of economic thought, New York 1911.
Williams, T. A. Intellectual precocity: comparison between Mill and the son of Boris Sidis. Pedagogical Seminary 18 1911.
Famous autobiographies. Edinburgh Rev 214 1911. Reply by M. Taylor, Nineteenth Century Feb 1912.
Archambault, P. Mill: choix de textes et étude du système philosophique. Paris [1912].
Beus, L. Der Begriff des Belief bei Mill. Bonn 1912.
Patten, S. N. Interpretation of Mill. Annals of American Acad of Political & Social Science 44 (suppl) 1912.
Phillips, M. A. Mill and Browning's Pauline. Cornhill Mag May 1912.
Freundlich, E. Mills Kausaltheorie. Düsseldorf [1913].
Krumme, E. Du libéralisme classique à l'individualisme social: la place de Mill dans l'histoire des doctrines économiques. Revue Internationale de Sociologie 21 1913.
Rey, L. Le roman de Mill. Paris 1913; tr as The romance of Mill, Nineteenth Century Sept 1913.
—— Mill en Avignon. Vaison 1921.
West, J. Mill. 1913, 1933 (Fabian Tract).
Degenfeld-Schonburg, F. G. von. Die Lohntheorie von Smith, Ricardo, Mill und Marx. Munich 1914.
Dugas, L. In his Penseurs libres et liberté de pensée, Paris 1914.
Gehrig, H. Mills als Sozialpolitiker. Jahrbüchern für Nationalökonomie und Statistik 3rd ser 47 1914.
Gotthelft, F. E. Mills sozialpolitische Wandlungen. Munich [1914]; rptd in Schmollers Jahrbuch 41 1917.
Ray, J. La méthode de l'économie politique d'après Mill. Paris 1914.
Wust, P. J. Mills Grundlegung der Geisteswissenschaften. Bonn 1914.
Davidson, W. L. In his Political thought in England: the Utilitarians from Bentham to Mill, 1915.
Kotarbinski, T. Utylitaryzm w etyce Milla y Spencera. Cracow 1915.
Oldershaw, L. R. F. Analysis of Mill's Principles. Oxford 1915.
Ashworth, M. The marriage of Mill. Englishwoman May 1916.
Crawford, J. F. The relation of inference to fact in Mill's logic. Chicago 1916.
Thwing, C. F. Education according to Mill. School & Society Jan 1916.
—— The grave of Mill. Nation Aug 1928.
Leeuw, H. J. van der. 700 stellingen van Mill, door een oudfabrikant. Rotterdam 1917.
Chouville, L. Un article de Mill sur Vigny. French Quart 1 1919.
Garnier, H. K. Mill and the philosophy of mediation. New York 1919.
Veblen, T. B. Preconceptions of economic science. In his Place of science in modern civilization, New York 1919.
Beer, M. In his History of British Socialism vol 2, 1920.
Dunning, W. A. In his History of political theories from Rousseau to Spencer, New York 1920.
Sorley, W. R. In his History of English philosophy, Cambridge 1920.
Fournier, G. Influencc de Coleridge sur Mill dans le problème de la liberté et de la nécessité. Revue de Philosophie 21 1921.
Graziani, A. Ricardo e Mill. Bari 1921.
Harley, C. Swedenborg and Mill. New Church Mag Sept–Oct 1921.
Marx, K. In his Theorien über den Mehrwert, ed K. Kautsky, Stuttgart 1921.
Turgeon, C. and C.-H. In their La valeur d'après les économistes anglais et français, Paris 1921 (2nd edn).
Warren, H. C. In his History of the association psychology, 1921.
Wentscher, E. Mill und die soziale Frage. Westmark 1 1921.
—— Das Problem des Empirismus dargestellt an Mill. Bonn 1922.
—— Mills Stellung zur Religion. Archiv für die gesamte Psychologie 77 1930.
Williams, S. T. Two Victorian boyhoods: Mill and Gosse. North Amer Rev 11 1922.
—— Mill and literature. London Mercury Feb 1929.
Anderson, W. Mill and the model city charter. Nat Municipal Rev 11 1922.
Becker, H. Mill. In his Zur Entwicklung der englischen Freihandelstheorie, Jena 1922.
Gazin, F. Les ensignements pédagogiques de Mill. Revue Pédagogique Feb–April 1922.
Gilman, B. I. What is liberty when two or more persons are concerned? International Jnl of Ethics 32 1922.
Rogers, A. K. In his English and American philosophy since 1800, 1922.
Diffenbaugh, G. L. Mrs Taylor seen through other eyes than Mill's. Sewanee Rev 31 1923.
Gonnard, R. Mill et sa théorie de l'état stationnaire. Questions Pratiques 19 1923.
Mercer, T. W. Mill and co-operation. Manchester 1923.
Thilly, R. The individualism of Mill. Philosophical Rev 32 1923.

Neff, E. E. Carlyle and Mill: mystic and utilitarian. New York 1924, 1926 (2nd edn rev as Carlyle and Mill: an introduction to Victorian thought).

Sée, H. Mill et la propriété foncière. Revue Internationale de Sociologie 32 1924.

Arias, G. Il pensiero economico di Mill. Annali di Economia 2 1925.

Jenks, E. A reply to Mill. Economica 5 1925. On the influence of lawyers.

Marshall, A. On Mill's theory of value. In Memorials of Marshall, ed A. C. Pigou 1925.

Wisniewski, J. Étude historique et critique de la théorie de la perception extérieure chez Mill et Taine. Paris 1925.

Schauchet, P. Individualistische und sozialistische Gedanken in den Lehren Mills. Giessen 1926.

Street, C. L. Individualism and individuality in the philosophy of Mill. Milwaukee 1926.

A Mill collection. Bulletin of Br Lib of Political & Economic Science 1926.

Bousquet, G.-H. Mill. In his Essai sur l'évolution de la pensée économique, Paris 1927.

Price, H. H. Mill's view of the external world. Proc Aristotelian Soc new ser 27 1927.

Ames, V. M. Kant and Mill visit an old lady. Open Court 42 1928.

Hertel, R. Die Erklärung der Krisen bei Mill und Marx. Cologne 1928.

Himes, N. E. The place of Mill and Owen in the history of English neo-Malthusianism. Quart Jnl of Economics 42 1928.

—— Mill's attitude towards neo-Malthusianism. Economic History (suppl to Economic Jnl) 1 1929.

Kennedy, G. The psychological empiricism of Mill. Amherst 1928.

Kinlock, T. F. In his Six English economists, 1928.

Abel, H. G. Mill and Socialism. Nation & Athenaeum Feb 1929.

—— Mill and Socialism. Fortnightly Rev Sept 1938.

Housman, L. Fire-lighters: a dialogue on a burning topic. London Mercury Jan 1929. Later turned into a drama on the burning of Carlyle's ms of the French Revolution by Mill's servant.

Murray, R. H. In his Studies in the English social and political thinkers of the nineteenth century vol 2, Cambridge 1929.

Ressler, A. Die beiden Mills. Ichenhausen 1929.

Tarozzi, G. Mill. 2 vols Milan 1929–31.

Roerig, F. Die Wandlungen in der Geistigen Grundhaltung Mills. Cologne 1930.

Turin, S. P. Chernyshevsky and Mill. [1930].

Apchié, M. Les sources françaises de certains aspects de la pensée économique de Mill. Paris 1931.

Cavanagh, F. A. James and J. S. Mill on education. Cambridge 1931.

Falco, S. E. de. Il quarto teoreme di Mill sul capitale. Giornale degli Economisti 46 1931.

McJarrow, J. S. Mill's On liberty. Holborn Rev Oct 1931.

Dower, R. S. Mill and the philosophical radicals. In Social and political ideas of some representative thinkers of the age of reaction and reconstruction, ed F. J. C. Hearnshaw 1932, 1949.

Kubitz, O. A. Development of Mill's System of logic. Urbana 1932.

Myers, G. C. How Wordsworth saved Mill from insanity. High School Teacher June 1932.

Brinton, C. C. In his English political thought in the nineteenth century, 1933.

Hamilton, M. A. Mill. 1933.

Cohen, M. R. and E. Nagel. In their An introduction to logic and scientific method, New York [1934].

Flugel, J. C. In his A hundred years of psychology, 1934.

Hales, G. T. The letters of Mill. BM Quart 9 1934.

Hippler, F. Staat und Gesellschaft bei Mill, Marx, Legarde. Berlin 1934.

McCallum, R. B. In Great democrats, ed A. B. Brown 1934.

Mévil, A. Un ami de Mill. Journal des Débats 41 1934.

Nesbitt, G. L. In his Benthamite reviewing: the first twelve years of the Westminster Review 1824–36, New York 1934.

Schörry, O. Lohnfondstheorie und ehernes Lohngesetz: eine Untersuchung der Lohntheorien von Smith, Malthus, Ricardo und Mill. Mannheim 1934.

Hull, A. The political ideas of Mill. Halifax 1935.

Levin, R. Der Geschichtsbegriff des Positivismus unter besonderer Berücksichtigung Mills und der rechtsphilosophischen Anschauungen Austins. Leipzig 1935.

Menger, C. In his Collected works vol 3, 1935.

Boegholt, C. M. Examination of Cohen and Nagel's reply to Mill in their Introduction to logic and scientific method. Jnl of Philosophy 33 1936.

Castell, A. Mill's logic of the moral sciences: a study of the impact of Newtonism on early nineteenth-century social thought. Chicago 1936.

De Ford, M. A. In British authors of the nineteenth century, ed S. J. Kunitz, New York 1936.

Gomperz, H. Cuius regio, illius opinio: considerations on the present crisis of the tolerance idea. International Jnl of Ethics 46 1936.

Grude-Oettli, N. Mill Zwischen Liberalismus und Sozialismus. Bleichrode-am-Harz 1936.

Morlan, G. America's heritage from Mill. New York 1936.

Jackson, R. Mill's joint method. Mind new ser 46–7 1937–8.

—— An examination of the deductive logic of Mill. 1941.

—— Mill's treatment of geometry: a reply to Jevons. Mind new ser 50 1941.

Sabine, G. H. In his History of political theory, 1937.

Véran, J. Le souvenir de Mill à Avignon. Revue des Deux Mondes Sept 1937.

Binkley, R. C. Mill's Liberty today. Foreign Affairs Sept 1938.

Heinemann, F. T. Gomperz und Mill. Belgrade 1938.

Hirst, W. A. The manuscript of Carlyle's French Revolution. Nineteenth Century Jan 1938.

Hülsman, P. In his Der wirtschaftsständische Gedanke in der englischen Literatur, Leipzig 1938.

Maxey, C. C. In his Political philosophies, New York 1938.

Villey, D. Sur la traduction par Dupont-White de la Liberté de Mill. Revue d'Histoire Economique et Social 24 1938.

Anschutz, R. P. Mill, philosopher of Victorianism. In 1840 and after, ed A. Sewell, Auckland 1939.

—— The logic of Mill. Mind new ser 58 1949.

—— The philosophy of Mill. Oxford 1953.

—— Mill, Carlyle and Mrs Taylor. Political Science 7 1955.

Beard, C. A. The idea of let us alone. Virginia Quart Rev 15 1939.

Catherwood, B. F. In his Basic theories of distribution, 1939.

Catlin, G. The later Utilitarians: James and J. S. Mill. In his History of the political philosophers, New York 1939, London 1950.

Cowley, M. The end of the reasoning man. New Republic Oct 1939.

Crossman, R. H. S. In his Government and the governed: a history of political ideas and political practice, 1939.

Everett, E. M. The party of humanity: the Fortnightly Review and its contributors 1865–74. Chapel Hill 1939.

Hübner, W. Wenderunkte des Freiheitsbegriffs: eine kritische Interpretation von Mills On liberty. Neuphilologische Monatsschrift 10 1939.

Schapiro, J. S. Utilitarianism and the foundations of English liberalism. Jnl of Social Philosophy 4 1939.

—— Mill, pioneer of democratic liberalism in England. JHI 4 1943.

Stocks, J. L. The empiricism of Mill. In his Reason and intuition, 1939.

Appadorai, A. In his Revision of democracy, 1940.
Grierson, H. In his Essays and addresses, 1940.
LeRossignol, J. E. Mill on machinery. Amer Economic Rev 30 1940.
Levi, A. W. A study in the social philosophy of Mill. Chicago 1940.
—— The mental crisis of Mill. Psychoanalytic Rev 32 1945.
—— The writing of Mill's Autobiography. Ethics 61 1951.
—— The idea of Socrates: the philosophic hero in the nineteenth century. JHI 17 1956.
—— The value of freedom: Mill's Liberty 1859–1959. Ethics 70 1959. Reply by H. A. Holloway, 71 1961.
Paden, W. D. Tennyson and the reviewers 1829–35. Univ of Kansas Stud in Eng 6 1940.
Emerson to Mill. More Books 14 1940.
Bladen, V. W. Mill to Marshall: the conversion of the economists. Jnl of Economic History (suppl 1) 1941.
—— The centenary of Marx and Mill. Jnl of Economic History (suppl 8) 1948.
—— Mill's Principles: a centenary estimate. Amer Economic Rev 39 1949.
Tuell, A. K. In his John Sterling, New York 1941.
Vaysset-Boutbien, R. Mill et la sociologie française contemporaine. Paris 1941.
Fain, J. T. Ruskin and the orthodox political economists. Southern Economic Jnl 10 1943.
—— Ruskin and Mill. MLQ 12 1951.
Haines, L. F. Reade, Mill and Zola: a study of the character and intention of Reade's realistic method. SP 40 1943.
—— Mill and Pauline: the review that retarded Browning's fame. MLN 59 1944.
Hayek, F. A. von. Rae and Mill: a correspondence. Economica new ser 10 1943.
—— Mill's correspondence. TLS 13 Feb 1943.
—— Letters of Mill. N & Q 24 April 1943.
—— In his Individualism and economic order, Chicago 1948.
—— Portraits of Mill. TLS Nov 1950.
—— Mill and Harriet Taylor: their friendship and subsequent marriage. Chicago 1951.
Linnenberg, C. C. Laissez-faire state in relation to the national economy. Southwestern Social Science Quart 24 1943.
O'Brien, G. Mill and Cairnes. Economica new ser 10 1943.
Huffer, E. J. E. Bij het eeuwfeest van een logica-boek. Algemeen Nederlands Tijdschrift voor Wijsbegeerte en Psychologie 37 1944.
Schmid, J. von. Mills Logica der Geesteswetenschappen. Ibid.
Harris, H. W. In his Caroline Fox, 1944.
Mineka, F. E. The dissidence of dissent: the Monthly Repository 1806–38. Chapel Hill 1944.
—— Mill: letters on the French revolution of 1830. Victorian Stud 1 1957.
—— The Autobiography and the lady. UTQ 32 1963.
Nogaro, B. Mill et le classicisme au milieu du XIXe siècle. In his Le développement de la pensée économique, Paris 1944.
Summers, R. Mill and liberty. Adelphi 20 1944.
Baumgardt, D. Bentham's censorial method. JHI 6 1945.
McCready, H. W. The defence of individualism. Queen's Quart 52 1945.
Popper, K. In his Open society and its enemies, 1945.
Shine, H. Mill and an open letter to the Saint-Simonian Society in 1832. JHI 6 1945.
Wenger, C. N. Sources of Mill's criticism of Pauline. MLN 60 1945.
Whitmore, C. E. Mill and mathematics: an historical note. JHI 6 1945.
Hainds, J. R. Mill and the Saint-Simonians. JHI 7 1946.
—— Mill's Examiner articles on art. JHI 11 1950.
Hyde, F. E. Utility and radicalism 1825–37: a note on the Mill-Roebuck friendship. Economic History Rev 16 1946.
Kohn, H. In his Prophets and peoples: studies in nineteenth-century nationalism, New York 1946.
La Nauze, J. A. A letter of Mill to Kingsley. Australian Quart 18 1946.
Irvine, W. Shaw, the Fabians and the Utilitarians. JHI 8 1947.
Stewart, H. L. Mill's Logic: a post-centenary appraisal. UTQ 17 1947.
Thompson, M. H. Mill's theory of truth: a study in metaphysics. Philosophical Rev 56 1947.
Brebner, J. B. Laissez-faire and state intervention in nineteenth-century Britain. Ibid.
Britton, K. The nature of arithmetic: a reconsideration of Mill's views. Proc Aristotelian Soc new ser 48 1948.
—— Mill, the ordeal of an intellectual. Cambridge Jnl 2 1948.
—— John Stuart Mill. 1953 (Pelican).
—— Mill: a debating speech on Wordsworth 1829. Cambridge Rev 8 March 1958.
—— Utilitarianism: the appeal to a first principle. Proc Aristotelian Soc 60 1960.
—— and J. M. Robson. Mill's debating speeches. Mill News Letter 1 1965.
Cole, M. In her Makers of the labour movement, 1948.
McRae, R. F. Phenomenalism and Mill's theory of causation. Philosophy and Phenomenological Research 9 1948.
Marchand, L. The Symington Collection. Jnl Rutgers Univ Lib 12 1948.
Marwick, J. D. Mill and liberty. Scottish Bankers' Mag April 1948.
Northrop, F. S. C. In his Logic of the sciences and the humanities, New York 1948.
Nyman, A. Leviathan och folkviljan, betraktelser över förstatligande byråkrati och skåttetryck, tellika en kommentar till Mills Om friheten. Stockholm 1948.
Letters of Bancroft, Froude, Gardiner, Kinglake, Mill, Morley, Rogers and others to Richard and George Bentley 1835–89. Bodleian Lib Record 2 1948.
Baudin, L. Mill, la codification de l'individualisme. In his Précis d'histoire des doctrines économiques, Paris 1949 (5th edn).
Brown, E. H. P. Prospects of labour. Economica new ser 16 1949.
Cadiou, R. La philosophie de Mill. Revue Philosophique new ser 74 1949.
Davy, G. L'explication sociologique et le recours à l'histoire, d'après Comte, Mill et Durkheim. Revue de Métaphysique et de Morale 54 1949.
Feuer, L. S. Mill and Marxian Socialism. JHI 10 1949. Reply by J. S. Schapiro, ibid.
—— In his Psychoanalysis and ethics, Springfield Mass 1955.
Hall, E. W. The proof of utility in Bentham and Mill. Ethics 60 1949. Reply by R. H. Popkin, 61 1950.
Hempel, C. G. Geometry and empirical science. In Readings in philosophical analysis, ed H. Feigl and W. Sellars, New York 1949.
Leavis, F. R. Mill, Beatrice Webb and the English School. Scrutiny 16 1949.
Mill, A. J. Mill's visit to Wordsworth 1831. MLR 44 1949.
—— The first ornamental Rector at St Andrews University. Scottish Historical Rev 43 1964.
—— Carlyle and Mill: two Scottish university Rectors. Edinburgh 1966.
Murphy, G. In his Historical introduction to modern psychology, New York 1949.
Pigou, A. C. Mill and the wages fund. Economic Jnl 59 1949.
Plamenatz, J. P. The English Utilitarians. Oxford 1949.

Ralph, P. L. Mo Ti and the English Utilitarians. Far Eastern Quart 9 1949.
Viner, J. Bentham and Mill: the Utilitarian background. Amer Economic Rev 39 1949.
— In his Long view and the short: studies in economic theory and policy, Glencoe Ill 1958.
Willey, B. In his Nineteenth-century studies, Coleridge to Arnold, 1949.
Buckley, J. H. The revolt from rationalism in the seventies. In Booker Memorial Studies, ed H. Shine, Chapel Hill 1950.
Mayer, J.-P. De Tocqueville and Mill. Listener 16 March 1950.
Ong, W. J. Mill's pariah poet. PQ 29 1950.
Popkin, R. H. A note on the proof of utility in Mill. Ethics 61 1950.
Sampson, R. V. Mill: an interpretation. Cambridge Jnl Jan 1950.
Samson, F. La conception doctrinale de Mill sur la coopérative de production et ses rapports avec les socialistes associationistes. Paris 1950.
Triceri, C. Il sistema filosofico-guiridico di Mill. Milan 1950.
Winkleman, P. H. De vrijheid sedert Mill. Groningen 1950.
Acton, H. B. Comte's Positivism and the science of society. Philosophy 26 1951.
Casellate, S. Mill e l'utilitarismo inglese. Padua 1951.
Nakhnikian, G. Value and obligation in Mill. Ethics 62 1951.
Pipping, H. E. Mill och Harriet Taylor. Nya Argus 44 1951.
Ulam, A. B. In his Philosophical foundations of English Socialism, Cambridge Mass 1951.
White, R. J. Mill. Cambridge Jnl 5 1951.
Ayer, A. J. and R. Winch (ed). In their British empirical philosophers, 1952. An anthology.
Christensen, P. A. On liberty in our time: Milton and Mill. Western Humanities Rev 6 1952.
Hammond, A. L. Euthyphro, Mill and Lewis. Jnl of Philosophy 49 1952.
Harris, R. T. Nature: Emerson and Mill. Western Humanities Rev 6 1952.
Kort, F. The issue of a science of politics in Utilitarian thought. Amer Political Science Rev 46 1952.
Leroux, R. Humbolt et Mill. Études Germaniques 6–7 1951–2.
Robbins, L. C. In his Theory of economic policy in English classical political economy, 1952.
Roellinger, F. X. Mill on education. Jnl of General Education 6 1952.
Trilling, D. Mill's intellectual beacon. Partisan Rev 19 1952.
Wedar, S. In his Duty and utility: a study in English moral philosophy, Lund 1952.
Zinkernagel, P. Revaluation of Mill's ethical proof. Theoria 18 1952.
Abrams, M. H. In his Mirror and the lamp: romantic theory and the critical tradition, New York 1953.
Bell, J. F. In his History of economic thought, New York 1953.
Blakely, R. J. Adult education—stalk or flower? Nat Education Assoc Jnl 42 1953.
Hutchison, T. W. Mill and the doctrine of the impossibility of general overproduction. In his Review of economic doctrines 1870–1929, Oxford 1953.
Jacobs, L. The Talmudic hermeneutical rule of binyan 'abh and Mill's method of agreement. Jnl of Jewish Stud 4 1953.
Perkins, M. and I. Singer. The definition of more valuable. Analysis 13 1953.
Preyer, R. The Utilitarian poetics: Mill. Univ of Kansas City Rev 19 1953.
Rinehart, K. Mill's Autobiography: its art and appeal. Ibid.
Urmson, J. O. The interpretation of the moral philosophy of Mill. Philosophical Quart 3 1953.
Ballhatchet, K. A. Mill and Indian education. Cambridge Historical Jnl 11 1954.
Borchard, R. Mill: the man and the thinker. Contemporary Rev Feb 1954.
— Mill the man. 1957.
Bowle, J. The liberal compromise: de Tocqueville and Mill. In his Politics and opinion in the nineteenth century, 1954.
Clark, P. M. Some difficulties in Utilitarianism. Philosophy 29 1954.
Magid, H. M. Mill and the problem of freedom of thought. Social Research 21 1954.
Packe, M. St J. Life of Mill. 1954.
Schumpeter, J. In his History of economic analysis, New York 1954.
Shumaker, W. In his English autobiography, its emergence, materials and form, Berkeley 1954.
Hampshire, S. Principia ethica. New Statesman 23 April 1955. Replies by I. Freed and Hampshire, ibid.
Keller, P. In his Dogmengeschichte des wohlstandspolitischen Interventionismus, Winterthur 1955.
Mack, M. P. The Fabians and Utilitarianism. JHI 16 1955.
Raphael, D. D. Fallacies in and about Mill's Utilitarianism. Philosophy 30 1955.
Russell, B. Mill. Proc Br Acad 41 1955.
— In his Portraits from memory, 1956.
Strong, E. W. Whewell and Mill: their controversy about scientific knowledge. JHI 16 1955.
Blaug, M. The empirical content of Ricardian economics. Jnl of Political Economy 64 1956.
— The half-way house of Mill. In his Ricardian economics, New Haven 1958.
Cranston, M. Illiberal tract [on social freedom] proved spurious: Mill exonerated. Manchester Guardian 9 June 1956.
— Mill on liberty, a revaluation. Listener 10 Jan 1957.
— Mill as a political philosopher. History Today Jan 1958.
— Mr and Mrs Mill on liberty. Listener 10 Sept 1959.
— In British writers and their work, ed B. Dobrée, vol 2, Lincoln Nebraska 1964.
Desai, S. S. M. Mill: restatement. In his Economic doctrines, Bombay 1956.
Fielding, K. J. Mill and Gradgrind. Nineteenth-Century Fiction 11 1956.
Harris, A. L. Mill's theory of progress. Ethics 66 1956.
— Mill: Liberalism, Socialism and laissez-faire. In his Economics and social reform, New York 1958.
— Mill on monopoly and Socialism. Jnl of Political Economy 67 1959.
— Mill: government and economy. Social Science Rev 37 1963.
— Mill: servant of the East India Company. Canadian Jnl of Economics & Political Science 30 1964.
Hourani, G. F. In his Ethical value, Ann Arbor 1956.
Levin, H. J. Standards of welfare in economic thought. Quart Jnl of Economics 70 1956.
Mabbot, J. D. Interpretations of Mill's Utilitarianism. Philosophical Quart 6 1956.
Magnino, B. In her Storia del positivismo, Rome 1956.
Mueller, I. W. Mill and French thought. Urbana 1956.
Pappé, H. O. The Mills and Harriet Taylor. Political Science 8 1956.
— Mill and the Harriet Taylor Myth. Melbourne 1960.
— Mill and Tocqueville. JHI 25 1964.
Patterson, J. E. A letter of Mill [to W. M. Dickson]. Yale Univ Lib Gazette 30 1956.
Rees, J. C. Mill and his early critics. Leicester 1956.
— A note on Macaulay and the Utilitarians. Political Stud 4 1956.
— A phase in the development of Mill's ideas on liberty. Political Stud 6 1958.

— A re-reading of Mill on liberty. Political Stud 8 1960.
— Was Mill for liberty? Political Stud 14 1966.
Rogin, L. In his Meaning and validity of economic theory, New York 1956.
Wethered, H. N. In his Curious art of autobiography from Cellini to Kipling, 1956.
Atkinson, R. F. Mill's proof of the principle of utility. Philosophy 32 1957.
Burns, J. H. Mill and democracy 1829–61. Political Stud 5 1957.
— Utilitarianism and democracy. Philosophical Quart 9 1959.
Ellegård, A. Darwinian theory and nineteenth-century philosophies of science. JHI 18 1957.
Hancock, R. Ethics and history in Kant and Mill. Ethics 68 1957.
Kotarbiński, T. L'utilitarisme dans le morale de Mill et de Spencer. In Mysli o działaniu, vol 1 of Wybor pism, Warsaw 1957.
Lindley, D. N. Mill: the second greatest influence. Victorian Newsletter no 11 1957.
Pankhurst, R. K. P. The Saint Simonians, Mill and Carlyle. 1957.
Ryle, G. The theory of meaning. In British philosophy in the mid-century, ed C. A. Mace, 1957.
Rudman, H. Mill on perpetual endowments. History of Ideas Newsletter 3 1957.
Sakai, N. Mill's conception of freedom. Zürich 1957.
Clive, J. More or less eminent Victorians: some trends in recent Victorian biography. Victorian Stud 2 1958.
de Selincourt, A. In his Six great thinkers, 1958.
Giulietti, G. La dottrina dell'induzione nel sistema di Mill. Verona 1958.
Greenberg, R. A. Mill on Bagehot and reform. N & Q Feb 1958.
Grenieski, H. Milla kanon zmian towarzyszaacych. Jnl of Symbolic Logic 23 1958.
Kaufmann, F. In his Methodology of the social sciences, New York 1958.
Kretzmann, N. Desire as proof of desirability. Philosophical Quart 8 1958.
Lennard, R. V. Mill and others on liberty. Hibbert Jnl 57 1958–9.
Myint, H. The classical theory of international trade and the under-developed countries. Economic Jnl 68 1958.
Quinton, A. The neglect of Victorian philosophy. Victorian Stud 1 1958.
Scanlan, J. P. Mill and the definition of freedom. Ethics 68 1958.
Senn, P. R. The earliest use of the term social science. JHI 19 1958. Replies by J. H. Burns and G. G. Iggers, 20 1959.
Winch, P. Mill's logic of the moral sciences. In his Idea of a social science and its relation to philosophy, 1958.
Belassa, B. A. Mill and the law of markets. Quart Jnl of Economics 73 1959. Reply by L. C. Hunter, 74 1960.
— Marx and Mill. Weltwirtschafliches Archiv 83 1959.
Clark, G. A. Mill's notorious analogy. Jnl of Philosophy 56 1959.
Dhar, T. N. On the possibility of optimum (unique) equilibrium in Mill's reciprocal demand. Indian Jnl of Economics 39 1959.
Hall, R. A virtually untapped source for dictionary quotations. N & Q Sept 1959.
— The diction of Mill. N & Q Jan 1964–Nov 1965.
Hart, H. L. A. and A. M. Honoré. Philosophical preliminaries. In their Causation in the law, Oxford 1959.
Havard, W. C. Sidgwick and late utilitarian political philosophy. Gainesville Florida 1959.
Krook, D. In her Three traditions of moral thought, Cambridge 1959.
Lancaster, L. W. In his Masters of political thought, 1959.
Lindquist, E. K. Mill's essay On liberty: a centennial review. Wichita Kansas 1959.
McCallum, R. B. The individual in the mass: Mill on liberty and the franchise. In 1859: entering an age of crisis, ed P. Appleman, W. A. Madden and M. Wolff, Bloomington 1959.
Powers, R. H. Mill: morality and inequality. South Atlantic Quart 58 1959.
Selem, A. La teoria dell' induzione di Mill. Studia Patavina 6 1959.
Stevenson, L. 1959: year of fulfillment. Centennial Rev 3 1959.
Stokes, E. In his English Utilitarians and India, Oxford 1959.
Ward, J. W. Mill, Marx and modern individualism. Virginia Quart Rev 35 1959.
Wellman, C. A reinterpretation of Mill's proof. Ethics 69 1959.
Annan, N. Landmarks of political thought: On liberty. Listener 28 Jan 1960.
— In The English mind, ed H. S. Davies and G. Watson, Cambridge 1964.
Cooney, S. Mill, poets and other men. Victorian Newsletter no 17 1960.
Cumming, I. A manufactured man: the education of Mill. Auckland 1960.
Giannotti, J. A. Mill e la crítica da evidência cartesiana. Anais do III Congresso Nacional de Filosofia (São Paulo) [1960?].
Holloway, H. Mill and Green on the modern welfare state. Western Political Quart 12 1960.
Kemp, M. C. The Mill-Bastable infant-industry dogma. Jnl of Political Economy 68 1960.
Kendall, W. The open society and its fallacies. Amer Political Science Rev 54 1960.
Qualter, T. H. Mill, disciple of de Tocqueville. Western Political Quart 13 1960.
Robson, J. M. Mill's theory of poetry. UTQ 29 1960.
— Mill and Arnold: liberty and culture—friends or enemies? Humanities Assoc Bull 34 1961.
— Victorian liberals. UTQ 31 1962.
— Mill and Bentham, with some observations on James Mill. In Essays in English literature from the Renaissance to the Victorian age presented to A. S. P. Woodhouse, ed M. MacLure and F. W. Watt, Toronto 1964.
— A note on Mill bibliography. UTQ 34 1964.
— Mill's Autobiography: the public and the private voice. College Composition & Communication 16 1965.
— and K. Britton. Mill's debating speeches. Mill News Letter 1 1965.
— Artist and scientist: Harriet Taylor and Mill. Queen's Quart 73 1966.
— Principles and methods in the collected edition of Mill. In Editing nineteenth-century texts, ed Robson, Toronto 1967.
Stillinger, J. The text of Mill's Autobiography. Bull of John Rylands Lib 43 1960.
Housing drive takes toll of history: Mill's house at Avignon. Times 31 Aug 1960.
Barber, W. J. The economics of affluence, South Atlantic Quart 60 1961.
Barton, M. N. Rare books and other bibliographical resources in Baltimore libraries. PBSA 55 1961.
Berlin, I. Mill and the ends of life. [1961].
Copi, I. M. Causal connections: Mill's methods of experimental inquiry. In his Introduction to logic, New York 1961.
Hacker, A. In his Political theory: philosophy, ideology, science, 1961.
Hanson, N. R. In his Patterns of discovery, Cambridge 1961.
Lakeman, E. Centennial: Mill's Representative government. Contemporary Rev April 1961.
Miller, K. E. Mill's theory of international relations. JHI 22 1961.
Spiegelberg, H. Mill on accident of birth. Ibid.

Woods, T. Poetry and philosophy: a study in the thought of Mill. 1961.
Carr, R. The religious thought of Mill: a study in reluctant scepticism. JHI 23 1962.
Cooney, S. The heart of that mystery: a note on Mill's theory of poetry. Victorian Newsletter no 21 1962.
Corry, B. A. In his Money, saving and investment in English economics 1800–50, 1962.
Hoffman, R. Note on Mill's method of residues. Jnl of Philosophy 59 1962.
Levine, G. Determinism and responsibility in the works of George Eliot. PMLA 77 1962.
Pap, A. In his An introduction to the philosophy of science, Glencoe Ill 1962.
Semmel, B. In his Governor Eyre controversy, 1962.
Swart, K. W. Individualism in the mid-nineteenth century. JHI 23 1962.
Waller, J. O. Mill and the American Civil War. BNYPL Oct 1962.
Walsh, H. T. Whewell and Mill on induction. Philosophy of Science 29 1962.
Bernard, M. Introduction à une sociologie des doctrines économiques, des Physiocrats à Mill. Paris 1963.
Blegvad, M. Mill, Moore, and the naturalistic fallacy. In Philosophical essays dedicated to Gunnar Aspelin, Lund 1963.
Cowling, M. Mill and Liberalism. Cambridge 1963.
Day, J. P. Mill on matter. Philosophy 38 1963.
— Mill. In A critical history of western philosophy, ed D. J. O'Connor 1964.
Durham, J. The influence of Mill's mental crisis on his thought. Amer Imago 20 1963.
Ludwig, M. Die Sozialethik des Mill. Zürich 1963.
McCloskey, H. J. Mill's Liberalism. Philosophical Quart 13 1963. Reply by A. Ryan, 14 1964.
Pike, R. In his Pioneers of social change, 1963.
Scheffler, I. In his Anatomy of inquiry, New York 1963.
Tanesse, G. La philosophie pratique de Mill. Revue de l'Enseignement Philosophique 14 1963.
Weinberg, A. T. Gomperz and Mill. Geneva 1963.
— A meeting of the Political Economy Club, 7 May 1857. Mill News Letter 1 1966.
Winch, D. N. Classical economics and the case for colonization. Economica 30 1963.
Cockshut, A. O. J. Mill, the half-circle. In his Unbelievers: English agnostic thought, 1964.
Cumming, R. D. Mill's history of his ideas. JHI 25 1964.
Ellery, J. B. Mill. New York 1964.
Hollander, S. Technology and aggregate demand in Mill's economic system. Canadian Jnl of Economics & Political Science 30 1964.
Juleus, N. The rhetorical theory and practice of Mill. Speech Monographs 1964.
— The rhetoric of opposites: Mill and Carlyle. Pennsylvania Speech Annual 1966.
Schwartz, P. Distribucion e instituciones en Mill. Annales de Economía new ser 8 1964.
— Mill y el laissez-faire. Moneda y Crédito 91 1964.
— Mill and laissez-faire: London water. Economica new ser 33 1966.
Alexander, E. Arnold and Mill. New York 1965.
— Mill's theory of culture: the wedding of literature and democracy. UTQ 35 1965.
Hamburger, J. Intellectuals in politics: Mill and the philosophic radicals. New Haven 1965.
Hyde, W. J. Theoretic and practical unconventionality in Jude the obscure. Nineteenth-Century Fiction 20 1965.
Karns, C. F. Causal analysis and rhetoric: a survey of the major philosophical conceptions of cause prior to Mill. Speech Monographs 32 1965.
Letwin, S. R. In her Pursuit of certainty: Hume, Bentham, Mill and B. Webb, Cambridge 1965.
Martin, P. E. Carlyle and Mill: the anti-self-consciousness theory. Thoth 6 1965.
Miyoshi, M. Mill and Pauline: the myth and some facts. Victorian Stud 11 1965.
Power, M. S. Democracy, representation and Mill. Susquehanna Univ Stud 11 1965.
Randall, J. H. Mill and the working-out of empiricism. JHI 26 1965.
— In his Career of philosophy, 2 vols New York 1966.
— Green: the development of English thought from Mill to Bradley. JHI 27 1966.
Ryan, A. Mill's art of living. Listener 22 Oct 1965.
— Mill and the naturalistic fallacy. Mind new ser 75 1966.
Schneewind, J. B. Moral problems and moral philosophy in the Victorian period. Victorian Stud 9 (suppl) 1965.
Sharpless, F. P. W. J. Fox and Mill's essays on poetry. Victorian Newsletter no 27 1965.
Shoul, B. Similarities in the work of Mill and Marx. Science & Soc 29 1965.
Stigler, G. The nature and role of originality in scientific progress. In his Essays in the history of economics, Chicago 1965.
West, E. G. Liberty and education: Mill's dilemma. Philosophy 40 1965.
Weinstein, W. L. The concept of liberty in nineteenth-century English political thought. Political Stud 13 1965.
Ayer, A. J. Science and philosophy. In Ideas and beliefs of the Victorians, New York 1966.
Bennett, J. R. Mill, F. W. Newman and Socialism: Mill's two argumentative voices. Mill News Letter 2 1966.
Ebel, H. 'The primaeval fountain of human nature': Mill, Carlyle and the French Revolution. Victorian Newsletter no 30 1966.
Friedman, R. B. A new exploration of Mill's On liberty. Political Stud 14 1966.
Govil, O. P. A note on Mill and Browning's Pauline. Victorian Poetry 4 1966.
Spitz, D. Pure tolerance: a critique of criticisms. Dissent 13 1966. Replies by M. Walzer and Spitz, ibid.
Feltes, N. N. Bentham and Coleridge: Mill's 'completing counterparts'. Mill News Letter 2 1967.

JOHN DANIEL MORELL
1816–91

Historical and critical view of the speculative philosophy of Europe in the nineteenth century. 2 vols 1846, Edinburgh 1847 (rev and enlarged).
On the philosophical tendencies of the age. 1848.
The philosophy of religion. 1849.
Elements of psychology, pt 1. 1853. All pbd.
Handbook of logic. [1855].
Modern German philosophy. [Manchester 1856].
Fichte's contributions to moral philosophy. 1860.
An introduction to mental philosophy on the inductive method. 1862.
Philosophical fragments, written during intervals of business. 1878.
Manual of the history of philosophy. [1884].
Also works on religion and education.

FREDERIC WILLIAM HENRY MYERS
1843–1901

See col 641, above.

RICHARD LEWIS NETTLESHIP

1846–92

Philosophical lectures and remains. Ed A. C. Bradley and G. R. Benson 2 vols 1897, 1901.
Memoir of T. H. Green. 1906.
The theory of education in Plato's Republic. Ed S. Leeson, Oxford 1935; tr Spanish, 1945.

JOHN HENRY NEWMAN

1801–90

An essay on the development of Christian doctrine. 1845, 1846; ed C. F. Harrold, New York 1949.
An essay in aid of a grammar of assent. 1870, 1892; ed C. F. Harrold, New York 1947.
See col 1311, above.

KARL PEARSON

1857–1936

Bibliographies

Morant, G. M. A bibliography of the statistical and other writings of Pearson. 1939.

§1

The Trinity: a nineteenth-century passion play. 1882. In verse.
Matter and soul. 1886.
The moral basis of Socialism. [1887].
Socialism: its theory and practice. [1887].
The ethic of freethought: a selection of essays and lectures. 1888, 1901 (rev).
The positive creed of freethought. [1888].
The grammar of science. 1892, 1900 (rev and enlarged), 1911 (rev and enlarged), 1937, New York 1957.
Reaction! a criticism of Balfour's attack on rationalism [1895].
The chances of death and other studies in evolution. 2 vols 1897.
National life from the standpoint of science. 1901, 1905 (with appendixes).
Nature and nurture: the problem of the future. 1910.
Social problems. 1912.
The life, letters and labours of Galton. 4 vols Cambridge 1914–30. Ed Pearson.
The science of man. 1920.
Galton: an appreciation. [1922].
Darwin: an appreciation. [1923].
Also works on statistics and biology.

§2

Pearson, E. S. Pearson. 1938. With bibliography.

JAMES ALLANSON PICTON

1832–1910

The mystery of matter, and other essays. 1873.
The religion of the universe. 1904.
Spinoza: a handbook to the Ethics. 1905, 1907.
Also works on religion.

CARVETH READ

1848–1931

On the theory of logic. 1878.
Logic: deductive and inductive. 1898, 1906 (enlarged), 1914 (4th edn enlarged and rewritten).
The metaphysics of nature. 1905, 1908 (with appendices).
Natural and social morals. 1909.
The origin of man and of his superstitions. Cambridge 1920, 2 vols Cambridge 1925 (rev).
Also works on psychology.

DAVID GEORGE RITCHIE

1853–1903

The rationality of history. In Essays in philosophical criticism, ed A. Seth and R. B. Haldane 1883.
Darwinism and politics. 1889, 1891 (enlarged), 1895, 1901.
The ultimate value of social effort. [1890].
Principles of state interference. 1891, 1896, 1902.
Darwin and Hegel, with other philosophical studies. 1893.
Natural rights. [1894].
Evolution and democracy. In Ethical democracy, ed S. Coit 1900.
Studies in political and social ethics. 1902.
Plato. New York 1902.
Philosophical studies. Ed R. Latta 1905. With memoir.

GEORGE CROOM ROBERTSON

1842–92

The senses. 1866.
Hobbes. Edinburgh 1886.
Philosophical remains. Ed A. Bain and T. Whittaker 1894.
Elements of general philosophy. Ed C. A. F. R. Davids 1896. From lecture notes.
Elements of psychology. Ed C. A. F. R. Davids 1896. From lecture notes.

GEORGE JOHN ROMANES

1848–94

§1

A candid examination of theism. Boston 1878, 1892 (3rd edn). By 'Physicus'.
Darwin. 1882.
The scientific evidences of organic evolution. 1882.
Animal intelligence. New York 1883, London 1886 (4th edn).
Mental evolution in animals. 1883; tr German, 1885.
Mental evolution in man. 1888; tr French, 1891; German, 1895.
Poems. 1889.
Darwin and after Darwin. Chicago 3 vols 1892–7.
An examination of Weismannism. 1893.
Mind and motion and monism. 1895.
Thoughts on religion. Ed C. Gore, Chicago 1895, 1897 (3rd edn).
Essays. Ed C. L. Morgan 1897.
Also works on psychology.

§2

Romanes, E. Life and letters of Romanes. 1896, 1902 (5th edn).

SIR JOHN ROBERT SEELEY

1834–95

David and Samuel, with other poems. 1859. By 'John Robertson'.
Classical studies as an introduction to the moral sciences. 1864.
Ecce homo: a survey of the life and work of Jesus Christ. 1866 (for 1865) etc; tr German, 1867; Italian nd.
Liberal education in universities. In F. W. Farrar, Essays on a liberal education, 1867.
Lectures and essays. 1870.
Natural religion. 1882, Boston 1882.
Goethe reviewed after sixty years. Boston 1893, London 1894.
Introduction to political science. Ed H. Sidgwick 1896.
Ethics and religion. 1900.
Also works on history; see col 1495, above.

ANDREW SETH, from 1898 PRINGLE-PATTISON

1856–1931

§1

The development from Kant to Hegel. 1882.
Essays in philosophical criticism. Ed Seth and R. B. Haldane 1883.
Scottish philosophy: a comparison of the Scottish and German answers to Hume. Edinburgh 1885.
Hegelianism and personality. Edinburgh 1887, 1893.
The present position of the philosophical sciences. Edinburgh 1891.
Two lectures on theism. New York 1897.
Man's place in the cosmos. Edinburgh 1897, 1902 (rev).
Philosophical works of Calderwood. In W. Calderwood and D. Woodside, Calderwood 1900.
The philosophical radicals, and other essays. Edinburgh 1907.
The idea of God in the light of recent philosophy. Aberdeen and Oxford 1917, 1920 (rev).
The idea of immortality. Oxford 1922.
The philosophy of history. [1924].
Haldane. 1930.
Studies in the philosophy of religion. Oxford 1930.
The Balfour lectures on realism. Ed G. F. Barbour, Edinburgh 1933. With memoir.

Articles

Hegel: an exposition and criticism. Mind 6 1881.
Contemporary records: mental philosophy. Contemporary Rev Feb 1884, Aug 1887.
Alexander's Moral order and progress. Mind 14 1889.
Hegel and his recent critics. Ibid.
Psychology, epistemology and metaphysics. Philosophical Rev 1 1892.
The problem of epistemology. Ibid.
Epistemology in Locke and Kant. Philosophical Rev 2 1893.
The epistemology of neo-Kantianism and subjective idealism. Ibid.
The new psychology and automatism. Contemporary Rev April 1893.
Man's place in the cosmos: Huxley on nature and man. Blackwood's Mag Dec 1893.
Epistemology and ontology. Philosophical Rev 3 1894.
Some epistemological conclusions. Ibid.
Hegelianism and its critics. Mind new ser 3 1894. Reply by D. G. Ritchie, ibid.
A new theory of the absolute. Contemporary Rev Nov–Dec 1894.
The term 'naturalism' in recent discussion. Philosophical Rev 5 1896.
Nietzsche. Blackwood's Mag Oct 1897.
The standpoint and method of ethics. Philosophical Rev 6 1897.
The opinions of Nietzsche. Contemporary Rev May 1898.
Scottish moral philosophy. Philosophical Rev 7 1898.
The venture of theism. Quart Rev 187 1898.
The utilitarian estimate of knowledge. Philosophical Rev 10 1901.
Martineau's philosophy. Hibbert Jnl 1 1903. Reply by G. Galloway, ibid.
A. C. Fraser. Proc Br Acad 6 1914.
The free man's worship: a consideration of Bertrand Russell's views on religion. Hibbert Jnl 12 1914.
Balfour's Theism and humanism. Hibbert Jnl 14 1916.
Do finite individuals possess a substantive or an adjectival mode of being? (symposium). Proc Aristotelian Soc 18 1918.
The idea of God: a reply to some criticisms. Mind new ser 28 1919.
Pragmatism and idealist ethics. Philosophical Rev 32 1923.

§2

Jones, A. H. Seth Pringle-Pattison's epistemological realism. Philosophical Rev 20 1911.
Rashdall, H. The religious philosophy of Pringle-Pattison. Mind new ser 27 1918.
Galloway, G. Idealism and the external world. Mind new ser 29 1920.
Capper, J. B. and J. B. Baillie. Pringle-Pattison. Proc Br Acad 17 1931.
Merrington, E. N. A Scottish thinker: Pringle-Pattison. Australasian Jnl of Psychology & Philosophy 9 1931.
Hallett, H. F. Seth Pringle-Pattison. Mind new ser 42 1933.
Gallagher, D. M. Pringle-Pattison's idea of God. Washington 1933.
Warren, W. P. Pantheism in neo-Hegelian thought. New Haven 1933.
Bertocci, P. A. The empirical argument for God in late British thought. Cambridge Mass 1939.

ALFRED SIDGWICK

1850–1943

Fallacies. 1883.
Distinction and the criticism of beliefs. 1892.
The process of argument. 1893.
The use of words in reasoning. 1901.
The application of logic. 1910.
Elementary logic. Cambridge 1914.

HENRY SIDGWICK

1838–1900

§1

The ethics of conformity and subscription. 1870.
The methods of ethics. 1874, 1877 (enlarged), 1884 (enlarged), 1907 (7th edn), 1962; tr German, 1909.
The incoherence of empirical philosophy. [1879].
Principles of political economy. 1883, 1901 (3rd edn), 1924.
The scope and method of economic science. 1885.
Outline of the history of ethics. 1886, 1888, 1892, 1896.
The elements of politics. 1891, 1897 (rev), 1919 (4th edn).
Practical ethics: a collection of addresses and essays. 1898.
The scope and limits of the work of an ethical society; the aims and methods of an ethical society. 1900.
Philosophy: its scope and relations. Ed J. Ward 1902.

Lectures on the ethics of Green, Spencer and Martineau. Ed E. E. C. Jones 1902.
The development of European polity. Ed E. M. Sidgwick 1903, 1920 (3rd edn).
Miscellaneous essays and addresses. Ed E. M. and A. Sidgwick 1904.
Lectures on the philosophy of Kant and other philosophical lectures and essays. Ed J. Ward 1905.

Articles

Ranke's History of England. Macmillan's Mag May 1861.
Alexis de Tocqueville. Macmillan's Mag Nov 1861.
Liberal education. Macmillan's Mag April 1867.
Verification of beliefs. Contemporary Rev July 1871.
Beale's life theories and their influence on religious thought. Academy Oct 1871.
Critique of Fraser's Berkeley. Athenaeum June 1871.
Lewes's History of philosophy. Academy Nov 1871.
Bree's exposition of fallacies in Darwin's hypothesis. Athenaeum July 1872. Replies by Bree, ibid; Sidgwick, Aug 1872.
Pleasure and desire. Contemporary Rev April 1872.
J. S. Mill. Academy May 1873.
On a passage in Plato's Republic. Jnl of Philology 5 1874.
Bradley's Ethical studies. Mind 1 1876. Replies by Bradley and Sidgwick, 2 1877.
Calderwood on intuitionism in morals. Mind 1 1876.
The theory of evolution in its application to practice. Ibid.
Philosophy at Cambridge. Ibid.
Grote's treatise on moral ideals. Mind 2 1877.
Hedonism and the ultimate good. Ibid. Reply by T. H. Green, ibid.
Reply to Barrett on the Suppression of egoism. Ibid.
Economic method. Fortnightly Rev Feb 1879.
The establishment of ethical first principles. Mind 4 1879.
The so-called idealism of Kant. Ibid.
On historical psychology. Nineteenth Century Feb 1880.
Kant's refutation of idealism. Mind 5 1880.
Spencer's ethical system. Ibid.
On the fundamental doctrines of Descartes. Mind 7 1882.
The incoherence of empirical philosophy. Ibid.
A criticism of the critical philosophy. Mind 8 1883. Reply by R. Adamson, ibid.
Kant's view of mathematical premisses and reasonings. Ibid.
Green's ethics. Mind 9 1884.
Bluntschli's theory of the state. EHR April 1886.
The historical method. Mind 11 1886.
Martineau's defence of types of ethical theory. Ibid.
Idiopsychological ethics. Mind 12 1887. Reply to J. Martineau, 10 1885.
Plato's Utilitarianism: a dialogue by J. Grote and Sidgwick. Classical Rev 3 1889.
Some fundamental ethical controversies. Mind 14 1889. Replies by T. Fowler and L. A. Selby-Bigge, 15 1890.
The morality of strife. International Jnl of Ethics 1 1890.
The definition of desire. Mind new ser 1 1892. Reply by H. R. Marshall, ibid.
The feeling-tone of desire and aversion. Ibid.
Spencer's Justice. Ibid.
Is the distinction between 'is' and 'ought' ultimate and irreducible? (symposium). Proc Aristotelian Soc 2 1892.
Unreasonable action. Mind new ser 2 1893. Reply by H. R. Marshall, 3 1894.
My station and its duties. International Jnl of Ethics 4 1893.
Conjectures on the constitutional history of Athens. Classical Rev 8 1894.
A dialogue on time and common sense. Mind new ser 3 1894.
Luxury. International Jnl of Ethics 5 1894.
The philosophy of common sense. Mind new ser 4 1895.
Theory and practice. Ibid.
Ritchie's Natural rights. Ibid.
The ethics of religious conformity. International Jnl of Ethics 6 1896. Reply by H. Rashdall, 7 1897.
Criteria of truth and error. Mind new ser 9 1900.
The philosophy of Green. Mind new ser 10 1901.
Sidgwick's ethical view: an auto-historical fragment. Ibid.

§2

Bain, A. Sidgwick's Methods. Mind 1 1876.
Calderwood, H. Sidgwick on intuitionism in morals. Ibid.
Bradley, F. H. Sidgwick's hedonism. 1877.
Green, T. H. In his Prolegomena to ethics, Oxford 1884 (2nd edn).
Martineau, J. In his Types of ethical theory, Oxford 1885.
Rashdall, H. Sidgwick's Utilitarianism. Mind 10 1885.
Ritchie, D. G. Sidgwick's Elements of politics. International Jnl of Ethics 2 1891.
Macmillan, M. Sidgwick and Schopenhauer on the foundations of morality. International Jnl of Ethics 8 1898.
Magill, R. Der rationale Utilitarismus Sidgwicks: oder seine Vereiningung des Intuitionismus und des Utilitarismus. Jena 1899.
Myers, F. W. Sidgwick. Proc Soc of Psychic Research 15 1900.
Albee, E. An examination of Sidgwick's proof of Utilitarianism. Philosophical Rev 10 1901. Replies by H. Barker and Albee, 11 1902.
— A history of English Utilitarianism. 1902.
Hayward, F. H. The ethical philosophy of Sidgwick. 1901.
— The true significance of Sidgwick's Ethics. International Jnl of Ethics 11 1901. Replies by E. E. C. Jones and Hayward, ibid.
Seth, J. The ethical system of Sidgwick. Mind new ser 10 1901.
Sorley, W. R. Sidgwick. International Jnl of Ethics 11 1901.
Stephen, L. Sidgwick. Mind new ser 10 1901.
Moore, G. E. In his Principia ethica, Cambridge 1903.
Bryce, J. In his Studies in contemporary biography, 1903.
— Sidgwick. Proc Br Acad 1 1904.
Jones, E. E. C. Sidgwick's Ethics. Proc Aristotelian Soc new ser 4 1904.
Seth, A. Sidgwick's philosophy: its scope and relations. Mind new ser 12 1903.
Sidgwick, E. M. and A. Memoir. 1906. With bibliography.
Barbour, G. F. Green and Sidgwick on the community of the good. Philosophical Rev 17 1908.
Broad, C. D. In his Five types of ethical theory, 1930.
— Sidgwick. Hibbert Jnl 37 1939.
— In his Ethics and the history of philosophy, 1952.
Havard, W. C. Sidgwick and later utilitarian political philosophy. Gainesville 1959. With bibliography.
Lacey, A. R. Sidgwick's ethical maxims. Philosophy 34 1959.
Melitz, J. Sidgwick's theory of international values. Economic Jnl 73 1963.
Mullins, T. Y. Sidgwick's concept of ethical science. JHI 24 1963.
Schneewind, J. B. First principles and common sense morality in Sidgwick's ethics. Archiv für Geschichte der Philosophie 45 1963.

WILLIAM HENRY SMITH
1808–72

See col 1610, below.

WILLIAM RITCHIE SORLEY

1855–1935

§1

The historical method. In A. Seth and R. B. Haldane, Essays in philosophic criticism, 1883.
On the ethics of naturalism. Edinburgh 1885, 1904 (rev).
Recent tendencies in ethics. Edinburgh 1904.
Agnosticism: its meanings and claims. 1908.
The moral life and moral worth. Cambridge 1911.
The interpretation of evolution. [1912].
The state and morality. In The international crisis: the theory of the state, 1916.
Moral values and the idea of God. Aberdeen and Cambridge 1918.
Spinoza. 1918.
A history of English philosophy. Cambridge 1920, 1965 (as A history of British philosophy to 1900). Based on CHEL.
Value and reality. In Contemporary British philosophy, ed J. H. Muirhead vol 2, 1925.
Tradition. Oxford 1926.

Articles

The morality of nations. International Jnl of Ethics 1 1891.
The philosophy of Herbert of Cherbury. Mind new ser 4 1895.
Betting and gambling. International Jnl of Ethics 13 1903.
The knowledge of good. Hibbert Jnl 3 1905.
The method of a metaphysic of ethics. Philosophical Rev 14 1905.
Ethical aspects of economics. International Jnl of Ethics 17 1907.
The interpretation of evolution. Proc Br Acad 4 1910.
The philosophical attitude. International Jnl of Ethics 20 1910.
Does religion need a philosophy? Hibbert Jnl 11 1913.
Time and reality. Mind new ser 32 1923.
Also works on religion and contributions on philosophy to CHEL.

§2

Tennant, F. R. Sorley. Proc Br Acad 22 1935.
Muirhead, J. H. Sorley. Philosophy 11 1936.
Stout, G. F. Sorley. Mind new ser 45 1936.

WILLIAM SPALDING

1809–59

See col 1401, above.

HERBERT SPENCER

1820–1903

§1

The proper sphere of government. 1843.
Social statics: or the conditions essential to human happiness specified. 1851, New York 1865, London 1876, 1892 (abridged and rev), 1910 (abridged and rev); tr Dutch, 1883; Italian, [1921?]; French, 1923.
A new theory of population. 1852.
Over-legislation. 1854; tr Spanish, 1895.
Railway morals and railway policy. 1855.
Essays scientific, political and speculative. Ser 1, 1858; ser 2, 1863; as Illustrations of universal progress, New York 1864, 3 vols 1868–74, 1 vol 1875 (new edn), 3 vols 1878 (3rd edn), 2 vols 1883, 3 vols 1885 (4th edn), 1891 (new edn enlarged); tr Russian, 1866; French, 1891 (3rd edn); Spanish, 1908.
Education: intellectual, moral and physical. 1861, New York 1864, 1883 (new edn), 1885, 1888, 1890, 1903, 1929, 1949; tr German, 1874; French, 1877, 1885; Spanish, 1879, 1884, [1906]; Dutch, 1887; Hungarian, [1895?]; Italian, 1901; Hebrew, 1908.
A system of synthetic philosophy. 10 vols 1860–96, 15 vols New York and London 1900; tr German, 1875–97; Hungarian, 1903. Vol 1, First principles of a new system of philosophy; vols 2–3, Principles of biology; vols 4–5, Principles of psychology; vols 6–8, Principles of sociology; vols 9–10, Principles of ethics (including The data of ethics, Justice, and Negative and positive beneficence). Separate vols tr into many languages.
The classification of the sciences. 1864, 1870, 1871; tr French, 1872. Pt 2 rev as Reasons for dissenting from the philosophy of Comte, 1884.
Spontaneous generation and the hypothesis of physiological units. New York 1870.
Recent discussions in science, philosophy and morals. New York 1871.
The study of sociology. 1873, 1874, 1874, 1880 (9th edn), 1897 (18th edn); tr German, 1875; French, 1894 (11th edn).
Descriptive sociology: or groups of sociological facts. 1873–81; tr Russian, 1878; (in part) Spanish, 1896, 1898. With D. Duncan et al.
Philosophy of style. New York 1873.
The morals of trade. 1874, 1891.
The data of ethics. 1879; tr Italian, 1881 (with introd by G. Serezi).
The man versus the State. 1884, 1885, 1909, 1940, 1950; tr French, 1885; Dutch, 1886; Italian, 1886 (with introd by G. Barzellotti); Spanish, 1904, [1930?].
Religion: a retrospect and a prospect. In The nature and reality of religion: a controversy between Harrison and Spencer, 1885, Boston 1885 (as The insuppressible book, a controversy between Spencer and Harrison).
The factors of organic evolution. 1887.
From freedom to bondage. 1891; tr German, 1891.
The inadequacy of natural selection. 1893.
A rejoinder to Weismann. 1893.
Weismannism once more. 1894. Replies by Weismann and Spencer, Contemporary Rev Sept 1895.
Against the metric system. 1896, 1904 (3rd edn enlarged).
Various fragments. 1897, 1900 (enlarged).
Facts and comments. 1902, 1914; tr Spanish, 1903.
Autobiography. 2 vols 1904, 1926; tr German, 1905.
Essays on education and kindred subjects. 1904, [1911], 1963.

Articles

Mental evolution. Contemporary Rev June 1871.
Martineau on evolution. Contemporary Rev June 1872.
Replies to criticisms. Fortnightly Rev 20 1873.
The comparative psychology of man. Mind 1 1876.
Consciousness under chloroform. Mind 3 1878.
Green's explanation. Contemporary Rev March 1881.
The militant type of society. Contemporary Rev Sept 1881.
The industrial type of society. Contemporary Rev Oct 1881.
Replies to criticisms on the Data of ethics. Mind 6 1881.
Goldwin Smith as a critic. Contemporary Rev March 1882.
The Americans: a conversation and a speech. Contemporary Rev Jan 1883.
Religion: a retrospect and prospect. Nineteenth Century Jan 1884.
Retrogressive religion. Nineteenth Century July 1884.
Last words about agnosticism. Nineteenth Century Nov 1884.

The ownership of land. In J. H. Levy, A symposium on the land question, 1890.
Our space-consciousness: a reply. Mind 15 1890. Reply by J. Watson, ibid.
The origin of music. Ibid. Replies by R. Wallaschek, J. Cattell and Spencer 16 1891; by Wallaschek, new ser 1 1892.
Weismann's theories. Contemporary Rev May 1893.
Professional institutions. Contemporary Rev May 1895–April 1896.
Balfour's dialectics. Fortnightly Rev June 1895.
Salisbury on evolution. Popular Science Monthly Feb 1896.
The relations of biology, psychology and sociology. Popular Science Monthly Dec 1896.

§2

Laugel, A. Spencer: les études philosophiques en Angleterre. Revue des Deux Mondes Feb 1864.
Atwater, L. Spencer's philosophy: atheism, pantheism and materialism. Princeton Rev 38 1865.
Jones, J. H. In his Know the truth, 1865.
Harris, W. T. Spencer. Jnl of Speculative Philosophy 1 1867.
Durkheim, E. In his De la division du travail social, Paris 1868.
Fiske, J. Spencer and the experts. Nation 8 1869.
Morris, G. S. In his British thought and thinkers, 1870.
Ribot, T. In his La psychologie anglaise contemporaine, Paris 1870; tr 1873, 1892.
Green, W. B. The facts of consciousness and the philosophy of Spencer. New York 1871.
Bowne, B. P. Spencer's laws of the unknowable. New Englander 31–2 1872–3.
—— Principles of psychology. New Englander 32 1873.
—— The philosophy of Spencer. New York 1874.
—— In his Kant and Spencer, Boston 1912.
Hodgson, S. H. The future of metaphysics. Contemporary Rev Nov 1872.
Pillon, F. Le sens moral selon Spencer. Critique Philosophique March 1873.
—— Examen des principes de psychologie de Spencer. Critique Philosophique May 1877–Sept 1878.
Leonard, W. A. A summary of Spencer's First principles. 1874.
Mivart, St. G. An examination of Spencer's psychology. Dublin Rev 75, 77, 80, 82–6 1874–5, 1877–80.
—— Spencer versus Balfour. Nineteenth Century Aug 1895.
Phelps, M. S. The general philosophy of Spencer. Bibliotheca Sacra 31 1874.
Porter, J. L. In his Science and revelation, Belfast 1874.
Youmans, E. L. Spencer and the doctrine of evolution. Popular Science Monthly Nov 1874.
—— Evolution philosophy of Spencer. North Amer Rev 129 1879.
—— Spencer on the Americans, and the Americans on Spencer. New York 1882.
—— Concerning the suppressed book. Popular Science Monthly Aug 1885.
Adams, L. The metaphysics of evolution. New Englander 34 1875.
—— Empirical dissent from Spencer's philosophy. New Englander 35 1876.
Fischer, E. L. Ueber das Gesetz der Entwicklung mit Rücksicht auf Spencer. Vienna 1875.
Watts, R. An examination of Spencer's biological hypothesis. Belfast 1875.
Bain, A. Spencer's Principles of sociology. Mind 1 1876.
—— Spencer's Data of ethics. Mind 4 1879.
—— Spencer's psychological congruities. Mind 6 1881.
Bascom, J. Philosophy of Spencer. Bibliotheca Sacra 33 1876.
Birks, T. R. Modern physical fatalism and the doctrine of evolution, including an examination of Spencer's First principles. 1876, 1882.
Kirkman, T. P. In his Philosophy without assumptions, 1876.
—— On Spencer's conquest of the problem of the universe. 1888.
Tylor, E. B. Spencer's Principles of sociology. Mind 2 1877. Replies by Spencer and Tylor, ibid.
Wright, C. Philosophical discussions. New York 1877.
Bobba, R. La dottrina della libertà secondo lo Spencer in rapporto colla morale. La Filosofia delle Scuole Italiane 18–9 1878–9.
Free notes on Spencer's First principles. Edinburgh 1878.
James, W. Remarks on Spencer's definition of mind as correspondence. Jnl of Speculative Philosophy 12 1878.
Vaihinger, H. Der Begriff des Absoluten mit Rücksicht auf Spencer. Vierteljahrsschrift für wissenschaftliche Philosophie 2 1878.
—— Der englische Realismus: Spencer. Deutsche Revue Feb 1878.
Watson, J. The world as force, with especial reference to the philosophy of Spencer. Jnl of Speculative Philosophy 12 1878.
—— In his Kant and his English critics, New York 1881.
—— Spencer's derivation of space. Mind 15 1890.
—— Comte, Mill and Spencer. Glasgow 1895.
—— In his Hedonistic theories from Aristippus to Spencer, 1895.
Coste, A. In his Les principes d'une sociologie objective, Paris 1879.
Fontana, B. Del sistema filosofico di Spencer. Imola 1879.
Funck-Bretano, T. In his Les sophistes grecs et les sophistes contemporains, Paris 1879.
Giner, F. Las buenas maneras y el filósofo Spencer. Revista de España March 1879.
Guthrie, M. On Spencer's formula of evolution, with a résumé and critique of the First principles. 1879.
—— On Spencer's unification of knowledge. 1882.
—— On Spencer's Data of ethics. 1884.
Guyau, M. In his La morale anglaise contemporaine, Paris 1879.
—— L'héridité morale et la théorie de Spencer. Revue Philosophique 7 1879.
Spruyt, C. B. Proeve van eene Geschiedenis van de Leer der aangeboren Begrippen. Leyden 1879.
Benn, A. W. Another view of Spencer's ethics. Mind 5 1880.
Calderwood, H. Spencer on the Data of ethics. Contemporary Rev Jan 1880.
—— Animal ethics as described by Spencer. Philosophical Rev 1 1892.
Means, D. M. G. The ethical method of evolution. Mind 5 1880.
Sidgwick, H. Spencer's ethical system. Ibid.
—— Spencer's Justice. Mind new ser 1 1892.
—— In his Lectures on the ethics of Green, Spencer and Martineau, 1902.
—— The philosophy of Spencer. In his Philosophy of Kant and other lectures, 1905.
Tarantino, G. Kant e Spencer. Giornale Napolitana di Filosofia 4 1880.
Wace, H. Spencer's Data of ethics. Contemporary Rev Aug 1880.
Beaussire, E. Examen de la morale évolutionniste de Spencer. Paris 1881.
Blanc, E. Les nouvelles bases de la morale d'après Spencer. Lyon 1881.
Brogialdi, A. Studii sulla psicologia di Spencer. Faenza 1881.
Fairbairn, A. M. Spencer and the philosophy of religion. Contemporary Rev July 1881.

Faraone, G. Esercizio intorno le basi della morale di Spencer. Naples 1881.
Mignardi, G. Spencer e la sua scuola condannati nella Regia Università di Genova. Macerata 1881.
Barnes, W. R. Political philosophy of Spencer. Chicago Dial 3 1882.
Barzellotti, G. Le basi della morale di Spencer. Rome 1882.
Clute, O. Spencer versus Spencer. Unitarian Rev 17 1882.
Greef, G. De. Abrégé de psychologie d'après Spencer. Brussels 1882.
Michelet, C. L. Spencer's System der Philosophie und sein Verhältnis zur deutschen Philosophie. Halle 1882.
Piola, G. Del fondamento della morale secondo Spencer e Hartmann. Rome 1882.
Rolph, W. H. Biologische Probleme zugleich als Versuch einer rationellen Ethik. Leipzig 1882.
Tiberghien, G. Krause et Spencer. Revue Belgique 41 1882.
Traina, T. La morale di Spencer. Turin 1882.
Beard, G. M. Spencer on American nervousness. 1883.
Cesca, G. L'evoluzionismo di Spencer. Verona 1883.
Craig, O. Philosophy and theism of Spencer. Presbyterian Rev 4–5 1883–4.
Graeff, J. E. Ultimatum of Spencer. New Englander 42 1883.
Ground, W. D. An examination of the structural principles of Spencer's philosophy. Oxford 1883.
Lacy, W. M. An examination of the philosophy of the unknowable as expounded by Spencer. Philadelphia 1883.
Maitland, F. W. Spencer's theory of society. Mind 8 1883.
Mercier, C. Spencer's classification of cognitions. Ibid.
Pellarin, C. La sociologie de Spencer. Critique Philosophique Nov 1883–Jan 1884.
Procter, R. A. Spencer's philosophy. GM Jan 1883.
Sewall, A. C. Spencer's Data of ethics. New Englander 42 1883.
Beeby, C. E. In his Woes of the Gospel, 1884.
Bonatelli, F. Alcune considerazioni critiche sopra una dottrina di Spencer. Atti del Reale Instituto Veneto 6th ser 2 1884.
Fairman, F. Spencer on Socialism. 1884.
Galasso, A. Della conciliazione dell'egoismo coll'altruismo secondo Spencer. Accademia di Scienza Morale e Politica di Napoli 18 1884.
Harrison, F. The ghost of religion. Nineteenth Century March 1884.
— Agnostic metaphysics. Nineteenth Century Sept 1884.
— Spencer. Oxford 1905.
Hyndman, H. M. In his Socialism and slavery, 1884.
Iverach, J. The philosophy of Spencer examined. 1884.
McCosh, J. E. Spencer's philosophy as culminated in his ethics. Edinburgh 1884.
Maguire, T. Agnosticism: Spencer and Harrison. Dublin 1884.
'Psychosis'. Our modern philosophers: Darwin, Bain and Spencer—a rhyme. 1884.
Signogne, E. Spencer. Revue Internationale 4 1884.
Sorley, W. R. In his On the ethics of naturalism, 1884.
— In his Ethics of naturalism, 1904.
Stephen, J. F. The unknowable and the unknown. Nineteenth Century June 1884.
'Wykehamist'. A short examination of Spencer's article entitled Religion, retrospect and prospect. 1884.
Arthur, W. Religion without God, and God without religion: pt 2, Agnosticism and Spencer. 1885.
Bennett, S. R. Spencer, Harrison and Arnold. Contemporary Rev Aug 1885.
Cathrein, V. Die Sittenlehre des Darwinismus: eine Kritik der Ethik Spencers. Freiburg 1885.
Fournière, E. Spencer et de Laveleye. Revue Socialiste Sept 1885.
Laveleye, E. de. The state versus the man. Contemporary Rev April 1885. Replies by Spencer and de Laveleye, ibid.
Naumann, A. Spencer wider Kant. Hamburg 1885.
Naville, E. La doctrine de l'évolution comme système philosophique. Revue Philosophique 20 1885.
Wing, J. Synthetic philosophy of Spencer. Amer Catholic Quart 10 1885.
Bridel, P. S. Les bases de la morale évolutionniste d'après Spencer. Paris 1886.
Goblet d'Alviella. Etudes d'histoire religieuse contemporaine: Harrison contre Spencer. Revue de l'Histoire des Religions 14 1886.
Green, T. H. Spencer and Lewes: their application of the doctrine of evolution to thought. In his Works vol 1, 1886.
Martineau, J. In his Types of ethical theory, Oxford 1886 (2nd edn).
— Science, nescience and faith. In his Essays vol 3, 1891.
Sala y Villaret, P. Opiniones religiosas de Spencer. Revista de España Dec 1886.
Sewall, H. Spencer as a biologist. Ann Arbor 1886.
Bobbio, A. Esposizione critica-esplicativa delle dottrine pedagogiche di Spencer. Turin 1887.
'Clergyman'. The answer to Spencer's theories of the evolution of ecclesiastical institutions. In his God in creation and in worship pt 1, 1887.
Drey, S. Spencer's theory of religion and morality. 1887.
Savage, M. J. Spencer: his influence on religion. Liverpool 1887.
Young, G. A. Whatever is, was. San Francisco 1887.
Barry, W. Agnosticism of Spencer. Dublin Rev 102 1888.
Collins, F. H. The ways of orthodox critics. Fortnightly Rev Feb 1888.
— An epitome of the synthetic philosophy. 1889.
Gaquoin, C. Die Grundlage der Spencerschen Philosophie. Berlin 1888.
Kindermann, C. Die Entwicklungslehre Spencers. 1888.
Lacy, G. In his Liberty and law, 1888.
Lilly, W. S. Spencer as a moralist. Fortnightly Rev March 1888.
— Our great philosopher. Contemporary Rev May 1889–Oct 1890.
Norström, V. Spencer's äsigt von sedligheten. Gothenburg 1888.
— Grunddragen af Spencers sedelära. Gothenburg 1889.
Roder, A. Der Weg zum Glück: auf Grund einer Darstellung der Entwickelungslehre Spencers. Leipzig 1888.
Watson, R. A. Gospels of yesterday: Drummond, Spencer. Glasgow 1888.
'Antaeus'. Imaginary conversation between Spencer and a poet. 1889.
Foley, G. C. Spencer's plea for religion. Church Rev 45 1889.
Laurens, C. L'évolution et Spencer. Lyons 1889.
Thompson, D. G. Spencer. New York 1889.
Tönnies, F. Spencer's sociologisches Werk. 1889.
Wright, G. F. Darwin on Spencer. Bibliotheca Sacra 46 1889.
Ball, W. P. In his Are the effects of use and disuse inherited?, 1890.
Gonsález, R. In his La idea racional, Mailand 1890.
Grosse, E. Spencer's Lehre von dem Unerkennbaren. Leipzig 1890.
MacMurray, F. M. Spencers Erziehungslehre. Gütersloh 1890.
Nöregaard, J. Studier over Spencer: Lotze og Grundtvig. Copenhagen 1890.
Spicker, G. Spencer's Ansicht über das Verhältnis der Religion zur Wissenschaft. Münster 1890.
Allara, G. Studio critico sopra I primi principii di Spencer. Casale 1891.

Janes, L. G. Philosophy of Spencer. Open Court 5 1891.
Ritchie, D. G. In his Principles of state interference, 1891.
Robertson, J. M. In his Modern humanists, 1891.
— In his Modern humanists reconsidered, 1927.
Skard, M. Spencers opdragelsestankar. Halmstad 1891.
Underwood, B. F. Spencer's Synthetic philosophy. New York 1891.
Wakeman, T. B. Latest phase of Spencer's philosophy. Open Court 5 1891.
Anzilotti, D. La scuola del diritto naturale nella filosofia giuridica contemporanea, a proposito del libro di Spencer Justice. 1892.
Cambareiu, J. La musique d'après Spencer. Revue Philosophique 34 1892.
Carus, P. Spencer on the ethics of Kant. Monist 2 1892.
— Kant and Spencer. Chicago 1899.
— Spencer's hedonism and Kant's ethics of duty. Monist 18 1908.
Hudson, W. H. Spencer. Arena 1892.
— Spencer and the synthetic philosophy. Popular Science Monthly May 1892.
— Introduction to the philosophy of Spencer. New York 1894.
— Spencer: the man and his work. Popular Science Monthly Feb 1897.
— Spencer. 1908, 1916.
Marret, R. R. The ethics of industrialism. Economic Rev 2 1892.
Parsons, F. In his Government and the law of equal freedom, 1892.
Saint-André, L. Simples notes sur la morale de Spencer. Paris 1892.
Shirreff, E. A. E. Moral training: Froebel and Spencer. 1892.
Weber, R. H. Die Philosophie von Spencer. Darmstadt 1892.
Weismann, A. Das Keimplasma. Jena 1892; tr 1893.
— Die Allmacht der Naturzüchtung. Leipzig 1893; tr Contemporary Rev Sept 1893.
— Neue Gedanken zur Vererbungsfrage. 1895.
Alexander, S. Spencer's Principles of ethics. Mind new ser 2–3 1893–4.
Barth, P. Kritik der Grundanschauungen der Sociologie Spencers. Vierteljahrsschrift für Wissenschaftliche Philosophie 17 1893.
Cattell, J. M. Survival of the fittest and sensation-areas. Mind new ser 2 1893.
George, H. A perplexed philosopher: being an examination of Spencer's various utterances on the land question. New York 1893.
Jones, J. L. Spencer as a teacher of ethics. [1893?].
Mironescu, A. Etica evoluţionistă şi etica creştină. Bucharest 1893.
Romanes, G. J. The Spencer-Weismann controversy. Contemporary Rev July 1893. Reply by Spencer, ibid.
Hartog, M. The Spencer-Weismann controversy. Ibid.
Wallace, A. R. The Spencer-Weismann controversy: are individually acquired characters inherited? Fortnightly Rev April–May 1893.
Arfridsson, H. D. Religion och vetenskap i deras ömsesidiga förhållande med särskild hänzyn till Spencers uppfattning af frågan. Lund 1894.
Benini, V. La morale e il diritto secondo Spencer. Rivista Italiana di Filosofia 1 1894.
Busse, K. Spencer's Philosophie der Geschichte. Leipzig 1894.
Chávez, E. A. Sintesis de los Principios de moral de Spencer. 1894.
Laws, T. C. The metaphysics of Spencer. Open Court 8 1894.
Masé-Dari, E. Le teorie darwiniana e spenceriana e l'economia politica. Archivio Giuridico 53 1894.
Roberty, E. de. Comte et Spencer. Paris 1894.
Ward, L. F. The political ethics of Spencer. Annals of Amer Acad 4 1894.
Delage, Y. In his La structure du protoplasma, Paris 1895.
Holländer, B. Spencer as a phrenologist. 1895.
Lucas, G. J. Agnosticism and religion: being an examination of Spencer's religion of the unknowable. 1895.
Bösch, J. M. Die Entwicklungstheoretische Idee socialer Gerechtigkeit. Zürich 1896.
Ferri, E. Socialisme et science positive. Paris 1896.
Morselli, E. La teoria d'evoluzione secondo Spencer. 1896.
Nicholson, J. A. The immorality of naturalism. 1896.
Sandeman, G. Problems of biology. 1896.
Tsimbouraky, A. I. Essai d'un plan de métaphysique. 1896; tr from Russian, 1896.
Vorländer, K. Spencer's Sociologie. Zeitschrift für Philosophie und philosophische Kritik 108 1896.
Zuccante, G. La dottrina della coscienza morale nello Spencer. Lonigo 1896.
— Condotta buona e condotta cattiva secondo lo Spencer. Rivista Italiana di Filosofia 12 1897.
Allen, G. Spencer and Darwin. Fortnightly Rev Feb 1897.
Campbell, G. D. Spencer and Salisbury on evolution. Nineteenth Century March–April 1897.
Carr, E. S. Philosophy of religion of Spencer. Bibliotheca Sacra 54 1897.
Didden, R. German appreciation of Spencer. Westminster Rev 148 1897.
Gaupp, O. Spencer. Stuttgart 1897.
Mikhailovsky, N. K. In his Qu'est-ce que le progrès? Paris 1897.
Pagnone, A. Le intuizioni morali e l'eredità nello Spencer. Turin 1897.
Vidari, G. Rosmini e Spencer. Milan 1897.
Allievo, G. La psicologia di Spencer. Turin 1898.
Ball, S. Spencer on industrial relations. International Jnl of Ethics 8 1898.
Mallock, W. H. Spencer in self-defence. Nineteenth Century Aug 1898. Reply by Spencer, Sept 1898.
Mercier, D. La philosophie de Spencer. Revue Néo-scolastique 17 1898.
Ardigò, R. La dottrina Spenceriana dell' inconoscibile. Rome 1899.
Dubois, J. Spencer et le principe de la morale. Paris 1899.
Ward, J. In his Naturalism and agnosticism, 1899.
Ferro, A. A. La critica della conoscenza in Kant e Spencer. Savona 1900.
Macpherson, H. C. Spencer: the man and his work 1900.
Nossig-Prochnik, F. Zur sociologischen Methodenlehre. Berne 1900.
Preston, S. T. Comparison of some views of Spencer and Kant. Mind new ser 9 1900. Replies by Spencer and Preston, 10 1901.
— Some physical conclusions in respect to space. Mind new ser 9 1900.
Salvadori, A. Spencer e l'opera sua. Florence 1900.
— La scienza economica e la teoria dell'evoluzione. Florence 1901.
— L'etica evoluzionista. Turin 1903.
Waite, C. B. Spencer and his critics. 1900.
Compayré, G. Spencer et l'éducation scientifique. 1901; tr 1907.
Halleux, J. L'évolutionnisme en morale: étude sur la philosophie de Spencer. 1901.
Roth, L. Schelling und Spencer. Berne 1901.
Kate, G. Spencer's theory of ethics in its evolutionary aspects. Philosophical Rev 11 1902.
Mellone, S. H. In his Leaders of religious thought in the nineteenth century, 1902.
Pekár, K. Darwin és Spencer. Budapest 1902.
Romano, M. Hobbes e Spencer. Avola 1902.

Borsdorf, A. T. W. In his Science of literature: on the literary theories of Taine and Spencer, 1903.
Nichols, J. B. Spencer's definition of evolution. Monist 13 1903.
Crespi, A. La religione nella filosofia di Spencer. Bologna 1904.
Dewey, J. The philosophical work of Spencer. Philosophical Rev 13 1904.
Duncan, D. An introduction to the philosophy of Spencer. 1904.
—— Life and letters of Spencer. 1908.
Fite, W. Spencer as a philosopher. Jnl of Philosophy 1 1904.
Giddings, F. H. The heart of Spencer's ethics. International Jnl of Ethics 14 1904. Reply by N. Wilde, Jnl of Philosophy 1 1904.
Höffding, H. Spencer. Tilskueren Jan 1904.
Mariupolsky, L. Die philosophische Begründung der Evolutionstheorie Spencers. Helsinki 1904.
Marvin, W. T. Appreciations of Spencer. Jnl of Philosophy 1 1904.
Royce, J. Spencer: an estimate and review. 1904.
Stoll, O. In his Grand survival, 1904.
Struve, H. Spencer i jego systemat filozofii syntetycznej. Warsaw 1904.
Swenson, D. F. The category of the unknowable. Jnl of Philosophy 2 1905.
Thouverez, E. Spencer. 1905.
Becker, F. C. The final edition of Spencer's First principles. Jnl of Philosophy 3 1906.
Papini, G. In his Il crepuscolo dei filosofi, Milan 1906.
Thomson, J. A. Spencer. 1906.
'Two'. Home life with Spencer. 1906.
Boutroux, E. Religion according to Spencer. 1907.
Laminne, J. La philosophie de l'inconnaissable. Brussels 1907.
Quesada, E. Spencer y sus doctrinas sociológicas. Buenos Aires 1907.
Sacerdote, S. La vita di Spencer ed I primi principii. Turin 1907.
Haeberlin, P. Spencers Grundlagen der Philosophie. Leizpig 1908.
Herbert, A. E. W. M. In his Voluntaryist creed, 1908.
Schwarze, C. Spencer. 1909.
Bourne, G. C. Spencer and animal evolution. 1910.
Groot, J. V. de. In his Denkers van onzen tijd, Amsterdam 1910.
Meldola, R. Evolution: Darwinian and Spencerian. 1910.
Shelton, H. S. Spencer as an ethical teacher. International Jnl of Ethics 20 1910.
—— Spencer's formula of evolution. Philosophical Rev 19 1910.
Tillett, A. W. Spencer refutes recent misrepresentations. 1910.
—— Spencer's synthetic philosophy: what it is all about. 1914.
—— Militancy versus civilization. 1915.
—— Spencer betrayed. 1939.
Chilesotti, O. L'evoluzione nella musica. Turin 1911.
Jordan, E. Spencer's unknowable. Philosophical Rev 20 1911. Replies by H. S. Shelton and Jordan 21 1912.
Morgan, C. L. Spencer's philosophy of science. 1913.
Stadler, A. Spencer. 1913.
Thompson, D'A. W. In his On Aristotle as a biologist, 1913.
Werner, E. T. C. Spencer. 1913.
Barker, E. Political thought in England from Spencer to the present day. 1915.
Herbert Spencer Lectures: decennial issue 1905–14. 10 pts Oxford 1916.
Elliot, H. S. R. Spencer. 1917.
Goddard, H. The coming bravery: a Spencerian dream. Jnl of Philosophy 15 1918.
Benso, M. G. L'educazione secondo Spencer. Biella 1919.
Bernard, L. L. Spencer's work in the light of his life. Monist 31 1921.
Bologna, V. I processi mentali nella psicologia di Spencer. Catania 1921.
Jaeger, M. Spencers Prinzipien der Ethik. Hamburg 1922.
Santayana, G. The unknowable. 1923.
Arenal de García Carrasco, C. La instrucción del Pueblo. Madrid 1929.
Guthmann, J. Entwicklung und Selbstentfaltung bei Spencer. Ochsenfurt 1930.
MacCarthy, D. In his Portraits, 1931.
Bradley, K. and E. Cooper ('Michael Field'). Spencer and Wilde. Cornhill Mag May 1932.
Kimball, E. P. In his Sociology and education, 1932.
Ramlow, L. Riehl und Spencer. Berlin 1933.
Rumney, J. Spencer's sociology. 1934.
Spencer. Dublin Rev 62 1936.
Asirvatham, E. Spencer's theory of social justice. New York 1936.
Hearnshaw, F. J. C. In his Some great political idealists of the Christian era, 1937.
—— Spencer and the individualists. In his Social and political ideas of some representative thinkers of the Victorian age, New York 1950.
Hill, T. W. The Spencer trust. TLS 6 Feb 1937.
Diaconide, E. Étude critique sur la sociologie de Spencer. Paris 1938.
Elwood, C. A. In his History of social philosophy, New York 1938.
Kral, J. La notion du consensus social chez Comte et la notion d'équilibre chez Spencer. Revue Internationale de Sociologie 47 1939.
Hook, S. In his Hero in history, New York 1943.
Schneider, H. W. The influence of Darwin and Spencer on American philosophical theology. JHI 6 1945.
Ensor, R. C. K. Some reflections on Spencer's doctrine that progress is differentiation. 1946.
d'Aurec, P. Du Bergson spencérien: ou Bergson de l'Essai. Archives de Philosophie 17 1948.
Lamar, L. B. Spencer and his father. SE 32 1953.
Harding, A. L. In his Origins of the natural law tradition, 1954.
Taylor, A. J. The originality of Spencer. SE 34 1955.
Burrow, J. W. Spencer, the philosopher of evolution. History Today 8 1958.
Munro, T. Evolution and progress in the arts: a reappraisal of Spencer's theory. Jnl of Aesthetics 18 1960.
—— Evolution in the arts and other theories of culture history. Cleveland 1964.
Simon, W. M. Spencer and the Social organism. JHI 21 1960.
Kardiner, A. and E. Preble. In their They studied man, Cleveland 1961.
Plochman, G. K. Darwin or Spencer? Science 130 1961.
Cockshut, A. O. J. Spencer, the scientific sage. In his Unbelievers: English agnostic thought 1840–90, 1964.
Burrow, J. W. In his Evolution and society, Cambridge 1966.

SIR JAMES FITZJAMES STEPHEN

1829–94

See col 1499, above.

SIR LESLIE STEPHEN

1832–1904

See col 1405, above.

JAMES HUTCHINSON STIRLING

1820–1909

§1

The secret of Hegel. 2 vols 1865, 1 vol Edinburgh [1897] (rev).
Hamilton: being the philosophy of perception. 1865.
De Quincey and Coleridge upon Kant. Fortnightly Rev Oct 1867.
Jerrold, Tennyson and Macaulay, with other critical essays. Edinburgh 1868.
Lectures on the philosophy of law. 1873.
Textbook to Kant, with commentary. 1881.
The community of property. Edinburgh 1885.
Of philosophy in the poets. Edinburgh 1885.
A brief estimate of Carlyle. In T. Carlyle, Counsels to a literary aspirant, 1886.
Philosophy and theology. Edinburgh 1890.
Darwinism: workmen and work. Edinburgh 1894.
What is thought? Edinburgh 1900.
The categories. Edinburgh 1903, 2 pts 1907.
Also works on biology.

§2

Stirling, A. H. Stirling: his life and work. 1911.

GEORGE FREDERICK STOUT

1860–1944

§1

Analytic psychology. 2 vols 1896.
A manual of psychology. 1899; ed C. A. Mace 1938 (5th rev and enlarged).
The groundwork of psychology. 1903, 1943 (3rd edn rev).
Studies in philosophy and psychology. 1930.
Mind and matter. Cambridge 1931. Partly rewritten in God and nature, below.
God and nature. Ed A. K. Stout, with memoir by J. A. Passmore. Cambridge 1952. With bibliography.

Articles

Many of Stout's articles are rptd in Analytic psychology *and* Studies in philosophy and psychology, *above.*
Is mind synonymous with consciousness? Proc Aristotelian Soc 1 1888.
The scope and method of psychology. Ibid.
Ladd on body and mind. Mind 13 1888.
Remarks on mental association. Ibid.
Herbart compared with English psychologists and Beneke. Mind 14 1889.
The psychological work of Herbart's disciples. Ibid.
Romanes's Mental evolution in man. Ibid.
The genesis of the cognition of physical reality. Mind 15 1890. Replies by J. Pikler and Stout, ibid; and J. M. Baldwin, 16 1891.
Is the distinction between feeling, cognition and conation valid as an ultimate distinction of the mental functions? (symposium). Proc Aristotelian Soc 1 1891.
Does our knowledge or perception of the ego admit of being analyzed? (symposium). Ibid.
A general analysis of presentations, with a view to their interaction. Proc Aristotelian Soc 2 1892.
Is the distinction between is and ought ultimate and irreducible? (symposium). Ibid.
Is human law the basis of morality or morality of human law? (symposium). Ibid.
The philosophy of Hodgson. Ibid.
The relation between thought and language (symposium). Proc Aristotelian Soc 2 1894.

Is the knowledge of space a priori? (symposium). Proc Aristototelian Soc 3 1895.
Relative suggestion. Ibid.
In what sense, if any, is it true that psychical states are extended? (symposium). Proc Aristotelian Soc 4 1896.
Reply to Angell's criticism of Analytic psychology. Philosophical Rev 7 1898.
Perception of change and duration. Mind new ser 9 1900. Replies by S. H. Hodgson and T. Loveday, ibid.
Alleged self-contradictions in the concept of relation: a criticism of Bradley. Proc Aristotelian Soc new ser 2 1902. Replies by H. W. Carr, S. H. Hodgson, J. Lindsay, ibid; by A. J. Finberg and Carr, 3 1903.
Error. In Personal idealism, ed H. Sturt 1903.
Primary and secondary qualities. Proc Aristotelian Soc new ser 4 1904.
Neo-Kantism as represented by Hicks. Proc Aristotelian Soc new ser 6 1906. Reply by G. D. Hicks, ibid.
Prichard's criticism of psychology. Mind new ser 16 1907.
The nature of mental activity (symposium). Proc Aristotelian Soc new ser 8 1908.
Are presentations mental or physical? Proc Aristotelian Soc new ser 9 1909.
Instinct and intelligence (symposium). Br Jnl of Psychology 3 1910.
Philosophy. In Votiva tabella, St Andrews 1911.
Can there be anything obscure or implicit in a mental state? (symposium). Proc Aristotelian Soc new ser 13 1913.
The status of sense data. Proc Aristotelian Soc new ser 14 1914.
Instinct and emotion (symposium). Proc Aristotelian Soc 15 1915.
Russell's theory of judgment. Ibid.
War and hatred. In The international crisis in its ethical and psychological aspects, ed E. M. Sidgwick 1915.
Do finite individuals possess a substantive or an adjectival mode of being? (symposium). Proc Aristotelian Soc new ser 18 1918.
Alexander's theory of sense perception. Mind new ser 31 1922. Replies by S. Alexander and J. E. Turner, 32 1923.
Are the characteristics of particular things universal or particular? (symposium). Proc Aristotelian Soc (suppl) 3 1923.
The nature of universals and propositions. Proc Br Acad 10 1923.
J. Ward on sense and thought. Mind new ser 35 1926. With M. Ward.
Ward as a psychologist. Monist 36 1926.
The nature of introspection (symposium). Proc Aristotelian Soc 7 (suppl) 1927.
Truth and falsity. Mind new ser 41 1932.
Self-evidence and matter of fact. Philosophy 9 1934.
Mechanical and teleological causation (symposium). Proc Aristotelian Soc (suppl) 14 1935.
Shand: a memoir. Proc Br Acad 22 1936.
Universals again. Proc Aristotelian Soc 15 (suppl) 1936.
Sorley. Mind new ser 45 1936.
Phenomenalism. Proc Aristotelian Soc new ser 39 1938.
Alexander: personal reminiscences. Mind new ser 49 1940.
The philosophy of Alexander. Ibid.
Things, predicates and relations. Australasian Jnl of Psychology & Philosophy 18 1940.
A criticism of Alexander's theory of mind and knowledge. Australasian Jnl of Psychology & Philosophy 22 1944.
Distributive unity as a category. Australasian Jnl of Psychology & Philosophy 25 1947.

§2

Marshall, H. R. Stout's algedonic theory. Mind new ser 7 1898.

Joseph, H. W. B. The psychological explanation of the development of the perception of external objects. Mind new ser 19 1910. Reply by Stout, 20 1911.
Hoernlé, R. F. A. Stout's theory of possibilities, truth and error. Mind new ser 40 1931.
Turner, J. E. Stout's realism: a criticism. Philosophy 7 1932.
Wisdom, J. In his Problems of mind and matter, 1934.
Knight, H. Stout on universals. Mind new ser 45 1936.
Passmore, J. A. Stout. Australasian Jnl of Psychology & Philosophy 22 1944.
Broad, C. D. Stout. Mind new ser 54 1945.
Mace, C. A. Stout. Proc Br Acad 31 1945.
— Stout. Br Jnl of Psychology 36 1946.
— Stout. Oxford 1948.
Knight, R. Stout. Br Jnl of Educational Psychology 16 1946.
O'Connor, D. J. Stout's theory of universals. Australasian Jnl of Psychology & Philosophy 27 1949.
Hughes, G. E. Stout's God and nature. Australasian Jnl of Psychology & Philosophy 31 1953.
Mabbott, J. D. Stout's God and nature. Mind new ser 62 1953.

ISAAC TAYLOR
1787–1865

Elements of thought. 1822.
Physical theory of another life. 1836.
The world of mind. 1857.
Logic in theology and other essays. 1859.
Ultimate civilization and other essays. 1860.
See col 1604, below.

THOMAS TAYLOR
1758–1835

Bibliographies

'J.J.W.' A brief notice of Taylor, with a complete list of his published works. 1831.
Axon, W. E. A. Taylor: a biographical and bibliographical sketch. 1890.
Balch, R. Taylor the Platonist: a list of his original works and translations. 1917.

§1

Proclus Diadochus: the philosophical and mathematical commentaries translated. 2 vols 1778, 1779.
A dissertation of the Eleusinian and Bacchic mysteries. Amsterdam [1790], 2 pts 1813; ed A. Wilder, New York 1875, 1891 (4th edn).
A vindication of the rights of brutes. 1792.
Plato's works. 5 vols 1804. Tr with F. Sydenham.
Miscellanies in prose and verse. 1805.
Collectanea: miscellanies from the European and Monthly Magazines. 1806.
Aristotle's works translated and illustrated. 10 vols 1806–12.
A dissertation on the philosophy of Aristotle. 1812.
Theoretic arithmetic. 1816.
Elements of a new arithmetical notation. 1823.
Also trns of many other classical works.

§2

Notopoulos, J. A. Shelley and Taylor. PMLA 51 1936.
Evans, F. B. Taylor: Platonist of the Romantic period. PMLA 55 1940.
Politella, J. 'Plato Taylor': a Greek born out of his time. Serif 3 1966.

WILLIAM THOMSON
1819–90

§1

An outline of the laws of thought. 1842, 1849 (enlarged), 1853 (enlarged).
Inaugural lecture, Yorkshire Philosophical Society. 1866.
The limits of philosophical inquiry. Edinburgh 1868.
Will and responsibility. [1875].
Word, work and will: collected papers. 1879.

§2

Thomson, E. H. Life and letters. 1919.

JOHN TULLOCH
1823–86

§1

Theism. 1855.
Rational theology and Christian philosophy in England in the seventeenth century. 2 vols Edinburgh 1872.
Pascal. 1878.
Modern theories in philosophy and religion. Edinburgh 1884.
Movements of religious thought in Britain during the nineteenth century. 1885.

§2

Oliphant, M. O. Memoir. 1888.
Also works on religion and education.

JOHN VEITCH
1829–94

§1

The Method, Meditations and selections from the Principles of Descartes translated. 1853, 1879 (6th edn with introd).
Speculative philosophy. 1864.
Memoir of Hamilton. Edinburgh 1869.
Lucretius and the atomic theory. Glasgow 1875.
The Tweed and other poems. Glasgow 1875.
The history and poetry of the Scottish border. Glasgow 1878.
Hamilton. Edinburgh 1882, 1883.
Institutes of logic. Edinburgh 1885.
The feeling for nature in Scottish poetry. 2 vols Edinburgh 1887.
Knowing and being: essays in philosophy, 1st series. Edinburgh 1889.
Merlin, and other poems. 1889.
Dualism and monism: essays in philosophy, 2nd series. Ed R. M. Wenley 1895.
Border essays [from Blackwood's Magazine]. 1896.

§2

Bryce, M. A. L. Memoir. 1896.

JOHN VENN
1834–1923

§1

The logic of chance, 1866, 1876 (rev and enlarged), 1888 (rev and enlarged), New York 1962.

On some of the characteristics of belief. 1870.
Symbolic logic. 1881, 1894 (rev).
The principles of empirical or inductive logic. 1889.
Also works on Cambridge.

§2

Francis, H. T. In memoriam John Venn. 1923.

WILLIAM WALLACE
1843–97

Logic of Hegel. 1874, Oxford 1894 (2nd edn rev as Prolegomena to the study of Hegel's philosophy and especially of his logic).
Epicureanism. 1880.
Kant. Edinburgh 1882.
Schopenhauer. 1890.
Hegel's Philosophy of mind, translated with introductory essays. 1894.
Lectures and essays on natural theology and ethics. Ed E. Caird, Oxford 1898.

JAMES WARD
1843–1925

Bibliographies

Titchener, E. B. and W. S. Foster. A list of the writings of Ward. Monist 36 1926.

§1

Naturalism and agnosticism. 2 vols 1899.
The realm of ends: or pluralism and theism. Cambridge 1911, 1912, 1920.
Heredity and memory. Cambridge 1913.
Psychological principles. Cambridge 1918, 1920.
A study of Kant. Cambridge 1922.
Psychology applied to education. Ed G. D. Hicks. Cambridge 1926.
Essays in philosophy. Ed W. R. Sorley and G. F. Stout, with memoir by O. Ward Campbell. Cambridge 1927.

Articles

An attempt to interpret Fechner's law. Mind 1 1876.
A general analysis of mind. Jnl of Speculative Philosophy 16 1882.
Objects and their interaction. Jnl of Speculative Philosophy 17 1883.
Psychological principles. Mind 8 1883, 12 1887.
Bradley's analysis of mind. Mind 12 1887.
The psychological theory of extension. Mind 14 1889.
The progress of philosophy. Mind 15 1890.
Mill's science of ethology. International Jnl of Ethics 1 1891.
Modern psychology: a reflexion. Mind new ser 2 1893.
Assimilation and association. Mind new ser 2–3 1893–4.
Bradley's Appearance and reality. Mind new ser 3 1894. Replies by Bradley and Ward, ibid.
On the definition of psychology. Br Jnl of Psychology 1 1904.
The present problems of general psychology. Philosophical Rev 13 1904.
Is black a sensation? Br Jnl of Psychology 1 1905.
Mechanism and morals. Hibbert Jnl 4 1906.
The nature of mental activity (symposium). Proc Aristotelian Soc new ser 8 1908.
Purpose and mechanism (discussion). Proc Aristotelian Soc new ser 12 1912.
Reconstruction: personality the final aim of social eugenics. Hibbert Jnl 15 1917.
Are the materials of sense affections of the mind? (symposium). Proc Aristotelian Soc new ser 17 1917.
Sense knowledge. Mind new ser 28–9 1919–20.
In the beginning.... Proc Aristotelian Soc new ser 20 1920.
Kant. Proc Br Acad 10 1923.
Bradley's doctrine of experience. Mind new ser 34 1925.
A theistic monadism. In Contemporary British philosophy, ed J. H. Muirhead, vol 2 1925. With partial bibliography.
The Christian ideas of faith and eternal life. Hibbert Jnl 24 1926.
An introduction to philosophy. Monist 36 1926.

§2

Bain, A. Ward on free will. Mind 5 1880.
—— Ward's psychology. Mind 11 1886.
—— Ward's Psychological principles. Mind 12 1887.
Jones, E. E. C. Ward's refutation of dualism. Mind new ser 9 1900.
Perry, R. B. Ward's philosophy of science. Jnl of Philosophy 1 1904.
—— Recent philosophical procedure with reference to science. Ibid. Reply by Ward, ibid.
Creighton, J. E. Perry's references to Ward's Naturalism and agnosticism. Ibid.
Muirhead, J. H. The last phase of Ward's philosophy. Mind new ser 22 1913.
Prasanna-Kumára, A. Second paper on Ward's psychology. 1919.
Hicks, G. D. Ward's Psychological principles. Mind new ser 30 1921.
—— Ward. Proc Aristotelian Soc new ser 25 1925.
—— The philosophy of Ward. Mind new ser 34 1925.
—— Ward and his philosophical approach to theism. Hibbert Jnl 24 1926.
—— The metaphysical systems of Bradley and Ward. Philosophy 1 1926.
Sorley, W. R. Ward. Hibbert Jnl 24 1926.
—— Ward's philosophy of religion. Monist 36 1926.
—— Ward. Proc Br Acad 12 1926.
Dowdall, H. C. The application of Ward's psychology to the legal problem of corporate identity. Monist 36 1926.
Laird, J. A. Ward's account of the ego. Ibid.
Lamprecht, S. P. Ward's critique of naturalism. Ibid.
Leroux, E. Ward's doctrine of experience. Ibid.
Stout, G. F. Ward as a psychologist. Ibid.
Turner, J. E. The ethical implications of Ward's philosophy. Ibid.
Ward, M. and G. F. Stout. Ward on sense and thought. Mind new ser 35 1926.
Oldenburger, T. Panpsychic philosophy of Ward. Grand Rapids Michigan 1934.
Murray, A. H. The philosophy of Ward. Cambridge 1937.
Bertocci, P. A. In his Empirical argument for God in late British thought, Cambridge Mass 1939.
De Marneffe, J. In his La preuve de l'absolu chez Bradley, Paris 1961.

WILLIAM GEORGE WARD
1812–82

§1

Can experience prove the uniformity of nature? [1872].
Essays on the philosophy of theism. Ed W. Ward 2 vols 1884.

§2

Ward, W. P. W. G. Ward and the Oxford movement. 1889.
—— W. G. Ward and the Catholic revival. 1893.

Ward, M. W. G. Ward and W. P. Ward. Dublin Rev 198 1936.
See col 1634, below.

RICHARD WHATELY
1787–1863

§1

Elements of logic. 1826, 1832 (4th edn rev), 1836 (6th edn rev), 1840 (rev), 1844 (rev), 1848 (rev).
Elements of rhetoric. 1828, 1836 (5th edn rev), 1846 (7th edn rev); ed D. Ehninger, Carbondale 1963.
Easy lessons on reasoning. 1843.
Address to the members of the Manchester Athenaeum. In The importance of literature to men of business, 1852.
Paley's Works. 1859. A lecture.
Miscellaneous lectures and reviews. 1861.

§2

Bentham, G. Outline of a new system of logic, with a critical examination of Whately's Elements. 1827.
Mill, J. S. Whately's Elements of logic. Westminster Rev 9 1828.
Whately, E. J. Life and correspondence. 2 vols 1866, 1875 (rev and enlarged).
See col 1307, above.

WILLIAM WHEWELL
1794–1866

§1

Boadicea: a poem. Cambridge 1820.
The history of the inductive sciences. 3 vols 1837, 1847 (rev, with suppl, 1857), 1857 (with addns), New York 1858; tr German, 1840–1.
On the foundation of morals. Cambridge [1838?].
The philosophy of the inductive sciences founded on their history. 2 vols 1840, 1847 (enlarged), 3 vols 1858 (pt 1 as History of scientific ideas; pt 2 enlarged as Novum organon renovatum).
Two introductory lectures to two courses of lectures on moral philosophy. Cambridge 1841.
On the fundamental antithesis of philosophy. Cambridge 1844.
A letter to Herschel. Cambridge [1844].
The elements of morality, including polity. 2 vols 1845, 1854 (enlarged), 1864 (4th edn enlarged).
Of a liberal education in general. 3 pts 1845–52.
Lectures on systematic morality. 1846.
Of induction, with especial reference to Mill's System of logic. 1849.
Lectures on the history of moral philosophy in England. 1852, Cambridge 1862 (enlarged).
Of the plurality of worlds. 1853, 1854.
On the influence of the history of science upon intellectual education. In Royal Institute of Gt Britain lectures on education, 1855.
On the philosophy of discovery. 1860.
Also works on science, mathematics and education.

§2

Mill, J. S. In his Dissertations and discussions vol 2, 1859.
Stirling, J. H. Whewell and Hegel. In his Lectures on the philosophy of law, 1873.
Todhunter, I. Whewell: an account of his writings with selections from his correspondence. 1876.
Douglas, J. M. Life and selections from the correspondence. 1882.
Blanché, R. Le rationalisme de Whewell. Paris 1935.
Seward, G. C. Die theoretische Philosophie Whewells und der kantische Einfluss. Tübingen 1938.
Ducasse, C. J. Whewell's philosophy of scientific discovery. Philosophical Rev 60 1951.
Wexler, P. J. The great nomenclator: Whewell's contributions to scientific terminology. N & Q Jan 1961.

JOHN WILSON, 'CHRISTOPHER NORTH'
1785–1854

See col 1308, above.

J. M. R.

X. RELIGION

A. THE LIBERAL THEOLOGIANS AND THE EVANGELICALS

(1) THE GROWTH OF LIBERAL THEOLOGY

General Studies

Taylor, J. J. A retrospect of the religious life of England. 1845, 1876. With an introductory chapter on recent developments by J. Martineau and a preface by H. E. Osler.
Lecky, W. E. H. History of the rise and influence of the spirit of rationalism in Europe. 2 vols 1865, 1865, [1869], 1910; tr Dutch, 1894; German, 1874.
Stephen, L. History of English thought in the eighteenth century. 2 vols 1876, 1881 (for 1880), 1902, 1927.
Martineau, H. Autobiography. 3 vols 1877, 1877, 1877.
Stoughton, J. Religion in England from 1800 to 1850: a history, with a postscript on subsequent events. 2 vols 1884.
Tulloch, J. Movements of religious thought in Britain during the nineteenth century. 1885.
Davidson, R. T. and W. Benham. Life of Archbishop Tait. 2 vols 1891.
Overton, J. H. The English Church in the nineteenth century 1800–33. 1894.
Hunt, J. Religious thought in England in the nineteenth century. 1896.
White, A. D. A history of the warfare of science with theology. 2 vols 1896, 1955.
Benn, A. W. The history of English rationalism in the nineteenth century. 2 vols 1906.
Robertson, J. M. A short history of freethought, ancient and modern. 1899, 2 vols 1906 (rewritten and greatly enlarged), 1915 (rev and expanded), 1936 (as A history of freethought).

Tuckwell, W. Pre-Tractarian Oxford: a reminiscence of the Oriel 'Noetics'. 1909.
Cornish, F. W. W. The English Church in the nineteenth century. 2 vols 1910.
Storr, V. F. The development of English theology in the nineteenth century 1800–60. 1913.
Mathieson, W. L. Church and reform in Scotland: a history from 1797 to 1843. Glasgow 1916.
Raven, C. E. Christian Socialism 1848–54. 1920.
Webb, C. C. J. A century of Anglican theology, and other lectures. 1923.
—— A study of religious thought in England from 1350. Oxford 1933.
Stewart, H. L. Modernism, past and present. 1932.
The Dean of Windsor [A. V. Baillie] and H. Bolitho. A Victorian dean: a memoir of Arthur Stanley, Dean of Westminster, with many new and unpublished letters. 1930.
Eden, G. R. and F. C. Macdonald (ed). Lightfoot of Durham: memories and appreciations. Cambridge 1932.
West, A. G. B. Memories of Brooke Foss Westcott. Cambridge 1936.
Jenkins, C. Frederick Denison Maurice and the New Reformation. 1938.
Sanders, C. R. Coleridge and the Broad Church Movement: studies in S. T. Coleridge, Dr Arnold of Rugby, J. C. Hare, Thomas Carlyle and F. D. Maurice. Durham NC 1942.
Higham, F. Frederick Denison Maurice. 1947.
Elliott-Binns, L. E. The development of English theology in the later nineteenth century. 1952.
—— English thought 1860–1900: the theological aspect. 1956.
Cowherd, R. G. The politics of English Dissent: the religious aspects of liberal and humanitarian reform movements from 1815 to 1848. New York 1956. On the Nonconformists.
Matthews, W. R. The religious philosophy of Dean Mansel. Oxford 1956.
Allchin, A. M. The silent revolution: Anglican religious communities 1845–1900. 1958.
Davies, G. C. B. The first Evangelical Bishop: some aspects of the life of Henry Ryder. 1958. A pamphlet.
Hennell, M. M. John Venn and the Clapham Sect. 1958.
Latourette, K. S. Christianity in a revolutionary age: a history of Christianity in the nineteenth and twentieth centuries. 5 vols New York 1958–, London 1959–63.
Sykes, J. The Quakers: a new look at their place in society. 1958. On the relationship between Quakerism and Evangelicism in the 19th century.
Brose, O. J. Church and Parliament: the reshaping of the Church of England 1828–1860. Stanford 1959.
Bullock, F. W. B. Evangelical conversion in Great Britain 1696–1845. St Leonard's-on-Sea 1959.
Cockshut, A. O. J. Anglican attitudes: a study of Victorian religious controversies. London 1959.
—— The unbelievers: English agnostic thought 1840–1890. 1964.
Carpenter, J. A. Gore: a study in Liberal Catholic thought. 1960.
Escott, H. A history of Scottish Congregationalism. Glasgow 1960.
Fox, A. Dean Inge. [1960].
Mechie, S. The Church and Scottish social development 1780–1870. Oxford 1960.
Routley, E. English religious dissent. Cambridge 1960.
Boulger, J. D. Coleridge as religious thinker. New Haven 1961.
Brandreth, H. R. T. Episcopi vagantes and the Anglican Church. 1961.
Brown, F. K. Fathers of the Victorians: the age of Wilberforce. Cambridge 1961. A study of William Wilberforce and his evangelical associates.
Chadwick, H. The vindication of Christianity in [Brooke Foss] Westcott's thought. 1961.
Davies, H. Worship and theology in England. Vol 3: From Watts to Wesley 1690–1850; vol 4: From Newman to Martineau 1850–1900. Princeton 1961.
Elliott-Binns, L. E. Religion in the Victorian era. 1964.
Orr, J. E. The light of the nations: evangelical renewal and advance in the nineteenth century. Exeter [1965].
Chadwick, O. The Victorian Church, part 1. 1966.

Principal Writers 1800–35

THOMAS ARNOLD

1795–1842

Sermons. 3 vols 1829–34; rev Mrs W. E. Forster 6 vols 1878.
Principles of Church reform. 1833 (3 edns); Postscript to Principles of Church reform, 1833 (in 4th edn).
Life and correspondence. Ed A. P. Stanley 2 vols 1844 (3 edns) etc, 1 vol 1901, 1903 (abridged); tr German, 1847.
Miscellaneous works. Ed A. P. Stanley 1845. *See col 1461, above.*

ROBERT ASPLAND

1782–1845

Causes of the slow progress of Christian truth. [1825].
Memoir of the life, works and correspondence. 1850.

THOMAS BELSHAM

1750–1829

A summary view of the evidence and practical importance of the Christian revelation. 1807.

JEREMY BENTHAM

1748–1832

Church of Englandism and its catechism examined. 1818.

WILLIAM ARCHER BUTLER

1814?–48

Letters on the development of Christian doctrine, in reply to Mr Newman's Essay [i.e. An Essay on the development of Christian doctrine]. Ed T. Woodward, Dublin 1850.
Sermons, doctrinal and practical: first series. Ed (with a memoir) T. Woodward, Dublin 1849; Dublin 1852; Cambridge 1855. Second series, ed J. A. Jeremie, Cambridge 1855.

THOMAS CHALMERS

1780–1847

A series of discourses on the Christian revelation, viewed in connection with the modern astronomy. Glasgow 1817, 1817, Glasgow and Edinburgh 1818, Andover Mass 1818 (with six sermons occasioned by the death of the Princess Charlotte of Wales), Glasgow 1822, 1830, Glasgow and London 1862, London [1870] (as Christian revelation viewed in connexion with modern astronomy), Edinburgh and London 1871 (Discourses on the Christian Revelation viewed in connexion with the modern astronomy), Glasgow [*c.* 1840] (as vol 7 of The works, with six additional discourses, entitled Astronomical discourses). Commonly known as Astronomical discourses.

The application of Christianity to the commercial and ordinary affairs of life, in a series of discourses. Glasgow 1820, 1820, 1820, 1820, Glasgow [*c.* 1840] (as vol 6 of The works, with seven additional discourses, entitled Commercial discourses), Edinburgh 1862 (as Discourses on the application of Christianity to the commercial and ordinary affairs of life); tr French, 1824. Commonly known as Commercial discourses.

The Bridgewater treatises on the power, wisdom and goodness of God as manifested in the Creation. Treatise 1: On the adaptation of external nature to the moral and intellectual constitution of man. 2 vols 1833, 1833, Glasgow [*c.* 1836] (as vols 1 & 2 of The works, entitled On natural theology); Edinburgh 1857 (as vol 5 of The select works).

Institutes of theology, with prelections on Hill's lectures in divinity etc. Ed W. Hanna 2 vols Edinburgh 1849, 1856.

Congregational sermons. Glasgow [*c.* 1840]. Vols 8, 9, 10 of The works, containing the Tron Church Sermons of 1819, with many additional sermons pbd for the first time.

SAMUEL TAYLOR COLERIDGE
1772–1834

Confessions of an enquiring spirit. Ed H. N. Coleridge 1840 (from ms).

Notes on English divines. Ed D. Coleridge 2 vols 1853.
See col 211, above.

JOHN DAVISON
1777–1834

Discourse on prophecy. 1824, 1825, 1839.

An inquiry into the origin and intent of primitive sacrifice. 1825.

THOMAS ERSKINE
1788–1870

Remarks on the internal evidence for the truth of revealed religion. 1820, 1821, 1821, 1821, 1823, 1823, 1827, 1829, 1878.

An essay on faith. 1822, 1822, 1823, 1825, 1829.

The unconditional freeness of the Gospel. 1828, 1828, 1879.

The brazen serpent: or life coming through death. 1831, 1879.

The doctrine of election. 1837, 1878.

The spiritual order and other papers. 1871.

Letters. Ed W. Hanna 2 vols 1877, 1878.

JOHN FOSTER
1770–1843

Essays. 2 vols 1805, 1806, 1 vol 1830.

Contributions to the Eclectic Review. 2 vols 1844.

Life and correspondence. Ed J. E. Ryland 2 vols 1846.
See also col 1281, above.

WILLIAM JOHNSON FOX
1786–1864

Christ and Christianity. 2 vols 1831.

On the religious ideas. 1849, 1907; tr French, 1877.

AUGUSTUS WILLIAM HARE
1792–1834
and
JULIUS CHARLES HARE
1795–1855

Guesses at truth, by two brothers. 1827; ser 2, 1848.
See also col 1282, above.

REGINALD HEBER
1783–1826

The personality and office of the Christian comforter. 1816.

Life of Bishop Jeremy Taylor. 1822 (in Whole works of Jeremy Taylor), 1828 (in Whole works), 1828 (separately).

Poetical works. 1841 etc.
See also col 382, above.

JOHN PYE SMITH
1774–1851

On the relation between the Holy Scriptures and some parts of geological science. 1839, 1840 (enlarged), 1843, 1848, 1852, 1852.

SYDNEY SMITH
1771–1845

Sermons preached at St Paul's. 1846.
See also col 1304, above, and A. Chevrillon, Smith et la renaissance des idées libérales en Angleterre, Paris 1894.

ISAAC TAYLOR
1787–1865

The natural history of enthusiasm. 1829 (anon), 1830 (anon), 1834 (anon), 1868.

The restoration of belief. [1852] (anon), 1853 (anon), 1864 (rev and enlarged).

The spirit of Hebrew poetry. 1861.

RICHARD WHATELY
1787–1863

Historic doubts relative to Napoleon Buonaparte. 1819 (anon), 1821, 1831, Cambridge Mass 1832, 1849, 1853, 1859, 1886, New York [1895].

The use and abuse of party-feeling in matters of religion. 1822, 1859 (enlarged).

Letters on the Church, by an Episcopalian. 1826.

The Kingdom of Christ delineated. 1841, 1842.

Life and correspondence. Ed E. J. Whately 2 vols 1866, 1868, 1875 (enlarged).
See also col 1307, above.

JOSEPH BLANCO WHITE,
formerly
JOSÉ MARIA BLANCO
1775–1841

Night and death. 1928. A sonnet.

Second travels of an Irish gentleman in search of a religion. 2 vols Dublin 1833 (anon). In answer to T. Moore, Travels of an Irish gentleman. 1833.

The life of, written by himself. Ed J. H. Thom 3 vols 1845.

Principal Writers, 1835–70

GEORGE DOUGLAS CAMPBELL, 8th DUKE OF ARGYLL
1823–1900

The reign of law. 1867 etc.
See also col 1512, above.

MATTHEW ARNOLD
1822–88

St Paul and Protestantism. 1870; ed R. H. Super, Ann Arbor 1968.
Literature and dogma. 1873 (3 edns); ed Super (with above); tr French, 1876.
God and the Bible. 1875, 1884.
Last essays on Church and religion. 1877.
See also col 465, above.

CHARLES BEARD
1827–88

Port Royal. 2 vols 1861, 1873.
The Reformation of the sixteenth century in its relation to modern thought and knowledge. 1883, 1927.

CHARLES BRAY
1811–84

The philosophy of necessity. 2 vols 1841, 1863 (rev), 1889 (rev and abridged).
Christianity viewed in the light of our present knowledge. [1876].
Phases of opinion and experience during a long life. [1884].

JOHN McLEOD CAMPBELL
1800–72

The nature of the Atonement. 1856, 1867 (with introd and notes), 1869 (for 1868), 1873.
Memorials. Ed D. Campbell. 2 vols 1877.

WALTER RICHARD CASSELS
1826–1907

Supernatural religion. 3 vols 1874–7 (anon), 1874–7, 2 vols 1874, 1874, 1875 (rev), 3 vols 1879, 1902, 1905.

ROBERT CHAMBERS
1802–71

Vestiges of the natural history of Creation. 1844 (anon), 1844 (anon), 1845 (anon), 1845 (anon), 1846 (anon), 1847 (anon), 1850 (anon), 1851 (anon), 1853 (anon), 1860 (anon); ed A. Ireland 1884; ed H. Morley 1887; tr German, 1851.
See col 1372, above.

ARTHUR HUGH CLOUGH
1819–61

Letters and remains. [Ed Mrs Clough] 1865 (priv ptd).
See also col 461, above.

JOHN WILLIAM COLENSO
1814–83

The Pentateuch and Book of Joshua critically examined. 7 pts 1862–79, 1862–4 (rev); pt 1, 1863 (rev); [1863] (extracts), 5 pts 1865, 1865 (preface and part of pt 5 only), 3 pts 1884, 1885.

SAMUEL COX
1826–93

Salvator mundi. 1877, 1879.

ROBERT WILLIAM DALE
1829–95

The Atonement. 1875, 1884.
The living Christ and the Four Gospels. 1890, 1890, 1891, 2 vols 1903.
A. W. W. Dale, Life of Dale. 1898.

SAMUEL DAVIDSON
1806–98

The text of the Old Testament considered. 1856.
Autobiography and diary, with an account of the Davidson controversy of 1857.

'GEORGE ELIOT'
1819–80

The life of Jesus critically examined, by D. F. Strauss. 3 vols 1846, 1 vol 1892. Anon trn.
The essence of Christianity, by Ludwig Feuerbach, translated by Marian Evans. 1854.
See col 899, above.

Essays and reviews [by F. Temple, Rowland Williams, Baden Powell, H. B. Wilson, C. W. Goodwin, Mark Pattison, B. Jowett]. 1860, 1861 (3 edns), 1862, 1862, 1865; ed F. H. Hedge, New York 1874.

ALEXANDER EWING
1814–73

Present-day papers on prominent questions in theology. [The Papers, originated and ed A. Ewing, were begun in Nov 1869 and the first 3 sers were pbd monthly until May 1871. The 4th ser was by F. Myers and ed H. Whitehead.] 4 vols 1870–4.
Revelation considered as light: a series of discourses. 1873.

FREDERIC WILLIAM FARRAR
1831–1903

The life of Christ. 1874, 2 vols 1874, [1876–8] (illustr), [1878] (illustr), [1880], 1881, 5 vols 1883, 1886, [1891?] (illustr), 1 vol [1887–89], [1890–1] (illustr), 1894 (illustr), 1894, 1896, 1898; ed W. Lefroy 1903; ed A. F. W. Ingram 1906; 1907, 1913, 1963 (reissue of edn of 1894); tr French, 1888.
Eternal hope. 1878, 1892 (with new preface).
See also col 1052, above.

THOMAS HILL GREEN
1836–82

The witness of God, and faith: two lay sermons. 1883.
See also col 1533, above.

WILLIAM RATHBONE GREG

1809–81

The creed of Christendom. 1851, 1863, 1874 (for 1873) (with new introd), 2 vols 1883 (with new introd); ed W. R. W. Sullivan 1905.
Enigmas of life. 1872, 1874 (with postscript), 1883, 1891 (with prefatory memoir).

RENN DICKSON HAMPDEN

1793–1868

The scholastic philosophy in its relation to Christian theology. 1833. *See* A concise history of the Hampden controversy, with documents, by H. Christmas, 1848.

EDWIN HATCH

1835–89

The organization of the early Christian churches. 1881, 1882, 1888.
The influence of Greek ideas and usages upon the Christian Church. 1890.

CHARLES CHRISTIAN HENNELL

1809–50

An inquiry concerning the origin of Christianity. 1838, 1841, 1870 (enlarged); tr German, 1840.

JAMES HINTON

1822–75

The mystery of pain. 1866 (anon), 1874, 1879, [1909]; ed R. H. Hutton [1911].

FENTON JOHN ANTHONY HORT

1828–92

The way, the truth, the life: Hulsean lectures. 1871; ed B. F. Westcott 1893, 1897.
Judaistic Christianity. 1894.
Life and letters. Ed A. F. Hort 2 vols 1896.
The Christian Ecclesia. Ed J. O. F. Murray 1897.

RICHARD HOLT HUTTON

1826–97

Essays theological and literary. 2 vols 1871, 1877 (for 1876) (rev and enlarged), 1888 (Theological essays only), 1895 (Theological essays only).
Essays on some of the modern guides of English thought in matters of faith. 1887.
Aspects of religious and scientific thought. 1899.
See also col 1389, above.

BENJAMIN JOWETT

1817–93

Epistles of St Paul to Thessalonians, Galatians and Romans: translation and commentary with essays and dissertations. 2 vols 1855, 1859; ed L. Campbell 2 vols 1894 (the trn and commentary, 'edited and condensed').

CHARLES KINGSLEY

1819–75

The good news of God: sermons. 1859.
What, then, does Dr Newman mean? 1864 (3 edns); ed W. Ward, Oxford 1913 (in J. H. Newman, Apologia pro vita sua).
Letters and memories of his life, ed by his wife. 2 vols 1877 (3 edns), 1 vol 1879 (for 1878) (abridged), 1883 (abridged); tr French, [c. 1905?].
See also col 935, above.

JOSEPH BARBER LIGHTFOOT

1828–89

Essays on the work entitled Supernatural religion. 1889.
Dissertations on the Apostolic Age. 1892. From his edns of St Paul's Epistles, 1865–75.

ROBERT WILLIAM MACKAY

1803–82

The progress of the intellect, as exemplified in the religious development of the Greeks and Hebrews. 2 vols 1850. *See* article by 'George Eliot', Westminster Rev 54 1851.
The Tübingen School and its antecedents. 1863.

HENRY LONGUEVILLE MANSEL

1820–71

The limits of religious thought examined. 1858, 1858, 1859, 1859, 1867; tr Danish, 1888.
See also col 1546, above.

JAMES MARTINEAU

1805–1900

The rationale of religious inquiry. 1836, 1844, 1845, [1908] (as What is Christianity?).
Endeavours after the Christian life. 2 sers 1843–7, 1 vol 1867, 1874, 1900, [1907]; ed J. E. Carpenter [1907], 1907, [1907].
Types of ethical theory. 2 vols Oxford 1885, 1886, 1889, 1891 (enlarged).
A study of religion. 2 vols 1888, 1889 (rev).
The seat of authority in religion. 1890.
Essays, reviews and addresses. 4 vols 1890–1.
See J. Drummond and C. B. Upton, Life and letters, 2 vols 1902; and J. Estlin Carpenter, Martineau: theologian and teacher, 1905.
See col 1547, above.

JOHN FREDERICK DENISON MAURICE

1805–72

The Kingdom of Christ, by a clergyman of the Church of England. [1837–8], 3 vols 1838, 2 vols 1842, 1883; [1906] (EL); ed A. R. Vidler 2 vols 1958, [1960].
Moral and metaphysical philosophy. 1845, 4 vols 1850–7, 2 vols 1871–2.
The religions of the world. 1847, 1848 (rev).
Theological essays. Cambridge 1853, 1853 (enlarged), 1854 (concluding essay and preface only), London 1871, 1957.
The doctrine of sacrifice. 1854.
The epistles of St John: lectures on Christian ethics. 1857.
The conscience: lectures on casuistry. 1868, 1872.
The friendship of books and other lectures. Ed T. Hughes 1874.

Life of Maurice, chiefly told in his own letters. Ed J. F. Maurice 2 vols 1884.
See col 1392, above.

JOHN STUART MILL
1806–73

Nature, the utility of religion and theism [3 essays on religion, with introductory notice by H. Taylor]. 1874, 1874, 1904.
See col 1552, above.

HUGH MILLER
1802–56

Footprints of the Creator. 1849 (anon); ed L. F. F. Miller, Edinburgh 1861 (with memoir).
The testimony of the rocks. Edingburgh 1857.

FREDERIC MYERS
1811–51

Catholic thoughts on the Church of Christ and the Church of England. 1834–41 (anon) (priv ptd), 1874; ed F. W. H. Myers 1883.
Catholic thoughts on the Bible and theology. 1841–8 (anon) (priv ptd), 1874.

FRANCIS WILLIAM NEWMAN
1805–97

The soul: her sorrows and her aspirations. 1849, 1852, 1905 (with memoir by C. B. Upton).
Phases of faith. 1850, 1907.
Memoir and letters. Ed I. G. Sieveking 1909.
See col 543, above.

MARK PATTISON
1813–84

Tendencies of religious thought in England 1688–1750. 1860 (in Essays and reviews).
Sermons. 1885.
Memoirs. Ed Mrs Pattison 1885.
Essays, collected by H. Nettleship. 2 vols Oxford 1889, London [1908] (containing 16 of the original 21 essays).
See col 1397, above.

BADEN POWELL
1796–1860

Tradition unveiled. 1839; Supplement, 1840.
Christianity without Judaism. 1857, 1866.

FREDERICK WILLIAM ROBERTSON
1816–53

Sermons preached at Trinity Chapel, Brighton. Ed S. E. Robertson 4 sers 1855–63, 1856–7 (sers 1–3), 1857 (sers 1–2), 1872 (4 sers); 5 sers 5 vols 1874–90, 1 vol 1898; 1904 (10 sermons); 1906 (12 sermons).
Lectures and addresses on literary and social topics. 1858; ed S. A. Brooke 1876 (enlarged).
Expository lectures on St Paul's Epistles to the Corinthians. 1859.
Life and letters, by S. A. Brooke, 2 vols 1865, 1866; 1 vol 1868, 1872, 1872, 2 vols 1873; tr German, 1888.

SIR JOHN ROBERT SEELEY
1834–95

Ecce homo. 1866 (for 1865) (anon), 1866, Boston 1866 etc; ed O. Lodge [1908]; ed J. E. Odgers 1910.
Natural religion, by the author of Ecce homo. 1882, 1891, 1895.
See also col 1495, below.

HENRY SIDGWICK
1838–1900

The ethics of conformity and subscription. 1870, 1898 (in Practical ethics).

WILLIAM HENRY SMITH
1808–72

Thorndale: or the conflict of opinions. Edinburgh 1857, 1858.
Gravenhurst: or thoughts on good and evil. 1862, 1875 (with memoir by his widow).

ARTHUR PENRHYN STANLEY
1815–81

Sermons and essays on the apostolical age. Oxford 1847, 1874, [1890].
Essays, chiefly on questions of Church and State. 1870, 1884.
Christian institutions. 1881, 1882, 1884.
See G. G. Bradley, Recollections, 1883; R. E. Prothero, Life and correspondence, 1893.

JOHN STERLING
1806–44

Essays and tales. Ed J. C. Hare 2 vols 1848. With memoir.
Twelve letters [to William Coningham]. Ed W. Coningham 1851, 1872.
See T. Carlyle, Life of Sterling, 1851, 1852; ed W. H. White, Oxford 1907 (WC).
See col 1306, above.

CONNOP THIRLWALL
1797–1875

Remains, literary and theological. Ed J. J. S. Perowne 3 vols 1877–8.
Letters, literary and theological. Ed J. J. S. Perowne and L. Stokes 1881, 1882.
See J. C. Thirlwall, Connop Thirlwall, 1936.
See col 1503, above.

JOHN HAMILTON THOM
1808–94

Laws of life after the mind of Christ. 2 sers 1883–6, 1901 (2nd ser only).
A spiritual faith, with memoir by J. Martineau. 1895, 1908 (abridged).

ROBERT ALFRED VAUGHAN
1823–57

Hours with the mystics. 2 vols 1856; ed R. Vaughan 2 vols 1860; ed W. Vaughan 2 vols [1880].
See col 1404, above.

BROOKE FOSS WESTCOTT
1825–1901

A general survey of the history of the canon of the New Testament. 1855, 1866, 1870, 1875 (with new preface), 1881, 1889, 1896.
An introduction to the study of the Gospels. 1860, 1867, 1872.
A general view of the history of the English Bible. 1868, 1872, 1905 (rev W. A. Wright).
Social aspects of Christianity. 1887.
Essays in the history of religious thought in the West. 1891.
Life and letters. Ed A. Westcott 2 vols 1903, 1 vol 1905 (abridged).

Principal Writers 1870–1900

EDWIN ABBOTT ABBOTT
1838–1928

Philochristus. 1878 (anon), 1916 (anon).
The kernel and the husk. 1886 (anon).
The spirit of the waters. 1897.

ISRAEL ABRAHAMS
1858–1928

Aspects of Judaism. 1895. With C. G. Montefiore.
Studies in Pharisaism and the Gospels. 2 sers Cambridge 1917–24.

STOPFORD AUGUSTUS BROOKE
1832–1916

Theology in the English poets. 1874, 1874, [1910] (EL).
See col 1422, above.

EDWARD CAIRD
1835–1908

The evolution of religion. 2 vols Glasgow 1893, 1894, 1899.
The evolution of theology in the Greek philosophers. 2 vols Glasgow 1904, 1923.
See A. W. Benn, History of English rationalism in the nineteenth century, 1906, and col 1526, above.

JOHN CAIRD
1820–98

An introduction to the philosophy of religion. Glasgow 1880.
Fundamental ideas of Christianity, with memoir by Edward Caird. 2 vols Glasgow 1899.

REGINALD JOHN CAMPBELL
1867–1956

A faith for to-day. 1900.
The new theology. 1907, [1909], [1909] (rev and enlarged, with speeches by Hall Caine and Bernard Shaw).
A spiritual pilgrimage. 1916.

JOSEPH ESTLIN CARPENTER
1844–1928

The first three Gospels. 1890, 1904; tr Dutch, [1892].
The Bible in the nineteenth century. 1903.
Studies in theology. 1903. With P. H. Wicksteed.

ROBERT HENRY CHARLES
1855–1931

A critical history of the doctrine of a future life. 1899, 1913 (rev and enlarged).

THOMAS KELLY CHEYNE
1841–1915

The origin and contents of the Psalter. 1891.
Founders of Old Testament criticism. 1893.
Encyclopaedia biblica. 4 vols 1899–1903, 1914. Joint editor with J. S. Black.

ANDREW BRUCE DAVIDSON
1831–1902

Biblical and literary essays. Ed J. A. Paterson 1902.

JOHN LLEWELYN DAVIES
1826–1916

Theology and morality. 1873.
Order and growth. 1891.

JAMES DENNEY
1856–1917

Studies in theology. 1894.
Jesus and the Gospel. 1908, 1909, 1913.

SAMUEL ROLLES DRIVER
1846–1914

An introduction to the literature of the Old Testament. 1891, 1894 (rev and with an appendix), 1897 (enlarged), 1909 (rev), 1913 (rev); tr German, 1896.

HENRY DRUMMOND
1851–97

Natural law in the spiritual world. 1883, 1902.
The Lowell lectures on the ascent of man. 1894.

JAMES DRUMMOND
1835–1918

Via, veritas, vita. 1894.

ANDREW MARTIN FAIRBAIRN
1838–1912

The place of Christ in modern theology. 1893. *See* W. B. Selbie, Life of Fairbairn, 1914.

PETER TAYLOR FORSYTH
1848–1927

Religion in recent art. 1889, 1901.
The principle of authority. [1912].

PERCY GARDNER

1846–1937

Exploratio evangelica. 1899, 1907.
Evolution in Christian doctrine. 1918.

ALFRED ERNEST GARVIE

1861–1945

The Ritschlian theology. 1899.

JAMES HASTINGS

1862–1922

A dictionary of the Bible. 5 vols Edinburgh 1898–1904, 1903–4, 1909. Ed Hastings et al.

WILLIAM RALPH INGE

1860–1954

Christian mysticism. 1899, 1912, 1933.
The philosophy of Plotinus. 2 vols 1918, 1923, 1929.
Outspoken essays. 1919; 2nd ser, 2 vols 1919 [22], 1921.
Christian ethics and modern problems. 1930.

LAWRENCE PEARSALL JACKS

1860–1955

Authority in religious belief. 1893 (in Religion and modern thought and other essays [by various authors]); [1894] (pbd separately in the Theological essays ser, vol 1 no 9); 1907 (in Authority in religious belief and other essays by L. P. Jacks et al). Previously separately pbd as Unitarian tracts.
The Hibbert journal. 1902–. Ed Jacks.
Writings. 6 vols 1916–17.
From authority to freedom. 1920.

JOHN SCOTT LIDGETT

1854–1953

The spiritual principle of the Atonement. 1897, 1898.
The fatherhood of God. 1902.

THOMAS MARTIN LINDSAY

1843–1914

Religious life in Scotland, from the Reformation to the present day. 1888. With others.
A history of the Reformation in Europe. 2 vols 1906–7.
Lux mundi: a series of studies in the religion of the Incarnation. 1889, 1890, 1891, 1904. Charles Gore (ed), W. J. H. Campion, H. Scott Holland, W. Lock, A. Lyttelton, J. R. Illingworth, R. C. Moberly, Aubrey Moore, R. L. Ottley, F. Paget and E. S. Talbot.

ROBERT MACKINTOSH

1858–1933

Essays towards a new theology. Glasgow 1889.

ALFRED WILLIAMS MOMERIE

1848–1900

Defects of modern Christianity. 1882; 1885.
The religion of the future. 1893.

CLAUDE JOSEPH GOLDSMID-MONTEFIORE

1858–1938

Lectures on the origin and growth of religion, as illustrated by the religion of the ancient Hebrews. 1892.
Liberal Judaism. 1903, 1918.
The Synoptic Gospels. 2 vols 1909, 1927. Ed Montefiore. A third vol of Additional notes by I. Abrahams was never pbd.

SIR WILLIAM MITCHELL RAMSAY

1851–1939

The Church in the Roman Empire before AD 170. 1893, 1895, 1900, 1903.
St Paul the traveller. 1895, 1896, 1897.
The teaching of Paul in terms of the present day. [1913].

HASTINGS RASHDALL

1858–1924

The universities of Europe in the Middle Ages. 2 vols 1895; rev F. M. Powicke and A. B. Emden 3 vols 1936, 1942.
Doctrine and development. 1898.
The theory of good and evil. 2 vols 1907, 1924.
The idea of Atonement in Christian theology. 1919.
See P. E. Matheson, Life of Rashdall, 1928.

GEORGE SALMON

1819–1904

The infallibility of the Church. 1888, 1890, 1914; abridged and ed H. F. Woodhouse 1952.
The human element in the Gospels. Ed N. J. D. White 1907.

WILLIAM SANDAY

1843–1920

Inspiration. 1893, 1896 (enlarged with new preface).
Christologies, ancient and modern. 1910.

FREDERIC SEEBOHM

1833–1912

The spirit of Christianity. 1876 (priv ptd); ed H. E. Seebohm 1916.

ANDREW SETH

1856–1931

from 1898 A. S. PRINGLE-PATTISON

Man's place in the cosmos. 1897, 1902 (rev and enlarged).
The idea of God in the light of recent philosophy. Aberdeen and Oxford 1917, New York 1920 (rev).
The idea of immortality. Oxford 1922.
See col 1579, above.

WILLIAM ROBERTSON SMITH

1846–94

The Old Testament in the Jewish Church. Edinburgh 1881, 1892 (enlarged).

The Prophets of Israel. Edinburgh 1882, 1895 (with introd and additional notes by T. K. Cheyne).
Lectures on the religion of the Semites. Edinburgh 1889, 1894 (rev and ed J. S. Black?); ed S. A. Cook 1927.

GEORGE TYRRELL

1861–1909

Nova et vetera: informal meditations. 1897, 1900; tr Italian, 1912.
Hard sayings. 1898.
External religion: its use and abuse. 1899.
The faith of the millions: essays. 2 sers 1901.
Oil and wine. 1902 (priv ptd), 1907 (with new preface).
The Church and the future. 1903 (priv ptd), 1910.
Lex orandi: or prayer and creed. 1903.
Lex credendi: a sequel to Lex orandi. 1906.
A much-abused letter. 1906.
Through Scylla and Charybdis. 1907.
Medievalism: a reply to Cardinal Mercier. 1908, 1909 (with addns).
Christianity at the cross-roads. 1909.
Versions and perversions of Heine and others. 1909.
Autobiography and life, arranged by M. D. Petre. 2 vols 1912.
Essays on faith and immortality, arranged by M. D. Petre. 1914.

JAMES WARD

1843–1925

Naturalism and agnosticism. 2 vols 1899, 1903, 1906, 1 vol 1915.
The realm of ends: or pluralism and theism. Cambridge 1911, 1912, 1920.
See col 1597, above.

MARY AUGUSTA WARD, née ARNOLD

1851–1920

Robert Elsmere. 3 vols 1888 (3 edns), 1 vol 1899, [1907], 1952; tr German, [1890].
A writer's recollections. 1918.
See col 1081, above.

(2) THE EVANGELICALS

General Studies

Stephen, J. Essays in ecclesiastical biography. 2 vols 1849, 1853, 1 vol 1860 (with a biographical notice of the author by J. F. Stephen), 2 vols 1907.
Gilfillan, G. In his Galleries of literary portraits, 2 vols 1856–7. For Chalmers, Dawson, R. Hall, Irving and other preachers.
Abbey, C. J. and J. H. Overton. The English Church in the eighteenth century. 2 vols 1878, 1 vol 1887 (abridged).
Seeley, Mary. The later evangelical fathers: John Thornton, John Newton, William Cowper etc. 1879, 1914 (with preface by H. C. G. Moule).
Dale, R. W. The evangelical revival and other sermons. 1880.
— The old evangelicalism and the new. 1889.
Stock, E. The history of the Church Missionary Society. 4 vols 1899–1916. A short version of this work in one vol, entitled One hundred years, was pbd in 1898, 1899, 1899.
Balleine, G. R. A history of the Evangelical Party in the Church of England. 1908, 1911, 1933, 1951.
Russell, G. W. E. A short history of the Evangelical Movement. 1915.
Tatlow, T. The story of the Student Christian Movement of Great Britain and Ireland. 1933.
Sloan, W. B. These sixty years: the story of the Keswick Convention. [1935].
Kellett, E. E. Religion and life in the early Victorian age. 1938.
Downer, A. C. A century of evangelical religion in Oxford. [1938].
Smyth, C. H. E. Simeon and Church Order: a study of the origins of the Evangelical revival in Cambridge in the eighteenth century. Cambridge 1940.
Storr, V. F. Freedom and tradition: a study of Liberal Evangelicism. 1940.
Bullock, F. W. B. The history of Ridley Hall, Cambridge. 2 vols Cambridge 1941–53.
Sandall, R. The history of the Salvation Army. 3 vols 1947–55.
Orr, J. E. The second evangelical awakening in Britain. 1949, 1955 (abridged, with an abridgement of The second evangelical awakening in America, as The second evangelical awakening etc).

Principal Writers 1800–35

RICHARD CECIL

1748–1810

The life, character and remains. Ed J. Pratt, 4 vols 1811, 1816, 1821 (Christian Lib), 1836, [1840?], Edinburgh 1854 (Christian's Fireside Lib), [1854] (with memoir by Mrs Cecil), [1854], 1876 (with introd by C. Cecil).

THOMAS CHALMERS

1780–1847

A series of discourses on the Christian revelation. Glasgow 1817, 1817, Andover Mass 1818 (enlarged), Edinburgh 1818, Glasgow 1822, 1830, London 1862, [1870], 1871.
The application of Christianity to the commercial and ordinary affairs of life. Glasgow 1820, 1820, Edinburgh 1862; tr French, 1824.
Works. 25 vols Glasgow [1836–42].
Posthumous works. Ed W. Hanna 9 vols Edinburgh 1847–9.
See W. Hanna, Memoirs of Chalmers, 4 vols Edinburgh 1849–52, 2 vols 1878; ed J. C. Moffat, Cincinatti 1853 (abridged).
See col 1602, above.

THOMAS GISBORNE

1758–1846

Poems, sacred and moral. 1798, 1799, 1803.
An enquiry respecting love as one of the divine attributes. 1838.

ROBERT HALL

1764–1831

Works, with a memoir by Olinthus Gregory and observations on his character. Ed O. Gregory 6 vols 1832 (for 1831–2), 3 vols New York 1832–3 (with memoir by J. Mackintosh and a sketch of his character by J. Foster), 6 vols 1836–41.

ROWLAND HILL
1744–1833

Village dialogues. 1801, 1801 (with corrections and addns), 3 vols 1824, 1 vol 1858 (abridged).
See E. Sidney, Life of Hill, 1834.

THOMAS HARTWELL HORNE
1780–1862

An introduction to the critical study of the Scriptures. 3 vols 1818–21, 1822, 4 vols 1822, 1825 (corrected), Philadelphia 1827, 1828 (corrected and enlarged), 1834, 1839, 5 vols 1846, 4 vols 1856 (rev), 1860–1.

ZACHARY MACAULAY
1768–1838

Editor of and contributor to Christian Observer 1802–16.

HENRY MARTYN
1781–1812

Journals and letters. Ed S. Wilberforce 2 vols 1837.

JOSEPH MILNER
1744–97

The history of the Church of Christ. Vols 1–3, York 1794–97. Continued by his brother Isaac (1750–1820): vol 4, York 1803; vol 5, York 1809; 5 vols 1810; ed I. Milner 5 vols 1816, 1824, 4 vols [1833?]; 1834, 5 vols 1842, 4 vols 1847 (rev and corrected by T. Grantham), ed T. Haweis 4 vols 1847, 1 vol 1834 (abridged as History of the Church of Christ), 1835 (excerpt ed as Reflections on ecclesiastical establishments).

HANNAH MORE
1745–1833

See vol 2.

JOHN OVERTON
1763–1838

The true churchmen ascertained. 1801, York 1802.

LEGH RICHMOND
1772–1827

Annals of the poor. 1814. Includes The dairyman's daughter, often ptd separately from 1809.

GRANVILLE SHARP
1735–1813

A dissertation on the supreme divine dignity of the Messiah. 1806.
See Prince Hoare, Memoirs of Sharp, 1820.

CHARLES SIMEON
1759–1836

An appeal to men of wisdom and candour. 1816.
Horae homilecticae. 11 vols 1819–20; appendix, 6 vols 1828; 21 vols 1832, 1833. A long ser beginning 1796.
See W. Carus, Memoirs, 1847, *and* H. C. G. Moule, Life of Simeon, 1892; ed J. R. S. Taylor 1948.

JOHN BIRD SUMNER
1780–1862

A treatise on the records of the Creation. 2 vols 1816, 1818, 1825 (corrected).
The evidence of Christianity, derived from its nature and reception. 1824, 1826, 1830, 1836, 1861 (rev with reference to current objections).

HENRY THORNTON
1760–1815

Family commentary. Ed R. H. Inglis 2 vols 1835–7.

WILLIAM WILBERFORCE
1759–1833

A practical view of the prevailing religious system of professed Christians. 1797, 1797, 1798, Boston 1803, London 1805, 1817, 1824, 1826 (with introd by D. Wilson), Edinburgh [1854], [1871], London 1888 (with prefatory memoir by W. B.), [1830?] (abridged as Nominal and real Christianity contrasted).
An appeal to the religion, justice and humanity of the inhabitants of the British Empire, in behalf of the negro slaves of the West Indies. 1823, 1823.
See Robert Isaac and Samuel Wilberforce (his sons), Life of William Wilberforce, 5 vols 1838, 1 vol 1843 (abridged); tr German, 1840 (full text).

CAROLINE WILSON, née FRY
1787–1846

The listener. 2 vols 1830, 1839, 1842, 1 vol 1856.

DANIEL WILSON
1778–1858

The evidences of Christianity. 2 vols 1828–30, 1832.
The sufficiency of Holy Scripture as the rule of faith. 1841, Calcutta 1841 (with appendix on Tract 90 by J. H. Newman).
Bishop Wilson's journal letters. Ed Daniel Wilson (his son) 1863.

Principal Writers 1835–70

HENRY ALFORD
1810–71

The school of the heart and other poems. 2 vols Cambridge 1835.
The Greek Testament, with a critical commentary. 4 vols 1849–61.
The Queen's English: stray notes on speaking and spelling. 1864 (for 1863), 1864 (as A plea for the Queen's English), 1870 (rev and enlarged); 1888 (Bohn's Shilling Lib).
See col 501, above.

EDWARD BICKERSTETH
1786–1850

Christian psalmody. 1833 (3 edns), 1834, 1835, 1836 (3 edns), 1839, [1841] (enlarged), [c. 1855] (enlarged). One of the earliest Church hymn-books, it formed the basis of his son, E. H. Bickersteth, Hymnal companion, 1870 etc.
See col 508, above.

THOMAS RAWSON BIRKS
1810–83

The Bible and modern thought. 2 pt [1861–2].
Modern physical fatalism and the doctrine of evolution. 1876, 1882 (with a preface in reply to the strictures of H. Spencer and C. Pritchard).

HENRY BLUNT
1794–1843

Eight lectures upon the history of Jacob. 1828.

JOHN JAMES BLUNT
1794–1855

Undesigned coincidences in the Old and New Testaments. 1847, 1850, 1859.

HORATIUS BONAR
1808–89

Hymns of faith and hope. 1857, 1858.
God's way of peace. 1862, 1862, 1920 (excerpts).
See col 511, above

ROBERT SMITH CANDLISH
1806–73

The fatherhood of God. 1865, 1865, 2 vols 1870 (supplementary vol containing reply to T. J. Crawford etc).

FRANCIS CLOSE
1797–1882

The footsteps of error. 1863.
The stage, ancient and modern: its tendencies on morals and religion. 1877.

WILLIAM JOHN CONYBEARE
1815–57
and
JOHN SAUL HOWSON
1816–85

The life and epistles of St Paul. 2 vols 1852, 1856 (rev), 1862 (with maps), 1864 (with maps and plates), 1864, 1 vol 1892 (with maps), 1901 (with maps).

GEORGE DAWSON
1821–76

The demands of the age upon the Church. 1847.
Biographical lectures. Ed G. St Clair 1886 (for 1885).

WILLIAM GOODE
1801–68

The divine rule of faith and practice. 2 vols 1842, 3 vols 1853 (rev and enlarged); ed A. E. Metcalfe 1903 (abridged).

THOMAS GUTHRIE
1803–73

The Gospel in Ezekiel. Edinburgh 1856, 1863.

EDWARD IRVING
1792–1834

Collected writings. Ed G. Carlyle 5 vols 1864–5.
See T. Carlyle, Fraser's Mag Jan 1835.

ANDREW JOHN JUKES
1810–1901

The second death and the restitution of all things, by M. A. [A. J. Jukes].

JOHN KITTO
1804–54

The pictorial Bible. To which are added original notes [by J. Kitto]. [Pbd in monthly pts anon] 3 vols 1836–8, 4 vols 1838–9, 1847–8, 1855–6, 58 pts [1871–6] (as The illustrated family Bible); tr Welsh, (Old Testament only) 3 vols 1844–50. Kitto's notes were issued separately, anon, in 5 vols in 1840 as The illustrated commentary on the Old and New Testament.

NORMAN MACLEOD the younger
1812–72

Editor of and contributor to Good Words *from 1860.*
Reminiscences of a Highland parish. 1867, [1910] (illustr).

HENRY MELVILL
1798–1871

The golden lectures 1850–6. 7 vols [1856–7], 1853 (as A selection from the lectures delivered at St Margaret's, Lothbury); ed author of Pietas privata 1856 (as Golden Counsels) (selection), 1876 (as Lectures etc) (selection).

EDWARD MONRO
1815–66

The dark mountains: an allegory. 1858.

BAPTIST WRIOTHESLEY NOEL
1798–1873

Essay on the Union of Church and State. 1848, 1849 (corrected), 1867 (abridged, as Influence of the Union of the Church with the State upon Christian Union and the progress of religion).

HENRY ROGERS

1806–77

The eclipse of faith. 1852 (anon), 1854, 1855, 1861.
Essays from the Edinburgh Review. 3 vols 1850–5, 1855.

JAMES SCHOLEFIELD

1789–1853

Scriptural grounds of union. Cambridge 1841.
The Christian altar. Cambridge 1842.

ROBERT BENTON SEELEY

1798–1886

Essays on the Church, by a layman. [R. B. Seeley]. 1834, 1834, 1836, 1840, 1859.

JAMES ELIMALET (ELISHAMA) SMITH

1801–57

Editor of The Shepherd *from 1834.*
See W. A. Smith, 'Shepherd' Smith the Universalist, 1892.

SAMUEL WALDEGRAVE

1817–69

New Testament Millennarianism. 1855, 1866.

Principal Writers 1870–1900

THOMAS DEHANEY BERNARD

1815–1904

The central teaching of Jesus Christ. 1892.

NATHANIEL DIMMOCK

1825–1909

The doctrine of the Sacraments. 1871 (anon); 1908.
The doctrine of the Death of Christ. [1890]; 1903 (rev).

HUGH MACMILLAN

1833–1903

Bible teachings in nature. 1867.
The ministry of nature. 1871.
The Isles and the Gospel, with memoir by George A. Macmillan. 1907.

FREDERICK MEYRICK

1827–1906

Doctrine of the Church of England restated, with a preface by E. H. Browne. 1885, 1888 (enlarged), 1891, 1899; tr Italian, 1891.
Memories of life at Oxford etc. 1905.

HANDLEY CARR GLYN MOULE

1841–1920

Veni creator. 1890, [1928].
Philippian studies. 1897.
Colossian studies. 1898, 1903, 1927 (for 1926).
Ephesian studies. 1900, 1908, 1927 (for 1926).
Imitations and translations, English, Latin and Greek. 1905 (for 1904).

CHARLES HADDON SPURGEON

1834–92

The treasury of David: containing an original exposition of the Book of Psalms etc. 7 vols 1870–85.

HENRY WACE

1836–1924

Christianity and morality. 1876.
Christianity and agnosticism. 1895.
An appeal to the first six centuries. 1905.

B. THE OXFORD MOVEMENT AND THE HIGH CHURCHMEN

General Studies

Perceval, A. P. A collection of papers connected with the theological movement of 1833. 1842, 1843.
Palmer, W. A narrative of events connected with the publication of the Tracts for the times. Oxford 1843, 1843, 1843 (with postscript), London 1883 (with introd and supplement to 1883).
Bricknell, W. S. The judgment of the Bishops upon Tractarian theology. Oxford 1845.
Newland, H. G. Three lectures on Tractarianism. 1852, 1855.
Browne, E. G. K. History of the Tractarian Movement. Dublin 1856, 1856, London 1861 (rev and priv ptd as Annals 1842 to 1860).
Oakeley, F. Historical notes on the Tractarian Movement 1833–45, 1865. This work, rptd from Dublin Rev, differs from Oakeley's Personal reminiscences of the Oxford Movement, 1855, which is only a lecture.
Mozley, T. Reminiscences chiefly of Oriel College and the Oxford Movement. 2 vols 1882, 1882.
Church, R. W. The Oxford Movement: twelve years 1833–45. 1891.
Worley, G. The Catholic Revival of the nineteenth century. 1894.
Overton, J. H. The Anglican revival. [1897].
Cruttwell, C. T. Six lectures on the Oxford Movement and its results on the Church of England. 1899.
Thureau-Dangin, P. La renaissance catholique en Angleterre au xixe siècle. 3 pts Paris 1899–1906; tr W. Wilberforce 2 vols 1914 (rev and re-edited).
Bodington, C. Devotional life in the nineteenth century. 1905.
Holland, H. S. The mission of the Oxford Movement. In his Personal studies, 1905; rptd from Lyra apostolica, ed H. C. Beeching 1899.
Hall, S. A short history of the Oxford Movement. 1906.
Hutchison, W. G. The Oxford Movement: selections from Tracts for the times. [1906].
Guibert, J. Le réveil du Catholicisme en Angleterre au xixe siècle. Paris 1907. With full bibliography, including French and English magazine articles.
Ward, W. P. The Oxford Movement. [1913].
Baring-Gould, S. The Church revival. 1914, [1915].
— The Evangelical revival. 1920.

Ollard, S. L. A short history of the Oxford Movement. 1915.
— The Oxford Movement. In vol 8 of Encyclopaedia of religion and ethics, ed J. Hastings, 1908–21.
— The Anglo-Catholic revival. 1925.
Brémond, H. L'inquiétude religieuse. Ser 1, Paris 1919.
Knox, W. L. The Catholic movement in the Church of England. 1923, 1930.
Webb, C. C. J. A century of Anglican theology and other lectures. 1923.
— Religious thought in the Oxford Movement. 1928.
Brilioth, Y. T. The Anglican revival: studies in the Oxford Movement. 1925.
Kaye-Smith, S. Anglo-Catholicism. 1925.
Stewart, H. L. A century of Anglo-Catholicism. 1929.
Shaw, P. E. The early Tractarians and the Eastern Church. [1930].
Embry, J. The Catholic movement and the Society of the Holy Cross. 1931.
Sparrow Simpson, W. J. The history of the Anglo-Catholic revival from 1845. 1932.
Clarke, C. P. S. The Oxford Movement and after. 1932.
Peck, W. G. The social implications of the Oxford Movement. 1933.
Knox, W. L. and A. R. Vidler. The development of modern Catholicism. 1933.
Morse-Boycott, D. The secret history of the Oxford Movement. 1933.
Faber, G. Oxford Apostles: a character study of the Oxford Movement. 1933, 1936, 1954 (Pelican).
Knox, E. A. The Tractarian Movement 1833–45. 1933, 1934.
Donovan, M. F. G. After the Tractarians: from the recollections of Athelstan Riley. 1933.
Upton, W. P. The churchman's history of the Oxford Movement. 1933.
Schaefer, P. Die katholische Wiedergeburt der englischen Kirche. Munich 1933; tr 1935.
Dawson, C. H. The spirit of the Oxford Movement. 1933.
Reckitt, M. B. Maurice to Temple: a century of the social movement in the Church of England. 1947.
Brandreth, H. R. T. The oecumenical ideals of the Oxford Movement. 1947.

Magazines

The British magazine. Ed H. J. Rose 1832–6; ed S. R. Maitland 1836–49.
The British critic. Ed J. H. Newman et al 1836–8; ed Newman 1838–41; ed T. Mozley 1841–3. Founded 1793 by W. Jones of Nayland.
The Christian remembrancer. Ed William Scott and Francis Garden 1841–4; ed Scott and J. B. Mozley 1844–54; ed Scott 1854–68.
The guardian. Founded Jan 1846 by R. W. Church, F. Rogers (Baron Blatchford) and M. Bernard.

Biographies and Memoirs

Churton, E. Memoir of Joshua Watson. 2 vols 1861.
Shutte, R. N. A memoir of Henry Newland. 1861.
Blomfield, A. A memoir of Charles James Blomfield, Bishop of London. 2 vols 1863, 1 vol 1864.
[Farrer, afterwards Lear, H. L.] Life of Robert Gray, Bishop of Capetown. Ed his son C. Gray. 2 vols 1876 (for 1875).
Fowler, J. R. W. Sibthorp: a biography told chiefly in his own correspondence; with appendix containing fragments of his earlier teaching. 1880.
Ornsby, R. Memoirs of James Robert Hope-Scott. 2 vols 1884.
[Trench, M.] Charles Lowder: a biography, by the author of the Life of St Teresa. 1881, 1883 ('ninth edition'; by the author of the Life of St Teresa).
Overton, J. H. and E. Wordsworth. Christopher Wordsworth, Bishop of Lincoln 1807–85. 1888, 1890.
T[owle], E. A. Alexander Heriot Mackonochie: a memoir. Ed F. F. Russell. 1890.
Bellasis, E. Memorials of Mr Bellasis 1800–73. 1893, 1895 (enlarged), 1923.
Carter, T. T. Richard Temple West: a record of life and work. 1895.
Letters of Frederic, Lord Blachford. Ed G. E. Marindin 1896.
B., A. J. [Butler, A. J. (ed)]. Life and letters of William John Butler, Dean of Lincoln. 1897.
Fowler, J. T. (ed). Life and letters of John Bacchus Dykes. 1897.
Purcell, E. S. Life and letters of Ambrose Phillipps de Lisle. Ed and finished by Edwin de Lisle 2 vols 1900.
Lake, K. Memorials of William Charles Lake, Dean of Durham 1869–94. Ed his widow Katharine Lake 1901.
Osborne, C. E. The life of Father Dolling. 1903, 1903, [1905].
Crouch, W. Bryan King and the riots at St George's-in-the-East, with a preface by G. W. E. Russell and a note by J. B. Knight. 1904.
Acland, J. E. A layman's life in the days of the Tractarian Movement: in memoriam Arthur Acland Troyte. 1904.
Kelway, A. C. George Rundle Prynne: a chapter in the early history of the Catholic Revival. 1905.
Kate, Mother. Old Soho days and other memories. 1906.
Paget, E. C. A year under the shadow of St Paul's. 1908.
Romanes, E. Charlotte Mary Yonge: an appreciation. 1908.
Bennett, F. The story of W. J. E. Bennett and of his part in the Oxford Church Movement of the nineteenth century etc. 1909.
Moberly, C. A. E. Dulce domum: George Moberly, his family and friends. 1911.
Hutton, W. H. et al. Robert Gregory 1819–1911: the autobiography. Ed W. H. Hutton 1912.
Mason, A. J. Life of William Edward Collins, Bishop of Gibraltar. 1912.
Paget, S. and J. M. C. Crum. Francis Paget, Bishop of Oxford. 1912.
Russell, G. W. E. Edward King, sixtieth Bishop of Lincoln: a memoir. 1912 (3 edns).
— Arthur Stanton: a memoir. 1917.
Watson, E. W. The life of Bishop John Wordsworth. 1915.
Congreve, G. and W. H. Longridge. Letters of Richard Meux Benson. 1916. *See* W. H. Longridge, Spiritual letters of Richard Meux Benson, 1924.
Randolph, B. W. and J. W. Townroe. The mind and work of Bishop King. 1918.
Newbolt, W. C. E. Years that are past. [1921].
Paget, S. Henry Scott Holland: memoir and letters. 1921.
Benson, A. C. The trefoil. 1923. On early life of Archbishop Benson.
Hine, J. E. Days gone by. 1924.
Talbot, E. S. Memories of early life. 1924.
Denison, H. P. Seventy-two years' Church recollections. 1925.
Otter, J. L. Nathaniel Woodard: a memoir. 1925.
Fullerton, T. G. Father Burn of Middlesbrough. 1927.
Coles, V. S. S. Letters, papers, addresses, hymns and verses with a memoir [by G. W. Borlase]. Ed J. F. Briscoe 1930.
Briscoe, J. F. and H. F. B. Mackay. A Tractarian at work: a memoir of Dean Randall. 1932.
Crosse, G. Charles Gore: a biographical sketch. 1932.
Gore, J. F. Charles Gore: father and son. 1932.
Ingram, K. John Keble. 1933.
Prestige, G. L. Pusey. 1933.
— The life of Charles Gore: a great Englishman. 1935.
Mansbridge, A. Edward Stuart Talbot and Charles Gore. 1935.
Lockhart, J. G. Charles Lindley, Viscount Halifax. 2 vols 1935–6.
Stephenson, G. Edward Stuart Talbot 1844–1934. 1936.

Middleton, R. D. Keble, Froude and Newman: short essays in the early history of the Oxford Movement. Canterbury [1933].
— Magdalen studies. 1936. Biographical essays on 10 men associated with the Oxford Movement.
— Newman and Bloxam: an Oxford friendship. 1947.
Clarke, C. P. S. Bishop Chandler: a memoir. 1940.
Cross, F. L. Darwell Stone: Churchman and counsellor. 1943.
Williams, T. J. Priscilla Lydia Sellon. 1950, 1965 (rev).
Nias, J. C. S. Gorham and the Bishop of Exeter. 1951.
Woodgate, M. V. Father Benson, founder of the Cowley Fathers. 1953.
Davies, G. C. B. Henry Phillpotts, Bishop of Exeter 1778–1869. 1954.

Principal Writings

Tracts for the Times, The Library of the Fathers, Plain Sermons, The Anglo-Catholic Library, The English Saints and Lyra Apostolica.

Tracts for the times. Ed J. H. Newman 6 vols 1833–41. 90 tracts were issued anon between 9 Sept 1833 (Three tracts) and 27 Feb 1841 (Tract no 90). 5 lists of the Tracts and their authors are extant: (1) appendix to H. P. Liddon's Life of Pusey vol 3, 1897, pp. 473–80; (2) Sir G. Prevost, Whitaker's almanack, 1883; (3) F. H. Rivington [based on information supplied by Newman in 1869], John Bull Sept 1890; (4) J. R. Bloxam, ms at Magdalen College Oxford; (5) W. J. Copeland (revision of list in Whitaker's almanack, 1883). In the case of 2 Tracts further evidence has come to light modifying these lists slightly. The contributors were: J. W. Bowden (nos 5, 29, 30, 56, 58); A. Buller (no 61); C. P. Eden (no 32); R. H. Froude (nos 8 (with J. H. Newman), 9, 59, 63); B. Harrison (nos 16, 17, 24, 49, 74 (with J. H. Newman), 81 (with E. B. Pusey)); John Keble (nos 4, 13, 40, 52, 54, 57, 60, 89); T. Keble (nos 12, 22, 43, 84 (with Sir G. Prevost)); H. E. Manning and C. Marriott (no 78); A. Menzies (no 14); J. H. Newman (nos 1–3, 6, 8 (with R. H. Froude), 10–11, 15 (with Sir W. Palmer), 19–21, 31, 33–4, 38, 41, 45, 47, 71, 73–4 (with B. Harrison), 75–6, 79, 82–3, 85, 88, 90); Sir W. Palmer (no 15 (with Newman)); A. P. Perceval (nos 23, 35, 36); Sir G. Prevost (no 84 (with T. Keble)); E. B. Pusey (nos 18, 66–70, 77, 81, (with B. Harrison)); I. Williams (nos 80, 86–7); R. F. Wilson (no 51). The remaining 17 tracts were reprints from older Anglican divines. There is some confusion about the numering of the Tracts after the 1st edn, when no 70 was enlarged and ptd as part of no 65 and Tracts 67–9 were reckoned as no 70.

Lyra apostolica. 1836; ed H. S. Holland and H. C. Beeching 1899. Poems originally ptd in Br Mag. Of the 179 pieces, Newman wrote 109, Keble 46, I. Williams 9, R. H. Froude 8, J. W. Bowden 6 and R. I. Wilberforce one. The authors used Greek letters as signatures: α=Bowden, β=Froude, γ=Keble, δ= Newman, ϵ=Wilberforce, ζ=Williams.

The library of the Fathers of the Holy Catholic Church, anterior to the division of the East and West. Ed J. Keble, J. H. Newman, E. B. Pusey and [1843–57] C. Marriott, 48 vols 1838–85. Included the works of 13 Fathers, e.g. St Chrysostom (16 vols), St Augustine (12 vols), St Athanasius (5 vols), St Gregory (4 vols). The prefaces were contributed by: C. Marriott (15), E. B. Pusey (12), J. H. Newman (4), J. Keble (2), P. E. Pusey (2), H. P. Liddon (1), H. G. Wilberforce (1), H. Browne (1). The translators included Keble, Newman, Pusey, R. W. Church, T. Keble, Sir G. Prevost, W. J. Copeland, J. B. Morris, Macmullen, P. E. Pusey and W. Bright. A complete list of the Library, with the translator and editor of each vol, so far as they are known, is ptd as an appendix to H. P. Liddon, Life of Pusey vol 1, 1893, ch 18.

Plain sermons by the contributors to the Tracts for the times. [Ed I. Williams and W. J. Copeland] 10 vols 1839–48. Preface to vol 1 by I. Williams, H. Jeffreys et al. On last p. of vol 10 it is stated that the sermons were the work, in various proportions carefully set out, of 7 authors designated by the first 7 letters of the alphabet. A=John Keble; B=Isaac Williams; C=E. B. Pusey; D=J. H. Newman; E=Thomas Keble; F=Sir George Prevost; G=R. F. Wilson. But a ms note in W. J. Copeland's copy of vol 7 assigns sermons 221–6 to him; and in Pusey's copy the same sermons are assigned to H. Copeland was not a contributor to the Tracts for the times and probably felt unable for that reason to appear among the authors of the series. It seems likely that the 6 sermons were substantially his but were adapted by J. Keble to enable them to be assigned to him. They appear among the contributions of A in the statement appended to vol 10.

The library of Anglo-Catholic theology. 88 vols 1841–63. Ed W. J. Copeland 1841–3, W. F. Audland 1843–7, C. L. Cornish 1847–54, J. Barrow 1854–63. The series was intended to include the principal post-Reformation divines, but the full programme was not carried out. The contributors included Keble, Edward Churton, W. H. Mill, C. P. Eden, A. W. Haddan, N. Pocock, J. Bliss and William Scott. Among the writers rptd were Bishop Andrewes, Archbishop Laud, Archbishop Bramhall, Bishop Cosin, Thorndike, Bishop Thomas Wilson and Bishop Hickes.

Lives of the English saints. 4 vols 1844–5; ed A. W. Hutton 6 vols 1900–1. Suggested by Newman, but he ceased to be editor after the first 2 Lives. The compilers of the 33 Lives were: R. W. Church (1), J. D. Dalgairns (7), T. Meyrick (4), M. Pattison (2), F. W. Faber (9), Newman (3), R. A. Coffin (1), R. Ornsby (1), J. A. Froude (1), J. Walker (1), F. Oakeley (1), J. Barrow (2). The list by A. W. Hutton in vol 6, Appendix 2 of the 1900 edns is correct except for its ascription of St Ninian (by Barrow) to Pattison and of St Bartholomew (by Dalgairns) to T. Mozley. A list corrected by Newman is among the Bloxam mss at Magdalen College Oxford.

Particular Authors

JOHN WILLIAM BOWDEN

1798–1844

St Bartholomew's Eve: a tale of the sixteenth century in two cantos. 1821 (anon). With J. H. Newman. The copy in BM contains ms notes by J. R. Bloxam, assigning the separate pts to the respective authors.
Tracts for the times. Nos 5, 29–30, 56, 58. 1833–5.
Lyra apostolica. 1836 etc. Poems signed α.
4 articles in Br Critic 1836, 1837, 1839, 1841.
Life and pontificate of Gregory the Seventh. 2 vols 1840.
Thoughts on the work of the six days of Creation. Oxford 1845. The editor's preface is signed JHN, i.e. J. H. Newman.

JOHN WILLIAM BURGON

1813–88

Petra: a prize poem recited in the Theatre, Oxford, June IV MDCCCXLV. Oxford 1845, 1846 (with shorter poems).
Poems 1840 to 1878. 1885.
The lives of twelve good men. 2 vols 1888, 1891 (with portraits). *See* E. M. Goulburn, Burgon: a biography, with extracts from his letters and early journals, 2 vols 1892.

EDWARD CASWALL

1814–78

Lyra catholica: containing all the breviary and missal hymns, with others from various sources. 1849, 1851, 1884, [1850?] (selected as A Catholic hymn-book for schools and private use). Tr Caswall.

See col 514, above.

RICHARD WILLIAM CHURCH

1815–90

§1

Lives of the English Saints: life of Wulstan. 1844 (anon), 1901.
Essays and reviews, collected from the British Critic and the Christian Remembrancer. 1854.
Sermons preached before the University of Oxford. 1868, 1880 (in The gifts of civilisation), [1913] with preface by the Bishop of London (as The gifts of civilisation).
Life of St Anselm. 1870, 1888 (as vol 3 in Miscellaneous writings).
Civilization before and after Christianity: two lectures. 1872, 1880 (in The gifts of civilisation).
On some influences of Christianity upon national character: three lectures. 1873, 1880 (in The gifts of civilisation).
The sacred poetry of early religions: two lectures. 1874, 1880 (in The gifts of civilisation).
The beginning of the Middle Ages. 1877, 1887, 1895 (as vol 7 in Miscellaneous writings).
Dante: an essay. Christian Remembrancer 1850; 1854 (in Essays and reviews); 1878 (with a trn of De Monarchia by F. J. Church), [1906] (essay on Dante, without the trn, but with Church's essays St Anselm and William Rufus and St Anselm and Henry I), [1910] (essay on Dante only).
Human life and its conditions: sermons preached before the University of Oxford in 1876–8 etc. 1878.
Spenser. 1880 (EML), 1888 (as vol 5 in Miscellaneous writings).
Bacon. 1884 (EML), 1888 (as vol 4 in Miscellaneous writings).
Discipline of the Christian character. 1885. Sermons.
Advent sermons. 1885, 1886.
[Miscellaneous writings.] 10 vols 1888 (uniform edn).
The Oxford Movement: twelve years 1833–45. 1891, 18 (as vol 6 in Miscellaneous writings).
Cathedral and University sermons. 1892.
Village sermons preached at Whatley. [1st ser] 1892; [2nd ser] 1894; [3rd ser] 1897; 1899 (1st ser); 1902 (2nd ser).
Pascal and other sermons. 1895.
The message of peace and other Christmas sermons. 1895, 1896, 1897.
Occasional papers 1846–90. [Ed M. C. Church] 2 vols 1897 (as vols 8–9 in Miscellaneous writings).

§2

Church, M. C. (ed). Life and letters of Dean Church. 1894, 1895, 18 (as vol 10 in Miscellaneous writings).
Donaldson, A. B. In his Five great Oxford leaders, 1900.
Holland, H. S. In his Personal studies, 1905.
Lathbury, D. C. Dean Church. 1905.
Cecil, A. In his Six Oxford thinkers, 1909.

JOHN DOBRÉE [BERNARD] DALGAIRNS

1818–76

Lives of the English saints: life of St Gilbert. 1844 (anon), 1901 (as vol 4 of The lives of the English saints).
Life of St Stephen Harding. 1844 (anon), 1900 (as vol 1 of The lives of the English saints); tr French, 1848.
Life of St Aelred. 1845 (anon), 1901 (as vol 5 in The lives of the English saints).
Life of St Richard. 1845 (anon), 1901 (as vol 6 in The lives of the English saints).
Lives of St Waltheof and St Robert of Newminster. 1845 (anon), 1901 (as vol 5 in The lives of the English saints).
The devotion to the heart of Jesus. 1853, 1854; ed A. Ross [1910].
The Holy Communion: its philosophy, theology and practice. 1861; ed A. Ross, 2 vols 1911.

AUBREY THOMAS de VERE

1814–1902

Essays, chiefly on poetry. 2 vols 1887.
Essays, chiefly literary and ethical. 1889, New York 1889.
Recollections. New York 1897.
See W. P. Ward, De Vere: a memoir, 1904.

DIGBY MACKWORTH DOLBEN

1848–67

Poems. Ed R. Bridges, Oxford 1911 (with a memoir), 1915 (rev and enlarged).

FREDERICK WILLIAM FABER

1814–63

See col 520, above.

ALEXANDER PENROSE FORBES

1817–75

A short explanation of the Nicene Creed. 1852.
Liber ecclesie Beati Terrenani de Arbuthnot: missale secundum usum ecclesiae Sancti Andreae in Scotia. [Ed A. P. Forbes.] Burntisland 1864.
An explanation of the Thirty-Nine Articles. 2 vols 1867–8.
Kalendars of Scottish saints. 1872.
Besides 4 vols of collected sermons, many pbd separately, lectures, manuals of devotion and articles in Edinburgh, Quart and North Br Rev and in Christian Remembrancer. List of Forbes's works in Memoir by D. J. Mackey, 1888, pp. 219–24. *See* J. O. Mowat, Bishop A. P. Forbes, 1925.

JAMES ANTHONY FROUDE

1818–94

See col 1468, above.

RICHARD HURRELL FROUDE

1803–36

Tracts for the times. Nos 9, 59, 63 and possibly part of 35 1833–5.
Lyra apostolica. 1836 etc. Poems signed β.
Remains: part 1. [Ed J. Keble and J. H. Newman] 2 vols 1838; part 2 [ed J. B. Mozley, preface by J. Keble] 2 vols 1839.
See L. I. Guiney, Hurrell Froude: memoranda and comments, 1904].

ELIZABETH FURLONG SHIPTON HARRIS

From Oxford to Rome, by a companion traveller. 1847 (anon), 1847 (rev).
Rest in the Church, by the author of From Oxford to Rome. 1848.

ROBERT STEPHEN HAWKER

1803–75

See col 524, above.

WALTER FARQUHAR HOOK

1798–1875

Five sermons preached before the University of Oxford. Oxford 1837.
Hear the Church: a sermon. Newcastle-upon-Tyne 1838, London 1841 (31st edn).
An ecclesiastical biography, containing the lives of the ancient Fathers and modern divines etc. 8 vols 1845–52.
Lives of the Archbishops of Canterbury [to Archbishop Juxon]. 12 vols 1860–76.
The Church and her ordinances [sermons]. Ed W. Hook 2 vols 1876.
Parish sermons. Ed W. Hook 1879.
And many other lectures, addresses and treatises.
See W. R. W. Stephens, Life and letters of Hook DD, FRS, 1878.

JOHN KEBLE

1792–1866

§1

The Christian year: thoughts in verse for the Sundays and Holydays throughout the year. 1827 (anon), 1827 (anon), 1828, 1829, 1832, 1834, 1835, 1840, 1841, 1848, 1849, 1850, 1858, 1866, 1868, 1868, [1873], 1873, 1973, [1873], 1873, [1874] (abridged), [1874] (with memoir by W. Temple); illustr F. Overbeck 1875; 1875, [1875] (authorized edn), 1876, 1877, 1878 (for 1877) (facs of original draft, with collation of the variations between draft and the pbd edns), 1878, [1879], 1879, [1880] (illustr), 1880, 1880, 1880, [1880?], 1881, 1882, 1882, 1883, 1883 (with memoir and portrait), 1884, [1884] (The Canterbury poets), [1885]; ed A. H. Grant [1886]; ed 'Pilgrim' (James Hogg) 1886 (with Collects, and a series of meditations and exhortations selected from the works of H. P. Liddon); introd H. Morley 1887; [1887], [1887], [1889], 1892, [1893], 1893 (illustr, including a portrait); 1894, [1895], 1895 (with introd and notes by W. Lock and five designs by R. Anning Bell; 1896 (authorized edn), 1897, 2 vols 1897 (facs of 1st edn with preface by Bishop of Rochester and a list of alterations made by the author in the text of later edns); ed W. Lock 1898, 1898; 1900, 1901, 1903 (Unit Lib); [1903] (Red Letter Lib), Guildford 1904, London [1906], [1907]; ed J. C. Sharp [1914], Oxford 1914 (WC), 1914 (with Lyra innocentium and other poems and the sermon National apostasy). Many of the hymns have been rptd separately and there has been a large number of vols composed of selections from the Christian year.
National apostasy considered in a sermon. Oxford 1833, 1847 etc (in Sermons, academical and occasional), 1914 (in The Christian year, Lyra innocentium and other poems etc); ed R. J. E. Boggis, Torquay [1931], London 1931.
Ode for the Encænia at Oxford. 1834 (anon), 1869 (in Miscellaneous poems).
Tracts for the times. Nos 4, 13, 40, 52, 54, 57, 60, 1834; no 89, 1841.
Lyra apostolica. 1836 etc. 46 poems signed γ.
Primitive tradition recognized in Holy Scripture: a sermon. 1836, 1837, 1837 (with postscript and Tract no 78 as appendix).
The Psalter or Psalms of David in English verse. 1839 (anon), 1840 (anon), 1869, 1904, 1906.
The case of Catholic subscription to the XXXIX articles. 1841 (priv ptd), 1865 (with Tract 90 by J. H. Newman), 1866.
Praelectiones poeticae. 1844.
Lyra innocentium: thoughts in verse on Christian children. Oxford 1846 (anon), 1846, 1846, 1851, 1867, 1884; ed W. Lock 1899; illustr B. Handler 1903; [1906], 1914 (with The Christian year and other poems and the sermon National apostasy).
Sermons, academical and occasional. Oxford 1847, 1848.
On Eucharistical adoration. Oxford 1857, 1859, 1867.
Sermons, occasional and parochial. 1868.
Miscellaneous poems. Ed G. Moberly 1869. Contains Ode for the Encœnia, the poems contributed to the Lyra apostolica, selections from The Christian year and Lyra innocentium, and Remains.
Village sermons on the baptismal service. [Ed E. B. Pusey] Oxford 1869 (for 1868).
Letters of spiritual counsel and guidance. Ed R. F. Wilson 1870, 1875 (enlarged); ed B. W. Randolph 1904.
Sermons for the Christian year [with an 'Advertisement' by E. B. P., i.e. E. B. Pusey]. 11 vols Oxford 1875–80.
Occasional papers and reviews. Ed E. B. Pusey, Oxford 1877. Includes Life of Sir Walter Scott; Sacred poetry; Unpublished papers of Bishop Warburton; Copleston's Praelectiones academicae; Miller's Bampton lectures etc.
Studia sacra. Ed J.P.N., i.e. J. P. Norris 1877.
Keble's lectures on poetry 1832–41. Translated from Latin by E. K. Francis. 2 vols Oxford 1912.
The Christian year, Lyra innocentium and other poems, together with National apostasy. 1914.

§2

Shairp, J. C. Keble: an essay on the author of the Christian year. Edinburgh 1866, 1868 (in Studies in poetry and philosophy).
Coleridge, J. T. A memoir of Keble. 1869, 2 vols 1869 (with corrections and addns), 1870 (with corrections and addns).
Yonge, C. M. Musings over the Christian year and Lyra innocentium, together with a few gleanings of recollections of Keble, gathered by several friends. 1871.
Lock, W. Keble: a biography. 1893. Appendix 2 contains complete list of Keble's pbd works.
Wood, E. F. L. (Earl of Halifax). John Keble. 1909, 1932.

THOMAS KEBLE

1793–1875

Tracts for the times. Nos 12, 22, 43, 84 (concluded by Sir G. Provost), 1833–8.
Plain sermons by contributors to the Tracts for the times. [Sermons signed E in vols 1–2, 4, 10].

ALEXANDER KNOX

1757–1831

Remains. [Ed J. J. Hornby] 4 vols 1834–37, 1836 (vols 1 and 2 only).
Thirty years' correspondence with J. Jebb, Bishop of Limerick. Ed C. L. Forster 1834.

HENRY PARRY LIDDON

1829–90

§1

Some words for God: being sermons preached before the University of Oxford 1863–5. 1865, 1869 (for 1868) (as Sermons preached before the University of Oxford); [1859–68], 1873, 1873, 1881, 1884; Second series [1868–79], 1879, 1880, 1883, 1887; First and second series, 2 vols in 1, 1891 (for 1890).

The divinity of Our Lord and Saviour Jesus Christ: the Bampton lectures for 1866, 1867, 1869, 1869, 1871, 1872, 1882 (rev), 1884 (rev), 1885 (rev) 1889, 1890, [1934] (abridged by G. Goodman); tr German, 1833.

The priest in his inner life. 1869.

Some elements of religion: Lent lectures 1870. 1872, 1873, 1881 (for 1880), 1883, 1885, 1890, 1904.

Sermons preached before the University of Oxford: second series. *See* Some words for God, above.

Thoughts on present Church troubles [4 sermons]. 1881, 1882 (for 1881).

Easter in St Paul's: sermons. 2 vols 1885, 1891 (for 1890).

Advent in St Paul's: sermons. 2 vols 1889 (for 1888), 1889 (rev), 1 vol 1891 (for 1890), 1906.

Christmastide in St Paul's: sermons. 1889.

The magnificat: sermons. 1889, 1890, 1891.

Passiontide sermons. 1891.

Sermons on Old Testament subjects. 1891.

Sermons on some words of Christ. 1892, 1898.

Essays and addresses. 1892.

Life of Edward Bouverie Pusey, by H. P. Liddon, edited and prepared for publication by J. O. Johnston and R. J. Wilson. Vols 1–2, 1893; vol 3, 1894; vol 4, ed J. O. Johnston and W. C. E. Newbolt 1897.

Explanatory analysis of St Paul's epistle to the Romans. 1893, 1897, 1899.

Clerical life and work: a collection of sermons with an essay. 1894.

Explanatory analysis of St Paul's first epistle to Timothy. 1897.

Sermons preached on special occasions 1860–89. 1897.

Sermons on some words of St Paul. 1898.

A list of Liddon's pbd works is given in the appendix to his Life and letters, (1904). *47 of these are sermons pbd separately between 1858 and 1890. Many of them appear to have been afterwards collected and rptd in various vols.*

§2

Donaldson, A. B. In Five great Oxford leaders, 1900.

Johnston, J. O. Life and letters of Liddon, with a concluding chapter by the Bishop of Oxford (Francis Paget). 1904.

Holland, H. S. In his Personal studies, 1905.

Russell, G. W. E. Dr Liddon. 1905, [1911].

Liddon: a centenary memoir [by various hands]. 1929.

HENRY EDWARD MANNING

1808–92

§1

The unity of the Church. 1842.

Sermons. 4 vols 1842–50, 1 vol 1844.

Sermons preached before the University of Oxford. 1844.

The temporal mission of the Holy Ghost. 1865, 1866, 1877, 1892.

Sermons on ecclesiastical subjects. 3 vols 1867–73.

Miscellanies. 3 vols 1877–88.

§2

Hutton, A. W. Cardinal Manning. 1892.

Jenkes, R. C. A few recollections of Cardinal Manning. [1892?] (priv ptd).

Purcell, E. S. Life of Cardinal Manning. 2 vols 1895, 1896, 1896, 1896.

Leslie, S. Manning: his life and labours. 1921.

CHARLES MARRIOTT

1811–58

Tracts for the times. No 78, 1837.

Sermons preached before the University and in other places. 1843.

Sermons preached in Bradfield Church, Berks, Oriel College Chapel and in other places. 1850.

JAMES BOWLING MOZLEY

1813–78

The theory of development: a criticism of Dr Newman's Essay. Christian Remembrancer Jan 1847, 1878.

Eight lectures on miracles: the Bampton lectures for 1865. 1865, 1872, 1878, 1880, 1883.

Sermons preached before the University of Oxford and on various occasions. 1876, 1876, 1879, 1883.

Ruling ideas in early ages etc. 1877, 1884.

Essays, historical and theological. 2 vols 1878, 1884 (with memoir by his sister, Anne Mozley, and at p. xxxix an anon notice by R. W. Church rptd from Guardian.

Sermons, parochial and occasional. 1879, 1882.

Lectures and other theological papers. 1883.

Letters of the Rev J. B. Mozley DD. Ed his sister [Anne Mozley]. 1885 (for 1884).

THOMAS MOZLEY

1806–93

Reminiscences, chiefly of Oriel College and the Oxford Movement. 2 vols 1882, 1882.

JOHN MASON NEALE

1818–66

See col 541, above.

JOHN HENRY NEWMAN

1801–90

See col 1311, above.

FREDERICK OAKELEY

1802–80

Sermons preached chiefly in the Chapel Royal at Whitehall. Oxford 1839.

Lives of the English saints: life of St Augustine of Canterbury. 1844 (anon), 1901 (in vol 3 of Lives of the English saints).

The order and ceremonial of the Mass. 1848, [1910?].

Historical notes on the Tractarian Movement. 1865.

Also some 38 pbd works, articles in Br Critic, Dublin Rev and Month.

FRANCIS EDWARD PAGET

1806–82

Caleb Kniveton. Oxford 1833.
St Antholin's: or old churches and new. 1841.
The Warden of Berkingholt. Oxford 1843.
The Owlet of Owlstone Edge. By the author of St Antholin's. 1856 (for 1855).
A student penitent of 1695. 1875.

WILLIAM PALMER

1811–79

Harmony of Anglican doctrine with the doctrine of the Catholic and Apostolic Church of the East. Aberdeen 1846. Anon.
Dissertations on subjects relating to the Orthodox or Eastern Catholic Communion. 1853.
Notes of a visit to the Russian Church in 1840, 1841. Ed J. H. Newman 1882.

SIR WILLIAM PALMER

1803–85

Origines liturgicae. 2 vols Oxford 1832, 1845; Supplement, 1845.
Tracts for the times. No 15, 1833 (rev and completed by J. H. Newman).
A treatise on the Church of Christ. 2 vols 1838, 1842 (rev and enlarged), 1840 (excerpt as The Church of Christ), 1841, 1857.
Letters to N. Wiseman DD on the errors of Romanism etc. Oxford 1842 (for 1841–2), 1851.
A narrative of events connected with the publications of the Tracts for the times. Oxford 1843, 1843, 1843 (with postscript), London 1883 (with introd and suppl).

ARTHUR PHILIP PERCEVAL

1799–1853

Tracts for the times. Nos 23, 35 (with R. H. Froude), 36, and possibly 17, 1833.
A vindication of the principles of the authors of the Tracts for the times. 1841, 1841.
A collection of papers connected with the theological movement of 1833. 1842, 1843.

JOHN HUNGERFORD POLLEN the elder

1820–1902

Letter to the parishioners of St Saviour's Leeds. Oxford 1851.
Narrative of five years at St Saviour's Leeds. Oxford 1851.
See A. Pollen, John Hungerford Pollen, 1912, *who lists Pollen's writings, pp. 377–8.*

EDWARD BOUVERIE PUSEY

1800–82

Tracts for the times. Nos 18, 66, 67, 68, 69, 70, 77, 81 and possibly 76, 1834–7.
A letter to the Archbishop of Canterbury. Oxford 1842, London 1842, 1843 (with notes); tr German 1843.
A letter to the Bishop of London. Oxford 1851, 1851, Hobart 1851.
Parochial sermons. 3 vols 1852–73.
The doctrine of the Real Presence. 1855.
The Real Presence. 1857.
Sermons preached before the University of Oxford 1859–72. Oxford 1872.
The minor prophets. 1860.
Daniel the prophet: nine lectures. 1864, 1868.
An eirenicon. Pt 1, 1865; pt 2 (1st letter to Dr Newman), 1869; pt 3 (Is healthful reunion impossible?), 1870.
Historical preface to [J. H. Newman's] Tract no 90. 1865, 1866.
Lenten sermons 1858–74. Oxford 1874.
What is of faith as to everlasting punishment? Oxford 1880, 1880, 1880.
Parochial and Cathedral sermons. 1883.
See H. P. Liddon, Life of Pusey, ed J. O. Johnston, R. J. Wilson and W. E. Newbolt 4 vols 1893–7; [M. Trench], The story of Dr Pusey's life, 1900§ G. W. E. Russell, Dr Pusey, 1907, [1913]. *A complete bibliography by F. Madan of Pusey's pbd works is given as appendix A in vol 4 of his Life by Liddon.*

HUGH JAMES ROSE

1795–1838

The state of the Protestant religion in Germany, in a series of discourses. Cambridge 1825; 2 pts 1829 (enlarged and with an appendix, first pbd separately in 1828, replying to critiques of the 1st edn).

MARTIN JOSEPH ROUTH

1755–1854

Reliquiae sacrae: sive auctorum fere jam perditorum secundi tertiique saeculi post Christum natum quae supersunt. Vols 1–4, Oxford 1814–18, 5 vols Oxford 1846–8.
Scriptorum ecclesiasticorum opuscula praecipua quaedam. 2 vols Oxford 1832, 1840, 1858 (rev W. Jacobson).
Tres breves tractatus. [Ed M. J. Routh] 1854.
See R. D. Middleton, Dr Routh, Oxford 1938.

WILLIAM SEWELL

1804–74

The plea of conscience for seceding from the Catholic Church to the Romish schism in England: a sermon. Oxford 1845, 1845, 1845, 1846 (with an Essay on the process of conscience prefixed).
A year's sermons to boys. 2 vols Oxford 1854–69.

RICHARD CHENEVIX TRENCH

1807–86

See col 556, above.

WILLIAM GEORGE WARD

1812–82

The ideal of a Christian Church considered in comparison with existing practice. 1844.
Ward edited Dublin Rev 1863–78. *See* W. Ward, Ward and the Oxford Movement, 1889, *and* Ward and the Catholic Revival, 1893, 1912.

HENRY WILLIAM WILBERFORCE

1807–73

Reasons for submitting to the Catholic Church: a farewell letter. 1851, 1855.

The Church and the empires. 1874. With memoir by J. H. Newman.
Owned and edited Catholic Standard (*later* Weekly Register) 1854–63.

ROBERT ISAAC WILBERFORCE

1802–97

Lyra apostolica. 1836 etc. Poem lettered ϵ.
The doctrine of the Incarnation of Our Lord Jesus Christ. 1848, 1852.
The doctrine of Holy Baptism. 1849.
The doctrine of the Holy Eucharist. 1853.
An inquiry into the principles of Church-authority. 1854, 1854.

ISAAC WILLIAMS

1802–65

See col 560, above.

NICHOLAS PATRICK STEPHEN WISEMAN

1802–65

Lectures on the doctrines and practices of the Roman Catholic Church. 1836 (ptd without the author's sanction), 2 vols 1836 (authorized edn as Lectures on the principal doctrines and practices etc), 1851; tr French, 2 vols 1854; German, 2 vols 1838; Spanish, 2 vols 1851.
High Church claims: or a series of papers on the Oxford controversy. 1841.
Essays on various subjects. 3 vols 1853; ed J. Murphy 1888.
Fabiola: or the Church of the Catacombs. 1855 (anon), [1855], [1896], [1904], [1906]; ed J. R. and A. C. Hagan 1932 (school edn); tr French, [1891], 1935.
Recollections of the last four Popes and of Rome in their times. 1858, [1859] (rev), 1936 (abridged).
See W. Ward, The life and times of Cardinal Wiseman, 2 vols 1897.

C. W.

XI. ENGLISH STUDIES

Scholars are listed in alphabetical order. Cross-references have not been included to the general section on Prose or to the section on History, above, though both include many writers who in the 19th century contributed incidentally to the study of English literature, notably W. D. Adams, S. A. Brooke, J. C. Collins, E. Dowden, W. Elwin, G. Gilfillan, W. P. Ker, Edmund Gosse, D. Masson, W. A. Raleigh, G. Saintsbury and Thomas Wright. For a history see D. J. Palmer, The rise of English studies, Hull 1965.

GEORGE ATHERTON AITKEN

1860–1917

The life of Richard Steele. 2 vols 1889.
The life and works of John Arbuthnot. Oxford 1892.
Poems and satires of Andrew Marvell. 2 vols 1892 (ML).
The poetical works of Robert Burns. Edited with a memoir 3 vols 1893.
The poetical works of Thomas Parnell. Edited with a memoir and notes 1894.
Richard Steele. 1894 (Mermaid Ser), 1903. Selected plays, with introd and appendixes.
Romances and narratives by Daniel Defoe. 16 vols 1895–6.
The critic by R. B. B. Sheridan. 1897.
The rivals by R. B. B. Sheridan. 1897.
The school for scandal by R. B. B. Sheridan. 1897.
The spectator, with introduction and notes. 8 vols 1898.
The tatler, with introduction and notes. 4 vols 1898–9.
The journal to Stella by J. Swift. 1901.
Journal of the Plague Year by Daniel Defoe. [1908].
Memoirs of a Cavalier by Daniel Defoe. [1908].
Notes on the bibliography of Pope. 1914.

EDWARD ARBER

1836–1912

English reprints. 30 vols 1868–71.
The first printed English New Testament, translated by William Tyndale, photolithographed from the unique fragment now in the Grenville Collection, British Museum. 1871.
Annotated reprints. 3 vols 1872–5.
A transcript of the Register of the Company of Stationers of London 1554–1640 AD. 5 vols 1875–94 (priv ptd).
An English garner: ingatherings from our history and literature. 8 vols 1877–96; ed and rearranged T. Seccombe 12 vols 1903. *See* H. Guppy, An analytical catalogue of the contents of the two editions of An English garner, 1909.
The English scholar's library of old and modern works. 16 vols 1878–84.
An introductory sketch to the Martin Marprelate controversy 1558–90. 1880. No 8 of English scholar's library, above.
The first three English books on America ?1511–55 AD: being chiefly translations, compilations, etc by Richard Eden. Birmingham 1885.
The war library. 2 vols Birmingham 1894.
The story of the Pilgrim Fathers 1606–23 AD as told by themselves, their friends and their enemies. 1897.
British anthologies. 10 vols 1899–1901.
The term catalogues 1668–1709 AD; with a number for Easter term 1711 AD, from the quarterly lists issued by the booksellers. 3 vols 1903–6 (priv ptd).
A Christian library: a popular series of religious literature. 3 vols 1907 (priv ptd).

THOMAS ARNOLD

1823–1900

A manual of English literature, historical and critical; with an appendix on English metres. 1862, 1867 (rev and enlarged), 1873, 1877, 1885, 1888, 1897 (all rev).
Chaucer to Wordsworth: a short history of English literature, from the earliest times to the present day. [1870], 2 vols 1875.

A Catholic dictionary. 1884, 1917, [1928], 1951. With W. E. Addis.

Editions

Select English works of John Wycliff 3 vols Oxford 1869–71.
Selections from Addison's papers contributed to the Spectator. 1875.
Beowulf: a heroic poem of the eighth century; with translation, notes and appendix. 1876.
Pope, selected poems: the Essay on criticism, the Moral essays, the Dunciad. 1876.
Henrici, Archidiaconi Huntendunensis, Historia Anglorum: the history of the English by Henry, Archdeacon of Huntingdon, from AC 55 to AD 1154. 1879 (Rolls Ser).
English poetry and prose: a collection of illustrative passages from the writings of English authors, commencing in the Anglo-Saxon period and brought down to the present time. 1882.
Symeonis monachi opera omnia. 2 vols 1882–5 (Rolls Ser).
Clarendon, History of the rebellion, book vi. 1886.
Dryden, An essay of dramatic poesy. 1889, 1903.
Memorials of St Edmund's Abbey. 1890.

WILLIAM BELOE

1756–1817

Poems and translations. 1788.
Incidents of youthful life: or the true history of William Langley. 1790, 1807. Children's tale.
Miscellanies: consisting of poems, classical extracts and oriental apologues. 3 vols 1795.
Julia: or last follies. 1795. Poems.
Anecdotes of literature and scarce books. 6 vols 1807–12.
The sexagenarian: or recollections of a literary life. 1817, 1818.

Editions and Translations

The rape of Helen, from the Greek of Coluthus. 1786.
A free translation of the preface to Bellendenus. 1788.
Alciphron's epistles, now first translated. 1791. With T. Munro.
The history of Herodotus. 4 vols 1791. 6 edns by 1830.
The British critic: a new review. May 1793–Oct 1826. Vols 1–42 ed Robert Nares and Beloe.
The Attic nights of Aulus Gellius. 3 vols 1795.
A new and general biographical dictionary. 15 vols 1798–1810. In this (3rd) edn vols 7, 9, 11, 13, 15 were ed Beloe.

WILLIAM BLADES

1824–90

The life and typography of William Caxton, England's first printer; with evidence of his typographical connection with Colard Mansion, the printer at Bruges. 2 vols 1861–3.
A catalogue of books printed by (or ascribed to the press of) William Caxton. 1865.
A list of medals, jettons, tokens, etc in connection with printers and the art of printing. 1869 (priv ptd).
How to tell a Caxton; with some hints where and how the same might be found. 1870.
A list of medals struck by order of the Corporation of London; with an appendix of other medals, struck privately or for sale, having reference to the same corporate body or its members. 1870 (priv ptd).
Typographical notes. [1870] (priv ptd).
Shakspere and typography: being an attempt to show Shakspere's personal connection with, and technical knowledge of, the art of printing; also remarks upon some common typographical errors, with especial reference to the text of Shakspere. 1872. A *jeu d'esprit*.
Some early type specimen books of England, Holland, France, Italy and Germany; with explanatory remarks. 1875.
The biography and typography of William Caxton. 1877. A different work from the Life, above.
The enemies of books. 1880, 1888 (rev and enlarged), 1896; tr French, 1883.
Numismata typographica: or the medallic history of printing, reprinted from the Printers' Register. 1883.
An account of the German morality-play entitled Depositio cornuti typographici; with a rhythmical translation of the German version of 1648. 1885.
Bibliographical miscellanies. 5 pts 1890. Pt 1: Signatures; pt 2: The chained library at Wimborne Minster; pts 3–5: Books in chains.
The Pentateuch of printing, with a chapter on Judges, with a memoir of the author, and list of his works, by T. B. Reed. 1891.
Blades also contributed many essays on printing and bibliography to periodicals and pbd several short papers; he edited Juliana Berners, Boke of St Albans; The dictes and sayings of the philosophers, Christine Pisan, Moral proverbes; *and he was a prime mover in the Caxton celebration of 1877.*

JAMES BOSWELL

1778–1822

A biographical memoir of the late Edmond Malone. 1814 (priv ptd). Rptd from GM June 1813; reissued in Catalogue of early English poetry by E. Malone, 1836.
A Roxburghe garland. 1817.
The plays and poems of William Shakespeare comprehending an enlarged history of the stage, by the late E. Malone. 21 vols 1821. The 3rd variorum edn; ed Boswell from Malone's mss.
Boswell also pbd the 6th (rev) edn of his father's Life of Johnson.

JOSEPH BOSWORTH

1789–1876

Grammars and Dictionaries

An introduction to Latin construing. 1821, 1846.
Latin construing. 1821, 1850.
The elements of Anglo-Saxon grammar. 1823.
A compendious grammar of the primitive English or Anglo-Saxon language. 1826.
Græcæ grammatices rudimenta by William Bosworth, with additions by Joseph Bosworth. 1830.
A dictionary of the Anglo-Saxon language. 1838, 4 vols Oxford 1898 (rev partly from Bosworth's mss by T. N. Toller), 1908–1921.
A compendious Anglo-Saxon and English dictionary. 1848, 1881, 1888.

Editions, Translations etc

The origin of the Dutch. 1836.
Scandinavian literature. 1839. Anthology.
The origins of the English, Germanic and Scandinavian languages and nations. 1848.
A literal English translation of King Alfred's Anglo-Saxon version of the Compendious history of the world by Orosius. 1855, 1859.
A description of Europe, and the voyages of Ohthere and Wulfstan, with Anglo-Saxon test and a literal English translation and notes. 1855.
The history of the Lauderdale manuscript of King Alfred's Anglo-Saxon version of Orosius. Oxford 1858.

King Alfred's Anglo-Saxon version of the Compendious history of the world by Orosius, containing facsimile specimens of the Lauderdale and Cotton manuscripts. 1859. The Anglo-Saxon text with notes and various readings.

The Gothic and Anglo-Saxon Gospels in parallel columns with the versions of Wycliffe and Tyndale. 1865.

HENRY BRADLEY
1845–1923

The Goths from the earliest times to the end of the Gothic dominion in Spain. 1888.

The making of English. 1904.

Changes in the language to the days of Chaucer. CHEL vol 1 1907.

The misplaced leaf of Piers the plowman. In J. M. Manly, Piers the plowman and its sequence, 1908 (EETS).

The authorship of Piers the plowman. 1910 (EETS).

English place names. 1910 (English Assoc).

On the relations between spoken and written language, with special reference to English. 1914; Proc Br Acad 8 1919.

The numbered sections in Old English poetical mss. 1916; Proc Br Acad 7 1918.

Shakespeare's English. In Shakespeare's England vol 2, 1916.

Sir James Murray 1837–1915. [1919]; Proc Br Acad 8 1919.

On the text of Abbo of Fleury's Quaestiones Grammaticales. [1922]; Proc Br Acad 10 1921.

The collected papers, with a memoir by Robert Bridges. Oxford 1928. With bibliography.

The 'Cædmonian' Genesis. E & S 6 1910.

Editions

A new English dictionary on historical principles, founded mainly on the materials collected by the Philological Society, edited by James A. H. Murray, Henry Bradley, William A. Craigie, C. T. Onions. 11 vols Oxford 1884–1933. Bradley was joint editor from 1889, and was responsible for E, F-G, L-M, S-SH, ST, W-WEZZON.

Stratmann, F. H. A Middle-English dictionary: new edition revised by Henry Bradley. Oxford 1894.

Morris, R. Historical outlines of English accidence, revised by L. Kellner with the assistance of Henry Bradley. 1895.

—— Elementary lessons in historical English grammar, revised by Henry Bradley. 1897.

Caxton, W. Dialogues in French and English. 1900 (EETS).

Stevenson, W. Gammer Gurton's Needle, edited with critical essay and notes. In Representative English comedies, ed C. M. Gayley vol 1, New York 1903.

HENRY BRADSHAW
1831–86

Discovery of the long lost Morland mss in the library of the University of Cambridge. In J. H. Todd, The books of the Vaudois, 1865.

The printer of the Historia S Albani. 1868.

The skeleton of Chaucer's Canterbury Tales: an attempt to distinguish the several fragments of the work as left by the author. 1868, [1871].

Notice of a fragment of the fifteen Oes and other prayers printed at Westminster by William Caxton about 1490, 91, preserved in the library of the Baptist College, Bristol. 1877.

The early collection of canons known as the Hibernensis: two unfinished papers. Ed F. J. H. Jenkinson, Cambridge 1893.

Bradshaw, who was University Librarian of Cambridge, also pbd other bibliographical papers, addresses and catalogues.

§2

Prothero, G. W. A memoir of Bradshaw. 1888.

Collected papers, comprising 1: Memoranda; 2: Communications read before the Cambridge Antiquarian Society; together with an article contributed to the Bibliographer and two papers not previously published. Ed F. J. H. Jenkinson, Cambridge 1889.

Newcombe, C. F. Some aspects of the work of Bradshaw. 1905.

Crone, J. S. Bradshaw: his life and work. [1931].

Leeper, A. A scholar-librarian. 1901.

ARTHUR HENRY BULLEN
1857–1920

Anthologies

A Christmas Garland: cards and poems from the fifteenth century to the present time. 1885.

Lyrics from the song-books of the Elizabethan age. 1887; More lyrics from the song-books of the Elizabethan age, 1888; 1889 (selected from the 2 preceding volumes).

Lyrics from the dramatists of the Elizabethan age. 1889.

Musa Proterva: love poems of the Restoration. 1889 (priv ptd).

Speculum amantis: love poems from rare song-books and miscellanies of the seventeenth century. 1889 (priv ptd).

Poems, chiefly lyrical, from romances and prose tracts of the Elizabethan age; with chosen poems of Nicholas Breton. 1890.

Shorter Elizabethan poems. 1903. Part of E. Arber, An English garner.

Some longer Elizabethan poems. 1903. Part of E. Arber, An English garner.

Editions and Reprints

The works of John Day. 7 pts 1881 (priv ptd).

A collection of old English plays. 4 vols 1882–5 (priv ptd). 16 rare Elizabethan-Jacobean plays.

The English dramatists. 14 vols 1885–7 (priv ptd). Marlowe, 3 vols; Middleton, 8 vols; Marston, 3 vols.

A collection of old English plays: new series. 3 vols 1887–90 (priv ptd). Dramatic works of Nobbes, Davenport et al.

Robert Burton's The anatomy of melancholy, with introduction. 1893, 1904, 1923.

The works of Francis Beaumont and John Fletcher: variorum edition. Vols 1–4 (all pbd), 1904–12. Bullen was general editor, each play being ed by a different hand.

Sonnets by William Shakespeare. Stratford-on-Avon 1905, 1921 (rev with memoir of Bullen by H. F. B. Brett-Smith).

The works of William Shakespeare. 10 vols Stratford-on-Avon 1910 (Stratford Town edn). Includes contributions by other scholars.

Bullen also issued edns of Peele, Campion, William Browne, Arden of Feversham, Davison's Poetical Rhapsody, Englands Helicon (1600), a selection from Drayton etc. He contributed largely to DNB and GM which he edited in 1906 and was general editor of ML.

Writings

The willow. Stratford-on-Avon 1916 (priv ptd). Poems.

Weeping-Cross. Stratford-on-Avon 1917 (priv ptd). Poems.

Weeping-Cross and other rimes. 1921.

Elizabethans. 1924. Critical essays.

ALEXANDER CHALMERS

1759–1834

A lesson in biography. 1798, Edinburgh 1887 (priv ptd). A parody of Boswell's Life of Samuel Johnson.
The Tatler, with prefaces, historical and biographical. 4 vols 1803.
The British essayists; with prefaces, historical and biographical. 45 vols 1803, 1817, 38 vols 1823, Boston 1856. With index.
The Spectator. 8 vols 1806.
The Guardian. 2 vols 1806.
Walker's classics. 45 vols 1808–12. Prefaces by Chalmers.
The British gallery of contemporary portraits. 2 vols 1809–16. Many lives by Chalmers.
A history of the Colleges, Halls and public buildings attached to the University of Oxford. 2 vols Oxford 1810.
The works of the English poets from Chaucer to Cowper. 21 vols 1810. A much expanded revision of Dr Johnson's collection, the additional lives all by Chalmers.
The Projector. 3 vols 1811. Periodical essays rptd from GM.
The general biographical dictionary. 32 vols 1812–17. Expanded by Chalmers from A new and general biographical dictionary, rev W. Tooke, R. Nares and W. Beloe 15 vols 1798–1810.
A dictionary of the English language. 1820. Dr Johnson's dictionary abridged.
The life of Martin Luther. 1857.
Chalmers also supervised edns of the following, generally with memoirs of some length : Beattie, Burns, Cruden, Fielding, Gibbon, Johnson, Milton, Paley, Edward Reynolds, Shakespeare.

JOHN PAYNE COLLIER

1789–1883

§1

Trilogy on the emendations of Shakespeare's text contained in Mr Collier's corrected folio, 1632, and employed by recent editors of the poet's works. 3 pts [1814].
Criticisms on the Bar, including strictures on the principal counsel, by Amicus Curiæ. 1819. Anon.
The poetical Decameron, or ten conversations on English poets and poetry, particularly of the reigns of Elizabeth and James I. 2 vols Edinburgh 1820.
The poet's pilgrimage: an allegorical poem. 1822, 1825, 1828.
Punch and Judy, accompanied by the dialogue of the puppet show, an account of its origin, and of puppet plays in England. 1828, 1870, 1944.
The history of English dramatic poetry to the time of Shakespeare, and annals of the stage to the Restoration. 3 vols 1831, 1879 (rev).
New facts regarding the life of Shakespeare. 1835.
New particulars regarding the works of Shakespeare. 1836.
A catalogue, bibliographical and critical, of early English literature, the property of Lord Francis Egerton. 1837.
Further particulars regarding Shakespeare and his works. 1839.
The Egerton papers: a collection of public and private documents, chiefly illustrative of the times of Elizabeth and James I, the property of Lord Francis Egerton. 1840.
Reasons for a new edition of Shakespeare's works. 1841, 1842 (expanded).
Memoirs of Edward Alleyn, including some new particulars respecting Shakespeare. 1841 (Shakespeare Soc). Contains some of the forgeries ascribed to Collier.
Memoirs of the principal actors in the plays of Shakespeare. 1846 (Shakespeare Soc).
Notes and emendations to the text of Shakespeare's plays from early mss corrections in a copy of the folio 1632 in the possession of J. P. Collier. 1852, 1853 (with preface).
Reply to Mr N. E. S. Hamilton's Inquiry into the imputed Shakespeare forgeries. 1860.
Illustrations of early English popular literature. 2 vols 1863–4 (priv ptd).
A bibliographical and critical account of the rarest books in the English language. 2 vols 1865.
Illustrations of Old English literature. 3 vols 1866 (priv ptd).
Odds and ends. 1870 (priv ptd).
An old man's diary, forty years ago. 4 pts 1871 (priv ptd).
Collier also made trns from Schiller 1824–5.

Editions

A select collection of old plays. 12 vols 1825–7. Dodsley's collection with additional plays by Collier.
Kynge Johan, by John Bale. 1838.
Patient Grisil, by Henry Chettle. 1841.
The school of abuse, by Stephen Gosson. 1841.
The works of William Shakespeare: the text formed from an entirely new collation of the old editions, with the various readings, notes, a life of the poet, and a history of the early English stage. 8 vols 1842–4.
Shakespeare's library: a collection of the romances [etc] used by Shakespeare. 2 vols [1843], 6 vols 1875 (rev).
Book entries of the stationers' register relating to the drama and popular literature to 1586. 1848–9 (Shakespeare Soc).
The diary of Philip Henslowe, from 1591 to 1609. 1848.
Seven lectures of Shakespeare and Milton by the late S. T. Coleridge. 1856. Collier's own ms notes, at first unjustly suspected to be forged.
Poems by Michael Drayton. 1856.
The works of Edmund Spenser. 5 vols 1862.
The firste (second) part of Churchyard's Chippes, by Thomas Churchyard. [1870].
Foure letters, by Gabriel Harvey. [1870].
Pierces supererogation, by Gabriel Harvey. [1870].
Have with you to Saffron-Walden, by Thomas Nash. [1870].
Epitaphes, epigrams, songs and sonetes, by George Turberville. [1870].
Collier also rptd, generally with introds, many Elizabethan and Stuart rarities (mainly dramatic and poetic), both independently and for the Camden, Percy and Shakespeare Socs and Roxburghe Club, including works by Thomas Heywood, Anthony Munday, and Thomas Wash. The BM possesses a number of books containing Collier's notes and annotations in ms.

§2

Singer, S. W. The text of Shakespeare vindicated from the interpolations and corruptions advocated by J. P. Collier. 1853.
Ingleby, C. M. The Shakespeare fabrications. 1859. With bibliography.
— A complete view of the Shakespeare controversy. 1861.
Hamilton, N. E. S. A. An inquiry into the genuineness of the ms corrections in Mr Payne Collier's Shakespeare folio. 1860.
Wheatley, H. B. Notes on the life of John Payne Collier, with a complete list of his works and an account of such Shakespeare documents as are believed to be spurious. 1884.

PETER CUNNINGHAM

1816–69

Poems upon several occasions. 1841 (priv ptd).
Westminster Abbey: its art, architecture and associations —a handbook for visitors. 1842.
Inigo Jones: a life of the architect by Peter Cunningham; remarks on some of his sketches for masques and dramas by J. R. Planché [etc]. 1848 (Shakespeare Soc).
A handbook for London, past and present. 2 vols 1849, 1851 (3rd edn, as Murray's handbook for modern London), [1866] (rev), [1867] (rev), 1879.
The story of Nell Gwynn, and the sayings of Charles II, related and corrected. 1852; ed H. B. Wheatley 1892; [1926], 1927.
Cunningham also wrote several annual handbooks on London.

Editions

The poems of William Drummond of Hawthornden, with life. 1833.
Extracts from the accounts of the Revels at Court, in the reigns of Queen Elizabeth and James I, from the original office books of the masters and yeomen, with an introduction and notes. 1842 (Shakespeare Soc).
Lives of the most eminent English poets, by Samuel Johnson; with notes, corrective and explanatory. 3 vols 1854.
The works of Oliver Goldsmith. 4 vols 1854.
The letters of Horace Walpole, now first chronologically arranged. 9 vols 1857–9, 1891.
Cunningham also edited 2 vols for the Percy Soc, Songs of England and Scotland, Specimens of the British poets, *and Pope's works; he was treasurer of the Shakespeare Soc and a contributor to Fraser's Mag, GM, Athenaeum etc.*

PETER AUGUSTIN DANIEL

Notes and conjectural emendations of certain doubtful passages in Shakespeare's plays. 1870.
Romeo and Juliet: parallel texts of the first two quartos. 1874 (New Shakespeare Soc).
Romeus and Juliet (written first in Italian by Bandell, and nowe in English) by A. Brooke; Rhomeo and Julietta (translated by W. Painter from the French paraphrase by P. Boasistuau, of Bandello's version of Romeo e Giulietta). 1875 (New Shakespeare Soc, originals and analogues pt 1).
The works of Francis Beaumont and John Fletcher: variorum edition. 4 vols 1904–12. General editor, A. H. Bullen; Daniel edited The maid's tragedy and Philaster in vol 1 and The Beggar's bush in vol 2.
Daniel also contributed introds to the following plays issued in the Shakespeare Quarto-Facs Ser: Romeo and Juliet, 1874; King Lear, 1885; Much ado, 1886; Henry V, 1887; Richard II, 1887; Richard III, 1888; Merry wives, 1888.

THOMAS FROGNALL DIBDIN

1776–1847

Poems. 1797.
An introduction to the knowledge of rare and valuable editions of the Greek and Roman classics. Gloucester 1802, 1804 (enlarged), 2 vols 1808 (rev), 1827 (greatly enlarged).
The Director; a weekly literary journal. 2 vols 1807. Ed Dibdin.
Specimen bibliothecae britannicae. 1808.
The bibliomania or book-madness, in an epistle addressed to Richard Heber. 1809, 1811 (enlarged), 2 pts 1842 (improved), 1876, 1905.

The typographical antiquities of Great Britain. Vols 1–4 (all pbd), 1810–19. A partial revision of Ames.
Bibliography, a poem: book I. [1812].
Bibliotheca Spenceriana: or a descriptive catalogue of the library of Earl Spencer. 4 vols 1814–15.
The bibliographical Decameron. 3 vols 1817.
A bibliographical antiquarian and picturesque tour in France and Germany. 3 vols 1821; tr French, 1825.
Aedes Althorpianae: or an account of the mansion, books and pictures at Althorp. 2 vols 1822.
A descriptive catalogue of the books lately of the library of the Duke di Cassana Serra and now of the Earl Spencer. 4 vols 1823.
The library companion. 2 vols 1824.
The Sunday library: a selection of sermons from eminent divines. 6 vols 1831.
Bibliophobia: remarks on the present languid state of literature and the book trade, by Mercurius Rusticus. 1832.
Reminiscences of a literary life. 2 pts 1836.
The bibliographical, antiquarian and picturesque tour in the northern counties of England and Scotland. 3 vols 1838.
Cranmer: a novel, by a member of the Roxburghe Club. 3 vols 1839.
Dibdin also pbd reprints of Tudor and Stuart rarities, mainly for the Roxburghe Club, as well as sermons, pamphlets etc.

FRANCIS DOUCE

1757–1834

The dance of death. [1794?] (anon), 1833 (enlarged). Ed Douce with elaborate dissertation.
Illustrations of Shakespeare and of ancient manners, with dissertation on the clowns and fools of Shakespeare. 2 vols 1807.
A catalogue of the Harleian mss in the British Museum. 1808–12. Revised by Douce.
A catalogue of the Lansdowne mss in the British Museum. 1819. With Sir H. Ellis.
Douce also pbd edns of Arnold's Chronicle, 1811; and a few ME texts for the Roxburghe Club. Bodley possesses numerous books annotated by Douce.

ALEXANDER DYCE

1798–1869

Editions

Specimens of British poetesses. 1825, 1827.
The poetical works of William Collins. 1827.
The works of George Peele. 3 vols 1828–39.
The works of John Webster. 4 vols 1830, 1857.
The dramatic works of Robert Greene. 2 vols 1831, 1861.
The dramatic works and poems of James Shirley. 6 vols 1833.
Specimens of English sonnets. 1833.
The works of Richard Bentley. 3 vols 1836–8.
The works of Thomas Middleton. 5 vols 1840.
The poetical works of John Skelton. 2 vols 1843, 1856.
The works of Beaumont and Fletcher. 11 vols 1843–6.
The works of Christopher Marlow. 3 vols 1850.
Recollections of the table talk of Samuel Rogers. 1856, 1887, 1903, 1952 (rev).
The works of Shakespeare: the text revised. 6 vols 1857, 9 vols 1864–7 (adds glossary), 1907.
The works of John Ford. 3 vols 1869.
Dyce also pbd the Aldine edns of Akenside, Beattie, Parnell, Pope and Shakespeare's poems, as well as several Elizabethan texts for the Camden, Percy and Shakespeare Socs.

Miscellaneous Writings

Select translations from the Greek of Quintus Smyrnaeus. 1821.

Remarks on Mr J. P. Collier's and Mr Charles Knight's editions of Shakespeare. 1844.

A few notes on Shakespeare with occasional remarks on Mr Collier's copy of the folio 1632. 1858, 1859.

JOHN EARLE
1824–1903

Gloucester fragments, legends of St Swithun and Sancta Maria Aegyptiaca. 1861.

Guide to Bath, ancient and modern. 1864.

Two of the Saxon chronicles parallel, with supplementary extracts from the others, edited with introduction, notes and a glossarial index. 1865, 1889, 1892.

A book for the beginner in Anglo-Saxon. 1866, 1902.

The philology of the English tongue. 1866, 1892.

Rhymes and reasons: essays by J. E. 1871.

English plant names. 1880.

Anglo-Saxon literature. 1884.

A handbook to the land charters and other Saxonic documents. 1888.

English prose: its elements, history and usage. 1890.

Deeds of Beowulf done into modern prose. 1892.

The Psalter of 1539. 1894.

Bath during British independence. 1895.

A simple grammar of English now in use. 1898.

Alfred as a writer. In Alfred the Great, ed A. Bowker 1899.

The Alfred jewel. 1901.

The place of English in education. In Furnivall miscellany, 1901.

ALEXANDER JOHN ELLIS
1814–90

Phonetics: a familiar system of the principles of that science, by A. J. E. 1844.

The essentials of phonetics: containing the theory of a universal alphabet, together with its practical application. 1848.

An extension of phonography to foreign languages: containing a complete phonographic alphabet; and hints towards the construction of a phonographic short hand for French and German. 1848.

Phonetic spelling familiarly explained, for the use of romanic readers: with numerous examples. 1849.

On early English pronunciation, with especial reference to Shakespeare and Chaucer; containing an investigation of the correspondence of writing with speech in England, from the Anglo-Saxon period to the present day, including a re-arrangement of F. J. Child's memoirs on the language of Chaucer and Gower. 5 pts 1869–89 (Chaucer Soc, Philolog Soc, EETS). Pt 5 a dialect survey of England.

On the sensations of tone as a physiological basis for the theory of music, by Hermann Ludwig von Helmholtz; translated from the third German edition, with additions and notes. 1875, 1885 (rev with addns). 'More than a third consisted of work by Ellis himself'–DNB.

The English, Dionysian and Hellenic pronunciations of Greek, considered in reference to school and college use. 1876.

An early English hymn to the Virgin, with notes on the Welsh phonetic copy. 1876 (English Dialect Soc).

The history of musical pitch, reprinted with corrections and an appendix, from the Journal of the Society of Arts. 1880.

Ellis also wrote many other papers and books on phonetics, phonography, music, mathematics, philosophy etc, and produced phonetic texts of the Bible, Macbeth, The Tempest, Bunyan's Pilgrim's Progress *etc. He edited* The Fonetic Frend 1849 *and* The Spelling Reformer 1849–50, *and was a significant figure in the movement for spelling reform.*

FREDERICK GARD FLEAY
1831–1909

Almond blossoms. 1857. Poems.

The poetry of Catallus rendered into English. 1864.

Shakespeare manual. 1876.

Guide to Chaucer and Spenser. 1877.

Introduction to Shakespearian study. 1877.

Marlow's tragedy of Edward the second, with introductory remarks and notes. 1877.

English sounds and English spelling. 1878.

The life and death of King John, by William Shakespeare, together with the troublesome reign of King John, edited with notes. 1878.

The logical English grammar. 1884.

A chronicle history of the life and work of William Shakespeare. 1886.

A chronicle history of the London stage 1559–1642. 1890.

A biographical chronicle of the English drama 1559–1642. 2 vols 1891.

Egyptian chronology: an attempt to conciliate the ancient schemes and to educe a rational system. 1899.

Fleay also produced several grammars and papers on education etc. He was editor of Spelling Reformer 1880–1, *and contributed to* Trans New Shakespeare Soc *many important papers and edns of* Pericles *and* Timon *without the non-Shakespearian scenes.*

HARRY BUXTON FORMAN
1842–1917

Editions

The works of Percy Bysshe Shelley, in verse and prose, edited with prefaces, notes and appendices. 8 vols [1876]–80. Also poems only, 4 vols 1876, and with memoir 5 vols 1892 (Aldine edn).

Letters of John Keats to Fanny Brawne, written in the years 1819 and 1820, with introduction and notes. 1878, 1889 (rev and enlarged).

The poetical works and other writings of John Keats, edited with notes and appendices. 4 vols 1883; supplement, 1890; [poems only] 1884.

The letters of John Keats: complete edition. 1895.

The complete works of John Keats. 5 vols Glasgow 1900–1.

The poetical works of John Keats, edited with an introduction and textual notes. Oxford 1906.

Note books of Percy Bysshe Shelley, deciphered, transcribed and edited, with a full commentary. 1911 (Boston Bibliophile Soc).

The life of Percy Bysshe Shelley, by Thomas Medwin, with an introduction and commentary. 1913.

Forman also supervised edns of separate poems by Shelley as well as works by Matthew Arnold, the Brownings et al.

Writings

Our living poets: an essay in criticism. 1871.

The Shelley library: an essay in bibliography. 1886.

The books of William Morris described, with some account of his doings in literature and in the allied crafts. 1897.

Forman also contributed to Literary anecdotes of the nineteenth century, ed Sir W. R. Nicoll and T. J. Wise 2 vols 1895–6, *as well as publishing papers on Shelley, Chatterton et al.*

FREDERICK JAMES FURNIVALL
1825–1910

§ 1

Editions
for the Ballad Society
(founded by Furnivall in 1868)

Ballads from manuscripts. 1868.
Captain Cox: his ballads and books. 1871.
Love poems and humerous ones 1614–19. 1874.

Editions
for the Chaucer Society
(founded by Furnivall in 1868)

A six-text print of Chaucer's Canterbury tales in parallel columns. [1868].
The Cambridge ms of Chaucer's Canterbury tales. 1868–79; The Corpus ms, 1868–79; The Ellesmere ms, 1868–79; The Hengwrt ms, 1868–79; The Lansdowne ms, 1868–79; The Petworth ms, 1868–79; The Harleian ms 7,334, 1885; The Cambridge ms Dd 4.24, completed by the Egerton ms 2726, 1901–2.
Essays on Chaucer: his words and works. [1868–94].
Odd texts of Chaucer's minor poems. 1868.
A parallel-text edition of Chaucer's minor poems. [1871]; Trial-forewords, 1871.
Supplementary parallel-texts of Chaucer's minor poems. [1871].
A one-text print of Chaucer's minor poems. [1871].
Originals of some of Chaucer's Canterbury tales. [1872].
Chaucer as valet and squire to Edward III. 1876.
Supplementary Canterbury Tales. 1876.
Animadversions uppon the annotacions and corrections of some imperfections of impressiones of Chaucers workes reprinted in 1598 sett downe by F. Thynne. 1876.
Autotypes of Chaucer's manuscripts. 1877.
A parallel-text print of Chaucer's Troilus and Criseyde. [1881].
Chaucer's Boecce. 1886.
John Lane's continuation of Chaucer's Squire's tale. 1887.
A one-text print of Chaucer's Troilus and Criseyde. 1894.
The romaunt of the rose. 1911.

Editions
for EETS
(founded by Furnivall in 1864)

Arthur: a short sketch of his life and history in English verse. 1864.
Thynne on Speght's Chaucer. 1865. With G. Kingsley.
The Wrights chaste wife, by Adam of Cobsam. 1865.
Political, religious and love poems. 1866, 1903.
The book of quinte essence. 1866.
Hymns to the Virgin and Christ; the Parliament of Devils. 1867.
The staciouns of Rome; and The pilgrim's sea-voyage; with Clene maydenhod. 1867.
The babees book, Aristotle's ABC, Urbanitatis [etc]. 1868.
Caxton's Book of curtesye. 1868.
Queene Elizabethes Achademy [etc], [by Sir H. Gilbert]. 1869.
Awdeley's Fraternitye of vacabondes, Harman's Caveat etc. 1869. With E. Viles.
The fyrste boke of the introduction of knowledge made by A. Borde [etc.]. [1870].
The minor poems of William Lauder. 1870.
A supplicacyon for the beggars, by Simon Fish. 1871.
The history of the Holy Grail, by Henry Lovelich from the French of Sir R. de Borron. 1874–8.
Emblemes and epigrames, by Francis Thynne. 1878.
Adam Davy's 5 dreams about Edward II [etc]. 1878.
The fifty earliest English wills in the Court of Probate 1387–1439. 1882.
The anatomie of the bodie of man, by Vicary. 1888.
The Curial made by maystere A. Charretier, translated by Caxton. 1888.
Caxton's Eneydos. 1890.
Hoccleve's works. 1892–7.
The three king's sons, englisht from the French. 1895.
The English conquest of Ireland AD 1166–85. 1897.
Child-marriages, divorces and ratifications in the diocese of Chester AD 1561–6. 1897.
Lydgate's Deguileville's Pilgrimage of the life of man. 1899–1901.
Robert of Brunne's Handlyng synne. 1901–3.
Minor poems of the Vernon ms. 1901.
The Macro plays. 1904.
The tale of Beryn etc. 1909. With W. G. Stone.
The Gild of St Mary, Lichfield. 1920.

Editions
for the New Shakespeare Society
(founded by Furnivall in 1873)

Stafford's Compendious examination of certayne complaints of divers of our countrymen. 1876.
Spalding's A letter on Shakespeare's authorship of the Two noble kinsmen. 1876.
Tell-trothes new-yeares gift etc. 1876.
Harrison's description of England in Shakespere's youth. 1877.
Stubbes's Anatomy of abuses. 1877.
The Digby mysteries. 1882.
A list of all the songs and passages in Shakspere which have been set to music. 1884. With J. Greenhill.
Some 300 fresh allusions to Shakspere. 1886.
Robert Laneham's letter. 1890, 1907.

Editions
for the Roxburghe Club

Seynt Graal: or the Sank Ryal, partly in English verse by Henry Lovelich and wholly in French prose by Robiers de Borron. 2 vols 1861–3.
Robert of Brunne's Handlyng Synne, William of Waddington's Le manuel des pechiez. 1862.
La queste del Saint Graal; in the French prose of Walter Map. 1864.
A royal historie of the excellent knight Generides. Hertford 1865.
The boke of nurture, by John Russell; The boke of kervynge, by Wynkyn de Worde; The boke of nurture, by Hugh Rhodes. 2 vols 1866.

Editions of Shakespeare

The Leopold Shakspere, in chronological order, from the text of Prof Delius. [1877].
Double text dallastype Shakespeare. 1895.
The works of William Shakespeare according to the orthography and arrangement of the more authentic quarto and folio versions. 1904 (Old Spelling Shakespeare).
The Century Shakespeare. 40 vols 1908. With introds and notes, and a vol on the life and work of Shakespeare, by Furnivall and J. J. Munro.
Cassell's illustrated Shakespeare. 1913.
Furnivall also edited a number of the plays separately.

Other Editions

Le Morte Arthur, edited from the Harleian ms 2,252 in the British Museum. 1864.
Bishop Percy's folio manuscript: ballads and romances. 1867. With J. W. Hales.
The boke of nurture by H. Rhodes. [1868?].
Mannyng of Brunne, Robert. The story of England AD 1338. 1887 (Rolls Ser).

Lamb's Tales from Shakespeare, with introduction and additions. 1901.

Many other works were written, edited or provided with introds by Furnivall, who founded the Wiclif Soc and the Browning Soc in 1881, and the same year compiled a Browning bibliography. In 1874 he contributed to Gervinus's commentaries on Shakspere an essay on metrical tests for the chronology of Shakespeare's works. In 1886 he founded the Shelley Soc. He was, as secretary of the Philological Soc, the proposer of the scheme for the New English Dictionary.

§2

An English miscellany presented to Dr Furnivall in honour of his seventy-fifth birthday. Oxford 1901.

Sidgwick, F. Frederick James Furnivall. Eng Illustr Mag 30 1904. A memoir with bibliography.

Dr Frederick James Furnivall. 1910. Obituary notices by Mrs C. C. Stopes and A. Brandl.

Ker, W. P. Memoir. Proc Br Acad 3 1909–10.

Furnivall: a volume of personal record. 1911. Reminiscences by forty-nine contributors, with a biography by J. J. Munro.

JOHN GENEST

1764–1839

Some account of the English stage from 1660 to 1830. 10 vols Bath 1832. Anon.

SIR ISRAEL GOLLANCZ

1863–1930

Pearl: an English poem of the fourteenth century, edited with a modern rendering. 1891, EETS 1923 (with Cleanness, Patience and Sir Gawain).

Cynewulf's Christ, edited with a modern rendering. 1892.

Charles Lamb's Specimens of English dramatic poets, now first edited anew. 1893.

The Exeter book, edited with a translation, notes and introduction. EETS 1895.

The parlement of the thre ages, edited with introduction, notes. 1897.

Hoccleve's works, vol 2: The minor poems in the Ashburnham ms addit 133. EETS 1897.

Marlowe's The tragical history of Doctor Faustus. 1897.

Hamlet in Iceland: being the Icelandic Ambales Saga, edited and translated. 1898.

Otway's Venice preserved. 1899.

Select early English poems. 1913.

A book of homage to Shakespeare. 1916. Gollancz was general editor.

Ich dene: some observations on a ms of the life and feats of arms of Edward Prince of Wales, the Black Prince, a metrical chronicle in French verse by the Herald of Sir John Chandos. 1921.

The Middle Ages in the lineage of English poetry. 1921.

Sir Gawayne and the Greene Knight, re-edited by R. Morris, revised. 1925, 1940.

The sources of Hamlet. 1926.

The Cædmon manuscripts of Anglo-Saxon Biblical poetry, Junius XI in the Bodleian Library. 1927.

Allegory and mysticism in Shakespeare: reports of three lectures. 1931 (priv ptd).

Gollancz was general editor of the following publishers' sers: The Temple Shakespeare, The Temple Classics, The King's Classics, The King's Novels, The Shakespeare Library. For memoir see F. G. Kenyon, Proc Br Acad 18 1932.

ALEXANDER BALLOCH GROSART

1835–99

Series of Reprints

The Fuller worthies library. 39 vols Edinburgh and Blackburn 1868–76 (priv ptd). Works of Sir John Davies, Fulke Greville, Henry Vaughan, Marvell, George Herbert; poems of Fuller, Crashaw, Donne, Southwell, Sidney et al.

Miscellanies of the Fuller worthies library. 4 vols Blackburn 1870–6 (priv ptd). Works of minor 16th- and 17th-century writers.

Occasional issues of unique and very rare books. 18 vols 1875–83 (priv ptd). 16th- and 17th-century rarities such as Robert Dover's Annalia Dubrensia, Robert Chester's Love's martyr, Willobie his Avisa etc.

The Chertsey worthies library, edited with memorial-introductions, notes, illustrations and facsimiles. 14 vols [Blackburn] 1876–80 (priv ptd). Works of Nicholas Breton, John Davies of Hereford, Joshua Sylvester, Francis Quarles, Joseph Beaumont, Henry More, Cowley.

Early English poets, edited with memorial-introductions and notes. 9 vols 1876–7 (priv ptd). Herrick, Sidney, Giles Fletcher, John Davies of Hereford.

The Huth library: or Elizabethan-Jacobean unique or very rare books, largely from the library of Henry Huth, edited with notes, introductions and illustrations. 29 vols 1881–6 (priv ptd). Works of Greene, Nashe, Gabriel Harvey, and Dekker's prose works.

Grosart also issued The complete works of Edmund Spenser, 9 vols 1882–4 (priv ptd) (*with contributions by E. Dowden, F. T. Palgrave et al*), The complete works of Samuel Daniel, 5 vols 1885–96 (priv ptd), The poetical works of George Herbert, 1891 (Aldine), *edns for Camden Soc, Roxburghe Club and Chetham Soc, and numerous other reprints including a number of 17th-century Puritan divines.*

Writings

Hymns. Liverpool 1868 (priv ptd).

Songs of the day and night: or three centuries of original hymns. Edinburgh 1890 (priv ptd), 1891.

Robert Ferguson. 1898.

Also numerous theological works, contributions to A. H. Miles, The poets and the poetry of the century, *many articles in periodicals, etc. For an appreciation see* O. Smeaton, A great Elizabethan, Westminster Rev 151 1899.

JOHN WESLEY HALES

1836–1914

Notes and essays on Shakespeare. 1884.

Folia litteraria: essays and notes on English literature. 1893.

Hales also pbd edns of Bishop Percy's Folio ms with F. J. Furnivall, Milton's Areopagitica, *and various works by Goldsmith, Gray, Johnson, Spenser and Malory. He was general editor of the* Handbooks of English literature ser 1895–1903.

JAMES ORCHARD HALLIWELL, later HALLIWELL-PHILLIPPS

1820–89

§1

Shakesperiana: a catalogue of the early editions of Shakespeare's plays and of the commentaries and other publications illustrative of his works. 1841.

A dictionary of archaic and provincial words, obsolete phrases, proverbs and ancient customs from the fourteenth century. 2 vols 1846–7, 6 edns by 1904.

The life of William Shakespeare; including many particulars respecting the poet and his family never before published. 1848.

Contributions to early English literature derived chiefly from rare books and ancient inedited manuscripts from the fifteenth to the seventeenth century. 6 pts 1849.

A new boke about Shakespeare and Stratford-on-Avon. 1850.

Observations on the Shakespeare forgeries at Bridgewater House, illustrative of a facsimile of the spurious letter of H.S. 1853 (priv ptd). On the John Payne Collier controversy.

A brief hand-list of books, manuscripts etc illustrative of the life and writings of Shakespeare, collected between the years 1842 and 1859. 1859 (priv ptd).

A dictionary of old English plays, existing either in print or in manuscript, from the earliest times to the close of the seventeenth century. 1860.

A brief hand-list of the records belonging to the Borough of Stratford-on-Avon showing their general character; with notes of a few of the Shakespearian documents in the same collection. 1862 (priv ptd).

A handlist of upwards of a thousand volumes of Shakespeariana added to the three previous collections of a similar kind. 1862 (priv ptd).

A descriptive calendar of the ancient manuscripts and records in the possession of the Corporation of Stratford-on-Avon; including notices of Shakespeare and his family, and of several persons connected with the poet. 1863 (priv ptd).

Illustrations of the life of Shakespeare in a discursive series of essays. 1874.

New lamps or old? a few additional words respecting the E and the A in the name of our national dramatist. Brighton 1880. Favours the spelling 'Shakespeare'.

Outlines of the life of Shakespeare. Brighton 1881 (priv ptd), 1882 (tripled in size), 2 vols 1887 (7th edn, enlarged). A different work from the Life of Shakespeare, above.

A calendar of the Shakespearean rarities, drawings and engravings, preserved at Hollingbury Copse. 1887 (priv ptd); ed E. E. Baker 1891 (enlarged).

Halliwell pbd many other bks and pamphlets, many of them in very small limited edns, dealing with Shakespearian topography, history, iconography etc; with 16th- and 17th-century literature and earlier literature; also catalogues, inventories etc.

Editions

The voiage and travaile of Sir John Maundevile, kt, reprinted from the edition of 1725, with an introduction, additional notes and glossary. 1839.

The harrowing of Hell: a miracle play, written in the reign of Edward the second, now first published from the original manuscript in the British Museum, with an introduction, translation and notes. 1840.

The first sketch of the Merry wives of Windsor. 1842 (Shakespeare Soc).

The nursery rhymes of England, obtained principally from oral tradition. 1842, 1843 (with addns), 1846 (4th edn, with addns) (Percy Soc).

Private diary of John Dee, and the catalogue of his library of manuscripts. 1842 (Camden Soc).

Nugae poeticae: select pieces of old English popular poetry, illustrating the manners and arts of the fifteenth century. 1844.

The Thornton romances: the early English metrical romances of Perceval, Isumbras, Eglamom and Degrevant, selected from manuscripts at Lincoln and Cambridge. 1844 (Camden Soc).

Letters of the Kings of England, now first collected from the originals, edited, with an historical introduction and notes. 2 vols 1846.

Morte Arthure: the alliterative romance of the death of King Arthur, now first printed from a manuscript in Lincoln Cathedral. 1847.

The poetry of witchcraft illustrated by copies of the plays on the Lancashire witches by Heywood, [Brome] and Shadwell. 1853 (priv ptd).

The works of William Shakespeare: the text formed from a new collation of the early editions; to which are added all the original novels and tales on which the plays are founded, copious archaeological annotations on each play; an essay on the formation of the text; and a life of the poet. 16 vols 1853–65 (150 copies ptd for the editor).

A glossary or collection of words, phrases, names and allusions to customs, proverbs etc which have been thought to require illustration in the works of the English authors, particularly Shakespeare and his contemporaries, by Robert Nares: a new edition, with considerable additions. 2 vols 1859. With Thomas Wright.

A treatyse of a galaunt; with the maryage of the fayre Pusell, the bosse of Byllyngesgate unto London Stone, from the unique edition printed by Wynkyn de Worde. 1860 (priv ptd).

Shakespearian facsimiles: a collection of curious and interesting documents, plans, signatures &c illustrative of the biography of Shakespeare and the history of his family, from the originals chiefly preserved at Stratford-on-Avon, facsimiled by E. W. Ashbee, selected by Halliwell. 1863 (priv ptd).

Those songs and poems from the excessively rare first edition of England's Helicon, 1600, which are connected with the works of Shakespeare. 1865 (25 copies).

Stratford-upon-Avon in the times of the Shakespeares, illustrated by extracts from the Council books of the Corporation, selected especially with reference to the history of the poet's father. 1864–5.

Halliwell edited some 150 works, mainly but not entirely in 17th century literature, and did much work for the Camden, Percy and Shakespeare Socs. In 1841–2, with Thomas Wright, he edited Archaeologist *and* Jnl of Antiquarian Science, *of which only 10 issues appeared.*

§2

Winsor, J. Halliwelliana: a bibliography of the publications of James Orchard Halliwell-Phillipps. Cambridge Mass 1881.

Wright, G. R. A brief memoir of the late Halliwell-Phillipps. 1889.

Obituary. Athenaeum 12 Jan 1889.

JOSEPH HASLEWOOD

1769–1833

Editions

The book containing the treatises of hawking, hunting, coat-armour, fishing and blasing of arms [by Juliana Berners]. 1810.

Ancient critical essays upon English poets and poësy. 2 vols 1811–15.

The first [and second] tome of the palace of pleasure [by William Painter]. 2 vols 1813.

Mirror for magistrates; collated with various editions. 2 vols 1815.

Barnabae itinerarium: or Barnabee's journal [by Richard Brathwait]. 1818, 2 vols 1820 (enlarged).

Also various rarities for the Roxburghe Club etc.

Miscellaneous Writings

Some account of the life and publications of the late Joseph Ritson. 1824.
Roxburghe Revels and other relative papers, including answers to the attack on the memory of the late Joseph Haslewood, with specimens of his literary productions. Ed J. Maidment, Edinburgh 1837 (priv ptd).
Haslewood also contributed largely to GM, *to* S. E. Brydges, Censura literaria, 1807–9, *and to* Bibliographer 1810–14.

WILLIAM CAREW HAZLITT
1834–1913

The history of the origin and rise of the Republic of Venice. 2 vols 1858, 1860 (enlarged).
Hand-book to the popular, poetical and dramatic literature of Great Britain, from the invention of printing to the Restoration. 1867.
Memoirs of William Hazlitt, with portions of his correspondence. 2 vols 1867.
Collections and notes. 4 sers and supplements 1876–1903. Catalogues of early English writings; general index by G. J. Gray 1893.
Schools, school-books and schoolmasters: a contribution to the history of educational development in Great Britain. 1888.
The Livery companies of the City of London. 1892.
A manual for the collector and amateur of old English plays. 1892.
The coinage of the European continent. 2 vols 1893–7.
The coin collector. 1896.
The confessions of a collector. 1897.
Four generations of a literary family: the Hazlitts 1725–1896. 2 vols 1897.
The Lambs: their lives, their friends and their correspondence. 1897.
Shakespeare. 1902, 1903 (rev), 1908 (recast and expanded).
The book-collector: a general survey of the pursuit. 1904.
The later Hazlitts. 1912 (priv ptd).
Hazlitt also pbd poems, essays, a novel, and several vols in H. B. Wheatley, Booklover's Library.

Editions

Old English jest-books. 3 vols 1864.
The Roxburghe Library. 8 vols 1868–70. Includes inedited tracts illustrating the manners, opinions and occupations of Englishmen during the sixteenth and seventeenth centuries, 1867; The English drama and stage 1543–1664, illustrated by a series of documents, 1869.
English proverbs and proverbial phrases collected from the most authentic sources. 1869, 1882 (enlarged), 1907.
Warton, Thomas. History of English poetry, edited with new notes and other additions. 4 vols 1871.
Prefaces, dedications, epistles selected from early English books 1540–1701. [1874] (priv ptd).
Dodsley, Robert. A select collection of old English plays, revised and enlarged. 15 vols 1874–6.
Fairy tales, legends and romances, illustrating Shakespeare and other early English writers. 1875.
Poetical and dramatic works of Thomas Randolph, now first collected. 2 vols 1875.
Shakespeare's library: a collection of the novels, romances, poems and histories used by Shakespeare, second edition greatly enlarged. 6 vols 1875. 1st edn by J. P. Collier.
Letters of Charles Lamb: an entirely new edition. 2 vols 1886.
Lamb and Hazlitt: further letters and records. 1900.
Hazlitt's editorial work also included reprints of Herrick, Suckling, William Hazlitt (his grandfather), an anthology of early popular poetry of England, and a trn of Montaigne.

GEORGE BIRKBECK NORMAN HILL
1835–1903

Dr Johnson, his friends and critics. 1878.
The life of Sir Rowland Hill. 2 vols 1880.
Footsteps of Dr Johnson (Scotland). 1890.
Writers and readers. 1892. Six lectures, 1–4 on revolutions in literary taste, 5–6 on the study of literature as a part of education.
Harvard College, by an Oxonian. New York 1894.
Talks about autographs. Boston 1896. Reminiscences of Lamb, Arnold, Froude et al.
Letters written by a grandfather, selected by Lucy Crump. 1903.
Letters, arranged by Lucy Crump. 1906. Arranged to form a complete memoir.

Editions

Boswell's Life of Johnson, including Boswell's Journal of a tour to the Hebrides and Johnson's diary of a journey into North Wales. 6 vols Oxford 1887, 1934.
The history of Rasselas, Prince of Abyssinia. Oxford 1887.
Wit and wisdom of Samuel Johnson. Oxford 1888.
Letters of David Hume to William Strahan. Oxford 1888.
Goldsmith, The traveller. Oxford 1888.
Select essays of Dr Johnson. 2 vols 1889.
Lord Chesterfield's Worldly wisdom: selections. Oxford 1891.
Letters of Dante Gabriel Rossetti to William Allingham. 1897.
Johnsonian miscellanies. 2 vols Oxford 1897.
Unpublished letters of Dean Swift. 1899.
The memoirs of the life of Edward Gibbon. 1900.
Lives of the English poets, by Samuel Johnson, edited by Hill, with brief memoir of Birkbeck Hill by Harold Spencer Scott. 3 vols Oxford 1905. Includes bibliography of Hill's writings.

JOSEPH HUNTER
1783–1861

Literary Studies and Editions

Who wrote Cavendish's Life of Wolsey? 1814, 1825.
Golden sentences [from Fuller, Sir Thomas Browne, Whichcote et al]. Bath 1826.
Life of Sir Thomas More by Cresacre More. 1828.
The diary of Ralph Thoresby. 2 vols 1830.
The Towneley mysteries. 1936 (Surtees Soc).
A disquisition on the scene, origin, date etc of Shakespeare's Tempest. 1839 (priv ptd).
The diary of Dr Thomas Cartwright. 1843 (Camden Soc).
New illustrations of the life, studies and writings of Shakespeare. 2 vols 1845.
Milton: a sheaf of gleanings after his biographers and annotators. 1850.
The great hero of the ancient minstrelsy of England, Robin Hood. 1852, Worksop 1883.
Pope: his descent and family connections. 1857.

Historical and Antiquarian Writings

Hallamshire: the history and topography of the parish of Sheffield. 1819.
South Yorkshire: the history and topography of the Deanery of Doncaster. 2 vols 1828–31.

The Hallamshire glossary. 1829.
English monastic libraries. 1831.
Gens Sylvestrina: memorials of some of my ancestors. 1846 (priv ptd).
Collections concerning the early history of the founders of New England. 1849.
Also edns of various rolls for the Public Records Commissioners. Hunter's contributions to Archaeologica *are listed in* Sylvester Hunter, A brief memoir of the late J. Hunter, 1861.

CLEMENT MANSFIELD INGLEBY
1823–86

The Shakespeare fabrications: or the ms notes of the Perkins folio shown to be of recent origin, with an appendix on the authorship of the Ireland forgeries. 1859. On the John Payne Collier controversy.
A complete view of the Shakespeare controversy, concerning the authenticity and genuineness of manuscript matter affecting the works and biography of Shakespeare, published by Mr J. Payne Collier as the fruits of his researches. 1861.
An introduction to metaphysics. 2 pts 1864–9.
Was Thomas Lodge an actor? an exposition touching the social status of the playwright in the time of Queen Elizabeth. 1868.
The still lion: an essay towards the restoration of Shakespeare's text, reprinted with additions from the second annual volume of the German Shakespeare Society. 1874, 1875 (enlarged as Shakespeare Hermeneutics).
Shakespeare—the man and the book: being a collection of occasional papers on the bard and his writings. 2 pts 1877–81.
Shakespeare's bones: a proposal to disinter them, considered in relation to their possible bearing on his portraiture: illustrated by instances on visits of the living to the dead. 1883.
Essays by the late C. M. Ingleby, edited by his son [Holcombe Ingleby]. 1888.
Ingleby also pbd several shorter papers, mainly on Shakespeare, and a number of books on philosophy and logic.

Editions

Shakespeare's allusion-books, pt 1. 1874.
Shakespeare's Centurie of prayse: being materials for a history of opinion on Shakespeare and his works, culled from writers of the first century after his rise. 1874, 1879 (rev with addns, for New Shakespeare Soc by L. T. Smith).
Shakespeare's Cymbeline: the text revised and annotated. 1886, 1889.

DAVID IRVING
1778–1860

The life of Robert Ferguson. Glasgow, 1799.
Lives of Scottish authors, viz Ferguson, Falconer and Russell. Edinburgh 1801.
The elements of English composition. Edinburgh 1801, 11 edns by 1841.
The lives of the Scotish poets. 2 vols Edinburgh 1804, London 1810 (rev).
Memoirs of the life and writings of George Buchanan. Edinburgh 1807, 1817 (rev).
Observations on the study of civil law. Edinburgh 1815.
A catalogue of the law books in the Advocates' Library. Edinburgh 1831.
Lives of Scotish writers. 2 vols Edinburgh 1839. Rptd from Encyclopaedia britannica 7th edn.
The history of Scotish poetry. Ed J. A. Carlyle, Edinburgh 1861. With memoir of Irving by David Laing.

Editions

The poetical works of R. Fergusson. Glasgow 1800.
Selden's table talk. 1819, 1854 (rev).
The poems of Alexander Montgomerie. Edinburgh 1821. With D. Laing.
The moral fables of Robert Henryson. Glasgow 1832 (Maitland Club).
Davidis Buchanani de scriptoribus scotis libri duo. Edinburgh 1837 (Bannatyne Club).
Also other works for the Maitland and Bannatyne Clubs.

JOHN JAMIESON
1759–1839

The use of sacred history. Edinburgh 1802, 2 vols Hartford 1810.
An etymological dictionary of the Scottish language. 2 vols Edinburgh 1808, 1818 (abridged by Author), 1867 (rev by J. Longmuir), 4 vols Paisley 1879–87 (rev by J. Longmuir and D. Donaldson).
An historical account of the ancient culdees of Iona. Edinburgh 1811, Glasgow 1890.
Hermes Scythius: or the radical affinities of the Greek and Latin languages to the Gothic. Edinburgh 1814.
The Bruce [by Barbour] and Wallace [by Blind Harry]. 2 vols Edinburgh 1820.
Jamieson also pbd 3 long poems 1789–98, sermons and theological works.

CHARLES KNIGHT
1791–1873

Arminius, or the deliverance of Germany: a tragedy. Windsor 1814.
The bridal of the Isles: a mask. 1817 (2nd edn).
A glossary; the lives of Tasso and Fairfax. Prefixed to 5th edn of E. Fairfax's Tasso, 2 vols Windsor 1817.
The menageries: the quadrupeds. 3 vols 1829–40 (Soc for Diffusion of Useful Knowledge). Anon.
The working man's companion, pt 1: The rights of industry—capital and labour. 1831 (Soc for the Diffusion of Useful Knowledge) (2nd edn); pt 2: The results of machinery, namely cheap production and increased employment, 1831 (Soc for the Diffusion of Useful Knowledge). Anon.
Trades' unions and strikes. 1834. Anon.
The pictorial edition of the works of Shakspere. 7 vols [1839–]41, 5 vols 1867 (rev).
Shakspere and his writings. In Knight's Store of knowledge, 1841.
London. 6 vols 1841–4; rev E. Walford 6 vols [1875–7]. Ed Knight, and contains many articles by him.
William Shakspere: a biography. 1842, 1850 (as Studies and illustrations of Shakspere vol 1).
William Caxton: a biography. 1844.
Studies of Shakspere, forming a companion volume to every edition of the text. 1849. Rptd from Pictorial and Library edns.
Studies and illustrations of the writings of Shakspere. 3 vols 1850.
The struggle of a book against excessive taxation. [1850] (2nd edn).
Once upon a time. 2 vols 1854, 1859, 1865.
The English cyclopaedia. 22 vols 1854–70. With A. Ramsay and J. Thorne.
The old printer and the modern press. 1854. Partly based on biography of Caxton, 1844.

The popular history of England. 8 vols 1856–62.

Passages of a working life, with a prelude of early reminiscences. 3 vols 1864–5, 1873, 1874.

Shadows of old booksellers. 1865, 1905, 1927.

Begg'd at Court: a legend of Westminster. 1867. A novel.

For life see A. A. Clowes, Charles Knight: a sketch, 1892 (with bibliography). *Knight pbd many edns of Shakespeare, including a facsimile edn, 1895, pbd, and wrote some of, Knight's Weekly Volumes, also several Cyclopaedias, and did much work for the Soc for the Diffusion of Useful Knowledge.*

DAVID LAING
1793–1878

Select remains of the ancient popular poetry of Scotland. Edinburgh 1822; ed J. Small, Edinburgh 1885 (with a memoir of Laing).

Various pieces of fugitive Scottish poetry. 2 vols Edinburgh 1823–5.

Early Scottish metrical tales. Edinburgh 1826, Paisley 1889.

The poems of William Dunbar. 2 vols Edinburgh 1834. Suppl of selections from minor Makars, 1865.

The letters and journals of Robert Abillie. 3 vols 1841–2 (Bannatyne Club).

The works of John Knox. 6 vols 1846–64 (Wodrow Soc and Bannatyne Club).

The poems and fables of Robert Henryson. Edinburgh 1865.

The poetical works of Sir David Lyndsay. 2 vols Edinburgh 1871, 3 vols Edinburgh 1879 (with bibliography).

In addition to over 100 papers in Proc Soc Antiquaries of Scotland, and various antiquarian books and pamphlets, Laing edited or assisted in editing many rarities (mainly Scottish) for the Abbotsford, Bannatyne, Hunterian and Spalding Clubs, and Shakespeare and Wodrow Socs, including 27 works for the Bannatyne Club alone. For details see T. G. Stevenson, Notices of David Laing with list of his publications, 1878 (priv ptd), *and* D. Murray, David Laing, antiquary and bibliographer, Scottish Historical Rev, July 1914.

SIR SIDNEY LEE
1859–1926

§1

Stratford-on-Avon, from the earliest times to the death of William Shakespeare. 1885, 1907.

The study of English literature: an address. 1893 (priv ptd).

A life of William Shakespeare. 1898, 1915 (rewritten and enlarged), 1925 (new preface).

Shakespeare's King Henry the Fifth: an account and an estimate. 1900, 1908.

Queen Victoria: a biography. 1902.

Great Englishmen of the sixteenth century. 1904. On Thomas More, Philip Sidney, Walter Ralegh, Spenser, Bacon, Shakespeare's career, foreign influences on Shakespeare.

Shakespeare and the modern stage, with other essays. 1906.

The French renaissance in England: an account of the literary relations of England and France in the sixteenth century. Oxford 1910.

Principles of biography: the Leslie Stephen lecture. Cambridge 1911.

The place of English literature in the modern university: a lecture. 1913.

King Edward VII: a biography. 2 vols 1925–7.

Elizabethan and other essays. Ed F. S. Boas, Oxford 1929 (with memoir).

Lee pbd other pamphlets, mainly on Elizabethan topics. He contributed to CHEL, Cambridge Modern History, Year's Work in English Studies 1921–3, Trans New Shakespeare Soc and other composite works.

Editions

The boke of Duke Huon of Burdeux, by Lord Berners. 4 pts EETS 1882–7.

The autobiography of Edward, Lord Herbert of Cherbury. 1886, 1906.

The dictionary of national biography, vol 27–end of suppl 2 1891–1917. In addition to editing the Dictionary, Lee contributed 820 articles, exclusive of his work in the supplements.

Shakespeare's comedies, histories and tragedies: being a reproduction in facsimile of the first folio edition, with introduction and census of copies. Oxford 1902. Similar facs reprints of Pericles, Sonnets, Venus and Adonis, Lucrece, 1905. Census also pbd separately; Notes and additions to the census, 1906.

Elizabethan sonnets, with an introduction. 2 vols 1904. A re-arrangement of parts of Arber's English garner.

Methuen's standard library. 40 vols 1905–6.

The works of William Shakespeare. 20 vols Cambridge Mass 1907–10 (Caxton edn). General introd only by Lee.

The chronicle history of King Leir. 1909. With introd.

Shakespeare's England. 2 vols Oxford 1916. Planned and partly ed Lee.

§2

Pollard, A. F. Lee and the Dictionary of national biography. Bull Inst of Historical Research June 1926.

Harrison, G. B. Sir Sidney Lee. London Mercury June 1930.

Firth, C. H. Sir Sidney Lee. 1931.

ROBERT WILLIAM LOWE

The fashionable tragedian. 1877. On Irving. Written with William Archer.

A bibliographical account of the English theatrical literature from the earliest times to the present day. 1888.

Thomas Betterton: a biography. 1891.

Lowe also edited Churchill's Rosciad and Apology, Cibber's Apology and J. Doran's Their Majesties' Servants, as well as a series of Dramatic essays by Hazlitt, Hunt, Lewes etc with Archer.

GEORGE CAMPBELL MACAULAY
1852–1915

Francis Beaumont: a critical study. 1883.

The history of Herodotus, translated. 2 vols 1890.

Poems by Matthew Arnold, selected and edited. 1896, 1928.

The complete works of John Gower, edited from the manuscripts with introductions, notes and glossaries. 4 vols Oxford 1899–1902.

Gower: selections from Confessio amantis. Oxford 1903.

James Thomson. 1908 (EML).

Also German, Greek and Latin text-books and edns of 4 of Tennyson's Idylls of the King and of Lord Berners' Froissart (Globe).

SIR FREDERIC MADDEN

1801–73

The ancient English romance of Havelok the Dane, accompanied by the French text; with an introduction, notes and a glossary. 1828 (Roxburghe Club).

Privy purse expenses of the Princess Mary, daughter of King Henry the eighth, afterwards Queen Mary, with a memoir of the Princess and notes. 1831.

The ancient English romance of William and the Werewolf; edited, with an introduction and glossary. 1832 (Roxburghe Club). With 2 letters on Werewolves by A. Herbert.

Illuminated ornaments, selected from manuscripts and early printed books from the sixth to the seventeenth centuries, drawn and engraved by H. Shaw; with descriptions by Madden. 1833.

The Olde English versions of the Gesta Romanorum, edited for the first time from manuscripts in the British Museum and University Library, Cambridge, with an introduction and notes. 1838 (Roxburghe Club).

Syr Gawayne: a collection of ancient romance-poems by Scottish and English authors, relating to that celebrated Knight of the Round Table, with an introduction, notes and a glossary. 1839 (Bannatyne Club).

Lazamon's Brut, or chronicle of Britain: a poetical semi-Saxon paraphrase of the Brut of Wace, now first published from the Cottonian manuscripts in the British Museum; accompanied by a literal translation, notes and a grammatical glossary. 3 vols 1847 (Soc of Antiquaries).

The Holy Bible in the earliest English versions made from the Latin Vulgate by John Wycliffe and his followers; edited by the Rev Josiah Forshall and Madden. 4 vols Oxford 1850. Contains glossary, with 2 distinct texts throughout.

Universal palaeography: or facsimiles of writings of all periods and nations, by J. B. Silvestre; accompanied by an historical and descriptive text by Champollion-Figeac and A. Champollion, translated from the French, and edited, with corrections and notes. 2 vols 1850.

Matthei Parisiensis, Monach Sancti Albani, Historia Anglorum, sive, ut vulgo dicitur, historia minor: item, ejusdem abbreviato chronicorum Angliae. 3 vols 1866–9 (Rolls Ser). To vol 3 is prefaced a life and criticism of Matthew Paris.

Madden was Keeper of mss at the BM from 1837, and produced various guides and catalogues for that department; his other edns included one of Warton's History of English poetry.

JAMES MAIDMENT

1795?–1879

A north countrie garland. Edinburgh 1824 (anon); ed T. G. Stevenson, Edinburgh 1868.

A [second; third] book of Scottish pasquils. 3 pts Edinburgh 1827–8, Edinburgh 1868 (enlarged).

Reliquiae Scoticae: Scotish remains in prose and verse. Edinburgh 1829. With R. Pitcairn.

Analecta Scotica: collections illustrative of the civil, ecclesiastical and literary history of Scotland. 2 vols Edinburgh 1834–7.

Fragmenta Scoto-dramatica 1715–58. Edinburgh 1835.

Bannatyniana: notices relative to the Bannatyne Club, including critiques on some of its publications. Edinburgh 1836.

Scotish elegiac verses on the principal nobility and gentry from 1629–1729. Edinburgh 1842.

A new book of old ballads. Edinburgh 1844; ed T. G. Stevenson, Edinburgh 1868, 1885.

Scotish ballads and songs. Edinburgh 1859, 1868.

Dramatists of the Restoration. 14 vols Edinburgh 1872–9. With W. H. Logan.

Maidment also pbd much, mainly Scottish antiquities, for the Abbotsford, Bannatyne, Hunterian and Maitland Clubs and the Spottiswoode Soc. For details see T. G. Stevenson, A bibliographical list of the various publications by James Maidment from 1817 to 1878, Edinburgh 1883.

RICHARD MORRIS

1833–94

The etymology of local names. Pt 1 (all pbd) 1857.

Historical outlines of English accidence, comprising chapters on the history and development of the language, and on word-formation. 1872; rev H. Bradley 1893.

Elementary lessons in historical English grammar. 1874; rev H. Bradley 1897.

English grammar. 1875. One of J. R. Green's Literature primers.

Notes and queries [on Pali lexicography]. [1887].

Also minor philological writings.

Editions

Rolle's Pricke of conscience. 1863.

Early English alliterative poems of the West Midlands dialect of the fourteenth century. EETS 1894, 1934.

Sir Gawayne and the Green Knight: an alliterative romance-poem. EETS 1864, 1925.

The story of Genesis and Exodus: an Early English song. EETS 1865, 1895.

Dan Michel's Ayenbite of Inwyt: or remorse of conscience. EETS 1866.

Specimens of early English AD 1250–AD 1400, with grammatical introduction, notes and glossary. Oxford 1867; rev W. W. Skeat, Oxford 1872.

Old English homilies and homiletic treatises of the twelfth and thirteenth centuries. EETS 2 sers 1868–73.

Chaucer's translation of Boethius's De consolatione philosophiae. EETS 1868, 1886.

Legends of the Holy Rood; symbols of the Passion and crosspoems. In Old English of the eleventh, fourteenth and fifteenth centuries, EETS 1871.

An Old English miscellany: containing a bestiary, Kentish sermons, Proverbs of Alfred, religious poems of the thirteenth century. EETS 1872.

Cursor mundi: the cursur of the world—a Northumbrian poem of the XIVth century in four versions. EETS 6 pts 1874–93.

The Blickling homilies of the tenth century. EETS 3 pts [1874–80].

Morris's other editorial work included the Aldine Chaucer, 1866, and the Globe Spenser, 1869.

SIR JAMES AUGUSTUS HENRY MURRAY

1837–1915

Editions

Sir David Lindesay's works: the minor poems. EETS 1863.

The complaynt of Scotlande, vyth ane exortatione to the thre estaits to be vigilante in the deffens of their public veil. EETS 1872.

The romance and prophecies of Thomas of Erceldoune, with illustrations from the prophetic literature of the 15th and 16th centuries. EETS 1875.

A new English dictionary on historical principles, founded mainly on materials collected by the Philological

Society. 11 vols Oxford 1884–1933, 13 vols Oxford 1933 (a corrected re-issue, with introd, suppl and bibliography, as The Oxford English Dictionary). Murray was chief creator of the NED, though his actual editorial responsibility covered only A-D, H-K, O, P, T.

Writings

The dialect of the southern counties of Scotland: its pronunciation, grammar and historical relations, with an appendix and a linguistical map of Scotland. 1873 (Philological Soc).

The Romanes lecture 1900: the evolution of English lexicography. Oxford 1900.

Also several short papers on philology, and a book on Orkney. For an appreciation see H. Bradley, Sir James Murray, Proc Br Acad 8 1919, *and* S. Baldwin, The Oxford English Dictionary 1884–1928: an address, [1928].

ROBERT NARES
1753–1829

Elements of Orthoepy, containing the whole analogy of the English language so far as it relates to pronunciation, accent and quantity. 1784, 1792 (as General rules for the pronunciation of the English language).

The British critic: a new review. May 1793–Oct 1826. Vols 1–42 ed Nares and William Beloe.

A new and general biographical dictionary. 15 vols 1798–1810. In this 3rd edn vols 6, 8, 10, 12, 14 were ed Nares.

Essays and other occasional compositions. 2 vols 1810.

A glossary, or collection of words, phrases, names and allusions to customs, proverbs etc which have been thought to require illustrations in the works of English authors, particularly Shakespeare and his contemporaries. 1822, 1825; rev J. O. Halliwell and T. Wright 2 vols 1859, 1882, 1905. For an appreciation *see* A book of words, TLS 1 June 1922.

Nares also pbd sermons and theological and miscellaneous works.

SIR NICHOLAS HARRIS NICOLAS
1799–1848

Life of William Davison, Secretary of State to Queen Elizabeth. 1823.

The history of the battle of Agincourt. 2 pts 1827, 1832.

History of the Orders of Knighthood of the British Empire. 4 vols 1841–2.

A history of the Royal Navy. 2 vols 1847.

Memoirs of the life and times of Sir Christopher Hatton. 1847.

Also antiquarian and heraldic works. Nicolas was a frequent contributor to GM and Archaeologia.

Editions

The literary remains of Lady Jane Grey. 1825.

The poetical rhapsody of Francis Davison. 2 vols 1826.

Private memoirs of Sir Kenelm Digby. 1827.

The retrospective review: second series. 1827–8. Ed Nicolas and H. Southern.

The letters of Joseph Ritson. 2 vols 1833. Includes memoir of Ritson by Nicolas.

The complete angler of Izaak Walton and Charles Cotton. 2 vols 1836.

In addition to various antiquarian edns and reprints, Nicolas was responsible for the Aldine edns of Burns, Chaucer, Collins, Cowper, Surrey and Wyatt, Thomson and Kirke White.

THOMAS PARK
1759–1834

Sonnets and other small poems. 1797.

Cupid turned volunteer; in a series of prints designed by the Princess Elizabeth, with poetical illustrations by Thomas Park. 1804.

Nugae modernae: morning thoughts and midnight musings in prose and verse. 1818.

Park also contributed to several of the literary and antiquarian works of Sir S. E. Brydges, G. Ellis, J. Nichols, J. Ritson, G. Steevens et al.

Editions and Revisions

The works of the British poets, collated with the best editions. 42 vols 1805–8; Supplement, 6 vols 1809.

Heliconia: comprising a collection of English poetry of the Elizabethan age 1575–1604. 3 vols 1815.

Facetiae: musarum deliciae. 1817. With E. Dubois.

Park also re-edited Sir John Harington, Nugae antiquae, 2 vols 1804; Horace Walpole, A catalogue of royal and noble authors, 5 vols 1806; The Harleian miscellany, 10 vols 1808–13; Thomas Percy, Reliques of ancient English poetry, 3 vols 1812; Joseph Ritson, A select collection of English songs, 3 vols 1813 (2nd edn). The BM possesses a number of his annotated books.

SAMUEL WELLER SINGER
1783–1858

Researches into the history of playing cards, with illustrations of the origin of printing and engraving on wood. 1816.

The text of Shakespeare vindicated from the interpolations and corruptions advocated by J. P. Collier. 1853.

Editions

Shakespeare's jest book. 3 pts 1814–15.

Diana: or the sonnets of H[enry] C[onstable]. 1818 (facs).

Anecdotes, observations and characters of books and men, by Joseph Spence. 1820.

The British poets. 100 vols Chiswick 1822. Many of the preliminary notices by Singer.

The dramatic works of William Shakespeare. 10 vols 1826 (4 edns by 1875.)

Singer also issued edns and rpts of the poems of Chalkhill, Chapman, Fairfax, Griffin, Herrick, Lodge, Lovelace, Marlowe and Marmion, as well as Bacon's Essays, Cavendish's Life of Wolsey, Selden's Table-Talk, and some French and Italian rarities etc.

WALTER WILLIAM SKEAT
1835–1912

Editions

The vision of William concerning Piers Plowman. EETS 4 pts 1867–85.

The Bruce, by John Barbour. EETS 4 pts 1870–89.

The Holy Gospels in Anglo-Saxon, Northumbrian and Old Mercian versions. 4 pts Cambridge 1871–87.

The poetical works of Thomas Chatterton. 1871, 1891.

Ælfric's Lives of the Saints. EETS 2 pts 1881–1900.

Wulfila's The gospel of Saint Mark. 1882.

Specimens of early English. 3 vols Oxford 1882. With R. Morris.

The Kingis quair. 1884, 1911 (Scottish Text Soc).

Twelve facsimiles of old English manuscripts. 1892.

The complete works of Geoffrey Chaucer. 7 vols Oxford 1894–7.
The student's Chaucer. Oxford 1895.
Skeat also edited many other early English texts, mainly for Chaucer Soc, EETS, Scottish Text Soc, and English Dialect Soc, which he founded.

Dictionaries and Philological Works

A Mœso-Gothic glossary. 1868.
An etymological dictionary of the English language, arranged on an historical basis. Oxford 1882, 1884 (corrected), 4 edns by 1910.
A concise etymological dictionary of the English language. Oxford 1882, 1886 (rev), 6 edns to 1936.
A concise dictionary of Middle English. 1888. With A. L. Mayhew.
A primer of English etymology. Oxford 1892, 6 edns to 1920.
A student's pastime. Oxford 1896. Articles from N & Q, including Skeats's autobiography.
Notes on English etymology, chiefly reprinted from the transactions of the Philological Society. Oxford 1901.
A primer of classical and English philology. Oxford 1905.
The science of etymology. Oxford 1912.
Skeat also pbd pamphlets on spelling-reform, place-names etc.

LUCY TOULMIN SMITH
1838–1911

The Maire of Bristowe is Kalendar, by Robert Ricart. 1872 (Camden Soc).
Gorboduc, or Ferrex and Porrex: a tragedy by Thomas Norton and Thomas Sackville, edited. Heilbronn 1883.
York plays: the plays performed by the crafts or mysteries, edited with introduction and glossary. Oxford 1885.
A common-place book of the fifteenth century, edited with notes. 1886.
A manual of the English grammar and language. [1886].
Les contes moralisés de Nicole Bozon. Paris 1889 (Société des Anciens Textes Français). With P. Meyer.
Expeditions to Prussia and the Holy Land made by Henry, Earl of Derby, afterwards King Henry IV. 1894 (Camden Soc).
The itinerary of John Leland, with an appendix of extracts from Leland's Collectanea. 5 vols 1906–10.
Lucy Toulmin-Smith also contributed to The Shakespeare allusion book *prepared by the New Shakespeare Soc, and translated* J. J. Jusserand, English wayfaring life.

HENRY SWEET
1845–1912

Readers and Editions

King Alfred's West-Saxon version of Gregory's Pastoral care. EETS 2 pts 1871–2.
An Anglo-Saxon reader in prose and verse, with grammatical introduction, notes and glossary. Oxford 1876, 8 edns by 1908 (rev Onions).
The Epinal glossary, edited with transliteration. 1883.
King Alfred's Orosius. EETS 1883; [extracts] Oxford 1885.
Ælfric, grammaticus, Abbot of Eynsham: selected homilies. Oxford 1885.
The oldest English texts. EETS 1885
A second Anglo-Saxon reader, archaic and dialectal. Oxford 1887.

Primers and Miscellaneous Writings

A history of English sounds. 1874 (English Dialect Soc). Rptd from Trans Philological Soc 1873–4.
A handbook of phonetics. Oxford 1877.
An Anglo-Saxon primer, with grammar, notes and glossary. Oxford 1882, 8 edns to 1896, 1953 (rev).
First Middle English primer: extracts from the Ancren Riwle and Ormulum; with grammar and glossary. Oxford 1884.
Elementarbuch des gesprochenen Englisch: Grammatik, Texte und Glossen. Oxford 1885; tr Oxford 1890 (as A primer of spoken English).
An Icelandic primer, with grammar, notes and glossary. Oxford 1886.
Second Middle English primer: extracts from Chaucer, with grammar and glossary. Oxford 1886.
A history of English sounds from the earliest period, with full word-lists. Oxford 1888.
A primer of phonetics. Oxford 1890, 4 edns by 1932.
A manual of current shorthand. Oxford 1892.
A new English grammar, logical and historical. 2 pts Oxford 1892–8.
A short historical English grammar. Oxford 1892.
A primer of historical English grammar. Oxford 1893.
First steps in Anglo-Saxon. Oxford 1897.
The student's dictionary of Anglo-Saxon. Oxford 1897.
The practical study of languages. 1899.
The history of language. 1900.
The sounds of English: an introduction to phonetics. Oxford 1908.
Collected papers, arranged by H. C. K. Wyld. Oxford 1913. Includes Words, logic and grammar; The practical study of language; Linguistic affinity; Progress of linguistic science (5 papers); History of English (4 papers); Shelley's nature-poetry; Phonetics and accounts of living languages (6 papers). Many rptd from Trans Philological Soc.

WILLIAM JOHN THOMS
1825–1910

The book of the Court, exhibiting the origin, peculiar duties, and privileges of the several ranks of the nobility and gentry, more particularly of the great Officers of State and members of the Royal Household. 1838, 1844.
Three notelets on Shakespeare: 1, Shakespeare in Germany; 2, Folk-lore of Shakespeare; 3, Was Shakespeare ever a soldier? 1865.
Hannah Lightfoot; Queen Charlotte and the Chevalier d'Eon; Dr Wilmot's Polish progress; Lord Chatham and the Princess Olive. 1867. Rptd with addns from N & Q.
Human longevity: its facts and fictions, including an inquiry into some of the more remarkable examples. 1873.

Editions

A collection of early prose romances. 3 vols 1827–8, 1858 (enlarged as Early English prose romances), 1904.
Lays and legends of various nations; illustrative of their traditions, popular literature, manners, customs and superstitions. 2 sers 1834. Ser 1: France, Spain, Tartary and Ireland; ser 2: Germany.
Anecdotes and traditions illustrative of early English history and literature from manuscript sources. 1839 (Camden Soc).
The history of Reynard the fox, from the edition printed by Caxton in 1481, with notes and an introductory sketch of the literary history of the romance. 1844 (Percy Soc).
Gammer Gurton's famous histories of Sir Guy of Warwick, Sir Bevis of Hampton, Tom Hickathrift, Friar Bacon, Robin Hood and the King and the cobbler, newly revised and amended by Ambrose Merton, Gent, FSA. [1846]. 'Merton' is Thoms.
Gammer Gurton's pleasant stories of Patient Grissel, the Princess Rosetta and Robin Goodfellow; and ballads of

The beggar's daughter, The babes in the wood, and Fair Rosamond, newly revised and amended by Ambrose Merton, Gent, FSA. [1846].

Notes and queries. Vol 1, no 1, 3 Nov 1849–Sept 1872. Planned and founded by Thoms, who had previously begun a similar series in Athenaeum 26 Aug 1846.

Thoms also pbd or edited various other papers, and translated J. J. A. Worsaal, Primeval antiquities of Denmark *from the Danish; he was Secretary of the Camden Soc 1838–73.*

BENJAMIN THORPE

1782–1870

Cædmon's metrical paraphrase of parts of the Holy Scriptures, in Anglo-Saxon. 1832 (Soc of Antiquaries) (with trn).

The Anglo-Saxon version of the story of Apollonius of Tyre. 1834 (with trn).

Analecta Anglo-Saxonica: a selection in prose and verse from Anglo-Saxon authors. Oxford 1834, 1846 (corrected).

Libri psalmorum versio antiqua Latina cum paraphrasi Anglo-Saxonica. Oxford 1835. Also ptd in Appendix B to Cooper's report on Rymer's Foedera, 1835.

Ancient laws and institutes of England. 2 vols 1840.

Codex Exoniensis: a collection of Anglo-Saxon poetry. 1842 (Soc of Antiquaries) (with trn).

Da halgan godspel on Englisc. Oxford 1842, 1846, 1851.

The homilies of the Anglo-Saxon Church. 2 vols 1844–6 (Ælfric Soc) (with trn).

Florence of Worcester's chronicle. 2 vols 1848–9.

Northern mythology, comprising the principal traditions of Scandinavia, North Germany and the Netherlands. 3 vols 1851.

Yule tide stories: a collection of Scandinavian tales. 1853, 1888.

The Anglo-Saxon poems of Beowulf, the Scöp or Gleeman's tale, and the Fight at Finnesburg, with a literal translation, notes and glossary. Oxford 1855.

The Anglo-Saxon chronicle. 2 vols 1861 (Rolls ser) (with trns).

Diplomatarium Anglicum aevi Saxonici: a collection of English charters. 1865.

Edda Sæmundar from the Old Norse. 2 pts 1866.

Thorpe also issued trns of Rask's Anglo-Saxon grammar, 1830, 1865, 1879; *Lappenberg's* A history of England under the Anglo-Saxon Kings, 2 vols 1845, *and* A history of England under the Norman Kings, 1857; and *Pauli's* Life of King Alfred, 1853 (which includes Thorpe's own version of Alfred's Orosius).

HENRY JOHN TODD

1763–1845

Some account of the Deans of Canterbury. Canterbury 1793.

A vindication of our authorized translation and translators of the Bible. 1819.

Memoirs of the life and writings of Bishop Brian Walton. 2 vols 1821.

The life of Archbishop Cranmer. 2 vols 1831.

Todd also pbd catalogues and minor theological works.

Editions

Comus: a mask by John Milton, with preliminary illustrations. 1798.

The poetical works of John Milton, with the principal notes of various commentators. 6 vols 1801, 1809, 1826. Vol 1 was also issued separately as An account of the life and writings of John Milton.

The works of Edmund Spenser, with the principal notes of the various commentators. 5 vols 1805, 1850.

Illustrations of the lives and writings of Gower and Chaucer. 1810.

Johnson's dictionary of the English language, with numerous corrections and additions. 4 vols 1818 (5 edns by 1839).

Cranmer's Defence of the true and Catholick doctrine of the Sacrament. 1825.

Selections from the metrical paraphrases on the Psalms by George Sandys. 1839.

DUNCAN CROOKES TOVEY

1842–1912

Gray and his friends. Cambridge 1890. Letters.

The poetical works of James Thomson. 1897. With memoir.

Reviews and essays in English literature. 1897. Teaching of English literature, More's Utopia, Fuller's Sermons, Letters of the Earl of Chesterfield, Arnold's Last essays, Waller, Gay, Ossian and his maker, Coventry Patmore, Elizabethan poetry, A Cambridge reminiscence (by M.T.).

Gray's English poems. 1898, 1922.

Verses. 1902.

The letters of Thomas Gray, including the correspondence of Gray and Masson. 3 vols 1909–12.

ARTHUR WILSON VERITY

1863–1937

The influence of Christopher Marlowe on Shakespere's earlier style: being the Harkness prize essay. Cambridge 1886.

The works of Sir George Etheredge. 1887.

Nero and other plays. 1888 (Mermaid Ser). Verity edited Field's Woman is a weathercock and Amends for ladies.

Thomas Heywood. 1888 (Mermaid Ser). 5 plays.

The Pitt Press Shakespeare for schools. 13 vols Cambridge 1890–1905. 13 plays.

The Cambridge Milton for schools. 11 vols Cambridge 1891–9.

The student's Shakespeare. 3 vols Cambridge 1902–5. 3 plays only.

WILLIAM SIDNEY WALKER

1795–1846

Gustavus Vasa and other poems. 1813.

The heroes of Waterloo: an ode. 1815.

Poems from the Danish, selected by Andreas Anderson Feldborg, translated into English verse. 1815.

The appeal of Poland: an ode. 1816.

Corpus poetarum latinorum. 1828, 1849, 1904.

The poetical remains of William Sidney Walker. Ed J. Moultrie 1852 (with memoir).

Shakespeare's versification and its apparent irregularities explained. Ed W. N. Lettsom 1854.

A critical examination of the text of Shakespeare, with remarks on his language and that of his contemporaries. Ed W. N. Lettsom 3 vols 1860.

Walker was also almost entirely responsible for the pbn of Milton's De ecclesia christiana, 1825, though the ostensible editor was C. R. Sumner.

SIR ADOLPHUS WILLIAM WARD

1837–1924

A history of English dramatic literature to the death of Queen Anne. 2 vols 1875, 3 vols 1899 (rev).

Chaucer. 1879 (EML).
Dickens. 1882 (EML).
The Counter-Reformation. 1886.
Sir Henry Wotton: a biographical sketch. 1898.
Great Britain and Hanover: being the Ford lectures. Oxford 1899; tr German, 1906.
The Electress Sophia and the Hanoverian Succession. 1903.
Germany 1815–90. 3 vols Cambridge 1916–18.
Collected papers, historical, literary, travel and miscellaneous. 5 vols Cambridge 1921. 97 rptd articles, 40 being literary (vols 3–4).

Editions

The poetical works of Alexander Pope. 1869.
Old English drama, select plays: Marlowe's Dr Faustus and Greene's Friar Bacon and Friar Bungay. Oxford 1887.
The spider and the flie. 1894 (Spenser Soc).
The poems of John Byrom. 3 vols 1894–1912 (Chetham Soc).
Heywood's A woman killed with kindness. 1897.
The Cambridge modern history, planned by Lord Acton. 14 vols Cambridge 1902–12, 1934. General editors: Ward, G. W. Prothero, S. Leathes. Ward contributed 16 chs.
The poems of George Crabbe. 3 vols Cambridge 1905–7.
The works of Mrs Gaskell. 8 vols 1906.
The Cambridge history of English literature. 14 vols Cambridge 1907–16. General editors Ward and A. R. Waller; Ward contributed 14 chs.
The London merchant, and Fatal curiosity, by George Lillo. Boston 1907.
For Ward's minor writings see A bibliography of Sir Adolphus William Ward by A. T. Bartholomew, with memoir by T. F. Tout, Cambridge 1926.

HENRY WILLIAM WEBER

1783–1818

The battle of Flodden field: a poem of the sixteenth century. 1808.
Metrical romances of the thirteenth, fourteenth and fifteenth centuries. 3 vols Edinburgh 1810.
The dramatic works of John Ford. 2 vols 1811. Also various correspondence relating to Ford.
Tales of the East. 3 vols Edinburgh 1812.
The works of Beaumont and Fletcher. 14 vols 1812.
Illustrations of northern antiquities, from the earlier Teutonic and Scandinavian romances. 1814. Assisted by Sir W. Scott and R. Jamieson.

HENRY BENJAMIN WHEATLEY

?–1917

Samuel Pepys and the world he lived in. 1880.
The book-lover's library. 1886–1902. Wheatley was general editor of the series. His own contributions were: How to form a library, 1886; The dedication of books, 1887; How to catalogue a library, 1889; Literary blunders, 1893; How to make an index, 1902.
A handbook of art industries in pottery and the precious metals. 2 pts 1886.
Remarkable bindings in the British Museum. 1889.
London past and present, based on the handbook of London by the late Peter Cunningham. 3 vols 1891.
Historical portraits: some notes on the painted portraits of celebrated characters of England, Scotland and Ireland. 1897.
Prices of books: an inquiry into the changes in the prices of books which have occurred in England at different periods. 1898.
Hogarth's London: pictures of the manners of the eighteenth century. 1909.

Editions

Diary of John Evelyn, with a life of the author. 4 vols 1879.
Chap-books and folk-lore tracts. 1885. With G. L. Gomme.
Reliques of ancient English poetry, edited with general introduction, additional prefaces, notes, glossary etc. 3 vols 1891.
The diary of Samuel Pepys, with Lord Braybrooke's notes, edited with additions. 10 vols 1893–9.
Also minor bibliographical and topographical works, and edns of 17th-century rarities.

SIMON WILKIN

1790–1862

A catalogue of the books belonging to the Public Library, and to the City Library of Norwich, methodically arranged. 4 pts Norwich 1825–32, 1 vol 1847.
A catechism of the use of the globes. 2 pts 1826.
Sir Thomas Browne's works, including his life and correspondence. 4 vols 1836, 3 vols 1852.
Joseph Kingdom of Norwich: a memoir. Norwich 1855. By M. H. Wilkin; preface and introductory ch by Simon Wilkin.

WILLIAM ALDIS WRIGHT

1831–1914

Bacon's Essays and Colours of good and evil, with notes and glossarial index. 1862.
The works of William Shakespeare. 9 vols Cambridge 1863–6. Vol 1 ed W. G. Clark and J. Glover; vols 2–9 by Clark and Wright.
The works of William Shakespeare. 1864, 1904 (Globe). With W. G. Clark.
The Bible word-book: a glossary of old English Bible words. 1866, 1884 (rev). With J. Eastwood.
Chaucer, The clerk's tale. 1867.
Shakespeare's select plays. 10 vols Oxford 1868–83. With W. G. Clark.
Bacon's Advancement of learning. 1869, 1875, 1880.
The pilgrimage of the lyf of the manhode, from the French of de Deguilleville. 1869 (Roxburghe Club).
Generydes: a romance in seven-line stanzas. EETS 2 pts 1873–8.
The metrical chronicle of Robert of Gloucester. 1887 (Rolls Ser).
Letters and literary remains of Edward FitzGerald. 1889; Letters, 1894; Letters to Fanny Kemble, 1895; Rubáiyát, 1899; Miscellanies, 1900; More letters, 1901.
Facsimile of the manuscript of Milton's minor poems. 1899.
Milton's poetical works. 1903.
Roger Ascham, English works. Cambridge 1904.
The authorised version of the English Bible 1611. Cambridge 1909.
Femina, now first printed from a unique ms in the Library of Trinity College Cambridge. 1909 (Roxburghe Club).
The Hexaplar Psalter: being the Book of Psalms in six English versions. 1911.
Wright also pbd biblical studies and was editor of the Jnl of Philology 1868–1913.

R. C. A.

XII. TRAVEL

(1) GENERAL

See Biography catalogue of the library of Royal Commonwealth Society, ed D. H. Simpson 1961; Cambridge history of the British Empire; J. N. L. Baker, History of geographical discovery and exploration, 1931.

Blakiston, Major John (1785–1867). Twelve years' military adventure in three quarters of the globe 1802–14. 1829.

Clarke, Edward Daniel (1769–1822). Travels in various countries of Europe, Asia, Africa. 6 vols 1810–23.

Franklin, Sir John (1786–1847). Narrative of a journey to the shores of the Polar Sea 1819–22. 1823.

— Narrative of a second expedition to the Polar Sea. 1828.

McCormick, Robert (1800–80). Voyages of discovery in the Arctic and Antarctic Seas, and round the world: being personal narratives of attempts to reach the North and South Poles [1827–]. 2 vols 1884.

Holman, James (1786–1857). Voyage round the world 1827–32. 1834–5.

Boteler, Capt John Harvey (1796–1885). Recollections of my sea-life from 1808 to 1830. Ed D. Bonner-Smith 1942.

Darwin, Charles Robert (1809–82). Journal of researches into the geology and natural history of the various countries visited by HMS Beagle from 1832–6. 1839. *See col 1364, above.*

Haley, Nelson Cole. Whale Hunt: the narrative of a voyage 1849–53. 1950.

Page, Charlotte A. Under sail and in port in the glorious 1850's. Ed A. P. Johnson 1950.

Buckingham, James Silk (1786–1855). Voyages, travels, adventures. 2 vols 1855.

McClintock, Sir Francis Leopold (1819–1907). Voyage of the Fox: discovery of the fate of Franklin. 1859.

MacGregor, John (1825–92). A thousand miles in the Rob Roy canoe. 1866.

— The Rob Roy on the Baltic. 1867.

— The Rob Roy on the Jordan, Nile, Red Sea etc. 1869.

Brassey, Lady Anne (1839–87). A voyage in the Sunbeam. 1878.

Bridges, Mrs F. D. Journal of a lady's travels round the world. 1883.

Palgrave, William Gifford (1829–88). Ulysses: scenes and studies in many lands. 1887.

(2) AFRICA

Barnard, Lady Anne (1750–1825). The Cape of Good Hope 1797–1802. Ed D. Fairbridge 1924.

Barrow, Sir John (1764–1848). Travels into the interior of S. Africa. 2 vols 1801–4.

Park, Mungo (1771–1806). The journal of a mission to the interior of Africa in the year 1805. 1815.

Salt, Henry (1780–1827). A voyage to Abyssinia, and travels into the interior of that country 1809–10. 1814.

Burckhardt, John Lewis (1784–1817). Travels in Nubia. 1819.

Daniell, Samuel (1775–1811). Sketches representing the native tribes, animals and scenery of S. Africa [with descriptive letterpress by William Somerville and Sir John Barrow]. 1820.

Moffat, Robert (1795–1883) and Mary (1795–1871). Apprenticeship at Kuruman 1820–38. Ed I. Shapera 1951.

— The Matabele journals 1829–60. Ed J. P. R. Wallis 2 vols 1945.

Burchell, William John (1781–1863). Travels in the interior of Southern Africa. 2 vols 1822–4.

Denham, Dixon (1786–1828). Travels and discoveries in Northern and Central Africa 1822–4. 1826.

Irby, Charles Leonard (1789–1845). Travels in Egypt and Nubia, Syria and the Holy Land. 1823. With J. Mangles.

Laing, Major Alexander Gordon (1793–1826). Travels in Timannee, Kooranko and Sodima.

— Countries in Western Africa. 1825.

— Mission to Timbuktu. 1826.

Bain, Andrew Geddes (1797–1864). Journals [S. Africa 1826–]. Ed M. H. Lister 1949.

Clapperton, Hugh (1788–1827). Journal of a second expedition into the interior of Africa from the Bight of Benin to Soccatoo. 1829.

Lander, Richard Lemon (1804–34) and J. Lander. Journal of an expedition to explore the course and termination of the Niger. 3 vols 1832.

Owen, Vice-Admiral William Fitzwilliam (1774–1857). Narrative of voyages to explore the shores of Africa, Arabia and Madagascar. 2 vols 1833.

Pringle, Thomas (1789–1834). Africa sketches. 1834.

— Narrative of a residence in S. Africa. 1835.

Smith, Sir Andrew (1797–1872). The diary of Sir Andrew Smith, Director of the 'Expedition for exploring Central Africa' 1834–6. 2 vols 1939–40.

Owen, Francis (d. 1854). The diary of a mission with Dingaan in 1837–8. Ed Sir G. E. Cory 1926.

Davidson, John (1797–1836). Notes taken during travels in Africa. 1839.

Tindall, Rev Joseph (1807–61). Journeys in South West Africa 1839–55. Ed B. A. Tindall 1959.

Meyrick, Henry Howard (1822–47). Life in the Bush 1840–7. Ed F. J. Meyrick 1939.

Merriman, Nathaniel James (1810–82). The Cape journals 1848–55. Ed D. H. Varley and H. M. Matthew 1957.

Saleman, Sir William Henry (1788–1856). A journey through the kingdom of Oudi in 1849–50. 2 vols 1858.

Galton, Sir Francis (1822–1911). Narrative of an exploration in tropical South Africa. 1853.

Parkyns, Mansfield. Life in Abyssinia. 1853.

Baikie, William Balfour (1825–64). Narrative of an exploring voyage up the rivers Kwo'ra and Bi'nue [i.e. Niger and Tsadda] in 1854. 1856.

Price, Elizabeth Lees (1839–1919). Journals written in Bechuanaland, Southern Africa 1854–83 with an epilogue: 1889 and 1900. Ed U. Long 1956.

Murray, Emma (1834–1905). Bloemfontein 1856–60. Ed J. Murray 2 vols 1954.

Burton, Sir Richard Francis (1821–90). First steps in East Africa. 1856.

— The lake regions of central equatorial Africa, with notices of the Lunar mountains and sources of the White Nile 1857–9. 2 vols 1860.

— The Nile Basin. 1864.

Livingstone, David (1813–73). Narrative of an expedition to the Zambesi and its tributaries 1858–64. 1865; ed J. P. R. Wallis 1956.

— Livingstone's travels. Ed J. I. McNair 1954.

— Private journals. Ed I. Schapera 1960.

Moffat, John Smith (1835–1918). The Matabele mission: a selection from the correspondence of John and Fanny Moffat, David Livingstone and others 1858–78. Ed J. P. R. Wallis 1945.

Buchanan, Nathaniel (1826–1901). Packhorse and waterhole; with the first overlanders to the Kimberley [1859–]. Ed G. Buchanan 1933.

Tristram, Henry Baker (1822–1906). The Great Sahara. 1860.

Stewart, Rev James (1831–1905). Zambesi journal 1862–3. Ed J. P. R. Wallis 1953.

Dobie, John Shedden (1819–1903). S. African journal 1862–6. Ed A. F. Hattersley 1945.

Speke, John Hanning (1827–64). Journal of discovery of the source of the Nile. 1863.

Grant, Lt Col James Augustus (1827–92). A walk across Africa: or domestic scenes from my Nile journal. 1864.

Leask, Thomas Smith (1839–1912). The South African diaries of Thomas Leask 1865–70. Ed J. P. R. Wallis 1954.

Baker, Sir Samuel White (1821–83). The Albert Nyanza great basin of the Nile and exploration of the Nile sources. 1866.

— The Nile tributaries of Abyssinia and the sword hunters of the Hamran Arabs. 1871.

— Ismailia: a narrative of the expedition to Central Africa for the suppression of the slave trade, organised by Ismail, Khediv of Egypt. 2 vols 1874.

Wingfield, Lewis Strange (1842–91). Under the palms in Algeria and Tunis. 2 vols 1868.

Hinderer, Mrs Anna (1827–70). Seventeen years in the Yoruba country. 1872.

Stanley, Sir Henry Morton (1841–1904). How I found Livingstone. 1872.

— Through the dark continent. 2 vols 1878.

— In darkest Africa. 2 vols 1890.

Reade, William Winwood (1838–75). African sketch-book. 2 vols 1873.

McKiernan, Gerald (1844–92). Narrative and journal in S.W. Africa 1875–9. Ed P. Serton 1934.

Baines, Thomas (1822–75). Northern goldfield diaries of 1877. Ed J. P. R. Wallis 1946.

Cameron, Verney Lovett (1844–94). Across Africa. 2 vols 1877.

Edwards, Amelia Blandford (1831–92). A thousand miles up the Nile. 1877.

Hooker, Sir Joseph Dalton (1817–1911). Journal of a tour in Morocco and the Great Atlas. 1878. With J. Ball.

Trollope, Anthony (1815–82). S. Africa. 1878.

Thomson, Joseph (1858–95). To the central African Lakes and back: the narrative of the Royal Geographical Society's East Central African Expedition 1878–80. 2 vols 1881.

— Through Masai land: a journey of exploration among the snow-clad volcanic mountains and strange tribes of E. Equatorial Africa. 1885.

Oliphant, Laurence (1829–88). The land of Khemi: up and down the middle Nile. 1882.

Johnston, Sir Harry Hamilton (1858–1927). The River Congo from its mouth to Bolobo. 1884.

— The Kilima-njavo expedition: a record of scientific exploration in Eastern Equatorial Africa. 1886.

Bousfield, Henry Brougham (1832–1902). Six years in the Transvaal: notes of the founding of the Church there. 1886.

Hore, Annie. To Lake Tanganyika in a bath-chair. 1886.

Smith, William Wilson Hind (b. 1869). A boy's scrambles: falls and mishaps in Morocco. 1886.

Bruce, George Windham Hamilton Knight (1852–96). Journey to the Zambesi in 1888. Ed C. E. Tripp 1939.

Harris, Walter Burton. The land of an African sultan: travels in Morocco. 1889.

Bent, James Theodore (1852–97). The ruined cities of Mashonaland. 1892.

— The sacred city of the Ethiopians. 1893.

— Southern Arabia, Soudan and Sokoto. 1900.

Macdonald, Col Sir Claude Maxwell (1852–1915). Up the Niger. 1892.

Bryce, James Viscount (1838–1922). Impressions of S. Africa. 1897.

Kingsley, Mary Henrietta (1862–1900). Travels in West Africa. 1897.

Cunningham-Graham, Robert Bontine (1852–1936). Mogreb el Acksa: a journey in Morocco 1898. 1921 (rev).

Stevenson, James Hamilton. Barotseland journal 1898–9. Ed J. P. R. Wallis 1954.

Carnegie, David Wynford (1871–1900). Letters from Nigeria 1899–1900. Ed Lady H. M. Carnegie 1902.

(3) AMERICA

North America

Thompson, David (1770–1857). Explorations in Western America 1784–1812. Ed J. B. Tyrrell 1916.

Harmon, Daniel Williams (1778–1845). Ten years in the Indian country 1800–16. Ed W. K. Lamb 1957.

Gordon, Daniel M. (1845–1925). Mountain and prairie: a journey from Victoria to Winnipeg via Peace River Pass. 1880.

Selkirk, Thomas Douglas, 5th Earl of (1771–1820). Journal of travels in British N. America and the north-eastern United States 1803–4. Ed P. C. T. White 1958.

Clark, William (1770–1838). Journals [1804–6]. Ed B. de Voto 1954.

Lambert, John. Travels through lower Canada and the United States of N. America in the years 1806, 1807 and 1808. 3 vols 1810.

Nuttall, Thomas (1786–1859). Travels in the old North-west in 1810. Ed J. E. Graustein 1951.

Ross, Sir John (1777–1856). A voyage of discovery for the purpose of exploring Baffin's Bay, and enquiring into the probability of a North-West Passage. 2 vols 1819.

Parry, Sir William Edward (1790–1855). Journal of a voyage for the discovery of a North-West Passage 1819–20. 2 vols 1821–4.

— Journal of a second voyage 1821–3. 1824.

— Journal of a third voyage 1824–5. 1826.

— Narrative of an attempt to reach the North Pole 1827. 1828.

Simpson, Sir George (1787–1860). Fur trade and empire 1824–5. Ed F. Merk 1931.

Ogden, Peter Skene (1794–1854). Snake country journals 1824–5 and 1825–6. Ed E. E. Rich, and A. M. Johnson 1950.

Hall, Basil (1788–1844). Travels in North America in 1827 and 1828. 1829.

Hall, Mrs Basil. The aristocratic journey: being outspoken letters written during a fourteen months' sojourn in America 1827–8. Ed U. Pope-Hennessy 1931.

Ross, Sir James Clark (1800–62). A second voyage in search of a northwest passage 1829–33. 1835.

Simpson, Thomas (1808–40). Narrative of the discoveries on the N. coast of America [1829–]. 1843.

Domett, Alfred. Journal of a tour in Canada, the United States and Jamaica 1833–5. Ed E. A. Horsman and L. R. Benson 1955.

Cather, Thomas (b. 1813–). Voyage to America in 1836. Ed T. Yoseloff 1961.

Sheridan, Francis. Galveston Island 1839–46. Ed W. W. Pratt 1954.

Dickens, Charles (1812–70). American notes for general circulation. 2 vols 1842.

Harris, Edward (1799–1863). Up the Missouri with Audubon. Ed J. F. McDermott 1951.
Le Froy, Major Gen Sir John Henry (1817–90). In search of the magnetic North: a soldier-surveyor's letters from the North-West 1843–4. Ed C. F. G. Stanley 1955.
Gregg, Josiah. Excursions in Mexico and California 1847–50. Ed M. G. Fulton 1944.
Hepburn, George (1802–83). Journal on his voyage from Scotland to Otago in 1850. Ed W. D. Stewart 1934.
Oliphant, Laurence. (1829–88) Minnesota and the Far West 1855.
Hind, Henry Youle (1823–1908). Narrative of the Canadian Red River exploring expedition of 1857 and of the Assinniboine and Saskatchewan exploring expedition of 1858. 2 vols 1860.
Palliser, John (1817–87). The exploration of that portion of British North America which lies between the western shore of Lake Superior and the Pacific Ocean 1857–60. 1863.
Carnegie, James 9th Earl of Southesk (1827–1905). Saskatchewan and the Rocky Mountains 1859–60. 1875.
Cheadle, Walter Butler (1835–1910). Journal of a trip across Canada 1862–3, with introduction and notes by A. G. Doughty and G. Lanctot. 1931.
— The North-West passage by land. 1865.
Burton, Sir Richard Francis (1821–90). The city of saints and across the Rocky Mountains to California. 1861.
Butler, Sir William Francis (1838–1910). The great lone land-travel in the North-West of America. 1872.
— The wild North land. 1873.
Quin, Windham Thomas Wyndham, Earl of Dunraven (1841–1926). The Great Divide: travels in Upper Yellowstone in the summer of 1874. 1876.
Bishop, Isabella Bird (1832–1904). A lady's life in the Rocky Mountains. 1879.

Latin America

Haynes, Gen Robert (1769–1851). Barbadian diary 1787–1836. Ed E. M. W. Cracknell 1934.
Nugent, Maria (1775–1834). Journal of a voyage to, and residence in, the island of Jamaica 1801–5. 2 vols 1839.
Hall, Basil (1788–1844). Extracts from journals written on the coasts of Chile, Peru and Mexico 1820–2. 2 vols 1824.
Hart, Miss. Letters from the Bahama Islands 1823–4. Ed R. Kent 1949.
Waterton, Charles (1782–1865). Wanderings in S. America 1825.
Bickford, Rev James (1860–95). An autobiography of Christian labour in the West Indies, Demerara, Victoria, New South Wales and South Australia 1836–88. 1890.
Miers, John (1789–1879). Travels in Chile and La Plata. 2 vols 1826.
Head, Sir Francis Bond (1793–1875). Rough notes taken during some rapid journeys across the pampas and among the Andes. 1846.
Wallace, Alfred Russel (1823–1913). Travels on the Amazon and Rio Negro. 1853.
Trollope, Anthony (1815–82). The West Indies and the Spanish Main. 1859.
Sill, Edward Roland. Around the Horn: December 1861 to March 1863. Ed T. Williams and B. Simison 1944.
Bates, Henry Walter (1825–92). The naturalist on the Amazons. 2 vols 1863.
Burton, Sir Richard Francis (1821–90). Explorations of the highlands of Brazil. 1869.
— Letters from the battle-fields of Paraguay. 1870.
Kingsley, Charles (1819–75). At last: a Christmas in the West Indies. 2 vols 1871.
Musters, George Chaworth (1841–79). At home with the Patagonians. 1871.
Dixie, Lady Florence Caroline (1857–1905). Across Patagonia. 1880.
Hudson, William Henry (1841–1922). The naturalist in La Plata. 1892.
— Idle days in Patagonia. 1893.
Whymper, Edward (1840–1911). Travels among the Great Andes of the Equator. 1892.
Fitzgerald, Edward Arthur (1871–1931). The highest Andes. 1899.

(4) ASIA

Daniell, Thomas (1749–1840) and William Daniell (1769–1837). Oriental scenery. 2 vols 1801.
— A picturesque voyage to India, by way of China. 1810.
Symes, Michael (1753?–1809). Journal of his second embassy to the court of Ava in 1802. [Burma]. Ed P. G. E. Hall 1955.
Barrow, Sir John (1764–1848). Travels in China. 1804.
— Voyage to Cochin-China. 1806.
Buchanan, Francis (1762–1829). A journey from Madras through the countries of Mysore, Canava and Malabar 1807. 2 vols 1870.
Morier, James Justinian (1780–1849). Journey through Persia, Armenia, and Asia Minor to Constantinople 1808–9. 1812.
— A second journey through Persia 1810–16. 1818.
Nugent, Maria (1775–1834). A journal from the year 1811 till the year 1815, including a voyage to and residence in India. 2 vols 1839.
Hall, Basil (1788–1844). Travels in India, Ceylon and Borneo [1812–]. Ed H. G. Rawlinson 1931.
— Account of voyage of discovery to the W. Coast of Corea. 1818.
— Fragments of voyages and travels. 9 vols 1831–3.
Porter, Sir Robert Ker (1777–1842). Travels in Georgia, Persia, Armenia, Babylonia etc in 1817–20. 2 vols 1821–2.
Gordon, Capt Peter (1790–1857). A tour through Persia in 1820. 1833.
Burckhardt, John Lewis (1784–1817). Travels in Syria and the Holy Land. 1822.
— Travels in Arabia. 2 vols 1829.
Irby, Charles Leonard (1789–1845). Travels in Egypt and Nubia, Syria and the Holy Land. 1823. With J. Mangles.
Leake, William Martin (1777–1860). Journal of a tour in Asia Minor. 1824.
Fenton, Mrs Michael (1800–75). Narrative of life in India 1826–30. 1901.
Fraser, James Baillie (1783–1856). Travels and adventures in the Persian Provinces on the southern banks of the Caspian Sea. 1826.
Brown, Samuel Sneade (1809–75). Home letters, written from India between the years 1828–41. 1848.
Crawford, John (1783–1868). Embassy to the Courts of Siam and Cochin-China. 2 vols 1828.
Malcolm, Sir John (1769–1833). Sketches of Persia. 1828.
Burnes, Lt Col Sir Alexander (1805–44). Cabool: being a personal narrative of a journey to, and residence in that city, in the years 1836, 1837 and 1838. 1842.
— Travels into Bokhara. 3 vols 1834.
Rich, Claudius James (1787–1820). Narrative of a residence in Koordistan. 2 vols 1836.
Wood, John (1811–71). A journey to the source of the Oxus. 1841.
Smith, Rev George (1815–71). A narrative of an explanatory visit to each of the consular cities of China and to the islands of Hong Kong and Chusan 1844–6. 1847.
Curzon, Robert (1810–73). Visits to monasteries in the Levant. 1849.

Oliphant, Laurence (1829–88). A journey to Katmandu. 1852.
— The land of Gilead. 1880.
— A trip to the north-east of Lake Tiberias. 1885.
Layard, Sir Austen Henry. Discoveries in the ruins of Nineveh and Babylon; with travels in Armenia, Kurdistan and the desert. 1853.
— Early adventures in Persia, Susiana and Babylonia. 2 vols 1887.
Danvers, Robert William (1833–58). Letters from India and China during the years 1854–8. 1898.
Hooker, Sir Joseph Dalton (1817–1911). Himalayan journals. 1854.
Burton, Sir Richard Francis (1821–90). Personal narrative of a pilgrimage to El-Medinah and Meccah. 3 vols 1855.
— Narrative of a year's journey through central and East Arabia. 1865.
— Sind re-visited. 1877.
— The gold-mines of Midian: a fortnight's tour in North West Arabia. 1878.
Bowring, Sir John (1792–1872). The kingdom and people of Siam 1855. 1857.
Porter, Rev J. L. Five years in Damascus. 1855.
— The giant cities of Bashan. 1865.
Yule, Henry (1820–89). Narrative of the mission to the court of Ava in 1855 [Burma]. 1858.
Baker, Sir Samuel White (1821–93). The rifle and hound in Ceylon. 1857 (2nd edn).
— Eight years in Ceylon. 1884.
Falkland, Amelia Cary, Viscountess (1803–58). Chow Chow: being selections from a journal kept in India, Egypt and Syria. 2 vols 1857.
Elsmie, George Robert (1838–1909). Thirty five years in the Punjab 1858–93. 1908.
Smith, Albert. To China and back. 1859.
Dixon, William Hepworth (1821–79). The Holy Land. 2 vols 1865.
Palgrave, William Gifford (1826–88). A year's journey through central and eastern Arabia. 2 vols 1865.
Wills, Charles James. In the land of the lion and sun: or modern Persia 1866–81. 1883.
Freshfield, Douglas W. (1845–1934). Travels in the central Caucasus and Bashan, including visits to Ararat and Tabreez etc. 1869.
— The exploration of the Caucasus. 2 vols 1896.
Bowring, Lewin Bentham (1824–1910). Eastern experiences. 1871.
Palmer, Edward Henry (1840–82). The desert of the Exodus. 1871.
Tristram, Henry Baker (1822–1906). The land of Moab. 1873.
Burton, Lady Isabel (1831–96). Inner life of Syria. 2 vols 1875.
— Arabia, Egypt and India. 1879.
Burnaby, Frederick Gustavius (1842–85). A ride to Khiva. 1876.
— On horse-back through Asia Minor. 2 vols 1877.
Cumming, Constance. From the Hebrides to the Himalays. 1876.
— A lady's cruise in a French man-of-war. 1882.
— Wanderings in China. 1886.
Bryce, James, Viscount (1838–1922). Trans-Caucasia and Ararat. 1877.
Low, Sir Hugh (1824–1905). Journal of Perak. 1877.
Conder, Claude Reignier (1848–1910). Tent work in Palestine. 1878.
O'Donovan, Edmund (1844–83). The Merv Oasis: travels and adventures east of the Caspian 1879–81. 2 vols 1882.
Bishop, Isabella Bird (1831–1904). Unbeaten tracks in Japan. 2 vols 1880.
— Journeys in Persia and Kurdistan. 2 vols 1891.
— Korea and her neighbours. 2 vols 1898.
— The Yangtze valley and beyond. 1899.
Blunt, Lady Anne Isabella (1837–1917). A pilgrimage to Nejd. 2 vols 1881.
Gill, William John (1843–82). The river of golden sand: a journey through China and Eastern Tibet to Burma. 2 vols 1882.
Hannington, James (1847–85). A journey through Palestine in 1884, and a journey through Masailand and U-Soga in 1885. Ed E. C. Dawson 1888.
Doughty, Charles Montagu (1843–1926). Travels in Arabia Deserta. 2 vols Cambridge 1888; ed T. E. Lawrence 2 vols 1921.
Younghusband, Sir George John. Eighteen hundred miles on a Burmese tat through Burmah, Siam and the E. Shan States. 1888.
— On short leave to Japan. 1894.
Wingfield, Lewis Strange (1842–91). Wanderings of a globe-trotter in the Far East. 2 vols 1889.
Browne, Edward Granville (1862–1925). A year amongst the Persians. 1893.
Harris, Walter Burton. Journey through the Yemen. 1893.
Marsden, Kate (1859–1931). On sledge and horseback to outcast Siberian Lepers. 1893.
Conway, Sir Martin (1856–1937). Climbing and exploration in the Karakoram-Himalays. 1894.
Dunmore, Charles Adolphus, 7th Earl of (1841–1907). The Pamirs: being a narrative of a year's expedition on horseback and on foot through Kashmir, to Tibet, Chinese Tartary and Russian Central Asia. 2 vols 1894.
Hogarth, David George (1862–1928). A wandering scholar in the Levant. 1896.

(5) AUSTRALASIA AND THE PACIFIC

Flinders, Matthew (1774–1814). A voyage to Terra Australis 1801–3. 2 vols 1814.
Lockerby, William (1782–1853). Journal of a sandalwood trader in the Fijian Islands 1808–9. 1925.
MacQuarie, Lachlan (1761–1824). Tours in New South Wales and Van Diemen's Land 1810–22. 1956.
Oxley, John Joseph William Molesworth (1783–1828). Journals of two expeditions into the interior of New South Wales 1817–18. 1820.
— Journal of a second expedition into the interior or Terra Incognita of New South Wales. 1818.
Hovell, William Hilton (1786–1875). Journey of discovery to Port Philip, New South Wales, in 1824 and 1825. 1831.
Fenton, Mrs Michael (c. 1800–75). Tasmania during the years 1826–30. 1901.
Dillon, Peter (1785?–1847). Successful voyage in the South Seas to ascertain the actual fate of La Pérouse's expedition. 2 vols 1829.
Markham, Edward. Voyage to Van Diemen's Land 1833. Ed K. R. von Stieglitz 1952.
Bunbury, Col Henry William St Pierre (1812–75). Early days in W. Australia: letters and journals [1834–7]. Ed Lt Col W. St Pierre Bunbury and W. P. Morrell 1930.
Bickford, Rev James (1806–95). An autobiography of Christian labour in the West Indies, Demarara, New South Wales and S. Australia 1836–88. 1890.
Franklin, Lady Jane (1792–1875). Visit to New South Wales 1839. 1943.
Eyre, Edward John (1815–1901). Journals of expeditions of discovery into central Australia and overland from Adelaide to King George's Sound in 1840–1. 1845.
Brooke, Sir James (1803–68). A letter from Borneo, with notices of the country and its inhabitants. 1842.
— The private letters of Sir James Brooke, Rajah of Sarawak, narrating the events of his life from 1838 to the present time. Ed C. Templar 3 vols 1853.

Sturt, Charles (1795–1869). Two expeditions into the interior of Southern Australia, during the years 1828–31. 2 vols 1833.
— Narrative of an expedition into Central Asia, performed under the authority of Her Majesty's Government, during the years 1844, 1845 and 1846. 2 vols 1849.
Brunner, Thomas. The great journey: an expedition to explore the interior of the Middle Island, New Zealand 1846–8. 1954.
Buckley, William (1780–1856). The life and adventures of Buckley, 32 years a wanderer amongst the aborigines of the then unexplored country round Port Philip, now the province of Victoria. 1852.
Baker, John Holland (1841–1930). A surveyor in New Zealand 1857–96. Ed N. Baker 1932.
Stuart, John McDouall (1815–66). Journals 1858–62 to fix the centre of the continent [Australia]. Ed W. Hardman 1865.
Bowring, Sir John (1792–1872). A visit to the Philippine islands. 1859.
Burke, Robert O'Hara (1821–61). The Australian exploring expedition of 1860. 1861.
Cracroft, Sophia. An account of the Hawaiian Kingdom 1861–6. Ed A. L. Korn 1958.
Wallace, Alfred Russel (1823–1913). The Malay archipelago. 2 vols 1869.
Macdonald, D. A year in the New Hebrides, Loyalty Islands and New Caledonia. 1873.
Strutt, William (1825–1915). Australian journal. Ed G. Mackaness 1958.
Stack, Rev James West (1835–1919). Early Maoriland adventures. Ed A. H. Reed 1935.
— More Maoriland adventures. Ed A. H. Reed 1935.
— Further Maoriland adventures. Ed A. H. Reed 1938.
Forbes, Henry Ogg (1851–1932). A naturalist's wanderings in the Eastern Archipelago. 1885.
Chalmers, James (1841–1901). Pioneering in New Guinea. 1887.
Stevenson, Mrs M. I. Letters from Samoa 1891–5. 1906.
Fitzgerald, Edward Arthur (1871–1931). Climbs in the New Zealand Alps. 1896.
Carnegie, David Synford (1871–1900). Spinfex and sand: a narrative of five years' pioneering and exploration in W. Australia. 1898.
Passfield, Sidney James Webb, Baron (1859–1947) and Lady Beatrice (1858–1943). Visit to New Zealand in 1898: Beatrice Webb's diary with entries by Sidney Webb. 1959.

(6) EUROPE

The Continent

MacNevin, William James (1763–1841). A ramble through Swisserland in the summer and autumn of 1802. 1803. *See* G. R. de Beer, Travellers in Switzerland, 1949.
Philips, John Burton. Continental travel in 1802–3. 1904.
Greatheed, Bertie (1759–1826). An Englishman in Paris 1803. Ed J. P. T. Bury and J. C. Barry 1953.
Thornton, Thomas (1757–1823). A sporting tour in France. 1806.
Lemaistre, J. G. Travels after the peace of Amiens through parts of France, Switzerland, Italy and Germany. 1806.
Sansom, J. Travels from Paris through Switzerland and Italy. 1807.
Byron, George Gordon Noel, 6th Baron (1788–1824). Letters written from Portugal, Spain, Greece and the shores of the Mediterranean 1809–11. [1824].
— The Ravenna journal 1821. Ed Lord Ernle 1928.
Porter, Sir Robert Ker (1777–1842). Travelling sketches in Russia and Sweden. 2 vols 1809.
Forsyth, Joseph (1763–1815). On antiquities, arts, letters in Italy. 1813.
Hobhouse, John Cam, Baron Broughton (1786–1869). Journey through Albania. 1813.
Bridges, George Windham. Alpine sketches by a member of the University of Oxford. 1814.
Shelley, Percy Bysshe (1792–1822). Visits to France, Switzerland and Savoy 1814. Ed C. S. Elton 1894.
Eustace, John Chetwode (1762?–1815). A classified tour through Italy. 1815.
Southey, Robert (1774–1843). Journal of a tour in the Netherlands in the autumn of 1815. 1902.
Waldie, Jane (1793–1826). Sketches descriptive of Italy in 1816–17. 1817.
Stoppard, John (1785–1879). Letters after a tour through some parts of France, Switzerland and Germany. 1817.
Clifford, Lady de. A picturesque tour through France, Switzerland, on the banks of the Rhine and through parts of the Netherlands. 1817.
Milford, John. A tour through the Pyrenees, south of France, Switzerland, Italy and the Netherlands. 1818.
Hookham, Thomas. A walk through Switzerland in September 1816. 1818.
Raffles, Thomas (1788–1863). A tour through some parts of France, Savoy, Switzerland and Germany, and the Netherlands. 1818.
Baillie, Marianne. First impressions on a tour on the Continent. 1819.
Bowring, Sir John (1792–1872). Observations on the state of religion and literature in Spain. 1819.
— Some account of the state of the prisons in Spain and Portugal. 1824.
Rose, Stewart. Letters from the north of Italy addressed to Henry Hallam. 1819.
Starke, Mrs Mariana (1762?–1838). Guide for travellers on the Continent. 1820.
Williams, Hugh William (1773–1829). Travels in Italy, Greece etc. 1820.
Cockburn, James Pattison (1779?–1847). Swiss scenery. 1820.
Journal of a tour in France, Switzerland and Lombardy. 1821. Anon.
Robinson, William (1804–27). Voyages up the Mediterranean and in the Indian seas [1821–6]. Ed J. A. Heraud 1837.
Scott, John (1783–1821). Sketches of manners, scenery etc in the French provinces, Switzerland and Italy. 1821.
Holman, James (1786–1857). Journey undertaken in 1819, 1820 and 1821 through France, Savoy, Switzerland etc. 1822.
Bakewell, Robert (1768–1843). Travels in the Tarentaisi and various parts of the Grecian and Pennine Alps and in Switzerland and Auvergne. 1823.
Tennant, Charles (1768–1838). A tour through parts of the Netherlands, Holland, Germany, Switzerland, Savoy and France. 1824.
Forbes, Murray. The diary of a traveller over Alps and Appenines. 1824.
Downes, George. Letters from continental countries. 1825.
Duppa, Richard (1770–1831). Miscellaneous observations and opinions on the Continent. 1825.
Lion hunting: or a summer's ramble through parts of Flanders, Germany and Switzerland. 1826. Anon.
Hazlitt, William (1778–1830). A journey through France and Italy. 1826.
A tour to Great St Bernard and round Mont Blanc. 1827. Anon.
Stevenson, Seth William (1784–1853). Tour in France, Savoy, N. Italy, Switzerland, Germany and the Netherlands. 1827.
Walter, W. Letters from the Continent. 1828.

Sinclair, J. D. An autumn in Italy. 1829.
Murray, John (1808–92). A glance at some of the beautiful sublimities of Switzerland. 1829.
Cobbett, J. P. Journal of a tour in Italy. 1830.
Inglis, Henry David (1795–1835). Spain in 1830. 1831.
— Switzerland, the south of France and the Pyrenees. 1837.
Roscoe, Thomas (1791–1871). The tourist in Switzerland and Italy. 1830.
Ritchie, Leitch (1800?–65). Travelling sketches in the north of Italy, the Tyrol and on the Rhine. 1832.
Liddiard, William (1774–1841). Three months' tour in Switzerland and France. 1832.
Forbes, James David (1809–68). Travels through the Alps [1832–50]. Ed W. A. B. Coolidge 1900.
— Norway and its glaciers. 1853.
Wilder, F. The journal of an economical tourist to France, Switzerland and Italy. 1833.
Bateman, Mrs. A summer's tour through Belgium up the Rhine and to the lakes of Switzerland. 1834.
Beckford, William Thomas (1759–1844). Italy, Spain and Portugal with an excursion to the monasteries of Alcobaça and Batalha. 2 vols 1834.
Dyke, T. (?1801–66). Tour through Belgium, Rhenish Prussia, Germany, Switzerland. 1834.
Hayward, Abraham (1801–84). A journey across the Alps. 1834.
Stanhope, Philip Henry, 5th Earl (1805–75). Letters from Switzerland. 1834.
A peep at the Continent: or six weeks' tour through parts of Belgium, Rhenish Prussia, Savoy, Switzerland and France. 1835. Anon.
Leake, William Martin (1777–1860). Travels in N. Greece. 4 vols 1835.
Rickman, E. S. Sketch of a pedestrian tour through Switzerland. 1835.
Thomson, William. Two journeys through Italy and Switzerland. 1835.
Wilkley, E. A ramble through France, Italy, Switzerland etc. 1836.
Laing, Samuel (1780–1868). Journal in Norway. 1836.
— Tour in Sweden. 1839.
— Notes on the social and political state of France, Prussia etc. 1842.
Atkins, Henry Martin (1818–42). Ascent to the summit of Mont Blanc. 1837.
O'Connor, Matthew (1773–1844). A tour through Belgium, Germany, France and Switzerland. 1837.
Bremner, Robert. Excursions in Russia. 2 vols 1839.
— Excursions in Denmark, Norway and Sweden. 2 vols 1840.
Clarke, Andrew. Tour in France, Italy and Switzerland during the years 1840 and 1841. 1841.
Fry, Elizabeth (1780–1845). Journeys on the Continent 1840–1. Ed R. Johnson 1931.
Chambers, William (1800–83). A tour in Switzerland. 1841.
Sedgwick, Miss. Letters from abroad. 1841.
Davy, John (1790–1868). Notes and observations in the Ionian island and Malta. 2 vols 1842.
Strutt, Mrs Elizabeth. Domestic residence in Switzerland. 1842.
Holmes, Mrs Dalkeith. A ride on horseback to Florence through France and Switzerland. 1842.
Yates, Mrs Ashton. Letters written during a journey to Switzerland. 1843.
Borrow, George (1803–81). The Bible in Spain. 3 vols 1843; suppl in Hand-book for travellers in Spain, 1913 (priv ptd).
Shelley, Mary Wollstonecraft (1797–1851). Rambles in Germany and Italy. 1844.
Buckingham, James Silk (1786–1855). Belgium, the Rhine, Switzerland and Holland. 1844.
Lamont, Martha Macdonald. Two years in France and Switzerland. 1844.

Snow, Robert. Memorials of a tour on the Continent. 1845.
Alexander, William Lindsay (1808–84). Switzerland and the Swiss churches. 1846.
Cheever, George Barrell. Wanderings of a pilgrim in the shadow of Mont-Blanc and the Jungfrau Alp. 1846.
Ford, Richard (1796–1858). Handbook for travellers in Spain. 2 vols 1845.
— Gatherings from Spain. 1846.
Lear, Edward (1812–88). Illustrated excursions in Italy. 1846.
— A tour in Sicily May–July 1847. Ed G. Proby 1938.
— Journal of a landscape painter in Albania, Illyria etc. 1851.
— Journal of a landscape painter in S. Calabria. 1852.
— Journal of a landscape painter in Corsica. 1870.
— Italian journal 1873–5. Ed R. Murphy 1953.
Massie, James William (1799–1869). A summer's ramble in Belgium, Germany and Switzerland. 1846.
Wilkinson, Sir John Gardner (1797–1875). Dalmatia and Montenegro. 2 vols 1848.
Morgan, John Minter (1782–1854). A tour through Switzerland and Italy 1846–7. 1850.
Smith, Albert. A month in Constantinople. 1850.
Townsend, Francis. Journal of a tour in Italy. 1850.
Sewell, Elizabeth Missing (1815–1906). Journal kept during a summer tour. 1851.
Cayley, George John (1826–78). Las Alforjas: or the bridle roads of Spain. 2 vols 1853.
Grant, James. Records of a run through continental countries. 1853.
Oliphant, Laurence (1829–88). The Russian shores of the Black Sea in the autumn of 1852. 1853.
Blackwell, Eardley, J. In Switzerland in 1854. 1855.
Headley, J. T. Travels among Alpine scenery. 1855.
Street, George Edmund (1824–81). Bricks and marble in the Middle Ages: notes of a tour in the north of Italy. 1855.
— Some account of Gothic architecture in Spain. 1865.
Wills, Alfred. Wanderings among the High Alps. 1856.
White, Walter (1811–93). On foot through the Tyrol. 1856.
Pestalozzi, Mrs Conrad. My travels abroad. 1856.
Travels in Switzerland, Italy and Dalmatia, by a lady. 1857. Anon.
Stephen, Sir Leslie (1832–1904). The playground of Europe [Switzerland 1857–69]. 1871.
Hinchcliff, Thomas Woodbine (1825–82). Summer months among the Alps. 1857.
— Peaks, passes and glaciers. 1859.
Clark, William George (1821–78). Peloponnesus: notes of study and travel. 1858.
King, Samuel William (1821–68). The Italian valleys of the Pennine Alps. 1858.
Coleman, Edmund Thomas. Scenes from the snowfields. 1859.
Tyndall, John (1820–93). Glaciers of the Alps. 1860.
— Hours of exercise in the Alps. 1871.
Whymper, Edward (1840–1911). Scrambles amongst the Alps [1860–5]. 1871.
Barrow, Sir John (1764–1848). Expeditions on the glaciers, including an ascent of Mont Blanc, Monte Rose, Col du Géant 1862. 1864.
Mackenzie, Georgina Mary Muir. Across the Carpathians. 1862. With A. P. Irby.
— Travels in the Slavonic provinces of Turkey in Europe. 1867.
Wordsworth, Christopher (1807–85). Journal of a tour in Italy. 1863.
McTear, Robert. Notes of a continental tour. 1865.
Rivington, Alexander. Notes of a travel in Europe. 1865.
Bradbury, J. Three weeks from home through France and Switzerland. 1866.
Coolidge, William Augustus Brevoort (1850–1926). Alpine Studies [1868–1905]. 1912.
Dowsing, William. Rambles in Switzerland. 1868.

Butler, Samuel (1835–1902). Alps and sanctuaries of Piedmont and the Canton Ticino [1869–]. 1881.
Girdlestone, Rev A. G. (b. 1842). The high Alps without guides. 1870.
Evill, William. A winter journey to Rome and back. 1871.
Vizard, John. A tour through France, Italy and Switzerland. 1872.
Carr, Alfred. Adventures with my alpenstock and knapsack: or a five weeks' tour in Switzerland in 1874. 1875.
Jackson, Lady Catherine Hannah Charlotte (d. 1891). Fair Lusitana. 1874. On Portugal.
Plunket, Frederica. Here and there among the Alps. 1875.
Freshfield, Douglas (1845–1934). Across country from Thonon to Trent. 1865.
— Italian Alps. 1875.
Green, John Richard (1837–83). Stray studies from England and Italy. 1876.
A Briton abroad. 1878. Anon.
Mahaffy, Sir John Pentland (1839–1919). Rambles and studies in Greece. 1878.
Stevenson, Robert Louis (1850–94). An inland voyage. 1878.
— Travels with a donkey in the Cévennes. 1879.
— Swiss notes 1880. In his Essays and criticisms, Edinburgh 1903.
Dixon, William Hepworth (1821–79). British Cyprus. 1879.
Mummery, Albert Frederick (1855–95). My climbs in the Alps and Caucasus [1879–]. 1895.
Farrer, Richard Ridley (b. 1856). A tour in Greece. 1880.
Capper, Samuel James. Shores and cities of the Bodensee. 1881.
Havergal, Frances Ridley (1836–79). Swiss letters. 1882.
Holworthy, S. M. Alpine scrambles and classic rambles. 1882.
Bryce, James Viscount (1838–1922). Memories of travel [Switzerland 1884]. 1923.
Tissot, Victor. Unknown Switzerland. 1889.
Gosse, Sir Edmund William (1849–1928). In Switzerland poetical and pictorial. 1893.
Layard, Sir Austen Henry. A handbook of Rome and its environs. 1894.
Marsh, Herbert. Two seasons in Switzerland. 1895.

Great Britain

Colt-Hoare, Richard (1758–1838). Northern tour. 1800. Cardiff Public Lib MS 3.127.5.
— Tour in S. Wales 1801. 1802. Cardiff Public Lib MS 3.127.2.1.
Heath, Charles. The excursion down the Wye from Ross to Monmouth. 1800.
Bristed, John. A pedestrian tour through part of the Highlands of Scotland in 1801. 2 vols 1803.
Evans, Thomas. Cambrian itinerary: or Welsh tourist. 1801.
Campbell, Alexander (1764–1824). A journey from Edinburgh through parts of North Britain. 2 vols 1802.
Barber, J. T. A tour through South Wales and Monmouthshire. 1803.
Hutton, William (1723–1815). Remarks upon North Wales. 1803.
Malkin, Benjamin Heath (1769–1842). The scenery, antiquities and biography of South Wales. 1804.
Denholm, James (1772–1818). A tour to the principal Scotch and English Lakes. 1804.
Evans, Rev John. A tour through South Wales. 1804.
— North Wales. 1812.
Fenton, Richard. Tours in Wales 1804–13. 1917 (Cambrian Archaeological Soc).
Pratt, Samuel Jackson (1749–1814). Gleanings in England. 3 vols 1804.
Thornton, Thomas (1757–1823). A sporting tour through the northern parts of England and Scotland. 1804.
Travers, Benjamin (1783–1858). A descriptive tour to the Lakes. 1804.
Donovan, Edward (1768–1837). Descriptive excursions through South Wales and Monmouthshire, in the year 1804 and the four preceding summers. 2 vols 1805.
Mawman, Joseph. An excursion to the Highlands of Scotland and the English Lakes. 1805.
Duke of Rutland, John Henry Manners, 5th Duke (1778–1857). A tour round the Southern coasts of England. 1805.
— A tour to the northern parts of Great Britain. 1813.
— A tour through North and South Wales. 1848.
Woodward, George Moutard (1760?–1809). Eccentric excursions in different parts of England and S. Wales. 1807.
Hutchinson, John. Tour through the High Peak of Derbyshire. 1809.
Dennis, Alexander. Journal of a tour through great part of England and Scotland in the year 1810. 1816.
Webb, Daniel Carless. Four excursions to various parts of Great Britain in 1810 and 1811. 1812.
Daniell, William (1769–1837). A voyage round Great Britain in the summer of 1813. 1814.
Ayton, Richard (1786–1823). A voyage round Great Britain in the summer of 1813. 2 vols 1814.
Horne, Thomas Hartwell (1780–1862). The Lakes of Lancashire, Westmorland and Cumberland. 1816.
Pugh, Edward. Cambria depicta. 1816.
Compton, Thomas. A tour through N. Wales. 1817.
Brown, John. Notes on an excursion into the Highlands of Scotland in autumn 1818. 1819.
Cromwell, Thomas Kitson (1792–1870). Excursions through England and Wales, Scotland and Ireland. 1818.
Sketch of a tour in the Highlands of Scotland, through Perthshire, Argyleshire and Inverness-shire. 1819. Anon.
Hassell, John (d. 1825). Tour of the Grand Junction Canal. 1819.
Southey, Robert (1774–1843). Tour in Scotland in 1819. Ed C. H. Herford 1929.
Selwyn, Mrs. Excursions through the most interesting parts of England, Wales and Scotland 1819–23. 1824.
Newell, Rev Robert Hasell. Letters on the scenery of Wales. 1821.
Wilkinson, Thomas. Tours to the British Mountains. 1824.
A summer ramble in the North Highlands. 1825. Anon.
Baines, Edward (1774–1848). A family tour to the Lakes of Cumberland, Westmorland and Lancashire. 1829.
Botfield, Beriah (1807–63). Journal of a tour through the Highlands of Scotland during the summer of 1829. 1830.
Cobbett, William (1762–1835). Rural rides. 1830.
Anderson, George. Guide to the Highlands and Islands of Scotland, including Orkney and Zetland. 1834.
Smith, B. P. A journal of an excursion round the south-eastern coast of England. 1834.
Head, Sir George. A home tour through the manufacturing districts of England in the summer of 1835. 1836.
— A home tour through various parts of the United Kingdom. 1837.
Smith, C. L. Excursions through the Highlands and Isles of Scotland in 1835 and 1836. 1837.
Roscoe, Thomas (1791–1871). Wanderings and excursions in North Wales. 1836.
Holland, John (1794–1872). The tour of the Don. 2 vols 1837.
Lauder, Sir Thomas Dick (1784–1848). Highland rambles. 2 vols 1837.
Turner, Thomas. Narrative of a journey associated with a fly, from Gloucester to Aberystwyth, and through North Wales in 1837. 1840.
Bennett, G. J. A pedestrian tour through North Wales. 1838.
Onwhyn, Joseph. Guide to the Highlands of Scotland. 1839.

Townshend, Chauncey Hare (1798–1868). A tour through part of the Western Highlands of Scotland. 1839.
Mackay, Charles (1814–89). The Thames and its tributaries. 2 vols 1840.
—— The scenery and poetry of the English Lakes. 1846.
Ritchie, Leitch (1800?–65). The Wye and its associations. 1841.
Evans, F. Furness and Furness Abbey: or a companion through the Lancashire part of the Lake District. 1842.
Maxwell, William Hamilton (1792–1850). Wanderings on the Scottish Border. 2 vols 1844.
'Ramble, Reuben'. Reuben Ramble's travels in the southern counties of England. 1845.
Hicklin, John. Excursions in North Wales. 1847.
Thorne, James (1815–81). Rambles by rivers: the Thames. 2 vols 1847–9; Handbook to the environs of London, 1876.
A six weeks' tour in the Highlands of Scotland, by a pedestrian. 1851. Anon.
Collins, William Wilkie (1824–89). Rambles beyond railways: or notes in Cornwall taken a-foot. 1851; ed A. Rowe 1948.
Sidney, Samuel (1813–83). Rides on railways leading to the Lakes and Derbyshire. 1851.
Borrow, George (1803–81). An expedition to the Isle of Man in 1855. Douglas 1915.
—— Wild Wales: its people, language and scenery. 3 vols 1862.
King, J. W. Journeyings through England and Wales. 1856.
Boase, J. J. A. A ramble in Scotland in 1857, starting from Oxford. BM add MSS 35.051. Vol 7, ff. 251.
A fortnight's ramble through some of the more beautiful counties of old England, by a Manchester clerk. 1859. Anon.
Halliwell, James Orchard (1820–89). Notes of family excursions in North Wales. 1860.
Pinks, W. J. Country trips. 1860.
Bradley, Edward ('Cuthbert Bede'). A tour in tartan-land. 1863.
Oxford to John O'Groats: what we saw and what we paid. 1866. Anon.
Houlding, Henry. From Lancashire to London on foot. 1867.
Douglas, J. P. A run through South Wales via the London and North-Western railway. 1868.
Thornbury, George Walter (1828–76). A tour round England. 2 vols 1870.
Roger, James Cruickshank (1820–99). Journal of a summer tour. 1898.

E. de W.

XIII. SPORT

Since the literature of 19th-century sport is large, it has not been possible to make this section comprehensive. Histories of particular sporting institutions e.g. yacht clubs, books on physical training, and wholly statistical works have, with one or two exceptions, been omitted.

(1) BIBLIOGRAPHIES

Slater, J. H. Illustrated sporting books: a descriptive survey. 1899.
Howard, H. L., Earl of Suffolk and Berkshire, H. Peek and F. G. Aflalo (ed). In their Encyclopaedia of sport. 2 vols 1897–8, 4 vols 1911. Bibliographies under each main heading.
Nevill, R. H. Old English sporting books. 1924.
Schwerdt, C. F. G. R. Hunting, hawking, shooting, illustrated in a catalogue of books, manuscripts, prints and drawings. 4 vols 1928–37.
Gee, E. R. The sportsman's library: being a descriptive list of the most important books on sport. New York 1940.
Darwin, B. Sporting writers of the nineteenth century. In Essays presented to Sir Humphrey Milford, Oxford 1948.

(2) PERIODICALS

The sporting magazine or monthly calendar of the transactions of the turf, the chace etc. 1792–1870.
Annals of sporting and farming gazette. 1822–8. Monthly.
Bell's life in London and sporting chronicle. 1822–86. Weekly.
Pierce Egan's life in London and sporting guide. 1824–7. Merged in 1827 with Bell's life in London, above. Weekly.
New sporting magazine. 1831–70. Monthly. From July 1846 identical except for title-page with Sporting magazine, above.
The sportsman. 1834–70. Monthly. From July 1846 identical except for title page with Sporting magazine, above.
The oracle of rural life: an almanack for sportsmen. 1839–44. 1841 as Sporting oracle; 1842–4 as Sporting almanack.
The sporting review. 1839–70. Monthly. From July 1846 identical except for title page with Sporting magazine, above.
The field. 1853–. Weekly.
The sporting life. 1859–. Daily. Originally 24 March–27 April 1859 as Penny Bell's life and sporting news.
Baily's monthly magazine of sports and pastimes. 1860–1926. From 1889 as Baily's magazine etc.
The sporting gazette. 1862–1905. Merged in 1905 with Land and water, below. Weekly. From 1880 as The county gentleman.
The sporting times ['the pink 'un']. 1865–. Weekly. *See also* J. G. Booth, Old pink 'un days, 1924 and Master [i.e. J. Corlett, the paper's owner] and men, 1926.
The sportsman. 1865–1924. Merged in 1924 with The sporting life. Daily.
Land and water. 1866–1920. Merged in 1920 with The field. Weekly. As The country gentleman and land and water 1905–15 apart from 2 nos, Aug 1914, appearing under original title.
Illustrated sporting and dramatic news. 1874–. Weekly.
The Badminton magazine of sports and pastimes. 1895–1923. Monthly.
Country life. 1895–. Weekly. Before 1897 appeared as Racing illustrated.

(3) GENERAL STUDIES

Strutt, J. Glig-gamena angel-ðeoð: or the sports and pastimes of the people of England. 1801, 1830; ed J. C. Cox [1903].

Taplin, W. The sporting dictionary and rural repository of general information upon every subject appertaining to the sports of the field. 2 vols 1803.

—— The sportsman's cabinet: or a correct delineation of the various dogs used in the sports of the field. 2 vols 1803–4. Under pseudonym 'A veteran sportsman'.

Egan, P. Sporting anecdotes original and select. 1804, [1808], 1820, 1825, 1827 (as P. E.'s anecdotes, original and selected).

—— P. E.'s book of sports and mirror of life. 1832.

Thornton, T. A sporting tour through the northern parts of England and the Highlands of Scotland. 1804.

—— A sporting tour through various parts of France. 2 vols 1805.

Howitt, S. et al. Foreign field sports, fisheries, sporting anecdotes. 1814. Plates with text.

Johnson, T. B. The complete sportsman. 1817. Under pseudonym 'T. H. Needham'.

—— The sportsman's cyclopaedia. 1831.

Mayer, J. The sportsman's directory. 1817.

Chafin, W. Anecdotes respecting Cranbourn Chase with the rural amusements it afforded our ancestors. 1818, 1818.

'Scott, W. H.' (J. Lawrence). British field sports. 1818.

'Careless, John'. The old English squire: a poem in ten cantos. 1821.

Hassell, J. Excursions of pleasure and sport on the Thames. 1823.

Armiger, C. The sportsman's vocal cabinet comprising original songs and ballads relative to field sports. 1830.

Maxwell, W. H. Wild sports of the west [of Ireland]. 1832; ed W. H. H. Quin 4th Earl of Dunraven 1924.

—— The field book: or sports and pastimes of the United Kingdom. 1833.

—— Wanderings in the Highlands and Islands. 2 vols 1844, 1853 (as Sports and adventures in the Highlands etc).

Walker, D. British manly exercises. 1834, 1835; ed 'Craven' [i.e. J. W. Carleton] 1847. Appendix as Games and sports, 1837.

—— Exercises for ladies. 1836, 1837.

—— Defensive exercises. 1840. Boxing, wrestling, fencing, shooting.

Harewood, H. (pseudonym?). A dictionary of sports containing explanations of every term applicable to racing, shooting, hunting, fishing, hawking, archery etc. 1835.

'Nimrod' (C. J. Apperley) (ed). Sporting. 1838. Contributions by various well known sporting writers.

—— Nimrod abroad. 2 vols 1842. Pbd under own name.

Blaine, D. P. An encyclopaedia of rural sports. 1840; ed 'Harry Hieover' (C. Bindley) 1852.

Colquhoun, J. The moor and the loch, containing minute instructions in all Highland sports. 1840, 2 vols 1878 (4th edn), 1888 (7th edn).

—— Salmon-casts and stray shots. 1858. On field sports in general.

—— Sporting days. 1866. On field sports.

Carleton, J. W. (ed). The sporting sketch book: a series of characteristic papers by the most distinguished sporting writers of the day. 1842.

—— Hyde Marston: or a sportsman's life. 3 vols 1844. Under pseudonym 'Craven'. A novel.

Mills, J. The sportsman's library. Edinburgh 1845. A general treatise on sport.

St John, C. W. G. Short sketches of the wild sports and natural history of the Highlands. 1846, 1893 (with memoir of the author); ed H. E. Maxwell 1919 as Sports and natural history of the Highlands.

—— A tour in Sutherlandshire with extracts from the field books of a sportsman. 2 vols 1849, 1884.

—— Natural history and sport in Moray. Edinburgh 1863.

Hall, H. B. Highland sports and Highland quarters. 2 vols [1847].

—— Scottish sports and pastimes. 1850.

—— The sportsman and his dog. 1850.

Lloyd, L. The English county gentleman: his sports and pastimes. 1849. Verse.

'Hieover, Harry' (C. Bindley). Sporting facts and sporting fancies. 1853.

—— The sportsman's friend in a frost. 1857. Essays on various sports.

—— The sporting world. 1858.

'Stonehenge' (J. H. Walsh). Manual of British rural sports. 1856, 1859, 1875, 1886 (16th edn).

Lennox, Lord W. P. Merrie England: its sports and pastimes. 1857.

—— Pictures of sporting life and character. 2 vols 1860.

—— Recreations of a sportsman. 2 vols 1862.

—— Sport at home and abroad. 1872.

Hamilton, J. P. Reminiscences of an old sportsman. 2 vols 1860. On field sports.

Miles, H. D. (ed). The book of field sports. 42 pts [1860–3].

—— The sportsman's companion. 12 pts [1863–4].

—— English country life: a work of reference for the gentleman, the sportsman, the farmer. [1868–9]. Largely sporting.

Dougall, J. D. Scottish field sports. Glasgow 1861.

Corbet, H. Tales and traits of sporting life. 1864.

Stretton, C. Sport and sportsmen: a book of recollections. 1866.

'Caw' (C. A. Wheeler) (ed). Sportascrapiana: cricket and shooting, pedestrian, equestrian, rifle and pistol doings, lion hunting and deer stalking. 1867.

Newton, G. W. Rural sports and how to enjoy them; with an appendix containing memories and characteristics of eminent sportsmen, 1867.

Egerton, T., Earl of Wilton. On the sports and pursuits of the English, as bearing upon their national character. 1868.

Trollope, A. (ed). British sports and pastimes. 1868.

'Old Shekarry' (H. A. Leveson). Sport in many lands. 2 vols 1876.

'Bagatelle' (A. G. Bagot). Sporting sketches at home and abroad. 1879, 1881 (as Sporting sketches in three continents).

'Rockwood' (T. Dykes). Stories of Scottish sports. Glasgow 1881.

—— All round sport with fish, fur and feather. 1887.

'Avon' (W. Kenrick). How I became a sportsman: being early reminiscences of a veteran sportsman. 1882.

Speedy, T. Sport in the Highlands and Lowlands of Scotland. Edinburgh 1884.

Bromley-Davenport, W. Sport. 1885. A treatise on field sports.

Gale, F. Modern English sports: their use and their abuse. 1885.

—— Sports and recreations in town and country. 1888.

Somerset, H. C. F., 8th Duke of Beaufort, and A. E. T. Watson (ed). The Badminton library of sports and pastimes. 28 vols 1885–96; Motors and motor-driving, 1902. Various contributors. Sports covered are listed in vol on The poetry of sport, an anthology which also contains introd giving history of the series. Most vols rev in subsequent edns. Vols on archery, big-game shooting, driving, fencing, hunting and swimming contain bibliographies.

Reynardson, C. T. S. B. Sports and anecdotes of bygone days. 1887.

'Ellangowan' (J. G. Bertram). Out of door sports in Scotland. 1889.

Stoddart, J. Sports and pastimes: men I have met. 2 vols Manchester [1889].

Corballis, J. H. Forty-five years of sport. Ed A. T. Fisher 1891.

Kennard, M. E. Sporting tales. 1893.

'Ubique' (P. Gillmore). Leaves from a sportsman's diary. 1893.

Watson, A. E. T. (ed). Fur, feather and fin series. 12 vols 1893–1906. Vols with sporting sections on the partridge, pheasant, hare, red deer, fox, salmon, grouse, trout, pike and perch, snipe and woodcock, rabbit, wildfowl.

Astley, Sir J. D. Fifty years of my life in the world of sport. 2 vols 1894.

Grimble, A. Highland sport. 1894.

Hartopp, E. C. C. Sport in England: past and present. 1894.

De Crespigny, Sir C. C. Memoirs. Ed G. A. B. Dewar 1896, 1910, 1925 (as Forty years of a sportsman's life). Includes accounts of ballooning, bull-fighting etc.

Pemberton, Sir M. (ed). The Isthmian library. 12 vols 1896–1902. Vols on Rugby football, ice sports, cycling, golf, rowing, boxing, figure-skating, croquet, hockey, tennis and racquets, small-boat sailing, athletics.

Howard, H. C., Earl of Suffolk and Berkshire, H. Peek and F. G. Aflalo. The encyclopaedia of sport. 2 vols 1897–8, 4 vols 1911.

Binstead, A. M. A pink 'un and a pelican: some random reminiscences, sporting or otherwise. 1898.

Gibbs, J. A. A Cotswold village: or country life and pursuits in Gloucestershire. 1898. Includes chs on field sports.

Haydon, T. Sporting reminiscences. 1898.

Kipling, Rudyard. An almanac of twelve sports. 1898. Verse.

Slaughter, F. E. (ed). The sportswoman's library. 2 vols 1898.

Aflalo, F. G. (ed). The cost of sport. 1899.

Manners, H. J. B., 8th Duke of Rutland and G. A. B. Dewar (ed). The Haddon Hall library. 9 vols 1899–1903. Vols on Fly-fishing, Our gardens, Wild life in Hampshire highlands [includes sport], Hunting, Our forests and woodlands [includes sport], Bird-watching, Outdoor games: cricket and golf, Shooting [includes chap on The literature of the gun], Farming.

Croome, A. C. M. et al (ed). Fifty years of sport at Oxford, Cambridge and the great public schools. 3 vols 1913–22. Vols 1–2, Oxford and Cambridge; vol 3, Eton, Harrow and Winchester.

Darwin, B. (ed). The game's afoot: an anthology of sports. 1926.

Colquhoun, Sir I. and H. W. Machell. Highland gatherings. 1927. Contains much history.

Parker, E. (ed). The Lonsdale anthology of sporting prose and verse. 1932 (Lonsdale Lib vol 12).

Hare, C. E. The language of sport. 1939, 1949 (as The language of field sports). On etymology of sporting terms.

Brander, M. The hunting instinct: the development of field sports over the ages. 1964.

(4) INDIVIDUAL SPORTS
(in alphabetical order)

Angling

Bibliographies

[Ellis, Sir H.] A catalogue of books on angling. 1811; ed W. Pickering 1836 (as Bibliotheca piscatoria) (issued separately and as appendix to Boosey's Piscatorial reminiscences, below).

Westwood, T. and T. Satchell. Bibliotheca piscatoria: a catalogue of books on angling, the fisheries and fish-culture. 1883. Expanded from earlier edn by Westwood 1861, suppl 1869. Suppl by R. B. Marston to 1883 edn as Appendix C in English catalogue of books vol 6, 1901.

Hampton, J. F. Modern angling bibliography from 1881 to 1945. 1947.

Robb, J. Notable angling literature. [1947].

Periodicals

The fishing gazette. 1865–. Weekly.

§ 1

Taylor, S. Angling in all its branches. 1800.

Mackintosh, A. The Driffield angler. Gainsborough [1806], Derby [1815?] (as The modern fisher). Treatise also contains sections on shooting and coursing.

Howitt, S. The angler's manual: or concise lessons of experience. Liverpool 1808.

Williamson, T. The complete angler's vade-mecum. 1808.

Salter, R. The modern angler. Oswestry [1811?].

Lascelles, R. A series of letters on angling shooting and coursing. 3 pts 1813–14.

Salter, T. F. The angler's guide. 1814, 1815, [1823], 1833.

—— The troller's guide. 1820, 1841.

Charleton, T. W. The art of fishing: a poem. North Shields 1819.

'Piscator' (T. P. Lathy). The angler: a poem in ten cantos. 1819. Largely plagiarism of The anglers, a poem pbd anon 1758 and attributed to Thomas Scott.

'An angler' (Sir Humphry Davy). Salmonia: or days of fly fishing. 1828, 1829, 1832; ed J. Davy 1851, 1869.

March, J. The jolly angler or waterside companion. [1831].

'Greendrake, Gregory' (J. Coad). The angling excursions of Gregory Greendrake esq [in Ireland]. Dublin 1832. Originally pbd in 3 pts Dublin 1824–6, this edn with addns by 'Geoffrey Greydrake' (T. Ettingsall) called the 4th.

Penn, R. Maxims and hints for an angler and miseries of fishing to which are added maxims and hints for a chess player. 1833 (anon), 1839, 1842 (as Maxims and hints on angling, chess, shooting and other matters).

Baddeley, J. The London angler's book. 1834.

[Bitton, W.] The angler in Ireland. 2 vols 1834. A description of a fishing tour.

[Chatto, W. A.] Scenes and recollections of fly-fishing. 1834. Under pseudonym 'S. Oliver'.

—— The angler's souvenir. 1835 (under pseudonym 'P. Fisher'); ed G. C. Davies [1877].

Hansard, G. A. Trout and salmon fishing in Wales. 1834.

Medwin, T. The angler in Wales: or days and nights of sportsmen. 2 vols 1834.

'An old angler and bibliopolist' (T. Boosey). Piscatorial reminiscences and gleanings; to which is added a catalogue of books on angling. 1835. *See* Ellis, *above*.

Stoddart, T. T. *See col 552 above*.

Jesse, E. An angler's rambles. 1836.

A collection of right merrie garlands, for North Country anglers. Newcastle-on-Tyne 1836, 1842; ed J. Crawhall 1864.

Ronalds, A. The fly-fisher's entomology. 1836; ed 'Piscator' (B. Smith) 1856 (5th edn); ed J. C. Carter 1901 (10th edn); ed H. E. Maxwell 2 vols Liverpool 1913; ed H. T. Sheringham 1921.

Hofland, T. C. The British angler's manual: or the art of angling in England, Scotland, Wales and Ireland, with some account of the principal rivers. 1839; ed E. Jesse 1848.

Younger, J. On river angling for salmon and trout. Edinburgh 1840, 1860, 1864.

Pulman, G. P. R. The vade mecum of fly-fishing for trout. London and Axminster 1841, London 1846, 1851.

—— Rustic sketches: being poems on angling. Taunton 1842.

Scrope, W. Days and nights of salmon fishing in the Tweed. 1843; ed H. T. Sheringham 1921.

Wayth, C. Trout fishing, or the river Darent: a rural poem. 1845.

Blakey, R. Hints on angling. 1846.

—— The angler's complete guide to the rivers and lakes of England. 1853, 1859.

—— The angler's complete guide to the rivers and lochs of Scotland. 1854.

—— Angling: or how to angle and where to go. 1854; ed W. Senior 1898 (with memoir of Blakey).

—— (ed). The angler's song book. 1855.

—— Historical sketches of the angling literature of all nations. 1856.

Akerman, J. Y. Spring-tide: or the angler and his friends. 1850. Fishing sketches.

Newland, Rev H. The Erne: its legends and its fly fishing. 1851. Fiction based on fact.

—— Forest scenes in Norway and Sweden: being extracts from the journal of a fisherman. 1854. Fiction based on fact.

'A North-Country angler' (T. Doubleday) (ed). The Coquet-Dale fishing songs. Edinburgh 1852. Mainly by R. Roxby with a memoir by Doubleday.

Badham, C. D. Prose halieutics: or ancient and modern fish tattle. 1854.

'Clericus' (W. Cartwright). Rambles and recollections of a fly-fisher. 1854.

—— Facts and fancies of salmon fishing. 1874.

Davy, J. The angler and his friend: or piscatory colloquies and fishing excursions. 1855.

—— The angler in the Lake District. 1857.

Stewart, W. C. The practical angler. Edinburgh 1857, 1861; ed W. E. Hodgson 1905.

—— A caution to anglers: or The practical angler and The modern practical angler compared. Edinburgh 1871. *See* Pennell, *below*.

Francis, F. The angler's register: a list of the come-at-able fisheries in England, Scotland, Ireland and Wales. 1858, [1859] (including Brittany and Belgium), [1860] (including Germany and the Tyrol).

—— A book on angling: being a complete treatise on the art of angling. 1867, 1867, 1872, 1880, 1885; ed H. E. Maxwell 1920.

—— By lake and river: an angler's rambles in the north of England and Scotland. 1874.

—— Hot pot: or miscellaneous papers [mainly on angling]. 1870.

—— Angling reminiscences. 1887.

Songs of the Edinburgh Angling Club. Edinburgh 1858, 1879; ed J. Smith 1900.

'Conway, James' (J. C. Walter). Letters from the Highlands: or two months among the salmon and the deer. 1859, 1861 (as Forays among salmon and deer).

Crawhall, J. The compleatest angling booke that ever was writ. Newcastle-on-Tyne 1859, 1881.

—— Chaplets from coquet-side. Newcastle 1873.

—— Border notes and mixty-maxty. Newcastle 1880.

Cliffe, J. H. Notes and recollections of an angler. 1860.

Smith, A. The Thames angler. 1860. Prose and verse.

Wilcocks, J. C. The sea-fisherman. Guernsey 1865, London 1868, 1875, 1884.

[Rooper, G.] The autobiography of the late Salmo Salar esq or Tweed salmon. 1867; rptd in his Flood, field and forest, 1869.

—— Thames and Tweed. 1870.

Pennell, H. C. The modern practical angler. [1870]. *See* Stewart, *above*.

—— (ed). Fishing gossip: or stray leaves from the note-books of several anglers. Edinburgh 1866.

Knox, A. E. Autumns on the Spey. 1872.

Kingsley, C. Chalk-stream studies. In his Prose idylls, 1873.

Senior, W. Waterside sketches: a book for wanderers and anglers. 1875.

—— By stream and sea: a book for wanderers and anglers. 1877.

—— Travel and trout in the Antipodes: an angler's sketches in Tasmania and New Zealand. 1880.

—— Near and far: an angler's sketches of home sport and colonial life. 1888.

Davies, G. C. Angling idylls. 1876. Prose.

Henderson, W. Notes and reminiscences of my life as an angler. 1876, 1879 (as My life as an angler).

Ellacombe, H. N. Shakespeare as an angler. 1883.

Froude, J. A. Cheneys and the house of Russell. In his Short studies on great subjects 4th ser, 1883.

International Fisheries Exhibition, London 1883. The Fisheries Exhibition literature [18 handbooks in 3 vols and index vol]. 1884. The following are relevant: vol 2, C. E. Fryer, The salmon fisheries; W. Senior, Angling in Great Britain; vol 3, J. P. Wheeldon, Angling clubs and preservation societies; J. J. Manley, Literature of sea and river fishing.

'Isys, Cotswold' (Rev R. H. Glover). An angler's strange experiences. 1883. Verse.

—— Lyra piscatoria: original lyrics. 1895.

Roscoe, E. S. Rambles with a fishing-rod. 1883, 1906.

'The amateur angler' (E. Marston). An amateur angler's days in Dovedale. 1884.

—— Fresh woods and pastures new. 1887.

—— Days in clover. 1892.

—— By meadow and stream. 1896.

—— On a sunshine holyday. 1897.

—— An old man's holidays. 1900.

Each of the above contains a number of angling essays and recollections.

Westwood, T. In memoriam Izaak Walton: twelve sonnets and an epilogue. [1884].

Bernnand, Sir F. C. (ed). The incomplete angler, after Master Izaak Walton. 1887.

'Bickerdyke, J.' (C. H. Cook). The book of the all-round angler. 1888, 1900, 1912, 1922 (5th edn).

—— Days in Thule with rod, gun and camera. 1894.

—— Days of my life on waters fresh and salt. 1895.

—— Practical letters to young sea fishers. 1898.

Roberts, Sir R. H. The silver trout and other stories. 1888.

Kennard, M. E. Landing a prize. 3 vols 1889. Novel.

Lang, A. Angling sketches. 1891.

Macvine, J. Sixty-three years angling, from the mountain streamlet to the mighty Tay. 1891.

Sandeman, F. By hook and by crook. 1892. Essays.

—— Angling travels in Norway. 1895.

Hopkins, F. P. Fishing experiences of half a century 1893.

Shrubsole, E. S. Long casts and sure rises. 1893.

Armistead, J. J. An angler's paradise and how to obtain it. Scarborough 1895.

Buchan, John (ed). Musa piscatrix. 1896. Anthology.

Maxwell, Sir H. E. and F. G. Aflalo (ed). The angler's library. 6 vols 1897–9. C. H. Wheeley, Coarse fish; F. G. Aflalo, Sea-fish; A. Jardine, Pike and perch; Sir H. E. Maxwell, Salmon and sea trout; G. A. B. Dewar, South country trout streams; J. Watson, The English lake fisheries.

Cadman, H. Harry Druidale: fisherman from Manxland to England. 1898.

Dewar, G. A. B. In pursuit of the trout. 1898.

Taylor, J. P. Fishing and fishers. [1898]. Includes chs on the literature of fishing.

Grimble, A. The salmon rivers of Scotland. 4 vols 1899–1900.

Durnford, Rev R. The fishing diary 1809–19 of R.D. Ed H. Nicoll, Winchester 1911.

§2

Parker, E. (ed). An angler's garland. 1920. Anthology.
Hills, J. W. A history of fly fishing for trout. 1921. Includes ch on literature of fly-fishing.
Taverner, E. Salmon fishing. 1931 (Lonsdale Lib vol 10). Includes 3 chs on the literature of salmon fishing.
Dickie, J. M. (ed). Great angling stories. London and Edinburgh 1941. Includes verse.
See also Lang *under* Cricket, *below;* Grimble, Jeans, 'Wildfowler' *under* Shooting, *below.*

Archery

Bibliographies

Walrond, H. In C. J. Longman and H. Walrond, Archery, 1894 (Badminton Lib).

Periodicals

The archer's register. 1864–6, 1877–. Annual.

§1

Roberts, T. The English bowman: or tracts on archery. 1801.
Waring, T. A treatise on archery. 1814.
Dodd, J. W. Ballads of archery, sonnets etc. 1818.
Hastings, T. The British archer. 1831.
'An old toxopholite'. The archer's guide; accompanied by a sketch of the history of the long-bow. 1833.
Harrison, A. P. The science of archery, showing its affinity to heraldry. 1834.
Warburton, R. E. E. The Hawkstone bow-meeting. Chester 1835. Verse.
—— Rhymes on the rules of the Cheshire bowmen. Northwich [1840?].
Hansard, G. A. The book of archery. 1840.
Ford, H. A. Archery: its theory and practice. 1856, 1859; ed W. Butt 1887 (as The theory and practice of archery).
'A toxopholite'. A history of the Royal Toxopholite Society. Taunton 1867 (priv ptd), 1870.
Paul, J. B. The history of the Royal Company of Archers. Edinburgh 1875.
Rushton, W. L. Shakespeare an archer. 1897.

§2

Burke, E. H. A history of archery. 1958.

Athletics

Periodicals

Athletic news. Manchester 1875–1931. Merged with Sporting chronicle. Weekly.

§1

Thorn, W. Pedestrianism: an account of the performances of celebrated pedestrians. Aberdeen 1813.

§2

Cook, Sir T. A. International sport: a short history of the Olympic movement. 1909.
Quercetani, R. L. A world history of track and field athletics. Oxford 1964.

Billiards

Bibliographies

'Crawley, Rawdon' (G. F. Pardon). Bibliographical catalogue of books on billiards. In his Billiard book, 1877 (2nd edn).

Periodicals

The billiard review. 1895–8. Irregular.

§1

White, E. A practical treatise on the game of billiards. 1807.
Kentfield, E. The game of billiards. 1839.
Roberts, J. Roberts on billiards. Ed H. Buck [1869], [1870].
Let us to billiards: prize essays on billiards as an amusement for all classes. Manchester 1873.
Bennett, J. Billiards. 1873. Includes short history of the game.
Cook, W. Billiards. Ed A. G. Payne [1884].
Buchanan, J. P. Hints on billiards. 1895.

Boxing

Bibliographies

Magriel, P. D. Bibliography of boxing: a chronological check list of books in English published before 1900. New York 1948.

Periodicals

The fancy, or true sportman's guide: being authentic memoirs of the lives, actions, prowess and battles of the leading pugilists. 55 nos 1821–5, 2 vols 1826. Irregular.

§1

A treatise on boxing. 1802.
Egan, P. Boxiana: or sketches of antient and modern pugilism. 1812, 1818–24 (with 3 additional vols).
Pancratia, or a history of pugilism: containing a full account of every battle of note from the time of Broughton and Slack down to the present day. 1812.
Mendoza, D. Memoirs of the life of Daniel Mendoza. 1816; ed P. D. Magriel 1951.
'One of the Fancy' (Thomas Moore). Tom Crib's memorial to congress. 1819. Boxing verse.
'Corcoran, Peter' (J. H. Reynolds). The fancy: a selection from the poetical remains of the late Peter Corcoran, with a brief memoir of his life. 1820; ed J. Masefield [1904].
Humphries, R. The memoirs of John Scroggins the pugilistic hero, with authentic annals of pugilism from the early days of Figg 1719 to those of Spring and Langan 1824. 1827.
Hazlitt, W. The fight. In his Literary remains vol 2, 1836.
[Dowling, F. D.] Fistiana or the oracle of the ring: comprising a defence of British boxing, a brief history of pugilism with chronological tables of prize battles from 1780–1840. 1841, 1842 etc (annual rev edn with suppl till 1870).
—— Fights for the championship and celebrated prize battles from the days of Figg and Broughton to the present time. 1855, 1860 (as The championship of England).
Borrow, G. H. In his Lavengro, 1851.
'Walker, Johnny' (J. Badman). The life and adventures of the renowned Johnny Walker. Winchester [1857].
Sayers, T. Memoirs of Tom Sayers champion of England. 1858.
History of the great international context between Heenan and Sayers at Farnborough on the 17th April 1860. 1860.
The fight of Sayerius and Heenanus: a lay of ancient London. Punch 28 April 1860.
Miles, H. D. Pugilistica: the history of British boxing. 1866, 3 vols [1880–1], Edinburgh 1906.
—— Tom Sayers, sometime champion of England: his life and pugilistic career. 1866.
Donnelly, 'Ned'. Self defence: or the art of boxing. [1879].

Shaw, G. B. Cashel Byron's profession. 1886, [1889], 1901 (Novels of his nonage 4; also includes The admirable Bashville, a play from the novel, and Note on modern prize-fighting).
Henning, F. W. J. Some recollections of the prize ring. 1888.
—— Fights for the championship: the men and their times. 2 vols [1902].
Doyle, A. Conan. Rodney Stone. 1896. Novel.
'Thormanby' (W. W. Dixon). Boxers and their battles: anecdotal sketches and personal recollections of famous pugilists. 1900.

§2

Bettinson, A. F. and W. O. Tristram (ed). The National Sporting Club past and present. 1901.
Sayers, H. Fights forgotten: a history of some of the chief English and American prize fights since the year 1788. [1909].
Wignall, T. C. The story of boxing. 1923.
Shepherd, T. B. (ed). The noble art: an anthology. 1950.
Deghy, G. Noble and manly: the history of the National Sporting Club. 1956.

Cards

Bibliographies

Horr, N. T. A bibliography of card-games and of the history of playing cards. Cleveland 1892.
Jessel, F. A bibliography of works in English on playing cards and gaming. 1905.
Hargrave, C. P. Bibliography of cards and gaming. In her History of playing cards, New York [1930].

§1

Mathews, T. Advice to the young whist-player. Bath 1804 etc. Author given as 'Matthews' until 1822 (13th edn).
The Faro table: or the gambling mothers. 2 vols 1808.
Singer, S. W. Researches into the history of playing cards. 1816.
Read, W. Rouge et noir: a poem in 6 cantos. 1821.
'Elia' (Charles Lamb). Mrs Battle's opinions on whist. In his Elia: essays which have appeared under that signature in the London Magazine [first series], 1823.
The St James' guide: or the sharper detected. 1825. Treatise exposing methods of cheating.
Garner, W. Garner's miscellaneous recitations: or whims of the loo table. 1827.
[Luttrell, H.] Crockford-house: a rhapsody in two cantos. 1827.
'An amateur' (G. F. Pardon). Whist: its history and practice. 1843.
Chatto, W. A. Facts and speculations on the origin and history of playing cards. 1848.
Pettigrew, J. J. On the origin and antiquity of playing cards. 1853.
'Cavendish' (H. Jones). The principles of whist. [1862], 1863 (5th edn as Laws and principles of whist), 1901 (24th edn).
—— Card essays. 1879.
Taylor, E. S. (ed). The history of playing cards. 1865.
Courtney, W. P. English whist and English whist players. 1894. Inlcudes 3 chs on the literature of whist.
'Portland' (J. Hogg) (ed). The whist table: a treasury of notes on the royal game. [1895].

Chess and other Board Games

Bibliographies

Simpson, R. Catalogue of books on the origin, history and practice of the game of chess. 1863.
Svendsen, K. Chess fiction in English to 1945: a bibliography. Langston 1950.

Bibliotheca Van der Linde-Niemeijeriana: a catalogue of the chess collection in the Royal Library, the Hague. Hague 1955.

Periodicals

The chess-monthly. 1879–96.
The chess-player's chronicle. 1841–56, 1859–62. Monthly.
British chess magazine. Huddersfield 1881–. Monthly.

§1

Sturges, J. Guide to the game of draughts. 1800.
[Pratt, P. (ed)]. Studies of chess. 2 vols 1803.
'An amateur' (Rev T. Pruen). An introduction to the history and study of chess. Cheltenham 1804.
Twiss, R. Pamphlets on chess and draughts. In his Miscellanies vol 2, 1805.
An easy introduction to the game of chess. 2 vols 1806.
Sarratt, J. H. A treatise on the game of chess. 1808; ed W. Lewis 1822.
—— A new treatise on the game of chess. 2 vols 1821, 1828.
Kenny, W. S. Practical chess grammar. 1817.
Peacock, Thomas Love. The chess dance. In his Melincourt vol 2 ch 28, 1817.
'An Oxford graduate'. Observations on the automaton chess player. 1819.
Playfair, P. The queen and her pawns against the king and his pieces: a poem. 1820.
Cochrane, J. A treatise on the game of chess. 1822. With a catalogue of writers on the game.
Lewis, W. Elements of the game of chess. 1822.
—— A treatise on the game of chess. 1844.
Dibdin, C. I. M. The Chessiad: a mock-heroic poem in five cantos. In his Comic tales and lyrical fancies, 1825.
Madden, F. Historical remarks on the introduction of the game of chess into Europe. Archaeologia 24 1832.
Walker, G. A new treatise on chess. 1832, 1833, 1841 (with full bibliography), 1846 (as The art of chess-play).
—— Chess and chess-play: original stories and sketches. 1850.
Staunton, H. The chess-player's handbook. 1847.
—— Chess praxis: a supplement to the Chess-player's handbook. 1860.
'An amateur' (S. S. Boden). A popular introduction to the study and practice of chess. 1851.
[Tomlinson, C.] Chess: a poem. 1854.
'A member of the Cambridge University Chess Club'. Chess: a poem. 1858.
'An Englishman' (F. M. Edge). Paul Murphy, the chess champion; with a history of chess and chess clubs in England. 1859.
'Captain Crawley' (G. F. Pardon). Backgammon: its theory and practice with something of its history. [1860].
Forbes, D. The history of chess. 1860.
Kennedy, H. A. Waifs and strays, chiefly from the chess-board. 1862, 1876.
'Carroll, Lewis' (C. L. Dodgson). Through the looking-glass, and what Alice found there. 1872.
Gossip, G. H. D. The chess-player's manual: a complete guide to chess. 1875.
MacDonnell, G. A. Chess life-pictures. 1883.
—— The knights and kings of chess. 1894. Essays on chess and chess-players.
Gould, J. The game of draughts. 1884.
Winter-Wood, E. J. The unexpected guest: a chess tale. In Chess souvenirs, 1886.
Tylor, L. Chess: a Christmas masque. 1888.
Bird, H. E. Chess history and reminiscences. [1893].

§2

Murray, H. J. R. A history of chess. Oxford 1913.
—— A history of board-games other than chess. Oxford 1952.

— A short history of chess. Oxford 1963.
Sergeant, P. W. A century of British chess. 1934.
See also Penn *under* Angling, *above*.

Cock-fighting

§1

Houston, T. The cock-fight. 1804.
The game cock, with an account of his origin. 1825.
Tregellas, J. T. The amusing adventures of Josee Cock, the Perran cock-fighter. 1857. Verse.
Cooper, J. W. Game fowls: their origin and history. 1869.
[Taylor, S. A.] Cocking and its votaries. 1885 (priv ptd).
Atkinson, H. The old English game-fowl. 1891, Idle 1899.
— Cock-fighting and game-fowl. Bath 1938.

§2

Scott, G. R. The history of cock-fighting. [1957]. With bibliography.

Coursing

'Sportsman'. A treatise on greyhounds. 1819.
Goodlake, T. The courser's manual or stud-book. 1828. With a contribution by Sir Walter Scott and a history of coursing.
— Continuation of the courser's manual. 1833.
Thacker, T. The courser's companion. Derby 1829, 2 vols 1834–5.
'Stonehenge' (J. H. Walsh). The greyhound: a treatise on breeding and training for public running. 1853, 1864, 1875.
Bullock, W. J. The coursing guide: or the Waterloo Cup made easy. [1873], [1874].
Brown, D. The history of coursing. In The greyhound stud book vol 3, 1884.
Jones, T. The courser's guide. 1896.
See also Lascelles, Mackintosh *under* Angling, *above*; 'The Druid' *under* Hunting, *below*.

Cricket

Bibliographies

Gaston, A. J. The bibliography of cricket. In Wisden's cricketers' almanack for 1892, 1894, 1900, 1923.
— Bibliography of cricket. 1895 (priv ptd). A separate work from the above.
Taylor, A. D. The catalogue of cricket literature. 1906.
Waghorn, H. T. Bibliography of cricket. In his The dawn of cricket, 1906.
Britton, C. J. Cricket books: the 100 best old and new. Birmingham 1929.
Goldman, J. W. Bibliography of cricket. 1937 (priv ptd).
Brodribb, A. G. N. Cricket in fiction: a bibliography. Canford 1950 (priv ptd).

Periodicals

John Wisden's cricketers' almanack. 1864–. 1864–9 as Cricketers' almanack; 1938 as Wisden cricketers' almanack. Index (to 1943) by R. Pogson, 1944.
Cricket. 1892–1914. Weekly. After 1913 as The world of cricket.

§1

Boxall, T. Rules and instructions for playing at the game of cricket. [1800], [1801], 1804.
Lambert, W. Instructions and rules for playing the noble game of cricket. Lewes 1816, 1830 (12th edn). Later edns variously as The cricketer's guide or Lambert's cricketer's guide. The 20th edn was pbd in 1829 before the 12th. The 13th–19th edns have not been traced. Originally a plagiarism of T. Boxall, Rules and instructions, above; *see also* G. B. Buckley, Lambert's cricketer's guide in Cricketer spring annual 1942; R. S. Rait Kerr, Lambert's cricketer's guide in Cricketer spring annual 1949.
Bentley, H. A correct account of all the cricket matches played by the Mary-le-bone Club and all other principal matches 1786–1822 inclusive. 1823. With suppls for 1823, 1824–5.
Mitford, Mary Russell. A country cricket-match. In her Our village vol 1, 1824.
Maunder, S. The game of life: or death among the cricketers. In Death's doings: verse and prose [by] various writers, 1826. Ed and illustr R. Dagley.
Nyren, John. The young cricketer's tutor; to which is added the cricketers of my time or recollections of the most famous old players. Ed C. Cowden Clarke 1833. Subsequent edns till 1858 (11th) as Nyren's cricketer's guide; ed C. Whibley 1893 (under original title); ed F. S. Ashley-Cooper 1902; ed E. V. Lucas 1907 (as The Hambledon men); ed J. Arlott 1948 (in his From Hambledon to Lords); ed N. Cardus 1948 (under original title). Original edn reviewed by John Mitford, GM July, Sept 1833; ed J. Arlott in his From Hambledon to Lords, 1948.
Pycroft, Rev J. The principles of scientific batting. Oxford 1833. Under pseudonym 'A gentleman'.
— The cricket field: or the history and science of cricket. 1851, 1873 (6th edn), 1887 (9th edn); ed F. S. Ashley-Cooper 1922; ed J. Arlott in his From Hambledon to Lords, 1948. *See also* L. E. S. Gutteridge, Bibliography of Pycroft's Cricket field in Cricket Soc News Letter 35 1954.
— The cricket tutor. 1862.
— Cricketana. 1865. Cricket articles rptd from London Soc Aug–Nov 1862, Jan, March, June 1863.
— Cricket reminiscences of the old players and observations on the young ones. 1868.
— Oxford memories. 2 vols 1886 (chs 21–5); ed J. Arlott in his Middle ages of cricket, 1949.
[Castelden, G.] Woburn Park: a fragment in rural rhyme. 1839, 1840. Pt 2 describes a match in some detail.
Lillywhite, F. W. Lillywhite's illustrated hand-book of cricket. 1844.
'Felix, N.' (N. Wanostrocht). Felix on the bat. 1845, 1850, 1855; with memoir by G. Brodribb 1962.
— How to play Clarke. 1852; ed F. S. Ashley-Cooper 1922.
— A cricket song. Ed F. S. Ashley-Cooper, Nottingham 1923. *See also* J. Arlott, Felix and some aspects of early cricket, in his Concerning cricket, 1949.
Denison, W. Cricket: sketches of the players. 1846; ed J. Arlott in his Middle ages of cricket, 1949.
Bolland, W. Cricket notes. 1851.
Gale, F. The public school matches and those we meet there. 1853 (under pseudonym 'Wykehamist'), 1896 (as Public school cricket matches forty years ago).
— Echoes from the old cricket fields: sketches of cricket and cricketers from the earliest history of the game. 1871, 1896.
— The life of the Hon Robert Grimston. 1885.
— The game of cricket. 1887.
'Chambers, C.' (T. Smith). The cricket match: a poem in two cantos. 1859.
Lillywhite, F. The English cricketers' trip to Canada and the United States. 1860.
— (ed). The guide to cricketers. Annual 1849–66. In 1867 merged with John Lillywhite's Cricketers' companion. 2 issues in 1849, 1860–1, 1861–2, 1862–3, 3 issues 1865–6. First 3 issues contain treatise by William Lillywhite; 2 issues of 1849 as The young cricketer's guide.
'Old cricketer' (C. Box?). The cricket-bat and how to use it. 1861.

Prowse, W. J. In memoriam [of the Kent cricketer Alfred Mynn]. Bell's Life in London 10 Nov 1861. Verse.

Haygarth, A. Frederick Lillywhite's cricket scores and biographies from 1746 [to 1878]. 15 vols 1862–1925. Vols 3–4 as Lillywhite's cricket scores etc, vols 4–5 and 14 as Arthur Haygarth's Cricket scores etc, vols 7–13 as Marylebone Club cricket scores etc, vol 15 ed F. S. Ashley-Cooper as MCC cricket scores etc but consisting only of biographies. Index to all first-class matches in scores and biographies vols 1–14 by J. B. Payne, Harrogate 1903.

Grace, E. M. The trip to Australia: scraps from the diary of one of the twelve. 1864. *See also* F. S. Ashley-Cooper, E.M.G. cricketer, 1916.

Payne, J. B. Scores and analyses [of matches not in Wisden] 1864–81. Harrogate [1904].

The Canterbury cricket week. Canterbury 1865.

John Lillywhite's cricketers' companion. 1865–85. In 1886 merged with James Lillywhite's cricketers' annual.

Fitzgerald, R. A. Jerks in from short-leg. 1866. Under pseudonym 'Quid'.

—— Wickets in the west: or the twelve in America. 1873.

Selkirk, G. H. Guide to the cricket ground. 1867. Practical treatise with ch on the history of the game.

Box, C. The theory and practice of cricket. 1868.

—— The English game of cricket. 1877. With anthology of cricket verse.

Gale, F. Echoes from the old cricket fields. 1871, 1896.

—— The game of cricket. 1887.

'Thomsonby' (H. P. Thomas). Cricketers in council. 1871. Practical treatise which includes some verse.

James Lillywhite's cricketers' annual. 1872–1900.

Compton, H. A colonial cricket match. In his Semi-tropical trifles, 1875.

'An old cricketer'. A cricketer's notebook. 1881. Verse and prose.

Trollope, Anthony. The cricket-match. In his Fixed period, 2 vols Edinburgh 1882.

Geering, T. Cricket on our common fifty years ago. In his Our parish: a medley, Hailsham 1884, London 1925 (with memoir by A. Beckett as Our Sussex parish).

Sapte, W. Cricketers guyed for 1886. [1885]. Humorous articles.

Shaw, A. and A. Shrewsbury. Cricket: Shaw and Shrewsbury's team in Australia. Nottingham 1885.

Bowen, E. E. Willow the King [and other verses on cricket]. In his Harrow songs, 1886.

Glover, W. Reminiscences of half a century. 1889. Includes chs on cricket.

Hutchinson, H. G. Cricketing saws and stories. 1889.

—— Peter Steele the cricketer. [1895]. A novel.

[Gale, N. R.] Cricket songs. Rugby 1890.

—— Cricket songs. 1894.

—— More cricket songs. 1905.

Dale, B. Some statistics of cricket: or the influence of the weather on the wicket. [1891].

Grace, W. G. Cricket. Bristol 1891.

—— Cricketing reminiscences and personal recollections. 1899.

—— W.G.'s little book. [1909]. Traces changes and developments in the game.

See also W. M. Brownlee, W.G.G.: a biography, 1887; M. B. Hawke (ed), The memorial biography of W.G.G., 1919; B. R. M. Darwin, W.G.G., 1934; C. Box, W.G.G., 1952; A. A. Thomson, The great cricketer, 1957.

Nelson, A. Comic cricket. [1891]. Humorous articles.

Lucas, E. V. Songs of the bat. 1892.

—— Willow and leather: a book of praise. Bristol [1898]. Anthology.

Standing, P. C. Gentlemen v. Players: with introduction and history of the contest since its origin in 1806. 1892.

—— Cricket of to-day and yesterday. 2 vols 1902.

—— The Hon F. S. Jackson [a biography]. 1906.

—— Anglo-Australian cricket 1862–1926. 1926.

Daft, R. Kings of cricket: reminiscences and anecdotes. Bristol [1893].

—— A cricketer's yarns. Ed F. S. Ashley-Cooper 1926.

Christian, E. B. V. At the sign of the wicket: essays on the glorious game. Bristol [1894]. Includes chs on cricket literature.

—— (ed). The light side of cricket: stories, sketches and verses. 1898.

Trew-Hay, J. The match of the season [Surrey v. Lancs Aug 16–18 1894]: a lay of the Oval. [1894].

Cobley, F. Black hats v. white hats: or Ilkley tradesmen at the wickes and around the festive board. Otley 1895. Verse and prose.

Pentelow, J. N. England v. Australia: the story of the test matches. 1895, 1904.

Cochrane, A. J. H. Lays from the pavilion and the links. In his Leviore plectro: occasional verses, 1896.

—— Told in the pavilion. Bristol 1896. Short stories.

Furniss, H. et al. How's that? including A century of Grace by H-F-, verses by E. J. Milliken and cricket sketches by E. B. V. Christian. Bristol [1896].

Read, W. W. Annals of cricket: a record of the game during the last twenty-three years. 1896.

Disney, T. Cricket lyrics. [1897].

Holmes, R. S. The county cricket championship 1873–96. Bristol [1897].

Moffat, D. Crickety cricket. 1897. Verse.

Ranjitsinhji, K. S. The Jubilee book of cricket. 1897. Reviewed by Francis Thompson in Academy 4 Sept 1897.

—— With Stoddart's team in Australia. 1898.

See also P. C. Standing, Ranjitsinhji: prince of cricket, 1903; R. Wild, The biography of Ranjitsinhji, 1934.

Ashley-Cooper, F. S. Stoddart's team in Australia 1897–8. [1898].

—— Curiosities of first-class cricket: descriptions of curious incidents arranged year by year from 1730–1901.

—— MCC match list: a summary of 8642 matches played in the UK by the MCC since 1787. 1930.

Bone, D. D. Fifty years' reminiscences of Scottish cricket. Glasgow 1898.

Giffen, G. With bat and ball: twenty-five years reminiscences of Australian and Anglo-Australian cricket. 1898.

Wells, H. G. The veteran cricketer. In his Certain personal matters, 1898.

Lyttelton, Hon R. H. Cricket. 1898.

—— (ed). Giants of the game. [1899].

Newbolt, Sir H. In vitaï Lampada. In his Island race, 1898.

Pullin, A. W. Talks with old Yorkshire cricketers. Leeds 1898.

—— Talks with old English cricketers. Edinburgh 1900.

—— (ed). Alfred Shaw, cricketer: his career and reminiscences. 1902.

[Barrie, J. M.] The Allahakbarrie book of Broadway cricket for 1899. [1899] (priv ptd), 1950 (as Allahakbarrie's CC 1899).

Caffyn, W. Seventy-one not out: reminiscences. Ed 'Mid-on' (R. P. Daft) 1899.

Fry, C. B. (ed). The book of cricket: a gallery of famous players. [1899].

Snaith, J. C. Willow the King: the story of a cricket match. [1899]. A novel.

Bayly, A. E. and W. Briscoe. Chronicles of a country cricket club. 1900. Fiction.

Bettesworth, W. A. The Walkers of Southgate: a famous brotherhood of cricketers. 1900.

—— Chats on the cricket field, with explanatory notes by F. S. Ashley-Cooper. [1910]. Interviews with c. 60 cricketers rptd from The cricket field and Cricket 1892–1906.

Ford, W. J. A cricketer on cricket. 1900.

Warner, Sir P. F. Cricket in many climes. 1900.
— Lord's 1787–1945. 1946.
— Gentlemen v. Players 1806–1949. 1950.
Thompson, Francis. At Lords [and other cricketing verse]. In A rhapsodist at Lord's, in E. V. Lucas, One day and another, 1909.
Lang, Andrew. Games and sport: cricket, golf, fishing. Pt 9 vol 2 of his Collected poems, ed L. B. Lang 4 vols 1923.

§2

Gordon, H. S. C. M. Cricket form at a glance showing the batting and bowling of every cricketer who has played in first class matches in any two seasons between 1878–1902, with every run scored for or against the Australians in England, the elevens they met, the results and that of every county match. 1902.
— Eton v. Harrow at Lord's: the story of the matches by Bernard Darwin and reminiscences of every match since 1861 by an actual player in each game. 1926.
Benson, E. F. and E. H. Miles. The cricket of Abel, Hirst and Shrewsbury. 1903.
Taylor, A. D. Annals of Lord's and history of the MCC. Bristol [1903].
Barlow, R. G. Forty seasons of first-class cricket: autobiography and reminiscences. Manchester [1908].
Toms, T. S. England v. Australia in the tests 1877–1908. [1909].
Harris, G. R. C. Baron Harris. Lord's and the MCC: a cricket chronicle of 137 years. 1914. With F. S. Ashley-Cooper.
— A few short runs. 1921. Cricketing reminiscences.
Altham, H. S. A history of cricket [with select bibliography]. 1926, 1938 (with E. W. Swanton), 1947, 1948, 2 vols 1962.
Parker, E. Between the wickets: an anthology of cricket. 1926.
— The history of cricket, 1950 (Lonsdale Lib of Sports vol 30).
Lewis, W. J. The language of cricket with illustrative extracts from the literature of the game. Oxford 1934.
Buckley, G. B. Fresh light on pre-Victorian cricket: a collection of cricket notices from 1709 to 1837. Birmingham 1937.
The MCC 1787–1937. 1937 (rptd from the Times MCC number). Includes Edmund Blunden, Some cricket books.
Brodribb, G. The English game: a cricket anthology. 1948.
— The book of cricket verse: an anthology. 1953.
Joy, N. Maiden over: a short history of women's cricket. 1950.
Kerr, R. S. Rait. The laws of cricket: their history and growth. 1950. Including list of edns of laws pbd 1744–1835.
Martineau, G. D. Bat, ball, wicket and all: an account of the origin and development of the implements, dress and appurtenances of the national game. 1950.
— The valiant stumper: a history of wicket-keeping. 1957.
Meynell, L. Famous cricket grounds: a brief history of some of the famous grounds in England. 1951.
Arlott, J. Cricket. 1953. Includes much history with extensive quotations from early cricket literature.
— and S. Brogden. The first test match: England v. Australia 1877. 1950.
Morrah, P. Alfred Mynn and the cricketers of his time. 1963. With bibliography.
Swanton, E. W. (ed). The world of cricket. 1966. With sections on literature.

Croquet

Prior, R. C. A. Notes on croquet: and some ancient bat and ball games related to it. 1872.

Lillie, A. Croquet: its history, rules and secrets. 1897.
— Croquet up to date. 1900.
See also Lawn tennis *under* Tennis, *below*.

Cycling

Bibliographies

Lightwood, J. T. Bibliography of cycling literature. In his Cyclists' touring club: the romance of 50 years cycling, 1928.

§1

Davis, A. The velocipede and how to use it. 1868.
— The velocipede: its history. 1869.
[Bottomley, J. F.] The velocipede: its past, its present and its future. 1869.
Jefferson, R. L. Awheel to Moscow and back: the record of a record cycle ride. 1895.
For details of the many books describing cycling tours pbd 1870–1900, see bibliography in Lightwood's Cyclists' touring club, 1928, *above*.
The humours of cycling. 1897. A selection of cycling stories by H. G. Wells, Jerome K. Jerome et al.
Waugh, A. Legends of the wheel. Bristol [1898]. Verse.
Jerome, Jerome K. Three men on the bummel. Bristol [1900].

Driving

Bibliographies

Somerset, H. C. F., 8th Duke of Beaufort. The bibliography of driving. In his Driving, 1889 (Badminton Lib).

§1

Cross, T. The autobiography of a stage-coachman. 3 vols 1861.
Reynardson, C. T. S. B. Down the road: or reminiscences of a gentleman coachman. 1875.
Lennox, Lord W. P. Coaching: with anecdotes of the road. 1876.
Malet, H. E. Annals of the road: or notes on mail and stage coaching in Great Britain. 1876.
Harris, S. Old coaching days. 1882.
— The coaching age. 1885.
Haworth, M. E. Road scrapings: coaches and coaching. 1882.
Maudslay, A. Highways and horses. 1888.
Tristram, W. O. Coaching days and coaching ways. 1888.
Corbett, E. An old coachman's chatter; with some practical remarks on driving. 1890.

§2

Shone, A. B. A century and a half of amateur driving. 1956.
See 'Cecil', 'Nimrod', Whitehurst *under* Hunting, *below*.

Falconry and Hawking

Bibliographies

Harting, J. E. Bibliotheca accipitraria: a catalogue of books ancient and modern relating to falconry. 1891.
Barber, R. H. A supplementary bibliography of hawking: books published in England between 1891 and 1943, together with a list of the most important books published prior to that period. 1943 (priv ptd).
Wood, C. A. and F. M. Fyfe. An annotated bibliography of ancient, medieval and modern falconry. In their Art of falconry: being the De arte venandi cum avibus of Frederick II of Hohenstaufen, Stanford 1943, Boston 1955.

§1

Sebright, Sir J. S. Observations upon hawking. 1826.
Belany, J. C. A treatise upon falconry. Berwick-on-Tweed 1841.

Burton, Sir R. F. Falconry in the valley of the Indus. 1852.
Salvin, F. H. and W. Brodrick. Falconry in the British Isles. 1855, 1873.
— and G. E. Freeman. Falconry: its claims, history and practice. 1859.
Freeman, G. E. Practical falconry; to which is added, How I became a falconer. 1869.
Fisher, C. H., G. E. Freeman et al. Prize essays on falconry. 1871.
Harting, J. E. The ornithology of Shakespeare. 1871. Contains much on falconry and hawking.
— Hints on the management of hawks. 1884, 1898 (with additional chs on falconry).
Michell, E. B. The art and practice of hawking. 1900.

Fencing

Bibliographies

Foster, F. W. A list of works on sword play. N & Q July–Dec 1875.
Castle, E. Bibliotheca artis dimicatoriae. In W. H. Pollock et al, Fencing: boxing; wrestling, 1889 (Badminton Lib).
Thimm, C. A. A complete bibliography of the art of fence. 1891.
— A complete bibliography of fencing and duelling. 1896.
Aylward, J. D. Some nineteenth-century fencing books. Connoisseur Oct 1950.

§1

Mathewson, T. Fencing familiarized. Salford 1805.
Roland, J. The amateur of fencing. 1809.
Angelo, H. C. W. A treatise on the utility and advantages of fencing. 1817.
— Reminiscences. 2 vols 1828, 1904 (with notes and memoir by H. L. Smith).
Martelli, C. An improved system of fencing. 1819.
Roland, G. A treatise on the theory and practice of the art of fencing. Edinburgh 1823.
— An introductory course of fencing. Edinburgh 1827.
Young, W. The fencer's manual. Chatham 1840.
Chapman, G. Foil practice: with a review of the art of fencing. 1861.
— Notes and observations on the art of fencing: a sequel to Foil practice. 1864.
Burton, Sir R. F. The book of the sword. 1884. All pbd of 3 projected vols.
— The sentiment of the sword: a country-house dialogue. Ed A. F. Sieveking 1911.
Castle, E. Schools and masters of fence. 1885, 1892.

§2

Aylward, J. de V. The house of Angelo: a dynasty of swordsmen. 1953.
— The English master of arms. 1956.
Baldick, R. The duel: a history of duelling. 1965.

Football: Association and Rugby

Bibliographies

Young, P. M. In his Manchester United, 1960.

Periodicals

The football annual. 1873–1908. Association and Rugby.

§1

Football: the first day of the sixth match. Rugby [1851].
'An old boy' (Thomas Hughes). In his Tom Brown's school days, Cambridge 1857.
Shearman, Sir M. and J. E. Vincent. Football: its history for five centuries. 1885.
Marshall, Rev F. (ed). Football: the Rugby union game. 1892, [1894]; ed L. R. Tosswill 1925.
The origin of Rugby football: report with appendices of the sub-committee of the Old Rugbeian Society. Rugby 1897.
'Tityrus' (J. A. H. Cotton). The rise of the Leaguers 1863–97. 1897.
— The real football: a sketch of the development of the Association game. 1900.
Jackson, N. L. et al. Association football. 1899.
Weddell, A. J. Handy guide to English league football. Liverpool 1899.

§2

Gibson, A. and W. Pickford. Association football and the men who made it. 4 vols [1905–6].
Sutcliffe, C. E. et al. The story of the football league 1888–1938. Preston 1938.
Green, G. The official history of the FA cup. 1949, 1960.
— et al. The history of the Football Association. 1953.
— and A. H. Fabian (ed). Association football. 4 vols 1960. Includes much on early history of the game.
Marshall, H. and J. P. Jordan. Oxford v. Cambridge: the story of the University Rugby match. 1951.
Owen, O. L. The history of the Rugby Football Union. 1955.
Pelmear, K. and J. E. Morpurgo. Rugby football: an anthology. 1958.
Thomas, J. B. G. Great rugger clubs. 1962.
Delaney, T. A century of soccer: a centenary publication of the Football Association. 1963.

Golf

Bibliographies

Lawless, P. A golfer's bibliography. In his Golfer's companion, 1937.
Hopkinson, C. Collecting golf-books 1743–1938. 1938.

Periodicals

The golfing annual. 1887–1910.
Golf. 1890–. Weekly. From 16 June 1899 as Golf illustrated.
Golfing. 1895–. Weekly. From 24 Feb 1897–30 June 1898 as Golfing and cycling illustrated. From 7 July–27 Oct 1898 as Golfing and cycling.

§1

[Cundell, J.] Rules of the Thistle Golf Club; with some historical notices relative to the progress of golf in Scotland. Edinburgh 1824; rptd in R. Clark, Golf, 1875.
Carnegie, G. F. Golfiana: or niceties connected with the game of golf. Leith 1833, Edinburgh 1833, 1842, 1867 (in Poems on golf), 1875 (in R. Clark, Golf).
'A keen hand' (H. B. Farnie). The golfer's manual: being an historical and descriptive account of the national game of Scotland. Cupar 1857, London 1947.
Chambers, R. A few rambling remarks on golf. 1862.
'A golfer' (G. Robb). Historical gossip about golf and golfers. Edinburgh 1863.
Poems on golf. Edinburgh 1867.
[Brown, T.] Golfiana: or a day at Gullane. [Edinburgh?] 1869; rptd in J. Kerr, The golf-book of East Lothian, 1896.
Marsh, T. Blackheath golfing lays. 1873.
Clark, R. (ed). Golf: a royal and ancient game. Edinburgh 1875, London 1893. Mainly an anthology of golf literature.
Hogg, W. T. M. Gullane: a poem. Edinburgh 1875.
Forgan, R. The golfer's handbook. Cupar 1881, London [1890], [1897] (as The golfer's manual).
Hutchinson, H. G. Hints on the game of golf. Edinburgh 1886, Edinburgh and London 1891 (6th edn).
— British golf links. 1897.
— The golfing pilgrim on many links. 1898.

— The book of golf and golfers. 1899.
— Aspects of golf. Bristol 1900.
— Fifty years of golf. [1919].
Jackson, D. Golf songs and recitations. Cupar 1886, Leven 1895.
Simpson, Sir W. G. The art of golf. Edinburgh 1887.
Stewart, J. L. Golfiana miscellanea: being a collection of interesting monographs on golf. 1887.
Lang, A. Two rhymes on golf. In On the links by W. A. Knight and T. T. Oliphant, Edinburgh 1889.
— et al. A batch of golfing papers. London and St Andrews 1892.
'Flint, Violet' (J. E. Thomson). A golfing idyll. St Andrews 1892. Verse.
'J.A.C.K.' Golf in the year 2000: or what we are coming to. 1892. A novel.
Stobart, M. A. Won at the last hole: a golfing romance. 1893. A novel.
Thomson, J. Golfing and other poems and songs. Glasgow 1893.
Kennard, M. E. The sorrows of a golfer's wife. 1896. A novel.
Mackern, L. (ed). Our lady of the green: a book of ladies' golf. 1899.
Low, J. L. F. G. Tait: a record, being his life, letters and golfing diary. [1900].

§2

Wood, H. B. Golfing curios and 'the like'. 1910. With bibliography.
Hilton, H. H. and G. G. Smith (ed). The royal and ancient game of golf. 1912.
Clapcott, C. B. The rules of golf of the ten oldest golf clubs 1754–1848. Edinburgh 1935.
Darwin, B. et al. A history of golf in Britain. 1952.
Mortimer, C. G. and F. J. C. Pignon. The story of the Open Golf Championship 1860–1950. 1952.
Browning, R. H.-K. A history of golf. 1955.
See also Cochrane, Lang *under* Cricket, *above*.

Hockey

Bibliographies

Malherbe, W. A. Bibliography of hockey. Kronsted 1956.

§1

Battersby, H. F. P. Hockey. 1895.
Solbé, F. de L. Hints on hockey. Edinburgh and London 1900.

Hunting, Racing, Riding

Bibliographies

Somerset, H. C. F., 8th Duke of Beaufort and M. Morris. Bibliography of hunting and hunters. In their Hunting, 1885 (Badminton Lib).
Huth, F. H. Works on horses and equitation: a bibliographical record of hippology [including some racing books]. 1887.
Higginson, A. H. British and American sporting authors: their writings and biographies, with a bibliography by S. R. Smith. 1951. Mainly concerned with hunting.
Allen, J. A. The steeplechaser's library: a bibliography. In Steeplechasing, ed J. H. P. Verney, Baron Willoughby de Broke 1954 (Lonsdale Lib vol 32).

Periodicals

The racing calendar. 1773–. Annual. *See also* C. M. Prior, The history of The racing calendar, 1926.
Racing times. 1851–64, 1866–8. Weekly.
Horse and hound. 1884–. Weekly.
The racing world. 1887–. Weekly.
Bailey's hunting directory. 1897–. Annual.

§1

Chifney, S. The narrative or address of S- C- to the public in general, but more particularly to such of them as are connected with the turf. 1800.
Adams, J. The analysis of horsemanship: teaching the whole art of riding. 3 vols 1805.
Hawkes, J. The Meynellian science: or fox-hunting upon system. [1808?], 1848; ed L. H. Irvine, Leicester 1932.
Lawrence, J. The history and delineation of the horse with a particular investigation of the character of the race-horse and the business of the turf. 1809.
Morland, T. H. The genealogy of the English race horse; with observations upon the present improved method of breeding for the turf. 1810.
Songs of the chace: containing an extensive collection relative to the sports of the field. 1811 (2nd edn).
Beard, J. A diary of fifteen years hunting, viz from 1796 to 1811. Bath 1813.
Lloyd, G. and R. Symes. The improved art of riding. [1815?].
Steward, C. A new and complete guide to the art of riding. 1821.
Allen, J. Principles of modern riding for ladies. 1825.
— Principles of modern riding for gentlemen. 1825.
Anecdotes on the origin and antiquity of horse-racing. 1825.
Cook, J. Observations on fox-hunting and the management of hounds. 1826; ed R. G. Verney 1922.
Johnson, T. B. The hunting directory. 1826. Prose work on all aspects of hunting.
Stanley, E. The young horsewoman's compendium of the modern art of riding. 1827.
Hood, Thomas. The Epping hunt. 1829. Verse.
Brown, T. Biographical sketches and authentic anecdotes of horses. 1830. Includes Charles Dibdin, The high-mettled racer, also pbd separately 1831.
'Nimrod' (Charles James Apperley). Remarks on the condition of hunters. 1831; ed C. Tongue 1855; ed F. T. Barton 1908.
— Nimrod's hunting tours. 1835; ed W. S. Sparrow 1926.
— The chace, the turf and the road. 1837; ed Sir H. E. Maxwell 1898; ed W. S. Sparrow 1927.
— Memoirs of the life of the late John Mytton. 1835, 1851 (with memoir of the author by Surtees).
— Nimrod's northern tour. 1838.
— The horse and the hound. Edinburgh 1842.
— Hunting reminiscences. 1843; ed W. S. Sparrow 1926.
— My life and times. Ed E. D. Cuming 1927. Taken in part from articles in Fraser's Mag 1842.
— My horses and other essays. Ed E. D. Cuming 1928. Miscellaneous contributions to periodicals.
Warburton, R. E. E. Hunting songs and ballads. Chester 1834, London 1846, 1859, 1860, 1873, 1877; ed H. Maxwell 1912.
'Caveat emptor' (Sir George Stephen). The adventures of a gentleman in search of a horse. 1835.
Hawke, Hon M.B.E. The Epwell hunt [and another hunting poem]. Cheltenham [1835?]; with two other hunting poems, [1840?].
— Poems on hunting [with a sketch of Hawke's sporting career by Nimrod]. Pontefract? 1842.
Peters, J. G. A treatise on equitation. 1835.
Smith, T. Extracts from the diary of a huntsman. 1838, 1841, 1921, 1933.
— The life of a fox written by himself. 1843 (under the pseudonym 'Wily'), 1896; ed R. G. Verney Lord Willoughby de Broke 1926.
[Surtees, R. S.] *See col 967, above.*
'Quis'. Shelton gorse. Bedford 1839.
Radcliffe, F. P. D. The noble science: a few general ideas on fox-hunting. 1839; ed W. C. A. Blew 1893; ed Blew and C. Bradley 2 vols 1911.
Whyte, J. C. History of the British turf. 2 vols 1840.

Mills, J. *See col 951, above.*
Vyner, R. T. Notitia venatica: a treatise on fox-hunting. 1841, [1871]; ed W. C. A. Blew 1892; ed Blew and C. Bradley 2 vols 1910. All edns illustr H. Alken.
Corbet, H. The steeple chase calendar: a consecutive chronicle of the sport in Great Britain 1826–44. 1845; Supplement, 1846.
'Hieover, Harry' (C. Bindley). Stable talk and table talk. 1845–6.
— The pocket and the stud. 1848.
— The hunting-field. 1850.
— Practical horsemanship. 1850.
— Bipeds and quadrupeds. 1853.
'Gêlert'. Fores's guide to the foxhounds and staghounds of England to which are added the otter-hounds and harriers of several counties. [1849], 1908 (as A guide to the foxhounds etc).
Hall, H. B. Exmoor. 1849. Sporting reminiscences of the area.
— Brooklands: a sporting biography. 2 vols 1852.
Rous, Hon H. J. The laws and practice of horse racing. 1850. *See also* T. H. Bird, Admiral Rous and the English turf 1795–1877, 1939.
Wayte, S. C. The equestrian's manual. 1850.
'Cecil' (Cornelius Tongue). The stud farm: or hints on breeding for the turf, the chase and the road. 1851, 1856, 1873.
— Stable practice: or hints on training for the turf, the chase and the road. 1852.
— Records of the chase and memoirs of celebrated sportsmen. 1854, 1877, 1922.
— Hunting tours. 1864.
'Martingale' (J. ? White). Turf characters: the officials and the subalterns. 1851.
'Scrutator' (K. W. Horlock). Letters on the management of hounds. 1852.
— Horses and hounds: a practical treatise on their management. 1855.
— The master of the hounds. 3 vols 1859. A novel.
— Recollections of a fox-hunter. 1861.
— The country gentleman. 3 vols 1862. A novel.
— The science of foxhunting. 1868.
Berkeley, Hon G. C. G. F. Reminiscences of a huntsman. 1854.
'The Druid' (H. H. Dixon). The post and the paddock, with recollections of George IV, Sam Chifney and other turf celebrities. [1856], [1856], [1857].
— Silk and scarlet. 1859.
— Scott and Sebright. 1862.
— Saddle and sirloin. 1870. Includes coursing.
The above 3 books all contain racing and hunting history and reminiscence.
See also J. B. Booth, Bits of character: a life of H. H. D., 1936.
Clarke, Mrs J. S. The habit and the horse: a treatise on female equitation. 1857.
Eardley-Wilmot, Sir J. E. Reminiscences of the late Thomas Assheton Smith esq, a famous fox-hunter. 1860, 1862; ed Sir H. E. Maxwell 1902 (6th edn).
Head, Sir F. B. The horse and his rider. 1860.
Whyte-Melville, G. J. *See col 971, above.*
Collyns, C. P. Notes on the chase of the wild red deer in the counties of Devon and Somerset. 1862.
Clarke, C. A box for the season. 2 vols 1864. A hunting novel.
— Which is the winner? 3 vols 1864. A racing novel.
— Crumbs from a sportsman's table. 2 vols 1865. A hunting novel.
— The flying scud. 2 vols 1867. A racing novel.
Trollope, A. Hunting sketches. 1865; ed J. Boyd 1934; ed L. Edwards 1952.
Lays of the Belvoir hunt. 1866, 1874.
'Meadows, Lindon' (C. B. Greatrex). Dame Perkins and her grey mare. 1866. Hunting verse.

Craven, W. G. The Margravine: a story of the turf. 2 vols 1870.
Bowers, G. Notes from a hunting box not in the shires. 1873.
'Old Calabor'. Over turf and stubble. 1873. A novel.
— Won in a canter. 3 vols 1874. A novel.
— Grey Abbey. 2 vols 1877. A novel with racing scenes.
Randall, J. Old sports and sportsmen, or the Willey country with sketches of Squire Forester and his whipper-in Tom Moody. 1873.
Sidney, S. The book of the horse and hints on horsemanship. 1874, 1881.
'Vieille Moustache' (R. Henderson). The barb and the bridle: a handbook of equitation for ladies. 1874.
Musters, J. C. The great run with J. C. M.'s foxhounds. Nottingham [1877]. Verse.
— Hunting songs and poems. Nottingham 1885.
Sewell, A. Black beauty: the autobiography of a horse. 1877.
Smart, H. Bound to win: a tale of the turf. 3 vols 1877.
'Triviator'. The West Union stag hounds and the Baytown run. [1877]. Verse.
'Brooksby' (E. P. Elmhirst). The hunting countries of England: their facilities, character and requirements. 2 vols 1878.
— The cream of Leicestershire. 1883. Articles selected and rptd from Field.
Fitt, J. N. Covert-side sketches: or thoughts on hunting. 1878.
Whitehurst, F. F. Tally-ho: sketches of hunting, coaching etc. 1878.
— Hark away: sketches of hunting, coaching etc. 1879.
Rice, J. History of the British turf. 2 vols 1879.
Webber, B. Pigskin and willow. 3 vols 1879.
'Blinkhoolie'. Angram, a hidden talent: the story of a wasted horse. York [1880].
— The tale of a horse. 1884.
Watson, A. E. T. Sketches in the hunting field. 1880.
— Racecourse and covert side. 1883. Sketches.
— Types of the turf: anecdotes and incidents. 1883. Under pseudonym 'Rapier'.
— Racing and 'chasing: a collection of sporting stories. 1897.
— The turf. 1898.
Bagot, A. G. Men we meet in the field. 1881.
Hayes, M. H. Riding on the flat and across country: a guide to practical horsemanship. 1881, 1882.
O'Donoghue, Mrs N. P. Ladies on horseback. 1881, 1891.
— The common sense of riding: riding for ladies with hints on the stable. 1887.
Mason, G. F. My day with the hounds and other stories. Cambridge [1882].
— Sporting recollections. 1885.
— Flowers of the hunt. 1889.
— The white hat and other stories. Bristol [1891].
— The tame fox, and other sketches. [1897].
— Heroes and heroines of the Grand National: containing a complete account of every race. 1907.
'Wanderer' (E. H. D'Avigdor). Across country. 1882. Short stories.
— Fair Diana. 1884. A hunting novel.
— Hunt-room stories and yachting yarns. 1885. Short stories.
— A loose rein. 1887. A hunting novel.
Kennard, M. E. The right sort: a romance of the shires. 3 vols 1883.
— The girl in the brown habit. 3 vols 1886.
— Killed in the open. 3 vols 1886.
— A real good thing. 3 vols 1887.
— A glorious gallop. 1888.
— Our friends in the hunting field. 1889. Prose sketches.
— That pretty little horse-breaker. 3 vols 1891.
— Wedded to sport. 3 vols 1892.
— The hunting girl. 3 vols 1893.

— The catch of the county. 3 vols 1894.
— A crack county. 3 vols 1894.
— At the tail of the hounds. 1897.
— Morals of the Midlands. 1899.
Day, W. Reminiscences of the turf. 1886.
— Turf celebrities I have known. 1891.
Hone, J. P. History of Newmarket and annals of the turf. 3 vols 1886.
Fortescue, Hon Sir J. W. Records of stag-hunting on Exmoor. 1887.
— The story of a red deer. 1897.
Roberts, Sir R. H. In the shires: a sporting novel. [1887].
— Curb and snaffle. 1888. A novel.
— Hard held. 1889. Sequel to preceding.
— High-flyer hall: Joshua Blewitt's sporting experiences. [1893]. A novel.
— Not in the betting. 1893. A novel.
Russell, F. Cross country reminiscences. 1887.
— In scarlet or silk: recollections of hunting and steeple-chase riding. 1896.
— The Haughtyshire hunt. 1897. A novel.
— Colonel Botcherby MSH. 1899. A novel.
Taunton, T. H. Portraits of celebrated racehorses 1702–1870, together with their respective pedigrees and performances recorded in full. 4 vols 1887–8.
'Thormanby' (W. W. Dixon). The horse and the rider: an anecdotic medley. 1888.
— Kings of the turf: memoirs and anecdotes. 1898.
— Kings of the hunting-field: memoirs and anecdotes. 1899.
Baden-Powell, R. S. S. Pigsticking: a complete account for sportsmen, 1889, 1924.
Thomson, J. A. Three great runs. 1889.
— Eighty years reminiscences. 2 vols 1904.
'Curzon, L. H.' (J. G. Bertram). The blue ribbon of the turf: a chronicle of the race for the Derby. 1890.
— A mirror of the turf: or the machinery of horse-racing revealed. 1892.
Black, R. The jockey club and its founders. 1891.
— Horse-racing in England [a history]. 1893.
Chetwynd, Sir G. Racing reminiscences and experiences of the turf. 2 vols 1891.
Kent, J. Racing life of Lord George Cavendish Bentinck. Ed Hon F. C. Lawley 1892.
Custance, H. Riding recollections and turf stories. 1894.
Underhill, G. F. The helterskelter hounds. 1894. A novel.
— Hunting. 1897.
— Gone to ground: a hunting novel. 1899.
— A century of English fox-hunting. 1900.
Williams, W. P. Poems in pink. Salisbury and London 1894.
— Plain poems. Salisbury and London 1896.
— Over the open. 1897. A novel.
— Rhymes in red. Salisbury and London 1899.
Fothergill, G. A. A riding retrospect. 1895.
Lutyens, F. M. Mr Spinks and his hounds: a hunting story. [1896].
Porter, J. Kingsclere. Ed B. Webber 1896. Trainer's reminiscences of famous stables.
Lister, T., 4th Baron Ribblesdale. The Queen's hounds and stag-hunting recollections. 1897.
Bradley, C. The reminiscences of Frank Gillard, huntsman, with the Belvoir hounds 1860–96. 1898.
Pease, Sir A. E. Hunting reminiscences. 1898.
Somerville, E. Œ. and Martin Ross (V. F. Martin). The silver fox. 1898.
— Some experiences of an Irish RM. 1899.
Anderson, T. S. Holloas from the hills. Jedburgh 1899. Verse.
Lyall, J. G. The merry gee-gee—how to breed, break and ride him for'ard away and the noble art of backing winners on the turf. 1899.

Cawthorne, G. J. and R. S. Herod. Royal Ascot: its history and its associations. 1900, 1902.
Dixon, W. S. The sport of kings. 1900. Articles on hunting.
Reeve, J. S. (ed). Lyra venatica: a collection of hunting songs [largely 19th century]. 1906.
Apperley, N. W. A hunting diary [1864–1920]. Ed E. D. Cuming 1926.
Osbaldeston, G. Squire Osbaldeston: his autobiography. Ed E. D. Cuming 1926.
Paget, G. and L. Irvine (ed). The flying parson and Dick Christian: incorporating chapters from Silk and scarlet and Post and paddock and letters from George Osbaldeston. 1934. With first pbn of hunting prose and verse by John Empson, the flying parson.

§2

Blew, W. C. A. A history of steeple-chasing. 1901.
Fletcher, J. S. The history of the St Leger stakes 1776–1901. 1902.
Aflalo, F. G. (ed). The hunting library: 1, Hare-hunting and harriers by H. A. Bryden; 2, Fox-hunting in the shires, by T. F. Dale; 3, The master of hounds by G. F. Underhill, with bibliography. 1903. All vols partly historical.
Cook, Sir T. A. A history of the English turf. 3 vols [1905].
Moorhouse, E. The romance of the Derby. 2 vols 1908.
Coaten, A. W. British hunting: a complete history of the national sport of Great Britain and Ireland. 1910.
Lattimer, R. B. The story of 'John Peel'. Cornhill Mag Oct 1919.
Verney, R. G., Lord Willoughby de Broke (ed). The sport of our ancestors: being a collection of prose and verse setting forth the sport of fox-hunting as they knew it. 1921.
Humphris, E. M. The life of Fred Archer. 1923.
— The life of Mathew Dawson. 1928.
Birkett, Lady D. N. Hunting lays and hunting ways: an anthology of the chase. 1924.
Machell, H. W. John Peel: famous in sport and song. 1926. Includes a history of the well known song with facsimiles of mss of words and music.
Munroe, D. H. The Grand National 1839–1931. 1931.
Higginson, A. H. The Meynell of the west: being a biography of James John Farquharson esqre, master of fox hounds 1806–58. 1936.
— Two centuries of foxhunting. 1946.
Biegel, P. (ed). Booted and spurred: an anthology of riding. 1949.
Orchard, V. R. Tattersalls: two hundred years of sporting history. 1953.
Eliot, Lady G. E. O. Portrait of a sport: a history of steeplechasing. 1957. With bibliography.
Mortimer, R. The Jockey Club. 1958. A history.
— The history of the Derby Stakes. 1962.
Murphy, G. (ed). The horse lover's treasury: an illustrated anthology of verse and prose. 1963.

Mountaineering

Bibliographies

Catalogue of books in the library of the Alpine Club. 1880, 1888, 1899, 1915.
Engel, C. E. La littérature alpestre en France et en Angleterre aux xviiie et xixe siècles. Paris 1931.
— In his A history of mountaineering in the Alps, 1950.
— In his They came to the hills [studies of famous mountaineers from Forbes to Smythe], 1952.
Porter, E. C. Library of mountaineering and exploration and travel. Chicago 1959.

Periodicals

The Alpine journal: a record of mountain adventure and scientific observation. 1863–. Monthly.

Scottish mountaineering club journal. Edinburgh 1890–. Thrice yearly.

§1

Wilkinson, T. Tours to the British mountains. 1824.
Forbes, J. D. Travels through the Alps. 1843, 1845; ed W. A. B. Coolidge 1900.
— Norway and its glaciers visited in 1851; followed by Journals of excursions in the high Alps. 1853, 1900 (Journals only, in Travels through the Alps). *See* J. C. Shairp et al, Life and letters of J. D. Forbes, 1873.
Smith, A. R. The story of Mont Blanc. 1853, 1854, 1860 (as Mont Blanc with a memoir of the author by E. Yates).
Hudson, Rev C. and E. S. Kennedy. Where there's a will there's a way: an ascent of Mont Blanc by a new route and without guides. 1856, 1856 ('with two ascents of Monte Rosa').
Wills, A. Wanderings among the high Alps. 1856, 1858.
— The eagle's nest: a summer home among the Alps, together with some excursions among the great glaciers. 1860.
Peaks, passes and glaciers: a series of excursions by members of the Alpine Club. Ed J. Ball 1859; ed E. S. Kennedy 2 vols 1862.
Tyndall, J. The glories of the Alps: being a narrative of excursions and ascents. 1860, 1896.
— Mountaineering in 1861: a vacation tour. 1862.
— Hours of exercise in the Alps. 1871; ed L. C. Tyndall 1899.
See also A. S. Eve and C. H. Creasey, The life and work of John Tyndall, 1945.
Galton, Sir F. (ed). Vacation tourists and notes of travel in 1860 [1861 and 1862–3]. 3 vols 1861–4. Includes accounts of mountaineering.
Ball, J. The Alpine guide. 3 pts 1863–8; ed W. A. B. Coolidge et al 4 pts 1898–1911.
Browne, Rev G. F. Ice-caves of France and Switzerland: a narrative of subterranean exploration. 1865.
Freshfield, D. W. Across country from Thonon to Trent: rambles and scrambles in Switzerland and the Tyrol. 1865.
— Travels in the central Caucasus, including ascents of Kazbek and Elbruz. 1869.
— Italian Alps. 1875. Accounts of many ascents.
— The exploration of the Caucasus. 2 vols 1896. Includes accounts of mountaineering.
Moore, A. W. The Alps in 1864. 1867; ed A. Kennedy, Edinburgh 1902; ed E. H. Stevens 2 vols Oxford 1939. Many ascents described.
— The Caucasus in 1874: from the original ms in the library of the Alpine Club. [c. 1950].
Girdlestone, Rev A. G. The high Alps without guides. 1870.
Stephen, Sir L. The playground of Europe. 1871, 1894, Oxford 1936.
Whymper, E. Scrambles amongst the Alps. 1871; ed H. E. G. Tyndale 1936 (6th edn) (with addns from Whymper's unpbd diaries).
— The ascent of the Matterhorn. 1880.
— Travels amongst the Great Andes of the Equator. 1892 (with separate pbn of appendix by various hands); ed F. S. Smythe 1949.
— The Alps revisited. Graphic 29 Sept–20 Oct 1894.
— Chamonix and the range of Mont Blanc: a guide. 1896.
— The valley of Zermatt and the Matterhorn: a guide. 1897.
See F. S. Smythe, Edward Whymper, 1940; R. W. Clark, The day the rope broke, 1965.
Wilson, H. S. Alpine ascents and adventures. 1878.
Burnaby, Mrs E. A. F. (afterwards Main, afterwards Le Blond). The high Alps in winter: or mountaineering in search of health. 1883.
— High life and towers of silence. 1886.
— My home in the Alps. 1892. Includes chs on mountaineering.
Barrow, J. Mountain ascents in Westmoreland and Cumberland. 1886.
Cunningham, C. D. and W. de W. Abney. The pioneers of the Alps. 1887.
Dent, C. T. Above the snow line: mountaineering sketches between 1870 and 1880. 1887.
— Can Mount Everest be ascended? Nineteenth Century Oct 1892.
Conway, W. M., Baron Conway. Conway and Coolidge's climbers' guides. 17 vols 1890–1910. With W. A. B. Coolidge.
— Climbing and exploration in the Karakoram-Himalayas. 3 vols 1894.
— The Alps from end to end. 1895.
— The first crossing of Spitsbergen: with descriptions of several mountain ascents. 1897.
— The Bolivian Andes: a record of climbing and exploration in the Cordillera Real in the years 1898 and 1900. 1901.
— Aconcagua and Tierra del Fuego: a book of climbing, travel and exploration [in 1898–9]. 1902.
— Mountain memories. 1920.
Davies, Rev J. S. Dolomite strongholds: the last untrodden Alpine peaks. 1894.
Smith, W. P. H. Climbing in the British Isles: England. 1894.
— and H. C. Hart. Climbing in the British Isles: Wales and Ireland. 1895.
Mummery, A. F. My climbs in the Alps and Caucasus. 1895, [1913]. With introd by M. Mummery and appreciation by J. A. Hobson.
Fitzgerald, E. A. (ed). Climbs in the New Zealand Alps. 1896.
— The highest Andes: a record of the first ascent of Aconcagua and Tupungato. 1899.
Weston, Rev W. Mountaineering and exploration in the Japanese Alps. 1896.
Wherry, G. E. Alpine notes and the climbing foot. Cambridge 1896.
Younghusband, Sir F. E. The heart of a continent: a narrative of travels in Manchuria, across the Gobi desert, through the Himalayas. 1896, 1937. Includes some mountaineering.
Jones, O. G. Rock climbing in the English Lake District. 1897, Keswick 1900 (with memoir of the author by W. M. Cook and an appendix by G. D. and A. Abraham), 1911.
Mathews, C. E. The annals of Mont Blanc. 1898.
Oppenheim, E. C. New climbs in Norway. 1898.
Gribble, F. H. The early mountaineers. 1899.
Slingsby, W. C. Norway, the northern playground: sketches of climbing in Norway between 1872 and 1903. Edinburgh 1904; ed E. Slingsby, Oxford 1941.
Coolidge, W. A. B. Alpine studies. 1912. Collection of mountaineering articles largely pbd before 1900.
See R. W. Clark, An eccentric in the Alps: the story of W.A.B.C. the great Victorian mountaineer, 1959.

§2

Lunn, A. (ed). The Englishman in the Alps: being a collection of English prose and poetry relating to the Alps. Oxford 1913.
— Switzerland and the English. 1944.
— A century of mountaineering 1857–1957. 1957.
Carr, H. R. C. and G. A. Lister (ed). The mountains of Snowdonia in history, the sciences, literature and sport. 1925, 1948.
Spencer, S. (ed). Mountaineering. 1934 (Lonsdale Lib). With bibliography.
de Beer, G. Travellers in Switzerland. Oxford 1949.
Clark, R. W. The Victorian mountaineers. 1953.

— and E. C. Pyatt. Mountaineering in Britain: a history from the earliest times to the present day. 1957.
Irving, R. L. G. A history of British mountaineering. 1955.
Mason, K. Abode of snow: a history of Himalayan exploration and mountaineering. 1955.

Polo

Miller, E. D. Modern polo. 1896.
Dale, T. F. The game of polo. [1897].
— Polo past and present. 1905.
Dryburgh, T. B. Polo. 1898, 1906.
Kipling, R. The Maltese cat. In his Day's work, 1898.

Rowing, Canoeing, Boating

Bibliographies

Brittain, F. Oar, scull and rudder: a bibliography of rowing. Oxford 1930.

Periodicals

The rowing almanack and oarsman's companion. 1861–1915, 1920–8. Annual.

§1

'A boating man'. A treatise on the art of rowing as practised at Cambridge. Cambridge 1842.
Shadwell, A. T. W. A treatise on steering. 1844.
'Oarsman' (A. T. W. Shadwell?). Principals of rowing. Cambridge 1846, Oxford [1857?].
[Bateman, J. F.] Aquatic notes: or sketches of the rise and progress of rowing at Cambridge. Cambridge 1852.
Mansfield, R. B. The log of the Water Lily. 1852. Account of a voyage on the Neckar, Maine, Moselle and Rhine.
— The Water Lily on the Danube: being a brief account of the perils of a pair-oar during a voyage from Lambeth to Perth. 1853. Both works rev in 1 vol 1854, 5th edn as The log of the Water Lily during three cruises, [1873] (with account of a third voyage on the Saône and Rhone).
'Argonaut' (E. D. Brickwood). The arts of rowing and training. 1866, 1876 (as Boat racing or the arts of rowing).
Macgregor, J. A thousand miles in the Rob Roy canoe on rivers and lakes of Europe. 1866, 1871 (7th edn).
— The Rob Roy on the Baltic. 1867.
— The Rob Roy on the Jordan, Nile, Red Sea and Gennesareth. 1869, 1880 (6th edn).
See E. Hodder, J. M., 'Rob Roy', 1894.
Macmichael, W. F. The Oxford and Cambridge boat races—from AD 1829 to AD 1869. Cambridge 1870.
Baden-Powell, W. Canoe travelling: log of a cruise on the Baltic. 1871.
Jerome, J. K. Three men in a boat (to say nothing of the dog). Bristol 1889.
Alcock, A. T. Hints on coxing. Cambridge 1895.
Peacock, W. The story of the inter-university boat race. 1900.
Sherwood, W. E. Oxford rowing: a history of boat-racing at Oxford. Oxford 1900.
Selwyn, T. K. Eton in 1829–30: a diary of boating and other events written in Greek edited with translation and notes by E. Warre. 1903.
Bourne, G. C. Memories of an Eton wet-bob of the seventies. [Ed R. C. Bourne], Oxford 1933.

§2

Steward, H. T. The records of Henley Royal Regatta from its institution in 1839 to 1902. 1903.
Cook, Sir T. A. and G. Nicholls. Thomas Doggett deceased. 1908. Pt 2 is a history of Doggett's 'Coat and badge' race.
Smith, L. C. (ed). Annals of public school rowing. Oxford 1919.
Burnell, R. D. The Oxford and Cambridge boat race 1829–1953. Oxford 1954.
— Henley Regatta: a history. Oxford 1957.
Ross, G. The boat race: the story of the first hundred races. 1954.
Cleaver, H. A history of rowing. 1957.

Shooting

Bibliographies

Phillipps-Wolley, Sir C. A short bibliography of big game shooting. In his Big game shooting, 1894 (Badminton Lib).
'Gerrare, Wirt' (W. Greener). A bibliography of guns and shooting. 1896.
Riling, R. Guns and shooting: a selected chronological bibliography. New York 1951.

Periodicals

Shooting times. 1882–. Weekly. 9 Sept 1882–11 April 1884 as Wildfowler's illustrated shooting times; 18 April–19 Sept 1884 as Illustrated shooting times.

§1

Thornhill, R. B. The shooting directory. 1804.
Williamson, T. Oriental field sports. 1807.
Vincent, J. Fowling: a poem. 1808.
Johnson, T. B. The shooter's guide [under pseudonym B. Thomas]. 1809, 1814 (4th edn), 1832 (9th edn).
— The shooter's companion. 1819, 1834.
— The sportsman and gamekeeper's directory. [1835?]; ed J. B. Johnson 1851.
— The shooter's preceptor. 1838.
'Markwell, Marmaduke'. Advice to sportsmen with anecdotes of the most renowned shots of the day. 1809.
Dobson, W. Kunopaedia: a practical essay on training the English spaniel with instructions for attaining the art of shooting flying. 1814.
Hawker, P. Instructions to young sportsmen [on guns and shooting]. 1814, 1816, 1824, 1825 (with addns pbd separately), [1825?], 1826, 1830 (with Abridgement of the new game laws pbd separately), 1831; ed P. W. L. Hawker 1854 (10th edn), 1859; ed E. Parker 1922.
— The diary of Colonel Peter Hawker. Ed R. Payne Gallwey 2 vols 1893; ed E. Parker 1931 (as Colonel Hawker's shooting diaries).
Alken, H. A cockney's shooting season in Suffolk. 1822.
Watt, W. Remarks on shooting to which are added a part of the game-laws both written in familiar verse. 1835, 1839.
'Oakleigh, Thomas' (A. K. Killmister). The Oakleigh shooting code: containing two hundred and twenty chapters of information relative to shooting. 1836.
— The shooter's handbook. Edinburgh 1842.
Rawstorne, L. Gamonia: or the art of preserving game. 1837; ed E. Parker 1929.
Harris, Sir W. C. Narrative of an expedition into Southern Africa during the years 1836 and 1837. Bombay 1838, London 1839 (as The wild sports of Southern Africa).
— Portraits of the game and wild animals of Southern Africa. 1840. Plates with extensive text. *See* E. C. Tabler, Captain Harris and his book: a biographical and bibliographical essay, Charleston 1944.
Peake, R. B. Snobson's seasons: being annals of cockney sports. [1838?], 1846 (as An evening's amusement).
Scrope, W. The art of deer-stalking. 1838, 1883 (as Days of deer stalking).
Harris, Sir W. C. The wild sports of Southern Africa. 1839.
Webber, A. Shooting: a poem. 1841.

Lacy, R. The modern shooter: containing poetical instructions and directions for every description of inland and coast shooting. 1842.
'Craven' (J. W. Carleton). Recreations in shooting. 1846.
'John Sobieski and Charles Edward Stuart' (J. C. and C. M. Allen, afterwards J. H. and C. S. H. Allan). Lays of the deer forest. 2 vols Edinburgh 1848.
Cumming, R. G. G. Five years of a hunter's life in South Africa. 2 vols 1850, 1 vol 1856 (as The lion hunter of South Africa).
Knox, A. E. Game birds and wild fowl. 1850.
'Hieover, Harry' (C. Bindley). Bipeds and quadrupeds. 1853.
Dougall, J. D. Shooting simplified: a concise treatise on the art of shooting. Glasgow 1857, London 1865.
Folkard, H. C. The wild-fowler: a treatise on ancient and modern wild-fowling historical and practical. 1859.
'Stonehenge' (J. H. Walsh). The shot-gun and sporting rifle. 1859.
— The modern sportsman's gun and rifle. 2 vols 1882–4.
Jeans, T. The Tommiebeg shootings: or a moor in Scotland. 1860. A novel about shooting and fishing.
'Marksman'. The dead shot or sportsman's complete guide: being a treatise on the use of the gun. 1860, 1892 (6th edn).
'Martingale' (C. White). Sporting scenes and country characters. 1860. Prose sketches mainly on shooting.
Baldwin, W. C. African hunting from Natal to the Zambesi. 1863.
[Robertson, W.] Forest sketches: deer-stalking in the Highlands fifty years ago. Edinburgh 1865.
Shirley, E. P. Some account of English deer parks with notes on the management of deer. 1867.
'Wildfowler' (L. Clements). Shooting and fishing trips in England [and other countries]. Ser 1, 2 vols 1876; ser 2, 2 vols 1879 (as Shooting adventures etc).
— Modern wildfowling. 1880.
— Public shooting quarters: being a descriptive list of localities where shooting can be obtained. 1881.
[Jefferies, J. R.] (Richard Jefferies). The gamekeeper at home. 1878.
— The amateur poacher. 1879.
Sanderson, G. P. Thirteen years among the wild beasts of India. 1878.
Manley, J. J. Notes on game and game shooting. [1880].
Greener, W. W. The gun and its development. [1881], [1884], [1885], 1896, 1907, 1910.
— Modern shot guns. 1888, 1891.
— Sharpshooting for sport and war. 1900.
Selous, F. C. A hunter's wanderings in Africa. 1881.
— Travel and adventure in south-east Africa. 1893.
Phillipps-Wolley, Sir C. Sport in the Crimea and Caucasus. 1881.
— A sportsman's Eden [British Columbia]. 1888.
Payne-Gallwey, Sir R. W. F. The fowler in Ireland. 1882.
— Letters to young shooters. Ser 1, 1890, 1899 (5th edn); ser 2, 1892, 1894 (with index to 1st–2nd sers); ser 3, 1896.
Whitehurst, F. F. On the Grampian hills: grouse and ptarmigan shooting. 1882. Prose sketches.
Grimble, A. Deer stalking. 1886.
— Shooting and salmon fishing: hints and recollections. 1892.
— The deer forests of Scotland. 1896, 1901 (with Deer stalking).
— Leaves from a game book. 1898.
Cookson, J. C. F. Tiger-shooting in the Doon and Ulwar. 1887.
Lancaster, C. An illustrated treatise on the art of shooting. 1889, 1924 (8th edn).
Macintyre, D. Hindu-Koh: wanderings and wild sport on and beyond the Himalayas. 1889.
'Purple heather' (W. A. Adams). Something about guns and shooting. 1890.
Watson, J. (ed). The confessions of a poacher. 1890.
— Poachers and poaching. 1891.
Buxton, E. N. Short stalks. 2 sers 1892–8.
Crealock, H. H. Deer-stalking in the Highlands of Scotland. Ed J. N. Crealock 1892.
Millais, J. G. Game birds and shooting—sketches. 1892.
— British deer and their horns. 1897. Includes chs on stalking.
Dixon, C. The game birds and wild fowl of the British islands. 1893.
Cornish, C. J. Nights with an old gunner. 1897.
Macpherson, H. A. A history of fowling. Edinburgh 1897.
Teasdale-Buckell, G. T. Experts on guns and shooting. 1900. On evolution of shooting in the 19th century.
Harris, J. E., 2nd Earl of Malmesbury. Half a century of sport in Hampshire [shooting journals 1798–1840]. Ed F. G. Aflalo 1905 (with memoir by the 5th Earl).
See also Bickerdyke, Conway, Lascelles, Mackintosh, Penn *under* Angling, *above*.

Skating, Tobogganing, Curling

Bibliographies

Foster, F. W. A bibliography of skating. 1898.

§1

[Ramsey, J.] An account of the game of curling. 1811 (priv ptd).
Frostiana: or a history of the river Thames in a frozen state, to which is added the art of skating. 1814.
Clay, T. Instructions on the art of skating. 1828.
Crawford, H. A descriptive and historical sketch of curling. 1828.
Brown, Sir R. Memorabilia curliana mabenensia. Dumfries 1830.
'A member of the Skating Club'. A skater's manual. 1831.
'Dove, Walter' (M. Whitelaw). The skater's monitor, instructor and evening companion. Edinburgh 1846.
'Cyclos' (G. Anderson). The art of skating. 1852.
Vandervell, H. E. and T. M. Witham. A system of figure-skating: being the theory and practice of the art in England, with a glance at its origin and history. 1869, 1889, 1893 (by Witham only).
Harwood, J. A. Rinks and rollers. [1876]. Includes history of roller skating.
Pycroft, J. On roller skating. Brighton [1876?].
Idyls of the rink. 1877. Verse.
Goodman, N. and A. Handbook of fen skating. 1882.
[Macnair, J.] The channel-stone: or sweeping frae the rinks. 4 sers Edinburgh 1883–4.
Monier-Williams, M. S. F. and S. F. Combined figure skating. 1883, 1892 (as Figure skating: simple and combined).
Taylor, J. Curling: the ancient Scottish game. 1884.
Kerr, J. The history of curling. Edinburgh 1890.
Cook, Sir T. A. Notes on tobogganing at St Moritz. 1894, 1896.
Fowler, G. H. On the outside edge: diversions in the history of skating. 1897.

§2

Bloom, A. The skaters of the Fens. Cambridge 1958.
Brown, N. Ice-skating: a history. 1959.

Swimming

Bibliographies

Thomas, R. H. Swimming: a bibliographical list of works. 1868, 1904.
Greenwood, F. A. Bibliography of swimming. New York 1940.

§1

Frost, J. Scientific swimming. 1816.

Hughes, T. The whole art of swimming. [1820].
Familiar hints on sea-bathing. 1838.
Richardson, C. Instructions on the art of swimming. 1857.
Swimming and swimmers; with an account of the progress of the art during the last twenty years. 1861.
Pearce, P. H. A treatise and poem on swimming. 1868.
'Piscator'. How to swim, float, plunge, bathe and dive. 1871.
'Dolphin' (J. T. Latey). The channel feats of Captain Webb and Captain Boyton. [1875].
Leahy, J. The art of swimming in the Eton style. 1875.
Randall, J. Captain Webb the intrepid champion Channel swimmer. Madeley 1875.
Webb, M. The art of swimming. Ed A. G. Payne [1875].
Wilson, W. Swimming, diving and how to save life. Glasgow 1876.
— The swimming instructor: a treatise on the arts of swimming and diving. 1883.
Brewster, F. W. How to avoid being drowned. 1885.

§2

Hedges, S. G. Swimming in literature. Chambers's Jnl Aug 1933.

Tennis, Lawn Tennis, Fives, Badminton

Bibliographies

Foster, F. W. A bibliography of lawn tennis 1874–97. Richmond 1897.

Periodicals

The lawn-tennis handbook 1888–. Annual.
Lawn tennis. 1896–. Weekly. 17 June–14 Oct 1891 nos 1–18; then fortnightly as Lawn tennis and croquet 27 April 1896–1 Nov 1899; as Lawn tennis and croquet and badminton 6 Dec 1899–25 April 1900.

§1

Hazlitt, W. Cavanagh the fives player. From The Indian jugglers. In his Table talk vol i, 1821.
[Lukin, R.] A treatise on tennis. 1822.
Wingfield, W. C. The game of sphairistike: or lawn tennis. 1874.
'Cavendish' (Henry Jones). The games of lawn tennis and badminton. 1876, 1890 (9th edn).
Latouche, J. Lawn tennis. New Quart Mag 5 1876.
Marshall, J. The annals of tennis. 1878. Real tennis.
— Tennis cuts and quips in prose and verse with rules and wrinkles. [1884].
Smythe, J. Lawn tennis. [1878].
Brownlee, W. M. Lawn tennis: its rise and progress. Bristol 1889.

§2

Noel, E. B. and J. O. M. Clark. A history of tennis. 2 vols Oxford 1924. Real tennis; includes ch on the literature of tennis.
Myers, A. W. Fifty years of Wimbledon. 1926.
Burrow, F. R. The 'last eights' at Wimbledon 1877–1926. [1927].
Bruce, M. G. L., 4th Baron Aberdare of Duffryn. The story of tennis. 1959. Real and lawn.

Yachting

Bibliographies

Hanson, H. J. (ed). The Cruising Association Library catalogue. [1927], 1931, 1954.

Periodicals

Hunt's universal yacht list. 1851–1914. Annual.
Hunt's yachting magazine. 1852–87. Monthly.
The yachtsman. 1891–1913. Continued as Yachting sailing and motor-boating. Weekly.
The yachting world. 1894–. Weekly.

§1

Folkard, H. C. The sailing boat: a description of English and foreign boats and practical directions for sailing. 1853, 1901 (5th edn).
Hughes, R. E. Two summer cruises with the Baltic fleet in 1854–5: being the log of the 'Pet' yacht. 1855.
Macmullen, R. T. Down Channel. 1869; ed D. Kemp 1893; with biographical foreword by A. Ransome 1931.
— Orion: or how I came to sail alone in a 19-ton yacht. 1878.
— An experimental cruise single handed in the 'Procyon' 7-ton lugger. 1880. Rev edns of these 2 works were incorporated into the 1893 edn of Down channel, *above*.
Middleton, E. E. The cruise of the Kate. 1870. Description of one of the first single-handed voyages.
Robinson, C. E. The cruise of the Widgeon: 700 miles in a ten-ton yawl from Swanage to Hambury. 1876.
Kemp, D. A manual of yacht and boat sailing. 1878; ed B. H. Smith 1900 (9th edn).
Watson, G. L. Progress in yachting and yacht-building In Lectures on naval architecture and engineering [given at the Glasgow naval and marine engineering exhibition 1880–1], 1881. A concise history of yachting and yacht-building in the 19th century.
Speed, H. F. Cruises in small yachts. 1883, 1926 (with More cruises by M. Speed).
Knight, E. F. The cruise of the Falcon: a voyage to South America in a 30-ton yacht. 2 vols 1884.
— The Falcon on the Baltic: a coasting voyage from Hammersmith to Copenhagen in a 3-ton yacht. 1889.
— The cruise of the Alerte [to Trinidad]. 1890.
— Reminiscences: the wanderings of a yachtsman. 1923.
Cowper, F. Sailing tours: the yachtsman's guide to the cruising waters of the English coast. 5 vols 1892–6.
— Jack-all-alone: his cruises. 1897.

§2

Gabe, J. Yachting: historical sketches of the sport. 1902. Includes short histories of the most important yacht clubs.
Guest, M. and W. B. Boulton. The Royal Yacht Squadron: memorials of its members, with an enquiry into the history of yachting and a complete list of members with their yachts from the foundation of the Club [in 1815] to the present time. 1903.
British yachts and yachtsmen: a complete history of British yachting from the middle of the sixteenth century to the present day. 1907.
Heaton, P. Yachting: a history. 1955.
Burnell, R. D. Races for the 'America's' cup. 1965.
See also 'Wanderer' *under* Hunting, *above*.

M. S.

XIV. EDUCATION

A. GENERAL SOURCES

Trimmer, Sarah. The oeconomy of charity. 1787, 1801.
— Reflections upon the education of children in Charity Schools. 1792.
— The Charity School spelling book. 1800, 1808 (2nd edn). Part 1, Words of one syllable; Part 2, Polysyllables.
— The guardian of education: a periodical work. 5 vols 1802–6.
— A comparative view of the new plan of education promulgated by Mr J. Lancaster. 1805.
The Edgeworths: R. L. Edgeworth; Maria Edgeworth. *See col 665, above.*
Bell, Andrew. An experiment in education made at the Male Asylum of Madras, suggesting a system by which a school or family may teach itself under the superintendence of the master or parent. 1797, 1814 (5th edn enlarged), 1807 (3rd edn as An analysis of the experiment).
— Instructions for conducting a school. 1808.
— Sketch of a National Institution. 1808.
— Elements of tuition, pt iii: Ludus literarius, the classical and grammar school. 1815.
— The wrongs of children. 1819. A periodical of which only 3 pts were issued; very rare.
— Letters to Sir John Sinclair on the Infant School Society at Edinburgh: the scholastic institutions of Scotland, with a scheme of a classical school for children of the richer classes. 1829.
See R. Southey (vol i) *and his son* Charles Cuthbert (vols 2–3), Life of the Rev Andrew Bell, 1844.
Meiklejohn, J. M. D. An old educational reformer, Dr Bell. 1891.
Salmon, D. The practical parts of Lancaster's improvements and Bell's experiment. Cambridge 1932.
Hamilton, Elizabeth. Letters on the elementary principles of education. 2 vols Bath 1801–2.
— Letters addressed to the daughter of a nobleman on the formation of principles, religious and moral. 2 vols 1806.
— Hints addressed to patrons and directors of schools to shew that the benefits derived from the new modes of teaching may be increased by a partial adoption of the plan of Pestalozzi. 1815.
Shaw, William. Suggestions respecting a plan of national education. Bath 1801.
Barrow, William. An essay on education particularly the merits and defects of the discipline and instruction in our academies. 2 vols 1802.
Bentham, Jeremy. Principles of penal law. 1802.
— Church of Englandism examined: strictures on the National Society's schools. 2 pts 1818. *See* Quart Rev 21 1819.
— Works. Ed J. Bowring 11 vols Edinburgh 1843. Papers relative to codification and public instruction in vol iv; Chrestomathia in vol viii; Memoirs and correspondence in vols x–xi. *See* J. P. Potter, Letter to John Hughes on the system of education proposed by the popular parties, 1828, Pamphleteer 29 1828, a reply to the Benthamite Chrestomathic School proposal.
Stephen, L. The English Utilitarians, vol i: Jeremy Bentham. 1900.
Halévy, E. The growth of philosophic radicalism, tr 1928, 1934 (rev).
Crabb, G. The order and method of instructing children. 1802.
Harrison, G. Some remarks relative to the present state of education among the Quakers. 1802.
— Education surest means to diminish crime. 1803.
Simons, T. Moral education the one thing needful. 1802; A sequel, 1805 (on Undenominationalism).
Lancaster, Joseph. Improvements in education as it respects the industrious classes. 1803.
— A letter to John Foster on the means of educating and employing the poor in Ireland. 1805.
— An appeal for justice in the case of ten thousand poor and orphan children. 1806.
— Improvements in education abridged. 1808.
— A remarkable establishment of education at Paris. 1809.
— Instructions for forming a society for the education of the labouring classes. 1809.
— Hints and directions for building, fitting up and arranging school-rooms. 1809.
— Address to the friends and superintendents of Sunday Schools. 1809.
— The British system of education. 1810.
— The school for girls on the Royal Lancasterian system. 1812.
— Oppression and persecution. Bristol 1816.
— Letters on national subjects. Washington 1820.
— The Lancasterian system with improvements. Baltimore 1821.
See David Salmon, Joseph Lancaster, 1904. Supplemented by many articles in the Educational Record 1905–29. *See under* Bell, *above.*
Benson, Maria. Thoughts on education. 1806.
Colquhoun, Patrick A. A new and appropriate system of education for the labouring people. 1806.
Bowles, John. A letter addressed to Samuel Whitbread. 1807; Second letter, 1808.
Ingram, Robert A. An essay on schools of industry and religious instruction. 1808.
Weyland, R. A. A letter to a country gentleman on the education of the lower orders. 1808.
Bernard, Sir Thomas. Of the education of the poor. 1809.
— The New School. 1809.
— The Barrington School. 1812.
See Reports of the Society for bettering the conditions and increasing the comforts of the poor, *under* Official Documents, *below.*
Smith, Sydney. Essay: too much Latin and Greek. 1809.
— Works. 2 vols 1859.
Also contributions to the Edinburgh Review, *of which he was co-founder; see also under* Education of Women and Girls, *below.*
Bouyer, Renynold Gideon A. A comparative view of the two new systems of education for the infant poor. 1811.
Ensor, J. On national education. 1811. *See* Quart Rev 6 1811.
Marsh, H. The national religion the foundation of national education. 1811. A sermon rptd in the Pamphleteer 1 1813. *See* Quart Rev 6 1811; Edinburgh Rev 19 1811, 21 1813.
— Vindication of Dr Bell's system. 1811.
The Philanthropist. Ed W. Allen 1811. Articles on Lancaster, popular education etc.
Hollingsworth, Nathaniel John. Address to the public in recommendation of the Madras system, with a comparison. 1812.
Mill, James. Schools for all, in preference to schools for Churchmen only. 1812.
— Education. In Supplement to the Encyclopaedia britannica, 4th, 5th and 6th edns (1816–24).

— State of the nation. Westminster Rev Oct 1826.
— Analysis of the human mind. 1829.
Stephen, L. The English Utilitarians, vol 2: James Mill 1900.
Halévy, E. The growth of philosophic radicalism, 1928, 1934 (rev).
Southey, Robert. Origin, nature and object of the new system of education. 1812.
See Lancaster, *above*, T. C. Scott, *below*; Quart Rev 6 1811, 8 1812, 19 1818, 39 1829, and Edinburgh Rev 19 1811, 21 1813, 33 1820.
Owen, Robert. A new view of society: or essays on the formation of the human character 1813. *See* Edinburgh Rev 32 1819.
Macnab, H. G. The new views of Mr Owen impartially examined. 1819.
Owen, R. D. Outline of the system of education at New Lanark. Glasgow 1824. By his son.
Poole, Rev John. The village school improved etc. 1812.
Babington, Thomas. Practical view of Christian education in its early stages. 1814.
Carpenter, Lant. Systematic education. 2 vols 1815. With Joyce and Shepherd.
— Principles of education. 1820. By Carpenter only.
Pestalozzi, John Henry. Address to the British public to aid a plan of preparing school-masters for the people. Yverdun 1817.
— Letters on early education addressed to J. P. Greaves, Secretary to the London Infant Society (with a memoir of Pestalozzi). 1827, 1850, 1851.
Many English trns and commentaries.
How Gertrude teaches her children, tr 1894, 1915 (3rd edn rev).
Pullen, P. H. The Mother's book exemplifying Pestalozzi's plan of awakening the understanding of children. 1820.
de Prati, J. The principles and practice of education illustrative of the Pestalozzian and Chrestomathic systems. 1829.
Biber, G. E. Pestalozzi and his plan. 1831.
Mayo, Charles. Pestalozzi and his Principles. 1837.
Russell, J. The student's Pestalozzi. 1888.
— Pestalozzi: his life and work. 1890, 1900, 1903 Trn of R. de Guimps, Histoire de Pestalozzi.
Hayward, F. H. The educational ideas of Pestalozzi. 1905.
Green, J. A. Educational ideas of Pestalozzi. 1905.
— Pestalozzi's educational writings. 1912.
Brown, S. A comparative view of the systems of Pestalozzi and Lancaster. 1925. *See* E. Hamilton, *above*; R. Dunning, J. Payne, *below*.
Brougham, Henry P. (Baron Brougham and Vaux). Letter to Sir Samuel Romilly. Pamphleteer 13 1818.
— Speech on the education of the poor, June 1820. Pamphleteer 40–1; Hansard vol 11, pp. 49–89.
See Edinburgh Rev 35 1821.
— Practical observations upon the education of the people addressed to the working classes and their employers. 1825. *See* E. W. Grinfield, A reply to Mr Brougham's Practical observations, Edinburgh Rev 42 1825, 45 1826, Quart Rev 32 1825.
— Inaugural discourse on being installed Lord Rector of Glasgow University. 1825. *See* Edinburgh Rev 42 1825.
— Speech in the House of Lords on the education of the people, 21 May 1835. Hansard vol 27 col 1293–1333. *See* 'M.A. Queen's College, Oxford', A letter to Henry Brougham on the best method of restoring decayed grammar schools, 1818. Pamphleteer 13 1818.
Ireland, J. A letter to Henry Brougham. 1819. Pamphleteer 14 1818, Edinburgh Rev 30–2 1818–19.
See Samuel Butler, *below*.
Dallaway, Miss R. C. Observations on the most important subjects in education. 1818.

Heberden, William. On education: a dialogue after the manner of Cicero. 1818.
Jardine, George. Outlines of philosophical education illustrated. Glasgow 1818, 1825.
Macnab, Henry Grey. Analysis and analogy recommended in education. Paris, 1818.
See Robert Owen, *above*.
Myers, T. Remarks on a course of education. 1818.
Arrowsmith, Joseph P. Art of instructing the infant deaf and dumb, with method of educating deaf mutes, by the Abbé de L'Épée. 1819. *See* Quart Rev 26 1822, Edinburgh Rev 102 1855.
Butler, Samuel. Thoughts on education of the poor: letter to Henry Brougham on certain changes in the Education Bill. 1820. *See* under Memoirs, *below*.
Knox, Vicesimus, Headmaster of Tonbridge School 1781–1812. Remarks on the tendency of certain clauses in a Bill now pending in Parliament to degrade grammar schools etc. 1820.
See Liberal Education 1781, 1795, Pamphleteer 19 1820.
Pullen, P. H. *See* Pestalozzi, *above*.
Bamford, Robert Walker. Essays on the discipline of children, particularly as regards their education. 1822.
Hill, Matthew Davenport. Public education: plans for the government and liberal instruction of boys in large numbers, drawn from experience. 1822, 1825 (2nd edn rptd 1894, in which 'drawn from experience' was replaced by 'as practised at Hazelwood School'). Reviewed by Jeffrey, Edinburgh Rev 1825, and by De Quincey, London Mag 1824. The original scheme was started in 1817.
Hoare, Louisa. Hints for the improvement of early education and nursery discipline. 1819, 1820, 1824, 1826 1877 (19th edn).
De Quincey, Thomas. Letters to a young man whose education has been neglected. London Mag 7 1823.
Pole, Thomas. Observations on infant schools. Bristol 1823. *See* Edinburgh Rev 38 1823 and under Adult Education, *below*.
Wilderspin, Samuel. The importance of educating the children of the poor. 1823, 1825 (as Infant education).
— Early discipline illustrated: or the infant system progressive and successful. 1832.
— A system for the education of the young. 1840, 1852 (8th edn rev as The infant system for developing the intellectual and moral powers of all children from one to seven years of age).
— and Terrington. A manual for the religious and moral instruction of young children in nursery and infant schools. 1845.
Montgomery, James. The chimney-sweeper's friend and mining boy's album. 1824. Illustrated by Cruikshank.
Goyder, David George. Manual of the system of instruction. Bristol 1824, 1825 (4th edn). Goyder complained that Stow had adopted his plan without acknowledgement.
— A treatise on the management of infant schools. 1826.
Wilson Rev William. The system of infants' schools. 2 vols 1825, 1826 (2nd edn).
— A manual of instruction for infants' schools. 1829.
— Advice to instructors of infant schools. nd. *See* Quart Rev 32 1825.
Daly, Robert. Observations upon the state of education in Ireland. Dublin 1826.
— On the proposed system of non-scriptural education of the poor in Ireland. 1831. With R. J. McGhie.
Mayo, Charles. Observations on the establishment and direction of infant schools. 1826. *See* Elizabeth Mayo, *below*.
Newnham, W. The principles of physical, intellectual, moral and religious education. 1827.

Ward, Valentine. Observations on Sunday schools. Leeds 1827.
Pillans, J. Principles of elementary teaching, chiefly in reference to the Parochial schools of Scotland. Edinburgh 1828.
—— Three lectures. 1836.
—— The rationale of discipline as exemplified in the High School. Edinburgh 1852.
—— Contributions to the cause of education. 1856.
—— Educational papers read before the Education Department of the Social Science Association. Edinburgh 1862.
Wood, John. Account of the Edinburgh Sessional School and other parochial institutes for education established in that city in the year 1812, with strictures on education in general. Edinburgh 1828.
Biber, George E. Christian education. 1830.
—— Pestalozzi and his plan. 1831. *See* Pestalozzi, *above*.
Mayo, Elizabeth. Lessons on objects to children in the Pestalozzian school at Cheam. 1830, 1831, 1859 (16th edn). *See* Quart Jnl of Education 1831.
—— Practical remarks on infant education. 1831. Contains 2 articles by Dr Charles Mayo and practical comment by Miss Mayo.
—— Lessons on objects by lessons on shells. 1833.
See Quart Jnl of Education 1833 *and* Charles Mayo, *above*. The formal memorizing of the Mayos was satirized by Charles Dickens in Mr Gradgrind of Hard times.
Sewell, William. An essay on the cultivation of the intellect by the study of dead languages. 1830.
—— A speech at the meeting of Friends of National Education at Willis's rooms, 7 Feb 1850. 1850.
See Special sources 1 and 6, *below*; L. James, A forgotten genius: Sewell of St Columba's and Radley, 1945.
Stow, David. Physical and moral training. 1831, 1840 (enlarged as The training system in the Glasgow Normal Seminary), 1859 (as The training system, the moral training school and the Normal Seminary).
Arnold, Thomas. Letter on education of the middle classes. 1832.
—— Miscellaneous works. 1845.
—— Collected sermons. 3 vols 1850–3.
Stanley, A. P. Life of Thomas Arnold. 1844, 1904 (popular edn).
Hughes, Thomas. Tom Brown's schooldays. Cambridge 1857. Anon.
Findlay, J. J. Dr Arnold of Rugby. Cambridge 1897.
Fitch, J. Thomas and Matthew Arnold. 1897, 1905.
Strachey, L. Dr Arnold. In his Eminent Victorians, 1918. This account is severely criticized by R. L. Archer in his Secondary education in the nineteenth century, Cambridge 1932.
Trilling, L. In his Matthew Arnold, New York 1939, 1955 (rev).
Wymer, N. G. Dr Arnold of Rugby. 1953.
Bamford, T. W. Thomas Arnold. 1960.
Frend, William. A plan of universal education. 1832.
Combe, George. Lectures on popular education. Edinburgh 1833.
—— Principles of physiology applied to physical and mental education. 1835.
—— Remarks on national education. Edinburgh 1847.
—— What should secular education embrace? Edinburgh 1848.
See Education: its principles and practice as developed by George Combe, collated and edited by W. Jolly, 1879; Discussions on education, 1893.
Duppa, Baldwin Francis. The education of the peasantry in England. 1834.
—— Industrial schools for the peasantry. 1837 (Central Soc of Education).
—— Lord Brougham's Bill for promoting education. 1838 (Central Soc of Education). First Bill proposing taxation for popular education.
—— Schools for the industrial classes: present state of education among the working classes. 1838 (Central Soc of Education).
—— Agricultural colleges: or schools for the sons of farmers. 1839.
Place, Francis. Improvement of the working people. 1834.
Simpson, James. Necessity of popular education as a national object. Edinburgh 1834.
Hull, J. The philanthropic repertory. 3 pts 1835. Pt 1: Hints and plans relating to popular education.
Maurice, Frederick Denison. The educational magazine. 1835–.
—— Has the Church or State power to educate the nation? 1839.
—— The Christian Socialist. 1851–.
—— National Education: a sermon at St Mark's College Chelsea. 1853.
—— Learning and working. 1855.
—— The workman and the franchise: chapters from English history on the representation and education of the people. 1866.
—— A few words on secular and denominational education. 1870.
See F. Maurice, Life of Maurice, 1884.
Reiner, Charles. Lessons on number and lessons on form. 1835 (pamphlet).
Whewell, William. Thoughts on the study of mathematics. Cambridge 1835. *See* Edinburgh Rev 62–3 1836.
See Universities, below.
Williamson, J. The diffusion of knowledge amongst the middle classes. 1835. *See* Edinburgh Rev 62 1836.
Gray, J. Thoughts on education with particular reference to the grammar school system. 1836.
Dunn, Henry. Popular education. 1837.
—— National education, the question of questions. 1837. *See* Edinburgh Rev 66 1838.
—— Calm thoughts on the recent Minutes of the Committee of Council. 1847.
Hoppus, J. Thoughts on academical education and degrees in arts. 1837.
—— Crisis of popular education. 1847.
Wyse, Sir Thomas. Educational reform or the necessity of a national system. 1837.
—— Education in the United Kingdom: its progress and prospects. 1837 (Central Soc of Education). Sir Thomas was one of the founders of the Society. *See* B. F. Foster, Eduaction reform: a review of Wyse, New York 1837.
—— Notes on education reform from the unpublished memoirs of Sir Thomas Wyse. Ed W. M. Wyse, Waterford 1901.
Boone, James S. The educational economy of England. Pt 1, 1838.
Horner, Leonard. On the state of education in Holland [with] measures to extend and improve education in Great Britain. 1838. A trn with addns of V. Cousin, De l'instruction publique en Hollande.
Martineau, Harriet. How to observe. 1838.
—— Household education. 1849, 1861, 1867, 1876.
Taylor, Isaac. Home education. 1838.
Kay-Shuttleworth, Sir James. Recent measures for the promotion of education in England. 1839.
—— The school in relation to the State, the Church and the Congregation. 1847.
—— Public education. 1853.
—— Four periods of public education. 1862. A reprint of earlier books and pamphlets.
—— Memorandum on popular education. 1865.
—— Some of the results of the Education Act and Code of 1870. Fortnightly Rev May 1876.

Kay-Shuttleworth, Sir James
See Official Documents, contribution to the Minutes of the Committee of Council on Education 1839–49; and F. Smith, The life and work of Kay Shuttleworth, 1923.

Russell, Lord John. National education: parliamentary speeches by Russell and the Marquess of Lansdowne and recent measures for the promotion of education in England, with statistical tables (1826–39). 1839.

Phillpots, Henry. Charge to the clergy of Exeter, Triennial Visitation 1839. On the State and religious education.

By a lady. The young lady's friend: a manual of practical advice and instructions to young females on their entering upon the duties of life after quitting school. 1840 (3rd edn).

L[ord ?], E. Discursive remarks on modern education. 1841.

Barwell, Mrs L. M. Letters from Hofwyl by a parent. 1842. *See* Pestalozzi, *above*.

Fenn, J. The school master's legacy and family monitor. 1843.

Hinton, J. H. Second letter to Sir James Graham on the educational clauses of the Factories Bill. 1843.

Owen, Sir Hugh. Letter to the Welsh people. 1843.

Wordsworth, W. The excursion. 1814. Bks 8–9, with Wordsworth's note in 1843 edn. *See* J. Fotheringham, Wordsworth Prelude as a study in education, 1899.

Skinner, S. Educational essays: practical observations on instruction, discipline, physical training. 1844.

Wordsworth, C. Discussions on public education. 1844.

— Diary in France mainly concerning education and the Church. 1845.

Parsons, B. Education the birthright of every human being. 1845.

Amos, Andrew. Four lectures on the advantages of a classical education as an auxiliary to a commercial education; with a letter to Whewell. 1846.

Angus, Joseph. Four lectures on the advantages of a classical education. 1846. 2 distinct essays written for two prizes offered by Henry Beaufoy; Angus won the first prize; James Pycroft, author of Oxford memories 1886, the second.

Baines, Sir Edward. Letters written to the Rt Hon Lord John Russell. 1846, 1848.

— The late struggle for the freedom of education. 1846.

— An alarm to the nation on the measure of State education. 1848.

— On the progress and efficiency of voluntary education. 1848.

— Strictures on the new Government Measure. 1853.

— National education. 1856.

— Our past educational improvement. 1857.

— Voluntary and religious education. 1857.

Booth, James. Education and educational institutions considered with reference to the present state of society. 1846.

— Examination the province of the State. 1847.

— On the influence of examination as an instrument of education. 1854.

— Systematic instruction and periodical examination. 1857. *See* Quart Rev 108 1860.

Kay, Joseph. Education of the poor in England and Europe. 1846.

— Social conditions and education of the people in England and Europe. 2 vols 1850.

— The condition and education of poor children in English and German towns. 1853.

Hamilton, Rev Richard Winter. Institutions of popular education. Leeds 1846. *See* R. V. Taylor, Biographia Leodiensis, Leeds 1865.

Hook, Dean Walter F. On the means of rendering more efficient the education of the people: a letter to the Bishop of St David's. 1846. *See* R. V. Taylor, *above*.

Mann, Horace. Report of an educational tour in Germany and parts of Great Britain and Ireland. 1846. With preface by Hodgson.

Binney, Thomas. Education. 1847.

Dawes, Richard. Hints on improved self-paying national education. 1847.

— Observations on the working of the Government scheme of education. 1847.

— Suggestive hints towards improved secular instruction, making it bear on practical life. 1849.

— Remarks occasioned by the present crusade against the Committee of Council on education. 1850.

— Schools and other similar institutions for the industrial classes. 1853.

— Remarks on the reorganisation of the Civil Service and its bearing on educational progress. 1854.

— Teaching of common things. 1854.

— Address to the Huddersfield Mechanics' Institute. 1856.

— Manual of educational requirements for the Civil Service, with a preface on its educational value and importance. 1856.

— Educational values and importance. 1856.

— Effective primary instruction the only sure road to success in secondary instruction. 1857.

— Lessons on the phenomena of industrial life. 1854, 1867 (3rd edn). *See* Minutes of the Committee of Council on education 1847–8 (report by Rev H. Moseley, HMI) and the general report of Matthew Arnold for 1853.

Henry, W. C. A biographical notice of the late Very Rev Richard Dawes MA, Dean of Hereford. 1867 (priv pbd).

Adamson, J. W. The illiterate Anglo-Saxon, ch ix. Cambridge 1946.

Curtis, S. J. and M. E. A. Boultwood. An introductory history of English education since 1800. 1960, 1964 (rev). Richard Dawes and King's Somborne, pp. 63–8. Dawes used a Project Method.

Dufton, J. National education: what it is and what it should be. 1847.

Kendall, Henry E. Designs for schools and school houses. 1847 (illustr). Kendall was the pioneer of a succession of school architects.

Porter, G. R. The influence of education shown by facts in the Criminal Tables for 1845 and 1846. 1847 (Br Assoc Report).

Pycroft, J. Four lectures on classical education as auxiliary to commercial. 1847.

Willm, J. The education of the people. Glasgow 1847.

Lectures on education. 1848 (Crosby Hall).

Woodard, Nathaniel. A plea for the middle classes. 1848. *See* under Memoirs, *below*.

Biggs, W. Lecture upon national education. Leicester 1849.

Emery, T. Educational economy: or State education vindicated. 1849.

Powell, B. State education. 1849.

Cooper, Thomas. Cooper's journal: or unfettered thinker. Jan–Oct 1850. A weekly.

Shirreff, Emily A. and M. G. Grey. Thoughts on self-culture. 2 vols 1850.

— Intellectual education. 1858.

Watts, John. On national education considered as a question of political and financial economy. 1850.

Couling, S. Our labouring classes, intellectual, social, moral condition. 1851.

Hare, Julius C. Education the necessity of mankind: sermon on the opening of Hurstpierpoint. 1851.

Inglis, Sir Robert H. The parochial schools of Scotland: a speech in the House of Commons, 4 June 1851.

Manchester and Salford Education Bill (1851–2).

Birley, W. A letter to Archdeacon Denison in reply to his strictures. 1851.

Close, F. National education: the secular system, the Manchester Bill and the Government scheme considered. 1852.

Denison, G. A. Supplement to Appendix B of a reply to the promoters of the Manchester and Salford Education Bill. 1852.
— Facts and considerations on the Manchester and Salford Education Bill. 1853.
Hinton, J. H. A review of the evidence in relation to the state of education in Manchester and Salford. 1852.
— A few plain words on the two Education Bills. 1852.
— Case of the Manchester educationists: state of education in Manchester and Salford. 2 pts 1852–4.
Newlands, H. Socinianism the inevitable result of the Manchester and Salford scheme of national education. 1851.
Richson, C. Sketch of some of the clauses which induced the abandonment of the voluntary system. 1851.
— Educational facts and statistics: evidence before the House of Commons. 1852.
See Parliamentary Papers under Official Documents, *below*.
Newman, Cardinal John Henry. *See* under Universities: General works, *below*.
Roth, Matthias D. Movements or exercises according to Ling's system for the due development and strengthening of the human body in childhood and in youth. 1852.
— The Gymnastic Free Exercises of P. H. Ling, arranged by H. Rothstein. Tr with addns by M. Roth 1853.
— A letter to the Earl of Granville, on the importance of rational gymnastics as a branch of national education. 1854.
— A plea for the compulsory teaching of the elements of physical education in our national elementary schools: or the claims of physical education to rank with reading, writing and arithmetic. 1870.
— On the neglect of physical education and hygiene by Parliament and the Education Department as the principal cause of the degeneration of the physique of the population. 1879.
— On school hygiene and scientific physical education. 1880.
Wilkinson, J. Popular education. 1852.
Whately, Richard. Address to the clergy on the recent changes in Irish national education. 1853.
Education of the blind. Edinburgh Rev 99 1854, 173 1891.
Nicholls, Sir George. History of the English Poor Law. 2 vols 1854, 1898. Vol 3, 'from 1834', by Mackay, 1899.
Tate, Thomas. The philosophy of education. 1854.
Conington, John. The academical study of Latin. 1855. *See* Edinburgh Rev 105 1857.
Morley, Henry. Infant Gardens: an article for Household Words. 1855. Written to draw attention to the work of Baroness von Bülow who visited England to introduce the Kindergarten system of Froebel.
Dickens, Charles. *See* his novels, especially Nicholas Nickleby, Dombey and Son, David Copperfield, Hard times.
See J. L. Hughes, Dickens as an educator, New York 1906; J. Manning, Dickens on education, Toronto 1959; P. Collins, Dickens and education, 1963.
Hill, Alexander. Hints on the discipline appropriate to schools. 1855. *See* Hazelwood School, under Special Sources: Schools, *below*, and G. B. Hill, Life of Sir Rowland Hill, 2 vols 1880.
Miller, J. C. Which? or neither? an examination of the Education Bills of Lord John Russell and Sir J. S. Pakington. 1855.
Dunning, R. A series of works on education after the methods of Pestalozzi. 1856.
Macleod, N. The Home School: hints on home education. Edinburgh 1856.
Temple, Frederick, Archbishop. National education. In Oxford essays contributed by members of the University, 1856.
— On apprenticeship and schools. 1858.

— The education of the world. In Essays and reviews, 1860. *See* Quart Rev 109 1861.
— Sermons preached in Rugby School Chapel in 1858, 1859, 1860. 3 further sermons, 1861–71.
— National schools. 1870.
— The true ideal of the educator. 1898. *See* J. G. Sheppard, *below*.
Currie, J. The principles and practice of infant school education. 1857.
— The principles and practice of common school education. Edinburgh 1861.
McCombie, W. On education in its constituents and issues. Aberdeen 1857.
Sheppard, J. G. Remarks on the Rev F. Temple's scheme for the extension of middle-class education. 1857.
Skeats, H. S. Results of government education. 1857, 1858.
Hawtrey, S. T. A letter containing an account of St Mark's School Windsor. 1859 (3rd edn).
— A narrative essay on a liberal education chiefly embodied in an attempt to give a liberal education to children of the working classes. 1868.
Arnold, Matthew. The popular education of France, with notices of that of Holland and Switzerland. 1861 (Report to Newcastle Commission).
— A French Eton. 1864, 1892 (with Schools and universities in France).
— Schools and universities on the Continent. 1868 (Report to the Schools Inquiry Commission).
— Culture and anarchy. 1869, 1875; ed J. D. Wilson, Cambridge 1932.
— Friendship's garland. 1871.
— (ed). A Bible-reading for schools. 1872.
— Report on higher schools and universities in Germany. 1874.
— 'Ecce, convertimur ad Gentes'. Fortnightly Rev Feb 1879.
— Special report on elementary education in Germany, Switzerland and France. 1886 (Cmd 4752). *See* Quart Rev 125 1868.
— Reports on elementary schools 1852–82. Ed F. Sandford 1889; ed F. S. Marvin 1908.
— Thoughts on education chosen from the writings of Arnold. Ed L. Huxley 1912.
Fitch, Sir J. Thomas and Matthew Arnold and their influence on English education. 1897.
Connell, W. F. The educational thought and influence Arnold. 1950.
See col 465, above.
Fitch, Sir Joshua. Public education: why is a new code wanted? 1861.
— Charity schools and the endowed schools commission. 1873.
— Lectures on teaching. 1881.
— Notes on American schools and training colleges. 1888.
— Educational aims and methods. 1900.
See under Thomas *and* Matthew Arnold, *above*.
Lilley, A. L. Sir Joshua Fitch. 1906.
Fraser, William. National education: reasons for the rejection in Britain of the Irish system—a brief exposition for Christian educationists. 1861. *See* Quart Rev 132 1872.
Hort, Rev F. J. A. Thoughts on the Revised Code of Education: its purposes and probable effects. 1861.
Senior, N. W. Suggestions on popular education. 1861.
Spencer, Herbert. Education, intellectual, moral and physical. 1861; ed F. A. Cavenagh, Cambridge 1932.
Compayre, G. Spencer et l'éducation scientifique. Paris 1901. *See* Memoirs, *below*.
Vaughan, Charles James. The revised code dispassionately considered. Cambridge 1861.
'One of practical experience'. Remarks on popular education in reference to the New Code. Bradford 1862.

Garfit, A. Some points of the education question, with outline of the progress of popular education. 1862.
— The conscience clause and the extension of education in the neglected districts practically considered. 1868.
Grant, A. R. Remarks on the revised code. Cambridge 1862.
Grote, John. A few words on the new educational code. 1862.
Grove, J. A few words on the new educational code and the report of the Education Commissioners. 1862.
Lowe, Robert (Viscount Sherbrooke). Speech of the Rt Hon Robert Lowe MP on the Revised Code of the Regulations of the Committee of the Privy Council on Education in the House of Commons. 13 Feb 1862.
— Primary and classical education. Edinburgh 1867.
— Middle class education: endowment or free-trade? 1868.
See Matthew Arnold, Reports on elementary education, *above*, *and under* Memoirs, *below*.
Randolph, E. J. The good properties of the Revised Code. 1862.
Gill, John. Introductory text-book to school education, method and school management. 1863 (9th edn).
— Systems of education: a history and criticism. 1876.
Ruskin, John. *See col 1340*, *above*.
Walter, J. Correspondence relative to the Resolutions on the Educational Grant to be moved, May 5th 1863. On the unaided schools.
The Museum and English journal of education. 5 vols 1864–9. Includes the Pupil teacher.
Thompson, D'A. W. Day-dreams of a schoolmaster. Edinburgh 1864.
— Wayside thoughts: desultory essays on education. 1868.
Thring, Edward. Education and school. 1864.
— Theory and practice of education. 1883.
— Sermons preached at Uppingham School. 2 vols 1886.
— Addresses. 1887.
See under Memoirs; *and* G. Hoyland, The man who made a school, 1946.
Education of the mentally defective. Edinburgh Rev 122 1865.
Laspée, Henry de. Calisthenics: or the elements of bodily culture on Pestalozzian principles. 1865.
Melville, D. The conscience clause; meaning, authority, use. 1865.
Menet, J. Letter on Mr Walter's motion. 1865. *See* Walter, *above*.
Sewell, Elizabeth M. Principles of education drawn from nature and revelation. 2 vols 1865.
Thompson, A. F. The English school-room: thoughts on private tuition. 1865.
Bruce, Henry Austin (Baron Aberdare). An address delivered to the National Association for the Promotion of Social Science. 1866.
Grant, P. The history of factory legislation 1802–50, with a warning by the Earl of Shaftesbury. Manchester 1866.
Pound, Rev William. Remarks upon English education in the nineteenth century. 1866.
Farrar, Frederic William, Dean, et al. Essays on a liberal education. 1867–8. By C. S. Parker, H. Sidgwick, J. Seeley, E. E. Bowen, F. W. Farrar, J. M. Wilson, H. W. Hales, W. Johnson and Lord Houghton.
— Observations on mental education. 1868.
Laurie, Simon Somerville. On primary intruction in relation to education. 1867.
— Institutes of education. Edinburgh 1868.
— John Amos Comenius. Cambridge 1881.
— Occasional addresses on educational subjects. 1888.
— Studies in the history of educational opinion from the Renaissance. Cambridge 1888, 1903 (rev).
— Training of teachers and methods of instruction. Cambridge 1902.

Almond, Hely Hutchinson. Mr Lowe's educational theories examined from a practical point of view. Edinburgh 1868.
Cooper, A. A. (Earl of Shaftesbury). Speeches relating to the labouring classes. 1868, *See* P. Grant, *above*.
Fraser, James, Bishop. National education: a sermon. 1868.
Hill, F. D. The children of the State: the training of juvenile paupers. 1868, 1889.
Hodgson, William B. Exaggerated estimates of reading and writing as means of education. 1868.
Markby, T. Practical essays on education. 1868.
Maxse, Frederick Augustus. The education of the agricultural poor. 1868.
— National education and its opponents. 1877.
Quick, Robert Hibert. Essays on educational reformers. 1868, 1902, 1929.
Storr, F. Life and remains of Quick. 1899.
Roby, H. J. The present state of the schools: the Law of Charities as affecting Endowed Schools. Chs ii, iv of the Schools Inquiry Commission. 1868.
Galton, Sir Francis. Hereditary genius: an enquiry into its laws and consequences. 1869, 1892.
— English men of science: their nature and nurture. 1874.
— Inquiries into human faculty and its development. 1883, 1907.
Maclaren, Archibald. A system of physical education. Oxford 1869, 1895.
— Training in theory and practice. 1896.
Norris, John P. The education of our people: weak points and strength. 1869.
'Outis' (J. L. Tupper). Hiatus: the void in modern education. 1869.
Quain, R. On some defects in general education: the Hunterian Oration. 1869, 1870.
Arnott, Neil. Fundamental principles of national education. 1869, 1870.
Campbell, H. Compulsory education. 1870.
Holland, H. W. Proposed national arrangements for primary education. 1870.
Playfair, Lyon. Primary education, technical education. Edinburgh 1870.
Rigg, G. H. History and present position of primary education in England and in connexion with Wesleyan Methodism. 1870.
Sproat, G. M. Education of the rural poor. 1870.
Wilson, James Maurice. Lecture on mathematical teaching. Rugby 1870.
— Morality in Public Schools. 1882. Rptd from Jnl of Education Nov 1881.
— Voluntary schools and State education. Manchester 1894.
— Education and popular control. 1898.
— The elementary education problem. Manchester 1898.
— Education and crime: a sermon. 1905.
— The day school and religious education: a sermon. 1907.
McCrie, J. Autopaedia: or instructions on personal education. 1871 (enlarged).
Fawcett, Henry and M. G. Essays and lectures on social and political subjects. Cambridge 1872. Contains 3 essays on educational subjects, all by M. G. Fawcett.
Jourdan, B. A. Essay on improvements in education during the eighteenth and nineteenth centuries. 1872.
Morley, John (Viscount). The struggle for national education. 1873.
Payne, Joseph. The true foundation of science teaching. 1873.
— The science and art of education. 1874.
— Pestalozzi: influence on elementary education. 1875.
— Froebel and the Kindergarten. 1876.
— A visit to German schools. 1876.
— Lectures on the science and art of education. 1880.
See Works of Payne, ed Dr J. F. Payne 2 vols 1883.

Todhunter, Isaac. The conflict of studies and other essays connected with education. 1873.
Grey, Mrs W. (Maria Georgina Shirreff). The study of education as a science: paper read at the British Association, Belfast. 1874.
— The ruling principle of method applied to education, by Antonio Rosmini Serbati. 1887, Boston 1889. Tr Mrs Grey.
— Last words to girls. 1889.
Mrs Grey with her sister was joint-author of Self-culture, 1850.
See E. A. Shirreff *and* M. G. Grey, *above*.
Kingsley, Charles. Health and education. 1874. *See col 935, above*.
Clarke, E. H. Sex in education. Boston 1875.
Leitch, J. H. Practical educationists and their systems of teaching. Glasgow 1875.
Fearon, Daniel Robert. School inspection. 1876. Also contributions to the Schools Inquiry Commission.
Lancaster, Henry Hill. Essays and reviews: prefatory notice by B. Jowett. Edinburgh 1876.
Stanley, Edward Lyulph (Baron Stanley). Three letters on Oxford University Reform. 1876.
— Our national education. 1890.
Latham, H. On examinations as a means of selection. Cambridge 1877. *See* Quart Rev 108 1860, Edinburgh Rev 139 1874.
Bain, Alexander. Education as a science. 1879.
Lyschinska, M. J. The Kindergarten principle: educational values and applications. 1880.
Rutherford, Mark. The autobiography of Mark Rutherford, dissenting minister. 1881. A novel.
— The early life of Mark Rutherford, by himself. 1913. Autobiography.
Craik, Sir Henry. The State and its relation to education. 1882.
Farrar, F. W. and R. B. Poole. General aims of the teacher and form management. Cambridge 1883.
Eve, H. W. and A. Sidgwick. The practice of education. Cambridge 1883.
Kay, D. Education and educators. 1883.
Froebel, Friedrich W. A. (1782–1852)
English translations:
Jarvis, Miss J. Fundamental principle of the education of man. New York 1885.
— Pedagogics of the Kindergarten. New York 1900.
— Education by development. New York 1905 (pt 2).
Hailmann, W. N. Fundamental principles of the education of man. New York 1887.
Michaelis, E. and H. Keatly Moore. Froebel's letters on the Kindergarten. 1891.
Bowen, H. C. Froebel and education by self activity. 1893.
Fletcher, S. S. F. and J. Welton. Froebel's writings on education rendered into English. 1912.
English commentaries:
Ronge, J. and B. Practical guide to the English Kindergarten. 1855.
Minutes of the Committee of Council on Education. 1855–6.
Barnard, H. Papers on Froebel's Kindergarten. New York 1881.
Shirreff, E. The Kindergarten principle of Froebel's system. 1897.
Herford, W. H. The student's Froebel. 1901.
Murray, E. R. Froebel as a pioneer in modern psychology. 1914.
Kilpatrick, W. H. Froebel's Kindergarten principle. New York 1916.
Priestman, B. O. Froebel education today. 1946.
Lawrence, E. (ed). Froebel and English education. 1952.
See J. Payne *and* M. J. Lyschinska, *above*.
Harrison, F. Politics and education: an address. 1887.
Bryant, Sophie. Educational ends. 1887.
— The teaching of morality in the family and the school. 1897.
Sidgwick, Henry. On stimulus. Cambridge 1888.
Findlay, Joseph John. Teaching as a career for university men. 1889.
— The principles of class teaching. 1898.
— The school: an introduction to the study of education. 1912.
— The children of England. 1923.
— The aims and organisation of education. 1925.
Herford, William Henry. The school: essay towards humane education. 1889.
Landon, J. School management. 1889.
James, William. Principles of psychology. 1890.
— Psychology: briefer course. 1892.
— Talks to teachers. 1899.
Paget, E. The spirit of discipline. 1891.
'The thirteen'. Thirteen essays on education. 1891.
Acland, Arthur H. D. and H. L. Smith (ed). Studies in secondary education. 1892.
Herbart, J. F.
English translations:
Felkin, H. M. and E. The science of education: its general principles deduced from its aims, and the aesthetic revelation of the world. 1892.
— Letters and lectures on education. 1898, 1901 (corrected).
Mulliner, B. A. The application of psychology to the science of education. 1898.
English commentaries:
Felkin, H. M. and E. An introduction to Herbart's science and practice of education. 1895, 1901 (corrected).
De Garmo, C. Herbart and the Herbartians. 1895.
Hayward, F. H. The reform of moral and biblical instruction on the lines of Herbartianism. 1902.
The critics of Herbartianism. 1903.
The meaning of education as interpreted by Herbart. 1907.
Davidson, A. New interpretation of Herbart's psychology. 1906.
See Sir John Adams, *below*.
Solomon, O. Theory of educational Sloyd. 1892.
Huxley, Thomas Henry. Science and education. In his Collected essays vol 3, 1893–4. *See* Quart Rev 123 1867.
Lyttleton, Hon E. Mothers and sons: or problems in the home training of boys. 1892.
Jolly, William Ruskin on education. 1894.
— Religious instruction in Board Schools. Edinburgh Rev 180 1894.
Gregory, Robert. Elementary education: some account of its rise and progress in England. 1895, 1905 (with appendix).
Sully, James. Studies of childhood. 1895.
Formby, C. W. Education and modern secularism. 1896. *See* Quart Rev 132 1872.
Hawtrey, M. The co-education of the sexes. 1896.
Rooper, T. G. A pot of green feathers, school and home life. 1896.
— On professional education. 1903.
— Selective writings. Ed R. G. Tatton 1907.
Adams, Sir John. Herbartian psychology applied to education. 1897.
— Exposition and illustration. 1909.
— The evolution of educational theory. 1912.
— The new teaching. 1918.
— Modern developments in educational practice. 1922.
— Errors in school. 1927.
Tuer, Andrew W. History of the horn-book. 1897. Dedicated by command to HM the Queen-Empress. The author claimed that 3 real horn-books were stowed away in the cover of each copy.
See P. Stone, When children read from horn-books, Country Life 19 Oct 1961.

Barnett, P. A. Teaching and organisation with special reference to secondary schools. 1897.
Armstrong, Henry Edward. The heuristic method of teaching or the art of making children think for themselves. In Special reports on educational subjects vol 2, 1898.
— The teaching of scientific method and other papers on education. 1903.
Cookson, C. (ed). Essays on secondary education. Oxford 1898.
Holman, Henry. English national education: a sketch of the rise of public elementary schools in England. 1898.
Churton, Annette. Kant on education. 1899.
Scott, R. P. What is secondary education? 1899.
Soulsby, L. H. M. Some thoughts for mothers and teachers. 1899.
— Stray thoughts on character. 1900.
Welton, James. The logical bases of education. 1899.
— Principles and methods of teaching. 1906.
— Educational theory. *See under* Education, Encyclopaedia britannica 1910 (11th edn).
— The psychology of education. 1911.
— What do we mean by education? 1915.
MacCunn, J. The making of character. 1900.
Ware, F. Education reform: the task of the Board of Education. 1900.
— Educational foundation of trade and industry. 1901.
Winch, W. H. Educational problems. 1900.

B. SPECIAL SOURCES

(1) THE UNIVERSITIES

General Works

'A graduate'. Enquiry into the studies in the universities preparatory to Holy Orders. 1824.
Considerations on the injuries arising from the course of education pursued in the universities and public schools. 1832.
Blakesley, J. W. The studies of the universities essentially general. Cambridge 1836.
— Thoughts on the recommendations of the Ecclesiastical Commission. 1836.
[Radnor, Earl]. An historical vindication of Earl Radnor's Bill to inquire respecting the statutes and administration of Oxford and Cambridge. 1837.
Whewell, William. Principles of English university education. 1837.
'A layman'. The independence of the universities and colleges. Oxford 1838.
Sewell, William. Collegiate reform: a sermon. Oxford 1838.
— The nation, the Church and the University of Oxford: two sermons. Oxford 1849.
Huber, V. A. The English universities. 2 vols in 3 1843 (abridged trn). *See* Quart Rev 72 1843, Edinburgh Rev 81 1845.
Quart Rev 73 1843, 124 1868, 134 1873.
Lyell, Sir Charles. Travels in North America. 2 vols 1845. Oxford and Cambridge: historical and critical, vol I pp. 271–316.
Pillans, James. A word for the universities of Scotland. Edinburgh 1848.
English universities and their reforms. Blackwood's Mag Feb 1849.
University reform. Edinburgh Rev 89 1849.
Christie, William Dougal. Two speeches in the House of Commons on the universities [25 May 1843, 10 April 1845]. 1850.
Hamilton, Sir William. Discussions on philosophy and literature, education and university reform. Edinburgh 1852, 1866 (3rd edn). *See* Education iii to vii, Appendix: Universities.
Newman, Cardinal John Henry. Discourses on the scope and nature of university education, addressed to the Catholics of Dublin. Dublin 1852, London 1859.
— Office and work of the universities. 1856.
— Lectures and essays on university subjects. 1859. All incorporated in The idea of a university defined and illustrated: I, in nine discourses addressed to the Catholics of Dublin; II, in occasional lectures and essays addressed to members of the Catholic University, 1873.
Lorimer, J. Universities of Scotland, past, present and possible. Edinburgh 1854.
See Scottish universities, Edinburgh Rev 81 1845, 143 1876; J. Pillans, *above*.
British universities. Edinburgh Rev 107 1858.
Campion, W. M. Commissioners and colleges. 1858.
Roby, H. J. Remarks on college reform. Cambridge 1858.
Emery, William. Past and present expenses and social conditions of university education. In British Association Report, 1862.
Seely, Sir John. Liberal education in universities. In Essays on a liberal education, 1867.
Griffiths, J. Enactments in Parliaments concerning the universities of Oxford and Cambridge. Oxford 1869.
Wilkins, A. Our national universities. 1871.
Fitch, Sir Joshua G. The universities and the training of teachers. Contemporary Rev Dec 1876. An anticipation of the Day Training Colleges.
Caird, J. University addresses on academic study. Glasgow 1899.
For the study of English and other modern literatures, see Quart Rev 156 1883, 164 1887; H. Nettleship, Study of modern European languages and literatures in Oxford, 1887; J. C. Collins, The study of English literature, 1891.

Admission of Dissenters

to the universities of Oxford, Cambridge and Durham

An address to Dissenters. 1834.
Dalby, W. The real question at issue. 1834.
Gray, J. H. The admission of Dissenters into the universities considered. Oxford 1834.
Hamilton, Sir William A. Bill to remove certain disabilities. Edinburgh Rev 60 1834.
Moberly, George. A few remarks on the proposed admission of Dissenters. Oxford 1834.
Pearson, G. Abrogating religious tests and subscriptions. Cambridge 1834.
Sedgwick, Adam. Admission of Dissenters to academical degrees. Cambridge Chron 9 June 1834. *See* H. J. Rose, Letter, Cambridge Chron 10 June 1834.
Selwyn, William. College examinations in Divinity. Cambridge 1834.
Sewell, S. Thoughts on the admission of Dissenters to the University of Oxford. Oxford 1834.
Turton, Thomas. Thoughts on the admission of persons, without regard to their religious opinions, to certain degrees in the universities of England. Cambridge 1834, 1835 (with A review of the principal dissenting colleges).
Lee, Samuel. Some remarks on the Dean of Peterborough's tract. Cambridge 1834.
Thirwall, Connor. A letter to the Revd Thos Turton on the admission of Dissenters to academical degrees. Cambridge 1834. A second letter followed the above.
Whewell, William. Additional remarks on some parts of Mr Thirwall's two letters. Cambridge 1834.
Also Quart Rev 52 1834, Edinburgh Rev 60 1834–5.

Wordsworth, Christopher. On the admission of Dissenters to reside and graduate. Cambridge 1834.

Manning, William Oke. Remarks upon religious tests at the English universities. 1846.

Arnold, Thomas et al. Opinions on the admission of Dissenters to the universities and on university reform. 1847.

Opinions on the admission of Dissenters and on university reform. 1847. By Palmerston, Lord John Russell, Sir W. Hamilton, J. S. Mill et al.

Smith, G. Plea for the abolition of tests in the university. Oxford 1864.

Young, Sir G. Series of letters to the Guardian, later published as a pamphlet under the title University tests. 1868.

Select Committee on University Tests: report to Parliament. 1870. Summarized in Cambridge Chron 6 May 1871.

Individual Universities

Aberdeen

Fasti Aberdonenses: selections from the records of the University and King's College of Aberdeen 1494–1854. 1854 (Spalding Club).

Grant Duff, Sir M. E. Inaugural addresses delivered to the University of Aberdeen. Edinburgh 1867.

Bulloch, J. M. History of the University of Aberdeen 1495–1895. 1895.

Aberdeen University studies. Aberdeen 1900.

Rectorial addresses delivered in the Universities of Aberdeen 1835–1900. Aberdeen 1902.

Birmingham

Smith, E. The educational work of the Birmingham and Midland Institute. 1870.

Lodge, Sir O. Addresses to students by the Principal. 1900.

See E. W. Vincent and P. Hinton, The University of Birmingham: its history and significance, Birmingham 1947.

Cambridge

See College histories, *the more important of which are listed in vol I*.

'Pembrochian'. Gradus ad Cantabrigiam: or a dictionary of the terms used at the University of Cambridge. 1803.

Wilson, J. Memorabilia Cantabrigiae. 1803.

Byron, George Gordon, Baron. Thoughts suggested by a College examination. 1806; Granta: a medley; 1806; in his Hours of idleness, 1807.

Wainewright, L. The literary and scientific studies pursued, encouraged and enforced in the University of Cambridge. 1815.

Quart Rev 19 1818. On the chair of Botany.

'Eubulus' (Samuel Butler of Shrewsbury). Thoughts on the present system of academic education. 1822.

—— A letter to Philograntus. 1822.

'Philograntus' (J. H. Monk). A letter on the additional examination of students. 1822. *See* 'Eubulus', *above*.

[Gooch, R.] The Cambridge tart, by Socius. 1823.

'A brace of Cantabs'. Gradus ad Cantabrigiam: or a new university guide to the academic customs and colloquial or cant terms. 1824.

Dyer, G. The privileges of the University of Cambridge. 1824.

[Wright, J. M. F.] Alma mater: or seven years at the University of Cambridge by a Trinity-man. 1827. *See* London Mag April 1827.

Gunning, Henry. The ceremonies observed in the Senate House Cambridge. 1828.

—— Letters from Cambridge illustrative of the studies, habits and peculiarities of the University. 1827.

Sedgwick, Adam. A discourse on the studies of the Universities. Cambridge 1833.

Selwyn, William. Extracts from college examinations in divinity with a letter to the lecturers and examiners. Cambridge 1835.

'Resident members of the University'. Hints for the introduction of an improved course of study in the University. Cambridge 1835.

[Le Grice, C. V.] Conversations at Cambridge: miscellaneous pieces. Cambridge 1836.

Walsh, B. D. A historical account of the University of Cambridge and its colleges, in a letter to the Earl of Radnor. 1837.

Cambridge University Magazine. March 1839–Nov 1840.

Peacock, George. Observations on the statutes of the university of Cambridge. 1841.

Whewell, William. Liberal education, with particular reference to the university of Cambridge. 1845.

Amos, A. Four lectures on the advantages of a classical education, with a letter to Whewell. 1846.

Alma mater: a satire dedicated to the collegiate dignitaries. 1848.

Bain, A. University education. Westminster Rev 69 1848. A review of Whewell, Liberal education, *above*.

Bristed, C. A. Five years in an English university. 2 vols New York 1852, 1 vol 1873.

Potts, Robert. Cantabrigiensis liber: aids afforded to poor students in the University, with maxims designed for learners. Cambridge 1855.

Cambridge essays contributed by members of the University. 4 vols 1855–8.

Mill, John Stuart. Dissertations and discussions. 4 vols 1859–75. On Adam Sedgwick, Discourse, *above*.

Everett, W. On the Cam: lectures on the University of Cambridge. 1866.

The Light Blue. 4 vols 1866–70.

Wilson, James Maurice. Letter to St John's College on sciences in relation to school and university. 1867.

[Rice, J.] The Cambridge freshman: or memoirs of Mr Golightly; by Martin Legrand. 1871.

Hilton, A. C. et al. The Light Green: a superior and high-class periodical. Cambridge 1872–3.

On the training of teachers. Cambridge Univ Reporter 2 Nov 1877, 20 Nov 1878; Teachers' training syndicate: first annual Report, 3 Dec 1880.

Burnand, F. C. Personal reminiscences of the ADC. 1880.

Whibley, C. In cap and gown: three centuries of Cambridge wit. 1889.

Lehmann, R. C. In Cambridge courts. 1891.

Atkinson, Thomas D. Cambridge described and illustrated. Cambridge 1897. Introd by J. W. Clark.

Stephen, J. K. Lapsus calami and other verses. Ed H. S., Cambridge 1898.

Stubbs, C. W. The story of Cambridge. 1905.

Leigh, A. A. A record of college reform. 1906.

Tillyard, A. I. A history of university reform from 1800. Cambridge 1913.

Winstanley, D. A. Early Victorian Cambridge. Cambridge 1940.

—— Later Victorian Cambridge. Cambridge 1947.

Dublin

Todd, James H. University of Dublin: remarks on some statements attributed to T. Wyse. 1844.

Taylor, W. B. S. History of the University of Dublin. 1845. *See* Edinburgh Rev 88 1848.

Vickers, R. Praelection on the university system of education. Dublin 1849.

Tyrrell, R. Y. et al. Kottabos: a college miscellany. Dublin 1869.

Hermathena: papers by members of T C D. Dublin 1874–.

Stubbs, J. M. History of the University of Dublin. Dublin 1889. *See* Quart Rev 175 1892.

Dixon, W. M. Trinity College Dublin. Dublin 1902.

Burtchaell, G. D. and T. U. Sadleir. Alumni dublienses 1593–1860. Dublin 1937.

Durham

The Thorp letters. 5 vols 1831–62.
Durham University Journal. 1876–.
Embleton, Dennis. History of the Medical School, afterwards the Durham College of Medicine. Newcastle 1890.
Turner, George Grey. A short history of the Durham University College of Medicine. Durham Univ Jnl 1896.
The student's guide to the University of Durham. 1897.
Fowler, J. T. Durham University: earlier foundations and present colleges. 1904.
Whiting, C. E. The University of Durham 1832–1932. 1932.

Edinburgh

Edinburgh essays. 1858.
Dazel, A. History of the University of Edinburgh. 2 vols Edinburgh 1862.
Geddes, P. et al. Viri illustres academiae Jacobi Sexti Scotiae regis anno CCCmo. Edinburgh 1884.
Grant, Sir Alexander. The story of the University of Edinburgh. 2 vols 1884.
Rectorial addresses delivered before the university 1859–99. Ed A. Stodart-Walker 1900.

Glasgow

Remarks on a pamphlet A memorial respecting the college of Glasgow. Glasgow 1835.
Inaugural addresses by Lord Rectors of the University. Ed J. B. Hay 1839.
Macaulay, Thomas Babington, Baron. Inaugural address as Lord Rector. 1849.
Munimenta alme universitatis glasguensis: records of the University till 1727. 3 vols in 4 Glasgow 1854 (Maitland Club).
Disraeli, Benjamin (Earl of Beaconsfield). Inaugural address delivered to the University of Glasgow. 1873. *See* Edinburgh Rev 139 1874.
Addison, W. I. et al. Roll of the graduates of the University of Glasgow 1727–1897 with biographical notes. Glasgow 1898.
Primrose, A. P. Inaugural address 1900. *See* Edinburgh Rev 195 1902.
Couts, I. History of the University of Glasgow. Glasgow 1909.
Morgan, A. Scottish university studies. Oxford 1933.

Ireland

'Nemo'. A few words on the new Irish Colleges. 1845.
Corrigan, D. J. University education in Ireland. Dublin 1865.
Sullivan, W. K. University education in Ireland. Dublin 1866.
Andrews, T. Address on education to the Social Science Association. 1867.
— Studium generale: a chapter of contemporary history. 1867. On the University of London, the new Irish universities, Maynooth.
Walsh, W. J. The Irish university question. Dublin 1890.
See Quart Rev 148 1879, 187 1898, 197 1903; Edinburgh Rev 135 1872, 137 1873, 187 1898, 195 1902.

Leeds

The Yorkshire College of Science: scheme for the foundation of a college. 1869.
Report of the inauguration of the Yorkshire College of Science. 1875.
The inauguration of the University of Leeds: a special issue of the Gryphon, the journal of the University of Leeds. 1904.
Smithells, A. From a modern university. Oxford 1921.
Curtis, S. J. The University of Leeds. Universities Rev 22 1949.
Brown, E. J. The private donor in the history of the University of Leeds. 1954.
Shimmin, A. N. The University of Leeds: the first half century. Cambridge 1954.

London

Campbell, Thomas. Times 9 Feb 1824. A letter.
— Suggestions respecting the plan of an University in London. New Monthly Mag 13 1825.
Edinburgh Rev 42 1825, 43 1826, 48 1828, 164 1886.
'An Oxonian'. Proposals for founding an University in London considered. 1825.
Quart Rev 33 1825.
London University: prospectus. London Mag Aug 1826.
'A subscriber'. Remarks to the provisional committee for the intended establishment of King's College London. 1828. *See* London Mag July 1828.
'Christianus'. Letter to Robert Peel on the London University. 1828. *See* Quart Rev 39 1829.
The London University Press: remarks upon a popular system of classical instruction. Bath 1828.
Stähele, A. Letter to the Council of the University of London. 1828.
The second statement of the Council explanatory of the plan of instruction. 1828. *See* Edinburgh Rev 48 1828.
Yates, James. Outlines of a constitution for the University of London. 1832.
Morgan, John M. Address to the proprietors of the University of London. 1833. Proposes a Chair of Education.
Sewell, William. A second letter to a dissenter on the opposition of the University of Oxford to the Charter of the London College. Oxford 1834. *See* Edinburgh Rev 42 1825.
London University. Quart Jnl of Education 7 1834.
Wetherall, Sir C. Substance for a speech on incorporating the University of London. 1834. In opposition, on behalf of Oxford.
E., E. (D. Edwards). The metropolitan university: remarks on a central university examining board. 1836.
De Morgan, Augustus. Thoughts suggested by the establishment of the University of London. 1837.
Hoppus, John. Thoughts on academic education and degrees in arts. 1837.
Letter to a member of the Senate relative to the BA examination. 1838.
Beattie, William. Life and letters of Thomas Campbell. 3 vols 1849. *See* vol 2 ch 14.
Jelf, Richard. W. Grounds for laying before the Council of King's College London theological essays by F. D. Maurice. 1853.
Andrews, Thomas. Studium generale. 1867. *See* T. Andrews *under* Ireland, *above*.
Beard, C. University College and Mr Martineau. 1867.
Bagehot, Walter. Matthew Arnold on the London University. Fortnightly Rev June 1868.
Grote, Harriet. The personal life of George Grote. 1873.
Prospectus of the Association for Promoting a Teaching University for London. 1886. *See* Edinburgh Rev 164 1886.
Quart Rev 164 1887, 191 1900.
The proposed teaching university for London. Times 31 Jan 1888.
London University Commission and Albert University Charter, by Sir J. G. Fitch. Quart Rev 174 1892.
Notes and memorials for the history of University College London. Ed W. P. Ker 1898.
Wilson, G. S. The University of London and its colleges. 1923.
Haldane, R. B. (Viscount). Birkbeck College centenary lectures. 1924.
Humberstone, T. L. University reform in London. 1926.
Bellot, H. H. L. University College London 1826–1926. 1929.

Hearnshaw, F. J. C. et al. The centenary history of King's College, London 1828–1928. 1929.
Collins, W. J. The University of London fifty years ago. Contemporary Rev Sept 1935.
Gledstone, M. Centenary of the Bedford College for Women. Universities Rev 21 1949.

Manchester (including Owens College and the Victoria University)

Essays and addresses by Professors of Owens College. 1874.
Thompson, Joseph. The Owens College: its foundation and growth and its connection with the Victoria University Manchester. Manchester 1886.
Hartog, Sir Philip. Owens College Manchester: a brief history of the College. 1900.
Fiddes, E. Chapters in the history of Owens College and of Manchester University (1857–1914). Manchester 1937.
Charlton, H. B. Portrait of a university 1851–1951. Manchester 1951.

Oxford

See the College histories, *the more important of which are listed in vol 1.*
Walker, J. Oxoniana. 4 vols 1807.
Edinburgh Rev 14 1809, 16 1810, 53 1831, 54 1831, 76 1843, 88 1848, 96 1852, 170 1889, 198 1903.
Copleston, E. A reply to the calumnies of the Edinburgh Review. Oxford 1810.
— A second reply. Oxford 1810.
— A third reply. Oxford 1811. *See* J. Davison, *below*; Quart Rev 4 1810; Edinburgh Rev 14 1808, 16 1810; D. K. Sandford to P. Elmslie, Pamphleteer 21 1822.
'A Nobleman'. Letters to his son at Eton and Oxford. 2 vols 1810.
[Tatham, E.] A new address to members of Convocation. Oxford 1810.
— An address to the Chancellor upon abuses. Oxford 1811. Both by the Rector of Lincoln College.
'A gentleman of the University'. A poetical essay on the existing state of things. [1811?].
'A Cambridge Master of Arts'. Oxoniana: a didactic poem. 1812.
[Boone, James S.] The Oxford spy: a dialogue in verse. Oxford 1818. With a prose appendix on studies.
Townsend, W. C. The paean of Oxford: a reply to the charges against the University. 1826.
Skelton, J. Pietas oxoniensis or records of Oxford founders. Oxford 1828.
Whittock, N. The microcosm of Oxford. 1828.
Ingram, James. Apologia academica. Oxford 1831.
— Memorials of Oxford. 3 vols 1837.
'A member of Convocation' (V. Thomas). The legality of the present academical system asserted against the new calumnies of the Edinburgh Review. Oxford 1831. *See* Edinburgh Rev 54 1831, *and under* Thomas, *below*.
— The legality [etc] reasserted. Oxford 1832.
Quart Jnl of Education 1–2, 4, 7 1831–4.
Academical abuses disclosed by Initiated. 1832.
Present state and future prospects of mathematical and physical studies in the University. Oxford 1832.
'A graduate'. Thoughts on reform at Oxford. Oxford 1833.
Quart Rev 52 1834, 61 1838, 137 1874.
Sewell, William. The attack upon the University of Oxford in a letter to Earl Grey. 1834 (2nd edn).
— Suggestions for the extension of the University. Oxford 1850.
— The university commission: or Lord John Russell's post-bag. Oxford 1850. Anon.
'A resident member of Convocation' (A. C. Tait). Hints on a plan for the revival of the professorial system. Oxford 1839.
Davidson, J. Remarks and occasional publications. Oxford 1840. Includes Review of replies to the calumnies of the Edinburgh Rev 1810. *See* J. H. Newman, Idea of a university: discourse vi, Liberal knowledge in relation to professional.
Bentham, Jeremy. Works. Ed J. Bowring 11 vols Edinburgh 1843. Vol 10 ch 2, Westminster School and Oxford.
[Caswell, E.] The art of pluck, by Scriblerus Redivivus. 1843.
Garbett, James. Dr Pusey and the University of Oxford. 1843.
Coleridge, John Duke (Baron). Memorials of Oxford. Oxford 1844. Verse.
Maurice, J. F. D. The New Statute and Mr Ward. Oxford 1845.
[Pycroft, J.] The collegian's guide: or recollections of college days, by the Revd — M A — College. 1845.
'Nema'. The Devil's return from Oxford. Oxford 1847.
'Country schoolmaster'. A letter to the authors of Suggestions for an improvement of the Examination Statute, Oxford 1848.
[Jowett, Benjamin and Arthur Penryn Stanley]. Suggestions for an improvement of the Examination Statute. Oxford 1848.
Walker, R. A letter on improvements in the present Examination Statute, and the studies of the University. Oxford 1848.
Grand university logic stakes. 1849.
'A member of the Oxford Convocation' [C. A. Row]. Letter to Lord John Russell on the constitutional defects of the University and Colleges of Oxford, with suggestions for a Royal Commission. 1850.
Price, B. Suggestions for the extension of professorial teaching. 1850.
Row, C. A. Letter to Sir Robert Inglis in reply to his speech on university reform. 1850.
'Bede, Cuthbert' (E. Bradley). The adventures of Mr Verdant Green, an Oxford freshman, 1853.
Thomas, V. The legality of the academic system asserted. 2 pts Oxford 1853. *See* Edinburgh Rev 96 1852, *and* A member of Convocation, *above*.
Tutors' Association Reports, Oxford 1853–4:
1. Recommendations respecting extension;
2. Recommendations respecting the constitution;
3. Recommendations relating to the professorial and tutorial systems;
4. Recommendations respecting College Statutes.

See F. H. Dickinson and E. A. Freeman, Suggestions with regard to certain proposed alterations, Oxford 1854; J. W. Aud and J. Patteson, Suggestions with regard to the possibility of legal education, Oxford 1854.
Barrow, T. The case of Queen's College Oxford. 1854.
Barry, H. B. Remarks on the three proposals for reforming the Constitution of the University. Oxford 1854.
Pusey, Edward Bouverie. Collegiate and professional teaching and discipline. 1854. *See* H. H. Vaugham, *below*.
Vaugham, H. H. Oxford reform and Oxford professors. 1854.
Wilson, H. B. A letter to the Chancellor of the University on university and college reforms. 1854.
'Members of the University'. Oxford essays. 1855, 1856, 1857.
'Clericus' (A. Clissold). A letter to the Vice-Chancellor on theology. 1858.
Acland, Sir Thomas Dyke. Some account of the origin and objects of the new examinations for the title of Associate in Arts. 1858.
Smith, G. Oxford University reforms. 1858.
— Reorganisation of the University. Oxford 1868.
— Oxford and her colleges. 1894.
Acland, H. W. and J. Ruskin. The Oxford Museum. 1859.
Rogers, J. E. T. Education in Oxford and its methods. 1861.

Hamilton, Sir William. Discussion on philosophy and literature, education and university reforms, chiefly from the Edinburgh Review. 1852, 1866 (3rd edn). *See under* Universities: General works, *above*; E. Moore, *below*.

Moore, E. Frugal education attainable under the existing collegiate system. Oxford 1867.

'Beta' (Thomas E. Brown). Christ Church servitors in 1853 by one of them. Macmillan's Mag 19 1868.

Pattison, Mark. Suggestions on academical organisation. Edinburgh 1868.

Mansel, H. L. The Phrontisterion: or Oxford in the nineteenth century. A skit on the Royal Commission of 1850–2. Ed H. W. Chandler 1873.

Essays on the endowment of research. 1876. By various writers.

Mozley, Thomas. Reminiscences chiefly of Oriel College and the Oxford Movement. 2 vols 1882. *See* Quart Rev 154 1882.

Brodrick, George Charles. A history of the University of Oxford. 1886.

English literature at the universities. Quart Rev 163 1886. Discusses Petition for a school of modern literature. Oxford 1886.

Burgon, John W. Historical notes of Oxford colleges. Oxford 1888.

Essays. Ed H. Nettleship 2 vols Oxford 1889.

Foster, Joseph. Alumni oxonienses 1500–1886. Oxford 1891.

Mackinder, H. J. and Sir M. E. Sadleir. University extension: has it a future? 1890, 1891 (enlarged as University extension past, present and future). *See* Quart Rev 172 1891.

Wells, J. et al. Oxford and Oxford life. 1892.

Our memories: shadows of old Oxford. 2 sers 1893–5.

Thompson, L. Christ Church. 1900.

Tuckwell, W. Reminiscences of Oxford. 1900.

—— Pre-Tractarian Oxford: a reminiscence of the Oriel Noetics. 1909. *See* Quart Rev 156 1883.

See C. Mallet, A history of the University of Oxford vol 3, 1927.

Reading

Childs, W. M. Making a university: an account of the university movement at Reading. 1933.

St Andrews

Rectorial addresses at St Andrews University 1863–1893. Ed W. Knight 1894.

Donaldson, Sir J. Addresses delivered in the University of St Andrews from 1886 to 1910. Edinburgh 1911.

Votiva tabella: memorial volume of St Andrews University 1411–1911. 1911.

Wales

Davies, W. C. and W. L. Jones. The University of Wales and its colleges. 1905.

(2) SCHOOLS, COLLEGES AND INSTITUTES

The standard school histories etc, which are listed in vols 1–2, have not usually been repeated here.

Ingram, Robert A. A sermon for the Charity School. Colchester 1788.

—— Parochial beneficence: the Baxted School of Industry. Colchester [1800].

—— An essay on Schools of Industry. [1808].

Cappe, C. An account of two Charity Schools in York. York 1800.

—— Observations on Charity Schools in York. York 1805.

Royal Military College: H M Warrants and Statutes. 1802.

Vincent, Rev W., Head Master of Westminster School. A defence of public education with an attempt to state fairly the question whether the religious instruction and moral conduct of the rising generation, are sufficiently provided for and effectually secured in our schools and universities. 1802. *See* Remarks on Vincent's Defence by a layman, 1802; and D. Morris, An attempted reply to the Master of Westminster School, 1802.

Byron, G. G. On a change of masters at a great public school. 1805.

—— On a distant view of Harrow. 1806.

—— In his Hours of idleness, 1807.

'A Carthusian' (Robert Smythe). Historical account of the Charterhouse. 1808.

Bernard, Sir Thomas. The new school. 1809.

—— Barrington School (Bishop Auckland): principles, practices and effects. 1812.

See Reports of the Society for Bettering the Conditions of the Poor, Official Documents, *below*.

Smith, Sydney. Edinburgh Rev 16 1810. Review of Remarks on the system of education in public schools, 1809.

The public schools. Edinburgh Rev 16 1810, 51 1830, 53 1831, 113 1861, 120 1864, 146 1877, 185 1897; Quart Rev 25 1821, 39 1829, 52 1834, 102 1857, 108 1860, 177 1893, 187 1898, 189 1899. *See* Sir J. T. Coleridge, *below*.

Harrison, R. Sermons on various important subjects, with life of the author by W. Harrison. Manchester 1813.

Poole, J. The village schools improved: the new system explained. 1813, Oxford 1815 (2nd edn).

Hill, Thomas Wright. The pupils of Hill-Top School Birmingham. Birmingham 1815. Hill-Top, 1803–19, was the predecessor of the Hill's Schools, Hazelwood etc.

Ackermann, Rudolph. The history of the Colleges of Winchester, Eton and Westminster, with the Charter-House, the Schools of St Paul's, Merchant Taylors, Harrow and Rugby, and the Free School of Christ's Hospital. 1816.

Lauphier, W. H. Upper Sunbury School Middlesex, for a limited number of persons of distinction and respectability. 1816.

The Trifler: a periodical paper. March–Sept 1817. *See* Vincent, *above*.

Bowles, William Lisle. Vindiciae wykehamicae: or a vindication of Winchester College in a letter to Henry Brougham. 1818, 1819.

Carlisle, Nicholas. A concise description of the Endowed Grammar Schools in England and Wales. 2 vols 1818. On the state of grammar schools in the early nineteenth century.

Rules for the government of the Westminster New Charity. 1818.

Grammar Schools and the education of the poor. Edinburgh Rev 32 1819.

Vindication of the Enquiry into Charitable Abuses with an exposure of the misrepresentation contained in the Quarterly Review. 1819.

Butler, Samuel. A letter to Henry Brougham esq. 1820.

Edinburgh Academical Institution: Milton's plan of education with the plan of the EAI founded thereon, by William Scott. Pamphleteer 17 1820.

The Etonian: a magazine. 1820–1, 1821–2, 1824 (4th edn). *See* Quart Rev 25 1821.

Quart Rev 25 1821, 52 1834, 171 1890, 187 1898. On Eton.

[Hill, Matthew Davenport]. Plans for the government and liberal instruction of boys in large numbers as practised at Hazelwood School. 1822, 1825 (as Public education plans etc), 1894. Ascribed to Arthur Hill et al. *See* F. Jeffrey, Edinburgh Rev 41 1825; T. de Quincey, London Mag April–May 1824.

Sheepshanks, Rev John. Brief history of Leeds Grammar School. 1822.

Churcher's College Petersfield and life of Churcher. Petersfield 1823.

The system pursued in the Pestalozzian Academy South Lambeth with some remarks on education. 1826. The author claims to have conversed daily with Pestalozzi at Yverdon.

Buckler, J. C. Sixty views of Endowed Grammar Schools. 1827.

Hill, Sir Roland and F. The laws of Hazelwood School. 1827.

Scots Parochial Schools. Edinburgh Rev 46 1827.

Ward, Valentine. Observations on Sunday Schools. Leeds 1827.

City of London Literary and Philosophical Institution. *See* Edinburgh Rev 47 1828.

Gilbert, Richard. Liber scholasticus. 1829, 1843 (as Parents' school and college guide). On emoluments at Oxford, Cambridge, Durham, the public and other endowed schools and from City companies.

Malet, Sir Alexander. Some account of the system of fagging at Winchester School, with remarks and a correspondence with Dr Williams, Head Master of that public school, on the late expulsions thence for resistance to the authority of the prefects. 1828. *See* Letter to Sir Alexander Malet by an old Etonian, 1829; Quart Rev 39 1829.

History of the Foundations in Manchester of Christ's College, Chetham's Hospital and the Free Grammar School. 3 vols Manchester 1828–9.

A very short letter from one Old Westminster to another. 1829.

'Etonensis'. Observations on an article in the last Edinburgh Review [51 1830] entitled Public schools of England. Eton 1830. *See* A few words in reply to Some remarks by Etonensis, 1834; The Eton system vindicated in reply to some recent publications, 1834; Quart Rev 52 1834.

A letter to the Edinburgh Review in answer to no CV [53 1831] respecting Westminster School. 1831.

Village schools of industry. 1831.

Eton College Magazine. Eton 1832 (8 issues).

[Hill, Arthur]. Sketch of the system of education at Bruce Castle, Tottenham and Hazelwood. 1833.

The kaleidoscope conducted by Eton boys. Eton 1833.

Statutes of Robert Johnson, Oakham and Uppingham. Uppingham 1837.

Coates, T. Visit to Borough Road Model School. In Central Society of Education, 1838 (2nd pbn).

Concio apud scholae Hergensis gubernatores habita xj Kal Jul. 1838.

Fry, A. Bruce Castle, Tottenham Junior School. In Central Society of Education, 1838 (2nd pbn).

Bruce Castle Magazine. 1839.

Westminster School of Industry. [An Ackermann colour-print. c. 1840].

Smith, A. J. A concise history of Berkhampstead. Hertford 1842.

Charter, Act of Parliament, By-laws and Regulations of the Foundling Hospital. 1843.

Liverpool Collegiate Institution: origin and progress. 1843.

Sandford, John. Parochialia: or church, school and parish. 1845.

[Williamson, R.] A short account of the discipline, studies and examinations, prizes etc of Westminster School. 1845. Anon; rptd from Quart Jnl of Education.

Confessions of an Etonian, by J.E.M. 1846.

The legacy of an Etonian. Ed R. Nolands, Cambridge 1846.

Wordsworth, Charles. Christian boyhood at a public school: a collection of sermons and lectures delivered at Winchester College. 2 vols 1846.

[Roper, W. J. D.]. Chronicles of Charterhouse, by a Carthusian. 1847.

Guthrie, Thomas. Plea for ragged schools. Edinburgh 1847.

—— Seed-time and harvest of ragged schools. Edinburgh 1860. *See* Edinburgh Rev 85 1847.

Murray, A. M. Remarks on education. 1847. On Charity Schools. Miss Murray co-operated in founding Queen's College London, 1848.

Creasy, Sir Edward Shepherd. Some account of Eton. 1848. *See* Edinburgh Rev 113 1861.

—— Memoirs of eminent Etonians, with notices on the early history of Eton College. 1850.

Steven, W. History of the High School of Edinburgh. 1849. *See* Edinburgh Rev 15 1812.

Manchester Free Grammar School, by an old scholar. 1849.

Notices on the early history of Eton College. 1850.

Reformatory schools. Edinburgh Rev 94 1851, 101 1855.

List of Queen's Scholars of St Peter's College Westminster since 1663. 1852.

Hall, Peter. An historical guide to Wimborne, with a particular account of Queen Elizabeth's Free Grammar School. 1848, 1853 (2nd edn).

Sarah Nowell's endowed charity school in Iffley. Oxford 1854.

Vaughan, Charles John. A letter to the Viscount Palmerston on the monitorial system of Harrow School. 1854; *see* Earl of Galloway, Observations on the abused reform of the monitorial, system 1854; Remarks addressed to Dr Vaughan by Anti-Monitor, 1854; A few words on the monitorial system, by one who was a monitor, 1854.

Sewell, William. A year's sermons preached in St Peter's College Radley. 2 vols Oxford 1854–69.

Close, Francis. High Church education, delusive and dangerous: being an exposition of the system adopted by W. Sewell. 1855.

Goulburn, Edward Heyrick. The book of Rugby School: history and daily life. 1856. *See* Quart Rev 102 1857.

Harper, A. History of the Cheltenham Grammar School from 1851. Cheltenham 1856.

Hasenbeth, F. C. Sedgley Park School: history. 1856.

Farrar, F. W. On some defects in public school education. 1857.

K.H. [Herbert Kynaston]. Lays of the seven half centuries. 1859.

Coleridge, Sir John Taylor. Public school education: a lecture at Tiverton. 1860. *See* Edinburgh Rev 113 1861; Quart Rev 108 1861; Paterfamilias, *below*.

The Eton observer: a miscellany conducted by present Etonians. Eton 1860.

Paterfamilias [Matthew G. Higgins, alias Jacob Omnium ?]. Letters. Cornhill Mag May, Dec 1860, March 1861.

Etonian. Thoughts on Eton suggested by Sir John Coleridge's speech at Tiverton. 1861.

Johnson, William [Cory]. Eton reform. 1861. *See* Edinburgh Rev 113 1861.

—— Hints for Eton Masters, 1862. 1898.

Moberly, George. Five short letters to Sir William Heathcote on the studies and discipline of public schools. 1861.

Social science: Cassell's prize essays by working men and women. 1861.

The Eton College Chronicle. No 1, 14 May 1863–no 1000, 5 March 1903.

Stapylton, H. E. C. Eton School lists 1791–1850. 1864; Appendix 1853–56–59, Eton 1868; Second appendix 1862–65–68, 1871–74–77, 1884.

School foundations and class education. 1865.

Sidebotham, J. S. Memorials of the King's School Canterbury. Canterbury 1865.

Staunton, Howard. The great schools of England. 1865.

[Collins, W. L.] The public schools; Winchester, Westminster, Shrewsbury, Harrow, Rugby. Edinburgh 1868.

'An old Cheltonian'. Reminiscences of Cheltenham College. 1868.

Haig Brown, W. (ed). Sertum Carthusainum floribus seculorum contextum 1620–1869. 1870.

Recollections of Eton, by an Etonian. 1870.

Mansfield, R. B. School-life at Winchester College. 1870.

Bedford, F. W. History of the George Heriot's Hospital. Edinburgh? 1872.

How not to do it as exemplified by the Skinners in their government of Tonbridge School, by an old Tonbridgean. [1873].

The endowed schools debate and the alleged neglect of the Skinners' scheme. [1874].

Maxwell Lyte, H. C. A history of Eton College. 1875.

Blanch, W. H. Dulwich College and Edward Alleyn. 1877.

Conybeare, J. C. To the Governors of Tonbridge School. [1877]. *See* Edinburgh Rev 36 1822.

Cox, T. History of the Heath Grammar School, Halifax. 1879.

Rowntree, T. S. A sketch of the history of Ackworth School. 1879.

Thompson, H. History of Ackworth School during its first hundred years. Ackworth 1879.

G[erard], J. Memorials of Stonyhurst College. 1881.

Rugby School Register 1675–1904. 3 vols 1881–1904.

Claridge, W. Origin and history of Bradford Grammar School from its foundation to Christmas 1882. Bradford 1882.

The leaflet, by members of Rugby School. Rugby 1883–87.

Gaskall, C. M. Records of an Eton schoolboy. 1883.

Seven years at Eton 1857–64. Ed J. B. Richards 1883.

Forshall, F. H. Westminster School, past and present. 1884.

A short account of the Marlyebone Charity School. 1885.

Cotterell, C. C. Suggestive reforms in public schools. 1885.

Mozley, Rev Thomas. Reminiscences chiefly of towns, villages and schools. 2 vols 1885.

Thornton, Percy M. Harrow School and its surroundings. 1885.

Bowen, Edward E. Harrow songs. 1886.

Pearman, A. J. Ashford: its College and Grammar School. 1886.

Clifton College Register 1862–87, compiled by E. M. Oakley. 1887, 1890. With preface by J. M. Wilson.

Graham, J. W. Our need of a new public school. 1887.

Gibbs, A. E. Historical records of St Albans, containing the history of the Grammar School. 1888.

Wilkinson, C. A. Reminiscences of Eton. 1888. On Keate's period.

Great public schools, by various authors. 1889.

History of Shrewsbury School from the Blakeway mss and many other sources. Shrewsbury 1889.

Young, W. The history of Dulwich College to 1857, with life of Edward Alleyn. 2 vols 1889.

Bousfield, W. et al. Elementary schools: how to increase their utility—six lectures. 1890.

Drage, Geoffrey. Eton and the Empire. Eton 1890.

—— Eton and the Labour question. 1894.

Mansfield College Oxford: origin and opening, by various authors. 1890.

Marlborough College Register 1843–89. 1890.

Moore, T. The education brief on behalf of voluntary schools. 1890.

Recollections of schooldays at Harrow. Manchester 1890.

Wrench, R. G. Winchester word book. Winchester 1891.

Peacock, Matthew Henry. History of the Free Grammar School of Queen Elizabeth at Wakefield. Wakefield 1892.

[Tucker, William Hill]. Eton of old: or eighty years since 1811–22, by an Old Colleger. 1892.

University College School London: register 1831–91, with historical introduction by T. Orme. 1892.

Barker, G. F. R. and A. H. Stenning. Westminster School Register 1764–1883. 1892.

Whitgift Grammar School: history and register. Croydon 1892.

The Whitgift Foundation: a sermon by E. H. Genge. Croydon 1892.

Lockwood, E. Early days of Marlborough College. 1893.

Magell, E. H. Educational institutes of the Religious Society of Friends. 1893.

Ward, B. History of St Edmunds College. 1893.

Winchester College and the Quarterly Review. Quart Rev 177 1893.

Cowie, George. Wyggeston's Hospital, Hospital Schools and Grammar Schools 1511–1893. Leicester 1893.

Hipkins, F. C. Repton: village, church, priory and school. Derby [1894], Repton 1899 (as Repton and its neighbourhood).

Danvers, F. C. et al. Williams 1894. *See* Edinburgh Rev 27 1816, Quart Rev 179 1894.

Uppingham School Roll 1824–94. *See* Statutes of Robert Johnson, *above*.

Eardley Wilmot, E. P. and E. C. Streatfield. Charterhouse, old and new. 1895.

Fitzgerald, P. H. Stonyhurst memories. 1895.

Coleridge, A. D. Eton in the Forties, by an old Colleger. 1896, 1898 (2nd edn).

Watney, J. Some account of Mercers' School. 1896.

Garstang, J. A history of Blackburn Grammar School. 1897.

John, W. [Cory]. Extracts from the letters and journals of William Cory, selected by F. W. Cornish. Oxford 1897. On Eton 1832–42, 1845–72; King's College Cambridge 1842–5.

Matthews, J. H. D. and V. Thompson. Leeds Grammar School Register 1820–96. 1897.

Morley, S. R. Studies in London Board Schools. 1897.

Sedbergh School and its Chapel. Leeds 1897.

Ford, Lionel. Public School athletics. In Essays on secondary education, ed C. Cookson, Oxford 1888.

Holman, H. English national education. 1898.

Houson, E. W. and G. T. Warner. Harrow School. 1898.

Kingswood School: history, registers of Woodhouse Grove School, by three old boys. 1898.

Minchin, J. G. Old Harrow days. 1898.

Rouse, W. H. D. A history of Rugby School. New York 1898.

—— Our public schools, their influence on English history: Charterhouse, Eton, Harrow, Merchant Taylors, Rugby, St Paul's, Westminster, Winchester. 1901.

St Botolph Aldgate: the story of a City parish. Ed A. G. B. Atkinson 1898. On Sir John Cass School.

Sargeant, John. Annals of Westminster School. 1898.

Sterry, W. Annals of Eton College. 1898.

Barletot, R. G. History of Crewkerne School. 1899.

Benson, Arthur C. Fasti Etonenses: a biological history of Eton. Eton 1899.

Butler, Henry Montague. Public school sermons. 1899.

Cardwell, J. H. Story of a charity school in Soho. 1899.

Cust, L. A history of Eton College. 1899.

Fisher, G. W. Annals of Shrewsbury School. 1899.

Leach, Arthur Francis. A history of Winchester College. 1899.

—— Early Yorkshire Schools. 2 vols 1899–1903.

—— A history of Bradfield College, Oxford. 1900.

—— History of Warwick School. 1906.

— Educational charters and documents 598–1909. Cambridge 1911.
— The schools of medieval England. 1915. *See* Fortnightly Rev Nov 1892.
Lubbock, A. Memories of Eton and Etonians, with boys' chances at Eton by Robert Lubbock. 1899.
Meade, L. T. A public school boy. 1899.
Spalding, T. A. The work of the London School Board. 1899.
Mockler-Ferryman, A. F. Annals of Sandhurst: a chronicle of the Royal Military College, with a sketch of the history of the Staff College. 1900.
Tod, A. H. Charterhouse. 1900.
Warner, T. R. Winchester. 1900.

(3) ADULT AND TECHNICAL EDUCATION

Pole, Thomas. History of the origin and progress of Adult Schools. 1814, 1816 (enlarged).
Winks, J. F. History of Adult Schools. Gainsborough 1821. Only known copy in Leicester City Library.
Place, Francis. Improvement of the working people. 1834.
Baker, C. Mechanics' Institutes and Libraries. 1837 (Central Soc of Education, 1st pbn). *See* Quart Rev 32 1825.
Duppa, B. F. A manual for Mechanics' Institutes. 1839. *See* T. Coates, *below*.
Coates, T. Report on the state of Mechanics' Institutes. 1841. *See* R. B. Litchfield, Working Men's College Mag 1860.
Ellis, William. Education as a means of preventing destitution, with exemplications from the teaching of the conditions of well-being and the principles of economic science at the Birkbeck Schools. 1851.
Hudson, J. W. History of adult education. 1851. With reasons for decline of Mechanics' Institutes in some areas.
Hole, J. History and management of Literary, Scientific and Mechanics' Institutes. 1853.
Report of the Society of Arts on industrial instruction. 1853.
Maurice, F. D. Learning and working. 1853.
— On the representation and education of the People. 1866. *See* The Working Men's College 1854–1904, ed J. L. Davies 1904.
Fitzwyram, J. Introduction of industrial work into village schools: an experiment at Shipsbourne Kent. 1859.
Jones, H. B. The Royal Institution: its founder and its first professors. 1871.
Galloway, R. Education, scientific and technical. 1881.
Godard, J. G. George Birkbeck: the pioneer of popular education. 1884.
Edwards, F. W. Technical education: its rise and progress, including recommendations to the Royal Commission. 1885. *See* Quart Rev 165 1887.
— Industrial education. 1888.
— Commercial education, including a review of commercial schools on the Continent. 1889.
Magnus, Sir Philip. Industrial education. 1888.
Mackinder, H. J. and M. E. Sadler. University extension, past, present and future. 1891.
Roberts, R. D. Eighteen years of university extension. 1891.
Sexton, A. H. The first Technical College. 1894.
White, W. (of Edgbaston). Our Jubilee year 1895: the story of the Severn Street and Priory Firstday schools, Birmingham. 1895. *See* Memoirs of Joseph Sturge; Alexander Peckover, Life of Joseph Sturge in Memoirs, *below*.

(4) EDUCATION OF WOMEN AND GIRLS

Lackington, James. Confessions. 1804.
[More, Hannah]. Hints towards forming the character of a young Princess. 2 vols 1805. *See* Edinburgh Rev 7 1805.
Broadhurst, T. Advice to young ladies on the improvement of the mind. 1808. *See* Edinburgh Rev 15 1810.
Smith, Sydney. Female education. 1810.
West, J. Letters to a young lady. 3 vols 1811.
'Domina' [Barbara Hofland?]. York House: conversations in a Ladies' School, principally founded on facts. 1813.
Remarks on female education adapted particularly to the regulation of schools. 1823.
'An experienced teacher'. The complete governess: a course of mental instruction for ladies. 1826.
Broadhurst, F. A word in favour of female schools. Pamphleteer 27 1826.
Sinclair, C. Modern accomplishments or the march of intellect. 1836, 1837.
— Modern society: conclusion of Modern accomplishments. 1837.
[Duppa, B. F.] Scottish Institution for the education of young ladies. 1837 (Central Soc of Education, 1st pbn).
Ellis, Lady M. The education of young ladies for other occupations than teaching. 1838 (Central Soc of Education, 2nd pbn).
Maurice, J. F. D. Queen's College London: its object and method. 1848. *See* Quart Rev 84 1848, 86 1850.
— A letter to the Bishop of London in reply to the article in no 172 [96 1850] of the Quarterly Review. 1850.
— Plan of a female college. Cambridge 1855.
— Lectures to ladies on practical subjects. 1855. Introductory lecture.
Grey, Mrs W. and E. A. E. Shirreff. Thoughts on self-culture addressed to women. 2 vols 1850.
Parkes, B. R. Remarks on the education of girls. 1854.
Booth, James. On the female education of the industrious classes. 1855.
[Bülow, Baroness M. von]. Women's educational mission: an explanation of Froebel's infant gardens. 1855.
Shirreff, E. A. E. Intellectual education and its influence on women. 1858.
— The Kindergarten: principles of Froebel's system and their bearing on the education of women. 1876. *See* Mrs W. Grey, *below*.
Women's education. Edinburgh Rev 109 1859.
Cobbe, F. P. Female education and how it would be effected by university examinations. 1862 (Social Science Congress).
— Life as told by herself. 1904.
Davies, Emily. On secondary instruction relating to girls. 1864.
— The application of funds to the education of girls. 1865.
— Higher education of women. 1866.
— Women in the universities of England and Scotland. Cambridge 1896.
— Thoughts on some questions relating to women 1860–1908. 1910. *See* B. Stephen, Emily Davies and Girton College, 1927.
Fitch, Sir Joshua. The education of women. Victoria Mag March 1864.
— Address on the College for Working Women. 1872.
— Women and the universities. Contemporary Rev Aug 1890.
— Reports on women's training colleges. 1886–93.
Hodgson, William B. The education of girls considered in connexion with university local examinations: a lecture. 1864.

Ruskin, J. Queens' Gardens. In his Sesame and lilies, 1865.

Sewell, E. M. Principles of education applied to female education in the upper classes. 2 vols 1865, 1 vol 1914 (abridged).

Beale, Dorothea. On the education of girls. 1866 (Social Science Congress).

— Reports issued by the Schools Inquiry Commission on the education of girls. 1869.

— On the organisation of girls' day schools. 1873 (Social Science Congress).

— Work and play in girls' schools. 1898, 1901. With L. H. M. Soulsby and J. F. Dove.

— Addresses to teachers. 1908.

See Cheltenham Ladies' College Mag 1890–1.

Raikes, E. Dorothea Beale of Cheltenham (1831–1905). 1908.

Shillito, E. H. Dorothea Beale. 1920.

Steadman, F. C. In the days of Miss Beale: a study of her work and influence. 1931.

Clarke, A. K. A history of the Cheltenham Ladies' College [1853–1953]. 1953.

Airy, George B. The history and position of the Blue Coat Girls' School, Greenwich. 1867.

Hill, Florence D. Children of the state: the training of juvenile paupers. 1868; ed F. Fowke 1889. *See* Edinburgh Rev 142 1875.

— Education of girls and employment of women of the upper classes. 1869 (2nd edn).

Mill, John Stuart. The subjection of women. 1869. *See* Edinburgh Rev 130 1869.

Wolstenholme, E. C. The education of girls: its present and future. In J. E. Butler, Women's work and women's culture, 1869.

Grey, Mrs W. [Maria Georgina Grey, born Shirreff]. The education of women. 1871.

Fawcett, M. G. Free education in its economic aspect: Schools Inquiry Commission on the education of girls—education of women. In H. and M. G. Fawcett, Essays and lectures on social and political subjects, Cambridge 1872.

Gurney, M. Are we to have education for middle-class girls? the history of Camden Collegiate Schools. 1872.

Somerville, Mary. Personal recollections and selections from correspondence. 1873. *See* Quart Rev 136 1874.

Maudsley, H. Sex and mind on education. 1874.

Anderson, E. G. Sex in education: a reply. 1874. *See* Edinburgh Rev 166 1887.

Bryant, Sophie. An account of the North London Collegiate School. 1886. *See* Edinburgh Rev 166 1887.

Pfeiffer, E. Women and work: relation to health and physical development of the Higher Education. 1888.

Ridley, A. E. Frances Mary Buss and her work for education. 1895. *See* F. M. Buss, Leaves from her note-book, by S. G. Toplis 1896; and E. M. Hill and S. Bryant, Frances Mary Buss Schools' Jubilee Record, 1900.

Bremner, G. S. Education of girls and women in Great Britain. 1897.

Frances, E. G. Countess of Warwick et al. Progress in women's education in the British Isles. In Report of the education section, Victorian era exhibition 1897–8.

Zimmern, Alice. Renaissance of girls' education in England. 1898.

(5) OFFICIAL DOCUMENTS

Education Acts and Bills

England and Wales

Health, and morals of apprentices Act (Sir Robert Peel the elder). 1802.

Parochial schools Bill (Samuel Whitbread). 1807.

Factory Bill to extend the provisions of the Act of 1802 (Sir Robert Peel, the elder). 1815. The Bill in a modified form was accepted as an Act, 1819.

Parish schools Bill (Henry Brougham) 1820. Withdrawn.

Act to make further provisions for the regulation of Cotton Mills and Factories (Sir John Cam Hobhouse). 1825.

Factory Act (consolidating Act). 1831.

Reform Act. 1832.

University of Durham Act. 1832.

Education Bill (J. A. Roebuck). 1833.

Education Act [£20,000 per annum voted for building schools in Great Britain]. 1833.

Factory Act (Lord Ashley, later Earl of Shaftesbury). 1833.

Wood's Bill to open universities to Dissenters. 1834.

Act to facilitate the conveyance of sites for school rooms. 1836.

Grammar school Act. 1840.

School sites Act (to afford further facilities for the Conveyance and Endowment of sites for schools). 1841.

Mines regulation Act. 1842.

Factory Bill (Sir James Graham). 1843. Modified and accepted in 1844.

School sites Act (extending Act of 1841). 1844.

Education Bill (W. J. Fox). 1850.

Factory Act (restricting hours of employment of women and young persons). 1850.

School sites Act (to extend and explain the provisions of earlier Acts). 1849.

Act to amend the granting of sites for Schools. 1851.

Charitable Trusts Act. 1853.

Factory Act (further regulations for the employment of children in factories). 1853.

Oxford University Act. 1854.

The Literary and Scientific Institutions Act (to give greater facilities for procuring and settling sites and buildings in trust for institutions established for the promotion of literature, science, or the fine arts, or for the diffusion of useful knowledge). 1854.

Education Bill (Sir John Pakington). 1855.

Cambridge University Act. 1856.

Act appointing a Vice-President of the Council of Education (repealed by the Board of Education Act 1899). 1856.

Act to bring the employment of women, young persons and children in bleaching works and dyeing works under the regulations of the Factory Acts. 1860.

Act to prohibit the employment of women and children during the night in certain operations connected with bleaching by the open-air process. 1862.

Act to amend the above Act. 1863.

The Factory Acts Extension Act. 1867.

Workshops Regulation Act (restricting age of employment of children to the age of 13 and obliging attendance at school for at least ten hours a week). 1867.

Public schools Acts. 1868.

Endowed schools Act. 1869.

Elementary schools Act (W. E. Forster). 1870. *See* National Education Union: a verbatim report with indexes of the debates in Parliament during the progress of the Elementary Education Bill 1870, together with a reprint of the Act, 1870.

Factory and Workshop Act. 1870. Extension of earlier Acts.

Factory Act for Jews (restricting employment on Sundays). 1871.

Act to amend the Acts relating to factories and workshops. 1871.

University tests Act. 1871.

Metalliferous mines regulation Act (prohibiting employment of boys under twelve, or of any female, below ground). 1872.
Agricultural children Act (prohibiting employment of a child under ten unless he had attended 250 times at a certified school within twelve months; exemption granted to children who held a certificate of having passed the Fourth Standard). 1873.
Elementary education (amendment) Act. 1873.
Further Factory Act (repealing former Acts, fixing hours of employment of children and extending the obligation of school attendance). 1874.
Education Act (Lord Sandon). 1876.
Oxford and Cambridge Act. 1877.
The canal boats Act (securing the education of children on such boats). 1877.
Factory and workshop consolidation Act. 1878.
Elementary education (industrial schools) Act. 1879.
Act to make further provision as to bye-laws under the elementary education Acts (requiring every local authority to make bye-laws). 1880.
Education Act (Mr Mundella). 1880.
City parochial charities Act. 1883.
Factory and workshop Act (amendment Act). 1883.
Canal boats amendment Act. 1884.
Coal mines regulation Act (extension of previous regulations). 1887.
Mortmain and charitable uses Act. 1888.
Victoria University Act (to enable graduates of the Victoria University to hold offices where previously only graduates of Oxford, Cambridge or London were eligible). 1888.
Welsh intermediate education Act. 1889.
Education Code Act (permitting extension of the curriculum of evening schools and to make Parliamentary grants in certain cases). 1890.
Technical education Act. 1889.
Schools for science and art Act (to facilitate transfer of such institutions to the School Boards). 1891.
Mortmain and charitable uses Act amended. 1891.
Factory and workshop Act (employment of children raised to 11 years). 1891.
Free education Act (extra grants made to schools in which fees were abolished). 1891.
Technical and industrial institutions Act (freeing such public institutions from the operation of the Mortmain and charitable uses Act). 1892.
Elementary education (school attendance) Act (raising the leaving age to 12). 1893.
Elementary education blind and deaf children Act. 1893.
The prevention of cruelty to children Act (to prevent boys under 14 and girls under 16 from begging or receiving alms under pretence of singing, playing, performing or offering goods for sale). 1894.
Education Bill (Sir John Gorst). 1896.
School Board Conference Act (expense of travelling to conferences chargeable upon the rates). 1897.
Voluntary school Act (special grants to Voluntary schools, freeing them from the payment of rates). 1897.
Elementary school teachers (superannuation) Act. 1898.
University of London Act. 1898.
Board of education Act. 1899.
Elementary education (school attendance) Act (raising leaving age to 12). 1899.
Elementary education (amendment) Act (amending the Free education Act of 1891). 1900.
Mines regulation Act (prohibition of child labour underground). 1900.
University of Birmingham established by Act of Parliament. 1900.

Scotland

Most of the Factory Acts applied to Scotland.
Scottish education Act (James IV). 1496.
Education Act (Scotland) (fixing salaries). 1803.
Parochial schools Act. 1829.
Act for endowing schools in the Highlands. 1838.
University (Scotland) Act. 1858.
Parochial and burgh schoolmasters Act. 1861.
Education (Scotland) Act. 1872.
Act instituting the Scotch [later Scottish] Education Department. 1878.
Educational endowments Act. 1882.
Act reorganising the Scottish Education Department. 1885.
Universities (Scotland) Act. 1889.

Reports of Royal Commissions

England and Wales

Royal Commission to inquire into educational charities (Brougham). 1818–37; Report, 44 vols 1819–42.
State, discipline, studies and revenues of the University and colleges of Oxford. 2 pts 1852. *See* Edinburgh Rev 96 1852.
Documents relating to the University and colleges of Cambridge. 3 vols 1852.
State, discipline etc of Cambridge. 2 pts 1853.
On popular education in England (Newcastle Commission). 6 vols 1861. Including reports by J. Fraser, Matthew Arnold and M. Pattison. *See* Edinburgh Rev 114 1861; Inquiry into the truth of the report on the state of popular education in the County of Durham, Durham 1862.
To inquire into the revenues and management of certain colleges and schools, and the studies pursued (Public Schools or Clarendon Commission). 4 vols 1864. *See* Quart Rev 108 1860, 116 1864; Edinburgh Rev 120 1864.
Schools inquiry or Taunton Commission: to inquire into the education given in schools not comprised within the Commissions on popular education and on public schools 1864–8. Report, 21 vols 1868. Matthew Arnold, vol vi; *see* Quart Rev 126 1869.
Schools inquiry commission on technical education. 1867.
On scientific instruction and the advancement of science (Devonshire Commission). 10 pts 1870–5. Full information respecting the whole range of instruction in science.
Report of the Lord's Commission on safeguards for the maintenance of religious instruction and worship in Oxford, Cambridge and Durham. 4 pts 1870–1. *See* Edinburgh Rev 135 1872.
On the property and income of Oxford and Cambridge. 3 vols 1873.
On technical instruction. 5 vols 1882–4. Led to the Technical instruction Act, 1889.
On the working of the elementary education Acts (Cross Commission). 10 vols 1886–8. *See* Quart Rev 165 1887; Edinburgh Rev 180 1894. The Report led to the establishment of Day Training Colleges in universities and university colleges after 1890.
University of London (Selborne Commission). 1888–9.
University of London (Gresham Commission). 3 vols 1892–4.
On secondary education (Bryce Commission). 9 vols 1895. *See* Quart Rev 1897; Edinburgh Rev 185 1897. Eventually led to the Board of Education Act 1899, and to the Education Act 1902.

Scotland

Inquiry into Scottish universities. 1826.
State of universities and colleges of Scotland. 4 vols 1837. *See* Edinburgh Rev 59 1834.
Analysis and review: the universities of King's College and Marischal College, Aberdeen. 1839.
Inquiry into all types of schools in Scotland (Argyll Commission). 1867.
Inquiry into the endowed institutions in Scotland (Colebrooke Commission). 1872.
Scottish universities. 1876.

Reports other than those of Royal Commissions

Reports of the Society for bettering the conditions and increasing the comforts of the poor. 1797–1805. Leading supporters were Sir Thomas Bernard and Count Rumford. The reports contain the following dealing with English education:

44. Extracts from an account of the asylum or school of instruction for the blind at Liverpool by Sir Thomas Bernard;
50. Extracts from an account of a provision for chimney sweepers' boys at Kingston upon Thames, by the Bishop of Durham;
61. Extracts from an account of the benefits of the Charity Schools at Chester, by Sir Thomas Bernard;
64. Extracts from an account of the Mendip school by Sir Thomas Bernard;
89. Extracts from an account of the School of Industry at Kendal, by Sir Thomas Bernard, with a copy of the plan of instruction at the Kendal schools of industry;
97. Extracts from an account of the schools for poor children at Weston near Bath by Miss Masters;
100. Account of the Free-Chapel schools in West Street, Seven Dials, by John Dougan;
107. An account of the Ladies' Schools and some other Charities at Leeds, by Sir Thomas Bernard;
111. Account of a Sunday school at Kirkstall, Leeds by Mrs Carr;
112. Account of a school for poor children at Fincham;
118. Account of a School in the Borough Road, by John Walker;
121. Account of a school near Hawkstone in the County of Salop, by Sir Thomas Bernard.

Appendices to vol 4, 1805:

6. Statement as to the reception and management of the children in the Foundling Hospital, London;
10. Copy of the agreement signed by the parents of the children learning the Straw Platt in the West-street schools;
12. Copy of a proposal for an enquiry into the present state of the schools for the education of the poor.

Poor Law Commission: annual reports. 1835 etc. *See* Sir W. Chance, Children under the Poor Law, 1897.

Committee of Council on Education (annual reports and minutes of the Committee, 1839–40 to 1857–8). *See* Edinburgh Rev 75 1842, 97 1853.

Committee of Council on Education (annual reports and minutes of the Committee, 1839–40 to 1857–8). *See* Edinburgh Rev 75 1842, 97 1853.

— Report by H. Moseley. 1845.

— Report of inquiry into the state of education in Wales. 1847. *See* Edinburgh Rev 97 1853.

— Reports of Matthew Arnold on elementary schools 1852–82. Ed F. Sandford 1889, 1908 (enlarged).

— Revised instructions to HM Inspectors. 1897.

Baines, Sir Edward. Second Report, Congregational Board of Education. 1846.

The educational record of the British and Foreign School Society. 1848 etc. *See* H. B. Binns, A century of education: being the centenary history of the British and Foreign School Society 1808–1908, 1908.

Report of the Northamptonshire Society for promoting and extending education in accordance with the principles of the Established Church, embracing parochial, training, reformatory and middle schools. Northampton 1856–65.

Annual reports of the Catholic Poor School Committee. 1848 etc.

National Society Church School Inquiry (1856–7).

Education Department Reports. 1858–9, 1898–9.

— Special reports on educational subjects. Vol i, 1896, vol ii, 1897, vol iii, 1898, vol iv, 1900. With reports by M. E. Sadler and Robert Morant.

— Report on religious teaching in Board Schools. 1895. *See* Edinburgh Rev 180 1894.

Technical education in various countries: letter from B. Samuelson to the Vice-President of the Education Department. 1867.

Scientific instruction: report of committee of the British Association. 1867–8.

Chambers of Commerce on technical education: letter from J. Behrens. 1868.

Technical and primary education: circular to HM representatives abroad with replies. 1868.

National Education League: first general meeting, Birmingham, Oct 1869.

National Education Union: congress held in Manchester. 1869.

London School Board report by Professor Huxley on curriculum. 1871.

— First report. 1873.

— Final report. 1904 (rev).

See T. A. Spalding et al, The work of the London School Board, [1900].

International conference on education. 1884.

Report of a conference on secondary education held at Oxford. Oxford 1893.

Resolutions of the Bradford Independent Labour Party. 1893. These 2 reports led to the Bryce Commission, 1895.

Parliamentary Papers

Reports of a Select Committee to inquire into the education of the lower orders (Brougham's Committee). 12 pts 1816–18. *See* Quart Rev 19 1818, Edinburgh Rev 30–31 1818–9.

Education inquiry (1833–5) (Lord Kerry's return). 3 vols 1835. Many of the statistics were unreliable.

Committee on providing useful education for the poorer classes. 1838.

Manchester and Salford, educational facts and statistics: evidence before the House of Commons. *See* Edinburgh Rev 95 1852.

Report of Select Committee on education in Manchester and Salford, with evidence, appendices and index. 2 pts 1852–3. On voluntary system, religious and secular instruction.

Return relating to endowed grammar schools in England and Wales. 1865.

Technical education. House of Commons Reports 54 1867–8.

Select Committee on university tests. 1870.

(6) MEMOIRS

Trimmer, Sarah. Some account of her life and writings with original letters. 2 vols 1814.

Edgeworth, Richard Lovell. Memoirs, begun by himself and concluded by Maria Edgeworth. 2 vols 1820.

Clarke, Edward Daniel. Life and remains, by W. Otter. 2 vols 1825.

Murray, Lindley. Memoirs in letters written by himself. York 1826.

Parr, Samuel. Aphorisms, opinions and reflections of the late Dr Parr. Ed E.B.H. 1826.
— Parriana. Ed E. H. Barker 2 vols 1828–9.
Pestalozzi, J. H. Memoir by C. Mayo. 1828 (2nd edn). Lecture delivered in 1826.
Lancaster, Joseph. Epitome of events and transactions in his life, and rise and progress of the Lancasterian system, by himself. New Haven 1833.
Romilly, Sir Samuel. Memoirs with selection of his correspondence, edited by his sons. 3 vols 1840.
Arnold, Thomas. Life and correspondence, by A. P. Stanley. 1844. *See* Edinburgh Rev 81 1845.
Findlay, J. J. Arnold of Rugby: his school life and contributions to education. Cambridge 1897.
Fitch, J. G. Thomas and Matthew Arnold and their influence on education. 1897.
Selfe, S. G. F. Dr Arnold of Rugby. 1899.
Strachey, L. In his Eminent Victorians, 1918.
Whitridge, A. Arnold of Rugby. 1928.
Trilling, L. In his Matthew Arnold, New York 1939, 1955 (rev).
Wymer, N. Dr Arnold of Rugby. 1953. Contains letters, diaries and journals written by Dr Arnold, Mrs Arnold and friends, relations and pupils.
Bell, Andrew. Life, comprising the history of the system of mutual tuition, by R. and C. C. Southey. 3 vols 1844.
An old educational reformer, Andrew Bell, by J. M. D. Meiklejohn. Edinburgh 1881.
Cooper, Thomas Cooper's journal. 1850.
— Life of Thomas Cooper written by himself. 1872.
Copleston, Edward. Memoir with selections from his diary and correspondence, by W. I. Copleston. 1851.
Owen, Robert. Life written by himself, with selections from his writings and correspondence. 1857.
Podmore, F. Robert Owen. 2 vols 1906.
Cole, G. D. H. Robert Owen. 1925. Ch 8, Ideas on education.
Shelley, Percy Bysshe. Life, by T. J. Hogg. 4 vols 1858. *See col 309, above.* Syon House Academy; Eton 1804–10; Oxford 1810–11.
Hill, Thomas Wright. Remains, with notices of his life (1763–1851), by himself and M. D. Hill. 1859. Hill-Top School Birmingham. *See* The pupils of Hill-Top School, B 2, above.
William Sewell in Ireland. Quart Rev 108 1860.
Henslow, John Stevens. Memoir by L. Henyns (afterwards Blomefield). 1862.
Clough, Arthur Hugh. Letters and remains. 1865. Rugby 1829–36; Oxford 1837–48; University Hall London 1849–52. *See col 461, above.*
Lennox, Lord William Pitt. Drawn on my memory. 2 vols 1866. Westminster School 1808–14.
Dawes, Richard. Biographical notice by W. C. Henry. 1867.
Stow, David. Memoir by W. Fraser. 1868.
Pryme, George. Autobiographical recollections. Ed A. Bayne, Cambridge 1870.
Brougham, Henry (Baron). Life and times, written by himself. 3 vols Edinburgh 1871.
Mill, John Stuart. Autobiography. Ed Helen Taylor [his step-daughter] 1873; ed R. Howson, New York 1924 (from ms). *See* Bentham, *below*, Quart Rev 136 1874, *and col 1551, above.*
Owen, Robert Dale. Threading my way. 1874.
Lovett, William. Life and struggles of William Lovett in pursuit of bread, knowledge and freedom, by himself. 1876.
Macaulay, Thomas Babington (Baron). Life and letters, by G. O. Trevelyan. 2 vols 1876. Trinity College Cambridge 1818–24.
Denison, George A. Notes of my life 1805–78. Oxford 1878, 1879.
— Middle class schools and the conscience clause. Oxford 1883.
Whewell, William. Life and correspondence, by Mrs Stair Douglas. 1881. Cambridge 1812–66, Master of Trinity College 1841–66.
Hodgson, William B. Life and letters, by J. M. D. Meiklejohn. 1883.
Birkbeck, George. Memoir and review, by J. G. Godard. 1884.
Maurice, Frederick Denison. Life, chiefly told in his own letters. Ed F. Maurice 2 vols 1884.
Pattison, Mark. Memoirs. 1885.
Froebel, Friedrich W. A. Autobiography. Tr E. Michaelis and H. K. Moore 1886.
Jevons, W. Stanley. Letters and journals, edited by his wife. 1886. University College School 1850–1; University College London 1851, 1859–80.
Fraser, James. Second Bishop of Manchester 1818–85, by Thomas Hughes QC 1887.
Bradshaw, Henry. Memoir, by G. W. Prothero. 1888. Eton 1843–50; King's College Cambridge 1850; University Librarian 1875–86.
Thomas Poole and his friends, by Mrs Henry Sandford. 2 vols 1888.
Rogers, W. Reminiscences compiled by R. H. Hadden. 1888.
Ellis, William. Life and some account of his writings for the improvement of education, by E. K. Blyth. 1889.
Forster, William Edward. Life, by T. Wemyss Reid. 1889.
Greton, F. E. Memory's harkback through half-a-century 1808–58. 1889. Shrewsbury 1814; Cambridge 1822.
Thring, Edward. A memory, by H. Skrine. 1889.
— Teacher and poet, by H. D. Rawnsley. 1889.
— Life, diary and letters, by Sir G. R. Parkin. 2 vols 1898, 1900 (abridged). *See* Quart Rev 187 1898.
Toynbee, Arnold. F. C. Montague and P. L. Gell, in Johns Hopkins University studies, Baltimore 1889. On Toynbee Hall.
Milnes, Richard Monckton (Baron Houghton). Life, letters and friendships, by T. Wemyss Reid. 2 vols 1890.
Peel, Sir Robert. From private papers and correspondence, by C. S. Parker. 3 vols 1891–9. Harrow 1801–4; Oxford 1805–8.
Sedgwick, Adam. Life and letters, by J. W. Clark and T. M. Hughes. Cambridge 1890. *See* Quart Rev 172 1891.
Tait, Archibald Campbell, Archbishop of Canterbury. Life, by R. T. Davidson and W. Benham. 2 vols 1891. Edinburgh High School and Academy 1821–7; Glasgow University 1827–30; Oxford 1830–42; Rugby 1842–50; Oxford University Commission 1850 etc.
Wordsworth, Charles. Annals of my early life 1806–46. 1891. Harrow, Oxford, Winchester.
— Annals of my life 1846–56. Ed W. E. Hodgson 1893. Trinity College; Glenalmond 1846–54.
Butler, George. Recollections 1819–90, by Josephine E. Butler. Bristol 1892. Harrow, Cambridge, Oxford, Durham, Liverpool.
Manning, Cardinal, by A. W. Hutton. 1892. Voluntary schools, ch 7.
— Life, by E. S. Purcell. 2 vols 1895. Harrow 1822–6; Oxford 1827–30. Vol 1, the Voluntary Schools in mid-century; vol 2, Education Act 1870; University College Kensington.
Lowe, Robert (Viscount Sherbrooke). Life and letters, by A. P. Martin. 2 vols 1893.
Stanley, Arthur Penrhyn, by R. E. Prothero and G. G. Bradley. 1893. Rugby 1829–34; Oxford 1834–63.
Hill, Frederic. An autobiography of fifty years in time of reforms. Ed C. Hill 1894.
Widgery, William Henry, schoolmaster, by W. K. Hill. 1894.
Freeman, Edward Augustus. Life and letters, by W. R. W. Stephens. 2 vols 1895. Cheam 1837–9; private tutor 1839–41; Oxford 1841; Regius Professor 1884–92.

Jowett, Benjamin. A personal memoir, by Lionel A. Tollemache. [1895].
— Life and letters, by E. Abbott and L. Campbell. 2 vols 1897.
Stephen, Sir James Fitzjames. Life, by L. Stephen. 1895. Eton 1842–5; King's College London 1845–7; Cambridge 1847–51. On the 'Apostles'.
Butler, Samuel. Life and letters, by Samuel Butler [his grandson]. 2 vols 1896. *See* Quart Rev 187 1898, *and col 1406, above.*
Hare, Augustus J. C. The story of my life. 6 vols 1896–1900. Harrow 1847–8; Oxford 1853–7.
Hawtrey, Edmund Craven. Headmaster and afterwards Provost of Eton, by F. St J. Thackeray. 1896. *See* Quart Rev 187 1898.
Lee, Samuel. A scholar of a past generation: a brief memoir of Samuel Lee, by A. M. Lee. 1896.
Palmer, Roundell (Earl of Selborne). Memorials. 2 vols in 4 pts 1896–8. Rugby 1823–5; Winchester 1825–30; Oxford 1830–7. University tests and Education Act 1870 in vol 1 pt 2; Oxford reform 1854 in vol 2 pt 2.
Clough, Anne Jemima. A memoir, by B. A. Clough. 1897. First Principal of Newnham College, Cambridge.
Cory [Johnson], William. Extracts from his letters and journals. Ed F. W. Cornish, Oxford 1897. Eton 1832–42.
Roebuck, John Arthur. Life and letters. Ed R. E. Leader 1897.
Benson, Edward White, Archbishop of Canterbury. By A. C. Benson. 2 vols 1899. Wellington College.
Gladstone, William Ewart. Life. Ed T. Wemyss Reid 1899. Eton and Christ Church Oxford, by A. F. Robbins; Oxford Union Society, by F. W. Hirst; Gladstone as scholar, by A. J. Butler.
— Life, by John Morley. 3 vols 1903. Vol 1, Eton 1821–7; Oxford 1828–31.
Liddell, Henry George. A memoir, by H. L. Thomson. 1899. Head Master, Westminster 1846–55; Dean of Christ Church, Oxford 1853–5.
Morris, William. Life, by J. W. Mackail. 2 vols 1899. Marlborough 1848–51; Exeter College Oxford 1853–5.
Playfair, Lyon. Memoirs and correspondence, by T. Wemyss Reid 1899.
Quick, Robert Herbert. Life and remains by F. Storr. 1899.
Brodrick, G. C. Memoirs and impressions 1831–1900. 1900. Balliol and Merton Colleges Oxford.
Huxley, Thomas Henry. Life and letters, by L. Huxley. 2 vols 1900.
Pearson, Charles Henry. Memorial by himself, his wife and his friends. Ed W. Stebbing 1900.
Besant, Sir Walter. An autobiography. 1902. Cambridge and the People's Palace.
Bowen, Edward Ernest. Memoir with essays, songs and verses, by W. E. Bowen. 1902. King's College London 1852–4; Harrow 1859–1901.
Acland, Sir Thomas Dyke. Memoir and letters. Ed A. H. D. Acland 1903.
Bain, Alexander. An autobiography. 1904.
Spencer, Herbert. An autobiography. 2 vols 1904.

S. J. C.

XV. NEWSPAPERS AND MAGAZINES

A. Technical development: Advertising; Management and distribution; Wages and conditions; Techniques of journalism.

B. The history of journalism: Memoirs and biographies of individual journalists, newspaper proprietors and publishers; The general history of the press; Lists of newspapers.

C. The daily and weekly press. The daily papers: London morning papers; London evening papers; Provincial daily papers; Scottish daily papers; Irish daily papers; London papers published more than once a week. The weekly papers: Sunday papers; General weekly papers; Illustrated papers; Unstamped and radical journals; Weekly literary reviews; Religious papers; Agricultural papers; Financial and commercial papers; Sporting papers; Humorous papers; Juvenile papers; Miscellaneous specialized papers; Accounts and studies of individual papers.

D. Magazines and reviews: Monthly magazines; Quarterly magazines; Accounts and studies of magazines and reviews.

E. School and university journalism.

F. Annuals and yearbooks.

A. TECHNICAL DEVELOPMENT

See also under Book Production and Distribution, col 25, above.

(1) ADVERTISING

Besides the returns of the Advertisement Duty (repealed in 1853) here listed, others issued together with the Stamp Duty will be found in col 1785 below. Important information may also be gleaned from the introductory matter to the Newspaper Advertisement Agents' Directories listed below.

[House of Commons: accounts and papers]. Abstract of account of sums paid for advertisements and proclamations in newspapers by the public offices. (470) xix 559 1822.
[House of Commons: accounts and papers]. Ireland: return of sums paid by the Stamp Office for advertisements. (588) xviii 465 1822.
[House of Commons: accounts and papers]. Amount of duty paid for advertisements by each provincial newspaper in England. (524) xxxii 617 1833.
[House of Commons: accounts and papers]. Ireland: sums paid by each newspaper in Ireland for stamps 1832–3, distinguishing sums paid for paper from those paid for advertisements. (658) xxxii 625 1833.
[House of Commons: accounts and papers]. Ireland: sums paid by the Irish Government to each newspaper in Ireland 1832–3, distinguishing sums paid to each for advertisements; duty or services for which paid, etc. (633) xxxii 629 1833.
[House of Commons: accounts and papers]. Number of advertisements which appeared in each of the newspapers published in London, 1831 to 1834; amount of duty paid by each during the period above-mentioned. (108) xxxvii 703 1835.
[House of Commons: accounts and papers]. Ireland: advertisement duty assessed on each paper in Ireland, 1834; sums paid monthly by each paper; arrears due for advertisement duty, Jan 5 1835. (265) xxxvii 695 1835.

Knight, C. Advertisements. In his London, 1843.
The advertising system. Edinburgh Rev 77 1843.
A guide to advertisers. 1852 (5 edns).
Advertisements. Quart Rev 97 1855.
Smith, W. Advertise: how? when? where? 1863.
Sampson, H. A history of advertising. 1874.
[Nicoll, D.] Publicity: an essay on advertising, by an adept of 35 years' experience. 1878.
Smith's advertising agency. T. Smith and J. H. Osborne, Successful advertising: its secrets explained. 1878, 1896 (17th edn), 1900 (20th edn), 1928.
Clay, A. The agony column of the Times 1800–70. 1881.
Sell, H. The philosophy of advertising. 1882. Later Sell's dictionary of the world's press.
Sinclair, A. Fifty years of newspaper life 1845–95. [c. 1897] (priv ptd).
Palmer, H. J. The march of the advertiser. Nineteenth Century Jan 1897.
Smith, T. 21 years in Fleet Street. 1899.
Stead, W. T. The art of advertising. 1899.
Street, E. and L. Jackson. Advertising. Jnl of Royal Soc of Arts 24 Jan 1913.
'On the road' one hundred years ago. Ed J. Cannon, Publishers' Circular 9 Feb–13 April 1935.
Roll call 1910. Statistical review of press advertising. April 1935. A chronological list of advertising agents.
Mansfield, F. J. The story of the advertiser. Journalist 21 1938.
Agents who used the provincial press 100 years ago. Newspaper World 12 Sept 1942.
Aspinall, A. Statistical accounts of the London newspapers 1800–36. EHR 65 1950. Advertisement duty returns.
Turner, E. S. The shocking history of advertising. 1953.
Elliott, B. B. A history of English advertising. 1962. Contains a section on the trade press.
Smyth, A. L. Youde's billposting journal. Manchester Rev 10 1963. Publicity for an attempt to monopolize bill-posting in Manchester in 1897.

Periodicals

The newspaper press directory. 1846, 1847, 1851 (3rd edn), 1854 (4th edn), 1856 (5th edn), 1857, 1858, 1859, 1860 onwards. Ed C. Mitchell 1846–59, W. Wellsman 1859–97. Annual.
The advertisers' guardian. no. 2 1855, No 4 1887–8, no 5 1889–90, 1891. [no more until] 1900, 1902. Ed. L. Collins to 1891, T. Dixon 1900–2. Annual.
Successful advertising. 1885 (7th edn), 1886, 1887, 1902 (21st edn), 1928 (Jubilee edn). Ed T. Smith 1885–6, T. Smith and J. H. Osborne 1887. Annual.
The advertising register. Nos 1–54, 12 Nov 1886–7 Oct 1887. Weekly.
The advertisers' ABC of official scales & charges. [1886], 1931 (45th annual issue). Ed T. B. Browne 1888–9. Annual.
Advertising. No 1, Oct 1891–Jan 1914. Ed J. H. Osborne. Monthly.
The advertisers' monthly circular. Nos 1–7, Jan–Nov 1895.
Advertising notes. No 1 Jan–Dec 1898. Continued as Profitable advertising, Jan 1899–Dec 1904. Monthly.
The advertiser's journal. No 1, June 1898.
The advertiser's review. No 1, 8 April 1899–24 Dec 1904. Incorporated in Advertising news, nos 1–66, 5 Feb 1904–Nov–Dec 1905. Amalgamated with Progressive advertising and outdoor publicity nos 1–13, 25 Oct 1901–Aug 1909.
Modern advertising. Nos 1–4, June 1900–April 1901.
Newspaper and poster advertising. Nos 1–58, 28 July 1900–21 Dec 1901. Incorporated in Advertiser's review, *above*.

(2) MANAGEMENT AND DISTRIBUTION

The commercial history of a penny magazine. Penny Mag Sept–Dec 1833.
[Grant, J.] Travels in town by the author of Random recollections. 2 vols 1839. Chs 7–8.
The bringing forth of the daily newspaper. Chambers's Jnl 26 Aug 1854.
King, H. Four and twenty hours in a newspaper office. Once a Week 26 Sept 1863, 6 Feb 1864.
Philbrick, F. A. and W. A. S. Westoby. The postage and telegraph stamps of Great Britain. 1881.
Sidman, W. A treatise on newspaper book-keeping. 1887.
Yeo, H. Newspaper management. Manchester 1891.
Maxwell, H. The life and times of the Rt Hon W. H. Smith MP. 2 vols Edinburgh 1893.
Newnes, George, Ltd. How popular periodicals are produced. [1894].
Norton, B. T. and G. T. Feasey. Newspaper accounts: being a practical treatise on the books and accounts in use in large and small newspaper offices. 1895.
Harmsworth, A. C. (Viscount Northcliffe). Making a modern newspaper: some secrets revealed. Harmsworth's Mag July 1898.
[Hepworth, T. C.] All about a London daily from the paper mill to the breakfast table. [1898].
Haywood, A. and Son. 1832–1899: a brief survey of the news trade. Manchester 1899.
Special newspaper trains, by Brunel Redivivus. Railway Mag Nov 1899.
Courtney, L. H. The making and reading of newspapers. 1901.
Ewen, H. L'E. Unadhesive postage stamps of the United Kingdom. 1905.
—— Newspaper and parcel stamps issued by the railway companies of the United Kingdom. 1906.
Given, J. L. Making a newspaper. 1913.
Pocklington, G. R. The story of W. H. Smith and Son. 1921, 1932 (rev F. K. Foat) (priv ptd).
Kitchin, F. H. Moberly Bell and his times. 1925.
Bell, E. H. C. M. The life and letters of C. F. Moberly Bell. 1927.
Aspinall, A. The circulation of newspapers in the early nineteenth century. RES 22 1946. On reading-rooms, the hiring-out of papers etc.
Colby, R. A. That he who rides may read: W. H. Smith and Son's railway library. Wilson Lib Bull 27 1952.
Bell, R. F. Gordon and Gotch, London: the story of the G. and G. century 1853–1953. 1953.
Haig, R. L. Circulation of some London newspapers, 1806–11: two documents. SB 7 1955.
Wadsworth, A. P. Newspaper circulations 1800–1954. Trans Manchester Statistical Soc 1955.
Chilston, Viscount. W. H. Smith. 1965.

Periodicals

The newsmen's weekly chronicle. Nos 1–7, 2 July–13 Aug 1837.
The newsvendor. No 1, Jan 1873–21 Feb 1883. Weekly after first 9 nos.
The newsagent and advertisers' record. Nos 1–15, July 1889–Dec 1890. Continued as Newsagent and booksellers' review, vol 4, no 1–vol 102, no 13, 31 Jan 1891–30 March 1940. Continued as News and book trade review and stationers' gazette, vol 102, no 14–vol 61, no 17, 6 April 1940–29 April 1950. Continued as Newsagents', booksellers' review and stationers' gazette, vol 61, no 18–vol 67, no 30, 6 May 1950–28 July 1956. Continued as Retail newsagent, bookseller and stationer, vol 67 no 31, 4 Aug 1956 onwards.

The newsagents' chronicle. Nos 1–75, 16 Feb 1895–26 Feb 1898. Fortnightly.

The newspaper owner and manager. 5 Jan 1898–11 Oct 1899. Continued as Newspaper owner and modern printer, 18 Oct 1899–20 May 1903. Continued as Master printer and newspaper owner, 27 May 1903–1 April 1905. Continued as The newspaper owner, 8 April 1905–28 June 1913. Continued as Newspaper world, 5 July 1913–28 Dec 1935. Continued as Newspaper world and advertising review, 4 Jan 1936–12 March 1953. Weekly. Prop and ed C. Baker.

Early days of the Newspaper world. Newspaper World 3 Jan 1948.

(3) WAGES AND CONDITIONS

The earlier portion of the Library of the London Society of Compositors is deposited at the St Bride Foundation.

Memorial of London Compositors addressed to proprietors of newspapers with a report of a meeting of the employers. [1809].

London Union of Compositors. The London scale of prices for compositors' work: agreed upon April 16th 1810, with explanatory notes, and the scales of Leeds, York, Dublin, Belfast and Edinburgh. [c. 1835] (4 edns).

London Trade Society of Compositors. Report of a committee appointed to draw up a statement of the regular mode of working on newspapers. 1820.

London Union of Compositors. Report of the proceedings of the delegated meeting of compositors, Dec 12 1833. [1833].

London Union of Compositors. Report of the General Trade Committee to the Compositors of London, March 4 & 11 1834. [1834].

London Union of Compositors. Report of the Trade Council on the mode of working the Times newspaper. [1835].

London Society of Compositors. Report of the journeymen members of the conference of master printers and compositors held in 1847. 1847, [1875], [1879], [1883].

London Association of Master Printers. The agreements made with the compositors, pressmen and machine-minders in Nov 1866. 1867.

London Society of Compositors. Report of the Special Committee appointed to revise the trade rules, examine the system of working in each office and frame a report upon the evidence that may come before them. 1868.

London Society of Compositors. Rules and regulations for news work. [1868].

Manchester Typographical Society. Regulations for piece-work on daily papers. Manchester 1873.

London Society of Compositors. Report of the Special Committee appointed to consider the best means for improving the conditions of newspaper compositors. 1874.

Glasgow Typographical Society. Newspaper time and piece scales of prices. Glasgow 1884.

The Vigilance Gazette: a monthly journal devoted to the interests of the London Society of Compositors. Nos 1–11 May 1888–May 1890. Continued as London printers' circular.

London Society of Compositors. News department: workmen's memorial to the newspaper proprietors. 1889.

London Society of Compositors. Fair and unfair religious and temperance weekly newspapers. 1890.

London Printing and Allied Trades Association. The London scale of prices for compositors' work. 1891.

London Society of Compositors. News department: report of the committee on the system of working in each office. 1891. Supplementary report of 1891 presented 11 Nov 1891.

The Institute of Journalists, by an old journalist. Nat Rev Oct 1892.

The Institute of Journalists. Proceedings. 1892–1912. Quarterly.

Society of Women Journalists. Annual report. [1894–5?]–1897–8–1914–15 (21st annual report)–?

London Society of Compositors. Rates and rules for working composing machines in London, agreed upon between representatives of the London newspapers and master printers and of the London Society of Compositors. 1896.

Dickson, J. J. Manchester Typographical Society and Branch of the Typographical Association centenary 1797–1897. Manchester 1897.

London Society of Compositors. Jubilee. A brief record of events prior to and since 1848. Ed C. W. Bowerman 1898.

Glasgow Typographical Society. Scale of prices for the working of composing machines in newspaper offices. Glasgow 1898.

The economic position of women in journalism, by a woman journalist. Humanitarian July 1900.

London Association of Correctors of the Press. Jubilee. 1854–1904. [1904].

MacDonald, J. R. Women in the printing trades: a sociological study, with a preface by F. Y. Edgeworth. 1904.

Murasken, E. Newswriters' unions in English-speaking countries. New York 1938.

Fifty years of Institute leadership. Inst of Journalists Jnl 27 1939.

Keefe, H. J. A century in print: the story of Hazell's 1839–1939. 1939.

Taylor, H. A. Through fifty years. Inst of Journalists Jnl 28 1940.

Howe, E. Newspaper printing in the nineteenth century. 1943.

—— The trade: passages from the literature of the printing craft 1550–1935. 1943.

—— The London compositor: documents relating to wages, working conditions and customs of the London printing trade 1785–1900. 1947 (Bibl Soc).

—— and H. E. Waite. The London Society of Compositors. 1948.

Hutchinson, W. The printer's devil: an account of the history and objects of the Printers' Pension Corporation. 1943.

Aspinall, A. The social status of journalists at the beginning of the nineteenth century. RES 21 1945.

Clowes, W. B. Family business 1803–1953. 1953.

(4) TECHNIQUES OF JOURNALISM

[Whitefoord, C.] Advice to the editors of newspapers. 1799.

[Copleston, E.] Advice to a young reviewer, with a specimen of the art. Oxford 1807.

Conder, J. Reviews reviewed: including an enquiry into the moral and intellectual effects of habits of criticism, and their influence on the general interests of literature; to which is subjoined a brief history of the periodical reviews published in England and Scotland by T. C. O'Reid. Oxford 1811.

Journalism. Westminster Rev 18 1833.

The newspapers. Metropolitan Mag Jan 1833.

Hughes, T. Anonymous journalism. Macmillan's Mag Dec 1861.
[Morley, J.] Anonymous journalism. Fortnightly Rev Sept 1867.
[House of Commons]. Special Report from the Select Committee on the Electric Telegraphs Bill. 1868.
Reed, T. A. The reporter's guide. 1869.
Modern newspaper enterprise. Fraser's Mag June 1876.
Whittaker, S. Parliamentary reporting in England, foreign countries and the colonies. Manchester 1877.
[House of Commons]. Report from the Select Committee on Parliamentary reporting. 1878.
Bussey, H. F. and T. W. Reid. The newspaper reader: the journals of the 19th century on the events of the day. 1879.
[House of Lords]. Report from the Select Committee on Parliamentary reporting. 1880.
Reade, A. A. Literary success: being a guide to practical journalism. [1880].
Davies, E. P. The reporter's handbook. 1884.
Dawson, J. Practical journalism. 1885.
Pendleton, J. Newspaper reporting in olden times and today. 1890.
—— How to succeed as a journalist. 1902.
Russell, P. The author's manual: a complete and practical guide to all branches of literary work. [1891].
Mackie, J. B. Modern journalism. 1894.
[Humboldt, W.] The compleat leader writer. Macmillan's Mag Sept 1894.
Phillips, E. How to become a journalist. 1895.
Baines, F. E. Forty years at the Post Office. 2 vols 1895.
Smith, L. A. Women's work in the London and provincial press. Newspaper Press Directory 1897.
Bennett, E. A. Journalism for women: a practical guide. 1898.
Kingston, A. Pitman's guide to journalism. 1898, 1904.
An Editor. How to write for the press: a practical handbook for beginners in journalism. 1899, 1904 (rev).
Lawrence, A. Journalism as a profession. 1903.
Wellcome, H. S. The evolution of journalism. 1909.
MacDonagh, M. The Reporters' Gallery. [1913].
Salmon, L. M. The newspaper and the historian. New York 1923.
Coronation reporting a century ago. Newspaper World 22 May 1937.
Mansfield, F. J. Social and Personal. Journalist 20 1937. On the rise of gossip and the 'personal column' as a newspaper staple.
Pollard, H. G. Novels in newspapers: some unpublished letters of Captain Mayne Reid. RES 18 1942. On syndication.
Maurer, O. Anonymity vs signature in Victorian reviewing. SE 27 1948.
Jump, J. D. Weekly reviewing in the eighteen-fifties. RES 24 1948.
—— Weekly reviewing in the eighteen-sixties. RES new ser 3 1952.
Snyder, L. and R. B. Morris. A treasury of great reporting. New York 1949.
Mathews, J. J. The genesis of newspaper war correspondence. Journalism Quart 29 1952.
Watson, M. R. Magazine serials and the essay tradition 1746–1820. Baton Rouge 1956. Includes a list of essay serials.
Fielding, K. J. The weekly serialisation of Dickens's novels. Dickensian 54 1958.
—— Monthly serialisations of Dickens's novels. Ibid.

Periodicals

London, provincial and colonial press news. No 1, 15 Jan 1866–Dec 1912. Ed C. W. Dorrington. Monthly.
The newspaper press. No 1, 1 Dec 1866–1 July 1872. Incorporated in Printers' register. Ed A. Andrews. Monthly.
The Fleet Street gazette: a journeyman's journal. Nos 1–7, 28 Feb–23 May 1874. Fortnightly.
The journalist: an illustrated phonographic magazine. Nos 1–21 Nov 1879–July 1881. Ed H. R. Evans. Monthly.
The journalist. No 1, 15 Oct 1886–May 1909.
Journalism. Nos 1–11, Nov 1887–Feb 1889.

Press Agencies

Whorlow, H. The Provincial Newspaper Society. 1886.
Hunt, W. Then and now. Hull 1887. With details on the Central Press and the Central News.
The Press Association. Chambers's Jnl Aug 1897.
The National Press Agency. Our silver anniversary 1873–1898. 1898.
Jones, R. International telegraphic news: a lecture at the University of London 23 May 1921. 1921.
—— News agencies and their work: address to the International Congress of the Press 6 July 1927. 1927.
Collins, M. H. From pigeon post to wireless. 1925. A history of Reuters'.
Pillars of the press. World's Press News June–July 1929. 4 articles on press agencies.
Central News Agency. Diamond jubilee souvenir. 1931.
D[avies], E. W. The Newspaper Society 1836–1936. 1936.
When telegraph companies collected and distributed news. Newspaper World 25 Feb 1939 (Press Assoc).
Storey, G. Reuters' century 1851–1951. 1951. *See* World's Press News 6–13 July 1951.

B. THE HISTORY OF JOURNALISM

For further information on policy and achievements of individual journalists, editors and proprietors, see the sections dealing with the histories and studies of the appropriate journals, below. Many biographical studies of journalists are to be found in The newspaper press directory *and in* The world's press news.

(1) MEMOIRS AND BIOGRAPHIES OF INDIVIDUAL JOURNALISTS, NEWSPAPER PROPRIETORS AND PUBLISHERS

À Beckett, A. W. (1844–1909: Punch)
The à Becketts of Punch. 1903.
The recollections of a humorist. 1907.
À Beckett, Gilbert (1811–56: Punch). *See col 1143, above.*
Adams, W. E. (b. 1832: Newcastle Weekly Chronicle)
Memoirs of a social atom. 2 vols 1903.
Ainsworth, William Harrison (1805–82: Ainsworth's Mag; Bentley's Miscellany; New Monthly Mag). *See col 911, above.*
Aird, A.
Reminiscences of editors, reporters and printers during the last sixty years. Glasgow 1890.
Alford, Henry (1810–71: Contemporary Rev). *See col 501, above.*
Allingham, William (1824–89: Fraser's Mag). *See col 502, above.*
Allon, Henry. (1818–92: British Quart Rev)
Letters to a Victorian editor. Ed A. Peel 1929.
Annand, James (1843–1906: Newcastle Daily Leader)

Hodgson, G. B. From smithy to senate: the life story of James Annand, journalist and politician. 1908.

Appleton, Charles E. C. B. (1841–79: Academy)
Appleton, J. H. and A. H. Sayce. Dr Appleton, his life and literary relics. 1881.

Arnold, William T. (1852–1904).
Ward, M. A. and C. E. Montague. William Thomas Arnold, journalist and historian. Manchester 1907.

Austin, Alfred (1835–1913: Nat Rev). *See col 608, above.*
Crowell, N. B. Alfred Austin, Victorian. Albuquerque 1953.

Bagehot, Walter (1826–77: Economist). *See col 1368, above.*
Buchan, A. The spare chancellor: the life of Bagehot. 1959.
Tener, R. H. and N. St J. Stevas. Bagehot and Bailey. TLS 8 Feb 1963.

Baines, Edward (1774–1848: Leeds Mercury)
Baines, E. The life of Baines by his son. 1851.

Baldwin, Charles (1774–1869: Standard)
Register & Mag of Biography April 1869. Memoir.

Baldwin, Walter (Clapham Observer)
Mursell, A. and C. Woods. Walter Baldwin. 1903.

Barclay, Thomas (b. 1853: Times)
Thirty years 1876–1906: Anglo-French reminiscences. 1914.

Barmby, J. Goodwin (1820–81: Promethean)
Armytage, W. H. G. The journalistic activities of J. Goodwin Barmby. N & Q April 1956.

Barnes, Thomas (1785–1841: Times)
Blunden, E. Thomas Barnes (1785–1841): Literary diversions of an editor. TLS 10 May 1941.
— Thomas Barnes. TLS 3 Aug 1946. *See also* 24 Aug and 5 Oct 1946.
Hudson, D. Thomas Barnes of the Times. Cambridge 1943.
Parker, W. M. Thomas Mitchell and Thomas Barnes. TLS 27 May 1944.
Aspinall, A. Thomas Barnes to Brougham: from friends to foes. TLS 27 July 1946. *See also* 7 Sept 1946.

Beatty-Kingston, William (1837–1900: Daily Telegraph)
A journalist's jottings. 2 vols 1890.
Men, cities and events. 1895.

Beeton, Samuel (1831?–77: Englishwoman's Domestic Mag; Boy's Own Jnl etc)
Spain, N. Mrs Beeton and her husband. 1948.
Hyde, H. M. Mr and Mrs Beeton. 1951.

Bell, John (1745–1831: Bell's Weekly Messenger)
Morison, S. John Bell. Cambridge 1930 (priv ptd).

Bell, John Browne (1779–1855: News of the World)
Berrey, R. P. The romance of a great newspaper. [c. 1933].

Bell, George (1814–90: Aunt Judy's Mag; N & Q etc)
Bell, E. George Bell, publisher. 1924 (priv ptd).

Bentley, Richard (1786–1860: Bentley's Miscellany; Temple Bar)
Gettmann, R. A. A Victorian publisher: a study of the Bentley papers. Cambridge 1960.

Bertram, J. G.
Some memories of books, authors and events. Westminster 1893.

Besant, Annie (1847–1933: National Reformer (1860), Link, Theosophist)
Nethercot, A. H. The first five lives of Annie Besant. 1961.
— The last four lives of Annie Besant. 1963.

Besant, Walter (1836–1901). *See col 1036, above.*
Autobiography. Ed S. Sprigge 1902.

Black, William (1841–98). *See col 1038, above.*
Reid, W. William Black, novelist: a biography. 1902.

Blanchard, E. L. Laman (1820–89: Chambers's London Jnl; Daily Telegraph etc). *See col 1145, above.*
Life and reminiscences. Ed C. Scott and C. Howard 1891.

Blanchard, Samuel Laman (1804–45: True Sun; Court Jnl; Courier; etc). *See col 510, above.*
Sketches from life; with a memoir of the author by Sir Edward Bulwer Lytton. 3 vols 1846.
Poetical works; with a memoir by Blanchard Jerrold. 1876.

Blatchford, Robert (1851–1943: Clarion)
My eighty years. 1931.
Thompson, L. Robert Blatchford: portrait of an Englishman. 1951.

Blowitz, Henri Stefan de (1832–1903: Times)
My memoirs. 1903.
Giles, F. A prince of journalists: the life and times of Henri Stefan Opper de Blowitz. 1962.
Mullen, T. E. Henri de Blowitz: the foreign correspondent and international affairs. Emory Univ Quart 21 1965.

Blumenfeld, Ralph D. (b. 1864: Daily Express)
R.D.B.'s diary 1887–1914. 1930.

Bodkin, M. M'. D. (b. 1850)
Recollections of an Irish judge. 1914.

Boon, John (1859–1928: Exchange Telegraph Co)
Victorians, Edwardians and Georgians: the impressions of a veteran journalist extending over forty years. 2 vols 1928.

Borthwick, Algernon (Baron Glenesk) (1830–1908: Morning Post)
Lucas, R. Lord Glenesk and the Morning Post. 1910.

Bottomley, Horatio (1860–1933: Youth etc)
Symons, J. Horatio Bottomley. 1955.

Bowles, Thomas Gibson (1842–1922: Vanity Fair)
Naylor, L. E. The irrepressible Victorian. 1965.

Bowring, John (1792–1872: Westminster Review). *See col 369, above.*
Autobiographical recollections. 1877.

Boyd, Frank M. (b. 1863: Pelican)
A pelican's tale: fifty years of London and elsewhere. 1919.

Boyle, Frederick (1841–83)
The narrative of an expelled correspondent. 1877.

Bradlaugh, Charles (1833–91: National Reformer)
Autobiography. 1873.
Bonner, H. B. and J. M. Robertson. The life of Charles Bradlaugh. 2 vols. 1894.
Champion of liberty: Charles Bradlaugh. Ed J. P. Gilmour 1933.

Brodrick, G. C. (1831–1903)
Memories and impressions 1831–1900. 1900.

Brooks, C. W. Shirley (1816–74: Punch). *See col 1147, above.*
Layard, G. S. A great Punch editor: being the life, letters and diaries of Shirley Brooks. 1907.

Brougham, Henry (1778–1868: Edinburgh Rev). *See col 1484, above.*

Buchanan, William (1781–1863: Edinburgh Courant)
The editorship of the Edinburgh Daily Courant. Edinburgh 1860.

Buckingham, James Silk (1786–1855: Athenaeum etc)
Specimens of newspaper literature, with personal memoirs. 2 vols Boston 1850.
Autobiography. 2 vols 1855.
Turner, R. E. J.S. Buckingham. 1934.

Burnand, F. C. (1836–1916: Punch)
Records and reminiscences. 2 vols [1904].

Busby, Thomas (1755–1838: Morning Post; Monthly Musical Jnl)
Boyle, A. Portraiture in Lavengro. N & Q 13, 27 Oct 1951.

Bussey, H. Findlater (d. 1919)
Sixty years of journalism. Bristol 1906.

Byrne, Nicholas (1761?–1833: Morning Post)
Herd, H. Seven editors. 1955.

Cadett, Herbert
The adventures of a journalist. 1900.

Campbell, Duncan (1824–90: Northern Chron [Inverness])
Reminiscences and reflections of an octogenarian Highlander, who was for over 26 years editor of the Northern Chronicle, Inverness. Inverness 1910.

Campbell, Thomas (1777–1844: New Monthly Mag). *See col 261, above.*
Beattie, William. The life and letters of Thomas Campbell. 3 vols 1848.
Redding, C. Literary reminiscences and memoirs of Thomas Campbell. 2 vols 1860.

Carlile, Richard (1790–1843: Republican). *See col 1272, above.*
Holyoake, G. J. The life and character of Richard Carlile. 1849.
Campbell, T. C. The battle of the press as told in the story of the life of Carlile by his daughter. 1899.
Centenary of Carlile, greatest fighter for press freedom. Journalism 26 1943.

Carnie, William (Aberdeen Herald)
Reporting reminiscences. 3 vols Aberdeen 1902–6 (priv ptd).

Carr, Emsley (News of the World)
Sir Emsley Carr: fifty years as editor. World's Press News 1 May 1941.

Cassell, The house of (Cassell's Mag; Quiver; Mag of Art etc)
Nowell-Smith, S. The house of Cassell 1848–1958. 1958.

Cassell, John (1817–65: Cassell's Illustr Family Paper; Quiver etc)
Pike, G. H. John Cassell. 1894.

Catling, Thomas (1838–1920: Lloyd's Weekly Newspaper)
My life's pilgrimage. 1911.

Chambers, Robert (1802–71. Chambers's Jnl). *See col 1372, above.*
Chambers, W. Memoirs of Robert Chambers; with autobiographical reminiscences of William Chambers. Edinburgh 1872.

Chambers, William (1800–83: Chambers's Jnl)
The story of a long and busy life. Edinburgh 1882.

Chapman, John (1821–94: Prospective Rev; Westminster Rev)
Haight, G. S. George Eliot and John Chapman, with Chapman's diaries. New Haven 1940.
Race, S. John Chapman. N & Q 26 April, 17 May 1941, May 1953.

Chatto & Windus, the house of (GM; Belgravia; Idler etc)
Low, D. M. A century of writers 1855–1955. 1955.

Clarke, William (1852–1901: Spectator; Daily Chron)
A collection of his writings, with a biographical sketch. Ed H. Burrows and J. A. Hobson 1908.

Cobbe, Frances Power (1822–1904: Echo). *See col 1376, above.*
The life of Frances Power Cobbe by herself. 2 vols 1894.

Cobbett, William (1762–1835: Political Register). *See col 1199, above.*
The life of Cobbett. Manchester 1835.
Smith, E. Cobbett: a biography. 2 vols 1878.
Carlyle, E. I. William Cobbett. 1904.
'Melville, Lewis' (L. S. Benjamin). The life and letters of Cobbett. 2 vols 1913.
Cole, G. D. H. The life of Cobbett. 1924.
Pemberton, W. B. William Cobbett. 1949.
Pearl, M. L. Cobbett: a bibliographical account. 1953. With information on his journalistic ventures.

Coleridge, S. T. (1772–1834: Morning Post). *See col 211, above.*
Gillman, J. The life of Coleridge vol 1. 1838 (all pbd). *See replies by* Daniel Stuart and H. N. Coleridge, GM May–Aug 1838.
Bourne, H. R. F. Coleridge among the journalists. GM Nov 1887.
See also under studies of the Morning Post, *below.*

Colles, Ramsay (1862–1919: Irish Figaro etc)
In castle and courthouse: being the reminiscences of thirty years in Ireland. 1911.

Conder, Josiah (1789–1855: Patriot). *See col 373, above.*
Conder, E. R. Josiah Conder: a memoir. 1857.

Cook, Edward Tyas (1857–1919: Pall Mall Gazette; Westminster Gazette)
Literary recreations. 1918.
Mills, J. S. Cook: a biography. 1921.

Cooper, Charles A. (1829–1916: Scotsman)
An editor's retrospect. 1896.

Cooper, Frederick Fox (1806–79: John Bull; Colored News).
Cooper, F. R. Nothing extenuate: the life of Cooper. 1964.

Cooper, Thomas (1805–1892: Cooper's Jnl). *See col 516, above.*
The life of Cooper, written by himself. 1872.
Conklin, R. J. Cooper, the Chartist. Manila 1935.

Courtney, Leonard H. (Baron Courtney) (1832–1918: Times etc)
Gooch, G. P. The life of Courtney. 1920.

Courtney, W. L. (1850–1928: Murray's Mag; Daily Telegraph; Fortnightly Rev).
The making of an editor 1850–1928. 1930.

Cowen, Joseph (1831–1900: Newcastle Chron)
Jones, E. R. The life and speeches of Cowen. 1885.
Duncan, W. The life of Cowen. 1904.

Croal, David.
The early recollections of a journalist 1832–1859. Edinburgh 1898.

Croker, John Wilson (1780–1857: Quart Rev etc). *See col 1275, above.*

Croly, George (1780–1860: Literary Gazette; Blackwood's Mag). *See col 375, above.*
Boyle, A. Portraiture in Lavengro. N & Q 27 Oct 1951.

Crosland, T. W. H. (1865–1924: Academy; Dome etc). *See col 619, above.*
Brown, W. S. The life and genius of Crosland. 1928.

Crowe, Joseph (1825–1896)
Reminiscences of thirty-five years of my life. 1895.

Dallas, Eneas Sweetland (1828–1879: Once a Week etc). *See col 1377, above.*

Dalziel, George (1815–1902 and Edward 1817–1905: Punch; Illustr London News; Cornhill Mag; Fun; Judy etc)
The brothers Dalziel: a record of fifty years' work 1840–1900. 1901.

Dangerfield, Edmund (1864?–1938: Cyclist)
Armstrong, A. C. Bouverie Street to Bowling Green Lane: fifty-five years of specialized publishing. 1946.

Delane, J. T. (1817–79: Times)
Dasent, A. I. John Thaddeus Delane, editor of the Times: his life and correspondence. 2 vols 1908.
Cook, E. T. Delane of the Times. 1915.

De Quincey, Thomas (1785–1859: Westmorland Gazette etc.)
See col 1238, above.
Pollitt, C. De Quincey's editorship of the Westmorland Gazette, with selections from his work on that journal from July 1818 to November 1819. Kendal 1890.
New essays by De Quincy: his contributions to the Edinburgh Saturday Post and the Edinburgh Evening Post 1827–8. Ed S. M. Towe, Princeton 1966.

Dickens, Charles (1812–70: Daily News; Household Words; All the Year Round etc). *See col 779, above.*
Lehmann, R. C. Dickens as editor: being the letters written by him to William Henry Wills, his sub-editor. 1912.
Ley, J. W. T. When Dickens led a reporters strike. Journalist 25 1942.
Grubb, G. G. Dickens's influence as an editor. SP 42 1945.

—— Dickens and the Daily News. In Booker memorial studies, Chapel Hill 1950; pts 2–4 in Nineteenth-Century Fiction 6–7 1952–3.
—— 'Dickens rejects'. Dickensian 52 1956.
See also under studies of the appropriate journals, below.

Dickens, John (1785?–1851: Daily News)
John Dickens, journalist. Dickensian 53 1957.

Dicks, John (1818–81: Bow Bells)
Summers, M. John Dicks, publishers. TLS 7 Nov 1942.

Dilke, Charles Wentworth (1789–1864: Athenaeum). *See col 1277, above.*
The papers of a critic, with a biographical sketch by Sir Charles Wentworth Dilke. 2 vols 1875.

Dixon, W. W. The spice of life: a medley of memoirs, by 'Thormanby'. 1911.

Downey, Edmund (b. 1856: Waterford News)
Twenty years ago: a book of anecdote illustrating literary life in London. 1905.

Dunlop, Andrew
Fifty years of Irish journalism. Dublin 1911.

Edwards, H. Sutherland (1828–1906)
Personal recollections. 1900.

Edwards, J. Passmore (1829–1911: Echo)
A few footprints. 1905 (priv ptd).

'Eliot, George' (1819–80: Westminster Rev). *See col 899, above.*
Pinney, Thomas. Essays of George Eliot. 1963. The introd describes her reviewing for several jnls and her editing for the Westminster.

Elwin, Whitwell (1816–1900: Quart Rev). *See col 1379, above.*
Some letters of Whitwell Elwin. TLS 18–25 Sept 1953.

Escott, T. H. S. (1844–1924: Fortnightly Rev)
Platform, press, politics and play. Bristol 1895.

Espinasse, Francis (1823?–1912: Edinburgh Courant)
Literary recollections and sketches. 1893.

Ewing, Juliana (1841–85: Aunt Judy's Mag). *See col 1049, above.*
Juliana Ewing's world. TLS 9 Aug 1941.
Maxwell, C. Mrs Gatty and Mrs Ewing. 1949.
Laski, M. Mrs Ewing, Mrs Molesworth and Mrs Hodgson Burnett. 1951.

Felbermann, Heinrich (1850–1925: Life)
The memoirs of a cosmopolitan life. 1936.

Finlay, George (1799–1875). *See col 1488, above.*
Miller, W. Finlay as a journalist. EHR 39 1924.

Fonblanque, Albany (1793–1872: Examiner)
Fonblanque, E. B. de. The life and letters of Fonblanque. 1874.

Forbes, Archibald (1838–1900)
Souvenirs of some continents. 1885.
Memoirs and studies of war and peace. 1895.

Forster, John (1812–76: Foreign Quart Rev; Daily News; Examiner). *See col 1379, above.*

Forsyth, William (1818–79: Aberdeen Jnl). *See col 1380, above.*
Selections from the writings of the late William Forsyth, with a memoir by Alexander Walker. Aberdeen 1882.

Foster, Ernest (1852–1919: Cassell's Saturday Jnl)
An editor's chair. 1909.

Fox, William Johnson (1786–1864: True Sun)
Garnett, R. The life of W. J. Fox. 1909.

Francis, John (1811–82: Athenaeum)
Francis, J. C. John Francis, publisher. 2 vols 1888.

Frost, John (1784?–1877: Welchman)
Williams, D. John Frost: a study in Chartism. Cardiff 1939.

Frost, Thomas (1821–1908)
Forty years' recollections: literary and political. 1880.
Reminiscences of a country journalist. 1886.

Froude, James Anthony (1818–94: Fraser's Mag etc). *See col 1468, above.*
Maurer, O. Froude and Fraser's Magazine 1860–74. SE 28 1949.
Dunn, W. H. James Anthony Froude. 2 vols Oxford 1961–3.

Furniss, Harry (1854–1925: Punch)
Confessions of a caricaturist. 1901.

Fyfe, H. Hamilton (b. 1869).
Sixty years of Fleet Street. 1949.

Gallenga, Antonio (1810–95: Times)
Episodes of my second life. 2 vols 1884.

Garrett, F. Edmund (1865–1907: Pall Mall Gazette; Westminster Gazette)
Cook, E. T. Garrett: a memoir. 1909.

Garvin, J. L. (1868–1947: Newcastle Chron)
Garvin, K. Garvin: a memoir. 1948.

Giffard, Stanley Lees (1788–1858: Standard; Morning Herald)
[Memoir]. Standard, 9 Nov 1858.

Gifford, William (1756–1826: Quart Rev).
Clark, B. R. Gifford, Tory satirist. New York 1930.

Gillies, R. P. (1788–1858)
Memoirs of a literary veteran. 3 vols 1851.

Greenwood, Frederick (1830–1909: Pall Mall Gazette)
[Memoir]. Blackwood's Mag Jan 1910.
See also J. W. Robertson Scott, The story of the Pall Mall Gazette, 1950.

Grove, George (1820–1900: Macmillan's Mag). *See col 1384, above.*

Hall, Anna Maria (1800–81: Juvenile Forget-me-not; Sharpe's Jnl; St James's Mag). *See col 932, above.*
See under S. C. Hall, *below.*

Hall, Samuel Carter (1800–89; New Monthly Mag)
A book of memories. 1871, 1877.
Retrospect of a long life 1815–83. 2 vols 1883.

Hammerton, J. A. (b. 1871)
Books and myself: memoirs of an editor. [1944].

Hannay, James (1827–73: Edinburgh Courant; Punch etc). *See col 1386, above.*
Reminiscences of a provincial editor. Temple Bar May 1868. *See also* April 1873.
Worth, G. J. Hannay: his life and works. Lawrence Kansas 1964.

Hardman, William (1828–90: Morning Post)
[Memoir]. Sell's World's Press 1891.

Harland, John (1806–68: Manchester Guardian)
Read, D. Harland: the father of provincial reporting. Manchester Rev 8 1958.

Harris, Frank (c. 1855–1931: Evening News; Fortnightly Rev; Saturday Rev)
Tobin, A. I. and E. Gertz. Harris: a study in black and white. Chicago 1931.
'Kingsmill, Hugh' (H. K. Lunn). Frank Harris. 1932.
Harris: his life and adventures. Ed G. Richards 1947.
Brome, V. Frank Harris. 1949.

Harris, Walter Burton (1866–1933: Times)
Mathews, J. J. Harris, Times correspondent in Morocco. Journalism Quart 17 1940.

Harvey, D. W. (1786–1863: Sunday Times; True Sun)
Redding, C. [Memoir]. Newspaper Press 1 Sept 1869.

Harwood, Philip (1809–87: Saturday Rev)
[Memoir]. Saturday Rev 17 Dec 1887.

Haynie, Henry
The captains and the kings: intimate reminiscences of notabilities. 1905.

Hayward, Abraham (1801–84)
A selection from the correspondence of Abraham Hayward, Q.C. from 1834 to 1884, with an account of his early life. 2 vols 1886.

Hazlitt, William (1778–1830: Examiner etc). *See col 1230, above.*
Howe, P. P. The life of Hazlitt. 1922.
Maclean, C. Born under Saturn. 1943.

Healy, Christopher
The confessions of a journalist. 1904.

Hedderwick, James (1814–97: Glasgow citizen)
Backward glances. Edinburgh 1891.

Helm, W. H. (1860–1936: Morning Post)
Memories. 1937.

Henley, William E. (1849–1903: Scots Observer; Mag of Art etc). *See col 629, above.*
Buckley, J. H. Henley: a study in the 'Counter-Decadence' of the nineties. Princeton 1945.
Connell, J. W. E. Henley. 1949.

Henty, G. A. (1832–1902: Union Jack). *See col 1094, above.*
G. A. Henty. TLS 28 Nov 1952.

Hetherington, Henry (1792–1849: Poor Man's Guardian etc)
Holyoake, G. J. The life of Hetherington. 1849.
Barker, A. G. Henry Hetherington 1792–1849. 1938.

Herzen, Alexander (1812–70)
Partridge, M. Herzen and the English press. Slavonic Rev 36 1958.

Hewlett, Henry G.
Autobiography, memoirs and letters. Ed H. F. Chorley 2 vols 1873.

Hibbert, H. G.
Fifty years of a Londoner's life. 1916.

Higgins, Matthew James (1810–68: New Monthly Mag; Morning Chron; Pall Mall Gazette etc)
'Jacob Omnium'. Essays on social subjects, with a memoir by W. S. Maxwell. 1875.

Hodder, George (d. 1870: Morning Post)
Memoirs of my time. 1870.

Hogg, James (1770–1835: Blackwood's Mag). *See col 267, above.*
Strout, A. L. Notes on Hogg. N & Q 2 April 1933, 29 Nov 1941.
—— Miscellaneous letters to, from and about Hogg. N & Q 13, 27 Dec 1941.
—— The life and letters of Hogg the Ettrick Shepherd. Vol 1 (1778–1825), Lubbock Texas 1946.

Holland, John (1794–1872: Sheffield Mercury etc)
Hudson, W. The life of Holland. 1874.

Hollingshead, John (1827–1904: Weekly Mail)
My lifetime. 2 vols 1895.

Holyoake, George Jacob (1817–1906: Reasoner etc)
Sixty years of an agitator's life. 1892.
Goss, C. W. F. A descriptive bibliography of the writings of Holyoake. 1908.
McCabe, J. The life and letters of Holyoake. 2 vols 1908.

Hone, William (1780–1842: Reformist's Register; Patriot). *See col 1284, above.*
Hackwood, F. W. Hone: his life and times. 1912.
Plummer, A. Hone: a centenary memoir. Jnl of SW Essex Technical College 1 1941.
Peterson, T. The fight of Hone for British press freedom. Journalism Quart 25 1948.
Sikes, H. M. Hone: Regency patriot, parodist and pamphleteer. Newberry Lib Bull 5 1961.

Hood, Thomas (1799–1845: London Mag; New Monthly Mag etc). *See col 359, above.*
Letters of Hood from the Dilke Papers in the British Museum. Ed L. A. Marchand, New Brunswick 1945.

Hook, Theodore (1788–1841: John Bull; New Monthly Mag etc). *See col 731, above.*
Barham, R. H. The life and remains of Hook. 2 vols 1849.
Hoaxer and wit: Hook. TLS 23 Aug 1941.

Howitt, William (1792–1879) and Mary (1799–1888): (Howitt's Jnl etc). *See col 1286, above.*
Woodring, C. R. Victorian samplers: William and Mary Howitt. Lawrence Kansas 1952.
Lee, A. Laurels and rosemary: the life of William and Mary Howitt. Oxford 1955.

Hunt, J. H. Leigh (1784–1859: Examiner etc). *See col 1216, above.*
Autobiography. 3 vols 1850; ed T. Hunt 1860 (by his eldest son); ed R. Ingpen 1903.
Blunden, E. Leigh Hunt: a biography. 1930.
Brewer, L. My Leigh Hunt library. Cedar Rapids Iowa 1932 (priv ptd).
Landré, L. Leigh Hunt. 2 vols Paris 1936.
Hunt's dramatic criticisms 1808–31. Ed L. H. and C. W. Houtchens, New York 1949.
Hunt's Literary criticism. Ed L. H. and C. W. Houtchens, New York 1956.
Hunt's political and occasional essays. Ed L. H. and C. W. Houtchens, New York 1962.

Hunt, Thornton (1810–1873: Constitutional; Leader; Daily Telegraph etc)
Blunden, E. Leigh Hunt's eldest son. Essays by Divers Hands new ser 19 1942.
See also N & Q 9, 23 Oct 1943.

Hunt, William (Eastern Morning News)
Then and now: or fifty years of newspaper work. Hull 1887.

Hutcheon, William (Morning Post)
Gentlemen of the press. 1933.

Hutton, Richard Holt (1826–97: Spectator; National Rev). *See col 1389, above.*
Hogben, John R. Hutton: a monograph. Edinburgh 1899.
LeRoy, G. C. Richard Holt Hutton. PMLA 561 941.
Tener, R. H. Hutton's Essays theological and literary: a bibliographical note. N & Q May 1960.
—— More articles by Hutton. BNYPL Jan 1962.

Jeffrey, Francis (1773–1850: Edinburgh Rev). *See col 1289, above.*
Greig, J. A. Jeffrey of the Edinburgh Review. 1948.

Jeffs, Harry (b. 1860: Evening Star (Wolverhampton); Christian World)
Press, preachers and politicians: reminiscences 1874–1932. 1933.

Jennings, H. J. (Birmingham Daily Mail; Financial News)
Chestnuts and small beer. 1920.

Jerdan, William (1782–1869: Sun; Literary Gazette)
Autobiography. 4 vols 1852–3.
Men I have known. 1866.
Ransom, H. Jerdan, editor and literary agent. SE 27 1948.
On a large collection of Jerdan papers, see Bodleian Lib Record 3 1950.

Jerome, Jerome Klapka (1859–1927: Idler; Today). *See col 1062, above.*
My life and times. 1926.

Jerrold, Douglas (1803–57: Lloyd's Illustr London News; Douglas Jerrold's Shilling Mag etc). *See col 1149, above.*
Jerrold, W. B. The life of Jerrold. 1859.
Jerrold, W. C. Jerrold and Punch. 1910.
—— Jerrold: dramatist and wit. 2 vols [1914].

Jeyes, Samuel Henry (1857–1911: Standard)
Low, S. Jeyes. 1915.

Jones, Kennedy (1865–1921: Evening News etc)
Fleet Street and Downing Street. [1920].

Keene, Charles (1823–91: Punch)
Layard, G. S. The life and letters of Keene. 1892.

Kemble, John Mitchell (1807–57: British & Foreign Rev).

Kingsley, Charles (1819–1875: Politics for the People). *See col 935, above.*

Kingsley, Henry (1830–1876: Edinburgh Daily Rev). *See col 939, above.*
Wolff, R. L. Henry Kingsley. Harvard Lib Bull 13 1959.

Kingston, W. H. G. (1814–80: Colonial Mag; Union Jack etc). *See col 940, above.*
Kingsford, M. R. The life, work and influence of Kingston. Toronto 1947.

Knight, Charles (1791–1873: Guardian; Knight's Quart Rev; Penny Mag etc). *See col 1656, above.*

Passages of a working life during half a century: with a prelude of early reminiscences. 3 vols 1864–5.

Knight, Joseph (1829–1907: N & Q). *See col 1390, above.*

Francis, J. C. Notes by the way; with memoirs of Knight etc. 1909.

Hale, B. F. R. Joseph Knight. N & Q 19 Oct 1949.

Knowles, James Thomas (1831–1908: Contemporary Rev; Nineteenth Century)

Brown, A. W. The Metaphysical Society: Victorian minds in crisis 1869–80. New York 1947.

Labouchere, Henry (1831–1912: Truth)

Thorold, A. L. The life of Labouchere. 1913.

Pearson, H. Labby. 1936.

West, E. J. An unappreciated Victorian dramatic critic: Labouchere. Quart Jnl of Speech 29 1943.

Lane, John (1854–1925: Yellow Book)

May, J. L. Lane and the nineties. 1936.

Lang, Andrew (1844–1912: Longman's Mag etc). *See col 1440, above.*

Salmond, J. B. Andrew Lang and journalism. 1950.

Latimer, Thomas (1803–88: Western Times)

Lambert, R. S. The Cobbett of the west: a study of Thomas Latimer and the struggle between pulpit and press at Exeter. 1939.

Leech, John (1817–64: Punch)

Frith, W. P. Leech's life and work. 2 vols 1891.

Kitton, F. G. John Leech. 1883, 1884 (rev).

Le Fanu, Joseph Sheridan (1814–73: Dublin Univ Mag). *See col 942, above.*

Lemon, Mark (1809–1870: Punch etc). *See col 1150, above.*

Hatton, J. With a show in the north. 1871.

Adrian, A. A. Mark Lemon: first editor of Punch. 1966.

Lennox, John (1794–1853: Greenock Newsclout)

Stewart, W. Lennox and the Greenock Newsclout. Glasgow 1918.

Levy, Joseph Moses (1812–1888: Daily Telegraph)

[Memoir] Daily Telegraph 13 Oct 1888.

Lewes, George Henry (1817–1878: Cornhill Mag; Fortnightly Rev). *See col 1542, above.*

Lewis, George Cornewall (1806–1863: Edinburgh Rev).

Linton, Eliza Lynn (1822–98: Saturday Rev etc). *See col 944, above.*

Layard, G. S. Mrs Lynn Linton: her life, letters and opinions. 1901.

Linton, William James (1812–98). *See col 533, above.*

Memories. 1895.

Ward Lock, the house of (Temple Bar; Boys' Own Mag; Windsor Mag etc)

Liveing, E. Adventures in publishing: the house of Ward Lock. 1954.

Longmans, Green etc, the house of (Edinburgh Rev; Longman's Mag etc)

Cox, H. and J. E. Chandler. The house of Longman 1724–1924. 1925 (priv ptd).

Lockhart, John Gibson (1794–1854: Quart Rev). *See col 1291, above.*

Low, Sidney (1857–1932: St James's Gazette)

Chapman-Huston, D. The lost historian: a memoir of Sir Sidney Low. 1936.

Lowe, Charles (1848–1931; Times)

The tale of a Times correspondent, Berlin 1878–1891. [1928].

Lowe, Robert (Viscount Sherbrooke) (1811–92: Times)

Martin, A. P. Life of Lowe. 2 vols 1893.

Lucas, Frederick (1812–55: Tablet)

Riethmüller, C. Frederick Lucas. 1862.

Lucas, E. The life of Frederick Lucas. 2 vols 1886.

Lucas, Samuel (1818–68: Times).

Mornings of the recess 1861–4. 2 vols 1864.

Lucy, Henry William (1845–1924: Daily News; Observer; Punch etc)

Sixty years in the wilderness. 1909.

Sixty years in the wilderness: a second series. 1912.

Nearing Jordan: being the third and last volume of sixty years. 1916.

The diary of a journalist: later entries. 1922.

Lytton, Edward George Earle Lytton Bulwer (Baron Lytton) (1802–73: New Monthly Mag). *See col 917, above.*

McCarthy, Justin (1830–1912: Morning Star). *See col 1491, above.*

An Irishman's story. 1904.

McCulloch, J. R. (1789–1864: Scotsman)

Reid, H. G. [Biographical notice] In McCulloch's Dictionary of commerce, 1869.

Macdonell, James (1842–79)

Nicoll, W. R. Macdonell: journalist. 1890.

Mackay, Charles (1814–1889: Morning Chron; Illustr London News). *See col 535, above.*

Forty years' recollections of life, literature and public affairs from 1830–70. 2 vols 1877.

Through the long day: or memorials of a literary life during half a century. 2 vols 1887.

Mackay, William

Bohemian days in Fleet Street, by a journalist. 1913.

Mackintosh, Alexander (1858–1948: Aberdeen Free Press)

Fifty-seven years in the Press Gallery. World's Press News 7 Apr 1938.

Macmillan, the house of (Macmillan's Mag; Nature; Eng Illustr Mag etc)

Morgan, C. The house of Macmillan 1843–1943. 1943.

Macmillan, Alexander (1818–96: Macmillan's Mag etc)

Letters. Ed G. A. Macmillan 1908 (priv ptd).

Graves, C. L. Life and letters of Macmillan. 1910.

Maginn, William (1793–1842: Blackwood's Mag etc). *See col 1293, above.*

Kenealy, E. V. William Maginn. Dublin Univ Mag Jan 1844.

Mahony, Francis Sylvester ('Father Prout'; 'Oliver Yorke') (1804–66: Fraser's Mag etc). *See col 1390, above.*

The works of Father Prout. Ed C. Kent 1881.

Mannin, E. Two studies in integrity. 1954.

Martineau, Harriet (1802–76: Daily News; Household Words; Westminster Rev etc). *See col 949, above.*

Harriet Martineau's autobiography, with memorials by M. W. Chapman. 3 vols 1877.

Wheatley, V. The life and works of Harriet Martineau. 1957.

Webb, R. K. Harriet Martineau. 1960.

Martineau, James (1805–1900: Prospective Rev; Nat Rev etc). *See col 1547, above.*

Drummond, J. and C. B. Upton. The life and letters of J. Martineau. 2 vols 1902.

Massingham, H. W. (1860–1924: Daily Chron)

H.W.M.: a selection from the writings of Massingham. Ed H. J. Massingham 1925.

Masson, David (1822–1907: Reader; Macmillan's Mag). *See col 1391, above.*

Maurice, J. Frederick Denison (1805–72: Athenaeum). *See col 1392, above.*

Mayo, Isabella Fyvie.

Recollections. 1910.

Merle, Gibbons (d. 1855: White Dwarf; Galignani's Messenger etc)

A newspaper editor's reminiscences. Fraser's Mag Nov 1839, Sept–Oct 1840, June 1841.

Miall, Edward (1809–81: Nonconformist)

Miall, A. The life of Edward Miall. 1881.

Mill, John Stuart (1806–1873: London Rev; Westminster Rev). *See col 1551, above.*

Macminn, N., J. R. Hainds and J. M. McCrimmon. Bibliography of the published writings of Mill, edited from his manuscript. Evanston 1945. With a record of Mill's contributions to many periodicals.

The earlier letters of Mill, 1812–48. Ed F. E. Mineka 2 vols Toronto 1963.

Miller, Hugh (1802–56: Witness). *See col 1395, above.*

Bayne, P. The life and letters of Miller. 2 vols 1871.

Mitchel, John (1815–75: United Irishman)
MacCall, S. Irish Mitchel: a biography. 1938.
Mitford, Mary Russell (1787–1855: New Monthly Mag; London Mag; Monthly Mag etc). *See col 748, above.*
Coles, W. A. Magazine and other contributions by Mary Russell Mitford and Thomas Noon Talfourd. SB 12 1959.
Montague, C. E. (1867–1928: Manchester Guardian)
Elton, O. C. E. Montague: a memoir. 1929.
Montgomery, James (1771–1854: Sheffield Iris). *See col 393, above.*
Holland, J. and J. Everett. The life of Montgomery. 7 vols 1854–6.
Moore, F. F. (b. 1855)
A journalist's note book. 1894.
Morley, John (1838–1923: Pall Mall Gazette; Fortnightly Rev; Macmillan's Mag). *See col 1447, above.*
My recollections. 2 vols 1917.
Hirst, F. W. The early life and letters of Lord Morley. 2 vols 1927.
Knickerbocker, F. W. Free minds: Morley and his friends. Cambridge Mass 1943.
Staebler, W. The liberal mind of Morley. Princeton 1943.
Morris, Mowbray (1847–1911: Macmillan's Mag; Times)
Bolitho, H. A late Victorian man of letters. Blackwood's Mag Jan 1950.
Morris, W. O'Connor (1824–1904: Times)
Memories and thoughts of a life. 1895.
Mudie, George (fl. 1822: Economist 1821–2)
Armytage, W. H. G. Mudie: journalist and utopian. N & Q May 1957.
Murray, David Christie (1847–1907)
Recollections. 1908.
Murray, Henry
A stepson of fortune: the memoirs, confessions and opinions of Murray. 1909.
Murray, John, the house of (Quart Rev; Representative; Academy; Murray's Mag)
Smiles, S. A publisher and his friends. 2 vols 1891.
'Paston, George' (E. M. Symonds). At John Murray's 1843–92. 1932.
Murray, John, II (1778–1843: Quart Rev; Representative)
Elwin, M. The founder of the Quarterly Review. Quart Rev 281 1943.
John Murray 1778–1843: 'the Anax of publishers'. TLS 26 June 1943.
Napier, Macvey (1776–1847: Edinburgh Rev)
Selection from the correspondence edited by his son. 1879.
Nevinson, Henry W. (1856–1941: Daily Chron)
Changes and chances. 1923.
Newman, John Henry (1801–90: Rambler; Br Critic). *See col 1311, above.*
Newnes, George (1851–1910: Tit-Bits; Rev of Reviews; Strand Mag; Westminster Gazette etc)
Bookman (London) May 1899.
Friedrichs, H. The life of Sir George Newnes .1911.
Nicoll, W. Robertson (1851–1923: Br Weekly; [London] Bookman)
A bookman's letters. 1913.
Parker, W. M. A great Scots journalist. Scots Mag 56 1951.
Northcliffe, Viscount (Alfred C. W. Harmsworth) (1865–1922: Daily Mail etc)
Pemberton, M. Lord Northcliffe: a memoir. 1922.
Wilson, R. M. Lord Northcliffe. 1927.
Fyfe, H. H. Northcliffe: an intimate biography. 1930.
Ryan, A. P. Lord Northcliffe. 1953.
Greenwall, H. J. Northcliffe: Napoleon of Fleet Street. 1957.
Pound, R. and G. Harmsworth. Northcliffe. 1959.
Oastler, Richard (1789–1861: Ashton Chron)
Driver, C. Tory radical: the life of Oastler. 1946.
O'Connor, T. P. (1848–1929: Sun; T.P.'s Weekly etc)
Memoirs of an old Parliamentarian. 2 vols 1929.
Fyfe, H. H. T. P. O'Connor. 1934.
O'Malley, William (b. 1853: Star)
Glancing backward. [1923].
O'Shea, J. A. (1839–1905: Standard)
Leaves from the life of a special correspondent. 2 vols 1885.
Owen, Robert (1771–1858: New Moral World). *See col 1295, above.*
Podmore, F. The life of Owen. 1906, 2 vols 1923.
A bibliography of Robert Owen. Aberystwyth 1914, 1925.
Paterson, James (1805–76)
Autobiographical reminiscences. Glasgow 1871.
Patmore, Peter George (1786–1855: Court Jnl; New Monthly Mag). *See col 1299, above.*
My friends and acquaintances. 3 vols 1854.
Memoirs and correspondence of Coventry Patmore. Ed B. Champneys 2 vols 1900.
Patmore, D. Portrait of my family. 1935.
Payn, James (1830–1898: Cornhill Mag; Chambers's Jnl). *See col 957, above.*
Some literary recollections. 1884.
Pearson, C. Arthur (1866–1921: Daily Express; Pearson's Weekly etc)
Dark, S. The life of Sir Arthur Pearson. 1922.
Phillips, Ernest
[Reminiscences]. Newspaper World 12, 19 Nov 1938
Phillips, Richard (1767–1840: Monthly Mag)
Memoirs of the public and private life of Sir Richard Phillips. 1808.
Timbs, J. Recollections of Sir Richard Phillips. In his Walks and talks about London, 1864.
Boyle, A. Portraiture in Lavengro. N & Q 12 May, 18 Aug, 15 and 29 Sept, 13 Oct 1951.
Prior, Melton (1845–1910: Illustr London News)
Campaigns of a war correspondent. Ed S. L. Bensusan 1912.
Ransome, Arthur (1884–1967)
Bohemia in London. 1907.
Redding, Cyrus (1785–1870: New Monthly Mag etc)
Fifty years' recollections. 3 vols 1858.
Yesterday and today: being a sequel to fifty years' recollections. 3 vols 1863.
Reeve, Henry (1813–95: Edinburgh Rev)
Laughton, J. K. Memoirs of the life and correspondence of Reeve. 2 vols 1898.
The letters of Reeve and Charles Greville. Ed A. H. Johnson 1924.
Reid, T. Wemyss (1842–1905: Speaker; Leeds Mercury).
Memoirs of Sir Wemyss Reid. Ed S. J. Reid 1905.
Reynolds, G. W. M. (1814–79: Reynolds' Miscellany; Reynolds' Weekly Newspaper). *See col 960, above.*
[Memoir]. Bookseller 8 July 1879.
Summers, M. G. W. M. Reynolds. TLS 4 July 1942.
Hunter, J. V. B. S. George Reynolds, sensational novelist and agitator. Book Handbook 4 1947.
Richardson, J. Hall (b. 1857)
From the City to Fleet Street. 1927.
Rintoul, Robert Stephen (1787–1858: Dundee Advertiser; Spectator)
[Memoir]. Dundee Advertiser 27 April 1858; Spectator 1 May 1858.
Ritchie, Leitch (1800–65: Chambers's Jnl; Era). *See col 961, above.*
Robinson, Henry Crabb (1775–1867: Times). *See col 1301, above.*
The diary, reminiscences and correspondence of Crabb Robinson. Ed T. Sadler 3 vols 1869.
Baker, J. M. Crabb Robinson of Bury, Jena, the Times and Russell Square. 1937.
Crabb Robinson in Germany 1800–5. Ed E. J. Morley 1929. With material on his contributions to the Monthly Register.

Robinson, John Richard (1828–1903: Daily News)
Thomas, F. M. Fifty years of Fleet Street: being the life and recollections of Sir J. R. Robinson. 1904.
Roche, Eugenius (1786–1829: Courier; Morning Post)
London in a thousand years. 1830.
Runciman, James (1852–91)
Sidelights; with a memoir by Grant Allen. 1893.
Russel, Alexander (1814–76: Scotsman)
Alexander Russel. Edinburgh 1876 (priv ptd).
Graham, H. G. In his Literary and historical essays, 1908.
Russell, Edward (1834–1920: Liverpool Daily Post)
That reminds me. 1899.
Russell, William Howard (1820–1907: Times)
The great war with Russia: a personal retrospect. 1895.
Atkins, J. B. The life of Russell. 2 vols 1911.
Furneaux, H. The first war correspondent, Russell of the Times. 1945.
Mathews, J. J. The father of war correspondents. Virginia Quart Rev 21 1945.
My diary north and south. Ed F. Pratt, New York 1954.
My Indian Mutiny diary, 1957.
Despatches from the Crimea 1854–6. Ed N. Bentley 1966.
Sala, George Augustus (1828–96: Temple Bar; Daily Telegraph). *See col 962, above.*
Things I have seen and people I have known. 2 vols 1895 (2nd edn).
The life and adventures of Sala, written by himself. 2 vols 1895.
Strauss, R. Sala: the portrait of an eminent Victorian. 1942.
Scott, C. P. (1846–1932: Manchester Guardian)
Hammond, J. L. C. P. Scott. 1934.
C. P. Scott 1846–1932: the making of the Manchester Guardian. 1946.
Scott, Clement (1841–1904: Theatre etc)
The wheel of life: a few memories and recollections. 1898.
Scott, Constance Margaret
Old days in Bohemian London. 1919.
Scott, John (1783–1821: Champion; London Mag)
Zeitlin, J. The editor of the London Magazine. JEGP 20 1921.
Hughes, T. R. John Scott: editor, author and critic. London Mercury April 1930.
Scott, J. W. Robertson (1866–1963: Pall Mall Gazette; Westminster Gazette)
Faith and works in Fleet Street. 1947.
The day before yesterday: memories of an uneducated man. 1951.
Scott, William (1813–72: Saturday Rev; Christian Remembrancer).
Shand, Alexander I. (1832–1907: Times)
Days of the past. 1905.
Shaw, George Bernard (1856–1950: Pall Mall Gazette; World; Star; Saturday Rev). *See col 1169, above.*
Shorter, Clement K. (1857–1929: Sphere etc)
C.K.S.: an autobiography. Ed J. M. Bulloch 1927 (priv ptd).
Simpson, Richard (1820–76: Rambler; Home & Foreign Rev).
Simpson, William (1823–99: Illustr London News)
Autobiography. Ed G. E. Todd 1903.
Sinclair, Alexander (Glasgow Herald)
Fifty years of newspaper life 1845–95. Glasgow [c. 1897] (priv ptd).
Smith, Charles Manby
The working man's way in the world: being the autobiography of a journeyman printer. 1854.
Smith, Ernest
Fields of adventure. 1923.
Smith, George Murray (1824–1901: Cornhill Mag; Pall Mall Gazette)
Lee, S. Memoir of George Smith. In DNB Supplement, 1901.
Huxley, L. The house of Smith Elder. 1923 (priv ptd).
Smith, Horatio (1779–1849: London Mag; New Monthly Mag)
A graybeard's gossip about his literary acquaintance. New Monthly Mag March–Dec 1847.
Smith, James Elimalet (1801–57: Shepherd)
Smith, W. A. 'Shepherd' Smith, the universalist. 1892.
Smith, Sydney (1771–1845: Edinburgh Rev). *See col 1304, above.*
Bullett, G. Sydney Smith: a biography and a selection. 1951.
Letters. Ed N. C. Smith 2 vols Oxford 1953.
Smith, Wareham (b. 1874)
Spilt ink. 1928.
Southey, Robert (1774–1843: Quart Rev). *See col 254, above.*
Graham, W. Southey as a Tory reviewer. PQ 2 1923.
Havens, R. D. Southey's contributions to the Foreign Review. RES 8 1932.
Spears, Robert (1825–99: Stockton Gazette; Christian Life)
Memorials of Robert Spears. Belfast 1903.
Spender, J. A. (1862–1942: Westminster Gazette)
Life, journalism and politics. 2 vols 1927.
Journalism in my time. Inst of Journalists' Jnl 28 1940.
Harris, W. J. A. Spender. 1946.
Stark, Malcolm (Glasgow Herald)
The pulse of the world. 1915.
Stead, William Thomas (1849–1912: Pall Mall Gazette; Rev of Reviews)
Waugh, B. William T. Stead: a life for the people. [1885].
Stead, E. My father. 1913.
Whyte, F. The life of Stead. 2 vols 1927.
Mansfield, F. J. Who started the New Journalism? World's Press News 3 March 1938.
Terrot, C. The maiden tribute: a study of the white slave traffic of the nineteenth century. 1959.
Baylen, J. O. Stead and the Boer War: the irony of idealism. Canadian Historical Rev 40 1959.
—— Stead, apologist for Imperial Russia 1870–80. Gazette (Amsterdam) 6 1960.
—— George Meredith and Stead: three unpublished letters. HLQ 24 1960.
—— A Victorian's 'crusade' in Chicago 1893–4. Jnl of Amer History 51 1964.
—— William Archer, Stead and the theatre: some unpublished letters. Univ of Mississippi Stud in Eng 5 1964.
—— W. T. Stead and the New Journalism. Emory Univ Quart 21 1965.
Baylen, J. O. and R. B. Holland. Whitman, Stead and the Pall Mall Gazette. Amer Lit 33 1961.
Hogan, P. G. and J. O. Baylen. G. Bernard Shaw and Stead: an unexplored relationship. Stud in Eng Lit 1 1961.
Stafford, A. The age of consent. 1964.
Steed, Henry Wickham (b. 1871: Times)
Through thirty years 1892–1922. 2 vols 1924.
Steevens, George Warrington (1869–1900)
Things seen, with a memoir by W. E. Henley. 1900.
Works: memorial edition. Ed G. S. Street and V. Blackburn 7 vols 1900–2.
Stephen, Leslie (1832–1904: Cornhill Mag). *See col 1405, above.*
Annan, N. Stephen: his thought and character in relation to his time. 1951.
Stephenson, Albert Frederick (1854–1934: Southport Critic; Halifax Guardian etc)
Stephenson, W. H. Albert Frederick Stephenson: a Lancashire newspaper man. Manchester 1937.

Sterling, Edward (1773–1847: Times)
Carlyle, T. The life of John Sterling. 1851.
Sterling, John (1806–44: Blackwood's Mag etc; Athenaeum etc). *See col 1306, above.*
Carlyle, T. The life of John Sterling. 1851.
Stillman, W. J. (1828–1901: Times)
The autobiography of a journalist. 2 vols 1901.
Strachey, John St Loe (1860–1927: Spectator)
The adventure of living. 1922.
Sanders, C. R. The Strachey family 1588–1932. Durham NC 1953.
Strachey, A. St Loe Strachey: his life and his paper. 1930.
Strahan, Alexander (Sunday Mag; Contemporary Rev; Good Words)
Twenty years of a publisher's life. Day of Rest Jan–Dec 1881.
Strauss, G. L. M. (1807–87: Grocer)
Reminiscences of an old Bohemian. 2 vols 1882.
Stuart, Daniel (1766–1846: Morning Post)
Reply to statements in James Gillman, Life of Coleridge, GM May June, Aug 1838.
Woof, R. S. Wordsworth's poetry and Stuart's newspapers 1797–1803. SB 15 1962.
Talfourd, Thomas Noon (1795–1854: New Monthly Mag; London Mag). *See col 1140, above.*
Watson, V. Talfourd and his friends. TLS 20–27 April 1956.
Coles, W. A. Magazine and other contributions by Mary Russell Mitford and Talfourd. SB 12 1959.
Taylor, John (1757–1832: Morning Post; Sun)
Records of my life. 2 vols 1832.
Taylor, John Edward (1791–1844: Manchester Guardian)
[Memoir]. Manchester Guardian 10 Jan 1844.
Taylor, Tom (1817–80: Punch). *See col 1157, above.*
Thackeray, W. M. (1811–1863: Constitutional; Cornhill Mag etc). *See col 855, above.*
Gulliver, H. S. Thackeray's literary apprenticeship. Valdosta Georgia 1934.
Dodds, J. W. Thackeray: a critical portrait. New York 1941.
The letters and private papers of Thackeray. Ed G. N. Ray 4 vols Cambridge Mass 1945–6.
Stevenson, L. The showman of Vanity Fair. New York 1947.
Ray, G. N. Thackeray. 2 vols New York 1955–8.
Thomas, William Beach (b. 1868)
A traveller in news. 1925.
Thomas, William Luson (1830–1900: Graphic)
[Memoir]. Graphic 20 Oct 1900.
Tillotson, W. F. (1844–89: Bolton Evening News)
Bolton's newspaper family. Newspaper World 14 Jan 1939.
Singleton, F. Tillotsons 1850–1950. 1951.
Tinsley, William (1831–1902: Tinsley's Mag etc)
Random recollections of an old publisher. 2 vols 1900.
Townsend, Meredith White (1831–1911: Spectator)
Asia and Europe. 1901.

Trollope, Anthony (1815–82: St Paul's Mag). *See col 882, above.*
Letters. Ed B. A. Booth, New York 1951.
Troup, George (1811–79: North Br Daily Mail)
Troup, G. E. The life of Troup, journalist. Edinburgh 1881.
Tulloch, John (1823–86: Fraser's Mag). *See col 1596, above.*
Tweedie, Mrs Alec
Thirteen years of a busy woman's life. 1912.
Urquhart, David (1805–77: Free Press)
Robinson, G. L. The life of Urquhart. Oxford 1932.
Vaughan, Robert (1795–1868: Br Quart Rev).
Venables, George Stovin (1810–88: Saturday Rev)
[Memoir]. Saturday Rev 13 Oct 1888.
Villiers, Frederick (1852–1922)
Pictures of many wars. 1902.
Vizetelly, Henry (1820–94: Illustr Times etc)
Glances back through 70 years. 2 vols 1893.
Wainewright, Thomas Griffiths (1794–1852: London Mag)
Wilde, O. Intentions. 1891, 1894.
Curling, J. Janus weathercock. 1938.
Lindsey, J. Suburban gentleman: the life of Wainewright: poet, painter and poisoner. 1942.
Wakeley, Thomas (1795–1862: Lancet)
Sprigge, S. The life and times of Wakeley. 1897.
Walford, Edward (1823–97: Once a Week; GM)
Buckler, W. E. Walford: a distressed editor. N & Q Dec 1953.
Watson, Aaron (1850–1926: Echo)
A newspaper man's memories. [1925].
Watson, James (1799–1874)
Linton, W. J. Watson: a memoir. 1880 (priv ptd).
Watts, Alaric (1797–1864: United Services Gazette). *See col 405, above.*
Watts, A. A. The life of Watts by his son. 2 vols 1884.
White, Joseph Blanco (1775–1841: London Rev (1829) etc). *See col 1604, above.*
Whiteing, Richard (1840–1928)
My harvest. 1915.
Wilde, Oscar (1854–1900: Woman's World). *See col 1182, above.*
Wilkinson, Henry Spenser (1853–1937)
Thirty-five years 1874–1909. 1933. Autobiography of a journalist and military expert.
Williams, F. C.
Journalistic jumbles. [1880?].
Wilson, John ('Christopher North') (1785–1854: Blackwood's Mag). *See col 1308, above.*
Wood, Ellen (Mrs Henry) (1814–87: Argosy). *See col 971, above.*
Yates, Edmund (1831–94: World). *See col 1083, above.*
Recollections and experiences. 2 vols 1884.
Yorke, Henry Redhead (1772–1813: H. R. Yorke's Political Rev)
Sykes, J. A. C. France in 1802. 1906.

(2) THE GENERAL HISTORY OF THE PRESS

Bibliographies

Besides the works cited below, several contemporary surveys occurred as articles in the monthly and quarterly reviews and magazines throughout the century. Further titles are cited by C. L. Cannon, below. See also Newspaper press directory.

Peel, H. W. A bibliography of journalism. 1915. Originally issued as part of the introd to Sell's World's press guide, 1915.

Cannon, C. L. Journalism: a bibliography. New York 1924 (New York Public Lib).

Bömer, K. Internationale Bibliographie des Zeitungswesens. Sammlung bibliothekwissenschaftlicher Arbeiten pt 43, Leipzig 1932.

Nafziger, R. International news and the press: an annotated bibliography. New York 1940.

Price, W. C. The literature of journalism: an annotated bibliography. Minneapolis 1959.

Stratman, C. J. A bibliography of British dramatic periodicals 1720–1960. New York 1962 (New York Public Lib).

—— Preparing a bibliography of British dramatic periodicals 1720–1960. BNYPL June 1962.

§1

Savage, J. An account of the London daily papers, and the manner in which they are conducted. 1811.

[Brougham, H.] Abuses of the press. Edinburgh Rev 22 1813.

Hankin, E. Letter to the Rt Hon the Earl of Liverpool on the licentiousness of the press. 1814.

Holt, F. L. The law of libel. 1816 (2nd edn).

[Poynder, J.] Observations on Sunday newspapers, tending to show the impiety of such a violation of the Sabbath, the religious and political evils consequent upon the practice, and the necessity which exists for its suppression. By a layman. 1820.

[House of Commons]. Return of the names of individuals sentenced for political libel (King's Bench and Scotland) 1808–21. Commons Journals 76 1821, pp. 1208–9.

[House of Commons: accounts and papers]. Return of persons prosecuted for libels, blasphemy and sedition. (379) xxi 399. 1821. [Ditto, 1823.] (562) xv 239 1823.

[House of Commons]. Return of details concerning nearly all prosecutions for libel (Great Britain without Ireland) 1813–22. Commons Journals, vol 78 1823, pp. 1082 ff.

[Salgues, J. B.] Les milles et une calomnies: ou extraits des correspondances privées insérés dans les journaux anglais et allemands pendant le ministère de M. le Duc Decazes. 2 vols Paris 1822.

[Hazlitt, W.] The periodical press. Edinburgh Rev 38 1823; rptd in Complete works of Hazlitt, ed P. P. Howe, vol 16 1933.

The periodical press of Great Britain and Ireland. 1824.

[Mill, James]. Periodical literature. Westminster Rev 1 1824.

Newspapers. Westminster Rev 2 1824.

[Westmacott, C. M.] The spirit of the public journals 1823–5. 3 vols 1824–6.

—— The Stamp Duties: serious considerations on the proposed alteration of the Stamp Duty on newspapers. 1836.

[Mudie, R.] Babylon the great. 2 vols 1825.

[Merle, G.] Newspaper press. Westminster Rev 10 1829.

—— Weekly newspapers. Ibid.

[House of Commons: accounts and papers]. Return of prosecutions for libels or misdemeanours in the reigns of Geo. 3 and Geo. 4, against members of the Government, or persons acting in official capacity, conducted in the Department of the Solicitor to the Treasury. (608) xxx 211 1830.

The influence of the newspapers. Fraser's Mag Sept–Oct 1831.

D., R.K. Letter to Viscount Althorp on the proposed reduction in the Newspaper Stamp and Advertisement Duties. 1831.

[House of Commons: accounts and papers]. Return of persons in confinement for non-payment of Penalties; prosecutions connected with the Paper Duties; and drawbacks allowed on the exportation of paper. (346) xv 539 1831.

Lamb, C. Newspapers thirty-five years ago. Englishman's Mag Oct 1831; rptd in his Last essays of Elia, 1833.

[House of Commons: accounts and papers]. Number of persons committed for selling unstamped publications since Dec 10 1831. (40) xxxiv 103 and (711) xxxiv 107 1832.

The companion to the newspaper. No 1, March 1833–47. Monthly paper pbd by Charles Knight, with the number of duty stamps issued to each paper.

[House of Commons: accounts and papers]. Return of prosecutions for libel since the accession of His present Majesty William IV, either by ex officio informations or indictment, conducted in the Department of the Solicitor to the Treasury. (202) xlviii 267 1834.

[House of Commons: accounts and papers]. Return of the names of individuals prosecuted for political libel etc from March 17 1821; Convictions in Great Britain, 1821–1831, for offences of blasphemy and sedition; Number of informations filed by the Attorney-General against persons accused of blasphemy or sedition 1821–1834. (410) xlviii 269 1834.

[Alison, A.] The influence of the press. Blackwood's Mag Sept 1834.

Influence of the press. Westminster Rev 21 1834.

Roebuck, J. A. The stamped press of London and its morality. [1835].

Fox, W. J. The morality of the press. 1835.

Advertising in Scotland. Tait's Mag March 1836.

[Knight, C.] The Newspaper Stamp and the duty on paper, viewed in relation to their effects upon the diffusion of knowledge, by the author of the Results of machinery. 1836.

Knight, C. London newspapers. [In his] London, 1843.

—— The old printer and the modern press. 1854.

The morning and evening papers. Fraser's Mag May 1836.

Crawfurd, J. The Newspaper Stamp and the newspaper postage compared. 1836.

[Grant, J.] The great metropolis. 2 vols 1837.

Grant, J. The newspaper press: its origin, progress and present history. 3 vols 1871, 1872.

[House of Commons: accounts and papers]. Effect upon the revenue by reduction of Stamp Duty on newspapers, and of legal proceedings relating to Stamp Duty on newspapers, and sale of unstamped papers. (291) xxxix 303 1837.

The religious periodical press. Fraser's Mag Sept 1838.

Newspapers and other publications found in the coffee, public and eating houses in Westminster. Jnl of Statistical Soc Dec 1838.

The fourth estate: or the moral influence of the press. 1839.

The spirit of the metropolitan conservative press: being a selection from the London conservative journals during the year 1839. 1840.

Simmonds, P. L. Statistics of newspapers in various countries. Jnl Statistical Soc July 1841.

[House of Commons: accounts and papers]. Numbers of newspapers to which stamps were issued, and the number issued to newspapers, 1836 to 1842; number of advertisements inserted in the London papers, the English provincial newspapers, the Irish papers etc 1836–42; amount of advertisement duty received in England, etc. Total for each year; rate of duty. (340) xxvi 613 1842.

[Evans, D. M.] City men and City manners. 1845, 1852.

The newspaper and periodical press of London. London Jnl, Vols 1–2 1845–6.

The power of the press: is it rightly employed? Facts, inquiries and suggestions addressed to members of Christian churches. 1847.

The provincial press of the United Kingdom. In Reynolds's miscellany, 1847.

Tilsley, H. Treatise on the Stamp laws in Great Britain and Ireland. 1849 (2nd edn).

Hunt, F. K. The fourth estate: contributions towards a history of newspapers, and of the liberty of the press. 2 vols 1850.

Munsell, J. The British press. [In his] Typographical miscellany, Albany 1850.

[House of Commons: accounts and papers]. Estimate of the annual expense of collecting the Stamp Duty on newspapers; stating the number and wages of persons employed at Somerset House, and in Edinburgh and Manchester, in stamping the paper; the annual cost of machinery, and the expense of clerks, including those who receive the money for the stamps. (211) xxxiii 571 1850.

[House of Commons]. Report from the Select Committee on Newspaper Stamps. (558) xvii 1 1851.

Barnes, E. Newspapers and the Stamp question. Br Quart Rev 15 1852. *See also* Edinburgh Rev 98 1853.

Smith, A. Press orders: being the opinions of the leading journals on the abolition of the newspaper privileges. 1853.

[Schlesinger, M.] Sauntering in London. 1853.

Urquhart, D. Public opinion and its organs. 1855.

[Greg, W. R.] The newspaper press. Edinburgh Rev 102 1855.

The London daily press. Westminster Rev 64, new ser 8, 1855.

Cockburn, H. Memorials of his time. Edinburgh 1856.

Clarigny, C. Histoire de la presse en Angleterre et aux Etats Unis. Paris 1857.

[Murray, E. C. G.] The press and the public service, by a distinguished writer. 1857.

A quarterly reviewer. The newspaper press reviewed. 1857.

[House of Commons: accounts and papers]. Return of correspondence on the subject of the registration of newspapers, and securities on the publication of newspapers and pamphlets. xxxiv 199 1857–8.

Andrews, A. The history of British journalism. 2 vols 1859.

Macintosh, C. A. Popular outlines of the press. 1859.

Amphlett, J. The newspaper press in part of the last century and up to 1860: recollections. 1860.

The newspaper press of the present day. 1860.

Grattan, C. J. The gallery: a sketch of the history of Parliamentary reporting and reporters. 1860.

Fontane, T. Aus England: Studien und Briefe über Londoner Theater, Kunst und Presse. Stuttgart 1860.

[Kirwan, A. V.] Editors and newspaper writers of the last generation, by an old apprentice of the law. Fraser's Mag Feb, May, July 1862.

Scott, J. A. The British newspaper: the penny theory and its solution. Dublin Univ Mag March 1863.

Bertrand, E. Le régime régal de la presse en Angleterre. Paris 1868.

Reid, H. G. The press. In J. Samuelson, The civilisation of our day, 1868.

Holtzendorff, F. von. Englands Presse. In Sammlung-Wissenschaftliche Vorträge, Berlin 1870.

[Marshall, T. W.] Protestant journalism, by the author of My clerical friends. 1874.

Murphy, A. The Tory press. Contemporary Rev April 1874.

Politics and the press. Fraser's Mag July 1875.

Routledge, J. Chapters in the history of popular progress, chiefly in relation to the freedom of the press and trial by jury 1660–1820, with an application to later years. 1876.

Webber, V. A. The English newspaper press and its influence. Ryde 1876.

[House of Commons]. Report from the Select Committee on the law of libel. 1879.

Paterson, J. The liberty of the press, speech and public worship. 1880.

English journalism. Nation (New York) 22–9 July, 12, 26 Aug, 16, 30 Sept, 14, 28 Oct 1880.

'Oldcastle, John' (Wilfred Meynell). Journals and journalism. 1880.

[Armstrong, R. A.] The story of nineteenth century reviewing. Modern Rev 1 1880.

The religious press. Dublin Rev 3rd ser 6 1881.

Pebody, C. English journalism and the men who have made it. 1882.

Hatton, J. Journalistic London. 1882.

R., G. The penny newspaper: the story of the cheap press. [1883].

Croker, J. W. The Croker papers 1809–30. Ed L. J. Jennings 3 vols 1884.

Elliott, G. The Newspaper Libel and Registration Act 1881. 1884.

Bowles, T. G. Newspapers. Fortnightly Rev July 1884.

Whorlow, H. The Provincial Newspaper Society: a jubilee retrospect. 1886.

Bourne, H. R. Fox. English newspapers: chapters in the history of journalism. 2 vols 1887.

Powell, A. The law specially affecting printers, publishers and newspaper proprietors. [1887].

B., H. A. About newspapers: chiefly English and Scottish; with an appendix containing an account of the periodical publications issued in connection with the Anglican Communion in Great Britain and Ireland. Edinburgh 1888.

Fraser, H. The law of libel in its relation to the press. 1889.

Kelly, R. S. The law of newspaper libel. 1889.

O'Connor, T. P. The New Journalism. New Rev Oct 1889.

Greenwood, F. The newspaper press. Nineteenth Century May 1890.

Baker, A. The newspaper world: essays on press history and work, past and present. 1890.

Quail, J. Our journals and journalists. Hull 1890.

Fisher, J. R. and J. A. Strahan. The law of the press: a digest of the law affecting newspapers in England, India and the Colonies. 1891.

Massingham, H. W. The London daily press. 1892.

Archer, T. The highway of letters and its echoes of famous footsteps. 1893.

Lucy, H. W. The power of the British press. North Amer Rev Aug 1896.

Smith, L. A. Woman's work in the London and provincial press. In Newspaper press directory, 1897.

Rose, J. H. The unstamped press 1815–36. EHR 12 1897.

Wellsman, W. The local press of London. 1898.

Taylor, F. The newspaper press as a power both in the expression and formation of public opinion. Oxford 1898.

Stead, W. T. A journalist on journalism. [1899].

Halewyck, M. Le régime régal de la presse en Angleterre. Louvain 1899.

Collet, C. D. History of the taxes on knowledge: their origin and repeal, with an introduction by G. J. Holyoake. 2 vols 1899, 1 vol 1933 (abridged).

Walpole, G. Some old Parliamentary reporters. 1899.

Duckworth, L. A complete summary of the law relating to the English newspaper press. 1899.

'Delta'. A generation of Scottish literature and journalism. Bookman (London) May–June, Aug–Sept 1900.

Tinsley, W. Random recollections of an old publisher. 2 vols 1900.

The progress of British newspapers in the 19th century. [1901]. Supplement to Sell's World's press guide, 1901.

Bennett, E. A. A note on the revolution in journalism. Academy 10 March 1900; rptd in his Fame and fiction, 1901.

Millar, J. H. A literary history of Scotland. 1903.

Leach, H. Fleet Street from within. Bristol 1905.

Lorensz, T. Die englische Presse. Halle 1907.

Couper, W. J. The Edinburgh periodical press. 2 vols Stirling 1908.

Adams, E. D. Great Britain and the American Civil War. 2 vols 1908.

Francis, J. C. Notes by the way. 1909.

Borsa, M. Il giornalismo inglese. Milan 1910.

Escott, T. H. S. Masters of English journalism. 1911.

Dibblee, G. B. The newspaper. 1912.

Bell, W. G. Fleet Street in seven centuries. 1912.

Chancellor, E. B. The annals of Fleet Street. 1912.

Scott-James, R. A. The influence of the press. 1913.

Symon, J. D. The press and its story: an account of the birth and development of journalism up to the present day, with the history of all the leading newspapers. 1914.

Bullard, F. L. Famous war correspondents. Boston 1914.

Mineau, G. Famous war correspondents. Madison 1915. With bibliography.

Simonis, H. The street of ink. 1917.
Birrell, A. Life, literature and literary journalism during the first half of the last century. London Mercury May 1920.
Martin, B. K. The triumph of Lord Palmerston. [1924].
Herd, H. The making of modern journalism. [1927].
— The march of journalism: the story of the British press from 1622 to the present day. 1952.
— Seven editors. 1955.
— A press gallery. 1958.
Wickwar, W. H. The struggle for the freedom of the press 1819–32. 1928.
Robbins, A. The press. [1928].
Hammond, J. L. and B. The age of the Chartists. [1930].
Jordan, D. and E. J. Pratt. Europe and the American Civil War. 1931.
Morison, S. The English newspaper 1622–1932. Cambridge 1932.
Stutterheim, K. von. Die englische Presse. Berlin 1933; tr 1934.
Cavour e l'Inghilterra: Carteggio di V.E. d'Azeglio. 3 pts Bologna 1933.
Weil, G. Le journal. Paris 1934.
Pollard, G. Serial fiction. In New paths in book collecting, ed J. Carter 1934; 1938 (separately).
Maccoby, S. English radicalism 1832–52. [1935].
— English radicalism 1853–86. 1938.
— English radicalism 1886–1914. 1953.
Grünbeck, M. Die Presse Grossbritanniens: ihr geistiger und wirtschaftlicher Aufbau. 2 vols Leipzig 1936. Vol 1: Geschichte und allgemeine Gegenwartsstrucktur der britischen Presse.
Sper, F. The periodical press of London, theatrical and literary 1800–30. Boston 1937.
Mansfield, F. J. Royal interest in the press. Newspaper World 8 May 1937.
Postgate, R. and A. Vallance. Those foreigners: the English people's opinions on foreign affairs as reflected in their newspapers since Waterloo (1815–1937). 1937.
Maitland, F. H. One hundred years of headlines 1837–1937. 1938.
Lefanu, W. R. British periodicals of medicine. Baltimore 1938.
Steed, H. W. The press. [1938].
Glicksberg, C. I. Henry Adams and the English and American press in 1861. Journalism Quart 16 1939.
Steed, W. British newspaper history. Listener 9 Feb 1939.
Bentley, E. G. Those days. 1940.
Innis, H. A. The newspaper in economic development. Jnl Economic History 2 (suppl) 1942.
— The English press in the nineteenth century: an economic approach. UTQ 15 1945.
Jaryc, M. Studies of 1935–42 on the history of the periodical press. Jnl of Modern History 15 1943.
Gohdes, C. The periodicals. [In his] American literature in nineteenth-century England, New York 1944. *See also* appendix, Representative articles on American literature appearing in British periodicals 1833–1901.
Hudson, D. British journalists and newspapers. 1945.
Aspinall, A. Politics and the press 1780–1850. 1949.
— The reporting and publishing of House of Commons debates 1771–1834. In Essays presented to Sir Lewis Namier, ed R. Pares and A. J. P. Taylor. 1956.
Altick, R. D. Nineteenth-century English periodicals. Newberry Lib Bull 2nd ser 9 1952.
— The English common reader: a social history of the mass reading public 1800–1900. Chicago 1957.
Shannon, E. F. jr. Tennyson and the reviewers 1827–51. Cambridge Mass 1952.
Dodds, J. W. The age of paradox: a biography of England 1841–51. New York 1952. Ch 3.
Symonds, R. V. The rise of English journalism. Exeter 1953.
Webb, R. K. The British working class reader 1790–1848. 1955.
— The Victorian reading public. Universities Quart 12 1957.
Andrews, J. S. The reception of Gotthelf in British and American nineteenth-century periodicals. MLR 51 1956.
— The reception of Fritz Reuter in Victorian England. MLR 56 1961.
Dalziel, M. Popular fiction 100 years ago. 1957.
Arundell, D. The critic at the opera. 1957.
Perkin, H. J. The origins of the popular press. History Today 7 1957.
Ellegård, A. The readership of the periodical press in mid-Victorian Britain. Gothenburg 1957.
— Darwin and the general reader: the reception of Darwin's theory of evolution in the British periodical press 1859–72. Gothenburg Stud in Eng 1958.
Appleman, P., W. A. Madden and M. Wolff. 1859: entering an age of crisis. Bloomington 1959. Includes R. D. Altick, The literature of an imminent democracy; and M. Wolff, Victorian reviewers and cultural responsibility.
Eye-witness: an anthology of British reporting. Ed J. Fisher 1960.
Worth, G. J. Popular culture and the seminal books of 1859. Victorian Newsletter no 19 1961.
Sowder, W. J. Emerson's early impact on England: a study in British periodicals. PMLA 77 1962.
Mayo, R. D. The English novel in the magazines 1740–1815. Evanston 1962.
James, L. Fiction for the working man 1830–50. Oxford 1963.
Stratman, C. J. Scotland's first dramatic periodical: the Edinburgh Theatrical Censor. Theatre Notebook 17 1963.

(3) LISTS OF NEWSPAPERS

Lists of Files now extant

British Museum catalogue of printed books. Supplement: newspapers published in Great Britain and Ireland 1801–1900. 1905. Also separately ptd.
[Muddiman, J. G.] Tercentenary handlist of English and Welsh newspapers, magazines and reviews 1620–1920. The most complete list available, based on the BM holdings, but not innocent of serious misprints.
Crane, R. S. and F. B. Kaye. A census of British newspapers and periodicals 1620–1800. Chapel Hill 1927. Records the files in American libraries, with supplementary summary list of those lacking.
Deutsches Institut für Zeitungskunde. Standortskatalog wichtiger Zeitungbestände in deutschen Bibliotheken. Leipzig 1933.
Stewart, A. The evolution of the English newspaper from its origins to the present day as illustrated by the catalogue of the Press Club collection. 1935 (priv ptd).
Gregory, W. Union list of serials in libraries of the United States and Canada. New York 1927, 1943; Supplement, ed G. B. Malikoff, New York 1945; Supplement, ed M. Franck, New York 1953.
Haskell, D. A checklist of cumulated indexes to individual periodicals in the New York Public Library. New York 1942. A guide to existing indexes to weeklies, monthlies and quarterlies listed in CBEL.
Ward, W. S. Index and finding list of serials published in the British Isles 1789–1832. Lexington Kentucky 1953.
British union catalogue of periodicals. 4 vols 1955–8; Supplement to 1960, 1962.

Library of Congress. Newspapers on microfilm. Washington 1953, 1963 (5th edn).

Government Returns of the Stamp Duties

The original returns of the Stamp Duty on Newspapers from about 1749 to 1855 were scheduled for destruction under the Public Record Office Act of 1877. Besides the official returns listed below from House of Commons Accounts & Papers, they were frequently cited in works on the press, e.g. Charles Knight's Companion to the Newspaper.

Account of all weekly newspapers published on Saturdays and Sundays. (445) xvi 387 and (579) xvi 391 1821.

Newspaper returns: an account of the number of stamps for newspapers for the year 1801; distinguishing the London from the provincial newspapers, and distinguishing the different London newspapers and the amount of duty received from each. (272) xxi 381 1822; rptd Inquirer Aug 1822 p. 300.

Account of stamps issued for newspapers, with the amount of the duties charged thereon from 1814 to 1824. (375) xxi 327 1825.

Ireland: account of the number of stamps issued to each newspaper from 1822 to 1826. (235) xxiii 383 1826.

Ireland: stamp duties on pamphlets, newspapers and advertisements in Ireland 1797–1826. (99) xvii 23 1827.

Stamps issued to each of the newspapers in England, Scotland and Wales (except those published in London) 1825 to 1829. (609) xxv 347 1830.

Ireland: stamp duties on newspapers and advertisements in Ireland, 1810 to 1830. (406) xxv 363 1830.

Stamps issued for the London newspapers, duty received, duty paid for advertisements, 1820 to 1829. (549) xxv 349 1830.

Ireland: stamps issued to each newspaper in Ireland 1826–9. (549) xxv 349 1830.

Number of stamps issued for newspapers and other publications 1821–31; number issued for London newspapers 1830; duties on pamphlets and advertisements 1830. (30) xxxiv 127 1832.

Ireland: stamps issued to each newspaper in Ireland 1830 to 1831. (242) xxxiv 123 1832.

Stamps issued for the London newspapers, duty received, duty paid for advertisements for 1831. (290) xxxiv 119 1832.

Number of square feet of surface of one copy of each of the daily newspapers, 1831; amount of stamp duty actually paid; rate of payment for each hundred square feet. (188) xxxiv 117 1832.

Scotland: number of stamps issued to each of the newspapers in Scotland 1831; amount of advertisement duty. (465) xxxiv 121 1832.

Number of stamps issued by the Stamp Office for London newspapers specifying each newspaper by name, and number of stamps issued to printers or publishers 1832–3. (758) xxxii 609 1833.

Number of stamps issued to each provincial newspaper in England 1832–3. (519) xxxii 613 1833.

Ireland: number of stamps issued to each newspaper in Ireland 1832–3. (503) xxxii 623 1833.

Ireland: a return of the number of stamps issued to each newspaper in Ireland respectively from 5 Jan 1833 to 5 April 1834; and the number of stamps cancelled by each newspaper respectively for the same period. (412) xlix 407. Ditto from 5 April to 5 July 1834 (510) xlix 409 1834.

Number of stamps issued to London newspapers 1833–5. (625) xxxvii 705 1835.

Number of stamps issued to newspapers in the United Kingdom 1835–6; amount of advertisement duty by London newspapers 1836. (294) xlv 345 1836.

Number of stamps issued monthly to each of the London newspapers from January to April 1837, and of the advertisement duty in the same period. (232) xxxix 321 1837.

Number of stamps issued monthly to each of the provincial papers in England and Wales from 1 Jan to 20 June 1837; of the number of advertisements published in each newspaper for the same period; and the amount of duty on advertisements paid by each paper for the same period. (In 526) xxxix 305 1837. Ditto from 1836 to 1838. (307) xxxvi 413 1838.

Number of stamps issued by the Stamp Office for all newspapers in Great Britain and Ireland from 30 June to 1 Dec 1837, specifying each newspaper by name, and number of stamps issued each month during that period to each newspaper. (73) xxxvi 393. Ditto 1–31 Dec 1837; similar return for each month of the quarter ended 31 March 1838. (368) xxxvi 403 1838.

Ireland: number of stamps issued to Irish newspapers in each year since 1824, distinguishing those printed in Dublin; newspapers existing in Ireland in 1824; newspapers which have ceased to exist since 1824; newspapers established since 1824, and which still exist. (In 488) viii 235 1838.

Number of stamps issued at 1d in the United Kingdom 1838–9, specifying each newspaper, and the number of stamps issued each month. (213) xxx 483. Ditto from April to June 1839. (449) xxx 493 1839.

Number of stamps at 1d issued to the several newspapers 1838, specifying each newspaper by name, and the number of stamps issued each month during that period to each newspaper; similar returns for Ireland. (15) xxix 483 1840.

Number of stamps issued to the several newspapers in Great Britain 1839, specifying each newspaper by name, and the number of stamps issued each month during the period to each newspaper. (266) xxix 503 1840.

Number of stamps issued to each newspaper in England and Wales 1839–40, specifying also the amount of advertisement duty paid by each newspaper in each of the above years; similar returns for Ireland and Scotland. (294) xxix 523 1840.

Number of stamps issued to the several newspapers in the United Kingdom April to June 1840, specifying each newspaper by name. (525) xxix 513 1840.

Number of newspaper stamps at 1d and ½d issued to the several newspapers in Great Britain 1 July to 1 Sept 1840, specifying each newspaper by name; number of stamps each month; similar returns for Ireland; similar returns from 1 Oct to 31 Dec 1840. (14) xiii 461 1841.

Number of stamps issued to each newspaper in England and Wales during each of the three years ending 5 Jan 1841, and similar returns for Scotland and Ireland; also return of number of newspaper stamps issued from 5 Jan to 31 March 1841. (407) xiii 481 1841.

Number of stamps issued to each of the newspapers in the United Kingdom; amount of advertisement duty paid. (26) ii 45 1841 (Sess 2); (44) xxvi 561 1842; (257) xxvi 587 1842; (572) xxvi 601 1842; (98) xxx 513 1843; (174) xxx 537 1843; (282) xxx 559 1843; (611) xxx 571 1843; (55) xxxii 419 1844.

Return of papers published in the metropolis, which are registered as newspapers, a portion whereof is published without stamps. (78) xxxiii 567 1850.

Return of names of newspapers in the United Kingdom to which halfpenny stamps were issued; number issued to each; and amount of duty paid, in 1852. lvii 573 1853.

Number of newspaper stamps at 1d issued to each newspaper in England, Ireland, Scotland and Wales in 1851, 1852 and 1853. xxxix 479 1854. Ditto in 1854 xxx 497 1855. Ditto, 1854 to 1 July 1855, xxx 509 1855; ditto, July–Dec 1855, xxxviii 511 1856.

Return of stamps at 1d issued to each newspaper published in London, Dublin and Edinburgh. Quarterly, 1851–4, xxxix 501 and 519 1854.

Return of registered newspapers and publications in the United Kingdom, and of the number of stamps issued to each quarterly 1855 to 1857. xxxiv 259 1858.

Lists in General Directories

The Post Office London directory for 1805 by B. Critchett. [1804] (6th edn). This edn first includes the London papers with days of issue; from the 15th edn 1814 onwards it contains the country papers as well. Annually to 1839.

Holden's triennial directory for 1805, 1806, 1807. [1805] (4th edn). Contains a list of London and country newspapers: this did not appear in the earlier edns, nor is it in the 10th edn for 1817, 1818, 1819, which was the first issued by Underhill after Holden's death.

Pigot and Co's London and provincial new commercial directory for 1822–3. [1822]. 2nd edn for 1823–4; 3rd edn for 1827–8; 6th edn for 1836–7; 7th edn Dec 1839.

Robson's London commercial directory for 1823. Also for 1839, 1840, 1843 (24th edn); the first edn for 1819 has no list. The lists in the later edns seem to have been supplied by Newton and Co; *see col* IIIII, *below*.

W. Kelly and Co. The Post Office London directory for 1840. 1839 onwards. The issues for the years from 1840–7 have opposite each paper the number of stamps issued to it for the second quarter of the preceding year; for the years 1842–7 they have the amount of advertisement duty paid as well. Annual.

Lists issued by Newspaper Advertisement Agents and others

These lists provide fuller information than the general directories, often giving the political complexion and particular area to which appeal is directed. The London Classified Directories (e.g. Robson's and Pigot's) give lists of agents for newspapers, and search in the larger libraries under the names there mentioned might reveal a number of lists not specified below.

Clarke and Lewis. Advertisements received by Clarke and Lewis, 4 Crown Court, Threadneedle Street, London. [Jan?] 1836, June 1836, Oct 1837. All single folio sheets ptd in 3 colours.

Newton and Co's general advertising country and London newspaper office, Warwick Square, Newgate Street. [c. 1840]. Single folio sheet.

Reid, J. & Co. An almanack of the British stamped press, including all stamped newspapers, literary or scientific journals, and commercial lists, for 1841. [1840].

Dawson, W. and Son. Advertisements and orders received by William Dawson and Son. [c. 1841]. Single folio sheet ptd in 3 colours.

—— W. Dawson and Son's London and country newspaper and advertising list. 1858 (9th edn). Single folio sheet ptd in 3 colours.

Lewis, Francis D. British and foreign newspaper and advertisement agent. 3 Castle Court, Cornhill, London. 30 June 1842. Single folio sheet.

Hammond's town and country advertising office. 27, Lombard Street, London. 1 Oct 1842. Single folio sheet.

Mitchell, Charles. The newspaper press directory. 1846, 1847, 1851, (3rd edn), 1854 (4th edn), 1856 (5th edn), 1857 onwards. Annual. Ed C. Mitchell 1846–59; W. Wellsman 1859–97. This is the fullest of the directories here listed, especially in the later issues.

A catalogue of London periodicals, newspapers, law reports and transactions of various societies. 1848–9. Continued as London catalogue of periodicals, newspapers and transactions etc, 1850–70. Annual.

Algar and Street. London, provincial and colonial advertising and newspaper agency office, 11 Clements Lane, Lombard Street, London. [Jan? 1855.] Single folio sheet.

Street Brothers. Advertising and newspaper agency office, 11 Serle Street, Lincoln's Inn, London. [Jan? 1855.] Single folio sheet.

Jack, Thomas C. Scottish newspaper directory and guide to advertisers: second edition, with an appendix containing the circulation of newspapers according to the Government Stamp Returns for 1854. Edinburgh 1855.

The newspaper record, containing a complete list of newspapers and periodicals in the United States, Canada and Great Britain. Ed W. T. Coggeshall, Philadelphia 1856.

William Thomas's universal newspaper and periodical list. 1863, 1864.

Frederick May. The London press dictionary and advertiser's handbook 1871. [1870].

Clarke, W. J. Newspaper list for the United Kingdom. 1873.

Eyre's guide containing a list of all newspapers and periodicals. [1873].

Street's list of newspapers published in Great Britain and Ireland. [1873].

Frederick May & Son. May's British and Irish press guide, and advertiser's handbook and dictionary. 1874. Annually to 1889. Continued as Willing's British and Irish press guide, 1890 onwards.

White, R. F. & Son. A list of the newspapers published in the United Kingdom, newly arranged and classified. 1878, 1882, 1884, 1887, 1889, 1891, 1895, 1897, 1912.

Deacon, S. & Co. Deacon's newspaper handbook and advertisers' guide. 1881 (5th edn), 1883, 1885, 1886, 1887, [c. 1890], 1893, 1894, 1895, 1904.

Sell, Henry. Sell's dictionary of the world's press 1884–1921. Annual, but none issued in 1911, 1913, 1916–18, 1920. Originally issued as The philosophy of advertising, 1882; then as The philosophy of advertising and newspaper register, 1883.

Alphabetical index of newspapers, the proprietors of which have been registered under the provisions of the Newspaper Libel and Registration Act 1881, at the Office of the Registrar of Joint Stock Companies in London. [1884].

Browne, T. B. (from 1888). Advertising ABC and advertisement press directory. 1887–1931 2. Annual.

—— Advertising in the provincial newspapers of Great Britain and Ireland. [1891].

Layton, Charles and Edwin. Handy newspaper list. [1890]–1915. Annual.

Street's list of newspapers published in Great Britain and Ireland. 1890–1917, 1920. Annual.

The annual index of periodicals and photographs for 1890. Continued as Index to the periodical literature of the world 1892 (for 1891), 1893 (for 1892). Continued as Index to the periodicals of 1894. Annually to 1901. Ed. W. T. Stead.

Ross, George and Co. The London signpost: shews the trade addresses of over 1,600 publishers and periodicals on sale at, or since Michaelmas 1893. [1893].

Mather and Crowther. Practical advertising. 1895–1923. Annual.

Walker, H. T. & Co. Walker's press directory. 1897.

Vickers's newspaper gazetteer: an annual reference book of the press for the United Kingdom, the Colonies etc 1900–16. Annual.

C. THE DAILY AND WEEKLY PRESS

Numbers and dates of periodicals in brackets are conjectural. Those without brackets are based on holdings recorded in Tercentenary handlist; Crane and Kaye; A census of British newspapers and periodicals; British Union catalogue of periodicals *or personal observation. In listing proprietors it has often been impossible to assign ultimate responsibility, especially in cases of multiple control.*

(1) DAILY PAPERS

London morning papers

The public ledger. No 1, 12 Jan 1760–14 Sept 1836. New ser no 1, 3 July 1837–11 July 1870. Continued as Public ledger evening report, 11 July 1870–2 May 1932. Continued as Evening report: the public ledger, 3 May 1932–27 July 1945. From 5 Sept 1836 to 1 July 1837 there appeared a separate paper, Constitutional and public ledger. *See col 1794, below.* Prop Lee Stevens. Ed Alexander Chalmers.

The morning chronicle. [No 1, 28 June 1769]–no 184, 3 Jan 1770–20 Dec 1862. Prop James Perry 1789–1821; William I. Clement 1822–34; John Easthope 1834–48(?); Duke of Newcastle, W. E. Gladstone, Sydney Herbert et al 1848 (?)–54; William Glover 1854–60(?); George Stiff 1860(?) –62. Ed James Perry 1789–1819, John Black 1819–43, Andrew Doyle 1843–8, J. D. Cook 1848–54, T. L. Holt, G. H. Francis.

The morning post. No 1, 2 Nov 1772–no 51561, 30 Sept 1937. Incorporated in Daily telegraph. Prop Daniel Stuart 1795–1803; Nicholas Byrne; C. E. Michele 1833–49; T. B. Crompton 1849–58; W. J. Rideout 1858–76; Algernon Borthwick 1876–1908. Ed Daniel Stuart 1795–1803, Nicholas Byrne (assisted by Eugenius Roche 1817–27) 1803–33, C. E. Michele 1833–49, Peter Borthwick 1849–52, Algernon Borthwick 1852–72, William Hardman 1872–90, Alexander Leys Moore 1890–4, Algernon Locker 1895–7, J. N. Dunn 1897–1905.

The morning herald. No 1, 1 Nov 1780–31 Dec 1869. Prop Henry Bate Dudley 1780–1824; ? Thwaites ?–1843; Edward Baldwin 1843–57; James Johnstone 1857–? Ed Alexander Chalmers, Thomas Wright (?), Edward Baldwin and S. L. Giffard 1843–6, Robert Knox 1846–57, Thomas Hamber 1857–?

The times. No 940, 1 Jan 1788 onwards. Started as Daily universal register, no 1, 1 Jan 1785; the original title was continued as a subtitle from 1 Jan to 17 March 1788. Prop John Walter I 1785–1803; John Walter II 1803–47; John Walter III 1847–94; Arthur Fraser Walter 1894–1908. Ed William Combe 1797–1808, Henry Crabb Robinson 1808–9, John Walter II, J. H. Stoddart 1814–17, Thomas Barnes 1817–41, J. T. Delane 1841–77, Thomas Chenery 1878–84, G. E. Buckle 1884–1912.

The oracle. No 1, 1 June 1789–28 Feb 1794. Amalgamated with Public advertiser and continued as Oracle and public advertiser, 1 March 1794–8 Sept 1798. Incorporated in Daily advertiser and continued as Oracle and daily advertiser, 10 Sept 1798–24 March 1802. Continued as Daily advertiser and oracle, 25 March 1802–8 June 1809. Prop John Bell 1789–96; Peter Stuart. Ed James Boaden.

The true Briton. No 1, 1 Jan 1793–no 3437, 31 Dec 1803. Incorporated in Daily advertiser and oracle. Ed John Heriot 1793–1803.

The morning advertiser. No 1, 8 Feb 1794 onwards. Prop The Licensed Victuallers' Association. Ed ? Anderson, John Scott, ? Sheridan, James Grant 1850–70, Alfred B. Richards 1870–6, Thomas Hamber 1876–86, Thomas Wright 1886–94, Frank G. Dovey.

The porcupine. No 1, 30 Oct 1800–31 Dec 1801. Incorporated in True Briton. Pop and ed William Cobbett.

The British press or morning literary advertiser. No 1, 1 Jan 1803–31 Oct 1826. Ed George Lane, Robert Heron, J. B. Capes.

The advertiser's daily magazine. [No 1, 29 Jan 1805]–no 9, 8 Feb 1805–?

The morning star. [1805]–no 58, 25 Jan 1806–?.

The aurora and British imperial reporter. No 1, 19 Jan–no 121, 8 June 1807–? Ed William Jerdan.

The day. No 1, 2 Jan 1809–no 2057, 20 April 1815–[1817]. Incorporated in New times. Ed Eugenius Roche 1809–11, John Scott, ? Hogan.

The new times. [1817]–1 Jan 1818–4 Oct 1828. Continued as Morning journal 6 Oct 1828–13 May 1830. Started before Easter 1817 and soon absorbed in Day; continued as Day and new times, but the first part of the title was dropped before the end of 1817. Ed J. H. Stoddart 1817–26. Eugenius Roche 1827–8, Robert Alexander and J. M. Gutch 1828–30.

The British statesman. No 1, 10 Feb–no 262, 11 Dec 1819.

The representative. No 1, 25 Jan–29 July 1826. Prop John Murray.

The tatler. No 1, 4 Oct 1830–13 Feb 1832. Ed J. H. Leigh Hunt.

The daily politician. No 1, 25 Jan–no 24, 20 Feb 1836. Another paper of the same name ran for a few days in Sept of the same year.

The constitutional and public ledger. No 1, 15 Sept 1836–1 July 1837. *See* Public ledger, above. Prop The Metropolitan Newspaper Co, a group of Radical sympathisers. Ed S. L. Blanchard assisted by Thornton Hunt.

The morning gazette. No 1, 2 Oct–no 54, 2 Dec 1837.

The iron times. No 1, 7 July 1845–no 264, 11 May 1846. Prop and ed T. L. Holt.

The daily news. No 1, 21 Jan 1846–31 May 1930. Amalgamated with Daily chronicle and continued as News-chronicle, 2 June 1930–17 Oct 1960. Prop Bradbury and Evans, Joseph Paxton, Joshua Walmsley et al; George Smith; Samuel Morley, Henry Labouchere, Henry Oppenheim et al. Ed Charles Dickens Jan 1846, John Forster Feb–Oct 1846, E. E. Crowe, Oct 1846–1851, F. Knight Hunt 1851–4, William Weir 1854–8, Thomas Walker 1858–69, Edward Dicey 1869, F. H. Hill 1870–85, H. W. Lucy Dec 1885–June 1887, John R. Robinson 1887–95, E. T. Cook 1895– 1901.

The London telegraph. No 1, 1 Feb–8 July 1848. Prop H. Ingram. Ed Thomas Hodgkin.

The daily telegraph. No 1, 29 June 1855 onwards. First pbd at 2d but in 1856 was the first daily newspaper to be sold at 1d. Prop A. B. Sleigh 1855; family company under J. M. Levy, Edward Lawson (Lord Burnham), Henry Lawson (Viscount Burnham) 1856–1927. Ed A. B. Richards 1855, Edward Lawson (Lord Burnham) 1856–1916(?) assisted by Thornton Hunt 1856–72 and Edwin Arnold 1873–1901.

The morning news. No 1, 3 March 1856–no 924, 29 June 1859. Ed Henry Mayhew.

The morning star. No 1, 17 March 1856–no 4251, 13 Oct 1869. Prop Samuel Lucas 1856–65. Ed Samuel Lucas 1856–65, J. McCarthy, J. Morley June–Oct 1869.

The standard. 29 June 1857–16 March 1916. Founded as an evening paper in 1827 (*see col* 1793, *below*), it was for many years run in conjunction with Morning herald; in 1857 it became a morning paper, though an evening edn continued to be pbd. Prop James Johnstone 1857–76; W. H. Mudford. Ed Thomas Hamber 1857–70, John Gorst 1870–74, W. H. Mudford 1874–1900, G. B. Curtis 1900–4.

The morning mail. 23 April 1864–21 July 1865. Continued as London general advertiser, 22 July 1865–1 Dec 1866.

The day. No 1, 19 March–4 May 1867.

The London daily reporter. [1869]–no 376, 2 Jan 1871–16 June 1871. Continued as London daily recorder, 17 June 1871–31 Dec 1872.

The financier. No 1, 1 March 1870–23 May 1924. Incorporated in Financial times.

The daily chronicle. No 3320, 25 Nov 1872–31 May 1930. Incorporated in News chronicle. Started weekly in 1855 as Clerkenwell news and general advertiser, nos 73–1200, 8 Oct 1856–5 Feb 1866; continued for a few issues daily, then twice weekly as Clerkenwell news and London times, nos 1201–2394, 7 Feb 1866–Dec 1869; then continued daily as Clerkenwell news and London daily chronicle, nos 2395–2779, 11 Dec 1869–5 March 1871; continued as London daily chronicle and Clerkenwell news, nos 2780–3319, 6 March 1871–23 Nov 1872. Prop Edward Lloyd. Ed Robert Whelan Boyle 1876–89, Alfred Ewen Fletcher 1889–94, H. W. Massingham 1894–9, W. H. Fisher 1899–1903.

The hour. No 1, 24 March 1873–11 Aug 1876. Prop D. Morier Evans. Ed Thomas Hamber.

The circle. No 1, 29 Jan–no 87, 9 May 1874. Ed William Saunders.

The echo. No 1 (of morning edition), 4 Oct 1875–31 May 1876. Run in connection with Echo (*see below under evening papers*). The first halfpenny morning daily. Prop Albert Grant. Ed Horace Voules.

The sportsman. 20 March 1876–22 Nov 1924. Incorporated in Sporting life. No 1, 2 Aug 1865 (twice weekly); thrice weekly in 1867. Ed Charles Russell 1867–75, Thomas Whitefoot 1878–85, A. Allison, S. Downing 1889–?

The daily express. Nos 1–101, 1 May–25 Aug 1877.

The continental times. [1878]–12 March 1881–15 Feb 1890. Pbd in London and Paris.

Sporting life. 23 March 1883 onwards. Started as Bell's penny life in London, no 1, 16 March 1859; continued twice weekly as Sporting life from no 12, 30 April 1859; in 1861 it absorbed Sporting telegraph (no 1, Feb 1860–6 March 1861); in April 1881 it was pbd 4 times weekly; on 23 March 1883 it became a daily paper; on 1 July 1886 it absorbed Bell's life in London, below. Prop George Maddick and S. O. Beeton; Edward Hulton 1885–? Ed Henry Fiest 1859–74, Charles W. Blake 1874–91, George S. Lowe 1891–?

The summary. No 1, 10 July 1883–11 Oct 1884. Pbd by Times.

The financial news. No 114, 1 July 1884 onwards. Absorbed Financial times and took over its title. Started as Financial and mining news, nos 1–113, 28 Jan–28 June 1884. Prop and ed Harry H. Marks.

The morning mail. Nos 1–69, 20 April–9 July 1885.

The journal. Nos 1–43, 1 Nov–20 Dec 1886.

The financial times. 13 Feb 1888 onwards. Started as London financial guide, no 1, Jan–Feb 1888. *See* Financial news *above*.

The daily oracle. Nos 1–840, 21 Nov 1889–27 Aug 1892. Ed T. P. Whittaker.

Galignani's messenger. No 23515, 1 Jan 1890–31 Dec 1895. Continued as Daily messenger, no 25679, 1 Jan 1896–30 July 1904. Started in Paris in 1814, thrice weekly and became daily in 1821. Ed Cyrus Redding 1815–8, James S. Bowes, Gibbons Merle 1830–55, J. C. Mackenzie, Horatio Bottomley 1896, Norman Angell.

The daily graphic. No 1, 4 Jan 1890–16 Oct 1926. An illustrated paper. Incorporated in Daily sketch. Prop William L. Thomas.

Morning. No 1, 21 May 1892–4 Sept 1898. Continued as London morning, no 1968, 5 Sept 1898–22 April 1899. Continued as Morning herald, no 1, 24 April 1899–1 Sept 1900. Incorporated in Daily express. Halfpenny paper. Ed Chester Ives.

The morning leader. No 1, 23 May 1892–11 May 1912. Incorporated in Daily news. Halfpenny paper. Ed F. W. Wilson.

The daily courier. Nos 1–98, 23 April–15 Aug 1896. Prop George Newnes. Ed W. Earl Hodgson.

The daily mail. No 1, 4 May 1896 onwards. Prop and ed Alfred Harmsworth.

The daily express. No 1, 24 April 1900 onwards. Prop C. A. Pearson. Ed Pearson 1900–4.

London evening papers

The star. No 1, 3 May 1788–15 Oct 1831. Incorporated in Albion and star. Prop Peter Stuart; Alexander Tilloch. Ed Andrew Macdonald, Alexander Tilloch, John Mayne, Rowland Nash.

The courier. [Sept 1792]–no 86, 31 Dec 1792–6 July 1842. Prop James Perry; Daniel Stuart 1799–1822. Ed Daniel Stuart 1803–11, Peter Street 1811–22, William Mudford 1827?, Eugenius Roche 1828?, John Galt 1830, James Stuart 1830–36, Samuel Laman Blanchard 1837–9.

The sun. No 1, 1 Oct 1792–15 April 1876. No 16042, 24 Jan 1844 gives this information: 'The sun is published every morning at five o'clock in time for the early trains and town delivery; a second edition (Evening sun) is published in time for the afternoon trains, and a third edition at seven o'clock for Post, containing Parliamentary and all other news in London up to that hour'. Prop Patrick Grant April 1826–1831; Murdo Young 1832–1850; Charles Kent 1850–? Ed John Heriot 1792–1806, Robert Clark 1806–7, William Jerdan 1813–7, John Taylor, Murdo Young, Patrick Grant, W. F. Deacon ?–1845, Charles Kent.

The albion and evening advertiser. [1799]–no 106, 7 Jan 1800–[1807]. Ed Allan M'Leod, John Fenwick.

The traveller. [1801]–no 5519, 1 Jan 1818–28 Dec 1822. Incorporated in Globe and traveller. Prop Robert Torrens. Ed Edward Quin, Walter Coulson.

The globe. [No 1, 1 Jan 1803]–no 1536, 8 Dec 1807–31 Dec 1922. Incorporated in Evening standard. It absorbed Traveller on 28 Dec 1822 and was called Globe and traveller, until 5 Feb 1921; it also absorbed Statesman, Feb 1824, Evening chronicle, March 1824, Nation, July 1824, and Argus, July 1828. Prop Richard Phillips and London booksellers; Robert Torrens 1822–64; Conservative syndicate under Stafford Northcote until 1866–75; George C. H. Armstrong 1875–1907. Ed George Lane 1803, Robert Heron 1803, Robert Torrens, Walter Coulson 1822–5, Gibbons Merle 1825–30, R. D. Hanson, George Stevenson, John Wilson 1834–?, ? Westcomb, R. H. Patterson, H. N. Barnett, Marwood Tucker 1868, George C. H. Armstrong 1871–89, Ponsonby Ogle, Algernon Locker 1891, George Elliot Armstrong 1895–1907.

The statesman. [No 1, 26 Feb 1806]–no 107, 30 June 1807–18 Feb 1824. Incorporated in Globe and traveller. Ed John Hunt 1806–9, W. M. Willett 1809, John Scott 1809–14, Daniel Lovell 1814–7, Sampson Perry 1817–9, David Carey 1819–24.

The pilot. [No 1, 1 Jan 1807]–no 687, 15 March 1809–31 Oct 1815. Ed E. Samuel, Herbert Compton, ? Fitzgerald.

The Alfred and Westminster gazette. [No 1, 17 April 1810]–no 22, 12 May 1810–23 April 1833. The second part of the title was soon dropped.

Cobbett's evening post. Nos 1–55, 29 Jan–1 April 1820. Prop and ed William Cobbett.

The true Briton. No 1, 1 July 1820–13 Nov 1822. Incorporated in Traveller.

The British traveller. No 1, 19 July 1821–no 3703, 25 May 1833. Ed W. M. Willett.

The new globe. No 1, 3 Feb–no 132, 5 July 1823.

The evening chronicle. Nos 1–30, 4 Feb–19 March 1824. Incorporated in Globe and traveller. Ed J. S. Buckingham.

The nation. Nos 1–65, 10 May–24 July 1824. Incorporated in Globe and traveller. Ed T. J. Wooler.

The evening times. Nos 1–46, 14 Nov 1825–5 Jan 1826.

The standard. No 1, 21 May 1827–29 June 1857. Continued as Evening standard, no 11179, 11 June 1860–13 March 1905. Continued as Evening standard and St James's gazette, 14 March 1905–23 Oct 1916. Continued as Evening standard, 24 Oct 1916 onwards. It absorbed Albion and star 1 Jan 1836. Prop Charles and Edward Baldwin 1827–57; James Johnstone 1857–76. Ed S. L. Giffard (assisted by A. A. Watts and William Maginn) 1827–45, Robert Knox 1846–57, ? Pritchard, Charles Williams 1860–3, Thomas Hamber 1863–70, John Gorst 1870–4, W. H. Mudford 1874–1900.

The argus. Nos 1–24, 30 June–26 July 1828. Incorporated in Globe and traveller. Ed J. S. Buckingham.

The albion. 15 Nov 1830–15 Oct 1831. Continued as Albion and star 17 Oct 1831–31 Dec 1835. Incorporated in Standard.

The true sun. No 1, 5 March 1832–23 Dec 1837. Prop Patrick Grant 1832; John Bell; Daniel Whittle Harvey 1833–7. Ed Patrick Grant, Samuel Laman Blanchard, John Bell, Daniel Whittle Harvey, W. J. Fox 1833 (?)–7.

The shipping gazette. Nos 1–557, 4 Jan 1836–13 Oct 1837. Continued as Shipping gazette and commercial advertiser, 14 Oct 1837–9 March 1838. Ed William Carpenter 1836.

Shipping and mercantile gazette. No 1, 12 March 1838–30 June 1884. Continued as Shipping and mercantile gazette and Lloyd's list, 1 July 1884–30 June 1914. Continued as Shipping and mercantile gazette and daily index, 1 July 1914–3 Feb 1916. Prop and ed William Mitchell.

The evening star. No 1, 25 July 1842–no 188, 28 Feb 1843.

The railway director. No 1, 3 Jan 1845–14 March 1846.

The express. No 1, 1 Sept 1846–30 April 1869. Run in conjunction with Daily news. Ed Thomas Elliott 1846–55, J. R. Robinson 1855–69.

The evening journal. No 1, 6 Oct 1851–14 April 1860.

The evening star. No 1, 17 March 1856–no 4251, 13 Oct 1869. Run in conjunction with Morning star. Ed F. W. Chesson.

The evening herald. No 1, 29 June 1857–no 2428, 27 May 1865. Run in conjunction with Standard.

The Pall Mall gazette. No 1, 7 Feb 1865–27 Oct 1923. Incorporated in Evening standard. Prop George Murray Smith 1865–May 1880; Henry Yates Thompson May 1880–1892; William Waldorf Astor 1892–1909. Ed Frederick Greenwood 1865–May 1880, Horace Voules May 1880–1, John Morley 1881–3, W. T. Stead 1883–9, E. T. Cook 1889–92, C. Kinloch Cooke 1892–3, H. C. Cust 1893–6, Douglas Straight 1896–1909.

The glow-worm. No 1, 5 June 1865–no 1152, 13 Feb 1869. Ed F. C. Burnand, A. W. à Beckett, T. H. S. Escott, T. W. Robertson.

The daily recorder (of commerce). [1866]–no 1982, 1 Jan 1873–20 Dec 1887. Incorporated in Evening post (i.e. Evening news).

The little times. No 1, 27 April–no 22, 22 May 1867. Ed Mayne Reid.

The echo. No 1, 8 Dec 1868–31 July 1905. In 1875 it ran a morning edn and its style was changed to Evening echo (*see col 1791, above*). The first halfpenny newspaper. Prop Cassell, Petter and Galpin 1868–75; Albert Grant 1875–6; J. Passmore Edwards 1876–1884; syndicate headed by Andrew Carnegie 1884–5; J. Passmore Edwards 1885–96. Ed Arthur Arnold 1868–75, Horace Voules 1875–6. J. Passmore Edwards 1876–84, Howard Evans, Aaron Watson, W. M. Crook 1898–?

The London Figaro. No 1, 17 May 1870–no 263, 11 March 1871. Ed J. Mortimer.

The public ledger and evening report. 11 July 1870–2 May 1932. Continued as Evening report: the public ledger, 3 May 1932–27 July 1945. *See col 1789 above under morning papers*. Not pbd Saturdays.

The St James's gazette. No 1, 31 May 1880–13 March 1905. Incorporated in Evening standard. Prop H. Huck Gibbs 1880–8; E. Steinkopff 1888–? Ed Frederick Greenwood 1880–8, Sidney Low 1888–97, Hugh Chisholm 1897–1900.

The evening news. No 1, 26 July 1881–Dec 1887. Continued as Evening post, no 1427, 21 Dec 1887–12 Jan 1889. Continued as Evening news and post, 13 Jan 1889–11 May 1889. Continued as Evening news, 12 May 1889 onwards. Halfpenny paper. Prop Coleridge Kennard ?–1894; Alfred Harmsworth 1894–? Ed Charles Williams 1881–4, John R. K. Ralph, ? Coplestone, Frank Harris 1889–92, Percy White, Louis Tracy 1894, Kennedy Jones 1894–1900.

The star. No 1, 17 Jan 1888–17 Oct 1960. Incorporated in Evening news. Halfpenny paper. Prop T. P. O'Connor. Ed T. P. O'Connor 1888–July 1890, H. W. Massingham July 1890–Jan 1891, James Stuart 1892–7, E. Parke.

The Westminster gazette. No 1, 31 Jan 1893–31 Jan 1928. Incorporated in Daily news. Prop George Newnes Ltd 1893–1908. Ed E. T. Cook 1893–6, J. A. Spender 1896–1922.

The sun. No 1, 27 June 1893–11 Oct 1906. Prop T. P. O'Connor. Ed T. P. O'Connor 1893–6, W. S. Johnstone.

The evening mail. No 1, 1 April 1896–9 Oct 1901.

Provincial Daily Papers

An asterisk before an entry indicates that no copy of the paper has been located. A valuable source of information on the proprietors of the provincial, Scottish and Irish press is Newspaper press directory, 1846 onwards.

*The mercantile gazette, and Liverpool and Manchester daily advertiser (Liverpool). No 1, 6 Aug 1811–?; expired before 1812. *See* A. Andrews, History of British journalism, vol 2, 1859, p 124. Ed ? Solomon.

*The northern express and Lancashire daily post (Manchester). No 1, 1 Dec 1821–Feb 1822. *See* A. Andrews, *above*. Pbd Henry Burgess.

Northern daily times (Liverpool). No 1, 24 Sept 1853–6 June 1857. Continued as Northern times, 7 June 1857–19 Feb 1860. Continued as Daily times, 20 Feb 1860–30 Jan 1861. Ed Charles Willmer.

The daily war telegraph (Manchester). No 2, 21 Oct 1854–29 Jan 1855. Continued as War telegraph, 30 Jan–20 March 1855. Continued as Daily telegraph, 22 March–7 April 1855. Continued as Manchester daily telegraph, 9 April–30 Nov 1855.

The war express and daily advertiser (Manchester). No 4, 24 Oct–no 46, 15 Dec 1854. Continued as Manchester express etc, 18 Dec 1854–8 June 1855.

The Manchester daily times. No 1, 12 Dec 1854–15 June 1855. Incorporated in Manchester examiner and times; *see below*.

The northern express (Darlington). No 1, 21 April–27 Oct 1855. Continued as Northern daily express (Newcastle), 30 Oct 1855–16 Oct 1886. Ed R. N. Worth 1866–7.

The Birmingham daily press. No 1, 7 May 1855–20 Nov 1858. Prop George Dawson, William Harris, James Freeman et al.

The Sheffield daily telegraph. No 1, 8 June 1855–14 July 1934. Continued as Sheffield telegraph, 16 July 1934–29 Oct 1938. Continued as Sheffield telegraph and daily independent, 31 Oct 1938–13 May 1939. Continued as Telegraph and independent, 15 May 1939–12 June 1942. Continued as Sheffield telegraph and independent, 13 June–14 July 1942. Continued as Sheffield telegraph, 15 July 1942 onwards. Prop William Leng and Frederick Clifford 1864; William Leng 1864–1902. Ed William Leng 1864–1902.

The daily post (Liverpool). No 1, 11 June 1855–28 Oct 1879. Continued as Liverpool daily post, 29 Oct 1879 onwards. Ed M. J. Whitty 1855–? Edward R. Russell 1869–? John Macleay.

The Birmingham daily mercury. No 1, 12 June 1855–22 Aug 1857. Incorporated in Birmingham daily press.

The Manchester examiner. 17 June 1855–10 March 1894. Started weekly, no 1, 10 Jan 1846; twice weekly at the beginning of 1854; and in Oct Manchester examiner extraordinary was issued on the four weekdays on which Manchester examiner itself did not appear; on 12 Dec this became Manchester daily times (*see above*); when this ceased 15 June 1855, Manchester examiner and times was continued daily under its old title; it was incorporated in Umpire (Manchester) in March 1894 (*see under Sunday papers below*). Prop Thomas Ballantyne, John Bright et al 1855–? Ed Thomas Ballantyne 1846, A. W. Paulton 1846–64, H. Dunckley 1864–88, J. S. R. Phillips 1889–91, W. M. Leslie, A. Ireland.

The morning news (Sheffield). No 1, 19 June–14 Nov 1855.

The Manchester guardian. 2 July 1855–22 Aug 1959. Continued as Guardian, 24 Aug 1959 onwards. Started weekly, no 1, 5 May 1821; twice weekly in Sept 1836. Prop J. E. Taylor I 1821–44; J. E. Taylor II 1844–1905. Ed J. E. Taylor I 1821–44, R. S. Taylor 1844–8, Jeremiah Garnett 1848–61, J. E. Taylor II 1861–72, C. P. Scott 1872–1930.

Stevenson's daily express (Nottingham). No 1, 2 July 1855–29 May 1856.

North and South Shields gazette. Daily telegraphic edition (South Shields). No 1, 2 July 1855–20 April 1860. Continued as North and South Shields gazette and daily telegraph, 21 April 1860–30 Dec 1876. Continued as North and South Shields daily gazette and shipping telegraph, 2 Jan 1877–26 Jan 1884. Continued as Shields daily gazette and shipping telegraph, 28 Jan 1884–2 April 1932. Continued as Shields gazette and shipping telegraph, 4 April 1932 onwards. Started weekly, no 1, 24 Feb 1849. Prop James Stevenson 1849–54; James Cochrane Stevenson 1854–83; Northern Press Co Ltd (with J. C. Stevenson as head) 1883–1905. Ed W. K. Kelly, D. M. McLennan ?–Oct 1861, ? Finlay, William Duncan 1865–78, James Annand 1878–85, Aaron Watson 1885–92.

The Hull morning telegraph. [1855?]–no 4921, 12 July 1869– 30 April 1880. Incorporated in Hull express.

The Sheffield daily news. No 1, 2 Dec 1856–27 Dec 1862.

The Liverpool daily mail. No 1, 17 March–no 19, 10 April 1857.

The Birmingham daily post. No 1, 4 Dec 1857–20 May 1918. Continued as Birmingham post, 21 May 1918–2 Nov 1956. Continued as Birmingham post and Birmingham gazette, 3 Nov 1956–23 Sept 1964. Continued as Birmingham post, 24 Sept 1964 onwards. Prop John F. Feeney and John Jaffray 1857–69; John Jaffray and John Feeney 1869–94; John Feeney 1894–1905. Ed John Jaffray 1857–61?, ? Silk, J. T. Bunce 1862–98, A. H. Poultney 1899–1905.

The Liverpool mercury. 1 Jan 1858–12 Nov 1904. Incorporated in Liverpool daily post. Started weekly, no 1, 5 July 1811; twice weekly in 1847. Ed Egerton Smith 1811–?, Thomas Ballantyne, John Maitland, John Lovell 1880–90, G. Wynne 1890–1904.

The daily chronicle and northern counties advertiser (Newcastle). No 1, 1 May 1858–30 Dec 1861. Continued as Newcastle daily chronicle and northern counties advertiser, 1 Jan 1862–16 March 1923. Continued as North mail and Newcastle daily chronicle. 19 March 1923–18 Sept 1939. Incorporated in Newcastle journal (*see below*, Newcastle daily journal). Started weekly as Newcastle chronicle, no 1, 24 March 1764. Prop Joseph Cowen 1858–1900. Ed Joseph Cowen, Langley Baxter, James Annand ?–1879, ? Ruddock, Aaron Watson 1885–93.

The western daily press (Bristol). No 1, 1 June 1858–30 Jan 1932. Continued as Western daily press and Bristol mirror, 2 Feb 1932 onwards. Incorporating Bristol times and mirror (*see below*, Daily Bristol times). Prop P. S. Macliver and Walter Reid 1858–91; Walter Reid 1891–? Ed Walter Reid 1858–?

The Sheffield daily argus. No 1, 11 May–No 20, 3 June 1859.

Willmer's Liverpool morning news. No 1, 16 July–no 104, 15 Nov 1859. Ed Charles Willmer.

The western morning news (Plymouth). No 1, 3 Jan 1860–31 Jan 1921. Continued as Western morning news and mercury, 1 Feb 1921 onwards. Ed William Saunders, Edward Spender 1860–78, Albert Groser 1878–94.

The Nottingham daily express. No 1, 4 Jan 1860–6 April 1918. Continued as Nottingham journal and express (incorporating the long dormant copyright of Nottingjam journal which had been purchased from William Bradshaw in 1887), 8 April 1918–5 Sept 1953. Amalgamated with Nottingham guardian and subsequently pbd as Guardian journal. Prop John W. Jevons 1860–4; Jevons and E. Renals 1864–? Ed J. Dods Shaw, D. Edwards. 1891–7.

The Bristol daily post. No 1, 24 Jan 1860–26 Jan 1878. Absorbed Bristol mercury and was continued as Bristol mercury and daily post, 27 Jan 1878–19 Dec 1901. Continued as Bristol daily mercury, 21 Dec 1901–30 Nov 1909. Ed Harold Lewis.

The daily western mercury (Plymouth). No 1, 2 June–25 Sept 1860. Continued as Western daily mercury, 26 Sept 1860–31 Jan 1921. Incorporated in Western morning news. Ed Isaac Latimer, Edwin Goadby 1866–74.

The Newcastle daily journal. 2 Jan 1861–29 March 1930. Continued as Newcastle journal, 31 March 1930–5 July 1958. Continued as Journal, 7 July 1958 onwards. Started weekly as Newcastle journal, no 1, 12 May 1832. Ed Robert Redpath, A. D. Murray.

The Cambrian daily leader (Swansea). No 1, 20–3 May 1861. Continued as Cambria daily leader, 24 May 1861–15 March 1930. Incorporated in South Wales daily post.

The Nottingham daily guardian. No 1, 1 July 1861–9 Oct 1905. Continued as Nottingham guardian, 10 Oct 1905–5 Sept 1953. Amalgamated with Nottingham journal and express and continued as Guardian journal. Ed J. R. Forman.

The Liverpool evening mercury. No 1, 26 Aug 1861–9 Jan 1863.

The Liverpool journal of commerce. No 1, Oct 1861–28 Feb 1873. Continued as Journal of commerce, March 1873–21 Aug 1880. Continued as Liverpool journal of commerce, 23 Aug 1880–Dec 1911. Continued as Journal of commerce, 1 Jan 1912 onwards. When it incorporated Liverpool shipping telegraph, no 11,908, 30 Dec 1899, was followed by no 22,846, 1 Jan 1900, as a result of its taking over the numbering of the latter. Prop Charles Birchall 1880–1905. Ed Thomas Ballantyne 1861 (?).

The Manchester courier. [1861]–28 Jan 1916. Started weekly, no 1, 1 Jan 1825. Prop Thomas Sowler 1871–April 1891. Ed A. A. Watts 1825–6, John Sowler, R. S. Sowler 1839, Thomas Sowler, Francis Hitchman.

The Leeds mercury. [1861]–19 Oct 1901. Continued as Leeds and Yorkshire mercury, 21 Oct 1901–4 Nov 1907. Continued as Leeds mercury, 5 Nov 1907–25 Nov 1939. Incorporated in Yorkshire post. Started weekly, no 1, May 1718; thrice weekly in July 1855. Prop Edward Baines I 1801–27; Edward Baines I and Edward Baines II 1827–37; Edward Baines I, Edward Baines II and Frederick Baines 1837–48; Edward Baines II and Frederick Baines 1848–?. Ed Edward Baines I, Edward Baines II, Thomas Baines ?–1887, T. Wemyss Reid May 1870–87, Talbot Baines 1887–97.

The Birmingham daily gazette. No 1, 12 May 1862–30

Jan 1904. Continued as Birmingham gazette and express, 1 Feb 1904–16 Nov 1912. Continued as Birmingham gazette, 18 Nov 1912–2 Nov 1956. Incorporated in Birmingham post. Started weekly as Aris's Birmingham gazette, no 1, 16 Nov 1741. Ed John Caldecott, J. T. Bunce, Dr J. A. Langford, Dr Sebastian Evans, A. W. Still 1860–1890–1904.

Exeter and Plymouth gazette daily telegrams. 7 Feb 1863–30 April 1885. Daily edition of Exeter and Plymouth gazette. Prop J. Salter.

The Sheffield daily advertiser. No 1, 24 Feb–no 60, 6 May 1863.

The daily courier (Liverpool). 21 April 1863–2 Oct 1882. Continued as Liverpool courier, 3 Oct 1882–2 Sept 1922. Continued as Daily courier, 9 Oct 1922–31 Dec 1929. Started weekly as Liverpool courier and commercial advertiser, no 1, 6 Jan 1808. Prop Thomas Kaye 1808–56; Charles Tinling 1856, subsequently joined by John A. Willox and R. Hadden to become C. Tinling & Co. Ed Thomas Kaye, Charles Tinling, John A. Willox.

The eastern morning news (Hull). No 1, 26 Jan 1864–8 Nov 1929. Ed William Saunders, William Hunt, J. A. Spender 1886–90.

The eastern evening news (Hull). No 1, 26 Jan 1864–30 April 1867.

The Shields daily news (North Shields). No 1, 22 Aug 1864–6 June 1933. Continued as Shields news, 7 June 1933–31 Dec 1937. Continued as Shields evening news, 1 Jan 1938–21 Aug 1959.

The Ipswich times. [1864]–no 380, 2 March 1866–9 Oct 1874. Continued as East Anglian daily times, 11 Oct 1874 onwards. Ed F. W. Wilson 1874–90.

The daily Bristol times and mirror. 5 Jan 1865–31 Dec 1883. Continued as Bristol times and mirror, 1 Jan 1884–29 Jan 1932. Incorporated in Western daily press. Started weekly as Bristol times and Bath advocate, no 1, 2 March 1839–26 March 1853; continued weekly as Bristol times and Felix Farley's Bristol journal, 2 April 1853–31 Dec 1864. Ed T. D. Taylor, Charles Pebody ?–1882.

The Sunderland daily shipping news. No 1, 6 Nov 1865–no 10,431, 31 Dec 1913.

The Sheffield evening star and daily times. [1865]–no 2,760, 21 April 1874–23 Jan 1888. Incorporated in Evening telegraph (Sheffield).

The northern evening express (Newcastle). No 1, 1 Aug 1866–16 Oct 1886. Ed William Saunders.

The Yorkshire post (Leeds). No 5,928, 2 July 1866 onwards. Amalgamated with Leeds intelligencer, 2 July 1754–no 5,927, 30 June 1866, a weekly. Prop Yorkshire Conservative Newspaper Company. Ed John R. K. Ralph 1866–82, Charles Pebody 1882–90, H. J. Palmer 1890–1903.

The western times (Exeter). [1866] onwards. Started as Exeter weekly times no 1, 6 Oct 1827; present title from 3 Jan 1829. Ed T. Latimer ?–23 Jan 1873, Hugh Latimer and Stephen Glanville.

The evening express of the Devon weekly times (Exeter). No 1, 19 Dec 1866–25 Oct 1873. Continued as Devon evening express, 27 Oct 1873–30 Sept 1904. Continued as Express and echo, 1 Oct 1904 onwards.

The Bolton evening news. No 1, 19 March 1867 onwards. Prop W. F. Tillotson 1867–1889; Tillotson and Son 1898–? Ed W. Brimelow 1867–1913.

The Bradford daily telegraph. No 1, 16 July 1868–15 Dec 1926. Continued as Bradford telegraph and argus, 16 Dec 1926–10 May 1930. Continued as Telegraph and argus 12 May 1930–3 Nov 1956. Continued as Telegraph and argus and Yorkshire observer, and eventually as Telegraph and argus when it dropped the rest of its title, 5 Nov 1956 onwards.

The Brighton daily news. No 1, 2 Nov 1868–31 May 1880. Incorporated in Argus (Brighton).

The western counties daily herald (Plymouth). No 1, 12 Nov 1868–13 Feb 1869.

The Manchester evening news. No 1, 10 Oct 1868–26 July 1963. Continued as Manchester evening news and chronicle, 29 July 1963 onwards. Prop W. Evans & Co. Ed John Astle.

The Bradford daily times. [1868]–no 813, 1 Jan–14 Sept 1871.

The Sussex daily news (Brighton). [1868]–no 1147, 2 July 1872–3 March 1956. Incorporated in Evening argus (Brighton).

The Bradford observer. [1868]–16 Nov 1901. Continued as Yorkshire daily observer, 17 Nov 1901–15 Jan 1909. Continued as Yorkshire observer, 16 Jan 1909–3 Nov 1956. Started weekly, no 1, 6 Feb 1834. Prop William Byles; W. P. Byles. Ed William Byles 1834–?, W. P. Byles, W. Harrison.

The western daily standard (Plymouth). No 1, 2 March 1869–5 March 1870.

The Oldham evening express. No 1, 5 April 1869–10 July 1889.

The western mail (Cardiff). No 1, 1 May 1869 onwards. Prop and ed Lascelles Carr.

The Leicester daily mail. No 1, 3 May 1869–19 Feb 1870. Continued as Leicester weekly express, nos 1–33, 26 Feb–1 Oct 1870.

The Newcastle daily telegraph. No 1, 19 June 1869–19 Nov 1870. Continued as Newcastle morning telegraph, 23 Nov 1870–7 June 1871. Continued as Newcastle evening telegraph, 8 June–23 Dec 1871.

The evening gazette for Middlesbrough. [8 Nov 1869]–6 Dec 1872. Continued as Daily gazette for Middlesbrough, 7 Dec 1872–10 June 1881. Continued as North eastern daily gazette (Middlesbrough), 11 June 1881–7 Nov 1936. Continued as North eastern gazette, 9 Nov 1936–13 Nov 1940. Continued as Evening gazette, 14 Nov 1940 onwards. Ed Hugh Gilzean Reid.

The northern echo (Darlington). No 1, 1 Jan 1870 onwards. Until 17 June 1870 it emanated from Hartlepool. Ed W. T. Stead 1871–80.

The Newcastle evening courant. No 1, 5 March 1870–Nov 1874. Continued as Newcastle daily courant, 26 Nov 1874–5 Feb 1876.

The evening telegram (Newport, Mon). No 1, 1 Aug 1870–12 July 1872. Continued as South Wales evening telegram, 13 July 1872–29 June 1876. Continued as South Wales daily telegram, 1 July 1876–13 Feb 1891. Continued as South Wales evening telegraph, 17 Feb–27 Nov 1891.

The Bolton morning news. No 1, 8 Aug–12 Nov 1870.

The evening news (Hull). No 54, 1 Oct 1870–6 July 1876. Continued as Hull express, 7 July 1876–25 May 1891. Incorporated in Hull daily news.

The eastern counties daily press (Norwich). No 1, 10 Oct 1870–2 May 1871. Continued as Eastern daily press, 3 May 1871 onwards. Ed J. Spilling 1873–97, A. Cozens-Hardy 1897–1937.

The Bolton daily chronicle. [1870]–no 705, 5 May 1873–July 1907. Continued as Bolton evening chronicle, 1 August 1907–21 Dec 1917.

The Birmingham daily mail. [1870]–no 154, 6 March 1871–16 May 1918. Continued as Birmingham mail, 17 May 1918–8 April 1963. Continued as Birmingham evening mail and despatch, 9 April 1963 onwards. Prop John Feeney and John Jaffray 1870–94; John Feeney 1894–1905. Ed H. J. Jennings 1870–80.

The evening express (Liverpool). [1870]–no 692, 2 June 1873–13 Oct 1958.

The Birmingham morning news. No 1, 4 Jan 1871–27 May 1876. Ed George Dawson.

The Huddersfield daily examiner. No 1, 28 Jan 1871 onwards. Ed Joseph Woodhead, Ernest Woodhead.

The Huddersfield daily chronicle. No 1, 30 Jan 1871–31 Dec 1915.

The sporting chronicle (Manchester). No 1, 14 Feb 1871 onwards. Prop Edward Hulton and E. O. Bleackley. Ed Edward Hulton.

The Liverpool daily Albion. [1871]–no 539, 21 July 1873–30 June 1875. Continued as Liverpool evening Albion, 1 July 1875–21 June 1879. Continued as Liverpool Albion, 23 June 1879–30 June 1883. Continued as Liverpool daily Albion, [July]–5 Oct–25 March 1887.

The Bolton evening guardian. [1871]–no 825, 1 Jan 1874–26 May 1893. Incorporated in Bolton evening news. Prop Thomas Cunliffe 1868–92.

The northern counties daily mail (Newcastle). No 1, 1 May–no 88, 10 Aug 1872.

The Leicester daily post. No 1, 1 Aug 1872–31 March 1921. Ed Angus Galbraith.

The Leicester evening news. [1872]–no 982, 12 June 1875–28 June 1878.

The Bradford evening mail. No 1, 18 Sept 1872–1 May 1875. Incorporated in Bradford chronicle.

The Bradford chronicle. No 1, 1 Oct 1872–18 June 1882. Absorbed Bradford evening mail and became Bradford daily chronicle and mail, 19 June 1882–25 Aug 1883.

The Leeds daily news. [1872]–no 148, 1 May 1873–29 May 1905. Continued as Yorkshire evening news, 1 June 1905–3 Dec 1963. Amalgamated with Yorkshire evening post. Prop Charles and Frank Macaskie c. 1880–?. Ed Charles Macaskie c. 1880–c. 1900.

The South Wales daily news (Cardiff). No 1, 7 Feb 1872–8 April 1918. Continued as South Wales news, 9 April 1918–24 Aug 1928. Amalgamated with Western mail. Ed John Astle 1872–4.

The Staffordshire daily sentinel (Hanley). No 2, 10 April 1873–30 Dec 1881. Continued as Staffordshire sentinel, 1 Jan 1882–16 March 1929. Continued as Evening sentinel, 18 March 1929 onwards.

The Sheffield post. No 19, 17 May 1873–25 July 1882. Continued as Sheffield daily post, 26 July 1882–19 July 1884. Continued as Sheffield post, 21 July 1884–28 May 1887.

The Sunderland daily echo and shipping gazette. No 1, 22 Dec 1873–3 Dec 1928. Continued as Sunderland echo and shipping gazette, 4 Dec 1928–2 May 1959. Continued as Sunderland echo (Echo Sunderland), 4 May 1959 onwards. Prop Samuel Storey.

The York herald. 1 Jan 1874–31 Dec 1889. Continued as Yorkshire herald, 1 Jan 1890–31 Dec 1936. Started weekly, no 1, 2 Jan 1790; reverted to this frequency, 2 Jan 1937–18 June 1954. Amalgamated with the Yorkshire gazette and continued weekly as Yorkshire gazette and herald, 25 June 1954 onwards. Ed William Hargrove 1813–46. W. Wallace Hargrove, Edwin N. Goadby 1874–87, A. H. Fletcher 1899–?.

The Manchester evening mail. No 1, 4 May 1874–10 July 1916. Ed Thomas Sowler.

The evening express telegram (Cheltenham). No 70, 6 July 1874–20 Jan 1875. Continued as Evening telegram and express, 21 Jan 1875–30 Dec 1882.

The East Anglian daily times (Ipswich). No 1, 13 Oct 1874 onwards. Begun weekly as Ipswich express, no 1, 13 Aug 1839.

The Wakefield evening herald. [1874]–no 4555, 5 Jan 1889–24 Dec 1890.

The Midland counties evening express (Wolverhampton). No 1, 2 Nov 1874–15 Jan 1876. Continued as Evening express, 17 Jan 1876–28 June 1884. Continued as Evening express and star, 30 June 1884–23 April 1889. Continued as Express and star, 24 April 1889 onwards. Prop Thomas Graham. Ed A. Meikle.

The Southport daily news. 3 May 1875–17 Nov 1877. Continued as Liverpool and Southport daily news, 19 Nov 1877–18 Feb 1881. Begun weekly as Southport independent, no 1, 4 July 1861. Prop Frederick M. Jones.

The Bath argus evening telegram. Nos 1–208, 17 May 1875–19 Jan 1876. Continued as Evening argus, nos 209–646, 20 Jan 1876–30 Oct 1877. Continued as Bath argus and West of England advertising register (daily edn), 647, 31 Oct 1877–30 April 1892. Continued as Bath daily argus, 2 May 1892–28 July 1893. Continued as Bath argus and West of England advertising register, 29 July 1893–10 April 1897. Continued as Bath daily argus, 11 April 1897–31 Jan 1900. Amalgamated with Bath daily chronicle to appear as Bath daily chronicle and argus. The first 646 nos were daily edns of the weekly Bath argus and West of England advertising register which began 23 July 1870.

The Birmingham evening news. No 1, 16 Aug 1875–no 119, 15 Jan 1876. Incorporated in Birmingham morning news.

The Scarborough daily post. No 1, 21 Feb 1876–24 May 1887. Continued as Scarborough post, 25 May 1887–12 May 1910. Continued as two: Scarborough daily post, 13 May 1910–29 Sept 1921; and Scarborough weekly post, 13 May 1910–27 Jan 1922. Continued as Scarborough post and weekly pictorial, 3 Feb 1922–7 Jan 1932.

The Brighton and Sussex daily post. No 1, 1 July 1876–8 July 1885. Continued as Brighton and Sussex evening post, 9 July 1885–7 Feb 1886.

The Sunderland daily times. No 1, 3 July 1876–3 Aug 1878. Incorporated in Sunderland daily echo.

The Sunderland daily post. No 1, 21 July 1876–3 Sept 1891. Incorporated in Sunderland daily herald.

The daily telegram (Wisbech). No 1, 24 April–no 123, 15 Sept 1877.

The Bristol evening news. No 1, 29 May 1877–30 Jan 1932. Ed T. Watkins.

The Warrington evening post. No 1, 17 May 1877–6 April 1878. Continued as Evening post, 8 April 1878–31 Dec 1880.

The evening post (Worcester). No 1, 4 June 1877–21 May 1881. Continued as Worcestershire evening post, 30 May 1881–3 March 1883. Continued as Worcestershire echo, 5 March 1883–3 Jan 1930.

The northern times (Oldham). No 1, 19 March 1877–11 June 1880. Continued as Oldham evening standard, 1880–2. Continued as Oldham daily standard, 9 Jan 1882–8 June 1917. Continued as Oldham evening standard, 11 June 1917–28 Dec 1928. Incorporated in Oldham evening chronicle.

The evening news (Portsmouth). [1877]–no 211, 1 Jan 1878–17 Jan 1959. Continued as News, 19 Jan 1959 onwards.

The Bath evening chronicle. No 2, 12 June 1877–4 August 1883. Continued as Bath daily chronicle, 7 Aug 1883–31 Jan 1900. Continued as Bath daily chronicle and argus, 1–14 Feb 1900. Continued as Daily chronicle and argus, 15 Feb 1900–7 Oct 1903. Continued as Bath daily chronicle and argus, 8 Oct 1903–15 Sept 1911. Continued as Bath and Wilts chronicle, 16 Sept 1911–11 April 1925. Continued as Bath and Wilts chronicle and herald, 14 April 1925–10 June 1961. Continued as Bath and Wilts evening chronicle, 12 June 1961 onwards.

The northern evening mail (West Hartlepool). [1877]–no 200, 18 Feb 1878–2 Oct 1883. Continued as Northern daily mail, 29 Oct 1883 onwards. Prop Samuel Storey.

The Swansea daily shipping register. [1877]–11 June 1888–3 July 1888. Continued as Swansea gazette, 4 July 1888–4 Jan 1913.

The evening star of Gwent and South Wales times (Newport, Mon). No 1, 10 Nov 1877–30 March 1889. Continued as South Wales daily times and star of Gwent, 1 April 1889–25 June 1892. Continued as South Wales daily star, 27 June 1892–6 Sept 1900. Continued as South Wales daily telegraph, 7 Sept 1900–24 Jan 1903. Continued as Newport and Monmouthshire evening telegraph, 12 Jan–10 July 1903. Between 12 and 24 Jan this existed as registration copies only.

The daily midland echo (Wolverhampton). No 1, 11 Dec 1877–2 Jan 1879. Continued as Midland echo, 8–15 Jan 1879.

The Grimsby express. No 1, 27 April 1878–25 May 1891. Incorporated in Hull daily news.

The Nottingham evening post. No 1, 1 May 1878–1 July 1963. Continued as Evening post and news, 2 July 1963 onwards.

The Gateshead and Tyneside echo (Gateshead). No 1, 24 April 1879–20 Jan 1880. Continued as Tyneside echo (Newcastle) until 30 Aug 1888.

The Derby daily telegraph and reporter. No 1, 28 July 1879–13 Oct 1881. Continued as Derby daily telegraph, 14 Oct 1881–29 Jan 1932. Continued as Derby daily telegraph and Derby daily express, 30 Jan–12 March 1932. Continued as Derby evening telegraph and Derby daily express, 14 March 1932–14 Aug 1933. Continued as Derby evening telegraph, 15 Aug 1933 onwards.

The Derby evening gazette. No 1, 28 July 1879–2 Oct 1880. Continued as Derby and Burton evening gazette, 4 Oct 1880–25 May 1881. Continued as Derby and Burton gazette, 27 May 1881–11 July 1884. Continued as Derby evening gazette, 12 July–30 Dec 1884.

The Liverpool echo. No 1, 27 Oct 1879 onwards. Ed Alexander G. Jeans.

The Worcester daily times and journal. No 1, 5 Jan 1880–30 Jan 1937. Continued as Worcester evening times, 1 Feb–30 Oct 1937. Continued as Evening news and times, 1 Nov 1937–21 Oct 1939. Continued as News and times, 23 Oct 1939–5 Oct 1941. Continued as Evening news and times, 7 Oct 1941–20 Oct 1962. Continued as Worcester evening news, 22 Oct 1962 onwards. Ed C. H. Birbeck.

The Northampton mercury daily reporter. No 1, 9 Feb 1880–30 July 1885. Continued as Northampton daily reporter, 1 Aug 1885–6 April 1908. Continued as Northampton daily echo, 13 April 1908–22 Aug 1919. Continued as Daily echo, 23 Aug 1919–31 Oct 1931. Continued as Chronicle and echo, 2 Nov 1931 onwards. Prop Mrs T. E. Dicey ?–1885; Samuel Smith Campion.

The evening herald (Northampton). No 1, 16 Feb 1880–31 July 1881. Continued as Northampton daily chronicle and evening herald, 1 Aug 1881–31 Oct 1931. Amalgamated with Daily echo (Northampton) and continued as Chronicle and echo, 2 Nov 1931 onwards.

The evening chronicle (Oldham). No 1, 17 March 1880–17 March 1882. Continued as Oldham evening chronicle, 20 March 1882 onwards. Prop ? Hirst and ? Rennie.

The argus (Brighton). No 1, 30 March 1880–24 Aug 1896. Continued as Evening argus, 25 Aug 1896 onwards.

The evening star (Wolverhampton). No 1, 28 June 1880–27 June 1884. Incorporated in Evening express (Wolverhampton). Ed Harry Jeffs.

The Sussex evening times (Brighton). No 1, 6 July 1880–30 April 1915.

The evening news (Norwich). No 1, 2 Jan–11 Feb 1882. Continued as Eastern evening news (Norwich), 13 Feb 1882 onwards.

The evening press (York). [1882]–20 March 1884–31 Dec 1904. Continued as Yorkshire evening press, 1 Jan 1905 onwards.

The Scarborough evening news. [1882]–no 908, 4 Jan 1886 onwards. Ed Meredith J. Whittaker.

The Stockport echo. No 1, 10 Feb 1883–25 June 1889. Continued as Cheshire echo, 1889–92; and as Cheshire evening echo, 1893–5; and as Cheshire daily echo, 1 Nov 1895–30 Sept 1939.

The Midland echo (Birmingham). No 1, 26 Feb 1883–1 March 1885. Incorporated in Evening express and star (Birmingham).

The evening times (Liverpool). No 1, 9 June 1883–9 June 1884. Continued as Liverpool and Bootle evening times, 10 June 1884–31 Dec 1894.

The evening mail (Portsmouth). No 1, 14 Jan 1884–8 June 1895. Continued as Mail, 1895–6; and as Southern daily mail, 23 March 1896–14 Jan 1905.

The Midland evening news (Wolverhampton). No 1, 3 April 1884–31 July 1915.

The Hull daily news. 21 Oct 1884–18 March 1914. Continued as Daily news, 19 March 1914–1 Feb 1916. Continued as Hull daily news, 2 Feb 1916–28 April 1923. Continued as Hull evening news, 30 April 1923–17 April 1930. Incorporated in Daily mail (Hull). Started weekly as Hull news, no 1, 3 Jan 1852.

The Derby express. No 1, 22 Oct 1884–27 Feb 1909. Continued as Derby daily express, 1 March 1909–29 Jan 1932. Incorporated in Derby daily telegraph.

The South Wales echo (Cardiff). [1884]–1 July 1889 onwards.

The Newcastle daily leader. No 1, 28 Sept 1885–31 Oct 1903. Ed James Annand, Aaron Watson.

The Hull daily mail. No 1, 29 Sept 1885–31 Dec 1895. Continued as Daily mail (Hull), Jan 1896 onwards.

The Nottingham evening news. No 1, 21 Oct 1885–30 Oct 1948. Continued as Evening news, 1 Nov 1948–23 Sept 1950. Continued as Nottingham evening news, 25 Sept 1950–1 July 1963. Incorporated in Nottingham evening post. Ed D. Edwards 1891–7.

The evening chronicle (Newcastle-on-Tyne.) No 1, 2 Nov 1885 onwards.

The Birmingham daily times. No 1, 4 Nov 1885–31 March 1890.

The evening post (Exeter). No 1, 12 Nov 1885–6 June 1902.

The Derby morning post. No 1, 16 Nov 1885–5 July 1887.

The Norfolk daily standard (Norwich). [1886]–no 695, 15 Dec 1887–31 Jan 1903. Continued as Norfolk evening standard. Incorporated in Eastern evening mail in 1905.

The Lancashire evening post (Preston). No 1, 16 Oct 1886–31 Dec 1892. Continued as Lancashire daily post, Jan 1893–1 Jan 1949. Continued as Lancashire evening post, 3 Jan 1949 onwards. Ed John Toulmin.

The northern daily telegraph (Blackburn). No 1, 26 Oct 1886–13 Oct 1956. Continued as Northern evening telegraph, 15 Oct–11 Dec 1956. Continued as Evening telegraph, 12 Dec 1956–31 Aug 1963. Continued as Lancashire evening telegraph, 2 Sept 1963 onwards.

The Sheffield evening telegraph. No 1, 4 June 1887–23 June 1888. Continued as Evening telegraph and star, 25 June 1888–17 Jan 1898. Continued as Yorkshire telegraph and star, Jan 1898–7 Oct 1937. Continued as Telegraph and star, 8 Oct 1937–12 Nov 1938. Continued as Star, 14 Nov 1938 onwards.

The Blackburn evening express. No 1, 29 Aug 1887–5 Oct 1888. Continued as Evening express and standard, 6 Oct 1888–26 April 1890. Continued as Lancashire evening express and standard, 28 April 1890–8 June 1895. Continued as Lancashire daily express and standard, 10 June 1895–3 March 1899.

The Cambridge daily news. No 1, 28 May 1888–29 Sept 1962. Continued as Cambridge news, 1 Oct 1962 onwards. Prop William F. Taylor 1888–?

The southern echo (Southampton). No 1, 20 Aug 1888–5 Sept 1891. Continued as Southern echo and Bournemouth telegraph, 7 Sept 1891–21 Feb 1901. Continued as Southern daily echo, 23 Feb 1901–30 June 1958. Continued as Southern evening echo, 1 July 1958 onwards. Prop J. Passmore Edwards Aug 1888–July 1891.

The Yorkshire evening post (Leeds). No 79, 1 Dec 1890 onwards. Ed Alexander Paterson, Alfred Turner.

The midland daily telegraph (Coventry). No 1, 9 Feb 1891–15 Nov 1941. Continued as Coventry evening telegraph, 17 Nov 1941 onwards.

The daily argus (Birmingham). No 1, 9 Nov 1891–30 June 1902. Incorporated in Birmingham evening dispatch.

The daily guardian (Warrington). No 1, 28 Nov 1891–8 Aug 1896. Continued as Warrington daily guardian, 10 Aug 1896–3 Oct 1903.

The daily independent press (Cambridge). No 1, 2 Jan–no 138, 31 July 1892.

The South Wales argus (Newport, Mon). No 1, 30 May 1892 onwards.

The Bradford daily argus. No 1, 16 June 1892–14 July 1923. Continued as Yorkshire evening argus, 16 July 1923–31 Dec 1925. Amalgamated with Bradford daily telegraph. Ed H. Fieldhouse.

The Leicester daily express. No 1, 20 June 1892–5 Oct 1895.

The Halifax evening courier. No 1, 21 June 1892–30 April 1921. Continued as Halifax daily courier and guardian, 2 May 1921 onwards.

The South Wales daily post (Swansea). No 1, 13 Feb 1893 –12 March 1932. Continued as South Wales evening post, 14 March 1932 onwards.

The Newcastle evening news. No 1, 2 Oct 1893–27 April 1899.

The Barrow evening echo. No 1, 21 March 1894–30 June 1898.

The eastern daily telegraph (Grimsby). No 1, 27 Feb 1897 –31 Dec 1898. Continued as Grimsby daily telegraph, Jan 1899–12 March 1932. Continued as Grimsby evening telegraph, 14 March 1932 onwards.

The Isle of Man daily times. No 1, 4 May 1897 onwards.

The Manchester evening chronicle. No 1, 10 May 1897–31 March 1914. Continued as Evening chronicle, 1 April 1914–26 July 1963. Incorporated in Manchester evening news. Founded by Edward Hulton and E. O. Bleackley.

The evening herald (Ipswich). No 1, 1 Sept–29 Dec 1897. Continued as Daily herald, 30 Dec 1897–30 July 1898. Incorporated in Evening star.

The north western daily mail (Barrow). No 1, 1 Jan 1898–31 Dec 1940. Continued as North-western evening mail, 1 Jan 1941 onwards.

The Newcastle morning mail. No 1, 23 May 1898–9 Feb 1901. Continued as Morning mail, 11 Feb–9 Aug 1901.

The Oxford and district morning echo. No 25, 22 Oct 1898–no 112, 3 Feb 1899. Continued as Oxford morning echo, 4 Feb 1899–30 Jan 1900.

The Sunderland morning mail. No 1, 14 Nov 1898–11 Feb 1901.

Scottish Daily Papers

An asterisk signifies that no copy has been found.

The day (Glasgow). Nos 1–112, 2 Jan–30 June 1832. Ed John Strang.

*The conservative (Edinburgh). No 1, 24 Feb 1837–?

North British daily mail (Glasgow). No 1, 14 April 1847–31 Dec 1900. Continued as Glasgow daily mail, 1 Jan–8 June 1901. Incorporated in Daily record (Glasgow). Ed George Troup 1847–8, Robert Somers 1849–59, C. Cameron 1860–73, James R. Manners.

Daily mail (Glasgow). [1848]–no 217, 17 March 1849–12 July 1851.

War telegraph (Edinburgh). No 1, 9 Oct 1854–no 53, 8 Dec 1854. Continued as Northern telegraph, no 54, 9 Dec 1854–no 77, 6 Jan 1855. Ed J. W. Finlay.

Northern telegraphic news (Aberdeen). No 1, 23 Jan 1855 –7 Oct 1876.

The Glasgow daily news. [No 1, 13 April 1855]–no 69, 30 June–no 111, 17 Aug 1855.

Morning bulletin (Glasgow). No 1, 26 May–no 12, 8 June 1855.

The daily express (Edinburgh). No 1, 23 June 1855–27 Aug 1859. Incorporated in Caledonian mercury. Ed W. H. Murray.

The Glasgow times. No 1, 25 June 1855–9 June 1869.

The Caledonian mercury (Edinburgh). 2 July 1855–20 April 1867. Incorporated in Scotsman. Started thrice weekly, no 1, 28 April 1720; later twice weekly; an evening paper from 14 July 1866. Prop Thomas Allan. Ed David Buchanan 1810–27, James Browne, J. G. Cochrane, J. D. White, W. D. Bruce, James Robie 1855–66, William Saunders 1866–7.

The daily Scotsman (Edinburgh). 2 July 1855–31 Dec 1859. Continued as Scotsman, 2 Jan 1860 onwards. Started weekly as Scotsman, no 1, 25 Jan 1817. Prop William Ritchie; John Ritchie 1847–70, J. R. Findlay 1870–98. Ed William Ritchie and Charles Maclaren 1817, J. R. McCulloch 1817–21, Charles Maclaren 1822–45, James Law 1845–9, Alexander Russel 1849–76, Robert Wallace 1876–80, Charles Cooper 1880–1906.

Daily bulletin (Glasgow). [July 1855]–no 1416, 9 Dec 1859–12 Feb 1861.

*The bawbee (Edinburgh). No 1, 19 Oct 1857–? Half-penny paper. Ed J. G. Bertram.

The Glasgow morning journal. No 1, 29 June–4 Sept 1858. Continued as Morning journal, 6 Sept 1858–11 Jan 1870. Continued as Daily express and morning journal, 12 Jan–19 Aug 1870. Incorporated in Star (Glasgow). Ed Robert Somers.

The Glasgow herald. 3 Jan 1859 onwards. Started weekly as Glasgow advertiser, no 1, 27 Jan 1783; twice weekly from 1 Nov 1802; thrice weekly in 1855. Present title adopted 23 Aug 1805. Ed John Mennons 1782–1803, Samuel Hunter 1803–37, George Outram 1837–56, James Pagan 1856–70, William Jack, J. H. Stoddart, Charles Russell 1887–1906.

The daily argus (Dundee). No 1, 23 May 1859–20 April 1861. Incorporated in Dundee courier.

The daily courant (Edinburgh). 2 Jan–31 Oct 1860. Continued as Edinburgh evening courant, 1 Nov 1860–15 Dec 1871. Continued as Edinburgh courant, 16 Dec 1871–6 Feb 1886. Incorporated in Scottish news (Glasgow). Started thrice weekly as Edinburgh evening courant, no 1, 15 Dec 1718. Ed George Houy 1826–7, David Buchanan 1827–48, Joseph Robertson 1849–53, William Buchanan 1853–60, James Hannay 1860–4, Francis Espinasse 1864–7, J. Scott Henderson 1867–72, James Mure, W. R. Lawson.

The daily review (Edinburgh). No 1, 2 April 1861–12 June 1886. Ed J. B. Manson 1861–8, Henry Kingsley 1868–71, T. B. Gillies 1871–4, George Smith 1874–7, William Mackie 1877–86.

The Dundee courier. 22 April 1861–15 Nov 1899. Continued as Courier and argus. 16 Nov 1899–4 May 1926. Incorporated in Dundee advertiser. Started as Dundee weekly courier, no 1, 20 Sep 1816. Ed ? Mitchell.

The Dundee advertiser. 1 May 1861–4 May 1926. Continued as Dundee advertiser and courier, 10 May–2 June 1926. Continued as Courier and advertiser, 3 June 1926 onwards. Started weekly, no 1, 16 Jan 1801; twice a week on 8 April 1845. Ed R. S. Rintoul, John Leng 1851–1900.

The Greenock telegraph. 24 Aug 1863 onwards. Started weekly in 1857. Prop J. F. Neilson and R. C. Mackenzie Ed W. H. Wylie.

Evening citizen (Glasgow). No 1, 8 Aug 1864–7 Aug 1914. Continued as Glasgow citizen, 8 Aug 1914–27 Oct 1923. Continued as Evening citizen, 29 Oct 1923 onwards. Started weekly as Glasgow citizen in 1842. Ed James Hedderwick 1842–97, Edwin C. Hedderwick.

The Glasgow evening mail. No 1, 24 April–30 Dec 1865.

The Glasgow evening herald. No 1, 29 April–30 Dec 1865.

The Glasgow evening post. No 1, 9 July 1866–31 Dec 1868. Continued as Evening journal, 1 Jan 1869–11 Jan 1870. Continued as Star, no 1, 12 Jan 1870–16 Feb 1872. Continued as Evening star, 17 Feb 1872–13 March 1875. Continued as Evening news and star, 15 March 1875–10 Feb 1888. Continued as Glasgow evening news, 11 Feb 1888–23 Sept 1905. Continued as Glasgow news, 25 Sept 1905–3 Oct 1915. Continued as Evening news, 4 Oct 1915–17 Jan 1957. Initially run in conjunction with Morning journal (Glasgow). Ed Frederick Wicks, J. Murray Smith, James Stephen Jeans.

Evening news (Greenock). No 1, 17 July 1866–11 Jan 1868. Continued weekly as Greenock news, 18 Jan 1868 –25 June 1870.

Greenock daily press. No 1, 5 March–27 April 1867. Continued weekly to 28 Dec 1867.

The Aberdeen daily free press. 4 May 1872–30 June 1874. Continued as Daily free press, 1 July 1874–31 Dec 1900. Continued as Aberdeen free press, 1 Jan 1901–30 Nov 1922. Amalgamated with Aberdeen journal and subsequently pbd as Aberdeen press and journal. Started weekly as North of Scotland gazette, no 1, 1 April 1845. Ed Henry Alexander.

The Edinburgh evening news. No 1, 27 May 1873 onwards. Ed Hector C. Macpherson.

The Glasgow news. No 1, 15 Sept 1873–6 Feb 1886. Continued as Scottish news, 7 Feb 1886–11 Feb 1888. Ed R. H. Patterson 1873–4.

The Paisley daily express. [No 1 Oct? 1874]–no 233, 1 June 1875 onwards.

Evening news (Dundee). No 1, 28 March 1876–12 March 1879.

Aberdeen journal, and general advertiser for the North of Scotland (daily edition). 24 April 1877–17 July 1901. Continued as Aberdeen daily journal, 18 July 1901–30 Nov 1922. Amalgamated with Aberdeen free press and subsequently pbd as Aberdeen press and journal. Started as Aberdeen journal and North-British magazine, no 1, 29 Dec 1747–5 Jan 1748. Ed William Forsyth 1849–79, David L. Pressly.

Evening telegraph (Dundee). No 1, 13 March 1877 onwards.

The Edinburgh evening telephone. No 1, 1 Nov 1878–no 79, 31 Jan 1879.

Aberdeen evening express. No 1, 20 Jan 1879–23 March 1899. Continued as Evening express, 24 March 1899 onwards. Ed David L. Pressly.

The evening express (Edinburgh). No 1, 6 March 1880–6 Feb 1886. Run in conjunction with Edinburgh courant.

Evening gazette (Aberdeen). No 1, 23 Jan 1882–30 Nov 1922. Incorporated in Evening express, Ed William Alexander 1882–94.

The Edinburgh evening dispatch. No 1, 4 Jan 1886–10 Dec 1921. Continued as Evening dispatch, 12 Dec 1921–18 Nov 1963. Incorporated in Edinburgh evening news. Run in conjunction with Scotsman.

The Scottish leader (Edinburgh). No 1, 3 Jan 1887–4 July 1894. Ed John Macfarlane, C. H. Hanson, J. H. Dalziel.

The daily record (Glasgow). No 1, 28 Oct 1895–8 June 1901. Continued as Daily record and daily mail, 10 June 1901–29 March 1902. Continued as Daily record and mail, 31 March 1902–12 March 1954. Continued as Record, 13 March 1954–.

Evening post (Dundee). No 1, 22 Jan 1900–16 May 1905.

Irish Daily Papers

Saunders's news-letter (Dublin). [June 1777]–4 June 1878. Continued as Saunders's Irish daily news, 5 June 1878–24 Nov 1879. Started thrice weekly in 1755. Prop James Potts, John Potts 1796–? Ed John Potts, J. T. Potts 1846–71.

The freeman's journal. [Before 1820]–20 Dec 1924. Started as Public register: or freeman's journal, no 1, 10 Sept 1763, twice weekly. Prop Francis Higgins 1783–1802; Philip Whitfield Harvey 1802–26; Henry Grattan 1826–30; Patrick Lavelle 1830–7; Mary Lavelle 1837–41; John Gray. Ed Francis Higgins 1783–1802, Philip Whitfield Harvey, Henry Grattan, Patrick Lavelle, John Gray, Edmund Dwyer Gray, Edward Byrne 1884–91.

The Cork daily advertiser. No 1, 1 Oct 1836–1 Jan 1837.

The daily express (Dublin). No 1, 3 Feb 1851–10 Feb 1917. Continued as Daily express and Irish daily mail, 12 Feb 1917–18 June 1921. Ed G. H. Francis, J. Robinson.

The Belfast daily Mercury. 19 April 1854–2 Nov 1861. Started as Belfast Mercury, no 1, 29 March 1851.

The southern reporter (Cork). 12 June 1855–16 June 1871. Continued as Irish daily telegraph, 1 July 1871–11 Dec 1873. Started weekly in June 1807.

The Belfast news-letter. 2 July 1855–1 Sept 1962. Continued as News letter, 3 Sept 1962 onwards. Started weekly, no 1, 1 Sept 1737. Ed Alexander Mackay 1796–1844, James A. Henderson 1845–83, Sir James Henderson.

The mail and Waterford daily express. No 1, 13 July 1855–30 June 1860.

The northern whig (Belfast). 1 Feb 1858 onwards. Started weekly in 1824. Ed F. D. Finlay 1824–?, E. M. Whitty, Thomas MacKnight.

The Irish times (Dublin). No 1, 29 March 1859 onwards. Ed G. B. Wheeler 1859–77, J. A. Scott 1877–99, Arthur Locker.

The morning news (Dublin). No 6, 2 May 1859–31 Dec 1864. Ed A. M. Sullivan.

The evening freeman (Dublin). [1859]–30 June 1871. Continued as Evening telegraph, no 1, 1 July 1861–19 Dec 1924. Started thrice weekly, no 1, 18 Jan 1831.

The Cork constitution. 2 Jan 1860–14 Aug 1925. Started thrice weekly in 1822.

The Cork daily herald. 2 March 1860–19 July 1901. Started weekly as Cork herald, no 1, 21 June 1856. Ed David A. Nagle.

The Dublin evening mail. 4 Feb 1861–1 Feb 1928. Continued as Evening mail, 2 Feb 1928–19 July 1962. Started thrice weekly, no 1, 3 Feb 1823. Prop Thomas Sheehan; J. S. Lefanu 1839–73. Ed Joseph T. Haydn 1823–?, Remigius Sheehan, H. Maunsell.

The Cork examiner. [1861] onwards. Started thrice weekly, no 1, 30 Aug 1841.

The Dublin evening post. 23 Jan 1865–21 Aug 1875. Started twice weekly, no 1, 10 June 1732. Ed John Magee ?–1809 (?), J. Magee jr ?–1814, F. W. Conway.

The evening Irish times (Dublin). [1865]–31 Oct 1921.

The morning mail (Dublin). [Feb 1870]–no 346, 17 March 1871–30 Aug 1912.

The Waterford daily mail. 24 May 1870–19 Sept 1908. Started weekly as Waterford mail, no 1, 16 Aug 1823. 'Daily' was omitted from the title from 30 Oct 1874 to 11 Dec 1886.

The Belfast evening telegraph. [Sept 1870]–no 171, 20 March 1871–18 April 1918. Continued as Belfast telegraph, 19 April 1918 onwards.

The daily examiner (Belfast). 16 Nov 1870–31 Dec 1872. Continued as Ulster examiner and northern star, 1 Jan 1873–22 July 1882. Incorporated in Morning news (Belfast). Started as Ulster examiner, no 1, 14 March 1868.

The evening press (Belfast), [July 1871]–no 520, 15 May 1873–21 May 1874.

The Belfast times. No 1, 1 Jan–31 May 1872. Continued as Belfast daily times, 1 June–10 Aug 1872.

The Belfast morning news. 20 Aug 1872–27 April 1882. Continued as Morning news, no 1, 1 May–no 72, 22 July 1882. Continued as Morning news and examiner, no 73, 24 July 1882–no 222, 18 Jan 1883. Continued as Morning news, vol 39, no 17, 19 Jan 1883–vol 39, no 8034, 27 Aug 1892. Incorporated in Irish news (Belfast). Started thrice weekly, no 1, 2 July 1855. Prop E. D. Gray May 1882–? Ed Daniel Reed.

The Ulster echo (Belfast). No 1, 26 May 1874–8 June 1916.

The Dublin sporting news. No 1, 5 Feb 1889–31 Dec 1901.

The Belfast evening star. No 1, 29 Jan–31 May 1890.

The Irish news (Belfast). No 1, 15 Aug 1891–27 Aug 1892. Continued as Irish news and Belfast morning news, 29 Aug 1892–31 Aug 1925; 1 Jan–29 March, 19 July–30 Sept, 11 Oct 1926 onwards.

The Irish daily independent (Dublin). No 1, 18 Dec 1891–31 Dec 1904. Continued as Irish independent, 2 Jan 1905 onwards. Ed Edward Byrne.

The evening herald (Dublin). No 1, 19 Dec 1891 onwards.

The evening echo (Cork). [1893]–no 825, 6 May 1896 onwards.

The daily nation (Dublin). 5 June 1897–31 Aug 1900. Incorporated in Irish daily independent. Started weekly, no 1, 15 Oct 1842. Ed A. M. Sullivan 1858–76, C. G. Duffy.

The evening news (Waterford). [1898]–no 288, 1 June 1899–31 Dec 1957.

London papers published more than once a week

The most important entries in this section are those London evening papers which were pbd three times a week; they were for the most part founded in the 18th century and were nearly extinct by 1850. There are 3 other kinds of paper which were pbd more than once a week: the London suburban press, various technical and trade journals and numerous provincial papers which existed as weeklies in 1800 and were pbd more frequently until they finally became dailies.

Tri-weekly: Monday, Wednesday and Friday

Lloyd's evening post and British chronicle. No 1, 22 July 1757–30 Dec 1805–[1815?]. Ed Robert Heron.

London packet: or new Lloyd's evening post. [Oct 1769]–no 91, 28 May 1770–no 11584, 30 Dec 1836. Incorporated in St James's chronicle. Prop Charles Baldwin.

The evening mail. [Feb 1789]–no 62, July 1789–27 June 1868. Continued as Mail, 30 June 1868–11 Oct 1922. Incorporated in Times weekly edition. Only twice a week from July 1868 to 1871. Run in conjunction with Times.

The mercantile chronicle. No 1, 20 July 1821–10 Jan 1823. Incorporated in London packet; or new Lloyd's evening post.

The evening chronicle. No 1, 31 Jan 1835–no 1940, 23 July 1847. Prop John Easthope. Ed George Hogarth.

The Hackney and Kingsland gazette. [1864]–no 277, 10 July 1867–19 May 1929. Continued as Hackney gazette and north London advertiser, 21 May 1926 onwards.

Tuesday, Thursday and Saturday

The London evening post. No 1, 1 Dec 1727–13 March 1806.

The general evening post. No 1, 2 Oct 1733–1 Feb 1822. Incorporated in St James's Chronicle. Ed Stephen Jones.

The London chronicle. No 1, 1 Jan 1757–28 April 1823. Incorporated in London packet: or new Lloyd's evening post.

The St James's chronicle. No 1, 12 March 1761–2 Aug 1866. Incorporated in Press. Prop Henry Baldwin; Charles Baldwin; James Johnstone; Charles Newdegate. Ed John MacDiarmid 1802, S. L. Giffard 1819–?, Thomas Ballantyne.

The English chronicle. No 1, 2 Jan 1779–30 Dec 1843. Ed William Radcliffe.

The inquisitor. [No 1, 18 Oct 1808]–no 129, 15 Aug 1809–? Ed John Browne Bell.

Bi-weekly (Tuesday and Friday unless otherwise noted)

The London gazette. No 1, 16 Nov 1665 at Oxford; from no 24, 5 Feb 1666 onwards in London. Ed Thomas Walker Oct 1869–Nov 1888.

The national adviser. No 1, 10 Aug 1811–no 138, 2 Dec 1812. Monday and Thursday.

The London evening chronicle. No 1, 2 Aug 1824–no 133, 7 Nov 1825.

The record. No 1, 1 Jan 1828–31 Dec 1948. Incorporated in Church of England newspaper and continued as Church of England newspaper and record, 7 Jan 1949 onwards. Frequency varied until it became a weekly, 31 March 1882. *See below under* Religious Papers.

The patriot. No 1, 22 Feb 1832–27 Dec 1866. Continued as English independent, 3 Jan 1867–24 Dec 1879. Frequency varied until it finally settled as a weekly, 6 Jan 1859. *See below under* Religious Papers.

The City press. No 1, 18 July 1857 onwards. Wednesday and Saturday. Ed William Hill Collingridge.

The East End news. [1859]–no 509, 17 July 1869–13 Sept 1899. Continued as East End news and London shipping chronicle, 16 Sept 1899–26 April 1963.

The south London press. No 1, 7 Jan 1865 onwards.

The south London observer, Camberwell and Peckham times. No 295, 6 June 1874–3 Dec 1948. Continued as South London observer, 10 Dec 1948 onwards. Started weekly in 1868 as Camberwell and Peckham times, no 74, 2 April 1870–no 294, 20 May 1874. Wednesday and Saturday.

(2) WEEKLY PAPERS

Besides the various types of papers here listed, one or more weekly papers were pbd in nearly every provincial town of any importance throughout the century. No attempt has been made to list them here, but they may be traced in the Lists of newspapers, *col 1783, above, and in* The provincial press, *col 1829, below.*

Sunday Papers

E. Johnson's Sunday monitor and British gazette. [No 1, 26 March 1780]–no 66, 24 June 1781–22 Sept 1805. Continued as Johnson's Sunday monitor and British gazette, 29 Sept 1805–20 Feb 1814. Continued as Sunday monitor, 27 Feb 1814–25 Jan 1829.

The London recorder. [No 1], 27 July 1783–no 1152, 9 July 1809. In 1796 it absorbed Sunday reformer and universal register (founded by George Ripley in 1793) and became London recorder and Sunday reformer.

The review and Sunday advertiser. No 1, 22 June 1789–1796–[?]. Continued as Sunday review [?]–no 574, 19 Aug 1798–19 March 1809.

The observer. No 1, 4 Dec 1791 onwards. Managed by Lewis Doxat 1804–57. Prop William I. Clement 1815–52; ?Beer ?–1880; F. A. Beer 1880–? Ed Lewis Doxat 1804–57, Joseph Snowe, ? M'Dermott, C. Kinloch Cooke, Edward Dicey 1870–89, H. D. Traill 1889–91, J. H. MacCarthy 1892–3, F. A. Beer 1894–1901.

The selector: or Say's Sunday reporter. [?Nov 1795]–no 161, 9 Dec 1798–no 569, 27 April 1806.

Bell's weekly messenger. No 1, 1 May 1796–28 March 1896. Continued as Country sport and messenger of agriculture, 4 April 1896–31 Dec 1904. Prop John Bell; John Edmund Cox. Ed John Bell 1796–1825, F. L. Holt, Thomas Wade, J. N. Lee, John Edmund Cox.

The weekly dispatch. No 1, 27 Sept 1801–24 June 1928. Continued as Sunday dispatch, 1 July 1928–11 June 1961. Prop Robert Bell 1801–15 and 1816–?; James Harmer 1821 (?)–?; George Stiff 1869–74; A. W. Dilke Jan 1875–83; George Newnes. Ed Robert Bell 1801–15 and 1816–?, George Kent 1815–16, James Harmer, Joseph Wrightson 1838–56, Sydney French 1856–62, T. J. Serle 1862–75, A. W. Dilke 1875–6, H. R. Fox Bourne 1876–87, W. A. Hunter, Charles J. Tibbits 1896–?.

The British Neptune. [? Jan 1803]–1 Dec 1805–12 May 1823. Ed Robert Heron 1805–6.

The Englishman. [No 1, 29 May 1803]–no 32, 8 Jan 1804–20 April 1834. Prop William I. Clement 1821–34.

The news. No 1, 19 May 1805–no 1768, 26 Aug 1839. Absorbed Sunday herald, 1829 and Sunday evening globe 1837. Ed John Hunt, John Scott.

The Sunday advertiser. [1807?]–no 555, 4 Jan 1818–5 Aug 1821. Absorbed Weekly register, 12 Aug 1812 and continued as Sunday advertiser and weekly register, 12 Aug 1821–5 Jan 1823. Continued as Weekly register, 12 Jan 1823–no 1073, 30 Dec 1827. Continued as Sunday herald, no 1074, 6 Jan 1828–8 Feb 1829. Incorporated in News. In 1822 it was run in conjunction with Morning post. Ed W. R. Macdonald 1828–9.

The independent Whig. [No 1, 5 Jan 1806]–no 6, 9 Feb 1806–no 793, 25 March 1821. Ed Henry White.

The examiner. No 1, 3 Jan 1808–26 Feb 1881. Prop John Hunt and J. H. Leigh Hunt 1808–25; Robert Fellowes 1828–30?; Albany Fonblanque 1830?–65; William McCullagh Torrens 1865–70; H. R. Fox Bourne 1870–73; P. A. Taylor 1873–8; Lord Rosebery 1878–81. Ed J. H. Leigh Hunt 1808–21, Albany Fonblanque 1830–47, John Forster 1847–55, M. W. Savage 1856–9, Henry Morley 1859–67, Robert Williams, William Minto 1874–8, Charles Williams.

The national register. No 1, 3 Jan 1808–12 May 1823. Prop John Browne Bell and J. de Camp; Eugenius Roche. Ed Eugenius Roche 1808–11.

The London and provincial Sunday gazette. [Aug 1808?]–no 488, 6 Jan 1818–no 589, 11 May 1823.

The anti-Gallican monitor and anti-Corsican chronicle. No 1, 27 Jan 1811–no 362, 4 Jan 1818. Continued as British monitor, 4 Jan 1818–10 April 1825. Incorporated in English gentleman. Ed Lewis Goldsmith.

The constitution. [Jan 1812 ?]–no 314, 4 Jan 1818–5 Jan 1823. Continued as Observer of the times and constitution, 12 Jan–6 April 1823. Incorporated in Englishman.

The champion. No 52, 2 Jan 1814–no 491, 2 June 1822. Started as Drakard's paper, no 1, 10 Jan–no 51, 26 Dec 1813. Continued as Investigator, 9 June 1822–[?]. Prop J. Clayton Jennings; R. D. Richards 1817; John Thelwall 1818. Ed John Scott.

Bell's Sunday dispatch. No 1, 16 April 1815–[?]. Continued as Weekly dispatch, [?]–no 54, 21 April 1816–[?]. Ed by Robert Bell on his exclusion from Weekly dispatch (1801), but dropped when he resumed control of the original paper.

The weekly intelligence. [Jan 1816?]–no 105, 4 Jan–no 143, 27 Sept 1818. Incorporated in British luminary and continued as Weekly intelligencer and British luminary, 30 July 1820–May 1821. Continued as British luminary and weekly intelligencer (see below).

The British luminary. [No 1, 4 Jan 1818]–no 3, 25 Jan 1818–8 June 1823. Absorbed Weekly intelligencer (*see above*). Ed George Glenny.

Wooler's British gazette (Manchester). No 1, 3 Jan 1819–no 259, 14 Dec 1823. Ed T. J. Wooler.

The guardian. No 1, 12 Dec 1819–25 April 1824. Prop Edward H. Locker; Edward H. Locker and Charles Knight June 1820–2. Ed Charles Knight June 1820–2.

John Bull. No 1, 17 Dec 1820–no 3739, 16 July 1892. Absorbed Britannia 19 April 1856. Prop ? Salomons and Samuel Phillips 1845–6. Ed Theodore Hook, H. F. Cooper, Samuel Phillips 1845–6, G. W. Turner, C. G. Prowett, G. H. Smith.

The observer of the times. No 1, 7 Jan 1821–no 103, 29 Dec 1822. Incorporated in Constitution.

The Brunswick, or true blue. No 1, 28 Jan–no 18, 28 May 1821.

The real John Bull. No 1, 21 Jan 1821–21 March 1824.

John Bull's British journal. No 1, 25 Feb–11 March 1821.

Aurora Borealis. No 1, 25 March–no 45, 30 Dec 1821. Incorporated in Observer of the times.

The representative. No 1, 6 Jan 1821–15 April 1823. Run in conjunction with Sun. Prop Patrick Grant.

Life in London. No 1, 13 Jan–no 23, 16 June 1822. Incorporated in Bell's life in London. Ed W. R. Macdonald.

Bell's life in London and sporting chronicle. No 1, 3 March 1822–29 May 1886. Incorporated in Sporting life. Prop Robert Bell 1822–4; William I. Clement 1825–52; William Charles Clement; Edward Hulton 1885. Ed Robert Bell, W. R. Macdonald, V. G. Dowling 1824–52, F. L. Dowling 1852–67, R. B. Wormald.

The Sunday times. No 1, 20 Oct 1822 onwards. Started as New observer, nos 1–6, 18 Feb–25 March 1821. Continued as Independent observer, no 1, 1 April 1821–no 85, 13 Oct 1822. Prop Daniel Whittle Harvey; ? Valpy; Henry Colburn; T. K. Chapman 1842; J. M. Levy 1855–6; E. T. Smith 1856–8; Edward Wilmot Seale 1858–67; Mrs F. A. Beer. Ed Henry White 1821, Daniel Whittle Harvey 1822–?, ? Clarkson, Thomas Gaspey 1828, William Carpenter 1854, J. M. Levy 1855–6, E. T. Smith 1856–8, Henry N. Barnett, Joseph Knight and Ashby Sterry, Joseph Hatton 1874–81, Philip Robinson 1887–90, A. W. à Beckett 1890–4, Mrs F. A. Beer 1894–7, F. G. Smale 1897–1904.

The weekly globe. No 1, 4 Jan 1824–20 March 1825. Incorporated in Common sense.

Pierce Egan's life in London and sporting guide. No 1, 1 Feb 1824–28 Oct 1827. Incorporated in Bell's life in London. Ed Pierce Egan.

The colonist and commercial weekly advertiser. Nos 1–8, 24 Feb–21 March 1824. Continued as Colonist and weekly courier, no 9, 28 March–no 39, 24 Oct 1824. Continued as Sunday herald, no 1, 31 Oct 1824–no 69, 22 May 1825.

Common sense. No 1, 1 Aug 1824–no 80, 5 Feb 1826. Absorbed Weekly globe and continued as Common sense and weekly globe, 28 March 1825–5 Feb 1826.

Old England. No 1, 14 Nov 1824–no 52, 6 Nov 1825.

The telescope. No 1, 12 Dec 1824–no 53, 11 Dec 1825.

The English gentleman. No 1, 19 Dec 1824–no 153, 18 Nov 1827. Continued as Nimrod, 25 Nov 1827–13 Jan 1828. Absorbed British monitor 17 April 1825.

The age. 15 May 1825–7 Oct 1843. Absorbed Argus and continued as Age and argus 16 Oct 1843–26 April 1845. Continued as English gentleman, no 1, 3 May 1845–no 73, 12 Sept 1846. Prop Charles M. Westmacott 1825–c. 1843; Thomas Holt, H. Bronder and G. Bronder 1843; Charles M. Westmacott Oct 1843–April 1845 (?). Ed Charles M. Westmacott, A. B. Richards, J. H. Stocqueler.

The atlas. No 1, 21 May 1826–29 Jan 1869. Prop H. J. Slack 1852. Ed R. S. Rintoul 1826–8 (?), Robert Bell, G. H. Francis, H. J. Slack 1852, Edmund Ollier 1859–60, J. B. Hopkins.

The weekly times. No 1, 3 June 1826–no 357, 5 May 1833. From 26 April–27 Dec 1829 it was called Liberal.

The sphynx. No 1, 8 July 1827–26 April 1829. Prop and ed J. S. Buckingham.

Pierce Egan's weekly courier. No 1, 4 Jan–26 April 1829. Ed Pierce Egan.

The United Kingdom. No 1, 30 Oct 1830–no 168, 12 Jan 1834–[?]. Absorbed Town, 27 July 1834.

The satirist: or censor of the times. No 1, 10 April 1831–no 924, 15 Dec 1849. Ed Barnard Gregory.

Bell's new weekly messenger. No 1, 1 Jan 1832–no 1288, 25 March 1855. Incorporated in News of the world. Prop and ed John Browne Bell.

The town. No 1, 1 Jan 1832–no 134, 20 July 1834. Incorporated in United Kingdom.

The weekly true sun. No 1, 10 Feb 1833–no 331, 29 Dec 1839. Continued as Statesman, no 332, 5 Jan 1840–no 394, 28 March 1841. Continued as British queen and statesman, no 395, 4 April 1841–19 Aug 1843. Prop Daniel Whittle Harvey. Ed W. J. Fox, Thomas Ballantyne Jan 1840–March 1841.

The new weekly dispatch. No 1, 8 Sept 1833–no 72, 18 Jan 1835. Continued as British and American intelligencer, no 1, 25 Jan–no 11, 5 April 1835.

The weekly times. No 16, 27 Dec 1835–no 53, 11 Sept 1836. Continued as London weekly times, nos 1–13, 18 Sept–18 Dec 1836.

The Sunday evening globe. No 1, 11 Sept 1836–no 32, 30 April 1837. Incorporated in News.

The champion. No 1, 18 Sept–no 9, 14 Nov 1836. Continued as Champion and weekly herald, no 10, 20 Nov 1836–no 189, 26 April 1840. Incorporated in Northern liberator (Newcastle). Ed Henry Hetherington, Richard Cobbett.

The weekly chronicle. No 1, 18 Sept 1836–15 June 1851. Continued as Weekly news and chronicle, 21 June 1851–30 Dec 1854. Continued as Weekly chronicle, 6 Jan–1 Sept 1855. Continued as Weekly chronicle and register, 8 Sept 1855–21 Dec 1867. Prop T. L. Holt and ? Marryat; H. G. Ward. Ed H. G. Ward 1836–49.

The London Mercury. No 1, 18 Sept 1836–no 53, 17 Sept 1837. Prop John Bell; J. B. Bernard; John Bell. Ed J. Bronterre O'Brien.

Cleave's London satirist and gazette of variety. No 1, 14 Oct–no 9, 9 Dec 1837. Continued as Cleave's penny gazette of variety, no 10, 16 Dec 1837–no 327, 20 Jan 1844. Unstamped. Ed John Cleave.

The Planet. No 1, 17 Dec 1837–no 310, 4 Feb 1844. Ed John Browne Bell.

The crown. No 1, 1 July 1838–no 42, 14 April 1839. Prop Renton Nicholson, Joseph Last and Charles Pitcher. Ed Renton Nicholson.

The operative. No 1, 4 Nov 1838–30 June 1839. Incorporated in London dispatch. Ed J. Bronterre O'Brien.

The charter. No 1, 27 Jan 1839–no 60, 15 March 1840. Incorporated in Statesman and weekly true sun. Ed William Carpenter.

The penny Sunday times and people's police gazette. [No 1, 5 April 1840]–no 2, 12 April 1840–[?]. Continued as Lloyd's penny Sunday times etc. [?]–no 171, 9 July 1843–no 529, 27 April 1850–[?]. Unstamped. Ed Edward Lloyd.

Tom Spring's life in London and sporting chronicle. [June? 1840]–no 17, 4 Oct 1840–18 June 1843–[?]. Pbd by W. M. Clark. Unstamped.

Bell's penny dispatch and penny Sunday chronicle. [Nov 1840?]–no 66, 27 Feb–no 97, 2 Oct 1842. Unstamped.

Lloyd's illustrated London newspaper. Nos 1–7, 27 Nov 1842–8 Jan 1843. Continued as Lloyd's weekly newspaper, no 8, 15 Jan 1843–26 May 1918. Continued as Lloyd's Sunday news, 2 June 1918–30 Sept 1923. Continued as Sunday news, 7 Oct 1923–9 Aug 1931. Incorporated in Sunday graphic. Prop Edward Lloyd. Ed Edward Lloyd, William Carpenter 1844, Douglas Jerrold 1852–7, Blanchard Jerrold 1857–84, Thomas Catling 1884–1907.

The news of the world. No 1, 1 Oct 1843 onwards. Absorbed Bell's new weekly messenger, April 1855. Prop John Browne Bell 1843–55; Lascelles Carr c. 1891. Ed John Browne Bell 1843–55, John William Bell 1855–77, Walter John and A. W. Bell 1877–91, Emsley Carr 1891–1941.

New Tom Spring's life in London and sporting times. No 1, 28 Oct 1843–no 59, 7 Dec 1844.

The family times. No 1, 6 June 1846–no 162, 26 June 1849.

The weekly times. No 1, 24 Jan 1847–27 Sept 1885. Continued as Weekly times and echo, no 1, 4 Oct 1885–29 Dec 1912. Prop George Stiff; John Hutton; J. Passmore Edwards. Ed F. G. Tomlins.

Reynolds's weekly newspaper. No 1, 5 May 1850–14 Sept 1924. Continued as Reynolds's illustrated news, 21 Sept 1924–23 Feb 1936. Continued as Reynolds's news, 1 March 1936–13 Aug 1944. Continued as Reynolds's news and Sunday citizen, 20 Aug 1944–16 Sept 1962. Continued as Sunday citizen, 23 Sept 1962–18 June 1967. Prop G. W. M. Reynolds. Ed G. W. M. Reynolds 1850–79, Edward Reynolds 1879–94 (assisted by Arthur Downing 1879–88 and William Thompson 1888–94), William Thompson 1894–?

Bell's news. No 1, 24 Feb 1855–no 118, 16 May 1857. Incorporated in Weekly star.

The penny newsman and Sunday morning mail and telegraph. No 1, 28 Jan 1860–10 July 1864. Continued as Newsman, etc. no 234, 17 July 1864–12 Feb 1865.

The London halfpenny newspaper. No 1, 11 Aug–no 4, 1 Sept 1861.

The Sunday gazette. No 1, 7 Jan 1866–24 Nov 1867.

The referee. No 1, 19 Aug 1877–9 Sept 1928. Continued as Sunday referee, 16 Sept 1928–4 June 1932. Incorporated in Sunday chronicle. Ed Henry Sampson 1877–91.

The people. No 1, 16 Oct 1881 onwards. Prop W. T. Madge and George C. H. Armstrong. Ed Sebastian Evans, Joseph Hatton 1892–1907.

The umpire (Manchester). No 1, 4 May 1884–25 May 1917. Continued as Empire, 1 April–15 July 1917. Continued as Empire news, 22 July 1917–26 Nov 1944. Continued as Sunday Empire news, 3 Dec 1944–1 Oct 1950. Continued as The Empire news and the umpire (Empire news incorporating Umpire), 8 Oct 1950–15 Feb 1953. Continued as Empire news, 22 Feb 1953 6 Nov 1955. Continued as Empire news and Sunday chronicle, 13 Nov 1955–16 Oct 1960. Incorporated in News of the world. In March 1894 absorbed Manchester examiner and times, which was for a time a daily paper.

The Sunday chronicle (Manchester). No 1, 23 Aug 1885–4 June 1939. Continued as Sunday chronicle and Sunday referee, 11 June 1939–26 Dec 1943. Continued as Sunday chronicle, 2 Jan 1944–6 Nov 1955. Incorporated in Empire news. A London edition, Sunday chronicle and Sunday referee, ran from 11 June 1939–9 March 1952. Prop Edward Hulton and E. O. Bleackley.

The Sunday sun. No 1, 10 May 1891–3 Jan 1909. Style changed to Weekly sun, and back again. Ed T. P. O'Connor.

The Sunday Mercury. No 1, 25 Oct 1891–23 April 1893.

The Sunday graphic. No 1, 30 July 1893–31 March 1901.

The Sunday mail. No 1, 17 May 1896–29 Dec 1914.

The Sunday special. No 1, 5 Dec 1897–27 Dec 1903. Ed George Wedlake.

General Weekly Papers

The Westminster journal and old British spy. [1794 ?]–no 3,368, 7 Sept 1805–26 Dec 1812. Continued as Westminster journal and imperial weekly gazette, 2 Jan 1813–1 Jan 1814–[?]. Continued as Imperial weekly gazette and Westminster journal, [?]–3 Jan 1818–22 Jan 1825. Started as New weekly miscellany, no 1, 18 July 1741 (*see vol 2*).

The craftsman: or Say's weekly journal. [July? 1758]–no 649, 5 Jan 1771–no 2,498, 16 June 1810. Incorporated in Baldwin's London journal, below. Pbd Charles Say, Mary Vint.

Baldwin's London journal or British chronicle. [No 1, 2 Jan 1762]–[?]. Continued as London journal, [?]–no 309, 31 Dec 1768. Continued as Baldwin's London weekly journal, no 400, 6 Jan 1769–no 3,968, 31 Dec 1836. Prop Henry Baldwin, Charles Baldwin, Robert Baldwin.

The county chronicle and weekly advertiser. [No 1, 29 May ? 1787]–no 37, 12 Feb 1788–no 4,051, 2 March 1841. Continued as County chronicle, Surrey herald and weekly advertiser for Kent etc, no 4,052, 9 March 1841–no 9068, 25 Dec 1869. Continued as County chronicle and Mark Lane journal, no 9,070, 1 Jan 1870–30 Dec 1902. Pbd in London and Guildford from Jan 1858 to Dec 1878 and in Lewes from Jan 1879 onwards.

The county herald and weekly advertiser. [1791 ?]–no 1,186, 16 April 1814–4 Oct 1873. Variations in subtitle. Pbd Guildford 1858–73.

The mirror of the times. [April? 1796]–no 92, 6 Jan 1798–no 1,391, 23 Feb 1823.

The philanthropic gazette. No 1, 1 Jan 1817–27 Aug 1823. Incorporated in Baldwin's London weekly journal.

The Christian reporter. No 1, 3 Jan 1820–11 Feb 1822. Incorporated in Philanthropic gazette.

The British freeholder and Saturday evening journal. No 1, 5 Feb 1820–no 175, 10 May 1823.

The London weekly gazette. No 1, 13 March 1822–no 68, 2 July 1823.

The weekly press. 23 Aug 1823–2 April 1831.

The British guardian and Protestant advocate. No 1, 7 Jan 1824–no 116, 22 March 1826.

The world. No 1, 4 May 1827–28 March 1832.

The olio: or museum of entertainment. Vols 1–11, 12 Jan 1828–20 July 1833.

The spectator. No 1, 5 July 1828 onwards. Prop R. S. Rintoul 1828–58; ? Scott 1858–61; Meredith Townsend and R. H. Hutton 1861–97; J. St Loe Strachey 1897–1925. Ed R. S. Rintoul 1828–58, Thornton Hunt 1858–61, Meredith Townsend and R. H. Hutton 1861–97, J. St Loe Strachey 1897–1925.

The Court journal. No 1, 2 May 1829–13 March 1925. Prop Henry Colburn. Ed P. G. Patmore 14 Oct 1831–32, William Carpenter 1848, Charles Taylor.

The country times. No 1, 4 Jan 1830–no 102, 26 Dec 1831.

The penny magazine. No 1, 31 March 1832–27 Dec 1845. Prop Society for the Diffusion of Useful Knowledge. Ed Charles Knight.

Old England. 14 April 1832–21 Feb 1842. No issue from 12 March 1836–15 June 1839.

Chambers's Edinburgh journal. Vols 1–12, 4 Feb 1832–30 Dec 1843. New series, vols 1–20, 6 Jan 1844–31 Dec 1853. Continued as Chambers's journal of popular literature, science and arts, vols 1–20, 7 Jan 1854–26 Dec 1863. 4th series, vols 1–20, 2 Jan 1864–29 Dec 1883. 5th series, vols 1–14, 5 Jan 1884–27 Nov 1897. Continued as Chambers's journal, 6th series, vols 1–13, 4 Dec 1897–26 Nov 1910. 7th series, vols 1–21, 3 Dec 1910–28 Nov 1931. Continued monthly, 8th series, vols 1–15, Jan 1932–Dec 1946. 9th series, vols 1–10, Jan 1947–Dec 1956. Prop William and Robert Chambers 1832–71 (assisted by Thomas Smibert 1837–41(?), W. H. Wills 1842(?)–44(?), Leitch Ritchie 1845(?)–59, James Payn 1858–73, Robert Chambers jr 1873–88, C. E. S. Chambers.

The Parliamentary review and family magazine. Vols 1–4, 1833–4, Continued as Parliamentary review, vols 1–2, 8 Feb–30 Aug 1834. Ed J. S. Buckingham.

The London dispatch. No 1, 17 Sept 1836–no 160, 6 Oct 1839.

The London journal. No 1, 17 Sept 1836–no 47, 2 Aug 1837.

The metropolitan Conservative journal. No 1, 8 Oct 1836–no 117, 29 Dec 1838. Continued as Conservative journal and Church of England gazette, no 118, 5 Jan 1839–no 320, 31 Dec 1842.

The penny satirist. No 1, 22 April 1837–25 April 1846. Continued as London pioneer, 1846–8. Ed Barnard Gregory.

The town. No 1, 3 June 1837–26 Jan 1842. Ed Renton Nicholson 3 June 1837–23 May 1840.

The Court gazette. No 1, 7 April 1838–no 438, 4 April 1846. Ed J. B. Torr.

The argus. No 1, 3 Feb 1839–30 Sept 1843. Incorporated in Age and argus.

Britannia. No 1, 20 April 1839–12 April 1856. Incorporated in John Bull. Ed D. T. Coulton 1839–50.

Chambers's London journal of history, literature, poetry, biography and adventure. Vols 1–3, 1841–3. Prop H. & H. Chambers. Ed E. L. Blanchard.

The family herald. No 1, 17 Dec 1842–22 June 1940. Monthly supplement issued from 1877–1940. Ed Mark Lemon.

The sentinel. No 1, 7 Jan 1843–no 179, 7 June 1846. Prop and ed Jonathan Duncan.

Lloyd's monthly [weekly] volume of amusing and instructive literature. Vols 1–22, 1845–6. Continued as Lloyd's weekly volume of amusing and instructive literature, new series, vols 1–7, [1847].

The London journal. No 1, 1 March 1845–no 2,029, 29 Dec 1883. New ser no 1, 5 Jan 1884–28 April 1906. Continued as New London journal, 3rd ser no 1, 5 May 1906–8 May 1909. Continued as London journal, 15 May 1909–27 Jan 1912. Incorporated in Spare moments. Prop George Stiff 1845–57; Herbert Ingram Oct 1857; George Stiff November (?) 1857; ? Johnson. Ed G. M. W. Reynolds 1846, W. H. D. Adams, Mark Lemon 1858–9.

The people's journal. No 1, 3 Jan 1846–June 1849. Amalgamated with Howitt's journal and continued as People's and Howitt's journal, July 1849–June 1851. Prop John Saunders, ? Turrell, William Howitt. Ed John Saunders, William Howitt.

The national. No 1, 14 March 1846–no 157, 10 March 1849.

Douglas Jerrold's weekly newspaper. No 1, 18 July 1846–no 129, 30 Dec 1848. Continued as Douglas Jerrold's weekly news and financial economist, no 130, 6 Jan 1849–no 181, 29 Dec 1849. Continued as Weekly news and financial economist, no 182, 6 Jan 1850–no 255, 31 May 1851.

Reynolds's miscellany. Vols 1–42, 7 Nov 1846–19 June 1869. Ed G. M. W. Reynolds.

Howitt's journal of literature and popular progress. 2 Jan 1847–24 June 1848. Amalgamated with People's journal (*see above*). Ed William and Mary Howitt.

The family friend. Begun monthly, vols 1–6, 1849–52. Continued weekly, new series, vols 1–21, 1852–Nov 1861. Enlarged series, vols 1–8, Jan 1862–Dec 1865. New series, 3 vols 1866–7. New series, with illustrations, vols 1–52, 1870–Sept 1921. New series, nos 1–8, 4 Feb–25 March 1929. Incorporated in Girls' mirror. Ed R. K. Philip 1849–52, W. Jones 1852–5.

The leader. No 1, 30 March 1850–no 536, 30 June 1860. Continued as Saturday analyst and leader, nos 537–557, 7 July–24 Nov 1860. Prop E. F. S. Pigott et al. Ed Thornton Hunt and G. H. Lewes 1850–September (?) 1854, Thornton Hunt, and Thomas Ballantyne.

Leigh Hunt's journal; a miscellany for the cultivation of the memorable, the progressive, and the beautiful. Nos 1–17, 7 Dec 1850–29 March 1851. Ed J. H. Leigh Hunt.

Chambers's papers for the people. Edinburgh. Vols 1–12, 1850–2.

The press. No 1, 7 May 1853–15 Nov 1884. Incorporated in English churchman. Prop B. Disraeli 1853–8; R. H. Patterson 1858–?, Ed Samuel Lucas 1853, D. T. Coulton 1854–7, R. H. Patterson 1858–?, G. H. Townsend.

The court circular. No 1, 26 April 1856–8 Feb 1911. Prop Edward Walford; W. H. Stephens. Ed H. Prendergast, Edward Walford June 1858–June 1859.

The Saturday review. No 1, 3 Nov 1856–23 July 1938. Prop A. J. B. Beresford Hope and J. D. Cook 1856–68; A. J. B. Beresford Hope 1868–87; P. Beresford Hope; Lewis H. Edmunds; Frank Harris 1894–8; 6th Earl of Hardwicke 1898–1904. Ed J. D. Cook 1856–68, Philip Harwood 1868–83, Walter H. Pollock 1884–94, Frank Harris 1894–8, Harold Hodge 1898–1913.

Town talk. No 1, 8 May 1858–no 56, 14 Nov 1859. Prop John Maxwell. Ed Edmund Yates.

The welcome guest. No 1, 1 May 1858–Sept 1861. Prop John Maxwell Nov 1859–Sept 1861. Ed G. A. Sala, R. Brough, W. F. Ainsworth.

Everybody's journal. No 1, 1 Oct 1859–no 18, 28 Jan 1860. Ed W. H. D. Adams.

The dial. No 1, 7 Jan 1860–2 June 1864. Ed David Thomas.

The London review and weekly journal. No 1, 7 July 1860–27 March 1869. Incorporated in Examiner. Ed Charles Mackay 1860, William Black.

Public opinion. No 1, 5 Oct 1861–22 June 1951. Ed Percy White 1880–90, P. Fisher.

Bow bells: a weekly magazine of general literature. Vols 1–2, 12 Nov 1862–27 July 1864. New series, vols 1–47,

3 Aug 1864–28 Dec 1887. Continued as Bow bells weekly: a journal of fiction, society, gossip, fashion, new series, vols 1–36, 6 Jan 1888–12 Feb 1897. Continued as Bow bells, a journal for the home, new series, 15–22 Feb 1897. Incorporated in Duchess novelette. Prop G. M. W. Reynolds and John Dicks. Ed G. M. W. Reynolds, Charles Shurey.

Happy hours. No 1, 16 March 1867–no 564, 29 Dec 1877.

Pall Mall budget. No 1, 3 Oct 1868–31 Dec 1920. Prop William Waldorf Astor. Ed C. L. Hind 1893–5.

Vanity Fair. No 1, 7 Nov 1868–June 1929. Ed T. Gibson Bowles.

The Queen's messenger. No 1, 21 Jan–no 25, 8 July 1869. Prop(?) and ed E. C. Grenville Murray.

The latest news. No 1, 28 Aug 1869–no 57, 25 Sept 1870. Ed Henry Sampson.

Figaro. No 1, 17 May 1870–31 Dec 1898. Ed James Mortimer.

The world. No 1, 8 July 1874–25 March 1922. Prop Edmund Yates and E. C. Grenville Murray July–Nov 1874; Edmund Yates Nov 1874–May 1894. Ed Edmund Yates July 1874–May 1894.

Light. No 1, 6 April–27 Oct 1876. Ed John Morley.

The Whitehall review. No 1, 20 May 1876–25 Oct 1912. Prop and ed Edward Legge.

Mayfair. 2 Jan 1877–14 Feb 1880. Ed H. W. Lucy.

Truth. No 1, 4 Jan 1877–27 Dec 1957. Prop Henry Labouchere 1877–1909. Ed Henry Labouchere assisted by Horace Voules 1877–97 (?), Horace Voules 1897(?)–1902.

The week. No 1, 5 Jan 1878–31 May 1879. Ed L. J. Jennings.

The citizen. No 1, 3 May 1878–24 June 1931. Incorporated in Insurance circular. Ed James Sutherland.

Life. No 1, 12 July 1879–15 Dec 1906. Prop Lord Rosebery. Ed H. P. Stephens, H. Felbermann, Charles Williams.

Society. [No 1, 2 May 1879]–no 45, 12 March 1880–31 Aug 1901. Prop and ed George Plant.

England. No 1, 27 March 1880–28 May 1898.

Tit-bits. No 1, 22 Oct 1881 onwards. Prop George Newnes. Ed George Newnes, P. Galloway Fraser.

St Stephen's review. No 1, 17 March 1883–no 502, 1 Dec 1892. Continued as Big Ben, 8 Dec 1892–30 March 1893.

Cassell's Saturday journal. No 1, 6 Oct 1883–19 Feb 1921. Ed E. Foster 1887–1907.

The outlook. No 1, 11 July 1885–Sept 1892. Incorporated in American settler.

The British weekly. No 1, 5 Nov 1886 onwards. From 1 Jan 1959 pbd in Edinburgh. Ed W. Robertson Nicoll.

The tattler. No 1, 7 July 1887–no 114, 26 Oct 1889. Continued as Pelican, 2 Nov 1889–April 1920. Ed F. M. Boyd.

The Scots observer (Edinburgh). No 1, 24 Nov 1888–15 Nov 1890. Continued in London as National observer, 22 Nov 1890–16 Oct 1897. Ed W. E. Henley Oct 1888–March 1894.

Answers to correspondents. No 1, 2 June 1888–no 82, 21 Dec 1889. Continued as Answers, 28 Dec 1889–18 Feb 1956. Prop Alfred Harmsworth. Ed Alfred Harmsworth.

The speaker. No 1, 4 Jan 1890–23 Feb 1907. Continued as Nation, 2 March 1907–21 Feb 1931. Incorporated in New statesman. Prop John Brunner 1890–9. Ed T. Wemyss Reid 1890–9.

Pearson's weekly. No 1, 26 July 1890–10 Sept 1938. Continued as New Pearson's and today, 17 Sept–19 Nov 1938. Continued as New Pearson's weekly, 26 Nov 1938–1 April 1939. Amalgamated with Tit-bits. Prop and ed C. A. Pearson.

To-day. No 1, 11 Nov 1893–19 July 1905. Ed Jerome K. Jerome 1893–7, Barry Pain 1897–9.

The new age. No 1, 4 Oct 1894–7 April 1938. Ed Frederick A. Atkins 1894–?, A. E. Fletcher.

Illustrated Papers

The mirror of literature, amusement and instruction. No 1, 22 Nov 1822–13 June 1847. Continued monthly to 1849. Ed John Timbs 1827–38, Thomas Byerley, P. B. St John.

The illustrated London news. No 1, 14 May 1842 onwards. Prop Nathaniel Cooke and Herbert Ingram 1842–8; Herbert Ingram 1848–60; William Ingram 1872–1900. Ed F. W. N. Bayley, William James Stewart, Charles Mackay 1848–58(?), John Latey 1858–90, C. K. Shorter 1891–1900. Sub-ed John Timbs 1842–58.

Lloyd's illustrated London newspaper. No 1, 27 Nov 1842–no 7, 8 Jan 1843. Continued as Lloyd's weekly newspaper. *See col 000, above.*

The illustrated weekly times. No 1, 11 March–no 6, 15 April 1843.

Illustrated London life. [No 1, 12 March]–no 5, 9 April–13 Aug 1843. Ed Renton Nicholson.

The pictorial times. No 1, 18 March 1844–3 Jan 1848. Incorporated in Lady's newspaper. Prop Andrew Spottiswoode 1844–5; Herbert Ingram 1845–8. Ed Henry Vizetelly, F. Knight Hunt.

The lady's newspaper. No 1, 2 Jan 1847–Jan 1848. Continued as Lady's newspaper and pictorial times, 15 Jan 1848–26 Dec 1863. Incorporated in Queen. Prop Herbert Ingram.

The historic times. No 1, 19 Jan–no 13, 13 April 1849. Continued as Illustrated historic times, no 14, 20 April 1849–no 89, 26 Sept 1850.

The field. No 1, 1 Jan 1853 onwards. Prop Bradbury and Evans Jan–Nov 1853; Benjamin Webster Nov 1853–Nov 1854; Edward William Cox 1854–79. Ed Mark Lemon 1853, Benjamin Webster Nov 1853–Nov 1854, J. H. Walsh 1858–88, Frederick Toms 1888–99, William Senior 1900–10.

Cassell's illustrated family paper. No 1, 31 Dec 1853–9 March 1867. Continued as Cassell's magazine, March 1867–Nov 1874, *below*. Prop John Cassell 1853–4; Petter and Galpin 1854–8; Cassell, Petter and Galpin. Ed John Cassell 1854–9, George William Petter 1859, William M. Thomas 1867–8, John Lovell, 1868–9, H. R. Haweis 1869–70, George Manville Fenn 1870–4.

Pen and pencil. No 1, 10 Feb–31 March 1855. Ed W. J. Linton.

The illustrated times. No 1, 9 June 1855–no 885, 2 March 1872. Absorbed by Zig-zag. Prop David Bogue and Henry Vizetelly 1855–?; Herbert Ingram. Ed Henry Vizetelly.

The picture times. No 1, 30 June 1855–12 April 1856. Incorporated in Illustrated times.

The coloured news. No 1, 4 Aug–no 9, 29 Sept 1855.

The illustrated news of the world. No 1, 6 Feb 1858–no 300, 31 Oct 1863. Ed J. Moir, John Tallis, J. E. Ritchie 1860–3.

The halfpenny journal. No 1, 1 July 1861–29 Jan 1866.

The welcome guest. No 1, 31 Aug 1861–17 Dec 1864. Incorporated in Halfpenny journal.

The queen. No 1, 7 Sept 1861 onwards. Prop S. O. Beeton 1861; Edward William Cox. Ed P. S. Cox.

The penny illustrated paper. No 1, 12 Oct 1861–24 May 1913. Continued as London life, 2 June 1913–July 1960. Title officially abbreviated to P.I.P., 4 Jan 1908–24 May 1913. Run in conjunction with Illustrated London news.

The illustrated weekly news. No 1, 12 Oct 1861–no 423, 30 Oct 1869.

The illustrated sporting news. [No 1, 15 March]–no 2, 22 March 1862–no 138, 29 Oct 1864. Continued as Illustrated sporting and theatrical news to 19 March 1870. Ed Henry Sampson 1869–70.

Land and water. No 1, 27 June 1866–16 Sept 1920. From 3 June 1905–30 Dec 1915 incorporated in County gentleman. Finally incorporated in Field.

The illustrated Midland news (Birmingham). No 1, 4 Sept 1869–no 80, 11 March 1871. Prop Joseph Hatton and R. W. Johnson.

The graphic. No 1, 4 Dec 1869–23 April 1932. Continued as National graphic, 28 April–14 July 1932. Incorporated in Sphere. Prop William L. Thomas. Ed Sutherland Edwards 1869–70, Arthur Locker 1870–91, Heath Joyce.

The illustrated newspaper. [1869]–no 81, 18 March–30 Dec 1871.

The illustrated sporting and dramatic news. [No 1,] 28 Feb 1874–22 Jan 1943. Continued as Sport and country, 5 Feb 1943–16 Oct 1957. Continued as Farm and country, 30 Oct 1957 onwards.

The pictorial world. No 1, 7 March 1874–9 July 1892. Incorporated in Black and white. Ed H. W. Cutts.

The penny pictorial news. No 1, 1 Sept 1877–10 Nov 1888. Continued as Pictorial news, 17 Nov 1888–27 Sept 1891. Continued as Penny pictorial weekly, no 736, 3 Oct 1891–4 June 1892. Ed Charles P. Sisley.

The lady's pictorial. No 1, 5 March 1881–26 Feb 1921. Incorporated in Eve. Ed Alfred Gibbons.

The lady. No 1, 19 Feb 1885 onwards. Prop Thomas Gibson Bowles. Ed Miss Stewart.

The daily graphic. No 1, 4 Jan 1890–16 Oct 1926. Incorporated in Daily sketch. Prop William L. Thomas. The first illustrated daily paper.

Black and white. No 1, 6 Feb 1891–13 Jan 1912. Incorporated in Sphere. Ed Oswald Crawfurd.

The sketch. No 1, 1 Feb 1893–17 June 1959. Prop William Ingram. Ed C. K. Shorter, John Latey.

Country life. No 1, 8 Jan 1897 onwards. Prop Edward Hudson.

The illustrated mail. No 1, 17 June 1899–1 June 1907. Continued as Weekly illustrated.

The sphere. No 1, 27 Jan 1900–27 Jan 1964. Ed C. K. Shorter 1900–26.

Unstamped and Radical Journals

This type of periodical, often issued in octavo, has usually been associated with a single personality, and by far the greater bulk are of pronounced radical tendency; for this reason Chartist, Socialist and trade union weekly papers have also been included in this section. Some unstamped Sunday papers of a similar kind but with more space given to news have already been noted above.

Cobbett's political register. No 1, 16 Jan 1802–20 Feb 1836. Prop W. Cobbett. Ed W. Cobbett 1802–35, W. Cobbett Jr. 1835–6.

Mr Redhead Yorke's weekly political review. No 1, 7 Dec 1805–6 July 1811. Continued as Weekly political and literary record, 13 July–28 Dec 1811. Ed H. R. Yorke.

The phoenix. No 1, 14 Feb–no 46, 25 Dec 1808. Ed F. W. Blagdon.

The anti-Cobbett: or weekly patriotic register. No 1, 15 Feb–no 8, 5 April 1817.

The black dwarf. No 1, 29 Jan 1817–Dec 1824. Ed T. J. Wooler.

The reformist's register and weekly commentary. No 1, 1 Feb–25 Oct 1817. Prop and ed William Hone.

The republican. No 1, 23 Feb–no 6, 30 March 1817. Continued as Sherwin's weekly political register, 5 April 1817–20 Aug 1819. Continued as Republican, vol 1, no 1, 28 Aug 1819–29 Dec 1826. Ed W. T. Sherwin, R. Carlile, J. A. St John.

The white dwarf. No 1, 29 Nov 1817–no 13, 21 Feb 1818. Tory. Ed Gibbons Merle 1817–18.

The yellow dwarf. No 1, 3 Jan–no 21, 23 May 1818. Ed John Hunt.

The Gorgon. No 1, 23 May 1818–24 April 1819. Ed J. Wade and Francis Place.

The deist: or moral philosopher. No 1, 1 Jan 1819–[?]. Ed R. Carlile.

The Medusa or penny politician. No 1, 20 Feb 1819–7 Jan 1820. Unstamped.

Shadgett's weekly review of Cobbett, Wooler, Sherwin and other democratic and infidel writers. No 1, 1 Feb 1818–no 78, 26 July 1819.

The true Briton (Boston). No 1, 9 June–no 20, 20 Oct 1819.

The theological comet or free thinking Englishman. No 1, 24 July–21 Aug 1819. Continued as Theological and political comet, 28 Aug–23 Nov 1819.

Edmond's weekly register (Birmingham). No 1, 28 Aug–30 Nov 1819.

The cap of liberty. No 1, 8 Sept 1819–5 Jan 1820. Incorporated in Medusa.

The democratic recorder and reformer's guide. No 1, 2 Oct–no 4, Nov 1819. Ed E. Edmonds.

The white hat. No 1, 16 Oct–11 Dec 1819.

The blue dwarf (Yarmouth). Nos 1–6, 1820.

The economist: a periodical paper explanatory of the New System of Society projected by Robert Owen. No 1, 27 Jan 1821–no 52, 9 March 1822. Ed George Mudie.

The lion. No 1, 4 Jan–25 Dec 1829. Ed R. Carlile.

The political letter and pamphlets, published for the avowed purpose of trying with the government the question of law, whether all publications containing news are liable to the imposition of the stamp duty. 1830–1. Unstamped. Ed William Carpenter.

The prompter. No 1, 13 Nov 1830–12 Nov 1831. Unstamped. Ed R. Carlile.

The poor man's guardian. No 1, 9 July 1831–26 Dec 1835. Ed Henry Hetherington 1831–2, Henry Hetherington and J. Bronterre O'Brien 1832–5.

The poor man's advocate (Manchester), No 1, 21 Jan 1832–no 50, 5 Jan 1833. Ed J. Doherty.

The working man's friend. No 1, 22 Dec 1832–no 33, 3 Aug 1833.

The Isis: a London weekly publication, edited by a lady. 1832. Ed Mrs Carlile.

The cosmopolite. No 1, 10 March 1832–no 55, 19 May 1833. Unstamped. Ed Rowland Detrosier.

The crisis. Vol 1, no 1, 14 April 1832–vol 4, no 20, 23 Aug 1834. Ed Robert Owen and J. E. Smith.

The destructive and poor man's conservative. No 1, 2 Feb 1833–no 53, 1 Feb 1834. Continued as People's conservative and trades union gazette, no 54, 8 Feb–no 74, June 1834. Ed J. Bronterre O'Brien 1833–4.

The gauntlet; a sound weekly republican newspaper. No 1, 9 Feb 1833–29 March 1834. Ed R. Carlile.

The shepherd. No 1, 30 Aug 1834–3 March 1838. Ed J. E. Smith.

Hetherington's twopenny dispatch and people's police register. [June 1834]–no 109, 9 July–no 118, 10 Sept 1836. Continued as London dispatch, no 1, 17 Sept 1836–no 160, 6 Oct 1839. Incorporated in Champion and weekly herald. Prop Henry Hetherington. Ed Augustus Beaumont, J. Bronterre O'Brien 1836–9.

The new moral world. No 1, 1 Nov 1834–10 Jan 1846. Pbd successively at London, Manchester, Birmingham and Leeds. Ed Robert Owen, G. A. Fleming.

The weekly herald. 18 Sept–13 Nov 1836. Incorporated in Champion.

Bronterre's national reformer. No 1, 7 Jan–no 11, 18 March 1837. Ed J. Bronterre O'Brien.

The northern liberator (Newcastle-on-Tyne). No 1, 21 Oct 1837–no 137, 23 May 1840. Continued as Northern liberator and champion, 30 May–19 Dec 1840. Ed A. H. Beaumont.

The northern star and Leeds general advertiser (Leeds). No 1, 18 Nov 1837–13 March 1852. Continued as Star and national trades journal, nos 750–5, 20 March–1 May 1852. Continued as Star of freedom, nos 1–16, 8 May–27 Nov 1852. Prop Feargus O'Connor; G. J. Harney 1852. Ed William Hill 1842, G. J. Harney 1847–50.

The national: a library for the people. No 1, 5 Jan–no 25, 29 June 1839. Ed W. J. Linton.

The Chartist. No 1, 2 Feb–no 23, 7 July 1839. 'Moral force'; Chartist.

The Chartist circular (Glasgow). No 1, 28 Sept 1839–no 84, 1 May 1841.

The English Chartist circular. No 1, 23 Jan 1841–no 153, 10 Jan 1844. Ed James Harris.

The London phalanx. No 1, 3 April 1841–30 April 1842. Continued monthly, June 1842–May 1843. Fourierist. Ed Hugh Doherty.

The oracle of reason. No 1, 6 Nov 1841–no 103, 2 Dec 1843. Ed Charles Southwell, G. J. Holyoake, Thomas Paterson, William Chilton.

The British statesman. No 1, 13 March 1842–no 46, 21 Jan 1843. Incorporated in British queen and statesman. Prop and ed J. Bronterre O'Brien June-Dec 1842.

The Dundee herald. No 1, 26 Aug 1842–[?]. Chartist. Ed Peter Brown.

The movement, anti-persecution gazette and register of progress. No 1, 16 Dec 1843–no 68, 2 April 1845. Ed G. J. Holyoake and M. Q. Ryall.

The league. No 1, 30 Sept 1843–4 July 1846. Organ of the Anti-Corn Law League. Ed A. W. Paulton.

The national reformer, and Manx weekly review of home and foreign affairs. No 1, Nov 1844–no 75, April 1846. No 76 (new ser no 1), 3 Oct 1846–no 110 (new ser no 35), 29 May 1847. Ptd at Douglas, Isle of Man, where no stamp was needed. Prop and ed J. Bronterre O'Brien.

The moral world. No 1, 30 Aug–no 11, 8 Nov 1845. Ed Robert Owen.

The herald of progress. No 1, 25 Oct 1845–no 16, 23 May 1846. Continued as Reasoner and herald of progress, no 1, 3 June 1846–no 788, 30 June 1861. Continued monthly as Secular world, no 789, June (?) 1863–no 826, Dec 1864. Continued as Reasoner and secular world, no 827, Jan 1865–no 838, Dec 1865–[no 910, 1872 irregularly]. Between Aug and Dec 1861 there appeared Counsellor on secular, co-operative and political questions. Ed G. J. Holyoake.

Politics for the people. No 1, 6 May–no 17, 29 July 1848. Christian Socialist. Prop J. W. Parker. Ed J. M. Ludlow and F. D. Maurice.

The spirit of the age. No 1, 1 July 1848–3 March 1849. Prop W. H. Ashurst. Ed Robert Buchanan.

The standard of freedom. No 1, 1 July 1848–no 171, 4 Oct 1851. Incorporated in Weekly news and chronicle. Prop John Cassell.

The spirit of the times. No 1, 10 March–29 Sept 1849. Continued as Weekly tribune, 6 Oct 1849–6 July 1850. Ed Robert Buchanan.

Reynolds's political instructor. No 1, 10 Nov 1849–11 May 1850. Ed G. W. M. Reynolds.

Cooper's journal. No 1, 5 Jan–no 30, 26 Oct 1850. Ed Thomas Cooper.

Robert Owen's weekly letter to the human race. [No 1]–no 18, May 1850.

The red republican. No 1, 22 June–no 24, 30 Nov 1850. Ed G. J. Harney.

The friend of the people. No 1, 7 Dec 1850–no 33, 26 July 1851. New ser no 1, 7 Feb–no 12, 24 April 1852. Ed G. J. Harney.

The operative. No 1, 4 Jan 1851–no 80, 10 July 1852.

The Christian Socialist. No 1, 2 Nov 1850–27 Dec 1851. Ed J. Townsend, F. D. Maurice.

Robert Owen's journal. No 1, 2 Nov 1851–23 Oct 1852.

The people's paper. No 1, 8 May 1852–4 Sept 1858. Ed Ernest Jones.

The friend of the people. No 1, 28 Jan 1860–20 Sept 1861.

The national reformer. No 1, 14 April 1860–vol 62, no 14 (new ser), 1 Oct 1893. Prop Charles Bradlaugh. Ed Charles Bradlaugh, Annie Besant.

The elector. No 1, 23 June 1860–no 142, 2 Aug 1862. Formerly Ballot, no 1, 19 Nov 1859–no 31, 16 June 1860.

The co-operator (Dewsbury and London). No 1, June 1860–Dec 1869. Continued as Co-operator and herald of health, 1 Jan–5 Feb 1870. Continued as Co-operator, anti-vaccinator and herald of health, 12 Feb–16 July 1870. Continued as Co-operator and anti-vaccinator, 23 July 1870–23 Sept 1871. Began as a monthly and continued as a fortnightly before becoming a weekly. Ed Edward Longfield 1869–?, Henry Pitman June 1861 (?)–1871.

The bee-hive. [1861]–no 404, 10 July 1869–no 794, 30 Dec 1876. Continued as Industrial review, 6 Jan 1877–28 Dec 1878. Prop Trades Newspaper Co and George Potter 1861–9; Daniel Pratt 1869–March 1873; George Potter July 1873–78. Ed George Stoup 1861–4, Robert Hartwell 1864–Dec 1868, George Potter Jan 1869–Feb 1870, Henry Solly assisted by George Potter Feb–Dec 1870, George Potter Jan 1871–Dec 1877.

British miner and general newsman. 13 Sept 1862–28 Feb 1863. Continued as Miner, 7 March–6 June 1863. Continued as Miner and workmen's advocate, 13 June 1863–Sept 1865. Continued as Workman's advocate, 9 Sept 1865–3 Feb 1866. Continued as Commonwealth, 10 Feb 1866–20 July 1867. Incorporated in Train (13 July 1866–?). The organ successively of British Miners' Benefit Association, International Working Men's Association and Reform League. Ed John Towers 7 March–6 June 1863, William Whitehorn.

The eastern post. No 1, 18 Oct 1868–29 Oct 1938.

The international herald. No 1, 2 March 1872–no 81, 18 Oct 1873. Continued as Republican herald, 1873–4. Organ of International Working Men's Association. Ed W. Harrison Riley.

The miners' advocate (Middlesbrough). No 1, 17 Jan 1873–31 Oct 1874.

The miner's weekly news (Coventry). No 1, 16 Aug 1873–no 23, 17 Jan 1874.

The union chronicle (Manchester, Leamington and Coventry). 1873–5. Continued as National agricultural labourers' chronicle, 1875–7. Continued as English labourers' chronicle, 1877–94.

Daylight (Norwich). No 1, 5 Oct 1878–1909.

The railway review. No 1, 16 July 1880 onwards.

The radical. 14 Dec 1880–July 1882. Ed Samuel Bennett.

The freethinker. No 1, May 1881 onwards. Ed G. W. Foote.

Justice. No 1, 19 Jan 1884–22 Jan 1925. Ed H. M. Hyndman 1884–6, H. Quelch 1886–1913.

The democrat. No 1, 15 Nov 1884–1 Sept 1890. Continued as Labour world, no 1, 21 Sept 1890–no 37, 22 March 1891. Continued as Sunday world, 29 March–31 May 1891. Ed Michael Davitt.

The commonweal. No 1, Feb 1885–12 May 1894. Ed William Morris.

Brotherhood. 28 April 1887–April 1903. Continued as a monthly. Organ of the Land Nationalization Society. Ed J. Bruce Wallace.

The leaflet newspaper. 4 Feb–23 June 1888. Continued as Socialist, 7 July–1 Sept 1888. Continued monthly to Feb–April 1889. Ed Thomas Bolas.

The link. No 1, 4 Feb–no 44, 1 Dec 1888. Organ of Law and Liberty League. Ed Annie Besant and W. T. Stead.

The Labour elector. No 10, 15 Dec 1888–July 1894. Started as a monthly, nos 1–5, June–Oct 1888. Continued fortnightly, nos 6–9, 1 Nov–3 Dec 1888. Suspended from April 1890–Jan 1893. Ed H. H. Champion.

The north and east London star. No 1, 30 March–11 May 1889. Continued as North London press and star, 18 May 1889–25 Jan 1890. Continued as People's press, 8 March 1890–28 Feb 1891. Prop Edward O. Adam March 1889–?; organ of several trade unions March 1890–Feb 1891. Ed Edward O. Adam March 1889–?, Shaw Maxwell March 1890–Feb 1891.

The workman's times (Huddersfield). No 1, 29 Aug 1890–7 March 1894. Pbd in London 1892–3 and Manchester 1893–4. Ed Joseph Burgess.

The trade unionist. No 1, 4 April–22 Aug 1891. New ser incorporating Docker's record, 29 Aug 1891–19 March 1892. Incorporated in Workman's times.

The labour leader. No 1, 10 Oct 1891–28 Sept 1922. Incorporated in New Leader.
The clarion. No 1, 12 Dec 1891–June 1932. Continued as New clarion, 11 June 1932–10 March 1934. Pbd in Manchester 12 Dec 1891–6 May 1893. Prop Robert and Montagu Blatchford, Edward Francis Fay. Ed Robert Blatchford.

Weekly Literary Reviews

The director: a weekly literary journal. No 1, 24 Jan–4 July 1807. Ed T. F. Dibdin.
The literary gazette. No 1, 25 Jan 1817–26 April 1862. Incorporated in Parthenon. Ed H. E. Lloyd and Miss Ross, William Jerdan 1817–50, L. A. Reeve 1850–8, J. M. Jephson 1858, C. W. Shirley Brooks Nov 1858–9, H. Christmas, W. R. Workman, F. Arnold, John Morley 1861, C. W. Goodwin.
The literary journal. No 1, 29 March 1818–19.
The county literary chronicle and weekly review. [1819]–no 59, 1 July 1820–no 260, 8 May 1823. Continued as Literary chronicle and weekly review, no 261, 15 May 1823–no 471, 24 May 1828. Incorporated in Athenaeum. Ed J. W. Dalby 1826–8.
The indicator. No 1, 13 Oct 1819–no 99, 30 Aug 1821. Ed J. H. Leigh Hunt nos 1–76, 13 Oct 1819–21 March 1821.
The literary examiner. Nos 1–27, 1823. Ed J. H. Leigh Hunt.
The Somerset House gazette, and literary museum. No 1, 11 Oct 1823–no 52, 2 Oct 1824. Ed Ephraim Hardcastle.
The Palladium. No 1, 6 Feb 1825–no 98, 17 Dec 1826.
The athenaeum. No 1, 2 Jan 1828–11 Feb 1921. Incorporated in Nation. Prop J. S. Buckingham and Henry Colburn Jan–July 1828; J. Sterling, F. D. Maurice et al July 1828–Jan 1830; James Holmes Jan–June 1830; James Holmes and J. H. Reynolds June 1830–32; C. W. Dilke 1832–64; C. W. Dilke II 1864–9; C. W. Dilke III 1869–?. Ed J. S. Buckingham Jan–July 1828 (assisted by H. Stebbing), F. D. Maurice July 1828–May 1829, John Sterling May 1829–June 1830, C. W. Dilke June 1830–46, T. K. Hervey 1846–53, W. H. Dixon Jan 1853–Aug 1869, John Doran 1869–71, N. MacColl 1871–1900.
The companion. No 1, 9 Jan–no 29, 23 July 1828. Ed J. H. Leigh Hunt.
Leigh Hunt's London journal. No 1, 2 April 1834, no 61, 30 May 1835. Merged with Printing Machine and continued as Leigh Hunt's London Journal and printing machine, no 62, 6 June–no 91, 26 Dec 1835. Ed J. H. Leigh Hunt.
Notes and queries. No 1, 3 Nov 1849 onwards. Ed W. J. Thomas 1849–Sept 1872, John Doran 1872–8 (assisted by H. F. Turle 1873–8), H. F. Turle 1878–83, Joseph Knight 1883–1907.
Household words. No 1, 30 March 1850–28 May 1859. Prop C. Dickens and Bradbury and Evans. Ed C. Dickens.
Once a week. No 1, 2 July 1859–May 1879. Prop Bradbury and Evans; James Rice ?–1873; George Manville Fenn 1873–?. Ed S. Lucas 1859–65, Edward Walford 1865–?, E. S. Dallas Jan 1868–July 1869, Mark Lemon, George Manville Fenn 1873–?.
All the year round. No 1, 30 April 1859–30 March 1895. Prop C. Dickens. Ed C. Dickens, C. Dickens jr.
The Parthenon. No 1, 3 May 1862–no 57, 30 May 1863. Ed C. W. Goodwin.
The reader. No 1, 3 Jan 1863–28 July 1866. Ed J. M. Ludlow, David Masson 1863–?, J. Dennis, T. Bendyshe.
The academy. No 1, 9 Oct 1869–11 Sept 1915. Began monthly and became weekly in 1874. Prop John Murray nos 1–12, 9 Oct 1869–10 Sept 1870; Charles Appleton et al Sept 1870–1873; Academy Co Ltd. 1873–8; Henry Villiers 1880–96; John Morgan Richards 1896–?. Ed Charles Appleton 1869–78, C. E. Dobell 1878–81, James Sutherland Cotton Jan 1881–Nov 1896, Charles Lewis Hind 1896–Oct 1903.
Sala's journal. No 1, 30 April 1892–11 April 1894. Ed G. A. Sala.
Literature. No 1, 23 Oct 1897–11 Jan 1902. Ed H. D. Traill 1897–1901.

Religious Papers

The record. No 1, 1 Jan 1828–31 Dec 1948. Incorporated in Church of England newspaper and continued as Church of England newspaper and the record, 7 Jan 1949 onwards. Frequency varied until it became a weekly 31 March 1882. Prop James Evans and Andrew Hamilton. Ed Henry Blunt, Edward Garbett 1854–67.
The Catholic vindicator. 5 Dec 1818–4 Dec 1819. Ed W. E. Andrews.
The Catholic advocate. No 1, 3 Dec 1820–no 34, 22 July 1821.
The world. No 1, 4 May 1827–28 March 1832. Incorporated in Patriot. Prop and ed Stephen Bourne.
The Catholic journal. No 1, 1 March 1828–no 55, 15 March 1829.
The Christian advocate. No 1, 7 Jan 1830–no 505, 2 Sept 1839.
The patriot. No 1, 22 Feb 1832–27 Dec 1866. Continued as English independent, 3 Jan 1867–24 Dec 1879. Incorporated in Nonconformist. Frequency varied until it finally settled as a weekly, 6 Jan 1859. Ed Stephen Bourne 1832, Josiah Conder 1833–55.
The watchman. No 1, 7 Jan 1835–31 Dec 1889. Wesleyan. Ed J. C. Rigg 1848–64.
The witness (Edinburgh). No 1, 15 Jan 1840–27 Feb 1864. Twice weekly. Ed Hugh Miller 1840–56.
The tablet. No 1, 16 May 1840–23 July 1842. *See below under* True tablet. Ed F. Lucas 1840–2, M. J. Quin 1842.
The Nonconformist. 14 April 1841–24 Dec 1879. Continued as Nonconformist and independent, 1 Jan 1880–18 Sept 1890. Continued as Independent and nonconformist, 26 Sept 1890–30 Dec 1897. Continued as Independent, 6 Jan 1898–29 March 1900. Incorporated in Examiner. Ed Edward Miall 1841 (?)–81.
The Jewish chronicle. [No 1, 12 Nov 1841]—new ser 6–20 May 1842. Suspended until 18 Oct 1844 when it resumed as Jewish chronicle and working man's friend–22 Dec 1854. Continued as Jewish chronicle and Hebrew observer–2 Aug 1869. Continued as Jewish chronicle Aug 1869 onwards. Fortnightly Oct 1844–Oct 1847. From 3 July 1865–2 Aug 1869 a penny abridged edn was issued concurrently. Prop Isaac Valentine 1841–20 May 1842; Joseph Mitchell and Isaac Valentine 18 Oct 1844–Aug 1854; Marcus Bresslau Aug 1854–Jan 1855; Abraham Benisch Jan 1855–Aug 1869; Lionel Cohen, Samuel Montagu and Lionel Van Oven Aug 1869–June 1875; Abraham Benisch June 1875–July 1878; Anglo-Jewish association; Israel Davis, Sydney Montagu Samuel, Asher Myers. Ed Moses Angel and David Meldola 1841–May 1842, Marcus Bresslau Oct 1848–Jan 1855, Abraham Benisch Jan 1855–Aug 1869, Michael Henry Aug 1869–June 1875, Abraham Benisch June 1875–July 1878, Asher Myers July 1878–1902.
The true tablet. 20 Feb–31 Dec 1842. Continued as Tablet, 7 Jan 1843 onwards. From 19 March–31 Dec 1842 True Tablet has two sets of enumeration, one derived from Tablet (1840–42). From 5 Jan 1850–11 Sept 1858 Tablet was pbd in Dublin. Prop F. Lucas 1842–Oct 1855; John Wallis; Cardinal Herbert Vaughan Nov 1868–? Ed F. Lucas 1842–55, John Wallis 1855–68, Herbert Vaughan Nov 1868–93 (?), J. G. Snead-Cox 1893 (?)–?
The English churchman. No 1, 5 Jan 1843 onwards. Ed D. W. Godfrey 1843–63.

The guardian. No 1, 12 Jan 1846–30 Nov 1951. Anglican. Ed Thomas Henry Haddan, M. R. Sharp 1859–83, J. Sharp 1883–95, W. H. Lathbury 1896–9.
The Christian times. No 1, 12 Aug 1848–no 528, 11 Aug 1858. Continued as Beacon and Christian times, no 1, 18 Aug 1858–no 54, 24 Aug 1859. Ed William Leask.
The Wesleyan times. No 1, 8 Jan 1849–29 July 1867. Continued as Methodist times, 5 Aug 1867–31 Dec 1869.
The Catholic standard. No 1, 13 Oct 1849–12 May 1855. Continued as Weekly register, 19 May 1855–14 March 1902. Prop H. W. Wilberforce 1854–63; ? De Lacy Towle 1880; Cardinal Manning 1880–1; Wilfred Meynell 1881–?. Ed H. W. Wilberforce 1854–63, Orby Shipley 1880–1, Wilfred Meynell 1881–?.
The freeman. No 1, 24 Jan 1855–no 2297, 17 Feb 1899. Continued as Baptist times and freeman, 24 Feb 1899 onwards.
The Christian world. No 1, 9 April 1857–28 Sept 1961. Low Church. Ed J. Whittemore 1857–60, James Clarke 1860–88, James G. Clarke.
The revival. No 1, 30 July 1859–27 Jan 1870. Incorporated in Christian, no 1, 3 Feb 1870 onwards. Low Church.
The universe. 8 Dec 1860–17 Sept 1909. Continued as Universe and Catholic weekly, 24 Sept 1909–14 June 1912. Continued as Universe, 14 June 1912–1 June 1962. Continued as Universe and Catholic times, 8 June 1962 onwards.
The Methodist recorder. No 1, 4 April 1861 onwards.
The Church times. No 1, 7 Feb 1863 onwards. High Church. Ed G. J. Palmer 1863–92, T. A. Lacey.
Sunday magazine. Vols 1–7, Oct 1864–Sept 1871. New ser, vols 1–35, Nov 1871–April 1906. Incorporated in Good words. Prop Alexander Strahan. Ed T. Guthrie 1864–73, W. G. Blaikie 1873–80, B. Waugh 1881–94.
The methodist. No 1, 1 Jan 1874–no 580, 27 Dec 1884.
The secular review. No 1, 6 Aug 1876–28 Jan 1877. Ed G. J. Holyoake.
The secular review. 9 June 1877–29 Dec 1888. Continued as Agnostic journal, 5 Jan 1889–15 June 1907. Ed G. W. Foote.
The war cry and official gazette of the Salvation Army. No. No 1, 27 Dec 1880 onwards.
The Christian commonwealth. No 1, 20 Oct 1881–24 Sept 1919.

Agricultural Papers

The farmer's journal. 15 Aug 1807–15 April 1809. Continued as Evans and Ruffy's farmer's journal, 22 April 1809–16 July 1832. Incorporated in Bell's weekly messenger.
Fleming's weekly express. No 1, 4 May 1823–no 167, 9 July 1826. Continued as Fleming's British farmer's chronicle, 10 July 1826–26 Jan 1829.
Exley, Dimsdale and Hopkinson's Corn Exchange circular. No 1, 1 Jan 1824–no 306, 28 Dec 1829.
The corn trade circular. No 1, 24 Oct 1825–no 402, 24 June 1833.
The Mark Lane express. No 1, 2 Jan 1832–31 March 1924. Continued as Farmer's express, 7 April 1924–29 July 1929. Incorporated in Farm, field and fireside. Prop Walter Darkin. Ed Peter Lund Simmonds 1841, Joseph Robertson, William Shaw.
The universal corn reporter. No 1, 6 Feb 1832–14 Jan 1870.
The new farmer's journal. No 1, 11 Feb 1833–no 58, 21 May 1834. Incorporated in Mark Lane express.
The magnet. No 1, 13 March 1837–no 2616, 27 Aug 1888. Ed John Browne Bell.
The farmer's journal. No 1, 9 Dec 1839–no 362, 28 Dec 1848.
The Scottish farmer and horticulturalist. No 1, 3 April 1861–11 Oct 1865. Continued as Farmer, 18 Oct 1865–26 Dec 1881. Continued as Farmer and the chamber of agriculture journal, 2 Jan 1882–5 Oct 1889. Continued as Farmer and stockbreeder and chamber of agriculture journal, 9 Oct 1889–13 July 1925. Continued as Farmer and stock-breeder and agricultural gazette, 20 July 1925 onwards.
The agricultural gazette. No 1, Jan 1874–17 July 1925. Incorporated in Farmer and stock-breeder. Ed J. C. Morton 1874–88.

Financial and Commercial Papers

The bankers' circular. No 1, 25 July–no 7, 5 Sept 1828. Continued as Circular to bankers, no 8, 12 Sept 1828–no 1417, 31 Dec 1853. Continued as Bankers' circular, 7 Jan 1854–9 Jan 1858. Continued as Monetary times and bankers' circular, 16 Jan 1858–31 Dec 1859. Continued as Bankers' circular and monetary times, 7 Jan–24 March 1860.
The London mercantile journal. No 1, 13 July 1830–22 March 1870.
Nicholson's weekly register. No 1, 1 Jan 1842–no 130, 22 June 1844. Continued as London commercial record, no 1, 29 June 1844–28 June 1940. Incorporated in London corn circular.
The economist. No 1, 2 Sept 1843 onwards. Prop James Wilson 1843–60; then his family to 1928. Ed James Wilson 1843–59 (assisted by Herbert Spencer 1843–53), Walter Bagehot 1859–77, R. H. Inglis-Palgrave and Daniel C. Lathbury 1877–83, Edward Johnstone 1883–1907.
The money market review. No 1, 9 June 1860–25 June 1921. Continued as Investors' chronicle and money market review, 2 July 1921 onwards.
The insurance record. No 1, 30 Jan 1863 onwards.
The investor's guardian. No 1, 22 Aug 1863 onwards.
The bullionist. No 1, 6 Jan 1866–5 Dec 1899. Continued as Daily bullionist, 7 Dec 1899–2 June 1900. Incorporated in Financier. Ed David Morier Evans, John Scott Henderson, Arthur Henry Evans 1883–?
The commercial world. [1874]–no 179, 1 Jan 1878–1 March 1939.
The statist. No 1, 12 March 1878–28 April 1967. Prop Robert Giffen 1878–1910; Thomas Lloyd 1878–1920. Ed Arthur Ellis 1878–80, Robert Giffen, George Paish.
The shipping world. No 1, May 1883 onwards.
The financial chronicle. [No 1, 19 June 1883]–no 1, new ser 19 June 1886–20 May 1931.
The capitalist. No 1, 16 Nov 1885–25 Dec 1926. Continued as Investor, 1 Jan 1927–March 1943.
The financial world. [1886]–27 April 1887 onwards.

Sporting Papers

Kent's weekly dispatch and sporting mercury. [1816]–no 98, 5 April 1818–no 192, 23 Jan 1820.
The racing times. [Feb 1851]–no 8, 16 April 1851–10 Aug 1868.
The sporting gazette. No 1, 1 Nov 1862–no 920, 27 Dec 1879. Continued as County gentleman, no 921, 3 Jan 1880–30 Dec 1915. Incorporated in Land and water.
The sporting times. No 1, 11 Feb 1865–5 Dec 1931. Prop John Corlett 1874–1912. Ed J. H. Shorthouse, John Corlett.
The sporting clipper. [1872]–18 April 1874–30 June 1894.
The athletic news (Manchester). [June 1875]–no 92, 3 March 1877–23 April 1917. Incorporated in Sporting chronicle. Prop Edward Hulton and E. O. Bleackley. Ed T. R. Sutton 1875–95.
The fishing gazette. No 1, 26 April 1877 onwards.
The bicycling times. No 1, 24 May 1877–25 Dec 1883. Continued as Cycling times, 1 Jan 1884–25 March 1887.
The cyclist. [1879]–no 12, 7 Jan 1880–11 Nov 1903. Continued as Cyclist trade review, 11 Nov 1903–4 May 1905. Continued as Cycle and motor trades review, 11 May

1905–19 Jan 1911. Amalgamated with Cycle trader and review. Prop William Iliffe. Ed Edmund Dangerfield, Henry Sturmey.

The sportsman's weekly guide to the turf. No 1, 21 Feb 1880–15 Nov 1884.

Horse and hound. No 1, 29 March 1884 onwards.

The racing world. No 1, 26 Feb 1887–26 July 1929.

The jockey. No 1, 18 April 1890–29 Dec 1956. Not pbd 8 Aug 1914–22 March 1919. Registration copies only from 26 Dec 1936.

Cycling. No 1, 27 Jan 1891 onwards. Ed Charles Sisley.

Humorous Papers

The quizzical gazette and merry companion. No 1, 27 Aug 1831–no 21, 14 Jan 1832. Ed John Mitford.

Figaro in London. No 1, 10 Dec 1831–9. Prop Thomas Lyttleton Holt. Ed G. A. à Beckett 1831–27 Dec 1834.

Punch: or the London Charivari. No 1, 17 July 1841 onwards. Prop Ebenezer Landells and Joseph Last 1841; Ebenezer Landells 1842; Bradbury and Evans. Ed Mark Lemon 1841–70, C. W. Shirley Brooks 1870–4, Tom Taylor 1874–80, F. C. Burnand 1880–1906.

Fun. No 1, 21 Sept 1861–Aug 1901. Incorporated in Sketchy bits. Prop Dalziel brothers. Ed Thomas Hood the younger 1861–74, Henry Sampson 1874–8, Charles Dalziel.

The comic news. No 1, 13 July 1863–14 March 1865. Ed H. J. Byron, Charles Collins.

Judy: or the London serio-comic journal. 1 May 1867–23 Oct 1907. Prop Charles Ross April 1869–?; Dalziel brothers. Ed Charles Ross.

The tomahawk. No 1, 11 May 1867–no 164, 25 June 1870. Ed A. à Beckett, M. S. Morgan.

Moonshine. July 1879–Aug 1902. Ed Arthur Clements.

Ally Sloper's half holiday. 3 May 1884–9 Sept 1916. Incorporated in London society. Prop Dalziel brothers. Ed Charles Ross.

Sketchy bits. No 1, 25 April 1893–9 May 1910.

Juvenile Papers

Boys of England. No 1, 24 Nov 1866–23 June 1899. Continued under various titles, Up-to-date boys, Boys of the Empire, Boys of our Empire, Boys of England, until 22 Dec 1906. Ed Charles Stevens, Edwin J. Brett.

The young Englishman's journal. No 1, 13 April 1867–73. Ed W. L. Emmett.

Young men of Great Britain. No 1, 29 Jan 1868–17 June 1889. Ed Edwin J. Brett, Vane St John.

The young Briton. No 1, 18 Sept 1869–77. Ed W. L. Emmett.

The gentleman's journal. No 1, 1 Nov 1869–Oct 1872. Ed George Frederick Pardon.

Our young folks' weekly budget. No 1, 2 Jan 1871–no 447, 28 June 1879. Continued as Young folks, no 448, 5 July 1879–no 733, 20 Dec 1884. Continued as Young folks' paper, 27 Dec 1884–28 June 1891. Continued as Old and young, 4 July 1891–11 Sept 1896. Continued as Folks at home, no 1, 18 Sept 1896–29 April 1897. Ed James Henderson.

The boys' standard. No 1, 6 Nov 1875–18 June 1892. Ed Charles Fox.

The boys' own paper. No 1, 18 Jan 1879–Feb 1967. Prop. Religious Tract Soc. Ed G. A. Hutchinson, J. Macaulay.

The boys' world. No 1, 14 April 1879–31 Jan 1883. Ed Ralph Rollington.

The Union Jack. No 1, 1 Jan 1880–25 Sept 1883. Prop Alfred Harmsworth. Ed W. H. Kingston, G. A. Henty.

The girl's own paper. No 1, 3 Jan 1880–26 Sept 1908.

The boys' newspaper. No 1, 15 Sept 1880–14 Aug 1882. Continued as Youth, 21 Aug 1882–25 April 1888. Prop Cassell Sept 1880–April 1881; William Ingram. Ed George Weatherly, Alfred Harmsworth.

The boys' illustrated news. No 1, 6 April 1881–no 61, 31 May 1882. Ed Mayne Reid.

The boys' comic journal. No 1, 17 March 1883–16 April 1898. Ed Edwin J. Brett.

Ching-Ching's own. No 1, 23 June 1888–17 June 1893. Ed E. Harcourt Burrage.

Comic cuts. No 1, 17 May 1890–12 Sept 1953. Incorporated in Knock-out. Prop Alfred Harmsworth. Ed Alfred Harmsworth.

Comic pictorial nuggets. No 1, 7 May–no 29, 19 Nov 1892. Continued as Nuggets, no 30, 26 Nov 1892–10 March 1905.

The world's comic. No 1, 6 July 1892–10 Nov 1908.

Chums. No 1, 12 Sept 1892–July 1932. Continued monthly to July 1934 and as an annual 1935–41. Prop Cassell. Ed Max Pemberton 1892–4, Ernest Foster 1894–1907.

Miscellaneous Specialized Papers

The military register. No 1, 30 March 1814–11 April 1821.

The united services gazette. No 1, 9 Feb 1833–29 Dec 1921. Ed A. A. Watts 1833–43.

The naval and military gazette. No 1, 9 Feb 1833–no 2774, 17 Feb 1886. Incorporated in Broad arrow.

The Civil Service gazette. No 1, 1 Jan 1853–Nov 1926. Ed John Bolger.

The army and navy gazette. No 1, 7 Jan 1860–26 Nov 1921. Continued as Army, navy and air force gazette, 3 Dec 1921–12 Nov 1936. Continued as United services review, 19 Nov 1936–April 1947. Continued as United services and Empire review, May 1947–Aug-Sept 1957. Not pbd between 28 Sept 1939 and Feb 1942. Ed W. H. Russell.

The broad arrow. No 1, 1 July 1868–18 April 1917.

The Admiralty and Horse Guards' gazette. No 1, 1 Nov 1884–19 Jan 1901.

The era. No 1, 30 Sept 1838–21 Sept 1939. Prop Licensed Victuallers' Association; Frederic Ledger 1850–74; E. Ledger. Ed William Carpenter 1838, William Henry Harrison 1845, Frederic Ledger 1850–74.

The London entr'acte. [1869]–no 27, 8 Jan 1870–no 137, 17 Feb 1872. Continued as Entr'acte, no 138, 24 Feb 1872–26 April 1907.

The stage. No 1, 25 March 1881 onwards. Begun monthly as Stage directory, no 1, Feb 1880–no 14, 1 March 1881.

The auction register and law chronicle. No 1, 7 Jan 1813–no 146, 23 Feb 1815. Continued as Law chronicle and estate advertiser, no 147, 2 March 1815–no 2747, 30 Dec 1847.

The law gazette. No 1, 15 Aug 1822–no 1146, 23 Dec 1847.

The jurist. No 1, 14 Jan 1837–no 939, 6 Jan 1855. New ser no 1, 13 Jan 1855–67. Ed John Jervis.

The law times. No 1, 8 April 1843–25 Oct 1965. Amalgamated with Law journal and continued as New law journal. Prop Edward William Cox. Ed Basil Crump.

The solicitor's journal. 3 Jan 1857 onwards.

The law journal. No 1, 19 Jan 1866–25 Oct 1965. Amalgamated with Law times and continued as New law journal. Ed W. D. I. Foulkes 1879–90.

The lancet. No 1, 5 Oct 1823 onwards. Ed Thomas Wakley 1823–62, James Wakley 1862–86, Thomas H. Wakley 1886–1905.

The medical times. 28 Sept 1839–26 Dec 1885. Prop Frederick Knight Hunt. Ed F. Knight Hunt 1839–?, T. P. Healey, J. S. Bushman.

The provincial medical and surgical journal. 3 Oct 1840–22 Dec 1852. Continued as Association medical journal, 7 Jan 1853–27 Dec 1856. Continued as British medical journal, 3 Jan 1857 onwards. Ed J. R. Cormack, A. Wynter 1855–60, W. O. Markham 1860–6, E. A. Hart

1866–94, E. A. Hart and Dawson Williams 1894–97, Dawson Williams and C. L. Taylor 1897–1916.

Nature: a weekly illustrated journal of science. No 1, Nov 1869 onwards. Prop Macmillan. Ed J. N. Lockyer.

The gardener's gazette. 7 Jan 1837–26 June 1847. Ed George Glenny.

The gardener's chronicle. No 1, 2 Jan 1841 onwards. Prop Bradbury and Evans. Ed John Lindley 1841–65, Maxwell T. Masters.

Amateur gardening. No 1, 3 May 1884 onwards.

The railway times. No 1, 29 Oct 1837–28 March 1914.

Bradshaw's railway gazette. No 1, 12 July 1845–no 103, 28 Nov 1846. Continued as Railway gazette, 5 Dec 1846–20 Jan 1872.

The railway news. No 1, 2 Jan 1864–30 Nov 1918. Incorporated in Railway gazette.

The mining journal. No 1, 29 Aug 1835 onwards. Ed T. W. Robertson.

The mechanics' magazine. 30 Aug 1823–28 Dec 1872. Continued as Iron, no 1, 18 Jan 1873–9 June 1893. Incorporated in Industries and iron. Ed I. C. Robertson 1823–June 1852, R. A. Brooman July 1852–July 1857, E. J. Reed July 1857–72.

The engineer. No 1, 4 Jan 1856 onwards. Ed Zerah Colburn 1859–66.

The colliery guardian. No 1, 2 Jan 1858 onwards. Ed H. K. Atkinson.

Engineering. No 1, 5 Jan 1866 onwards. Ed Zerah Colburn.

Griffith's iron trade exchange. 28 March 1873–June 1874. Continued as London iron trade exchange, 27 June 1874–24 Sept 1877. Continued as Iron and steel trades journal and mining engineer, no 1477, 1 Oct 1877–31 Dec 1920. Incorporated in Foundry trade journal.

The builder. No 1, 31 Dec 1842 onwards. Prop J. A. Hanson. Ed George Godwin 1842–83.

The builder's weekly reporter. No 2, 17 March 1856–23 July 1886. Continued as Builder's reporter and engineering times, 30 July 1886–31 Oct 1906. Incorporated in Building trade.

The freehold land times and building news. No 3, 1 April–no 20, 15 Dec 1854. Continued as Land and building news, 1 Jan 1855–27 Dec 1856. Continued as Building news, 2 Jan 1857–12 March 1926. Incorporated in Architect. Prop George Maddox; J. Passmore Edwards 1862–?.

The architect. No 1, 2 Jan 1869 onwards. Ed ? Hobart.

The educational times. 2 Oct 1847–Dec 1923. Continued as Educational outlook, Jan 1924–1937. Continued as Educational times, Sept 1946–Nov 1951. Continued as Education today, Jan 1952 onwards. Prop College of Preceptors.

The photographic news. No 1, 10 Sept 1858–8 May 1908. Incorporated in Amateur photographer. Prop Cassell; G. Wharton Simpson 1868–? Ed William Crooks 1858–Jan 1860, G. Wharton Simpson Jan 1862–Jan 1880.

The grocer. No 1, 4 Jan 1862 onwards. Prop W. Reed and L. M. Reed. Ed G. L. M. Strauss.

The accountant. No 1, Oct 1874 onwards. Weekly from 2 Jan 1875.

The draper's record. No 1, 6 Aug 1887 onwards.

Weldon's ladies' journal of dress, fashion, etc. July 1879–March 1954. Continued as Weldon's home journal, April 1954–Sept 1955. Continued as Home, Oct 1955–Oct 1963. Incorporated in Homes and gardens.

Home chat. No 1, 23 March 1895–25 April 1959. Incorporated in Woman's weekly. Prop Alfred Harmsworth. Ed Maud Bown.

Woman. No 1, 3 Jan 1890–7 Aug 1912. Ed Arnold Bennett 1896–1900.

(3) ACCOUNTS AND STUDIES OF INDIVIDUAL PAPERS

Brief summaries of many centenary numbers by J. C. Francis are to be found in N & Q 1898–1914. Useful notices, apart from those cited, may be found in Newspaper world.

London Morning Papers

Morning Chronicle [1769]

When Dickens quarrelled with the Morning Chronicle. World's Press News 23 June 1938.

Carlton, W. J. Charles Dickens, dramatic critic. Dickensian 56 1960.

Morning Post 1772

Francis, J. C. The Morning Post 1772–1916. N & Q 14–28 Oct, 25 Nov 1916.

Ferguson, M. T. The Morning Post 1772–1921. 1922.

Hindle, W. H. The Morning Post 1772–1937. 1937.

'Journalist'. The Morning Post. Nat Rev Sept 1937.

Colgate, W. Death at 164: the portrait of a newspaper. Queens Quart 45 1938.

Glickfield, C. W. Coleridge's prose contributions to the Morning Post. PMLA 69 1954.

Times 1788

Stephen, L. The Times on the American war: a historical study. 1865, New York 1915.

Marchant, J. History through the Times: a collection of leading articles on important events 1800–1937. 1937.

The history of the Times. Vol 1, 'The Thunderer' in the making 1785–1841. 1935; vol 2, The tradition established 1841–84, 1939; vol 3, The twentieth century test 1884–1912, 1947; vol 4, The 150th anniversary and beyond, 2 pts 1952.

Morning Advertiser 1794

Centenary number. 8 Feb 1894.

Daily News 1846

McCarthy, J. and J. R. Robinson. The Daily News jubilee. 1896.

Cruikshank, R. J. The roaring century 1846–1946. 1946.

World's Press News 17 Jan 1946; Newspaper World 19 Jan 1946. Centenary articles.

Grubb, G. G. Dickens and the Daily News. In Booker Memorial studies. Chapel Hill 1950; Pts 2–4 in Nineteenth Century Fiction 6–7 1951–2.

Daily Telegraph 1855

Rhode, D. The social relationships of the Daily Telegraph. New Century Rev April 1898.

Jubilee number. 17 Sept 1905.

Burnham, Lord. Peterborough Court: the story of the Daily Telegraph. 1955.

Coulling, S. M. Matthew Arnold and the Daily Telegraph. RES new ser 12 1961.

Standard 1857

Notes on the history of the Standard. People Jan 1906.

Financial News 1884

Twentieth anniversary number 23 Jan 1904.

Daily Mail 1896

Harmsworth, A. C. (Viscount Northcliffe). The romance of the Daily Mail. 1903.

McKenzie, F. A. The mystery of the Daily Mail 1896–1921. 1921.

News in our time 1896–1946: Golden Jubilee book of the Daily Mail. 1946.

London Evening Papers

Sun 1792
Grant, P. Statement of facts regarding the Sun newspaper. [1832].

Globe [1803]
Atlay, J. B. The Globe centenary: a sketch of its history. 1903.

True Sun 1832
Vivian, C. H. Dickens, the True Sun and Samuel Laman Blanchard. Nineteenth-Century Fiction 4 1950.

Pall Mall Gazette 1865
Stead, W. T. The Pall Mall Gazette. Rev of Reviews Feb 1893.
10,000th number. 14 April 1897.
Last number. 27 Oct 1923.
Booth, B. A. Trollope and the Pall Mall Gazette. Nineteenth-Century Fiction 4 1949.
Collins, J. P. The boy who saved a famous paper. Chambers's Jnl Sept 1951.
Scott, J. W. Robertson. The story of the Pall Mall Gazette. 1950.
—— The life and death of a newspaper. 1952.
—— 'We' and me: memoirs of four eminent editors. 1956. Includes material on J. A. Spender's editorship.
Laurence, D. H. Bernard Shaw and the Pall Mall Gazette: an identification of his unsigned contributions. Shaw Bull 5–6 1954.
Neiman, F. Some newly attributed contributions of Matthew Arnold to the Pall Mall Gazette. MP 55 1957.

Echo 1868
The staff of the Echo. Bookman (London) July 1898.
30th Birthday. Double no 8 Dec 1898.

St James's Gazette 1880
Green, R. L. Lewis Carroll and the St James's Gazette. N & Q 7 April 1945.

Star 1888
Shaw, G. B. London music in 1888–9 as heard by Corno di Bassetto. 1937. Musical criticisms first pbd in Star.
The story of the Star 1883–1938. 1938.

The Provincial Press: General Studies of more than one Paper

Hunt, W. Hull newspapers. Hull 1880.
Morley, J. C. The newspaper press and periodical literature of Liverpool. Liverpool 1887.
Wightman, H. A list of the newspapers in Lancashire, Yorkshire and Cheshire. Liverpool 1887.
Edwards, F. A. The early newspaper press of Hampshire. Southampton 1889.
Smith, C. F. The press of Essex 1837–97. Essex Rev July 1897.
Patterson, A. Yorkshire journalism past and present. Barnsley 1901.
The Gazette's precursors: Tyneside newspapers half a century ago. Shields Daily Gazette 24 Feb 1899.
Willox, J. The press of Liverpool. Liverpool Courier 6 Jan 1908.
Burton, G. H. Stamford Mercury 17, 24 April 1914. Articles on Lincolnshire newspapers and journalists.
Slade, J. J. and H. Richardson. Wiltshire newspapers past and present. Wiltshire Archaeological & Natural History Mag 40–1 1917–22.
Jones, I. A history of printers and printing in Wales to 1810 and of successive and related printers to 1923. Cardiff 1925.
Fenton, W. A. Cambridge periodicals 1750–1931. Cambridge Public Lib Record & Book List March 1931.
Sunderland and Portsmouth. Newspaper World 11 Feb 1939.
Cambridge's weekly newspapers. Newspaper World 12 Aug 1939.
Watson, S. F. Some materials for a history of printing and publishing in Ipswich. Proc Suffolk Inst of Archaeology & Natural History 24 1948.
Briggs, A. Press and public in nineteenth-century Birmingham. Dugdale Soc Occasional Papers 8 1950.
The Norwich Post: its contemporaries and successors. Norwich 1951. 250 years of Norwich newspapers.
Burton, K. G. The early newspaper press in Berkshire 1723–1855. Reading 1954.
Desmond, R. G. C. Our local press: a short historical account of the newspapers of Walthamstow. Walthamstow 1955.
Read, D. North of England newspapers c. 1700–c. 1900 and their value to historians. Proc Leeds Philosophical & Literary Soc, Literary & Historical Section 8 1957.
—— Press and people 1790–1850: opinion in three English cities [Leeds, Manchester and Sheffield]. 1961.
Laughton, G. E. and L. R. Stephen. Yorkshire newspapers: a bibliography with locations. 1960.
Cranfield, G. A. The development of the provincial newspaper 1700–60. Oxford 1962. The early history of many nineteenth-century journals.
Sewell, G. Echoes of a century: the centenary history of Southern Newspapers Ltd 1864–1964. Southampton 1964.
Smith, R. E. G. Newspapers first published before 1900 in Lancashire, Cheshire and the Isle of Man. 1965.

Provincial Dailies

Sheffield Daily Telegraph 1855
Shepherdson, W. Reminiscences in the career of a newspaper. 1876.
Jubilee 1855–1905. Sheffield 1905.

Manchester Guardian 1855
Mills, W. H. A century of history. 1921.
Musson, A. E. Newspaper printing in the Industrial Revolution. Economic History Rev 10 1957–8. Material drawn exclusively from Guardian.

Shields Daily Gazette 1855
Jubilee number. 24 Feb 1899.
The oldest evening paper. Newspaper World 1 April 1939.

The Birmingham Post 1857
Jubilee number 4 Dec 1907.
Centenary supplement. 4 Dec 1957.
Whates, H. R. G. The Birmingham Post 1857–1957. Birmingham 1957.

Liverpool Daily Mercury 1858; Liverpool Daily Post 1855
Liverpool Daily Post jubilee number. 13 June 1905.
The centenary of the Liverpool Post and Mercury: a record of the progress of Liverpool and its leading newspaper. Liverpool 1911.
Trollope, A. Tireless traveller: twenty letters to the Liverpool Mercury. 1875. Ed B. A. Booth, Cambridge 1941.

Newcastle Chronicle 1858
Dolman, F. The Newcastle Chronicle and its editor, Joseph Cowen. Young Man Aug 1895.

Western Daily Press (Bristol) 1858
Great provincial newspapers II. Caxton Mag Oct 1901.
The first daily in the west. Newspaper World 22 April 1939.

Western Morning News (Plymouth) 1860
Great provincial newspapers IV. Caxton Mag Dec 1901.

Nottingham Daily Express 1860
The oldest provincial daily. Newspaper World 8 April 1939.

Bristol Mercury (Bristol Daily Post 1860)
Lewis, H. The history of the Bristol Mercury 1715–1886. Bristol [1887?]

Western Daily Mercury (Plymouth) 1860
Walling, R. A. J. The Western Daily Mercury. Cornish Mag Jan 1899.

Leeds Mercury [1861]
A champion of reform. Newspaper World 27 May 1939.
Liverpool Journal of Commerce 1861
Liverpool's shipping daily. Newspaper World 11 March 1939.
Birmingham Gazette 1862
Birmingham's oldest newspaper. Newspaper World 5 Aug 1939.
Liverpool Courier 1863
Centenary number. 6 Jan 1908.
Daily Bristol Times and Mirror 1865
Wells, C. The history of the Bristol Times and Mirror. 1913.
Yorkshire Post 1866
The Leeds Intelligencer–Yorkshire Post. Newspaper World 19 Aug 1939.
Gibb, M. A. and F. Beckwith. The Yorkshire Post: two centuries. [Leeds] 1954.
Yorkshire Observer (Bradford Observer 1868)
75 years retrospect. Yorkshire Observer 6 Feb 1909.
Huddersfield Examiner 1871
A fair name. Newspaper World 21 Jan 1939.
Yorkshire Herald (York) 1874
Jubilee number 2 Jan 1905.
Liverpool Echo 1879
Morning and evening at Liverpool. Newspaper World 25 Feb 1939.
Wolverhampton Express and Star 1880; Midland Counties Evening Express 1874
Wolverhampton's evening paper. Newspaper World 24 Dec 1938.

Provincial Weeklies

Berkshire Chronicle
The Berkshire Chronicle. Newspaper World 16 Aug 1939.
Berrow's Worcester Journal
The oldest English newspaper. Worcester 1890.
Britain's oldest weekly. Newspaper World 18 March 1938.
Griffiths, I. Berrow's Worcester Journal, Worcester 1941.
Blackburn Times
Jubilee number. 3 June 1905.
Blackpool Gazette
From visitors' list to daily paper. Newspaper World 17 Dec 1938.
Bury Times
Jubilee number. 8 July 1905.
Cardiff Times
Jubilee number. 15 Oct 1887.
Chester Courant
A nursery of journalists. Newspaper World 1 July 1939.
Coventry Mercury and Standard
The Coventry Mercury and Standard. Newspaper World 29 July 1939.
Derby Mercury
The chronicler of Derby. Newspaper World 8 July 1939.
Doncaster Gazette
Yorkshire Journal–Doncaster Gazette. Newspaper World 28 Oct 1939.
Falkirk Herald
The jubilee of the Falkirk Herald 1846–96. Falkirk 1896.
Gloucester Journal
Chance, H. G. The bicentenary of the Gloucester Journal. Gloucester 1922.
Grantham Journal
Quilter, H. H. Mid-Victorian Grantham: a commentary on the earliest numbers of the Grantham Journal. Grantham 1937.

Hampshire Advertiser (Southampton)
Centenary number. 28 July 1923.
Hereford Times
The British Chronicle–Hereford Times. Newspaper World 6 May 1939.
Huddersfield Examiner
Our jubilee: a brief sketch of the history of the Examiner. Huddersfield Examiner 6 Sept 1901.
Impartial Reporter (Enniskillen)
The Trimbles of Enniskillen. Newspaper World 2 Sept 1939.
Ipswich Journal
The history of the Ipswich Jnl for 150 years. [Ipswich 1875].
Isle of Man Times (Douglas)
The jubilee of the Isle of Man Times: the story of its first half century. Douglas 1911.
Kentish Gazette
222 years in Canterbury. Newspaper World 20 May 1939.
Kentish Express and Ashford News (Ashford)
Jubilee. July 14 1855–July 15 1905. Ashford 1905.
Lancaster Guardian
History of the paper and reminiscences by 'Old Hands'. [Lancaster 1897] (priv ptd).
Lincoln, Rutland and Stamford Mercury
Burton, G. H. Notes on newspapers. Stamford Mercury 20 March 1914.
Evans, F. H. Brief sketch . . . Lincoln. Rutland and Stamford Mercury. 1938.
Newton, D. Mercury story: a brief record of the Lincoln, Rutland and Stamford Mercury. Stamford 1962.
Macclesfield Courier and Herald
Centenary number. 4 Feb 1911.
Middlesex Chronicle (Hounslow)
Jubilee number and supplement. 9 Jan 1909.
Newcastle Journal
228 years on Tyneside. Newspaper World 15 April 1939.
Norfolk News (Norwich)
Round a newspaper office: Norfolk News Co. [Norwich 1902].
North British Advertiser (Edinburgh)
The case of Mr John Gray, the founder of the North British Advertiser. Edinburgh 1831.
Northampton Mercury
1720–1901. [Northampton 1901].
Hadley, W. W. The bicentenary record of the Northampton Record. Northampton 1920.
It flourisheth by circulation. Newspaper World 3 June 1939.
Norwich Mercury
The Norwich Mercury. Newspaper World 13 May 1939.
Preston Chronicle
Spencer, J. H. The Dobson family of the Preston Chronicle. Preston Herald 29 Dec 1950.
Reading Mercury
Noble engine of freedom. Newspaper World 17 June 1939.
Rochdale Observer
Jubilee number. 17 Feb 1906.
Salisbury and Winchester Journal
Richardson, H. 1729–1929. Supplement 7 June 1929.
The Salisbury and Winchester Journal. Newspaper World 24 June 1939.
Scarborough Mercury
Jubilee number. 21 July 1905.
Shrewsbury Chronicle
The Shrewsbury Chronicle–Salop's first newspaper. Newspaper World 7 Oct 1939.
Staffordshire Advertiser (Stafford)
A centenary history of the Staffordshire Advertiser. Stafford 1895.

Stirling Observer
90 years' progress 1836–1926. Stirling 1926.
Trowbridge and Wiltshire Advertiser
Three generations at Trowbridge. Newspaper World 29 April 1939.
Wakefield Express
Jubilee 1852–1902. Souvenir. [Wakefield 1902].
Wellington Journal
Advertising and literature. Newspaper World 10 June 1939.
Western Gazette
Flying Post–Western Gazette. Newspaper World 22 July 1939.
Windsor and Eton Express and General Advertiser
Bebbington, W. G. The most remarkable man of his age: Byron in the Windsor and Eton Express and General Advertiser. Keats-Shelley Memorial Bull 7 1956.

The Scottish Press: General Studies of more than one Paper

The newspaper press of Scotland. Fraser's Mag May, July–Aug 1938.
M'Bain, J. M. Bibliography of Arbroath periodical literature and political broadsides. Arbroath 1889.
Norrie, W. Edinburgh newspapers past and present. Earlestown 1891.
Concerning three northern newspapers: their rise and progress 1748–1900: Aberdeen Daily Journal, Aberdeen Weekly Journal, Aberdeen Evening Express. Aberdeen 1900.
Noble, J. A bibliography of Inverness newspapers and periodicals. Ed J. Whyte, with appendix by W. Mackay, Stirling 1903.
Graham, M. The early Glasgow press. Glasgow 1906.
Couper, W. J. The Edinburgh periodical press. 2 vols Stirling 1908.
Stewart, W. The Glasgow press in 1840. Glasgow 1921 (priv ptd).

Scottish Daily Papers

Scotsman (Edinburgh) 1855
The story of the Scotsman. Edinburgh 1886 (priv ptd).
Centenary number. 25 Jan 1917.
Ritchie, Findlay and Law. Newspaper World 28 Jan 1939.
Jones, S. Hazlitt in Edinburgh: an evening with Mr Ritchie of the Scotsman. Etudes anglaises 17 1964.
150th anniversary supplement. 24 Jan 1967.
Glasgow Herald 1859
Stewart, W. The Glasgow Herald: the story of a great newspaper from 1783 to 1911. Glasgow 1911.
Dundee Advertiser 1861
Millar, A. H. The Dundee Advertiser 1801–1901: a centenary memoir. Dundee 1901.
Dundee Courier 1861
Great provincial newspapers I. Caxton Mag Aug 1901.
Edinburgh Evening News 1873
Fifty years 1873–1923. Edinburgh 1923.
Aberdeen Journal 1877
The Aberdeen Journal and its history; the men who made it. Aberdeen 1894.
Our 150th year. Aberdeen 1897.
Mitchell, W. A. Or was it yesterday? 1947.
The Evening Telegraph (Dundee)1877
Silver Jubilee number. 13 March 1902.

The Irish Press: General Studies of more than one paper

Madden, R. R. The history of Irish periodical literature from the end of the seventeenth to the middle of the nineteenth century. 2 vols 1867.

Proprietors for 143 years. Newspaper World 7 Jan 1939. Belfast papers.
Baird's. Newspaper World 4 March 1939. Belfast papers.
Dublin's Newspaper family. Newspaper World 15 July 1939.
Inglis, B. The freedom of the press in Ireland 1784–1841. 1954.

London Papers Published more than once a Week

London Gazette 1865
The cost of printing and publishing the London, Edinburgh and Dublin Gazettes in each of the years 1846, 1847, 1848 and 1849, exclusive of stamps and paper, with balance sheets for each of the said years, showing the profit and loss. House of Commons Accounts & Papers (677) xxxiii 429 1850.
Handover, P. M. A history of the London Gazette 1665–1965. 1965.
City Press 1857
Jubilee number. 13 July 1907.

Weekly Papers: Sunday

Observer 1791
1791–1921: a short record of 130 years. 1921.
175th anniversary supplement. 4 Dec 1966.
The Observer of the nineteenth century. Ed M. Miliband 1966.
Weekly Dispatch: Sunday Dispatch 1801
The Weekly Dispatch: special centenary number. 9 June 1901.
The Sunday Dispatch: 150th anniversary number. 23 Sept 1951.
Examiner 1808
Blunden, E. Leigh Hunt's Examiner examined: comprising an account of that celebrated newspaper's contents 1808–25. 1928.
Graham, W. Shelley's debt to Leigh Hunt and the Examiner. PMLA 40 1925.
Johnson, R. B. Shelley-Leigh Hunt: how friendship made history. 1929.
Stout, G. D. The political history of Leigh Hunt's Examiner together with an account of 'The Books'. Washington Univ Stud new ser (Lang & Lit) 19 1949.
Champion 1814
Parker, W. M. and D. Hudson. Thomas Barnes and the Champion. TLS 1, 15 Jan 1944.
Jones, L. M. Keats's theatrical reviews in the Champion. Keats-Shelley Jnl 3 1954.
Sunday Times 1822
100 years of history. 1920.
Newspaper World 16 April 1938.
Lloyd's Weekly News (Lloyds Illustrated Newspaper 1842)
Diamond jubilee number. 30 Nov 1902.
News of the World 1843
Through four reigns: the romance of a great newspaper. [1928].
Berrey, R. P. The romance of a great newspaper. [c. 1933].
Centenary article. World's Press News 30 Sept 1943.
Reynolds' Newspaper 1850
Jubilee number. 27 May 1900. *See* 1 March 1936.
Weekly Sun 1891
[Opinions on by eminent men. Ed T. P. O'Connor] 1896.

General Weekly Papers

Spectator 1828
Thomas, W. B. The story of the Spectator 1828–1928. 1928.
6,000th number. 25 June 1943.
125th anniversary number. 15 May 1953.

Colby, R. A. 'How it strikes a contemporary': the Spectator as critic. Nineteenth-Century Fiction 11 1957.
Tener, R. H. Swinburne as a reviewer. TLS 25 Dec 1959.
— The Spectator records 1847–97. Victorian Newsletter 1960.
— Spectatorial Strachey. TLS 31 Dec 1964.
Paden, W. D. Swinburne, the Spectator in 1862 and Walter Bagehot: six studies in nineteenth century English literature and thought. Ed H. Orel and G. G. Worth, Lawrence Kansas 1962.
Waller, J. O. Edward Dicey and the American negro in 1862: an English working journalist's view. BNYPL Jan 1962.

Chambers's Journal 1832
Chambers, R. Essays familiar and humorous, reprinted from Chambers's Journal. [1866].
— Tales from Chambers's Journal. 11 vols [1884–5].
Chambers, W. Our jubilee year. Chambers's Jnl 28 Jan 1882.
Gray, W. F. A hundred years old. Chambers's Jnl Feb 1932.

Press 1853
A sketch of the political history of the last three years in connection with the Press newspaper, and the part it has taken on the leading questions of the time. 1856.

Saturday Review 1856
Grant, J. The Saturday Review: its origin and progress. 1873.
Bevington, M. M. The Saturday Rev 1855–68: representative educated opinion in Victorian England. New York 1941.

Everybody's Journal
N & Q 30 Sept 1939.

London Rev 1860
Books, R. L. Matthew Arnold and the London Review. PMLA 76 1961.

Bow Bells 1862
Lloyd-Jones, A. Bow Bells. N & Q. 22 Nov 1952.

Queen's Messenger 1869
G., A. M. The spleen of Mr Murray. Blackwood's Mag Feb 1951.

Truth 1877
Mr Labouchere and Truth. Bookman (London) Sept 1892.

Illustrated Papers

Jackson, M. The pictorial press: its origin and progress. 1885.
Blackburn, H. The Cantor lectures on the art of book and newspaper illustration. 1894.
Gamble, W. Newspaper illustrations. Penrose's Pictorial Annual 3 1897.
— Pictorial telegraphy. Penrose's Pictorial Annual 4 1898.
Shorter, C. K. Illustrated journalism: its past and future. Contemporary Rev April 1899.

Illustrated London News 1842
Centenary number. 16 May 1942. Historical material also in issue of 10 June 1951.

Field 1853
Centenary number. 22 Nov 1952.
Rose, R. N. The Field 1853–1953: a centenary volume. 1953.

Daily Graphic 1890
21 years of progress of the pioneer illustrated daily newspaper. Daily Graphic 4 Jan 1911 (supplement).

County Life 1897
70th anniversary number. 12 Jan 1967.

Unstamped and Radical Journals

Berguer, L. T. A warning letter to HRH the Prince Regent. 1819 (3rd edn).
Standard 10 Sept 1833.
Gammage, R. G. The history of the Chartist movement 1837–54. Newcastle 1854, 1894 (rev).
Rose, J. H. The unstamped press 1815–36. EHR 12 1897.
Menger, A. The right to the whole produce of labour. Tr 1899.
Dierlamm, G. Die Flugschriftenliteratur der Chartistenbewegung in der öffentlichen Meinung. Tübingen 1909.
Kovalev, Y. V. The literature of Chartism. Victorian Stud 2 1958.
Cole, G. D. H. Chartist portraits. Ed A. Briggs 1965.

Cobbett's Political Register 1802
Birrell, T. A. The Political Register: Cobbett and English literature. English Stud 45 (Supplement) 1964.

Yellow Dwarf 1818
Marshall, W. H. Pulpit oratory I-III: essays by J. H. Reynolds in imitation of William Hazlitt. Lib Chron 28 1962.

Northern Star 1837
Glasgow, E. The establishment of the Northern Star newspaper. History 39 1954.

Bee-Hive [1861]
Coltham, S. The Bee-Hive newspaper: its origins and early struggles. In Essays in labour history, ed A. Briggs and J. Saville 1960.
— George Potter, the Junta and the Bee-Hive. International Rev of Social History 9–10 1964–5.

Weekly Literary Reviews

Literary Gazette 1817
Duncan, R. W. Byron and the London Literary Gazette. Boston Univ Stud in Eng 2 1956.
— The London Literary Gazette and American writers. Papers on English Lang & Lit Spring 1965.

Athenaeum 1828
Francis, J. C. John Francis, publisher of the Athenaeum. 2 vols 1888.
Marchand, L. A. The Athenaeum: a mirror of Victorian culture. Chapel Hill 1940.

Leigh Hunt's London Journal 1834
Marchand, L. A. Leigh Hunt's London Journal. Jnl Rutgers Univ Lib 6 1943.

Notes and Queries 1849
N & Q 29 June, 7 Sept 1946, 4 Oct 1947, 19 Aug 1950.
Periodical July 1947.

Household Words 1850: All the Year Round 1859
Grubb, G. G. Dickens's pattern of weekly serialization. ELH 9 1942.
— Dickens's editorial methods. SP 40 1943.
— The editorial policies of Charles Dickens. PMLA 58 1943.
— The American edition of All the Year Round. PBSA 47 1953.
— Dickens the paymaster once more. Dickensian 51 1955.
Hopkins, A. B. Dickens and Mrs Gaskell. HLQ 9 1946.
Gomme, G. J. L. T. B. Aldrich and Household Words. PBSA 42 1948.
Buckler, W. E. Dickens's success with Household Words. Dickensian 46 1950.
— Dickens the paymaster. PMLA 66 1951.
— Household Words in America. PBSA 45 1951.
Morley, M. Plays from the Christmas numbers of Household Words. Dickensian 51 1955.
— All the Year Round plays. Dickensian 52 1956.
Collins, P. A. W. Keep Household Words imaginative. Ibid.
— Dickens's periodicals: articles on education; an annotated bibliography. Univ of Leicester Vaughan College Papers 3 1957.
— Dickens as editor: some uncollected fragments. Dickensian 56 1960.
— The significance of Dickens's periodicals. REL 2 1961.

—— Inky fishing nets: Dickens as editor. Dickensian 61 1965.
Adrian, A. A. Dickens as verse editor. MP 58 1960.
Hunter, R. A. and I. Macalpine. Dickens and Conolly: an embarrassed editor's disclaimer. TLS 11 Aug 1961.
Lohrli, A. Dickens's Household Words on American English. Amer Speech 37 1962.
—— Household Words and its 'office book'. Princeton Univ Lib Chron 26 1964.
Easson, A. Dickens, Household Words and a double standard. Dickensian 60 1964.

Once a Week 1859
Buckler, W. E. E. S. Dallas's appointment as editor of Once a Week. N & Q 24 June 1950.
—— Once a Week under Samuel Lucas 1859–65. PMLA 67 1952.
Gettmann, R. A. Serialization and Evan Harrington. PMLA 64 1949.
—— Serialization of Reade's A good fight. Nineteenth-Century Fiction 6 1952.

Academy 1869
Roll-Hansen, D. Matthew Arnold and the Academy: a note on English criticism in the eighteen-seventies. PMLA 68 1953.
—— The Academy 1869–79: Victorian intellectuals in revolt. Copenhagen 1957.

Religious Papers

Fletcher, J. R. Early Catholic periodicals in England. Dublin Rev 198 1936. Includes valuable bibliography of nineteenth-century Catholic papers.

Jewish Chronicle 1841
The Jewish Chronicle 1841–1941: a century of newspaper history. 1950.

Christian World 1857
Farningham, M. Some personal reminiscences. Christian World 11 April 1907.

Universe 1860
Seventieth anniversary. 5 Dec 1930.

Agricultural Papers

Mark Lane Express 1832
70th birthday number. 31 March 1902.

Financial and Commercial Papers

Skinner, H. The early background to financial journalism. World's Press News 20 July 1942.

Economist 1843
Centenary issue. 4 Sept 1943.
The Economist 1843–1943: a centenary volume. 1943.
Gordon, S. The London Economist and the high tide of laissez-faire. Jnl of Political Economy 63 1955.

Sporting Papers

Sporting Times 1865
3,000th number. 19 March 1921.
Booth, K. B. Sporting Times: the 'Pink 'Un' world. 1938.

Humorous Papers

Spielmann, M. H. The rivals of Punch: a glance at the illustrated comic press of half a century. Nat Rev July 1895.
Roe, F. G. The lighter side of collecting some 'comics' of yesteryear. Connoisseur 108 1941.

Punch 1841
Mr Punch: his origin and career, with a facsimile of his original prospectus in the handwriting of Mark Lemon. [c. 1870].
Spielmann, M. H. The history of Punch. 1895.
Mr Punch's pageant 1841–1908: a souvenir catalogue. 1909.
Dickensian peeps into Punch. Dickensian 31–35 1935–39. Cartoons etc with Dickensian associations.
Falconer, J. W. A hundred years of Punch. Dalhousie Rev 21 1941.
Horton-Smith, L. G. H. Punch: have you a complete set? N & Q 25 Jan, 15 Feb 1947. On the 'suppressed' issue of 7 Feb 1885.
Ray, G. N. Thackeray and Punch: 44 newly identified contributions. TLS 1 Jan 1949.
Darwin, B. Christmas and Mr Punch. Nat Rev Dec 1950. Xmas drawings 1864–1900.
Williams, R. E. A centenary of Punch. 1956. A collection of cartoons.
Price, R. G. G. A history of Punch. 1957.
Maurer, O. Punch on slavery and the Civil War in America. Victorian Stud 1 1957.
—— Punch and the Opera War 1847–67. Texas Stud in Lang & Lit 1 1959.
Adburgham, A. A Punch history of manners and modes 1841–1940. 1961.
Pulling, C. Mr Punch and the police. 1964.
Altick, R. D. Our gallant colonel in Punch and Parliament. BNYPL Sept 1965.

Judy 1867
Peyrouton, N. C. Dickens and the Judy magazine. Dickensian 62 1966.

Moonshine 1879
The staff of Moonshine: portraits and facts concerning the celebrated weekly paper. 1900.

Juvenile Papers

Rollington, R. A brief history of boys' journals with interesting facts about the writers of boys' stories. Leicester 1913.
Dexter, W. Boys' periodicals of the nineties. Chambers's Jnl Dec 1943.
Turner, E. S. Boys will be boys. 1949.
Egoff, S. A. Children's periodicals of the nineteenth century: a survey and bibliography. 1951.
Enough of blood. TLS 4 Dec 1959. The battle to counter the penny-dreadfuls.

Young Folks 1871
McCleary, G. F. Stevenson in Young Folks. Fortnightly Rev Feb 1949.

Miscellaneous Specialized Papers

Ulrich, C. F. and K. Küp. Books and printing: a selected list of periodicals 1800–1942. Woodstock Vermont 1943.
Casson, H. One hundred years of architectural journalism. Builder 11 June 1948.

Lancet 1823
Centenary number 6 Oct 1923.

Builder 1842
Centenary issues 1–8 June 1943.

D. MAGAZINES AND REVIEWS

See headnote cols 1789–90, above

(1) MONTHLY MAGAZINES

The gentleman's magazine: or monthly intelligencer. Vols 1–5, Jan 1731–Dec 1735. Continued as Gentleman's magazine and historical chronicle, vols 6–77, Jan 1736–Dec 1807. New series, vols 78–103, Jan 1808–Dec 1833. Continued as Gentleman's magazine: new series vols 1–45, Jan 1834–June 1856. Continued as Gentleman's magazine and historical review: new series, vols 1–19, July 1856–Dec 1865. New ser ,vols 1–5, Jan 1866–May 1868. Continued as Gentleman's magazine, entirely new series, vols 1–16, June 1868–June 1876. From July 1876, vol 17, no 1747, returns to consecutive numbering from the beginning. Vols 240–72, Jan 1877–Sept (?) 1907. From Oct 1907 to 1922 covers only were ptd to retain copyright of the title. Gentleman's annual: being the New Year supplement of the Gentleman's magazine, 1870 etc. Indexes: General index to first 20 vols, 1753. Index from 1731 to 1786, by S. Ayscough, 2 vols 1789. From 1787 to 1818, by J. Nichols, vols 3–4 1821. A list of the plates, maps etc from 1731 to 1813, 1814. A list of the plates and woodcuts from 1731 to 1818 by C. St Barbe jr, vol 5, 1821. Prop John Nichols and J. B. Nichols 1792–1856; John Henry Parker 1856–65; Bradbury, Evans and Co 1865–May 1868; Chatto and Windus 1868–1906. Ed Edward Cave 1731–54, R. Cave 1754–66, D. Henry 1754–92, J. Nichols 1778–1826, J. B. Nichols 1826–33, John Mitford 1834–50, J. G. Nichols 1851–6, John Henry Parker 1856–65, Edward Walford 1866–7, Bolton Corney, Joseph Hatton 1867–74, Joseph Knight 1887–1905.

The Scots magazine. Vols 1–65, Jan 1739–Dec 1803. Continued as Scots magazine and Edinburgh literary miscellany, vols 66–79, Jan 1804–July 1817. Continued as Edinburgh magazine and literary miscellany: a new series of the Scots magazine, vols 1–18, Aug 1817–June 1826. Prop Constable. Ed Thomas Pringle and James Cleghorn 1817–?

The universal magazine of knowledge and pleasure. Vols 1–113, June 1747–Dec 1803. Continued as Universal magazine: new series, vols 1–21, Jan 1804–June 1814. Continued as New universal magazine: new series, vols 1–3, July 1814–Sept 1815.

The monthly review. Vols 1–2, May 1749–April 1750. Continued as Monthly review: or new literary journal, vols 3–4, May 1750–May 1751. Continued as Monthly review; or literary journal, vols 5–81, June 1751–Dec 1789. Enlarged series, vols 1–108, Jan 1790–Nov 1825. Continued as Monthly review (new and improved series), vols 1–15, Jan 1826–Dec 1830. New and improved series, vols 1–?, Jan 1831–Dec 1844 (?). Indexes: A general index from the commencement to the end of the 70th vol, by S. Ayscough, 2 vols, 1786. A continuation of the general index from vol 71 to 81, by S. Ayscough, 1796. A general index from the commencement of the new series [Jan 1790] to the end of the 81st volume [Dec 1816], [by J.C.], 2 vols 1818. Ed Ralph Griffiths 1749–1803, G. E. Griffiths 1803–25, M. J. Quin 1825–32.

The critical review: or annals of literature. 1756–1817: 1st ser, vols 1–70; 2nd ser extended and improved: a new arrangement, 39 vols 1791–1803; 3rd ser 24 vols 1804–11; 4th ser 6 vols 1812–14; 5th ser 5 vols 1815–17. Incorporated in Monthly review. Ed Tobias Smollett, ? Guthrie, Percival Stockdale, George Gregory, Samuel Hamilton.

The lady's magazine: or entertaining companion for the fair sex. Vols 1–50, 1770–Dec 1819. New ser, vols 1–10, Jan 1820–29. Improved ser, vols 1–4, 1830–2. Incorporated in Ladies' museum and continued as Lady's magazine and museum of belles lettres: improved series, enlarged, vols 1–11, 1832–7. Incorporated in Court magazine and monthly critic, and continued as Court magazine and monthly critic and ladies' magazine and museum of belles lettres, vols 12–31, Jan 1838–47.

The Hibernian magazine: or companion of entertaining knowledge. Dublin. Feb 1771–April 1785. Continued as Walker's Hibernian magazine, May 1785–July 1812.

The Arminian magazine. Vols 1–20, Jan 1778–Dec 1797. Continued as Methodist magazine, vols 21–44, Jan 1798–Dec 1821. Continued as Wesleyan-Methodist magazine, 3rd ser vols 1–136, Jan 1822–Dec 1913. Continued as Magazine for the home, vol 137, Jan-Dec 1914. Continued as Magazine of the Wesleyan Methodist Church, vols 138–149, Jan 1915–Dec 1926. Continued as Methodist magazine, vol 150, Jan 1927 onwards. Wesleyan Methodist magazine, 6th edn, vols 1–5, 1861–5. Wesleyan Methodist magazine, abridged edn, new set vols 1–5, 1866–70. Ed John Wesley 1778–91, George Story 1791–6 (?), Joseph Benson 1796–1821, Jabez Bunting 1821–3, Thomas Jackson 1823–42, G. Cubitt, L. Thornton, W. H. Rule, Benjamin Frankland and Benjamin Gregory 1868–76, Benjamin Gregory 1876–93.

The European magazine and London review, by the Philological Society of London. Vols 1–87, April (?) 1782–July 1825. From vol 51, Jan–June 1807, 'by the Philological Society of London' omitted. New series, vols 1–2, 1825–6. Incorporated in Monthly magazine. Ed James Perry.

The Edinburgh magazine: or literary miscellany. Vols 1–13, June 1785–June 1791. New ser, vols 1–22, Jan 1793–Dec 1803. Incorporated in Scots magazine.

The botanical magazine: or, flower-garden displayed. Vols 1–14, 1787–1800. Continued as Curtis's botanical magazine, vols 15–53, 1801–26. New ser vols 1–70, 1827–44. 3rd ser vols 71–130, Jan 1845–1904. 4th series 1905 etc onwards. Now quarterly. Indexes: A general index to the Latin names and synonyms for the plants depicted in vols 1–107 of Curtis's botanical magazine, by E. Tonks, 1883. A new and complete index to the Botanical magazine, 1787–1904, to which is prefixed a history of the magazine by I. W. B. Hemsley. 1906. Prop S. Curtis 1799–1846 (?). Ed William Curtis 1787–99, John Sims 1800–26, W. J. Hooker 1827–67, J. D. Hooker 1866–1904.

The sporting magazine: or monthly calendar of the transactions of the turf, the chace etc. Vols 1–50, Oct 1792–1817. New ser vols 51–75, 1817–29. 2nd (really 3rd) ser, vols 76–100, 1829–42. 3rd [4th] ser, 56 vols 1843–70. From July 1846 onwards this is identical, except for title-pages, with New sporting magazine, Sportsman and Sporting review. Index of engravings 1792–1870. 1892.

The Evangelical magazine. Vols 1–20, July 1793–1812. Continued as Evangelical magazine and missionary chronicle, vols 21–30, 1813–Dec 1822. New ser vols 1–36, Jan 1823–Dec 1858. 3rd ser vols 1–10, Jan 1859–Dec 1868. New [4th] ser vols 1–21 (old ser vol 100), Jan 1869–92. New [5th] ser vols 1–12 (old ser vols 101–12), 1893–1904. Index to first 24 vols, July 1793–Dec 1816. 1817. Ed John Eyre and Matthew Wilks 1793–?, ? Fuller, Dr Haweis, E. Williams, ? Greatheed ?–1823, George Burder, John Morison 1843–?, H. F. Burder, J. Stoughton, John Kennedy and Josiah Viney 1889–90, D. B. Hooke 1891–1904.

The British critic: a new review. Vols 1–42, May 1793–Dec 1813. New series, 23 vols Jan 1814–June 1825. 3rd series, 3 vols Oct 1825–Oct 1826. Incorporated in Quarterly theological review and continued as British critic, quarterly theological review and ecclesiastical record. *See under quarterlies, col 1855, below*. Index: A general index to the first 20 vols, by S. Ayscough. 2 pts 1804. General index to vols 21–40, 1st ser, by F. W. Blagden 1815. Ed W. Beloe, R. Nares, T. F. Middleton, W. R. Lyall et al.

The repertory of arts and manufactures. Vols 1–16, 1794–1802. Continued as Repertory of arts, manufactures and agriculture, 2nd series, vols 1–46, June 1802–June 1825. Continued as Repertory of patent inventions and other discoveries and improvements in arts, manufactures and agriculture, vols 1–6, July 1825–June 1828. Continued as Repertory of patent inventions, and other discoveries and improvements in arts, manufactures and agriculture, vols 7–16, July 1828–Dec 1833. New ser, vols 1–18, Jan 1834–Dec 1842. Enlarged series, vols 1–40, Jan 1843–Dec 1862. Indexes: An analytical index to the sixteen vols of the 1st series and of all patents granted for inventions 1795–1802. 1806. A general index to the 25 vols of the 2nd series, including all patents 1806–15. 1815. Index to all patents granted in England 1815–45. 1846. Appendix to index. 1815–45. 1849. Index to the Repertory 1846–50. 1851. Index for 1851. [1852].

The monthly magazine and British register. Vols 1–63, Feb 1796–Jan 1826. Continued as Monthly magazine: or British register of literature, sciences and belles lettres, new series, vols 1–18, 1826–34. New ser vol 19, 1835. Continued as Monthly magazine of politics, literature and the belles lettres, vols 20–26, 1835–8. Continued as Monthly magazine, 9 vols 1839–43. Prop Richard Phillips; ? Holland. Ed John Aiken 1796–1806, George Gregory 1806–8, Richard Phillips, ? Holland ?–1836, James Grant 1836–?, Francis F. Barham and Abraham Heraud July 1839–May 1840, Abraham Heraud May 1840–?

The Gospel magazine and theological review. 1796 onwards. Ed W. Row 1796–1839.

The journal of natural philosophy, chemistry and the arts. Vols 1–5, April 1797–Dec 1801. New ser vols 1–36, Jan 1802–Dec 1813. Incorporated in Philosophical magazine. Prop and ed William Nicholson.

The Anti-Jacobin review and magazine: or monthly political and literary censor. Vols 1–35, July 1798–April 1810. Continued as Antijacobin review, and true churchman's magazine: or monthly political and literary censor, vols 36–50, May 1810–Aug 1817. Continued as Antijacobin review; True churchman's magazine and Protestant advocate: or monthly political and literary censor, vols 51–5, Sept 1817–Feb 1819. Continued as Antijacobin review; and Protestant advocate: or monthly political and literary censor, vols 56–61, March 1819–Dec 1821. Ed 'John Gifford' (John Richards Green).

The philosophical magazine. Vols 1–68, June 1798–Dec 1826. Continued as Philosophical magazine: or annals of chemistry, mathematics, astronomy, natural history and general science, vols 1–11, Jan 1827–June 1832. Continued as London and Edinburgh philosophical magazine and journal of science, vols 1–16, July 1832–June 1840. Continued as London, Edinburgh and Dublin philosophical magazine and journal of science, vols 17–37, July 1840–Dec 1850. 4th ser ,vols 1–50, Jan 1851–Dec 1875. 5th ser, vols 1–50, Jan 1876–Dec 1900. 6th ser, vols 1–50, Jan 1901–Dec 1925. 7th ser, vols 1–35, Jan 1926–Dec 1944. Continued as Philosophical magazine, vol 36, Jan 1945 onwards. Index: General index to vols 1–11 of 2nd ser 1827–32. 1835. Ed Alexander Tilloch 1797–Dec 1813, Alexander Tilloch and William Nicholson Jan 1814–June 1822, Alexander Tilloch, William Nicholson and Richard Taylor July 1822–June 1825, Richard Taylor July 1825–Dec 1826, Richard Taylor and Richard Phillips Jan 1827–June 1832, Richard Taylor, Richard Phillips and David Brewster July 1832–June 1840, Richard Taylor, Richard Phillips, David Brewster and Robert Kane July 1840–Dec 1850, Richard Taylor, Richard Phillips, David Brewster, Robert Kane and William Francis Jan–Dec 1851, Richard Taylor, David Brewster, Robert Kane and William Francis Jan 1852–Dec 1853, Richard Taylor, David Brewster, Robert Kane, William Francis and John Tyndall, Jan 1854–Dec 1858, David Brewster, Robert Kane, William Francis and John Tyndall Jan 1859–Dec 1863, David Brewster, Robert Kane and William Francis Jan 1864–June 1868, Robert Kane and William Francis July–Dec 1868, Augustus Mathieson, Robert Kane and William Francis Jan 1869–June 1870, Robert Kane and William Francis July 1870–July 1871, Robert Kane, William Francis and William Thomson August 1871–89, William Francis and William Thomson 1889–1890, William Francis, William Thomson and George Fitzgerald 1890–1, William Francis, George Fitzgerald and Lord Kelvin 1892–1904.

The lady's monthly museum: or polite repository of amusement and instruction. Vols 1–16, July 1798–June 1806. New series, vols 1–17, July 1806–Dec 1814. Improved series, vols 1–28, Jan 1815–Dec 1828. Continued as Ladies' museum, vols 1–3, 1829–32. Amalgamated with Ladies' magazine.

The general Baptist repository. Vols 1–10, Oct(?) 1802–21. Continued as General Baptist repository and missionary observer, vols 1–6 [3rd] ser, Jan 1822–Dec 1859. Continued as General Baptist magazine and missionary observer, new ser [4th], vols 1–4, Jan 1860–Dec 1863. Continued as General Baptist magazine, Jan 1864–Dec 1891. Continued as Baptist Union magazine, vols 1–2, Jan–Dec 1893. New ser, vols 1–2, Jan 1894–Dec 1895. Continued as Church and household, Jan 1896–Dec 1901. Ed J. Goadby 1833–59, J. J. Goadby 1859–June 1867, W. Underwood, W. R. Stevenson, J. C. Pike July–Dec 1867, W. Underwood Jan 1867–Dec 1869, John Clifford Jan 1870–Dec 1883, R. W. Stevenson and J. Fletcher Jan 1884–Aug 1889, J. Fletcher Sept 1889–1891, J. Clifford and G. Hawker 1892–95, D. Davies 1896–1901.

The Christian observer. Vols 1–74, 1802–74. Continued as Christian observer and advocate, vols 75–7, 1875–7. Ed J. Pratt 1802, Z. Macaulay 1802–16, S. C. Wilks 1816–50, J. W. Cunningham 1850–8, J. B. Marsden 1859–69.

The literary journal: a review of literature, science, manners and politics. Vols 1–4, [Jan 1803]–Dec 1804. Continued as Literary journal; or universal review of literature domestic and foreign, vol 5 vols 1–2 (2nd ser), 1805–6. Ed James Mill.

The imperial review or London [Edinburgh] and Dublin literary journal. Vols 1–5, 1804–5. The last 2 vols only have 'Edinburgh' in the title.

The eclectic review. Vols 1–10, Jan 1805–Dec 1813. New ser vols 1–30, Jan 1814–Dec 1828. 3rd ser, vols 1–16, Jan 1829–Dec 1836. New [4th] ser, vols 1–28, Jan 1837–Dec 1850. New [5th] ser, vols 1–12, Jan 1851–Dec 1856. New [6th] ser, vols 1–4, Jan 1857–Dec 1858. New [7th] ser, vols 1–5, Jan 1859–June 1861. New [8th] ser July 1861–Dec 1868. Prop Josiah Conder 1814–36 ?. Ed S. Greatheed, D. Parker, T. Williams 1805–13, Josiah Conder 1814–36, T. Price 1837–50, T. Price and W. H. Stowell 1851–4, J. E. Ryland 1855–6, Edwin Paxton Hood 1850(?)–8.

La belle assemblée; or Bell's court and fashionable magazine. Vols 1–8, Feb 1806–10. New and improved ser vols 1–30, 1810–24. 3rd ser, vols 1–15, 1825–June 1832. Continued as Court magazine and belle assemblée, vols 1–9, July 1832–37. Continued as Court magazine and monthly critic, vols 10–11, 1837. Continued as Court magazine and monthly critic and lady's magazine, and museum of the belles-lettres, music etc., united series, Jan 1838. Prop John Bell 1806–21. Ed Mrs Norton 1832–7.

The monthly repository of theology and general literature. Vols 1–21, Jan 1806–Dec 1826. Continued as Monthly repository and review, new series, vols 1–11, Jan 1827–June 1837. Continued as Monthly repository, enlarged series, vols 1–2(?), July 1837–April 1838. Prop Robert Aspland 1806–26; British and Foreign Unitarian Association Book Committee 1827–31; W. J. Fox 1831–June 1837; J. H. Leigh Hunt July 1837–April 1838. Ed Robert Aspland 1806–26, W. J. Fox 1828–36, R. H. Horne June 1836–June 1837, J. H. Leigh Hunt July 1837–April 1838.

The literary panorama: a review of books, register of events, magazine of varieties. Vols 1–2, Oct 1806–Sept 1807. Continued as Literary panorama, being a review of books, magazine of varieties and annual register, vols 3–9, Oct 1807–June 1811. Continued as Literary panorama: being a compendium of national papers and Parliamentary reports . . . a review of books, and magazine of varieties, forming an annual register, vols 10–15, July 1811–Sept 1814. Continued as Literary panorama, and national register, new series, vols 1–9, Oct 1814–July 1819. Incorporated in New monthly magazine. Vols 1–4, new series, rptd Boston 1816–17.

Flower's political review, and monthly register. Vols 1–9, Jan 1807–July 1811. Ed B. Flower.

The cabinet: or monthly report of polite literature. Vols 1–4, Feb-March 1807–Dec 1808.

The satirist, or monthly meteor. Vols 1–14, Oct 1807–June 1814.

The Belfast monthly magazine. Vols 1–13, Sept 1808–Dec 1814.

The London review. Vols 1–2, Feb–Nov 1809. Ed Richard Cumberland.

The poetical magazine. Vols 1–4, May 1809–April 1811. Prop and ed Rudolph Ackermann.

The Baptist magazine. Vols 1–96, Jan 1809–Dec 1904. Prop Baptist Missionary Society; William Groser 1838–56; Samuel Manning Jan 1857–1860. Ed William Groser 1838–56, D. Katterns, W. G. Lewis, C. H. Spurgeon 1861–?, W. G. Lewis 1866–80, J. P. Barnett 1881–4, Stephen A. Swaine 1886(?)–March 1889, James Stuart 1890–1904.

The Edinburgh Christian instructor. Vols 1–30, July 1810–Dec 1831. New ser, vols 1–4, Jan 1832–Dec 1835. New ser [3rd] vols 1–2, Jan 1836–Dec 1837. Continued as Edinburgh Christian instructor, and Colonial religious register, new ser [4th] vols 1–3, Jan 1838–Dec 1840. Ed Andrew Thomson 1810–30(?), Marcus Dods 1831(?)–35, Archibald Bennie 1835–7.

The British review and London critical journal. Vols 1–23, March 1811–Nov 1825. Ed William Roberts.

The scourge: or monthly expositor of imposture and folly. Vols 1–10, Jan 1811–Dec 1815.

The entertaining magazine: or repository of general knowledge. Vols 1–3, Jan 1813–Dec 1815.

The annals of philosophy: or magazine of chemistry, mineralogy, mechanics, natural history, agriculture and the arts. Vols 1–16, Jan 1813–Dec 1820. New ser, 12 vols Jan 1821–Dec 1826. Incorporated in Philosophical magazine. Ed Thomas Thomson 1813–20, Richard Phillips and Edward William Brayley 1821–6.

The new monthly magazine, and universal register. Vols 1–14, Jan 1814–Dec 1820. Continued as New monthly magazine and literary journal, vols 15–48, Jan 1821–Dec 1836. Continued as New monthly magazine and humourist, vols 49–149, Jan 1837–Dec 1871. Continued as New monthly magazine, new series, vols 1–15, Jan 1872–June 1879. New [3rd] ser, vols 1–5, July 1879–Dec 1881. Continued as New monthly, vols 6–7, Jan? 1882–4. Prop Henry Colburn and Frederic Shoberl 1814–June 1845; W. H. Ainsworth 1845–70; W. F. Ainsworth 1870–84. Ed Frederic Shoberl, ? Watkins, Alaric Watts, Thomas Campbell Jan 1821–Dec 1830 (assisted by Cyrus Redding 1821–Aug 1830 and Samuel Carter Hall Sept–Dec 1830), Samuel Carter Hall Jan–Nov 1831, E. G. Bulwer-Lytton Nov 1831–Aug 1833 (assisted by Samuel Carter Hall), Samuel Carter Hall Sept 1833–35, Theodore Hook 1836–Aug 1841, Thomas Hood Sept 1841–Aug 1843 (assisted by Frederic Shoberl), O. E. Williams, P. G. Patmore 1841–5(?), W. H. Ainsworth 1845–70, W. F. Ainsworth 1871–9.

The Asiatic journal and monthly register for British India and its dependencies. Vols 1–28, Jan 1816–Dec 1829. Continued as Asiatic journal and monthly register for British and foreign India, China and Australasia, new ser, vols 1–40, Jan 1830–April 1843. Continued as Asiatic journal and monthly miscellany, 3rd ser, vols 1–4, May 1843–April 1845. Continued as Asiatic quarterly review, vol 1, Jan 1886 onwards. Ed D. Boulger.

Blackwood's Edinburgh magazine. Begun as Edinburgh monthly magazine, nos 1–6, April–Sept 1817. Continued as Blackwood's Edinburgh magazine, Oct 1817–Dec 1905. Continued as Blackwood's magazine, Jan 1906 onwards. Index: General index to vols 1–50. Edinburgh 1855. Prop Blackwood (with John Murray summer 1818–winter 1819). Ed Thomas Pringle and James Cleghorn April–Sept 1817, William Blackwood Oct 1817–Sept 1834, Alexander Blackwood Oct 1834–April 1845 (Robert Blackwood 1836–7 during Alexander's illness), John Blackwood May 1845–Oct 1879, William Blackwood III Nov 1879–?

The new bon ton magazine: or telescope of the times. Vols 1–6, May 1818–April 1821.

The pocket magazine of classic and polite literature. Vols 1–13, Jan 1818–June(?) 1824. Continued as Arliss' pocket magazine of classic and polite literature, new ser, vols 1–5, July(?) 1824–6. Continued as Pocket magazine. Robin's series, 4 vols Jan 1827–Dec 1828. Continued as Pocket magazine, [1829–31]–Jan 1832–3.

The tickler: or monthly compendium of good things. Vols 1–6, no 6, Dec 1818–June 1824.

The Christian remembrancer: or the churchman's biblical, ecclesiastical and literary miscellany. Vols 1–22, Jan 1819–Dec 1840. Continued as Christian remembrancer: a monthly magazine and review, new series, vols 1–8, Jan 1841–Dec 1844. Continued as Christian remembrancer: a quarterly review, vols 9–56, Jan 1845–Oct 1868. Ed William Scott and Francis Garden 1841–4, William Scott and J. B. Mozley 1844–54, William Scott 1854–68.

The Edinburgh monthly review. Edinburgh. Vols 1–5, Jan 1819–June 1821. Continued as New Edinburgh review, vols 1–4, July 1821–April 1823.

The London magazine. Vols 1–10, Jan 1820–Dec 1824. New ser, vols 1–10, Jan 1825–March 1828. 3rd ser, vols 1–3, April 1828–June 1829. Prop Baldwin, Cradock and Joy Jan 1820–June 1821; John Taylor and James Hessey July 1821–Sept 1825; Henry Southern Sept 1825–March 1828; Charles Knight April 1828–June 1829. Ed John Scott 1820–Jan 1821, John Taylor July 1821–4, Henry Southern July 1825–March 1828, Charles Knight April 1828–June 1829.

The Newcastle magazine. Sept 1820–July 1821. New ser, vols 1–10, Jan 1822–March 1831. Ed William Andrew Mitchell.

The drama: or theatrical pocket magazine. Vols 1–7, May 1821–May 1825. New ser 1 vol 1825.

The annals of sporting and fancy gazette. Vols 1–13, Jan 1822–June 1828.

The new European magazine. Vols 1–4, July 1822–June 1824.

The world of fashion and continental feuilletons. Vols 1–28, 1824–51. Continued as Ladies' monthly magazine. The world of fashion, vols 29–56, 1852–79. Continued as Le monde élégant, or the world of fashion, vols 57–68, 1880–91. Prop and ed John Browne Bell 1824–51.

The Newgate monthly magazine: or calendar of men, things and opinions. 2 vols Sept 1824–Aug 1826. Ed William Campion.

The oriental herald and colonial review. Vols 1–23, Jan 1824–Dec 1829. Ed J. S. Buckingham.

The Dublin and London magazine. Vols 1–2, March 1825–Dec 1826. Continued as Robins's London and Dublin magazine, 1 vol Jan–June 1827. Continued as Dublin and London magazine, Feb–June 1828. Suspended from July 1827–Feb 1828. Ed M. J. Whitty.

The gardener's magazine. Vols 1–19, March 1826–43. Ed J. C. Loudon.

The united service journal, and naval and military magazine. Jan 1829–Dec 1841. Continued as United service magazine and naval and military journal, Jan 1842–April 1843. Continued as Colburn's united service magazine and naval and military journal, May 1843–March 1890. Continued as United service magazine, April 1890–June 1920. Incorporated in Army quarterly. Prop Henry Colburn.

The magazine of natural history, and journal of zoology, botany, mineralogy, geology and meteorology. Vols 1–9, May 1829–Dec 1836. New ser, vols 1–4, Jan 1837–Aug 1840. From vol 2, new ser, title became Magazine of natural history. Ed J. C. Loudon 1829–31, John Denison 1831–6, Edward Charlesworth 1837–40.

The British magazine. Vols 1–2, Jan–Dec 1830.

Fraser's magazine for town and country. Vols 1–80, Feb 1830–Dec 1869. New ser, vols 1–26, Jan 1870–Oct 1882. Replaced by Longman's magazine below. Prop J. W. Parker and Son 1847–63; Longman's 1863–82. Ed William Maginn 1830–6 (assisted by John Heraud 1830–3), Francis Mahony 1836–40(?), George William Nickisson 1841–7, J. W. Parker II 1847–60, J. A. Froude 1860–74, William Allingham 1874–9, John Tulloch 1879–81.

The national magazine. Vol 1, July-Dec 1830. Continued as National magazine and Dublin literary gazette, vol 2, Jan-April 1831(?) Begun weekly as Dublin literary gazette: or weekly chronicle of criticism, belles lettres, and fine arts, 2 Jan–26 June 1830. Ed S. Lover 1830, P. D. Hardy 1831.

Cobbett's twopenny trash: or politics for the poor. Vols 1–2, July 1830–July 1832. Prop and ed W. Cobbett.

The diamond magazine. 2 vols 1831–2.

The magazine of the beau monde. Vols 1–12, 1831–42.

The metropolitan: a monthly journal of literature, science and the fine arts. Vols 1–5, May 1831–Dec 1832. Continued as Metropolitan magazine, vols 6–57, Jan 1833–April 1850. Prop Thomas Campbell(?); F. Marryat; James Grant. Ed Thomas Campbell, F. Marryat 1832–5, James Grant.

The ladies' cabinet of fashion, music and romance. [1832]–vol 5, Jan 1834–vol 14, Dec 1838. New ser, vols 1–10, Jan 1839–Dec 1843. [New ser] vol 1, Jan 1844 [vol 17, June 1852]. Continued as Ladies' cabinet of fashion (incorporated with New monthly belle assemblée), new ser, vols 1–37, July 1852–Dec 1870. From Oct 1852 this is identical, except for title-pages, with New monthly belle assemblée and Ladies' companion. Ed Margaret and Beatrice de Courcy.

Tait's Edinburgh magazine. Vols 1–4, April 1832–Jan 1834. New ser, vols 1–27, Feb 1834–Jan 1861. New ser, 1 vol May 1861. Absorbed Johnstone's Edinburgh magazine June 1834. Prop William Tait 1832–4; William Tait and Christian Isobel Johnstone 1834–46; George Troup and Archibald Alison 1846–61. Ed William Tait 1832–4, Christian Isobel Johnstone 1834–46(?), George Troup.

Chambers's historical newspaper, a monthly record of intelligence. Nos 1–39, Nov 1832–Jan 1836. Prop and ed R. and W. Chambers.

The Dublin University magazine. Vols 1–90, Jan 1833–Dec 1877. Continued as University magazine: a literary and philosophic review, vols 1–5, Jan 1878–June 1882. 2 further quarterly nos pbd Sept and Dec 1882. Prop Digby Pilot Starkey and Cheyne Brady Jan–Oct 1856; Cheyne Brady Nov 1856–June 1861; J. S. Le Fanu July 1861–June 1870; Charles F. Adams July 1870–May 1873; Durham Dunlop 1873–? Ed Charles S. Stanford Jan 1833–July 1834, Isaac Butt Aug 1834–41(?), James McGlashan(?), James Wills(?) 1841–March 1842, Charles Lever April 1842–Jan 1846, James Francis Waller? Feb 1846–Jan 1854?, Durham Dunlop(?), Percy Boyd(?), James McGlashan(?), Digby Pilot Starkey(?) and Cheyne Brady(?) Jan–Oct 1856, Cheyne Brady(?) Nov 1856–June 1861, J. S. Le Fanu July 1861–June 1870, James Francis Waller(?) July 1870–May 1873, Durham Dunlop(?) June 1873–(?), Keningale Cook (?)–1877.

The companion to the newspaper; and journal of facts in politics, statistics and public economy. Vols 1–4, March 1833–Jan 1837. Under the superintendence of Society for the Diffusion of Political Knowledge. Ed Charles Knight.

The family magazine. Vols 1–4, Aug 1834–Dec 1837. Incorporated in Ward's miscellany. Ed J. Belcher.

The architectural magazine, and journal of improvement in architecture, building and furnishing, and in the various arts and trades connected therewith. Vols 1–5, March 1834–Jan 1839. Ed J. C. Loudon.

The sportsman. Began weekly, vol 1, Aug 1833–May 1834. Continued monthly, vol 2, June 1834–Jan 1835. Continued as Sportsman and veterinary recorder, vols 1–3, Jan 1835–July 1836. Continued as Sportsman, new series, vols 1–6, July 1836–June 1839. 2nd series, vols 1–53, July 1839–Dec 1870. From July 1846 the vols of this periodical are identical, with the exception of the title-pages, with New sporting magazine, Sporting magazine and Sporting review.

The Christian lady's magazine. Vols 1–31, Jan 1834–June 1849. Ed Charlotte Elizabeth Tonna [formerly Phelan] 1834–46.

Blackwood's lady's magazine and gazette of the fashionable world. Vols 1–49 1836–60.

Bentley's miscellany. Vols 1–64, Jan 1837–Dec 1868. Prop Richard Bentley 1837–54; W. H. Ainsworth 1854–68. Ed Charles Dickens 1837–Jan 1839, W. H. Ainsworth 1839–41, George Bentley, Albert Smith.

The magazine of zoology and botany. Began bi-monthly. Vols 1–2, Feb 1837–1838. Continued as Annals of natural history; or magazine of zoology, botany and geology, vols 1–5, March 1838–Aug 1840. Continued as Annals and magazine of natural history, including zoology, botany and geology (including Charlesworth's magazine of natural history), vols 6–20, Sept 1840–Dec 1847). 2nd series, vols 1–20 (including supplementary number, Jan 1858), Jan 1848–Dec 1857. 3rd series, vols 1–20, Jan 1858–Dec 1867. 4th series, Jan 1868–Dec 1877. 5th ser etc, Jan 1878 onwards.

The monthly chronicle: a national journal of politics, literature, science and art. Vols 1–7, March 1838–June 1841. Prop D. Lardner and Bulwer Lytton. Ed D. Lardner, Bulwer Lytton and Robert Bell.

The servant's magazine, under the superintendence of Committee of the London Female Mission. Vols 1–3, April(?) 1838–40. Continued as Servants' magazine, or female domestics' instructor, vols 4–25, 1841–Dec 1862. New ser, vols 1–4, Jan 1863–Dec 1866. Continued as Servants' magazine; or, the friend of the household workers, vols 1–3, Jan 1867–Dec 1869.

The Wesleyan Methodist Association magazine. Vols 1–20, [1838]–Dec 1857. Continued as United Methodist Free Churches' magazine, new ser, vols 1–34 Jan 1858–Dec 1891. Continued as Methodist monthly, new ser, vols 1–16, Jan 1892–Dec 1907. Ed M. Miller 1872–7, J. S. Withington.

The art-union. A monthly journal of the fine arts. Vols 1–5, Feb 1839–Dec 1843. Continued as Art-union, monthly journal of the fine arts, and the arts decorative and ornamental, vols 6–9, Jan 1844–Nov(?) 1847. Continued as Art-union monthly journal of the arts, vol 10, Jan-Nov 1848. Continued as Art-journal, vols 11–74,

Jan 1849–Feb 1912. Prop Samuel Carter Hall 1839–51. Ed Samuel Carter Hall 1839–80, Marcus Huish.

The sporting review: a monthly chronicle of the turf, the chase and rural sports in all their varieties. Vols 1–54, Jan 1839–Dec 1870. From 1845 the vols of this periodical are identical, except for the title-pages, with New sporting magazine and Sportsman. Ed 'Craven' (John William Carleton).

Peter Parley's magazine. Vols 1–24(?), Jan 1840–March 1863.

The colonial magazine and commercial-maritime journal. Vols 1–8, Jan 1840–June 1842. Ed Robert M. Martin.

Bradshaw's Manchester journal. Began weekly. Vol 1, May–Oct 1841. Continued as Bradshaw's journal: a miscellany of literature, science and art, vols 2–3, Nov 1841–Oct 1842. Continued as Bradshaw's journal: a monthly miscellany of literature etc, vol 4, Dec 1842–May 1843. Ed George Falkner Dec 1842–May 1843.

The north of England magazine: a monthly journal of politics, literature, science and art. Vols 1–2, Feb 1842–May 1843. Continued as North of England magazine, and Bradshaw's journal of politics, literature, science and art, vol 3, June–Sept 1843.

Magazine for the young. Vols 1–34, Jan 1842–Dec 1875. Ed John and Charles Mozley.

Ainsworth's magazine. Vols 1–26, Feb 1842–Dec 1854. Prop and ed W. H. Ainsworth.

The illuminated magazine. Vols 1–4, May 1843–April 1845. New ser, 1 vol (7 nos), 1845. Prop Ebenezer Landells. Ed Douglas Jerrold 1843–5, W. J. Linton 1845.

Tegg's magazine of knowledge and amusement. Vol 1, nos 1–12, May 1843–April 1844.

The English journal of education. Vols 1–4, Jan 1843–Dec 1846. New ser, Jan 1847–Feb 1864. Incorporated in Museum. Ed G. Moody 1843–7.

The national temperance chronicle. July 1843–Dec 1850. New ser, vols 1–4, July 1851–Dec 1856. Organ of National Temperance Society. Ed Thomas Spencer July 1851–Feb 1853.

Hood's magazine and comic miscellany. Vols 1–3, Jan 1844–June 1845. Continued as Hood's magazine, vols 4–10, July 1845–Dec 1848. Continued as Hood's magazine and literary, scientific and dramatic journal, new ser, vol 1, Jan 1849. Ed Thomas Hood.

Simmonds's colonial magazine and foreign miscellany. Vols 1–15, Jan 1844–Dec 1848. Continued as Colonial magazine and East India review, vols 16–23, Jan 1849–June 1852. Continued as Colonial and Asiatic review, [new series], vols 1–2, July 1852–June 1853. Ed P. L. Simmonds 1844–8, W. H. G. Kingston 1849–52.

The musical times and singing class circular. June 1844–Dec 1902. Continued as Musical times, Jan 1903 onwards. Between Feb 1854 and July 1855, fortnightly.

Wade's London review: a critical journal and magazine. Vols 1–3, 16 nos Oct 1844(?)–Jan 1846. Ed T. Wade.

The Wesleyan juvenile offering: a miscellany of missionary information for young persons. Vols 1–23, Jan 1844–Dec 1866. New series, vols 1–12, Jan 1867–Dec 1878.

The British mothers' magazine. Vols 1–11, Jan 1845–Dec 1855. Continued as British mothers' journal, Jan 1856–Dec 1859. Continued as British mothers' journal and domestic magazine, 1860–Dec 1863. Continued as British mothers' family magazine, Jan–Dec 1864. Ed Mrs J. Bakewell.

Douglas Jerrold's shilling magazine. Vols 1–7, Jan 1845–June 1848. Prop and ed Douglas Jerrold.

Hogg's weekly instructor. [Vol 1, 1845]–vol 2, Aug 1845–21 Feb 1846. New series, vols 1–2, 1848–9. Continued as Hogg's instructor, vols 3–10, 1849–53. New series, vols 1–6, July 1853–June 1856. Continued as Titan, a monthly magazine. Conjoined series, vols 23–9, 1856–9.

The Oxford and Cambridge review. Vols 1–5, July 1845–Dec 1847.

Sharpe's London magazine: a journal of entertainment and instruction for general reading. Began weekly, 1 Nov 1845–vol 5 (no 113), 24 Dec 1847. Monthly, vols 5–8, Jan 1848–Feb 1849. Continued as Sharpe's London journal of entertainment and instruction, vols 9–15, March 1849–June 1852. Continued as Sharpe's London magazine of entertainment and instruction for general reading, new ser, vols 1–37, July 1852–Dec 1870. From 1858, this is identical, except for the title-pages, with Ladies' companion, New monthly belle assemblée, Ladies' cabinet and Illustrated London magazine. Prop Bethel Henry Strousberg. Ed 'Frank Fairlegh' (Francis E. Smedley) 1847–52, Mrs S. C. Hall 1852–3, Bethel Henry Strousberg 1854, Alfred W. Cole.

The almanack of the month: a review of everything and everybody. Vols 1–2, Jan–Dec 1846. Ed Gilbert à Beckett.

The labourer: a monthly magazine of politics, literature, poetry etc. Vols 1(?–)4, 1847–8. Ed Feargus O'Connor and Ernest Jones.

The rambler: a journal of home and foreign literature, politics, science, music and the fine arts. Began weekly Jan–Aug(?) 1848. Continued monthly, vols 3–12, Sept 1848–Dec 1853. New series, vols 1–11, Jan 1854–Feb 1859. New ser, bi-monthly, vols 1–6, May 1859–May 1862. Continued as Home and foreign review. *See col below, under quarterlies.* Prop John Moore Capes 1848–57; Richard Simpson, Frederick Capes and John Acton 1858–62. Ed John Moore Capes 1848–52, James Spencer Northcote 1852–4, John Moore Capes 1854–Oct 1957, Richard Simpson Nov 1857–Feb 1859, John Henry Newman Mar–July 1859, John Acton Sept 1859–May 1862.

The democratic review. June 1849–Sept 1850. Ed G. J. Harney.

The ladies' companion at home and abroad. Vols 1–2, 29 Dec 1849–25 Dec 1850 (weekly). Continued monthly as Ladies' companion and monthly magazine, Feb 1851–Dec 1852–1870. From Oct 1852, this is identical, except for the title-pages, with Ladies' cabinet and New monthly belle assemblée. Ed Mrs Loudon 1850–1.

The household narrative of current events ('for the year 1850' etc): being a monthly supplement to Household words. Vols 1–6 Jan 1850–Dec 1855. Prop C. Dickens and Bradbury and Evans. Ed C. Dickens.

The germ: thoughts towards nature in poetry, literature and art. Nos 1 & 2, Jan & Feb 1850. Continued as Art and poetry: being thoughts towards nature conducted principally by artists, nos 3 & 4, March & May 1850; rptd Portland Maine 1898; ed W. M. Rossetti 1901 (facs).

Papers for the schoolmaster. March 1851–Dec 1864. New series, vols 1–7, Jan 1865–Dec 1871. Succeeded by Schoolmaster (organ of the National Union of Teachers) 6 Jan 1872 onwards. Now Teacher. Ed C. H. Bromby.

The gentleman's herald of fashion: containing all the newest French and English costumes with models and patterns. Oct 1851–Sept 1862.

The monthly packet of evening readings for the younger members of the English church. Vols 1–30, Jan 1851–Dec 1865. Continued as Monthly packet of evening readings for the members of the English church, new series, vols 1–30, Jan 1866–Dec 1880. 3rd series, vols 1–20, Jan 1881–Dec 1890. 4th series, vols 1–17, Jan 1891–June 1899. Ed Charlotte M. Yonge 1871–91, Christabel R. Coleridge 1891–?, Arthur Innes.

The American magazine. Oct 1851–Feb 1852. Ed H. H. Paul.

The leisure hour: a family journal of instruction and recreation. Began weekly, Jan 1852–Dec 1880. Continued monthly, 1881–Oct 1905. Index to first 25 vols, 1852–76, [1878]. Ed W. H. Miller 1852–8, James Macaulay 1858–95, William Stevens 1895–1900.

Chambers's pocket miscellany. Edinburgh. Vols 1–24, 1852–3.

The Englishwoman's domestic magazine. 8 vols 1852–[9]. New series, 9 vols [1860–4]. New series, 25 vols [1865–77]. Continued as Illustrated household journal and Englishwoman's domestic magazine, 3 vols [1880–1]. Incorporated in Milliner, dressmaker and draper.

The charm: a magazine for boys and girls. May 1852–April 1854.

Chambers's repository of instructive and amusing tracts. Edinburgh. Vols 1–12, 1853–4.

Bentley's monthly review: or literary argus. 1 vol May 1853–April 1854. Continued as Bentley's monthly review, new series, May-June 1854. Continued as New monthly review, vol 1, July–Oct 1854.

The illustrated London magazine: a monthly journal. Vols 1–4, July 1853–1855. New series, vols 1–30, 1856–1870. From 1857, this is identical, except for the title-pages, with Ladies' companion, New monthly belle assemblée and Ladies' cabinet. Ed R. B. Knowles 1853–5.

The free press. Sheffield. Vols 1–14, 13 Oct 1855–June 1866. Continued as Diplomatic review vol 14 (no 6)–25 July 1866–Jan 1877. Frequency varies: began weekly, Oct 1855–March 1858; continued bi-weekly, April-May 1858; continued monthly, June 1858–July 1870; continued quarterly, Oct 1870–Jan 1877. Beginning Jan 1866 there were 2 edns, one entirely in English, the other including material in French. Ed D. Urquhart.

The boy's own magazine. Vols 1–8, Jan 1855–Dec 1862.

The national magazine. Vols 1–15, Nov 1856–May 1864. Ed John Saunders and Westland Marston.

The train. Jan 1856–Jan 1858. Ed Edmund Yates.

Gossip for the garden, a handbook for the florist and suburban horticulturist. Vols 1–8, March 1856–Dec 1863. Ed E. S. Dodwell, J. Edwards, W. Dean, John Sladden.

The ladies' treasury: an illustrated magazine of entertaining literature, education, fine art, domestic economy etc. Vols 1–9, April 1857–Dec 1865. New ser, Jan 1866–1895. Ed Mrs Warren.

The Englishwoman's review and drawing-room journal of social progress, literature and art. Vol 1, March-Aug 1857. New series, vols 1–2, Sept 1857–Sept 1859.

The Englishwoman's journal. Vols 1–3, March 1858–Aug 1859.

The geologist: a popular monthly magazine of geology. Vols 1–7, Jan 1858–June 1864. Ed S. J. Mackie.

Macmillan's magazine. Cambridge and London. Vols 1–59, Nov 1859–Oct 1907. Prop Macmillan. Ed David Masson Nov 1859–April 1868, George Grove May 1868–April 1883, John Morley May 1883–Sept 1885, Mowbray Morris Oct 1885–1907.

The what-not: or, ladies' handy-book and monthly magazine of literature. 1859–66.

The Cornhill magazine. Jan 1860–Dec 1939. Resumed Jan 1944–6. Continued quarterly 1947 onwards. Prop George Murray Smith 1860–1901. Ed W. M. Thackeray Jan 1860–May 1862, Frederick Greenwood and G. H. Lewes and George Murray Smith 1862–64(?), Frederick Greenwood and George Murray Smith 1864(?)–8(?), Edward Dutton Cook and G. H. Lewes and George Murray Smith 1868(?)–March 1871, Leslie Stephen April 1871–Dec 1882, James Payn Jan 1883–June 1896, J. St Loe Strachey July 1896–Dec 1897, Reginald John Smith Jan 1898–Dec 1916.

Good words. Edinburgh. Jan 1860–April 1906. Amalgamated with Sunday magazine and continued weekly, May 1906–10 and pbd in London. Prop Alexander Strahan. Ed Norman Macleod, Donald Macleod.

Temple Bar: a London magazine for town and country readers. Vols 1–132, Dec 1860–Dec 1905. New series, vols 1–2, Jan–Dec 1906. Index: Alphabetical list of the titles of all articles appearing in the previous 99 vols, vol 100, April 1894. Prop George Sala 1860–6; Richard and George Bentley 1866–95; Richard Bentley II 1895–8, Macmillan 1898–1906. Ed George Sala 1860–3, Edmund Yates 1863–7, George Bentley 1867–95.

Duffy's Hibernian magazine: a monthly journal of literature, science and art. Vols 1–3, July 1860–Dec 1861. Continued as Duffy's Hibernian sixpenny magazine, new series, vols 1–5, Jan 1862–June 1864. Continued as Hibernian magazine, 3rd series, vol 1, July 1864.

Once a month: original tales by the most popular authors. Nos 1–14, 1861–2. New series, nos 15–17, 1862.

The quiver. Vols 1–6, Sept 1861–Sept 1864. New series, vols 1–2, Oct 1864–Oct 1865. New series, 1866–June 1956. Prop Cassell 1861–1926. Ed John Cassell, C. H. H. Wight, John Willis Clarke 1864, Thomas T. Shore 1865, H. G. Bonavia Hunt 1865–1905.

The sixpenny magazine: a miscellany for all classes and seasons. Vols 1–14, July 1861–May 1867. New series, vols 1–2, June 1867–March 1868.

The St James's magazine. Vols 1–21, April 1861–March 1868. New series, April 1868–[1882]. Prop John Maxwell. Ed Mrs S. C. Hall 1861–2, Mrs Braddon, Mrs J. H. Riddell, Edward Walford 1870, W. J. Morgan.

The Victoria magazine. 1863–vol 28, Dec 1876–[1880]. Ed Emily Faithfull.

The month: an illustrated magazine of literature, science and art. Vols 1–11, July 1864–Dec 1869. New ser vols 12 (new ser)–186, Jan 1870–Dec 1948. New ser, vol 1, Jan 1949 onwards. Issued twice monthly 1871–3, resumed monthly 1874 as Month and Catholic review, 1874–81; continued as Month, a Catholic magazine and review, 1882–90; continued as Month, a Catholic magazine 1890–1913; continued as Month 1914 onwards. Index 1864–1908. 1909. Prop Frances Taylor 1864–June 1865; Society of Jesus 1865 onwards. Ed Frances Taylor 1864–5, Henry J. Coleridge 1865–81, Richard F. Clarke 1882–Feb 1894, John Gerard 1894–97, Sidney F. Smith 1897–1901.

The shilling magazine. Illustrated: a miscellany of literature, social science, fiction, poetry etc. Vols 1–4, May 1865–[67]. Ed S. Lucas.

The fortnightly review. No 1, 15 May 1865–Dec 1954. Incorporated in Contemporary review. Pbd twice monthly to no 35, 15 Oct 1866. Thereafter monthly. Prop Chapman and Hall. Ed G. H. Lewes 1865–6, John Morley 1867–82, T. H. S. Escott 1882–6(?), Frank Harris 1887(?)–94, W. L. Courtney 1894–1928.

The argosy: a magazine of tales, travels, essays and poems. Vols 1–75, Dec 1865–Dec 1901. Prop Mrs Henry Wood 1867–87. Ed Mrs Henry Wood 1865–June 1887, Charles W. Wood July 1887–?.

The young Englishwoman: a magazine of fiction and fashions. Vols 1–4, 1865–66. New series, 3 vols 1867–9. New series 8 vols 1870–77. Continued as Sylvia's home journal. 14 vols 1878–91. Continued as Sylvia's journal, 3 vols 1892–4. Prop Samuel Orchart Beeton. Ed John Tillotson.

Merry and wise: a magazine for young people edited by Old Merry. Vols 1–5, Jan 1865–Dec 1869. New series, vols 1–2, Jan 1870–Dec 1871. Continued as Old Merry's monthly, Jan–Dec 1872.

Gilead. Vols 1–7, June 1865–Dec 1876. Continued as Wayside words, vols 8–35, Jan 1877–Dec 1904. Ed T. H. Gregg 1865–Dec 1872, F. Harper Jan 1873–1904.

The contemporary review. Jan 1866 onwards. Prop Alexander Strahan 1866–Jan 1877; 'Strahan and Co Ltd' (Samuel Morley, Francis Peek, John Paton Brown) Feb 1877–?. Ed Henry Alford Jan 1866–March 1870, James Thomas Knowles April 1870–Jan 1877, Alexander Strahan Feb 1877–82, Percy William Bunting 1882–1911 (John Paton Brown 'consulting editor' 1882–8).

Belgravia. Nov 1866–June 1899. Prop John Maxwell. Ed M. E. Braddon. 1866–93.

The Englishwoman's review: a journal of woman's work. Began quarterly, Oct 1866–July 1869. New series, Jan 1870–Dec 1875. Continued monthly at least by Jan–Dec 1876. Continued as Englishwoman's review of social and industrial questions, Jan 1877–July 1910. Ed Jessie Boucherett, C. A. Biggs, Helen Blackburn.

Aunt Judy's magazine. Vols 1–19, May 1866–Oct 1881. New ser, vols 1–4, Nov 1881–Oct 1885. Ed Mrs Alfred Gatty 1866–73, H. K. F. Gatty and J. H. Ewing 1873–6, H. K. F. Gatty 1877–85.

Tinsley's magazine. Vols 1–42, Aug 1867–May 1889. New series, vols 43–8, June 1889–March 1892. Continued as Novel review: with which is incorporated Tinsley's magazine, 1 vol 1892. Ed Edmund Yates 1867–9.

The St Paul's: a monthly magazine. Vols 1–14, Oct 1867–March 1874. Prop Alexander Strahan (?). Ed A. Trollope Oct 1867–March 1870.

The Broadway annual. Vol 1, Sept 1867–Aug 1868. Continued as Broadway, new series, vols 1–4, Sept 1868–July 1870. New series, vols 1–5, Aug 1870–Dec 1872.

Once a month: a monthly magazine of general and amusing literature. Vols 1–2, Nov 1868–Dec 1869. Continued as Once a month: a London magazine of romance, literature, politics, music and the drama, new series, vol 1, Jan 1871. Continued as Once a month: an illustrated magazine of romance, general literature etc. New series, vols 1–2, March 1872–Aug 1873. Ed Joseph Collins 1872–3.

The portfolio: an artistic periodical. Jan 1870–Dec 1893. 3rd series, vols 1–48, 1894–1907. Ed P. G. Hamerton.

Cope's tobacco plant: a monthly periodical interesting to the manufacturer, the dealer and the smoker. Liverpool. March 1870–Jan 1881. Ed John Fraser.

National Society for Women's Suffrage journal. Manchester. Vol 1, nos 1–6, March–Aug 1870. Continued as Women's suffrage journal, vol 1, no 7–vol 21, Sept 1870–June 1890. Ed Lydia E. Becker.

The traveler: an international monthly of real estate, agriculture, mineral, financial, educational, statistical, market and general reports in Great Britain and the United States. Birmingham. Vols 1–2, April 1871–Nov 1872.

The transatlantic: a magazine of American periodical literature conducted by the editor of 'The Anglo-American times'. Vols 1–4, Aug 1872–Aug 1875.

The Irish monthly magazine. Vols 1–2, July 1873–Nov 1874. Continued as Irish monthly, vols 3–83, Dec 1874–Sept 1954. Ed Father Matthew Russell.

The British architect: a national record of the aesthetic and constructive arts; and business journal of the building community. Vols 1–88, Jan 1874–April 1919. Incorporated in Builder.

The Argonaut: a monthly magazine. Vols 1–7, no 50, Jan 1874–8. Ed George Gladstone 1874–7, Edwin Paxton Hood 1877–8.

Cassell's family magazine. Dec 1874–Nov 1897. Continued as Cassell's magazine, Dec 1897–Mar 1912. Continued as Cassell's magazine of fiction (and popular literature), April 1912–June 1919. Continued as Cassell's (magazine), July 1919–Dec 1932. Incorporated in Story-teller. Began weekly, 1853. *See col 1816, above*, Prop Cassell. Ed H. G. Bonavia Hunt 1874–96, Max Pemberton 1896.

The Celtic magazine: a monthly periodical devoted to the literature, history, antiquities of the Celt at home and abroad. Inverness. Vols 1–13, Nov 1875–Oct 1888. Ed Alexander Mackenzie and Alexander Macgregor 1875–6, Alexander Mackenzie 1876–86, Alexander Macbain 1886–8.

The poet's magazine. Vols 1–6, 1876–9. Continued as Lloyd's magazine, with which is incorporated the poet's magazine, vols 7–11, 1879–81. Continued as Authors and artists, 1881. Continued as Lloyd's London magazine, 1882–6. Continued quarterly as Lloyd's quarterly magazine, 1886–8. Continued as Modern poets, 1892–4. Continued as Modern authors, 1895. Continued as Lloyd's magazine, 1895–June 1900. Ed L. Lloyd.

The quaver, with which is published 'Choral harmony'. Vols 1–6, Jan 1876–March 1885.

The nineteenth century. Vols 1–48, March 1877–Dec 1900. Continued as Nineteenth century and after, Jan 1901–Dec 1950. Continued as Twentieth century, Jan 1951 onwards. Index: Catalogue of contributors and contributions. 1877–1901. By James Knowles [1904].

The theatre: a weekly critical review. 3 vols 1877–8. Continued as Theatre: a monthly review and magazine, new series, vols 1–3, Aug 1878–9. New series, 6 vols, 1880–2. New series, 30 vols, 1883–Dec 1907. Ed Clement Scott 1880–9, B. E. J. Capes 1890, B. E. J. Capes and Charles Eglington 1891–2, Charles Eglington 1893, Addison Bright 1894–7.

The welcome hour: an illustrated monthly magazine. [1877]–vol 2, no 7, Jan 1878–vol 17, Sept? 1893. Ed Percy Russell 1891–3.

The magazine of art illustrated. Vols 1–25, May 1878–Oct 1902. New series, vols 1–2, Nov 1902–July 1904. Prop Cassell. Ed Arthur Trendell 1878–80, Eric Robertson 1880–1, W. E. Henley Oct 1881–Aug 1886, Sidney Galpin 1886, M. H. Spielmann 1887–1904.

Time: a monthly miscellany of interesting and amusing literature. Vol 1, April 1879–[1891]. Ed Edmund Yates 1879–81, E. M. Abdy Williams 1885–6, Walter Sichel 1888–9, E. B. Bax 1890–1.

Modern thought. Vols 1–6, Feb 1879–Jan 1884. Ed J. Westby-Gibson.

The biograph and review. Vols 1–6, Jan 1879–Dec 1881. New series, vol 1, Jan 1882–June 1882. Ed 'Guy Roslyn' (Joshua Hatton).

Celebrities of the day: British and foreign. Vols 1–3, April 1881–Dec 1882. Ed S. E. Thomas.

The national Temperance mirror. Vols 1–27, Jan 1881–April 1907.

Longman's magazine. Vols 1–46. Nov 1882–Oct 1905. Successor to Fraser's magazine. Prop Longman. Ed Charles J. Longman.

The English illustrated magazine. Vols 1–49, Oct 1883–Aug 1913. Prop Macmillan 1882–93; William Ingram. Ed J. W. Comyns Carr, C. Kinloch Cooke, Clement Shorter and William Ingram 1893–1900.

The national review. Vols 1–134, March 1883–May 1950. Continued as National and English review, vols 135–154, June 1950–June 1960. Prop Leopold James Maxse 1893–1932. Ed Alfred Austin, W. J. Courthope, Leopold James Maxse 1893–1929.

Merry England: an illustrated magazine. Vols 1–24, May 1883–March 1895. Ed Wilfred Meynell.

Progress: a monthly magazine of advanced thought. Vols 1–7, Jan 1883–Dec 1887. Ed G. W. Foote.

Eastward Ho! Vols 1–7, May 1884–April 1888. Ed Freeman Wills.

The monthly magazine of fiction. Nos 1–504, [1885–1927]. Continued as Magazine of fiction, series nos 505–22, [1927–8]. Continued as Magazine of fiction and complete story teller, nos 523–60, [1928–31]. Continued as Magazine of fiction: the complete story teller monthly, nos 561–79, [1931–3]. Continued as Complete story-teller etc, nos 580–673, [1933–41].

The lady's world: a magazine of fiction and society. 1 vol Nov 1886–Oct 1887. Continued as Woman's world, vols 1–3, Nov 1887–Oct 1890. Ed Oscar Wilde Nov 1887–autumn 1889.

Murray's magazine: a home and colonial periodical. Vols 1–2, Jan–Dec 1887. Continued as Murray's magazine: a home and colonial periodical for the general reader, vols 3–10, Jan 1888–Dec 1891. Prop John Murray. Ed Edward Arnold.

Scottish notes and queries (Aberdeen). Vols 1–12, June 1887–June 1899. 2nd series, vols 1–8, July 1899–June 1907. 3rd series, vols 1–13, Jan 1923–Dec 1935. General index to 1st series 1887–1899. 1901. Ed John Bulloch.

Atalanta. [For girls]. Vols 1–11, Oct 1887–Sept 1898. Ed L. T. Meade and Alicia A. Leith 1887–8, L. T. Meade and John C. Staples 1888–91 (?), L. T. Meade 1891 (?)–2,

L. T. Meade and A. B. Symington 1892–3, A. B. Symington 1893–6, Edwin Oliver 1896–8.

Beeton's boy's own magazine. [1888]–new series, vols 1–6, Dec 1888–Nov 1890. Ed G. A. Henty.

Lucifer: a theosophical monthly. Vols 1–11, 1887–97. Continued as Theosophical review, 11 vols, 1897–1907. Ed H. P. Blavatsky, Mabel Collins, Annie Besant, G. R. S. Mead.

The universal review. Vols 1–8, May 1888–Dec 1890. Ed H. Quilter.

Art and letters; an illustrated review. 8 vols, Jan 1888–Dec 1889. English edn of Les lettres et les arts. Ed Frédéric Masson.

The new review. Vols 1–17, June 1889–Dec 1897. Ed Archibald Grove 1889–94, W. E. Henley Jan 1895–1897.

The Newbery House magazine: a monthly review for churchmen and churchwomen. Vols 1–11, July 1889–Dec 1894.

The expository times. Oct 1889 onwards. Index to vols 1–20, 1889–1909. By James Donald. [1910]. Prop and ed James Hastings.

The monthly record of eminent men. Vols 1–4, Jan 1890–Dec 1891. Ed George Potter.

The review of reviews. Vols 1–87, Jan 1890–Feb 1936. Continued as World review of reviews, 1 vol, March–Aug 1936. Continued as World review, Sept 1936–May 1953. Prop George Newnes and W. T. Stead Jan–April 1890; W. T. Stead April 1890–1912. Ed W. T. Stead 1890–1912.

Lambert's monthly. Vols 1–2, Jan 1890–May 1891. Ed G. E. Campbell.

The author. Vols 1–29, May 1890–April 1919. Continued quarterly, vol 29, July 1919 onwards. Organ of the Incorporated Society of Authors. Ed Walter Besant 1890–1901.

The King's own: a monthly magazine for the study and the home. Vols 1–9, Jan 1890–Oct 1898. Prop and ed John Urquhart.

The Strand magazine: an illustrated monthly. Jan 1891–March 1950. Incorporated in Men only. Prop George Newnes. Ed George Newnes 1891–?, H. Greenough Smith.

The Ludgate monthly. Vols 1–6, May 1891–Jan 1894. Continued as Ludgate illustrated magazine, vols 6–9, Feb 1894–Oct 1895. Continued as Ludgate, new series, vols 1–11, Nov 1895–Feb 1901. Ed Phil May 1891–?, A. M. De Beck.

The bookman: a monthly journal for book readers. Vols 1–87, Oct 1891–Dec 1934. Amalgamated with London Mercury. Ed William Robertson Nicoll (assisted by Ernest Hodder-Williams 1899–1903).

The idler magazine. Vols 1–38, Feb 1892–March 1911. Prop Robert Barr and J. K. Jerome. Ed J. K. Jerome and Robert Barr Feb 1892–July 1894, J. K. Jerome Aug 1894–Nov 1897, Arthur Lawrence and S. H. Sime May 1899–Jan 1900, S. H. Sime Sept 1900–Jan 1901.

The Albemarle. Vols 1–2, Jan–Sept 1892. Ed Hubert Crackanthorpe and W. H. Wilkins.

The butterfly. Nos 1–10, May 1893–4. New series, nos 1–12, 1899–1900. Ed L. Raven-Hill and Arnold Golsworthy.

The studio. Vol 1, April 1893 onwards. Index: General index to the first 21 vols, 1893–1901. 1911. Prop Charles Holme. Ed J. Gleeson White 1893, Charles Holme, C. Geoffrey Holme.

The Pall Mall magazine. Vols 1–54, May 1893–Sept 1914. New series, vols 1–5, May 1927–Sept 1929. From Oct 1914 to April 1927, and again from Oct 1929 to Sept 1937 amalgamated with Nash's magazine as Nash's and Pall Mall magazine. Incorporated in Good housekeeping. Prop William Waldorf Astor 1893–1910(?). Ed Douglas Straight and Frederic Hamilton 1893–6, Frederic Hamilton 1896–1900.

The free review: a monthly magazine. Vols 1–7, Oct 1893–March 1897. Continued as University magazine and free review, vols 8–10, April 1897–Sept 1898. Ed John M. Robertson 1893–5, G. Astor Singer 1896–March 1897, 'Democritus' (George Bedborough?) 1897.

The Positivist review. Vols 1–31, Jan 1893–Dec 1923. Continued as Humanity, vols 32–3, Jan 1924–Dec 1925. Ed E. S. Beesley 1893–1900.

The Bohemian, a monthly magazine and review of literature, drama and art. Vols 1–6, June 1893–Oct 1899. Ed S. L. Bensusan 1893–June 1894(?), Charles W. Forward, H. S. Muller.

The Englishwoman. An illustrated magazine. Vols 1–10, March 1895–Dec 1899. Ed E. Hepworth Dixon.

The Windsor magazine. Vols 1–90, Jan 1895–Sept 1939. Ed David Williamson.

The Savoy. Nos 1–2, Jan and April 1896 (quarterly). Continued monthly, nos 3–8, July–Dec 1896. Prop Leonard Smithers. Ed Arthur Symons.

The architectural review for the artist and craftsman. Magazine issue of Builder's journal. July 1896 onwards.

The Temple magazine. Vols 1–3, Oct 1896–Sept 1899. Continued as Temple magazine for home and sundry reading, vol 4, Oct 1899–Sept 1900. Ed Frederick A. Atkins 1896–8, John Foster Fraser 1899–1900.

To-morrow: a monthly review. Vols 1–5, no 1, Jan 1896–Jan 1898. Ed J. T. Grein.

Pearson's magazine. Vols 1–88, 1896–Nov 1939. Prop C. A. Pearson.

The new century review. Vols 1–8, Jan 1897–Dec 1900. Ed Douglas Story Aug–Dec 1900.

The railway magazine. July 1897 onwards.

The royal magazine. Vols 1–44, Nov 1898–Nov 1930. Continued as New royal magazine, vols 1–2, Dec 1930–May 1932. Continued as Royal pictorial, vols 2–4, June 1932–Dec 1934. Continued as Royal screen pictorial, 1 vol, Jan–June 1935. Continued as Screen pictorial, July 1935–Sept 1939. Ed Peter Keary.

The wide world magazine. Vols 1–135, April 1898–Dec 1965. Incorporated in Geographical magazine. Prop George Newnes. Ed W. Fitzgerald.

The girl's realm. Vols 1–17, Nov 1898–Nov 1915.

The Harmsworth monthly pictorial magazine. Vols 1–4, July 1898–July 1900. Continued as Harmsworth magazine, vols 5–6, Aug 1900–July 1901. Continued as Harmsworth London magazine, vols 7–10, Aug 1901–July 1903. Continued as London magazine, vols 11–65, Aug 1903–Oct 1930. Continued as New London magazine, new series, vols 1–6, Nov 1930–May 1933. Incorporated in Story-teller.

The British Empire review. July 1899–Sept 1939.

The monthly review. Vols 1–27, Oct 1900–June 1907. Ed H. Newbolt 1900–7.

The imperial and colonial magazine and review illustrated. Vols 1–3, Nov 1900–[May] 1901. Ed 'Celt' and E. F. Benson.

(2) QUARTERLY MAGAZINES

The Edinburgh review: or critical journal. Edinburgh. Vol 1, Oct 1802–Oct 1929. Indexes: R. Ryland, vols 1–27, Oct 1802–Nov 1812, Edinburgh 1813; vols 28–50, April 1813–Jan 1830, Edinburgh 1832; vols 51–80, April 1830–Oct 1844, 1850; vols 81–110, Jan 1845–Oct 1859, 1862; vol 111–140, Jan 1860–Oct 1874, 1876. Prop Constable 1802–26; Longman 1826–1929. Ed Sydney Smith Oct 1802, Francis Jeffrey Jan 1803–June 1829, Macvey Napier Oct 1829–Jan 1847, William Empson April 1847–Oct 1852, George C. Lewis Jan 1853–Jan

1855, George C. Lewis and Henry Reeve April 1855, Henry Reeve July 1855–Oct 1895, Arthur R. D. Elliot Jan 1896–1923.

The quarterly review. Feb 1809 onwards. No issues between April 1824 and March 1825. Indexes: vols 1–19, Quart Rev 20 1820; vols 21–39, Quart Rev 40 1831; vols 41–59, Quart Rev 60 1839; vols 61–79, Quart Rev 80 1850; vols 81–99, Quart Rev 100 1858; vols 101–120, Quart Rev 121 1867; vols 122–139, Quart Rev 140 1876; vols 141–159, Quart Rev 160 1885; vols 161–180, Quart Rev 181 1895; vols 182–200, Quart Rev 201 1905 etc. Prop John Murray. Ed William Gifford Feb 1809–April 1824, John Taylor Coleridge March-Dec 1825, John G. Lockhart March 1826–June 1853, Whitwell Elwin Sept 1853–July 1860, William Macpherson Oct 1860–Jan 1867, William Smith April 1867–July 1893, John Murray (1851–1928) Oct 1893–Jan 1894, Rowland E. Protherto April 1894–Jan 1899, George W. Prothero April 1899–1922.

The reflector. Nos 1–4, 1811–2. Ed J. H. Leigh Hunt.

Annals of the fine arts. Vols 1–5, July 1817–Dec(?) 1820.

The quarterly musical magazine and review. Vols 1–10, 1818–28. Ed R. M. Bacon.

The Edinburgh philosophical journal. Edinburgh. Vols 1–14, June 1819–April 1826. Continued as Edinburgh new philosophical journal, vols 1–57, April 1826 sic–July 1854. New series, vols 1–19, Jan 1855–April 1864. Ed David Brewster and Robert Jameson 1819–24, Robert Jameson 1824–April 1854, Laurence Jameson, J. Anderson, W. Jardine, J. H. Balfour 1855–64.

The retrospective review. Vols 1–14, 1820–6. New series, vols 1–2, 1827–8. Ed Henry Southern 1820–6, Henry Southern and H. Nicolas 1827–8.

Ollier's literary miscellany in prose and verse. No 1, 1820.

The liberal: verse and prose from the south. 2 vols 1822–3. Ed J. H. Leigh Hunt.

The album. Vols 1–4, 1822–5. Ed F. B. St Leger.

Knight's quarterly magazine. Vols 1–3, June 1823–Nov 1824. Continued as Quarterly magazine, vol 1, no 1, Aug 1825. Ed Charles Knight.

The Westminster review. Vols 1–24, Jan 1824–Jan 1836. Continued as London and Westminster review, vols 25–33, April 1836–March 1840. Continued as Westminster review, vols 34–45, June 1840–June 1846. Continued as Westminster and foreign quarterly review, vols 46–56, Oct 1846–Oct 1851. Continued as Westminster review: new series, vols 1–71, Jan 1852–April 1887. Continued monthly, vols 128 (resumption of numbering from 1824)–181, April 1887–Jan 1914. General index Jan 1824–Jan 1836, Westminster Rev 24; July 1835–March 1840 (including 2 vols of London Rev), Westminster Rev 33. Prop Jeremy Bentham et al 1824–9; T. Perronet Thompson 1829–35; William Molesworth 1836–40; W. E. Hickson 1840–51; John Chapman 1852–60; George Manwaring 1860–1; Trubner & Co. Ed Henry Southern and John Bowring 1824–7, John Bowring 1827–9, T. Perronet Thompson 1829–35, John Stuart Mill 1836–40, W. E. Hickson 1840–51, John Chapman 1852–94 (assisted by 'George Eliot' 1852–July 1854), Mrs John Chapman 1894–1914.

The Edinburgh journal of science. Edinburgh .Vols 1–10, April 1824–April 1829. New series, vols 1–6, July 1829–April 1832. Incorporated in Philosophical Magazine. Ed David Brewster.

The British critic, quarterly theological review and ecclesiastical record. Vols 1–34, Jan 1827–Oct 1843. Prop Francis Rivington. Ed Edward Smedley Jan 1827–Oct 1833, James Shergold Boone Jan 1834–Nov 1837, S. R. Maitland Jan 1838, John Henry Newman July 1838–April 1841, Thomas Mozley July 1841–Oct 1843.

The foreign quarterly review. Vols 1–37, July 1827–July 1846. Incorporated in Westminster review. Ed Robert Pearse Gillies 1827 (nominal ed until June 1830), John George Cochrane 1828–34, Frederic Shoberl(?) 1835–7, Benjamin Edward Pote 1838–Jan 1840, James William Worthington April 1840–April 1842, John Forster July 1842–Oct 1843, John R. Beard 1844–?, ? Kelly.

The foreign review and continental miscellany. Vols 1–5, 1828–30.

The law magazine: or quarterly journal of jurisprudence. Vols 1–55, Oct 1828–Feb 1856. Continued as Law magazine and law review, vols 1–31, May 1856–Nov 1871. Continued as Law magazine and review, vols 1–4, Feb 1872–Aug 1875. Continued as Law magazine and review and quarterly digest of all reported cases, vols 1–23, Nov 1875–Aug 1898. 5th series, vols 24–40, Nov 1898–Aug 1915.

The London review. Nos 1–2, 1829. Prop Nassau W. Senior. Ed Joseph Blanco White.

The quarterly journal of education. Vols 1–10, Jan 1831–Oct 1835. Organ of the S.D.U.K.

The Freemasons' quarterly review. Vols 1–9, April 1834–Dec 1842. New series, vols 1–7, March 1843–Dec 1849. Continued as Freemasons' quarterly magazine and review, vols 1–3, March 1850–Dec 1852. Continued as Freemasons' magazine: new series, 2 vols March 1853–Oct 1854. Continued monthly as Freemason's monthly magazine, vol 1, Jan–Dec 1855. Continued as Freemasons' magazine and Masonic mirror, vols 2–6, Jan 1856–June 1859. New series, vols 1–25 (no 2), 9 July 1859–26 Aug 1871. Weekly from 6 Jan 1858.

The London review. Vols 1–2, April 1835–Jan 1836. Incorporated in Westminster review. Prop William Molesworth. Ed John Stuart Mill.

The British and foreign review: or European quarterly journal. Vols 1–8, July 1835–44. Ed ? Wallace July 1835, G. A. Young Oct 1835–Jan 1836, Wentworth Beaumont April–July 1836, John Mitchell Kemble 1836–Oct 1844.

The Christian teacher. Vols 1–4, Jan 1835–June 1838 (monthly). New series, vols 1–6, July 1839–Oct 1844. Issued quarterly from vol 2, 1840. Continued as Prospective review, vols 1–10, Feb 1845–Aug 1854, plus a separate no 41, for Feb 1855. Ed John R. Beard, William Johns and G. Buckland 1835–8, J. H. Thom 1839–44, J. H. Thom, James Martineau, J. J. Tayler and Charles Wicksteed 1845–55.

The British and foreign medical review and quarterly journal of practical medicine and surgery. Vols 1–24, Jan 1836–Oct 1847. Index to first 24 vols. By R. Bower, vol 25, 1848. Ed J. Forbes and J. Conolly.

The Dublin review. May 1836 onwards. Index: complete list of articles pbd May 1836–April 1936. 1936. Prop Nicholas Wiseman 1837–62; Henry Edward Manning 1863–79; Herbert Vaughan 1879–1903(?). Ed M. J. Quin May-July 1836, M. A. Tierney Dec 1836, James Smith April–July 1837, Nicholas Wiseman 1837–63 (assisted by C. W. Russell, with H. R. Bagshaw as sub-editor), W. G. Ward 1864–78 (with Cashel Hoey as sub-editor), J. C. Hedley 1879–85 (with W. E. Driffield as sub-editor), Herbert Vaughan 1885–91, James Moyes 1892–?.

The Church of England quarterly review. Vols 1–44, Jan 1837–Nov 1858. Ed E. Thompson.

The foreign and colonial quarterly review. Vols 1–3, Jan 1843–April 1844. Continued as New quarterly review: or home, foreign and colonial journal, vols 4–8, no 1, July 1844–July 1846. Ed James William Worthington.

The English review: or quarterly journal of ecclesiastical and general literature. Vols 1–19, April 1844–April 1853.

The North British review. Vols 1–53, May 1844–Jan 1871. No issue May 1857. Prop T. and T. Clark; group of liberal Catholics under John Acton 1869–71. Ed David Welsh 1844–May 1845, Edward F. Maitland Aug 1845–Nov 1846, William Hanna Feb 1847–Feb 1850, A. C. Fraser May 1850–Feb 1857, John Duns Aug 1857–May

1860, ? Forster Aug 1860, W. G. Blaikie Nov 1860–Aug 1863, David Douglas Nov 1863–July 1869, T. F. Wetherell Oct 1869–Jan 1871.

The law review and quarterly journal of British and foreign jurisprudence. Vols 1–23, Nov 1844–Feb 1856. Incorporated in Law magazine.

The British quarterly review. Vols 1–53, Feb 1845–April 1886. Ed Robert Vaughan 1845–65, Henry Allon and Robert Reynolds 1865–74, Henry Allon 1875–86.

The prospective review. 1845–55. *See above, under* Christian teacher.

The Irish quarterly review. Dublin. Vols 1–9, March 1851–Jan 1860.

The new quarterly review and digest of current literature. Nos 1–41, 1852–62.

The Scottish review: a quarterly journal of social progress and general literature. Glasgow. Vols 1–10 and one no, Jan 1853–Jan 1863. Organ of the Scottish Temperance League.

The London quarterly review. Sept 1853–Jan 1932. Continued as London quarterly and Holborn review, April 1932 onwards. Prop Methodist Connexion. Ed Thomas M'Nicoll 1853–9, William Burt Pope 1860–83, William Burt Pope and James Harrison Rigg 1883–6, James Harrison Rigg 1886–98, William L. Watkinson 1898–1904.

The national review. Vols 1–18, July 1855–April 1864. Ed Walter Bagehot and R. H. Hutton 1855–62, Walter Bagehot and C. H. Pearson 1862–4.

Meliora: a quarterly review of social science. Vols 1–12, April 1858–Oct 1869. Ed Henry Septimus Sutton 1859–69.

The Atlantis: a register of literature and science conducted by members of the Catholic University of Ireland. Vol 1, nos 1–2, Jan, July 1858; vol 2, nos 3–4, Jan, July 1859; vol 3, nos 5–6, Jan 1860, Jan 1862; vol 4, nos 7–8, 1863; vol 5, no 9, Feb 1870. Prop John Henry Newman. Ed John Henry Newman and W. K. Sullivan 1858, W. K. Sullivan and P. Le Page Renouf.

The ibis: a magazine of general ornithology. Vols 1–6, Jan 1859–Oct 1864. New series, 6 vols Jan 1865–Oct 1870. 3rd series, 6 vols Jan 1871–Oct 1876. 4th series, Jan 1877–Oct 1882. 5th series, 6 vols Jan 1883–Oct 1888. 6th series, 6 vols Jan 1889–Oct 1894. 7th series, 6 vols Jan 1895–Oct 1900. 8th series, Jan 1901–Oct 1906 ... 14th series, vol 6, 1942. Then vol 85 1943 onwards. Indexes: Index of genera and species referred to, and to the plates [series 1–3] 1859–76, 1879; Index of genera etc. [series 4–6] 1877–94, 1897; Index of genera series 7–9, 1895–1912, 1916; General subject index series 1–6 1859–94. Ed O. Salvin 1871–76, O. Salvin and P. L. Sclater 1877–82, P. L. Sclater and H. Saunders 1883–8, P. L. Sclater 1889–94, P. L. Sclater and H. Saunders 1895–1900.

Bentley's quarterly review. Vols 1–2, March 1859–Jan 1860. Prop Richard Bentley. Ed John Douglas Cook ('director'), William Scott and Robert Cecil.

The natural history review. Vols 1–5, Jan 1861–Oct 1865. Ed T. H. Huxley et al.

The fine arts quarterly review. Vols 1–3, May 1863–Jan 1865. New series, vols 1–2, July 1866–June 1867. Ed B. B. Woodward 1863–5.

The Alpine journal: a record of mountain adventure and scientific observation. [By members of the Alpine Club.] March 1863 onwards. Now twice a year. Index to vols 1–15. By F. A. Walroth, 1892. Ed H. B. George 1863–7, A. T. Malkin 1868, Leslie Stephen 1868–71, D. W. Freshfield, W. A. B. Coolidge, A. J. Butler, W. M. Conway, G. Yeld.

The home and foreign review. Vols 1–4, July 1862–April 1864. Prop John Acton and Richard Simpson July–Dec 1862; John Acton 1863–4. Ed John Acton (assisted by Thomas Wetherell 1862–4 and P. Le Page Renouf Oct 1863–April 1864).

The quarterly journal of science. Vols 1–7, Jan 1864–Oct 1870. New series, vols 8–15, Jan 1871–Oct 1878. Continued as Journal of science, 3rd series, vols 1–7, Jan 1879–Dec 1885. Ed J. Samuelson and W. Crookes 1864–70, W. Crookes 1871–85.

The theological review: a journal of religious thought and life. Begun bi-monthly, vols 1–2, March 1864–Nov 1865. Continued quarterly, vols 3–12, Jan 1866–Dec 1875. Continued as Theological review: a quarterly journal of religious thought and life, vols 13–16, Jan 1876–Oct 1879. Ed C. Beard.

The Friends' quarterly examiner. Jan 1867–Oct 1946. Continued as Friends' quarterly, new series, Jan 1947 onwards. Ed W. C. Westlake.

The new quarterly magazine. Vols 1–10, Oct 1873–Oct 1878. New series, vols 1–3, Jan 1879–April 1880. Ed O. J. F. Crawfurd 1873–Jan 1878, Francis Hueffer April–Oct 1878, C. Kegan Paul Jan 1879–April 1880.

The church quarterly review. Oct 1875 onwards. Ed A. R. Ashwell 1876–9.

Mind: a quarterly review of psychology and philosophy. Jan 1876 onwards. Ed George Croom Robertson 1876–92, G. F. Stout 1892–1920.

Brain: a journal of neurology. April 1878 onwards. Index: General index to vols 1–23, 1878–1900. 1902. Prop Macmillan. Ed J. C. Bucknill, J. Crichton-Browne, D. Fevrier, J. Hughlings-Jackson 1878–83, J. C. Bucknill, J. Crichton-Browne, D. Fevrier, J. Hughlings-Jackson, A. de Watteville 1883–5, A. de Watteville plus editorial committee 1885–1900.

The modern review. Vols 1–5, Jan 1880–Oct 1884. Ed R. A. Armstrong.

The law quarterly review. Jan 1885 onwards. Ed F. Pollock 1885–1919.

The English historical review. Jan 1886 onwards. Ed Mandell Creighton 1886–91, S. R. Gardiner 1891–5, S. R. Gardiner and R. L. Poole 1895–1901.

The century guild hobby horse. Vols 1–7, Jan 1886–Oct 1892. Continued as Hobby horse, 3 nos. 1893–4. Ed H. P. Horne and A. H. Mackmurdo 1886–7, H. P. Horne 1888–91, A. H. Mackmurdo 1892, H. P. Horne 1893–4.

The Jewish quarterly review. Vols 1–20, Oct 1888–July 1908. New series edited for Dropsie College for Hebrew and Cognate Learning, Philadelphia, 1910 onwards. Ed Israel Abrahams and Claude Montefiore Oct 1888–July 1908.

The archaeological review. Vols 1–4, March 1888–Jan 1890. Incorporated in Folklore. Ed G. L. Gomme.

The Downside review. July 1880 onwards. Originally 3 times a year, now quarterly. Index to vols 1–25, vol 25 1906. Ed Alfred Maskell, Dom Edmund Ford, Abbot Gasquet, Abbot Butler.

Folklore. 1890 onwards.

The yellow book. Vols 1–13, April 1894–April 1897. Prop John Lane. Ed Aubrey Beardsley and Henry Harland.

The Savoy. *See col 000, above, under Monthly magazines.*

The quarto. Irregular. 2 nos 1896; 3rd no 1897; 4th no 1898. Ed John Bernard Holborn.

The dome: a quarterly containing examples of all the arts. Nos 1–5, March 1897–May 1898. 1 issue gratis Aug 1898. Continued monthly, new series, vols 1–7, Oct 1898–July 1900. Prop and ed Ernest J. Oldmeadow.

Beltaine: the organ of the Irish literary theatre. Irregular. No 1, May 1899; no 2, Feb 1900; no 3, April 1900. Ed W. B. Yeats.

The Anglo-Saxon review. June 1899–Sept 1910. Ed Lady Randolph S. Churchill.

(3) ACCOUNTS AND STUDIES OF MONTHLY AND QUARTERLY MAGAZINES

Basic to the study of Victorian periodicals is W. E. Houghton (ed), The Wellesley index to Victorian periodicals, *which includes identification of authorship and tables of contents in British monthlies and quarterlies 1824–1900 with bibliographies of contributors. Evidence is cited for every attribution.* Vol 1, Toronto 1966, *covers Blackwood's Mag, Contemporary Rev, Cornhill Mag, Edinburgh Rev (with an initial section covering 1802–23), Home & Foreign Rev, Macmillan's Mag, North Br Rev, and Quart Rev.* Vol 2 *will deal with a further 15 of the most important monthlies and quarterlies.*

Accounts and Studies covering several Monthlies and Quarterlies

Brown, A. W. The Metaphysical Society: Victorian minds in crisis 1869–80. New York 1947.

Lockhart, J. G. John Bull's letter to Lord Byron. Ed A. L. Strout, Norman Oklahoma 1947.

Houghton, W. E. British periodicals of the Victorian age: bibliographies and indexes. Lib Trends 7 1959.

Morrison, J. L. The Oxford Movement and the British periodicals. Catholic Historical Rev 45 1959.

Maurer, O. 'My squeamish public': some problems of Victorian magazine publishers and editors. SB 12 1959.

Amarasinghe, U. Dryden and Pope in the early nineteenth century: a study of changing literary taste 1800–30. Cambridge 1962.

Fielding, K. J. American notes and some English reviewers MLR 59 1964.

Fetter, F. W. Economic controversy in the British reviews 1802–50. Economica 32 1965.

Gordon, B. J. Say's Law, effective demand and the contemporary British periodicals 1820–50. Economica 32 1965.

Accounts and Studies of Monthly Magazines

Mayo, R. D. The Gothic short story in the magazines. MLR 37 1942.

— The Gothic romance in the magazines [1770–1820]. PMLA 65 1950.

Smith, J. Magazines of the nineties. Chambers's Jnl Jan 1945.

Ward, W. S. Some aspects of the conservative attitude towards poetry in English criticism 1798–1820. PMLA 60 1945.

Morgan, B. Q. and A. R. Hohlfeld. German literature in British magazines 1750–1860. Madison 1949.

Gentleman's magazine 1731

A selection of curious articles from the Gentleman's magazine. Ed J. Walker 4 vols 1814 (3rd edn).

The autobiography of Sylvanus Urban. GM July–Sept, Nov–Dec 1856, Jan–April 1857.

The Gentleman's magazine library: being a classified collection of the chief contents of the Gentleman's magazine from 1731 to 1868. Ed G. L. Gomme 1883.

Bullen, A. H. GM Feb 1906.

Blunden, E. The Gentleman's magazine 1731–1907. In his Votive tablets, 1931.

Buckley, W. E. Henry Kingsley and the Gentleman's Magazine. JEGP 50 1951.

Monthly review 1749

Robberds, J. W. A memoir of the life and writings of William Taylor. 1843.

Nangle, B. C. The Monthly review: second series 1790–1815–indexes of contributors and articles. Oxford 1955.

Critical review 1756

Roper, D. The politics of the Critical review 1756–1817. Durham Univ Jnl 22 1961.

Arminian magazine 1778

Blacket, J. The oldest religious periodical in the world. Methodist Mag Jan–March 1927.

Botanical magazine 1787

Curtis's botanical magazine dedications 1827–1927: portraits and biographical notes by E. Nelmes and W. Cuthbertson. 1931.

A new and complete index, to which is prefaced a history of the magazine by I. W. B. Hemsley. 1906.

Hooker, W. J. Companion to the Botanical magazine: being a journal containing such interesting information as does not come within the limits of the magazine. Vols 1–2, 1835–7. Incorporated in the Annals of natural history.

Sporting magazine 1792

Index of engravings in Sporting magazine 1792–1870. [1892].

Monthly magazine 1796

Dowden, W. S. A Jacobin journal's view of Lord Byron. SP 48 1951.

Carnall, G. The monthly magazine. RES new ser 5 1954.

Eclectic review 1805

Remarks on the principles of the Eclectic review with reference to civil and ecclesiastical subjects illustrated by extracts from that publication. 1817.

Foster, J. Contributions, biographical, literary and philosophical to the Eclectic review. 2 vols 1844.

The controversy between the Eclectic review and Mr James Grant: reprinted from the Morning Chronicle. 1856 (10 edns).

Monthly repository 1806

Mineka, F. E. The dissidence of dissent: the Monthly repository 1806–38. Chapel Hill 1944.

British review 1811

Ward, W. S. Lord Byron and 'my grandmother's review'. MLN 64 1949.

New monthly magazine 1814

Redding, C. Literary reminiscences and memoirs of Thomas Campbell. 2 vols 1860.

Sadleir, M. Bulwer and his wife. 1933.

Rollins, H. E. Letters of Horace Smith to his publisher Colburn. Harvard Lib Bull 3 1949.

Strickland, G. (ed). Selected journalism from the English reviews by Stendhal, with translations of other critical writings. 1959. On his work as French correspondent of New monthly magazine.

Sikes, H. M. 'The infernal Hazlitt', the New Monthly Magazine and the Conversations of James Northcote RA. Essays in History & Lit 5 1965.

Blackwood's Edinburgh magazine 1817

Wilson, John. The recreations of Christopher North. 3 vols 1842.

— Essays critical and imaginative. 4 vols 1866.

Eagles, J. The sketcher. 1856.

— Essays contributed to Blackwood's magazine. 1857.

Tales from Blackwood. 12 vols Edinburgh 1858–61. New series, 12 vols Edinburgh 1878–80. 3rd series 6 vols Edinburgh 1889–90.

Travel, adventure and sport from Blackwood's Magazine. 6 vols Edinburgh 1889–90.

Gordon, M. Christopher North: a memoir. 1862.

Shand, A. I. Magazine writers. Blackwood's Mag Feb 1879.

Douglas, G. B. S. The Blackwood group. 1897.

Oliphant, M. O. Annals of a publishing house: William Blackwood and his sons: their magazine and friends. 2 vols 1897.

Porter, M. Annals of a publishing house: John Blackwood. Edinburgh 1898. A continuation of the previous entry.
Strout, A. L. Hunt, Hazlitt and Maga. ELH 4 1937.
— Walter Scott and Maga. TLS 5 Feb 1938.
— Blackwood's magazine, Lockhart and John Scott: a Whig satirical broadside. N & Q 11 Jan 1941.
— 'Timothy Tickler' of Blackwood's magazine. N & Q 25 Jan 1941.
— A study in periodical patchwork: John Wilson's re-creations of Christopher North 1842. MLR 38 1943. Compares original text in Blackwood's with that of the collected edn.
— George Croly and Blackwood's Magazine. TLS 6 Oct 1950.
— Lockhart: champion of Shelley. TLS 12 Aug 1955.
— William Maginn as gossip. N & Q June 1955.
— A bibliography of articles in Blackwood's magazine 1817–25. Texas Technological College Lit Bull 5 1959. This important bibliography complements the section on Blackwood's in the Wellesley index, giving attributions of articles 1817–1900. It also contains a select bibliography.
— Some miscellaneous letters, concerning Blackwood's magazine. N & Q March, July 1954.
Wardle, R. M. The motive for Byron's George Russell of A. MLN 65 1950.
Parker, W. M. Anthony Trollope and Maga. Blackwood's Mag Jan 1945.
Nolte, E. A. Michael Scott and Blackwood's magazine: some unpublished letters. Library 5th ser 8 1953.
Tredrey, F. D. The House of Blackwood 1804–1954. Edinburgh 1954.
Cooke, Mrs A. K. William Maginn on John Keats. N & Q March 1956.
Fetter, F. W. The economic articles in Blackwood's Edinburgh magazine and their authors 1817–53. Scottish Jnl of Political Economy 7 1960.

London Magazine 1820
Blunden, E. Keats' publisher. 1936.
Wendland, I. Der Einfluss der Politik auf das London magazine und seine Hauptbeiträger. Emsdetten 1937.
Hennig, J. Early English translations of Goethe's essays on Byron. MLR 44 1949.
Brooks, E. L. Coleridge's second packet for Blackwood's magazine. PQ 30 1951. Speculates on Coleridge's authorship of certain articles in London magazine.
— Was William Hazlitt a news reporter? N & Q Aug 1954. On possibility that Hazlitt contributed more than Table Talk and dramatic criticism.
— Byron and the London magazine. Keats-Shelley Jnl 5 1956.
Bauer, J. The London magazine 1820–9. Copenhagen 1953.
Patmore, D. A literary duel. Princeton Univ Lib Chron 16 1954. On duel between John Scott and J. G. Lockhart.
House, H. In his All in due time, 1955.
Morgan, P. F. Taylor and Hessey: aspects of their conduct of the London Magazine. Keats-Shelley Jnl 7 1958.
Strickland, G. (ed). Selected journalism from the English reviews by Stendhal, with translations of other critical writings. 1959. On his work as French correspondent of London Magazine.
Sikes, H. M. Hazlitt, the London magazine and the 'anonymous reviewer'. BNYPL March 1961.
Prance, C. A. Peppercorn papers. Cambridge 1964 (priv ptd).

Fraser's magazine 1830
A gallery of illustrious literary characters 1830–8 drawn by D. Maclise, accompanied by notices chiefly by W. Maginn: republished from Fraser's magazine. Ed W. Bates [1873].
Mahony, F. S. (Father Prout). The works of Father Prout, edited with biographical introduction and notes by C. Kent. 1892.
Thrall, M. M. H. Rebellious Fraser's 1830–40. New York 1934.
Our past and our future. Fraser's Mag July 1879.
Sampson, M. Fraser's magazine: 'Regina'. N & Q 31 Aug 1940.
Maurer, O. Froude and Fraser's magazine 1860–74. SE 28 1949.
White, E. N. Thackeray's contributions to Fraser's magazine. SB 19 1966.

Dublin University magazine 1833
Sadleir, M. The Dublin University magazine: its history, contents and bibliography. Pbns of Bibl Soc of Ireland 5 1938.

Bentley's miscellany 1837
Tales from Bentley. 4 vols 1860, 1865.
Dexter, W. Bentley's Miscellany. Dickensian 33 1937.
Littlewood, L. M. A Victorian magazine. Contemporary Rev March 1937.
Rickels, M. The humorists of the old southwest in the London Bentley's miscellany. Amer Lit 27 1950.
Gettmann, R. A. Barham and Bentley. JEGP 56 1957.

Art Journal (Art-union 1839)
Fifty years of art 1849–99: being articles and illustrations selected from the Art journal. Ed D. C. Thomson 1900.

Musical times 1844
Scholes, P. A. The mirror of music 1844–1944: a century of musical life in Britain as reflected in the pages of the Musical Times. 2 vols 1948.

Sharpe's London magazine 1845
Boase, G. C. Sharpe's London Magazine. N & Q 12 April 1879.
'Bede, Cuthbert' (E. Bradley) Sharpe's London Magazine. N & Q 26 April 1879.

Rambler 1848
Altholz, J. L. The liberal Catholic movement in England: the Rambler and its contributors. 1962.
— A bibliographical note on the Rambler. PBSA 56 1962.

Macmillan's magazine 1859
Buckler, W. E. Tennyson's Lucretius bowdlerized? RES new ser 5 1954.
Gurr, A. J. Macmillan's magazine. REL 6 1965.

Cornhill Magazine 1860
The Cornhill gallery, containing 100 engravings by F. Leighton, J. E. Millais etc. 1865.
Maurer, O. L. Stephen and the Cornhill Magazine 1871–82. SE 32 1953.
Scott, J. W. Robertson. The story of the Pall Mall Gazette. 1950.
Smith, P. The Cornhill Magazine number 1. REL 4 1963.

Temple Bar 1860
The one hundredth volume of Temple Bar magazine: being an alphabetical list of all articles appearing in the previous ninety-nine volumes. Temple Bar April 1894.
de Baun, V. C. Temple Bar: index of Victorian middle-class thought. Jnl Rutgers Univ Lib 19 1955.

Month 1864
Gerard, J. A 'century' and a retrospect. Month Dec 1902.
Jubilee issues. Month Jan, June 1914.
75th anniversary issue. Month July 1939.
Martindale, C. C. Newman and the Month. Month Dec 1950.
Thomas, A. The Month: attribution of articles. N & Q June 1954.

Fortnightly Review 1865
Waugh, A. The biography of a periodical. Fortnightly Rev Oct 1929.
— A hundred years of publishing. 1930.
Everett, E. M. The party of humanity: the Fortnightly Review and its contributors 1865–74. Chapel Hill 1939.

Contemporary review 1866
Strahan, A. Account in Day of Rest Jan-Dec 1881.
Lowe, R. L. Matthew Arnold and Percy William Bunting: some new letters 1884–7. SB 7 1955.
Aunt Judy's Magazine 1866
Twenty years with Aunt Judy. TLS 7 Dec 1946.
Cope's tobacco plant 1870
Altick, R. D. Cope's tobacco plant: an episode in Victorian journalism. PBSA 45 1951.
Nineteenth century 1877
Sixty years ago. Nineteenth Century. March 1937.
Fairchild, H. N. 'La Saisiaz' and the Nineteenth Century. MP 48 1950. On a symposium in the magazine 1877.
75th anniversary number. Twentieth Century March 1952.
Goodwin, M. Nineteenth century opinion: an anthology of extracts from the first fifty volumes of the Nineteenth century 1877–1901. 1952 (Pelican).
Time 1879
Mumby, F. A. and F. H. Stallybrass. From Swann Sonnenschein to George Allen and Unwin Ltd. 1955.
Longman's magazine 1882
Reid, F. Andrew Lang and Longman's. London Mercury March 1938.
Parker, W. M. Land and Longman's. Scots Mag new ser March 1944.
Maurer, O. Andrew Lang and Longman's Magazine 1882–1905. SE 34 1955.
Blagden, C. Longman's Magazine. REL 4 1963.
National review 1883
Milner, V. Fifty-five years: an historical note. Nat Rev Oct 1948.
See historical material in last issue, June 1960.
Woman's world 1887
Wyndham, H. When Oscar Wilde was editor. Life & Letters Dec 1947.
— 'Edited by Oscar Wilde'. Lib Rev 12 1949.
Expository times 1889
Jubilee number. Oct 1939.
Strand magazine 1891
The 100th number of the Strand magazine: a chat about its history by Sir George Newnes, Bart. Strand Mag April 1899.
Dawson, A. An interview with Sir George Newnes. Bookman (London) May 1899.
Pound, R. The Strand magazine 1891–1950. 1966.
Savoy 1896
Garbáty, T. The French coterie of the Savoy 1896. PMLA 75 1960.
Harris, W. Innocent decadence: the poetry of the Savoy. PMLA 77 1962.

Accounts and Studies of Quarterly Magazines

Cox, R. G. The great reviews. Scrutiny 6 1937.
Welker, J. J. The position of the quarterlies on some classical dogmas. SP 37 1940.
Lloréns, V. Colaboraciones de emigrados españoles en revistas inglesas 1824–34. Hispanic Rev 19 1951.
Edinburgh Review 1802
'Scipio, C.' A sketch of the politics of the Edinburgh Review. 1807.
Selections from the Edinburgh Review comprising the best articles in that journal from its commencement to the present time, and explanatory notes. Ed M. Cross 4 vols 1833, 6 vols Paris 1835–6.
Macaulay, T. B. Critical and historical essays contributed to the Edinburgh Review. 3 vols 1843, 1887 (complete); ed F. C. Montague 3 vols 1903.
Jeffrey, F. Contributions to the Edinburgh Review. 4 vols 1844, 1853.
Rogers, H. Essays selected from contributions to the Edinburgh Review. 3 vols 1850–55.
Brougham, H. Contributions to the Edinburgh Review. 3 vols 1856.
Smith, S. Essays rptd from the Edinburgh Review 1802–18. 1874, 1880 (with addns up to 1827).
Constable, T. Archibald Constable and his literary correspondents. 3 vols Edinburgh 1873.
Eliot, A. R. D. The Edinburgh Review. Edinburgh Rev 196 1902.
Griggs, E. L. Southey and the Edinburgh Review. MP 30 1933.
Schneider, E. Thomas Moore and the Edinburgh review. MLN 61 1946.
— Tom Moore and the Edinburgh review of Christabel. PMLA 77 1962. Contains an account and bibliography of the whole controversy.
Clive, J. The Earl of Buchan's kick: a footnote to the history of the Edinburgh review. Harvard Lib Bull 5 1951.
— The Scotch reviewers: the Edinburgh Review 1802–15. 1957.
Karminski, A. The Edinburgh Review after 150 years. Listener 30 Oct 1952.
Fetter, F. W. The authorship of economic articles in the Edinburgh Review 1802–47. Jnl of Political Economy 61 1953.
Crawford, T. The Edinburgh Review and romantic poetry 1802–29. Auckland Univ Coll Bull no 47 (Eng ser no 8). 1955.
Collins, P. Dickens and the Edinburgh Review. RES 14 1963.
Quarterly review 1809
Centenary article. Quart rev 210 1909.
Graham, W. Tory criticism in the Quarterly review 1809–53. New York 1921.
Strout, A. L. Lockhart and Croker. TLS 30 Aug, 13 Sept 1941. Letters on Lockhart's appointment as editor.
— Unpublished letters of Lockhart to Croker. N & Q 11 Sept 1943, 9 and 23 March, 20 April, 4 and 18 May, 1 and 15 June 1946.
Shine, H. and H. C. The Quarterly review under Gifford: identification of contributors 1809–24. Chapel Hill 1949.
Lochhead, M. Lockhart, the Quarterly review and the Tractarians. Quart rev 291 1953.
— Miss Rigby and the Quarterly review: pioneer woman journalist. Quart rev 298 1960.
Johnson, R. V. Pater and the Victorian anti-Romantics. EC 4 1954.
Parker, W. M. Dean Milman and the Quarterly Review. Quart Rev 293 1955.
— Gladstone as a Quarterly review contributor. Ibid.
Fetter, F. W. The economic articles in the Quarterly Review and their authors. Jnl of Political Economy 66 1958.
Liberal 1822
A critique on the Liberal. 1822.
Lord Byron, Leigh Hunt and the Liberal. Ed L. P. Pickering 1925. Selections.
Dilke, C. W. The Liberal. N & Q 1 July 1893. On C. A. Browne's marked file.
Marshall, W. H. Byron, Shelley, Hunt and the Liberal. Philadelphia 1960.
Knight's quarterly magazine 1823
Sadleir, M. Bulwer and his wife. 1933.
Westminster review 1824
Blyth, E. K. Life of William Ellis. 1889.
Nesbitt, G. L. Benthamite reviewing: the first twelve years of the Westminster Review 1824–36. New York 1934.
Fraiberg, L. The Westminster Review and American literature 1824–85. Amer Lit 24 1952.
Johnson, L. G. General T. Perronet Thompson 1783–1869. 1957.

Haight, G. S. George Meredith and the Westminster Review. MLR 53 1958.

Daniels, E. A. Collaboration of Mazzini on an article in the Westminster Review. BNYPL Nov 1961.

Fetter, F. W. Economic articles in the Westminster Review and their authors 1824–51. Jnl of Political Economy 70 1962.

Morgan, P. F. Francis Place's copy of the Westminster Review. N & Q Sept 1966.

British critic 1827

Mozley, T. Reminiscences chiefly of Oriel College and the Oxford Movement. 2 vols 1882.

Houghton, E. R. The British critic and the Oxford Movement. SB 16 1963.

British and Foreign Review 1835

Winegarner, L. Thackeray's contributions to British and foreign review. JEGP 47 1948.

Dublin review 1836

Centenary article 198 1936.

McLaughlin, P. J. Dr Russell and the Dublin review. Studies 41 1952.

North British review 1844

The story of the North British Review. Scottish Rev 3 Jan 1907.

British quarterly review 1845

Osbourn, R. V. The British quarterly review. RES new ser 1 1950.

London quarterly review 1853

See historical material. Oct 1943.

Yellow book 1894

The Yellow book: a selection. Ed N. Denny 1950.

Townsend, J. B. The Yellow book. Princeton Univ Lib Chron 16 1955.

Egerton, G. and T. de V. White. A leaf from the Yellow book: the correspondence of George Egerton. 1958.

Mix, K. L. A study in yellow: the Yellow book and its contributors. 1960.

Huntley, J. Aline and Henry Harland, Aubrey Beardsley and the Yellow book: a verification of some evidence. N & Q March 1962.

Weintraub, S. The Yellow book: a reappraisal. Jnl of General Education 16 1964.

Dome 1897

West, P. The Dome: an aesthetic periodical of the 1890's. Book Collector 6 1957.

Ziegler, A. P. The Dome and its editor publisher: an exploration. Amer Book Collector 15 1965.

E. SCHOOL AND UNIVERSITY JOURNALISM

Cambridge

The Galvanist, by Hydra Polycephalus Esq. Nos 1–11, 1804. By W. D. Whittington et al.

The Cambridge monthly repository or literary miscellany. No 1, Dec 1819.

The Cambridge quarterly review and academical register. Nos 1–3, March–Oct 1824.

The snob: a literary and scientific journal, not conducted by members of the University. Nos 1–11, 9 April–18 June 1829. Continued as Gownsman, vol 2, no 17, 5 Nov 1829–25 Feb 1830. By W. M. Thackeray, Edward FitzGerald et al.

Punch in Cambridge. Vols 1–3, 7 Feb 1832–30 Dec 1834.

Toby in Cambridge. Vols 1–4, Oct 1832–12 Sept 1836.

The Cambridge quarterly review and magazine of literature, arts, sciences. Nos 1–3, 1 July 1833–Jan 1834. By Sheridan Knowles, Douglas Jerrold et al.

The Cambridge University magazine. Nos 1, 2, 1835.

The freshman. Nos 1–6, 5 March–9 April 1836.

The fellow. Nos 1–11, 6 Oct–15 Dec 1836.

The individual. Nos 1–16, 25 Oct 1836–11 April 1837.

The Cambridge University magazine. Vol 1, no 1–vol 3, no 1, 1840–3. The wrappers of the first 5 nos bore the title 'The symposium'. Ed George Brimley, C. B. Wilcox, W. M. W. Call.

Cambridge essays contributed by members of the University. 4 vols, 1855–8.

Academica. No 1, May 1858. Ed R. P. O'Hara.

The lion university magazine. Nos 1–3, May–Oct 1858. Ed H. R. Haweis.

The bear university magazine. No 1, Oct 1858. By G. O. Trevelyan.

The Cambridge terminal magazine. Nos 1–3, Dec 1858–April 1859.

The light blue. Vol 1, no 1–vol 4, 1866–71. Ed J. C. Ross, C. Greene, E. S. Shuckburgh, R. K. Miller.

Momus: a semi-occasional university periodical. Nos 1–3, 1866–9. Ed E. H. Palmer, G. A. Critchett, W. H. Pollock.

The Cambridge undergraduates' journal. No 1, 14 Oct 1868–6 Nov 1874. Incorporated in Oxford and Cambridge undergraduates' journal.

The Cambridge University gazette. Nos 1–33, 28 Oct 1868–15 Dec 1869.

The Cambridge University reporter. No 1, 19 Oct 1870 onwards.

The Moslem in Cambridge. Nos 1–3, Nov 1870–April 1871. Ed G. S. Davies.

The lantern of the Cam. Nos 1–4, 1871.

The tatler in Cambridge. Nos 1–80, 26 April 1871–15 June 1872.

The light green. Nos 1–2, May, Nov 1872; rptd 1882, 1890. Ed A. C. Hilton.

The Cantab. Nos 1–2, 1873.

The light blue incorporated with the light green. Nos 1–4, May 1873–May 1874.

Light greens. No 1, July 1875.

The Cambridge tatler. Nos 1–10, 6 March–29 May 1877.

The Cambridge review. No 1, 15 Oct 1879 onwards.

The Cambridge meteor. Nos 1–7, 7–14 June 1882. Ed G. N. Bankes, J. A. Fabb, J. K. Stephen.

Ye true blue. Nos 1–2, [1883]. Ed E. M. Maxwell.

The blue 'un. Vol 1, no 1, 31 May 1884.

The May bee. Nos 1–7, 4–11 June 1884.

The Cambridge University magazine. Nos 1–13, 6 May–7 Dec 1886. Ed J. J. Withers.

The reflector. Vol 1, nos 1–4, 1–22 Jan 1888. Ed J. K. Stephen.

The Cambridge fortnightly. Vol 1, nos 1–5, 24 Jan–13 March 1888. Ed N. Wedd and Roger Fry.

The gadfly. No 1, 15 Nov 1888. By W. M. Guthrie and R. B. Ross.

The Granta. No 1, 18 Jan 1889 onwards. In term time. Suspended from June 1914 to May 1919 and from June 1939 to March 1946. Ed R. C. Lehmann 1889–95, C. F. G. Masterman 1898.

The wasp. Nos 1–4, 12–16 June 1891.

The Cambridge observer. Nos 1–21, 3 May 1892–7 March 1893. Ed S. Makower.

The Cambridge A.B.C. Nos 1–4, 8–12 June 1892. Ed R. Austen Leigh and H. Warre Cornish.

The 'K.P.' illustrated. No 1, 1 Feb 1893–4(?)

The Cantab. Jan 1898–Dec 1899.

The bubble. No 0, 10 June 1898.

The Cambridge gazette. No 1, 15 Oct 1898–6 Oct 1900.

The Cambridge magazine. Nos 1–15, 27 April–30 Nov 1899.

The snarl. Nos 1–2, 31 Oct, 14 Nov 1899.

Alma mater. Nos 1–5, 1900.

College magazines

St John's
The eagle. Lent term 1858 onwards.
Christ's
Fleur-de-lys. Nos 10–11, 20 May, 7 June 1871.
The Christ's College magazine. No 1, Easter term 1886 onwards. Ed J. R. Seeley.
Girton
The Girton review. No 1, 1882 onwards.
Jesus
The chanticleer. No 1–21, Oct 1885–92. Continued as Chanticlere no 22, 1892 onwards.
The rag. 6 nos 1896.
Corpus Christi
The benedict. Nos 1–59, 1898–1928.
Trinity
The trident. Nos 1–6 (7 nos), June 1889–Nov 1892.
Emmanuel
Emmanuel College magazine. Nos 1–31, May 1889–1938.
Trinity Hall
The silver crescent. Nos 1–48, Nov 1890–1907.
The brass halo. Nos 1–3, 1893–4. Ed J. W. Murison.
Gonville and Caius
The Caian. 1891 onwards.
Pembroke
The Pem. Nos 1–13, March 1893–97. New series, no 1, March 1897 onwards.
Peterhouse
The Peterhouse magazine. No 1, March 1893.
The sex. 1897 onwards. Organ of the Peterhouse sexcentenary club.
King's
Basileona. No 1, June 1900–March 1903. Continued as Basileon, 1907–14, 1919–25, 1928–9, 1931, 1934–5, 1937, 1940 onwards.

London

The London University magazine. Vols 1–2, 1829–30.
The London University chronicle. No 1, 26 April 1830–? Ed F. Lucas.
The marauder. 1830.
The London University inquirer. 1833.
The adventurer or London University magazine. 1833.
The London University magazine. Nos 1–3, 1842.
The King's College magazine, conducted by the students of King's College, London. 1842.
The London University College magazine. Vol 1, 1849.
The King's College literary and scientific magazine. 1849–50. Continued as King's College magazine, 1850–1.
The London University magazine. Vols 1–3, 1856–9. New series, nos 1–5, 1859.
The London student. Vol 1, nos 1–5, April–Oct 1868. Ed J. R. Seeley.
The London students' gazette: a monthly chronicle of student opinion and student news. Nos 1–8, 1872.
The King's College magazine. Vols 1–4, 1877–81.
The University College London gazette. Vol 1, nos 1–12, Oct 1886–Nov 1887(?)–[1889?] Ed Henry Morley.
The privateer. Nos 1–11, 1892–3. Ed E. V. Lucas.
The University College gazette. No 1, 30 Nov 1895–1904. Continued as UCL Union magazine. 1904–19. Continued as University College magazine, 1919 onwards.
The King's College magazine (ladies' dept). Nos 1–52. Michaelmas term, 1896–1914.

Oxford

The Oxford review: or literary censor. Vols 1–3, no 3, 1807–8.
The farrago: or the lucubrations of Councillor Bickerton Esquire. Nos 1–2, 1816.
Il vagabondo: a terminal miscellany. Nos 1–8, 1816.
The Oxonian. Nos 1–3, 1817.
The undergraduate. Nos 1–6, 1819.
The Oxford miscellany. Nos 1–2, [1820].
The Oxford quarterly magazine. Vol 1, 1825.
The Oxford literary gazette, and classical and foreign journal. Nos 1–4, 11 March–20 May 1829.
The Oxford University magazine. Vol 1, 1834.
The Oxford magazine. No 1, 1845.
The Oxonian. No 1, 1847.
Oxford essays, contributed by members of the University. 1855–8.
The Oxford and Cambridge magazine, conducted by members of the two universities. Nos 1–12, 1856. Ed William Fulford.
Undergraduate papers. Nos 1–2 (4 pts), 3 Dec 1857–April 1858. Ed John Nichol.
The Oxford critic and university magazine (contributed chiefly by undergraduate members of the University). Nos 1–3, [1857].
Great Tom: a university magazine. Nos 1–4, [1861]. Ed Bertram Montgomery.
College rhymes, contributed by members of the universities of Oxford and Cambridge. Vols 1–14, 1861–74. Ed F. E. Weatherley.
The Milton magazine. Nos 1–2, 1866.
The Oxford undergraduates journal. No 1, 31 Jan 1866–Oct 1875. Continued as Oxford and Cambridge undergraduates journal, 21 Oct 1875–30 Nov 1882. Continued as Oxford review, 7 Dec 1882–14 June 1883. Continued as Oxford and Cambridge undergraduates journal, 18 Oct 1883–4 Dec 1884. Continued as Oxford review, Jan 1885–19 June 1914.
Dark blue: an Oxford University magazine. No 1, [1867].
The Oxford spectator. 1868. By R. S. Copleston, E. Nolan, T. H. Ward.
The Radcliffe. Nos 1–10, 27 Feb–9 June 1869.
The Oxford University magazine and review. Nos 1–2, 1869.
The Oxford University gazette. No 1, 28 Jan 1870 onwards.
The dark blue. Vols 1–4, 1871–3. Ed J. C. Freund.
The Shotover papers: or echoes from Oxford. Vol 1, 1874–5. Ed W. E. W. Morrison, F. G. Stokes, F. S. Pulling.
The public schools magazine: conducted by the university men. Vol 1, nos 1–4, 1875.
Ye roonde table: an Oxford and Cambridge magazine. Vol 1, nos 1–6, 2 Feb–June 1878.
Waifs and strays: a terminal magazine of Oxford poetry. Nos 1–10, [1879–82].
The Oxford magazine: a weekly newspaper and review. 1883 onwards. Ed R. Lodge, P. E. Matheson, C. Cannan, J. E. King, A. D. Godley, D. G. Hogarth, R. Carter, J. Fischer Williams, A. J. Carlyle, C. G. Robertson.
The rattle. Vol 1, no 1–vol 3, no 6, 25 Feb 1886–30 May 1888.
The undergraduate. Nos 1–21, 24 Jan–6 Dec 1888.
The new rattle. Vol 1, no 1, 1890–3. Annual.
The Isis. No 1, 27 April 1892 onwards. Ed T. M. Pigott, W. K. Stride.
The spirit lamp. Vol 1, no 1–vol 4, no 2 (15 nos), 6 May 1892–6 June 1893. Ed Sandys Mason, Lord Alfred Douglas.
Fritillary: magazine of the Oxford women's colleges. Nos 1–37, 1893–June 1931.
The ephemeral. Nos 1–6, 1893. Ed Lord Alfred Douglas.
The chameleon. Vol 1, no 1, Dec 1894. Ed J. F. Bloxam.
The octopus. Nos 1–6, May 1895. Ed Comyns Carr.
The procter. No 1, 5 March 1896.
The bulldog. Vol 1, no 1, 28 Feb 1896.
The JCR. Vol 1, no 1, Feb 1897–June 1899.
Ye tea-potte. Vol 1, no 1, 1898. Ed A. F. R. Abbott and L. L. Morell.
The bump. Vol 1, no 1, 21 May 1898.
The X: an unknown quantity. Vol 1, no 1, 10 Nov 1898–6 Dec 1900.
The quad. Nos 1–4, 1900–1. Ed C. Scott Moncrieff.

College magazines

Jesus
The druid. Nos 1–6, 1862–3.
Corpus Christi
The Pelican record. 1891 onwards.
Wadham
The Wadham College gazette. 1897 onwards. Ed F. E. Smith et al.

Edinburgh

The new lapsus linguae: or the college tattler, session 1824–5, edited by Criticus, student of medicine and Justus, student of law. 1825.
The cheiliad, or university coterie: being violent ebullitions of graphomaniacs affected by cacoethes scribendi and famae sacra fames. Nos 1–16, 1827.
The university squib. Nos 1–2, 1833.
The Edinburgh University journal and critical review. Nos 1–12, 1833. Ed A. Miller.
The university maga. Vols 1–2, Jan–March 1835, 1 Dec 1837–23 March 1838.
The Edinburgh University souvenir. 1835.
The Edinburgh University magazine. Nos 1–3, 1839.
Edinburgh essays by members of the University. 1857.
The Edinburgh University magazine. Nos 1–3, 1866.
The Edinburgh University magazine. Vol 1, nos 1–4, Jan–April 1871. Ed R. L. Stevenson, J. W. Ferrier et al.
The student: a casual. 1887. Continued as Student, 1887.

Aberdeen

The Aberdeen University magazine. Vol 1, Jan–Aug 1836.
The King's College miscellany. Nos 1–8, 1846–7.
The Aberdeen Universities' magazine. Dec 1849–April 1850.
The academic. Nos 1–7. New series, nos 1–8, 1877–8.
Alma mater. 28 Nov 1883 onwards.

St Andrews

St Andrews University magazine. No 1, Cupar 1863.
The tomahawk. Nos 1–4, Cupar [1874].
St Andrews University news sheet. 1886–9.
College echoes. 1889.

Glasgow

The collegian, conducted by students in the University of Glasgow. 13 Dec 1826–7 March 1827.
The college album: a selection of original pieces edited by students in the University of Glasgow. 1828, 1830, 1832. Continued as Glasgow University album for 1836 (1838–40, 1843, 1845, 1847, 1851, 1854, 1858, 1859), edited by the students. Continued as Old college, being the Glasgow University album for MDCCCLXIX, edited by students. 1869. Continued as New college: Glasgow University album. 1874.
The Glasgow University magazine. 1889 onwards.

Dublin

The Dublin University review and quarterly magazine. Vol 1, pts 1–3, Jan–June 1833.
The Dublin University magazine. 90 vols Jan 1833–Dec 1877. Continued as University magazine: a literary and philosophical review. 5 vols Jan 1878–June 1882. Monthly; two further quarterly nos pbd in Sept and Dec 1882. *See col 1845, above*, under Monthly Magazines.
The Catholic University gazette. Vol 1, 1854–6.
Kottabos: a college miscellany. Vols 1–3, 1868–81. 2nd series, 1881–91. 3rd series, 1895. Ed R. Y. Tyrrell 1868–81, J. B. Bury 1888–95.
Hermathena: a series of papers on literature, science and philosophy by members of Trinity College, Dublin. 1873 onwards. Index of contributors to Hermathena 1873–1943, by J. G. Smyly [1944]. Ed J. K. Ingram, B. Williamson, J. P. Mahaffy, R. Y. Tyrrell. Annual; postgraduate.
The Dublin University review. 1885–7.

Eton

The microcosm: a periodical by Gregory Griffin. 2 vols 6 Nov 1786–30 July 1787. Various edns to 1827. By R. Smith, George Canning, J. H. Frere et al.
The miniature: a periodical paper, by Solomon Grildrig of the college of Eton. Nos 1–34, 23 April 1804–1 April 1805. By T. Rennell, H. G. Knight, G. Canning the younger et al.
The college magazine. 1819. Ed W. B[lunt].
The salt-bearer: a periodical work by an Etonian [T. W. Helps]. May 1820–April 1821.
The Etonian. 2 vols Oct 1820–Aug 1821. Ed W. Blunt and W. M. Praed.
The Eton miscellany, by Bartholomew Bouverie. 2 vols 1827. By W. E. Gladstone, G. A. Selwyn, P. A. Pickering et al.
The oppidan. Nos 1–2, Oct 1828.
The Eton College magazine. Nos 1–8, June–Nov 1832. By J. Wickens, G. W. Lyttelton, C. G. Wynne et al.
The kaleidoscope. Nos 1–9, 1833. By A. J. Ellis, T. B. Charlton, G. W. Lyttelton, F. H. Doyle et al.
The Eton bureau. Nos 1–7, 1842. By C. W. Johnson, W. Johnson (later Cory), J. D. Coleridge et al.
The Eton School magazine. Vol 1, nos 1–6, 1847–8.
Porticus etonensis. Nos 1–2, 1859. Ed M. Lubbock and M. Hankey.
The Eton observer: a miscellany conducted entirely by present Etonians. Vol 1, no 1–vol 2, no 10, 21 Feb–21 Sept 1860. By V. S. Coles, V. C. Amcotts, W. Pollock et al.
The phoenix. Nos 1–5, [1860–1]. Ed V. C. Amcotts.
Etonensia. Nos 1–2, 1862. By V. S. Coles, V. C. Amcotts and Lord Francis Hervey.
The Eton College chronicle. 14 May 1863 onwards.
The Eton scrap book. Nos 1–7, 1865. Ed H. Maxwell Lyte and E. H. Primrose.
The adventurer. Nos 1–29, 1867–72. By R. Shute, C. W. Bell, A. A. Tilley, E. C. Selwyn, G. C. Macaulay et al.
The Eton review. Nos 1–6, 1867–8.
The phœnix. No 1, 1874.
The salt-hill papers: or vindiciae Etonenses by two Etonians. 4 June 1875. By J. K. Stephen and H. E. Ryle.
The sugar-loaf papers, by three Etonians. 1875. By J. K. Stephen, H. E. Ryle and M. T. Tatham.
The Etonian. Nos 1–30, 19 May 1875–2 Aug 1876. By G. N. Curzon, S. Sandbach, H. St C. Fielden, J. K. Stephen et al.
The Eton rambler. Nos 1–6, 1880. By A. C. Benson and S. Leathes.
The Mosleian. Nos 1–2, 1882. Continued as Vanitas, no 3, 1882. By A. W. M. Bosville.
The rambler. No 1, 27 Jan 1883. By A. W. M. Bosville.
The Etonian. Nos 1–29, 1883–5. By E. D. Hildyard, W. J. Seton, R. C. Devereux et al.
The Eton review. Nos 1–10, 1886. By H. C. Dawkins and J. H. Hope.
The Eton fortnightly. Nos 1–10, 1887. By A. Clutton Brock, J. A. C. Tilley, A. B. Lowry et al.
The Eton observer. Nos 1–2, 1887. By I. Z. Malcolm and M. M. MacNaughton.
The present Etonian. Nos 1–15, 1888. Ed J. R. L. Rankin.
The Eton review. Nos 1–10, 1889. Ed Lord Elmley (Earl Beauchamp).
The parachute. Nos 1–3, 22 June–30 July, 1889. By R. S. Bosanquet, F. M. S. Parker and Lord Warkworth.
The rocket. No 1, 31 March 1890. Ed J. S. Arkwright.

The student's humour. No 1, 4 June 1891. By V. R. Hoare, C. C. Bigham, J. S. Arkwright, H. T. G. Watkins et al.
The mayfly. Nos 1–3, 16 May–24 June 1891. By A. B. Ramsay and H. T. G. Watkins.
The Eton idler. Nos 1–7, 22 May–1 Aug 1893. By H. E. S. Fremantle and C. W. E. Cotton.
The Eton spectator. Nos 1–3, 1893. Ed A. S. Ward.
The new Etonian. Nos 1–4, 1895. Ed A. S. Ward.
The amphibian. Nos 1–9, 1898–9.
The bantling. Nos 1–9, 1900.
The gnat. Nos 1–3, 1900.

Harrow

The Harrovian. Nos 1–6, 1828. A collection of poems, essays and trns.
The triumvirate. Vols 1–2, [1860–1].
The Harrovian. Vols 1–3, 16 Oct 1869–6 July 1872.
The Harrovian. Nos 1–26, 21 Nov 1878–30 July 1881.
Harrow notes: a school newspaper, edited by an old Harrovian. Vols 1–5, 1883–87. Continued as Harrovian, vol 1, 2 Feb 1888 onwards.

Rugby

The Rugby magazine. 2 vols 1835–7. Ed A. H. Clough.
The Rugbaean. Vol 1, 1840.
The Rugby miscellany. Nos 1–10, 1846.
The new Rugbeian. Vols 1–3, 1858–Dec 1861.
The meteor. Vol 1, 1867(?) onwards.
The leaflet, edited by members of Rugby School. Nos 1–6; new series nos 1–26, 1883–87.
The sibyl. Nos 1–24, 1890–5.

Rossall

Rossall news. Nos 1–14, 1850.
Rossall herald. Nos 1–6, 1850.
The Rossallian. Vol 1, 1870 onwards.

Marlborough

The Marlburian. 20 Sept 1865 onwards.

Winchester

The Wykehamist. Oct 1866 onwards.
The Winchester review. Nos 1–2, 1880.

Wellington

Wellingtonia. Vol 1, nos 1–6, 1866–7.
The Wellingtonian. 1868 onwards.

Repton

The Reptonian. May 1866 onwards.

Clifton

The Cliftonian. Dec 1867 onwards.

Haileybury

The Haileyburyian. March 1868 onwards.

Cheltenham

The Cheltenham College magazine. Vols 1–4, 1869–74. Continued as Cheltonian, 1874 onwards.

Malvern

The Malvernian. Nov 1869 onwards.

Shrewsbury

The Salopian. 1876 onwards.

Working Men's College

The Working Men's College magazine. Nos 1–37, Jan 1859–Jan 1862. Ed R. B. Litchfield.
The Working Men's College journal: the monthly organ of the Working Men's College. Vols 1–22, Feb 1890–1932. Continued as Journal, vol 23, 1933 onwards.

School and University Journalism: Accounts and Studies

Marillier, H. C. University magazines and their makers. 1899 (priv ptd), 1902 (enlarged).
Russell, G. W. E. Collections and recollections. 1903 (new edn).

Cambridge

Gray, G. J. Cambridge University periodicals. Cambridge Rev 10 March 1886.
Bowes, R. A catalogue of the books printed at, or relating to the University, town and county of Cambridge 1521–1893. Cambridge 1894. Index by E. J. Worman, 1894.
Bartholomew, A. T. Catalogue of books and papers bequeathed to the University of Cambridge by J. W. Clark. Cambridge 1912.
The Cambridge tart: epigrammatic and satiric poetical effusions etc. Dainty morsels served up by Cantabs on various occasions, dedicated to members of the University of Cambridge by Socius. 1823.
Calverly, C. S. Verses and translations. 1862.
— The literary remains with a memoir by W. J. Sendall. 1885.
[Bankes, G. N.] Cambridge trifles. 1881.
Seaman, O. Paulopostprandials. 1883.
— Horace at Cambridge. 1894.
Trevelyan, G. The ladies in Parliament and other pieces. 1888; rev in Interludes in prose and verse, 1905.
In cap and gown. Ed C. Whibley 1889, 1898 (3rd edn with new preface).
S[tephen], J. K. Quo musa tendis? 1891.
— Lapsus calami. 1891, 1896 (enlarged).
Pain, B. In a Canadian canoe. 1891, 1898.
— Playthings and parodies. 1892, 1896.
Lehmann, R. C. In Cambridge courts. 1891, 1897.
Kellett, E. E. Book of Cambridge verse. 1911.
Nicholson, R. A. The don and the dervish: a book of verse, original and translated. 1911.
Cambridge University Magazine
 Characters of freshmen and other papers, reprinted from the Cambridge University magazine. 1848.
Cambridge Review
 The book of the Cambridge review 1879–97. 1898.
Light Green
 Hilton, A. C. Works. Ed R. P. Edgecumbe 1904.
Granta
 Rice, F. A. The Granta and its contributors 1889–1914. 1924.
 Philip, J., J. Simpson and N. Snowman, The best of Granta 1889–1966, 1967.

London

Hawgood, J. A. University College and its magazine. Univ College Mag June 1927.
Bellot, H. H. University College London 1826–1926. 1929.
University College London Gazette
 Solly, H. S. The life of Henry Morley. 1898.
Sleuth
 'Sleuth'. King's College magazine. N & Q 10 March 1945.

Oxford

G[odley], A. D. Verses to order. 1892, 1904 (enlarged).
— The casual ward: academic and other oddments. 1912.
Seccombe, T. and H. S. Scott. In praise of Oxford: an anthology in prose and verse. Vol 2, 1912.
Symon, J. D. The earlier Oxford magazines. Oxford & Cambridge Rev 13 1911.
Oxford Magazine
 Echoes from the Oxford magazine: being reprints of seven years. 1890.
 More echoes from the Oxford Magazine: being a second series of reprints of seven years. 1896.

Oxonian 1817
Fair-play: or no 1 of the Oxonian exposed by a member of the University of Oxford. 1817.

Isis
Pigott, T. M. Two on a tour and other papers from the Isis. 1895.

Edinburgh

Edinburgh University Magazine
The new Amphion: being the book of the Edinburgh University Union Fancy Fair. 1886.

Student
Famous Edinburgh students. 1914. Mainly rptd from Student.

Aberdeen

Smith, R. H. A village propaganda. 1889.

Donaldson, J. The Aberdeen Universities' magazine 1849–50. Aberdeen Univ Rev 1 1913.

Leask, W. K. The story of the University magazine 1836–1914. Aberdeen Univ Rev 4 1914.

St Andrews

Murray, R. F. The scarlet gown. 1891, 1932 (with memoir by Andrew Lang).

Dublin

Kottabos
Echoes from Kottabos. Ed R. Y. Tyrrell and E. Sullivan 1906.

Eton

Harcourt, L. V. An Eton bibliography. 1902.

Rugby

C., G.A.F.M. Matthew Arnold and the Rugby Magazine 1837. N & Q 28 March 1942. Evidence that Arnold did not contribute.

F. ANNUALS AND YEAR BOOKS

(1) LITERARY ANNUALS

The spirit of the public journals: being an impartial selection of the most exquisite essays and jeux d'esprit etc. 29 vols 1798 (for 1797) to 1823 (for 1822). New series, 3 vols 1824 (for 1823) to 1826 (for 1825).

The annual anthology. 2 vols 1799–1800. Bristol. Ed Robert Southey.

The poetical register, and repository of fugitive poetry for 1801, 1802, 1803, 1804, 1805, 1806–7, 1808–9, 1810–11. 8 vols 1802–14.

Flowers of literature for 1801 & 1802: or characteristic sketches of human nature and modern manners. 1803, 1804, 1805, 1806, 1807. 6 vols 1803–8. Ed F. Prevost and Francis W. Blagdon, vols 1–2. Francis W. Blagdon, vols 3–6.

The annual review: and history of literature for 1802, 1803, 1804, 1805, 1806, 1807, 1808. 7 vols 1803–9.

Forget me not: a Christmas and New Year's present. 25 vols 1823–47. Prop Rudolph Ackermann. Ed Frederic Shoberl.

Friendship's offering. 21 vols 1824–44. In 1833 absorbed Winter's wreath and continued as Friendship's offering and winter's wreath: a Christmas and New Year's present, until 1843. Continued as Friendship's offering of sentiment and mirth, 1844. Ed T. K. Hervey 1826, T. K. Hervey and B. E. Pote 1827, Charles Knight 1828, Thomas Pringle 1829–33, H. Inglis 1834; W. H. Harrison 1835, Leitch Ritchie 1842–4.

The Graces: or literary souvenir for 1824. 1824.

Blossoms at Christmas and first flowers of the New Year. 2 vols 1825–6.

Homage aux dames. 1825.

The literary souvenir: or cabinet of poetry and romance. 10 vols 1825–34. Continued as Literary souvenir and cabinet of modern art. New series, 1 vol 1835. Continued as Cabinet of modern art and literary souvenir, 2nd-3rd series, 1836, 1837. Prop Alaric A. Watts 1826–37. Ed Alaric A. Watts.

Janus: or the Edinburgh literary almanac. 1826. Ed John Wilson and J. G. Lockhart.

The ladies' pocket magazine. 15 vols 1826–39.

The amulet: or Christian and literary remembrancer. 11 vols 1826–36. Ed Samuel Carter Hall.

The pledge of friendship. 3 vols 1826–8.

A wreath from the Emerald Isle: a New Year's gift. Dublin 1826. Ed P. D. Hardy.

The every day book forming a complete history of the year, months and seasons. 2 vols 1826–7. Each vol issued in weekly pts during the preceding year. Ed William Hone.

The table book. 1828. Issued in weekly pts for the preceding year. Successor to the Every day book. Ed William Hone.

The keepsake. 30 vols 1828–57. Ed W. H. Ainsworth 1828, F. M. Reynolds 1829–35, Caroline Norton 1836, Lady E. Stuart Wortley 1837, F. M. Reynolds 1839, Lady E. Stuart Wortley 1840, Countess of Blessington 1841–50, Marguerite Power 1851–7.

The winter's wreath: or a collection of original contributions in prose and verse. 5 vols 1828–32. Absorbed in Friendship's offering. Ed W. B. Chorley.

The bijou: or annual of literature and the arts. 3 vols 1828–30. Ed W. Fraser.

Affection's offering: designed as a Christmas and New Year's gift. 4 vols 1829–[32].

The talisman. 2 vols 1829–31. Ed Elam Bliss, Zillah Watts.

The treasure of knowledge, literature, instruction and amusement. 2 vols 1829–30.

The anniversary: or poetry and prose for 1829. Ed Allan Cunningham.

Le petit bijou. 1829. Ed H. D'Emden.

The gem: a literary annual. 4 vols 1829–32. Ed Thomas Hood 1829.

Affection's gift. 5 vols 1830–3, 1844.

The anthology: an annual reward book for Midsummer and Christmas. 1830. Ed J. D. Parry.

The comic annual. 11 vols 1830–9, 1842. Ed Thomas Hood.

The landscape annual. 5 vols 1830–4. Continued as Jennings' landscape annual: or tourist in Spain. 3 vols 1835–7. Continued as Jennings' landscape annual, 1838. Continued as Jennings' landscape annual: or tourist in Portugal, 1839. Ed T. Roscoe 1835–8, W. H. Harrison 1839.

Mr Mathew's comic annual for 1830, with humorous cuts and other embellishments; as published (1830; 'performed', 1831–3) by him at the Adelphi Theatre. 4 vols 1830–3.

The zoological keepsake: or zoology, and the garden and museum of the Zoological Society. 1830.

The sacred offering: a poetical annual. 8 vols Liverpool 1831–8. Ed M. A. Jevons.

The iris: a literary and religious offering. 2 vols 1831(?)–2(?). Ed Thomas Dale.

The comic offering: or ladies' melange of literary mirth. 5 vols 1831–5. Ed Louisa H. Sheridan.

The cabinet annual register, and historical, political, biographical and miscellaneous chronicle. 3 vols 1831–3.

The new comic annual. 1831. Dedication and preface refer to it as Falstaff's annual.
The cameo. 1831. Largely rptd from Bijou, above. Ed William Pickering.
The remembrance. 13(?) vols 1831–[43]. Only vols for 1831, 1834, 1838 and 1843 have been noted. Ed T. Roscoe 1831 and 1834, T. Albin 1843.
The talisman. 1831. Largely rptd from Iris, above. Ed Zillah Watts.
Fisher's drawing-room scrap book. 21 vols 1832–52. Ed L. E. Landon 1832–9, L. E. Landon and Mary Howitt 1840, Mary Howitt 1841, Sarah Ellis 1844–5, Caroline Norton 1846–9, Charles Mackay 1850–2.
Heath's picturesque annual. 14 vols 1832–45. The vols for 1844 and 1845 were also issued as Cattermole's historical annual. Ed Leitch Ritchie 1832–9, Catherine Gore 1840, T. Roscoe 1841, Jules Janin and Catherine Gore 1842, Catherine Gore 1843, R. Cattermole 1844–5.
The amethyst: or Christian's annual. 3 vols 1832–4. Ed Richard Huie and R. K. Greville.
The musical gem. 3(?) vols 1832[–45]. Ed N. Mori and W. Ball.
The bouquet: a collection of tales, essays and poems, original and select. 3 vols 1832[–4].
The pocket album and literary scrap book. 1832.
The botanic annual. 1832. Ed Robert Mudie.
The year book of daily recreation and information. 1832. Ed William Hone.
The Continental annual and romantic cabinet. 1832. Ed W. Kennedy.
The Yorkshire literary annual. Leeds. 1832. Ed C. F. Edgar.
The Easter gift. 1832, [1836], 1838. Ed L. E. Landon.
The Easter offering. 1832. Ed Joseph Booker.
Heath's book of beauty. 15 vols 1833[–47]. Continued as Book of beauty; or regal gallery, 2 vols 1848[–9]. Ed L. E. Landon 1833, Countess of Blessington 1834–47.
The Christian keepsake and missionary annual. 8 vols 1833[–40]. Ed W. Ellis.
Turner's annual tour. 3 vols 1833[–5]. Written by Leitch Ritchie; illustr J. M. W. Turner.
The landscape album. [2 vols 1832–4.] Written by Thomas Moule; illustr W. Westall. Ed Charles Tilt.
The aurora borealis. Newcastle-on-Tyne. 1833. Ed William Howitt.
The oriental annual, or scenes in India: containing a series of tales, legends and historical romances. 3 vols 1834–6. New series 2 vols 1837–8; 1839–40. Ed Hobart Caunter 1834–6, T. Bacon 1839–40; illustr W. Daniell 1834–6, and by engravings by W. and E. Finden after T. Bacon and Meadows Taylor 1839–40.
The album wreath and bijou littéraire. 1834. Ed J. Francis.
The white rose of York: a midsummer annual. 1834. Ed G. Hogarth.
The Continental landscape annual. 3 vols 1835, [1837–8]. Ed F. Fergusson.
Gems of beauty. 5 vols 1936[–40]. Ed Countess of Blessington; illustr E. Corbould.
The squib annual of poetry, politics and personalities. 1836.
Affection's keepsake: original poetry. 11(?) vols 1836–46. Ed T. Albin.
The Scottish annual. Glasgow. 1836. Ed W. Weir.
The sportsman's annual: 1st series, Dogs. 1836. Illustr E. Landseer, A. Cooper and C. Hancock.
Flowers of loveliness. 1836–41(?) Ed Countess of Blessington et al.
Findens' tableaux. 5 vols 1837–41. Ed Mrs S. C. Hall 1837, Mary Russell Mitford 1838–41; illustr with engravings by W. and E. Finden after W. Perring etc.
The pictorial album: or cabinet of painting. 1837. Illustr-George Baxter.
The scenic annual for 1838. Ed Thomas Campbell.
Portraits of the children of the nobility. 3 vols 1838[–41]. Ed Louisa Fairlie. Parodied in Children of the mobility, 1841; illustr John Leech.
The hunter's annual. 2 vols 1838[–9]. Ed A. H. Baily.
The Christmas library: birds and flowers, and other country things. 1838. Ed Mary Howitt.
The amaranth: a miscellany of original prose and verse. 1839. Ed T. K. Hervey.
The annual of British landscape scenery. 1839. Ed L. A. Twamley; illustr with engravings after Fielding, Cox, Warren and Radclyffe.
Album wreath of music and literature. 1840.
The Lilliputian picturesque annual. 1841. Ed B. Crecerelle.
The Protestant annual. 1841. Ed Charlotte Elizabeth Tonna (formerly Phelan).
The Renfrewshire annual. 2 vols Paisley 1841–2. Ed Mrs Maxwell.
A love gift. 4 vols 1842[–5].
The Christian souvenir. 1842. Ed C. B. Tayler.
The comic album: a book for every table. 2 vols 1843–4.
The holly branch. 1843. Ed E. Davis.
The gem of loveliness. 1843. Ed H. I. and W. Stevens.
The Catholic keepsake. 1843.
The Victoria annual. 1844.
The ball room annual. 1844.
George Cruikshank's table book. 1845. Ed Gilbert à Beckett.
The comic miscellany. 1845. Ed J. Poole.
The coronal. 1846. Ed E. Lacey.
The golden annual. 1848.
The annual miscellany. 1848.
Portraits of the female aristocracy. Vols 1–2, 1849.
The Christian keepsake. 1850. Ed Mrs Ellet.
The Cheltenham literary annual. 1857. Ed Mrs H. Chetwynd.
The Scottish annual. Glasgow 1859. Ed C. R. Brown.

Many annuals were issued from 1860 onwards which form an integral part of many of the weekly and monthly periodicals listed in the preceding sections. These were either extra numbers or enlarged forms of the June and Dec issues.

Accounts and Studies of Literary Annuals

Tales of adventure and stories of travel [from the annuals] of fifty years ago. 1893.
Tallent-Bateman, C. T. Drawing room annuals. Papers of Manchester Literary Club 1897.
Faxon, F. W. Literary annuals and gift-books. Boston 1912. The bibliography of English annuals draws on the work of Tallent-Bateman; it contains many items not listed above.
A cabinet of gems: short stories from the English annuals. Ed B. A. Booth, Berkeley 1938.
Weitenkampf, F. The keepsake in 19th century art. Boston Public Lib Quart 4 1952.
Bose, A. The verse of the English annuals. RES new ser 4 1953.
Renier, A. Friendship's offering: an essay on the annuals and gift books of the 19th century. 1964.
Boyle, A. An index to the annuals 1820–50. Vol 1: Authors. Worcester 1967.

A partial list of the French annuals of the same period, many of which were trns from the English and vice versa, will be found in J. Brivois, Bibliographie des ouvrages illustrés du 19me siècle, Paris 1883; *and* L. Carteret, Le trésor du bibliophile romantique et moderne, 3 vols and index, Paris 1924–7. *The American annuals are listed by Faxon, above, and* R. Thompson, American literary annuals and gift-books 1825–65, New York 1936.
Annual Anthology 1799
Curry, K. The contributors to the Annual anthology. PBSA 42 1948.

Annual Review 1803
Curry, K. Southey's contributions to the Annual review. Bull of Bibl 16 1939.
Table book 1827
Barnett, G. L. Dating Lamb's contributions to the Table book. PMLA 60 1945.

Drawing-room scrap book 1832
The drawing-room scrap book: being a selection edited by the Hon Mrs Norton and Charles Mackay. 4 vols [1853-4].

(2) JUVENILE ANNUALS

The Christmas box: an annual present for children. 1828-9. Continued as Christmas box and annual present for young persons, 1829. Ed T. C. Croker.
The juvenile keepsake. 2 vols 1829-30. Ed T. Roscoe.
The juvenile forget me not. 9 vols 1829-37. Ed Mrs S. C. Hall. Juvenile. Forget-me-not, 1833-7.
Ackermann's juvenile forget me not. 3 vols 1830-2. Absorbed in Juvenile forget-me-not in 1833. Ed Frederic Shoberl.
The New Year's gift and juvenile souvenir. 8 vols 1829-36. Ed Zillah Watts.
The excitement: or a book to induce young people to read. 8 vols Edinburgh [1830-7]. *See* also New excitement 8 vols 1838-[45]. Ed Robert Jamieson.
Marshall's Christmas box: a juvenile annual. 2 vols 1831-2. Ed W. Marshall.
The infant annual. Liverpool 1835. Ed H. M. Marshall.
The New Year's token: or Christmas present. 2 vols 1835 [-6].
The nursery offering: or children's gift. 2 vols Edinburgh 1835-6.
Fisher's juvenile scrapbook. 15 vols 1836-50. Ed Bernard Barton 1836, Bernard Barton and Agnes Strickland 1837-9, Sarah Ellis 1840-8, Jane Strickland 1849, Mrs Milner 1850.
The new juvenile keepsake. 1839. Ed L. E. Landon.
Peter Parley's annual: a Christmas and New Year's present for young people. 1839-89(?) Ed W. Martin.
The recreation: a gift book for young readers. 6 vols Edinburgh 1842[-8].
The child's own annual. 2 vols 1843[-4].
The juvenile missionary keepsake. 1846.
The juvenile offering. 1848.
My own treasury: a gift book for boys and girls. [1850]. Ed Mark Merriwell.
Beeton's annual: a book for the young. 1866. Ed S. O. Beeton and J. G. Wood.
The children's annual. 3 vols 1869[-71].

Numerous juvenile annuals were issued from 1860 onwards as an integral part of juvenile magazines. Thus Boys own annual *and* Girls own annual *are the issues of each paper for the whole year put up in cloth bindings. Other magazines issued an extra number at Christmas which is described as annual, sometimes under a totally different title. Frequently, however, the annuals of this period are enlarged or double numbers of the December issue in an elaborately coloured cover.*

(3) YEAR BOOKS

General

The annual register: or a view of the history, politicks and literature of the year 1758 onwards. In 1790 the stock and copyright were sold: the first was bought by Otridge and the second by Rivington; each party issued a distinct continuation. Rivington's ran from 1791 to 1800, new series 1801 to 1827. General index 1758-80, 1783; 2nd edn 1784; 3rd edn with addns; General index 1781-92, 2 vols 1799. General index 1758-1819, 1826.
The new annual register: or general repository of history, politics and literature for the year 1780-1825. Vols 1-45.
The Asiatic annual register for the year 1799-1811. Vols 1-12. Ed L. D. Campbell 1804-6, E. Samuel 1810-11.
The Edinburgh annual register. 1808-27. Vols 1-19. Ed Robert Southey 1809-15.
The annual chronology and historical record of important and interesting events in 1827, by Tell-Tale Time. 1828.
Arcana of science and art. 6 vols 1828-38. Continued as Year-book of facts in science and art. 29 vols 1839-1880 (for 1879). Ed John Timbs 1839-73, C. W. Vincent 1874-5, J. Mason 1876-9.
The British almanac of the Society for the Diffusion of Useful Knowledge. 1828-1914. Ed Charles Knight.
The companion to the [British] almanack 1828-56. A complete index to the Companion to the almanack, 1828-43, 1843.
The annual historian: a sketch of the chief historical events of the world for the year 1831. 1832. Ed J. Cobbin.
The British annual and epitome of the progress of science for 1837-9. 3 vols Ed R. D. Thomson.
The annual scrap book: a selection of paragraphs which have appeared in the newspapers and periodicals. 1838-41.
The annual mirror for 1845: an historical register. Vol 1. Ed W. Lurcott.
The British year book for the country for 1856. Ed C. MacIntosh and T. L. Kemp.
The photographic news almanac for 1860 with which is included Photographic almanac. 1859(?)-63. Continued as Year-book of photography, 1864-1907/8. Ed G. W. Simpson 1865-1880, H. B. Pritchard 1881-4, T. Bolas 1885-9, T. C. Hepworth 1892-5, E. J. Wall 1897-1900, P. R. Salmon 1901-?
The statesman's year book: a statistical, genealogical and historical account of the states and sovereigns of the civilised world for 1864 onwards. Ed Frederick Martin 1864-1882, J. S. Keltie 1883-? (assisted by I. Renwick from 1895).
Whitaker's almanack for 1869. [1868] onwards. Ed Joseph Whitaker 1868-95.
The Era almanack. Annual register of dramatick and musical events 1868-1919. Ed Edward Ledger 1868-1905.
The year book of women's work. 6 vols 1875-1880. Continued as Englishwoman's year book for 1881. 35 vols 1881-1916. Ed L. M. Hubbard 1875-98, E. Jones 1899-1916.
The year's art. 1880 onwards. Ed Marcus Huish.
The annual summary: a complete chronicle of events at home and abroad. 2 vols 1875-6 (also for 1876-7). Ed J. Mason.
The constitutional year book and politician's guide. 1885-1939.

Biographical

The annual necrology for 1797-8; including also various articles of neglected biography. 1800.
Public characters of 1798-1810. 10 vols. Vol 1 rptd 4 times.
The annual biography and obituary for the year 1817-37. Vols 1-21.
The annual biography: being lives of eminent or remarkable persons who have died within the year 1842. 1843. Ed C. R. Dod.

Who's who in 1849. 1849 onwards. Ed H. R. Addison 1849, C. H. Oakes 1851–64, W. J. Lawson 1865–9, Douglas Sladen 1897–9.

Men of the time. 1852, 1853, 1856, 1857, 1862, 1865, 1868, 1872, 1875, 1879, 1884, 1887. Continued as Men and women of the time, 1891, 1895, 1899 (15th edn). Ed A. A. Watts 1856, E. Walford 1862, G. H. Townsend 1868, Thompson Cooper 1872–84, T. H. Ward 1887, G. W. Moon 1891, V. G. Plarr 1895–9.

The biographical magazine. Vols 1–7, 1852–7. Monthly. Ed J. P. Edwards.

The military obituary for 1853, 1854. Continued as The annual military obituary for 1855, 1856. 4 vols. Ed H. S. Smith.

The annual Royal Naval obituary for 1855.

Hardwicke's annual biography for 1856–7: containing memoirs of celebrated characters who have died during the year 1855–6. 2 vols. Ed E. Walford.

Celebrities of the day, British and foreign: a monthly repertoire of contemporary biography. Vols 1–3, 1881–2. Monthly. Ed S. E. Thomas.

The Peerage

The present peerage of the United Kingdom. 25 vols 1808–32. Pbd by Stockdale.

The royal blue book: or fashionable directory, and canvassing guide for 1822. 1822–1940. In 1900 Royal blue book, court and parliamentary guide.

A general and heraldic dictionary of the peerage and baronetage of the United Kingdom. Triennial. 1826 onwards. Continued also as Burke's genealogical and heraldic dictionary etc. Ed John Burke 1826–46, John B. Burke 1840–?

The annual peerage of the British Empire. 4 vols 1827–9. Prop and ed Anne, Eliza and Maria Innes.

The peerage of the British Empire: to which is added the baronetage of the three kingdoms. Vols 1–27, 1832–58. Continued as Peerage and baronetage of the British Empire, vols 28–81, 1859–1912. Edmund Lodge lent his name; in reality prop and ed Anne, Eliza and Maria Innes to death of survivor, Maria, in 1862.

Webster's royal red book: or court and fashionable register. 1847–1939. From May 1925 incorporated Boyle's court guide and fashionable register.

Debrett's illustrated baronetage and knightage of the United Kingdom of Great Britain and Ireland. 1865 onwards. Ed R. H. Mair.

Debrett's illustrated peerage of the United Kingdom of Great Britain and Ireland. 1865 onwards. For the years 1866, 1867 and 1868 this and the previous entry were issued in one volume. Ed R. H. Mair.

The upper ten thousand: an alphabetical list of all members of noble families. 3 vols 1875–7. Continued as Kelly's handbook of the upper ten thousand for 1878–9, 2 vols. Continued as Kelly's handbook to the titled, landed and official classes. 1880 onwards. Ed A. B. Thom 1875–7.

Official

[Perrin, W. G.] Admiralty library: subject catalogue of printed books. Pt I, 1912.

A list of the general and field officers as they rank in the army. 1754–1868.

List of the officers of the several regiments and corps of militia. 1793–1825.

The monthly army list. Jan 1798–Feb 1809. Continued as Army list etc, March 1809 onwards.

The new annual army list (and militia list). 1840–1916. A quarterly edn was started in 1897. Ed H. G. Hart.

The official army list etc. 1880 onwards. Quarterly from 1913; semi-annual from 1923.

An alphabetical list of the commission officers of His Majesty's Fleet etc. 1748–1846.

A list of the flag officers of HM Fleet. 1749–1846.

Steel's original and correct list of the Royal Navy. 1783–1816. Monthly during war, and quarterly during peace.

The Navy list. Feb 1814 onwards. Quarterly; then monthly.

The new Navy list. 1839–56. Quarterly; half-yearly from 1846. Ed Charles Haultain 1839–45, J. Allen 1846–56.

The Royal Navy list. 1878 onwards. Quarterly; annual since 1914. Ed C. E. Warren 1878–81, Francis Lean 1878–1906.

The Naval annual 1886–1911. Ed Lord Brassey 1886–9, T. A. Brassey 1890–1911.

The East India register and directory for 1803–44. Semi-annual. Continued as East India register and army list for 1845–60. Continued as Indian Army and Civil Service List, 1861–76. Continued as India list, civil and military, 1877–95. Replaced by India Office list and Indian Army list. Ed J. Mathison, A. W. Mason, J. S. Kingston, G. Owen, G. H. Brown, F. Clark.

The British imperial calendar and Civil Service list. 1810 onwards. Suspended from 1920 to 1925. Ed B. P. Capper 1810–14, R. Capper 1816–17, J. Debrett 1818–22.

The parliamentary pocket companion for 1833 onwards. Now styled Dod's parliamentary pocket companion. Ed C. R. Dod 1841–55, R. P. Dod 1856–?

A general police and constabulary list and analysis of criminal and police statistics. Sept 1844.

Shaws' union officers' manual of duties etc. 1846 onwards. Now Local government manual.

The mercantile navy list. 1850 onwards. Ed J. H. Brown 1850–62, I. I. Mayo 1863–?

The Foreign Office list for 1852 onwards. Ed F. W. H. Cavendish and E. Hertslet.

The Colonial Office list: or general register of the colonial dependencies of Great Britain. 1862–1925. Continued as Dominions Office and Colonial Office list for 1926. 1926–1940. Ed W. C. Sargeaunt and A. N. Birch.

Religious

The ecclesiastical and university annual register. 3 vols 1809–11.

The missionary register for the year 1813[–55] containing an abstract of the proceedings of the principal missionary and Bible societies throughout the world. 43 vols.

The annual monitor: or new letter case memorandum book. Nos 1–30, York 1813–41. New ser, Annual monitor: or obituary of the members of the Society of Friends. York 1842 onwards. Index for the years 1813–32, York 1833.

Minutes of several conversations between the Methodist Ministers at their 86th annual conference. 1829 onwards.

The Catholic directory etc. 1838 onwards.

The clergy list for 1841. 1841–1917.

The Congregational year book for 1846 onwards. Ed J. Blackburn 1846–7, R. Ashton and W. S. Palmer 1848–52, R. Ashton.

The Churchman's year book for 1852[–7]: or ecclesiastical annual register. 6 vols.

The clerical directory: a biographical and statistical book of reference for facts relating to the clergy and the Church. 2 vols 1858–9. Continued as Crockford's clerical directory for 1860 onwards.

General Baptist year book for 1866. 1865–91.

The Christian year book. 2 vols 1867–8.

The clergy directory and parish guide: an alphabetical list of the clergy of the Church of England. 1872.

The official year book of the Church of England. 1883 onwards.

Educational

The Cambridge University calendar. 1796 onwards. Ed John Beverley, B. C. Raworth, J. W. Clark.

The Oxford University calendar for the year 1810 onwards. Ed J. Walker, P. Bliss.
The London University calendar for the year 1844 onwards.
The literary and educational year book for 1859 and 1860. 2 vols.
Crockford's scholastic directory for 1861.
The public schools calendar. 2 vols 1865[-6]. Ed C. E. Pascoe.
The institute register and handbook of reference. 1868.
A practical handbook to the principal schools of England. 2 vols 1877-8. Ed C. E. Pascoe.
Year-book of the scientific and learned societies of Great Britain and Ireland. 1884-1939; 1950 onwards.

Professional

The new law list. 5 vols 1798-1802. Continued as Clarke's new law list, 38 vols 1803-40. Continued as Law list, 1841 onwards. Ed J. Hughes 1798-1802, S. Hill 1803-19, S. Cockell 1820-48, W. Powell 1849-58, W. W. Dalbiac 1859-71, W. H. Cousins 1872-83, J. S. Purcell.
The lawyer's companion for 1848, containing a list of the English Bar. 1848 onwards. Ed W. F. Finlason 1855-60, H. Moore.
The medical annual for 1831-4. 4 vols. Ed R. Reece.
The medical directory of Great Britain and Ireland for 1845.
The London medical directory. 3 vols 1845-7. Incorporated in Provincial medical directory and continued as London and provincial medical directory, 1848 onwards. In 1861 it absorbed Medical directory for Scotland and Medical directory for Ireland.
The provincial medical directory. 1847.
The medical directory for Scotland. 9 vols 1852-60.
The medical directory for Ireland. 9 vols 1852-60.
The London medical guide: containing a complete directory of the names of all qualified medical practitioners residing in London and the suburbs. 1872.

Miscellaneous Commercial

The Post Office London directory for 1799-1839. 41 vols. Continued as W. Kelly and Co, The Post Office London directory for 1840 onwards.
The British postal guide: containing the chief public regulations of the Post Office. 1856-79. Quarterly. Continued as Post Office guide, 1880 onwards. Quarterly.
Bradshaw's railway time tables. No 1, 19 Oct-no 3, 18 Nov 1839. Continued as Bradshaw's railway companion, 1 Jan 1840-Nov 1840. Continued as Bradshaw's railway guide, [no 1] Dec 1841-no 6, May 1842. Continued as Bradshaw's monthly general railway and steam navigation guide etc, no 7, June 1842-June 1961.
Osborne's railway time table and literary companion. Birmingham Nov 1839-67.
The ABC: or alphabetical railway guide. Oct 1853 onwards. Monthly.
Cook's excursionist and international tourist advertiser. 1864-70. Ed Thomas Cook.
The municipal corporations directory, 1866; or official guide to the counties and municipal boroughs of England and Wales. 1866.
Cook's continental time tables and tourist's handbook. 1873 onwards.
Dickens's dictionary of continental railways, steamboats, diligences etc: being an easy guide for travellers. 1880-1. Continued as Dickens's continental ABC railway guide, 1881-7. Ed Charles Dickens jr.
The British tariff for 1829-30[1862-3]. 34 vols. Ed R. Ellis 1829-47, E. Beedell 1847-63.

The yearly journal of trade for 1836-46. 11 vols. Ed Charles Pope.
The exporter's directory: an index to merchandise shipped to Australia, New Zealand, India, Africa, N. and S. America etc 1878-81.
The international mercantile directory (Collingwood's). 1881-1930.
The banking almanac, directory and year book. 1845-1919. Continued as Banker's almanac, 1920 onwards. Ed D. Morier Evans 1856-?, R. H. Inglis Palgrave 1876(?).
The Stock Exchange year book. 1874 onwards.
The directory of directors. 1880 onwards. Ed T. Skinner
The newspaper press directory. 1846 onwards. Ed C. Mitchell. *See col 000, above.*
The brown book: a book of ready reference to the hotels, libraries, post offices, cab stands, in the metropolis. 3 vols 1864-7.
London in 1880 [etc] illustrated with birds-eye views of the principal streets; also its chief suburbs and environs. 1880-9. Ed H. Fry.
The municipal corporations companion, diary and year book of statistics. 1877-1914. At end: County councils, municipal corporations and local authorities companion. Ed J. R. S. Vine 1877-89.
The brewer's annual for 1841-3. 3 vols. Ed G. Amsinck.
The licensed victualler's year book for 1874-1940. Ed H. D. Miles.
Duncan's manual of British and foreign brewery companies. 1889-1900. Continued as Manual of British and foreign brewery companies for 1902 onwards. Known as Brewery manual. Ed W. W. Duncan 1889-?

Sport

The racing calendar; containing an account of the plates, matches and sweepstakes run for in 1773 etc onwards. Since 1846 there have been 2 vols for each year with the same serial no; Races past and races to come. Ed J. Weatherby 1773-93, E. and J. Weatherby 1794-1830, E. and C. Weatherby 1831-5, E., C. and J. Weatherby 1836-9, C. and J. Weatherby 1840-58, E. C. and J. Weatherby 1859-67, C. J., E. and J. P. Weatherby.
Guide to the turf: or pocket racing companion. 1842-53. Continued as Ruff's guide to the turf, 1854 onwards. In 1869 including Baily's turf guide. Ed W. Ruff 1842-53, W. H. Langley 1854-6.
The cricketer's manual for 1849, by 'Bat'.
The guide to cricketers. 14 vols 1853-66. Incorporated in John Lillywhite's cricketers' companion. Ed F. Lillywhite.
The cricket chronicle for the season 1863. 1864. Ed W. Bayly.
The archer's register: a year book of facts for 1864. 1864-6 1877-1915. Ed J. Sharp 1864-88, F. T. Follett 1889-97, H. Walrond 1898-1915.
The cricketer's almanack. 1864-9. Continued as John Wisden's cricketer's almanack. 1870 onwards.
Mantz's cricket directory, with the laws of cricket as revised by the Marylebone Club. [1865].
The cricketer's handbook for 1865. Manchester 1865.
J. Lillywhite's cricketer's companion for 1865-73. 9 vols. Continued as J. Lillywhite's cricketer's annual for 1874-85. Ed J. Lillywhite 1865-73, C. W. Alcock 1873-85.
The football annual. 1873-1908. Ed C. W. Alcock.
The football calendar, containing laws of both sections of the game, list of clubs, playing grounds, and fixtures for the season 1875-6. 1875-94. Ed G. H. West.
The bicycle annual for 1879-83. 5 vols. Continued as cycling annual for 1884-? Ed C. W. Nairn 1879-83, and C. J. Fox 1879-?
The lawn tennis annual. 1882. Ed L. S. F. Winslow.

The Field lawn tennis calendar. 1882–91. Ed B. C. Evelegh.

The year's sport: a review of British sports and pastimes for 1885. 1886. Ed A. E. T. Watson.

The golfing annual. 1888–1910. Ed C. R. Bauchope, John Bauchope.

The yachting racing calendar and review for 1888. 1888–95. Ed Dixon Kemp.

Baily's fox-hunting directory. 1897–8. Continued as Baily's hunting directory 1898–9 onwards.

Studies of year books

Dring, E. H. Early railway time tables. Library 4th ser 2 1921.

Gosse, C. W. F. The London directories 1677–1855. 1932.

Annual Register 1758

H., A.M. The annual register: a bibliographical note. N & Q 13 Feb 1943.

Todd, W. B. A bibliographical account of the Annual Register 1758–1825. Library 5th ser 16 1961.

H. M. R. and S. K. R.

6. ANGLO-IRISH LITERATURE

Section I deals with the Gaelic sources of Anglo-Irish literature. Section II describes general works on Anglo-Irish literature. Sections III (Poets), IV (Yeats and Synge), and V (Dramatists) are continued into the twentieth century. There is no separate section for prose, since this was largely a later development, though some prose writers are listed under Poets. Such Irish novelists as the Banims, Lever, Le Fanu, George Moore et al will be found under Novel, col 657 f., above.

I. GAELIC SOURCES

(1) BIBLIOGRAPHIES

O'Reilly, E. A chronological account of nearly 400 Irish writers commencing with the earliest accounts of Irish history and carried down to 1750. Trans Iberno-Celtic Soc 1 pt 1 1820.

O'Curry, E. Lectures on the manuscript materials of ancient Irish history. Dublin 1861.

O'Hart, J. Irish pedigrees. 2 vols Dublin 1876–8.

Webb, A. Compendium of Irish biography. Dublin 1878.

Dottin, G. Notes bibliographiques sur l'ancienne littérature chrétienne de l'Irlande. Revue d'Histoire et de Littérature Religieuses 5 1900.

Dix, E. and J. Cassedy. List of books, pamphlets etc printed wholly or partly in Irish from the earliest period to 1820. Dublin 1905.

d'Arbois de Jubainville, H. Essai d'un catalogue de la littérature épique de l'Irlande. Paris 1883. Addns by K. Meyer, Revue Celtique 6 1884; suppl by G. Dottin 33 1912.

Best, R. I. Bibliography of Irish philology and of printed Irish literature. Dublin 1913.

—— Bibliography of Irish philology and manuscript literature publications 1913–41. Dublin 1942.

O'Grady, S. H. Catalogue of Irish manuscripts in the British Museum. Vol 1, 1926. For vols 2–3 *see* under Flower, *and* Flower and Dillon, *below*.

Flower, R. Catalogue of Irish manuscripts in the British Museum. Vol 2, 1926.

—— and M. Dillon. Catalogue of Irish manuscripts in the British Museum. Vol 3, 1953.

Kennedy, J. F. The sources for the early history of Ireland. Vol 1, New York 1929. Vol 2 unpbd.

Farrar, C. and A. Evans. Bibliography of English translations from medieval sources. New York 1946.

(2) HISTORIES

Walker, J. Historical memoirs of the Irish bards. Dublin 1786.

O'Grady, S. J. Early bardic literature: Ireland. 1879.

d'Arbois de Jubainville, H. Introduction à l'étude de la littérature celtique. Paris 1883.

—— The Irish mythological cycle and Celtic mythology. Tr Dublin 1903.

—— Tain bo Cualnge: enlèvement des vaches de Cooley. Paris 1907.

—— Supplément à l'essai d'un catalogue de la littérature épique de l'Irlande. Revue Celtique 33 1912.

Zimmer, H. The Irish element in medieval culture. New York 1891.

Nutt, A. Voyage of Bran. Vol 1, The happy otherworld; vol 2, The Celtic doctrine of rebirth. 1895–7.

—— Ossian and the Ossianic literature. 1899, 1910 (rev).

Hyde, D. The last three centuries of Gaelic literature. Dublin 1894.

—— The story of early Gaelic literature. 1895.

—— A literary history of Ireland from the earliest times to the present day. 1899, 1901, 1906, 1967.

Dottin, G. La littérature gaélique de l'Irlande. Revue de Synthèse Historique 3 1901; tr 1906 (priv ptd).

—— Manuel pour servir à l'étude de l'antiquité celtique. Paris 1913 (2nd edn).

Windisch, E. Introd to his Die altirische Heldensage Tain bo Cualnge, Leipzig 1905.

Hull, E. A text book of Irish literature. 2 pts Dublin 1906–8.

MacNeill, E. Introd to his Duanaire Finn, 1908.

Seymour, St J. Irish visions of the otherworld. 1920.

Thurneysen, R. Die irische Helden- und Königsage. Halle 1921.

Corkery, D. The hidden Ireland: a study of Gaelic Munster in the eighteenth century. Dublin 1925, 1941.

—— The fortunes of the Irish language. Dublin 1954.

De Blacam, A. Gaelic literature surveyed. Dublin 1929.

—— A first book of Irish literature, from the earliest times to the present day. Dublin 1936.

Hubert, H. Les Celtes depuis l'époque de la Tène et la civilisation celtique. Paris 1932.

Jackson, K. Studies in early Celtic nature poetry. Cambridge 1935.

Raglan, Lord. The hero. Oxford 1937. On mythological aspects of Cuchulain.

Sjoestedt, M. Dieux et heros des Celtes. Paris 1940; tr 1949.

O'Rahilly, T. Early Irish history and mythology. Dublin 1946.

Dillon, M. The cycles of the kings. Oxford 1946.

—— Early Irish literature. Chicago 1948.

—— The archaism of Irish tradition. 1947. Rptd from Proc Br Acad 33 1947.

Flower, R. The Irish tradition. Oxford 1947.

Saul, G. The shadow of the three queens: a handbook introduction to traditional Irish literature and its backgrounds. Harrisburg Pa 1953.

Early Irish society. Ed M. Dillon, Dublin 1954. Thos Davis lectures by the editor et al.

Murphy, G. The Ossianic lore and romantic tales of medieval Ireland. Dublin 1955.

—— Saga and myth in ancient Ireland. Dublin 1955.

—— Early Irish lyrics. 1956.

Knott, E. Irish classical poetry, commonly called Bardic poetry. Dublin 1957.

Rivoallan, A. Présence des Celtes. Paris 1957. On the Irish sagas.

Heppenstall, R. The children of Gomer. TLS 17 Oct 1958. Comments, 31 Oct, 7, 14 Nov; rptd in his Fourfold tradition, 1961. Questions current concepts of Celticism.

Rees, A. and B. Rees. Celtic heritage: ancient tradition in Ireland and Wales. 1961.

Seven centuries of Irish learning 1000–1700. Ed B. O'Cuiv, Dublin 1961. Thos Davis lectures by the editor et al.

(3) SCHOLARS AND HISTORIANS

EDMUND SPENSER

c. 1552–1599

A view of the present state of Ireland. Ed J. Ware, Dublin 1633. *See vol i, above.*

LUGHAIDH O'CLERY

fl. 1609

Life of Aodh Ruadh O'Donnell. Ed E. O'Reilly 1820.

MICHAEL O'CLERY

1575–1643

Annales Dungallenses, or Annala Rioghachta Eireann, or Annals of the four masters, compiled by O'Clery and three others. Ed J. O'Donovan, Dublin 1848–51.

Martyrologium sanctorum Hiberniae (The Martyrology of Donegal). Ed J. O' Donovan, J. Todd and W. Reeves, Dublin 1864.

JAMES USSHER

1581–1656

Of the original and first institution of Corbes, Herenaches and Termon lands. 1609.

A discourse of the religion anciently professed by the Irish and British. Dublin 1631.

Veterum Epistolarum Hibernicarum Sylloge. Dublin 1632.

Brittanicarum ecclesiarum antiquitates. Dublin 1639.

Works. 17 vols Dublin 1847–64.

DUALD MacFIRBIS

1585–1670

Chronicum Scotorum. Ed W. M. Hennessy 1866. Introd.

PHILIP O'SULLIVAN BEARE

c. 1590–1660

Historia Catholicae Iberniae compendium. Lisbon 1621.

JOHN COLGAN

d. 1657?

Acta sanctorum veteris et majoris Scotiae seu Hibernia. Louvain 1645.

Trias thaumaturga. Louvain 1647. Contains lives of Saints Patrick, Columba and Bridget.

SIR THOMAS STAFFORD

fl. 1633

Pacata Hibernia. 1663, 2 vols Dublin 1810.

SIR JAMES WARE

1594–1666

De scriptoribus Hiberniae. Dublin 1639; tr 2 vols 1705.

De Hibernia et antiquitatibus ejus: disquisitiones. 1654, 1658 (rev).

S Patricio adscripta opuscula. 1656.

Rerum hibernicarum annales 1485–1558. Dublin 1664.

De praesulibus Hiberniae: commentarius. Dublin 1665.

The whole works of Ware concerning Ireland. Ed. W. Harris 2 vols Dublin 1739–64.

JOHN LYNCH

1599?–1673

Cambrensis eversus: sive potius historica fides in rebus Hibernicis Giraldo Cambrensi abrogata. [St Malo?] 1652; tr Theophilus O'Flanagan, Dublin 1795; ed M. Kelly 3 vols Dublin 1848–52.

RODERIC O'FLAHERTY

1629–1718

Ogygia: seu rerum Hibernicarum chronologia. 1685: tr J. Hely, Dublin 1793.

Ogygia vindicated against the objections of Sir George Mackenzie. [Ed C. O'Conor?], Dublin 1775.

A chorographical description of west or H-Iar Connaught. Ed J. Hardiman, Dublin 1846.

DERMOD O'CONNOR

fl. 1712–29

The general history of Ireland. Tr Geoffrey Keating, Dublin 1723, 1723, Westminster 1726, 1732, 1738, Dublin 1854.

JOHN O'BRIEN

d. 1767

Focalŏir Gaoidhilge-Sax-Bhearla: or an English-Irish dictionary. Paris 1768; ed R. Daly and M. McGinty, Dublin 1832; rptd in Collectanea de rebus hibernicis, ed C. Vallancey 1770–1804.

CHARLES O'CONNOR

1710–1791

Dissertations on the ancient history of Ireland. 1753, 1766; rptd in R. O'Flaherty, Ogygia vindicated, 1775 and in Collectanea de rebus hibernicis, ed C. Vallancey 1770–1804.

CHARLES VALLANCEY

1721–1812

Collectanea de rebus hibernicis. 6 vols 1770–1804. Ed Vallancey with contributions by others.

An essay on the antiquity of the Irish language. Dublin 1772.

A grammar of the Iberno-Celtic or Irish language. Dublin 1773.

A vindication of the ancient history of Ireland. Dublin 1786. Collectanea no 14, above.

SYLVESTER O'HALLORAN

1728–1807

Insula sacra. 1770.

An introduction to the study of the history and antiquities of Ireland. 1772.

Ierne defended. 1774.
General history of Ireland from the earliest accounts to the close of the 12th century. 1778.

CHARLOTTE BROOKE

1740–93

Reliques of Irish poetry. Dublin 1789.

JOSEPH WALKER

1762?–1810

Historical memoirs of the Irish bards. Dublin 1786.
Historical essay on the dress of ancient and modern Irish. Dublin 1788.

EDWARD BUNTING

1773–1843

A general collection of the ancient Irish music. Dublin 1796, 1807, 1840.

THOMAS MOORE

1779–1852

Irish melodies. 1821.
The history of Ireland. 4 vols 1835–46.

GEORGE PETRIE

1789–1866

The history and antiquities of Tara hill. Trans Royal Irish Acad 17 1837.
Inquiry into the origins and uses of the round towers of Ireland. Trans Royal Irish Acad 20 1845. Re-issued as The ecclesiastical architecture of Ireland, 1845.
Ancient music of Ireland. 2 vols Dublin 1855–82.
Christian inscriptions in the Irish language. Ed M. Stokes 2 vols Dublin 1872–8.
The complete collection of Irish music as noted by George Petrie. Ed C. Stanford 1905.

JAMES HARDIMAN

1790?–1855

The history of the town and county of Galway. Dublin 1820, Galway 1958.
Irish minstrelsy: or bardic remains of Ireland, with English poetical translations. 2 vols 1831.

EDWARD O'REILLY

d. 1829

An Irish-English dictionary. Dublin 1817, 1864 (rev John O'Donovan), 1901 (corrected).
A chronological account of nearly four hundred Irish writers. Trans Iberno-Celtic Soc 1 pt 1 1820.
An essay on the nature and influence of the ancient Irish institute commonly called Brehon laws. Dublin 1824.

EUGENE O'CURRY

1796–1862

§1

Lectures on the manuscript material of ancient Irish history. Dublin 1861.
On the manners and customs of the ancient Irish. Ed W. Sullivan 3 vols 1873.
The fate of the children of Tuirenn. Atlantis 4 1863; rptd Gaelic Jnl 2 1884.

§2

Atkinson, S. Essays. Dublin 1896.

JOHN DALY

1800–78

Reliques of Irish Jacobite poetry. 2 pts Dublin 1844, 1866. Ed Daly, with metrical versions by E. Walsh.
Poets and poetry of Minster. Dublin 1849, 1925. Ed Daly, with metrical versions by J. Mangan.

JAMES HENTHORN TODD

1805–69

Irish version of the Historia Britonum of Nennius. Dublin 1847.
Liber Hymnorum: or Book of hymns of the ancient church of Ireland. 1855, 1869.
St. Patrick, apostle of Ireland. Dublin 1864.
Cogadh Gaedhel re Gallaibh: the war of the Gaedhil with the Gaill, or the invasions of Ireland by the Danes and other Norsemen. 1867 (Rolls Ser).

EDWARD WALSH

1805–50

See under III, below.

JOHN O'DONOVAN

1809–61

The circuit of Ireland by Muircheartach MacNeill. 1841 (Irish Archaeological Soc).
The banquet of Dun na nGedh and the battle of Magh Rath. 1842 (Irish Archaeological Soc).
The tribes and customs of Hy-Many. 1843 (Irish Archaeological Soc).
The genealogies, tribes and customs of Hy Fiachrach. Dublin 1844.
Grammar of the Irish language. Dublin 1845.
Irish charters in the Book of Kelts. Dublin 1846.
Annals of Ireland, 1443 to 1468. In Irish Archaeological Soc miscellany, 1846.
The book of rights. 1847 (Celtic Soc).
'The annals of the four masters.' 7 vols Dublin 1848–51.
Annals of Ireland 571–913: three fragments copied from ancient sources by Dubhaltach MacFirbisigh. 1860 (Irish Archaeological & Celtic Soc.)
The topographical poems of John O'Dubhagain and Giolla na naomh O'Huidhrin. 1862 (Royal Irish Acad).
The martyrology of Donegal. Tr John O'Donovan, ed J. Todd and W. Reeves 1864 (Irish Archaeological & Celtic Soc).
The ancient laws of Ireland. 5 vols 1865–79. Various editors; texts and trns in most cases by O'Donovan. Vol 5 ed R. Atkinson with trn based on that of O'Donovan and O'Curry.

SIR SAMUEL FERGUSON

1810–86

See under III, below.

SIR WILLIAM WILDE

1815–76

The beauties of the Boyne and the Blackwater. Dublin 1849.
Catalogue of the contents of the museum of the Royal Irish Academy. 3 vols 1857–62.
Lough Corrib and Lough Mask. Dublin 1867, 1872, 1936 (rev C. O. Lochlainn), 1955.
The ancient races of Ireland. 1874; rptd in Lady Wilde, Ancient legends of Ireland vol 2, 1887.

WILLIAM REEVES

1815–92

Ecclesiastical antiquities of Down, Connor and Dromore. Dublin 1847.
Acts of Archbishop Colton. 1850 (Irish Archaeological Soc).
Life of Saint Columba, founder of Hy, written by Adamnan. 1857 (Irish Archaeological & Celtic Soc).

MATTHEW ARNOLD

1822–88

§1

On the study of Celtic literature. 1867; ed R. H. Super, in Complete prose works of Arnold vol 3, Ann Arbor 1962.

§2

Kelleher, J. V. Arnold and the Celtic revival. In Perspectives in criticism, ed H. Levin, Cambridge Mass 1950.
Faverty, F. E. Arnold the ethnologist. Evanston 1951.

ERNEST RENAN

1823–95

The poetry of the Celtic races. Tr W. Hutchinson 1896. From his Essais de morale et de critique, Paris 1859.

JANE FRANCESCA, LADY WILDE

1826–96

See under III, below.

PATRICK WESTON JOYCE

1827–1910

The origin and history of Irish names and places. 2 sers Dublin 1869–75.
Irish local names explained. Dublin nd.
Old Celtic romances. 1891, 1894.
A social history of ancient Ireland. 2 vols Dublin 1903, 1913, 1920.
English as we speak it in Ireland. 1910.

HENRI d'ARBOIS de JUBAINVILLE

1827–1910

Cours de littérature celtique. Paris 1883–99. Vol 2 tr R. I. Best as The Irish mythological cycle and Celtic mythology, Dublin 1903.

SIR THOMAS GILBERT

1829–98

Facsimiles of national manuscripts of Ireland. 4 pts Dublin 1874.

WHITLEY STOKES

1830–1909

Best, R. Bibliography of the publications of Whitley Stokes. 1911.

§1

The voyage of Mael Duin. Revue Celtique 9–10 1888–9. Text and trn.
Lives of the saints from the Book of Lismore. Oxford 1890.
The second battle of Mag Tured. Revue Celtique 12 1891.
The destruction of Da Derga's hostel. Revue Celtique 22–3 1901–2.

STANDISH HAYES O'GRADY

1832–1915

Catalogue of Irish manuscripts in the British Museum. Vol 1, 1926.

§1

The pursuit of Diarmuid and Grainne. Ed with trn Trans Ossianic Soc 3 1857.
Silva Gadelica. 2 vols 1892.
The Tain Bo Cuailnge. In E. Hull in Cuchulinn saga, 1898. Analysis and extracts.

§2

Hull, E. Standish Hayes O'Grady. Studies March 1916.
Flower, R. Catalogue of Irish manuscripts in the British Museum. Vol 2, 1926. Preface on O'Grady's life.

ROBERT ATKINSON

1839–1908

The yellow book of Lecan. Dublin 1896. Facs introd famous for its adverse criticism of the value of medieval Irish literature.

GEORGE SIGERSON

1839–1925

See under III, below.

STANDISH JAMES O'GRADY

1846–1928

O'Hegarty, P. A bibliography of books written by O'Grady. Dublin 1930 (priv ptd from Dublin Mag 4 1930).
McKenna, J. The O'Grady collection at Colby College: a check list. Colby Lib Quart 4 1958.

§1

History of Ireland. Vol 1, The heroic period. Dublin 1878; vol 2, Cuculain and his contemporaries, Dublin 1880.
Early bardic literature [of] Ireland. 1879.
History of Ireland, critical and philosophical. Vol 1, 1881. Only vol 1 pbd.
Cuculain: an epic. 1882. 'A kind of condensation from my first two books, History of Ireland vols 1 and 2'.
The crisis in Ireland. Dublin 1882.
Toryism and the Tory democracy. 1886.
Red Hugh's captivity: a picture of Ireland, social and political, in the reign of Queen Elizabeth. 1889.

Finn and his companions. 1892 (illustr Jack Yeats), New York 1892, Dublin [1921], Dublin [1927].
The bog of stars, and other stories of Elizabethan Ireland. 1893, 1893, Dublin nd.
The story of Ireland. 1894.
The coming of Cuculain: a romance of the heroic age of Ireland. 1894, Dublin 1920 (introd by AE), New York [1920]; tr Irish, 1933.
Lost on Du Corrig. 1894.
The chain of gold: a tale of adventure on the west coast of Ireland. 1895.
In the wake of King James: or Dun-Randal on the sea. 1896, 1897.
Ulrick the ready; or the chieftain's last rally. 1896, Dublin [1921].
The flight of the eagle. 1897, Dublin 1897, 1908; tr Irish, 1933. 'The final form of Red Hugh's captivity'.
All Ireland. Dublin 1898.
The queen of the world, by 'Luke Netterville'. 1900.
In the gates of the north. Kilkenny 1901, London [1919].
Hugh Roe O'Donnell: a sixteenth century Irish historical play. Belfast 1902.
The masque of Finn. Dublin 1907, [1927].
The departure of Dermot. Dublin 1917.
The passing of Cuculain. Dublin 1917.
The triumph of Cuculain. Dublin 1917.
Selected essays and passages. Dublin [1918]. Introd by E. Boyd with bibliography.
The triumph and passing of Cuculain. Dublin [1919?].
O'Grady edited Scintilla Shelliana: Shelley's attitude towards religion explained and defended by himself, Dublin 1875; Pacata Hibernia: or a history of the wars in Ireland during the reign of Queen Elizabeth under the government of Sir George Carew, compiled by his direction, 2 vols 1896; All Ireland Review 1–7 1900–6.

§2

Boyd, E. The father of the revival: O'Grady. In his Ireland's literary renaissance, 1916.
—— A Fenian unionist: O'Grady. In his Appreciations and depreciations, Dublin 1918.
O'Grady, H. O'Grady, the man and the writer. Dublin 1929.
Clarke, A. Standish James O'Grady. Dublin Mag 22 1947.
Mercier, V. Standish James O'Grady. Colby Lib Quart 4 1958.

KUNO MEYER

1859–1919

The vision of MacConglinne. 1892.
The voyage of Bran. 1895.
King and Hermit. 1901.
Liadain and Curithir. 1902.
Four Old Irish songs of summer and winter. 1903.
The death-tales of the Ulster heroes. 1906 (Royal Irish Acad).
Fianaigecht. 1910 (Royal Irish Acad).
Selections from ancient Irish poetry. 1911.
For a full list of Meyer's pbns see R. Best, Zeitschrift für Celtische Philologie 14 1924.

DOUGLAS HYDE

1860–1949

See under III, below.

(4) LEARNED JOURNALS

Gaelic Society of Dublin. 1808–.
Iberno-Celtic Society. 1820–.
Irish Archaeological Society and Celtic Society. 1841.
Celtic Society. 1847. Merged with Irish Archaeological Society.
Journal of the Royal Society of Antiquaries of Ireland. Successor to Journal of the Royal Historical and Archaeological Society of Ireland and to Journal of the Kilkenny Archaeological Society, 1849–.
Ulster Journal of Archaeology. 1853–.
Ossianic Society. 1854–.
Revue Celtique. 1870–1934.
The Celtic Magazine. 1875–.
Society for the Preservation of the Irish Language. 1876–.
The Gaelic Journal. 1882–.
Waterford and South-east of Ireland Archaeological Society. 1895.
Zeitschrift für Celtische Philologie. 1897–.
The Gaelic League. 1897–.
The Irish Texts Society. 1898–.
Archiv für Celtische Philologie. 1898–.
Eriu. 1904.
The Celtic Review. 1904–.
Études Celtiques. 1934–. Interrupted 1940–8.
Journal of Celtic Studies. 1949–58. 2 vols pbd.
Ogam. 1949–.
Studia Hibernica. 1961–.

(5) ANTHOLOGIES

Sigerson, G. The poets and poetry of Munster: a selection of Irish songs, with metrical translations. Dublin 1860.
—— Bards of the Gael and Gall: examples of the poetic literature of Erinn, done into English. 1897, 1907 (rev and enlarged), New York 1907, Dublin 1925 (with memorial preface by D. Hyde).
Hull, E. The Cuchullin saga, translated from the Irish by various scholars. 1898.
Hyde, D. The love-songs of Connacht. 1893, 1895, Dundrum 1904, Dublin 1963. Texts and trns.
—— The religious songs of Connacht. 2 vols Dublin 1906. Texts and trns.
Gregory, I. A., Lady. Cuchulain of Muirthemne. 1902. Stories from the Ulster cycle reworked from literal trns by others.
—— Gods and fighting men. 1904. Stories from the Fenian cycle reworked from literal trns by others.
Leahy, A. H. Heroic romances of Ireland. 2 vols 1905–6.
Flower, R. Love's bitter sweet. Dublin 1925.
—— Poems and translations. 1931.
'Frank O'Connor' (M. F. O'Donovan). The wild bird's nest. Dundrum 1932.
—— Three old brothers and other poems. 1936.
—— Lords and Commons. Dundrum 1938.
—— Kings, Lords and Commons: an anthology from the Irish. New York 1959, London 1961.
Cross, T. and C. Slover. Ancient Irish tales. New York 1936. The most comprehensive anthology of trns from Old and Middle Irish narratives.
O'Faolain, S. The silver branch: a collection of the best Old Irish lyrics variously translated. New York 1938.
Longford, Earl of. Poems from the Irish. Dublin 1944.
—— More poems from the Irish. Dublin 1945.

— The dove in the castle. Dublin 1946.
Hoagland, K. 1,000 years of Irish poetry. New York 1947.
Jackson, K. A Celtic miscellany: translations from the Celtic literatures. Cambridge Mass 1951.
Greene, D. H. An anthology of Irish literature. New York 1954.
Murphy, G. Early Irish lyrics. 1956. Texts and trns.
For trns by Brook, O'Donovan, Stokes, S. H. O'Grady and Meyer, *see* above.

(6) FOLKLORE

Croker, T. Fairy legends and traditions of the south of Ireland. 1825–8, 1929 (as Fairy tales of Old Ireland).
— Legends of the lakes. 1829.
— Popular songs of Ireland. 1839, 1886 (with introd by H. Morley).
Kennedy, P. Legendary fictions of the Irish Celts. 1866.
— The bardic stories of Ireland. Dublin 1871.
Yeats, W. B. Fairy and folk tales of the Irish peasantry. 1888.
— Irish fairy tales. 1892, New York 1892.
— Irish fairy and folk tales. 1893, New York 1895. Text identical with Fairy and folk tales of the Irish peasantry, above.
Curtin, J. Myths and folk-lore of Ireland. Boston 1890, London 1890, 1911.
— Hero tales of Ireland. Boston 1894.
— Tales of the fairies and of the ghost-world, collected from oral tradition in southwest Munster. Boston 1895.
— Irish folk-tales. Ed S. O'Duillarga, Dublin 1960 (4th edn).
Hyde, D. Beside the fire. 1890.
— An sgealuidhe gaedhealeach. 1901.
— Oscar au Fléau. Revue Celtique 13 1892. Irish text and French trn.
Larminie, W. West Irish folk-tales and romances. 1893.
Wood-Martin, W. Pagan Ireland. 1895.
— Traces of the elder faiths of Ireland. 2 vols 1902.
Joyce, P. A social history of ancient Ireland. 2 vols 1903, 1913, 1920.
Westropp, T. A folklore survey of County Clare. 1910–12.
MacCulloch, J. The religion of the ancient Celts. Edinburgh 1911.
— Celtic mythology. Boston 1918.
Hull, E. Folklore of the British Isles. 1928.
Arensburg, C. The Irish countryman: an anthopological study. New York 1937, 1950.
— and S. Kimball. Family and community in Ireland. Cambridge Mass 1940, 1948.
Evans, R. Irish heritage. Dundalk 1942.
— Mourne country. Dundalk 1951.
— Irish folkways. 1957, New York 1957.
O'Sullivan, S. A handbook of Irish folklore. Dublin 1942.
— Folktales of Ireland. 1965.
— and T. Christansen. The types of the Irish folktale. 1963.
MacCarthy, B. Thomas Crofton Croker. Studies 32 1943.
DeLargy, J. The Gaelic storyteller, with some notes on Gaelic folk tales. Proc Br Acad 31 1945.
— Notes on the oral tradition of Thomond. Jnl Royal Soc of Antiquaries 95 1965.
Flower, R. The western island: or the great Blasket. 1944, New York 1945, 1946.
— The Irish tradition. Oxford 1947.
Cross, T. P. Motif-index of early Irish literature. Bloomington 1952.
Colum, P. A treasury of Irish folklore. New York 1954.
Campbell, J. Legends of Ireland. 1955.
Danaher, K. In Ireland long ago. Cork 1962.
— Gentle places and simple things. Cork 1964.
MacNeill, M. The festival of Lugnasa: a study of the survival of the Celtic festival of the beginning of harvest. Dublin 1962.

II. GENERAL WORKS

(1) BIBLIOGRAPHIES

A list of books and pamphlets written by the members of the National Literary Society Dublin. Jnl Nat Literary Soc of Ireland 1 1900.
Brown, S. A reader's guide to Irish fiction. 1910, Dublin 1916 (rev and enlarged as Ireland in fiction), 1919.
— A guide to books on Ireland. Dublin 1912.
— Irish historical fiction. Studies 4 1915.
— Ireland in books. Irish Monthly April 1946.
O'Donoghue, D. J. The poets of Ireland. Dublin 1912.
Bibliographies of Irish writers series. 1919–.
O'Neill, J. Bibliographical account of Irish theatrical literature. Dublin 1920.
Irish literature in English 1900–9. 1929 (2nd edn).
O'Hegarty, P. Bibliography: Abbey theatre plays. Dublin Mag 22 1947.
Kiely, B. Modern Irish fiction: a critique. Dublin 1950. Contains a bibliography of Irish fiction.
Saul, G. Ancient and medieval Irish literature: an introductory bibliography. BNYPL Aug 1954.
— Introductory bibliography in Anglo-Irish literature. BNYPL Sept 1954.
Leclaire, L. A general analytical bibliography of the regional novelists of the British Isles 1800–1950. Clermont-Ferrand 1954.
Anderson, J. British novels of the twentieth century. Cambridge 1959.
Eager, A. A guide to Irish bibliographical material. Dublin 1964.

(2) CRITICAL AND HISTORICAL WORKS

MacCarthy, D. The poets and dramatists of Ireland, with an introduction on the early religion and literature of the Irish people. Dublin 1846.
McGee, T. D. Gallery of Irish writers: the Irish writers of the seventeenth century. Dublin 1846.
Brook, S. The need and use of getting Irish literature into the English tongue. 1893.
Ryan, W. The Irish literary revival. 1894.
'Eglinton, John' (W. K. Magee). Literary ideals in Ireland. 1899. With W. B. Yeats, AE and W. Larminie.

— Anglo-Irish essays. Dublin 1917.
Beltaine. Organ of the Irish literary theatre. Ed W. B. Yeats 3 nos 1899–1900.
Gregory, I. A., Lady. Ideals in Ireland. 1901. Contributions by Yeats et al.
— Our Irish theatre: a chapter of autobiography. New York 1913.
Samhain, edited for the Irish literary theatre by W. B. Yeats. 6 nos Dublin 1901–6.
Krans, H. Irish life in Irish fiction. New York 1903.
Bickley, F. J. M. Synge and the Irish dramatic movement. 1912.
Weygandt, C. Irish plays and playwrights. Boston 1913.
MacDonagh, T. Literature in Ireland. [1916].
Boyd, E. Ireland's literary renaissance. Dublin, London and New York 1916, New York 1922. With bibliography.
— Appreciations and depreciations. Dublin 1917. Essays on AE, John Eglinton, Dunsany, Dowden and S. J. O'Grady.
— The contemporary drama of Ireland. Boston 1917, Dublin 1918.
Hogan, J. The English language in Ireland. Dublin 1916.
Morris, L. The Celtic dawn. New York 1917.
O'Conor, N. Changing Ireland: literary backgrounds of the Irish Free State 1889–1922. Cambridge Mass 1924.
Law, H. Anglo-Irish literature. 1926.
Byrne, D. The story of Ireland's National Theatre. Dublin 1929.
Malone, A. The Irish Theatre. 1929.
Morton, D. The renaissance of Irish poetry. New York 1929.
Seymour, St J. Anglo-Irish literature 1200–1582. Cambridge 1929.
Fay, W. and C. Carswell. The Fays of the Abbey Theatre. 1935.
Gwynn, S. Irish literature and drama in the English language: a short history. 1936.
Duggan, G. The stage Irishman: a history. 1937.
The Abbey theatre: lectures delivered during the Abbey theatrefestival in Dublin in 1938. Ed L. Robinson 1939. Lectures by the editor et al.
Ellis-Fermor, U. The Irish dramatic movement. 1939, 1954 (rev).
Byrne, J. Sound in modern Irish poetry. Queens Quart 47 1940.
Rivoallan, A. La Littérature irlandaise contemporaine. Paris [1940].
Alspach, R. A consideration of the poets of the literary revival in Ireland 1889–1929. Philadelphia 1942.
— Irish poetry from the English invasion to 1798. Philadelphia 1943, 1959 (rev).
Enright, D. J. A note on Irish literature and the Irish tradition. Scrutiny 10 1942.
Kavanagh, P. The Irish theatre. Tralee 1946.
— The story of the Abbey theatre from its origins in 1899 to the present. New York 1950.
MacCarthy, B. Irish regional novelists of the early nineteenth century. Dublin Mag new ser 21 1946.
Robinson, L. Pictures in a theatre: a conversation piece. Dublin [1946].
— Ireland's Abbey theatre: a history 1899–1951. [1951].
Farren, R. The course of Irish verse in English. New York 1947.
O'Lochlainn, C. Anglo-Irish songwriters since Moore. Dublin 1947.
Scott, F. Teg–the stage Irishman. MLR 35 1942, 42 1947.
Colum, P. Ibsen in Irish writing. Irish writing 1949.
— Early days of the Irish theatre. Dublin Mag 24–5 1949–50.
MacNamara, B. Abbey plays 1899–1948, including the productions of the Irish Literary Theatre. Dublin 1949. Dates and places of performances, with casts.
MacLiammoir, M. Theatre in Ireland. Dublin 1950.
Strong, L. A. G. Francis Sylvester Mahony–Father Prout. Irish Writing 1950.
Kiely, B. Modern Irish fiction: a critique. Dublin 1950.
Clarke, A. Poetry in modern Ireland. Dublin 1951.
MacManus, M. Adventures of an Irish bookman. Dublin 1952.
Kelly, B. The voice of the Irish. New York 1952.
Marriner, E. Fifty years of the Cuala press. Colby Lib Quart ser 3 1953.
Saul, G. The shadow of the three queens: a handbook introduction to traditional Irish literature and its backgrounds. Harrisburg Pa [1953].
Taylor, E. The modern Irish writers. Lawrence Kansas 1954.
Black, H. The theatre in Ireland before 1900. Threshold 1 1957.
Fay, G. The Abbey theatre: cradle of genius. 1958.
Howarth, H. The Irish writers 1880–1940: literature under Parnell's star. [1958]. George Moore, Lady Gregory, Yeats, AE, Synge, Joyce.
Flanagan, T. The Irish novelists 1800–50. New York 1959.
Kain, R. Dublin in the age of William Butler Yeats and James Joyce. Norman Oklahoma 1962.
Mercier, V. The Irish comic tradition. Oxford 1962.
O'Faolain, S. Fifty years of Irish writing. Studies 51 1962.
Blythe, E. The Abbey theatre. Dublin 1963.
Adams, G., J. Braidwood and R. Gregg. Ulster dialects: an introductory symposium. Holywood Co Down 1964.
Loftus, R. Nationalism in Anglo-Irish poetry. Madison 1964.
Mercier, V. The Irish short story and oral tradition. In The Celtic cross, ed R. Browne, W. Roscelli and R. Loftus, Lafayette Indiana 1964.
Skelton, R. Twentieth-century Irish literature and the private press tradition: Dun Emer, Cuala, and Dolmen presses 1902–63. Mass Rev 5 1964.

(3) BIOGRAPHIES

Stokes, W. The life and labours in art and archaeology of George Petrie LlD. 1868.
Webb, A. Compendium of Irish biography. Dublin 1878.
Ferguson, M. (Lady Ferguson). Sir Samuel Ferguson and the Ireland of his day. 2 vols Edinburgh 1896.
Moore, G. Hail and farewell. 3 vols 1911–14.
McSweeney, P. A group of nation builders. Dublin 1913.
Figgis, D. AE: George W. Russell. Dublin 1916.
Mitchell, S. George Moore. Dublin 1916.
O'Cobhthaigh (Coffey), D. Douglas Hyde. 1917.
— Douglas Hyde, President of Ireland. Dublin 1938.
Crone, J. A concise dictionary of Irish biography. Dublin 1928.
Hone, J. Thomas Davis. Dublin 1934.
'Eglinton, John' (W. K. Magee). Irish literary portraits. 1935.
MacCarthy, B. Thomas Crofton Croker. Studies 32 1943.
Maguire, W. Irish literary figures: biographies in miniature. Dublin 1945–.
Ahern, J. Thomas Davis and his circle. Waterford 1945.
Wilson, T. Victorian doctor: being the life of Sir William Wilde. New York 1946.
Strong, L. A. G. Francis Sylvester Mahony–Father Prout. Irish Writing 1950.
Wyndham, H. Speranza: a biography of Lady Wilde. 1951.
Byrne, P. The Wildes of Merrion Square. 1953.
Mannin, E. Two studies in integrity. 1954. Gerald Griffin and 'Father Prout'.
Coxhead, E. Daughters of Erin. 1965. Biographical essays on Maud Gonne, Constance Markievicz, Sarah Purser, Sarah Allgood and Maire O'Neill. For biographies of Yeats and Synge *see below*.

(4) ANTHOLOGIES

O'Duffy, C. G. Ballad poetry of Ireland. Dublin 1843.
Macmahon, T. The casket of Irish pearls: a selection of prose and verse. Dublin 1846.
Murray, J. The prose and poetry of Ireland: a collection. New York 1877.
Reade, C. and T. P. O'Connor. The cabinet of Irish literature. 4 vols 1879, 1893; rev K. Tynan Hinkson 1903.
O'Sullivan, D. Popular songs and ballads of the Emerald Isle. New York 1880.
Brooke, S. and T. W. Rolleston. A treasury of Irish poetry in the English tongue. 1900.
McCarthy, J. Irish literature. 10 vols Chicago 1904.
Cooke, J. The Dublin book of Irish verse. 1909.
The spirit of the nation. Dublin 1913.
Colum, P. Broad-sheet ballads. Dublin 1913.
— An anthology of Irish verse: the poetry of Ireland from mythological times to the present. New York 1922, 1948.
Gregory, P. Modern Anglo-Irish verse. 1914.
Graves, A. A book of Irish poetry. Dublin 1915.
Walters, L. Irish poets of today: an anthology. [1921].
Robinson, L. A golden treasury of Irish verse. 1925.
— A little anthology of modern Irish verse. Dundrum 1928.
— and D. MacDonagh. The Oxford book of Irish verse. Oxford 1958.
Canfield, C. Plays of the Irish renaissance 1880–1930. New York 1929.
— Plays of changing Ireland. New York 1936.
O'Lochlainn, C. Irish street ballads. Dublin 1939.
Nathan, G. Five great modern Irish plays. New York [1941].
Stamm, R. Three Anglo-Irish plays. Berne 1941. Synge, Riders to the sea; Yeats, Deirdre; Lady Gregory, The rising of the moon.
Daiken, L. They go, the Irish: a miscellany of war-time writing. [1944].
Greacen, R. Northern harvest: an anthology of Ulster writing. Belfast 1944.
— Irish harvest: an anthology of prose and poetry. Dublin 1946.
— and V. Iremonger. Contemporary Irish poetry. [1949].
MacDonagh, D. Poems from Ireland. Dublin 1944, 1945. Poems rptd from Irish Times.
Russell, D. The portable Irish reader. New York 1946, 1948.
Irvine, J. The flowering branch: an anthology of Irish poetry past and present. Belfast 1945.
Hoagland, K. 1,000 years of Irish poetry. New York 1947.
Garrity, D. New Irish poets. New York 1948.
— 44 Irish short stories: an anthology of Irish short fiction from Yeats to Frank O'Connor. New York 1955.
— Irish stories and tales. New York 1957.
— The Mentor book of Irish poetry. New York 1965.
Taylor, G. Irish poets of the nineteenth century. 1951.
Mercier, V. and D. H. Greene. 1,000 years of Irish prose pt 1: the literary revival. New York 1952.
Greene, D. H. An anthology of Irish literature. New York 1954.
MacDonagh, D. and L. Robinson. The Oxford book of Irish verse XVIIth century–XXth century. Oxford 1958.
Browne, E. Three Irish plays. 1959 (Penguin). D. Johnston, The moon in the yellow river; J. O'Conor, The iron harp; D. MacDonagh, Step-in-the-hollow.
'O'Connor, Frank' (M. F. O'Donovan). A book of Ireland. 1959.
Barnet, S., M. Berman and W. Burto. The genius of the Irish theatre. New York 1960.
Skelton, R. Six Irish poets. Oxford 1962. A. Clarke, R. Kell, T. Kinsella, J. Montague, R. Murphy, R. Weber.
Saul, G. Age of Yeats: the golden age of Irish literature. New York 1964.
Mercier, V. Great Irish short stories. New York 1964.

III. POETS

RICHARD A. MILLIKEN

1767–1815

The river-side. Cork 1807.
Poetical fragments. 1823. With memoir.
The groves of Blarney. Waterford [1830?].

JEREMIAH J. CALLANAN

1795–1829

§1

The recluse of Inchidony, and other poems. 1830.
The poems. Cork 1847, Dublin 1861.

§2

MacCarthy, B. Jeremiah J. Callanan. Studies 35 1946.
Taylor, G. In his Irish poets of the nineteenth century, selected with introductions, 1951.
Gems of the Cork poets, comprising the complete works of Callanan and others. Cork [1883].

JAMES CLARENCE MANGAN

1803–49

Bibliographies

O'Hegarty, P. A bibliography of Mangan. Dublin 1941. Rptd from Dublin Mag.

Collections

Poems, original and translated: being a selection from his contributions to Irish periodicals. [Dublin] 1852. Christmas supplement to Nation 25 Dec 1852.
Poems. Ed J. Mitchel, New York 1859, 1870.
Irish and other poems, with a selection from his translations. Dublin 1886.
Irish poetic gems, from Mangan, Moore and Griffin. Dublin 1887.
Selected poems. Ed L. Guiney 1897.
Poems. Ed D. O'Donoghue, Dublin 1903. Introd by J. Mitchel.
Prose writings. Ed D. O'Donoghue, Dublin 1904. With essay by Lionel Johnson.
Dark Rosaleen [etc]. Dublin [1923].
Poems. Dublin 1931.

§ 1

Anthologia germanica. 2 vols Dublin 1845. Trns from German.
The poets and poetry of Munster. Dublin 1849 (trns from Irish with Irish texts, ed J. O'Daly), 1850; ser 2 1860, 189–? (Irish texts rev by W. Hennessey and ed C. Meehan).
Romances and ballads of Ireland. Ed H. Ellis, Dublin 1850. With contributions by Mangan.
The tribes of Ireland: a satire by Aenghus O'Daly. Dublin 1852. Irish texts with trn by Mangan.

§ 2

Ingram, J. James Clarence Mangan. Dublin Univ Mag 90 1877.
Fragment of an unpublished autobiography. Irish Monthly Nov 1882.
MacColl, J. The life of Mangan. Dublin [1887].
O'Donoghue, D. The life and writings of Mangan. Edinburgh 1897, Chicago 1897.
Graves, A. James Clarence Mangan. Cornhill Mag March 1898.
Nevinson, H. The dark Rosaleen. North Amer Rev Aug 1904.
Duffy, C. Personal memories of Mangan. Dublin Rev 142 1908.
Cain, H. Mangan and the Poe-Mangan question. Washington 1929.
Joyce, James. James Clarence Mangan. [1930], [1930]. Rptd from St Stephen's (Dublin) May 1902. Rptd in James Joyce Rev 1 1957 and in The critical writings of Joyce, ed E. Mason and R. Ellmann, New York 1959.
Colum, P. James Clarence Mangan. Commonweal 17 1932.
Sheridan, J. James Clarence Mangan. Dublin [1937].
Hess, M. Mangan: a story of triumph. Catholic World 169 1949.
Thompson, F. Poe and Mangan. Dublin Mag 25 1950.
Jeffares, A. N. The Irish contribution: Mangan. Envoy 4 1951.
Taylor, G. In his Irish poets of the nineteenth century, selected with introductions, 1951.
Magalaner, M. Mangan and Joyce's Dedalus family. PQ 31 1952.
Thompson, F. Mangan in America 1850–60. Dublin Mag 27 1952.

EDWARD WALSH

1805–50

Reliques of Irish Jacobite poetry. Ed J. Daly with English metrical versions by Walsh, Dublin 1844, 1866.
Irish popular songs, with English metrical translations by Walsh. Dublin 1847.

SIR SAMUEL FERGUSON

1810–86

§ 1

The Cromlech on Howth: a poem. [1861], [1864].
Lays of the western Gael, and other poems. 1865; ed A. Williams, Dublin 1888.
Congal: a poem in five books. Dublin 1872, 1907. Introd by Lady Ferguson.
Leabhar Breac. Dublin 1872–6. Lithographic reproduction of the Irish ms, with preface by Ferguson.
Deirdre. Dublin 1880.
Poems. Dublin 1880.
The forging of the anchor: a poem. 1883.
Hibernian nights' entertainments. 3 vols Dublin 1887. Rptd from Dublin Univ Mag.
Ogham inscriptions in Ireland, Wales and Scotland. Edinburgh 1887.
Remains of St Patrick: the Confessio and Epistle to Coroticus, translated into English blank verse. 1888.
Lays of the Red Branch. Dublin 1897. Introd by Lady Ferguson.
Poems. Dublin [1918]. Introd by A. Graves.
Aideen's grave. Dublin 1925.
Selected poems, with life and notes. Dublin 1931.
Poems. Dublin 1963. Introd by P. Colum.

§ 2

[Stokes, M.] Obituary. Blackwood's Mag Nov 1886.
O'Hagan, J. The poetry of Ferguson. Dublin 1887.
Williams, A. In his Studies in folk-song and popular poetry, Boston 1894.
Ferguson, M. (Lady Ferguson). Ferguson in the Ireland of his day. 2 vols Edinburgh 1896. A biography.
Deering, A. Ferguson, poet and antiquarian. Philadelphia 1931.
O'Lochlainn, C. Ferguson and John T. Gilbert. Irish Book Lover 30 1948.
Taylor, G. In his Irish poets of the nineteenth century, selected with introductions, 1951.

THOMAS OSBORNE DAVIS

1814–45

§ 1

The poems, now first collected, with notes and historical illustrations. Dublin 1846.
The life of the Right Hon J. P. Curran. Dublin 1846.
Literary and historical essays. Ed C. G. Duffy, Dublin 1846.
The speeches of the right honourable John Philpot Curran. Ed Davis 1847 (with memoir).
Poems. Ed J. Mitchel, New York 1868.
Prose writings. Ed T. Rolleston [1889].
The patriot parliament of 1689, with its statutes, votes and proceedings. Ed C. G. Duffy 1893.
National and other poems. Dublin 1907.
Essays, literary and historical. Dundalk 1914. With preface and notes by D. O'Donoghue and an essay by J. Mitchel.
Selections from his prose and poetry. Ed T. Rolleston 1914.
Davis the thinker and teacher: the essence of his writings in prose and poetry. Ed A. Griffith, Dublin 1914.
Essays and poems, with a centenary memoir. Dublin 1945.
Songs, ballads and poems. Dublin 1945.

§ 2

The poems of Davis. Irish Quart Rev 5 1852.
Duffy, C. G. Davis: the memoirs of an Irish patriot 1840–6. 1890.
—— Short life of Davis 1840–6. 1895.
Schiller, J. Davis: ein irischer Freiheitssänger. Vienna 1915. With bibliography.
Hone, J. Thomas Davis. Dublin 1934.
Ahern, J. Davis and his circle. Waterford 1945.
Quigley, M. Pictorial record: centenary of Davis and Young Ireland. Dublin 1945.
Davis and Young Ireland. Ed M. MacManus, Dublin 1945.
Tierney, M. Thomas Davis. Studies 34 1945.
Moody, T. Thomas Davis. Dublin 1945.
Yeats, W. B. Tribute to Davis, with an account of the Davis centenary meeting held in Dublin on November 20 1914. Cork 1947.

Gwynn, D. Denny Lane and Thomas Davis. Studies 38 1949.
— John E. Pigot and Thomas Davis. Ibid.

AUBREY THOMAS de VERE

1814–1902

Bibliographies

Winckler, P. and W. Stone. De Vere: a bibliography. Victorian Newsletter no 10 1956.

Collections

Poems. 1855.
Poetical works. 6 vols 1884–98. Vol 2 rptd London and New York 1895, vols 4–6 rptd London and New York 1897–8.
De Vere's poems: a selection. Ed J. Dennis 1890.
Selections from the poems. Ed G. Woodberry, New York 1894.
Poems from the works of de Vere. Ed M. Dombile 1904.

§1

The Waldenses, or the fall of Rora: a lyrical sketch, with other poems. Oxford 1842.
The search after Proserpine; Recollections of Greece and other poems. Oxford 1843.
English misrule and Irish deeds: four letters from Ireland addressed to an English Member of Parliament. 1848.
Picturesque sketches in Greece and Turkey. 2 vols 1850, Philadelphia 1850.
May carols: or ancilla domini. 1857, New York 1866, London 1870 (with addns), 1881 (with addns).
The sisters, Inisfail and other poems. 1861.
Inisfail: a lyrical chronicle of Ireland. Dublin 1863.
The month of Mary. 1864. A selection from May carols, above.
The infant bridal and other poems. 1864, 1876.
The Church settlement of Ireland: or Hibernia pacanda. 1866, 1866.
The Church Establishment in Ireland, illustrated exclusively by Protestant authorities. 1867.
Ireland's church property, and the right use of it. 1867.
Pleas for secularization. 1867.
Reply to certain strictures by Myles O'Reilly Esq. 1868.
Ireland's Church question: five essays. 1868. Collects The Church settlement of Ireland; The Church Establishment in Ireland; Ireland's church property; Pleas for secularization; Reply to certain strictures by Myles O'Reilly Esq, above.
Irish odes and other poems. New York 1869.
The legends of Saint Patrick. 1872, 1889, 1905.
Alexander the Great: a dramatic poem. 1874.
St Thomas of Canterbury: a dramatic poem. 1876.
Antar and Zara: an eastern romance; Inisfail and other poems. 1877.
The fall of Rora, The search after Proserpine and other poems. 1877.
Proteus and Amadeus: a correspondence [with W. S. Blunt]. Ed A. T. de Vere 1878.
Legends of the Saxon saints. 1879, 1893.
The children of Lir: an Irish legend. [New York] [1881].
Constitutional and unconstitutional political action. Limerick 1881.
The foray of Queen Maeve, and other legends of Ireland's heroic age. 1882.
Ireland and proportionate representation. Dublin 1885.
Essays, chiefly on poetry. 2 vols 1887.
Legends and records of the Church and the empires. 1887.
Saint Peter's chains, or Rome and the Italian revolution: a series of sonnets. 1888.
Essays, chiefly literary and ethical. 1889, New York 1889.
Medieval records and sonnets. 1893.
Religious problems of the nineteenth century: essays. Ed J. Wenham 1893.
The search after Proserpine and other poems. 1896.
Recollections. New York 1897.

§2

Taylor, H. In his Notes from books, 1849.
[Dixon, W.] The poetry of the de Veres. Quart Rev 183 1896; rptd in his In the republic of letters, 1898.
Towle, E. Recollections of de Vere. Sewanee Rev 7 1899.
Woodberry, G. De Vere on poetry. In his Makers of literature, New York 1900.
— In his Studies of a littérateur, New York 1921.
Ward, W. P. De Vere: a memoir based on his unpublished diaries and correspondence. 1904.
Gosse, E. Memories of de Vere. Independent 54 1902; rptd in his Portraits and sketches, New York 1914.
Gunning, J. De Vere: a memoir. Limerick 1902.
Schney, G. De Veres Alexandertragödie: eine Quellenstudie. Strasbourg 1914.
Russell, M. Unpublished letters of de Vere. Irish Monthly Aug-Oct 1911, Jan-Feb 1912, Nov 1914, April 1915.
— The centenary of de Vere. Irish Monthly May 1914.
Parsons, J. Aubrey de Vere. America 19 1918.
Pijpers, T. De Vere as a man of letters. Nijmegen 1941.
Taylor, G. Aubrey de Vere. Bell 4 1942.
— In his Irish poets of the nineteenth century, selected with introductions, 1951.
Hess, M. Poet of the Catholic revival. America 82 1949.
Reilly, S. De Vere: Victorian observer. Lincoln Nebraska [1953], Dublin [1956].

DENIS FLORENCE MacCARTHY

1817–82

The book of Irish ballads. Ed D. F. MacCarthy, Dublin 1846, 1853, 1861, 1869 (rev and enlarged), 1874 (rev and enlarged).
The poets and dramatists of Ireland. Dublin 1846. With contribution by MacCarthy.
Ballads, poems and lyrics, original and translated. Dublin 1850.
The bell-founder and other poems. 1857.
Under glimpses and other poems. 1857.
Irish legends and lyrics, with poems of the imagination and fancy. Dublin 1858.
The poets and poetry of Ireland. New York 1868. With contribution by MacCarthy.
The centenary of Moore, May 28th, 1879; an ode. 1880.
Poems. Dublin 1882.
Poems. Dublin 1931.
MacCarthy also translated the plays of Calderon.
The poems of MacCarthy. Dublin Rev 28 1850.
The poems of MacCarthy. Irish Quart Rev 7 1858.
Taylor, G. Notes towards an anthology. Bell 3 1942.

JOHN KELLS INGRAM

1823–1907

Bibliographies

Lyster, T. Bibliography of the writings of Ingram. Dublin 1909. With a chronology.

§1

Who fears to speak of ninety-eight? Nation (Dublin) 1 April 1843; rptd in The spirit of the Nation, 1843 and in his Sonnets and other poems, 1900, below.

Considerations on the state of Ireland: an address. Dublin 1863.
Sonnets and other poems. 1900.

§2

Falkiner, C. A memoir of the late Ingram. Jnl of Statistical & Social Inquiry Soc of Ireland 12 1908.
Proc Royal Irish Acad Abstract of Minutes 1907–8.

JANE FRANCESCA ELGEE, LADY WILDE

1826–96

§1

Jacta alea est. Nation (Dublin) 29 July 1848; rptd as appendix in H. Wyndham, Speranza: a biography of Lady Wilde, 1951.
Poems. Dublin 1864, Glasgow [1871].
The American Irish. Dublin [187–?]. A pamphlet; rptd as an appendix in H. Wyndham, Speranza: a biography of Lady Wilde, 1951.
Driftwood from Scandinavia. 1884.
Ancient legends, mystic charms and superstitions of Ireland. 2 vols 1887.
Ancient cures, charms and usages of Ireland. 1890.
Notes on men, women and books. 1891.
Social studies. 1893.
Essays and stories. 1907, Boston 1909, 1910.

§2

Hamilton, C. In her Notable Irishwomen, Dublin [1904].
Wilson, T. Victorian doctor. New York 1946.
Wyndham, H. Speranza: a biography of Lady Wilde. 1951.
Byrne, P. The Wildes of Merrion Square. 1953.

ROBERT DWYER JOYCE

1830–83

Ballads, romances and songs. Dublin 1861.
A much-admired song called the Drian-naun Don. [1865?]. Anon.
Legends of the wars in Ireland. Boston 1868.
Ballads of Irish chivalry: songs and poems. Boston 1872; ed P. Joyce 1908.
Deirdrè. Boston 1876, Dublin 1877.
Blanid. Boston 1879.
Russell, M. Robert Dwyer Joyce. Irish Monthly Jan 1878.

GEORGE SIGERSON

1839–1925

§1

The poets and poetry of Munster: a selection of Irish songs, with metrical translations. Dublin 1860.
History of the land tenures and land classes of Ireland, with an account of the various secret agrarian confederacies. 1871.
Political prisoners at home and abroad. 1890.
Irish literature: its origin, environment and influence. In The revival of Irish literature: addresses by Sir C. G. Duffy, Dr G. Sigerson and Dr D. Hyde, 1894.
Bards of the Gael and Gall: examples of the poetic literature of Erinn, done into English. 1897, 1907 (rev and enlarged), New York 1907, Dublin 1925 (with memorial preface by D. Hyde).
The saga of King Lir. Dublin 1913.
The last independent parliament of Ireland. Dublin 1918.
Sedulius: the Easter song. Dublin 1922. Tr Sigerson.
Songs and poems. Dublin 1927. Introd by P. Colum.

§2

Colum, P. An Irish poet-scholar. Commonweal 6 1927.
Garnier, C. George Sigerson 1925. Revue Anglo-américaine 3 1925.

JOHN TODHUNTER

1839–1916

Alcestis: New York 1874, London 1879.
Laurella and other poems. 1876.
A study of Shelley. 1880.
Forest songs, and other poems. 1881.
The true tragedy of Rienzi, tribune of Rome. 1881.
Helena in Troas. 1886.
The banshee and other poems. 1888, Dublin 1891.
A Sicilian idyll: a pastoral play. 1890.
How dreams come true: a dramatic sketch in two scenes. [1890] (priv ptd).
The legend of Stauffenberg: a dramatic cantata. Dublin 1890. Words by Todhunter, music by J. Culwick.
The black cat: a play in three acts. 1895.
Life of Patrick Sarsfield, Earl of Lucan; with a short narrative of the principal events of the Jacobite war in Ireland. 1895.
Three Irish bardic tales: being metrical versions of the three tales known as the three sorrows of storytelling. 1896.
Ye minutes of ye CLXXVIIth meeting of ye Sette of odd volumes, extracted from ye diary of Samuel Pepys. [1896] (priv ptd).
An essay upon essays, written by command of his oddship brother Francis Elgar and read before the sette of odd volume Jan 4 1895. 1896 (priv ptd).
A riverside walk: an easy-going essay by a peripatetic philosopher. 1898 (priv ptd).
An essay in search of a subject, written by command of his oddship brother Silvanus Thompson magentiser and read before the sette of odd volumes May 31st 1904. 1904 (priv ptd).
Sounds and sweet airs. 1905.
Heine's Book of songs. 1907. Tr Todhunter.
From the land of dreams: Irish poems. 1918. Introd by T. Rolleston.
Essays. 1920. Foreword by S. J. O'Grady.
Goethe's Faust, first part. Oxford 1924. Tr Todhunter.
Isolt of Ireland: a legend in a prologue and three acts; and The poison flower. 1929. Blank verse plays.
Trivium amoris; and The wooing of Artemis. 1927.
Selected poems. Ed D. Todhunter and A. Graves 1929. With biographical sketch by T. Rolleston.

ARTHUR WILLIAM EDGAR O'SHAUGHNESSY

1844–81

§1

An epic of women, and other poems. 1870.
Lays of France. 1872, 1874.
Music and moonlight: poems and songs. 1874.
Toyland. 1875. With E. O'Shaughnessy.
Songs of a worker. Ed A. Deacon 1881.
Lyrics. Bibelot (Portland Maine) 16 1910.
Poems. Ed W. Percy, New Haven 1923. Selections.

§2

Forman, H. In his Our living poets, 1871.
Moulton, L. O'Shaughnessy: his life and work, with selections from his poems. 1894.

Turquet-Milnes, G. In her Influence of Baudelaire, 1913.
A pathetic love episode in a poet's life: being letters [from Helen Snee] to O'Shaughnessy; also a letter from him containing a dissertation on love. [1916].
Porter, A. Arthur O'Shaughnessy. Spectator 11 Aug 1923.
O'Shaughnessy's poems. Contemporary Rev July 1924.
Broenner, O. Das Leben O'Shaughnessys. Heidelberg 1933.
Evans, B. In his English poetry in the later nineteenth century, 1933, 1966 (rev).
Anderson, G. Marie de France and O'Shaughnessy: a study in Victorian adaptation. SP 36 1939.
Fairchild, H. Rima's mother. PMLA 68 1953.

EMILY LAWLESS
1845–1913

§1

A Chelsea householder. New York 1883.
A millionaire's cousin. 1885.
Hurrish: a study. 1886, Edinburgh1 887, 1902, London 1902.
Major Lawrence, FLS. New York 1887, London 1888. A novel.
Ireland, with additions by A. Bronson. 1887, New York 1888 (as The story of Ireland), New York 1908, London 1912 (rev and enlarged).
Plain Frances Mowbray and other tales. 1889.
With Essex in Ireland: extracts from a diary kept in Ireland during 1599. New York 1890, London 1902. With contribution by E. Lawless.
Grania. 1892, 1892 (2 vols), New York 1892.
Maelcho: a sixteenth-century narrative. 1894, 1902.
With Essex in Ireland. 1890, 1902. An historical novel.
Traits and confidences. 1898. Stories and sketches.
A garden diary. 1901.
With the wild geese. 1902. Introd by S. Brooke.
Maria Edgeworth. 1904, New York 1904 (EML).
The book of Gilly. 1906. A novel.
The point of view: some talks and disputations. 1909 (priv ptd).
The race of Castlebar: a narrative. 1913. With Shan E. Bullock.
The inalienable heritage, and other poems. 1914.

§2

Sichel, E. Emily Lawless, poetess. Nineteenth Century July 1914.

ALFRED PERCIVAL GRAVES
1846–1932

Songs of Killarney. 1873.
Irish songs and ballads. Manchester 1880.
Father O'Flynn and other Irish lyrics. 1889.
Songs of Irish wit and humour. 1884.
The Irish song book. 1895 (2nd edn). Ed Graves.
The Irish poems of Graves. 2 vols Dublin 1908.
Father O'Flynn and Ould Doctor Mack. 1908.
The Irish fairy book. 1909.
Welsh poetry, old and new, in English verse. 1912.
Irish literary and musical studies. 1913.
The reciter's treasury of Irish verse and prose, compiled and edited by Graves and G. Pertwee. [1915].
Poems of Sir Samuel Ferguson. Dublin. [1916]. Ed Graves.
A Celtic psaltery: being mainly renderings in English verse from Irish and Welsh poetry. 1917.
Songs of the Gael. Dublin [1925].
English verse translations of the Welsh poems of Ceiriog Hughes. 1926.
Irish Doric in song and story. 1926.
The Celtic song book: being representative folk songs of the six Celtic nations, chosen by Graves. 1928.
The progenitors, or our first parents, a morality: an Old Irish religious poem done into English verse. Oxford 1929.
To return to all that: an autobiography. 1930. With bibliography.

WILLIAM LARMINIE
1849–1900

§1

Glanula and other poems. 1889.
Fand and other poems. Dublin 1892.
West Irish folk-tales and romances. 1893. Collected and tr Larminie.
Legends as material for literature. In J. Eglinton et al, Literary ideals in Ireland, 1899.

§2

'Eglinton, John' (W. K. Magee). William Larminie. Dublin Mag 19 1944.
O'Meara, J. William Larminie 1849–1900. Studies 36 1947.

JANE BARLOW
1857–1917

§1

Bog-land studies. 1892, 1893 (enlarged), 1894.
Irish idylls. 1892, New York 1893, 1894, 1897, 1898.
Kerrigan's quality. New York 1894.
The battle of the frogs and mice, rendered into English. 1894.
The end of Elfintown. 1894.
Maureen's fairing and other stories. 1895, New York 1895.
Strangers at Lisconnel: a second series of Irish idylls. 1895, New York 1895.
Mrs Martin's company and other stories. 1896, New York 1896.
A creel of Irish stories. 1897, New York 1898.
From east unto the west. 1898, 1905.
From the land of the shamrock. 1900, New York 1900.
Ghost-bereft, with other stories and studies in verse. 1901.
At the back of beyond. New York 1902.
The founding of fortunes. 1902, New York 1902, London 1906.
By beach and bog-land. 1905.
Irish neighbours. 1907.
The mockers, and other verses. 1908.
Irish ways. 1909.
Flaws: a novel. 1911.
Mac's adventures. 1911.
Doings and dealings. 1913.
Between doubting and daring: verses. Oxford 1916.
In Mio's youth: a novel. 1917.

§2

MacArthur, J. Jane Barlow. Critic 24 1894.
Tynan, K. Jane Barlow. Catholic World 69 1899.
— Jane Barlow. Living Age 295 1917.

THOMAS WILLIAM HAZEN ROLLESTON
1857–1920

§ 1

Deirdre: the feis ceoil prize cantata. Dublin 1897, Edinburgh [1897].
Prose writings of Thomas Davis. 1889, 1914. Ed Rolleston.
A treasury of Irish poetry in the English tongue. New York 1900, 1910, 1923, 1932. Ed with S. Brooke.
Imagination and art in Gaelic literature; being notes on some recent translations from the Gaelic. [1900].
Parallel paths: a study in biology, ethics and art. 1908.
Sea spray: verses and translations. Dublin 1909.
The high deeds of Finn, and other bardic romances of ancient Ireland. 1910, New York 1911. Introd by S. Brooke.
Myths and legends of the Celtic race. 1911, New York 1911.
Ireland and Poland: a comparison. 1917, New York 1917.
Ireland's vanishing opportunity. Dublin 1919.
Whitman and Rolleston: a correspondence. Ed H. Frenz, Dublin 1952.

§ 2

Rolleston, C. Portrait of an Irishman. 1939. A biography.

DOUGLAS HYDE
1860–1949

Bibliographies

O'Hegarty, P. A bibliography of Hyde. Dublin 1939.

§ 1

Beside the fire. 1890.
The love songs of Connacht. Dublin 1893, 1895, Dundrum 1904, Dublin 1963.
The revival of Irish literature: addresses by Hyde and others. 1894.
The last three centuries of Gaelic literature. Dublin 1894.
The three sorrows of story-telling and Ballads of St Columkille. 1895.
The story of early Gaelic literature. 1895.
A literary history of Ireland from the earliest times to the present day. 1899, New York 1899, London 1903.
Irish poetry: an essay in Irish with translation in English. Dublin 1902.
Songs ascribed to [Anthony] Raftery. 1903. Collected and tr Hyde.
The religious songs of Connacht. 2 vols Dublin 1906.
The poor house. 1906. With Lady Gregory.
The twisting of the rope, translated from Irish by Lady Gregory. Dublin nd.
Beside the fire: a collection of Irish Gaelic folk stories. 1910.
Legends of saints and sinners, collected and translated by Hyde. [1915].
Mayo stories told by Thomas Casey, collected, edited and translated by Hyde. Dublin 1939.
Poems from the Irish. Dublin 1963. Introd by M. Gibbon.

§ 2

Cary, E. Hyde, a Gaelic poet and dreamer. Lamp 28 1904.
Coffey, D. Douglas Hyde. Dublin 1917.
—— Hyde, president of Ireland. Dublin 1938.
Weygandt, C. Hyde and his Songs of Connacht. In his Tuesdays at ten, Philadelphia 1928.
Madden, R. Hyde, saviour of Gaelic Ireland. Catholic World 1938.
Stewart, H. Hyde: the first president of Eire. Dalhousie Review 18 1938.
Lennon, M. Douglas Hyde. Bell 16 1951.

'MOIRA O'NEILL', NESTA HIGGINSON, later SKRINE

§ 1

An Easter vacation. 1893, New York 1894.
The elf-errant. 1895, 1902.
Songs of the glens of Antrim. Edinburgh 1900, New York 1910, 1922 (with More songs of the glens of Antrim, below).
More songs of the glens of Antrim, 1921, New York 1922 (with songs of the glens of Antrim, above).
From two points of view. Edinburgh 1924.
Collected poems. Edinburgh 1933.

§ 2

Nesta Higginson ('Moira O'Neill'). Book Buyer 11 1895.
A school of Irish poetry. Edinburgh Rev 209 1909.

KATHARINE TYNAN, later HINKSON
1861–1931

Collections

Twenty one poems, selected by W. B. Yeats. Dundrum 1907.
The flower of place: a collection of the devotional poetry of Katharine Tynan. 1914.
Collected poems. 1930.
Twenty-four poems. 1931.
Poems of Katharine Tynan. Dublin 1963. Introd by M. Gibbon.

§ 1

Louise de la Vallière, and other poems. 1885.
Shamrocks. 1887.
A nun, her friends and her order: being a sketch of the life of Mother Xaveria Fallon. 1891.
Ballads and lyrics. 1891.
Irish love-songs, selected by Katharine Tynan. 1892, New York 1892.
Cuckoo songs. 1894.
Miracle plays: Our Lord's coming and childhood. 1895, Chicago 1895.
An isle in the water. 1895. Stories.
Land of mist and mountain. [1895]. Stories.
The way of a maid. 1895.
A lover's breast-knot. 1896.
An isle in the water. 1896.
Oh, what a plague is love! 1896.
The wind in the trees: a book of country verse. 1898.
The dear Irish girl. 1899.
The handsome Brandons: a story for girls. 1899, Chicago 1900.
Led by a dream, and other stories. 1899.
A daughter of the fields. 1900.
Poems. 1901.
The queen's page: a story of the days of Charles I of England. New York [c. 1902].
A girl of Galway. 1902.
Innocencies: a book of verse. 1905.
A little book for John O'Mahony's friends. 1906 (priv ptd), Portalnd Maine 1909.
The rhymed life of St Patrick. 1907.
A little book of xxiv carols. Portland Maine 1907, 1916.
Experiences. 1908.
Lauds. 1909.

Ireland. 1909.
Peggy the daughter. 1909.
New poems. 1911.
Irish poems. 1913, 1914.
The wild harp: a selection from Irish poetry by Katharine Tynan. 1913.
Twenty-five years: reminiscences. 1913, New York [1913].
The house of the foxes. 1915.
Flower of youth: poems in war-time. 1915.
Countrymen all. 1915.
Lord Edward: a study in romance. 1916.
The holy war. 1916.
The middle years. 1916, Boston 1917.
Book of Irish history. Dublin [1917].
Late songs. 1917.
Kit. 1917.
Kitty at school and college. Dublin [1917?].
Herb O'Grace: poems in war-time. 1918.
The years of the shadow. 1919, Boston 1919.
The man from Australia. [1919].
The wandering years. 1922.
Evensong. Oxford 1922.
Memories. 1924.
Life in the occupied area. [1925].
Twilight songs. Oxford 1927, New York 1927.
The river. 1929.

§2

The poems of Katharine Tynan. Irish Monthly Dec 1884.
Bregy, K. The poetry of Katharine Tynan Hinkson. Catholic World 97 1913.
Alspach, R. The poetry of Katharine Tynan Hinkson. Ireland Amer Rev 4 1940.
Hinkson, P. Katharine Tynan. Irish Lib Bull 2 1941.
Yeats, W. B. Letters to Katharine Tynan. Ed R. McHugh, Dublin [1953].

FREDERIC HERBERT TRENCH
1865–1923

Collections

Collected works. Ed H. Williams 3 vols 1924.
Selected poems. Ed H. Williams 1924.

§1

Deirdre wed, and other poems. 1901.
New poems: Apollo and the seaman, The queen of Gothland, Stanzas to Tolstoy and other lyrics. 1907, New York 1908.
All that matters: a play. [1911].
Lyrics and narrative poems. [1911].
Ode from Italy in time of war: night on Mottarone. Florence 1915 (priv ptd).
Poems, with fables in prose. 2 vols 1918.
Napoleon: a play. 1919.

§2

Clarke, A. The poetry of Trench. London Mercury 10 1924.
George, R. The poetry of Mr Trench. Contemporary Rev July 1924.
Chevalley, A. Trench, poète anglais: notice sur sa vie et ses oeuvres. Paris 1925.

DORA SIGERSON, later SHORTER
1866–1918

Collections

Collected poems. 1907, New York 1907. Introd by G. Meredith.

§1

Verses. 1893.
The fairy changeling and other poems. 1898.
My lady's slipper and other verses. 1898, New York 1899.
Ballads and poems. 1899.
The father confessor: stories of death and danger. 1900.
The woman who went to Hell and other ballads and lyrics. [1902], New York [1902].
As the sparks fly upward: poems and ballads. [1903].
The country-house party. 1905 (2nd edn).
The story and song of Black Roderick. 1906, New York 1906.
Through wintry terrors. 1907.
The troubadour and other poems. 1910.
New poems. Dublin 1912, 1921 (3rd edn).
Madge Lindsey and other poems. Dublin 1913.
Do-well and do-little: a fairy tale. [1913].
Comfort the women: a prayer in time of war. [1915] (priv ptd).
Love of Ireland: poems and ballads. Dublin 1914, London 1916, Dublin 1916 (with poems of the Irish rebellion, 1916).
An old proverb: 'it will be all the same in a thousand years'. [London] 1916 (priv ptd).
The sad years [and other poems]. 1918, New York 1918, 1918 (priv ptd). Introd by K. Tynan.
A legend of Glendalough and other ballads. Dublin 1919.
Sixteen dead men and other poems of Easter week. New York 1919.
A dull day in London and other sketches. [1920]. Prefatory note by Thomas Hardy.
The tricolour: poems of the Irish revolution. Dublin 1922.
Twenty-one poems. 1926.

§2

Colum, P. The poetry of Dora Sigerson Shorter. Bookman (New York) 1919.
In memoriam Dora Sigerson 1918–23. 1923 (priv ptd). Poems by various writers.

'A.E.' or 'AE', GEORGE WILLIAM RUSSELL
1867–1935

Most of AE's mss and letters are in the National Library Dublin, the Lilly Library of Indiana Univ and at Colby College, Waterville Maine and Yale Univ. There are notebooks in the County Museum Armagh and the Congressional Library Washington. Letters and rare pamphlets are at Harvard and in the Berg Collection of the New York Public Library.

Bibliographies

[MacManus, M. J.] Bibliography of AE, George Russell. Dublin Mag Jan 1930. Addns, Oct 1935.
Kindilien, C. The Russell collection at Colby college: a check list. Colby Lib Quart ser 4 1955.
Denson, A. Printed writings by George W. Russell (AE): a bibliography. Evanston 1961. Contributions by P. Colum, M. Bonn and T. Bodkin.

Collections

Collected poems. 1913, 1913, 1914, New York 1915 (in part), London 1917, 1919 (enlarged), 1920, 1926 (enlarged), 1927, 1928, 1930 (in part), 1931 (in part), 1935 (enlarged).
Selected poems. 1935, New York 1935, London 1951, New York 1951.

§ 1

To the fellows of the Theosophical Society. Dublin 1894. A letter.
Homeward: songs by the way. Dublin 1894, 1895, London 1896, 1901, 1908, Portland Maine 1895 (enlarged), 1895, 1904, 1904.
The future of Ireland and the awakening of the fires. [Dublin 1897]. Rptd from Irish Theosophist.
Ideals in Ireland: priest or hero? Dublin [1897].
The earth breath and other poems. [1897], New York [1897], 1906, New York 1906.
Cooperative credit. Dublin [1898], 1898 (in I.A.O.S. Annual report for 1898); tr Irish, 1899.
An artist of Gaelic Ireland. [Dublin 1902, 1902, 1902]. Rptd from Freeman's Jnl. Rptd in Jack Yeats, Catalogue of sketches of life in the west of Ireland, nd.
The nuts of knowledge: lyrical poems, old and new. Dundrum 1903.
Deirdre: a drama in three acts. Dublin 1903, (rptd from All-Ireland, rev, and from Irish Homestead), 1907, 1922.
The divine vision and other poems. 1904, New York 1904.
Controversy in Ireland: an appeal to Irish journalists. Dublin [1904]. Two articles rptd from Dana and The Leader.
The mask of Apollo, and other stories. Dublin [1905], London [1905].
Some Irish essays. Dublin 1906.
By still waters: lyrical poems old and new. Dundrum 1906.
Ireland and tariff reform, by 'Libra'. Dublin [1909].
The hero in man. [1909], 1910, Bombay [1945].
The building up of a rural civilisation. Dublin 1910. An address.
The renewal of youth. 1911.
Cooperation and nationality: a guide for rural reformers from this to the next generation. Dublin 1912, New York 1913, Chicago and New York 1940; tr Finnish, 1912.
The rural community: an address to the American commission of agricultural inquiry. Dublin 1913.
To the masters of Dublin: an open letter. [Dublin 1913]. Rptd from Irish Times 7 Oct 1913; rptd in 1,000 years of Irish prose, ed V. Mercier and D. H. Greene, New York 1952, 1961.
The tragedy of labour in Dublin. [London 1913]. Rptd from Times 13 Nov 1913.
The Dublin strike. 1913, Dublin [1913]. A speech; rptd in 1,000 years of Irish prose, ed V. Mercier and D. H. Greene, New York 1952, 1961.
Oxford university and the co-operative movement. Oxford 1914.
Ireland, agriculture and the war. Dublin 1915.
Gods of war, with other poems. Dublin 1915 (priv ptd).
Imaginations and reveries, 1915, Dublin 1915, New York 1916, London 1921, Dublin 1921, London 1925, New York 1932.
Talks with an Irish farmer. Jan-Sept 1916 (Irish Homestead leaflets nos 1-12).
The national being: some thoughts on an Irish polity, Dublin 1916, 1918, 1918, Madras 1923, London 1925. New York 1930.
Templecrone: a record of co-operative effort. Dublin [1917]. Rptd from Irish Homestead.
Salutation: a poem on the Irish rebellion of 1916. 1917 (priv ptd).
Thoughts for a convention: memorandum on the state of Ireland. 1917, 1917, Dublin 1917, 1917, 1918, London 1918.
Conscription for Ireland: a warning to England. Dublin [1918]. Rptd from a letter pbd in Manchester Guardian 11 May 1918.
The candle of vision. 1918, 1918, 1919, 1919, 1919, New York 1919, London 1920, 1927, 1931.
Literary imagination. Dublin [1919]. Rptd from Irish Homestead.
Michael. Dublin 1919 (priv ptd).
A plea for justice, being a demand for a public enquiry into the attacks on co-operative societies in Ireland. Dublin [1920], Dublin [1921] (with addns).
The economics of Ireland and the policy of the British government. New York 1920, 1920, 1921.
Thoughts for British co-operators: being a further demand for a public enquiry into the attacks on co-operative societies in Ireland. Dublin [1921].
The inner and the outer Ireland. Dublin 1921, 1921, London 1921. Rptd from Pearson's Mag: tr French, [1921]; Spanish, [1922].
Ireland and the Empire at the court of conscience. Dublin 1921. Rptd from Manchester Guardian.
Ireland, past and future. 1922.
The interpreters. 1922, New York 1923.
Voices of the stones. 1925, New York 1925, London 1931.
Midsummer Eve. New York 1928.
Dark weeping; with designs by P. Nash. 1929, 1929 (no 19 of Ariel poems).
Enchantment, and other poems. New York 1930.
Vale, and other poems. 1931, New York 1931, 1931, London 1931.
Song and its fountains. 1932, New York 1932.
Verses for friends. Dublin 1932 (priv ptd).
The avatars: a futurist fantasy. 1933, New York 1933.
The house of the Tirans, and other poems. 1934, New York 1934.
The living torch: AE. Ed M. Gibbon 1937, New York 1938. Mainly articles and reviews rptd from Irish Statesman.
A gold standard for literature. Norton Mass 1939. Rptd from Living Torch, above.

Letters

Some passages from the letters of AE to W. B. Yeats. Dublin 1936.
AE's letters to Minanlabain. Ed L. Porter, New York 1937. Letters to the editor and her husband, written 1930-5.
The letters of AE. Ed Alan Denson [1961]. Foreword by M. Gibbon.

Contributions to Books

Literary ideals in Ireland, by J. Eglinton, W. B. Yeats and G. Russell. 1899. With essays by Russell.
Ideals in Ireland. Ed Lady Gregory 1901, New York 1901. With essay by Russell.
New songs. London and Dublin 1904, 1904, [1904], [1904]. Poems by P. Colum, E. Gore Booth et al; selection and preface by Russell.
Lyrics, by 'Seumas O'Sullivan' (J. S. Starkey). Portland Maine 1910. Selection and preface by Russell.
The United Irishwomen: their place, work and ideals. Dublin 1911, 1911. With essay by Russell.
Rural reconstruction in Ireland, by L. Smith-Gordon and C. Staples. 1917. Preface by Russell.
Essays, Irish and American, by J. B. Yeats. Dublin 1918. An appreciation by Russell.
Secret springs of Dublin song. Ed S. Mitchell, Dublin 1918. Poem entitled Y- - -s by Russell.
The coming of Cuchulain, by S. J. O'Grady. Dublin and London 1919. Introd by Russell.
An Irish commune, by E. T. Craig. Dublin [1920]. Introd by Russell.
The government of Ireland, by Mrs J. R. Green. 1921. Foreword by Russell.
Mors et vita [Poems], by Shan F. Bullock. 1923. Foreword by Russell.
Guilds and co-operatives in Italy, by O. Por. 1923. Introd by Russell.
Island blood, by F. R. Higgins. 1925. Foreword by Russell.

Anglo-Irish literature, by H. Law. 1926. Foreword by Russell.
Living India, by S. Zimand. Dublin 1928. Introd by Russell.
Agin the governments: memories and adventures, by F. Fletcher-Vane. 1929. Foreword by Russell.
Standish James O'Grady: the man and the writer, by H. O'Grady. Dublin 1929. A tribute by Russell; includes 8 poems by Russell wrongly attributed to O'Grady.
Collected poems, by K. Hinkson [Tynan]. 1930. Foreword by Russell.
First hymn to Levin and other poems by 'Hugh MacDiarmid' [C. M. Grieve]. 1931. Introd by Russell.
The wild bird's nest: poems translated from the Irish, by 'Frank O'Connor' [Michael O'Donovan]. Dundrum 1932. With essay by Russell.
Twenty-five lyrics. by 'Seumas O'Sullivan' [J. S. Starkey]. Flansham Sussex 1933. Introd by Russell.
Selected poems, by Oliver St J. Gogarty. New York [1933], London 1938 (as Others to adorn). Foreword by Russell.
The valley of the bells and other poems, by I. Haugh. Oxford 1933. Introd by Russell.
Land under England, by J. O'Neill. 1935. Foreword by Russell.

§2

Ford, J. AE, the neo-Celtic mystic. Poet-Lore 16 1905.
Weygandt, C. AE, the Irish Emerson. Sewanee Rev 15 1907.
A school of Irish poetry. Edinburgh Rev 209 1909. On Yeats, M. O'Neill and Colum.
Boyd, E. AE–mystic and economist. North Amer Rev 202 1915.
—— In his Appreciation and depreciations, Dublin 1918.
Figgis, D. AE–George W. Russell: a study of a man and of a nation. Dublin 1916.
Colum, P. AE, poet, painter and economist. New Republic 15 1918.
Ervine, St J. In his Some impressions of my elders, 1923.
Speakman, H. Dublin hours with AE. Bookman (New York) Nov 1925.
'Eglinton, John' (W. K. Magee). AE and his story. Dial 82 1927.
—— A memoir of AE. 1937.
—— A note on AE's The avatars. Dublin Mag 16 1941.
—— The poetry of AE. Dublin Mag 26 1951.
Garnier, C. Tagore et George Russell. Revue Anglo-américaine 7 1929.
—— George Russell, AE: poète du sommeil, avec fragments de lettres inédites. Etudes Anglaises 3 1939.
Biens, F. AE: sein Leben und Werk im Lichte seiner theosophischen Weltanschauung. Greifswald 1934.
Clyde, W. AE. [1935]. Foreword by 'Seumas O'Sullivan' (J. S. Starkey). A lecture.
Curran, C. P. George Russell. Studies 24 1935.
Finlay, T. AE: in memoriam. Dublin Mag 10 1935.
Hopfl, H. AE: Dichtung und Mystik: Versuch einer Deutung von AE's mystischer Weltanschauung. Bonn 1935.
Tierney, M. A prophet of mystic nationalism: AE. Studies 26 1937.
Jameson, G. Irish poets of today and Blake. PMLA 53 1938. Influence of Blake on AE and Yeats.
Cassidy, C. Some less-known chapters in the life of AE. Dublin 1939 (priv ptd). A lecture.
'O'Connor, Frank' (M. O'Donovan). Two friends: Yeats and AE. Yale Rev 29 1939.
O'Faolain, S. AE and W.B. Virginia Quart Rev 15 1939.
Plass, M. Mystische Lyrik und politische Prosa im Werk Russells. Würzburg 1940.
Byrne, J. AE, poet and man. Poet-Lore 47 1941.
Russell, D. AE. Atlantic Monthly Feb 1943.
—— AE. Irish Writing 1951.
Bose, A. Three mystic poets: W. B. Yeats, AE and Rabindranath Tagore. Kolhapur 1945.
De Blacam, A. Talks with AE. Irish Bookman 1 1947.
Gogarty, O. Mourning becomes Mrs Spendlove. New York 1948.
—— An angelic anarchist. Colby Lib Quart 4 1955.
O'Casey, S. Dublin's glittering guy. In his Inisfallen fare thee well, 1949.
McFadden, R. The bard of Armagh: a note on AE. Rann (Belfast) 1952.
Kindilien, C. Russell and the Colby Library collection. Colby Library Quart 4 1955.
Wallace, H. AE: a prophet out of an ancient age. Ibid.
Gibbon, M. AE. The years of mystery. Dublin Mag 31 1956.
—— AE and the early days of theosophy in Dublin. Dublin Mag 32 1957.
—— AE and the Homestead. Dublin Mag 33 1958.
Watson, V. AE to E.H.W. Meyerstein. English 12 1959.
Fréchet, R. A propos d'AE, l'Irlandais et libre fidèle. Etudes Anglaises 15 1962.
Loftus, R. In his Nationalism in modern Anglo-Irish poetry, Madison 1964.

NORA HOPPER, later CHESSON

1871–1906

Ballads in prose. 1894.
Under quicken boughs. 1896.
Songs of the morning. 1900.
Aquamarines. 1902.
Mildred and her mills, and other poems. [1903].
Selected poems. 5 vols 1906.

IV. YEATS AND SYNGE

WILLIAM BUTLER YEATS

1865–1939

Most of Yeats's mss and personal papers are in the possession of his family. There are mss and letters in the National Library Dublin, the Berg Collection of the New York Public Library and the Univ of Texas. Many others are in private hands.

Bibliographies etc

Wade, A. A bibliography of the writings of Yeats. In Collected works in verse and prose of Yeats vol 8, Stratford-on-Avon 1908, below.
—— A bibliography of the writings of Yeats. 1951, 1958 (rev). Addns by R. Alspach, Irish Book 2 1963.
Symons, A. J. A. A bibliography of the first editions of books by Yeats. 1924.

Roth, W. Catalogue of English and American first editions of Yeats. New Haven 1939.
O'Hegarty, P. Notes on the bibliography of Yeats. Dublin Mag Oct-Dec 1939, Jan-March 1940.
[Dougan, R.] Yeats: manuscripts and printed books exhibited in the library of Trinity College Dublin. Dublin 1956.
Gerstenberger, D. Yeats and the theatre: a selected bibliography. Modern Drama 6 1963.
Parrish, S. M. A concordance to the poems of Yeats. Ithaca 1963.

Collections

Poems. 1895, Boston 1895, London 1899, 1901, 1904, 1908, 1912, 1913, 1927, 1929 (all rev).
The poetical works in two volumes: vol 1 Lyrical poems, 1906; vol 2 Dramatical poems, 1907, 1912 (rev).
The collected works in verse and prose. Stratford-on-Avon 1908. Vol 1 Poems lyrical and narrative; vol 2 The king's threshold, On Baile's strand, Deirdre, The shadowy waters; vol 3 The countess Cathleen, The land of heart's desire. The unicorn from the stars; vol 4 The hour glass, Cathleen Ni Houlihan, The golden helmet, The Irish dramatic movement; vol 5 The Celtic twilight, Stories from Red Hanrahan; vol 6 Ideas of good and evil; vol 7 The secret rose, Rosa alchemica, The tables of the law, The adoration of the magi, John Sherman, Dhoya; vol 8 Discoveries, Edmund Spenser, Poetry and tradition and other essays. Vol 8 contains Wade's bibliography, above. The countess Cathleen tr Polish, [1912]; Italian, 1914; Swedish, 1923.
Poems: second series. Stratford-on-Avon 1909.
A selection from the poetry of Yeats. Leipzig 1913. Selection by Yeats.
Selected poems. New York 1921.
Collected edition of the works: vol 1 Later poems. 1922, New York 1924; vol 2 Plays in prose and verse written for an Irish theatre, and generally with the help of a friend, 1922, New York 1924; vol 3 Plays and controversies, 1923, New York 1924; vol 4 Essays, 1924, New York 1924; vol 5 Early poems and stories, 1925, New York 1925; vol 6 Autobiographies: Reveries over childhood and youth and The trembling of the veil. 1926, New York 1927.
Selected poems: lyrical and narrative. 1929, 1951.
The collected poems. New York 1933, London 1933, 1950 (enlarged with author's final corrections), New York 1951, 1957, 1960, London [1961].
The collected plays. 1934, New York 1935, (with first pbn of Oedipus at Colonus), London 1952 (enlarged), New York 1953, New York [1963].
Nine one-act plays. 1937.
Selected poems. Ed A. Holst, Amsterdam 1939.
The poems of Yeats. 2 vols 1949. Definitive edn with author's final corrections and revisions.
The variorum edition of the poems. Ed P. Allt and R. Alspach, New York 1957.
Selected poems and two plays. Ed M. Rosenthal, New York 1962.
Poems. Ed A. N. Jeffares 1963 (selection); Selected prose, ed Jeffares 1964; Selected plays, ed Jeffares 1964; selected criticism, ed Jeffares 1964.
Poèmes choisis. Ed and tr L. Cazamian, Aubier [1954]. English and French texts.
Poèmes. Tr A. Audra, Paris [1956].
Poemas. Tr J. Ferran, Madrid 1957. English and Spanish texts.

§ 1

Mosada: a dramatic poem, reprinted from the Dublin University Review [June 1886]. Dublin 1886, Dundrum 1943.
The wanderings of Oisin and other poems. 1889, 1892.
Ganconagh. John Sherman and Dhoya. 1891, 1891, 1892, New York [1891]. 'Ganconagh' is Yeats's pseudonym.
The Countess Cathleen and various legends and lyrics. 1892, 1892, Boston 1892.
The Celtic twilight: men and women, dhouls and fairies. 1893, New York 1894, London 1902 (rev and enlarged), New York [1902], Dublin 1905, London and Stratford-on-Avon 1912.
The land of heart's desire. 1894, Chicago 1894, Portland Maine 1903 (two edns rptd from Bibelot 9 1903), New York 1909, London 1912, Boston [1918 or later], Boston 1920, London 1924 (with the Countess Cathleen), San Francisco 1926; tr German, 1911, 1933; Italian, 1914, 1945; Swedish, 1924.
The secret rose, with illustrations by J. B. Yeats. 1897, New York 1897, Dublin 1905; tr Swedish (in part), 1924; German (in part), 1927.
The tables of the law; The adoration of the magi. 1897 (priv ptd), 1904, Stratford-on-Avon 1914.
The wind among the reeds. 1899, New York 1899, London 1900, New York 1902, 1905, Cambridge Mass 1911.
The shadowy waters. 1900 (rptd from North Amer Rev May 1900), 1901, New York 1901, 1901, 1905; acting version, 1907; tr Italian, 1914, 1945; Swedish, 1923; Danish, 1924; German, 1933.
Is the order of R.R. & A.C. [Rubidae Rosae and Aurae Crucis] to remain a magical order? by D.E.D.I. 1901 (priv ptd). A postscript by D.E.D.I. 1901. D.E.D.I. is Yeas's pseudonym.
There are seven that pull the thread: song in act 1 Grania and Diarmid, the verse written by Yeats, the music composed by Edward Elgar. 1902. Rptd from A broad sheet, 1902.
Cathleen ni Houlihan. 1902, 1902 (rptd from Samhain Oct 1902); theatre edns 1906, 1909, Stratford-on-Avon 1911; tr Irish, 1905; Italian, 1914, 1945; Swedish, 1923; German, 1933.
Where there is nothing: a play in five acts. Dublin 1902 (issued as special suppl to The United Irishman 1 Nov 1902), New York 1902, 1902 (priv ptd for J. Quinn), London 1903, New York 1903.
Ideas of good and evil. 1903, 1903, New York 1903 (3 edns), Dublin 1905, London 1907, 1914; tr Japanese, 1914; German (in part), 1916.
In the seven woods: being poems chiefly of the Irish heroic age. Dundrom 1903, New York 1903; tr Danish, 1924.
The hour glass: a morality. 1903 (rptd from North Amer Rev Sept 1903); theatre edn 1907; Dundrum 1914 (a new version, partly in verse and partly in prose rptd from Mask (Florence) April 1913. Two separate versions, one in verse and one in prose, appeared in vol 2 Collected edition of the works, 1922, above; tr Swedish, 1923; German, 1933; Italian, 1944.
The hour-glass and other plays, being volume two of plays for an Irish theatre. New York 1904, London 1904 (entitled The hour-glass, Cathleen ni Houlihan, The pot of broth, being volume two of plays for an Irish theatre), Dublin 1905.
The king's threshold. New York 1904 (priv ptd for J. Quinn), London 1904 (with On Baile's strand), Dublin 1905; theatre edn, Stratford-on-Avon 1911, 1915, London 1937; tr German, 1933.
On Baile's strand. Dublin 1905, London 1907 (rev); tr Swedish, 1923; German, 1933.
Stories of Red Hanrahan. Dundrum 1905. Stories from The secret rose, above, rewritten with the help of Lady Gregory.
The pot of broth. 1905, 1911 (rptd from The hour glass and other plays, New York 1904, above); tr Swedish, 1923.
Poems 1899–1905. 1906.
Deirdre. 1907, Stratford-on-Avon 1911 (rev), London 1914; tr German 1933. A four-page leaflet of 'alterations' was issued in 1908.
Discoveries: a volume of essays (rev). Dundrum 1907.

The unicorn from the stars and other plays, with Lady Gregory. New York 1908. The unicorn tr Swedish, 1924; German, 1933.
The golden helmet. New York 1908 (priv ptd for J. Quinn); tr German, 1933.
The green helmet and other poems. Dundrum 1910, New York 1911, London 1912 (enlarged).
The green helmet: an heroic farce. Stratford-on-Avon 1911; tr Danish, 1924.
Synge and the Ireland of his time, with a note concerning a walk through Connemara with him by Jack Butler Yeats. Dundrum 1911.
Plays for an Irish theatre: Deirdre, The green helmet, On Baile's strand, The king's threshold, The shadowy waters, The hour glass, Cathleen ni Houlihan. 1911.
The Countess Cathleen. 1912 (rev version of the text in vol 3 of Collected works 1908, above), 1924 (with The land of heart's desire); tr Danish, 1924; German, 1925, 1933; Italian, 1944.
The cutting of an agate. New York 1912, London 1919 (enlarged).
Stories of Red Hanrahan, the secret rose, rosa alchemica. 1913, New York 1914.
A selection from the love poetry of Yeats. Dundrum 1913.
Poems written in discouragement 1912–13. Dundrum 1913.
Nine poems chosen from the works of Yeats. [New York] 1914 (priv ptd for J. Quinn).
Responsibilities: poems and a play. Dundrum 1914; tr Danish, 1924.
Reveries over childhood and youth. Dundrum 1915, New York 1916, London 1916.
Eight poems by Yeats transcribed by Edward Pay, published by Form [Magazine]. 1916.
Responsibilities and other poems. 1916, New York 1916.
Easter 1916. 1916 (priv ptd for C. Shorter).
The wild swans at Coole, other verses and a play in verse. Dundrum 1917, London 1919 (enlarged), New York 1919.
Per amica silentia lunae. 1918, New York 1918.
Nine poems. 1918 (priv ptd for C. Shorter).
Two plays for dancers. Dundrum 1919. The dreaming of the bones, The only jealousy of Emer.
Michael Robartes and the dancer. Dundrum 1920 (for 1921); tr Danish, 1924.
Four plays for dancers. 1921, New York 1921. At the hawk's well, The only jealousy of Emer, The dreaming of the bones, Calvary.
Seven poems and a fragment. Dundrum 1922.
The trembling of the veil. 1922 (priv ptd).
The player queen. 1922; tr Swedish, 1924.
The lake isle of Innisfree, with a facsimile of the poem in the poet's handwriting. [San Francisco?] 1924 (priv ptd).
The cat and the moon and certain poems. Dundrum 1924.
A vision: an explanation of life founded upon the writings of Giraldus and upon certain doctrines attributed to Kusta Ben Luka. 1937 (priv ptd). *See* below.
Poems. 1929. Early poems only.
The Augustan books of English poetry: second series no 4 1927. Selected poems.
October blast. Dundrum 1929.
Stories of Red Hanrahan and The secret rose, illustrated by N. McGuiness. 1927. Text of the 6 Red Hanrahan stories rev with Lady Gregory's help in 1904.
The tower. 1928, New York 1928.
Sophocles' King Oedipus: a version for the modern stage. 1928, New York 1928.
A packet for Ezra Pound. Dundrum 1929.
The winding stair. New York 1929.
Three things, with drawings by G. Spencer. 1929, 1929. Rptd from New Republic 2 Oct 1929.
Stories of Michael Robartes and his friends: an extract from a record made by his pupils and a play in prose. Dundrum 1931 (for 1932).
Words for music perhaps and other poems. Dundrum 1932.
The winding stair and other poems. 1933, New York 1933.
The words upon the window pane: a play in one act, with notes upon the play and its subject. Dundrum 1934.
Wheels and butterflies. 1934, New York 1935.
The king of the great clock tower: commentaries and poems. Dundrum 1934, New York 1935.
The singing head and the lady. 1934 (priv ptd by F. Prokosch). Rptd from Spectator 7 Dec 1934.
A full moon [in March]. 1935.
Dramatis personae. Dundrum 1935.
Poems. Dundrum 1935. 9 poems.
Leda and the swan. Florence. 1935 (priv ptd by F. Prokosch). Rptd from The cat and the moon, above.
Dramatis personae 1896–1902, Estrangement, The death of Synge, The bounty of Sweden. New York 1936, London 1936.
A vision. 1937, New York 1938, 1956 (with author's final corrections), London 1962, 1962. A substantially new version of A vision, 1925, above.
Essays 1931 to 1936. Dundrum 1937.
The herne's egg: a stage play. 1938; tr French, 1950.
The herne's egg and other plays. New York 1938.
New poems. Dundrum 1938.
The autobiography of Yeats, consisting of Reveries over childhood and youth, The trembling of the veil and Dramatis personae. New York 1938. Enlarged as Autobiographies, below.
Last poems and two plays. Dundrum 1939.
On the boiler. Dundrum 1939, Dublin 1939.
Last poems and plays. 1940, New York 1940.
If I were four-and-twenty. Dundrum 1940.
Autobiographies. 1955. Contains Reveries over childhood and youth, The trembling of the veil, Dramatis personae, Estrangement, The death of Synge, The bounty of Sweden.
Essays and introductions. 1961. Contains Ideas of good and evil, The cutting of an agate, later essays and introds.
Explorations. 1962. Essays, introds, articles etc selected by Mrs Yeats.
Mythologies. 1962. Contains The Celtic twilight, The secret rose, Stories of Red Hanrahan, Rosa alchemica, The tables of the law, The adoration of the magi, Per amica silentia lunae.

Letters, Diaries, Speeches etc

Letters

Letters to the new island. Ed H. Reynolds, Cambridge Mass 1934. Rptd from Boston Pilot & Providence Sunday Jnl 1889–91.
Letters on poetry from Yeats to Dorothy Wellesley. Oxford 1940, New York 1940.
Florence Farr, Bernard Shaw and W. B. Yeats. Ed C. Bax, Dundrum 1941, New York 1942, London 1946.
Some letters from Yeats to John O'Leary and his sister, from originals in the Berg Collection. Ed A. Wade, New York 1953.
Yeats and T. Sturge Moore: their correspondence 1901–37. Ed U. Bridge, Oxford 1953.
Letters to Katharine Tynan. Ed R. McHugh, Dublin 1953, New York 1953.
The letters of Yeats. Ed A. Wade 1954, New York 1955. First complete edn.
Some new letters from Yeats to Lady Gregory. Ed D. Torchiana and G. O'Malley, REL 4 1963. *See also Häusermann under* §2, *below*.

Diaries

Four years. Dundrum 1921. Rptd from London Mercury and Dial 1921.

Estrangement: being some fifty thoughts from a diary kept by Yeats in the year nineteen hundred and nine. Dundrum 1926.
The death of Synge, and other passages from an old diary. Dundrum 1928.
Pages from a diary written in nineteen hundred and thirty. Dundrum 1940.

Speeches

'98 Centennial Association of Great Britain and France: report of speeches delivered at inaugural banquet April 13 1898. Dublin 1898. Speech by Yeats, The union of the Gael.
Royal Society of Literature. Addresses of reception to J. Masefield and others by W. Raleigh and others. Oxford 1914. Contains Yeats's address on the award of the Polignac prize to J. Stephens.
Seanad Eireann. Disboireachtai Parliminte [Parliamentary debates]. Official report of Yeats's utterances in the Irish Senate. 10 vols Dublin 1922–8. Rptd in Senate speeches, below.
Les prix Nobel en 1923. Stockholm 1924. Yeats's lecture before the Royal Swedish Academy. Rptd in The bounty of Sweden, below.
Coinage of Saorstat Eireann. Dublin 1928. Yeats contributed What we did or tried to do. Rptd in Senate speeches, below.
The bounty of Sweden: a meditation and a lecture delivered before the Royal Swedish Academy. Dundrum 1925.
Reale Accademia d'Italia. The Irish national theatre. Rome 1934. Text of a lecture by Yeats.
Modern poetry. 1936. BBC broadcast of 11 Oct 1936; rptd from Listener 14 Oct 1936.
A speech [before the Irish Academy of Letters] and two poems. Dublin 1937 (priv ptd).
The Senate speeches of Yeats. Ed D. Pearce, Bloomington 1960.

Books edited by Yeats

Fairy and folk tales of the Irish peasantry. 1888; tr Japanese (in part), 1925. With contributions by Yeats.
Stories from Carleton. 1889. Introd by Yeats.
Representative Irish tales. New York 1891. Introd and notes by Yeats.
Irish fairy tales. 1892, New York 1892 (introd and notes by Yeats); tr German, 1894.
The works of William Blake. 3 vols 1893, 1893. With E. Ellis.
The poems of William Blake. 1893, 1893, 1905, 1910 (with rev introd), New York nd (Modern Lib). Introd and notes by Yeats.
Irish fairy and folk tales. Illustr J. Torrance 1893, New York 1895. Text identical with that of Fairy and folk tales of the Irish peasantry, above.
A book of Irish verse selected from modern writers. 1895, 1900 (rev). Introd and notes by Yeats.
A book of images, drawn by W. Horton. 1898. Introd by Yeats.
Beltaine: an occasional publication. 3 nos 1899–1900, 1900. Contributions by Yeats.
Samhain, edited for the Irish Literary Theatre. 7 nos Dublin 1901–1908. Contributions by Yeats.
Irish fairy and folk tales. New York 1902, nd. Contents substantially the same as Fairy and folk tales of the Irish peasantry, above.
Twenty-one poems written by Lionel Johnson. Dundrum 1904. Without introd by Yeats.
Some essays and passages by John Eglinton. Dundrum 1905. Without introd by Yeats.
Sixteen poems by William Allingham. Dundrum 1905. Without introd by Yeats.
Poems of Spenser. Edinburgh 1906. Introd by Yeats.
The arrow. 5 nos Dublin 1906–1909. Contributions by Yeats.
Twenty-one poems by Katharine Tynan. Dundrum 1907. Without introd by Yeats.
British Association visit: Abbey Theatre special programme. Dublin 1908. Contribution by Yeats.
Poetry and Ireland: essays by Yeats and Lionel Johnson. Dundrum 1908. Yeats's contribution, Poetry and patriotism, appeared also in Collected works in verse and prose vol 8, above.
Poems and translations by John M. Synge. Dundrum 1909, New York 1909 (priv ptd for J. Quinn). Preface by Yeats.
Deirdre of the sorrows: a play by John M. Synge. Dundrum 1910, New York 1910 (priv ptd for J. Quinn). Preface by Yeats.
Selections from the writings of Lord Dunsany. Dundrum 1912. Introd by Yeats.
Irish fairy and folk tales. New York [1918] (Modern Lib). Contributions by Yeats identical with those to Fairy and folk tales of the Irish peasantry, above.
Broadsides: a collection of old and new songs. Dundrum 1935. With F. Higgins. Contributions by Yeats et al.
The Oxford book of modern verse 1892–1935. Oxford 1936, New York 1936. Introd and poems by Yeats.
The ten principal Upanishads, put into English by Shree Purohit Swami and Yeats. 1937, New York 1937. Yeats also contributed preface.
Broadsides: a collection of new Irish and English songs. Dundrum 1937. With D. Wellesley. Contributions by Yeats et al.

Contributions to Books

Poems and ballads of Young Ireland. Dublin 1888. Poems by Yeats.
Irish minstrelsy. Ed H. Sparling 1888. Poem by Yeats.
The book of the Rhymers' Club. 1892, 1892. Poems by Yeats.
The poets and the poetry of the century. Ed A. Miles, vols 5 and 7 1892. Entries on Allingham and E. O'Leary by Yeats.
The second book of the Rhymers' Club. 1894. Poems by Yeats.
The pageant. Ed C. Shannon and J. White 1896. Story by Yeats.
Roma. In Recueil artistique international, publié par le comité, Rome 1897. Poem by Yeats.
Literary ideals in Ireland, by J. Eglinton, Yeats and AE. 1899. Essays by Yeats.
A treasury of Irish poetry in the English tongue. Ed S. Brooke and T. Rolleston 1900, New York 1900. Essays and poems by Yeats.
Ideals in Ireland. Ed Lady Gregory 1901, New York 1901. Essays by Yeats.
Cuchulain of Muirthemne, arranged and put into English by Lady Gregory. 1904, New York 1904. Preface by Yeats.
Gods and fighting men, arranged and put into English by Lady Gregory. 1904, New York 1904. Preface by Yeats.
The love songs of Connacht, collected and translated by D. Hyde. Dundrum 1904. Preface by Yeats.
Irish literature. Ed J. McCarthy 10 vols Philadelphia 1904. Yeats contributed an essay, Modern Irish poetry, to vol 3 and is listed as one of the authors of Biographies and literary appreciations.
Wayfarer's love: contributions from living poets. Ed Duchess of Sutherland 1904. Poem by Yeats.
The well of the saints, by J. M. Synge. 1905. Introd by Yeats.
A bibliography of the writings of Yeats, by A. Wade. Stratford-on-Avon 1908. Poem and prologue to The King's threshold by Yeats.

Gitanjali, by R. Tagore. 1912, 1913, New York 1914. Introd by Yeats. *See* Gitanjali, below.
Our Irish theatre, by Lady Gregory. New York 1913. Contains Yeats's Advice to playwrights who are sending plays to the Abbey, Dublin.
The post office, by R. Tagore. Dundrum 1914, London 1914. Preface by Yeats.
Catholic anthology 1914–15. 1915. Poem by Yeats.
The book of the homeless. Ed A. Wharton 1916. Poem by Yeats.
Certain noble plays of Japan, by E. Fenollosa and E. Pound. Dundrum 1916. Introd by Yeats.
Gitanjali and fruit gathering, by R. Tagore. 1919. Introd by Yeats, rptd from Gitanjali, above.
Visions and beliefs in the west of Ireland, by Lady Gregory. New York 1920. Essays and notes by Yeats.
The John Keats memorial volume. 1921. Yeats contributed A letter about the book.
The complete works of Oscar Wilde, vol 3. Garden City NY 1923. Introd by Yeats.
Early memories: some chapters of autobiography by John Butler Yeats. Dundrum 1923. Preface by Yeats.
An offering of swans, by O. Gogarty. Dundrum 1923 (for 1924), London 1924. Preface by Yeats.
Axel, by V. de l'Isle-Adam. 1925. Preface by Yeats.
The midnight court and The adventures of a luckless fellow, translated from the Gaelic by P. Assher. 1926, New York 1926. Introd by Yeats.
Songs of innocence, by W. Blake. 1927. Prefatory letter by Yeats.
Wild apples, by O. Gogarty. Dundrum 1930. Preface by Yeats.
Bishop Berkeley, by J. Hone and M. Rossi. 1931. Introd by Yeats.
The golden book of Tagore. Ed R. Chatterjee, Calcutta 1931. Yeats contributed A letter to Tagore.
Coole, by Lady Gregory. Dundrum 1931. Poem by Yeats.
The new keepsake, by M. Baring and others. 1931. Poem by Yeats.
An Indian monk, by P. Swami. 1932. Introd by Yeats.
Spectator's gallery. Ed P. Fleming 1932 (for 1933). Essays and poems by Yeats rptd from Spectator.
The holy mountain, by B. Hamsa. Introd and biographical note by Yeats.
Selections from the poems of Dorothy Wellesley. 1936. Introd by Yeats.
The lemon tree, by M. Ruddock. Introductory poem and footnotes by Yeats.
Others to adorn, by O. Gogarty. 1938. Preface by Yeats.
Aphorisms of Yoga, by B. Patanjali. 1938. Introd by Yeats.
A poet's life, by H. Munroe. New York 1938. Letters and speech by Yeats.
Lightning flash, by M. O'Leary. 1949. Letter by Yeats to L. Robinson dated 16 April 1929.
Lady Gregory's journals 1916–30. Ed L. Robinson 1946. Poems by Yeats.
Selected poems, by D. Wellesley. 1949. Introd by Yeats rptd from Selections from the poems of D. Wellesley, above.
Bread out of stone, by S. Iris. Chicago 1953. Preface by Yeats dated 1934.

Miscellaneous

The speckled bird. Ed J. Hone. Bell March 1941. Part of ch from the unfinished novel.
Tribute to Thomas Davis; with an account of the Thomas Davis centenary meeting held in Dublin on November 20th, 1914. Cork 1947. Text of Yeats's Thomas Davis rptd from New Ireland 17 July 1915.
Diarmuid and Grania: a play in three acts by George Moore and Yeats. Dublin 1951. Rptd from Dublin Mag April-June 1951.
The speckled bird: a novel by Yeats—section from the novel with a note by Curtis Bradford. Irish Writing 31 1955.

§2

Johnson, L. The poetry of Yeats. Academy 1 Oct 1892.
Archer, W. In his Poets of the younger generation, 1902.
'Macleod, Fiona' (William Sharp). The later work of Yeats. North Amer Rev 175 1902.
Krans, H. Yeats and the Irish literary revival. 1904.
More, P. E. Two poets of the Irish movement. In his Shelburne essays ser 1, New York 1904.
Symons, A. In his Studies in prose and verse, 1904.
Elton, O. Living Irish literature. In his Modern studies, 1907.
Gwynn, S. Poetry and the stage. Fortnightly Rev Feb 1909.
Moore, G. Hail and farewell: ave. 1911.
—— Yeats, Lady Gregory and Synge. Eng Rev 16 1914.
Chesterton, G. K. Efficiency in elfland. Littell's Living Age 274 1912.
Hinkson, K. (Tynan). Twenty-five years. 1913.
—— The middle years. 1916.
—— Letters from Yeats. Yale Rev 29 1930.
Weygandt, C. Mr Yeats. In his Irish plays and playwrights, New York 1913.
Gregory, Lady. Our Irish theatre. 1914.
Reid, F. Yeats: a critical study. 1915.
Gurd, P. The early poetry of Yeats. Lancaster Pa 1916.
Hone, J. Yeats: the poet in contemporary Ireland. Dublin 1916.
—— Yeats 1865–1939. 1941. A biography.
Pound, E. In his Pavanes and divisions, New York 1918.
Wrenn, C. Yeats: a literary study. Durham 1920.
Ervine, St J. In his Some impressions of my elders, 1923.
Colum, P. Mr Yeats's plays and later poems. Yale Rev 14 1925.
—— Poet's progress: Yeats in the theatre. Theatre Arts Monthly Dec 1935.
—— Yeats's lyrical poems. Irish Writing 2 [1947].
Russell, G. (AE). Yeats's early poems. Littell's Living Age Nov 1925.
'Eglinton, John' (W. K. Magee). Yeats and his story. Dial 80 1926.
—— Irish literary portraits. 1935.
—— A memoir of AE. 1937.
Richards, I. A. In his Science and poetry, 1926.
—— In his Principles of literary criticism, 1934.
Dubois, L. M. Yeats et le mouvement poétique en Irlande. Revue des Deux Mondes Oct 1929.
McGreevy, T. Mr Yeats as a dramatist. Revue Anglo-américaine 7 1929.
Empson, W. In his Seven types of ambiguity, 1930, 1953 (rev with addns). On Who goes with Fergus.
—— Mr Wilson on the Byzantium poems. REL 1 1960.
Williams, C. In his Poetry at present, Oxford 1930.
Wilson, E. In his Axel's castle, New York 1931.
Jackson, G. Mysticism in AE and Yeats in relation to Oriental and American thought. Columbus Ohio 1932.
Leavis, F. R. In his New bearings in English poetry, 1932, 1950 (with addns).
Strong, L. A. G. A letter to Yeats. 1932.
—— Yeats: an appreciation. Cornhill Mag July 1937.
—— In his Personal remarks, 1953.
Eliot, T. S. In his After strange gods, 1934.
—— A commentary. Criterion 14 1935.
—— The poetry of Yeats. Southern Rev 7 1941; rptd in The permanence of Yeats, below.
—— In his On poetry and poets, 1957.
Matthiessen, F. O. Yeats and four American poets. Yale Rev 23 1934.
—— The crooked road. Southern Rev 7 1941.
Murry, J. M. Mr Yeats's swan song. In his Aspects of literature, 1934 (rev); rptd in The permanence of Yeats, below.

Shaw, F. The Celtic twilight. Studies 23 1934.
Sitwell, E. In her Aspects of modern poetry, 1934.
Spender, S. Yeats as a realist. Criterion 14 1934; rptd in The permanence of Yeats, below.
— The destructive element. 1935.
Thunless, P. In his Modern poetic drama, Oxford 1934.
Tillyard, E. M. W. In his Poetry direct and oblique, 1934.
O'Faolain, S. W. B. Yeats. Eng Rev 60 1935.
— AE and WB. Virginia Quart Rev 15 1939.
— Yeats and the younger generation. Horizon Jan 1942.
Pollock, J. William Butler Yeats. 1935.
Rhys, E. Yeats: early recollections. Fortnightly Rev July 1935.
Saul, G. B. Literary parallels: Yeats and Coppard. N & Q 4 May. 1935
— Yeats's Hare. TLS 11 Jan 1947. Reply 18 Oct 1947.
— Yeats, Noyes and Day Lewis. N & Q June 1950.
— Yeats and his poems. TLS 31 March 1950.
— Jeffares on Yeats. MLN 66 1951.
— The winged image: a note on birds in Yeats's poems. BNYPL 58 1954.
— Prolegomena to the study of Yeats's poems. Philadelphia 1957.
— Prolegomena to the study of Yeats's plays. Philadelphia 1958.
— Yeats's verse before Responsibilities. Arizona Quart 16 1960.
— Coda: the verse of Yeats's last five years. Arizona Quart 17 1961.
— The short stories of Yeats. Poet Lore 57 1962.
— A frenzy of concentration: Yeats's verse from Responsibilities to the King of the great clock tower. Arizona Quart 20 1964.
Barnes, T. Yeats, Synge, Ibsen and Strindberg. Scrutiny 5 1936.
Passages from the letters of AE to Yeats. Dundrum 1936.
Zabel, M. D. Yeats at thirty and seventy. Poetry 47 1936.
— The thinking of the body: Yeats in the Autobiographies. Southern Rev 7 1941.
Bush, D. In his Mythology and the romantic tradition, Cambridge Mass 1937.
Gilomen, W. George Moore and his friendship with Yeats. E Studies 19 1937.
Gogarty, O. As I was walking down Sackville Street. 1937.
— Yeats: a memoir. Dublin 1963. Preface by M. Dillon.
Hoare, A. The works of Morris and Yeats in relation to early saga literature. Cambridge 1937.
Lewis, C. D. In his A hope for poetry, 1937.
— A note on Yeats and the aristocratic tradition. In Scattering branches, ed S. Gwynn 1940.
Bogan, L. William Butler Yeats. Atlantic Monthly May 1938.
Brooks, C. The vision of Yeats. Southern Rev 4 1938; rptd in his Modern poetry and the tradition, Chapel Hill 1939, 1948 (rev).
— Yeats and his deep rooted blossomer. In his Well wrought urn, New York 1947.
— In his Hidden god, New Haven 1963.
Ellmann, R. Yeats, magician. Western Rev 12 1938.
— Robartes and Aherne: two sides of a penny. Kenyon Rev 10 1948.
— Black magic against white: Aleister Crowley versus W. B. Yeats. Partisan Rev 15 1948.
— Yeats: the man and the masks. New York 1948.
— Joyce and Yeats. Kenyon Rev 12 1950.
— The art of Yeats: affirmative capability. Kenyon Rev 15 1953.
— The identity of Yeats. Oxford 1954.
— Yeats without analogue. Kenyon Rev 26 1964.
— Yeats and Eliot. Encounter July 1965.
Jameson, G. Irish poets of today and Blake. PMLA 53 1938.
MacBride, M. (Gonne). A servant of the Queen. 1938.
Brash, W. W. B. Yeats. London Quart 164 1939.
Bronowski, J. In his Poet's defence, Cambridge 1939.
Cattaui, G. Rencontres avec Yeats. Nouvelles Littéraires 4 Feb 1939.
— Trois poètes: Hopkins, Yeats, Eliot. Paris 1947.
Cazamian, M. William Butler Yeats. Etudes Anglaises 3 1939.
Clarke, A. W. B. Yeats. Dublin Mag 14 1939.
Clarke, E. William Butler Yeats. Dublin Rev 204 1939.
Colum, M. Memories of Yeats. Saturday Rev of Lit 25 Feb 1939.
Edgar, P. The enigma of Yeats. Queen's Quart 46 1939.
Ellis-Fermor, U. In her Irish dramatic movement, 1939, 1954 (rev).
Gillet, L. W. B. Yeats. Revue des Deux Mondes 1 March 1939.
Higgins, F. Yeats and poetic drama in Ireland. In The Irish theatre, ed L. Robinson 1939.
Hogan, J. W. B. Yeats. Studies 28 1939.
'O'Connor, Frank' (M. F. O'Donovan). Two friends: Yeats and AE. Yale Rev 29 1939.
— The old age of a poet. Bell Feb 1941.
— Quarrelling with Yeats: a friendly recollection. Esquire Dec 1964.
O'Donnell, J. Sailing to Byzantium: a study in the development of the later style and symbolism in the poetry of Yeats. Cambridge Mass 1939.
O'Hegarty, P. Yeats and the revolutionary Ireland of his time. Dublin Mag 14 1939.
Ransom, J. C. Yeats and his symbols. Kenyon Rev 1 1939; rptd in The permanence of Yeats, below.
— The Irish, the Gaelic and the Byzantine. Southern Rev 7 1941.
Richardson, D. Yeats of Bloomsbury. Life & Letters 21 1939.
Rivoallan, A. William Butler Yeats. Langues Modernes 37 1939.
Scott-James, R. The farewell to Yeats. London Mercury March 1939.
Smith, A. A poet young and old: Yeats. Toronto 1939. Rptd from UTQ 8 1939.
Whitridge, A. Yeats 1865–1939. Dalhousie Rev 19 1939.
Auden, W. H. Yeats: master of diction. Saturday Rev of Lit 8 June 1940.
— In memory of Yeats. In his Collected poetry, New York 1945. A poem.
— The public vs the late William Butler Yeats. In Partisan reader 1934–44, New York 1946; and in Foundations of modern literary judgement, ed M. Schorer, New York 1948.
— Yeats as an example. Kenyon Rev 10 1948; rptd in The permanence of Yeats, below.
Blackmur, R. P. The later poetry of Yeats. In his Expense of greatness, New York 1940. Rptd from Southern Rev 2 1936.
— Between myth and philosophy: fragments of Yeats. Southern Rev 7 1941.
Daiches, D. In his Poetry and the modern world, Chicago 1940; rptd in The permanence of Yeats, below.
Fay, W. G. The poet and the actor. In Scattering branches, ed S. Gwynn 1940.
Lipski, W. Note sur le symbolisme de Yeats. Etudes Anglaises 4 1940.
Masefield, J. Some memories of Yeats. Dublin 1940.
Pauly, M. Yeats et les symbolistes français. Revue de Littérature Comparée 20 1940.
Robinson, L. The man and the dramatist. In Scattering branches, below.
Scattering branches: tributes to the memory of Yeats. Ed S. Gwynn 1940. Contributions by M. Gonne, W. Rothenstein, L. Robinson, W. G. Fay, E. Dulac, F. R. Higgins, C. Day Lewis, L. A. G. Strong and the editor.
Allt, P. W. B. Yeats. Theology 42 1941.
— Yeats and the revision of his early verse. Hermathena 64–5 1944–5.
— Yeats, religion and history. Sewanee Rev 60 1952.

— Lady Gregory and Yeats's cult of aristocracy. Irish Writing 31 1955.
Baker, H. Domes of Byzantium. Southern Rev 7 1941.
Brenner, R. In his Poets of our time, New York 1941.
Burke, K. On motivation in Yeats. Southern Rev 7 1941; rptd in The permanence of Yeats, below.
— The problem of the intrinsic. In his Grammar of motives, New York 1945.
Church, R. In his Eight for immortality, 1941.
Davidson, D. Yeats and the centaur. Southern Rev 7 1941; rptd in The permanence of Yeats, below.
— Still rebels, still Yankees and other essays, Baton Rouge 1957.
Gregory, H. Yeats and the mask of Jonathan Swift. Southern Rev 7 1941; rptd in his Shield of Achilles, New York 1944.
Jarrell, R. The development of Yeats's sense of reality. Southern Rev 7 1941.
Knights, L. C. Yeats: the assertion of values. Southern Rev 7 1941; rptd in his Explorations, 1946.
MacNeice, L. The poetry of Yeats. Oxford 1941.
Mizener, A. The romanticism of Yeats. Southern Rev 7 1941.
Schwartz, D. An unwritten book. Ibid.
Southern Review 7 1941: Yeats memorial issue. Contributions from H. Baker, R. P. Blackmur, K. Burke, D. Davidson, T. S. Eliot, H. Gregory, R. Jarrell, L. C. Knights, F. O. Matthiessen, A. Mizener, J. C. Ransom, A. Schwartz, A. Tate, A. Warren, M. D. Zabel.
Tate, A. Yeats's romanticism: notes and suggestions. Ibid.
— Winter mask: to the memory of Yeats. Chimera 1 1943. A poem.
Warren, A. Religio poetae. Southern Rev 7 1941.
Killen, A. Some French influences in the works of Yeats at the end of the nineteenth century. Comparative Lit Stud 8 1942.
Menon, V. The development of Yeats. 1942, 1960 (rev).
Olson, E. Sailing to Byzantium: prolegomena to a poetics of the lyric. Univ of Kansas City Rev 8 1942.
Alspach, R. Some sources of Yeats's The wanderings of Oisin. PMLA 58 1943.
— Yeats's first two published poems. MLN 58 1943. Song of the fairies and Voices.
— The use by Yeats and other Irish writers of the folklore of Patrick Kennedy. Jnl of Amer Folklore 59 1946.
— Two songs of Yeats. MLN 61 1946. Red Hanrahan and Song of wandering Aengus.
— Yeats's Maid quiet. MLN 65 1950.
— Yeats's The grey rock. Jnl of Amer Folklore 63 1950.
— Some textual problems in Yeats. SB 9 1957.
Bowra, C. M. In his Heritage of symbolism, 1943.
Clemens, K. Some recollections of Yeats. Mark Twain Quart 6 1943.
Hackett, J. Shaw and Yeats. Studies 32 1943.
Houghton, W. Yeats and Crazy Jane: the hero in old age. MP 40 1943. Rptd in The permanence of Yeats, below.
MacLiammoir, M. Yeats, Lady Gregory, Denis Johnston. Bell 6 1943.
J. B. Yeats: letters to his son W. B. Yeats and others 1869–1922. Ed J. Hone 1944.
Savage, D. S. In his Personal principle, 1944.
— Two prophetic poems. Adelphi 22 1946.
Bose, A. Three mystic poets. Kolhapur 1945.
Burke, K. The problem of the intrinsic. In his A grammar of motives, New York 1945.
Edwards, O. Yeats and Ulster. Northman 13 1945.
Howarth, R. Yeats and Hopkins. N & Q 20 Oct 1945.
Notopoulos, J. Sailing to Byzantium. Classical Jnl Nov 1945.
Tindall, W. Y. The symbolism of Yeats. Accent 5 1945.
— In his Forces in modern British literature, New York 1947.
Bentley, E. In his Playwright as thinker, New York 1946.
— Yeats as playwright. Kenyon Rev 10 1948.
— On staging Yeats's plays. New Republic 128 1953.

Häusermann, H. W. Yeats's idea of Shelley. In The mint, ed G. Grigson 1946.
— Yeats's criticism of Ezra Pound. E Studies 29 1948.
— Yeats and W. J. Turner 1935–37. E Studies 40–1 1959–60. With unpbd letters.
Healy, J. Yeats and his imagination. Sewanee Rev 54 1946.
Jeffares, A. N. Yeats and his methods of writing verse. Nineteenth Century March 1946.
— Gyres in the poetry of Yeats. E Studies 27 1946.
— Yeats: man and poet. 1949. A biography.
— Yeats's The gyres: sources and symbolism. HLQ 15 1952.
— Yeats: the poems. 1961.
— The poems of Yeats. 1962.
— Yeats's Byzantine poems and the critics. Eng Stud in Africa 5 1962.
Murray, T. C. The casting out of Shaw and Yeats. Bell 12 1946.
'Orwell, George' (E. Blair). In his Critical essays, 1946.
Peacock, R. In his Poet in the theatre, 1946.
Seiden, M. A psychoanalytical essay on Yeats. Accent spring 1946. On The cap and bells.
— Yeats as a playwright. Western Humanities Rev 13 1959.
— Yeats: the poet as a myth-maker 1865–1939. East Lansing 1961.
Ure, P. Towards a mythology: studies in the poetry of Yeats. Liverpool 1946.
— The statues: a note on the meaning. RES 15 1949.
— The integrity of Yeats. Cambridge Jnl 3 1949.
— Yeats's Demon and beast. Irish Writing 31 1955.
— Yeats's supernatural songs. RES new ser 7 1956.
— A source of Yeats's Parnell's funeral. E Studies 39 1958.
— Yeats's Christian mystery plays. RES new ser 11 1960.
— Yeats's Deirdre. E Studies 42 1961.
— Yeats's hero-fool in The herne's egg. HLQ 24 1961.
— The evolution of Yeats's The Countess Cathleen. MLR 57 1962.
— Yeats the playwright: a commentary on character and design in the major plays. 1963.
— Yeats. Edinburgh 1963 (Writers & Critics).
— Yeats and the two harmonies. Modern Drama 7 1964.
Witt, M. The critical significance of biographical evidence: Yeats. Eng Inst Essays (New York) 1946.
— A note on Joyce and Yeats. MLN 63 1948.
— A competition for eternity: Yeats's review of his later poems. PMLA 64 1949.
— The making of an elegy: Yeats's In memory of Major Robert Gregory. MP 48 1950.
— Yeats on the poet laureateship. MLN 66 1951.
— Great art beaten down: Yeats on censorship. College Eng 13 1952.
— W. B. Yeats. TLS 11 April 1952.
— Yeats's The song of the happy shepherd. PQ 32 1953.
— An unknown Yeats poem. MLN 70 1955.
— A note on Yeats and Symons. N & Q Dec 1960.
— Yeats 1865–1965. PMLA 80 1965.
Alexander, I. Valéry and Yeats: the rehabilitation of time. Scottish Periodical 1 1947.
Freyer, G. The politics of Yeats. Politics & Letters 1 1947.
Frye, N. Yeats and the language of symbolism. UTQ 17 1947.
Hayden, H. The last of the romantics: an introduction to the symbolism of Yeats. Sewanee Rev 55 1947.
Stauffer, D. The modern myth of the modern myth. English Inst Stud (New York) 1947.
— Yeats and the medium of poetry. ELH 15 1948.
— The golden nightingale: essays on some principles of poetry in the lyrics of Yeats. New York 1949.
Henn, T. R. The return to the valley. Irish Lib Bull 9 1948.
— The lonely tower: studies in the poetry of Yeats. 1950.
— Yeats and the Irish background. Yale Rev 42 1953.

— The accent of Yeats's Last poems. E & S 9 1956.
Mercier, V. Speech after long silence. Irish Writing 6 1948.
— Yeats and the Fisherman. TLS 6 June 1958.
— In defence of Yeats. Modern Drama 8 1965.
Stamm, R. The sorrow of love. E Studies 29 1948.
Weeks, D. Image and idea in Yeats's The second coming. PMLA 63 1948.
Bradford, C. Journeys to Byzantium. Virginia Quart Rev 25 1949.
— Yeats's Byzantium poems: a study of their development. PMLA 75 1960.
— The order of Yeats's last poems. MLN 76 1961.
— Yeats at work. Carbondale 1965.
Dulac, E. Yeats as I knew him. Irish Writing 8 1949.
Hough, G. A study of Yeats. Cambridge Jnl 2 1949.
— In his Last romantics, 1949.
Rajan, B. Yeats and the unity of being. Nineteenth Century Sept 1949.
Stein, A. Yeats: a study in recklessness. Sewanee Rev 57 1949.
Bjersby, B. The interpretation of the Cuchulain legend in the works of Yeats. Upsala 1950.
Goldgar, H. Axël de Villiers de l'Isle-Adam et The shadowy waters de Yeats. Revue de Littérature Comparée 24 1950.
— Yeats and the black centaur in French. Western Rev 15 1951.
Graves, R. In his Common asphodel, 1950. On the Lake isle of Innisfree.
Heath-Stubbs, J. In his Darkling plain, 1950. On Purgatory.
Parkinson, T. Yeats: a poet's stagecraft 1899–1911. ELH 17 1950.
— Yeats: self-critic. Berkeley 1951.
— The individuality of Yeats. Pacific Spectator 6 1952.
— The sun and the moon in Yeats's early poetry. MP 50 1952.
— Yeats and Pound: the illusion of influence. Comparative Lit 6 1954.
— Vestiges of creation. Sewanee Rev 69 1961.
— Yeats: the later poetry. Berkeley 1963.
Smith, G. Yeats's Cat and the moon. N & Q 21 Jan 1950.
The permanence of Yeats: selected criticism. Ed J. Hall and M. Steinmann, New York 1950. *See* above.
Thompson, F. Poetry and politics: Yeats. Hopkins Rev 3 1950.
Watts, H. Yeats: theology bitter and gay. South Atlantic Quart 49 1950.
— Yeats and lapsed mythology. Renascence 3 1951.
Cronin, A. Some aspects of Yeats and his influence. Bell 16 1951.
Koch, V. Yeats: the tragic phase–a study of the last poems. 1951.
Pearce, D. Dublin's National Literary Society 1892. N & Q 12 May 1951.
— Philosophy and phantasy: notes on the growth of Yeats's system. Univ of Kansas City Rev 18 1952.
— Yeats and the romantics. Shenandoah 8 1957.
— Yeats's last plays: an interpretation. ELH 18 1957.
Whalley, G. Yeats's quarrel with old age. Queen's Quart 58 1951.
Benson, C. Yeats and Balzac's Louis Lambert. MP 49 1952.
— Yeats's The cat and the moon. MLN 68 1953.
Block, H. Flaubert, Yeats and the National Library. MLN 67 1952.
— Yeats's The King's threshold: the poet and society. PQ 34 1955.
Davenport, A. Yeats and the Upanishads. RES new ser 3 1952.
Dume, T. Yeats's golden tree and birds in the Byzantium poems. MLN 67 1952.
Fraser, G. S. Yeats and the new criticism. Colonnade 1 1952.
— Yeats and T. S. Eliot. In T. S. Eliot: a symposium for his seventieth birthday, ed N. Braybrooke 1958.
— Yeats's Byzantium. CQ 2 1960.
— W. B. Yeats. 1962.
— A Yeats borrowing [of a phrase in Easter 1916 from M. Ebbutt, Hero-myths and legends of the British race]. TLS 25 Feb 1965.
McHugh, R. Yeats, Synge and the Abbey Theatre. Studies 41 1952.
— Yeats and Irish politics. Texas Quart 5 1962.
Usher, A. Three great Irishmen: Shaw, Yeats, Joyce. New York 1952.
Adams, R. Now that my ladder's gone: Yeats without myth. Accent 13 1953.
Becker, W. The mask mocked: or farce and the dialectic of self. Sewanee Rev 61 1953.
Glick, W. Yeats's early reading of Walden. Boston Public Lib Quart 5 1953.
Glicksberg, C. Yeats and the hatred of science. Prairie Schooner 28 1953.
Gwynn, F. Yeats's Byzantium and its sources. PQ 32 1953.
Masson, D. Word and sound in Yeats's Byzantium. ELH 20 1953.
— The musical form of Yeats's Byzantium. N & Q Sept 1953.
Reid, J. Leda, twice assaulted. Jnl of Aesthetics 11 1953.
Rudd, M. Divided image: a study of William Blake and Yeats. 1953.
Blenner-Hassett, R. Yeats's use of Chaucer. Anglia 72 1954.
Bloom, E. Yeats's Second coming: an experiment in analysis. Univ of Kansas City Rev 21 1954.
Greene, D. Yeats's Byzantium and Johnson's Lichfield. PQ 33 1954.
Moore, V. The unicorn: Yeats's search for reality. New York 1954.
Taylor, E. The modern Irish writers. Lawrence Kansas 1954.
Trowbridge, H. Leda and the Swan: a Longinian analysis. MP 51 1954. Comment by L. Spitzer, ibid.
Adams, H. Blake and Yeats: the contrary vision. New York 1955.
— Yeats's country of the young. PMLA 72 1957.
— The Yeats collection at Texas. Univ of Texas Lib Chron 6 1957.
— Yeatsian art and mathematic form. Centennial Rev 4 1960.
— Yeats scholarship and criticism: a review of research. Texas Stud in Lit & Lang 3 1962.
Campbell, H. Yeats's Sailing to Byzantium. MLN 70 1955.
Davie, D. A. Yeats and Pound. Dublin Mag 31 1955.
— Yeats, Berkeley and romanticism. Irish Writing 31 1955.
Iremonger, V. Yeats as a playwright. Ibid.
Kenner, H. The sacred book of the arts. Ibid; rptd in Sewanee Rev 64 1956.
Mills, J. W. B. Yeats and Noh. Japan Quart 2 1955.
Noon, W. Yeats and the human body. Thought 30 1955.
Rubenstein, J. Three misprints in Yeats's Collected poems. MLN 70 1955.
Suss, I. Yeatsian Drama and the Dying hero. South Atlantic Quart 54 1955.
Wain, J. Yeats's Among school children. In Interpretations: essays on twelve English poems, ed Wain 1955.
Wildi, M. The influence and poetic development of Yeats. E Studies 36 1955.
Melchiori, G. Leda and the swan: the genesis of Yeats's poem. Eng Miscellany (Rome) 7 1956.
— Yeats's beast and the unicorn: a study in the development of an image. Durham Univ Jnl 20 1959.
— The whole mystery of art: pattern into poetry in the work of Yeats. 1960.

Rosenthal, M. Sources in myth and magic. Nation (New York) 182 1956.
— Yeats and the modern mind. In his Modern poets: a critical introduction, Oxford 1960.
— On Yeats and the cultural symbolism of modern poetry. Yale Rev 49 1960.
Alvarez, A. Eliot and Yeats: orthodoxy and tradition. Twentieth Century Sept 1957.
— In his Shaping spirit, 1958.
Beerbohm, M. First meetings with Yeats. Atlantic Monthly Sept 1957.
Cohane, J. Cowley and Yeats. TLS 10 May 1957.
Eberhart, R. Memory of meeting Yeats, AE, Gogarty, James Stephens. Literary Rev 1 1957.
Fletcher, I. Leda and St Anne. Listener 21 Feb 1957.
Holroyd, S. Emergence from chaos. Boston 1957.
Kermode, F. In his Romantic image, 1957.
Lees, F. Yeats's Byzantium, Dante and Shelley. N & Q 1 July 1957.
Mazzaro, J. Apple imagery in Yeats's The song of wandering Aengus. MLN 72 1957.
Miner, E. R. A poem by Swift and Yeats's Words upon the windowpane. MLN 72 1957.
— An aristocratic form: Japan in the thought and writing of Yeats. In his Japanese tradition, Princeton 1958.
Partridge, E. Yeats's The three bushes: genesis and structure.
Pirkhofer, A. Zur Bildersprache von Blake und Yeats. Anglia 75 1957.
Rouyer, A. In quest of Yeats. Threshold 1 1957.
Thwaite, A. Yeats and the Noh. Twentieth Century Sept 1957.
Wilson, F. A. C. Patterns in Yeats's imagery: The herne's egg. MP 55 1957.
— Yeats and tradition. 1958.
— Yeats's iconography. 1960.
Clark, D. Yeats's Deirdre: the rigour of logic. Dublin Mag 34 1958.
— Yeats and the modern theatre. Threshold 4 1960.
— Aubrey Beardsley's drawing of the shadows in Yeats's The shadowy waters. Modern Drama 7 1964.
— Nishikigi and Yeats's The dreaming of the bones. Ibid.
— Yeats and the drama of vision. Arizona Quart 20 1964.
— Yeats and the theatre of desolate reality. Dublin 1965.
Hewitt, J. Irish poets, learn your trade. Threshold 3 1958.
Howarth, H. In his Irish writers: literature and nationalism 1880–1939, New York 1958.
Kiernan, T. Lady Gregory and Yeats. Dalhousie Rev 38 1958.
Martin, C. Yeats: an unpublished letter. N & Q 1 June 1958.
Nelick, F. Yeats, Bullen and the Irish drama. Modern Drama 1 1958.
Newton, N. Yeats as dramatist: The player queen. EC 8 1958.
Raine, K. A traditional language of symbols. Listener 9 Oct 1958.
Read, H. Poetry in my time. Texas Quart 1 1958.
Reid, B. Yeats and tragedy. Hudson Rev 11 1958.
Shanley, J. Thoreau's geese and Yeats's swans. Amer Lit 30 1958.
Vickery, J. Three modes and a myth. Western Humanities Rev 12 1958.
Chittick, V. Yeats the dancer. Dalhousie Rev 39 1959.
Cohen, J. In memory of Yeats—and Wilfred Owen. JEGP 58 1959.
Donoghue, D. Yeats and the clean outline. In his Third voice: modern British and American verse drama, Princeton 1959.
— The vigour of its blood: Yeats's Words for music perhaps. Kenyon Rev 21 1959.
— (ed). The integrity of Yeats. Cork 1964. Thomas Davis lectures by A. N. Jeffares, T. R. Henn, F. Kermode, D. Davie and the editor.
Fixler, M. The affinities between J. K. Huysmans and the Rosicrucian stories of Yeats. PMLA 74 1959.
Gibbon, M. The masterpiece and the man: Yeats as I knew him. New York 1959.
Greene, D. H. Recordings of Yeats. Evergreen Rev 2 1959.
Orel, H. Dramatic values, Yeats and the Countess Cathleen. Modern Drama 2 1959.
Popkin, H. Yeats as dramatist. Tulane Drama Rev 3 1959.
Raines, C. Yeats's metaphors of permanence. Twentieth Century Lit 5 1959.
Rexroth, K. The plays of Yeats. In his Bird in the bush, New York 1959.
Senior, J. In his Way down and out: the occult in symbolist literature, 1959.
Sharp, W. Yeats: a poet not in the theatre. Tulane Drama Rev 4 1959.
Snow, W. A Yeats-Longfellow parallel. MLN 74 1959.
Unterecker, J. A reader's guide to Yeats. New York 1959.
— A fair chance of a disturbed Ireland: Yeats to Mrs J. Duncan. Mass Rev 6 1964.
— The shaping force in Yeats's plays. Modern Drama 7 1964.
Whitaker, T. The dialectic of Yeats's vision of history. MP 57 1959.
— The early Yeats and the pattern of history. PMLA 75 1960.
— Yeats's alambric. Sewanee Rev 68 1960.
— Yeats's dove or swan. PMLA 76 1961.
Youngblood, S. A reading of the Tower. Twentieth-Century Lit 5 1959.
Allen, J. Yeats's bird-soul symbolism. Twentieth-Century Lit 6 1960.
— Yeats's use of the serious pun. Southern Quart 1 1963.
Cosman, M. Mannered passion: Yeats and the Ossianic myths. Western Humanities Rev 14 1960.
Faulkner, P. Yeats and William Morris. Threshold 1960.
Gose, E. The lyric and the philosophic in Yeats's Calvary. Modern Drama 2 1960.
Keith, W. Yeats's Arthurian black tower. MLN 75 1960.
Lakin, R. Unity and strife in Yeats's tower symbol. Midwestern Quart 1 1960.
Loftus, R. Yeats and the Easter Rising: a study in ritual. Arizona Quart 16 1960.
— In his Nationalism in modern Anglo-Irish poetry, Madison 1964.
MacLeish, A. In his Poetry and experience, Boston 1960.
[MacLochloinn, A.]. An unrecorded Yeats item. Irish Book 1 1960. Memorial to T. W. Lyster.
Moore, G. The Nō and the dance plays of Yeats. Japan Quart 7 1960.
Stock, A. A vision (1925 and 1937). Indian Jnl of Eng Stud (Calcutta) 1 1960.
— Yeats: his poetry and thought. Cambridge 1961.
Watson, T. The French reputation of Yeats. Comparative Lit 12 1960.
Winters, Y. The poetry of Yeats. Twentieth-Century Lit 6 1960; Denver 1960.
Wright, G. The poet in the poem: the personae of Eliot, Yeats and Pound. Berkeley 1960.
Zwerdling, A. Yeats: variations on the visionary quest. UTQ 30 1960.
— Yeats and the heroic ideal. New York 1965.
— Tame swan at Coole. TLS 17 Feb 1961.
Beum, R. Yeats's octaves. Texas Stud in Lit & Lang 3 1961.
Davis, E. Yeats's early contacts with French poetry. Pretoria 1961.
Diskin, P. A source for Yeats's The black tower. N & Q March 1961.
Dunseath, T. Yeats and the genesis of supernatural song. ELH 28 1961.

Engelberg, E. Picture and gesture in the Yeatsian aesthetic. Criticism 3 1961.
— Passionate reverie: Yeats's tragic correlative. UTQ 31 1962.
— The vast design: pattern in Yeats's aesthetic. Toronto 1964.
Hahn, M. Yeats's The wild swans at Coole: meaning and structure. College Eng 22 1961.
Hutchins, P. Yeats and Pound in England. Texas Quart 4 1961.
Martin, G. Fine manners, liberal speech: a note on the public poetry of Yeats. EC 11 1961.
Moore, J. Yeats as a last romantic. Virginia Quart Rev 37 1961.
— Cuchulain, Christ and the queen of love: aspects of Yeatsian drama. Tulane Drama Rev 6 1962.
— An old man's tragedy: Yeats's Purgatory. Modern Drama 5 1963.
— Cold passion: a study of The herne's egg. Modern Drama 7 1964.
Reid, B. Yeats: the lyric of tragedy. Norman Oklahoma 1961.
Reiman, D. Yeats's Deirdre. E Studies 42 1961.
Rose, W. A letter from Yeats on Rilke. German Life & Letters 15 1961.
Sandberg, A. The anti-theater of Yeats. Modern Drama 4 1961.
Sanesi, R. Lapis lazuli. Osservatore Politico Letterario 7 1961.
Schramm, R. The line unit: studies in the later poetry of Yeats. Ohio Univ Rev 3 1961.
Southam, B. C. Yeats: life and the creator in The long legged fly. Twentieth-Century Lit 6 1961.
Staub, A. The unpopular theatre of Yeats. Quart Jnl of Speech 47 1961.
Torchiana, D. Senator Yeats, Burke and able men. Newberry Lib Bull 5 1961.
— Yeats, Jonathan Swift and liberty. MP 61 1963.
— Yeats and Georgian Ireland. Evanston 1965.
Yeats: images of a poet. Ed D. Gordon, Manchester 1961. Contributions by I. Fletcher, F. Kermode, R. Skelton and the editor.
Berkelman, R. The poet, the swan and the woman. Univ of Kansas City Rev 28 1962. On Leda and the swan.
Farag, F. Yeats's daimon. Cairo Stud in Eng 1962.
Faulkner, P. William Morris and Yeats. Dublin 1962.
— Yeats as critic. Criticism 4 1962.
— Yeats, Ireland and Ezra Pound. Threshold no 18 1963.
Gaskell, R. Purgatory. Modern Drama 4 1962.
Gullans, C. Leda and the swan. TLS 9 Nov 1962. Reply by C. Madge 16 Nov 1962. *See* Madge, below.
Hardy, J. The curious frame: seven poems in text and context. Notre Dame 1962. On A prayer for my daughter.
Leach, E. Yeats's A friend's illness and Herbert's Vertue. N & Q June 1962.
Madge, C. Leda and the swan. TLS 20 July 1962. Replies by G. Melchiori 3 Aug and by H. Williamson 31 Aug 1962.
Nathan, L. Yeats's experiments with an influence. Victorian Stud 6 1962.
— The tragic drama of Yeats: figures in a dance. New York 1965.
Nist, J. In defence of Yeats. Arizona Quart 18 1962.
Parish, J. The tone of Yeats's After long silence. Western Humanities Rev 16 1962.
Rhynehart, J. Wilde's comments on early works of Yeats. Irish Book 1 1962.
Sidnell, M. Manuscript versions of Yeats's The Countess Cathleen. PBSA 56 1962.
Spanos, W. Sacramental imagery in the middle and late poetry of Yeats. Texas Stud in Lit & Lang 4 1962.
Unger, L. Yeats and Milton. South Atlantic Quart 41 1962.
Watkins, V. Yeats: the religious poet. Texas Stud in Lit & Lang 3 1962.
Bushrui, S. The King's threshold: a defence of poetry. REL 4 1963.
— Yeats's verse plays: the revisions 1900–10. Oxford 1965.
Cambon, G. La lotta con Proteo. Milan 1963.
Linebarger, J. Yeats's Among school children and Shelley's Defence of poetry. N & Q 10 1963.
Mayhew, G. A corrected typescript of Yeats's Easter 1916. HLQ 27 1963.
Parks, L. The hidden aspect of Sailing to Byzantium. Etudes Anglaises 16 1963.
Quin, C. W. B. Yeats and Irish tradition. Hermathena no 97 1963.
Stallworthy, J. Between the lines: Yeats's poetry in the making. Oxford 1963.
— Two of Yeats's last poems. REL 4 1963.
Stanford, W. Yeats in the Irish senate. Ibid.
Stemmler, T. Yeats's Song of the happy shepherd und Shelley's Defence of poetry. Neophilologus 47 1963.
Stewart, J. I. M. In his Eight modern writers, Oxford 1963 (OHEL vol 12).
Vendler, H. Yeats's Vision and the later plays. Cambridge Mass 1963.
— Yeats's changing metaphors for the other world. Modern Drama 7 1964.
Wall, R. and R. Fitzgerald. Yeats and Jung: an ideological comparison. Lit & Psychology 13 1963.
Wind, E. Raphael: the dead child on a dolphin. TLS 25 Oct 1963. Replies 7–12 Nov 1963.
Yeats: a collection of critical essays. Ed J. Unterecker, Englewood Cliffs NJ 1963.
Fallon, G. Profiles of a poet. Modern Drama 7 1964.
Hurwitz, H. Yeats and Tagore. Comparative Lit 16 1964.
Kostelanetz, A. Irony in Yeats's Byzantine poems. Tennessee Stud in Lit 9 1964.
Levin, G. The Yeats of the Autobiographies: a man of phase 17. Texas Stud in Lit & Lang 6 1964.
Michie, D. A man of genius and a man of talent. Ibid. On Yeats and Moore.
Mortenson, R. Yeats's Vision and the Two trees. SB 17 1964.
Murphy, D. Yeats and Lady Gregory: a unique dramatic collaboration. Modern Drama 7 1964.
Scanlon, A. The sustained metaphor in the Only jealousy of Emer. Modern Drama 7 1964.
Warchausky, S. Yeats's purgatorial plays. Ibid.
In excited reverie: a centenary tribute to Yeats 1865–1939. Ed A. N. Jeffares and K. Cross 1965. Contributions by C. O'Brien, J. Stallworthy et al.
Salvadori, C. Yeats and Castiglione. Dublin 1965.

EDMUND JOHN MILLINGTON SYNGE

1871–1909

Synge's mss, diaries, notebooks etc are in Dublin, in the possession of his estate. Most of his letters to 'Marie O'Neill' (Molly Allgood) are held by the estate, others are privately owned in London; some letters are in the Berg Collection of the New York Public Library. Typescript copies of the Playboy of the western world *and* Deirdre of the sorrows*–made by Synge, but not the only such typescripts of these plays–are in the libaries of Indiana Univ and the Univ of Texas respectively.*

Bibliographies

Bourgeois, M. General bibliography. Appendix A in his Synge and the Irish theatre, 1913.
MacManus, M. Bibliographies of Irish authors: Synge. Dublin Mag Oct-Dec 1930.
O'Hegarty, P. Some notes on the bibliography of Synge. Dublin Mag Jan-March 1942.
MacPhail, I. Synge: some bibliographical notes. Irish Book 1 1959.

— and M. Pollard. Synge 1871–1909: a catalogue of an exhibition held at Trinity College Dublin on the occasion of the fiftieth anniversary of his death. Dublin 1959.

Collections

[Works]. 4 vols Dublin 1910, 5 vols Dublin 1911, 4 vols Boston 1912, 1 vol New York [1935] (not complete; contains unrev version of act 3 of The well of the saints); ed E. Rhys [1941] (EL) (with unrev version of act 3 of The well of the saints); ed M. MacLiammoir 1958 (EL).

[Plays]. 4 vols Dublin 1911, Dublin and London 1915, Leipzig 1922, London 1924, 1929, Leipzig 1931 (with The shadow of the glen and Riders to the sea), London [1932] (contains rev version of act 3 of The well of the saints and other unpbd material), 1938, 1949, 2 vols 1941 (Guild Books), 1952 (Penguin), Tokyo 1954, Oxford 1962 (WC) (4 plays and The Aran islands), London [1963] (with poems); Two plays (The playboy and Deirdre), Dublin 1911; Four plays (Riders to the sea, The shadow of the glen, The tinker's wedding, The well of the saints), Dublin 1911.

Collected works. Ed R. Skelton et al 5 vols Oxford 1962–.

Plays and poems. Ed T. R. Henn 1963.

§1

In the shadow of the glen: a play in one act. New York 1904 (priv ptd for J. Quinn, rptd from Samhain Dec 1904), London 1905 (with Riders to the sea), 1911, Boston 1911, 1911, Portland Maine 1913 (in Bibelot 19 no 8); tr French, 1913; Danish, 1925; Welsh nd.

Riders to the sea. 1905 (with In the shadow of the glen; rptd from Samhain Oct 1903), 1911, Boston 1911, Portland Maine 1913 (in Bibelot 19 no 7), Oxford 1936 (set to music by R. V. Williams), Boston 1951, London 1961 (with The playboy); tr French, 1913; Spanish, 1920; Danish, 1925; Turkish, 1940; Irish, 1945; Welsh [1939].

The well of the saints. Dublin 1905, London 1905 (with introd by W. B. Yeats), New York 1905 (priv ptd for J. Quinn), Dublin 1907, Boston 1911, 1911, Dublin 1911, London 1924; tr German, 1906; Dutch, 1912.

The playboy of the western world. Dublin 1907, 1907, New York 1907 (act 2 priv ptd for J. Quinn), Dublin 1909, Boston 1911, 1911, Dublin 1911, London 1927 (illustr J. Keating), New York 1935, London 1957; tr German, 1912; French, 1920.

The Aran islands. Dublin 1907 (with drawings by Jack Yeats), Dublin 1911, 1912, Boston 1911 (with drawings by Jack Yeats), 2 vols Dublin and London 1912, 1921, Leipzig 1926, London 1934, New York 1962 (with In Wicklow, West Kerry and Connemara, Under ether, and 15 unrptd essays and reviews), Oxford 1962 (WC) (with 4 plays); tr French, 1921.

The tinker's wedding. Dublin 1907, Boston 1911, Dublin 1911 (with Riders to the sea, The shadow of the glen), London 1924 (with Riders to the sea, The shadow of the glen).

Poems and translations. Dundrum 1909 (with preface by W. B. Yeats), New York 1909 (priv ptd for J. Quinn), Dublin 1911, 1911, London 1924, 1950, Oxford 1962. Vol 1 of Collected works, with unpbd verse.

Deirdre of the sorrows. Dundrum 1910, New York 1910 (priv ptd for J. Quinn), Boston 1911, Dublin 1911, 1912, London 1924; tr French, 1921; Irish, 1932.

In Wicklow, West Kerry and Connemara. Dublin 1911 (with drawings by Jack Yeats, rptd from vol 4 of Works, Dublin 1910), 1912, Dublin and London 1921, New York 1962 (with The Aran islands and some essays and reviews).

With Petrarch: twelve sonnets. Larchmont NY 1928. Prose trns by Synge.

Translations. Ed R. Skelton [Dublin 1961]. Contains unpbd material.

Letters, Diaries etc

Letters of Synge, from material supplied by Max Meyerfeld. Yale Rev 13 1924.

Some unpublished letters and documents of Synge formerly in the possession of Mr Lawrence Wilson of Montreal and now for the first time published for him. Montreal 1959.

Synge to Mackenna: the mature years. Ed A. Saddlemeyer, Mass Rev 1964.

The autobiography of Synge, constructed from the manuscripts by Alan Price with 14 photographs by Synge and an essay on Synge and the photography of his time by P. J. Pocock. Dublin 1965.

§2

Yeats, W. B. Introduction. In his Well of the saints, 1905.

— Preface. In his Poems and translations, Dundrum 1909.

— Synge and the Ireland of his time, with a note concerning a walk through Connemara with him by Jack Yeats. 1911.

— A memory of Synge. Irish Statesman July 1924.

— The death of Synge and other passages from an old diary. Dundrum 1928.

Elton, O. Living Irish literature. In his Modern studies, 1907.

Bickley, F. The art of Synge. Nation (London) 5 1909.

— Synge and the drama. New Quart 1910.

— Synge and the Irish dramatic movement. 1912.

Connell, F. John Millington Synge. Eng Rev 2 1909.

Masefield, J. In Dictionary of national biography, suppl 2 1901–11.

— Synge: a few personal rceollections with biographical notes. Dundrum 1915. Rptd from Contemporary Rev April 1911.

Blake, W. Synge and his plays. Dial (Chicago) Jan 1911.

— An Irish playwright. Independent (New York) April 1911.

O'Donoghue, D. The Synge boom: foreign influences. Daily Independent (Dublin) 21 Aug 1911.

Maguire, M. (Mary Colum). John Synge. Irish Rev 1 1911.

Montague, C. Dramatic values. 1911.

Bennett, C. The plays of Synge. Yale Rev 1 1912.

Figgis, D. The art of Synge. In his Studies and appreciations, 1912.

Howe, P. Synge: a critical study. 1912.

Jackson, H. The work of Synge. In his All manner of falk, 1912.

Lowther, G. Synge and the Irish revival. Oxford & Cambridge Rev Nov 1912.

Sherman, S. John Synge. Nation (New York) 95 1912.

Van Hamel, A. On Anglo-Irish syntax. E Studien 45 1912. Contains an analysis of Synge's language.

Bourgeois, M Synge and Loti. Westminster Rev 179 1913.

— Synge and the Irish theatre. 1913. With bibliography.

Weygandt, C. Irish plays and playwrights. 1913.

Gregory, Lady. Our Irish theatre: a chapter of autobiography. 1914.

Moore, G. Yeats, Lady Gregory and Synge. Eng Rev 16 1914.

— Hail and farewell: vale. 1914.

Boyd, E. Ireland's literary renaissance. New York 1916.

— The contemporary drama of Ireland. Dublin 1918.

Krieger, H. Synge: ein Dichter der keltischen Renaissance. Marburg 1916.

Morris, L. The Celtic dawn. New York 1917.

Sherman, S. On contemporary literature. New York 1917.

Lynd, R. Old and new masters. 1919.

Jameson, S. Modern drama in Europe.

Colum, P. Memories of Synge. Literary Rev 2 1921.

Schoepperle, G. Synge and his Old French farce: de la Vigne's L'aveugle et le boiteux, a moralité. North Amer Rev 214 1921.
Thorning, J. Synge: en moderne irsk dramatiker. Copenhagen 1921.
Ervine, St J. Bernard Shaw and Synge. In his Some impressions of my elders, 1923.
H., C.H. (Cherrie Houghton). Synge as I knew him. Irish Statesman 5 July 1924.
Fausset, H. I'A. Synge and tragedy. Fortnightly Rev Feb 1924.
O'Conor, N. Changing Ireland. Cambridge Mass 1924.
Téry, S. J. M. Synge et son oeuvre. Revue Anglo-américaine 2 1924.
Law, H. Anglo-Irish literature. Dublin 1926.
Stephens, J. I remember Synge. Radio Times 23 March 1928.
Malone, A. The Irish drama. 1929.
Empson, W. In his Seven types of ambiguity, 1930, 1953 (rev). On Deirdre of the sorrows.
Corkery, D. Synge and Anglo-Irish literature: a study. Cork 1931.
Strong, L. A. G. John Millington Synge. Bookman (New York) 73 1931.
Frenzel, H. Synge's work as a contribution to Irish folklore and to the psychology of primitive tribes. Bonn 1932.
Synge, S. Letters to my daughter: memories of Synge. Dublin [1932].
Zabel, M. Synge and the Irish. Poetry 62 1933.
Aufhauser, A. Sind die Dramen von Synge durch französische Vorbilder beeinflusst? Würzburg 1935.
Alspach, R. Synge's Well of the saints. TLS 28 Dec 1935.
Colum, M. Shaw and Synge. Forum 94 1935.
— From these roots. New York 1938.
Paul-Dubois, L. Le théâtre irlandais: Synge. Revue des Deux Mondes 1 June 1935.
Fay, W. and C. Carswell. The Fays of the Abbey Theatre. 1935.
Barnes, T. Yeats, Synge, Ibsen and Strindberg. Scrutiny 5 1936.
Gwynn, S. Irish literature and drama. 1936.
Journal and letters of Stephen MacKenna. Ed E. R. Dodds 1936.
Riva, S. La tradizione celtica e la moderna letteratura irlandese, i: Synge. Rome 1937.
Casey, H. Synge's use of the Anglo-Irish idiom. Eng Jnl (college edn) Nov 1938.
Conacher, W. The Irish literary movement. Queen's Quart Rev 45 1938.
Ellis-Fermor, U. The Irish dramatic movement. 1939, 1954 (rev).
Estill, A. The sources of Synge. Philadelphia 1939.
'O'Connor, Frank' (M. F. O'Donovan). Synge. In The Abbey theatre, ed L. Robinson 1939. A lecture.
Strong, L. A. G. John Millington Synge. 1941.
Greene, D. H. An adequate text of Synge. MLN 61 1946.
— The shadow of the glen and the widow of Ephesus. PMLA 62 1947.
— The tinker's wedding: a revaluation. Ibid.
— The playboy and Irish nationalism. JEGP 46 1947.
— Synge's unfinished Deirdre. PMLA 63 1948.
— Synge and the Irish. Colby Lib Quart 1957.
— Synge and the Celtic revival. Modern Drama 4 1962.
Peacock, R. In his Poet in the theatre, 1946.
Collins, R. The distinction of Riders to the sea. Univ of Kansas City Rev 13 1948.
Freyer, G. The little world of Synge. Politics & Letters 1948.
White, H. O. John Millington Synge. Irish Writing 1949.
Henn, T. R. In his Lonely tower: studies in the poetry of W. B. Yeats, 1950.
Kavanagh, P. The story of the Abbey Theatre. New York 1950.
Quinn, O. No garland for Synge. Envoy 3 1950.
Price, A. A consideration of Synge's The shadow of the glen. Dublin Mag 26 1951.
— Synge and Anglo-Irish drama. 1961.
Robinson, L. Ireland's Abbey Theatre: a history 1899–1951. 1951.
Setterquist, J. Ibsen and the beginnings of Anglo-Irish drama, i: Synge. Upsala [1951].
Davie, D. The poetic diction of Synge. Dublin Mag 27 1952.
McHugh, R. Yeats, Synge and the Abbey Theatre. Studies 41 1952.
Ottaway, D. Riders to the sea [music drama version]. Musical Times 93 1952.
Suss, I. The Playboy riots. Irish Writing 1952.
Williams, R. Synge. In his Drama from Ibsen to Eliot, 1952, 1965 (rev).
Podhoretz, N. Synge's Playboy: morality and the hero. EC 3 1953.
MacLean, H. The hero as Playboy. Univ of Kansas City Rev 21 1954.
Taylor, E. The modern Irish writers. Lawrence Kansas 1954.
Donoghue, D. Too immoral for Dublin: Synge's The tinker's wedding. Irish Writing 1955.
— Riders to the sea: a study. Univ Rev 1 1955.
— Flowers and timber: a note on Synge's poems. Threshold 1 1957.
Kenny, E. The splendid years: recollections of Maire Nic Shiubhlaigh, as told to Edward Kenny. Dublin 1955.
Lokhurst, E. Toneelkroniek: teleurstelling en voldoening. De Gids 119 1956.
Mercier, V. Irish comedy: the probable and the wonderful. Univ Rev 1 1956.
— The Irish comic tradition. Oxford 1962.
Dysinger, R. The Synge collection at Colby College. Colby Lib Quart 4 1957; adds, ibid.
Fay, G. The Abbey Theatre. Dublin 1958.
Howarth, H. In his Irish writers, 1958.
Leyburn, E. The theme of loneliness in the plays of Synge. Modern Drama 1 1958.
Greene, D. H. and E. Stephens. J. M. Synge 1871–1909. New York 1959. Authorized biography.
Mercer, C. Stephen Dedalus' vision and Synge's peasant girl. N & Q Dec 1960.
Murphy, D. The reception of Synge's Playboy in Ireland and America. BNYPL 64 1961.
Coxhead, E. Synge and Lady Gregory. 1962 (Br Council pamphlet).
Cusack, C. A player's reflections on Playboy. Modern Drama 4 1962.
Krause, D. The outrageous Ossean: patron-hero of Synge and O'Casey. Ibid.
Orel, H. Synge's last play: and a story will be told forever. Ibid.
Skelton, R. The poetry of Synge. Poetry Ireland 1962.
Spacks, P. The making of the Playboy. Modern Drama 4 1962.
Ayling, R. Synge's first love. Irish Times 21 Feb 1963; rptd in Modern Drama 6 1964.
Bayman, R. Synge and Irish folklore. Southern Folklore Quart 27 1963.
Gaskell, R. The realism of Synge. CQ 5 1963.
Lucas, R. The drama of Chekhov, Synge, Yeats and Pirandello. [1963].
O'Neill, M. Holloway on Synge's last days. Modern Drama 6 1963.
Gerstenberger, D. John Millington Synge. New York [1965]. With bibliography.

V. DRAMATISTS

WILLIAM BOYLE

1853–1922

A kish of brogues. 1899.
Comic capers. [1903]. Illustr H. Neilson, verses by Boyle.
Christmas at the zoo. [1904]. Illustr H. Neilson, verses by Boyle.
The building fund: a play in three acts. Dublin 1905.
The eloquent Dempsey: a comedy in three acts. Dublin 1907, London 1911, Dublin 1917.
The mineral workers: a play in four acts. Dublin 1907, London 1910, Dublin 1916.
Family failing: a comedy in three acts. Dublin 1912.

EDWARD MARTYN

1859–1923

§1

Morgante the lesser: his notorious life and wonderful deeds, arranged and narrated for the first time by Sirius. 1890.
The heather field; and Maeve. 1899 (introd by George Moore). Both plays rptd separately in 1917; Maeve rptd in C. Canfield, Plays of the Irish renaissance 1880–1930, New York 1929.
The tale of a town; and An enchanted sea. Kilkenny 1902. G. Moore's The bending of the bough was an adaptation of The tale of a town.
The place-hunters. Leader 26 July 1902. A one-act comedy.
Elliott, R. Art and Ireland. 1906. Preface by Martyn.
Romulus and Remus: or the makers of delights. In the Christmas suppl to The Irish people, ed W. O'Brien 21 Dec 1907.
Grangecolman: a domestic drama in three acts. Dublin 1912.
The dream physician: a play in five acts. Dublin [1914], New York 1918.
O'Hanlon, H. The all-alone. Dublin 1922. Preface by Martyn.

§2

Moore, G. In his Hail and farewell, 3 vols 1911–14.
Gwynn, D. Martyn and the Irish revival. 1930.
—— Edward Martyn. Studies (St Louis) 19 1930.
Courtney, M. Martyn and the Irish theatre. New York 1956.
Ryan, S. P. An unpublished letter of Martyn. N & Q July 1960.

ISABELLA AUGUSTA, LADY GREGORY

1859–1932

§1

Mr Gregory's letter box 1813–30. 1898. Ed Lady Gregory.
Ideals in Ireland. 1901. Ed Lady Gregory, with contributions by AE, D. Moran, G. Moore, D. Hyde, S. O'Grady, W. B. Yeats.
Cuchulain of Muirthemine: the story of the men of the Red Branch of Ulster. 1902, New York 1903. With preface and note by W. B. Yeats.
Poets and dreamers: studies and translations from the Irish. Dublin 1903.

Gods and fighting men: the story of the Tuatha de Danaan and of the Fianna of Ireland. 1904, New York 1904, London 1910, 1919.
Kincora. Dublin 1905, 1905, London 1912 (in Irish folk-history plays ser 1).
Spreading the news, The rising of the moon, by Lady Gregory; The poorhouse, by Lady Gregory and Douglas Hyde. Dublin 1906. Spreading the news and Rising of the moon rptd Dublin 1909, London 1923 (in Seven short plays); tr Italian, 1916.
A book of saints and wonders put down here by Lady Gregory according to the old writings and the memory of the people of Ireland. Dundrum 1906, London 1907, 1908.
The unicorn from the stars, and other plays, by W. B. Yeats and Lady Gregory. 1908, 1915. Contains also Cathleen ni Houlihan and The hourglass.
The workhouse ward. Dublin [1909?].
Seven short plays. Dublin 1909, [1911], London [1923], New York [1923?]. Spreading the news, Hyacinth Halvey, The rising of the moon, The jackdaw, The Workhouse ward, The travelling man, The gaolgate; all rptd separately Dublin 1918. Hyacinth Halvey and The travelling man tr Italian, 1916.
The Kiltartan history book. Dublin 1909, London 1926.
The image: a play in three acts. Dublin 1910, London 1922 (with Hanrahan's oath, Shanwalla, The wrens).
The Kiltartan wonder book. Dublin [1910], New York [1911].
The full moon: a comedy in one act. Dublin 1911 (priv ptd).
Irish folk-history plays. Ser 1, The tragedies (Grania, Kincora, Dervorgilla); ser 2, The tragi-comedies (The Canavans, The white cockade, The deliverer). 2 vols 1912, New York 1912, [1923].
New comedies: The bogie men, The full moon, Coats, Damer's gold, McDonough's wife. 1913; all rptd separately [1923].
Our Irish theatre: a chapter of autobiography. 1913.
Commedie irlandesi: versione e proemio di Carlo Linati. Milan 1916. Spreading the news, The rising of the moon, Hyacinth Halvey, The travelling man.
The golden apple: a play for Kiltartan children. 1916, New York 1916.
The Kiltartan poetry book: prose translations from the Irish. New York 1919.
Visions and beliefs in the west of Ireland, collected and arranged by Lady Gregory, with two essays and notes by W. B. Yeats. 2 vols 1920.
The dragon: a wonder play in three acts. Dublin 1920, London 1920; rptd in Three wonder plays, [1923].
Hugh Lane's life and achievement, with some account of the Dublin galleries. 1921.
Three wonder plays. [1922]. The dragon, Aristotle's bellows, The jester.
The story brought by Brigit: a passion play in three acts. 1924, 1924.
On the race course. New York [1925]. In One-act plays for stage and study, ser 2, 1926. A rewriting of Lady Gregory's unpbd but produced play Twenty-five, [1926].
Case for the return of Sir Hugh Lane's pictures to Dublin. Dublin 1926.
Three last plays. 1928. Sancho's master, Dave, The would-be gentleman (from Molière).
My first play. 1930. Colman and Guaire.
Coole. Dundrum. 1931. With an introductory poem by Yeats.
Journals 1916–30. Ed L. Robinson 1946, New York 1947.

Selected plays. Ed E. Coxhead [1962], New York 1963. Introd by Sean O'Casey.

§2

Quinn, J. Lady Gregory and the Abbey theater. Outlook (USA) 16 Dec 1911.
Tennyson, C. Irish plays and playwrights. Quart Rev 215 1911.
Lady Gregory's Irish plays. Contemporary Rev Oct 1912.
Moore, G. Yeats, Lady Gregory and Synge. Eng Rev Jan–Feb 1914.
Toksvig, S. A visit to Lady Gregory. North Amer Rev 214 1921.
Malone, A. The plays of Lady Gregory. Yale Rev 14 1925.
—— Lady Gregory. Dublin Mag 8 1933.
Bowen, A. Lady Gregory's use of proverbs in her plays. South Folklore Quart 3 1939.
Klenze, H. Lady Gregory: Leben und Werk. Bochum 1940.
MacLiammoir, M. Yeats, Lady Gregory, Denis Johnston. Bell 6 1943.
Henchy, P. The origins of the Workhouse ward. Irish Book 1 1959.
Ayling, R. Charwoman of the Abbey. Shaw Rev 4 1961.
Coxhead, E. Lady Gregory: a library portrait. New York 1961.
—— J. M. Synge and Lady Gregory. [1962] (Br Council pamphlet).

'RUTHERFORD MAYNE', SAMUEL WADDELL

1878–

§1

The turn of the road: a play in two scenes and an epilogue. Dublin 1907.
The drone: a play in three acts. Dublin 1909, Boston 1912.
The troth: a play in one act. Dublin 1909.
The drone and other plays. Dublin 1912. The turn of the road, The drone, The troth, Red turf.
Phantoms: a comedy or tragedy in one act. Dublin Mag 1 1923.
Bridgehead: play in three acts. 1939.
Peter: a comedy in three acts and a prologue. Dublin 1944.

§2

'The Bellman'. Meet Rutherford Mayne. Bell 4 1942.

GEORGE FITZMAURICE

1877–1963

§1

The country dressmaker: a play in three acts. Dublin 1914.
Five plays. 1914. The country dressmaker, The moonlighters (misprinted throughout as The moonlighter), The piedish, The magic glasses, The dandy dolls. The dandy dolls rptd in C. Canfield, Plays of the Irish Renaissance 1880–1930, New York 1929.
The Linnaun Shee. Dublin Mag 2 1924.
The green stone: a comedy in one act. Dublin Mag new ser 1 1926.
'Twixt the Giltinans and the Carmodys. Dublin Mag 18 1943.
There are tragedies and tragedies. Dublin Mag 23 1948.
One evening gleam. Dublin Mag 24 1949.
The coming of Ewn Andzale. Dublin Mag 33 1954.
The enchanted land: play in three acts. Dublin Mag 32 1957.

§2

Clarke, A. The dramatic fantasies of Fitzmaurice. Dublin Mag 1940.
Miller, L. Fitzmaurice: a bibliographical note. Irish Writing 1951.
Kennedy, M. Fitzmaurice: sketch for a portrait. Ibid.
Riley, J. The plays of Fitzmaurice. Dublin Mag 31 1955.

PADRAIC COLUM

b. 1881

Collections

Collected poems. New York 1932, 1953 (enlarged).
Ten poems. Dublin 1957.
The poet's circuit: collected poems of Ireland. Oxford 1960.

§1

Broken soil. Performed Dublin, 3 Dec 1903, but not pbd.
The land: a play in three acts. Dublin 1905, 1909 (with The fiddler's house, below), 1917 (in Three plays, below); rptd in Plays of the Irish renaissance, ed C. Canfield, New York 1929.
Wild earth: a book of verse. Dublin 1907, New York 1916 (enlarged).
The fiddler's house: a play in three acts. Dublin 1907, 1909 (with The land, above), 1917 (in Three plays, below).
Studies. Dublin 1907.
The miracle of the corn: a miracle play in one act. Dublin 1907 (in Studies, above), 1922 (in Dramatic legends and other poems, below).
Thomas Muskerry: a play in three acts. Dublin 1910, 1917 (in Three plays, below).
Eyes of youth, with S. Leslie and others. [1910].
My Irish year. [1912].
The desert. 1912.
Broadsheet ballads. Dublin [1913]. Introd by Colum.
A boy in Eirinn. [1913]; tr Irish, 1934.
Poems of the Irish revolutionary brotherhood. Ed P. Colum, Boston 1916.
Three plays. Boston 1916, Dublin 1917, 1963. The land, Thomas Muskerry, The fiddler's house.
The King of Ireland's son. 1916.
Mogu, the wanderer, or the desert: a fantastic comedy in three acts. Boston 1917.
The girl who sat by the ashes. New York 1919.
The children of Odin. New York [1920].
The boy apprenticed to an enchanter. New York 1920.
The golden fleece and the heroes who lived before Achilles. New York 1921.
Anthology of Irish verse. New York 1922, [1948] (enlarged). Ed with introd by Colum.
Dramatic legends and other poems. New York 1922.
The grasshopper. Performed Dublin, 24 Oct 1922, but not pbd.
Castle conquer. New York 1923; tr Irish, 1939.
At the gateways of the day. New Haven 1924.
The island of the mighty: being the hero stories of Celtic Britain retold from the Mabinogion. New York 1924.
The bright islands. New Haven 1925.
The road round Ireland. New York 1926.
Creatures. New York 1927.
The voyagers: being legends and romances of Atlantic discovery. New York 1927, 1930.
The fountain of youth. New York 1927.
The adventures of Odysseus and the Tale of Troy. New York [1928].
Balloon. New York 1929.
Balloon: a comedy in four acts. New York 1929.
Orpheus: myths of the world. New York 1930.

Cross roads in Ireland. New York 1930.
Old pastures. New York 1930, 1931.
Poems. 1932, New York 1932.
The peep-show man. New York 1932.
A half-day's ride: or estates in Corsica. New York 1932.
The betrayal. In One-act plays of to-day ser 4, ed J. Marriott [1939].
The white sparrow. New York 1933.
The children who followed the piper. New York 1933.
The big tree of Bunlahy: stories of my own countryside. New York 1933.
The boy who knew what the birds said. New York 1934.
The legend of Saint Columba. New York 1935.
The King of Ireland's son. [New York 1916]; tr Irish, 1935.
The story of Lowry Maen. New York 1937.
Legends of Hawaii. New Haven and Oxford 1937.
Flower pieces: new poems. Dublin 1938.
The jackdaw. [Dublin 1942].
The frenzied prince: being heroic stories of ancient Ireland. Philadelphia [1943].
Wild earth: poems. Dublin [1950].
The vegetable kingdom. [Bloomington 1954].
A treasury of Irish folklore. New York [1954].
The flying swans. New York [1957].
Our friend James Joyce, with M. Colum. Garden City NY 1958, London 1959.
Irish elegies. Dublin 1958, 1961.
Ulysses in nightgown, adapted from J. Joyce and dramatized and transposed by M. Barkentin under the supervision of P. Colum. In The off-Broadway theatre, ed R. Cordell and L. Matson, [New York 1959].
Arthur Griffith. Dublin [1959], New York 1959 (as Ourselves alone: the story of Arthur Griffith and the origin of the Irish Free State, New York [1959]).
Irish elegies. Dublin 1961.
Jonathan Swift, Poems. New York [1962]. Introd by Colum.
Moytura: a play for dancers. [Dublin 1963].
Three plays. Dublin 1963.

§2

Fiacc, P. Padraic Colum. Irish Bookman 1 1947.
Strong, L. A. G. Padraic Colum. Irish Writing 1950.
Loftus, R. Colum: the peasant nation. In his Nationalism in modern Anglo-Irish poetry, Madison 1964.

LENNOX ROBINSON
1886–1958

§1

The cross-roads: a play in a prologue and two acts. Dublin [1909].
Two plays: Harvest and The Clancy name. Dublin 1911.
Patriots: a play in three acts. Dublin 1912.
The dreamers: a play in three acts. 1915.
A young man from the south. Dublin 1917.
The lost leader: a play in three acts. Dublin 1918.
Eight short stories. Dublin [1919?].
The whiteheaded boy: a play in three acts. 1920, New York 1921 (introd by E. Blythe), New York 1924; tr Welsh, 1928; Irish, 1934.
The round table: a comic tragedy in three acts. 1924, 1928 (in Plays, below).
Crabbed youth and age: a little comedy. 1924, 1928 (in Plays, below).
Never the time and place. Performed Dublin, 8 April 1924, but not pbd.
A golden treasury of Irish verse. Ed L. Robinson 1925, New York 1925, 1932.
The white blackbird, and Portrait. Dublin [1926?], 1928 (in Plays, below).
A little anthology of modern Irish verse. Ed L. Robinson, Dublin 1928.
The big house: four scenes in its life. 1928, 1928 (in Plays, below).
Give a dog: a play in three acts. 1928, 1928 (in Plays, below).
Plays. 1928. The round table. Crabbed youth and age, Portrait, The white blackbird, The big house and Give a dog.
Ever the twain. 1930.
The far-off hills: a comedy in three acts. 1931, New York 1932.
Is life worth living? an exaggeration in three acts. 1933, 1939 (in Killycreggs in twilight, and other plays, below), Dublin 1953 (as Drama at Imish). First performed as Drama at Imish.
More plays. 1935. All's over, then? and Church street.
Three homes: Lennox Robinson, Tom Robinson and Nora Dorman. [1938]. An autobiography written with his brother and sister.
The Irish theatre: lectures delivered during the Abbey Theatre Festival held in Dublin in August 1938. Ed L. Robinson 1938. Contributors: A. Malone, F. O'Connor, F. Higgins, T. C. Murray, W. Starkie, E. Blythe, M. MacLiammoir and the editor.
Killycreggs in twilight, and other plays. 1939. Includes Is life worth living and Bird's nest.
Forget me not. Performed Dublin, 26 Dec 1941, but not pbd.
Curtain up: an autobiography. 1942.
Towards an appreciation of the theatre. Dublin 1945.
Lady Gregory's journals 1916–30. Ed L. Robinson 1946, New York 1947.
Pictures in a theatre: a conversation piece. Dublin [1946].
The lucky finger. Performed Dublin, 23 Aug 1948, but not pbd.
Ireland's Abbey Theatre: a history 1899–1951. [1951].
The demon lover. Performed Dublin 21 June 1954, but not pbd.
Church street: a play. Belfast 1955.
I sometimes think. Dublin [1956].
The Oxford book of Irish verse. Ed D. MacDonagh and L. Robinson, Oxford 1958.

§2

'M.R.' Lennox Robinson. Bell 5 1943.
Spinner, K. Die alte Dame sagt: nein! drei irische Dramatiker: Lennox Robinson, Sean O'Casey, Denis Johnston. Berne 1961.
O'Neill, M. Lennox Robinson. New York [1964].

THOMAS CORNELIUS MURRAY
1873–1959

§1

Birthright: a play in two acts. Dublin 1911, London 1928 (with The pipe in the fields, below); tr Irish, 1931.
Maurice Harte: a play in two acts. Dublin 1912, 1934 (with A stag at bay).
Spring and other plays. Dublin 1917. Spring, Sovereign love and The briery gap. Sovereign is a revision of The wheel o' fortune, performed Cork 1909 but not pbd.
Aftermath: a play in three acts. Dublin 1922.
Autumn fire: a play in three acts. 1925, Boston 1926, London [1952]; tr Irish, 1930.
The pipe in the fields, and Birthright. 1928.
The blind wolf. Performed Dublin, 30 April 1928 but not pbd.
A flutter of wings. Performed Dublin 1930 but not pbd.
Michaelmas Eve: a play in three acts. 1932.
Maurice Harte, and A stag at bay. 1934.

Spring horizon: a novel. [1937].
A spot in the sun. Performed Dublin, 14 Feb 1938 but not pbd.
Illumination. Performed Dublin, 31 July 1939 but not pbd.

§2

Hogan, J. Thomas Cornelius Murray. Studies 38 1949.
Hogan, T. T. C. Murray. Envoy 3 1950.
Oh-Aodha, M. Murray and some critics. Studies 48 1958.
Conlin, M. The tragic effect in Autumn fire and Desire under the elms. Modern Drama 1 1959.
— Murray: Ireland on the stage. Renascence 13 1961.

ST JOHN ERVINE
b. 1883

§1

Mixed marriage: a play in four acts. Dublin 1912, London 1914 (rptd in Four Irish plays, below).
The magnanimous lover: a play in one act. Dublin 1912.
Jane Clegg: a play in three acts. 1914, 1914 (rptd in Four Irish plays, below).
Four Irish plays. 1914. Mixed marriage, The critics, Jane Clegg, The Orangemen.
John Ferguson: a play in four acts. Dublin 1915.
Some impressions of my elders. New York 1922, London 1923.
The ship: a play in three acts. 1922.
The lady of Belmont: a play in five acts. 1923.
Mary, Mary, quite contrary: a light comedy in four acts. 1923.
The organized theatre. New York 1924.
Anthony and Anna: a comedy in three acts. 1925, 1936 (rev).
Four one-act plays. 1928. Ole George comes to tea, Progress, She was no lady.
The first Mrs Fraser. 1929.
People of our class: a comedy. 1936.
Boyd's shop: a comedy. 1936.
Robert's wife: a comedy. 1938.
The island of saints. Performed Dublin, 12 Oct 1920, but apparently not pbd.
Friends and relations. 1947.
Private enterprise. 1948.
The Christies. 1949.
My brother Tom. 1952.
William John Mawhinney. Performed Dublin, 23 March 1940 but not pbd.

§2

St John Ervine, Ulster realist. Outlook (USA) 125 1920.
McQuilland, L. Mr St John Ervine and his work. Living Age 305 1920.
Lothian, A. The plays and novels of St John Ervine. North Amer Rev 215 1922.
Aas, L. Tre engelske dramatikere. Tilskueren 46 1929.
Ireland, D. Red brick city and its dramatist: a note on St John Ervine. Envoy 3 1950.

EDWARD JOHN MORETON DRAX PLUNKETT, 18th BARON DUNSANY
1878–1957

Bibliographies

Danielson, H. In his Bibliographies of modern authors ser 1, [1925].

§1

The gods of Pegāna. 1905, 1911, Boston [1916?].

Time and the gods. 1906, Boston [1913].
The sword of Welleran, and other stories. 1908, Boston [1916?].
A dreamer's tales. 1910, Boston [1911?], New York 1919 (introd by P. Colum).
The book of wonder: a chronicle of little adventures at the edge of the world. 1912, Boston [1915?], New York [1918?], London 1919, New York (Modern Lib).
Selections from the writings of Lord Dunsany. Dundrum 1912. Preface by W. B. Yeats.
The sphinx at Gizeh. Tripod (Cambridge) May 1912.
Five plays. 1914, New York 1914, Boston 1916, 1917, 1918, 1919, 1921, 1925. The gods of the mountain, The golden doom, King Argimines and the unknown warrior, The glittering gate, The lost silk hat.
Fifty-one tales. 1915, New York 1915, Boston 1917, 1920.
A night at an inn: a play in one act. New York 1916, London 1925, 1917 (in Plays of gods and men).
Tales of wonder. 1916, 1917.
The last book of wonder. Boston [1916].
Plays of gods and men. Dublin 1917, London 1917, Boston [1917], Dublin 1918, New York 1923. The laughter of the gods (rptd 1918), The Queen's enemies, The tents of the Arabs, A night at an inn.
Tales of war. Boston 1918, Dublin [1918], Boston 1919.
Nowadays. Boston 1918, 1920.
Tales of three hemispheres. Boston [1919], London 1920.
Unhappy far-off things. 1919, Boston 1919, New York 1924.
If: a play in four acts. 1921, 1922, New York [1923].
The chronicles of Rodriguez. [1922], New York 1922 (as Don Rodriguez: chronicles of Shadow Valley).
Plays of near and far. [1922], New York 1923. The compromise of the King of the golden isles, The flight of the Queen, Cheezo, A good bargain, If Shakespeare lived to-day, Fame and the poet.
The laughter of the gods. [1922].
The compromise of the king of the golden isles. New York 1924.
The King of Elfland's daughter. New York and London 1924.
The amusements of Khan Kharuda. [1925].
The evil kettle. London and New York [1925].
The old King's tale. London and New York [1925].
The charwoman's shadow. New York and London 1926.
The blessing of Pan. New York and London [1927], [1928].
Seven modern comedies. [1928], New York 1929. Atalanta in Wimbledon, The raffle, The journey of the soul, In holy Russia, His sainted grandmother, The hopeless passion of McBunyon, The jest of Hahalaba.
Fifty poems. London and New York [1929].
The old folk of the centuries: a play. 1930.
The travel tales of Mr Joseph Jorkens. New York 1931.
Lord Adrian: a play in three acts. 1933.
The curse of the wise woman. [1933], New York 1933.
Lord Adrian: a play in three acts. Waltham Saint Lawrence, Berkshire [1933].
Building a sentence. New York [1934?]. Rptd from Atlantic Monthly Dec 1933.
Jorkens remembers Africa. New York and London 1934.
If I were dictator: the pronouncements of the Grand Macaroni. [1934].
Mr Jorkens remembers Africa. [1934].
Mr Faithful. 1935.
Up in the hills. [1935].
Mr Faithful: a comedy in three acts. [1935].
My talks with Dean Spanley. [1936], New York 1936.
Rory and Bran. [1936], New York 1937.
My Ireland. [1937], New York 1937, London [1950].
Plays for earth and air. 1937. Plays for earth: Fame comes late, A matter of honour, Mr Sliggen's hour, The pumpkin; Plays for air: The use of man, The bureau de change, The seventh symphony, Golden dragon city, Time's joke, Atmospherics.

Patches of sunlight. [1938], New York 1938. An autobiography.
Mirage water. [1938].
The story of Mona Sheehy. [1939], New York 1940.
Jorkens has a large whiskey. [1940].
War poems. 1941.
A journey. 1943.
Wandering songs. 1943.
The Donellan lectures 1943, delivered at Trinity College Dublin. 1945.
Guerilla. 1944.
While the sirens slept. 1944. An autobiography.
A glimpse from a watchtower: a series of essays. 1945.
The sirens wake. 1945.
The year. 1946.
The fourth book of Jorkens. [1947?].
The odes of Horace, translated by Lord Dunsany. [1947].
To awaken Pegasus, and other poems. Oxford [1949].
The man who ate the phoenix. [1949].
The strange journeys of Colonel Polders. [1950].
The last revolution: a novel. [1951].
His fellow men: a novel. [1952].
Jorkens borrows another whiskey. [1954].

§2

Bierstadt, E. Dunsany the dramatist. Boston 1917.
Boyd, E. In his Appreciations and depreciations, Dublin 1918.
Lovecraft, H. Marginalia. Sauk City 1944.
Smith, H. Lord Dunsany, king of dreams: a personal portrait. New York [1959].
Wilson, W. Future and fortune in A night at an inn. PBSA 58 1964.

D. H. G.

INDEX

To volume 3, containing the names of primary authors together with certain headings. Numerals refer to columns. Volume 5 will eventually provide a more detailed index to the whole of New CBEL.